PRENTICE HALL

LITERATURE

TEACHER'S EDITION • GRADE 9

COMMON CORE EDITION ©

ISBN-13: 978-0-13-319058-8
ISBN-10: 0-13-319058-7
5 6 7 8 9 10 V011 15 14 13 12

Preparing Students for College and Career

Literature opens minds. It should also open doors to a student's future. *Prentice Hall Literature Common Core Edition* is a comprehensive literacy program that teaches the new standards and helps students become better readers, better writers, and better thinkers so they're better prepared for college, careers, and beyond. You can be confident that what you are teaching meets the Common Core framework.

Common Core in *Prentice Hall Literature*

- Leveled support and scaffolding for understanding increasingly complex texts
- Informational texts across content areas
- Emphasis on writing argumentative, informative/explanatory, and narrative texts
- Critical thinking and higher-order thinking skills presented in instruction
- Traditional and performance-based assessments
- Best-in-class digital resources
- Teacher training to implement the new standards

Builds Better Readers

Prentice Hall Literature provides a scaffolded approach to rigorous instruction, enabling students to build a solid literary foundation that is necessary for success in college and careers.

Exposure to rich literature selections with increasing text complexity across genres builds students' literary and cultural knowledge, so they become comfortable reading different text structures and understand the elements that appear in the selections.

Leveled Selection Pairs in the Student Edition let you choose the right text without skipping essential skills.

Text Complexity Rubrics guide you in choosing the selection that's appropriate for your students' abilities.

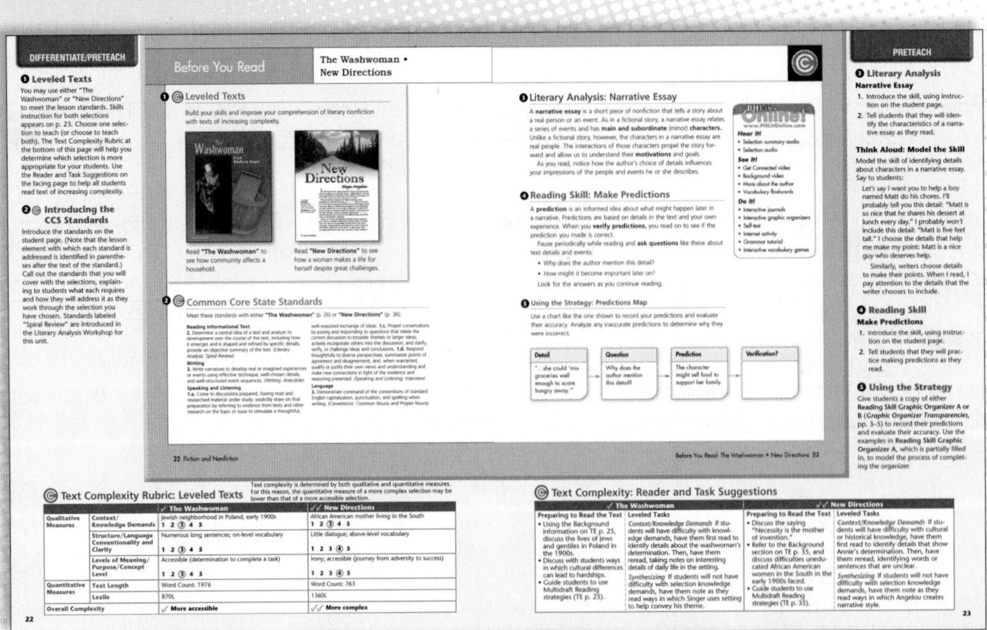

DIFFERENTIATE/PRETEACH

1 Leveled Texts

You may use either "The Washwoman" or "New Directions" to meet the lesson standards. Skills instruction for both selections appears on p. 23. Choose one selection to teach (or choose to teach both). The Text Complexity Rubric at the bottom of this page will help you determine which selection is more appropriate for your students. Use the Reader and Task Suggestions on the facing page to help all students read text of increasing complexity.

2 Introducing the CCS Standards

Introduce the standards on the student page. (Note that the lesson element with which each standard is addressed is identified in parentheses after the text of the standard.) Call out the standards that you will cover with the selections, explaining to students what each requires and how they will address it as they work through the selection you have chosen. Standards labeled "Spiral Review" are introduced in the Literary Analysis Workshop for this unit.

Before You Read | The Washwoman • New Directions

1 Leveled Texts

Build your skills and improve your comprehension of literary nonfiction with texts of increasing complexity.

Read **"The Washwoman"** to see how community affects a household.

Read **"New Directions"** to see how a woman makes a life for herself despite great challenges.

2 Common Core State Standards

Meet these standards with either **"The Washwoman"** (p. 26) or **"New Directions"** (p. 36).

Reading Informational Text
2. Determine a central idea of a text and analyze its development over the course of the text, including how it emerges and is shaped and refined by specific details; provide an objective summary of the text. *(Literary Analysis: Spiral Review)*

Writing
3. Write narratives to develop real or imagined experiences or events using effective technique, well-chosen details, and well-structured event sequences. *(Writing: Anecdote)*

Speaking and Listening
1.a. Come to discussions prepared, having read and researched material under study; explicitly draw on that preparation by referring to evidence from texts and other research on the topic or issue to stimulate a thoughtful, well-reasoned exchange of ideas. **1.c.** Propel conversations by posing and responding to questions that relate the current discussion to broader themes or larger ideas; actively incorporate others into the discussion; and clarify, verify, or challenge ideas and conclusions. **1.d.** Respond thoughtfully to diverse perspectives, summarize points of agreement and disagreement, and, when warranted, qualify or justify their own views and understanding and make new connections in light of the evidence and reasoning presented. *(Speaking and Listening: Interview)*

Language
2. Demonstrate command of the conventions of standard English capitalization, punctuation, and spelling when writing. *(Conventions: Common Nouns and Proper Nouns)*

22 Fiction and Nonfiction

3 Literary Analysis: Narrative Essay

A **narrative essay** is a short piece of nonfiction that tells a story about a real person or an event. As in a fictional story, a narrative essay relates a series of events and has **main and subordinate** (minor) **characters.** Unlike a fictional story, however, the characters in a narrative essay are real people. The interactions of those characters propel the story forward and allow us to understand their **motivations** and goals.

As you read, notice how the author's choice of details influences your impressions of the people and events he or she describes.

4 Reading Skill: Make Predictions

A **prediction** is an informed idea about what might happen later in a narrative. Predictions are based on details in the text and your own experience. When you **verify predictions,** you read on to see if the prediction you made is correct.

Pause periodically while reading and **ask questions** like these about text details and events:

- Why does the author mention this detail?
- How might it become important later on?

Look for the answers as you continue reading.

5 Using the Strategy: Predictions Map

Use a chart like the one shown to record your predictions and evaluate their accuracy. Analyze any inaccurate predictions to determine why they were incorrect.

Detail	Question	Prediction	Verification?
"...she could 'mix groceries well enough to scare hungry away.'"	Why does the author mention this detail?	The character might sell food to support her family.	

PHLit Online! www.PHLitOnline.com

Hear It!
- Selection summary audio
- Selection audio

See It!
- Get Connected video
- Background video
- More about the author
- Vocabulary flashcards

Do It!
- Interactive journals
- Interactive graphic organizers
- Self-test
- Internet activity
- Grammar tutorial
- Interactive vocabulary games

Before You Read: The Washwoman • New Directions 23

PRETEACH

3 Literary Analysis
Narrative Essay

1. Introduce the skill, using instruction on the student page.
2. Tell students that they will identify the characteristics of a narrative essay as they read.

Think Aloud: Model the Skill

Model the skill of identifying details about characters in a narrative essay. Say to students:

Let's say I want you to help a boy named Matt do his chores. I'll probably tell you this detail: "Matt is so nice that he shares his dessert at lunch every day." I probably *won't* include this detail: "Matt is five feet tall." I choose the details that help me make my point: Matt is a nice guy who deserves help.

Similarly, writers choose details to make their points. When I read, I pay attention to the details that the writer chooses to include.

4 Reading Skill
Make Predictions

1. Introduce the skill, using instruction on the student page.
2. Tell students that they will practice making predictions as they read.

5 Using the Strategy

Give students a copy of either **Reading Skill Graphic Organizer A or B** (*Graphic Organizer Transparencies,* pp. 3–5) to record their predictions and evaluate their accuracy. Use the examples in **Reading Skill Graphic Organizer A,** which is partially filled in, to model the process of completing the organizer.

Text Complexity Rubric: Leveled Texts

Text complexity is determined by both qualitative and quantitative measures. For this reason, the quantitative measure of a more complex selection may be lower than that of a more accessible selection.

		✓ The Washwoman	✓✓ New Directions
Qualitative Measures	Context/Knowledge Demands	Jewish neighborhood in Poland, early 1900s 1 2 ③ 4 5	African American mother living in the South 1 2 ③ 4 5
	Structure/Language Conventionality and Clarity	Numerous long sentences; on-level vocabulary 1 2 ③ 4 5	Little dialogue; above-level vocabulary 1 2 3 ④ 5
	Levels of Meaning/Purpose/Concept Level	Accessible (determination to complete a task) 1 2 ③ 4 5	Irony; accessible (journey from adversity to success) 1 2 3 ④ 5
Quantitative Measures	Text Length	Word Count: 1976	Word Count: 763
	Lexile	870L	1360L
Overall Complexity		✓ More accessible	✓✓ More complex

22

Text Complexity: Reader and Task Suggestions

✓ The Washwoman: Preparing to Read the Text	✓ The Washwoman: Leveled Tasks	✓✓ New Directions: Preparing to Read the Text	✓✓ New Directions: Leveled Tasks
• Using the Background information on TE p. 25, discuss the lives of Jews and gentiles in Poland in the 1900s. • Discuss with students ways in which cultural differences can lead to hardships. • Guide students to use Multidraft Reading strategies (TE p. 25).	*Context/Knowledge Demands* If students will have difficulty with knowledge demands, have them first read to identify details about the washwoman's determination. Then, have them reread, taking notes on interesting details of daily life in the setting. *Synthesizing* If students will not have difficulty with selection knowledge demands, have them note as they read ways in which Singer uses setting to help convey his theme.	• Discuss the saying "Necessity is the mother of invention." • Refer to the Background section on TE p. 35, and discuss difficulties uneducated African American women in the South in the early 1900s faced. • Guide students to use Multidraft Reading strategies (TE p. 35).	*Context/Knowledge Demands* If students will have difficulty with cultural or historical knowledge, have them first read to identify details that show Annie's determination. Then, have them reread, identifying words or sentences that are unclear. *Synthesizing* If students will not have difficulty with selection knowledge demands, have them note as they read ways in which Angelou creates narrative style.

23

Reader and Task Suggestions offer support to ensure all readers meet achievable challenges.

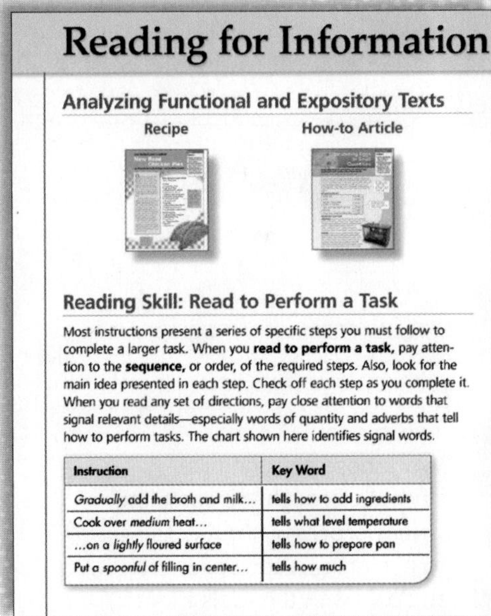

Reading for Information

Analyzing Functional and Expository Texts

Recipe

How-to Article

Reading Skill: Read to Perform a Task

Most instructions present a series of specific steps you must follow to complete a larger task. When you **read to perform a task,** pay attention to the **sequence,** or order, of the required steps. Also, look for the main idea presented in each step. Check off each step as you complete it. When you read any set of directions, pay close attention to words that signal relevant details—especially words of quantity and adverbs that tell how to perform tasks. The chart shown here identifies signal words.

Instruction	Key Word
Gradually add the broth and milk…	tells how to add ingredients
Cook over *medium* heat…	tells what level temperature
…on a *lightly* floured surface	tells how to prepare pan
Put a *spoonful* of filling in center…	tells how much

Informational texts provide context for learning and allow for the application of knowledge across science, social studies, and math.

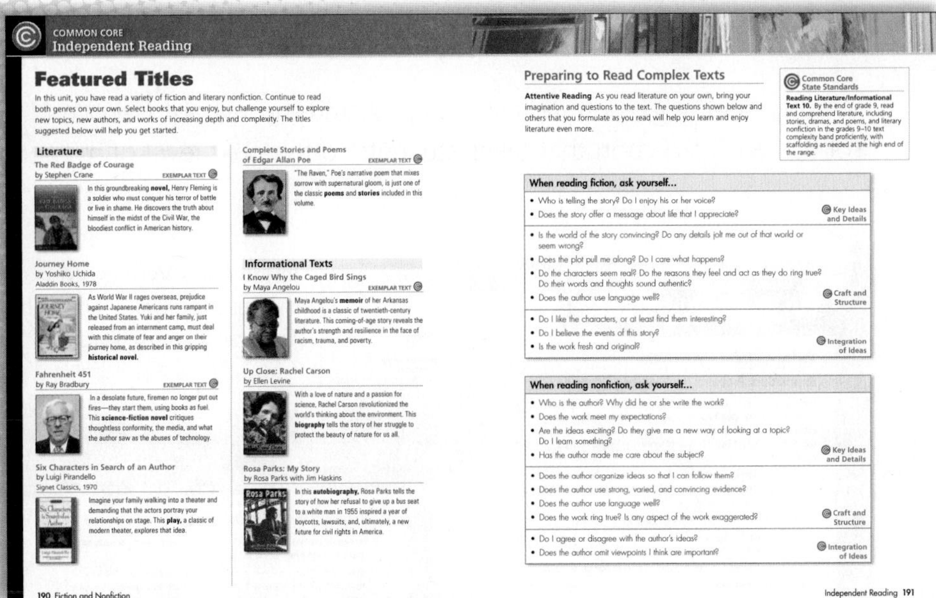

COMMON CORE Independent Reading

Featured Titles

In this unit, you have read a variety of fiction and literary nonfiction. Continue to read both genres on your own. Select books that you enjoy, but challenge yourself to explore new topics, new authors, and works of increasing depth and complexity. The titles suggested below will help you get started.

Literature

The Red Badge of Courage by Stephen Crane — EXEMPLAR TEXT

In this groundbreaking **novel,** Henry Fleming is a soldier who must conquer his terror of battle or live in shame. He discovers the truth about himself in the midst of the Civil War, the bloodiest conflict in American history.

Journey Home by Yoshiko Uchida, Aladdin Books, 1978

As World War II rages overseas, prejudice against Japanese Americans runs rampant in the United States. Yuki and her family, just released from an internment camp, must deal with this climate of fear and anger on their journey home, as described in this gripping **historical novel.**

Fahrenheit 451 by Ray Bradbury — EXEMPLAR TEXT

In a desolate future, firemen no longer put out fires—they start them, using books as fuel. This **science-fiction novel** critiques thoughtless conformity, the media, and what the author saw as the abuses of technology.

Six Characters in Search of an Author by Luigi Pirandello, Signet Classics, 1970

Imagine your family walking into a theater and demanding that the actors portray your relationships on stage. This **play,** a classic of modern theater, explores that idea.

Complete Stories and Poems of Edgar Allan Poe — EXEMPLAR TEXT

"The Raven," Poe's narrative poem that mixes sorrow with supernatural gloom, is just one of the classic **poems** and **stories** included in this volume.

Informational Texts

I Know Why the Caged Bird Sings by Maya Angelou — EXEMPLAR TEXT

Maya Angelou's **memoir** of her Arkansas childhood is a classic of twentieth-century literature. This coming-of-age story reveals the author's strength and resilience in the face of racism, trauma, and poverty.

Up Close: Rachel Carson by Ellen Levine

With a love of nature and a passion for science, Rachel Carson revolutionized the world's thinking about the environment. This **biography** tells the story of her struggle to protect the beauty of nature for us all.

Rosa Parks: My Story by Rosa Parks with Jim Haskins

In this **autobiography,** Rosa Parks tells the story of how her refusal to give up a bus seat to a white man in 1955 inspired a year of boycotts, lawsuits, and, ultimately, a new future for civil rights in America.

Preparing to Read Complex Texts

Attentive Reading As you read literature on your own, bring your imagination and questions to the text. The questions shown below and others that you formulate as you read will help you learn and enjoy literature even more.

Common Core State Standards

Reading Literature/Informational Text 10. By the end of grade 9, read and comprehend literature, including stories, dramas, and poems, and literary nonfiction in the grades 9–10 text complexity band proficiently, with scaffolding as needed at the high end of the range.

When reading fiction, ask yourself...

- Who is telling the story? Do I enjoy his or her voice?
- Does the story offer a message about life that I appreciate? (Key Ideas and Details)
- Is the world of the story convincing? Do any details jolt me out of that world or seem wrong?
- Does the plot pull me along? Do I care what happens?
- Do the characters seem real? Do the reasons they feel and act as they do ring true? Do their words and thoughts sound authentic?
- Does the author use language well? (Craft and Structure)
- Do I like the characters, or at least find them interesting?
- Do I believe the events of this story?
- Is the work fresh and original? (Integration of Ideas)

When reading nonfiction, ask yourself...

- Who is the author? Why did he or she write the work?
- Does the work meet my expectations?
- Are the ideas exciting? Do they give me a new way of looking at a topic? Do I learn something?
- Has the author made me care about the subject? (Key Ideas and Details)
- Does the author organize ideas so that I can follow them?
- Does the author use strong, varied, and convincing evidence?
- Does the author use language well?
- Does the work ring true? Is any aspect of the work exaggerated? (Craft and Structure)
- Do I agree or disagree with the author's ideas?
- Does the author omit viewpoints I think are important? (Integration of Ideas)

190 Fiction and Nonfiction

Independent Reading 191

Wide and deep independent readings of increasing complexity challenge learners. Support for reading complex texts is aligned to the Common Core.

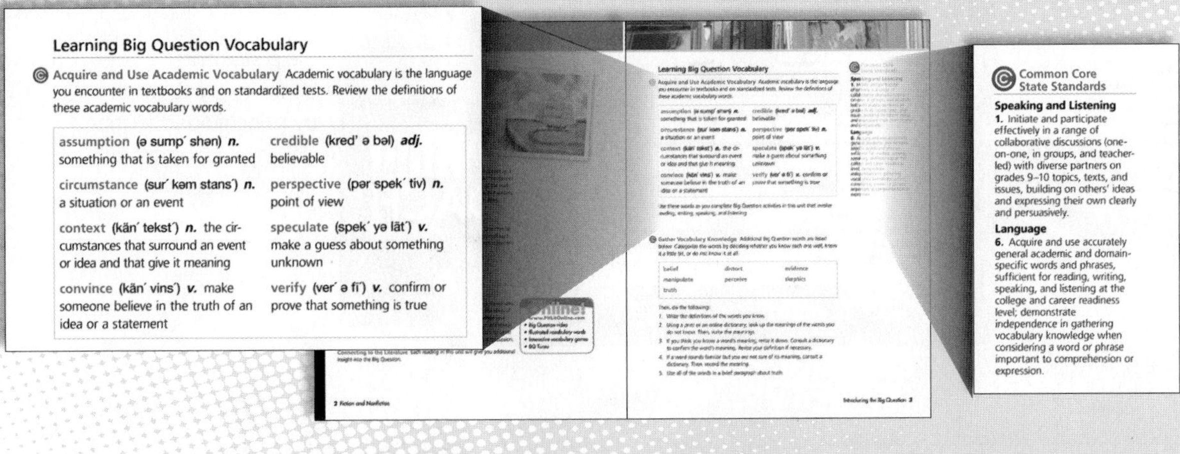

Learning Big Question Vocabulary

Acquire and Use Academic Vocabulary Academic vocabulary is the language you encounter in textbooks and on standardized tests. Review the definitions of these academic vocabulary words.

assumption (ə sump′ shən) ***n.*** something that is taken for granted

circumstance (sur′ kəm stans′) ***n.*** a situation or an event

context (kän′ tekst′) ***n.*** the circumstances that surround an event or idea and that give it meaning

convince (kän′ vins′) ***v.*** make someone believe in the truth of an idea or a statement

credible (kred′ ə bəl) ***adj.*** believable

perspective (pər spek′ tiv) ***n.*** point of view

speculate (spek′ yə lāt′) ***v.*** make a guess about something unknown

verify (ver′ ə fī′) ***v.*** confirm or prove that something is true

Common Core State Standards

Speaking and Listening

1. Initiate and participate effectively in a range of collaborative discussions (one-on-one, in groups, and teacher-led) with diverse partners on grades 9–10 topics, texts, and issues, building on others' ideas and expressing their own clearly and persuasively.

Language

6. Acquire and use accurately general academic and domain-specific words and phrases, sufficient for reading, writing, speaking, and listening at the college and career readiness level; demonstrate independence in gathering vocabulary knowledge when considering a word or phrase important to comprehension or expression.

Extensive practice with general and domain-specific vocabulary builds vocabulary knowledge and prepares students for success.

Digital Resources Target Practice with Customized Instruction

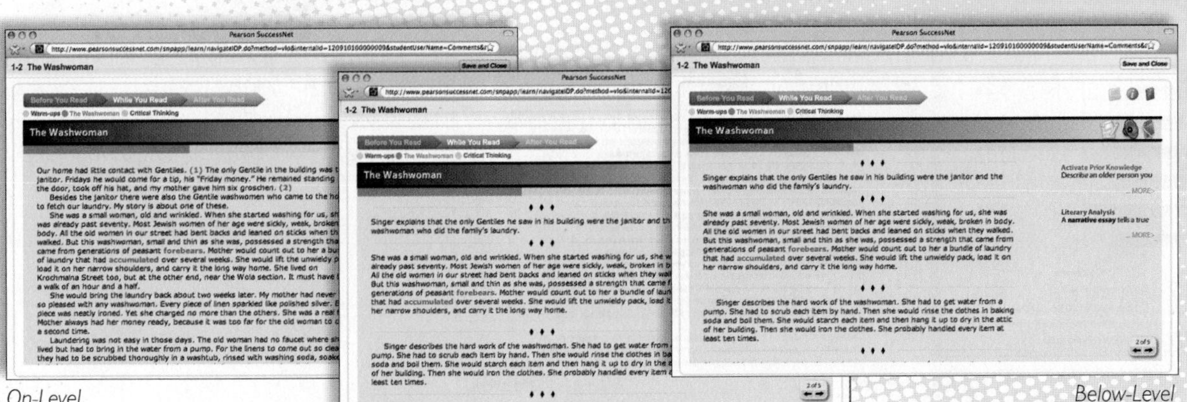

On-Level

English Learner

Below-Level

Online instruction instantly responds to students' needs with precise practice and scaffolding. PHLitOnline automatically assigns learner levels based on Diagnostic Test results.

Better Writers, Better Thinkers

Writing, speaking, and listening are integrated throughout *Prentice Hall Literature* with rigorous, robust skill instruction that takes students to the next level of mastery.

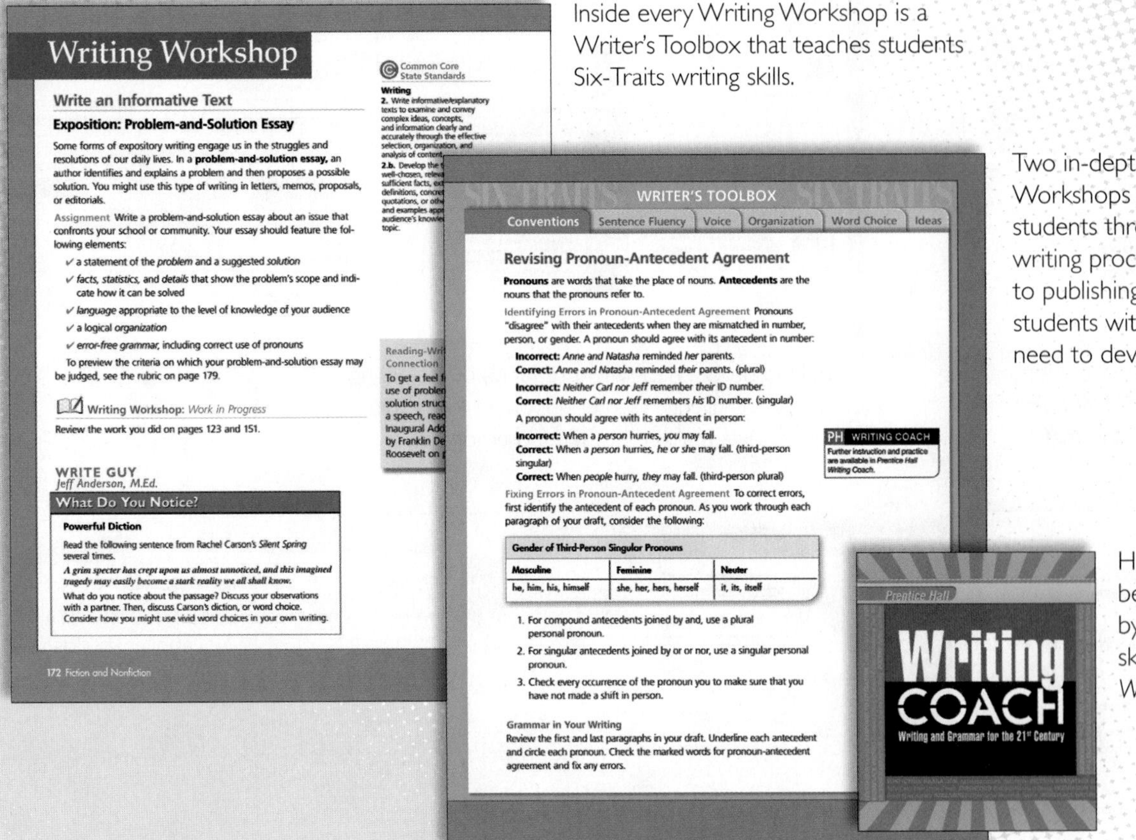

Inside every Writing Workshop is a Writer's Toolbox that teaches students Six-Traits writing skills.

Two in-depth Writing Workshops per unit take students through the complete writing process—from drafting to publishing—equipping students with the tools they need to develop as writers.

Help students become great writers by using guided writing skill instruction from *Writing Coach.*

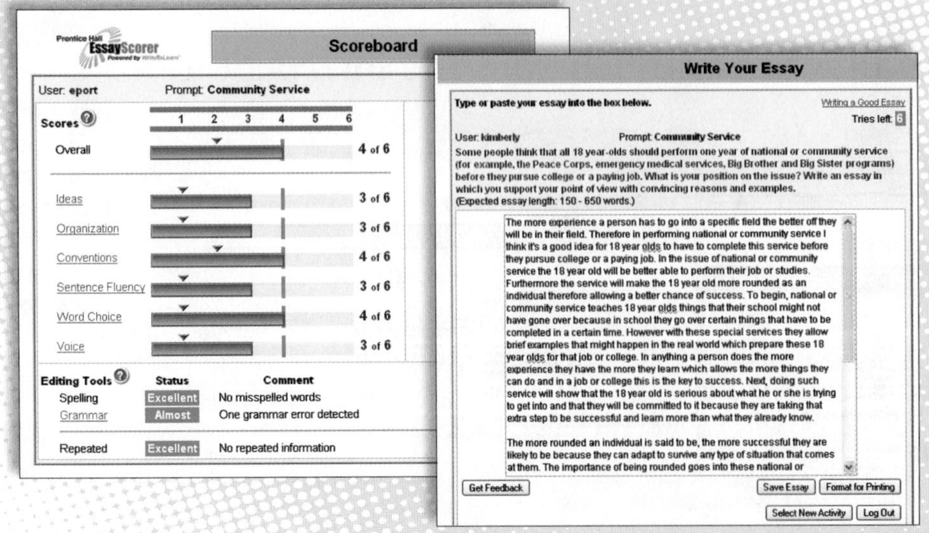

EssayScorer saves you hundreds of hours grading papers by providing students instant feedback on their writing.

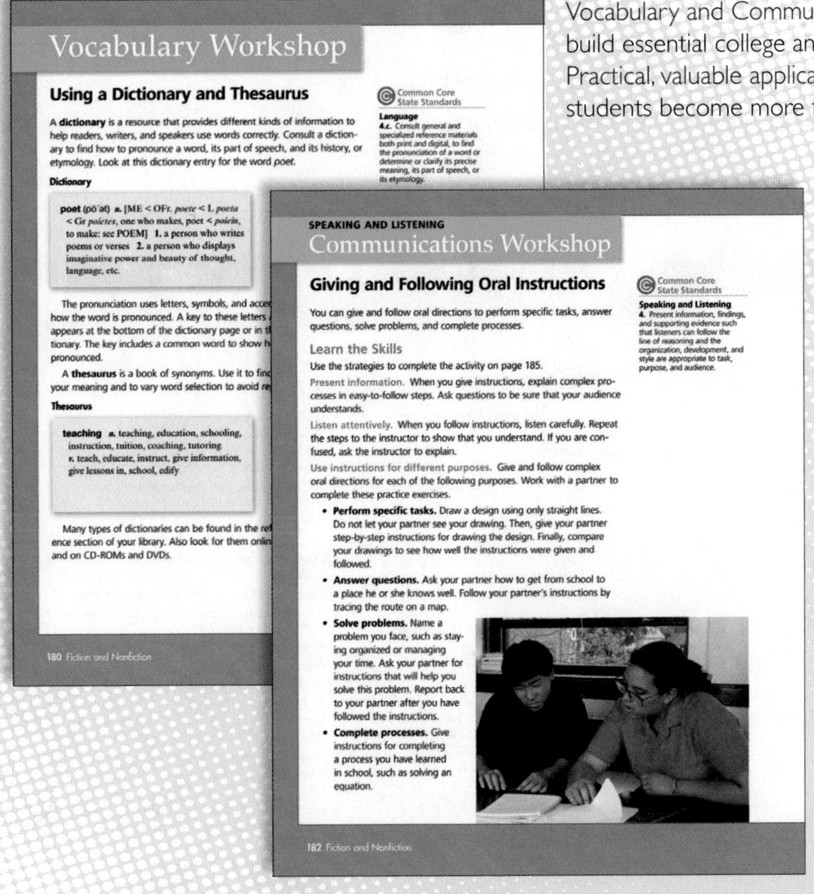

Vocabulary Workshop

Using a Dictionary and Thesaurus

A **dictionary** is a resource that provides different kinds of information to help readers, writers, and speakers use words correctly. Consult a dictionary to find how to pronounce a word, its part of speech, and its history, or etymology. Look at this dictionary entry for the word *poet*.

Common Core State Standards

Language
4.c. Consult general and specialized reference materials both print and digital, to find the pronunciation of a word or determine or clarify its precise meaning, its part of speech, or its etymology.

Dictionary

poet (pō′ət) *n.* [ME < OFr. *poete* < L *poeta* < Gr *poietes*, one who makes, poet < *poiein*, to make: see POEM] **1.** a person who writes poems or verses **2.** a person who displays imaginative power and beauty of thought, language, etc.

The pronunciation uses letters, symbols, and acce… how the word is pronounced. A key to these letters… appears at the bottom of the dictionary page or in t… tionary. The key includes a common word to show h… pronounced.

A **thesaurus** is a book of synonyms. Use it to fin… your meaning and to vary word selection to avoid re…

Thesaurus

teaching *n.* teaching, education, schooling, instruction, tuition, coaching, tutoring *v.* teach, educate, instruct, give information, give lessons in, school, edify

Many types of dictionaries can be found in the ref… ence section of your library. Also look for them onli… and on CD-ROMs and DVDs.

180 Fiction and Nonfiction

SPEAKING AND LISTENING

Communications Workshop

Giving and Following Oral Instructions

You can give and follow oral directions to perform specific tasks, answer questions, solve problems, and complete processes.

Common Core State Standards

Speaking and Listening
4. Present information, findings, and supporting evidence such that listeners can follow the line of reasoning and the organization, development, and style are appropriate to task, purpose, and audience.

Learn the Skills

Use the strategies to complete the activity on page 185.

Present information. When you give instructions, explain complex processes in easy-to-follow steps. Ask questions to be sure that your audience understands.

Listen attentively. When you follow instructions, listen carefully. Repeat the steps to the instructor to show that you understand. If you are confused, ask the instructor to explain.

Use instructions for different purposes. Give and follow complex oral directions for each of the following purposes. Work with a partner to complete these practice exercises.

- **Perform specific tasks.** Draw a design using only straight lines. Do not let your partner see your drawing. Then, give your partner step-by-step instructions for drawing the design. Finally, compare your drawings to see how well the instructions were given and followed.
- **Answer questions.** Ask your partner how to get from school to a place he or she knows well. Follow your partner's instructions by tracing the route on a map.
- **Solve problems.** Name a problem you face, such as staying organized or managing your time. Ask your partner for instructions that will help you solve this problem. Report back to your partner after you have followed the instructions.
- **Complete processes.** Give instructions for completing a process you have learned in school, such as solving an equation.

182 Fiction and Nonfiction

Vocabulary and Communications Workshops build essential college and career-ready skills. Practical, valuable applications are used to help students become more fluent in these skills.

Speaking and Listening are emphasized to help students develop the career-ready skills they need for life and work.

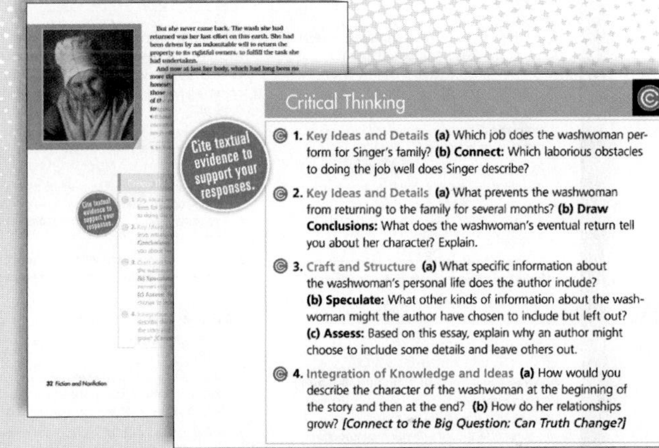

Critical Thinking

Cite textual evidence to support your responses.

1. Key Ideas and Details **(a)** Which job does the washwoman perform for Singer's family? **(b) Connect:** Which laborious obstacles to doing the job well does Singer describe?
2. Key Ideas and Details **(a)** What prevents the washwoman from returning to the family for several months? **(b) Draw Conclusions:** What does the washwoman's eventual return tell you about her character? Explain.
3. Craft and Structure **(a)** What specific information about the washwoman's personal life does the author include? **(b) Speculate:** What other kinds of information about the washwoman might the author have chosen to include but left out? **(c) Assess:** Based on this essay, explain why an author might choose to include some details and leave others out.
4. Integration of Knowledge and Ideas **(a)** How would you describe the character of the washwoman at the beginning of the story and then at the end? **(b)** How do her relationships grow? *[Connect to the Big Question: Can Truth Change?]*

Critical Thinking questions build learning skills by helping students apply their reading.

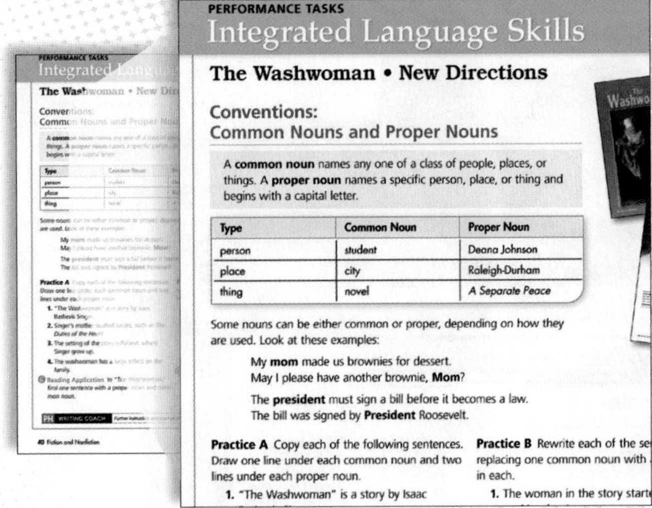

PERFORMANCE TASKS

Integrated Language Skills

The Washwoman • New Directions

Conventions: Common Nouns and Proper Nouns

A **common noun** names any one of a class of people, places, or things. A **proper noun** names a specific person, place, or thing and begins with a capital letter.

Type	Common Noun	Proper Noun
person	student	Deona Johnson
place	city	Raleigh-Durham
thing	novel	*A Separate Peace*

Some nouns can be either common or proper, depending on how they are used. Look at these examples:

My **mom** made us brownies for dessert.
May I please have another brownie, **Mom**?

The **president** must sign a bill before it becomes a law.
The bill was signed by **President** Roosevelt.

Practice A Copy each of the following sentences. Draw one line under each common noun and two lines under each proper noun.

1. "The Washwoman" is a story by Isaac

Practice B Rewrite each of the se… replacing one common noun with… in each.

1. The woman in the story start…

Integrated Language Skills offers full coverage of grammar, writing, speaking and listening, and research.

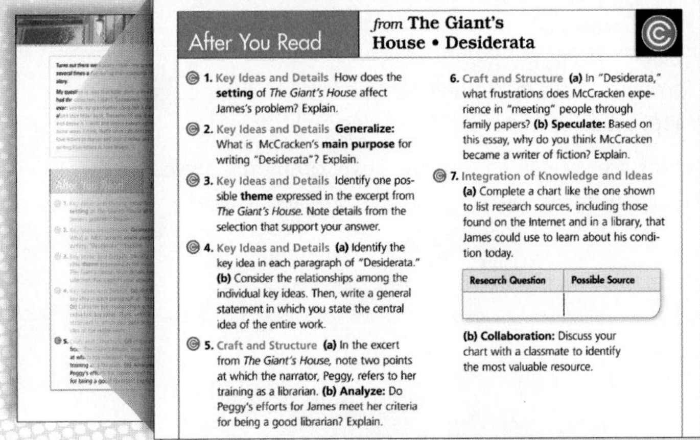

After You Read

from The Giant's House • Desiderata

1. Key Ideas and Details How does the **setting** of *The Giant's House* affect James's problem? Explain.
2. Key Ideas and Details **Generalize:** What is McCracken's **main purpose** for writing "Desiderata"? Explain.
3. Key Ideas and Details Identify one possible **theme** expressed in the excerpt from *The Giant's House*. Note details from the selection that support your answer.
4. Key Ideas and Details **(a)** Identify the key idea in each paragraph of "Desiderata." **(b)** Consider the relationships among the individual key ideas. Then, write a general statement in which you state the central idea of the entire work.
5. Craft and Structure **(a)** In the excerpt from *The Giant's House*, note two points at which the narrator, Peggy, refers to her training as a librarian. **(b) Analyze:** Do Peggy's efforts for James meet her criteria for being a good librarian? Explain.
6. Craft and Structure **(a)** In "Desiderata," what frustrations does McCracken experience in "meeting" people through family papers? **(b) Speculate:** Based on this essay, why do you think McCracken became a writer of fiction? Explain.
7. Integration of Knowledge and Ideas **(a)** Complete a chart like the one shown to list research sources, including those found on the Internet and in a library, that James could use to learn about his condition today.

Research Question	Possible Source

(b) Collaboration: Discuss your chart with a classmate to identify the most valuable resource.

Every selection is followed by critical thinking questions aligned to the organizational structure of the Common Core Reading Domain.

Ensure Mastery

The new standards require new assessments. *Prentice Hall Literature* provides traditional assessments along with new performance-based assessments as called for by the Common Core. Students are given opportunities to apply critical thinking to demonstrate mastery of the standards.

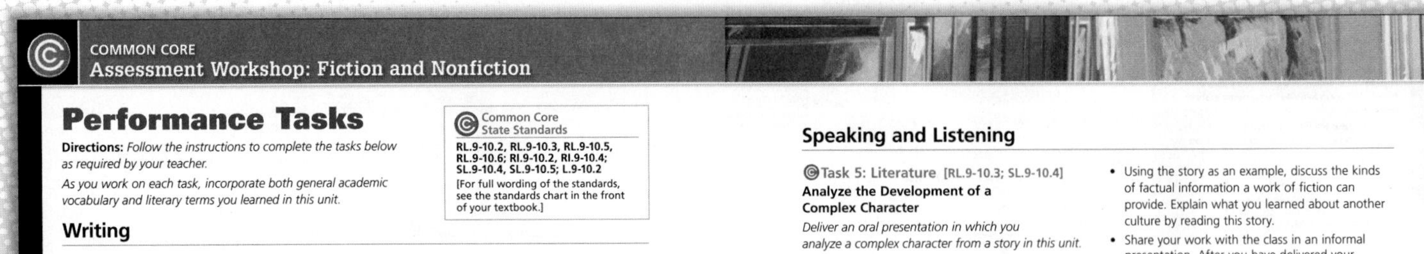

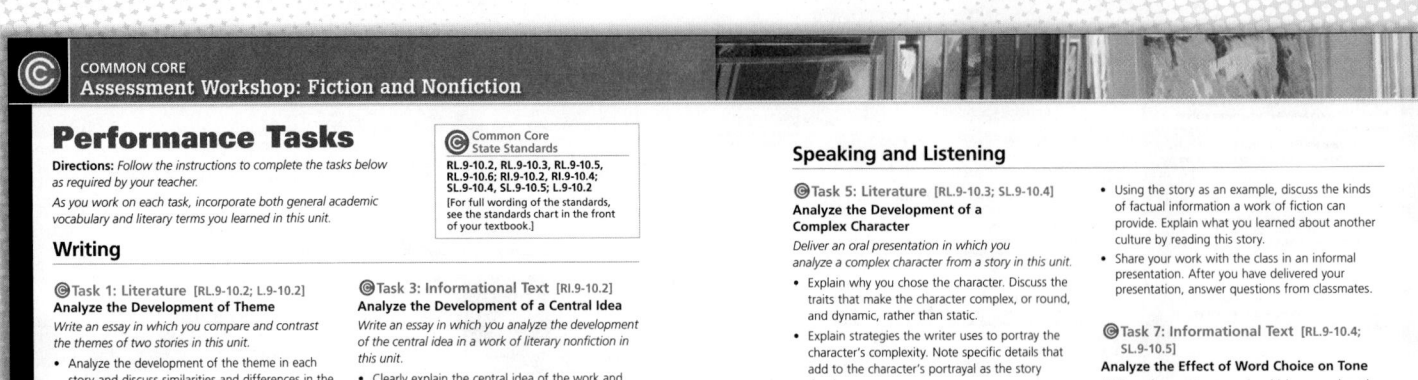

COMMON CORE
Assessment Workshop: Fiction and Nonfiction

Performance Tasks

Directions: *Follow the instructions to complete the tasks below as required by your teacher.*

As you work on each task, incorporate both general academic vocabulary and literary terms you learned in this unit.

Common Core State Standards
RL.9-10.2, RL.9-10.3, RL.9-10.5, RL.9-10.6; RI.9-10.2, RI.9-10.4; SL.9-10.4, SL.9-10.5; L.9-10.2
[For full wording of the standards, see the standards chart in the front of your textbook.]

Writing

Task 1: Literature [RL.9-10.2; L.9-10.2]
Analyze the Development of Theme

Write an essay in which you compare and contrast the themes of two stories in this unit.

- Analyze the development of the theme in each story and discuss similarities and differences in the message each expresses.
- Note specific strategies each author uses to introduce and develop the theme.
- Discuss specific details that contribute to the development of each theme. Explain what each detail adds.
- To ensure that readers understand your analysis, include an objective summary of each story.
- Capitalize proper nouns, including characters' and authors' names, correctly.

Task 2: Literature [RL.9-10.5]
Analyze the Effects of Structure in a Story

Write an essay in which you explain how the structure of a story in this unit leads to a specific emotional effect, such as tension or suspense.

- Identify the story's main conflict and summarize the narrative.
- Describe specific structural choices the writer makes. For example, discuss how much exposition the author provides and how he or she introduces the conflict. Also describe any use of plot devices, such as foreshadowing.
- Finally, explain how the story affects you as a reader and how the author's choices regarding structure contribute to that effect.
- Cite textual evidence to support your assertions.

Task 3: Informational Text [RI.9-10.2]
Analyze the Development of a Central Idea

Write an essay in which you analyze the development of the central idea in a work of literary nonfiction in this unit.

- Clearly explain the central idea of the work and discuss how it emerges or is introduced by the author.
- Identify specific details that shape and refine the central idea. Consider various types of evidence and explain what each adds to the development of the central idea.
- To ensure that readers understand your analysis, include an objective summary of the work.

Task 4: Informational Text [RI.9-10.6]
Analyze an Author's Purpose and Use of Rhetoric

Write an essay in which you determine an author's purpose and point of view and analyze his or her uses of rhetoric in a work of nonfiction in this unit.

- Explain the topic of the work and determine both the author's general and specific purposes for writing.
- Analyze the author's perspective or point of view on the topic. For example, explain whether the author has a positive or negative perspective or expresses a particular attitude toward the topic.
- Note specific examples of the author's uses of rhetoric. For example, identify examples of parallel structure or repetition. Then, explain how those uses of rhetoric work to advance the author's purpose and point of view.

Speaking and Listening

Task 5: Literature [RL.9-10.3; SL.9-10.4]
Analyze the Development of a Complex Character

Deliver an oral presentation in which you analyze a complex character from a story in this unit.

- Explain why you chose the character. Discuss the traits that make the character complex, or round, and dynamic, rather than static.
- Explain strategies the writer uses to portray the character's complexity. Note specific details that add to the character's portrayal as the story develops.
- Describe how the character's complexity, including his or her emotions, motivations, actions, and reactions, advances the plot and contributes to the story's theme.
- Present your analysis and evidence logically so that listeners can follow your line of reasoning. Make sure your overall approach, including both content and style, is appropriate for a classroom presentation on an academic topic.

Task 6: Literature [RL.9-10.6; SL.9-10.5]
Analyze a Cultural Perspective

Present a visual essay in which you analyze a cultural perspective reflected in a story in this unit.

- A visual essay combines images and text to explain an idea. The visual part of your essay may take the form of a slideshow, poster, or other format.
- Choose a story from this unit that reflects a cultural perspective from outside the United States. Explain how that cultural perspective is reflected in the setting and events as well as in characters' thoughts, emotions, actions, and reactions.
- Using the story as an example, discuss the kinds of factual information a work of fiction can provide. Explain what you learned about another culture by reading this story.
- Share your work with the class in an informal presentation. After you have delivered your presentation, answer questions from classmates.

Task 7: Informational Text [RI.9-10.4; SL.9-10.5]
Analyze the Effect of Word Choice on Tone

Write and present an essay in which you analyze the cumulative effect of word choice on tone in a work of literary nonfiction in this unit.

- Choose a work of literary nonfiction from this unit that offers a clear and distinct tone. Explain your choice.
- Identify specific word choices that contribute to the creation of that tone.
- Illustrate your analysis by creating a graphic organizer or chart that captures your ideas visually.
- Present your essay, including charts or graphic organizers, to the class. Use technology to display graphics, or distribute them as handouts.

Can truth change?
At the beginning of Unit 1, you participated in a discussion about the Big Question. Now that you have completed the unit, write a response to the question. Discuss how your initial ideas have either changed or been reinforced. Cite specific examples from the literature in this unit, from other subject areas, and from your own life to support your ideas. Use Big Question vocabulary words (see page 3) in your response.

188 Fiction and Nonfiction

Assessment Workshop 189

Performance Tasks in the unit Assessment Workshops call for the application of higher-level thinking skills.

Students are assessed across the key Common Core domains of reading, writing, speaking and listening, and language.

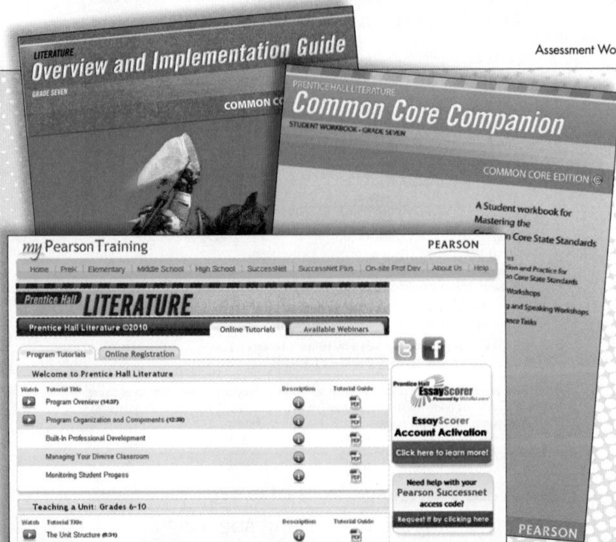

Prentice Hall Literature offers additional resources to ensure a successful implementation.

COMMON CORE
Assessment Workshop: Fiction and Nonfiction

Cumulative Review

I. Reading Literature

Directions: *Read the passage. Then, answer each question that follows.*

Common Core State Standards
RL.9-10.2, RL.9-10.3, RL.9-10.5; L.9-10.4.a
[For the full wording of the standards, see the standards chart in the front of your textbook.]

I was born in Brooklyn, New York and lived there until I was eleven. I had never really been outside the city. Sure, I had been to Long Island for beach days with my family, but I had never been to the country. My mother got a job Upstate, and suddenly my parents were planning the move. They said that living in the country would be a great experience for all of us, but I was miserable. In August, as we drove the long winding country roads to our new home, I barely said a word.

Many things were lacking in the country. There was no basketball game to pick up. There was no Thai food. There was no skateboarding. There was no sitting on the stoop. Most importantly, there were no old friends. I was so lonely—and bored. It was just my mom, my dad, and me. We were in the middle of nowhere with the closest neighbor over a mile away. Life as I had known it came to an end that August day.

Dad tried to get me to go fishing, but I thought the whole idea was disgusting. Mom tried to get me to walk in the woods, but I didn't like all the bugs, and the brambles scratched my legs. I wanted to go back to Brooklyn in the worst way. All of that would soon change.

I was petrified when I walked into my homeroom. Everyone there knew everyone else, and I did not know anyone. I was set apart from all the other boys by my pale skin and long hair. I sat in the back, and no one said anything to me. The teacher came in and introduced herself.

"Class, we have two new students with us this year." My ears perked up at the word *two,* and I scanned the room for another outsider.

"First, I want to introduce Dave from Brooklyn." The teacher pointed to me. My face flushed as I said "Hi."

"Next, meet Alexis from Washington, D.C."

"Call me Al," she said to the class, looking as lost as I felt.

I had been staring at the back of her head. Her hair was as short as mine was long. I knew immediately that this was not only the year of the Big Move, but it was also the year of the New Best Friend.

1. From which **point of view** is this story told?
   A. first person
   B. second person
   C. third-person limited
   D. third-person omniscient

2. Which element from the passage helped you determine the **point of view**?
   A. The narrator directly addresses his audience, the reader.
   B. The narrator refers to himself as *I* and *me.*
   C. The narrator knows only one person's thoughts.
   D. The narrator has insight into all the people's thoughts.

3. Which word best describes the **author's voice**?
   A. formal
   B. casual
   C. friendly
   D. sarcastic

4. Which of the following sentences is an example of **foreshadowing**?
   A. All of that would soon change.
   B. I had never really been outside of the city.
   C. I wanted to go back to Brooklyn in the worst way.
   D. The teacher pointed to me.

5. Which event occurs during the **rising action** of the narrative?
   A. Dave is born in Brooklyn.
   B. Dave makes a new friend.
   C. Dave's mom gets a job Upstate.
   D. Dave meets Alexis.

6. Which event is the turning point, or **climax,** of the narrative?
   A. Dave moves in August.
   B. Dave wants to move back to Brooklyn.
   C. Dave refuses to go fishing.
   D. Dave hears the teacher say "two."

7. **Vocabulary** Which word is closest in meaning to the underlined word *petrified*?
   A. angry
   B. terrified
   C. annoyed
   D. disturbed

8. How is the conflict in the story resolved?
   A. Dave makes a new friend in the city.
   B. Dave wants to return to Brooklyn.
   C. Dave's mom does not like her job.
   D. Dave goes fishing with his dad.

9. In what way does the choice of narrator affect the description of the country in paragraph 2?
   A. Life in the country seems frightening.
   B. The country appears to offer lots of fun activities.
   C. Moving to the country sounds like a good idea.
   D. The country seems to lack a lot of things that life in the city has to offer.

Timed Writing

10. In a well-developed essay, **identify** the conflict in this story. **Explain** how the author of the text establishes the conflict. Cite evidence from the text to support your analysis. [20 minutes]

GO ON

Traditional Cumulative Review prepares students for high-stakes testing.

Pearson SuccessNet | Home | Content | Planning | Classes | Reports | About My Account Log out Help
Lesson Progress Test Scores Mastery Item Analysis Self Assessments

Classroom Test Reports — Success Tracker

Save as Spreadsheet | Save

Class/Group: 1 - Period 1 Grade 6 ; PHLitOnlinel Grade 6
View by: Common Core Standards

Legend: ● Mastered × Not mastered – Not assessed

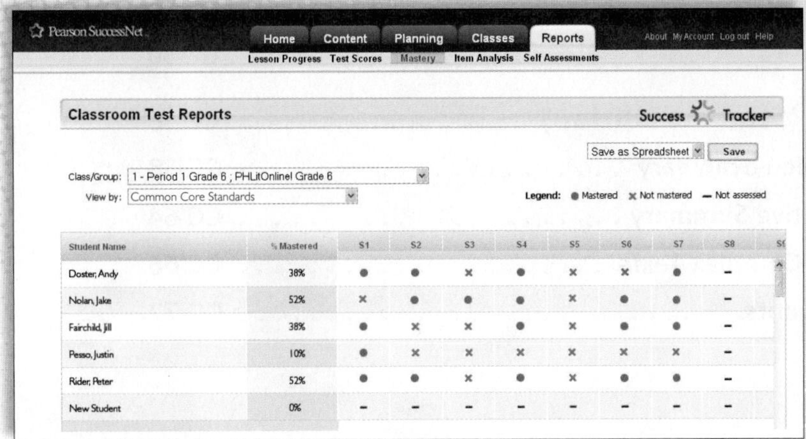

Student Name	% Mastered	S1	S2	S3	S4	S5	S6	S7	S8	S
Doster, Andy	38%	●	●	×	●	×	×	●	–	
Nolan, Jake	52%	×	●	●	●	×	●	●	–	
Fairchild, Jill	38%	●	×	×	●	×	●	●	–	
Pesso, Justin	10%	●	×	×	×	×	×	×	–	
Rider, Peter	52%	●	●	×	●	×	●	●	–	
New Student	0%	–	–	–	–	–	–	–	–	

SuccessTracker® includes reporting tools to make progress monitoring easier.

COMMON CORE
Teacher's Edition Table of Contents

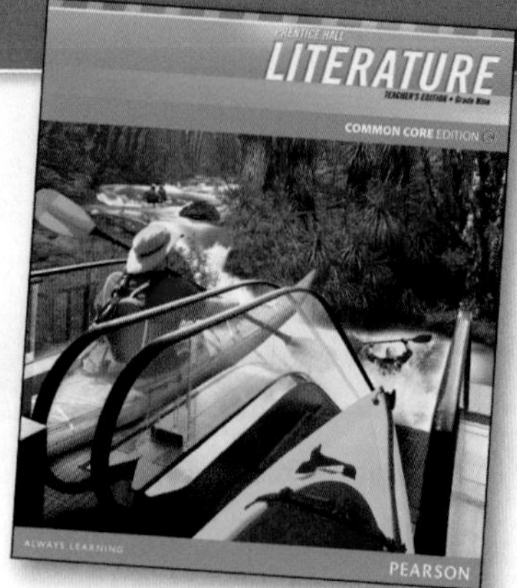
LITERATURE
PEARSON

Research Bibliography

Reading and Concept-Driven Instruction

Alexander, Patricia A., and Tamara Jetton. "Learning from Text: A Multidimensional and Developmental Perspective." *Handbook of Reading Research*, vol. 3. Ed. M. L. Kamil, P. B. Mosenthal, P. D. Pearson, and R. Barr, 285–310. Mahwah, NJ: Lawrence Erlbaum Associates, 2000.

Blau, Sheridan. *The Literature Workshop: Teaching Texts and Their Readers.* Portsmouth: Heinemann Press, 2003.

Buehl, Doug, Judith L. Irvin, and Ronald M. Klemp. *Reading and the High School Student: Strategies to Enhance Literacy.* Boston: Allyn and Bacon, 2007.

Buehl, Doug, Judith L. Irvin, and Barbara J. Radcliffe. *Strategies to Enhance Literacy and Learning in Middle School Content Area Classrooms.* Boston: Allyn and Bacon, 2007.

Daniels, Harvey. *Literature Circles: Voice and Choice in Book Clubs and Reading Groups.* Portland: Stenhouse Publishers, 2002.

———*Mini-Lessons for Literature Circles.* Portsmouth: Heinemann Press, 2005.

Gallagher, Kelly. *Reading Reasons: Motivational Mini-Lessons for the Middle and High School.* Portland: Stenhouse Publishers, 2003.

Guthrie, John T. and Allan Wigfield. "Engagement and Motivation in Reading." *Handbook of Reading Research*, vol. 3, eds. M. L. Kamil, P. B. Mosenthal, P. D. Pearson, and R. Barr, 403–422. Mahwah: Lawrence Erlbaum Associates, 2000.

Harvey, Stephanie, and Anne Goudvis. "Determining Importance in Text: The Nonfiction Connection." *Strategies That Work: Teaching Comprehension to Enhance Understanding.* Portland: Stenhouse Publishers, 2000.

Langer, Judith. "Beating the Odds: Teaching Middle and High School Students to Read and Write Well," 1999. Center on English Learning and Achievement. May 2003.<http://cela.albany.edu/eie2/main.html>

National Reading Panel. *Teaching Children to Read: An Evidence-Based Assessment of the Scientific Research on Reading and Its Implications for Reading Instruction.* NIH Publication 00–4769. Bethesda: U.S. Department of Health and Human Services, 2000.

Pressley, Michael. "What Should Comprehension Instruction Be the Instruction Of?" *Handbook of Reading Research*, vol. 3, eds. M. L. Kamil, P. B. Mosenthal, P. D. Pearson, and R. Barr, 545–562. Mahwah: Lawrence Erlbaum Associates, 2000.

Scieszka, Jon. *Guys Write for Guys Read.* New York: Penguin Group, 2005.

Wiggins, Grant P., and Jay McTighe. *Understanding by Design.* Alexandria: Association for Supervision and Curriculum Development, 2006.

Vocabulary, Writing, and Grammar

Anderson, Jeff. *Mechanically Inclined: Building Grammar, Usage, and Style into Writer's Workshop.* Portland: Stenhouse Publishers, 2005.

Baumann, J. F., and E. J. Kame'enui. *Vocabulary Instruction: From Research to Practice.* New York: Guilford Press, 2004.

Blachowicz, Camille, and Peter Fisher. *Teaching Vocabulary in All Classrooms*, Second Edition. Upper Saddle River: Merrill, 2002.

Feber, Jane. *Creative Book Reports: Fun Projects With Rubrics for Fiction and Nonfiction.* Gainesville: Maupin House Publishing, Inc., 2004.

———*Active Word Play.* Gainesville: Maupin House Publishing, Inc., 2008.

Kinsella, Kate. "Strategies to Teach Academic Vocabulary." *Strategies to Promote Academic Literacy for Second Language Learners Within the English Language Arts Classroom.* 2005.

Kinsella, Kate and Kevin Feldman. *Narrowing the Language Gap: The Case for Explicit Vocabulary Instruction.* New York: Scholastic, 2005.

Marzano, Robert J. "The Developing Vision of Vocabulary Instruction." In Baumann and Kame'enui, *Vocabulary Instruction: From Research to Practice.* New York: Guilford Press, 2004.

Differentiated Instruction for Universal Access

Allington, Richard L. *What Really Matters for Struggling Readers: Designing Research Based Programs.* New York: Longman, 2001.

Download the research report at pearsonschool.com/phlit

Armbruster, Bonnie, and Thomas H. Anderson. "On Selecting 'Considerate' Content Area Textbooks." *Remedial and Special Education*, 9.1 (1988): 47–52.

Balderrama, María V., and Lynne T. Díaz-Rico. *Teacher Performance Expectations for Educating English Learners*. Boston: Allyn and Bacon, 2006.

Ball, Arnetha F. and Ted Lardner. *African American Literacies Unleashed: Vernacular English and the Composition Classroom*. Carbondale: Southern Illinois University Press, 2005.

Carnie, Douglas, Jerry Silbert, and Edward J. Kame'enui. *Direct Instruction Reading*. 3rd ed. Upper Saddle River: Prentice Hall, 1997.

Deshler, Donald D., Keith B. Lenz, and Brenda R. Kissam. *Teaching Content to All: Evidence-Based Inclusive Practices in Middle and Secondary Schools*. Boston: Allyn and Bacon, 2004.

Francis, David, Mabel Rivera, Nonie Lesaux, Michael Kieffer, and Hector Rivera. *Practical Guidelines for the Education of English Language Learners*. Portsmouth: RMC Research Corporation, Center on Instruction, 2006.

Vaughn, Sharon, Candace S. Bos, and Jeanne Shay Schumm. *Teaching Exceptional, Diverse, and At-Risk Students in the General Education Classroom*. Boston: Allyn and Bacon, 2002.

Pearson Prentice Hall Literature: A Rich Tradition of Learning Success

The Research Process

Since 1988, *Pearson Prentice Hall Literature* has been at the forefront of language arts instruction, providing teachers and their students with quality instruction and assessment tools to ensure success. Each successive edition builds on the strong heritage of the program. Our research comprised these three design stages:

1. EXPLORATORY NEEDS ASSESSMENT

In conjunction with Pearson Prentice Hall authors, we conducted research proven to explore educational reading methodologies. This research was incorporated into our instructional strategy and pedagogy to create a more effective literature program. This stage included:

- reading research
- review of state standards
- teacher interviews

2. FORMATIVE RESEARCH, DEVELOPMENT, AND FIELD-TESTING

During this phase of the research, we developed and field-tested prototype material with students and teachers. Results informed revisions to the final design and pedagogy. Formative research included:

- field-testing of prototypes in classroom pilots
- classroom observations
- teacher reviews
- supervisor reviews
- educator advisory panels

3. SUMMATIVE RESEARCH AND VALIDATION RESEARCH

Finally, we have conducted and will continue to conduct longer-term research under actual classroom conditions. Research at this phase includes:

- pilot-testing
- prepublication learner verification research
- postpublication validation studies, including validation of test questions
- evaluation of results on standardized tests

Harvey Daniels
Voice and Choice

Excerpts from "Using Leveled Selections" and "Leveled Reading Selections, A Key to Differentiation" by Harvey Daniels

"With leveled texts, all students can understand their selection—and no one is left behind."

We have all watched it unfold.

You select a wonderful book or article for your class to read. You hand it out to the students and what happens? The text is way too hard for some kids, and far too easy for others, and "boring" to still others. Not a good feeling.

Using Leveled Readings. Happily, research on differentiated instruction shows us a better way: leveled selections. **Prentice Hall Literature** offers two levels of text. All students can understand and enjoy their selection and still learn the same required skills—and no one is left behind.

Why are leveled selections so important?

- If we expect kids to grow as readers, they must spend part of each day reading *text they can read.* As the Common Core State Standards put it: "Students need opportunities to stretch their reading abilities but also to experience the satisfaction and pleasure of easy, fluent reading, both of which the Standards allow for."
- A *choice* of texts means that more students will have the background knowledge to understand and enjoy the chosen selection.
- All students need to read increasingly challenging text as the school year unfolds, but every student does not need to read the same texts. As the Common Core standards explain: "Teachers who have had success using particular texts that are easier than those required for a given grade band should feel free to continue to use them, so long as the general movement during a given school year is toward texts of higher levels of complexity."

These are the reasons **Prentice Hall Literature** offers two leveled selections for almost every lesson—one more accessible and one more challenging. Every student can be challenged at his or her own level, from lesson to lesson, throughout the school year.

"When we make accommodations like leveled selections, we often find that such accommodations make learning work better for everyone."

Harvey Daniels is known for his passionate work on literacy and student-led book clubs. He is the author of *Literature Circles: Voice and Choice in Book Clubs and Reading Groups* and *Mini-lessons for Literature Circles.* He has been a classroom teacher, writing project director, author, and university professor.

Read the full text of Harvey Daniels's articles at PHLitOnline.

Grant Wiggins
Better Big Questions

Excerpts from "Teaching Literature by Design: Introducing the Big Questions" by Grant Wiggins

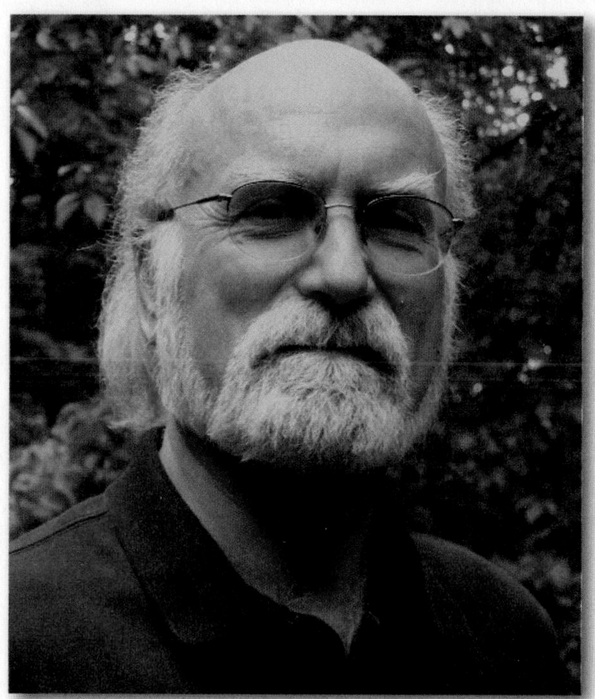

"... our methods have to foster that questioning and meaning-making."

Grant Wiggins is the co-author of *Understanding By Design,** published by ASCD. He is also the president of Authentic Education in Hopewell, New Jersey. He consults with schools, districts, and state education departments on a variety of reform issues. His work has been supported by the Pew Charitable Trusts, the Geraldine R. Dodge Foundation, and the National Science Foundation.

Read the full text of Grant Wiggins's article at PHLitOnline.

*The Association for Supervision of Curriculum Development (ASCD), publisher of the "Understanding by Design Handbook" co-authored by Grant Wiggins and registered owner of the trademark "Understanding by Design," has not authorized, approved, or sponsored this work and is in no way affiliated with Pearson or its products.

A Big Question is different from many of the questions teachers typically ask students in class.

A Big Question is more of a *why?* or a *so what?* question rather than a *what?* or a *where?* question. We are not looking for an answer, really; we are inviting inquiry and reflection. The Big Questions awaken curiosity and thus provide a purpose for reading.

What Makes a Question "Big"?

"Big" connotes "substantial"—occupying a considerable amount of space and time. A question is "big" or "weighty" if it has significant depth and breadth—occupying a good deal of our psychic space, such as our thoughts and feelings. Another aspect of "bigness" is the time it consumes. Vital issues and inquiries remain alive over days, months, and years, unlike simple or superficial queries. Important questions recur over and through time, as we rethink and reflect on our present and past experiences. **Prentice Hall Literature** provides Big Questions that meet the criteria in ways that others do not.

- The questions cannot be answered with a list or a single answer.
- The questions are designed to allow answers to change to accommodate new information or experience.
- The questions are designed to encourage answers that change over time.

Why Ask Big Questions? The teacher has a different intent when asking a "big" as opposed to an "academic" question. If we want students to end up asking Big Questions on their own, then our courses have to be designed "backward" from that goal. If we want students to learn from their reading, our methods have to foster that questioning and meaning-making.

"Important questions occur over and through time."

Kelly Gallagher
Multidraft Reading

Excerpts from "The Value of Second Draft Reading" and "Powerful, Purposeful Reading" by Kelly Gallagher

"In our classrooms, we are the 'tour guides.'"

Where do adolescents get the idea that they can read complex text one time and get it? More importantly, how can we help our students to understand that much of our deepest thinking comes when we reread? How can we teach our students to recognize the value of second-draft reading?

The Importance of Rereading The principal strategy that good readers employ when confronted by difficult text is to reread it. If the text is particularly difficult, you might have students read the text first with the sole purpose of monitoring where they were confused. Use the blue dots in the student edition of **Prentice Hall Literature** to help students "chunk" the text into passages with logical pause points to stop, reread, and clarify.

Multi-Lens Reading Students often read difficult text better when they have been provided a purpose for their reading. In our classrooms, we are the "tour guides." We create student tours by first determining the purpose for each reading. Providing students with a specific purpose gives them a more focused, meaningful reading experience.

Prentice Hall Literature provides the tools for multiple reading purposes.

When students read with a purpose in mind, their anxiety is lowered, their comprehension deepens, and they are given the confidence to approach works they might have otherwise shunned.

"Providing students with a specific purpose gives them a more focused, meaningful reading experience."

Kelly Gallagher is a full-time English teacher at Magnolia High School in Anaheim, California, where he has taught for twenty-two years. He is the author of several books:

- *Reading Reasons: Motivational Mini-Lessons for the Middle and High School*
- *Deeper Reading: Comprehending Challenging Texts*
- *Teaching Adolescent Writers*
- *Readicide*

Read the full text of Kelly Gallagher's article at PHLitOnline.

Elfrieda H. Hiebert

What Is Text Complexity?

"... greater focus on text complexity will help ... prepare students for the increasing demands of required reading in college and the workplace."

The Common Core State Standards cite research that shows that the difficulty of texts used in elementary and secondary classrooms in the United States has decreased over the past 50 years, while the difficulty of college texts has not. As a result, students entering post-secondary education are not prepared for the level of text complexity required to be successful.

To address this issue, the Standards have identified text complexity grade bands (K–1, 2–3, 4–5, 6–8, 9–10, 11–12), in which students read increasingly complex texts within a defined spectrum. Ultimately, greater focus on text complexity will help close the gap that exists between secondary and post-secondary education and prepare students for the increasing demands of required reading in college and the workplace.

The Common Core State Standards identify a three-part model for measuring a text's complexity. This model, as detailed below, includes quantitative and qualitative measures as well as variables of individual readers.

Quantitative Dimensions

Quantitative dimensions are aspects of text complexity that can be measured with traditional readability formulas, such as the Lexile measure. These formulas measure such aspects of a text as word length and frequency, total number of words, average sentence length, and text cohesion.

Qualitative Dimensions

Qualitative dimensions consist of "those aspects of text complexity best measured or only measurable by an attentive human reader." Qualitative measures include categories such as a student's familiarity with a text's structure, levels of meaning, language clarity and conventionality, and knowledge demands, or what the reader needs to know to access the text.

Reader and Task Considerations

Reader and task considerations include an evaluation of student variables, such as the reader's motivation, background knowledge, experience, and cognitive abilities. Evaluating text complexity is best done by the classroom teacher, who brings to bear professional judgments concerning subject matter and individual students.

"... students read increasingly complex texts ..."

Dr. Elfrieda "Freddy" H. Hiebert is the President and CEO of TextProject, Inc. Her model of accessible texts for beginning and struggling readers—TEXT—has been used to develop several reading programs. Most recently, Dr. Hiebert served on the Common Core State Standards development team focused on text complexity. Dr. Hiebert has published more than 130 research articles, chapters in edited volumes, and books. In particular, Hiebert's interests lie in how fluency, vocabulary, and knowledge can be fostered through appropriate texts.

Text Complexity: Building Capacity for All Students

To better gauge a text's difficulty, Dr. Elfrieda Hiebert has created a Text Complexity Multi-Index. In this model, four comprehensive measures and considerations are taken into account to determine a text's appropriateness for a student or group of students.

The four parts of Dr. Hiebert's model expand upon the Common Core State Standards' three-part model for measuring text complexity. A critical component of both models is that qualitative measures and reader-task considerations are balanced with quantitative measures to achieve an overall text complexity recommendation. By measuring text complexity, both quantitative and qualitative, teachers can challenge students to read more complex texts as they move toward college and career readiness.

In Dr. Hiebert's Multi-Index, quantitative measures consist of Overall Text Difficulty and Specifics of Text Difficulty. Qualitative Measures include Themes and Knowledge Demands. Reader and Task in the Common Core aligns with Purpose and Task in Dr. Hiebert's index. These four parts of Dr. Hiebert's Text Complexity Multi-Index are explained below.

Text Complexity Multi-Index

❶ Themes and Knowledge Demands

- The reader's familiarity with the theme of a text and the concept presented must be considered as part of the assessment of text complexity.
- Knowledge demands are based on the background knowledge students need to bring to a given text. Teachers can assess background knowledge through informal classroom discussions.

❷ Specifics of Text Difficulty

- Readability scores are based on quantitative variables, such as average sentence length and overall word frequency.
- Sentence length is determined by averaging the number of words in each sentence in a selection. Formulaically speaking, shorter sentences should mean easier reading. However, teachers must consider conceptual and thematic complexity of a selection to accurately assess a text's difficulty.
- Word frequency refers to how often the same words appear in a text. A low score indicates that the text most likely has words that students may not have encountered. This is especially true when dealing with informational texts that may address unfamiliar content and concepts.

❸ Overall Quantitative Text Difficulty

- Overall quantitative text difficulty can be determined by a readability formula. Frequently used readability formulas include Lexile, Dale-Chall, and Spache.

❹ Purpose and Task

- Purpose and task refer to the why and what of reading—questions such as "Why am I reading this text?" and "What tasks are involved before, during, and after reading to build knowledge?"
- To address purpose and task, teachers use professional judgment to assess reader and task compatibility.

The Text Complexity Rubric in *Prentice Hall Literature*

The following rubric is a sample from the Grade 9, Unit 1 Teacher's Edition. The leveled texts "The Washwoman" and "New Directions" are featured in Unit 1 of this grade level. The leveling of these selections relies on many factors as depicted in the measures outlined here.

Analyze the Qualitative and Quantitative measures to determine the complexity of these texts.

Text Complexity Rubric: Leveled Texts

Text complexity is determined by both qualitative and quantitative measures. For this reason, the quantitative measure of a more complex selection may be lower than that of a more accessible selection.

			✓ The Washwoman	✓✓ New Directions
1	Qualitative Measures	Context/ Knowledge Demands	Jewish neighborhood in Poland, early 1900s 1 2 ③ 4 5	African American mother living in the South 1 2 ③ 4 5
		Structure/Language Conventionality and Clarity	Numerous long sentences; on-level vocabulary 1 2 ③ 4 5	Little dialogue; challenging vocabulary 1 2 3 ④ 5
		Levels of Meaning/ Purpose/Concept Level	Accessible concept (determination to complete a task) 1 2 ③ 4 5	Irony; accessible concept (journey from adversity to success) 1 2 3 ④ 5
2	Quantitative Measures	Text Length	Word Count: 1,976	Word Count: 763
		Lexile	870L	1360L
3	Overall Complexity		✓ More accessible	✓✓ More complex

1 Themes and Knowledge Demands

Context/Knowledge Demands: The accessibility of texts is dependent in part on the range of students' experiences and their background knowledge.

Structure/Language Conventionality and Clarity: Conventional and unconventional structures as well as domain-specific language and vocabulary all affect the ability of students to access text.

Levels of Meaning/Purpose/Concept Level: An author's use of either single or multiple levels of meaning impacts the accessibility of a text's concepts.

2 Specifics of Text Difficulty

Pearson has provided two quantitative measures of text complexity—text length and Lexile score. Use these measures in tandem with qualitative measures to make informed choices.

3 Overall Quantitative Text Difficulty

Based on the criteria cited above for Themes and Knowledge Demands and Specifics of Text Difficulty, texts can be deemed either more accessible or more complex.

Text Complexity: Reader and Task Suggestions

	✓ The Washwoman		✓✓ New Directions	
4	**Preparing to Read the Text**	**Leveled Tasks**	**Preparing to Read the Text**	**Leveled Tasks**
	• Using the Background information on TE p. 25, discuss the lives of Jews and gentiles in Poland in the 1900s. • Discuss with students ways in which cultural differences can lead to hardships. • Guide students to use Multidraft Reading strategies (TE p. 25).	*Knowledge Demands* If students will have difficulty with knowledge demands, have them first read to identify details about the washwoman's determination. Then, have them reread, taking notes on interesting details of daily life in the setting. *Synthesizing* If students will not have difficulty with selection knowledge demands, have them note as they read ways in which Singer uses setting to help convey his theme.	• Discuss the saying "Necessity is the mother of invention." • Refer to the Background section on TE p. 35, and discuss difficulties uneducated African-American women in the South in the early 1900s faced. • Guide students to use Multidraft Reading strategies (TE p. 35).	*Knowledge Demands* If students will have difficulty with cultural or historical knowledge, have them first read to identify details that show Annie's determination. Then, have them reread, identifying words or sentences that are unclear. *Synthesizing* If students will not have difficulty with selection knowledge demands, have them note as they read ways in which Angelou creates narrative style.

4 Purpose and Task

Specific pre-reading suggestions are given in "Preparing to Read the Text." These are followed by "Leveled Tasks" that will help you guide students' comprehension as they analyze, synthesize, or evaluate the concept development of selections. Teachers may adapt the leveled tasks, as needed, to suit the needs of their students.

Jim Cummins
Second Language Learning

Excerpts from "The Challenge of Learning Academic English" by Jim Cummins

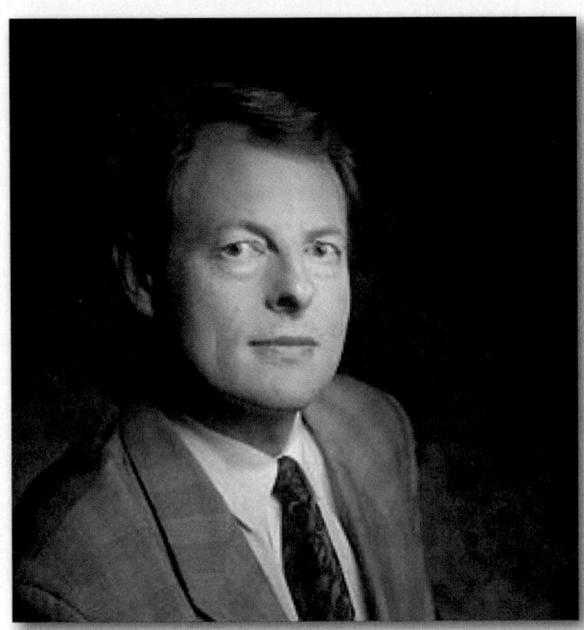

"Students who gain a sense of control over language will want to use it for powerful purposes."

Learning difficulties faced by struggling readers can derive from a variety of sources. This is true regardless of whether their home language is English or a language other than English. Intervention should address the specific difficulties they are experiencing.

Scaffold Instruction We can promote literacy engagement among ELL students and struggling readers by using "scaffolds" or supports to make the input more comprehensible (e.g., through graphic organizers, demonstrations, etc.). It is also important to scaffold students' use of language.

Build Background Effective instruction for ELL students and struggling readers will also activate students' prior knowledge and build background knowledge as needed. Learning can be defined as the integration of new knowledge or skills with the knowledge or skills we already possess. Therefore, it is crucial to activate ELL students' preexisting knowledge so that they can relate new information to what they already know.

Validate Culture Identity affirmation is also crucial for literacy engagement. Students who feel their culture and identity validated in the classroom are much more likely to engage with literacy than those who perceive their culture and identity ignored or devalued.

Literacy engagement among ELL students and struggling readers also requires that teachers across the curriculum explain how language works and stimulate students' curiosity about language. Students who gain a sense of control over language will want to use it for powerful purposes.

"Students who feel their culture and identity validated in the classroom are much more likely to engage with literacy. . . ."

Jim Cummins's research focuses on literacy development in multilingual school contexts as well as English Language Learners' academic trajectories. He has been a recipient of the International Reading Association's Albert J. Harris award, and has published in *Educational Researcher, International Education Journal, NABE Journal, and TESOL Quarterly.*

Read the full text of Jim Cummins's article at PHLitOnline.

Sharroky Hollie
Culturally Responsive Instruction

Excerpts from "Expanding Academic Home Language" and "Navigating Cultural Discourse Styles" by Sharroky Hollie

"By capitalizing on the student's own resources, a teacher ensures success."

Sharroky Hollie is the Executive Director of the Center for Culturally Responsive Teaching and Learning. He is an assistant professor at California State University and a visiting professor at Webster University in St. Louis. His work focuses on African American education and on second language methodology. In addition to his university teaching, Dr. Hollie also teaches professional development courses, and he is the co-founding director of the Culture and Language Academy of Success, an independent charter school in Los Angeles.

Read the complete texts of Sharroky Hollie's articles on PHLitOnline.

Students entering the classroom bring with them a variety of experiences, traditions, interpretive frameworks, and learning styles. Culturally responsive instruction begins when a teacher acknowledges this variety as a positive resource for education. By capitalizing on the student's own resources, a teacher ensures success.

What is Culturally Responsive Instruction?

To make academic progress, a student must build on one success to another. How do we ensure that we are teaching to and through students' personal and cultural strengths and prior accomplishments?

- Build bridges from what students already know or have experienced to new knowledge and skills.
- Create a cooperative learning environment rich in affirmations of students' heritages.
- Build not just on individual strengths, but on the new strength that emerges when individuals join together in a community that respects their diversity.

Building on Strength

A key premise for culturally responsive pedagogy is that education proceeds from students' strengths and not students' weaknesses. **Prentice Hall Literature** consistently supports culturally responsive instruction with each selection in the anthology. Integrated throughout each lesson plan are the strategies for using what students bring with them into the classroom to enrich learning and foster success.

"... education proceeds from students' strengths and not students' weaknesses."

William G. Brozo
Response to Intervention

"Within RTI, the frontline of prevention is Tier 1, or the general education classroom, where every student regardless of ability is to receive high-quality instruction. What's revolutionary about these new standards is that they situate literacy and language development squarely within the content areas....Common core proponents assert that prevailing literacy curriculum needs to shift from a focus on developing reading skills and building fluency with simple narratives toward reading and writing to gain knowledge and express new understandings with informational text."

William G. Brozo, "The Role of Content Literacy in an Effective RTI Program," *The Reading Teacher,* (64) 2, pp. 147–150

Donald J. Leu
21st-Century Solutions

"The good news about the Common Core State Standards is that we are going to increasingly support higher-level thinking, reasoning, and comprehension. Locating, evaluating, integrating, and communicating information – all these skills are essential to students' success in the future. We need to help students think in deeper, more complex ways as they read a wider variety of texts, both print and digital."

Karen K. Wixson
The Goal: College and Career Readiness

"The ELA Common Core State Standards are meant to be read as an integrated English Language Arts program beginning with College and Career Readiness Anchor Standards. It is absolutely essential that teachers and administrators look first at the anchor standards, next the appendices, and lastly at the grade-level standards."

Expanded essays by these authors are available at PHLitOnline.com.

Master Teacher Board

Contributing Authors

The contributing authors guided the direction and philosophy of Pearson Prentice Hall Literature. *Working with the development team, they helped to build the pedagogical integrity of the program and to ensure its relevance for today's teachers and students.*

Grant Wiggins, Ed.D., is the President of Authentic Education in Hopewell, New Jersey. He earned his Ed.D. from Harvard University and his B.A. from St. John's College in Annapolis. Grant consults with schools, districts, and state education departments on a variety of reform matters; organizes conferences and workshops; and develops print materials and Web resources on curricular change. He is the coauthor, with Jay McTighe, of *Understanding by Design* and *The Understanding by Design Handbook,* the award-winning and highly successful materials on curriculum published by ASCD. His work has been supported by the Pew Charitable Trusts, the Geraldine R. Dodge Foundation, and the National Science Foundation. *The Association for Supervision of Curriculum Development (ASCD), publisher of the "Understanding by Design Handbook" co-authored by Grant Wiggins and registered owner of the trademark "Understanding by Design," has not authorized, approved, or sponsored this work and is in no way affiliated with Pearson or its products.*

Jeff Anderson has worked with struggling writers and readers for almost 20 years. Anderson's specialty is the integration of grammar and editing instruction into the processes of reading and writing. He has published two books, *Mechanically Inclined: Building Grammar, Usage, and Style into Writer's Workshop* and *Everyday Editing: Inviting Students to Develop Skill and Craft in Writer's Workshop,* as well as a DVD, *The Craft of Grammar.* Anderson's work has appeared in *English Journal.* Anderson won the NCTE Paul and Kate Farmer Award for his *English Journal* article on teaching grammar in context.

Arnetha F. Ball, Ph.D., is a Professor at Stanford University. Her areas of expertise include language and literacy studies of diverse student populations, research on writing instruction, and teacher preparation for working with diverse populations. Dr. Ball has also served as an academic specialist for the United States Information Services Program in South Africa. She is the author of *African American Literacies Unleashed* with Dr. Ted Lardner, and *Multicultural Strategies for Education and Social Change.*

Sheridan Blau is Professor of Education and English at the University of California, Santa Barbara, where he directs the South Coast Writing Project and the Literature Institute for Teachers. He has served in senior advisory roles for such groups as the National Board for Professional Teaching Standards, the College Board, and the American Board for Teacher Education. Blau served for twenty years on the National Writing Project Advisory Board and Task Force, and is a former president of NCTE. Blau is the author of *The Literature Workshop: Teaching Texts and Their Readers,* which was named by the Conference on English Education as the 2004 Richard Meade Award winner for outstanding research in English education.

William G. Brozo, Ph.D., is a Professor of Literacy at George Mason University in Fairfax, Virginia. He has taught reading and language arts in junior and senior high school and is the author of numerous texts on literacy development. Dr. Brozo's work focuses on building capacity among teacher leaders, enriching the literate culture of schools, enhancing the literate lives of boys, and making teaching more responsive to the needs of all students. His recent publications include *Bright Beginnings for Boys: Engaging Young Boys in Active Literacy* and the *Adolescent Literacy Inventory.*

Doug Buehl is a teacher, author, and national literacy consultant. He is the author of *Classroom Strategies for Interactive Learning* and coauthor of *Reading and the High School Student: Strategies to Enhance Literacy;* and *Strategies to Enhance Literacy and Learning in Middle School Content Area Classrooms.*

Jim Cummins, Ph.D., is a professor in the Modern Language Centre at the University of Toronto. He is the author of numerous publications, including *Negotiating Identities: Education for Empowerment in a Diverse Society.* Cummins coined the acronyms BICS and CAPT to help differentiate the type of language ability students need for success.

Harvey Daniels, Ph.D., has been a classroom teacher, writing project director, author, and university professor. "Smokey" serves as an international consultant to schools, districts, and educational agencies. He is known for his work on student-led book clubs, as recounted in *Literature Circles: Voice and Choice in Book Clubs & Reading Groups* and *Mini Lessons for Literature Circles.* Recent works include *Subjects Matter: Every Teacher's Guide to Content-Area Reading* and *Content Area Writing: Every Teacher's Guide.*

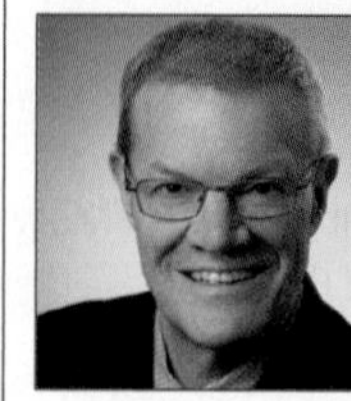

Jane Feber taught language arts in Jacksonville, Florida, for 36 years. Her innovative approach to instruction has earned her several awards, including the NMSA Distinguished Educator Award, the NCTE Edwin A. Hoey Award, the Gladys Prior Award for Teaching Excellence, and the Florida Council of Teachers of English Teacher of the Year Award. She is a National Board Certified Teacher, past president of the Florida Council of Teachers of English and is the author of *Creative Book Reports* and *Active Word Play*.

Danling Fu, Ph.D., is Professor of Language and Culture in the College of Education at the University of Florida. She researches and provides inservice to public schools nationally, focusing on literacy instruction for new immigrant students. Fu's books include *My Trouble is My English* and *An Island of English* addressing English language learners in the secondary schools. She has authored chapters in the *Handbook of Adolescent Literacy Research* and in *Adolescent Literacy: Turning Promise to Practice*.

Kelly Gallagher is a full-time English teacher at Magnolia High School in Anaheim, California. He is the former co-director of the South Basin Writing Project at California State University, Long Beach. Gallagher wrote *Reading Reasons: Motivational Mini-Lessons for the Middle and High School, Deeper Reading: Comprehending Challenging Texts 4-12,* and *Teaching Adolescent Writers.* Gallagher won the Secondary Award of Classroom Excellence from the California Association of Teachers of English—the state's top English teacher honor.

Sharroky Hollie, Ph.D., is an assistant professor at California State University, Dominguez Hills, and an urban literacy visiting professor at Webster University, St. Louis. Hollie's work focuses on professional development, African American education, and second language methodology. He is a contributing author in two texts on culturally and linguistically responsive teaching. He is the Executive Director of the Center for Culturally Responsive Teaching and Learning and the co-founding director of the Culture and Language Academy of Success, an independent charter school in Los Angeles.

Dr. Donald J. Leu, Ph.D., teaches at the University of Connecticut and holds a joint appointment in Curriculum and Instruction and in Educational Psychology. He directs the New Literacies Research Lab and is a member of the Board of Directors of the International Reading Association. Leu studies the skills required to read, write, and learn with Internet technologies. His research has been funded by groups including the U.S. Department of Education, the National Science Foundation, and the Bill & Melinda Gates Foundation.

Jon Scieszka founded GUYS READ, a nonprofit literacy initiative for boys, to call attention to the problem of getting boys connected with reading. In 2008, he was named the first U.S. National Ambassador for Young People's Literature by the Library of Congress. Scieszka taught from first grade to eighth grade for ten years in New York City, drawing inspiration from his students to write *The True Story of the 3 Little Pigs!, The Stinky Cheese Man*, the *Time Warp Trio* series of chapter books, and the *Trucktown* series of books for beginning readers.

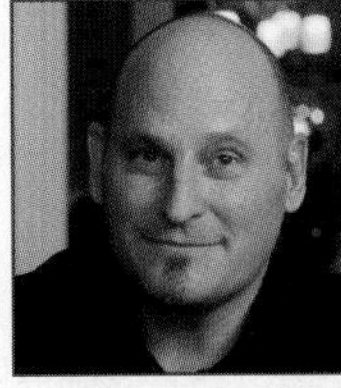

Sharon Vaughn, Ph.D., teaches at the University of Texas at Austin. She is the previous Editor-in-Chief of the *Journal of Learning Disabilities* and the co-editor of *Learning Disabilities Research and Practice.* She is the recipient of the American Education Research Association SIG Award for Outstanding Researcher. Vaughn's work focuses on effective practices for enhancing reading outcomes for students with reading difficulties. She is the author of more than 100 articles and numerous books designed to improve research-based practices in the classroom.

Karen K. Wixson is Dean of the School of Education at the University of North Carolina, Greensboro. She has published widely in the areas of literacy curriculum, instruction, and assessment. Wixson has been an advisor to the National Research Council and helped develop the National Assessment of Educational Progress (NAEP) reading tests. She is a past member of the IRA Board of Directors and co-chair of the IRA Commission on RTI. Recently, Wixson served on the English Language Arts Work Team that was part of the Common Core State Standards Initiative.

COMMON CORE
Contents in Brief

Each unit addresses a BIG Question to enrich exploration of literary concepts and reading strategies.

COMMON CORE

Unit 1 ▪ Fiction and Nonfiction

THE BIG ?
Can truth change?

Six units per grade explore specific genres while focusing on a Big Question.

Robust Literary Analysis Workshops enable students to perform in-depth exploration of genres and standards.

Reading for Information texts appear twice per unit.

★ INFORMATIONAL TEXT HIGHLIGHTED

Student Edition Pages

Comparing
Points of View

A robust mix of literary and informational texts provides a wide range of reading.

Author's Purpose
Voice

Author's Purpose
Character

Leveled selection pairs let you choose text that is appropriate for your students' abilities without skipping essential skills.

Interactive resources provide personalized instruction and activities online.

All program resources are available online for classroom presentation or individual study.

Assessment practice includes writing on demand activities.

Professional authors model their own revision strategies.

Vocabulary Workshops provide robust instruction and multiple practice opportunities.

The Assessment Workshops provide both multiple-choice tests and performance tasks.

Student Edition Pages

Skills at a Glance

This page provides a quick look at the skills you will learn and practice in Unit 1.

Each unit develops reading and literary skills, teaching them to mastery.

Reading Skills

Make Predictions
- Ask Questions
- Reread or Read Ahead to Verify Your Predictions

Author's Purpose
- Preview the Text Before You Read
- Reflect

Reading for Information

- Read to Perform a Task
- Analyze Structure and Format

Literary Analysis

Theme
Central Idea
Narrative Essay
Plot
Comparing Points of View
Voice
Character
Comparing Themes
Independent Reading

Vocabulary

Big Question Vocabulary
Prefixes: *fore-*, *con-*
Suffixes: *-ate*, *-tion*, *-able*, *-ive*
Roots: *-fin-*, *-term-*
Using a Dictionary and Thesaurus

Conventions

Common and Proper Nouns
Abstract and Concrete Nouns
Revising to Correct Use of Possessive Nouns
Personal Pronouns and Reflexive Pronouns
Relative, Interrogative, and Indefinite Pronouns
Revising Pronoun-Antecedent Agreement

Writing

Writing About the Big Question
Anecdote
Critique
Journal Entry
Character Profile
Timed Writing
Writing Workshop: Narrative Text: Autobiographical Narrative
Writing Workshop: Argument: Problem-and-Solution Essay

Speaking and Listening

Interview
Retelling
Giving and Following Oral Instructions

Research and Technology

Introduction for a Multimedia Presentation
Learning Log

Common Core State Standards Addressed in This Unit

Reading Literature RL.9-10.1, RL.9-10.2, RL.9-10.3, RL.9-10.5, RL.9-10.6, RL.9-10.7, RL.9-10.10

Reading Informational Text RI.9-10.2, RI.9-10.3, RI.9-10.6, RI.9-10.7, RI.9-10.10

Writing W.9-10.1, W.9-10.1.a-1.e, W.9-10.2, W.9-10.2.a, W.9-10.2.b, W.9-10.2.d, W.9-10.2.f, W.9-10.3, W.9-10.3.a–d, W.9-10.4, W.9-10.5, W.9-10.6, W.9-10.9, W.9-10.9.a, W.9-10.9.b, W.9-10.10

Speaking and Listening SL.9-10.1, SL.9-10.1.a, SL.9-10.1.c, SL.9-10.1.d, SL.9-10.4, SL.9-10.5

Language L.9-10.1, L.9-10.2, L.9-10.2.c, L.9-10.3, L.9-10.4.a–c, L.9-10.5, L.9-10.5.b, L.9-10.6

[For the full wording of the standards, see the standards chart in the front of your textbook.]

The Common Core State Standards are addressed throughout the unit.

THE BIG
Is conflict necessary?

Academic Vocabulary related to the Big Question is taught at the beginning of each unit.

Frequent progress monitoring catches small learning problems before they become big ones.

★ INFORMATIONAL TEXT HIGHLIGHTED

Student Edition Pages

www.PHLitOnline.com
Interactive resources provide personalized instruction and activities online.

COMMON CORE
Unit 2 ▪ Short Stories

The "What Do You Notice?" feature leads to in-depth exploration of ways in which authors use language.

Independent Reading suggestions offer opportunities for students to read complex texts independently.

Student Edition Pages

Skills at a Glance

This page provides a quick look at the skills you will learn and practice in Unit 2.

Reading Skills

Make Inferences
- Use Details as Clues
- Use Your Own Prior Knowledge and Experience

Cause and Effect
- Ask Questions
- Visualize the Action to Analyze Cause and Effect

Reading for Information

- Critique the Logic of Functional Documents
- Analyze Structure and Format

Literary Analysis

Character, Plot, and Theme
Text Structure
Plot
Story
Conflict
Irony
Comparing Setting
Characterization
Dialogue and Dialect
Comparing Symbolism and Allegory
Independent Reading

Key vocabulary skills are taught throughout the program.

Vocabulary

Big Question Vocabulary
Prefixes: *de-, inter-*
Suffixes: *-esque, -ant, -ity, -ous*
Roots: *-bene-, -jec(t)-*
Word Origins

Conventions

The Principal Parts of Regular Verbs
Irregular Verbs
Subjects and Predicates
Active and Passive Voice
Revising Inconsistent Verb Tense
Revising to Correct Faulty Subject-Verb Agreement

Writing

Writing About the Big Question
Alternative Ending
News Report
Written Presentation
Informal Letter
Timed Writing
Writing Workshop: Narrative Text: Short Story
Writing Workshop: Explanatory Text: Cause-and-Effect Essay

Speaking and Listening

Oral Presentation
Debate
Dialogue
Evaluating a Speech

Research and Technology

Informative Brochure

Common Core State Standards Addressed in This Unit

Reading Literature RL.9-10.1, RL.9-10.3, RL.9-10.4, RL.9-10.6, RL.9-10.10

Reading Informational Text RI.9-10.3, RI.9-10.10

Writing W.9-10.2, W.9-10.2.a–c, W.9-10.2.f, W.9-10.3, W.9-10.3.a–e, W.9-10.4, W.9-10.5, W.9-10.9.a, W.9-10.10

Speaking and Listening SL.9-10.1, SL.9-10.1.b, SL.9-10.2, SL.9-10.3, SL.9-10.4

Language L.9-10.1, L.9-10.2.c, L.9-10.4, L.9-10.4.b, L.9-10.4.c, L.9-10.6

[For the full wording of the standards, see the standards chart in the front of your textbook.]

The Common Core State Standards are addressed throughout the unit.

COMMON CORE
Unit 3 ▪ Types of Nonfiction

THE BIG ?
Is knowledge the same as understanding?

Development of Ideas
Word Choice and Tone
Point of View and Purpose

Exemplar texts appear throughout the program.

FOCUS ON POINT OF VIEW AND PURPOSE

Main Idea
Author's Style

Leveled selection pairs let you choose text that is appropriate for your students' abilities without skipping essential skills.

Main Idea
Expository Essay

Grammar, Writing, Speaking and Listening, and Research activities link to selection content.

Generate Relevant Questions

★ INFORMATIONAL TEXT HIGHLIGHTED

Student Edition Pages

Comparing Biographical Writing

The Writer's Toolbox focuses on six traits.

FOCUS ON ARGUMENT

Students are presented with an extended focus on argument.

www.PHLitOnline.com
Interactive resources provide personalized instruction and activities online.

All program resources are available online for classroom presentation or individual study.

COMMON CORE
Unit 3 ▪ Types of Nonfiction

A perfect mix of classic and contemporary selections provides a rich variety of choices.

Professional authors model their own revision strategies.

Independent Reading suggestions offer opportunities for students to read complex texts independently.

UNIT 3

Skills at a Glance

This page provides a quick look at the skills you will learn and practice in Unit 3.

Each unit develops reading and literary skills, teaching them to mastery.

Reading Skills

Main Idea
- Generate Questions Prior to Reading
- Reread

Evaluate Persuasion
- Reread
- Read Aloud to Hear the Effect

Reading for Information

- Generate Relevant Questions
- Evaluate Credibility

Literary Analysis

Development of Ideas
Word Choice and Tone
Point of View and Purpose
Author's Style
Expository Essay
Comparing Biographical Writing
Persuasive Essay
Persuasive Speech
Comparing Humorous Writing
Independent Reading

Vocabulary

Big Question Vocabulary
Roots: *-viv-, -dur-, -nov-, -temp-, -potens-, -sum-, -cred-, -duct-*
Words With Multiple Meanings

Conventions

Direct and Indirect Objects
Predicate Nominatives and Predicate Adjectives
Revising to Combine Choppy Sentences
Adjectives
Adverbs
Revising to Create Parallelism

Writing

Writing About the Big Question
Book Jacket Copy
Script
Journal Entries
Abstract
Proposal
Timed Writing
Writing Workshop: Informative Text: Business Letter
Writing Workshop: Argument: Editorial

Speaking and Listening

Panel Discussion
Radio News Report
Delivering a Persuasive Speech

Research and Technology

Journal Entries
Comparative Chart / Persuasive Speech

Common Core State Standards Addressed in This Unit

Reading Literature RL.9-10.6, RL.9-10.10
Reading Informational Text RI.9-10.1, RI.9-10.2, RI.9-10.3, RI.9-10.4, RI.9-10.5, RI.9-10.6, RI.9-10.8, RI.9-10.9, RI.9-10.10
Writing W.9-10.1, W.9-10.1.a–e, W.9-10.2, W.9-10.2.a, W.9-10.2.d–f, W.9-10.4, W.9-10.5, W.9-10.6, W.9-10.7, W.9-10.8, W.9-10.9, W.9-10.9.b, W.9-10.10
Speaking and Listening SL.9-10.1, SL.9-10.3, SL.9-10.4, SL.9-10.5, SL.9-10.6
Language L.9-10.1, L.9-10.1.a, L.9-10.3, L.9-10.4, L.9-10.4.a, L.9-10.4.b, L.9-10.4.d, L.9-10.5, L.9-10.5.b, L.9-10.6
[For the full wording of the standards, see the standards chart in the front of your textbook.]

Common Core State Standards are integrated throughout the units.

THE BIG ?
How does communication change us?

Robust Literary Analysis Workshops enable students to perform in-depth exploration of genres and standards.

Poetry is organized in collections to allow students to practice skills with either group.

Literature in Context notes provide point-of-use cross-curricular nonfiction links to selections.

★ INFORMATIONAL TEXT HIGHLIGHTED

Student Edition Pages

A robust mix of literary and informational texts provides a wide range of reading.

Grammar, Writing, Speaking and Listening, and Research activities link to selection content.

COMMON CORE
Unit 4 ▪ Poetry

Assessment practice includes writing on demand activities.

Communications Workshops enable students to practice speaking and listening skills for the twenty-first century.

Student Edition Pages

Skills at a Glance

This page provides a quick look at the skills you will learn and practice in Unit 4.

Reading Skills

Read Fluently
- Read in Sentences or Units of Meaning
- Read Poems Several Times

Paraphrase
- Picture the Action
- Break Down Long Sentences

Reading for Information

- Follow Technical Directions
- Paraphrase a Text: Main Idea

Literary Analysis

Poetic Language
Tone
Figurative Language
Sound Devices
Comparing Imagery
Narrative Poetry
Rhyme and Meter
Comparing Lyric Poetry
Independent Reading

Each unit develops reading and literary skills, teaching them to mastery.

Vocabulary

Big Question Vocabulary
Prefixes: *ana-*, *mono-*, *pre-*, *im-*
Suffixes: *-ment*, *-ion*
Roots: *-fer-*, *-vert-*
Connotation and Denotation

Conventions

Prepositions
Prepositional Phrases
Revising to Vary Sentence Patterns
Appositive Phrase
Infinitives
Using Quotations

Writing

Writing About the Big Question
Description of a Scene
Editorial
Poem
Timed Writing
Writing Workshop: Informative Text: Descriptive Essay
Writing Workshop: Argument: Response to Literature

Speaking and Listening

Impromptu Speech
Illustrated Presentation
Dialogue
Panel Discussion
Oral Interpretation of Literature

Common Core State Standards Addressed in This Unit

Reading Literature RL.9-10.2, RL.9-10.4, RL.9-10.5, RL.9-10.7, RL.9-10.10

Reading Informational Text RI.9-10.2, RI.9-10.4, RI.9-10.5, RI.9-10.10

Writing W.9-10.1, W.9-10.2, W.9-10.2.a, W.9-10.2.b, W.9-10.2.d, W.9-10.2.e, W.9-10.3.d, W.9-10.4, W.9-10.5, W.9-10.9.a, W.9-10.10

Speaking and Listening SL.9-10.1, SL.9-10.1.a–d, SL.9-10.4, SL.9-10.5, SL.9-10.6

Language L.9-10.1, L.9-10.1.b, L.9-10.3, L.9-10.5, L.9-10.6

[For the full wording of the standards, see the standards chart in the front of your textbook.]

The Common Core State Standards are addressed throughout the unit.

THE BIG ? Do our differences define us?

Dramatic Structure

Character, Plot, and Theme

Extended Studies enable students to perform an in-depth exploration of key literary works.

Summarize Dialogue and Stage Directions

Frequent progress monitoring catches small learning problems before they become big ones.

★ INFORMATIONAL TEXT HIGHLIGHTED

Student Edition Pages

Analyzing Text Information

Reading for Information texts appear twice per unit.

Comparing Archetypal Themes

The Writer's Toolbox focuses on six traits.

www.PHLitOnline.com
Interactive resources provide personalized instruction and activities online.

COMMON CORE
Unit 5 ▪ Drama

Evaluating Sources

Comparing Satire

Literature in Context notes provide point-of-use cross-curricular nonfiction links to selections.

Professional authors model their own revision strategies.

Vocabulary Workshops provide robust instruction and multiple practice opportunities.

Student Edition Pages

Skills at a Glance

This page provides a quick look at the skills you will learn and practice in Unit 5.

Reading Skills

- Summarize
  - Use Text Aids
  - Read in Sentences
  - Paraphrase
  - Break Down Long Sentences
  - Identify Causes and Effects
- Draw Conclusions
  - Dialogue and Stage Directions

Reading for Information

- Analyze Text Information
- Evaluate Sources

Literary Analysis

- Dramatic Structure
- Character, Plot, and Theme
- Dialogue and Stage Directions
- Blank Verse
- Dramatic Speeches
- Dramatic Irony
- Tragedy and Motive
- Comparing Archetypal Themes
- Comedy
- Comparing Satire
- Independent Reading

Vocabulary

- Big Question Vocabulary
- Prefixes: *trans-*, *pro-*, *en-*, *ambi-*
- Roots: *-loque-*, *-nym-*, *-nom-*
- Borrowed and Foreign Words

Conventions

- Participles and Participial Phrases
- Gerunds and Gerund Phrases
- Revising to Combine Sentences With Phrases
- Main and Subordinate Clauses
- Revising to Combine Sentences Using Adverb Clauses

Writing

- Writing About the Big Question
- Editorial
- Persuasive Letter
- Play
- Timed Writing
- Writing Workshop: Explanatory Text: How-to Essay
- Writing Workshop: Informative Text: Research Report

Speaking and Listening

- Staged Performance
- Mock Trial

Research and Technology

- Annotated Flowchart
- Film Review
- Multimedia Presentation
- Informational Chart
- Multimedia Presentation of a Research Report

Common Core State Standards Addressed in This Unit

Reading Literature RL.9-10.2, RL.9-10.3, RL.9-10.4, RL.9-10.5, RL.9-10.7, RL.9-10.9, RL.9-10.10

Reading Informational Text RI.9-10.3, RI.9-10.10

Writing W.9-10.1, W.9-10.1.c, W.9-10.2, W.9-10.2.a, W.9-10.2.b, W.9-10.3, W.9-10.5, W.9-10.7, W.9-10.8, W.9-10.9.a, W.9-10.10

Speaking and Listening SL.9-10.1.b, SL.9-10.5

Language L.9-10.1, L.9-10.1.b, L.9-10.3, L.9-10.4, L.9-10.4.c, L.9-10.4.d, L.9-10.5.a, L.9-10.6

[For the full wording of the standards, see the standards chart in the front of your textbook.]

The Common Core State Standards are addressed throughout the unit.

COMMON CORE
Unit 6 ▪ Themes in Literature: Heroism

★ INFORMATIONAL TEXT HIGHLIGHTED

Student Edition Pages

Comparing Contemporary Interpretations

Writing Workshops provide step-by-step instruction in the writing process.

Comparing and Contrasting Characters Protagonist and Antagonist

Comparing and Contrasting Philosophical Assumptions

Grammar, Writing, Speaking and Listening, and Research activities link to selection content.

www.PHLitOnline.com
Interactive resources provide personalized instruction and activities online.

All program resources are available online for classroom presentation or individual study.

COMMON CORE
Unit 6 ▪ Themes in Literature: Heroism

Analyzing Primary Sources

Comparing Tall Tale and Myth

The "What Do You Notice?" feature leads to in-depth exploration of ways in which authors use language.

Independent Reading suggestions offer opportunities for students to read complex texts independently.

Student Edition Pages

Skills at a Glance

This page provides a quick look at the skills you will learn and practice in Unit 6.

Reading Skills

- Historical and Cultural Context
  - Use Background and Prior Knowledge
  - Identify Influences on Your Own Reading and Responses
- Comparing and Contrasting Characters
  - Generate Questions
  - Use Self-Monitoring Techniques

Reading for Information

- Identify Characteristics of Various Types of Text
- Analyze Primary Sources

Literary Analysis

Each unit develops reading and literary skills, teaching them to mastery.

- Theme
- Social and Cultural Context
- Point of View and Cultural Experience
- Epic Hero
- Epic Simile
- Comparing Contemporary Interpretations
- Protagonist and Antagonist
- Philosophical Assumptions
- Comparing Tall Tale and Myth

Vocabulary

- Big Question Vocabulary
- Prefixes: *be-*, *dis-*
- Roots: *-min-*, *-spect-*, *-merg-*, *-fer-*
- Idioms, Jargon, and Technical Terms

Conventions

- Simple and Compound Sentences
- Complex and Compound-Complex Sentences
- Revising to Correct Fragments and Run-ons
- Using Commas and Dashes
- Colons, Semicolons, and Ellipsis Points
- Varying Sentence Structure and Length

Writing

- Writing About the Big Question
- Everyday Epic
- Biography
- Journal Entries
- Letter
- Timed Writing
- Writing Workshop: Explanatory Text: Technical Document
- Writing Workshop: Informative Text: Comparison-and-Contrast Essay

Speaking and Listening

- Conversation
- Debate
- Oral Report
- Panel Discussion
- Comparing Media Coverage

Common Core State Standards Addressed in This Unit

Reading Literature RL.9-10.2, RL.9-10.3, RL.9-10.4, RL.9-10.6, RL.9-10.7, RL.9-10.10

Reading Informational Text RI.9-10.3, RI.9-10.6, RI.9-10.7, RI.9-10.10

Writing W.9-10.2, W.9-10.2.a, W.9-10.2.b, W.9-10.3, W.9-10.3.a, W.9-10.3.b, W.9-10.5, W.9-10.9, W.9-10.9.a, W.9-10.10

Speaking and Listening SL.9-10.1.a, SL.9-10.1.c, SL.9-10.2

Language L.9-10.1, L.9-10.1.b, L.9-10.2, L.9-10.2.a, L.9-10.2.b, L.9-10.4.b, L.9-10.4.c, L.9-10.5, L.9-10.5.a, L.9-10.6

[For the full wording of the standards, see the standards chart in the front of your textbook.]

Common Core State Standards are integrated throughout the units.

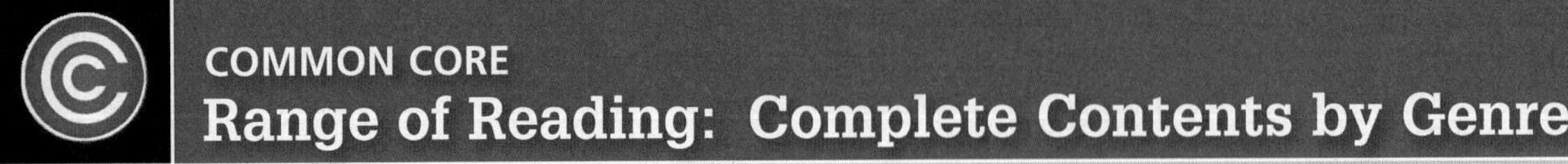

COMMON CORE

Range of Reading: Complete Contents by Genre

Literature

▶ Stories

▶ Drama

▶ Poetry

Epics

Lyrical Poems

Narrative and Dramatic Poems

Sonnets and Haiku

COMMON CORE
Range of Reading: Complete Contents by Genre

Informational Text

Arguments

Opinion Pieces

Speeches

Exposition

Biographies

Content-Area Essays and Articles

Historical Accounts

Memoirs

Narrative Essays

Personal Essays

Reflective Essays

Functional Text

Literature in Context—Reading in Content Areas

COMMON CORE

Comparing Literary Works

COMMON CORE Skills Workshops

Writing Workshops

Vocabulary Workshops

Communications Workshops

Student Edition Pages

Introductory Unit

COMMON CORE
Workshops

Building Academic Vocabulary

Writing an Objective Summary

Comprehending Complex Texts

Analyzing Arguments

Common Core State Standards

Reading Literature 2, 10
Reading Informational Text 6, 8, 9, 10
Writing 1a, 1b, 1e
Language 6

Building Academic Vocabulary

Common Core State Standards

Language 6. Acquire and use accurately general academic and domain-specific words and phrases, sufficient for reading, writing, speaking, and listening at the college and career readiness level; demonstrate independence in gathering vocabulary knowledge when considering a word or phrase important to comprehension or expression.

Academic vocabulary is the language you encounter in textbooks and on standardized tests and other assessments. Understanding these words and using them in your classroom discussions and writing will help you communicate your ideas clearly and effectively.

There are two basic types of academic vocabulary: general and domain-specific. **General academic vocabulary** includes words that are not specific to any single course of study. For example, the general academic vocabulary word *analyze* is used in language arts, math, social studies, art, and so on. **Domain-specific academic vocabulary** includes words that are usually encountered in the study of a specific discipline. For example, the words *factor* and *remainder* are most often used in mathematics classrooms and texts.

General Academic Vocabulary

Word	Definition	Related Words	Word in Context
ambiguous (am BIHG yoo uhs) *adj*	having more than one meaning; unclear	ambiguity	The story's uncertain ending was ambiguous.
appreciate (uh PREE shee ayt) *v.*	be aware of the value of	appreciative appreciating	Once I read Frost's poem, I learned to appreciate his use of symbols.
argument (AHR gyuh muhnt) *n.*	persuasive message	argue argumentative	The argument in the essay is well supported.
articulate (ahr TIHK yuh layt) *v.*	express an idea clearly	articulating articulated	The writer was able to articulate his ideas clearly.
articulate (ahr TIHK yuh liht) *adj.*	able to express clearly	articulating articulated	It is important to be articulate when giving a speech.
assumption (uh SUHMP shuhn) *n.*	something taken for granted	assume assuming	My assumption that the character was telling the truth proved wrong.
character (KAR ihk tuhr) *n.*	qualities that make a person unique	characteristic characteristically	Jenny's character became clear through her actions and words.
circumstance (SUR kuhm stans) *n.*	situation; event		In that circumstance, I would have done the same thing as that character.

Ordinary Language:
I **like** poems with strong rhymes and rhythms.

Academic Language:
I **appreciate** poems with strong rhymes and rhythms.

Word	Definition	Related Words	Word in Context
clarify (KLAR uh fy) *v.*	make something more clear or understandable	clarification	More details were needed to clarify the writer's ideas about pollution.
compete (kuhm PEET) *v.*	battle against; try to win	competition competitor	The two characters compete in a battle of wits.
competition (kom puh TIHSH uhn) *n.*	rivalry; act of competing	compete competitor	There seemed to be a competition between the mother and daughter.
comprehend (kom prih HEHND) *v.*	understand	comprehension	It was easy to comprehend the character's motives.
comprehension (kom prih HEHN shuhn) *n.*	act of understanding something	comprehend	My comprehension of the poem was hampered by the use of archaic language.
concept (KON sehpt) *n.*	idea; notion	conceive conceptualize	The concept of freedom is explored in this essay.
context (KON tehkst) *n.*	surrounding text; situation	contextual	In this context, the word *democracy* takes on new meaning.
controversy (KON truh vur see) *n.*	discussion of a question in which opposing opinions clash	controversial	The essayist explores the controversy that brewed in the heartland.
convince (kuhn VIHNS) *v.*	persuade by argument or evidence	convincing	The writer tries to convince her audience to change their ways.
credible (KREHD uh buhl) *adj.*	believable	creed credibility	I found the story's plot to be credible.
defend (dih FEHND) *v.*	protect against attack	defense	The writer tries to defend his notions about fairness.
determine (dih TUR muhn) *v.*	cause something to happen in a certain way	determination	The character's actions determine his fate.
differentiate (dihf uh REHN shee ayt) *v.*	see or express what makes two or more things different from each other	differ different	In this essay, the writer differentiates between students and scholars.

Word	Definition	Related Words	Word in Context
discriminate (dihs KRIHM uh nayt) *v.*	see the differences between things; act against someone because of prejudice	discrimination	The character was unable to discriminate loyal friends from disloyal ones.
discuss (dihs KUHS) *v.*	talk about; write about	discussion	Discuss your ideas in your response.
identify (ahy DEHN tuh fy) *v.*	say who someone or something is	identification	I will identify three key factors in the story's success.
illuminate (ih LOO muh nayt) *v.*	light up; make something clearer	illumination	Here is my attempt to illuminate my ideas.
imitate (IHM uh tayt) *v.*	copy the actions of another	imitation imitator	The poet uses onomatopoeia to imitate the sounds of a rooster.
informed (ihn FAWRMD) *v.*	gave someone information	inform information	The character informed his teacher that he had finished his test.
interpret (ihn TUR priht) *v.*	understand or explain the meaning of something	interpreter interpretation	How do you interpret the title of this poem?
interpretation (ihn tur pruh TAY shuhn) *n.*	explanation of the meaning of something	interpreter interpret	My interpretation of the theme differs from that of my friend.
involvement (ihn VOLV muhnt) *n.*	state of being included in something	involve	The character's involvement in sports propels the plot.
perspective (puhr SPEHK tihv) *n.*	point of view		The story is told from the perspective of a three-year-old.
speculate (SPEHK yuh layt) *v.*	think about or make up theories about a subject; guess at	speculative	Speculate about the author's reasons for setting this story in the tundra.
standard (STAN duhrd) *n.*	idea or thing to which other things are compared	standardize	Shakespeare sets the standard by which many playwrights are judged.
standard (STAN duhrd) *adj.*	normal; average	standardize substandard	It is standard practice for stories to center on conflict.
unique (yoo NEEK) *adj.*	one of a kind	uniqueness	The poet has a unique style.
verify (VEHR uh fy) *v.*	make sure something is true; confirm	verification	You should verify the facts before you accept them.

Ordinary Language: In this essay, I will **talk about** the story's theme.

Academic Language: In this essay, I will **discuss** the story's theme.

Practice

Examples of various kinds of domain-specific academic vocabulary appear in the charts below. On a separate piece of paper, create your own domain-specific academic vocabulary charts for each domain in which you enter new academic vocabulary words as you learn them.

Social Studies: Domain-Specific Academic Vocabulary

Word	Definition	Related Words	Word in Context
entrepreneurship (ahn truh pruh NUR ship) *n.*	willingness to assume the risk and responsibility of starting a business	entrepreneur entrepreneurial	The scholarship rewards entrepreneurship.
sovereignty (SOV rin tee) *n.*	independence and self-government	sovereign	The country fought for its sovereignty.
capitalism (KAP i tl iz uhm) *n.*	an economic system based on private investment and ownership	capitalist	With capitalism, private individuals or corporations control the wealth.
populist (POP yuh list) *adj.*	favoring common people over the wealthy and elite	populism	The politician tried to sway populist groups.
impeach (im PEECH) *v.*	accuse a public official of misconduct in office	impeached impeachment	The people will impeach a corrupt official.

Create a chart for these social studies academic vocabulary words: *enterprise, landmass, ecosystem, market,* and *opportunity.*

Mathematics: Domain-Specific Academic Vocabulary

Word	Definition	Related Words	Word in Context
theorem (THEE er uhm) *n.*	an assertion that can be proved true using the rules of logic	theory	The scientist worked hard to prove her theorem.
permutation (pur myoo TAY shuhn) *n.*	an ordered arrangement of a set of objects	permuting	The teacher formed a permutation by rearranging the letters.
congruent (KONG groo uhnt) *adj.*	exactly equal in size and shape	congruous congruity	The triangles are congruent.
logarithm (LAW guh rith uhm) *n.*	the power to which a constant must be raised to equal a specified number	logarithmic	2 is the logarithm of 100 to the base 10.
inverse (in VURS) *adj.*	containing terms of which an increase in one causes a decrease in another	invert	The inverse functions mirrored each other.

Create a chart for these mathematics academic vocabulary words: *graph, slope, triangle, quadrilateral,* and *diagram.*

Science: Domain-Specific Academic Vocabulary

Word	Definition	Related Words	Word in Context
meiosis (mahy OH sis) *n.*	process of cell division that halves the number of chromosomes	meiotic	The biology video included a section about meiosis.
ion (AHY uhn) *n.*	an atom or a group of atoms that has an electric charge	ionic	An ion can carry a positive or negative charge.
catalyst (KAT I ist) *n.*	a substance that starts or speeds up a chemical reaction	catalytic	The chemical served as a catalyst in the experiment.
power (POU er) *n.*	the rate at which work is done, or energy expended, per unit time	powered powerful	The work done per second is called the power.
work (wurk) *n.*	the product of the force applied to a body and the resulting distance the body moves	worked working	How much work needs to be done to pick up the box?

Create a chart for these science academic vocabulary words: *glacier, tsunami, atomic, tectonic,* and *fracture.*

Art: Domain-Specific Academic Vocabulary

Word	Definition	Related Words	Word in Context
abstract (ab STRAKT) *adj.*	not depicting recognizable scenes or objects	abstraction abstractly	The artist was known for his abstract paintings.
tone (tohn) *n.*	a slight modification of a given color	tonal	He chose a tone that matched the color of the leaves.
monochrome (MON uh krohm) *adj.*	in the shades of a single color	monochromatic	The red painting was monochromatic.
complementary (kom pluh MEN tuh ree) *adj.*	perceived as enhancing each other or another	complement complementariness	The colors in the painting are complementary.
proportion (pruh PAWR shuhn) *n.*	relation between parts	proportional proportioned	The figures are drawn in correct proportion.

Create a chart for these art academic vocabulary words: *outline, still life, sketch, contrast,* and *repetition.*

Technology: Domain-Specific Academic Vocabulary

Word	Definition	Related Words	Word in Context
byte (byt) *n.*	a unit of computer information consisting of eight bits	megabyte gigabyte	The storage device can hold many bytes.
processor (PROS es er) *n.*	electronic device that responds to instructions that drive a computer	process processing	The computer processor quickly performs calculations.
pixel (PIK suhl) *n.*	any of a number of very small picture elements that make up a picture	pixelated	I could see a single pixel in the magnified picture.
application (ap li KAY shuhn) *n.*	software designed to help a user perform specific tasks	apply	The computer application will track the information.
streaming (STREE ming) *n.*	technique for transferring data as a continuous stream	stream	The presenter was live streaming a video.

Create a chart for these technology academic vocabulary words: *graphic, format, copyright, scanner,* and *browser.*

Increasing Your Word Knowledge

Increase your word knowledge and chances of success by taking an active role in developing your vocabulary. Here are some tips for you.

To own a word, follow these steps:

Steps to Follow	Model
1. Learn to identify the word and its basic meaning.	The word *examine* means "to look at closely."
2. Take note of the word's spelling.	*Examine* begins and ends with an *e*.
3. Practice pronouncing the word so that you can use it in conversation.	The *e* on the end of the word is silent. Its second syllable gets the most stress.
4. Visualize the word and illustrate its key meaning.	When I think of the word *examine,* I visualize a doctor checking a patient's health.
5. Learn the various forms of the word and its related words.	*Examination* and *exam* are forms of the word *examine*.
6. Compare the word with similar words.	*Examine, peruse,* and *study* are synonyms.
7. Contrast the word with similar words.	*Examine* suggests a more detailed study than *read* or *look at*.
8. Use the word in various contexts.	"I'd like to *examine* the footprints more closely." "I will *examine* the use of imagery in this poem."

Building Your Speaking Vocabulary

Language gives us the ability to express ourselves. The more words you know, the better able you will be to get your points across. There are two main aspects of language: reading and speaking. Using the steps above will help you to acquire a rich vocabulary. Follow these steps to help you learn to use this rich vocabulary in discussions, speeches, and conversations.

Steps to Follow	Tip
1. Practice pronouncing the word.	Become familiar with pronunciation guides to allow you to sound out unfamiliar words. Listening to audio books as you read the text will help you learn pronunciations of words.
2. Learn word forms.	Dictionaries often list forms of words following the main word entry. Practice saying word families aloud: "generate," "generated," "generation," "regenerate," "generator."
3. Translate your thoughts.	Restate your own thoughts and ideas in a variety of ways, to inject formality or to change your tone, for example.
4. Hold discussions.	With a classmate, practice using academic vocabulary words in discussions about the text. Choose one term to practice at a time, and see how many statements you can create using that term.
5. Record yourself.	Analyze your word choices by listening to yourself objectively. Note places your word choice could be strengthened or changed.

Writing an Objective Summary

The ability to write objective summaries is key to success in college and in many careers. Writing an effective objective summary involves recording the key ideas of a text while demonstrating your understanding.

Common Core State Standards

Literature 2. Determine a theme or central idea of a text and analyze in detail its development over the course of the text, including how it emerges and is shaped and refined by specific details; provide an objective summary of the text.

What Is an Objective Summary?

An effective objective summary is a concise, complete, and accurate overview of a text. Following are key elements of an objective summary:

- A good summary focuses on the main theme or central idea of a text and specific, relevant details that support that theme or central idea, while unnecessary supporting details are left out.
- Effective summaries are brief, although the writer must take care not to misrepresent the text by leaving out key elements.
- A summary should accurately capture the essence of the longer text it is describing.
- Finally, the writer must take care to remain objective, or to refrain from inserting his or her own opinions, reactions, or personal connections into the summary.

What to Avoid in an Objective Summary

- Avoid simply copying a collection of sentences or paragraphs from the original source.
- An objective summary should also not be a long recounting of every event, detail, or point in the original text.
- Finally, a good summary does not include evaluative comments, such as the reader's overall opinion of or reaction to the piece. An objective summary is not the reader's interpretation or critical analysis of the work.

INFORMATIONAL TEXT

Model Objective Summary

Note the elements of an effective objective summary, called out in the yellow sidenotes. Then, write an objective summary of a text you have recently read. Review your summary, and delete any unnecessary details, opinions, or evaluations.

Summary of "Thank You, M'am"

"Thank You, M'am" by Langston Hughes is a~~n amusing~~ story of a young boy who tries to steal a large purse from Mrs. Luella Bates Washington Jones, but he gets more than he expected.

The story begins with a description of a large woman with a heavy purse walking alone at night. A boy tries to snatch her purse, but the weight of the purse causes him to fall on the ground. The woman kicks the boy and then grabs his shirt, picking him up off the ground.

Then, the woman asks the boy if he will run if she lets go. He says yes, so she doesn't let go. The boy tells her he is sorry, and the woman responds by stating that his face is dirty. She begins to drag him down the street, declaring that his face will be washed this evening. ~~The boy looks to be fourteen years old.~~

The boy tells the woman that he just wants to be let go, and the woman responds that he put himself in contact with her, and that contact is going to last awhile. She tells him that he will remember Mrs. Luella Bates Washington Jones.

The boy begins to struggle, but Mrs. Jones pins his arm up and drags him to her room. She asks the boy his name, and he tells her: Roger. She lets go of Roger and commands him to go wash his face. Even though the door is open, he goes to the sink.

Mrs. Jones then asks if Roger tried to steal her purse because he was hungry. He explains that he wanted a pair of blue suede shoes. Mrs. Jones tells him he didn't have to snatch her purse for shoes, but that he could have asked her.

After a long pause, during which Roger once again thinks of running away, Mrs. Jones reveals that she once wanted things she could not get, and she had done things she would not talk about. Mrs. Jones leaves Roger alone with her purse as she goes behind a screen to prepare food. Roger wants her to trust him, so he moves to where she can see him.

After dinner, she gives him ten dollars to buy blue suede shoes and tells him not to steal anymore.

Mrs. Jones then walks him to the door and wishes him good night. Roger is unable to say anything, even "Thank you, M'am" before Mrs. Jones shuts the door. Mrs. Jones was right: the unexpected kindness she showed him means Roger will never forget Mrs. Luella Bates Washington Jones.

A one-sentence synopsis highlighting the theme or central idea of the story can be an effective start to a summary.

The adjective *amusing* marks an opinion and should not be included in an objective summary.

Relating the development of the text in chronological order makes a summary easy to follow.

Unnecessary details should be eliminated.

Not using the woman and the boy's names until this point keeps with the essence of the story.

A key phrase at the end of the story is included in the summary.

The writer's interpretations should not appear in an objective summary.

Comprehending Complex Texts

Over the course of your academic years, you will be required to read increasingly complex texts as preparation for college and the workplace. A complex text can be loosely described as a text that contains challenging vocabulary; long, complex sentences; figurative language; multiple levels of meaning; or unfamiliar settings and situations.

The texts in this textbook provide you with a range of readings, from short stories to autobiographies, poetry, drama, myths, and even science and social studies texts. Some of these texts will fall within your comfort zone; others will most likely be more challenging.

Common Core State Standards

Literature 10. By the end of grade 9, read and comprehend literature, including stories, dramas, and poems, in the grades 9–10 text complexity band proficiently, with scaffolding as needed at the high end of the range.

Informational Text 10. By the end of grade 9, read and comprehend literary nonfiction in the grades 9–10 text complexity band proficiently, with scaffolding as needed at the high end of the range.

Strategy 1: Multidraft Reading

Good readers develop the habit of revisiting texts in order to comprehend them completely. Just as a musician returns over and over again to a song in order to master it, good readers return to texts to more fully enjoy and comprehend them. To fully understand a text, try this multidraft reading strategy:

1st Reading

The first time you read a text, read to gain the basic meaning of the text. If you are reading a narrative text, look for some of the story basics: who did what to whom. If the text is nonfiction, look for the main ideas. If you are reading poetry, read first to get a sense of who the speaker is. Also take note of the setting and situation.

2nd Reading

During your second reading of a text, focus on the artistry or effectiveness of the writing. Look for text structures and think about why the author chose those organizational patterns. Then, examine the author's creative uses of language and the effects of that language. For example, has the author used rhyme, figurative language, or words with negative connotations?

3rd Reading

After your third reading, compare and contrast the text with others of its kind you have read. For example, if you read a poem in sonnet form, think of other sonnets you have read, and think of ways the poems are alike or different. Evaluate the text's overall effectiveness and its central idea or theme.

Independent Practice

As you read this poem, practice the multidraft reading strategy by completing a chart like the one below.

"Memory" by Margaret Walker

I can remember wind-swept streets of cities
on cold and blustery nights, on rainy days;
heads under shabby felts and parasols
and shoulders hunched against a sharp concern;
seeing hurt bewilderment on poor faces,
smelling a deep and sinister unrest
these brooding people cautiously caress;
hearing ghostly marching on pavement stones
and closing fast around their squares of hate.
I can remember seeing them alone,
at work, and in their tenements at home.
I can remember hearing all they said:
their muttering protests their whispered oaths,
and all that spells their living in distress.

Multidraft Reading Chart

	My Understanding
1st Reading Look for key ideas and details that unlock basic meaning.	
2nd Reading Read for deeper meanings. Look for ways in which the author used text structures and language to create effects.	
3rd Reading Read to integrate your knowledge and ideas. Connect the text to others of its kind and to your own experience.	

Strategy 2: Close Read the Text

Complex texts require close reading, a careful analysis of the words, phrases, and sentences. When you close read, use the following tips to comprehend the text:

Tips for Close Reading
1. **Break down long sentences** into parts. Look for the subject of the sentence and its verb. Then, identify which parts of the sentence modify, or give more information about, its subject.
2. **Reread passages** to confirm that you understand their meaning.
3. **Look for context clues,** such as **a.** restatement of an idea. For example, in this sentence, "utter defeat" restates the noun *rout*. The rugby team celebrated its **rout,** its utter defeat, of its arch rival. **b.** definition of sophisticated words. In this sentence, the underlined information defines the word *fealty*. **Fealty** is a pledge of support and allegiance between one person and another. **c.** examples of concepts and topics. In the following passage, the underlined text provides examples of the adjective *serendipitous*. Discovering a treasure when cleaning out an attic or bumping into an old friend when taking shelter from a rain storm—these **serendipitous** events never fail to bring a smile to one's face. **d.** contrasts of ideas and topics. **Altruism,** unlike selfishness, is a rare quality.
4. **Identify pronoun antecedents.** If long sentences contain pronouns, reread the text to make sure you know to what the pronouns refer.
5. **Look for conjunctions,** such as *and*, *or*, and *yet,* to understand relationships between ideas.
6. **Paraphrase,** or restate in your own words, passages of difficult text in order to check your understanding. Remember that a paraphrase is a restatement of an original text; it is not a summary.

Close-Read Model

As you read this document, take note of the sidenotes that model ways to unlock meaning in the text.

from *The Federalist* No. 2 by John Jay

To the People of the State of New York:

WHEN the people of America reflect that they are now called upon to decide a question, which, in its consequences, must prove one of the most important that ever engaged their attention, the propriety of their taking a very comprehensive, as well as a very serious, view of it, will be evident. Nothing is more certain than the indispensable necessity of government, and it is equally undeniable, that whenever and however it is instituted, the people must cede to it some of their natural rights in order to vest it with requisite powers. It is well worthy of consideration therefore, whether it would conduce more to the interest of the people of America that they should, to all general purposes, be one nation, under one federal government, or that they should divide themselves into separate confederacies, and give to the head of each the same kind of powers which they are advised to place in one national government.

It has until lately been a received and uncontradicted opinion that the prosperity of the people of America depended on their continuing firmly united, and the wishes, prayers, and efforts of our best and wisest citizens have been constantly directed to that object. But politicians now appear, who insist that this opinion is erroneous, and that instead of looking for safety and happiness in union, we ought to seek it in a division of the States into distinct confederacies or sovereignties. However extraordinary this new doctrine may appear, it nevertheless has its advocates; and certain characters who were much opposed to it formerly, are at present of the number. Whatever may be the arguments or inducements which have wrought this change in the sentiments and declarations of these gentlemen, it certainly would not be wise in the people at large to adopt these new political tenets without being fully convinced that they are founded in truth and sound policy.

Break down this long sentence into parts. The text highlighted in yellow conveys the basic meaning of the sentence. The text highlighted in blue provides additional information.

Look for antecedents. In this sentence, the noun, *government*, is replaced by the pronoun *it*.

The conjunction *or* indicates that two options are being presented.

Search for context clues. The words in blue are context clues that help you figure out the meaning of the words in yellow.

Strategy 3: Ask Questions

Be an attentive reader by asking questions as you read. Throughout this textbook, we have provided questions for you following each selection. These questions are sorted into three basic categories that build in sophistication and lead you to a deeper understanding of the texts you read.

Here is an example from this text:

Some questions are about **Key Ideas and Details** in the text. To answer these questions, you will need to locate and cite explicit information in the text or draw inferences from what you have read.

Some questions are about **Craft and Structure** in the text. To answer these questions, you will need to analyze how the author developed and structured the text. You will also look for ways in which the author artfully used language and how those word choices impacted the meaning and tone of the work.

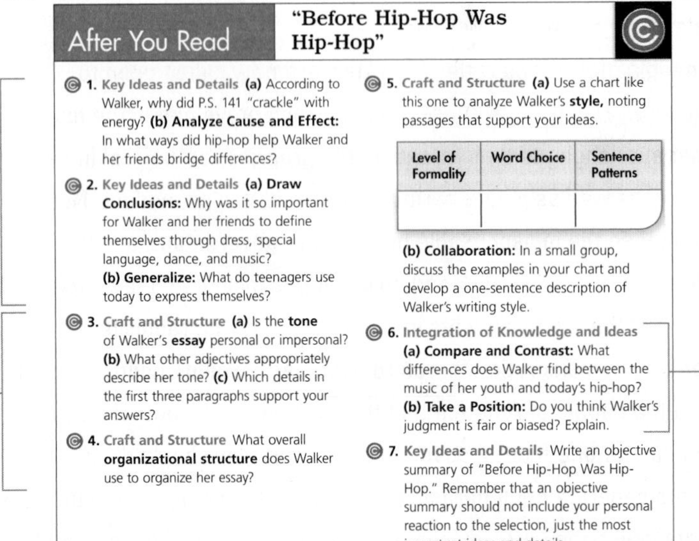

After You Read "Before Hip-Hop Was Hip-Hop"

1. **Key Ideas and Details (a)** According to Walker, why did P.S. 141 "crackle" with energy? **(b) Analyze Cause and Effect:** In what ways did hip-hop help Walker and her friends bridge differences?
2. **Key Ideas and Details (a) Draw Conclusions:** Why was it so important for Walker and her friends to define themselves through dress, special language, dance, and music? **(b) Generalize:** What do teenagers use today to express themselves?
3. **Craft and Structure (a)** Is the **tone** of Walker's **essay** personal or impersonal? **(b)** What other adjectives appropriately describe her tone? **(c)** Which details in the first three paragraphs support your answers?
4. **Craft and Structure** What overall **organizational structure** does Walker use to organize her essay?
5. **Craft and Structure (a)** Use a chart like this one to analyze Walker's **style,** noting passages that support your ideas.

Level of Formality	Word Choice	Sentence Patterns

(b) Collaboration: In a small group, discuss the examples in your chart and develop a one-sentence description of Walker's writing style.

6. **Integration of Knowledge and Ideas (a) Compare and Contrast:** What differences does Walker find between the music of her youth and today's hip-hop? **(b) Take a Position:** Do you think Walker's judgment is fair or biased? Explain.
7. **Key Ideas and Details** Write an objective summary of "Before Hip-Hop Was Hip-Hop." Remember that an objective summary should not include your personal reaction to the selection, just the most important ideas and details.

Some questions are about the **Integration of Knowledge and Ideas.** These questions ask you to evaluate a text in many different ways, such as comparing texts, analyzing arguments in the text, and using many other methods of thinking critically about a text's ideas.

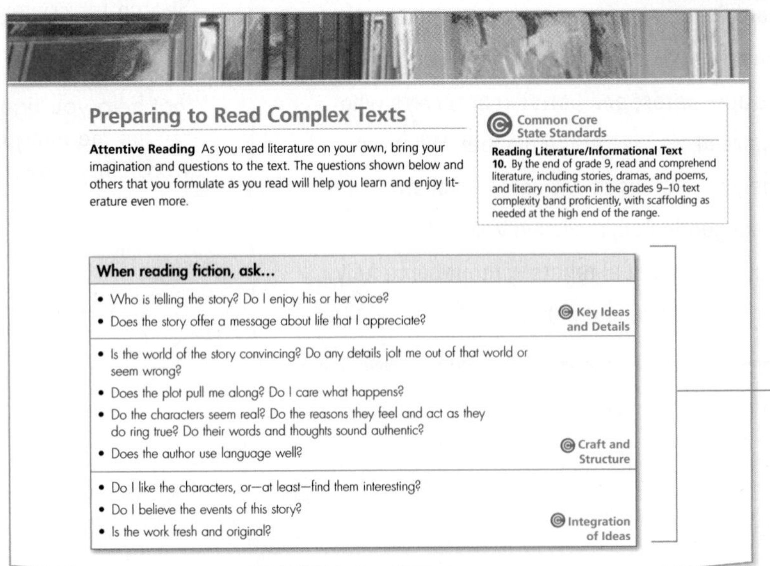

Preparing to Read Complex Texts

Attentive Reading As you read literature on your own, bring your imagination and questions to the text. The questions shown below and others that you formulate as you read will help you learn and enjoy literature even more.

Common Core State Standards

Reading Literature/Informational Text
10. By the end of grade 9, read and comprehend literature, including stories, dramas, and poems, and literary nonfiction in the grades 9–10 text complexity band proficiently, with scaffolding as needed at the high end of the range.

When reading fiction, ask...

- Who is telling the story? Do I enjoy his or her voice?
- Does the story offer a message about life that I appreciate?

Key Ideas and Details

- Is the world of the story convincing? Do any details jolt me out of that world or seem wrong?
- Does the plot pull me along? Do I care what happens?
- Do the characters seem real? Do the reasons they feel and act as they do ring true? Do their words and thoughts sound authentic?
- Does the author use language well?

Craft and Structure

- Do I like the characters, or—at least—find them interesting?
- Do I believe the events of this story?
- Is the work fresh and original?

Integration of Knowledge and Ideas

As you read independently, ask similar types of questions to ensure that you fully enjoy and comprehend texts you read for school and for pleasure. We have provided sets of questions for you on the Independent Reading pages at the end of each unit.

INFORMATIONAL TEXT

Model

Following is an example of a complex text. The sidenotes show sample questions that an attentive reader might ask while reading.

from "Farewell Address" by General Douglas MacArthur

. . . I have just left your fighting sons in Korea. . . . It was my constant effort to preserve them and end this savage conflict honorably and with the least loss of time and a minimum sacrifice of life. . . . Those gallant men will remain often in my thoughts and in my prayers always.

I am closing my fifty-two years of military service. . . . The world has turned over many times since I took the oath on the plain at West Point . . . but I still remember the refrain of one of the most popular barracks ballads of that day which proclaimed most proudly that old soldiers never die; they just fade away. And like the old soldier of that ballad, I now close my military career and just fade away, an old soldier who tried to do his duty as God gave him the light to see that duty. Good-by.

Sample questions:

Integration of Knowledge and Ideas What do I know about the Korean War? What can I learn from the General's comments?

Key Ideas and Details What ideas are introduced in the first paragraph? How is the second paragraph different in topic? How are the two paragraphs related?

Craft and Structure How is the last paragraph a good conclusion? How does the General feel about the Korean War? How does he feel about his career?

INFORMATIONAL TEXT

Independent Practice

Write three to five questions you might ask yourself as you read this passage from a speech delivered by Andrew Johnson shortly after the death of Abraham Lincoln.

from "State of the Union Address" by Andrew Johnson

. . . To express gratitude to God in the name of the people for the preservation of the United States is my first duty in addressing you. Our thoughts next revert to the death of the late President by an act of parricidal treason. The grief of the nation is still fresh. It finds some solace in the consideration that he lived to enjoy the highest proof of its confidence by entering on the renewed term of the Chief Magistracy to which he had been elected; that he brought the civil war substantially to a close; that his loss was deplored in all parts of the Union, and that foreign nations have rendered justice to his memory. His removal cast upon me a heavier weight of cares than ever devolved upon any one of his predecessors. To fulfill my trust I need the support and confidence of all who are associated with me in the various departments of Government and the support and confidence of the people.

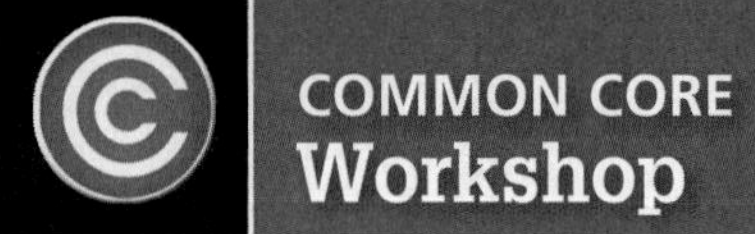

Analyzing Arguments

The ability to evaluate an argument, as well as to make one, is an important skill for success in college and in the workplace.

What Is an Argument?

When you think of the word *argument,* you might think of a disagreement between two people, but an argument is more than that. An argument is a logical way of presenting a belief, conclusion, or stance. A good argument is supported with logical reasoning and relevant evidence.

Purposes of Argument

There are three main purposes for writing a formal argument:

- to change the reader's mind
- to convince the reader to accept what is written
- to motivate the reader to take action, based on what is written

Elements of Argument

Claim (assertion)—what the writer is trying to prove or the call to action
Example: Harold would make a good student council president.

Grounds (evidence)—the support used to convince the reader
Example: He participates in several extracurricular activities, volunteers locally, and earns good grades.

Justification—the link between the grounds and the claim; why the grounds are credible
Example: School and community involvement suggest he knows his school and town well; good grades indicate intelligence.

Addressing the Opposition

While it might be tempting to ignore the opposing side of an issue because you don't agree with it, it is important to present a balanced argument. You can make your argument stronger by refuting the opposition's claim or by demonstrating that you understand it, or perhaps even accept a part or parts of it. When calling someone to action, it is important to address barriers to that action, or to point out ways that the person has already moved in that direction.

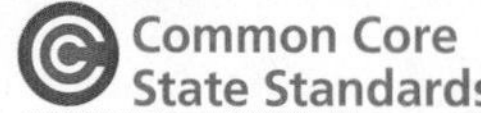
Common Core State Standards

Informational Text 6. Determine an author's point of view or purpose in a text and analyze how an author uses rhetoric to advance that point of view or purpose.

Informational Text 8. Delineate and evaluate the argument and specific claims in a text, assessing whether the reasoning is valid and the evidence is relevant and sufficient; identify false statements and fallacious reasoning.

Informational Text 9. Analyze seminal U.S. documents of historical and literary significance (e.g., Washington's Farewell Address, the Gettysburg Address, Roosevelt's Four Freedoms speech, King's "Letter from Birmingham Jail"), including how they address related themes and concepts.

Language 6. Acquire and use accurately grade-appropriate general academic and domain-specific words and phrases; gather vocabulary knowledge when considering a word or phrase important to comprehension or expression.

INFORMATIONAL TEXT

Model Argument

The excerpted speech includes the common elements of arguments.

from "Remarks on East-West Relations at the Brandenburg Gate in West Berlin," June 12, 1987 by Ronald Reagan

...Behind me stands a wall that encircles the free sectors of this city, part of a vast system of barriers that divides the entire continent of Europe. From the Baltic, south, those barriers cut across Germany in a gash of barbed wire, concrete, dog runs, and guardtowers. Farther south, there may be no visible, no obvious wall. But there remain armed guards and checkpoints all the same—still a restriction on the right to travel, still an instrument to impose upon ordinary men and women the will of a totalitarian state....

The first part of the argument describes the setting and context for the call to action.

...Yet I do not come here to lament. For I find in Berlin a message of hope, even in the shadow of this wall, a message of triumph...

...Where four decades ago there was rubble, today in West Berlin there is the greatest industrial output of any city in Germany—busy office blocks, fine homes and apartments, proud avenues, and the spreading lawns of park land. Where a city's culture seemed to have been destroyed, today there are two great universities, orchestras and an opera, countless theaters, and museums. Where there was want, today there's abundance—food, clothing, automobiles ...From devastation, from utter ruin, you Berliners have, in freedom, rebuilt a city that once again ranks as one of the greatest on Earth...

...In the 1950s, Khrushchev predicted: "We will bury you." But in the West today, we see a free world that has achieved a level of prosperity and well-being unprecedented in all human history. In the Communist world, we see failure, technological backwardness, declining standards of health, even want of the most basic kind-too little food. Even today, the Soviet Union still cannot feed itself. After these four decades, then, there stands before the entire world one great and inescapable conclusion: Freedom leads to prosperity...

Grounds: The free West achieved prosperity, while the Communist East remained in decline.

Justification: A country achieves prosperity when its people have economic freedom. (The grounds support this idea with the example of the free West vs. the Communist East.)

And now the Soviets themselves may, in a limited way, be coming to understand the importance of freedom. We hear much from Moscow about a new policy of reform and openness. Some political prisoners have been released. Certain foreign news broadcasts are no longer being jammed. Some economic enterprises have been permitted to operate with greater freedom from state control. Are these the beginnings of profound changes in the Soviet state?...

The opposition's claim is refuted; later, the opposition is acknowledged for the steps they have already taken.

There is one sign the Soviets can make that would be unmistakable, that would advance dramatically the cause of freedom and peace. General Secretary Gorbachev, ...if you seek prosperity for the Soviet Union and Eastern Europe... Come here to this gate! Mr. Gorbachev, open this gate! Mr. Gorbachev, tear down this wall!

Claim: The wall dividing West and East Berlin should be torn down.

The speaker gives a specific call to action.

The Art of Argument: Rhetorical Devices and Persuasive Techniques

Rhetorical Devices

Rhetoric is the art of using language in order to make a point or to persuade listeners. Rhetorical devices such as the ones listed below are accepted elements of argument. Their use does not invalidate or weaken an argument. Rather, the use of rhetorical devices is regarded as a key part of an effective argument.

Rhetorical Devices	Examples
Repetition The repeated use of certain words, phrases, or sentences	What we long for is freedom. Freedom to work. Freedom to learn.
Parallelism The repeated use of similar grammatical structures	Good writing entertains; great writing inspires.
Rhetorical Question Calling attention to an issue by implying an obvious answer	Is there no reasonable solution to this problem?
Sound Devices The use of alliteration, assonance, rhyme, or rhythm	The path before them was dark, dangerous, and daunting.
Simile and Metaphor Comparison of two like things or asserting that one thing is another	We are caged birds, unable to fly free.

Persuasive Techniques

The persuasive techniques below are often found in advertisements and in other forms of informal persuasion. Although techniques like the ones below are sometimes found in formal arguments, these techniques are usually avoided.

Persuasive Techniques	Examples
Bandwagon Approach/Anti-Bandwagon Approach Appeals to a person's desire to belong/Encourages or celebrates individuality	You have to buy one; everyone has one. Be yourself; don't give into peer pressure.
Emotional Appeal Capitalizes on people's fear, anger, or desire	Without a home security system, your family is in danger.
Endorsement/Testimony Employs a well-known person to promote a product or idea	I use this product every time before I compete, and it has helped me win.
Loaded Language Uses words charged with emotion	They live in abject squalor, their hovels not fit for human inhabitation.
"Plain Folks" Appeal Shows a connection to everyday, ordinary people	I grew up in a hard-working community just like this one.
Hyperbole Exaggerates to make a point	There are a thousand reasons why I'm right.

Model Speech

The excerpted speech below includes examples of rhetorical devices and persuasive techniques.

from "Remarks to the Senate in Support of a Declaration of Conscience" by Margaret Chase Smith

Mr. President:

I would like to speak briefly and simply about a serious national condition. It is a national feeling of fear and frustration that could result in national suicide and the end of everything that we Americans hold dear...

> This emotional language appeals to national pride.

...The United States Senate has long enjoyed worldwide respect as the greatest deliberative body in the world. But recently that deliberative character has too often been debased to the level of a forum of hate and character assassination sheltered by the shield of congressional immunity....

...I think that it is high time for the United States Senate and its members to do some soul-searching—for us to weigh our consciences—on the manner in which we are performing our duty to the people of America—on the manner in which we are using or abusing our individual powers and privileges. I think that it is high time that we remembered that we have sworn to uphold and defend the Constitution. I think that it is high time that we remembered that the Constitution, as amended, speaks not only of the freedom of speech but also of trial by jury instead of trial by accusation....

> The repetition of the first few words in each sentence gives the speech rhythm.

Whether it be a criminal prosecution in court or a character prosecution in the Senate, there is little practical distinction when the life of a person has been ruined.

Those of us who shout the loudest about Americanism in making character assassinations are all too frequently those who, by our own words and acts, ignore some of the basic principles of Americanism:

The right to criticize;

The right to hold unpopular beliefs;

The right to protest;

The right of independent thought.

The exercise of these rights should not cost one single American citizen his reputation or his right to a livelihood nor should he be in danger of losing his reputation or livelihood merely because he happens to know someone who holds unpopular beliefs. Who of us doesn't? Otherwise none of us could call our souls our own. Otherwise thought control would have set in...

> The rhetorical question assumes that all people listening would answer in the same way.

...The American people are sick and tired of seeing innocent people smeared and guilty people whitewashed...

> The parallelism created by repeated grammatical structures adds to the rhythm of the speech.

Composing an Argument

Choosing a Topic

You should choose a topic that matters to people—and to you. Brainstorm topics you would like to write about; then, choose the topic that most interests you.

Once you have chosen a topic, you should check to make sure you can make an arguable claim. Ask yourself:

1. What am I trying to prove?
2. Are there people who would disagree with my claim?
3. Do I have evidence to support my claim?

If you are able to put into words what you want to prove and answered "yes" to questions 2 and 3, you have an arguable claim.

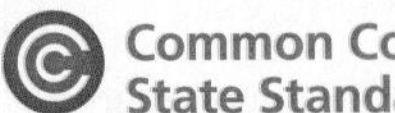

Writing 1.a. Introduce precise, knowledgeable claim(s), distinguish the claim(s) from alternate or opposing claims, and create an organization that establishes clear relationships among claim(s), counterclaims, reasons, and evidence.

Writing 1.b. Develop claim(s) and counterclaims fairly, supplying evidence for each while pointing out the strengths and limitations of both in a manner that anticipates the audience's knowledge level and concerns.

Writing 1.e. Provide a concluding statement or section that follows from and supports the argument presented.

Introducing the Claim and Establishing Its Significance

Before you begin writing, you should consider your audience and how much you think they already know about the topic you have chosen to write about. Then, provide only as much background information as necessary. Remember that you are not writing a summary of the issue—you are crafting an argument.

Once you have provided context for your argument, you should clearly state your claim, or thesis. A written argument's claim often appears in the first paragraph.

Developing Your Claim with Reasoning and Evidence

Now that you have made your claim, you must support it with evidence, or grounds. A good argument should have at least three solid pieces of evidence to support the claim.

Evidence can range from personal experience to researched data or expert opinion. Knowing your audience's knowledge level, concerns, values, and possible biases can help inform your decision on what kind of evidence will have the strongest impact. Make sure your evidence is up to date and comes from a credible source, and don't forget to credit your sources. *(See page R36 for guidelines on citing sources.)*

You should also address the opposing counterclaim within the body of your argument. Consider points you have made or evidence you have provided that a person might challenge. Decide how best to respond to these counterclaims.

Writing a Concluding Statement or Section

Restate your claim in the conclusion (not necessarily word for word) and synthesize the evidence you have provided. Make your conclusion compelling enough to be memorable to the reader; leave him or her with something to think about.

Practice

Complete an outline like the one below to help you plan your own argument.

Brainstorming for Topics:

____

____

The Topic That Most Interests Me Is ______________________ because

____

Arguable Claim (Thesis): ______________________

What I Already Know About the Issue: ______________________

What I Need to Find Out About the Issue:

____

Who Is My Audience and How Much Does My Audience Know About the Issue?

____

Possible Sources of Evidence: ______________________

Grounds to Support My Claim (at least three strong pieces of evidence):

1. ______________________
2. ______________________
3. ______________________

Justifications for My Grounds (why my grounds are allowed to stand as evidence):

1. ______________________
2. ______________________
3. ______________________

Opposing Viewpoints to Consider: ______________________

Correlation to Prentice Hall Literature © 2012

The following correlation shows points at which focused, sustained instruction is provided in the Student Edition. The standards are spiraled and revisited throughout the program, and the Teacher's Edition provides further opportunity to address standards.

Key
SE/TE: Student Edition/Teacher's Edition
CCC: Common Core Companion

Grade 9 Reading Standards for Literature			Prentice Hall Literature © 2012, Grade 9
Key Ideas and Details	RL.1	Cite strong and thorough textual evidence to support analysis of what the text says explicitly as well as inferences drawn from the text.	**SE/TE:** 210, 256, 966; see also After You Read Critical Thinking question banks in Units 1, 2, 4, 5, and 6 **CCC:** 2, 3, 9
	RL.2	Determine a theme or central idea of a text and analyze in detail its development over the course of the text, including how it emerges and is shaped and refined by specific details; provide an objective summary of the text.	**SE/TE:** xlix, 5, 6, 42, 124, 160, 718, 800, 832, 860, 892, 912, 1031, 1032, 1040 **CCC:** 15, 16, 22
	RL.3	Analyze how complex characters (e.g., those with multiple or conflicting motivations) develop over the course of a text, interact with other characters, and advance the plot or develop the theme.	**SE/TE:** 124, 197, 198, 312, 346, 781, 782, 800, 832, 860, 892, 944, 966, 1040, 1144 **CCC:** 28, 29
Craft and Structure	RL.4	Determine the meaning of words and phrases as they are used in the text, including figurative and connotative meanings; analyze the cumulative impact of specific word choices on meaning and tone (e.g., how the language evokes a sense of time and place; how it sets a formal or informal tone).	**SE/TE:** 290, 346, 382, 607, 608, 616, 642, 676, 692, 718, 986, 1086 **CCC:** 35, 36, 42
	RL.5	Analyze how an author's choices concerning how to structure a text, order events within it (e.g., parallel plots), and manipulate time (e.g., pacing, flashbacks) create such effects as mystery, tension, or surprise.	**SE/TE:** 42, 197, 198, 199, 210, 692, 748, 800, 832, 860, 892, 966, 1040 **CCC:** 48, 49
	RL.6	Analyze a particular point of view or cultural experience reflected in a work of literature from outside the United States, drawing on a wide reading of world literature.	**SE/TE:** 80, 290, 572, 1031, 1032, 1040, 1086 **CCC:** 55, 56
Integration of Knowledge and Ideas	RL.7	Analyze the representation of a subject or a key scene in two different artistic mediums, including what is emphasized or absent in each treatment (e.g., Auden's "Musée des Beaux Arts" and Breughel's *Landscape with the Fall of Icarus*).	**SE/TE:** 718, 912, 935, 1126, 1216 **CCC:** 62, 63
	RL.8	(Not applicable to literature)	
	RL.9	Analyze how an author draws on and transforms source material in a specific work (e.g., how Shakespeare treats a theme or topic from Ovid or the Bible or how a later author draws on a play by Shakespeare).	**SE/TE:** 944, 1126, 1216 **CCC:** 69, 70
Range of Reading and Level of Text Complexity	RL.10	By the end of grade 9, read and comprehend literature, including stories, dramas, and poems, in the grades 9–10 text complexity band proficiently, with scaffolding as needed at the high end of the range.	**SE/TE:** xlix, 191, 421, 601, 775, 1025, 1253 **CCC:** 76, 77

Grade 9 Reading Standards for Informational Text			Prentice Hall Literature © 2012, Grade 9
Key Ideas and Details	RI.1	Cite strong and thorough textual evidence to support analysis of what the text says explicitly as well as inferences drawn from the text.	**SE/TE:** 440, 594; see also After You Read Critical Thinking question banks in Units 1,3, and 6 **CCC:** 84, 85, 91
	RI.2	Determine a central idea of a text and analyze its development over the course of the text, including how it emerges and is shaped and refined by specific details; provide an objective summary of the text.	**SE/TE:** 5, 7, 22, 100, 160, 440, 464, 742 **CCC:** 97, 98, 104
	RI.3	Analyze how the author unfolds an analysis or series of ideas or events, including the order in which the points are made, how they are introduced and developed, and the connections that are drawn between them.	**SE/TE:** 74, 154, 284, 427, 428, 464, 498, 938, 980, 1192 **CCC:** 110, 111
Craft and Structure	RI.4	Determine the meaning of words and phrases as they are used in a text, including figurative, connotative, and technical meanings; analyze the cumulative impact of several word choices on meaning and tone (e.g., how the language of a court opinion differs from that of a newspaper).	**SE/TE:** 427, 429, 464, 572, 670 **CCC:** 117, 124
	RI.5	Analyze in detail how an author's ideas or claims are developed and refined by particular sentences, paragraphs, or larger portions of a text (e.g., a section or chapter).	**SE/TE:** 427, 428, 492, 670 **CCC:** 130, 131
	RI.6	Determine an author's point of view or purpose in a text and analyze how an author uses rhetoric to advance that point of view or purpose.	**SE/TE:** xlix, 100, 427, 429, 440, 518, 538, 566, 1120, 1192, 1210 **CCC:** 137, 138, 144
Integration of Knowledge and Ideas	RI.7	Analyze various accounts of a subject told in different mediums (e.g., a person's life story in both print and multimedia), determining which details are emphasized in each account.	**SE/TE:** 100, 1244 **CCC:** 150, 151
	RI.8	Delineate and evaluate the argument and specific claims in a text, assessing whether the reasoning is valid and the evidence is relevant and sufficient; identify false statements and fallacious reasoning.	**SE/TE:** xlix, 518, 538, 566 **CCC:** 157, 158
	RI.9	Analyze seminal U.S. documents of historical and literary significance (e.g., Washington's Farewell Address, the Gettysburg Address, Roosevelt's Four Freedoms speech, King's "Letter from Birmingham Jail"), including how they address related themes and concepts.	**SE/TE:** xlix, 538, 566 **CCC:** 164, 165
Range of Reading and Level of Text Complexity	RI.10	By the end of grade 9, read and comprehend literary nonfiction in the grades 9–10 text complexity band proficiently, with scaffolding as needed at the high end of the range.	**SE/TE:** xlix, 191, 421, 601, 775, 1025, 1253 **CCC:** 171, 172

Grade 9 Writing Standards			Prentice Hall Literature © 2012, Grade 9
Text Types and Purposes	W.1	Write arguments to support claims in an analysis of substantive topics or texts, using valid reasoning and relevant and sufficient evidence.	**SE/TE:** 172, 284, 538, 563, 582, 642, 667, 800, 912 **CCC:** 179, 180, 181, 182, 183, 184, 185, 186, 187, 188, 189
	W.1.a	Introduce precise claim(s), distinguish the claim(s) from alternate or opposing claims, and create an organization that establishes clear relationships among claim(s), counterclaims, reasons, and evidence.	**SE/TE:** xlix, 174, 582, 584, 1120 **CCC:** 179, 180, 181, 182, 183, 184, 185, 186, 187, 188, 189
	W.1.b	Develop claim(s) and counterclaims fairly, supplying evidence for each while pointing out the strengths and limitations of both in a manner that anticipates the audience's knowledge level and concerns.	**SE/TE:** xlix, 584 **CCC:** 179, 180, 181, 182, 183, 184, 185, 186, 187, 188, 189
	W.1.c	Use words, phrases, and clauses to link the major sections of the text, create cohesion, and clarify the relationships between claim(s) and reasons, between reasons and evidence, and between claim(s) and counterclaims.	**SE/TE:** 176, 586, 912, 933 **CCC:** 179, 180, 181, 182, 183, 184, 185, 186, 187, 188, 189
	W.1.d	Establish and maintain a formal style and objective tone while attending to the norms and conventions of the discipline in which they are writing.	**SE/TE:** 172, 176, 584 **CCC:** 179, 180, 181, 182, 183, 184, 185, 186, 187, 188, 189
	W.1.e	Provide a concluding statement or section that follows from and supports the argument presented.	**SE/TE:** xlix, 174, 176, 584 **CCC:** 179, 180, 181, 182, 183, 184, 185, 186, 187, 188, 189
	W.2	Write informative/explanatory texts to examine and convey complex ideas, concepts, and information clearly and accurately through the effective selection, organization, and analysis of content.	**SE/TE:** 160, 290, 382, 402, 440, 463, 464, 489, 498, 512, 572, 670, 676, 686, 756, 938, 944, 960, 986, 1126, 1138, 1192, 1207, 1216, 1234 **CCC:** 190, 191, 192, 193, 194, 195, 196, 197, 198, 199, 200, 201
	W.2.a	Introduce a topic; organize complex ideas, concepts, and information to make important connections and distinctions; include formatting (e.g., headings), graphics (e.g., figures, tables), and multimedia when useful to aiding comprehension.	**SE/TE:** 80, 402, 404, 512, 514, 686, 688, 748, 960, 962, 986, 1126, 1138, 1140, 1216, 1236 **CCC:** 190, 191, 192, 193, 194, 195, 196, 197, 198, 199, 200, 201
	W.2.b	Develop the topic with well-chosen, relevant, and sufficient facts, extended definitions, concrete details, quotations, or other information and examples appropriate to the audience's knowledge of the topic.	**SE/TE:** 402, 404, 758, 960, 986, 1138, 1192, 1207, 1210, 1236 **CCC:** 190, 191, 192, 193, 194, 195, 196, 197, 198, 199, 200, 201
	W.2.c	Use appropriate and varied transitions to link the major sections of the text, create cohesion, and clarify the relationships among complex ideas and concepts.	**SE/TE:** 406, 962, 1238 **CCC:** 190, 191, 192, 193, 194, 195, 196, 197, 198, 199, 200, 201
	W.2.d	Use precise language and domain-specific vocabulary to manage the complexity of the topic.	**SE/TE:** 514, 686, 688, 760, 960, 962, 1138, 1238 **CCC:** 190, 191, 192, 193, 194, 195, 196, 197, 198, 199, 200, 201
	W.2.e	Establish and maintain a formal style and objective tone while attending to the norms and conventions of the discipline in which they are writing.	**SE/TE:** 404, 512, 772, 1140, 1192, 1207 **CCC:** 190, 191, 192, 193, 194, 195, 196, 197, 198, 199, 200, 201
	W.2.f	Provide a concluding statement or section that follows from and supports the information or explanation presented (e.g., articulating implications or the significance of the topic).	**SE/TE:** 406, 514, 960 **CCC:** 190, 191, 192, 193, 194, 195, 196, 197, 198, 199, 200, 201
	W.3	Write narratives to develop real or imagined experiences or events using effective technique, well-chosen details, and well-structured event sequences.	**SE/TE:** 22, 41, 94, 256, 306, 966, 977, 1040, 1085 **CCC:** 202, 203, 204, 205, 206, 207, 208, 209, 210, 211, 212

Grade 9 Writing Standards			Prentice Hall Literature © 2012, Grade 9
	W.3.a	Engage and orient the reader by setting out a problem, situation, or observation, establishing one or multiple point(s) of view, and introducing a narrator and/or characters; create a smooth progression of experiences or events.	**SE/TE:** 94, 306, 308, 346, 373, 966, 977, 1040, 1085 **CCC:** 202, 203, 204, 205, 206, 207, 208, 209, 210, 211, 212
	W.3.b	Use narrative techniques, such as dialogue, pacing, description, reflection, and multiple plot lines, to develop experiences, events, and/or characters.	**SE/TE:** 96, 308, 966, 977, 1040, 1085 **CCC:** 202, 203, 204, 205, 206, 207, 208, 209, 210, 211, 212
	W.3.c	Use a variety of techniques to sequence events so that they build on one another to create a coherent whole.	**SE/TE:** 94, 256, 281, 308, 966, 977, 1040, 1085 **CCC:** 202, 203, 204, 205, 206, 207, 208, 209, 210, 211, 212
	W.3.d	Use precise words and phrases, telling details, and sensory language to convey a vivid picture of the experiences, events, setting, and/or characters.	**SE/TE:** 94, 308, 616, 641, 1040, 1144, 1191 **CCC:** 202, 203, 204, 205, 206, 207, 208, 209, 210, 211, 212
	W.3.e	Provide a conclusion that follows from and reflects on what is experienced, observed, or resolved over the course of the narrative.	**SE/TE:** 96, 210, 255, 306 **CCC:** 202, 203, 204, 205, 206, 207, 208, 209, 210, 211, 212
Production and Distribution of Writing	W.4	Produce clear and coherent writing in which the development, organization, and style are appropriate to task, purpose, and audience.	**SE/TE:** 100, 123, 124, 151, 312, 345, 512, 518, 537, 686, 688, 692, 717, 718, 739, 756, 800, 912, 933, 960, 1086, 1117 **CCC:** 213, 214
	W.5	Develop and strengthen writing as needed by planning, revising, editing, rewriting, or trying a new approach, focusing on addressing what is most significant for a specific purpose and audience.	**SE/TE:** 94, 402, 406, 586, 758, 760, 962, 1002, 1006, 1138, 1234 **CCC:** 220, 221
	W.6	Use technology, including the Internet, to produce, publish, and update individual or shared writing products, taking advantage of technology's capacity to link to other information and to display information flexibly and dynamically.	**SE/TE:** 124, 151, 514, 1006 **CCC:** 227, 228
Research to Build and Present Knowledge	W.7	Conduct short as well as more sustained research projects to answer a question (including a self-generated question) or solve a problem; narrow or broaden the inquiry when appropriate; synthesize multiple sources on the subject, demonstrating understanding of the subject under investigation.	**SE/TE:** 464, 489, 582, 800, 966, 977, 1002, 1004, 1144, 1191 **CCC:** 234, 235, 238
	W.8	Gather relevant information from multiple authoritative print and digital sources, using advanced searches effectively; assess the usefulness of each source in answering the research question; integrate information into the text selectively to maintain the flow of ideas, avoiding plagiarism and following a standard format for citation.	**SE/TE:** 464, 489, 582, 1002, 1004, 1008 **CCC:** 241, 242, 243, 244, 245, 246, 247, 248, 249, 250, 251, 252, 253, 254
	W.9	Draw evidence from literary or informational texts to support analysis, reflection, and research.	**SE/TE:** 42, 71, 1126 **CCC:** 255, 256, 259, 260
	W.9.a	Apply grades 9–10 Reading standards to literature (e.g., "Analyze how an author draws on and transforms source material in a specific work [e.g., how Shakespeare treats a theme or topic from Ovid or the Bible or how a later author draws on a play by Shakespeare].").	**SE/TE:** 418, 756, 1250 **CCC:** 255, 256, 259, 260
	W.9.b	Apply grades 9–10 Reading standards to literary nonfiction (e.g., "Delineate and evaluate the argument and specific claims in a text, assessing whether the reasoning is valid and the evidence is relevant and sufficient; identify false statements and fallacious reasoning.").	**CCC:** 255, 256, 259, 260

Grade 9 Writing Standards			Prentice Hall Literature © 2012, Grade 9
Range of Writing	W.10	Write routinely over extended time frames (time for research, reflection, and revision) and shorter time frames (a single sitting or a day or two) for a range of tasks, purposes, and audiences.	**SE/TE:** 756; See these features in Units 1, 2, 3, 4, 5, and 6: Integrated Language Skills; Reading for Information: Comparing Informational Texts; Comparing Literary Works; Writing Workshops **CCC:** 263, 264, 265, 266, 269, 270, 271, 272

Grade 9 Speaking and Listening Standards			Prentice Hall Literature © 2012, Grade 9
Comprehension and Collaboration	SL.1	Initiate and participate effectively in a range of collaborative discussions (one-on-one, in groups, and teacher-led) with diverse partners on *grades 9–10 topics, texts, and issues,* building on others' ideas and expressing their own clearly and persuasively.	**SE/TE:** 3, 42, 71, 440, 463, 605, 642, 667, 779, 800, 912, 935, 1029, 1040, 1085, 1086, 1117 **CCC:** 274, 275, 276, 277, 278, 279, 280, 281
	SL.1.a	Come to discussions prepared, having read and researched material under study; explicitly draw on that preparation by referring to evidence from texts and other research on the topic or issue to stimulate a thoughtful, well-reasoned exchange of ideas.	**SE/TE:** 22, 41, 42, 71, 692, 717, 718, 739, 1040, 1085, 1192, 1207 **CCC:** 274, 275, 276, 277, 278, 279, 280, 281
	SL.1.b	Work with peers to set rules for collegial discussions and decision-making (e.g., informal consensus, taking votes on key issues, presentation of alternate views), clear goals and deadlines, and individual roles as needed.	**SE/TE:** 195, 425, 692, 717, 1040, 1085 **CCC:** 274, 275, 276, 277, 278, 279, 280, 281
	SL.1.c	Propel conversations by posing and responding to questions that relate the current discussion to broader themes or larger ideas; actively incorporate others into the discussion; and clarify, verify, or challenge ideas and conclusions.	**SE/TE:** 22, 41, 692, 717, 718, 739, 1192, 1207 **CCC:** 274, 275, 276, 277, 278, 279, 280, 281
	SL.1.d	Respond thoughtfully to diverse perspectives, summarize points of agreement and disagreement, and, when warranted, qualify or justify their own views and understanding and make new connections in light of the evidence and reasoning presented.	**SE/TE:** 22, 718, 739, 1016 **CCC:** 274, 275, 276, 277, 278, 279, 280, 281
	SL.2	Integrate multiple sources of information presented in diverse media or formats (e.g., visually, quantitatively, orally) evaluating the credibility and accuracy of each source.	**SE/TE:** 312, 345,1144 **CCC:** 282, 283
	SL.3	Evaluate a speaker's point of view, reasoning, and use of evidence and rhetoric, identifying any fallacious reasoning or exaggerated or distorted evidence.	**SE/TE:** 412, 538, 563, 592, 1086, 1117, 1191 **CCC:** 286, 287, 290
Presentation of Knowledge and Ideas	SL.4	Present information, findings, and supporting evidence clearly, concisely, and logically such that listeners can follow the line of reasoning and the organization, development, substance, and style are appropriate to purpose, audience, and task.	**SE/TE:** 182, 210, 255, 256, 281, 346, 373, 464, 489, 518, 537, 592, 616, 641, 800, 912, 935 **CCC:** 293, 294, 297
	SL.5	Make strategic use of digital media (e.g., textual, graphical, audio, visual, and interactive elements) in presentations to enhance understanding of findings, reasoning, and evidence and to add interest.	**SE/TE:** 100, 123, 592, 642, 667, 1016, 1144, 1191 **CCC:** 300, 301
	SL.6	Adapt speech to a variety of contexts and tasks, demonstrating command of formal English when indicated or appropriate.	**SE/TE:** 592, 766 **CCC:** 302, 303, 306

Grade 9 Language Standards			Prentice Hall Literature © 2012, Grade 9
Conventions of Standard English	L.1	Demonstrate command of the conventions of standard English grammar and usage when writing or speaking.	**SE/TE:** 100, 123, 124, 151, 210, 255, 256, 281, 346, 373, 440, 463, 518, 537, 616, 641, 642, 667, 800, 966, 1040, 1085, 1086, 1117, 1140 **CCC:** 310, 311, 312, 313
	L.1.a	Use parallel structure.	**SE/TE:** 586 **CCC:** 310, 311
	L.1.b	Use various types of phrases (noun, verb, adjectival, adverbial, participial, prepositional, absolute) and clauses (independent, dependent; noun, relative, adverbial) to convey specific meanings and add variety and interest to writing or presentations.	**SE/TE:** 688, 692, 717, 718, 739, 912, 933, 962, 966, 977, 1008, 1238 **CCC:** 312, 313
	L.2	Demonstrate command of the conventions of standard English capitalization, punctuation, and spelling when writing.	**SE/TE:** 22, 41, 1140, 1144, 1191, 1192, 1207 **CCC:** 314, 315, 316, 317, 318, 319
	L.2.a	Use a semicolon (and perhaps a conjunctive adverb) to link two or more closely related independent clauses.	**CCC:** 314, 315
	L.2.b	Use a colon to introduce a list or quotation.	**SE/TE:** 756, 760 **CCC:** 316, 317
	L.2.c	Spell correctly.	**SE/TE:** 178, 408, 588, 690, 1142 **CCC:** 318, 319
Knowledge of Language	L.3	Apply knowledge of language to understand how language functions in different contexts, to make effective choices for meaning or style, and to comprehend more fully when reading or listening.	**SE/TE:** 71, 538, 563, 670, 764, 1014 **CCC:** 320, 321
	L.3.a	Write and edit work so that it conforms to the guidelines in a style manual (e.g., *MLA Handbook, Turabian's Manual for Writers*) appropriate for the discipline and writing type.	**SE/TE:** 1006, 1008, 1012 **CCC:** 320, 321
Vocabulary Acquisition and Use	L.4	Determine or clarify the meaning of unknown and multiple-meaning words and phrases based on *grades 9–10 reading and content,* choosing flexibly from a range of strategies.	**SE/TE:** 410, 590 **CCC:** 322, 323, 324, 325, 326, 327, 328, 329
	L.4.a	Use context (e.g., the overall meaning of a sentence, paragraph, or text; a word's position or function in a sentence) as a clue to the meaning of a word or phrase.	**SE/TE:** 124, 590 **CCC:** 322, 323
	L.4.b	Identify and correctly use patterns of word changes that indicate different meanings or parts of speech (e.g., *analyze, analysis, analytical; advocate, advocacy*).	**SE/TE:** 74, 154, 284, 566, 1120, 1210 **CCC:** 324, 325
	L.4.c	Consult general and specialized reference materials (e.g., dictionaries, glossaries, thesauruses), both print and digital, to find the pronunciation of a word or determine or clarify its precise meaning, its part of speech, or its etymology.	**SE/TE:** 180, 376, 410, 938, 1014, 1210, 1242 **CCC:** 326, 327
	L.4.d	Verify the preliminary determination of the meaning of a word or phrase (e.g., by checking the inferred meaning in context or in a dictionary).	**SE/TE:** 590, 1014 **CCC:** 328, 329
	L.5	Demonstrate understanding of figurative language, word relationships, and nuances in word meanings.	**SE/TE:** 42, 518, 616, 641, 642, 667, 686, 1144 **CCC:** 330, 331, 332, 333
	L.5.a	Interpret figures of speech (e.g., euphemism, oxymoron) in context and analyze their role in the text.	**SE/TE:** 892, 1242 **CCC:** 330, 331
	L.5.b	Analyze nuances in the meaning of words with similar denotations.	**SE/TE:** 180, 582, 764 **CCC:** 332, 333

Grade 9 Language Standards			Prentice Hall Literature © 2012, Grade 9
Vocabulary Acquisition and Use	L.6	Acquire and use accurately general academic and domain-specific words and phrases, sufficient for reading, writing, speaking, and listening at the college and career readiness level; demonstrate independence in gathering vocabulary knowledge when considering a word or phrase important to comprehension or expression.	**SE/TE:** xlix, 3, 42, 74, 100, 123, 124, 151, 176, 195, 210, 255, 312, 345, 346, 373, 376, 425, 440, 492, 538, 605, 670, 742, 779, 938, 980, 1029, 1086, 1120, 1192 **CCC:** 334, 335

Grade 9 Language Progressive Skills The following skills are particularly likely to require continued attention in higher grades as they are applied to increasingly sophisticated writing and speaking.			Prentice Hall Literature © 2012, Grade 9
Conventions of Standard English	L.3.1.f	Ensure subject-verb and pronoun-antecedent agreement.	177, 345, 407, 587
	L.4.1.f	Produce complete sentences, recognizing and correcting inappropriate fragments and run-ons.	1141
	L.4.1.g	Correctly use frequently confused words (e.g., *to/too/two; there/their*).	763
	L.5.1.d	Recognize and correct inappropriate shifts in verb tense.	309
	L.6.1.c	Recognize and correct inappropriate shifts in pronoun number and person.	123, 151, 177
	L.7.1.c	Place phrases and clauses within a sentence, recognizing and correcting misplaced and dangling modifiers.	963
	L.6.1.d	Recognize and correct vague pronouns (i.e., ones with unclear or ambiguous antecedents).	177
	L.8.1.d	Recognize and correct inappropriate shifts in verb voice and mood.	372, 514
	L.6.1.e	Recognize variations from standard English in their own and others' writing and speaking, and identify and use strategies to improve expression in conventional language.	412, 413, 593, 641
	L.6.2.a	Use punctuation (commas, parentheses, dashes) to set off nonrestrictive/parenthetical elements.	1190, 1206
Knowledge of Language	L.3.3.a	Choose words and phrases for effect.	539, 586, 588, 687
	L.4.3.b	Choose punctuation for effect.	760
	L.6.3.a	Vary sentence patterns for meaning, reader/listener interest, and style.	345, 515, 517, 963
	L.6.3.b	Maintain consistency in style and tone.	515, 517
	L.7.3.a	Choose language that expresses ideas precisely and concisely, recognizing and eliminating wordiness and redundancy.	425, 641, 687, 717

Key Features of the Standards

The following summary of key features is from the Introduction to the Common Core State Standards for English Language Arts © 2010, National Governors Association for Best Practices and Council of Chief State School Officers. All rights reserved.

Reading

Text Complexity and the Growth of Comprehension

The Reading standards place equal emphasis on the sophistication of what students read and the skill with which they read. Standard 10 defines a grade-by-grade "staircase" of increasing text complexity that rises from beginning reading to the college and career readiness level. Whatever they are reading, students must also show a steadily growing ability to discern more from and make fuller use of text, including making an increasing number of connections among ideas and between texts, considering a wider range of textual evidence, and becoming more sensitive to inconsistencies, ambiguities, and poor reasoning in texts.

Writing

Text Types, Responding to Reading, and Research

The Standards acknowledge the fact that whereas some writing skills, such as the ability to plan, revise, edit, and publish, are applicable to many types of writing, other skills are more properly defined in terms of specific writing types: arguments, informative/explanatory texts, and narratives. Standard 9 stresses the importance of the writing-reading connection by requiring students to draw upon and write about evidence from literary and informational texts. Because of the centrality of writing to most forms of inquiry, research standards are prominently included in this strand, though skills important to research are infused throughout the document.

Speaking and Listening

Flexible Communication and Collaboration

Including but not limited to skills necessary for formal presentations, the Speaking and Listening standards require students to develop a range of broadly useful oral communication and interpersonal skills. Students must learn to work together, express and listen carefully to ideas, integrate information from oral, visual, quantitative, and media sources, evaluate what they hear, use media and visual displays strategically to help achieve communicative purposes, and adapt speech to context and task.

Language

Conventions, Effective Use, and Vocabulary

The Language standards include the essential "rules" of standard written and spoken English, but they also approach language as a matter of craft and informed choice among alternatives. The vocabulary standards focus on understanding words and phrases, their relationships, and their nuances and on acquiring new vocabulary, particularly general academic and domain-specific words and phrases.

Introductory Unit	Standards Addressed
• **Building Academic Vocabulary**	Language 6
• **Writing an Objective Summary**	Literature 2
• **Comprehending Complex Texts**	Literature 10, Informational Text 10
• **Analyzing Arguments**	Informational Text 6, Informational Text 8, Informational Text 9, Writing 1.a, Writing 1.b, Writing 1.e, Language 6

	Literary Analysis Workshop	Writing Workshop	Vocabulary Workshop
Unit 1	Literary Analysis Workshop: **Fiction and Nonfiction**	**Narrative Text: Autobiographical Narrative,** pp. 94–99 **Work in Progress:** pp. 41, 71 **Argument: Problem-and-Solution Essay,** pp. 172–179 **Work in Progress:** pp. 123, 151	**Using a Dictionary and Thesaurus,** pp. 180–181
Unit 2	Literary Analysis Workshop: **Short Stories**	**Narrative Text: Short Story,** pp. 306–311 **Work in Progress:** pp. 255, 281 **Explanatory Text: Cause-and-Effect Essay,** pp. 402–409 **Work in Progress:** pp. 345, 373	**Etymology: Words from Mythology,** pp. 410–411
Unit 3	Literary Analysis Workshop: **Types of Nonfiction**	**Informative Text: Business Letter,** pp. 512–517 **Work in Progress:** pp. 463, 489 **Argument: Editorial,** pp. 582–589 **Work in Progress:** pp. 537, 563	**Words With Multiple Meanings,** pp. 590–591
Unit 4	Literary Analysis Workshop: **Poetry**	**Informative Text: Descriptive Essay,** pp. 686–691 **Work in Progress:** pp. 641, 667 **Argument: Response to Literature,** pp. 756–763 **Work in Progress:** pp. 717, 739	**Connotation and Denotation,** pp. 764–765
Unit 5	Literary Analysis Workshop: **Drama**	**Explanatory Text: How-to-Essay,** pp. 960–965 **Work in Progress:** p. 933 **Informative Text: Research Report,** pp. 1002–1013 **Work in Progress:** p. 977	**Borrowed and Foreign Words,** pp. 1014–1015
Unit 6	Literary Analysis Workshop: **Themes in Literature: Heroism**	**Explanatory Text: Technical Document,** pp. 1138–1143 **Work in Progress:** pp. 1085, 1117 **Informative Text: Comparison-and-Contrast Essay,** pp. 1234–1241 **Work in Progress:** pp. 1191, 1207	**Idioms, Jargon, and Technical Terms,** pp. 1242–1244

Common Core State Standards appear in red throughout the Skills Navigator.

Communications Workshop	Independent Reading	Assessment Practice
Giving and Following Oral Instructions, pp. 182–183	**Independent Reading,** pp. 190–191	**Test Practice: Cumulative Review,** pp. 184–187 **Performance Tasks,** pp. 188–189
Evaluating a Speech, pp. 412–413	**Independent Reading,** pp. 420–421	**Test Practice: Cumulative Review,** pp. 414–417 **Performance Tasks,** pp. 418–419
Delivering a Persuasive Speech, pp. 592–593	**Independent Reading,** pp. 600–601	**Test Practice: Cumulative Review,** pp. 594–597 **Performance Tasks,** pp. 598–599
Oral Interpretation of Literature, pp. 766–767	**Independent Reading,** pp. 774–775	**Test Practice: Cumulative Review,** pp. 768–771 **Performance Tasks,** pp. 772–773
Multimedia Presentation of a Research Report, pp. 1016–1017	**Independent Reading,** pp. 1024–1025	**Test Practice: Cumulative Review,** pp. 1018–1021 **Performance Tasks,** pp. 1022–1023
Comparing Media Coverage, pp. 1244–1245	**Independent Reading,** pp. 1252–1253	**Test Practice: Cumulative Review,** pp. 1246–1249 **Performance Tasks,** pp. 1250–1251

COMMON CORE

UNIT 1 ▪ Skills Navigator: Fiction and Nonfiction

		Selection	Page	Reading Skill	Literary Analysis	Word Study
LITERARY ANALYSIS WORKSHOP		***from*** **I Stand Here Ironing** Tillie Olsen	9–11		**Determining Themes in Fiction,** p. 6 RL.2 **Determining Central Ideas in Nonfiction,** p. 7 RI.2 **Close Read: Theme in Fiction,** pp. 8–11 **Close Read: Central Idea in Nonfiction,** pp. 16–21	**Introducing the Big Question,** pp. 2–3 L.6
		from **The Giant's House** Elizabeth McCracken	12–15			
		from **State of the Union Address (1941)** Franklin D. Roosevelt	17			
		Desiderata Elizabeth McCracken	18–21			
READING FOCUS MAKE PREDICTIONS	MA	**The Washwoman** Isaac Bashevis Singer	26	**Make Predictions,** pp. 23, 30, 31, 33, 37, 39; **UR** pp. 36, 54	**Narrative Essay,** pp. 23, 27, 33, 39; **UR** pp. 35, 53 **Spiral Review,** pp. 28, 38	**Old English prefix** ***fore-,*** pp. 24, 33 **Latin Prefix** ***con-,*** pp. 34, 39
	MC	**New Directions** Maya Angelou	36			
	MA	**Sonata for Harp and Bicycle** Joan Aiken	46	**Make Predictions,** pp. 43, 49, 53, 54, 56, 57, 62, 67, 69; **UR** pp. 75, 93	**Plot,** pp. 43, 48, 50, 51, 53, 57, 64, 69; **UR** pp. 74, 92 RL.5 **Spiral Review,** pp. 48, 68	**Latin suffix** ***-ate,*** pp. 44, 57 **Latin suffix** ***-tion,*** pp. 58, 69
	MC	**The Cask of Amontillado** Edgar Allan Poe	60			
		Reading for Information Recipe/How-to Article	74	**Read to Perform a Task,** p. 74 RI.3		
		Comparing Literary Works **Checkouts** Cynthia Rylant **The Girl Who Can** Ama Ata Aidoo	82 86		**Comparing Literary Works: Point of View,** pp. 80, 83, 84, 85, 87, 89, 93; **UR** p. 113 RL.6 **Spiral Review,** p. 91	**UR** p. 114
READING FOCUS AUTHOR'S PURPOSE	MA	***from*** **A White House Diary** Lady Bird Johnson	104	**Author's Purpose,** pp. 101, 105, 109, 111, 118, 121; **UR** pp. 141, 159 RI.7, RI.9	**Voice,** pp. 101, 105, 110, 111, 116, 117, 120, 121; **UR** pp. 140, 158 RI.7, RI.9 **Spiral Review,** pp. 106, 116	**Latin root** ***-fin-,*** pp. 102, 111 **Latin root** ***-term-,*** pp. 112, 121
	MC	**My English** Julia Alvarez	114			
	MA	**The Secret Life of Walter Mitty** James Thurber	128	**Author's Purpose,** pp. 125, 129, 135, 143, 144, 149; **UR** pp. 180, 198	**Character,** pp. 125, 130, 134, 135, 141, 144, 146, 149; **UR** pp. 179, 197 RL.3 **Spiral Review,** pp. 133, 142	**Latin suffix** ***-able,*** pp. 126, 135 **Latin suffix** ***-ive,*** pp. 136, 149
	MC	**Uncle Marcos** Isabel Allende	138			
		Reading for Information Train Schedule/Brochure	154	**Analyze Structure and Format,** p. 154 RI.3		
		Comparing Literary Works **I Forget Thee, Oh Earth . . .** Arthur C. Clarke **from** ***Silent Spring*** Rachel Carson	162 167		**Comparing Literary Works: Theme,** pp. 160, 162, 163, 165, 166, 167, 170, 171; **UR** p. 218 RL.2, RI.2	**UR** p. 219

Key: UR: *Unit Resources* **MA:** More Accessible **MC:** More Complex Indicates an Exemplar Text

Writing	Conventions	Extension Activity	Assessment
Narrative Text: Anecdote, p. 41; **UR** p. 58 W.3 **Writing Workshop: Work in Progress:** Prewriting for an Autobiographical Narrative, p. 41	**Common and Proper Nouns,** p. 40; **UR** p. 57 L.2	• **Speaking and Listening: Interview,** p. 41; **UR** p. 59 SL.1.a, SL.1.c, SL.1.d	**Selection Tests,** **UR** pp. 42–47; 63–68
Explanatory Text: Critique, p. 71; **UR** p. 97 W.9 **Writing Workshop: Work in Progress:** Prewriting for an Autobiographical Narrative, p. 71	**Abstract and Concrete Nouns,** p. 70; **UR** p. 96 L.3	• **Speaking and Listening: Retell,** p. 71; **UR** p. 98 SL.1, SL.1.a	**Test Practice: Reading,** pp. 72–73 **Selection Tests,** **UR** pp. 81–86; 102–107
Timed Writing: Explanatory Text: Essay, p. 79 W.2			
Timed Writing: Explanatory Text: Essay, p. 93; **UR** p. 115 W.2.a			**Selection Tests,** **UR** pp. 119–124
Narrative Text: Journal Entry, p. 123; **UR** p. 163 W.4 **Writing Workshop: Work in Progress:** Prewriting for Problem-Solution Essay, p. 123	**Pronouns,** p. 122; **UR** p. 162 L.1	• **Research and Technology: Multimedia Presentation,** p. 123; **UR** p. 164 SL.5	**Selection Tests,** **UR** pp. 147–152; 168–173
Informational Text: Character Profile, p. 151; **UR** p. 202 W.4, W.6 **Writing Workshop: Work in Progress:** Prewriting for Problem-Solution Essay, p. 151	**Pronouns,** p. 150; **UR** p. 201 L.1	• **Research and Technology: Scene,** p.151; **UR** p. 203 W.6	**Test Practice: Reading,** pp. 152–153 **Selection Tests,** **UR** pp. 186–191; 207–212
Timed Writing: Explanatory Text: Description, p. 159 W.2			
Timed Writing: Reflective Text: Essay, p. 171; **UR** p. 220 W.2			**Selection Tests,** **UR** pp. 224–229 **Cumulative Review,** pp. 184–187 **Performance Tasks,** pp. 188–189

COMMON CORE

UNIT 2 ▪ Skills Navigator: Short Stories

Section	Level	Selection	Page	Reading Skill	Literary Analysis	Word Study
LITERARY ANALYSIS WORKSHOP		**Old Man at the Bridge,** Ernest Hemingway **The Jade Peony** Wayson Choy	201 203		**Analyzing Character,** p. 198 RL.3, RL.5 **Analyzing Structure and Theme,** p. 199 RL.5 **Close Read: Elements of a Short Story,** pp. 200–209	**Introducing the Big Question,** pp. 194–195 RL.6
READING FOCUS **MAKE INFERENCES**	MA	**The Most Dangerous Game** Richard Connell	214	**Make Inferences,** pp. 211, 219, 220, 223, 226, 227, 228, 231, 237, 242, 247, 250, 253; **UR** pp. 29, 47	**Conflict,** pp. 211, 216, 218, 222, 224, 225, 226, 228, 232, 235, 237, 245, 246, 249, 251, 252, 253; **UR** pp. 28, 46 RL.3 **Spiral Review,** pp. 231, 246	**Latin suffi x *-esque*,** pp. 212, 237 **Latin suffi x *-ant*,** pp. 238, 253 **UR** pp. 30, 48
	MC	**American History** Judith Ortiz Cofer	240			
	MA	**The Gift of the Magi** O. Henry	260	**Make Inferences,** pp. 257, 261, 267, 272, 276, 279; **UR** pp. 68, 86 RL.1	**Irony,** pp. 257, 265, 267, 273, 274, 276, 277, 278, 279; **UR** pp. 67, 85 **Spiral Review,** pp. 266, 277	**Latin prefix *de-*,** pp. 258, 267 **Latin prefix *inter-*,** pp. 268, 279 **UR** pp. 69, 87
	MC	**The Interlopers** Saki	270			
		Reading for Information Signs and Instructions/ Technical Instructions	284	**Critique the Logic of Functional Documents,** p. 284 RI.3		
		Comparing Literary Works **The Man to Send Rain Clouds** Leslie Marmon Silko **Old Man of the Temple** R. K. Narayan	 292 298		**Comparing Literary Works: Setting,** pp. 290, 293, 294, 296, 297, 300, 303, 304, 305; **UR** p. 106 RL.3; **Spiral Review,** p. 294	**UR** p. 107
READING FOCUS **CAUSE AND EFFECT**	MA	**Rules of the Game** Amy Tan	316	**Cause and Effect,** pp. 313, 320, 323, 324, 326, 328, 329, 334, 335, 340, 341, 343; **UR** pp. 133, 151	**Characterization,** pp. 313, 318, 319, 320, 321, 324, 329, 333, 334, 336, 339, 343; **UR** pp. 132, 150 RL.3; **Spiral Review,** pp. 318, 341	**Latin root *-bene-*,** pp. 314, 329 **Latin root *-jec(t)-*,** pp. 330, 343 **UR** pp. 134, 152
	MC	**The Necklace** Guy de Maupassant	332			
	MA	**Blues Ain't No Mockin Bird** Toni Cade Bambara	350	**Cause and Effect,** pp. 347, 351, 356, 358, 359, 365, 369, 370, 371; **UR** pp. 172, 190	**Dialogue and Dialect,** pp. 347, 351, 352, 355, 359, 367, 371; **UR** pp. 171, 189 RL.4 **Spiral Review,** pp. 352, 366	**Latin suffix *-ity*,** pp. 348, 359 **Latin suffix *-ous*,** pp. 360, 371; **UR** pp. 173, 191
	MC	**The Invalid's Story** Mark Twain	362			
		Reading for Information User Guide/Application	376	**Analyze Structure and Format,** p. 376		
		Comparing Literary Works **The Scarlet Ibis** James Hurst **The Golden Kite, the Silver Wind** Ray Bradbury	 384 396		**Comparing Literary Works: Symbolism and Allegory,** pp. 382, 384, 385, 387, 388, 390, 391, 393, 394, 395, 397, 398, 400, 401; **UR** p. 210 RL.4; **Spiral Review,** pp. 394, 399	**UR** p. 211

Key: UR: *Unit Resources* **MA:** More Accessible **MC:** More Complex ⓔ Indicates an Exemplar Text

Writing	Conventions	Extension Activity	Assessment
Narrative Text: Alternative Ending, p. 255; **UR** p. 51 W.3.e **Writing Workshop: Work in Progress:** Prewriting for Narration: Short Story, p. 255	**Regular Verbs,** p. 254; **UR** p. 50 L.1	• **Speaking and Listening: Oral Presentations,** p. 255; **UR** p. 52 SL.4	**Selection Tests, UR** pp. 35–40; 56–61
Narrative Text: News Report, p. 281; **UR** p. 90 W.3, W.3.c **Writing Workshop: Work in Progress:** Prewriting for Narration: Short Story, p. 281	**Irregular Verbs,** p. 280; **UR** p. 89	• **Speaking and Listening: Debate,** p. 281; **UR** p. 91 SL.4	**Test Practice: Reading,** pp. 282–283 **Selection Tests, UR** pp. 74–79; 95–100
Timed Writing: Explanatory Text: Speech, p. 289 W.2			
Timed Writing: Explanatory Text: Essay, p. 305; **UR** p. 108 W.2			**Selection Tests, UR** pp. 112–117
Informative Text: Written Presentation, p. 345; **UR** p. 155 W.4 **Writing Workshop: Work in Progress:** Prewriting for Exposition: Cause-and-Effect Essay, p. 345	**Subjects and Predicates,** p. 344; **UR** p. 154	• **Research and Technology: Brochure,** p. 345; **UR** p. 156 SL.2	**Selection Tests, UR** pp. 139–144; 160–165
Narrative Text: Informal Letter, p. 373; **UR** p. 194 W.3.a **Writing Workshop: Work in Progress:** Prewriting for Exposition: Cause-and-Effect Essay, p. 373	**Active and Passive Voice,** p. 372; **UR** p. 193	• **Speaking and Listening: Dialogue,** p. 373; **UR** p. 195 SL.2	**Test Practice: Reading,** pp. 374–375 **Selection Tests, UR** pp. 178–183, 199–204
Timed Writing: Explanatory Text: Report, p. 381 W.2			
Timed Writing: Explanatory Text: Essay, p. 401; **UR** p. 212 W.2			**Selection Tests, UR** pp. 216–221 **Cumulative Review,** pp. 414–417 **Performance Tasks,** pp. 418–419

All selections are supported in the *Reader's Notebooks.*

UNIT 3 ▪ Skills Navigator: Types of Nonfiction

Section	Level	Selection	Page	Reading Skill	Literary Analysis	Word Study
LITERARY ANALYSIS WORKSHOP		**I Am an American Day Address** ⓒ Learned Hand	431		**Analyzing the Development and Organization of Ideas,** p. 428 RI.3, RI.5 **Analyzing Word Choice and Rhetoric,** p. 429 RI.4, RI.6 **Close Read: Development of Ideas,** pp. 430–439	**Introducing the Big Question,** pp. 424–425 L.6
		Speech to the Virginia Convention Patrick Henry	432			
		Before Hip-Hop Was Hip-Hop Rebecca Walker	435			
READING FOCUS MAIN IDEA	MA	**A Celebration of Grandfathers** Rudolfo A. Anaya	444	**Main idea,** pp. 441, 448, 453, 458, 461; **UR** pp. 29, 47 RI.1, RI.2	**Author's Style,** pp. 441, 445, 446, 449, 453, 457, 458, 460, 461; **UR** pp. 28, 46 **Spiral Review,** pp. 446, 458	**Latin root *-viv-*,** pp. 442, 453 **Latin root *-dur-*,** pp. 454, 461 **UR** pp. 30, 48
	MC	**On Summer** Lorraine Hansberry	456			
	MA	**Single Room, Earth View** Sally Ride	468	**Main idea,** pp. 465, 470, 475, 481, 486, 487; **UR** pp. 68, 86 RI.1, RI.2, RI.3	**Expository Essay,** pp. 465, 471, 472, 475, 479, 480, 483, 485, 487; **UR** pp. 67, 85 **Spiral Review,** pp. 471, 485	**Latin root *-nov-*,** pp. 466, 475 **Latin root *-temp-*,** pp. 476, 487 **UR** pp. 69, 87
	MC	**The News** Neil Postman	478			
		Reading for Information Technical Document/ Web Article	492	**Generate Relevant Questions,** p. 492 RI.5		
		Comparing Literary Works ***from* A Lincoln Preface** Carl Sandburg	500		**Comparing Literary Works: Biographical Writing,** pp. 498, 503, 504, 506, 507, 510, 511; **UR** p. 106 RI.4; **Spiral Review,** pp. 504, 510	**UR** p. 107
		Arthur Ashe Remembered John McPhee	508			
READING FOCUS EVALUATE PERSUASION	MA	**Carry Your Own Skis** Lian Dolan	522	**Evaluate Persuasion,** pp. 519, 525, 526, 527, 535; **UR** pp. 133, 151 RI.8	**Persuasive Essay,** pp. 519, 523, 525, 527, 531, 535; **UR** pp. 132, 150 **Spiral Review,** pp. 526, 534	**Latin root *-potens-*,** pp. 520, 527 **Latin root *-sum-*,** pp. 528, 535 **UR** pp. 134, 152
	MC	**Libraries Face Sad Chapter** Pete Hamill	530			
	MA	**I Have a Dream** Martin Luther King, Jr.	542	**Evaluate Persuasion/ Persuasive Techniques,** pp. 539, 546, 549, 554, 561; **UR** pp. 172, 190 RI.6, RI.8	**Persuasive Speech,** pp. 539, 543, 544, 545, 546, 549, 555, 556, 559, 561; **UR** pp. 171, 189 RI.9; **Spiral Review,** pp. 543, 556	**Latin root *-cred-*,** pp. 540, 549 **Latin root *-duct-*,** pp. 550, 561; **UR** pp. 173, 191
	MC	**First Inaugural Address** Franklin D. Roosevelt	552			
		Reading for Information *from* Nothing to Fear/ *from* Address of the President	566	**Evaluate Credibility,** p. 566 RI.6, RI.8, RI.9		
		Comparing Literary Works **The Talk** Gary Soto	574		**Comparing Literary Works: Humorous Writing,** pp. 572, 575, 576, 578, 580, 581; **UR** p. 210 RL.6, RI.1; **Spiral Review,** 575, 579	**UR** p. 211
		Talk Harold Courlander and George Herzog	577			

Key: UR: *Unit Resources* **MA:** More Accessible **MC:** More Complex ⓒ Indicates an Exemplar Text

Writing	Conventions	Extension Activity	Assessment
Informative Text: Book Jacket Copy, p. 463; **UR** p. 51 W.2 **Writing Workshop: Work in Progress:** Prewriting for Business Letters, p. 463	**Direct and Indirect Objects,** p. 462; **UR** p. 50 L.3	• **Speaking and Listening: Panel Discussion,** p. 463; **UR** p. 52 SL.1	**Selection Tests,** pp. 35–40; 56–61
Argument: Script, p. 489; **UR** p. 90 W.2, W.4 **Writing Workshop: Work in Progress:** Prewriting for Business Letters, p. 489	**Predicate Nominatives and Predicate Adjectives,** p. 488; **UR** p. 89	• **Research and Technology: Journal Entries,** p. 489; **UR** p. 91 W.7, W.8	**Test Practice: Reading,** pp. 490–491 **Selection Tests, UR** pp. 74–79; 95–100
Timed Writing: Informational Text: Explanation, p. 497 W.2.a			
Timed Writing: Explanatory Text: Essay, p. 511; **UR** p. 108 W.2			**Selection Tests, UR** pp. 112–117
Informative Text: Abstract, p. 537; **UR** p. 155 W.4 **Writing Workshop: Work in Progress:** Prewriting for Editoral, p. 537	**Adjectives,** p. 536; **UR** p. 154 L.1	• **Research and Technology: Comparative Chart,** p. 537; **UR** p. 156 SL.4	**Selection Tests, UR** pp. 139–144; 160–165
Argument: Proposal, p. 563; **UR** p. 194 W.1 **Writing Workshop: Work in Progress:** Prewriting for Editorial, p. 563	**Adverbs,** p. 562; **UR** p. 193 L.3	• **Speaking and Listening: Radio News Report,** p. 563; **UR** p. 195 SL.3	**Test Practice: Reading,** pp. 564–565 **Selection Tests, UR** pp. 178–183, 199–204
Timed Writing: Argument: Essay, p. 571 W.1			
Timed Writing: Explanatory Text: Essay, p. 581; **UR** p. 212 W.2			**Selection Tests, UR** pp. 216–221 **Cumulative Review,** pp. 594–597 **Performance Tasks,** pp. 598–599

All selections are supported in the *Reader's Notebooks.*

UNIT 4 ▪ Skills Navigator: Poetry

		Selection	Page	Reading Skill	Literary Analysis	Word Study
LITERARY ANALYSIS WORKSHOP		**Barter** ◎ Sara Teasdale **We grow accustomed to the dark—** ◎ Emily Dickinson **Uncoiling** **A Voice** Pat Mora	611 612 613 614		**Analyzing Poetic Language,** pp. 608–609 RL.4 **Close Read: Poetic Language and Meaning,** pp. 610–615	**Introducing the Big Question,** pp. 604–605 L.6
READING FOCUS **READ FLUENTLY**	MA	**Poetry Collection 1**	620	**Read Fluently,** p. 617, 621, 623, 629, 634, 639; **UR** pp. 29, 47	**Figurative Language,** p. 617, 625, 627, 629, 633, 637, 639; **UR** pp. 28, 46 RL.4; Spiral Review, pp. 627, 633	**Latin root *-fer-*,** pp. 618, 629 **Latin root *-vert-*,** pp. 630, 639 **UR** pp. 30, 48
	MC	**Poetry Collection 2**	632			
	MA	**Poetry Collection 3**	646	**Read Fluently,** pp. 643, 649, 651, 659, 665; **UR** pp. 68, 86	**Sound Devices,** pp. 643, 649, 651, 656, 657, 659, 661, 663, 665; **UR** pp. 67, 85 Spiral Review, pp. 649, 655	**Greek prefix *ana-*,** pp. 644, 651 **Greek prefix *mono-*,** pp. 652, 665
	MC	**Poetry Collection 4**	654			
		Reading for Information Technical Directions/ News Article	670	**Follow Technical Directions,** p. 670 RI.4, RI.5		
		Comparing Literary Works **There Is No Word for Goodbye,** Mary TallMountain, **Daily,** Naomi Shihab Nye, **Hope,** David T. Hilbun, **The Day of the Storm,** Tyroneca "Ty" Booker	678 679 680 682		**Comparing Literary Works: Imagery,** pp. 676, 678, 679, 680, 683, 684, 685; **UR** p. 106 RL.4	**UR** p. 107
READING FOCUS **PARAPHRASE**	MA	**Poetry Collection 5**	696	**Paraphrase,** pp. 693, 699, 702, 703, 707, 709, 711, 712, 715; **UR** pp. 133, 151	**Narrative Poetry,** pp. 693, 697, 698, 703, 706, 708, 711, 713, 714, 715; **UR** pp. 132, 150 RL.5; Spiral Review, pp. 698, 712	**Latin prefix *pre-*,** pp. 694, 703 **Latin prefix *im-*,** pp. 704, 715 **UR** pp. 134, 152
	MC	**Poetry Collection 6**	706			
	MA	**Poetry Collection 7**	724	**Paraphrase,** pp. 721, 725, 727, 729, 737; **UR** pp. 172, 190 RL.2	**Rhyme and Meter,** pp. 719, 725, 726, 729, 732, 735, 737; **UR** pp. 171, 189 Spiral Review, p. 735	**Latin suffix *-ment*,** pp. 722, 729 **Latin suffix *-ion*,** pp. 730, 737 **UR** p. 211
	MC	**Poetry Collection 8**	732			
		Reading for Information Case Study/News Article	742	**Paraphrase a Text: Main Idea,** p. 742 RI.2		
		Comparing Literary Works **I Hear America Singing,** Walt Whitman, **Three Haiku,** Bashō and Chiyojo, **Women,** Alice Walker, **Sonnet 30,** William Shakespeare	750 751 752 754		**Comparing Literary Works:** Lyric Poetry, pp. 748, 750, 751, 753, 755; **UR** p. 210 RL.4, RL.5	**UR** p. 211

Key: UR: *Unit Resources* **MA:** More Accessible **MC:** More Complex ◎ Indicates an Exemplar Text

Writing	Conventions	Extension Activity	Assessment
Informative Text: Description of a Scene, p. 641; **UR** p. 51 W.3.d **Writing Workshop: Work in Progress:** Prewriting for Descriptive Essay, p. 641	**Prepositions,** p. 640; **UR** p. 50 L.1	• **Speaking and Listening: Impromptu Speech,** p. 641; **UR** p. 52 SL.4	**Selection Tests, UR** pp. 35–40, 56–61
Argument: Editorial, p. 667; **UR** p. 90 W.1 **Writing Workshop: Work in Progress:** Prewriting for Descriptive Essay, p. 667	**Prepositional Phrases,** p. 666; **UR** p. 89 L.1	• **Speaking and Listening: Illustrated Presentation,** p. 667; **UR** p. 91 SL.1	**Test Practice: Reading,** pp. 668–669 **Selection Tests, UR** pp. 74–79, 95–100
Timed Writing: Explanatory Text: Letter, p. 675 W.2.a			
Timed Writing: Explanatory Text: Essay, p. 685; **UR** p. 108 W.2			**Selection Tests, UR** pp. 112–117
Informative Text: Description of a Scene, p. 717; **UR** p. 155 **Writing Workshop: Work in Progress:** Prewriting for a Response to Literature, p. 717 W.4	**Appositive Phrases,** p. 716; **UR** p. 154 L.1.b	• **Speaking and Listening: Dialogue,** p. 717; **UR** p. 156 SL1.a, SL.1.b, SL.1.c	**Selection Tests, UR** pp. 139–144; 160–165
Poetry: Poem, p. 739; **UR** p. 194 W.4 **Writing Workshop: Work in Progress:** Prewriting for a Response to Literature, p. 739	**Infinitives,** p. 738; **UR** p. 193 L.1.b	• **Speaking and Listening: Panel Discussion,** p. 739; **UR p. 195** SL.1.a, SL.1.c, SL.1.d	**Test Practice: Reading,** pp. 740–741 **Selection Tests, UR** pp. 178–183; 199–204
Timed Writing: Argument: Persuasive Essay, p. 747 W.1			
Timed Writing: Explanatory Text: Essay, p. 755; **UR** p. 212 W.2			**Selection Tests, UR** pp. 216–221 **Cumulative Review,** pp. 768–771 **Performance Tasks,** pp. 772–773

All selections are supported in the *Reader's Notebooks.*

Section	Level	Selection	Page	Reading Skill	Literary Analysis	Word Study
LITERARY ANALYSIS WORKSHOP		*from* **The Glass Menagerie** Tennessee Williams *from* **The Shakespeare Stealer** Gary L. Blackwood	785 787		**Analyzing Character Development,** pp.782–783 RL.3 **Close Read: Character, Plot, and Theme,** pp. 784–797	**Introducing the Big Question,** pp. 778–779 L.6
READING FOCUS SUMMARIZE	MC	**The Tragedy of Romeo and Juliet, Act I**	806	**Summarize,** pp. 801, 809, 811, 816, 820, 824, 831; **UR** p. 29 RL.2	**Dialogue and Stage Directions,** pp. 801, 808, 813, 817, 819, 821, 822, 824, 826, 827, 828, 829, 831; **UR** p. 28 RL.5; **Spiral Review,** p. 825	**Latin prefix *trans-*,** pp. 804, 831
	MC	**The Tragedy of Romeo and Juliet, Act II**	834	**Summarize,** pp. 833, 839, 844, 853, 859; **UR** p. 47 RL.2	**Blank Verse,** pp. 833, 836, 837, 839, 841, 843, 845, 847, 849, 850, 853, 855, 856, 859; **UR** p. 46 RL.5; **Spiral Review,** p. 852	**Latin prefix *pro-*,** pp. 832, 859
	MC	**The Tragedy of Romeo and Juliet, Act III**	862	**Summarize,** pp. 861, 864, 868, 873, 875, 877, 881, 882, 884, 888, 891; **UR** p. 65 RL.2	**Dramatic Speeches,** pp. 861, 864, 870, 871, 874, 878, 885, 886, 887, 890, 891; **UR** p. 64 RL.5; **Spiral Review,** p. 871	**Latin root *-loque-*,** pp. 860, 891 **UR** pp. 30, 48, 66
	MC	**The Tragedy of Romeo and Juliet, Act IV**	895	**Summarize,** pp. 893, 901, 903, 911; **UR** p. 83 RL.2	**Dramatic Irony,** pp. 893, 896, 897, 899, 900, 904, 905, 906, 908, 910, 911; **UR** p. 82 RL.5; L.5.a; **Spiral Review,** p. 901	**Latin prefix *en-*,** pp. 892, 911
	MC	**The Tragedy of Romeo and Juliet, Act V**	915	**Summarize,** pp. 913, 919, 922, 927, 931; **UR** p. 101 RL.2	**Tragedy and Motive,** pp. 913, 916, 919, 920, 921, 922, 925, 926, 928, 930, 931; **UR** p. 100 **Spiral Review,** p. 919	**Latin prefix *ambi-*,** pp. 912, 931
		Reading for Information Atlas Entry/Travel Brocure	938	**Analyze Text Information,** p. 938 RI.3		**UR** p. 123
		Comparing Literary Works **Pyramus and Thisbe,** Ovid *from* **A Midsummer Night's Dream,** William Shakespeare	 946 950		**Comparing Literary Works: Archetypal Themes,** pp. 944, 947, 948, 949, 952, 955, 957, 959; **UR** p. 122	
READING FOCUS DRAW CONCLUSIONS	MA	***The Inspector-General*** Anton Chekhov	970	**Draw Conclusions,** pp. 967, 971, 974, 975; **UR** p. 153 RL.1	**Comedy,** pp. 967, 972, 975; **UR** p. 152 RL.5 **Spiral Review,** p. 973	**Latin root *-nym-* and *-nom-*,** pp. 968, 975 **UR** p. 154
		Reading for Information Web Site/Web Encyclopedia Entry	980	**Evaluate Sources,** p. 980 RI.3		
		Comparing Literary Works *from* **The Importance of Being Earnest,** Oscar Wilde *from* **Big Kiss,** Henry Alford	 988 996		**Comparing Literary Works: Satire,** pp. 986, 989, 990, 991, 992, 993, 994, 995, 996, 997, 998, 1000, 1001; **UR** p. 173 RL.4 **Spiral Review,** pp. 993, 997	**UR** p. 174

Key: UR: *Unit Resources* **MA:** More Accessible **MC:** More Challenging  Indicates an Exemplar Text

Writing	Conventions	Extension Activity	Assessment
Argumentative Text: Editorial, p. 933; **UR** p. 105 W.4 **Writing Workshop: Work in Progress:** Prewriting for How-to Essay, p. 933	**Particles and Participial Phrases, Gerunds and Gerund Phrases;** p. 932; **UR** p. 104 L.1, L.1.b	• **Speaking and Listening: Staged Performance,** p. 934; **UR** p. 106 • **Research and Technology: Annotated Flowchart,** p. 935; **UR** p. 107 W.7; SL.1, SL.4	**Selection Tests, UR** pp. 35–40; 53–58; 71–76; 89–94; 111–116
Argumentative Text: Persuasive Letter, p. 933; **UR** p. 105 W.1		• **Research and Technology: Multimedia Presentation,** p. 935; **UR** p. 107 W.7; SL.1, SL.4 • **Research and Technology: Film Review,** p. 935; **UR** p. 107 • **Speaking and Listening: Mock Trial,** p. 934; **UR** p. 106 SL.1	**Test Practice: Reading,** pp. 936–937
Timed Writing: Explanatory Text: Essay, p. 943 W.2.a			
Timed Writing: Explanatory Text: Essay, p. 959; **UR** p. 124 W.2			**Selection Tests, UR** pp. 132–137
Narrative Text: Play, p. 977; **UR** p. 157 W.3, W.3.a, W.3.b **Writing Workshop: Work in Progress:** Prewriting for Research Report, p. 977	**Main and Subordinate Clauses,** p. 976; **UR** p. 156 L.1, L.1.b	• **Research and Technology: Informational Chart,** p. 977; **UR** p. 158 W.7	**Test Practice: Reading,** pp. 978–979 **Selection Tests, UR** pp. 162–167
Timed Writing: Argument: Evaluation, p. 985 W.1			
Timed Writing: Explanatory Text: Essay, p. 1001; **UR** p. 175 W.2, W.2.a, W.2.b			**Selection Tests, UR** pp. 179–184 **Cumulative Review,** pp. 1018–1021 **Performance Tasks,** pp. 1022–1023

All selections are supported in the *Reader's Notebooks*.

UNIT 6 ▪ Skills Navigator: Themes in Literature: Heroism

Section	Level	Selection	Page	Reading Skill	Literary Analysis	Word Study
LITERARY ANALYSIS WORKSHOP		**from *The Ramayana*** R. K. Narayan **Play Hard; Play Together; Play Smart, from *The Carolina Way*** Dean Smith	1035 1037		**Determining Themes,** p. 1032 **RL.2** **Analyzing Point of View and Cultural Experience,** p. 1033 **RL.6** **Close Read: Theme and Point of View,** pp.1034–1039	**Introducing the Big Question,** pp. 1028–1029 **L.6**
READING FOCUS **HISTORICAL AND CULTURAL CONTEXT**	MC	***from the* Odyssey, Part 1** Homer	1044	**Historical and Cultural Context,** pp. 1041, 1048, 1050, 1052, 1056, 1062, 1064, 1067, 1068, 1072, 1076, 1083; **UR** p. 29 **RL.6**	**Epic Hero,** pp. 1041, 1047, 1048, 1049, 1051, 1052, 1053, 1054, 1057, 1059, 1060, 1063, 1071, 1072, 1074, 1076, 1077, 1079, 1081, 1082, 1083; **UR** p. 28 **RL.3; Spiral Review,** pp. 1060, 1073	**Old English prefix *be-*,** pp. 1042, 1083 **UR** p. 30
	MC	***from the* Odyssey, Part 2** Homer	1089	**Historical and Cultural Context,** pp. 1087, 1092, 1094, 1097, 1098, 1099, 1101, 1107, 1108, 1110, 1115; **UR** p. 50 **RL.6**	**Epic Simile,** pp. 1087, 1093, 1109, 1111, 1112, 1114, 1115; **UR** p. 49 **RL.6; Spiral Review,** pp. 1092, 1100	**Latin prefix *dis-*,** pp. 1088, 1115 **UR** p. 51
		Reading for Information Commentary/Movie Review	1120	**Identify Characteristics of Various Types of Text,** p. 1120 **RI.6**		
		Comparing Literary Works **An Ancient Gesture** Edna St. Vincent Millay **Siren Song,** Margaret Atwood **Prologue and Epilogue *from the* Odyssey,** Derek Walcott **Ithaca,** Constantine Cavafy	 1128 1130 1132 1134		**Comparing Literary Works: Contemporary Interpretations,** pp. 1126, 1129, 1130, 1131, 1132, 1133, 1136, 1137; **UR** p. 70 **RL.7, RL.9 Spiral Review,** p.1133	**UR** p. 71
READING FOCUS **COMPARE AND CONTRAST**	MA	**Three Skeleton Key** George G. Toudouze	1148	**Comparing and Contrasting Characters,** pp. 1145, 1150, 1152, 1153, 1154, 1155, 1158, 1160, 1162, 1163, 1167, 1168, 1171, 1172, 1173, 1176, 1179, 1182, 1185, 1186, 1189; **UR** pp. 98, 116 **RL.3**	**Protagonist and Antagonist,** pp. 1145, 1150, 1154, 1155, 1157, 1158, 1161, 1163, 1167, 1170, 1174, 1176, 1177, 1178, 1184, 1185, 1187, 1188, 1189; **UR** pp. 97, 115 **RL.3; Spiral Review,** pp. 1161, 1184	**Latin root *-min-*,** pp. 1146, 1163 **UR** pp. 99, 117 **Latin root *-spect-*,** pp. 1164, 1189
	MC	**The Red-headed League** Sir Arthur Conan Doyle	1166			
	MA	**There Is a Longing** Chief Dan George	1196	**Comparing and Contrasting,** pp. 1193, 1199, 1202, 1205; **UR** pp. 137, 153 **RL.2**	**Philosophical Assumptions,** pp. 1193, 1198, 1199, 1205; **UR** pp. 136, 152 **RI.6 Spiral Review,** p. 1203	**Latin root *-merg-*,** pp. 1194, 1199; **UR** pp. 138, 154 **Latin root *-fer-*,** pp. 1200, 1205
	MC	**Glory and Hope** Nelson Mandela	1202			
		Reading for Information News Article/Primary Source	1210	**Analyze Primary Sources,** p. 1210 **RI.6**		
		Comparing Literary Works **Pecos Bill: The Cyclone** Harold W. Felton **Perseus** Edith Hamilton	 1218 1225		**Comparing Literary Works: Tall Tale and Myth,** pp. 1216, 1218, 1219, 1220, 1223, 1224, 1226, 1229, 1230, 1232, 1233; **UR** p. 171 **RL.7, RL.9; Spiral Review,** pp. 1221, 1230	**UR** p. 172

Key: UR: *Unit Resources* **MA:** More Accessible **MC:** More Challenging Ⓔ Indicates an Exemplar Text

Writing	Conventions	Extension Activity	Assessment
Narrative Text: Everyday Epic, p. 1085; **UR** p. 33 **W.3, W.3.a, W.3.b, W.3.c, W.3.d** **Writing Workshop: Work in Progress:** Prewriting for Technical Document, p. 1085	**Simple and Compound Sentences,** p. 1084; **UR** p. 32	• **Speaking and Listening: Improvise a Conversation,** p. 1085; **UR** p. 34 **SL.1, SL.1.a, SL.1.b**	**Selection Tests, UR** pp. 38–43
Narrative Text: Biography of Odysseus, p. 1117; **UR** p. 54 **W.4** **Writing Workshop: Work in Progress:** Prewriting for Technical Document, p. 1117	**Complex and Compound-Complex Sentences,** p. 1116; **UR** p. 53 **L.1**	• **Speaking and Listening: Debate,** p. 1117; **UR** p. 55 **SL.1, SL.3**	**Test Practice: Reading,** pp. 1118–1119 **Selection Tests, UR** pp. 59–64
Timed Writing: Argumentative Text: Critique, p. 1125 **W.1**			
Timed Writing: Explanatory Text: Essay, p. 1137; **UR** p. 72 **W.2, W.2.a, W.9**			**Selection Tests, UR** pp. 76–81
Narrative Text: Journal Entries, p. 1191; **UR** p. 120 **W.3.d** **Writing Workshop: Work in Progress:** Prewriting for Comparison-and-Contrast Essay, p. 1191	**Using Commas and Dashes,** p. 1190; **UR** p. 119 **L.2**	• **Research and Technology: Oral Report,** p. 1191; **UR** p. 121 **W.7**	**Selection Tests, UR** pp. 104–109, 125–130
Informative Text: Letter, p. 1207; **UR** p. 157 **W.2, W.2.b, W.2.e** **Writing Workshop:** Work in Progress: Prewriting for Comparison-and-Contrast Essay, p. 1207 **Timed Writing: Explanatory Text: Expository Essay,** p. 1215 **W.2**	**Colons, Semicolons and Ellipsis Points,** p. 1206; **UR** p. 156 **L.2**	• **Speaking and Listening: Panel Discussion,** p. 1207; **UR** p. 158 **SL.1.a, SL.1.c**	**Test Practice: Reading,** pp. 1208–1209 **Selection Tests, UR** pp. 143–146, 162–165
Timed Writing: Explanatory Text: Essay, p. 1233; **UR** p. 173 **W.2, W.2.a**			**Selection Tests, UR** pp. 177–182 **Cumulative Review,** pp. 1246–1249 **Performance Tasks,** pp. 1250–1251

All selections are supported in the *Reader's Notebooks.*

1 Where Do I Start?

Right here! These pages will guide you through the program's unique organization and describe the many resources that will enrich your teaching.

2 How Do I Teach the Unit?

Begin each unit with **Introducing the Big Question** to present an overarching big idea that will guide students' reading. Have students use the academic vocabulary to think, talk, and write about this question throughout the unit.

Assign the related question in the Performance Tasks feature at the end of each unit. This assignment will help students explore how their ideas about the Big Question have deepened or changed as a result of their reading.

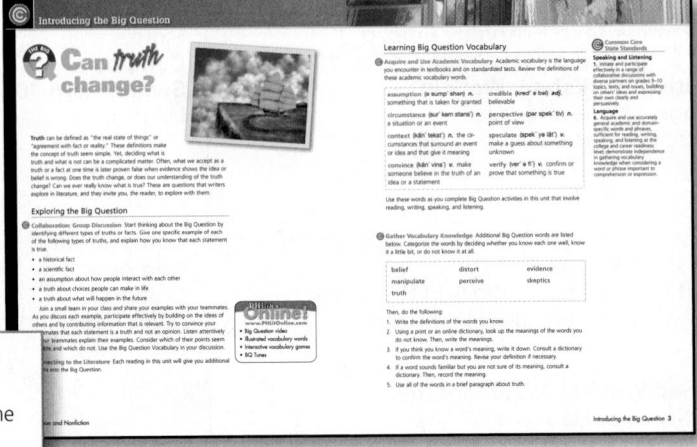

Can truth change?
At the beginning of Unit 1, you participated in a discussion about the Big Question. Now that you have completed the unit, write a response to the question. Discuss how your initial ideas have either changed or been reinforced. Cite specific examples from the literature in this unit, from other subject areas, and from your own life to support your ideas. Use Big Question vocabulary words (see page 3) in your response.

Each of the six units focuses on a different genre. The **Literary Analysis Workshops** provide in-depth exploration of each genre by introducing important characteristics, key concepts, and literary terms.

Then, in the **Model Selection,** students are shown how to apply their understanding of the literary forms and concepts. The Independent Practice selections that follow the models enable students to immediately practice what they have learned. The standards that are introduced and modeled in the introductions are developed and reinforced through spiraled instruction throughout the unit.

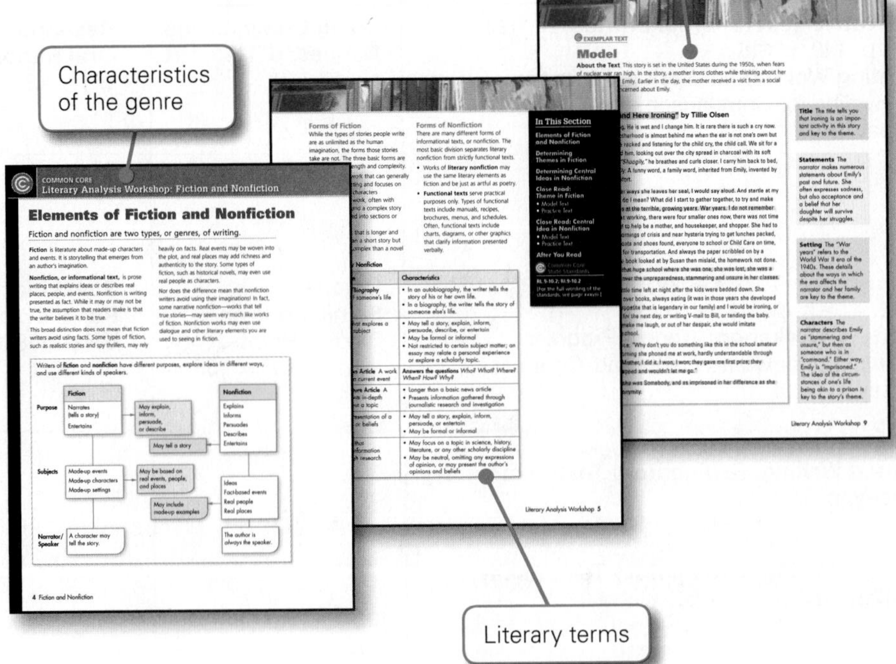

3 What Should I Use to Plan and Prepare?

Start your planning with the **Pacing Plan** at the beginning of each unit and the **Time and Resource Manager** that precedes every leveled selection pairing.

The Time and Resource Manager provides

- a detailed lesson plan.
- a list of the standards covered in the lesson.
- suggestions for incorporating program resources into your instruction.

For an at-a-glance look at selection resources, see the **Visual Guide to Featured Selection Resources** that precedes each leveled selection pairing.

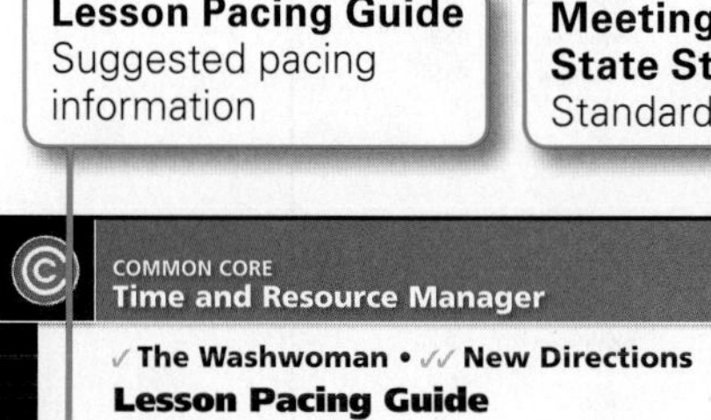

Lesson Pacing Guide
Suggested pacing information

Meeting Common Core State Standards
Standard-coverage information

Resources
Suggested resources for differentiated instruction

COMMON CORE
Time and Resource Manager

✓ The Washwoman • ✓✓ New Directions
Lesson Pacing Guide

DAY 1 Preteach
- Administer the Reading and Vocabulary Warm-ups (*Unit 1 Resources,* pp. 30–33 or 48–51) as necessary.
- Introduce the Reading Skill: Make Predictions.
- Introduce the Literary Analysis concept: Narrative Essay.
- Distribute copies of the appropriate graphic organizer for the Reading Skill (*Graphic Organizer Transparencies,* pp. 3–5).
- Distribute copies of the appropriate graphic organizer for Literary Analysis (*Graphic Organizer Transparencies,* pp. 6–8).
- Teach the selection vocabulary.
- Introduce the Word Study skill.

DAYS 2–3 Preteach/Teach
- Build background with the Background feature.
- Develop thematic vocabulary and thematic thinking with Writing About the Big Question.
- Prepare students to read with the Activating Prior Knowledge activities (TE).
- Informally monitor comprehension while students read.
- Use the Reading Check questions to confirm comprehension.
- Develop students' ability to make predictions, using the Reading Skill questions.
- Develop students' understanding of narrative essays, using the Literary Analysis questions.
- Reinforce vocabulary with the Vocabulary notes.
- Reinforce unit focus standards using the Spiral Review prompts.

DAY 4 Assess
- Assess students' comprehension and mastery of the skills by having them answer the Critical Thinking, Reading Skill, and Literary Analysis questions.
- Have students complete the Vocabulary Practice activities.
- Have students complete the Word Study activities.

DAY 5 Extend/Assess
- Have students complete the Conventions lesson.
- Have students complete the Writing activity and write an anecdote. (You may assign as homework.)
- Extend learning by having students complete the Speaking and Listening activity, an interview. As an alternative, assign them "As Long as They Can Play" or "Riding the Waves" in *Reality Central.*
- Administer Selection Test A or B (*Unit 1 Resources,* pp. 42–47 or 63–68).

Common Core State Standards

Unit Focus Standards Introduced on pp. 4–7.

Reading Literature 2. Determine a theme or central idea of a text and analyze in detail its development over the course of the text, including how it emerges and is shaped and refined by specific details.

Reading Informational Text
2. Determine a central idea of a text and analyze its development over the course of the text, including how it emerges and is shaped and refined by specific details.

Additional Standards Supported

Writing 3. Write narratives to develop real or imagined experiences or events using effective technique, well-chosen details, and well-structured event sequences.

Speaking and Listening 1.a. Come to discussions prepared, having read and researched material under study; explicitly draw on that preparation by referring to evidence from texts and other research on the topic or issue to stimulate a thoughtful, well-reasoned exchange of ideas.
1.c. Propel conversations by posing and responding to questions that relate the current discussion to broader themes or larger ideas; actively incorporate others into the discussion; and clarify, verify, or challenge ideas.
1.d. Respond thoughtfully to diverse perspectives, summarize points of agreement and disagreement, and, when warranted, qualify or justify their own views and understanding.

Language 2. Demonstrate command of the conventions of standard English capitalization, punctuation, and spelling when writing.

Additional Standards Practice
Common Core Companion,
pp. 15–22; 97–104

Daily Block Scheduling
Each day in this Lesson Pacing Guide represents a 40–50 minute period. Teachers using block scheduling may combine days to revise pacing. In addition, teachers may differentiate and support core instruction by integrating components for extended and intensive support as students require. See the Guide to Selected Leveled Resources (facing page).

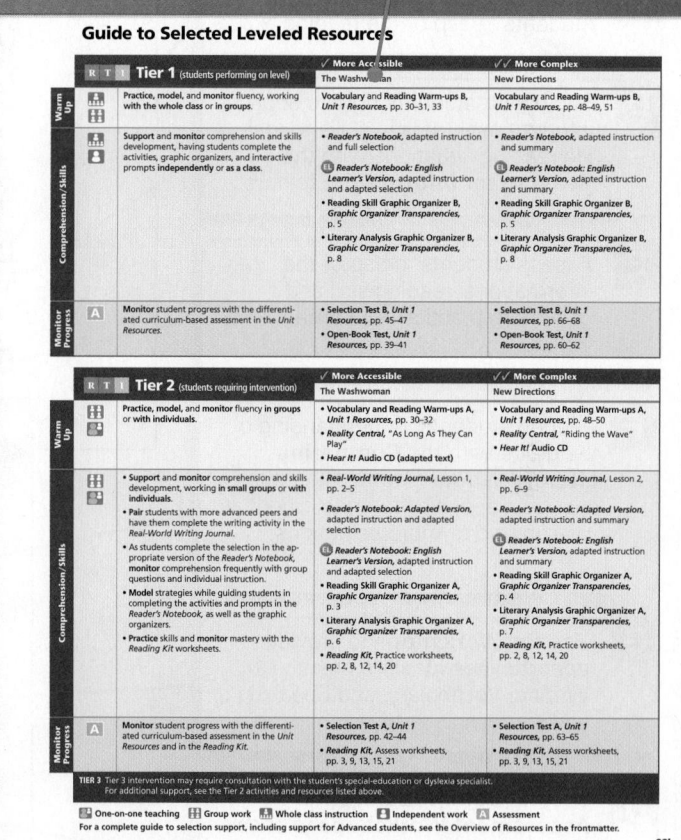

22a

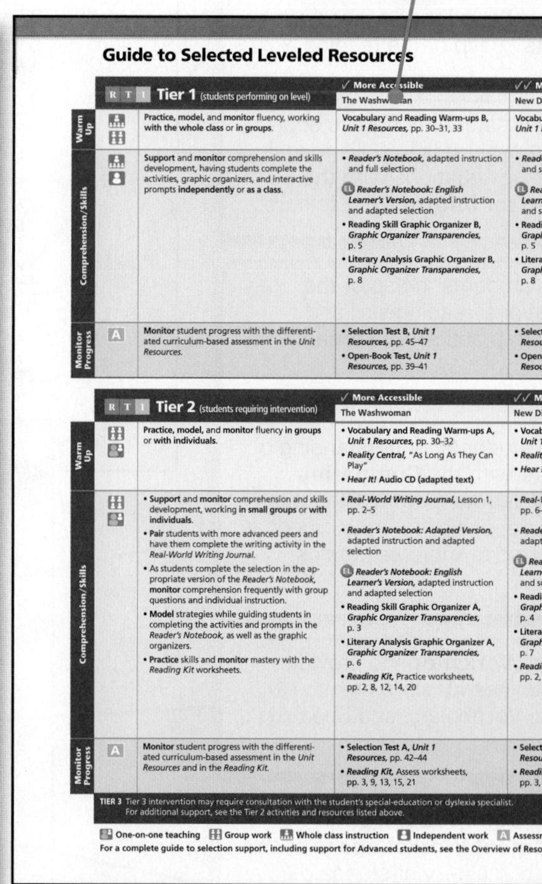

Guide to Selected Leveled Resources

	RTI Tier 1 (students performing on level)	✓ More Accessible The Washwoman	✓✓ More Complex New Directions
Warm Up	**Practice, model,** and **monitor** fluency, working **with the whole class** or **in groups.**	**Vocabulary** and **Reading Warm-ups B,** ***Unit 1 Resources,*** pp. 30–31, 33	**Vocabulary** and **Reading Warm-ups B,** ***Unit 1 Resources,*** pp. 48–49, 51
Comprehension/Skills	**Support** and **monitor** comprehension and skills development, having students complete the activities, graphic organizers, and interactive prompts **independently** or **as a class.**	• ***Reader's Notebook,*** adapted instruction and full selection EL ***Reader's Notebook: English Learner's Version,*** adapted instruction and adapted selection • **Reading Skill Graphic Organizer B, *Graphic Organizer Transparencies,*** p. 5 • **Literary Analysis Graphic Organizer B, *Graphic Organizer Transparencies,*** p. 8	• ***Reader's Notebook,*** adapted instruction and summary EL ***Reader's Notebook: English Learner's Version,*** adapted instruction and summary • **Reading Skill Graphic Organizer B, *Graphic Organizer Transparencies,*** p. 5 • **Literary Analysis Graphic Organizer B, *Graphic Organizer Transparencies,*** p. 8
Monitor Progress	**Monitor** student progress with the differentiated curriculum-based assessment in the *Unit Resources.*	• **Selection Test B, *Unit 1 Resources,*** pp. 45–47 • **Open-Book Test, *Unit 1 Resources,*** pp. 39–41	• **Selection Test B, *Unit 1 Resources,*** pp. 66–68 • **Open-Book Test, *Unit 1 Resources,*** pp. 60–62

	RTI Tier 2 (students requiring intervention)	✓ More Accessible The Washwoman	✓✓ More Complex New Directions
Warm Up	**Practice, model,** and **monitor** fluency **in groups** or **with individuals.**	• **Vocabulary and Reading Warm-ups A, *Unit 1 Resources,*** pp. 30–32 • ***Reality Central,*** "As Long As They Can Play" • ***Hear It!* Audio CD (adapted text)**	• **Vocabulary and Reading Warm-ups A, *Unit 1 Resources,*** pp. 48–50 • ***Reality Central,*** "Riding the Wave" • ***Hear It!* Audio CD**
Comprehension/Skills	• **Support** and **monitor** comprehension and skills development, working **in small groups** or **with individuals.** • **Pair** students with more advanced peers and have them complete the writing activity in the *Real-World Writing Journal.* • As students complete the selection in the appropriate version of the *Reader's Notebook,* **monitor** comprehension frequently with group questions and individual instruction. • **Model** strategies while guiding students in completing the activities and prompts in the *Reader's Notebook,* as well as the graphic organizers. • **Practice** skills and **monitor** mastery with the *Reading Kit* worksheets.	• ***Real-World Writing Journal,*** Lesson 1, pp. 2–5 • ***Reader's Notebook: Adapted Version,*** adapted instruction and adapted selection EL ***Reader's Notebook: English Learner's Version,*** adapted instruction and adapted selection • **Reading Skill Graphic Organizer A, *Graphic Organizer Transparencies,*** p. 3 • **Literary Analysis Graphic Organizer A, *Graphic Organizer Transparencies,*** p. 6 • ***Reading Kit,*** Practice worksheets, pp. 2, 8, 12, 14, 20	• ***Real-World Writing Journal,*** Lesson 2, pp. 6–9 • ***Reader's Notebook: Adapted Version,*** adapted instruction and summary EL ***Reader's Notebook: English Learner's Version,*** adapted instruction and summary • **Reading Skill Graphic Organizer A, *Graphic Organizer Transparencies,*** p. 4 • **Literary Analysis Graphic Organizer A, *Graphic Organizer Transparencies,*** p. 7 • ***Reading Kit,*** Practice worksheets, pp. 2, 8, 12, 14, 20
Monitor Progress	**Monitor** student progress with the differentiated curriculum-based assessment in the *Unit Resources* and in the *Reading Kit.*	• **Selection Test A, *Unit 1 Resources,*** pp. 42–44 • ***Reading Kit,*** Assess worksheets, pp. 3, 9, 13, 15, 21	• **Selection Test A, *Unit 1 Resources,*** pp. 63–65 • ***Reading Kit,*** Assess worksheets, pp. 3, 9, 13, 15, 21

TIER 3 Tier 3 intervention may require consultation with the student's special-education or dyslexia specialist. For additional support, see the Tier 2 activities and resources listed above.

One-on-one teaching Group work Whole class instruction Independent work Assessment
For a complete guide to selection support, including support for Advanced students, see the Overview of Resources in the frontmatter.

22b

4 How Does the Program Help Me With Pacing?

The program is organized into three-week instructional blocks, with each block focusing on core skills and standards. This consistent organization ensures thorough skills coverage presented in manageable chunks. A benchmark test is provided at the middle and end of each unit, allowing you to administer assessment at 3-, 6-, or 9-week intervals. This systematic, logical organization with built-in progress monitoring allows you to make sound instructional choices for your class without skipping or missing any skills or standards.

5 How Do I Use Each Feature in a Unit?

A Use the **Literary Analysis Workshop** to provide rigorous study of a genre and related Common Core standards.

B Choose a selection from the **leveled selection pairing** to teach and practice core skills and strategies. See p. CC 103 for how to choose the most appropriate selection for your class.

C Use **Test Practice** to assess students' grasp of the reading skill.

D Show your students how to apply informational reading skills to real-life reading situations with the **Reading for Information** feature.

E Assess students' grasp of the informational reading skill and give them practice with timed writing.

F Deepen students' understanding of the genre with the **Comparing Literary Works** feature. Students analyze a specific literary element at work in two or more selections.

G Use the **Workshops** to provide opportunities for skills practice in Writing, Vocabulary, and Speaking and Listening.

H Use the **Common Core Assessment Workshops** to check students' mastery of standards taught in the unit. Performance Tasks allow for hands-on application of skills as called for by the Common Core framework.

I Develop students' abilities to read independently through this end-of-unit feature. Selected titles include Exemplar Texts and strategies for reading complex texts.

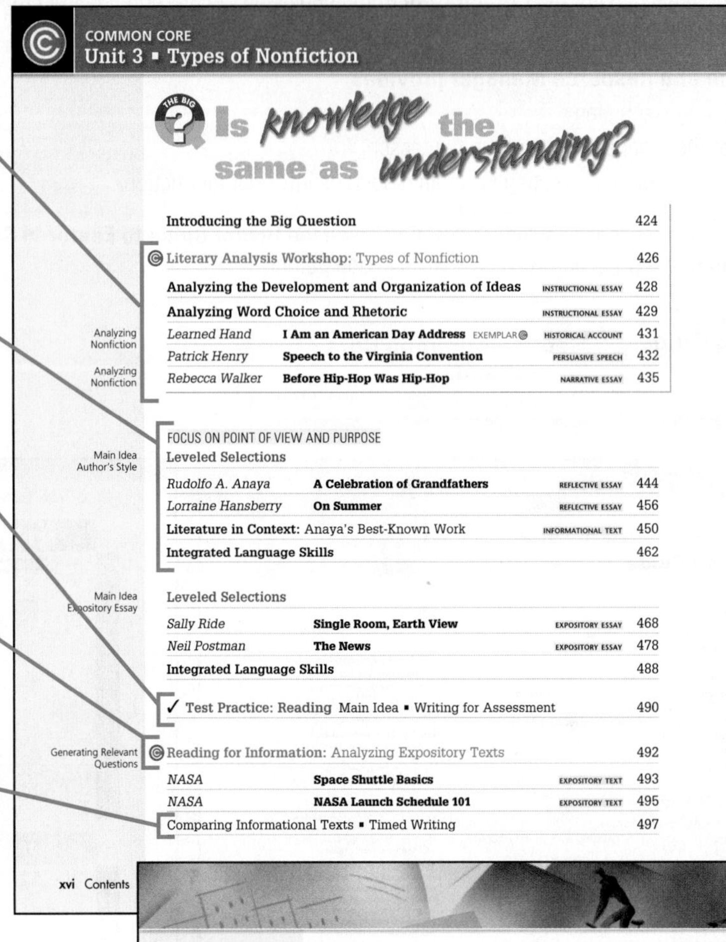
COMMON CORE
Unit 3 ▪ Types of Nonfiction

Is knowledge the same as understanding?

PHLit Online!
www.PHLitOnline.com
Interactive resources provide personalized instruction and activities online.

Contents xvii

6 How Do I Use the Leveled Selection Pairs?

Pearson Prentice Hall Literature addresses the challenges of today's mixed-ability classrooms through its unique combination of differentiated instruction, online activities, and skills support. When planning lessons for a diverse group of students, consult the **Text Complexity Rubric** on the Before You Read pages. (See pages CC 16 and CC 17 for more information.) Take advantage of the following useful features:

The rubric provides a **Lexile** score. Lexile uses factors such as sentence length and vocabulary difficulty to determine a score that can help you predict student comprehension.

This rubric also provides a variety of qualitative measures to help you make informed choices about literature assignments.

Text Complexity Rubric: Leveled Texts

Text complexity is determined by both qualitative and quantitative measures. For this reason, the quantitative measure of a more complex selection may be lower than that of a more accessible selection.

		✓ The Washwoman	✓✓ New Directions
Qualitative Measures	**Context/ Knowledge Demands**	Jewish neighborhood in Poland, early 1900s 1 2 ③ 4 5	African American mother living in the South 1 2 ③ 4 5
	Structure/Language Conventionality and Clarity	Numerous long sentences; on-level vocabulary 1 2 ③ 4 5	Little dialogue; above-level vocabulary 1 2 3 ④ 5
	Levels of Meaning/ Purpose/Concept Level	Accessible (determination to complete a task) 1 2 ③ 4 5	Irony; accessible (journey from adversity to success) 1 2 3 ④ 5
Quantitative Measures	**Text Length**	Word Count: 1976	Word Count: 763
	Lexile	870L	1360L
Overall Complexity		✓ **More accessible**	✓✓ **More complex**

Use the **Overall Complexity** as the final tool for deciding which selection to assign to your students.

7 How Do I Differentiate Instruction?

Pearson Prentice Hall Literature provides unprecedented opportunities for differentiated instruction:

- **Teacher's Edition:** Use the strategies and techniques geared toward a variety of reading levels and learning styles.
- **Reader's Notebooks:** Customize instruction with reading support for struggling readers and English learners.
- **Leveled Vocabulary and Reading Warm-ups:** For each selection, build background, fluency, and vocabulary.
- **Leveled Selection Tests:** Choose from two tests for each selection, according to your students' ability levels.
- **Graphic Organizers:** Give struggling readers additional support with completed versions of all organizers in the Student Edition.

Differentiated Instruction for Universal Access

Culturally Responsive Instruction

Culture Focus Point out how deeply upset Della is at not being able to afford a nice Christmas present for Jim. Note that in the United States, Christmas is an important holiday to which people look forward for months in advance. People spend a great deal of time and thought to find the perfect Christmas present.

Many cultures do not celebrate Christmas, but almost all have some special occasion on which it is very important to give the perfect gift. Invite students to share their knowledge and experience of important occasions in their home culture or family's country of origin.

PHLitOnline provides a customized learning experience for students. Learner levels are assigned to students based on Diagnostic Test results. All selections and support provided are based on that level, creating a truly personalized learning experience!

8 When Do I Teach Writing?

This program incorporates opportunities in every unit for both process writing and writing for assessment.

Writing Process: To help students prepare for every **Writing Workshop,** *Work in Progress* features appear with each leveled selection pair. These focused prewriting activities encourage students to practice prewriting strategies such as these:

- choosing and narrowing a topic
- gathering details
- preparing a thesis statement

Twice per unit, a **Writing Workshop** with step-by-step instruction guides students to develop their ideas into full-length compositions, addressing these key stages in the writing process:

- Prewriting
- Drafting
- Revising
- Editing and Proofreading
- Publishing and Presenting

Timed Writing: To address the call for writing in the Common Core State Standards, the program provides several opportunities for students to practice writing for assessment. Each **Reading for Information** and **Comparing Literary Works** feature concludes with an annotated timed-writing prompt that includes a step-by-step planner to help students complete the assignment.

Finally, to facilitate your teaching of writing, **Prentice Hall EssayScorer** provides instant scoring and feedback, plus tips for revision. You save time, and your students become better writers!

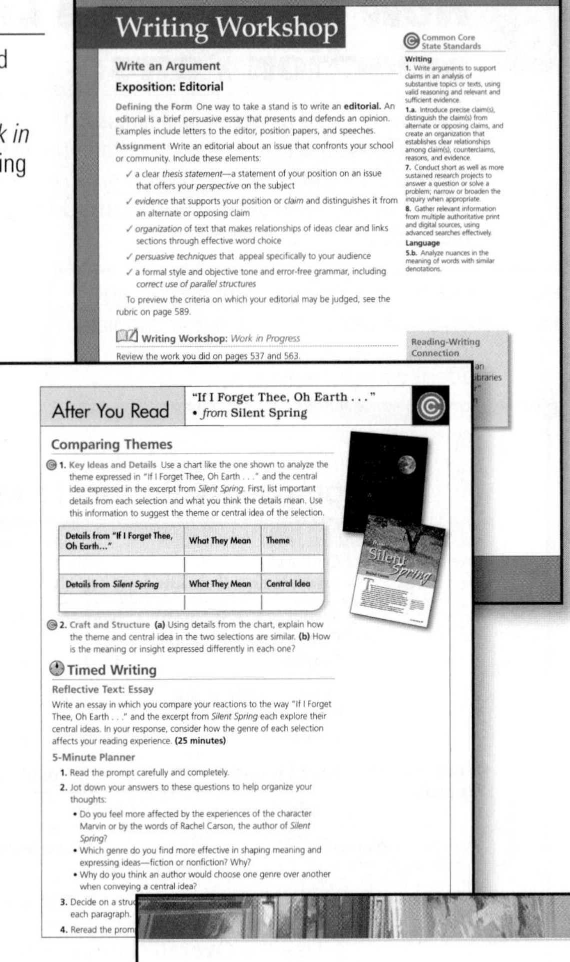

Writing Workshop

Common Core State Standards

Writing
1. Write arguments to support claims in an analysis of substantive topics or texts, using valid reasoning and relevant and sufficient evidence.
1.a. Introduce precise claim(s), distinguish the claim(s) from alternate or opposing claims, and create an organization that establishes clear relationships among claim(s), counterclaims, reasons, and evidence.
7. Conduct short as well as more sustained research projects to answer a question or solve a problem; narrow or broaden the inquiry when appropriate.
8. Gather relevant information from multiple authoritative print and digital sources, using advanced searches effectively.

Language
5.b. Analyze nuances in the meaning of words with similar denotations.

Write an Argument

Exposition: Editorial

Defining the Form One way to take a stand is to write an **editorial.** An editorial is a brief persuasive essay that presents and defends an opinion. Examples include letters to the editor, position papers, and speeches.

Assignment Write an editorial about an issue that confronts your school or community. Include these elements:

✓ a clear *thesis statement*—a statement of your position on an issue that offers your *perspective* on the subject
✓ *evidence* that supports your position or *claim* and distinguishes it from an alternate or opposing claim
✓ *organization* of text that makes relationships of ideas clear and links sections through effective word choice
✓ *persuasive techniques* that appeal specifically to your audience
✓ a formal style and objective tone and error-free grammar, including *correct use of parallel structures*

To preview the criteria on which your editorial may be judged, see the rubric on page 589.

Writing Workshop: *Work in Progress*

Review the work you did on pages 537 and 563.

Reading-Writing Connection

After You Read

"If I Forget Thee, Oh Earth . . ." • *from* Silent Spring

Comparing Themes

1. Key Ideas and Details Use a chart like the one shown to analyze the theme expressed in "If I Forget Thee, Oh Earth . . ." and the central idea expressed in the excerpt from *Silent Spring*. First, list important details from each selection and what you think the details mean. Use this information to suggest the theme or central idea of the selection.

Details from "If I Forget Thee, Oh Earth..."	What They Mean	Theme

Details from *Silent Spring*	What They Mean	Central Idea

2. Craft and Structure **(a)** Using details from the chart, explain how the theme and central idea in the two selections are similar. **(b)** How is the meaning or insight expressed differently in each one?

Timed Writing

Reflective Text: Essay

Write an essay in which you compare your reactions to the way "If I Forget Thee, Oh Earth . . ." and the excerpt from *Silent Spring* each explore their central ideas. In your response, consider how the genre of each selection affects your reading experience. **(25 minutes)**

5-Minute Planner

1. Read the prompt carefully and completely.
2. Jot down your answers to these questions to help organize your thoughts:
   - Do you feel more affected by the experiences of the character Marvin or by the words of Rachel Carson, the author of *Silent Spring*?
   - Which genre do you find more effective in shaping meaning and expressing ideas—fiction or nonfiction? Why?
   - Why do you think an author would choose one genre over another when conveying a central idea?
3. Decide on a stru... each paragraph.
4. Reread the prom...

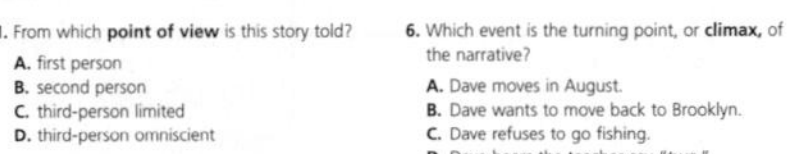

1. From which **point of view** is this story told?
   A. first person
   B. second person
   C. third-person limited
   D. third-person omniscient
2. Which element from the passage helped you determine the **point of view**?
   A. The narrator directly addresses his audience, the reader.
   B. The narrator refers to himself as *I* and *me*.
   C. The narrator knows only one person's thoughts.
   D. The narrator has insight into all the people's thoughts.
3. Which word best describes the **author's voice**?
   A. formal
   B. casual
   C. friendly
   D. sarcastic
4. Which of the following sentences is an example of **foreshadowing**?
   A. All of that would soon change.
   B. I had never really been outside of the city.
   C. I wanted to go back to Brooklyn in the worst way.
   D. The teacher pointed to me.
5. Which event occurs during the **rising action** of the narrative?
   A. Dave is born in Brooklyn.
   B. Dave makes a new friend.
   C. Dave's mom gets a job Upstate.
   D. Dave meets Alexis.
6. Which event is the turning point, or **climax,** of the narrative?
   A. Dave moves in August.
   B. Dave wants to move back to Brooklyn.
   C. Dave refuses to go fishing.
   D. Dave hears the teacher say "two."
7. **Vocabulary** Which word is closest in meaning to the underlined word *petrified*?
   A. angry
   B. terrified
   C. annoyed
   D. disturbed
8. How is the conflict in the story resolved?
   A. Dave makes a new friend in the city.
   B. Dave wants to return to Brooklyn.
   C. Dave's mom does not like her job.
   D. Dave goes fishing with his dad.
9. In what way does the choice of narrator affect the description of the country in paragraph 2?
   A. Life in the country seems frightening.
   B. The country appears to offer lots of fun activities.
   C. Moving to the country sounds like a good idea.
   D. The country seems to lack a lot of things that life in the city has to offer.

Timed Writing

10. In a well-developed essay, **identify** the conflict in this story. **Explain** how the author of the text establishes the conflict. Cite evidence from the text to support your analysis. [20 minutes]

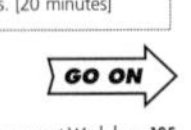

Assessment Workshop 185

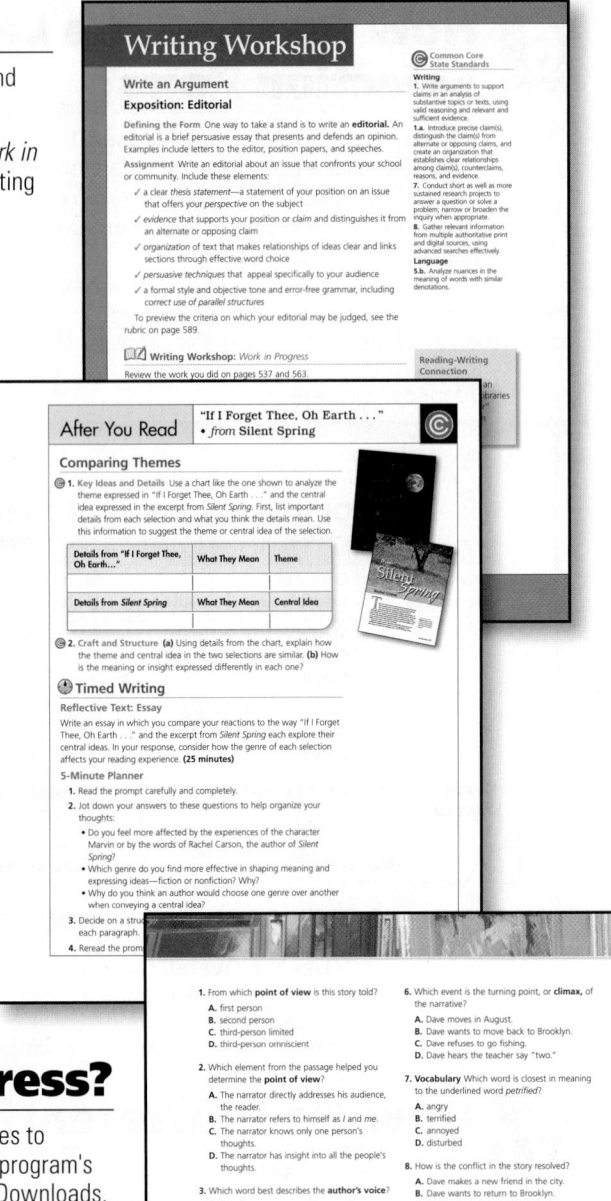

9 How Do I Monitor Student Progress?

Pearson Prentice Hall makes progress monitoring easy with frequent opportunities to evaluate student progress and to reteach material. For more information on the program's assessments, see the Assessment Roadmap in PHLitOnline under Resources & Downloads.

- The **Beginning-of-Year Benchmark Test** assesses students' skills and deficiencies at the onset of the year. Test results allow you to tailor your instruction to students.
- Use the **Diagnostic Tests** at the beginning of the school year to determine entry-level reading skills. You will find frequent **reading checks** and suggestions in the Teacher's Edition for monitoring student progress during reading. If tests are taken online, learner levels are assigned automatically, based on test results.
- After reading selections, use the **Open Book Tests** and leveled **Selection Tests** to assess comprehension and mastery of the literary, reading, and vocabulary skills.
- As you teach the unit, use the **Cumulative Review** pages in standardized-test format to give students practice in applying core unit skills and in writing for assessment under test-taking conditions.
- Use the **Benchmark Tests** to monitor progress at regular, frequent intervals. For your convenience, both mid-unit and end-of-unit tests are provided. If taken online, remediation for skills missed is assigned automatically!
- **Mid-Year Tests** and **End-of-Year Summative Tests** provide a measure of student achievement over a longer period of time.

Use the electronic test generator to customize assessment.

10 How Can I Use Technology in My Classroom?

PHLitOnline allows you to teach the entire program without using the print products. Here, you will find the components of the program in one central location—PLUS integrated videos, animations, interactive practice activities, songs, and audio. You will navigate through the program by using the Table of Contents, exactly as you would in the textbook.

You can choose to use PHLitOnline only, or you may choose to use it in conjunction with the print program. Supporting resources such as videos, audio, online assessments, lesson planning, and reporting are just what you need to teach literature to your 21st Century students!

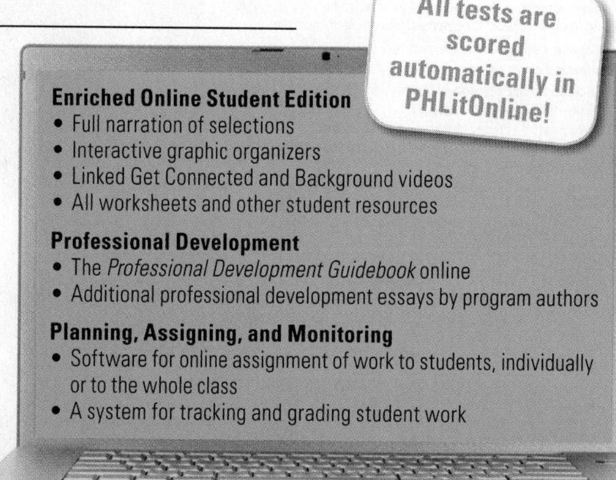

All tests are scored automatically in PHLitOnline!
Enriched Online Student Edition
• Full narration of selections
• Interactive graphic organizers
• Linked Get Connected and Background videos
• All worksheets and other student resources
Professional Development
• The Professional Development Guidebook online
• Additional professional development essays by program authors
Planning, Assigning, and Monitoring
• Software for online assignment of work to students, individually or to the whole class
• A system for tracking and grading student work

11 How Can PHLitOnline Help Me in the Classroom?

The **PHLitOnline Teacher Center** has digital and print tools you can use to reach your students, manage your teaching resources, and meet the Common Core State Standards. You can

- provide personalized diagnosis, instruction, and remediation to all students.
- tailor instruction for the right level of support for each student's specific needs.
- create customized assignments.
- correlate lessons to the Common Core State Standards.
- plan with easy-to-use tools.
- access all print resources online.

The **PHLitOnline Student Center** allows students to access the complete program from computers in the classroom or at home. In addition to all print and activity-based materials, the PHLitOnline Student Center offers videos, animations, interactive practice activities, "sticky" notes, songs, and audio features.

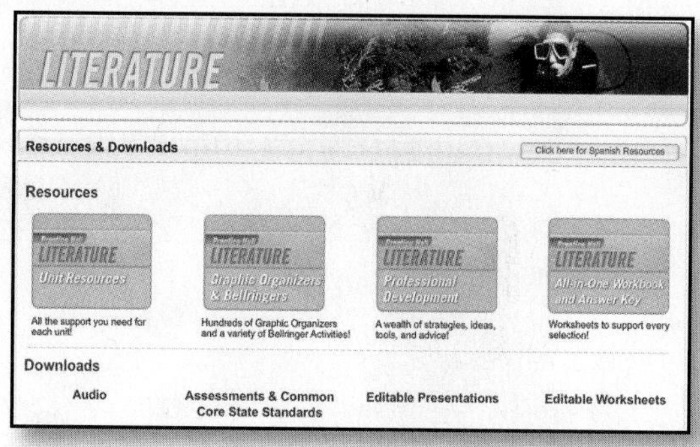

12 How Can PHLitOnline Help Me Personalize Instruction?

PHLitOnline provides personalized differentiated support with **Diagnostic** and **Benchmark** tests. The program can assess, diagnose, and auto-assign reading materials and practice at each student's level. And, since you know your students better than anyone, you have the flexibility to change the learner level as needed!

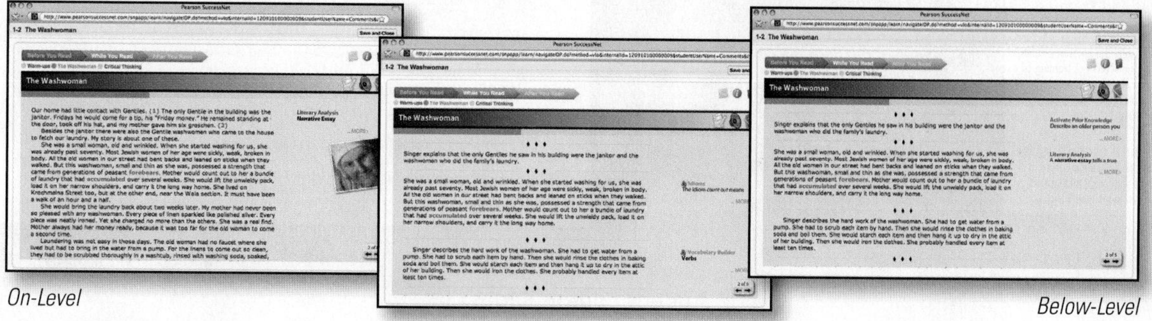

On-Level

English Learner

Below-Level

Students are assigned a learner level—On-Level, Below-Level, or English Learner.

Full-size versions of these Media Literacy Handbook pages can be found in the Student Edition.

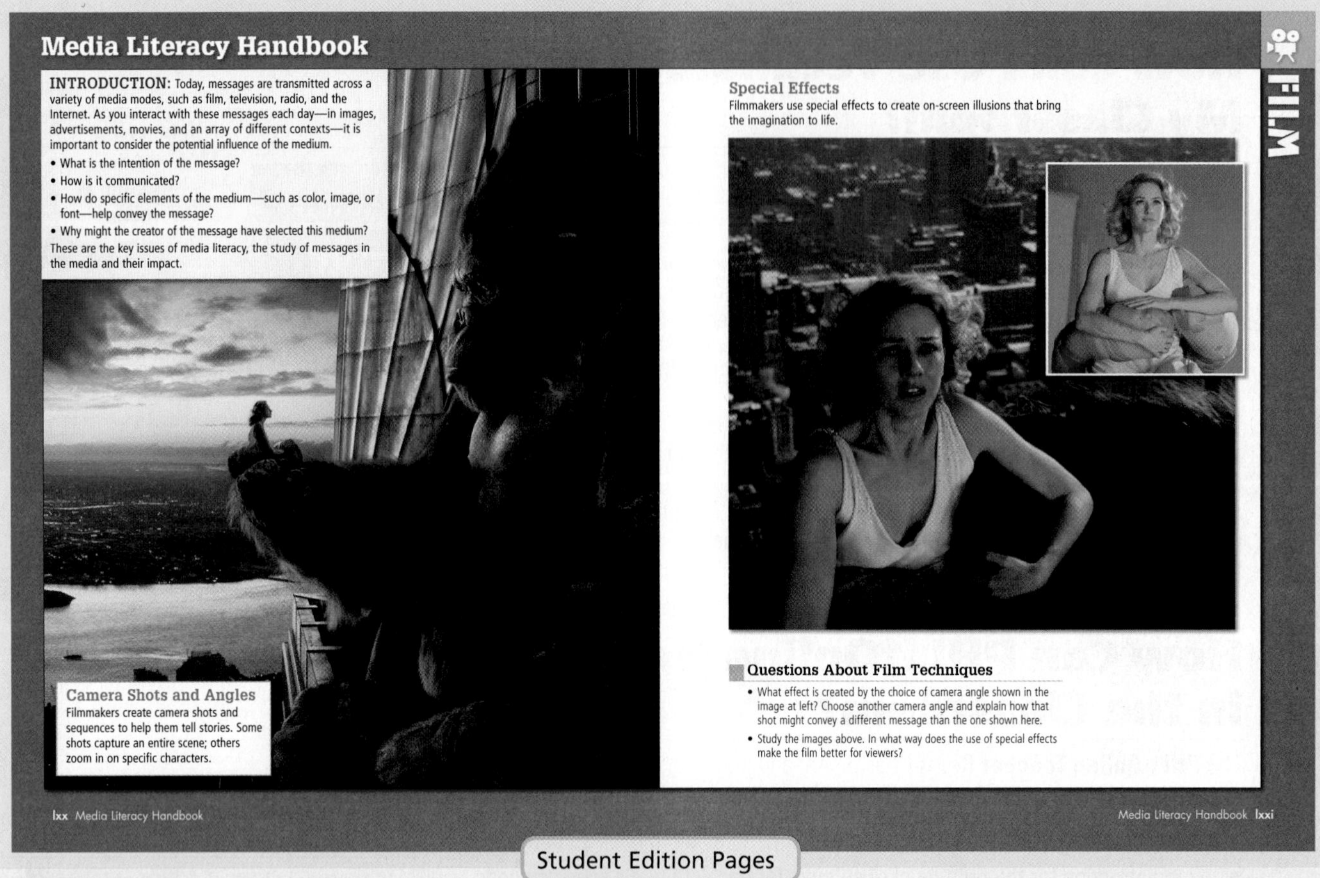

Media Literacy Handbook

INTRODUCTION: Today, messages are transmitted across a variety of media modes, such as film, television, radio, and the Internet. As you interact with these messages each day—in images, advertisements, movies, and an array of different contexts—it is important to consider the potential influence of the medium.

- What is the intention of the message?
- How is it communicated?
- How do specific elements of the medium—such as color, image, or font—help convey the message?
- Why might the creator of the message have selected this medium?

These are the key issues of media literacy, the study of messages in the media and their impact.

Camera Shots and Angles

Filmmakers create camera shots and sequences to help them tell stories. Some shots capture an entire scene; others zoom in on specific characters.

Special Effects

Filmmakers use special effects to create on-screen illusions that bring the imagination to life.

Questions About Film Techniques

- What effect is created by the choice of camera angle shown in the image at left? Choose another camera angle and explain how that shot might convey a different message than the one shown here.
- Study the images above. In what way does the use of special effects make the film better for viewers?

FILM

lxx Media Literacy Handbook

Media Literacy Handbook lxxi

Student Edition Pages

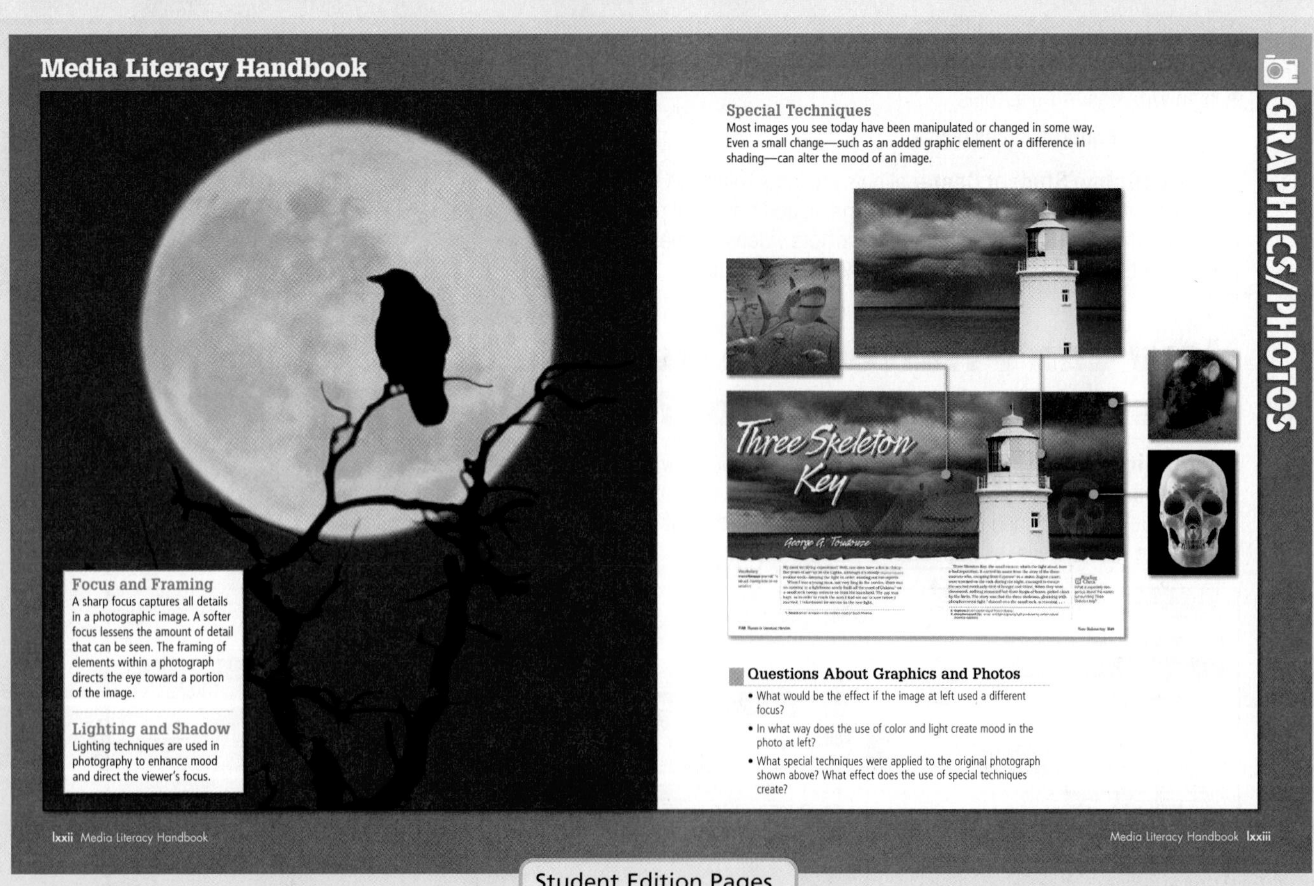

Media Literacy Handbook

Focus and Framing

A sharp focus captures all details in a photographic image. A softer focus lessens the amount of detail that can be seen. The framing of elements within a photograph directs the eye toward a portion of the image.

Lighting and Shadow

Lighting techniques are used in photography to enhance mood and direct the viewer's focus.

Special Techniques

Most images you see today have been manipulated or changed in some way. Even a small change—such as an added graphic element or a difference in shading—can alter the mood of an image.

Questions About Graphics and Photos

- What would be the effect if the image at left used a different focus?
- In what way does the use of color and light create mood in the photo at left?
- What special techniques were applied to the original photograph shown above? What effect does the use of special techniques create?

GRAPHICS/PHOTOS

lxxii Media Literacy Handbook

Media Literacy Handbook lxxiii

Student Edition Pages

Media Literacy Handbook

PRINT MEDIA

Persuasive Techniques
Advertisements use carefully selected visual elements to appeal to the viewer's emotions.

Text and Graphics
Newspaper and magazine layouts are constructed to capture the eye and quickly convey the important ideas of a story. The use of type fonts, images, and page space direct the eye to portions of the printed page.

Questions About Print Media

- What image or graphic dominates the advertisement at left? How does the image make the advertisement more effective?
- Which of the above grabs your attention: the image or the text on the magazine cover? Explain.
- What do you notice first on the newspaper's front page? What overall effect does the use of type size and fonts create?

lxxiv Media Literacy Handbook

Media Literacy Handbook lxxv

Student Edition Pages

How is this book organized?

- **There are six units, each focusing on a specific genre.**
- **Each unit has a Big Question to get you thinking about important ideas and to guide your reading.**
- **A Literary Analysis Workshop begins each unit, providing instruction and practice for essential skills.**

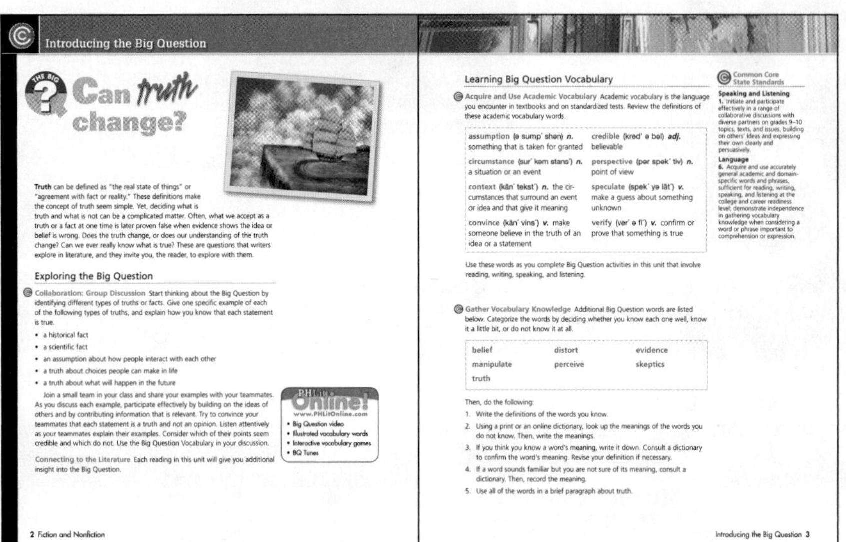

Introducing the Big Question

THE BIG Q Can truth change?

Truth can be defined as "the real state of things" or "agreement with fact or reality." These definitions make the concept of truth seem simple. Yet, deciding what is truth and what is not can be a complicated matter. Often, what we accept as a truth or a fact at one time is later proven false when evidence shows the idea or belief is wrong. Does the truth change, or does our understanding of the truth change? Can we ever really know what is true? These are questions that writers explore in literature, and they invite you, the reader, to explore with them.

Exploring the Big Question

Collaboration: Group Discussion Start thinking about the Big Question by identifying different types of truths or facts. Give one specific example of each of the following types of truths, and explain how you know that each statement is true.

- a historical fact
- a scientific fact
- an assumption about how people interact with each other
- a truth about choices people can make in life
- a truth about what will happen in the future

Join a small team in your class and share your examples with your teammates. As you discuss each example, participate effectively by building on the ideas of others and by contributing information that is relevant. Try to convince your teammates that each statement is a truth and not an opinion. Listen attentively as your teammates explain their examples. Consider which of their points seem credible and which do not. Use the Big Question Vocabulary in your discussion.

Connecting to the Literature Each reading in this unit will give you additional insight into the Big Question.

PHLit Online! www.PHLitOnline.com
- Big Question video
- Illustrated vocabulary words
- Interactive vocabulary games
- BQ Tunes

2 Fiction and Nonfiction

Learning Big Question Vocabulary

Acquire and Use Academic Vocabulary Academic vocabulary is the language you encounter in textbooks and on standardized tests. Review the definitions of these academic vocabulary words.

assumption (ə sump' shən) *n.* something that is taken for granted
circumstance (sur' kəm stans') *n.* a situation or an event
context (kän' tekst') *n.* the circumstances that surround an event or idea and that give it meaning
convince (kän' vins') *v.* make someone believe in the truth of an idea or a statement
credible (kred' ə bəl) *adj.* believable
perspective (pər spek' tiv) *n.* point of view
speculate (spek' yə lāt') *v.* make a guess about something unknown
verify (ver' ə fī') *v.* confirm or prove that something is true

Use these words as you complete Big Question activities in this unit that involve reading, writing, speaking, and listening.

Gather Vocabulary Knowledge Additional Big Question words are listed below. Categorize the words by deciding whether you know each one well, know it a little bit, or do not know it at all.

belief, distort, evidence, manipulate, perceive, skeptics, truth

Then, do the following:

1. Write the definitions of the words you know.
2. Using a print or an online dictionary, look up the meanings of the words you do not know. Then, write the meanings.
3. If you think you know a word's meaning, write it down. Consult a dictionary to confirm the word's meaning. Revise your definition if necessary.
4. If a word sounds familiar but you are not sure of its meaning, consult a dictionary. Then, record the meaning.
5. Use all of the words in a brief paragraph about truth.

Common Core State Standards

Speaking and Listening
1. Initiate and participate effectively in a range of collaborative discussions with diverse partners on grades 9–10 topics, texts, and issues, building on others' ideas and expressing their own clearly and persuasively.

Language
6. Acquire and use accurately general academic and domain-specific words and phrases, sufficient for reading, writing, speaking, and listening at the college and career readiness level; demonstrate independence in gathering vocabulary knowledge when considering a word or phrase important to comprehension or expression.

Introducing the Big Question 3

◀ At the beginning of the unit, **Introducing the Big Question** provides a reading focus for the entire unit. Use **academic vocabulary** to think, talk, and write about this question.

A **Literary Analysis Workshop** provides an overview of the unit genre, an in-depth exploration of Common Core State Standards, as well as models and practice opportunities. ▶

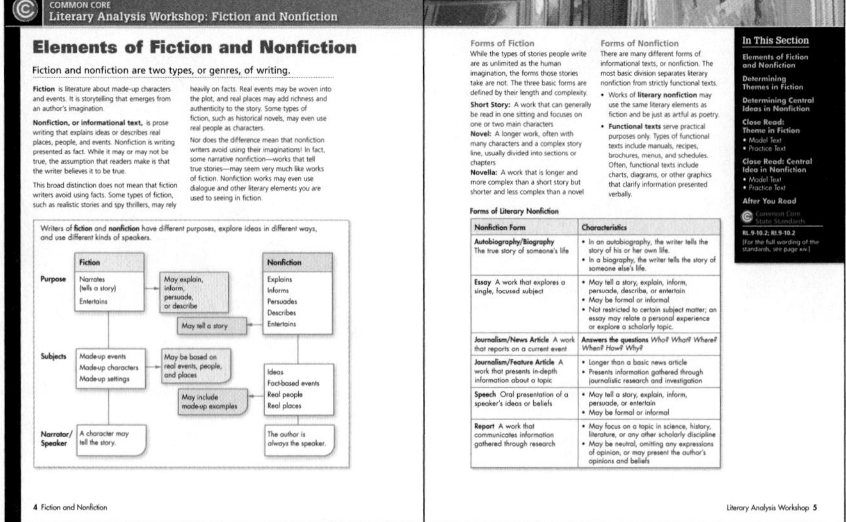

COMMON CORE
Literary Analysis Workshop: Fiction and Nonfiction

Elements of Fiction and Nonfiction

Fiction and nonfiction are two types, or genres, of writing.

Fiction is literature about made-up characters and events. It is storytelling that emerges from an author's imagination.

Nonfiction, or informational text, is prose writing that explains ideas or describes real places, people, and events. Nonfiction is writing presented as fact. While it may or may not be true, the assumption that readers make is that the writer believes it to be true.

This broad distinction does not mean that fiction writers avoid using facts. Some types of fiction, such as realistic stories and spy thrillers, may rely heavily on facts. Real events may be woven into the plot, and real places may add richness and authenticity to the story. Some types of fiction, such as historical novels, may even use real people as characters.

Nor does the difference mean that nonfiction writers avoid using their imaginations! In fact, some narrative nonfiction—works that tell true stories—may seem very much like works of fiction. Nonfiction works may even use dialogue and other literary elements you are used to seeing in fiction.

Writers of **fiction** and **nonfiction** have different purposes, explore ideas in different ways, and use different kinds of speakers.

4 Fiction and Nonfiction

Forms of Fiction

While the types of stories people write are as unlimited as the human imagination, the forms those stories take are not. The three basic forms are defined by their length and complexity.

Short Story: A work that can generally be read in one sitting and focuses on one or two main characters
Novel: A longer work, often with many characters and a complex story line, usually divided into sections or chapters
Novella: A work that is longer and more complex than a short story but shorter and less complex than a novel

Forms of Nonfiction

There are many different forms of informational texts, or nonfiction. The most basic division separates literary nonfiction from strictly functional texts.

- Works of **literary nonfiction** may use the same literary elements as fiction and be just as artful as poetry.
- **Functional texts** serve practical purposes only. Types of functional texts include manuals, recipes, brochures, menus, and schedules. Often, functional texts include charts, diagrams, or other graphics that clarify information presented verbally.

Forms of Literary Nonfiction

Nonfiction Form	Characteristics
Autobiography/Biography The true story of someone's life	• In an autobiography, the writer tells the story of his or her own life. • In a biography, the writer tells the story of someone else's life.
Essay A work that explores a single, focused subject	• May tell a story, explain, inform, persuade, describe, or entertain • May be formal or informal • Not restricted to certain subject matter; an essay may relate a personal experience or explore a scholarly topic.
Journalism/News Article A work that reports on a current event	**Answers the questions** *Who? What? Where? When? How? Why?*
Journalism/Feature Article A work that presents in-depth information about a topic	• Longer than a basic news article • Presents information gathered through journalistic research and investigation
Speech Oral presentation of a speaker's ideas or beliefs	• May tell a story, explain, inform, persuade, or entertain • May be formal or informal
Report A work that communicates information gathered through research	• May focus on a topic in science, history, literature, or any other scholarly discipline • May be neutral, omitting any expressions of opinion, or may present the author's opinions and beliefs

In This Section

- Elements of Fiction and Nonfiction
- Determining Themes in Fiction
- Determining Central Ideas in Nonfiction
- Close Read: Theme in Fiction
  - Model Text
  - Practice Text
- Close Read: Central Idea in Nonfiction
  - Model Text
  - Practice Text
- After You Read

Common Core State Standards
RL.9-10.2; RI.9-10.2
[For the full wording of the standards, see page xiv.]

Literary Analysis Workshop 5

How are the literary selections organized?

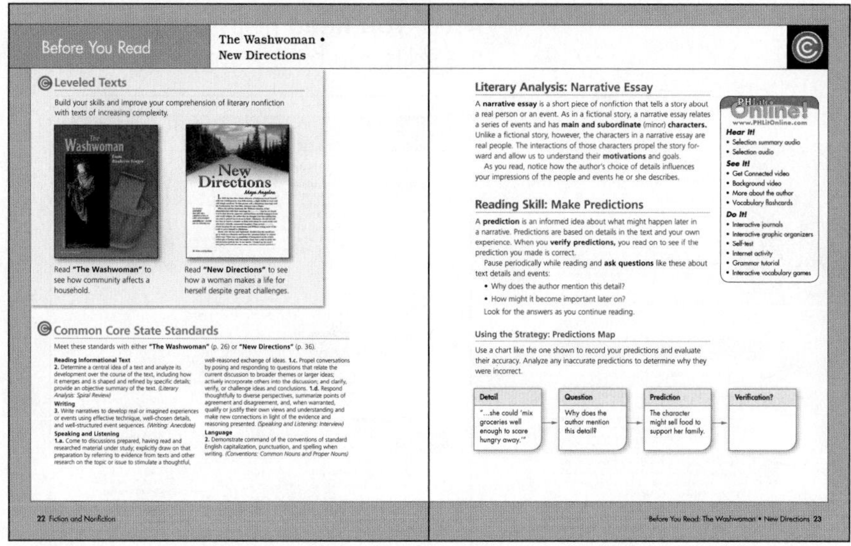

◀ **Before You Read** introduces two selection choices that both teach the same skills. Your teacher will help you choose the selection that is right for you.

Writing About the Big Question is a quick-writing activity that helps you connect the Big Question to the selection you are about to read.

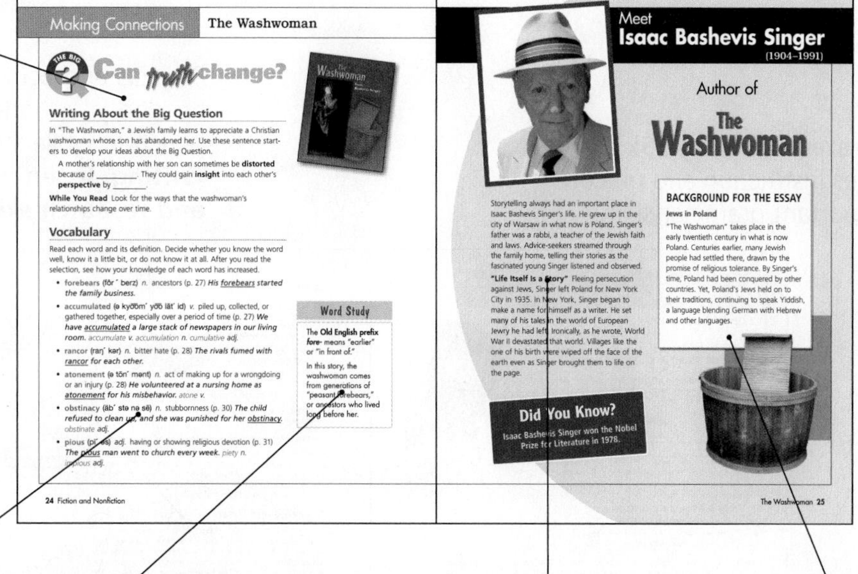

Vocabulary and Word Study introduce important selection vocabulary words and teach you about prefixes, suffixes, and roots.

Meet the Author and Background teach you about the author's life and provide information that will help you understand the selection.

How are the literary selections organized? *(continued)*

After You Read helps you practice the skills you have learned. ▼

Critical Thinking questions help you reflect on what you have read and apply the Big Question to the selection.

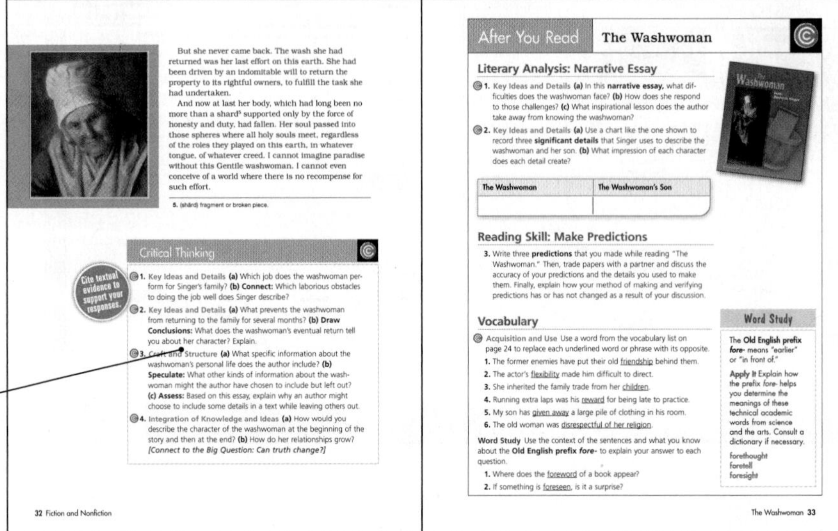

But she never came back. The wash she had returned was her last effort on this earth. She had been driven by an indomitable will to return the property to its rightful owners, to fulfill the task she had undertaken.

And now at last her body, which had long been no more than a shard[5] supported only by the force of honesty and duty, had fallen. Her soul passed into those spheres where all holy souls meet, regardless of the roles they played on this earth, in whatever tongue, of whatever creed. I cannot imagine paradise without this Gentile washwoman. I cannot even conceive of a world where there is no recompense for such effort.

5. (shärd) fragment or broken piece.

Critical Thinking

Cite textual evidence to support your responses.

1. **Key Ideas and Details (a)** Which job does the washwoman perform for Singer's family? **(b) Connect:** Which laborious obstacles to doing the job well does Singer describe?
2. **Key Ideas and Details (a)** What prevents the washwoman from returning to the family for several months? **(b) Draw Conclusions:** What does the washwoman's eventual return tell you about her character? Explain.
3. **Craft and Structure (a)** What specific information about the washwoman's personal life does the author include? **(b) Speculate:** What other kinds of information about the washwoman might the author have chosen to include but left out? **(c) Assess:** Based on this essay, explain why an author might choose to include some details in a text while leaving others out.
4. **Integration of Knowledge and Ideas (a)** How would you describe the character of the washwoman at the beginning of the story and then at the end? **(b)** How do her relationships grow? *[Connect to the Big Question: Can truth change?]*

32 Fiction and Nonfiction

After You Read The Washwoman

Literary Analysis: Narrative Essay

1. **Key Ideas and Details (a)** In this **narrative essay,** what difficulties does the washwoman face? **(b)** How does she respond to those challenges? **(c)** What inspirational lesson does the author take away from knowing the washwoman?
2. **Key Ideas and Details (a)** Use a chart like the one shown to record three **significant details** that Singer uses to describe the washwoman and her son. **(b)** What impression of each character does each detail create?

The Washwoman	The Washwoman's Son

Reading Skill: Make Predictions

3. Write three **predictions** that you made while reading "The Washwoman." Then, trade papers with a partner and discuss the accuracy of your predictions and the details you used to make them. Finally, explain how your method of making and verifying predictions has or has not changed as a result of your discussion.

Vocabulary

Acquisition and Use Use a word from the vocabulary list on page 24 to replace each underlined word or phrase with its opposite.

1. The former enemies have put their old friendship behind them.
2. The actor's flexibility made him difficult to direct.
3. She inherited the family trade from her children.
4. Running extra laps was his reward for being late to practice.
5. My son has given away a large pile of clothing in his room.
6. The old woman was disrespectful of her religion.

Word Study Use the context of the sentences and what you know about the **Old English prefix *fore-*** to explain your answer to each question.

1. Where does the foreword of a book appear?
2. If something is foreseen, is it a surprise?

Word Study

The **Old English prefix *fore-*** means "earlier" or "in front of."

Apply It Explain how the prefix *fore-* helps you determine the meanings of these technical academic words from science and the arts. Consult a dictionary if necessary.

forethought
foretell
foresight

The Washwoman 33

Projects and activities help you deepen your understanding of the selection while strengthening your **writing, listening, speaking, and research skills.**

Integrated Language Skills provides instruction and practice for important grammar skills.

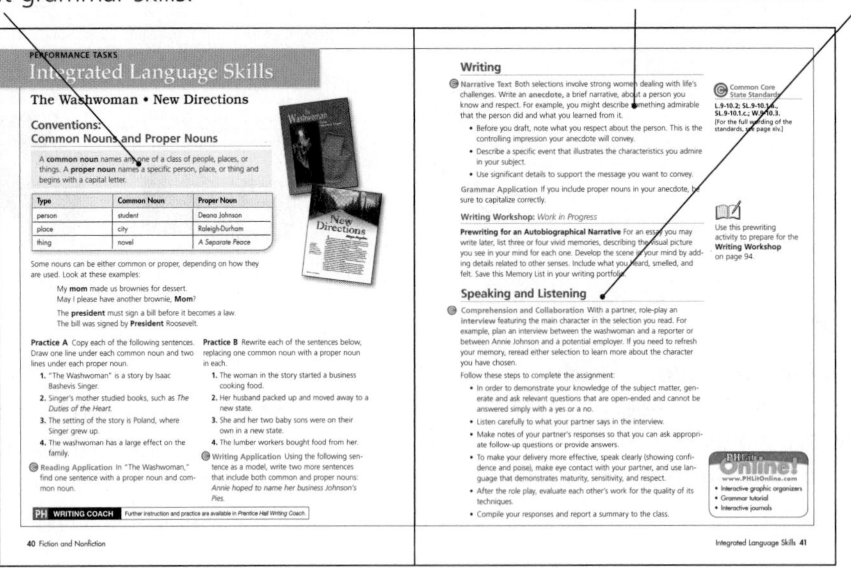

PERFORMANCE TASKS

Integrated Language Skills

The Washwoman • New Directions

Conventions: Common Nouns and Proper Nouns

A **common noun** names any one of a class of people, places, or things. A **proper noun** names a specific person, place, or thing and begins with a capital letter.

Type	Common Noun	Proper Noun
person	student	Deana Johnson
place	city	Raleigh-Durham
thing	novel	*A Separate Peace*

Some nouns can be either common or proper, depending on how they are used. Look at these examples:

My **mom** made us brownies for dessert.
May I please have another brownie, **Mom**?

The **president** must sign a bill before it becomes a law.
The bill was signed by **President** Roosevelt.

Practice A Copy each of the following sentences. Draw one line under each common noun and two lines under each proper noun.

1. "The Washwoman" is a story by Isaac Bashevis Singer.
2. Singer's mother studied books, such as *The Duties of the Heart.*
3. The setting of the story is Poland, where Singer grew up.
4. The washwoman has a large effect on the family.

Reading Application In "The Washwoman," find one sentence with a proper noun and common noun.

Practice B Rewrite each of the sentences below, replacing one common noun with a proper noun in each.

1. The woman in the story started a business cooking food.
2. Her husband packed up and moved away to a new state.
3. She and her two baby sons were on their own in a new state.
4. The lumber workers bought food from her.

Writing Application Using the following sentence as a model, write two more sentences that include both common and proper nouns: *Annie hoped to name her business Johnson's Pies.*

PH WRITING COACH Further instruction and practice are available in *Prentice Hall Writing Coach.*

40 Fiction and Nonfiction

Writing

Narrative Text Both selections involve strong women dealing with life's challenges. Write an **anecdote,** a brief narrative, about a person you know and respect. For example, you might describe something admirable that the person did and what you learned from it.

- Before you draft, note what you respect about the person. This is the controlling impression your anecdote will convey.
- Describe a specific event that illustrates the characteristics you admire in your subject.
- Use significant details to support the message you want to convey.

Grammar Application If you include proper nouns in your anecdote, be sure to capitalize correctly.

Writing Workshop: *Work in Progress*

Prewriting for an Autobiographical Narrative For an essay you may write later, list three or four vivid memories, describing the visual picture you see in your mind for each one. Develop the scene in your mind by adding details related to other senses. Include what you heard, smelled, and felt. Save this Memory List in your writing portfolio.

Speaking and Listening

Comprehension and Collaboration With a partner, role-play an **interview** featuring the main character in the selection you read. For example, plan an interview between the washwoman and a reporter or between Annie Johnson and a potential employer. If you need to refresh your memory, reread either selection to learn more about the character you have chosen.

Follow these steps to complete the assignment:

- In order to demonstrate your knowledge of the subject matter, generate and ask relevant questions that are open-ended and cannot be answered simply with a yes or a no.
- Listen carefully to what your partner says in the interview.
- Make notes of your partner's responses so that you can ask appropriate follow-up questions or provide answers.
- To make your delivery more effective, speak clearly (showing confidence and poise), make eye contact with your partner, and use language that demonstrates maturity, sensitivity, and respect.
- After the role play, evaluate each other's work for the quality of its techniques.
- Compile your responses and report a summary to the class.

Common Core State Standards
L.9-10.2; SL.9-10.1.a., SL.9-10.1.c.; W.9-10.3.
[For the full wording of the standards, see page xiv.]

Use this prewriting activity to prepare for the **Writing Workshop** on page 94.

PHLit Online!
www.PHLitOnline.com
- Interactive graphic organizers
- Grammar tutorial
- Interactive journals

Integrated Language Skills 41

What special features will I find in this book?

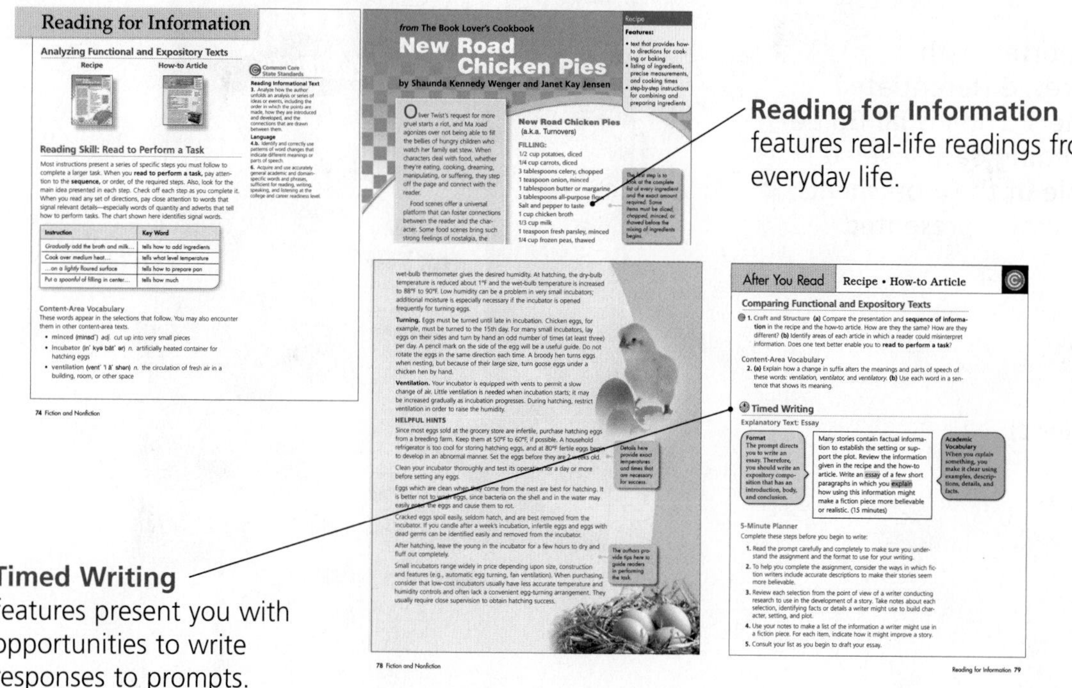

Reading for Information features real-life readings from everyday life.

Timed Writing features present you with opportunities to write responses to prompts.

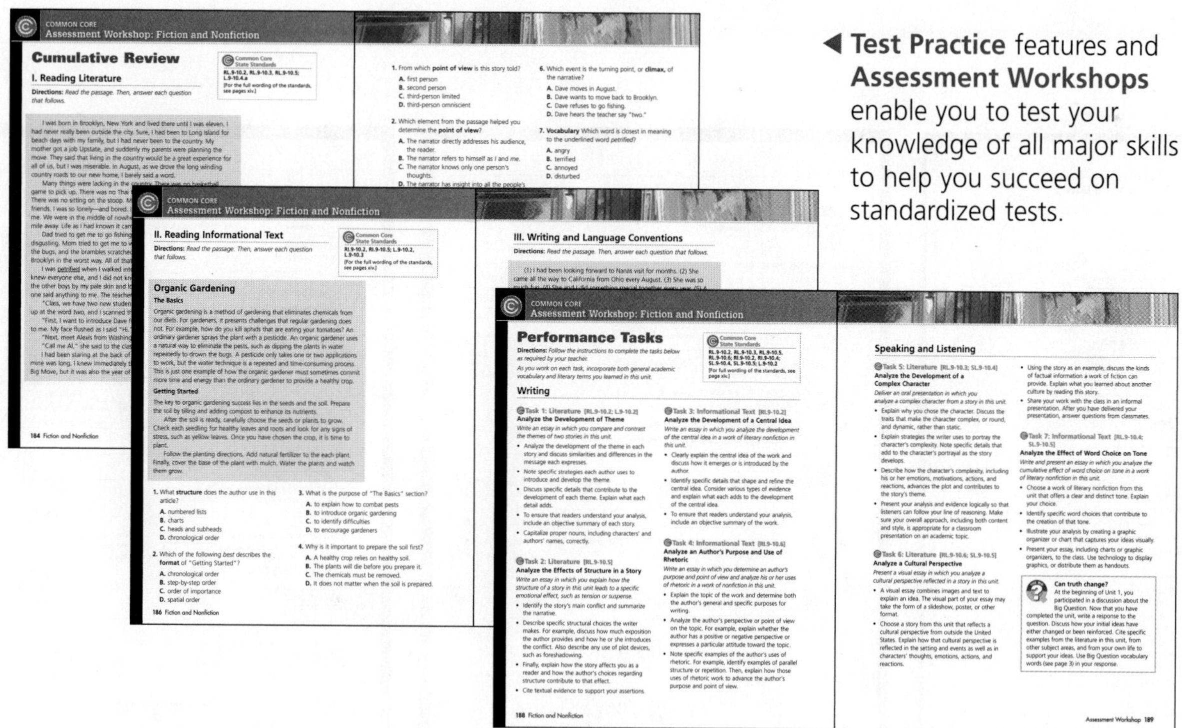

◀ **Test Practice** features and **Assessment Workshops** enable you to test your knowledge of all major skills to help you succeed on standardized tests.

Selection and Skills Support

Every selection is fully supported with worksheets in *Unit Resources*, differentiated for various groups of learners. The Visual Guide to Selected Resources preceding each leveled selection pair gives a sample of the worksheets available. The full complement is presented on these pages.

RESOURCES FOR:

- **L1 Special-Needs Students**
- **L2 Below-Level Students (Tier 2)**
- **L3 On-Level (Tier 1)**
- **L4 Advanced Students (Tier 1)**
- **EL English Learners**
- **All All Students**

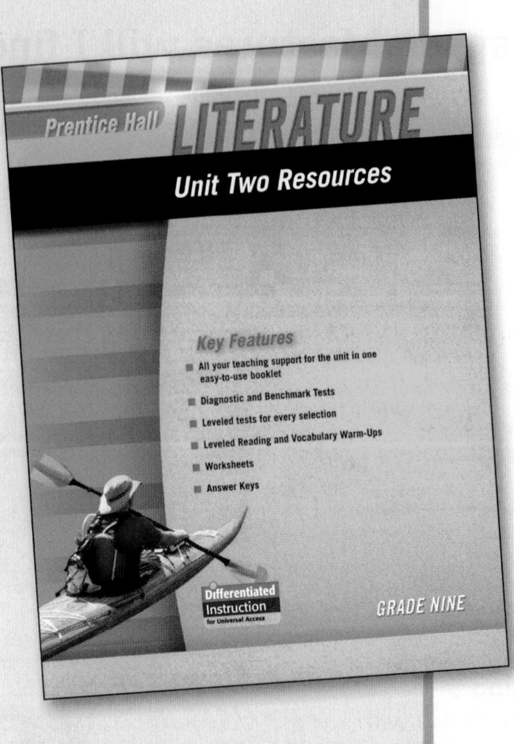

Prentice Hall LITERATURE
Unit Two Resources
Key Features
All your teaching support for the unit in one easy-to-use booklet
Diagnostic and Benchmark Tests
Leveled tests for every selection
Leveled Reading and Vocabulary Warm-Ups
Worksheets
Answer Keys
Differentiated Instruction for Universal Access
GRADE NINE

"**The Most Dangerous Game**" by Richard Connell

Vocabulary Warm-up Word Lists

Study these words from "The Most Dangerous Game." Then, complete the activities.

Word List A

acknowledge [ak NAHL ij] *v.* to admit something is true or real
After our defeat, we had to acknowledge that we were not a strong team.

bewilderment [bee WIL der ment] *n.* strong feeling of confusion
Not knowing the customs of a place can create bewilderment.

complicated [KAHM pli kay tid] *adj.* having many parts; complex
The report was complicated and required a great deal of research.

consideration [kuhn sid uh RAY shuhn] *n.* thoughtful concern for others
Please show consideration and do not talk during the movie.

grisly [GRIZ lee] *adj.* horrible in an extreme way
Movies that show a lot of blood are too grisly for me to watch.

particularly [pahr TIK yoo ler lee] *adv.* to a great degree
All my relatives are fun, but I particularly like my oldest cousin.

superstition [soo per STI shuhn] *n.* irrational but deep-seated belief
It may be a superstition, but I think my four-leaf clover brings me luck.

vivid [VIV id] *adj.* very bright; very clear
The sky was a vivid blue, with not a cloud in sight.

Word List B

apprehensive [ap ree HEN siv] *adj.* worried about what may happen
After three lost games, everyone is apprehensive about this one.

enthusiastically [en thoo zee AS tik lee] *adv.* with great interest
She is so popular that everyone responds enthusiastically to her ideas.

inspiration [in spuh RAY shuhn] *n.* sudden bright idea
Inventors often start with an inspiration that comes out of the blue.

jagged [JAG id] *adj.* sharp and uneven
The thought of a shark's jagged teeth near me in the water is terrifying.

obstacle [AHB stuh kuhl] *n.* something or someone in the way
If you give up too soon, you become an obstacle to your own success.

postponing [pohst POHN ing] *v.* putting off until later; delaying
We are postponing our trip because will have more time next month.

precision [pri SIZH uhn] *n.* exactness or accuracy
Precision is key in making clocks to ensure they tell the right time.

trait [TRAYT] *n.* quality or characteristic of a person or an animal
The trait I like best in cats is their independence.

Unit 2 Resources: Short Stories

41

EL L1 L2 Vocabulary Warm-ups A and B

vocabulary and reading practice for lower-level students and English learners

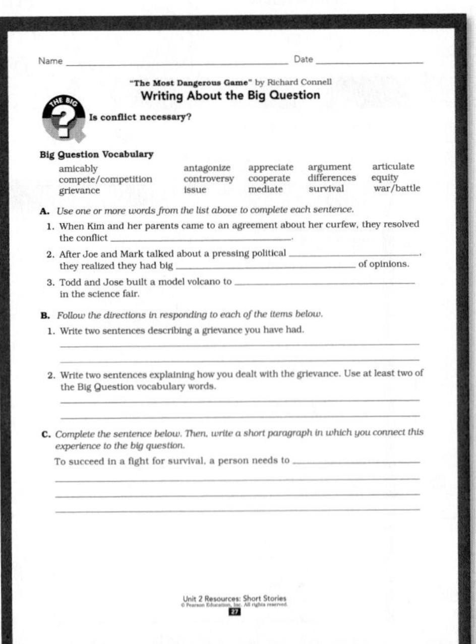

Name ____________ Date ____________

"**The Most Dangerous Game**" by Richard Connell

Writing About the Big Question

THE BIG ? **Is conflict necessary?**

Big Question Vocabulary

amicably	antagonize	appreciate	argument	articulate
compete/competition	controversy	cooperate	differences	equity
grievance	issue	mediate	survival	war/battle

A. *Use one or more words from the list above to complete each sentence.*

1. When Kim and her parents came to an agreement about her curfew, they resolved the conflict ____________.
2. After Joe and Mark talked about a pressing political ____________, they realized they had big ____________ of opinions.
3. Todd and Jose built a model volcano to ____________ in the science fair.

B. *Follow the directions in responding to each of the items below.*

1. Write two sentences describing a grievance you have had.
2. Write two sentences explaining how you dealt with the grievance. Use at least two of the Big Question vocabulary words.

C. *Complete the sentence below. Then, write a short paragraph in which you connect this experience to the big question.*

To succeed in a fight for survival, a person needs to ____________

Unit 2 Resources: Short Stories

27

All Writing About the Big Question

thematic vocabulary and thought-provoking activities centered around the unit Big Question

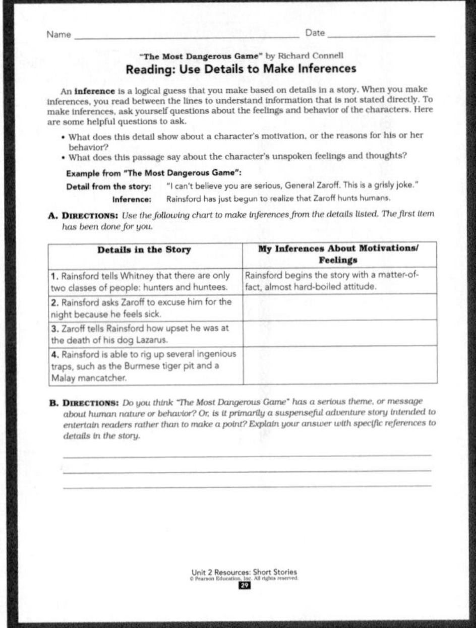

Name ____________ Date ____________

"**The Most Dangerous Game**" by Richard Connell

Reading: Use Details to Make Inferences

An **inference** is a logical guess that you make based on details in a story. When you make inferences, you read between the lines to understand information that is not stated directly. To make inferences, ask yourself questions about the feelings and behavior of the characters. Here are some helpful questions to ask.

- What does this detail show about a character's motivation, or the reasons for his or her behavior?
- What does this passage say about the character's unspoken feelings and thoughts?

Example from "The Most Dangerous Game":

Detail from the story: "I can't believe you are serious, General Zaroff. This is a grisly joke."

Inference: Rainsford has just begun to realize that Zaroff hunts humans.

A. Directions: *Use the following chart to make inferences from the details listed. The first item has been done for you.*

Details in the Story	My Inferences About Motivations/ Feelings
1. Rainsford tells Whitney that there are only two classes of people: hunters and huntees.	Rainsford begins the story with a matter-of-fact, almost hard-boiled attitude.
2. Rainsford asks Zaroff to excuse him for the night because he feels sick.	
3. Zaroff tells Rainsford how upset he was at the death of his dog Lazarus.	
4. Rainsford is able to rig up several ingenious traps, such as the Burmese tiger pit and a Malay mancatcher.	

B. Directions: *Do you think "The Most Dangerous Game" has a serious theme, or message about human nature or behavior? Or, is it primarily a suspenseful adventure story intended to entertain readers rather than to make a point? Explain your answer with specific references to details in the story.*

Unit 2 Resources: Short Stories

29

All Reading

a full page of support for the Reading Skill taught with the selection

All teacher resources are available online at www.PHLitOnline.com

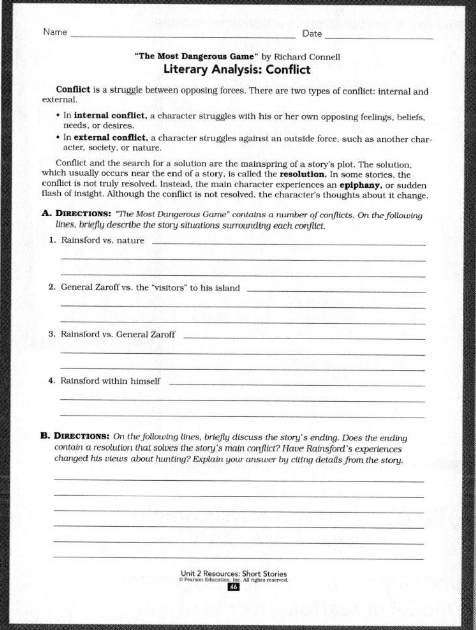

Name ____ Date ____

"The Most Dangerous Game" by Richard Connell

Literary Analysis: Conflict

Conflict is a struggle between opposing forces. There are two types of conflict: internal and external.

- In **internal conflict,** a character struggles with his or her own opposing feelings, beliefs, needs, or desires.
- In **external conflict,** a character struggles against an outside force, such as another character, society, or nature.

Conflict and the search for a solution are the mainspring of a story's plot. The solution, which usually occurs near the end of a story, is called the **resolution.** In some stories, the conflict is not truly resolved. Instead, the main character experiences an **epiphany,** or sudden flash of insight. Although the conflict is not resolved, the character's thoughts about it change.

A. Directions: *"The Most Dangerous Game" contains a number of conflicts. On the following lines, briefly describe the story situations surrounding each conflict.*

1. Rainsford vs. nature ____
2. General Zaroff vs. the "visitors" to his island ____
3. Rainsford vs. General Zaroff ____
4. Rainsford within himself ____

B. Directions: *On the following lines, briefly discuss the story's ending. Does the ending contain a resolution that solves the story's main conflict? Have Rainsford's experiences changed his views about hunting? Explain your answer by citing details from the story.*

Unit 2 Resources: Short Stories
© Pearson Education, Inc. All rights reserved.
46

All Literary Analysis

a full page of support for the Literary Analysis concept taught with the selection

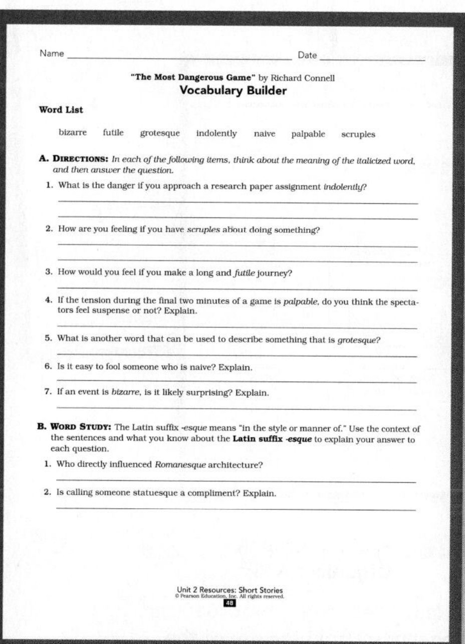

Name ____ Date ____

"The Most Dangerous Game" by Richard Connell

Vocabulary Builder

Word List

bizarre futile grotesque indolently naive palpable scruples

A. Directions: *In each of the following items, think about the meaning of the italicized word, and then answer the question.*

1. What is the danger if you approach a research paper assignment *indolently?*
2. How are you feeling if you have *scruples* about doing something?
3. How would you feel if you make a long and *futile* journey?
4. If the tension during the final two minutes of a game is *palpable,* do you think the spectators feel suspense or not? Explain.
5. What is another word that can be used to describe something that is *grotesque?*
6. Is it easy to fool someone who is naive? Explain.
7. If an event is *bizarre,* is it likely surprising? Explain.

B. Word Study: The Latin suffix *-esque* means "in the style or manner of." Use the context of the sentences and what you know about the **Latin suffix *-esque*** to explain your answer to each question.

1. Who directly influenced *Romanesque* architecture?
2. Is calling someone statuesque a compliment? Explain.

Unit 2 Resources: Short Stories
© Pearson Education, Inc. All rights reserved.
48

All Vocabulary Builder

selection vocabulary and Word Study skill practice

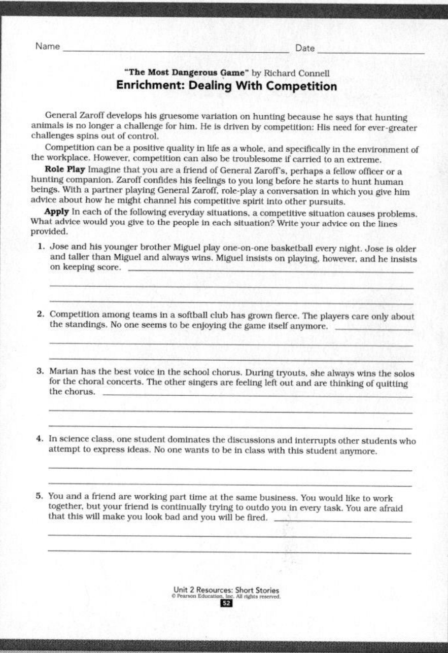

Name ____ Date ____

"The Most Dangerous Game" by Richard Connell

Enrichment: Dealing With Competition

General Zaroff develops his gruesome variation on hunting because he says that hunting animals is no longer a challenge for him. He is driven by competition: His need for ever-greater challenges spins out of control.

Competition can be a positive quality in life as a whole, and specifically in the environment of the workplace. However, competition can also be troublesome if carried to an extreme.

Role Play Imagine that you are a friend of General Zaroff's, perhaps a fellow officer or a hunting companion. Zaroff confides his feelings to you long before he starts to hunt human beings. With a partner playing General Zaroff, role-play a conversation in which you give him advice about how he might channel his competitive spirit into other pursuits.

Apply In each of the following everyday situations, a competitive situation causes problems. What advice would you give to the people in each situation? Write your advice on the lines provided.

1. Jose and his younger brother Miguel play one-on-one basketball every night. Jose is older and taller than Miguel and always wins. Miguel insists on playing, however, and he insists on keeping score. ____
2. Competition among teams in a softball club has grown fierce. The players care only about the standings. No one seems to be enjoying the game itself anymore. ____
3. Marian has the best voice in the school chorus. During tryouts, she always wins the solos for the choral concerts. The other singers are feeling left out and are thinking of quitting the chorus. ____
4. In science class, one student dominates the discussions and interrupts other students who attempt to express ideas. No one wants to be in class with this student anymore.
5. You and a friend are working part time at the same business. You would like to work together, but your friend is continually trying to outdo you in every task. You are afraid that this will make you look bad and you will be fired. ____

Unit 2 Resources: Short Stories
© Pearson Education, Inc. All rights reserved.
52

L4 Enrichment

a selection-related challenge for advanced learners

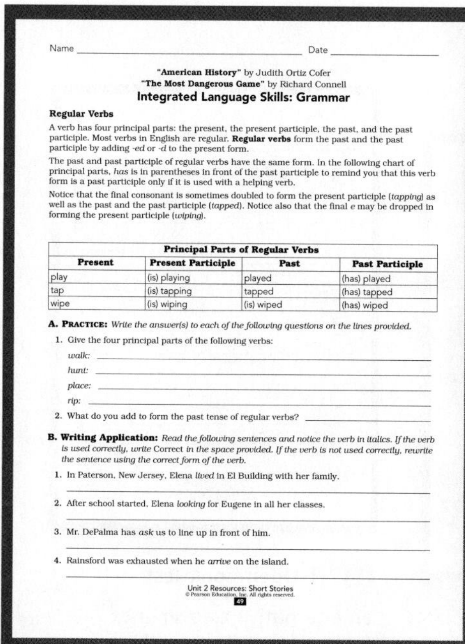

Name ____ Date ____

"American History" by Judith Ortiz Cofer
"The Most Dangerous Game" by Richard Connell

Integrated Language Skills: Grammar

Regular Verbs

A verb has four principal parts: the present, the present participle, the past, and the past participle. Most verbs in English are regular. **Regular verbs** form the past and the past participle by adding *-ed* or *-d* to the present form.

The past and past participle of regular verbs have the same form. In the following chart of principal parts, *has* is in parentheses in front of the past participle to remind you that this verb form is a past participle only if it is used with a helping verb.

Notice that the final consonant is sometimes doubled to form the present participle (*tapping*) as well as the past and the past participle (*tapped*). Notice also that the final *e* may be dropped in forming the present participle (*wiping*).

Principal Parts of Regular Verbs			
Present	**Present Participle**	**Past**	**Past Participle**
play	(is) playing	played	(has) played
tap	(is) tapping	tapped	(has) tapped
wipe	(is) wiping	(is) wiped	(has) wiped

A. Practice: *Write the answer(s) to each of the following questions on the lines provided.*

1. Give the four principal parts of the following verbs:
   walk: ____
   hunt: ____
   place: ____
   rip: ____
2. What do you add to form the past tense of regular verbs? ____

B. Writing Application: *Read the following sentences and notice the verb in italics. If the verb is used correctly, write* Correct *in the space provided. If the verb is not used correctly, rewrite the sentence using the correct form of the verb.*

1. In Paterson, New Jersey, Elena *lived* in El Building with her family.
2. After school started, Elena *looking* for Eugene in all her classes.
3. Mr. DePalma has *ask* us to line up in front of him.
4. Rainsford was exhausted when he *arrive* on the island.

Unit 2 Resources: Short Stories
© Pearson Education, Inc. All rights reserved.
49

L3 L4 Grammar

more practice with the grammar skill taught with the selection

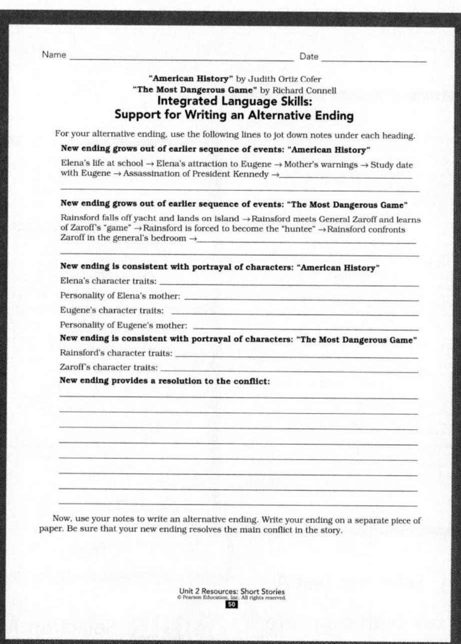

Name ____ Date ____

"American History" by Judith Ortiz Cofer
"The Most Dangerous Game" by Richard Connell

Integrated Language Skills: Support for Writing an Alternative Ending

For your alternative ending, use the following lines to jot down notes under each heading.

New ending grows out of earlier sequence of events: "American History"

Elena's life at school → Elena's attraction to Eugene → Mother's warnings → Study date with Eugene → Assassination of President Kennedy → ____

New ending grows out of earlier sequence of events: "The Most Dangerous Game"

Rainsford falls off yacht and lands on island → Rainsford meets General Zaroff and learns of Zaroff's "game" → Rainsford is forced to become the "huntee" → Rainsford confronts Zaroff in the general's bedroom → ____

New ending is consistent with portrayal of characters: "American History"

Elena's character traits: ____
Personality of Elena's mother: ____
Eugene's character traits: ____
Personality of Eugene's mother: ____

New ending is consistent with portrayal of characters: "The Most Dangerous Game"

Rainsford's character traits: ____
Zaroff's character traits: ____

New ending provides a resolution to the conflict:

Now, use your notes to write an alternative ending. Write your ending on a separate piece of paper. Be sure that your new ending resolves the main conflict in the story.

Unit 2 Resources: Short Stories
© Pearson Education, Inc. All rights reserved.
50

L3 L4 Writing

support for the Writing activity accompanying the selection

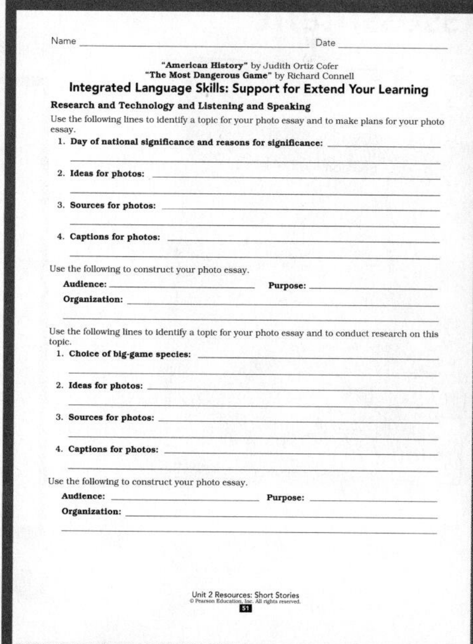

Name ____ Date ____

"American History" by Judith Ortiz Cofer
"The Most Dangerous Game" by Richard Connell

Integrated Language Skills: Support for Extend Your Learning

Research and Technology and Listening and Speaking

Use the following lines to identify a topic for your photo essay and to make plans for your photo essay.

1. **Day of national significance and reasons for significance:** ____
2. **Ideas for photos:** ____
3. **Sources for photos:** ____
4. **Captions for photos:** ____

Use the following to construct your photo essay.

Audience: ____ **Purpose:** ____
Organization: ____

Use the following lines to identify a topic for your photo essay and to conduct research on this topic.

1. **Choice of big-game species:** ____
2. **Ideas for photos:** ____
3. **Sources for photos:** ____
4. **Captions for photos:** ____

Use the following to construct your photo essay.

Audience: ____ **Purpose:** ____
Organization: ____

Unit 2 Resources: Short Stories
© Pearson Education, Inc. All rights reserved.
51

L3 L4 Extend Your Learning

customized support for the Listening and Speaking or Research and Technology activity related to the selection

Selection Support

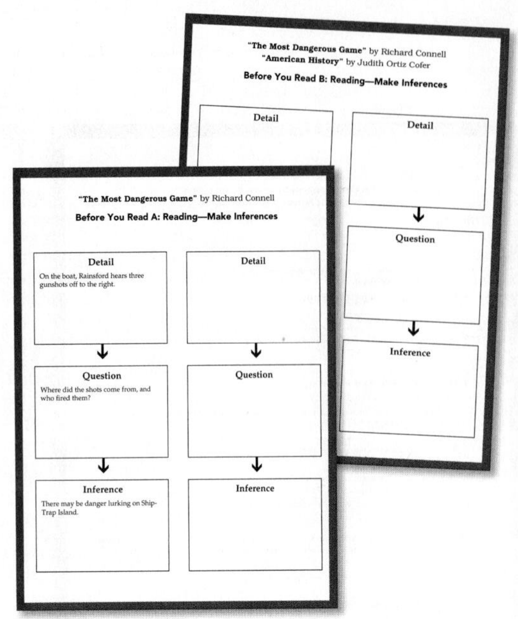

"The Most Dangerous Game" by Richard Connell
"American History" by Judith Ortiz Cofer
Before You Read B: Reading—Make Inferences

Detail | Detail
Question
Inference

"The Most Dangerous Game" by Richard Connell
Before You Read A: Reading—Make Inferences

Detail	Detail
On the boat, Rainsford hears three gunshots off to the right.	

Question	Question
Where did the shots come from, and who fired them?	

Inference	Inference
There may be danger lurking on Ship-Trap Island.	

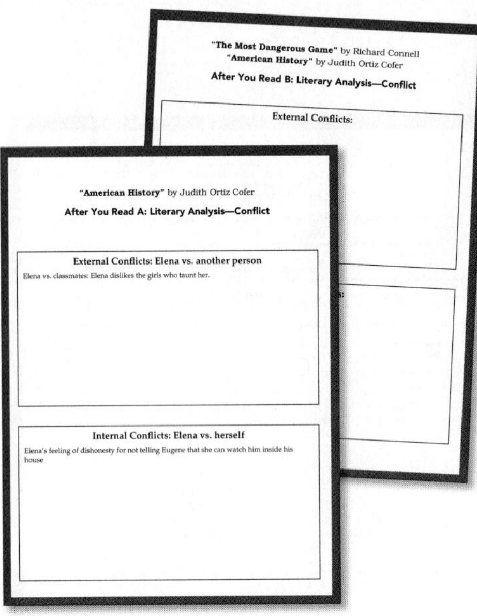

"The Most Dangerous Game" by Richard Connell
"American History" by Judith Ortiz Cofer
After You Read B: Literary Analysis—Conflict

External Conflicts:

"American History" by Judith Ortiz Cofer
After You Read A: Literary Analysis—Conflict

External Conflicts: Elena vs. another person
Elena vs. classmates: Elena dislikes the girls who taunt her.

Internal Conflicts: Elena vs. herself
Elena's feeling of dishonesty for not telling Eugene that she can watch him inside his house

EL L1 L2 Reading Graphic Organizer A

a partially filled-in graphic organizer to model or scaffold the use of the organizer

L3 Reading Graphic Organizer B

the blank version of the organizer

EL L1 L2 Literary Analysis Graphic Organizer A

a partially filled-in graphic organizer to model or scaffold the use of the organizer

L3 Literary Analysis Organizer B

the blank version of the organizer

Assessment

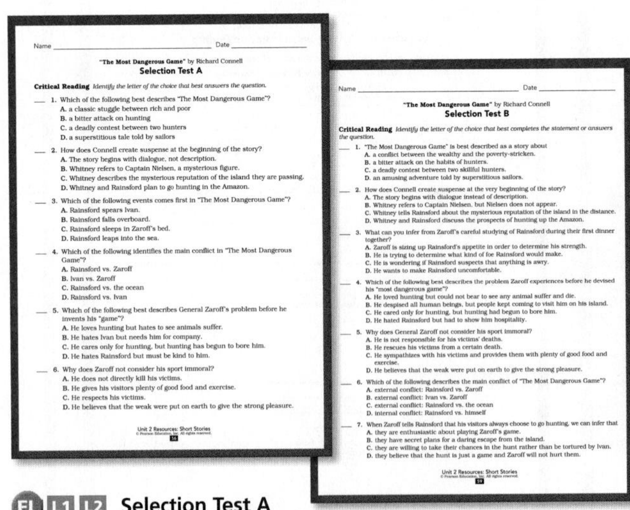

Name ______________________ Date ____________

"The Most Dangerous Game" by Richard Connell
Selection Test A

Critical Reading *Identify the letter of the choice that best answers the question.*

___ 1. Which of the following best describes "The Most Dangerous Game"?
A. a classic stuggle between rich and poor
B. a bitter attack on hunting
C. a deadly contest between two hunters
D. a superstitious tale told by sailors

___ 2. How does Connell create suspense at the beginning of the story?
A. The story begins with dialogue, not description.
B. Whitney refers to Captain Nielsen, a mysterious figure.
C. Whitney describes the mysterious reputation of the island they are passing.
D. Whitney and Rainsford plan to go hunting in the Amazon.

___ 3. Which of the following events comes first in "The Most Dangerous Game"?
A. Rainsford spears Ivan.
B. Rainsford falls overboard.
C. Rainsford sleeps in Zaroff's bed.
D. Rainsford leaps into the sea.

___ 4. Which of the following identifies the main conflict in "The Most Dangerous Game"?
A. Rainsford vs. Zaroff
B. Ivan vs. Zaroff
C. Rainsford vs. the ocean
D. Rainsford vs. Ivan

___ 5. Which of the following best describes General Zaroff's problem before he invents his "game"?
A. He loves hunting but hates to see animals suffer.
B. He hates Ivan but needs him for company.
C. He cares only for hunting, but hunting has begun to bore him.
D. He hates Rainsford but must be kind to him.

___ 6. Why does Zaroff not consider his sport immoral?
A. He does not directly kill his victims.
B. He gives his visitors plenty of good food and exercise.
C. He respects his victims.
D. He believes that the weak were put on earth to give the strong pleasure.

Unit 2 Resources: Short Stories
56

Name ______________________ Date ____________

"The Most Dangerous Game" by Richard Connell
Selection Test B

Critical Reading *Identify the letter of the choice that best completes the statement or answers the question.*

___ 1. "The Most Dangerous Game" is best described as a story about
A. a conflict between the wealthy and the poverty-stricken.
B. a bitter attack on the habits of hunters.
C. a deadly contest between two skillful hunters.
D. an amusing adventure told by superstitious sailors.

___ 2. How does Connell create suspense at the very beginning of the story?
A. The story begins with dialogue instead of description.
B. Whitney refers to Captain Nielsen, but Nielsen does not appear.
C. Whitney tells Rainsford about the mysterious reputation of the island in the distance.
D. Whitney and Rainsford discuss the prospects of hunting up the Amazon.

___ 3. What can you infer from Zaroff's careful studying of Rainsford during their first dinner together?
A. Zaroff is sizing up Rainsford's appetite in order to determine his strength.
B. He is trying to determine what kind of foe Rainsford would make.
C. He is wondering if Rainsford suspects that anything is awry.
D. He wants to make Rainsford uncomfortable.

___ 4. Which of the following best describes the problem Zaroff experiences before he devised his "most dangerous game"?
A. He loved hunting but could not bear to see any animal suffer and die.
B. He despised all human beings, but people kept coming to visit him on his island.
C. He cared only for hunting, but hunting had begun to bore him.
D. He hated Rainsford but had to show him hospitality.

___ 5. Why does General Zaroff not consider his sport immoral?
A. He is not responsible for his victims' deaths.
B. He rescues his victims from a certain death.
C. He sympathizes with his victims and provides them with plenty of good food and exercise.
D. He believes that the weak were put on earth to give the strong pleasure.

___ 6. Which of the following describes the main conflict of "The Most Dangerous Game"?
A. external conflict: Rainsford vs. Zaroff
B. external conflict: Ivan vs. Zaroff
C. external conflict: Rainsford vs. the ocean
D. internal conflict: Rainsford vs. himself

___ 7. When Zaroff tells Rainsford that his visitors always choose to go hunting, we can infer that
A. they are enthusiastic about playing Zaroff's game.
B. they have secret plans for a daring escape from the island.
C. they are willing to take their chances in the hunt rather than be tortured by Ivan.
D. they believe that the hunt is just a game and Zaroff will not hurt them.

Unit 2 Resources: Short Stories
59

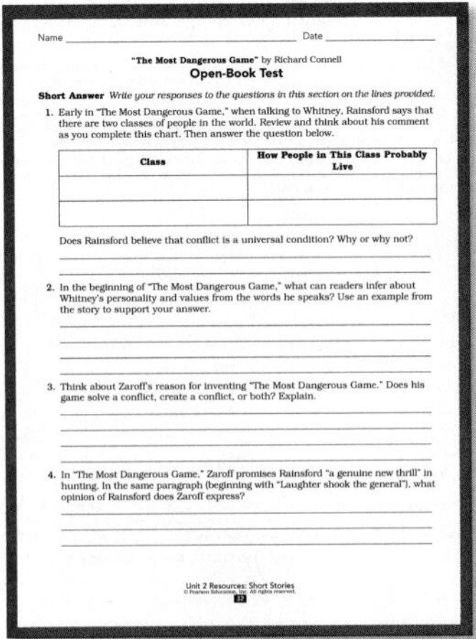

Name ______________________ Date ____________

"The Most Dangerous Game" by Richard Connell
Open-Book Test

Short Answer *Write your responses to the questions in this section on the lines provided.*

1. Early in "The Most Dangerous Game," when talking to Whitney, Rainsford says that there are two classes of people in the world. Review and think about his comment as you complete this chart. Then answer the question below.

Class	How People in This Class Probably Live

Does Rainsford believe that conflict is a universal condition? Why or why not?

2. In the beginning of "The Most Dangerous Game," what can readers infer about Whitney's personality and values from the words he speaks? Use an example from the story to support your answer.

3. Think about Zaroff's reason for inventing "The Most Dangerous Game." Does his game solve a conflict, create a conflict, or both? Explain.

4. In "The Most Dangerous Game," Zaroff promises Rainsford "a genuine new thrill" in hunting. In the same paragraph (beginning with "Laughter shook the general"), what opinion of Rainsford does Zaroff express?

Unit 2 Resources: Short Stories
52

EL L1 L2 Selection Test A

selection test with complete skills coverage, adapted for lower-level students and English learners

EL L3 L4 Selection Test B

selection test with complete skills coverage, including multiple choice and essay items

L3 L4 Open-Book Test

an alternative assessment format for on-level and advanced students

All teacher resources are available online at www.PHLitOnline.com

Common Core Companion

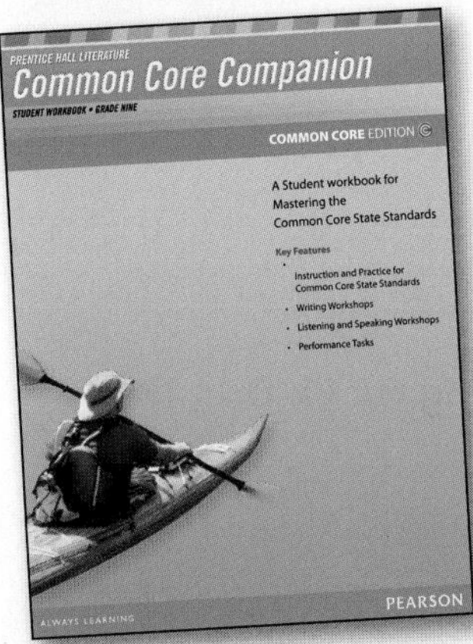

The Common Core Companion student workbook provides instruction and practice for all Common Core State Standards. Here is a closer look at this workbook.

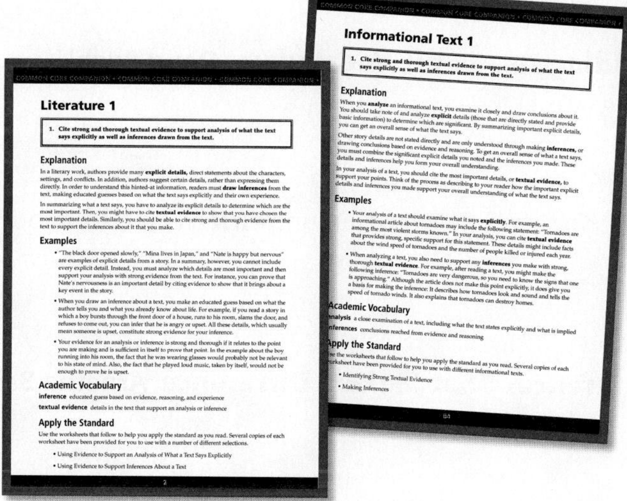

All Literature and Informational Text

Direct instruction and practice for each Common Core State Standard. Standards requiring writing or presentation outcomes are supported through process workshops.

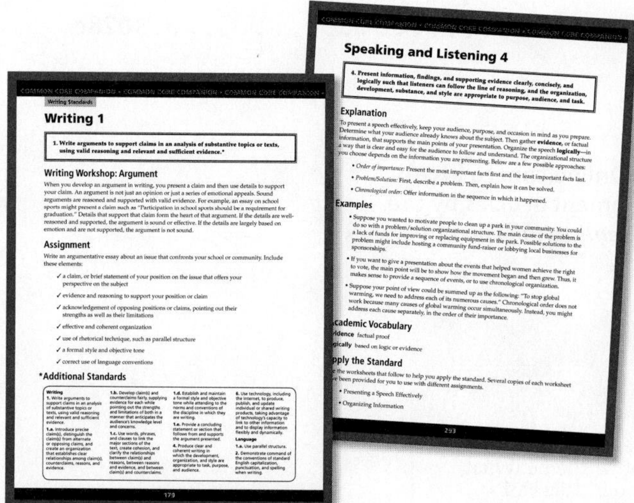

All Writing and Speaking and Listening

Full writing process workshops are supported with direct instruction and worksheets. Writing process standards are integrated with Speaking and Listening activities.

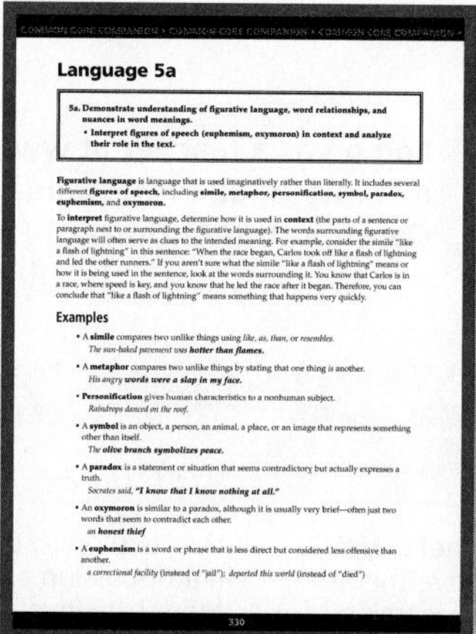

All Language

Explicit instruction supports each Language standard. Practice worksheets and graphic organizers provide additional opportunities for mastery.

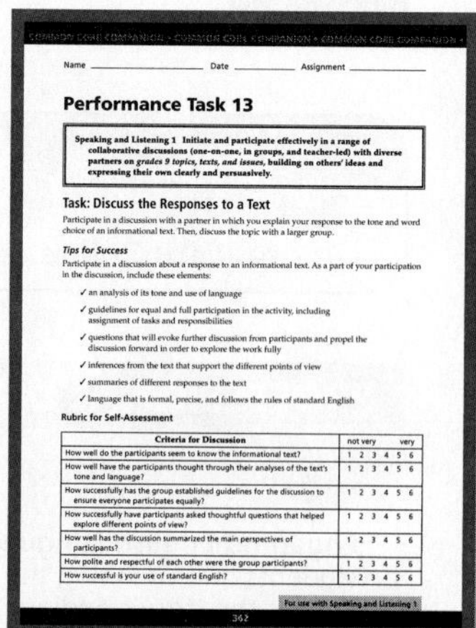

All Performance Tasks

Assessment opportunities are provided for each reading standard, along with tips for success and rubrics.

Each unit in this Teacher's Edition begins with a professional development essay by a program author. For more professional development essays, visit www.PHLitOnline.com.

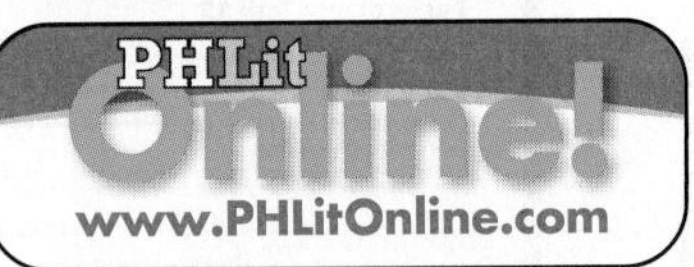

Log on as a teacher at www.PHLitOnline.com to access a library of all Professional Development articles by the Contributing Authors of *Pearson Prentice Hall Literature.*

PROFESSIONAL DEVELOPMENT | **Danling Fu**

Apply the Strategy

Engaging English Language Learners: After students finish reading the story, have them discuss the story's ending. Ask the following questions: *Are the characters satisfied or disappointed with the gifts they receive? What is the real gift they present to each other?* Encourage students to share personal stories about what their parents and relatives sacrificed for their families by leaving their country of origin.

After exploring this theme, guide students in a discussion about another theme: What does "true love" mean in our daily life?

For more of Danling Fu's strategies, see her Professional Development essay, pp. 194c–194d.

Authors give concrete applications for the strategies they discuss in their essays at point of use in the Teacher's Edition.

PRENTICE HALL

LITERATURE

GRADE 9

COMMON CORE EDITION ©

Upper Saddle River, New Jersey

Boston, Massachusetts

Chandler, Arizona

Glenview, Illinois

LWAYS LEARNING

PEARSON

Student Edition Pages

Cover: (Bkgd) ©Ted Mead/Getty Images, (L) ©James Forte/Getty Images, (B) ©Tom Merton/OJO Images/Getty Images, (TL, BC) ©Blaine Harrington III/CORBIS, (CR) ©Uli Wiesmeier/zefa/CORBIS

Acknowledgments appear on page R72, which constitutes an extension of this copyright page.

PEARSON

ISBN-13: 978-0-13-319555-2
ISBN-10: 0-13-319555-4
2 3 4 5 6 7 8 9 10 15 14 13 12 11

Student Edition Pages

PRENTICE HALL

LITERATURE

TEACHER'S EDITION • GRADE 9

COMMON CORE EDITION 

ALWAYS LEARNING

PEARSON

Unit 1 Features Overview

Unit Genre and Unit Big Question

In this unit, students will analyze fiction and nonfiction. As they read they will discuss responses to the unit Big Question: Can truth change?

Unit 1 Selections

Teach Selections are presented in leveled pairs. To teach the skills and meet the objectives, you need to assign only one selection in each pair.

Differentiate and Reinforce Choose the selection in a pair that is best suited for your students, based on the Text Complexity box shown on the next page. You may use the other selection to reinforce skills or provide enrichment.

Integrate Skills Each selection presents students with a reading strategy, a literary analysis concept, a vocabulary skill, and grammar instruction. Students can extend learning in the writing and extension activities.

Additional Unit Features

Literary Analysis Workshop Teach and model the Unit Focus standards. Spiral Review notes enable students to revisit these skills over the course of the unit.

Reading for Information Students analyze functional, expository, and argumentative texts and complete Timed Writing activities.

Comparing Literary Works Students study two literary works either within or across genres.

Test Practice: Reading This feature provides extra practice in utilizing reading skills to master assessments.

Writing Workshops Two writing workshops appear in each unit, along with rubrics and instruction in the writing process.

Assessment Workshop Cumulative Skill Review and Performance Tasks provide a range of assessment opportunities.

Independent Reading Students broaden their knowledge as they read longer works of increasing complexity.

THE BIG ?
Can truth change?

PHLit Online!
www.PHLitOnline.com

Teaching From Technology

Log on at this address for the following:

Enriched Online Student Edition

- full narration of selections
- interactive graphic organizers
- linked **Get Connected!** and **Background** videos
- all worksheets and other student resources

Professional Development

- the *Professional Development Guidebook* online
- additional professional development essays by program authors

Planning, Assigning, and Monitoring

- software for online assignment of work to students, individually or to the whole class
- a system for tracking and grading student work

Unit 1

Fiction and Nonfiction

PHLit Online!

www.PHLitOnline.com

Hear It!
- Selection summary audio
- Selection audio
- BQ Tunes

See It!
- Author videos
- Big Question video
- Get Connected videos
- Background videos
- More about the authors
- Illustrated vocabulary words
- Vocabulary flashcards

Do It!
- Interactive journals
- Interactive graphic organizers
- Grammar tutorials
- Interactive vocabulary games
- Test practice

1

Instructional Resources

Unit 1 Resources supports unit skills with pages of the following types:

- **Benchmark Tests** assess and monitor student progress at mid-unit and at unit's end.
- **Vocabulary and Reading Warm-ups** provide additional vocabulary support, based on Lexile rankings of words, for each selection. **"A" Warm-ups** are for students reading two grades below level. **"B" Warm-ups** are for students reading one grade below level.
- **Selection Support** These practice pages are available for each selection:
  - Reading Skill
  - Literary Analysis
  - Writing About the Big Question
  - Vocabulary
  - Support for Writing
  - Support for Extend Your Learning
  - Enrichment

PHLit Online!

All worksheets and other student resources are also available online at **www.PHLitOnline.com.**

Text Complexity: Accessibility for Various Ability Levels

This chart gives a general text complexity rating to help you decide which selection in each leveled pair is more appropriate for your students. **Choose one selection in each pair, or choose to teach both.** You will meet the objectives for the pair when you teach either of the two selections. For additional guidance on factors that affect the complexity of each selection, see the Leveled Texts page for each selection set.

	✓ More Accessible	✓✓ More Complex
Pair 1	The Washwoman	New Directions
Pair 2	Sonata for Harp and Bicycle	Cask of Amontillado
Pair 3	*from* A White House Diary	My English
Pair 4	The Secret Life of Walter Mitty	Uncle Marcos

Accessibility for English Learners

This icon indicates support for English learners at point of use in this Teacher's Edition.

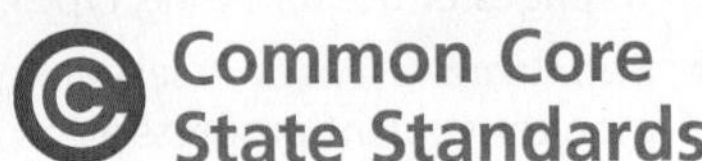

Common Core State Standards

Unit 1 Focus Standards
- **Reading Literature 2**
- **Reading Informational Text 2**

Additional Activities and Assessments
- **Speaking and Listening 1, 5**
- **Language 1, 2, 4, 5, 6**
- **Reading Literature 5**
- **Reading Informational Text 6**
- **Writing 4, 6, 9**

	Week 1					Week 2					Week 3				
	1	2	3	4	5	1	2	3	4	5	1	2	3	4	5
Administer the Diagnostic Test (*Unit 1 Resources*, pp. 1–6).	●														
Introduce the Unit Big Question (pp. 2–3).	●														
Introduce the Unit author and the Unit forms, fiction and nonfiction (pp 4–5).		●													
Teach the Model selections (pp. 6–21).		●	●												
Teach one selection from Pairing 1 (pp. 22–41).			●	●	●	●	●								
Teach one selection from Pairing 2 (pp. 42–71).							●	●	●	●	●				
Complete the Test Practice: Reading (pp. 72–73).										●					
Teach Reading for Information (pp. 74–79).											●				
Teach Comparing Literary Works (pp. 80–93).												●	●		
Have students complete the Writing Workshop (pp. 94–99).											●	●	●	●	●
Administer **Benchmark Test 1** (*Unit 1 Resources*, pp. 127–133).														●	
Reteach skills, judging which skills to reteach by evaluating students' performance on **Benchmark Test 1**.															●

Independent Reading

Have students choose a full-length work from the Independent Reading feature at the end of the unit and read it while working on this unit.

Pacing Suggestions
- Have students read their chosen work for homework.
- Devote parts of class periods in each school week to Literature Circles in which students reading the same work discuss it.

	Week 4					Week 5					Week 6				
	1	2	3	4	5	1	2	3	4	5	1	2	3	4	5
Teach one selection from Pairing 3 (pp. 100–123).	●	●	●	●	●										
Teach one selection from Pairing 4 (pp. 124–151).					●	●	●	●	●						
Complete the Test-Practice: Reading (pp. 152–153).								●							
Teach Reading for Information (pp. 154–159).									●						
Teach Comparing Literary Works (pp. 160–171).										●	●				
Have students complete the Writing Workshop (pp. 172–179).									●	●	●	●	●		
Have students complete Applying the Big Question (pp. 180–181).											●				
Have students complete the Vocabulary Workshop (pp. 180–181).												●			
Have students complete the Communications Workshop (pp. 182–183).													●		
Complete the Test Practice: Unit 1 Review (pp. 184–187).													●	●	●
Administer **Benchmark Test 2** (***Unit 1 Resources***, pp. 235–240).														●	
Reteach skills, judging which skills to reteach by evaluating students' performance on **Benchmark Test 2**.															●

- Cover the focus standards with independent readings and abbreviate review of the focus standards with student-edition selections.
- Do not assign extension activities for selections (day 5 of main selection lessons), except as needed for full standards coverage.
- If students demonstrate reading proficiency, consider omitting Test Practice: Reading features in the unit.

Block and Daily Scheduling

The assignments and activities in this Unit planner are organized by week. You may adjust them to your daily or block schedule. The Time and Resource Manager for each selection set gives specific pacing suggestions, or you may use the comprehensive lesson planning support online at **www.PHLitOnline.com.**

Monitoring Progress

Diagnose Each main selection pairing in the Unit contains a more accessible and a more complex selection. To determine which selection to assign to students, administer the **Diagnostic Test, *Unit 1 Resources,*** pp. 1–6. Use the **Interpretation Guide** to interpret the results of the test.

Preteach and Prepare As indicated by the diagnostic, prepare students for reading by assigning the **Vocabulary Practice** and **Reading Warm-ups** for the selections you assign.

Teach Follow this Pacing Plan and use the resources to teach the skills and selections. For specific pacing suggestions and a list of resources, see the Time and Resource Manager and the Visual Guide to Featured Selection Resources preceding each selection pairing.

Classroom Management

For classroom management suggestions for using leveled texts in a mixed-ability classroom, see Harvey Daniels's professional development essay "Leveled Reading Selections," online at **www.PHLitOnline.com.**

Assess After students have completed the first half of the Unit, administer **Benchmark Test 1**. Administer **Benchmark Test 2** at the end of the Unit. **Note:** For the most accurate diagnosis of students who score in the middle range of the diagnostic portion of the test, administer the additional diagnostic questions online at **www.PHLitOnline.com.**

Intervention and Reteach After administering each test, use the **Interpretation Guide** for the tests to determine which reteaching pages, if any, you should assign from the ***Reading Kit.*** The appropriate pages are also available through the online Progress Monitoring software.

CLASSROOM STRATEGIES

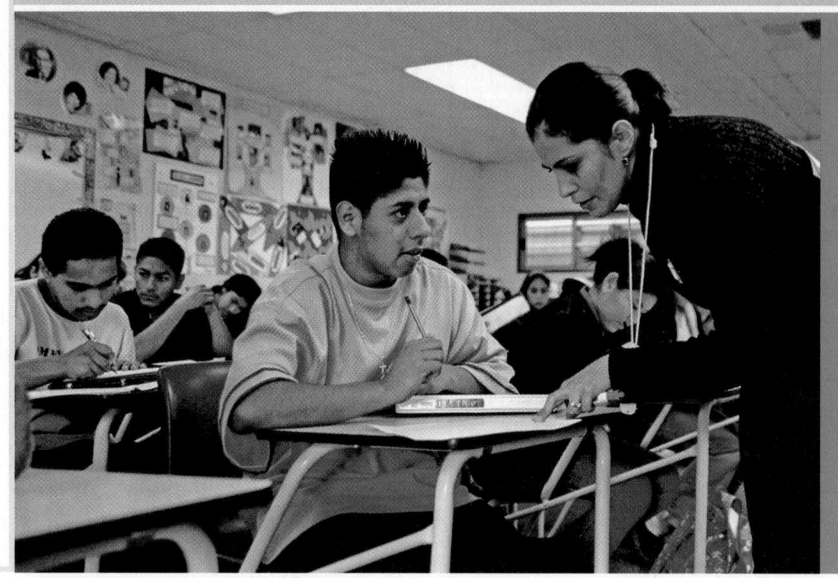

> Students versed in the language of a discipline will have deeper and more precise academic knowledge to apply to their reading and learning.

What's the difference between *infer* and *imply*? What could your students tell you? Teachers generally focus vocabulary instruction on words students encounter in written texts—words used by authors. But an undercurrent of classroom talk features language we use to think about and discuss written texts. In many cases, teachers assume students possess a deep understanding of this foundational language (words like *infer* and *imply*). However, although students encounter such language on an ongoing basis during instruction, it is often left for students to *infer* what these words mean, leaving confusions about some of the essential vocabulary used for classroom learning.

Vocabulary and Academic Discourse

Marzano (2004) argued that academic knowledge is largely vocabulary driven; students versed in the language of a discipline will have deeper and more precise academic knowledge to apply to their reading and learning. Academic vocabulary is related to the concept of "discourse," which refers to expected ways of communicating and interacting (Gee, 2000). Students who have mastered the language of academic discourse are better positioned to meet the reading, writing, speaking, and listening demands of school subjects. Academic vocabulary also encompasses what Beck, McKeown, and Kucan (2002) identified as "tier 3 words"—words used nearly exclusively within a specific academic discipline. *Heterotrophic* (science) and *onomatopoeia* (language arts) are examples of tier 3 words that are integral to learning within a discipline and need to be developed extensively as concepts.

Teaching the Language of "Language Arts"

Selecting Words for Instruction Which academic vocabulary is most worthy of instructional time? Feldman and Kinsella (2004) recommend the following guidelines:

- **Big Idea words**—tier 3 terms that are the core of the academic language of a specific discipline. In Language Arts, key conceptual terms like *figurative language, verb,* and *protagonist* qualify for focused attention.
- **Academic Tool Kit words**—vocabulary students meet again and again, across the curriculum. Words such as *contrast, verify,* and *perspective* pop up continuously in learning contexts; yet these words are typically not taught. As a result students develop hazy or imprecise meanings of highly crucial and recurring vocabulary.
- **Disciplinary Tool Kit words**—words common to the study of an academic discipline. Terms like *infer* and *imply* are words that students may have to figure out totally on their own, and as a result accrue only indistinct meanings.

- **Multiple Meaning words**—words that may have both a general meaning and a very specific application in an academic discipline. *Root, meter,* and *symbol* have distinct meanings in language arts that contrast with their general usage.

Don't Define; Explain! Instruction of academic vocabulary needs to extend beyond mere provision of a "definition." Beck, McKeown, and Kucan recommend student-friendly explanations that feature "you," "someone," and "something" in extended everyday language: *When you infer something, you have to use clues to figure it out.* Continue developing a meaningful understanding with additional examples: *If you normally are cheerful and today you are scowling, I could infer that something is bothering you.* For further elaboration request students to supply their own examples: *Think of times outside of school when you have to infer something.* Challenge students to generate examples that involve different contexts from the ones that have been mentioned so far. Visual representations of a new word can be especially powerful. Ask students to quickly sketch an image that crystallizes their understanding of the word, or some key aspect of it.

Integrating Academic Vocabulary into Classroom Conversations

Putting Words "In Play" Academic vocabulary is often perceived as "teacher talk." Students also need to develop confidence becoming regular users of academic vocabulary in their speaking and writing. Prompt students to put these words 'in play' in discussions and written activities. For example, when a student comments she *"realized that,"* interject targeted academic vocabulary into your response: *"So what did the author say that helped you infer . . ."* This ongoing gentle modeling and persistent use of academic language encourages students to integrate these words into their working vocabularies.

Connected, Not Isolated, Word Study Teach academic vocabulary in conjunction with other related terms, rather than as "stand-alone" knowledge. Our opening example of *infer* and *imply* illustrates that both terms can be best learned in relationship to each other. Readers and listeners must *infer* what writers and speakers *imply* but do not explicitly say. Terms such as *sarcasm* and *irony* can be best understood if explained as companion terms: *"Sarcasm is saying the opposite of what you mean; it is using humor to belittle you or put you down. Irony is also saying the opposite of what you mean; but usually for a humorous effect rather than as ridicule. Whether a statement is sarcastic or ironic depends on the intent of the speaker."*

Modeled Strategy

See pp. 63 and 129 for point-of-use notes modeling these strategies.

Teacher Resources

- ***Professional Development Guidebook***
- ***Classroom Strategies and Teaching Routines* cards**

Log on as a teacher at **www.PHLitOnline.com** to access a library of all Professional Development articles by the Contributing Authors of Pearson Prentice Hall *Literature.*

Doug Buehl

Doug Buehl is a teacher, author, and national literacy consultant. His 33 years with the Madison Metropolitan School District, Madison, WI, included experiences as a reading teacher and district adolescent literacy support teacher.

Supporting Research

Beck, I., McKeown, M. & Kucan, L., (2002). *Bringing words to life: Robust vocabulary instruction.* New York: Guilford Press.

Feldman, K., & Kinsella, K. (2004). *Narrowing the language gap: The case for explicit vocabulary instruction.* Scholastic Professional Paper. New York: Scholastic Inc.

Gee, J. P. (2000). Discourse and sociocultural studies in reading. In Kamil, M., Mosenthal, P., Pearson, P. D., & Barr, R. Edited. *Handbook of Reading Research (Vol. 3)* Mahwah, NJ: Lawrence Erlbaum Associates, 195–207.

Marzano, R. (2004). *Building background knowledge for academic achievement.* Alexandria, VA: ASCD

Common Core State Standards

- **Speaking and Listening 1**
- **Language 6**

1  Introducing the Big Question

1. Read aloud the first paragraph.
2. Provide an example of a truth that was later proven false. (Pluto is no longer considered a planet.) **Ask:** Is truth the same for everyone? (**Possible responses:** Yes, because it is based in fact. No, because people may have different views of it.) **Ask** students why a belief might be confused with a truth. (**Possible response:** People may believe something without having any proof that it is true.)
3. Have students consider whether the stories reinforce or challenge their first answers to the Big Question as they read.

2 Exploring the Big Question

Collaboration: Group Discussion

1. Introduce the activity, using the instruction on the student page.
2. What might one say when confronting a choice involving uncertainty? (**Sample response:** "Better safe than sorry.")

   What might people say when a good deal seems to change in a situation, but the basics remain the same? (**Sample response:** "The more things change, the more they remain the same.")
3. Review the Big Question vocabulary on page 3, following the teaching suggestions. Have students use the vocabulary as they complete the activity on page 2.

Connecting to the Literature

Explain the Big Question strand in the unit, referring to the box at right.

Introducing the Big Question

1 THE BIG ?

Can *truth* change?

Truth can be defined as "the real state of things" or "agreement with fact or reality." These definitions make the concept of truth seem simple. Yet, deciding what is truth and what is not can be a complicated matter. Often, what we accept as a truth or a fact at one time is later proven false when evidence shows the idea or belief is wrong. Does the truth change, or does our understanding of the truth change? Can we ever really know what is true? These are questions that writers explore in literature, and they invite you, the reader, to explore with them.

2 Exploring the Big Question

Collaboration: Group Discussion Start thinking about the Big Question by identifying different types of truths or facts. Give one specific example of each of the following types of truths, and explain how you know that each statement is true.

- a historical fact
- a scientific fact
- an assumption about how people interact with each other
- a truth about choices people can make in life
- a truth about what will happen in the future

Join a small team in your class and share your examples with your teammates. As you discuss each example, participate effectively by building on the ideas of others and by contributing information that is relevant. Try to convince your teammates that each statement is a truth and not an opinion. Listen attentively as your teammates explain their examples. Consider which of their points seem credible and which do not. Use the Big Question Vocabulary in your discussion.

Connecting to the Literature Each reading in this unit will give you additional insight into the Big Question.

PHLit Online!
www.PHLitOnline.com
- Big Question video
- Illustrated vocabulary words
- Interactive vocabulary games
- BQ Tunes

Applying Understanding by Design Principles

The Big Question

Explain to students that they will continue to consider the Big Question as they work through Unit 1.

- At the beginning of each selection, they will write a response to a Writing About the Big Question sentence frame.
- As they read the selection, they will look for details related to the Big Question.
- At the end of the selection, they will answer a Critical Thinking Question that is related to the Big Question.
- Tell students that their goal will be to gain a deeper understanding of literature and a more sophisticated way of discussing the Big Question.

❸ Learning Big Question Vocabulary

Common Core State Standards

Speaking and Listening
1. Initiate and participate effectively in a range of collaborative discussions with diverse partners on grades 9–10 topics, texts, and issues, building on others' ideas and expressing their own clearly and persuasively.

Language
6. Acquire and use accurately general academic and domain-specific words and phrases, sufficient for reading, writing, speaking, and listening at the college and career readiness level; demonstrate independence in gathering vocabulary knowledge when considering a word or phrase important to comprehension or expression.

Acquire and Use Academic Vocabulary Academic vocabulary is the language you encounter in textbooks and on standardized tests. Review the definitions of these academic vocabulary words.

assumption (ə sump′ shən) ***n.*** something that is taken for granted

circumstance (sur′ kəm stans′) ***n.*** a situation or an event

context (kän′ tekst′) ***n.*** the circumstances that surround an event or idea and that give it meaning

convince (kän′ vins′) ***v.*** make someone believe in the truth of an idea or a statement

credible (kred′ ə bəl) ***adj.*** believable

perspective (pər spek′ tiv) ***n.*** point of view

speculate (spek′ yə lāt′) ***v.*** make a guess about something unknown

verify (ver′ ə fī′) ***v.*** confirm or prove that something is true

Use these words as you complete Big Question activities in this unit that involve reading, writing, speaking, and listening.

Gather Vocabulary Knowledge Additional Big Question words are listed below. Categorize the words by deciding whether you know each one well, know it a little bit, or do not know it at all.

belief	**distort**	**evidence**
manipulate	**perceive**	**skeptics**
truth		

Then, do the following:

1. Write the definitions of the words you know.
2. Using a print or an online dictionary, look up the meanings of the words you do not know. Then, write the meanings.
3. If you think you know a word's meaning, write it down. Consult a dictionary to confirm the word's meaning. Revise your definition if necessary.
4. If a word sounds familiar but you are not sure of its meaning, consult a dictionary. Then, record the meaning.
5. Use all of the words in a brief paragraph about truth.

❸ Learning Big Question Vocabulary

Acquire and Use Academic Vocabulary

1. Introduce the academic vocabulary words in the first word bank on the student page. Have students preview the words.
2. For each word, have students say the word aloud. Then, use the word in a sentence that defines the word.

Gather Vocabulary Knowledge

1. With the class, review the steps in the activity on the student page. Have students complete the activity independently, with partners, or in small groups.
2. Before students complete the last step, review the words and their meanings as a class. (Definitions appear below on the left.) Then, have students complete their paragraphs.

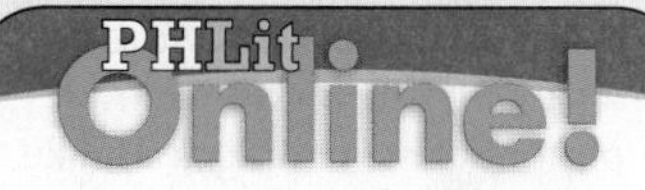

Show the Big Question video, online at **www.PHLitOnline.com.**

Gather Vocabulary Knowledge: Definitions

belief (bə lēf′) *n.* trust in the truth of a statement or idea

distort (di stôrt′) *v.* to change in a way that gives a false meaning

evidence (ev′ə dəns) *n.* proof

manipulate (mə nip′yo͞o lāt′) *v.* to influence a person or situation in a way that is intended to mislead

perceive (pər sēv′) *v.* to understand or become aware of

skeptics (skep′tiks) *n.* doubters or disbelievers

truth (tro͞oth) *n.* a fact or idea that agrees with reality

❶ Elements of Fiction and Nonfiction

1. Introduce the genres of fiction and nonfiction, using the instruction on the student page.

   Referring to the chart on the student page, discuss with students the purposes, subjects, and speakers characteristic of fiction and nonfiction. For each purpose and subject listed, **ask** students for examples from their own reading.

   Sample responses: Fiction— Purpose: Charles Dickens tells the story of Scrooge in "A Christmas Carol" to teach a lesson; Subject: The story is about made-up characters and events. **Nonfiction—** Purpose: To give information, a social studies textbook chapter explains the causes of the Great Depression; Subjects: The chapter is about events that actually occurred in the past.
2. Have students review the shaded boxes in the center of the chart. **Ask** students for an example of nonfiction writing that, like fiction, tells a story.

   Sample response: Autobiographical writing, such as a memoir, tells a story.
3. **Ask** students what storytelling techniques such a work might have in common with fiction.

   Sample response: An autobiography might use description to paint a picture of a place.
4. Discuss each of the other overlapping characteristics listed in the chart.

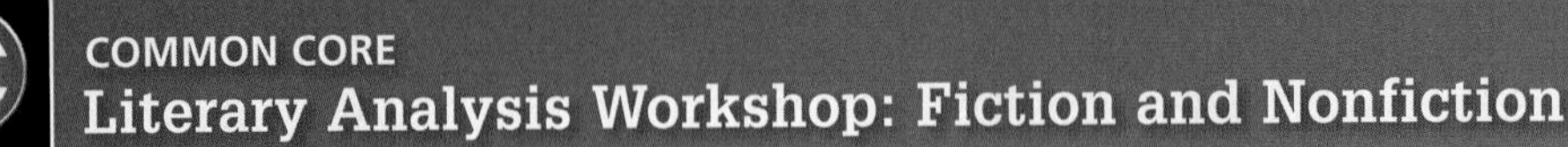

❶ Elements of Fiction and Nonfiction

Fiction and nonfiction are two types, or genres, of writing.

Fiction is literature about made-up characters and events. It is storytelling that emerges from an author's imagination.

Nonfiction, or informational text, is prose writing that explains ideas or describes real places, people, and events. Nonfiction is writing presented as fact. While it may or may not be true, the assumption that readers make is that the writer believes it to be true.

This broad distinction does not mean that fiction writers avoid using facts. Some types of fiction, such as realistic stories and spy thrillers, may rely heavily on facts. Real events may be woven into the plot, and real places may add richness and authenticity to the story. Some types of fiction, such as historical novels, may even use real people as characters.

Nor does the difference mean that nonfiction writers avoid using their imaginations! In fact, some narrative nonfiction—works that tell true stories—may seem very much like works of fiction. Nonfiction works may even use dialogue and other literary elements you are used to seeing in fiction.

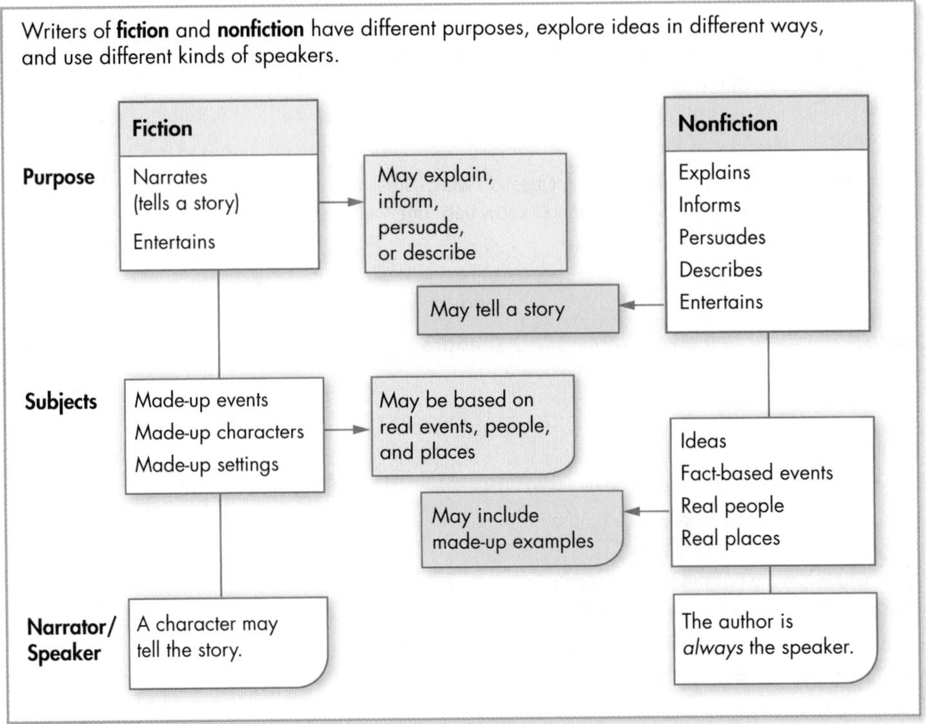

Writers of **fiction** and **nonfiction** have different purposes, explore ideas in different ways, and use different kinds of speakers.
Fiction
Nonfiction
Purpose
Narrates (tells a story)
Entertains
May explain, inform, persuade, or describe
May tell a story
Explains
Informs
Persuades
Describes
Entertains
Subjects
Made-up events
Made-up characters
Made-up settings
May be based on real events, people, and places
May include made-up examples
Ideas
Fact-based events
Real people
Real places
Narrator/ Speaker
A character may tell the story.
The author is *always* the speaker.

Teaching Resources

- All *Common Core Companion,* pp. 15–27, 97–109
- All *Unit 1 Resources,* pp. 3–9
  Professional Development Guidebook, p. 33
- All *See It!* DVD
  Elizabeth McCracken, Segments 1 and 2
- All *Graphic Organizer Transparencies,* pp. 1, 2
- All Enriched Online Student Edition
- L2 L3 *Reader's Notebook*
- L1 *Reader's Notebook: Adapted Version*
- EL *Reader's Notebook: English Learner's Version*
- L2 EL *Hear It!* Audio CD
- L1 EL *Hear It!* Audio CD (adapted text)

PHLit Online! All resources, including print and video, are available online at **www.PHLitOnline.com.**

❷ Forms of Fiction

While the types of stories people write are as unlimited as the human imagination, the forms those stories take are not. The three basic forms are defined by their length and complexity.

Short Story: A work that can generally be read in one sitting and focuses on one or two main characters

Novel: A longer work, often with many characters and a complex story line, usually divided into sections or chapters

Novella: A work that is longer and more complex than a short story but shorter and less complex than a novel

❸ Forms of Nonfiction

There are many different forms of informational texts, or nonfiction. The most basic division separates literary nonfiction from strictly functional texts.

- Works of **literary nonfiction** may use the same literary elements as fiction and be just as artful as poetry.
- **Functional texts** serve practical purposes only. Types of functional texts include manuals, recipes, brochures, menus, and schedules. Often, functional texts include charts, diagrams, or other graphics that clarify information presented verbally.

Forms of Literary Nonfiction

Nonfiction Form	Characteristics
Autobiography/Biography The true story of someone's life	• In an autobiography, the writer tells the story of his or her own life. • In a biography, the writer tells the story of someone else's life.
Essay A work that explores a single, focused subject	• May tell a story, explain, inform, persuade, describe, or entertain • May be formal or informal • Not restricted to certain subject matter; an essay may relate a personal experience or explore a scholarly topic.
Journalism/News Article A work that reports on a current event	**Answers the questions** *Who? What? Where? When? How? Why?*
Journalism/Feature Article A work that presents in-depth information about a topic	• Longer than a basic news article • Presents information gathered through journalistic research and investigation
Speech Oral presentation of a speaker's ideas or beliefs	• May tell a story, explain, inform, persuade, or entertain • May be formal or informal
Report A work that communicates information gathered through research	• May focus on a topic in science, history, literature, or any other scholarly discipline • May be neutral, omitting any expressions of opinion, or may present the author's opinions and beliefs

❹ In This Section

Elements of Fiction and Nonfiction

Determining Themes in Fiction

Determining Central Ideas in Nonfiction

Close Read: Theme in Fiction
- Model Text
- Practice Text

Close Read: Central Idea in Nonfiction
- Model Text
- Practice Text

After You Read

Common Core State Standards

RL.9-10.2; RI.9-10.2

[For the full wording of the standards, see the standards chart in the front of your textbook.]

❷ Forms of Fiction

1. Introduce the forms, using the instruction on the student page.
2. Explore students' knowledge of different types of fiction. **Ask** students to name novels, novellas, and short stories that they have read.

❸ Forms of Nonfiction

1. Introduce the forms, using the instruction and the chart on the student page.
2. Explain that a work of nonfiction may include one or more types of nonfiction. For example, a feature article might include biographical passages.
3. **Ask:** What type of nonfiction is a manual for programming a cell phone?

   Answer: The manual is functional nonfiction.
4. **Ask:** What type of nonfiction is a book about the life of famous chef Julia Child?

   Answer: This type of book is a biography, a form of literary nonfiction.

❹ In This Section

Explain that in the remainder of this Literary Analysis Workshop, students will analyze an important element of each genre: theme in the case of fiction, central idea in the case of nonfiction. After reviewing the concepts, students will then see them applied in an analysis of two Model texts. Finally, they will apply what they have learned to two Independent Practice texts.

Differentiated Instruction for Universal Access

Support for Special-Needs Students

Have students read the **Exploring Fiction and Nonfiction** pages in the ***Reader's Notebook: Adapted Version***. This version provides a basic-level introduction to fiction and nonfiction.

Support for Less Proficient Readers

Have students read the **Exploring Fiction and Nonfiction** pages in the ***Reader's Notebook***. This version provides a basic-level introduction to fiction and nonfiction.

EL Support for English Learners

Have students read the **Exploring Fiction and Nonfiction** pages in the ***Reader's Notebook: English Learner's Version***. This version provides a basic-level introduction to fiction and nonfiction.

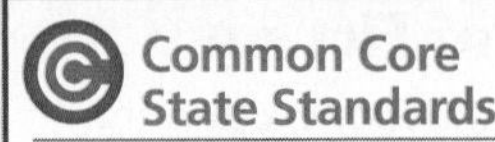

Unit 1 Focus Standards

- **Reading Literature 2**
- **Reading Informational Text 2**

These standards spiral through the unit.

❶ Determining Themes in Fiction

1. Introduce the concept of theme, using the instruction on the student page.
2. Emphasize that in fiction, writers often suggest their themes rather than state them directly. For example, an author might show the value of self-reliance—a theme—through contrasts between the fate of two characters: one self-reliant, the other dependent on others.
3. Review with students the notions of universal and multiple themes, defined on the student page.
4. Lead students in a discussion of the three interpretations of the theme of "Beauty and the Beast." **Ask:** In what way does the story support each interpretation?

   Sample response: The first interpretation is justified by the fact that the Beast's ugly appearance is transformed to match his noble nature. The second is justified by the fact that the woman loves the Beast despite his outward appearance. The fact that the woman's love undoes the curse supports the idea that the theme is "True love heals."
5. Remind students that in this Workshop, they will read a model analysis of the theme of a passage and then perform their own analysis of a second passage.

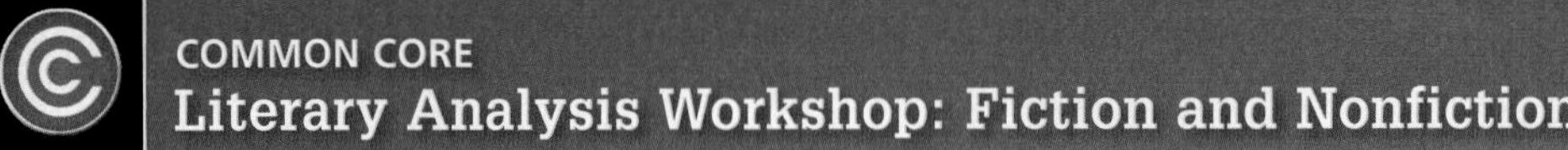

❶ Determining Themes in Fiction

Works of fiction express themes—messages or insights about life.

Reading Literature
2. Determine a theme or central idea of a text and analyze in detail its development over the course of the text, including how it emerges and is shaped and refined by specific details; provide an objective summary of the text.

A story may take you to whole new worlds, rich with amazing characters, events, and settings. That journey, full of drama, suspense, and intrigue, is a critical element of fiction. However, the true heart of a story is its deeper, underlying meaning—its theme. The theme is not the subject of the story. Rather, it is the insight with which the author explores the subject. This insight can often be expressed as a generalization about people or life.

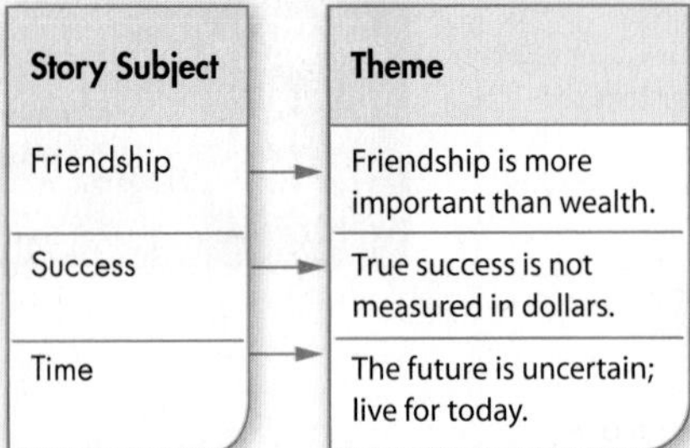

Story Subject
Friendship
Success
Time
Theme
Friendship is more important than wealth.
True success is not measured in dollars.
The future is uncertain; live for today.

Universal Themes Some themes are timeless, appearing in the literature of nearly all cultures and eras. Such universal themes express fundamental aspects of the human experience, such as the power of love or the danger of greed. Folk tales, fairy tales, epics, and legends often address universal themes, but so do contemporary novels, movies, and even video games.

Multiple Themes The length and complexity of some literary works may allow writers to explore more than one unifying thematic insight. Novels, full-length plays, and epic poems may have multiple themes, while short stories usually express a single theme.

Multiple Interpretations of Theme Writers use all the details of a story to develop the theme. However, your interpretation of those details and the theme they develop may be very different from someone else's. For example, consider just three of the ways you might interpret the theme of the traditional fairy tale "Beauty and the Beast":

Example: Beauty and the Beast
A poor but beautiful young woman falls in love with a rich prince who has been cursed to look like a horrible beast. Her love frees him from the curse, and the two live happily ever after.

Interpretation of Theme
1. Real beauty comes from a noble heart.
2. True love sees through outward appearances.
3. True love heals; it frees people from pain.

While all three interpretations center on related ideas—those of beauty, love, and suffering—the particular insight each expresses is slightly different. With more complex texts, such as those that involve multiple characters, locations, and events, interpretations may differ more widely. The best interpretation of a theme will take into account all of a story's critical details. It will show how an author has woven those details together into the unifying pattern of meaning that we call a theme.

Think Aloud

Theme

To model the skill of analyzing theme, use the following "think aloud." Say to students:

> To figure out the theme of a story, I look for significant patterns of events and connections between ideas. For example, when I read that the Beast begins the story with a horrible outward appearance but that the curse is lifted at the end, I am struck by the "before-and-after" contrast. It makes a significant pattern.
>
> The young woman's love for him despite his appearance is another striking story element. I can connect this story element, her love, to the first significant pattern, outward appearances. I draw the conclusion that the story shows that "True love sees through outward appearances." To check my conclusion, I look at the fact that the two live happily ever after. This story ending reinforces the idea that love has triumphed over outward appearances.

❷ Determining Central Ideas in Nonfiction

Works of literary nonfiction express **central, or main, ideas.**

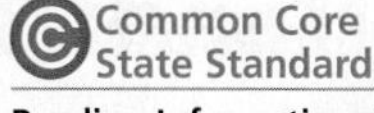
Common Core State Standards

Reading Informational Text
2. Determine a central idea of a text and analyze its development over the course of the text, including how it emerges and is shaped and refined by specific details; provide an objective summary of the text.

Central, or Main, Ideas Central ideas are the key arguments, positions, or points writers communicate in works of literary nonfiction. Regardless of the form of the literary work or the subject it addresses, the central idea provides the focus for the writing. All of the other details work to develop and support that idea.

Author's Purpose and Central Ideas The author's purpose is his or her main reason for writing. The three main purposes for writing are **to inform or explain, to entertain**, and **to persuade**. Nonfiction writers also have specific purposes for writing. For example, a writer does not merely seek to inform readers in some general way, he or she seeks to inform them about a specific topic. At an even deeper level, the writer seeks to inform readers about a specific idea within the larger topic. That specific idea is the central idea of the text.

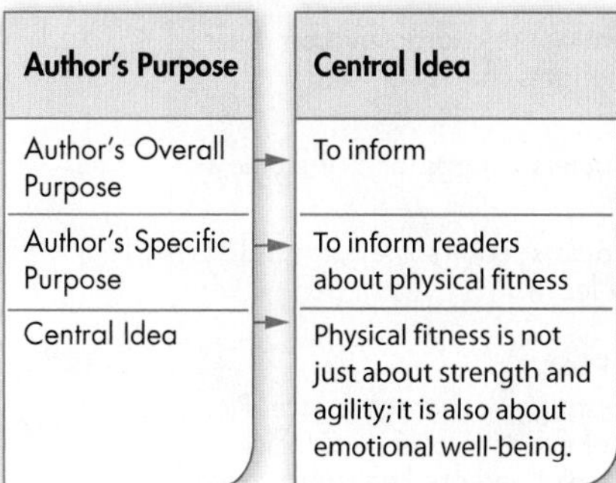

Author's Purpose	Central Idea
Author's Overall Purpose	To inform
Author's Specific Purpose	To inform readers about physical fitness
Central Idea	Physical fitness is not just about strength and agility; it is also about emotional well-being.

Central ideas drive all the decisions a writer makes, including how to structure a text to introduce the idea and how to develop, shape, and refine the idea through the use of specific details.

Central Ideas in Academic Writing In academic and scholarly writing, such as formal essays and research reports, the writer's overall purpose is usually to inform or to persuade. Often, the writer seeks to do both.

> **Example:**
> **History Report:** The American Revolution inspired other revolutions throughout the world, including those in France and Haiti.
> **Literary Criticism** (essay): The novel's darkest conflict pits two brothers against each other in a battle neither can win.
> **Science Report:** Although people have studied nature since antiquity, modern science did not truly begin until 1543, when Copernicus published *On the Revolutions of the Celestial Spheres.*

Central Ideas in Nonacademic Writing Magazine articles, memoirs, blogs, and other types of nonfiction may also inform or persuade. Usually, however, at least one purpose is to entertain. The writer's choices of content and structure, including the central ideas and the details that support them, reflect those combined purposes.

> **Example:**
> **Celebrity Profile:** With dazzling performances in four movies this year alone, she has become the most bankable young actress in Hollywood.
> **Memoir:** Raised by a stand-up comedian, I had a childhood that was often exciting but not always funny.

❷ Determining Central Ideas in Nonfiction

1. Introduce the concept of central, or main, idea, using the instruction on the student page.
2. **Ask** students to identify the likely author's purpose and the likely central idea in each of the following examples:

   (a) *In a history of baseball, the writer links the outlawing of spitballs to the emergence of the powerhouse hitter, including such celebrities as Babe Ruth.*

   (b) *In a profile of a rap star, the writer contrasts the star's humble origins with his current wealth and celebrity, noting how hard the star worked to achieve his success.*

   Sample responses: (a) *Possible author's purpose*—To inform readers about trends in the history of baseball. *Possible central idea*—The nature of baseball can be altered by a small change in the rules. **(b)** *Possible author's purpose*—To inform readers about a rap star's rise to success. *Possible central idea*—Through determination and hard work, it is possible to overcome adversity.
3. Explore with students the contrast between central ideas in academic and nonacademic writing, discussed on the student page. Emphasize for students that writers of works in either category often have combined purposes. Academic writers often seek to persuade readers of the merits of their ideas or explanations as well as to inform readers about their subject. Nonacademic writers typically seek to entertain readers while informing them.
4. Remind students that in this Workshop, they will read a model analysis of the central idea of a passage and then perform their own analysis of a second passage.

Differentiated Instruction for Universal Access

Enrichment for Advanced Readers

Challenge students with the concept of "creative nonfiction," a genre that has become popular in recent years. Lee Gutkind, the founding editor of the journal *Creative Nonfiction,* defines the genre as follows: "The word 'creative' refers simply to the use of literary craft in presenting nonfiction—that is, factually accurate prose about real people and events—in a compelling, vivid manner. To put it another way, creative nonfiction writers do not make things up; they make ideas and information that already exist more interesting and, often, more accessible."

Lead students in a discussion of this definition and of the genre itself. Have them consider questions such as these: Is it possible to "make ideas and information . . . more interesting" without making things up? Is the term *creative nonfiction* unnecessary because we can just refer to *narrative nonfiction,* which means the same thing?

PRETEACH

❸ Close Read: Theme in Fiction

1. Remind students that the theme of a work is the central insight, message, or question about life that it expresses.
2. Review with the class the Clues to Theme chart. Discuss ways in which each element might contribute to the expression of a theme. For example, if the setting of a novel is divided between the country estate of a family and the city homes of their cousins, the setting might contribute to a theme about family relationships.
3. Divide students into groups. Write the following theme on the board:

   Humanity will never truly conquer nature.

   Then, have members of each group work together to describe an element in each category that might help convey this theme.

   Have groups then share their work with the class. **Sample responses:** *Title*—"Cold Spell"; *Setting*—a snowbound mountain; *Symbols*—a radio symbolizing a connection to civilization; *Statements and Observations*—A human being is not built by nature to survive temperatures below freezing; *Characters*—a hiker; the forest ranger who comes to his rescue; *Conflict and Plot*—The hiker is determined to climb the mountain in the middle of winter; he comes into conflict with the ranger, who does not want him to make the climb; he comes into conflict with the elements when he is trapped in a snow storm. At the end, the ranger rescues him using modern technology, and the hiker agrees with him that nature is fundamentally hostile to humanity.
4. Point out examples of highlighted text in the model on page 9. Explain that in each case, the color of the highlighting matches the color of the category in the chart. Details that illustrate a given category are highlighted in the color of that category.

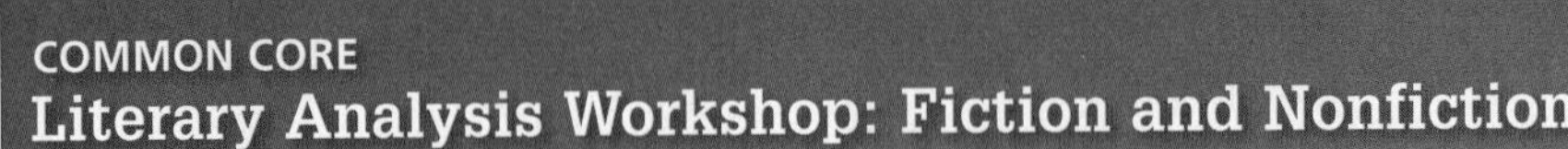

❸ Close Read: Theme in Fiction

All the elements of a story, from the title to the characters to individual words, may be clues to the theme.

Authors of serious fiction almost never state themes directly. Instead, they suggest the theme by weaving meaningful details into the narrative. Reading for theme, then, is like being a detective solving a mystery. You must notice details and analyze how they relate to one another. These relationships may include contrasts, comparisons, repetitions, or other connections.

Clues to Theme

Title
The title is the name of a story. Sometimes, the chapters of a novel or sections of a story have their own titles. Titles may give you information about a story's characters, setting, events, and theme. As you read, consider whether the title
- points to a character, an event, an object, or a location in the story;
- suggests emotions or abstract ideas;
- has more than one possible meaning.

Statements and Observations
A statement or an observation asserts an idea. Characters or the narrator may make statements that suggest or even reveal the theme. As you read, notice
- whether a character or the narrator sums up the story's events;
- whether a character or the narrator makes general observations about characters' emotions.

Setting
The setting is the time and location of the action in a story. In some stories, the setting is just a backdrop. However, in other stories, the setting can shed light on the theme. As you read, consider
- the importance of the setting to the characters and events;
- whether descriptions of the setting include words with strong emotional associations.

Characters
Characters are the people who take part in the action of a story. Their motivations, experiences, and reactions almost always relate to the theme. As you read, notice
- what you learn about characters from their statements, thoughts, behavior, and appearance;
- whether characters change and, if so, how they change;
- whether characters learn something and, if so, what they learn.

Symbols
A symbol is any story element, whether an object, a person, an animal, a place, an action, or an image, that has both a literal and a deeper meaning. Symbols often relate directly to themes. As you read,
- notice story elements that repeat or that have strong emotional content;
- think about the deeper meanings these elements suggest.

Conflict and Plot
Conflicts are the struggles characters face. Plot is the sequence of events in a story. Conflicts always spark the plot and are key to the theme. As you read, identify
- the problems characters face;
- how or if the conflicts are resolved;
- how characters feel about the resolution.

Vocabulary Development

Ⓒ CCSS Language 6

Domain-Specific Words: Literature

Reinforce comprehension of the literary terms on this page by having students complete these "show-you-know" sentences. The second part of each clarifies the first, as in the example:

Example: The swan was a good *symbol* for the characters' marriage; swans are thought to mate for life.

1. The *setting* of the story—an immigrant community in America—helps develop the *conflict* between the mother and daughter about how to dress; _______

   Sample response: the mother's ideas about dress come from her traditional culture, while the daughter has adopted modern American ideas.
2. The main character's feelings about the ring he has inherited shows that the ring is a *symbol* of family pride; _______

   Sample response: he takes pride in the ring, just as he takes pride in his family.

EXEMPLAR TEXT

4 Model

About the Text This story is set in the United States during the 1950s, when fears of nuclear war ran high. In the story, a mother irons clothes while thinking about her teenage daughter Emily. Earlier in the day, the mother received a visit from a social worker who is concerned about Emily.

5 from "I Stand Here Ironing" by Tillie Olsen

Ronnie is calling. He is wet and I change him. It is rare there is such a cry now. That time of motherhood is almost behind me when the ear is not one's own but must always be racked and listening for the child cry, the child call. We sit for a while and I hold him, looking out over the city spread in charcoal with its soft aisles of light. *"Shoogily,"* he breathes and curls closer. I carry him back to bed, asleep. *Shoogily.* A funny word, a family word, inherited from Emily, invented by her to say: *comfort.*

6 In this and other ways she leaves her seal, I say aloud. And startle at my saying it. What do I mean? What did I start to gather together, to try and make coherent? I was at the terrible, growing years. War years. I do not remember them well. 7 I was working, there were four smaller ones now, there was not time for her. She had to help be a mother, and housekeeper, and shopper. She had to set her seal. Mornings of crisis and near hysteria trying to get lunches packed, hair combed, coats and shoes found, everyone to school or Child Care on time, the baby ready for transportation. And always the paper scribbled on by a smaller one, the book looked at by Susan then mislaid, the homework not done. Running out to that huge school where she was one, she was lost, she was a drop; suffering over the unpreparedness, stammering and unsure in her classes.

There was so little time left at night after the kids were bedded down. She would struggle over books, always eating (it was in those years she developed her enormous appetite that is legendary in our family) and I would be ironing, or preparing food for the next day, or writing V-mail to Bill, or tending the baby. Sometimes, to make me laugh, or out of her despair, she would imitate happenings or types at school. 8

I think I said once: "Why don't you do something like this in the school amateur show?" One morning she phoned me at work, hardly understandable through the weeping: "Mother, I did it. I won, I won; they gave me first prize; they clapped and clapped and wouldn't let me go."

Now suddenly she was Somebody, and as imprisoned in her difference as she had been in anonymity.

5
Title The title tells you that ironing is an important activity in this story and key to the theme.

6
Statements The narrator makes numerous statements about Emily's past and future. She often expresses sadness, but also acceptance and a belief that her daughter will survive despite her struggles.

7
Setting The "War years" refers to the World War II era of the 1940s. These details about the ways in which the era affects the narrator and her family are key to the theme.

8
Characters The narrator describes Emily as "stammering and unsure," but then as someone who is in "command." Either way, Emily is "imprisoned." The idea of the circumstances of one's life being akin to a prison is key to the story's theme.

Differentiated Instruction for Universal Access

Strategy for Less Proficient Readers

Guide students in making inferences and connections as they read:

- Have them reread the first paragraph. Guide them to see that Ronnie is the narrator's son.
- Read aloud this sentence from the second paragraph: "She had to help be a mother, and housekeeper, and shopper." Guide students in finding details illustrating Emily's responsibilities during the war years. (**Sample response:** "get lunches packed")

EL Strategy for English Learners

Preteach the following words from page 9, using visuals and the help of students fluent in English who share students' home language: *motherhood, invented, seal, housekeeper, crisis, mislaid, suffering,* and *unpreparedness.* Read the first two paragraphs aloud as students track. Repeat, and then ask volunteers to explain who Emily is and to name things she did for the family. (**Sample responses:** Emily is the speaker's daughter. She helped care for and raise her brother Ronnie and her sister Susan.)

TEACH

4 Reading the Model

1. Discuss the About the Text note. Explain further that the passage students are about to read gives the speaker's thoughts as she thinks them. Students will be able to reconstruct her situation based on the clues she gives.
2. Have students read the passage (pp. 9–11). Discuss, clarifying as necessary. Then, guide students in reviewing the annotations.

5 Title

Read aloud the Title annotation. **Ask:** To which details in the passage does the title relate?

Possible response: Emily says her mother is always ironing: ironing is connected to the responsibilities that prevent the mother from giving her more. At the end, the iron appears as a symbol of the forces that shape people's lives.

6 Statements

Read aloud the bracketed passage and Statements annotation. Have students look at the highlighted yellow text on pages 9–11 and find a statement expressing sadness and one expressing confidence.

Possible response: The statement "there was not time for her" expresses sadness. "[She] leaves her sad" and "She will find her way" (p. 10) express the mother's confidence.

7 Setting

Read aloud the Setting annotation and the bracketed text. **Ask:** How might the war have contributed to the family's hardships?

Possible response: Certain goods may have been scarce, and friends and family members may have faced danger overseas.

8 Characters

Have a volunteer read aloud the blue highlighted text on pages 9–10 and the Characters annotation. **Ask:** In what two ways has Emily been imprisoned?

Possible response: She was "imprisoned" in her anonymity. Then, she was "imprisoned" in others' perception of her as talented.

9 Setting

1. Have a volunteer read aloud the bracketed passage.
2. Explain to students that in 1945, at the end of World War II, the United States dropped two atomic bombs on Japan, with devastating results. After the war, the world's rival superpowers, the United States and the Soviet Union, pursued an arms race in which each competed to stockpile the most powerful nuclear arsenal.
3. Then, read aloud the Setting annotation and the text highlighted in green. **Ask:** In the 1950s, why might someone doubt whether he or she truly had a future?

   Possible response: Someone of the time might fear that the growing stockpiles of nuclear weapons might be used in a war, destroying the Earth.

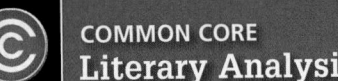

Model continued

She began to be asked to perform at other high schools, even colleges, then at city and statewide affairs. The first one we went to, I only recognized her that first moment when thin, shy, she almost drowned herself into the curtains. Then: Was this Emily? The control, the command, the convulsing and deadly clowning, the spell, then the roaring, stamping audience, unwilling to let this rare and precious laughter out of their lives.

Afterwards: You ought to do something about her with a gift like that—but without money or knowing how, what does one do? We have left it all to her, and the gift has as often eddied inside, clogged and clotted, as been used and growing.

She is coming. She runs up the stairs two at a time with her light graceful step, and I know she is happy tonight. Whatever it was that occasioned your call did not happen today.

"Aren't you ever going to finish the ironing, Mother? Whistler painted his mother in a rocker. I'd have to paint mine standing over an ironing board." This is one of her communicative nights and she tells me everything and nothing as she fixes herself a plate of food out of the icebox.

She is so lovely. Why did you want me to come in at all? Why were you concerned? She will find her way.

9 She starts up the stairs to bed. "Don't get me up with the rest in the morning." "But I thought you were having midterms." "Oh, those," she comes back in, kisses me, and says quite lightly, "in a couple of years when we'll all be atom-dead they won't matter a bit."

9 Setting The 1950s setting plays a key role: The daughter believes she has no future. Her certainty pains the mother, who cannot accept such hopelessness.

She has said it before. She *believes* it. But because I have been dredging the past, and all that compounds a human being is so heavy and meaningful in me, I cannot endure it tonight.

10 I will never total it all. I will never come in to say: She was a child seldom smiled at. Her father left me before she was a year old. I had to work her first six years when there was work, or I sent her home and to his relatives. There were tears she had care she hated. She was dark and thin and foreign-looking in a world where the prestige went to blondness and curly hair and dimples, she was slow where glibness was prized. She was a child of anxious, not proud, love. We were poor and could not afford for her the soil of easy growth. I was a young mother, I was a distracted mother. There were other children pushing up, demanding. Her younger sister seemed all that she was not. There were years she did not want me to touch her. She kept too much in herself, her life was such she had to keep too much in herself. My wisdom came too late. She has

Vocabulary Development

CCSS Language 6

Thematic Vocabulary: The Big Question

As students discuss the excerpt from "I Stand Here Ironing," encourage them to use the thematic vocabulary presented in Introducing the Big Question, pages 2–3. Help them with sentence starters such as these:

1. One *circumstance* that shapes Emily's childhood is the fact that . . .
2. The mother's view (is/is not) *credible* because . . .
3. *Evidence* that Emily may face further challenges includes the fact that . . .

10 much to her and probably nothing will come of it. She is a child of her age, of depression, of war, of fear.

11 Let her be. So all that is in her will not bloom—but in how many does it? There is still enough left to live by. Only help her to know—help make it so there is cause for her to know—that she is more than this dress on the ironing board, helpless before the iron.

10 **Characters** The daughter's pain is not hers alone. The theme relates both to individual suffering and to that of the entire society.

11 **Symbols** In this final sentence, we learn that the ironing is symbolic: The narrator does not want her daughter to feel as powerless as a dress "before the iron."

12 **Determining the Theme** By combining details about the impact of the historical setting on the characters and the hopes that the mother has for her daughter, you might interpret the story's theme in this way: *While historical events and personal circumstances may make life difficult and unfair, people survive.*

Differentiated Instruction for Universal Access

Strategy for Special Needs Students
Pair students, and have them create a T-chart graphic organizer. Have partners take turns reading each paragraph on page 10 aloud. At the conclusion of each paragraph, have them determine what they have learned about Emily and her circumstances. Instruct partners to list any positive aspects of her character and circumstances in the left column of the T-chart. Have them list negative aspects in the right column.

When students have completed their charts, have them exchange charts with another pair. Have pairs circle any points in the other pair's chart that they did not include in their own chart. Then, have them review the selection to find evidence for these circled points. Discuss charts as a class, collating pairs' points in a master T-chart on the board.

10 Characters

Have a volunteer read aloud the bracketed text and the Characters annotation. **Ask:** How does her childhood mirror her historical period?

Possible response: The time is one "of war, of fear," factors mirrored in Emily's anxious childhood.

11 Symbols

1. Have students reread the final paragraph. **Ask:** What is the relationship between iron and dress in this concluding image?

   Possible response: The dress is "helpless before the iron"; it will be pressed into shape by the iron's force.

2. Next, **ask:** What does the mother mean in wishing that "there is cause for her to know—that she is more than this dress"?

   Possible response: The mother hopes that Emily will experience life as shaped by her own choices, not just by circumstances.

12 Determining the Theme

1. Review with the class the elements discussed in the annotations for the Model. Have students offer words and phrases that sum up these elements.

   Possible response: Students may say "talent versus responsibility," "powerlessness, or the future."

2. Have students read the Determining the Theme note. Then, **ask** them to evaluate the interpretation of the story's theme, citing story elements in support of their views.

   Possible response: I think the interpretation is valid because the passage shows how difficult Emily's circumstances are but also shows that she has a good chance for a happy life.

⓭ Introducing the Independent Practice

1. Explain to students that they will analyze the theme of the Independent Practice selection.
2. Discuss the About the Selection note, and have students read the selection. Then, direct them to go back through and respond to the side-column prompts. As necessary, guide students in answering the prompts, using the teaching notes. Conclude by having students answer the After You Read questions for the selection, on page 21.

⓮ Setting

1. Have students reread the first second and third paragraphs. Then, have them identify the types of books James wants to find.

   Answer: He wants to find books about "people like me"—tall people.
2. **Ask** the Setting question.

   Possible response: Thematic ideas include the desire for self-knowledge and concern about being different.

⓯ Conflict

1. Read aloud the bracketed text. **Ask** the first Conflict question.

   Answer: She is embarrassed to address his difference directly.
2. **Ask** the second Conflict question.

   Answer: He is impatient because his great height clearly sets him apart from others.

⓰ Character

1. Read the highlighted sentence aloud. **Ask** the first Character question.

   Answer: Because of his height, James has difficulty walking.
2. **Ask** the second Character question.

   Possible response: James's difficulty shows that his difference from others has far-ranging consequences.

⓭ Independent Practice

About the Selection This is an excerpt from a novel by Elizabeth McCracken. Set in a small town during the 1950s, the story revolves around James Sweatt, the world's tallest boy. The story is told by Peggy, the town librarian.

⓮ **Setting** This section of the story takes place in the library. Identify the types of books James wants to find. What thematic ideas does his search introduce to the story?

⓯ **Conflict** Why is the narrator cautious in answering James? How does James's reaction suggest a conflict?

⓰ **Character** The narrator says that James "leaned on the desk, and pushed off." What does her observation tell you about the difficulties James faces simply in moving? How does this add to an emerging theme about normality and difference?

from *The Giant's House* by Elizabeth McCracken

James took out books on astronomy, ornithology:[1] sciences at once about tininess and height. He approached the desk with books he'd liked and asked for more—he knew it was easier to find more books with a good example in hand.

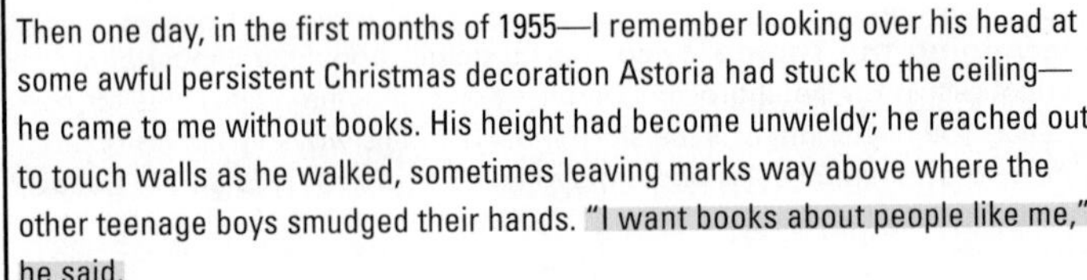

⓮ Then one day, in the first months of 1955—I remember looking over his head at some awful persistent Christmas decoration Astoria had stuck to the ceiling—he came to me without books. His height had become unwieldy; he reached out to touch walls as he walked, sometimes leaving marks way above where the other teenage boys smudged their hands. "I want books about people like me," he said.

I thought I knew what he was talking about, but I wanted to be cautious. "What exactly about you?" I asked. I made myself think of all the things he could have meant: Boy Scouts, basketball players. Never jump to conclusions when trying to answer a reference question. Interview the patron.

⓯ "Tall people," he said.

"Tall people? Just tall people in general?"

"Very tall people. Like me," he said, clearly exasperated with my playing dumb. "What they do."

"Okay," I told him. "Try the card catalog. Look in the big books on the table—see those books?" I pointed. "Those are books of subject headings for the card catalog. Look under words that you think describe your topic." James was used to me doing this: I gave directions but would not pull the books off the shelf for him. My job was to show people—even people I liked—how to use the library, not to use it for them. "Dig around," I said. "Try height, try stature. Then look in the catalog for books."

⓰ He nodded, leaned on the desk, and pushed off.

An hour later he headed out the door.

"Did you find what you needed?" I asked.

"There isn't anything," he said. "There was one book that sort of was about it, but I couldn't find it on the shelf."

1. **astronomy, ornithology** Astronomy is the study of the stars and planets. Ornithology is the study of birds.

Think Aloud

Vocabulary: Using Context

Direct students' attention to the word *stature* on this page. Using a think-aloud process, model how to use context to infer the meaning of an unknown word. Say to students:

> I'm going to think aloud to show you how I figure out the meaning of *stature* from its context.
>
> James is looking for information about people like him. The librarian suggests that he search using the word *stature*. We know that the most unusual thing about James is that he is so tall. He is likely to be looking for information about people who are tall. *Stature* may have something to do with being tall. Peggy also tells James to search using the term *height*. So I think the word *stature* refers to a person's or thing's height.

"There's something," I told him. "Come back. We'll look for it together."

That night after closing, I hunted around myself. The only thing under *stature* was a book about growth and nutrition. I tried our two encyclopedias under height and found passing references. Not much.

In truth, my library was a small-town place, and this was a specialized topic. Still, I was certain I could find more. I got that familiar mania—there is information somewhere here, and I can find it, I have to. A good librarian is not so different from a prospector, her whole brain a divining rod. She walks to books and stands and wonders: here? Is the answer here? The same blind faith in finding, even when hopeless. If someone caught me when I was in the throes of tracking something elusive, I would have told them: but it's out there. I can feel it. God *wants* me to find it.

That night I wandered the reference department, eyed the bindings of the encyclopedias, dictionaries, atlases. James was so big I almost expected to locate him in the gazetteer.[2] I set my hands upon our little card catalog, curled my fingers in the curved handles of the drawers. Then I went to the big volumes of subject headings.

Looking under *height* and *stature* turned up nothing; *anthropometry* was not quite right. Then I realized the word I was looking for: *Giant.* 17

Giant described him. *Giant,* I knew, would lead me to countless things—not just the word, located in indexes and catalogs and encyclopedias, but the idea of Giant, the knowledge that the people that James wanted to read about, people who could be described as like him, were not just tall but giants. I sat in a spindle-backed chair in the reference room, waiting for a minute. Then I checked the volume of the Library of Congress headings. *Giant. See also: dwarfs.*

We did not have a book, but I found several encyclopedia entries. Nowadays I could just photocopy; but that night I wrote down the page and volume numbers, thinking I could not bear to tell him the word to look under. Most of the very tall people mentioned in the encyclopedia had worked in the circus as professional giants, so I went to our books on the circus. 18

The photographs showed enormous people. Not just tall, though of course they were that, often with an ordinary person posed beside them. The tall people looked twice as big as the ambassador from the normal-sized, as if they were an entirely different race. The books described weak stomachs and legs and bones. Sometimes what made them tall showed in their faces: each feature looked like something disturbed in an avalanche, separate from the others, in danger of slipping off. 19

2. **gazetteer** (gaz′ ə tir′) *n.* dictionary or index of geographical names.

17

Symbol What shades of meaning does the word *"Giant"* convey? How might the narrator's discovery of this word point to a theme?

Conflict Why is the narrator so worried about telling James to find works under the category "Giant"?

Statements and Observations How does the narrator's description of giants help develop a theme? In particular, consider her use of the word *ambassador* to describe the normal-sized people in the photographs.

17 Symbol

1. Read aloud the bracketed text. **Ask** students the first Symbol question.

   Possible response: In addition to conveying the idea of large size, the word has some negative associations. In fairy tales, giants are often cruel or stupid.

2. **Ask** students the second Symbol question.

   Possible response: The discovery of the word is both a step towards self-knowledge and confirmation of his difference from others. The word reinforces the idea that self-knowledge may be a mixed blessing.

18 Conflict

Have a volunteer read aloud the bracketed passage. **Ask:** the Conflict question.

Answer: She is concerned that the negative associations of the word will hurt him.

19 Statements and Observations

Have students reread the last paragraph on the student page. **Ask:** the Statements and Observations question.

Possible response: The narrator's description of giants suggests a theme of difference and the idea that self-knowledge is a double-edged sword. The theme of difference is reinforced by the use of the word *ambassadors,* which suggests that giants are another people, not really a part of the community of ordinary-sized human beings.

Differentiated Instruction for Universal Access

Support for Special-Needs Students
Have students read the adapted version of the excerpt from *The Giant's House* in the ***Reader's Notebook: Adapted Version.*** They may also listen to the adapted version on the ***Hear It!* Audio CD.**

Support for Less Proficient Readers
Have students read the excerpt from *The Giant's House* in the ***Reader's Notebook.*** After students finish the selection in the ***Reader's Notebook,*** have them complete the questions and activities in the Student Edition.

EL Support for English Learners
Have students read the excerpt from *The Giant's House* in the ***Reader's Notebook: English Learner's Version.*** English learners may also read the selection as they listen to the recorded version on the ***Hear It!* Audio CD.**

PHLit Online!

Enriched Online Student Edition
To have students read the selection in interactive format, with narration and point-of-use interactive graphic organizers, go online at **www.PHLitOnline.com.**

20 Symbols

1. **Ask** students: What view of giants do the books on the circus seem to promote?

   Answer: The giants in these books are associated with amazing facts and surprising eccentricity or even gruesome detail. They are also clearly human, as in the story of the couple who fall in love and have children.

2. Have students reread the bracketed paragraph. **Ask:** In what way is the book *Medical Curiosities* different from the books on the circus?

   Possible response: It discusses giants as medical "abnormalities." It probably does not paint pictures of them as full people.

3. **Ask** students the Symbols question.

   Possible response: They seem to suggest that he will be perceived and treated either as a wonder—something to be astonished by—or as an abnormality—something to pity or to be horrified by.

4. Remind students that a symbol in a literary work is an object, person, place, and so on that stands for something else. Point out that James's gigantism raises questions about his future, about his relations with others, and about his control over his own life that are related to general questions that any person might ask about life. **Ask:** What general aspect of becoming an adult or of life in general might James's struggle with his gigantism stand for?

   Possible responses: His gigantism might symbolize the parts of our own life we cannot control or choose; it might symbolize the differences that can divide each individual from others.

Practice continued

Anna Swann, the Nova Scotia Giantess, married Captain Bates, the Kentucky Giant. As a young woman at Barnum's Dime Museum in New York, Miss Swann had been in two fires; in the second she had to be lifted out by a crane. No ordinary over-the-shoulder rescue for a woman better than seven feet tall. She and her husband retired to Ohio, to a specially made house. Their church installed an extra-large pew.

Byrne, the Irish Giant, lived in fear of a certain doctor who lusted after his skeleton; he imagined the doctor's giant kettle ready to boil his bones.

Jack Earle was over seven feet tall, traveled with the circus for years; after his retirement he wrote poetry.

I took comfort in Anna Swann and her husband. They were solid-looking people. Respectable. They'd had two children, though neither survived. The book described them as *in love*, and you could believe that from the pictures: their complementary heights were just a lovely coincidence to their love affair. I found myself that late night a little jealous of Anna Swann and her handsome, bearded captain.

The books said that giants tended to exaggerate their heights for exhibition purposes. I did not know it then, but every person I read about was shorter than James grew to be.

20 Symbols The narrator finds two different types of books for James. What do these two categories of books suggest about James's situation in life?

The worst book was called *Medical Curiosities*. I say worst now. That is hindsight. The night I looked, I thought, in fact, that it was the best book—not because it was good or even accurate, but because it had the most pages on the subject I was researching. I found it under the subject heading *Abnormalities, human*. A terrible phrase, and one I knew I could not repeat to James. (20) It was a late-nineteenth-century medical book, described two-headed people and parasitic twins and dwarfs. And giants. Not exactly information, but interesting: giants who had enormous or usual appetites; ones who grew throughout their lives or only after adolescence; professional giants and private citizens.

So I took that book, and the circus books, marked the pertinent places with the old catalog cards I used for scrap, and set them aside. Ready for him, so that he did not have to look in the index, or wander through the pages at all.

"Your tall friend is here," Astoria said to me the next week. I was in my office, reading reviews. "He's looking for you."

James waited for me at the circ desk. "You said we could—"

"I looked," I said. I'd stowed the books beneath the shelf. "Try these out."

He took them to the big table in the front room. Read them. He made the sturdy chair, the same chair I'd sat in the night before, seem tiny.

Think Aloud

Symbolism

To model the skill of identifying and analyzing symbolism, use the following "think aloud." Say to students:

I know that any literary element, such as a character, object, or image, can serve as a symbol if it receives special emphasis.

In the excerpt, James's struggle with being a giant looks as if it will be a main part of the conflict in the book. However, the sheer unusualness of James's condition, as well as its fantastical or grotesque associations, sets off a big "symbol alert" for me.

To see what symbolic meanings James's gigantism might have, I list both the literal consequences of his condition as well as the emotional associations: growing uncontrollably taller, being different, fearing the feeling of being abnormal, having an uncertain future. I realize that experiences resembling these may be part of growing up for anyone.

I conclude that James's gigantism may have symbolic significance. As I read further, I will look for additional details that support my interpretation.

Afterward he came up to me.

"How were they?" I asked. "Would you like to take them home?"

He shook his head.

"No," he said. "Thanks."

"Nothing useful here at all?"

"No," he said.

I tried to catch his eye. "Close?"

"Close. I guess." He pointed at *Medical Curiosities.* "I guess that's close."

I picked up the book and opened it to where the marker was, but he'd moved it to another page. A line drawing of a double-bodied baby looked up at me. Horrible. I snapped the book shut.

"I meant medical books," he said. "But new ones. Ones that say what goes wrong. How to cure it."

21 "Cures," I said. "Oh." Cures for giants? No such thing. No cure for height. Only preventive medicine. I said it as a question. "Cures? For tall people?"

"Yes," he said.

All I wanted was for him to explain it to me. It seemed presumptuous to come to any conclusions myself. I knew what he was talking about. I did. But what he wanted, I couldn't help him with.

Darla, the shelver, came rattling up with her metal cart. "Shelve these?" she said, pointing at the books. The catalog cards I'd used stuck out from the pages; James had lined them up, like a pack of cards he'd shuffled into them. "Hi, Jim," she said.

"Hi." He squinted down at her.

She stared at me; I waited for her to get back to shelving.

"Peggy. Shelve them, or not?"

"Not yet," I said. She sighed and pushed the cart off.

James stood in silence on the other side of the desk. He looked ready to leave.

"You mean how to stop growing," I said.

"Yes." Now he looked at me. "Medicine, or operations, or something."

"I'm not sure we have anything here," I said. That was a lie. I knew we didn't. "A medical library somewhere, perhaps. Or a university library. But really—" I started pulling the bookmarks from the books. I tried to sound gentle. "Really, you should ask your doctor."

"I have," he said. "I've asked a lot of doctors."

21

Character What does James want? What does his desire tell you about the story's theme?

22

Theme How do the characters of the narrator and James help point to a theme about human nature? Explain a possible story theme and cite textual evidence to support your response.

21 Character

1. Review with students the fact that James's size affects his ability to walk. Discuss the books' negative representations of giants as abnormal or "different." Then, have a volunteer read aloud the highlighted text.
2. **Ask** students the first Character question.

   Answer: He wants to be cured of his gigantism.
3. Review ideas of the story's theme that students have already discussed, such as the desire for self-knowledge and the problem of an individual's feeling different from everyone else. Then, **Ask** the second Character question.

   Possible responses: His desire shows that the story's theme is not just about the desire for self-knowledge, but about the desire to use knowledge to change oneself and one's fate.

22 Theme

Ask the Theme question.

Possible response: The story's theme is not just about feeling different from others, but about the desire in human nature to overcome that difference and to fit in with the rest of society by being "normal." James's desire to change and the narrator's attempts not to hurt him by using certain words, such as *giant,* both support that theme.

Fluency

Have students work in pairs. Distribute copies of page 14. Direct partners to take turns reading, starting with "The worst book was called . . ." and ending with the last paragraph on the page. Have the partner who is listening mark any words or phrases with which the reader has difficulty. Collect and review students' copies. Look for these problem spots:

- If students have difficulty with the word *curiosities,* explain that the word is plural because its ending is *-ies.* Direct students to say the word in its singular form, then in its plural form. Have students read the sentence again to check for fluency.
- If students have difficulty with the phrase "*parasitic twins,*" ask them what part of speech *parasitic* is (an adjective—indicated by its *-ic* ending). Then, have a volunteer tell what a parasite is (an organism that lives on or inside another and receives nourishment from its host). Explain that the phrase is a term for conjoined twins who share some of their body parts and internal organs.

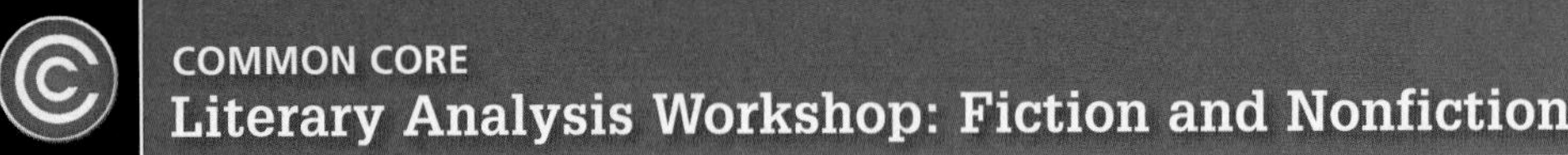

23 Close Read: Central Idea in Nonfiction

1. Ensure that students understand that the central idea in a work of nonfiction is the main point that the author wishes to convey. Each specific detail in the work should contribute to this central idea.
2. Explain that, when reading a text with an implied central idea, the reader must analyze the relationships among the key points and draw a conclusion about the main idea that they all support.
3. Provide this example:

   In the 1940s, there were only sixteen baseball teams. Now, there are thirty, so it is harder for fans to keep track of them. In the 1940s, players tended to play with the same team for many years. It was more enjoyable to root for a team when you knew who each player was. In more recent times, baseball players play for whichever team will pay them the most.

   Ask students: What central idea might be supported by each of these details?

   Possible response: It was more enjoyable to be a baseball fan in the 1940s, when baseball was easy to follow, than it is now.
4. Review the Types of Supporting Details chart with the class. **Ask** students: In what cases might personal experience be a more powerful form of support than statistics? When might statistics be the stronger form of support?

   Possible response: A report of a personal experience might be stronger when the point concerns how something, such as staying in a certain hotel, feels. Statistics might be stronger support for general claims, such as claims about the success rate of a given medical procedure.
5. Point out examples of highlighted text in the model on page 17. Explain that in each case, the color of the highlighting matches the color of a category in the chart. Details that illustrate a given category are highlighted in the color for that category.

23 Close Read: Central Idea in Nonfiction

The central idea is often stated or implied early in a work. Supporting details develop that idea.

Central Idea The central idea is the author's main point in a work of nonfiction. The term also refers to key ideas in individual paragraphs or sections of a work. The main ideas expressed in paragraphs work to develop the central idea of the work as a whole.

Stated Central Idea In some nonfiction, the author expresses the central idea in a direct statement. The title of a work may also state the central idea directly.

Example:
Here, the author states the central idea in the first sentence:
My acting career began early, long before I could actually act. As a baby, I wore elf suits, snowsuits, bunny suits, and my birthday suit to crawl through movie scenes.

Implied Central Idea The author may also imply a central idea through a series of related details. You can determine the central idea by identifying how individual details relate to one another. The central idea can then be expressed as a broad statement that accounts for all of the details.

Example:
Human beings, eagles, owls, hawks, and other predators hunt rabbits for food. Mother rabbits spend only a few minutes in the nest each day, so the babies are often unprotected. Wild rabbits also fall victim to disease and starvation.
In each sentence, the author discusses a different threat to wild rabbits. The inferred central idea might be stated as follows: Wild rabbits face many dangers.

Types of Supporting Details

Writers develop and refine central ideas by using supporting details of many different types. As you read, distinguish between the supporting details and the central concepts they help to shape.

Facts are statements that can be proved true. *Example: Most grocery stores carry a variety of fruits and vegetables.*	**Observations** are eyewitness accounts of experiments or events. *Example: Adding vinegar to baking soda causes a chemical reaction.*
Statistics are numerical data. *Example: Girls account for 47 percent of all high school soccer players.*	**Personal experience** is the author's own lived experience. *Example: Riding the rapids was a great adventure.*
Expert testimony is information provided by an authoritative person. *Example: Biologist George Tillman estimates that 50,000 species go extinct every year.*	**Anecdotes** are brief stories that illustrate a point. *Example: My mother insisted I get out on the ice and skate. "Falling down is part of life," she said.*
Examples are specific illustrations of a general concept. *Example: Hybrid flowers are popular. The "Peace" rose is a favorite among gardeners.*	**Analogies** are comparisons of seemingly unlike situations to show similarities. *Example: Alice's moods are like a rocket. They go from warm to explosive in seconds.*

Vocabulary Development

CCSS Language 6

Thematic Vocabulary: The Big Question

As students discuss the speech, encourage them to use the thematic vocabulary presented in Introducing the Big Question, pages 2–3. Help them with sentence starters such as these:

1. One belief that defines Roosevelt's *perspective* is that . . .
2. One piece of *evidence* for his view might be that . . .
3. The idea that the political and economic system should provide for a "constantly rising standard of living" (is/is not) *credible* because . . .

EXEMPLAR TEXT

24 Model

President Franklin Delano Roosevelt delivered this address, known as "The Four Freedoms Speech," at the beginning of his second term in office. Although the United States was not yet involved in World War II, the speech anticipates the ideals for which the nation would fight in that conflict.

from "State of the Union Address (1941)"
by Franklin D. Roosevelt

For there is nothing mysterious about the foundations of a healthy and strong democracy. The basic things expected by our people of their political and economic systems are simple. They are:

Equality of opportunity for youth and for others.

Jobs for those who can work.

25 Security for those who need it.

The ending of special privilege for the few.

The preservation of civil liberties for all.

The enjoyment of the fruits of scientific progress in a wider and constantly rising standard of living.

These are the simple, basic things that must never be lost sight of in the turmoil and unbelievable complexity of our modern world. The inner and abiding strength of our economic and political systems is dependent upon the degree to which they fulfill these expectations.

Many subjects connected with our social economy call for immediate improvement. As examples:

We should bring more citizens under the coverage of old-age pensions and unemployment insurance.

26 We should widen the opportunities for adequate medical care.

We should plan a better system by which persons deserving or needing gainful employment may obtain it.

27 I have called for personal sacrifice. I am assured of the willingness of almost all Americans to respond to that call.

25 **Observations** Roosevelt begins this section of his address with the observation that the elements of a healthy and strong democracy are those people intuitively understand.

Examples Roosevelt cites specific examples of how to improve the social economy.

27 **Expert Testimony** Roosevelt's expression of confidence in the American people carries all the authority of his office. This statement supports his central idea that the nation can meet the challenges of the day.

TEACH

24 Reading the Model

1. Discuss the introductory paragraph. Explain further that Roosevelt came to office during the Great Depression, when banks and the stock market had collapsed and the people suffered from widespread unemployment.
2. Have students read the passage. Discuss, clarifying as needed. Then, guide students in reviewing the annotations.

25 Observations

Have a volunteer read aloud the bracketed passage and the annotation. Discuss whether these elements are still held as expectations by people today.

Possible response: Responses may vary; however, most students will probably agree that people today have these same expectations.

26 Examples

Have a volunteer read aloud the highlighted passage and the annotation. Ask students to connect each improvement to the expectation listed above that the improvement will address.

Possible response: Old-age pensions relate to "security." Increased opportunities for medical care relate to a "constantly rising standard of living." A system for finding people jobs relates to the expectation of "jobs for those who can work."

27 Expert Testimony

Have a volunteer read aloud the bracketed passage and the annotation. **Ask:** What is the effect of Roosevelt's shift to the first-person pronoun I?

Possible response: It makes his request for self-sacrifice personal, emphasizing that it is a matter of individual commitment.

Differentiated Instruction for Universal Access

Strategy for Less Proficient Readers

To build background before students read, explain that Roosevelt spoke during the Great Depression. Review these facts about the period:

- Many people lost their jobs.
- Because the banks and the stock market were in trouble, many people lost their savings. Elderly people, however, depended on their savings for their retirement. As students read, guide them in finding details related to these two facts.

EL Strategy for English Learners

Preteach the following words from page 17, using visuals, mime, gestures, and the help of students fluent in English who share students' home language, as appropriate: *foundations, democracy, expect/expectations, employment/unemployment, pensions,* and *sacrifice.* On the board, draw a diagram of the foundations of democracy. Then, guide students in restating each of Roosevelt's expectations and adding it to the diagram as part of this foundation.

28 Introducing the Independent Practice

1. Explain to students that they will analyze the central idea and supporting details of the Independent Practice selection.
2. Discuss the About the Selection note, and have students read the selection. Then, direct them to go back through and respond to the side-column prompts. As necessary, guide students in answering the prompts, using the teaching notes. Conclude by having students answer the After You Read questions for the selection, on page 21.

29 Fact

Have students review the bracketed passage and the annotation. Point out that the author defines *desiderata* in her first sentence. **Ask** the Fact question.

Possible response: It helps establish McCracken's topic: the need or desire that leads her to collect the items in her archive and her thoughts about what might be missing from it.

30 Examples

1. Review the second and third paragraphs with the class. **Ask** students: What are three sources of documents McCracken draws on for her collection?

   Answer: McCracken has her grandfather McCracken's history of the family, his wife's stories and poems, and her other grandmother's collection of letters, including letters from her mother's nanny, Martha.
2. **Ask** the Examples question.

   Possible response: All of the details in these paragraphs elaborate on the main idea in the first sentence: McCracken is assembling an archive of documents needed to give a complete picture of her family.

28 Independent Practice

About the Selection Elizabeth McCracken wrote this personal essay in response to a request from her publisher. The title, "Desiderata," means "something wanted, needed, or desired."

Fact In her first sentence, McCracken provides a definition, which is a type of fact. Why is this supporting detail important?

Examples Which details in the second and third paragraphs support the main idea that McCracken states in the yellow highlighted sentence?

"Desiderata" by Elizabeth McCracken

29 Desiderata, I learned in library science school, were the items you needed for an archive to make it useful. Useful, not complete, because there is no such thing as a complete archive. There's always a letter out there you want and need, either in someone else's collection or in an attic or just unfound. You need and want things you don't even know exist. That's how collections work.

30 I come from a family strong on documents. I have a small archive myself. My grandfather McCracken was a genealogist—I have his history of the McCrackens, a lovely compilation of research on early ancestors and personal remembrances of his own relatives. His wife, my grandmother, wrote stories and poems; I have copies of those, and remember once opening a drawer full of letters she wrote to God, part prayer and part daily correspondence to Someone dear. I have my grandmother Jacobson's collection of family letters; she had 11 brothers and sisters, some who wrote often and some just now and then. I have diplomas of relatives I never met. I have diaries and laundry lists. I love anything written by a relative, any evidence of what they really thought.

And I read these documents fairly regularly. Besides letters from her family, my grandmother also saved letters from Martha, her children's nanny. My mother, who says she had the happiest childhood on record, remembers Martha and her letters as lovely and slightly daffy. Her twin sister, my aunt Carolyn, remembers the letters and the woman as dark and Dickensian,[1] longing for a time that never really existed. I'd always assumed that the truth was somewhere in the middle, but I have the letters and now know that Martha was, at best, weird. She wrote to my travelling grandmother that the twins—The Dollies, she called them—didn't miss her at all. She reported that she took them out to her mother's farm, and couldn't understand why the girls were so upset to be served for dinner the chicken they'd met earlier. She reported on The Dollies' toilet training as if it were grand opera, and the Dollies heroines who wanted only, desperately, to triumph. 31

I'm glad to know this, I think. Certainly, it's a whole different Martha than the one I knew from my mother's stories. I know Martha now because of all that she reveals of herself, not knowing she was doing it, in her letters.

1. **Dickensian** of or relating to English novelist Charles Dickens (1812–1870).

Think Aloud

Implied Central Idea

To model the skill of identifying and analyzing an implied central idea, use the following "think aloud." Say to students:

> To interpret an implied, or unstated central idea, I need to determine what general idea the details in the work "point to." When I read the title of the work, "Desiderata," and McCracken's definition of the word, I realize the notion of "desiderata" is a main clue to the central idea: The essay will be about "things needed for a collection."
>
> As I read, I quickly find details relating to McCracken's collection of family documents. When I read on page 19 her statement that "the major frustration is how incomplete everything is," I begin to understand that McCracken's central idea involves both what she collects and why. I will state the central idea as follows: "I value and collect family documents out of my always unsatisfied desire for a complete picture of my family." As I read further, I will look for additional details supporting this interpretation.

31 Still, there are many frustrations to family papers. First of all, you may learn things you don't want to know. For instance: some of my grandmother's sisters wanted to sue the widow of one of their brothers. Even in letters from the litigious[2] sisters themselves, this comes across as merely petty and vindictive. There are letters that can break your heart: my Aunt Edna, writing to my grandmother, lamented how poor her health was, how the doctors told her to slow down; I know from the dates that Edna died two weeks later, of a heart attack.

32 But the major frustration is how incomplete everything is, how incomplete *people* are if you try to meet them this way. The great-aunt who wanted to sue only happened to write it down; maybe she gave up the idea. Maybe she was suffering otherwise—her life was continually tragic in small ways, I know that. Some of the great-aunts I barely know, because they barely wrote. Or rather, I *think* they barely wrote—my grandmother saved every letter some years, and selected letters others. Perhaps those great-aunts simply never made it into the collection.

And then there's my grandmother Jacobson herself. She was a wonderful and complex woman, an attorney and small businessperson who died at home at the age of 90. The pieces of paper I have from her don't conjure her up at all. Her diary (which I don't own but have read) is a very careful record of daily events, nothing more. She doesn't detail worries or doubts, and the fact is she was a worried and somewhat doubtful person. I think she knew that we'd read it, eventually, and didn't want to tell us in her diary anything she hadn't told us already.

One piece of paper I do have: a post-it note from late in her life, which she used to mark a recipe in *The Jewish Cookbook*. It says:

coffee
bananas
bread
milk
33 wax beans?

and then, in the corner, written diagonally and underlined,

lottery ticket.

I know that this dates to a time when she was both worried about money and had become very serious about luck. I don't know how superstitious she'd previously been, but about two years before she died, she began to see luck

2. **litigious** (li tij´ əs) *adj.* given to carrying out lawsuits; quarrelsome.

Anecdote What idea do the anecdotes about the sisters of the narrator's grandmother and the narrator's Aunt Edna help to shape?

Observations How does this observation help shape the central idea of McCracken's work? Explain.

Observation What idea is developed by McCracken's observations about her grandmother's note?

31 Anecdote

Have a volunteer read aloud the bracketed text on pages 18–19. **Ask** the Anecdote question.

Possible response: The central idea is that exploring family memorabilia is not just an affirmative experience. It may bring to light unpleasant things.

32 Observations

1. Have a volunteer read the highlighted text. **Ask** the first Observation question.

   Possible response: This observation supports the idea that what is left behind can only hint at the reality of the past.

2. **Ask** How much does the literal meaning of the grandmother's note reveal about her as an individual?

   Possible response: The note reveals practically nothing about her; it might be anyone's list.

33 Observations

1. **Ask** the second Observation question.

   Possible response: These observations show how much the meaning and value of collectibles lie in the desires and knowledge of the collector.

2. Then, read aloud the text from the paragraph beginning "I know that this dates . . ." through the paragraph on the next page, beginning "I love that little green piece of paper." **Ask** students: What does McCracken's knowledge of her grandmother allow her to see in the note?

   Possible response: In the mention of the lottery ticket, she sees the difficulty her grandmother was having with money at the time, the superstition that she adopted near her death, and the affirmation that the ticket represented to her.

Differentiated Instruction for Universal Access

Support for Special-Needs Students

Have students read the adapted version of "Desiderata" in the ***Reader's Notebook: Adapted Version.*** They may also listen to the adapted version on the ***Hear It!* Audio CD.**

Support for Less Proficient Readers

Have students read "Desiderata" in the ***Reader's Notebook.*** After students finish the selection in the ***Reader's Notebook,*** have them complete the questions and activities in the Student Edition.

EL Support for English Learners

Have students read "Desiderata" in the ***Reader's Notebook: English Learner's Version.*** English learners may also read the selection as they listen to the recorded version on the ***Hear It!* Audio CD.**

34 Anecdote

1. Have a volunteer read the highlighted text aloud. **Ask:** Why is McCracken surprised by the letter?

   Answer: While she has known her grandparents as "quiet people," the letter reveals the depths of their love and shows her grandfather to have been quite passionate.

2. **Ask** the Anecdote question.

   Possible response: McCracken refines the idea that these family documents hold insights about the family. She needed to know something about her grandmother to understand the full significance of the reference to a lottery ticket on the note, and here is the document that gives her fuller, deeper knowledge of her family.

35 Central Idea

Ask the Central Idea question on page 21.

Possible response: Human beings want to hold onto their past and that of their family. That is why they desire memorabilia, incomplete as it is.

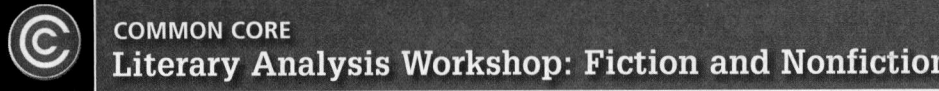

Practice continued

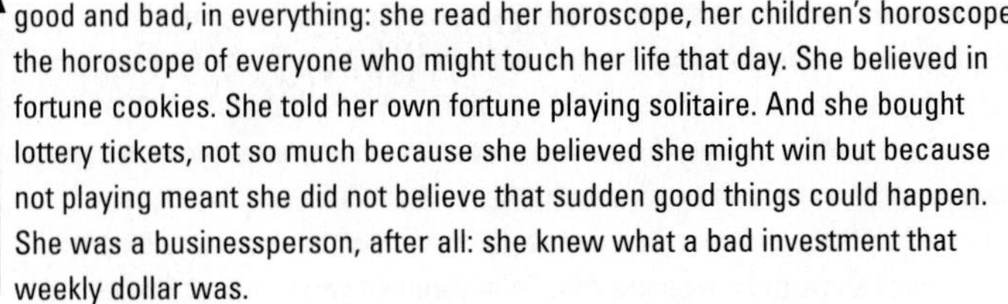

33 good and bad, in everything: she read her horoscope, her children's horoscope, the horoscope of everyone who might touch her life that day. She believed in fortune cookies. She told her own fortune playing solitaire. And she bought lottery tickets, not so much because she believed she might win but because not playing meant she did not believe that sudden good things could happen. She was a businessperson, after all: she knew what a bad investment that weekly dollar was.

I love that little green piece of paper. *Desideratum* to me, though less than ephemera[3] to anyone else.

I could tell dozens of other stories from the pages of family papers: my aunt Blanche's pell-mell record of taking care of her favorite sister, Elizabeth, who was dying of Alzheimer's; Blanche has that disease herself now, and you can see the early signs in these notes. My great-uncles' cheery letters from Europe during World War II. A letter my brother wrote to my grandmother when I was four and he was six, thanking her for a gift and then recording that I was resisting writing a thank-you note myself.

34 **Anecdote** What idea does McCracken refine with this anecdote about her grandparents' love letters?

34 Here's a last story. My father's parents were, when I knew them, quiet people. I know now that my version of them is different from anyone else's, but they were my grandparents and I never questioned who I understood them to be. After their deaths, I inherited a cherry chest-of-drawers from their house. I owned this imposing piece of furniture for a few years before I lifted some paper lining from one of the drawers and found a letter. Part of a letter, actually, written by my grandfather to my grandmother before their marriage.

It was one of the most beautiful love letters I've ever read, full of delight for her person and for their love together. It was passionate and thrilled and almost disbelieving of his great fortune, to have found her. I never imagined my grandfather, my quiet careful grandfather, was the sort of man who'd write any kind of love letter, never mind this kind. Wrong again. And my grandmother had saved it for more than fifty years. I wondered whether she took it out and reread it from time to time, or whether she'd forgotten where she'd put it.

My parents were out of town that weekend, and as it happened I'd agreed to pick them up at the airport. I brought the letter to give to my father—if it meant that much to me, I couldn't imagine what it would mean to him. And so, sitting on a bench in Logan,[4] I gave it to him. "Look what I found," I said.

"Oh," he said, perfectly pleased but not surprised. "Another letter. I'll put it with the others."

3. **ephemera** (e fem′ ər ə) *n.* something, often printed material, meant to last for only a short time.
4. **Logan** Boston's Logan International Airport, named for General Edward Lawrence Logan.

Think Aloud

Vocabulary: Using Context

To model the skill of using context to infer the meaning of an unfamiliar word, use the following "think aloud." Say to students:

When I read McCracken's description of her aunt's "pell-mell record of taking care of her favorite sister," I realize that *pell-mell* is an adjective modifying *record.* It tells "what kind of record." I look for clues to its meaning and find: "Blanche has [Alzheimer's] disease herself now, and you can see the early signs in these notes."

I know that Alzheimer's disease involves memory loss. If her notes show the early signs of this disease, she may repeat herself in them, forget to explain key details, or jot them down in an unorganized way. I conclude that *pell-mell* means "in a state of disorder." I will check my inference in a dictionary. There, I find that *pell-mell* means "in a jumbled, confused mass or manner."

Turns out there were many more—my grandparents had written each other several times a day during their courtship. Which makes it, of course, a happier story.

My question is: was that letter more a *desideratum* for me, or my father? He had the collection, I didn't. Sometimes I regret giving it to him. I've forgotten the exact words my grandfather used, but it doesn't seem right to ask for someone else's love letter back. Someday I'll see it again, I know. Meanwhile, I need it and desire it. I need and desire everything that belongs to my family, and in some ways, I think, that's what I do with my days, writing fiction. I am writing love letters to diaries and post-it notes and telegrams and birthday cards. I am writing love letters to love letters.

Central Idea What central idea about desiderata in general and human nature specifically can be supported with the key ideas and details in this work?

After You Read

from The Giant's House • Desiderata

1. **Key Ideas and Details (a)** Write a summary of the excerpt from *The Giant's House.* A summary is a brief version of a text that relates the most important ideas in your own words and in a logical order. Your summary should be understood by someone who has not read the selection. **(b)** Write a summary of "Desiderata."
2. **Key Ideas and Details** What is McCracken's **main purpose** for writing "Desiderata"? Explain.
3. **Key Ideas and Details** Identify one possible **theme** expressed in the excerpt from *The Giant's House.* Note details from the selection that support your answer.
4. **Key Ideas and Details (a)** Identify the key idea in each of the final seven paragraphs of "Desiderata." **(b)** Consider the relationships among the individual key ideas. Then, write a general statement in which you express the central idea of the entire work. Remember that each of the key ideas will support the work's central idea.
5. **Key Ideas and Details (a)** In the excerpt from *The Giant's House,* note two points at which the narrator, Peggy, refers to her training as a librarian. **(b) Analyze:** Do Peggy's efforts for James meet her criteria for being a good librarian? Explain.
6. **Integration of Knowledge and Ideas (a)** In "Desiderata," what frustrations does McCracken experience in "meeting" people through family papers? **(b) Speculate:** Based on this essay, why do you think McCracken became a writer of fiction? Explain.
7. **Integration of Knowledge and Ideas (a)** Complete a chart like the one shown to list sources, including those found on the Internet and in a library, that James could use if he were researching his condition today.

Research Question	Possible Source

(b) Collaboration: Discuss your chart with a classmate to identify the most valuable resource.

Assessment Resources

The following resources can be used to assess students' knowledge and skills.

Unit 1 Resources

L1 L2 EL **Selection Test A,** pp. 24–26

L3 L4 EL **Selection Test B,** pp. 27–29

L3 L4 **Open Book Test,** pp. 21–23

PHLit Online! Students may use the **Self-test,** online at **www.PHLitOnline.com,** to prepare for **Selection Test A** or **Selection Test B.**

ASSESS/EXTEND

Answers

1. Students' summaries may vary but should state only key ideas and be logically organized.
2. **Possible responses:** McCracken's purpose is to reflect on the importance of family documents and to understand her motivation for writing fiction.
3. **Possible response:** One theme relates to James's desperate quest for normality. He wants to learn about "Medicine, or operations, or something" that can stop him from growing.
4. **(a) Possible response:** Key ideas include the following:
   - 6th paragraph—My major frustration with my archive is that it is incomplete.
   - 17th paragraph—My fiction writing may be inspired by my fascination with my family's documents.

   (b) The urge to complete a story hinted at by an incomplete record may be one inspiration for writing fiction.
5. **Possible response: (a)** Peggy says, "Never jump to conclusions when trying to answer a reference question. Interview the patron." She also says, a bit later, "My job was to show people—even people I liked—how to use the library, not use it for them." **(b)** By hunting for books herself, she goes beyond her role as a librarian and perhaps becomes a friend.
6. **Possible response: (a)** She is frustrated that the record is incomplete. **(b)** McCracken may write fiction because gaps in her family's history inspire her to imagine what happened.
7. **Possible response: (a)** Research Question—What has modern science learned about cures for gigantism? Possible Sources—up-to-date health stories on gigantism from a reputable newspaper; current articles in a specialized journal such as *Journal of the American Medical Association;* Web sites on the subject sponsored by reputable educational organizations. **(b)** Partners should support their points with evidence and reasoning.

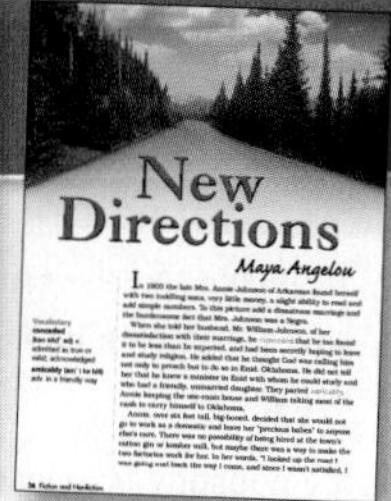

✓ The Washwoman • ✓✓ New Directions

Lesson Pacing Guide

DAY 1 Preteach

- Administer the Reading and Vocabulary Warm-ups (*Unit 1 Resources,* pp. 30–33 or 48–51) as necessary.
- Introduce the Reading Skill: Make Predictions.
- Introduce the Literary Analysis concept: Narrative Essay.
- Distribute copies of the appropriate graphic organizer for the Reading Skill (*Graphic Organizer Transparencies,* pp. 3–5).
- Distribute copies of the appropriate graphic organizer for Literary Analysis (*Graphic Organizer Transparencies*, pp. 6–8).
- Teach the selection vocabulary.
- Introduce the Word Study skill.

DAYS 2–3 Preteach/Teach

- Build background with the Background feature.
- Develop thematic vocabulary and thematic thinking with Writing About the Big Question.
- Prepare students to read with the Activating Prior Knowledge activities (TE).
- Informally monitor comprehension while students read.
- Use the Reading Check questions to confirm comprehension.
- Develop students' ability to make predictions, using the Reading Skill questions.
- Develop students' understanding of narrative essays, using the Literary Analysis questions.
- Reinforce vocabulary with the Vocabulary notes.
- Reinforce unit focus standards using the Spiral Review prompts.

DAY 4 Assess

- Assess students' comprehension and mastery of the skills by having them answer the Critical Thinking, Reading Skill, and Literary Analysis questions.
- Have students complete the Vocabulary Practice activities.
- Have students complete the Word Study activities.

DAY 5 Extend/Assess

- Have students complete the Conventions lesson.
- Have students complete the Writing activity and write an anecdote. (You may assign as homework.)
- Extend learning by having students complete the Speaking and Listening activity, an interview. As an alternative, assign them "As Long as They Can Play" or "Riding the Waves" in *Reality Central.*
- Administer Selection Test A or B (*Unit 1 Resources,* pp. 42–47 or 63–68).

Common Core State Standards

Reading Informational Text
2. Determine a central idea of a text and analyze its development over the course of the text, including how it emerges and is shaped and refined by specific details.

Writing 3. Write narratives to develop real or imagined experiences or events using effective technique, well-chosen details, and well-structured event sequences.

Speaking and Listening 1.a. Come to discussions prepared, having read and researched material under study; explicitly draw on that preparation by referring to evidence from texts and other research on the topic or issue to stimulate a thoughtful, well-reasoned exchange of ideas.
1.c. Propel conversations by posing and responding to questions that relate the current discussion to broader themes or larger ideas; actively incorporate others into the discussion; and clarify, verify, or challenge ideas.
1.d. Respond thoughtfully to diverse perspectives, summarize points of agreement and disagreement, and, when warranted, qualify or justify their own views and understanding.

Language 2. Demonstrate command of the conventions of standard English capitalization, punctuation, and spelling when writing.

Additional Standards Practice
Common Core Companion,* *pp. 15–22; 97–104

Daily Block Scheduling
Each day in this Lesson Pacing Guide represents a 40–50 minute period. Teachers using block scheduling may combine days to revise pacing. In addition, teachers may differentiate and support core instruction by integrating components for extended and intensive support as students require. See the Guide to Selected Leveled Resources (facing page).

Guide to Selected Leveled Resources

RTI Tier 1 (students performing on level)		✓ More Accessible The Washwoman	✓✓ More Complex New Directions
Warm Up	**Practice, model,** and **monitor** fluency, working **with the whole class** or **in groups.**	**Vocabulary** and **Reading Warm-ups B,** ***Unit 1 Resources,*** pp. 30–31, 33	**Vocabulary** and **Reading Warm-ups B,** ***Unit 1 Resources,*** pp. 48–49, 51
Comprehension/Skills	**Support** and **monitor** comprehension and skills development, having students complete the activities, graphic organizers, and interactive prompts **independently** or **as a class.**	• ***Reader's Notebook,*** adapted instruction and full selection EL ***Reader's Notebook: English Learner's Version,*** adapted instruction and adapted selection • **Reading Skill Graphic Organizer B,** ***Graphic Organizer Transparencies,*** p. 5 • **Literary Analysis Graphic Organizer B,** ***Graphic Organizer Transparencies,*** p. 8	• ***Reader's Notebook,*** adapted instruction and summary EL ***Reader's Notebook: English Learner's Version,*** adapted instruction and summary • **Reading Skill Graphic Organizer B,** ***Graphic Organizer Transparencies,*** p. 5 • **Literary Analysis Graphic Organizer B,** ***Graphic Organizer Transparencies,*** p. 8
Monitor Progress	**Monitor** student progress with the differentiated curriculum-based assessment in the *Unit Resources.*	• **Selection Test B,** ***Unit 1 Resources,*** pp. 45–47 • **Open-Book Test,** ***Unit 1 Resources,*** pp. 39–41	• **Selection Test B,** ***Unit 1 Resources,*** pp. 66–68 • **Open-Book Test,** ***Unit 1 Resources,*** pp. 60–62

RTI Tier 2 (students requiring intervention)		✓ More Accessible The Washwoman	✓✓ More Complex New Directions
Warm Up	**Practice, model,** and **monitor** fluency **in groups** or **with individuals.**	• **Vocabulary and Reading Warm-ups A,** ***Unit 1 Resources,*** pp. 30–32 • ***Reality Central,*** "As Long As They Can Play" • ***Hear It!*** **Audio CD (adapted text)**	• **Vocabulary and Reading Warm-ups A,** ***Unit 1 Resources,*** pp. 48–50 • ***Reality Central,*** "Riding the Wave" • ***Hear It!*** **Audio CD**
Comprehension/Skills	• **Support** and **monitor** comprehension and skills development, working **in small groups** or **with individuals.** • **Pair** students with more advanced peers and have them complete the writing activity in the *Real-World Writing Journal.* • As students complete the selection in the appropriate version of the *Reader's Notebook,* **monitor** comprehension frequently with group questions and individual instruction. • **Model** strategies while guiding students in completing the activities and prompts in the *Reader's Notebook,* as well as the graphic organizers. • **Practice** skills and **monitor** mastery with the *Reading Kit* worksheets.	• ***Real-World Writing Journal,*** Lesson 1, pp. 2–5 • ***Reader's Notebook: Adapted Version,*** adapted instruction and adapted selection EL ***Reader's Notebook: English Learner's Version,*** adapted instruction and adapted selection • **Reading Skill Graphic Organizer A,** ***Graphic Organizer Transparencies,*** p. 3 • **Literary Analysis Graphic Organizer A,** ***Graphic Organizer Transparencies,*** p. 6 • ***Reading Kit,*** Practice worksheets, pp. 2, 8, 12, 14, 20	• ***Real-World Writing Journal,*** Lesson 2, pp. 6–9 • ***Reader's Notebook: Adapted Version,*** adapted instruction and summary EL ***Reader's Notebook: English Learner's Version,*** adapted instruction and summary • **Reading Skill Graphic Organizer A,** ***Graphic Organizer Transparencies,*** p. 4 • **Literary Analysis Graphic Organizer A,** ***Graphic Organizer Transparencies,*** p. 7 • ***Reading Kit,*** Practice worksheets, pp. 2, 8, 12, 14, 20
Monitor Progress	**Monitor** student progress with the differentiated curriculum-based assessment in the *Unit Resources* and in the *Reading Kit.*	• **Selection Test A,** ***Unit 1 Resources,*** pp. 42–44 • ***Reading Kit,*** Assess worksheets, pp. 3, 9, 13, 15, 21	• **Selection Test A,** ***Unit 1 Resources,*** pp. 63–65 • ***Reading Kit,*** Assess worksheets, pp. 3, 9, 13, 15, 21

TIER 3 Tier 3 intervention may require consultation with the student's special-education or dyslexia specialist. For additional support, see the Tier 2 activities and resources listed above.

One-on-one teaching **Group work** **Whole class instruction** **Independent work** **A Assessment**

For a complete guide to selection support, including support for Advanced students, see the Overview of Resources in the frontmatter.

✓The Washwoman
✓✓New Directions

The Washwoman
Isaac Bashevis Singer
26 Fiction and Nonfiction

New Directions
Maya Angelou

In 1903 the late Mrs. Annie Johnson of Arkansas found herself
with two toddling sons, very little money, a slight ability to read and
add simple numbers. To this picture add a disastrous marriage and
the burdensome fact that Mrs. Johnson was a Negro.
When she told her husband, Mr. William Johnson, of her
dissatisfaction with their marriage, he conceded that he too found
it to be less than he expected, and had been secretly hoping to leave
and study religion. He added that he thought God was calling him
not only to preach but to do so in Enid, Oklahoma. He did not tell
her that he knew a minister in Enid with whom he could study and
who had a friendly, unmarried daughter. They parted amicably,
Annie keeping the one-room house and William taking most of the
cash to carry himself to Oklahoma.
Annie, over six feet tall, big-boned, decided that she would not
go to work as a domestic and leave her "precious babes" to anyone
else's care. There was no possibility of being hired at the town's
cotton gin or lumber mill, but maybe there was a way to make the
two factories work for her. In her words, "I looked up the road I
was going and back the way I come, and since I wasn't satisfied, I

36 Fiction and Nonfiction

RESOURCES FOR:

- **L1 Special-Needs Students**
- **L2 Below-Level Students (Tier 2)**
- **L3 On-Level Students (Tier 1)**
- **L4 Advanced Students (Tier 1)**
- **EL English Learners**
- **All All Students**

Vocabulary/Fluency/Prior Knowledge

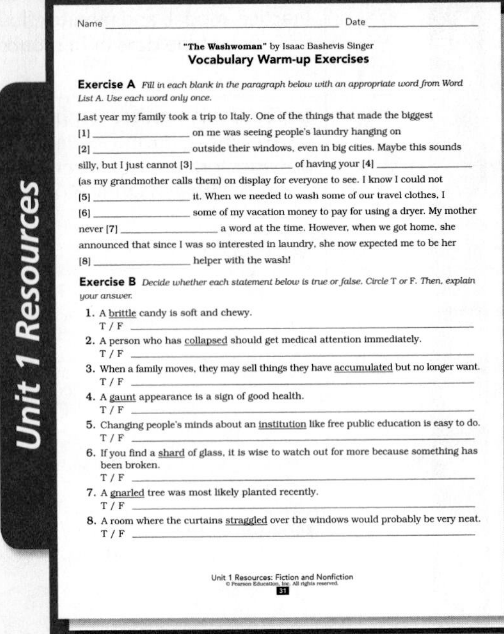

Name ______________________ Date ______________

"The Washwoman" by Isaac Bashevis Singer
Vocabulary Warm-up Exercises

Exercise A *Fill in each blank in the paragraph below with an appropriate word from Word List A. Use each word only once.*

Last year my family took a trip to Italy. One of the things that made the biggest [1] ______________ on me was seeing people's laundry hanging on [2] ______________ outside their windows, even in big cities. Maybe this sounds silly, but I just cannot [3] ______________ of having your [4] ______________ (as my grandmother calls them) on display for everyone to see. I know I could not [5] ______________ it. When we needed to wash some of our travel clothes, I [6] ______________ some of my vacation money to pay for using a dryer. My mother never [7] ______________ a word at the time. However, when we got home, she announced that since I was so interested in laundry, she now expected me to be her [8] ______________ helper with the wash!

Exercise B *Decide whether each statement below is true or false. Circle T or F. Then, explain your answer.*

1. A brittle candy is soft and chewy.
   T / F ______________
2. A person who has collapsed should get medical attention immediately.
   T / F ______________
3. When a family moves, they may sell things they have accumulated but no longer want.
   T / F ______________
4. A gaunt appearance is a sign of good health.
   T / F ______________
5. Changing people's minds about an institution like free public education is easy to do.
   T / F ______________
6. If you find a shard of glass, it is wise to watch out for more because something has been broken.
   T / F ______________
7. A gnarled tree was most likely planted recently.
   T / F ______________
8. A room where the curtains straggled over the windows would probably be very neat.
   T / F ______________

Unit 1 Resources: Fiction and Nonfiction
© Pearson Education, Inc. All rights reserved.
31

EL L1 L2 Vocabulary Warm-ups A and B, pp. 30–31, 48–49

Also available for these selections:

EL L1 L2 Reading Warm-ups A and B, pp. 32–33, 50–51

All Writing About the Big Question, pp. 34, 52

All Vocabulary Builder, pp. 37, 55

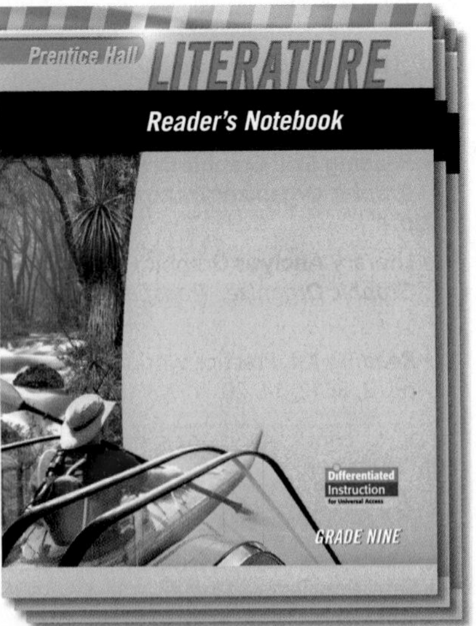

Reader's Notebooks

Pre- and postreading pages for both selections, as well as "The Washwoman," appear in an interactive format in the *Reader's Notebooks*. Each *Notebook* is differentiated for a different group of learners.

The selections in the Adapted and English Learner's versions are abridged.

- **L2 L3 *Reader's Notebook***
- **L1 *Reader's Notebook: Adapted Version***
- **EL *Reader's Notebook: English Learner's Version***
- **EL *Reader's Notebook: Spanish Version***

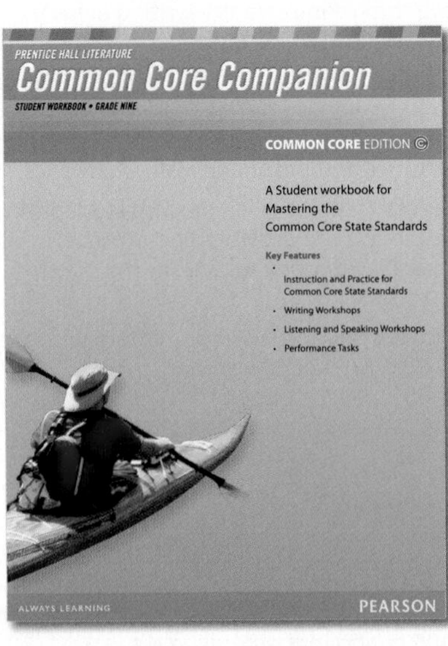

Common Core Companion

Additional instruction and practice for each Common Core State Standard

Selection Support

Graphic Organizer Transparencies

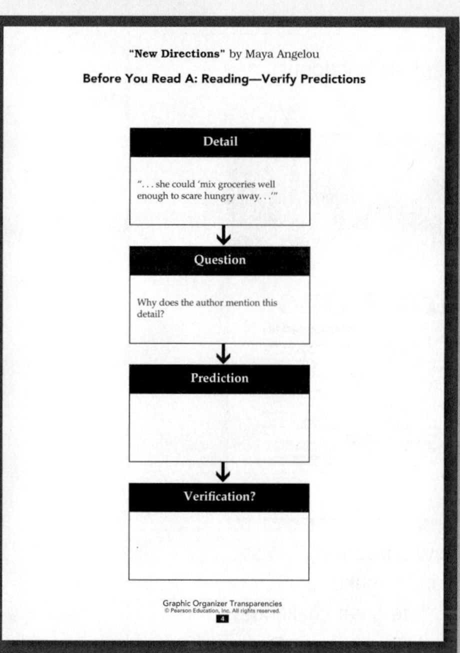

"New Directions" by Maya Angelou

Before You Read A: Reading—Verify Predictions

Detail

". . . she could 'mix groceries well enough to scare hungry away . . .'"

Question

Why does the author mention this detail?

Prediction

Verification?

Graphic Organizer Transparencies

4

EL L1 L2 **Reading: Graphic Organizer A,** pp. 3, 4 (partially filled in)

Also available for these selections:

EL L3 **Reading: Graphic Organizer B,** p. 5

EL L1 L2 **Literary Analysis: Graphic Organizer A,** pp. 6, 7 (partially filled in)

EL L3 **Literary Analysis: Graphic Organizer B,** p. 8

Skills Development/Extension

Unit 1 Resources

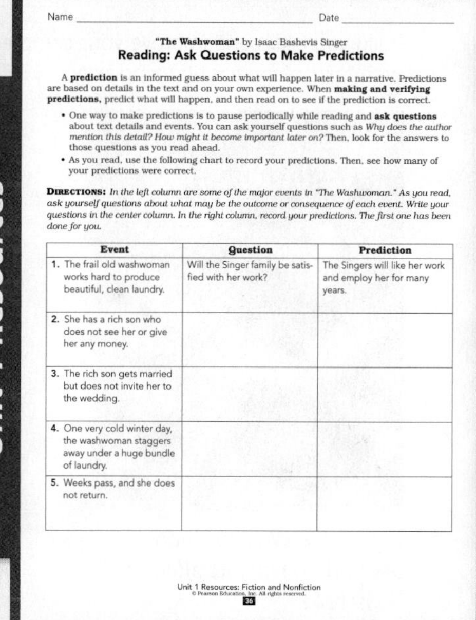

Name ______________________ Date ____________

"The Washwoman" by Isaac Bashevis Singer

Reading: Ask Questions to Make Predictions

A **prediction** is an informed guess about what will happen later in a narrative. Predictions are based on details in the text and on your own experience. When **making and verifying predictions,** predict what will happen, and then read on to see if the prediction is correct.

- One way to make predictions is to pause periodically while reading and **ask questions** about text details and events. You can ask yourself questions such as *Why does the author mention this detail? How might it become important later on?* Then, look for the answers to those questions as you read ahead.
- As you read, use the following chart to record your predictions. Then, see how many of your predictions were correct.

Directions: *In the left column are some of the major events in "The Washwoman." As you read, ask yourself questions about what may be the outcome or consequence of each event. Write your questions in the center column. In the right column, record your predictions. The first one has been done for you.*

Event	Question	Prediction
1. The frail old washwoman works hard to produce beautiful, clean laundry.	Will the Singer family be satisfied with her work?	The Singers will like her work and employ her for many years.
2. She has a rich son who does not see her or give her any money.		
3. The rich son gets married but does not invite her to the wedding.		
4. One very cold winter day, the washwoman staggers away under a huge bundle of laundry.		
5. Weeks pass, and she does not return.		

Unit 1 Resources: Fiction and Nonfiction

36

All **Reading: Make Predictions,** pp. 36, 54

Also available for these selections:

All **Literary Analysis: Narrative Essay,** pp. 35, 53

L4 **Enrichment,** pp. 38, 56

EL L3 L4 **Grammar,** p. 57

EL L3 L4 **Support for Writing,** p. 58

L3 L4 **Support for Extend Your Learning,** p. 59

Assessment

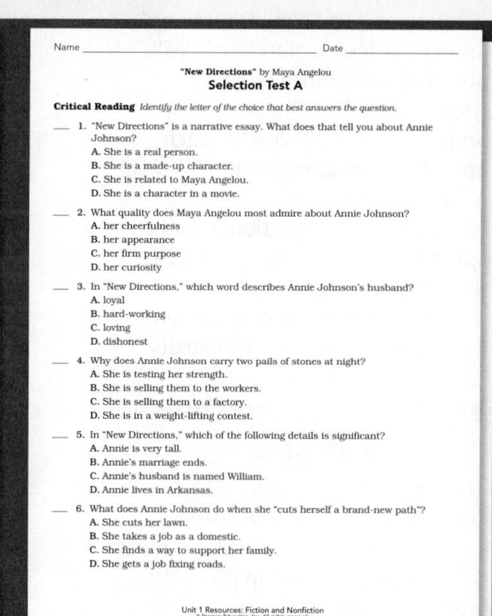

Name ______________________ Date ____________

"New Directions" by Maya Angelou

Selection Test A

Critical Reading *Identify the letter of the choice that best answers the question.*

____ 1. "New Directions" is a narrative essay. What does that tell you about Annie Johnson?
A. She is a real person.
B. She is a made-up character.
C. She is related to Maya Angelou.
D. She is a character in a movie.

____ 2. What quality does Maya Angelou most admire about Annie Johnson?
A. her cheerfulness
B. her appearance
C. her firm purpose
D. her curiosity

____ 3. In "New Directions," which word describes Annie Johnson's husband?
A. loyal
B. hard-working
C. loving
D. dishonest

____ 4. Why does Annie Johnson carry two pails of stones at night?
A. She is testing her strength.
B. She is selling them to the workers.
C. She is selling them to a factory.
D. She is in a weight-lifting contest.

____ 5. In "New Directions," which of the following details is significant?
A. Annie is very tall.
B. Annie's marriage ends.
C. Annie's husband is named William.
D. Annie lives in Arkansas.

____ 6. What does Annie Johnson do when she "cuts herself a brand-new path"?
A. She cuts her lawn.
B. She takes a job as a domestic.
C. She finds a way to support her family.
D. She gets a job fixing roads.

Unit 1 Resources: Fiction and Nonfiction

63

EL L1 L2 **Selection Test A,** pp. 42–44, 63–65

Also available for these selections:

L3 L4 **Open-Book Test,** pp. 39–41, 60–62

EL L3 L4 **Selection Test B,** pp. 45–47, 66–68

PHLit Online!
www.PHLitOnline.com

- complete narrated selection text
- a thematically related video with writing prompt
- an interactive graphic organizer
- highlighting feature
- access to all student print resources, adapted to individual student needs
- Spanish and English summaries
- adapted selection translations in Spanish

Online Resources: All print materials are also available online.

Background Video

Also available:

Get Connected! (thematic video with writing prompt)

All videos are available in Spanish.

Vocabulary Central (tools, activities, and songs for studying vocabulary)

Also available:

Writer's Journal (with graphics feature)

DIFFERENTIATE/PRETEACH

❶ Leveled Texts

You may use either "The Washwoman" or "New Directions" to meet the lesson standards. Skills instruction for both selections appears on p. 23. Choose one selection to teach (or choose to teach both). The Text Complexity Rubric at the bottom of this page will help you determine which selection is more appropriate for your students. Use the Reader and Task Suggestions on the facing page to help all students read text of increasing complexity.

❷ Introducing the CCS Standards

Introduce the standards on the student page. (Note that the lesson element with which each standard is addressed is identified in parentheses after the text of the standard.) Call out the standards that you will cover with the selections, explaining to students what each requires and how they will address it as they work through the selection you have chosen. Standards labeled "Spiral Review" are introduced in the Literary Analysis Workshop for this unit.

Before You Read

The Washwoman • New Directions

❶ Leveled Texts

Build your skills and improve your comprehension of literary nonfiction with texts of increasing complexity.

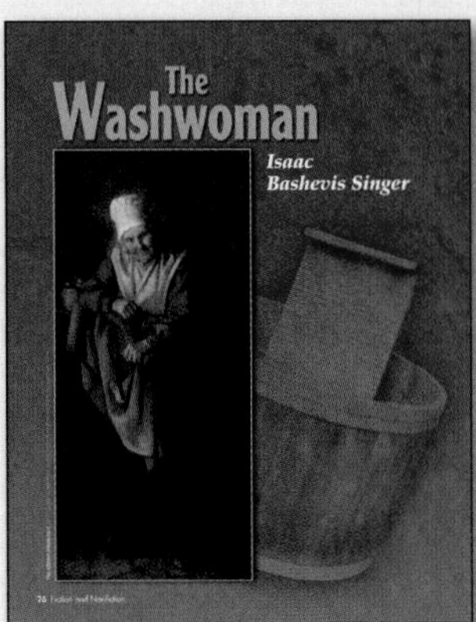

Read **"The Washwoman"** to see how community affects a household.

Read **"New Directions"** to see how a woman makes a life for herself despite great challenges.

❷ Common Core State Standards

Meet these standards with either **"The Washwoman"** (p. 26) or **"New Directions"** (p. 36).

Reading Informational Text
2. Determine a central idea of a text and analyze its development over the course of the text, including how it emerges and is shaped and refined by specific details; provide an objective summary of the text. *(Literary Analysis: Spiral Review)*

Writing
3. Write narratives to develop real or imagined experiences or events using effective technique, well-chosen details, and well-structured event sequences. *(Writing: Anecdote)*

Speaking and Listening
1.a. Come to discussions prepared, having read and researched material under study; explicitly draw on that preparation by referring to evidence from texts and other research on the topic or issue to stimulate a thoughtful, well-reasoned exchange of ideas. **1.c.** Propel conversations by posing and responding to questions that relate the current discussion to broader themes or larger ideas; actively incorporate others into the discussion; and clarify, verify, or challenge ideas and conclusions. **1.d.** Respond thoughtfully to diverse perspectives, summarize points of agreement and disagreement, and, when warranted, qualify or justify their own views and understanding and make new connections in light of the evidence and reasoning presented. *(Speaking and Listening: Interview)*

Language
2. Demonstrate command of the conventions of standard English capitalization, punctuation, and spelling when writing. *(Conventions: Common Nouns and Proper Nouns)*

Text Complexity Rubric: Leveled Texts

Text complexity is determined by both qualitative and quantitative measures. For this reason, the quantitative measure of a more complex selection may be lower than that of a more accessible selection.

		✓ The Washwoman	✓✓ New Directions
Qualitative Measures	**Context/ Knowledge Demands**	Jewish neighborhood in Poland, early 1900s 1 2 ③ 4 5	African American mother living in the South 1 2 ③ 4 5
	Structure/Language Conventionality and Clarity	Numerous long sentences; on-level vocabulary 1 2 ③ 4 5	Little dialogue; challenging vocabulary 1 2 3 ④ 5
	Levels of Meaning/ Purpose/Concept Level	Accessible concept (determination to complete a task) 1 2 ③ 4 5	Irony; accessible concept (journey from adversity to success) 1 2 3 ④ 5
Quantitative Measures	**Text Length**	Word Count: 1,976	Word Count: 763
	Lexile	870L	1360L
Overall Complexity		✓ **More accessible**	✓✓ **More complex**

❸ Literary Analysis: Narrative Essay

A **narrative essay** is a short piece of nonfiction that tells a story about a real person or an event. As in a fictional story, a narrative essay relates a series of events and has **main and subordinate** (minor) **characters.** Unlike a fictional story, however, the characters in a narrative essay are real people. The interactions of those characters propel the story forward and allow us to understand their **motivations** and goals.

As you read, notice how the author's choice of details influences your impressions of the people and events he or she describes.

❹ Reading Skill: Make Predictions

A **prediction** is an informed idea about what might happen later in a narrative. Predictions are based on details in the text and your own experience. When you **verify predictions,** you read on to see if the prediction you made is correct.

Pause periodically while reading and **ask questions** like these about text details and events:

- Why does the author mention this detail?
- How might it become important later on?

Look for the answers as you continue reading.

❺ Using the Strategy: Predictions Map

Use a chart like the one shown to record your predictions and evaluate their accuracy. Analyze any inaccurate predictions to determine why they were incorrect.

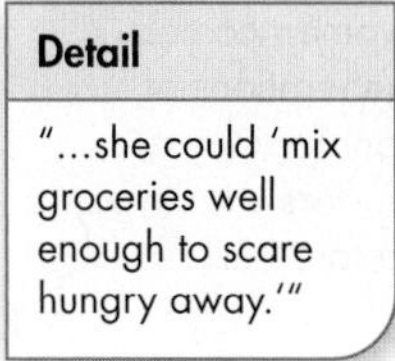

Detail	Question	Prediction	Verification?
"...she could 'mix groceries well enough to scare hungry away.'"	Why does the author mention this detail?	The character might sell food to support her family.	

PHLit Online!
www.PHLitOnline.com

Hear It!
- Selection summary audio
- Selection audio

See It!
- Get Connected video
- Background video
- More about the author
- Vocabulary flashcards

Do It!
- Interactive journals
- Interactive graphic organizers
- Self-test
- Internet activity
- Grammar tutorial
- Interactive vocabulary games

PRETEACH

❸ Literary Analysis

Narrative Essay

1. Introduce the skill, using instruction on the student page.
2. Tell students that they will identify the characteristics of a narrative essay as they read.

Think Aloud: Model the Skill

Model the skill of identifying details about characters in a narrative essay. Say to students:

Let's say I want you to help a boy named Matt do his chores. I'll probably tell you this detail: "Matt is so nice that he shares his dessert at lunch every day." I probably *won't* include this detail: "Matt is five feet tall." I choose the details that help me make my point: Matt is a nice guy who deserves help.

Similarly, writers choose details to make their points. When I read, I pay attention to the details that the writer chooses to include.

❹ Reading Skill

Make Predictions

1. Introduce the skill, using instruction on the student page.
2. Tell students that they will practice making predictions as they read.

❺ Using the Strategy

Give students a copy of either **Reading Skill Graphic Organizer A or B** (*Graphic Organizer Transparencies,* pp. 3–5) to record their predictions and evaluate their accuracy. Use the examples in **Reading Skill Graphic Organizer A,** which is partially filled in, to model the process of completing the organizer.

Ⓒ Text Complexity: Reader and Task Suggestions

✓ The Washwoman		✓✓ New Directions	
Preparing to Read the Text	**Leveled Tasks**	**Preparing to Read the Text**	**Leveled Tasks**
• Using the Background information on TE p. 25, discuss the lives of Jews and gentiles in Poland in the 1900s. • Discuss with students ways in which cultural differences can lead to hardships. • Guide students to use Multidraft Reading strategies (TE p. 25).	*Knowledge Demands* If students will have difficulty with knowledge demands, have them first read to identify details about the washwoman's determination. Then, have them reread, taking notes on interesting details of daily life in the setting. *Synthesizing* If students will not have difficulty with selection knowledge demands, have them note as they read ways in which Singer uses setting to help convey his theme.	• Refer to the Background section on TE p. 35, and discuss difficulties uneducated African American women in the South in the early 1900s faced. • Discuss the saying "Necessity is the mother of invention." • Guide students to use Multidraft Reading strategies (TE p. 35).	*Knowledge Demands* If students will have difficulty with cultural or historical knowledge, have them first read to identify details that show Annie's determination. Then, have them reread, identifying words or sentences that are unclear. *Synthesizing* If students will not have difficulty with selection knowledge demands, have them note as they read ways in which Angelou creates narrative style.

PRETEACH

❶ Writing About the Big Question

1. Review the assignment with the class.
2. Remind students that their *perspective* is the way in which they look at or think about something. Ask students to remember a personal experience and to think about how their perspective might have differed from others'.
3. Have students complete the sentence starters. Review responses as a class.

   (**Possible response:** A mother's relationship with her son can sometimes be distorted because of their age difference. They could gain insight into each other's perspective by speaking openly and honestly about their opinions.)
4. Remind students that their answers will help them think about the Big Question, "Can truth change?"

While You Read

Tell students that as they read, they should look for how the washwoman's situations change over time.

❷ Vocabulary

1. Have students preview the selection vocabulary.
2. For each word, have students say the word aloud.
3. Then, use the word in a sentence that defines the word.
4. Finally, repeat your definitional sentence or a similar sentence with the word missing and have the class "fill in the blank" chorally. Here are some examples:

   Forebears are ancestors. My father said that John Adams is one of our [students say "forebears"].

   Atonement is a way of making amends or restitution. In some faiths, people pray on special days of [students say "atonement"].

❸ Word Study

1. Introduce the skill, using the instruction in the box.
2. Write the words *foreground* and *forefather* on the board. Invite volunteers to state the definition of the words, using "earlier" or "in front of" in their definitions.

Making Connections | **The Washwoman**

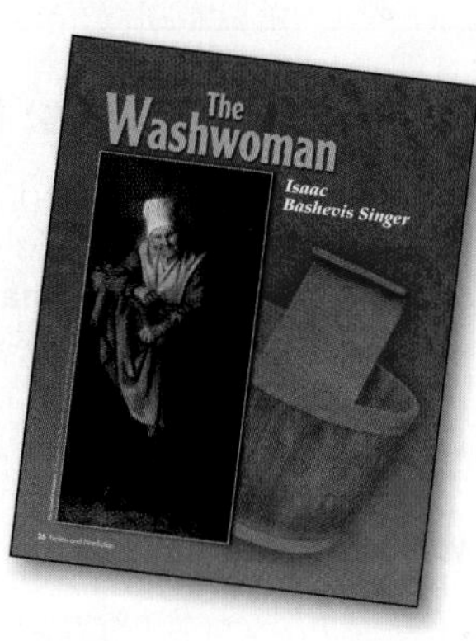

Can truth change?

❶ Writing About the Big Question

In "The Washwoman," a Jewish family learns to appreciate a Christian washwoman whose son has abandoned her. Use these sentence starters to develop your ideas about the Big Question.

A mother's relationship with her son can sometimes be **distorted** because of __________. They could gain **insight** into each other's **perspective** by ________.

While You Read Look for the ways that the washwoman's relationships change over time.

❷ Vocabulary

Read each word and its definition. Decide whether you know the word well, know it a little bit, or do not know it at all. After you read the selection, see how your knowledge of each word has increased.

- **forebears** (fôr´ berz) *n.* ancestors (p. 27) *His forebears started the family business.*
- **accumulated** (ə kyo͞om´ yo͞o lāt´ id) *v.* piled up, collected, or gathered together, especially over a period of time (p. 27) *We have accumulated a large stack of newspapers in our living room.* *accumulate v. accumulation n. cumulative adj.*
- **rancor** (raŋ´ kər) *n.* bitter hate (p. 28) *The rivals fumed with rancor for each other.*
- **atonement** (ə tōn´ mənt) *n.* act of making up for a wrongdoing or an injury (p. 28) *He volunteered at a nursing home as atonement for his misbehavior.* *atone v.*
- **obstinacy** (äb´ stə nə sē) *n.* stubbornness (p. 30) *The child refused to clean up, and she was punished for her obstinacy.* *obstinate adj.*
- **pious** (pī´ əs) *adj.* having or showing religious devotion (p. 31) *The pious man went to church every week.* *piety n. impious adj.*

❸

Word Study

The **Old English prefix *fore-*** means "earlier" or "in front of."

In this story, the washwoman comes from generations of "peasant **forebears**," or ancestors who lived long before her.

Vocabulary Development

Vocabulary Knowledge Rating Chart

Create a **Vocabulary Knowledge Rating Chart** (*Professional Development Guidebook*, p. 33) for this selection. Include the selection vocabulary and the forms of the Big Question words that appear in the Writing About the Big Question sentence starter on this page. (The Big Question vocabulary is introduced on pp. 2–3.)

Give students a copy of the chart. Read the words aloud, and have students mark their rating in the Before Reading column. Urge them to be alert to these words as they read and discuss the selection.

Tally how many students think they know a word to gauge how much instruction to provide. As students read and discuss the selection, point out the words and their context.

Vocabulary Central, featuring tools, activities, and songs for studying vocabulary, is available online at **www.PHLitOnline.com.**

Meet Isaac Bashevis Singer (1904–1991)

Author of

The Washwoman

❹

Storytelling always had an important place in Isaac Bashevis Singer's life. He grew up in the city of Warsaw in what now is Poland. Singer's father was a rabbi, a teacher of the Jewish faith and laws. Advice-seekers streamed through the family home, telling their stories as the fascinated young Singer listened and observed.

"Life Itself Is a Story" Fleeing persecution against Jews, Singer left Poland for New York City in 1935. In New York, Singer began to make a name for himself as a writer. He set many of his tales in the world of European Jewry he had left. Ironically, as he wrote, World War II devastated that world. Villages like the one of his birth were wiped off the face of the earth even as Singer brought them to life on the page.

Did You Know?

Isaac Bashevis Singer won the Nobel Prize for Literature in 1978.

BACKGROUND FOR THE ESSAY

Jews in Poland

"The Washwoman" takes place in the early twentieth century in what is now Poland. Centuries earlier, many Jewish people had settled there, drawn by the promise of religious tolerance. By Singer's time, Poland had been conquered by other countries. Yet, Poland's Jews held on to their traditions, continuing to speak Yiddish, a language blending German with Hebrew and other languages.

Daily Bellringer

For each class during which you will teach this selection, have students complete one of the five Quick Write activities for Week 1 in the ***Daily Bellringer Activities*** booklet.

❹ Background

Jews in Poland

It is not certain when the first Jewish people arrived in Poland, but many came during the 1300s when anti-Semitism was especially strong across much of Europe. Poland, in contrast, offered Jewish people sanctuary and legal rights that were unusual for the time period. By 1500, more than half of the world's Jewish population lived in Poland—a percentage that remained more or less constant until World War II. Although their legal rights and privileges varied over the centuries, Polish Jews often enjoyed security and freedom that were difficult to find in other countries.

Multidraft Reading

This icon ● marks natural pauses in the selection. To assist struggling readers and to deepen reading for all, assign the text in "chunks," following the icons, and apply multidraft reading protocols. For each reading, have students set the purpose indicated:

- **First reading**—identifying key ideas and details and answering any Reading Checks.
- **Second reading**—analyzing craft and structure and responding to the side-column prompts.
- **Third reading**—integrating knowledge and ideas, connecting to other texts and the world, and answering the end-of-selection questions.

For more guidance, refer to the ***Classroom Strategies and Teaching Routines*** card on multidraft reading.

Differentiated Instruction — Additional Instruction

EL Extended Support—English Learners

Have students complete the **Reading and Vocabulary Warm-ups, *Unit 1 Resources*,** pp. 30–33, before they read. Assign the prereading pages and the adapted selection in the ***Reader's Notebook: English Learner's Version.*** Then, have students listen to portions of the selection on the ***Hear It!* Audio CD.**

L1 L2 Extended Support—Struggling Readers

Have students complete the **Reading and Vocabulary Warm-ups, *Unit 1 Resources*,** pp. 30–33, before they read. Assign the prereading pages and the adapted selection in the ***Reader's Notebook: Adapted Version.*** Then, have students listen to portions of the selection on the ***Hear It!* Audio CD** (adapted text).

Extended Support—Reluctant Readers

To build motivation and engagement before assigning the selection, have students read "As Long As They Can Play," a thematically related selection in ***Reality Central.*** Then, use the questions at the conclusion of the related selection to guide discussion.

PHLit Online!

For more about the author, practice with the selection vocabulary, or more background, go online at **www.PHLitOnline.com.**

TEACH

❶ Activating Prior Knowledge

1. Prepare an **Anticipation Guide** (see ***Professional Development Guidebook,*** pp. 36–38) with the following statements:
   - The type of work a person does reveals his or her character.
   - Working hard is its own reward.
   - People contribute less to society as they age.
   - A person can become wealthy if he or she works hard enough.
2. Give students a copy of the prepared **Anticipation Guide** and have students mark their responses in the appropriate columns.
3. For further guidance, use the ***Classroom Strategies and Teaching Routines*** card: **Using an Anticipation Guide.**

Concept Connector

Students will return to the **Anticipation Guide** after completing "The Washwoman."

Individual Activity

The washwoman in this essay says very little. As students read, have them "listen" to her silence. What effect does this silence have on them? Have students write a sentence.

❷ About the Selection

In "The Washwoman," Singer recalls the woman who did his family's laundry when he was a child in Poland. Singer never forgets her courage and endurance.

❸ Humanities

The Oldest Inhabitant, 1876, by Julian Alden Weir

American painter Julian Alden Weir (1852–1919) was one of a family of artists and teachers. Weir studied art at the École des Beaux-Arts in Paris. Use this question for discussion:

How would you describe the painter's attitude toward his subject?
Possible response: The dignity of her pose and the soft lighting suggest that the painter respected and admired the woman.

1
2
The Washwoman

3

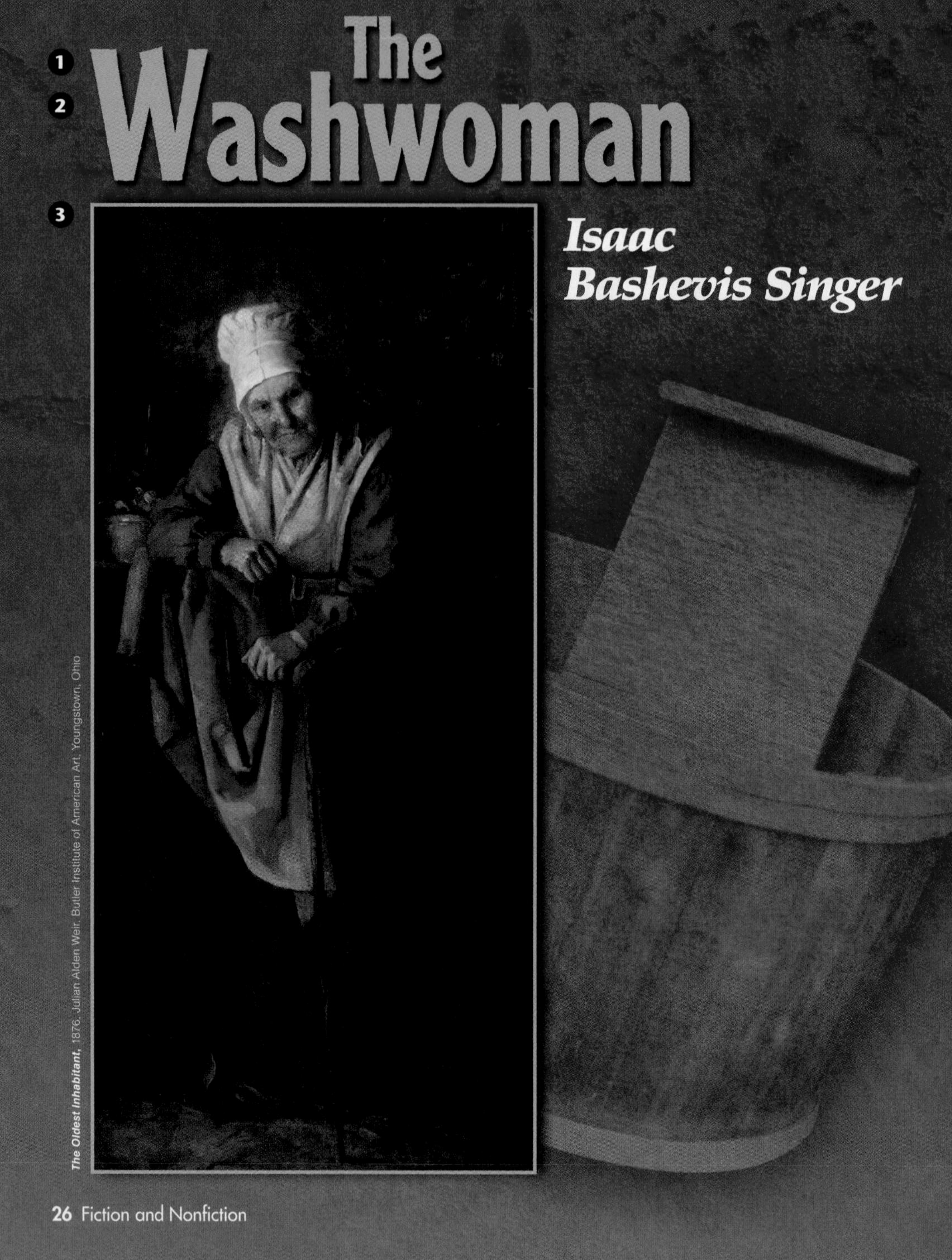

The Oldest Inhabitant, 1876, Julian Alden Weir. Butler Institute of American Art, Youngstown, Ohio

Isaac Bashevis Singer

Vocabulary Development

CCSS Language 6

Thematic Vocabulary: The Big Question

As students are discussing "The Washwoman," encourage them to use the thematic vocabulary presented in Introducing the Big Question, pp. 2–3. You might encourage them with sentence starters like these:

1. One *circumstance* that makes the washwoman's job difficult is . . .
2. When the washwoman does not return with the large load of laundry, Singer and his mother *speculate* that . . .
3. As Singer explores the *truth* about the differences between Jews and Gentiles, he suggests that . . .
4. Singer and his family *verify* that the washwoman has died when . . .

4 Our home had little contact with Gentiles.[1] The only Gentile in the building was the janitor. Fridays he would come for a tip, his "Friday money." He remained standing at the door, took off his hat, and my mother gave him six groschen.[2]

Besides the janitor there were also the Gentile washwomen who came to the house to fetch our laundry. My story is about one of these.

She was a small woman, old and wrinkled. When she started washing for us, she was already past seventy. Most Jewish women of her age were sickly, weak, broken in body. All the old women in our street had bent backs and leaned on sticks when they walked. But this washwoman, small and thin as she was, possessed a strength that came from generations of peasant **forebears**. Mother would count out to her a bundle of laundry that had **accumulated** over several weeks. She would lift the unwieldy pack, load it on her narrow shoulders, and carry it the long way home. She lived on Krochmalna Street too, but at the other end, near the Wola section. It must have been a walk of an hour and a half.

She would bring the laundry back about two weeks later. My mother had never been so pleased with any washwoman. Every piece of linen sparkled like polished silver. Every piece was neatly ironed. Yet she charged no more than the others. She was a real find. Mother always had her money ready, because it was too far for the old woman to come a second time.

Laundering was not easy in those days. The old woman had no faucet where she lived but had to bring in the water from a pump. For the linens to come out so clean, they had to be scrubbed thoroughly in a washtub, rinsed with washing soda, soaked, boiled in an enormous pot, starched, then ironed. Every piece was handled ten times or more. And the drying! It could not be done outside because thieves would steal the laundry. The wrung-out wash had to be carried up to the attic and hung on clotheslines. In the winter it would become as brittle as glass and almost break when touched. And there was always a to-do with other housewives and washwomen who wanted the attic clothesline for their own use. Only God knows all the old woman had to endure each time she did a wash!

1. **Gentiles** (jen′ tīls) *n.* any persons not Jewish; here, specifically Christians.
2. **groschen** (grō′ shən) *n.* Austrian cent or penny.

Literary Analysis
Narrative Essay
Which detail in the first paragraph helps you identify this as a narrative essay?

Vocabulary
forebears (fôr′ berz′) *n.* ancestors
accumulated (ə kyo͞om′ yo͞o lāt′ id) *v.* piled up, collected, or gathered together, especially over a period of time

▲ Iron, end of 19th century

5 
Reading Check
According to Singer, what is the washwoman's physical appearance?

4 Literary Analysis
Narrative Essay

1. Have students consider the title of the essay and the main ideas in the bracketed text. **Ask** students to identify the subject of the essay.
   Answer: The subject is the washwoman.
2. **Ask:** Why does Singer begin the story with details about the janitor?
   Answer: The details help make the point that the narrator and his family had little contact with Gentiles, so readers know that the essay is about an unusual woman. This information creates interest and sets the plot in motion.
3. Draw students' attention to the second paragraph. **Ask** them to respond to the Literary Analysis question: Which detail in this paragraph helps you identify this as a narrative essay?
   Answer: The author says that he is telling a story about a washwoman.

5 Reading Check
Answer: The washwoman is old and wrinkled, small and thin, but strong.

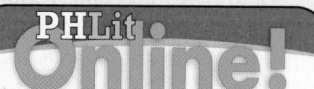

PHLit Online!

This selection is available in interactive format in the **Enriched Online Student Edition, www.PHLitOnline.com,** which includes a thematically related video with writing prompt and an interactive graphic organizer.

Fluency

Distribute copies of page 27, and pair students. Have partners take turns reading paragraphs aloud. While one partner reads, the other should mark any words with which the one reading has difficulty. Circulate to monitor the fluency of students' reading. Collect students' marked-up copies, and review difficult words and passages with the class. Look for these problem spots:

- If a student reads a particular sentence or passage laboriously or word by word, practice echo reading. Have the student track (point to each word) as you read the passage fluently and with appropriate expression. Then, have the student read the text aloud by himself or herself.
- If students have difficulty with the unfamiliar words *groschen*, *Krochmalna*, and *Wola*, tell students that these words come from a different language. Students should read the footnote for *groschen*, but they shouldn't worry about the pronunciation or meaning of *Krochmalna* or *Wola*. What matters is that *Krochmalna* is the name of a street, and *Wola* is a section of town.

Spiral Review

Central Idea

1. Remind students that they studied the concept of central idea in Unit 1 (pp. 4–21).
2. **Ask** students the first Spiral Review question.

   Answer: Despite her son's cold, disrespectful treatment of her, the washwoman speaks of him without resentment. Her love for her son is strong enough to survive his disrespect. The author's mother also dedicates her life to her children, and her love for them seems also to know no bounds. The author's mother, however, is deeply disturbed by the washwoman's son's behavior and is led to question whether any mother's sacrifices are truly appreciated.
3. Then, **ask** the second question in the Spiral Review prompt.

   Possible response: The author seems to be developing a central idea of loyalty or duty that defines a person and that transcends rewards or acknowledgment.

She could have begged at the church door or entered a home for the penniless and aged. But there was in her a certain pride and love of labor with which many Gentiles have been blessed. The old woman did not want to become a burden, and so she bore her burden. ●

My mother spoke a little Polish, and the old woman would talk with her about many things. She was especially fond of me and used to say I looked like Jesus. She repeated this every time she came, and Mother would frown and whisper to herself, her lips barely moving, "May her words be scattered in the wilderness."

Vocabulary
rancor (raŋ´ kər)
n. bitter hate

The woman had a son who was rich. I no longer remember what sort of business he had. He was ashamed of his mother, the washwoman, and never came to see her. Nor did he ever give her a groschen. The old woman told this without rancor. One day the son was married. It seemed that he had made a good match. The wedding took place in a church. The son had not invited the old mother to his wedding, but she went to the church and waited at the steps to see her son lead the "young lady" to the altar.

Spiral Review
Central Idea Compare the washwoman's reaction to her son's faithlessness with the author's description of his mother's reaction to this news. What central idea do these differing reactions suggest the author is developing?

The story of the faithless son left a deep impression on my mother. She talked about it for weeks and months. It was an affront not only to the old woman but to the entire institution of motherhood. Mother would argue, "Nu, does it pay to make sacrifices for children? The mother uses up her last strength, and he does not even know the meaning of loyalty."

And she would drop dark hints to the effect that she was not certain of her own children: Who knows what they would do some day? This, however, did not prevent her from dedicating her life to us. If there was any delicacy in the house, she would put it aside for the children and invent all sorts of excuses and reasons why she herself did not want to taste it. She knew charms that went back to ancient times, and she used expressions she had inherited from generations of devoted mothers and grandmothers. If one of the children complained of a pain, she would say, "May I be your ransom and may you outlive my bones!" Or she would say, "May I be the atonement for the least of your fingernails." When we ate she used to say, "Health and marrow in your bones!" The day before the new moon she gave us a kind of candy that was said to prevent parasitic worms. If one of us had something in his eye, Mother would lick the eye clean with her tongue. She also fed us rock candy against coughs, and from time to time she would take us to be blessed against the evil eye. This did not prevent her from studying *The Duties of the Heart, The Book of the Covenant*, and other serious philosophic works.

Vocabulary
atonement (ə tōn´ mənt)
n. act of making up for a wrongdoing or an injury

Think Aloud

Make Predictions

Draw students' attention to these sentences in the third paragraph: "The woman had a son who was rich. . . . He was ashamed of his mother, the washwoman, and never came to see her." Use the following "think aloud" to model the process of making a prediction:

When I read these sentences, I wonder why the author decided to introduce the washwoman's son. It makes me suspect that the son will have a role later in the essay. Will the son change his mind? Will he realize that his mother is a good person, as the author has described her? Or will he hurt her even more?

Now I'll recall what I know about mothers and children. I can see why a son would be ashamed of his mother, but I can't imagine why he would reject her completely. I predict that the son will show some love for his mother. I will read further to verify my prediction.

But to return to the washwoman. That winter was a harsh one. The streets were in the grip of a bitter cold. No matter how much we heated our stove, the windows were covered with frostwork and decorated with icicles. The newspapers reported that people were dying of the cold. Coal became dear. The winter had become so severe that parents stopped sending children to cheder,[3] and even the Polish schools were closed.

On one such day the washwoman, now nearly eighty years old, came to our house. A good deal of laundry had accumulated during the past weeks. Mother gave her a pot of tea to warm herself, as well as some bread. The old woman sat on a kitchen chair trembling and shaking, and warmed her hands against the teapot. Her fingers were gnarled from work, and perhaps from arthritis too. Her fingernails were strangely white. These hands spoke of the stubbornness of mankind, of the will to work not only as one's strength permits but beyond the limits of one's power. Mother counted and wrote down the list: men's undershirts, women's vests, long-legged drawers, bloomers, petticoats, shifts, featherbed covers, pillowcases, sheets, and the men's fringed garments. Yes, the Gentile woman washed these holy garments as well.

3. **cheder** (khā´ dər) religious school.

7 ▲ **Critical Viewing**
How does this picture of a neighborhood in Poland compare with how you imagine the Singers' neighborhood to look? **[Compare]**

8 
How did the winter weather affect the neighborhood?

6 Humanities

In the Jewish Quarter Kazimierz in Cracow, artist unknown

For centuries, generations of Jewish families called the Kazimierz district in Cracow, Poland, home. The community was nearly destroyed during the Holocaust, but today it has become a monument to Jewish culture and history. Use these questions for discussion:

1. What does the painting suggest about the Jewish people who lived in such neighborhoods in Poland?

   Possible responses: They were hardworking but poor. They lived close together, so they knew their neighbors well.

2. How does the depiction of laundry in the picture compare to Singer's description of it in "The Washwoman"?

   Answer: In the picture, the laundry is hung outside to dry. Singer says this could not be done in his community because the laundry would be stolen.

7 Critical Viewing

Possible response: The neighborhoods seem similar. As in the washwoman's neighborhood, the picture shows that water comes from an outside well, people live in large apartment buildings, and women carry heavy loads.

8 Reading Check

Answer: Some people died. Coal was scarce, and children stopped going to school.

Differentiated Instruction for Universal Access

Strategy for Less Proficient Readers

Display **Reading Skill Graphic Organizer B** (***Graphic Organizer Transparencies,*** p. 5), and review the process of making and verifying predictions. Fill in the first box of the organizer with the following sentences from this page: "But to return to the washwoman. That winter was a harsh one."

Guide students as they list questions that they might ask about the second sentence. For example, How will the harsh winter affect the washwoman? Will the cold weather get even worse? With students' input, choose a question for the second box of the organizer.

Next, tell students to think about what they have read and what they know about older people. Have students brainstorm for predictions and write them on sheets of paper. At the end of the selection, have students confirm or revise their predictions.

9 Literary Analysis

Character

1. Have a volunteer read aloud the bracketed passage. **Ask:** Physically, how suited is the washwoman to her burden? Which details help you know?

   Answer: The washwoman is barely able to carry the bundle; it is large enough to cover her completely, and when she first takes it on she sways as if she is about to fall. However, she is able to carry it.

2. **Ask** the Literary Analysis question.

   Possible response: The washwoman's refusal to be defeated by her heavy load comes from her sense of human dignity. This sense of dignity, and the dedication that comes from it, shows that she acts for reasons beyond mere pain or pleasure. Human beings might be called "the crown of creation" in part because of their ability to act out of "higher" motives.

10 Connecting to the Big Question

1. Have students read the bracketed text. **Ask:** What is happening with the washwoman in this passage?

   Answer: She has not returned to Singer's home with the laundry. It seems as if something terrible happened to her.

2. **Ask:** How is this situation different from what happens earlier?

   Possible response: Up until now, the washwoman always showed up.

3. **Ask:** What does this change in the washwoman's situation suggest about whether truth can change?

   Possible response: It suggests that the truth of the washwoman's strength or character might have changed. Mother's conviction that the washwoman must be ill or dead, however, suggests that the washwoman's character would never change.

Vocabulary
obstinacy (äb′ stə nə sē) *n.* stubbornness

Literary Analysis
Character What qualities does the author describe in the washwoman that show she is "a human being, the crown of creation"? Explain.

The bundle was big, bigger than usual. When the woman placed it on her shoulders, it covered her completely. At first she swayed, as though she were about to fall under the load. But an inner **obstinacy** seemed to call out: No, you may not fall. A donkey may permit himself to fall under his burden, but not a human being, the crown of creation.

It was fearful to watch the old woman staggering out with the enormous pack, out into the frost, where the snow was dry as salt and the air was filled with dusty white whirlwinds, like goblins dancing in the cold. Would the old woman ever reach Wola?

She disappeared, and Mother sighed and prayed for her. 9

Usually the woman brought back the wash after two or, at the most, three weeks. But three weeks passed, then four and five, and nothing was heard of the old woman. We remained without linens. The cold had become even more intense. The telephone wires were now as thick as ropes. The branches of the trees looked like glass. So much snow had fallen that the streets had become uneven, and sleds were able to glide down many streets as on the slopes of a hill. Kindhearted people lit fires in the streets for vagrants[4] to warm themselves and roast potatoes in, if they had any to roast.

At first she swayed, as though she were about to fall under the load.

10 For us the washwoman's absence was a catastrophe. We needed the laundry. We did not even know the woman's address. It seemed certain that she had collapsed, died. Mother declared she had had a premonition, as the old woman left our house that last time, that we would never see our things again. She found some old torn shirts and washed and mended them. We mourned, both for the laundry and for the old, toil-worn woman who had grown close to us through the years she had served us so faithfully.

More than two months passed. The frost had subsided, and then a new frost had come,

4. **vagrants** (vā′ grənts) *n.* people who wander from place to place, especially those without regular jobs.

Vocabulary Development

Vocabulary Knowledge Rating

When students have completed reading and discussing "The Washwoman," have them take out their **Vocabulary Knowledge Rating Chart** for this selection. Read the words aloud once more and have students rate their knowledge of the words again in the After Reading column. Clarify any words that are still problematic. Have students write their own definition and example or sentence in the appropriate column. Then have students complete the Vocabulary Practice activities at the end of the selection. Encourage students to use the words in further discussion and written work about this selection. Remind them that they will be accountable for these words on the **Selection Test, *Unit 1 Resources,*** pp. 42–44 or 45–47.

a new wave of cold. One evening, while Mother was sitting near the kerosene lamp mending a shirt, the door opened and a small puff of steam, followed by a gigantic bundle, entered. Under the bundle tottered the old woman, her face as white as a linen sheet. A few wisps of white hair straggled out from beneath her shawl. Mother uttered a half-choked cry. It was as though a corpse had entered
11 the room. I ran toward the old woman and helped her unload her pack. She was even thinner now, more bent. Her face had become more gaunt, and her head shook from side to side as though she were saying no. She could not utter a clear word, but mumbled something with her sunken mouth and pale lips.

After the old woman had recovered somewhat, she told us that she had been ill, very ill. Just what her illness was, I cannot remember. She had been so sick that someone had called a doctor, and the doctor had sent for a priest. Someone had informed the son, and he had contributed money for a coffin and for the funeral. But the Almighty had not yet wanted to take this pain-racked soul to Himself. She began to feel better, she became well, and as soon as she was able to stand on her feet once more, she resumed her washing. Not just ours, but the wash of several other families too.

"I could not rest easy in my bed because of the wash," the old woman explained. "The wash would not let me die."

"With the help of God you will live to be a hundred and twenty," said my mother, as a benediction.

"God forbid! What good would such a long life be? The work becomes harder and harder . . . my strength is leaving me . . . I do not want to be a burden on anyone!" The old woman muttered and crossed herself, and raised her eyes toward heaven.

Fortunately there was some money in the house and Mother counted out what she owed. I had a strange feeling: the coins in the old woman's washed-out hands seemed to become as worn and clean and pious as she herself was. She blew on the coins and tied them in a kerchief. Then she left, promising to return in a few weeks for a new load of wash.

Reading Skill
Make Predictions
Was your earlier prediction about the old woman accurate? Why or why not?

12
◄ **Critical Viewing**
What do you think it would be like to wash clothes using a washboard and tub like these? **[Speculate]**

Vocabulary
pious (pī′ əs) *adj.* having or showing religious devotion

13
Reading Check
Why does the washwoman do other people's laundry?

11 Reading Skill
Make Predictions

1. **Ask** students the Reading Skill question: Was your earlier prediction about the old woman accurate? Why or why not?

   Possible response: The prediction was not accurate; the old woman did not die.
2. Have students share their experiences with making predictions about the essay. Encourage them to tell which predictions proved accurate and which did not.
3. Discuss with students how making predictions affected their response to the narrative.

12 Critical Viewing
Possible response: This chore would be time-consuming and physically exhausting.

13 Reading Check
Possible response: She feels she cannot die until she fulfills her responsibility to do their laundry.

Concept Connector

Anticipation Guide
Have students return to their **Anticipation Guides** and respond to the statements again in the After Reading column. Then, lead a class discussion, probing for what students have learned that confirms or invalidates each statement.

Writing About the Big Question
Have students compare their responses to the sentence starter they completed before reading the essay with their ideas afterwards. Ask them to explain whether their thoughts have changed.

Reading Skill Graphic Organizer
Have students review the graphic organizers they completed to make and verify predictions while reading. Show them **Reading Skill Graphic Organizer A** (*Graphic Organizer Transparencies,* p. 3) as an example. Then, have students share the graphic organizers they did and the predictions they made about the essay.

ASSESS

Answers

Critical Thinking

Before students respond, you may wish to have them write a brief objective summary of the selection. As they answer the questions below, remind them to support their answers with evidence from the text.

1. (a) She does the laundry. (b) Singer cites the need to haul water and to compete for drying space in the attic.
2. (a) The washwoman is ill. (b) She is dedicated to her work, and it is important for her to finish what she starts.
3. (a) She is poor and has been abandoned by her son, who is ashamed of her and does not help her. She is not bitter toward him. (b) Singer says nothing about her family history or what she does in the present besides laundry. (c) Singer wanted the focus on the washwoman's working life. Including other details would not support this main idea.
4. (a) **Possible response:** At the beginning of the essay, the washwoman is old and thin but strong. She has a strong work ethic. She might be a bit lonely because her son has abandoned her, and she is eager to talk with Singer's mother in Polish. At the end, the washwoman is older and weaker. She is still determined to do her work, but she does not want to burden anyone by being unable to fulfill her responsibility. (b) **Possible response:** The washwoman's relationship with Singer's mother gets stronger, as the two speak their common language of Polish. Singer himself admires the washwoman more and more as he sees how noble and hardworking she is. Her relationship with her son also changes. When she gets sick, her son contributes money for the coffin and funeral. The truths of the washwoman's character remain the same, but her relationships—and her health—change.

But she never came back. The wash she had returned was her last effort on this earth. She had been driven by an indomitable will to return the property to its rightful owners, to fulfill the task she had undertaken.

And now at last her body, which had long been no more than a shard[5] supported only by the force of honesty and duty, had fallen. Her soul passed into those spheres where all holy souls meet, regardless of the roles they played on this earth, in whatever tongue, of whatever creed. I cannot imagine paradise without this Gentile washwoman. I cannot even conceive of a world where there is no recompense for such effort.

5. (shärd) fragment or broken piece.

Critical Thinking

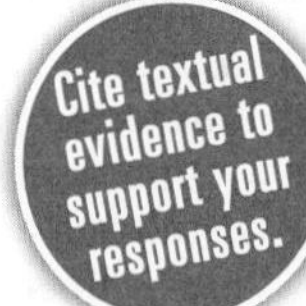
Cite textual evidence to support your responses.

1. **Key Ideas and Details** **(a)** Which job does the washwoman perform for Singer's family? **(b) Connect:** Which laborious obstacles to doing the job well does Singer describe?
2. **Key Ideas and Details** **(a)** What prevents the washwoman from returning to the family for several months? **(b) Draw Conclusions:** What does the washwoman's eventual return tell you about her character? Explain.
3. **Craft and Structure** **(a)** What specific information about the washwoman's personal life does the author include? **(b) Speculate:** What other kinds of information about the washwoman might the author have chosen to include but left out? **(c) Assess:** Based on this essay, explain why an author might choose to include some details in a text while leaving others out.
4. **Integration of Knowledge and Ideas** **(a)** How would you describe the character of the washwoman at the beginning of the story and then at the end? **(b)** How do her relationships grow? *[Connect to the Big Question: Can truth change?]*

Assessment Resources

Unit 1 Resources

L1 L2 EL **Selection Test A,** pp. 42–44. Administer Test A to less advanced readers.

L3 L4 EL **Selection Test B,** pp. 45–47. Administer Test B to on-level and more advanced students.

L3 L4 **Open-Book Test,** pp. 39–41. As an alternative, give the Open-Book Test.

All **Customizable Test Bank**

All **Self-tests**
Students may prepare for the **Selection Test** by taking the **Self-test** online.

PHLit Online! All assessment resources are available at **www.PHLitOnline.com.**

After You Read The Washwoman 

Literary Analysis: Narrative Essay

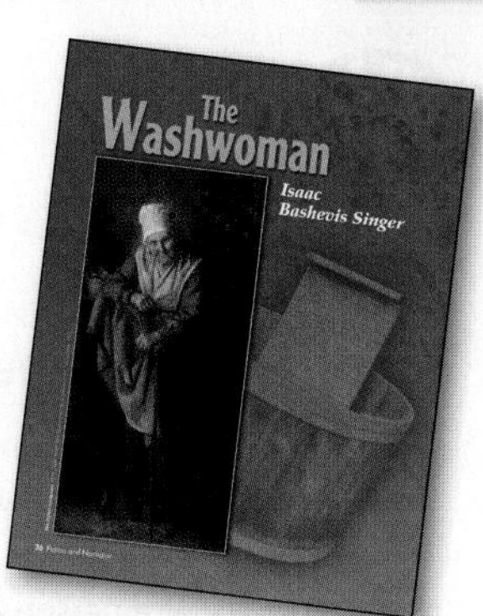

1. **Key Ideas and Details** **(a)** In this **narrative essay,** what difficulties does the washwoman face? **(b)** How does she respond to those challenges? **(c)** What inspirational lesson does the author take away from knowing the washwoman?
2. **Key Ideas and Details** **(a)** Use a chart like the one shown to record three **significant details** that Singer uses to describe the washwoman and her son. **(b)** What impression of each character does each detail create?

The Washwoman	The Washwoman's Son

Reading Skill: Make Predictions

3. Write three **predictions** that you made while reading "The Washwoman." Then, trade papers with a partner and discuss the accuracy of your predictions and the details you used to make them. Finally, explain how your method of making and verifying predictions has or has not changed as a result of your discussion.

Vocabulary

Acquisition and Use Use a word from the vocabulary list on page 24 to replace each underlined word or phrase with its opposite.

1. The former enemies have put their old friendship behind them.
2. The actor's flexibility made him difficult to direct.
3. She inherited the family trade from her children.
4. Running extra laps was his reward for being late to practice.
5. My son has given away a large pile of clothing in his room.
6. The old woman was disrespectful of her religion.

Word Study Use the context of the sentences and what you know about the **Old English prefix *fore-*** to explain your answer to each question.

1. Where does the foreword of a book appear?
2. If something is foreseen, is it a surprise?

Word Study

The **Old English prefix *fore-*** means "earlier" or "in front of."

Apply It Explain how the prefix *fore-* helps you determine the meanings of these technical academic words from science and the arts. Consult a dictionary if necessary.

forethought
foretell
foresight

ASSESS/EXTEND

Answers

Literary Analysis

1. (a) She faces poverty. She has to work under very difficult conditions to make a living. She suffers exhaustion and illness. (b) Despite the hardships of the weather and the heavy loads, she remains positive and without bitterness. She is determined to do her duty. (c) In spite of a difficult and unappreciated life, the old washwoman proves that people can endure, find satisfaction in their work, and remain positive about life.
2. (a) **Possible response: The Washwoman:** She is small, old, and wrinkled; she does her work conscientiously and charges no more than others; she is not bitter toward her son. **The Washwoman's Son:** He is wealthy; he is ashamed of his mother; he does not invite her to his wedding. (b) She is hardworking, honest, and determined; she still cares for her son. He is snobbish and self-centered.

For other sample answers, see ***Graphic Organizer Transparencies,*** **Literary Analysis Graphic Organizer A,** p. 6, and the **Additional Answers** section.

Reading Skill

3. **Possible response:** The washwoman will survive her walk home in the severe weather. The family will not see the washwoman or their laundry again. The washwoman will ask her son to help her with the last load of laundry. Students should explain how their methods of making predictions have changed as a result of their discussions.

Vocabulary

Acquisition and Use

Sample answers:

1. rancor
2. obstinacy
3. forebears
4. atonement
5. accumulated
6. pious

Word Study

Sample answers:

1. The prefix *fore-* means "earlier," and a *foreword* is an introductory passage found in the front of a book.
2. No; the prefix *fore-* means "earlier," and *foreseen* means "known in advance." If something is known in advance, it is not a surprise.

Word Study: Apply It

Sample answers:

To give *forethought* is to consider something beforehand or earlier. To *foretell* something is to predict an action earlier than it happens. Someone with *foresight* can see the future in advance or earlier.

PRETEACH

*Skills instruction for the **Reading Skill** and the **Literary Analysis** concept appears on p. 23.*

1 Writing About the Big Question

1. Review the assignment with the class.
2. Ask students to think about the meaning of the word *truth*. Is truth relative or absolute—or can it be both?
3. Have students complete the sentence starters. Review responses as a class. (**Possible response:** The truth about a person can change as a result of the specific situation a person finds him- or herself in. We see things differently as circumstances change because being in a different position makes us understand new things.)
4. Remind students that their answers will help them think about the Big Question, "Can truth change?"

While You Read

Tell students that as they read, they should look for the way Annie Johnson's situation changes.

2 Vocabulary

1. Have students preview the selection vocabulary.
2. For each word, have students say the word aloud.
3. Then, use the word in a sentence that defines the word.
4. Finally, repeat your definitional sentence or a similar sentence with the word missing, and have the class "fill in the blank" chorally. Here is an example:

   Something unpalatable is extremely distasteful. I think clams are slimy and foul-tasting, so I find them [students say "unpalatable"].

3 Word Study

1. Introduce the skill, using the instruction in the box.
2. Ask students to name a *con-* word that means "to come together." (**Answer:** *converge*)

1

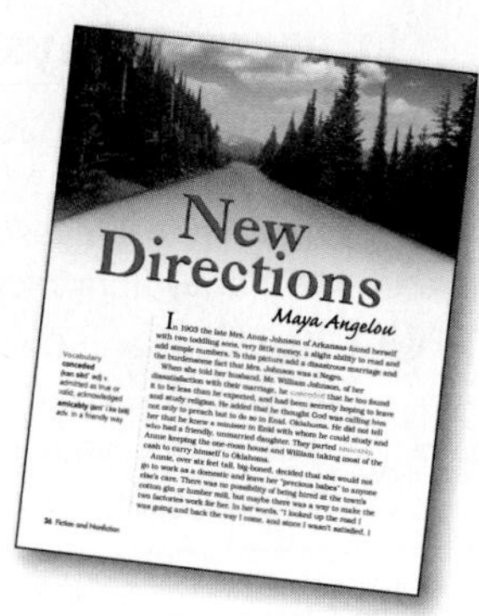

Writing About the Big Question

In "New Directions," Mrs. Annie Johnson finds herself on her own with two young children. Use these sentence starters to develop your ideas about the Big Question.

The **truth** about a person can change as a result of ________.

We see things differently as **circumstances** change because ________.

While You Read Look for the ways Annie Johnson's situation changes over time, and decide whether she really has set off in a new direction.

2 Vocabulary

Read each word and its definition. Decide whether you know the word well, know it a little bit, or do not know it at all. After you read, see how your knowledge of each word has increased.

- **conceded** (kən sēd′ əd) *v.* admitted as true or valid; acknowledged (p. 36) *Julie conceded that she had made an awful mistake.* concede *v.* concession *n.*
- **amicably** (am′ i kə blē) *adv.* in a friendly way (p. 36) *Luckily, they settled their disagreements amicably before the problem escalated into something violent.* amicable *adj.*
- **meticulously** (mə tik′ yo͞o ləs lē) *adv.* very carefully and precisely (p. 37) *She meticulously applied her makeup.* meticulous *adj.*
- **balmy** (bäm′ ē) *adj.* having the qualities of balm; soothing, mild, pleasant (p. 38) *It was a balmy spring day with sunshine and a warm breeze.* balm *n.* balminess *n.*
- **ominous** (äm′ ə nəs) *adj.* threatening (p. 38) *The sound of the thunder seemed ominous.* ominously *adv.* omen *n.*
- **unpalatable** (un pal′ it ə bəl) *adj.* distasteful; unpleasant (p. 38) *She thought changing soiled diapers was her most unpalatable chore.* palate *n.* palatable *adj.*

3 Word Study

The **Latin prefix *con-*** means "with" or "together."

If a person **concedes,** he or she yields to or gives in. In the story, Annie Johnson's husband *concedes* that their marriage is not going to work.

Vocabulary Development

Vocabulary Knowledge Rating

Create a **Vocabulary Knowledge Rating Chart** (***Professional Development Guidebook***, p. 33) for this selection. Include the selection vocabulary from this page and the forms of the Big Question words that appear in the Writing About the Big Question sentence starters on this page. (The Big Question vocabulary is introduced on pp. 2–3.)

Give students a copy of the chart. Read the words aloud, and have students mark their rating in the Before Reading column. Urge them to be alert to these words as they read the selection because they will rate their knowledge again.

Tally how many students think they know a word to gauge how much instruction to provide. As students read and discuss the selection, point out the words and their context.

Vocabulary Central, featuring tools, activities, and songs for studying vocabulary, is available at **www.PHLitOnline.com.**

Meet
Maya Angelou
(b. 1928)

Author of
New Directions

Maya Angelou's life is a story of overcoming hardships and succeeding. She was raised in rural, segregated Arkansas. In 1940, she moved to San Francisco, where she worked as a waitress, cook, and dancer. In the 1950s, Angelou went to New York, where she discovered her talents as a writer.

"I am human, and nothing human can be alien to me." Angelou wrote these words, and she lives by them. She went on to become a poet, a playwright, an editor, an actress, a director, and a teacher. Her many literary honors include a nomination for a Pulitzer Prize. She also read one of her poems at President Bill Clinton's inauguration in January 1993.

4

BACKGROUND FOR THE STORY

Limited Options

In the early 1900s, job opportunities were limited for many Americans—particularly African Americans like Annie Johnson, the main character in "New Directions." At that time, the most common jobs available for African American women were cleaning, child care, and general household labor. For women who had families, caring for someone else's household was an extra burden.

DID YOU KNOW?

Angelou's first name is Marguerite. Her brother gave her the nickname Maya when she was a child.

Daily Bellringer

For each class during which you will teach this selection, have students complete one of the five Quick Write activities for Week 1 in the *Daily Bellringer Activities* booklet.

4 Background

Limited Options In the early 1900s, African Americans in the South faced extreme prejudice and hatred. During Reconstruction, federal soldiers protected the rights of the newly freed slaves. African Americans voted and served in government. When the troops withdrew, legal maneuvering, intimidation, and other tactics stripped African Americans of their rights and opportunities. At the turn of the twentieth century, opportunities for African Americans were at a low point. Many began migrating north in the hope of finding better living and working conditions. Those who stayed behind struggled to survive. In general, only the most menial tasks were open to them.

Multidraft Reading

This icon ● marks natural pauses in the selection. To assist struggling readers and to deepen reading for all, assign the text in "chunks," following the icons, and apply multidraft reading protocols. For each reading, have students set the purpose indicated:

- **First reading**—identifying key ideas and details and answering any Reading Checks.
- **Second reading**—analyzing craft and structure and responding to the side-column prompts.
- **Third reading**—integrating knowledge and ideas, connecting to other texts and the world, and answering the end-of-selection questions.

For more guidance, refer to the *Classroom Strategies and Teaching Routines* card on multidraft reading.

Differentiated Instruction — Additional Instruction

EL Extended Support—English Learners
Have students complete the **Reading and Vocabulary Warm-ups, *Unit 1 Resources,*** pp. 48–51, before they read. Assign the prereading pages and the adapted selection in the ***Reader's Notebook: English Learner's Version.*** Then, have students listen to portions of the selection on the ***Hear It!* Audio CD.**

L1 L2 Extended Support—Struggling Readers
Have students complete the **Reading and Vocabulary Warm-ups, *Unit 1 Resources,*** pp. 48–51, before they read. Assign the prereading pages and the adapted selection in the ***Reader's Notebook: Adapted Version.*** Then, have students listen to portions of the selection on the ***Hear It!* Audio CD** (adapted text).

Extended Support—Reluctant Readers
To build motivation and engagement before assigning the selection, have students read "Riding the Waves," a thematically related selection in ***Reality Central.*** Then, use the questions at the conclusion of the related selection to guide discussion.

PHLit Online!
For more about the author, practice with the selection vocabulary, or more background, go online at **www.PHLitOnline.com.**

❶ Activating Prior Knowledge

1. Prepare an **Anticipation Guide** (see ***Professional Development Guidebook,*** pp. 36–38) with the following statements:
   - Success depends upon being in the right place at the right time.
   - If you think too much about making a change, you will lose your nerve.
   - All it takes to succeed in business is one good idea.
   - Change is best made quickly and spontaneously.
2. Give students a copy of the prepared **Anticipation Guide,** and have them fill in their responses.
3. For further guidance, use the ***Classroom Strategies and Teaching Routines*** card: **Using an Anticipation Guide.**

Concept Connector

Students will return to the **Anticipation Guide** after completing "New Directions."

Individual Activity

Angelou does not tell us what Annie Johnson is feeling and rarely uses Annie's own words. As students read the essay, invite them to put themselves in Annie's place. Have students list words and phrases that describe what Annie may be thinking and feeling at different points in the essay.

❷ About the Selection

"New Directions" is more than a biographical sketch of one woman's road from adversity to success; it is about choices. Annie Johnson is temporarily the victim of circumstances. She could give up, but she does not. Instead, she shows us that success follows those who are courageous, creative, and flexible in their decisions.

❶ ❷ New Directions

Maya Angelou

In 1903 the late Mrs. Annie Johnson of Arkansas found herself with two toddling sons, very little money, a slight ability to read and add simple numbers. To this picture add a disastrous marriage and the burdensome fact that Mrs. Johnson was a Negro.

When she told her husband, Mr. William Johnson, of her dissatisfaction with their marriage, he conceded that he too found it to be less than he expected, and had been secretly hoping to leave and study religion. He added that he thought God was calling him not only to preach but to do so in Enid, Oklahoma. He did not tell her that he knew a minister in Enid with whom he could study and who had a friendly, unmarried daughter. They parted amicably, Annie keeping the one-room house and William taking most of the cash to carry himself to Oklahoma.

Annie, over six feet tall, big-boned, decided that she would not go to work as a domestic and leave her "precious babes" to anyone else's care. There was no possibility of being hired at the town's cotton gin or lumber mill, but maybe there was a way to make the two factories work for her. In her words, "I looked up the road I was going and back the way I come, and since I wasn't satisfied, I

Vocabulary
conceded (kən sēd´ əd) *v.* admitted as true or valid; acknowledged
amicably (am´ i kə blē) *adv.* in a friendly way

Vocabulary Development

Vocabulary Knowledge Rating

When students have completed reading and discussing "New Directions," have them take out their **Vocabulary Knowledge Rating Chart** for this selection. Read the words aloud once more and have students rate their knowledge of the words again in the After Reading column. Clarify any words that are still problematic. Have students write their own definition and example or sentence in the appropriate column. Then, have students complete the Vocabulary Practice activities at the end of the selection. Encourage students to use the words in further discussion and written work about this selection. Remind them that they will be accountable for these words on the **Selection Test, *Unit 1 Resources,*** pp. 63–65 or 66–68.

decided to step off the road and cut me a new path." She told herself that she wasn't a fancy cook but that she could "mix groceries well enough to scare hungry away and from starving a man."

3 She made her plans meticulously and in secret. One early evening to see if she was ready, she placed stones in two five-gallon pails and carried them three miles to the cotton gin. She rested a little, and then, discarding some rocks, she walked in the darkness to the saw mill five miles farther along the dirt road. On her way back to her little house and her babies, she dumped the remaining rocks along the path.

That same night she worked into the early hours boiling chicken and frying ham. She made dough and filled the rolled-out pastry with meat. At last she went to sleep.

The next morning she left her house carrying the meat pies, lard, an iron brazier,[1] and coals for a fire. Just before lunch she appeared in an empty lot behind the cotton gin. As the dinner noon bell rang, she dropped the savors into boiling fat and the aroma rose and floated over to the workers who spilled out of the gin, covered with white lint, looking like specters.

4 Most workers had brought their lunches of pinto beans and biscuits or crackers, onions and cans of sardines, but they were tempted by the hot meat pies which Annie ladled out of the fat. She wrapped them in newspapers, which soaked up the grease, and offered them for sale at a nickel each. Although business was slow, those first days Annie was determined. She balanced her appearances between the two hours of activity.

1. **brazier** (brā′ zhər) *n.* A brazier is a pan or bowl that holds burning coals or charcoal as a heat source for cooking. In some braziers, food is placed on a grill directly over the flames. Johnson uses hers to heat a pot of boiling fat so that she can deep-fry her pies.

Vocabulary
meticulously (mə tik′ yo͞o ləs lē) *adv.* very carefully and precisely

Reading Skill
Make Predictions
What prediction can you make about Annie's plans? Why?

As the dinner noon bell rang, she dropped the savors into boiling fat and the aroma rose....

5
◀ **Critical Viewing**
Judging from this photograph, why do you think Annie Johnson felt that lumber workers would want to buy her pies? **[Draw Conclusions]**

3 Reading Skill
Make Predictions

Ask the Reading Skill question: What prediction do you make about Annie's plans? Why?

Possible response: Annie is going to use her cooking skills to open a food stand for the workers. I predict this because she tests the distance to the cotton gin and then cooks some food.

▶ **Monitor Progress:** As students share predictions, have them point to the phrase or phrases in the text that led them to their answer.

▶ **Reteach:** If students have difficulty supporting their predictions, have them reread the bracketed text with a partner and discuss predictions that spring from the text.

4 Connecting to the Big Question

1. Have students read the bracketed text. **Ask:** What happens in this passage?
   Answer: The workers begin to buy meat pies from Annie.
2. **Ask:** How has Annie's situation changed?
   Possible response: At the beginning of the essay she has no job, but now she works for herself.
3. **Ask:** What does Annie's new situation suggest about whether truth can change?
   Possible response: The truth about a person can change when that person decides to take a new path in life. Change may be slow, but it can happen.

5 Critical Viewing

Possible response: Because of their intense physical labor, lumber workers would get very hungry.

Concept Connector

Anticipation Guide
Have students return to their **Anticipation Guides** and respond to the statements again in the After Reading column. Then, lead a class discussion, probing for what students have learned that confirms or invalidates each statement.

Writing About the Big Question
Have students compare their responses to the sentence starter they completed before reading the essay with their ideas afterwards. Ask them to explain whether their thoughts have changed.

Reading Skill Graphic Organizer
Have students review the graphic organizers they completed to make and verify predictions while reading. Show them **Reading Skill Graphic Organizer A** (*Graphic Organizer Transparencies*, p. 6) as an example. Then, have students share the graphic organizers they did and the predictions they made about the essay.

PHLit Online!
This selection is available in interactive format in the **Enriched Online Student Edition, www.PHLitOnline.com,** which includes a thematically related video with writing prompt and an interactive graphic organizer.

Spiral Review

Central Idea

1. Remind students that they studied the concept of central idea in Unit 1 (pp. 4–21).
2. **Ask** the Spiral Review question.
Answer: The author gives the example of Annie Johnson's success and expresses her opinion that people have "the right and the responsibility" to choose their own path. These details reinforce the central idea: Solving a problem may require people to forge their own paths.

ASSESS

Answers

Critical Thinking

Remind students to support their answers with evidence from the text.

1. (a) Annie is a single mother, and her husband took most of their money when they divorced.
(b) She does not want to leave her children in someone else's care. (c) Annie is a devoted mother.
2. (a) Annie sells her homemade meat pies to the workers at the cotton gin and the lumber mill.
(b) **Possible response:** Annie is a smart businessperson; she knows how to plan ahead and how to attract customers.
3. (a) Annie builds a stall between the two factories, and eventually the stall becomes a store. (b) It suggests that people can rise above circumstances.
4. (a) **Possible response:** Annie begins the essay as a single, recently divorced mother with no source of income. By the end of the essay, she is a successful businesswoman. The truth of her life challenges the constraints of her background and gender.
(b) **Possible response:** Yes, I think taking a new direction is worth the risk of failure. I believe that being happy and being challenged are important in life. If I never take risks, I will never get a chance to do what would make me truly happy.

Vocabulary

balmy (bäm′ ē) *adj.* having the qualities of balm; soothing, mild, pleasant

ominous (äm′ ə nəs) *adj.* threatening

unpalatable (un pal′ it ə bəl) *adj.* distasteful; unpleasant

So, on Monday if she offered hot fresh pies at the cotton gin and sold the remaining cooled-down pies at the lumber mill for three cents, then on Tuesday she went first to the lumber mill presenting fresh, just-cooked pies as the lumbermen covered in sawdust emerged from the mill.

For the next few years, on balmy spring days, blistering summer noons, and cold, wet, and wintry middays, Annie never disappointed her customers, who could count on seeing the tall, brown-skin woman bent over her brazier, carefully turning the meat pies. When she felt certain that the workers had become dependent on her, she built a stall between the two hives of industry and let the men run to her for their lunchtime provisions.

She had indeed stepped from the road which seemed to have been chosen for her and cut herself a brand-new path. In years that stall became a store where customers could buy cheese, meal, syrup, cookies, candy, writing tablets, pickles, canned goods, fresh fruit, soft drinks, coal, oil, and leather soles for worn-out shoes.

Each of us has the right and the responsibility to assess the roads which lie ahead, and those over which we have traveled, and if the future road looms ominous or unpromising, and the roads back uninviting, then we need to gather our resolve and, carrying only the necessary baggage, step off that road into another direction. If the new choice is also unpalatable, without embarrassment, we must be ready to change that as well.

Spiral Review
Central Idea In this section, how does the author interweave personal examples with factual information to support the central idea?

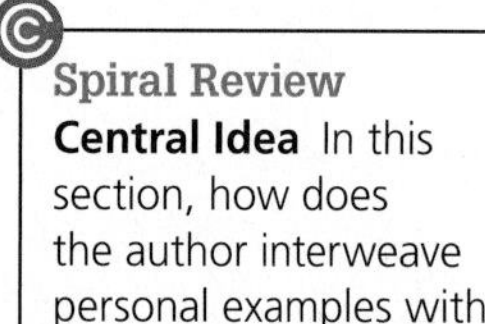
Cite textual evidence to support your responses.

Critical Thinking

1. **Key Ideas and Details** **(a)** Why does Annie Johnson have to find a source of income? **(b)** Why does she decide against a job as a domestic? **(c) Infer:** What does Annie Johnson's decision suggest about the kind of mother she is?
2. **Key Ideas and Details** **(a)** What does Annie Johnson decide to do to earn a living? **(b) Evaluate:** How would you describe Annie Johnson's abilities as a businessperson? Explain your response.
3. **Craft and Structure** **(a)** What details in the text show that Annie Johnson's business grows? **(b) Draw Conclusions:** What does her achievement suggest about the human spirit in general?
4. **Integration of Knowledge and Ideas** **(a)** How does the truth of Annie's life change? **(b)** Do you think that taking a "new direction" in life is worth the risk of failure? Explain. *[Connect to the Big Question: Can truth change?]*

Assessment Resources

Unit 1 Resources

L1 L2 EL **Selection Test A,** pp. 63–65. Administer Test A to less advanced readers.

L3 L4 EL **Selection Test B,** pp. 66–68. Administer Test B to on-level and more advanced students.

L3 L4 **Open-Book Test,** pp. 60–62. As an alternative, give the Open-Book Test.

All **Customizable Test Bank**

All **Self-tests**
Students may prepare for the **Selection Test** by taking the **Self-test** online.

PHLit Online!

All assessment resources are available at **www.PHLitOnline.com.**

After You Read | New Directions

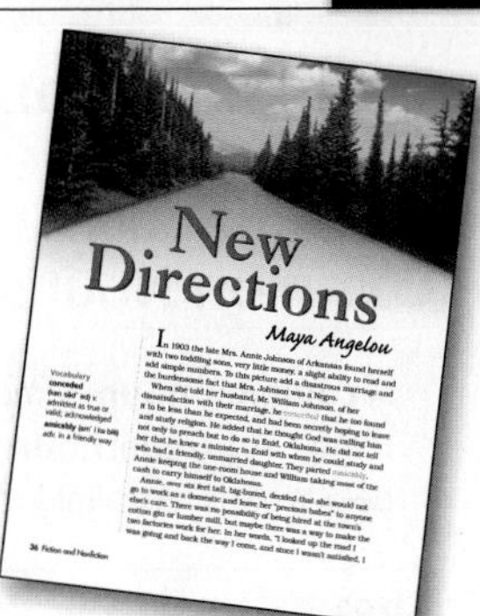

Literary Analysis: Narrative Essay

1. **Key Ideas and Details** **(a)** In this **narrative essay,** what problem sets the story in motion? **(b)** How is the problem overcome?
2. **Key Ideas and Details** **(a)** Use a chart like the one shown to record three **significant details** Angelou uses to describe Annie Johnson and her husband. **(b)** What impression of each character does each of these details create?

Annie Johnson	Annie Johnson's Husband

Reading Skill: Make Predictions

3. Write three **predictions** that you made while reading "New Directions." Then, trade papers with a partner and discuss the accuracy of your predictions and the details you used to make them. Finally, explain how your method of making and verifying predictions has or has not changed as a result of your discussion.

Vocabulary

Acquisition and Use Use a word from the vocabulary list on page 34 to replace each underlined word or phrase with its opposite.

1. When people act in a friendly manner, they behave viciously.
2. Some people think that spinach is delicious.
3. The rumble of a volcano is an encouraging sound.
4. You can avoid mistakes on tests by checking your work carelessly.
5. Ralph finally did not admit his participation in the prank.
6. A chilly wind was blowing on that summer day.

Word Study Use the context of the sentences and what you know about the **Latin prefix** ***con-*** to explain your answer to each question.

1. What does it mean if something is concentrated?
2. How does a person contend with problems?

Word Study

The **Latin prefix** ***con-*** means "with" or "together."

Apply It Explain how the prefix *con-* helps you determine the meanings of these technical academic words from science and social studies. Consult a dictionary if necessary.

convex
concentric
confederate

ASSESS/EXTEND

Answers

Literary Analysis

1. (a) Annie faces the problem of how to support herself and her children. (b) Annie overcomes the problem by starting a business selling meat pies to factory workers.
2. (a) **Possible response: Annie Johnson:** She will not leave her children; she is a good cook; she makes meticulous plans for her business. **Annie Johnson's Husband:** He wants to study religion and preach; he is interested in studying with a minister who has an unmarried daughter; he takes most of the family's money when he leaves. (b) **Possible response:** Annie is strong, skilled, intelligent, and business-savvy. Annie's husband is hypocritical, selfish, and irresponsible.

For other sample answers, see ***Graphic Organizer Transparencies,*** **Literary Analysis Graphic Organizer A, p. 7,** and the **Additional Answers** section.

Reading Skill

3. **Possible response:** She will make food and sell it to the factory workers. The factory workers will not be able to resist the smell of the fresh meat pies. Annie will build a successful business. Students should use details from their discussions to explain why their method of making predictions has or has not changed.

Vocabulary

Acquisition and Use

Sample answers:

1. amicably
2. unpalatable
3. ominous
4. meticulously
5. conceded
6. balmy

Word Study

Sample answers:

1. The prefix *con-* means "with" or "together." *Concentrated* means "clustered or gathered together."
2. The prefix *con-* means "with" or "together." To *contend* is to "deal with." A person contends with his problems by figuring out how to solve them.

Word Study: Apply It

Sample answers:

Convex comes from *convexus,* which means arched, or coming together. *Concentric* circles are circles with the same center. *Confederate* countries or people join together for a special purpose.

Conventions

Introduce the skill, using the instruction on the student page. Discuss the definitions and the examples in the chart.

Teaching the Skill

1. Use *girl, city,* and *landmark* as examples of common nouns and have students name a proper noun to take each one's place. **Possible responses:** *Carmen, San Francisco,* and *Statue of Liberty*
2. Give students example sentences in which proper nouns are used as adjectives, such as *Our Thanksgiving vacation begins on Tuesday.*

PH WRITING COACH Grade 9

Students will find further instruction on common and proper nouns in Chapter 13, Section 1.

Practice A

1. "The Washwoman" is a story by Isaac Bashevis Singer.
2. Singer's mother studied books, such as *The Duties of the Heart.*
3. The setting of the story is Poland, where Singer grew up.
4. The washwoman has a large effect on the family.

Reading Application

Sample answer: My mother [C] spoke a little Polish, [P] and the old woman [C] would talk with her about many things [C].

Practice B

Sample answers:

1. Annie started a business cooking food.
2. Her husband packed up and moved away to Oklahoma.
3. She and her two baby sons were on their own in Arkansas.
4. The lumber workers bought food from Annie.

Writing Application

Answer: Annie Johnson and her family were from Arkansas. William took most of his family's money to Oklahoma.

PERFORMANCE TASKS

Integrated Language Skills

The Washwoman • New Directions

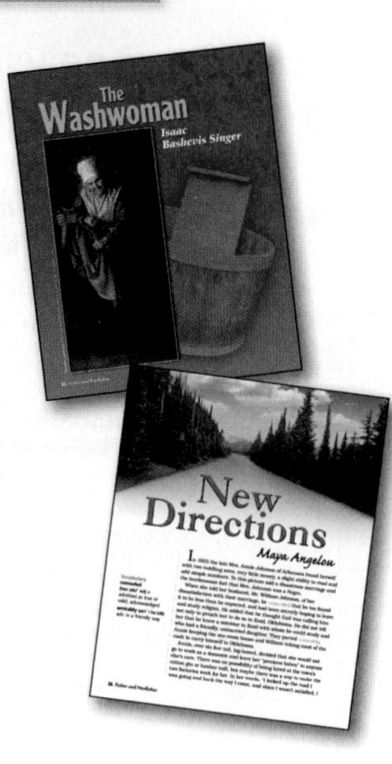

Conventions: Common Nouns and Proper Nouns

A **common noun** names any one of a class of people, places, or things. A **proper noun** names a specific person, place, or thing and begins with a capital letter.

Type	Common Noun	Proper Noun
person	student	Deana Johnson
place	city	Raleigh-Durham
thing	novel	*A Separate Peace*

Some nouns can be either common or proper, depending on how they are used. Look at these examples:

My **mom** made us brownies for dessert.
May I please have another brownie, **Mom**?

The **president** must sign a bill before it becomes a law.
The bill was signed by **President** Roosevelt.

Practice A Copy each of the following sentences. Draw one line under each common noun and two lines under each proper noun.

1. "The Washwoman" is a story by Isaac Bashevis Singer.
2. Singer's mother studied books, such as *The Duties of the Heart.*
3. The setting of the story is Poland, where Singer grew up.
4. The washwoman has a large effect on the family.

Reading Application In "The Washwoman," find one sentence with a proper noun and common noun.

Practice B Rewrite each of the sentences below, replacing one common noun with a proper noun.

1. The woman in the story started a business cooking food.
2. Her husband packed up and moved away to a new state.
3. She and her two baby sons were on their own in a new state.
4. The lumber workers bought food from her.

Writing Application Using the following sentence as a model, write two more sentences that include both common and proper nouns: *Annie hoped to name her business Johnson's Pies.*

PH WRITING COACH Further instruction and practice are available in *Prentice Hall Writing Coach.*

Extend the Lesson

Sentence Modeling

Choose the sentence given from the selection students have read:

This did not prevent her from studying *The Duties of the Heart, The Book of the Covenant,* and other serious philosophic works. ("The Washwoman")

He added that he thought God was calling him not only to preach but to do so in Enid, Oklahoma. ("New Directions")

Ask students what they notice about the sentence. Elicit from them that the sentence contains both common and proper nouns. Then, ask how the proper nouns add impact to the sentence. Guide students to recognize that the proper nouns make the sentence more specific and realistic.

Have students imitate the sentence in a sentence on a topic of their own choosing. Have students first write the sentence using proper nouns, and then rewrite it without any proper nouns. Collect the sentences and share them with the class.

Writing

Narrative Text Both selections involve strong women dealing with life's challenges. Write an **anecdote,** a brief narrative, about a person you know and respect. For example, you might describe something admirable that the person did and what you learned from it.

- Before you draft, note what you respect about the person. This is the controlling impression your anecdote will convey.
- Describe a specific event that illustrates the characteristics you admire in your subject.
- Use significant details to support the message you want to convey.

Grammar Application If you include proper nouns in your anecdote, be sure to capitalize correctly.

Writing Workshop: *Work in Progress*

Prewriting for an Autobiographical Narrative For an essay you may write later, list three or four vivid memories, describing the visual picture you see in your mind for each one. Develop the scene in your mind by adding details related to other senses. Include what you heard, smelled, and felt. Save this Memory List in your writing portfolio.

Speaking and Listening

Comprehension and Collaboration With a partner, role-play an **interview** featuring the main character in the selection you read. For example, plan an interview between the washwoman and a reporter or between Annie Johnson and a potential employer. If you need to refresh your memory, reread either selection to learn more about the character you have chosen.

Follow these steps to complete the assignment:

- In order to demonstrate your knowledge of the subject matter, generate and ask relevant questions that are open-ended and cannot be answered simply with a yes or a no.
- Listen carefully to what your partner says in the interview.
- Make notes of your partner's responses so that you can ask appropriate follow-up questions or provide answers.
- To make your delivery more effective, speak clearly (showing confidence and poise), make eye contact with your partner, and use language that demonstrates maturity, sensitivity, and respect.
- After the role play, evaluate each other's work for the quality of its techniques.
- Compile your responses and report a summary to the class.

Common Core State Standards

L.9-10.2; W.9-10.3; SL.9-10.1.a, SL.9-10.1.c
[For the full wording of the standards, see page 22.]

Use this prewriting activity to prepare for the **Writing Workshop** on page 94.

www.PHLitOnline.com
- Interactive graphic organizers
- Grammar tutorial
- Interactive journals

EXTEND/ASSESS

Writing

1. Review the assignment, using the instruction on the student page.
2. To guide students in writing an anecdote, give them **Support for Writing,** p. 58 in ***Unit 1 Resources.***
3. To evaluate students' anecdotes, use the **Descriptive Essay** rubrics, pp. 220–221 in ***Professional Development Guidebook.*** In addition, you might evaluate how well students use significant details in the structuring of their anecdotes.

Grammar Application

Have students check their drafts for correct capitalization of proper nouns.

Six Traits Focus

✓	Ideas		Word Choice
✓	Organization		Sentence Fluency
	Voice		Conventions

PH WRITING COACH Grade 9

Students will find guidance on narrative writing in Chapter 5.

Writing Workshop
Work in Progress

Have students save their completed Memory List in their portfolios. They will use the Memory List later as they continue this Work-in-Progress assignment (see p. 41). These assignments prepare them to complete the Writing Workshop assignment (see pp. 94–99).

Speaking and Listening

1. Review the assignment, using the instruction on the student page.
2. To support students' work on the assignment, have students complete the **Support for Extend Your Learning** page (***Unit 1 Resources,*** p. 59).

Teaching Resources

All *Unit 1 Resources*
L3 L4 EL **Integrated Language Skills: Grammar,** p. 57
L3 L4 EL **Support for Writing,** p. 58
L3 L4 **Support for Extend Your Learning,** p. 59
L4 **Enrichment,** pp. 38 and 56

All **Enriched Online Student Edition**
Available under After You Read for this selection:
All **Interactive Grammar Tutorial**
L3 L4 **Internet Research Activity**

Professional Development Guidebook
Rubrics for Descriptive Essay, pp. 220–221

PHLit Online! All print and digital resources are available online at **www.PHLitOnline.com**. Online resources accessible by students are noted on the student page.

✓ Sonata for Harp and Bicycle • ✓✓ The Cask of Amontillado

Lesson Pacing Guide

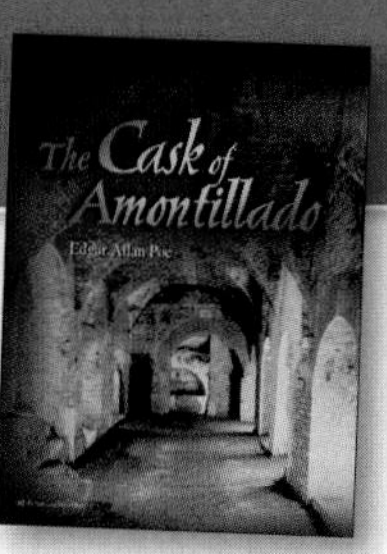

DAY 1 Preteach

- Administer the Reading and Vocabulary Warm-ups (*Unit 1 Resources,* pp. 69–72 or 87–90) as necessary.
- Introduce the Reading Skill: Make Predictions.
- Introduce the Literary Analysis concept: Plot.
- Distribute copies of the appropriate graphic organizer for the Reading Skill (*Graphic Organizer Transparencies,* pp. 9–11).
- Distribute copies of the appropriate graphic organizer for Literary Analysis (*Graphic Organizer Transparencies,* pp. 12–14).
- Teach the selection vocabulary.
- Introduce the Word Study skill.

DAYS 2–3 Preteach/Teach

- Build background with the Background feature.
- Develop thematic vocabulary and thematic thinking with Writing About the Big Question.
- Prepare students to read with the Activating Prior Knowledge activities (TE).
- Informally monitor comprehension while students read.
- Use the Reading Check questions to confirm comprehension.
- Develop students' ability to make predictions, using the Reading Skill questions.
- Develop students' understanding of plot, using the Literary Analysis questions.
- Reinforce vocabulary with the Vocabulary notes.
- Reinforce unit focus standards using the Spiral Review prompts.

DAY 4 Assess

- Assess students' comprehension and mastery of the skills by having them answer the Critical Thinking, Reading Skill, and Literary Analysis questions.
- Have students complete the Vocabulary Practice activities.
- Have students complete the Word Study activities.

DAY 5 Extend/Assess

- Have students complete the Conventions lesson.
- Have students complete the Writing activity and write a critique. (You may assign as homework.)
- Extend learning by having students complete the Speaking and Listening activity, a retelling from another point of view. As an alternative, assign them "Is Anybody Out There?" or "Whose Justice Is It?" in *Reality Central.*
- Administer Selection Test A or B (*Unit 1 Resources*, pp. 81–86 or 102–107).

Common Core State Standards

Reading Literature 2. Determine a theme or central idea of a text and analyze in detail its development over the course of the text, including how it emerges and is shaped and refined by specific details.
5. Analyze how an author's choices concerning how to structure a text, order events within it, and manipulate time create such effects as mystery, tension, or surprise.

Writing 9. Draw evidence from literary or informational texts to support analysis, reflection, and research.

Speaking and Listening 1. Initiate and participate effectively in a range of collaborative discussions with diverse partners.
1.a. Come to discussions prepared, having read and researched material under study; explicitly draw on that preparation by referring to evidence from texts and other research on the topic or issue.

Language 5. Demonstrate understanding of figurative language, word relationships, and nuances in word meanings.
6. Acquire and use accurately general academic and domain-specific words and phrases, sufficient for reading and listening at the college and career readiness level.

Additional Standards Practice
Common Core Companion,
pp. 15–22; 97–104

Daily Block Scheduling
Each day in this Lesson Pacing Guide represents a 40–50 minute period. Teachers using block scheduling may combine days to revise pacing. In addition, teachers may differentiate and support core instruction by integrating components for extended and intensive support as students require. See the Guide to Selected Leveled Resources (facing page).

Guide to Selected Leveled Resources

RTI Tier 1 (students performing on level)		✓ More Accessible Sonata for Harp and Bicycle	✓✓ More Complex The Cask of Amontillado
Warm Up	**Practice, model,** and **monitor** fluency, working **with the whole class** or **in groups.**	**Vocabulary** and **Reading Warm-ups B,** ***Unit 1 Resources,*** pp. 69–70, 72	**Vocabulary** and **Reading Warm-ups B,** ***Unit 1*** **Resources,** pp. 87–88, 90
Comprehension/Skills	**Support** and **monitor** comprehension and skills development, having students complete the activities, graphic organizers, and interactive prompts **independently** or **as a class.**	• ***Reader's Notebook,*** adapted instruction and full selection EL ***Reader's Notebook: English Learner's Version,*** adapted instruction and adapted selection • **Reading Skill Graphic Organizer B,** ***Graphic Organizer Transparencies,*** p. 11 • **Literary Analysis Graphic Organizer B,** ***Graphic Organizer Transparencies,*** p. 14	• ***Reader's Notebook,*** adapted instruction and summary EL ***Reader's Notebook: English Learner's Version,*** adapted instruction and summary • **Reading Skill Graphic Organizer B,** ***Graphic Organizer Transparencies,*** p. 11 • **Literary Analysis Graphic Organizer B,** ***Graphic Organizer Transparencies,*** p. 14
Monitor Progress	**Monitor** student progress with the differentiated curriculum-based assessment in the Unit Resources.	• **Selection Test B,** ***Unit 1 Resources,*** pp. 84–86 • **Open-Book Test,** ***Unit 1 Resources,*** pp. 78–80	• **Selection Test B,** ***Unit 1 Resources,*** pp. 105–107 • **Open-Book Test,** ***Unit 1 Resources,*** pp. 99–101
Assess/ Screen	**Assess** student progress using Benchmark Test 1.	• **Benchmark Test 1,** ***Unit 1 Resources,*** pp. 127–133	• **Benchmark Test 1,** ***Unit 1 Resources,*** pp. 127–133

RTI Tier 2 (students requiring intervention)		✓ More Accessible Sonata for Harp and Bicycle	✓✓ More Complex The Cask of Amontillado
Warm Up	**Practice, model,** and **monitor** fluency **in groups** or **with individuals.**	• **Vocabulary and Reading Warm-ups A,** ***Unit 1 Resources,*** pp. 69–71 • ***Reality Central,*** "Is Anybody Out There?" • ***Hear It!*** **Audio CD (adapted text)**	• **Vocabulary and Reading Warm-ups A,** ***Unit 1 Resources,*** pp. 87–89 • ***Reality Central,*** "Whose Justice Is It?" • ***Hear It!*** **Audio CD**
Comprehension/Skills	• **Support** and **monitor** comprehension and skills development, working **in small groups** or **with individuals.** • **Pair** students with more advanced peers and have them complete the writing activity in the *Real-World Writing Journal.* • As students complete the selection in the appropriate version of the *Reader's Notebook,* **monitor** comprehension frequently with group questions and individual instruction. • **Model** strategies while guiding students in completing the activities and prompts in the *Reader's Notebook,* as well as the graphic organizers. • **Practice** skills and **monitor** mastery with the *Reading Kit* worksheets.	• ***Real-World Writing Journal,*** Lesson 3, pp. 10–13 • ***Reader's Notebook: Adapted Version,*** adapted instruction and adapted selection EL ***Reader's Notebook: English Learner's Version,*** adapted instruction and adapted selection • **Reading Skill Graphic Organizer A,** ***Graphic Organizer Transparencies,*** p. 9 • **Literary Analysis Graphic Organizer A,** ***Graphic Organizer Transparencies,*** p. 12 • **Reading Kit,** Practice worksheets, pp. 4, 8, 12, 16, 22	• ***Real-World Writing Journal,*** Lesson 4, pp. 14–17 • ***Reader's Notebook: Adapted Version,*** adapted instruction and summary EL ***Reader's Notebook: English Learner's Version,*** adapted instruction and summary • **Reading Skill Graphic Organizer A,** ***Graphic Organizer Transparencies,*** p. 10 • **Literary Analysis Graphic Organizer A,** ***Graphic Organizer Transparencies,*** p. 13 • **Reading Kit,** Practice worksheets, pp. 4, 8, 12, 16, 22
Monitor Progress	**Monitor** student progress with the differentiated curriculum-based assessment in the *Unit Resources* and in the *Reading Kit.*	• **Selection Test A,** ***Unit 1 Resources,*** pp. 81–83 • **Reading Kit,** Assess worksheets, pp. 5, 9, 13, 17, 23	• **Selection Test A,** ***Unit 1 Resources,*** pp. 102–104 • **Reading Kit,** Assess worksheets, pp. 5, 9, 13, 17, 23
Assess/ Screen	**Assess** student progress using Benchmark Test 1.	• **Benchmark Test 1,** ***Unit 1 Resources,*** pp. 127–133	• **Benchmark Test 1,** ***Unit 1 Resources,*** pp. 127–133

TIER 3 Tier 3 intervention may require consultation with the student's special-education or dyslexia specialist. For additional support, see the Tier 2 activities and resources listed above.

One-on-one teaching **Group work** **Whole class instruction** **Independent work** **A Assessment**

For a complete guide to selection support, including support for Advanced students, see the Overview of Resources in the frontmatter.

Visual Guide to Featured Selection Resources

✓Sonata for Harp and Bicycle
✓✓The Cask of Amontillado

RESOURCES FOR:

- L1 Special-Needs Students
- L2 Below-Level Students (Tier 2)
- L3 On-Level Students (Tier 1)
- L4 Advanced Students (Tier 1)
- EL English Learners
- All All Students

Vocabulary/Fluency/Prior Knowledge

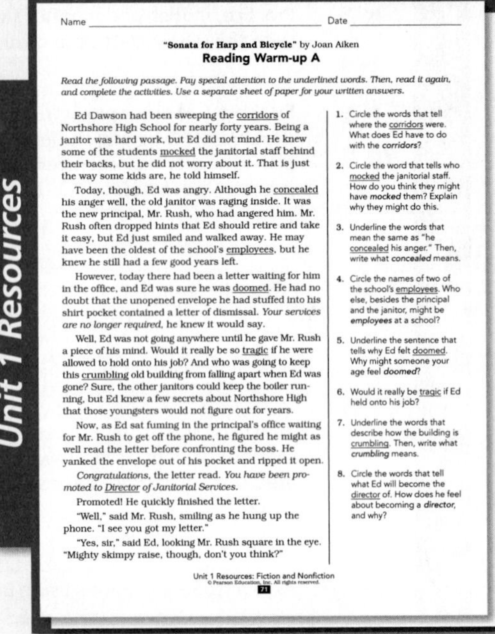

Unit 1 Resources

Name ____________________ Date ____________

"Sonata for Harp and Bicycle" by Joan Aiken

Reading Warm-up A

Read the following passage. Pay special attention to the underlined words. Then, read it again, and complete the activities. Use a separate sheet of paper for your written answers.

Ed Dawson had been sweeping the corridors of Northshore High School for nearly forty years. Being a janitor was hard work, but Ed did not mind. He knew some of the students mocked the janitorial staff behind their backs, but he did not worry about it. That is just the way some kids are, he told himself.

Today, though, Ed was angry. Although he concealed his anger well, the old janitor was raging inside. It was the new principal, Mr. Rush, who had angered him. Mr. Rush often dropped hints that Ed should retire and take it easy, but Ed just smiled and walked away. He may have been the oldest of the school's employees, but he knew he still had a few good years left.

However, today there had been a letter waiting for him in the office, and Ed was sure he was doomed. He had no doubt that the unopened envelope he had stuffed into his shirt pocket contained a letter of dismissal. *Your services are no longer required,* he knew it would say.

Well, Ed was not going anywhere until he gave Mr. Rush a piece of his mind. Would it really be so tragic if he were allowed to hold onto his job? And who was going to keep this crumbling old building from falling apart when Ed was gone? Sure, the other janitors could keep the boiler running, but Ed knew a few secrets about Northshore High that those youngsters would not figure out for years.

Now, as Ed sat fuming in the principal's office waiting for Mr. Rush to get off the phone, he figured he might as well read the letter before confronting the boss. He yanked the envelope out of his pocket and ripped it open.

Congratulations, the letter read. *You have been promoted to Director of Janitorial Services.*

Promoted! He quickly finished the letter.

"Well," said Mr. Rush, smiling as he hung up the phone. "I see you got my letter."

"Yes, sir," said Ed, looking Mr. Rush square in the eye. "Mighty skimpy raise, though, don't you think?"

1. Circle the words that tell where the corridors were. What does Ed have to do with the *corridors*?
2. Circle the word that tells who mocked the janitorial staff. How do you think they might have *mocked* them? Explain why they might do this.
3. Underline the words that mean the same as "he concealed his anger." Then, write what *concealed* means.
4. Circle the names of two of the school's employees. Who else, besides the principal and the janitor, might be *employees* at a school?
5. Underline the sentence that tells why Ed felt doomed. Why might someone your age feel *doomed*?
6. Would it really be tragic if Ed held onto his job?
7. Underline the words that describe how the building is crumbling. Then, write what *crumbling* means.
8. Circle the words that tell what Ed will become the director of. How does he feel about becoming a *director*, and why?

Unit 1 Resources: Fiction and Nonfiction

71

EL L1 L2 **Reading Warm-ups A and B,** pp. 71–72, 89–90

Also available for these selections:

EL L1 L2 **Vocabulary Warm-ups A and B,** pp. 69–70, 87–88

All **Writing About the Big Question,** pp. 73, 91

All **Vocabulary Builder,** pp. 76, 94

Reader's Notebooks

Pre- and postreading pages for both selections, as well as "Sonata for Harp and Bicycle," appear in an interactive format in the *Reader's Notebooks.* Each *Notebook* is differentiated for a different group of learners. The selections in the Adapted and English Learner's versions are abridged.

L2 L3 ***Reader's Notebook***

L1 ***Reader's Notebook: Adapted Version***

EL ***Reader's Notebook: English Learner's Version***

EL ***Reader's Notebook: Spanish Version***

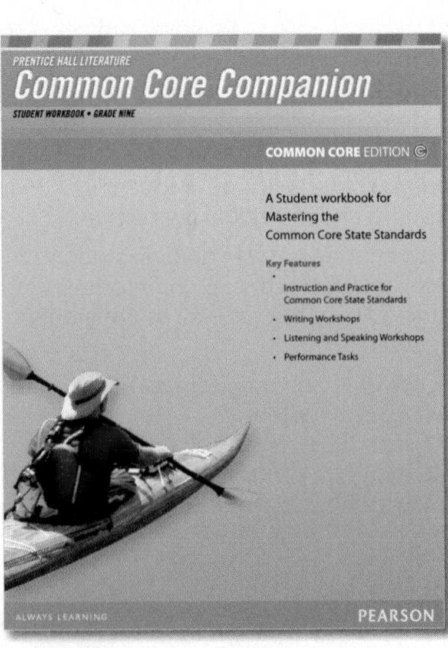

Common Core Companion

Additional instruction and practice for each Common Core State Standard

Selection Support

Graphic Organizer Transparencies

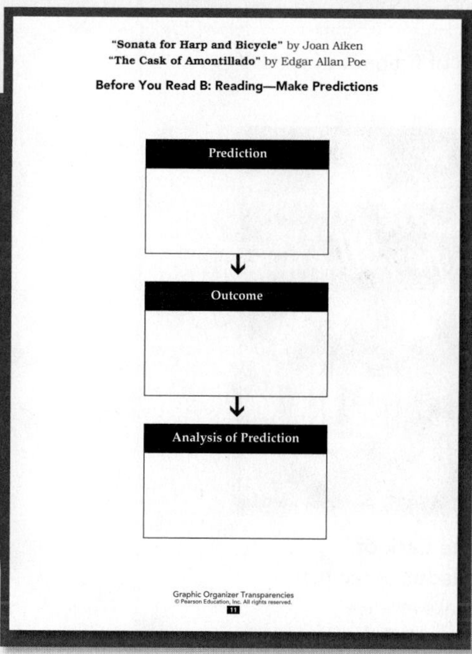
"Sonata for Harp and Bicycle" by Joan Aiken
"The Cask of Amontillado" by Edgar Allan Poe

Before You Read B: Reading—Make Predictions

Prediction

Outcome

Analysis of Prediction

Graphic Organizer Transparencies
© Pearson Education, Inc. All rights reserved.
11

EL L3 **Reading: Graphic Organizer B,** p. 11

Also available for these selections:

EL L1 L2 **Reading: Graphic Organizer A,** pp. 9, 10 (partially filled in)

EL L1 L2 **Literary Analysis: Graphic Organizer A,** pp. 12, 13 (partially filled in)

EL L3 **Literary Analysis: Graphic Organizer B,** p. 14

Skills Development/Extension

Unit 1 Resources

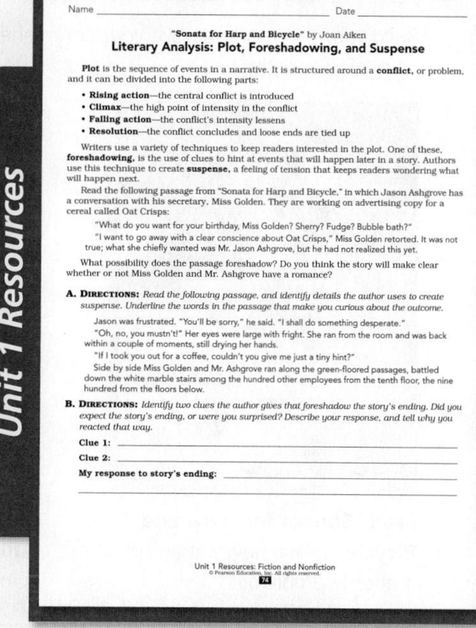
Name ______________________ Date ______________

"Sonata for Harp and Bicycle" by Joan Aiken

Literary Analysis: Plot, Foreshadowing, and Suspense

Plot is the sequence of events in a narrative. It is structured around a **conflict**, or problem, and it can be divided into the following parts:

- **Rising action**—the central conflict is introduced
- **Climax**—the high point of intensity in the conflict
- **Falling action**—the conflict's intensity lessens
- **Resolution**—the conflict concludes and loose ends are tied up

Writers use a variety of techniques to keep readers interested in the plot. One of these, **foreshadowing**, is the use of clues to hint at events that will happen later in a story. Authors use this technique to create **suspense**, a feeling of tension that keeps readers wondering what will happen next.

Read the following passage from "Sonata for Harp and Bicycle," in which Jason Ashgrove has a conversation with his secretary, Miss Golden. They are working on advertising copy for a cereal called Oat Crisps:

"What do you want for your birthday, Miss Golden? Sherry? Fudge? Bubble bath?"

"I want to go away with a clear conscience about Oat Crisps," Miss Golden retorted. It was not true; what she chiefly wanted was Mr. Jason Ashgrove, but he had not realized this yet.

What possibility does the passage foreshadow? Do you think the story will make clear whether or not Miss Golden and Mr. Ashgrove have a romance?

A. Directions: *Read the following passage, and identify details the author uses to create suspense. Underline the words in the passage that make you curious about the outcome.*

Jason was frustrated. "You'll be sorry," he said. "I shall do something desperate."

"Oh, no, you mustn't!" Her eyes were large with fright. She ran from the room and was back within a couple of moments, still drying her hands.

"If I took you out for a coffee, couldn't you give me just a tiny hint?"

Side by side Miss Golden and Mr. Ashgrove ran along the green-floored passages, battled down the white marble stairs among the hundred other employees from the tenth floor, the nine hundred from the floors below.

B. Directions: *Identify two clues the author gives that foreshadow the story's ending. Did you expect the story's ending, or were you surprised? Describe your response, and tell why you reacted that way.*

Clue 1: ______________________

Clue 2: ______________________

My response to story's ending: ______________________

Unit 1 Resources: Fiction and Nonfiction
© Pearson Education, Inc. All rights reserved.
74

All **Literary Analysis: Plot,** pp. 74, 92

Also available for these selections:

All **Reading: Make Predictions,** pp. 75, 93

L4 **Enrichment,** pp. 77, 95

EL L3 L4 **Grammar,** p. 96

EL L3 L4 **Support for Writing,** p. 97

L3 L4 **Support for Extend Your Learning,** p. 98

Assessment

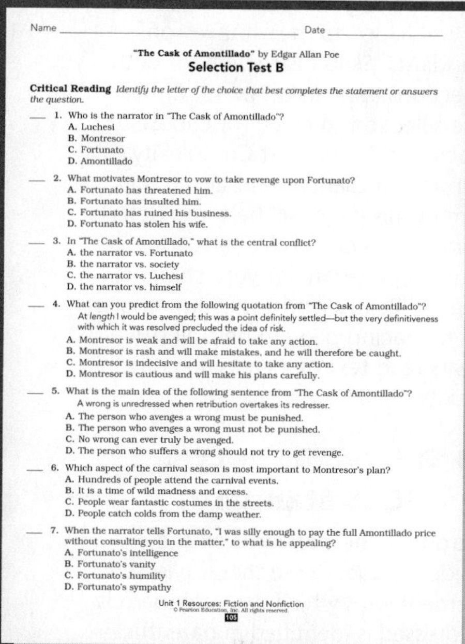
Name ______________________ Date ______________

"The Cask of Amontillado" by Edgar Allan Poe

Selection Test B

Critical Reading *Identify the letter of the choice that best completes the statement or answers the question.*

___ 1. Who is the narrator in "The Cask of Amontillado"?
A. Luchesi
B. Montresor
C. Fortunato
D. Amontillado

___ 2. What motivates Montresor to vow to take revenge upon Fortunato?
A. Fortunato has threatened him.
B. Fortunato has insulted him.
C. Fortunato has ruined his business.
D. Fortunato has stolen his wife.

___ 3. In "The Cask of Amontillado," what is the central conflict?
A. the narrator vs. Fortunato
B. the narrator vs. society
C. the narrator vs. Luchesi
D. the narrator vs. himself

___ 4. What can you predict from the following quotation from "The Cask of Amontillado"?
At *length* I would be avenged; this was a point definitely settled—but the very definitiveness with which it was resolved precluded the idea of risk.
A. Montresor is weak and will be afraid to take any action.
B. Montresor is rash and will make mistakes, and he will therefore be caught.
C. Montresor is indecisive and will hesitate to take any action.
D. Montresor is cautious and will make his plans carefully.

___ 5. What is the main idea of the following sentence from "The Cask of Amontillado"?
A wrong is unredressed when retribution overtakes its redresser.
A. The person who avenges a wrong must be punished.
B. The person who avenges a wrong must not be punished.
C. No wrong can ever truly be avenged.
D. The person who suffers a wrong should not try to get revenge.

___ 6. Which aspect of the carnival season is most important to Montresor's plan?
A. Hundreds of people attend the carnival events.
B. It is a time of wild madness and excess.
C. People wear fantastic costumes in the streets.
D. People catch colds from the damp weather.

___ 7. When the narrator tells Fortunato, "I was silly enough to pay the full Amontillado price without consulting you in the matter," to what is he appealing?
A. Fortunato's intelligence
B. Fortunato's vanity
C. Fortunato's humility
D. Fortunato's sympathy

Unit 1 Resources: Fiction and Nonfiction
© Pearson Education, Inc. All rights reserved.
105

EL L3 L4 **Selection Test B,** pp. 84–86, 105–107

Also available for these selections:

L3 L4 **Open-Book Test,** pp. 78–80, 99–101

EL L1 L2 **Selection Test A,** pp. 81–83, 102–104

PHLit Online!
www.PHLitOnline.com

Online Resources: All print materials are also available online.

- complete narrated selection text
- a thematically related video with writing prompt
- an interactive graphic organizer
- highlighting feature
- access to all student print resources, adapted to individual student needs
- Spanish and English summaries
- adapted selection translations in Spanish

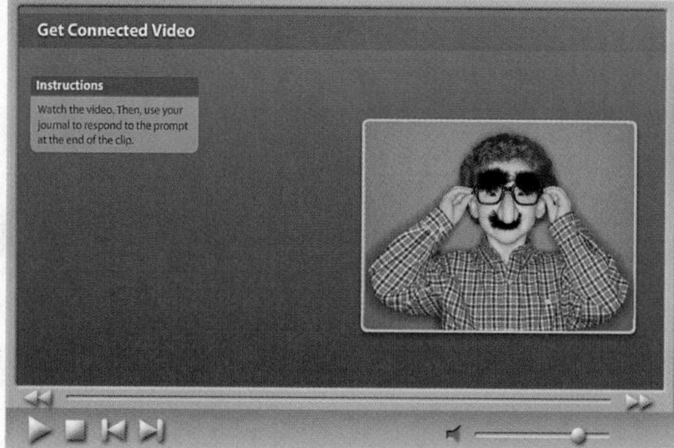

Get Connected! (thematic video with writing prompt)

Also available:

Background Video

All videos are available in Spanish.

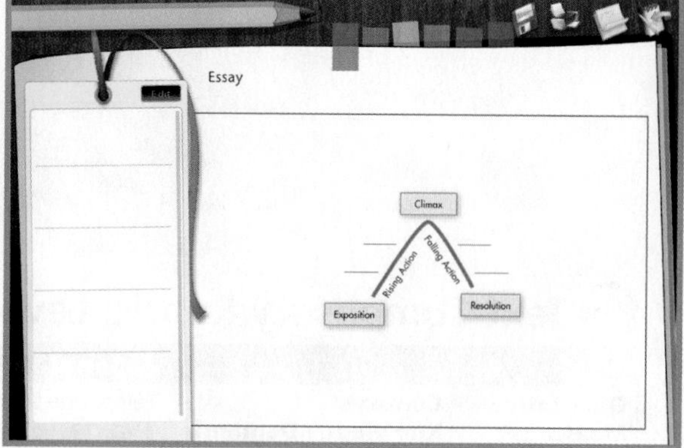

Writer's Journal (with graphics feature)

Also available:

Vocabulary Central (tools, activities, and songs for studying vocabulary)

❶ Leveled Texts

You may use either "Sonata for Harp and Bicycle" or "The Cask of Amontillado" to meet the lesson standards. Skills instruction for both selections appears on p. 43. Choose one selection to teach (or choose to teach both). The Text Complexity Rubric at a Glance chart at the bottom of this page will help you determine which of the two selections is more appropriate for your students. Use the Reader and Task Suggestions on the facing page to help all students read text of increasing complexity.

❷ Introducing the CCS Standards

Introduce the standards on the student page. (Note that the lesson element with which each standard is addressed is identified in parentheses after the text of the standard.) Call out the standards that you will cover with the selections, explaining to students what each requires and how they will address it as they work through the selection you have chosen. Standards labeled "Spiral Review" are introduced in the Literary Analysis Workshop for this unit.

Before You Read

Sonata for Harp and Bicycle • The Cask of Amontillado

❶ Leveled Texts

Build your skills and improve your comprehension of fiction with texts of increasing complexity.

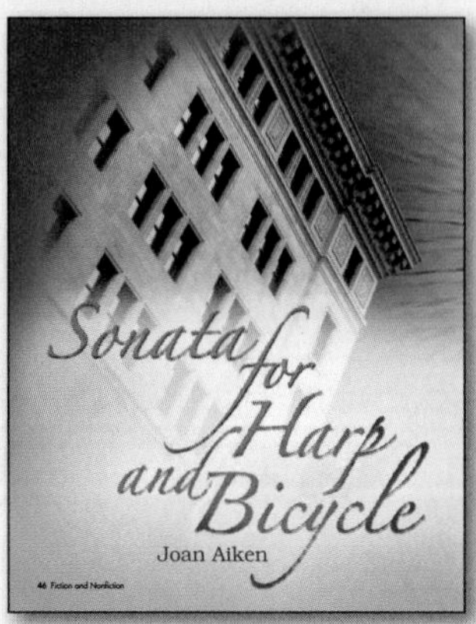

Read **"Sonata for Harp and Bicycle"** to see how a man solves a ghostly problem.

Read **"The Cask of Amontillado"** to see how a man seeks revenge.

❷ Common Core State Standards

Meet these standards with either **"Sonata for Harp and Bicycle"** (p. 46) or **"The Cask of Amontillado"** (p. 60).

Reading Literature
5. Analyze how an author's choices concerning how to structure a text, order events within it, and manipulate time create such effects as mystery, tension, or surprise. *(Literary Analysis: Plot)*

Spiral Review: RL.9-10.2

Writing
9. Draw evidence from literary or informational texts to support analysis, reflection, and research. *(Writing: Critique)*

Speaking and Listening
1. Initiate and participate effectively in a range of collaborative discussions with diverse partners, building on others' ideas and expressing their own clearly and persuasively. **1.a.** Come to discussions prepared, having read and researched material under study; explicitly draw on that preparation by referring to evidence from texts and other research on the topic or issue to stimulate a thoughtful, well-reasoned exchange of ideas. *(Speaking and Listening: Retell a Story)*

Language
5. Demonstrate understanding of figurative language, word relationships, and nuances in word meanings. *(Vocabulary: Analogy)*
6. Acquire and use accurately general academic and domain-specific words and phrases, sufficient for reading and listening at the college and career readiness level; demonstrate independence in gathering vocabulary knowledge when considering a word or phrase important to comprehension or expression. *(Vocabulary: Word Study)*

Text Complexity Rubric: Leveled Texts

Text complexity is determined by both qualitative and quantitative measures. For this reason, the quantitative measure of a more complex selection may be lower than that of a more accessible selection.

		✓ Sonata for Harp and Bicycle	✓✓ The Cask of Amontillado
Qualitative Measures	**Context/ Knowledge Demands**	Telephone switchboard; electric typewriter 1 2 ③ 4 5	Gothic; eighteenth-century Italy; catacombs 1 2 ③ 4 5
	Structure/Language Conventionality and Clarity	On-level vocabulary; conversational dialogue 1 2 ③ 4 5	Numerous long sentences; difficult diction 1 2 3 ④ 5
	Levels of Meaning/ Purpose/Concept Level	Accessible concept (character's determination to solve a mystery and win love) 1 2 ③ 4 5	Challenging concept (ghastly quest for revenge) 1 2 3 ④ 5
Quantitative Measures	**Text Length**	Word Count: 3,141	Word Count: 1,976
	Lexile	960L	800L
Overall Complexity		✓ **More accessible**	✓✓ **More complex**

❸ Literary Analysis: Plot

Plot is the sequence of events in a narrative. It is structured around a **conflict,** or problem, and it can be divided into the following parts:

- **Exposition:** characters and setting are introduced
- **Rising Action:** central conflict begins
- **Climax:** high point of intensity in the conflict is reached
- **Falling Action:** conflict's intensity lessens
- **Resolution:** conflict concludes and loose ends are tied up

Writers use a variety of techniques, or *stylistic devices,* to keep readers interested in the plot. One of these devices, **foreshadowing,** is the use of clues to hint at events that will happen later in a story. Authors use this technique to create **suspense,** a feeling of tension that keeps readers wondering what will happen next.

❹ Reading Skill: Make Predictions

A **prediction** is an idea you develop about what will happen later in a narrative. It is based on details in the text combined with your own experience. As you read, notice details that may foreshadow future events. Next, make predictions based on those details, and then **read ahead to verify your predictions.** If a prediction turns out to be wrong, evaluate your reasoning by asking questions like these:

- Did you misread details?
- Did the author purposely create false expectations in order to surprise you later in the story?

Revise, or change, your prediction based on your evaluation.

❺ Using the Strategy: Predictions Map

Use a chart like the one shown to record and evaluate your predictions. Analyze any inaccurate predictions to determine why they were incorrect.

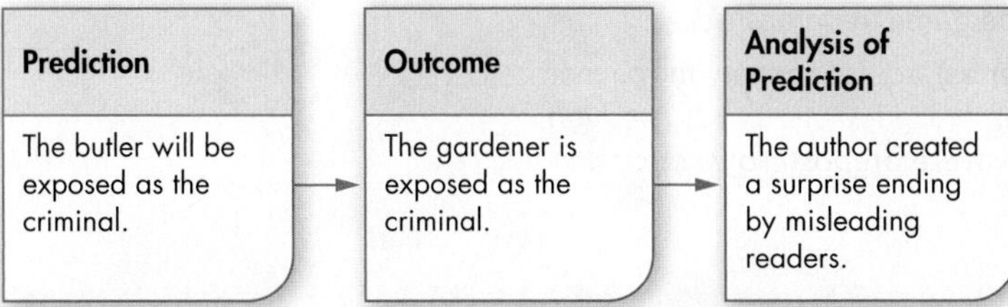

Prediction	Outcome	Analysis of Prediction
The butler will be exposed as the criminal.	The gardener is exposed as the criminal.	The author created a surprise ending by misleading readers.

PHLit Online!
www.PHLitOnline.com

Hear It!
- Selection summary audio
- Selection audio

See It!
- Get Connected video
- Background video
- More about the author
- Vocabulary flashcards

Do It!
- Interactive journals
- Interactive graphic organizers
- Self-test
- Internet activity
- Grammar tutorial
- Interactive vocabulary games

PRETEACH

❸ Literary Analysis

Plot

1. Introduce the skill, using instruction on the student page.
2. Tell students that they will identify plot elements as they read.

Think Aloud: Model the Skill

Model the skill of identifying plot elements. Say to students:

> Imagine I'm reading a story about a mountain climber. His preparations for the big climb make up the exposition. At this point, a minor slip at home might foreshadow a major stumble on the mountain.
>
> As he climbs, the terrain becomes difficult and the weather worsens—this is the rising action. In the climax, he has a mishap near the top and nearly dies, but somehow reaches the summit. In the falling action and resolution, the climber makes it down safely and reflects on how the experience has changed his life.

❹ Reading Skill

Make Predictions

1. Introduce the skill, using instruction on the student page.
2. Tell students that they will make predictions as they read.

❺ Using the Strategy

Give students a copy of either **Reading Skill Organizer A** or **B** (***Graphic Organizer Transparencies,*** pp. 9–11) to record their predictions as they read. Use the examples in **Reading Skill Graphic Organizer A,** which is partially filled in, to model the process of completing the organizer.

Ⓒ Text Complexity: Reader and Task Suggestions

✓ Sonata for Harp and Bicycle		✓✓ The Cask of Amontillado	
Preparing to Read the Text	**Leveled Tasks**	**Preparing to Read the Text**	**Leveled Tasks**
• Review strategies for understanding the meaning of unfamiliar words. Refer to Vocabulary: Using Context on TE p. 48. • Discuss ways in which an author develops characters and creates drama. • Guide students to use Multidraft Reading strategies (TE p. 45).	*Levels of Meaning* If students will have difficulty with meaning, have students read the story and identify details about Jason's actions. Then, have them reread and take notes on how the setting affects his actions. *Synthesizing* If students will not have difficulty with meaning, have them note as they read examples showing how Aiken uses language to develop the characters and to create drama. Discuss as a class.	• Refer to the Background note on TE p. 59 and discuss the catacombs and the historical setting. • Discuss the concept of revenge. Ask students how the desire for revenge affects people's thoughts and actions. • Guide students to use Multidraft Reading strategies (TE p. 59).	*Levels of Meaning* If students will have difficulty with meaning, have them read to identify details of Montresor's plot for vengeance. Then, have them reread and note his reasons for wanting revenge. *Analyzing* If students will not have difficulty with levels of meaning, have them note as they read ways in which the setting helps create mystery and a feeling of dread. Discuss students' conclusions with the class.

PRETEACH

❶ Writing About the Big Question

1. Review the assignment with the class.
2. Have students provide examples of times when evidence has changed their views of a situation, such as when they unexpectedly liked—or didn't like—a movie after seeing it.
3. Have students complete the sentence starters. Review responses as a class. (**Possible responses:** You can change your own fate by making careful choices. Evidence can change our beliefs because it may contradict those beliefs.)
4. Remind students that their answers will help them think about the Big Question, "Can truth change?"

While You Read

Tell students that as they read, they should look for ways the main character takes charge of his life.

❷ Vocabulary

1. Have students preview the selection vocabulary.
2. For each word, have students say the word aloud.
3. Then, use the word in a sentence that defines the word.
4. Finally, repeat your definitional sentence or a similar sentence with the word missing and have the class "fill in the blank" chorally. Here are some examples:

   Something that is furtive is sneaky or secretive. As the man climbed in through a broken window, he looked over his shoulder with an expression that was sneaky, or [students say "furtive"].

   To reciprocate means to give in return. Carla gave me a beautiful gift for my birthday, so when I take her to lunch I will [students say "reciprocate"].

❸ Word Study

1. Introduce the skill, using the instruction in the box.
2. Have students think of an *-ate* word that means "to go faster and faster." (*accelerate*)

Making Connections | Sonata for Harp and Bicycle

THE BIG ? Can truth change?

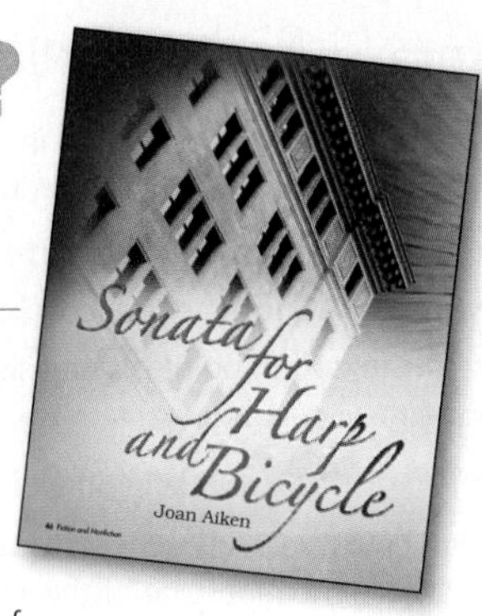

❶ Writing About the Big Question

In "**Sonata for Harp and Bicycle,**" miscommunication leads to tragedy and a curse on a building. Use these sentence starters to develop your ideas about the Big Question:

You can change your own fate by ________________.

Evidence can change our **beliefs** because ________________.

While You Read Look for the ways the main character takes charge of his life to change the truth of his situation.

❷ Vocabulary

Read each word and its definition. Decide whether you know the word well, know it a little bit, or do not know it at all. After you have read the selection, see how your knowledge of each word has increased.

- **encroaching** (en krōch′ iŋ) *adj.* intruding (p. 47) *The encroaching weeds are taking over the lawn.* encroach *v.* encroachment *n.*
- **tantalizingly** (tan′ tə līz′ iŋ lē) *adv.* in a teasing way (p. 48) *He held the ball tantalizingly out of reach.* tantalize *v.* tantalizing *adj.*
- **furtive** (fur′ tiv) *adj.* sneaky; hidden (p. 50) *With a furtive wink, he let his best friends in on the joke.* furtively *adv.*
- **menacing** (men′ əs iŋ) *adj.* threatening (p. 51) *The menacing cat stalked the little bird.* menace *v.* menace *n.*
- **reciprocate** (ri sip′ rə kāt′) *v.* return (p. 52) *Because Julio invited Mary to the party, she decided to reciprocate the offer by asking him to the game.* reciprocal *adj.*
- **preposterous** (prē päs′ tər əs) *adj.* so contrary to common sense as to be laughable; absurd; ridiculous (p. 53) *The high ticket prices for the show were preposterous.* preposterously *adv.*

❸ Word Study

The **suffix** ***-ate*** means "to become or form," and it often indicates the word is a verb.

In this story, the main character **reciprocates** the love of his admirer, forming a reciprocal, or shared, relationship.

Vocabulary Development

Vocabulary Knowledge Rating

Create a **Vocabulary Knowledge Rating Chart** (*Professional Development Guidebook,* p. 33) for this selection. Include the selection vocabulary from this page and the forms of the Writing About the Big Question words that appear in the Writing About the Big Question sentence starter on this page. (The Big Question vocabulary is introduced on pp. 2–3.)

Give students a copy of the chart. Read the words aloud, and have students mark their rating in the Before Reading column. Urge them to be alert to these words as they read and discuss the selection.

Tally how many students think they know a word to gauge how much instruction to provide. As students read and discuss the selection, point out the words and their context.

Vocabulary Central, featuring tools, activities, and songs for studying vocabulary, is available online at **www.PHLitOnline.com.**

Meet Joan Aiken (1924–2004)

Author of *Sonata for Harp and Bicycle*

The daughter of an American poet, Conrad Aiken, and a Canadian mother, Jessie MacDonald, Joan Aiken was born in England and grew up there. She lived with her family in an eerie old house, an experience that helped foster her fascination with mystery and the unexplained. Her mother's second husband was another writer, Martin Armstrong. Not surprisingly, Aiken knew when she was very young that she would become a writer someday.

The "Family Trade" Aiken began writing when she was five and published her first story at sixteen. After spending some time working in London for a magazine, an advertising agency, and the United Nations, she decided to pursue what she called "the family trade." Her many literary works include novels, poems, plays, and stories for both children and adults.

Did You Know?

Aiken did not attend a school until she was twelve. Before then, she was taught at home.

4 BACKGROUND FOR THE STORY

Sonata

A sonata (sə nät′ ə) is a musical composition in several movements, or parts. Sonatas are often written for solo piano or for piano and another instrument. In titling her story "Sonata for Harp and Bicycle," Joan Aiken playfully suggests a musical structure that will, like a sequence of chords, be resolved harmoniously at the end.

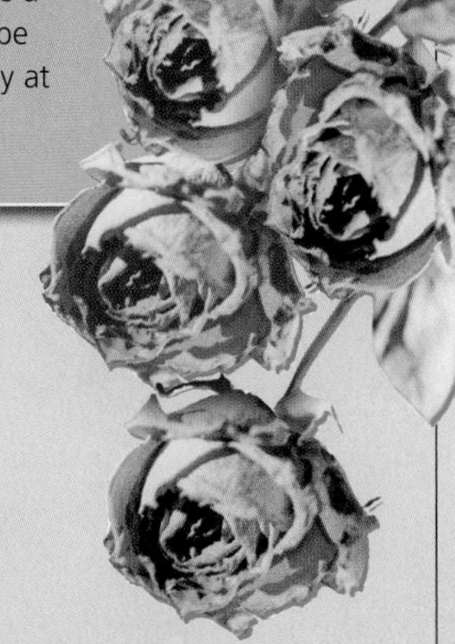

Daily Bellringer

For each class during which you will teach this selection, have students complete one of the five Sentence Modeling activities for Week 2 in the ***Daily Bellringer Activities*** booklet.

4 Background

Sonatas The musical structure of a sonata can be compared to a story's plot structure. It begins with an *exposition* (conflict introduced), which introduces a main and a secondary theme. Next comes the *development* (rising action), which freely plays with and spins out the two themes of the exposition until it reaches a climax. The next stage is the *recapitulation* (falling action), which repeats the exposition, often varying it somewhat. The sonata ends with the *coda* (resolution), which is a kind of comment on or summary of the previous stages. The coda is often much shorter than the other three sections.

Multidraft Reading

This icon marks natural pauses in the selection. To assist struggling readers and to deepen reading for all, assign the text in "chunks," following the icons, and apply multidraft reading protocols. For each reading, have students set the purpose indicated:

- **First reading**—identifying key ideas and details and answering any Reading Checks.
- **Second reading**—analyzing craft and structure and responding to the side-column prompts.
- **Third reading**—integrating knowledge and ideas, connecting to other texts and the world, and answering the end-of-selection questions.

For more guidance, refer to the ***Classroom Strategies and Teaching Routines*** card on multidraft reading.

Differentiated Instruction — Additional Instruction

EL Extended Support—English Learners
Have students complete the **Reading and Vocabulary Warm-ups, *Unit 1 Resources,*** pp. 69–72, before they read. Assign the prereading pages and the adapted selection in the ***Reader's Notebook: English Learner's Version.*** Then, have students listen to portions of the selection on the ***Hear It!* Audio CD.**

L1 L2 Extended Support—Struggling Readers
Have students complete the **Reading and Vocabulary Warm-ups, *Unit 1 Resources,*** pp. 69–72, before they read. Assign the prereading pages and the adapted selection in the ***Reader's Notebook: Adapted Version.*** Then, have students listen to portions of the selection on the ***Hear It!* Audio CD** (adapted text).

Extended Support—Reluctant Readers
To build motivation and engagement before assigning the selection, have students read "Is Anybody Out There?" a thematically related selection in ***Reality Central.*** Then, use the questions at the conclusion of the related selection to guide discussion.

PHLit Online!
For more about the author, practice with the selection vocabulary, or more background, go online at **www.PHLitOnline.com.**

❶ Activating Prior Knowledge

Tell students that Aiken's story is about an advertising copywriter who goes to work at a company that seems very ordinary, except for one thing: All employees are hurried out of the building each evening at five o'clock. The reason for this policy is a secret that employees do not learn until they have been with the company a long time. The copywriter is intrigued by this odd situation and sets out to unravel the mystery. Challenge students to predict what the secret might be.

Concept Connector

Students will return to this discussion after reading the selection.

Small-Group Activity

Share the background information on sonatas on p. 45 of this Teacher's Edition. Have students work in small groups to see whether this story is in any sense written in sonata form. You might start them off by pointing out that the story is in three long sections followed by a final short paragraph. Have them compare this structure to a sonata's exposition, development, recapitulation, and coda. Remind students that *theme* is both a musical and a literary term. Have groups take notes on their observations.

❷ About the Selection

"Sonata for Harp and Bicycle" combines the elements of mystery, romance, and the supernatural—with a wink at Greek mythology included. A hero challenges the absurd rules of his office and the fears of his co-workers by entering the office building after dark—a forbidden act. He uses his problem-solving skills to rid the building of two ghosts and to ensure a triumph for love. Students will enjoy the skill with which Aiken uses visual and musical imagery to build suspense, as well as the touches of humor that lighten this modern-day ghost story.

❶ ❷

Sonata for Harp and Bicycle

Joan Aiken

Vocabulary Development

Ⓒ CCSS Language 6

Thematic Vocabulary: The Big Question

As students are discussing "Sonata for Harp and Bicycle," encourage them to use the thematic vocabulary presented in Introducing the Big Question, pp. 2–3. You might encourage them with sentence starters like these:

1. Jason tries to *convince* Berenice Golden to reveal . . .
2. Many parts of the story are not *credible* because . . .
3. When Jason goes into the Grimes Buildings for the second time, he plans to *manipulate* . . .
4. *Skeptics* might predict that Heron will . . .

"No one is allowed to remain in the building after five o'clock," Mr. Manaby told his new assistant, showing him into the little room that was like the inside of a parcel.

"Why not?"

"Directorial policy," said Mr. Manaby. But that was not the real reason.

❸ Gaunt and sooty, Grimes Buildings lurched up the side of a hill toward Clerkenwell.[1] Every little office within its dim and crumbling exterior owned one tiny crumb of light—such was the proud boast of the architect—but toward evening the crumbs were collected as by an immense vacuum cleaner, absorbed and demolished, yielding to an uncontrollable mass of dark that came tumbling in through windows and doors to take their place. Darkness infested the building like a flight of bats returning willingly to roost.

"Wash hands, please. Wash hands, please," the intercom began to bawl in the passages at a quarter to five. Without much need of prompting, the staff hustled like lemmings along the corridors to green- and blue-tiled washrooms that mocked with an illusion of cheerfulness the encroaching dusk.

"All papers into cases, please," the voice warned, five minutes later. "Look at your desks, ladies and gentlemen. Any documents left lying about? Kindly put them away. Desks must be left clear and tidy. Drawers must be shut."

A multitudinous shuffling, a rustling as of innumerable bluebottle flies might have been heard by the attentive

1. **Clerkenwell** district of London.

Vocabulary
encroaching
(en krōch′ iŋ) *adj.*
intruding

❹ 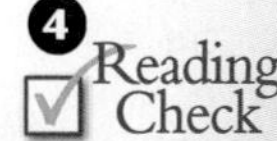

What is the new assistant told about being in the building after five o'clock?

❸ Critical Thinking

Infer

1. Have students reread the bracketed text. **Ask** them to summarize what has happened.

   Answer: Night brings darkness to an office building. The employees wash their hands, clean off their desks, and leave the building in response to orders from a voice on an intercom.

2. **Ask** students how the employees respond to the directions.

   Answer: They follow them without hesitation.

3. Challenge students to make inferences about the policy and practice of emptying the building.

   Possible response: This is a long-standing practice. Existing employees are familiar with it, and the orders come from a powerful source, so nobody asks questions.

4. **Ask** students how the contrast between the existing employees' responses and the new assistant's response contributes to the mood of Aiken's story.

   Possible response: The contrast creates a sense of mystery because nobody seems to know the answer to the new assistant's question, yet there must be a reason for the policy. It also creates a sense of fright because the employees might be scared of the building's director.

❹ Reading Check

Answer: The new assistant is told that no one is allowed to remain in the building after five o'clock.

PHLit Online!

This selection is available in interactive format in the **Enriched Online Student Edition, www.PHLitOnline.com,** which includes a thematically related video with writing prompt and an interactive graphic organizer.

Differentiated Instruction for Universal Access

Support for Special-Needs Students

Lead a quick tour of the selection, pointing out the title and eliciting students' associations with the illustrations. Then, remind students of the elements of plot. Give them a copy of the partially completed **Literary Analysis Graphic Organizer A** (*Graphic Organizer Transparencies,* p. 12) and model how to record information in it. Urge students to track the story's plot as they read for added understanding.

Strategy for Advanced Readers

Point out Aiken's blend of mystery, horror, and humor. For example, the order to empty the building by five o'clock is mysterious. The darkness of the building evokes horror. Humor appears in the reference to the staff as "lemmings." Ask students to analyze this mix of elements and evaluate whether Aiken combines them effectively throughout the story.

5 Literary Analysis

Plot

1. Remind students that the conflict is the central problem in a story. Then, have students reread the bracketed text.
2. **Ask** students to respond to the Literary Analysis question: What problem is introduced in Jason's conversation with Miss Golden?

   Answer: Jason wants to find out why no one is allowed in the building after five o'clock, but no one will tell him.
3. Call students' attention to the description of Miss Golden's "terrified" eyes when she tells Jason to "Hush!" **Ask** students how these lines foreshadow events to come.

   Answer: They suggest that the answer to Jason's question is frightening.
4. Discuss how the foreshadowing builds suspense. Remind students that the suspense will continue to build until the climax is reached.

Spiral Review

Theme

1. Remind students that they studied the concept of theme in the Unit 1 Literary Analysis Workshop (pp. 4–21).
2. **Ask** students the first Spiral Review question.

   Answer: Details that hint at the secret love between the characters are the tantalizing way Miss Golden answers Jason; the narrator's description of her lips, hair, lashes and eyes; Jason's question about what she wants for her birthday; and the narrator's comment that what Miss Golden really wants is Jason, although he doesn't know it yet.
3. **Ask** students the second Spiral Review question.

   Possible response: These details suggest the theme that love is a force that cannot be ignored.

Literary Analysis
Plot What problem is introduced in Jason's conversation with Miss Golden? 5

Vocabulary
tantalizingly (tan′ tə līz′ iŋ lē) *adv.* in a teasing way

Spiral Review
Theme Which details hint that Jason and Miss Golden are secretly in love? What theme, or insight into people, is suggested by these details? 6

ear after this injunction, as the employees of Moreton Wold and Company thrust their papers into cases, hurried letters and invoices into drawers, clipped statistical abstracts together and slammed them into filing cabinets, dropped discarded copy into wastepaper baskets. Two minutes later, and not a desk throughout Grimes Buildings bore more than its customary coating of dust.

"Hats and coats on, please. Hats and coats on, please. Did you bring an umbrella? Have you left any shopping on the floor?" At three minutes to five the homegoing throng was in the lifts[2] and on the stairs; a clattering, staccato-voiced flood darkened momentarily the great double doors of the building, and then as the first faint notes of St. Paul's[3] came echoing faintly on the frosty air, to be picked up near at hand by the louder chimes of St. Biddulph's-on-the-Wall, the entire premises of Moreton Wold stood empty.

"But why is it?" Jason Ashgrove, the new copywriter, asked his secretary one day. "Why are the staff herded out so fast? Not that I'm against it, mind you; I think it's an admirable idea in many ways, but there is the liberty of the individual to be considered, don't you think?"

"Hush!" Miss Golden, the secretary, gazed at him with large and terrified eyes. "You mustn't ask that sort of question. When you are taken onto the Established Staff you'll be told. Not before."

"But I want to know now," Jason said in discontent. "Do you know?"

"Yes, I do," Miss Golden answered tantalizingly. "Come on, or we shan't have finished the Oat Crisp layout by a quarter to." And she stared firmly down at the copy in front of her, lips folded, candyfloss hair falling over her face, lashes hiding eyes like peridots,[4] a girl with a secret.

Jason was annoyed. He rapped out a couple of rude and witty rhymes which Miss Golden let pass in a withering silence.

"What do you want for your birthday, Miss Golden? Sherry? Fudge? Bubble bath?"

"I want to go away with a clear conscience about Oat Crisps," Miss Golden retorted. It was not true; what she chiefly wanted was Mr. Jason Ashgrove, but he had not realized this yet.

"Come on, don't tease! I'm sure you haven't been on the Established Staff all that long," he coaxed her. "What happens when one is taken on, anyway? Does the Managing Director have us up for a confidential chat? Or are we given a little book called *The Awful Secret of Grimes Buildings?*"

2. **lifts** *n.* British term for elevators.
3. **St. Paul's** famous church in London.
4. **peridots** (per′ i däts′) *n.* yellowish-green gems.

Think Aloud

Vocabulary: Using Context

Direct students' attention to the word *conscience* near the bottom of page 48. Using a think-aloud process, model how to use context to infer the meaning of an unknown word. Say to students:

> I'm going to think aloud to show you how I would figure out the meaning of *conscience* based on its context.
>
> In this sentence, Miss Golden says she wants to leave work with a clear (pure) conscience. Jason has been trying to distract Miss Golden from their work by offering her luxurious birthday gifts. In Miss Golden's short "retort," I get the feeling she wants to focus on work because she feels guilty about flirting with Jason. This suggests that *conscience* has something to do with what you are feeling about yourself. It tells you that your actions are either wrong or right. Miss Golden wants to leave work with a clear mind.

Miss Golden wasn't telling. She opened her drawer and took out a white towel and a cake of rosy soap.

"Wash hands, please! Wash hands, please!"

Jason was frustrated. "You'll be sorry," he said. "I shall do
6 something desperate."

"Oh no, you mustn't!" Her eyes were large with fright. She ran from the room and was back within a couple of moments, still drying her hands.

"If I took you out for a coffee, couldn't you give me just a tiny hint?"

Side by side Miss Golden and Mr. Ashgrove ran along the green-floored passages, battled down the white marble stairs among the hundred other employees from the tenth floor, the nine hundred from the floors below.

He saw her lips move as she said something, but in the clatter of two thousand feet the words were lost.

"—fire escape," he heard, as they came into the momentary hush of the carpeted entrance hall. And "—it's to do with a bicycle. A bicycle and a harp."

"I don't understand."

Now they were in the street, chilly with the winter dusk smells of celery on carts, of swept-up leaves heaped in faraway parks, and cold layers of dew sinking among the withered evening primroses in the bombed areas. London lay about them wreathed in twilit mystery and fading against the barred and smoky sky. Like a ninth wave the sound of traffic overtook and swallowed them.

"Please tell me!"

But, shaking her head, she stepped onto a scarlet homebound bus and was borne away from him.

Jason stood undecided on the pavement, with the crowds dividing around him as around the pier of a bridge. He scratched his head, looked about him for guidance.

An ambulance clanged, a taxi hooted, a drill stuttered, a siren wailed on the river, a door slammed, a brake squealed, and close beside his ear a bicycle bell tinkled its tiny warning.

A bicycle, she had said. A bicycle and a harp.

Jason turned and stared at Grimes Buildings.

8 Somewhere, he knew, there was a back way in, a service entrance. He walked slowly past the main doors, with their tubs of

Reading Skill
Make Predictions
Which text clue leads you to predict that a romance will develop between Jason and Miss Golden? Explain.

7 **Reading Check**
What question does Jason Ashgrove want Miss Golden to answer?

6 Reading Skill

Make Predictions

1. Have students reread the bracketed text.
2. **Ask** students the Reading Skill question: Which text clue leads you to predict that a romance will develop between Jason and Miss Golden? Explain.

   Answer: One text clue is that Miss Golden "chiefly wanted" Jason, although Jason doesn't know it yet. The *yet* suggests that something more will develop between them. Another text clue is that when Jason says he "shall do something desperate," Miss Golden says, "Oh no, you mustn't!" with eyes "large with fright." Miss Golden's words suggest that she cares about Jason. Then, Jason asks Miss Golden out for coffee, which suggests that he is interested in seeing her outside of work.
3. Point out how these text clues both foreshadow events and invite readers to make predictions.
4. Allow students time to write their predictions in **Reading Skill Graphic Organizer B** (*Graphic Organizer Transparencies,* p. 11). Remind students to verify and revise their predictions as they read.

7 Reading Check

Answer: Jason wants to know why the staff is forced to leave the building so abruptly.

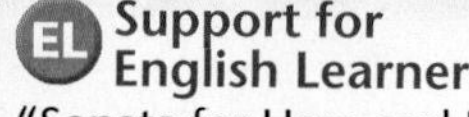

Differentiated Instruction for Universal Access

EL Support for English Learners

"Sonata for Harp and Bicycle" is a gripping story to hear as well as to read. You may want to play the ***Hear It!* Audio CD** for students. Play the CD to the point when Jason is about to enter Grimes Buildings after hours. (This is the conclusion of the first movement of the sonata.) After students have listened to the passage, replay a portion of it and have students read along. Encourage them to duplicate the intonations and pacing of the reader. Coach them in the technique of giving a dramatic reading.

Continue with the CD as students progress through the selection. Allow them to practice their oral reading skills by giving them more opportunities to read with the CD.

8 Literary Analysis
Plot

1. Have students summarize the action in the bracketed text, which begins on page 49.
2. **Ask** students the Literary Analysis question: How do Jason's actions increase the suspense of the narrative?

   Answer: His actions increase the suspense because readers know something mysterious is going on in the building. At every footstep, they expect something terrifying to happen to Jason.
3. **Ask** students how they can tell these events are still part of the rising action.

   Answer: The tension and excitement keep increasing; the climax has not occurred yet.

9 Critical Viewing

Possible response: A bicycle would make it faster to patrol the corridors. In addition, a bicycle would enable a guard to catch a criminal more quickly.

Vocabulary
furtive (fur´ tiv) *adj.* sneaky; hidden

Literary Analysis
Plot
How do Jason's actions increase the suspense of the narrative?

▼ Critical Viewing
What advantages would patrolling corridors on a bicycle offer as opposed to patrolling on foot? **[Evaluate]**

snowy chrysanthemums, and up Glass Street. A tiny **furtive** wedge of darkness beckoned him, a snicket, a hacket, an alley carved into the thickness of the building. It was so narrow that at any moment, it seemed, the overtopping walls would come together and squeeze it out of existence.

Walking as softly as an Indian, Jason passed through it, slid by a file of dustbins,[5] and found the foot of the fire escape. Iron treads rose into the mist, like an illustration to a Gothic[6] fairy tale.

He began to climb.

When he had mounted to the ninth story he paused for breath. It was a lonely place. The lighting consisted of a dim bulb at the foot of every flight. A well of gloom sank beneath him. The cold fingers of the wind nagged and fluttered at the tails of his jacket, and he pulled the string of the fire door and edged inside.

Grimes Buildings were triangular, with the street forming the base of the triangle, and the fire escape the point. Jason could
see two long passages coming toward him, meeting at an acute 8
angle where he stood. He started down the left-hand one, tiptoeing in the cavelike silence. Nowhere was there any sound, except for the faraway drip of a tap. No night watchman would stay in the building; none was needed. Burglars gave the place a wide berth.

Jason opened a door at random; then another. Offices lay everywhere about him, empty and forbidding. Some held lipstick-stained tissues, spilled powder, and orange peels; others were still foggy with cigarette smoke. Here was a Director's suite of rooms—a desk like half an acre of frozen lake, inch-thick carpet, roses, and the smell of cigars. Here was a conference room with scattered squares of doodled blotting paper. All equally empty.

He was not sure when he first began to notice the bell. Telephone, he thought
at first, and then he 10
remembered that all the outside lines were disconnected at five. And

5. **dustbins** *n.* British term for garbage cans.
6. **Gothic** *adj.* mysterious.

Vocabulary Development
Ⓒ CCSS Language 6

Expressive Vocabulary
To help students broaden their expressive vocabulary, encourage them to use the following words as they discuss the selection: *anticipate, comprehend, confirm, eliminate,* and *expose.* Have them complete these sentence starters:

1. Jason is able to *anticipate* . . .
2. Jason cannot *comprehend* . . .
3. Jason asks Miss Golden to *confirm* . . .
4. Jason wants to *eliminate* . . .
5. Jason hopes to *expose* . . .

this bell, anyway, had not the regularity of a telephone's double ring: there was a tinkle, and then silence; a long ring, and then silence; a whole volley of rings together, and then silence.

Jason stood listening, and fear knocked against his ribs and shortened his breath. He knew that he must move or be paralyzed by it. He ran up a flight of stairs and found himself with two more

10 endless green corridors beckoning him like a pair of dividers.

Another sound now: a waft of ice-thin notes, riffling up an arpeggio[7] like a flurry of snowflakes. Far away down the passage it echoed. Jason ran in pursuit, but as he ran the music receded. He circled the building, but it always outdistanced him, and when he came back to the stairs he heard it fading away to the story below.

Literary Analysis
Plot
What earlier details foreshadowed this mysterious ringing?

He hesitated, and as he did so heard again the bell; the bicycle bell. It was approaching him fast, bearing down on him, urgent, menacing. He could hear the pedals, almost see the shimmer of an invisible wheel. Absurdly, he was reminded of the insistent clamor of an ice-cream vendor, summoning children on a sultry Sunday afternoon.

Vocabulary
menacing (men´ əs iŋ) *adj.* threatening

There was a little fireman's alcove beside him, with buckets and pumps. He hurled himself into it. The bell stopped beside him, and then there was a moment while his heart tried to shake itself loose in his chest. He was looking into two eyes carved out of expressionless air; he was held by two hands knotted together out of the width of dark.

He hesitated, and as he did so heard again the bell; the bicycle bell.

"Daisy, Daisy?" came the whisper. "Is that you, Daisy? Have you come to give me your answer?"

Jason tried to speak, but no words came.

"It's not Daisy! Who are you?" The sibilants[8] were full of threat. "You can't stay here. This is private property."

He was thrust along the corridor. It was like being pushed by a whirlwind—the fire door opened ahead of him without a touch, and he was on the openwork platform, clutching the slender railing. Still the hands would not let him go.

"How about it?" the whisper mocked him. "How about jumping? It's an easy death compared with some."

Jason looked down into the smoky void. The darkness nodded to him like a familiar.[9]

"You wouldn't be much loss, would you? What have you got to live for?"

11 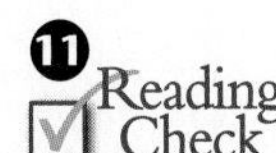
Reading Check
What makes the ringing sound that Jason hears inside the Grimes Buildings?

---

7. **arpeggio** (är pej´ ō) *n.* notes of a chord played one after the other instead of together.
8. **sibilants** (sib´ əl əntz) *n.* hissing sounds.
9. **a familiar** *n.* a spirit.

10 Literary Analysis
Plot

1. Have students read the bracketed text, which begins on page 50. **Ask** them to describe Jason's feelings at this point in the story.

   Possible response: Jason is becoming more and more frightened. He does not understand what is happening.

2. **Ask** students to respond to the Literary Analysis question: What earlier details foreshadowed this mysterious ringing?

   Answer: First, Miss Golden says that the mystery involves a bicycle. Then, while Jason stands on the sidewalk after Miss Golden leaves, a bicycle bell tinkles nearby, giving Jason a "tiny warning."

3. **Ask** students how the ringing bell contributes to the plot.

   Answer: The bell signals a new complication. The ringing is a new mystery for Jason—and the reader—to investigate.

11 Reading Check

Answer: A bicycle bell makes the ringing sound.

Differentiated Instruction for Universal Access

Culturally Responsive Instruction

Culture Focus Point out the ringing that Jason hears, and note the clues at the top of page 51 that help him identify the sound as a bicycle bell. Then, highlight the memory that the sound recalls for Jason: He is reminded of an ice-cream vendor's bell on a hot summer afternoon. Explain that sounds call to mind common experiences of a culture. Someone with a cultural background different from Jason's might not relate this particular sound to a childhood memory about ice-cream vendors. Ask students to describe sounds that they associate with hot summer days, with transportation, or with bicycles. Have them explain the roles of these sounds in their home culture or their family's country of origin.

12 Connecting to the Big Question

1. Stress with students that sometimes we need courage to take our own path when other people are urging us to follow theirs. One person's truth might be different from another person's. Invite students to think of ways they have struggled to take charge of their own lives.
2. Have students reread the first bracketed text on page 52.

   Ask: What does Jason do to take charge of his life?

   Answer: He remembers Miss Golden and refuses to jump to his death. He escapes from the hands and runs from the building.
3. **Ask:** What is the truth for Jason in this moment? How does finding that truth affect the outcome of the story?

   Possible response: Jason's truth is that Miss Golden would miss him, and he cares about her so much that he doesn't want her to experience loss. Miss Golden makes life worth living. Recognizing this gives Jason the courage to take charge and save his own life.

13 Critical Viewing

Possible response: It would make a soft, clear, rippling sound.

Miss Golden, Jason thought. She would miss me. And the syllables Berenice Golden lingered in the air like a chime. Drawing on some unknown deposit of courage he shook himself loose from the holding hands and ran down the fire escape without looking back.

Next morning when Miss Golden, crisp, fragrant, and punctual, shut the door of Room 492 behind her, she stopped short of the hat-pegs with a horrified gasp.

"Mr. Ashgrove, your hair!"

"It makes me look more distinguished, don't you think?" he said.

It had indeed this effect, for his impeccable dark cut had turned to a stippled silver which might have been envied by many a diplomat.

"How did it happen? You've not—" her voice sank to a whisper—*"you've not been in Grimes Buildings after dark?"*

"Miss Golden—Berenice," he said earnestly. "Who was Daisy? Plainly you know. Tell me the story."

"Did you see him?" she asked faintly.

"Him?"

"William Heron—The Wailing Watchman. Oh," she exclaimed in terror, "I can see you did. Then you are doomed—doomed!"

"If I'm doomed," said Jason, "let's have coffee, and you tell me the story quickly."

13

▶ **Critical Viewing**
The harp is an important part of this mystery. Describe the sound you think this instrument would make.
[Speculate]

"It all happened over fifty years ago," said Berenice, as she spooned out coffee powder with distracted extravagance. "Heron was the night watchman in this building, patrolling the corridors from dusk to dawn every night on his bicycle. He fell in love with a Miss Bell who taught the harp. She rented a room—this room—and gave lessons in it. She began to reciprocate his love, and they used to share a picnic supper every night at eleven, and she'd stay on a while to keep him company. It was an idyll,[10] among the fire buckets and the furnace pipes.

Vocabulary
reciprocate (ri sip′ rə kāt′) *v.* return

10. **idyll** (ī′ dəl) *n.* romantic scene, usually in the country.

Think Aloud

Plot

Draw students' attention to the scene after the text break: "Next morning when Miss Golden . . ." Explain that this scene occurs on the morning after Jason's encounter with the bicycle rider. Use the following "think aloud" to model the process of identifying plot elements:

When I read this passage, I realize that the story's mood has changed abruptly. If I compare this passage to the previous passage on the fire escape, I see that the writer has broken the tension and suspense. This makes me wonder if the climax just happened.

Then, I ask myself if the main conflict has been resolved. It hasn't, because I still don't know who the ghost is or why he is haunting the Grimes Buildings. Neither do I know whether Jason and Miss Golden will become romantically involved.

When I read further, Miss Golden tells Jason that he is doomed. I sense the tension building again, which means I am still reading part of the rising action. The climax is yet to come.

"On Halloween he had summoned up the courage to propose to her. The day before he had told her he was going to ask her a very important question, and he came to the Buildings with a huge bunch of roses and a bottle of wine. But Miss Bell never turned up.

He fell in love with a Miss Bell who taught the harp.

"The explanation was simple. Miss Bell, of course, had been losing a lot of sleep through her nocturnal romance, and so she used to take a nap in her music room between seven and ten, to save going home. In order to make sure that she would wake up, she persuaded her father, a distant relative of Graham Bell,[11] to attach an alarm-waking fixture to her telephone which called her
14 every night at ten. She was too modest and shy to let Heron know that she spent those hours in the building, and to give him the pleasure of waking her himself.

"Alas! On this important evening the line failed, and she never woke up. The telephone was in its infancy at that time, you must remember.

"Heron waited and waited. At last, mad with grief and jealousy, having called her home and discovered that she was not there, he concluded that she had betrayed him; he ran to the fire escape, and cast himself off it, holding the roses and the bottle of wine.

"Daisy did not long survive him but pined away soon after. Since that day their ghosts have haunted Grimes Buildings, he vainly patrolling the corridors on his bicycle, she playing her harp in the room she rented. But they never meet. And anyone who meets the ghost of William Heron will himself, within five days, leap down from the same fatal fire escape."

She gazed at him with tragic eyes.

"In that case we must lose no time," said Jason, and he enveloped her in an embrace as prompt as it was ardent. Looking down at the gossamer hair sprayed across his pin-stripe, he added, "Just the same it is a **preposterous** situation. Firstly, I have no intention of
15 jumping off the fire escape—" here, however, he repressed a shudder as he remembered the cold, clutching hands of the evening before—"and secondly, I find it quite nonsensical that those two inefficient ghosts have spent fifty years in this building without coming across each other. We must remedy the matter, Berenice. We must not begrudge our new-found happiness to others."

He gave her another kiss so impassioned that the electric typewriter against which they were leaning began chattering to itself in a frenzy of enthusiasm.

11. **Graham Bell** Alexander Graham Bell (1847–1922), the inventor of the telephone.

Literary Analysis
Plot
How does this new information increase the suspense of the narrative?

Reading Skill
Make Predictions
What do you think Jason might do to "remedy the matter"?

Vocabulary
preposterous (prē päs´ tər əs) *adj.* so contrary to common sense as to be laughable; absurd; ridiculous

16

Reading Check

According to Berenice, what happens to anyone who meets the ghost of William Heron?

14 Literary Analysis
Plot

1. Read aloud the first bracketed text, which begins on page 52.
2. Point out to students that the story of Heron and Daisy has its own plot. **Ask** students to identify the story's conflict, rising action, and climax.

   Answer: The conflict is Heron's wish to marry Daisy. The rising action includes the picnics, Daisy's use of the phone alarm to wake her, and Heron's plans for proposing. The climax occurs when Daisy fails to meet Heron and Heron jumps from the fire escape.
3. **Ask** students the Literary Analysis question: How does this new information increase the suspense of the narrative?

   Answer: The information makes Jason's situation much more serious; he must now try to survive a fatal curse.

15 Reading Skill
Make Predictions

1. Have students share the predictions they have made so far. Talk about the reasons students had for making them. Then, have students read the second bracketed text.
2. **Ask** students the Reading Skill question: What do you think Jason might do to "remedy the matter"?

   Possible response: Since the central problem Jason faces is that the two ghosts have never met, he probably plans to arrange a meeting between them.

16 Reading Check

Answer: The person is doomed to leap from the fire escape within five days.

Differentiated Instruction for Universal Access

EL Pronunciation for English Learners

To help students pronounce initial *h*, post these words: *hair, air, heel, eel, harm, arm.* Pronounce each word, stressing the initial consonant and the breath expelled to make the /h/ sound. Have students echo, placing a hand in front of their mouth to feel the breath when *h* is pronounced. Call out words at random as volunteers circle them on the board. Discuss incorrect choices and clarify.

Enrichment for Gifted/Talented Students

Point out that by naming her protagonists "Jason" and "Miss Golden," Aiken likely references the Greek myth "Jason and the Golden Fleece." Have students read the myth and then draw or act out the quest, obstacles, and dangers that each hero faces. Have students share their creations and tell how the reference adds to their understanding of the plot and characters of Aiken's story.

17 Reading Skill

Make Predictions

Have students read the bracketed text and identify what Jason carries into the building. Then, **ask** them the Reading Skill question: What do you predict Jason will do with the two bunches of roses? Why?

Possible response: Jason will probably give one to Heron and Daisy and the other to Berenice. He wants to create romance for two couples.

▶ **Monitor Progress: Ask** students to explain how they made their predictions.

Possible response: Berenice says that Heron brought a bottle of wine and a bunch of roses to give to Daisy when he proposed. So it is logical that one of the bunches of roses and one bottle of wine are for Heron and Daisy. Jason and Berenice are also in love, so it is possible that Jason has brought the other roses and wine for Berenice.

▶ **Reteach:** If students have difficulty with this prediction, remind them of the romance between Jason and Berenice. Tell them to reread the story about Heron and Daisy on pp. 52–53 and to look for references to the roses and wine. Then, have students use the information to reevaluate their predictions. Follow up with students after they finish reading the story.

"This very evening," he went on, looking at his watch, "we will put matters right for that unhappy couple and then, if I really have only five more days to live, which I don't for one moment believe, we will proceed to spend them together, my bewitching Berenice, in the most advantageous manner possible."

She nodded, spellbound.

"Can you work a switchboard?" he added. She nodded again. "My love, you are perfection itself. Meet me in the switchboard room then, at ten this evening. I would say, have dinner with me, but I shall need to make one or two purchases and see an old R.A.F.[12] friend. You will be safe from Heron's curse in the switchboard room if he always keeps to the corridors."

"I would rather meet him and die with you," she murmured.

"My angel, I hope that won't be necessary. Now," he said, sighing, "I suppose we should get down to our day's work."

Strangely enough the copy they wrote that day, although engendered from such agitated minds, sold more packets of Oat Crisps than any other advertising matter before or since.

Reading Skill
Make Predictions
What do you predict Jason will do with the two bunches of roses? Why?

17 That evening when Jason entered Grimes Buildings he was carrying two bottles of wine, two bunches of red roses, and a large canvas-covered bundle. Miss Golden, who had concealed herself in the switchboard room before the offices closed for the night, eyed these things with surprise.

"Now," said Jason, after he had greeted her, "I want you first to ring our own extension."

"No one will reply, surely?"

"I think she will reply."

Sure enough, when Berenice rang Extension 170 a faint, sleepy voice, distant and yet clear, whispered, "Hullo?"

"Is that Miss Bell?"

"Yes."

Berenice went a little pale. Her eyes sought Jason's and, prompted by him, she said formally, "Switchboard here, Miss Bell. Your ten o'clock call."

"Thank you," the faint voice said. There was a click and the line went blank.

"Excellent," Jason remarked. He unfastened his package and slipped its straps over his shoulders. "Now plug into the intercom."

Berenice did so, and then said, loudly and clearly, "Attention. Night watchman on duty, please. Night watchman on duty. You have

12. **R.A.F.** Royal Air Force.

Vocabulary Development

Vocabulary Knowledge Rating

When students have completed reading and discussing "Sonata for Harp and Bicycle," have them take out their **Vocabulary Knowledge Rating Chart** for this selection. Read the words aloud once more and have students rate their knowledge of the words again in the After Reading column. Clarify any words that are still problematic. Have students write their own definition and example or sentence in the appropriate column. Then, have students complete the Vocabulary Practice activities at the end of the selection. Encourage students to use the words in further discussion and written work about this selection. Remind them that they will be accountable for these words on the **Selection Test, *Unit 1 Resources,*** pp. 81–83 or 84–86.

an urgent summons to Room 492. You have an urgent summons to Room 492." The intercom echoed and reverberated through the empty corridors, then coughed itself to silence.

"Now we must run. You take the roses, sweetheart, and I'll carry the bottles."

18 Together they raced up eight flights of stairs and along the passages to Room 492. As they neared the door a burst of music met them—harp music swelling out, sweet and triumphant. Jason took a bunch of roses from Berenice, opened the door a little way, and gently deposited them, with a bottle, inside the door. As he closed it again Berenice said breathlessly, "Did you see anyone?"

"No," he said. "The room was too full of music." She saw that his eyes were shining.

They stood hand in hand, reluctant to move away, waiting for they hardly knew what. Suddenly the door opened again.

20 Neither Berenice nor Jason, afterward, would speak of what they saw but each was left with a memory, bright as the picture on a Salvador Dali[13] calendar, of a bicycle bearing on its saddle a harp, a bottle of wine, and a bouquet of red roses, sweeping improbably down the corridor and far, far away.

13. **Salvador Dali** (sal′ və dôr′ dä′ lē) (1904–1989) modern artist famous for his unusual pictures.

19 
Reading Check

What is Jason carrying as he enters the Grimes Buildings?

18 Critical Thinking

Compare and Contrast

1. Have students read the bracketed text, and **ask** them to summarize what happens. **Answer:** They go to Room 492 to see what happens with Miss Bell and Heron. They hear beautiful harp music coming from the room. They place roses and a bottle of wine inside the room.
2. **Ask:** How do the events in this passage differ from the original story of Miss Bell and Heron? **Answer:** In the original story, Miss Bell and Heron never meet. Heron kills himself out of grief. In the version that Jason and Berenice engineer, Heron finds Miss Bell in Room 492. Miss Bell plays beautiful music on her harp, and we are led to believe that Heron proposes marriage. The events of the original story are tragic, while the events in this passage are joyful.

19 Reading Check

Answer: Jason is carrying two bottles of wine, two bunches of red roses, and a canvas-covered bundle.

Concept Connector

Activating Prior Knowledge

Have students return to their predictions of the secret the copywriter attempts to unravel. Have volunteers share what they predicted and discuss which predictions were the most accurate.

Writing About the Big Question

Have students compare their responses to the sentence starters they completed before reading the story with their ideas afterwards. Ask them to explain whether their thoughts have changed.

Reading Skill Graphic Organizer

Have students review the graphic organizers they completed to make and verify predictions while reading. Show them **Reading Skill Graphic Organizer A** (*Graphic Organizer Transparencies*, p. 9) as an example. Then, have students share the graphic organizers they did and the predictions they made about the story.

⓴ Reading Skill

Make Predictions

Ask students the Reading Skill question.

Possible response: Students' predictions will vary, but they should provide details from the story to support their predictions.

ASSESS

Answers

Critical Thinking

Before students respond, you may wish to have them write a brief objective summary of the selection. As they answer the questions below, remind them to support their answers with evidence from the text.

1. (a) Miss Golden drops hints about a fire escape, a bicycle, and a harp. (b) Jason finds the fire escape and uses it to get into the building.
2. (a) In the main plot, Jason Ashgrove and Miss Berenice Golden are in love. In the subplot, the night watchman William Heron and the harp teacher Daisy Bell are in love. (b) Jason encounters Heron's ghost, inadvertently dooming himself and his relationship with Miss Golden. After Miss Golden explains what happened between Heron and Miss Bell, Jason is determined to reunite the ghost lovers and so that they can share the happiness that he and Miss Golden now enjoy.
3. He jumps off the fire escape but does so securely strapped in a parachute.
4. (a) He becomes determined to undo the curse and to change its outcome. (b) **Possible response:** By cleverly changing the outcome of the original story of the ghosts, Jason creates a new truth: Heron and Miss Bell, as well as Jason and Berenice, end up together and happy.

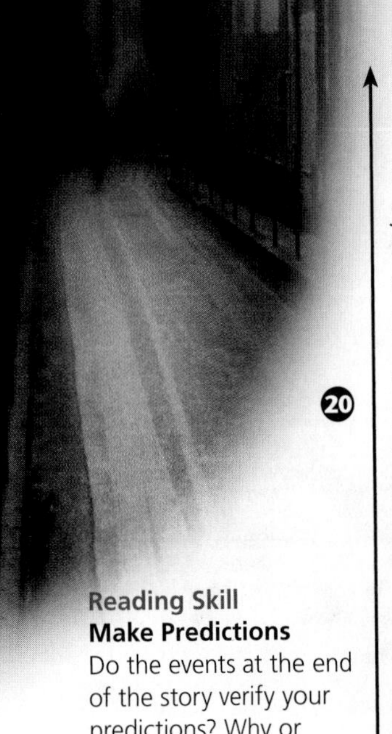

"We can go now," Jason said.

He led Berenice to the fire door, tucking the bottle of Médoc in his jacket pocket. A black wind from the north whistled beneath them as they stood on the openwork platform, looking down.

⓴ "We don't want our evening to be spoiled by the thought of a curse hanging over us," he said, "so this is the practical thing to do. Hang onto the roses." And holding his love firmly, Jason pulled the rip cord of his R.A.F. friend's parachute and leaped off the fire escape.

A bridal shower of rose petals adorned the descent of Miss Golden, who was possibly the only girl to be kissed in midair in the district of Clerkenwell at ten minutes to midnight on Halloween.

Reading Skill
Make Predictions
Do the events at the end of the story verify your predictions? Why or why not?

Critical Thinking

Cite textual evidence to support your responses.

1. **Key Ideas and Details** **(a)** What three important objects does Miss Golden mention to Jason as they leave the Grimes Buildings at five o'clock? **(b) Connect:** How does he use this information?
2. **Craft and Structure** **(a)** Who is in love in the main plot of the story? In the ghost-story subplot? **(b) Analyze:** How do these two love plots connect?
3. **Key Ideas and Details** What actions does Jason take to avoid the curse that awaits those who see Heron's ghost?
4. **Integration of Knowledge and Ideas** **(a)** How does Jason react to the news of the curse? **(b) Analyze Cause and Effect:** How do his actions help change the "truth"? *[Connect to the Big Question: Can truth change?]*

Assessment Resources

Unit 1 Resources

L1 L2 EL **Selection Test A,** pp. 81–83. Administer Test A to less advanced readers.

L3 L4 EL **Selection Test B,** pp. 84–86. Administer Test B to on-level and more advanced students.

L3 L4 **Open-Book Test,** pp. 78–80. As an alternative, give the Open-Book Test.

All **Customizable Test Bank**

All **Self-tests**
Students may prepare for the **Selection Test** by taking the **Self-test** online.

All assessment resources are available at **www.PHLitOnline.com.**

After You Read

Sonata for Harp and Bicycle

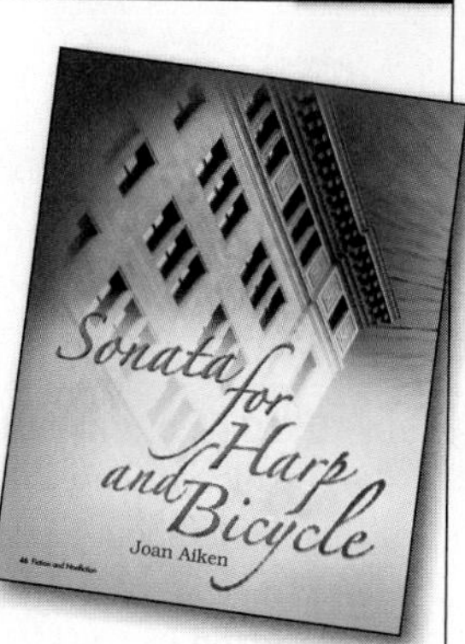

Literary Analysis: Plot

1. **Key Ideas and Details** Using a chart like this one, identify two key events in the **rising action,** one that marks the **climax,** and one in the **falling action.** Discuss your choices with a partner.

2. **Craft and Structure (a)** Identify a passage that **foreshadows** Jason's entering the Grimes Buildings after hours. **(b)** Explain how foreshadowing increases the story's **suspense.**

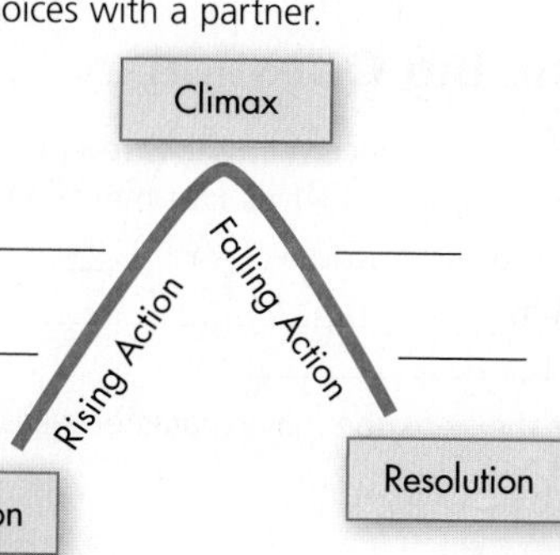

Reading Skill: Make Predictions

3. What **prediction** did you make when Jason entered the Grimes Buildings after closing and heard a bicycle bell? **(b)** What details helped you make your prediction?
4. Was your prediction **verified** by later story events? Explain.

Vocabulary

Acquisition and Use An **analogy** shows the relationship between pairs of words. Use a word from the vocabulary list on page 44 to complete each analogy. For each case, your choice should create a word pair that matches the relationship between the first two words.

1. angry : shout :: ______ : whisper
2. steal : take :: ______ : give
3. hopelessly : far :: ______ : near
4. ending : concluding :: ______ : infringing
5. criticizing : praising :: ______ : comforting
6. funny : serious :: ______ : reasonable

Word Study Use the context of the sentences and what you know about the **suffix *-ate*** to explain your answer to each question.

1. What does someone do if they *participate* in an activity?
2. If a question is *complicated*, is it easy?

Word Study

The **suffix *-ate*** means "to become or form."

Apply It Explain how the suffix *-ate* contributes to the meaning of these words. Use a dictionary if necessary.

depreciate
captivate
duplicate

ASSESS/EXTEND

Answers

Literary Analysis

1. **Possible response: Rising Action:** Jason hears hints about the fire escape, bicycle, and harp; Jason enters the building and meets the ghost of Heron. **Climax:** Jason places the bunch of roses and bottle of wine inside the room where the ghosts of Heron and Daisy are meeting. **Falling Action:** Jason and Miss Golden leap from the fire escape.

For other sample answers, see ***Graphic Organizer Transparencies,* Literary Analysis Graphic Organizer A,** p. 12, and the **Additional Answers** section.

2. (a) **Possible response:** Jason's decision is foreshadowed by his vow to "do something desperate" when Miss Golden refuses to explain the secret of Grimes Buildings. (b) It increases suspense by creating anticipation for a desperate action.

Reading Skill

3. (a) **Possible response:** Students may have predicted that someone was haunting the building and riding a bike. (b) **Possible response:** Students may have based the prediction on the way workers leave the building hurriedly each night and the fact that Miss Golden says the mystery involves a bicycle.
4. **Possible response:** Students' predictions may have been verified when they discovered that the watchman's ghost rides his bicycle through the building each night.

Vocabulary

Acquisition and Use

Sample answers:

1. furtive
2. reciprocate
3. tantalizingly
4. encroaching
5. menacing
6. preposterous

Word Study

Sample answers:

1. The suffix *-ate* means "to become," and *participate* means "to become part of." Someone who *participates* takes part in an activity.
2. No; the suffix *-ate* means "to become," and *complicated* means "to become complex." A *complicated* question is hard to answer.

Word Study: Apply It

Sample answers:

To *depreciate* is to become less valuable. To *captivate* is to cause to become interested. To *duplicate* is to form a second copy.

PRETEACH

Skills instruction for the ***Reading Skill*** *and the* ***Literary Analysis*** *concept appears on p. 43.*

1 Writing About the Big Question

1. Review the assignment with the class.
2. Have students provide examples of times when they discovered the truth by verifying evidence. Ask them what factors in the situation could have distorted the truth.
3. Have students complete the sentence starters. Review responses as a class. (**Possible response:** The truth about a person can be discovered when all the information is known. It can either be verified by that information or distorted by false information.)
4. Remind students that their answers will help them think about the Big Question, "Can truth change?"

While You Read

Tell students that as they read, they should look for ways the main character takes charge of his life.

2 Vocabulary

1. Have students preview the selection vocabulary.
2. For each word, have students say the word aloud.
3. Then, use the word in a sentence that defines the word.
4. Finally, repeat your definitional sentence or a similar sentence with the word missing, and have the class "fill in the blank" chorally. Here is an example:

   Something explicit is expressed clearly. We managed not to get lost because our directions were specific and [students say "explicit"].

3 Word Study

1. Introduce the skill, using the instruction in the box.
2. Use the word *inform* to model the process of creating a noun from a verb by adding *-tion*. Have student pairs take turns suggesting verbs and adding *-tion* to create nouns.

Making Connections **The Cask of Amontillado**

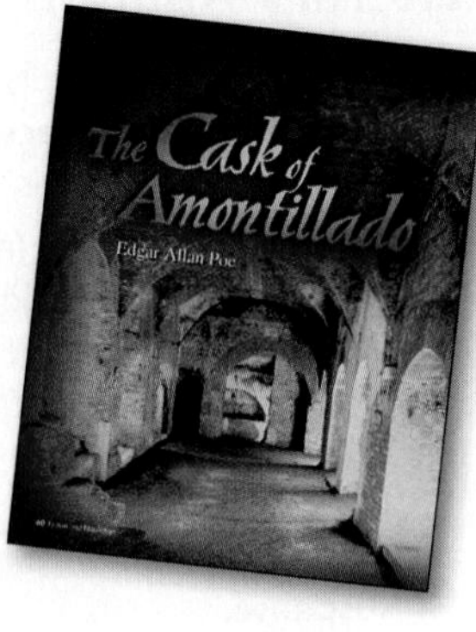

1 Writing About the Big Question

In "The Cask of Amontillado," a wronged man seeks revenge. Use these sentence starters to develop your ideas about the Big Question.

The **truth** about a person can be discovered when ______________.
It can either be **verified** by ______________ or **distorted** by ______________.

While You Read Look for the ways the main character takes charge of his life.

2 Vocabulary

Read each word and its definition. Decide whether you know the word well, know it a little bit, or do not know it at all. After you have read the selection, see how your knowledge of each word has increased.

- **precluded** (prē klo͞od′ id) *v.* prevented (p. 61) *When his injury precluded any chance of victory, the fans lost hope.* *preclude v. include v.*
- **retribution** (re′ trə byo͞o′ shən) *n.* payback; punishment for a misdeed (p. 61) *He wanted retribution for an insult he had received.* *tribute n.*
- **afflicted** (ə flikt′ əd) *v.* suffering or sickened (p. 63) *The old man was afflicted with a rare type of pneumonia.* *affliction n. afflict v.*
- **explicit** (eks plis′ it) *adj.* clearly stated (p. 63) *I could not ignore her explicit refusal.* *explicate v.*
- **recoiling** (ri koil′ iŋ) *v.* staggering back (p. 65) *Wendy, recoiling in horror, shrieked at the rattlesnake in her path.* *recoil v. recoil n.*
- **subsided** (səb sīd′ əd) *v.* settled down; became less active or intense (p. 67) *As we walked away from the beach, the sound of the waves subsided.* *subside v. subsidiary n.*

3 Word Study

The **suffix *-tion*** means "the act of." It usually indicates the word is a noun.

In this story, the ghost seeks **retribution**, or the act of revenge, for his lost life and love.

58 Fiction and Nonfiction

Vocabulary Development

Vocabulary Knowledge Rating

Create a **Vocabulary Knowledge Rating Chart** (***Professional Development Guidebook***, p. 33) for this selection. Include the selection vocabulary from this page and the forms of the Big Question words that appear in the Writing About the Big Question sentence starter on this page. (The Big Question vocabulary is introduced on pp. 2–3.)

Give students a copy of the chart. Read the words aloud, and have students mark their rating in the Before Reading column. Tell students that they will rate their knowledge again.

Tally how many students think they know a word to gauge how much instruction to provide. As students read and discuss the selection, point out the words and their context.

Vocabulary Central, featuring tools, activities, and songs for studying vocabulary, is available online at **www.PHLitOnline.com.**

Meet Edgar Allan Poe

(1809–1849)

Author of *The Cask of Amontillado*

One of the first great American storytellers, Edgar Allan Poe made the most of a short, tragic life. Orphaned at the age of three, Poe was raised by foster parents, the Allans, from whom he took his middle name. The Allans were good to Poe and gave him an education, but he had to leave college when his foster father refused to pay Poe's gambling debts. Poe found some happiness when he married Virginia Clemm. However, her early death from tuberculosis in 1847 caused Poe to become increasingly antisocial. In 1849, he was discovered in a delirious condition on a Baltimore street, and three days later he was dead.

An Inspiration to Later Generations

Like few others, Poe blazed trails for future writers. His work helped to define the short story, and his dark imagination helped establish the genre of horror literature now popularized by writers like Stephen King.

4

BACKGROUND FOR THE STORY

Catacombs

Much of the action in this story takes place in catacombs—underground tunnels that house tombs. These long, often complex passageways stretch out like cities of the dead. In past centuries, some wealthy European families held funerals in catacombs beneath the family manor. The dead were laid to rest surrounded by the bones of their ancestors.

Did You Know?

Poe invented the genre of the detective story with his tale "The Murders in the Rue Morgue."

Daily Bellringer

For each class during which you will teach this selection, have students complete one of the five Sentence Modeling activities for Week 2 in the ***Daily Bellringer Activities*** booklet.

4 Background

Catacombs From before Roman times, people across the Mediterranean region built catacombs as places of burial. Greeks and Romans ordinarily used cremation, but Christians and Jewish people buried their dead. The catacombs were begun on a single level, with separate chambers or galleries laid out like a honeycomb. As the chambers filled, additional levels were dug deeper down and connected by stairs. Some catacombs had as many as five levels.

Multidraft Reading

This icon ● marks natural pauses in the selection. To assist struggling readers and to deepen reading for all, assign the text in "chunks," following the icons, and apply multidraft reading protocols. For each reading, have students set the purpose indicated:

- **First reading**—identifying key ideas and details and answering any Reading Checks.
- **Second reading**—analyzing craft and structure and responding to the side-column prompts.
- **Third reading**—integrating knowledge and ideas, connecting to other texts and the world, and answering the end-of-selection questions.

For more guidance, refer to the ***Classroom Strategies and Teaching Routines*** card on multidraft reading.

For more about the author, practice with the selection vocabulary, or more background, go online at **www.PHLitOnline.com.**

Differentiated Instruction — Additional Instruction

EL Extended Support—English Learners

Have students complete the **Reading and Vocabulary Warm-ups, *Unit 1 Resources,*** pp. 87–90, before they read. Assign the prereading pages for the selection in the ***Reader's Notebook: English Learner's Version.*** Then, have students listen to portions of the selection on the ***Hear It!* Audio CD.**

L1 L2 Extended Support—Struggling Readers

Have students complete the **Reading and Vocabulary Warm-ups, *Unit 1 Resources,*** pp. 87–90, before they read. Assign the prereading pages for the selection in the ***Reader's Notebook: Adapted Version.*** Then, have students listen to portions of the selection on the ***Hear It!* Audio CD** (adapted text).

Extended Support—Reluctant Readers

To build motivation and engagement before assigning the selection, have students read "Whose Justice Is It?" a thematically related selection in ***Reality Central.*** Then, use the questions at the conclusion of the related selection to guide discussion.

❶ Activating Prior Knowledge

Students will discover that this horrifying tale of revenge is as gripping as any horror movie they've seen. Give them a verbal "trailer" of the story by reading aloud the following excerpts:

"We . . . stood together upon the damp ground of the catacombs of the Montresors."

"We had passed through long walls of piled skeletons, with casks and puncheons intermingling, into the inmost recesses. . . ."

Have students discuss these images. What do they think will happen in the catacombs?

Whole-Class Activity

Have students note the many sound effects and sound-imitating words that Poe uses in his description of the events that take place in the catacombs. In a class discussion, have students answer the following questions: How does Poe use words to create sounds? How does he help readers hear the scene? What do the sound effects add to the story's mood? Which verbs and adjectives re-create sounds for the reader?

❷ About the Selection

"The Cask of Amontillado" illustrates how a person can become so obsessed with revenge that he or she descends into madness and commits unspeakable acts. The main character, Montresor, has vowed to avenge the unnamed insults of Fortunato, an old acquaintance. With a mix of flattery and reverse psychology, Montresor lures and traps Fortunato in the catacombs below Montresor's house.

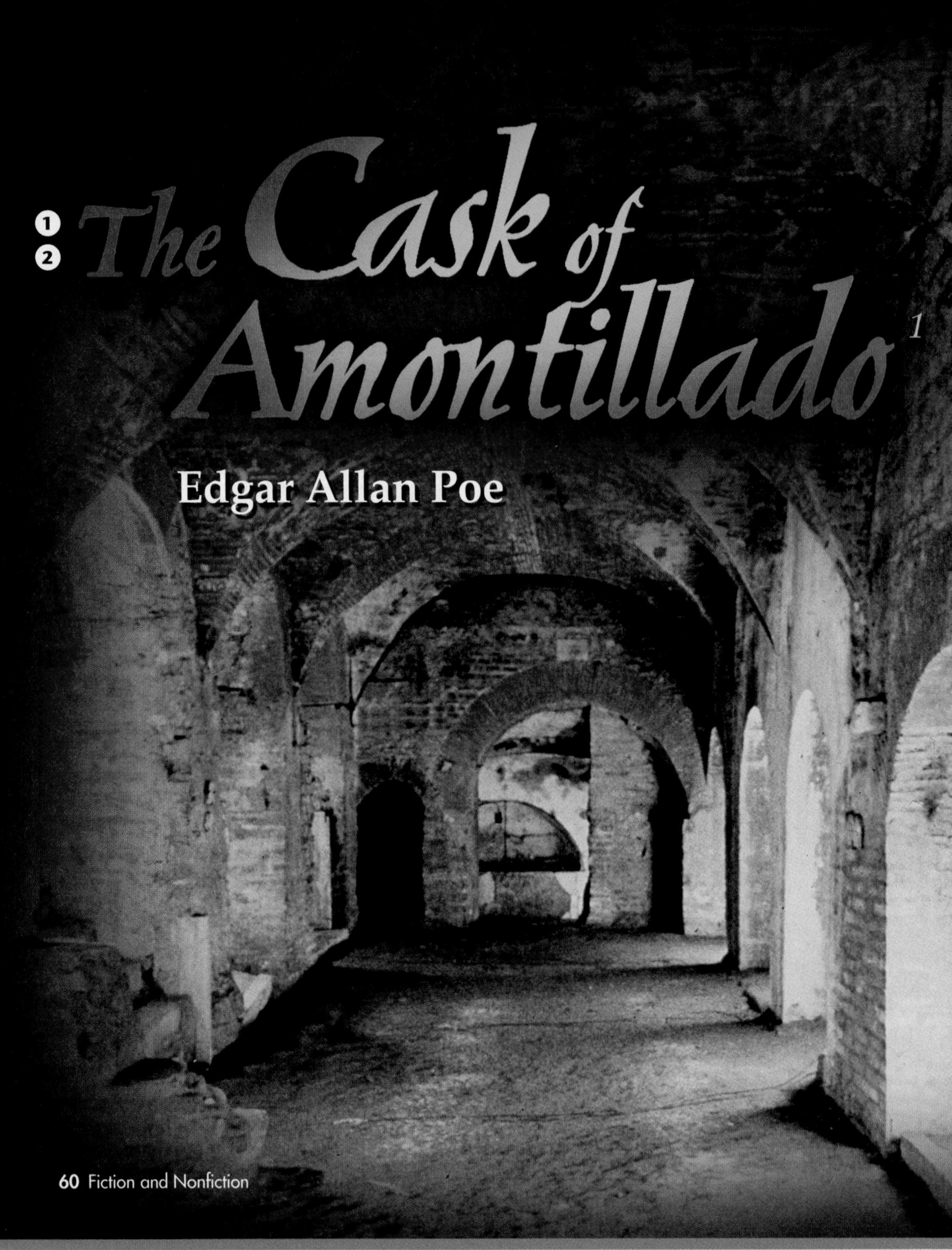

❶ ❷ The Cask of Amontillado[1]

Edgar Allan Poe

Vocabulary Development

Ⓒ CCSS Language 6

Thematic Vocabulary: The Big Question

As students are discussing "The Cask of Amontillado," encourage them to use the thematic vocabulary presented in Introducing the Big Question, pp. 2–3. You might encourage them with sentence starters like these:

1. Montresor is able to *manipulate* Fortunato by . . .
2. Fortunato never tries to *distort* . . .
3. Fortunato's cough is *evidence* that . . .
4. As they walk through the catacombs, it is Fortunato's *belief* that . . .
5. Montresor attempts to *verify* that he is a mason by . . .

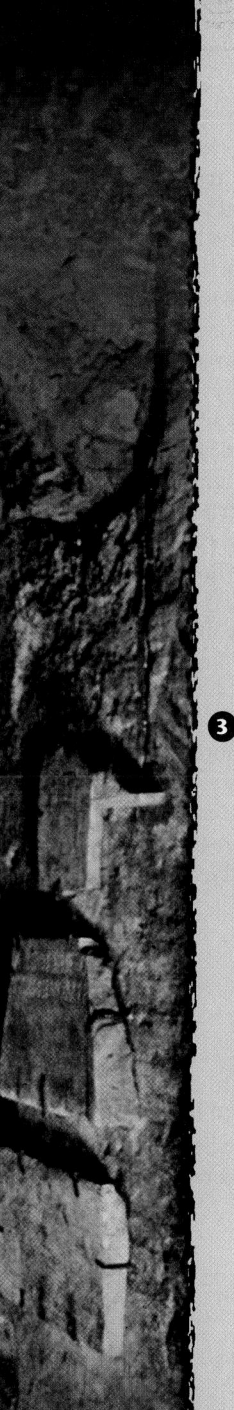

The thousand injuries of Fortunato I had borne as I best could, but when he ventured upon insult I vowed revenge. You, who so well know the nature of my soul, will not suppose, however, that I gave utterance to a threat. At *length* I would be avenged; this was a point definitely settled—but the very definitiveness with which it was resolved **precluded** the idea of risk. I 3 must not only punish but punish with impunity.[2] A wrong is unredressed when **retribution** overtakes its redresser. It is equally unredressed when the avenger fails to make himself felt as such to him who has done the wrong.

It must be understood that neither by word nor deed had I given Fortunato cause to doubt my good will. I continued, as was my wont, to smile in his face, and he did not perceive that my smile *now* was at the thought of his immolation.[3]

1. **Amontillado** (ə män′ tə yä′ dō) *n.* a pale, dry sherry.
2. **impunity** (im pyo͞o′ nə tē′) *n.* freedom from consequences.
3. **immolation** (im′ ə lā′ shən) *n.* destruction.

Vocabulary
precluded (prē klo͞od′ id) *v.* prevented
retribution (re′ trə byo͞o′ shən) *n.* payback; punishment for a misdeed

4 

Why does the narrator vow revenge on Fortunato?

3 Connecting to the Big Question

1. Point out that in this story, the narrator speaks directly to the audience and shares the "truth" of his actions. He distorts this truth when dealing with Fortunato.
2. Have students reread the bracketed text. **Ask:** What does the narrator promise? How does he take charge of his life with this promise?
   Possible response: He promises to take revenge on Fortunato for a series of injuries. He says that he will no longer accept the injuries and is going to do something about them. He is taking charge of his future relationship with Fortunato, and perhaps he is deciding never to let *anyone* hurt him again.
3. **Ask:** Does the "truth" that the narrator reveals to you as the reader change your view of the character? Would it change Fortunato's view if he knew the truth? Explain.
   Possible response: Yes, knowing that the narrator plans to seek revenge and that he is tricking Fortunato makes me suspicious and critical of him. Yes, Fortunato would surely view the narrator differently if he knew the narrator's true intentions. He would know that the narrator is being falsely friendly.

4 Reading Check

Answer: The narrator believes that Fortunato has injured and insulted him.

PHLit Online!
This selection is available in interactive format in the **Enriched Online Student Edition, www.PHLitOnline.com,** which includes a thematically related video with writing prompt and an interactive graphic organizer.

Differentiated Instruction for Universal Access

Strategy for Special-Needs Students
Read aloud the first two paragraphs of the story. Have students identify details that show the narrator's state of mind. List their suggestions on the board, and discuss their significance. As students read independently, they should continue to note actions and words that reveal the narrator's mental condition.

EL Pronunciation for English Learners
To help students pronounce the short *i* vowel sound, post these words: *did, deed; lid, lead;* and *ship, sheep.* Pronounce each word in turn, stressing the vowel sound, and have students echo. Pair English learners with fluent speakers to practice discriminating short *i* from long *e.* If English learners make mistakes, fluent speakers should pronounce the word carefully, leading the way to the correct pronunciation.

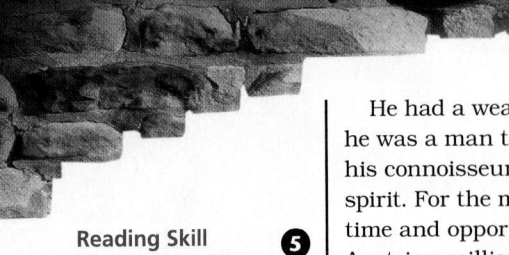

5 Reading Skill

Make Predictions

1. Have students consider the relationship between predicting and foreshadowing. **Ask:** How can a writer's use of foreshadowing help readers make predictions as they read?

   Answer: Foreshadowing is the writer's use of clues to hint at future events in a story. These hints can help readers make predictions about what may happen.
2. Discuss what the bracketed text foreshadows, and encourage students to base their predictions on such details.
3. **Ask** students the Reading Skill question: What role do you predict Fortunato's "weak point" will play in the narrator's revenge?

   Possible response: Fortunato has great pride in his knowledge of wine, so the narrator will probably use this arrogance to trap Fortunato and get revenge.
4. Have students write their predictions on copies of **Reading Skill Graphic Organizer B** (***Graphic Organizer Transparencies***, p. 11). Tell them to read on to find out whether their predictions were accurate.

Reading Skill 5
Make Predictions
What role do you predict Fortunato's "weak point" will play in the narrator's revenge?

He had a weak point—this Fortunato—although in other regards he was a man to be respected and even feared. He prided himself on his connoisseurship[4] in wine. Few Italians have the true virtuoso[5] spirit. For the most part their enthusiasm is adopted to suit the time and opportunity, to practice imposture upon the British and Austrian millionaires. In painting and gemmary, Fortunato, like his countrymen, was a quack, but in the matter of old wines he was sincere. In this respect I did not differ from him materially; I was skillful in the Italian vintages myself, and bought largely whenever I could.

It was about dusk, one evening during the supreme madness of the carnival season, that I encountered my friend. He accosted me with excessive warmth, for he had been drinking much. The man wore motley.[6] He had on a tight-fitting parti-striped dress, and his head was surmounted by the conical cap and bells. I was so pleased to see him that I thought I should never have done wringing his hand.

I said to him, "My dear Fortunato, you are luckily met. How remarkably well you are looking today. But I have received a pipe[7] of what passes for Amontillado, and I have my doubts."

"How?" said he. "Amontillado? A pipe? Impossible! And in the middle of the carnival!"

"I have my doubts," I replied: "and I was silly enough to pay the full Amontillado price without consulting you in the matter. You were not to be found, and I was fearful of losing a bargain."

"Amontillado!"

"I have my doubts."

"Amontillado!"

"And I must satisfy them."

"Amontillado!"

"As you are engaged, I am on my way to Luchesi. If any one has a critical turn it is he. He will tell me—"

"Luchesi cannot tell Amontillado from sherry."

"And yet some fools will have it that his taste is a match for your own."

6 ↓ "Come, let us go."

4. **connoisseurship** (kän′ ə sʉr′ ship) *n.* expert judgment.
5. **virtuoso** (vʉr′ cho͞o ō′ sō) *adj.* masterly skill in a particular field.
6. **motley** (mät′ lē) *n.* a clown's multicolored costume.
7. **pipe** (pīp) *n.* large barrel, holding approximately 126 gallons.

Think Aloud

Vocabulary: Using Context

Direct students' attention to the word *surmounted* in the second paragraph of page 62. Using a think-aloud process, model how to use context to infer the meaning of an unknown word. Say to students:

> I'm going to think aloud to show you how I would figure out the meaning of *surmounted* based on its context.
>
> In this sentence, Fortunato's head is *surmounted* by a "conical cap and bells." At this point of the story it is carnival season, which means people are likely to wear costumes. In the sentence before the one in which *surmounted* appears, I find out that Fortunato is, in fact, wearing a costume: "a tight-fitting parti-striped dress." I know that a cap is something that you wear on top of your head. So, *surmounted* must mean "topped"—Fortunato is wearing a cap and bells on top of his head.

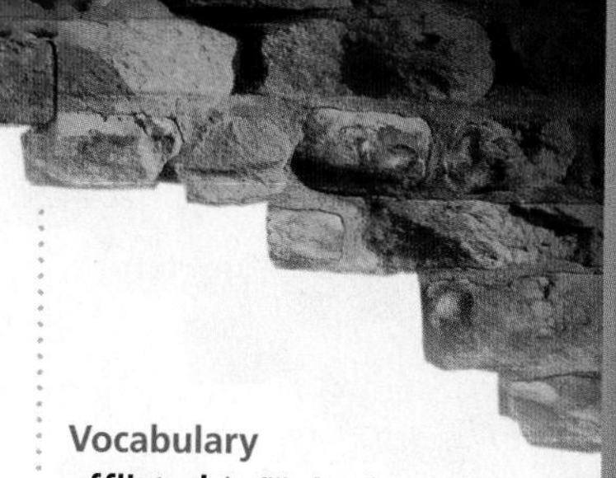

"Whither?"

"To your vaults."

"My friend, no; I will not impose upon your good nature. I perceive you have an engagement. Luchesi—"

6 "I have no engagement—come."

"My friend, no. It is not the engagement, but the severe cold with which I perceive you are **afflicted**. The vaults are insufferably damp. They are encrusted with niter."

"Let us go, nevertheless. The cold is merely nothing. Amontillado! You have been imposed upon. And as for Luchesi, he cannot distinguish sherry from Amontillado."

Thus speaking, Fortunato possessed himself of my arm; and putting on a mask of black silk and drawing a *roquelaure*[8] closely about my person, I suffered him to hurry me to my palazzo.

There were no attendants at home; they had absconded to make merry in honor of the time. I had told them that I should not return until the morning, and had given them **explicit** orders not to stir from the house. These orders were sufficient, I well knew, to insure their immediate disappearance, one and all, as soon as my back was turned.

I took from their sconces two flambeaux, and giving one to Fortunato, bowed him through several suites of rooms to the archway that led into the vaults. I passed down a long and winding staircase, requesting him to be cautious as he followed. We came at length to the foot of the descent, and stood together upon the damp ground of the catacombs of the Montresors.

The gait of my friend was unsteady, and the bells upon his cap jingled as he strode.

"The pipe," he said.

"It is farther on," said I; "but observe the white webwork which gleams from these cavern walls."

He turned towards me, and looked into my eyes with two filmy orbs that distilled the rheum of intoxication.

"Niter?" he asked, at length.

"Niter," I replied. "How long have you had that cough?"

8. ***roquelaure*** (räk´ ə lôr) *n.* knee-length cloak.

Vocabulary

afflicted (ə flikt´ əd) *v.* suffering or sickened

Vocabulary

explicit (eks plis´ it) *adj.* clearly stated

It was about dusk, one evening during the supreme madness of the carnival season, that I encountered my friend.

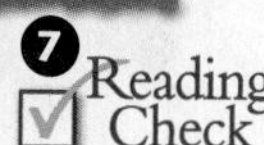

7 **Reading Check**

What common interest does the narrator share with Fortunato?

6 Critical Thinking

Analyze

1. Ask two volunteers to read aloud the dialogue in the bracketed text, which begins on p. 62. Have students give their impressions of the two characters.
2. Point out that the narrator's words do not accurately reflect his thoughts and intentions. **Ask** how this affects students' impressions of the narrator's character.

Possible responses: It shows that he is very self-controlled. It shows that he finds it easy to lie and act a part. It shows that he is not impulsive; he does not speak without thinking.

7 Reading Check

Answer: The narrator and Fortunato share an interest in wines.

PROFESSIONAL DEVELOPMENT | Doug Buehl

Apply the Strategy

Student-Friendly Explanations Model a "student-friendly explanation" of the vocabulary word *explicit* and the related term *implicit*. After reading the story, have students reread the sentence in which *explicit* appears (p. 63) and review the provided definition. Then, explain:

> When something is *explicit*, it is out in the open. For example, when the narrator says he "had given them *explicit* orders not to stir from the house," I know the narrator had told them exactly what to do.
>
> Something *implicit*, however, is implied or suggested. If the narrator had simply locked the doors, that would be *implicit* instruction.

Ask students for further examples where they might find something *explicit*. Reinforce students' use of the word with each example. Then, ask them to contrast with *implicit* examples.

For more of Doug Buehl's strategies, see his Professional Development essay, pp. 2c–2d.

8 Literary Analysis

Plot

1. Point out to students how the suspense continues to increase as Fortunato and Montresor walk deeper into the catacombs.
2. Call students' attention to the conversation in the bracketed text, and **ask** them the Literary Analysis question: What fate does this conversation foreshadow for Fortunato?

   Answer: It foreshadows Fortunato's death by means other than an illness.
3. **Ask** students how this conversation affects the story's plot.

   Answer: The rising action continues to build. The reader feels increasing fear and concern for Fortunato.

"Ugh! ugh! ugh!—ugh! ugh! ugh!—ugh! ugh! ugh!—ugh! ugh! ugh!—ugh! ugh! ugh!"

My poor friend found it impossible to reply for many minutes.

"It is nothing," he said, at last.

"Come," I said, with decision, "we will go back; your health is precious. You are rich, respected, admired, beloved; you are happy, as once I was. You are a man to be missed. For me it is no matter. We will go back; you will be ill, and I cannot be responsible. Besides, there is Luchesi—"

"Enough," he said; "the cough is a mere nothing; it will not kill me. I shall not die of a cough."

"True—true," I replied; "and, indeed, I had no intention of alarming you unnecessarily—but you should use all proper caution. A draft of this Médoc will defend us from the damps."

Literary Analysis
Plot
What fate does this conversation foreshadow for Fortunato?

Here I knocked off the neck of a bottle which I drew from a long row of its fellows that lay upon the mold.

"Drink," I said, presenting him the wine.

He raised it to his lips with a leer. He paused and nodded to me familiarly, while his bells jingled. 8

"I drink," he said "to the buried that repose around us."

"And I to your long life."

He again took my arm, and we proceeded.

"These vaults," he said, "are extensive."

"The Montresors," I replied, "were a great and numerous family."

"I forget your arms."

"A huge human foot d'or, in a field azure; the foot crushes a serpent rampant whose fangs are imbedded in the heel."

"And the motto?"

"Nemo me impune lacessit."[9]

"Good!" he said.

The wine sparkled in his eyes and the bells jingled. My own fancy grew warm with the Médoc. We had passed through long walls of piled skeletons, with casks and puncheons[10] intermingling, into the inmost recesses of the catacombs. I paused again, and this time I made bold to seize Fortunato by an arm above the elbow.

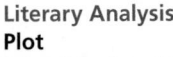

▼ **Casks for storing wine**

9. ***Nemo me impune lacessit*** Latin for "No one attacks me with impunity."
10. **puncheons** (pun´ chənz) *n.* large barrels.

Vocabulary Development

© CCSS Language 6

Expressive Vocabulary

To help students broaden their expressive vocabulary, encourage them to use the following words as they discuss Poe's eerie description of the catacombs: *contributes, interpret, participate, devious, lure,* and *obsessive.* Have them complete these sentence starters:

1. The sound of Fortunato's cough *contributes* to . . .
2. Fortunato does not correctly *interpret* . . .
3. Montresor wants Fortunato to *participate* . . .
4. Montresor's *devious* plan . . .
5. To *lure* Fortunato, Montresor has to . . .
6. Montresor is *obsessive* about . . .

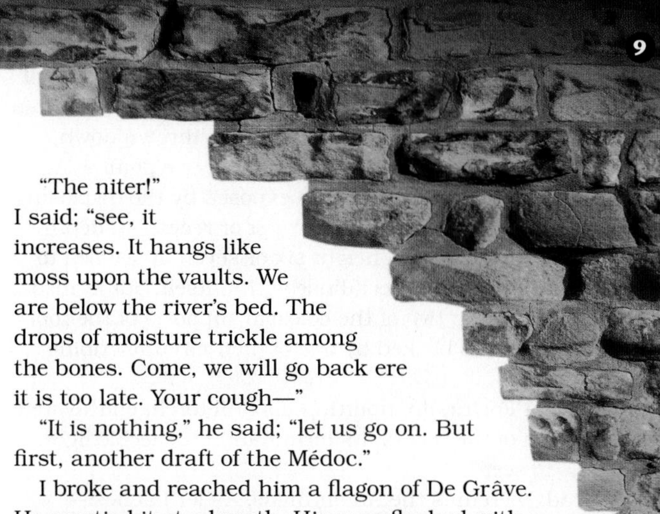

"The niter!" I said; "see, it increases. It hangs like moss upon the vaults. We are below the river's bed. The drops of moisture trickle among the bones. Come, we will go back ere it is too late. Your cough—"

"It is nothing," he said; "let us go on. But first, another draft of the Médoc."

I broke and reached him a flagon of De Grâve. He emptied it at a breath. His eyes flashed with a fierce light. He laughed and threw the bottle upwards with a gesticulation I did not understand.

I looked at him in surprise. He repeated the movement—a grotesque one.

"You do not comprehend?" he said.

"Not I," I replied.

"Then you are not of the brotherhood."

"How?"

"You are not of the masons."[11]

"Yes, yes," I said; "yes, yes."

"You? Impossible! A mason?"

"A mason," I replied.

"A sign," he said, "a sign."

"It is this," I answered, producing from beneath the folds of my *roquelaure* a trowel.

"You jest," he exclaimed, **recoiling** a few paces. "But let us proceed to the Amontillado."

"Be it so," I said, replacing the tool beneath the cloak and again offering him my arm. He leaned upon it heavily. We continued our route in search of the Amontillado. We passed through a range of low arches, descended, passed on, and descending again, arrived at a deep crypt, in which the foulness of the air caused our flambeaux rather to glow than flame.

At the most remote end of the crypt there appeared another less spacious. Its walls had been lined with human remains,

11. masons *n.* the Freemasons, an international secret society.

9 **LITERATURE IN CONTEXT**

Literature Connection

Poe and the Gothic Tradition

The literary genre known as gothic fiction emerged in England in the late 1700s in works like *Castle of Otranto* (1765) by Horace Walpole and *The Mysteries of Udolpho* (1794) by Ann Radcliffe. The word *gothic* was originally used to describe a style of building that was common in the late Middle Ages. To writers in the eighteenth century, the cold chambers and secret passages of such buildings suggested mystery and dark tales of vengeance and passion.

Edgar Allan Poe translated the imagery and atmosphere of British gothic fiction to an American landscape, pioneering an American gothic tradition. Contemporary writers like Stephen King and Anne Rice, as well as countless filmmakers, carry on that tradition today.

Connect to the Literature

What qualities of gothic fiction do you find in "The Cask of Amontillado"? Explain.

Vocabulary

recoiling (ri koil′ iŋ) *v.* staggering back

10 

Reading Check

Where does Montresor bring Fortunato?

9 Literature in Context

Literature Connection Point out that originally, gothic literature was set in medieval castles and ancient structures such as the catacombs that Poe describes. Modern gothic literature is often placed in other settings, but the goal of the writing remains the same—to create a combined sense of unknown horror and empathy for the character involved in the situation. Gothic literature is not defined so much by setting, characterization, or plot but by its ability to create a mood and tone that evoke deep emotions in the reader.

Connect to the Literature Have students read the Literature in Context feature, and present the additional background information above. Then, **ask** students to cite other contemporary writers and directors who carry on the gothic tradition. **Ask** the Connect to the Literature question: What qualities of gothic fiction do you find in "The Cask of Amontillado"? Explain.

Possible responses: Students may cite the dank, eerie setting of the vaults; the foul atmosphere; and Montresor's devious, demented revenge plot.

10 Reading Check

Answer: Montresor brings Fortunato to the deepest and farthest part of the catacombs.

Fluency

Distribute copies of page 65, and pair students. While one partner reads from the beginning of the page to the end of the last full paragraph, the other should mark any words with which the student reading has difficulty. Circulate to monitor the fluency of students' reading. Collect students' marked-up copies of the story, and review difficult words and passages with the class. Look for these problem spots:

- If students struggle to follow the unlabeled dialogue, read it aloud, beginning with "You do not comprehend?" and ending with "You jest." At each line, pause to help students identify and label who is speaking.
- If students stumble over the varied sentence types, review and model the correct intonation for sentences ending with question marks and exclamation marks. Have students echo you.
- If students have difficulty with repeated words, such as *I, yes,* and *a sign,* read the pertinent sentences aloud slowly to model fluency. Have students echo until they read fluently.

⓫ Critical Viewing

Possible response: A mask can't change its expression, and it has no eyes, only holes for the wearer's eyes. Lack of expression can make any face seem sinister because the person's actions are hard to predict.

⓬ Critical Thinking

Analyze

1. Have a volunteer read the first bracketed text aloud. Then, **ask** students to summarize the events.

   Answer: The narrator grabs Fortunato and chains him to the back of the niche. Fortunato expresses surprise.

2. **Ask** students to describe the mood (general feeling) of the passage. They should cite details from the text to support their description.

   Possible response: The mood is tense and exciting. Words and phrases such as *interrupted, immediately, "a moment more,"* and *astounded* convey the rapid action and tension of the moment.

3. Direct students' attention to Montresor's comment, "But I must first render you all the little attentions in my power." **Ask:** What does this sentence suggest about the mood of the text yet to be read?

   Answer: Montresor's remark suggests that he will torture Fortunato even more, and the mood of the story will continue to be tense and dark as the two characters struggle.

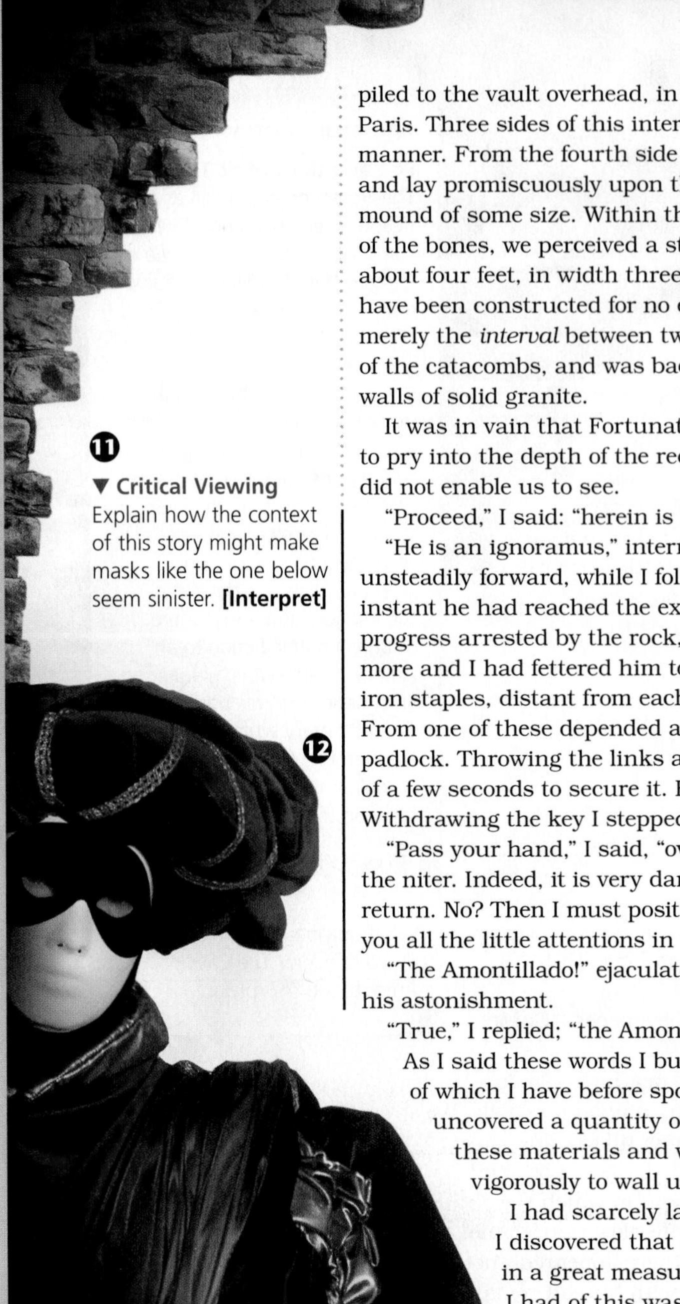

⓫

▼ **Critical Viewing**
Explain how the context of this story might make masks like the one below seem sinister. **[Interpret]**

piled to the vault overhead, in the fashion of the great catacombs of Paris. Three sides of this interior crypt were still ornamented in this manner. From the fourth side the bones had been thrown down, and lay promiscuously upon the earth, forming at one point a mound of some size. Within the wall thus exposed by the displacing of the bones, we perceived a still interior crypt or recess, in depth about four feet, in width three, in height six or seven. It seemed to have been constructed for no especial use within itself, but formed merely the *interval* between two of the colossal supports of the roof of the catacombs, and was backed by one of their circumscribing walls of solid granite.

It was in vain that Fortunato, uplifting his dull torch, endeavored to pry into the depth of the recess. Its termination the feeble light did not enable us to see.

⓬

"Proceed," I said: "herein is the Amontillado. As for Luchesi—"

"He is an ignoramus," interrupted my friend, as he stepped unsteadily forward, while I followed immediately at his heels. In an instant he had reached the extremity of the niche, and finding his progress arrested by the rock, stood stupidly bewildered. A moment more and I had fettered him to the granite. In its surface were two iron staples, distant from each other about two feet, horizontally. From one of these depended a short chain, from the other a padlock. Throwing the links about his waist, it was but the work of a few seconds to secure it. He was too much astounded to resist. Withdrawing the key I stepped back from the recess.

"Pass your hand," I said, "over the wall; you cannot help feeling the niter. Indeed, it is very damp. Once more let me implore you to return. No? Then I must positively leave you. But I must first render you all the little attentions in my power."

"The Amontillado!" ejaculated my friend, not yet recovered from his astonishment.

"True," I replied; "the Amontillado."

As I said these words I busied myself among the pile of bones of which I have before spoken. Throwing them aside, I soon uncovered a quantity of building stone and mortar. With these materials and with the aid of my trowel, I began vigorously to wall up the entrance of the niche.

I had scarcely laid the first tier of the masonry when I discovered that the intoxication of Fortunato had in a great measure worn off. The earliest indication I had of this was a low moaning cry from the depth of the recess. It was not the cry of a drunken man. There was then a long and obstinate silence. I laid

Vocabulary Development

Vocabulary Knowledge Rating

When students have completed reading and discussing "The Cask of Amontillado," have them take out their **Vocabulary Knowledge Rating Chart** for this selection. Read the words aloud once more and have students rate their knowledge of the words again in the After Reading column. Clarify any words that are still problematic. Have students write their own definition and example or sentence in the appropriate column. Then have students complete the Vocabulary Practice activities at the end of the selection. Encourage students to use the words in further discussion and written work about this selection. Remind them that they will be accountable for these words on the **Selection Test,** ***Unit 1 Resources,*** pp. 102–104 or 105–107.

the second tier, and the third, and the fourth; and then I heard the furious vibrations of the chain. The noise lasted for several minutes, during which, that I might hearken to it with the more satisfaction, I ceased my labors and sat down upon the bones. When at last the clanking **subsided**, I resumed the trowel, and finished without interruption the fifth, the sixth, and the seventh tier. The wall was now nearly upon a level with my breast. I again paused, and holding the flambeaux over the masonwork, threw a few feeble rays upon the figure within.

13 A succession of loud and shrill screams, bursting suddenly from the throat of the chained form, seemed to thrust me violently back. For a brief moment I hesitated, I trembled. Unsheathing my rapier, I began to grope with it about the recess; but the thought of an instant reassured me. I placed my hand upon the solid fabric of the catacombs, and felt satisfied. I reapproached the wall; I replied to the yells of him who clamored. I reechoed, I aided, I surpassed them in volume and in strength. I did this, and the clamorer grew still.

It was now midnight, and my task was drawing to a close. I had completed the eighth, the ninth, and the tenth tier. I had finished a portion of the last and the eleventh; there remained but a single stone to be fitted and plastered in. I struggled with its weight; I placed it partially in its destined position. But now there came from out the niche a low laugh that erected the hairs upon my head. It was succeeded by a sad voice, which I had difficulty in recognizing as that of the noble Fortunato. The voice said—

"Ha! ha! ha!—he! he! he!—a very good joke, indeed—an excellent jest. We will have many a rich laugh about it at the palazzo—he! he! he!—over our wine—he! he! he!"

"The Amontillado!" I said.

"He! he! he!—he! he! he!—yes, the Amontillado. But is it not getting late? Will not they be awaiting us at the palazzo, the Lady Fortunato and the rest? Let us be gone."

"Yes," I said, "let us be gone."

"For the love of God, Montresor!"

Vocabulary
subsided (səb sīd´ əd) *v.* settled down; became less active or intense

Reading Skill
Make Predictions
Does this scene in which Montresor imprisons Fortunato verify your earlier predictions? Explain.

14 
Reading Check
How does Fortunato become locked in the chains so easily?

It was now midnight, and my task was drawing to a close.

13 Reading Skill
Make Predictions

1. **Ask** students whether making predictions helps them concentrate on their reading. Have them explain their answers.

   Possible response: Most students will say that making predictions helps them concentrate because they are looking for clues and verification of their predictions.

2. Have students read the bracketed text, which begins on page 66. **Ask** the Reading Skill question: Does this scene in which Montresor imprisons Fortunato verify your earlier predictions? Explain.

   Possible response: Students might have predicted this outcome based on clues such as Montresor's deep-seated desire for revenge, Fortunato's statement that the cough "will not kill me," and the fact that Montresor was carrying a trowel.

▶ **Monitor Progress:** Review students' graphic organizers to ensure that they have been making and verifying predictions effectively.

▶ **Reteach:** If students have difficulty making predictions, ask them to review the story and list clues that foreshadow Fortunato's final imprisonment. List the clues on the board, and discuss how they foreshadow the final scene.

14 Reading Check

Possible response: Fortunato is intoxicated, which dulls his senses and reaction time. In addition, when they arrive at a blank wall in the catacombs, Fortunato is bewildered and perplexed. This distraction allows Montresor to chain Fortunato to the wall with no resistance.

Concept Connector

Writing About the Big Question
Have students compare their responses to the sentence starter they completed before reading the story with their ideas afterwards. Ask them to explain whether their thoughts have changed.

Reading Skill Graphic Organizer
Have students review the graphic organizers they prepared to make and verify predictions while reading. Show them **Reading Skill Graphic Organizer A** (*Graphic Organizer Transparencies,* p. 10) as an example. Then, have students share the graphic organizers they did and the predictions they made about the story.

Spiral Review

Theme

1. Remind students that they studied the concept of theme in Unit 1 (pp. 4–21).
2. **Ask** students the first Spiral Review question.

   Answer: Fifty years have passed.
3. **Ask** students the second Spiral Review question.

   Possible response: This detail suggests that for some people, the need for revenge never dies. This insight is emphasized by Montresor's comment, *In pace requiescat,* which means "May he rest in peace."

ASSESS

Answers

Critical Thinking

1. (a) Montresor describes Fortunato as vain and not perceptive enough to see that Montresor is his enemy. (b) Fortunato's pride in his wine expertise make him receptive to Montresor's flattery.
2. (a) Montresor wears a mask and a cloak so that no one will recognize him. He makes sure his servants are out of the house. He remembers to bring a trowel. (b) He knows that the more he urges a return, the more a vain Fortunato will insist on proceeding.
3. (a) At the end, Montresor hesitates, suggesting that he might have some regret. (b) Montresor's character is flawed, but not beyond redemption. He does recognize that revenge is wrong.
4. **Possible response:** No, I do not think Montresor sees the truth. Montresor's truth is distorted by his anger and sense of injury. I do not think he acts appropriately when he takes revenge. He should find a better way to deal with Fortunato. Truth can change when you have a wide perspective, but Montresor's perspective is narrow.

"Yes," I said, "for the love of God!"

But to these words I hearkened in vain for a reply. I grew impatient. I called aloud—

"Fortunato!"

No answer. I called again—

"Fortunato!"

No answer still. I thrust a torch through the remaining aperture and let it fall within. There came forth in return only a jingling of the bells. My heart grew sick; it was the dampness of the catacombs that made it so. I hastened to make an end of my labor. I forced the last stone into its position; I plastered it up. Against the new masonry I reerected the old rampart of bones. For the half of a century no mortal has disturbed them. *In pace requiescat!*[12]

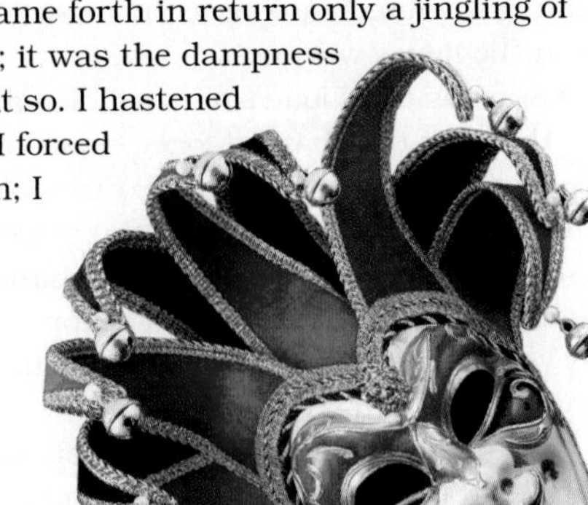

Spiral Review

Theme How many years have passed since Montresor took revenge on Fortunato? What insight into revenge does this detail suggest? Explain.

12. ***In pace requiescat!*** Latin for "May he rest in peace!"

Critical Thinking

Cite textual evidence to support your responses.

1. **Key Ideas and Details (a)** How does Montresor describe Fortunato's strengths and weaknesses early in the story? **(b) Analyze:** Which character traits make Fortunato easy prey for Montresor?
2. **Key Ideas and Details (a)** What specific steps does Montresor take to ensure that his plan works? **(b) Interpret:** Why does Montresor keep urging Fortunato to turn back?
3. **Craft and Structure (a) Assess:** Does Montresor express any regret or ever question whether this punishment is fair, just, or rational? **(b) Evaluate:** What does your answer tell you about Montresor's character?
4. **Integration of Knowledge and Ideas** Montresor acts as both victim and judge in this story. Do you think that Montresor sees the truth and acts appropriately? Explain. ***[Connect to the Big Question: Can truth change?]***

Assessment Resources

Unit 1 Resources

L1 L2 EL **Selection Test A,** pp. 102–104. Administer Test A to less advanced readers.

L3 L4 EL **Selection Test B,** pp. 105–107. Administer Test B to on-level and more advanced students.

L3 L4 **Open-Book Test,** pp. 99–101. As an alternative, give the Open-Book Test.

All **Customizable Test Bank**

All **Self-tests**
Students may prepare for the **Selection Test** by taking the **Self-test** online.

PHLit Online!

All assessment resources are available at **www.PHLitOnline.com.**

After You Read The Cask of Amontillado

Literary Analysis: Plot

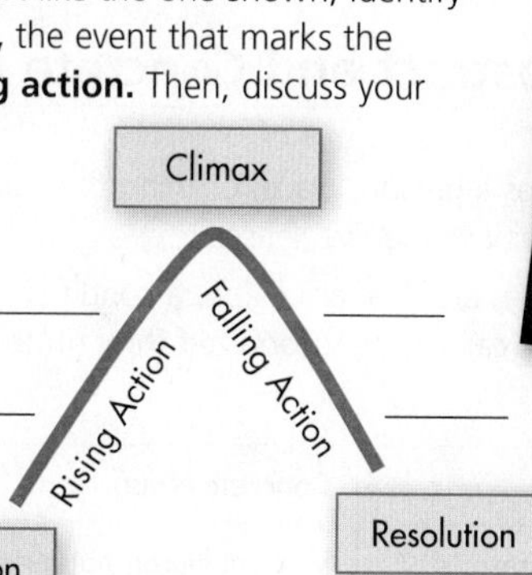

1. **Key Ideas and Details** Using a chart like the one shown, identify two key events in the **rising action,** the event that marks the **climax,** and one event in the **falling action.** Then, discuss your choices with a partner.
2. **Craft and Structure** **(a)** Identify a passage that **foreshadows** Fortunato's fate. **(b)** Explain how the foreshadowing adds to the story's **suspense**.

Climax
Rising Action
Falling Action
Exposition
Resolution

Reading Skill: Make Predictions

3. **(a)** What **prediction** did you make after reading about Montresor's and Fortunato's shared interest in wine?
   (b) What details helped you make your prediction?
4. Was your prediction **verified** by later story events? Explain.

Vocabulary

Acquisition and Use An **analogy** shows the relationship between pairs of words. Use a word from the vocabulary list on page 58 to complete each analogy. For each case, your choice should create a word pair that matches the relationship between the first two words.

1. conversation: dialogue :: ______ : revenge
2. harmed : helped :: ______ : allowed
3. delicious : food :: ______ : instructions
4. graceful : awkward :: ______ : increased
5. humor : laughing :: disgust : ______
6. enormous : gigantic :: troubled : ______

Word Study Use the context of the sentences and what you know about the **suffix *-tion*** to explain your answer to each question.

1. What is audience *participation?*
2. If you make a *contribution* to a cause, what have you done?

Word Study

The **suffix *-tion*** means "the act of."

Apply It The suffix *-tion* often indicates that a word is a noun. Identify another form of each word below by changing the suffix.

reconciliation
compensation
induction

ASSESS/EXTEND

Answers

Literary Analysis

1. **Possible response:** Rising **Action:** Montresor invites Fortunato to the vaults to try his wine; Montresor chains Fortunato to the wall. **Climax:** Montresor thrusts his torch into the crypt and hears only the jingling of the bells on Fortunato's costume. **Falling Action:** Montresor replaces the bones to cover the crypt's entrance.

For other sample answers, see ***Graphic Organizer Transparencies,*** **Literary Analysis Graphic Organizer A,** p. 13, and the **Additional Answers** section.

2. (a) Montresor declares himself a "mason" and shows Fortunato a trowel that he has hidden under his cloak. (b) **Possible response:** Foreshadowing makes readers anxious about what Montresor is going to do. Clues suggest that he is planning something horrible, so readers anticipate it with uncertainty and dread.

Reading Skill

3. (a) **Possible response:** Students may have predicted that Montresor would use Fortunato's interest in wine to exact his revenge. (b) Clues include Montresor's stated desire for revenge and his comment that wine is Fortunato's weakness.
4. **Possible response:** Yes, my prediction was verified. Fortunato goes into the catacombs believing he is going to taste some wine.

Vocabulary

Acquisition and Use

Sample answers:

1. retribution
2. precluded
3. explicit
4. subsided
5. recoiling
6. afflicted

Word Study

Sample answers:

1. The suffix *-tion* means "the act of," and *participation* means "the act of participating." Making comments is audience *participation.*
2. The suffix *-tion* means "the act of," and *contribution* means "the act of contributing." Donating money or time is making a *contribution.*

Word Study: Apply It

Sample answers:

reconcile, compensatory, inductive

EXTEND/ASSESS

Answers

Conventions

Introduce the skill, using the instruction on the student page.

Think Aloud: Model the Skill

Say to students:

To distinguish concrete and abstract nouns, I ask myself if I can see or touch what the noun names. Consider the sentence, "I use words to describe my thoughts." I can see *words* because I can write them down, so *words* is a concrete noun. I can't see *thoughts* because they're in my head, so *thoughts* is an abstract noun.

PH WRITING COACH Grade 9

Students will find further instruction on concrete and abstract nouns in Chapter 13, Section 1.

Practice A

1. concrete; The new assistant, Jason, was unaware of the policy.
2. abstract; To Jason, the reason for the policy was a mystery.
3. abstract; Jason felt no fear of going into the building at night.
4. abstract; While at work, Jason fell in love with Miss Golden.
5. abstract; He was willing to take a big risk to be with her.

Reading Application

Students' should find one sentence with a concrete noun and one with an abstract noun.

Practice B

1. abstract: *vengeance;* concrete: *heart;* A desire for vengeance nearly always leads to problems.
2. abstract: *falsehood;* concrete: *catacombs;* Catacombs are dark and damp places.
3. abstract: *search;* concrete: *men;* You must use careful thinking when conducting a search.
4. abstract: *fate;* concrete: *Fortunato;* Fortunato loved wine.
5. abstract: *remorse;* concrete: *Montresor;* Montresor is the narrator of "The Cask of Amontillado."

Writing Application

Students should write two sentences that follow the pattern of presenting and describing nouns.

PERFORMANCE TASKS

Integrated Language Skills

Sonata for Harp and Bicycle • The Cask of Amontillado

Conventions: Abstract and Concrete Nouns

A **concrete noun** names a person, place, or thing that can be seen or recognized through any of the five senses.

An **abstract noun** names an idea, an action, a condition, or a quality—something that cannot be recognized through the senses.

Abstract Noun	Concrete Noun
Fortunato discovered Montresor's *intention*, but it was too late.	William Heron patrolled the halls on a *bicycle*.

Practice A Tell whether the underlined word in each sentence is a concrete noun or an abstract noun. Then, use the word in an original sentence about the story.

1. Mr. Manaby instructed Jason, the new assistant, to leave at five.
2. What went on in the building after five was a mystery to Jason.
3. He did not seem to have fear of the curse.
4. He wanted to know why he could not stay later at work.
5. He found answers by taking a tremendous risk.

Reading Application In "Sonata for Harp and Bicycle," find one sentence with a concrete noun and one with an abstract noun.

Practice B Identify an abstract and a concrete noun in each sentence. Then, use one of the words in an original sentence.

1. Montresor held vengeance in his heart.
2. He lured Fortunato to the catacombs with a falsehood.
3. The men were supposedly on the search for a cask of wine.
4. Instead, Fortunato met a horrid fate after reading Montresor's letters.
5. Montresor felt no remorse after carrying out his plan.

Writing Application Using these two sentences as models, write two more sentences that follow the pattern of presenting and describing nouns: *The wine sparkled in his eyes and bells jingled. The joy glowed on his face and his keys jangled.*

PH WRITING COACH Further instruction and practice are available in *Prentice Hall Writing Coach.*

Extend the Lesson

Sentence Modeling

Choose the sentence given from the selection students have read:

An ambulance clanged, a taxi hooted, a drill stuttered, a siren wailed on the river, a door slammed, a brake squealed, and close beside his ear a bicycle bell tinkled its tiny warning. ("Sonata for Harp and Bicycle")

He turned towards me, and looked into my eyes with two filmy orbs that distilled the rheum of intoxication. ("The Cask of Amontillado")

Ask students what they notice about the sentence. Elicit that the sentence contains abstract and concrete nouns. Then, ask what else they notice. ("Sonata for Harp and Bicycle": The abstract noun *warning* turns the bell into a symbol. "The Cask of Amontillado": Poe uses a metaphor combining abstract and concrete nouns.) Have students imitate the sentence, matching each grammatical and stylistic feature discussed. Have students share their sentences.

Writing

 **Explanatory Text** Each of these stories presents readers with a compelling plot. Write a **critique** analyzing and evaluating the suspense and the ending of either "Sonata for Harp and Bicycle" or "The Cask of Amontillado."

- Before you draft, list the qualities a suspenseful story should have. Then, list the qualities that make a satisfactory ending for you.
- Use your lists to evaluate the suspense, the ending of the story, and the author's use of devices, such as foreshadowing. Note specific details from the story that demonstrate your ideas.
- As you write your critique, consult your checklists, using them as evidence to support your analysis.

Grammar Application As you write, consider your noun choices. Use abstract nouns to describe ideas or qualities and concrete nouns to refer to physical things.

Writing Workshop: *Work in Progress*

Prewriting for an Autobiographical Narrative Review the Memory List in your writing portfolio. Next to each scene description, **describe your reaction** in the situation. Save this Reaction Work in your writing portfolio.

Common Core State Standards

L.9-10.3; W.9-10.9; SL.9-10.1, SL.9-10.1.a

[For the full wording of the standards, see page 42.]

Use this prewriting activity to prepare for the **Writing Workshop** on page 94.

Speaking and Listening

Comprehension and Collaboration With a partner, **retell** one of the stories from another point of view. For example, you might tell "Sonata for Harp or Bicycle" from Miss Golden's point of view or "The Cask of Amontillado" from Fortunato's point of view. Refresh your memory by rereading your chosen selection. Follow these steps to complete the assignment.

- Identify an audience and the type of information they will need.
- Make language choices appropriate for the audience and the story, using words and expressions consistent with the narrator's character.
- As you speak, use facial expressions and body movements effectively to convey the narrator's personality.
- Make eye contact with your audience to engage them in the story.
- Vary your intonation to reflect the emotions of the narrator.
- After you and your partner have presented your work, evaluate each other's presentations in a thoughtful, well-reasoned discussion.

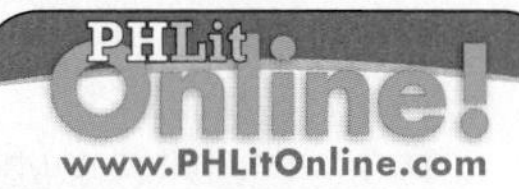

www.PHLitOnline.com

- Interactive graphic organizers
- Grammar tutorial
- Interactive journals

EXTEND/ASSESS

Writing

1. Review the assignment, using the instruction on the student page.
2. To give students guidance for writing a critique, give them **Support for Writing,** p. 97 in ***Unit 1 Resources.***
3. To evaluate students' critiques, use the **Response to Literature** rubrics, pp. 224–225 in ***Professional Development Guidebook.*** In addition, you might place emphasis on using evidence from the story to support students' ideas.

Grammar Application

Have students check their drafts for correct capitalization of proper nouns.

Six Traits Focus

✓	Ideas		Word Choice
	Organization		Sentence Fluency
✓	Voice		Conventions

PH WRITING COACH Grade 9

Students will find guidance on writing a response to literature in Chapter 10.

Writing Workshop
Work in Progress

Have students save their completed Memory Lists in their portfolios. They will use the Memory List later as they complete the Writing Workshop assignment (see pp. 94–99).

Speaking and Listening

1. Review the assignment, using the instruction on the student page.
2. To support students' work on the assignment, have students complete the **Support for Extend Your Learning** page (*Unit 1 Resources,* p. 98).

Teaching Resources

All *Unit 1 Resources*

L3 L4 EL **Integrated Language Skills: Grammar,** p. 96

L3 L4 EL **Support for Writing,** p. 97

L3 L4 **Support for Extend Your Learning,** p. 98

L4 **Enrichment,** pp. 77, 95

All **Enriched Online Student Edition**
Available under After You Read for this selection:

All **Interactive Grammar Tutorial**

L3 L4 **Internet Research Activity**

Professional Development Guidebook
Rubrics for Response to Literature, pp. 224–225

PHLit Online! All print and digital resources are available online at **www.PHLitOnline.com**. Online resources accessible by students are noted on the student page.

MONITORING PROGRESS

Using the Test Practice

In this two-page Test Practice, students apply the reading skill for the first half of Unit 1 to a passage of fiction and a passage of nonfiction.

Review this skill, making predictions, then administer the test. For more guidance, consult the ***Classroom Strategies and Teaching Routines*** card, **Formally Assessing Students.**

ASSESS

Answers

Answers With Explanations

1. **C**—The title and first sentence together suggest that Martina will learn to skateboard. *Incorrect answers:* A—The story is about skateboarding, not Martina's relationship with her brother. B—The story is unlikely to address the history of skateboarding. D—The story might have a competition, but focusing on Martina learning to skateboard is more likely.
2. **B**—Martina's mother had confidence in her because of her determination. *Incorrect answers:* A—One person's skill in an activity does not always predict that of a sibling. C—This answer does not reflect her determination. D—This comment comes after Martina has already learned skateboarding.
3. **A**—This answer is likely; he said this previously. *Incorrect answers:* B—This would be a surprise, as he never agreed to her using it before. C—His typical response is to deny it outright rather than to use sarcasm. D—She does not have to ask their mother because it is his board.
4. **A**— From the title and Martina's behavior, she will probably ride well. *Incorrect answers:* B—Since she has been practicing, we know she is unlikely to fall. C—From the next-to-last sentence, we know she uses his board. D—She wants to demonstrate her skill, not anger him.

Test Practice: Reading

Make Predictions

Fiction Selection

Directions: *Read the selection. Then, answer the questions.*

The Great Skate

All Martina ever wanted was to learn how to ride a skateboard. Despite Martina's pleading, any attempt at using her older bother's board would invite a shrieking response. "Don't touch that!" he would shout. Seeing her determination, Martina's mother bought her a skateboard. Practicing secretly every day, Martina built her skills and her confidence. When she finally felt ready to prove her ability, Martina asked one last time to use her brother's board. Surprisingly, he gave in to the request but with little encouragement. "Okay, little girl, give it your best shot," he laughed. Martina smiled as her hands gripped the rough edges of the board. She knew she would skate away his sarcasm.

1. Based on clues in the title and the first sentence, which would be the best prediction?
- **A.** The story will be about a rivalry between Martina and her brother.
- **B.** The story will be about the history of skateboarding.
- **C.** The story will be about Martina learning to ride a skateboard.
- **D.** The story will be about Martina competing on a skateboard.

2. Which clue from the text supports the prediction that Martina will learn to skateboard well?
- **A.** Her older brother was so good he competed.
- **B.** Her mom gave Martina her own board because she was so determined.
- **C.** One day, she begged her brother to let her try his board.
- **D.** Martina hated it when her brother called her "little girl."

3. Based on clues in the text, what did you predict Martina's brother would say when she asked one last time to try his board?
- **A.** "Don't touch that!"
- **B.** "Sure. No problem."
- **C.** "What board?"
- **D.** "You'd better ask Mom."

4. Based on clues in the text, what do you predict will happen once Martina takes her brother's board?
- **A.** She will ride well and impress him.
- **B.** She will fall as he expects her to.
- **C.** She will tell him she has her own board.
- **D.** She will break his skateboard.

Writing for Assessment

In a brief paragraph, explain your thinking process in predicting what will happen when Martina takes the board. Which details from the text support your prediction?

Writing for Assessment

Students' answers should mention Martina's determination to ride a skateboard, her hours of practice, and her desire to surprise her brother.

Strategies for Test Taking

Because time is often a factor in standardized tests, point out to students that they should answer the questions they know first and then go back and work on the remaining questions. This way they will receive credit for what they know and then can make educated guesses on the rest of the items.

Nonfiction Selection

Directions: *Read the selection. Then, answer the questions.*

Skateboarding grew out of surfing. Surfers had to depend on the weather and the perfect conditions to catch a wave. Instead of waiting for the perfect wave, they invented the skateboard and started "surfing" on land. The first skateboards were difficult to steer and ride. The wheels were also very hard, so the ride was bumpy. Over the years, many improvements have been made to skateboards. Even though the popularity of skateboarding declined for a while, it is now very popular again. Skateboarding is even considered to be an extreme sport.

1. Based on the first sentence in the selection, which is the best prediction about its content?
A. It will be about skateboarding history.
B. It will be about surfing history.
C. It will be about a famous skateboarder.
D. It will give specific instructions on how to skateboard.

2. What information would support a prediction about the safety of the original skateboards?
A. Skateboarding grew out of surfing.
B. The first skateboards were difficult to steer and ride.
C. They invented the skateboard and started "surfing" on land.
D. Skateboarding is even considered to be an extreme sport.

3. Which information would support a prediction about the decline in popularity of skateboarding?
A. Skateboards were easier to maneuver.
B. Skate parks closed because of accidents.
C. Rollerblades became popular.
D. People's interest in skateboarding grew.

4. Based on the information in the text, which is the best prediction for the future of skateboarding?
A. People will lose interest in skateboarding as a sport.
B. Skateboarding will be eliminated from extreme sports.
C. Skateboarding will continue to progress in popularity.
D. Skateboarders will stick with the inventions they now have.

Writing for Assessment

Connect Across Texts
If Martina and her brother had been alive when skateboards were first invented, do you think that would have affected Martina's ability to learn how to skateboard? Write a paragraph, in which you use details from the two passages to support your answer.

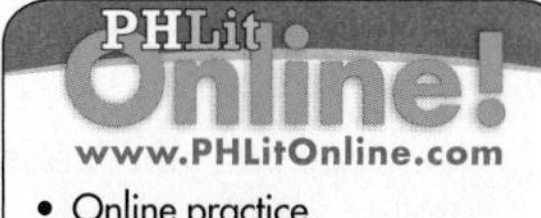

www.PHLitOnline.com
- Online practice
- Instant feedback

ASSESS

Answers

Answers With Explanations

1. **A**—The sentence tells how skateboarding began, so the passage is probably about the sport's history. *Incorrect answers:* B—Surfing appears only in relation to skateboarding. C—The first sentence focuses on history, so that is likely to be the thrust of the passage. D—same explanation as for C.
2. **B**—Since the article mentions the skateboards' limitations, it is reasonable to predict that they will have safety issues. *Incorrect answers:* A—This answer does not raise safety issues. C—same explanation as for A. D—same explanation as for A.
3. **C**—Rising popularity of a different sport could explain the decline in skateboarding, and a subsequent decline in the popularity of rollerblading could help explain why skateboarding gained popularity again. *Incorrect answers:* A—This positive characteristic is unlikely to lead to a decline in popularity. B—Although this could be true, it could not explain why skateboarding became popular again. D—If people's interest grew, skateboarding would not have become less popular.
4. **C**—Since skateboarding has undergone improvements, it will probably become more popular. *Incorrect answers:* A—The upbeat tone of the article suggests that this is not a reasonable prediction. B—The article does not examine what makes a sport extreme. D—Given past innovations, more are likely in the future.

Writing for Assessment

Students may suggest that unless Martina and her brother were surfers, they both may have had difficulty learning to skateboard. Early skateboards were hard to steer and ride. Also, Martina's mother may have been less eager to buy her a skateboard if it seemed dangerous.

Students may take the test in interactive format with instant feedback online at **www.PHLitOnline.com.**

Differentiated Instruction for Universal Access

EL Strategy for English Learners

Review the skill of making predictions by walking students through item 3. First, point out that if something "declines in popularity," people are no longer interested in it. Reread the passage with students. Explain that they will use the process of elimination to determine why skateboarding became less popular.

- A—Is it probable that skateboarding would decline in popularity if boards were easier to maneuver? (Eliminate.)
- B—Skateboarders do not need parks in order to skateboard. (Eliminate.)
- C—Could skateboarding became unpopular if another sport rose in popularity? This answer could be correct.
- D—If people's interest in skateboarding grew, skateboarding would be more popular, not less so. (Eliminate.)

Have students go back over the answers and determine that **C** is correct.

PRETEACH

Common Core State Standards

- Reading Informational Text 3
- Language 4.b; 6

Reading Skill

1. Introduce the skill, using the instruction on the student page.
2. Review the chart.
3. Tell students they will read instructions to perform a task.

Think Aloud: Model the Skill

Model the skill of reading to perform a task. Say to students:

As I look over the chart on page 74, I notice signal words that will help me prepare the recipe. The signal word *gradually* tells me how to add ingredients; *medium* tells me the temperature to use; *lightly* instructs me on how to prepare the surface; and *spoonful* tells me the amount of an ingredient to use.

Multidraft Reading

Have students follow a multidraft reading protocol.

- **First reading**—Have students read to identify key ideas and details.
- **Second reading**—Have students read to identify the structure of the text.
- **Third reading**—Have students read to integrate knowledge and ideas by connecting the text to the world, their own experiences, and other texts.

Content-Area Vocabulary

1. Have students say each word.
2. Next, use each word in a sentence that defines it.
3. Finally, repeat your definitional sentence or a similar sentence with the word missing and have the class "fill in the blank" chorally.

Reading for Information

Analyzing Functional and Expository Texts

Recipe

How-to Article

Common Core State Standards

Reading Informational Text

3. Analyze how the author unfolds an analysis or series of ideas or events, including the order in which the points are made, how they are introduced and developed, and the connections that are drawn between them.

Language

4.b. Identify and correctly use patterns of word changes that indicate different meanings or parts of speech.

6. Acquire and use accurately general academic and domain-specific words and phrases, sufficient for reading, writing, speaking, and listening at the college and career readiness level.

Reading Skill: Read to Perform a Task

Most instructions present a series of specific steps you must follow to complete a larger task. When you **read to perform a task,** pay attention to the **sequence,** or order, of the required steps. Also, look for the main idea presented in each step. Check off each step as you complete it. When you read any set of directions, pay close attention to words that signal relevant details—especially words of quantity and adverbs that tell how to perform tasks. The chart shown here identifies signal words.

Instruction	Key Word
Gradually add the broth and milk…	tells how to add ingredients
Cook over *medium* heat…	tells what level temperature
…on a *lightly* floured surface	tells how to prepare pan
Put a *spoonful* of filling in center…	tells how much

Content-Area Vocabulary

These words appear in the selections that follow. You may also encounter them in other content-area texts.

- **minced** (minsd´) *adj.* cut up into very small pieces
- **incubator** (in´ kyə bāt´ ər) *n.* artificially heated container for hatching eggs
- **ventilation** (vent´ 'l ā´ shən) *n.* the circulation of fresh air in a building, room, or other space

Can truth change?

Have students consider how outcomes might differ if directions are not followed precisely.

Differentiated Instruction for Universal Access

Reading Support

Give students reading support with the appropriate version of the ***Reader's Notebooks:***

- L2 L3 *Reader's Notebook*
- L1 *Reader's Notebook: Adapted Version*
- EL *Reader's Notebook: English Learner's Version*

from The Book Lover's Cookbook

New Road Chicken Pies

by Shaunda Kennedy Wenger and Janet Kay Jensen

Recipe

Features:

- text that provides how-to directions for cooking or baking
- listing of ingredients, precise measurements, and cooking times
- step-by-step instructions for combining and preparing ingredients

Oliver Twist's request for more gruel starts a riot, and Ma Joad agonizes over not being able to fill the bellies of hungry children who watch her family eat stew. When characters deal with food, whether they're eating, cooking, dreaming, manipulating, or suffering, they step off the page and connect with the reader.

Food scenes offer a universal platform that can foster connections between the reader and the character. Some food scenes bring such strong feelings of nostalgia, the experience between the fiction of the story, the reality of the present, and the memories of the past blur to the point where we question, Could I have known this author? Could I have known this character?

This recipe links the real-life experience of preparing and eating delicious meat-pies to the characters and events in Maya Angelou's story "New Directions."

The introduction describes the way in which a recipe can connect readers to literary characters.

New Road Chicken Pies

(a.k.a. Turnovers)

FILLING:

1/2 cup potatoes, diced
1/4 cup carrots, diced
3 tablespoons celery, chopped
1 teaspoon onion, **minced**
1 tablespoon butter or margarine
3 tablespoons all-purpose flour
Salt and pepper to taste
1 cup chicken broth
1/3 cup milk
1 teaspoon fresh parsley, minced
1/4 cup frozen peas, thawed
1 1/2 cups chicken, cooked & diced

PASTRY DOUGH:

2/3 cup shortening or margarine
2 cups all-purpose flour
1/2 teaspoon salt
5 to 7 tablespoons water
1 egg white
1 teaspoon water

The first step is to look at the complete list of every ingredient and the exact amount required. Some items must be *diced, chopped, minced,* or *thawed* before the mixing of ingredients begins.

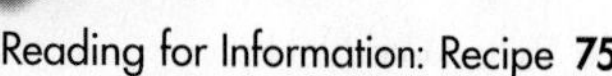

About Recipes

1. Review the list of recipe features shown in the box at the top of page 75.
2. Discuss different ways to read a recipe. Point out that people may casually read recipes to decide whether they want to make a particular dish. **Ask:** How is reading a recipe casually different from reading a recipe as you prepare it?

   Possible response: When you read a recipe casually, you read the ingredients and think about how the food will look and taste. When you read a recipe as you prepare it, you carefully follow the steps in the instructions.

Read to Perform a Task

1. Have a volunteer read the name of the recipe. Tell students that *a.k.a.* stands for "also known as" and that *Turnovers* is another name for this recipe.
2. Have students skim the ingredients. **Ask:** What do you notice about the list of ingredients?

   Possible response: It is divided into two parts: filling ingredients and pastry dough ingredients.
3. Remind students that sometimes you need to prepare ingredients before using them. Have a volunteer read the filling ingredients. **Ask:** What additional preparations do you need to make?

   Answer: You need to dice the potatoes and carrots, chop the celery, mince the onion and parsley, thaw the peas, and cook and dice the chicken.
4. Tell students that having all the ingredients prepared and measured enables you to be ready to follow the instructions to make the recipe.

Differentiated Instruction for Universal Access

Strategy for Less Proficient Readers

Organize students into groups. Have them work together to find images of each ingredient in the recipe. Then have them label the images and sort them into filling ingredients and pastry dough ingredients. If students have difficulty finding particular images, suggest that they illustrate the ingredients. Finally, have students write on the image any additional preparation needed for ingredients, such as "dice" on the image of the potatoes.

Strategy for Advanced Readers

Have students research turnover recipes used in other cultures. Many cultures prepare recipes in which a piece of dough is wrapped around a filling. Have students choose another culture's recipe and compare and contrast its ingredients with the ingredients for the recipe shown on this page. Have students research occasions when the recipes are prepared and present their results to the class.

Read to Perform a Task

1. Tell students that it is helpful to read completely through the recipe before making it. Then have students read the recipe. **Ask:** Why do you think it is useful to read completely through the recipe before making it?

   Possible response: When you read completely through the recipe, you find out what other materials you need, such as bowls and saucepans, and you can have them ready.
2. Point out the note explaining that the recipe instructions are given in a particular order. **Ask:** What do you do first: cook the vegetables or make the sauce?

   Answer: Cook the vegetables.
3. **Ask:** After you have made the pastry dough, cut it into circles, and placed a spoonful of filling in each circle, what do you do?

   Answer: Fold the circle to a half-moon shape and press the edges together to make a seam.
4. Discuss the final steps in preparing the New Road Chicken Pies. **Ask:** For how long do you bake the turnovers?

   Answer: Bake them for 15 to 20 minutes or until golden brown.
5. Explain that recipes often tell the number of servings they make so that you can plan the appropriate amount for your guests.

New Road Chicken Pies

continued

Boil the potatoes, carrots, celery, and onions until tender, about 6 to 8 minutes. Drain and set aside. In a separate saucepan, melt the butter or margarine over medium heat. Whisk in the flour, salt, and pepper. Gradually add the broth and milk, whisking continually to keep sauce smooth. Cook over medium heat until thickened. Stir in the cooked vegetables, parsley, peas, and chicken and continue cooking until warmed through.

The recipe gives instructions in a specific order. First the vegetables must be cooked, and then they can be added to the sauce.

Prepare pastry by mixing the shortening or margarine, sugar, flour, and salt in a bowl with a fork or pastry blender until the mixture is crumbly. Add water 1 tablespoon at a time until dough is pliable. Work dough into a ball with hands after last tablespoon of water is added.

With a rolling pin, roll the pastry dough out to a 1/4-inch thickness on a lightly floured surface. Cut 4-inch or 5-inch-diameter circles from the dough. Put a spoonful of filling in center of each circle. Fold to a half-moon shape. Press edges together to make a seam. Crimp edges with a fork, dipping tines in flour as needed to keep from sticking to dough.

In a small bowl, whisk together egg white and 1 teaspoon water. Brush egg white mixture onto the tops of the turnovers with a pastry brush. Cut a small slit in the top of each turnover. Bake on ungreased cookie sheet at 375° for 15 to 20 minutes or until golden brown.

MAKES 8 TO 10 TURNOVERS

The last line provides the number of servings the recipe makes. If you want to make 16–20 turnovers, you would double the quantities of the ingredients.

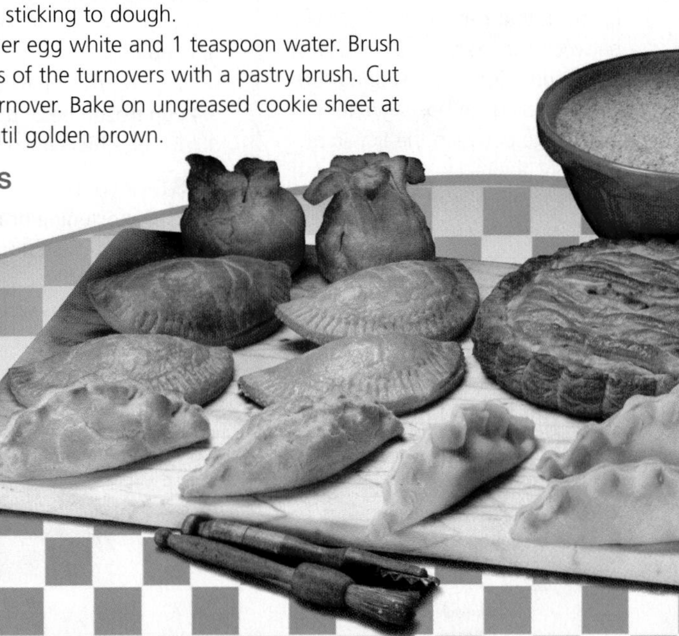

Vocabulary Development

CCSS Language 6

Content-Area Vocabulary: Family and Consumer Science

Point out that recipes often use vocabulary that is specific to food preparation and cooking equipment. Guide students to understand the meaning of these terms:

crimp: to press tightly together so as to form ridges

diced: cut into small cubes

minced: cut into tiny pieces

pastry blender: a kitchen utensil having a handle and several semicircular-shaped wires, used to mix dough

rolling pin: a cylinder-shaped utensil with handles on both ends, used to flatten or shape dough

thawed: defrosted or become unfrozen

tines: thin, pointed ends of a fork

whisk: to lightly and rapidly stir a liquid

PHLit Online! All student resources are also available online at **www.PHLitOnline.com.**

Incubating Eggs in Small Quantities

How-to Article

Features:

- text that identifies the steps necessary to perform a task
- information presented in step-by-step order
- headings and subheadings for clarity
- text that is written for a specific audience

Ursula K. Abbott, Professor Emerita; Ralph A. Ernst, Extension Poultry Specialist; and Francine A. Bradley, Extension Poultry Specialist

Department of Animal Science, University of California, Davis

To hatch a small number of eggs, buy or build an **incubator** that provides controlled conditions. You might want a model with transparent sides or top so you can watch the hatching. An alternative that is frequently overlooked is natural incubation under a broody hen. Each hen can cover 12 to 14 chicken eggs, 9 to 11 duck eggs, or 4 to 6 goose eggs. General purpose breeds like New Hampshires and Plymouth Rocks make better setters than Leghorns.

The authors provide relevant details about a variety of incubators to help readers decide which type would best suit their needs.

INCUBATION PERIODS

Japanese quail	17-18 days
Chicken	21 days
Pheasants, Chukar partridge, Bobwhite and Valley quail	24 days
Turkeys, guinea fowl, peafowl, most ducks	28 days
Most geese	30 days
Muscovy ducks, Canadian and Egyptian geese	35 days

This chart of the various incubation periods tells readers what to expect from each type of egg.

INCUBATING CONDITIONS

Read this section carefully to ensure that you understand the details about temperature and humidity.

Temperature. Incubators with fans are set at 99 1/2°F to 99 3/4°F; incubators with gravity **ventilation** are set at temperatures of 101°F to 103°F as measured at the top of the egg. Lethal temperatures are 103°F in fan-ventilated incubators, and 107°F in gravity-ventilated incubators. To regulate temperature, humidity, etc., follow the manufacturer's directions if available.

Humidity. During incubation, a relative humidity of about 60 percent is satisfactory; at hatching it should be raised to about 70 percent. Trays of water inside the incubator furnish these humidity levels. In fan-ventilated machines, humidity is measured indirectly but quite accurately by a wet-bulb thermometer (a thermometer with its bulb wrapped in a damp cloth). At 99.5°F dry bulb, a reading of 85°F to 86°F on the

Differentiated Instruction for Universal Access

Strategy for Special-Needs Students

Invite students to give a class demonstration that explains how to perform a task. Have students bring to class an object that they have made and ask them to show the class how they created it. Students might bring a craft project, such as a scrapbook or a woven belt. Allow time for students to give their presentations to the class.

Strategy for Gifted/Talented Students

Students may be interested in exploring a hands-on activity with incubators. Have students research organizations or companies that carry the necessary equipment. Then have students work with an adult experienced in poultry farming. Students should decide what type of eggs they are going to incubate and work with the adult throughout the incubation process. Have students present their results to the class.

About How-to Articles

1. Discuss how-to articles with students. Tell them that a how-to article explains how to perform a particular task. Point out the features of how-to articles shown in the box at the top of page 77.
2. **Ask:** What types of how-to articles have you read?

   Possible responses: How to build a model airplane; how to sew a dress.
3. Tell students that this how-to article explains how to incubate small quantities of eggs. **Ask:** Who might need to know this information?

   Possible responses: A poultry farmer might need this information.

Read to Perform a Task

1. Discuss the meaning of *incubate*, "to keep eggs at a suitable temperature so that they will develop."
2. Direct students' attention to the note beside the first paragraph of text. Point out that the note explains the author's purpose for including this information.
3. Have students read "Incubating Eggs in Small Quantities."
4. Discuss the chart with students. Explain that the chart tells the incubation periods of different types of poultry eggs. **Ask:** How long do chicken eggs need to incubate?

   Answer: They need 21 days to incubate.
5. **Ask:** What are two incubating conditions that need to be controlled? How do you know?

   Answer: Temperature and humidity need to be controlled. I know because I see the subheadings "Temperature" and "Humidity" beneath the heading "Incubating Conditions."
6. **Ask:** After reading the paragraphs about temperature and humidity, what equipment do you learn that you will need to use in an incubator?

   Possible responses: Students may say that equipment might include a fan, a thermometer, a damp cloth, or trays for water.

Read to Perform a Task

1. Discuss with students the additional incubating conditions listed on page 78. **Ask:** How do you know that incubating eggs is time consuming?

   Possible responses: Eggs have to be turned at least three times a day, and some of them must be turned for up to 15 days. Some eggs have to be turned by hand, which takes a lot of time.

2. **Ask:** What are some of the points that are covered in "Helpful Hints"?

   Possible responses: "Helpful Hints" includes information about how to store eggs, how to set eggs, how to choose eggs, how to care for chicks after hatching, and tips on purchasing an incubator.

3. **Ask:** Why is it important to know what to look for when buying an incubator?

   Possible responses: Successful hatching often depends on accurate temperature and humidity controls. Buying an incubator with good controls means that your eggs will have a better chance of hatching.

wet-bulb thermometer gives the desired humidity. At hatching, the dry-bulb temperature is reduced about 1°F and the wet-bulb temperature is increased to 88°F to 90°F. Low humidity can be a problem in very small incubators; additional moisture is especially necessary if the incubator is opened frequently for turning eggs.

Turning. Eggs must be turned until late in incubation. Chicken eggs, for example, must be turned to the 15th day. For many small incubators, lay eggs on their sides and turn by hand an odd number of times (at least three) per day. A pencil mark on the side of the egg will be a useful guide. Do not rotate the eggs in the same direction each time. A broody hen turns eggs when nesting, but because of their large size, turn goose eggs under a chicken hen by hand.

Ventilation. Your incubator is equipped with vents to permit a slow change of air. Little ventilation is needed when incubation starts; it may be increased gradually as incubation progresses. During hatching, restrict ventilation in order to raise the humidity.

HELPFUL HINTS

Since most eggs sold at the grocery store are infertile, purchase hatching eggs from a breeding farm. Keep them at 50°F to 60°F, if possible. A household refrigerator is too cool for storing hatching eggs, and at 80°F fertile eggs begin to develop in an abnormal manner. Set the eggs before they are 2 weeks old.

Details here provide exact temperatures and times that are necessary for success.

Clean your incubator thoroughly and test its operation for a day or more before setting any eggs.

Eggs which are clean when they come from the nest are best for hatching. It is better not to wash eggs, since bacteria on the shell and in the water may easily enter the eggs and cause them to rot.

Cracked eggs spoil easily, seldom hatch, and are best removed from the incubator. If you candle after a week's incubation, infertile eggs and eggs with dead germs can be identified easily and removed from the incubator.

After hatching, leave the young in the incubator for a few hours to dry and fluff out completely.

The authors provide tips here to guide readers in performing the task.

Small incubators range widely in price depending upon size, construction and features (e.g., automatic egg turning, fan ventilation). When purchasing, consider that low-cost incubators usually have less accurate temperature and humidity controls and often lack a convenient egg-turning arrangement. They usually require close supervision to obtain hatching success.

Vocabulary Development

CCSS Language 6

Vocabulary for How-to Articles

Point out that how-to articles use vocabulary that is specific to the task being performed and to the end product. The author explains in detail how to complete the task. How-to articles generally include the equipment that the reader needs, along with a step-by-step guide to achieve success.

In "Incubating Eggs in Small Quantities" the vocabulary is specific to this task. Point out to students how the authors laid out the task. The authors include a chart that lists the various types of poultry and their incubation periods.

The authors also describe kinds of incubators, types of ventilation methods, the necessary temperature readings, and methods of egg turning.

Discuss the words that readers should become familiar with if they are interested in incubating eggs. *(incubator, ventilation, thermometer, lethal, relative humidity, hatching, nesting, infertile)*

Remind students that how-to articles often include specialized vocabulary.

After You Read | Recipe • How-to Article

Comparing Functional and Expository Texts

1. **Craft and Structure (a)** Compare the presentation and **sequence of information** in the recipe and the how-to article. How are they the same? How are they different? **(b)** Identify areas of each article in which a reader could misinterpret information. Does one text better enable you to **read to perform a task**?

Content-Area Vocabulary

2. **(a)** For each of the following words, explain how a change in suffix alters the meanings and parts of speech of the base word *ventilate*: *ventilation, ventilator,* and *ventilating*. **(b)** Use each word in a sentence that shows its meaning.

Timed Writing

Explanatory Text: Essay

Format
The prompt directs you to write an essay. Therefore, you should write an expository composition that has an introduction, body, and conclusion.

Many stories contain factual information to establish the setting or support the plot. Review the information given in the recipe and the how-to article. Write an essay of a few short paragraphs in which you explain how using this information might make a fiction piece more believable or realistic. (15 minutes)

Academic Vocabulary
When you *explain* something, you make it clear using examples, descriptions, details, and facts.

5-Minute Planner

Complete these steps before you begin to write:

1. Read the prompt carefully and completely to make sure you understand the assignment and the format to use for your writing.
2. To help you complete the assignment, consider the ways in which fiction writers include accurate descriptions to make their stories seem more believable.
3. Review each selection from the point of view of a writer conducting research to use in the development of a story. Take notes about each selection, identifying facts or details a writer might use to build character, setting, and plot.
4. Use your notes to make a list of the information a writer might use in a fiction piece. For each item, indicate how it might improve a story.
5. Consult your list as you begin to draft your essay.

ASSESS/EXTEND

Answers

Comparing Functional and Expository Texts

1. (a) **Possible response:** In both the recipe and the how-to article, a process is described in step-by-step order. In the recipe, the ingredients are listed first, followed by the steps of the process. The recipe is intended for a general audience. In the how-to article, the authors present the materials and the essential information needed to incubate eggs. The article is intended for a specialized audience. (b) **Possible response:** The recipe contains terms that might be confusing to an inexperienced cook, such as *pliable* and *crimp*. The how-to article is vague in some places, as in how to regulate temperature and humidity. Overall, the recipe is easier to understand if one has never performed the task before.
2. (a) The *-ion* suffix in *ventilation* indicates "the act or condition of"—in this case, the act or process of circulating air. The *-or* suffix in *ventilator* indicates "the person or thing that does something"—here, the person or thing that ventilates. The *-ory* suffix in *ventilatory* means "having the nature of"; something that is ventilatory has the nature of or pertains to ventilation. The first two suffixes create nouns; the third, adjectives. (b) **Sample response:** The room is stuffy because of poor ventilation. I would find it easier to breathe if I could install a ventilator in the window. Two windows that create a cross-breeze have a ventilatory function.

Timed Writing

1. Before students complete the activity, guide them in identifying and analyzing key words and phrases in the prompt, highlighted on the student page.
2. Work with students to draw up guidelines for their explanations based on the key words.
   - **Focus** The essay should explain how including factual information would make a piece of fiction more realistic.
   - **Organization** The essay should identify facts from the recipe and the how-to article, and then indicate how those facts might improve a story.
   - **Elaboration** The writer should suggest a plot that might be enhanced by details from the recipe or the incubator directions.
   - **Style** The audience is not specified, so a formal style is appropriate.
3. Have students use the 5-Minute Planner to structure their time.
4. Allow students 15 minutes to complete the assignment. Evaluate their work using the guidelines they have developed.

Common Core State Standards

- Reading Literature 6
- Writing 2.a.

1 Comparing Points of View

Narrative Point of View

1. Introduce the skill, using the instruction on the student page.
2. Give students a copy of **Comparing Points of View Graphic Organizer B** (*Graphic Organizer Transparencies,* p. 16) to compare points of view as they read.

Think Aloud: Model the Skill

Model a way of understanding point of view. Say to students:

To understand third-person point of view, I study how much information a narrator provides. For instance, the sentence, "He thought that Anna looked worried" suggests a limited narrator who knows the thoughts of only one character. Similarly, the text, "She felt apprehensive. He sensed her worry and tried to ease it" suggests an omniscient narrator who knows what both characters are experiencing. Clues like this help me identify the kind of point of view in a text.

Cultural Perspective

1. Introduce the skill, using the instruction on the student page.
2. Point out that cultural beliefs and customs, some of which are made explicit by the author and some of which are suggested or assumed, influence what characters say, do, and think.
3. Explain that when characters seem to place special emphasis on aspects of behavior or appearances, they may be reflecting cultural perspectives.

Comparing Literary Works

Checkouts • The Girl Who Can

1 Comparing Points of View

Narrative point of view is the perspective from which a story is narrated, or told.

- **First-person point of view:** The narrator is a character who participates in the action and uses the first-person pronouns *I* and *me.*
- **Third-person point of view:** The narrator is not a character in the story but a voice outside it. The narrator uses the third-person pronouns *he, she, him, her, they,* and *them* to refer to all characters. There are two kinds of third-person point of view. In the **third-person omniscient point of view,** the narrator knows everything, including the thoughts of all the characters. In the **third-person limited point of view,** the narrator sees and reports things through one character's eyes.

These selections are written using different points of view. As you read, complete a Venn diagram like this one to compare and contrast how the point of view affects the way you understand the characters and the plot of each story.

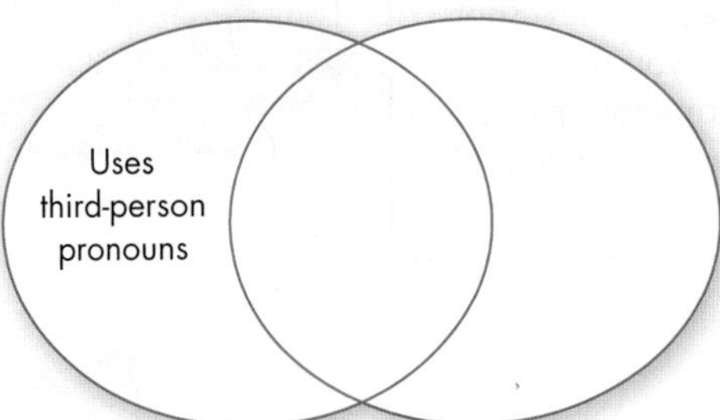

Common Core State Standards

Reading Literature

6. Analyze a particular point of view or cultural experience reflected in a work of literature from outside the United States, drawing on a wide reading of world literature.

Writing

2.a. Introduce a topic; organize complex ideas, concepts, and information to make important connections and distinctions; include formatting, graphics, and multimedia when useful to aiding comprehension.

Cultural perspective is another, related, element of many literary works. A character's perspective or outlook may also be referred to as point of view. This perspective can be strongly influenced by the customs and beliefs of the place and time in which he or she lives. Notice how the perspective of the girl in each story is affected by her culture's ideas and attitudes about the roles of women.

www.PHLitOnline.com

- Vocabulary flashcards
- Interactive journals
- More about the authors
- Selection audio
- Interactive graphic organizers

Vocabulary Development

Vocabulary Knowledge Rating

Create a **Vocabulary Knowledge Rating Chart (Professional Development Guidebook,** p. 33) for these words from the selections:

reverie (p. 83)	*fertile* (p. 87)
dishevelment (p. 84)	*comprehension* (p. 88)
perverse (p. 85)	*humble* (p. 89)

Give students a copy of the chart, and read the words aloud. Have students mark their rating of each in the Before You Read column. To gauge how much instruction to provide, tally the students who think they know each word.

Explain that the words are defined in the margin at the point where they appear in the selection. Urge students to be alert to these words as they read the selections. They will rate their knowledge again when they finish.

❷ Writing About the Big Question

Although the characters in these stories seem sure of certain things, when circumstances change, new possibilities—and new questions—emerge. Use these sentence starters to develop your ideas about the Big Question.

People may have **assumptions** about others or themselves based on ___________.

Those **beliefs** can be changed when ___________.

Meet the Authors

Cynthia Rylant (b. 1954)

Author of "Checkouts"

Cynthia Rylant spent four years as a child living with her grandparents in a small town in West Virginia. With no public library and little money to buy books, she started reading comic books. Once in college, she discovered great literature, but she did not consider becoming a writer until she took a job as a librarian and began reading children's books.

Writing About Her Life In her work, Rylant draws upon her experiences as a young adult. "The best writing," she says, "is that which is most personal, most revealing." She has written many award-winning stories, poems, and novels.

Ama Ata Aidoo (b. 1942)

Author of "The Girl Who Can"

Ama Ata Aidoo was born in Ghana, Africa, where her father was a village chief. He wanted his daughter to have a Western education and sent her to a university in Cape Coast, Ghana. Aidoo earned her bachelor's degree in English and later taught at universities in Ghana and the United States.

Works and Themes Aidoo has written plays, short stories, poetry, and novels. Her fiction, written in English, often explores the conflicts between Western and African cultures and the roles of women in modern society.

Daily Bellringer

For each class during which you will teach this selection, have students complete one of the five Vocabulary activities for Week 3 in the *Daily Bellringer Activities* booklet.

❷ Writing About the Big Question

1. Read the assignment with the class.
2. Help students discuss assumptions that people make about others or about the world.
3. Have students complete the sentence starters. Review responses as a class. (**Possible response:** People may have assumptions about others or themselves based on their past experiences. Those beliefs can be changed when people gain a new perspective.)
4. Remind students that their answers will help them think about the Big Question, "Can truth change?"

Concept Connector

Students will return to their responses to the sentence starters after they have finished reading "Checkouts" and "The Girl Who Can."

Multidraft Reading

To assist struggling readers and to deepen reading for all, apply multidraft reading protocols. For each reading, have students set the purpose indicated:

- **First reading**—identifying key ideas and details and answering any Reading Checks.
- **Second reading**—analyzing craft and structure and responding to the side-column prompts.
- **Third reading**—integrating knowledge and ideas, connecting to other texts and the world, and answering the end-of-selection questions.

For more guidance, see ***Classroom Strategies and Teaching Routines*** card on multidraft reading.

PHLit Online!

For more about the authors and practice with the selection vocabulary, go online at **www.PHLitOnline.com.**

Teaching Resources

- All *Unit 1 Resources,* pp. 108–124
- All *Graphic Organizer Transparencies,* pp. 15–18
- All **Enriched Online Student Edition**
- All *Common Core Companion,* pp. 55–56

PHLit Online! All resources, including print and audio, are available online at **www.PHLitOnline.com.**

TEACH

❶ Background

Work Experiences In many cultures, work experiences are a way that young adults learn more about their abilities, interests, strengths, and weaknesses. Rural teens may perform work that requires them to drive farm machinery and trucks. Suburban and urban teens often work in retail, in malls or supermarkets. The bag boy in "Checkouts" has one of the more common jobs for teenagers.

❷ Activating Prior Knowledge

In class, have five students form a panel to discuss briefly their opinions about what can happen when people fall in love or develop a strong infatuation at first sight. Then, open up the discussion to comments and questions from the rest of the class. Explain that "Checkouts" describes one course that love at first sight can take.

Concept Connector →

Students will follow up on this activity after completing "Checkouts."

❸ About the Selection

In "Checkouts," a girl and a boy fall in love at first sight, but never actually meet. Readers might expect such a missed opportunity to lead to a sad ending, but the plot takes a different turn. For both characters, the unrealized romance leads to new opportunities, not only for friendships and romance, but also for self-discovery.

❶ ❷ ❸

Checkouts

Cynthia Rylant

Her parents had moved her to Cincinnati, to a large house with beveled glass[1] windows and several porches and the history her mother liked to emphasize. You'll love the house, they said. You'll be lonely at first, they admitted, but you're so nice you'll make friends fast. And as an impulse tore at her to lie on the floor, to hold to their ankles and tell them she felt she was dying, to offer anything, anything at all, so they might allow her to finish growing up in the town of her childhood, they firmed their mouths and spoke from their chests and they said, It's decided.

They moved her to Cincinnati, where for a month she spent the greater part of every day in a room full of beveled glass windows, sifting through photographs of the life she'd lived and left behind. But it is difficult work, suffering, and in its own way a kind of art, and finally she didn't have the energy for it anymore, so she emerged from the beautiful house and fell in love with a bag boy at the supermarket. Of course, this didn't happen all at once, just like that, but in the sequence of things that's exactly the way it happened.

She liked to grocery shop. She loved it in the way some people love to drive long country roads, because doing it she could think and relax and wander. Her parents wrote up the list and handed it to her and off she went without complaint to perform what they regarded as a great sacrifice of her time and a sign that she was indeed a very nice girl. She had never told them how much she loved grocery shopping, only that she was "willing" to do it. She had an intuition which told her that her parents were not safe for sharing such strong, important facts about herself. Let them think they knew her.

1. **beveled** (bev´ əld) **glass** *n.* glass having angled or slanted edges.

© Text Complexity Rubric

Checkouts		
Qualitative Measures	**Context / Knowledge Demands**	Contemporary setting and situation 1 (2) 3 4 5
	Structure / Language Conventionality and Clarity	Informal tone; accessible sentence structure; challenging vocabulary 1 2 3 (4) 5
	Levels of Meaning / Purpose / Concept Level	Nuanced characterization; challenging concept (we sometimes reject what we want) 1 2 3 4 (5)
Quantitative Measures	**Text Length**	Word Count: 1,475
	Lexile	1350L

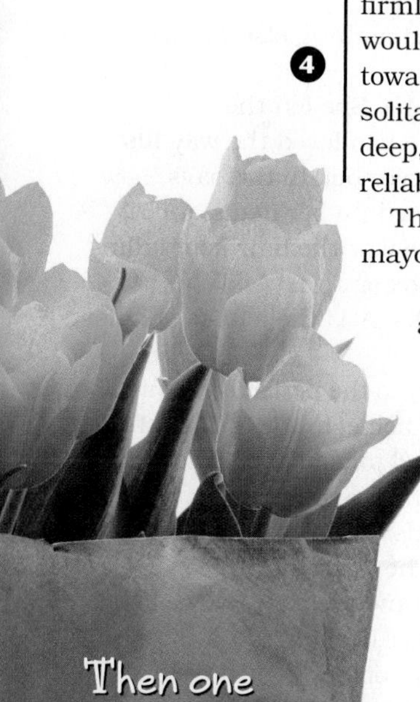

Once inside the supermarket, her hands firmly around the handle of the cart, she would lapse into a kind of reverie and wheel toward the produce. Like a Tibetan monk in solitary meditation, she calmed to a point of deep, deep happiness; this feeling came to her, reliably, if strangely, only in the supermarket. ❹

Then one day the bag boy dropped her jar of mayonnaise and that is how she fell in love.

He was nervous—first day on the job—and along had come this fascinating girl, standing in the checkout line with the unfocused stare one often sees in young children, her face turned enough away that he might take several full looks at her as he packed sturdy bags full of food and the goods of modern life. She interested him because her hair was red and thick, and in it she had placed a huge orange bow, nearly the size of a small hat. That was enough to distract him, and when finally it was her groceries he was packing, she looked at him and smiled and he could respond only by busting her jar of mayonnaise on the floor, shards of glass and oozing cream decorating the area around his feet.

❼ She loved him at exactly that moment, and if he'd known this perhaps he wouldn't have fallen into the brown depression he fell into, which lasted the rest of his shift. He believed he must have looked the fool in her eyes, and he envied the sureness of everyone around him: the cocky cashier at the register, the grim and harried store manager, the bland butcher, and the brazen bag boys who smoked in the warehouse on their breaks. He wanted a second chance. Another chance to be confident and say witty things to her as he threw tin cans into her bags, persuading her to allow him to help her to her car so he might learn just a little about her, check out the floor of the

Then one day the bag boy dropped her jar of mayonnaise and that is how she fell in love.

Literary Analysis
Point of View How does the use of pronouns in this paragraph show that this story is being told from the third-person point of view?

Vocabulary
reverie (rev´ ə rē) *n.* dreamy thinking and imagining

Literary Analysis
Point of View Whose thoughts and feelings are expressed in this paragraph?

❻ 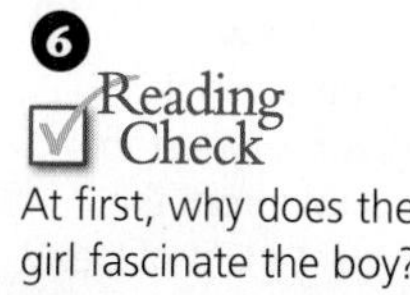

At first, why does the girl fascinate the boy?

❹ Literary Analysis

Point of View

1. Remind students to examine the pronouns used in a story to help identify the point of view.
2. **Ask** the first Literary Analysis question: How does the use of pronouns in this paragraph show that this story is being told from the third-person point of view?
   Answer: The pronouns *her* and *she* indicate that the story is being told from the third-person point of view.
3. **Ask** which pronouns indicate first-person point of view.
   Answer: Pronouns such as *I, my,* and *me* would indicate the first-person point of view.

❺ Literary Analysis

Point of View

1. Recall that there are two types of third-person narrators: omniscient and limited. **Ask** volunteers to define each type.
   Answer: In third-person omniscient, the narrator tells the thoughts and feelings of all the characters. In limited, the narrator sees events through a single character's perspective.
2. **Ask** students the second Literary Analysis question: Whose thoughts and feelings are expressed in this paragraph?
   Answer: The paragraph describes the thoughts and feelings of the bag boy.
3. Have students contrast this passage with the first bracketed text.
   Answer: The first passage is told from the girl's perspective, whereas this passage is told from the perspective of the bag boy.

❻ Reading Check

Answer: The boy is fascinated by her thick red hair with the huge orange bow. Also, she distracts him from his boring job.

This selection is available in interactive format in the **Enriched Online Student Edition**, at **www.PHLitOnline.com**, which includes an interactive graphic organizer.

Ⓒ Text Complexity: Reader and Task Suggestions

Checkouts	
Preparing to Read the Text • Preteach the vocabulary, using the Vocabulary Development box on TE p. 80. • Explain that the story concerns a "crush at first sight." Discuss the symptoms of this experience, such as nervousness. Then, guide students in applying their prior knowledge in interpreting the story. Practice with the sentence containing the clause "he could respond only by busting her jar of mayonnaise on the floor," on p. 83. • Guide students in using Multidraft Reading strategies to deepen their comprehension (TE p. 81).	**Leveled Tasks** *Levels of Meaning* If students will have difficulty with the levels of meaning in the selection, have them first read to identify details about the romantic attraction. Then, have them reread to identify reasons the romance does not succeed. Discuss nuances of characterization. *Synthesizing* If students will not have difficulty interpreting levels of meaning in the selection, have them note as they read ways in which the author creates style and ways in which her style supports the story's cultural perspective. (For example, students may conclude that Rylant's dry observations support an individualistic perspective on romance.)

7 Literary Analysis

Point of View

1. Remind students that the narrator previously stated that the girl fell in love with the bag boy at the exact moment that he dropped the mayonnaise. Explain that this passage details the boy's thoughts and feelings about the same moment.
2. **Ask** the Literary Analysis question: What does the narrator reveal about the boy's regrets?

   Answer: The narrator reveals that the boy regrets not having made more of an effort to get to know the girl. He wishes he could have impressed her with confidence and clever conversation.

8 Connecting to the Big Question

1. Emphasize to students that a person's outlook, or belief, can change when he or she experiences new situations.
2. Invite a volunteer to read the bracketed passage. Then, **ask:** How do the narrator and the bag boy feel about their situations before they see one another in the supermarket? **Possible response:** The narrator hates her new life in Cincinnati. The bag boy struggles through boring work shifts.
3. **Ask:** How has their brief encounter changed their outlooks? **Possible response:** Instead of believing that their situations are hopeless, each finds joy in the possibility of seeing one another again.

9 Literary Analysis

Point of View

1. After students read the bracketed passage, **ask** them how the characters react to finally seeing each other again.

   Answer: The characters pretend not to notice each other and even make a point to avoid contact.
2. **Ask** the Literary Analysis question.

   Answer: The paragraph discusses the thoughts and feelings of both the girl and the boy. In the third-person omniscient point of view the narrator knows everything, so the narrator can reveal the inner thoughts of multiple characters.

Literary Analysis
Point of View 7
What does the narrator reveal about the boy's regrets?

car for signs of hobbies or fetishes and the bumpers for clues as to beliefs and loyalties.

But he busted her jar of mayonnaise and nothing else worked out for the rest of the day.

Strange, how attractive clumsiness can be. She left the supermarket with stars in her eyes, for she had loved the way his long nervous fingers moved from the conveyor belt to the bags, how deftly (until the mayonnaise) they had picked up her items and placed them in her bags. She had loved the way the hair kept falling into his eyes as he leaned over to grab a box or a tin. And the tattered brown shoes he wore with no socks. And the left side of his collar turned in rather than out.

Vocabulary
dishevelment
(di shev′ əl ment) *n.* disorder; messiness

The bag boy seemed a wonderful contrast to the perfectly beautiful house she had been forced to accept as her home, to the history she hated, to the loneliness she had become used to, and she couldn't wait to come back for more of his awkwardness and **dishevelment**.

Incredibly, it was another four weeks before they saw each other again. As fate would have it, her visits to the supermarket never coincided with his schedule to bag. Each time she went to the store, her eyes scanned the checkouts at once, her heart in her mouth. And each hour he worked, the bag boy kept one eye on the door, watching for the red-haired girl with the big orange bow.

Strange, how attractive clumsiness can be.

Yet in their disappointment these weeks there was a kind of ecstasy. It is reason enough to be alive, the hope you may see again some face which has meant something to you. The anticipation of meeting the bag boy eased the girl's painful transition into her new and jarring life in Cincinnati. It provided for her an anchor amid all that was impersonal and unfamiliar, and she spent less time on thoughts of what she had left behind as she concentrated on what might lie ahead. And for the boy, the long and often tedious hours at the supermarket which provided no challenge other than that of showing up the following workday . . . these hours became possibilities of mystery and romance for him as he watched the electric doors for the girl in the orange bow. 8

Literary Analysis
Point of View 9
Which details in this paragraph suggest the story is told from the omniscient point of view? Explain.

And when finally they did meet up again, neither offered a clue to the other that he, or she, had been the object of obsessive thought for weeks. She spotted him as soon as she came into the store, but she kept her eyes strictly in front of her as she pulled out a cart and wheeled it toward the produce. And he, too, knew the instant she came through the door—though the orange bow was gone, replaced by a small but bright yellow flower instead—and he never once turned his head in her direction but watched her from the corner of his vision as he tried to swallow back the fear in his throat.

It is odd how we sometimes deny ourselves the very pleasure we have longed for and which is finally within our reach. For

---

Vocabulary Development

CCSS Language 6

Thematic Vocabulary: The Big Question

As students are discussing "Checkouts," ask them to use the thematic vocabulary presented in Introducing the Big Question, pp. 2–3. You might encourage them with sentence starters like these:

1. The girl's parents make the *assumption* that she will quickly make friends after . . .
2. The girl does not *perceive* the new house as . . .
3. Due to a chance *circumstance,* the girl falls in love with . . .
4. The girl and boy never reveal the *truth* about . . .
5. Some readers might think the story is *credible* because . . .

some perverse reason she would not have been able to articulate,
9 the girl did not bring her cart up to the bag boy's checkout when her shopping was done. And the bag boy let her leave the store, pretending no notice of her.

This is often the way of children, when they truly want a thing, to pretend that they don't. And then they grow angry when no one tried harder to give them this thing they so casually rejected, and they soon find themselves in a rage simply because they cannot say yes when they mean yes. Humans are very complicated. (And perhaps cats, who have been known to react in the same way, though the resulting rage can only be guessed at.)

The girl hated herself for not checking out at the boy's line, and
10 the boy hated himself for not catching her eye and saying hello, and they most sincerely hated each other without having ever exchanged even two minutes of conversation.

Eventually—in fact, within the week—a kind and intelligent boy who lived very near her beautiful house asked the girl to a movie and she gave up her fancy for the bag boy at the supermarket. And the bag boy himself grew so bored with his job that he made a desperate search for something better and ended up in a bookstore where scores of fascinating girls lingered like honeybees about a hive. Some months later the bag boy and the girl with the orange bow again crossed paths, standing in line with their dates at a movie theater, and, glancing toward the other, each smiled slightly, then looked away, as strangers on public buses often do, when one is moving off the bus and the other is moving on.

Vocabulary
perverse (pər vʉrs′) *adj.* different from what is considered right or reasonable

Literary Analysis
Point of View
Which details in this paragraph might be omitted if the story were told from the third-person limited point of view? Explain.

Critical Thinking

1. **Key Ideas and Details** **(a)** What do the boy and girl think about while they are apart? **(b) Speculate:** How do you think the two characters feel when they see each other at the movie theater?
2. **Key Ideas and Details** **Draw Conclusions:** Does the experience described in the story seem like a missed opportunity or a necessary outcome? Explain.
3. **Key Ideas and Details** **(a) Summarize:** Why do the boy and girl never act on their feelings? **(b) Make a Judgment:** Do you agree that "humans are very complicated"? Explain, using details from the story.
4. **Integration of Knowledge and Ideas** **(a)** Is the situation described in this story a common cultural experience for American teenagers? Explain. **(b) Speculate:** How might the story be different if it were set in a culture that limits the independence of teenage girls? *[Connect to the Big Question: Can truth change?]*

Cite textual evidence to support your responses.

Differentiated Instruction for Universal Access

Vocabulary for Special-Needs Students
Ask students to use the given definition and the context of the vocabulary word on this page to answer the following extension questions: What was *perverse* about the girl's decision to not go to the bag boy's checkout? What other types of decisions might be considered *perverse?* Why?

Enrichment for Gifted/Talented Students
Suggest that students imagine themselves to be the character of the red-haired girl or the bag boy when the two characters finally see each other for a second time. Have each student compose a diary entry describing what happened as he or she lived through the experience. Students may describe their actions, thoughts, and feelings. They should conclude their diary entry by answering this question: What did this experience teach me about myself?

10 Literary Analysis
Point of View

Ask the Literary Analysis question.
Answer: In the third-person limited point of view, one of the character's feelings would be omitted.

Concept Connector

Have students return to the Activating Prior Knowledge activity on p. 82. Ask students to discuss how the story's end compares to other love-at-first-sight stories. In addition, have students compare their Writing About the Big Question responses before reading the story with their ideas afterwards.

ASSESS
Answers

Remind students to support their answers with evidence from the text.

1. (a) They think about each other. (b) **Possible response:** Students might say that they view each other the way strangers do.
2. **Possible responses:** It is a necessary outcome because if they had really wanted to meet, they would have made a bigger effort. It was a missed opportunity because it is hard to find someone similar in disposition.
3. (a) They are pretending not to want what they most desire. (b) **Possible response:** Yes, the behavior of the boy and girl confirms that humans are "complicated."
4. (a) **Possible response:** Some students may say it is a common experience for American teenagers because many teens are naturally shy about approaching people to whom they are attracted. (b) **Possible response:** If the story were set in a culture that limits the independence of teenage girls, the girl might feel attracted to a young man but would not even have a choice or chance to approach him on her own.

PHLit Online!
This selection is available in interactive format in the **Enriched Online Student Edition**, at **www.PHLitOnline.com**, which includes an interactive graphic organizer.

⓫ Background

Women in Africa In rural African villages, a woman's traditional role has been to give birth and raise children. In recent years, many people have challenged this notion of women's role in society, advocating equality between men and women. Writers like Ama Ata Aidoo have been instrumental in promoting feminism within Africa and beyond.

⓬ Activating Prior Knowledge

Explain that in "The Girl Who Can," the narrator's grandmother hopes that the girl will one day be able to have children. Ask students to share some of the hopes and expectations that adults typically have for their children or grandchildren. Compare and contrast students' responses with those of the grandmother in the story.

Concept Connector ➡

Students will follow up on this activity after completing "The Girl Who Can."

⓭ About the Selection

In "The Girl Who Can," seven-year-old Adjoa challenges her grandmother's views about a woman's place in society. Convinced that Adjoa's legs are too thin for childbearing, the grandmother often worries about Adjoa's future. Adjoa's success as a runner convinces her grandmother that there are other things she can accomplish in life besides motherhood. In this story, readers witness how traditional views and progressive notions about women can intersect across generations.

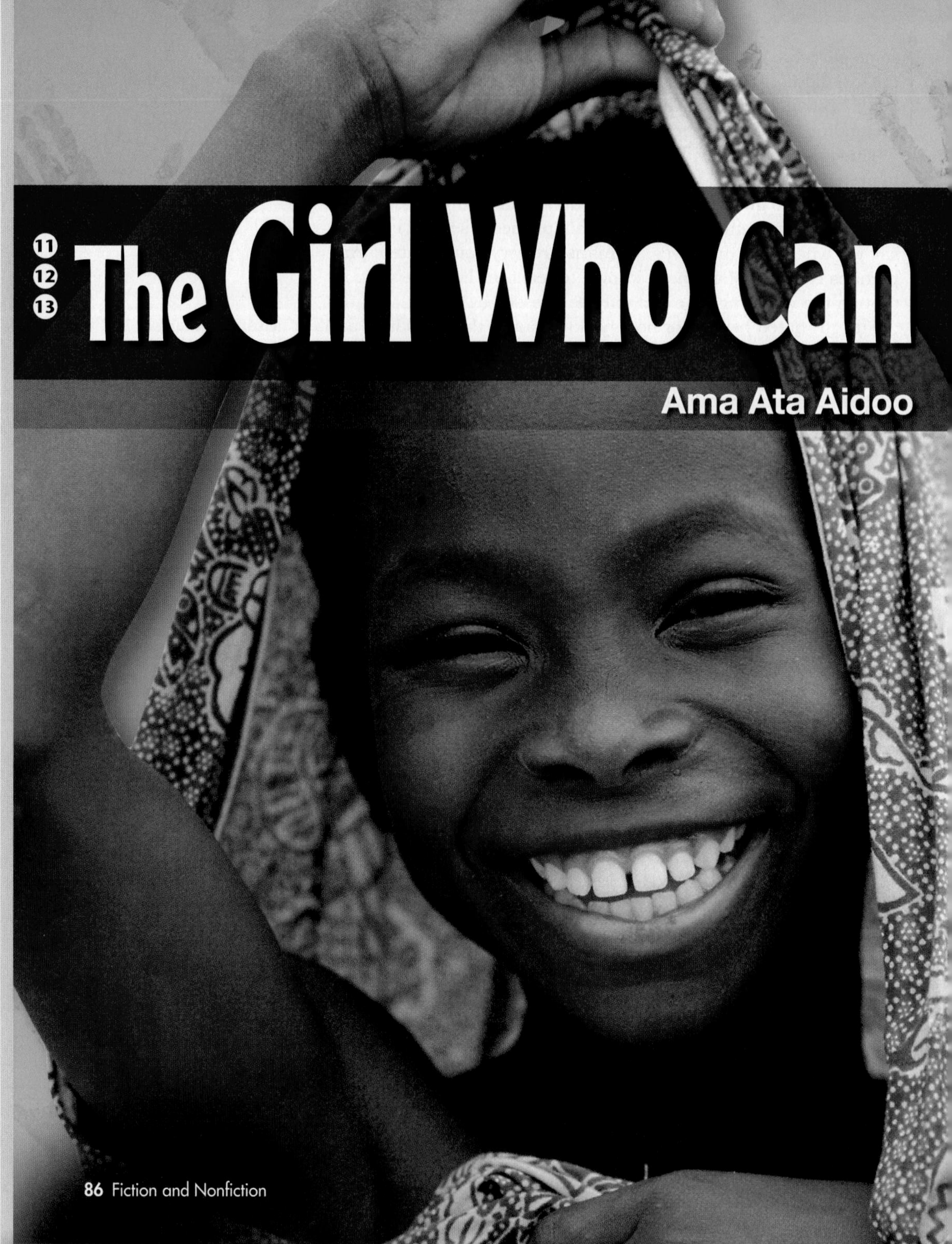

⓫ ⓬ ⓭ The Girl Who Can

Ama Ata Aidoo

Ⓒ Text Complexity Rubric

The Girl Who Can		
Qualitative Measures	**Context/ Knowledge Demands**	Small village in Ghana, Africa; explores traditional and modern views of women's roles **1 2 ③ 4 5**
	Structure/ Language Clarity and Conventionality	Informal, conversational style; told by a young girl; on-level vocabulary **1 ② 3 4 5**
	Levels of Meaning/ Purpose/Concept Level	Accessible concept (main character succeeds despite cultural mores) **1 2 ③ 4 5**
Quantitative Measures	**Text Length**	Word Count: 2,235
	Lexile	870L

They say that I was born in Hasodzi; and it is a very big village in the central region of our country, Ghana. They also say that when all of Africa is not choking under a drought, Hasodzi lies in a very fertile lowland in a district known for its good soil. Maybe that is why any time I don't finish eating my food, Nana says, "You Adjoa, you don't know what life is about . . . you don't know what problems there are in this life . . ."

As far as I could see, there was only one problem. And it had nothing to do with what I knew Nana considered as "problems," or what Maami thinks of as "the problem." Maami is my mother. Nana is my mother's mother. And they say I am seven years old. And my problem is that at this seven years of age, there are things I can think in my head, but which, maybe, I do not have the proper language to speak them out with. And that, I think, is a very serious problem because it is always difficult to decide whether to keep quiet and not say any of the things that come into my head, or say them and get laughed at. Not that it is easy to get any grown-up to listen to you, even when you decide to take the risk and say something serious to them.

Take Nana. First, I have to struggle to catch her attention. Then I tell her something I had taken a long time to figure out. And then you know what always happens? She would at once stop whatever she is doing and, mouth open, stare at me for a very long time. Then, bending and turning her head slightly, so that one ear comes down towards me, she'll say in that voice: "Adjoa, you say what?" After I have repeated whatever I had said, she would either, still in that voice, ask me "never, never, but NEVER to repeat THAT," or she would immediately burst out laughing. She would laugh and laugh and laugh, until tears run down her cheeks and she would stop whatever she is doing and wipe away the tears with the hanging edges of her cloth. And she would continue laughing until she is
15 completely tired. But then, as soon as another person comes by, just to make sure she doesn't forget whatever it was I had said, she would repeat it to her. And then, of course, there would be two old people laughing and screaming with tears running down their faces. Sometimes this show continues until there are three, four or even more of such laughing and screaming tear-faced grownups. And all that performance for whatever I'd said? I find something quite confusing in all this. That is, no one ever explains to me why sometimes I shouldn't repeat some things I say; while at other times, some other things I say would not only be all right, but would be considered so funny they would be repeated so many times for so many people's enjoyment. You see how neither way of hearing me out can encourage me to express my thoughts too often?

◀ **Critical Viewing**
Describe the feelings the girl in the photograph expresses. **[Interpret]**

Vocabulary
fertile (furt´ 'l) *adj.* rich in nutrients that promote growth

Literary Analysis
Point of View
Which pronouns in this paragraph show that this story is being told from the first-person point of view?

16 

Reading Check

What does the narrator say is her problem?

14 Critical Viewing

Possible response: The girl seems happy and energetic.

15 Literary Analysis

Point of View

1. Remind students that identifying pronouns can help them determine the point of view of a story.
2. **Ask** students to respond to the Literary Analysis question: Which pronouns in this paragraph show that this story is being told from the first-person point of view?

   Answer: The pronouns *I* and *me* indicate a first-person narrator.
3. **Ask** students how the first-person point of view in this story differs from the third-person omniscient point of view in the previous story.

   Answer: In first-person point of view, the narrator participates in the story and tells the story from his or her viewpoint. In third-person omniscient point of view, the narrator does not participate in the story and is able to reveal the thoughts and feelings of multiple characters.

16 Reading Check

Answer: The narrator has difficulty expressing her thoughts, and this makes it difficult for her to determine when to speak her mind and when to keep her thoughts to herself.

PHLit Online!

This selection is available in interactive format in the **Enriched Online Student Edition**, at **www.PHLitOnline.com**, which includes an interactive graphic organizer.

Text Complexity: Reader and Task Suggestions

The Girl Who Can	
Preparing to Read the Text • Using the Background information on TE p. 86, discuss the traditional roles of women in rural African villages. • Discuss the ways in which traditions can restrict a person's potential. Tie it to ways in which cultural traditions change over time. • Guide students to use Multidraft Reading strategies (TE p. 81).	**Leveled Tasks** *Knowledge Demands* If students have difficulty with knowledge demands, have them first read the story to identify the expected roles of women in Ghanaian society. Then, have them reread and list ways in which the main character doesn't fit that role. Discuss their notes. *Evaluating* If students will not have difficulty understanding the roles of women in society, have them note as they read ways in which the main character changes the perceptions of others in the society. As a class, discuss how cultural expectations change when a strong individual sets an example.

17 Literary Analysis

Point of View

1. Remind students that the story is told from Adjoa's point of view. Point out that she is seven years old, so her thoughts and words represent a child's perspective.
2. **Ask** students what details about the narrator's reaction to older people reveal about her.

   Answer: Adjoa's mystification about the behavior of adults suggests that she is very young and naïve.
3. Point out that the reader can only gain insight into the mother's and grandmother's thoughts and feelings through what Adjoa reports. **Ask** students what they think the advantages and disadvantages of first-person point of view are.

   Possible response: The advantage is that the reader becomes very familiar with Adjoa and the way she thinks and feels. It makes the story more personal and real. The disadvantage is that the reader's knowledge of other characters is limited; the reader only learns about them through Adjoa's perspective, which is biased.

18 Connecting to the Big Question

1. Remind students a person's idea of the truth can change as circumstances change.
2. Read the bracketed text.

   Ask: What does Nana believe to be true?

   Answer: Nana believes that Adjoa's legs are too thin and too long.
3. **Ask:** Do you think that Nana will always believe that Adjoa's legs are abnormal? Explain.

   Possible response: No, if Nana were shown that long, thin legs were useful, she would change her mind about Adjoa's legs.

19 Critical Viewing

Possible response: Like Adjoa and her elders, the women and children in the photograph seem affectionate and close. The women probably want the best for their children, as Adjoa's elders want for her.

Vocabulary
comprehension
(käm′ prē hen′ shen) *n.* understanding

17 Like all this business to do with my legs. I have always wanted to tell them not to worry. I mean Nana and my mother. It did not have to be an issue for my two favorite people to fight over. I didn't want to be told not to repeat it or for it to be considered so funny that anyone would laugh at me until they cried. After all, they were my legs . . . When I think back on it now, those two, Nana and my mother must have been discussing my legs from the day I was born. What I am sure of is that when I came out of the land of sweet, soft silence into the world of noise and **comprehension**, the first topic I met was my legs.

That discussion was repeated very regularly.

18 Nana: "Ah, ah, you know, Kaya, I thank my God that your very first child is female. But Kaya, I am not sure about her legs. Hm . . . hm . . . hm . . ."

And Nana would shake her head.

Maami: "Mother, why are you always complaining about Adjoa's legs? If you ask me . . ."

Nana: "They are too thin. And I am not asking you!"

Nana has many voices. There is a special one she uses to shut everyone up.

"Some people have no legs at all," my mother would try again with all her small courage.

"But Adjoa has legs," Nana would insist; "except that they are too thin. And also too long for a woman. Kaya, listen. Once in a while, but only once in a very long while, somebody decides — nature, a child's spirit mother, an accident happens, and somebody gets born without arms, or legs, or both sets of limbs. And then let me touch wood; it is a sad business. And you know, such things are not for talking about every day. But if any female child decides to come into this world with legs, then they might as well be legs."

20 "What kind of legs?" And always at that point, I knew from her voice that my

19 ▼ **Critical Viewing** Might these mothers and children have relationships similar to those between Adjoa and her elders? Explain. **[Connect]**

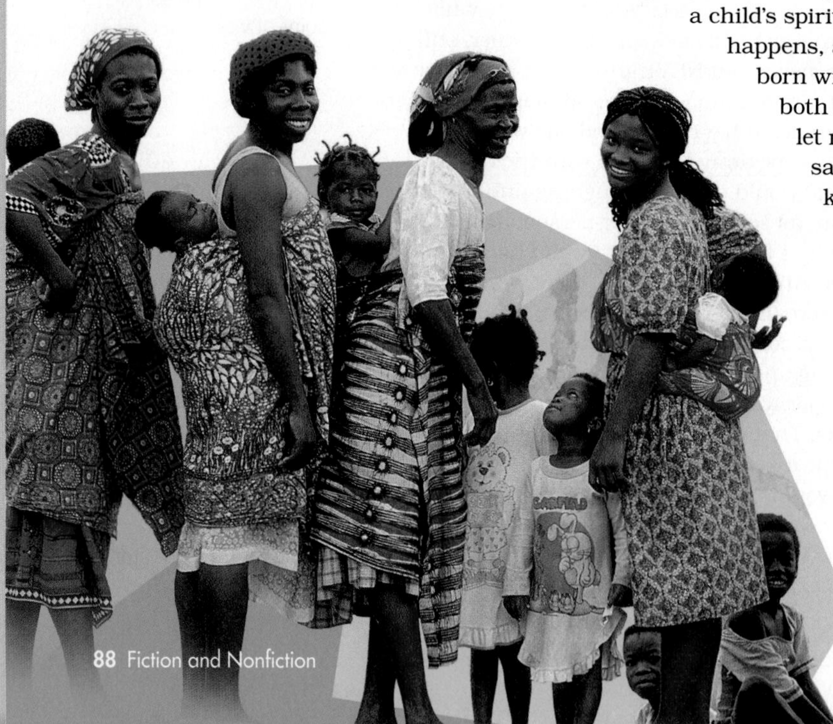

Vocabulary Development

CCSS Language 6

Selection Vocabulary Reinforcement

To reinforce and assess students' comprehension of selection vocabulary words, give them sentences using the words in which the word may or may not be used correctly. Students must tell whether the use is correct and explain their answer. Use these sentences:

1. The *fertile* land produced excellent crops this year.
   Answer: Yes, *fertile* is used correctly. It means "able to make plants grow."
2. Ryan felt that he had full *comprehension* of the case study, but he still didn't understand it.
   Answer: No, *comprehension* is not used correctly. It means "understanding."
3. Despite his riches and fame, the prince was quite *humble*.
   Answer: Yes, *humble* is used correctly. It means "modest."

20 mother was weeping inside. Nana never heard such inside weeping. Not that it would have stopped Nana even if she had heard it. Which always surprised me. Because, about almost everything else apart from my legs, Nana is such a good grown-up. In any case, what do I know about good grown-ups and bad grown-ups? How could Nana be a good grown-up when she carried on so about my legs? All I want to say is that I really liked Nana except for that.

Nana: "As I keep saying, if any woman decides to come into this world with her two legs, then she should select legs that have meat on them: with good calves. Because you are sure such legs would support solid hips. And a woman must have solid hips to be able to have children."

"Oh, Mother." That's how my mother would answer. Very, very quietly. And the discussion would end or they would move on to something else.

Sometimes, Nana would pull in something about my father:

How, "Looking at such a man, we have to be **humble** and admit that after all, God's children are many . . ."

How, "After one's only daughter had insisted on marrying a man like that, you still have to thank your God that the biggest problem you got later was having a granddaughter with spindly legs that are too long for a woman, and too thin to be of any use."

The way she always added that bit about my father under her breath, she probably thought I didn't hear it. But I always heard it. Plus, that is what always shut my mother up for good, so that even if I had not actually heard the words, once my mother looked like even her little courage was finished, I could always guess what Nana had added to the argument.

"Legs that have meat on them with good calves to support solid hips . . . to be able to have children."

So I wished that one day I would see, for myself, the legs of any woman who had had children. But in our village, that is not easy. The older women wear long wrap-arounds[1] all the time. Perhaps if they let me go bathe in the river in the evening, I could have checked. But I never had the chance. It took a lot of begging just to get my mother and Nana to let me go splash around in the shallow end of the river with my friends, who were other little girls like me. For proper baths, we used the small bathhouse behind our hut. Therefore, the only naked female legs I have ever really seen are those of other little girls like me, or older girls in the school. And those of my mother and Nana: two pairs of legs which must surely belong to the approved kind; because Nana gave birth to my mother

1. **wrap-arounds** (rap′ ə rŏundz′) *n.* a type of garment that is open down the side and is wrapped around the body.

Literary Analysis
Point of View
What do we learn about the narrator's inner feelings from the words in this paragraph?

Vocabulary
humble (hum′ bəl) *adj.* modest; having humility

When I think back on it now, those two, Nana and my mother must have been discussing my legs from the day I was born.

21 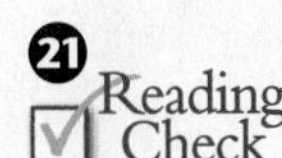

According to the narrator, which topic makes the mother weep inside?

20 Literary Analysis
Point of View

1. **Ask** students to respond to the Literary Analysis question: What do we learn about the narrator's inner feelings from the words in this paragraph?

   Answer: Readers learn that the narrator can tell when her mother is sad, an insight that her grandmother apparently does not possess. Readers also learn that Adjoa loves her grandmother but does not like how she treats Adjoa's mother.

2. **Ask** students how the revelation of these feelings influences their view of Adjoa's character.

   Possible response: Students might say that the feelings surprised them because they did not expect a seven-year-old to have such insight into her elders.

21 Reading Check

Answer: Adjoa's legs is the topic that upset her mother.

Differentiated Instruction for Universal Access

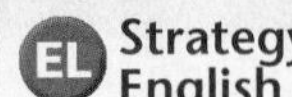

EL Strategy for English Learners

To give students a context for the story and to model how to compare points of view, show them **Comparing Points of View Graphic Organizer A** (*Graphic Organizer Transparencies,* p. 15). The partially completed graphic organizer will give students insight into the process of comparing points of view. They can use it as a model for making their own observations as they read.

Strategy for Advanced Readers

The selection describes three generations of women—Adjoa, her mother, and Nana—and their views regarding the role of women in society. Ask students to write a brief essay that compares and contrasts each character's viewpoint on this issue. Remind students to use evidence from the story to support their ideas.

㉒ Literary Analysis

Point of View

1. Remind students that first-person narrators can tell readers about their own thoughts and feelings, but they can only guess about other characters' interior lives by observing what the characters say and do.
2. Read aloud the bracketed text, and point out that Adjoa makes several observations about her grandmother's and mother's opinions regarding school. **Ask** students how Adjoa knows their opinions on this issue.

   Answer: Adjoa has overheard their discussions.
3. **Ask** what Adjoa's observations reveal about her mother's and grandmother's expectations for her.

   Answer: Nana thinks school is a waste because Adjoa will grow up to be a mother and will have no use for an education. Adjoa's mother hopes that getting an education will allow Adjoa to become more than just a mother.

㉓ Critical Viewing

Possible responses: Students might say that the girls in the image match their image of Adjoa. Others might have pictured Adjoa in a different-looking school uniform.

and my mother gave birth to me. In my eyes, all my friends have got legs that look like legs, but whether the legs have got meat on them to support the kind of hips that . . . that I don't know.

㉒ According to the older boys and girls, the distance between our little village and the small town is about five kilometers. I don't know what five kilometers mean. They always complain about how long it is to walk to school and back. But to me, we live in our village, and walking those kilometers didn't matter. School is nice. School is another thing Nana and my mother discussed often and appeared to have different ideas about. Nana thought it would be a waste of time. I never understood what she meant. My mother seemed to know—and disagreed. She kept telling Nana that she—that is, my mother—felt she was locked into some kind of darkness because she didn't go to school. So that if I, her daughter, could learn to write and read my own name and a little besides—perhaps be able to calculate some things on paper—that would be good. I could always marry later and maybe . . .

㉓ ▼ **Critical Viewing** How does your image of the narrator compare to the girls in this photograph? **[Compare]**

Nana would just laugh. "Ah, maybe with legs like hers, she might as well go to school."

Running with our classmates on our small sports field and winning first place each time never seemed to me to be anything about which to tell anyone at home. This time it was different. I don't know how the teachers decided to let me run for the junior section of our school in the district games. But they did.

When I went home to tell my mother and Nana, they had not believed it at first. So Nana had taken it upon herself to go and "ask into it properly." She came home to tell my mother that it was really true. I was one of my school's runners.

"Is that so?" exclaimed my mother. I know her. Her mouth moved as though she was going to tell Nana, that, after all, there was a secret about me she couldn't be expected to share with anyone. But then Nana herself looked so pleased, out of surprise, my mother shut her mouth up. In any case, since the first time they heard the news, I have often caught Nana staring at my legs with a strange look on her face, but still pretending like she was not looking. All this week, she has been washing my school uniform herself. That is a big surprise. And she didn't stop at that,

Think Aloud

Vocabulary: Using Context

Direct students' attention to the word *sheen* in the first full paragraph on page 91. Using a think-aloud process, model how to use context to infer the meaning of an unknown word. Say to students:

> I am going to think aloud to show you how I would figure out the meaning of *sheen* from its context.

In this sentence, *sheen* is said to be a part of Adjoa's school uniform. We know that she is outside on a sunny day, and the phrases *caught the rays of the sun* and *shone brighter* are clues that it becomes more pronounced when exposed to sunlight. The next sentence shows that it is something that people would notice, so I think *sheen* refers to a part of her school uniform that has a shiny finish.

24 **LITERATURE IN CONTEXT**

Social Studies Connection

Country Profile: Ghana

Location: southern coast of West Africa bordering the Atlantic Ocean

Climate: tropical; wet in the south and dry in the north

Terrain: low fertile plains and plateaus

Population: 20.2 million

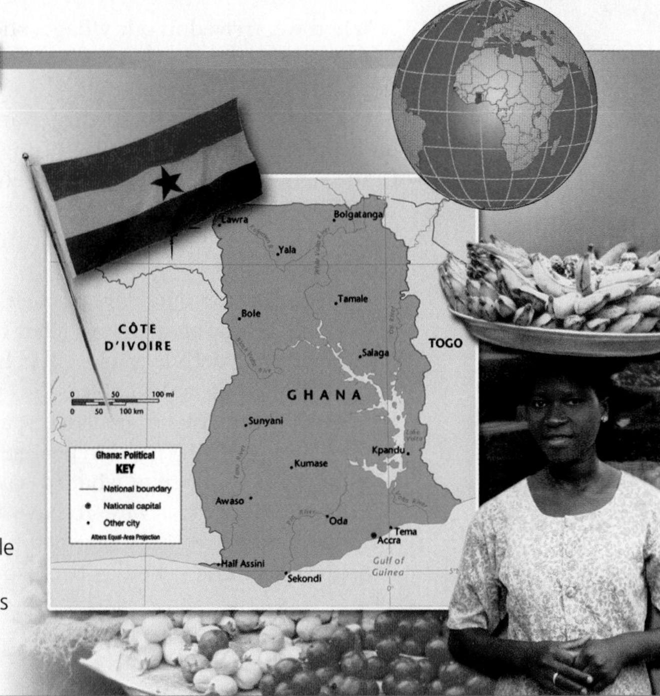

Connect to the Literature

Adjoa says that she lives in a fertile lowland of central Ghana. What benefits and challenges might this region's climate and terrain present for a runner like Adjoa?

she even went to Mr. Mensah's house and borrowed his charcoal pressing iron. Each time she came back home with it and ironed and ironed and ironed the uniform, until, if I had been the uniform, I would have said aloud that I had had enough.

Wearing my school uniform this week has been very nice. At the parade, on the first afternoon, its sheen caught the rays of the sun and shone brighter than anybody else's uniform. I'm sure Nana saw that too, and must have liked it. Yes, she has been coming into town with us every afternoon of this district sports week. Each afternoon, she has pulled one set of fresh old cloth from the big brass bowl to wear. And those old clothes are always so stiffly starched, you can hear the cloth creak when she passes by. But she walks way behind us schoolchildren. As though she was on her own way to some place else.

Yes, I have won every race I ran for my school, and I have won the cup for the best all-round junior athlete. Yes, Nana said that she didn't care if such things are not done. She would do it. You know what she did? She carried the gleaming cup on her back. Like they do with babies, and other very precious things. And this time, not taking the trouble to walk by herself.

Spiral Review

Theme How does Nana's behavior toward Adjoa connect to a possible theme?

25

Reading Check

After learning about her running talent, what does Nana do with the narrator's uniform?

Differentiated Instruction for Universal Access

Culturally Responsive Instruction

Culture Focus Point out how deeply concerned Nana is with the possibility that Adjoa's thin legs and schooling will prohibit her from fulfilling her womanly duties. Note that in many cultures, men and women are expected to follow particular gender roles for the culture they live in. These roles exist in the home, the workplace, and in educational facilities. Typically, a woman's traditional role has always included child-bearing, keeping a clean house, and preparing meals, while excluding a woman's ability to secure employment or attend school.

In contrast to the traditional roles of women, males have been expected to be the breadwinner, or financial supporter and provider. In the United States, gender roles have been challenged and revised over the past century. Today, women have the opportunity to thrive in the workforce, and share equal rights, though some discrimination and biases still exist. Invite students to share their knowledge and experience of gender roles in their home culture or family's country of origin.

24 Literature in Context

Point of View

Social Studies Connection Ghana has been an independent country since 1957, when it broke away from Great Britain, which had possessed it as a colony. Since then, Ghana has not been able to harness its earning potential from agriculture. While the fertile terrain ensures plentiful natural resources, the country remains relatively impoverished. Better technology might help Ghana to become more financially independent in the future.

Connect to the Literature Point out that Adjoa lives in a tropical climate, which is hot year-round.

Ask students the Connect to the Literature question: Adjoa says that she lives in a fertile lowland of central Ghana. What benefits and challenges might this region's climate and terrain present for a runner like Adjoa?

Answer: The hot climate might be difficult for a runner, who might become overheated. However, the flat, grassy land would provide an excellent surface for running.

Spiral Review

Theme

1. Remind students that they studied the concept of theme in the Unit 1 Literary Analysis Workshop (pp. 4–21).
2. **Ask** students the Spiral Review question.

   Possible response: Often, a change in a character's thinking or behavior is a clue to a story's theme. Nana's newfound respect for the school uniform, as evidenced by her reverent and repeated ironing of it, suggests that she now sees value in school, in running, and in activities for young women that are not necessarily directly related to childbearing and motherhood. These changes in Nana's thinking relate to the theme of women's changing roles in society.

25 Reading Check

Answer: Nana repeatedly irons the uniform.

Concept Connector

Have students return to the Activating Prior Knowledge exercise. Ask students to discuss how the grandmother's aspirations for Adjoa changed over the course of the story. Then, have them connect their Writing About the Big Question responses to the story.

ASSESS

Answers

Remind students to support their answers with evidence from the text.

1. (a) Nana worries that the narrator's legs are too thin. (b) Nana fears that Adjoa will not be able to bear children.
2. (a) Nana thinks that school is unnecessary. (b) The narrator's mother believes that school is valuable. (c) In Ghana women are expected to bear and raise children, not to become educated and work in a profession.
3. (a) Nana seems surprised that Adjoa's legs are good for something. (b) Nana is proud of Adjoa.
4. (a) Adjoa has acted out her belief that her legs are worth more than just supporting hips for childbearing. (b) **Possible response:** Students may agree that it was better because Adjoa's actions provided irrefutable evidence of her belief; saying it aloud would have been the mere opinion of a child, and Nana probably would have laughed at her.
5. **Possible response:** At the beginning of the story, Adjoa's legs are a problem in the view of Nana, and as a result, a source of discomfort for Adjoa and sadness for her mother. At the end of the story, her ability to run has shown that her legs are valuable or useful, even to Nana.

Oh, grown-ups are so strange.

When we arrived in our village, she entered our compound to show the cup to my mother before going to give it back to the headmaster.

Oh, grown-ups are so strange. Nana is right now carrying me on her knee, and crying softly. Muttering, muttering, muttering that: "saa, thin legs can also be useful . . . thin legs can also be useful . . ." that "even though some legs don't have much meat on them, to carry hips . . . they can run. Thin legs can run . . . then who knows? . . ."

I don't know too much about such things. But that's how I was feeling and thinking all along. That surely, one should be able to do other things with legs as well as have them because they can support hips that make babies. Except that I was afraid of saying that sort of thing aloud. Because someone would have told me never, never, but NEVER to repeat such words. Or else, they would have laughed so much at what I'd said, they would have cried.

It's much better this way. To have acted it out to show them, although I could not have planned it.

As for my mother, she has been speechless as usual.

Critical Thinking

Cite textual evidence to support your responses.

1. **Key Ideas and Details** **(a)** Why does Nana criticize the narrator's legs? **(b) Draw Conclusions:** How does this criticism reveal Nana's fears for the narrator's future? Explain.
2. **Integration of Knowledge and Ideas** **(a)** What are Nana's feelings about the narrator going to school? **(b) Compare and Contrast:** How do the mother's feelings about school differ from Nana's? **(c) Make Generalizations:** Based on these details, what kind of lives do you think many women in Ghana are expected to lead?
3. **Key Ideas and Details** **(a) Infer:** After Adjoa is chosen for the district games, why does Nana keep staring at her legs? **(b) Draw Conclusions:** Why does Nana iron Adjoa's school uniform so carefully?
4. **Key Ideas and Details** **(a) Analyze:** At the end of the story, Adjoa says it was much better to "have acted it out to show them." What has she acted out? **(b) Evaluate:** Was it "better," as Adjoa says? Explain.
5. **Integration of Knowledge and Ideas** Do the narrator's legs mean the same thing to her and her family at the end of the selection as they do at the beginning? Use details to support your answer. ***[Connect to the Big Question: Can truth change?]***

Vocabulary Development

Vocabulary Knowledge Rating

When students have completed reading and discussing "Checkouts" and "The Girl Who Can," have them take out their **Vocabulary Knowledge Rating Chart.** Read the words aloud once more and have students rate their knowledge of the words again in the After Reading column. Clarify any words that are still problematic. Have students write their own definition and example or sentence in the appropriate column. Then have students complete the Vocabulary Practice activities on the next page. Encourage students to use the words in further discussion and written work about the selections. Remind them that they will be accountable for these words on the **Selection Test** (*Unit 1 Resources,* pp. 119–121 or 122–124).

After You Read

Checkouts • The Girl Who Can

Comparing Points of View

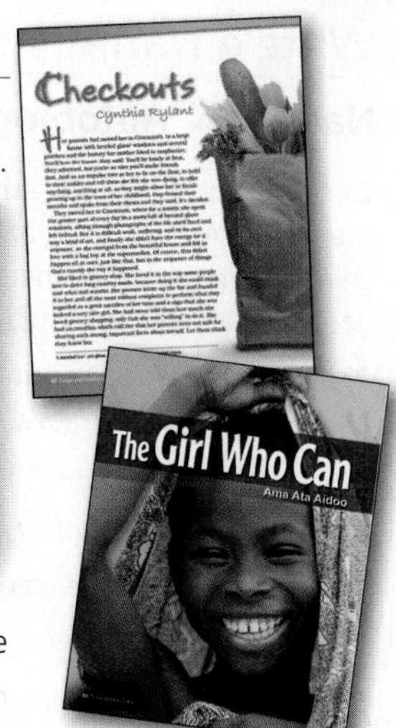

1. **Key Ideas and Details** Use a chart like the one shown to note the actions, thoughts, and feelings of the listed characters in both stories.

Checkouts	Actions	Thoughts	Feelings
Girl			
Boy			
The Girl Who Can	**Actions**	**Thoughts**	**Feelings**
Nana			
Adjoa			

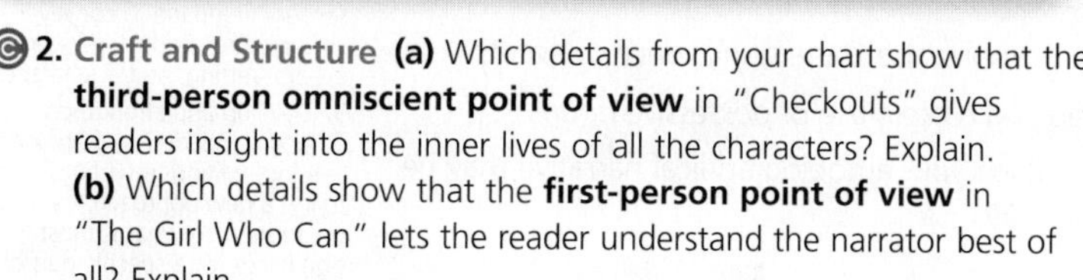

2. **Craft and Structure** **(a)** Which details from your chart show that the **third-person omniscient point of view** in "Checkouts" gives readers insight into the inner lives of all the characters? Explain. **(b)** Which details show that the **first-person point of view** in "The Girl Who Can" lets the reader understand the narrator best of all? Explain.

Timed Writing

Explanatory Text: Essay

Compare and contrast the main character in "Checkouts" with the narrator in "The Girl Who Can." In an essay, analyze the way in which the development of each character is shaped by the narrative point of view. Also, consider the cultural perspectives that contribute to the portrayal of each character. **(30 minutes)**

5-Minute Planner

1. Read the prompt carefully and completely.
2. Organize your ideas to make important connections by answering these questions:
   - Who are the narrators in the two stories?
   - How do you know what each girl is thinking?
   - Do both narrators seem equally reliable? Why or why not?
   - How does each girl's culture influence her perspective?
3. Reread the prompt, and then draft your essay.

ASSESS

Answers

Comparing Points of View

1. **Sample answer:** **Checkouts—Character:** Boy **Actions:** Dropping the mayonnaise **Thoughts:** I look like a fool. **Feelings:** Depression and shame

   For other sample answers, see ***Graphic Organizer Transparencies,*** **Comparing Points of View Graphic Organizer A**, p. 17, and the **Additional Answers** section.
2. (a) The thoughts and feelings of both the girl and the boy are listed. If the third-person limited or first-person points of view had been used, readers would know the thoughts and feelings of only one character. (b) The chart lists the thoughts and feelings of Adjoa, whereas Nana's thoughts and feelings can only be inferred.

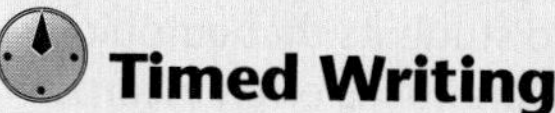

Timed Writing

1. Review the prompt with students.
2. Have students use the 5-Minute Planner to structure their time. Guide them in answering the bulleted questions. For example, point out that the third bulleted item might prompt them to focus on Adjoa's age and understanding of adults.
3. Allow students 30 minutes to complete the assignment.
4. As students prewrite and draft, have them refer to their completed **Comparing Points of View Graphic Organizer** or to their completed version of the chart on this page.

Six Traits Focus

✔	Ideas	Word Choice
✔	Organization	Sentence Fluency
	Voice	Conventions

Assessment Resources

Unit 1 Resources

L1 L2 EL **Selection Test A**, pp. 119–121.
L3 L4 EL **Selection Test B**, pp. 122–124.
L3 L4 **Open-Book Test**, pp. 116–118.

PHLit Online! All assessment resources are available at **www.PHLitOnline.com**.

PRETEACH

Common Core State Standards

- Writing 3, 3.a, b, c, d, e; 5

Introducing the Writing Assignment

Review the assignment and the criteria, using the instruction on the student page.

Connecting to Real-Life Writing

Point out to students that autobiographical narration is often incorporated into other types of writing. For example, speeches frequently include autobiographical segments.

Writing Workshop
Work in Progress

If students have completed the Work-in-Progress assignments on pp. 41 and 71, suggest that they try to develop their Work-in-Progress ideas in an autobiographical narrative.

TEACH

Prewriting/Planning Strategy

1. Introduce the prewriting strategy, using the instruction given.
2. Have students apply the strategy.

Six Traits Focus

✓	Ideas		Word Choice
✓	Organization		Sentence Fluency
	Voice		Conventions

Writing Workshop

Write a Narrative

Narration: Autobiographical Narrative

Defining the Form An **autobiographical narrative** describes real events in the writer's life and shares the lessons or wisdom the writer gained from the experiences. You might use elements of autobiographical narration in letters, journals, reflective essays, or persuasive essays.

Assignment Write an autobiographical narrative about an event that taught you a valuable lesson. Include the following elements:

✓ a *sequence of events* involving you, the writer

✓ a *problem, or conflict,* and a lesson you learned from it

✓ details that locate scenes and incidents in specific places

✓ your thoughts, feelings, or views about the significance of events

✓ error-free grammar, including *correct use of possessive nouns*

To preview the criteria on which your autobiographical narrative may be judged, see the rubric on page 99.

Writing Workshop: *Work in Progress*

Review the work you did on pages 41 and 71.

Common Core State Standards

Writing

3. Write narratives to develop real or imagined experiences or events using effective technique, well-chosen details, and well-structured event sequences.

3.a. Engage and orient the reader by setting out a problem, situation, or observation, establishing one or multiple point(s) of view, and introducing a narrator and/or characters; create a smooth progression of experiences or events.

3.c. Use a variety of techniques to sequence events so that they build on one another to create a coherent whole.

3.d. Use precise words and phrases, telling details, and sensory language to convey a vivid picture of the experiences, events, setting, and/or characters.

5. Develop and strengthen writing as needed by planning, revising, editing, rewriting, or trying a new approach, focusing on addressing what is most significant for a specific purpose and audience.

Prewriting/Planning Strategy

Structure the sequence. Create a detailed record of events by making a timeline like the one shown. Write down the first incident related to your subject and record subsequent incidents in the order and place in which they occurred. Note the significance of each event so that you will be able to communicate it to your audience in your essay.

Reading-Writing Connection

To get a feel for autobiographical narratives, read "My English" by Julia Alvarez on page 114.

Timeline

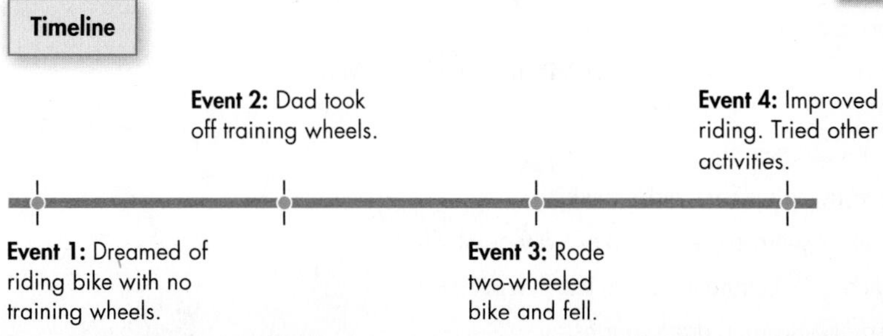
Event 1: Dreamed of riding bike with no training wheels.
Event 2: Dad took off training wheels.
Event 3: Rode two-wheeled bike and fell.
Event 4: Improved riding. Tried other activities.

Teaching Resources

The following resources can be used to enrich or extend the instruction.

All *Unit 1 Resources*
Writing Workshop, pp. 125–126

All *Common Core Companion,*
pp. 202–212; 220–221

All *Professional Development Guidebook*
Rubrics for Self-Assessment: Autobiographical Narrative, pp. 222–223

All *Graphic Organizer Transparencies*
Rubric for Self-Assessment: Autobiographical Narrative, p. 19

All resources are available online at **www.PHLitOnline.com**.

SIX TRAITS

WRITER'S TOOLBOX

Word Choice | Ideas | Conventions | Sentence Fluency | Voice | Organization

Painting a Picture with Words

Word choice is the specific language a writer uses to tell a story. By choosing the right words in your narrative, you can make the people, places, and events you describe as real for your reader as they are for you.

Choosing Details Remember that your readers can only see what you show them with words. As you write, do not just list events; use details to show readers what happened and how it felt. Add life to your story with precise descriptions. The chart shown below gives a spectrum of tips that will help you elaborate further on an idea.

Story Element	Elaboration Tip
Experience	Explain its main effect on you.
Time and Place	Describe impressions using sensory details.
Suspense	Add details that raise the tension and heighten the story's problem.
Main Events of Story	Include thoughts or feelings that occurred to you at the time of the events.
Story Outcome	Consider other possible outcomes of events.

Avoiding Vague Language A good story not only describes an event; it makes readers feel as if they were there. To be sure that your readers understand what you are trying to communicate, avoid words that are vague. Instead, use language that creates a clear image in readers' minds.

Vague: There was a *beautiful* tree in the playground.

Precise: In the playground stood an *old oak* tree with *thick branches that stretched at least twenty feet in every direction.*

Vague: It was a *hot* day.

Precise: It was the kind of day *when the sun is so bright that it hurts your eyes and the sidewalk scorches your feet if you walk barefoot.*

Evaluating Word Choice Check your writing to be sure you have used precise words. If you find that a word you are using does not capture the meaning you are trying to communicate, use a *thesaurus* to find a more precise word. Then, check a *dictionary* to be sure that you are using the new word correctly.

Painting a Picture with Words

1. Introduce the writing skill, using the instruction on the student page.
2. Discuss the chart and the strategies for choosing words.

Teaching the Writing Skill

1. Remind students that a writer can control the picture in readers' minds by carefully selecting words. Provide an example. First, **ask** students to draw a picture that comes to mind when you say the word *dog.* (Students' drawings should show a variety of different types of dogs.). Then **ask** students to draw the picture that comes to mind when you say the phrase *huge, shaggy collie.* (Students' drawings should resemble huge, shaggy collies.) Invite volunteers to share their drawings with the class. Point out that using precise words in descriptions helps readers visualize what is happening in a narrative.
2. Tell students that they can break down a particular event into specific steps to help them create a detailed picture of the event. Discuss how using vivid details helps to develop reader interest.
3. Review using a thesaurus. Remind students that each word listed in a thesaurus entry may have different connotations. Point out the importance of checking a dictionary for the precise meaning of a word.

Prentice Hall EssayScorer

A writing prompt for this mode of writing can be found on the ***Prentice Hall Essay Scorer*** at **www.PHLitOnline.com.**

Differentiated Instruction for Universal Access

EL Strategy for English Learners

Help English language learners identify specific and precise language. Select groups of words with similar meanings and provide pictures that illustrate each word. For example, provide pictures of an *apartment, house, castle, cottage, mansion, townhouse,* and *suburban home.* Work with students to label each picture. Use the pictures to point out the differences in meaning between the words.

Strategy for Advanced Writers

Provide students with a group of words, such as *dark, bold, curious, careful,* and *timid.* Have students generate a list of synonyms for each word that displays the nuances of language. For example, given the word *dark,* students may come up with *dim, dusky, gloomy, inky.* Encourage students to use their own knowledge and to consult a dictionary and thesaurus for additional ideas.

Drafting Strategies

1. Introduce the drafting strategies.
2. Have students apply the strategies.

Teaching the Strategies

1. Have students review their timelines and delete details that do not reinforce their main points.
2. Encourage students to write a sentence or two about how they personally felt about each event.

Six Traits Focus

✓	Ideas		Word Choice
✓	Organization		Sentence Fluency
	Voice		Conventions

Revising Strategy

1. Introduce the revision strategy.
2. Have students apply the strategy.

Teaching the Strategy

1. Work with students to evaluate their sentence beginnings.
2. Invite volunteers to share their original sentence beginnings and the rewritten versions.

Six Traits Focus

	Ideas	✓	Word Choice
✓	Organization	✓	Sentence Fluency
	Voice		Conventions

Drafting Strategies

Identify your main point. As you draft, think about why this experience matters to you. To convey that importance to readers, clearly state the main problem you faced and what you learned from it. Then, organize your details to highlight the significance of that main point.

Pace the action. Details and description add substance to your essay, but too much can slow the pace, or flow, of the story. Be sure that every detail you include has a clear purpose and keeps the reader engaged.

- Emphasize the central conflict that sets the story in motion.
- Create suspense by withholding some details until later in the narrative.
- Conclude by reflecting on the experience and telling what you learned from it.

Use a flow chart like the one shown below to help you decide which details to include in your narrative and the most effective time to reveal them.

Detail	Purpose	Best Use of Detail
I put my good-luck penny in my pocket the first time I rode without training wheels, but it fell out while I was riding.	This detail shows that it was courage and hard work, not luck, that helped me ride without training wheels.	Reveal that I put the penny in my pocket early in the narrative. Delay revealing that it fell out until the end, when I explain what I learned.

Common Core State Standards

Writing

3.b. Use narrative techniques, such as dialogue, pacing, description, reflection, and multiple plot lines, to develop experiences, events, and/or characters.

3.e. Provide a conclusion that follows from and reflects on what is experienced, observed, or resolved over the course of the narrative.

Revising Strategy

Vary your sentence beginnings. Even though your narrative is about you, avoid beginning every sentence with *I*. Circle the first word in each sentence in your draft. Then, consider varying sentence beginnings to make your story more interesting.

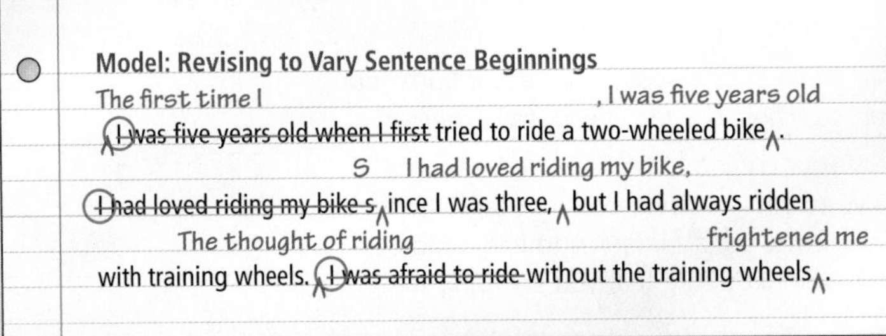

Model: Revising to Vary Sentence Beginnings
The first time I
, I was five years old
I was five years old when I first tried to ride a two-wheeled bike.
S
I had loved riding my bike,
I had loved riding my bike since I was three, but I had always ridden
The thought of riding
frightened me
with training wheels. I was afraid to ride without the training wheels.

Applying Understanding by Design Principles

Clarifying Expected Outcomes: Using Rubrics

- Before students begin working on this assignment, have them preview the Rubric for Self-Assessment (p. 99) to learn what qualities their autobiographical narratives must have. A copy of this rubric appears in ***Graphic Organizer Transparencies,*** p. 19.
- Review the criteria in the Rubric with the class. Before students use the Rubric to assess their writing, work with them to rate the Student Model (p. 98) using the Rubric.
- If you wish to assess students' autobiographical narratives with either a 4-point or a 6-point scoring rubric, see ***Professional Development Guidebook,*** pp. 222–223.

WRITER'S TOOLBOX

Conventions | Sentence Fluency | Voice | Organization | Word Choice | Ideas

Revising to Correct Use of Possessive Nouns

Possessive nouns show to whom places or things belong. A possessive noun is usually formed by adding an apostrophe and an *s* ('s) to a noun.

Noun	Possessive Noun
the homework of the *student*	the *student's* homework

Because they modify other nouns, possessive nouns function in sentences as adjectives.

Forming Possessive Nouns Correctly

Singular Nouns

- Add an apostrophe and an *s* to show the possessive case of most singular nouns.

  the radiator of the car ⟶ the car's radiator

- When a singular noun ends in *s*, you may still be able to add an apostrophe and *s*. However, if the apostrophe and *s* make the word difficult to pronounce, the apostrophe may be used alone.

  the sleeve of the dress ⟶ the dress's sleeve
  the poetry of Burns ⟶ Burns' poetry

Plural Nouns

- Add an apostrophe to show the possessive case of plural nouns ending in *s* or *es:* the *representatives'* decision.
- Add an apostrophe and *s* to show the possessive case of plural nouns that do not end in *s* or *es:* the *men's* books.

Compound Nouns

- Add an apostrophe and *s* to the last word of a compound noun: the *Prime Minister's* visit.
- Add only an apostrophe if the last word of a compound noun ends in *s:* the *House of Representatives'* decision.

Grammar in Your Writing

Review the draft of your autobiographical narrative, highlighting all the possessive nouns. Check that you have used singular possessives and plural possessives correctly. Correct any errors you find.

PH WRITING COACH

Further instruction and practice are available in *Prentice Hall Writing Coach*.

Differentiated Instruction for Universal Access

EL Strategy for English Learners

Point out to students that possession can also be shown using the preposition *of*, as in this example:

The trees of the forest were tall and thick.

Trees is a noun and *forest* is the object of the preposition, but together this construction shows possession. An apostrophe is not used.

Emphasize that this construction is primarily used with things, but almost never with people. Therefore, students might use this sentence: *Brian's house is white.* Students would probably not use this sentence: *The house of Brian is white.*

Have students go through their drafts to make sure that they have not used any "of constructions" with people as objects of their prepositions.

Revising Use of Possessive Nouns

1. Introduce the grammar skill, using the instruction on the student page.
2. Discuss the examples and the strategies for forming possessive nouns correctly.
3. Have students follow the instruction under Grammar in Your Writing to correct errors in their drafts.

Teaching the Grammar Skill

1. Tell students to be careful not to confuse the plural, the singular possessive, and the plural possessive forms of a noun. Give them the following examples:

   Two girls *waited to play the game.* (plural)

   The older girl's *father gave her a quarter.* (singular possessive)

   Both girls' *pockets were full of the tickets that they had won.* (plural possessive)

2. Write the following paragraph on the board. Call on students to correct the possessive forms of words.

   Sasha Walker dog barked at a cat that bolted across the yard. The dogs continuous barking alerted all of the neighbors dogs, and they started barking too. All of the dogs noise woke the neighbors. Peoples heads poked out of windows. My neighbors wife, Sara Jones, knocked on our door. Her familys dog had run away. Now the Joneses children were worried about their dog.

   Answer: *Sasha Walker's dog barked at a cat that bolted across the yard. The dog's continuous barking alerted all of the neighbors' dogs, and they started barking too. All of the dogs' noise woke the neighbors. People's heads poked out of windows. My neighbor's wife, Sara Jones, knocked on our door. Her family's dog had run away. Now the Joneses' children were worried about their dog.*

PH WRITING COACH Grade 9

Students will find practice with and guidance on possessive nouns in Chapter 23.

Student Model

Review the Student Model with the class, using the annotations to analyze the writer's use of the elements of an autobiographical narrative.

Teaching the Grammar Skill

1. Explain that the student model is a sample and that narratives may be longer.
2. Write the following sentences on the board:

   Fiona waited for her brother at the top of the basement stairs. She peered down into the musty darkness, took a few steps back, and then yelled for her brother to hurry.

   Ask students to use dialogue to make this passage more real and vivid. Have volunteers write responses on the board.

   Possible response:

   Fiona waited for her brother at the top of the basement stairs. She peered down into the musty darkness, took a few steps back, and then yelled, "Jeremiah, this is ridiculous! Hurry up!"
3. **Ask** students how the description of the sleeping bag helps establish the conflict.

   Answer: The details reveal the sleeping bag's appeal, showing readers why the siblings were fighting over it.
4. **Ask** students what details the writer gives to show that the conflict had intensified.

   Answer: Their fight was lasting into the weekend, and she brought others into the fight.
5. Remind students that an autobiographical narrative provides a personal insight gained from the experience described. **Ask** students what lesson Jonathan learned.

   Answer: He learned that, even when angry, he shouldn't abandon his friends.

Connecting to Real-Life Writing

Emphasize that autobiographical writing is not limited to school assignments. Explain to students that they will be asked to write about their experiences for college and job applications.

Student Model: Jonathan Chan, Royersford, PA

True Friend

Late one Thursday night in July, my sister and I were packing for our upcoming trip to youth camp. This was my first time attending the camp, but it would be my older sister Phoebe's third experience. Everything was running smoothly until my mother called from downstairs, "Don't forget to grab a sleeping bag from my closet!" Our mother never dreamed such a simple statement would start a desperate dash by both of us to seize the most coveted sleeping bag in our household.

Jonathan's use of dialogue helps to make this opening scene more real and vivid.

The night-sky blue, extra long, brand new, one hundred percent fleece sleeping bag with a built-in pillow was one-of-a-kind. By comparison, the old sleeping bag, with a broken zipper and a small hole forming at the bottom, looked even worse. Phoebe and I reached for the beautiful new bag at the exact same moment. Insulting remarks sailed from our lips as we each grabbed it. Our stomps and yells attracted our parents to the fight scene. I began to argue that I had reached the bag first, when my sister simply let go, returned to her room, and slammed the door. She was so thoroughly angry we did not speak again that night.

The detailed description of the sleeping bag helps to establish the conflict.

As the weekend progressed, our relationship did not improve. Even worse, she had shared the story with her friends. Phoebe's words were so moving, they convinced her friends to embark on a personal voyage to "get me." As a result, I spent the getaway with a target on my back.

Here, the conflict intensifies.

As the skinny new kid at the camp, terror struck my heart when I heard a rumor about the plot against me. By Sunday morning, the plan, "Operation Little Brother," was all set. My sister's friends were on a mission.

Jonathan uses specific details to paint a picture of the problem he faces.

I was shooting hoops in the gym that morning when my sister's friends appeared. I looked frantically for an escape but was quickly surrounded. The assailants closed to within inches of me when a familiar voice echoed through the emptiness of the open gymnasium. My sister walked calmly between her friends and me and said, "Do not bother him or you will feel the wrath of Phoebe." I was in awe. With this statement, "Operation Little Brother" came to an abrupt end. The sister I was feuding with had just saved me. Her friends never bothered me again.

The dialogue and description help to convey the drama of the moment and make it seem real.

On the trip home I asked her to explain her unlikely action. She simply replied, "I still don't like you, but I would dislike myself even more if I ever abandoned a friend in trouble." Since then, I have often modeled my actions to emulate my sister's behavior that day. I have learned that even when I am angry, I must stand up for my friends. My sister has taught me many things, but the most important lesson is how to be a true friend.

Jonathan concludes by drawing an important lesson from his experience.

Strategies for Test Taking

When students are taking a test that requires them to respond to a narrative writing prompt, they should devote the majority of their time to the drafting stage of the writing process. Tell students that the key to effective writing (and to making the most of the allotted time) is to organize their thoughts in the drafting stage. Students should pay careful attention to the main points of their essays and provide adequate support for these points. They should also remember that their time, and probably their space, is limited. Therefore, it is vital for them to include important ideas and eliminate unnecessary details. If students follow these suggestions during drafting, revision will be a smoother, less time-consuming process.

Editing and Proofreading

Check your draft for errors in grammar, spelling, and punctuation.

Focus on Dates and Facts. Review your manuscript to make sure you have provided accurate factual information. Capitalize the proper names of people or places and use correct punctuation when including dates.

Spiral Review

Earlier in the unit, you learned about **common and proper nouns** (p. 40) and **abstract and concrete nouns** (p. 70). Check the capitalization of the common and proper nouns in your narrative. Review your essay to be sure you have used these types of nouns correctly.

Publishing and Presenting

Consider one of the following ways to share your writing.

Present an oral narrative. Mark up a copy of your autobiographical narrative, underlining any thoughts or conversations that you believe your audience would enjoy. As you present to your classmates, emphasize those passages. Be sure to pace the presentation of actions to accommodate changes in time or mood. When you are done, gracefully accept your classmates' applause and praise.

Post your essay. With your classmates, create a bulletin board display of the narratives. Have each writer supply a short comment about the event or idea that inspired his or her writing.

Reflecting on Your Writing

Writer's Journal Jot down your answers to this question:
How did writing about events help you to understand them better?

Rubric for Self-Assessment

Find evidence in your writing to address each category. Then, use the rating scale to grade your work.

Criteria	Rating Scale (not very — very)
Focus: How central are you to the action of the story?	1 2 3 4 5
Organization: How clearly organized is the sequence of events?	1 2 3 4 5
Support/Elaboration: How powerfully are sensory details used to locate scenes in specific places?	1 2 3 4 5
Style: How clearly do you convey your insights, thoughts, and feelings?	1 2 3 4 5
Conventions: How correct is your grammar—especially your use of possessive nouns?	1 2 3 4 5
Word Choice: How precise is the language used to describe the people, places, and events in your narrative?	1 2 3 4 5

Editing and Proofreading

1. Introduce the editing and proofreading focus, using the instruction on the student page.
2. Have students edit and proofread their narratives, correcting grammar, spelling, punctuation, and word choice. Make sure they check for errors of the type noted on the student page.

Teaching the Editing Focus

1. Encourage students to use highlighters to identify dates and facts in their narratives before checking the accuracy of the information.
2. Have students circle all of their possessive nouns. Have partners check each other's work for correct use of possessive nouns.

Six Traits Focus

	Ideas		Word Choice
	Organization		Sentence Fluency
	Voice	✓	Conventions

ASSESS

Publishing and Presenting

1. As students practice their oral narratives, tell them to think about how they can use tone, pacing, gestures, and facial expressions to emphasize their marked passages.
2. Encourage students to supplement their bulletin board displays with photographs or related objects.

Reflecting on Your Writing

1. Have students consider the significance of the events they described. Ask students the following questions: *Has writing an autobiographical narrative changed your opinion of the event? What did you learn about the significance of the event?*
2. Have students reflect on the personal nature of an autobiographical narrative. Ask students whether they enjoyed writing a narrative focused on themselves.

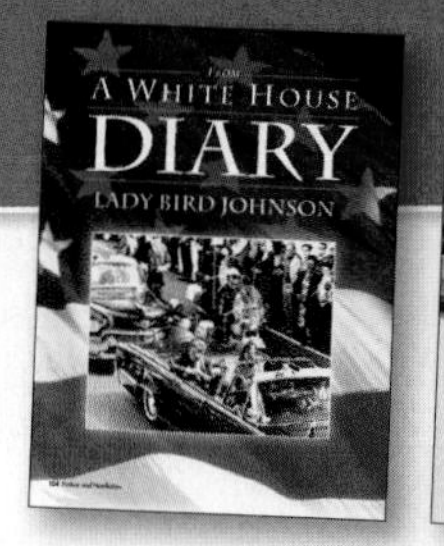

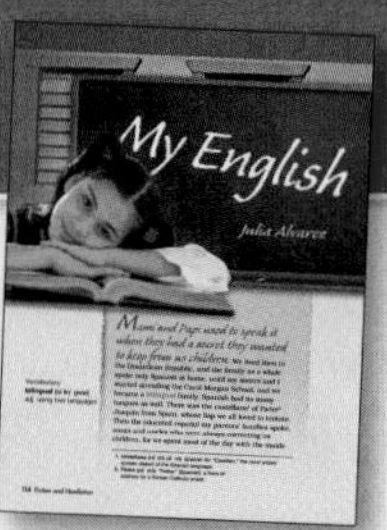

✓ from A White House Diary • ✓✓ My English

Lesson Pacing Guide

DAY 1 Preteach

- Administer the Reading and Vocabulary Warm-ups (*Unit 1 Resources,* pp. 135–138 or 153–156) as necessary.
- Introduce the Reading Skill: Author's Purpose.
- Introduce the Literary Analysis concept: Voice.
- Distribute copies of the appropriate graphic organizer for the Reading Skill (*Graphic Organizer Transparencies*, pp. 20–22).
- Distribute copies of the appropriate graphic organizer for Literary Analysis (*Graphic Organizer Transparencies,* pp. 23–25).
- Teach the selection vocabulary.
- Introduce the Word Study skill.

DAYS 2–3 Preteach/Teach

- Build background with the Background feature.
- Develop thematic vocabulary and thematic thinking with Writing About the Big Question.
- Prepare students to read with the Activating Prior Knowledge activities (TE).
- Informally monitor comprehension while students read.
- Use the Reading Check questions to confirm comprehension.
- Develop students' ability to determine the author's purpose, using the Reading Skill questions.
- Develop students' understanding of voice, using the Literary Analysis questions.
- Reinforce vocabulary with the Vocabulary notes.
- Reinforce unit focus standards using the Spiral Review prompts.

DAY 4 Assess

- Assess students' comprehension and mastery of the skills by having them answer the Critical Thinking, Reading Skill, and Literary Analysis questions.
- Have students complete the Vocabulary Practice activities.
- Have students complete the Word Study activities.

DAY 5 Extend/Assess

- Have students complete the Conventions lesson.
- Have students complete the Writing activity and write a journal entry. (You may assign as homework.)
- Extend learning by having students complete the Research and Technology activity, introduction for a multimedia presentation. (You may assign as homework.) As an alternative, assign them "Judging Eyewitness Accounts" or "Shifting Gears on Language" in *Reality Central.*
- Administer Selection Test A or B (*Unit 1 Resources,* pp. 147–152 or 168–173).

Common Core State Standards

Reading Informational Text
2. Determine a central idea of a text and analyze its development over the course of the text, including how it emerges and is shaped and refined by specific details; provide an objective summary of the text.
6. Determine an author's point of view or purpose in a text and analyze how an author uses rhetoric to advance that point of view or purpose.
7. Analyze various accounts of a subject told in different mediums, determining which details are emphasized in each account.

Writing 4. Produce clear and coherent writing in which the development, organization, and style are appropriate to task, purpose, and audience.

Speaking and Listening 5. Make strategic use of digital media in presentations to enhance understanding of findings, reasoning, and evidence and to add interest.

Language 1. Demonstrate command of the conventions of standard English grammar and usage when writing or speaking.
6. Acquire and use accurately grade-appropriate general academic and domain-specific words and phrases; gather vocabulary knowledge when considering a word or phrase important to comprehension or expression.

Additional Standards Practice
Common Core Companion,
pp. 15–22; 97–104

Daily Block Scheduling
Each day in this Lesson Pacing Guide represents a 40–50 minute period. Teachers using block scheduling may combine days to revise pacing. In addition, teachers my differentiate and support core instruction by integrating components for extended and intensive support as students require. See the Guide to Selected Leveled Resources (facing page).

Guide to Selected Leveled Resources

RTI **Tier 1** (students performing on level)		✓ More Accessible *from* A White House Diary	✓✓ More Complex My English
Warm Up	**Practice, model,** and **monitor** fluency, working **with the whole class** or **in groups.**	**Vocabulary** and **Reading Warm-ups B,** ***Unit 1 Resources,*** pp. 135–136, 138	**Vocabulary** and **Reading Warm-ups B,** ***Unit 1 Resources,*** pp. 153–154, 156
Comprehension/Skills	**Support** and **monitor** comprehension and skills development, having students complete the activities, graphic organizers, and interactive prompts **independently** or **as a class.**	• ***Reader's Notebook,*** adapted instruction and full selection EL ***Reader's Notebook: English Learner's Version,*** adapted instruction and adapted selection • **Reading Skill Graphic Organizer B,** ***Graphic Organizer Transparencies,*** p. 22 • **Literary Analysis Graphic Organizer B,** ***Graphic Organizer Transparencies,*** p. 25	• ***Reader's Notebook,*** adapted instruction and summary EL ***Reader's Notebook: English Learner's Version,*** adapted instruction and summary • **Reading Skill Graphic Organizer B,** ***Graphic Organizer Transparencies,*** p. 22 • **Literary Analysis Graphic Organizer B,** ***Graphic Organizer Transparencies,*** p. 25
Monitor Progress	**Monitor** student progress with the differentiated curriculum-based assessment in the *Unit Resources.*	• **Selection Test B,** ***Unit 1 Resources,*** pp. 150–152 • **Open-Book Test,** ***Unit 1 Resources,*** pp. 144–146	• **Selection Test B,** ***Unit 1 Resources,*** pp. 171–173 • **Open-Book Test,** ***Unit 1 Resources,*** pp. 165–167

RTI **Tier 2** (students requiring intervention)		✓ More Accessible *from* A White House Diary	✓✓ More Complex My English
Warm Up	**Practice, model,** and **monitor** fluency **in groups** or **with individuals.**	• **Vocabulary and Reading Warm-ups A,** ***Unit 1 Resources,*** pp. 135–137 • ***Reality Central,*** "Judging Eyewitness Accounts" • ***Hear It!*** **Audio CD (adapted text)**	• **Vocabulary and Reading Warm-ups A,** ***Unit 1 Resources,*** pp. 153–155 • ***Reality Central,*** "Shifting Gears on Language" • ***Hear It!*** **Audio CD**
Comprehension/Skills	• **Support** and **monitor** comprehension and skills development, working **in small groups** or **with individuals.** • **Pair** students with more advanced peers and have them complete the writing activity in the *Real-World Writing Journal.* • As students complete the selection in the appropriate version of the *Reader's Notebook,* **monitor** comprehension frequently with group questions and individual instruction. • **Model** strategies while guiding students in completing the activities and prompts in the *Reader's Notebook,* as well as the graphic organizers. • **Practice** skills and **monitor** mastery with the *Reading Kit* worksheets.	• ***Real-World Writing Journal,*** Lesson 5, pp. 18–21 • ***Reader's Notebook: Adapted Version,*** adapted instruction and adapted selection EL ***Reader's Notebook: English Learner's Version,*** adapted instruction and adapted selection • **Reading Skill Graphic Organizer A,** ***Graphic Organizer Transparencies,*** p. 20 • **Literary Analysis Graphic Organizer A,** ***Graphic Organizer Transparencies,*** p. 23 • ***Reading Kit,*** Practice worksheets, pp. 26, 32, 36, 38, 46	• ***Real-World Writing Journal,*** Lesson 6, pp. 22–25 • ***Reader's Notebook: Adapted Version,*** adapted instruction and summary EL ***Reader's Notebook: English Learner's Version,*** adapted instruction and summary • **Reading Skill Graphic Organizer A,** ***Graphic Organizer Transparencies,*** p. 21 • **Literary Analysis Graphic Organizer A,** ***Graphic Organizer Transparencies,*** p. 24 • ***Reading Kit,*** Practice worksheets, pp. 26, 32, 36, 38, 46
Monitor Progress	**Monitor** student progress with the differentiated curriculum-based assessment in the *Unit Resources* and in the *Reading Kit.*	• **Selection Test A,** ***Unit 1 Resources,*** pp. 147–149 • ***Reading Kit,*** Assess worksheets, pp. 27, 33, 37, 39, 47	• **Selection Test A,** ***Unit 1 Resources,*** pp. 168–170 • ***Reading Kit,*** Assess worksheets, pp. 27, 33, 37, 39, 47

TIER 3 Tier 3 intervention may require consultation with the student's special-education or dyslexia specialist. For additional support, see the Tier 2 activities and resources listed above.

One-on-one teaching | Group work | Whole class instruction | Independent work | A Assessment

For a complete guide to selection support, including support for Advanced students, see the Overview of Resources in the frontmatter.

✓*from* A White House Diary
✓✓My English

RESOURCES FOR:

- L1 Special-Needs Students
- L2 Below-Level Students (Tier 2)
- L3 On-Level Students (Tier 1)
- L4 Advanced Students (Tier 1)
- EL English Learners
- All All Students

Vocabulary/Fluency/Prior Knowledge

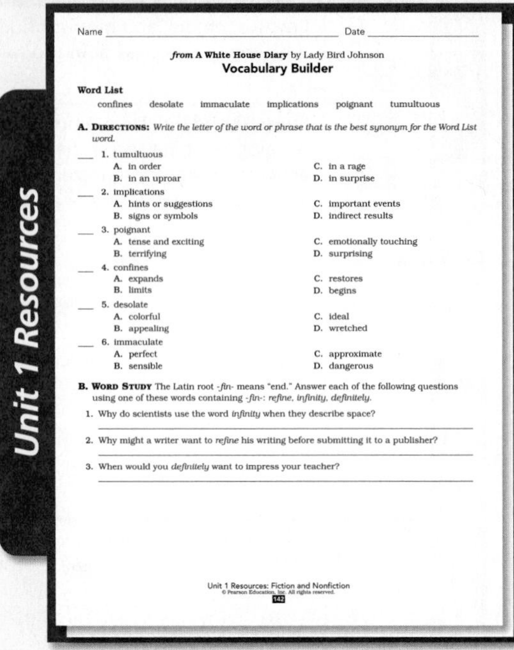

Name ______ Date ______

from **A White House Diary** by Lady Bird Johnson
Vocabulary Builder

Word List

confines desolate immaculate implications poignant tumultuous

A. Directions: *Write the letter of the word or phrase that is the best synonym for the Word List word.*

___ 1. tumultuous
A. in order C. in a rage
B. in an uproar D. in surprise

___ 2. implications
A. hints or suggestions C. important events
B. signs or symbols D. indirect results

___ 3. poignant
A. tense and exciting C. emotionally touching
B. terrifying D. surprising

___ 4. confines
A. expands C. restores
B. limits D. begins

___ 5. desolate
A. colorful C. ideal
B. appealing D. wretched

___ 6. immaculate
A. perfect C. approximate
B. sensible D. dangerous

B. Word Study The Latin root *-fin-* means "end." Answer each of the following questions using one of these words containing *-fin-*: *refine, infinity, definitely.*

1. Why do scientists use the word *infinity* when they describe space?
2. Why might a writer want to *refine* his writing before submitting it to a publisher?
3. When would you *definitely* want to impress your teacher?

Unit 1 Resources: Fiction and Nonfiction
© Pearson Education, Inc. All rights reserved.
142

All **Vocabulary Builder,** pp. 142, 160

Also available for these selections:

EL L1 L2 **Vocabulary Warm-ups A and B,** pp. 135–136, 153–154

EL L1 L2 **Reading Warm-ups A and B,** pp. 137–138, 155–156

All **Writing About the Big Question,** pp. 139, 157

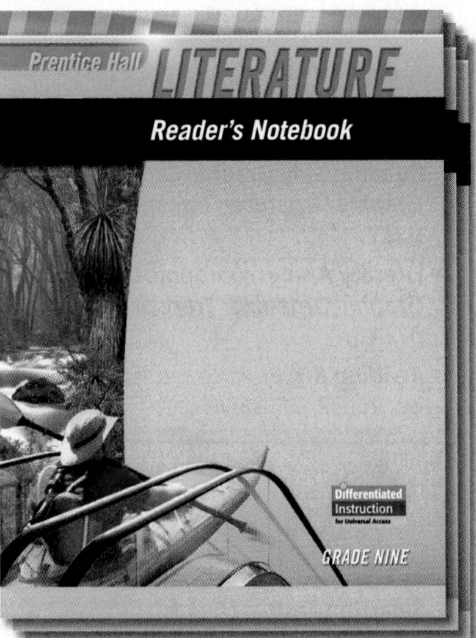

Reader's Notebooks

Pre- and postreading pages for both selections, as well as selections from *A White House Diary*, appear in an interactive format in the *Reader's Notebooks*. Each *Notebook* is differentiated for a different group of learners.

The selections in the Adapted and English Learner's versions are abridged.

L2 L3 ***Reader's Notebook***

L1 ***Reader's Notebook: Adapted Version***

EL ***Reader's Notebook: English Learner's Version***

EL ***Reader's Notebook: Spanish Version***

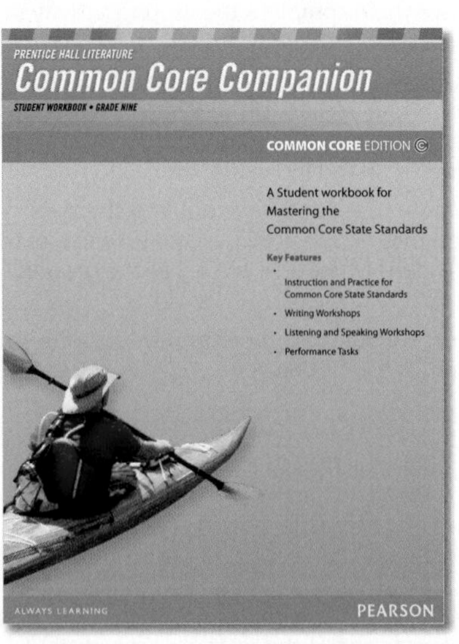

Common Core Companion

Additional instruction and practice for each Common Core State Standard

Selection Support

Graphic Organizer Transparencies

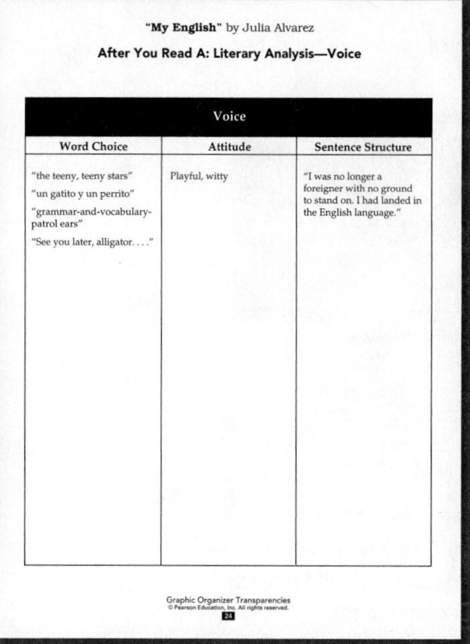

"My English" by Julia Alvarez

After You Read A: Literary Analysis—Voice

Voice		
Word Choice	**Attitude**	**Sentence Structure**
"the teeny, teeny stars" "un gatito y un perrito" "grammar-and-vocabulary-patrol ears" "See you later, alligator. . . ."	Playful, witty	"I was no longer a foreigner with no ground to stand on. I had landed in the English language."

Graphic Organizer Transparencies

24

EL L1 L2 **Literary Analysis: Graphic Organizer A,** pp. 23, 24 (partially filled in)

Also available for these selections:

EL L1 L2 **Reading: Graphic Organizer A,** pp. 20, 21 (partially filled in)

EL L3 **Reading: Graphic Organizer B,** p. 22

EL L3 **Literary Analysis: Graphic Organizer B,** p. 25

Skills Development/Extension

Unit 1 Resources

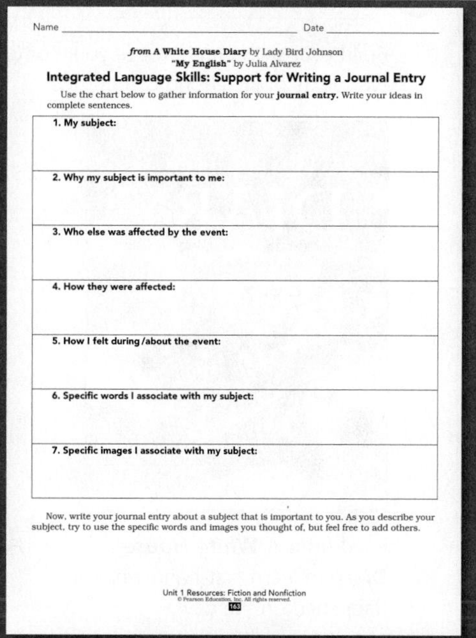

Name ______________________ Date ____________

from **A White House Diary** by Lady Bird Johnson
"My English" by Julia Alvarez

Integrated Language Skills: Support for Writing a Journal Entry

Use the chart below to gather information for your **journal entry.** Write your ideas in complete sentences.

1. **My subject:**
2. **Why my subject is important to me:**
3. **Who else was affected by the event:**
4. **How they were affected:**
5. **How I felt during /about the event:**
6. **Specific words I associate with my subject:**
7. **Specific images I associate with my subject:**

Now, write your journal entry about a subject that is important to you. As you describe your subject, try to use the specific words and images you thought of, but feel free to add others.

Unit 1 Resources: Fiction and Nonfiction

163

EL L3 L4 **Support for Writing,** p. 163

Also available for these selections:

All **Literary Analysis: Voice,** pp. 140, 158

All **Reading: Author's Purpose,** pp. 141, 159

L4 **Enrichment,** pp. 143, 161

EL L3 L4 **Grammar,** p. 162

L3 L4 **Support for Extend Your Learning,** p. 164

Assessment

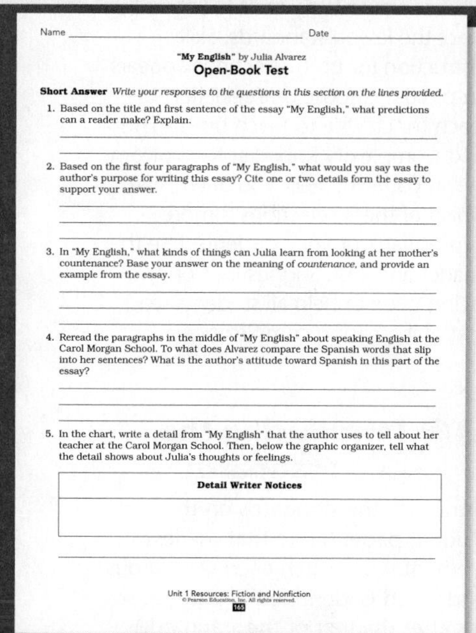

Name ______________________ Date ____________

"My English" by Julia Alvarez

Open-Book Test

Short Answer *Write your responses to the questions in this section on the lines provided.*

1. Based on the title and first sentence of the essay "My English," what predictions can a reader make? Explain.
2. Based on the first four paragraphs of "My English," what would you say was the author's purpose for writing this essay? Cite one or two details form the essay to support your answer.
3. In "My English," what kinds of things can Julia learn from looking at her mother's countenance? Base your answer on the meaning of *countenance,* and provide an example from the essay.
4. Reread the paragraphs in the middle of "My English" about speaking English at the Carol Morgan School. To what does Alvarez compare the Spanish words that slip into her sentences? What is the author's attitude toward Spanish in this part of the essay?
5. In the chart, write a detail from "My English" that the author uses to tell about her teacher at the Carol Morgan School. Then, below the graphic organizer, tell what the detail shows about Julia's thoughts or feelings.

Detail Writer Notices

Unit 1 Resources: Fiction and Nonfiction

165

L3 L4 **Open-Book Test,** pp. 144–146, 165–167

Also available for these selections:

EL L1 L2 **Selection Test A,** pp. 147–149, 168–170

EL L3 L4 **Selection Test B,** pp. 150–152, 171–173

PHLit Online!
www.PHLitOnline.com

- complete narrated selection text
- a thematically related video with writing prompt
- an interactive graphic organizer
- highlighting feature
- access to all student print resources, adapted to individual student needs
- Spanish and English summaries
- adapted selection translations in Spanish

Online Resources: All print materials are also available online.

Background Video

Also available:

Get Connected! (thematic video with writing prompt)

All videos are available in Spanish.

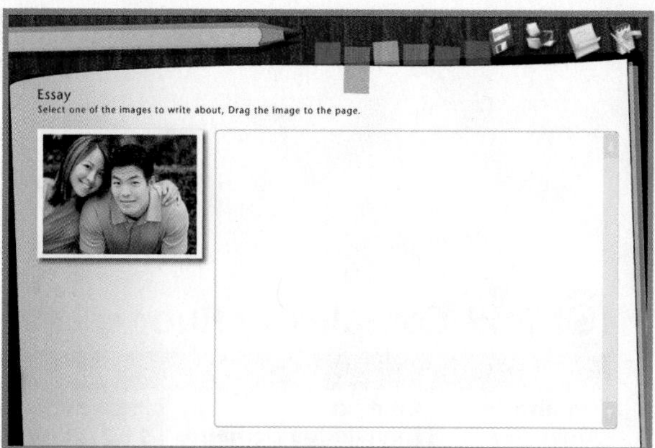

Writer's Journal (with graphics feature)

Also available:

Vocabulary Central (tools, activities, and songs for studying vocabulary)

❶ Leveled Texts

You may use either the selection from *A White House Diary* or "My English" to meet the lesson standards. Skills instruction for both selections appears on p. 101. Choose one selection to teach (or choose to teach both). The Text Complexity Rubric at the bottom of this page will help you determine which of these selections is more appropriate for your students. Use the Reader and Task Suggestions on the facing page to help all students read text of increasing complexity.

❷ Introducing the CCS Standards

Introduce the standards on the student page. (Note that the lesson element with which each standard is addressed is identified in parentheses after the text of the standard.) Call out the standards that you will cover with the selections, explaining to students what each requires and how they will address it as they work through the selection you have chosen. Standards labeled "Spiral Review" are introduced in the Literary Analysis Workshop for this unit.

Before You Read

from A White House Diary • My English

❶ Leveled Texts

Build your skills and improve your comprehension of narrative nonfiction with texts of increasing complexity.

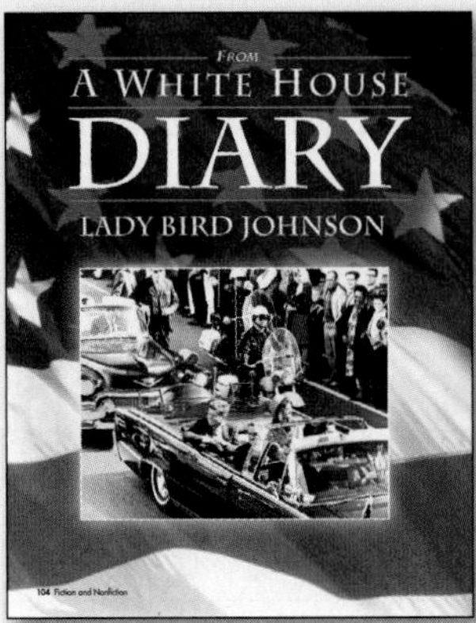

Read from ***A White House Diary*** to learn first-hand what happened on the day a president was assassinated.

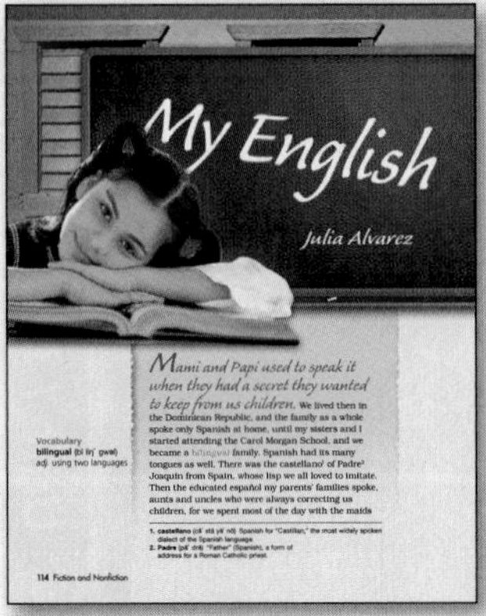

Read **"My English"** to learn how a Spanish-speaking child makes English her language.

❷ Common Core State Standards

Meet these standards with either the excerpt from ***A White House Diary*** (p. 104) or **"My English"** (p. 114).

Reading Informational Text

6. Determine an author's point of view or purpose in a text and analyze how an author uses rhetoric to advance that point of view or purpose. *(Literary Analysis: Voice; Reading Skill: Author's Purpose)*

7. Analyze various accounts of a subject told in different mediums, determining which details are emphasized in each account. *(Analyze Media)*

Spiral Review: RI.9-10.2

Writing

4. Produce clear and coherent writing in which the development, organization, and style are appropriate to task, purpose, and audience. *(Writing: Journal Entry)*

Speaking and Listening

5. Make strategic use of digital media in presentations to enhance understanding of findings, reasoning, and evidence and to add interest. *(Research and Technology: Multimedia Presentation Introduction)*

Language

1. Demonstrate command of the conventions of standard English grammar and usage when writing or speaking. *(Conventions: Pronouns)*

6. Acquire and use accurately grade-appropriate general academic and domain-specific words and phrases; gather vocabulary knowledge when considering a word or phrase important to comprehension or expression. *(Vocabulary: Word Study)*

Text Complexity Rubric: Leveled Texts

Text complexity is determined by both qualitative and quantitative measures. For this reason, the quantitative measure of a more complex selection may be lower than that of a more accessible selection.

		✓ *from* A White House Diary	✓✓ My English
Qualitative Measures	**Context/ Knowledge Demands**	President Kennedy's assassination 1 2 (3) 4 5	Learning the English language 1 2 3 (4) 5
	Structure/Language Conventionality and Clarity	Formal language; on-level vocabulary; descriptive passages 1 2 (3) 4 5	Challenging vocabulary; Spanish words are footnoted 1 2 3 (4) 5
	Levels of Meaning/ Purpose/Concept Level	Accessible concept (witnessing a tragedy; performing in a crisis) 1 2 (3) 4 5	Accessible concept (adapting to new situations; learning a new skill) 1 2 (3) 4 5
Quantitative Measures	**Text Length**	Word Count: 1,631	Word Count: 2,233
	Lexile	820L	1070L
Overall Complexity		✓ **More accessible**	✓✓ **More complex**

❸ Literary Analysis: Voice

Voice is the way a writer sounds on the page. It is related to both the author's *point of view*—his or her unique way of seeing a topic—and his or her *style*, or distinct way of using language. For example, a writer's voice may be sophisticated, blunt, or breathless. The following elements contribute to an author's voice:

- *word choice:* the kinds of words the author chooses
- *tone,* or *attitude:* the way the writer feels about the subject
- *sentence structure:* the arrangement of words in sentences

Voice is a key element in all literature. However, it may be particularly evident in **autobiographical writing,** in which the author relates his or her own life story. As you read, notice how details capture the author's voice, or personality, on the page.

❹ Reading Skill: Author's Purpose

An **author's purpose** is his or her main reason for writing. General purposes for writing are to inform, to persuade, and to narrate. Authors also have specific purposes for writing. For example, an author may write to expose a social problem or to describe an adventure. The author's purpose shapes the decisions he or she makes about every element of the work. To better understand what you read, **preview the text** to identify the author's purpose.

- Notice information or ideas conveyed in the title.
- Look for any organizing features, such as subheads.
- Identify the subject of photos, illustrations, or diagrams.

❺ Using the Strategy: Author's Purpose Map

As you preview, use an organizer like the one shown to jot down ideas about the author's specific purpose. Later, as you read the full text, confirm whether your ideas are correct.

Text Feature	Insight About Purpose

PHLit Online!
www.PHLitOnline.com

Hear It!
- Selection summary audio
- Selection audio

See It!
- Get Connected video
- Background video
- More about the author
- Vocabulary flashcards

Do It!
- Interactive journals
- Interactive graphic organizers
- Self-test
- Internet activity
- Grammar tutorial
- Interactive vocabulary games

PRETEACH

❸ Literary Analysis

Voice

1. Introduce the skill, using the instruction on the student page.
2. Tell students that they will practice assessing the writer's voice as they read.

Think Aloud: Model the Skill

Model a way of assessing a writer's voice. Say to students:

> While I read, I imagine that I am "hearing" the writer's words, not just reading them. For example, if a writer uses words such as *dark, moody, somber,* and *resigned,* I imagine a sad person talking to me. If her sentences are long and disconnected, I imagine a person revealing her thoughts exactly as they occur to her. My imagination helps me "hear" this writer's melancholy, contemplative **voice.**

❹ Reading Skill

Author's Purpose

1. Introduce the skill, using the instruction on the student page.
2. Tell students that they will practice identifying the author's purpose as they read.

❺ Using the Strategy

Give students a copy of either **Reading Skill Graphic Organizer A** or **B** (*Graphic Organizer Transparencies,* pp. 20–22) to record their ideas about author's purpose in an autobiographical selection as they read. Use the examples in **Reading Skill Graphic Organizer A,** which is partially filled in, to model the process of completing the organizer.

Text Complexity: Reader and Task Suggestions

✓ *from* A White House Diary		✓✓ My English	
Preparing to Read the Text	**Leveled Tasks**	**Preparing to Read the Text**	**Leveled Tasks**
• Using the Background information on TE p. 103, discuss the assassination of President Kennedy. • Discuss the impact of President Kennedy's death on Americans at that time. • Guide students to use Multidraft Reading strategies (TE p. 103).	*Knowledge Demands* If students will have difficulty with context and knowledge demands, have them first examine the photographs and read the accompanying text. Then, have them reread the entire selection. *Synthesizing* If students will not have difficulty with context, have them note the similarities in how those close to the event responded during the tragedy. As a class, discuss the impact of Kennedy's death.	• Using the Background information on TE p. 113, discuss Alvarez's two nationalities. • Discuss the challenges everyone faces when learning some difficult new skill. • Guide students to use Multidraft Reading strategies (TE p. 113).	*Levels of Meaning* If students will have difficulty with meaning, have them read the selection, taking notes about the challenges the author faced while learning English. Then, have them reread the selection and add notes about how she overcame those challenges. *Synthesizing* If students will not have difficulty with meaning, have them read and take note of how the author uses humor to tell her story.

PRETEACH

1 Writing About the Big Question

1. Review the assignment with the class.
2. Invite students to think of a time when they had made exciting plans that were canceled at the last minute. How did students feel? How long did it take them to accept this change in circumstances?
3. Have students complete the sentence starters. Review responses as a class. (**Possible response:** Abrupt changes in circumstances can disprove old truths and reveal new ones. Accepting the truth of these changes can be difficult because it may not be the same as what we want to believe.)
4. Remind students that their answers will help them think about the Big Question, "Can truth change?"

While You Read

Tell students that as they read, they should think about Johnson's recollections and if the truth changes in her retelling as events occurred.

2 Vocabulary

1. Have students preview the selection vocabulary.
2. For each word, have students say the word aloud.
3. Then, use the word in a sentence that defines the word.
4. Finally, repeat your definitional sentence or a similar sentence with the word missing and have the class "fill in the blank" chorally. Here are some examples:

   Something that is poignant is often touching, or sad. Parents often think of their children's wedding day as [students say "poignant"].

   Something tumultuous is loud, noisy, or agitated. At the pep rally, students roared as they gave the team a [students say "tumultuous"] *send-off.*

3 Word Study

1. Introduce the skill, using the instruction in the box.
2. Have students use a *-fin-* word in a sentence. (**Sample answer:** I will eat after I finish my book.)

Making Connections *from* A White House Diary

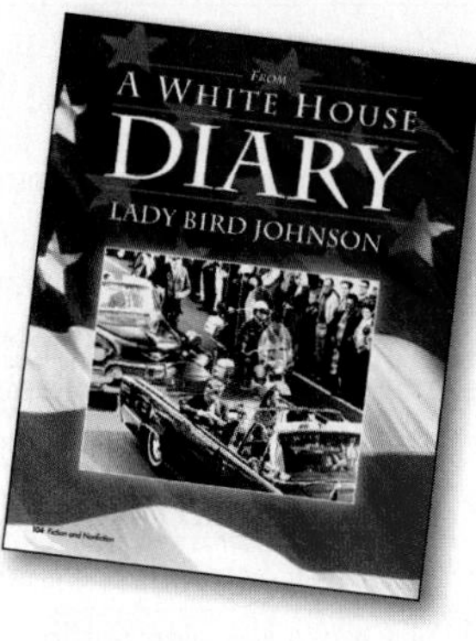

1 Writing About the Big Question

In this passage from *A White House Diary,* Lady Bird Johnson recalls details about the day President John F. Kennedy was assassinated. Use these sentence starters to develop your ideas about the Big Question.

Abrupt changes in **circumstances** can ______________________.

Accepting the **truth** of these changes can be difficult because ______________________.

While You Read Look for details that show how the author's feelings and attitudes shift as a result of her eyewitness observations during these historic days.

2 Vocabulary

Read each word and its definition. Decide whether you know the word well, know it a little bit, or do not know it at all. After you read, see how your knowledge of each word has increased.

- **tumultuous** (to͞o mul´ cho͞o əs) *adj.* greatly disturbed; in an uproar (p. 107) *The year we moved cross-country was a tumultuous one for the whole family.* tumult *n.*
- **implications** (im´ pli kā´ shənz) *n.* indirect results (p. 108) *He did not think about the implications of his decision to change jobs.* implicate *v.* imply *v.*
- **confines** (kän´ fīnz) *n.* boundaries or bounded region; border; limit (p. 109) *Please, stay within the confines of this yard.* confine *v.* confinement *n.* confined *adj.*
- **desolate** (des´ ə lit) *adj.* forlorn; wretched (p. 109) *Living alone on a desolate mountain top would make most people feel lonely.* desolate *v.* desolation *n.*
- **poignant** (poin´ yənt) *adj.* emotionally touching (p. 109) *The moment of farewell is often very poignant.* poignancy *n.*
- **immaculate** (i mak´ yə lit) *adj.* perfectly correct; without a flaw, fault, or error (p. 109) *My mother kept an immaculate house, with nothing out of place.* immaculately *adv.*

3 Word Study

The **Latin root *-fin-*** means "end."

In this selection, the author describes the **confines** of a plane, emphasizing the tight, enclosed space on board the aircraft.

Vocabulary Development

Vocabulary Knowledge Rating Chart

Create a **Vocabulary Knowledge Rating Chart** (*Professional Development Guidebook,* p. 33) for this selection. Include the selection vocabulary and the Big Question words that appear in the Writing About the Big Question sentence starters on this page. (The Big Question vocabulary is introduced on pp. 2–3.)

Give students a copy of the chart. Read the words aloud, and have students mark their rating in the Before Reading column. Urge them to be alert to these words as they read and discuss the selection.

Tally how many students think they know a word to gauge how much instruction to provide. As students read and discuss the selection, point out the words and their context.

Vocabulary Central, featuring tools, activities, and songs for studying vocabulary, is available at **www.PHLitOnline.com.**

Meet
Lady Bird Johnson
(1912–2007)

Author of

A WHITE HOUSE DIARY

Texas-born Claudia Alta Taylor received her nickname when a nurse said the two-year-old was "as pretty as a lady bird." A graduate of the University of Texas, Lady Bird met and married Lyndon Johnson, then a young congressional aide, in 1934. Even though she was a shy woman, Lady Bird was a valued advisor and effective campaigner for her husband, who said that voters "would happily have elected her over me."

Living History When President Kennedy was assassinated, Vice President Lyndon Johnson became president, and Lady Bird became First Lady of the United States. In this role, she made many contributions to her husband's agenda, including the launch of Head Start, a project that makes early childhood education available to all children.

4

BACKGROUND FOR THE MEMOIR

The Assassination of JFK

President John F. Kennedy was a young, vibrant, and popular leader who had been elected in 1960. His assassination on November 22, 1963, was a stunning and unforgettable event. As the news media reported the tragedy, people wept openly in the streets. A mournful nation agreed with Lyndon B. Johnson, JFK's successor, when he said, "We have suffered a loss that cannot be weighed."

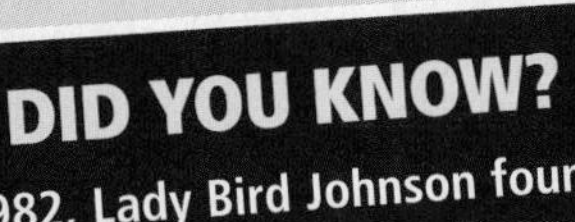

DID YOU KNOW?

In 1982, Lady Bird Johnson founded the National Wildflower Research Center in Austin, Texas.

Daily Bellringer

For each class during which you will teach this selection, have students complete one of the five Revision activities for Week 4 in the ***Daily Bellringer Activities*** booklet.

4 Background

The Assassination of JFK

Shortly after President Kennedy's assassination, Lee Harvey Oswald, a supporter of Communist Cuba, was arrested for the crime. Two days later, during a transfer between jails, Oswald was fatally shot by a nightclub owner named Jack Ruby, who soon thereafter died of cancer. Neither man lived to stand trial.

Newly sworn-in President Johnson ordered a committee formed to investigate the assassination. The committee found no evidence of a conspiracy to assassinate John F. Kennedy, nor any link connecting Oswald to Ruby.

Despite the committee's findings, conspiracy theories still exist. However, no person has ever confessed to involvement in such a conspiracy, nor has any hard evidence contradicted the committee's findings.

Multidraft Reading

This icon ● marks natural pauses in the selection. To assist struggling readers and to deepen reading for all, assign the text in "chunks," following the icons, and apply multidraft reading protocols. For each reading, have students set the purpose indicated:

- **First reading**—identifying key ideas and details and answering any Reading Checks.
- **Second reading**—analyzing craft and structure and responding to the side-column prompts.
- **Third reading**—integrating knowledge and ideas, connecting to other texts and the world, and answering the end-of-selection questions.

For more guidance, refer to the ***Classroom Strategies and Teaching Routines*** card on multidraft reading.

PHLit Online!

For more about the author, practice with the selection vocabulary, and more background, go online at **www.PHLitOnline.com.**

Differentiated Instruction — Additional Instruction

EL Extended Support—English Learners
Have students complete the **Reading and Vocabulary Warm-ups, *Unit 1 Resources*,** pp. 135–138, before they read. Assign the prereading pages and the adapted selection in the ***Reader's Notebook: English Learner's Version.*** Then, have students listen to portions of the selection on the ***Hear It!* Audio CD.**

L1 L2 Extended Support—Struggling Readers
Have students complete the **Reading and Vocabulary Warm-ups, *Unit 1 Resources*,** pp. 135–138, before they read. Assign the prereading pages and the adapted selection in the ***Reader's Notebook: Adapted Version.*** Then, have students listen to portions of the selection on the ***Hear It!* Audio CD** (adapted text).

Extended Support—Reluctant Readers
To build motivation and engagement before assigning the selection, have students read "Judging Eyewitness Accounts," a thematically related selection in ***Reality Central.*** Then, use the questions at the conclusion of the related selection to guide discussion.

❶ Activating Prior Knowledge

1. Prepare an **Anticipation Guide** (see ***Professional Development Guidebook***, pp. 36–38) with the following statements:
   - The greatest tragedies occur when they are least expected.
   - If certain precautions are taken, tragedy can always be avoided.
   - People can remain calm and objective in the worst of times.
   - When life takes an unexpected turn, people should always step back and take a break.
2. Give students a copy of the prepared **Anticipation Guide** and have students mark their responses in the Me column. Have students discuss the statements in pairs or groups and mark the Guides again in the Group column.
3. For further guidance, use the ***Classroom Strategies and Teaching Routines*** card: **Using an Anticipation Guide.**

Concept Connector →

Students will return to the **Anticipation Guide** after completing the selection from *A White House Diary*.

Small-Group Activity

Lady Bird Johnson gives an objective yet personal account of the day that President Kennedy was assassinated. She also talks about what other people were experiencing, thinking, and feeling that day. Urge students to pay attention to the insights Lady Bird Johnson reveals while observing and interacting with other people.

Put students into small groups and have them list Lady Bird's insights.

❷ About the Selection

In this excerpt from *A White House Diary*, Lady Bird Johnson recalls the day President John F. Kennedy was shot in Dallas, Texas. Johnson, wife of the vice president, was in Kennedy's motorcade when the shots rang out. She describes the feelings of shock, horror, and helplessness at the event and recalls details of the somber plane flight back to Washington.

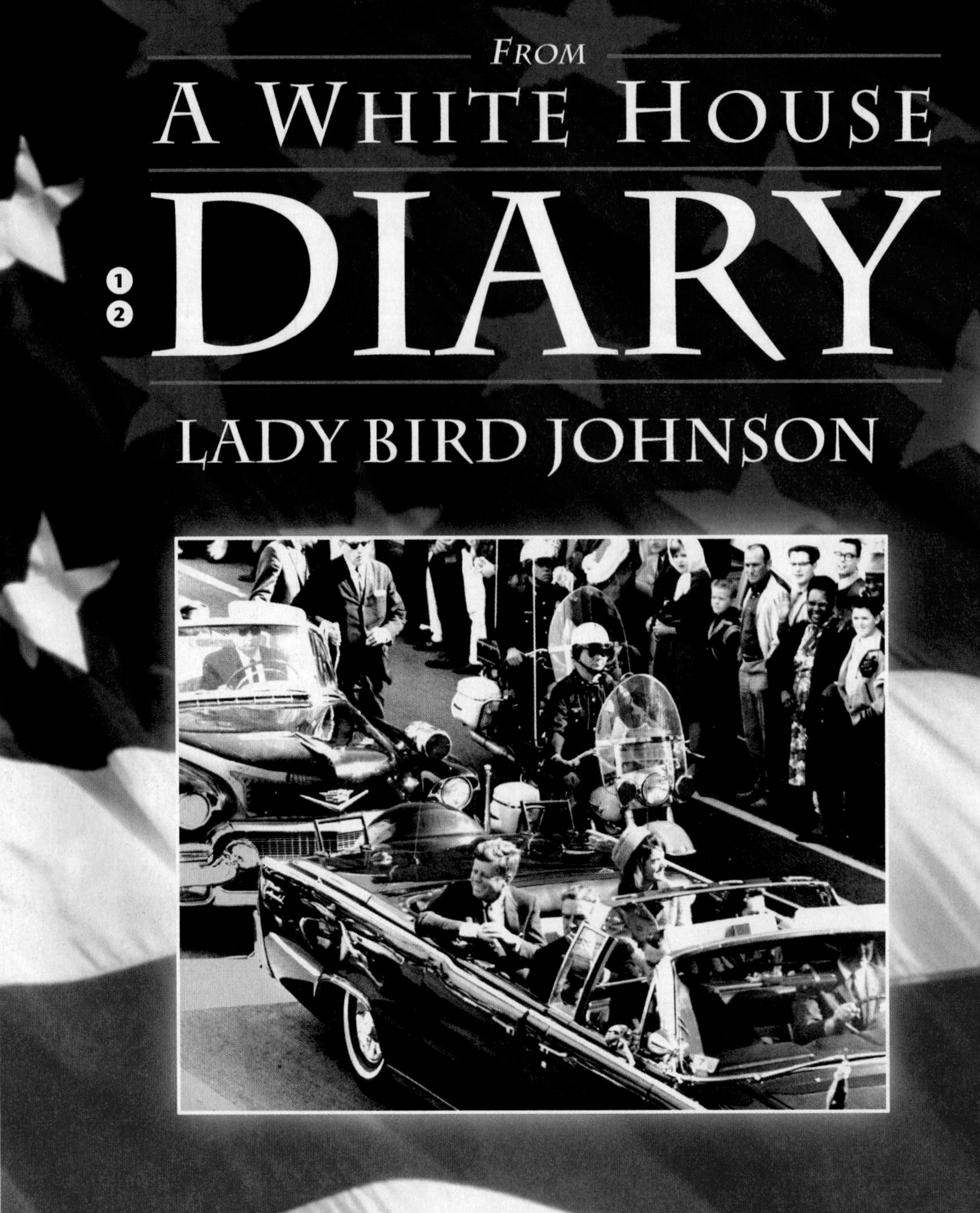

Vocabulary Development

CCSS Language 6

Thematic Vocabulary: The Big Question

As students are discussing *A White House Diary*, encourage them to use the thematic vocabulary presented in Introducing the Big Question, pp. 2–3. You might encourage them with sentence starters like these:

1. As the motorcade passed and shots rang out, people had to *convince* themselves . . .
2. Even at such a public event, police officers had to *verify* that . . .
3. Lady Bird held on to the *belief* that . . .
4. As time went by, the police hoped that *credible* . . .
5. Even though the assassination took place in front of thousands of people, there was little *evidence* to . . .

Dallas, Friday, November 22, 1963

3 It all began so beautifully. After a drizzle in the morning, the sun came out bright and clear. We were driving into Dallas. In the lead car were President and Mrs. Kennedy, John and Nellie Connally,[1] a Secret Service[2] car full of men, and then our car with Lyndon and me and Senator Ralph Yarborough.

The streets were lined with people—lots and lots of people—the children all smiling, placards, confetti, people waving from windows. One last happy moment I had was looking up and seeing Mary Griffith leaning out of a window waving at me. (Mary for many years had been in charge of altering the clothes which I purchased at Neiman-Marcus.)

4 Then, almost at the edge of town, on our way to the Trade Mart for the Presidential luncheon, we were rounding a curve, going down a hill, and suddenly there was a sharp, loud report. It sounded like a shot. The sound seemed to me to come from a building on the right above my shoulder. A moment passed, and then two more shots rang out in rapid succession. There had been such a gala air about the day that I thought the noise must come from firecrackers—part of the celebration. Then the Secret Service men were suddenly down in the lead car. Over the car radio system, I heard "Let's get out of here!" and our Secret Service man, Rufus Youngblood, vaulted over the front seat on top of Lyndon, threw him to the floor, and said, "Get down."

1. **John and Nellie Connally** John Connally, then governor of Texas, and his wife, Nellie.
2. **Secret Service** division of the U.S. Treasury Department, responsible for protecting the president.

Reading Skill
Author's Purpose
What does this subhead tell you about the author's purpose in this part of the diary?

Literary Analysis
Voice
What do the details about firecrackers tell you about the writer's attitude toward the events she describes?

5
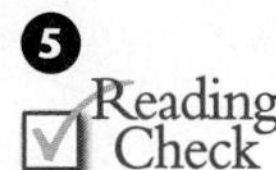

What was Lady Bird Johnson's last happy moment on this day?

November 22, 1963
President John F. Kennedy and his wife, Jackie, arrive in Dallas, Texas.

November 22, 1963
The President, First Lady, and Texas Governor Connally ride through Dallas.

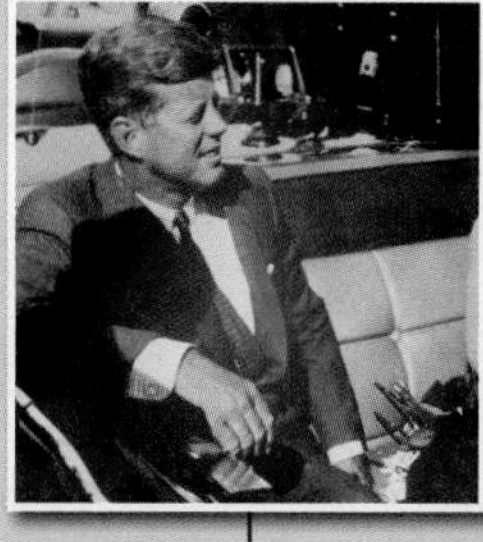

November 22, 1963
President Kennedy smiles at the crowd in his last moments.

3 Reading Skill
Author's Purpose

1. Have students read the subhead that begins this page, and then **ask** them to respond to the Reading Skill question: What does this subhead tell you about the author's purpose in this part of the diary?
   Answer: It tells me that she wants to report the events of one day.
2. Read the bracketed text. **Ask** students how these details contribute to the writer's purpose.
   Answer: The details set the scene and help the author report the events of the day vividly.

4 Literary Analysis
Voice

1. **Ask** students to define autobiographical writing and to explain the details usually included in this type of work.
   Answer: Autobiographical writing is a work in which the author tells all or part of his or her own life story. The author usually includes details to show what he or she notices, thinks, and feels.
2. Draw students' attention to the bracketed text. **Ask** them to respond to the Literary Analysis question: What do the details about firecrackers tell you about the writer's attitude toward the events she describes?
   Answer: When she heard the sound, her attitude was festive. She did not expect anything sinister to happen, and so she interpreted the shots as firecrackers.

5 Reading Check
Answer: Lady Bird Johnson saw an acquaintance, Mary Griffith, waving at her.

PHLit Online!
This selection is available in interactive format in the **Enriched Online Student Edition**, at **www.PHLitOnline.com**, which includes a thematically related video with writing prompt and an interactive graphic organizer.

Differentiated Instruction for Universal Access

Strategy for Special-Needs Students
After students read the first paragraph, create a chart on the board for students listing each of the people mentioned. As students continue reading, have them provide details that identify each person and his or her role in the event described. Have students make a copy of the chart for study and review.

Strategy for Less Proficient Readers
Help students better understand the author's purpose by showing them **Reading Skill Graphic Organizer A** (*Graphic Organizer Transparencies,* p. 20). Review the general purposes for writing and discuss the answers provided in the organizer. Encourage students to use these ideas to think about the author's purpose as they continue reading.

Spiral Review

Central Idea

1. Remind students that they studied the concept of central idea in the Unit 1 Literary Analysis Workshop (pp. 4–21).
2. **Ask** students the Spiral Review question.

   Possible response: The central idea is the sense of urgency with which the Secret Service responded after the shots were fired, combined with a sense of shock and disbelief.

6 Literature in Context

History Connection In October 1962, the United States government discovered that the Soviet Union was building nuclear missile launchers in Cuba, which is only 90 miles away from Florida. The president had to decide if he should ignore the missiles or confront the Soviet Union, essentially risking nuclear war. President Kennedy chose an aggressive approach; he used the navy to block Soviet ships from delivering military supplies to Cuba. After thirteen fearful, uneasy days, the Cuban Missile Crisis ended when the Soviet Union agreed to remove the missiles. In turn, President Kennedy publicly promised that the United States would not invade Cuba and secretly agreed to remove American missiles from Turkey. President Kennedy's decisions prevented Soviet missiles in Cuba, averted nuclear war, and paved the way for a slowing of the nuclear arms race.

Connect to the Literature Point out to students that President Kennedy built this legacy in less than one complete presidential term. **Ask** students the Connect to the Literature question: How does information about President Kennedy's ideas help explain the intense grief most Americans felt at his death?
Possible response: Americans mourned not only his death, but also the death of his influence on the future of the United States.

Spiral Review
Central Idea What is the central, or most important, idea conveyed so far?

Senator Yarborough and I ducked our heads. The car accelerated terrifically—faster and faster. Then, suddenly, the brakes were put on so hard that I wondered if we were going to make it as we wheeled left and went around the corner. We pulled up to a building. I looked up and saw a sign, "HOSPITAL." Only then did I believe that this might be what it was. Senator Yarborough kept saying in an excited voice, "Have they shot the President? Have they shot the President?" I said something like, "No, it can't be."

As we ground to a halt—we were still the third car—Secret Service men began to pull, lead, guide, and hustle us out. I cast one last look over my shoulder and saw in the President's car a bundle of pink, just like a drift of blossoms, lying on the back seat. It was Mrs. Kennedy lying over the President's body.

The Secret Service men rushed us to the right, then to the left, and then onward into a quiet room in the hospital—a very small room. It was lined with white sheets, I believe.

People came and went—Kenny O'Donnell, the President's top aide, Congressman Homer Thornberry, Congressman Jack Brooks. Always there was Rufe right there and other Secret Service agents—Emory Roberts, Jerry Kivett, Lem Johns, and Woody Taylor. People spoke of

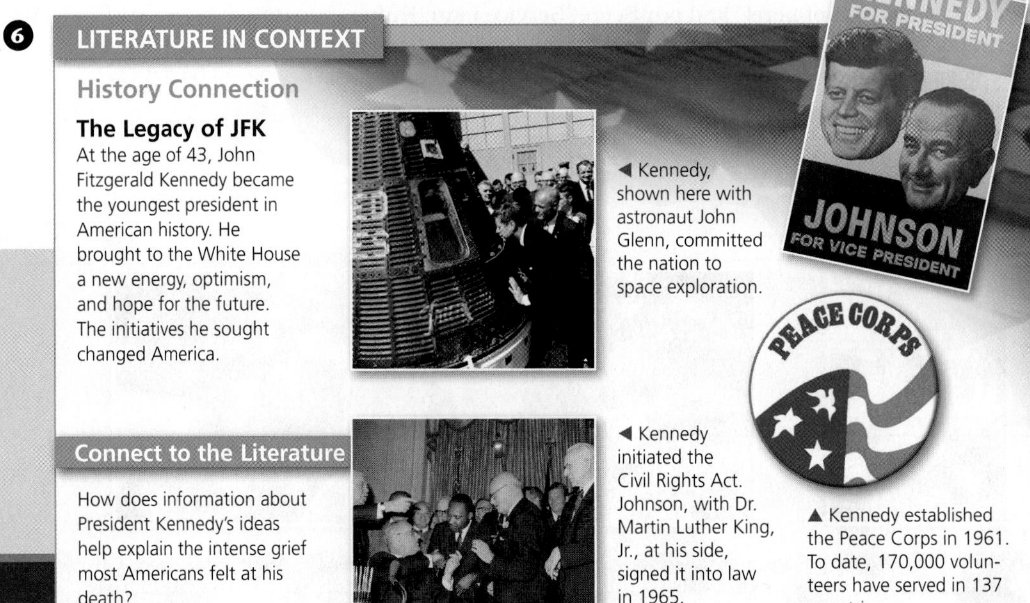

6 **LITERATURE IN CONTEXT**

History Connection

The Legacy of JFK
At the age of 43, John Fitzgerald Kennedy became the youngest president in American history. He brought to the White House a new energy, optimism, and hope for the future. The initiatives he sought changed America.

◀ Kennedy, shown here with astronaut John Glenn, committed the nation to space exploration.

◀ Kennedy initiated the Civil Rights Act. Johnson, with Dr. Martin Luther King, Jr., at his side, signed it into law in 1965.

▲ Kennedy established the Peace Corps in 1961. To date, 170,000 volunteers have served in 137 countries.

Connect to the Literature

How does information about President Kennedy's ideas help explain the intense grief most Americans felt at his death?

Vocabulary Development

CCSS Language 6

Multiple Meanings

Point out the word *ground* in the first sentence of the second paragraph, and ask students to define the word as it is used here. ("moved with difficulty or friction"—past tense of *grind*) Then explain that *ground* is a word with multiple meanings. Write these sentences on the board, and ask student pairs to write definitions for each use of *ground*.

1. We live on the *ground* floor.
2. The *ground* was covered with leaves.
3. The army planned a *ground* attack.

Answers: 1. bottom; 2. the solid surface of the earth; 3. operating on land

Ask students to write more sentences showing the multiple meanings of *ground.*

how widespread this might be. There was talk about where we would go—to the plane, to our house, back to Washington.

Through it all Lyndon was remarkably calm and quiet. He suggested that the Presidential plane ought to be moved to another part of the field. He spoke of going back out to the plane in unmarked black cars. Every face that came in, you searched for the answer. I think the face I kept seeing the answer on was the face of Kenny O'Donnell, who loved President Kennedy so much.

It was Lyndon who spoke of it first, although I knew I would not leave without doing it. He said, "You had better try to see Jackie and Nellie." We didn't know what had happened to John.

I asked the Secret Service if I could be taken to them. They began to lead me up one corridor and down another. Suddenly I found myself face to face with Jackie in a small hallway. I believe it was right outside the operating room. You always think of someone like her as being insulated, protected. She was quite alone. I don't think I ever saw anyone so much alone in my life. I went up to her, put my arms around her, and said something to her. I'm sure it was something like "God, help us all," because my feelings for her were too **tumultuous** to put into words.

And then I went to see Nellie. There it was different, because Nellie and I have gone through so many things together since 1938. I hugged her tight and we both cried and I said, "Nellie, John's going to be all right." And Nellie said, "Yes, John's going to be all right." Among her many other fine qualities, she is also strong.

I turned and went back to the small white room where Lyndon was. Mac Kilduff, the President's press man on this trip, and Kenny O'Donnell were coming and going. I think it was from Kenny's face that I first knew the truth and from Kenny's voice that I first heard

7 ▼ Analyze Media
Based on the photos shown below and Mrs. Johnson's account, explain how different types of media can emphasize different aspects of an event.
[Analyze]

Vocabulary
tumultuous
(to͞o mul′ cho͞o əs) *adj.* greatly disturbed; in an uproar

8 Reading Check
Where were the Johnsons taken after the shots were fired?

Dealey Plaza
This is the site of JFK's assassination.

November 22, 1963
Spectators drop to the ground moments after shots are fired at President Kennedy.

November 22, 1963
Mourners lay flowers along the street, weeping for their fallen president.

7 Critical Viewing

Possible response: In the three photographs, the mood changes from neutral to frenetic to mournful. This shows that mood can change quickly and dramatically.

8 Reading Check

Answer: The Johnsons were taken to a small room in the hospital.

Differentiated Instruction for Universal Access

Culturally Responsive Instruction

Culture Focus Explain to students that President Kennedy was a young and vigorous president who challenged Americans with goals and ideals that gripped their imaginations. He appealed to American cultural values such as justice, innovation, personal integrity, and individualism. He stood up to the power of the Soviet Union in 1962 when that country placed missiles with nuclear warheads in Cuba. Later, he promoted the space program and set a goal of placing a man on the Moon by 1969. He was active in civil rights legislation and enforcement. Kennedy's leadership inspired Americans, and his early and tragic death was devastating to the nation. The event immediately became a landmark in the lives of Americans living at the time. Even decades later, many Americans remember where they were and what they were doing at the exact moment they heard of the assassination of President Kennedy.

9 Analyze Media

Possible response: Johnson was concerned about the various problems he would now have to solve. He was also sad and shocked about the loss of President Kennedy. He felt this way because he wasn't prepared to take on such an enormous duty, and he couldn't help being sad after the tragic death of a much-loved leader.

10 Connecting to the Big Question

1. Point out that a time of crisis can change the truth of people's lives dramatically and irreversibly. Invite students to think of moments that changed the truth of people's lives forever. If students have difficulty responding, suggest September 11, 2001, as a possibility.
2. Have students reread the bracketed passage. **Ask:** What dramatic change does this passage describe? **Answer:** With Kennedy's death, Lyndon Johnson immediately became president of the United States.
3. **Ask:** How did Lady Bird's feelings and attitudes shift as a result of these events? **Possible response:** Her feelings shifted from shock and disbelief to awe at the "enormity" of the situation. She probably felt a new attitude of responsibility as the new first lady.
4. **Ask:** What truths changed as a result of the events? **Possible response:** The truth of Lady Bird's life—as well as the lives of her husband and the American people—changed completely. The Johnsons took on new roles, and the American people had a new leader.

9 ▼ **Analyze Media** The central photo below and the first paragraph on page 109 address the same moment. Do you learn different things about that moment from the two texts? **[Analyze]**

Vocabulary
implications (im′ pli kā′ shənz) *n.* indirect results

the words "The President is dead." Mr. Kilduff entered and said to Lyndon, "Mr. President."

It was decided that we would go immediately to the airport. Hurried plans were made about how we should get to the cars and who was to ride in which car. Our departure from the hospital and approach to the cars was one of the swiftest walks I have ever made.

We got in. Lyndon told the agents to stop the sirens. We drove along as fast as we could. I looked up at a building and there, already, was a flag at half-mast. I think that was when the enormity of what had happened first struck me.

When we got to the field, we entered *Air Force One*[3] for the first time. There was a TV set on and the commentator was saying, "Lyndon B. Johnson, now President of the United States." The news commentator was saying the President had been shot with a 30-30 rifle. The police had a suspect. They were not sure he was the assassin.

On the plane, all the shades were lowered. We heard that we were going to wait for Mrs. Kennedy and the coffin. There was a telephone call to Washington—I believe to the Attorney General.[4]

It was decided that Lyndon should be sworn in here as quickly as possible, because of national and world implications, and because we did not know how widespread this was as to intended victims. Judge Sarah Hughes, a Federal Judge in Dallas—and I am glad it was she—was called and asked to come in a hurry to administer the oath.

3. ***Air Force One*** name of the airplane officially assigned to transport the president of the United States.
4. **Attorney General** chief law officer of the nation, head of the U.S. Department of Justice; at the time, the position was held by Robert Kennedy, JFK's brother.

November 22, 1963
Vice President Johnson responds to the news of Kennedy's death.

November 22, 1963
Lyndon B. Johnson is sworn in as the thirty-sixth U.S. president.

November 22, 1963
The coffin of John F. Kennedy is removed from Air Force One.

Vocabulary Development

Vocabulary Knowledge Rating

When students have completed reading and discussing the excerpt from *A White House Diary,* have them take out their **Vocabulary Knowledge Rating Chart** for this selection. Read the words aloud once more and have students rate their knowledge of the words again in the After Reading column. Clarify any words that are still problematic. Have students write their own definition and example or sentence in the appropriate column. Then have students complete the Vocabulary Practice activities at the end of the selection. Encourage students to use the words in further discussion and written work about this selection. Remind them that they will be accountable for these words on the **Selection Test, *Unit 1 Resources,*** pp. 147–149 or 150–152.

Mrs. Kennedy had arrived by this time, as had the coffin. There, in the very narrow confines of the plane—with Jackie standing by Lyndon, her hair falling in her face but very composed, with me beside him, Judge Hughes in front of him, and a cluster of Secret Service people, staff, and Congressmen we had known for a long time around him—Lyndon took the oath of office.

11 It's odd the little things that come to your mind at times of utmost stress, the flashes of deep compassion you feel for people who are really not at the center of the tragedy. I heard a Secret Service man say in the most desolate voice—and I hurt for him: "We never lost a President in the Service." Then, Police Chief Curry of Dallas came on the plane and said, "Mrs. Kennedy, believe me, we did everything we possibly could." That must have been an agonizing moment for him.

We all sat around the plane. The casket was in the corridor. I went in the small private room to see Mrs. Kennedy, and though it was a very hard thing to do, she made it as easy as possible. She said things like, "Oh, Lady Bird, we've liked you two so much. . . . Oh, what if I had not been there. I'm so glad I was there."

I looked at her. Mrs. Kennedy's dress was stained with blood. One leg was almost entirely covered with it and her right glove was caked, it was caked with blood—her husband's blood. Somehow that was one of the most poignant sights—that immaculate woman exquisitely dressed, and caked in blood.

I asked her if I couldn't get someone in to help her change and she said, "Oh, no. Perhaps later I'll ask Mary Gallagher but not right now." And then with almost an element of fierceness—if a person

Vocabulary

confines (kän′ fīnz) *n.* boundaries or bounded region; border; limit

desolate (des′ ə lit) *adj.* forlorn; wretched

poignant (pɔin′ yənt) *adj.* emotionally touching

immaculate (i mak′ yə lit) *adj.* perfectly correct; without a flaw, fault, or error

Reading Skill
Author's Purpose
What is the writer's purpose in including the comments of the Secret Service man?

12
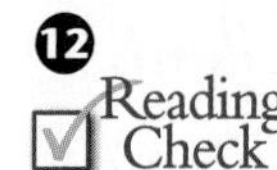

How did Mrs. Johnson first know that the President was dead?

November 22, 1963
President Johnson prepares to make his first address to a grieving nation.

November 25, 1963
John F. Kennedy, Jr., salutes his father's coffin.

A Nation Mourns
The flag on the White House is lowered to half-mast.

11 Reading Skill
Author's Purpose

1. Point out that Johnson holds her emotions back during most of the story, telling only the facts. In recalling the Secret Service man and the police chief's apology, she allows herself to express sympathy.
2. **Ask** students to respond to the Reading Skill question: What is the writer's purpose in including the comments of the Secret Service man?
   Possible response: Johnson may have wanted to show how this tragedy affected different people.
3. Remind students that this is a diary entry. Point out, however, that the diaries of famous people are often written with an expectation that sooner or later their diaries will become public. Invite students to **speculate** on how this idea may or may not have influenced Johnson's purpose in writing her account of this event.
   Possible response: Johnson's diary is not a private document. As a public figure, she wrote it knowing that it would be published and be read by a wide audience. Her purposes in writing were most likely to share with other Americans an insider's look at a tragic historical incident and to go on record with accurate details about the events of that day.

12 Reading Check

Answer: She learned the news from Kenny O'Donnell's facial expression, then his words.

Concept Connector

Anticipation Guide
Have students return to their **Anticipation Guides** and respond to the statements again in the After Reading column. Then, lead a class discussion, probing for what students have learned that confirms or invalidates each statement.

Writing About the Big Question
Have students compare their responses to the sentence starters they completed before reading the excerpt with their ideas afterwards. Ask them to explain whether their thoughts have changed.

Reading Skill Graphic Organizer
Ask students to review the graphic organizers they completed to identify the author's purpose while reading. Show them **Reading Skill Graphic Organizer A** (*Graphic Organizer Transparencies,* p. 20) as an example. Then have students share the graphic organizers they did and the author's purpose that they identified.

⓭ Literary Analysis

Voice

Have students read the bracketed text. Then, **ask** students the Literary Analysis question.

Answer: It reveals that Mrs. Johnson was deeply moved by Mrs. Kennedy's loss and was concerned about how she was holding up. Mrs. Johnson cared about Mrs. Kennedy very much.

ASSESS

Answers

Critical Thinking

Before students respond, you may wish to have them write a brief objective summary of the selection. As they answer the questions below, remind them to support their answers with evidence from the text.

1. (a) She says, "I want them to see what they have done to Jack." (b) She wants the nation to see evidence of the brutality of the assassination. (c) **Possible responses:** It is a powerful comment that helps define Mrs. Kennedy's feelings and qualities.
2. (a) She remembers that she had said that "he's a good man in a tight spot." (b) **Possible response:** This comment suggests that President Johnson reacts well under pressure. This was an important quality for him to possess, considering the circumstances under which he became president. (c) **Possible response:** Mrs. Johnson's calmness, concern for others, and awareness of her public responsibilities in an extreme situation show that she is also a good person in a tight spot.
3. Yes, because she gives a vivid account that includes other people's feelings.
4. **Possible response:** The events of November 22, 1963, changed Lady Bird Johnson's relationships as well as her role in life. Before that day she was the wife of the vice president. After that day, she was the First Lady of the United States, and she was responsible for helping her friends—and the entire nation—mourn their fallen leader.

that gentle, that dignified, can be said to have such a quality—she said, "I want them to see what they have done to Jack."

⓭ I tried to express how we felt. I said, "Oh, Mrs. Kennedy, you know we never even wanted to be Vice President and now, dear God, it's come to this." I would have done anything to help her, but there was nothing I could do, so rather quickly I left and went back to the main part of the airplane where everyone was seated.

Literary Analysis
Voice
What does this passage reveal about Mrs. Johnson's attitude toward Mrs. Kennedy?

The flight to Washington was silent, each sitting with his own thoughts. One of mine was a recollection of what I had said about Lyndon a long time ago—he's a good man in a tight spot. I remembered one little thing he had said in that hospital room—"Tell the children to get a Secret Service man with them."

Finally we got to Washington, with a cluster of people waiting and many bright lights. The casket went off first, then Mrs. Kennedy, and then we followed. The family had come to join her. Lyndon made a very simple, very brief, and, I think, strong statement to the people there. Only about four sentences. We got in helicopters, dropped him off at the White House, and I came home in a car with Liz Carpenter.[5]

The flight to Washington was silent, each sitting with his own thoughts.

5. **Liz Carpenter** Mrs. Johnson's press secretary.

Critical Thinking

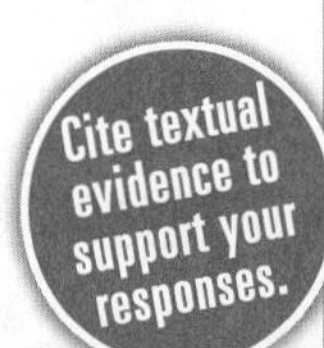
Cite textual evidence to support your responses.

1. **Key Ideas and Details (a)** What does Mrs. Kennedy say when Mrs. Johnson offers to find someone to help her change her clothes? **(b) Interpret:** What does Mrs. Kennedy mean? **(c) Analyze:** Why do you think Mrs. Johnson reports this detail?
2. **Key Ideas and Details (a)** What comment about her husband does Mrs. Johnson recall on the flight back to Washington? **(b) Interpret:** What character traits does this comment suggest President Johnson possesses? Explain. **(c) Support:** Which details from the selection show that Mrs. Johnson possesses similar character traits?
3. **Craft and Structure Evaluate:** Do you think Mrs. Johnson effectively expresses what it felt like to live through this historic incident? Explain.
4. **Integration of Knowledge and Ideas** How do the events of November 22, 1963, change what Lady Bird Johnson thinks of as her everyday reality? *[Connect to the Big Question: Can truth change?]*

Assessment Resources

Unit 1 Resources

- L1 L2 EL **Selection Test A,** pp. 147–149. Administer Test A to less advanced readers.
- L3 L4 EL **Selection Test B,** pp. 150–152. Administer Test B to on-level and more advanced students.
- L3 L4 **Open-Book Test,** pp. 144–146. As an alternative, give the Open-Book Test.
- All **Customizable Test Bank**
- All **Self-tests** Students may prepare for the **Selection Test** by taking the **Self-test** online.

PHLit Online!

All assessment resources are available at **www.PHLitOnline.com.**

After You Read *from* A White House Diary

Literary Analysis: Voice

1. **Craft and Structure** **(a)** Complete a chart like the one shown to find examples of Johnson's **word choice, attitude,** and **sentence structure.**

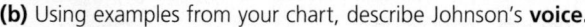

Voice		
Word Choice	Attitude	Sentence Structure

(b) Using examples from your chart, describe Johnson's **voice.**

2. **Key Ideas and Details** **(a)** What details about Lyndon Johnson are emphasized in Lady Bird Johnson's **autobiographical writing?** **(b)** What are two other details that reflect Mrs. Johnson's perspective?

Reading Skill: Author's Purpose

3. Review the notes you made in your **preview** of the excerpt. Which of your ideas about the **author's purpose** were confirmed as you read the selection? Which were not? Explain.
4. **(a)** What general purpose do you think Mrs. Johnson had in writing this portion of *A White House Diary*? Explain. **(b)** What more specific purpose do you think she had? Explain.

Vocabulary

Acquisition and Use An **analogy** shows the relationship between pairs of words. To complete each analogy, use a word from the vocabulary list on page 102. Your choice should create a word pair that matches the relationship between the first two words given.

1. weak : strong :: calm : ______
2. rain : flood :: choice : ______
3. laughter : humorous :: sadness : ______
4. troubled : carefree :: ______ : delighted
5. steep : precipitous :: ______ : perfect
6. vital : necessary :: ______ : bounds

Word Study Use the context of the sentences and what you know about the **Latin root *-fin-*** to explain your answer to each question.

1. If you have a *definite* opinion, are you uncertain?
2. Do you think of the *infinity* of space as limitless?

Word Study

The **Latin root *-fin-*** means "end."

Apply It Explain how the root *-fin-* contributes to the meanings of these words. Consult a dictionary if necessary.

finish
final
refine

Literary Analysis

1. (a) **Possible response: Word Choice:** "that immaculate woman exquisitely dressed, and caked in blood"; **Attitude:** "I went up to her, put my arms around her"; **Sentence Structure:** "We got in. Lyndon told the agents to stop the sirens. We drove along as fast as we could." (b) **Possible response:** Her voice is vivid, factual, specific, and empathetic. The words "immaculate woman exquisitely dressed, and caked in blood" show how vivid and specific her details are. "We got in. Lyndon told the agents to stop the sirens. We drove along as fast as we could" is an example of her delivering a factual, objective account. Putting her arms around Mrs. Kennedy is an example of Mrs. Johnson's empathy and compassion.

   For other sample answers, see ***Graphic Organizer Transparencies,* Literary Analysis Graphic Organizer A,** p. 23, and the **Additional Answers** section.
2. (a) She says that he is calm and quiet, but he also takes command readily and is considerate of others. (b) **Possible response:** She notices the Secret Service man's anguish and Mrs. Kennedy's subtle anger.

Reading Skill

3. **Possible response:** Students may have expected the purpose to be to describe the assassination. They may not have expected such a personal, emotional account.
4. (a) Her general purpose is to inform readers about the assassination. She gives details about events, the setting, and people's feelings. (b) She wants readers to understand the experiences of those at the scene. She tells about the sorrow on the faces of President Kennedy's advisors and about how Mrs. Kennedy reacted.

Vocabulary

Acquisition and Use

1. tumultuous
2. implications
3. poignant
4. desolate
5. immaculate
6. confines

Word Study

Sample answers:

1. No. The root *-fin-* means "end" or "final," so if you have a *definite* opinion, your thoughts are final and unchanging.
2. Yes. The root *-fin-* means "end" and the prefix *in-* means "not." So, the *infinity* of space is without end or limit.

Word Study: Apply It

Sample answers:

Finish means "end." When you finish something, you've reached the end of it. *Final* means "last" or "end." Something that is *final* comes at the end. *Refine* means "to improve or make better." If you refine something, you end its imperfections or impurities.

PRETEACH

*Skills instruction for the **Reading Skill** and **Literary Analysis** concept appears on p. 101.*

❶ Writing About the Big Question

1. Read the assignment with the class.
2. Ask volunteers to describe a time when their feelings or reactions about something changed as they learned more about it.
3. Have students complete the sentence starters. Review responses as a class. (**Possible response:** Learning a language can affect our perspective because we see things from a different point of view. We may make assumptions about people from other cultures because we have little first-hand knowledge of the culture.)
4. Remind students that their answers will help them think about the Big Question, "Can truth change?"

While You Read

Tell students that as they read, they should track how learning English increased the author's self-confidence.

❷ Vocabulary

1. Have students preview the selection vocabulary.
2. For each word, have students say the word aloud.
3. Then, use the word in a sentence that defines the word.
4. Finally, repeat your definitional sentence or a similar sentence with the word missing, and have the class "fill in the blank" chorally. Here are some examples:

   Bilingual means able to speak two languages. Because my mother speaks English and Mandarin, she is [students say "bilingual"].

   Interminably means unending or incessant. After an hour I realized that the speaker would go on [students say "interminably"].

❸ Word Study

1. Introduce the skill, using the instruction in the box.
2. Have students use a *-term-* word in a sentence. (**Sample answer:** Many diseases are no longer considered *terminal* illnesses.)

❶ Writing About the Big Question

In "My English," Alvarez describes how her view of her place in the world changes as she learns English. Use these sentence starters to develop your ideas about the Big Question.

Learning a language can affect our **perspective** because___________.

We may make **assumptions** about people from other cultures because ___________.

While You Read Look for details that show how the author's confidence in herself changes as she learns English.

❷ Vocabulary

Read each word and its definition. Decide whether you know the word well, know it a little bit, or do not know it at all. After you read, see how your knowledge of each word has increased.

- **bilingual** (bī liŋ′ gwəl) *adj.* using two languages (p. 114) ***The bilingual student speaks Spanish and English.*** *linguistics n.*
- **countenance** (koun′ tə nəns) *n.* face (p. 116) ***The child's overjoyed countenance showed her relief at being home.***
- **ponderously** (pän′ dər əs lē) *adv.* in a labored, boring, and serious way (p. 117) ***The telemarketer ponderously explained the rules of the service contract.*** *ponderous adj. ponder v.*
- **enumerated** (ē no͞o′ mər āt id) *v.* named one by one; specified, as in a list (p. 118) ***Joel enumerated the names of video games he likes to play.*** *enumerate v. enumerable adj. numeral n.*
- **interminably** (in tʉr′ mi nə blē) *adv.* endlessly (p. 119) ***To the tired audience, the speaker seemed to go on interminably.*** *interminable adj. terminal adj. terminal n. terminate v.*
- **accentuated** (ak sen′ cho͞o āt id) *v.* emphasized; heightened the effect of (p. 119) ***Her new haircut accentuated her graceful neck.*** *accentuate v. accent n.*

❸ Word Study

The **Latin root *-term-*** means "limit, end, boundary."

The teacher in this essay does not make the class diagram sentences **interminably,** or in a way that has no end.

Vocabulary Development

Vocabulary Knowledge Rating

Create a **Vocabulary Knowledge Rating Chart** (***Professional Development Guidebook,*** p. 33) for this selection. Include the selection vocabulary and the Big Question words that appear in the Writing About the Big Question sentence starters on this page. (The Big Question vocabulary is introduced on pp. 2–3.)

Give students a copy of the chart. Read the words aloud, and have students mark their rating in the Before Reading column. Urge them to be alert to these words as they read and discuss the selection.

Tally how many students think they know a word to gauge how much instruction to provide. As students read and discuss the selection, point out the words and their context.

Vocabulary Central, featuring tools, activities, and songs for studying vocabulary, is available at **www.PHLitOnline.com.**

Meet Julia Alvarez

(b. 1950)

Author of

My English

When her family fled the Dominican Republic and returned to New York, Julia Alvarez was ten years old, and Spanish was her primary language. Painfully aware of not fitting in, Julia took refuge in reading and making up stories. She says, "I landed, not in the United States, but in the English language. That became my new home."

"I write to find out who I am." Alvarez attended Middlebury College, where she won several poetry awards. She later earned a master's degree in creative writing from Syracuse University. Alvarez says that writing is "a way to understand yourself." Her writing has been praised for its humor, sensitivity, and insight.

Did You Know?

One of Julia Alvarez's books, *In the Time of the Butterflies,* was made into a film starring Salma Hayek.

BACKGROUND FOR THE AUTOBIOGRAPHY

Alvarez's Two Nationalities

Julia Alvarez, the author of "My English," was born in New York but grew up in the Dominican Republic, a small Caribbean nation. An independent state since 1844, the Dominican Republic has often struggled with foreign conquest, political unrest, and dictatorship. Alvarez's family was forced to return to New York in 1960 because her father had participated in a movement against the brutal Dominican dictator Raphael Trujillo.

Daily Bellringer

For each class during which you will teach this selection, have students complete one of the five Revision activities for Week 4 in the *Daily Bellringer Activities* booklet.

4 Background

Alvarez's Two Nationalities

Rafael Trujillo was a brutal dictator who came to power in the Dominican Republic in 1930. He repressed human rights and ran the country as if it were his personal estate. As a result, a small but active opposition arose, Alvarez's father among them. He and his family fled the country twice. In 1960, the family returned to New York City. Trujillo was assassinated in 1961, but Alvarez's family remained in New York. Alvarez grew up in a city in which many nationalities thrived, including large numbers of Hispanics. More than half a million Dominicans live in New York today.

Multidraft Reading

This icon ● marks natural pauses in the selection. To assist struggling readers and to deepen reading for all, assign the text in "chunks," following the icons, and apply multidraft reading protocols. For each reading, have students set the purpose indicated:

- **First reading**—identifying key ideas and details and answering any Reading Checks.
- **Second reading**—analyzing craft and structure and responding to the side-column prompts.
- **Third reading**—integrating knowledge and ideas, connecting to other texts and the world, and answering the end-of-selection questions.

For more guidance, refer to the ***Classroom Strategies and Teaching Routines*** card on multidraft reading.

Differentiated Instruction — Additional Instruction

EL Extended Support—English Learners

Have students complete the **Reading and Vocabulary Warm-ups, *Unit 1 Resources,*** pp. 153–156, before they read. Assign the prereading pages for the selection in the ***Reader's Notebook: English Learner's Version.*** Then, have students listen to portions of the selection on the ***Hear It!* Audio CD.**

L1 L2 Extended Support—Struggling Readers

Have students complete the **Reading and Vocabulary Warm-ups, *Unit 1 Resources,*** pp. 153–156, before they read. Assign the prereading pages and the adapted selection in the ***Reader's Notebook: Adapted Version.*** Then, have students listen to portions of the selection on the ***Hear It!* Audio CD** (adapted text).

Extended Support—Reluctant Readers

To build motivation and engagement before assigning the selection, have students read "Shifting Gears on Language," a thematically related selection in ***Reality Central.*** Then, use the questions at the conclusion of the related selection to guide discussion.

PHLit Online!

For more about the author, practice with the selection vocabulary, or more background, go online at **www.PHLitOnline.com.**

TEACH

❶ Activating Prior Knowledge

1. Prepare an **Anticipation Guide** (***Professional Development Guidebook,*** pp. 36–38) with the following statements:
   - People who do not grow up speaking English never truly master the language.
   - Learning a new skill can be intimidating but is rewarding if enough time and effort are invested.
   - Children learn languages effortlessly.
   - Good teachers can inspire students to discover and develop their talents.
2. Give students a copy of the prepared **Anticipation Guide** and have them mark their responses in the Me column. Have students discuss the statements in pairs or groups and mark the Guides again in the Group column.
3. For further guidance, use the ***Classroom Strategies and Teaching Routines*** card: **Using an Anticipation Guide.**

Concept Connector

Students will return to the **Anticipation Guide** after completing "My English."

Individual Activity

As students read, have them look for situations in which Alvarez uses language to bridge the two cultures in which she lives. Tell them to make a list of examples to share after they have finished reading the selection.

❷ About the Selection

In "My English," Julia Alvarez describes her introduction to English and the slow process of learning the language, first picking up a few words and then gradually absorbing more and more. Her vocabulary soon combines Spanish and English words in a hybrid language she calls Spanglish. It is only after considerable effort—and the inspiration of master teachers—that her command of English becomes complete.

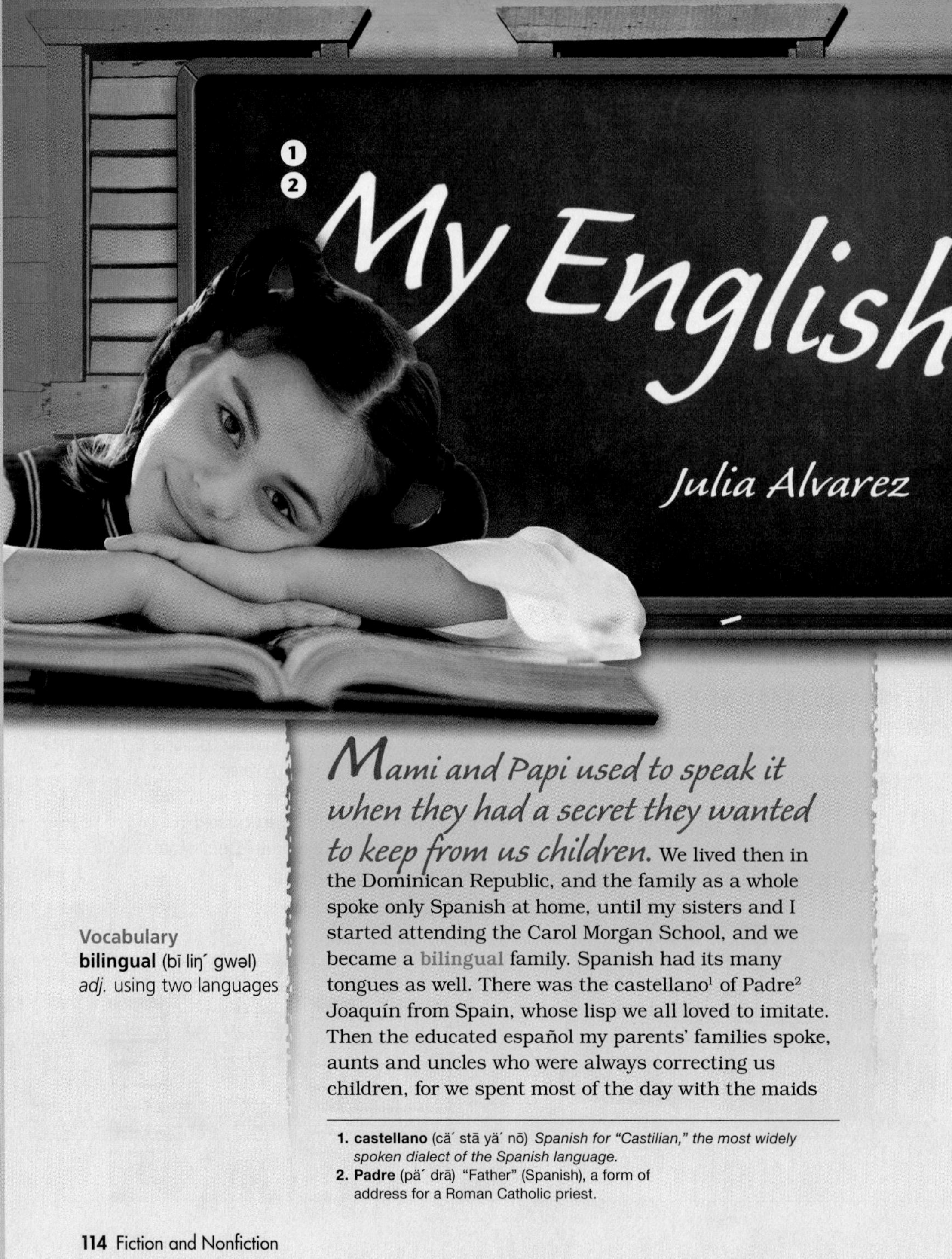

❶ ❷

My English

Julia Alvarez

Mami and Papi used to speak it when they had a secret they wanted to keep from us children. We lived then in the Dominican Republic, and the family as a whole spoke only Spanish at home, until my sisters and I started attending the Carol Morgan School, and we became a bilingual family. Spanish had its many tongues as well. There was the castellano[1] of Padre[2] Joaquín from Spain, whose lisp we all loved to imitate. Then the educated español my parents' families spoke, aunts and uncles who were always correcting us children, for we spent most of the day with the maids

Vocabulary
bilingual (bī liŋ′ gwəl)
adj. using two languages

1. **castellano** (cä′ stä yä′ nō) *Spanish for "Castilian," the most widely spoken dialect of the Spanish language.*
2. **Padre** (pä′ drā) "Father" (Spanish), a form of address for a Roman Catholic priest.

Vocabulary Development

© CCSS Language 6

Thematic Vocabulary: The Big Question

As students are discussing "My English," encourage them to use the thematic vocabulary presented in Introducing the Big Question, pp. 2–3. You might encourage them with sentence starters like these:

1. Alvarez was under the *assumption* that English was just "harder Spanish" because . . .
2. Alvarez *perceived* her mother's facial expressions as being "Spanish" because . . .
3. The *truth* about the English language was revealed to Alvarez when . . .
4. "My English" suggests that a person's *perspective* on another language might change when . . .

and so had picked up their "bad Spanish." Campesinas,[3] they spoke a lilting, animated campuno,[4] ss swallowed, endings chopped off, funny turns of phrases. This campuno was my true mother tongue, not the Spanish of Calderón de la Barca or Cervantes or even Neruda,[5] but of Chucha and Iluminada and Gladys and Ursulina from Juncalito and Licey and Boca de Yuma and San Juan de la Maguana.[6] Those women yakked as they cooked, they storytold, they gossiped, they sang—boleros, merengues, canciones, salves.[7] Theirs were the voices that belonged to the rain and the wind and the teeny, teeny stars even a small child could blot out with her thumb.

Besides all these versions of Spanish, every once in a while another strange tongue emerged from my papi's mouth or my mami's lips. What I first recognized was not a language, but a tone of voice, serious, urgent, something important and top secret being said, some uncle in trouble, someone divorcing, someone dead. *Say it in English so the children won't understand.* I would listen, straining to understand, thinking that this was not a different language but just another and harder version of Spanish. *Say it in English so the children won't understand.* From the beginning, English was the sound of worry and secrets, the sound of being left out.

I could make no sense of this "harder Spanish," and so I tried by other means to find out what was going on. I knew my mother's face by heart. When the little lines on the corners of her eyes crinkled, she was amused. When her nostrils flared and she bit her lips, she was trying hard not to laugh. She held her head down, eyes glancing up, when she thought I was lying. Whenever she spoke that gibberish English, I translated the general content by watching the Spanish expressions on her face.

3. **Campesinas** (cäm pā sē´ näs) simple rural women; peasant women (Spanish).
4. **campuno** (cäm po͞o´ nō) Spanish dialect spoken in rural areas of the Dominican Republic.
5. **Calderón de la Barca** (cäl de rôn´ dā lä bär´ cä) . . . **Cervantes** (ser vän´ tes) . . . **Neruda** (nā ro͞o´ dä) important literary figures.
6. **Juncalito** (ho͞oŋ cä lē´ tō) . . . **Licey** . . . **Boca de Yuma** (bō´ cä dā yo͞o´ mä) . . . **San Juan de la Maguana** (sän hwän´ dā lä mä gwä´ nä) small rural villages in the Dominican Republic.
7. **boleros** (bō ler´ ōs) . . . **merengues** (mə reŋ´ gās) . . . **canciones** (cän sē ō´ nes) . . . **salves** (säl´ ves) Spanish and Latin American songs and dances.

❸ LITERATURE IN CONTEXT

Social Studies Connection

The Dominican Republic
The Dominican Republic occupies the eastern portion of the Caribbean island of Hispaniola, which it shares with the Republic of Haiti. Located about 600 miles southeast of Florida, this area was one of the landing points of Christopher Columbus's first voyage in 1492. The dominant language and culture are Spanish.

Connect to the Literature

Considering the distance between the Dominican Republic and the United States, why do you think knowing both Spanish and English would be useful?

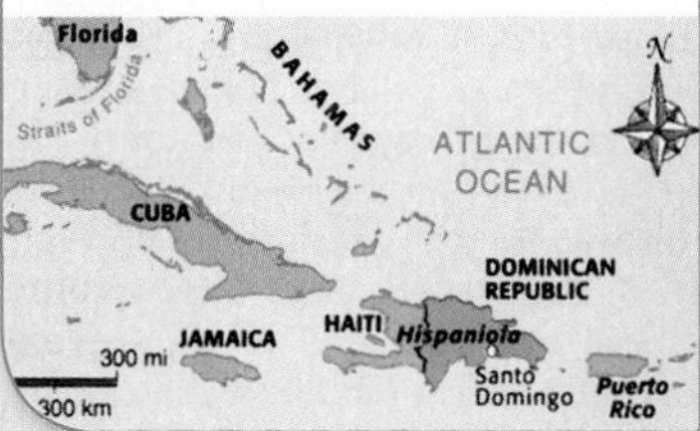

❹ 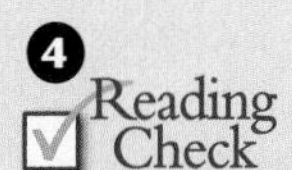
Reading Check

According to Alvarez, how does English sound?

❸ Literature in Context

Social Studies Connection The Dominican Republic, which is about twice the size of the state of New Hampshire, occupies two-thirds of the island of Hispaniola. The nation has a history of nonrepresentative government. The last dictator lost power in 1966, but questionable election practices compromised representative government. Since 1996, however, regular, competitive elections have brought the Dominican Republic a more representative government. Since democracy took hold in 1996, the Dominican Republic has enjoyed one of the fastest-growing economies in the Caribbean region.

Connect to the Literature Tell students that the United States has a large Dominican population, partly because of people who have immigrated for political reasons.

Ask the Connect to the Literature question: Considering the distance between the Dominican Republic and the United States, why do you think knowing both Spanish and English would be useful?

Answer: The close proximity of the Dominican Republic to the United States has allowed a high volume of travel between the two countries. Knowledge of both Spanish and English would make communication for tourism, business dealings, and friendship much easier.

❹ Reading Check

Answer: According to Alvarez, English sounds like "worry" and "secrets" and "being left out" because her parents spoke English when they didn't want her to understand their adult conversation.

PHLit Online!

This selection is available in interactive format in the **Enriched Online Student Edition**, at **www.PHLitOnline.com**, which includes a thematically related video with writing prompt and an interactive graphic organizer.

Differentiated Instruction for Universal Access

Strategy for Special-Needs Students
To help students better understand the author's purpose in writing "My English," show them **Reading Skill Graphic Organizer A** (***Graphic Organizer Transparencies,*** p. 21). Discuss the partially completed organizer and explain how the details lead to an understanding of the author's purpose. Have them use the organizer as a model as they continue to study Alvarez's purpose for writing.

Culturally Responsive Instruction
Culture Focus Invite students to share their own experiences in learning a new language and in building a bridge between two cultures. Ask them to talk about the challenge of keeping their two languages separated. Have they experienced Spanglish or some other version of a blended language? Encourage classmates to ask questions about the linguistic and cultural transition. As students progress through the selection, pause at appropriate points to discuss moments of culture clash.

5 Literary Analysis

Voice

1. Remind students that voice is how the writer sounds and that it is created by word choice, attitude, and sentence length and structure.
2. **Ask** students to respond to the Literary Analysis question: Which words and phrases here convey the writer's uncertainty about English and her unwillingness to learn it?

   Answer: Alvarez uses words like *strangest* and *strange,* suggesting that she was not comfortable with the other students and her books. She also writes about "a whole new language" that is just "for school and for books," indicating that she did not see why she needed to learn English, especially when her teacher taught her "double the amount of words" she needed to know.
3. Point out to students that Alvarez uses a wide range of sentence lengths and structures. Ask volunteers to give examples. Then **ask** what this variety indicates about voice.

   Possible response: It indicates that Alvarez is confident and at ease with English.

Spiral Review

Central Idea

1. Remind students that they studied the concept of central idea in the Unit 1 Literary Analysis Workshop (pp. 4–21).
2. **Ask** the Spiral Review question.

   Answer: Alvarez conveys the idea that although she did not see the value in learning English and was confused by it, her parents considered it a right and a responsibility. To reinforce this idea, her mother says things such as "it's quite the place for you and me" and that it was very important to learn "our English."

Literary Analysis
Voice
Which words and phrases here convey the writer's uncertainty about English and her unwillingness to learn it?

Spiral Review
Central Idea What central idea does Alvarez convey here?

Vocabulary
countenance
(koun´ tə nəns) *n.* face

Soon, I began to learn more English, at the Carol Morgan School. That is, when I had stopped gawking. The teacher and some of the American children had the strangest coloration: light hair, light eyes, light skin, as if Ursulina had soaked them in bleach too long, to' deteñío.[8] I did have some blond cousins, but they had deeply tanned skin, and as they grew older, their hair darkened, so their earlier paleness seemed a phase of their acquiring normal color. Just as strange was the little girl in my reader who had a *cat* and a *dog,* that looked just like un gatito y un perrito. Her mami was *Mother* and her papi *Father.* Why have a whole new language for school and for books with a teacher who could speak it teaching you double the amount of words you really needed? 5

Butter, butter, butter, butter. All day, one English word that had particularly struck me would go round and round in my mouth and weave through all the Spanish in my head until by the end of the day, the word did sound like just another Spanish word. And so I would say, "Mami, please pass la mantequilla." She would scowl and say in English, "I'm sorry, I don't understand. But would you be needing some butter on your bread?"

Why my parents didn't first educate us in our native language by enrolling us in a Dominican school, I don't know. Part of it was that Mami's family had a tradition of sending the boys to the States to boarding school and college, and she had been one of the first girls to be allowed to join her brothers. At Abbot Academy,[9] whose school song was our lullaby as babies ("Although Columbus and Cabot[10] never heard of Abbot, it's quite the place for you and me"), she had become quite Americanized. It was very important, she kept saying, that we learn our English. She always used the possessive pronoun: *your* English, an inheritance we had come into and must wisely use. Unfortunately, my English became all mixed up with our Spanish.

Mix-up, or what's now called Spanglish, was the language we spoke for several years. There wasn't a sentence that wasn't colonized by an English word. At school, a Spanish word would suddenly slide into my English like someone butting into line. Teacher, whose face I was learning to read as minutely as my mother's, would scowl but no smile played on her lips. Her pale skin made her strange **countenance** hard to read, so that I often misjudged how much I could get away with. Whenever I made a

8. **to' deteñío** (tō dā tān yē´ ō) all washed out; completely colorless (Spanish).
9. **Abbot Academy** boarding school for girls in Andover, Massachusetts; merged in 1973 with the neighboring boys' school, Phillips Academy.
10. **Cabot** (kab´ ət) John Cabot (1450–1499), Italian explorer who sailed in the service of England and was the first European to discover the coast of North America in 1497.

Think Aloud

Vocabulary: Using Context

Direct students' attention to the word *minutely* in the fourth paragraph. Using a think-aloud process, model how to use context to infer the meaning of an unknown word. Say to students:

I'm going to think aloud to show you how I would figure out the meaning of *minutely* based on its context.

In this sentence, *minutely* describes the way in which Alvarez read her teacher's face. I know from earlier in the selection that Alvarez watched her mother's face very carefully and knew the face "by heart." If Alvarez was learning to read her teacher's face "as *minutely* as my mother's," *minutely* must mean "in great detail."

mistake, Teacher would shake her head slowly, "In English, YU-LEE-AH, there's no such word as *columpio.* Do you mean a *swing?*"

I would bow my head, humiliated by the smiles and snickers of the American children around me. I grew insecure about Spanish. My native tongue was not quite as good as English, as if words like *columpio* were illegal immigrants trying to cross a border into another language. But Teacher's discerning grammar-and-vocabulary-patrol ears could tell and send them back.

Literary Analysis
Voice
How would you describe the author's voice, based on her examples of idiomatic expressions?

6 Soon, I was talking up an English storm. "Did you eat English parrot?" my grandfather asked one Sunday. I had just enlisted yet one more patient servant to listen to my rendition of "Peter Piper picked a peck of pickled peppers" at breakneck pace. "Huh?" I asked impolitely in English, putting him in his place. *Cat got your tongue? No big deal! So there! Take that! Holy Toledo!* (Our teacher's favorite "curse word.") *Go jump in the lake! Really dumb. Golly. Gosh.* Slang, clichés, sayings, hotshot language that our teacher called, ponderously, idiomatic expressions. Riddles, jokes, puns, conundrums. *What is yellow and goes click-click? Why did the chicken cross the road? See you later, alligator.* How wonderful to call someone an alligator and not be scolded for being disrespectful. In fact, they were supposed to say back, *In a while, crocodile.*

Vocabulary
ponderously
(pän′ dər əs lē) *adv.*
in a labored, boring, and serious way

There was also a neat little trick I wanted to try on an English-speaking adult at home. I had learned it from Elizabeth, my smart-alecky friend in fourth grade, whom I alternately worshiped and resented. I'd ask her a question that required an explanation, and she'd answer, "Because . . ." "Elizabeth, how come you didn't go to Isabel's birthday party?" "Because . . ." "Why didn't you put your name in your reader?" "Because . . ." I thought that such a cool way to get around having to come up with answers. So, I practiced saying it under my breath, planning for the day I could use it on an unsuspecting English-speaking adult.

One Sunday at our extended family dinner, my grandfather sat down at the children's table to chat with us. He was famous, in fact, for the way he could carry on adult conversations with his grandchildren. He often spoke to us in English so that we could practice speaking it outside the classroom. He was a Cornell[11] man, a United Nations representative from our country. He gave speeches in English. Perfect English, my mother's phrase. That

7 Reading Check
Which language did Alvarez learn to speak first—English or Spanish?

11. **Cornell** Cornell University in Ithaca, New York.

6 Literary Analysis

Voice

1. Read aloud the bracketed text. Have students translate the idioms and slang, and invite them to give other examples. Discuss how idioms, slang, and various colloquial expressions can pose an extra challenge to new speakers of English. Explain that most of these phrases make no sense if a reader or listener tries to decode them word by word. Also point out that most of them cannot be found in a standard dictionary.
2. **Ask** students how an English learner could find out the meaning of these terms.

   Possible response: An English learner could ask an English speaker to define the terms.
3. **Ask** students to respond to the Literary Analysis question: How would you describe the author's voice, based on her examples of idiomatic expressions?

   Possible response: Her voice is relaxed and playful.

7 Reading Check

Answer: She learned to speak Spanish first.

Differentiated Instruction for Universal Access

Strategy for Special-Needs Students
This selection can be especially challenging for some students due to the difficulty of the language in general and the intermingling of Spanish words and phrases. Even with footnoted translations, these terms can pose obstacles to understanding. You may want to preview difficult words prior to students' reading each page. As students read, have them pause for sentences containing Spanish text or puzzling English words, and help them paraphrase the meaning.

Strategy for Advanced Readers
Explain to students that part of Alvarez's voice is displayed through humor. Have students go through the selection and identify specific passages where she uses humor to show her voice. Ask students how this reflects Alvarez's attitude toward her subject.

8 Reading Skill

Author's Purpose

1. Project **Reading Skill Graphic Organizer B** (*Graphic Organizer Transparencies,* p. 22), and discuss the scene at the dinner table in which Tío Gus gives his demonstration with a grain of salt. Then read aloud the scene with Mami. Have students suggest details to add to the organizer. Then **ask** students the Reading Skill question: Why do you think the writer includes these details about Mami's comments?

   Answer: It illustrates Alvarez's learning process and her growing understanding of the power of words.

2. Add students' comments on the significance of the details to the organizer. Then point out that this explains Alvarez's purpose in writing this scene—to show how learning English is a process that does not happen quickly.

9 Connecting to the Big Question

1. Have students reread the second bracketed passage (the passage continues on page 119). **Ask:** What change occurred in Alvarez? **Answer:** She began to understand English in a more comfortable way.
2. **Ask:** What happened to Alvarez's confidence in herself as she experienced this change? **Answer:** She became more confident within her new language, as well as her new culture.
3. **Ask:** What new truth about English seemed to be developing within Alvarez? **Possible response:** English can make just as much sense as Spanish; it's a matter of time and comfort within a new cultural context.

Sunday, he asked me a question. I can't even remember what it was because I wasn't really listening but lying in wait for my chance. "Because . . .," I answered him. Papito waited a second for the rest of my sentence and then gave me a thumbnail grammar lesson, "*Because* has to be followed by a clause."

"Why's that?" I asked, nonplussed.[12]

"Because," he winked. "Just because."

A beginning wordsmith, I had so much left to learn; sometimes it was disheartening. Once Tío[13] Gus, the family intellectual, put a speck of salt on my grandparents' big dining table during Sunday dinner. He said, "Imagine this whole table is the human brain. Then this teensy grain is all we ever use of our intelligence!" He enumerated geniuses who had perhaps used two grains, maybe three: Einstein, Michelangelo, da Vinci, Beethoven. We children believed him. It was the kind of impossible fact we thrived on, proving as it did that the world out there was not drastically different from the one we were making up in our heads. 8

Vocabulary
enumerated (ē no͞o′ mər āt id) *v.* named one by one; specified, as in a list

Later, at home, Mami said that you had to take what her younger brother said "with a grain of salt." I thought she was still referring to Tío Gus's demonstration, and I tried to puzzle out what she was saying. Finally, I asked what she meant. "Taking what someone says with a grain of salt is an idiomatic expression in English," she explained. It was pure voodoo is what it was—what later I learned poetry could also do: a grain of salt could symbolize both the human brain and a condiment for human nonsense. And it could be itself, too: a grain of salt to flavor a bland plate of American food.

Reading Skill
Author's Purpose
Why do you think the writer includes these details about Mami's comments?

"Taking what someone says **with a grain of salt** *is an idiomatic expression in English," she explained.*

When we arrived in New York, I was shocked. A country where everyone spoke English! These people must be smarter, I thought. Maids, waiters, taxi drivers, doormen, bums on the street, all spoke this difficult language. It took some time before I understood that Americans were not necessarily a smarter, superior race. It was as natural for them to learn their mother tongue as it was for a little Dominican baby to learn Spanish. It came with "mother's milk," my mother explained, and for a while I thought a mother tongue was a mother tongue because you got it from your mother's milk along with proteins and vitamins.

Soon it wasn't so strange that everyone was speaking in English instead of Spanish. I learned not to hear it as English, but as sense. I no longer strained to understand, I understood. I relaxed in this second language. Only when someone with a heavy southern or 9

12. **nonplussed** (nän plüst′) *v.* confused; baffled.
13. **Tío** (tē′ ō) "Uncle" (Spanish).

Vocabulary Development

Vocabulary Knowledge Rating

When students have completed reading and discussing "My English," have them take out their **Vocabulary Knowledge Rating Chart** for this selection. Read the words aloud once more and have students rate their knowledge of the words again in the After Reading column. Clarify any words that are still problematic. Have students write their own definition and example or sentence in the appropriate column. Then have students complete the Vocabulary Practice activities at the end of the selection. Encourage students to use the words in further discussion and written work about this selection. Remind them that they will be accountable for these words on the **Selection Test,** ***Unit 1 Resources,*** pp. 168–170 or 171–173.

9 British accent spoke in a movie, or at church when the priest droned his sermon—only then did I experience that little catch of anxiety. I worried that I would not be able to understand, that I wouldn't be able to "keep up" with the voice speaking in this acquired language. I would be like those people from the Bible we had studied in religion class, whom I imagined standing at the foot of an enormous tower[14] that looked just like the skyscrapers around me. They had been punished for their pride by being made to speak different languages so that they didn't understand what anyone was saying.

But at the foot of those towering New York skyscrapers, I began to understand more and more—not less and less—English. In sixth grade, I had one of the first in a lucky line of great English teachers who began to nurture in me a love of language, a love that had been there since my childhood of listening closely to words. Sister Maria Generosa did not make our class **interminably** diagram sentences from a workbook or learn a catechism[15] of grammar rules. Instead, she asked us to write little stories imagining we were snowflakes, birds, pianos, a stone in the pavement, a star in the sky. What would it feel like to be a flower with roots in the ground? If the clouds could talk, what would they say? She had an expressive, dreamy look that was **accentuated** by the wimple[16] that framed her face.

Supposing, just supposing . . . My mind would take off, soaring into possibilities, a flower with roots, a star in the sky, a cloud full of sad, sad tears, a piano crying out each time its back was tapped, music only to our ears.

14. **enormous tower** a reference to the Tower of Babel in Genesis 11:1–9. According to Genesis, early Babylonians tried to build a tower to heaven, but they were thwarted when God caused them to speak many languages rather than one.
15. **catechism** (kat´ ə kiz´ əm) *n.* short book written in question-and-answer format.
16. **wimple** (wim´ pəl) *n.* cloth worn around the head, neck, and chin by some nuns.

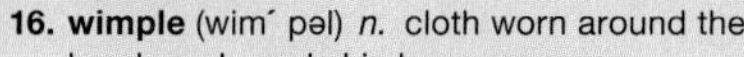

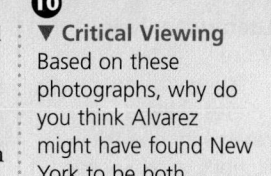

10 ▼ **Critical Viewing**
Based on these photographs, why do you think Alvarez might have found New York to be both intimidating and exciting? **[Analyze]**

Vocabulary

interminably (in tʉr´ mi nə blē) *adv.* endlessly

accentuated (ak sen´ cho͞o āt id) *v.* emphasized; heightened the effect of

11 **Reading Check**
To what city does Alvarez's family relocate?

10 Critical Viewing

Possible response: The tall, crowded buildings are intimidating and overwhelming. They could cause a person to feel small and insignificant. However, the majesty and grace of the welcoming Statue of Liberty suggest limitless opportunities and new things to do and see.

11 Reading Check

Answer: Alvarez's family relocates to New York City.

Concept Connector

Anticipation Guide

Have students return to their **Anticipation Guides** and respond to the statements again in the After Reading column. Then, lead a class discussion, probing for what students have learned that confirms or invalidates each statement.

Writing About the Big Question

Have students compare their responses to the sentence starters they completed before reading the selection with their ideas afterwards. Ask them to explain whether their thoughts have changed.

Reading Skill Graphic Organizer

Ask students to review the graphic organizers they completed to identify the author's purpose while reading. Show them **Reading Skill Graphic Organizer A** (*Graphic Organizer Transparencies,* p. 21) as an example. Then have students share the graphic organizers they did and the author's purposes that they identified.

⓬ Literary Analysis

Voice

Point out an author's word choice and sentence structure can lead to a poetic voice. **Ask** the Literary Analysis question: Which words and phrases in this paragraph give the author's voice a poetic quality?

Possible response: The following phrases sound poetic: "her whole habit shaking with the swing of her arm," "her hand tap-tap-tapping," and "her wimple poked up."

ASSESS

Answers

Critical Thinking

Before students respond, you may wish to have them write a brief objective summary of the selection. As they answer the questions below, remind them to support their answers with evidence from the text.

1. (a) Alvarez's parents used English when they were having discussions that were inappropriate for children to hear. (b) English kept her out of their conversation.
2. (a) Sister Generosa had students add colorful details to sentences and write creative stories. (b) The teacher at Carol Morgan School emphasized vocabulary and grammar. (c) Alvarez prefered Sister Generosa's method because it appealed to her creative side and inspired her.
3. **Possible response:** She does an excellent job because she shows her relationship with English in different periods of her life. For example, she shows how she becomes more comfortable with the language when she moves to New York City and is surrounded by English speakers. This helps the reader imagine Alvarez's relationship with English changing and growing.
4. **Possible response:** As Alvarez learned English, she began to feel more like the language was accessible to her—even a part of her. The language was no longer a symbol of her status as a foreigner or an outsider. She began to believe that English made sense.

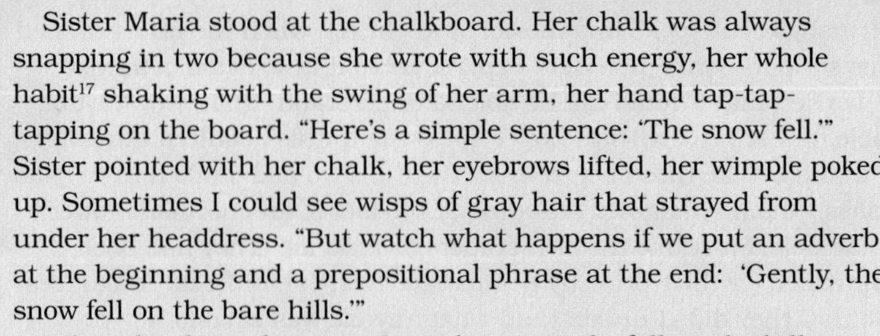

Literary Analysis
Voice
⓬ Which words and phrases in these paragraphs give the author's voice a poetic quality?

Sister Maria stood at the chalkboard. Her chalk was always snapping in two because she wrote with such energy, her whole habit[17] shaking with the swing of her arm, her hand tap-tap-tapping on the board. "Here's a simple sentence: 'The snow fell.'" Sister pointed with her chalk, her eyebrows lifted, her wimple poked up. Sometimes I could see wisps of gray hair that strayed from under her headdress. "But watch what happens if we put an adverb at the beginning and a prepositional phrase at the end: 'Gently, the snow fell on the bare hills.'"

I thought about the snow. I saw how it might fall on the hills, tapping lightly on the bare branches of trees. Softly, it would fall on the cold, bare fields. On toys children had left out in the yard, and on cars and on little birds and on people out late walking on the streets. Sister Marie filled the chalkboard with snowy print, on and on, handling and shaping and moving the language, scribbling all over the board until English, those verbal gadgets, those tricks and turns of phrases, those little fixed units and counters, became a charged, fluid mass that carried me in its great fluent waves, rolling and moving onward, to deposit me on the shores of my new homeland. I was no longer a foreigner with no ground to stand on. I had landed in the English language.

I was no longer a foreigner with no ground to stand on. I had landed in the English language.

17. **habit** (hab´ it) *n.* robe or dress worn by some nuns.

Critical Thinking

Cite textual evidence to support your responses.

1. **Key Ideas and Details (a)** When Julia Alvarez was young, at what times did her parents speak English at home? **(b) Infer:** Why do you think Alvarez says that English was the "sound of being left out"?
2. **Key Ideas and Details (a)** What method does Sister Maria Generosa use to teach Alvarez English? **(b) Compare and Contrast:** How does this method differ from the way she was taught at the Carol Morgan School? **(c) Assess:** Which method does Alvarez prefer? Why?
3. **Craft and Structure Evaluate:** How well do you think Alvarez succeeds in portraying the growth of her relationship with the English language? Use details from the text to support your answer.
4. **Integration of Knowledge and Ideas** How do Alvarez's ideas about English change as she learns the language? *[Connect to the Big Question: Can truth change?]*

Assessment Resources

Unit 1 Resources

L1 L2 EL **Selection Test A,** pp. 168–170. Administer Test A to less advanced readers.

L3 L4 EL **Selection Test B,** pp. 171–173. Administer Test B to on-level and more advanced students.

L3 L4 **Open-Book Test,** pp. 165–167. As an alternative, give the Open-Book Test.

All **Customizable Test Bank**

All **Self-tests**
Students may prepare for the **Selection Test** by taking the **Self-test** online.

All assessment resources are available at **www.PHLitOnline.com.**

After You Read **My English**

Literary Analysis: Voice

1. **Craft and Structure (a)** Complete a chart like the one shown to find examples of Alvarez's **word choice, attitude,** and **sentence structure. (b)** Using examples from your chart, describe Alvarez's **voice** in this work of nonfiction.

Voice		
Word Choice	**Attitude**	**Sentence Structure**

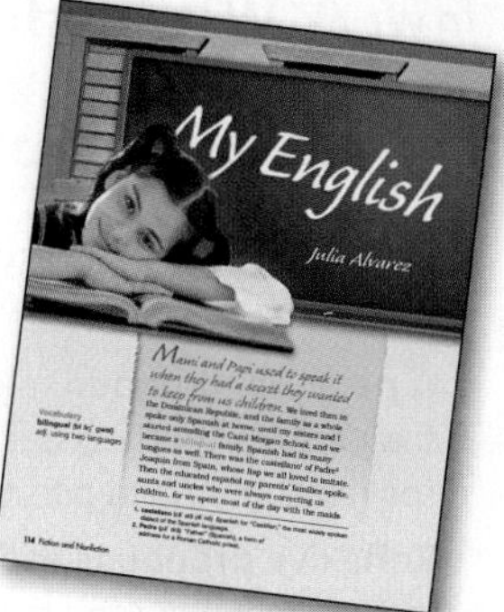

2. **Key Ideas and Details (a)** Which aspects of learning English does the author emphasize in this example of **autobiographical writing? (b)** Note two details that reflect her individual point of view.

Reading Skill: Author's Purpose

3. Review the notes you made in your **preview** of "My English." Which of your ideas about the **author's purpose** were confirmed as you read the selection? Which were not? Explain.
4. **(a)** What general purpose do you think Alvarez had in writing this essay? Explain. **(b)** What more specific purpose or purposes do you think she had for writing? Support your answer.

Vocabulary

Acquisition and Use An **analogy** shows the relationship between pairs of words. To complete each analogy, use a word from the vocabulary list on page 112. For each case, your choice should create a word pair that matches the relationship between the first two words given.

1. happily : sadly :: ______ : quickly
2. bipartisan : party :: ______ : language
3. frame : photograph :: ______ : expression
4. counted : tally :: ______ : list
5. terrific : great :: ______ : highlighted
6. boldly : meekly :: ______ : lightly

Word Study Use the context of the sentences and what you know about the **Latin root *-term-*** to explain your answer to each question.

1. If you are *determined*, are you likely to quit?
2. If a worker is *terminated*, has he or she been fired?

Word Study

The **Latin root *-term-*** means "limit, end, boundary."

Apply It Explain how the root contributes to the meanings of these words. Consult a dictionary if necessary.

terminal
exterminate
determination

ASSESS/EXTEND

Answers

Literary Analysis

1. (a) **Possible response:** Word Choice: "a strange tongue emerged from my papi's mouth or my mami's lips"; **Attitude:** "Supposing, just supposing . . . My mind would take off, soaring into possibilities. . . ."; **Sentence Structure:** "I thought about the snow. I saw how it might fall on the hills, tapping lightly on the bare branches of trees."
   (b) **Possible response:** Alvarez's voice is playful when she describes the "strange tongue" that came from her "papi's mouth." It is exultant, as when she describes her mind "soaring into possibilities." It is thoughtful, as when she describes thinking about the snow.
   For other sample answers see ***Graphic Organizer Transparencies,*** **Literary Analysis Graphic Organizer A**, p. 24, and the **Additional Answers** section.
2. (a) Alvarez stresses that learning English is a process that grows into an automatic understanding of the language. (b) **Possible response:** She grew up in a bilingual household. Despite understanding the language, she still had occasional fears of comprehension.

Reading Skill

3. **Possible response:** Students may have expected Alvarez to describe or teach English. They should explain which of their ideas were confirmed and which were not.
4. (a) Her purpose is to entertain and to inform. She wants to show the humor in a confusing situation, and she wants to inform readers of all cultures about the difficulties of learning a new language. (b) **Possible response:** She wants readers to learn compassion for those who do not yet know English well.

Vocabulary

Acquisition and Use

Sample answers:

1. interminably
2. bilingual
3. countenance
4. enumerated
5. accentuated
6. ponderously

Word Study

Sample answers:

1. No. The root *-term-* means "limit" or "boundary." A *determined* person tries to push beyond boundaries and will not quit.
2. Yes. The root *-term-* means "limit" or "end." If a worker is *terminated,* he or she has been fired, meaning his or her employment has ended.

Word Study: Apply It

Sample answers:

Terminal can mean a place that is at the end of a line or it can mean a disease that ends in death. *Exterminate* means to put an end to. *Determination* means to have firmness or courage to achieve an end.

EXTEND/ASSESS

Answers

Conventions

1. Introduce the skill, using the instruction on the student page.
2. Discuss the definitions and the examples in the chart.

Think Aloud: Model the Skill

Model the skill of using personal and reflexive pronouns. Say to students:

I know that personal pronouns refer to the person who is speaking, spoken to, or spoken about. *I, you, he,* and *she* are examples of personal pronouns. But not all pronouns are personal. Some are reflexive. Those are pronouns like *himself* or *ourselves*. I use reflexive pronouns when I describe something that someone or something performed, as in I took a long look at *myself* and I didn't like what I saw.

PH WRITING COACH Grade 9

Students will find out more about pronouns in Chapters 13 and 18.

Practice A

1. herself—reflexive
2. I, them, they—personal
3. you—personal

Reading Application

Sample answer:

As we ground to a halt—we were still the third car—Secret Service men began to pull, lead, guide, and hustle us out. Suddenly I found myself face to face with Jackie in a small hallway.

Practice B

1. themselves—reflexive
   Both of her parents were well-educated.
2. herself—reflexive
   Alvarez was in a class where her writing was encouraged.
3. She—personal

Writing Application

Possible responses:

Julia Alvarez describes how her parents often spoke English between themselves, but not to her.

Julia spoke English to herself so that she could become more accustomed to her new language.

PERFORMANCE TASKS

Integrated Language Skills

from A White House Diary • My English

Conventions: Pronouns

A **pronoun** is a word that stands for a noun or for a word that takes the place of a noun.

A **personal pronoun** refers to the person speaking (first person), the person spoken to (second person), or the person or thing spoken about (third person).

Reflexive pronouns end in *-self* or *-selves* and are used to indicate that someone or something performs an action to, for, or upon himself, herself, or itself.

	First Person	Second Person	Third Person
Personal Pronouns	**Singular:** I, me, my, mine **Plural:** we, us, our, ours	**Singular:** you, your, yours **Plural:** you, your, yours	**Singular:** he, she, him, her, his, hers, it, its **Plural:** they, them, their, theirs
Reflexive Pronouns	**Singular:** myself **Plural:** ourselves	**Singular:** yourself **Plural:** yourselves	**Singular:** himself, herself, itself **Plural:** themselves

Practice A Identify the pronouns in each sentence and indicate whether they are personal or reflexive. Look for a word, or antecedent, to which the pronoun refers.

1. At first, Lady Bird Johnson was herself unsure of what had happened.
2. Mrs. Kennedy said, "I want them to see what they have done to Jack."
3. If you were alive in 1963, you would still remember the events of November 22.

Reading Application In *A White House Diary*, find one sentence that uses a personal pronoun and one that uses a reflexive pronoun.

Practice B Identify the pronouns in each sentence and indicate whether they are personal or reflexive. Rewrite sentences with reflexive pronouns to eliminate the reflexive pronoun.

1. Her parents were themselves well educated.
2. Alvarez found herself in a class where her writing was encouraged.
3. She enjoyed talking to her grandfather.

Writing Application Using this sentence as a model, write two or more sentences that include both personal and reflexive pronouns: *Julia Alvarez writes about her parents speaking English between themselves.*

PH WRITING COACH Further instruction and practice are available in *Prentice Hall Writing Coach.*

122 Fiction and Nonfiction

Extend the Lesson

Sentence Modeling

Choose the sentence given from the selection students have read:

I went up to her, put my arms around her, and said something to her. (from *A White House Diary*)

I saw how it might fall on the hills, tapping lightly on the bare branches of trees. ("My English")

Ask students what they notice about the sentence. Elicit from them that the sentence contains personal pronouns. Then, **ask** what else they notice. (from *A White House Diary:* The pronouns are *I, her,* and the possessive pronoun *my.* Repetitive use of the phrase "to her" gives the sentence a lulling, comforting quality. "My English": The pronouns are *I* and *it.* Alvarez uses alliteration—repetition of the initial *b*—in the phrase "bare branches.")

Have students imitate the sentence in a sentence on a topic of their own choosing, matching each grammatical and stylistic feature discussed. Collect the sentences and share them with the class.

Writing

Narrative Text Both selections deal with the experience of going through a tough time. Write a **journal entry** about an event or subject of importance to you. Model your writing on either *A White House Diary* or "My English." As you prepare to write, consider these questions about your topic:

- Who was affected by the event, and in what way?
- What specific words, images, sights, sounds, or smells does this event call to mind?
- Has this subject always been important to you? Why or why not?
- How does this subject influence your outlook on the world?

Grammar Application Use personal, reflexive, and reciprocal pronouns correctly in your writing.

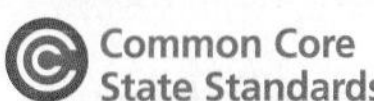

L.9-10.1, L.9-10.6; W.9-10.4; SL.9-10.5

[For the full wording of the standards, see page 100.]

Writing Workshop: *Work in Progress*

Prewriting for Problem-Solution Essay Think of issues that concern people in your school or community. Jot down several problems. As you write, use a narrative format, describing events in the order they occurred. Put these Problem Notes in your writing portfolio for development later.

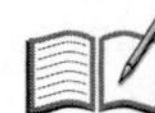

Use this prewriting activity to prepare for the **Writing Workshop** on page 172.

Research and Technology

Build and Present Knowledge Each of these selections is based on actual historical events. Using presentation software, prepare an **introduction for a multimedia presentation** about one of these two topics suggested by the reading:

- First ladies in American history and how the role of the first lady has changed over time
- Immigration to the United States since 1800, the reasons people left their home countries, and what they sought in the United States

Follow these steps to complete the assignment:

- Choose your topic and conduct research to learn more.
- Identify the main idea and key points of your presentation.
- Create a strong opening statement that captures your audience's interest and introduces the main idea of your topic.
- Choose appropriate media to present your topic. Use available technologies to achieve your purpose, displaying information on charts, maps, or graphs when appropriate.
- Provide an overview of your presentation so your audience knows what your focus will be.

PHLit Online!
www.PHLitOnline.com
- Interactive graphic organizers
- Grammar tutorial
- Interactive journals

Writing

1. Review the assignment, using the instruction on the student page.
2. To guide the students in writing their notes, give them **Support for Writing**, p. 163 in ***Unit 1 Resources.***
3. To evaluate students' journal entries, use the Autobiographical Narrative rubrics, pp. 222–223 in ***Professional Development Guidebook.*** In addition, you might place emphasis on using only significant details.

Grammar Application

Have students check their drafts for correct use of pronouns.

Six Traits Focus

✓	Ideas	✓	Word Choice
	Organization		Sentence Fluency
✓	Voice		Conventions

PH WRITING COACH Grade 9

Students will find guidance on autobiographical writing in Chapter 5.

Writing Workshop
Work in Progress

Have students save their completed list of problems in their portfolios. They will use these notes later as they continue this Work-in-Progress assignment (see p. 151). The assignment prepares them to complete the Writing Workshop (see pp. 172–179).

Research and Technology

1. Review the assignment, using the instruction on the student page.
2. Have students complete the **Support for Extend Your Learning** page (***Unit 1 Resources,*** p. 164).

Teaching Resources

Unit 1 Resources

L3 L4 EL **Integrated Language Skills: Grammar,** p. 162

L3 L4 EL **Support for Writing,** p. 163

L3 L4 **Support for Extend Your Learning,** p. 164

L4 **Enrichment,** pp. 143, 161

Enriched Online Student Edition

Available under After You Read for this selection:

All **Interactive Grammar Tutorial**

L3 L4 **Internet Research Activity**

Professional Development Guidebook

Rubrics for Self-Assessment: Autobiographical Narrative, pp. 222–223

PHLit Online! All print and digital resources are available at **www.PHLitOnline.com.** Online resources accessible by students are noted on the student page.

✓ The Secret Life of Walter Mitty • ✓✓ Uncle Marcos

Lesson Pacing Guide

DAY 1 Preteach

- Administer the Reading and Vocabulary Warm-ups (*Unit 1 Resources,* pp. 174–177 or 192–195) as necessary.
- Introduce the Reading Skill: Author's Purpose.
- Introduce the Literary Analysis concept: Character.
- Distribute copies of the appropriate graphic organizer for the Reading Skill (*Graphic Organizer Transparencies*, pp. 26–28).
- Distribute copies of the appropriate graphic organizer for Literary Analysis (*Graphic Organizer Transparencies,* pp. 29–31).
- Teach the selection vocabulary.
- Introduce the Word Study skill.

DAYS 2–3 Preteach/Teach

- Build background with the Background feature.
- Develop thematic vocabulary and thematic thinking with Writing About the Big Question.
- Prepare students to read with the Activating Prior Knowledge activities (TE).
- Informally monitor comprehension while students read.
- Use the Reading Check questions to confirm comprehension.
- Develop students' ability to determine the author's purpose, using Reading Skill questions.
- Develop students' understanding of character, using the Literary Analysis questions.
- Reinforce vocabulary with the Vocabulary notes.
- Reinforce unit focus standards using the Spiral Review prompts.

DAY 4 Assess

- Assess students' comprehension and mastery of the skills by having them answer the Critical Thinking, Reading Skill, and Literary Analysis questions.
- Have students complete the Vocabulary Practice activities.
- Have students complete the Word Study activities.

DAY 5 Extend/Assess

- Have students complete the Conventions lesson.
- Have students complete the Writing activity and write a character profile. (You may assign as homework.)
- Extend learning by having students complete the Research and Technology activity, a learning log. (You may assign as homework.) As an alternative, assign them "Secret Lives" or "Telling Tales" in *Reality Central.*
- Administer Selection Test A or B (*Unit 1 Resources,* pp. 186–191 or 207–212).

Common Core State Standards

Reading Literature 2. Determine a theme or central idea of a text and analyze in detail its development over the course of the text, including how it emerges and is shaped and refined by specific details; provide an objective summary of the text.
3. Analyze how complex characters develop over the course of a text, interact with other characters, and advance the plot or develop the theme.

Writing 4. Produce clear and coherent writing in which the development, organization, and style are appropriate to task, purpose, and audience.
6. Use technology, including the Internet, to produce, publish, and update individual or shared writing products, taking advantage of technology's capacity to link to other information and to display information flexibly and dynamically.

Language 1. Demonstrate command of the conventions of standard English grammar and usage when writing or speaking.
4.a. Use context as a clue to the meaning of a word or phrase.
6. Acquire and use accurately general academic and domain-specific words and phrases, sufficient for reading and listening at the college and career readiness level.

Additional Standards Practice
Common Core Companion,* *pp. 15–22; 97–104

Daily Block Scheduling
Each day in this Lesson Pacing Guide represents a 40–50 minute period. Teachers using block scheduling may combine days to revise pacing. In addition, teachers may differentiate and support core instruction by integrating components for extended and intensive support as students require. See the Guide to Selected Leveled Resources (facing page).

Guide to Selected Leveled Resources

RTI **Tier 1** (students performing on level)			✓ More Accessible The Secret Life of Walter Mitty	✓✓ More Complex Uncle Marcos
Warm Up	Whole class instruction; Group work	**Practice, model,** and **monitor** fluency, working **with the whole class** or **in groups.**	**Vocabulary** and **Reading Warm-ups B,** ***Unit 1 Resources,*** pp. 174–175, 177	**Vocabulary** and **Reading Warm-ups B,** ***Unit 1 Resources,*** pp. 192–193, 195
Comprehension/Skills	Whole class instruction; Independent work	**Support** and **monitor** comprehension and skills development, having students complete the activities, graphic organizers, and interactive prompts **independently** or **as a class.**	• ***Reader's Notebook,*** adapted instruction and full selection EL ***Reader's Notebook: English Learner's Version,*** adapted instruction and adapted selection • **Reading Skill Graphic Organizer B,** ***Graphic Organizer Transparencies,*** p. 28 • **Literary Analysis Graphic Organizer B,** ***Graphic Organizer Transparencies,*** p. 31	• ***Reader's Notebook,*** adapted instruction and summary EL ***Reader's Notebook: English Learner's Version,*** adapted instruction and summary • **Reading Skill Graphic Organizer B,** ***Graphic Organizer Transparencies,*** p. 28 • **Literary Analysis Graphic Organizer B,** ***Graphic Organizer Transparencies,*** p. 31
Monitor Progress	A	**Monitor** student progress with the differentiated curriculum-based assessment in the *Unit Resources.*	• **Selection Test B,** ***Unit 1 Resources,*** pp. 189–191 • **Open-Book Test,** ***Unit 1 Resources,*** pp. 183–185	• **Selection Test B,** ***Unit 1 Resources,*** pp. 210–212 • **Open-Book Test,** ***Unit 1 Resources,*** pp. 204–206
Assess/ Screen	A	• **Assess** student progress using Benchmark Test 2. • **Preassess** instructional needs using the Vocabulary in Context section of the test.	• **Benchmark Test 2,** ***Unit 1 Resources,*** pp. 235–243, including Vocabulary in Context diagnostic items	• **Benchmark Test 2,** ***Unit 1 Resources,*** pp. 235–243, including Vocabulary in Context diagnostic items

RTI **Tier 2** (students requiring intervention)			✓ More Accessible The Secret Life of Walter Mitty	✓✓ More Complex Uncle Marcos
Warm Up	Group work; One-on-one teaching	**Practice, model,** and **monitor** fluency **in groups** or **with individuals.**	• **Vocabulary and Reading Warm-ups A,** ***Unit 1 Resources,*** pp. 174–176 • ***Reality Central,*** "Secret Lives" • ***Hear It!*** **Audio CD (adapted text)**	• **Vocabulary and Reading Warm-ups A,** ***Unit 1 Resources,*** pp. 192–194 • ***Reality Central,*** "Telling Tales" • ***Hear It!*** **Audio CD**
Comprehension/Skills	Group work; One-on-one teaching	• **Support** and **monitor** comprehension and skills development, working **in small groups** or **with individuals.** • **Pair** students with more advanced peers and have them complete the writing activity in the *Real-World Writing Journal*. • As students complete the selection in the appropriate version of the *Reader's Notebook,* **monitor** comprehension frequently with group questions and individual instruction. • **Model** strategies while guiding students in completing the activities and prompts in the *Reader's Notebook,* as well as the graphic organizers. • **Practice** skills and **monitor** mastery with the *Reading Kit* worksheets.	• ***Real-World Writing Journal,*** Lesson 7, pp. 26–29 • ***Reader's Notebook: Adapted Version,*** adapted instruction and adapted selection EL ***Reader's Notebook: English Learner's Version,*** adapted instruction and adapted selection • **Reading Skill Graphic Organizer A,** ***Graphic Organizer Transparencies,*** p. 26 • **Literary Analysis Graphic Organizer A,** ***Graphic Organizer Transparencies,*** p. 29 • ***Reading Kit,*** Practice worksheets, pp. 28, 32, 36, 40, 48	• ***Real-World Writing Journal,*** Lesson 8, pp. 30–33 • ***Reader's Notebook: Adapted Version,*** adapted instruction and summary EL ***Reader's Notebook: English Learner's Version,*** adapted instruction and summary • **Reading Skill Graphic Organizer A,** ***Graphic Organizer Transparencies,*** p. 27 • **Literary Analysis Graphic Organizer A,** ***Graphic Organizer Transparencies,*** p. 30 • ***Reading Kit,*** Practice worksheets, pp. 28, 32, 36, 40, 48
Monitor Progress	A	**Monitor** student progress with the differentiated curriculum-based assessment in the *Unit Resources* and in the *Reading Kit.*	• **Selection Test A,** ***Unit 1 Resources,*** pp. 186–188 • ***Reading Kit,*** Assess worksheets, pp. 29, 33, 37, 41, 49	• **Selection Test A,** ***Unit 1 Resources,*** pp. 207–209 • ***Reading Kit,*** Assess worksheets, pp. 29, 33, 37, 41, 49
Assess/ Screen	A	• **Assess** student progress using Benchmark Test 2. • **Preassess** instructional needs using the Vocabulary in Context section of the test.	• **Benchmark Test 2,** ***Unit 1 Resources,*** pp. 235–243, including Vocabulary in Context diagnostic items	• **Benchmark Test 2,** ***Unit 1 Resources,*** pp. 235–243, including Vocabulary in Context diagnostic items

TIER 3 Tier 3 intervention may require consultation with the student's special-education or dyslexia specialist. For additional support, see the Tier 2 activities and resources listed above.

One-on-one teaching · Group work · Whole class instruction · Independent work · A Assessment

For a complete guide to selection support, including support for Advanced students, see the Overview of Resources in the frontmatter.

✓The Secret Life of Walter Mitty
✓✓Uncle Marcos

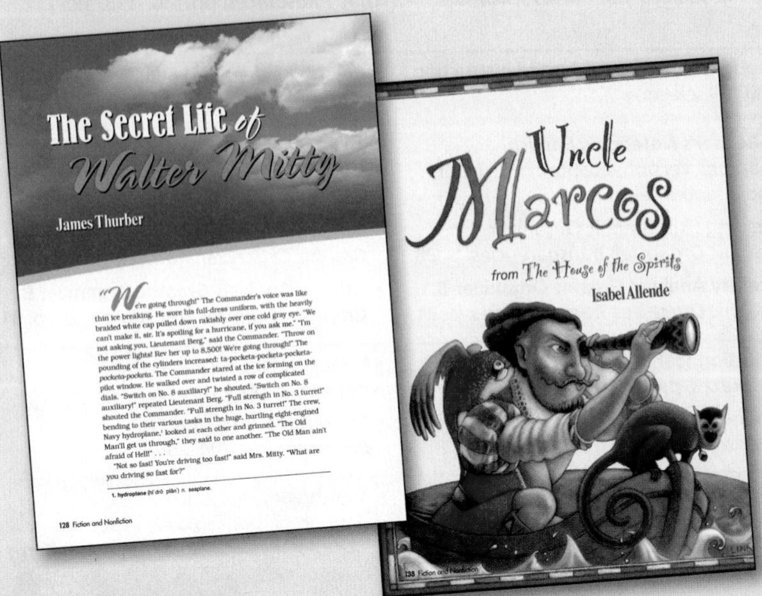
The Secret Life of Walter Mitty

James Thurber

"We're going through!" The Commander's voice was like thin ice breaking. He wore his full-dress uniform, with the heavily braided white cap pulled down rakishly over one cold gray eye. "We can't make it, sir. It's spoiling for a hurricane, if you ask me." "I'm not asking you, Lieutenant Berg," said the Commander. "Throw on the power lights! Rev her up to 8,500! We're going through!" The pounding of the cylinders increased: ta-pocketa-pocketa-pocketa-pocketa-pocketa. The Commander stared at the ice forming on the pilot window. He walked over and twisted a row of complicated dials. "Switch on No. 8 auxiliary!" he shouted. "Switch on No. 8 auxiliary!" repeated Lieutenant Berg. "Full strength in No. 3 turret!" shouted the Commander. "Full strength in No. 3 turret!" The crew, bending to their various tasks in the huge, hurtling eight-engined Navy hydroplane,[1] looked at each other and grinned. "The Old Man'll get us through," they said to one another. "The Old Man ain't afraid of Hell!" . . .

"Not so fast! You're driving too fast!" said Mrs. Mitty. "What are you driving so fast for?"

1. hydroplane (hī′ drō plān′) n. seaplane.

128 Fiction and Nonfiction

Uncle Marcos

from The House of the Spirits

Isabel Allende

138 Fiction and Nonfiction

RESOURCES FOR:

- L1 Special-Needs Students
- L2 Below-Level Students (Tier 2)
- L3 On-Level Students (Tier 1)
- L4 Advanced Students (Tier 1)
- EL English Learners
- All All Students

Vocabulary/Fluency/Prior Knowledge

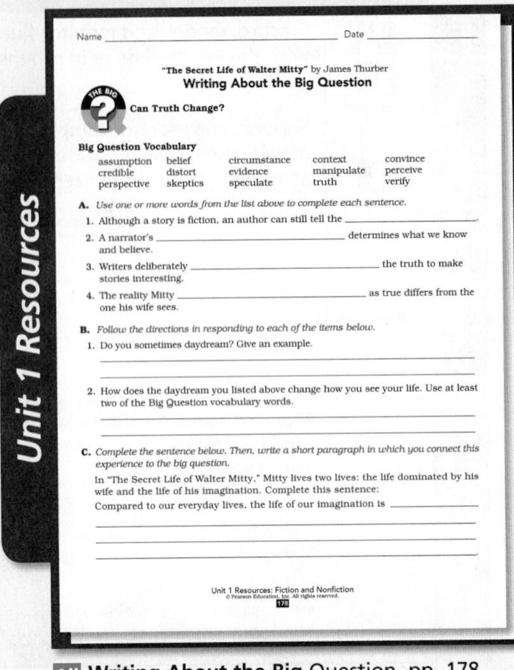

Name ______ Date ______

"The Secret Life of Walter Mitty" by James Thurber
Writing About the Big Question

THE BIG ? **Can Truth Change?**

Big Question Vocabulary

assumption	belief	circumstance	context	convince
credible	distort	evidence	manipulate	perceive
perspective	skeptics	speculate	truth	verify

A. *Use one or more words from the list above to complete each sentence.*

1. Although a story is fiction, an author can still tell the ______.
2. A narrator's ______ determines what we know and believe.
3. Writers deliberately ______ the truth to make stories interesting.
4. The reality Mitty ______ as true differs from the one his wife sees.

B. *Follow the directions in responding to each of the items below.*

1. Do you sometimes daydream? Give an example.
2. How does the daydream you listed above change how you see your life. Use at least two of the Big Question vocabulary words.

C. *Complete the sentence below. Then, write a short paragraph in which you connect this experience to the big question.*

In "The Secret Life of Walter Mitty," Mitty lives two lives: the life dominated by his wife and the life of his imagination. Complete this sentence:

Compared to our everyday lives, the life of our imagination is ______

Unit 1 Resources: Fiction and Nonfiction
© Pearson Education, Inc. All rights reserved.
178

All **Writing About the Big** Question, pp. 178, 196

Also available for these selections:

- EL L1 L2 **Vocabulary Warm-ups A and B,** pp. 174–175, 192–193
- EL L1 L2 **Reading Warm-ups A and B,** pp. 176–177, 194–195
- All **Vocabulary Builder,** pp. 181, 199

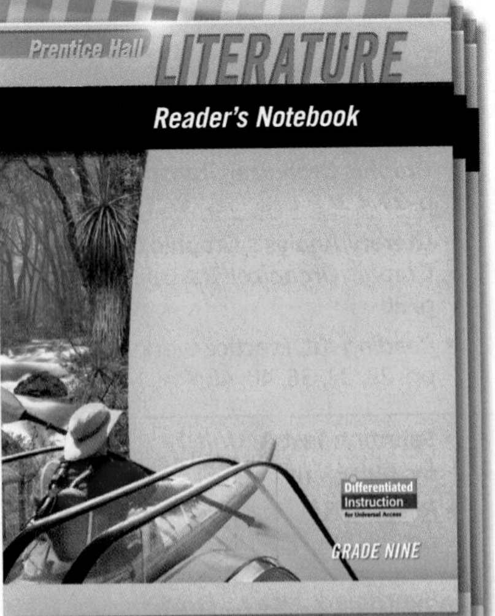

Reader's Notebooks

Pre- and postreading pages for both selections, as well as "The Secret Life of Walter Mitty," appear in an interactive format in the *Reader's Notebooks*. Each *Notebook* is differentiated for a different group of learners. The selections in the Adapted and English Learner's versions are abridged.

- L2 L3 ***Reader's Notebook***
- L1 ***Reader's Notebook: Adapted Version***
- EL ***Reader's Notebook: English Learner's Version***
- EL ***Reader's Notebook: Spanish Version***

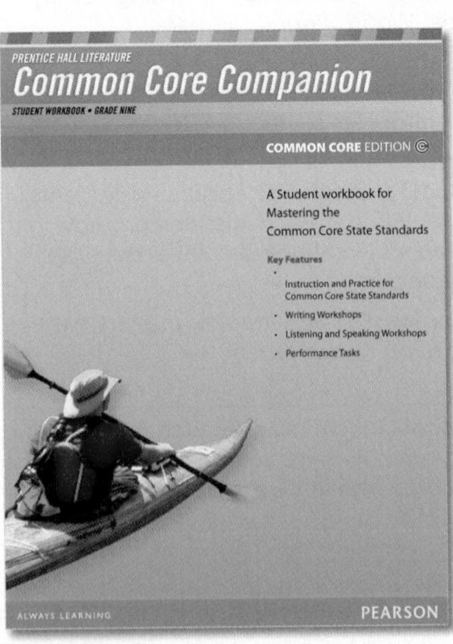

Common Core Companion

Additional instruction and practice for each Common Core State Standard

Selection Support

Graphic Organizer Transparencies

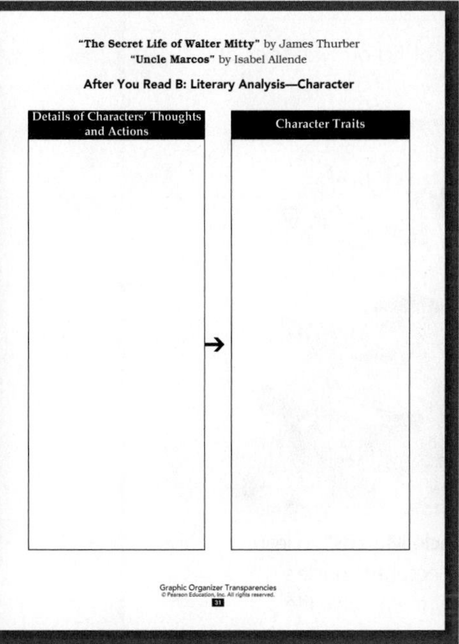
"The Secret Life of Walter Mitty" by James Thurber
"Uncle Marcos" by Isabel Allende
After You Read B: Literary Analysis—Character

Details of Characters' Thoughts and Actions	→	Character Traits

Graphic Organizer Transparencies
© Pearson Education, Inc. All rights reserved.
31

EL L3 **Literary Analysis: Graphic Organizer B,** p. 31

Also available for these selections:

EL L1 L2 **Reading: Graphic Organizer A,** pp. 26, 27 (partially filled in)

EL L3 **Reading: Graphic Organizer B,** p. 28

EL L1 L2 **Literary Analysis: Graphic Organizer A,** pp. 29, 30 (partially filled in)

Skills Development/Extension

Unit 1 Resources

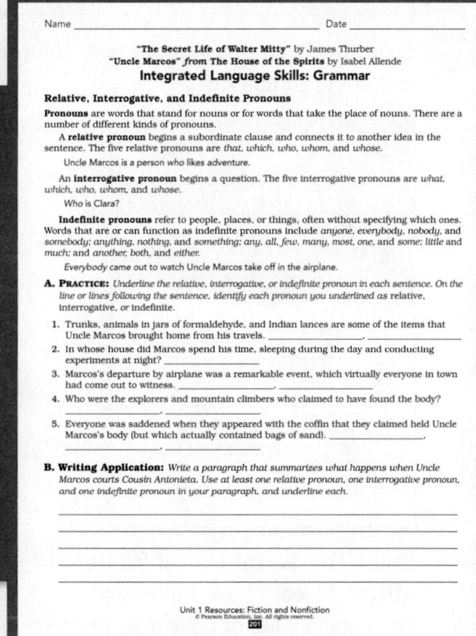
Name ______________________ Date ______________

"The Secret Life of Walter Mitty" by James Thurber
"Uncle Marcos" *from* The House of the Spirits by Isabel Allende
Integrated Language Skills: Grammar

Relative, Interrogative, and Indefinite Pronouns

Pronouns are words that stand for nouns or for words that take the place of nouns. There are a number of different kinds of pronouns.

A **relative pronoun** begins a subordinate clause and connects it to another idea in the sentence. The five relative pronouns are *that, which, who, whom,* and *whose.*

Uncle Marcos is a person *who* likes adventure.

An **interrogative pronoun** begins a question. The five interrogative pronouns are *what, which, who, whom,* and *whose.*

Who is Clara?

Indefinite pronouns refer to people, places, or things, often without specifying which ones. Words that are or can function as indefinite pronouns include *anyone, everybody, nobody,* and *somebody; anything, nothing,* and *something; any, all, few, many, most, one,* and *some; little* and *much;* and *another, both,* and *either.*

Everybody came out to watch Uncle Marcos take off in the airplane.

A. Practice: *Underline the relative, interrogative, or indefinite pronoun in each sentence. On the line or lines following the sentence, identify each pronoun you underlined as* relative, interrogative, *or* indefinite.

1. Trunks, animals in jars of formaldehyde, and Indian lances are some of the items that Uncle Marcos brought home from his travels. ____________, ____________
2. In whose house did Marcos spend his time, sleeping during the day and conducting experiments at night? ____________
3. Marcos's departure by airplane was a remarkable event, which virtually everyone in town had come out to witness. ____________, ____________
4. Who were the explorers and mountain climbers who claimed to have found the body? ____________, ____________
5. Everyone was saddened when they appeared with the coffin that they claimed held Uncle Marcos's body (but which actually contained bags of sand). ____________, ____________, ____________

B. Writing Application: *Write a paragraph that summarizes what happens when Uncle Marcos courts Cousin Antonieta. Use at least one relative pronoun, one interrogative pronoun, and one indefinite pronoun in your paragraph, and underline each.*

Unit 1 Resources: Fiction and Nonfiction
© Pearson Education, Inc. All rights reserved.
201

EL L3 L4 **Grammar,** p. 201

Also available for these selections:

All **Literary Analysis: Character,** pp. 179, 197

All **Reading: Author's Purpose,** pp. 180, 198

L4 **Enrichment,** pp. 182, 200

EL L3 L4 **Support for Writing,** p. 202

L3 L4 **Support for Extend Your Learning,** p. 203

Assessment

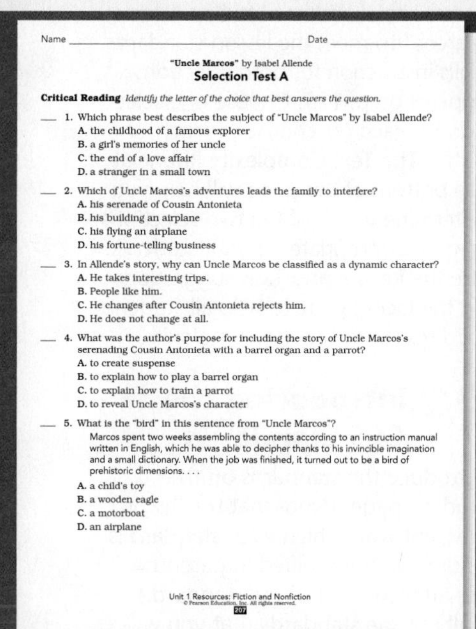
Name ______________________ Date ______________

"Uncle Marcos" by Isabel Allende
Selection Test A

Critical Reading *Identify the letter of the choice that best answers the question.*

___ 1. Which phrase best describes the subject of "Uncle Marcos" by Isabel Allende?
A. the childhood of a famous explorer
B. a girl's memories of her uncle
C. the end of a love affair
D. a stranger in a small town

___ 2. Which of Uncle Marcos's adventures leads the family to interfere?
A. his serenade of Cousin Antonieta
B. his building an airplane
C. his flying an airplane
D. his fortune-telling business

___ 3. In Allende's story, why can Uncle Marcos be classified as a dynamic character?
A. He takes interesting trips.
B. People like him.
C. He changes after Cousin Antonieta rejects him.
D. He does not change at all.

___ 4. What was the author's purpose for including the story of Uncle Marcos's serenading Cousin Antonieta with a barrel organ and a parrot?
A. to create suspense
B. to explain how to play a barrel organ
C. to explain how to train a parrot
D. to reveal Uncle Marcos's character

___ 5. What is the "bird" in this sentence from "Uncle Marcos"?
Marcos spent two weeks assembling the contents according to an instruction manual written in English, which he was able to decipher thanks to his invincible imagination and a small dictionary. When the job was finished, it turned out to be a bird of prehistoric dimensions. . . .
A. a child's toy
B. a wooden eagle
C. a motorboat
D. an airplane

Unit 1 Resources: Fiction and Nonfiction
© Pearson Education, Inc. All rights reserved.
207

EL L1 L2 **Selection Test A,** pp. 186–188, 207–209

Also available for these selections:

L3 L2 **Open-Book Test,** pp. 183–185, 204–206

EL L3 L4 **Selection Test B,** pp. 189–191, 210–212

PHLit Online!
www.PHLitOnline.com

- complete narrated selection text
- a thematically related video with writing prompt
- an interactive graphic organizer
- highlighting feature
- access to all student print resources, adapted to individual student needs
- Spanish and English summaries
- adapted selection translations in Spanish

Online Resources: All print materials are also available online.

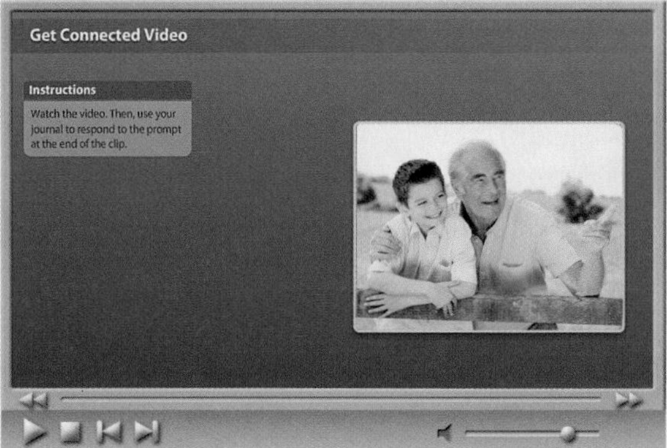

Get Connected! (thematic video with writing prompt)

Also available:

Background Video

All videos are available in Spanish.

Vocabulary Central (tools, activities, and songs for studying vocabulary)

Also available:

Writer's Journal (with graphics feature)

DIFFERENTIATE/PRETEACH

1 Leveled Texts

You may use either the selection "The Secret Life of Walter Mitty" or "Uncle Marcos" to meet the lesson standards. Skills instruction for both selections appears on p. 125. Choose one selection to teach (or choose to teach both). The Text Complexity Rubric at the bottom of this page will help you determine which of the two selections is more appropriate for your students. Use the Reader and Task Suggestions on the facing page to help all students read text of increasing complexity.

2 Introducing the CCS Standards

Introduce the standards on the student page. (Note that the lesson element with which each standard is addressed is identified in parentheses after the text of the standard.) Call out the standards that you will cover with the selections, explaining to students what each requires and how they will address it as they work through the selection you have chosen. Standards labeled "Spiral Review" are introduced in the Literary Analysis Workshop for this unit.

Before You Read

The Secret Life of Walter Mitty • Uncle Marcos

1 Leveled Texts

Build your skills and improve your comprehension of fiction with texts of increasing complexity.

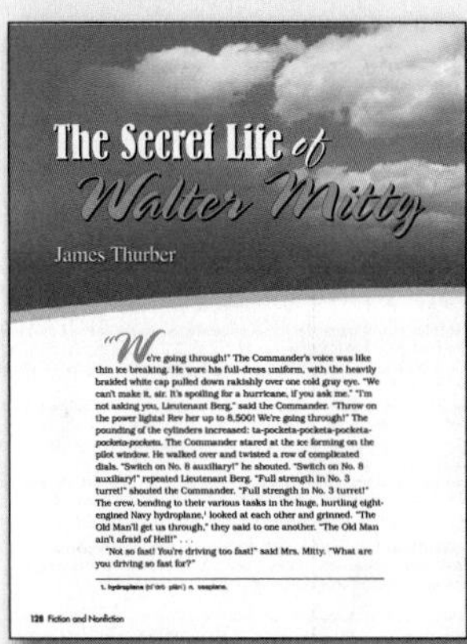

Read **"The Secret Life of Walter Mitty"** to learn how a man lives an imaginary life of adventure in his own mind.

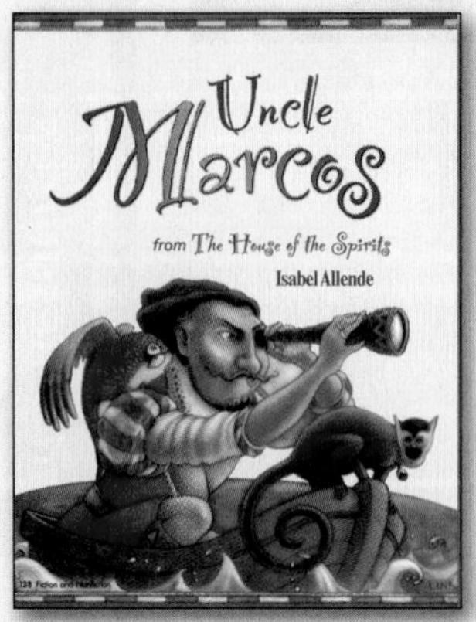

Read **"Uncle Marcos"** to learn about an eccentric uncle's fabulously memorable life.

2 Common Core State Standards

Meet these standards with either **"The Secret Life of Walter Mitty"** (p. 128) or **"Uncle Marcos"** (p. 138).

Reading Literature
3. Analyze how complex characters develop over the course of a text, interact with other characters, and advance the plot or develop the theme. *(Literary Analysis: Character)*

Spiral Review: RL.9-10.2

Writing
4. Produce clear and coherent writing in which the development, organization, and style are appropriate to task, purpose, and audience. *(Writing: Character Profile)*
6. Use technology, including the Internet, to produce, publish, and update individual or shared writing products, taking advantage of technology's capacity to link to other information and to display information flexibly and dynamically. *(Research and Technology: Learning Log)*

Language
1. Demonstrate command of the conventions of standard English grammar and usage when writing or speaking. *(Conventions: Pronouns)*
4.a. Use context as a clue to the meaning of a word or phrase. *(Vocabulary: Word Study)*
6. Acquire and use accurately general academic and domain-specific words and phrases, sufficient for reading and listening at the college and career readiness level; demonstrate independence in gathering vocabulary knowledge when considering a word or phrase important to comprehension or expression. *(Vocabulary: Word Study)*

124 Fiction and Nonfiction

Text Complexity Rubric: Leveled Texts

Text complexity is determined by both qualitative and quantitative measures. For this reason, the quantitative measure of a more complex selection may be lower than that of a more accessible selection.

		✓ The Secret Life of Walter Mitty	✓✓ Uncle Marcos
Qualitative Measures	**Context/ Knowledge Demands**	Alternate settings in a character's life 1 ② 3 4 5	Latin America, before the advent of the airplane 1 2 3 ④ 5
	Structure/Language Conventionality and Clarity	Use of nonsense and real words in unrelated contexts; interrupted narrative (dreams interrupt real events) 1 ② 3 4 5	Numerous long sentences with embedded clauses; challenging vocabulary 1 2 3 ④ 5
	Levels of Meaning/ Purpose/Concept Level	Accessible concept (desire to escape reality) 1 ② 3 4 5	Challenging concept (character sketch of an eccentric relative) 1 2 3 ④ 5
Quantitative Measures	**Text Length**	Word Count: 2,053	Word Count: 3,632
	Lexile	640L	1440L
Overall Complexity		✓ **More accessible**	✓✓ **More complex**

❸ Literary Analysis: Character

A **character** is a person or an animal who takes part in the action of a literary work. You can learn about a character through the character's words and actions, the author's narration, and what others say about the character.

- A **round character** is complex, showing many different qualities—revealing faults as well as virtues. In contrast, a **flat character** is one-dimensional, showing a single trait.
- A **dynamic character** develops, changes, and learns something during the course of a story—unlike a **static character,** who remains the same.

The main character of a story tends to be a round character and usually is a dynamic one. The main character's development and growth are often central to a story's plot and theme. As you read, consider the traits that make characters seem round or flat, dynamic or static.

PHLit Online!
www.PHLitOnline.com

Hear It!
- Selection summary audio
- Selection audio

See It!
- Get Connected video
- Background video
- More about the author
- Vocabulary flashcards

Do It!
- Interactive journals
- Interactive graphic organizers
- Self-test
- Internet activity
- Grammar tutorial
- Interactive vocabulary games

❹ Reading Skill: Author's Purpose

An **author's purpose** is his or her main reason for writing. In fiction, the specific purpose is often expressed in the story's theme, message, or insight. Pause periodically while reading and **reflect** on the story's details and events to determine the author's purpose for relating this particular story. Ask questions such as the following:

- *What significance might this event have?*
- *Why does the author include this detail?*

Based on your reflections, formulate ideas about what the author's purpose might be.

❺ Using the Strategy: Author's Purpose Map

Use a chart like the one shown to organize your thoughts.

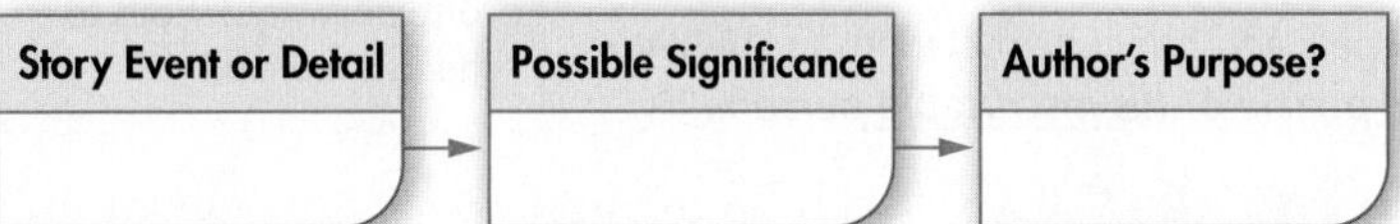

PRETEACH

❸ Literary Analysis

Character

1. Introduce the skill, using the instruction on the student page.
2. Tell students that they will practice categorizing characters as they read.

Think Aloud: Model the Skill

Model the skill of categorizing characters. Say to students:

As I read, I categorize characters by analyzing their actions and traits. For example, Dorothy in *The Wizard of Oz* is a round character because she shows both good and bad qualities, such as bravery and naiveté. She is a dynamic character because she learns to appreciate home. The Wicked Witch of the West is a flat, static character because she has a single trait—evil intentions—and does not change.

❹ Reading Skill

Author's Purpose

1. Introduce the skill, using the instruction on the student page.
2. Tell students that they will practice reflecting on a story's details and events to determine the author's purpose as they read.

❺ Using the Strategy

Give students a copy of either **Literary Analysis Graphic Organizer** A or B (*Graphic Organizer Transparencies,* pp. 26–28) to record their ideas about recognizing the author's purpose as they read. Use the examples in **Literary Analysis Graphic Organizer A,** which is partially filled in, to model the process of completing the organizer.

Ⓒ Text Complexity: Reader and Task Suggestions

✓ The Secret Life of Walter Mitty		✓✓ Uncle Marcos	
Preparing to Read the Text	**Leveled Tasks**	**Preparing to Read the Text**	**Leveled Tasks**
• Using the Background information on TE p. 127, discuss how people sometimes interrupt real-world activities to daydream. • Discuss with students why people sometimes want to escape everyday reality. • Guide students to use Multidraft Reading strategies (TE p. 127).	*Levels of Meaning* If students will have difficulty with the concept of the integration of dreams with reality, have them first read the story to get an overview of the plot. Then, have them write descriptions of each event. *Synthesizing* If students will not have difficulty with the concept of the integration of dreams with reality, have them note reasons why Mitty wants to escape reality. Discuss how those reasons reveal his character.	• Using the Background information on TE p. 137, discuss how magical realism can convey the magic of everyday life. • Discuss with students how eccentric people can open our eyes to new possibilities. • Guide students to use Multidraft Reading strategies (TE p. 137).	*Levels of Meaning* If students will have difficulty with ambiguous meaning, have them first read the story and note important plot events. Then, have them reread the story and note improbable events. *Synthesizing* If students will not have difficulty with ambiguous meaning, have them take notes as they read about how Clara and other characters respond to Uncle Marcos. Discuss their findings with the class.

PREACH

❶ Writing About the Big Question

1. Read the assignment with the class.
2. Ask students how often they day-dream. What do they daydream about? How does the imaginary world of their daydreams compare to their everyday life?
3. Have students complete the sentence starters. Review responses as a class. (**Possible responses:** Compared to our everyday life, the life of our imagination is often fanciful and unrealistic. Truth can change in our imagination because our minds can get carried away.)
4. Remind students that their answers will help them think about the Big Question, "Can truth change?"

While You Read

Tell students that as they read, they should look for details that show the importance of Mitty's imagination in his daily life.

❷ Vocabulary

1. Have students preview the selection vocabulary.
2. For each word, have students say the word aloud.
3. Then, use the word in a sentence that defines the word.
4. Finally, repeat your definitional sentence or a similar sentence with the word missing and have the class "fill in the blank" chorally. Here are some examples:

   If something terrible happened to you, you might be distraught. After my cat ran away I couldn't eat. I was so [students say "distraught"].

   Someone who is insolent is rude or disrespectful. After a second episode, I was sent to Study Hall because Mr. Brady said I was [students say "insolent"].

❸ Word Study

1. Introduce the skill, using the instruction in the box.
2. Define the following words by using "can or will" or "capable of being": affordable, maneuverable, breakable, readable.

Making Connections | The Secret Life of Walter Mitty

Can truth change?

❶ Writing About the Big Question

In "The Secret Life of Walter Mitty," Mitty lives two lives: the one dominated by his wife and the one of his imagination. Use these sentence starters to develop your ideas about the Big Question.

Compared to our everyday life, the life of our imagination is ________.
Truth can change in our imagination because ________.

While You Read Look for details in the text that show how important Mitty's imagination is in his daily life.

❷ Vocabulary

Read each word and its definition. Decide whether you know the word well, know it a little bit, or do not know it at all. After you read, see how your knowledge of each word has increased.

- **distraught** (di strôt′) *adj.* very troubled or confused (p. 130) ***She was distraught over losing her wallet.***
- **insolent** (in′ sə lənt) *adj.* boldly disrespectful (p. 130) ***Her insolent words offended the guests.*** *insolence n. insolently adv.*
- **insinuatingly** (in sin′ yo͞o āt′ iŋ lē) *adv.* suggesting indirectly (p. 131) ***My friend looked at me insinuatingly, as if she thought I had taken the money from her purse.*** *insinuate v. insinuation n.*
- **pandemonium** (pan′ də mō′ nē əm) *n.* any place or scene of wild disorder, noise, or confusion (p. 132) ***When the band left the stage, the crowd erupted into pandemonium.***
- **derisive** (di rī′ siv) *adj.* showing contempt or ridicule (p. 134) ***With a derisive laugh, the bully pushed the little boy off the swing.*** *derision n. deride v.*
- **inscrutable** (in skro͞ot′ ə bəl) *adj.* baffling; mysterious (p. 134) ***No one has ever solved the puzzle of his inscrutable personality.***

❸

Word Study

The **Latin suffix *-able*** means "can or will" or "capable of being."

Thurber closes the story by describing Mitty as **inscrutable** to the end. The word choice indicates that Mitty is able to remain mysterious to the last moment.

126 Fiction and Nonfiction

Vocabulary Development

Vocabulary Knowledge Rating

Create a **Vocabulary Knowledge Rating Chart** (*Professional Development Guidebook,* p. 33) for this selection. Include the selection vocabulary and the Big Question word that appears in the Writing About the Big Question sentence starters on this page. (The Big Question vocabulary is introduced on pp. 2–3.)

Give students a copy of the chart. Read the words aloud, and have students mark their rating in the Before Reading column. Urge them to be alert to these words as they read and discuss the selection.

Tally how many students think they know a word to gauge how much instruction to provide. As students read and discuss the selection, point out the words and their context.

Vocabulary Central, featuring tools, activities, and songs for studying vocabulary, is available at **www.PHLitOnline.com.**

Meet James Thurber

(1894–1961)

Author of The Secret Life of Walter Mitty

James Thurber was a rare writer who expressed his comic genius in both words and pictures. He wrote stories, plays, essays, and poems, and he was also a great cartoonist. Born in Ohio, he joined the staff of *The New Yorker* magazine in 1927. "The Secret Life of Walter Mitty" was published in that magazine in 1939, becoming an instant success.

Humor and Anxiety Many of Thurber's stories and sketches grew directly out of his own life. As he put it, "Humor is a kind of emotional chaos told about calmly and quietly in retrospect." Thurber's characters try to stand up to the surprises of the modern world. Whether they succeed or fail, they always strike readers as authentic and very funny.

4

BACKGROUND FOR THE STORY

Reality and Imagination

Psychologists say that a person's thoughts are often a series of seemingly unconnected reflections. An event in the real world can prompt unpredictable mental responses, such as memories, snippets of songs, or daydreams. In Thurber's story, random events cause Walter Mitty's thoughts to jump back and forth between his exciting "secret" life and his humdrum everyday existence.

Did You Know?

Thurber offered a Hollywood producer $10,000 not to make a movie about Walter Mitty. The movie was made anyway in 1947. A new version is in development.

Daily Bellringer

For each class during which you will teach this selection, have students complete one of the five Research activities for Week 5 in the ***Daily Bellringer Activities*** booklet.

4 Background

Reality and Imagination

Most scientists say that daydreams fill much the same function as dreams. Daydreams relate to what is bothering us or to what we want to be doing. In the past, scientists believed that daydreams were unnecessary and counterproductive because they draw our attention away from the matter at hand; however, most scientists today suggest that daydreams are signs of a healthy psychological state.

Multidraft Reading

This icon ● marks natural pauses in the selection. To assist struggling readers and to deepen reading for all, assign the text in "chunks," following the icons, and apply multidraft reading protocols. For each reading, have students set the purpose indicated:

- **First reading**—identifying key ideas and details and answering any Reading Checks.
- **Second reading**—analyzing craft and structure and responding to the side-column prompts.
- **Third reading**—integrating knowledge and ideas, connecting to other texts and the world, and answering the end-of-selection questions.

For more guidance, refer to the ***Classroom Strategies and Teaching Routines*** card on multidraft reading.

For more about the author, practice with the selection vocabulary, or more background, go online at **www.PHLitOnline.com.**

Differentiated Instruction Additional Instruction

EL Extended Support—English Learners
Have students complete the **Reading and Vocabulary Warm-ups, *Unit 1 Resources,*** pp. 174–177, before they read. Assign the prereading pages and the adapted selection in the ***Reader's Notebook: English Learner's Version.*** Then, have students listen to portions of the selection on the ***Hear It!* Audio CD.**

L1 L2 Extended Support—Struggling Readers
Have students complete the **Reading and Vocabulary Warm-ups, *Unit 1 Resources,*** pp. 174–177 before they read. Assign the prereading pages and the adapted selection in the ***Reader's Notebook: Adapted Version.*** Then, have students listen to portions of the selection on the ***Hear It!* Audio CD** (adapted text).

Extended Support—Reluctant Readers
To build motivation and engagement before assigning the selection, have students read "Secret Lives," a thematically related selection in ***Reality Central.*** Then, use the questions at the conclusion of the related selection to guide discussion.

TEACH

❶ Activating Prior Knowledge

Engage students in a discussion about the importance of dreams. Point out that our dreams often tell us about our wishes and hopes, as well as our deepest fears. Tell students that they will read about a famous dreamer named Walter Mitty. As they read, have them look for the differences between the dream and the reality of the character.

Whole-Class Activity

Walter Mitty's daydreams are full of action. Students may wish to act out some of the verbs they find as they read. Examples from this page, listed here in present participle form, include pounding, twisting, switching, bending, hurtling, grinning, and driving. Invite volunteers to demonstrate one or more of these actions.

❷ About the Selection

In "The Secret Life of Walter Mitty," James Thurber creates a vivid image of an ineffectual person who cannot cope with the world around him. Feeling powerless and picked-on by everyone—-from his wife to parking-lot attendants to anonymous passersby—Mitty retreats into a daydream world where he becomes dashing, powerful, and in control.

❶ ❷ The Secret Life of Walter Mitty

James Thurber

"We're going through!" The Commander's voice was like thin ice breaking. He wore his full-dress uniform, with the heavily braided white cap pulled down rakishly over one cold gray eye. "We can't make it, sir. It's spoiling for a hurricane, if you ask me." "I'm not asking you, Lieutenant Berg," said the Commander. "Throw on the power lights! Rev her up to 8,500! We're going through!" The pounding of the cylinders increased: ta-pocketa-pocketa-pocketa-*pocketa-pocketa*. The Commander stared at the ice forming on the pilot window. He walked over and twisted a row of complicated dials. "Switch on No. 8 auxiliary!" he shouted. "Switch on No. 8 auxiliary!" repeated Lieutenant Berg. "Full strength in No. 3 turret!" shouted the Commander. "Full strength in No. 3 turret!" The crew, bending to their various tasks in the huge, hurtling eight-engined Navy hydroplane,[1] looked at each other and grinned. "The Old Man'll get us through," they said to one another. "The Old Man ain't afraid of Hell!" . . .

"Not so fast! You're driving too fast!" said Mrs. Mitty. "What are you driving so fast for?"

1. **hydroplane** (hī′drō plān′) *n.* seaplane.

Vocabulary Development

© CCSS Language 6

Thematic Vocabulary: The Big Question

As students are discussing "The Secret Life of Walter Mitty," encourage them to use the thematic vocabulary presented in Introducing the Big Question, pp. 2–3. You might encourage them with sentence starters like these:

1. A *circumstance* that generates one of Walter's daydreams is . . .
2. By considering the events of Walter's daydreams, we can *speculate* that his life is . . .
3. By looking at the *context* of Walter's daydreams, it is clear that he wishes to be . . .
4. Throughout the story, Walter tries to *distort* reality by . . .

3 "Hmm?" said Walter Mitty. He looked at his wife, in the seat beside him, with shocked astonishment. She seemed grossly unfamiliar, like a strange woman who had yelled at him in a crowd. "You were up to fifty-five," she said. "You know I don't like to go more than forty. You were up to fifty-five." Walter Mitty drove on toward Waterbury in silence, the roaring of the SN202 through the worst storm in twenty years of Navy flying fading in the remote, intimate airways of his mind. "You're tensed up again," said Mrs. Mitty. "It's one of your days. I wish you'd let Dr. Renshaw look you over."

Walter Mitty stopped the car in front of the building where his wife went to have her hair done. "Remember to get those overshoes while I'm having my hair done," she said. "I don't need overshoes," said Mitty. She put her mirror back into her bag. "We've been all through that," she said, getting out of the car. "You're not a young man any longer." He raced the engine a little. "Why don't you wear your gloves? Have you lost your gloves?" Walter Mitty reached in a pocket and brought out the gloves. He put them on, but after she had turned and gone into the building and he had driven on to a red light, he took them off again. "Pick it up, brother!" snapped a cop as the light changed, and Mitty hastily pulled on his gloves and lurched ahead. He drove around the streets aimlessly for a time, and then he drove past the hospital on his way to the parking lot.

Reading Skill
Author's Purpose
Pause to reflect. What does the phrase "intimate airways of his mind" suggest about the author's purpose in writing this story?

4
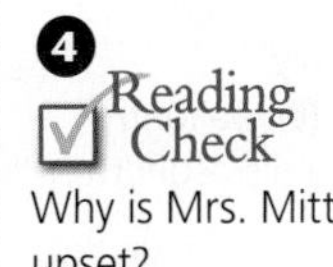

Why is Mrs. Mitty upset?

3 Reading Skill

Author's Purpose

1. Have students **describe** what is happening in the bracketed text.

   Answer: Mrs. Mitty's words pull Walter out of his daydream and back to reality, where he is driving a car.
2. Remind students that reflecting on details in the story can help them determine an author's purpose. Show students how to use **Reading Skill Graphic Organizer B** (***Graphic Organizer Transparencies,*** p. 28) to organize their thoughts.
3. **Ask** students to respond to the Reading Skill question: Pause to reflect. What does the phrase "intimate airways of his mind" suggest about the author's purpose in writing this story?

   Answer: The phrase suggests that the author's purpose is to reveal the differences between the real world and the unseen, imaginary landscape of Mitty's mind.

4 Reading Check

Answer: Mrs. Mitty is upset because she thinks Mitty is driving too fast.

PHLit Online!

This selection is available in interactive format in the **Enriched Online Student Edition**, at **www.PHLitOnline.com,** which includes a thematically related video with writing prompt and an interactive graphic organizer.

PROFESSIONAL DEVELOPMENT | **Doug Buehl**

Apply the Strategy

After reading the story, ask students to reread the sentences that contain the words *distraught, insolent,* and *inscrutable,* and to review the provided definitions. Then, pair students. Give each pair one of the words. Provide these instructions: For *distraught:* Identify conditions that could make someone *distraught;* list behaviors that imply someone is *distraught.* For *insolent:* Identify things a person might be *insolent* about; list how an *insolent* person might act. For *inscrutable:* Identify situations in which someone may be *inscrutable;* list how an *inscrutable* person might act.

Have pairs share their ideas with the class. Then, ask them for examples of how the words might connect—for example, I am *distraught* that my friend is *insolent.*
For more of Doug Buehl's strategies, see his Professional Development essay, pp. 2c–2d

5 Literary Analysis

Character

1. **Ask** students to explain the difference between a round and a flat character.

   Answer: A round character is complex and has many different qualities. A flat character is one-dimensional, usually identified to the reader through a single characteristic or trait.

2. Have students read the bracketed text and then **identify** where each paragraph takes place.

   Answer: The first paragraph takes place in Mitty's fantasy life. The second paragraph takes place in Mitty's real life.

3. **Ask** the Literary Analysis question: How does this shift in scenes show that Walter Mitty is a multidimensional character?

   Answer: The shift reveals that Mitty is able to shift back and forth between his real-world personality and his daydream characters. This shows that he is a round character because there is more than one aspect to his personality.

4. Remind students that characters can also be dynamic or static. **Ask** students whether Mitty shows signs of being dynamic or static. Have them give reasons for their opinions.

   Possible response: So far, Mitty is a static character. Although he switches from daydreaming to reality, there is no evidence that his character is changing or growing in any way.

Vocabulary
distraught (di strôt′) *adj.* very troubled or confused

. . . "It's the millionaire banker, Wellington McMillan," said the pretty nurse. "Yes?" said Walter Mitty, removing his gloves slowly. "Who has the case?" "Dr. Renshaw and Dr. Benbow, but there are two specialists here, Dr. Remington from New York and Mr. Pritchard-Mitford from London. He flew over." A door opened down a long, cool corridor and Dr. Renshaw came out. He looked distraught and haggard. "Hello, Mitty," he said. "We're having the devil's own time with McMillan, the millionaire banker and close personal friend of Roosevelt. Obstreosis of the ductal tract.[2] Tertiary. Wish you'd take a look at him." "Glad to," said Mitty.

Someone handed him a fountain pen.

In the operating room there were whispered introductions: "Dr. Remington, Dr. Mitty. Mr. Pritchard-Mitford, Dr. Mitty." "I've read your book on streptothricosis," said Pritchard-Mitford, shaking hands. "A brilliant performance, sir." "Thank you," said Walter Mitty. "Didn't know you were in the States, Mitty," grumbled Remington. "Coals to Newcastle,[3] bringing Mitford and me up here for tertiary." "You are very kind," said Mitty. A huge, complicated machine, connected to the operating table, with many tubes and wires, began at this moment to go pocketa-pocketa-pocketa. "The new anesthetizer is giving way!" shouted an intern. "There is no one in the East who knows how to fix it!" "Quiet, man!" said Mitty, in a low, cool voice. He sprang to the machine, which was now going pocketa-pocketa-queep-pocketa-queep. He began fingering delicately a row of glistening dials. "Give me a fountain pen!" he snapped. Someone handed him a fountain pen. He pulled a faulty piston out of the machine and inserted the pen in its place. "That 5
will hold for ten minutes," he said. "Get on with the operation." A nurse hurried over and whispered to Renshaw, and Mitty saw the man turn pale. "Coreopsis has set in," said Renshaw nervously. "If you would take over, Mitty?" Mitty looked at him and at the craven figure of Benbow, who drank, and at the grave, uncertain faces of the two great specialists. "If you wish," he said. They slipped a white gown on him; he adjusted a mask and drew on thin gloves; nurses handed him shining . . .

Literary Analysis
Character How does this shift in scenes show that Walter Mitty is a multidimensional character?

"Back it up, Mac! Look out for that Buick!" Walter Mitty jammed on the brakes. "Wrong lane, Mac," said the parking-lot attendant, looking at Mitty closely. "Gee. Yeh," muttered Mitty. He began cautiously to back out of the lane marked "Exit Only." "Leave her sit there," said the attendant. "I'll put her away." Mitty got out of the car. "Hey, better leave the key." "Oh," said Mitty, handing the man the ignition key. The attendant vaulted into the car, backed it up with insolent skill, and put it where it belonged.

Vocabulary
insolent (in′ sə lənt) *adj.* boldly disrespectful

2. **obstreosis of the ductal tract** Thurber has invented this and other medical terms.
3. **coals to Newcastle** The proverb "bringing coals to Newcastle" means bringing things to a place unnecessarily—Newcastle, England, was a coal center and so did not need coal brought to it.

Think Aloud

Author's Purpose

Draw students' attention to the last sentence on this page: "The attendant vaulted . . . where it belonged." Use the following "think aloud" to model the process of reflecting on story details to determine the author's purpose:

When I read this sentence, I pause to reflect about why the author decided to use the word *insolent* to describe the parking-lot attendant's actions. The phrase "insolent skill" seems to emphasize the opposite quality in Mitty: his ineptitude and distraction as he drives in the "Exit Only" lane. *Insolent* also illustrates the attendant's disrespect toward the bungling Mitty.

Now I'll think about how this detail helps reveal the author's purpose. I think Thurber is trying to show how the disrespect and negativity that Mitty receives from people in the real world only encourage him to escape to his daydreams. Thurber may be suggesting that the world is a cruel place that drives eccentric people to become even more eccentric.

They're so cocky, thought Walter Mitty, walking along Main Street; they think they know everything. Once he had tried to take his chains off, outside New Milford, and he had got them wound around the axles. A man had had to come out in a wrecking car and unwind them, a young, grinning garageman. Since then Mrs. Mitty always made him drive to a garage to have the chains taken off. The next time, he thought, I'll wear my right arm in a sling; they won't grin at me then. I'll have my right arm in a sling and they'll see I couldn't possibly take the chains off myself. He kicked at the slush on the sidewalk. "Overshoes," he said to himself, and he began looking for a shoe store.

When he came out into the street again, with the overshoes in a box under his arm, Walter Mitty began to wonder what the other thing was his wife had told him to get. She had told him, twice, before they set out from their house for Waterbury. In a way he hated these weekly trips to town—he was always getting something wrong. Kleenex, he thought, Squibb's, razor blades? No. Toothpaste, toothbrush, bicarbonate, carborundum, initiative and referendum?[4] He gave it up. But she would remember it. "Where's the what's-its-name?" she would ask. "Don't tell me you forgot the what's-its-name." A newsboy went by shouting something about the Waterbury trial.

. . . "Perhaps this will refresh your memory." The District Attorney suddenly thrust a heavy automatic at the quiet figure on the witness stand. "Have you ever seen this before?" Walter Mitty took the gun and examined it expertly. "This is my Webley-Vickers 50.80," he said calmly. An excited buzz ran around the courtroom. The Judge rapped for order. "You are a crack shot with any sort of firearms, I believe?" said the District Attorney, insinuatingly. "Objection!" shouted Mitty's attorney. "We have shown that the defendant

4. **carborundum** (kär´ bə run´ dəm), **initiative** (i ni´ shē ə tiv) **and referendum** (ref´ ə ren´ dəm) Thurber is purposely making a nonsense list; *carborundum* is a hard substance used for scraping, *initiative* is a process by which citizens may introduce ideas for laws, and *referendum* is a process by which citizens may vote on laws.

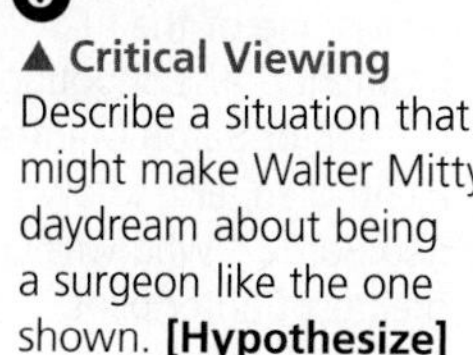

6 ▲ **Critical Viewing**
Describe a situation that might make Walter Mitty daydream about being a surgeon like the one shown. **[Hypothesize]**

Vocabulary
insinuatingly
(in sin´ yo͞o āt´ iŋ lē)
adv. suggesting indirectly

7 

Reading Check
Why does Mitty say that next time he will wear his arm in a sling?

6 Critical Viewing

Possible response: Walter Mitty's daydreams reflect a way to overcome any recent experience that embarrasses or humiliates him. A daydream about being a successful surgeon might result after Mitty has failed at something or has been made to feel like a failure by others.

7 Reading Check

Answer: Mitty thinks that if he has his arm in a sling, the garageman will not expect him to be able to take off the car chains without help.

Differentiated Instruction for Universal Access

EL Pronunciation for English Learners

Recite the following for students and have them repeat after you: *take, tape, taste.* Have each student draw a visual depiction of each word. Then pair English learners with fluent speakers and have students share their work with their partner. If students note discrepancies in their drawings, guide fluent speakers to model pronunciation of each word and point to the drawing that correctly depicts each word.

Strategy for Advanced Readers

Ask students to make charts of all the characters that Mitty assumes in his daydreams. Have them describe the traits that each character exhibits. Then have them discuss as a group what all of the characters have in common. Guide their discussion with this question: What void in Mitty's real personality do these fictitious characters fill?

8 Literature in Context

Social Studies Connection With the introduction of airplanes for military purposes during World War I, fighter pilots quickly became international heroes. Germany's Baron von Richthofen—The Red Baron—was considered the best of them. He shot down eighty Allied planes before his death on April 21, 1918. An Australian anti-aircraft gun shot down Richthofen while he was chasing an inexperienced RAF pilot. The RAF buried Richthofen with full military honors.

In World War II, Germany sought to invade Great Britain, but they had to gain control of the air first. The RAF, although initially overmatched, put up a staunch defense and eventually took command of the air. They won the Battle of Britain, saving their country from invasion and ultimately giving the Allies the advantage to win World War II.

Connect to the Literature The flying aces of the RAF were among the wars' most glamorous and popular heroes. **Ask** the Connect to the Literature question: What elements of life in the RAF would Mitty enjoy? **Answer:** As a member of the RAF, Mitty would enjoy having the admiration of others, and he would relish the thrills and dangers of that lifestyle.

9 Connecting to the Big Question

1. Have a volunteer read aloud the bracketed text. **Ask:** Which sentence shows that Mitty returns to his daydream temporarily? **Answer:** "The greatest pistol shot in the world thought a moment."
2. **Ask:** Why do you think Mitty returns to his daydream at this moment? **Possible response:** He is gathering confidence as he interacts with the clerk and tries to remember the correct biscuit brand.
3. **Ask:** What does Mitty's quick shift into his fantasy world suggest about the role of his imagination in his daily life? **Answer:** Mitty relies on his imagination both to escape real-world situations and to bolster his confidence as he tries to interact with people effectively.

8 **LITERATURE IN CONTEXT**

Social Studies Connection

The Royal Air Force

Although he is American, Mitty fantasizes about being a brave and handsome English officer, a bomber pilot in the Royal Air Force (RAF). The RAF was officially formed in 1918 and distinguished itself in numerous air battles during World War I. RAF pilots would earn even greater distinction in the Battle of Britain during World War II. The reference to "Von Richtman's circus" recalls one of the RAF's finest moments—the shooting down in 1918 of Baron Manfred von Richthofen, also known as "The Red Baron," who was Germany's greatest fighter pilot.

Connect to the Literature

What elements of life in the RAF would Mitty enjoy?

could not have fired the shot. We have shown that he wore his right arm in a sling on the night of the fourteenth of July." Walter Mitty raised his hand briefly and the bickering attorneys were stilled. "With any known make of gun," he said evenly, "I could have killed Gregory Fitzhurst at three hundred *feet with my left hand.*" **Pandemonium** broke loose in the courtroom. A woman's scream rose above the bedlam and suddenly a lovely, dark-haired girl was in Walter Mitty's arms. The District Attorney struck at her savagely. Without rising from his chair, Mitty let the man have it on the point of the chin. "You miserable cur!" . . .

"Puppy biscuit," said Walter Mitty. He stopped walking and the buildings of Waterbury rose up out of the misty courtroom and surrounded him again. A woman who was passing laughed. "He said 'Puppy biscuit,'" she said to her companion. "That man said 'Puppy biscuit' to himself." Walter Mitty hurried on. He went into an A. & P., not the first one he came to but a smaller one farther up the street. "I want some biscuit for small, young dogs," he said to the clerk. "Any special brand, sir?" The greatest pistol shot in the world thought a moment. "It says 'Puppies Bark for It' on the box," said Walter Mitty. 9

His wife would be through at the hairdresser's in fifteen minutes, Mitty saw in looking at his watch, unless they had trouble drying it; sometimes they had trouble drying it. She didn't like to get to the hotel first;

Vocabulary
pandemonium
(pan′ də mō′ nē əm)
n. any place or scene of wild disorder, noise, or confusion

Vocabulary Development

Vocabulary Knowledge Rating

When students have completed reading and discussing "The Secret Life of Walter Mitty," have them take out their **Vocabulary Knowledge Rating Chart** for this selection. Read the words aloud once more and have students rate their knowledge of the words again in the After Reading column. Clarify any words that are still problematic. Have students write their own definition and example or sentence in the appropriate column. Then have students complete the Vocabulary Practice activities at the end of the selection. Encourage students to use the words in further discussion and written work about this selection. Remind them that they will be accountable for these words on the **Selection Test,** ***Unit 1 Resources,*** pp. 186–188 or 189–191.

she would want him to be there waiting for her as usual. He found a big leather chair in the lobby, facing a window, and he put the overshoes and the puppy biscuit on the floor beside it. He picked up an old copy of *Liberty* and sank down into the chair. "Can Germany Conquer the World Through the Air?" Walter Mitty looked at the pictures of bombing planes and of ruined streets.

. . . "The cannonading has got the wind up in young Raleigh,[5] sir," said the sergeant. Captain Mitty looked up at him through tousled hair. "Get him to bed," he said wearily. "With the others. I'll fly alone." "But you can't, sir," said the sergeant anxiously. "It takes two men to handle that bomber and the Archies[6] are pounding hell out of the air. Von Richtman's circus[7] is between here and Saulier." "Somebody's got to get that ammunition dump," said Mitty. "I'm going over. Spot of brandy?" He poured a drink for the sergeant and one for himself. War thundered and whined around the dugout and battered at the door. There was a rending of wood and splinters flew through the room. "A bit of a near thing," said Captain Mitty carelessly. "The box barrage is closing in," said the sergeant. "We only live once, Sergeant," said Mitty, with his faint, fleeting smile. "Or do we?" He poured another brandy and tossed it off. "I never see a man could hold his brandy like you, sir," said the sergeant. "Begging your pardon, sir." Captain Mitty stood up and strapped on his huge Webley-Vickers automatic. "It's forty kilometers through hell, sir," said the sergeant. Mitty finished one last brandy. "After all," he said softly, "what isn't?" The pounding of the cannon increased; there was the rat-tat-tatting of machine guns, and from somewhere came the menacing pocketa-pocketa-pocketa of the new flame-throwers. Walter Mitty walked to the door of the dugout humming "Auprés de Ma Blonde."[8] He turned and waved to the sergeant. "Cheerio!" he said. . . .

Something struck his shoulder. "I've been looking all over this hotel for you," said Mrs. Mitty. "Why do you have to hide in this old chair? How did you expect me to find
11 you?" "Things close in," said Walter Mitty vaguely. "What?" Mrs. Mitty said. "Did you get the what's-its-name? The puppy biscuit? What's in that box?" "Overshoes," said Mitty. "Couldn't you have put them on in the store?"

5. **has got the wind up in young Raleigh** has made young Raleigh nervous.
6. **Archies** slang term for antiaircraft guns.
7. **Von Richtman's circus** a fictional German airplane squadron.
8. **"Auprès de Ma Blonde"** (ō prā′ də mä blôn′ də) "Next to My Blonde," a popular French song.

Spiral Review
Theme What insight into daily life is suggested by the contrast between Mitty's daydreams and his reality?

"We only live once, Sergeant," said Mitty, with his faint, fleeting smile.

10 Reading Check
What triggers Mitty's daydream about being a military Captain?

Spiral Review

Theme

1. Remind students that they studied the concept of theme in the Unit 1 Literary Analysis Workshop (pp. 4–21).
2. **Ask** the Spiral Review question: What insight into daily life is suggested by the contrast between Mitty's daydreams and his reality?

   Possible response: The contrast between Mitty's successful, powerful, dynamic fantasy life and his unfulfilling, ineffective, bland real life suggests the theme that dreams offer people an escape from the mundane and, sometimes, disappointing reality of daily life.

10 Reading Check

Answer: Mitty picks up a copy of *Liberty* magazine and reads an article called "Can Germany Conquer the World Through the Air?" This triggers Mitty to launch into a reverie about being a daring military captain.

Concept Connector

Writing About the Big Question

Have students compare their responses to the sentence starters they completed before reading the story with their ideas afterwards. Ask them to explain whether their thoughts have changed.

Reading Skill Graphic Organizer

Have students review the graphic organizers they completed to determine the author's purpose while reading. Then show them **Reading Skill Graphic Organizer A** (*Graphic Organizers Transparencies,* p. 26) as an example. Have students share the graphic organizers they did and the details they identified that support their conclusions about the author's purpose.

⓫ Literary Analysis

Character

Ask students the Literary Analysis question.

Possible response: His response that "Things close in" reveals emotions deeply affected by his dull, oppressive life. "Does it ever occur to you . . . ?" reveals a hidden inner life and shows his rebellious side. These qualities make him a round character.

ASSESS

Answers

Critical Thinking

Before students respond, you may wish to have them write a brief objective summary of the selection. As they answer the questions below, remind them to support their answers with evidence from the text.

1. (a) His wife tells him that he is driving too fast. (b) In his daydream, Mitty is a bold leader; in real life, he is meek.
2. (a) Mitty drops Mrs. Mitty at the hairdresser, buys overshoes, picks up dog food, and waits for his wife. (b) Mitty is landing a plane, doing surgery, testifying in court, fighting a war, and facing a firing squad. (c) The tasks of his daily life are boring and dull. The tasks of his fantasy life are exciting.
3. (a) Mitty's low self-esteem and his weariness at being patronized by his wife trigger his final daydream. (b) Mitty has stood up to his wife, and he may be anticipating what will happen to him when they get home.
4. (a) **Possible response:** His daydreams help him survive a humdrum life. For example, his daydreams give him confidence to interact effectively with the store clerk, entertain him while waiting for Mrs. Mitty, and help him stand up to Mrs. Mitty. (b) Students should compare and contrast their responses.
5. **Possible response:** He uses his daydreams to replace his humdrum everyday life with exciting, heroic truths of his "characters'" lives. The excitement of his daydreams then creeps into his real-life interactions and goals.

Vocabulary
derisive (di rī′siv) *adj.* showing contempt or ridicule

Literary Analysis
Character
How do Walter Mitty's responses in this paragraph indicate that he is a complex character? ⓫

Vocabulary
inscrutable (in skro͞ot′ ə bəl) *adj.* baffling; mysterious

"I was thinking," said Walter Mitty. "Does it ever occur to you that I am sometimes thinking?" She looked at him. "I'm going to take your temperature when I get you home," she said.

They went out through the revolving doors that made a faintly **derisive** whistling sound when you pushed them. It was two blocks to the parking lot. At the drugstore on the corner she said, "Wait here for me. I forgot something. I won't be a minute." She was more than a minute. Walter Mitty lighted a cigarette. It began to rain, rain with sleet in it. He stood up against the wall of the drugstore, smoking. . . . He put his shoulders back and his heels together. "To hell with the handkerchief," said Walter Mitty scornfully. He took one last drag on his cigarette and snapped it away. Then, with that faint, fleeting smile playing about his lips, he faced the firing squad; erect and motionless, proud and disdainful, Walter Mitty the Undefeated, **inscrutable** to the last.

Critical Thinking

Cite textual evidence to support your responses.

1. **Key Ideas and Details (a)** What distraction jars Mitty out of his first daydream? **(b) Compare and Contrast:** Explain how Mitty's behavior in this daydream differs from his behavior in real life.
2. **Key Ideas and Details (a)** In the "real world," what tasks are Mitty and his wife carrying out? **(b) Infer:** What deeds is Mitty attempting to accomplish in his fantasy life? **(c) Compare and Contrast:** How do the tasks of his daily life compare to those of his fantasy life?
3. **Key Ideas and Details (a) Infer:** Which aspects of Mitty's personality trigger his final daydream? **(b) Draw Conclusions:** In what ways is this daydream a comment on his fate in real life?
4. **Key Ideas and Details (a) Evaluate:** Do Mitty's daydreams help him in any way or do they hurt him? Identify three details from the story that support your evaluation. **(b) Discuss:** Share your responses with a small group and discuss the differences and similarities among them.
5. **Integration of Knowledge and Ideas** Does Walter Mitty rely on daydreams to change the truth of his everyday life? *[Connect to the Big Question: Can truth change?]*

Assessment Resources

Unit 1 Resources

L1 L2 EL **Selection Test A,** pp. 186–188. Administer Test A to less advanced readers.

L3 L4 EL **Selection Test B,** pp. 189–191. Administer Test B to on-level and more advanced students.

L3 L4 **Open-Book Test,** pp. 183–185. As an alternative, give the Open-Book Test.

All **Customizable Test Bank**

All **Self-tests**
Students may prepare for the **Selection Test** by taking the **Self-test** online.

All assessment resources are available at **www.PHLitOnline.com.**

After You Read

The Secret Life of Walter Mitty

Literary Analysis: Character

1. **Key Ideas and Details** Mitty wants to be like the heroes in his daydreams. **(a)** Using a chart like the one shown, identify one detail from each of Mitty's daydreams and the quality that each detail reveals.

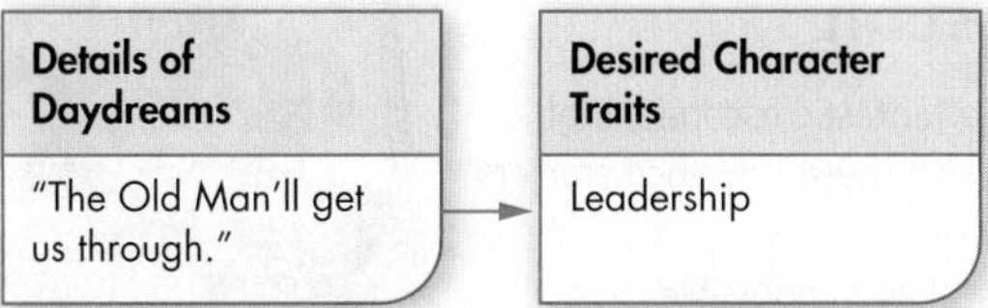

(b) Briefly describe the **character** of the man Mitty wants to be.

2. **Craft and Structure** Review the characters of Walter and Mrs. Mitty. **(a)** Determine whether each character is **round** or **flat.** Explain your responses. **(b)** Determine whether each character is **static** or **dynamic.** Explain.

Reading Skill: Author's Purpose

3. **(a)** What specific **purpose** might James Thurber have had for creating the character of Walter Mitty? **(b)** Identify three details from the story that support your responses, and explain how **reflecting** on them helped you determine Thurber's purpose.

Vocabulary

Acquisition and Use Review the vocabulary list for "The Secret Life of Walter Mitty" on page 126. Then, decide whether each of the following statements is true or false. Explain your answers.

1. Someone who is *distraught* is likely to behave in a calm manner.
2. Coaches encourage their players to be *insolent*.
3. *Inscrutable* handwriting is difficult to interpret.
4. If you speak *insinuatingly*, you say exactly what you mean.
5. A *derisive* comment shows great kindness.
6. *Pandemonium* might result if you gave unlimited candy to kindergarten students.

Word Study Use the context of sentences and what you know about the **Latin suffix *-able*** to explain your answer to each question.

1. Should you give up when facing an *achievable* goal?
2. If two bicycles are *comparable*, are they much alike?

Word Study

The **Latin suffix *-able*** means "can or will" or "capable of being."

Apply It Explain how the suffix contributes to the meanings of these words. Consult a dictionary if necessary.

unpalatable
interminable
portable

EXTEND/ASSESS

Answers

Literary Analysis

1. (a) **Details of Daydreams:** "Give me a fountain pen"; Mitty let the man have it. . . . "We only live once, Sergeant." He faced the firing squad. **Desired Character Traits:** resourcefulness; gallantry; fearlessness; heroism.
   For other sample answers, see ***Graphic Organizer Transparencies,*** **Literary Analysis Graphic Organizer A,** p. 29, and the **Additional Answers** section.
   (b) **Possible response:** Mitty wants to be a brilliant and heroic leader—a man who knows what to do and has the courage to do it.
2. (a) Mitty is a round character. He is capable of seeing himself in different roles, with different skills, responding to challenges. Mrs. Mitty is a flat character. She is revealed only as a controlling wife. (b) Both characters are static. Neither changes or learns anything in the story.

Reading Skill

3. (a) **Possible response:** Thurber's purpose might have been to show the positive, self-affirming effects of imagination. (b) **Possible response:** When his wife makes him wear gloves, Mitty dreams of saving a life. When he does not park the car well, he dreams of being a star witness. When he speaks up to his wife, he imagines he is before a firing squad. Reflecting on these details showed me that all of Mitty's daydreams are positive and self-affirming. They help him cope with a mundane life and a nagging wife, and they give him confidence.

Vocabulary

Acquisition and Use

Sample answers:

1. False. Someone who is *distraught* is troubled or confused, not calm.
2. False. A coach wants players to be obedient and respectful, not rude or disrespectful
3. True. *Inscrutable* handwriting would be difficult to read.
4. False. *Insinuatingly* means to suggest something indirectly, not directly.

Answers Continued:

5. False. A *derisive* comment is something said to ridicule another person.
6. True. *Pandemonium,* or wild disorder, might happen if five-year-olds had too much candy.

Word Study: Apply It

Sample answers: When something is *unpalatable*, you are not capable of standing its taste. When something is *interminable,* you are not capable of ending it. When something is *portable,* it is capable of being moved.

Word Study

Sample answers:

1. No. The suffix *-able* means "can or will," and *achievable* means "can be achieved."
2. Yes. The suffix *-able* means "can or will," and *comparable* means "can be compared" or "similar." Two such bicycles are very much alike.

PRETEACH

*Skills instruction for the **Reading Skill** and **Literary Analysis** concept appears on p. 125.*

1 Writing About the Big Question

1. Review the assignment with the class.
2. Ask students to consider the pros and cons of being imaginative or practical. Ask them which they would rather be: overly practical or overly imaginative. Why?
3. Have students complete the sentence starters. Review responses as a class. (**Possible response:** A person who believes strongly in impractical and impossible things may become disappointed in reality. Manipulating the truth can be dangerous because it could harm others).
4. Remind students that their answers will help them think about the Big Question, "Can truth change?"

While You Read

Tell students while they read to look for details showing how Uncle Marcos created his own realities.

2 Vocabulary

1. Have students preview the selection vocabulary.
2. For each word, have students say the word aloud.
3. Then, use the word in a sentence that defines the word.
4. Repeat your definitional sentence or a similar sentence with the word missing, and have the class "fill in the blank" chorally. Here are some examples:

   Pallid means pale. After a week in the hospital, his face was [students say "pallid"].

   Disconsolately means unhappily. After losing the championship game, the team walked home [students say "disconsolately"].

3 Word Study

1. Introduce the skill, using the instruction in the box.
2. Choose a word ending in *-ive.* Define the word using "of, belonging to, or quality of." Then based on your definition, have students identify the word.

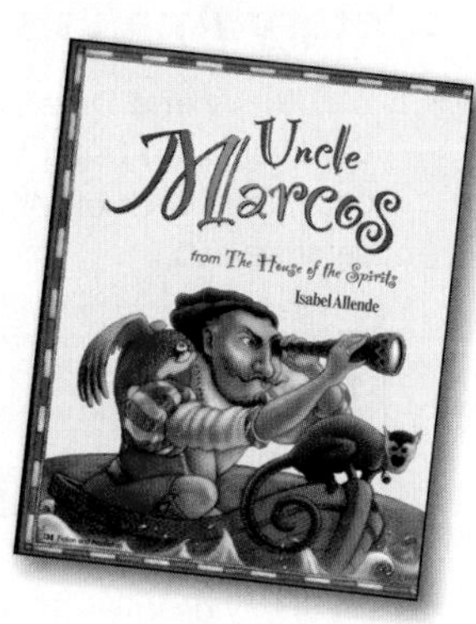

Uncle Marcos
from The House of the Spirits
Isabel Allende

1 Writing About the Big Question

In "Uncle Marcos," the narrator describes the fantastic escapades of an uncle who is not satisfied with the ordinary. Use these sentence starters to develop your ideas about the Big Question.

A person who **believes** strongly in impractical and impossible things may ____________.

Manipulating the **truth** can be __________ because __________ .

While You Read Look for details that show how Uncle Marcos created his own realities.

2 Vocabulary

Read each word and its definition. Decide whether you know the word well, know it a little bit, or do not know it at all. After you read, see how your knowledge of each word has increased.

- **pallid** (pal′ id) *adj.* pale (p. 139) ***The flu gave him a weak and pallid appearance.*** *pallidness n. pallidly adv. pallor n.*
- **impassive** (im pas′ iv) *adj.* showing no emotion (p. 141) ***She wanted to cry, but her face remained impassive as she watched her daughter leave for college.*** *passive adj.*
- **conspicuous** (kən spik′ yo͞o əs) *adj.* attracting attention by being unexpected, unusual or outstanding (p. 141) ***Renee felt conspicuous in her red coat and hat.*** *inconspicuous adj.*
- **disconsolately** (dis kän′ sə lit lē) *adv.* very unhappily (p. 144) ***He gazed disconsolately as his friends drove to the game without him.*** *disconsolate adj. consolation n. console v.*
- **pertinent** (pʉrt′ ′n ənt) *adj.* relevant; to the point (p. 146) ***Your outrageous comments are not at all pertinent to our discussion.*** *pertinence n. impertinent adj.*
- **unrequited** (un ri kwīt′ id) *adj.* not returned or repaid (p. 146) ***Romance novels sometimes describe the sadness of unrequited love.***

3 Word Study

The **Latin suffix *-ive*** means "of, belonging to, or quality of."

In this story, Uncle Marcos cannot believe that any woman could remain **impassive** when listening to a barrel organ. He thinks the organ must surely evoke the quality of passion.

Vocabulary Development

Vocabulary Knowledge Rating

Create a **Vocabulary Knowledge Rating Chart** (***Professional Development Guidebook,*** p. 33) for this selection. Include the selection vocabulary and the forms of the Big Question words that appear in the Writing About the Big Question sentence starters on this page. (The Big Question vocabulary is introduced on pp. 2–3.)

Give students a copy of the chart. Read the words aloud, and have students mark their rating in the Before Reading column. Urge them to be alert to these words as they read and discuss the selection.

Tally how many students think they know a word to gauge how much instruction to provide. As students read and discuss the selection, point out the words and their context.

Vocabulary Central, featuring tools, activities, and songs for studying vocabulary, is available at **www.PHLitOnline.com.**

Meet Isabel Allende

(b. 1942)

Author of Uncle Marcos

4

The daughter of diplomats, Isabel Allende grew up in the South American country of Chile. Her uncle was the Chilean president Salvador Allende. When his government was overthrown in 1973, Allende fled to Venezuela. She lived there in exile until 1988, when she moved to California.

Family and Fiction "Uncle Marcos" is excerpted from Allende's first novel, *The House of the Spirits*, which was inspired by her own remarkable family. Allende's family stories, however, are usually told with large helpings of imagination. She delights in blending the real and the imaginary. Allende once summed up her profession by quoting her granddaughter. Asked what it means to have a great imagination, the child replied, "You can remember what never happened."

BACKGROUND FOR THE STORY

Magical Realism

Imagine a world in which people float in the air and rain falls continuously for years. Such fantastic details fill stories and novels by a group of writers, including Isabel Allende, who are called magical realists. Works of magical realism blend fantastic details with realistic ones to stretch the boundaries of readers' imaginations.

Did You Know?

Allende's first novel, *The House of the Spirits*, began as a letter to her 100-year-old grandfather.

Daily Bellringer

For each class during which you will teach this selection, have students complete one of the five Research activities for Week 5 in the *Daily Bellringer Activities* booklet.

4 Background

Magical Realism

The name "magical realism" shows the contrast on which this literary style is based—it highlights and reveals magical occurrences in everyday life. Magic realism is a style most readers associate with modern and contemporary Latin American writers, but it is an international style. Magic realists include Salman Rushdie, Milan Kundera, and a number of other European and Eastern writers.

Multidraft Reading

This icon ● marks natural pauses in the selection. To assist struggling readers and to deepen reading for all, assign the text in "chunks," following the icons, and apply multidraft reading protocols. For each reading, have students set the purpose indicated:

- **First reading**—identifying key ideas and details and answering any Reading Checks.
- **Second reading**—analyzing craft and structure and responding to the side-column prompts.
- **Third reading**—integrating knowledge and ideas, connecting to other texts and the world, and answering the end-of-selection questions.

For more guidance, refer to the *Classroom Strategies and Teaching Routines* card on multidraft reading.

PHLit Online!

For more about the author, practice with the selection vocabulary, or more background, go online at **www.PHLitOnline.com.**

Differentiated Instruction Additional Instruction

EL Extended Support—English Learners
Have students complete the **Reading and Vocabulary Warm-ups,** ***Unit 1 Resources,*** pp. 192–195, before they read. Assign the prereading pages for the selection in the ***Reader's Notebook: English Learner's Version.***

L1 L2 Extended Support—Struggling Readers
Have students complete the **Reading and Vocabulary Warm-ups,** ***Unit 1 Resources,*** pp. 192–195, before they read. Assign the prereading pages for the selection in the ***Reader's Notebook: Adapted Version.***

Extended Support—Reluctant Readers
To build motivation and engagement before assigning the selection, have students read "Telling Tales," a thematically related selection in ***Reality Central.*** Then, use the questions at the conclusion of the related selection to guide discussion.

❶ Activating Prior Knowledge

Have students create a detailed character sketch based on the following rough description of the central character from "Uncle Marcos": an eccentric inventor and world adventurer whose relatives find him peculiar and at times embarrassing. Have students read the story to see whether the character they've come up with is as interesting as the one Isabel Allende developed.

Concept Connector →

Students will follow up on this activity after completing "Uncle Marcos."

Individual Activity

As students read "Uncle Marcos," have them consider the point of view of Clara, the narrator. Ask students to think about how the story would be different if it were told from Uncle Marcos's point of view. Challenge students to write brief summaries of the story from Uncle Marcos's point of view.

❷ About the Selection

In this excerpt from *The House of the Spirits*, Clara del Valle recalls her eccentric Uncle Marcos. Laughed at by some, but loved by many, Uncle Marcos impresses his community with his daring adventures in courtship, flight, rebirth, and clairvoyance. Through Clara's eyes, Uncle Marcos earns the renown he had gained only fitfully in his lifetime. The story conveys an important message about how individuals can be misjudged or underappreciated by some people but beloved by others.

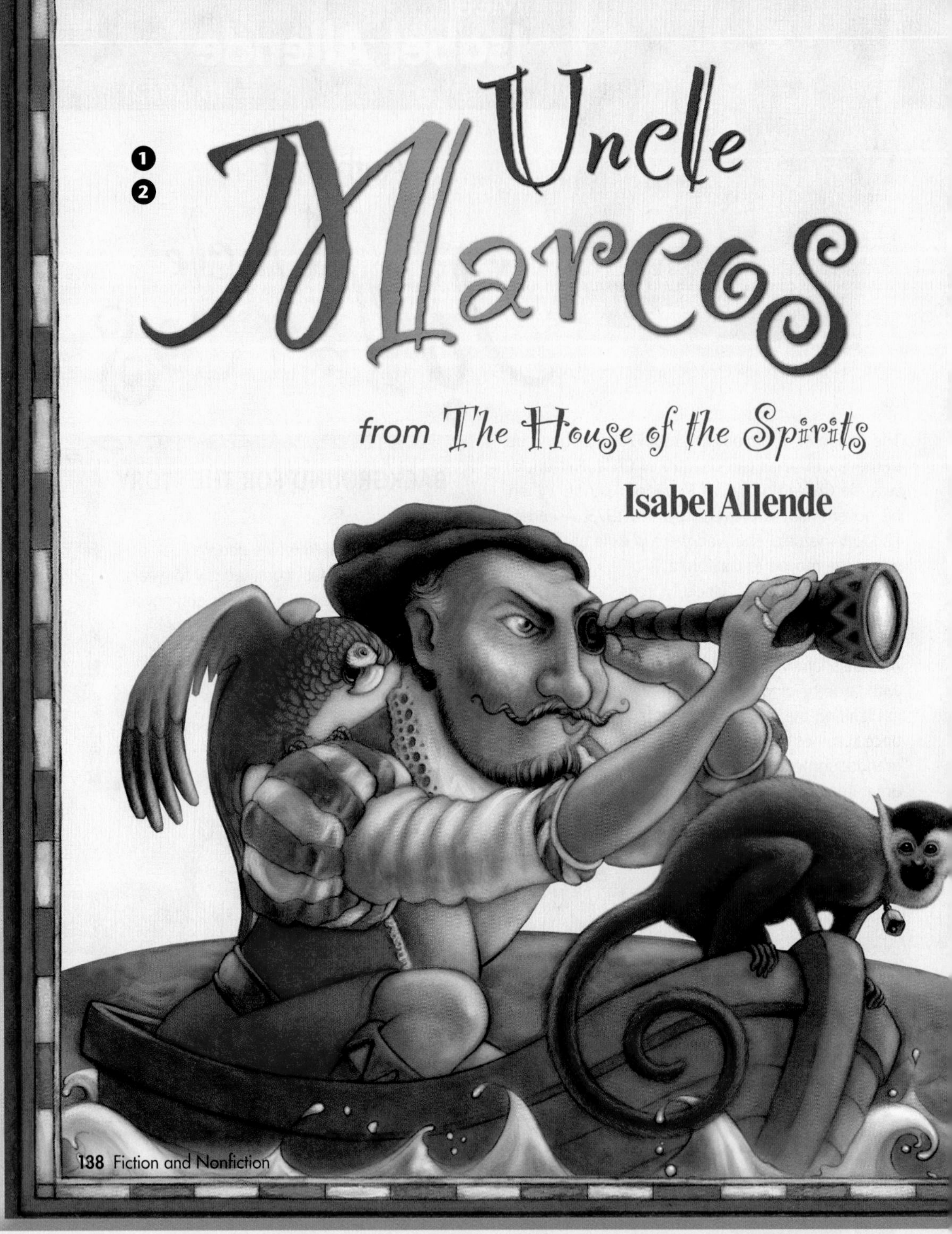

Vocabulary Development

ⓒ CCSS Language 6

Thematic Vocabulary: The Big Question

As students are discussing "Uncle Marcos," encourage them to use the thematic vocabulary presented in Introducing the Big Question, pp. 2–3. You might encourage them with sentence starters like these:

1. Uncle Marcos hopes that the barrel organ will help him *convince* Cousin Antonieta . . .
2. Many people *perceive* Uncle Marcos to be . . .
3. People are *skeptical* of Uncle Marco's flying machine because . . .
4. After Uncle Marcos flies away, people begin to *speculate* that . . .

...It had been two years since Clara had last seen her Uncle Marcos, but she remembered him very well. His was the only perfectly clear image she retained from her whole childhood, and in order to describe him she did not need to consult the daguerreotype[1] in the drawing room that showed him dressed as an explorer leaning on an old-fashioned double-barreled rifle with his right foot on the neck of a Malaysian tiger, the same triumphant position in which she had seen the Virgin standing between plaster clouds and pallid angels at the main altar, one foot on the vanquished devil. All Clara had to do to see her uncle was close her eyes and there he was, weather-beaten and thin, with a pirate's mustache through which his strange, sharklike smile peered out at her. It seemed impossible that he could be inside that long black box that was lying in the middle of the courtyard.

Each time Uncle Marcos had visited his sister Nivea's home, he had stayed for several months, to the immense joy of his nieces and nephews, particularly Clara, causing a storm in which the sharp lines of domestic order blurred. The house became a clutter of trunks, of animals in jars of formaldehyde,[2] of Indian lances and sailor's bundles. In every part of the house people kept tripping over his equipment, and all sorts of unfamiliar animals appeared that had traveled from remote lands only to meet their death beneath Nana's irate broom in the farthest corners of the house. Uncle Marcos's manners were those of a cannibal, as Severo put it. He spent the whole night making incomprehensible movements in the drawing room; later they turned out to be exercises designed to perfect the mind's control over the body and to improve digestion. He performed alchemy[3] experiments in the kitchen, filling the house with fetid smoke and ruining pots and pans with solid substances that stuck to their bottoms and were impossible to remove. While

1. **daguerreotype** (də ger´ ō tīp´) *n.* early type of photograph.
2. **formaldehyde** (for mal´ də hīd´) *n.* solution used as a preservative.
3. **alchemy** (al´ kə mē) *n.* early form of chemistry with philosophic and magical associations.

Vocabulary
pallid (pal´ id) *adj.* pale

4 

What happens to the order of the house when Uncle Marcos visits?

3 Critical Thinking

Infer

1. Have students read the bracketed text, and then **ask** what they can infer about Uncle Marcos's character. Have them identify details that support their answers. **Possible response:** The picture with the rifle and tiger suggests that Uncle Marcos is brave and adventurous. The pirate's mustache and sharklike smile create a rascally impression.
2. **Ask:** What does the comparison between Marcos's photograph and the statue of the Virgin suggest?

   Possible response: It suggests that Marcos is somehow good in spirit, despite his adventurous nature, or that he has special powers.

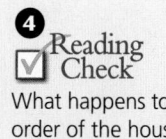

4 Reading Check

Answer: The household becomes a jumble of confusion, disorder, and clutter.

PHLit Online!

This selection is available in interactive format in the **Enriched Online Student Edition,** at **www.PHLitOnline.com,** which includes a thematically related video with writing prompt and an interactive graphic organizer.

Differentiated Instruction for Universal Access

Strategy for Less Proficient Readers

The long paragraphs and sentences in "Uncle Marcos" may challenge some students. Preview the reading with them, page by page. Help them find the main idea in each paragraph, and then have them use this list to summarize Marcos's adventures. When students have finished reading, have them go back over the text and note how the details of each paragraph support and illuminate the main ideas.

EL Support for English Learners

If any students are native speakers of Spanish or are fluent in that language, encourage them to locate and read this excerpt in Spanish, the original language of *The House of the Spirits (La casa de los espíritus).* Challenge students to choose any two-paragraph section of the excerpt and translate it into English. Then have them compare and contrast their versions with the one in the textbook.

5 Connecting to the Big Question

1. Tell students that some people make their surroundings adjust to them rather than adjusting to their surroundings. In this way, people create their own realities—and truths.
2. Have students read the bracketed text. **Ask:** What is happening in this passage? **Answer:** Marcos has become bored with life at the house, so he has created a new scheme. He fixes up a barrel organ and intends to use it to court Cousin Antonieta and to tell people's fortunes.
3. **Ask:** What details in this passage show how Marcos creates his own realities? **Answer:** By fixing up the barrel organ, he escapes the activities and pressures at home and creates his own way to spend time, to win love, and to make money—all on his own terms. He also creates his own reality by teaching a South American parrot to speak Spanish. Students may suggest that Marcos determines his own truths in life, regardless of what other people think he should do or be.

▲ Barrel organ

the rest of the household tried to sleep, he dragged his suitcases up and down the halls, practiced making strange, high-pitched sounds on savage instruments, and taught Spanish to a parrot whose native language was an Amazonic dialect. During the day, he slept in a hammock that he had strung between two columns in the hall, wearing only a loincloth that put Severo in a terrible mood but that Nivea forgave because Marcos had convinced her that it was the same costume in which Jesus of Nazareth had preached. Clara remembered perfectly, even though she had been only a tiny child, the first time her Uncle Marcos came to the house after one of his voyages. He settled in as if he planned to stay forever. After a short time, bored with having to appear at ladies' gatherings where the mistress of the house played the piano, with playing cards, and with dodging all his relatives' pressures to pull himself together and take a job as a clerk in Severo del Valle's law practice, he bought a barrel organ and took to the streets with the hope of seducing his Cousin Antonieta and entertaining the public in the bargain. The machine was just a rusty box with wheels, but he painted it with seafaring designs and gave it a fake ship's smokestack. It ended up looking like a coal stove. The organ played either a military march or a waltz, and in between turns of the handle the parrot, who had managed to learn Spanish although he had not lost his foreign accent, would draw a crowd with his piercing shrieks. He also plucked slips of paper from a box with his beak, by way of selling fortunes to the curious. The little pink, green, and blue papers were so clever that they always divulged the exact secret wishes of the customers. Besides fortunes there were little balls of sawdust to amuse the children. The idea of the organ was a last desperate attempt to win the hand of Cousin Antonieta after more conventional means of courting her had failed. Marcos thought no

> The organ played either a military march or a waltz...

Think Aloud

Vocabulary: Using Context

Point out the word *practice* in the middle of this page. Using a "think-aloud" process, model how to use context to infer the appropriate definition of the word. Say to students:

I'm going to think aloud to show you how I would figure out the correct dictionary definition of *practice* by using context clues. The dictionary says that *practice* can mean 1. a repeated or customary action; 2. systematic exercise that creates proficiency; 3. a professional business.

In this paragraph, Marcos's relatives are encouraging him to take a job as a clerk in a "law practice." Since the narrator is talking about a potential job, and I know that law is a profession, I think definition 3 would fit. "A professional business" is best for this context.

woman in her right mind could remain impassive before a barrel-organ serenade. He stood beneath her window one evening and played his military march and his waltz just as she was taking tea with a group of female friends. Antonieta did not realize the music was meant for her until the parrot called her by her full name, at which point she appeared in the window. Her reaction was not what her suitor had hoped for. Her friends offered to spread the news to every salon[4] in the city, and the next day people thronged the downtown streets hoping to see Severo del Valle's brother-in-law playing the organ and selling little sawdust balls with a motheaten parrot, for the sheer pleasure of proving that even in the best of families there could be good reason for embarrassment. In the face of this stain to the family reputation, Marcos was forced to give up organ grinding and resort to less conspicuous ways of winning over his Cousin Antonieta, but he did not renounce his goal. In any case, he did not succeed, because from one day to the next the young lady married a diplomat who was twenty years her senior; he took her to live in a tropical country whose name no one could recall, except that it suggested negritude,[5] bananas, and palm trees, where she managed to recover from the memory of that suitor who had ruined her seventeenth year with his military march and his waltz. Marcos sank into a deep depression that lasted two or three days, at the end of which he announced that he would never marry and that he was embarking on a trip around the world. He sold his organ to a blind man and left the parrot to Clara, but Nana secretly poisoned it with an overdose of cod-liver oil, because no one could stand its lusty glance, its fleas, and its harsh, tuneless hawking of paper fortunes and sawdust balls.

That was Marcos's longest trip. He returned with a shipment of enormous boxes that were piled in the far courtyard, between the chicken coop and the woodshed, until the winter was over. At the first signs of spring he had them transferred to the parade grounds, a huge park where people would gather to watch the soldiers file by on Independence Day, with the goosestep they had learned from the Prussians. When the crates were opened, they were found to contain

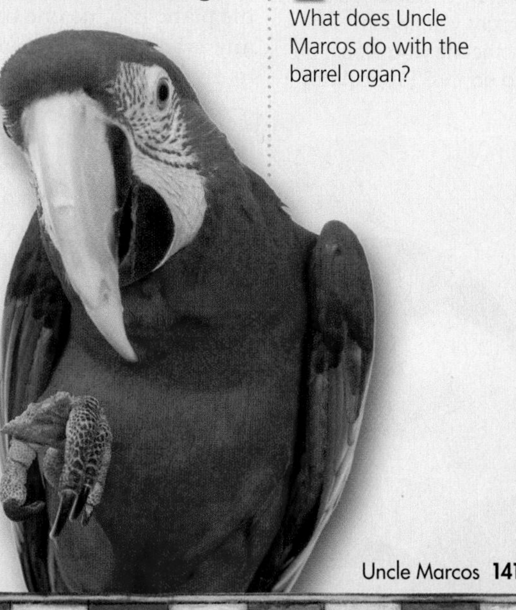

4. **salon** (sə län′) *n.* regular gathering of distinguished guests that meets in a private home.
5. **negritude** (neg′ rə to͞od′) *n.* blacks and their cultural heritage.

Vocabulary
impassive (im pas′ iv) *adj.* showing no emotion

Literary Analysis
Character In what way does Uncle Marcos's behavior suggest that he is a multidimensional character?

Vocabulary
conspicuous (kən spik′ yo͞o əs) *adj.* attracting attention by being unexpected, unusual or outstanding

7 **Reading Check**
What does Uncle Marcos do with the barrel organ?

6 Literary Analysis

Character

1. Remind students that characters can be round or flat and dynamic or static. Have students keep these aspects of character in mind as they read the bracketed text.
2. **Ask** students to respond to the Literary Analysis question: In what way does Uncle Marcos's behavior suggest that he is a multidimensional character?

   Answer: His behavior suggests that there are many aspects to his personality. He is beloved by his nieces and nephews, a world traveler and adventurer, a collector of strange animals, a performer of unusual exercises, an alchemist, a musician, and a man who sleeps in a hammock and teaches a parrot to speak Spanish.
3. **Ask** students whether, at this point in the story, they think Uncle Marcos is a static or dynamic character. Have them explain their answers.

   Possible response: Uncle Marcos is dynamic because he changes, moving from one emotional state to another. Having failed in his courtship of Antonieta, he becomes depressed, then shakes himself out of his depression and embarks on a trip around the world.

7 Reading Check

Answer: He sells it to a blind man.

Differentiated Instruction for Universal Access

Strategy for Special-Needs Students
To give students a context for the story and to model how to determine an author's purpose, show them **Reading Skill Graphic Organizer A** (***Graphic Organizer Transparencies***, p. 27). The partially completed graphic organizer will give students insight into the process of reflecting to determine an author's purpose. They can use it as a model for organizing their thoughts about author's purpose as they read.

Enrichment for Gifted/Talented Students
Point out that Allende creates vivid descriptions of Uncle Marcos's extravagances, such as the way he disrupts the house by bringing in trunks, Indian lances, and animals in jars. She also describes his eccentric devices, such as the barrel organ. Have students take a passage and create one or more drawings to illustrate the setting and the things that Uncle Marcos has collected.

8 Critical Thinking

Compare and Contrast

1. Have students review the text on p. 141 about Marcos's experience as an organ grinder.
2. **Ask** students to compare and contrast how the townspeople treat Marcos when he is an organ grinder with how they treat him in the first bracketed text.
   Possible response: As an organ grinder, the townspeople laugh at Marcos and view him as a "stain" on his family's reputation. In this passage the townspeople view Marcos with interest and curiosity, especially after he announces his flight.

Spiral Review

Theme

1. Remind students that they studied the concept of theme in the Unit 1 Literary Analysis workshop (pp. 4–21).
2. **Ask** the Spiral Review question.
   Possible response: The various reactions to Uncle Marcos and his giant bird suggest that people are intrigued by and drawn to the new and daring, even if the new and daring makes no sense. After Uncle Marcos builds the giant bird, people plan Sunday outings to see it. After he announces he will try to fly it, journalists and others flock to see it, even when it is apparent the huge contraption could never fly, "much less take flight across the snow peaks." In fact, when Marcos announces his plane trip, the narrator says that "no one believed that his contraption could be put to any practical use." Nevertheless, crowds of people come to watch Marcos try to fly.

9 Critical Viewing

Possible response: Someone who would try to build a flying machine would be inventive, creative, ambitious, adventuresome, and whimsical.

---

loose bits of wood, metal, and painted cloth. Marcos spent two weeks assembling the contents according to an instruction manual written in English, which he was able to decipher thanks to his invincible imagination and a small dictionary. When the job was finished, it turned out to be a bird of prehistoric dimensions, with the face of a furious eagle, wings that moved, and a propeller on its back. It caused an uproar. The families of the oligarchy[6] forgot all about the barrel organ, and Marcos became the star attraction of the season. People took Sunday outings to see the bird; souvenir vendors and strolling photographers made a fortune. Nonetheless, the public's interest quickly waned. But then Marcos announced that as soon as the weather cleared he planned to take off in his bird and cross the mountain range. The news spread, making this the most talked-about event of the year. The contraption lay with its stomach on terra firma,[7] heavy and sluggish and looking more like a wounded duck than like one of those newfangled airplanes they were starting to produce in the United States. There was nothing in its appearance to suggest that it could move, much less take flight across the snowy peaks. Journalists and the curious flocked to see it. Marcos smiled his immutable[8] smile before the avalanche of questions and posed for photographers without offering the least technical or scientific explanation of how he hoped to carry out his plan. People came from the provinces to see the sight. Forty years later his great-nephew Nicolás, whom Marcos did not live to see, unearthed the desire to fly that had always existed in the men of his lineage. Nicolás was interested in doing it for commercial reasons, in a gigantic hot-air sausage on which would be printed an advertisement for carbonated drinks. But when Marcos announced his plane trip, no one believed that his contraption could be put to any practical use. The appointed day dawned full of clouds, but so many people had turned out that Marcos did not want to disappoint them. He showed up punctually at the appointed spot and did not once look up at the sky, which was growing darker and darker with thick gray clouds. The astonished crowd filled all the nearby streets, perching on rooftops and the balconies of the nearest houses and squeezing into the park.

8

Spiral Review

Theme What insights into human nature are suggested by the various reactions to Uncle Marcos and his giant bird? Explain.

9

▼ Critical Viewing

In this story, a man builds a flying machine. Which character traits might you find in someone who would try to do this? **[Speculate]**

6. **oligarchy** (äl´ i gar´ kē) *n.* government ruled by a few.
7. **terra firma** (ter´ a fur´ ma) *n.* Latin term meaning "firm earth; solid ground."
8. **immutable** (im myo͞ot´ ə bəl) *adj.* never changing.

Vocabulary Development

CCSS Language 6

Word Analysis

Call students' attention to the words *invincible* near the top of p. 142 and *invisible* near the bottom of p. 143. Explain that each word begins with the prefix *in-*, which means "not."

Explain that *vincible* is an adjective that means "able to be defeated." So *invincible* means "not able to be defeated." Marcos's imagination cannot be defeated. Explain in the same way that *visible* means "able to be seen" and *invisible* means "not able to be seen."

Have students brainstorm for other words that use the prefix *in-*. Ask them to decode the words by combining the meaning of the base word with what they have learned about the prefix *in-*.

No political gathering managed to attract so many people until half a century later, when the first Marxist candidate attempted, through strictly democratic channels, to become President. Clara would remember this holiday as long as she lived. People dressed in their spring best, thereby getting a step ahead of the official opening of the season, the men in white linen suits and the ladies in the Italian straw hats that were all the rage that year. Groups of elementary-school children paraded with their teachers, clutching flowers for the hero. Marcos accepted their bouquets and joked that they might as well hold on to them and wait for him to crash, so they could take them directly to his funeral. The bishop himself, accompanied by two incense bearers, appeared to bless the bird without having been asked, and the police band played happy, unpretentious music that pleased everyone. The police, on horseback and carrying lances, had trouble keeping the crowds far enough away from the center of the park, where Marcos waited dressed in mechanic's overalls, with huge racer's goggles and an explorer's helmet. He was also equipped with a compass, a telescope, and several strange maps that he had traced himself based on various theories of Leonardo da Vinci and on the polar knowledge of the Incas.[9] Against all logic, on the second try the bird lifted off without mishap and with a certain elegance, accompanied by the creaking of its skeleton and the roar of its motor. It rose flapping its wings and disappeared into the clouds, to a send-off of applause, whistlings, handkerchiefs, drumrolls, and the sprinkling of holy water. All that remained on earth were the comments of the amazed crowd below and a multitude of experts, who attempted to provide a reasonable explanation of the miracle. Clara continued to stare at the sky long after her uncle had become invisible. She thought she saw him ten minutes later, but it was only a migrating sparrow. After three days the initial euphoria that had accompanied the first airplane flight in the country died down and no one gave the episode another thought, except for Clara, who continued to peer at the horizon.

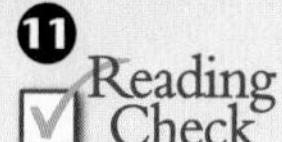
Against all logic, on the second try the bird lifted off without mishap...

Reading Skill
Author's Purpose
What does the statement "Clara would remember this holiday as long as she lived" suggest about the author's purpose in this story?

11 Reading Check
Where does Uncle Marcos plan to fly in his flying machine?

9. **Leonardo da Vinci** (lē′ ə när′ dō də vin′ chē) . . . **Incas** Leonardo da Vinci (1452–1519) was an Italian painter, sculptor, architect, and scientist. The Incas were Native Americans who dominated ancient Peru until the Spanish conquest.

10 Reading Skill
Author's Purpose

1. **Ask** students to define an author's purpose and to explain how readers can determine this.
   Answer: An author's purpose is his or her main reason for writing. Readers can determine an author's purpose by reflecting on story details and events.
2. Write the following sentence on the board: "Clara would remember this holiday as long as she lived." Have students discuss what this event means to Clara.
3. **Ask** students the Reading Skill Question: What does the statement "Clara would remember this holiday as long as she lived" suggest about the author's purpose in this story?
   Answer: The author wants to emphasize the affection and admiration Clara has for her uncle.

11 Reading Check
Answer: He plans to cross the mountain range.

Fluency

Distribute copies of page 143, and pair students. Have partners take turns reading paragraphs aloud. While one partner reads, the other should mark any words with which the student reading has difficulty. Circulate to monitor the fluency of students' reading. Collect students' marked-up copies of the page, and review difficult words and passages with the class. Look for these problem spots:

- If students have difficulty with the word *unpretentious,* remind them to use context clues. Point out that if they read the rest of the sentence containing the word, clues such as *happy* and *that pleased everyone* will help them figure out what the word means.
- If students have difficulty pronouncing the word *roar,* say the word aloud correctly three times and have students repeat. Suggest that student write on scratchpads the following words with the same letter pattern and sound: *soar, boar,* and *oar.*
- If students have limited sight vocabulary, show pictures that illustrate concepts represented by words such as *democratic, bouquets, bless, traced,* and *logic.*

⓬ Reading Skill

Author's Purpose

1. Have students **summarize** the bracketed text.

   Answer: Uncle Marcos has returned from his flight. Even though the plane went down and he had to walk back, Uncle Marcos is in high spirits.

2. **Ask** students the Reading Skill question: What do the narrator's observations about Marcos suggest about the author's purpose?

   Possible response: The author's purpose is to cast the situation in a humorous light and to show Marcos as an eternal optimist.

3. Guide a discussion of how these details contribute to Allende's overall purpose, which is to entertain her readers.

▶ **Monitor Progress:** Review students' graphic organizers to make sure that they are correctly determining the author's purpose.

▶ **Reteach:** If students have trouble determining author's purpose, review the instruction on p. 125. Recall a writing assignment that students have done recently. Ask them why they wrote the piece. What did they want to achieve? What details helped them achieve that purpose?

⓭ Literary Analysis

Character

1. **Ask** students what business Marco and Clara start together and why they decide to quit.

   Answer: Marcos and Clara tell people's fortunes. They quit the business because they realize that they have too much power over people. They are worried that someone might do something foolish as a result of one of their predictions.

2. **Ask** students to respond to the Literary Analysis question: Which details in this passage indicate that Marcos has changed since the beginning of the story?

   Answer: At the beginning of the story, Marcos seems indifferent to the people around him. Now he seems to genuinely care for others.

3. Have students identify the aspects of character that this information reveals about Uncle Marcos.

   Answer: This information reveals that Uncle Marcos is a round, dynamic character.

After a week with no word from the flying uncle, people began to speculate that he had gone so high that he had disappeared into outer space, and the ignorant suggested he would reach the moon. With a mixture of sadness and relief, Severo decided that his brother-in-law and his machine must have fallen into some hidden crevice of the cordillera,[10] where they would never be found. Nivea wept disconsolately and lit candles to San Antonio, patron of lost objects. Severo opposed the idea of having masses said, because he did not believe in them as a way of getting into heaven, much less of returning to earth, and he maintained that masses and religious vows, like the selling of indulgences, images, and scapulars,[11] were a dishonest business. Because of his attitude, Nivea and Nana had the children say the rosary,[12] behind their father's back for nine days. Meanwhile, groups of volunteer explorers and mountain climbers tirelessly searched peaks and passes, combing every accessible stretch of land until they finally returned in triumph to hand the family the mortal remains of the deceased in a sealed black coffin. The intrepid traveler was laid to rest in a grandiose funeral. His death made him a hero and his name was on the front page of all the papers for several days. The same multitude that had gathered to see him off the day he flew away in his bird paraded past his coffin. The entire family wept as befit the occasion, except for Clara, who continued to watch the sky with the patience of an astronomer. One week after he had been buried, Uncle Marcos, a bright smile playing behind his pirate's mustache, appeared in person in the doorway of Nivea and Severo del Valle's house. Thanks to the surreptitious[13] prayers of the women and children, as he himself admitted, he was alive and well and in full possession of his faculties, including his sense of humor. Despite the noble lineage of his aerial maps, the flight had been a failure. He had lost his airplane and had to return on foot, but he had not broken any bones and his adventurous spirit was intact. This confirmed the family's eternal devotion to San Antonio, but was not taken as a warning by future generations, who also tried to fly, although by different means. Legally, however, Marcos was a corpse. Severo del Valle was obliged to use all his legal ingenuity to bring his brother-in-law back to life and the full rights of citizenship. When the coffin was pried open in the presence of the appropriate authorities, it was found to contain a bag of sand. This discovery ruined the

Vocabulary
disconsolately
(dis kän′ sə lit lē) *adv.* very unhappily

⓬ **Reading Skill**
Author's Purpose
What do the narrator's observations about Marcos suggest about the author's purpose?

⓭ **Literary Analysis**
Character
Which details in this passage indicate that Marcos has changed since the beginning of the story?

10. **cordillera** (kôr′ dil yer′ ə) *n.* system or chain of mountains.
11. **indulgences, images, and scapulars** (skap′ yə lərz) Indulgences are pardons for sins; images are pictures or sculptures of religious figures; scapulars are garments worn by Roman Catholics as tokens of religious devotion.
12. **say the rosary** use a set of beads to say prayers.
13. **surreptitious** (sər′ əp tish′ əs) *adj.* secretive.

Vocabulary Development

Ⓒ CCSS Language 6

Expressive Vocabulary

To help students broaden their expressive vocabulary, encourage them to use the following words as they discuss the selection: *enhance, alters, distort, evolves,* and *generate.* Have them complete these sentence starters:

1. To *enhance* his life, Uncle Marcos . . .
2. Uncle Marcos *alters* the barrel organ by . . .
3. The townspeople *distort* . . .
4. The relationship between Uncle Marcos and Clara *evolves* . . .
5. Among the townspeople, Uncle Marcos's exploits *generate* . . .

Challenge students to use these words as you continue to discuss the story.

reputation, up till then untarnished, of the volunteer explorers and mountain climbers, who from that day on were considered little better than a pack of bandits.

Marcos's heroic resurrection made everyone forget about his barrel-organ phase. Once again he was a sought-after guest in all the city's salons and, at least for a while, his name was cleared. Marcos stayed in his sister's house for several months. One night he left without saying goodbye, leaving behind his trunks, his books, his weapons, his boots, and all his belongings. Severo, and even Nivea herself, breathed a sigh of relief. His visit had gone on too long. But Clara was so upset that she spent a week walking in her sleep and sucking her thumb. The little girl, who was only seven at the time, had learned to read from her uncle's storybooks and been closer to him than any other member of the family because of her prophesying powers. Marcos maintained that his niece's gift could be a source of income and a good opportunity for him to cultivate his own clairvoyance.[14] He believed that all human beings possessed this ability, particularly his own family, and that if it did not function well it was simply due to a lack of training. He bought a crystal ball in the Persian bazaar, insisting that it had magic powers and was from the East (although it was later found to be part of a buoy from a fishing boat), set it down on a background of black velvet, and announced that he could tell people's fortunes, cure the evil eye, and improve the quality of dreams, all for the modest sum of five centavos.[15] His first customers were the maids from around the neighborhood. One of them had been accused of stealing, because her employer had misplaced a valuable ring. The crystal ball revealed the exact location of the object in question: it had rolled beneath a wardrobe. The next day there was a line outside the front door of the house. There were coachmen, storekeepers, and milkmen; later a few municipal employees and distinguished ladies made a discreet appearance, slinking along the side walls of the house to keep from being recognized. The customers were

After a week with no word from the flying uncle, people began to speculate that he had gone so high that he had disappeared into outer space...

14. **clairvoyance** (kler voi´ əns) *n.* supposed ability to perceive unseen things.
15. **centavos** (sen tä´ vōs) *n.* coins equal to 1/100 of a *cruzeiro*, the basic monetary unit of Brazil.

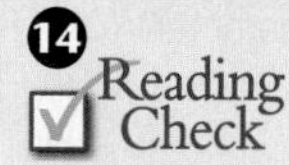

What power does Marcos believe Clara holds?

14 Reading Check

Answer: Marcos believes that Clara has the power to see the future.

Differentiated Instruction for Universal Access

Enrichment for Advanced Readers

Review Magical Realism with students. Then have them meet in a group and discuss the elements of magic in "Uncle Marcos." Ask them to consider the following questions:

- Do the magical elements contribute to or detract from the story?
- How do the magical elements contribute to your understanding of Marcos and of Clara?
- How do the magical elements contribute to the theme?
- How does the magical realism of "Uncle Marcos" compare to that used in other magical realist stories that you have read?

Have students present a summary of their ideas to the class.

15 Literary Analysis

Character

1. **Ask** students what they have learned about Clara's character throughout the story.

   Possible response: Clara has clairvoyant powers, and she loves and admires her uncle so much that she sleepwalks and sucks her thumb when he leaves.

2. **Ask** the Literary Analysis question: Which details in this paragraph indicate that Clara, like Marcos, is a complex character?

   Answer: Details that indicate Clara is a complex character include her interest in Uncle Marcos's stories, how she memorizes words from different Indian dialects, how she knows the exact way in which certain Indians pierced their lips and earlobes, and how she remembers the unpronounceable names of flora and fauna.

3. Emphasize to students that just because a character is round does not mean the character is also dynamic. **Ask** students whether they think Clara is dynamic or static and to explain their reasoning.

   Answer: Clara is static. Although the reader learns about different aspects of Clara's character, there is no evidence that she changes or grows as a result of her experiences.

received by Nana, who ushered them into the waiting room and collected their fees. This task kept her busy throughout the day and demanded so much of her time that the family began to complain that all there ever was for dinner was old string beans and jellied quince.[16] Marcos decorated the carriage house with some frayed curtains that had once belonged in the drawing room but that neglect and age had turned to dusty rags. There he and Clara received the customers. The two divines wore tunics "color of the men of light," as Marcos called the color yellow. Nana had dyed them with saffron powder, boiling them in pots usually reserved for rice and pasta. In addition to his tunic, Marcos wore a turban around his head and an Egyptian amulet around his neck. He had grown a beard and let his hair grow long and he was thinner than ever before. Marcos and Clara were utterly convincing, especially because the child had no need to look into the crystal ball to guess what her clients wanted to hear. She would whisper in her Uncle Marcos's ear, and he in turn would transmit the message to the client, along with any improvisations of his own that he thought **pertinent**. Thus their fame spread, because all those who arrived sad and bedraggled at the consulting room left filled with hope.

Vocabulary
pertinent (purt´ 'n ənt) *adj.* relevant; to the point
unrequited (un ri kwīt´ id) *adj.* not returned or repaid

Unrequited lovers were told how to win over indifferent hearts, and the poor left with foolproof tips on how to place their money at the dog tracks. Business grew so prosperous that the waiting room was always packed with people, and Nana began to suffer dizzy spells from being on her feet so many hours a day. This time Severo had no need to intervene to put a stop to his brother-in-law's venture, for both Marcos and Clara, realizing that their unerring guesses could alter the fate of their clients, who always followed their advice to the letter, became frightened and decided that this was a job for swindlers. They abandoned their carriage-house oracle and split the profits, even though the only one who had cared about the material side of things had been Nana.

Literary Analysis
Character
Which details in this paragraph indicate that Clara, like Marcos, is a complex character?

Of all the del Valle children, Clara was the one with the greatest interest in and stamina for her uncle's stories. She could repeat each and every one of them. She knew by heart words from several dialects of the Indians, was acquainted with their customs, and could describe the exact way in which they pierced their lips and earlobes with wooden shafts, their initiation rites, the names of the most poisonous snakes, and the appropriate antidotes for each. Her uncle was so eloquent that the child could feel in her own skin the burning sting of snakebites, see reptiles slide across the carpet between the legs of the jacaranda[17] room divider, and hear the

16. **quince** (kwins) hard, gold or greenish-yellow apple-shaped fruit.
17. **jacaranda** (jak´ ə ran´ də) type of tropical American tree.

Vocabulary Development

Vocabulary Knowledge Rating

When students have completed reading and discussing "Uncle Marcos," have them take out their **Vocabulary Knowledge Rating Chart** for this selection. Read the words aloud once more and have students rate their knowledge of the words again in the After Reading column. Clarify any words that are still problematic. Have students write their own definition and example or sentence in the appropriate column. Then have students complete the Vocabulary Practice activities at the end of the selection. Encourage students to use the words in further discussion and written work about this selection. Remind them that they will be accountable for these words on the **Selection Test,** ***Unit 1 Resources,*** pp. 207–209 or 210–212.

shrieks of macaws behind the drawing-room drapes. She did not hesitate as she recalled Lope de Aguirre's search for El Dorado,[18] or the unpronounceable names of the flora and fauna her extraordinary uncle had seen; she knew about the lamas who take salt tea with yak lard and she could give detailed descriptions of the opulent women of Tahiti, the rice fields of China, or the
5 white prairies of the North, where the eternal ice kills animals and men who lose their way, turning them to stone in seconds. Marcos had various travel journals in which he recorded his excursions and impressions, as well as a collection of maps and books of stories and fairy tales that he kept in the trunks he stored in the junk room at the far end of the third courtyard. From there they were hauled out to inhabit the dreams of his descendants, until they were mistakenly burned half a century later on an infamous pyre.

Now Marcos had returned from his last journey in a coffin. He had died of a mysterious African plague that had turned him as yellow and wrinkled as a piece of parchment. When he realized he was ill, he set out for home with the hope that his sister's ministrations and Dr. Cuevas's knowledge would restore his health and youth, but he was unable to withstand the sixty days on ship and died at the latitude of Guayaquil,[19] ravaged by fever and hallucinating about musky women and hidden treasure. The captain of the ship, an Englishman by the name of Longfellow, was about to throw him overboard wrapped in a flag, but Marcos, despite his savage appearance and his delirium, had made so many friends on board and seduced so many women that the

18. **Lope de Aguirre's** (lō´ pā dā ä gĕr´ räs) . . . **El Dorado** Lope de Aguirre was a Spanish adventurer (1518–1561) in colonial South America who searched for a legendary country called El Dorado, which was supposedly rich in gold.
19. **Guayaquil** (gwī´ ä kēl´) seaport in western Ecuador.

16

LITERATURE IN CONTEXT

Humanities Connection

Magical Realists

The literary movement known as Magical Realism is most closely associated with the wonder-filled novels and short stories of a group of twentieth-century Latin American authors. Isabel Allende is an important writer in this group. The great Argentinian writer Jorge Luis Borges is another. His style often combines realistic characters and events with details that seem to come out of dreams and myths. Gabriel García Márquez of Colombia is often considered the central figure of the movement. His works chronicle the lives of passionate and sympathetic characters who experience miraculous happenings and strange, unearthly events.

Connect to the Literature

What elements of "Uncle Marcos" confirm that it belongs to the literary movement known as Magical Realism?

17

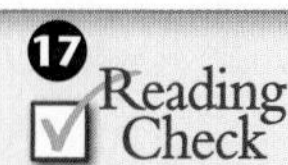

Who loves hearing Marcos's stories the most?

16 Literature in Context

Humanities Connection Magical Realism, as represented by writers such as Allende and Marquez, challenges readers with a paradox by mixing mundane, everyday reality with magical events that are treated like common, everyday occurrences. Only the reader perceives that events have slipped into the supernatural. Although generally considered to have originated in South America, Magical Realism is also practiced by such diverse writers as Ben Okri of Nigeria, Toni Morrison of the United States, and Syl Cheney-Coker of Sierra Leone. The Nobel Prizes awarded to both Marquez and Morrison are evidence of Magical Realism's international acceptance and appreciation.

Connect to the Literature Point out the matter-of-fact language of "Uncle Marcos"; neither the narrator nor the characters seem surprised by the magical events that happen. **Ask** students the Connect to the Literature question: What elements of "Uncle Marcos" confirm that it belongs to the literary movement known as Magical Realism?

Answer: The story intermingles the common occurrences of everyday life with magical, extraordinary events, such as Marcos's flight and Clara's clairvoyance. None of the characters seem to think these events are odd or miraculous.

17 Reading Check

Answer: Clara loves hearing Marcos's stories the most.

Concept Connector

Activating Prior Knowledge
Have students return to the character sketch they created before reading "Uncle Marcos." Guide a discusion about how the sketches compared to the characters in the story.

Writing About the Big Question
Have students compare their responses to the sentence starters they completed before reading the excerpt with their ideas afterwards. Ask them to explain whether their thoughts have changed.

Reading Skill Graphic Organizer
Have students review the graphic organizers they completed to determine the author's purpose while reading. Then show them **Reading Skill Graphic Organizer A** (***Graphic Organizer Transparencies,*** p. 27) as an example. Have students share the graphic organizers they did and the details they identified that support their conclusions about the author's purpose.

ASSESS

Answers

Critical Thinking

Before students respond, you may wish to have them write a brief objective summary of the selection. As they answer the questions below, remind them to support their answers with evidence from the text.

1. (a) He serenades her with a barrel organ. (b) No, his efforts produce the opposite of what he intended. Antonieta does not even realize the serenade is for her. Antonieta marries and leaves for a faraway place.
2. (a) He makes a flying machine. (b) Students may say that Marcos seeks risk and adventure in front of a huge audience.
3. (a) Clara never doubts that Marcos will return alive; Severo feels sad but relieved; Nivea feels sad. (b) Clara has faith that Uncle Marcos has not failed and is still alive, which indicates her loyalty and the strong bond she feels for him.
4. (a) Possible response: People should live their lives with good humor, confidence, and a sense of adventure. (b) Students should discuss the lessons that readers might learn from Marcos. (c) Students may find that they have seen new sides of Marcos as a result of the discussion.
5. (a) **Possible response:** Uncle Marcos creates his own reality and does not let other people's priorities and judgments prevent him from keeping his life exciting and adventurous. The narrator and other characters lead more conventional lives and let their surroundings dictate their reality. (b) **Possible response:** I think Uncle Marcos's reality is truer because he remains true to himself, and he lives life to the fullest more effectively than the other characters.

passengers prevented him from doing so, and Longfellow was obliged to store the body side by side with the vegetables of the Chinese cook, to preserve it from the heat and mosquitoes of the tropics until the ship's carpenter had time to improvise a coffin. At El Callao[20] they obtained a more appropriate container, and several days later the captain, furious at all the troubles this passenger had caused the shipping company and himself personally, unloaded him without a backward glance, surprised that not a soul was there to receive the body or cover the expenses he had incurred. Later he learned that the post office in these latitudes was not as reliable as that of far-off England, and that all his telegrams had vaporized en route. Fortunately for Longfellow, a customs lawyer who was a friend of the del Valle family appeared and offered to take charge, placing Marcos and all his paraphernalia in a freight car, which he shipped to the capital to the only known address of the deceased: his sister's house. . . .

20. El Callao (kə yä´ ō) seaport in western Peru.

Critical Thinking

Cite textual evidence to support your responses.

1. **Key Ideas and Details (a)** What does Uncle Marcos do to try to win the hand of Cousin Antonieta? **(b) Connect:** Is her reaction what Uncle Marcos expects? Use details from the text to explain.
2. **Key Ideas and Details (a)** What does Uncle Marcos make from the materials he brings back in "enormous boxes"? **(b) Infer:** What do you think motivates Uncle Marcos to undertake this project?
3. **Key Ideas and Details (a) Compare and Contrast:** Compare and contrast Clara's reaction to her uncle's disappearance with those of the others. **(b) Interpret:** What does Clara's reaction show about her personality and relationship to Uncle Marcos? Explain.
4. **Key Ideas and Details (a) Draw Conclusions:** What life lessons can people learn from the character of Uncle Marcos? **(b) Discuss:** Share your responses with a group and discuss similarities and differences among them. **(c) Reflect:** How has the discussion affected your response?
5. **Integration of Knowledge and Ideas (a)** How is Uncle Marcos's reality different from that of the narrator and other characters? **(b)** Which reality do you think is truer? Defend your answers. *[Connect to the Big Question: Can truth change?]*

Assessment Resources

Unit 1 Resources

L1 L2 EL **Selection Test A,** pp. 207–209. Administer Test A to less advanced readers.

L3 L4 EL **Selection Test B,** pp. 210–212. Administer Test B to on-level and more advanced students.

L3 L4 **Open-Book Test,** pp. 204–206. As an alternative, give the Open-Book Test.

All **Customizable Test Bank**

All **Self-tests**
Students may prepare for the **Selection Test** by taking the **Self-test** online.

All assessment resources are available at **www.PHLitOnline.com.**

After You Read | Uncle Marcos 

Literary Analysis: Character

1. **Key Ideas and Details (a)** Using a chart like the one shown, list at least three of Uncle Marcos's projects or adventures. Then, identify a quality that each project or adventure reveals.

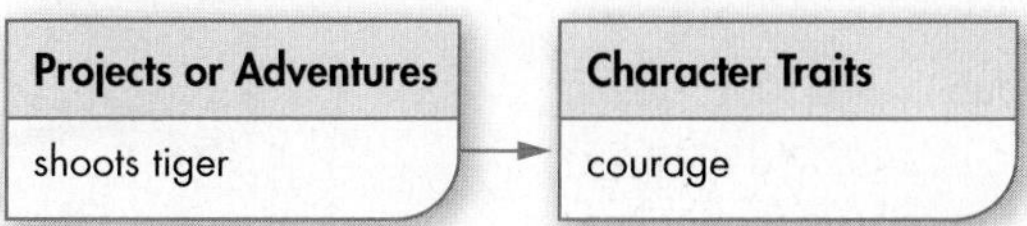

(b) Based on his projects and adventures, summarize the **character** of Uncle Marcos in a few sentences.

2. **Craft and Structure** Review the characters of Clara and Uncle Marcos. **(a)** Determine whether each character is **round** or **flat.** Explain your responses. **(b)** Explain whether each character is **static** or **dynamic.**

Reading Skill: Author's Purpose

3. **(a)** What specific **purpose** might Isabel Allende have had for creating the character of Uncle Marcos? **(b)** Identify three details from the story that support your response and explain how **reflecting** on them helped you determine Allende's purpose.

Vocabulary

Acquisition and Use Review the vocabulary list for "Uncle Marcos" on page 136. Then, decide whether each of the following statements is true or false. Explain your answers.

1. Something that looks *pallid* is full of color.
2. Sighing *disconsolately* is a good way to express enthusiasm.
3. *Unrequited* love is symbolized by a wedding.
4. Standing on your head in public would be considered *conspicuous*.
5. A *pertinent* detail has absolutely nothing to do with the topic.
6. You can easily read the mood of an *impassive* person.

Word Study Use the context of the sentences and what you know about the **Latin suffix *-ive*** to explain your answer to each question.

1. Do *permissive* parents allow their children their freedom?
2. If people are *cooperative*, will they refuse to work together?

Word Study

The **Latin suffix *-ive*** means "of, belonging to, or quality of."

Apply It Explain how the suffix contributes to the meanings of these words. Consult a dictionary if necessary.

derisive
collective
festive

ASSESS/EXTEND

Answers

Literary Analysis

1. (a) **Possible response:** Projects or Adventures—Character Traits: performs alchemy—curiosity; takes trip around world—adventurousness; builds flying machine—inventiveness

   For other sample answers, see ***Graphic Organizer Transparencies,*** **Literary Analysis Graphic Organizer A,** p. 30, and the **Additional Answers** section.

   (b) Marcos is an eccentric and adventurous man who takes chances. He is inventive and imaginative, and he has the courage to follow through with his dreams and ideas.

2. (a) Marcos and Clara are both round. Readers see different sides of their personalities. They learn, for example, that both characters have varied interests and feelings. (b) Marcos is a dynamic character, because he changes and develops during the story. For example, his emotions shift when he believes he can win Antonieta and when she rejects him. Clara is a static character; readers do not see her change.

Reading Skill

3. (a) Allende's purpose was to produce a memorable character whom readers will admire—or at least find intriguing—for his imagination, spirit, and energy. (b) The details of the wooing of Antonieta, the trip around the world, and the displays of clairvoyance make Marcos a vivid and unique presence for the reader. Reflecting on these details helped me realize that Allende must have wanted to make Marcos stand out against other characters, both in the story and in her readers' lives.

Vocabulary

Acquisition and Use

Sample answers:

1. False. Something that is *pallid* lacks color.
2. False. *Disconsolately* means sadly or unhappily, so it does not express enthusiasm.
3. False. *Unrequited* love is not returned.

Answers Continued:

4. True. Standing on one's head in public attracts attention, so it is *conspicuous*.
5. False. A *pertinent* detail is relevant.
6. False. An *impassive* person expresses little emotion.

Word Study

Sample answers:

1. Yes. The suffix *-ive* means "of, belonging to, or quality of," and *permissive* means "possessing the quality of permission." Permissive parents give children their freedom.
2. No. The suffix *-ive* means "of, belonging to, or quality of," and *cooperative* means "possessing the quality of cooperation." People who cooperate work together.

Word Study: Apply It

Sample answers:

Something *derisive* has the quality of deriding; Something *collective* has the quality of being collected; Something *festive* has the quality of a festival.

EXTEND/ASSESS

Answers

Conventions

1. Introduce the skill, using the instruction on the student page.
2. Discuss the definitions and the examples in the chart.

Teach the Skill

1. Remind students that pronouns are words that take the place of nouns.
2. Point out relative, interrogative and indefinite pronouns and give the students examples.
3. Name a type of pronoun and call on a student to use that type in a sentence. Give students opportunities to use both singular and plural pronouns.

PH WRITING COACH Grade 9

Students will find further instruction on and practice with relative, interrogative, and indefinite pronouns in Chapter 13, Section 1.

Practice A

1. No one; indefinite
2. Who; interrogative
3. who; relative
4. whose; relative

Reading Application

Sample answers:

Relative: She seemed grossly unfamiliar, like a strange woman <u>who</u> had yelled at him in a crowd.
Interrogative: 'Who has the case?'
Indefinite: <u>Something</u> struck his shoulder.

Practice B

Sample answers:

1. anybody
2. who
3. that
4. some

Writing Application

In their sentences, students should be sure to use the same part of speech as the italicized word or words.

PERFORMANCE TASKS

Integrated Language Skills

The Secret Life of Walter Mitty • Uncle Marcos

Conventions: Pronouns

A **pronoun** is a word that stands for a noun.

- A **relative pronoun** begins a subordinate clause and connects it to another idea in the sentence. The five relative pronouns are *that, which, who, whom,* and *whose.*
- An **interrogative pronoun** is used to begin a question. The five interrogative pronouns are *what, which, who, whom,* and *whose.*
- **Indefinite pronouns** refer to people, places, or things, often without specifying which ones.

Indefinite Pronouns

Singular				Plural	Singular or Plural	
another	either	much	one	both	all	most
anybody	everybody	neither	other	few	any	none
anyone	everyone	nobody	somebody	many	more	some
anything	everything	no one	someone	others		
each	little	nothing	something	several		

Practice A Identify the pronouns in each sentence, and tell whether each one is relative, interrogative, or indefinite.

1. No one knew about Mitty's daydreams.
2. Who doesn't daydream occasionally?
3. Mitty was a courageous pilot who saved his crew from certain death.
4. Mitty, whose wife was getting her hair done, waited quietly in the hotel.

Reading Application Find an example of sentences using a relative, an interrogative, and an indefinite pronoun in "The Secret Life of Walter Mitty."

Practice B Complete each sentence by adding a relative, an interrogative, or an indefinite pronoun that makes sense.

1. Has _________ heard Uncle Marcos's stories?
2. People _________ listen to him find him hard to believe.
3. The adventures _________ Uncle Marcos had sometimes embarrassed his family.
4. _________ of them were surprised by his flying.

Writing Application Use this sentence as a model to write five sentences. Substitute the italicized word or words with the same part speech.
<u>Many</u> of them came from a country <u>that</u> is in Asia.

PH WRITING COACH Further instruction and practice are available in *Prentice Hall Writing Coach.*

150 Fiction and Nonfiction

Extend the Lesson

Sentence Modeling

Choose the sentence given from the selection students have read:

She seemed grossly unfamiliar, like a strange woman who had yelled at him in a crowd. ("The Secret Life of Walter Mitty")

After three days the initial euphoria that had accompanied the first airplane flight in the country died down and no one gave the episode another thought, except for Clara, who continued to peer at the horizon. ("Uncle Marcos")

Ask students what they notice about the sentence. Elicit that the sentence contains pronouns. Have students identify the pronouns and their types. Then, **ask** what else they notice. ("The Secret Life of Walter Mitty": The relative pronoun *who* introduces a clause that helps visualize Mrs. Mitty. "Uncle Marcos": The relative pronouns *that* and *who* introduce a clause that helps readers visualize the flight and Clara.)

Have students imitate the sentence, matching each grammatical and stylistic feature discussed.

Writing

Ⓒ **Informational Text** Both of these selections present memorable characters who entertain readers. Using details from the story you read, write a **character profile.** If you read "The Secret Life of Walter Mitty," choose one of the heroic personalities in Mitty's daydreams. If you read "Uncle Marcos," write a profile of Uncle Marcos.

- Begin by jotting down details that capture the character's appearance, personality, and achievements.
- Decide on a single impression to convey about the character.
- Organize and present details to create an impression.
- Maintain a consistent tone and focus throughout the piece.

Grammar Application Check your character profile to be sure that you have used relative, interrogative, and indefinite pronouns correctly.

Common Core State Standards

L.9-10.1, L.9-10.6; W.9-10.4, W.9-10.6
[For the full wording of the standards, see page 124.]

Writing Workshop: *Work in Progress*

Prewriting for Problem-Solution Essay Review the Problem Notes you created in your writing portfolio. To build on this work, provide three specific examples of the problem and three examples of solutions. Put these Problem/Solution Notes in your writing portfolio.

Use this prewriting activity to prepare for the **Writing Workshop** on page 172.

Research and Technology

Ⓒ **Build and Present Knowledge** Literature often suggests great topics for further research. Use a variety of sources from both the library and the Internet to research information for a **learning log,** a written record of information you learn about a topic. Use any available reliable sources, including speeches, journals, and news sources. Follow reliable links within sources to locate additional useful information. Analyze the information to compare your findings to details and descriptions in the story you read.

- If you read "The Secret Life of Walter Mitty," research scientific facts and theories about daydreams. Record your research in a learning log. Decide whether Mitty's daydreams reflect the facts you have learned.
- If you read "Uncle Marcos," research the history of human flight. Look for historic details that can be compared to the descriptions of flight given in the story. Record your research in a learning log. Decide if Allende's description of flight is realistic or fantastic.

If possible, incorporate graphics, visuals, or audio files into your log. Then, present the log to a small group, explaining how you researched and created it.

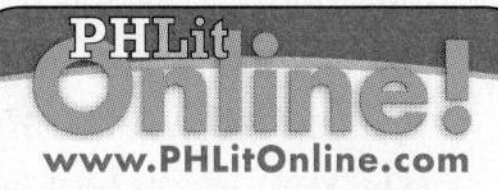

www.PHLitOnline.com

- Interactive graphic organizers
- Grammar tutorial
- Interactive journals

EXTEND/ASSESS

Writing

1. Review the assignment, using the instruction on the student page.
2. To guide students in writing a character profile, give them **Support for Writing,** p. 202 in ***Unit 1 Resources.***
3. To evaluate students' character profiles, use the Descriptive Essay rubrics, pp. 220–221 in ***Professional Development Guidebook.***

Grammar Application

Have students check their drafts for correct use of pronouns.

Six Traits Focus

✔	Ideas	✔	Word Choice
✔	Organization		Sentence Fluency
	Voice		Conventions

PH WRITING COACH Grade 9

Students will find guidance on descriptive writing in Chapter 6.

Writing Workshop
Work-in-Progress

Have students save their completed Problem/Solution Notes in their portfolios. They will use the Problem/Solution Notes later as they complete the Writing Workshop Assignment (see pp. 172–179).

Research and Technology

1. Review the assignment, using the instruction on the student page.
2. To support students' work on the assignment, have students complete the **Support for Extend Your Learning** page (***Unit 1 Resources,*** p. 203).

Teaching Resources

Unit 1 Resources

L3 L4 EL **Integrated Language Skills: Grammar,** p. 201
L3 L4 EL **Support for Writing,** p. 202
L3 L4 **Support for Extend Your Learning,** p. 203
L4 **Enrichment,** pp. 182, 200

Enriched Online Student Edition
Available under After You Read for this selection:
All **Interactive Grammar Tutorial**
L3 L4 **Internet Research Activity**

Professional Development Guidebook
Rubrics for Descriptive Essay, pp. 220–221

All print and digital resources are available at **www.PHLitOnline.com.** Online resources accessible by students are noted on the student page.

MONITORING PROGRESS

Using the Test Practice

In this two-page Test Practice, students apply the reading skill for the second half of Unit 1 to a passage of fiction and a passage of nonfiction.

Review the skill, determining an author's purpose, and then administer the test. For more guidance, consult the ***Classroom Strategies and Teaching Routines*** card, **Formally Assessing Students.**

ASSESS

Answers

Answers With Explanations

1. **A**—This thought shows that Juan is concerned about how much garbage he sees. *Incorrect answers:* B—Juan is concerned about the garbage before he connects it to the science fair. C—The exclamation about the garbage is unrelated to the science fair. D—The passage has already said that he is walking home.
2. **B**—Seeing the garbage gives Juan the inspiration for his project. *Incorrect answers:* A—Unless the garbage figured in the story further, its inclusion would not add interest. C—The setting is not really significant to the story. D—It only shows that Juan is observant.
3. **C**—The description shows that Juan has been struck with an idea. *Incorrect answers:* A—The word *hit* is used figuratively. B—The passage says nothing about prizes. D—The garbage solved his problem of what to do for the science fair.
4. **C**—The details show how a real science fair project might be constructed. *Incorrect answers:* A—The passage is not humorous. B—The passage is not particularly long. D—The passage does not describe how to recycle.
5. **A**—Juan and his family discover how much of their garbage can be recycled. *Incorrect answers:* B—The passage is not about garbage collection. C—This passage does not exhort students to complete homework. D—The passage does not make this link.

Test Practice: Reading

Author's Purpose

Fiction Selection

Directions: *Read the selection. Then, answer the questions.*

Juan slowly walked home from school, wondering what he could possibly do for his science fair project. As he ambled down his block, he noticed the gigantic mounds of garbage on the curb waiting to be taken to a landfill. "Something's got to be done about all this garbage!" Juan thought, and the idea for his science project hit him. He decided to prepare a presentation on recycling. First, he weighed how much garbage his family threw out in a week. Then, Juan and his family removed the recyclable glass and plastic from their trash and weighed it again. Finally, they took out the paper they were throwing away and weighed the remaining trash. Juan and his family were shocked by the difference in the weight of their garbage.

1. The author most likely includes the line, "Something's got to be done about this garbage!" to show that Juan is—
A. genuinely concerned about the garbage.
B. going to win first prize at the science fair.
C. wondering what to do for his project.
D. walking home from school.

2. Why does the author include the description of Juan seeing the mounds of garbage?
A. It adds realism and interest to the story.
B. It gives Juan's inspiration for his project.
C. It provides crucial details about the setting.
D. It shows that Juan is conscientious.

3. The author says, "the idea for his science fair project hit him" to show that Juan has—
A. tripped over the mounds of garbage.
B. created a prize-winning presentation.
C. decided what to study for the science fair.
D. given up on his science fair project.

4. For what purpose does the author describe the steps in Juan's project?
A. to entertain the reader with humor
B. to make the story longer
C. to make the story realistic
D. to show how to recycle

5. What is the author's main purpose in writing this story?
A. to inspire people to recycle
B. to call for more garbage collection
C. to persuade us to complete science projects
D. to show the importance of science on the environment

Writing for Assessment

How do you think Juan feels about the environment? Write a brief paragraph and use details from the text to support your response.

Writing for Assessment

Students should identify how Juan feels about the environment and give details from the story to support their answer.

Strategies for Test Taking

Tell students that if they are unsure about an answer for any item, they should eliminate any answers that are obviously incorrect. Doing so narrows their choices and saves time. Then they should reread the question and evaluate the remaining answers.

Nonfiction Selection

Directions: *Read the selection. Then, answer the questions.*

Recycling saves on the amount of garbage we make and helps us keep our planet healthy. Even if you recycle just a small amount of material, you can have a positive impact on the environment. Some materials can be reused in their present state, such as using a tire for a flower planter. Other materials can be recycled into new products. Plastic, for example, is processed and reused to create new plastic items. Whatever way you choose to recycle, you do the earth a favor. Recycling helps lower greenhouse gases and decreases the space we need for landfills. Overall, recycling is a friend to the environment. You can make a difference. Why not recycle something today?

1. What is the general purpose of this article?
- **A.** to entertain
- **B.** to reflect
- **C.** to describe
- **D.** to persuade

2. Why do you think the author ends the article with a question?
- **A.** to call the audience to action
- **B.** to make the audience look for an answer
- **C.** to teach the audience about landfills
- **D.** to eliminate the need for questioning the author

3. For what purpose does the author give examples of how materials can be recycled?
- **A.** to provide ideas for recycling plastic
- **B.** to explain how recycling works
- **C.** to convince the reader to do Earth a favor
- **D.** to show the advantages of reusing products

4. Which sentence *best* reveals the author's purpose in this selection?
- **A.** Some materials can be reused in their present state, such as using a tire for a flower planter.
- **B.** Other materials can be recycled into new products.
- **C.** Whatever way you choose to recycle, you do the earth a favor.
- **D.** Recycling is expensive and unnecessary.

5. What would be the *best* title for this article?
- **A.** The Environment
- **B.** Recycling Saves Lives
- **C.** How I Started Recycling
- **D.** Why Everyone Should Recycle

Writing for Assessment

Connecting Across Texts

In what ways would this article be helpful to Juan as he completes his science fair project? Write a paragraph in which you use specific details from both passages to explain why Juan should read this article as he prepares his presentation on recycling.

PHLit Online!
www.PHLitOnline.com
- Online practice
- Instant feedback

Differentiated Instruction for Universal Access

Strategy for Less Proficient Readers

Help students prepare for the test by walking them through item 1. Ask a volunteer to read it aloud. Guide students to see that the key word is *general.* The correct answer must describe the purpose of the passage *as a whole.* Next, guide students in evaluating answer choices:

- A—The passage does not really provide entertainment or humor. (Eliminate)
- B—The author discusses the benefits of recycling, but does not really explore his or her own feelings. (Eliminate)
- C—There is description in the passage, but the overall impression is the author's desire to get people to act. (Eliminate)
- D—The author hopes to prompt action; he or she is trying to persuade. (Correct.)

Guide students in seeing that **D** is the best choice. Encourage students to apply a similar strategy to the remaining items: First, define key terms in the prompt and then eliminate incorrect choices.

ASSESS

Answers

Answers With Explanations

1. **D**—The writer tells readers their actions can make a difference to persuade them to recycle. *Incorrect answers:* A—The article is not entertaining. B—The author does not reflect on an important event or issue. C—Description is secondary in importance to persuasion.
2. **A**—The author hopes to move readers to act. *Incorrect answers:* B—The author has already given several reasons for recycling. C—The point of the question is to urge recycling, not to discuss landfills. D—The question addresses readers' behavior, not the author's ideas.
3. **D**—The examples show the benefits of recycling. *Incorrect answers:* A—The article mentions other materials as well. B—In this persuasive passage, a persuasive purpose is a better response. C—In this part of the passage, the author is focusing on the benefits of recycling.
4. **C**—The main idea is that any kind of recycling is good. *Incorrect answers:* A—This is a detail, not the main idea. B—same explanation as for A. D—The article argues the opposite.
5. **D**—The author urges everyone to recycle. *Incorrect answers:* A—The focus of the article is on recycling in particular. B—The article does not make this claim. C—The author does not reveal his or her recycling history.

Writing for Assessment

Students may suggest that Juan could use the information from the nonfiction selection to develop graphics or examples for his science fair project.

Students may take the test in interactive format with instant feedback online at **www.PHLitOnline.com.**

Common Core State Standards

- Reading Informational Text 3
- Language 4.b

Reading Skill

1. Introduce the skill, using the instruction on the student page.
2. Review the chart, pointing out examples of each bulleted item.
3. Tell students that they will analyze the structure and format of a schedule and a brochure.

Think Aloud: Model the Skill

Model the skill of analyzing structure and format. Say to students:

When I analyze a schedule or a brochure, I look at how it is organized. I look for pictures, titles, headings, and tables or charts. For example, when I read the title on page 155 ("Pascack Valley Line Train Schedule") and the heading on the table ("To Hoboken Monday – Friday"), I know that this schedule shows the times that trains run on weekdays to Hoboken.

Multidraft Reading

Have students follow a multidraft reading protocol.

- **First reading**—Have students read to identify key ideas and details.
- **Second reading**—Have students read to identify the structure of the text.
- **Third reading**—Have students read to integrate knowledge and ideas by connecting the text to the world, their own experiences, and other texts.

Content-Area Vocabulary

1. Have students say each word.
2. Next, use each word in a sentence that defines it.
3. Finally, repeat your definitional sentence or a similar sentence with the word missing and have the class "fill in the blank" chorally.

Reading for Information

Analyzing Functional Texts

Schedule

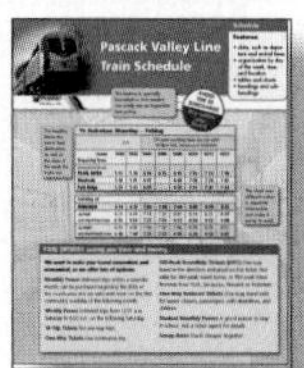

Brochure

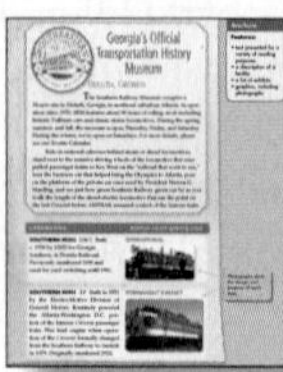

Common Core State Standards

Reading Informational Text
3. Analyze how the author unfolds an analysis or series of ideas or events, including the order in which the points are made, how they are introduced and developed, and the connections that are drawn between them.

Language
4.b. Identify and correctly use patterns of word changes that indicate different meanings or parts of speech.

Reading Skill: Analyze Structure and Format

The structure of a text is the way in which it is organized. Format refers to the layout and other features that clarify the structure. When you **analyze structure and format,** you identify organizational elements in a text and consider how they help convey information. In functional texts, such as schedules and brochures, information might be presented in graphic formats, such as tables or charts. Understanding how such features connect with verbal elements can help you locate useful information.

The following chart shows some common structural features and the purposes they achieve.

Structural Features of Schedules	Structural Features of Brochures
• **headings:** show where to find categories of information • **rows and columns:** formatted information allows for easy scanning across and down the page • **graphics:** call attention to important information	• **headings and subheadings:** help readers to locate information on a topic • **lists:** provide a quick way to reference essential information • **photographs and other images:** convey visual information

Content-Area Vocabulary

These words appear in the selections that follow. You may also encounter them in other content-area texts.

- **obstructions** (əb struk′shən) *n.* objects that block access; obstacles
- **complement** (kom plə ment′) *n.* object or action that makes something else whole or complete
- **cosmetic** (koz met′ik) *adj.* dealing with physical beauty or outward appearances

The Big Question: Can truth change?

Have students consider which facts in the train schedule and brochure might change.

Differentiated Instruction for Universal Access

Reading Support
Give students reading support with the appropriate version of the *Reader's Notebooks:*

- L2 L3 *Reader's Notebook*
- L1 *Reader's Notebook: Adapted Version*
- EL *Reader's Notebook: English Learner's Version*

Pascack Valley Line Train Schedule

Schedule

Features:

- data, such as departure and arrival times
- organization by day of the week, time, and location
- tables and charts
- headings and subheadings

NJTRANSIT The Way To Go.

This feature is specially formatted so that readers can easily see an important fare policy.

AVOID THE $5 SURCHARGE Buy before you board

The heading shows the train's final destination, as well as the days of the week the trains run.

To Hoboken Monday – Friday

	AM		Off-peak roundtrip fares are not valid to New York, Secaucus or Hoboken					
TRAINS Departing from:	1600	1602	1604	1606	1608	1610	1612	1614
METRO-NORTH STATION **PEARL RIVER**	5 15	5 38	6 04	6 35	6 45	7 05	7 24	7 38
Montvale	5 18	5 41	6 07		6 48	7 08	7 28	7 41
Park Ridge	5 20	5 43	6 09		6 50	7 11	7 30	7 44
Arriving at:								
HOBOKEN	**6 14**	**6 37**	**7 07**	**7 18**	**7 49**	**8 07**	**8 19**	**8 41**
via PATH	6 24	6 44	7 14	7 32	8 01	8 19	8 31	8 49
arrive World Trade Center	**6 34**	**6 54**	**7 25**	**7 43**	**8 12**	**8 30**	**8 42**	**9 00**
via FERRY	6 30	6 50	7 16	7 32	7 56	8 20	8 28	8 52
arrive World Financial Center	**6 40**	**7 00**	**7 26**	**7 42**	**8 06**	**8 30**	**8 38**	**9 02**

The chart uses different colors to separate information and make it easier to read.

FARE OPTIONS saving you time and money

We want to make your travel convenient and economical, so we offer lots of options:

Monthly Passes Unlimited trips within a calendar month; can be purchased beginning the 20th of the month prior and are valid until noon on the first commuting weekday of the following month.

Weekly Passes Unlimited trips from 12:01 a.m. Saturday to 6:00 a.m. on the following Saturday.

10-Trip Tickets Ten one-way trips.

One-Way Tickets One continuous trip.

Off-Peak Roundtrip Tickets (ORT) One-way travel in the direction indicated on the ticket. Not valid for AM peak travel to/via, or PM peak travel from/via New York, Secaucus, Newark or Hoboken.

One-Way Reduced Tickets One-way travel valid for senior citizens, passengers with disabilities, and children.

Student Monthly Passes A good reason to stay in school. Ask a ticket agent for details.

Group Rates Travel cheaper together.

Differentiated Instruction for Universal Access

Strategy for Less Proficient Readers

Review how numbers are displayed in standard text. Remind students that prices are shown with a dollar sign and a decimal point. Tell students that time is usually shown with a colon between the hour and the minutes. Point out that in this train schedule, the times shown do not contain colons. Instead, a space separates the numbers that indicate the hour and the minutes.

Strategy for Advanced Readers

Have students obtain a bus or train schedule for the local public transportation system and analyze it. Have them compare it to the Pascack Valley Line Train Schedule. Tell students to look for similarities in headings, train numbers, times, and descriptions of fare options. Then, have them make a compare and contrast chart to show how their local system differs from the Pascack Valley Line. Ask volunteers to share their findings with the class.

TEACH

About Schedules

1. Review the list of features of schedules in the box on page 155.
2. Invite students to tell about schedules they have used, such as class schedules, sports activity schedules, or bus schedules.
3. **Ask:** What features on the list do you recognize from the schedules you are familiar with?

   Possible response: Details about time, organization by day of the week, tables and charts.
4. Talk to students about how to approach a schedule, including how to check the schedule for A.M. and P.M. times.

Analyze Structure and Format

1. Remind students that a roundtrip ticket is for travel that begins at one station, goes to another, and then returns to the original station.
2. Help students understand the schedule. Point out that the numbers in a row across the top, 1600, 1602, 1604, and so on, are the identifying numbers of each train, not times or prices.
3. Tell students that they can find out when a train leaves by reading across from left to right. **Ask:** If you were leaving from Pearl River and going to Montvale, at what times could you take a train?

   Answer: You could take a train at 5:15, 5:38, 6:04, 6:45, 7:05, 7:24, and 7:38.

   Ask: Why couldn't you take the 6:35 train?

   Answer: It doesn't stop at Montvale.
4. Draw students' attention to the Fare Options box at the bottom of the page. Discuss the different options and why someone might choose to purchase one fare option instead of another. **Ask:** If you rode the train to work and then back home each day, what fare option would be easiest to manage?

   Possible response: The Monthly Pass would be easiest.

Analyze Structure and Format

1. Tell students that this page of the train schedule uses headings, icons, and graphics to organize information. Point out that the headings help the reader notice the main topics. Then direct students' attention to the icons. **Ask:** Where else have you seen icons used?

   Possible response: Icons are used in books and on computers. Textbooks use icons to point out common features that show up frequently. Software programs use icons as task buttons.

2. **Ask:** What topics do the icons on this schedule give information about?

   Answer: They give information about personal items, pets, smoking, electronic devices and cell phones, bicycles, and accessibility for mobility assist devices.

3. Make sure students understand that although the graphic of the Pascack Valley Line shows a straight line, the train route is not necessarily straight. **Ask:** How many stations are on the Pascack Valley Line? How many stations are accessible to people using mobility assist devices?

   Answer: There are eighteen stations; seven have access for mobility assist devices.

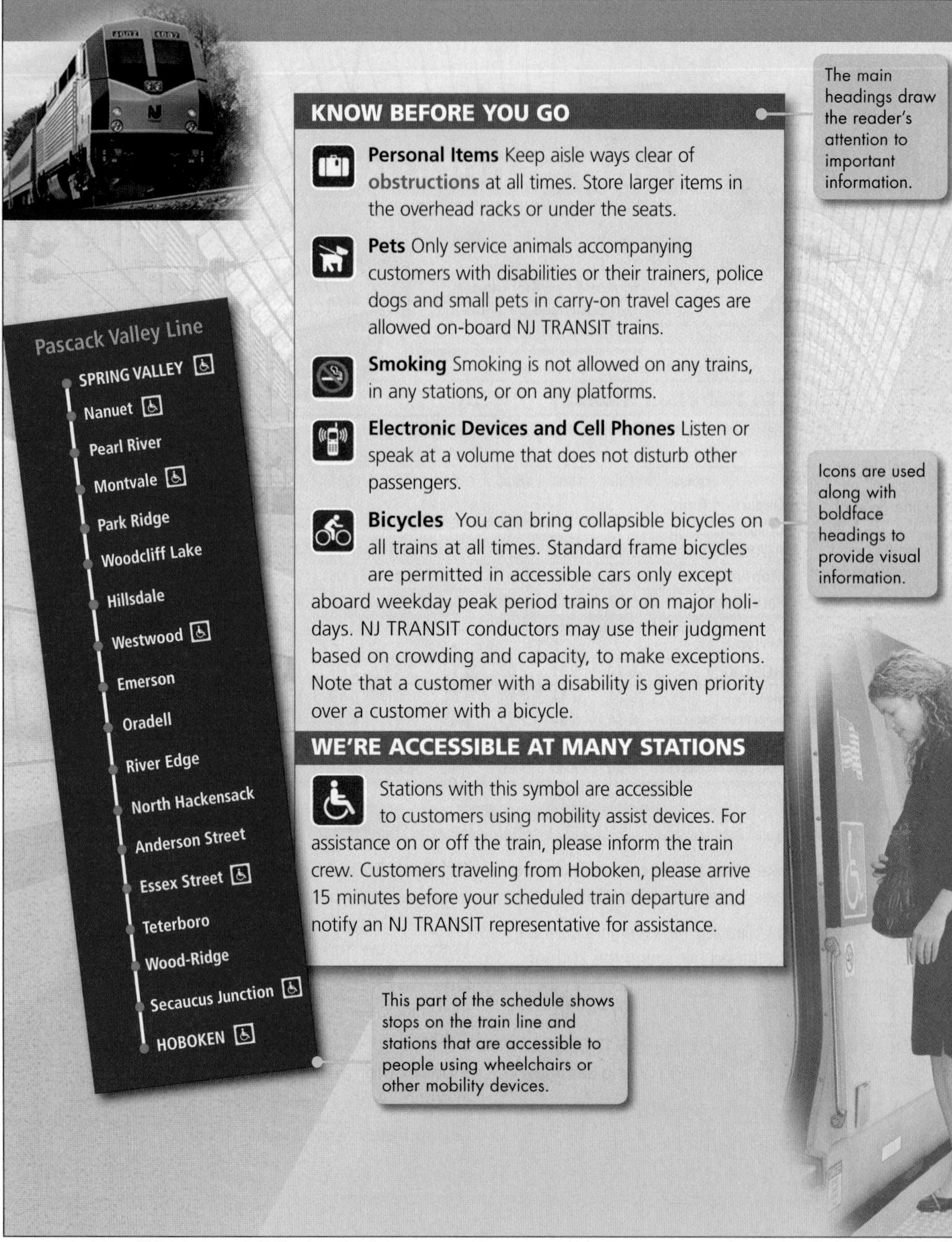

KNOW BEFORE YOU GO
Personal Items Keep aisle ways clear of **obstructions** at all times. Store larger items in the overhead racks or under the seats.
Pets Only service animals accompanying customers with disabilities or their trainers, police dogs and small pets in carry-on travel cages are allowed on-board NJ TRANSIT trains.
Smoking Smoking is not allowed on any trains, in any stations, or on any platforms.
Electronic Devices and Cell Phones Listen or speak at a volume that does not disturb other passengers.
Bicycles You can bring collapsible bicycles on all trains at all times. Standard frame bicycles are permitted in accessible cars only except aboard weekday peak period trains or on major holidays. NJ TRANSIT conductors may use their judgment based on crowding and capacity, to make exceptions. Note that a customer with a disability is given priority over a customer with a bicycle.
WE'RE ACCESSIBLE AT MANY STATIONS
Stations with this symbol are accessible to customers using mobility assist devices. For assistance on or off the train, please inform the train crew. Customers traveling from Hoboken, please arrive 15 minutes before your scheduled train departure and notify an NJ TRANSIT representative for assistance.
Pascack Valley Line
SPRING VALLEY
Nanuet
Pearl River
Montvale
Park Ridge
Woodcliff Lake
Hillsdale
Westwood
Emerson
Oradell
River Edge
North Hackensack
Anderson Street
Essex Street
Teterboro
Wood-Ridge
Secaucus Junction
HOBOKEN
The main headings draw the reader's attention to important information.
Icons are used along with boldface headings to provide visual information.
This part of the schedule shows stops on the train line and stations that are accessible to people using wheelchairs or other mobility devices.

Vocabulary Development

CCSS Language 6

Vocabulary from Social Studies

Point out that schedules often use vocabulary that is specific to traveling. Guide students to understand the meaning of the following words or phrases that are used on this schedule.

accessible: able to be reached or entered

fare: the price of a ticket

mobility assist devices: wheeled devices that allow disabled people to get around

off-peak: less busy times, when fewer people are traveling

Georgia's Official Transportation History Museum

DULUTH, GEORGIA

The Southern Railway Museum occupies a 34-acre site in Duluth, Georgia, in northeast suburban Atlanta. In operation since 1970, SRM features about 90 items of rolling stock including historic Pullman cars and classic steam locomotives. During the spring, summer, and fall, the museum is open Thursday, Friday, and Saturday. During the winter, we're open on Saturdays. For more details, please see our Events Calendar.

Ride in restored cabooses behind steam or diesel locomotives, stand next to the massive driving wheels of the locomotive that once pulled passenger trains to Key West on the "railroad that went to sea," tour the business car that helped bring the Olympics to Atlanta, pose on the platform of the private car once used by President Warren G. Harding, and see just how green Southern Railway green can be as you walk the length of the diesel-electric locomotive that ran the point on the last *Crescent* before AMTRAK assumed control of the famous train.

Brochure

Features:

- text presented for a variety of reading purposes
- a description of a facility
- a list of exhibits
- graphics, including photographs

LOCOMOTIVE	STATUS AS OF SPRING 2006
SOUTHERN #8202 SW-7 Built c. 1950 by EMD for Georgia Southern, & Florida Railroad. Previously numbered 1100 and used for yard switching until 1981.	**OPERATIONAL** 
SOUTHERN #6901 E8 Built in 1951 by the Electro-Motive Division of General Motors. Routinely powered the Atlanta-Washington D.C. portion of the famous *Crescent* passenger train. Was lead engine when operation of the *Crescent* formally changed from the Southern Railway to Amtrak in 1979. Originally numbered 2924.	**PERMANENT EXHIBIT** 

Photographs show the design and purpose of each train.

Differentiated Instruction for Universal Access

Strategy for Special-Needs Students
Brochures present information in an unfamiliar format. Many readers struggle to process the text because they are overwhelmed by the visual content. Suggest that students cover images while reading text so they are not distracted. Then, when viewing the images, students can think about how the images relate to the words they just read.

Strategy for Gifted/Talented Students
Challenge students to sketch out a two-sided brochure promoting your school or an area attraction. Remind students that the purpose of the brochure is to entice others to want to visit and to communicate vital information clearly. Allow time for students to present their brochures in class.

About Brochures

1. Have students read the features of brochures found in the box at the top right on page 157.
2. Ask volunteers to describe brochures they have seen for attractions such as zoos, theme parks, or state parks.
3. **Ask:** How did the information differ from a story or article about a place?

   Possible responses: A story has more words and it tells about something happening from beginning to end. It does not have headings and pictures with captions.
4. **Ask:** What do you like or dislike about reading brochures?

   Possible responses: Brochures have short paragraphs, and they are usually detailed and concise. However, sometimes brochures do not tell you everything you would like to know about a topic.

Analyze Structure and Format

1. Remind students that to evaluate text formats, they will analyze text and design features. Text features include headings, word choice, and word placement. Design features include images, charts, graphs, color, and font choices.
2. Review the chart on page 154 with students. Explain that designers work closely with writers to create brochures. The text and design features can be equally important in evaluating the overall format of the brochure.
3. Point out that this page shows only the front of the brochure about Georgia's Official Transportation History Museum, along with a description of the activities available there.
4. **Ask:** What activities can you participate in at Georgia's Official Transportation History Museum?

   Answer: A visitor can ride in restored cabooses, tour train cars, and walk the length of a diesel-electric locomotive.
5. **Ask:** How do the images on the page help you understand what the museum offers?

   Answer: The pictures show trains that are part of the museum collection.

Analyze Structure and Format

1. Have students look at the reverse side of the brochure. **Ask:** What words attract your attention? Why?

   Possible response: My attention is drawn to the pictures of the different trains. The bold headings are easy to read.

2. Have students analyze the brochure. **Ask:** Based on the information presented in the brochure, what do you think you would see and do at Georgia's Official Transportation Museum?

   Possible response: Students may say that they would see some of the important trains from Georgia's history that the museum has restored. They may also explore and ride the trains.

LOCOMOTIVE **STATUS AS OF SPRING 2006**

SOUTHERN FT B-UNIT #960604 STEAM HEAT & TRAINLINE POWER Constructed as a **complement** to the full diesel locomotive ("A" unit), these "B" units are essentially locomotives without cabs. Originally containing both diesel engines and steam generators (for passenger car heating), this unit has been modified to hold only steam generation equipment.

EXHIBIT

NEW YORK, ONTARIO, AND WESTERN #104 (FORMERLY HARTWELL #5) GE 44-TON Built 1941 by General Electric for the New York, Ontario & Western Railroad as #104. The museum staff completed a **cosmetic** restoration of the locomotive in 2005.

Here's the engine's previous paint scheme →

OPERATIONAL, NORMAL POWER FOR TRAIN RIDE

The headings allow readers to easily locate information about particular exhibits.

GEORGIA RAILROAD #1026 EMD GP 7 Acquired by the museum in 2004 from Tennessee Valley Railway Museum, the locomotive was repainted to it's original 1950 paint scheme before being delivered in January 2006.

EXHIBIT

Vocabulary Development

CCSS Language 6

Vocabulary for Brochure Planning

Tell students that special terms are used when creating a brochure. Guide students to understand the meanings of the following words in this article:

restoration: a renovation or an improvement of an object or a historical artifact

locomotive: train engine

steam generators: engine that creates electricity using steam

After You Read | Schedule • Brochure

Comparing Functional and Expository Texts

1. **Key Ideas and Details** **(a)** Summarize the information you learn from the maps and charts of the train schedule. **(b)** What information is conveyed in the visual elements of the brochure? **(c) Analyze:** What purposes do the graphic elements in each document serve? **(d) Evaluate:** Which graphics do you find more effective in meeting their intended purpose? Explain.

Content-Area Vocabulary

2. **(a)** For each of the following words, explain how a change in suffix alters the meaning and part of speech of the base word *obstruct*: *obstruction, obstructive,* and *obstructed.* **(b)** Use each word in a sentence that reveals its meaning.

Timed Writing

Explanatory Text: Description

Format
The prompt directs you to write a description of a scene. Therefore, be sure your response is specific to the situation as it is described in the prompt.

Write a description of a scene at a train station. Describe what you would see if you were on the station's platform waiting to board a train. Use the information in the train schedule for ideas about what kinds of details to include. (20 minutes)

Academic Vocabulary
When you *describe* something, you use words and details to create a vivid picture in your readers' minds.

5-Minute Planner

Complete these steps before you begin to write:

1. Read the prompt to be sure you understand the assignment.
2. Review the train schedule to find details that you can include in your description. **TIP** Use structural features such as subheadings and boldface type to quickly locate information in the document.
3. Make a list of the details that you want to use in your writing. Then, make a quick sketch of the train station scene as you picture it in your mind, including details from your list.
4. Use your sketch and your list of details for your description.

ASSESS/EXTEND

Answers

Comparing Functional and Expository Texts

1. (a) **Possible response:** Arrival and departure times, station stops, rules and regulations, and fare options

   (b) **Possible response:** Photographs show the design and purpose of each train. The bulleted lists and headings help the reader find important details.

   (c) **Possible response:** The graphic elements serve to communicate important information in each document by making it easy for the reader to locate.

   (d) Answers will vary but should show an understanding of the function and effectiveness of the graphics in each document.

2. (a) The *-ion* suffix in *obstruction* means "the condition of"—in this case, the condition of blocking. The *-ive* suffix means "tending toward an action"; something obstructive tends to obstruct, or block. The suffix *-ism* means "the act of." *Obstructionism* is the intentional act of delaying a process. The prefix *non-* means "not"; *nonobstructive* means "not blocking or stopping." The suffixes *-ion* and *-ism* create nouns. The suffix *-ive* creates adjectives.
   (b) **Sample response:** The candidate did not consider her young age an *obstruction* to getting elected. Her opponent's *obstructive* tactics could not slow her growing popularity. "If elected, I vow to end the *obstructionism* delaying the passage of important laws," she said. "My *nonobstructive* position will lead to progress."

Timed Writing

1. Before students complete the activity, guide them in identifying and analyzing key words and phrases in the prompt, highlighted on the student page.
2. Work with students to draw up guidelines for their descriptions based on the key words:
   - **Focus** The description should concentrate on a scene at a train station.
   - **Organization** The description should establish the scene and then introduce the details.
   - **Elaboration** The description should include details that relate to information from the train schedule.
   - **Style** The audience is not specified, so a formal style is appropriate.
3. Have students use the 5-Minute Planner to structure their time.
4. Allow students 20 minutes to complete the assignment. Evaluate their work using the guidelines they have developed.

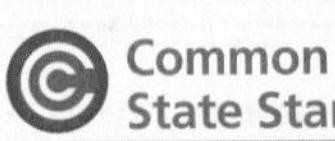

Common Core State Standards

- Reading Literature 2
- Reading Informational Text 2
- Writing 2

❶ Comparing Themes

Narrative Point of View

1. Introduce the skill, using the instruction on the student page.
2. Give students a copy of **Comparing Themes Graphic Organizer B, *Graphic Organizer Transparencies,*** p. 33, to fill in with details about theme as they read.

Think Aloud: Model the Skill

Model a way of understanding theme. Say to students:

> Sometimes, I need to think about characters' actions and thoughts to figure out the theme, or central message, of a story. Suppose I read about a boy who feels sad on his birthday despite receiving a long-awaited present. Then, his father arrives home early from a business trip and the boy becomes happy. From these details, I can figure out that the theme of the story is that family closeness is very important to a child's happiness.

Comparing Literary Works

"If I Forget Thee, Oh Earth . . ." • *from* Silent Spring

❶ Comparing Themes

Theme is the message or insight about life that is conveyed in a short story, a play, or another literary work. Sometimes it is explicit, or stated directly. More often, it is implicit, or expressed indirectly, through the words and actions of the characters or the events of a story. The way theme is developed depends in part on the **genre,** or form, of the work.

- **Nonfiction:** In nonfiction literature, such as essays or articles, the meaning or insight is usually referred to as the **central idea.** The central idea is generally stated directly. A thesis statement expressing that idea may appear at the beginning of the work. Key ideas and supporting details presented throughout the work develop the central idea in a systematic way.
- **Fiction and poetry:** In fiction and poetry, the theme is often implicit. Readers can figure it out by looking at story events, the words and actions of characters, and patterns of related images and ideas called *motifs.* As readers make connections between various literary elements, the thematic message emerges.

Works of nonfiction and fiction can express similar central ideas and themes. Nonfiction and fiction can address the same concerns and subjects.

The following selections share a similar basic topic: the effects of human behavior on the environment. However, "If I Forget Thee, Oh Earth . . ." is a short story, and *Silent Spring* is nonfiction. Because they represent two different genres, the two works develop meaning in different ways. As you read, complete a Venn diagram like the one shown to analyze how theme and central ideas develop.

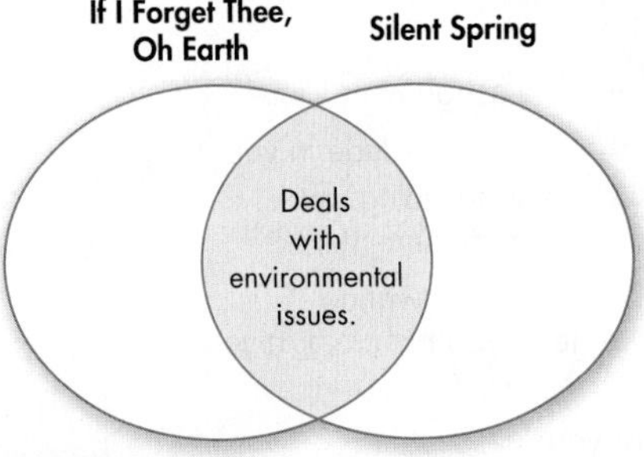

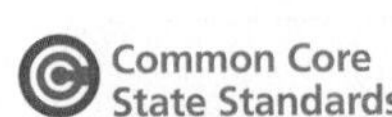

Reading Literature
2. Determine a theme or central idea of a text and analyze its development over the course of the text, including how it emerges and is shaped and refined by specific details; provide an objective summary of the text.

Reading Informational Text
2. Determine a central idea of a text and analyze its development over the course of the text, including how it emerges and is shaped and refined by specific details.

Writing
2. Write informative/explanatory texts to examine and convey complex ideas, concepts, and information clearly and accurately through the effective selection, organization, and analysis of content.

- Vocabulary flashcards
- Interactive journals
- More about the authors
- Selection audio
- Interactive graphic organizers

Vocabulary Development

Vocabulary Knowledge Rating

Create a **Vocabulary Knowledge Rating Chart** (***Professional Development Guidebook,*** p. 33) for these words from the selections:

purged (p. 162) *maladies* (p. 168)
perennial (p. 165) *moribund* (p. 168)
blight (p. 168)

(These words are glossed in the selection side columns.) Include as well the Big Question words that appear in the Writing About the Big Question sentence starters on the next page. (The Big Question vocabulary is introduced on pp. 2–3.)

Give students a copy of the chart. Read the words aloud, and have students mark their rating in the Before Reading column. Urge them to be alert to these words as they read and discuss the selection.

Tally how many students think they know a word to gauge how much instruction to provide. As students read and discuss the selection, point out the words and their context.

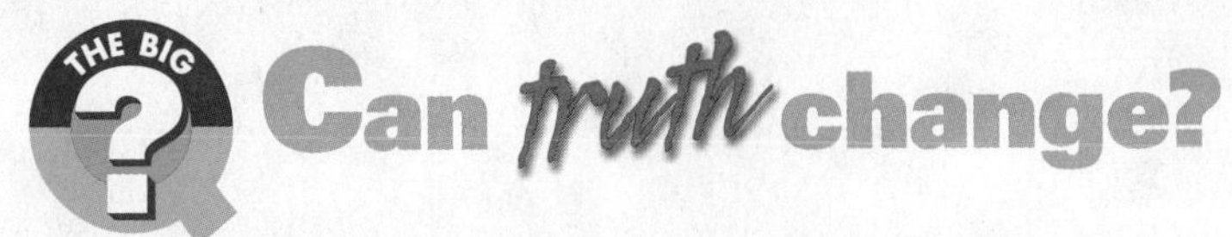

❷ Writing About the Big Question

Some people feel that the condition of Earth is a constant, unchangeable truth. Use these sentence starters to develop your ideas about the Big Question.

I **speculate** that in 100 years, Earth will be ____________________.

My **assumptions** are based on ____________________.

Meet the Authors

Arthur C. Clarke (1917–2008)

Author of "If I Forget Thee, Oh Earth . . ."

Born in England, Arthur C. Clarke was both a writer and a scientist. He wrote his first science-fiction stories during his teens, and he later published more than fifty works of fiction and nonfiction.

A True Scientist Although best known for his science fiction, Clarke was a serious scientist as well. In 1945, he published a technical article called "Extra-Terrestrial Relays" in which he established the principles of the satellite communications system we have today.

Rachel Carson (1907–1964)

Author of *Silent Spring*

Even as a young girl, Rachel Carson thought of herself as a writer, and she entered college to pursue that goal. Once there, she renewed an interest in nature and switched her major to marine biology. She later earned a master's degree in zoology.

Environmental Activist Carson had long been worried about the overuse of pesticides. "Everything which meant most to me as a naturalist was being threatened," she said, and she felt that the most important thing she could do was publicize the facts. *Silent Spring* became one of the most influential environmental books ever written. Carson died of cancer before she witnessed the major impact of her book.

Teaching Resources

- All *Unit 1 Resources,* pp. 213–229
- All *Authors in Depth,* Rachel Carson
- All *Graphic Organizer Transparencies,* pp. 33, 35
- All *Common Core Companion,* pp. 15–22; 97–104; 190–201
- All **Enriched Online Student Edition**
- L2 EL *Hear It!* **Audio CD**

All resources, including print (except *Authors in Depth*) and audio, are available at **www.PHLitOnline.com.**

Daily Bellringer

For each class during which you will teach this selection, have students complete one of the five Sentence Combining activities for Week 6 in the ***Daily Bellringer Activities*** booklet.

❷ Writing About the Big Question

1. Read the assignment with the class.
2. Recall ways that life on Earth has changed since 1910 and how it might change in the future. Ask students to consider what assumptions they make about people's actions and the impact of these on Earth's future.
3. Have students complete the sentence starters. Review responses as a class. (**Possible response**: I speculate that in 100 years, the Earth will be a healthier place. My assumptions are based on the focus on renewable energy.)
4. Remind students that their answers will help them think about the Big Question. Tell students to look for warnings about Earth's future as they read.

Concept Connector

Students will return to their responses to the sentence starters they completed before reading.

Multidraft Reading

To assist struggling readers and to deepen reading for all, apply multidraft reading protocols. For each reading, have students set the purpose indicated:

- **First reading**—identifying key ideas and details and answering any Reading Checks.
- **Second reading**—analyzing craft and structure and responding to the side-column prompts.
- **Third reading**—integrating knowledge and ideas, connecting to other texts and the world, and answering the end-of-selection questions.

For more guidance, refer to the ***Classroom Strategies and Teaching Routines*** card on multidraft reading.

For more about the authors and practice with the selection vocabulary, go online at **www.PHLitOnline.com.**

TEACH

1 Background

The title of "If I Forget Thee, Oh Earth. . ." draws on a quotation from Psalm 137:

If I forget thee, O Jerusalem, let my right hand forget her cunning.

This vow expresses the emotion of the ancient Hebrews, after they were forced into exile in Babylon in 597 B.C. The exiles in Arthur C. Clarke's story are the humans who live on the moon, the only humans still alive after all human life on Earth was destroyed in a nuclear holocaust.

2 Activating Prior Knowledge

Direct students to the image on the selection page. Ask them to think about films, television shows, or stories they have seen or read that focus on space travel. Have them offer examples of how each genre depicts modes of and reasons for space travel in the future. Do these depictions correspond with students' understanding of space travel?

Concept Connector →

Students will follow up on this activity after completing "If I Forget Thee, Oh Earth. . . ."

3 About the Selection

Ten-year-old Marvin lives on a space station and is taken on a special trip by his father to the outside world. This trip is the first time Marvin has even ventured outside the station. His father brings him to a valley from which they can see an object in the sky. Marvin's father tells his son that they are seeing the Earth, once home to humans but now a wasteland destroyed in a nuclear war. He wants Marvin to know what happened so the story can be passed on until the day that humans can once again set foot on Earth.

4 Literary Analysis

Theme

1. Remind students that details can often help them determine a story's theme.
2. **Ask** the Literary Analysis question.
   Possible response: Marvin is in a building with many levels. The Farmlands is an area with plants on the top level.

1 2 3

"If I Forget Thee, Oh Earth. . ."

Arthur C. Clarke

Literary Analysis
Theme What information about Marvin's environment appears in this description of the Farmlands?

4

Vocabulary
purged (purjd) *v.* cleansed

When Marvin was ten years old, his father took him through the long, echoing corridors that led up through Administration and Power, until at last they came to the uppermost levels of all and were among the swiftly growing vegetation of the Farmlands. Marvin liked it here: it was fun watching the great, slender plants creeping with almost visible eagerness toward the sunlight as it filtered down through the plastic domes to meet them. The smell of life was everywhere, awakening inexpressible longings in his heart: no longer was he breathing the dry, cool air of the residential levels, purged of all smells but the faint tang of ozone.[1] He wished he could stay here for a little while, but Father would not let him. They went onward until they had reached the entrance to the Observatory, which he had never visited: but they did not stop, and Marvin knew

1. **ozone** (ō' zōn') *n.* form of oxygen with a sharp odor.

Text Complexity Rubric

If I Forget Thee, Oh Earth . . .		
Qualitative Measures	**Context/ Knowledge Demands**	Space colony on the Moon; nuclear war; space travel 1 2 (3) 4 5
	Structure/ Language Clarity and Conventionality	Long sentences; challenging vocabulary 1 2 3 (4) 5
	Levels of Meaning/ Purpose/Concept Level	Challenging concepts (end of civilization on Earth; survival on the Moon) 1 2 3 (4) 5
Quantitative Measures	**Text Length**	Word Count: 1,773
	Lexile	1220L

4 with a sense of rising excitement that there could be only one goal left. For the first time in his life, he was going Outside.

There were a dozen of the surface vehicles, with their wide balloon tires and pressurized cabins, in the great servicing chamber. His father must have been expected, for they were led at once to the little scout car waiting by the huge circular door of the airlock. Tense with expectancy, Marvin settled himself down in the cramped cabin while his father started the motor and checked the controls. The inner door of the lock slid open and then closed behind them: he heard the roar of the great air pumps fade slowly away as the pressure dropped to zero. Then the "Vacuum" sign flashed on, the outer door parted, and before Marvin lay the land which he had never yet entered.

5 He had seen it in photographs, of course: he had watched it imaged on television screens a hundred times. But now it was lying all around him, burning beneath the fierce sun that crawled so slowly across the jet-black sky. He stared into the west, away from the blinding splendor of the sun—and there were the stars, as he had been told but had never quite believed. He gazed at them for a long time, marveling that anything could be so bright and yet so tiny. They were intense unscintillating points, and suddenly he remembered a rhyme he had once read in one of his father's books:

Twinkle, twinkle, little star,
How I wonder what you are.

Well, he knew what the stars were. Whoever asked that question must have been very stupid. And what did they mean by "twinkle"? You could see at a glance that all the stars shone with the same steady, unwavering light. He abandoned the puzzle and turned his attention to the landscape around him.

They were racing across a level plain at almost a hundred miles an hour, the great balloon tires sending up little spurts of dust behind them. There was no sign of the Colony: in the few minutes while he had been gazing at the stars, its domes and radio towers had fallen below the horizon. Yet there were other indications of man's presence, for about a mile ahead Marvin could see the curiously shaped structures clustering round the head of a mine. Now and then a puff of vapor would emerge from a squat smokestack and would instantly disperse.

8 They were past the mine in a moment: Father was driving with a reckless and exhilarating skill as if—it was a strange thought to come into a child's mind—he were trying to escape from something. In a few minutes they had reached the edge of the plateau on which the Colony had been built. The ground fell sharply away beneath them in a dizzying slope whose lower stretches were lost in shadow.

Literary Analysis
Theme What do the words "burning beneath the fierce sun" suggest about what Marvin is observing?

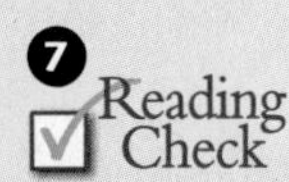

What astronomical bodies does Marvin see for the first time?

5 Literary Analysis

Theme

1. Have students **contrast** information about the Farmlands at the story's beginning with the environment described in the bracketed text.

   Answer: This environment is harsher and less inviting than the Farmlands, which seem fresh and energizing.

2. **Ask** the Literary Analysis question: What do the words "burning beneath the fierce sun" suggest about what Marvin is observing?

   Answer: The description suggests a severe, unwelcoming environment.

6 Connecting to the Big Question

1. Remind students that the "truth" as people understand it evolves as people gain experience.
2. Read the first paragraph of the bracketed text. **Ask:** How does Marvin's experience seeing the stars affect his understanding of them?

   Answer: Marvin sees that, contrary to the familiar rhyme in his father's books, stars do not twinkle.

3. Guide a discussion about the value of experience versus secondhand knowledge. **Ask:** How else does Marvin's experience affect him in a way that books and television did not? **Possible response:** His direct experience helps him to more fully appreciate the sun and stars.
4. **Ask:** What does this passage suggest about people's perceptions of the truth? **Possible response:** People often do not fully understand or appreciate something until they experience it for themselves.

7 Reading Check

Answer: Marvin sees the stars for the first time.

Text Complexity: Reader and Task Suggestions

If I Forget Thee, Oh Earth . . .	
Preparing to Read the Text • Use the Background information on TE p. 162 to discuss the concept of nuclear holocaust and what it might be like to live in space. • Discuss with students why it is important to learn about historical events. • Guide students to use Multidraft Reading strategies (TE p. 161).	**Leveled Tasks** *Levels of Meaning* If students will have difficulty with levels of meaning in the story, first have them read to identify details about the main character's life in the space station. Then, have them reread, taking notes on how the colony came to be isolated. Discuss their notes, offering clarification. *Synthesizing* If students will not have difficulty with the levels of meaning, have them take notes as they read, showing how the main character changes in his awareness of the predicament and its significance for him. As a class, discuss why the character changes.

PHLit Online!

This selection is available in interactive format in the **Enriched Online Student Edition**, at **www.PHLitOnline.com**, which includes an interactive graphic organizer.

8 Critical Thinking

Interpret

1. Read aloud the bracketed text, which begins on p.163. **Ask** students to identify details that describe the setting and to explain what effect these details have on the reader.
   Possible response: Details such as a "dizzying slope," a "jumbled wasteland," and mountain crests that "burn" in the setting sun have an ominous effect on the reader.
2. **Ask** students whether they can deduce the Colony's location from the details given so far. If they have no idea, explain that Clarke has not invented this description; it is an accurate description of an actual place.
   Possible response: Students might associate the word "craters" with the moon.

9 Literature in Context

Science Connection The International Space Station generates its own electric power through the use of giant solar panels. Still, the ISS is not entirely self-contained; it depends on the "home planet" for many supplies, including oxygen, food, fuel, and other consumables. The astronauts stay connected to life on Earth in other ways. The crew uses videophones and e-mail to stay in touch with their loved ones. Also, astronauts can watch DVDs and use other media tools to stay connected with current events and popular culture.

Connect to the Literature Point out that Marvin's space colony was entirely self-contained, with no connections to the uninhabited Earth. **Ask** students the Connect to the Literature question: How do you think the astronauts' feelings about living in outer space compare to Marvin's feelings?
Possible response: ISS astronauts are probably comforted by their connections with Earth, whereas Marvin is angered and saddened by Earth's destruction.

9 **LITERATURE IN CONTEXT**

Science Connection

International Space Station
In Arthur C. Clarke's story, a space colony is all that remains of the human species. If the idea of a space colony seems implausible, consider the fact that a small colony is being developed directly over your head in the form of an International Space Station. Sixteen nations are contributing scientific and technological resources to build the Station, which has been under construction since 1998. The Space Station will be used for experiments and research, and it will also provide insight into the way humans can learn to live and work in outer space. The first astronaut crew arrived at the Station in November of 2000, and since then, people have lived and worked continuously at the Station, more than 200 miles above Earth.

Connect to the Literature

How do you think the astronauts' feelings about living in outer space compare to Marvin's feelings?

Ahead, as far as the eye could reach, was a jumbled wasteland of craters, mountain ranges, and ravines. The crests of the mountains, catching the low sun, burned like islands of fire in a sea of darkness: and above them the stars still shone as steadfastly as ever.

There could be no way forward—yet there was. Marvin clenched his fists as the car edged over the slope and started the long descent. Then he saw the barely visible track leading down the mountainside, and relaxed a little. Other men, it seemed, had gone this way before.

Night fell with a shocking abruptness as they crossed the shadow line and the sun dropped below the crest of the plateau. The twin searchlights sprang into life, casting blue-white bands on the rocks ahead, so that there was scarcely need to check their speed. For hours they drove through valleys and past the foot of mountains whose peaks seemed to comb the stars, and sometimes they emerged for a moment into the sunlight as they climbed over higher ground.

And now on the right was a wrinkled, dusty plain, and on the left, its ramparts and terraces rising mile after mile into the sky, was a wall of mountains that marched into the distance until its peaks sank from sight below the rim of the world. There was no sign that men had ever explored this land, but once they passed the skeleton of a crashed rocket, and beside it a stone cairn[2] surmounted by a metal cross.

It seemed to Marvin that the mountains stretched on forever: but at last, many hours later, the range ended in a towering, precipitous headland[3] that rose steeply from a cluster of little hills. They drove down into a shallow valley that curved in a great arc toward the far side of the mountains: and as they did so, Marvin slowly realized that something very strange was happening in the land ahead.

The sun was now low behind the hills on the right: the valley before them should be in total darkness. Yet it was awash with a cold white radiance that came spilling over the crags beneath which they were driving. Then, suddenly, they were out in the open plain, and the source of the light lay before them in all its glory.

2. **cairn** (kern) *n.* a cone-shaped pile of stones built as a monument.
3. **precipitous headland** (prē sip′ ə təs hed′ land′) *n.* steep cliff that juts out over water.

Vocabulary Development

CCSS Language 6

Selection Vocabulary Reinforcement

Students will benefit from additional examples and practice with the selection vocabulary words. Reinforce their comprehension with "show-you-know" sentences. The first part of the sentence uses the vocabulary word in an appropriate context. The second part of the sentence—the "show-you-know" part—clarifies the first. Model the strategy with this example for *distribute*:

She asked Paul to *distribute* the newspaper in his neighborhood; he gave each neighbor a copy later that day.

Then give students these sentence prompts, and coach them in creating the clarification part:

1. Sarah *purged* her closet of the clothes she didn't wear anymore; _______.
   Sample answer: when she was finished, she donated the clothes to charity.
2. Pizza was a *perennial* favorite in the school cafeteria; _______.
   Sample answer: students and staff requested it time and time again.

It was very quiet in the little cabin now that the motors had stopped. The only sound was the faint whisper of the oxygen feed and an occasional metallic crepitation as the outer walls of the vehicle radiated away their heat. For no warmth at all came from the great silver crescent that floated low above the far horizon and flooded all this land with pearly light. It was so brilliant that minutes passed before Marvin could accept its challenge and look steadfastly into its glare, but at last he could discern the outlines of continents, the hazy border of the atmosphere, and the white islands of cloud. And even at this distance, he could see the glitter of sunlight on the polar ice.

It was beautiful, and it called to his heart across the abyss of space. There in that shining crescent were all the wonders that he had never known—the hues of sunset skies, the moaning of the sea on pebbled shores, the patter of falling rain, the unhurried benison of snow. These and a thousand others should have been his rightful heritage, but he knew them only from the books and ancient records, and the thought filled him with the anguish of exile.

10 Why could they not return? It seemed so peaceful beneath those lines of marching cloud. Then Marvin, his eyes no longer blinded by the glare, saw that the portion of the disk that should have been in darkness was gleaming faintly with an evil phosphorescence[4] and he remembered. He was looking upon the funeral pyre of a world—upon the radioactive aftermath of Armageddon.[5] Across a quarter of a million miles of space, the glow of dying atoms was still visible, a perennial reminder of the ruinous past. It would be centuries yet before that deadly glow died from the rocks and life could return again to fill that silent, empty world.

And now Father began to speak, telling Marvin the story which until this moment had meant no more to him than the fairy tales he had once been told. There were many things he could not understand: it was impossible for him to picture the glowing, multicolored pattern of life on the planet he had never seen. Nor could he comprehend the forces that had destroyed it in the end, leaving the Colony, preserved by its isolation, as the sole survivor. Yet he could share the agony of those final days, when the Colony had learned at last that never again would the supply ships come flaming down through the stars with gifts from home. One by one the radio stations had ceased to call: on the shadowed globe the lights of the cities had dimmed and died, and they were alone at last, as no men had ever been alone before, carrying in their hands the future of the race.

4. **phosphorescence** (fäs´ fə res´ əns) *n.* emission of light resulting from exposure to radiation.
5. **Armageddon** (är´ mə ged´ ′n) *n.* in the Bible, the place where the final battle between good and evil is to be fought.

Literary Analysis
Theme Which details in these paragraphs provide an insight into what Marvin and others in his colony have lost?

Vocabulary
perennial (pə ren´ ē əl) *adj.* happening over and over; perpetual

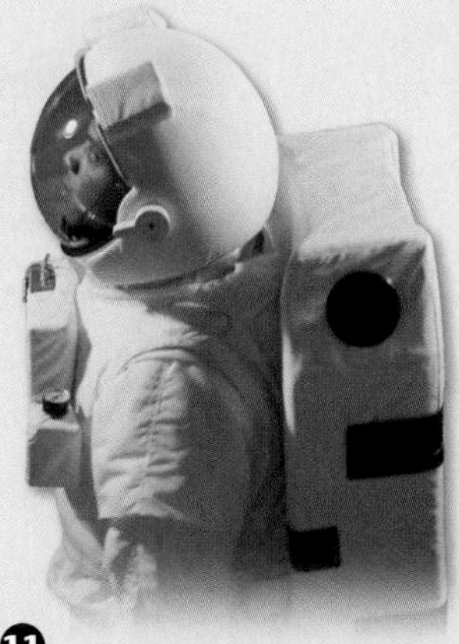

11 **Reading Check**
What does Marvin notice in a portion of the disk?

10 Literary Analysis

Theme

1. Tell students to focus on adjectives in the first paragraph of the bracketed text. Discuss how the words differ from the previous descriptions of Marvin's surroundings. Then, **ask** students to infer the identity of the "shining crescent."
   Answer: It is Earth.
2. Direct students' attention to the description of Earth in the second paragraph of the bracketed text. Discuss the contrasts between the two paragraphs. **Ask** students what warning is implied in the description of Earth in the second paragraph of the bracketed text.
   Answer: The description implies a warning of the dangers of nuclear weapons. Clarke describes an Earth glowing with radiation and says it will be uninhabitable for centuries to come.
3. **Ask** the Literary Analysis question: Which details in these paragraphs provide an insight into what Marvin and others in his colony have lost?
   Answer: Details that describe the beauty and appeal of Earth—the sunsets, the sounds of rain and the ocean, the gentle fall of snow—provide a poignant reminder of everything the Colony members have lost.

11 Reading Check

Answer: Marvin notices that a portion of the disk is glowing with radiation.

Differentiated Instruction for Universal Access

Strategy for Special-Needs Students

Have students create two-column charts, with one column labeled Colony and the other column labeled Earth. Then, in each column, tell students to write adjectives from the story that describe the setting. After students finish their charts, have them write sentences summarizing each setting.

EL Strategy for English Learners

Tell students that certain words can be signals of a statement of opinion. In the story, words such as *beautiful, strange, fun, cramped, curiously, reckless,* and *exhilarating* express a person's feelings, not facts. Have students look for these and similar "signals of opinion" as they read. Discuss how the author's word choices impact the theme of the story.

12 Literary Analysis

Theme

Ask the Literary Analysis question.

Answer: The message is that if Earth is destroyed by radiation, it will be uninhabitable. It is a warning against the use of nuclear weapons.

Concept Connector

Have students return to the Activating Prior Knowledge activity. Ask them to compare the portrayal of space travel in the text with the previously mentioned genres. Then, have students compare their Writing About the Big Question responses with their ideas after reading the selection.

ASSESS

Answers

Remind students to support their answers with evidence from the text.

1. (a) Marvin determines to take this trip one day with his own child. (b) Marvin's father wanted to share his dream that future generations could return to Earth.
2. (a) The dusty, cratered surface and airless atmosphere suggest a lunar setting. (b) The accurate description of the moon's surface and its nearness to Earth make the story seem more realistic.
3. (a) Nuclear war destroyed Earth. (b) **Possible response:** Clarke might have suggested that nations settle differences peacefully.
4. **Possible response:** Marvin's experience helps him to appreciate Earth's tragedy and want to preserve the colony and reclaim his heritage on Earth. This experience makes the truth more real to him.

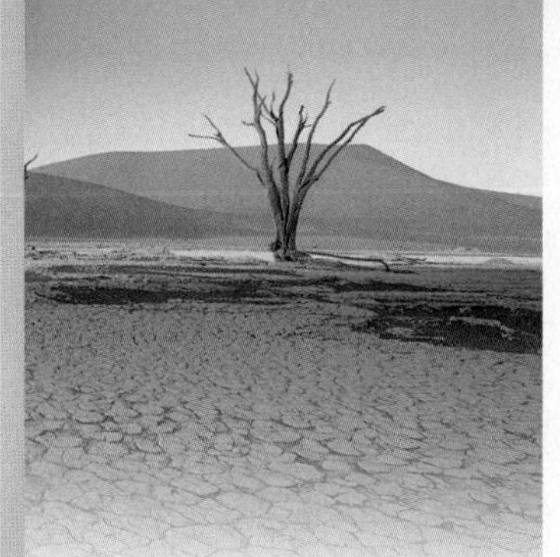

Then had followed the years of despair, and the long-drawn battle for survival in their fierce and hostile world. That battle had been won, though barely: this little oasis of life was safe against the worst that Nature could do. But unless there was a goal, a future toward which it could work, the Colony would lose the will to live, and neither machines nor skill nor science could save it then.

So, at last, Marvin understood the purpose of this pilgrimage. He would never walk beside the rivers of that lost and legendary world, or listen to the thunder raging above its softly rounded hills. Yet one day—how far ahead?—his children's children would return to claim their heritage. The winds and the rains would scour the poisons from the burning lands and carry them to the sea, and in the depths of the sea they would waste their venom until they could harm no living things. Then the great ships that were still waiting here on the silent, dusty plains could lift once more into space, along the road that led to home.

Literary Analysis
Theme What message about the future is conveyed through the details in this paragraph?

That was the dream: and one day, Marvin knew with a sudden flash of insight, he would pass it on to his own son, here at this same spot with the mountains behind him and the silver light from the sky streaming into his face.

He did not look back as they began the homeward journey. He could not bear to see the cold glory of the crescent Earth fade from the rocks around him, as he went to rejoin his people in their long exile.

Critical Thinking

Cite textual evidence to support your responses.

1. **Key Ideas and Details (a)** At the end of the story, what does Marvin realize? **(b) Draw Conclusions:** What was the purpose of Marvin's trip with his father?
2. **Craft and Structure (a) Infer:** What evidence from the text indicates that the story is set on the moon? **(b) Analyze:** How does the choice of setting make the story more realistic?
3. **Integration of Knowledge and Ideas (a) Infer:** How did Earth come to be destroyed? **(b) Speculate:** What suggestions do you think Clarke might have offered today to prevent a situation like this from occurring?
4. **Integration of Knowledge and Ideas** How does the truth about the moon and Earth shift for Marvin after his trip with his father? *[Connect to the Big Question: Can truth change?]*

Think Aloud

Vocabulary: Using Context

Direct students' attention to the word *pilgrimage* in the bracketed text on this page. Using a think-aloud process, model how to use context to infer the meaning of an unknown word. Say to students:

I'm going to think aloud to show you how I would figure out the meaning of the word *pilgrimage* from its context.

In the first sentence, the author refers to it as "this pilgrimage," so I know that he is talking about something that happened in the story. We know that the only thing that happened to Marvin in the story was the trip on which his father took him to the spot where he could see Earth and hear about its history. From the context of the story, then, I can figure out that a *pilgrimage* is a journey of some sort. Since Marvin thinks about the "purpose" of the pilgrimage, I conclude that a pilgrimage is a journey to a specific place that has a special meaning

PHLit Online!

This selection is available in interactive format in the **Enriched Online Student Edition**, online at **www.PHLitOnline.com**, which includes an interactive graphic organizer.

13 14 15

from Silent Spring

Rachel Carson

There was once a town in the heart of America where all life seemed to live in harmony with its surroundings. The town lay in the midst of a checkerboard of prosperous farms, with fields of grain and hillsides of orchards where, in spring, white clouds of bloom drifted above the green fields. In autumn, oak and maple and birch set up a blaze of color that flamed and flickered across a backdrop of pines. Then foxes barked in the hills and deer silently crossed the fields, half hidden in the mists of the fall mornings.

Along the roads, laurel, viburnum and alder, great ferns and wildflowers delighted the traveler's eye through much of the year. Even in winter the roadsides were places of beauty, where

Literary Analysis
Central Idea Which details in this paragraph paint a picture of the beauty and energy of nature? Explain.

13 Background

Pesticides Pesticides are chemical compounds intended to destroy crop-eating insects. Pesticides can be lethal to many species besides the insects they are intended to kill. Partly because of the publication of *Silent Spring*, the United States began phasing out the pesticide DDT in 1970 and banned it entirely in 1972.

14 Activating Prior Knowledge

Ask students to think carefully about the selection title. Pose the following questions to students: Is spring normally a silent season? What sounds do you associate with spring? What might it mean if these sounds were no longer heard?

Concept Connector

Students will follow up on this activity after completing *Silent Spring*.

15 About the Selection

In this excerpt from the landmark book *Silent Spring*, Rachel Carson sounds a warning about how the indiscriminate use of pesticides threatens our environment. At the time Carson wrote, most people had little idea about the unintended harm of these chemicals. In the tradition of many writers who have a lesson to teach, Carson introduces her ideas in the form of a fable.

16 Literary Analysis

Theme

1. **Ask** the Literary Analysis question: Which details in this paragraph paint a picture of the beauty and energy of nature? Explain.
   Possible response: Vibrant details that convey the pleasantness of the natural setting.

Text Complexity Rubric

from Silent Spring	
Qualitative Measures	
Context/ Knowledge Demands	Written before many knew dangers of pesticides 1 2 (3) 4 5
Structure/ Language Clarity	Conversational; some challenging vocabulary 1 2 (3) 4 5
Levels of Meaning	Accessible concept (the dangers of pesticides) 1 2 (3) 4 5
Quantitative Measures	
Text Length	Word Count: 1,657
Lexile	1080L

Reader and Task Suggestions

Preparing to Read the Text

- Using the Background note on TE p. 167, discuss pesticides and the dangers they pose to the environment.
- Explain that although this is a nonfiction selection, the first part is told as a fable. Explain what a fable is and how it can present difficult concepts.
- Guide students to use Multidraft Reading strategies (TE p. 161).

Leveled Tasks

Levels of Meaning Have students read the essay and list the changes in the environment described in the fable. Have them reread and note how pesticides caused those changes.

Synthesizing If students will not have difficulty with levels of meaning in the essay, have them note how Carson conveys her message effectively.

17 Connecting to the Big Question

1. Explain to students that in the past, humans did not have a firm understanding of the impact their actions had on the environment.
2. Invite a volunteer to read the bracketed text aloud. Then, **ask:** How does this paragraph compare to the previous positive description of the town?

   Answer: A land full of bustling life and health has become a landscape of death and destruction. Plants and animals have died, and people have died or become ill.
3. **Ask** students what new truth is revealed as a result of the "strange blight."

   Possible answer: The pestilence reveals that introducing foreign substances into the environment has devastating consequences. The Earth is a sensitive environment that humans need to be conscious of in order to avoid further negative ramifications.

18 Critical Viewing

Possible response: There are no animals visible in the photograph, and the land appears lifeless, covered with dead trees and brown grass.

This selection is available in interactive format in the **Enriched Online Student Edition**, online at **www.PHLitOnline.com**, which includes an interactive graphic organizer.

countless birds came to feed on the berries and on the seed heads of the dried weeds rising above the snow. The countryside was, in fact, famous for the abundance and variety of its bird life, and when the flood of migrants was pouring through in spring and fall people traveled from great distances to observe them. Others came to fish the streams, which flowed clear and cold out of the hills and contained shady pools where trout lay. So it had been from the days many years ago when the first settlers raised their houses, sank their wells, and built their barns.

Vocabulary
blight (blīt) *n.* something that destroys or prevents growth
maladies (mal′ ə dēz) *n.* diseases

Then a strange blight crept over the area and everything began to change. Some evil spell had settled on the community: mysterious maladies swept the flocks of chickens; the cattle and sheep sickened and died. Everywhere was a shadow of death. The farmers spoke of much illness among their families. In the town the doctors had become more and more puzzled by new kinds of sickness appearing among their patients. There had been several sudden and unexplained deaths, not only among adults but even among children, who would be stricken suddenly while at play and die within a few hours.

Vocabulary
moribund (môr′ i bund′) *adj.* slowly dying

There was a strange stillness. The birds, for example—where had they gone? Many people spoke of them, puzzled and disturbed. The feeding stations in the backyards were deserted. The few birds seen anywhere were moribund; they trembled violently and could not fly. It was a spring without voices. On the mornings that had once throbbed with the dawn chorus of robins, catbirds, doves, jays, wrens, and scores of other bird voices there was now no sound; only silence lay over the fields and woods and marsh.

On the farms the hens brooded, but no chicks hatched. The farmers complained that they were unable to raise any pigs—the litters were small and the young survived only a few days. The apple trees were coming into bloom but no bees droned among the blossoms, so there was no pollination and there would be no fruit.

The roadsides, once so attractive, were now lined with browned and withered vegetation as though swept by fire. These, too, were silent, deserted by all living things. Even

18 ▶ **Critical Viewing** What details in this picture indicate that a "strange blight" may have affected this area? **[Connect]**

19

⓳ Visual Connections

Whole-Class Activity

1. **Ask** students to look at the picture and describe what they see.

   Possible response: I see the remains of a farm. The building and the fence are weathered and collapsing. The grass and shrubbery look dead.

2. Then, have students think about Carson's description of the town following the arrival of the "strange blight." **Ask** students to compare and contrast Carson's description with the picture.

   Possible response: The picture is a clear representation of Carson's description. All life has abandoned the farm, leaving behind that which the white granular powder could not poison.

3. Now, **ask** students what mood, or tone, the picture presents.

   Possible responses: The picture presents a somber mood. Death and despair have replaced life. There is a feeling of solitude in the old, forsaken farmland.

Small-Group Activity

1. Have students form small groups. Post the following sentence starter: "This farmland once . . ." Have groups discuss the sentence starter and speculate about the farm's function before the picture was taken. Ask groups to write a response in the form of a brief story.
2. Ask one student from each group to record the group's story.
3. Have a volunteer from each group read the story aloud. Record similarities and differences of the stories on the board. To model the process of speculation, choose one of the ideas and discuss how the picture supports it.

Individual Activity

1. Briefly discuss the picture with the class.
2. Ask students to write a response to the picture that examines what they see, think, and feel.
3. Tell students to reread their responses, either in class or at home, and make any appropriate revisions.
4. Display each student response in the classroom. Urge students to share their responses.

Differentiated Instruction for Universal Access

Enrichment for Advanced Readers

Suggest that students read additional works by Rachel Carson. Provide students with **Authors In Depth,** Gold Level, which contains the following selections:

- from *The Sea Around Us* (p. 93)
- from *Always Rachel* (p. 97)
- "An Island I Remember" (p. 99)
- from *Under the Sea-Wind* (p. 104)

After students have read these or other works by Carson, have them form discussion groups in which they compare and contrast the selections. Suggest criteria for comparison, such as setting, theme, characters, and author's purpose. To extend the activity, have volunteers present to the class brief oral reports on their favorite Carson selections.

20 Literary Analysis

Theme

Ask the first Literary Analysis question.

Possible response: Students might say that the disturbing surprise they feel shows that the author wants to highlight the fact that humans are destroying life and to bring readers to reject this destruction.

21 Literary Analysis

Theme

Ask the second Literary Analysis question.

Answer: The theme is stated directly. Carson directly addresses her readers when she says that the use of pesticides can turn her imagined fable into reality.

Concept Connector

Have students recall the Activating Prior Knowledge exercise and compare their responses before reading. Then, have them connect their Writing About the Big Question responses to the story.

ASSESS

Answers

Remind students to support their answers with evidence from the text.

1. (a) Life is idyllic. The world is clean, beautiful, and fruitful. (b) The condition of life changes for the worse. Animals and people get sick and die.
2. (a) They sicken and die. (b) Carson's reference to "white granular powder" indicates that the source of the problem is chemicals.
3. (a) The town does not exist. (b) **Possible response:** By using a fictional town, Carson creates a more vivid example.
4. (a) Carson blames people for causing the problem. (b) **Possible response:** People should respect the environment.
5. **Possible response:** Some students may say that most Americans are definitely more aware of environmental issues because of the efforts of the media to educate the public about protecting our environment and because of government agencies, such as the US Environmental Protection Agency, which promote programs and laws dedicated to preserving the environment.

Literary Analysis
Central Idea How might your reaction to this sudden change suggest the author's message?

the streams were now lifeless. Anglers[1] no longer visited them, for all the fish had died.

20 In the gutters under the eaves and between the shingles of the roofs, a white granular powder still showed a few patches; some weeks before it had fallen like snow upon the roofs and the lawns, the fields and streams.

No witchcraft, no enemy action had silenced the rebirth of new life in this stricken world. The people had done it themselves.

Literary Analysis
Central Idea Is the central idea stated directly here or is it implied? Explain.

21 This town does not actually exist, but it might easily have a thousand counterparts in America or elsewhere in the world. I know of no community that has experienced all the misfortunes I describe. Yet every one of these disasters has actually happened somewhere, and many real communities have already suffered a substantial number of them. A grim specter has crept upon us almost unnoticed, and this imagined tragedy may easily become a stark reality we all shall know.

1. **anglers** (aŋ´ glərz) *n.* people who fish with a line and hook.

Critical Thinking

Cite textual evidence to support your responses.

1. **Key Ideas and Details (a)** What is the condition of life at the beginning of this excerpt? **(b) Compare and Contrast:** How does the condition of life change as the narrative continues?
2. **Key Ideas and Details (a)** What happens to the farm animals and the vegetation? **(b) Infer:** What causes this sudden change?
3. **Craft and Structure (a)** What information about the town does Carson reveal at the end of the excerpt? **(b) Speculate:** Do you think the narrative would be more effective if the town was real? Why or why not?
4. **Integration of Knowledge and Ideas (a)** According to Carson, who caused the environmental problems? **(b) Speculate:** What suggestions do you think Carson would make to people today?
5. **Integration of Knowledge and Ideas** Do you think most Americans' understanding of environmental issues has changed since Carson first wrote *Silent Spring*? Why or why not? *[Connect to the Big Question: Can truth change?]*

Vocabulary Development

Vocabulary Knowledge Rating

When students have completed reading and discussing "If I Forget Thee, O Earth…" and the excerpt from *Silent Spring*, have them take out their **Vocabulary Knowledge Rating Chart.** Read the words aloud once more and have students rate their knowledge of the words again in the After Reading column. Clarify any words that are still problematic. Have students write their own definition and example or sentence in the appropriate column. Then have students complete the Vocabulary Practice activities on the next page. Encourage students to use the words in further discussion and written work about the selections. Remind them that they will be accountable for these words on the **Selection Test** (*Unit 1 Resources*, pp. 224–226 or 227–229.)

After You Read

"If I Forget Thee, Oh Earth . . ." • *from* Silent Spring

ASSESS

Answers

Comparing Themes

1. **Key Ideas and Details** Use a chart like the one shown to analyze the theme expressed in "If I Forget Thee, Oh Earth . . ." and the central idea expressed in the excerpt from *Silent Spring.* First, list important details from each selection and what you think the details mean. Use this information to suggest the theme or central idea of the selection.

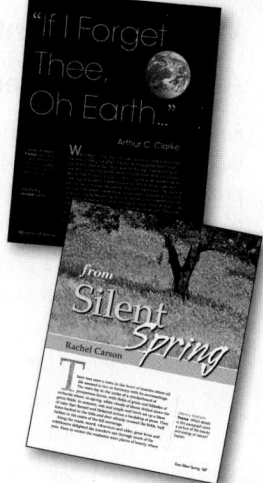

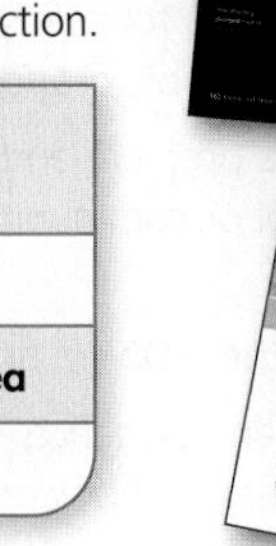

Details from "If I Forget Thee, Oh Earth..."	What They Mean	Theme
Details from *Silent Spring*	**What They Mean**	**Central Idea**

2. **Craft and Structure (a)** Using details from the chart, explain how the theme and central idea in the two selections are similar. **(b)** How is the meaning or insight expressed differently in each one?

Timed Writing

Reflective Text: Essay

Write an essay in which you compare your reactions to the way "If I Forget Thee, Oh Earth . . ." and the excerpt from *Silent Spring* explore a theme and a central idea. In your response, consider how the genre of each selection affects your reading experience. **(25 minutes)**

5-Minute Planner

1. Read the prompt carefully and completely.
2. Jot down your answers to these questions to help organize your thoughts:
   - Do you feel more affected by the experiences of the character Marvin or by the words of Rachel Carson, the author of *Silent Spring?*
   - Which genre do you find more effective in shaping meaning and expressing ideas—fiction or nonfiction? Why?
   - Why do you think an author would choose one genre over another when conveying an important insight or idea?
3. Decide on a structure for your essay. Plan the points you will cover in each paragraph.
4. Reread the prompt and then draft your essay.

Comparing Themes

1. **Possible response:** Detail from **"If I Forget Thee, Oh Earth . . .":** "It would be centuries yet before that deadly glow died . . ." **What It Means:** Earth has become radioactive. **Theme:** Humans have the ability to destroy themselves as well as the Earth. **Detail from *Silent Spring*:** "Then a strange blight crept over the area. . . . [C]attle and sheep sickened and died." **What It Means:** An unknown source breeds sickness and death. **Central Idea:** People have polluted their environment, making it toxic to life.

For other sample answers see ***Graphic Organizer Transparencies,* Comparing Themes Graphic Organizer A (After You Read),** p. 34, and the **Additional Answers** section.

2. (a) Both selections use imagined visions of the future to warn readers about the consequences of harming Earth. (b) Clarke's story belongs to the science-fiction genre. Rachel Carson grounds her piece in reality by describing a town that could exist anywhere in the world.

Timed Writing

1. Review the prompt with students.
2. Have students use the 5-Minute Planner to structure their time. Guide them in answering the bulleted questions.
3. Allow students 30 minutes to complete the assignment.
4. As students prewrite and draft, have them refer to a completed version of the **Identifying Strong Textual Evidence Graphic Organizer, Summarizing the Text Graphic Organizer, Analyzing the Central Idea Graphic Organizer,** or to a completed version of the chart on this page.

Six Traits Focus

✔	Ideas		Word Choice
✔	Organization		Sentence Fluency
	Voice		Conventions

Assessment Resources

Unit 1 Resources

L1 L2 EL **Selection Test A,** pp. 224–226.
L3 L4 EL **Selection Test B,** pp. 227–229.
L3 L4 **Open-Book Test,** pp. 221–223.

PHLit Online! All assessment resources are available at **www.PHLitOnline.com.**

Common Core State Standards

- Writing 1, 1.a, b, c, d, e
- Language 2.c, 6

Introducing the Writing Assignment

Review the assignment and the criteria, using the instruction on the student page.

Elizabeth McCracken on Word Choice

Show students Segment 3 on Elizabeth McCracken on the *See It!* DVD or from this page in the **Enriched Online Student Edition** at **www.PHLitOnline.com.** Discuss the difference between writing a story and writing a problem-and-solution essay.

Writing Workshop *Work in Progress*

If students have completed the Work-in-Progress assignments on pp. 123 and 151, suggest that they consider developing their Work-in-Progress ideas in a problem-and-solution essay.

What Do You Notice?

1. Have a volunteer read the question aloud.
2. **Ask** students what they notice about the sentences. (**Possible response:** Rachel Carson has used personification; her word choice is vivid; she uses the verb form *shall.*)
3. Guide students to understand that Carson's diction helps her to achieve a specific purpose: to persuade her audience. The vivid words she has chosen (*grim specter, crept, tragedy, stark*) stand out within a seemingly simple and direct statement.

Writing Workshop

Write Arguments

Argument: Problem-and-Solution Essay

Some forms of writing engage us in the struggles and resolutions of our daily lives. In a **problem-and-solution essay,** an author identifies a problem and then argues for a possible solution. You might use this type of writing in letters, memos, proposals, or editorials.

Assignment Write a problem-and-solution essay about an issue that confronts your school or community. Your essay should feature the following elements:

✓ a statement of the *problem* and a suggested *solution*

✓ *valid reasoning* and *evidence*, such as *facts* and *expert opinions*, that show the problem's scope and support an effective solution

✓ formal and objective *language* appropriate to your audience

✓ logical *organization* and a *concluding statement* or section that supports your argument

✓ *error-free grammar,* including correct use of pronouns

To preview problem-and-solution essay criteria, see page 179.

Writing Workshop: *Work in Progress*

Review the work you did on pages 123 and 151.

WRITE GUY
Jeff Anderson, M.Ed.

What Do You Notice?

Powerful Diction

Read the following sentences from Rachel Carson's *Silent Spring* several times.

A grim specter has crept upon us almost unnoticed, and this imagined tragedy may easily become a stark reality we all shall know.

What do you notice about the passage? Discuss your observations with a partner. Then, discuss Carson's diction, or word choice. Consider how you might use vivid word choices in your own writing.

Common Core State Standards

Writing

1. Write arguments to support claims in an analysis of substantive topics or texts, using valid reasoning and relevant and sufficient evidence.

1.b. Develop claim(s) and counterclaims fairly, supplying evidence for each while pointing out the strengths and limitations of both in a manner that anticipates the audience's knowledge level and concerns.

1.d. Establish and maintain a formal style and objective tone while attending to the norms and conventions of the discipline in which they are writing.

Reading-Writing Connection

To get a feel for the use of problem-and-solution structure in a speech, read "First Inaugural Address" by Franklin Delano Roosevelt on page 552.

Teaching Resources

The following resources can be used to enrich or extend the instruction.

All *Unit 1 Resources*
Writing Workshop, pp. 230–231

All *Common Core Companion,*
pp. 190–201; 213–214

All *Professional Development Guidebook*
Rubrics for Self-Assessment: Problem-and-Solution Essay,
pp. 244–245

All *Graphic Organizer Transparencies*
Rubric for Self-Assessment: Problem-and-Solution Essay,
p. 36

All *See It! DVD*
Elizabeth McCracken,
Segments 3 and 4

All resources, including print and video, are also available at **www.PHLitOnline.com.**

Prewriting/Planning Strategies

Choose a topic. To select a topic for your problem-and-solution essay, use one of the following strategies:

- **Media Scan** Review local newspapers and television news programs for items about issues and problems in your community. List problems for which you can imagine practical solutions, and select one as your topic.
- **Sentence Starters** Complete the following sentence starters and jot down any associated ideas that come to mind. Then, choose one of the issues generated by the sentence starters as your topic.

One issue that needs to be addressed is ____
The biggest problem people my age face is ____
Life would be better in my community if ____
The world would be a much better place if ____

PHLit Online!
www.PHLitOnline.com
- Author video: Writing Process
- Author video: Rewards of Writing

Create a problem profile. Once you have chosen a topic, create a profile like the one shown to help you focus your essay on a specific aspect of the problem. Answer the following questions about the problem:

- Who is affected by the problem?
- What causes the problem to occur?
- Is there more than one cause of the problem?
- What are some possible solutions to the problem?

Problem Profile
Problem: Litter is creating an unsafe and unsightly environment.
Who is affected? Everyone on Earth
What causes the problem? Lack of: • responsibility • environmental education • sense of ownership
What are the possible solutions? Stiffer fines, more policing, more environmental education, volunteer trash pickup

Consider your audience. Once you have clearly defined the problem, collect the details and information you will need to start your draft. Assess all possible solutions and weed out the less practical ones. Then, determine whom you want to reach with your essay and which aspects of the problem affect them most. For example, if you are trying to reach community leaders, you may shape your message differently than if you are trying to reach a peer group. As you narrow your focus, identify the ideas that will have the strongest impact on your target audience.

Applying Understanding by Design Principles

Clarifying Expected Outcomes: Using Rubrics

- Before students begin working on this assignment, have them preview the Rubric for Self-Assessment (p. 179) to learn what qualities their problem-and-solution essays must have. A copy of this rubric appears in ***Graphic Organizer Transparencies***, p. 36.
- Review the criteria in the rubric with the class. Before students use the rubric to assess their writing, work with them to rate the Student Model (p. 178) using the rubric.
- If you wish to assess students' problem-and-solution essays with either a 4-point or a 6-point scoring rubric, see ***Professional Development Guidebook***, pp. 244–245.

Prewriting/Planning Strategies

1. Introduce the prewriting strategies, using the instruction on the student page.
2. Have students apply the strategies to choose a topic.

Teaching the Strategies

1. Have students bring in newspapers and magazines to browse.
2. Give students the example problem of a deteriorating community playground and have them make a class problem profile.

   Possible response: Who is affected: *children and parents.* Causes of problem: *outdated playground equipment, lack of funds to improve or replace equipment.* Possible solutions: *implement new tax, have fund-raiser, lobby local businesses for funds and materials.*

Think Aloud: Model Considering Your Audience

Model the strategy, using the following "think aloud":

For the playground problem, my target audience is the whole community, not just children and parents. If I suggest a new tax, taxpayers who aren't parents may disapprove. Instead, I can suggest a fundraiser so that helping is optional.

Six Traits Focus

✓	Ideas		Word Choice
	Organization		Sentence Fluency
	Voice		Conventions

Prentice Hall EssayScorer

A writing prompt for this mode of writing can be found on the ***Prentice Hall Essay Scorer*** at **www.PHLitOnline.com.**

Drafting Strategies

1. Introduce the drafting strategies, using the instruction on the student page.
2. Have the students apply the strategies as they draft.

Teaching the Strategies

1. Take the class example of the community playground, and have volunteers think of ways to start the essay with a personal example, an anecdote, and a scenario.

   Possible responses: Personal example: *I took my younger brother to the playground, but we had to leave because the playground was unsafe.* Anecdote: *Most parents drive across town to another playground when their children want to play.* Scenario: *The outdated equipment could cause injuries, which increases the likelihood of lawsuits.*

2. Give students these examples for providing elaboration on the community playground example: Statistics: *57% of community members have children;* Expert opinion: *a lawyer's appraisal of playground injury lawsuits;* Comparable situation: *a nearby community's fundraiser for rebuilding its playground.*

Think Aloud: Model Addressing Readers' Concerns

Model the strategy, using the following "think aloud":

> Suppose that my essay suggests holding an art fair to raise money for a new playground. I'll include skeptical questions that readers may ask, such as "Where will we get artworks to sell?" Then, in my essay, I address the readers' concerns by including an answer, such as, "We'll ask local artists to donate works to support this worthy cause."

Six Traits Focus

✓	Ideas		Word Choice
✓	Organization		Sentence Fluency
	Voice		Conventions

Drafting Strategies

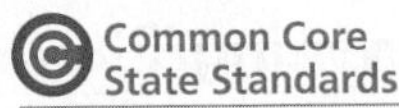

Common Core State Standards

Writing

1.a. Introduce precise claim(s), distinguish the claim(s) from alternate or opposing claims, and create an organization that establishes clear relationships among claim(s), counterclaims, reasons, and evidence.

1.e. Provide a concluding statement or section that follows from and supports the argument presented.

Engage your audience immediately. To make the problem real to your audience, consider one of these strategies for starting your essay:

- **Personal example:** Provide a detail from your own experience.
- **Anecdote:** Give a factual account of how the problem has already affected others.
- **Scenario:** Present a hypothetical but realistic picture of future consequences if the problem is not addressed.

Outline the problem clearly. Use an organizer like the one shown to display aspects of the central problem, their causes, and their direct effects on people's lives. Then, select and develop only those details that will make the problem clear, significant, and urgent to your audience.

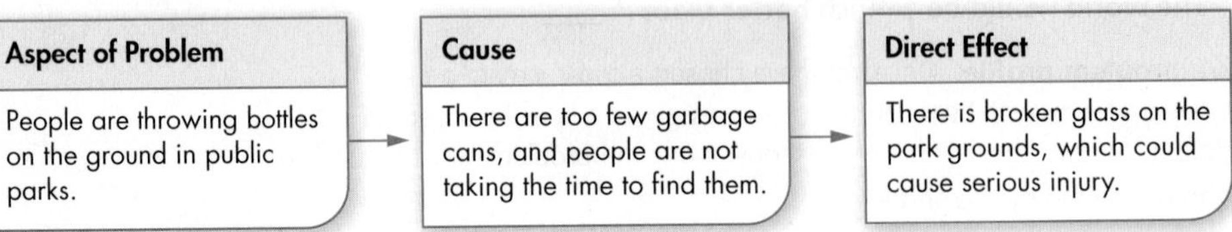

Aspect of Problem
People are throwing bottles on the ground in public parks.
Cause
There are too few garbage cans, and people are not taking the time to find them.
Direct Effect
There is broken glass on the park grounds, which could cause serious injury.

Select convincing details. You cannot "prove" your solution in advance, but you can persuade the audience that your proposal is likely to work by using the following types of evidence. Make sure that you research your evidence using reliable sources.

- **Statistics:** Provide relevant numerical data.
- **Expert opinions:** Include the advice of those who have training or experience related to your topic problem. Integrate quotations and citations from experts to support the evidence.
- **Comparable situations:** Describe other real-life difficulties that were resolved by actions similar to the ones you propose.

Use primary and secondary sources that are appropriate to your purpose and audience. To maintain the flow of ideas, explain the value of each quotation you include and make sure that you establish clear connections among the various types of evidence you use.

Address readers' concerns. Anticipate arguments that you might get from people with differing opinions. Include one or two skeptical questions to show you know both sides of the issue. Then, provide well-supported answers and a concluding statement that supports your argument.

Strategies for Test Taking

Point out that students may be asked to identify a problem and solution in a reading passage on a standardized test. Explain that students can ask themselves one question to identify the problem (What's wrong?) and another question to identify the solution (How does the writer propose to fix what's wrong?).

Writers on Writing

Elizabeth McCracken On Word Choice

Elizabeth McCracken is the author of *The Giant's House* (p. 12) and "Desiderata" (p. 18).

One of the best things about writing my novel *Niagara Falls All Over Again,* which tells the story of a comedy team, was that I could watch videotapes of old TV shows and movies, and claim that I was working. My favorite tapes were old episodes of a show that my beloved comic duo Abbott and Costello hosted once a month. This passage is basically just a description of what I saw when I was "working," watching *The Colgate Comedy Hour.*

"Write about your most beloved obsessions."
—Elizabeth McCracken

Professional Model:

from *Niagara Falls All Over Again*

We broke into television as the once-a-month hosts of a weekly hour-long live variety show. By 1951, our movie career was mostly over, and we were back where we'd begun, except famous, rich, and middle-aged: a thin man and a fat man on a stage, willing to do anything for a laugh. We were shameless. We insulted the band leader, we knocked down scenery on purpose, we tried to crack each other up. We broke props we'd need later, just so we could improvise first about the breakage, and then about the lack of props. Our old wheezing vaudeville jokes were new again, thanks to the postwar baby boom: the country was full of brand-new people with blissfully unsophisticated senses of humor. You could see Rocky search for the red light that told us which camera was paying attention, doing a slow burn and then saying, "Watch me, camera two," and tipping his hat. . . .

I have a weakness for repetition, both straight repeats (like all the *We's*) and slight variations, like *break, broke.*

Some writers say, Avoid adverbs. It's true that some people use adverbs to do the work that verbs and adjectives should do, but I use *blissfully* here as a joke—most people wouldn't see a lack of sophistication as *blissful.*

He's wearing a bowler hat. I draw my characters' clothing when I write (though I'm a very poor artist). I know them better if I know what they wear.

Elizabeth McCracken on Word Choice

Review the passage on the student page with the class, using McCracken's comments to deepen students' understanding of the process of choosing words.

Teaching From the Professional Model

1. Show students Segment 3 on Elizabeth McCracken on *See It!* **DVD** or from this page in the **Enriched Online Student Edition** at **www.PHLitOnline.com.** Discuss how McCracken uses word choice to add to the emotional effect of her writing.
2. Point out to students McCracken's statement about adverbs. Write these two sentences on the board:

   After falling on the ice, Devon slowly walked to the car.

   After falling on the ice, Devon limped to the car.

   Point out to students that the first sentence has an adverb that does the work of the verb, which allows the writer to use a general, weak verb. Point out to students that the second sentence deletes the adverb and uses a more specific verb.
3. Have students go through their essays and look for adverbs that do the work of the verbs or adjectives near them. Tell them to delete these adverbs and use more specific verbs or adjectives.
4. Point out to students McCracken's comment about how she "draws (her) characters' clothing." Explain to students that this means she uses specific details to give readers a vivid mental picture of the clothing.
5. Have students go through their essays and look for any descriptions or details that could be developed further to give more vivid mental pictures. Have students enhance their essays by adding more specific details to these parts.

Revising Strategies

1. Introduce the revision strategies, using the instruction on the student page.
2. Have students apply the strategies as they revise their essays.

Teaching the Strategies

1. Write this paragraph on the board:

   The community playground needs to be replaced. The playground is located down the street from me. The metal bars are covered in rust, and the wood is flaking and full of splinters. The slide is warped with age. The swing set wobbles dangerously when used. A new playground is desperately needed.

   Have students revise the paragraph, putting a star next to the topic sentence and eliminating unnecessary sentences. Have a volunteer write the revised paragraph on the board.

   Sample answer: *The community playground needs to be replaced. The metal bars are covered in rust, and the wood is flaking and full of splinters. The slide is warped with age. The swing set wobbles dangerously when used.*

2. Write the following sentences on the board:

   Stray dogs roam the streets constantly.

   Stray dogs run around all the time.

   Tell students that one sentence has a general audience and the other has a third-grade audience. Have a volunteer note which sentence applies to which audience, and explain why.

   Answer: The first sentence is for a general audience; the second is for a third-grade audience. The vocabulary in the first sentence is more advanced.

Six Traits Focus

	Ideas	✓	Word Choice
✓	Organization		Sentence Fluency
✓	Voice		Conventions

Revising Strategies

Support your generalizations. Look at each paragraph in your essay to be certain that the details you have used support or explain the main idea that is expressed in the topic sentence. Use the following strategy to revise your paragraphs:

1. Highlight your topic sentence, the general statement in which you summarize the main idea of the paragraph.
2. Underline the sentences that develop and support this idea.
3. Eliminate any sentences that do not support the main idea or that simply restate it.

Model: Revising to Support Generalizations

Litter can be dangerous, as well as unsightly. <u>When glass bottles are left on the ground, they eventually break into tiny, sharp pieces. These pieces of glass are hard to see and could easily cut someone walking barefoot or diving for a soccer ball.</u> ~~Also, broken bottles are more difficult to recycle.~~

Evaluate your vocabulary. Review your draft as if you were a member of your target audience. Find specialized or technical terms that need to be defined. Look for vocabulary that seems too difficult or easy for your readers. Then, adjust your language so that it is appropriate for your target audience. Be sure to maintain a formal style and objective tone. Use resources and reference materials to select more effective and precise language. Even if you simplify your language to address the needs of your audience, make sure to maintain a formal, academic style and objective tone.

General Audience	Target Audience of Experts
Another way to fight fatigue is to exercise.	Another way to raise low levels of blood sugar is to get more exercise.

Peer Review

Exchange drafts with a partner. Review each other's work, circling words that are either too specialized and technical or too simple and basic for your target audiences. Use reference materials such as a dictionary or thesaurus to suggest more effective and precise language. Review your concluding section, and make sure it sums up your argument and supports the evidence you presented. Discuss your decisions with your partner and make the revisions you think will improve your writing.

Common Core State Standards

Writing

1.c. Use words, phrases, and clauses to link the major sections of the text, create cohesion, and clarify the relationships between claim(s) and reasons, between reasons and evidence, and between claim(s) and counterclaims.

1.d. Establish and maintain a formal style and objective tone while attending to the norms and conventions of the discipline in which they are writing.

1.e. Provide a concluding statement or section that follows from and supports the argument presented.

Language

6. Acquire and use accurately general academic and domain-specific words and phrases, sufficient for reading, writing, speaking, and listening at the college and career readiness level; demonstrate independence in gathering vocabulary knowledge when considering a word or phrase important to comprehension or expression.

Strategies for Test Taking

Tell students that word choice is critical in any form of expository writing. To be successful, students must use clear and concise language. Remind students that a word is only effective when used in the proper context. Also point out that using fewer words often allows a clearer meaning to emerge.

Show or assign the video online at **www.PHLitOnline.com.**

SIX TRAITS WRITER'S TOOLBOX SIX TRAITS

Conventions | Sentence Fluency | Voice | Organization | Word Choice | Ideas

Revising Pronoun-Antecedent Agreement

Pronouns are words that take the place of nouns. **Antecedents** are the nouns that the pronouns refer to.

Identifying Errors in Pronoun-Antecedent Agreement. Pronouns "disagree" with their antecedents when they are mismatched in number, person, or gender. A pronoun should agree with its antecedent in number:

Incorrect: *Anne and Natasha* reminded *her* parents.
Correct: *Anne and Natasha* reminded *their* parents. (plural)

Incorrect: *Neither Carl nor Jeff* remember *their* ID number.
Correct: *Neither Carl nor Jeff* remembers *his* ID number. (singular)

A pronoun should agree with its antecedent in person:

Incorrect: When a *person* hurries, *you* may fall.
Correct: When *a person* hurries, *he or she* may fall. (third-person singular)
Correct: When *people* hurry, *they* may fall. (third-person plural)

PH WRITING COACH
Further instruction and practice are available in *Prentice Hall Writing Coach.*

Fixing Errors in Pronoun-Antecedent Agreement. To correct errors, first identify the antecedent of each pronoun. As you work through each paragraph of your draft, consider the following:

Gender of Third-Person Singular Pronouns

Masculine	Feminine	Neuter
he, him, his, himself	she, her, hers, herself	it, its, itself

1. For compound antecedents joined by *and,* use a plural personal pronoun.
2. For singular antecedents joined by *or* or *nor,* use a singular personal pronoun.
3. Check every occurrence of the pronoun *you* to make sure that you have not made a shift in person.

Grammar in Your Writing
Review the first and last paragraphs in your draft. Underline each antecedent and circle each pronoun. Check the marked words for pronoun-antecedent agreement and fix any errors.

Strategies for Using Technology in Writing

Remind students that many word-processing programs have grammar checkers, but they are usually unreliable. They often call out errors in sentences that are actually grammatically correct, and they are likely to miss real errors. Grammar checkers are especially unreliable with complex sentences. Students should never rely on them when proofreading their writing, but should always read each sentence carefully and identify their own errors.

Revising Pronoun-Antecedent Agreement

1. Introduce the grammar skill, using the instruction on the student page.
2. Discuss the examples and the strategies for identifying and fixing errors in pronoun-antecedent agreement.
3. Have students follow the instruction under Grammar in Your Writing to correct errors in their drafts.

Teaching the Grammar Skill

1. Read the following sentences aloud, and have students identify the pronouns and the antecedents:

   Alicia lost her necklace.
   Answer: pronoun: *her;* antecedent: *Alicia*

   If Marcus had run, he could have caught the bus.
   Answer: pronoun: *he;* antecedent: *Marcus*
2. Tell students that errors in pronoun-antecedent agreement often occur when words are widely separated.
3. Write the following sentences on the board, and have students identify which sentence has pronoun-antecedent agreement:

   Thomas lost his watch.

   Faith and Verona washed her dogs.

   Answer: The first sentence has agreement.
4. Write the following sentences on the board, and have volunteers correct the pronoun-antecedent errors:

   Jakeem or Roger is going to read their report today.
   Answer: his report
   When a student does well on a test, they should feel proud.
   Answer: he or she should feel proud

PH WRITING COACH Grade 9

Students will find practice with and guidance on pronoun-antecedent agreement in Chapter 19, Section 2.

Student Model

Review the Student Model with the class, using the annotations to analyze the writer's use of the elements of a problem-and-solution essay.

Teaching From the Student Model

1. Explain that the Student Model is a sample and that essays may be longer.
2. Ask students to paraphrase the author's general statement of the problem.

   Possible response: Although they may not be aware of it, people who litter harm the environment.
3. Ask students to identify the paragraph in which the author gives more details about the problem.

   Answer: The author gives more details in the third paragraph.
4. Have students identify the proposed solution to the problem.

   Answer: The proposed solution is to create a feeling of ownership of public spaces.
5. Ask students to share their opinions on the effectiveness of the author's proposed solution.

   Possible response: This is a good solution because people care about places that they own and public parks are really owned by everyone, so they should be everyone's responsibility.

Connecting to Real-Life Writing

If students have concerns about problems in their own places of work, they can use their problem-and-solution essays to address concerns and to suggest solutions. Workplace suggestions are likely to be taken more seriously if a thorough analysis and a supported solution are submitted.

Student Model: Naomi Barrowclough, Maplewood, NJ

Common Core State Standards

Language
2.c. Spell correctly.

Environmental Un-Consciousness

During a recent Earth Day cleanup, I became disgusted by the amount of trash I picked up within a two-hour period. People had thrown little papers, bits of plastic, and candy wrappers until the mess formed a multicolored carpet over the green grass. Those who litter may not realize that litter creates serious environmental problems.

In the opening paragraph, Naomi provides a general statement of the problem.

We've all been told not to litter, but it does not seem to sink in. One person may think his or her contribution is only a microscopic addition when viewed against the whole. But if every person shared this sense of irresponsibility, Earth would soon be overwhelmed by pollution.

Litter is harmful for many reasons. For one, roadside litter eventually washes into waterways and oceans—water we use for drinking and recreation. Also, animals might entangle themselves or mistake trash for food and swallow it. In our public spaces, children spend a great deal of time in areas where they could be physically harmed by the pollution caused by litter.

Here, the author provides greater detail to explain the problem more fully.

There is no simple solution to the problem of litter, only an array of possible solutions with one strategy in common: Create a feeling of ownership over public spaces. Some of the most popular sites for litter are beaches and parks because people feel no sense of ownership over these places. These same people would never litter in their own homes.

Naomi introduces a general solution here.

To create a feeling of ownership, it is necessary to educate children early about the environmental consequences of littering. According to research done by Keep America Beautiful, a non-profit organization, most people do not feel responsible for public spaces. They think "someone else" will clean up. To change this attitude, schools could lead field trips to local beaches or parks where students pick up trash and test water quality. If kids have to fish two shopping carts from the side of a stream, as I did, they might think twice about throwing something else on the ground. If they see that contaminated water is harmful to both humans and wildlife, they might stop someone they see littering.

In this paragraph, specific strategies for achieving the solution are introduced.

There is no easy way to stop littering. Fines and policing alone will not do the trick because people will just look before they litter. Until people understand that littering is irresponsible and has devastating environmental consequences, they will continue to litter. The solution lies in education and creating a sense of ownership about our public spaces.

In the final paragraph, Naomi addresses a potential concern and then restates her solution.

Editing and Proofreading

Check your draft for errors in spelling, grammar, and punctuation.

Focus on spelling. As you proofread, circle any words that you are not sure how to spell, frequently misspell, or seldom use. Then, use reference resources, such as a dictionary or a thesaurus, to confirm the correct spelling. Follow these steps to find spellings in a dictionary:

- **Check the first letters of a word.** Think of homophones for that sound.
- **Check the other letters.** Once you spell the first sound correctly, try sounding out the rest of the word. Look for likely spellings in the dictionary. If you do not find your word, look for more unusual spellings of the sound.

Spiral Review

Earlier in this unit, you learned about **personal and reflexive pronouns** (p. 122) and **relative, interrogative, and indefinite pronouns** (p. 150). Check your essay to be sure that you have used these pronouns correctly.

Publishing and Presenting

To make the best use of your problem-and-solution essay, share it with people who can help you make a difference.

Send a letter. Send your essay to the appropriate government official, agency, or organization. When you receive a response, share it with your classmates in a presentation. Save both the essay and response in your portfolio.

Make a speech. Deliver your essay as a speech to a group from your school or a community that shares your concerns about the problem. Then, lead a question-and-answer session. Be sure to restate your answers if the audience seems confused. Report any consequences of your speech to your classmates.

PH WRITING COACH

Further instruction and practice are available in *Prentice Hall Writing Coach*.

Reflecting on Your Writing

Writer's Journal. Jot down your answers to this question.

How did writing about the problem help you to better understand it?

Rubric for Self-Assessment

Find evidence in your writing to address each category. Then, use the rating scale to grade your work.

Criteria	Rating Scale (not very – very)
Focus: How adequately do you explore the problem in the essay?	1 2 3 4 5
Organization: How well do you organize the steps of the solution?	1 2 3 4 5
Support/Elaboration: How convincing are your facts, details, and reasons?	1 2 3 4 5
Style: How appropriate is the language for the audience's knowledge level?	1 2 3 4 5
Conventions: How correct is your grammar, especially your use of pronouns?	1 2 3 4 5

Differentiated Instruction for Universal Access

Strategy for English Learners

English learners may be nervous about delivering speeches. Point out that by preparing well, they can avoid the need to improvise ways to express complex ideas in English. They can use dictionaries to find appropriate words, and then memorize their speeches. They can also anticipate questions that may be asked and write down these answers as well. If students plan well, they are less likely to be caught off guard by a question.

Strategy for Gifted and Talented Students

If students feel passionate about the problems they explored in their essays, they may want to do more to get their messages out to the world. Suggest that they create Web sites to encourage others to help with their causes. They can include letters and mailing addresses for important government officials. Visitors to the Web sites can print out the letters, sign them, and mail them to the appropriate government officials.

Editing and Proofreading

1. Introduce the editing and proofreading focus, using the instruction on the student page.
2. Have students edit and proofread their essays, correcting grammar, spelling, punctuation, and word choice. Make sure they look for errors of the type noted in the lesson focus and the Spiral Review.

Teaching the Editing Focus

Have students write on the board any words that they are not sure how to spell. Have a volunteer look up each word in a dictionary or thesaurus and correct its spelling if necessary. Discuss ways to remember odd or difficult spellings.

Six Traits Focus

	Ideas		Word Choice
✓	Organization		Sentence Fluency
	Voice	✓	Conventions

ASSESS

Publishing and Presenting

1. Assist students in finding appropriate agencies or organizations.
2. Discuss the additional information conveyed when a message is delivered as a speech or presentation. Tell students that body language can show how confident you are, vocal intonations can stress specific points, and eye contact can keep the audience engaged. Encourage students to be aware of these factors when speaking.

Reflecting on Your Writing

1. Ask students whether it was difficult for them to find convincing details to show the merit of their solutions. Did students feel as if they acquired enough evidence to prove their solutions?
2. Ask students how difficult it was to write for their target audiences.

PH WRITING COACH Grade 9

Students will find additional information on the writing process in Chapter 3.

Common Core State Standards

- Language 4.c; 5.b

Using a Dictionary and Thesaurus

1. Introduce the skill, using the instruction on the student page.
2. Review the definitions and examples in the boxes.
3. Remind students of the importance of checking the precise meaning of synonyms they choose from a thesaurus.

Think Aloud: Model the Skill

Model using a dictionary and thesaurus. Say to students:

When I look up the word *poet* in the dictionary, I see that it has two syllables. The accent mark after the first syllable tells me that the first syllable is emphasized, "PO et". The letter *n* followed by a period tells me the part of speech. *N* stands for "noun," so I know that the word *poet* is a noun. The number 1 indicates the most common meaning of the word. I read that *poet* means "a person who writes poems or verses." I see there is a second, less common, meaning for *poet*. It also means "a person who displays imaginative power and beauty of thought, language, etc."

Now let's say I'd like to find a synonym for the word *teaching* in this sentence: *The students gave Professor Elmore's teaching the highest rating.* I look up *teaching* in the thesaurus and I see that the entry shows synonyms for both the noun *teaching* and the verb *teaching*. I am looking for synonyms for the noun. So I read the listings after the *n.*: "teaching, education, schooling, instruction, tuition, coaching, and tutoring." I choose *instruction* because its meaning fits best with the meaning of my sentence.

Vocabulary Workshop

Using a Dictionary and Thesaurus

Common Core State Standards

Language

4.c. Consult general and specialized reference materials, both print and digital, to find the pronunciation of a word or determine or clarify its precise meaning, its part of speech, or its etymology.

5.b. Analyze nuances in the meanings of words with similar denotations.

A **dictionary** is a resource that provides different kinds of information to help readers, writers, and speakers use words correctly. Consult a dictionary to find how to pronounce a word, its part of speech, and its history, or etymology. Look at this dictionary entry for the word *poet.*

Dictionary

poet (pō´ət) ***n.*** [ME < OFr. *poete* < L *poeta* < Gr *poietes*, one who makes, poet < *poiein*, to make: see POEM] **1.** a person who writes poems or verses **2.** a person who displays imaginative power and beauty of thought, language, etc.

The pronunciation uses letters, symbols, and accent marks to show how the word is pronounced. A key to these letters and symbols usually appears at the bottom of the dictionary page or in the front of the dictionary. The key includes a common word to show how the symbols are pronounced.

A **thesaurus** is a book of synonyms. Use it to find the exact word to fit your meaning and to vary word selection to avoid repetition. A thesaurus can also help you locate words that share **denotations,** or dictionary definitions, but have different **connotations,** or shades of meaning.

Thesaurus

teaching ***n.*** teaching, education, schooling, instruction, tuition, coaching, tutoring ***v.*** teach, educate, instruct, give information, give lessons in, school, edify

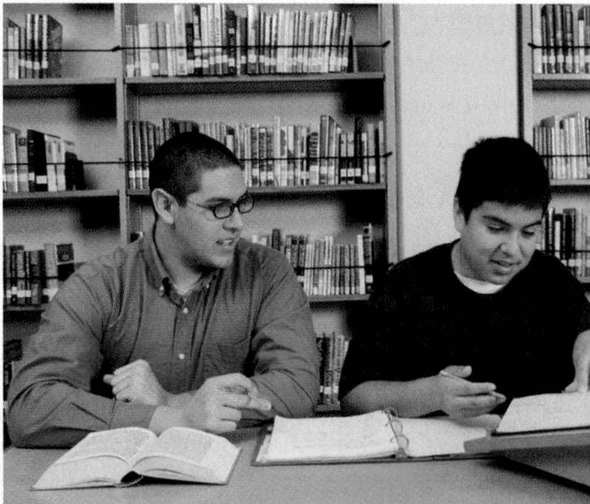

Many types of dictionaries can be found in the reference section of your library. Also look for them online and on CD-ROMs and DVDs.

Teaching Resources

Unit 1 Resources
Using a Dictionary and Thesaurus, pp. 232, 233

Practice A Look up each word in a dictionary. Write the part of speech and the first definition for each word.

1. eminent **2.** misconstrue **3.** anecdote
4. illiterate **5.** diversion **6.** perceive

Practice B Use a dictionary to answer questions 1 through 8.

1. Which syllable receives the heaviest accent in the word *integrity*?
2. Can *wane* be properly used as a noun? If so, what does it mean?
3. What word can be used to replace *agitate* in this sentence? "Jonathan began to *agitate* the fish tank."
4. What is the adverb form of the word *dire*?
5. What part of speech is *expire*?
6. Does the vowel sound in *fray* sound like the vowel in *at, ate,* or *car*?
7. Which syllable of *upheaval* receives the heaviest accent?
8. **(a)** Note two words with similar denotations you might use to replace *melancholy* in this sentence. "At the end of her vacation, Alice felt melancholy." **(b)** For each word, explain how the connotations of the replacement words change the overall meaning of the sentence.

Activity Form a small group with classmates. Write a sentence about a story that you know. Then, pass your sentence to another student. That student should change the sentence that he or she receives by replacing one word with a synonym. See how long your group can keep passing the sentence on and coming up with new words while keeping the original sentence's meaning. Group members may use a thesaurus if they need help.

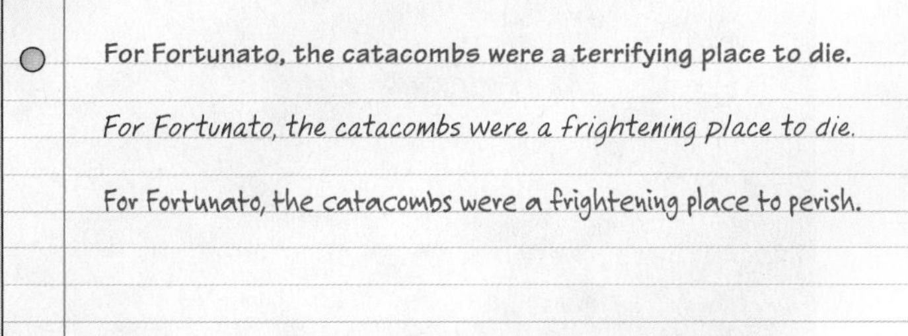

For Fortunato, the catacombs were a terrifying place to die.
For Fortunato, the catacombs were a frightening place to die.
For Fortunato, the catacombs were a frightening place to perish.

PHLit Online!
www.PHLitOnline.com

- Illustrated vocabulary words
- Interactive vocabulary games
- Vocabulary flashcards

Comprehension and Collaboration

How do you pronounce these words: *feint, insignia, valise*? Look up each word in a dictionary, study the pronunciation, and practice saying it. Then, compare your pronunciations of the words with those of three other students. If you disagree, review the pronunciation key and decide who's correct.

ASSESS/EXTEND

Answers

Practice A

Answers:

1. *eminent*—adjective; famous and respected
2. *misconstrue*—verb; misunderstand
3. *anecdote*—noun; a short account of an incident
4. *illiterate*—adjective; unable to read and write
5. *diversion*—noun; the act of turning aside
6. *perceive*—verb; to become aware of

Practice B

Answers:

1. The second syllable in *integrity* receives the heaviest accent.
2. Yes, *wane* can properly be used as a noun. As a noun, *wane* means " the act of decreasing or lessening."
3. The word *stir* can replace *agitate.*
4. *Direly* is the adverb form of *dire.*
5. *Expire* is a verb.
6. The vowel sound in *fray* sounds like the vowel sound in *ate.*
7. The second syllable in *upheaval* receives the heaviest accent.
8. **(a)** Sad, glum. **(b)** The connotations of the replacement words do not change the overall meaning of the sentence because they are synonyms to *melancholy.*

Activity

Divide the class into groups. Provide a thesaurus for each group. Give students a set amount of time in which to do the activity. When time is up, have one student in each group read aloud the original sentence and the final sentence. Have the class determine if the new words enhanced the meaning of the sentence.

Comprehension and Collaboration

Provide students with dictionaries. In their responses, students should correctly pronounce *feint, insignia,* and *valise.*

Differentiated Instruction for Universal Access

Less Proficient Students
Have students work in pairs to give them extra practice using a dictionary and thesaurus. Have partners write sentences using each of the six words given in Practice A. Then have partners take turns using a thesaurus to write a list of synonyms for each of the six words. Partners then work together to choose a synonym to replace each of the original words in their sentences. Finally, have partners use the dictionary to check the meaning of each substituted synonym and confirm that its meaning makes sense in the sentence.

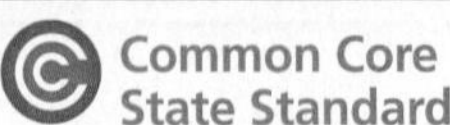
Common Core State Standards

• Speaking and Listening 4

Learn the Skills

1. Introduce the workshop, including the activity on page 183.
2. Emphasize the importance of making directions complete and clear. Read and discuss two versions of one step in the process of making a peanut butter and jelly sandwich:

   A: Put the two pieces of bread together.

   B: Put the two pieces of bread together, placing the peanut butter on one slice against the jelly on the other.

   Ask students which version is complete and clear and which is not. Have students explain why.

   Answer: Option B is clear because it specifies how to assemble the two slices of bread. Option A is incomplete; someone following this description might place the peanut butter and jelly sides of each slice on the outside of the sandwich.
3. Suggest that students take notes on instructions while listening to them. The act of writing can help make them more memorable. Also, the notes provide a resource they can refer to later, when following the instructions.
4. Give students examples of each type of purpose:
   - To perform specific tasks: An athletic coach explaining what each player should do on a particular play.
   - To answer questions: A science teacher describing how to conduct an experiment.
   - To solve problems: A math teacher explaining how to calculate probabilities.
   - To complete processes: An English teacher outlining the writing process.

SPEAKING AND LISTENING

Communications Workshop

Giving and Following Oral Instructions

You can give and follow oral directions to perform specific tasks, answer questions, solve problems, and complete processes.

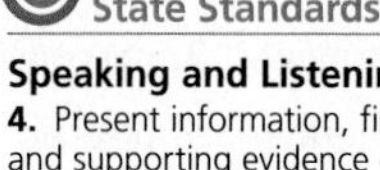
Common Core State Standards

Speaking and Listening
4. Present information, findings, and supporting evidence clearly, concisely, and logically such that listeners can follow the line of reasoning and the organization, development, and style are appropriate to task, purpose, and audience.

Learn the Skills

Use the strategies to complete the activity on page 183.

Present information. When you give instructions, explain complex processes in easy-to-follow steps. Ask questions to be sure that your audience understands.

Listen attentively. When you follow instructions, listen carefully. Repeat the steps to the instructor to show that you understand. If you are confused, ask the instructor to explain.

Use instructions for different purposes. Give and follow complex oral directions for each of the following purposes. Work with a partner to complete these practice exercises.

- **Perform specific tasks.** Draw a design using only straight lines. Do not let your partner see your drawing. Then, give your partner step-by-step instructions for drawing the design. Finally, compare your drawings to see how well the instructions were given and followed.
- **Answer questions.** Ask your partner how to get from school to a place he or she knows well. Follow your partner's instructions by tracing the route on a map.
- **Solve problems.** Name a problem you face, such as staying organized or managing your time. Ask your partner for instructions that will help you solve this problem. Report back to your partner after you have followed the instructions.
- **Complete processes.** Give instructions for completing a process you have learned in school, such as solving an equation.

Strategies for Giving and Following Directions

Give students these additional strategies for following directions:

- Advise students that, after writing a draft of a set of steps describing how to perform a process, they actually perform the process following the steps. If problems arise, they can then revise the steps as necessary.
- Remind students when giving instructions to use specific names for objects or processes and to consistently use those names whenever referring to the same object or process.
- Point out that demonstrating how to do a process can help clarify a series of steps. Students might need to bring relevant materials so they can perform appropriate steps, using those steps to show listeners as well as tell them.
- Encourage students to pause occasionally when giving instructions and to ask if listeners have any questions. Taking this step might encourage those reluctant to ask questions by showing a willingness to receive them.

Practice the Skills

Presentation of Knowledge and Ideas Use what you've learned in this workshop to perform the following task.

ACTIVITY: Give Complex Oral Instructions

Choose a specific task or process that would help your classmates solve a problem that they face. Give complex oral instructions that tell the class how to perform this task. Answer the following questions in your presentation:

- What are you teaching your classmates to do?
- How could your directions help your classmates solve a problem?
- What materials will your classmates need to follow the directions?
- How will your classmates know when they have completed the process correctly?
- What are the steps in the task or process?

As your classmates make their presentations, follow their directions. Use the Presentation Checklist below to analyze their presentations, and let your classmates use the checklist to analyze your presentation.

Presentation Checklist

Presentation Content

Does the presentation meet all of the requirements of the activity? Check all that apply.

- ❑ It gives listeners instructions to complete a task or process.
- ❑ It helps listeners solve a problem.
- ❑ It answers the questions outlined in the activity assignment.

Presentation Delivery

Did the speaker give the instructions clearly? Check all that apply.

- ❑ The speaker gave instructions in logical, easy-to-follow steps.
- ❑ The speaker asked questions to check that the audience understood the steps.
- ❑ The speaker gave clear answers to questions asked by the audience.

Comprehension and Collaboration After your presentation, ask your classmates to tell you how they rated you on the Presentation Checklist. While your classmates give their presentations, follow their instructions and use the checklist to rate them. As a group, discuss which presentations were the easiest to follow and why.

EXTEND/ASSESS

Practice the Skills

1. Review the assignment with students. Make sure that they understand that the instructions they give should cover a task or process that classmates could follow to solve a problem. They should choose tasks that students can perform while they speak, such as drawing a map of the school or making a form that can be used to analyze Internet sites.
2. Explain to students that they should use a copy of the Presentation Checklist to evaluate their own presentation and the presentations made by classmates.
3. Before students give their presentations to the class, remind listeners to ask questions if any points are unclear. To maintain order, encourage them to raise their hands and wait to be acknowledged by the presenter before stating their questions. Suggest that students making presentations scan the classroom from time to time so they will notice any students who have questions.

Evaluate the Activity

1. Evaluate students' presentations on the basis of the clarity and completeness of their instructions, the logic of the organization of those instructions, and their use of questions and responses to ensure listeners' comprehension.
2. When the class discusses the presentations that were easiest to follow, encourage students to make note of the features of those presentations that made them effective and to incorporate those techniques in their future presentations.

Differentiated Instruction for Universal Access

Strategy for English Learners
Dictate directions for a simple line drawing. Then, ask questions about the general meaning, main points, and important details of the directions. Encourage students to monitor their comprehension of the directions and to seek clarification for any unfamiliar language or contexts.

Strategy for Less Proficient Learners
Pair students and have them practice presenting instructions to each other. Partners should fill out a copy of the Presentation Checklist evaluating their partner's work. Encourage them to offer constructive criticism to help presenters improve the content and delivery of their presentations.

Cumulative Review

In this Common Core Assessment Workshop (pp. 184–189), students apply and reinforce their mastery of the Common Core State Standards and the skills taught in Unit 1. The practice is divided into four sections, including a section of Performance Tasks addressing CCS Reading standards.

1. Before assigning each section, review the relevant Common Core State Standards and unit skills with students.
2. Set a time limit for the multiple-choice items in each section, allowing a little over one minute per question. Allow twenty minutes for any Timed Writing questions.
3. Administer each of the first three sections of the Cumulative Review (pp. 184–187).
4. Use the Performance Tasks on pages 188–189 to assess the depth of students' mastery of standards taught in the unit. Follow the suggestions on teacher pages 188–189 for assigning tasks and for supporting and evaluating student performance.

Reteaching Skills

1. For each practice, use the Reteach chart on the same page as the answers to determine which skills require reteaching, based on which items students answered incorrectly.
2. Reteach these skills prior to assigning the **Benchmark Test** for the second half of Unit 1 (***Unit 1 Resources,*** pp. 235–240).

Cumulative Review

Common Core State Standards

RL.9-10.2, RL.9-10.3, RL.9-10.5; L.9-10.4.a

[For the full wording of the standards, see the standards chart in the front of your textbook.]

I. Reading Literature

Directions: *Read the passage. Then, answer each question that follows.*

I was born in Brooklyn, New York and lived there until I was eleven. I had never really been outside the city. Sure, I had been to Long Island for beach days with my family, but I had never been to the country. My mother got a job Upstate, and suddenly my parents were planning the move. They said that living in the country would be a great experience for all of us, but I was miserable. In August, as we drove the long winding country roads to our new home, I barely said a word.

Many things were lacking in the country. There was no basketball game to pick up. There was no Thai food. There was no skateboarding. There was no sitting on the stoop. Most importantly, there were no old friends. I was so lonely—and bored. It was just my mom, my dad, and me. We were in the middle of nowhere with the closest neighbor over a mile away. Life as I had known it came to an end that August day.

Dad tried to get me to go fishing, but I thought the whole idea was disgusting. Mom tried to get me to walk in the woods, but I didn't like all the bugs, and the brambles scratched my legs. I wanted to go back to Brooklyn in the worst way. All of that would soon change.

I was <u>petrified</u> when I walked into my homeroom. Everyone there knew everyone else, and I did not know anyone. I was set apart from all the other boys by my pale skin and long hair. I sat in the back, and no one said anything to me. The teacher came in and introduced herself.

"Class, we have two new students with us this year." My ears perked up at the word *two,* and I scanned the room for another outsider.

"First, I want to introduce Dave from Brooklyn." The teacher pointed to me. My face flushed as I said "Hi."

"Next, meet Alexis from Washington, D.C."

"Call me Al," she said to the class, looking as lost as I felt.

I had been staring at the back of her head. Her hair was as short as mine was long. I knew immediately that this was not only the year of the Big Move, but it was also the year of the New Best Friend.

Differentiated Instruction for Universal Access

Strategy for Less Proficient Readers

Review the parts of a plot with students. Then, walk students through item 6. Read the passage with students, helping them summarize it. Then, ask a volunteer to read item 6 aloud. Call on students to define the *climax*. (**Answer:** The climax is the moment of greatest tension or the moment when the outcome is determined.) Guide students in eliminating incorrect answer choices.

- A—As the move happens near the beginning of the story, it cannot be the climax. (Eliminate.)
- B—Dave wants to move back to Brooklyn, but that desire does not affect the story's outcome. (Eliminate.)
- C—Dave refuses to go fishing with his father, but that event is not pivotal to the story. (Eliminate.)
- D—When Dave hears the teacher say "two," he immediately knows that he is not alone and his situation is going to change. (Correct.)

Guide students in seeing that D is the correct choice. Have them complete the remaining items, encouraging them to apply a similar strategy to each.

1. From which **point of view** is this story told?

A. first person
B. second person
C. third-person limited
D. third-person omniscient

2. Which element from the passage helped you determine the **point of view**?

A. The narrator directly addresses his audience, the reader.
B. The narrator refers to himself as *I* and *me*.
C. The narrator knows only one person's thoughts.
D. The narrator has insight into all the people's thoughts.

3. Which word best describes the **author's voice**?

A. formal
B. casual
C. friendly
D. sarcastic

4. Which of the following sentences is an example of **foreshadowing**?

A. All of that would soon change.
B. I had never really been outside of the city.
C. I wanted to go back to Brooklyn in the worst way.
D. The teacher pointed to me.

5. Which event occurs during the **rising action** of the narrative?

A. Dave is born in Brooklyn.
B. Dave makes a new friend.
C. Dave's mom gets a job Upstate.
D. Dave meets Alexis.

6. Which event is the turning point, or **climax,** of the narrative?

A. Dave moves in August.
B. Dave wants to move back to Brooklyn.
C. Dave refuses to go fishing.
D. Dave hears the teacher say "two."

7. **Vocabulary** Which word is closest in meaning to the underlined word *petrified*?

A. angry
B. terrified
C. annoyed
D. disturbed

8. How is the conflict in the story resolved?

A. Dave makes a new friend in the city.
B. Dave wants to return to Brooklyn.
C. Dave's mom does not like her job.
D. Dave goes fishing with his dad.

9. In what way does the choice of narrator affect the description of the country in paragraph 2?

A. Life in the country seems frightening.
B. The country appears to offer lots of fun activities.
C. Moving to the country sounds like a good idea.
D. The country seems to lack a lot of things that life in the city has to offer.

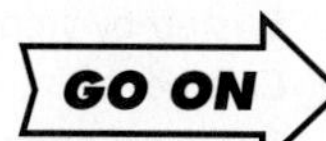

Timed Writing

10. In a well-developed essay, **identify** the conflict in this story. **Explain** how the author of the text establishes the conflict. Cite evidence from the text to support your analysis. [20 minutes]

GO ON

Answers

I. Reading Literature

Answers With Explanations

1. A—The narrator is talking about himself. *Incorrect answers:* B—Second person is not used to tell a story. C—The story has a first-person narrator. D—same explanation as for C.
2. B—First-person pronouns are used throughout the story. *Incorrect answers:* A—A third-person narrator could directly address the reader as well. C—This answer does not address the question. D—The narrator only knows his own thoughts.
3. C—The passage is written in a friendly, matter-of-fact manner. *Incorrect answers:* A—The voice is conversational, not formal. B—A casual voice would contain more slang. D—A sarcastic voice would be more caustic.
4. A—The sentence signals that Dave will reach a turning point. *Incorrect answers:* B—This does not hint at any event. C—Since Dave does not return to Brooklyn, this does not foreshadow anything. D—This simply describes the teacher's actions.
5. C—The story is put in motion with Dave's mom's new job. *Incorrect answers:* A—This event took place long before the story began. B—Dave's making friends with Alexis takes place after the story. D—Dave will meet Alexis in the future.
6. D—When Dave finds out he is not the only new student, he cheers up. *Incorrect answers:* A—This event happens at the beginning of the story. B—This is a feeling, not a part of the plot. C—This is part of the narration.
7. B—Like *petrified, terrified* reflects extreme fear. *Incorrect answers:* A—Being angry is not being fearful. C—Being annoyed is not being fearful. D—Being disturbed is not being fearful.
8. A—Dave knows that he and Alexis will become best friends. *Incorrect answers:* B—This feeling is not part of the resolution. C—The story does not say this. D—This event does not happen.

Continued from right column

9. D—The activities Dave cites are those that a teen who grew up in the city might enjoy. *Incorrect answers:* A—The narrator paints country life as boring, not frightening. B—The narrator does not see country activities as fun. C—The narrator thinks the move is a disastrous change.

Timed Writing

10. Students should explain Dave's unhappiness at moving to the country using details from the text.

Reteach

Question	Instructional Pages to Reteach
1	80
2	80
3	101
4	43
5	43
6	43
8	43
9	101

II. Reading Informational Text

Answers With Explanations

1. C—The two subheads organize the information in the article. *Incorrect answers:* A—The article has no lists. B—The article has no charts. D—The article does not describe events in time order.
2. B—The article describes the procedure to follow. *Incorrect answers:* A—The article does not describe events in chronological order. C—The article takes a step-by-step approach. D—The article does not describe the layout.
3. B—This section gives an overview of organic gardening. *Incorrect answers:* A—This is one detail, but not the subject of the paragraph as a whole. C—same explanation as for A. D—The paragraph is descriptive, not encouraging.
4. D—The article states that seeds are one key to successful organic gardening. *Incorrect answers:* A—This is a result of successful gardening, not the first step in it. B—This is one step in the process, but not the first. C—same explanation as for B.

Reteach

Question	Pages to Reteach
1	154
2	154
3	154
4	74

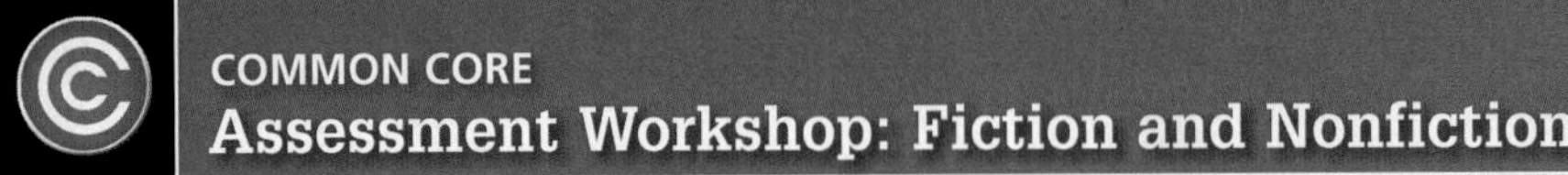

COMMON CORE
Assessment Workshop: Fiction and Nonfiction

II. Reading Informational Text

Directions: *Read the passage. Then, answer each question that follows.*

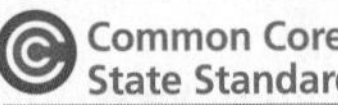

Common Core State Standards

RI.9-10.2, RI.9-10.5; L.9-10.2, L.9-10.3

[For the full wording of the standards, see the standards chart in the front of your textbook.]

Organic Gardening

The Basics

Organic gardening is a method of gardening that eliminates chemicals from our diets. For gardeners, it presents challenges that regular gardening does not. For example, how do you kill aphids that are eating your tomatoes? An ordinary gardener sprays the plant with a pesticide. An organic gardener uses a natural way to eliminate the pests, such as dipping the plants in water repeatedly to drown the bugs. A pesticide only takes one or two applications to work, but the water technique is a repeated and time-consuming process. This is just one example of how the organic gardener must sometimes commit more time and energy than the ordinary gardener to provide a healthy crop.

Getting Started

The key to organic gardening success lies in the seeds and the soil. Prepare the soil by tilling and adding compost to enhance its nutrients.

After the soil is ready, carefully choose the seeds or plants to grow. Check each seedling for healthy leaves and roots and look for any signs of stress, such as yellow leaves. Once you have chosen the crop, it is time to plant.

Follow the planting directions. Add natural fertilizer to the each plant. Finally, cover the base of the plant with mulch. Water the plants and watch them grow.

1. What **structure** does the author use in this article?
   A. numbered lists
   B. charts
   C. heads and subheads
   D. chronological order

2. Which of the following *best* describes the **format** of "Getting Started"?
   A. chronological order
   B. step-by-step order
   C. order of importance
   D. spatial order

3. What is the purpose of "The Basics" section?
   A. to explain how to combat pests
   B. to introduce organic gardening
   C. to identify difficulties
   D. to encourage gardeners

4. Why is it important to prepare the soil first?
   A. A healthy crop relies on healthy soil.
   B. The plants will die before you prepare it.
   C. The chemicals must be removed.
   D. It does not matter when the soil is prepared.

Strategies for Test Taking

Often the anxiety surrounding test taking causes students to skim (or even skip) the instructions. Tell students that carefully reading the instructions for each section is essential to performing well. A misreading might cause them to answer every question in a section incorrectly.

III. Writing and Language Conventions

Directions: *Read the passage. Then, answer each question that follows.*

(1) I had been looking forward to Nanas visit for months. (2) She came all the way to California from Ohio every August. (3) She was so much fun. (4) She and I did something special together every year. (5) A week before her visit, my cousin invited me to come with his family to Yellowstone National Park. (6) I had never been there before, and I couldn't believe I had the chance to go. (7) Only after the phone call did I realize that the trip was the exact same week Nana was coming. (8) In the end, I weighed the pros and cons and decided to stay for Nana. (9) I only saw her twice a year. (10) Besides, Yellowstone will always be there for me to visit. (11) I had to make a decision.

1. Which revision corrects the illogical **sequence of events**?

A. Combine sentences 1 and 2.
B. Eliminate sentence 3.
C. Break sentence 6 into two sentences.
D. Move sentence 11 after sentence 7.

2. Which **detail** would most vividly support sentence 4?

A. She taught me to fish, to cook, and to sew.
B. She spent a lot of time with Mom.
C. We didn't do much but talk.
D. She traveled alone all the way there.

3. Which revision would you make to sentences 2, 3, and 4 to make the writing more interesting?

A. Change the verb tense.
B. Vary the sentence beginnings.
C. Put them in a different order.
D. Add punctuation.

4. What is the correct way to form the **possessive** in sentence 1?

A. Nanas
B. Nana's
C. Nanas'
D. Nana

5. Which revision is the most effective way to vary the beginning of sentence 4?

A. We did something special every year.
B. Her and I did something special every year.
C. Every year, we did something special.
D. Special things were done by us every year.

6. Which is the proper **possessive** form of the **plural** noun *families*?

A. familys'
B. familie's
C. family's
D. families'

Differentiated Instruction for Universal Access

Strategy for Less Proficient Readers

Review skills and warm up for the test by walking students through item 2. First, read the passage with students, helping them summarize it. Then ask a volunteer to read item 2 aloud. Help students define *detail* (specific information that clarifies or illustrates a general statement). Next, guide students in eliminating incorrect answer choices.

- **A**—The three activities stated here are details that could be related to the general statement in sentence 4. (Correct.)
- **B**—This statement gives a detail, but not one that would explain what the narrator and Nana do together. (Eliminate.)
- **C**—This statement gives a detail of how people can spend time together, but it would contradict, rather than support, sentence 4. (Eliminate.)
- **D**—This statement has no connection to the statement in sentence 4. (Eliminate.)

Guide students in seeing that **A** is the best choice. Have them complete the remaining items, encouraging them to apply a similar strategy to each. First, define key terms in the prompt, and then eliminate incorrect choices.

III. Writing and Language Conventions

Answers With Explanations

1. **D**—The narrator must choose whether to take the trip or stay for Nana's visit. *Incorrect answers:* A—This change would not affect the sequence of events. B—same explanation as for A. C—same explanation as for A.
2. **A**—Since the narrator and Nana do things together, this answer explains what they might do. B—This isn't something that Nana does with the narrator. C—The narrator says they do things. D—This detail is not related to things they do together.
3. **B**—Varying the sentence beginnings would add interest. *Incorrect answers:* A—A change in verb tense does not add interest. C—The repetition of the simple sentence structure makes the sentences dull. D—Punctuation does not add liveliness to sentences.
4. **B**—The singular possessive is formed with an apostrophe followed by an *–s*. *Incorrect answers:* A—This is a plural form. C—This is a plural possessive form. D—This is a singular form.
5. **A**—"We" is a simple way of saying "She and I." *Incorrect answers:* B—"Her and I" is an incorrect grammatic structure. C—This sentence is awkward. D—The passive voice is not an improvement.
6. **D**—The plural possessive is formed by adding an apostrophe after the *–s*. *Incorrect answers:* A—The plural form of *family* is *families*. B—The plural possessive is formed by adding an apostrophe after the *–s*. C—same as for B.

Reteach

Question	Pages to Reteach
1	94
2	95
3	96
4	97
5	96
6	97

Performance Tasks

Assigning Tasks/Reteaching Skills

Use the chart below to choose appropriate Performance Tasks by identifying which tasks assess lessons in the textbook that you have taught. Use the same lessons for reteaching when students' performance indicates a failure to fully master a standard. For additional instruction and practice, assign the *Common Core Companion* pages indicated for each task.

Task	Where Taught/ Pages to Reteach	*Common Core Companion* Pages
1	5–8, 160	2–14, 314–319
2	8, 43	48–54
3	7, 16	97–109
4	101, 125	137–149
5	8, 125	28–34, 293–299
6	80	55–61, 300–301
7	101	35–47, 300–301

Assessment Pacing

In assigning the Writing Tasks on this student page, allow a class period for the completion of a task. As an alternative, assign tasks as homework. In assigning the Speaking and Listening Tasks on the facing page, consider having students do any required preparation as a homework assignment. Then, allow a class period for the presentations themselves.

Evaluating Performance Tasks

Use the rubric at the bottom of this Teacher Edition page to evaluate students' mastery of the standards as demonstrated in their Performance Task responses. Review the rubric with students before they begin work so they know the criteria by which their work will be evaluated.

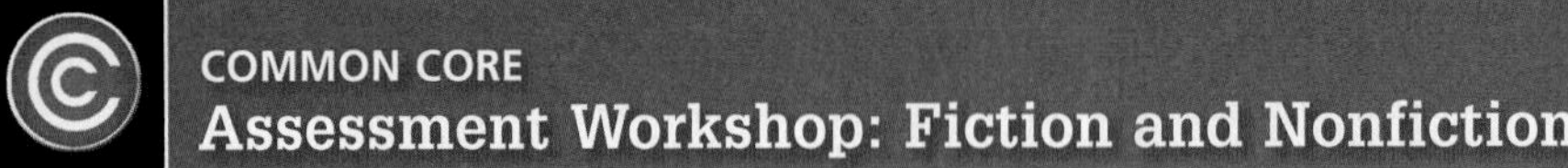

Performance Tasks

Directions: *Follow the instructions to complete the tasks below as required by your teacher.*

As you work on each task, incorporate both general academic vocabulary and literary terms you learned in this unit.

Common Core State Standards

RL.9-10.2, RL.9-10.3, RL.9-10.5, RL.9-10.6; RI.9-10.2, RI.9-10.4; SL.9-10.4, SL.9-10.5; L.9-10.2

[For full wording of the standards, see the standards chart in the front of your textbook.]

Writing

Task 1: Literature [RL.9-10.2; L.9-10.2]

Analyze the Development of Theme

Write an essay in which you compare and contrast the themes of two stories in this unit.

- Analyze the development of the theme in each story and discuss similarities and differences in the message each expresses.
- Note specific strategies each author uses to introduce and develop the theme.
- Discuss specific details that contribute to the development of each theme. Explain what each detail adds.
- To ensure that readers understand your analysis, include an objective summary of each story.
- Capitalize proper nouns, including characters' and authors' names, correctly.

Task 2: Literature [RL.9-10.5]

Analyze the Effects of Structure in a Story

Write an essay in which you explain how the structure of a story in this unit leads to a specific emotional effect, such as tension or suspense.

- Identify the story's main conflict and summarize the narrative.
- Describe specific structural choices the writer makes. For example, discuss how much exposition the author provides and how he or she introduces the conflict. Also describe any use of plot devices, such as foreshadowing.
- Finally, explain how the story affects you as a reader and how the author's choices regarding structure contribute to that effect.
- Cite textual evidence to support your assertions.

Task 3: Informational Text [RI.9-10.2]

Analyze the Development of a Central Idea

Write an essay in which you analyze the development of the central idea in a work of literary nonfiction in this unit.

- Clearly explain the central idea of the work and discuss how it emerges or is introduced by the author.
- Identify specific details that shape and refine the central idea. Consider various types of evidence and explain what each adds to the development of the central idea.
- To ensure that readers understand your analysis, include an objective summary of the work.

Task 4: Informational Text [RI.9-10.6]

Analyze an Author's Purpose and Use of Rhetoric

Write an essay in which you determine an author's purpose and point of view and analyze his or her uses of rhetoric in a work of nonfiction in this unit.

- Explain the topic of the work and determine both the author's general and specific purposes for writing.
- Analyze the author's perspective or point of view on the topic. For example, explain whether the author has a positive or negative perspective or expresses a particular attitude toward the topic.
- Note specific examples of the author's uses of rhetoric. For example, identify examples of parallel structure or repetition. Then, explain how those uses of rhetoric work to advance the author's purpose and point of view.

Performance Task Rubric: Standards Mastery	Rating Scale (*not very* – *very*)
Critical Thinking: How clearly and consistently does the student pursue the specific mode of reasoning or discourse required by the standard, as specified in the prompt (e.g., comparing and contrasting, analyzing, explaining)?	1 2 3 4 5
Focus: How well does the student understand and apply the focus concepts of the standard, as specified in the prompt (e.g., development of theme or of complex characters, effects of structure, and so on)?	1 2 3 4 5
Support/Elaboration: How well does the student support points with textual or other evidence? How relevant, sufficient, and varied is the evidence provided?	1 2 3 4 5
Insight: How original, sophisticated, or compelling are insights the student achieves by applying the standard to the text(s)?	1 2 3 4 5
Expression of Ideas: How well does the student organize and support ideas? How well does the student use language, including word choice and conventions, in the expression of ideas?	1 2 3 4 5

Speaking and Listening

Task 5: Literature [RL.9-10.3; SL.9-10.4]

Analyze the Development of a Complex Character

Deliver an oral presentation in which you analyze a complex character from a story in this unit.

- Explain why you chose the character. Discuss the traits that make the character complex, or round, and dynamic, rather than static.
- Explain strategies the writer uses to portray the character's complexity. Note specific details that add to the character's portrayal as the story develops.
- Describe how the character's complexity, including his or her emotions, motivations, actions, and reactions, advances the plot and contributes to the story's theme.
- Present your analysis and evidence logically so that listeners can follow your line of reasoning. Make sure your overall approach, including both content and style, is appropriate for a classroom presentation on an academic topic.

Task 6: Literature [RL.9-10.6; SL.9-10.5]

Analyze a Cultural Perspective

Present a visual essay in which you analyze a cultural perspective reflected in a story in this unit.

- A visual essay combines images and text to explain an idea. The visual part of your essay may take the form of a slideshow, poster, or other format.
- Choose a story from this unit that reflects a cultural perspective from outside the United States. Explain how that cultural perspective is reflected in the setting and events as well as in characters' thoughts, emotions, actions, and reactions.
- Using the story as an example, discuss the kinds of factual information a work of fiction can provide. Explain what you learned about another culture by reading this story.
- Share your work with the class in an informal presentation. After you have delivered your presentation, answer questions from classmates.

Task 7: Informational Text [RI.9-10.4; SL.9-10.5]

Analyze the Effect of Word Choice on Tone

Write and present an essay in which you analyze the cumulative effect of word choice on tone in a work of literary nonfiction in this unit.

- Choose a work of literary nonfiction from this unit that offers a clear and distinct tone. Explain your choice.
- Identify specific word choices that contribute to the creation of that tone.
- Illustrate your analysis by creating a graphic organizer or chart that captures your ideas visually.
- Present your essay, including charts or graphic organizers, to the class. Use technology to display graphics, or distribute them as handouts.

Can truth change?
At the beginning of Unit 1, you participated in a discussion about the Big Question. Now that you have completed the unit, write a response to the question. Discuss how your initial ideas have either changed or been reinforced. Cite specific examples from the literature in this unit, from other subject areas, and from your own life to support your ideas. Use Big Question vocabulary words (see page 3) in your response.

Differentiated Instruction for Universal Access

Strategy for Less Proficient Readers
Assign a Performance Task, and then have students meet in groups to review the standard assessed in that task. Remind students of the selections or independent readings to which they have previously applied the standard. Have groups summarize what they learned in applying the standard and then present their summaries. Discuss, clarifying any points of confusion. After students have completed their tasks, have groups meet again to evaluate members' work. Encourage members to revise their work based on the feedback they receive.

EL Strategy for English Learners
For each assigned Performance Task, review the instructions with students. Clarify the meaning of any unfamiliar vocabulary, emphasizing routine classroom words such as *topic, presentation,* and *evidence* and academic vocabulary such as *discuss.* Next, have students note ideas for their responses. Pair students, and have them review each other's notes, asking questions to clarify meaning and suggesting improvements. Encourage students to ask for your assistance in supplying English words or expressions they may require.

Supporting Speaking and Listening

1. Consider having students work with partners or in groups to complete Performance Tasks involving listening and speaking. For tasks that you assign for individual work, you may still wish to have students rehearse with partners, who can provide constructive feedback.
2. As students rehearse, have them keep in mind these tips:
   - Present findings and evidence clearly and concisely.
   - Observe conventions of standard English grammar and usage.
   - Be relaxed and friendly but maintain a formal tone.
   - Make eye contact with the audience, pronounce words clearly, and vary your pace.
   - When working with a group, respond thoughtfully to others' positions, modifying your own response to new evidence.

Linking Performance Tasks to Independent Reading

If you wish to cover the standards with students' independent reading, adapt Performance Tasks of your choice to the works they have selected. (Independent reading suggestions appear on the next page.)

Can truth change?

1. Remind students that the unit Big Question is "Can truth change?"
2. Have students complete their responses to the prompt on the student page. Point out that they have read selections in this unit about different approaches to or views of truth and that they should draw on these selections in their responses. Remind them that they can also draw on their own experiences and what they have learned in other subject areas in formulating their answers.

EXTEND

Independent Reading

Titles featured on the Independent Reading pages at the end of each unit represent a range of reading, including stories, dramas, and poetry, as well as literary nonfiction and other types of informational text. Throughout, labels indicate the works that are CCSS Exemplar Texts. Choosing from among these featured titles will help students read works at increasing levels of text complexity in the grades 9–10 text complexity band.

Independent Reading and Pacing

See the Unit Overview and Pacing Plan, pp. 2a–2b, for suggestions on integrating independent reading with work in the Student Edition.

Using Literature Circles

A literature circle is a temporary group in which students independently discuss a book.

Use the guidance in the *Professional Development Guidebook*, pp. 47–49, as well as the teaching notes on the facing page, for additional suggestions for literature circles.

Meeting Unit 1 CCS Focus Standards

Students can use books listed on this page to apply and reinforce their mastery of the CCS Focus Standards covered in this unit. (The Focus Standards are introduced on pp. 4–7.)

Introducing Featured Titles

Have students choose a book or books for independent reading. Assist them by previewing the titles, noting their subject matter and level of difficulty. **Note:** Before recommending a work to students, preview it, taking into account the values of your community as well as the maturity of your students.

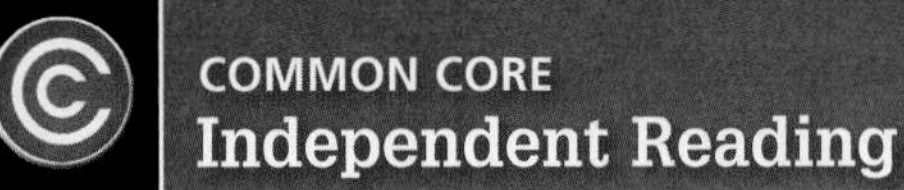

COMMON CORE
Independent Reading

Featured Titles

In this unit, you have read a variety of fiction and literary nonfiction. Continue to read both genres on your own. Select books that you enjoy, but challenge yourself to explore new topics, new authors, and works of increasing depth and complexity. The titles suggested below will help you get started.

Literature

The Red Badge of Courage
by Stephen Crane

In this groundbreaking **novel,** Henry Fleming is a soldier who must conquer his terror of battle or live in shame. He discovers the truth about himself in the midst of the Civil War, the bloodiest conflict in American history.

Journey Home
by Yoshiko Uchida
Aladdin Books, 1978

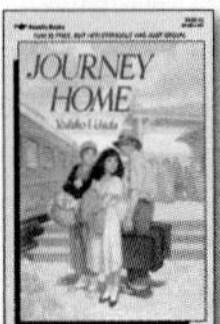

As World War II rages overseas, prejudice against Japanese Americans runs rampant in the United States. Yuki and her family, just released from an internment camp, must deal with this climate of fear and anger on their journey home, as described in this gripping **historical novel.**

Fahrenheit 451
by Ray Bradbury

EXEMPLAR TEXT

In a desolate future, firemen no longer put out fires—they start them, using books as fuel. This **science-fiction novel** critiques thoughtless conformity, the media, and what the author saw as the abuses of technology.

Six Characters in Search of an Author
by Luigi Pirandello
Signet Classics, 1970

Imagine your family walking into a theater and demanding that the actors portray your relationships on stage. This **play,** a classic of modern theater, explores that idea.

Complete Stories and Poems of Edgar Allan Poe
EXEMPLAR TEXT

"The Raven," Poe's narrative poem that mixes sorrow with supernatural gloom, is just one of the classic **poems** and **stories** included in this volume.

Informational Texts

I Know Why the Caged Bird Sings
by Maya Angelou
EXEMPLAR TEXT

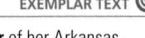

Maya Angelou's **memoir** of her Arkansas childhood is a classic of twentieth-century literature. This coming-of-age story reveals the author's strength and resilience in the face of racism, trauma, and poverty.

Up Close: Rachel Carson
by Ellen Levine

With a love of nature and a passion for science, Rachel Carson revolutionized the world's thinking about the environment. This **biography** tells the story of her struggle to protect the beauty of nature for us all.

Rosa Parks: My Story
by Rosa Parks with Jim Haskins

In this **autobiography,** Rosa Parks tells the story of how her refusal to give up a bus seat to a white man in 1955 inspired a year of boycotts, lawsuits, and, ultimately, a new future for civil rights in America.

Text Complexity: Aligning Texts With Readers and Tasks

TEXTS	READERS AND TASKS
• *Journey Home* (Lexile: 890L) • *Fahrenheit 451* (Lexile: 890L)	**Below-Level Readers** Allow students to focus on reading for content, and challenge them to interpret multiple perspectives.
• *The Red Badge of Courage* (Lexile: 920L) • *Rosa Parks: My Story* (970L) • *"The Raven"* (NP) • *Up Close: Rachel Carson* (Lexile: 1060L)	**Below-Level Readers** Challenge students as they read for content. **On-Level Readers** Allow students to focus on reading for content, and challenge them to interpret multiple perspectives. **Advanced Readers** Allow students to focus on interpreting multiple perspectives.
• *I Know Why the Caged Bird Sings* (Lexile: 1070L) • *Six Characters in Search of an Author* (NP)	**On-Level Readers** Challenge students as they read for content. **Advanced Readers** Allow students to focus on reading for content, and challenge them to interpret multiple perspectives.

Preparing to Read Complex Texts

Attentive Reading As you read literature on your own, bring your imagination and questions to the text. The questions shown below and others that you formulate as you read will help you learn and enjoy literature even more.

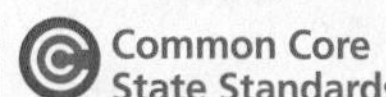

Reading Literature/Informational Text 10. By the end of grade 9, read and comprehend literature, including stories, dramas, and poems, and literary nonfiction in the grades 9–10 text complexity band proficiently, with scaffolding as needed at the high end of the range.

When reading fiction, ask yourself...	
• Who is telling the story? Do I enjoy his or her voice? • Does the story offer a message about life that I appreciate?	Key Ideas and Details
• Is the world of the story convincing? Do any details jolt me out of that world or seem wrong? • Does the plot pull me along? Do I care what happens? • Do the characters seem real? Do the reasons they feel and act as they do ring true? Do their words and thoughts sound authentic? • Does the author use language well?	Craft and Structure
• Do I like the characters, or at least find them interesting? • Do I believe the events of this story? • Is the work fresh and original?	Integration of Ideas

When reading nonfiction, ask yourself...	
• Who is the author? Why did he or she write the work? • Does the work meet my expectations? • Are the ideas exciting? Do they give me a new way of looking at a topic? Do I learn something? • Has the author made me care about the subject?	Key Ideas and Details
• Does the author organize ideas so that I can follow them? • Does the author use strong, varied, and convincing evidence? • Does the author use language well? • Does the work ring true? Is any aspect of the work exaggerated?	Craft and Structure
• Do I agree or disagree with the author's ideas? • Does the author omit viewpoints I think are important?	Integration of Ideas

Text Complexity: Reader and Task Support Suggestions

INDEPENDENT READING

Increased Support Suggest that students choose a book that they feel comfortable reading and one that is a bit more challenging. Pair a more proficient reader with a less proficient reader and have them work together on the more challenging text. Partners can prepare to read the book by reviewing questions on this student page. They can also read difficult passages together, sharing questions and insights. They can use the questions on the student page to guide after-reading discussion.

Increased Challenge Encourage students to integrate knowledge and ideas by combining the Big Question and the Unit Focus concepts in their approach to two or more featured titles.

For example, students might consider how the speakers' experiences of internal "truth" and external "reality" conflict in *Journey Home* and *I Know Why the Caged Bird Sings*. In addition, students can focus on similarities and differences in the ways authors develop a theme in fiction and a central idea in nonfiction.

Preparing to Read Complex Texts

1. Tell students they can be attentive readers by bringing their experience and imagination to the texts they read and by actively questioning those texts. Explain that the questions they see on the student page are examples of questions to ask about works of fiction and nonfiction.
2. Point out that, like writing, reading is a "multidraft" process, involving several readings of complete works or passages, revising and refining one's understanding each time.

Key Ideas and Details

3. As an example, review and amplify the first bulleted item under fiction. **Ask:** What key ideas and details could you cite as evidence that you enjoy the speaker's voice?

   Possible response: You might point out that the speaker's voice is entertaining or that the speaker provided interesting information to support the main idea.

Craft and Structure

4. **Ask:** What details of craft and structure would you cite as evidence that an author uses language well?

   Possible response: You might cite an author's use of vocabulary or devices like metaphors that help you form mental images as you read.

Integration of Ideas

5. **Ask:** How would you determine that a short story is fresh or original?

   Possible response: You would compare and contrast the short story with others you have read by evaluating elements like theme, plot, and characters.
6. Finally, explain to students that they should cite key ideas and details, examples of craft and structure, or instances of the integration of ideas as evidence to support their points during a book discussion. After hearing the evidence, the group might reach a consensus or might agree to disagree.

Unit 2 Features Overview

Unit Genre and Big Question

In this unit, students will analyze short stories. As they read they will discuss responses to the unit Big Question: Is conflict necessary?

Unit 2 Selections

Teach Selections are presented in leveled pairs. To teach the skills and meet the objectives, you need to assign only one selection in each pair.

Differentiate and Reinforce Choose the selection in a pair that is best suited for your students, based on the Text Complexity box shown on the next page. You may use the other selection to reinforce skills or provide enrichment.

Integrate Skills Each selection presents students with a reading strategy, a literary analysis concept, a vocabulary skill, and grammar instruction. Students can extend learning in the writing and extension activities.

Additional Unit Features

Literary Analysis Workshop Teach and model the Unit Focus standards. Spiral Review notes enable students to revisit these skills over the course of the unit.

Reading for Information Students analyze functional, expository, and argumentative texts and complete Timed Writing activities.

Comparing Literary Works Students study two literary works either within or across genres.

Test Practice: Reading This feature provides extra practice in utilizing reading skills to master assessments.

Writing Workshops Two writing workshops appear in each unit, along with rubrics and instruction in the writing process.

Assessment Workshop Cumulative Skill Review and Performance Tasks provide a range of assessment opportunities.

Independent Reading Students broaden their knowledge as they read longer works of increasing complexity.

THE BIG ? Is conflict necessary?

Teaching From Technology

www.PHLitOnline.com

Log on at this address for the following:

Enriched Online Student Edition

- full narration of selections
- interactive graphic organizers
- linked **Get Connected!** and **Background** videos
- All worksheets and other student resources

Professional Development

- the *Professional Development Guidebook* online
- additional professional development essays by program authors

Planning, Assigning, and Monitoring

- software for online assignment of work to students, individually or to the whole class
- a system for tracking and grading student work

Unit 2

Short Stories

PHLit Online!

www.PHLitOnline.com

Hear It!

- Selection summary audio
- Selection audio
- BQ Tunes

See It!

- Author videos
- Big Question video
- Get Connected videos
- Background videos
- More about the authors
- Illustrated vocabulary words
- Vocabulary flashcards

Do It!

- Interactive journals
- Interactive graphic organizers
- Grammar tutorials
- Interactive vocabulary games
- Test practice

193

Instructional Resources

Unit 2 Resources supports Unit skills with pages of the following types:

- **Benchmark Tests** assess and monitor student progress at mid-Unit and at Unit's end.
- **Vocabulary and Reading Warm-ups** provide additional vocabulary support, based on Lexile rankings of words, for each selection. **"A" Warm-ups** are for students reading two grades below level. **"B" Warm-ups** are for students reading one grade below level.
- **Selection Support** These practice pages are available for each selection:
  - Reading Skill
  - Literary Analysis
  - Writing About the Big Question
  - Vocabulary
  - Support for Writing
  - Support for Extend Your Learning
  - Enrichment

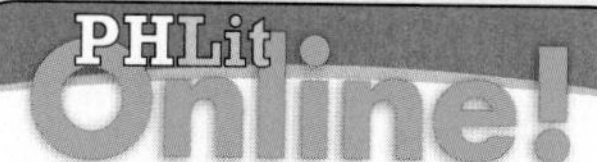

All worksheets and other student resources are also available online at **www.PHLitOnline.com.**

Text Complexity: Accessibility for Various Ability Levels

This chart gives a general text complexity rating to help you decide which selection in each leveled pair is more appropriate for your students. **Choose one selection in each pair, or choose to teach both.** You will meet the objectives for the pair when you teach either of the two selections. For additional guidance on factors that affect the complexity of each selection, see the Leveled Texts page for each selection set.

Accessibility for English Learners

This icon indicates support for English learners at point of use in this Teacher's Edition.

	✓ More Accessible	✓✓ More Complex
Pair 1	The Most Dangerous Game	American History
Pair 2	The Gift of the Magi	The Interlopers
Pair 3	Rules of the Game	The Necklace
Pair 4	Blues Ain't No Mockin Bird	The Invalid's Story

Common Core State Standards

Unit 2 Focus Standards
- Reading Literature 3, 5

Additional Activities and Assessments
- Writing 3, 4
- Speaking and Listening 2, 4
- Language 1, 6
- Reading Literature 1, 4

	Week 1					Week 2					Week 3				
	1	2	3	4	5	1	2	3	4	5	1	2	3	4	5
Introduce the Unit Big Question (pp. 194–195).	●														
Introduce the Unit author and the Unit genre, short stories, (pp. 196–199).	●														
Teach the Model selection (pp. 198–209).	●	●													
Teach one selection from Pairing 1 (pp. 210–255).		●	●	●	●	●									
Teach one selection from Pairing 2 (pp. 256–281).						●	●	●	●	●					
Complete the Test Practice: Reading (pp. 282–283).									●						
Teach Informational Texts (pp. 284–289).										●					
Teach Comparing Literary Works (pp. 290–305).											●	●			
Have students complete the Writing Workshop (pp. 306–311).										●	●	●	●	●	
Administer **Benchmark Test 3** (***Unit 2 Resources***, pp. 120–125).														●	
Reteach skills, judging which skills to reteach by evaluating students' performance on **Benchmark Test 3**.															●

Independent Reading

Have students choose a full-length work from the Independent Reading feature at the end of the unit and read it while working on this unit.

Pacing Suggestions
- Have students read their chosen work for homework.
- Devote parts of class periods in each school week to Literature Circles in which students reading the same work discuss it.

	Week 4					Week 5					Week 6				
	1	2	3	4	5	1	2	3	4	5	1	2	3	4	5
Teach one selection from Pairing 3 (pp. 312–345).	●	●	●	●	●										
Teach one selection from Pairing 4 (pp. 346–373).					●	●	●	●	●						
Complete the Test Practice: Reading (pp. 374–375).								●							
Teach Informational Texts (pp. 376–381).									●						
Teach Comparing Literary Works (pp. 382–401).										●	●				
Have students complete the Writing Workshop (pp. 402–409).									●	●	●	●	●		
Have students complete the Vocabulary Workshop (pp. 410–411).												●			
Have students complete the Communications Workshops (pp. 412–413).													●		
Have students complete the first three sections of the Assessment Workshop: Short Stories (pp. 414–417).													●	●	●
Have students complete the selected Performance Tasks in the Assessment Workshop (pp. 418–419).														●	
Administer **Benchmark Test 4** (***Unit 2 Resources***, pp. 227–235).														●	
Reteach skills, judging which skills to reteach by evaluating students' performance on **Benchmark Test 4**.															●

- Cover the focus standards with independent readings, and abbreviate review of the focus standards with student-edition selections.
- Do not assign extension activities for selections (day 5 of main selection lessons), except as needed for full standards coverage.
- If students demonstrate reading proficiency, consider omitting Test Practice: Reading features in the unit.

Block and Daily Scheduling

The assignments and activities in this Unit planner are organized by week. You may adjust them to your daily or block schedule. The Time and Resource Manager for each selection set gives specific pacing suggestions, or you may use the comprehensive lesson planning support online at **www.PHLitOnline.com.**

Monitoring Progress

Diagnose Each main selection pairing in the Unit contains a more accessible and a more challenging selection. To determine which selection in each pairing to assign, refer to students' results on the Vocabulary in Context section of **Benchmark Test 2, *Unit 1 Resources,*** pp. 238–240 (administered at the end of the previous Unit). Use the **Interpretation Guide** to interpret the results of this diagnostic portion of the test. **Note:** For the most accurate diagnosis of students who score in the middle range of the diagnostic portion of the test, administer the additional diagnostic questions online at **www.PHLitOnline.com.**

Preteach and Prepare As indicated by the diagnostic, prepare students for reading by assigning the **Vocabulary** and **Reading Warm-ups** for the selections you assign.

Teach Follow this Pacing Plan and use the resources to teach the skills and selections. For specific pacing suggestions and a list of resources, see the Time and Resource Manager and the Visual Guide to Featured Selection Resources preceding each selection pairing.

Assess After students have completed the first half of the Unit, administer **Benchmark Test 3**. Administer **Benchmark Test 4** at the end of the Unit.

Intervention and Reteach After administering each test, use the **Interpretation Guide** for the tests to determine which reteaching pages, if any, you should assign from the ***Reading Kit.*** The appropriate pages are also available through the online Progress Monitoring software.

CLASSROOM STRATEGIES

Multifaceted Student Engagement in Classroom Learning Danling Fu

> Studies show that academic achievement is associated with engagement in reading and classroom-related activities.

Numerous studies have shown that student engagement in school learning drops considerably as students get older. By the time they reach high school, lack of interest in schoolwork becomes increasingly apparent in more and more students (Brewster & Fager, 2000). Attempting to build skills of disengaged adolescents is a futile enterprise. Students who are motivated to learn, on the other hand, can succeed in less-than-optimal environments. Studies show that academic achievement is associated with engagement in reading and classroom-related activities (Blackowicz and Ogle, 2001). To make literacy instruction effective in the English classroom, efforts must be made to engage adolescent learners.

Multifaceted Engagement

Research tells us that the teachers who are most successful in engaging students develop activities with students' basic psychological and intellectual needs in mind (Anderman & Midgley, 1998; Strong et al., 1995). In general, students need work that

- develops their sense of competency,
- allows them to develop connections with their peers,
- gives them some degree of autonomy and
- makes learning personally relevant to their life and interest.

Developing Students' Sense of Competency

Research Tasks that seem impossible easily discourage learners, as do those tasks that are rote and repetitive (Dev, 1997). Remedial programs that limit students to repetitive basic skills activities actually "prompt students' lack of engagement in their schoolwork and frequently result in limited achievement" (Policy Studies Associates, 1995). Students need to feel successful and that they've earned success.

How to Apply It Assign challenging but achievable tasks for all students, including at-risk, remedial, and learning-disabled students and English language learners. Students in a class can have a wide range of abilities, interests, and learning styles. Teachers need to assign tasks that reach all students' potential. For instance, encouraging students to make connections with the text read is a way not only to demonstrate their comprehension but also to push them to go beyond the text boundary to higher-level thinking. Teachers can suggest different connections students may make in their reading: text to self, text to text, and text to the world. Students may choose to make any connections to present their understanding.

Allowing Students to Develop Connections with Peers

Research Adolescents' self-esteem and confidence can be heavily influenced by their peers. Teachers need to design projects that allow students to build their boundaries with their peers through sharing new knowledge with each other (Strong, Silver & Robison, 1995). Forming a collaborative relationship rather than a competing relationship among peers is a key to building a supportive learning community.

How to Apply It Projects are more engaging when students share what they are learning in reciprocal relationships. Literature circle is a highly recommended structure to use in book discussions. In a literature circle, each member focuses on a certain part, such as characters, settings, background of the story and unique techniques the author used. Each student in a group of four is an expert in his/her part, and the students need each other's knowledge to form a holistic understanding of the text read.

Giving Students Some Degree of Autonomy

Research Adolescents are at the growing stage that strives for independence from adults. Research shows that when given responsibility in their own learning, students are more engaged as learners and are willing to actively participate in class activities (Anderman & Midgley, 1998).

How to Apply It Give students their choice of different assignments or of different ways to present their learning. For instance, students can choose to use art, drama, or a narrative format to present their understanding of a text read. For group work, teachers can minimize their supervision over group projects by letting students monitor and evaluate their own progress or by letting them choose to work with a partner or independently.

Making Learning Relevant

Research Schoolwork should be meaningful to students outside the school building, as well as within. Students are more engaged in activities when they build on their prior knowledge and draw clear connections between what they are learning and the world they live in. They also need to feel that "school work is significant, valuable, and worthy of their efforts" (Policy Studies Associates, 1995).

How to Apply It Teachers should get to know their students as individuals first: what they care about, their interests, their neighborhood communities where they live, and their lifestyle. In teaching, teachers should use this information about their students to link the texts with their students' interests and life experiences, and help students see personal values in the stories they read and in the assignment they do. For example, in discussion of a story character, teachers should help students compare the complexity of a character in the story with people they know in their lives. If students realized reading a story is reading their world, they would see more value in literature study.

Modeled Strategy

See pp. 225 and 263 for point-of-use notes modeling these strategies.

Teacher Resources

- ***Professional Development Guidebook***
- ***Classroom Strategies and Teaching Routines* cards**

Log on as a teacher at **www.PHLitOnline.com** to access a library of all Professional Development articles by the Contributing Authors of Pearson Prentice Hall *Literature*.

Danling Fu, Ph.D

Danling Fu, Ph.D, is a Professor of Literacy, Language, and Culture, College of Education at the University of Florida. She researches and provides in-service and consultancy to public schools nationally on literacy issues.

Supporting Research

Anderman, L.H., & Midgley, C. (1998). *Motivation and middle school students* [ERIC digest]. Champaign, IL: ERIC Clearinghouse on Elementary and Early Childhood Education. (ERIC Document Reproduction Service No. ED421281)

Blackowicz, C., & Ogle, D. (2001). *Reading comprehension: Strategies for independent learners.* New York: Guilford Press.

Brewster, C., & Fager, J. (2000). *Increasing student engagement and motivation: From time-on-task to home work.* Northwest Regional Education Laboratory. Retrieved on October, 2000, from http://www.nwrel.org/request/oct00/textonly.html

Dev. P.C. (1997). Intrinsic motivation and academic achievement: What does their relationship imply for the classroom teachers? *Remedial and Special Education, 18*(1), 12–19.

Policy Studies Associates. (1995). *Raising the educational achievement of secondary school students: Vol. I, Summary of promising practices.* Washington, DC: U.S. Department of Education. Retrieved Oct. 4, 2000, from http://www.ed.gov/pubs/Raising/vol1/

Strong, R., Silver, H.F., & Robison, A. (1995). What do students want? *Educational Leadership,* 53(1), 8–12.

INTRODUCE

Introducing the Big Question

Common Core State Standards

- Speaking and Listening 1.b
- Language 6

1 Introducing the Big Question

1. Have students read the introductory paragraph.
2. Guide students in a discussion about why conflicts occur.
3. **Ask** students how conflicts can be resolved? (**Possible responses:** People can come to peaceful agreements. People can come up with new solutions.)
4. **Ask** students the Big Question, "Is conflict necessary?" (**Possible responses:** Yes, because people will always disagree. No, because people can work out their differences.)
5. Point out that the stories in this unit describe how people deal with conflicts. Remind students that as they read, they should consider whether the stories reinforce or challenge their first answers to the Big Question.

2 Exploring the Big Question

Collaboration: Group Discussion

1. Introduce the activity, using the instruction on the student page.
2. Have students work individually to list examples for each subject-area specified. Ask students to discuss the positive aspects of conflict as it pertains to Bob Dylan's "Blowin' in the Wind."
3. Review the Big Question vocabulary on page 195, following the teaching suggestions. Have students use the vocabulary as they complete the activity on page 194.

Connecting to the Literature

Explain the Big Question strand in the unit, referring to the box at right.

1 THE BIG ? Is *conflict* necessary?

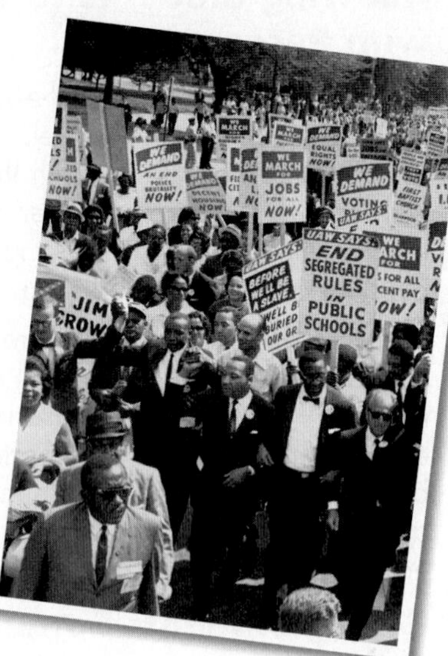

A **conflict** is a struggle between opposing forces. A conflict might be as small as an argument between friends or as large as a war between nations. It might also involve just one person who faces a personal challenge or a hard decision. Conflicts occur frequently in literature and in life, but are they necessary? Conflicts can be difficult for the people involved in them, but can a conflict also have a positive outcome?

2 Exploring the Big Question

Collaboration: Group Discussion Start thinking about the Big Question by identifying different types of conflicts and what can happen as a result of them. Make a list of some different conflicts you have either read about or experienced. Describe one specific example of each of the following:

- An argument or a disagreement between friends
- A contest or competition between teams
- A struggle to make a decision
- A controversy in the news
- A problem that must be solved

Share your examples with a group. Talk about both the causes and the effects of each conflict. Consider the positive and negative effects that each conflict might have for each person involved.

Before you begin the discussion, establish rules that will allow you to manage conflicts within your own group. For example, agree upon specific goals you want to achieve, how you will handle disagreements, and timeframes for completing your objectives. Write down the rules and refer to them as needed as you conduct your discussion.

Connecting to the Literature Each reading in this unit will give you additional insight into the Big Question.

www.PHLitOnline.com
- Big Question video
- Illustrated vocabulary words
- Interactive vocabulary games
- BQ Tunes

Applying Understanding by Design Principles

The Big Question

Explain to students that they will continue to consider the Big Question as they work through Unit 2.

- At the beginning of each selection, they will write a response to a Writing About the Big Question sentence starter.
- As they read the selection, they will look for details related to the Big Question.
- At the end of the selection, they will answer a Critical Thinking Question that is related to the Big Question.
- Tell students that their goal will be to gain a deeper understanding of literature and a more sophisticated way of discussing the Big Question.

❸ Learning Big Question Vocabulary

Acquire and Use Academic Vocabulary Academic vocabulary is the language you encounter in textbooks and on standardized tests. Review the definitions of these academic vocabulary words.

appreciate (ə prē′ shē āt′) ***v.*** be aware of the value of something

argument (är′ gyo͞o mənt) ***n.*** disagreement; dispute

articulate (är tik′yo͞o lāt′) ***v.*** express clearly

compete (kəm pēt′) ***v.*** try to win

competition (käm′ pə tish′ ən) ***n.*** contest or match

controversy (kän′trə vur′ sē) ***n.*** disagreement, often public

Use these words as you complete Big Question activities that involve reading, writing, speaking, and listening.

Gather Vocabulary Knowledge Additional Big Question words are listed below. Categorize the words by deciding whether you know each one well, know it a little bit, or do not know it at all.

amicably	**equity**	**mediate**
antagonize	**grievance**	**survival**
cooperate	**issue**	**war/battle**
differences		

Then, do the following:

1. Write the definitions of the words you know.
2. Consult a dictionary to confirm the word's meaning. Revise your definition if necessary.
3. Using a print or an online dictionary, look up the meanings of the words you do not know. Then, write the meanings.
4. If a word sounds familiar but you are not sure of its meaning, consult a dictionary. Then, record the meaning.
5. Use all of the words in a brief paragraph about the necessity of conflict. Choose punctuation for effect.

Common Core State Standards

Speaking and Listening
1.b. Work with peers to set rules for collegial discussions and decision-making, clear goals and deadlines, and individual roles as needed.

Language
6. Acquire and use accurately general academic and domain-specific words and phrases, sufficient for reading, writing, speaking, and listening at the college and career readiness level; demonstrate independence in gathering vocabulary knowledge when considering a word or phrase important to comprehension or expression.

❸ Learning Big Question Vocabulary

Acquire and Use Academic Vocabulary

1. Introduce the academic vocabulary words in the first word bank on the student page. Have students preview the words.
2. For each word, have students say the word aloud. Then, use the word in a sentence that defines the word.

Gather Vocabulary Knowledge

1. With the class, review the steps in the activity on the student page. Have students complete the activity independently, with partners, or in small groups.
2. Before students complete the last step, review the words and their meanings as a class. (Definitions appear below on the left.) Then, have students complete their paragraphs.

Show the Big Question video, online at **www.PHLitOnline.com.**

Gather Vocabulary Knowledge: Definitions

amicably (am′i kə blē) *adv.* in a friendly manner
antagonize (an tag′ə nīz′) *v.* to act in a hostile manner toward someone
cooperate (ko äp′ər āt′) *v.* to work together to achieve a goal
differences (dif′ər əns′ ez) *n.* disputes
equity (ek′wit ē) *n.* the quality of being fair
grievance (grēv′əns) *n.* an actual or imagined wrong over something thought to be unfair
issue (ish′o͞o) *n.* a subject for debate or discussion
mediate (mē′dē āt′) *v.* to bring about agreement between people who disagree
survival (sər vī′vəl) *n.* the state of continuing to exist
war / battle (wôr) / (bat′l) *n.* an armed conflict

❶ Elements of a Short Story

1. Introduce the elements of a short story, using the instruction on the student page.
2. **Ask** students for an example of a character who went through a change in a story they read.
   Sample response: The narrator/mother went through a change in her feelings about her daughter in "I Stand Here Ironing."
3. **Ask** students to give an example of a short story setting they thought was important to the story.
   Sample response: The setting of "Checkouts" was important because the characters could meet without really meeting.
4. **Ask** students to summarize the plot of one of the stories they have read.
   Sample response: In "New Directions," Mrs. Annie Johnson is left on her own to raise her sons, so she cooks pies to sell to workers and becomes successful.
5. **Ask** students to give examples of internal and external conflict from their reading or life experience.
   Sample response: External: Two people want the same job. Internal: A person is tempted to steal.
6. **Ask** students to imagine a short story in which a stop sign functions as a symbol. What could it represent, and what might the theme of the story be?
   Sample response: The stop sign might represent things that keep us from getting what we want. The theme might be that there might be a reason to stop and think.
7. Lead a discussion on how the elements of a short story interrelate, based on the chart.

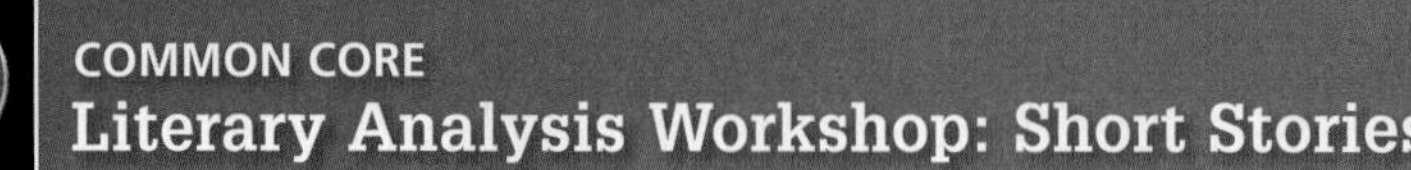

❶Elements of a Short Story

In a short story, elements such as characters, setting, plot, and conflict combine to create a unified impression, or main effect.

Short stories are brief fictional narratives intended to be read in a single sitting. Because of a short story's length, the narration and character portrayals must be focused and compressed, adding a special energy and depth to the form. As a result, a good short story leaves the reader with a unified, strong impression—its **main effect.** Each element of a story can contribute to this effect.

Characters The **characters** are the people or animals who take part in the action of the story. Details in the story help readers understand characters' **traits,** or qualities, and **motives,** or reasons for acting. The main effect of a story often involves a change or revelation experienced by a character.

Setting The **setting** of a story is the time and place of its action. Often, a short story takes place in a single, unified setting. The setting often contributes to a story's **mood**—the general feeling the story conveys.

Plot The **plot** of a story is the sequence of events it tells. Plot often contributes to the unified effect of a story by building toward a **climax,** or turning point, in which a character reaches an insight or undergoes a change.

Conflict A plot is driven by a **conflict,** or struggle between two opposing forces. Short stories usually focus on one central conflict.

- An **internal conflict** takes place in the mind of a character. The character struggles to make a decision or overcome feelings.
- An **external conflict** takes place between a character and an outside force, such as another character or a force of nature.

Theme and Symbols As the elements of a story combine to create a unified effect, they also suggest a **theme,** or insight into life. Most often, readers come to understand the theme by making inferences from key elements, including symbols. A **symbol** is an object or a story element that stands for a larger meaning.

The elements of a short story are interrelated and contribute to a unified effect.

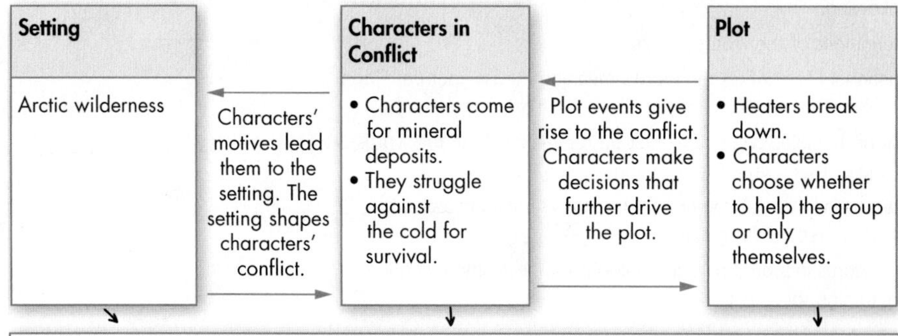

Setting
Arctic wilderness
Characters' motives lead them to the setting. The setting shapes characters' conflict.
Characters in Conflict
• Characters come for mineral deposits.
• They struggle against the cold for survival.
Plot events give rise to the conflict. Characters make decisions that further drive the plot.
Plot
• Heaters break down.
• Characters choose whether to help the group or only themselves.

Main Effect: Characters' fear and greed create a sickening sense of chaos until one character rallies them.

Teaching Resources

- All *Common Core Companion,* pp. 28–34, 48–54
- All *Unit 2 Resources,* pp. 7–22
- All *Professional Development Guidebook,* pp. 33, 36–38
- All *See It!* DVD Wayson Choy, Segments 1 and 2
- All *Graphic Organizer Transparencies,* pp. 37, 38
- All **Enriched Online Student Edition**
- L2 L3 *Reader's Notebook*
- L1 *Reader's Notebook: Adapted Version*
- EL *Reader's Notebook: English Learner's Version*
- L2 EL *Hear It!* Audio CD
- L1 EL *Hear It!* Audio CD (adapted text)

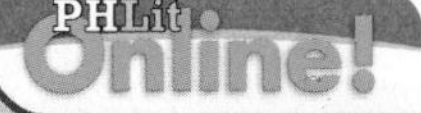

All resources, including print and video, are available online at **www.PHLitOnline.com.**

❷ Plot Structure in a Short Story

No matter what tales short stories tell, many stories share a basic plot structure. Understanding this structure can help you appreciate how a short story builds to a satisfying conclusion.

In the section of the plot called the **exposition,** the author introduces the setting and the characters. This section often includes an **inciting event**—an event that establishes the **conflict,** or struggle between opposing forces, that drives the story. Types of conflicts include

- a struggle between two characters;
- a struggle between a character and an outside force, such as nature;
- a struggle within the mind of a character, such as a struggle with guilt.

The next part of a typical plot is the **rising action,** which includes events and complications that intensify the conflict. The rising action leads to the **climax,** which is the turning point in the story—the moment of highest tension or suspense. The climax is the part of the story that makes readers want to read on to find out what happens next.

The **falling action** sets up the story's ending. The intensity of the conflict lessens and events wind down, leading to the **resolution,** or **denouement,** which shows the outcome of the conflict. In some stories, the conflict is settled, meaning that the central problem is solved; in other stories, the conflict may be left unsettled. In still other stories, the ending may revisit the characters after time has passed to show how the situation changes after the conflict is resolved. Look at the example in the chart below.

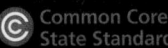

Example: Plot Structure

1. Exposition
The author describes a farm family in the Old West. *Inciting incident:* A nearby rancher wants the family's land and tells them to move.

→

2. Rising Action
Roughnecks hired by the rancher harass the family. The family asks a stranger for help.

→

3. Climax
The stranger confronts the rancher and reveals that he is the rancher's long lost brother. He reminds the rancher of the lessons their father taught them.

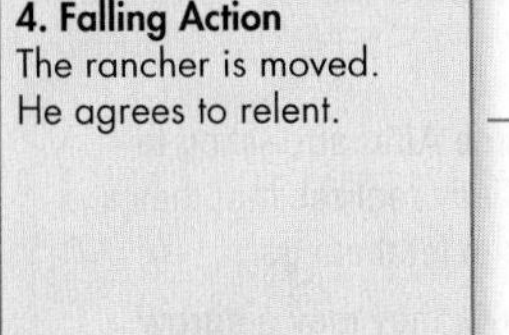

4. Falling Action
The rancher is moved. He agrees to relent.

→

5. Resolution/Denouement
The humbled rancher apologizes to the farm family.

A month later, the rancher pays a friendly social call on the farm family.

❸ In This Section

Elements of a Short Story

Analyzing Character

Analyzing Structure and Theme

Close Read: Elements of a Short Story
- Model Text
- Practice Text

After You Read

Common Core State Standards

RL.9-10.3, RL.9-10.5

[For the full wording of the standards, see the standards chart in the front of your textbook.]

❷ Plot Structure in a Short Story

1. Introduce the basic plot structure that is characteristic of many short stories, using the material on the student page.
2. **Ask** students to explain why the exposition would be important to a short story.

   Sample response: It's important to know who the characters are going to be and what their situation is. Then what happens in the rest of the story has a context.
3. **Ask** students how important they think the question "What will happen next?" might be in the rising action.

   Sample response: The rising action needs to keep the reader interested, so the question of what is going to happen next is very important.
4. **Ask** students whether they think a good plot must have a good climax.

   Sample response: In some stories, plot is not very important. But a good plot needs a good climax so that a reader will feel satisfied.

❸ In This Section

Explain that in the remainder of this Literary Analysis Workshop, students will learn about important elements of character, text structure, and theme. After reviewing the concepts, they will then see them applied in an analysis of a Model text. Finally, they will apply what they have learned to an Independent Practice text.

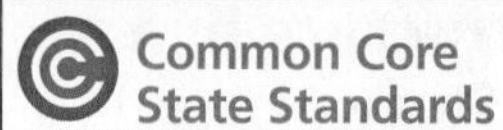

Common Core State Standards

Unit 2 Focus Standards

- **Reading Literature 3, 5**

These standards spiral through the unit.

❶ Analyzing Character

Review the concept of character, using the instruction on the student page.

1. Emphasize that complex characters make stories more interesting, in part because their actions, and therefore the various elements of the story, are unpredictable.
2. Have students focus on the character example in the first box. **Ask:** In what way does the contradiction in Bob's personality with regard to organization affect whether you can predict the end of the story?

   Sample response: The contradiction in Bob's personality makes it much more difficult to predict what will happen.
3. Have students review the second box. **Ask** students to explain why Cindy's action in going to the game with Matilda increases the conflict.

   Sample response: It makes Staci and Ashley jealous and angry.
4. Have students review the third box on the page. **Ask** students to explain how the change in Cindy's feelings about her friends develops the story's theme.

   Sample response: The change in her feelings indicates that what she values has changed.

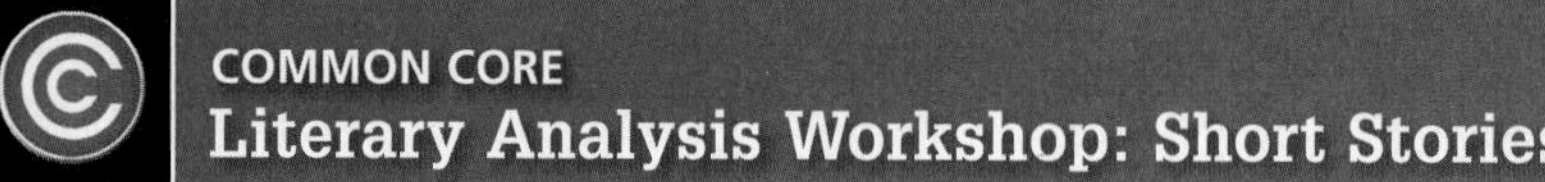

❶Analyzing Character

An author develops characters in ways that advance a story's plot.

Common Core State Standards

Reading Literature

3. Analyze how complex characters develop over the course of a text, interact with other characters, and advance the plot or develop the theme.

5. Analyze how an author's choices concerning how to structure a text, order events within it, and manipulate time create such effects as mystery, tension, or surprise.

Developing Complex Characters

In the best short stories, the main characters are interesting and **complex,** or well-rounded. Complex characters share these qualities:

- They show multiple or even contradictory **traits,** or qualities.
- They struggle with conflicting **motivations,** or reasons for acting as they do.
- They may change by the end of the story.

Example: Complex Character

Contradictory Traits Bob's ability to organize ideas leads the debate team to victory—but his room is a mess.

Conflicting Motives After high school, Bob wants to stay near his friends; he also wants to go to the best college he can.

Change After making a new friend on a trip, Bob decides he will move away for college.

Characterization To create and **develop** a character, a writer will use techniques of **characterization.**

- In **direct characterization,** the narrator makes direct statements about a character's personality:
  Afshin focused on just one thing at a time, but the depth of his focus was remarkable. Before a race, his single-minded trance could only be broken by the sound of the starter's whistle.
- In **indirect characterization,** readers learn what characters are like by analyzing what they say and do as well as how other characters respond to them:
  Summer or winter, in sun, wind, or rain, Jess rose before dawn and jogged the two-mile loop around the reservoir. After a quick shower and two chocolate donuts, she always felt ready to face the day.

How Characters Advance a Story

Characters Advance the Plot As characters interact with one another and struggle to overcome problems, their choices move the story along. A character's action—or decision *not* to take action—can lead to new plot developments and may intensify the conflict, heightening tension or suspense in the story.

Example:

Conflict Cindy is friendly with Matilda. Cindy's friends Staci and Ashley do not like Matilda and put pressure on Cindy to shun her.

Characters' Interactions Cindy decides that Staci and Ashley are being unfair and makes a point of attending a school game with Matilda.

Result: Intensified Conflict Staci and Ashley invite everyone to their party except Cindy.

Characters Develop Theme As in real life, a character's struggles with a situation can teach a general lesson. In this way, characters help develop a story's **theme**—the central insight that it conveys. As you read a short story, pay close attention to the ways that characters change and to the lessons that they learn. These details will point you toward the story's theme.

Example:

Character's Experience After struggling to please her friends, Cindy realizes that they are shallow and decides to let them go.

Theme As people grow, they may outgrow their friendships with others.

❷ Analyzing Structure and Theme

An author **structures** a story in ways that create interest and help develop the **theme.**

Reading Literature

5. Analyze how an author's choices concerning how to structure a text, order events within it, and manipulate time create such effects as mystery, tension, or surprise.

Structuring a Text for Effect

The way in which an author structures or organizes information in a story can create effects like tension, mystery, and surprise.

Plot Structure Authors make decisions about the order in which to present information as well as the pacing of events.

- **Openings** The opening establishes the general feeling of a story.

Examples of Some Story Openings
Focus on Setting: *The hospital waiting room was empty at that hour of the night. It was so quiet I could hear the second hand on the large wall clock toll each passing second.*
Focus on Character: *I'll never forget my grandfather. He was the most charming man I ever met.*
in medias res (Latin for "in the middle of things"): *"Someone call for help!" shouted a man at the side of the road.*

- **Sequence** Narrators tell plot events mainly in **chronological order**—the order in which events occurred. However, they may break from chronological order for effect. **Flashbacks** are sections of a narrative that describe a time before the present time of the story. A flashback might give insight into a character's motivations. **Foreshadowing** gives readers hints about what will happen later in the story, as when a narrator says, "That would be the last time they spoke." Foreshadowing can create **suspense,** or a reader's feeling of anxious uncertainty about the outcome.
- **Pacing** refers to the "speed" with which a narrator relates events. For example, by describing a scene at length and giving many descriptive details, the narrator "slows down" the pace. This effect can be used to heighten suspense, as in the following example:

Example: Slow Pace

Beads of sweat stood out on Agent Vole's forehead. As he struggled with the ropes that bound him, he could hear each beat of his heart, rapid but distinct. Ba-dum, ba-dum. With each beat, the second hand on the timing device clicked one notch closer to catastrophe.

- A narrative can also create a sensation of "speed" and excitement by moving quickly from one idea to another in a scene that is loaded with tension.

Point of View The **point of view,** or narrative perspective, from which a story is told determines the information an author includes. There are three main points of view:

- **Third-person omniscient:** The narrator is outside the events of the story and tells the thoughts and feelings of all characters.
- **Third-person limited:** The narrator is outside the story but tells the thoughts and feelings of only one character.
- **First-person:** The narrator is a character in the story and uses the pronouns *I* and *me.*

Point of view can be used to achieve striking effects. For example, if the first-person narrator is naive, or unsophisticated, the reader may know more about what is going on than the narrator, creating an effect known as **dramatic irony.**

❷ Analyzing Stucture and Theme

1. Review the concepts of structure and theme, using the instruction on the student page.
2. Have students review the examples of story openings in the chart. **Ask** students to describe the general feeling they get from each of the three story openings.

   Sample responses: (a) There is a feeling of quiet tension and concern about who is in the hospital and why. **(b)** There is a friendly, cheerful feeling that you're going to hear about an interesting person. **(c)** The feeling here is exciting and immediately involving.
3. Lead a discussion about why a writer might use elements that break out of chronological order, such as flashbacks and foreshadowing.
4. Have students review the box in column 2. Then, have them consider how the pace might change when Agent Vole gets out of the ropes. **Ask** students to describe a fast-paced climax to Agent Vole's story.

   Sample response: He breaks the ropes, runs across the room, grabs the bomb with its timing device, runs as hard and fast as he can to the edge of a lake, and throws the bomb forcefully into the water.
5. Remind students that in this Workshop, they will read a model analysis of the central idea of a passage and then carry out their own analysis of a second passage.

Differentiated Instruction for Universal Access

Support for Special-Needs Students
Have students read the **Exploring Short Stories** pages in the ***Reader's Notebook: Adapted Version***. This version provides a basic-level introduction to the short story.

Support for Less Proficient Readers
Have students read the **Exploring Short Stories** pages in the ***Reader's Notebook***. This version provides a basic-level introduction to the short story.

EL Support for English Learners
Have students read the **Exploring Short Stories** pages in the ***Reader's Notebook: English Learner's Version***. This version provides a basic-level introduction to the short story.

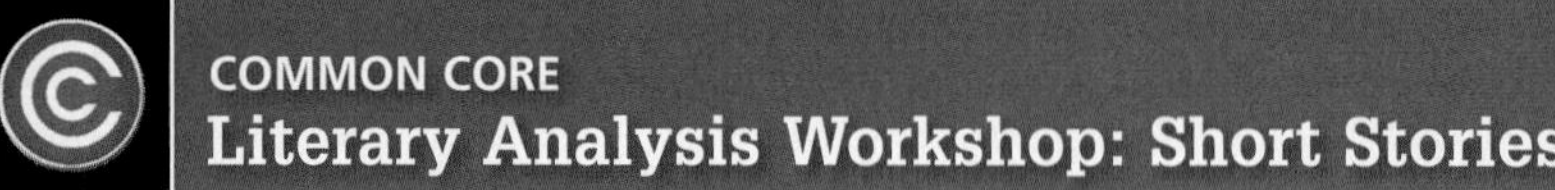

3 Close Read: Elements of a Short Story

1. Remind students that the elements of a short story work together to move the story forward.
2. Review with the class the Tips for Analyzing Elements of Short Stories chart. Discuss ways in which each element might interact with the others. For example, if the setting of a short story is a cabin snowed in by a storm, the characters might show their worst qualities under the strain.
3. Divide students into groups. Write the following theme on the board:

   There's more than one way to be happy.

   Then, discuss as a class how the different elements of a short story might work together to convey this theme. For example, a girl who wants to be on the track team (character) in an inner-city school (setting) tells her own story (point of view) about losing in tryouts for the dash (plot and conflict). Then she turns to the shot put and finds a place on the team.
4. Point out examples of highlighted text in the model on page 201. Explain that in each case, the color of the highlighting matches the color of the category in the chart. Details that illustrate a given category are highlighted in the color of that category.

3 Close Read: Elements of a Short Story

Short stories create a main effect and convey a theme by telling how complex characters interact and struggle to resolve a conflict.

A short story is like a small but powerful machine. Conflict, the motor, drives events of the plot toward a resolution, brought about by the characters' actions. Along the way, characters may grow or change. As you read a short story, use these tips to analyze its elements.

Tips for Analyzing Elements of Short Stories	
Plot and Conflict The plot is the sequence of events. Plot events are driven by a conflict, or struggle between opposing forces. As you read, identify • how the story begins and ends; • the main conflict and how events intensify it; • breaks from chronological order, including flashbacks (shifts to the past) or foreshadowing (hints of future events); • how the conflict is resolved.	**Characters** The characters are the people who take part in the action of the story. As you read, think about • characters' actions, thoughts, statements, and appearance; • how complex, or many-sided, they are; • whether characters learn something and if so, what they learn; • how their actions drive the plot; • how their experiences develop the theme.
Point of View Point of view is the perspective from which a story is told. As you read, determine • whether the story is told from third-person omniscient, third-person limited, or first-person point of view; • how the point of view shapes the story, either by excluding certain information or by making certain information available.	**Setting** The setting is the time and place of the story. It may simply be the backdrop against which actions take place, or it may be a crucial element of the conflict. As you read, consider • the conflict and where it takes place; • whether the setting affects what the characters say and do.
Main Effect The elements of a well-constructed short story combine to create one main effect. Notice • the feeling that accompanies the climax—horror, amusement, pity, and so on; • how the story impacts your understanding or view of a situation or character.	**Theme and Symbols** The theme, or insight, a story conveys may be reinforced by a symbol—an object or story element that stands for a larger idea. Think about • what the characters learn about themselves or life; • whether or not characters change; • whether elements in the story are treated as symbols, and if so, what they stand for.

Vocabulary Development

CCSS Language 6

Domain-Specific Words: Literature

Reinforce comprehension of the literary terms on this page by having students complete these "show-you-know" sentences using those terms.

1. If I wanted to write about how a modern girl would get along in the 1800s, I would be dealing with the element of _______.
2. If I wrote a story in which three different people told their versions of the same event, I would be dealing with _______.
3. If I wrote a story exploring the feelings of a talented young boy, I would be focused on _______.
4. If I wrote a story about someone forced to make a hard decision, I would be dealing with an internal _______.

❹ Model

About the Text Nobel Prize-winning author Ernest Hemingway (1899–1961) pioneered a distinctive narrative style in his fiction. In 1938, Hemingway went to Spain as a reporter to cover events in the Spanish Civil War (1936–1939), a bloody conflict that divided the country and drew the attention of the world. He originally wrote this story as a news dispatch, but later rewrote it as a short story.

"Old Man at the Bridge" by Ernest Hemingway

❺ An old man with steel rimmed spectacles and very dusty clothes sat by the side of the road. There was a pontoon bridge across the river and carts, trucks, and men, women and children were crossing it. The mule-drawn carts staggered up the steep bank from the bridge with soldiers helping push against the spokes of the wheels. The trucks ground up and away heading out of it all and the peasants plodded along in the ankle deep dust. But the old man sat there without moving. He was too tired to go any farther.

❻ It was my business to cross the bridge, explore the bridgehead beyond and find out to what point the enemy had advanced. I did this and returned over the bridge. There were not so many carts now and very few people on foot, but the old man was still there.

❼ "Where do you come from?" I asked him.

"From San Carlos," he said, and smiled.

That was his native town and so it gave him pleasure to mention it and he smiled.

"I was taking care of animals," he explained.

"Oh," I said, not quite understanding.

"Yes," he said, "I stayed, you see, taking care of animals. I was the last one to leave the town of San Carlos."

He did not look like a shepherd nor a herdsman and I looked at his black dusty clothes and his gray dusty face and his steel rimmed spectacles and said, "What animals were they?"

"Various animals," he said, and shook his head. "I had to leave them."

❽ I was watching the bridge and the African looking country of the Ebro Delta and wondering how long now it would be before we would see the enemy, and listening all the while for the first noises that would signal that ever mysterious event called contact, and the old man still sat there.

"What animals were they?" I asked.

"There were three animals altogether," he explained. "There were two goats and a cat and then there were four pairs of pigeons."

"And you had to leave them?" I asked.

"Yes. Because of the artillery. The captain told me to go because of the artillery."

❺ **Setting** This description of wartime activities establishes the setting.

❻ **Point of View** The story is told by a first-person narrator. While he can share his own thoughts and feelings, he does not know those of the old man, adding to the old man's mystery.

❼ **Characters** The old man's pleasure at naming his hometown conveys his simplicity and innocence.

❽ **Plot and Conflict** The narrator's expectation of the enemy's arrival—and the implication that violence is imminent—contrasts with the old man's passivity. The contrast heightens the conflict.

TEACH

❹ Reading the Model

1. Discuss the About the Text note. Explain further that the passage students are about to read is a short story based on a real experience.
2. Have students read the passage (pp. 201–202). Discuss, clarifying as necessary. Then, guide students in reviewing the annotations.

❺ Setting

Read aloud the Setting annotation. **Ask:** What can you tell about the setting of the story?

Possible response: The setting is a place by a river where there is a pontoon bridge. The road is dusty. It is a time and place in which people used both trucks and mules.

❻ Point of View

Read aloud the bracketed passage and Point of View annotation. **Ask:** How do you know this is a first-person narrator?

Answer: The narrator used the personal pronoun *I*.

❼ Characters

Read aloud the Characters annotation and the bracketed text. **Ask:** At this point in the story, what do you know about the man by the bridge?

Possible response: He is old and tired. He is from San Carlos, which he takes pleasure in talking about. He was taking care of animals.

❽ Plot and Conflict

Have a volunteer read aloud the bracketed passage and the Plot and Conflict annotation. **Ask:** How is the old man reacting to the conflict of war?

Possible response: He does not seem to be concerned about it.

❾ Theme

Have a volunteer read aloud the passage highlighted in yellow. Explain to students that in a civil war, there is no clear distinction between the battlefield and civilian area. Every place is dangerous and everyone is in danger. This is one of the reasons it does not matter that the old man is without politics.

❿ Plot and Conflict

Read aloud the Plot and Conflict annotation and the text highlighted in pink. **Ask:** What seems to be the main conflict for the old man?

Possible response: He is in conflict about whether he should have left the animals.

⓫ Main Effect

Have a volunteer read aloud the passage highlighted in aqua. **Ask:** What parallel does Hemingway draw between the old man and the animals?

Possible response: The old man could not save the animals, and the narrator cannot save him.

⓬ Theme

Have a volunteer read aloud the passage highlighted in yellow. **Ask:** How does the narrator use the idea of luck to emphasize the theme?

Possible response: The examples of luck are so small that it is clear they scarcely count.

Model continued

Theme The old man describes himself as "without politics." His statement develops the theme: War affects even those who do not take sides.

Plot and Conflict The repetitive dialogue heightens the conflict between the old man's lack of action and the narrator's concern. It advances the plot by showing that the narrator has done all that he can.

Main Effect Through the old man's incomprehension of the danger facing him, Hemingway achieves his main effect: a glimpse of the dull horror of war.

⓬

Theme This conclusion points to a theme: *War has innocent victims. It displaces, disorients, and may even destroy them.*

"And you have no family?" I asked, watching the far end of the bridge where a few last carts were hurrying down the slope of the bank.

"No," he said, "only the animals I stated. The cat, of course, will be all right. A cat can look out for itself, but I cannot think what will become of the others."

"What politics have you?" I asked.

❾ "I am without politics," he said. "I am seventy-six years old. I have come twelve kilometers now and I think now I can go no further."

"This is not a good place to stop," I said. "If you can make it, there are trucks up the road where it forks for Tortosa."

"I will wait a while," he said, "and then I will go. Where do the trucks go?"

"Towards Barcelona," I told him.

"I know no one in that direction," he said, "but thank you very much. Thank you again very much."

He looked at me very blankly and tiredly, then said, having to share his worry with some one, "The cat will be all right, I am sure. There is no need to be unquiet about the cat. But the others. Now what do you think about the others?" ❿

"Why they'll probably come through it all right."

"You think so?"

"Why not," I said, watching the far bank where now there were no carts.

"But what will they do under the artillery when I was told to leave because of the artillery?"

"Did you leave the dove cage unlocked?" I asked.

"Yes."

"Then they'll fly."

"Yes, certainly they'll fly. But the others. It's better not to think about the others," he said.

"If you are rested I would go," I urged. "Get up and try to walk now."

"Thank you," he said and got to his feet, swayed from side to side and then sat down backwards in the dust.

⓫ "I was taking care of animals," he said dully, but no longer to me. "I was only taking care of animals."

There was nothing to do about him. It was Easter Sunday and the Fascists[1] were advancing toward the Ebro. It was a gray overcast day with a low ceiling so their planes were not up. That and the fact that cats know how to look after themselves was all the good luck that old man would ever have. ⓬

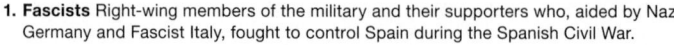

1. **Fascists** Right-wing members of the military and their supporters who, aided by Nazi Germany and Fascist Italy, fought to control Spain during the Spanish Civil War.

⓭ Independent Practice

About the Text Wayson Choy (b. 1939) is a contemporary Canadian writer. During World War II, while Choy's immigrant parents worked, he was cared for by Chinatown's village elders in Vancouver, Canada. The vivid myths that they shared during his childhood inspired him to tell his own tales.

"The Jade Peony"[1] by Wayson Choy

⓮ When Grandmama died at 83 our whole household held its breath. She had promised us a sign of her leaving, final proof that her present life had ended well. My parents knew that without any clear sign, our own family fortunes could be altered, threatened. My stepmother looked endlessly into the small cluttered room the ancient lady had occupied. Nothing was touched; nothing changed. My father, thinking that a sign should appear in Grandmama's garden, looked at the frost-killed shoots and cringed: *no, that could not be it.*

⓯ My two older teenage brothers and my sister, Liang, age 14, were embarrassed by my parents' behavior. What would all the white people in Vancouver[2] think of us? We were Canadians now, *Chinese-Canadians,* a hyphenated reality that my parents could never accept. So it seemed, for different reasons, we all held our breath waiting for *something.*

I was eight when she died. For days she had resisted going into the hospital . . . *a cold, just a cold . . .* and instead gave constant instruction to my stepmother and sister on the boiling of ginseng roots mixed with bitter extract. At night, between wracking coughs and deadly silences, Grandmama had her back and chest rubbed with heated camphor oil and sipped a bluish decoction of an herb called Peacock's Tail. When all these failed to abate her fever, she began to arrange the details of her will. This she did with my father, confessing finally: "I am too stubborn. The only cure for old age is to die."

⓰ My father wept to hear this. I stood beside her bed; she turned to me. Her round face looked darker, and the gentleness of her eyes, the thin, arching eyebrows, seemed weary. I brushed the few strands of gray, brittle hair from her face; she managed to smile at me. Being the youngest, I had spent nearly all my time with her and could not imagine that we would ever be parted. Yet when she spoke, and her voice hesitated, cracked, the somber shadows of her room chilled me. Her wrinkled brow grew wet with fever, and her small body seemed even more diminutive.

"I—I am going to the hospital, Grandson." Her hand reached out for mine. "You know, Little Son, whatever happens I will never leave you." Her palm felt plush and warm, the slender, old fingers boney and firm, so magically strong was her grip that I could not imagine how she could ever part from me. Ever.

⓮ **Plot and Conflict** What information does the narrator give readers in the opening paragraph?

⓯ **Point of View** From what point of view is the story told? How does this point of view determine the information the narrator can share?

⓰ **Characters** How does the physical description of Grandmama contribute to your understanding of her character?

1. **Jade Peony** (pē´ ə nē) jade is a hard, dense gemstone; a peony is a common garden flower, the Chinese variety of which produces large, single blossoms in early summer.
2. **Vancouver** (van ko͞o´ vər) large city in the province of British Columbia, Canada.

⓭ Independent Practice

1. Discuss the About the Text note. Explain further that the passage students are about to read is a short story based on a real experience.
2. Have students read the passage (pp. 203–209). Discuss, clarifying as necessary. Then, guide students in reviewing the annotations.

⓮ Plot and Conflict

Have a volunteer read aloud the passage highlighted in pink. **Ask** the Plot and Conflict question.

Possible response: The family is superstitious.

⓯ Point of View

Have a volunteer read aloud the passage highlighted in tan. **Ask** the Point of View questions.

Possible response: The story is told from the point of view of a young person who does not know everything about the adult world.

⓰ Characters

Have a volunteer read aloud the passage highlighted in blue. **Ask** the Characters question.

Possible response: She is a very old, frail woman who manages to smile anyway.

PHLit Online!

To have students read the selection in interactive format, with narration and point-of-use interactive graphic organizers, go to **www.PHLitOnline.com.**

Differentiated Instruction for Universal Access

Strategy for Special-Needs Students
Have students read the adapted version of "The Jade Peony" in the ***Reader's Notebook: Adapted Version.*** They may also listen to the adapted version on the ***Hear It!* Audio CD.**

Support for Less Proficient Readers
Have students read "The Jade Peony" in the ***Reader's Notebook.*** After students finish the selection in the ***Reader's Notebook,*** have them complete the questions and activities in the Student Edition.

EL Support for English Learners
Have students read "The Jade Peony" in the ***Reader's Notebook: English Learner's Version.*** English learners may also read the selection as they listen to the recorded version on the ***Hear It!* Audio CD.**

17 Plot

Have a volunteer read aloud the passage highlighted in pink. **Ask** the Plot question.

Possible response: Grandmama was once loved by an actor and juggler who promised to return to her.

18 Symbols

Have a volunteer read aloud the passage highlighted in yellow. **Ask** the Symbols questions.

Possible response: Grandmama cherishes it and keeps it always with her. It was once part of a windchime.

19 Setting

Have a volunteer read aloud the passage highlighted in green. **Ask** the Setting question.

Possible response: The setting is modern-day Canada, where her behavior is not accepted.

20 Conflict

Have a volunteer read aloud the passage highlighted in pink. **Ask** the Conflict question.

Possible response: The family is embarrassed by Grandmama.

21 Theme and Symbols

Have a volunteer read aloud the passage highlighted in yellow. **Ask** the Theme and Symbols questions.

Possible response: His reaction develops the theme of respect for tradition, which is symbolized by the Jade Peony.

Practice continued

Plot What important information do you learn in this passage, which flashes back to events before the beginning of the story and then returns to the present?

Symbols How do you know the jade peony is an important symbol? What is its connection to the windchimes?

Setting How does the setting influence the characters' reactions to Grandmama's quest?

Conflict What conflict between Grandmama and other family members is established here?

Theme and Symbols What theme concerning tradition and the past does the father's reaction develop? How is it connected to the symbol of the jade peony?

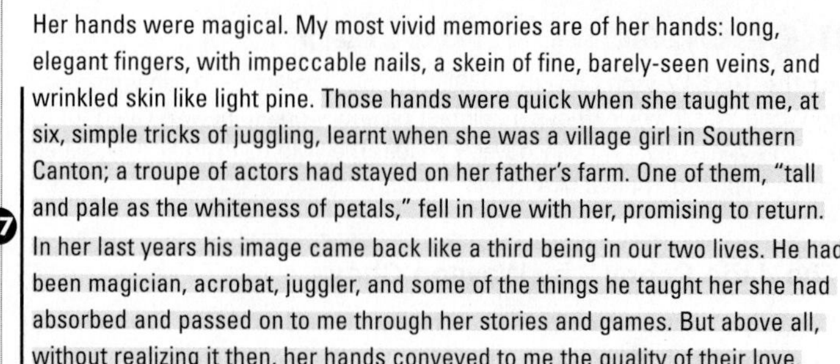

Her hands were magical. My most vivid memories are of her hands: long, elegant fingers, with impeccable nails, a skein of fine, barely-seen veins, and wrinkled skin like light pine. Those hands were quick when she taught me, at six, simple tricks of juggling, learnt when she was a village girl in Southern Canton; a troupe of actors had stayed on her father's farm. One of them, "tall
17 and pale as the whiteness of petals," fell in love with her, promising to return. In her last years his image came back like a third being in our two lives. He had been magician, acrobat, juggler, and some of the things he taught her she had absorbed and passed on to me through her stories and games. But above all, without realizing it then, her hands conveyed to me the quality of their love.

Most marvelous for me was the quick-witted skill her hands revealed in making windchimes for our birthdays: windchimes in the likeness of her lost friend's only present to her, made of bits of string and scraps, in the center of which once hung a precious jade peony. This wondrous gift to her broke apart years ago, in China, but Grandmama kept the jade pendant in a tiny red silk envelope, and kept it always in her pocket, until her death.

18 These were not ordinary, carelessly made chimes, such as those you now find in our Chinatown stores, whose rattling noises drive you mad. But making her special ones caused dissension in our family, and some shame. Each one that she made was created from a treasure trove of glass fragments and castaway costume jewelry, in the same way that her first windchime had been made.

The problem for the rest of the family was in the fact that Grandmama looked for these treasures wandering the back alleys of Keefer and Pender Streets,
19 peering into our neighbors' garbage cans, chasing away hungry, nervous cats and shouting curses at them.

"All our friends are laughing at us!" Older Brother Jung said at last to my father, when Grandmama was away having tea at Mrs. Lim's.

"We are not poor," Oldest Brother Kiam declared, "Yet she and Sek-Lung poke
20 through those awful things as if—" he shoved me in frustration and I stumbled against my sister, "—they were beggars!"

"She will make Little Brother crazy!" Sister Liang said. Without warning, she punched me sharply in the back; I jumped. "You see, look how *nervous* he is!"

I lifted my foot slightly, enough to swing it back and kick Liang in the shin. She yelled and pulled back her fist to punch me again. Jung made a menacing move towards me.

"Stop this, all of you!" My father shook his head in exasperation. How could he dare tell the Grand Old One, his aging mother, that what was somehow
21 appropriate in a poor village in China, was an abomination here. How could he prevent me, his youngest, from accompanying her? If she went walking into those alleyways alone she could well be attacked by hoodlums. "She is not a beggar looking for food. She is searching for—for. . . ."

Think Aloud

Vocabulary: Using Context

Direct students' attention to the word *hoodlums* at the bottom of this page. Using a think-aloud process, model how to use context to infer the meaning of an unknown word. Say to students:

I'm going to think aloud to show you how I would figure out the meaning of *hoodlums* based on its context.

In this sentence, Sek-Lung is discussing his father's fear that Grandmama might be attacked by *hoodlums*. I know that Sek-Lung's father is angry that Grandmama and Sek-Lung are looking for garbage in the alleyways. My first context clue about the meaning of *hoodlums* is that if they might attack an elderly woman, they are probably bad people. My second clue is that alleyways are considered dangerous places in which a respectable person probably would not want to go. If *hoodlums* lurk in dark places like alleyways, they must be dangerous. Based on these clues, I think *hoodlums* are violent people who lurk in out-of-the-way places.

My stepmother attempted to speak, then fell silent. She, too, seemed perplexed and somewhat ashamed. They all loved Grandmama, but she was *inconvenient,* unsettling. 22

As for our neighbors, most understood Grandmama to be harmlessly crazy, others that she did indeed make lovely toys but for what purpose? *Why?* they asked, and the stories she told me, of the juggler who smiled at her, flashed in my head.

Finally, by their cutting remarks, the family did exert enough pressure so that Grandmama and I no longer openly announced our expeditions. Instead, she took me with her on "shopping trips," ostensibly for clothes or groceries, while in fact we spent most of our time exploring stranger and more distant neighborhoods, searching for splendid junk: jangling pieces of a vase, cranberry glass fragments embossed with leaves, discarded glass beads from Woolworth[3] necklaces. . . . We would sneak them all home in brown rice sacks, folded into small parcels, and put them under her bed. During the day when the family was away at school or work, we brought them out and washed every item in a large black pot of boiling lye[4] and water, dried them quickly, carefully, and returned them, sparkling, under her bed. 24

Our greatest excitement occurred when a fire gutted the large Chinese Presbyterian Church, three blocks from our house. Over the still-smoking ruins the next day, Grandmama and I rushed precariously over the blackened beams to pick out the stained glass that glittered in the sunlight. Small figure bent over, wrapped against the autumn cold in a dark blue quilted coat, happily gathering each piece like gold, she became my spiritual playmate: "There's a good one! *There!"*

Hours later, soot-covered and smelling of smoke, we came home with a carton full of delicate fragments, still early enough to steal them all into the house and put the small box under her bed. "These are special pieces," she said, giving the box a last push, "because they come from a sacred place." She slowly got up and I saw, for the first time, her hand begin to shake. But then, in her joy, she embraced me. Both of our hearts were racing, as if we were two dreamers. I buried my face in her blue quilt, and for a moment, the whole world seemed silent.

"My juggler," she said, "he never came back to me from Honan[5]. . . perhaps the famine. . . ." Her voice began to quake. "But I shall have my sacred windchime . . . I shall have it again." 25

One evening, when the family was gathered in their usual places in the parlor, Grandmama gave me her secret nod: a slight wink of her eye and a flaring of her nostrils. There was *trouble* in the air. Supper had gone badly, school examinations were due, father had failed to meet an editorial deadline at the *Vancouver Chinese Times.* A huge sigh came from Sister Liang.

Characters How do other characters' reactions to Grandmama add to your understanding of her personality?

23 **Characters** How do the interactions of characters advance the plot in this section?

24 **Point of View** How does the narrator's point of view determine which information is presented and how?

Plot In what ways do Grandmama's musings both flash back to earlier events and foreshadow the future?

3. **Woolworth** a variety store belonging to the chain founded by Frank Woolworth in 1879.
4. **lye** (lī) *n.* substance derived from wood ashes, commonly used in making soap or for washing.
5. **Honan** (hō´ nän´) province in east central China.

22 Characters

Have a volunteer read aloud the bracketed passage. **Ask** the first Characters question.

Possible response: Their reactions make clear that she is loved in spite of her oddness in that culture.

23 Characters

Have a volunteer read aloud the bracketed passage. **Ask** the second Characters question.

Possible response: Because the family objects to their expeditions, Grandmama and Sek-Lung begin to hide their purposes and their finds.

24 Point of View

Have a volunteer read aloud the bracketed passage. **Ask** the Point of View question.

Possible response: Because Sek-Lung is the narrator, the information about Grandmama's secrets is presented with sympathy.

25 Plot

Have a volunteer read aloud the bracketed passage. **Ask** the Plot question.

Possible response: The flashback reminds us what Grandmama is waiting for and hints that she might get it.

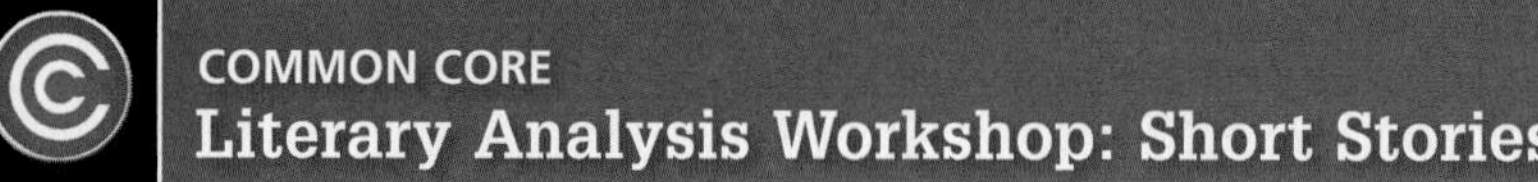

㉖ Characters

Have a volunteer read aloud the bracketed passage. **Ask** the Characters question.

Possible response: There is a little bit of room in the family for argument, but in the end Father rules.

㉗ Plot

Have a volunteer read aloud the bracketed passage. **Ask** the Plot question.

Possible response: The reason he is not at school is not as important as the other things he talked about first.

㉘ Setting

Have a volunteer read aloud the bracketed passage. **Ask** the Setting questions.

Possible response: Grandmama's belongings are traditional and beautiful, which reveals what she values. Sek-Lung might have absorbed some of those values.

Practice continued

"But it is useless this Chinese they teach you!" she lamented, turning to Stepmother for support. Silence. Liang frowned, dejected, and went back to her Chinese book, bending the covers back.

"Father," Oldest Brother Kiam began, waving his bamboo brush in the air, "you must realize that this Mandarin only confuses us. We are Cantonese[6] speakers. . . ."

"And you do not complain about Latin, French or German in your English school?" Father rattled his newspaper, a signal that his patience was ending.

"But, Father, those languages are *scientific*," Kiam jabbed his brush in the air. "We are now in a scientific, logical world."

Father was silent. We could all hear Grandmama's rocker.

Characters What do you learn about Older Brother and Father from this dialogue?

㉖ "What about Sek-Lung?" Older Brother Jung pointed angrily at me. "He was sick last year, but this year he should have at least started Chinese school, instead of picking over garbage cans!"

"He starts next year," Father said, in a hard tone that immediately warned everyone to be silent. Liang slammed her book.

Grandmama went on rocking quietly in her chair. She complimented my mother on her knitting, made a remark about the "strong beauty" of Kiam's brushstrokes which, in spite of himself, immensely pleased him. All this babbling noise was her family torn and confused in a strange land: everything here was so very foreign and scientific.

Plot The narrator goes back in time to explain why he was not yet attending school. Why do you think he gives this information now, rather than at the beginning of the story?

㉗ The truth was, I was sorry not to have started school the year before. In my innocence I had imagined going to school meant certain privileges worthy of all my brothers' and sister's complaints. The fact that my lung infection in my fifth and sixth years, mistakenly diagnosed as TB,[7] earned me some reprieve, only made me long for school the more. Each member of the family took turns on Sunday, teaching me or annoying me. But it was the countless hours I spent with Grandmama that were my real education. Tapping me on my head she would say, "Come, Sek-Lung, we have *our* work," and we would walk up the stairs to her small crowded room. There, in the midst of her antique shawls, the old ancestral calligraphy and multi-colored embroidered hangings, beneath the mysterious shelves of sweet herbs and bitter potions, we would continue doing what we had started that morning: the elaborate windchime for her death.

Setting How does the description of Grandmama's room reflect her values? How might spending time in this room have influenced Sek-Lung?

"I can't last forever," she declared, when she let me in on the secret of this one. "It will sing and dance and glitter," her long fingers stretched into the air, pantomiming the waving motion of her ghost chimes; "My spirit will hear its sounds and see its light and return to this house and say goodbye to you."

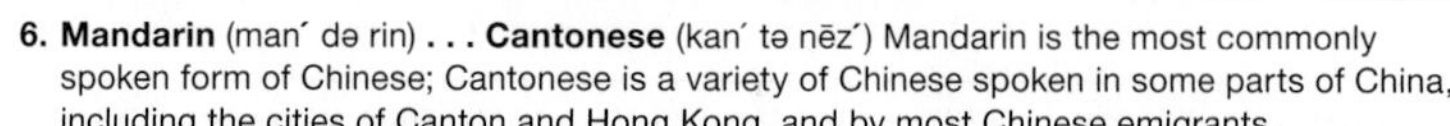

6. **Mandarin** (man′ də rin) **. . . Cantonese** (kan′ tə nēz′) Mandarin is the most commonly spoken form of Chinese; Cantonese is a variety of Chinese spoken in some parts of China, including the cities of Canton and Hong Kong, and by most Chinese emigrants.
7. **TB** (tē′ bē′) *n.* abbreviation for tuberculosis, a contagious disease that begins in the lungs.

Deftly she reached into the carton she had placed on the chair beside me. She picked out a fish-shape amber piece, and with a long needle-like tool and a steel ruler, she scored[8] it. Pressing the blade of a cleaver against the line, with the fingers of her other hand, she lifted up the glass until it cleanly *snapped* into the exact shape she required. Her hand began to tremble, the tips of her fingers to shiver, like rippling water.

"You see that, Little One?" She held her hand up. "That is my body fighting with Death. He is in this room now." (29)

My eyes darted in panic, but Grandmama remained calm, undisturbed, and went on with her work. Then I remembered the glue and uncorked the jar for her. Soon the graceful ritual movements of her hand returned to her, and I became lost in the magic of her task: she dabbed a cabalistic[9] mixture of glue on one end and skillfully dropped the braided end of a silk thread into it. This part always amazed me: the braiding would slowly, *very* slowly, *unknot,* fanning out like a prized fishtail. In a few seconds the clear, homemade glue began to harden as I blew lightly over it, welding to itself each separate silk strand.

Each jam-sized pot of glue was precious; each large cork had been wrapped with a fragment of pink silk. I remember this part vividly, because each cork was treated to a special rite. First we went shopping in the best silk stores in Chinatown for the perfect square of silk she required. It had to be a deep pink, a shade of color blushing toward red. And the tone had to match—as closely as possible—her precious jade carving, the small peony of white and light-red jade, her most lucky possession. In the center of this semi-translucent carving, no more than an inch wide, was a pool of pink light, its veins swirling out into the petals of the flower.

"This color is the color of my spirit," she said, holding it up to the window so I could see the delicate pastel against the broad strokes of sunlight. She dropped her voice, and I held my breath at the wonder of the color. "This was given to me by the young actor who taught me how to juggle. He had four of them, and each one had a center of this rare color, the color of Good Fortune." The pendant seemed to pulse as she turned it: "Oh, Sek-Lung! He had white hair and white skin to *his toes!* It's *true*, I saw him bathing." She laughed and blushed, her eyes softened at the memory. The silk had to match the pink heart of her pendant: the color was magical for her, to hold the unraveling strands of her memory. . . . (30)

It was just six months before she died that we really began to work on her last windchime. Three thin bamboo sticks were steamed and bent into circlets; 30 exact lengths of silk thread, the strongest kind, were cut and braided at both ends and glued to stained glass. Her hands worked on their own command, each hand racing with a life of its own: cutting, snapping, braiding, knotting. . . .

(29) **Theme** What possible theme is developed through the contrast between Grandmama's and Sek-Lung's responses to the thought of death?

(30) **Symbols** How does this description connect the jade peony with Grandmama's spirit in youth and old age?

(31) **Plot** How does this discussion bring the story full circle, back to the beginning discussion of "signs"?

8. **scored** (skôrd) *v.* put a notch or groove in.
9. **cabalistic** (kab´ ə lis´ tik) *adj.* relating to a secret or mystical belief or practice.

(29) Theme

Have a volunteer read aloud the bracketed passage. **Ask** the Theme question.

Possible response: Age and wisdom lessen fear of death.

(30) Symbols

Have a volunteer read aloud the bracketed passage. **Ask** the Symbols question.

Possible response: Grandmama says that the deep pink at the center of the jade peony is the color of her spirit.

(31) Plot

Have a volunteer read aloud the bracketed passage. **Ask** the Plot question.

Possible response: The story begins with Grandmama's death and now comes back to it.

Fluency

Distribute copies of pages 206–207, and pair students. Have partners take turns reading paragraphs aloud. While one partner reads, the other should mark any words with which the student reading has difficulty. Circulate to monitor the fluency of students' reading. Collect students' marked-up copies of the page and review difficult words and passages with the class. Look for these problem spots:

- If students have difficulty with the word *lamented* (p. 206), point out the context of the word. Ask students to think about what Liang is doing when she says what she says. Then, ask them to replace *lamented* with another word that would make sense, such as *complained.*
- If students have difficulty with the word *undisturbed* (p. 207), point out that the word has a common prefix, *un-*, and a common suffix, *-ed*. Have students cover up parts of the word with their thumbs to sound out each syllable in turn. Explain that *undisturbed* means "not moved or touched."

32 Plot and Conflict

Have a volunteer read aloud the bracketed passage. **Ask** the Plot and Conflict question.

Possible answer: She is facing death and needs to finish her windchime first.

33 Main Effect

Have a volunteer read aloud the bracketed passage. **Ask** the Main Effect question.

Possible answer: The passage contributes to the main effect of the love between Grandmama and Sek Lung.

34 Symbols

Have a volunteer read aloud the bracketed passage. **Ask** the Symbols questions.

Possible answer: They react in fear. Their reactions suggest that the cat symbolizes death.

35 Plot and Conflict

Have a volunteer read aloud the bracketed passage. **Ask** the Plot and Conflict question.

Possible answer: Grandmama is now ready for death.

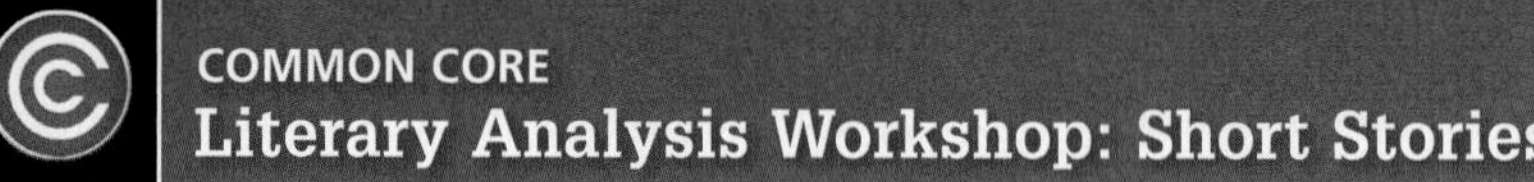

Practice continued

Plot and Conflict What conflict does Grandmama face?

Sometimes she breathed heavily and her small body, growing thinner, sagged against me. *Death,* I thought, *He is in this room,* and I would work harder alongside her. For months Grandmama and I did this every other evening, a half dozen pieces each time. The shaking in her hand grew worse, but we said nothing. Finally, after discarding hundreds, she told me she had the necessary 30 pieces. But this time, because it was a sacred chime, I would not be permitted to help her tie it up or have the joy of raising it. "Once tied," she said, holding me against my disappointment, "not even I can raise it. Not a sound must it make until I have died."

"What will happen?"

"Your father will then take the center braided strand and raise it. He will hang it against my bedroom window so that my ghost may see it, and hear it, and return. I must say goodbye to this world properly or wander in this foreign land forever."

Main Effect To what main effect of the story does this passage contribute? Explain.

33 "You can take the streetcar!" I blurted, suddenly shocked that she actually meant to leave me. I thought I could hear the clear-chromatic chimes, see the shimmering colors on the wall: I fell against her and cried, and there in my crying I knew that she would die. I can still remember the touch of her hand on my head, and the smell of her thick woolen sweater pressed against my face. "I will always be with you, Little Sek-Lung, but in a different way . . . you'll see."

Symbols How do the characters react to the white cat? What do their reactions suggest about the cat's symbolic meaning?

Months went by, and nothing happened. Then one late September evening, when I had just come home from Chinese School, Grandmama was preparing supper when she looked out our kitchen window and saw a cat—a long, lean white cat—jump into our garbage pail and knock it over. She ran out to chase it away, shouting curses at it. She did not have her thick sweater on and when she came back into the house, a chill gripped her. She leaned against the door: "That was 34 not a cat," she said, and the odd tone of her voice caused my father to look with alarm at her. "I can not take back my curses. It is too late." She took hold of my father's arm: "It was all white and had pink eyes like sacred fire."

My father started at this, and they both looked pale. My brothers and sister, clearing the table, froze in their gestures.

"The fog has confused you," Stepmother said. "It was just a cat."

35

Plot and Conflict How does Grandmama's reaction suggest a resolution to the central conflict she has faced throughout the story?

35 But Grandmama shook her head, for she knew it was a sign. "I will not live forever," she said. "I am prepared."

The next morning she was confined to her bed with a severe cold. Sitting by her, playing with some of my toys, I asked her about the cat: "Why did father jump at the cat with the pink eyes? He didn't see it, you did."

"But he and your mother know what it means."

"What?"

"My friend, the juggler, the magician, was as pale as white jade, and he had pink eyes." I thought she would begin to tell me one of her stories, a tale of enchantment or of a wondrous adventure, but she only paused to swallow; her eyes glittered, lost in memory. She took my hand, gently opening and closing her fingers over it. "Sek-Lung," she sighed, "*he* has come back to me."

Vocabulary Development

Vocabulary Knowledge Rating

When students have completed reading and discussing "The Jade Peony," have them take out their **Vocabulary Knowledge Rating Chart** for this selection. Read the words aloud once more and have students rate their knowledge of the words again in the After Reading column.

Clarify any words that are still problematic. Have students write their own definition and example sentence in the appropriate column. Encourage students to use the words in further discussion and written work about the selection.

Then Grandmama sank back into her pillow and the embroidered flowers lifted to frame her wrinkled face. I saw her hand over my own, and my own began to tremble. I fell fitfully asleep by her side. When I woke up it was dark and her bed was empty. She had been taken to the hospital and I was not permitted to visit. A few days after that she died of the complications of pneumonia. Immediately after her death my father came home and said nothing to us, but walked up the stairs to her room, pulled aside the drawn lace curtains of her window and lifted the windchimes to the sky. 36

I began to cry and quickly put my hand in my pocket for a handkerchief. Instead, caught between my fingers, was the small, round firmness of the jade peony. In my mind's eye I saw Grandmama smile and heard, softly, the pink center beat like a beautiful, cramped heart. 37

Plot How does the pacing accelerate at the end of the story? What is the effect of this acceleration?

Theme and Symbols What theme is emphasized by the final paragraph of the story? How does the symbol of the jade peony help convey this theme?

After You Read | The Jade Peony

1. **Key Ideas and Details (a) Explain:** Citing details from the story, explain who gave the grandmother her first windchime. **(b) Infer:** Why do you think the making of windchimes was such a meaningful activity in the grandmother's later years?

2. **Key Ideas and Details (a) Compare and Contrast:** How do Sek-Lung's reactions to his grandmother's activities differ from those of the other family members? **(b) Analyze:** How do you explain these differing attitudes?

3. **Craft and Structure (a) Identify:** Who is the narrator of the story? **(b) Analyze:** How does the narrator's unique perspective on events help develop the character of the grandmother and the characters of other family members? **(c) Analyze:** How does the narrator's perspective help develop the conflict between the grandmother and other family members?

4. **Key Ideas and Details (a) Collaborate:** With a partner, complete a chart like the one shown to examine key details and symbols in the story. List events, actions, or descriptions that seem important.

What It Says	What It Means	Why It Is Important

(b) Interpret: Based on your chart, draw a conclusion about the underlying theme, or message, of this story. Support your answer with story details.

5. **Integration of Knowledge and Ideas Evaluate:** Does the theme of the story apply to everyone, or is it limited to people in certain situations? Explain.

36 Plot

Have a volunteer read aloud the bracketed passage. **Ask** the Plot question.

Possible response: Things happen quickly, which indicates that the important part of the story is over.

37 Theme and Symbols

Have a volunteer read aloud the bracketed passage. **Ask** the Theme and Symbols questions.

Possible response: Grandmama will remain with Sek-Lung. The jade peony now symbolizes her presence in his life.

ASSESS/EXTEND

Answers

1. **Possible response: (a)** The albino acrobat gave it to her. The narrator says she made windchimes in the likeness of his gift to her. **(b)** It connected her to her past.
2. **Possible response: (a)** Sek-Lung supports Grandmama's activities. It bothers the father that she is not more modern. The rest of the family is embarrassed. **(b)** They represent different generations and ages and therefore different points of view.
3. **Possible response: (a)** Sek-Lung is the narrator. **(b)** He knew the grandmother in a different way than the others did. **(c)** He is able to represent Grandmama's side of the conflict.
4. **Possible response: (a)** The albino acrobat gives her the windchime. It means that he will return. It is important because she is waiting for it before she dies. **(b)** Students should support their interpretation with details from the story.
5. **Possible response:** The theme of the story applies to everyone because we all have memories.

Assessment Resources

The following resources can be used to assess students' knowledge and skills.

Unit 2 Resources

L1 L2 EL **Selection Test A,** pp. 17–19.
L3 L4 EL **Selection Test B,** pp. 20–22.
L3 L4 **Open-Book Test,** pp. 14–16.

PHLit Online! Students may use the **Self-test,** at **www.PHLitOnline.com,** to prepare for **Selection Test A** or **Selection Test B.**

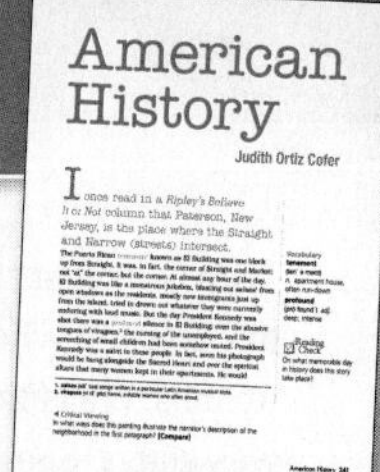

✓ The Most Dangerous Game • ✓✓ American History

Lesson Pacing Guide

DAY 1 Preteach

- Administer the Reading and Vocabulary Warm-ups (*Unit 2 Resources*, pp. 23–26 or 41–44) as necessary.
- Introduce the Reading Skill: Make Inferences.
- Introduce the Literary Analysis concept: Conflict.
- Distribute copies of the appropriate graphic organizer for the Reading Skill (*Graphic Organizer Transparencies*, pp. 39–41).
- Distribute copies of the appropriate graphic organizer for Literary Analysis (*Graphic Organizer Transparencies*, pp. 42–44).
- Teach the selection vocabulary.
- Introduce the Word Study skill.

DAYS 2–3 Preteach/Teach

- Build background with the Background feature.
- Develop thematic vocabulary and thematic thinking with Writing About the Big Question.
- Prepare students to read with the Activating Prior Knowledge activities (TE).
- Informally monitor comprehension while students read.
- Use the Reading Check questions to confirm comprehension.
- Develop students' ability to make inferences using the Reading Skill questions.
- Develop students' understanding of conflict, using the Literary Analysis questions.
- Reinforce vocabulary with the Vocabulary notes.
- Reinforce unit focus standards using the Spiral Review prompts.

DAY 4 Assess

- Assess students' comprehension and mastery of the skills by having them answer the Critical Thinking, Reading Skill, and Literary Analysis questions.
- Have students complete the Vocabulary Practice activities.
- Have students complete the Word Study activities.

DAY 5 Extend/Assess

- Have students complete the Conventions lesson.
- Have students complete the Writing activity and write an alternative ending. (You may assign as homework.)
- Extend learning by having students complete the Speaking and Listening activity, an oral presentation. As an alternative, assign them "The Survival Game Controversy" or "Rebuilding What Is Broken" in *Reality Central*.
- Administer Selection Test A or B (*Unit 2 Resources*, pp. 35–40 or 56–61).

Common Core State Standards

Reading Literature 1. Cite strong and thorough textual evidence to support analysis of what the text says explicitly as well as inferences drawn from the text.
3. Analyze how complex characters (e.g., those with multiple or conflicting motivations) develop over the course of a text, interact with other characters, and advance the plot or develop the theme.
5. Analyze how an author's choices concerning how to structure a text, order events within it (e.g., parallel plots), and manipulate time (e.g., pacing, flashbacks) create such effects as mystery, tension, or surprise.

Writing 3.e. Provide a conclusion that follows from and reflects on what is experienced, observed, or resolved over the course of the narrative.

Speaking and Listening 4. Present information, findings, and supporting evidence clearly, concisely, and logically such that listeners can follow the line of reasoning and the organization, development, substance, and style are appropriate to purpose, audience, and task.

Language 1. Demonstrate command of the conventions of standard English grammar and usage when writing or speaking.
6. Acquire and use accurately grade-appropriate general academic and domain-specific words and phrases; gather vocabulary knowledge when considering a word or phrase important to comprehension or expression.

Additional Standards Practice
Common Core Companion,
pp. 28–29; 48–49

Daily Block Scheduling
Each day in this Lesson Pacing Guide represents a 40–50 minute period. Teachers using block scheduling may combine days to revise pacing. In addition, teachers may differentiate and support core instruction by integrating components for extended and intensive support as students require. See the Guide to Selected Leveled Resources (facing page).

Guide to Selected Leveled Resources

RTI Tier 1 (students performing on level)			✓ More Accessible The Most Dangerous Game	✓✓ More Complex American History
Warm Up	Whole class instruction; Group work	**Practice, model,** and **monitor** fluency, working **with the whole class** or **in groups.**	**Vocabulary** and **Reading Warm-ups B,** ***Unit 2 Resources,*** pp. 23–24, 26	**Vocabulary** and **Reading Warm-ups B,** ***Unit 2 Resources,*** pp. 41–42, 44
Comprehension/Skills	Whole class instruction; Independent work	**Support** and **monitor** comprehension and skills development, having students complete the activities, graphic organizers, and interactive prompts **independently** or **as a class.**	• ***Reader's Notebook,*** adapted instruction and full selection EL ***Reader's Notebook: English Learner's Version,*** adapted instruction and adapted selection • **Reading Skill Graphic Organizer B,** ***Graphic Organizer Transparencies,*** p. 41 • **Literary Analysis Graphic Organizer B,** ***Graphic Organizer Transparencies,*** p. 44	• ***Reader's Notebook,*** adapted instruction and summary EL ***Reader's Notebook: English Learner's Version,*** adapted instruction and summary • **Reading Skill Graphic Organizer B,** ***Graphic Organizer Transparencies,*** p. 41 • **Literary Analysis Graphic Organizer B,** ***Graphic Organizer Transparencies,*** p. 44
Monitor Progress	A	**Monitor** student progress with the differentiated curriculum-based assessment in the *Unit Resources.*	• **Selection Test B,** ***Unit 2 Resources,*** pp. 38–40 • **Open-Book Test,** ***Unit 2 Resources,*** pp. 32–34	• **Selection Test B,** ***Unit 2 Resources,*** pp. 59–61 • **Open-Book Test,** ***Unit 2 Resources,*** pp. 53–55

RTI Tier 2 (students requiring intervention)			✓ More Accessible The Most Dangerous Game	✓✓ More Complex American History
Warm Up	Group work; One-on-one teaching	**Practice, model,** and **monitor** fluency **in groups** or **with individuals.**	• **Vocabulary and Reading Warm-ups A,** ***Unit 2 Resources,*** pp. 23–25 • ***Reality Central,*** "The Survival Game Controversy" • ***Hear It!*** **Audio CD (adapted text)**	• **Vocabulary and Reading Warm-ups A,** ***Unit 2 Resources,*** pp. 41–44 • ***Reality Central,*** "Rebuilding What Is Broken" • ***Hear It!*** **Audio CD**
Comprehension/Skills	Group work; One-on-one teaching	• **Support** and **monitor** comprehension and skills development, working **in small groups** or **with individuals.** • **Pair** students with more advanced peers and have them complete the writing activity in the *Real-World Writing Journal*. • As students complete the selection in the appropriate version of the *Reader's Notebook,* **monitor** comprehension frequently with group questions and individual instruction. • **Model** strategies while guiding students in completing the activities and prompts in the *Reader's Notebook,* as well as the graphic organizers. • **Practice** skills and **monitor** mastery with the *Reading Kit* worksheets.	• ***Real-World Writing Journal,*** Lesson 1, pp. 36–39 • ***Reader's Notebook: Adapted Version,*** adapted instruction and adapted selection EL ***Reader's Notebook: English Learner's Version,*** adapted instruction and adapted selection • **Reading Skill Graphic Organizer A,** ***Graphic Organizer Transparencies,*** p. 39 • **Literary Analysis Graphic Organizer A,** ***Graphic Organizer Transparencies,*** p. 42 • ***Reading Kit,*** Practice worksheets, pp. 52, 58, 62, 64, 70	• ***Real-World Writing Journal,*** Lesson 2, pp. 40–43 • ***Reader's Notebook: Adapted Version,*** adapted instruction and summary EL ***Reader's Notebook: English Learner's Version,*** adapted instruction and summary • **Reading Skill Graphic Organizer A,** ***Graphic Organizer Transparencies,*** p. 40 • **Literary Analysis Graphic Organizer A,** ***Graphic Organizer Transparencies,*** p. 43 • ***Reading Kit,*** Practice worksheets, pp. 52, 58, 62, 64, 70
Monitor Progress	A	**Monitor** student progress with the differentiated curriculum-based assessment in the *Unit Resources* and in the *Reading Kit.*	• **Selection Test A,** ***Unit 2 Resources,*** pp. 35–37 • ***Reading Kit,*** Assess worksheets, pp. 53, 59, 63, 65, 71	• **Selection Test A,** ***Unit 2 Resources,*** pp. 56–58 • ***Reading Kit,*** Assess worksheets, pp. 53, 59, 63, 65, 71

TIER 3 Tier 3 intervention may require consultation with the student's special-education or dyslexia specialist. For additional support, see the Tier 2 activities and resources listed above.

One-on-one teaching **Group work** **Whole class instruction** **Independent work** **A Assessment**

For a complete guide to selection support, including support for Advanced students, see the Overview of Resources in the frontmatter.

✓The Most Dangerous Game
✓✓American History

American History

Judith Ortiz Cofer

I once read in a *Ripley's Believe It or Not* column that Paterson, New Jersey, is the place where the Straight and Narrow (streets) intersect. The Puerto Rican tenement known as El Building was one block up from Straight. It was, in fact, the corner of Straight and Market; not "at" the corner, but the corner. At almost any hour of the day, El Building was like a monstrous jukebox, blasting out salsas[1] from open windows as the residents, mostly new immigrants just up from the island, tried to drown out whatever they were currently enduring with loud music. But the day President Kennedy was shot there was a profound silence in El Building; even the abusive tongues of viragoes,[2] the cursing of the unemployed, and the screeching of small children had been somehow muted. President Kennedy was a saint to these people. In fact, soon his photograph would be hung alongside the Sacred Heart and over the spiritist altars that many women kept in their apartments. He would

Vocabulary
tenement (ten′ ə mənt) *n.* apartment house, often run-down
profound (prō found′) *adj.* deep; intense

Reading Check
On what memorable day in history does this story take place?

1. **salsas** (säl′ səs) songs written in a particular Latin American musical style.
2. **viragoes** (vi rā′ gōz) fierce, irritable women who often shout.

◀ Critical Viewing
In what ways does this painting illustrate the narrator's description of the neighborhood in the first paragraph? **[Compare]**

American History 241

RESOURCES FOR:

- L1 Special-Needs Students
- L2 Below-Level Students (Tier 2)
- L3 On-Level Students (Tier 1)
- L4 Advanced Students (Tier 1)
- EL English Learners
- All All Students

Vocabulary/Fluency/Prior Knowledge

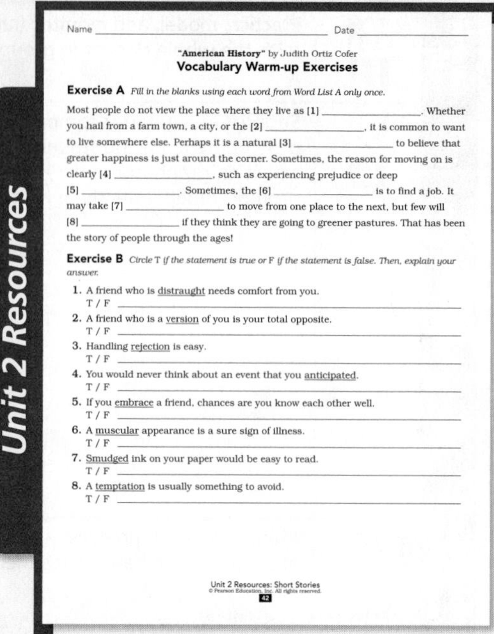

Name ________________ Date ________________

"American History" by Judith Ortiz Cofer
Vocabulary Warm-up Exercises

Exercise A *Fill in the blanks using each word from Word List A only once.*

Most people do not view the place where they live as [1] ________. Whether you hail from a farm town, a city, or the [2] ________, it is common to want to live somewhere else. Perhaps it is a natural [3] ________ to believe that greater happiness is just around the corner. Sometimes, the reason for moving on is clearly [4] ________, such as experiencing prejudice or deep [5] ________. Sometimes, the [6] ________ is to find a job. It may take [7] ________ to move from one place to the next, but few will [8] ________ if they think they are going to greener pastures. That has been the story of people through the ages!

Exercise B *Circle T if the statement is true or F if the statement is false. Then, explain your answer.*

1. A friend who is distraught needs comfort from you.
   T / F ________
2. A friend who is a version of you is your total opposite.
   T / F ________
3. Handling rejection is easy.
   T / F ________
4. You would never think about an event that you anticipated.
   T / F ________
5. If you embrace a friend, chances are you know each other well.
   T / F ________
6. A muscular appearance is a sure sign of illness.
   T / F ________
7. Smudged ink on your paper would be easy to read.
   T / F ________
8. A temptation is usually something to avoid.
   T / F ________

Unit 2 Resources: Short Stories
42

EL L1 L2 **Vocabulary Warm-ups A and B,** pp. 23–24, 41–42

Also available for these selections:

EL L1 L2 **Reading Warm-ups A and B,** pp. 25–26, 43–44

All **Writing About the Big Question,** pp. 27, 45

All **Vocabulary Builder,** pp. 30, 48

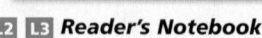

L2 L3 ***Reader's Notebook***

L1 ***Reader's Notebook: Adapted Version***

EL ***Reader's Notebook: English Learner's Version***

EL ***Reader's Notebook: Spanish Version***

Reader's Notebooks

Pre- and postreading pages for both selections, as well as "The Most Dangerous Game," appear in an interactive format in the *Reader's Notebooks.* Each *Notebook* is differentiated for a different group of learners. The selections in the Adapted and English Learner's versions are abridged.

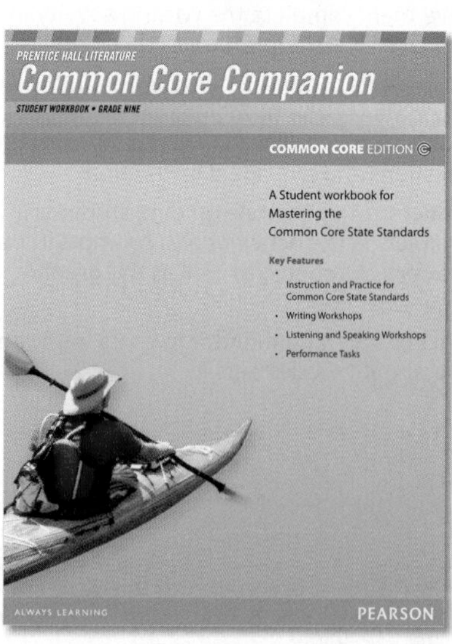

Common Core Companion

Additional instruction and practice for each Common Core State Standard

Selection Support

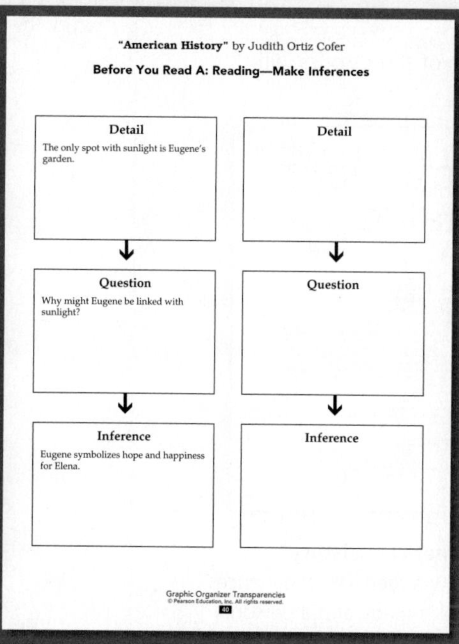
"American History" by Judith Ortiz Cofer

Before You Read A: Reading—Make Inferences

Detail	Detail
The only spot with sunlight is Eugene's garden.	
Question	**Question**
Why might Eugene be linked with sunlight?	
Inference	**Inference**
Eugene symbolizes hope and happiness for Elena.	

Graphic Organizer Transparencies

40

Graphic Organizer Transparencies

EL L1 L2 **Reading: Graphic Organizer A,** pp. 39, 40 (partially filled in)

Also available for these selections:

EL L3 **Reading: Graphic Organizer B,** p. 41

EL L1 L2 **Literary Analysis: Graphic Organizer A,** pp. 42, 43 (partially filled in)

EL L3 **Literary Analysis: Graphic Organizer B,** p. 44

Skills Development/Extension

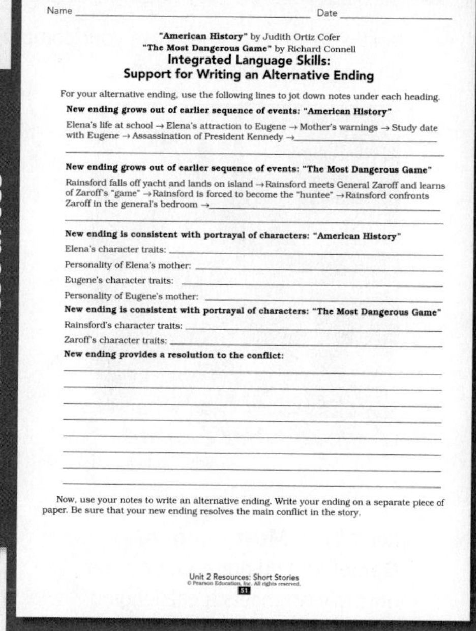
Name ______________________ Date ____________

"American History" by Judith Ortiz Cofer
"The Most Dangerous Game" by Richard Connell

Integrated Language Skills:
Support for Writing an Alternative Ending

For your alternative ending, use the following lines to jot down notes under each heading.

New ending grows out of earlier sequence of events: "American History"

Elena's life at school → Elena's attraction to Eugene → Mother's warnings → Study date with Eugene → Assassination of President Kennedy → ______________

New ending grows out of earlier sequence of events: "The Most Dangerous Game"

Rainsford falls off yacht and lands on island → Rainsford meets General Zaroff and learns of Zaroff's "game" → Rainsford is forced to become the "huntee" → Rainsford confronts Zaroff in the general's bedroom → ______________

New ending is consistent with portrayal of characters: "American History"

Elena's character traits: ______________

Personality of Elena's mother: ______________

Eugene's character traits: ______________

Personality of Eugene's mother: ______________

New ending is consistent with portrayal of characters: "The Most Dangerous Game"

Rainsford's character traits: ______________

Zaroff's character traits: ______________

New ending provides a resolution to the conflict:

Now, use your notes to write an alternative ending. Write your ending on a separate piece of paper. Be sure that your new ending resolves the main conflict in the story.

Unit 2 Resources: Short Stories

51

Unit 2 Resources

EL L3 L4 **Support for Writing,** pp. 51

Also available for these selections:

All **Literary Analysis: Conflict** pp. 28, 46

All **Reading: Make Inferences,** pp. 29, 47

L4 **Enrichment,** pp. 31, 49

EL L3 L4 **Grammar,** p. 50

L3 L4 **Support for Extend Your Learning,** p. 52

Assessment

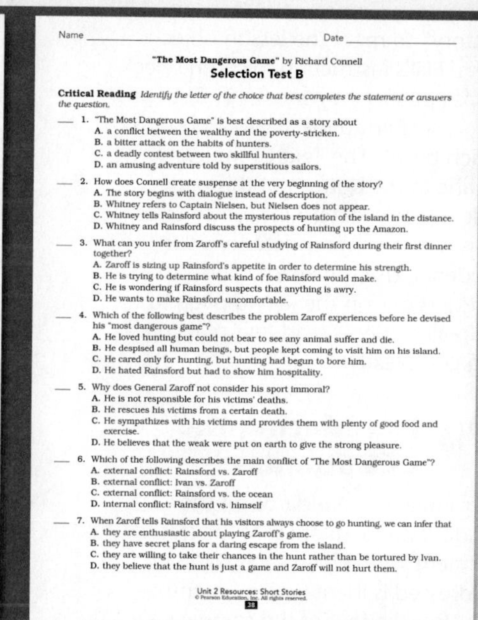
Name ______________________ Date ____________

"The Most Dangerous Game" by Richard Connell

Selection Test B

Critical Reading *Identify the letter of the choice that best completes the statement or answers the question.*

___ 1. "The Most Dangerous Game" is best described as a story about
A. a conflict between the wealthy and the poverty-stricken.
B. a bitter attack on the habits of hunters.
C. a deadly contest between two skillful hunters.
D. an amusing adventure told by superstitious sailors.

___ 2. How does Connell create suspense at the very beginning of the story?
A. The story begins with dialogue instead of description.
B. Whitney refers to Captain Nielsen, but Nielsen does not appear.
C. Whitney tells Rainsford about the mysterious reputation of the island in the distance.
D. Whitney and Rainsford discuss the prospects of hunting up the Amazon.

___ 3. What can you infer from Zaroff's careful studying of Rainsford during their first dinner together?
A. Zaroff is sizing up Rainsford's appetite in order to determine his strength.
B. He is trying to determine what kind of foe Rainsford would make.
C. He is wondering if Rainsford suspects that anything is awry.
D. He wants to make Rainsford uncomfortable.

___ 4. Which of the following best describes the problem Zaroff experiences before he devised his "most dangerous game"?
A. He loved hunting but could not bear to see any animal suffer and die.
B. He despised all human beings, but people kept coming to visit him on his island.
C. He cared only for hunting, but hunting had begun to bore him.
D. He hated Rainsford but had to show him hospitality.

___ 5. Why does General Zaroff not consider his sport immoral?
A. He is not responsible for his victims' deaths.
B. He rescues his victims from a certain death.
C. He sympathizes with his victims and provides them with plenty of good food and exercise.
D. He believes that the weak were put on earth to give the strong pleasure.

___ 6. Which of the following describes the main conflict of "The Most Dangerous Game"?
A. external conflict: Rainsford vs. Zaroff
B. external conflict: Ivan vs. Zaroff
C. external conflict: Rainsford vs. the ocean
D. internal conflict: Rainsford vs. himself

___ 7. When Zaroff tells Rainsford that his visitors always choose to go hunting, we can infer that
A. they are enthusiastic about playing Zaroff's game.
B. they have secret plans for a daring escape from the island.
C. they are willing to take their chances in the hunt rather than be tortured by Ivan.
D. they believe that the hunt is just a game and Zaroff will not hurt them.

Unit 2 Resources: Short Stories

38

EL L3 L4 **Selection Test B,** pp. 38–40, 59–61

Also available for these selections:

EL L1 L2 **Selection Test A,** pp. 35–37, 56–58

L3 L4 **Open-Book Test,** pp. 32–34, 53–55

PHLit Online!
www.PHLitOnline.com

Online Resources: All print materials are also available online.

- complete narrated selection text
- a thematically related video with writing prompt
- an interactive graphic organizer
- highlighting feature
- access to all student print resources, adapted to individual student needs
- Spanish and English summaries
- adapted selection translations in Spanish

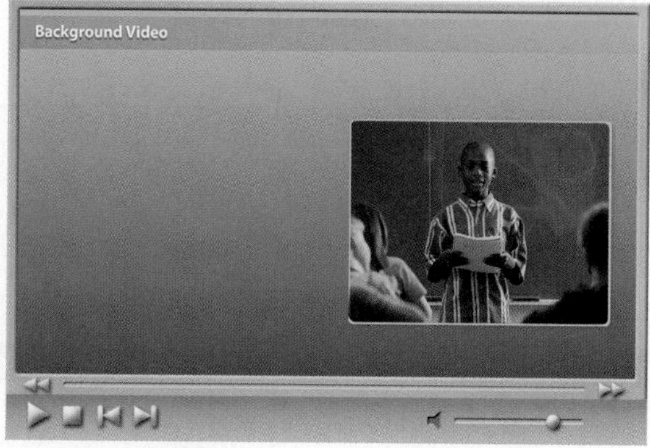

Background Video

Also available:

Get Connected! (thematic video with writing prompt)

All videos are available in Spanish.

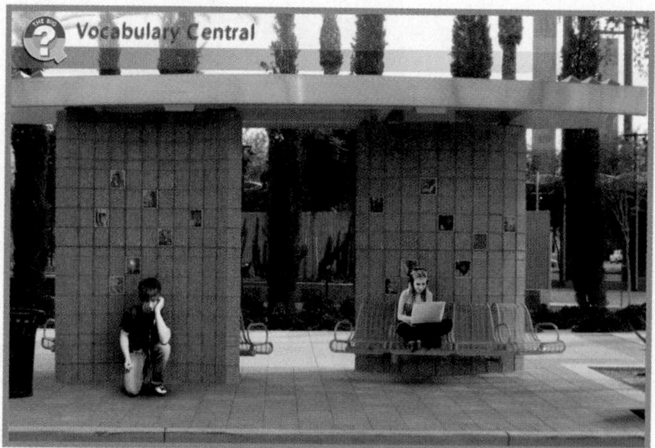

Vocabulary Central (tools, activities, and songs for studying vocabulary)

Also available:

Writer's Journal (with graphics feature)

DIFFERENTIATE/PRETEACH

❶ Leveled Texts

You may use either "The Most Dangerous Game" or "American History" to meet the lesson objectives. Skills instruction for both selections appears on page. 211. Choose one selection to teach (or choose to teach both). The Text Complexity Rubric at the bottom of this page will help you determine which selection is more appropriate for your students. Use the Reader and Task Suggestions on the facing page to help all students read text of increasing complexity.

❷ Introducing the CCS Standards

Introduce the standards on the student page. (Note that the lesson element with which each standard is addressed is identified in parentheses after the text of the standard.) Call out the standards that you will cover with the selections, explaining to students what each requires and how they will address it as they work through the selection you have chosen. Standards labeled "Spiral Review" are introduced in the Literary Analysis Workshop for this unit.

Before You Read

The Most Dangerous Game • American History

❶ Leveled Texts

Build your skills and improve your comprehension of short stories with texts of increasing complexity.

Read **"The Most Dangerous Game"** to find out about a great hunter who meets a challenging opponent.

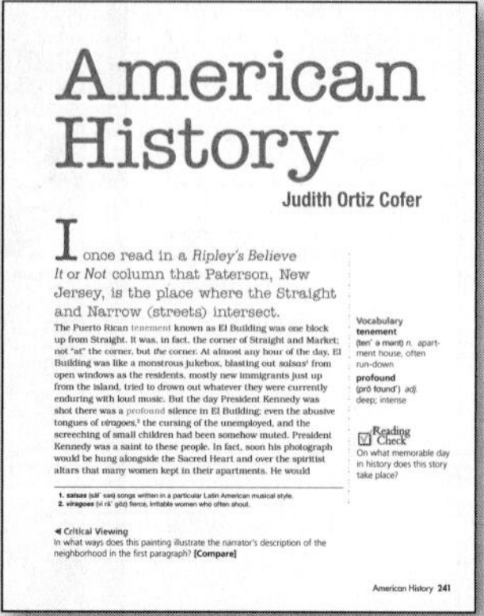

American History

Judith Ortiz Cofer

I once read in a *Ripley's Believe It or Not* column that Paterson, New Jersey, is the place where the Straight and Narrow (streets) intersect.

The Puerto Rican tenement known as El Building was one block up from Straight. It was, in fact, the corner of Straight and Market; not "at" the corner, but *the* corner. At almost any hour of the day, El Building was like a monstrous jukebox, blasting out *salsas*[1] from open windows as the residents, mostly new immigrants just up from the island, tried to drown out whatever they were currently enduring with loud music. But the day President Kennedy was shot there was a profound silence in El Building; even the abusive tongues of *viragoes*,[2] the cursing of the unemployed, and the screeching of small children had been somehow muted. President Kennedy was a saint to these people. In fact, soon his photograph would be hung alongside the Sacred Heart and over the spiritist altars that many women kept in their apartments. He would

Vocabulary
tenement (ten' ə mənt) *n.* apartment house, often run-down
profound (prō found') *adj.* deep; intense

Reading Check
On what memorable day in history does this story take place?

1. **salsas** (säl' səs) songs written in a particular Latin American musical style.
2. **viragoes** (vi rä' gōz) fierce, irritable women who often shout.

◄ **Critical Viewing**
In what ways does this painting illustrate the narrator's description of the neighborhood in the first paragraph? **[Compare]**

American History 241

Read **"American History"** to see how a teenager experiences a national tragedy and a personal crisis.

❷ Common Core State Standards

Meet these standards with either **"The Most Dangerous Game"** (p. 214) or **"American History"** (p. 240).

Reading Literature

1. Cite strong and thorough textual evidence to support analysis of what the text says explicitly as well as inferences drawn from the text. *(Reading Skill: Make Inferences)*

5. Analyze how an author's choices concerning how to structure a text, order events within it, and manipulate time create such effects as mystery, tension, or surprise. *(Literary Analysis: Spiral Review)*

Writing

3.e. Provide a conclusion that follows from and reflects on what is experienced, observed, or resolved over the course of the narrative. *(Writing: Alternative Ending)*

Speaking and Listening

4. Present information, findings, and supporting evidence clearly, concisely, and logically such that listeners can follow the line of reasoning and the organization, development, substance, and style are appropriate to purpose, audience, and task. *(Speaking and Listening: Oral Presentation)*

Language

1. Demonstrate command of the conventions of standard English grammar and usage when writing or speaking. *(Conventions: Regular Verbs)*

6. Acquire and use accurately grade-appropriate general academic and domain-specific words and phrases; gather vocabulary knowledge when considering a word or phrase important to comprehension or expression. *(Vocabulary: Context Clues)*

Text Complexity Rubric: Leveled Texts

Text complexity is determined by both qualitative and quantitative measures. For this reason, the quantitative measure of a more complex selection may be lower than that of a more accessible selection.

		✓ The Most Dangerous Game	✓✓ American History
Qualitative Measures	**Context/ Knowledge Demands**	Small jungle island in Caribbean 1 (2) 3 4 5	New Jersey tenement house, early 1960s 1 2 (3) 4 5
	Structure/Language Conventionality and Clarity	Challenging vocabulary; vocabulary is footnoted 1 2 (3) 4 5	Accessible vocabulary; Spanish words are footnoted 1 2 (3) 4 5
	Levels of Meaning/ Purpose/Concept Level	Accessible concept (hunter finds himself the prey in a hunt) 1 2 (3) 4 5	Challenging concept (young girl sees firsthand the reality of prejudice) 1 2 3 (4) 5
Quantitative Measures	**Text Length**	Word Count: 7,942	Word Count: 3,490
	Lexile	740L	1000L
Overall Complexity		✓ More accessible	✓✓ More complex

3 Literary Analysis: Conflict

Conflict is a struggle between opposing forces.

- In an **external conflict,** a character clashes with an outside force—for example, another character, society, or nature.
- In an **internal conflict,** a character grapples with his or her own opposing feelings, beliefs, needs, or desires.

Conflict drives the plot of most stories. Its solution usually occurs near the end of the story, in the **resolution.** When a story's conflict is left unresolved, the character may have an **epiphany,** or sudden flash of insight, that changes his or her feelings about the conflict. Some epiphanies can also lead to a plot's resolution, or result from one. As you read, analyze the conflicts that characters face and decide which ones truly are resolved.

PHLit Online!
www.PHLitOnline.com

Hear It!
- Selection summary audio
- Selection audio

See It!
- Get Connected video
- Background video
- More about the author
- Vocabulary flashcards

Do It!
- Interactive journals
- Interactive graphic organizers
- Self-test
- Internet activity
- Grammar tutorial
- Interactive vocabulary games

4 Reading Skill: Make Inferences

Inferences are logical assumptions about information or ideas that are not directly stated in a piece of writing.

When you make inferences, you use details as clues to develop ideas about unstated information and concepts in a text. To make inferences as you read a story, for example, ask questions such as these about characters' feelings and behavior:

- What does this detail show about the reasons for a character's actions or words?
- What does this passage say about the character's unstated feelings?

5 Using the Strategy: Inferences Chart

Use an **inferences chart** like this one to track your thinking as you read.

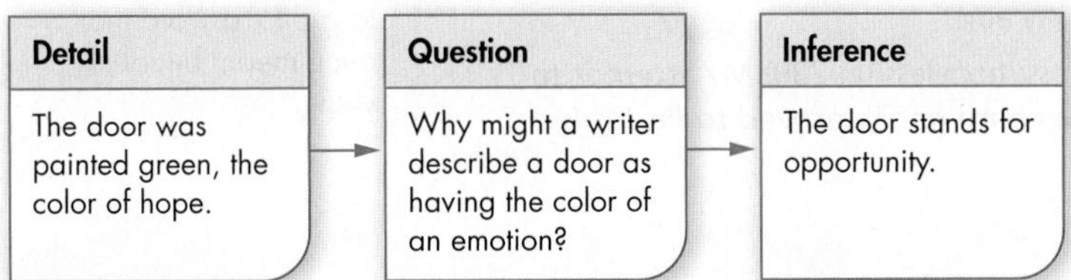

Detail
The door was painted green, the color of hope.
Question
Why might a writer describe a door as having the color of an emotion?
Inference
The door stands for opportunity.

PRETEACH

3 Literary Analysis

Conflict

1. Introduce the skill, using instruction on the student page.
2. Tell students that they will practice analyzing conflict as they read.

Think Aloud: Model the Skill

Model a way to analyze conflict. Say to students:

Literary conflicts are just like real-life struggles. For example, if my volleyball team is about to play a big game, I am in conflict with an external force—the other team. If I'm watching a game and can't decide whether to root for my home team or my best friend's team, I am experiencing internal conflict between my loyalty to my hometown and my wish to support my friend.

Now, suppose my friend gets injured during the game. I have an epiphany that changes my view of the conflict. I realize that it doesn't matter who wins as long as my friend is okay. This epiphany resolves my inner conflict.

4 Reading Skill

Make Inferences

1. Introduce the skill, using the instruction on the student page.
2. Tell students that they will practice making inferences as they read.

5 Using the Strategy

Give students a copy of either **Reading Skill Graphic Organizer A or B** (*Graphic Organizer Transparencies,* pp. 39–41) to record details and inferences. Use the examples in **Reading Skill Graphic Organizer A,** which is partially filled in, to model the process of completing the organizer.

Text Complexity: Reader and Task Suggestions

✓ The Most Dangerous Game		✓✓ American History	
Preparing to Read the Text	**Leveled Tasks**	**Preparing to Read the Text**	**Leveled Tasks**
• Using the Background information on TE p. 213, discuss big game hunting and why some people feel challenged by hunting. • Discuss the two kinds of conflict in this story. • Guide students to use Multidraft Reading strategies (TE p. 213).	*Levels of Meaning* Have students first read to identify the main events of the plot. Then, have them reread, taking notes on the motivations of the characters. *Synthesizing* If students will not have difficulty with meaning, have them note the similarities and differences between Rainsford and General Zaroff, and how these similarities and differences affect events.	• Using the Background information on TE p. 239, discuss the assassination and its emotional impact on people. • Using the Think Aloud on TE p. 242, engage students in a discussion about prejudice. • Guide students to use Multidraft Reading strategies (TE p. 239).	*Levels of Meaning* If students will have difficulty with the concept of prejudice, have them first read and list examples of situations in which Elena experiences prejudice. Then, have them reread and list ways in which prejudice affects her. *Analyzing* Have students note the different ways in which the assassination of Kennedy affects the characters. Then, discuss as a class.

PREACH

❶ Writing About the Big Question

1. Review the assignment with the class.
2. **Ask** students to give examples of times when people were up against what looked like insurmountable odds. What happened? What qualities make it possible for people to overcome enormous obstacles and achieve?
3. Have students complete the sentence starters. Review responses as a class. (**Possible response:** To succeed in a fight for survival, a person needs to know his opponent because it makes it easier to form a strategy. Competition is important for our personal growth because it makes us push ourselves.)
4. Remind students that their answers will help them think about the Big Question, "Is conflict necessary?"

While You Read

Tell students that as they read they should note the ways the hunter tries to ensure his survival.

❷ Vocabulary

1. Have students preview the selection vocabulary.
2. For each word, have students say the word aloud.
3. Then, use the word in a sentence that defines the word.
4. Finally, repeat your definitional sentence or a similar sentence with the word missing and have the class "fill in the blank" chorally. Here are some examples:

   Scruples are doubts that keep someone from doing something wrong. Manny knew playing a prank would be wrong so he didn't go along with it because of his [students say "scruples"].

   Futile means "hopeless." If there is no hope for solving the problem, any effort to solve it is [students say "futile"]

❸ Word Study

1. Introduce the skill, using the instruction in the box.
2. Ask students for another *-esque* word meaning "graceful like a statue" (**Answer:** Statuesque)

Making Connections | **The Most Dangerous Game**

❶ Writing About the Big Question

In "The Most Dangerous Game," a hunter faces a life-threatening conflict. Use these sentence starters to develop your ideas about the Big Question.

To succeed in a fight for **survival,** a person needs to _____________ because _____________.

Competition is important for our personal growth because _______.

While You Read Consider the conflict at the heart of hunting. Keep track of the ways in which the hunter tries to ensure his survival.

❷ Vocabulary

Read each word and its definition. Decide whether you know the word well, know it a little bit, or do not know it at all. After you have read the selection, see how your knowledge of each word has increased.

- **palpable** (pal′ pə bəl) *adj.* able to be felt; easily perceived (p. 215) ***The tension during the exam was palpable.*** *palpate v.*
- **indolently** (in′ də lənt lē) *adv.* lazily; idly (p. 217) ***The sleepy cat yawned indolently.*** *indolent adj. indolence n.*
- **naive** (nä ēv′) *adj.* unsophisticated (p. 225) ***How naive you are to trust everyone you meet!*** *naiveté n. naively adv.*
- **scruples** (scro͞o′ pəlz) *n.* misgivings about something one feels is wrong (p. 225) ***Her scruples prevented her from lying.*** *scrupulous adj. unscrupulous adj.*
- **grotesque** (grō tesk′) *adj.* having a strange, bizarre design; shocking or offensive (p. 227) ***The disease can cause grotesque lumps under the skin.*** *grotesquely adv.*
- **futile** (fyo͞ot′ ′l) *adj.* useless; hopeless (p. 230) ***My attempt to catch the mouse with my bare hands proved to be futile.*** *futility n. futilely adv.*

❸ Word Study

The **Latin suffix *-esque,*** which forms adjectives, means "in the style or manner of."

In this story, the hunter sees many **grotesque** things—things that remind him of death—on the island he visits. *Grotesque* is related to *grotto,* a word that once meant burial vault.

Vocabulary Development

Vocabulary Knowledge Rating

Create a **Vocabulary Knowledge Rating Chart *(Professional Development Guidebook,*** p. 33) for this selection. Include the selection vocabulary and the Big Question words that appear in the Writing About the Big Question sentence starters on this page. (The Big Question vocabulary is introduced on pp. 194–195.)

Give students a copy of the chart. Read the words aloud, and have students mark their rating in the Before Reading column. Urge them to be alert to these words as they read and discuss the selection.

Tally how many students think they know a word to gauge how much instruction to provide. As students read and discuss the selection, point out the words and their context.

Vocabulary Central, featuring tools, activities, and songs for studying vocabulary, is available at **www.PHLitOnline.com.**

Meet Richard Connell

(1893–1949)

Author of *The Most Dangerous Game*

Richard Connell seemed destined to become a writer: he was a sports reporter at the age of ten! At sixteen, he was editing his father's newspaper, the *Poughkeepsie News-Press,* in upstate New York. Connell attended Harvard University, where he worked on the *Daily Crimson* and the *Lampoon,* an early version of the humor magazine *National Lampoon.* During World War I, Connell edited his army division's newspaper.

From Page to Screen In 1924, Connell published "The Most Dangerous Game." In 1936, he settled in Beverly Hills, California, where he started working as a screenwriter. Twice nominated for Academy Awards, he became one of the most successful screenwriters of his day.

4

BACKGROUND FOR THE STORY

Tests of Survival

As civilizations advance, people no longer need to struggle for their basic survival. Nevertheless, some people still enjoy testing their bravery and physical skills in competitions. Today, computer games sometimes feature death-defying challenges. As this story shows, the sport of big-game hunting once served a similar purpose.

Did You Know?

When "The Most Dangerous Game" was first published, it won the prestigious O. Henry Memorial Award for short fiction.

Differentiated Instruction

Additional Instruction

EL Extended Support—English Learners
Have students complete the **Reading and Vocabulary Warm-ups, *Unit 2 Resources,*** pp. 23–26, before they read. Assign the prereading pages and the adapted selection in the ***Reader's Notebook: English Learner's Version.*** Then, have students listen to portions of the selection on the ***Hear It!*** **Audio CD.**

L1 L2 Extended Support—Struggling Readers
Have students complete the **Reading and Vocabulary Warm-ups, *Unit 2 Resources,*** pp. 23–26, before they read. Assign the prereading pages and the adapted selection in the ***Reader's Notebook: Adapted Version.*** Then, have students listen to portions of the selection on the ***Hear It!*** **Audio CD** (adapted text).

Extended Support—Reluctant Readers
To build motivation and engagement before assigning the selection, have students read "The Survival Game Controversy," a thematically related selection in ***Reality Central.*** Then, use the questions at the conclusion of the related selection to guide discussion.

Daily Bellringer

For each class during which you teach this selection, have students complete one of the five Quick Write activities for Week 7 in the ***Daily Bellringer Activities*** booklet.

4 Background

Tests of Survival

One of the best-known of all big-game hunters was Theodore Roosevelt (1858–1919), president of the United States from 1901 to 1909. Though sickly as a child, Roosevelt became a vigorous outdoorsman. He traveled the world to hunt big game; on one year-long African safari, he shot nine lions, eight elephants, and thirteen rhinos. Today, governments carefully limit hunting to preserve animal populations and protect habitats. Roosevelt himself played a huge role in America's conservation movement. As president, he set aside 194 million acres in the United States as protected land, doubled the number of national parks, and founded 51 wildlife reserves.

Multidraft Reading

This icon ● marks natural pauses in the selection. To assist struggling readers and to deepen reading for all, assign the text in "chunks," following the icons, and apply multidraft reading protocols. For each reading, have students set the purpose indicated:

- **First reading**—identifying key ideas and details and answering any Reading Checks.
- **Second reading**—analyzing craft and structure and responding to the side-column prompts.
- **Third reading**—integrating knowledge and ideas, connecting to other texts and the world, and answering the end-of-selection questions.

For more guidance, refer to the ***Classroom Strategies and Teaching Routines*** card on multidraft reading.

PHLit Online!

For more about the author, practice with the selection vocabulary, and more background, go online at **www.PHLitOnline.com.**

❶ Activating Prior Knowledge

1. Prepare an **Anticipation Guide** (***Professional Development Guidebook***, pp. 36–38) with the following statements:
   - Those who perform well under pressure tend to succeed.
   - A person's character is revealed during intense competition.
   - The first impression you have of someone is always correct.
2. Give students a copy of the prepared **Anticipation Guide** and have students mark their responses in the Me column. Have students discuss the statements in pairs or groups and mark the Guides in the Group column.
3. For further guidance, use the ***Classroom Strategies and Teaching Routines*** card: **Using an Anticipation Guide**.

Concept Connector

Students will return to the Anticipation Guide after completing "The Most Dangerous Game."

Whole-Class Activity

"The chase"—one person pursuing another—is the basis for many active games, from tag to hide-and-seek to paintball. Ask students whether it is more exciting to chase or to be chased. After a group discussion, have students write brief journal entries about how they felt during games of pursuit. Have them apply this knowledge as they read the story of the "game" Zaroff forces Rainsford to play.

❷ About the Selection

In addition to keeping readers on the edges of their seats, "The Most Dangerous Game" asks an important question about human nature: Are human beings really civilized? The author contrasts Zaroff, whose style of living reflects highly cultured tastes but who hunts other human beings for sport, with Rainsford, who is horrified at the idea of taking a human life. However, when Rainsford is forced into the role of a "beast at bay," the primitive side of his nature emerges.

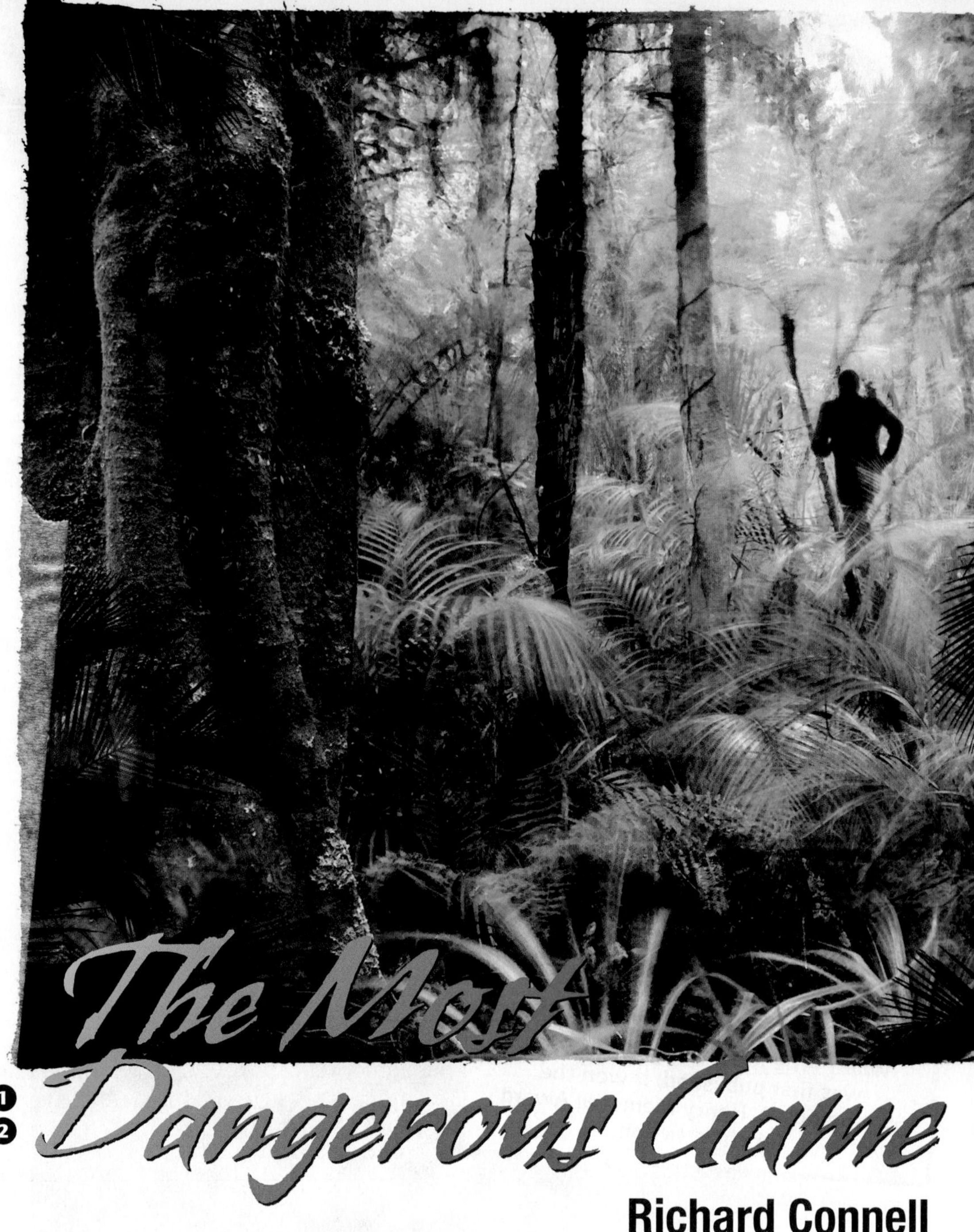

❶ ❷ The Most Dangerous Game

Richard Connell

Vocabulary Development

CCSS Language 6

Thematic Vocabulary: The Big Question

As students are discussing "The Most Dangerous Game," encourage them to use the thematic vocabulary presented in Introducing the Big Question, pp. 194–195. You might encourage them with sentence starters like these:

1. Some of the *differences* between the characters of Rainsford and Whitney are . . .
2. Whitney wants to *cooperate* with Rainsford, but . . .
3. Rainsford sparks *controversy* with General Zaroff when . . .
4. Once General Zaroff begins the hunt, Rainsford decides that his only hope for *survival* is . . .

"Off there to the right—somewhere—is a large island," said Whitney. "It's rather a mystery—"

"What island is it?" Rainsford asked.

"The old charts call it 'Ship-Trap Island,'" Whitney replied. "A suggestive name, isn't it? Sailors have a curious dread of the place. I don't know why. Some superstition—"

"Can't see it," remarked Rainsford, trying to peer through the dank tropical night that was palpable as it pressed its thick warm blackness in upon the yacht.

"You've good eyes," said Whitney, with a laugh, "and I've seen you pick off a moose moving in the brown fall bush at four hundred yards, but even you can't see four miles or so through a moonless Caribbean[1] night."

"Not four yards," admitted Rainsford. "Ugh! It's like moist black velvet."

"It will be light in Rio," promised Whitney. "We should make it in a few days. I hope the jaguar guns have come from Purdey's. We should have some good hunting up the Amazon. Great sport, hunting."

"The best sport in the world," agreed Rainsford.

5 "For the hunter," amended Whitney. "Not for the jaguar."

"Don't talk rot, Whitney," said Rainsford. "You're a big-game hunter, not a philosopher. Who cares how a jaguar feels?"

1. **Caribbean** (kar′ ə bē′ ən) the Caribbean Sea, a part of the Atlantic Ocean, bounded by the north coast of South America, Central America, and the West Indies.

3 ◀ **Critical Viewing**
Based on the details in this image, what do you think this story will be about? **[Speculate]**

Vocabulary
palpable (pal′ pə bəl) *adj.* able to be felt; easily perceived

4 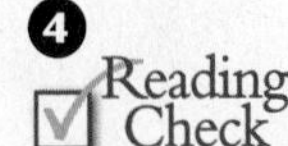
Reading Check
What do Rainsford and Whitney see from the ship?

3 Critical Viewing

Possible response: The story will be about an escaped prisoner or someone hiding in the jungle.

4 Reading Check

Answer: Students should infer that while Whitney and Rainsford cannot see through the darkness, they are looking in the direction of Ship-Trap Island.

PHLit Online!

This selection is available in interactive format in the **Enriched Online Student Edition,** at **www.PHLitOnline.com,** which includes a thematically related video with writing prompt and an interactive graphic organizer.

Differentiated Instruction for Universal Access

Strategy for Special-Needs Students
Have students choose partners with whom to read the story's dialogue aloud. One student can play Rainsford, and the other can play both Whitney and Zaroff. Reading the dialogue aloud will help students comprehend the conflicts and the plot. It will also help them relate to the characters.

Enrichment for Gifted/Talented Students
Have two students expand the dialogue that Whitney and Rainsford have about hunting. Encourage each student to be either Whitney or Rainsford and to debate the issues presented by elaborating with more details to support each position. Encourage the students to summarize their debate for the class.

5 Literary Analysis

Conflict

1. Read the bracketed text aloud. Have students consider what it means to be a hunter and what it means to be hunted. **Ask** students what Rainsford means when he says that Whitney is a hunter and not a philosopher.

   Answer: Rainsford means that Whitney should simply enjoy what he does and not think about the consequences of hunting.

2. **Ask** students if they agree with Whitney that animals can understand fear.

   Possible response: Yes, animals are able to understand fear because it is linked to survival. Like humans, animals feel fear if their lives are threatened.

3. **Ask** students the Literary Analysis question: How does Rainsford's attitude about hunting differ from Whitney's?

   Answer: Whitney recognizes the feelings of his prey, but Rainsford has no sympathy for the animals he hunts.

6 Critical Viewing

Answer: The image is different because it is not "as flat as a plate-glass window"; it is tumultuous. It is similar to the image in the story because it suggests a dark and dangerous rocky coast like the shore of Ship-Trap Island.

Literary Analysis
Conflict How does Rainsford's attitude about hunting differ from Whitney's?

"Perhaps the jaguar does," observed Whitney.

"Bah! They've no understanding."

"Even so, I rather think they understand one thing—fear. The fear of pain and the fear of death."

"Nonsense," laughed Rainsford. "This hot weather is making you soft, Whitney. Be a realist. The world is made up of two classes—the hunters and the huntees. Luckily, you and I are the hunters. Do you think we've passed that island yet?"

"I can't tell in the dark. I hope so."

"Why?" asked Rainsford.

"The place has a reputation—a bad one."

"Cannibals?" suggested Rainsford.

"Hardly. Even cannibals wouldn't live in such a God-forsaken place. But it's gotten into sailor lore, somehow. Didn't you notice that the crew's nerves seemed a bit jumpy today?"

"They were a bit strange, now you mention it. Even Captain Nielsen—"

"Yes, even that tough-minded old Swede, who'd go up to the devil himself and ask him for a light. Those fishy blue eyes held a look I never saw there before. All I could get out of him was: 'This place has an evil name among sea-faring men, sir.' Then he said to me, very gravely: 'Don't you feel anything?'—as if the air about us was actually poisonous. Now, you mustn't laugh when I tell you this—I did feel something like a sudden chill.

"There was no breeze. The sea was as flat as a plate-glass window. We were drawing near the island then. What I felt was a—a mental chill; a sort of sudden dread."

"Pure imagination," said Rainsford. "One superstitious sailor can taint the whole ship's company with his fear."

6

▼ **Critical Viewing**
In what ways does this image differ from the Caribbean Sea as it is described in the story? In what ways is it similar? **[Compare and Contrast]**

Vocabulary Development

CCSS Language 6

Expressive Vocabulary

To help students broaden their expressive vocabulary, encourage them to use the following words as they discuss the selection: *contemplate, render, simulate,* and *utilize.* Have them complete these sentence starters:

1. Whitney would *contemplate* what an animal feels when . . .
2. To *render* an animal harmless, the hunters . . .
3. The color and pattern of their clothes would *simulate* . . .
4. As experienced hunters, they know how to *utilize* . . .

“Maybe. But sometimes I think sailors have an extra sense that tells them when they are in danger. Sometimes I think evil is a tangible thing—with wave lengths, just as sound and light have. An evil place can, so to speak, broadcast vibrations of evil. Anyhow, I'm glad we're getting out of this zone. Well, I think I'll turn in now, Rainsford.”

“I'm not sleepy,” said Rainsford. “I'm going to smoke another pipe on the afterdeck.”

“Good night, then, Rainsford. See you at breakfast.”

“Right. Good night, Whitney.”

There was no sound in the night as Rainsford sat there, but the muffled throb of the engine that drove the yacht swiftly through the darkness, and the swish and ripple of the wash of the propeller.

Rainsford, reclining in a steamer chair, **indolently** puffed on his favorite brier. The sensuous drowsiness of the night was on him. “It's so dark,” he thought, “that I could sleep without closing my eyes; the night would be my eyelids—”

An abrupt sound startled him. Off to the right he heard it, and his ears, expert in such matters, could not be mistaken. Again he heard the sound, and again. Somewhere, off in the blackness, someone had fired a gun three times.

Rainsford sprang up and moved quickly to the rail, mystified. He strained his eyes in the direction from which the reports had come, but it was like trying to see through a blanket. He leaped upon the rail and balanced himself there, to get greater elevation; his pipe, striking a rope, was knocked from his mouth. He lunged for it; a short, hoarse cry came from his lips as he realized he had reached too far and had lost his balance. The cry was pinched off short as the blood-warm waters of the Caribbean Sea closed over his head.

Vocabulary
indolently (in′ də lənt lē) *adv.* lazily; idly

7

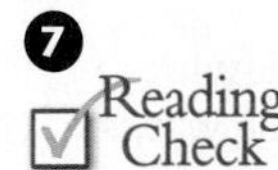

What “two classes” does Rainsford believe make up the world?

7 Reading Check

Answer: Rainsford believes that the world is made up of hunters and the hunted.

Differentiated Instruction for Universal Access

Strategy for Less Proficient Readers
Display **Reading Skill Graphic Organizer B** (***Graphic Organizer Transparencies***, p. 41), and show students how to make an inference by asking questions about details.

1. In the details box, write *Ship-Trap Island's reputation.*
2. Tell students that the following question is one that could be used to make an inference: *What might have happened in the past to give Ship-Trap island its reputation?* Write the question in the second box.
3. Have students answer the question and put the best inference in the third box. If students have trouble creating a suitable inference, write the following: *Ship-Trap Island could have earned its reputation because sailors have either been harmed or have died there.* As students continue reading, tell them to look for details that yield useful inferences.

8 Literary Analysis

Conflict

1. Remind students that a character can face an external conflict with another character, an animal, or nature itself. Then, have students read the first bracketed text.
2. **Ask** students the Literary Analysis question: With what external conflict is Rainsford suddenly confronted?

   Answer: He is battling for his life against the sea.
3. Discuss with students the fact that, just as in life, characters often do not choose their external conflicts. Conflicts may arise suddenly and force a character to marshal all possible resources in order to endure.

9 Critical Viewing

Possible response: The island is remote and is covered with a dense forest of trees. It appears to be a jungle. It also looks mountainous and unpopulated.

Literary Analysis
Conflict With what external conflict is Rainsford suddenly confronted?

He struggled up to the surface and tried to cry out, but the wash from the speeding yacht slapped him in the face and the salt water in his open mouth made him gag and strangle. Desperately he struck out with strong strokes after the receding lights of the yacht, but he stopped before he had swum fifty feet. A certain cool-headedness had come to him; it was not the first time he had been in a tight place. There was a chance that his cries could be heard by someone aboard the yacht, but that chance was slender, and grew more slender as the yacht raced on. He wrestled himself out of his clothes, and shouted with all his power. The lights of the yacht became faint and ever-vanishing fireflies; then they were blotted out entirely by the night.

Rainsford remembered the shots. They had come from the right, and doggedly he swam in that direction, swimming with slow, deliberate strokes, conserving his strength. For a seemingly endless time he fought the sea. He began to count his strokes; he could do possibly a hundred more and then—

Rainsford heard a sound. It came out of the darkness, a high screaming sound, the sound of an animal in an extremity of anguish and terror.

He did not recognize the animal that made the sound; he did not try to; with fresh vitality he swam toward the sound. He heard it again; then it was cut short by another noise, crisp, staccato.

"Pistol shot," muttered Rainsford, swimming on.

9
▶ **Critical Viewing** What does the wildness of the island in the picture tell you about the island itself? **[Infer]**

Ten minutes of determined effort brought another sound to his ears—the most welcome he had ever heard—the muttering and growling of the sea breaking on a rocky shore. He was almost on the rocks before he saw them; on a night less calm he would have been shattered against them. With his remaining strength he dragged himself from the swirling waters. Jagged crags appeared to jut into the opaqueness, he forced himself upward, hand over hand. Gasping, his hands raw, he reached a flat place at the top. Dense jungle came down to the very edge of the cliffs. What perils that tangle of trees and underbrush might hold for him did not concern Rainsford just then. All he knew was that he was safe from his enemy, the sea, and that utter weariness was on him. He flung himself down at the jungle edge and tumbled headlong into the deepest sleep of his life.

When he opened his eyes he knew from the position of the sun that it was late in the afternoon. Sleep had given him new vigor; a sharp hunger was picking at him. He looked about him, almost cheerfully.

"Where there are pistol shots, there are men. Where there are men, there is food," he thought. But what kind of men, he

Think Aloud

Vocabulary: Using Context

Direct students' attention to the word *crags* on this page. Using a think-aloud process, model how to use context to infer the meaning of an unknown word. Say to students:

> I'm going to think aloud to show you how I would figure out the meaning of *crags* from its context.
>
> *Crags* is the subject of the sentence and, therefore, a noun. The paragraph says that the shoreline is rocky and that the rocks are dangerous. This suggests that the rocks are jagged. The story refers to "jagged crags"; therefore, *crags* must refer to these dangerous rocks.

10 wondered, in so forbidding a place? An unbroken front of snarled and ragged jungle fringed the shore.

He saw no sign of a trail through the closely knit web of weeds and trees; it was easier to go along the shore, and Rainsford floundered along by the water. Not far from where he had landed, he stopped.

Some wounded thing, by the evidence a large animal, had thrashed about in the underbrush; the jungle weeds were crushed down and the moss was lacerated; one patch of weeds was stained crimson. A small, glittering object not far away caught Rainsford's eye and he picked it up. It was an empty cartridge.

"A twenty-two," he remarked. "That's odd. It must have been a fairly large animal too. The hunter had his nerve with him to tackle it with a light gun. It's clear that the brute put up a fight. I suppose the first three shots I heard was when the hunter flushed his quarry and wounded it. The last shot was when he trailed it here and finished it."

Reading Skill
Make Inferences
What inferences does Rainsford make based on the evidence of pistol shots?

11 

As Rainsford swims for shore, what sounds does he hear coming out of the darkness?

10 Reading Skill

Make Inferences

1. Point out to students that sometimes characters themselves make inferences—that is, they make logical guesses based on details. For example, detectives often make inferences in mystery stories.
2. **Ask** students how Rainsford's experience as a hunter facilitates his skill at making inferences.

   Possible response: An experienced hunter, Rainsford knows how to track his prey, which involves making inferences based on details he observes. For example, he can draw inferences from broken brush, tracks, and other clues an animal leaves behind. His experience hunting in jungles, savannahs, and other wild places also helps him know what to expect in a wide variety of settings. This, in turn, helps him draw inferences from details around him. For example, he might perceive the presence of danger long before an inexperienced person could make a similar inference.
3. Read the bracketed text, which begins on p. 218, aloud. **Ask** the Reading Skill question: What inferences does Rainsford make based on the evidence of pistol shots?

   Answer: Rainsford infers from the pistol shots that men are present on the island. He also infers that the men must have food.

11 Reading Check

Answer: He hears an animal's scream and a pistol shot.

Fluency

Distribute copies of pp. 218–219, and pair students. Have partners take turns reading paragraphs aloud. While one partner reads, the other should mark any words with which the student reading has difficulty. Circulate to monitor the fluency of students' reading. Collect students' marked-up copies of the page, and review difficult words and passages with the class. Look for these problem spots:

- If students read a passage in a choppy, repetitious, or slow way, practice repeated reading. Pair the struggling student with a fluent reader. Have the fluent reader read the passage aloud. Then, have the struggling reader repeat until his or her fluency improves.
- If students have difficulty recognizing roots, prefixes, and suffixes in the words *cool-headedness* (p. 218), *doggedly* (p. 218), *weariness* (p. 218), and *underbrush* (p. 219), help students use their thumbs to cover up parts of the words to recognize individual components.
- If English learners have difficulty with the concepts of anguish (*anguish*, p. 218) or laceration (*lacerated*, p. 219), tell stories to help students grasp the meaning.

⓬ Reading Skill
Make Inferences

1. Tell students that when examining characters to make inferences, they should pay attention to all relevant details. Tell students that they should examine a character's physical appearance, actions, dialogue, and thoughts.
2. Have the students read the bracketed text, which continues onto p. 221. **Ask** students the Reading Skill question: Which details here lead you to infer that the two men Rainsford meets have a shared military past? Explain.

   Answer: The giant man, who stands rigidly holding a gun, is dressed in a uniform, clearly indicating that he is or was part of a military unit. Then, as the slender man approaches, the giant makes a military salute and clicks his heels.
3. Tell students that the giant man's salute references an old, formal European military style.

He examined the ground closely and found what he had hoped to find—the print of hunting boots. They pointed along the cliff in the direction he had been going. Eagerly he hurried along, now slipping on a rotten log or a loose stone, but making headway; night was beginning to settle down on the island.

Bleak darkness was blacking out the sea and jungle when Rainsford sighted the lights. He came upon them as he turned a crook in the coast line, and his first thought was that he had come upon a village, for there were many lights. But as he forged along he saw to his great astonishment that all the lights were in one enormous building—a lofty structure with pointed towers plunging upward into the gloom. His eyes made out the shadowy outlines of a palatial château;[2] it was set on a high bluff, and on three sides of it cliffs dived down to where the sea licked greedy lips in the shadows.

"Mirage," thought Rainsford. But it was no mirage, he found, when he opened the tall spiked iron gate. The stone steps were real enough; the massive door with a leering gargoyle[3] for a knocker was real enough; yet about it all hung an air of unreality.

He lifted the knocker, and it creaked up stiffly, as if it had never before been used. He let it fall, and it startled him with its booming loudness. He thought he heard steps within; the door remained closed. Again Rainsford lifted the heavy knocker, and let it fall. The door opened then, opened as suddenly as if it were on a spring, and Rainsford stood blinking in the river of glaring gold light that poured out. The first thing Rainsford's eyes discerned was the largest man Rainsford had ever seen—a gigantic creature, solidly made and black-bearded to the waist. In his hand the man held a long-barreled revolver, and he was pointing it straight at Rainsford's heart.

Out of the snarl of beard two small eyes regarded Rainsford.

"Don't be alarmed," said Rainsford, with a smile which he hoped was disarming. "I'm no robber. I fell off a yacht. My name is Sanger Rainsford of New York City."

⓬ The menacing look in the eyes did not change. The revolver pointed as rigidly as if the giant were a statue. He gave no sign that he understood Rainsford's words, or that he had even heard them. He was dressed in uniform, a black uniform trimmed with gray astrakhan.[4]

"I'm Sanger Rainsford of New York," Rainsford began again. "I fell off a yacht. I am hungry."

The man's only answer was to raise with his thumb the hammer of his revolver. Then Rainsford saw the man's free hand go to his forehead in a military salute, and he saw him click his heels together and stand at attention. Another man was coming down

Reading Skill
Make Inferences
Which details here lead you to infer that the two men Rainsford meets have a shared military past? Explain.

2. **palatial** (pə lā′ shəl) *château* (sha tō′) a mansion as luxurious as a palace.
3. **gargoyle** (gär′ goil′) *n.* strange and distorted animal form projecting from a building.
4. **astrakhan** (as′ trə kən) *n.* loosely curled fur made from the skins of very young lambs.

Vocabulary Development
Ⓒ CCSS Language 6

Word Forms

Expand students' vocabulary by helping them learn related forms of the selection vocabulary words. Give students a blank **Word Form Chart** (***Professional Development Guidebook***, p. 42), with *palpable, indolently, scruples,* and *futile* in the correct columns. Work with the class, or have students work with a partner, to determine the related forms.

Noun	Verb	Adjective	Adverb
palpability		**palpable**	palpably
indolence		indolent	**indolently**
scruples	scruple	scrupulous	scrupulously
futility		**futile**	futilely

12 the broad marble steps, an erect, slender man in evening clothes. He advanced to Rainsford and held out his hand.

In a cultivated voice marked by a slight accent that gave it added precision and deliberateness, he said: "It is a very great pleasure and honor to welcome Mr. Sanger Rainsford, the celebrated hunter, to my home."

Automatically Rainsford shook the man's hand.

"I've read your book about hunting snow leopards in Tibet, you see," explained the man. "I am General Zaroff."

Rainsford's first impression was that the man was singularly handsome; his second was that there was an original, almost bizarre quality about the general's face. He was a tall man past middle age, for his hair was a vivid white; but his thick eyebrows and pointed military mustache were as black as the night from which Rainsford had come. His eyes, too, were black and very bright. He had high cheek bones, a sharp-cut nose, a spare, dark face, the face of a man used to giving orders, the face of an aristocrat. Turning to the giant in uniform, the general made a sign. The giant put away his pistol, saluted, withdrew.

"Ivan is an incredibly strong fellow," remarked the general, "but he has the misfortune to be deaf and dumb. A simple fellow, but, I'm afraid, like all his race, a bit of a savage."

"Is he Russian?"

"He is a Cossack," said the general, and his smile showed red lips and pointed teeth. "So am I."

"Come," he said, "we shouldn't be chatting here. We can talk later. Now you want clothes, food, rest. You shall have them. This is a most restful spot."

Ivan had reappeared, and the general spoke to him with lips that moved but gave forth no sound.

"Follow Ivan, if you please, Mr. Rainsford," said the general. "I was about to have my dinner when you came. I'll wait for you. You'll find that my clothes will fit you, I think."

It was to a huge, beam-ceilinged bedroom with a canopied bed big enough for six men that Rainsford followed the silent giant. Ivan laid out an evening suit, and Rainsford, as he put it on, noticed that it came from a London tailor who ordinarily cut and sewed for none below the rank of duke.

The dining room to which Ivan conducted him was in many ways remarkable. There was a medieval magnificence about it; it suggested a baronial hall of feudal times with its oaken panels,

13

LITERATURE IN CONTEXT

History Connection

Cossacks

Ivan and Zaroff are Cossacks, members of a people from southern Russia who also made up a special Russian military unit. As a group, Cossacks were famous for their fierceness, and the soldiers enjoyed a privileged status. Because of their elite position, these soldiers were also fiercely independent. When the czar—the ruler of Russia—was overthrown in the Russian Revolution of 1917, Cossacks like Zaroff were executed or forced into exile. As a Cossack, Zaroff is unwilling to acknowledge that the rules of ordinary people apply to him.

Connect to the Literature

What traits does Zaroff exhibit that might be due, in part, to his having been a Cossack?

◀ **Czar Nicholas II, overthrown in the Russian Revolution of 1917**

14

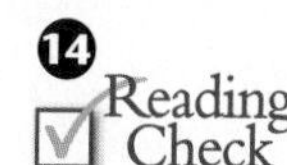

Reading Check

What type of building does Rainsford encounter on the island he reaches?

13 Literature in Context

History Connection *Cossack* comes from a Turkish word meaning "adventurer" or "free man." Early Cossacks included Tartar nomads and runaway serfs; they established several independent strongholds within Russia. Gradually, Cossacks allied themselves to the czar and joined Russian armies as elite cavalry units. Cossacks became famous for their skill as horsemen, for their loyalty to the czar, and for their ferocity in battle.

Connect to the Literature

1. Have students read the Literature in Context feature, and present the additional background information above. Tell students to **compare** the qualities of Cossacks to the qualities of Zaroff.

   Answer: Both are fierce and fiercely independent.

2. **Ask** students the Connect to the Literature question: What traits does Zaroff exhibit that might be due, in part, to his having been a Cossack?

   Answer: Zaroff behaves toward Ivan as a strict military commander who is used to being obeyed instantly. He expects absolute loyalty from Ivan. He acts toward Rainsford like a man completely independent of outside authority and supremely confident of his skills.

14 Reading Check

Answer: He encounters an enormous mansion.

Differentiated Instruction for Universal Access

EL Strategy for English Learners

Have students list the place names mentioned in the story, such as Rio and the Amazon on p. 215. Have students identify these places in their home languages, then find out where they are and learn one or two facts about them. Have students work together to make a set of flash cards that give clues to each place on the front and identify it on the back. Students can use the cards to learn the place names.

Enrichment for Gifted/Talented Students

Have students work together to make two classroom maps of Rainsford's adventures. The first map should be a long-distance view of the area where Rainsford falls overboard; the second, a close-up map of the island, showing Death Swamp, Zaroff's chateau, and other important locations. Students can search the story for geographical clues and use an atlas to help them with the first map.

⓯ Literary Analysis

Conflict

1. Remind students that a character can face an external and an internal conflict at the same time.
2. Point out that the external conflict and the internal conflict may arise from the same source.
3. Point out the bracketed text and **ask** students what questions might be running through Rainsford's mind during this conversation with Zaroff.

   Possible responses: Can I trust this man? Is this just a pleasant dinner, or am I in real danger?
4. **Ask** students the Literary Analysis question: Explain how Rainsford's discomfort in this passage is both an internal and an external conflict.

   Answer: Rainsford's discomfort is an internal conflict because he is struggling to understand why he feels uncomfortable. His discomfort is an external conflict because the source of his concern is Zaroff, who keeps looking at Rainsford strangely.

its high ceiling, its vast refectory table where twoscore men could sit down to eat. About the hall were the mounted heads of many animals—lions, tigers, elephants, moose, bears; larger or more perfect specimens Rainsford had never seen. At the great table the general was sitting, alone.

"You'll have a cocktail, Mr. Rainsford," he suggested. The cocktail was surpassingly good; and, Rainsford noted, the table appointments were of the finest—the linen, the crystal, the silver, the china.

They were eating *borsch,* the rich, red soup with whipped cream so dear to Russian palates. Half apologetically General Zaroff said: "We do our best to preserve the amenities of civilization here. Please forgive any lapses. We are well off the beaten track, you know. Do you think the champagne has suffered from its long ocean trip?"

Literary Analysis ⓯
Conflict Explain how Rainsford's discomfort in this passage is both an internal and an external conflict.

"Not in the least," declared Rainsford. He was finding the general a most thoughtful and affable host, a true cosmopolite.[5] But there was one small trait of the general's that made Rainsford uncomfortable. Whenever he looked up from his plate he found the general studying him, appraising him narrowly.

"Perhaps," said General Zaroff, "you were surprised that I recognized your name. You see, I read all books on hunting published in English, French, and Russian. I have but one passion in my life, Mr. Rainsford, and it is the hunt."

"You have some wonderful heads here," said Rainsford as he ate a particularly well cooked filet mignon. "That Cape buffalo is the largest I ever saw."

"Oh, that fellow. Yes, he was a monster."

"Did he charge you?"

"Hurled me against a tree," said the general. "Fractured my skull. But I got the brute."

"I've always thought," said Rainsford, "that the Cape buffalo is the most dangerous of all big game."

For a moment the general did not reply; he was smiling his curious red-lipped smile. Then he said slowly: "No. You are wrong, sir. The Cape buffalo is not the most dangerous big game." He sipped his wine. "Here in my preserve on this island," he said in the same slow tone, "I hunt more dangerous game."

Rainsford expressed his surprise. "Is there big game on this island?"

The general nodded. "The biggest."

"Really?"

"Oh, it isn't here naturally, of course. I have to stock the island."

"What have you imported, general?" Rainsford asked. "Tigers?"

The general smiled. "No," he said. "Hunting tigers ceased to

---

5. **cosmopolite** (käz mäp′ ə līt′) *n.* person at home in all parts of the world.

Think Aloud

Vocabulary: Using Content

Direct students' attention to the word *amenities* on this page. Using a think-aloud process, model how to use context to infer the meaning of an unknown word. Say to students:

> I'm going to think aloud to show you how I would figure out the meaning of *amenities* from its context.
>
> *Amenities* is a plural noun in this sentence. The general says that *amenities* are part of civilization; therefore the term would refer to something unlike the jungle environment. The general also says that he does his "best to preserve the amenities." This statement tells me that *amenities* are likely very nice "things" that can be preserved. The two men are eating with china, crystal, and silver, and they are drinking champagne. Therefore, *amenities* must mean "pleasant or elegant things."

interest me some years ago. I exhausted their possibilities, you see. No thrill left in tigers, no real danger. I live for danger, Mr. Rainsford."

The general took from his pocket a gold cigarette case and offered his guest a long black cigarette with a silver tip; it was perfumed and gave off a smell like incense.

"We will have some capital hunting, you and I," said the general. "I shall be most glad to have your society."

"But what game—" began Rainsford.

"I'll tell you," said the general. "You will be amused, I know. I think I may say, in all modesty, that I have done a rare thing. I have invented a new sensation. May I pour you another glass of port, Mr. Rainsford?"

"Thank you, general."

16 The general filled both glasses, and said: "God makes some men poets. Some He makes kings, some beggars. Me He made a hunter. My hand was made for the trigger, my father said. He was a very rich man with a quarter of a million acres in the Crimea,[6] and he was an ardent sportsman. When I was only five years old he gave me a little gun, specially made in Moscow for me, to shoot sparrows with. When I shot some of his prize turkeys with it, he did not punish me; he complimented me on my marksmanship. I killed my first bear in the Caucasus[7] when I was ten. My whole life has been one prolonged hunt. I went into the army—it was expected of noblemen's sons—and for a time commanded a division of Cossack cavalry, but my real interest was always the hunt. I have hunted every kind of game in every land. It would be impossible for me to tell you how many animals I have killed."

The general puffed at his cigarette.

"After the debacle[8] in Russia I left the country, for it was imprudent for an officer of the Czar to stay there. Many noble Russians lost everything. I, luckily, had invested heavily in American securities, so I shall never have to open a tea room in Monte Carlo or drive a taxi in Paris. Naturally, I continued to hunt—grizzlies in your Rockies, crocodiles in the Ganges, rhinoceroses in East Africa. It was in Africa that the Cape buffalo hit me and laid me up for six months. As soon as I recovered I started for the Amazon to hunt jaguars, for I had heard they were unusually cunning. They weren't." The Cossack sighed. "They were no match at all for a hunter with his wits about him, and a high-

6. **Crimea** (krī mē´ ə) region in southwestern Ukraine extending into the Black Sea.
7. **Caucasus** (kô´ kə səs) mountain range between the Black and Caspian seas.
8. **debacle** (di bä´ kəl) *n.* bad defeat (Zaroff is referring to the Russian Revolution of 1917, a defeat for upper-class Russians like himself).

"Here in my preserve on this island," he said in the same slow tone, "I hunt more dangerous game."

Reading Skill
Make Inferences
How do the details about Zaroff's life support the inference that he feels neither guilt nor fear concerning hunting?

17 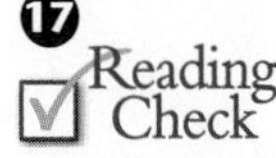
Why does Zaroff recognize Rainsford's name?

16 Reading Skill
Make Inferences

1. Remind students that most characters do not speak directly about their own qualities. Very few heroes, for example, say, "I am brave." Very few villains say, "I am evil." Their thoughts, actions, and conversations indirectly reveal their beliefs, likes, dislikes, hopes, and fears.
2. Tell students that readers can also infer from a character's words the traits that he or she does not have.
3. Read the bracketed text aloud. **Ask** students the Reading Skill question: How do the details about Zaroff's life support the inference that he feels neither guilt nor fear concerning hunting?

   Answer: Zaroff says he speaks modestly, but he is actually proud of inventing a new hunting sensation. He brags about hunting during his childhood, killing a bear at ten, and hunting every kind of animal. His self-description betrays no guilt; in fact, he justifies himself by saying God created him to be a hunter. He is not afraid of any animal, even the fierce Cape buffalo and the jaguar.

17 Reading Check

Answer: Zaroff recognizes Rainsford's name because he has read Rainsford's book about hunting snow leopards in Tibet.

Differentiated Instruction for Universal Access

Enrichment for Advanced Readers

On this page, Zaroff refers to "the debacle in Russia." He is speaking of the Bolshevik Revolution that ended the Russian monarchy and gave birth to the Soviet Union.

From the 1500s until 1917, Russia was ruled by monarchs called czars. The word *czar* is derived from Caesar, the first emperor of Rome. For most of the time, the Romanov family ruled the country. In 1905, a rebellion robbed the czar, Nicholas II, of much of his absolute power and made him a constitutional monarch. In March 1917, a moderate socialist government came to power. The radical Bolsheviks were not satisfied, however, and in October they seized power and established a communist government that would last until 1991. Zaroff's comment that "it was imprudent for an officer of the Czar to stay" in Russia was quite true; many Russian aristocrats became refugees.

Have students research the locations to which the Russian aristocrats fled. Why did they decide to settle in certain places? How were their lives changed by having to leave Russia?

18 Literary Analysis

Conflict

1. Briefly review Zaroff's career as a hunter. **Ask:** Why did Zaroff become bored with hunting?

   Answer: Hunting became too easy for Zaroff. As he says, animal instinct is "no match" for human reason.

2. Have students reread the bracketed text. **Ask** students the Literary Analysis question: How was the "tragic moment" Zaroff refers to the sign of an internal conflict?

   Answer: Zaroff was torn between two emotions: his passion for hunting and his growing boredom with it.

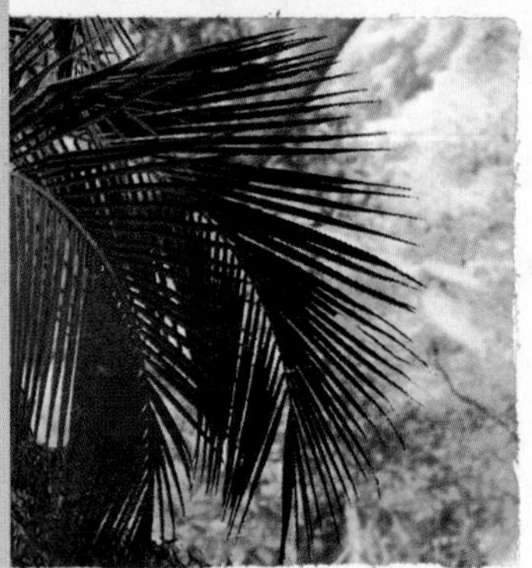

powered rifle. I was bitterly disappointed. I was lying in my tent with a splitting headache one night when a terrible thought pushed its way into my mind. Hunting was beginning to bore me! And hunting, remember, had been my life. I have heard that in America business men often go to pieces when they give up the business that has been their life."

"Yes, that's so," said Rainsford.

The general smiled. "I had no wish to go to pieces," he said. "I must do something. Now, mine is an analytical mind, Mr. Rainsford. Doubtless that is why I enjoy the problems of the chase."

"No doubt, General Zaroff."

"So," continued the general, "I asked myself why the hunt no longer fascinated me. You are much younger than I am, Mr. Rainsford, and have not hunted as much, but you perhaps can guess the answer."

"What was it?"

"Simply this: hunting had ceased to be what you call 'a sporting proposition.' It had become too easy. I always got my quarry. Always. There is no greater bore than perfection."

The general lit a fresh cigarette.

Literary Analysis 18
Conflict How was the "tragic moment" Zaroff refers to the sign of an internal conflict?

"No animal had a chance with me any more. That is no boast; it is a mathematical certainty. The animal had nothing but his legs and his instinct. Instinct is no match for reason. When I thought of this it was a tragic moment for me, I can tell you."

Rainsford leaned across the table, absorbed in what his host was saying.

"It came to me as an inspiration what I must do," the general went on.

"And that was?"

The general smiled the quiet smile of one who has faced an obstacle and surmounted it with success. "I had to invent a new animal to hunt," he said.

"A new animal? You're joking."

"Not at all," said the general. "I never joke about hunting. I needed a new animal. I found one. So I bought this island, built this house, and here I do my hunting. The island is perfect for my purpose—there are jungles with a maze of trails in them, hills, swamps—"

"But the animal, General Zaroff?"

"Oh," said the general, "it supplies me with the most exciting hunting in the world. No other hunting compares with it for an instant. Every day I hunt, and I never grow bored now, for I have a quarry with which I can match my wits."

Rainsford's bewilderment showed in his face.

Vocabulary Development

CCSS Language 6

Word Origin

On p. 225, General Zaroff tells Rainsford that his "scruples are quite ill founded." Tell students that *scruple* is derived from the Latin for "pebble" and originally referred to a tiny unit of weight. **Ask** students to speculate with you how the meaning of *scruple* might have developed into its current sense of "moral concern or caution."

Possible response: A tiny unit of weight may be associated with preciseness and carefulness. Over time this meaning came to include a sense of moral carefulness, of carefully "weighing" the consequences of actions.

"I wanted the ideal animal to hunt," explained the general. "So I said: 'What are the attributes of an ideal quarry?' And the answer was, of course: 'It must have courage, cunning, and, above all, it must be able to reason.'"

"But no animal can reason," objected Rainsford.

"My dear fellow," said the general, "there is one that can."

"But you can't mean—" gasped Rainsford.

"And why not?"

19 "I can't believe you are serious, General Zaroff. This is a grisly joke."

"Why should I not be serious? I am speaking of hunting."

"Hunting? General Zaroff, what you speak of is murder."

The general laughed with entire good nature. He regarded Rainsford quizzically. "I refuse to believe that so modern and civilized a young man as you seem to be harbors romantic ideas about the value of human life. Surely your experiences in the war—"

"Did not make me condone cold-blooded murder," finished Rainsford stiffly.

Laughter shook the general. "How extraordinarily droll you are!" he said. "One does not expect nowadays to find a young man of the educated class, even in America, with such a **naive**, and, if I may say so, mid-Victorian point of view.[9] It's like finding a snuff-box in a limousine. Ah, well, doubtless you had Puritan ancestors. So many Americans appear to have had. I'll wager you'll forget your notions when you go hunting with me. You've a genuine new thrill in store for you, Mr. Rainsford."

"Thank you, I'm a hunter, not a murderer."

"Dear me," said the general, quite unruffled, "again that unpleasant word. But I think I can show you that your **scruples** are quite ill founded."

"Yes?"

"Life is for the strong, to be lived by the strong, and, if need be, taken by the strong. The weak of the world were put here to give the strong pleasure. I am strong. Why should I not use my gift? If I wish to hunt, why should I not? I hunt the scum of the earth—sailors from tramp ships—lascars,[10] blacks, Chinese, whites, mongrels—a thoroughbred horse or hound is worth more than a score of them."

"But they are men," said Rainsford hotly.

"Precisely," said the general. "That is why I use them. It gives me pleasure. They can reason, after a fashion. So they are dangerous."

"But where do you get them?"

The general's left eyelid fluttered down in a wink. "This island is called Ship-Trap," he answered. "Sometimes an angry god of the

9. **mid-Victorian point of view** a point of view emphasizing proper behavior and associated with the time of Queen Victoria of England (1819–1901).

10. **lascars** (las′ kərz) *n.* Indian or East Indian sailors, employed on European ships.

Literary Analysis
Conflict What does Rainsford suddenly understand about Zaroff?

Vocabulary
naive (nä ēv′) *adj.* unsophisticated

scruples (skrōō′ pəlz) *n.* misgivings about something one feels is wrong

20 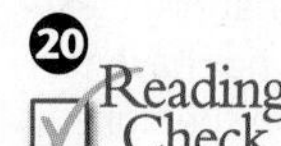

What does Zaroff do to ease his boredom with hunting?

19 Literary Analysis
Conflict

1. Remind students that an epiphany is a moment of sudden insight or revelation—a flash of understanding—that a character, and often the reader, experience.
2. Have volunteers read the bracketed text aloud. **Ask** students the Literary Analysis question: What does Rainsford suddenly understand about Zaroff?

   Answer: Rainsford suddenly understands that Zaroff hunts men; Zaroff is mentally unbalanced and a savage murderer.

20 Reading Check
Answer: Zaroff hunts human beings.

PROFESSIONAL DEVELOPMENT | **Danling Fu**

Apply the Strategy

Deepening Understanding Have students reread the general's words in the middle of the next page, "Life is for the strong, to be lived by the strong, and, if needed be, taken by the strong…," and discuss what the general means by "being strong" here and what the general's perception of "being strong" manifests about a certain kind of human nature. Then, help students extend their connections to the historical people in the world who resemble this character, such as Stalin, Hitler, etc. If possible, help students make connections between this story and J. Conrad's *Heart of Darkness*, which also vividly depicts the dark and greedy side of human nature, which is the cause of wars within and across countries.

For more of Danling Fu's strategies, see the Professional Development essay, pp. 194c–194d.

21 Reading Skill

Make Inferences

1. Have students read the first bracketed text. Point out to students that Zaroff uses the example of the electric lights in the channel as a demonstration that he is civilized. He wants Rainsford to infer that he is a sophisticated, intelligent, modern man.
2. **Ask** students the Reading Skill question: Based on this description, what can you infer about the method Zaroff uses to lure his quarry to the island?

   Possible response: Zaroff uses lights to lure ships onto the rocks, where the ships are destroyed and the men either drown or become stranded; Zaroff calculatingly destroys people and property for his own personal pleasure.
3. Have students **discuss** Zaroff's comment that he is civilized because he uses electricity to lure the ships.

   Possible response: Zaroff has only a technological, material definition of civilization. Morally, he is a barbarian.

22 Literary Analysis

Conflict

1. Read the second bracketed text aloud. Tell students that just as Zaroff uses false lights to create the illusion of a channel and destroy ships, he also uses false reasoning to create the illusion that he is a fair and civilized man.
2. **Ask** students the Literary Analysis question: Is Zaroff's statement that his captives do not have to participate in the hunt true? Explain.

   Possible response: Captives do not have to participate, but the other option that they are given is even more undesirable. The captives can choose to have a faint chance of escape in the hunt or to face certain death at the hands of the brutal Ivan.

high seas sends them to me. Sometimes, when Providence is not so kind, I help Providence a bit. Come to the window with me."

Rainsford went to the window and looked out toward the sea.

"Watch! Out there!" exclaimed the general, pointing into the night. Rainsford's eyes saw only blackness, and then, as the general pressed a button, far out to sea Rainsford saw the flash of lights.

Reading Skill
Make Inferences Based on this description, what can you infer about the method Zaroff uses to lure his quarry to the island?

21 The general chuckled. "They indicate a channel," he said, "where there's none: giant rocks with razor edges crouch like a sea monster with wide-open jaws. They can crush a ship as easily as I crush this nut." He dropped a walnut on the hardwood floor and brought his heel grinding down on it. "Oh, yes," he said, casually, as if in answer to a question, "I have electricity. We try to be civilized here."

"Civilized? And you shoot down men?"

A trace of anger was in the general's black eyes, but it was there for but a second, and he said, in his most pleasant manner: "Dear me, what a righteous young man you are! I assure you I do not do the thing you suggest. That would be barbarous. I treat these visitors with every consideration. They get plenty of good food and exercise. They get into splendid physical condition. You shall see for yourself tomorrow."

"What do you mean?"

"We'll visit my training school," smiled the general. "It's in the cellar. I have about a dozen pupils down there now. They're from the Spanish bark San Lucar that had the bad luck to go on the rocks out there. A very inferior lot, I regret to say. Poor specimens and more accustomed to the deck than to the jungle."

He raised his hand, and Ivan, who served as waiter, brought thick Turkish coffee. Rainsford, with an effort, held his tongue in check.

"It's a game, you see," pursued the general blandly. "I suggest to one of them that we go hunting. I give him a supply of food and an excellent hunting knife. I give him three hours' start. I am to follow, armed only with a pistol of the smallest caliber and range. If my quarry eludes me for three whole days, he wins the game. If I find him"—the general smiled—"he loses."

"Suppose he refuses to be hunted?"

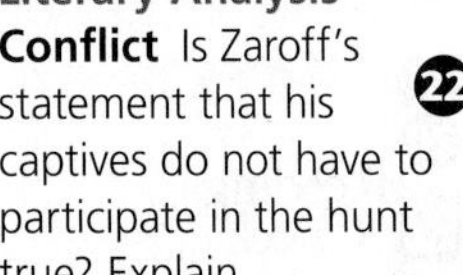

Literary Analysis
Conflict Is Zaroff's statement that his captives do not have to participate in the hunt true? Explain.

22 "Oh," said the general, "I give him his option, of course. He need not play the game if he doesn't wish to. If he does not wish to hunt, I turn him over to Ivan. Ivan once had the honor of serving as official knouter[11] to the Great White Czar, and he has his own ideas of sport. Invariably, Mr. Rainsford, invariably they choose the hunt."

"And if they win?"

The smile on the general's face widened. "To date I have not lost," he said.

11. **knouter** (nout´ ər) *n.* someone who beats criminals with a leather whip, or knout.

Think Aloud

Make Inferences

Draw students' attention to the paragraph beginning "'It's a game, you see . . .'" Use the following "think aloud" to model the process of making inferences:

> As I read this passage, I make inferences about what Zaroff is saying. At the end of the paragraph, he states that if he finds his quarry within three days, his quarry "loses." Based on Zaroff's revelation that he hunts men, I can safely infer that "losing" the game means being shot and killed. Zaroff does not state this directly, however.
>
> I also make another, more subtle inference. Zaroff says that he plays the game with a weapon inferior to that which he is used to using. He also gives his opponent an excellent hunting knife. I ask myself, "Why would Zaroff downgrade his weapon and at the same time give his opponent an 'excellent' weapon?" Based on Zaroff's earlier statements about being bored of hunting because it is too easy for him, I infer that Zaroff is arrogantly looking for a challenge. This is why he chooses the weapons.

Then he added, hastily: "I don't wish you to think me a braggart, Mr. Rainsford. Many of them afford only the most elementary sort of problem. Occasionally I strike a tartar.[12] One almost did win. I eventually had to use the dogs."

"The dogs?"

"This way, please. I'll show you."

The general steered Rainsford to a window. The lights from the windows sent a flickering illumination that made grotesque patterns on the courtyard below, and Rainsford could see moving about there a dozen or so huge black shapes; as they turned toward him, their eyes glittered greenly.

"A rather good lot, I think," observed the general. "They are let out at seven every night. If anyone should try to get into my house—or out of it—something extremely regrettable would occur to him." He hummed a snatch of song from the Folies Bergère.[13]

24 "And now," said the general, "I want to show you my new collection of heads. Will you come with me to the library?"

"I hope," said Rainsford, "that you will excuse me tonight, General Zaroff. I'm really not feeling at all well."

"Ah, indeed?" the general inquired solicitously. "Well, I suppose that's only natural, after your long swim. You need a good, restful night's sleep. Tomorrow you'll feel like a new man, I'll wager. Then we'll hunt, eh? I've one rather promising prospect—"

Rainsford was hurrying from the room.

"Sorry you can't go with me tonight," called the general. "I expect rather fair sport—a big, strong black. He looks resourceful—Well good night, Mr. Rainsford; I hope you have a good night's rest."

The bed was good, and the pajamas of the softest silk, and he was tired in every fiber of his being, but nevertheless Rainsford could not quiet his brain with the opiate of sleep. He lay, eyes wide open. Once he thought he heard stealthy steps in the corridor outside his room. He sought to throw open the door; it would not

12. **tartar** (tärt´ ər) *n.* stubborn, violent person.
13. **Folies** (fô´ lē) **Bergère** (ber zher') musical theater in Paris.

23
▲ Critical Viewing
Why might Zaroff have used dogs like these on his hunts? **[Connect]**

Vocabulary
grotesque (grō tesk´) *adj.* having a strange, bizarre design; shocking or offensive

Reading Skill
Make Inferences
What kind of heads do you think Zaroff wants to show Rainsford? Explain.

25
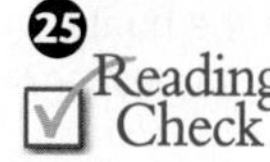

Who are the "pupils" in Zaroff's cellar?

23 Critical Viewing

Answer: The dogs' ferocity, size, and speed would intimidate Zaroff's victims and would make them fear being tracked down and torn apart.

24 Reading Skill

Make Inferences

1. **Ask** students to recall how Zaroff decorates his dining hall.
   Answer: He decorates it with the heads of the animals he has killed.
2. **Ask** students what Rainsford has learned about Zaroff's interest in hunting since their conversation began.
   Answer: Rainsford has learned that Zaroff sees no difference between hunting animals and hunting humans.
3. Invite a volunteer to read the bracketed text aloud. **Ask** students the Reading Skill question: What kind of heads do you think Zaroff wants to show Rainsford? Explain.
   Answer: Zaroff wants to show Rainsford his collection of human heads in the library. They are mounted like the heads of the animals in the dining room. It is reasonable to infer that the heads are human because Zaroff refers to them as his "new collection," and we know he hunts people.

25 Reading Check

Answer: The "pupils" are sailors from the Spanish bark San Lucar, which Zaroff lured onto the rocks.

Differentiated Instruction for Universal Access

Strategy for Less Proficient Readers

To help students understand the horrific character of Zaroff, have them listen carefully to the conversation between Zaroff and Rainsford on the ***Hear It!* Audio CD.** Have them follow along with the text as they listen. Point out that Zaroff speaks in a polite, sophisticated, and gentlemanly way about matters that are violent and cruel. Help students make a list of the expressions Zaroff uses that are much more depraved than they seem to be. For example, when Zaroff says "training school" on p. 226, he really means prison. Other expressions include the following:

"some capital hunting" (p. 223)
"a new sensation" (p. 223)
"invent a new animal" (p. 224)
"that unpleasant word" (p. 225)
"play the game" (p. 226)
"something extremely regrettable" (p. 227)

26 Literary Analysis

Conflict

1. Point out that the intensity of a conflict will change throughout a story. In addition, as a story develops, internal and external conflicts affect each other.
2. **Ask** students to explain the common expression "a matter of life or death."

   Answer: A matter of life or death means an issue or event that can cause someone's death if it is not avoided or resolved.
3. **Ask** students if they think that, in most cases, an external conflict that is "a matter of life or death" is more serious than an internal conflict.

   Possible response: Most students will agree that an external conflict that is a matter of life or death is more serious than any internal conflict.
4. Read the first bracketed text aloud. **Ask** students the Literary Analysis question: How does Rainsford's statement about wishing to leave make his internal conflict an external one?

   Answer: His statement shows that he is no longer struggling internally with the issue of whether or not to trust Zaroff. His feelings are now out in the open and will prompt Zaroff's response, most likely creating an external conflict.

27 Reading Skill

Make Inferences

1. Have students read the second bracketed text. **Ask** students what choice Zaroff gives his captives.

   Answer: They can either be hunted by Zaroff or be tortured and killed by Ivan.
2. **Ask** students the Reading Skill question: What inference can you make about the hunting trip Zaroff is suggesting?

   Answer: Rainsford is not going on the hunting trip as a companion for Zaroff; he is the prey.

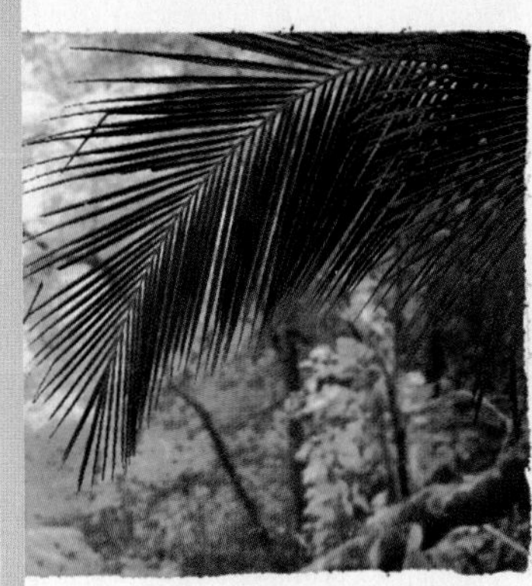

open. He went to the window and looked out. His room was high up in one of the towers. The lights of the château were out now, and it was dark and silent, but there was a fragment of sallow moon, and by its wan light he could see, dimly, the courtyard; there, weaving in and out in the pattern of shadow, were black, noiseless forms; the hounds heard him at the window and looked up, expectantly, with their green eyes. Rainsford went back to the bed and lay down. By many methods he tried to put himself to sleep. He had achieved a doze when, just as morning began to come, he heard, far off in the jungle, the faint report of a pistol.

General Zaroff did not appear until luncheon. He was dressed faultlessly in the tweeds of a country squire. He was solicitous about the state of Rainsford's health.

"As for me," sighed the general, "I do not feel so well. I am worried, Mr. Rainsford. Last night I detected traces of my old complaint."

To Rainsford's questioning glance the general said: "Ennui. Boredom."

Then, taking a second helping of crêpes suzette, the general explained: "The hunting was not good last night. The fellow lost his head. He made a straight trail that offered no problems at all. That's the trouble with these sailors; they have dull brains to begin with, and they do not know how to get about in the woods. They do excessively stupid and obvious things. It's most annoying. Will you have another glass of Chablis, Mr. Rainsford?"

Literary Analysis
Conflict How does Rainsford's statement about wishing to leave make his internal conflict an external one? 26

"General," said Rainsford firmly, "I wish to leave this island at once."

The general raised his thickets of eyebrows; he seemed hurt. "But, my dear fellow," the general protested, "you've only just come. You've had no hunting—"

"I wish to go today," said Rainsford. He saw the dead black eyes of the general on him, studying him. General Zaroff's face suddenly brightened.

He filled Rainsford's glass with venerable Chablis from a dusty bottle.

Reading Skill 27
Make Inferences What inference can you make about the hunting trip Zaroff is suggesting?

"Tonight," said the general, "we will hunt—you and I."

Rainsford shook his head. "No, general," he said. "I will not hunt."

The general shrugged his shoulders and delicately ate a hothouse grape. "As you wish, my friend," he said. "The choice rests entirely with you. But may I not venture to suggest that you will find my idea of sport more diverting than Ivan's?"

He nodded toward the corner to where the giant stood, scowling, his thick arms crossed on his hogshead of chest.

"You don't mean—" cried Rainsford.

Think Aloud

Vocabulary: Using Context

Direct students' attention to the word *deplorable* on p. 229. Using a think-aloud process, model how to use context to infer the meaning of an unknown word. Say the following to students:

> I'm going to think aloud to show you how I would figure out the meaning of *deplorable* from its context. *Deplorable* is an adjective, describing the part of Zaroff's experience in which his favorite dog dies. Because Zaroff was obviously fond of this dog, *deplorable* must describe something "unfortunate" or "regrettable."

㉘ Reading Check

Answer: Zaroff suggests that Rainsford wear moccasins and avoid Death Swamp.

"My dear fellow," said the general, "have I not told you I always mean what I say about hunting? This is really an inspiration. I drink to a foeman worthy of my steel—at last."

The general raised his glass, but Rainsford sat staring at him.

"You'll find this game worth playing," the general said enthusiastically. "Your brain against mine. Your woodcraft against mine. Your strength and stamina against mine. Outdoor chess! And the stake is not without value, eh?"

"And if I win—" began Rainsford huskily.

"I'll cheerfully acknowledge myself defeated if I do not find you by midnight of the third day," said General Zaroff. "My sloop will place you on the mainland near a town."

The general read what Rainsford was thinking.

"Oh, you can trust me," said the Cossack. "I will give you my word as a gentleman and a sportsman. Of course you, in turn, must agree to say nothing of your visit here."

"I'll agree to nothing of the kind," said Rainsford.

"Oh," said the general, "in that case— But why discuss that now? Three days hence we can discuss it over a bottle of Veuve Cliquot, unless—"

The general sipped his wine.

Then a businesslike air animated him. "Ivan," he said to Rainsford, "will supply you with hunting clothes, food, a knife. I suggest you wear moccasins; they leave a poorer trail. I suggest too that you avoid the big swamp in the southeast corner of the island. We call it Death Swamp. There's quicksand there. One foolish fellow tried it. The deplorable part of it was that Lazarus followed him. You can imagine my feelings, Mr. Rainsford. I loved Lazarus; he was the finest hound in my pack. Well, I must beg you to excuse me now. I always take a siesta after lunch. You'll hardly have time for a nap, I fear. You'll want to start, no doubt. I shall not follow till dusk. Hunting at night is so much more exciting than by day, don't you think? Au revoir,[14] Mr. Rainsford, au revoir."

General Zaroff, with a deep, courtly bow, strolled from the room.

From another door came Ivan. Under one arm he carried khaki hunting clothes, a haversack of food, a leather sheath containing a long-bladed hunting knife; his right hand rested on a cocked revolver thrust in the crimson sash about his waist. . . .

Rainsford had fought his way through the bush for two hours. "I must keep my nerve. I must keep my nerve," he said through tight teeth.

"My dear fellow," said the general, "have I not told you I always mean what I say about hunting?"

㉘  Reading Check

What two suggestions does Zaroff give Rainsford before they begin the hunt?

14. Au (ō') **revoir** (rə vwär') French for "until we meet again."

Differentiated Instruction for Universal Access

Strategy for Special-Needs Students

As the hunt begins, be sure students understand what is going to happen. Help students fill in a spider map graphic organizer, with "the hunt for Rainsford" at the center. Have students supply the following information on the branches of the spider map:

- the "prize" Zaroff wants
- the "prize" Rainsford wants
- Zaroff's advantages
- Rainsford's disadvantages
- the time limit

Support for Less Proficient Readers

Point out that the writer provides three clues near the bottom of this page to indicate the important passing of time:

- the use of an ellipsis after the words *about his waist*
- the beginning of a new paragraph
- the phrase *for two hours*

Be sure students understand that an ellipsis indicates that something has been omitted. In this case, the author has omitted a description of the first two hours of Rainsford's run through the bush.

29 Critical Viewing

Answer: The dense jungle would make it impossible for Rainsford to outrace pursuit, especially by dogs.

30 Connecting to the Big Question

1. Point out that Zaroff and Rainsford use many different strategies as they engage in the conflict of the hunt.
2. Have a volunteer read the bracketed text aloud. **Ask:** What is Rainsford doing in this passage?

   Answer: He is making a complex series of paths in the jungle.
3. **Ask:** How is Rainsford's strategy a way in which he tries to ensure his survival? **Possible response:** He is trying to throw Zaroff off his trail. This might help Rainsford survive because he can wait for Zaroff and kill him as he follows the fake trail.

He had not been entirely clear-headed when the château gates snapped shut behind him.

His whole idea at first was to put distance between himself and General Zaroff, and, to this end, he had plunged along, spurred on by the sharp rowels of something very like panic. Now he had got a grip on himself, had stopped, and was taking stock of himself and the situation.

Vocabulary
futile (fyo͞ot´ 'l) *adj.* useless; hopeless

He saw that straight flight was futile; inevitably it would bring him face to face with the sea. He was in a picture with a frame of water, and his operations, clearly, must take place within that frame.

▼ Critical Viewing How does this picture support Rainsford's thought that straight flight through the jungle is futile? **[Support]**

"I'll give him a trail to follow," muttered Rainsford, and he struck off from the rude paths he had been following into the trackless wilderness. He executed a series of intricate loops; he doubled on his trail again and again, recalling all the lore of the fox hunt, and all the dodges of the fox. Night found him leg-weary, with his hands 30

Vocabulary Development

CCSS Language 6

Words That Build Conflict

Tell students that an author may use words that enhance the conflict in a story. Such words convey tension, the struggle of opposing forces, physical or mental strain, fear, doubt, and danger. Point out the following four words and explain how each word helps to build the conflict.

- *panic* (p. 230) Rainsford feels "something very like panic" because he is literally playing a game for his life.
- *flight* (p.230) Rainsford considers "straight flight" because the desire to escape is a natural response to conflict.
- *apprehensive* (p. 231) The "apprehensive night" is full of fear because Rainsford himself is fearful.
- *tensed* (p. 231) Rainsford has "every muscle tensed" because he is coiled to spring like an attacking animal.

and face lashed by the branches, on a thickly wooded ridge. He knew it would be insane to blunder on through the dark, even if he had the strength. His need for rest was imperative and he thought: "I have played the fox, now I must play the cat of the fable." A big tree with a thick trunk and outspread branches was nearby, and, taking care to leave not the slightest mark, he climbed up into the crotch, and stretching out on one of the broad limbs, after a fashion, rested. Rest brought him new confidence and almost a feeling of security. Even so zealous a hunter as General Zaroff could not trace him there, he told himself; only the devil himself could follow that complicated trail through the jungle after dark. But, perhaps, the general was a devil—

An apprehensive night crawled slowly by like a wounded snake, and sleep did not visit Rainsford, although the silence of a dead world was on the jungle. Toward morning when a dingy gray was varnishing the sky, the cry of some startled bird focused Rainsford's attention in that direction. Something was coming through the bush, coming slowly, carefully, coming by the same winding way Rainsford had come. He flattened himself down on the limb, and through a screen of leaves almost as thick as tapestry, he watched. The thing that was approaching was a man.

It was General Zaroff. He made his way along with his eyes fixed in utmost concentration on the ground before him. He paused, almost beneath the tree, dropped to his knees and studied the ground. Rainsford's impulse was to hurl himself down like a panther, but he saw the general's right hand held something metallic—a small automatic pistol.

The hunter shook his head several times, as if he were puzzled. Then he straightened up and took from his case one of his black cigarettes; its pungent incense-like smoke floated up to Rainsford's nostrils.

Rainsford held his breath. The general's eyes had left the ground and were traveling inch by inch up the tree. Rainsford froze there, every muscle tensed for a spring. But the sharp eyes of the hunter stopped before they reached the limb where Rainsford lay; a smile spread over his brown face. Very deliberately he blew a smoke ring into the air; then he turned his back on the tree and walked carelessly away, back along the trail he had come. The swish of the underbrush against his hunting boots grew fainter and fainter.

The pent-up air burst hotly from Rainsford's lungs. His first thought made him feel sick and numb. The general could follow a trail through the woods at night; he could follow an extremely difficult trail; he must have uncanny powers; only by the merest chance had the Cossack failed to see his quarry.

Spiral Review

Pacing The author shows Rainsford resting and waiting. How does the slower pace of this scene help to create tension in the story?

Reading Skill

Make Inferences Which details in the description of Zaroff's searching the tree suggest that he knows Rainsford is there?

32 

On the first night of the hunt, where does Rainsford attempt to hide from Zaroff?

Spiral Review

Pacing

1. Remind students that they studied the concept of pacing in the Unit 2 Literary Analysis workshop (pp. 196–209).
2. **Ask** students the Spiral Review question.

   Possible response: The slower pace increases the tension because it suspends the action; in addition to making readers wait longer to learn the outcome, this scene builds tension through Rainsford's inactivity. Readers feel anxious because he is not moving.

31 Reading Skill

Make Inferences

1. Have students read the bracketed text, which continues onto p. 232. **Ask** students what they can infer about Zaroff from the fact that he arrives at the tree in which Rainsford is hiding.

   Answer: The inference is that Zaroff is a tremendously skilled hunter and tracker.
2. **Ask** students the Reading Skill question: Which details in the description of Zaroff's searching the tree suggest that he knows Rainsford is there?

   Answer: Zaroff's eyes stop before they reach the branch Rainsford is on. He smiles, blows a smoke ring very deliberately, turns his back, and walks away.
3. **Ask** students what inference Rainsford makes from Zaroff's actions.

   Answer: Rainsford knows that Zaroff knows where he is and that the hunter is just playing with his prey.

32 Reading Check

Answer: He tries to hide in a tree.

Differentiated Instruction for Universal Access

Strategy for Less Proficient Readers

Struggling readers may have difficulty following Zaroff's actions as he tracks Rainsford. To reinforce understanding of the text and to appeal to kinesthetic learners, have one student read aloud the text beginning "Something was coming through the bush . . ." and ending ". . . grew fainter and fainter." As the student reads, two other students should mime the actions of Rainsford (in the tree) and Zaroff (pursuing Rainsford).

Enrichment for Advanced Readers

Point out Zaroff's emphasis on being civilized: He is always polite and well-dressed and has surrounded himself with luxuries. Have students consider what they think it means to be civilized. Ask whether, according to their definitions, animals are not more civilized than human beings (they do not kill for sport, they do not fight wars, they do not destroy the environment). Have students choose sides and stage a debate on the issue.

33 Literary Analysis
Conflict

1. Discuss with students the let-down Rainsford must feel when his trap does not succeed. **Ask:** What must Rainsford think are his chances for survival?

   Possible response: Rainsford has put all his thought and effort into the trap, and it has failed to kill Zaroff. It is likely that he is demoralized and pessimistic about his chances of survival.

2. **Read the second bracketed text which continues onto p. 233, aloud. Ask** students the Literary Analysis question: Who seems to be winning the conflict at this point in the story? Explain.

   Answer: At this point, Zaroff seems to be winning. He has survived the trap and is confident that he will return and easily find Rainsford. Rainsford is now in a "desperate, hopeless flight."

3. **Have students speculate** which man they think will win and why they think so.

   Possible responses: Students may say that Rainsford will win because he is clearly the hero, and the story has emphasized the skill, tenacity, and bravery with which he has faced a sadistic opponent. Other students may suggest that Rainsford may destroy Zaroff but he may have to give up his life to do so.

31 Rainsford's second thought was even more terrible. It sent a shudder of cold horror through his whole being. Why had the general smiled? Why had he turned back?

Rainsford did not want to believe what his reason told him was true, but the truth was as evident as the sun that had by now pushed through the morning mists. The general was playing with him! The general was saving him for another day's sport! The Cossack was the cat; he was the mouse. Then it was that Rainsford knew the full meaning of terror.

"I will not lose my nerve. I will not."

He slid down from the tree, and struck off again into the woods. His face was set and he forced the machinery of his mind to function. Three hundred yards from his hiding place he stopped where a huge dead tree leaned precariously on a smaller, living one. Throwing off his sack of food, Rainsford took his knife from its sheath and began to work with all his energy.

The job was finished at last, and he threw himself down behind a fallen log a hundred feet away. He did not have to wait long. The cat was coming again to play with the mouse.

Following the trail with the sureness of a bloodhound, came General Zaroff. Nothing escaped those searching black eyes, no crushed blade of grass, no bent twig, no mark, no matter how faint, in the moss. So intent was the Cossack on his stalking that he was upon the thing Rainsford had made before he saw it. His foot touched the protruding bough that was the trigger. Even as he touched it, the general sensed his danger and leaped back with the agility of an ape. But he was not quite quick enough; the dead tree, delicately adjusted to rest on the cut living one, crashed down and struck the general a glancing blow on the shoulder as it fell; but for his alertness, he must have been smashed beneath it. He staggered, but he did not fall; nor did he drop his revolver. He stood there, rubbing his injured shoulder, and Rainsford, with fear again gripping his heart, heard the general's mocking laugh ring through the jungle.

"Rainsford," called the general, "if you are within the sound of my voice, as I suppose you are, let me congratulate you. Not many men know how to make a Malay mancatcher. Luckily, for me, I too have hunted in Malacca. You are proving interesting, Mr. Rainsford. I am going now to have my wound dressed; it's only a slight one. But I shall be back. I shall be back."

Literary Analysis
Conflict Who seems to be winning the conflict at this point in the story? Explain.

33 When the general, nursing his bruised shoulder, had gone, Rainsford took up his flight again. It was flight now, a desperate, hopeless flight, that carried him on for some hours. Dusk came, then darkness, and still he pressed on. The ground grew softer

Vocabulary Development

CCSS Language 6

Thematic Vocabulary: The Big Question

As students continue to read the story, use a graphic organizer to practice the thematic vocabulary presented in Introducing the Big Question, pp. 194–195. Write the word *antagonize* on the board and draw a circle around it. This is the center of a word web. Draw three short lines extending away from the circle like spokes on a wheel. Then draw a circle at the end of each new line. **Ask:** In what ways does Zaroff *antagonize* Rainsford during the hunt? Write each answer in one of the blank circles.

Possible responses: Zaroff smiles and blows a smoke ring in the air to show that he knows where Rainsford is. Zaroff also taunts Rainsford about the failure of the Malay mancatcher.

Ask: What does it mean to *antagonize* someone?

Answer: It means "to act against."

34 LITERATURE IN CONTEXT

History Connection

World War I Trenches

When Rainsford digs himself in, he is drawing on his experiences as a soldier. During World War I (1914–1918), European armies on both sides dug hundreds of miles of deep, narrow ditches. The soldiers lived in these trenches, from where they would charge the enemy's trenches.

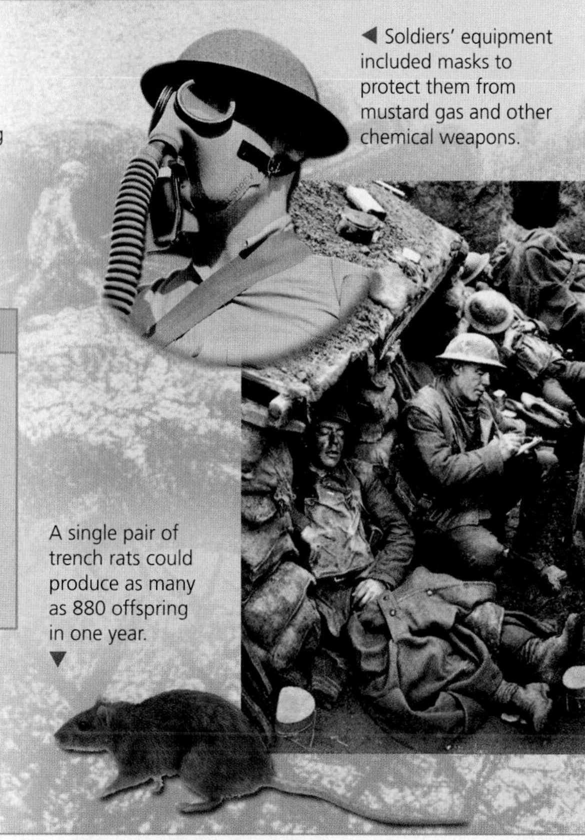

◀ Soldiers' equipment included masks to protect them from mustard gas and other chemical weapons.

LIFE IN THE TRENCHES

- Throughout the war, approximately seven thousand British soldiers were killed, wounded, or disabled every day while serving in the trenches.
- Soldiers living in trenches were plagued by lice, rats, beetles, and frogs.
- The trenches smelled terrible due to dead bodies, overflowing latrines, and unwashed men.

A single pair of trench rats could produce as many as 880 offspring in one year. ▼

Connect to the Literature

Rainsford says his time in the trenches was "placid" compared to his experience on the island. How does this information about trenches clarify his fear?

under his moccasins; the vegetation grew ranker, denser; insects bit him savagely. Then, as he stepped forward, his foot sank into
33 the ooze. He tried to wrench it back, but the muck sucked viciously at his foot as if it were a giant leech. With a violent effort, he tore his foot loose. He knew where he was now. Death Swamp and its quicksand.

His hands were tight closed as if his nerve were something tangible that someone in the darkness was trying to tear from his grip. The softness of the earth had given him an idea. He stepped back from the quicksand a dozen feet or so, and, like some huge prehistoric beaver, he began to dig.

Rainsford had dug himself in in France when a second's delay meant death. That had been a placid pastime compared to his digging now. The pit grew deeper; when it was above his shoulders, he climbed out and from some hard saplings cut stakes and

35

Reading Check

What toll does Rainsford's trap take on Zaroff?

34 Literature in Context

History Connection Modern artillery, machine guns, and barbed wire drastically changed the face of combat in World War I—but generals were slow to change their tactics. Massive assaults by hundreds of thousands of soldiers produced horrific casualties, but little or no gain on the battlefield. On the first day of the First Battle of the Somme, for example, nearly 60,000 British soldiers were killed or wounded. That Rainsford was able to survive trench warfare may help explain his abilities in his combat with Zaroff.

Connect to the Literature Have students read the Literature in Context feature, and present the additional background information above. Explain further that some synonyms for *placid* are *calm*, *peaceful*, and *serene*. Then, **ask** the Connect to the Literature question: Rainsford says his time in the trenches was "placid" compared to his experience on the island. How does this information about trenches clarify his fear?

Answer: To call his experience in the horrific trenches "placid" in comparison to his island experience means that Rainsford is incredibly frightened.

35 Reading Check

Answer: The Malay mancatcher bruises Zaroff's shoulder.

Differentiated Instruction for Universal Access

Strategy for Less Proficient Readers

In 1932, RKO Studios in Hollywood began work on two films: *The Most Dangerous Game* and the more famous *King Kong*. Since the films were being shot at the same time, the studio saved money by using the same jungle sets and casting several of the same actors in both films. Have students gather for a screening of *The Most Dangerous Game*. Seeing the story brought to life on screen will help students follow the story's plot and themes. After seeing the film, have students compare and contrast it with the story. What are the obvious differences? Why do students think the filmmakers made these changes? Was the story or the film more exciting? more dramatic? more believable? Students can address these questions in a group discussion.

36 Critical Thinking

Hypothesize

1. Have students read the bracketed text. **Ask:** How is Zaroff's behavior in this passage different from his behavior earlier in the hunt?

   Answer: Zaroff is moving quickly and less carefully.

2. **Ask:** Imagine that Zaroff had to play his "dangerous game" in a desert instead of on Ship-Trip Island. Based on this passage, as well as what you already know about Zaroff's skill as a hunter, how do you think the desert game would go for Zaroff?

   Possible response: Zaroff would be much less successful. He is used to the island's dense jungle landscape. In the barren desert, he wouldn't be able to rely on his tried-and-true strategies. In addition, he would not have access to his dogs, as they wouldn't be able to survive in a hot, dry climate. In this passage, Zaroff shows evidence of tiring or becoming too complacent. A different environment would unseat him.

sharpened them to a fine point. These stakes he planted in the bottom of the pit with the points sticking up. With flying fingers he wove a rough carpet of weeds and branches and with it he covered the mouth of the pit. Then, wet with sweat and aching with tiredness, he crouched behind the stump of a lightning-charred tree.

He knew his pursuer was coming; he heard the padding sound of feet on the soft earth, and the night breeze brought him the perfume of the general's cigarette. It seemed to Rainsford that the general was coming with unusual swiftness; he was not feeling his way along, foot by foot. Rainsford, crouching there, could not see the general, nor could he see the pit. He lived a year in a minute. Then he felt an impulse to cry aloud with joy, for he heard the sharp crackle of the breaking branches as the cover of the pit gave way; he heard the sharp scream of pain as the pointed stakes found their mark. He leaped up from his place of concealment. Then he cowered back. Three feet from the pit a man was standing, with an electric torch in his hand. 36

"You've done well, Rainsford," the voice of the general called. "Your Burmese tiger pit has claimed one of my best dogs. Again you score. I think, Mr. Rainsford, I'll see what you can do against my whole pack. I'm going home for a rest now. Thank you for a most amusing evening."

At daybreak Rainsford, lying near the swamp, was awakened by a sound that made him know that he had new things to learn about fear. It was a distant sound, faint and wavering, but he knew it. It was the baying of a pack of hounds.

Rainsford knew he could do one of two things. He could stay where he was and wait. That was suicide. He could flee. That was postponing the inevitable. For a moment he stood there, thinking. An idea that held a wild chance came to him, and, tightening his belt, he headed away from the swamp.

Vocabulary Development

Vocabulary Knowledge Rating

When students have completed reading and discussing "The Most Dangerous Game," have them take out their **Vocabulary Knowledge Rating Chart** for this selection. Read the words aloud once more and have students rate their knowledge of the words again in the After Reading column. Clarify any words that are still problematic. Have students write their own definition and example or sentence in the appropriate column. Then have students complete the Vocabulary Practice activities at the end of the selection. Encourage students to use the words in further discussion and written work about this selection. Remind them that they will be accountable for these words on the **Selection Test,** ***Unit 2 Resources,*** pp. 35–37 or 38–40.

The baying of the hounds drew nearer, then still nearer, nearer, ever nearer. On a ridge Rainsford climbed a tree. Down a watercourse, not a quarter of a mile away, he could see the bush moving. Straining his eyes, he saw the lean figure of General Zaroff; just ahead of him Rainsford made out another figure whose wide shoulders surged through the tall jungle weeds; it was the giant Ivan, and he seemed pulled forward by some unseen force; Rainsford knew that Ivan must be holding the pack in leash.

37 They would be on him any minute now. His mind worked frantically. He thought of a native trick he had learned in Uganda. He slid down the tree. He caught hold of a springy young sapling and to it he fastened his hunting knife, with the blade pointing down the trail; with a bit of wild grapevine he tied back the sapling. Then he ran for his life. The hounds raised their voices as they hit the fresh scent. Rainsford knew now how an animal at bay feels.

He had to stop to get his breath. The baying of the hounds stopped abruptly, and Rainsford's heart stopped too. They must have reached the knife.

He shinnied excitedly up a tree and looked back. His pursuers had stopped. But the hope that was in Rainsford's brain when he climbed died, for he saw in the shallow valley that General Zaroff was still on his feet. But Ivan was not. The knife, driven by the recoil of the springing tree, had not wholly failed.

"Nerve, nerve, nerve!" he panted, as he dashed along. A blue gap showed between the trees dead ahead. Ever nearer drew the hounds. Rainsford forced himself on toward that gap. He reached it. It was the shore of the sea. Across a cove he could see the gloomy gray stone of the château. Twenty feet below him the sea rumbled and hissed. Rainsford hesitated. He heard the hounds. Then he leaped far out into the sea. . . .

When the general and his pack reached the place by the sea, the Cossack stopped. For some minutes he stood regarding the blue-green expanse of water. He shrugged his shoulders. Then he sat down, took a drink of brandy from a silver flask, lit a perfumed cigarette, and hummed a bit from *Madame Butterfly*.[15]

General Zaroff had an exceedingly good dinner in his great paneled dining hall that evening. With it he had a bottle of Pol Roger and half a bottle of Chambertin. Two slight annoyances kept him from perfect enjoyment. One was the thought that it would be difficult to replace Ivan; the other was that his quarry had escaped him; of course the American hadn't played the game—so thought the general as he tasted his after-dinner liqueur. In his library he

15. ***Madame Butterfly*** an opera by Giacomo Puccini.

Literary Analysis
Conflict What new internal conflict does the sound of the baying dogs create for Rainsford?

38

What does Rainsford do when he reaches the edge of the cliff?

37 Literary Analysis
Conflict

1. Point out that in many games and sports the conflict between opponents is made more intense when time limits are added. **Ask** students for examples of such games.

   Possible responses: football, basketball, soccer.

2. Have students read the bracketed text. **Ask** students the Literary Analysis question: What new internal conflict does the sound of the baying dogs create for Rainsford?

   Answer: Rainsford must now struggle to control his panic because he knows the dogs are drawing nearer and that he has a limited amount of time to think of a tactic.

3. **Ask** students why they think poise and self-control—grace under pressure—are highly respected traits found in athletes, military leaders, and those in life-saving professions.

   Possible response: It is easy to give in to panic; maintaining calm shows the ability to control circumstances instead of being controlled by them. It is an ingredient of genuine heroism.

38 Reading Check
Answer: He leaps into the sea.

Concept Connector

Anticipation Guide
Have students return to their **Anticipation Guides** and respond to the statements again in the After Reading column. They may do this individually or in their original pairs or groups. Then, lead a class discussion, probing for what students have learned that confirms or invalidates each statement. Encourage students to cite specific details, quotations, or other evidence from the text to support their responses to each statement.

Writing About the Big Question
Have students compare their responses to the sentence starters they completed before reading the story with their ideas afterwards. Ask them to explain whether their thoughts have changed.

Reading Skill Graphic Organizer
Ask students to review the graphic organizers they completed to make inferences. Then have students share the graphic organizers they did and the inferences they made.

ASSESS

Answers

Critical Thinking

Before students respond, you may wish to have them write a brief objective summary of the selection. As they answer the questions below, remind them to support their answers with evidence from the text.

1. (a) Zaroff believes that human beings are the most dangerous game. (b) Since he is a sadist and murderer, students probably will not find Zaroff civilized.
2. (a) Zaroff says, "You have won the game." (b) Rainsford fights with and kills Zaroff.
3. If Rainsford hunts, he will certainly think about his prey's experience. This is because he now knows what it is like to be the prey instead of the hunter.
4. (a) **Possible response:** The idea of hunting is to track, outwit, and overcome the quarry. The prey faces the hunter in a classic case of external conflict. (b) **Possible response:** Zaroff has become obsessed with finding an opponent that challenges his well-honed hunting ability. Increased conflict is "necessary" for him to experience even slight satisfaction.

read, to soothe himself, from the works of Marcus Aurelius.[16] At ten he went up to his bedroom. He was deliciously tired, he said to himself, as he locked himself in. There was a little moonlight, so, before turning on his light, he went to the window and looked down at the courtyard. He could see the great hounds, and he called: "Better luck another time," to them. Then he switched on the light.

A man, who had been hiding in the curtain of the bed, was standing there.

"Rainsford!" screamed the general. "How in God's name did you get here?"

"Swam," said Rainsford. "I found it quicker than walking through the jungle."

The general sucked in his breath and smiled. "I congratulate you," he said. "You have won the game."

Rainsford did not smile. "I am still a beast at bay," he said, in a low, hoarse voice. "Get ready, General Zaroff."

The general made one of his deepest bows. "I see," he said. "Splendid! One of us is to furnish a repast for the hounds. The other will sleep in this very excellent bed. On guard, Rainsford. . . ."

He had never slept in a better bed, Rainsford decided.

16. **Marcus Aurelius** (ô rē′ lē əs) Roman emperor and philosopher (A.D. 121–180).

Critical Thinking

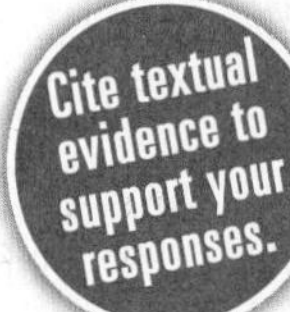
Cite textual evidence to support your responses.

1. **Key Ideas and Details** **(a)** According to Zaroff, what is the most dangerous game? **(b) Make a Judgment:** Based on this attitude, would you call Zaroff "civilized"? Why or why not?
2. **Key Ideas and Details** **(a)** Near the end, with what words does Zaroff congratulate Rainsford? **(b) Infer:** What action does Rainsford then take?
3. **Integration of Knowledge and Ideas** **Speculate:** How might Rainsford's experience on the island change him? Use evidence from the text to support your answer.
4. **Integration of Knowledge and Ideas** **(a)** In what sense is conflict a "necessary" part of the hunting experience? **(b)** Why does Zaroff consider it necessary to increase the conflict in his hunts? *[Connect to the Big Question: Is conflict necessary?]*

Assessment Resources

Unit 2 Resources

L1 L2 EL **Selection Test A,** pp. 35–37. Administer Test A to less advanced readers.

L3 L4 EL **Selection Test B,** pp. 38–40. Administer Test B to on-level and more advanced students.

L3 L4 **Open-Book Test,** pp. 32–34. As an alternative, give the Open-Book Test.

All **Customizable Test Bank**

All **Self-tests**
Students may prepare for the **Selection Test** by taking the **Self-test** online.

PHLit Online!

All assessment resources are available at **www.PHLitOnline.com.**

After You Read | The Most Dangerous Game

Literary Analysis: Conflict

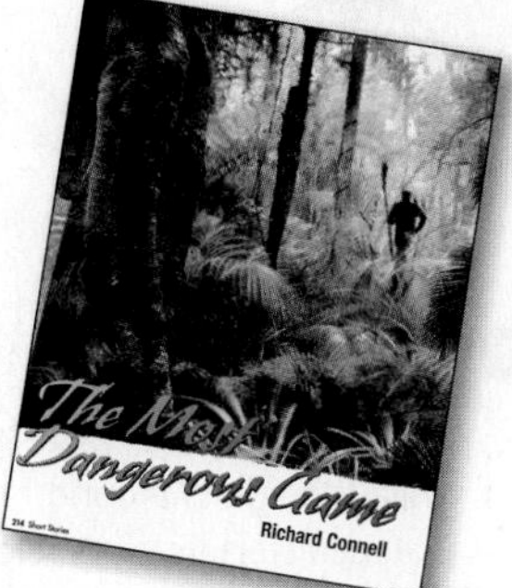

1. **Key Ideas and Details** **(a)** What is the main **conflict** in this story? Explain. **(b)** Is the main conflict primarily **internal** or **external**? Explain.
2. **Key Ideas and Details** Use a chart like the one shown to provide specific details that reveal conflicts other than the main conflict.

Rainsford vs. Nature	Rainsford vs. Himself

3. **Integration of Knowledge and Ideas** Is there a **resolution** in this story or does Rainsford experience an **epiphany** with no real end to the conflict? Support your answer.

Reading Skill: Make Inferences

4. **(a)** Identify three **inferences** you made while reading this story and the details you used to make them. **(b)** Did making inferences improve your understanding of the story? Explain your response.
5. **(a)** Write two **inferences** you made about Whitney. Compare the inferences you made with a partner's inferences. **(b)** Based on your ideas, discuss how the story would be different if it had been Whitney on the island with Zaroff.

Vocabulary

Acquisition and Use Use a word from the vocabulary list on page 212 to fill in the blank in each sentence. Then, explain the **context clues,** or key words and phrases, in each sentence that helped you.

1. His cheating at the game demonstrated a lack of ______.
2. At the wedding, the joy in the air seemed ______.
3. She tried to climb, but her high heels made her efforts ______.
4. The lazy sloth hung ______ from the tree branch.
5. Only a very ______ person would believe in the Tooth Fairy.
6. The ______ necklace was made of beads that looked like skulls.

Word Study Use the context of the sentences and what you know about the **Latin suffix *-esque*** to explain your answer to each question.

1. Why do people like to visit *picturesque* places?
2. If a film is called *Disneyesque,* whose movies does it resemble?

Word Study

The **Latin suffix *-esque*** means "in the style or manner of."

Apply It Explain how the suffix *-esque* contributes to the meanings of these words. Consult a dictionary if necessary.

statuesque
Lincolnesque
tabloidesque

ASSESS/EXTEND

Answers

Literary Analysis

1. (a) The main conflict is a life-or-death "game" between Rainsford and Zaroff. (b) The main conflict is external because it is between two characters.
2. **Possible response:** Rainsford **vs. nature**—almost drowning at start of story; almost dying in jungle and swamp. **Rainsford vs. himself:** not panicking when thrown from boat; controlling his anxiety during hunt.

   For other sample answers, see ***Graphic Organizer Transparencies,*** **Literary Analysis Graphic Organizer A,** p. 42, and the **Additional Answers** section.
3. The main conflict has a resolution; Rainsford wins the hunt and kills Zaroff.

Reading Skill

4. **Possible responses:** Zaroff is barbaric because he hunts humans; Zaroff knows Rainsford is in the tree because he smiles and blows a smoke ring; Rainsford sleeps in Zaroff's bed because he has killed Zaroff. (b) **Possible response:** Students may answer that inferences give them a better understanding of the characters and events.
5. (a) **Possible response:** Whitney's desire to relate to the animals shows that he is a more sensitive man than Rainsford; Whitney has a vivid imagination, which becomes apparent when he says he feels a "mental chill" and believes in "vibrations of evil." (b) **Possible response:** If Whitney had been on the island, his sensitivity and active imagination would have added to his fear, making him easier prey for Zaroff.

Vocabulary

Acquisition and Use

1. scruples
2. palpable
3. futile
4. indolently
5. naïve
6. grotesque

Word Study

Sample answers:

1. The suffix *-esque* means "in the style or manner of," and *picturesque* means "in the style of a picture." People like to visit picturesque places because they are as pretty as something they've seen in a picture.
2. The suffix *-esque* means "in the style or manner of," so a *Disneyesque* movie would resemble movies made by the Disney studios.

Word Study: Apply It

Sample answers:

Statuesque means tall, quiet, or stately in the manner of a statue.

Lincolnesque means having the qualities of or in the manner of President Lincoln.

Tabloidesque refers to something that would appear or be in the style of a tabloid newspaper.

PREPEACH

Skills instruction for the ***Reading Skill*** *and* ***Literary Analysis*** *concept appears on p. 211.*

❶ Writing About the Big Question

1. Review the assignment with the class.
2. **Ask** volunteers to give examples of a situation when someone might face a conflict in which his or her life is at stake. (Accept examples that describe a situation between humans and humans; nature and humans; or animals and animals.)
3. Have students complete the sentence starters. Review responses as a class. (**Possible responses:** For both individuals and countries, historic events often involve conflict because they depend on one country overtaking another. Fighting the same battle allows people to overlook the differences among them because they are working toward the same goal.)
4. Remind students that their answers will help them think about the Big Question, "Is conflict necessary?"

While You Read

Tell students that as they read they should think about how Elena prioritizes her thoughts.

❷ Vocabulary

1. Have students preview the selection vocabulary.
2. For each word, have students say the word aloud.
3. Then, use the word in a sentence that defines the word.
4. Repeat your definitional sentence or a similar sentence with the word missing, and have the class "fill in the blank" chorally. Here is an example:

   To be vigilant means to be alert to possible danger. For the past year, the army patrol has been on 24-hour alert and continues to be [students say "vigilant"].

❸ Word Study

1. Introduce the skill, using the instruction in the box.
2. Ask students for another *-ant* word with a meaning lacking certainty or doubtful. (**Answer:** hesitant)

Making Connections | American History

❶ Writing About the Big Question

In "American History," a teenage girl wrestles with personal feelings while the adults around her try to grasp a tragic historic event. Use these sentence starters to develop your ideas about the Big Question.

For both individuals and countries, historic events often involve conflict because ________________.

Fighting the same **battle** allows people to overlook the **differences** among them because ________________.

While You Read Think about how Elena prioritizes the thoughts that compete for her attention.

❷ Vocabulary

Read each word and its definition. Decide whether you know the word well, know it a little bit, or do not know it at all. After you read, see how your knowledge of each word has increased.

- **tenement** (ten′ ə mənt) *n.* apartment house, often run-down (p. 241) ***Many families lived in the large tenement.***
- **profound** (prō found′) *adj.* deep; intense (p. 241) ***Mia felt profound sorrow when her dog died.*** *profoundly adv.*
- **discreet** (di skrēt′) *adj.* careful about one's actions; prudent; keeping silent or preserving confidences (p. 244) ***Please, be discreet when you talk to the press about our agreement.*** *discreetly adv. discretion n. indiscreet adj. indiscretion n.*
- **vigilant** (vij′ ə lənt) *adj.* watchful (p. 245) ***The bodyguard kept a vigilant eye on the candidate.*** *vigil n. vigilance n.*
- **elation** (ē lā′ shən) *n.* exultant joy or pride; high spirits (p. 249) ***She danced with elation when she saw the new puppy.*** *elate v. elated adj.*
- **dilapidated** (də lap′ ə dāt′ əd) *adj.* broken down (p. 250) ***The old furniture was dilapidated and worn.***

❸

Word Study

The **Latin suffix *-ant*** is often used to form adjectives. It usually means "performing an action."

In this story, a mother is **vigilant** about her daughter. She watches closely—keeps vigil—to make sure her daughter focuses on the right things.

Vocabulary Development

Vocabulary Knowledge Rating

Create a **Vocabulary Knowledge Rating Chart** (***Professional Development Guidebook***, p. 33) for this selection. Include the selection vocabulary and the Big Question words that appear in the Writing About the Big Question sentence starters on this page. (The Big Question vocabulary is introduced on pp. 194–195.)

Give students a copy of the chart. Read the words aloud, and have students mark their rating in the Before Reading column. Urge them to be alert to these words as they read and discuss the selection.

Tally how many students think they know a word to gauge how much instruction to provide. As students read and discuss the selection, point out the words and their context.

Vocabulary Central, featuring tools, activities, and songs for studying vocabulary, is available at **www.PHLitOnline.com.**

Meet
Judith Ortiz Cofer
(b. 1952)

Author of
American History

Judith Ortiz Cofer spent her childhood in two different cultures. Born in Puerto Rico, she moved with her parents to Paterson, New Jersey, when she was four years old. She grew up mostly in Paterson, but she also spent time in Puerto Rico with her *abuela* (grandmother).

The Art of Storytelling It was from her grandmother that Ortiz Cofer learned the art of storytelling. "When my *abuela* sat us down to tell a story," she says, "we learned something from it, even though we always laughed. That was her way of teaching." In her own work, Ortiz Cofer teaches readers about the richness and difficulty of coming of age in two cultures at once.

4

BACKGROUND FOR THE STORY

The Kennedy Assassination

On November 22, 1963, President John F. Kennedy was shot and killed in Dallas, Texas, and the United States was plunged into mourning. Most people who lived through that time can still remember where they were when they heard the news. Kennedy's assassination and the nation's grief defined a generation. Key events in "American History" take place on that fateful day.

Did You Know?

Ortiz Cofer teaches for Operation Homecoming, a writing program for U.S. military personnel.

Daily Bellringer

For each class during which you teach this selection, have students complete one of the five Quick Write activities for Week 7 in the ***Daily Bellringer Activities*** booklet.

4 Background

The Kennedy Assassination

The shock of the Kennedy assassination appeared in the faces and behavior of Americans from all walks of life—from bus drivers to Hollywood actors, from factory workers to university professors. Famous television news reporters cried on live television, and radio announcers found it difficult to speak. Schools and businesses were shut down, and the nation's daily routines were suspended. The Kennedy White House had been considered by many to be an American "Camelot," and Americans reacted as if an almost mythical leader such as King Arthur had been killed. This disturbing disruption of the ordered adult world is reflected in what the young narrator sees and hears in "American History."

Multidraft Reading

This icon marks natural pauses in the selection. To assist struggling readers and to deepen reading for all, assign the text in "chunks," following the icons, and apply multidraft reading protocols. For each reading, have students set the purpose indicated:

- **First reading**—identifying key ideas and details and answering any Reading Checks.
- **Second reading**—analyzing craft and structure and responding to the side-column prompts.
- **Third reading**—integrating knowledge and ideas, connecting to other texts and the world, and answering the end-of-selection questions.

For more guidance, refer to the ***Classroom Strategies and Teaching Routines*** card on multidraft reading.

PHLit Online!

For more about the author, practice with the selection vocabulary, and more background, go online at **www.PHLitOnline.com.**

Differentiated Instruction

Additional Instruction

EL Extended Support—English Learners
Have students complete the **Reading and Vocabulary Warm-ups,** *Unit 2 Resources,* pp. 41–44 before they read. Assign the prereading pages in the ***Reader's Notebook: English Learner's Version.*** Then, have students listen to portions of the selection on the ***Hear It!*** **Audio CD.**

L1 L2 Extended Support—Struggling Readers
Have students complete the **Reading and Vocabulary Warm-ups,** *Unit 2 Resources,* pp. 41–44, before they read. Assign prereading pages for the selection in the ***Reader's Notebook: Adapted Version.*** Then, have students listen to portions of the selection on the ***Hear It!*** **Audio CD** (adapted text).

Extended Support—Reluctant Readers
To build motivation and engagement before assigning the selection, have students read "Rebuilding What Is Broken," a thematically related selection in ***Reality Central.*** Then, use the questions at the conclusion of the related selection to guide discussion.

❶ Activating Prior Knowledge

1. Prepare an **Anticipation Guide** (***Professional Development Guidebook***, pp. 36–38) with the following statements:
   - Major world events shape people's lives.
   - Personal struggles are always less painful than societal struggles.
   - Conflict is necessary in life.
2. Give students a copy of the prepared Anticipation Guide and have students mark their responses in the appropriate columns.
3. For further guidance, use the ***Classroom Strategies and Teaching Routines*** card: **Using an Anticipation Guide.**

Concept Connector →

Students will return to the Anticipation Guide after completing "American History."

Individual Activity

Ask students to pay attention to the descriptions of the buildings in "American History." Have students draw Elena's vantage point from her fire escape.

❷ About the Selection

Elena, a Puerto Rican girl living in a tenement in New Jersey, becomes friends with a boy named Eugene. Elena struggles to control her feelings of elation about Eugene, so different from the nation's anguish on the day of the assassination of President John F. Kennedy. When Eugene's mother turns her away at their doorstep, Elena experiences a personal sorrow more intense than her feelings about Kennedy.

❸ Humanities

Sunday Afternoon by Ralph Fasanella

In this painting, kids play a game of stickball on a city street. Fasanella (1914–1997) grew up in an Italian American neighborhood. His colorful paintings depict working-class life.

Ask: Based on this painting, what do you think the setting of the story will be?

Possible response: A crowded urban area.

❸ ***Sunday Afternoon - Stickball Game,*** 1953, Ralph Fasanella. Courtesy A.C.A. Galleries, N.Y.

Vocabulary Development

Ⓒ **CCSS** Language 6

Thematic Vocabulary: The Big Question

As students are discussing "American History," encourage them to use the thematic vocabulary presented in Introducing the Big Question, pp. 194–195. You might encourage them with sentence starters like these:

1. Elena doesn't seem to *appreciate* her relationship with her mother because . . .
2. Elena feels she cannot *compete* with the girls playing jump rope because . . .
3. Eugene's friendship with Elena seems to *antagonize* his mother because . . .
4. Elena begins to question the realities of racial *equity* when . . .

❶ ❷

American History

Judith Ortiz Cofer

I once read in a *Ripley's Believe It or Not* column that Paterson, New Jersey, is the place where the Straight and Narrow (streets) intersect.

The Puerto Rican tenement known as El Building was one block up from Straight. It was, in fact, the corner of Straight and Market; not "at" the corner, but *the* corner. At almost any hour of the day, El Building was like a monstrous jukebox, blasting out *salsas*[1] from open windows as the residents, mostly new immigrants just up from the island, tried to drown out whatever they were currently enduring with loud music. But the day President Kennedy was shot there was a profound silence in El Building; even the abusive tongues of *viragoes*,[2] the cursing of the unemployed, and the screeching of small children had been somehow muted. President Kennedy was a saint to these people. In fact, soon his photograph would be hung alongside the Sacred Heart and over the spiritist altars that many women kept in their apartments. He would

Vocabulary

tenement (ten′ ə mənt) *n.* apartment house, often run-down

profound (prō found′) *adj.* deep; intense

❺

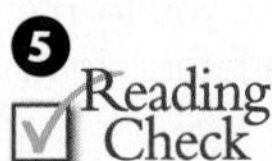
Reading Check

On what memorable day in history does this story take place?

1. ***salsas*** (säl′ səs) songs written in a particular Latin American musical style.
2. ***viragoes*** (vi rä′ gōz) fierce, irritable women who often shout.

❹

◀ **Critical Viewing**
In what ways does this painting illustrate the narrator's description of the neighborhood in the first paragraph? **[Compare]**

❹ Critical Viewing

Answer: The neighborhood is filled with people living in crowded apartment houses. The residents are talking and playing in the streets, as if to "drown out whatever they were currently enduring."

❺ Reading Check

Answer: The story takes place on the day President John F. Kennedy was assassinated.

PHLit Online!

This selection is available in interactive format in the **Enriched Online Student Edition, www.PHLitOnline.com,** which includes a thematically related video with writing prompt and an interactive graphic organizer.

Differentiated Instruction for Universal Access

Strategy for Less Proficient Readers

To help students understand how to make inferences as they read, show them **Reading Skill Graphic Organizer A** (***Graphic Organizer Transparencies,*** p. 40). The partially completed graphic organizer will give students insight into the process of asking and answering questions to make inferences. They can use the graphic organizer as a model for making their own inferences as they read.

EL Background for English Learners

Assist students by explaining the following cultural expressions and idioms:

- *Ripley's Believe It or Not*—a newspaper feature about amazing facts
- *Straight and Narrow*—description of the path that virtuous people follow in life

Then, ask students to share with the class any expressions or idioms with similar meaning in their home languages.

❻ Critical Viewing

Possible response: The scene is similar to my school because students are walking down a long, crowded hallway lined with lockers. It is different from my school because the students are dressed like they're in the 1960s, and they are all white.

❼ Reading Skill

Make Inferences

1. **Ask** students to summarize how the narrator says she feels about going to school and living in the city in winter.

   Answer: She says that she hates the school, and she hates the city in winter.

2. Have students **speculate** why the narrator might be especially in need of a friend.

   Possible responses: The narrator seems angry, lonely, and depressed. The school, the weather, and the other girls on the playground contribute to her distress and feelings of humiliation.

3. Have students read the bracketed text. **Ask** the Reading Skill question: Which details in this passage lead you to infer that the narrator is fond of Eugene?

   Answer: The narrator, who is badly in need of a friend, considers Eugene a "source of beauty and light," and she looks forward to seeing him in school. She loves to read while sitting on the fire escape and looking down into his yard.

become part of the hierarchy of martyrs they prayed to for favors that only one who had died for a cause would understand.

On the day that President Kennedy was shot, my ninth grade class had been out in the fenced playground of Public School Number 13. We had been given "free" exercise time and had been ordered by our P.E. teacher, Mr. DePalma, to "keep moving." That meant that the girls should jump rope and the boys toss basketballs through a hoop at the far end of the yard. He in the meantime would "keep an eye" on us from just inside the building.

It was a cold gray day in Paterson. The kind that warns of early snow. I was miserable, since I had forgotten my gloves, and my knuckles were turning red and raw from the jump rope. I was also taking a lot of abuse from the black girls for not turning the rope hard and fast enough for them.

"Hey, Skinny Bones, pump it, girl. Ain't you got no energy today?" Gail, the biggest of the black girls who had the other end of the rope, yelled, "Didn't you eat your rice and beans and pork chops for breakfast today?"

❻ ▶ **Critical Viewing** In what ways is this school scene similar to your school? In what ways is it different? **[Compare and Contrast]**

The other girls picked up the "pork chops" and made it into a refrain: "pork chop, pork chop, did you eat your pork chop?" They entered the double ropes in pairs and exited without tripping or missing a beat. I felt a burning on my cheeks and then my glasses fogged up so that I could not manage to coordinate the jump rope with Gail. The chill was doing to me what it always did, entering my bones, making me cry, humiliating me. I hated the city, especially in winter. I hated Public School Number 13. I hated my skinny flat-chested body, and I envied the black girls who could jump rope so fast that their legs became a blur. They always seemed to be warm while I froze.

Reading Skill
Make Inferences Which details in this passage lead you to infer that the narrator is fond of Eugene? ❼

There was only one source of beauty and light for me that school year. The only thing I had anticipated at the start of the semester. That was seeing Eugene. In August, Eugene and his family had moved into the only house on the block that had a yard and trees. I could see his place from my window in El Building. In fact, if I sat on the fire escape I was literally suspended above Eugene's backyard. It was my favorite spot to read my library books in the summer. Until that August the house had been occupied by an old Jewish couple. Over the years I had become part of their family, without their knowing it, of course. I had a view of their kitchen and their backyard, and though I could not hear what they said, I knew when they were arguing, when one of them was sick, and many other things. I knew all this by watching them at mealtimes. I could see their kitchen table, the sink, and the stove. During good times, he sat at the table and read his newspapers while she

Think Aloud

Conflict

Draw students' attention to the passage beginning "'Hey, Skinny Bones . . .'" and ending "warm while I froze." Use the following "think aloud" to model the process of analyzing conflict:

As I read this passage, I look for ways in which the main character, Elena, struggles with an external or internal force. In this passage, a group of African American girls insults and humiliates Elena. This is clear evidence of an external conflict. I wonder if Elena will resolve the conflict by becoming more confident and standing up to the girls.

Later in the passage, Elena talks about how much she hates the cold of winter, the city, and her school. Here I see evidence of a more subtle internal conflict within Elena. She is struggling with her own negative attitude toward the life she is living. Again, I wonder if Elena will resolve her conflict. Perhaps she will find a way to overcome her hatred.

fixed the meals. If they argued, he would leave and the old woman would sit and stare at nothing for a long time. When one of them was sick, the other would come and get things from the kitchen and carry them out on a tray. The old man had died in June. The last week of school I had not seen him at the table at all. Then one day I saw that there was a crowd in the kitchen. The old woman had finally emerged from the house on the arm of a stocky, middle-aged woman, whom I had seen there a few times before, maybe her daughter. Then a man had carried out suitcases. The house had stood empty for weeks. I had had to resist the temptation to climb down into the yard and water the flowers the old lady had taken such good care of.

By the time Eugene's family moved in, the yard was a tangled mass of weeds. The father had spent several days mowing, and

8 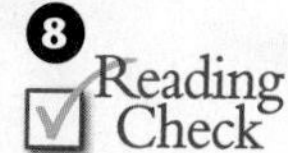
Reading Check
Who is Eugene, and how does the narrator become aware of him?

There was only one source of beauty and light for me that school year.

8 Reading Check

Answer: Eugene is a boy whose family recently moved into a house in the narrator's neighborhood. She becomes aware of him by looking out her window and watching him from her fire escape.

Differentiated Instruction for Universal Access

Strategy for Special-Needs Students

Students may be confused by the way the narrator relates the unfolding of events in a nonlinear fashion: The story begins with the assassination of President Kennedy, and then the narrator describes events that occurred prior to that day. Help students make a simple timeline to track the events of the story. Have students identify on their timelines the calendar indicators in the story, such as "that August," "in June," and "once school started." The timeline might look like this:

June—old Jewish man dies
July—"for weeks" house stands empty
August—Eugene and family move in
September—school starts; narrator meets Eugene
October—"in the weeks that followed," friendship grows
November—Kennedy assassination; narrator is turned away from Eugene's home

9 Humanities

Brownstones by Patti Mollica

Patti Mollica is a contemporary American artist from Syracuse, New York, who sells her paintings throughout the world. She started painting with her babysitter when she was about eight years old. Mollica never attended art school. "I consider myself largely self-taught," she says. "No one can really teach you how to find your own voice." **Ask:** What does the painting suggest about Mollica's background?

Possible response: It suggests that Mollica spent some time living in, or visiting, cities. It also suggests that she finds beauty in what some might consider a harsh urban environment.

10 Critical Viewing

Answer: The painting suggests the description of Elena's fire escape outside El Building, from which she could see Eugene's yard. The dark, muted colors in the painting suggest bleak winter.

9 10

▲ **Critical Viewing**
Which description from the selection does this painting suggest? **[Connect]**

when he finished, from where I sat, I didn't see the red, yellow, and purple clusters that meant flowers to me. I didn't see this family sit down at the kitchen table together. It was just the mother, a red-headed tall woman who wore a white uniform—a nurse's, I guessed it was; the father was gone before I got up in the morning and was never there at dinner time. I only saw him on weekends when they sometimes sat on lawn chairs under the oak tree, each hidden behind a section of the newspaper; and there was Eugene. He was tall and blond, and he wore glasses. I liked him right away because he sat at the kitchen table and read books for hours. That summer, before we had even spoken one word to each other, I kept him company on my fire escape.

Vocabulary
discreet (di skrēt′) *adj.* careful about one's actions; prudent; keeping silent or preserving confidences

Once school started I looked for him in all my classes, but P.S. 13 was a huge, overpopulated place and it took me days and many discreet questions to discover that Eugene was in honors classes for all his subjects; classes that were not open to me because English was not my first language, though I was a straight A
11 student. After much maneuvering, I managed "to run into him" in

Vocabulary Development

CCSS Language 6

Word Forms

Expand students' vocabulary by helping them learn related forms of the selection vocabulary words. Three of the selection vocabulary words for "American History" have related forms. Give students a blank **Word Form Chart** (***Professional Development Guidebook***, p. 42) with *profound, discreet,* and *vigilant* in the correct columns. Work with the class, or have students work with a partner, to determine the related forms. The final chart should look like the one shown.

Noun	Verb	Adjective	Adverb
profundity		**profound**	profoundly
discretion		**discreet**	discreetly
vigilance		**vigilant**	vigilantly

11 the hallway where his locker was—on the other side of the building from mine—and in study hall at the library, where he first seemed to notice me but did not speak; and finally, on the way home after school one day when I decided to approach him directly, though my stomach was doing somersaults.

I was ready for rejection, snobbery, the worst. But when I came up to him, practically panting in my nervousness, and blurted out: "You're Eugene. Right?" he smiled, pushed his glasses up on his nose, and nodded. I saw then that he was blushing deeply. Eugene liked me, but he was shy. I did most of the talking that day. He nodded and smiled a lot. In the weeks that followed, we walked home together. He would linger at the corner of El Building for a few minutes then walk down to his two-story house. It was not until Eugene moved into that house that I noticed that El Building blocked most of the sun, and that the only spot that got a little sunlight during the day was the tiny square of earth the old woman had planted with flowers.

I did not tell Eugene that I could see inside his kitchen from my bedroom. I felt dishonest, but I liked my secret sharing of his evenings, especially now that I knew what he was reading since we chose our books together at the school library.

One day my mother came into my room as I was sitting on the windowsill staring out. In her abrupt way she said: "Elena, you are acting 'moony.' " *Enamorada* [3] was what she really said, that is—like a girl stupidly infatuated. Since I had turned fourteen . . . my mother had been more **vigilant** than ever. She acted as if I was going to go crazy or explode or something if she didn't watch me and nag me all the time about being a *señorita*[4] now. She kept talking about virtue, morality, and other subjects that did not interest me in the least. My mother was unhappy in Paterson, but my father had a good job at the blue jeans factory in Passaic and soon, he kept assuring us, we would be moving to our own house there. Every Sunday we drove out to the suburbs of Paterson, Clifton, and Passaic, out to where people mowed grass on Sundays in the summer, and where children made snowmen in the winter from pure white snow, not like the gray slush of Paterson which seemed to fall from the sky in that hue. I had learned to listen to my parents' dreams, which were spoken in Spanish, as fairy tales, like the stories about life in the island paradise of Puerto Rico before I was born. I had been to the island once as a little girl, to grandmother's funeral, and all I remembered was wailing women in black, my mother becoming hysterical and being given a pill that

Literary Analysis
Conflict What internal conflict does the narrator experience as she prepares to approach Eugene?

Vocabulary
vigilant (vij′ ə lənt) *adj.* watchful

12

According to her mother, how does Elena seem to feel about Eugene?

3. **Enamorada** (ā nä′ mō rä′ dä) Spanish for "enamored; lovesick."
4. **señorita** (se′ nyô rē′ tä) *n.* Spanish for "young lady."

11 Literary Analysis
Conflict

1. Have students reread the bracketed text, which begins on p. 244. **Ask** them what the narrator wants to do.
   Answer: She wants to meet Eugene.
2. **Discuss** with students what the narrator says she is afraid will happen.
   Answer: She is afraid that Eugene will reject her, act like a snob, or humiliate her in some way.
3. **Ask** students the Literary Analysis question: What internal conflict does the narrator experience as she prepares to approach Eugene?
   Answer: The narrator assumes that Eugene is different from her and will probably reject her. However, she also wants very much to meet him. Her fear and her desire are in conflict.
4. Have students **identify** the visible signs of Elena's inner conflict.
   Answer: Elena's visible nervousness and blurting out are outward signs of her internal conflict.

12 Reading Check
Answer: Elena's mother says Elena is *enamorada*—infatuated—with Eugene.

Differentiated Instruction for Universal Access

Enrichment for Gifted/Talented Students
Have students create a soundscape, a collection of music and sound effects that reflects the different scenes and moods of "American History." Students might follow these steps:

1. Reread the story, taking notes on the various sounds and sound effects that might be included.
2. Identify scenes for the soundscape, such as a typical day in El Building, the schoolyard, the walk home on November 22, and the scene with Eugene's mother.
3. Find short excerpts of songs, music, and sound effects that capture the mood of each scene or that might be appropriate background music.
4. Make a recording of the songs, music, and sound effects in the correct order of the scenes they accompany.
5. Play the soundscape for the class. If time permits, read excerpts from the story to accompany the soundscape.

13  Connecting to the Big Question

1. Have a volunteer read aloud the first bracketed text. **Ask:** What does Elena talk about in this passage? **Answer:** First, she talks about her parents' dream to retire to a house on the beach in Puerto Rico. Then she talks about her future goals of becoming a teacher and entering Eugene's house.
2. **Ask:** Based on this passage, what two types of thoughts compete for Elena's attention? **Answer:** Her parents' future dreams and her own desires for the present and future compete for Elena's attention.
3. **Ask:** How does Elena prioritize these thoughts? **Answer:** She puts her parents' wishes at the back of her mind and concentrates on her own goals and dreams.

Spiral Review

Plot Devices

1. Remind students that they studied the concept of plot devices in the Unit 2 Literary Analysis workshop (pp. 196–209).
2. **Ask** students the Spiral Review question.

   Possible response: One story line is from personal history and the other is public.

14 Literary Analysis

Conflict

1. Discuss with students some of the most common sources of external conflict, such as fear, ignorance, greed, and desire for power.
2. **Ask** students why they think some people mock and humiliate people who are new to their community.

   Possible response: Some people fear newcomers, and they try to feel more secure and important by making fun of newcomers.

made her sleep two days, and me feeling lost in a crowd of strangers all claiming to be my aunts, uncles, and cousins. I had actually been glad to return to the city. We had not been back there since then, though my parents talked constantly about buying a house on the beach someday, retiring on the island—that was a common topic among the residents of El Building. As for me, I was going to go to college and become a teacher.

13 **Spiral Review**
Plot Devices This story can be seen as having a parallel plot structure. What are the two story lines that the author develops?

But after meeting Eugene I began to think of the present more than of the future. What I wanted now was to enter that house I had watched for so many years. I wanted to see the other rooms where the old people had lived, and where the boy spent his time. Most of all, I wanted to sit at the kitchen table with Eugene like two adults, like the old man and his wife had done, maybe drink some coffee and talk about books. I had started reading *Gone with the Wind.* I was enthralled by it, with the daring and the passion of the beautiful girl living in a mansion, and with her devoted parents and the slaves who did everything for them. I didn't believe such a world had ever really existed, and I wanted to ask Eugene some questions since he and his parents, he had told me, had come up from Georgia, the same place where the novel was set. His father worked for a company that had transferred him to Paterson. His mother was very unhappy, Eugene said, in his beautiful voice that rose and fell over words in a strange, lilting way. The kids at school called him "the hick" and made fun of the way he talked. I knew I was his only friend so far, and I liked that, though I felt sad for him sometimes. "Skinny Bones" and the "Hick" was what they called us at school when we were seen together.

14 **Literary Analysis**
Conflict What external conflict does Eugene experience at school?

The day Mr. DePalma came out into the cold and asked us to line up in front of him was the day that President Kennedy was shot. Mr. DePalma, a short, muscular man with slicked-down black hair, was the science teacher, P.E. coach, and disciplinarian at P.S. 13. He was the teacher to whose homeroom you got assigned if you were a troublemaker, and the man called out to break up playground fights, and to escort violently angry teenagers to the office. And Mr. DePalma was the man who called your parents in for "a conference."

That day, he stood in front of two rows of mostly black and Puerto Rican kids, brittle from their efforts to "keep moving" on a November day that was turning bitter cold. Mr. DePalma, to our complete shock, was crying. Not just silent adult tears, but really sobbing. There were a few titters from the back of the line where I stood shivering.

"Listen," Mr. DePalma raised his arms over his head as if he were about to conduct an orchestra. His voice broke, and he covered his

Vocabulary Development

CCSS Language 6

Multiple Meanings

The word *common* has several meanings that students can learn to distinguish by paying attention to the different contexts in which they are used.

- When Elena discusses a "*common* topic among the residents of El Building," the word *common* is an adjective that means "happening frequently." A daily habit is a *common* activity because it happens frequently. The use of the word *common* suggests that many of the residents of El Building want to retire to Puerto Rico, and they talk about it frequently.
- Something relating to a community at large is also called *common*. For example, police officers work for the *common* safety of the citizens in their town.
- The word *common* can also be a noun meaning "a public open area in a city." People gather on their town *common* to listen to a concert or to attend a demonstration.

Ask students to write a sentence for each meaning of the word *common*.

face with his hands. His barrel chest was heaving. Someone giggled behind me.

"Listen," he repeated, "something awful has happened." A strange gurgling came from his throat, and he turned around and spat on the cement behind him.

"Gross," someone said, and there was a lot of laughter.

"The president is dead, you idiots. I should have known that wouldn't mean anything to a bunch of losers like you kids. Go home." He was shrieking now. No one moved for a minute or two, but then a big girl let out a "Yeah!" and ran to get her books piled up with the others against the brick wall of the school building. The others followed in a mad scramble to get to their things before somebody caught on. It was still an hour to the dismissal bell.

A little scared, I headed for El Building. There was an eerie feeling on the streets. I looked into Mario's drugstore, a favorite hangout for the high school crowd, but there were only a couple of old Jewish men at the soda bar talking with the short order cook in tones that sounded almost angry, but they were keeping their voices low. Even the traffic on one of the busiest intersections in Paterson—Straight Street and Park Avenue—seemed to be moving slower. There were no horns blasting that day. At El Building, the usual little group of unemployed men were not hanging out on the front stoop making it difficult for women to enter the front door. No music spilled out from open doors in the hallway. When I walked into our apartment, I found my mother sitting in front of the grainy picture of the television set.

She looked up at me with a tear-streaked face and just said: "*Dios mío*,"[5] turning back to the set as if it were pulling at her eyes. I went into my room.

Though I wanted to feel the right thing about President Kennedy's death, I could not fight the

5. ***Dios mío*** (dē´ ōs mē´ ō) Spanish for "My God!"

"Listen," he repeated, "something awful has happened."

Reading Skill
Make Inferences
Which details in Elena's description of her walk home let you infer the anguish people feel over the assassination of the president?

◀ **Critical Viewing**
What lines in the story help you to understand this image? **[Connect]**

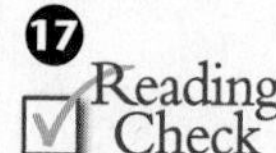

How does Mr. DePalma's reaction to the news of Kennedy's assassination differ from the students' reaction?

15 Reading Skill

Make Inferences

1. Remind students of the description of the noisy tenement building at the beginning of the story. Point out the contrast between the usual loud sounds of the building and the amazing quiet of the day President Kennedy is shot.
2. Then have students read the bracketed text that describes Elena's walk home.
3. **Ask** students the Reading Skill question: Which details in Elena's description of her walk home let you infer the anguish people feel over the assassination of the president?

   Answer: Details include "an eerie feeling on the streets," only two men in the soda-bar talking in low voices, traffic moving slower than usual, no horns blasting, no men hanging out on the front stoop of El Building, no music from open doors, and Elena's mother crying in front of the television set.

16 Critical Viewing

Possible response: "He would become part of the hierarchy of martyrs they prayed to for favors that only one who had died for a cause would understand" (pp. 241–242). "His voice broke, and he covered his face with his hands. His barrel chest was heaving" (pp. 246–247). "There was an eerie feeling on the streets. . . . She looked up at me with a tear-streaked face and just said: '*Dios mio*'" (p. 247).

17 Reading Check

Answer: Mr. DePalma is clearly upset and disturbed, while the students are unaffected—they are just happy to leave school early.

Differentiated Instruction for Universal Access

Enrichment for Advanced Readers

Elena begins reading *Gone with the Wind*, a best-selling novel by Margaret Mitchell published in 1936 and winner of the Pulitzer Prize. Like Cofer's story, Mitchell's novel unfolds against a background of painful events in American history. Ask students to research the novel's basic plot, setting, and characters. Have a group of students present an oral report on their findings, with emphasis on why Cofer has Elena read this particular novel. Students might use the following questions to organize their report:

1. Elena mentions the mansion and slavery in the novel. What other details of the novel's setting are different from Elena's world?
2. What questions might Elena want to ask Eugene about life in Georgia?
3. What is the main external conflict?
4. What is the internal conflict of the novel's heroine, Scarlett O'Hara?
5. What qualities of Scarlett O'Hara would Elena probably admire?

18 Visual Connections

Whole-Class Activity

1. Review background information on painter Patti Mollica on p. 244. Then, **ask** students to describe what they see in the painting, *Midtown Mayhem* (1999).

   Possible response: I see taxis parked and moving on a city street. I cannot see any people inside the taxis. There is a traffic light at the top, which suggests the scene is at an intersection. A person is walking on the street. The colors are dark and muted. It appears to be nighttime.
2. **Ask:** What word would you use to describe the mood in the painting? **Possible responses:** The mood is somber, dark, lonely, peaceful, quiet, contemplative, depressing, suspenseful, or melancholy.
3. **Ask:** What details would you change if you wanted to make the painting joyous and energetic?

   Possible response: I would make the colors brighter and the lines sharper. I would also add more people and put smiles on their faces.

Small-Group Activity

1. Organize students in small groups. Tell students to imagine themselves in the painting and discuss who they are and how they are feeling.
2. Ask one person from each group to summarize the group's ideas.
3. Have the designated students share the results of their groups' discussions. To model the process of making connections to an image, choose one response and analyze how the painting supports it.

Individual Activity

1. As a class, briefly discuss the painting.
2. Ask students to imagine that they are the man in the painting and to write a two-paragraph journal entry about what they are doing and feeling.
3. In class or for homework, have students edit and proofread their journal entries.
4. Post the entries in the room. Invite students to read each other's work.

18

Vocabulary Development — CCSS Language 6

Selection Vocabulary Reinforcement

Students will benefit from additional examples and practice with the selection vocabulary words. Reinforce their comprehension with "show-you-know" sentences. The first part of the sentence uses the vocabulary word in an appropriate context. The second part of the sentence—the "show-you-know" part—clarifies the first. Model the strategy with this example for *elation*:

> We were not surprised at the intensity of the jockey's *elation*; he had won the horse race by five lengths.

Then give students these sentence prompts, and coach them in creating the clarification part:

1. It takes something really exciting for me to experience *elation*; ____________.

Sample answer: normally I do not have strong emotions.

2. By the end of the morning, Carla was filled with *elation*; ____________.

Sample answer: she had won first prize in the spelling bee.

feeling of elation that stirred in my chest. Today was the day I was to visit Eugene in his house. He had asked me to come over after school to study for an American history test with him. We had also planned to walk to the public library together. I looked down into his yard. The oak tree was bare of leaves and the ground looked gray with ice. The light through the large kitchen window of his house told me that El Building blocked the sun to such an extent that they had to turn lights on in the middle of the day. I felt ashamed about it. But the white kitchen table with the lamp hanging just above it looked cozy and inviting. I would soon sit there, across from Eugene, and I would tell him about my perch just above his house. Maybe I should.

In the next thirty minutes I changed clothes, put on a little pink lipstick, and got my books together. Then I went in to tell my mother that I was going to a friend's house to study. I did not expect her reaction.

"You are going out *today?* " The way she said "today" sounded as if a storm warning had been issued. It was said in utter disbelief.
19 Before I could answer, she came toward me and held my elbows as I
clutched my books.

"*Hija*,[6] the president has been killed. We must show respect. He was a great man. Come to church with me tonight."

She tried to embrace me, but my books were in the way. My first impulse was to comfort her, she seemed so distraught, but I had to meet Eugene in fifteen minutes.

"I have a test to study for, Mama. I will be home by eight."

"You are forgetting who you are, *Niña*.[7] I have seen you staring down at that boy's house. You are heading for humiliation and

6. ***Hija*** (ē´ hä) Spanish for "daughter."
7. ***Niña*** (nē´ nyä) Spanish for "child."

Vocabulary
elation (ē lā´ shən) *adj.* exultant joy or pride; high spirits

Literary Analysis
Conflict On the evening of the assassination, how do Elena's plans conflict with her mother's?

20

Reading Check
How does Elena feel about studying with Eugene?

"*Hija*, the president has been killed. We must show respect. He was a great man."

19 Literary Analysis
Conflict

1. **Ask** students what they think is important to Elena.

   Possible response: Elena's growing friendship and affection for Eugene is the most important aspect of her emotional life at this time.

2. Have students reread the bracketed text. **Ask** students the Literary Analysis question: On the evening of the assassination, how do Elena's plans conflict with her mother's?

   Answer: Elena's mother thinks it is inappropriate for Elena to go out on the day of the president's death. Instead, she wants Elena to come to church with her.

3. **Ask** students how Elena's reaction to her mother's embrace reveals the conflict.

   Answer: Elena does not move her books as her mother embraces her. This suggests a barrier between Elena's and her mother's views over the importance of the president's assassination; Elena's personal wishes overshadow the public significance of events that day.

20 Reading Check

Answer: Elena is extremely excited about studying with Eugene.

Differentiated Instruction for Universal Access

Culturally Responsive Instruction

Culture Focus On this page, Elena's mother encourages Elena to attend church on the night President Kennedy is shot. Point out to students that people of different cultures have unique ways of seeking solace in times of crisis and of mourning the death of a treasured person. People of Puerto Rican origin commonly practice the religion of Catholicism, and the church plays a central role in family and community life. Elena's mother's actions reflect a cultural belief that it is wrong to go out and spend time with friends when a "great man" has died.

Discuss students' own cultural beliefs and practices about how to respond to a tragedy and to mourn a person's death. What kind of clothing do they wear? Do they take time off from school and work—for example, do they sit shiva for seven days as Jewish families do? Is it considered disrespectful to show happiness and joy? From which community or religious leaders do students seek comfort?

21 Critical Viewing

Possible response: Everyone is completely engrossed in reading the newspaper. The headline screams "ASSASSINATED!" The men's expressions look serious and stunned. The background lights are also striking.

22 Reading Skill

Make Inferences

1. Read the bracketed text aloud. Point out that all the adults who are emotionally affected by the national tragedy of the president's assassination will likely reveal their emotions. Asking questions about why a character is acting in a particular manner helps the reader make inferences about how the character's outward behavior reflects his or her inner pain and turmoil.
2. **Ask** students the Reading Skill question: Based on the description of the woman's face, what do you think she was doing before Elena arrived?

   Possible response: The woman was crying because of the Kennedy assassination.

- **Monitor Progress:** Monitor students' abilities to make inferences by evaluating their responses to this Reading Skill question.
- **Reteach:** If students have difficulty understanding how to make inferences, explain this alternative approach: Making an inference is like being a literary detective—looking at evidence, asking questions, and solving a mystery. When you read you notice details, and then you ask questions to try to figure out people's motives, thoughts, feelings, and even actions based on those details. Point out that when you make inferences you use a combination of logic, common sense, and everyday experience.

21 ▲ **Critical Viewing** What is striking about this image? **[Respond]**

pain." My mother said this in Spanish and in a resigned tone that surprised me, as if she had no intention of stopping me from "heading for humiliation and pain." I started for the door. She sat in front of the TV holding a white handkerchief to her face.

I walked out to the street and around the chain-link fence that separated El Building from Eugene's house. The yard was neatly edged around the little walk that led to the door. It always amazed me how Paterson, the inner core of the city, had no apparent logic to its architecture. Small, neat, single residences like this one could be found right next to huge, dilapidated apartment buildings like El Building. My guess was that the little houses had been there first, then the immigrants had come in droves, and the monstrosities had been raised for them—the Italians, the Irish, the Jews, and now us, the Puerto Ricans and the blacks. The door was painted a deep green: *verde,* the color of hope, I had heard my mother say it: *Verde-Esperanza.*[8]

Vocabulary
dilapidated (də lap′ə dāt′ əd) *adj.* broken down

I knocked softly. A few suspenseful moments later the door opened just a crack. The red, swollen face of a woman appeared. She had a halo of red hair floating over a delicate ivory face—the face of a doll—with freckles on the nose. Her smudged eye makeup made her look unreal to me, like a mannequin seen through a warped store window.

22 **Reading Skill**
Make Inferences
Based on the description of the woman's face, what do you think she was doing before Elena arrived?

"What do you want?" Her voice was tiny and sweet-sounding, like a little girl's, but her tone was not friendly.

"I'm Eugene's friend. He asked me over. To study." I thrust out my books, a silly gesture that embarrassed me almost immediately.

8. **Verde-Esperanza** (ver′ dā es pä rän′ zä) Spanish for "green-hope."

Vocabulary Development

Vocabulary Knowledge Rating

When students have completed reading and discussing "American History," have them take out their **Vocabulary Knowledge Rating Chart** for this selection. Read the words aloud once more and have students rate their knowledge of the words again in the After Reading column. Clarify any words that are still problematic. Have students write their own definition and example or sentence in the appropriate column. Then have students complete the Vocabulary Practice activities at the end of the selection. Encourage students to use the words in further discussion and written work about this selection. Remind them that they will be accountable for these words on the **Selection Test,** ***Unit 2 Resources,*** pp. 56–58 or 59–61.

"You live there?" She pointed up to El Building, which looked particularly ugly, like a gray prison with its many dirty windows and rusty fire escapes. The woman had stepped halfway out and I could see that she wore a white nurse's uniform with "St. Joseph's Hospital" on the name tag.

"Yes. I do."

She looked intently at me for a couple of heartbeats, then said as if to herself, "I don't know how you people do it." Then directly to me: "Listen. Honey. Eugene doesn't want to study with you. He is a smart boy. Doesn't need help. You understand me. I am truly sorry if he told you you could come over. He cannot study with you. It's nothing personal. You understand? We won't be in this place much longer, no need for him to get close to people—it'll just make it harder for him later. Run back home now."

I couldn't move. I just stood there in shock at hearing these things said to me in such a honey-drenched voice. I had never heard an accent like hers, except for Eugene's softer version. It was as if she were singing me a little song.

"What's wrong? Didn't you hear what I said?" She seemed very angry, and I finally snapped out of my trance. I turned away from the green door, and heard her close it gently.

Our apartment was empty when I got home. My mother was in someone else's kitchen, seeking the solace she needed. Father would come in from his late shift at midnight. I would hear them talking softly in the kitchen for hours that night. They would not discuss their dreams for the future, or life in Puerto Rico, as they often did; that night they would talk sadly about the young widow and her two children, as if they were family. For the next few days, we would observe *luto*[9] in our apartment; that is, we would practice restraint and silence—no loud music or laughter. Some of the women of El Building would wear black for weeks.

That night, I lay in my bed trying to feel the right thing for our dead president. But the tears that came up from a deep source inside me were strictly for me. When my mother came to the door, I pretended to be sleeping. Sometime during the night, I saw from my bed the streetlight come on. It had a pink halo around it. I went to my window and pressed my face to the cool glass. Looking up

Literary Analysis
Conflict How do Eugene's mother's comments change the story's conflict?

The door was painted a deep green: *verde*, the color of hope, I had heard my mother say it: *Verde-Esperanza.*

24

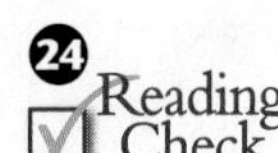

How does Eugene's mother react to Elena's visit to their house?

9. ***luto*** (lo͞o′ tō) Spanish for "mourning."

23 Literary Analysis

Conflict

1. Point out to students that not every story resolves a conflict. In many stories, the conflict or struggle continues after the story ends. Then, remind students that an *epiphany* is a sudden flash of insight by a character in a story.
2. Have students reread the bracketed text. **Ask** students the Literary Analysis question: How do Eugene's mother's comments change the story's conflict?

   Answer: Eugene's mother doesn't want him associating with Elena. Now the conflict is between Elena and Eugene's mother—and the racism she represents—instead of between Elena and her own mother. Students may mention that Eugene's mother's words bring about an epiphany in Elena.
3. **Ask** students to explain how Elena's epiphany might be the shocking awareness that she is part of a conflict that has never before touched her in such a profound way.

   Possible response: Elena's insight is that discrimination and rejection can be based on racial prejudice, which is a reality that she may confront throughout her life.

24 Reading Check

Answer: She is angry that Elena would even consider trying to enter her house. She sends Elena away.

Concept Connector

Anticipation Guide

Have students return to their **Anticipation Guides** and respond to the statements again in the After Reading column. They may do this individually or in their original pairs or groups. Then, lead a class discussion, probing for what students have learned that confirms or invalidates each statement. Encourage students to cite specific details, quotations, or other evidence from the text to support their responses to each statement.

Writing About the Big Question

Have students compare their responses to the sentence starters they completed before reading the story with their ideas afterwards. Ask them to explain whether their thoughts have changed.

Reading Skill Graphic Organizer

Have students review the graphic organizers they completed to make inferences while reading. Then have students share the graphic organizers they did and the inferences they made about the story and its characters.

25 Literary Analysis

Conflict

1. Read the bracketed text. **Ask** students the Literary Analysis question.
2. **Possible response:** The white snow reflects Elena's caring for Eugene, while the contrasting gray snow represents her disappointment and sadness at a missed opportunity for friendship.

ASSESS

Answers

Critical Thinking

Before students respond, you may wish to have them write a brief objective summary of the selection. As they answer the questions below, remind them to support their answers with evidence from the text.

1. (a) Elena describes her building as a "tenement" that is "like a monstrous jukebox." (b) She describes Eugene's house as small and neat. (c) Elena feels her home is large and noisy; Eugene's home is quiet and comfortable.
2. (a) They are going to study American history. (b) **Possible response:** The title suggests that Elena's experience of prejudice and rejection is a part of the national experience.
3. (a) She is seeking comfort in someone else's kitchen. (b) **Possible response:** Her tears are for herself because she feels her personal pain more intensely than she feels the pain of the national tragedy.
4. (a) Elena's personal conflict is much more important to her than the national one.
   (b) **Possible response:** Yes, these conflicts are necessary for Elena's growth and understanding. Without them, she would never learn about realities that will likely affect her in the future—deep-seated discrimination and racism, as well as senseless violence such as the assassination of a president. Experiencing conflict firsthand prepares Elena to face the world in an informed, rather than naïve, way.

Literary Analysis 25
Conflict How does the contrast between the white snow falling and the gray snow touching the ground reflect Elena's feelings for Eugene?

at the light I could see the white snow falling like a lace veil over its face. I did not look down to see it turning gray as it touched the ground below.

Critical Thinking

Cite textual evidence to support your responses.

1. **Key Ideas and Details (a)** In the first paragraph, what words does Elena use to describe her building? **(b)** How does she describe Eugene's house from her fire escape? **(c) Compare and Contrast:** Based on these descriptions, explain the contrast in Elena's feelings toward her own home and toward Eugene's house.
2. **Key Ideas and Details (a)** What subject is Elena going to study with Eugene? **(b) Interpret:** What other reasons might Ortiz Cofer have for calling this story "American History"?
3. **Key Ideas and Details (a) Analyze:** Where is Elena's mother and what is she doing when Elena returns from Eugene's house? **(b) Analyze:** In the last scene of the story, why does Elena say that her tears are just for herself?
4. **Integration of Knowledge and Ideas (a)** For Elena, which problem in the story—the national one or the personal one—is more important? **(b)** Are these conflicts necessary for Elena's personal growth and understanding of the world? Explain your response. *[Connect to the Big Question: Is conflict necessary?]*

Assessment Resources

Unit 2 Resources

L1 L2 EL **Selection Test A**, pp. 56–58. Administer Test A to less advanced readers.

L3 L4 EL **Selection Test B**, pp. 59–61. Administer Test B to on-level and more advanced students.

L3 L4 **Open-Book Test**, pp. 53–55. As an alternative, give the Open-Book Test.

All **Customizable Test Bank**

All **Self-tests**
Students may prepare for the **Selection Test** by taking the **Self-test** online.

All assessment resources are available at **www.PHLitOnline.com.**

After You Read American History

Literary Analysis: Conflict

1. **Key Ideas and Details** **(a)** What is the main **conflict** in this story? Explain. **(b)** Is the main conflict primarily **internal** or **external**? Explain your response.
2. **Key Ideas and Details** Use a chart like the one shown to provide specific details that reveal conflicts other than the main conflict.

Elena vs. Another Person	Elena vs. Herself

3. **Key Ideas and Details** **(a)** What realization about life's disappointments does Elena come to at the end of the story? **(b)** Does this **epiphany** lead to a clear **resolution?** Support your answer with details from the story.

Reading Skill: Make Inferences

4. **(a)** Identify three **inferences** you made while reading this story. **(b)** Identify the details you used in order to make those inferences.
5. Explain how making inferences improved your understanding of the story.

Vocabulary

Acquisition and Use Use a word from the "American History" vocabulary list on page 238 to fill in each blank. Then, explain the **context clues,** or key words and phrases, in each sentence that helped you.

1. During the blackout, the guard was more ______ than usual.
2. The ______ car had no wheels and was covered in rust.
3. She felt a ______ sense of pride as she graduated with honors.
4. The serene garden contrasted with the bustling ______.
5. We shouted with ______ when our team won the game.
6. I remained ______, even though I was desperate to tell the secret.

Word Study Use the context of the sentences and what you know about the **Latin suffix *-ant*** to explain your answer to each question.

1. Would it be easy to get along with a *compliant* person?
2. Why is a baby *reliant* upon her parents?

Word Study

The **Latin suffix *-ant*** often means "performing an action."

Apply It Explain how the suffix *-ant* contributes to the meanings of these words. Consult a dictionary if necessary.

defiant
repentant
errant

ASSESS/EXTEND

Answers

Literary Analysis

1. (a) **Possible response:** The main conflict is Elena's struggle to find happiness by becoming a part of Eugene's life. (b) The conflict is primarily internal because it focuses on Elena's feelings.
2. **Possible response:** Elena vs. another person—Elena's conflict with her mother's expectations of her occurs when Elena chooses to visit Eugene instead of attending church with her mother. **Elena vs. herself**—Elena is bothered by her inability to "feel the right thing" for the dead president.

For other sample answers, see ***Graphic Organizer Transparencies,* Literary Analysis Graphic Organizer A**, p. 43, and the **Additional Answers** section.

3. (a) Elena realizes that social issues, such as prejudice, can crush her private hopes and dreams. (b) This epiphany does not lead to a clear resolution: It ends with Elena crying after her rejection by Eugene's mother, with no clear way for her to resolve the larger social conflict she has entered.

Reading Skill

4. (a) **Possible response:** Inferences might include the ideas that the people love the president, that Elena respects learning, and that Eugene's mother is prejudiced. (b) **Possible response:** The people feel anguish about the president's assassination, Elena is interested in reading, and Eugene's mother does not want Eugene to study with Elena.
5. **Possible response:** Making inferences gives readers a more in-depth look into characters and events.

Vocabulary

Acquisition and Use

1. vigilant
2. dilapidated
3. profound
4. tenement
5. elation
6. discreet

Word Study

Sample answers:

1. Yes. The suffix *-ant* means "performing an action" and *compliant* means "performing the action of compliance." A *compliant* person is easily swayed.
2. The suffix *-ant* means "performing an action" and *reliant* means "performing the action of reliance." A baby is *reliant* upon her parents because babies are helpless and can't do anything for themselves.

Word Study: Apply It

Sample answers:

If you are *defiant,* you are performing an act of defiance such as breaking the law. If you are *repentant*, you are performing an act of repentance or penance. Someone who is *errant* is performing the act of wandering.

EXTEND/ASSESS

Answers

Conventions

1. Introduce the skill, using the instruction on the student page.
2. Discuss the definitions and the examples in the chart.

Think Aloud: Model the Skill

Model a way to form the principal parts of regular verbs. Say to students:

I know that a verb expresses what a subject is or does. Suppose I want to describe something Carolina does now. I use a present tense verb such as *walk, talk, expect,* or *observe.* If I want to describe something Carolina is in the middle of doing, I use a present participle verb such as *is walking* or *is talking.* If I want to describe what Carolina did yesterday, I use past or past participle verbs such as *walked* or *has walked.* Sometimes I have to double a final consonant or drop a final *e* before adding an ending, as in *stopped* or *living.*

PH WRITING COACH Grade 9

Students will find instruction on and practice with active and passive voice in Chapter 17, section 4.

Practice A

1. discover
2. awaken
3. run
4. confront

Reading Application

Sample answers:

1. Not four yards, admitted Rainsford; "I admit, not four yards," said Rainsford.
2. Don't talk rot; He talked rot.
3. He strained his eyes in the direction . . .; He is straining his eyes in the direction . . .
4. He struggled up to the surface . . . .; He is struggling up to the surface . . .

Practice B

1. saddened
2. thinking
3. moved
4. study

Writing Application

Sample answers:

1. Each man is reading a newspaper.
2. Papers sold out that awful day.
3. Headlines scream "Assassinated!"
4. He has read the news with horror.

PERFORMANCE TASKS

Integrated Language Skills

The Most Dangerous Game • American History

Conventions: Regular Verbs

The **principal parts** of a verb are the present, the present participle, the past, and the past participle.

Most verbs in the English language are **regular verbs** that use predictable patterns. By using various **principal parts,** you can show how actions take place in time and add variety and interest to sentences.

The **present** tense describes action happening now or in the future. The **present participle** is formed by adding *-ing* to the present form. The **future** tense is achieved by adding *will* to the present form as a helping verb. The **past** tense describes events that happened already. To form the past and **past participle,** add *-ed* to the present form (the participle uses *have, has,* or *had* as a helping verb). If the present form ends in *-e,* that *-e* is usually dropped when adding an ending. Finally, the **present progressive** shows continuing action and uses a form of *be* as a helping verb.

Present	Present Participle	Past	Past Participle
inspect	(is) inspecting	inspected	(has) inspected
race	(is) racing	raced	(has) raced

Practice A Identify the principal part of each underlined verb.

1. Rainsford <u>discovered</u> a mysterious island.
2. The gunshots had <u>awakened</u> the night.
3. Now he is <u>running</u> toward a cliff.
4. Soon, he will <u>confront</u> the foe in his fight.

Reading Application Find four sentences in "The Most Dangerous Game" that use regular verbs. Change each sentence by using a different principal part.

Practice B Complete each sentence with a regular verb, using the form in parentheses.

1. Kennedy's death (past) Elena's mother.
2. Elena is (present participle) about Eugene.
3. Eugene's family has (past participle) next door.
4. Elena will (future) with him after school.

Writing Application Look back to the image on page 250 in "American History." Write four sentences about it using a different principal part for each.

PH WRITING COACH Further instruction and practice are available in *Prentice Hall Writing Coach.*

Extend the Lesson

Sentence Modeling

Choose the sentence given from the selection students have read:

He struggled up to the surface and tried to cry out, but the wash from the speeding yacht slapped him in the face and the salt water in his open mouth made him gag and strangle. ("The Most Dangerous Game")

They entered the double ropes in pairs and exited without tripping or missing a beat. ("American History")

Ask students what they notice about the sentence.

Elicit that the sentence contains several verbs. Have students identify each verb's principal part. Then, ask what else they notice. ("The Most Dangerous Game": The conjunctions *and* and *but* pile up actions in a compound sentence.) ("American History": The opposite verbs—*entered* and *exited*—provide symmetry when describing the jump roping.)

Have students imitate the sentence in a sentence on a topic of their own choosing, matching each grammatical and stylistic feature discussed. Collect the sentences, and share them with the class.

Writing

Narrative Text Each of these stories may leave readers with more questions than answers. Write an **alternative ending** to "American History" or "The Most Dangerous Game."

- Create an ending that flows logically from earlier events.
- Focus on presenting a satisfactory resolution to the conflict.
- Make your ending consistent with your understanding of the characters.
- Include dialogue and details to show how the characters feel and think.

Grammar Application As you write, use the principal parts of verbs correctly to show actions as they occur in time.

Writing Workshop: *Work in Progress*

Prewriting for Narration: Short Story To prepare for writing a short story, create a Character Profile. Name a character and develop information about his or her gender, age, appearance, background, interests, and longings. Save the profile in your portfolio.

Speaking and Listening

Presentation of Ideas In a group, prepare an **oral presentation** using print and nonprint media.

- If you read "American History," discuss the effect of President Kennedy's assassination upon the American public.
- If you read "The Most Dangerous Game," discuss two or three big-game species mentioned in the story. Include key facts about each one, including any threats that the species faces today.

Follow these steps to write a speech on the topic:

- Choose questions that the speech should answer. Then, gather information from primary and secondary sources.
- Organize the information that you wish to share. You may need to do additional research to supplement what you already have.
- Write an introduction and conclusion for the speech. The introduction should grab the audience's attention and the conclusion should summarize key points in a memorable way.
- Use vivid language to make the speech interesting.
- Gather images, either print or nonprint, that illustrate the speech and decide how you want to display them.

Practice your presentation. Rehearse to make sure that you can operate multimedia equipment. If necessary, revise your presentation so that points will be clearer or more interesting.

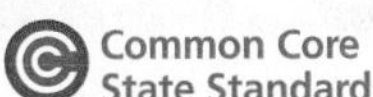

L.9-10.1, L.9-10.6; W.9-10.3.e; SL.9-10.4
[For the full wording of the standards, see page 210.]

Use this prewriting activity to prepare for the **Writing Workshop** on page 306.

www.PHLitOnline.com

- Interactive graphic organizers
- Grammar tutorial
- Interactive journals

EXTEND/ASSESS

Writing

1. Review the assignment, using the instruction on the student page.
2. To guide students in writing an alternative ending, give them **Support for Writing**, p. 51 in ***Unit 2 Resources.***
3. To evaluate students' presentations, use the rubrics for **Short Story**, pp. 226–227 in ***Professional Development Guidebook.*** In addition, you might evaluate how well students respond to the characters' plight and in what way they decide to resolve the conflict.

Grammar Application

Have students check their drafts to make sure they have formed the principle parts of regular verbs correctly.

Six Traits Focus

✓	Ideas		Word Choice
✓	Organization		Sentence Fluency
	Voice		Conventions

PH WRITING COACH Grade 9

Students will find instruction on and practice with narration and short story writing in Chapter 6.

Writing Workshop
Work in Progress

Have students save their completed Character Profiles in their portfolios. They will use their profiles later as they continue this Work in Progress assignment (see p. 281). The assignment prepares them to complete the Writing Workshop (see pp. 306–311).

Speaking and Listening

1. Review the assignment, using the instruction on the student page.
2. To support students' work on the assignment, have them complete the **Support for Extend Your Learning** page (***Unit 2 Resources,*** p. 52).

Teaching Resources

Unit 2 Resources

L3 L4 EL **Integrated Language Skills: Grammar,** p. 50

L3 L4 EL **Support for Writing,** p. 51

L3 L4 **Support for Extend Your Learning,** p. 52

L4 **Enrichment,** pp. 31, 49

Enriched Online Student Edition
Available under After You Read for this selection:

All **Interactive Grammar Tutorial**

L3 L4 **Internet Research Activity**

Professional Development Guidebook
Rubrics for Self-Assessment: Short Story, pp. 226–227

PHLit Online! All print and digital resources are available at **www.PHLitOnline.com.** Online resources accessible by students are noted on the student page.

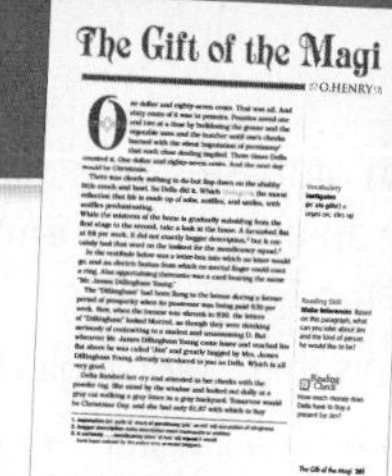
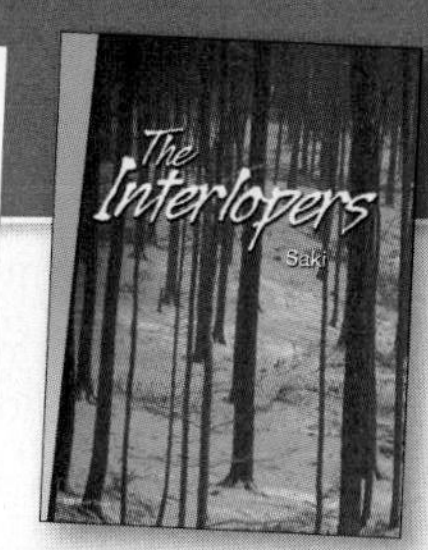

✓ The Gift of the Magi • ✓✓ The Interlopers

Lesson Pacing Guide

DAY 1 Preteach

- Administer the Reading and Vocabulary Warm-ups (*Unit 2 Resources*, pp. 62–65 or 80–83) as necessary.
- Introduce the Reading Skill: Make Inferences.
- Introduce the Literary Analysis concept: Irony.
- Distribute copies of the appropriate graphic organizer for the Reading Skill (*Graphic Organizer Transparencies*, pp. 45–47).
- Distribute copies of the appropriate graphic organizer for Literary Analysis (*Graphic Organizer Transparencies*, pp. 48–50).
- Teach the selection vocabulary.
- Introduce the Word Study skill.

DAYS 2–3 Preteach/Teach

- Build background with the Background feature.
- Develop thematic vocabulary and thematic thinking with Writing About the Big Question.
- Prepare students to read with the Activating Prior Knowledge activities (TE).
- Informally monitor comprehension while students read.
- Use the Reading Check questions to confirm comprehension.
- Develop students' ability to make inferences, using the Reading Skill questions.
- Develop students' understanding of Irony, using the Literary Analysis questions.
- Reinforce vocabulary with the Vocabulary notes.
- Reinforce unit focus standards using the Spiral Review prompts.

DAY 4 Assess

- Assess students' comprehension and mastery of the skills by having them answer the Critical Thinking, Reading Skill, and Literary Analysis questions.
- Have students complete the Vocabulary Practice activities.
- Have students complete the Word Study activities.

DAY 5 Extend/Assess

- Have students complete the Conventions lesson.
- Have students complete the Writing activity and write a news report. (You may assign as homework.)
- Extend learning by having students complete the Speaking and Listening activity, a debate. As an alternative, assign them "Buy Me This, Buy Me That" or "The Possibility of Peace" in *Reality Central*.
- Administer Selection Test A or B (*Unit 2 Resources*, pp. 74–79 or 95–100).

Common Core State Standards

Reading Literature 1. Cite strong and thorough textual evidence to support analysis of what the text says explicitly as well as inferences drawn from the text.

Writing 3. Write narratives to develop real or imagined experiences or events using effective technique, well-chosen details, and well-structured event sequences.
3.c. Use a variety of techniques to sequence events so that they build on one another to create a coherent whole.

Speaking and Listening 4. Present information, findings, and supporting evidence clearly, concisely, and logically such that listeners can follow the line of reasoning and the organization, development, substance, and style are appropriate to purpose, audience, and task.

Language 1. Demonstrate command of the conventions of standard English grammar and usage when writing or speaking.

Additional Standards Practice
***Common Core Companion*, pp. 28–29; 48–49**

Daily Block Scheduling
Each day in this Lesson Pacing Guide represents a 40–50 minute period. Teachers using block scheduling may combine days to revise pacing. In addition, teachers may differentiate and support core instruction by integrating components for extended and intensive support as students require. See the Guide to Selected Leveled Resources (facing page).

Guide to Selected Leveled Resources

RTI Tier 1 (students performing on level)		✓ More Accessible The Gift of the Magi	✓✓ More Complex The Interlopers
Warm Up	**Practice, model,** and **monitor** fluency, working **with the whole class** or **in groups.**	**Vocabulary** and **Reading Warm-ups B,** ***Unit 2 Resources,*** pp. 62–63, 65	**Vocabulary** and **Reading Warm-ups B,** ***Unit 2 Resources,*** pp. 80–81, 83
Comprehension/Skills	**Support** and **monitor** comprehension and skills development, having students complete the activities, graphic organizers, and interactive prompts **independently** or **as a class.**	• ***Reader's Notebook,*** adapted instruction and full selection EL ***Reader's Notebook: English Learner's Version,*** adapted instruction and adapted selection • **Reading Skill Graphic Organizer B,** ***Graphic Organizer Transparencies,*** p. 47 • **Literary Analysis Graphic Organizer B,** ***Graphic Organizer Transparencies,*** p. 50	• ***Reader's Notebook,*** adapted instruction and summary EL ***Reader's Notebook: English Learner's Version,*** adapted instruction and summary • **Reading Skill Graphic Organizer B,** ***Graphic Organizer Transparencies,*** p. 47 • **Literary Analysis Graphic Organizer B,** ***Graphic Organizer Transparencies,*** p. 50
Monitor Progress	**Monitor** student progress with the differentiated curriculum-based assessment in the *Unit Resources.*	• **Selection Test B,** ***Unit 2 Resources,*** pp. 77–79 • **Open-Book Test,** ***Unit 2 Resources,*** pp. 71–73	• **Selection Test B,** ***Unit 2 Resources,*** pp. 98–100 • **Open-Book Test,** ***Unit 2 Resources,*** pp. 92–94
Assess/ Screen	**Assess** student progress using Benchmark Test 3.	• **Benchmark Test 3,** ***Unit 2 Resources,*** pp. 120–125	• **Benchmark Test 3,** ***Unit 2 Resources,*** pp. 120–125

RTI Tier 2 (students requiring intervention)		✓ More Accessible The Gift of the Magi	✓✓ More Complex The Interlopers
Warm Up	**Practice, model,** and **monitor** fluency **in groups** or **with individuals.**	• **Vocabulary and Reading Warm-ups A,** ***Unit 2 Resources,*** pp. 62–64 • ***Reality Central,*** "Buy Me This, Buy Me That" • ***Hear It!*** **Audio CD (adapted text)**	• **Vocabulary and Reading Warm-ups A,** ***Unit 2 Resources,*** pp. 80–82 • ***Reality Central,*** "The Possibility of Peace" • ***Hear It!*** **Audio CD**
Comprehension/Skills	• **Support** and **monitor** comprehension and skills development, working **in small groups** or **with individuals.** • **Pair** students with more advanced peers and have them complete the writing activity in the *Real-World Writing Journal.* • As students complete the selection in the appropriate version of the *Reader's Notebook,* **monitor** comprehension frequently with group questions and individual instruction. • **Model** strategies while guiding students in completing the activities and prompts in the *Reader's Notebook,* as well as the graphic organizers. • **Practice** skills and **monitor** mastery with the *Reading Kit* worksheets.	• ***Real-World Writing Journal,*** Lesson 3, pp. 44–47 • ***Reader's Notebook: Adapted Version,*** adapted instruction and adapted selection EL ***Reader's Notebook: English Learner's Version,*** adapted instruction and adapted selection • **Reading Skill Graphic Organizer A,** ***Graphic Organizer Transparencies,*** p. 45 • **Literary Analysis Graphic Organizer A,** ***Graphic Organizer Transparencies,*** p. 48 • ***Reading Kit,*** Practice worksheets, pp. 54, 58, 62, 66, 72	• ***Real-World Writing Journal,*** Lesson 4, pp. 48–51 • ***Reader's Notebook: Adapted Version,*** adapted instruction and summary EL ***Reader's Notebook: English Learner's Version,*** adapted instruction and summary • **Reading Skill Graphic Organizer A,** ***Graphic Organizer Transparencies,*** p. 46 • **Literary Analysis Graphic Organizer A,** ***Graphic Organizer Transparencies,*** p. 49 • ***Reading Kit,*** Practice worksheets, pp. 54, 58, 62, 66, 72
Monitor Progress	**Monitor** student progress with the differentiated curriculum-based assessment in the *Unit Resources* and in the *Reading Kit.*	• **Selection Test A,** ***Unit 2 Resources,*** pp. 74–76 • ***Reading Kit,*** Assess worksheets, pp. 55, 59, 63, 67, 73	• **Selection Test A,** ***Unit 2 Resources,*** pp. 95–97 • ***Reading Kit,*** Assess worksheets, pp. 55, 59, 63, 67, 73
Assess/ Screen	**Assess** student progress using Benchmark Test 3.	• **Benchmark Test 3,** ***Unit 2 Resources,*** pp. 120–125	• **Benchmark Test 3,** ***Unit 2 Resources,*** pp. 120–125

TIER 3 Tier 3 intervention may require consultation with the student's special-education or dyslexia specialist. For additional support, see the Tier 2 activities and resources listed above.

One-on-one teaching   Group work   Whole class instruction   Independent work   A Assessment

For a complete guide to selection support, including support for Advanced students, see the Overview of Resources in the frontmatter.

✓The Gift of The Magi
✓✓The Interlopers

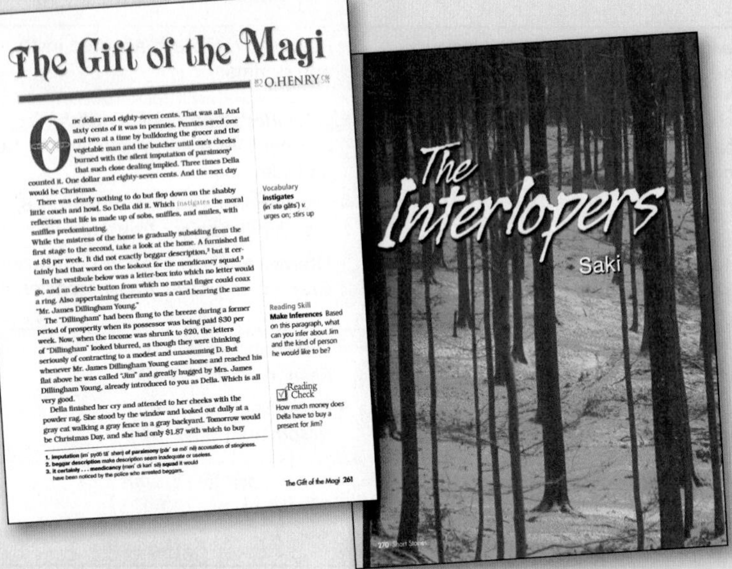

RESOURCES FOR:

- L1 Special-Needs Students
- L2 Below-Level Students (Tier 2)
- L3 On-Level Students (Tier 1)
- L4 Advanced Students (Tier 1)
- EL English Learners
- All All Students

Vocabulary/Fluency/Prior Knowledge

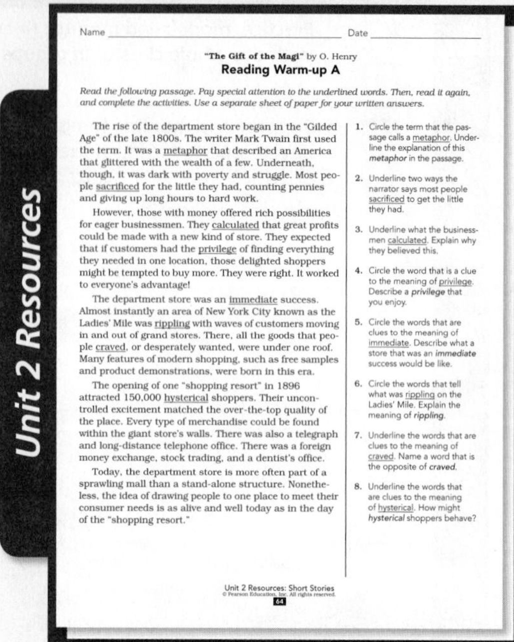

EL L1 L2 **Reading Warm-ups A and B,** pp. 64–65, 82–83

Also available for these selections:

EL L1 L2 **Vocabulary Warm-ups A and B,** pp. 62–63, 80–81

All **Writing About the Big Question,** pp. 66, 84

All **Vocabulary Builder,** pp. 69, 87

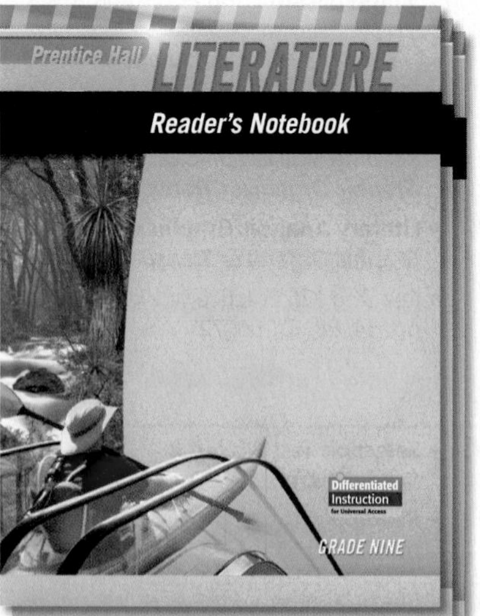

Reader's Notebooks

Pre- and postreading pages for both selections, as well as "The Gift of the Magi," appear in an interactive format in the *Reader's Notebooks.* Each *Notebook* is differentiated for a different group of learners. The selections in the Adapted and English Learner's versions are abridged.

L2 L3 ***Reader's Notebook***

L1 ***Reader's Notebook: Adapted Version***

EL ***Reader's Notebook: English Learner's Version***

EL ***Reader's Notebook: Spanish Version***

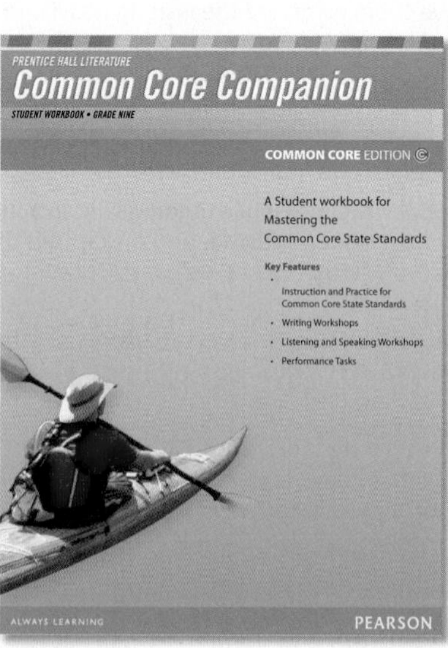

Common Core Companion

Additional instruction and practice for each Common Core State Standard

Selection Support

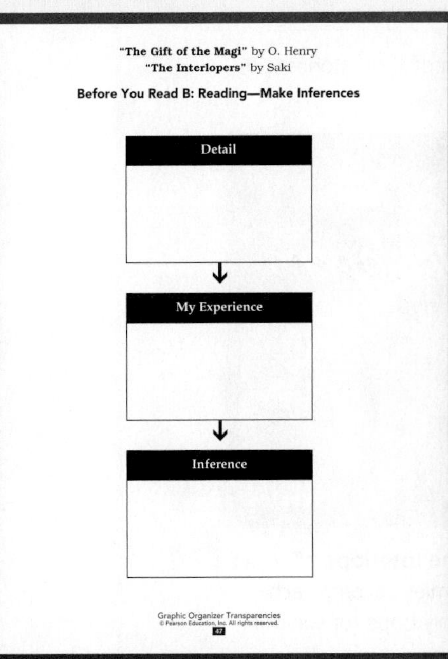
Graphic Organizer Transparencies

"The Gift of the Magi" by O. Henry
"The Interlopers" by Saki

Before You Read B: Reading—Make Inferences

Detail

My Experience

Inference

Graphic Organizer Transparencies
© Pearson Education, Inc. All rights reserved.
47

EL L3 **Reading: Graphic Organizer B,** p. 47

Also available for these selections:

EL L1 L2 **Reading: Graphic Organizer A,** pp. 45, 46 (partially filled in)

EL L1 L2 **Literary Analysis: Graphic Organizer A,** pp. 48, 49 (partially filled in)

EL L3 **Literary Analysis: Graphic Organizer B,** p. 50

Skills Development/Extension

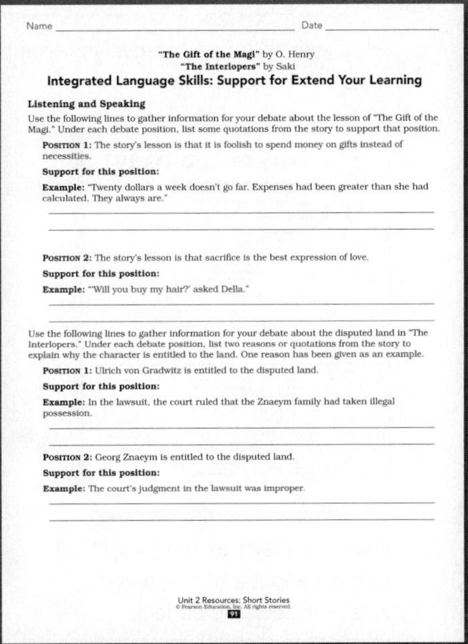
Unit 2 Resources

Name ______________ Date ______________

"The Gift of the Magi" by O. Henry
"The Interlopers" by Saki

Integrated Language Skills: Support for Extend Your Learning

Listening and Speaking

Use the following lines to gather information for your debate about the lesson of "The Gift of the Magi." Under each debate position, list some quotations from the story to support that position.

Position 1: The story's lesson is that it is foolish to spend money on gifts instead of necessities.

Support for this position:

Example: "Twenty dollars a week doesn't go far. Expenses had been greater than she had calculated. They always are."

Position 2: The story's lesson is that sacrifice is the best expression of love.

Support for this position:

Example: "Will you buy my hair?" asked Della."

Use the following lines to gather information for your debate about the disputed land in "The Interlopers." Under each debate position, list two reasons or quotations from the story to explain why the character is entitled to the land. One reason has been given as an example.

Position 1: Ulrich von Gradwitz is entitled to the disputed land.

Support for this position:

Example: In the lawsuit, the court ruled that the Znaeym family had taken illegal possession.

Position 2: Georg Znaeym is entitled to the disputed land.

Support for this position:

Example: The court's judgment in the lawsuit was improper.

Unit 2 Resources: Short Stories
© Pearson Education, Inc. All rights reserved.
91

L3 L4 **Support for Extend Your Learning,** p. 91

Also available for these selections:

All **Literary Analysis: Irony,** pp. 67, 85

All **Reading: Make Inferences,** pp. 68, 86

L4 **Enrichment,** pp. 70, 88

EL L3 L4 **Grammar,** p. 89

EL L3 L4 **Support for Writing,** p. 90

Assessment

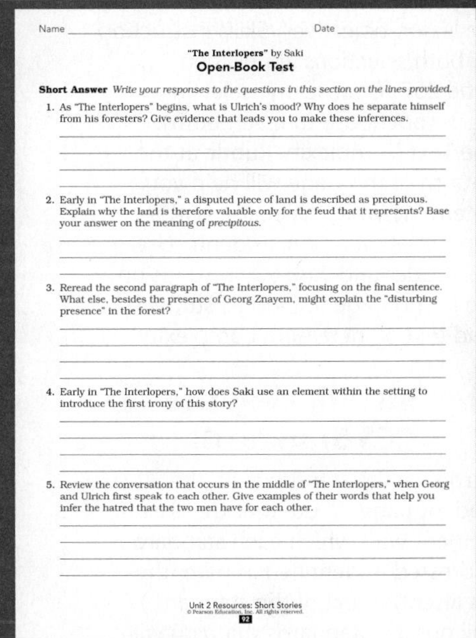
Name ______________ Date ______________

"The Interlopers" by Saki
Open-Book Test

Short Answer *Write your responses to the questions in this section on the lines provided.*

1. As "The Interlopers" begins, what is Ulrich's mood? Why does he separate himself from his foresters? Give evidence that leads you to make these inferences.

2. Early in "The Interlopers," a disputed piece of land is described as precipitous. Explain why the land is therefore valuable only for the feud that it represents? Base your answer on the meaning of *precipitous.*

3. Reread the second paragraph of "The Interlopers," focusing on the final sentence. What else, besides the presence of Georg Znayem, might explain the "disturbing presence" in the forest?

4. Early in "The Interlopers," how does Saki use an element within the setting to introduce the first irony of this story?

5. Review the conversation that occurs in the middle of "The Interlopers," when Georg and Ulrich first speak to each other. Give examples of their words that help you infer the hatred that the two men have for each other.

Unit 2 Resources: Short Stories
© Pearson Education, Inc. All rights reserved.
92

L3 L4 **Open-Book Test,** pp. 71–73, 92–94

Also available for these selections:

EL L1 L2 **Selection Test A,** pp. 74–76, 95–97

EL L3 L4 **Selection Test B,** pp. 77–79, 98–100

PHLit Online!
www.PHLitOnline.com

- complete narrated selection text
- a thematically related video with writing prompt
- an interactive graphic organizer
- highlighting feature
- access to all student print resources, adapted to individual student needs
- Spanish and English summaries
- adapted selection translations in Spanish

Online Resources: All print materials are also available online.

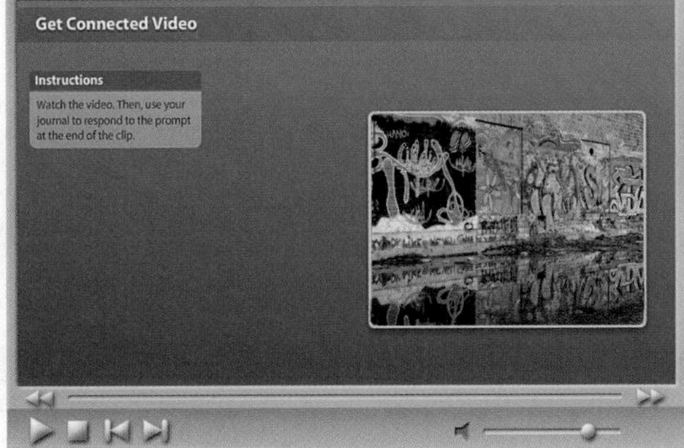

Get Connected! (thematic video with writing prompt)

Also available:

Background Video

All videos are available in Spanish.

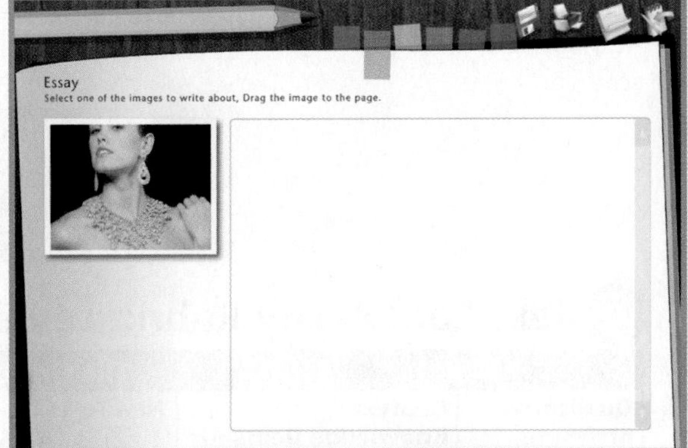

Writer's Journal (with graphics feature)

Also available:

Vocabulary Central (tools, activities, and songs for studying vocabulary)

DIFFERENTIATE/PRETEACH

❶ Leveled Texts

You may use either "The Gift of the Magi" or "The Interlopers" to meet the lesson objectives. Skills instruction for both selections appears on page 257. Choose one selection to teach (or choose to teach both). The Text Complexity Rubric at the bottom of this page will help you determine which selection is more appropriate for your students. Use the Reader and Task Suggestions on the facing page to help all students read text of increasing complexity.

❷ © Introducing the CCS Standards

Introduce the standards on the student page. (Note that the lesson element with which each standard is addressed is identified in parentheses after the text of the standard.) Call out the standards that you will cover with the selections, explaining to students what each requires and how they will address it as they work through the selection you have chosen. Standards labeled "Spiral Review" are introduced in the Literary Analysis Workshop for this unit.

Before You Read

The Gift of the Magi • The Interlopers

❶ © Leveled Texts

Build your skills and improve your comprehension of short stories with texts of increasing complexity.

EXEMPLAR TEXT

The Gift of the Magi

O. HENRY

Read **"The Gift of the Magi"** to learn about a husband and wife who seek the perfect present for each other.

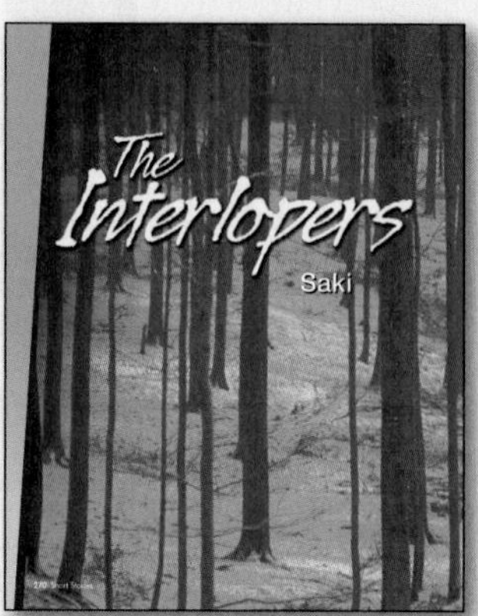

Read **"The Interlopers"** to see how enemies become each other's only hope for survival.

❷ © Common Core State Standards

Meet these standards with either **"The Gift of the Magi"** (p. 260) or **"The Interlopers"** (p. 270).

Reading Literature

1. Cite strong and thorough textual evidence to support analysis of what the text says explicitly as well as inferences drawn from the text. *(Reading Skill: Make Inferences)*

Writing

3. Write narratives to develop real or imagined experiences or events using effective technique, well-chosen details, and well-structured event sequences. *(Writing: News Report)*

3.c. Use a variety of techniques to sequence events so that they build on one another to create a coherent whole.

Speaking and Listening

4. Present information, findings, and supporting evidence clearly, concisely, and logically such that listeners can follow the line of reasoning and the organization, development, substance, and style are appropriate to purpose, audience, and task. *(Speaking and Listening: Debate)*

Language

1. Demonstrate command of the conventions of standard English grammar and usage when writing or speaking. *(Conventions: Irregular Verbs)*

256 Short Stories

© Text Complexity Rubric: Leveled Texts

Text complexity is determined by both qualitative and quantitative measures. For this reason, the quantitative measure of a more complex selection may be lower than that of a more accessible selection.

		✓ The Gift of the Magi	✓✓ The Interlopers
Qualitative Measures	**Context/ Knowledge Demands**	New York City, early 1900s 1 (2) 3 4 5	Carpathian Mountains in Central Europe, early 1900s 1 (2) 3 4 5
	Structure/Language Conventionality and Clarity	Period-specific vocabulary is footnoted; short sentences 1 (2) 3 4 5	Challenging vocabulary; long, complicated sentences 1 2 3 (4) 5
	Levels of Meaning/ Purpose/Concept Level	Accessible concept (material sacrifices made for love) 1 2 (3) 4 5	Accessible concept (bitter family feud over land) 1 2 (3) 4 5
Quantitative Measures	**Text Length**	Word Count: 2,066	Word Count: 2,153
	Lexile	890L	1230L
Overall Complexity		✓ **More accessible**	✓✓ **More complex**

❸ Literary Analysis: Irony

Irony is a *contradiction* between appearance and reality—it is the difference between what is expected and what actually happens.

In **situational irony,** something happens in the story that contradicts the expectations of a character or the reader. For example, a runner who trains hard would be expected to do well in a race. It would be ironic if she trained so hard that she overslept and missed the race.

A **surprise ending** often presents a situational irony. The turn of events may be startling, but writers using irony usually build clues into the story that make the ending logical, just the same.

Ironies and surprise endings usually help convey the story's *theme*, or message. As you read, watch for surprises and think about what each one may mean.

❹ Reading Skill: Make Inferences

An **inference** is a logical assumption that you make based on details in a text. The author may state some information directly, but most of the ideas in a story are suggested through details. When reading short stories, **use your own prior knowledge and experience** to make inferences. As you learn, watch movies and plays, and observe the world every day, you gather knowledge and experiences.

- When you read something new, look for ways in which the characters and situations resemble ones you have seen before.
- Then, apply that knowledge and experience to make inferences.

❺ Using the Strategy: Inferences Chart

Use a **flowchart** like this one to make inferences as you read.

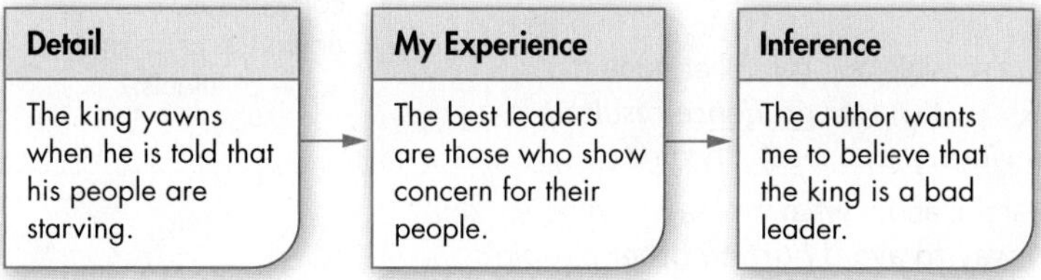

Detail
The king yawns when he is told that his people are starving.
My Experience
The best leaders are those who show concern for their people.
Inference
The author wants me to believe that the king is a bad leader.

PHLit Online!
www.PHLitOnline.com

Hear It!
- Selection summary audio
- Selection audio

See It!
- Get Connected video
- Background video
- More about the author
- Vocabulary flashcards

Do It!
- Interactive journals
- Interactive graphic organizers
- Self-test
- Internet activity
- Grammar tutorial
- Interactive vocabulary games

PRETEACH

❸ Literary Analysis

Irony

1. Introduce the skill, using the instruction on the student page.
2. Tell students that they will recognize different types of irony as they read.

Think Aloud: Model the Skill

Model the skill of understanding irony. Say to students:

To help me understand irony, I think of a disaster movie. If people are trapped under rubble after a disaster, they might look to the strongest character to help them escape. Now suppose the weakest and most frightened character uses careful thinking instead of strength to find an escape. Since this is not what the characters or I expect to happen, this surprise ending is ironic. When I read short stories, I look for ironies to appreciate.

❹ Reading Skill

Make Inferences

1. Introduce the skill, using the instruction on the student page.
2. Tell students that they will practice making inferences.

❺ Using the Strategy

Give students a copy of either **Reading Skill Graphic Organizer A** or **B** (*Graphic Organizer Transparencies*, pp. 45–47) to record details and inferences. Use the examples in **Reading Skill Graphic Organizer A,** which is partially filled in, to model the process of completing the organizer.

Ⓒ Text Complexity: Reader and Task Suggestions

✓ The Gift of the Magi		✓✓ The Interlopers	
Preparing to Read the Text	**Leveled Tasks**	**Preparing to Read the Text**	**Leveled Tasks**
• Using the Background information on TE p. 259, discuss how the value of money has changed since in the early 1900s. • Discuss the emphasis our culture places on giving expensive gifts. • Guide students to use Multidraft Reading strategies (TE p. 259).	*Levels of Meaning* If students will have difficulty with meaning, ask them to first read to identify what each character gives up and what each purchases as a gift. Then, have them reread to identify how the characters felt about the gifts they bought. *Synthesizing* If students will not have difficulty with meaning, have students take notes on how O. Henry develops the theme of self-sacrifice. Have them make a connection to the title.	• Referring to the Background note on TE p. 269, discuss how feuds develop and how they can affect families in unexpected ways. • Review strategies for reading long and complex sentences. • Guide students to use Multidraft Reading strategies (TE p. 269).	*Structure/Language* If students will have difficulty with long complex sentences, have them read and note sentences that were difficult to understand due to their length or complexity. Review sentences, offering clarification. *Analyzing* If students will not have difficulty with long, complex sentences, have them define the word *interloper* and then decide whom or what the story title refers to.

PRETEACH

❶ Writing About the Big Question

1. Review the assignment with the class.
2. **Ask** students to give examples of times when they or someone they know wanted to buy a special gift and didn't have enough money.
3. Have students complete the sentence starters. (**Possible response:** When money is tight, it may be hard to show you appreciate others because you cannot afford to buy them gifts. To resolve this problem, you might try to get more money or give a gift of time.) Review responses as a class.
4. Remind students that their answers will help them think about the Big Question, "Is conflict necessary?"

While You Read

Tell students that as they read, they should think about the similarities in the ways that Della and Jim overcome their Christmastime conflict.

❷ Vocabulary

1. Have students preview the selection vocabulary.
2. For each word, have students say the word aloud.
3. Then, use the word in a sentence that defines the word.
4. Finally, repeat your definitional sentence or a similar sentence with the word missing and have the class "fill in the blank" chorally. Here are some examples:

   Instigates means starts or stirs up. Fights don't usually start on their own; rather, they are something that a person starts, or [students say "instigates"].

   Depreciate means to decrease in value. Diamonds and gold are good investments because they usually do not lose value, or [students say "depreciate"].

❸ Word Study

1. Introduce the skill, using the instruction in the box.
2. Ask students to use the meaning of the prefix *de-* to define *depreciate*. (**Answer:** The prefix *de-* means "down" and something that *depreciates* goes down in value.)

Making Connections | The Gift of the Magi

❶ Writing About the Big Question

In "The Gift of the Magi," Jim and Della want to exchange Christmas presents, but money is an issue. Use these sentence starters to develop your ideas about the Big Question.

When money is tight, it may be hard to show you **appreciate** others because __________. To resolve this problem, you might ______ or ______.

While You Read Think about the similarities in the ways that Della and Jim try to overcome their Christmastime conflict.

❷ Vocabulary

Read each word and its definition. Decide whether you know the word well, know it a little bit, or do not know it at all. After you read, see how your knowledge of each word has increased.

- **instigates** (in′ stə gāts′) *v.* urges on; stirs up (p. 261) ***When he is not watched carefully, he instigates trouble.*** *instigation n.*
- **depreciate** (dē prē′ shē āt′) *v.* reduce in value (p. 262) ***Items that do not depreciate are good investments.*** *depreciation n.*
- **cascade** (kas kād′) *n.* a small steep waterfall; anything suggesting such a waterfall (p. 262) ***Her hair flowed down her back like a cascade.*** *cascade v. cascading v.*
- **faltered** (fôl′ tərd) *v.* acted hesitantly; showed uncertainty (p. 262) ***The manager faltered in her decision to hire the inexperienced worker.*** *falter v.*
- **prudence** (pro͞o′ dəns) *n.* a sensible and careful attitude that makes you avoid some risks (p. 263) ***Her prudence resulted in a substantial amount of savings.*** *prudent adj. imprudence n.*
- **discreet** (di skrēt′) *adj.* careful about what one says or does (p. 265) ***Being discreet is a good way to avoid hurting other people's feelings.*** *discretion n. indiscreet adj. indiscretion adj.*

❸ Word Study

The **Latin prefix *de-*** has various meanings, including "down."

In this story, Della's hair is said to **depreciate** a queen's treasures. Her hair is so lovely that, by comparison, it brings down the price and value of jewels.

Vocabulary Development

Vocabulary Knowledge Rating

Create a **Vocabulary Knowledge Rating Chart** (***Professional Development Guidebook***, p. 33) for this selection. Include the selection vocabulary and the Big Question word that appears in the Writing About the Big Question sentence starters on this page. (The Big Question vocabulary is introduced on pp. 194–195.)

Give students a copy of the chart. Read the words aloud, and have students mark their rating in the Before Reading column. Urge them to be alert to these words as they read and discuss the selection.

Tally how many students think they know a word to gauge how much instruction to provide. As students read and discuss the selection, point out the words and their context.

Vocabulary Central, featuring tools, activities, and songs for studying vocabulary, is available at **www.PHLitOnline.com.**

Meet O. Henry (1862–1910)

Author of The Gift of the Magi

William Sydney Porter, better known as O. Henry, dropped out of school at sixteen to work in his uncle's drugstore. In 1882, he left his home in North Carolina to seek his fortune in Texas. He worked on a ranch, then at a bank, and eventually started writing sketches. He became a reporter, columnist, and cartoonist for the *Houston Post.*

Writing Stories in Prison In 1896, Porter was jailed for his involvement in a bank scandal. While in prison, he began writing stories. When he was released, Porter changed his name to O. Henry, moved to New York City, and developed into one of America's most celebrated writers of short fiction.

Did You Know?

Since 1919, the O. Henry Awards for short fiction have been given to the best short stories written each year.

❹

BACKGROUND FOR THE STORY

The Value of Money

In a story written years ago, prices may seem unrealistically low. The reason is inflation—the steady increase in the prices of most things over time. In this story, written around 1905, $32 is roughly one month's rent for Della and Jim. For most people today, $32 would not even cover one week's rent.

Daily Bellringer

For each class during which you will teach this selection, have students complete one of the five Sentence Modeling activities for Week 8 in the ***Daily Bellringer Activities*** booklet.

❹ Background

The Value of Money

Explain to students that in order to convert the sums of money in this story to present-day prices, they will have to multiply them by anywhere from 10 to 100. The story is set in New York City in about 1905. In that time and place, a newspaper cost from 1¢ to 3¢, and a ride on the brand-new subway cost 5¢. In 2005, the daily *New York Times* cost $1, and the subway fare was $2. The monthly rent of many one-room Manhattan apartments was close to 50 times more than the $32 Jim and Della pay.

Multidraft Reading

This icon marks natural pauses in the selection. To assist struggling readers and to deepen reading for all, assign the text in "chunks," following the icons, and apply multidraft reading protocols. For each reading, have students set the purpose indicated:

- **First reading**—identifying key ideas and details and answering any Reading Checks.
- **Second reading**—analyzing craft and structure and responding to the side-column prompts.
- **Third reading**—integrating knowledge and ideas, connecting to other texts and the world, and answering the end-of-selection questions.

For more guidance, refer to the ***Classroom Strategies and Teaching Routines*** card on multidraft reading.

Differentiated Instruction — Additional Instruction

EL Extended Support—English Learners

Have students complete the **Reading and Vocabulary Warm-ups, *Unit 2 Resources*,** pp. 62–65, before they read. Assign the prereading pages and the adapted selection in the ***Reader's Notebook: English Learner's Version.*** Then, have students listen to portions of the selection on the ***Hear It!* Audio CD.**

L1 L2 Extended Support—Struggling Readers

Have students complete the **Reading and Vocabulary Warm-ups, *Unit 2 Resources*,** pp. 62–65, before they read. Assign the prereading pages and the adapted selection in the ***Reader's Notebook: Adapted Version.*** Then, have students listen to portions of the selection on the ***Hear It!* Audio CD** (adapted text).

Extended Support—Reluctant Readers

To build motivation and engagement before assigning the selection, have students read "Buy Me This, Buy Me That," a thematically related selection in ***Reality Central.*** Then, use the questions at the conclusion of the related selection to guide discussion.

PHLit Online!

For more about the author, practice with the selection vocabulary, and more background, go online at **www.PHLitOnline.com.**

TEACH

❶ Activating Prior Knowledge

1. Prepare an **Anticipation Guide** (***Professional Development Guidebook***, pp. 36–38) with the following statements:
   - People who love each other won't make huge sacrifices.
   - People with limited means can't buy anything to express their love.
   - The love that inspires someone to buy a gift is more important than the gift itself.
   - Modern society puts too much emphasis on giving expensive gifts.
2. Give students a copy of the prepared **Anticipation Guide** and have students mark their responses in the Me column. Have students discuss the statements in pairs or groups and mark the Guides again in the Group column.
3. For further guidance, use the ***Classroom Strategies and Teaching Routine*** card: **Using an Anticipation Guide**.

Concept Connector

Students will return to the **Anticipation Guide** after completing "The Gift of the Magi."

Individual Activity

Point out to students that the woman in the picture is performing a common nightly ritual—brushing her long, flowing hair. Ask students to describe a present-day, daily or regular ritual that many people perform.

❷ About the Selection

"The Gift of the Magi" is a story of self-sacrificing love—and its ironic consequences. On Christmas Eve, Della Young decides to sell her beautiful knee-length brown hair to buy Jim a platinum chain for his prized gold watch. When he sees her hair, he stops dead in the doorway, then slowly gives her his Christmas gift—a set of ornamental combs for her hair.

The title alludes to the wise men, or Magi, who brought gifts to the infant Jesus.

1
2

260 Short Stories

Vocabulary Development

CCSS Language 6

Thematic Vocabulary: The Big Question

As students are discussing "The Gift of the Magi," encourage them to use the thematic vocabulary presented in Introducing the Big Question, pp. 194–195. You might encourage them with sentence starters like these:

1. One of the major *differences* between life in Della and Jim's time and now was . . .
2. Neighbors had to *cooperate* with one another because . . .
3. Then, like now, money could become an *issue* when . . .
4. Hard work made people *appreciate* . . .

EXEMPLAR TEXT

The Gift of the Magi

O. HENRY

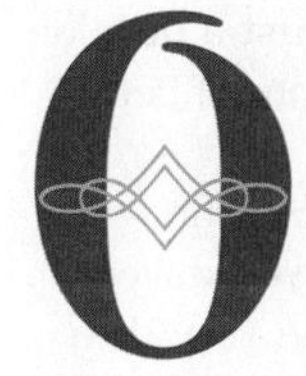

One dollar and eighty-seven cents. That was all. And sixty cents of it was in pennies. Pennies saved one and two at a time by bulldozing the grocer and the vegetable man and the butcher until one's cheeks burned with the silent imputation of parsimony[1] that such close dealing implied. Three times Della counted it. One dollar and eighty-seven cents. And the next day would be Christmas.

There was clearly nothing to do but flop down on the shabby little couch and howl. So Della did it. Which instigates the moral reflection that life is made up of sobs, sniffles, and smiles, with sniffles predominating.

While the mistress of the home is gradually subsiding from the first stage to the second, take a look at the home. A furnished flat at $8 per week. It did not exactly beggar description,[2] but it certainly had that word on the lookout for the mendicancy squad.[3]

In the vestibule below was a letter-box into which no letter would go, and an electric button from which no mortal finger could coax a ring. Also appertaining thereunto was a card bearing the name "Mr. James Dillingham Young."

3 The "Dillingham" had been flung to the breeze during a former period of prosperity when its possessor was being paid $30 per week. Now, when the income was shrunk to $20, the letters of "Dillingham" looked blurred, as though they were thinking seriously of contracting to a modest and unassuming D. But whenever Mr. James Dillingham Young came home and reached his flat above he was called "Jim" and greatly hugged by Mrs. James Dillingham Young, already introduced to you as Della. Which is all very good.

Della finished her cry and attended to her cheeks with the powder rag. She stood by the window and looked out dully at a gray cat walking a gray fence in a gray backyard. Tomorrow would be Christmas Day, and she had only $1.87 with which to buy

1. **imputation** (im´ pyo͞o tā´ shən) **of parsimony** (pär´ sə mō´ nē) accusation of stinginess.
2. **beggar description** make description seem inadequate or useless.
3. **it certainly . . . mendicancy** (men´ di kən´ sē) **squad** it would have been noticed by the police who arrest beggars.

Vocabulary
instigates (in´ stə gāts´)
v. urges on; stirs up

Reading Skill
Make Inferences Based on this paragraph, what can you infer about Jim and the kind of person he would like to be?

How much money does Della have to buy a present for Jim?

3 Reading Skill

Make Inferences

1. **Ask** students what they can infer about Della from her actions thus far in the story.

   Answer: Della is very frugal and deeply concerned about the little money she has. She is humiliated by the way she must deal with tradespeople, and she is worried about not having enough money to buy her husband a decent Christmas gift.

2. **Ask** students what they think the detail of the mailbox card reveals about Jim.

   Answer: The name on the mailbox card sounds much more elegant than Jim's actual financial circumstances would confirm.

3. Read the bracketed text aloud. **Ask** students the Reading Skill question: Based on this paragraph, what can you infer about Jim and the kind of person he would like to be?

   Answer: Jim has had high hopes for a career, but now he is facing reduced income and difficulties making ends meet. He would like to be much more financially successful. Nevertheless, he loves his wife and she him.

4 Reading Check

Answer: She has $1.87.

PHLit Online!

This selection is available in interactive format in the **Enriched Online Student Edition, www.PHLitOnline.com,** which includes a thematically related video with writing prompt and an interactive graphic organizer.

Differentiated Instruction for Universal Access

Culturally Responsive Instruction

Culture Focus Point out how deeply upset Della is at not being able to afford a nice Christmas present for Jim. Note that in the United States, Christmas is an important holiday to which people look forward for months in advance. People spend a great deal of time and thought to find the perfect Christmas present.

Many cultures do not celebrate Christmas, but almost all have some special occasion on which it is very important to give the perfect gift. Invite students to share their knowledge and experience of important occasions in their home culture or family's country of origin.

❺ Humanities

Hairdresser's Window, by John Sloan

John Sloan (1871–1951) was one of a group of young painters known as The Eight. Most had known one another during their student days in Philadelphia. While they worked toward fame and success, they supported themselves as magazine and newspaper illustrators. Eventually, they gravitated toward New York City.

Sloan and other members of The Eight did not sentimentalize city life, but painted what they saw in all its liveliness, vividness, and warmth. Their frequent depictions of poor neighborhoods earned them the nickname "Ashcan School." Use these questions for discussion:

- This painting shows New York City at the period of this story. How does it help you understand what Della's everyday life is like?

  Possible response: The city is crowded. The colors are drab. There is little privacy. People stare at one another with curiosity rather than sympathy.

- What details in the picture teach you something about the story's setting?

  Possible response: The painting shows the hairstyles and styles of hats and clothing people wore, the prevalence of advertising signs, the mix of businesses in one block, and the atmosphere of a crowded city neighborhood.

❻ Critical Viewing

Possible responses: Della may have felt afraid, nervous, confused, or self-conscious.

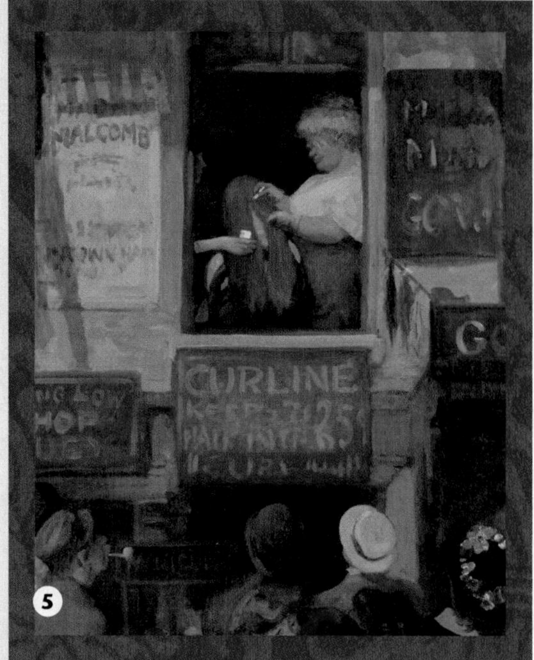

❻ ▲ **Critical Viewing** How do you think Della felt in a street like this one as she approached Madame Sofronie's shop? **[Analyze]**

Jim a present. She had been saving every penny she could for months, with this result. Twenty dollars a week doesn't go far. Expenses had been greater than she had calculated. They always are. Only $1.87 to buy a present for Jim. Her Jim. Many a happy hour she had spent planning for something nice for him. Something fine and rare and sterling—something just a little bit near to being worthy of the honor of being owned by Jim.

There was a pier glass between the windows of the room. Perhaps you have seen a pier glass in an $8 flat. A very thin and very agile person may, by observing his reflection in a rapid sequence of longitudinal strips, obtain a fairly accurate conception of his looks. Della, being slender, had mastered the art.

Suddenly she whirled from the window and stood before the glass. Her eyes were shining brilliantly, but her face had lost its color within twenty seconds. Rapidly she pulled down her hair and let it fall to its full length.

Now, there were two possessions of the James Dillingham Youngs in which they both took a mighty pride. One was Jim's gold watch that had been his father's and his grandfather's. The other was Della's hair. Had the Queen of Sheba lived in the flat across the airshaft, Della would have let her hair hang out the window some day to dry just to depreciate Her Majesty's jewels and gifts. Had King Solomon been the janitor, with all his treasures piled up in the basement, Jim would have pulled out his watch every time he passed, just to see him pluck at his beard from envy.

So now Della's beautiful hair fell about her rippling and shining like a cascade of brown waters. It reached below her knee and made itself almost a garment for her. And then she did it up again nervously and quickly. Once she faltered for a minute and stood still while a tear or two splashed on the worn red carpet.

On went her old brown jacket; on went her old brown hat. With a whirl of skirts and with the brilliant sparkle still in her eyes, she fluttered out the door and down the stairs to the street.

Where she stopped the sign read: "Mme. Sofronie. Hair Goods of All Kinds." One flight up Della ran, and collected herself, panting. Madame, large, too white, chilly, hardly looked the "Sofronie."

Vocabulary

depreciate (dē prē´ shē āt´) *v.* reduce in value

cascade (kas kād´) *n.* a small steep waterfall; anything suggesting such a waterfall

faltered (fôl´ tərd) *v.* acted hesitantly; showed uncertainty

Think Aloud

Vocabulary: Allusions

Point out the references to "the Queen of Sheba" and to "King Solomon" on this page. Model how to use context to understand unfamiliar allusions. Say to students:

> If I have never heard of the Queen of Sheba or King Solomon, I use context to improve my understanding. I read in the first sentence of this paragraph: The couple has "two possessions . . . in which they both took a mighty pride"—Jim's watch and Della's hair. I see that the references to the Queen of Sheba and King Solomon are meant to illustrate this pride. Jim and Della are so proud that they would show off the watch and hair to a king and a queen. I know it is unlikely that a king and a queen would live among poor people like Jim and Della, so I guess that they are not characters in the story. Instead, O. Henry is making an *allusion*, or reference to a widely known figure. He is saying, Jim and Della's pride was so great, they would show off even to these two legendary wealthy people.

"Will you buy my hair?" asked Della.

"I buy hair," said Madame. "Take yer hat off and let's have a sight at the looks of it."

Down rippled the brown cascade.

"Twenty dollars," said Madame, lifting the mass with a practiced hand.

"Give it to me quick," said Della.

Oh, and the next two hours tripped by on rosy wings. Forget the hashed metaphor. She was ransacking the stores for Jim's present.

She found it at last. It surely had been made for Jim and no one else. There was no other like it in any of the stores, and she had turned all of them inside out. It was a platinum fob chain simple and chaste in design, properly proclaiming its value by substance alone and not by meretricious ornamentation—as all good things should do. It was even worthy of The Watch. As soon as she saw it she knew that it must be Jim's. It was like him. Quietness and value—the description applied to both. Twenty-one dollars they took from her for it, and she hurried home with the 87 cents. With that chain on his watch Jim might be properly anxious about the time in any company. Grand as the watch was he sometimes looked at it on the sly on account of the old leather strap that he used in place of a chain.

When Della reached home her intoxication gave way a little to **prudence** and reason. She got out her curling irons and lighted the gas and went to work repairing the ravages made by generosity added to love. Which is always a tremendous task, dear friends—a mammoth task.

Within forty minutes her head was covered with tiny, close-lying curls that made her look wonderfully like a truant schoolboy. She looked at her reflection in the mirror long, carefully, and critically.

7 LITERATURE IN CONTEXT

Cultural Connection

Watch Fob Chain

A fob chain is central to the plot of "The Gift of the Magi." The word *fob* probably entered the English language from the German dialect word *fuppe,* meaning "pocket." Before the wristwatch became common, a man would carry a pocket watch that fit in a special vest pocket. To keep the watch from falling or becoming lost, it was fastened to the vest by means of a strap or chain (sometimes with an ornament, or a fob, at the end) that was attached to a pin with a locking clasp, making it secure. Sometimes, as pictured here, a chain's finely detailed metalwork elevated the piece to a work of art.

Connect to the Literature

A pocket watch was often handed down from father to son, as was Jim Young's in O. Henry's story. Why might this fact alone make a fob chain and watch precious to its owner despite its modest cash value?

Vocabulary

prudence (proo͞′ dəns) *n.* a sensible and careful attitude that makes you avoid some risks

8 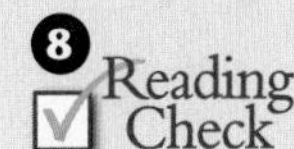

What does Della sell for twenty dollars?

7 Literature in Context

Culture Connection The wristwatch was invented at about the time of this story, but it was regarded as a woman's accessory until World War I. Since soldiers' uniforms did not provide watch pockets, men's wristwatches became popular during the war years. In O. Henry's day, all men's suits included waistcoats or vests that had watch pockets. Today, the two-piece suit (jacket and trousers only) is more popular. The rise in popularity of the wristwatch and the decline of the waistcoat combined to make the pocket watch a rarity.

Connect to the Literature After students read the Literature in Context feature, present the additional background information above. Then, remind students of details earlier in the story that suggest Jim is unhappy about the contrast between his current financial status and his desires. **Ask** students to speculate about how these feelings might be reinforced in Jim's daily life.

Answer: Jim cannot afford the types of clothing he wants, so he may not be happy with his appearance. As a poor man, he may feel that he is not treated with respect by shopkeepers or those he meets in business. He may feel ashamed of his poverty and wish to hide it from others.

Then, **ask** the Connect to the Literature question: A pocket watch was often handed down from father to son, as was Jim Young's in O. Henry's story. Why might this fact alone make a fob chain and watch precious to its owner despite its modest cash value?

Answer: A fob chain and watch would be precious because it was a reminder of a much-loved parent.

8 Reading Check

Answer: She sells her hair.

PROFESSIONAL DEVELOPMENT | **Danling Fu**

Apply the Strategy

Engaging English Learners: After students finish reading the story, have them discuss the story's ending. Ask the following questions: *Are the characters satisfied or disappointed with the gifts they receive? What is the real gift they present to each other?* Encourage students to share personal stories about what their parents and relatives sacrificed for their families by leaving their country of origin.

After exploring this theme, guide students in a discussion about another theme: What does "true love" mean in our daily life?

For more of Danling Fu's strategies, see her Professional Development essay, pp. 194c–194d.

9 Connecting to the Big Question

1. Point out that sometimes internal conflicts, such as between a desire to show love and a lack of money, lead to actions such as Della cutting her hair.
2. Have students read the bracketed text on pages 264–265. **Ask** students: How are both Della's and Jim's actions similar? What emotion do both characters show with their actions? **Possible response:** Both have bought the other a present. They both show their love for the other.
3. **Ask:** How is Della's conflict between desire to buy Jim a gift and lack of money necessary to the story? **Possible response:** Without that conflict, she would not have sold her hair. Jim would not be surprised, and apparently upset by her action.

"If Jim doesn't kill me," she said to herself, "before he takes a second look at me, he'll say I look like a Coney Island[4] chorus girl. But what could I do—oh! what could I do with a dollar and eighty-seven cents?"

At 7 o'clock the coffee was made and the frying-pan was on the back of the stove hot and ready to cook the chops.

Jim was never late. Della doubled the fob chain in her hand and sat on the corner of the table near the door that he always entered. Then she heard his step on the stair away down on the first flight, and she turned white for just a moment. She had a habit of saying little silent prayers about the simplest everyday things, and now she whispered: "Please God, make him think I am still pretty."

The door opened and Jim stepped in and closed it. He looked thin and very serious. Poor fellow, he was only twenty-two—and to be burdened with a family! He needed a new overcoat and he was without gloves.

Jim stopped inside the door, as immovable as a setter at the scent of quail. His eyes were fixed upon Della, and there was an expression in them that she could not read, and it terrified her. It was not anger, nor surprise, nor disapproval, nor horror, nor any of the sentiments that she had been prepared for. He simply stared at her fixedly with that peculiar expression on his face.

Della wriggled off the table and went for him.

"Jim, darling," she cried, "don't look at me that way. I had my hair cut off and sold it because I couldn't have lived through Christmas without giving you a present. It'll grow out again—you won't mind, will you? I just had to do it. My hair grows awfully fast. Say 'Merry Christmas!' Jim, and let's be happy. You don't know what a nice—what a beautiful, nice gift I've got for you."

> *"...I couldn't have lived through Christmas without giving you a present."*

"You've cut off your hair?" asked Jim, laboriously, as if he had not arrived at that patent fact yet even after the hardest mental labor.

"Cut it off and sold it," said Della. "Don't you like me just as well, anyhow? I'm me without my hair, ain't I?"

Jim looked about the room curiously.

"You say your hair is gone?" he said, with an air almost of idiocy.

4. **Coney** (kō′ nē) **Island** beach and amusement park in Brooklyn, New York.

Vocabulary Development

Vocabulary Knowledge Rating

When students have completed reading and discussing "The Gift of the Magi," have them take out their **Vocabulary Knowledge Rating Charts** for this selection. Read the words aloud once more and have students rate their knowledge of the words again in the After Reading column. Clarify any words that are still problematic. Have students write their own definitions and examples or sentences in the appropriate column. Then have students complete the Vocabulary Practice at the end of the selection. Encourage students to use the words in further discussion and written work about this selection. Remind them that they will be accountable for these words on the **Selection Test**, ***Unit 2 Resources***, pp. 74–76 or 77–79.

"You needn't look for it," said Della. "It's sold, I tell you—sold and gone, too. It's Christmas Eve, boy. Be good to me, for it went for you. Maybe the hairs of my head were numbered," she went on with a sudden serious sweetness, "but nobody could ever count my love for you. Shall I put the chops on, Jim?"

Out of his trance Jim seemed quickly to wake. He enfolded his Della. For ten seconds let us regard with discreet scrutiny some inconsequential object in the other direction. Eight dollars a week or a million a year—what is the difference? A mathematician or a wit would give you the wrong answer. The Magi brought valuable gifts, but that was not among them. This dark assertion will be illuminated later on.

Jim drew a package from his overcoat pocket and threw it upon the table.

"Don't make any mistake, Dell," he said, "about me. I don't think there's anything in the way of a haircut or a shave or a shampoo that could make me like my girl any less. But if you'll unwrap that package you may see why you had me going a while at first."

White fingers and nimble tore at the string and paper. And then an ecstatic scream of joy; and then, alas! a quick feminine change to hysterical tears and wails, necessitating the immediate employment of all the comforting powers of the lord of the flat.

For there lay The Combs—the set of combs, side and back, that Della had worshipped for long in a Broadway window. Beautiful combs, pure tortoise shell, with jeweled rims—just the shade to wear in the beautiful vanished hair. They were expensive combs, she knew, and her heart had simply craved and yearned over them without the least hope of possession. And now, they were hers, but the tresses that should have adorned the coveted adornments were gone.

But she hugged them to her bosom, and at length she was able to look up with dim eyes and a smile and say: "My hair grows so fast, Jim!"

And then Della leaped up like a little singed cat and cried, "Oh, oh!"

Jim had not yet seen his beautiful present. She held it out to him eagerly upon her open palm. The dull precious metal seemed to flash with a reflection of her bright and ardent spirit.

Vocabulary
discreet (di skrēt′) *adj.* careful about what one says or does

Literary Analysis
Irony In what way does Jim's gift to Della create an ironic situation?

11

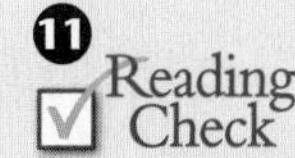

How does Jim react to Della's newly cut hair?

10 Literary Analysis

Irony

1. Remind students that an ironic situation is one in which situations are not what they seem to be or expectations are overturned or disappointed.
2. Have students read the second bracketed passage. Then, **ask** students what response Jim expected to his Christmas gift.

   Answer: He expected his gift of combs to be a perfect match for Della's hair and to make Della extremely happy.
3. **Ask** students the Literary Analysis question: In what way does Jim's gift to Della create an ironic situation?

   Answer: The situation is ironic in that Della's generous sacrifice has unknowingly rendered his gift useless. What he expected has not occurred.

▶ **Monitor Progress:** Ask each student to describe an example of situational irony. Examples can be real or fictional.

▶ **Reteach:** If necessary, remind students that in an ironic situation, there is a stark contrast between what is expected and what happens. For instance, if a student expects to do well on a test and ends up doing poorly, the situation is not ironic because there is no stark contrast. However, if the student boasted to friends about his mastery of the material and then failed the test, there is a stark contrast and the situation is ironic.

11 Reading Check

Answer: He is stunned, then upset, by Della's newly cut hair.

Concept Connector

Anticipation Guide

Have students return to their **Anticipation Guides** and respond to the statements again in the After Reading column. They may do this individually or in their original pairs or groups. Then, lead a class discussion, probing for what students have learned that confirms or invalidates each statement. Encourage students to cite specific details, quotations, or other evidence from the text to support their responses to each statement.

Writing About the Big Question

Have students compare their responses to the sentence starters they completed before they read the story with their ideas afterwards. Ask them to explain whether their thoughts have changed.

Reading Skill Graphic Organizer

Ask students to review the graphic organizers they completed to identify the persuasive appeals while reading. Show them **Reading Skill Graphic Organizer A** (*Graphic Organizer Transparencies*, p. 45) as an example. Then have students share the graphic organizers they did and the inferences they made.

Literary Analysis

Surprise Ending

1. **Ask** students the Literary Analysis question.

   Answer: Neither Della nor the reader knows, until the end, that Jim has sold his watch.

2. Have students **speculate** about why the author adds one final paragraph after the revelation of the surprise ending.

   Possible response: The author takes the opportunity to add a thought about the meaning of this ironic situation.

Spiral Review

Narrator

1. Students studied point of view in the Unit 2 Literary Analysis Workshop (pp. 196–209).
2. **Ask** students the Spiral Review question.

   Possible response: The narrator's attitude toward the characters is respectful and admiring. By first calling them naïve and foolish, he reflects his attitude that society does not value the right things, but he directly addresses readers in a confidential and friendly tone.

ASSESS

Answers

Critical Thinking

Remind students to support their answers with evidence from the text.

1. (a) Della sells her hair. (b) She is generous and self-sacrificing.
2. (a) Jim is stunned. (b) Della fears that Jim no longer finds her attractive.
3. **Possible response:** Wisdom is the understanding that some things, such as love, generosity, and kindness, are more important than money or coveted gifts.
4. **Possible responses:** (a) Jim and Della each want to buy the other a wonderful Christmas gift, but neither of them has enough money. (b) Yes, it is a necessary conflict. It reflects the selflessness and the love they each feel for the other.

Literary Analysis
Surprise Ending Explain why the ending is a surprise to both the characters and the reader.

Spiral Review
Narrator Based on this final paragraph, how would you describe the narrator's attitude toward both the characters and the reader? Explain.

"Isn't it a dandy, Jim? I hunted all over town to find it. You'll have to look at the time a hundred times a day now. Give me your watch. I want to see how it looks on it."

Instead of obeying, Jim tumbled down on the couch and put his hands under the back of his head and smiled.

"Dell," said he, "let's put our Christmas presents away and keep 'em a while. They're too nice to use just at present. I sold the watch to get the money to buy your combs. And now suppose you put the chops on."

The Magi, as you know, were wise men—wonderfully wise men—who brought gifts to the Babe in the manger. They invented the art of giving Christmas presents. Being wise, their gifts were no doubt wise ones, possibly bearing the privilege of exchange in case of duplication. And here I have lamely related to you the uneventful chronicle of two foolish children in a flat who most unwisely sacrificed for each other the greatest treasures of their house. But in a last word to the wise of these days let it be said that of all who give gifts these two were the wisest. Of all who give and receive gifts, such as they are wisest. Everywhere they are wisest. They are the magi.

Critical Thinking

Cite textual evidence to support your responses.

1. **Key Ideas and Details** **(a)** What does Della do to get money for Jim's present? **(b) Infer:** What does her action suggest about her character?
2. **Key Ideas and Details** **(a)** How does Jim react when he first sees that Della has cut her hair? **(b) Analyze:** Why does Della misunderstand Jim's reaction?
3. **Integration of Knowledge and Ideas** **Draw Conclusions:** O. Henry says that these "two foolish children" were "the wisest." How do you think he would define wisdom? Explain your response.
4. **Integration of Knowledge and Ideas** **(a)** What internal conflict occurs for both Jim and Della? **(b)** Do you think that this is a necessary conflict? Explain. ***[Connect to the Big Question: Is conflict necessary?]***

Assessment Resources

Unit 2 Resources

L1 L2 EL **Selection Test A,** pp. 74–76. Administer Test A to less advanced students.

L3 L4 EL **Selection Test B,** pp. 77–79. Administer Test B to on-level and more advanced students.

L3 L4 **Open-Book Test,** pp. 71–73. As an alternative, give the Open-Book Test.

All **Customizable Test Bank**

All **Self-tests**
Students may prepare for the **Selection Test** by taking the **Self-test** online.

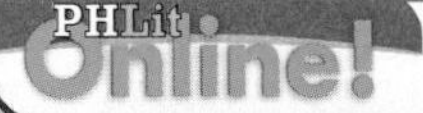

All assessment resources are available at **www.PHLitOnline.com**.

After You Read The Gift of the Magi

Literary Analysis: Irony

1. **Key Ideas and Details (a)** Identify **irony** in the story by using a chart like the one shown. In the first box, note the outcome that Jim and Della expect when they present their gifts to each other. In the second box, describe what actually happens.

What Characters Expect	What Actually Happens

(b) What message about life does this situational irony convey?

2. **Craft and Structure (a)** Which details in the story make its **surprise ending** seem like a logical outcome of events? **(b)** Why do you think surprise endings are such a popular device in literature and movies?

Reading Skill: Make Inferences

3. **(a)** What **inferences** do you think O. Henry intended readers to make about the characters of Jim and Della? **(b)** Which details in the text support your inferences?
4. In what ways do your prior knowledge and experience of characters like Jim and Della help you make inferences about them? Use details from the text to explain your response.

Vocabulary

Acquisition and Use Explain why each statement below is true or false.

1. One who *instigates* conflict might be called a "problem solver."
2. After six years of hard use, a car will *depreciate* in value.
3. Only a *discreet* person should be trusted with a secret.
4. It is a sign of *prudence* to drive a car before you have your license.
5. In a fireworks display, a shell might create a sparkling *cascade.*
6. The horse *faltered* in the home stretch and won as a result.

Word Study Use the context of the sentences and what you know about the **Latin prefix *de-*** to explain your answer to each question.

1. If you were to *depress* a friend, would he feel better?
2. What happens to food when people *devour* it?

Word Study

The **Latin prefix *de-*** has various meanings, including "down."

Apply It Explain how the prefix *de-* contributes to the meanings of these words. Consult a dictionary if necessary.

descend
decline
depose

Word Study: Apply It
Sample answers:
Descend means to go down. *Decline* means to go down in value, or to turn down. *Depose* means to remove from office, or take down.

Word Study
Sample answers:
1. No, the prefix *de-* means "down." If you said something to *depress* a friend, his or her mood would go down, and he or she would feel worse, not better.
2. The prefix *de-* means "down." When people devour food, they eat all of it and the quantity goes down.

Answers Continued
4. F. Someone who shows prudence is sensible and careful; therefore, that person wouldn't drive a car without a license.
5. T. Fireworks often resemble light falling down, or cascading, from the sky like a waterfall.
6. F. If a horse faltered, it would fall down or stumble and probably not win the race.

Answers

Literary Analysis

1. (a) **What characters expect**—Their gifts will be perfect and much appreciated. **What actually happens**—Both of their gifts are useless.

   (b) This situational irony conveys the idea that life is not predictable and that gifts are not the most reliable means for expressing love.
2. (a) The emphasis on the appearance, the history, and the value of the watch sets up the surprise and makes Jim's selling of his watch just as believable as Della's selling of her hair. (b) **Possible response:** Surprise endings are popular because people love surprises and admire clever manipulations of plot events.

For other sample answers, see ***Graphic Organizer Transparencies,*** **Literary Analysis Graphic Organizer A**, p. 48, and the **Additional Answers** section.

Reading Skill

3. **Possible response:** (a) O. Henry probably intended readers to infer that Jim and Della are both deeply in love, that they are willing to sacrifice greatly to express their love, and that their relationship is strong enough to survive hardships. (b) Details include the sacrifices of the watch and the hair, the concern each shows for the other's feelings, and Jim's final gesture of putting his hands behind his head and smiling.
4. **Possible responses:** I am familiar with characters that were in love from books, television, and movies, and I understand how much these characters were willing to sacrifice for each other.

Vocabulary

Acquisition and Use
Sample answers:
1. F. Someone who instigates conflict is a trouble maker, not a problem solver.
2. T. A car will depreciate, or lose value, after years of hard use.
3. T. A discreet person is careful about what he or she says, so a secret is safe with him or her.

PRETEACH

Skills instruction for the ***Reading Skill*** *and* ***Literary Analysis*** *concept appears on p. 257.*

1 Writing About the Big Question

1. Review the assignment with the class.
2. **Ask** volunteers to describe family feuds that they have either read or heard about. Feuds can be real or fictional.
3. Have students complete the sentence starters. Review the responses as a class. (**Possible response:** In a longtime feud, the people involved may struggle to resolve their issues amicably because anger has built up between them. Those in competition often antagonize each other because they each see the other as the enemy.)
4. Remind students that their answers will help them think about the Big Question, "Is conflict necessary?"

While You Read

Tell students as they read they should consider the men's reasons for continuing the feud and for ending it.

2 Vocabulary

1. Have students preview the selection vocabulary.
2. For each word, have students say the word aloud.
3. Then, use the word in a sentence that defines the word.
4. Repeat your definitional sentence or a similar sentence with the word missing, and have the class "fill in the blank" chorally. Here is an example:

   Precipitous means steep. The road sits next to a cliff, so the descent to the water below is steep and [students say "precipitous"].

3 Word Study

1. Introduce the skill, using the instruction in the box.
2. Ask students for another *inter-* word with a meaning of "between races." (*interracial*)

1 Writing About the Big Question

In "The Interlopers," men from feuding families face a situation that makes them rethink their hatred for each other. Use these sentence starters to develop your ideas about the Big Question.

In a longtime feud, the people involved may struggle to resolve their **issues amicably** because ___________.

Those in **competition** often **antagonize** each other because ___________.

While You Read Consider the men's reasons for continuing the feud and their reasons for ending it.

2 Vocabulary

Read each word and its definition. Decide whether you know the word well, know it a little bit, or do not know it at all. After you read, see how your knowledge of each word has increased.

- **precipitous** (prē sip′ ə təs) *adj.* steep; sheer (p. 272) ***At the edge of the cliff, you will face a precipitous drop.*** *precipice n.*
- **acquiesced** (ak′ wē est′) *v.* agreed quietly without protest or enthusiasm (p. 272) ***The boy sullenly acquiesced to the demand that he take out the garbage.*** *acquiescence n.*
- **feud** (fyo͞od) *n.* a long and violent quarrel, especially between clans or families, often characterized by killing (p. 272) ***The feud between the Hatfields and the McCoys lasted for almost 30 years.*** *feud v.*
- **disputed** (di spyo͞ot′ id) *adj.* contested; argued about (p. 272) ***The disputed border between the yards had been a source of conflict for many years.*** *dispute n. dispute v.*
- **condolences** (kən dō′ lən səz) *n.* expressions of sympathy with another in grief (p. 274) ***The mourners shared their condolences.***
- **interlopers** (in′ tər lō′ pərz) *n.* people who intrude or meddle in other peoples' business or lives (p. 275) ***Even though we had been invited to the party, we felt like unwelcome interlopers.***

3

Word Study

The **Latin prefix *inter-*** means "between."

This is the story of **interlopers,** describing those who leap or intrude into each other's affairs and find themselves unwelcome.

Vocabulary Development

Vocabulary Knowledge Rating

Create a **Vocabulary Knowledge Rating Chart** (***Professional Development Guidebook,*** p. 33) for this selection. Include the selection vocabulary and the Big Question words that appear in the Writing About the Big Question sentence starters on this page. (The Big Question vocabulary is introduced on pp. 194–195.)

Give students a copy of the chart. Read the words aloud, and have students mark their rating in the Before Reading column. Urge them to be alert to these words as they read and discuss the selection.

Tally how many students think they know a word to gauge how much instruction to provide. As students read and discuss the selection, point out the words and their context.

Vocabulary Central, featuring tools, activities, and songs for studying vocabulary, is available at **www.PHLitOnline.com.**

Meet Saki (1870–1916)

Author of *The Interlopers*

Saki is the pen name of the British writer H. H. Munro. Munro was born in Burma and sent at age two to live in England. As a young adult, he returned to Burma to serve in the police force. However, poor health forced him to return to England, where he began work as a journalist.

Talent and Tragedy In 1904, Munro published a collection of short stories entitled *Reginald.* He went on to write several more collections of stories and two novels. The abrupt ending of Saki's own life was as shocking as one of his plot twists: When World War I broke out, he enlisted in the British army and was killed fighting in France.

4

BACKGROUND FOR THE STORY

Family Feuds

A feud is a bitter, prolonged fight, typically between families or clans, that may continue for years or even generations. The brutality of a feud can make for gripping drama, as it does in "The Interlopers."

Did You Know?

Munro's pen name is thought to have been taken from a character in *The Rubaiyat*, by Persian poet Omar Khayyam.

Daily Bellringer

For each class during which you will teach this selection, have students complete one of the five Sentence Modeling activities for Week 8 in the *Daily Bellringer Activities* booklet.

4 Background

Family Feuds

The feud between the Hatfields, who lived on the West Virginia side of a stream that divides West Virginia and Kentucky, and the McCoys, who lived on the Kentucky side, has fascinated the public since the 1880s. It has passed into legend as the bloodiest disagreement among neighbors in American history.

Bad feelings had existed between the families since the Civil War, but it was a legal dispute over two hogs that led to the first shootings in 1878. Perhaps the climax of the feud came in 1888, when at least six people were killed, including one young McCoy woman and the Hatfield man convicted and executed for her murder. The two family patriarchs who began the feud lived to great old age.

Multidraft Reading

This icon marks natural pauses in the selection. To assist struggling readers and to deepen reading for all, assign the text in "chunks," following the icons, and apply multidraft reading protocols. For each reading, have students set the purpose indicated:

- **First reading**—identifying key ideas and details and answering any Reading Checks.
- **Second reading**—analyzing craft and structure and responding to the side-column prompts.
- **Third reading**—integrating knowledge and ideas, connecting to other texts and the world, and answering the end-of-selection questions.

For more guidance, refer to the ***Classroom Strategies and Teaching Routines*** card on multidraft reading.

PHLit Online!

For more about the author, practice with the selection vocabulary, and more background, go online at **www.PHLitOnline.com.**

Differentiated Instruction — Additional Instruction

EL Extended Support—English Learners

Have students complete the **Reading and Vocabulary Warm-ups, *Unit 2 Resources,*** pp. 80–83, before they read. Assign the prereading pages in the ***Reader's Notebook: English Learner's Version.*** Then, have students listen to portions of the selection on the ***Hear It!*** **Audio CD.**

L1 L2 Extended Support—Struggling Readers

Have students complete the **Reading and Vocabulary Warm-ups, *Unit 2 Resources,*** pp. 80–83, before they read. Assign the prereading pages in the ***Reader's Notebook: Adapted Version.*** Then, have students listen to portions of the selection on the ***Hear It!*** **Audio CD** (adapted text).

Extended Support—Reluctant Readers

To build motivation and engagement before assigning the selection, have students read "The Possibility of Peace," a thematically related selection in ***Reality Central.*** Then, use the questions at the conclusion of the related selection to guide discussion.

TEACH

❶ Activating Prior Knowledge

1. Prepare an **Anticipation Guide** (***Professional Development Guidebook***, pp. 36–38) with the following statements:
   - Serious arguments can begin over trivial matters.
   - People who quarrel for a long time often forget why they started fighting in the first place.
   - Arguments always weaken as time goes by.
   - When arguing you should never give in or show weakness.
2. Give students copies of the prepared **Anticipation Guide** and have them mark their responses in the Me column. Have students discuss the statements in pairs or groups and mark their Guides again in the Group column.
3. For further guidance, use the ***Classroom Strategies and Teaching Routines*** card: Using an **Anticipation Guide**.

Concept Connector

Students will return to the **Anticipation Guide** after completing "The Interlopers."

Individual Activity

As students read "The Interlopers," have them identify points in the story at which the feuding families might have resolved their disagreement, as well as specific ways they might have gone about it. Ask students to invent the constructive dialogue Ulrich von Gradwitz and Georg Znaeym might have had that would have ended their feud.

❷ About the Selection

"The Interlopers" shows that a feud not only fuels feelings of hatred and bitterness, but also has the power to destroy feuding parties. The story begins at the climax of a generations-long feud, as two of the antagonists find themselves face to face in the forest. As they are about to destroy each other, a tree crashes down and traps them. During the time they are trapped, they agree to reconcile. As the story ends, however, it appears that their decision has come too late.

❶
❷

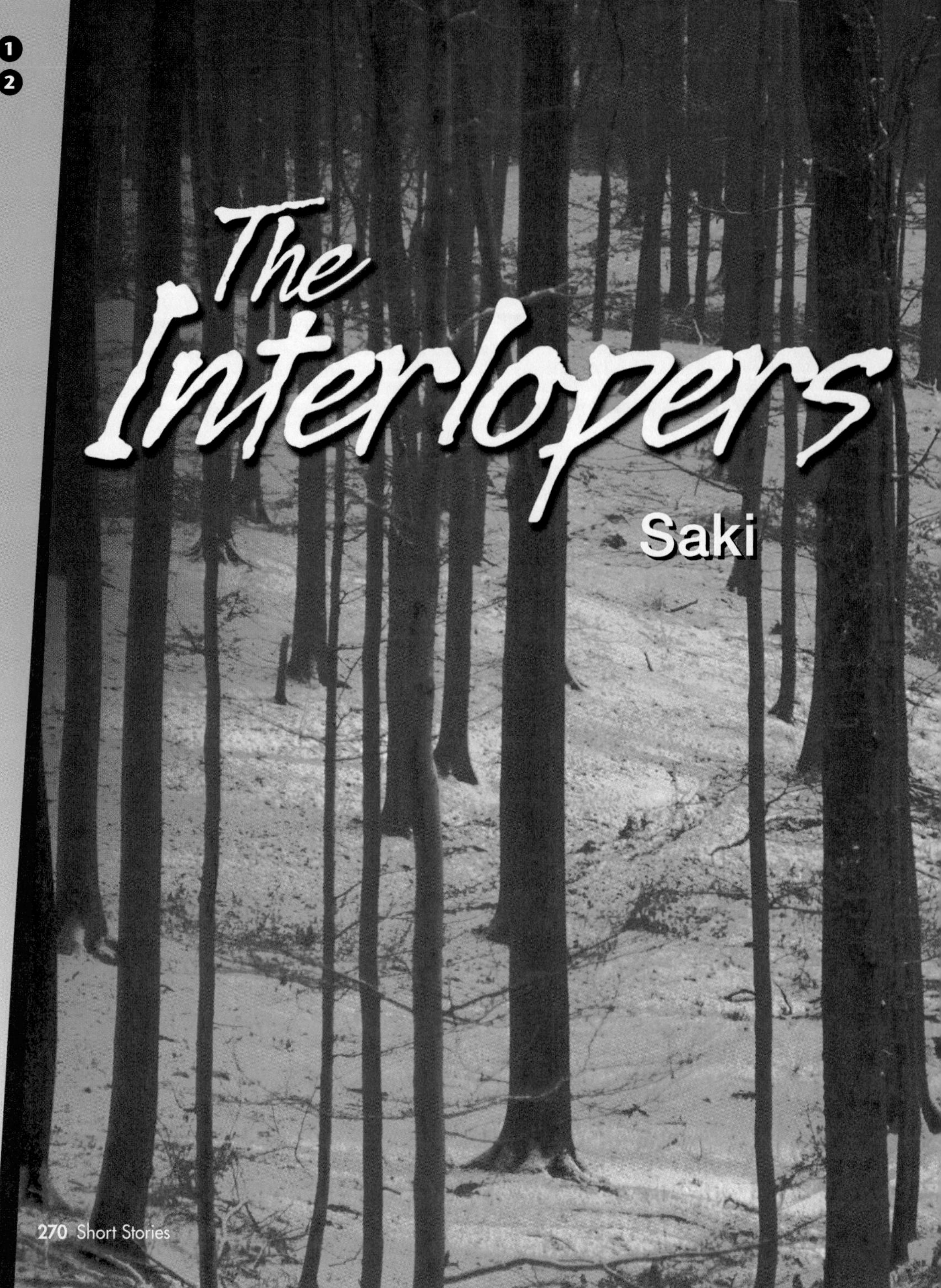

270 Short Stories

Vocabulary Development

CCSS Language 6

Thematic Vocabulary: The Big Question

As students are discussing "The Interlopers," encourage them to use the thematic vocabulary presented in Introducing the Big Question, pp. 194–195. You might encourage them with sentence starters like these:

1. When neighbors do not *cooperate* with each other, they become . . .
2. Ulrich and Georg need to put aside their *grievances* and . . .
3. If they can't *mediate* their *differences*, they should . . .
4. In ending a feud, each side needs to *articulate* its . . .

3 In a forest of mixed growth somewhere on the eastern spurs of the Carpathians,[1] a man stood one winter night watching and listening, as though he waited for some beast of the woods to come within the range of his vision, and, later, of his rifle. But the game for whose presence he kept so keen an outlook was none that figured in the sportsman's calendar as lawful and proper for the chase: Ulrich von Gradwitz (o͞ol rik fôn gräd´ vitz) patrolled the dark forest in quest of a human enemy.

1. **Carpathians** (kär pā´ thē ənz) mountains in central Europe.

4

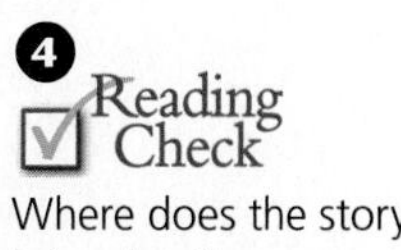

Where does the story take place?

3 Critical Thinking

Classify/Analyze

1. Point out that the beginning of a short story serves two functions: It sets the scene for what will happen, and it captures the reader's interest. To set the scene, it introduces one or more of the elements of short stories.
2. Ask a volunteer to give a dramatic reading of the text on page 271, using appropriate body language and tone of voice. Have students listen for the elements of short stories and think about how Saki captures their interest.
3. **Ask** students to identify the short story elements in the passage and to describe each.

   Answer: The setting is a forest on a winter night. There are two characters: a violent, hateful hunter, and his enemy whom we know nothing about yet. His desire to hurt his enemy introduces an external conflict and a theme of hatred and violence.
4. **Ask:** How does Saki capture the reader's interest?

   Possible responses: He captures readers' interest by painting a vivid picture and by building suspense. He surprises readers by describing a hunter stalking a beast, then revealing that the prey is actually human. He makes readers wonder why Ulrich hates his enemy so much.

4 Reading Check

Answer: The story takes place in a forest in the eastern Carpathian Mountains in central Europe.

Differentiated Instruction for Universal Access

EL Support for English Learners

As students read the story, have them choose several words they would like to make part of their spoken and written vocabularies. Have them practice saying the words. Then, ask them to make a flash card for each word by writing the word on one side of an index card and the meaning and a context sentence on the other.

Enrichment for Advanced Readers

As students read the story, have them consider how Saki's choice of words contributes to the mood and tone of "The Interlopers." Have them each write a short paper on the topic of Saki's word choice in "The Interlopers." They should include examples of words and phrases from the story.

PHLit Online!

This selection is available in interactive format in the **Enriched Online Student Edition, www.PHLitOnline.com,** which includes a thematically related video with writing prompt and an interactive graphic organizer.

5 Reading Skill

Make Inferences

1. Have students reread the first bracketed passage. **Ask** what the phrase "jealously guarded" suggests about Ulrich.

   Answer: Ulrich is a possessive man who feels the need to ensure no one intrudes on his territory.

2. **Ask** what the words "embittered" and "detested" indicate about the two men's relationship.

   Answer: The men hate each other intensely.

3. **Ask** students the first Reading Skill question: What can you infer about the characters from their unwillingness to compromise?

   Answer: Both men are extremely strong-willed and stubborn, each refusing to admit weakness or defeat.

6 Reading Skill

Make Inferences

1. Read the second bracketed passage aloud, continuing onto p. 273. Remind students that a feud can often be between two people as well as between two families.

2. **Ask** students what the words "with none to witness" indicate about Ulrich's desire?

   Answer: He hopes to be able to kill his enemy and not be publicly accused of murder or punished by the law.

3. **Ask** students the second Reading Skill question: How does your knowledge of feuds help you infer the reason Ulrich hopes to meet Znaeym?

   Answer: Because a family feud generates intense personal hatred, Ulrich hopes to kill Znaeym personally. He would thus gain the satisfaction of revenge, defend his family's honor, and hopefully avoid an involvement with the law.

Vocabulary

precipitous (prē sip′ ə təs) *adj.* steep; sheer

acquiesced (ak′ wē est′) *v.* agreed quietly without protest or enthusiasm

feud (fyo͞od) *n.* a long and violent quarrel, especially between clans or families

disputed (di spyo͞ot′ əd) *adj.* contested; argued about

The forest lands of Gradwitz were of wide extent and well stocked with game; the narrow strip of **precipitous** woodland that lay on its outskirt was not remarkable for the game it harbored or the shooting it afforded, but it was the most jealously guarded of all its owner's territorial possessions. A famous lawsuit, in the days of his grandfather, had wrested it from the illegal possession of a neighboring family of petty landowners; the dispossessed party had never **acquiesced** in the judgment of the Courts, and a long series of poaching affrays[2] and similar scandals had embittered the relationships between the families for three generations. The neighbor **feud** had grown into a personal one since Ulrich had come to be head of his family; if there was a man in the world whom he detested and wished ill to it was Georg Znaeym (gà′ ôrg znä′ im), the inheritor of the quarrel and the tireless game-snatcher and raider of the **disputed** border-forest. The feud might, perhaps, have died down or been compromised if the personal ill will of the two men had not stood in the way; as boys they had thirsted for one another's blood, as men each prayed that misfortune might fall on the other, and this wind-scourged winter night Ulrich had banded together his foresters to watch the dark forest, not in quest of four-footed quarry, but to keep a lookout for the prowling thieves whom he suspected of being afoot from across the land boundary. The roebuck which usually kept in the sheltered hollows during a storm wind, were running like driven things tonight, and there was movement and unrest among the creatures that were wont to sleep through the dark hours. Assuredly there was a disturbing element in the forest, and Ulrich could guess the quarter from whence it came.

Reading Skill
Make Inferences What can you infer about the characters from their unwillingness to compromise?

He strayed away by himself from the watchers whom he had placed in ambush on the crest of the hill, and wandered far down the steep slopes amid the wild tangle of undergrowth, peering through the tree trunks and listening through the whistling and skirling of the wind and the restless beating of the branches for

Reading Skill
Make Inferences How does your knowledge of feuds help you infer the reason Ulrich hopes to meet Znaeym? 6

2. **poaching** (pōch′ iŋ) **affrays** (ə frāz′) disputes about hunting on someone else's property.

Think Aloud

Make Predictions

Draw students' attention to the description that begins "And before the moment of hesitation . . ." on p. 273. Use the following "think aloud" to model the process of making predictions (introduced on p. 23):

> When I read the paragraph, I use text clues and my own life experiences to make predictions about character's emotions and experiences. I visualize Ulrich and Georg pinned beneath the tree branch together. Then I connect to my own experience by remembering a time when I fell on my bike and it landed on top of me. I couldn't get up and someone I didn't like very much came to my rescue. After that incident, I felt completely differently about that person. I can predict that Ulrich and Georg will have similar reactions from being pinned under the tree together. I will read on to see if my prediction is correct.

sight or sound of the marauders. If only on this wild night, in this dark, lone spot, he might come across Georg Znaeym, man to man, with none to witness—that was the wish that was uppermost in his thoughts. And as he stepped round the trunk of a huge beech he came face to face with the man he sought.

6

The two enemies stood glaring at one another for a long silent moment. Each had a rifle in his hand, each had hate in his heart and murder uppermost in his mind. The chance had come to give full play to the passions of a lifetime. But a man who has been brought up under the code of a restraining civilization cannot easily nerve himself to shoot down his neighbor in cold blood and without word spoken, except for an offense against his hearth and honor. And before the moment of hesitation had given way to action a deed of Nature's own violence overwhelmed them both. A fierce shriek of the storm had been answered by a splitting crash over their heads, and ere they could leap aside a mass of falling beech tree had thundered down on them. Ulrich von Gradwitz found himself stretched on the ground, one arm numb beneath him and the other held almost as helplessly in a tight tangle of forked branches, while both legs were pinned beneath the fallen mass. His heavy shooting-boots had saved his feet from being crushed to pieces, but if his fractures were not as serious as they might have been, at least it was evident that he could not move from his present position till someone came to release him. The descending twigs had slashed the skin of his face, and he had to wink away some drops of blood from his eyelashes before he could take in a general view of the disaster. At his side, so near that under ordinary circumstances he could almost have touched him, lay Georg Znaeym, alive and struggling, but obviously as helplessly pinioned down as himself. All round them lay a thick-strewn wreckage of splintered branches and broken twigs.

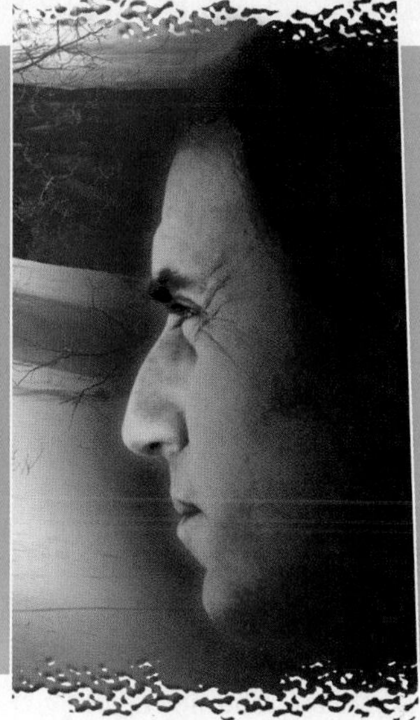

Relief at being alive and exasperation at his captive plight brought a strange medley of pious thank-offerings and sharp

The two enemies stood glaring at one another for a long silent moment.

7 **Literary Analysis**
Irony Each character wishes harm to the other. What is the irony in how the wish is fulfilled?

8 
Reading Check

What happens to the two men when the tree falls?

7 Literary Analysis

Irony

1. Have students read aloud the sentence at the top of the second bracketed passage: "And before the moment of hesitation had given way to action a deed of Nature's own violence overwhelmed them both."
2. **Ask** students why they think the word "Nature" is capitalized.

   Possible response: Nature is capitalized because it is personified—that is, it is given human characteristics.
3. **Ask** students what human characteristics or intentions seem to be given to Nature at this point in the story.

   Answer: The story says that Nature is capable of committing its "own violence," far greater than the violence that the men can commit. Nature, after all, is the true "owner" of the land, and the story suggests that Nature, as a third party, has stepped in to resolve the feud between the two men.
4. Have students read the rest of the second bracketed passage. Then, **ask** the Literary Analysis question: Each character wishes harm to the other. What is the irony in how the wish is fulfilled?

   Answer: The irony is that they each got what they wanted, but both are now injured and in a dire situation.

8 Reading Check

Answer: The tree injures and pins both men.

Differentiated Instruction for Universal Access

Strategy for Less Proficient Readers

To give students a context for the story and to model how to make inferences using prior knowledge and experience, show them **Reading Skill Graphic Organizer A** (***Graphic Organizer Transparencies,*** p. 46). The partially completed graphic organizer will give students insight into the process of making inferences. They can use it as a model for making their own inferences as they read.

Enrichment for Gifted/Talented Students

Challenge students to demonstrate their understanding of the story and its irony by writing a ballad about the long and destructive feud between the von Gradwitz and Znaeym families. Have students base their ballads on the natural setting of the story, the two main characters, and the irony of the plot. Ask students to perform their ballads for the class, with or without musical accompaniment.

❾ Literary Analysis

Irony

1. Remind students that, up to this point in their long feud, the two men have expressed only hatred toward one another. **Ask** students what the two men have been out hunting for.

   Answer: They have been hunting for each other.
2. Have students read the first bracketed passage aloud. **Ask** them to describe both men's situations.

   Answer: Both men have been injured and caught by the falling tree.
3. **Ask** students why Georg is happy.

   Answer: He's happy that Ulrich is caught.

   Ask students the Literary Analysis question: What is ironic about Georg's joy over catching Ulrich?

   Answer: Georg's joy is ironic because he is just as caught as Ulrich is.

❿ Connecting to the Big Question

1. Review the conflict between the two men. Point out that conflicts tend to self-perpetuate unless something happens to stop them.
2. Have students read the bracketed text beginning at the bottom of page 274. **Ask** students: What reasons does Ulrich give for his hate toward Georg? **Possible response:** Ulrich says Georg has been poaching on his lands.
3. **Ask:** Is the feud between the two men avoidable? For example, what could Georg do to change Ulrich's view of him? **Possible response:** Yes, the feud is avoidable. Georg could meet Ulrich's anger with a calm explanation of why he believes the land and its game belong to him. He could offer a compromise.

curses to Ulrich's lips. Georg, who was nearly blinded with the blood which trickled across his eyes, stopped his struggling for a moment to listen, and then gave a short, snarling laugh.

Literary Analysis ❾
Irony What is ironic about Georg's joy over catching Ulrich?

"So you're not killed, as you ought to be, but you're caught, anyway," he cried; "caught fast. Ho, what a jest, Ulrich von Gradwitz snared in his stolen forest. There's real justice for you!"

And he laughed again, mockingly and savagely.

"I'm caught in my own forest land," retorted Ulrich. "When my men come to release us you will wish, perhaps, that you were in a better plight than caught poaching on a neighbor's land, shame on you."

Georg was silent for a moment; then he answered quietly:

"Are you sure that your men will find much to release? I have men, too, in the forest tonight, close behind me, and *they* will be here first and do the releasing. When they drag me out from under these branches it won't need much clumsiness on their part to roll this mass of trunk right over on the top of you. Your men will find you dead under a fallen beech tree. For form's sake I shall send my condolences to your family."

Vocabulary
condolences (kən dō′ lən səz) *n.* expressions of sympathy with another in grief

"It is a useful hint," said Ulrich fiercely. "My men had orders to follow in ten minutes' time, seven of which must have gone by already, and when they get me out—I will remember the hint. Only as you will have met your death poaching on my lands I don't think I can decently send any message of condolence to your family."

❿ "Good," snarled Georg, "good. We fight this quarrel out to the

Vocabulary Development

CCSS Language 6

Word Analysis

- Ulrich remarks sneeringly that he cannot send a message of condolence to Georg's family. Write the word *condolence* on the board and point out that it is based on the Latin root *-dol-* which means "pain." The Latin word *dolere* means "to suffer."
- Ask students to think of other words with this root, and then work as a class to provide brief definitions.

Possible answers: *doldrums,* "period of stagnation or unhappy listlessness"; *doleful,* "full of sadness caused by pain"; *dolorous,* "marked by sorrow or pain."

- Have a volunteer look up in a dictionary any words that no one can define confidently.

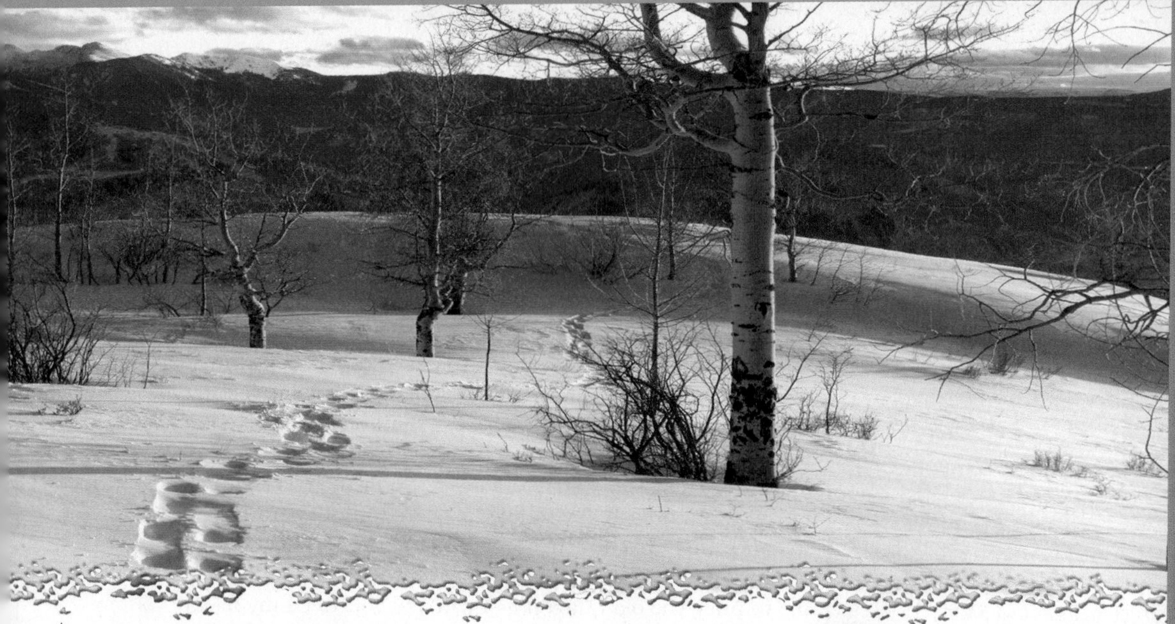

10 death, you and I and our foresters, with no cursed **interlopers** to come between us. Death and damnation to you, Ulrich von Gradwitz."

"The same to you, Georg Znaeym, forest-thief, game-snatcher."

Both men spoke with the bitterness of possible defeat before them, for each knew that it might be long before his men would seek him out or find him; it was a bare matter of chance which party would arrive first on the scene.

Both had now given up the useless struggle to free themselves from the mass of wood that held them down; Ulrich limited his endeavors to an effort to bring his one partially free arm near enough to his outer coat pocket to draw out his wine flask. Even when he had accomplished that operation it was long before he could manage the unscrewing of the stopper or get any of the liquid down his throat. But what a heaven-sent draft it seemed! It was an open winter, and little snow had fallen as yet, hence the captives suffered less from the cold than might have been the case at that season of the year; nevertheless, the wine was warming and reviving to the wounded man, and he looked across with something like a throb of pity to where his enemy lay, just keeping the groans of pain and weariness from crossing his lips.

"Could you reach this flask if I threw it over to you?" asked Ulrich suddenly; "there is good wine in it, and one may as well be as comfortable as one can. Let us drink, even if tonight one of us dies."

11

▲ Critical Viewing
What are some dangers the characters might face in a setting like this one? **[Analyze]**

Vocabulary
interlopers (in´ tər lō´ pərz) *n.* people who intrude or meddle in other peoples' business or lives

12

Reading Check

What is each man's hope for rescue?

11 Critical Viewing

Possible responses: Dangers include freezing to death, starving to death, being attacked by wild animals, and getting lost.

12 Reading Check

Answer: Each man hopes that his men—his foresters—will seek and find him before the other man's foresters arrive.

Fluency

Distribute copies of pages 274–275, and pair students. Have listeners mark text with which readers struggle. Circulate to monitor students' fluency. Collect students' marked up pages, then review difficult words and passages. Look for these problem issues:

- If students stumble over the word *Ho* (p. 274), explain that it is an interjection. Model the tone with which it is spoken, and have students echo.
- If students are confused by the italic text in *they* (p. 274), explain that it suggests emphasis. Have students read the surrounding text for context, then read the pertinent sentence aloud chorally.
- If students have difficulty with hyphenated adjectives such as *forest-thief, game-snatcher,* or *heaven-sent* (all on p. 275), explain that these terms should be read as one word, with little to no pause between them.

⓭ Reading Skill

Make Inferences

1. **Ask** students what they can infer about someone who is silent during a time of stress or crisis.

   Possible response: Someone who is silent at such a time may be thinking about matters of great importance, reconsidering past decisions, or vowing to change.

2. Have students read the first bracketed passage. **Ask** what they can infer about Ulrich from his statement beginning with "Neighbor."

   Possible response: Ulrich is experiencing a turning point in his life. His attitude toward himself and his enemy is changed from one of conflict to one of common humanity, and he realizes the foolishness of the feud.

3. **Ask** students the Reading Skill question: What can you infer that Georg is considering during this long silence?

   Possible response: He may be recognizing the time and energy wasted on the feud.

▶ **Monitor Progress:** Check that students try to use prior knowledge or experience to choose inferences founded on details in the story.

▶ **Reteach:** If necessary, remind students to ask themselves a question that begins, "Have I ever known or heard of someone who . . . ?" Urge students to record details and prior knowledge or experience in their Inferences Chart.

⓮ Literary Analysis

Irony

1. Remind students that the two men had just considered interlopers to be any outsiders who interfered in their feud. Then have them read the second bracketed passage.

2. **Ask** students the Literary Analysis question: What is surprising about this new meaning of interlopers?

   Answer: Now the "interlopers" are those who might *prevent* the two men from reconciling.

3. **Ask** students why this change is ironic.

   Answer: The change is ironic because it is the opposite of what the two men have always wanted and it is completely unexpected.

"No, I can scarcely see anything; there is so much blood caked round my eyes," said Georg, "and in any case I don't drink wine with an enemy."

Ulrich was silent for a few minutes, and lay listening to the weary screeching of the wind. An idea was slowly forming and growing in his brain, an idea that gained strength every time that he looked across at the man who was fighting so grimly against pain and exhaustion. In the pain and languor that Ulrich himself was feeling the old fierce hatred seemed to be dying down.

⓭ "Neighbor," he said presently, "do as you please if your men come first. It was a fair compact. But as for me, I've changed my mind. If my men are the first to come you shall be the first to be helped, as though you were my guest. We have quarreled like devils all our lives over this stupid strip of forest, where the trees can't even stand upright in a breath of wind. Lying here tonight, thinking, I've come to think we've been rather fools; there are better things in life than getting the better of a boundary dispute. Neighbor, if you will help me to bury the old quarrel I—I will ask you to be my friend."

Reading Skill
Make Inferences What can you infer that Georg is considering during this long silence?

Georg Znaeym was silent for so long that Ulrich thought, perhaps, he had fainted with the pain of his injuries. Then he spoke slowly and in jerks.

Literary Analysis
Irony What is surprising about this new meaning of interlopers?

⓮ "How the whole region would stare and gabble if we rode into the market square together. No one living can remember seeing a Znaeym and a von Gradwitz talking to one another in friendship. And what peace there would be among the forester folk if we ended our feud tonight. And if we choose to make peace among our people there is none other to interfere, no interlopers from outside . . . You would come and keep the Sylvester night beneath my roof, and I would come and feast on some high day at your castle . . . I would never fire a shot on your land, save when you invited me as a guest; and you should come and shoot

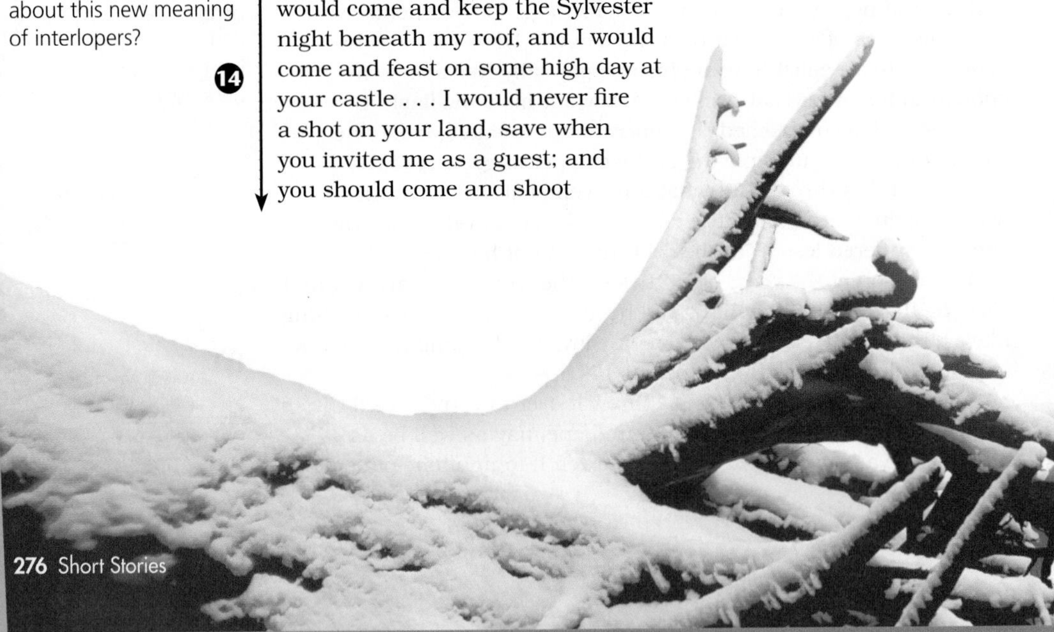

Vocabulary Development

Vocabulary Knowledge Rating

When students have completed reading and discussing "The Interlopers," have them take out their **Vocabulary Knowledge Rating Charts** for this selection. Read the words aloud once more and have students rate their knowledge of the words again in the After Reading column. Clarify any words that are still problematic. Have students write their own definitions and examples or sentences in the appropriate column. Then, have students complete the Vocabulary Practice at the end of the selection. Encourage students to use the words in further discussion and written work about this selection. Remind them that they will be accountable for these words on the **Selection Test**, ***Unit 2 Resources***, pp. 95–97 or 98–100.

4 with me down in the marshes where the wildfowl are. In all the countryside there are none that could hinder if we willed to make peace. I never thought to have wanted to do other than hate you all my life, but I think I have changed my mind about things too, this last half-hour. And you offered me your wine flask . . . Ulrich von Gradwitz, I will be your friend."

For a space both men were silent, turning over in their minds the wonderful changes that this dramatic reconciliation would bring about. In the cold, gloomy forest, with the wind tearing in fitful gusts through the naked branches and whistling round the tree trunks, they lay and waited for the help that would now bring release and succor to both parties. And each prayed a private prayer that his men might be the first to arrive, so that he might be the first to show honorable attention to the enemy that had become a friend.

5 Presently, as the wind dropped for a moment, Ulrich broke silence.

"Let's shout for help," he said; "in this lull our voices may carry a little way."

"They won't carry far through the trees and undergrowth," said Georg, "but we can try. Together, then."

The two raised their voices in a prolonged hunting call.

"Together again," said Ulrich a few minutes later, after listening in vain for an answering halloo.

"I heard something that time, I think," said Ulrich.

"I heard nothing but the pestilential wind," said Georg hoarsely.

There was silence again for some minutes, and then Ulrich gave a joyful cry.

"I can see figures coming through the wood. They are following in the way I came down the hillside."

Both men raised their voices in as loud a shout as they could muster.

"They hear us! They've stopped. Now they see us. They're running down the hill toward us," cried Ulrich.

"How many of them are there?" asked Georg.

"I can't see distinctly," said Ulrich; "nine or ten."

"Then they are yours," said Georg; "I had only seven out with me."

Spiral Review
Conflict What contrast in this paragraph hints that the men's friendship may be short lived?

Literary Analysis
Irony In what way is the two men's cooperation an ironic situation?

In the cold, gloomy forest, with the wind tearing in fitful gusts through the naked branches and whistling round the tree trunks...

16 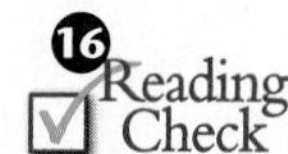

What do the men agree to do?

Spiral Review

Conflict

1. Remind students that they studied the concept of conflict in the Unit 2 Literary Analysis workshop (pp. 196–209).
2. **Ask** students the Spiral Review question.

   Possible response: The contrast between the warmth and peacefulness of the men's newfound friendship and the cold and bitter weather suggests that although their conflict with each other has ended, their conflict with nature is still a problem.

15 Literary Analysis

Irony

1. Remind students that an ironic situation is one in which things are not what they seem to be or expectations are overturned or disappointed.
2. Have students reread the second bracketed passage. **Ask** students what the two men are doing now that they have never done before.

   Answer: The two men are each considering showing "honorable attention" to the other, cooperating, and sharing hope and joy.
3. **Ask** students the Literary Analysis question: In what way is the two men's cooperation an ironic situation?

   Answer: Their cooperation is ironic because they had set out to kill each other. What they expected is the opposite of what is occurring.

16 Reading Check

Answer: They agree to work together, and to shout for help.

Concept Connector

Anticipation Guide

Have students return to their **Anticipation Guides** and respond to the statements again in the After Reading column. They may do this individually or in their original pairs or groups. Then, lead a class discussion, probing for what students have learned that confirms or invalidates each statement. Encourage students to cite specific details, quotations, or other evidence from the text to support their responses to each statement.

Writing About the Big Question

Have students compare their responses to the sentence starters they completed before they read the story with their ideas afterwards. Ask them to explain whether their thoughts have changed.

Reading Skill Graphic Organizer

Ask students to review the graphic organizers they completed to make inferences. Show them **Reading Skill Graphic Organizer A** (*Graphic Organizer Transparencies*, p. 46) as an example. Then have students share their graphic organizers and inferences.

17 Literary Analysis

Irony

1. Read the bracketed passage aloud. **Ask** students the Literary Analysis question: In what way does the story's surprise ending make the title ironic?

   Answer: The surprise ending conveys the irony that, even though they have reconciled with each other, unexpected interlopers—the wolves—will bring a lethal end to their plans. In a further ironic twist, it is the men's cries for help that summon their killers.
2. Point out to students that part of irony is the tone, or attitude, it adds to a story.
3. **Ask** students what final tone they think the author conveys with this ironic surprise ending.

   Answer: The ironic ending adds a tone of sympathy for the men as well as a deep regret for all that they have lost by wasting a great deal of their lives in hatred and violence. It is now too late for them to enjoy their friendship.

ASSESS

Answers

Critical Thinking

Before students respond, you may wish to have them write a brief objective summary of the selection. As they answer the questions below, remind them to support their answers with evidence from the text.

1. (a) Ulrich's family won possession of the land. (b) Georg does not accept the court's decision.
2. (a) The tree pins and injures both men. (b) Their difficult circumstances help the men realize the futility of their dispute.
3. (a) **Possible response:** Some students may believe that the men deserved their fate because of their stubborn hatred.

   (b) **Possible response:** Students may note that the story made them realize more intensely that people should resolve their differences.
4. **Possible responses:** (a) Three generations (b) The feud has lasted for generations and is widely known in the community.

Literary Analysis
Irony In what way does the story's surprise ending make the title ironic?

"They are making all the speed they can, brave lads," said Ulrich gladly.

"Are they your men?" asked Georg. "Are they your men?" he repeated impatiently as Ulrich did not answer.

17 "No," said Ulrich with a laugh, the idiotic chattering laugh of a man unstrung with hideous fear.

"Who are they?" asked Georg quickly, straining his eyes to see what the other would gladly not have seen.

"*Wolves.*"

Critical Thinking

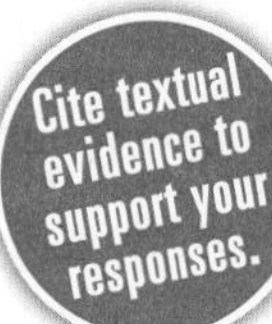
Cite textual evidence to support your responses.

1. **Key Ideas and Details (a)** Whose family won possession of the disputed land in the lawsuit? **(b) Interpret:** Why does Georg not consider himself a poacher?
2. **Key Ideas and Details (a)** In what condition does the fallen tree leave each man? **(b) Draw Conclusions:** Why do the men decide finally to end their feud?
3. **Integration of Knowledge and Ideas (a) Evaluate:** Considering the cause of their predicament, do you think the two men deserved their fate? Why or why not? **(b) Discuss:** Share your ideas with a partner and then explain how your answer has grown or changed.
4. **Integration of Knowledge and Ideas (a)** How long has the controversy between Ulrich and Georg been going on? **(b)** Why does it take special courage for Ulrich and Georg to consider the conflict no longer "necessary"? *[Connect to the Big Question: Is conflict necessary?]*

Assessment Resources

Unit 2 Resources

L1 L2 EL **Selection Test A,** pp. 95–97. Administer **Selection Test A** to less advanced students and English learners.

L3 L4 EL **Selection Test B,** pp. 98–100. Administer Test B to on-level and more advanced students.

L3 L4 **Open-Book Test,** pp. 92–94. As an alternative, administer the Open Book Test.

All **Customizable Test Bank**

All **Self-tests**
Students may prepare for the **Selection Test** by taking the **Self-test** online.

PHLit Online!

All assessment resources are available at **www.PHLitOnline.com.**

After You Read The Interlopers

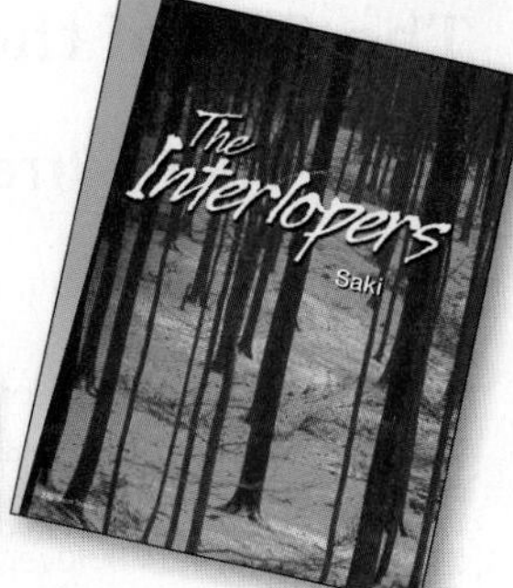

Literary Analysis: Irony

1. **Key Ideas and Details (a)** Identify **irony** in the story by using a chart like the one shown. In the first box, note the outcome that Ulrich and Georg expect when they first confront each other in the forest. In the second box, describe what actually happens.

What Characters Expect	→	What Actually Happens

(b) What message about life does this **situational irony** convey?

2. **Craft and Structure (a)** Which **nuances,** or subtle details, in "The Interlopers" make its **surprise ending** seem like a logical outcome of events? **(b)** Is the ending certain, or is it ambiguous—open to many interpretations? Explain your response.

Reading Skill: Make Inferences

3. **(a)** What **inferences** do you think Saki intended readers to make about the characters of Ulrich and Georg? **(b)** Which details in the text support your inferences?
4. In what ways do your prior knowledge and experience of characters help you to make inferences about Ulrich and Georg?

Vocabulary

Acquisition and Use Explain why each statement is true or false.

1. A beach generally has a *precipitous* slope down to the water.
2. It is proper to express *condolences* to one who has suffered a loss.
3. *Interlopers* are people who are always welcome.
4. A *feud* between powerful families could endanger a community.
5. People involved in a *disputed* matter enjoy each other's company.
6. If protesters did not obey a curfew, they would have *acquiesced.*

Word Study Use the context of the sentences and what you know about the **Latin prefix *inter-*** to explain your answer to each question.

1. Does an *international* crisis affect more than one country?
2. Where is an *intertidal* zone located?

Word Study

The **Latin prefix *inter-*** means "between."

Apply It Explain how the prefix *inter-* contributes to the meanings of these words. Consult a dictionary if necessary.

intercept
intermission
interstate

Answers

Literary Analysis

1. (a) **What characters expect—** Each man expects that there will be a fight to the death and that he will be victorious. **What actually happens—** A tree falls and pins them down; they reconcile but are discovered by wolves.

   For other sample answers, see ***Graphic Organizer Transparencies,*** **Literary Analysis Graphic Organizer A,** p. 49, and the **Additional Answers** section.

   (b) The situational irony conveys the idea that life isn't guaranteed and people should resolve issues with one another before it's too late.
2. (a) Details include the wildness and danger of the forest and references to the "beast of the woods" and "four-footed quarry." (b) **Possible response:** The ending is ambiguous. Wolves are running toward the men, but their foresters should be nearby and might be able to scare off the wolves and rescue the men.

Reading Skill

3. (a) **Possible response:** Saki probably intended readers to infer that the men are proud and stubborn, and that their change at the end gives them a glimpse of the lives they could have led. (b) Details include their insults, their intention to kill each other, and their vision of reconciliation.
4. **Possible response:** Students may say that they have read stories and seen movies about people in conflict, thus understanding how fiercely people can hate each other.

Vocabulary

Acquisition and Use

Sample answers:

1. F. A beach slopes gently down to the water, so it is not precipitous.
2. T. Condolences are expressions of sorrow, so you would offer them to someone who has suffered a loss.
3. F. Interlopers are people who meddle in people's business; they are seldom welcome.

Answers Continued

4. T. A long-standing quarrel, or feud, between powerful families could endanger a community by causing violence.
5. F. A disputed, or contested, matter can bring about bad feelings between people, so they wouldn't enjoy being around each other.
6. F. If the protestors didn't obey the curfew, they didn't agree without protest, or acquiesce, to it.

Word Study

Sample answers:

1. Yes, the prefix *inter-* means "between," so an international crisis affects several countries.
2. The prefix *inter-* means "between," so an intertidal zone is located between high and low tide levels.

Word Study: Apply It

Sample answers: To intercept means to stop someone or something between one place and another. An intermission is a break between acts. Something that runs interstate runs between states.

EXTEND/ASSESS

Answers

Conventions

1. Introduce the skill, using the instruction on the student page.
2. Discuss the chart.

Think Aloud: Model the Skill

Use the following "think aloud" to model forming irregular past tense verbs. Say to students:

Since irregular verbs don't follow the usual rules, I have to memorize their past tenses. Still, I can sometimes use general similarities to help me. For example, many irregular verbs form the past tense by changing the internal vowel instead of adding *-ed* to the end. This means that *hang* becomes *hung* and *drive* becomes *drove* and *win* becomes *won*. When I form an irregular past tense verb, I try different interior vowels and then check a dictionary if I'm still not sure.

PH WRITING COACH Grade 9

Students will find instruction on and practice with irregular verbs in Chapter 17, section 1.

Practice A

1. written
2. sold; buy
3. chose
4. spoken; seen

Reading Application

Possible responses:

1. see, is seeing, saw, has/have seen
2. am, is being, was/were, has been
3. fall, is falling, fell, has/have fallen
4. go, is going, went, has/have gone
5. run, is running, ran, has/have run

Practice B

1. spoke
2. has chosen
3. saw
4. given

Writing Application

1. took cover
2. were afraid
3. spoke quietly
4. wrote wills

PERFORMANCE TASKS

Integrated Language Skills

The Gift of the Magi • The Interlopers

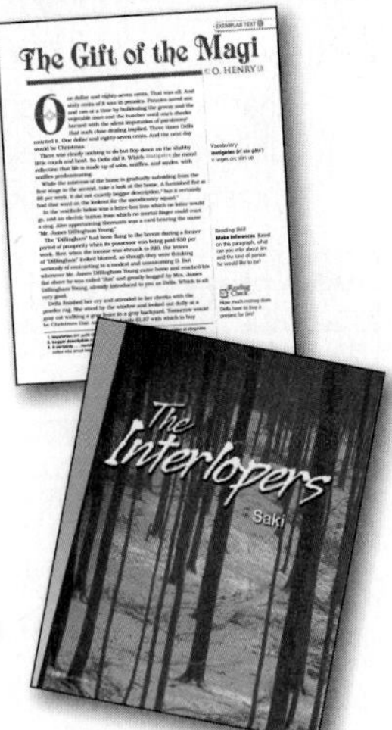

Conventions: Irregular Verbs

Irregular verbs form their principal parts in a variety of ways.

Regular verbs form the present participle by adding *-ing* to the present form. They form the past and past participle by adding *-ed* to the present form. **Irregular verbs** also form the present participle by adding *-ing* to the present form. However, they form the past and past participle in a variety of ways. Here are a few of the most common examples:

Present	Past	Past Participle
be (am, is, are)	was, were	(has) been
buy	bought	(has) bought
choose	chose	(has) chosen
come	came	(has) come
give	gave	(has) given
go	went	(has) gone
have	had	(has) had
see	saw	(has) seen
sell	sold	(has) sold
speak	spoke	(has) spoken
take	took	(has) taken
write	wrote	(has) written

Practice A Use the correct form of each verb in parentheses.

1. O. Henry has (write) a great story.
2. Della (sell) her hair to (buy) Jim a watch fob.
3. Jim (choose) a set of combs for Della.
4. By the end, the husband and wife have (speak) of their love and have (see) its power.

Reading Application Find five irregular verbs that appear in "The Gift of the Magi." Write the principal parts of each.

Practice B Revise each sentence by correcting the mistakes in the principal parts of verbs.

1. In the forest, Ulrich speaked to himself.
2. Georg has chose to trespass on my land.
3. Suddenly, Ulrich seen Georg, rifle in hand.
4. What cause for hatred have these men gave?

Writing Application Rewrite the following sentence, replacing the underlined words with these phrases: take cover, be afraid, speak quietly, write wills. *While they waited for the wolves, they* *became* *friends*.

PH WRITING COACH Further instruction and practice are available in *Prentice Hall Writing Coach*.

280 Short Stories

Extend the Lesson

Sentence Modeling

Choose the sentence given from the selection students have read:

"Perhaps you have seen a pier glass in an $8 flat." ("The Gift of the Magi")

"Could you reach this flask if I threw it over to you?" ("The Interlopers")

Ask students what they notice about the sentence. Elicit from them that the sentence contains an irregular verb. Ask students to give the present, present progressive, past, and past participle of each verb (see, is/am seeing, saw, has/have seen; throw, is/am throwing, threw, has/have thrown). Then, ask students what else they notice. ("The Gift of the Magi": The author is speaking directly to the reader. "The Interlopers": This is a polite way to ask the question.)

Have students imitate the sentence by writing sentences on topics of their own choosing, matching each grammatical and stylistic feature discussed. Have students share their sentences with the class.

Writing

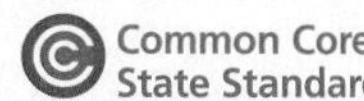

Narrative Text These selections present conflicts that end in irony. Write a **news report** about the experiences characters face in either story.

- First, gather facts by asking the questions *Who? What? Where? When? Why?* and *How?* Write an opening paragraph or lead that summarizes events and grabs the reader's interest.
- Include quotations to show characters' reactions. Choose logical points where quotations will integrate smoothly into the narrative.
- Read your lead paragraph to a classmate. Revise unclear parts.
- Add several more paragraphs, providing details that tell the rest of the story.

Grammar Application Make sure to form the principal parts of irregular verbs correctly.

Writing Workshop: *Work in Progress*

Prewriting for Narration: Short Story Using the Character Profile from your portfolio, write a letter from your character to a best friend, telling about an important event. Describe the event in detail and show why it is important. Save this letter in your portfolio.

Common Core State Standards

L.9-10.1; W.9-10.3, W.9-10.3.c.; SL.9-10.4
[For the full wording of the standards, see page 256.]

Use this prewriting activity to prepare for the **Writing Workshop** on page 306.

Speaking and Listening

Presentation of Ideas With a group of classmates, use your persuasive skills to present a **debate.**

- If you read "The Gift of the Magi," debate whether sacrifice is the best expression of love.
- If you read "The Interlopers," debate which character is entitled to the disputed land.

Follow these steps to complete the assignment:

- Prepare an argument that expresses your opinion.
- Choose supporting evidence. Look for specific ways in which the story supports your claim. Find events, quotations from dialogue, comments from the narrator, and so on. If necessary, do additional research to find outside evidence, such as statistics or quotations from experts to back up your ideas.
- Anticipate opposing arguments. Consider what the other side may say. Be ready with a response and evidence to support it.
- After the teams have debated, ask the audience to evaluate the presentation and decide which team was more persuasive.

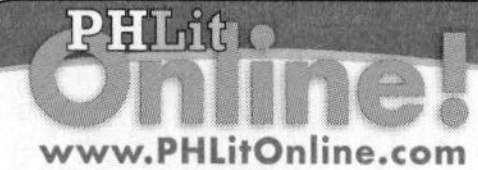

www.PHLitOnline.com

- Interactive graphic organizers
- Grammar tutorial
- Interactive journals

EXTEND/ASSESS

Writing

1. Review the assignment, using the instruction on the student page.
2. To give students guidance for writing a news story, give them **Support for Writing,** p. 90, in ***Unit 2 Resources.***
3. To evaluate students' news stories, use the Short Story rubrics, pp. 226–227 in ***Professional Development Guidebook.***

Grammar Application

Have students check their drafts to make sure they have used irregular verbs correctly.

Six Traits Focus

✔	Ideas		Word Choice
✔	Organization		Sentence Fluency
	Voice		Conventions

PH WRITING COACH Grade 9

Students will find instruction on and practice with narrative writing in Chapters 5 and 6.

Writing Workshop
Work in Progress

Have students save their completed letters in their portfolios. They will use their letters later as they complete the Writing Workshop assignment (see pp. 306–311).

Speaking and Listening

1. Review the assignment, using the instruction on the student page.
2. Have students complete the **Support for Extend Your Learning** page (***Unit 2 Resources,*** p. 91).

Teaching Resources

Unit 2 Resources

- L3 L4 EL **Integrated Language Skills: Grammar,** p. 89
- L3 L4 EL **Support for Writing,** p. 90
- L3 L4 **Support for Extend Your Learning,** p. 91
- L4 **Enrichment,** p. 88

Enriched Online Student Edition
Available under After You Read for this selection:

- All **Interactive Grammar Tutorial**
- L3 L4 **Internet Research Activity**

Professional Development Guidebook
Rubrics for Self-Assessment: Short Story, pp. 226–227

PHLit Online! All print and digital resources are available at **www.PHLitOnline.com**. Online resources accessible by students are noted on the student page.

MONITORING PROGRESS

Using the Test Practice

In this two-page Test Practice, students apply the reading skill for the first half of Unit 2 to a passage of fiction and a passage of nonfiction.

Review this skill, making inferences, then administer the test. For more guidance, consult the ***Classroom Strategies and Teaching Routines*** card, **Formally Assessing Students.**

ASSESS

Answers

Answers With Explanations

1. C—The Departures board, lines, and metal detector are all details you would find at an airport. *Incorrect answers:* A—Carmen is going to Phoenix, but has not yet left her parents. B—There is no evidence that the passage is set in a home. D—Carmen is getting ready to board an airplane, but she is not yet on it.
2. B—Carmen swallows hard, feels alone, and her mother is reassuring her. *Incorrect answers:* A—Carmen does not apologize for anything. C—Carmen does not act in a proud manner. D—Carmen is nervous but not disappointed.
3. A—Mama's is speaking of her father, who would be Carmen's grandfather, so *abuelo* means "grandfather." *Incorrect answers:* B—This statement gives no context for the meaning of *abuelo.* C—This statement does not mention *abuelo* at all. D—same explanation as for B.
4. B—Everything Mama says is meant to reassure Carmen in her fear of flying alone. *Incorrect answers:* A—There is no evidence of this in the passage. C—Mama enjoys the fact that her father will tell Carmen a joke. D—There is no evidence of this in the passage.

Test Practice: Reading

Make Inferences

Fiction Selection

Directions: *Read the selection. Then, answer the questions.*

Carmen stared at the Departures board and swallowed hard. In about an hour, she would be taking her first airplane flight. "Everything will be fine, *querida,*" Mama whispered. "Your *abuelo* will be waiting for you in Phoenix—ready with a joke, I'm sure." Mama smiled the way she only did when she spoke of her father. "You need to go through security on your own now and wait at gate 23. Please call me on your cell phone if you have any problems. Have fun in Phoenix!" Mama kissed Carmen on the cheek and then stepped back. Carmen turned. Feeling more alone than she ever had felt before, Carmen put her bag on the conveyer belt and stepped through the metal detector.

1. It would be reasonable to infer that events in this passage take place
- **A.** in Phoenix, Arizona.
- **B.** in Carmen's home.
- **C.** at an airport.
- **D.** on an airplane.

2. Based on details in the passage, how do you think Carmen feels about making this trip?
- **A.** apologetic
- **B.** nervous
- **C.** proud
- **D.** disillusioned

3. Which detail is most helpful in making an inference about the meaning of *abuelo*?
- **A.** Mama smiles the way she only does when she is speaking of her father.
- **B.** In a little while, *abuelo* will see Carmen in Phoenix.
- **C.** Carmen feels very alone as she steps through the metal detector.
- **D.** *Abuelo* will probably tell Carmen a joke when she arrives in Phoenix.

4. From the tone of Mama's words, which of the following would be a reasonable inference?
- **A.** Mama does not want Carmen to go to Phoenix.
- **B.** Mama wants to help Carmen feel more comfortable flying alone.
- **C.** Mama thinks that making jokes is a waste of time.
- **D.** Mama wishes that she was going to Phoenix to see *abuelo.*

Writing for Assessment

What might readers **infer** about Carmen's thoughts as her plane departs for Phoenix? Write a one paragraph journal entry from Carmen's point of view describing what she is thinking and feeling at the beginning of the flight. Use details from the passage to develop your ideas.

Writing for Assessment

Students should use details from the selection to develop their ideas and draw inferences. Journal entries might describe Carmen's nervousness and her anticipation of seeing her *abuelo.*

Strategies for Test Taking

Remind students to read questions and answer choices carefully. For example, in item 3, a quick reading of choice A might lead a reader to think that *abuelo* means "father," because Mama is speaking of her father. In sentence 4, however, Mama says "your *abuelo*" to Carmen, which would make the word *abuelo* mean "grandfather."

Nonfiction Selection

Directions: *Read the selection. Then, answer the questions.*

The career of Bessie Coleman, the first African American pilot, began with a joke. When her brother John came home after World War I, he laughed about French women who were pilots. Inspired, Coleman went to France in 1920 and finished the ten-month training course in seven months. Coleman soon was performing in air shows in the United States, attracting crowds with her stunts. She also started plans for a flight school for African Americans. A test plane's malfunction ended her life in 1926, but Coleman's dream of a flight school was fulfilled by others.

1. Which of the following details helps readers infer that there were few women pilots in the 1920s?
A. Bessie Coleman became the first African American pilot.
B. Bessie Coleman performed in air shows.
C. World War I, in Europe, had just ended.
D. John Coleman treated the idea of women pilots as a joke.

2. Details about Coleman's training help readers infer that Coleman—
A. wanted to become a pilot as quickly as possible.
B. hoped to become a commercial pilot, not a stunt pilot.
C. was the only woman in her class to earn a pilot's license.
D. often was made fun of by her classmates.

3. Which of the following would *not* be a reasonable inference, based on the passage?
A. Coleman wanted to help other people fulfill their dreams.
B. Since Coleman's time, other African Americans have become pilots.
C. After World War I, the only jobs for pilots were in air shows.
D. It takes several months of training for a person to become a pilot.

4. Which word *best* describes Bessie Coleman, based on details in the passage?
A. impractical
B. creative
C. determined
D. thoughtless

Writing for Assessment

Connecting Across Texts

Suppose that Bessie Coleman and Carmen had a conversation about flying. What might they say to each other? Write a **dialogue** of at least ten lines between Bessie and Carmen. Incorporate details from the two passages.

www.PHLitOnline.com

- Online practice
- Instant feedback

Differentiated Instruction for Universal Access

Strategy for Special-Needs Students

Walk students through item 1 on page 282 to reinforce making inferences. Guide students in eliminating incorrect answer choices.

- A—If Carmen's grandfather will be waiting for her *in* Phoenix, Arizona, the passage cannot be set in Phoenix. (Eliminate.)
- B—There is no evidence that Mama and Carmen are in anyone's home. (Eliminate.)
- C—There are several details about airports. In addition, it is most logical that Carmen's mother would stay with her all the way to the airport, rather than sending her off on her first lain ride from some other place. (Possible answer.)
- D—Carmen and her mother are still on the public side of the security detector. There are no details to suggest that Carmen is already on the airplane. (Eliminate)

Help students to understand that **C** is the correct answer.

ASSESS

Answers

Answers With Explanations

1. D—John laughs at French women pilots because there are so few of them. *Incorrect answers:* A—Given the discrimination against African Americans at the time, there could have been many white women pilots before there was the first African American woman pilot. B—This detail reveals Coleman's skill rather than the scarcity of women pilots. C—This choice says nothing about women pilots in the 1920s.
2. A—Since Coleman finished the ten-month training course in seven months, she clearly was motivated to learn quickly. *Incorrect answers:* B—The passage does not even mention commercial pilots. C—This choice is not supported by the passage. D—same explanation as for C.
3. C—Bessie Coleman flew in air shows, but there is no reason to infer that this was the only job for pilots. *Incorrect answers:* A—Coleman's desire to start a flight school shows her interest in helping others learn to fly. B—The passage states that Coleman's flight school became a reality. D—The passage states that Coleman's training was a ten-month course, so there is no need to make this inference.
4. C—Coleman's refusal to let the attitudes of the time stand in her way and her completing her training early attest to her determination. *Incorrect answers:* A—Coleman took practical steps to become a pilot and plan a flight school. B—There is no evidence in the passage of this quality. D—same explanation as for B.

Writing for Assessment

Students' dialogues should reflect what they know about Carmen's nervousness about flying and what they can infer from Coleman's biography of her pleasure in that activity.

Students may take the test in interactive format with instant feedback online at **www.PHLitOnline.com.**

Reading for Information

Common Core State Standards

- Reading Informational Text 3
- Writing 1
- Language 4.b

Reading Skill

1. Introduce the skill, using the instruction on the student page.
2. Tell students they will critique the logic of functional documents as they read.

Think Aloud: Model the Skill

Model critiquing the logic of functional documents. Say to students:

The directory for a mall is a type of functional document. Directories use different sizes of type to show more and less important information. They also use colors to highlight different kinds of stores. When I think about *why* directories are set up as they are, I realize that their purpose is to make it easy for people to gather information quickly.

Multidraft Reading

Have students follow a multidraft reading protocol.

- **First reading**—Have students read to identify key ideas and details.
- **Second reading**—Have students read to identify the structure of the text.
- **Third reading**—Have students read to integrate knowledge and ideas by connecting the text to the world, their own experiences, and other texts.

Content-Area Vocabulary

1. Have students say each word.
2. Next, use each word in a sentence that defines it.
3. Finally, repeat your definitional sentence or a similar sentence with the word missing and have the class "fill in the blank" chorally.

Analyzing Functional and Expository Texts

Signs and Instructions

Technical Instructions

Common Core State Standards

Reading Informational Text
3. Analyze how the author unfolds an analysis or series of ideas or events, including the order in which the points are made, how they are introduced and developed, and the connections that are drawn between them.

Writing
1. Write arguments to support claims in an analysis of substantive topics or texts, using valid reasoning and relevant and sufficient evidence.

Language
4.b. Identify and correctly use patterns of word changes that indicate different meanings or parts of speech.

Reading Skill: Critique the Logic of Functional Documents

Because instructions give important information or help people perform a task, they should be clear and logical. To **critique the logic** of functional documents, look at how the writer identifies the steps in a process and the order in which each one should be completed. Consider whether the organization suits the information. Also, notice how the writer uses text features, such as the ones listed in the chart, to clarify ideas.

Text Features	Description
Subheads	Boldfaced words that identify the main idea of each section
Highlighted text	Boldfaced, italicized, uppercase words that emphasize important information
Charts, graphs, maps	Graphic organizers that order information in a clear, easy-to-understand form
Illustrations and diagrams	Graphic organizers that show ideas described in the text
Captions	Brief information that describes an illustration, diagram, or other graphic organizer

Content-Area Vocabulary

These words appear in the selections that follow. You may also encounter them in other content-area texts.

- **generated** (jen´ ə rāt´ d) *v.* caused to be; brought into being; produced
- **carabiners** (ker ə 'bē nərz) *n.* hooks used for climbing
- **substantial** (səb stan´ shəl) *adj.* large; important; ample

Is conflict necessary?

Have students discuss the importance of being prepared when encountering potentially dangerous situations.

Differentiated Instruction for Universal Access

Reading Support
Give students reading support with the appropriate version of the ***Reader's Notebooks:***

 L2 L3 *Reader's Notebook*

 L1 *Reader's Notebook: Adapted Version*

EL *Reader's Notebook: English Learner's Version*

Signs and Instructions

BEACH SAFETY GUIDE

HIGH SURF SIGN

Features:

- essential information
- symbols and text features
- brief sentences

WARNING

HIGH SURF

CAN CAUSE SERIOUS INJURIES OR DROWNING

IF IN DOUBT, DON'T GO OUT

It is logical that *warning* is the boldest word on the sign. The background for the word is orange—a color often used on warning signs and safety devices.

A simple picture illustrates the danger.

WARNING LEVEL: *DANGEROUS...*a potential for loss of *life* or *limb* exists.

CONDITION: Large powerful waves are **generated** by winds and storms at sea, sometimes thousands of miles from the Hawaiian Islands. Seasonal high surf occurs on all shores of Oahu. Typically, shorelines facing North, East and West receive high surf during winter months. Shores facing Southeast and Southwest receive high surf during summer months. Surf on the North shore may reach heights of twenty-five feet plus—on the West shore, *fifteen* feet plus!

INSTRUCTIONS: If you're uncertain of your abilities, don't go into the ocean during high surf; heed all posted high surf warnings!

The uppercase red letters in each heading let readers know that they are reading important information.

Differentiated Instruction for Universal Access

Strategy for Less Proficient Readers
Ask students to write a sentence telling what is happening in the picture on the *high surf* sign. Ask how many of their sentences included something about a person being tossed by a wave. Point out that carefully studying the pictures on signs can help you make sense of the words.

Enrichment for Gifted/Talented Students
Discuss that, because of safety issues, the *high surf* and *strong current* signs include a lot of words. Point out that most signs have few words so that the whole sign can be read at a glance. Also, explain that choosing the most meaningful and clear words for a sign can be challenging. Ask students to design a sign that would be useful in your school, such as ones about cell phone usage or proper locker usage. Have students work together to design the sign using five or fewer words.

TEACH

About Signs and Instructions

1. Review the features of signs and instructions on page 285 with students. **Ask** students what they would consider to be "essential information."

   Possible response: Students may say that details explaining a law or providing critical safety information are essential.
2. Discuss occasions when students have seen signs or brief instructions meant to ensure people's safety. Have them describe where they saw the signs and how the signs were helpful.
3. Point out to students that we often see signs and instructions in public places, such as along streets and highways, on airplanes and ships, and at parks and tourist attractions. Explain that many toys and other products for children also have warning labels about how the items should be used.

Critique the Logic of Functional Documents

1. Tell students that they are likely to encounter signs and instructions where their safety is at risk. Point out that such signs explain what dangers are present and how people should act to stay safe.
2. Have students read the document and the side notes.
3. Remind students that visual aids are used to make sure that everyone gets the message being communicated. **Ask:** Why does this sign use a simple graphic?

   Possible responses: This sign uses the graphic to communicate the message at a glance. The graphic also communicates the basic message to people who cannot read the sign.
4. **Ask** students what other features of the "beach safety guide" help direct readers' attention to important points.

   Possible responses: The orange background and the large type of the word "WARNING" call people's attention to the sign. The same is true of the large type and capital letters below the graphic. The red headings in the text also signal important information.

Critique the Logic of Functional Documents

1. Remind students that signs, like other visual aids, use images, color, and typeface to clearly communicate an important message in a small area. Tell students to glance at the sign quickly and then look away. **Ask:** What words did you read at a glance?

   Possible response: Students are likely to say "Strong Current." Point out that on signs with many words, the most important words are often the biggest.

2. **Ask:** Do you think the picture on the *STRONG CURRENT* sign is effective enough to be able to determine the danger at a glance? Or do you think you would need to read more to understand what the warning is about?

   Possible response: It is difficult to determine exactly what the danger is solely from the picture, but there is a sense of urgency. The words make it clear that this is a warning for a dangerous situation.

3. **Ask:** What should you do if you are caught in a strong current?

   Answer: Try to remain calm. If possible, swim at a diagonal to the current rather than against it. If you are not able to swim out of the current, signal for help by waving one or both arms and calling for help.

4. **Ask:** How do you know that information?

   Answer: The section of the "Beach Safety Guide" headed "Instructions" states it.

BEACH SAFETY GUIDE

STRONG CURRENT SIGN

WARNING
STRONG CURRENT
YOU COULD BE SWEPT AWAY FROM SHORE AND COULD DROWN
IF IN DOUBT, DON'T GO OUT

A specific warning message is stated briefly and clearly. The most important words are printed in the largest letters.

WARNING LEVEL: *DANGEROUS...a potential for loss of life or limb exists.*

CONDITION: These are swift moving channels of water against which it is difficult to swim. Strong currents frequently accompany high surf and rapid tide changes and can be recognized as a turbulent channel of water between areas where waves are breaking.

The information in the instructions is logically and simply stated.

INSTRUCTIONS: When caught in a strong current —Try to keep a level head. Don't panic! Wave one or both hands in the air, and scream or call for help. Swim diagonally to the current, not against it.

OCEAN SAFETY TIPS:

The tips reinforce warnings and instructions and clear up any misunderstandings readers might have.

- Swim in Lifeguarded Areas.
- Never Swim Alone.
- Don't Dive Into Unknown Water or Into Shallow Breaking Waves.
- Ask a Lifeguard About Beach and Surf Conditions Before Swimming.
- If You Are Unable to Swim Out of a Strong Current, Signal for Help.
- Rely on Your Swimming Ability Rather Than a Flotation Device.
- Look For, Read and Obey All Beach Safety Signs and Symbols.
- If In Doubt, Just Stay Out!

Vocabulary Development

CCSS Language 6

Vocabulary from Science

Point out that signs and instructions often use vocabulary that is specific to one particular setting, in this case, a beach. Guide students to understand the meaning of the following words that are used in the signs and instructions in this selection:

current: flow in the water marked by force or strength
channel: a narrow path of water
turbulent: agitated or disturbed
flotation: having the ability to float
surf: the swell of the sea

ROCK CLIMBING EQUIPMENT AND TECHNIQUES

Technical Instructions

Features:

- how-to information
- symbols and text features
- brief, to-the-point

THE FOLLOWING DESCRIBES one way of using ropes and equipment to climb safely. It also describes how to descend after climbing.

Top-Roping and Belaying

Subheads identify the content of each segment of the instructions.

In top-roping, a rope from the top of the climb always holds the climber, making most slips off the climb harmless. As shown above, the climber is attached to one end of the rope, the middle is passed through an anchor at the top of the climb, and the other end is held by the belayer.

The anchor at the top of the climb is assembled from loops of webbing connected to **carabiners** attached securely to the rock. The rope is passed through some of the carabiners, and the others are attached to either pieces of protection, wedged into a convenient crack, or bolts, which other climbers have drilled into the rock.

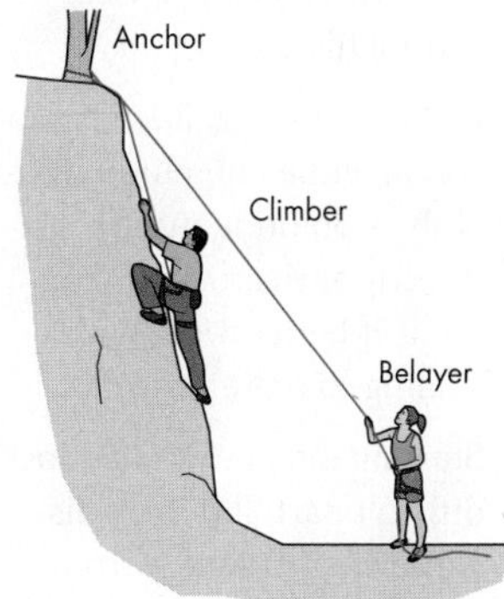

The anchor's carabiners with the rope passing through are suspended below the top of the climb to prevent the rope from rubbing. When bolts or protection are far from the top of the climb, **substantial** lengths of webbing are needed to place the carabiners correctly.

Not all climbs can be top-roped because of two requirements:

1. There must be a safe way to the top to set the anchor before the climber starts. Most popular top-roped climbs have an easy way to hike to the top.
2. The climb may be no longer than half the length of the rope; when the climber starts, the rope must cross the full length of the climb twice.

Numbered points explain an important idea so the reader will not misunderstand the instructions.

About Technical Instructions

1. Have students read the list of features of Technical Instructions in the box on page 287. **Ask** where students have seen symbols in technical instructions.

   Possible response: Students might mention the icons used in instructions for digital devices.
2. Explain to students that technical instructions contain detailed information. Information is presented in text and may be supplemented by diagrams or charts.
3. Invite students to share experiences they have had with technical documents. Have them explain what kinds of technical documents they have read and whether they were easy or difficult to understand.
4. **Ask:** What did the technical instructions look like?

   Possible response: The instructions were in list form with charts and different type styles and sizes to draw attention to the most important information.

Critique the Logic of Functional Documents

1. Tell students that technical documents include features such as charts, pictures, lists, and different font styles and sizes. Point out that looking at pictures is a good way to make sure that directions are clear.
2. Have students read the document. **Ask:** What information did you find in the instructions, and why was this a good format for presenting the information?

   Possible response: The instructions provide a detailed explanation of how to climb safely. The information works well in a technical instruction because it gives serious safety information along with explanations for dealing with the most difficult parts of the sport.
3. Have students review the page again. **Ask:** Who might find this information the most useful?

   Possible response: A person who is interested in learning to rock climb would find it most useful.

Differentiated Instruction for Universal Access

EL Vocabulary for English Learners

You might want to provide help with vocabulary and concept development. Be particularly careful to focus students' attention on the purpose of the instructions. Point out that technical instructions often use vocabulary that is specific to one particular setting, in this case the sport of rock climbing. Guide students to understand the meaning of the following words that are used in the document.

belayer: the person holding the rope at the bottom of the rock
webbing: ropes or strong support fabric
carabiners: sturdy oval shaped hooks that can be easily clipped to ropes
rappeling: a scheme of lowering yourself with a rope
slack: looseness in a stretch of rope
abrade: scrape or rub

Critique the Logic of Functional Documents

1. Direct students' attention to the diagram on page 288. **Ask** why technical instructions include diagrams.

   Possible response: Some processes are hard for readers to visualize and understand based only on a written description.

2. Point out that the author uses transitional words such as *unlike*, *moreover*, *since*, and *once* to help the reader understand the instructions. **Ask:** How do these words help clarify the instructions?

   Possible response: The words create signposts in the order of steps to clarify how some information is related to other information.

3. Identify the label in the diagram. **Ask:** How is a label helpful for understanding the diagram?

   Possible response: The label makes it easy to understand what is happening.

The belayer stops the rope with a belay device attached to his harness if the climber slips. The belay device makes it easy to apply enough friction to stop a falling climber. If there is some danger of the belayer being lifted into the air, he can be anchored down.

The belayer must keep the slack in the rope to a minimum since when a climber slips, any slack must be taken up before the rope can stop the fall. To take up this slack, the belayer pulls the rope downward as the climber climbs. While doing this, the belayer must never release the rope fully to ensure the climber could never fall far.

Rappeling

Rappeling is a scheme for lowering yourself with the rope. As shown above, the center of the rope is passed through an anchor at the top of the climb. The person descending wears a harness and attaches himself to the rope with a belay device, which he uses to control his descent.

Unlike climbing, it is best to be nearly horizontal while rappeling. In this position, the body is pointing more directly at the rock, giving the feet better friction and leading to more control.

Starting a rappel is the most difficult part. It is very disconcerting to switch from standing to being supported completely by the rope. Moreover, it is necessary to get below the anchor before the rope can help. If the anchor is below the top of the climb, climbing down is necessary.

Anchor

Diagrams illustrate the descriptions in the text, making it easy for readers to understand the technique. Labels identify important parts of the equipment.

Instructions outline the sequence of steps necessary to complete the task safely.

Once everybody has descended, the rope is recovered by pulling it through the anchor. The anchor cannot be recovered, but this is not usually a problem. In many cases, other climbers have placed a permanent anchor at the top, often a pair of bolts drilled into the rock connected to a ring with some chains. Another possibility is to use the base of a tree as an anchor. Since the rope is under little tension when it is pulled through the anchor, this abrades the rope and tree only slightly, and can be done occasionally.

A single rope can only be used to descend half a rope-length, but two ropes can be tied together to rappel a full rope-length. This is useful, for example, when descending a multi-pitch lead climb via the same route used for the ascent. The belay stations, usually spaced a full rope-length, can be used as rappel anchors. Three or more ropes cannot be used to rappel in this manner, since doing so would require rappeling past a knot and pulling a knot through the anchor, which are generally impossible.

288 Short Stories

Think Aloud

Critiquing Logic

To model the skill of critiquing the logic of functional documents, have students look at the section on rappeling. Then, use the following "think aloud." Say to students:

When I think about using functional documents, I think about how I can combine the information in images and text. I start by looking at the pictures. In this case, I see that the person is going up or down the rocks by holding onto the rope. That looks like a difficult task, so I wonder how he can accomplish it. I realize that the text looks quite detailed, so I turn to it to learn more about this technique.

The pictures prepare me for what I am about to read, and they raise questions in my mind. Then, once I read the text, the pictures and text together explain to me what I need to know about the topic.

After You Read

Signs and Instructions • Technical Instructions

Comparing Functional and Expository Texts

1. **Craft and Structure** **(a)** How is the organization of the information used in the signs and instructions document different from the organization used in the technical instructions? **(b) Critique the logic** of the organization of each document by explaining how it does or does not suit the information.
2. **Craft and Structure** For each document, identify specific text features that clarify the order of ideas or help draw connections among them.

Content-Area Vocabulary

3. **(a)** Explain how a change in prefix or suffix alters the meanings and parts of speech of the base word *generate*: *generation, generative,* and *regenerate*. **(b)** Use each word in a sentence that shows its meaning.

Timed Writing

Argumentative Text: Speech

Format and Audience
The prompt directs you to write a brief speech for your community, so your remarks should be three to five paragraphs long and should address the concerns of your audience.

People are often injured when they take unintentional risks. Write a brief speech for your community, urging people to observe safety signs and to follow equipment instructions exactly. Use the information in the signs and technical instructions to support your ideas. (25 minutes)

Academic Vocabulary
When you *support* your ideas, you use details and examples to show that your ideas are reasonable and correct.

5-Minute Planner

Complete these steps before you begin to write:

1. Read the prompt carefully. Look for key words and instructions that tell what you should include in your speech.
2. Review the signs and technical instructions. Consider the importance of the details presented, including the sequence of the information.
3. Jot down the main ideas you will cover in outline form.
4. Use your outline to organize your ideas as you write. **TIP:** Check your outline and make sure you have put new ideas in the best place.

Answers

Comparing Functional and Expository Texts

1. (a) **Possible response:** In the signs and instructions document, the most important information is presented prominently at the top of the sign. In the technical instructions, the information is presented in a sequence of steps with graphics. (b) **Possible response:** In the signs and instructions, it is logical to include the boldfaced, large headings and clear graphics so that all people, even those who cannot read or understand English, can understand them. In the technical instructions, it is logical to present the information in a sequence of steps with graphics so that the reader can understand them and follow along easily.
2. **Possible response:** In "Beach Safety Guide," red, uppercase subheads let the reader know the information is important. In "Rock Climbing Equipment and Techniques," illustrations show the techniques being described.
3. (a) **Sample response:** Prefixes and suffixes have their own meaning, and when added to a word, change the meaning of that word. The suffix *-ation* means "that which is" and changes the word to a noun. The suffix *-ive* means "like" and changes a word to an adjective. The prefix *re-* means "back or again."
(b) **Sample response:** The advancing technology created a new generation of electronics. Sunlight and water have a generative effect on plants. Food helped to regenerate the runners after the race.

Timed Writing

1. Before students complete the activity, guide them in identifying and analyzing key words and phrases in the prompt, highlighted on the student page.
2. Work with students to draw up guidelines for their speeches based on the key words:
   - **Focus** The speech should clearly explain why it is important for people in the community to pay attention to safety signs and equipment instructions.
   - **Organization** The speech should begin with a strong statement so that the audience will understand the speaker's position immediately. The statement should be followed with three or more reasons for the position.
   - **Support** The speech should use information from the signs and technical instructions to support its ideas.
   - **Style** The speech is argumentative, so it should include opinions and emotional language.
3. Have students use the 5-Minute Planner to structure their time.
4. Allow students 25 minutes to complete the assignment. Evaluate their work using the guidelines they have developed.

PREACHTEACH

Common Core State Standards

- **Reading Literature 4, 6**
- **Writing 2**

❶ Comparing Setting

Setting

1. Introduce the skill, using the instruction on the student page.
2. Give students a copy of **Comparing Setting Graphic Organizer B, *Graphic Organizer Transparencies,*** p. 52 to complete as they compare the selections.

Think Aloud: Model the Skill

Model a way to think about setting. Say to students:

As I read a story, I pay attention to details that tell me about the setting. These details are especially important in stories set in another country because the culture of that place affects characters' feelings, decisions, and actions. For example, a child on a Greek farm will face different choices and situations than will a child in a Chinese city. Thinking about the setting helps me recognize cultural clues, which in turn helps me understand the characters.

Cultural Perspective

1. Introduce the skill, using the instruction on the student page.
2. Point out that the setting can influence the way a character acts and speaks. Characters' actions will be affected by the ideas of their time period and the details of their physical environment. Characters from different places may speak different languages.
3. Explain that when characters seem to place special emphasis on aspects of behavior or appearances, they may be reflecting cultural perspectives.

Comparing Literary Works

The Man to Send Rain Clouds • Old Man of the Temple

❶ Comparing Setting

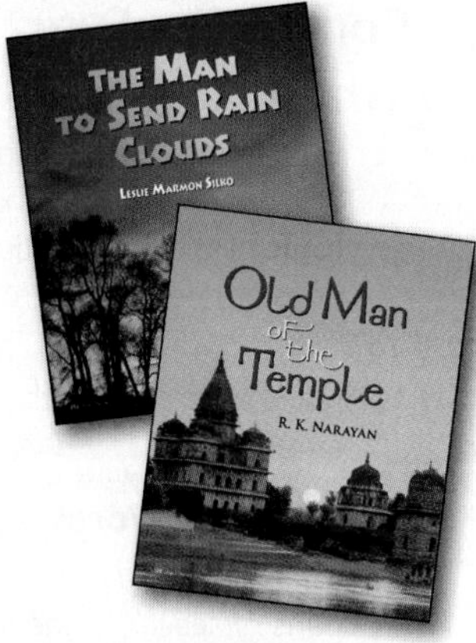

The **setting** of a story is the time and place in which it occurs. The time may include not only the *historical period* but also a year or an hour. "Place" may mean the social, economic, or *cultural environment*, not just the location. Cultural aspects of setting may be present in a variety of ways:

- the values and beliefs the characters hold
- the details of daily life, such as characters' work, food, or clothing
- the types of language, such as non-English words or slang, that characters use. To build setting, a writer may include *idioms*, or phrases whose meanings differ from those of the individual words.
- the themes and issues of the historical period

The importance of setting varies from story to story. Sometimes, the setting is only a backdrop for the action. In such a story, the setting could change, but events would remain the same. However, in some stories, the setting shapes the characters and plot. For example, cultural expectations may cause characters to take specific actions. Vivid descriptive details that focus on setting often create a story's mood, or emotional atmosphere, and even hint at what may happen to characters as the plot unfolds.

These two stories are set in very different places. However, culture and belief systems play a role in both. Use a chart like this to identify details suggesting the place, time, issues, and culture of each story.

	Place:	Time:	Culture:
The Man to Send Rain Clouds			
Old Man of the Temple			

Cultural Perspectives An author may express a distinct point of view, or attitude, toward the cultural setting of a story. That perspective may be positive, negative, mixed, or neutral. For example, an author may show that certain cultural values limit or complicate characters' lives. As you read, consider whether the author expresses a particular point of view toward the culture reflected in each story.

Common Core State Standards

Reading Literature

4. Determine the meaning of words and phrases as they are used in the text, including figurative and connotative meanings; analyze the cumulative impact of specific word choices on meaning and tone.

6. Analyze a particular point of view or cultural experience reflected in a work of literature from outside the United States, drawing on a wide reading of world literature.

Writing

2. Write informative/explanatory texts to examine and convey complex ideas, concepts, and information clearly and accurately through the effective selection, organization, and analysis of content.

- Vocabulary flashcards
- Interactive journals
- More about the authors
- Selection audio
- Interactive graphic organizers

Vocabulary Development

Vocabulary Knowledge Rating

Create a **Vocabulary Knowledge Rating Chart *(Professional Development Guidebook,*** p. 33) featuring the words glossed in the selections:

penetrated (p. 296)
perverse (p. 296)
venture (p. 304)

Give students a copy of the chart, and read the words aloud. Have students mark their rating of each in the Before You Read column. To gauge how much instruction to provide, tally the students who think they know each word.

Explain that the words are defined in the margin at the point where they appear in the selection. Urge students to be alert to these words as they read the selections. They will rate their knowledge again when they finish.

Vocabulary Central, featuring tools, activities, and songs for studying vocabulary, is available at **www.PHLitOnline.com.**

❷ Writing About the Big Question

In both of these stories, the authors show the modern world in conflict with traditional ways. Use these sentence starters to develop your ideas:

The modern world sometimes **competes** with traditional ways because ________________.

When these **differences** can be resolved, ________________.

Meet the Authors

Leslie Marmon Silko (b. 1948)

Author of "The Man to Send Rain Clouds"

Storytelling has always been an important part of Leslie Marmon Silko's life. Raised on the Laguna Pueblo reservation in New Mexico, she grew up listening to tribal stories told by her great-grandmother and great aunts. She has said that the oral tradition is "a collective memory and depends upon the whole community."

The Old and the New In her stories, novels, and poems, Silko explores what life is like for Native Americans in today's world. Many of her works capture the contrast between traditional values and beliefs and elements of modern life.

R. K. Narayan (1906–2001)

Author of "Old Man of the Temple"

R. K. Narayan was born in the city of Madras in southern India. He was one of nine children in a middle-class family. After briefly working as a teacher, he became a writer. In 1960, his novel *The Guide* won India's highest literary honor.

Combining Themes Within a career that spanned nearly seventy years, Narayan wrote more than fifteen novels—as well as collections of short stories and essays. His works skillfully combine Western plots and themes with Indian subject matter.

Teaching Resources

- All *Unit 2 Resources,* pp. 101–117
- All *Graphic Organizer Transparencies,* pp. 51–54
- All *Professional Development Guidebook,* p. 33
- All Enriched Online Student Edition
- L2 EL *Hear It!* Audio CD
- All *Common Core Companion,* pp. 35–47, 55–61, 190–201

All resources, including print and audio, are available online at **www.PHLitOnline.com.**

For more about the authors and practice with the selection vocabulary, go online at **www.PHLitOnline.com.**

Daily Bellringer

For each class during which you will teach this selection, have students complete one of the five vocabulary activities for Week 9 in the *Daily Bellringer Activities* booklet.

❷ Writing About the Big Question

1. Review the assignment with the class.
2. **Ask** students why they think people can feel so strongly about their cultural traditions, and why this might lead to conflicts.
3. Have students complete the sentence starters. Review their responses as a class. (**Possible responses:** The modern world sometimes competes with traditional ways because logic is stressed over tradition. When these differences can be resolved, people from all cultures can get along better.)
4. Remind students that their answers will help them think about the Big Question, "Is conflict necessary?"

Concept Connector

Tell students that they will return to their sentence starters after they have concluded reading.

Multidraft Reading

To assist struggling readers and to deepen reading for all, apply multidraft reading protocols. For each reading, have students set the purpose indicated:

- **First reading**—identifying key ideas and details and answering any Reading Checks.
- **Second reading**—analyzing craft and structure and responding to the side-column prompts.
- **Third reading**—integrating knowledge and ideas, connecting to other texts and the world, and answering the end-of-selection questions.

For more guidance, see the *Classroom Strategies and Teaching Routines* card on multidraft reading.

TEACH

❶ Background

History of the Pueblos "The Man to Send Rain Clouds" explores the traditions of the Pueblo people of the southwestern United States. The Pueblos have lived in the southwestern United States for nearly 2,000 years. They first came into contact with Europeans when the Spanish arrived in the 1500s. In modern times, the Pueblos have incorporated many aspects of the industrial world into their traditional lives. There are many Pueblo peoples, including the Hopi, Zuni, and Taos, who speak differing languages yet share a common heritage.

❷ Activating Prior Knowledge

Ask students to name movies or television shows that depict death as honorable, humorous, frightening, sad, or mythical. List students' responses on the board, and then point out the ways in which death can provoke such different responses. Tell students that the selection they are about to read describes traditions and attitudes toward death with which students may not be familiar.

Concept Connector

Students will follow up on this activity after completing "The Man to Send Rain Clouds."

❸ About the Selection

In "The Man to Send Rain Clouds," the death of an elderly Native American, Teofilo, serves as a backdrop to illuminate the actions, reactions, and interactions of the living. Although characters lead their lives according to centuries-old cultural rules and beliefs, these customs have been modified by outside influences. The funeral rites for Teofilo demonstrate how combining Native American and Christian traditions can create an enriching and redefining experience.

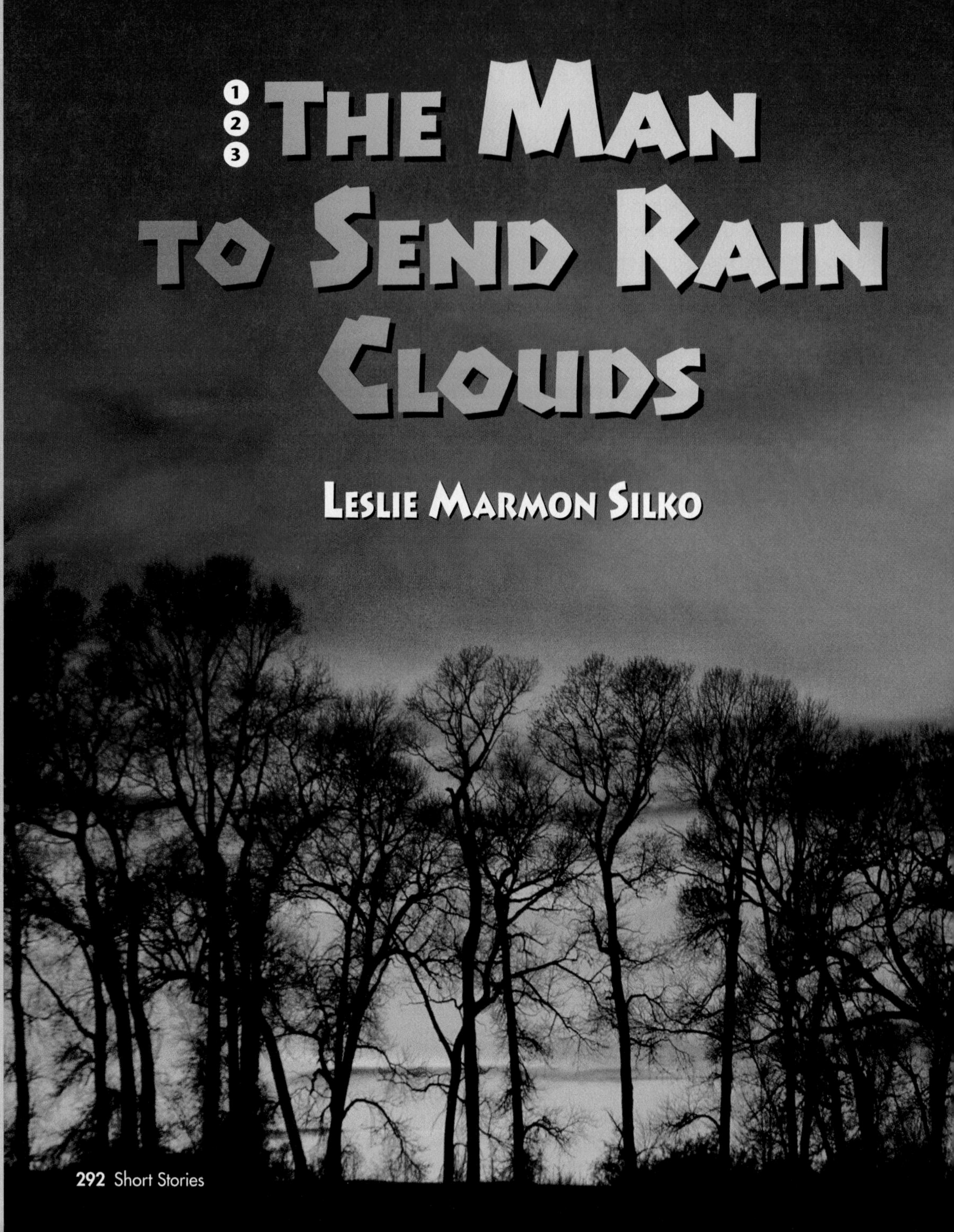

❶ ❷ ❸ The Man to Send Rain Clouds

Leslie Marmon Silko

Text Complexity Rubric

The Man to Send Rain Clouds		
Qualitative Measures	Context/ Knowledge Demands	Native American community in the Southwest; death and burial traditions 1 2 (3) 4 5
	Structure/ Language Clarity and Conventionality	Cultural terms explained in footnotes; on-level vocabulary 1 (2) 3 4 5
	Levels of Meaning/ Purpose/Concept Level	Accessible concept (burial of a family member) 1 (2) 3 4 5
Quantitative Measures	Text Length	Word Count: 1,721
	Lexile	920L

They found him under a big cottonwood tree. His Levi jacket and pants were faded light blue so that he had been easy to find. The big cottonwood tree stood apart from a small grove of winterbare cottonwoods which grew in the wide, sandy arroyo.[1] He had been dead for a day or more, and the sheep had wandered and scattered up and down the arroyo. Leon and his brother-in-law,
4 Ken, gathered the sheep and left them in the pen at the sheep camp before they returned to the cottonwood tree. Leon waited under the tree while Ken drove the truck through the deep sand to the edge of the arroyo. He squinted up at the sun and unzipped his jacket—it sure was hot for this time of year. But high and northwest the blue mountains were still in snow. Ken came sliding down the low, crumbling bank about fifty yards down, and he was bringing the red blanket.

Before they wrapped the old man, Leon took a piece of string out of his pocket and tied a small gray feather in the old man's long white hair. Ken gave him the paint. Across the brown wrinkled forehead he drew a streak of white and along the high cheekbones
5 he drew a strip of blue paint. He paused and watched Ken throw pinches of corn meal and pollen into the wind that fluttered the small gray feather. Then Leon painted with yellow under the old man's broad nose, and finally, when he had painted green across the chin, he smiled.

"Send us rain clouds, Grandfather." They laid the bundle in the back of the pickup and covered it with a heavy tarp before they started back to the pueblo.

They turned off the highway onto the sandy pueblo road. Not long after they passed the store and post office they saw Father Paul's car coming toward them. When he recognized their faces he slowed his car and waved for them to stop. The young priest rolled down the car window.

"Did you find old Teofilo?" he asked loudly.

Leon stopped the truck. "Good morning, Father. We were just out to the sheep camp. Everything is O.K. now."

"Thank God for that. Teofilo is a very old man. You really shouldn't allow him to stay at the sheep camp alone."

"No, he won't do that any more now."

"Well, I'm glad you understand. I hope I'll be seeing you at Mass[2] this week—we missed you last Sunday. See if you can get old Teofilo to come with you." The priest smiled and waved at them as they drove away.

1. **arroyo** (ə roi′ ō) *n.* a dry gully or hollow in the earth's surface.
2. **Mass** (mas) *n.* church service celebrated by Roman Catholics.

Literary Analysis
Setting What do the details about the trees, mountains, and sheep reveal about the characters' way of life?

6 
Reading Check

How do Leon and Ken prepare the old man's body before they move it?

4 Literary Analysis

Setting

1. Remind students that the setting of a story includes where and when the action takes place. **Ask** them to identify words from the first bracketed text that relate to setting.

   Answer: Setting-related words include "cottonwood tree," "sandy arroyo," "sheep," "hot," "mountains," and "snow."

2. **Ask** students to use these words to draw conclusions about the story's time and place.

   Possible response: The place is somewhere in the Southwest or another desert environment. The time is probably late winter or early spring.

3. **Ask** the students the Literary Analysis question: What do the details about the trees, mountains, and sheep reveal about the characters' way of life?

   Answer: These details reveal that the characters live and work in a rural, desert environment and have important ties to nature.

5 Critical Thinking

Make Inferences

1. Read aloud the second bracketed text.
2. **Ask** students to think about the actions that are taken when someone in their family or community dies. Then, **ask** them why Leon and Ken might be performing these actions.

   Answer: They are performing a funeral ritual of their culture.

6 Reading Check

Answer: Leon and Ken tie a feather into Teofilo's hair and mark his face with streaks of paint.

PHLit Online!

This selection is available in interactive format in the **Enriched Online Student Edition, www.PHLitOnline.com,** which includes an interactive graphic organizer.

Text Complexity: Reader and Task Suggestions

The Man to Send Rain Clouds

Preparing to Read the Text	Leveled Tasks
• Refer to the Background note on TE p. 292 and discuss the Pueblo people, guiding students to appreciate the history and traditions that influence these people today. • Using the Activating Prior Knowledge note on TE p. 292, discuss different attitudes toward death and burial traditions. • Guide students to use Multidraft Reading strategies (TE p. 291).	*Knowledge Demands* If students will have difficulty with context and knowledge demands, ask them to first read and take notes about details of what the characters do with Teofilo's body. Then, have them reread and take notes on the attitude of Teofilo's relatives during the process. *Analyzing* If students will not have difficulty with knowledge demands, ask them to read and take notes comparing the different views of death taken by the Pueblo relatives of Teofilo and the priest. Encourage students to contribute their ideas to discussion.

7 Literary Analysis

Setting

1. Remind students that an important aspect of setting is the cultural environment in which a story takes place.
2. Read the first bracketed text aloud. **Ask** the Literary Analysis question.

   Answer: The church bells marking the noon hour.
3. **Ask** students to predict how these cultural elements have affected the characters' way of life.

   Possible response: The characters' lives are probably a combination of Catholic and Pueblo beliefs and traditions.

Spiral Review

Character

1. Remind students that they studied the concept of character in the Unit 2 Literary Analysis workshop (pp. 196–209)
2. **Ask** students the Spiral Review question.

   Possible response: She is a static character, because she herself does not change or grow.

8  Connecting to the Big Question

1. **Ask** students to name a behavior, perhaps fidgeting or mumbling, that people may display if they feel conflicted inside. Discuss why moments of life passage, such as funerals, might lead people to feel conflicted inside.
2. Have students read the bracketed text on page 294. **Ask** students: What does Louise ask Leon to do? How does she speak? **Possible response:** She asks Leon to get the priest to sprinkle holy water for Grandpa. She speaks so quietly that Leon can hardly hear her.
3. **Ask:** Why does Louise feel so conflicted about asking for the priest? Is her conflict necessary? Explain. **Possible response:** She feels conflicted because they have just buried Grandpa with traditional ways, but she also wants to have the Christian priest. Her conflict is unavoidable because both traditions are important to her.

Louise and Teresa were waiting. The table was set for lunch, and the coffee was boiling on the black iron stove. Leon looked at Louise and then at Teresa.

"We found him under a cottonwood tree in the big arroyo near sheep camp. I guess he sat down to rest in the shade and never got up again." Leon walked toward the old man's bed. The red plaid shawl had been shaken and spread carefully over the bed, and a new brown flannel shirt and pair of stiff new Levi's were arranged neatly beside the pillow. Louise held the screen door open while Leon and Ken carried in the red blanket. He looked small and shriveled, and after they dressed him in the new shirt and pants he seemed more shrunken.

Literary Analysis
Setting Which detail here is a reminder of the Christian influence in the characters' lives? 7

It was noontime now because the church bells rang the Angelus.[3] They ate the beans with hot bread, and nobody said anything until after Teresa poured the coffee.

Ken stood up and put on his jacket. "I'll see about the gravediggers. Only the top layer of soil is frozen. I think it can be ready before dark."

Leon nodded his head and finished his coffee. After Ken had been gone for a while, the neighbors and clanspeople came quietly to embrace Teofilo's family and to leave food on the table because the gravediggers would come to eat when they were finished.

Spiral Review
Character Based on what you know about Louise and her role in this story, would you consider her a static character or a dynamic character? Explain. 8

The sky in the west was full of pale yellow light. Louise stood outside with her hands in the pockets of Leon's green army jacket that was too big for her. The funeral was over, and the old men had taken their candles and medicine bags[4] and were gone. She waited until the body was laid into the pickup before she said anything to Leon. She touched his arm, and he noticed that her hands were still dusty from the corn meal that she had sprinkled around the old man. When she spoke, Leon could not hear her.

"What did you say? I didn't hear you."

"I said that I had been thinking about something."

"About what?"

"About the priest sprinkling holy water for Grandpa. So he won't be thirsty."

Leon stared at the new moccasins that Teofilo had made for the ceremonial dances in the summer. They were nearly hidden by the red blanket. It was getting colder, and the wind pushed gray dust down the narrow pueblo road. The sun was approaching the long mesa where it disappeared during the winter. Louise stood there shivering and watching his face. Then he zipped up his jacket and opened the truck door. "I'll see if he's there."

3. **Angelus** (an′ jə ləs) *n.* bell rung at morning, noon, and evening to announce a prayer.
4. **medicine bags** bags containing objects that were thought to have special powers.

Vocabulary Development

CCSS Language 6

Thematic Vocabulary: The Big Question

As students are discussing "The Man to Send Rain Clouds," encourage them to use the thematic vocabulary presented in Introducing the Big Question, pp. 194–195. You might encourage them with sentence starters like these:

1. Leon and Ken *cooperate* easily in preparing Grandpa under the tree because . . .
2. They speak *amicably* to the priest, but they do not tell him . . .
3. After Grandpa is buried, Louise struggles to *articulate* . . .
4. Leon is willing to blend burial traditions, but the priest sees important *differences* between . . .

9
10

Ken stopped the pickup at the church, and Leon got out: and then Ken drove down the hill to the graveyard where people were waiting. Leon knocked at the old carved door with its symbols of the Lamb.[5] While he waited he looked up at the twin bells from the king of Spain with the last sunlight pouring around them in their tower.

The priest opened the door and smiled when he saw who it was. "Come in! What brings you here this evening?"

The priest walked toward the kitchen, and Leon stood with his cap in his hand, playing with the earflaps and examining the living room—the brown sofa, the green armchair, and the brass lamp that hung down from the ceiling by links of chain. The priest dragged a chair out of the kitchen and offered it to Leon.

"No thank you, Father. I only came to ask you if you would bring your holy water to the graveyard."

12 The priest turned away from Leon and looked out the window at the patio full of shadows and the dining-room windows of the nuns' cloister[6] across the patio. The curtains were heavy, and the light

5. **the Lamb** Jesus Christ, as the sacrificial Lamb of God.
6. **cloister** (kloisʹ tər) *n.* place devoted to religious seclusion.

▲ **Critical Viewing**
How does the scene depicted in this painting compare to the images described in the story? **[Compare and Contrast]**

11

What do the old men take with them when the funeral is over?

9 Humanities

Feast Day, San Juan Pueblo, 1921, by William Penhallow Henderson

Henderson's painting illustrates the presence of Catholicism in a Native American community. The looming church evokes an air of mystery and secrecy. In contrast, the villagers are gathering for their feast day in a circle of warmth and light. Use the following questions for discussion:

1. How does the painting depict the relationship between the Catholic church and the community?

   Answer: The church has a strong presence in the village scene, but it is separated from the main square by trees and buildings.

2. How does this relationship compare to the church-community relationship described in the story?

   Possible response: As in the painting, a Catholic presence is evident, but not all of the people in the community seem to be strong followers of it.

10 Critical Viewing

Answer: Red rock formations, adobe homes, desert roads, and a Catholic church are all part of the New Mexico landscape that serves as the setting for the story.

11 Reading Check

Answer: The old men take their candles and medicine bags with them.

Differentiated Instruction for Universal Access

EL Strategy for English Learners

Point out that the artwork can help students identify words in the story that are related to setting. Using the art on this page as a guide, have students list words from the story that relate to the image. Explain that these words help the reader use his or her imagination to picture where the story is taking place.

Strategy for Less Proficient Readers

Point out the text breaks in Silko's story, and explain that these indicate a change in time, place, or situation. Suggest that students work in pairs to identify how the setting changes at each of the text breaks. For example, the paragraph at the top of p. 294—before the first story break—takes place at lunchtime, before the funeral. **Ask:** Where are the characters on the other side of the story break? What time of day is it? **Answer:** The characters are at the graveside. It is sunset.

⓬ Literary Analysis

Setting

1. Have students **identify** the cultural and environmental elements of the setting as described in the bracketed text which begins on p. 295.

   Answer: The cultural setting explores the intersection of Catholic and Pueblo beliefs. The environmental setting is the dry New Mexico land.

2. **Ask** the Literary Analysis question: What details of Leon's request to the priest combine Christian and Pueblo beliefs?

   Answer: The priest believes that the Last Rites were necessary for Teofilo to have a Christian burial. Leon believes that all Teofilo needs from the priest is a sprinkling of holy water so that he will not be thirsty.

3. **Ask** students: Which cultural element (Catholic or Pueblo) becomes dominant by the end of the passage? Explain.

   Possible response: The Native American beliefs become dominant, because Leon is willing to leave the priest rather than be persuaded that Teofilo should have a Catholic burial.

Vocabulary
penetrated (pen´ i trāt´ əd) *v.* broke through

Literary Analysis
Setting What details of Leon's request to the priest combine Christian and Pueblo beliefs?

Vocabulary
perverse (pər vurs´) *adj.* deviating from what is considered right

from within faintly penetrated; it was impossible to see the nuns inside eating supper. "Why didn't you tell me he was dead? I could have brought the Last Rites[7] anyway."

Leon smiled. "It wasn't necessary, Father."

The priest stared down at his scuffed brown loafers and the worn hem of his cassock. "For a Christian burial it was necessary."

His voice was distant, and Leon thought that his blue eyes looked tired.

"It's O.K. Father, we just want him to have plenty of water."

The priest sank down into the green chair and picked up a glossy missionary magazine. He turned the colored pages full of lepers and pagans[8] without looking at them.

"You know I can't do that, Leon. There should have been the Last Rites and a funeral Mass at the very least."

Leon put on his green cap and pulled the flaps down over his ears. "It's getting late, Father. I've got to go."

When Leon opened the door Father Paul stood up and said, "Wait." He left the room and came back wearing a long brown overcoat. He followed Leon out the door and across the dim churchyard to the adobe steps in front of the church. They both stooped to fit through the low adobe entrance. And when they started down the hill to the graveyard only half of the sun was visible above the mesa.

The priest approached the grave slowly, wondering how they had managed to dig into the frozen ground; and then he remembered that this was New Mexico, and saw the pile of cold loose sand beside the hole. The people stood close to each other with little clouds of steam puffing from their faces. The priest looked at them and saw a pile of jackets, gloves, and scarves in the yellow, dry tumbleweeds that grew in the graveyard. He looked at the red blanket, not sure that Teofilo was so small, wondering if it wasn't some perverse Indian trick—something they did in March to ensure a good harvest—wondering if maybe old Teofilo was actually at sheep camp corraling the sheep for the night. But there he was, facing into a cold dry wind and squinting at the last sunlight, ready to bury a red wool blanket while the faces of his parishioners were in shadow with the last warmth of the sun on their backs.

His fingers were stiff, and it took him a long time to twist the lid off the holy water. Drops of water fell on the red blanket and soaked into dark icy spots. He sprinkled the grave and the water disappeared almost before it touched the dim, cold sand; it reminded him of something—he tried to remember what it was,

7. **Last Rites** religious ceremony for a dying person or for someone who has just died.
8. **pagans** (pā´ gənz) *n.* people who are not Christians, Muslims, or Jews.

Vocabulary Development

Ⓒ CCSS Language 6

Selection Vocabulary Reinforcement

To reinforce and assess students' comprehension of selection vocabulary words, give them sentences using the words in which the word may or may not be used correctly. Students must tell whether the use is correct and explain their answer. Use these sentences:

1. He carefully screwed the lid onto the jar, making sure that it *penetrated.*
   Answer: No, *penetrated* is not used correctly. It means "found a way through." A lid only covers a jar; it doesn't go through it.
2. Amy's decision to spend her birthday touring cemeteries seemed *perverse.*
   Answer: Yes, *perverse* is used correctly. Most people would want to do something celebratory on their birthdays.

because he thought if he could remember he might understand this. He sprinkled more water; he shook the container until it was empty, and the water fell through the light from sundown like August rain that fell while the sun was still shining, almost evaporating before it touched the wilted squash flowers.

HE SPRINKLED THE GRAVE AND THE WATER DISAPPEARED ALMOST BEFORE IT TOUCHED THE DIM, COLD SAND...

The wind pulled at the priest's brown Franciscan robe[9] and swirled away the corn meal and pollen that had been sprinkled on the blanket. They lowered the bundle into the ground, and they didn't bother to untie the stiff pieces of new rope that were tied around the ends of the blanket. The sun was gone, and over on the highway the eastbound lane was full of headlights. The priest walked away slowly. Leon watched him climb the hill, and when he had disappeared within the tall, thick walls, Leon turned to look up at the high blue mountains in the deep snow that reflected a faint red light from the west. He felt good because it was finished, and he was happy about the sprinkling of the holy water; now the old man could send them big thunderclouds for sure.

9. **Franciscan** (fran sis´ kən) **robe** robe worn by a member of the Franciscan religious order, founded in 1209 by Saint Francis of Assisi.

Literary Analysis
Setting Which details in the last paragraph reflect Native American practices and beliefs? Explain.

Critical Thinking

Cite textual evidence to support your responses.

1. **Key Ideas and Details** **(a)** What do Leon and Ken find at the beginning of the story? **(b) Infer:** Why does Leon avoid telling Father Paul about Teofilo?
2. **Key Ideas and Details** **Infer:** What insight into the Pueblo people does Father Paul gain during the ceremony?
3. **Integration of Knowledge and Ideas** **(a) Draw Conclusions:** What do Leon's thoughts after Teofilo's burial reveal about his views of death? **(b) Compare and Contrast:** What does the ending reveal about the contrasts between Pueblo and Christian beliefs?
4. **Integration of Knowledge and Ideas** Why does Father Paul decide that the conflict over modern and traditional death rituals is not "necessary"? *[Connect to the Big Question: Is conflict necessary?]*

13 Literary Analysis
Setting

1. **Ask** students to summarize the action occurring in the last paragraph of the story.

   Answer: Teofilo is lowered into the ground; the priest walks away; Leon watches him climb the hill; and Leon looks at the mountain and feels happy.
2. **Ask** the Literary Analysis question: Which details in the last paragraph reflect Native American practices and beliefs? Explain.

   Answer: Leon's emotions reflect the Native American attitude toward death; the natural setting reflects their closeness with the land; and Leon convincing the priest to use holy water reflects the belief that the dead man can deliver rain to the dry region.

Concept Connector

Have students return to the Activating Prior Knowledge activity on p. 292. Compare beliefs and practices surrounding death in the selection with those previously discussed. Then, have students compare their Writing About the Big Question responses before reading the selection with their ideas afterwards.

ASSESS
Answers

Remind students to support their answers with evidence from the text.

Critical Thinking

1. (a) Leon and Ken find Teofilo's body. (b) Leon wants to give Teofilo a Native American burial.
2. He learns that the Pueblo people honor those who die and believe that the deceased can help the living.
3. (a) He believes that life continues after death. (b) **Possible response:** The story suggests that contrasting cultures do not have to clash.
4. **Possible response:** The priest felt that the Native American's traditions were as important as his own, so he allowed both and sprinkled the holy water over the grave.

Differentiated Instruction for Universal Access

Enrichment for Gifted/Talented Students
To give students a context for the story and to model how to make inferences using prior knowledge and experience, show them **Reading Skill Graphic Organizer A** (*Graphic Organizer Transparencies,* p. 51). The partially completed graphic organizer will give students insight into the process of making inferences. They can use it as a model for making their own inferences as they read.

Strategy for Advanced Readers
Have students write brief reports explaining the importance of the setting in "The Man to Send Rain Clouds." Remind students to address all aspects of setting—time, place, and culture—and to describe how each element contributes to the story's meaning. Suggest that students use their in-process **Comparing Setting Graphic Organizer B** (*Graphic Organizer Transparencies,* p. 52) as a starting point for writing.

⓮ Background

Universal Themes Most of Narayan's stories take place in the fictional town of Malgudi. While Malgudi is a distinctly southern Indian place, the tales that Narayan tells about it are universal. If the backdrop of any of Narayan's tales changed to a modern American town, the characters' struggles, plans, hopes, and dreams would still apply. It is his universal appeal to human experience that makes Narayan's writing so special.

⓯ Activating Prior Knowledge

Point out to students that ideas about ghosts vary from culture to culture. In some cultures, ghosts are dead ancestors, angry because they have been excluded from paradise. Some are upset over unfinished work. Others return to contact relatives, friends, or enemies. Write the following passage from the selection on the board, or read it aloud:

> *"Dead! Dead!" he said. "Don't talk nonsense. How can I be dead when you see me before you now? If I am dead how can I be saying this and that?"*

Have students discuss what kind of ghost is speaking and whom he may be addressing.

Concept Connector →

Students will follow up on this activity after completing "Old Man of the Temple."

⓰ About the Selection

In "Old Man of the Temple," the Talkative Man describes a long-ago encounter with the ghost of an old man. The ghost has temporarily taken over the body of the Talkative Man's driver, Doss. The Talkative Man helps the ghost find its way to a permanent departure. The story explores a timeless theme: people's inability to let go of the past.

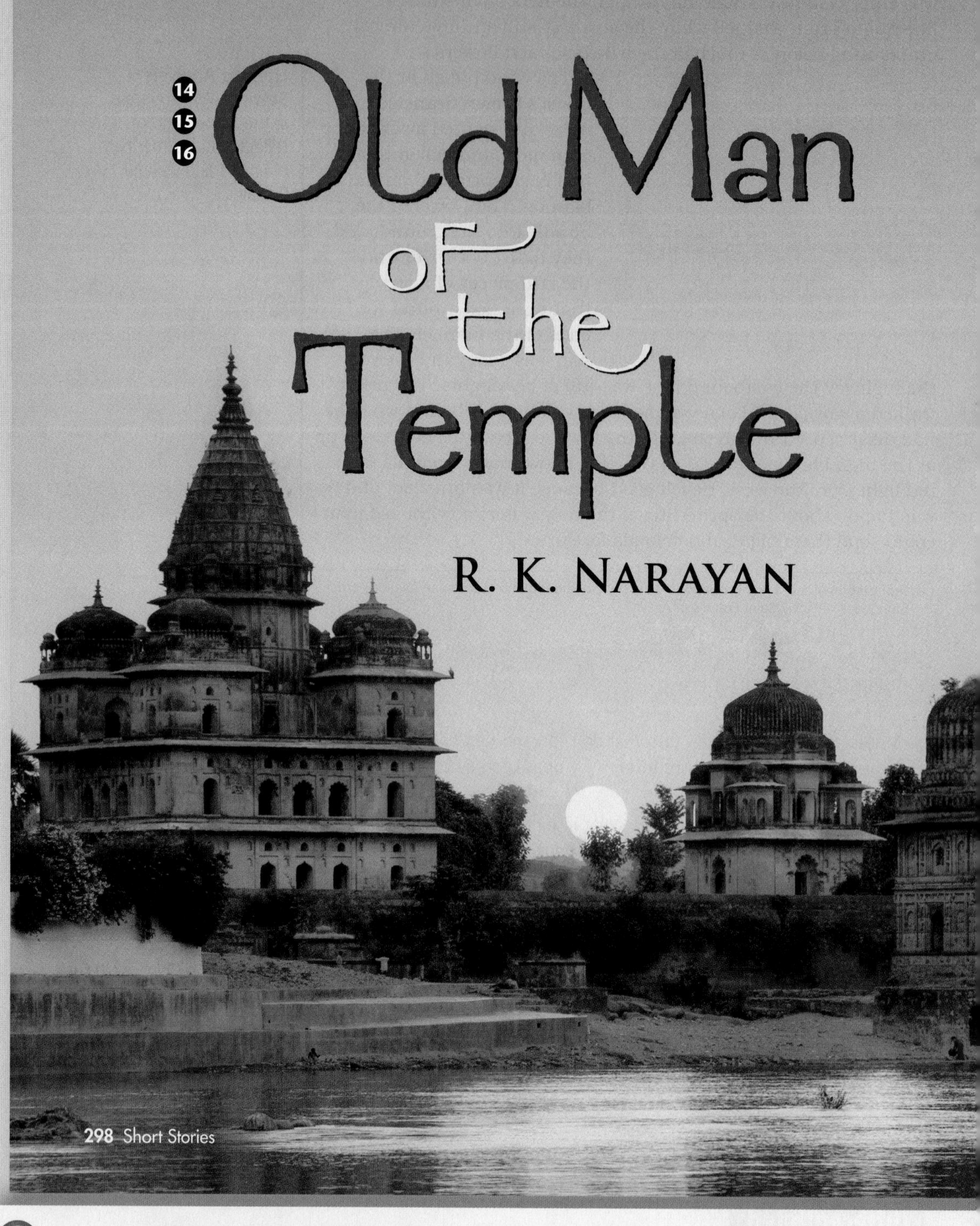

⓮ ⓯ ⓰

Old Man of the Temple

R. K. NARAYAN

Text Complexity Rubric

Old Man of the Temple		
Qualitative Measures	**Context/ Knowledge Demands**	Ghost story that alternates elements of reality and fantasy; set in India 1 2 ③ 4 5
	Structure/ Language Clarity and Conventionality	Heavy dialogue; historical and cultural terms 1 2 ③ 4 5
	Levels of Meaning/ Purpose/Concept Level	Accessible concept (coming to terms with past) 1 2 ③ 4 5
Quantitative Measures	**Text Length**	Word Count: 2,109
	Lexile	560L

17 Critical Viewing

Possible response: Ghosts or demons might lurk inside the temple. The architecture is so exotic that almost anything might happen.

This selection is available in interactive format in the **Enriched Online Student Edition, www.PHLitOnline.com,** which includes an interactive graphic organizer.

The Talkative Man said:

It was some years ago that this happened. I don't know if you can make anything of it. If you do, I shall be glad to hear what you have to say; but personally I don't understand it at all. It has always mystified me. Perhaps the driver was drunk; perhaps he wasn't.

I had engaged a taxi for going to Kumbum, which, as you may already know, is fifty miles from Malgudi.[1] I went there one morning and it was past nine in the evening when I finished my business and started back for the town. Doss [däs], the driver, was a young fellow of about twenty-five. He had often brought his car for me and I liked him. He was a well-behaved, obedient fellow, with a capacity to sit and wait at the wheel, which is really a rare quality in a taxi driver. He drove the car smoothly, seldom swore at passers-by, and exhibited perfect judgment, good sense, and sobriety; and so I preferred him to any other driver whenever I had to go out on business.

1. **Malgudi** (mäl go͞o′ dē) fictional town about which Narayan often writes.

17 ◂ Critical Viewing
What mysterious events might occur in a temple like this? **[Speculate]**

Text Complexity: Reader and Task Suggestions

Old Man of the Temple	
Preparing to Read the Text • Using the background note on TE p. 298, discuss the universality of ghost stories. • Refer to the Differentiated Instruction note on TE p. 303 and discuss cultural interpretations meant to explain why dead people might be seen or heard. • Guide students to use Multidraft Reading strategies (TE p. 291).	**Leveled Tasks** *Knowledge Demands* If students will have difficulty distinguishing between reality and fantasy in the story, ask them to first read and note each time the characters of Doss and the old man appear. Then have them reread and take notes about the traits of each character. Discuss notes and clarify meaning. *Synthesizing* If students will not have difficulty distinguishing between reality and fantasy in the story, ask them to read and take notes about how the setting influences events and characters. Discuss the importance of setting in the development of the characters and plot.

18 Literary Analysis

Setting

1. Explain that writers often use details about setting to make their writing seem more realistic or life-like. Tell students to keep this in mind as they read the bracketed text.
2. **Ask** students the Literary Analysis question: Which details in this paragraph describe the place and the time in which the story occurs?

   Answer: The details "the dark half of the month," "swallowed up in the night," "the street was deserted," and "stars overhead sparkled brightly" indicate that the place and time of the story is a deserted village street at nighttime.
3. **Ask** students to predict how the place and time will affect the events of the story.

   Possible response: Because it is dark and deserted, the story events will probably seem unsettling or frightening.
4. Encourage students to think about how the mood of the story would be different if the setting were, for example, a sunny Monday afternoon on a busy city street. Tell students that writers often use setting to help set the mood of a story.

Spiral Review

Character

1. Remind students that they studied the concept of Character in the Unit 2 Literary Analysis workshop (pp. 196-209).
2. **Ask** students the Spiral Review question.

   Possible response: The many details the narrator observes and describes suggest details of his background. His language and reactions also give him the distinct and unique voice of a complex character.

Literary Analysis
Setting Which details in this paragraph describe the place and the time in which the story occurs?

It was about eleven when we passed the village Koopal [ko͞o päl′], which is on the way down. It was the dark half of the month and the surrounding country was swallowed up in the night. The village street was deserted. Everyone had gone to sleep; hardly any light was to be seen. The stars overhead sparkled brightly. Sitting in the back seat and listening to the continuous noise of the running wheels, I was half lulled into a drowse.

All of a sudden Doss swerved the car and shouted: "You old fool! Do you want to kill yourself ?"

I was shaken out of my drowse and asked: "What is the matter?"

Doss stopped the car and said, "You see that old fellow, sir. He is trying to kill himself. I can't understand what he is up to."

I looked in the direction he pointed and asked, "Which old man?"

"There, there. He is coming towards us again. As soon as I saw him open that temple door and come out I had a feeling, somehow, that I must keep an eye on him."

Spiral Review
Character Which details suggest that the narrator is a round, or complex, character rather than a flat character?

I took out my torch, got down, and walked about, but could see no one. There was an old temple on the roadside. It was utterly in ruins; most portions of it were mere mounds of old brick; the walls were awry; the doors were shut to the main doorway, and brambles and thickets grew over and covered them. It was difficult to guess with the aid of the torch alone what temple it was and to what period it belonged.

"The doors are shut and sealed and don't look as if they had been opened for centuries now," I cried.

"No, sir," Doss said coming nearer. "I saw the old man open the doors and come out. He is standing there; shall we ask him to open them again if you want to go in and see?"

I said to Doss, "Let us be going. We are wasting our time here."

We went back to the car. Doss sat in his seat, pressed the self-starter, and asked without turning his head, "Are you permitting this fellow to come with us, sir? He says he will get down at the next milestone."

"Which fellow?" I asked.

Doss indicated the space next to him.

"What is the matter with you, Doss? Have you had a drop of drink or something?"

"I have never tasted any drink in my life, sir," he said, and added, "Get down, old boy. Master says he can't take you."

"Are you talking to yourself?"

"After all, I think we needn't care for these unknown fellows on the road," he said.

"Doss," I pleaded. "Do you feel confident you can drive? If you feel dizzy don't drive."

Vocabulary Development

CCSS Language 6

Expressive Vocabulary
To help students broaden their expressive vocabulary, encourage them to use the following words as they discuss the selection: *challenges, emphasizes, benefit,* and *examine*. Have them complete these sentence starters:

1. The ghost *challenges* . . .
2. The setting of the story *emphasizes* . . .
3. The ghost might *benefit* from . . .
4. The narrator approaches the temple to *examine* . . .

Challenge students to use these words as you continue to discuss the story.

"Thank you, sir," said Doss. "I would rather not start the car now. I am feeling a little out of sorts." I looked at him anxiously. He closed his eyes, his breathing became heavy and noisy, and gradually his head sank.

19 "Doss, Doss," I cried desperately. I got down, walked to the front seat, opened the door, and shook him vigorously. He opened his eyes, assumed a hunched-up position, and rubbed his eyes with his hands, which trembled like an old man's.

"Do you feel better?" I asked.

"Better! Better! Hi! Hi!" he said in a thin, piping voice.

"What has happened to your voice? You sound like someone else," I said.

"Nothing. My voice is as good as it was. When a man is eighty he is bound to feel a few changes coming on."

"You aren't eighty, surely," I said.

"Not a day less," he said. "Is nobody going to move this vehicle? If not, there is no sense in sitting here all day. I will get down and go back to my temple."

"I don't know how to drive," I said. "And unless you do it, I don't see how it can move."

"Me!" exclaimed Doss. "These new chariots! God knows what they are drawn by, I never understand, though I could handle a pair of bullocks[2] in my time. May I ask a question?"

"Go on," I said.

"Where is everybody?"

"Who?"

"Lots of people I knew are not to be seen at all. All sorts of new fellows everywhere, and nobody seems to care. Not a soul comes near the temple. All sorts of people go about but not one who cares to stop and talk. Why doesn't the king ever come this way? He used to go this way at least once a year before."

"Which king?" I asked.

"Let me go, you idiot," said Doss, edging towards the door on which I was leaning. "You don't seem to know anything." He pushed me aside, and got down from the car. He stooped as if he had a big hump on his back, and hobbled along towards the temple. I followed

2. **bullocks** (bo͝ol′ əks) *young bulls.*

20 ▲ **Critical Viewing**
How does the man in this picture compare to your vision of the old man in the story? **[Compare and Contrast]**

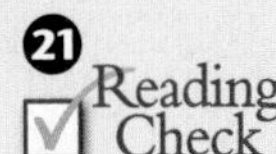

21 Reading Check
How old does Doss say he is when he wakes up?

19 Connecting to the Big Question

1. Share examples from films or books in which a character changes identity. **Ask** students what problems this can cause for the character and those around him or her.
2. Have students read the bracketed text on page 301. **Ask** students: How is Doss different now than before he fell asleep? **Possible response:** He thinks he's eighty years old and doesn't know how to drive, whereas before he was a young man who worked as a driver.
3. **Ask:** What conflict is developing for the narrator? What might he have to do to resolve that conflict? Explain. **Possible response:** Without the original Doss, the narrator is alone without a driver in an unfamiliar place. The narrator will have to solve the problem of getting back to town or solve the problem of getting Doss back to his earlier self.

20 Critical Viewing

Possible responses: Some students may say that this image does resemble their vision of the old man who has taken over Doss's body. However, others may say that they picture Doss, not the old ghost. Doss is a young man who may wear modern, Western clothes.

21 Reading Check

Answer: Doss says that he is eighty years old.

Differentiated Instruction for Universal Access

Strategy for Less Proficient Readers

Tell students that the story provides details about two settings: the setting of the narrator and the setting remembered by Krishna Battar. Ask students to record details about each setting in two-column charts. Then, have each student write a sentence that compares the settings and a sentence that contrasts the settings.

Enrichment for Gifted/Talented Students

Have students use details from the story to sketch two images of Doss: one as Doss the taxi driver and one as Doss overtaken by the spirit of Krishna Battar. Have students compare images with partners and discuss which story details each student used in his or her drawings.

㉒ Literature in Context

Cultural Connection The word *Hinduism* comes from a term coined by ancient Greeks to describe the inhabitants of the Indus Valley. Indians did not use the word *Hindu* until the sixteenth century, and then only to identify their origin rather than their religion. Veda, or Vedic religion, are the Indian terms for what westerners call Hinduism. In modern times, however, Indians have accepted this term to designate their religion.

Hindus believe that everyone's view of the truth is affected by his or her time, place, origins, experiences, gender, age, and other factors. This view is conducive to a broad, all-embracing view of religious truth.

Connect to the Literature Have the students read the Literature in Context feature, and present the additional background information above. Then, point out that because of their respect for a variety of points of view, Hindus believe that the supreme religious virtue is tolerance. **Ask** students the Connect to the Literature question: Which aspects of Hinduism does Narayan include in his story?

Answer: The story suggests that death and life are intertwined through the dead man's possession of Doss. The narrator's patience with the old man and his fantastical stories reflects the Hindu belief in tolerance and reincarnation.

㉒ LITERATURE IN CONTEXT

Culture Connection

Hinduism

Hinduism is the religion of the majority of people in India, the setting for "Old Man of the Temple." Drawing from a set of beliefs that are thousands of years old, Hinduism teaches that death is a temporary stage in an endless cycle of reincarnation, or rebirths. The actions that someone performs in one life, good and bad, will determine the conditions of future rebirths.

Connect to the Literature

Which aspects of Hinduism does Narayan include in this story?

him, hardly knowing what to do. He turned and snarled at me: "Go away, leave me alone. I have had enough of you."

"What has come over you, Doss?" I asked.

"Who is Doss, anyway? Doss, Doss, Doss. What an absurd name! Call me by my name or leave me alone. Don't follow me calling 'Doss, Doss.'"

"What is your name?" I asked.

"Krishna Battar [krish′ nə bə tar′], and if you mention my name people will know for a hundred miles around. I built a temple where there was only a cactus field before. I dug the earth, burnt every brick, and put them one upon another, all single-handed. And on the day the temple held up its tower over the surrounding country, what a crowd gathered! The king sent his chief minister . . ."

"Who was the king?"

"Where do you come from?" he asked.

"I belong to these parts certainly, but as far as I know there has been only a collector at the head of the district. I have never heard of any king."

"Hi! Hi! Hi!" he cackled, and his voice rang through the gloomy silent village. "Fancy never knowing the king! He will behead you if he hears it."

"What is his name?" I asked.

This tickled him so much that he sat down on the ground, literally unable to stand the joke any more. He laughed and coughed uncontrollably.

"I am sorry to admit," I said, "that my parents have brought me up in such utter ignorance of worldly affairs that I don't know even my king. But won't you enlighten me? What is his name?"

"Vishnu Varma [vish′ no͞o vär′ mə], the emperor of emperors . . ."

I cast my mind up and down the range of my historical knowledge but there was no one by that name. Perhaps a local chief of pre-British days, I thought.

"What a king! He often visited my temple or sent his minister for the Annual Festival of the temple. But now nobody cares."

"People are becoming less godly nowadays," I said. There was silence for a moment. An idea occurred to me, I can't say why. "Listen to me," I said. "You ought not to be here any more."

"What do you mean?" he asked, drawing himself up, proudly.

"Don't feel hurt; I say you shouldn't be here any more because you are dead."

Think Aloud

Vocabulary: Using Context

Direct students' attention to the word *snarled* at the top of this page. Using a think-aloud process, model how to use context to infer the meaning of an unknown word. Say to students:

> I'm going to think aloud to show you how I would figure out the meaning of *snarled* from its context.
>
> In this sentence, *snarled* is being used to describe the way that Doss/Krishna Battar speaks to the narrator. We know from Doss's previous behavior that he is frustrated because he calls the narrator an idiot and pushes him. In the next few sentences, Doss seems to be enraged. He is clearly fed up with the narrator, so I think *snarled* means "spoke angrily or harshly."

"Dead! Dead!" he said. "Don't talk nonsense. How can I be dead when you see me before you now? If I am dead how can I be saying this and that?"

"I don't know all that," I said. I argued and pointed out that according to his own story he was more than five hundred years old, and didn't he know that man's longevity was only a hundred? He constantly interrupted me, but considered deeply what I said.

He said: "It is like this . . . I was coming through the jungle one night after visiting my sister in the next village. I had on me some money and gold ornaments. A gang of robbers set upon me. I gave
23 them as good a fight as any man could, but they were too many for me. They beat me down and knifed me; they took away all that I had on me and left thinking they had killed me. But soon I got up and tried to follow them. They were gone. And I returned to the temple and have been here since . . ."

I told him, "Krishna Battar, you are dead, absolutely dead. You must try and go away from here."

"What is to happen to the temple?" he asked.

"Others will look after it."

"Where am I to go? Where am I to go?"

"Have you no one who cares for you?" I asked.

"None except my wife. I loved her very much."

"You can go to her."

"Oh, no. She died four years ago . . ."

Four years! It was very puzzling. "Do you say four years back from now?" I asked.

"Yes, four years ago from now." He was clearly without any sense of time.

So I asked, "Was she alive when you were attacked by thieves?"

"Certainly not. If she had been alive she would never have allowed me to go through the jungle after nightfall. She took very good care of me."

"See here," I said. "It is imperative you should go away from here. If she comes and calls you, will you go?"

"How can she when I tell you that she is dead?"

I thought for a moment. Presently I found myself saying, "Think of her, and only of her, for a while and see what happens. What was her name?"

"Seetha [sē´ thə], a wonderful girl . . ."

"Come on, think of her." He remained in deep thought for a while. He suddenly screamed, "Seetha is coming! Am I dreaming or what? I will go with her . . ." He stood up, very erect; he appeared to have

"Don't feel hurt; I say you shouldn't be here any more because you are dead."

Literary Analysis
Setting What details of setting are revealed through the old man's story of the robbery?

24

Based on the old man's story, how old does the narrator think the old man is?

23 Literary Analysis

Setting

1. Have students **look** for details about Krishna Battar's setting in the bracketed text. Point out that the descriptions of the dead man's surroundings make him seem more realistic and believable.
2. **Ask** the Literary Analysis question: What details of setting are revealed through the old man's story of the robbery?

   Answer: The old man describes a jungle between two villages. Also, the robbery suggests that the social setting was dangerous and volatile.

24 Reading Check

Answer: The narrator calculates that the old man is more than five hundred years old.

Differentiated Instruction for Universal Access

Culturally Responsive Instruction

Culture Focus Point out to students that the main conflict in this story occurs because Krishna Battar is dead but still wandering his village in other people's bodies. Note that many cultures have beliefs to explain what happens to people who have died with a problem unresolved. Some cultures describe this as haunting, for example, and create stories about haunted houses, communities, or families. Other cultures feature reincarnation, in which a person's soul returns in different forms until peace is achieved. Invite students to share their own knowledge of beliefs and traditions about what happens to people after they die, and how unresolved problems might change the process.

25 Literary Analysis
Setting

1. Read the bracketed text aloud. **Ask** the Literary Analysis question: What do the villagers' words reveal about the culture and belief system at work in the story?

   Answer: The villagers' words indicate that the spirit world is a part of everyday life. They are not frightened by the knocking.

2. **Ask** students how villagers from another culture might have acted in a similar situation.

   Possible response: In a culture that does not believe in the spirit world, the villagers might have been afraid or confused.

Concept Connector

Have students return to the Activating Prior Knowledge activity on p. 298. Ask volunteers to share their original thoughts about the ghost. Discuss what students have learned about the ghost through the writer's use of setting. In addition, have students compare their Writing About the Big Question responses before reading the selection with their ideas afterwards.

ASSESS
Answers

Remind students to support their answers with evidence from the text.

1. (a) Doss sees an old man. (b) The narrator can't see anyone.
2. (a) Doss falls heavily asleep and awakens as an old man. (b) The narrator is bewildered at first.
3. The narrator suggests that the old man think about his wife.
4. Some students might try to explain what happened to the narrator. Others might simply rate the quality of his tall tale.
5. **Possible response:** The story teaches that we must review the past in order to resolve old conflicts. Only then can we go forward in the present.

lost all the humps and twists he had on his body. He drew himself up, made a dash forward, and fell down in a heap.

Doss lay on the rough ground. The only sign of life in him was his faint breathing. I shook him and called him. He would not open his eyes. I walked across and knocked on the door of the first cottage. I banged on the door violently.

25 Someone moaned inside, "Ah, it is come!"

Someone else whispered, "You just cover your ears and sleep. It will knock for a while and go away." I banged on the door and shouted who I was and where I came from.

I walked back to the car and sounded the horn. Then the door opened, and a whole family crowded out with lamps. "We thought it was the usual knocking and we wouldn't have opened if you hadn't spoken."

Literary Analysis
Setting What do the villagers' words reveal about the culture and belief system at work in the story?

"When was this knocking first heard?" I asked.

"We can't say," said one. "The first time I heard it was when my grandfather was living; he used to say he had even seen it once or twice. It doesn't harm anyone, as far as I know. The only thing it does is bother the bullock carts passing the temple and knock on the doors at night . . ."

I said as a venture, "It is unlikely you will be troubled any more."

Vocabulary
venture (ven′ chər) *n.* a risky action

It proved correct. When I passed that way again months later I was told that the bullocks passing the temple after dusk never shied now and no knocking on the doors was heard at nights. So I felt that the old fellow had really gone away with his good wife.

Critical Thinking

Cite textual evidence to support your responses.

1. **Key Ideas and Details** **(a)** Early in the story, what does Doss say he sees when the car swerves? **(b) Analyze:** Why doesn't the narrator believe Doss?
2. **Key Ideas and Details** **(a) Summarize:** Describe Doss's transformation. Use details. **(b) Analyze:** How does the narrator react to these changes?
3. **Key Ideas and Details** **(a) Summarize:** How does the narrator finally get the ghost to leave?
4. **Integration of Knowledge and Ideas** **Evaluate:** How would you respond to the narrator's invitation to "hear what you have to say" about his story?
5. **Integration of Knowledge and Ideas** Use details from the story to explain what this story teaches about conflicts between the past and the present. *[Connect to the Big Question: Is conflict necessary?]*

Vocabulary Development

Vocabulary Knowledge Rating

When students have completed reading and discussing "The Man to Send Rain Clouds" and "Old Man of the Temple," have them take out their **Vocabulary Knowledge Rating Chart.** Read the words aloud once more and have students rate their knowledge of the words again in the After Reading column. Clarify any words that are still problematic. Have students write their own definition and example or sentence in the appropriate column. Then have students complete the vocabulary practice activities on the next page. Encourage students to use the words in further discussion and written work about the selections. Remind them that they will be accountable for these words on the **Selection Test** (*Unit 2 Resources*, pp. 112–114 or pp. 115–117).

After You Read

The Man to Send Rain Clouds • Old Man of the Temple

Comparing Setting

1. **Key Ideas and Details** **(a)** Describe the place, time, and culture of each story. **(b)** For each story, note at least two details that describe specific aspects of the setting—the geographical location, the time, and the cultural environment. As you reread, use a chart like the one shown to record specific details. Pay particular attention to the cultural experiences reflected in each work.

	Place:	Time:	Culture:
The Man to Send Rain Clouds			
Old Man of the Temple			

2. **Key Ideas and Details** If the setting were changed, could either story take place without being totally different? Explain.

Timed Writing

Explanatory Text: Essay

In an essay, compare and contrast the way the setting in each story, including the values and attitudes held by people in that time and place, influences the characters and story events. Support your analysis with the details about the setting you gathered while reading. **(40 minutes)**

5-Minute Planner

1. Read the prompt carefully and completely.
2. Gather your ideas. Consider these questions before you write.
   - How do the characters in each story live?
   - What cultural values, themes, and issues are present in each story?
   - Does the setting itself affect the events in each story?
   - Do any characters in either story change their thinking or behavior because of the setting? Explain.
3. Use the details from your chart to consider the similarities and differences.
4. Reread the prompt, and then draft your essay.

ASSESS
Answers

Comparing Setting

1. **Possible response:** (a) For "The Man to Send Rain Clouds," the place is New Mexico. The time is one day in early spring, from morning until dusk. The cultural setting includes both Pueblo and Catholic cultures. (b) For "Old Man of the Temple," the place is Malgudi, a fictional town in India. The time is an unspecified day in the past, late at night. The cultural setting relates to Hinduism.
2. **Possible response:** In "The Man to Send Rain Clouds," the land and the culture of Native Americans contribute heavily to the meaning of the story. Changing the context would result in a very different story. In "Old Man of the Temple," setting is less important but still effective. The temple lends the story an air of mystery, and the Hindu culture helps explain the characters' reactions to the ghost.

Timed Writing

1. Review the prompt with students.
2. Have students use the 5-Minute Planner to structure their time. Guide them in answering the bulleted questions. For example, point out that the bulleted items help them focus on the reasons for the choices each writer made about how to develop the plot.
3. Allow students 40 minutes to complete the assignment.
4. As students prewrite and draft, have them refer to their completed Comparing Setting Graphic Organizer.

Six Traits Focus

✓	Ideas		Word Choice
✓	Organization		Sentence Fluency
	Voice		Conventions

Assessment Resources

Unit 2 Resources

L1 L2 EL **Selection Test A,** pp. 112–114

L3 L4 EL **Selection Test B,** pp. 115–117

L3 L4 **Open Book Test,** pp. 109–111

PHLit Online! All assessment resources are available at **www.PHLitOnline.com**.

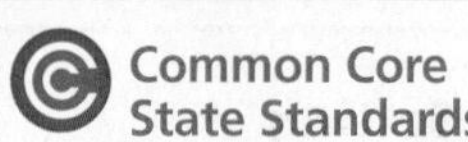

PRETEACH

Common Core State Standards

- **Writing 3, 3.a, b, c, d, e**
- **Language 2.c**

Introducing the Writing Assignment

Review the assignment and the criteria.

Connecting to Real-Life Writing

Point out that short stories are used for a variety of purposes. For example, a brief short story can illustrate a main point in an essay.

Writing Workshop *Work in Progress*

If students have completed the Work-in-Progress assignments on pp. 255 and 281, suggest that they try to develop their Work-in-Progress ideas in a short story.

TEACH

Prewriting/Planning Strategy

1. Introduce the prewriting strategy.
2. Have students apply the strategy.

Six Traits Focus

✓	Ideas	Word Choice
✓	Organization	Sentence Fluency
	Voice	Conventions

Writing Workshop

Write a Narrative

Narration: Short Story

Defining the Form Stories are one of the oldest and most familiar forms of literature. A traditional **short story** is a brief fictional narrative composed of plot, setting, and characters. You might use elements of this type of writing in science fiction, mysteries, and autobiographies.

Assignment Write a short story that presents characters in a specific setting and engaged in a specific conflict that is resolved. Include these elements:

- ✓ a *main character* who takes part in the action
- ✓ details that establish a particular *time, place,* and *mood*
- ✓ a *conflict,* or problem, that is introduced, developed, and resolved, including a smooth progression of experiences or events
- ✓ a central *theme,* or message about life
- ✓ *dialogue* between characters
- ✓ a narrator's *point of view*
- ✓ error-free grammar, including *correct use of verbs*

To preview story criteria, see the rubric on page 311.

Writing Workshop: *Work in Progress*

Review the work you did on pages 255 and 281.

Prewriting/Planning Strategy

Develop characters. Use a chart like the one shown to help you think about each character and the conflict he or she might face. Match a character with a conflict to begin generating ideas for a story. Then, consider how you would have the conflict play out in the character's life.

Potential Characters	Potential Conflicts
A business man	loses family heirloom
An elderly woman	wins lottery
A teenage girl	cheats on exam
A mechanic	loses job
A sports player	moves to a new town

Common Core State Standards

Writing

3. Write narratives to develop real or imagined experiences or events using effective technique, well-chosen details, and well-structured event sequences.

3.a. Engage and orient the reader by setting out a problem, situation, or observation, establishing one or multiple point(s) of view, and introducing a narrator and/or characters; create a smooth progression of experiences or events.

3.e. Provide a conclusion that follows from and reflects on what is experienced, observed, or resolved over the course of the narrative.

Teaching Resources

The following resources can be used to enrich or extend the instruction.

All *Unit 2 Resources*
Writing Workshop, pp. 118–119

All *Common Core Companion,*
pp. 202–212

All *Professional Development Guidebook*
Rubric for Self-Assessment: Short Story, pp. 226–227

All *Graphic Organizer Transparencies*
Rubric for Self-Assessment: Short Story, p. 55

All resources are available online at **www.PHLitOnline.com.**

SIX TRAITS WRITER'S TOOLBOX SIX TRAITS

Organization | Word Choice | Ideas | Conventions | Sentence Fluency | Voice

Developing the Plot

The **organization** of a story includes several elements, which are often presented in a particular order. The major building blocks of a story's plot include the following:

Exposition: introduction of the characters, setting, and basic situation

Inciting Incident: introduction of a central conflict

Rising Action: development of the conflict

Climax: the high point of interest or suspense

Falling Action: winding down of the conflict

Resolution: general insight about or change in the main character

Decide who and what your story is about. Think about the characters, the setting, and the basic situation. Then, introduce these elements in the exposition of your story.

Identify the conflict, or problem. Consider your main character and his or her feelings about the basic situation of the story. Ask yourself these questions to develop the conflict:

- How does he or she react to the conflict?
- How does his or her reaction lead to the development of the conflict?
- What external circumstances add to the character's reactions and actions?

Use your answers to plan the inciting incident and rising action.

Decide how the conflict will play out. After the development of the inciting incident and rising action, think about the most interesting and effective way for the conflict to be developed and resolved. Consider what will be the high point of anxiety or the possible turning point in the conflict. Use these considerations to construct the climax of your story.

Decide what will happen in the end. Everything that happens after the climax is a simple wrapping up of the loose ends. This part of the story is also a place where you can express the moral or lesson of the story. You might present this insight both indirectly through the events and directly through narration. Think about what your character learned through the conflict and use that knowledge to express the insight he or she gained.

Developing the Plot

1. Introduce the writing skill, using the instruction on the student page.
2. Discuss the tips and strategies for planning and organizing a short story.

Teaching the Writing Skill

1. Remind students that a story's plot is the sequence of events in the story. Explain that each story has a basic situation, a central conflict, and a resolution of the conflict.
2. Review the six major building blocks of a story's plot, using the definitions on the student page. Tell students that they will work together as a class to develop each of the six building blocks for a "class story."
3. Have students begin by identifying a main character and describing his or her personality. Record the character traits on the board. Next, work together with students to describe a conflict that the character faces. Discuss with students how the character would react to the conflict. Record the character's reaction on the board.
4. **Ask:** *How does the character's reaction add to, or further, the conflict?* Record students' responses on the board. Explain that this is the plot's rising action. Then divide students into small groups and have them come up with the story's climax, falling action, and resolution. Allow time for groups to share their ideas with the class.
5. Tell students that they can use this same process to develop their own individual short stories.

Prentice Hall EssayScorer

A writing prompt for this mode of writing can be found on the ***Prentice Hall Essay Scorer*** at **www.PHLitOnline.com**.

Differentiated Instruction for Universal Access

Strategy for Less Proficient Writers
As students consider ideas for their main characters, they may benefit from browsing through images. Provide magazines, newspapers, or computer access, and ask students to find a picture of someone who would make a good main character. Have students use the picture to help them describe the personality traits of their character.

Strategy for Advanced Writers
Remind students that a story's setting can be used to augment plot development. Have students use sensory details from the five senses to develop a descriptive setting for their stories. Challenge them to create an atmosphere that adds to the development of the story's conflict.

Drafting Strategies

1. Introduce the drafting strategies.
2. Have students apply the strategies.

Teaching the Strategies

1. Tell students that they must stick to a consistent point of view throughout the story.
2. Remind students that they can use dialogue to reveal important character traits. Explain that using details can help them show, rather than tell, the setting.

Six Traits Focus

	Ideas	✓	Word Choice
✓	Organization		Sentence Fluency
✓	Voice		Conventions

Revising Strategies

1. Introduce the revision strategies.
2. Have students apply the strategies.

Six Traits Focus

✓	Ideas	✓	Word Choice
✓	Organization	✓	Sentence Fluency
✓	Voice		Conventions

Drafting Strategies

Develop the narrator's point of view. Decide how your story will be told. The narrator may be a character within the story or someone who simply reports on the action. Your narrator may be biased toward one character or outcome. Think about all of these options as you begin crafting your story. It is important to give your narrator a consistent voice to relate the story's events and to express his or her observations.

Create realistic dialogue between characters. Effective dialogue does not sound stiff and unnatural. It should sound like real people speaking to one another. Try writing a dialogue between characters. Then, read the dialogue aloud with a friend or by yourself. As you listen, decide whether your dialogue sounds natural.

Show, don't tell. Use descriptions, dialogue, movements, gestures, and *characters' interior monologues* to make events and characterization vivid for your readers. For example, do not simply report that a street was noisy—provide details that help readers hear the commotion. You might write that the character thought, "How can I possibly think with all these blaring horns?" Additionally, you can add *sensory details*—words that appeal to the senses of sight, smell, taste, touch, and hearing. Appeal to as many senses as possible to bring the scene to life for readers.

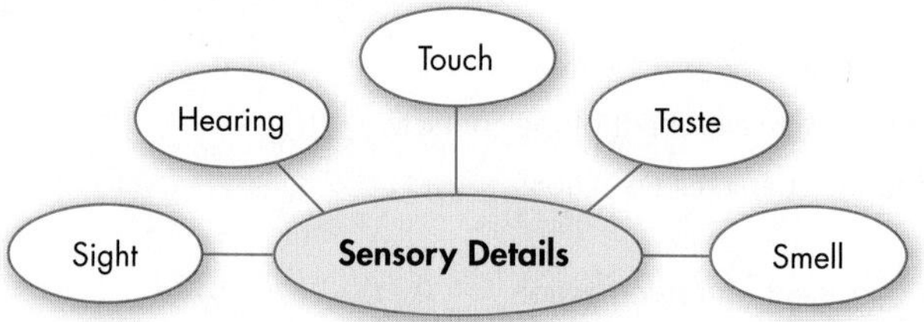

Common Core State Standards

Writing

3.a. Engage and orient the reader by setting out a problem, situation, or observation, establishing one or multiple point(s) of view, and introducing a narrator and/or characters; create a smooth progression of experiences or events.

3.b. Use narrative techniques, such as dialogue, pacing, description, reflection, and multiple plot lines, to develop experiences, events, and/or characters.

3.c. Use a variety of techniques to sequence events so that they build on one another to create a coherent whole.

3.d. Use precise words and phrases, telling details, and sensory language to convey a vivid picture of the experiences, events, setting, and/or characters.

Revising Strategies

Maintain an effective sequence of events. Every detail in your story should deepen your portrayal of the characters or increase the tension of the conflict. Review your draft, noting any interruptions to the momentum of your plot. Consider modifying or deleting such interruptions.

Use active language. To create dynamic sentences, choose the active voice instead of the passive voice. Make sure that the subjects in your sentences perform the actions.

- **Passive Voice:** The problem was solved by Curtis.
- **Active Voice:** Curtis solved the problem.

Applying Understanding by Design Principles

Clarifying Expected Outcomes: Using Rubrics

- Before students begin working on this assignment, have them preview the Rubric for Self-Assessment (p. 311) to learn what qualities their short stories must have. A copy of this rubric appears in ***Graphic Organizer Transparencies,*** p. 55.
- Review the criteria in the Rubric with the class. Before students use the Rubric to assess their writing, work with them to rate the Student Model (p. 310) using the Rubric.
- If you wish to assess students' short stories with either a 4-point or a 6-point scoring rubric, see ***Professional Development Guidebook,*** pp. 226–227.

SIX TRAITS WRITER'S TOOLBOX SIX TRAITS

Conventions | Sentence Fluency | Voice | Organization | Word Choice | Ideas

Revising Inconsistent Verb Tenses

A **tense** is a form of a verb that expresses the time of an action. The six verb tenses are present, present perfect, past, past perfect, future, and future perfect. Inconsistent use of verb tenses causes confusion in a story.

Uses of Past and Future Perfect Tense	
Past action of condition completed before another	I had been to the museum before it was remodeled.
Future action of condition completed before another	I will have seen that movie before it will be on television.
Continuing past action interrupted by another	I had been on the telephone when you rang the doorbell.
Continuing future action interrupted by another	By the time I will graduate, I will have been in school for thirteen years.

Identifying Inconsistent Verb Tenses Inconsistent verb tense occurs when a sentence begins in one tense and incorrectly switches to another. Shifts in tense should always reflect a logical sequence.

Incorrect: I *will be* on time today, and I *was* on time tomorrow.
Correct: I *was* on time today, and I *will be* on time tomorrow.
Perfect tenses can clarify a sequence of actions.

Unclear: By the time she *will arrive*, we *will start* the meeting.
Clear: By the time she *will arrive*, we *will have started* the meeting.

Fixing Errors Scan your draft for shifts in tense.

1. **Identify the reason for each shift.** Correct unnecessary shifts.
2. **Determine which actions happened first.** When two actions occur at different times in the past, use the past perfect tense for the earlier action. When two actions will occur at different times in the future, use the future perfect tense for the earlier action.

Grammar in Your Writing

Review a passage of your draft that includes both narrative and dialogue. Underline any shifts in tense that you find. Be sure that the shift represents a clear and logical time order. Fix any inconsistent tenses.

PH WRITING COACH
Further instruction and practice are available in *Prentice Hall Writing Coach.*

Revising Inconsistent Verb Tenses

1. Introduce the grammar skill, using the instruction on the student page.
2. Discuss the examples and the strategies for making verb tenses consistent.
3. Have students follow the instruction under Grammar in Your Writing to correct errors in their drafts.

Teaching the Grammar Skill

1. Emphasize to students that not all shifts in tense are incorrect. For example, in this sentence, the shift in tense shows that the actions occurred at two different times.

   Babe Ruth set a home run record that we still admire.

2. Tell students to choose a tense that makes sense and then to use it consistently throughout their stories, changing tenses only to show that one event comes before or after another event.
3. Have students make the verb tenses in this paragraph consistent.

   I had trouble sleeping last night. The dog barked all night, which wakes me two or three times. My father had forgotten to shut the tool-shed door, and the wind keeps blowing it open. By the time the sun shines through my window, I give up on getting a good night's sleep.

   Answer: *I had trouble sleeping last night. The dog barked all night, which woke me two or three times. My father had forgotten to shut the tool-shed door, and the wind kept blowing it open. By the time the sun shone through my window, I had given up on getting a good night's sleep.*

PH WRITING COACH Grade 9

Students will find practice with and guidance on verb tenses in Chapter 17.

Differentiated Instruction for Universal Access

Strategy for Less Proficient Writers
Have students select the three longest paragraphs in their drafts and circle all of the verbs. Next, have students identify the tense of each verb. Tell students to make sure that any change in tense is made for a logical reason.

Strategy for Advanced Writers
Review the use of perfect tenses with students, reminding students that these forms can precisely establish the time-order relationship of two or more events. Have students circle the verbs in their drafts, looking for ways to use present and past perfect tenses to clarify time sequence.

Student Model

Review the Student Model with the class, using the annotations to analyze the writer's use of the elements of a short story.

Teaching from the Student Model

1. Give students an example of a graveyard setting. Have students give a detailed description of the setting.

   Possible response: *We walked into the graveyard by the light of the moon, which highlighted the chipped and broken tombstones. Wind whipped and whistled through the long grass that surrounded the ancient tombstones.*

2. Tell students to use distinct names for characters in their stories. Tell them that memorable, telling names will enhance their stories.
3. Tell students that the use of dialogue helps place the reader in the story.
4. Point out to students how the writing on the wall intensifies the conflict. Ask students to read on and identify what other details intensify the conflict further.
   Answer: The door slams shut and they find out that Uno wrote the threats and that he wants the treasure for himself.

Connecting to Real-Life Writing

Explain to students that when writing letters or e-mails to friends or relatives, they often incorporate stories. A student may tell about a funny thing that happened to her in the grocery store or about a scary moment at softball practice. Point out that they can use the principles within this workshop to enhance their stories, giving their readers vividly portrayed and highly enjoyable stories to read.

Student Model: Randy Hays, Clackamas, OR

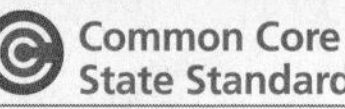
Common Core State Standards

Language
2.c. Spell correctly.

The Oil Slick

The Oil Slick is a place where I play baseball with a bunch of friends. We call the field the "Oil Slick" because a boat carrying gallons of oil once sailed by. The boat sprang a leak, polluting the water around it. The Oil Slick also has a big hole in the outfield. . . .

> Randy starts the story with a detailed description of an interesting setting.

My nickname is Giant. It suits me because I am the tallest player on the team. . . . I only know the nicknames of the others on my team. They're called Ant, Dash, Rip, X-Ray, Target, Eye, Animal, Uno, and Cover. . . .

> The characters' quirky nicknames help the writer create a sense of what each one is like.

This morning, I headed out to the Oil Slick, ready to play. However, before we started, Uno held a meeting. "As you know," he said, "there is a hole in the outfield."

"Who can tell me why the hole is there?" There was silence until Uno spoke again. "That's what I thought," he said. "Some people say there's treasure buried on this field. Somebody probably tried to dig for it, and they left that hole behind. I thought maybe we should dig, too, but then I figured that'd be stupid. It's probably just a rumor. We wouldn't find anything, diggin' holes."

> Randy uses dialogue to introduce the mystery of the hole in the field—the source of the story's conflict. Notice the correct use of punctuation to show Uno's direct words.

Silence again until someone shouted. "Let's play already!" Everyone went to their positions and the game started. . . .

Rip hit the ball and it flew past the right-fielder, Eye. Concentrating on the ball, Eye ran toward the hole. He didn't know when to stop and he fell. . . .

We all ran and looked down the hole. Nobody had ever bothered to really look before, and it was deep—much deeper than we thought. Hoping to find Eye, we jumped in. . . .

When we saw what the hole truly was, we forgot about Eye. We had expected dirt, rocks—the usual stuff you'd find in a hole. Instead, we saw smooth walls, stretching into the distance. All this time, without ever suspecting it, we had been playing above a maze of tunnels. . . .

We headed down the tunnel to our right. . . .These weren't ordinary tunnels. They had the names of famous baseball players carved right into the walls. Then, we noticed something strange. There were other, different words painted on the wall, and what they said scared us all: "Your friend is here. Don't try to find him. Or else."

> The conflict intensifies here.

We continued through the tunnels until we emerged in a room which . . . had a sign that said, "You Found Him." Sure enough, there was Eye, leaning against a wall. He saw us and shouted, "Go! Now!"

But it was too late. A door slammed shut and we were trapped. Then, we heard a familiar voice. "You saw the warnings, but you didn't stop. Now you are trapped and the treasure is mine!". . .

Strategies for Revising

Encourage students to use the "Save As" feature on their computers to save different versions of their drafts in case they want to refer to earlier versions as they write. Students might find that they can use sentences or descriptions from earlier drafts, even if they cannot reuse entire paragraphs.

Editing and Proofreading

Check your draft for errors in spelling, punctuation, and grammar.

Focus on spelling. Often, the addition of a suffix does not require a spelling change to the base word. Sometimes, though, spelling changes are required. For example, you may need to drop final e's or change final *y*'s to *i*. The final consonant in a word or its internal spelling may also need to change, as in *suspend-suspension* and *maintain-maintenance*. Consult a dictionary to double-check your spelling.

Use punctuation for effect. Use a style guide to be sure you have correctly punctuated dialogue in your story. In addition, occasionally use punctuation to emphasize characters' emotions. For example, exclamation points suggest excitement while ellipses (a series of three periods) suggest hesitation or wandering thoughts.

Spiral Review

Earlier in the unit, you learned about **regular verbs** (p. 254) and **irregular verbs** (p. 280). Check the use of all verbs in your narrative to be sure you have used them consistently and correctly.

Publishing and Presenting

Consider one of the following ways to share your writing:

Deliver an oral presentation. Read your story aloud to your classmates. Get feedback from your classmates and make necessary revisions.

Create an anthology. Work with your class to illustrate and collect your stories in a single binder. Contribute the anthology to the school library.

Reflecting on Your Writing

Writer's Journal Jot down your answer to this question:

How might your experience writing a story help with other writing you do?

Rubric for Self-Assessment

Find evidence in your writing to address each category. Then, use the rating scale to grade your work.

Criteria	Rating Scale (not very — very)
Focus: How clear is the story's theme or message?	1 2 3 4 5
Organization: How clearly do you introduce, develop, and resolve the conflict?	1 2 3 4 5
Support/Elaboration: How well do you use details to establish time, place, and mood?	1 2 3 4 5
Style: How well do you describe the characters and setting?	1 2 3 4 5
Conventions: How correct is your grammar, especially your use of verb tenses?	1 2 3 4 5

Editing and Proofreading

1. Introduce the editing and proofreading focus, using the instruction on the student page.
2. Have students edit and proofread their short stories, correcting grammar, spelling, punctuation, and word choice. Make sure they check for errors of the type noted on the student page.

Teaching the Editing Focus

Remind students that the spelling of a word sometimes changes when a suffix is added. Review the rules for adding suffixes. Then, ask students to read their stories and highlight each word that contains a suffix. Have students verify that their highlighted words are spelled correctly.

Six Traits Focus

	Ideas		Word Choice
	Organization		Sentence Fluency
	Voice	✓	Conventions

ASSESS

Publishing and Presenting

1. Tell students to consider changing the pace of their readings or altering tone of voice to reflect actions, suspense, or mood.
2. Students might ask classmates to read lines for characters in their stories.

Reflecting on Your Writing

Ask students to respond to these additional questions as they reflect on their writing:

1. *What did you find most difficult about writing a short story?*
2. *What would you do differently the next time you write a short story?*

Lead a discussion about the connection between reading short stories and writing them.

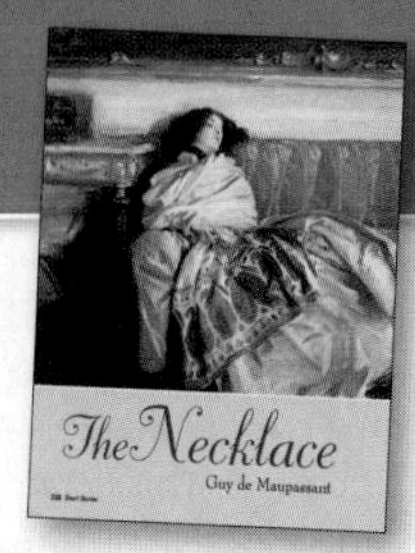

✓ Rules of the Game • ✓✓ The Necklace

Lesson Pacing Guide

DAY 1 Preteach

- Administer the Reading and Vocabulary Warm-ups (*Unit 2 Resources*, pp. 127–130 or 145–148) as necessary.
- Introduce the Reading Skill: Cause and Effect.
- Introduce the Literary Analysis concept: Characterization.
- Distribute copies of the appropriate graphic organizer for the Reading Skill (*Graphic Organizer Transparencies*, pp. 59–61).
- Distribute copies of the appropriate graphic organizer for Literary Analysis (*Graphic Organizer Transparencies*, pp. 56–58).
- Teach the selection vocabulary.
- Introduce the Word Study skill.

DAYS 2–3 Preteach/Teach

- Build background with the Background feature.
- Develop thematic vocabulary and thematic thinking with Writing About the Big Question.
- Prepare students to read with the Activating Prior Knowledge activities (TE).
- Informally monitor comprehension while students read.
- Use the Reading Check questions to confirm comprehension.
- Develop students' ability to determine cause and effect, using the Reading Skill questions.
- Develop students' understanding of characterization, using the Literary Analysis questions.
- Reinforce vocabulary with the Vocabulary notes.
- Reinforce unit focus standards using the Spiral Review prompts.

DAY 4 Assess

- Assess students' comprehension and mastery of the skills by having them answer the Critical Thinking, Reading Skill, and Literary Analysis questions.
- Have students complete the Vocabulary Practice activities.
- Have students complete the Word Study activities.

DAY 5 Extend/Assess

- Have students complete the Conventions lesson.
- Have students complete the Writing activity and create a written presentation. (You may assign as homework.)
- Extend learning by having students complete the Research and Technology activity, an informative brochure. (You may assign as homework.) As an alternative, assign them "Competing to Win" or "Wrongfully Accused?" in *Reality Central*.
- Administer Selection Test A or B (*Unit 2 Resources*, pp. 139–144 or 160–165).

Common Core State Standards

Reading Literature 3. Analyze how complex characters (e.g., those with multiple or conflicting motivations) develop over the course of a text, interact with other characters, and advance the plot or develop the theme.

Writing 4. Produce clear and coherent writing in which the development, organization, and style are appropriate to task, purpose, and audience.

Speaking and Listening 2. Integrate multiple sources of information presented in diverse media or formats, evaluating the credibility and accuracy of each source.

Language 6. Acquire and use accurately grade-appropriate general academic and domain-specific words and phrases; gather vocabulary knowledge when considering a word or phrase important to comprehension or expression.

Additional Standards Practice
***Common Core Companion*, pp. 28–29; 48–49**

Daily Block Scheduling
Each day in this Lesson Pacing Guide represents a 40–50 minute period. Teachers using block scheduling may combine days to revise pacing. In addition, teachers may differentiate and support core instruction by integrating components for extended and intensive support as students require. See the Guide to Selected Leveled Resources (facing page).

Guide to Selected Leveled Resources

RTI **Tier 1** (students performing on level)		✓ **More Accessible** Rules of the Game	✓✓ **More Complex** The Necklace
Warm Up	**Practice, model,** and **monitor** fluency, working **with the whole class** or **in groups.**	**Vocabulary** and **Reading Warm-ups B,** ***Unit 2 Resources,*** pp. 127–128, 130	**Vocabulary** and **Reading Warm-ups B,** ***Unit 2 Resources,*** pp. 145–146, 148
Comprehension/Skills	**Support** and **monitor** comprehension and skills development, having students complete the activities, graphic organizers, and interactive prompts **independently** or **as a class.**	• ***Reader's Notebook,*** adapted instruction and full selection EL ***Reader's Notebook: English Learner's Version,*** adapted instruction and adapted selection • **Reading Skill Graphic Organizer B,** ***Graphic Organizer Transparencies,*** p. 58 • **Literary Analysis Graphic Organizer B,** ***Graphic Organizer Transparencies,*** p. 61	• ***Reader's Notebook,*** adapted instruction and summary EL ***Reader's Notebook: English Learner's Version,*** adapted instruction and summary • **Reading Skill Graphic Organizer B,** ***Graphic Organizer Transparencies,*** p. 58 • **Literary Analysis Graphic Organizer B,** ***Graphic Organizer Transparencies,*** p. 61
Monitor Progress	**Monitor** student progress with the differentiated curriculum-based assessment in the *Unit Resources.*	• **Selection Test B,** ***Unit 2 Resources,*** pp. 142–144 • **Open-Book Test,** ***Unit 2 Resources,*** pp. 136–138	• **Selection Test B,** ***Unit 2 Resources,*** pp. 163–165 • **Open-Book Test,** ***Unit 2 Resources,*** pp. 157–159

RTI **Tier 2** (students requiring intervention)		✓ **More Accessible** Rules of the Game	✓✓ **More Complex** The Necklace
Warm Up	**Practice, model,** and **monitor** fluency **in groups** or **with individuals.**	• **Vocabulary and Reading Warm-ups A,** ***Unit 2 Resources,*** pp. 127–129 • ***Reality Central,*** "Competing to Win" • ***Hear It!*** **Audio CD (adapted text)**	• **Vocabulary and Reading Warm-ups A,** ***Unit 2 Resources,*** pp. 145–147 • ***Reality Central,*** "Wrongfully Accused?" • ***Hear It!*** **Audio CD**
Comprehension/Skills	• **Support** and **monitor** comprehension and skills development, working **in small groups** or **with individuals.** • **Pair** students with more advanced peers and have them complete the writing activity in the *Real-World Writing Journal.* • As students complete the selection in the appropriate version of the *Reader's Notebook,* **monitor** comprehension frequently with group questions and individual instruction. • **Model** strategies while guiding students in completing the activities and prompts in the *Reader's Notebook,* as well as the graphic organizers. • **Practice** skills and **monitor** mastery with the *Reading Kit* worksheets.	• ***Real-World Writing Journal,*** Lesson 3, pp. 52–55 • ***Reader's Notebook: Adapted Version,*** adapted instruction and summary EL ***Reader's Notebook: English Learner's Version,*** adapted instruction and summary • **Reading Skill Graphic Organizer A,** ***Graphic Organizer Transparencies,*** p. 59 • **Literary Analysis Graphic Organizer A,** ***Graphic Organizer Transparencies,*** p. 56 • ***Reading Kit,*** Practice worksheets, pp. 76, 82, 86, 88, 96	• ***Real-World Writing Journal,*** Lesson 6, pp. 56–59 • ***Reader's Notebook: Adapted Version,*** adapted instruction and adapted selection EL ***Reader's Notebook: English Learner's Version,*** adapted instruction and adapted selection • **Reading Skill Graphic Organizer A,** ***Graphic Organizer Transparencies,*** p. 60 • **Literary Analysis Graphic Organizer A,** ***Graphic Organizer Transparencies,*** p. 57 • ***Reading Kit,*** Practice worksheets, pp. 76, 82, 86, 88, 96
Monitor Progress	**Monitor** student progress with the differentiated curriculum-based assessment in the *Unit Resources* and in the *Reading Kit.*	• **Selection Test A,** ***Unit 2 Resources,*** pp. 139–141 • ***Reading Kit,*** Assess worksheets, pp. 77, 83, 87, 89, 97	• **Selection Test A,** ***Unit 2 Resources,*** pp. 160–162 • ***Reading Kit,*** Assess worksheets, pp. 77, 83, 87, 89, 97

TIER 3 Tier 3 intervention may require consultation with the student's special-education or dyslexia specialist. For additional support, see the Tier 2 activities and resources listed above.

One-on-one teaching **Group work** **Whole class instruction** **Independent work** **A Assessment**

For a complete guide to selection support, including support for Advanced students, see the Overview of Resources in the frontmatter.

✓Rules of the Game
✓✓The Necklace

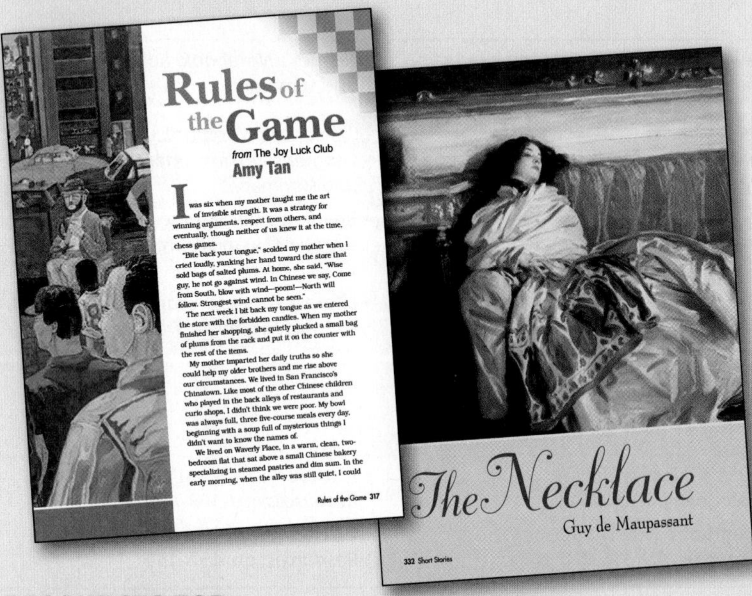

Rules of the Game

from The Joy Luck Club
Amy Tan

I was six when my mother taught me the art of invisible strength. It was a strategy for winning arguments, respect from others, and eventually, though neither of us knew it at the time, chess games.

"Bite back your tongue," scolded my mother when I cried loudly, yanking her hand toward the store that sold bags of salted plums. At home, she said, "Wise guy, he not go against wind. In Chinese we say, Come from South, blow with wind—poom!—North will follow. Strongest wind cannot be seen."

The next week I bit back my tongue as we entered the store with the forbidden candies. When my mother finished her shopping, she quietly plucked a small bag of plums from the rack and put it on the counter with the rest of the items.

My mother imparted her daily truths so she could help my older brothers and me rise above our circumstances. We lived in San Francisco's Chinatown. Like most of the other Chinese children who played in the back alleys of restaurants and curio shops, I didn't think we were poor. My bowl was always full, three five-course meals every day, beginning with a soup full of mysterious things I didn't want to know the names of.

We lived on Waverly Place, in a warm, clean, two-bedroom flat that sat above a small Chinese bakery specializing in steamed pastries and dim sum. In the early morning, when the alley was still quiet, I could

Rules of the Game 317

The Necklace

Guy de Maupassant

332 Short Stories

RESOURCES FOR:

- L1 **Special-Needs Students**
- L2 **Below-Level Students (Tier 2)**
- L3 **On-Level Students (Tier 1)**
- L4 **Advanced Students (Tier 1)**
- EL **English Learners**
- All **All Students**

Vocabulary/Fluency/Prior Knowledge

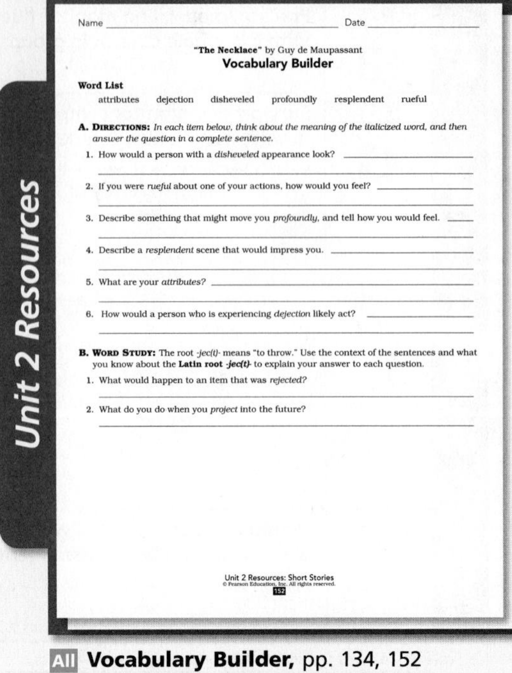

Name ______________________ Date ______________

"The Necklace" by Guy de Maupassant
Vocabulary Builder

Word List

attributes dejection disheveled profoundly resplendent rueful

A. Directions: *In each item below, think about the meaning of the italicized word, and then answer the question in a complete sentence.*

1. How would a person with a *disheveled* appearance look? ______________
2. If you were *rueful* about one of your actions, how would you feel? ______________
3. Describe something that might move you *profoundly*, and tell how you would feel. ______________
4. Describe a *resplendent* scene that would impress you. ______________
5. What are your *attributes?* ______________
6. How would a person who is experiencing *dejection* likely act? ______________

B. Word Study: The root *-jec(t)-* means "to throw." Use the context of the sentences and what you know about the **Latin root** ***-jec(t)-*** to explain your answer to each question.

1. What would happen to an item that was *rejected?* ______________
2. What do you do when you *project* into the future? ______________

Unit 2 Resources: Short Stories
© Pearson Education, Inc. All rights reserved.
152

All **Vocabulary Builder,** pp. 134, 152

Also available for these selections:

EL L1 L2 **Vocabulary Warm-ups A and B,** pp. 127–128, 145–146

EL L1 L2 **Reading Warm-ups A and B,** pp. 129–130, 147–148

All **Writing About the Big Question,** pp. 131, 149

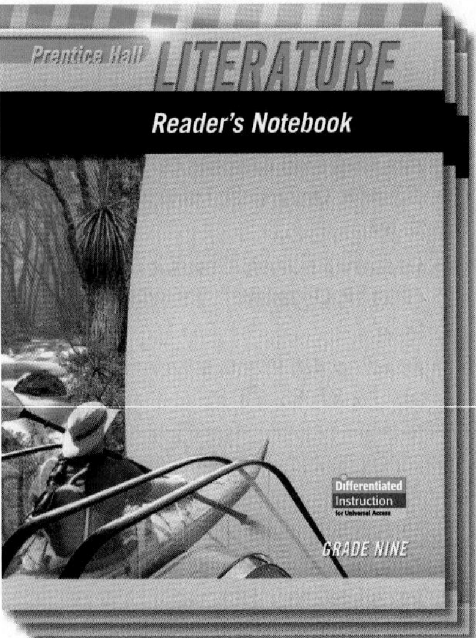

Reader's Notebooks

Pre- and postreading pages for both selections, as well as "Rules of the Game" appear in an interactive format in the *Reader's Notebooks.* Each *Notebook* is differentiated for a different group of learners. The selections in the Adapted and English Learner's versions are abridged.

L2 L3 ***Reader's Notebook***

L1 ***Reader's Notebook: Adapted Version***

EL ***Reader's Notebook: English Learner's Version***

EL ***Reader's Notebook: Spanish Version***

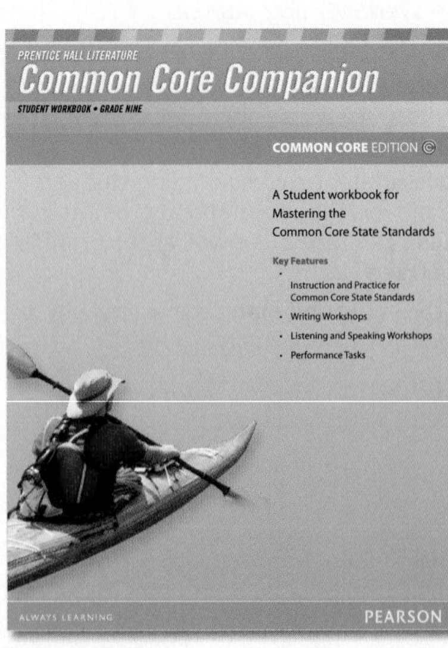

Common Core Companion

Additional instruction and practice for each Common Core State Standard

Selection Support

Graphic Organizer Transparencies

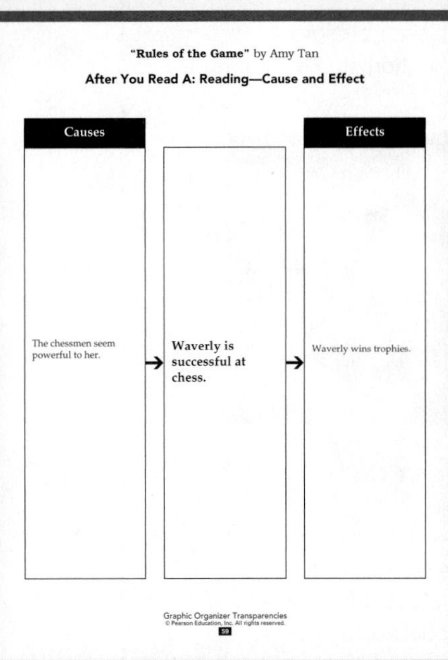
"Rules of the Game" by Amy Tan

After You Read A: Reading—Cause and Effect

Causes		Effects
The chessmen seem powerful to her.	→ Waverly is successful at chess. →	Waverly wins trophies.

Graphic Organizer Transparencies

59

EL L1 L2 **Reading: Graphic Organizer A,** pp. 59, 60 (partially filled in)

Also available for these selections:

EL L1 L2 **Literary Analysis: Graphic Organizer A,** pp. 56, 57 (partially filled in)

EL L3 **Literary Analysis: Graphic Organizer B,** p. 58

EL L3 **Reading: Graphic Organizer B,** p. 61

Skills Development/Extension

Unit 2 Resources

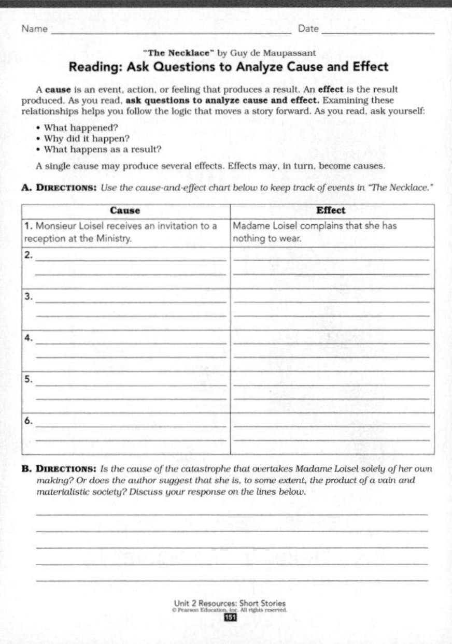
Name ______________________ Date ____________

"The Necklace" by Guy de Maupassant

Reading: Ask Questions to Analyze Cause and Effect

A **cause** is an event, action, or feeling that produces a result. An **effect** is the result produced. As you read, **ask questions to analyze cause and effect.** Examining these relationships helps you follow the logic that moves a story forward. As you read, ask yourself:

- What happened?
- Why did it happen?
- What happens as a result?

A single cause may produce several effects. Effects may, in turn, become causes.

A. Directions: *Use the cause-and-effect chart below to keep track of events in "The Necklace."*

Cause	Effect
1. Monsieur Loisel receives an invitation to a reception at the Ministry.	Madame Loisel complains that she has nothing to wear.
2.	
3.	
4.	
5.	
6.	

B. Directions: *Is the cause of the catastrophe that overtakes Madame Loisel solely of her own making? Or does the author suggest that she is, to some extent, the product of a vain and materialistic society? Discuss your response on the lines below.*

Unit 2 Resources: Short Stories

151

L3 **Reading: Cause and Effect,** pp. 133, 151

Also available for these selections:

All **Literary Analysis: Characterization,** pp. 132, 150

L4 **Enrichment,** pp. 135, 153

EL L3 L4 **Grammar,** p. 154

EL L3 L4 **Support for Writing,** p. 155

L3 L4 **Support for Extend Your Learning,** p. 156

Assessment

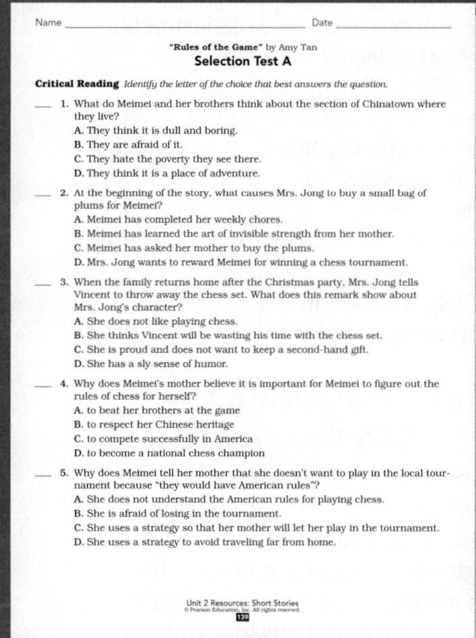
Name ______________________ Date ____________

"Rules of the Game" by Amy Tan

Selection Test A

Critical Reading *Identify the letter of the choice that best answers the question.*

___ 1. What do Meimei and her brothers think about the section of Chinatown where they live?
A. They think it is dull and boring.
B. They are afraid of it.
C. They hate the poverty they see there.
D. They think it is a place of adventure.

___ 2. At the beginning of the story, what causes Mrs. Jong to buy a small bag of plums for Meimei?
A. Meimei has completed her weekly chores.
B. Meimei has learned the art of invisible strength from her mother.
C. Meimei has asked her mother to buy the plums.
D. Mrs. Jong wants to reward Meimei for winning a chess tournament.

___ 3. When the family returns home after the Christmas party, Mrs. Jong tells Vincent to throw away the chess set. What does this remark show about Mrs. Jong's character?
A. She does not like playing chess.
B. She thinks Vincent will be wasting his time with the chess set.
C. She is proud and does not want to keep a second-hand gift.
D. She has a sly sense of humor.

___ 4. Why does Meimei's mother believe it is important for Meimei to figure out the rules of chess for herself?
A. to beat her brothers at the game
B. to respect her Chinese heritage
C. to compete successfully in America
D. to become a national chess champion

___ 5. Why does Meimei tell her mother that she doesn't want to play in the local tournament because "they would have American rules"?
A. She does not understand the American rules for playing chess.
B. She is afraid of losing in the tournament.
C. She uses a strategy so that her mother will let her play in the tournament.
D. She uses a strategy to avoid traveling far from home.

Unit 2 Resources: Short Stories

139

EL L1 L2 **Selection Test A,** pp. 139–141, 160–162

Also available for these selections:

L3 L4 **Open-Book Test,** pp. 136–138, 157–159

EL L3 L4 **Selection Test B,** pp. 142–144, 163–165

PHLit Online!
www.PHLitOnline.com

- complete narrated selection text
- a thematically related video with writing prompt
- an interactive graphic organizer
- highlighting feature
- access to all student print resources, adapted to individual student needs
- Spanish and English summaries
- adapted selection translations in Spanish

Online Resources: All print materials are also available online.

Background Video

Also available:

Get Connected! (thematic video with writing prompt)

All videos are available in Spanish.

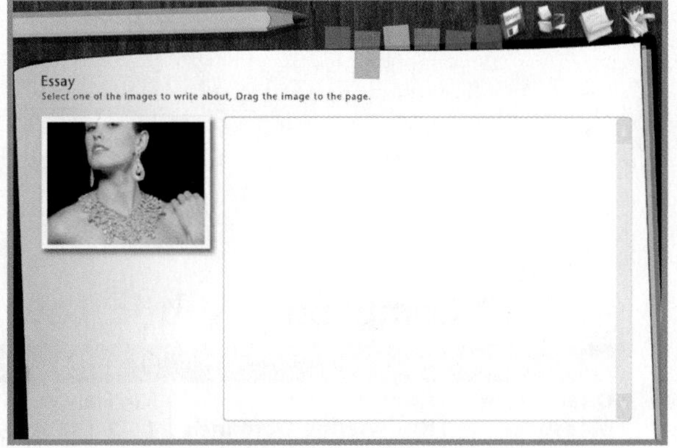

Writer's Journal (with graphics feature)

Also available:

Vocabulary Central (tools, activities, and songs for studying vocabulary)

DIFFERENTIATE/PRETEACH

❶ Leveled Texts

You may use either "Rules of the Game" or "The Necklace" to meet the lesson objectives. Skills instruction for both selections appears on page 313. Choose one selection to teach (or choose to teach both). The Text Complexity Rubric at the bottom of this page will help you determine which selection is more appropriate for your students. Use the Reader and Task Suggestions on the facing page to help all students read text of increasing complexity.

❷ Introducing the CCS Standards

Introduce the standards on the student page. (Note that the lesson element with which each standard is addressed is identified in parentheses after the text of the standard.) Call out the standards that you will cover with the selections, explaining to students what each requires and how they will address it as they work through the selection you have chosen. Standards labeled "Spiral Review" are introduced in the Literary Analysis Workshop for this unit.

Before You Read

Rules of the Game • The Necklace

❶ Leveled Texts

Build your skills and improve your comprehension of short stories with texts of increasing complexity.

Read **"Rules of the Game"** to learn how a daughter's success leads to a new set of problems.

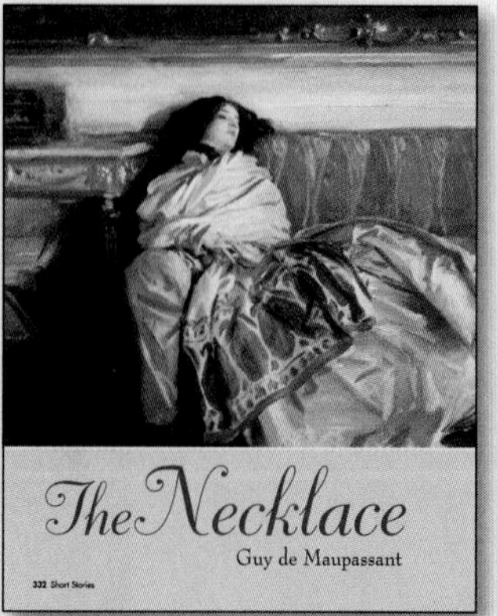

Read **"The Necklace"** to see the disastrous effects of a woman's wish for social acceptance.

❷ Common Core State Standards

Meet these standards with either **"Rules of the Game"** from *The Joy Luck Club* (p. 316) or **"The Necklace"** (p. 332).

Reading Literature
3. Analyze how complex characters develop over the course of a text, interact with other characters, and advance the plot or develop the theme. *(Literary Analysis: Characterization)*

Writing
4. Produce clear and coherent writing in which the development, organization, and style are appropriate to task, purpose, and audience. *(Writing: Written Presentation)*

Speaking and Listening
2. Integrate multiple sources of information presented in diverse media or formats evaluating the credibility and accuracy of each source. *(Research and Technology: Informative Brochure)*

Language
6. Acquire and use accurately grade-appropriate general academic and domain-specific words and phrases; gather vocabulary knowledge when considering a word or phrase important to comprehension or expression. *(Vocabulary: Latin Roots)*

Text Complexity Rubric: Leveled Texts

Text complexity is determined by both qualitative and quantitative measures. For this reason, the quantitative measure of a more complex selection may be lower than that of a more accessible selection.

		✓ Rules of the Game	✓✓ The Necklace
Qualitative Measures	**Context/ Knowledge Demands**	San Francisco's Chinatown; chess 1 2 (3) 4 5	France in 1800s 1 2 (3) 4 5
	Structure/Language Conventionality	On-level vocabulary; relatively short sentences and clauses; some dialogue in nonstandard English. 1 (2) 3 4 5	Numerous long, complex sentences; period language; pronunciation provided for French words 1 2 3 (4) 5
	Levels of Meaning/ Purpose/Concept Level	Accessible concept (mother/daughter relationship; struggle to fit in) 1 2 (3) 4 5	Challenging concept (irony of outcome) 1 2 3 (4) 5
Quantitative Measures	**Text Length**	Word Count: 4,486	Word Count: 2,866
	Lexile	1000L	910L
Overall Complexity		✓ **More accessible**	✓✓ **More complex**

❸ Literary Analysis: Characterization

A **character** is a person, an animal, or even an object that participates in the action and experiences the events of a literary work. Writers communicate a character's traits and personality through these **characterization** techniques:

- **Direct characterization:** The writer (speaking through a narrator) simply tells readers about a character.
- **Indirect characterization:** The writer gives clues to a character by presenting the character's actions, words, and thoughts and by showing how others react to the character.

❹ Using the Strategy: Characterization Chart

Use a **characterization chart** like this one to explore characters as they are developed over the course of the story.

Story Details	What They Show About the Character
Narrator's comments	
Character's thoughts and words	
Character's actions	
Character's appearance	
What others say or think about character	

PHLit Online!
www.PHLitOnline.com

Hear It!
- Selection summary audio
- Selection audio

See It!
- Get Connected video
- Background video
- More about the author
- Vocabulary flashcards

Do It!
- Interactive journals
- Interactive graphic organizers
- Self-test
- Internet activity
- Grammar tutorial
- Interactive vocabulary games

❺ Reading Skill: Cause and Effect

A **cause** is an event, action, or feeling that produces a result. An **effect** is the result produced. A single cause may produce several effects. For example, a poor student starts to do well in school. Her success results in greater self-esteem. Effects, in turn, may become causes. For example, that same student's new confidence leads her to audition for a play.

As you read, ask questions like these to analyze cause and effect:

- What happened?
- Why did it happen?
- What happens as a result?
- Does that result cause something else to happen?

PRETEACH

❸ Literary Analysis

Characterization

1. Introduce the skill, using the instruction on the student page.
2. Tell students that they will identify *direct* and *indirect* characterization as they read.

Think Aloud: Model the Skill

Model ways to identify direct and indirect characterization. Say to students:

> Let's say I'm describing Brad. I say that he's tall, he often wears red, and he reads a lot. I'm directly telling you about Brad. In writing, this is called direct characterization.
>
> Now, suppose I tell you that Brad's friends are all shorter than he is and that Brad says "Wow" often. I also describe smiling when he trips on my front steps. Now you're learning about Brad indirectly by picturing his actions, his words, and others' responses to him. In writing, this is called indirect characterization.

❹ Using the Strategy

Give students a copy of either **Literary Analysis A or B** (***Graphic Organizer Transparencies,*** pp. 56–58) to record characterization details as they read. Use the examples in **Literary Analysis Graphic Organizer A,** which is partially filled in, to model the process of completing the organizer.

❺ Reading Skill

Cause and Effect

1. Introduce the skill, using the instruction on the student page.
2. Tell students that they will identify causes and effects as they read.

Ⓒ Text Complexity: Reader and Task Suggestions

✓ Rules of the Game		✓✓ The Necklace	
Preparing to Read the Text	**Leveled Tasks**	**Preparing to Read the Text**	**Leveled Tasks**
• Using the Background information on TE p. 315, discuss the background and objective of the game of chess. • Discuss with students how it can be a struggle to fit into a new group or culture. • Guide students to use Multidraft Reading strategies (TE p. 315).	*Levels of Meaning* If students will have difficulty with meaning, ask them to first read and take notes on how the characters try to fit into the new culture. Then, have them tell what the characters learn from these encounters. *Synthesizing* If students will not have difficulty with meaning, have them note as they read the ways in which Tan uses chess as an avenue to explore the struggle to fit in and as a means to achieve it.	• Refer to the Background note on TE p. 331 and discuss the bourgeoisie class of France in the 1800s. • Review strategies for reading long, complex sentences. • Guide students to use Multidraft Reading strategies (TE p. 331).	*Structure/Language* If students will have difficulty with language, ask them to first read and identify passages that describe the bourgeoisie of France. Then have them reread, identifying sentences that are difficult for them to understand. *Analyzing* If students will not have difficulty with long, complex sentences, have them read and take notes on how Maupassant introduces details to create an ironic ending.

PRETEACH

1 Writing About the Big Question

1. Review the assignment with the class.
2. Remind students that a conflict is a struggle between opposing forces; an internal conflict is a struggle between forces within oneself. For example, in a competition you might struggle between wanting to win and being concerned for your opponent's feelings.
3. Have students complete the sentence starters. Review responses as a class. (**Possible responses:** Competition can cause internal conflicts because we want to win but also have other concerns. Overcoming conflict while playing a game can help us battle through other real–life struggles because we learn to make difficult decisions under pressure.)
4. Remind students that their answers will help them think about the Big Question, "Is conflict necessary?"

While You Read

Tell students that as they read, they should look for ways that Waverly treats her mother like a chess opponent.

2 Vocabulary

1. Have students preview the selection vocabulary.
2. For each word, have students say the word aloud.
3. Then, use the word in a sentence that defines the word.
4. Finally, repeat your definitional sentence or a similar sentence with the word missing and have the class "fill in the blank" chorally. Here is an example:

   If something is pungent, it has a strong smell. I knew my mother was making pizza sauce, because the strong smell of garlic was very [students say "pungent"].

3 Word Study

1. Introduce the skill, using the instruction in the box.
2. Ask students for another *-bene-* word that means "something that has a good effect." (**Answer:** *benefit*)

Making Connections | Rules of the Game

Is conflict necessary?

1 Writing About the Big Question

In "Rules of the Game," a girl learns some important life lessons while working to master chess. Use these sentence starters to develop your ideas about the Big Question:

Competition can cause internal conflicts because ________________.
Overcoming conflict while playing a game can help us **battle** through other real-life struggles because ________________________.

While You Read Look for ways in which Waverly starts treating her mother like a chess opponent.

2 Vocabulary

Read each word and its definition. Decide whether you know the word well, know it a little bit, or do not know it at all. After you read, see how your knowledge of each word has increased.

- **pungent** (pun´ jənt) *adj.* producing a sharp smell (p. 318) ***We could smell the pungent Indian spices as we walked into the apartment.*** *pungency n. pungently adv.*
- **benevolently** (bə nev´ ə lənt lē) *adv.* in a well-meaning way (p. 322) ***The helpful officer smiled benevolently at the children.*** *benevolent adj. benevolence n.*
- **retort** (ri tôrt´) *n.* sharp or clever reply (p. 322) ***Her quick retort silenced her critic.*** *retort v.*
- **prodigy** (präd´ ə jē) *n.* person who is amazingly talented or intelligent, especially a child of unusual genius (p. 324) ***The six-year-old concert pianist was a prodigy.***
- **malodorous** (mal ō´ dər əs) *adj.* having a bad smell (p. 325) ***The bag was filled with malodorous garbage.*** *malodorously adv. malodorousness n. odor n.*
- **concessions** (kən sesh´ ənz) *n.* things given or granted as privileges (p. 326) ***I had to make a lot of concessions to get my brother to give me his game tickets.*** *concede v. concessionary adj.*

3 Word Study

The **Latin root *-bene-*** means "well."

In this story, an elderly man who is playing chess in the park smiles **benevolently** at Waverly. His smile shows that he wishes her well.

Vocabulary Development

Vocabulary Knowledge Rating

Create a **Vocabulary Knowledge Rating Chart *(Professional Development Guidebook,*** p. 33) for this selection. Include the selection vocabulary and the Big Question words that appear in the Writing About the Big Question sentence starters on this page. (The Big Question vocabulary is introduced on pp. 194–195.)

Give students a copy of the chart. Read the words aloud, and have students mark their rating in the Before Reading column. Urge them to be alert to these words as they read and discuss the selection.

Tally how many students think they know a word to gauge how much instruction to provide. As students read and discuss the selection, point out the words and their context.

Vocabulary Central, featuring tools, activities, and songs for studying vocabulary, is available at **www.PHLitOnline.com.**

Meet Amy Tan (b. 1952)

Author of Rules of the Game

As a child, Amy Tan did not imagine that she would become a successful novelist. Her parents, who had emigrated from China to the San Francisco Bay area, wanted her to become a doctor. Doubting her abilities in science, Tan instead majored in English in college. She went on to become a successful business writer.

Finding Herself in Fiction When she reached her mid-thirties, Tan began writing stories. While she was surprised by the pleasure writing fiction gave her, she was even more surprised by the content of her work. Tan had tried to play down her ethnicity, but in her fiction, she found herself exploring the experiences of Chinese American women. In 1985, Tan wrote "Rules of the Game," which she later included in her best-selling first novel, *The Joy Luck Club.*

Did You Know?

When she was eight years old, Tan's essay "What the Library Means to Me" won first prize in a local contest.

4

BACKGROUND FOR THE STORY

The Game of Chess

A game of strategy, chess resembles a battle between two armies, each led by a figurehead king and a powerful queen. Chess may have started in India. After it spread to Persia (present-day Iran), Arab invaders introduced it to other lands. Today, it is played throughout the world.

Daily Bellringer

For each class during which you will teach this selection, have students complete one of the five Revision activities for Week 10 in the *Daily Bellringer Activities* booklet.

4 Background

The Game of Chess The game of chess was originally known as *chaturanga*, a name that referred to the four divisions of the Indian army of the sixth century: elephants, horses, chariots, and foot soldiers. During the Middle Ages, games of chess became part of courtship rituals between knights and ladies.

Multidraft Reading

This icon ● marks natural pauses in the selection. To assist struggling readers and to deepen reading for all, assign the text in "chunks," following the icons, and apply multidraft reading protocols. For each reading, have students set the purpose indicated:

- **First reading**—identifying key ideas and details and answering any Reading Checks.
- Second reading—analyzing craft and structure and responding to the side-column prompts.
- Third reading—integrating knowledge and ideas, connecting to other texts and the world, and answering the end-of-selection questions.

For more guidance, refer to the ***Classroom Strategies and Teaching Routines*** card on multidraft reading.

PHLit Online!

For more about the author, practice with the selection vocabulary, and more background, go online at **www.PHLitOnline.com.**

Differentiated Instruction — Additional Instruction

EL Extended Support—English Learners
Have students complete the **Reading and Vocabulary Warm-ups,** ***Unit 2 Resources,*** pp. 127–130, before they read. Assign the prereading pages for the selection in the ***Reader's Notebook: English Learner's Version.*** Then, have students listen to portions of the selection on the ***Hear It!*** **Audio CD.**

L1 L2 Extended Support — Struggling Readers
Have students complete the **Reading and Vocabulary Warm-ups,** ***Unit 2 Resources,*** pp. 127–130, before they read. Assign the prereading pages for the selection in the ***Reader's Notebook: Adapted Version.*** Then, have students listen to portions of the selection on the ***Hear It!*** **Audio CD** (adapted text).

Extended Support—Reluctant Readers
To build motivation and engagement before assigning the selection, have students read "Competing to Win," a thematically related selection in ***Reality Central.*** Then, use the questions at the conclusion of the related selection to guide discussion.

TEACH

❶ Activating Prior Knowledge

1. Prepare an **Anticipation Guide** (*Professional Development Guidebook*, pp. 36–38) with the following statements:
    - People with special talents should get special recognition.
    - People should put the needs of their family before their own individual needs.
    - Parents have a right to take credit for their children's accomplishments.
    - Even if people rise in circumstances, they should keep their family's traditional values.
2. Give students a copy of the prepared **Anticipation Guide** and have them respond in the Me column. Have them discuss the statements in groups and mark the Guides again in the Group column.
3. For further guidance, use the ***Classroom Strategies and Teaching Routines*** card: **Using an Anticipation Guide.**

Concept Connector →

Students will return to the **Anticipation Guide** after completing "Rules of the Game."

Small-Group Activity

Discuss different types of board games and what they have in common: rules, movable pieces, and a board on which to play. Now have small groups create a new board game, with rules, board and pieces. Invite students to share their board games with the class.

❷ About the Selection

"Rules of the Game" focuses on the relationship between a mother who was born and raised in China and her daughter, born in America. As the girl succeeds as a chess champion, the two clash over their generational and cultural differences, but behind these conflicts are their similarities: pride, intelligence and stubbornness.

Vocabulary Development

CCSS Language 6

Thematic Vocabulary: The Big Question

As students are discussing "The Rules of the Game," encourage them to use the thematic vocabulary presented in Introducing the Big Question, pp. 194–195. You might encourage them with sentence starters like these:

1. Waverly and her mother's *arguments* centered around . . .
2. For Waverly, chess became a *battle* between . . .
3. The main *issue* was Waverly's love of the game and . . .
4. In the end, Waverly was able to *articulate* . . .

EXEMPLAR TEXT

❶ ❷ Rules of the Game

from The Joy Luck Club

Amy Tan

I was six when my mother taught me the art of invisible strength. It was a strategy for winning arguments, respect from others, and eventually, though neither of us knew it at the time, chess games.

"Bite back your tongue," scolded my mother when I cried loudly, yanking her hand toward the store that sold bags of salted plums. At home, she said, "Wise guy, he not go against wind. In Chinese we say, Come from South, blow with wind—poom!—North will follow. Strongest wind cannot be seen."

The next week I bit back my tongue as we entered the store with the forbidden candies. When my mother finished her shopping, she quietly plucked a small bag of plums from the rack and put it on the counter with the rest of the items.

My mother imparted her daily truths so she could help my older brothers and me rise above our circumstances. We lived in San Francisco's Chinatown. Like most of the other Chinese children who played in the back alleys of restaurants and curio shops, I didn't think we were poor. My bowl was always full, three five-course meals every day, beginning with a soup full of mysterious things I didn't want to know the names of. ❸

We lived on Waverly Place, in a warm, clean, two-bedroom flat that sat above a small Chinese bakery specializing in steamed pastries and dim sum. In the early morning, when the alley was still quiet, I could

❸ Critical Thinking

Analyze

1. Have students read the bracketed text. Then **ask** them what culture the narrator is describing.

   Answer: The narrator is describing Chinese culture.

2. Have students **identify** which elements in this description are more universal and which elements are associated more with Chinese culture.

   Possible response: The struggle between parent and child over control and over access to treats, as well as the narrator's childhood unawareness of poverty, are more universal. The salted plums, mysterious soups, five-course meals, and Chinese baked goods are associated with Chinese culture.

Differentiated Instruction for Universal Access

Strategy for Special-Needs Students

Prepare students for reading by giving them a brief preview of the selection.

1. Have students read aloud the selection title, and then discuss its meaning.
2. Ask students to describe the images and what the images suggest.
3. Review the footnoted vocabulary words and other terms that may confuse students.
4. Finally, help students understand the conflict between traditional Chinese culture and American culture.

Strategy for Less Proficient Readers

To give students a context for the selection and to model how to identify and interpret details of characterization, show them **Literary Analysis Graphic Organizer A** (***Graphic Organizer Transparencies,*** p. 56). The partially completed graphic organizer will give students insight into characterization. They can use it as a model for identifying and interpreting their own details of characterization as they read.

Spiral Review

Setting

1. Remind students that they studied the concept of setting in the Unit 2 Literary Analysis workshop (pp. 196–209).
2. **Ask** students the Spiral Review question.

   Possible response: The details about the conversation, foods, and markets indicate that the narrator grew up in a setting that had many features of traditional Chinese culture.

4 Literary Analysis

Characterization

1. Ask a volunteer to read aloud the bracketed text, and then tell students that the sanddab is a fish commonly found in San Francisco Bay.
2. **Ask** students why the sanddab reminds the narrator of her mother's story.

   Answer: The fish looks like it has been smashed flat, like the girl in the mother's story.
3. Draw students' attention to the last sentence in the passage. **Ask** them to respond to the Literary Analysis question: What does this quotation reveal about the narrator's mother?

   Possible response: The quotation reveals that the mother does not speak English well and that her native language most likely is Chinese. She probably holds traditional Chinese cultural values as well.

smell fragrant red beans as they were cooked down to a pasty sweetness. By daybreak, our flat was heavy with the odor of fried sesame balls and sweet curried chicken crescents. From my bed, I would listen as my father got ready for work, then locked the door behind him, one-two-three clicks.

At the end of our two-block alley was a small sandlot playground with swings and slides well-shined down the middle with use. The play area was bordered by wood-slat benches where old-country people sat cracking roasted watermelon seeds with their golden teeth and scattering the husks to an impatient gathering of gurgling pigeons. The best playground, however, was the dark alley itself. It was crammed with daily mysteries and adventures. My brothers and I would peer into the medicinal herb shop, watching old Li dole out onto a stiff sheet of white paper the right amount of insect shells, saffron-colored seeds and pungent leaves for his ailing customers. It was said that he once cured a woman dying of an ancestral curse that had eluded the best of American doctors. Next to the pharmacy was a printer who specialized in gold-embossed wedding invitations and festive red banners.

Vocabulary
pungent (pun´ jənt) *adj.* producing a sharp smell

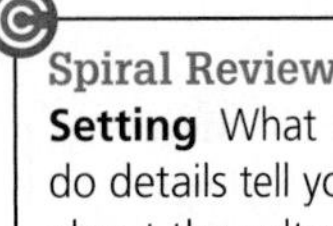

Spiral Review
Setting What do details tell you about the cultural environment in which the narrator grew up?

Farther down the street was Ping Yuen Fish Market. The front window displayed a tank crowded with doomed fish and turtles struggling to gain footing on the slimy green-tiled sides. A hand-written sign informed tourists, "Within this store, is all for food, not for pet." Inside, the butchers with their bloodstained white smocks deftly gutted the fish while customers cried out their orders and shouted, "Give me your freshest," to which the butchers always protested, "All are freshest." On less crowded market days, we would inspect the crates of live frogs and crabs which we were warned not to poke, boxes of dried cuttlefish, and row upon row of iced prawns, squid, and slippery fish. The sanddabs made me shiver each time; 4 their eyes lay on one flattened side and reminded me of my mother's story of a careless girl who ran into a crowded street and was crushed by a cab. "Was smash flat," reported my mother.

Literary Analysis
Characterization What does this quotation reveal about the narrator's mother?

At the corner of the alley was Hong Sing's, a four-table cafe with a recessed stairwell in front that led to a door marked "Tradesmen." My brothers and I believed the bad people emerged from this door at night. Tourists never went to Hong Sing's,

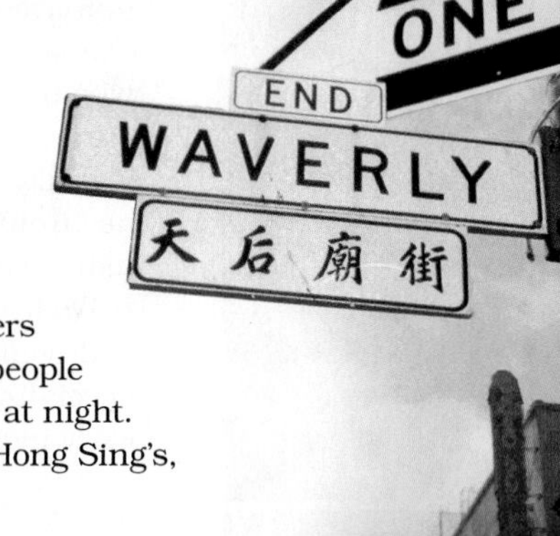

Vocabulary Development

CCSS Language 6

Selection Vocabulary Reinforcement

Students will benefit from additional examples and practice with the selection vocabulary words. Reinforce their comprehension with "show-you-know" sentences. The first part of the sentence uses the vocabulary word in an appropriate context. The second part of the sentence—the "show-you-know" part—clarifies the first. Model the strategy with this example for *pungent*:

> The *pungent* smell of fried chicken wafted from the restaurant; the strong aroma made me hungry.

Then, give students these sentence prompts, and coach them in creating the clarification part.

1. The meaning of her *retort* was unmistakable; ________

   Sample answer: its sharpness told me that she was very angry.
2. The old trench coat was *malodorous*; ________

   Sample answer: they could never get it to smell pleasant again.

since the menu was printed only in Chinese. A Caucasian man with a big camera once posed me and my playmates in front of the restaurant. He had us move to the side of the picture window so the photo would capture the roasted duck with its head dangling from a juice-covered rope. After he took the picture, I told him he should go into Hong Sing's and eat dinner. When he smiled and asked me what they served, I shouted, "Guts and duck's feet and octopus gizzards!" Then I ran off with my friends, shrieking with laughter as we scampered across the alley and hid in the entryway grotto of the China Gem Company, my heart pounding with hope that he would chase us.

My mother named me after the street that we lived on: Waverly Place Jong, my official name for important American documents. But my family called me Meimei [mā´ mā´], "Little Sister," I was the youngest, the only daughter. Each morning before school, my mother would twist and yank on my thick black hair until she had formed two tightly wound pigtails. One day, as she struggled to weave a hard-toothed comb through my disobedient hair, I had a sly thought.

I asked her, "Ma, what is Chinese torture?" My mother shook her head. A bobby pin was wedged between her lips. She wetted her palm and smoothed the hair above my ear, then pushed the pin in
5 so that it nicked sharply against my scalp.

"Who say this word?" she asked without a trace of knowing how wicked I was being. I shrugged my shoulders and said, "Some boy in my class said Chinese people do Chinese torture."

"Chinese people do many things," she said simply. "Chinese people do business, do medicine, do painting. Not lazy like American people. We do torture. Best torture."

My older brother Vincent was the one who actually got the chess set. We had gone to the annual Christmas party held at the First Chinese Baptist Church at the end of the alley. The missionary ladies had put together a Santa bag of gifts donated by members of another church. None of the gifts had names on them. There were separate sacks for boys and girls of different ages.

One of the Chinese parishioners had donned a Santa Claus costume and a stiff paper beard with cotton balls glued to it. I think the only children who thought he was the real thing were too young to know that Santa Claus was not Chinese. When my turn came up, the Santa man asked me how old I was. I thought it was a trick question; I was seven according to the American formula and eight by the Chinese calendar. I said I was born on March 17, 1951. That seemed to satisfy him. He then solemnly asked if I had been a very,

Literary Analysis
Characterization What does Mrs. Jong's response to the accusation that Chinese people do torture reveal about her personality?

6

What gift does Vincent receive at the Christmas party?

5 Literary Analysis

Characterization

1. Have students read the bracketed text. **Ask:** Why does Waverly ask her mother about Chinese torture, and what does the question reveal about Waverly's character?

   Possible response: She probably wants to give her mother a hard time. The question reveals that Waverly is mischievous and has a sense of humor.

2. **Ask** students to respond to the Literary Analysis question: What does Mrs. Jong's response to the accusation that Chinese people do torture reveal about her personality?

   Possible response: Her response reveals that she is proud of her culture. It also reveals that she knows Waverly is baiting her and trying to make her defensive. Her response turns the tables on Waverly and demonstrates Mrs. Jong's sense of humor and intelligence.

6 Reading Check

Answer: Vincent receives a used chess set.

Fluency

Distribute copies of page 319, and pair students. Have listeners mark words with which their reading partner struggles. Circulate to monitor students' fluency, then collect the marked up pages. Review difficult words and passages, such as these:

- If students struggle to syllabicate *disobedient*, model how to cover parts of the word, pronounce each part, and then blend the parts together. Read the word aloud and have students echo to confirm.
- If students have difficulty with Mrs. Jong's English, pair them with fluent partners to listen to and repeat the text until they are reading it fluently.
- If students pronounce, but do not understand the word *donned*, use gestures to demonstrate its meaning. Then reinforce by pointing out context clues such as *costume* and *stiff paper beard*. Stress that students should try to figure out meaning separately from learning to pronounce a word.

7 Literary Analysis

Characterization

1. Refer students to the first bracketed text. **Ask:** What is Waverly attempting to do as she analyzes the size and shape of the gifts?

   Answer: She is trying to determine which package contains a nice gift.

2. **Ask** students to respond to the Literary Analysis question: What does Waverly's thought process in this paragraph reveal indirectly about her character?

   Possible response: She is very careful and practical; she is analytical and calculating.

8 Reading Skill

Cause and Effect

1. Have students read the second bracketed text, continuing onto page 321. **Ask** students why Waverly thinks the chessmen are so powerful.

   Answer: The patterns of the chessboard and the strategic puzzle of the chessmen's movements are loaded with meaning and mystery for Waverly. Her response suggests she has a strong affinity for the game.

2. **Ask** students to respond to the Reading Skill question: What effect does the gift of the chess board have on Waverly?

   Possible response: She is fascinated by it and wants to learn its secrets.

3. **Ask** students what Waverly's interest in the chess set causes her to do.

   Answer: It causes her to beg for her brother's permission to play.

very good girl this year and did I believe in Jesus Christ and obey my parents. I knew the only answer to that. I nodded back with equal solemnity.

Literary Analysis
Characterization
What does Waverly's thought process in this paragraph reveal indirectly about her character?

7 Having watched the other children opening their gifts, I already knew that the big gifts were not necessarily the nicest ones. One girl my age got a large coloring book of biblical characters, while a less greedy girl who selected a small box received a glass vial of lavender toilet water. The sound of the box was also important. A ten-year-old boy had chosen a box that jangled when he shook it. It was a tin globe of the world with a slit for inserting money. He must have thought it was full of dimes and nickels, because when he saw that it had just ten pennies, his face fell with such undisguised disappointment that his mother slapped the side of his head and led him out of the church hall, apologizing to the crowd for her son who had such bad manners he couldn't appreciate such a fine gift.

As I peered into the sack, I quickly fingered the remaining presents, testing their weight, imagining what they contained. I chose a heavy, compact one that was wrapped in shiny silver foil and a red satin ribbon. It was a twelve-pack of Life Savers and I spent the rest of the party arranging and rearranging the candy tubes in the order of my favorites. My brother Winston chose wisely as well. His present turned out to be a box of intricate plastic parts; the instructions on the box proclaimed that when they were properly assembled he would have an authentic miniature replica of a World War II submarine.

Vincent got the chess set, which would have been a very decent present to get at a church Christmas party except it was obviously used and, as we discovered later, it was missing a black pawn and a white knight. My mother graciously thanked the unknown benefactor, saying, "Too good. Cost too much." At which point, an old lady with fine white, wispy hair nodded toward our family and said with a whistling whisper, "Merry, merry Christmas."

When we got home, my mother told Vincent to throw the chess set away. "She not want it. We not want it," she said, tossing her head stiffly to the side with a tight, proud smile. My brothers had deaf ears. They were already lining up the chess pieces and reading from the dog-eared instruction book.

Reading Skill
Cause and Effect
What effect does the gift of the chess board have on Waverly?

8 I watched Vincent and Winston play during Christmas week. The chess board seemed to hold elaborate secrets waiting to be untangled. The chessmen were more powerful than Old Li's magic herbs that cured ancestral curses. And my brothers wore such serious faces that I was sure something was at stake that was greater than avoiding the tradesmen's door to Hong Sing's.

Vocabulary Development

CCSS Language 6

Expressive Vocabulary
To help students broaden their expressive vocabulary, encourage them to use the following words as they discuss the selection: *induce*, *evoke*, *initiate*, and *generate*. Have them complete these sentence starters.

1. Waverly had a tough time trying to *induce* . . .
2. When one of the brothers lost a game of chess, it seemed to *evoke* . . .
3. Discussion of the rules of the game was sure to *initiate* . . .
4. Waverly found that the challenge of learning to play began to *generate* . . .

8 "Let me! Let me!" I begged between games when one brother or the other would sit back with a deep sigh of relief and victory, the other annoyed, unable to let go of the outcome. Vincent at first refused to let me play, but when I offered my Life Savers as replacements for the buttons that filled in for the missing pieces, he relented. He chose the flavors: wild cherry for the black pawn and peppermint for the white knight. Winner could eat both. As our mother sprinkled flour and rolled out small doughy circles for the steamed dumplings that would be our dinner that night, Vincent explained the rules, pointing to each piece. "You have sixteen pieces and so do I. One king and queen, two bishops, two knights, two castles, and eight pawns. The pawns can only move forward one step, except on the first move. Then they can move two. But they can only take men by moving crossways like this, except in the beginning, when you can move ahead and take another pawn."

"Why?" I asked as I moved my pawn. "Why can't they move more steps?"

"Because they're pawns," he said.

"But why do they go crossways to take other men? Why aren't there any women and children?"

9 "Why is the sky blue? Why must you always ask stupid questions?" asked Vincent. "This is a game. These are the rules. I didn't make them up. See. Here. In the book." He jabbed a page with a pawn in his hand. "Pawn. P-A-W-N. Pawn. Read it yourself."

My mother patted the flour off her hands. "Let me see book," she said quietly. She scanned the pages quickly, not reading the foreign English symbols, seeming to search deliberately for nothing in particular.

"This American rules," she concluded at last. "Every time people come out from foreign country, must know rules. You not know, judge say, Too bad, go back. They not telling you why so you can use their way go forward. They say, Don't know why, you find out yourself. But they knowing all the time. Better you take it, find out why yourself." She tossed her head back with a satisfied smile.

I found out about all the whys later. I read the rules and looked up all the big words in a dictionary. I borrowed books from the Chinatown library. I studied each chess piece, trying to absorb the power each contained.

Literary Analysis
Characterization
What do you learn about Vincent based on this conversation?

10 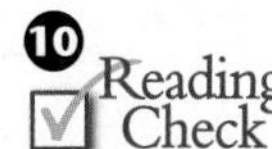
Reading Check
How does Waverly convince Vincent to let her play chess?

9 Literary Analysis

Characterization

1. Have students read aloud the second bracketed passage and then **describe** Vincent's attitude and the reasons for it.

   Answer: Vincent is aggravated because his sister is asking so many questions.

2. **Ask** students to respond to the Literary Analysis question: What do you learn about Vincent based on this conversation?

   Possible responses: He is irritable and easily frustrated; he finds his sister annoying; he is satisfied to accept rules and not question them.

10 Reading Check

Answer: She offers her Life Savers as replacements for the missing chess pieces.

Differentiated Instruction for Universal Access

EL Support for English Learners

Students might benefit by recasting some of the phrases spoken by Mrs. Jong and the other Chinese characters into Standard English. Point out to students that people learning English or any other new language often start out using phrases in which the basic ideas are stated—and usually understood by English speakers—but often they are not stated in grammatically correct form.

For example, write this sign text on the board: "Within this store, is all for food, not for pet." Ask students how they would communicate the meaning of this sign in Standard English. (**Possible response:** The animals in this store are sold as food, not as pets.)

Encourage students to flesh out the main ideas in phrases throughout the selection, such as "Was smash flat" (p. 318) and "She not want it. We not want it" (p. 320).

⓫ Literature in Context

Cultural Connection In a typical endgame, both players have lost their queens and have limited resources. They attempt to checkmate each other's king, trapping the king in a position where no move is possible. Note to students that the terms *endgame* and *checkmate* are frequently applied beyond the game of chess—especially in military, political, and athletic contests.

Connect to the Literature Have students read the Literature in Context feature, and present the additional background information above. Point out that chess masters develop their mastery over time and with discipline. Then **ask** students the Connect to the Literature question: Why might it be difficult for a young beginning chess player like Waverly to master the endgame?
Answer: It is the most difficult part of the game, when mistakes can have more serious consequences. Waverly might not have the maturity or experience for this.

⓫ **LITERATURE IN CONTEXT**

Cultural Connection

Endgame
Endgame describes a tense period in a chess game when the end seems close at hand. With fewer pieces left, lines of attack and defense become clearer to both players. Mistakes are magnified in an endgame, when victory and defeat can be determined by a single ill-considered move. In this story, Waverly develops a keen awareness of the strategies needed to secure a victory in the endgame.

Connect to the Literature

Why might it be difficult for a young beginning chess player like Waverly to master the endgame?

I learned about opening moves and why it's important to control the center early on; the shortest distance between two points is straight down the middle. I learned about the middle game and why tactics between two adversaries are like clashing ideas; the one who plays better has the clearest plans for both attacking and getting out of traps. I learned why it is essential in the endgame to have foresight, a mathematical understanding of all possible moves, and patience; all weaknesses and advantages become evident to a strong adversary and are obscured to a tiring opponent. I discovered that for the whole game one must gather invisible strengths and see the endgame before the game begins.

I also found out why I should never reveal "why" to others. A little knowledge withheld is a great advantage one should store for future use. That is the power of chess. It is a game of secrets in which one must show and never tell.

I loved the secrets I found within the sixty-four black and white squares. I carefully drew a handmade chessboard and pinned it to the wall next to my bed, where at night I would stare for hours at imaginary battles. Soon I no longer lost any games or Life Savers, but I lost my adversaries. Winston and Vincent decided they were more interested in roaming the streets after school in their Hopalong Cassidy cowboy hats.

On a cold spring afternoon, while walking home from school, I detoured through the playground at the end of our alley. I saw a group of old men, two seated across a folding table playing a game of chess, others smoking pipes, eating peanuts, and watching. I ran home and grabbed Vincent's chess set, which was bound in a cardboard box with rubber bands. I also carefully selected two prized rolls of Life Savers. I came back to the park and approached a man who was observing the game.

"Want to play?" I asked him. His face widened with surprise and he grinned as he looked at the box under my arm.

"Little sister, been a long time since I play with dolls," he said, smiling **benevolently**. I quickly put the box down next to him on the bench and displayed my **retort**.

Lau Po, as he allowed me to call him, turned out to be a much better player than my brothers. I lost many games and many Life

Vocabulary
benevolently (bə nev′ ə lənt lē) *adv.* in a well-meaning way
retort (ri tôrt′) *n.* sharp or clever reply

Think Aloud

Vocabulary: Using Context
Direct students' attention to the word *etiquette* on p. 323. Using a think-aloud process, model how to use context to infer the meaning of an unknown word. Say to students:

I'm going to think aloud to show you how I would figure out the meaning of *etiquette* from its context.

In this sentence, *etiquette* is a noun and is being used in relation to a game of chess. At first it might seem that the word refers to a chess strategy, since the previous paragraph lists strategies. However, the following sentences list examples of etiquette—keep men in rows, never say "check" with vanity, do not throw pieces in the sandbox after losing a game. These are examples of what one should not do and are examples of poor behavior or poor manners. So, I think *etiquette* must refer to good manners.

Savers. But over the weeks, with each diminishing roll of candies, I added new secrets. Lau Po gave me the names. The Double Attack from the East and West Shores. Throwing Stones on the Drowning Man. The Sudden Meeting of the Clan. The Surprise from the Sleeping Guard. The Humble Servant Who Kills the King. Sand in the Eyes of Advancing Forces. A Double Killing Without Blood.

There were also the fine points of chess etiquette. Keep captured men in neat rows, as well-tended prisoners. Never announce "Check" with vanity, lest someone with an unseen sword slit your throat. Never hurl pieces into the sandbox after you have lost a game, because then you must find them again, by yourself, after apologizing to all around you. By the end of the summer, Lau Po had taught me all he knew, and I had become a better chess player.

By the end of summer, Lau Po had taught me all he knew . . .

A small weekend crowd of Chinese people and tourists would gather as I played and defeated my opponents one by one. My mother would join the crowds during these outdoor exhibition games. She sat proudly on the bench, telling my admirers with proper Chinese humility, "Is luck."

A man who watched me play in the park suggested that my mother allow me to play in local chess tournaments. My mother smiled graciously, an answer that meant nothing. I desperately
12 wanted to go, but I bit back my tongue. I knew she would not let me play among strangers. So as we walked home I said in a small voice that I didn't want to play in the local tournament. They would have American rules. If I lost, I would bring shame on my family.

"Is shame you fall down nobody push you," said my mother.

During my first tournament, my mother sat with me in the front row as I waited for my turn. I frequently bounced my legs to unstick them from the cold metal seat of the folding chair. When my name was called, I leapt up. My mother unwrapped something in her lap. It was her chang, a small tablet of red jade which held the sun's fire. "Is luck," she whispered, and tucked it into my dress pocket. I turned to my opponent, a fifteen-year-old boy from Oakland. He looked at me, wrinkling his nose.

Reading Skill
Cause and Effect
What does Waverly anticipate would be the effect of her expressing her desire to play in local chess tournaments?

13
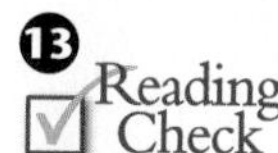

How does Waverly's mother respond to Waverly's admirers in the park?

12 Reading Skill

Cause and Effect

1. Have students read the bracketed text. **Ask** them to describe how the suggestion that Waverly play in a tournament affects Mrs. Jong.
   Answer: Mrs. Jong smiles and says nothing.
2. **Ask** students how Waverly interprets her mother's response.
   Answer: She thinks her mother does not want Waverly to play in tournaments.
3. **Ask** students to respond to the Reading Skill question: What does Waverly anticipate would be the effect of her expressing her desire to play in local chess tournaments?
   Possible response: Waverly thinks that if she pleads to be allowed to play, her mother will almost certainly say no.
4. **Ask** students how Waverly practices "invisible strength" with her mother and what the effect of that is.
   Answer: Waverly tells her mother that she does not want to play in a tournament because if she loses it will bring shame on her family. Her mother responds that Waverly should play.

13 Reading Check

Answer: She tells them that Waverly wins because of luck.

Differentiated Instruction for Universal Access

EL Pronunciation for English Learners

To help students pronounce the initial "p" sound, post these word pairs: *park, bark; post, boast;* and *pill, bill.* Pronounce each word in turn, stressing the initial consonant, as students echo. Pair English learners with fluent speakers to practice discriminating the initial "p" sound from the initial "b" sound. If English learners err, fluent speakers should pronounce the word carefully, leading the way to the correct pronunciation.

Enrichment for Gifted/Talented Students

Encourage chess-playing students to bring in a chess set and demonstrate the basics of the game. They might also create diagrams, charts, or other visuals to demonstrate chess moves or to explain chess terminology from the story. Direct students to chess contests in an available newspaper or magazine, and suggest that students try to solve the contests.

14 Reading Skill

Cause and Effect

1. Read the first bracketed text aloud to students.
2. **Ask** students to describe Waverly's mindset.

   Answer: She is concentrating very deeply.
3. **Ask** students what Waverly's concentration allows her to do.

   Answer: She blocks out her opponent and sees only the game pieces.
4. **Ask** students to respond to the Reading Skill question: How does Waverly's mindset affect the outcome of the match?

   Possible response: Waverly's mindset allows her to see the way to victory, so it helps her win the match.

15 Literary Analysis

Characterization

1. Have students read the second bracketed text, and then **identify** the conflict between Waverly and her mother.

   Answer: Her mother does not understand how the game of chess is played; Waverly gets exasperated with her for insisting that it is better to lose fewer pieces.
2. **Ask** students to respond to the Literary Analysis question: What do Waverly's mother's comments here reveal indirectly about her ambitions for Waverly?

   Possible responses: She wants Waverly to continue to improve and win; she wants Waverly to be successful.

▶ **Monitor Progress:** Use students' answers to the previous question to gauge their understanding of characterization.

▶ **Reteach:** If students are having difficulty identifying and interpreting details of characterization, show them **Literary Analysis Graphic Organizer A *(Graphic Organizer Transparencies,* p. 56).** Point out how the details listed tell something about the character.

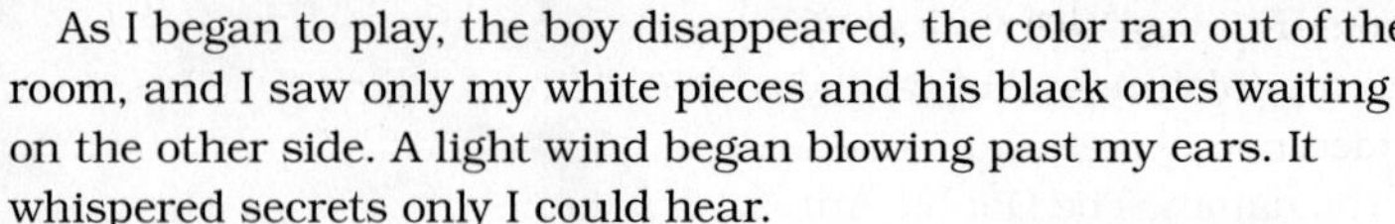

As I began to play, the boy disappeared, the color ran out of the room, and I saw only my white pieces and his black ones waiting on the other side. A light wind began blowing past my ears. It whispered secrets only I could hear.

"Blow from the South," it murmured. "The wind leaves no trail." I saw a clear path, the traps to avoid. The crowd rustled. "Shhh! Shhh!" said the corners of the room. The wind blew stronger. "Throw sand from the East to distract him." The knight came forward ready for the sacrifice. The wind hissed, louder and louder. "Blow, blow, blow. He cannot see. He is blind now. Make him lean away from the wind so he is easier to knock down."

"Check," I said, as the wind roared with laughter. The wind died down to little puffs, my own breath.

Reading Skill
Cause and Effect
How does Waverly's mindset affect the outcome of the match?

My mother placed my first trophy next to a new plastic chess set that the neighborhood Tao society had given to me. As she wiped each piece with a soft cloth, she said, "Next time win more, lose less."

"Ma, it's not how many pieces you lose," I said. "Sometimes you need to lose pieces to get ahead."

"Better to lose less, see if you really need."

At the next tournament, I won again, but it was my mother who wore the triumphant grin.

"Lost eight piece this time. Last time was eleven. What I tell you? Better off lose less!" I was annoyed, but I couldn't say anything.

Literary Analysis
Characterization
What do Waverly's mother's comments here reveal indirectly about her ambitions for Waverly?

I attended more tournaments, each one farther away from home. I won all games, in all divisions. The Chinese bakery downstairs from our flat displayed my growing collection of trophies in its window, amidst the dust-covered cakes that were never picked up. The day after I won an important regional tournament, the window encased a fresh sheet cake with whipped-cream frosting and red script saying, "Congratulations, Waverly Jong, Chinatown Chess Champion." Soon after that, a flower shop, headstone engraver, and funeral parlor offered to sponsor me in national tournaments. That's when my mother decided I no longer had to do the dishes. Winston and Vincent had to do my chores.

"Why does she get to play and we do all the work," complained Vincent.

"Is new American rules," said my mother. "Meimei play, squeeze all her brains out for win chess. You play, worth squeeze towel."

By my ninth birthday, I was a national chess champion. I was still some 429 points away from grand-master status, but I was touted as the Great American Hope, a child prodigy and a girl to boot. They ran a photo of me in *Life* magazine next to a quote in

Vocabulary
prodigy (präd′ ə jē) *n.* person who is amazingly talented or intelligent, especially a child of unusual genius

Think Aloud

Make Inferences

Draw students' attention to the second bracketed text on page 324. Use the following "think aloud" to model the process of making an inference (introduced on p. 211).

When I read Mrs. Jong's comment, "Next time win more, lose less," I realize that it is a comment on Waverly's playing. Waverly's response—an explanation for why players must sometimes lose pieces—suggests that she thinks her mother's comment is wrong.

Then, I read that Mrs. Wong is still happy when Waverly loses fewer pieces, despite the explanation. Waverly's reaction—she is annoyed—suggests that now she thinks her mother is really wrong. These clues help me make inferences about Mrs. Wong: She doesn't listen very well. She's either very stubborn or not very smart. I will keep reading to see if my inferences are proven by other clues.

16 which Bobby Fischer[1] said, "There will never be a woman grand master." "Your move, Bobby," said the caption.

The day they took the magazine picture I wore neatly plaited braids clipped with plastic barrettes trimmed with rhinestones. I was playing in a large high school auditorium that echoed with phlegmy coughs and the squeaky rubber knobs of chair legs sliding across freshly waxed wooden floors. Seated across from me was an American man, about the same age as Lau Po, maybe fifty. I remember that his sweaty brow seemed to weep at my every move. He wore a dark, **malodorous** suit. One of his pockets was stuffed with a great white kerchief on which he wiped his palm before sweeping his hand over the chosen chess piece with great flourish.

In my crisp pink-and-white dress with scratchy lace at the neck, one of two my mother had sewn for these special occasions, I would clasp my hands under my chin, the delicate points of my elbows poised lightly on the table in the manner my mother had shown me for posing for the press. I would swing my patent leather shoes back and forth like an impatient child riding on a school bus. Then I would pause, suck in my lips, twirl my chosen piece in midair as if undecided, and then firmly plant it in its new threatening place, with a triumphant smile thrown back at my opponent for good measure.

1. **Bobby Fischer** (1943–2008), this American chess prodigy attained the top rank of grandmaster in 1958.

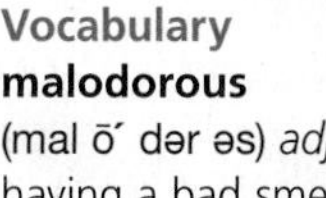

Vocabulary
malodorous
(mal ō´ dər əs) *adj.* having a bad smell

17 
Reading Check
Why does Waverly no longer have to do her chores?

16 Critical Thinking

Analyze

1. Have students read the bracketed text that begins at the bottom of page 324 and the footnote on page 325.
2. **Ask** students why Waverly's picture is placed next to Bobby Fischer's.

   Answer: Like Bobby Fischer, Waverly is a child prodigy at chess. She is near to disproving his statement that a girl could never be a grandmaster.
3. **Ask** students why Waverly's picture is in *Life* magazine.

   Answer: There has never been a female grandmaster in chess, and Waverly is seen as someone who might achieve this status.

17 Reading Check

Answer: Mrs.Jong wants her to spend all her energy on playing chess.

Differentiated Instruction for Universal Access

Culturally Responsive Instruction:
Culture Focus Point out that Waverly uses the stories her mother has told her about the wind to guide her play and to help her to win. Stress that stories offering guidance on how to live are present in most cultures. Invite students to describe stories from their own culture that provide lessons on ways to live, or have students describe a family member who uses stories to convey ideas about how to live.

Enrichment for Advanced Readers
Ask students to imagine that they are journalists working for *Life* magazine. Have them write articles to accompany the photo of Waverly and the quotation by Bobby Fischer. The article might trace Waverly's development as a chess champion and include an interview with Waverly and with Waverly's mother.

Urge students to add imaginative details and dialogue, but to ensure that additions accurately reflect the characters from the selection. Have students share their articles with the class.

⓲ Reading Skill

Cause and Effect

1. Have students read the bracketed text which continues onto p. 327. **Ask** what happens when Waverly complains about a noisy bedroom.

   Answer: Her brothers are forced to sleep in the living room.

2. **Ask** students how they think Waverly's brothers felt about having to give up their bedroom.

   Answer: They were probably angry and resentful.

3. **Ask** students how Waverly feels about her mother introducing her to strangers.

   Answer: She is embarrassed and resentful.

4. **Ask** students to respond to the Reading Skill question: In what ways does Waverly's success at chess affect her family life? Explain.

   Possible response: On the positive side, Waverly is treated respectfully, allowed freedom, and given special privileges; her mother is very proud of her. On the negative side, her brothers' lives are disrupted, and they are probably resentful; Waverly is embarrassed and resentful at having her mother show her off.

I no longer played in the alley of Waverly Place. I never visited the playground where the pigeons and old men gathered. I went to school, then directly home to learn new chess secrets, cleverly concealed advantages, more escape routes.

But I found it difficult to concentrate at home. My mother had a habit of standing over me while I plotted out my games. I think she thought of herself as my protective ally. Her lips would be sealed tight, and after each move I made, a soft "Hmmmmph" would escape from her nose.

"Ma, I can't practice when you stand there like that," I said one day. She retreated to the kitchen and made loud noises with the pots and pans. When the crashing stopped, I could see out of the corner of my eye that she was standing in the doorway. "Hmmmmph!" Only this one came out of her tight throat.

Vocabulary
concessions (kən sesh′ ənz) *n.* things given or granted as privileges

My parents made many **concessions** to allow me to practice. One time I complained that the bedroom I shared was so noisy that I couldn't think. Thereafter, my brothers slept in a bed in the living room facing the street. I said I couldn't finish my rice; my head didn't work right when my stomach was too full. I left the table with half-finished bowls and nobody complained. But there was one duty I couldn't avoid. I had to accompany my mother on Saturday market days when I had no tournament to play. My mother would proudly walk with me, visiting many shops, buying very little. "This my daughter Wave-ly Jong," she said to whoever looked her way.

Reading Skill
Cause and Effect
In what ways does Waverly's success at chess affect her family life? Explain.

⓲ One day, after we left a shop I said under my breath, "I wish you wouldn't do that, telling everybody I'm your daughter." My mother stopped walking. Crowds of people with heavy bags pushed past us on the sidewalk, bumping into first one shoulder, then another.

"Aiii-ya. So shame be with mother?" She grasped my hand even tighter as she glared at me.

I looked down. "It's not that, it's just so obvious. It's just so embarrassing."

"Embarrass you be my daughter?" Her voice was cracking with anger.

"That's not what I meant. That's not what I said."

"What you say?"

I knew it was a mistake to say anything more, but I heard my voice speaking. "Why do you have to use me to show off? If you

Vocabulary Development

Vocabulary Knowledge Rating

When students have completed reading and discussing "Rules of the Game," have them take out their **Vocabulary Knowledge Rating Chart** for this selection. Read the words aloud once more and have students rate their knowledge of the words again in the After Reading column. Clarify any words that are still problematic. Have students write their own definition and example or sentence in the appropriate column. Then have students complete the Vocabulary Practice activities at the end of the selection. Encourage students to use the words in further discussion and written work about this selection. Remind them that they will be accountable for these words on the **Selection Test, *Unit 2 Resources,*** pp. 139–141 or 142–144.

18 want to show off, then why don't you learn to play chess?" My mother's eyes turned into dangerous black slits. She had no words for me, just sharp silence.

I felt the wind rushing around my hot ears. I jerked my hand out of my mother's tight grasp and spun around, knocking into an old woman. Her bag of groceries spilled to the ground.

"Aii-ya! Stupid girl!" my mother and the woman cried. Oranges and tin cans careened down the sidewalk. As my mother stooped to help the old woman pick up the escaping food, I took off.

I raced down the street, dashing between people, not looking back as my mother screamed shrilly, "Meimei! Meimei!" I fled down an alley, past dark curtained shops and merchants washing the grime off their windows. I sped into the sunlight, into a large street crowded with tourists examining trinkets and souvenirs. I ducked into another dark alley, down another street, up another alley. I ran until it hurt and I realized I had nowhere to go, that I was not running from anything. The alleys contained no escape routes.

My breath came out like angry smoke. It was cold. I sat down on an upturned plastic pail next to a stack of empty boxes, cupping my chin with my hands,
19 thinking hard. I imagined my mother, first walking briskly down one street or another looking for me, then giving up and returning home to await my arrival. After two hours, I stood up on creaking legs and slowly walked home.

The alley was quiet and I could see the yellow lights shining from our flat like two tiger's eyes in the night. I climbed the sixteen steps to the door, advancing quietly up each so as not to make any warning sounds. I turned the knob; the door was locked. I heard a chair moving, quick steps, the locks turning—click! click! click!—and then the door opened.

"About time you got home," said Vincent. "Boy, are you in trouble."

He slid back to the dinner table. On a platter were the remains of a large fish, its fleshy head still connected to bones swimming upstream in vain escape. Standing there waiting for my
21 punishment, I heard my mother speak in a dry voice.

"We not concerning this girl. This girl not have concerning for us."

Nobody looked at me. Bone chopsticks clinked against the insides of bowls being emptied into hungry mouths.

I walked into my room, closed the door, and lay down on my bed. The room was dark, the ceiling filled with shadows from the dinnertime lights of neighboring flats.

My mother had a habit of standing over me while I plotted out my games.

20 

Reading Check

What do Waverly and her mother argue about at the market?

19 Connecting to the Big Question

1. Point out that sometimes conflicts motivate people to work hard or to struggle to reach goals.
2. Have students read the bracketed text on page 327, beginning "I raced down the street...."

   Ask: How does Waverly's reaction after her argument with her mother remind you of her behavior toward chess playing and chess opponents? How is it different from her behavior as a chess player?

   Possible response: As she does when playing chess, Waverly thinks about moves and escape routes, as well as what her opponent (Mrs. Jong) will do. Unlike when she plays chess, here Waverly is too upset to think clearly so she cannot find an escape route.
3. **Ask** students: Did Waverly need to get angry with her mother and run away? Explain.

   Possible response: Yes, she was tired of her mother telling her what to do; she needed to share that anger and show her independence from her mother.

20 Reading Check

Answer: Waverly doesn't like it when her mother brags about being Waverly's mother.

Concept Connector

Anticipation Guide

Have students return to their **Anticipation Guides** and respond to the statements again in the After Reading column. Then, lead a class discussion, probing for what students have learned that confirms or invalidates each statement.

Writing About the Big Question

Have students compare their responses to the sentence starters they completed before reading the selection with their ideas afterward. Ask them to explain whether their thoughts have changed.

Literary Analysis Graphic Organizer

Have students review the graphic organizers they completed to identify and interpret details of characterization while reading. Show them the partially-completed **Literary Analysis Graphic Organizer A** *(Graphic Organizer Transparencies,* p. 56) as an example. Then have students share the graphic organizers they did and the details they identified in the selection.

21 Reading Skill

Cause and Effect

1. Have students read the bracketed text, which begins at the top of p. 327, then **speculate** about why Waverly runs away.

   Possible responses: She is upset with her mother for embarrassing her; she feels that her mother regards her as a personal trophy.

2. **Ask** students to respond to the Reading Skill question.

   Possible response: Waverly's mother is angry because she feels Waverly is being disrespectful; Waverly feels that her mother is too controlling.

ASSESS

Answers

Critical Thinking

Before students respond, you may wish to have them write a brief objective summary of the selection. As they answer the questions below, remind them to support their answers with evidence from the text.

1. (a) Waverly wants salted plums; her mother tells her to keep her needs secret. (b) Her mother buys the plums another day. (c) She learns to hide her feelings to get what she wants.
2. (a) She gives the rules of behavior in the form of Chinese sayings. (b) She learns to give the appearance of one thing while actually doing another. She is able to hide the true meaning of her moves until it is too late for her opponent to launch a defense. (c) She manipulates her mother by pretending not to want things.
3. **Possible response:** Waverly will win the game of doing what she wants to do. She has learned from her mother.
4. **Possible response:** (a) No, Waverly could have chosen a less public place to oppose her mother; however, Waverly probably wanted people to witness her opposition. (b) Waverly's mother is her natural opponent, because, despite their common heritage, Waverly is also American. Superior chess playing is the only way she can resist her mother's control.

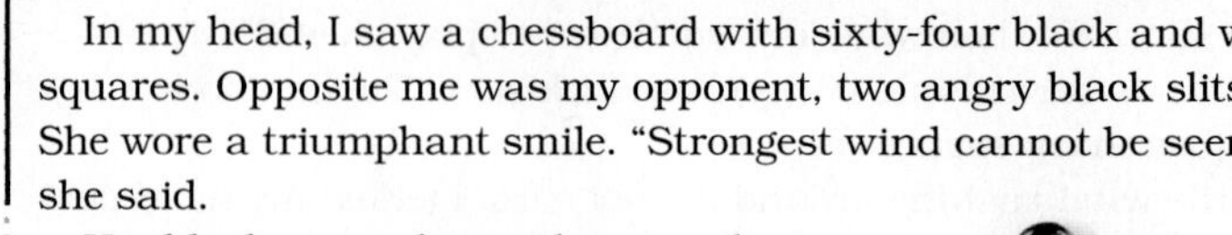

Reading Skill
Cause and Effect
Why do you think Waverly and her mother stop speaking to each other?

"Strongest wind cannot be seen."

21 In my head, I saw a chessboard with sixty-four black and white squares. Opposite me was my opponent, two angry black slits. She wore a triumphant smile. "Strongest wind cannot be seen," she said.

Her black men advanced across the plane, slowly marching to each successive level as a single unit. My white pieces screamed as they scurried and fell off the board one by one. As her men drew closer to my edge, I felt myself growing light. I rose up into the air and flew out the window. Higher and higher, above the alley, over the tops of tiled roofs, where I was gathered up by the wind and pushed up toward the night sky until everything below me disappeared and I was alone.

I closed my eyes and pondered my next move.

Critical Thinking

Cite textual evidence to support your responses.

1. **Key Ideas and Details** **(a)** Early in the story, what happens when Waverly asks for a bag of salted plums? **(b) Connect:** What happens when she stops asking? **(c) Apply:** How does Waverly later apply that strategy to her desire to play chess competitively?
2. **Key Ideas and Details** **(a)** How does Mrs. Jong teach Waverly rules of behavior? **(b) Connect:** How does Waverly translate these rules into strategies for winning at chess? **(c) Extend:** How does she use these rules against her mother?
3. **Integration of Knowledge and Ideas** **Speculate:** Who do you think will "win" the game between Waverly and her mother? Use details from the text to explain.
4. **Integration of Knowledge and Ideas** **(a)** Is it necessary for Waverly to oppose her mother at the market? **(b)** How do their personal and cultural differences make it "necessary" for Waverly to see her mother on the other side of the chess board? *[Connect to the Big Question: Is conflict necessary?]*

Assessment Resources

Unit 2 Resources

L1 L2 EL **Selection Test A,** pp. 139–141. Administer Test A to less advanced readers.

L3 L4 EL **Selection Test B,** pp. 142–144. Administer Test B to on-level and more advanced students.

L3 L4 **Open-Book Test,** pp. 136–138. As an alternative, give the Open-Book Test.

All **Customizable Test Bank**

All **Self-tests**
Students may prepare for the **Selection Test** by taking the **Self-test** online.

All assessment resources are available at **www.PHLitOnline.com.**

After You Read — Rules of the Game 

Literary Analysis: Characterization

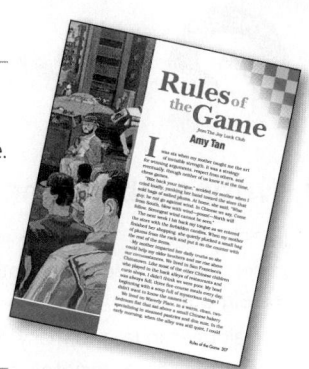

1. **Key Ideas and Details** Describe the **character** of Waverly. Support your response with examples of her actions, behavior, words, and thoughts, along with details about the effect she has on other people.
2. **Craft and Structure** **(a)** Is the conversation in which Waverly and Mrs. Jong discuss Chinese torture an example of **direct** or **indirect characterization?** Explain your response. **(b)** What do you learn about Mrs. Jong's character from this exchange?

Reading Skill: Cause and Effect

3. Use a chart like the one shown to **analyze cause and effect** in this story. **(a)** Note two causes for Waverly's success with chess. **(b)** List three effects of her success.

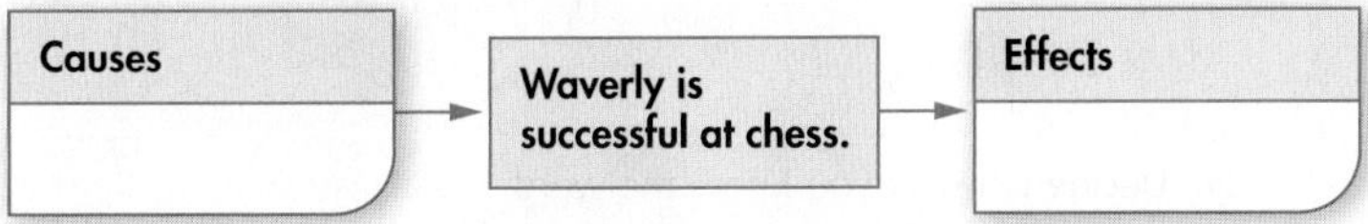

4. **(a)** Why does Mrs. Jong give Waverly special privileges? **(b)** How do these privileges affect Waverly and her relationship with her mother? Use details from the text to explain your response.

Vocabulary

Acquisition and Use Tell whether each sentence below makes sense. Use the meaning of the italicized vocabulary word to explain your answer.

1. The *pungent* scent of the baking pie drew the hungry crowd.
2. The girl was wary when the lady *benevolently* distributed cookies.
3. The audience was bored by the comedian's brilliant *retort*.
4. He gave his wife a bottle of expensive, *malodorous* perfume.
5. During play rehearsals, Mom made some *concessions* regarding my homework.
6. With his average talent, the violin *prodigy* amazed no one.

Word Study Use the context of the sentences and what you know about the **Latin root *-bene-*** to explain your answer to each question.

1. Would you appreciate what a *benefactor* would do for you?
2. What are some of the *benefits* of exercise?

Word Study

The **Latin root *-bene-*** means "well."

Apply It Explain how the root *-bene-* contributes to the meanings of these words. Consult a dictionary if necessary.

beneficial
benediction
beneficiary

ASSESS/EXTEND

Answers

Literary Analysis

1. **Possible responses:** Waverly is a strong-minded and intelligent girl. **Actions:** She quickly masters the game of chess. **Behavior:** She uses "invisible strength" to get her way; she is competitive at chess. **Words:** Waverly stands up to her mother when she tells her not to introduce her to anyone who looks her way. **Thoughts:** She uses Life Savers to join the chess game with her brothers. **Effect:** Waverly's parents allow her many concessions, and her chess skills earn her wide respect.
2. (a) The discussion of Chinese torture is an example of indirect characterization. The characters reveal themselves through their words. (b) Mrs. Jong is a strong, intelligent woman from a demanding culture.

Reading Skill

3. **Possible responses: Causes**—Two causes for her success are her raw talent and her mother's teachings. **Effects**—Three effects of her success are increases in self-confidence, in her status, and in her mother's pride.

   For other sample answers, see ***Graphic Organizer Transparencies,* Reading Skill Graphic Organizer A**, p. 59, and the **Additional Answers** section.
4. (a) Mrs. Jong gives Waverly special privileges to encourage her to succeed. (b) Waverly becomes more independent and challenges her mother. Waverly tells her mother not to show her off when they are out shopping.

Vocabulary

Acquisition and Use

Sample answers:

1. Yes, the pungent, or sharp, smell of a baking pie might draw a crowd.
2. Yes, people are often suspicious of those who act benevolently, or kindly.
3. No, an audience wouldn't be bored if a comedian used a quick and clever retort.

Answers Continued

4. No, a bottle of expensive perfume would have a pleasant, not malodorous, smell.
5. Yes, in a busy time, parents might make concessions, or allow exceptions, about homework.
6. No, a violin prodigy would have a superior, not an average, talent.

Word Study

Sample answers:

1. Yes, a *benefactor* adds to people's wellness.
2. *Benefits* are good results, such as improved wellness from exercise.

Word Study: Apply It

Sample answers: Something *beneficial* adds wellness. A *benediction* prays all goes well. A *beneficiary* receives benefits, such as improved wellness.

PRETEACH

Skills instruction for the ***Reading Skill*** *and* ***Literary Analysis*** *concepts appears on p. 313.*

❶ Writing About the Big Question

1. Review the assignment with the class.
2. Start a list of emotions that might cause internal conflict, such as jealousy. **Ask** students to contribute and describe the potential conflicts.
3. Have students complete the sentence starters. Review responses as a class. (**Possible responses:** Jealousy can lead to many conflicts because people want what others have. Learning to appreciate who we are and what we have can help us avoid conflict because we will not want what others have.)
4. Remind students that their answers will help them think about the Big Question, "Is conflict necessary?"

While You Read

Tell students that as they read, they should consider how a jealous attitude leads to conflicts.

❷ Vocabulary

1. Have students preview the selection vocabulary.
2. For each word, have students say the word aloud.
3. Then, use the word in a sentence that defines the word.
4. Repeat your definitional sentence or a similar sentence with the word missing, and have the class "fill in the blank" chorally. Here is an example:

   When something is disheveled, it is messy or untidy. The desk was covered in books, crumpled paper, and empty coffee cups, so we said it was [students say "disheveled"].

❸ Word Study

1. Introduce the skill, using the instruction in the box.
2. Ask students for a *-jec(t)-* word with a meaning nearly opposite of *dejection.* (**Answer:** *projection*)

Making Connections | The Necklace

❶ Writing About the Big Question

In "The Necklace," a woman is jealous of people with greater wealth and social standing. Use these sentence starters to develop your ideas about the Big Question.

Jealousy can lead to many conflicts because____________________.

Learning to **appreciate** who we are and what we have can help us avoid conflict because ____________________.

While You Read Consider how a jealous attitude creates both internal and external conflict.

❷ Vocabulary

Read each word and its definition. Decide whether you know the word well, know it a little bit, or do not know it at all. After you read, see how your knowledge of each word has increased.

- **rueful** (ro͞o′ fəl) *adj.* feeling sorrow or regret (p. 333) ***With a rueful sigh, she picked up the pieces of the broken dish.*** *rue v.*
- **resplendent** (ri splen′ dənt) *adj.* shining brightly (p. 336) ***The winner's face was resplendent as he accepted the prize.*** *splendor n. splendid adj.*
- **dejection** (dē jek′ shən) *n.* lowness of spirits; depression (p. 339) ***I suffered dejection when I lost the spelling bee.*** *deject v. dejected adj.*
- **fortitude** (fôrt′ ə to͞od′) *n.* the strength to bear misfortune and pain (p. 340) ***Lucy met each problem with fortitude and a sense of humor.*** *forte n.*
- **disheveled** (di shev′ əld) *adj.* untidy (p. 341) ***Val's disheveled hair showed that it was very windy outside.*** *dishevel v.*
- **profoundly** (prō found′ lē) *adv.* deeply (p. 342) ***We were all profoundly moved by the long-lost brothers' reunion.*** *profound adj.*

❸ Word Study

The **Latin root** ***-jec(t)-*** means "to throw."

In this story, the Loisels feel **dejection.** A problem has made them feel gloomy; literally, it has thrown them down emotionally.

Vocabulary Development

Vocabulary Knowledge Rating

Create a **Vocabulary Knowledge Rating Chart** (***Professional Development Guidebook***, p. 33) for this selection. Include the selection vocabulary and the Big Question word that appears in the Writing About the Big Question sentence starters on this page. (The Big Question vocabulary is introduced on pp. 194–195.)

Give students a copy of the chart. Read the words aloud, and have students mark their rating in the Before Reading column. Urge them to be alert to these words as they read and discuss the selection.

Tally how many students think they know a word to gauge how much instruction to provide. As students read and discuss the selection, point out the words and their context.

Vocabulary Central, featuring tools, activities, and songs for recording and studying vocabulary, is available at **www.PHLitOnline.com.**

Meet
Guy de Maupassant
(1850–1893)

Author of
The Necklace

Perhaps the best-known short-story writer in the world, Guy de Maupassant (gē´ də mō pä sän´) wrote tales that are realistic and pessimistic, and often offer surprise endings.

Friendship with Writers Following his army service, Maupassant settled in Paris, where he began to develop his skills as a writer, guided by the famous French author Gustave Flaubert. Maupassant also joined a circle of writers led by French novelist Emile Zola. With Zola's encouragement, Maupassant published his first short story, "Ball of Fat," in 1880. The story earned him immediate fame and freed him to write full time. "The Necklace" is perhaps his most widely read story.

4
BACKGROUND FOR THE STORY

European Society

During the nineteenth century, the old social order in Europe changed. Previously, society had been divided into two main classes: nobles, who owned land, and peasants, who farmed it. However, as industry spread, a new middle class emerged and people could rise—or sink—in social position. Some sought to own material goods as a mark of higher social standing.

Did You Know?

Maupassant wrote more than 300 short stories, six novels, and other books.

Daily Bellringer

For each class during which you will teach this selection, have students complete one of the five Revision activities for Week 10 in the *Daily Bellringer Activities* booklet.

4 Background
European Society

The fictional Monsieur and Madame Loisel in "The Necklace" represent the bourgeoisie, or middle class—the social class between the working class and the very wealthy in nineteenth-century France. These characters are ordinary, middle-class people, with no inherited position or wealth. They live on M. Loisel's salary from his government job. The word *bourgeois* has come to mean conventional or ordinary, respectable but unimaginative, and, sometimes, selfishly materialistic.

Multidraft Reading

This icon ● marks natural pauses in the selection. To assist struggling readers and to deepen reading for all, assign the text in "chunks," following the icons, and apply multidraft reading protocols. For each reading, have students set the purpose indicated:

- **First reading**—identifying key ideas and details and answering any Reading Checks.
- Second reading—analyzing craft and structure and responding to the side-column prompts.
- Third reading—integrating knowledge and ideas, connecting to other texts and the world, and answering the end-of-selection questions..

For more guidance, refer to the ***Classroom Strategies and Teaching Routines*** card on multidraft reading.

Differentiated Instruction — Additional Instruction

EL Extended Support—English Learners

Have students complete the **Reading and Vocabulary Warm-ups,** ***Unit 2 Resources,*** pp. 145–148, before they read. Assign the prereading pages and the adapted selection in the ***Reader's Notebook: English Learner's Version.*** Then, have students listen to portions of the selection on the ***Hear It!*** **Audio CD**.

L1 L2 Extended Support—Struggling Readers

Have students complete the **Reading and Vocabulary Warm-ups,** ***Unit 2 Resources,*** pp. 145–148, before they read. Assign the prereading pages and the adapted selection in the ***Reader's Notebook: Adapted Version.*** Then, have students listen to portions of the selection on the ***Hear It!*** **Audio CD** (adapted text).

Extended Support—Reluctant Readers

To build motivation and engagement before assigning the selection, have students read "Wrongfully Accused?" a thematically related selection in ***Reality Central.*** Then, use the questions at the conclusion of the related selection to guide discussion.

PHLit Online!

For more about the author, practice with the selection vocabulary, or more background, go online at **www.PHLitOnline.com.**

TEACH

❶ Activating Prior Knowledge

1. Prepare an **Anticipation Guide** (**Professional Development Guidebook**, pp. 36–38) with the following statements:
   - Having expensive possessions is a sign of success.
   - A person's physical appearance reveals his or her personality.
   - People get what they deserve in life.
   - People should repay their debts at all costs.
2. Give students a copy of the prepared **Anticipation Guide** and have students mark their responses in the Me column. Have students discuss the statements in pairs or groups and mark the Guides again in the Group column.
3. For further guidance, use the ***Classroom Strategies and Teaching Routines*** card: **Using an Anticipation Guide.**

Concept Connector

Students will return to the **Anticipation Guide** after completing "The Necklace."

Individual Activity

Suggest that students look at the picture on p. 332 to gain a clearer sense of the clothing the characters wore and the type of world in which they lived. Ask students to suggest adjectives to describe the clothing.

❷ About the Selection

In "The Necklace," Madame Loisel loses a borrowed diamond necklace. The replacement necklace takes her and her husband ten years of hard work to pay off. After they have done so, Madame Loisel learns that the original was a fake.

❶ ❷ The Necklace

Guy de Maupassant

Vocabulary Development

CCSS Language 6

Thematic Vocabulary: The Big Question

As students are discussing "The Necklace," encourage them to use the thematic vocabulary presented in Introducing the Big Question, pp. 194–195. You might encourage them with sentence starters such as these:

1. Mme. Loisel noticed and dwelled on the *differences* between . . .
2. She nursed her *grievance* against . . .
3. Mme. Loisel went to her friend and managed to *articulate* her . . .
4. Mme. Forestier said that loaning the necklace wasn't an *issue* and . . .

She was one of those pretty, charming young women who are born, as if by an error of Fate, into a petty official's family.

She had no dowry,[1] no hopes, not the slightest chance of being appreciated, understood, loved, and married by a rich and distinguished man; so she slipped into marriage with a minor civil servant at the Ministry of Education.

3 Unable to afford jewelry, she dressed simply: but she was as wretched as a déclassée, for women have neither caste nor breeding—in them beauty, grace, and charm replace pride of birth. Innate refinement, instinctive elegance, and suppleness of wit give them their place on the only scale that counts, and these qualities make humble girls the peers of the grandest ladies.

She suffered constantly, feeling that all the attributes of a gracious life, every luxury, should rightly have been hers. The poverty of her rooms—the shabby walls, the worn furniture, the ugly upholstery—caused her pain. All these things that another woman of her class would not even have noticed, tormented her and made her angry. The very sight of the little Breton girl who cleaned for her awoke **rueful** thoughts and the wildest dreams in her mind. She dreamt of thick-carpeted reception rooms with Oriental hangings, lighted by tall,

1. **dowry** (dou′ rē) *n.* property that a woman brought to her husband at marriage.

Literary Analysis
Characterization
What does the author tell you directly about the young woman in the first two paragraphs?

Vocabulary
rueful (ro͞o′ fəl) *adj.* feeling sorrow or regret

4 **Reading Check**
Why does the woman suffer constantly?

3 Literary Analysis

Characterization

1. Refer students to the first sentence in the bracketed text. **Ask** students what they think the author means by saying that the character was born "as if by an error of Fate, into a petty official's family."

   Answer: The author is suggesting that the character should have been born into a wealthy or important family, where her charm and beauty would have allowed her to attract affluent suitors.

2. **Ask** the Literary Analysis question: What does the author tell you directly about the young woman in the first two paragraphs?

   Answer: She is equal in beauty, charm, and wit to the grandest of women; however, she is married to a civil servant and cannot afford lavish clothing or jewelry.

4 Reading Check

Answer: She believes that she should be living a life of wealth and luxury.

PHLit Online!

This selection is available in interactive format in the **Enriched Online Student Edition, www.PHLitOnline.com,** which includes a thematically related video with writing prompt and an interactive graphic organizer.

Fluency

Distribute copies of page 333, and pair students. Have listeners mark words with which reading partners struggle. Circulate to monitor students' fluency, then collect the marked up pages. Review difficult words and passages, such as these:

- If students struggle to pronounce *déclassée*, point out the accents and model pronunciation (day′ klah′ *say′*). Read the word aloud again and have students echo to confirm.
- If students have difficulty with the word *caste*, explain that the *e* is silent but does not create a long vowel. Have students cover the *e*, then read the word as *cast* to achieve correct pronunciation.
- If students stumble over the dashes, explain that these punctuation marks function like commas but indicate a slightly longer pause. Ask fluent readers to model the pauses indicated by dashes, then have mixed-fluency groups read to reinforce.

❺ Literary Analysis

Characterization

1. Draw students' attention to the first bracketed text. **Ask** students why they think the author mentions the "three-day-old cloth."

   Answer: The fact that a tablecloth has been in use for three days suggests that the couple does not have the money for fine linens to be changed daily. He is pointing out that the characters are not living luxuriously.

2. **Ask:** Do you think the husband notices the "three-day-old cloth"? Why or why not?

   Answer: He probably does not notice it because he seems happy with the meal and his life in general.

3. **Ask** students to respond to the Literary Analysis question: What does the husband's comment in this paragraph reveal indirectly about his character?

   Answer: It reveals that he is content and easily pleased; he is not interested in material possessions.

❻ Reading Skill

Cause and Effect

1. Have students read the second bracketed text and then **describe** how they think the woman's life is different from her friend's life.

   Answer: Madame Loisel lives in a shabby home with worn furniture; she dresses simply and has no expensive jewelry. Her friend is rich and able to afford the things Madame Loisel dreams of having, such as a large home with plush furnishings and expensive clothing and jewelry.

2. **Ask** students the Reading Skill question: Why do visits to her rich friend always fill the young woman with despair?

   Answer: The woman sees elegance in her friend's life where there is poverty in her own; she sees all her friend's expensive possessions, which she believes she is entitled to as well.

bronze torches, and with two huge footmen in knee breeches, made drowsy by the heat from the stove, asleep in the wide armchairs. She dreamt of great drawing rooms upholstered in old silks, with fragile little tables holding priceless knick-knacks, and of enchanting little sitting rooms redolent of perfume, designed for tea-time chats with intimate friends—famous, sought-after men whose attentions all women longed for.

Literary Analysis
Characterization ❺ What does the husband's comment in this paragraph reveal indirectly about his character?

When she sat down to dinner at her round table with its three-day-old cloth, and watched her husband opposite her lift the lid of the soup tureen and exclaim, delighted: "Ah, a good homemade beef stew! There's nothing better . . ." she would visualize elegant dinners with gleaming silver amid tapestried walls peopled by knights and ladies and exotic birds in a fairy forest; she would think of exquisite dishes served on gorgeous china, and of gallantries whispered and received with sphinx-like smiles while eating the pink flesh of trout or wings of grouse.

She had no proper wardrobe, no jewels, nothing. And those were the only things that she loved—she felt she was made for them. She would have so loved to charm, to be envied, to be admired and sought after.

Reading Skill
Cause and Effect ❻ Why do visits to her rich friend always fill the young woman with despair?

She had a rich friend, a schoolmate from the convent she had attended, but she didn't like to visit her because it always made her so miserable when she got home again. She would weep for whole days at a time from sorrow, regret, despair, and distress.

Then one evening her husband arrived home looking triumphant and waving a large envelope.

"There," he said, "there's something for you."

She tore it open eagerly and took out a printed card which said:

"The Minister of Education and Madame Georges Ramponneau [ma dam′ zhôrzh ram pə nō̃′] request the pleasure of the company of M. and Mme. Loisel [lwa zel′] at an evening reception at the Ministry on Monday, January 18th."

❼ Instead of being delighted, as her husband had hoped, she tossed the invitation on the table and muttered, annoyed:

"What do you expect me to do with that?"

"Why, I thought you'd be pleased, dear. You never go out and this would be an occasion for you, a great one! I had a lot of trouble getting it. Everyone wants an invitation; they're in great demand and there are only a few reserved for the employees. All the officials will be there."

She looked at him, irritated, and said impatiently:

"I haven't a thing to wear. How could I go?"

Vocabulary Development

Ⓒ CCSS Language 6

Expressive Vocabulary

To help students broaden their expressive vocabulary, encourage them to use the following words as they discuss the selection: *obtain, impress, exceed,* and *identify*. Have them complete these sentence starters:

1. M. Loisel thought his wife would be happy that he was able to *obtain* . . .
2. Madame Loisel was eager to *impress* . . .
3. The cost of a new dress would *exceed* . . .
4. As she searched through the box of jewelry, she tried to *identify* . . .

It had never even occurred to him. He stammered:

"But what about the dress you wear to the theater? I think it's lovely. . . ."

He fell silent, amazed and bewildered to see that his wife was crying. Two big tears escaped from the corners of her eyes and rolled slowly toward the corners of her mouth. He mumbled:

"What is it? What is it?"

But, with great effort, she had overcome her misery; and now she answered him calmly, wiping her tear-damp cheeks:

"It's nothing. It's just that I have no evening dress and so I can't go to the party. Give the invitation to one of your colleagues whose wife will be better dressed than I would be."

He was overcome. He said:

"Listen, Mathilde [ma tēld′], how much would an evening dress cost—a suitable one that you could wear again on other occasions, something very simple?"

She thought for several seconds, making her calculations and at the same time estimating how much she could ask for without eliciting an immediate refusal and an exclamation of horror from this economical government clerk.

At last, not too sure of herself, she said:

"It's hard to say exactly but I think I could manage with four hundred francs."

He went a little pale, for that was exactly the amount he had put aside to buy a rifle so that he could go hunting the following summer near Nanterre, with a few friends who went shooting larks around there on Sundays.

However, he said:

"Well, all right, then. I'll give you four hundred francs. But try to get something really nice."

As the day of the ball drew closer, Madame Loisel seemed depressed, disturbed, worried—despite the fact that her dress was ready. One evening her husband said:

"What's the matter? You've really been very strange these last few days."

And she answered:

"I hate not having a single jewel, not one stone, to wear. I shall look so dowdy.[2] I'd almost rather not go to the party."

> *She had no proper wardrobe, no jewels, nothing. And those were the only things that she loved—she felt she was made for them.*

Reading Skill
Cause and Effect
Why is the husband surprised by his wife's reaction to the party invitation?

8 

What does Monsieur Loisel give up to make his wife happy?

2. **dowdy** (dou′dē) *adj.* shabby.

7 Reading Skill

Cause and Effect

1. Have students read the bracketed text, beginning on page 334, and then **ask** how they expected Madame Loisel to respond to the invitation.

   Answer: Students will probably say that they expected her to be ecstatic about the invitation.

2. **Ask** students to describe her reaction to the invitation.

   Answer: She is annoyed and irritated.

3. **Ask** students to respond to the Reading Skill question: Why is the husband surprised by his wife's reaction to the party invitation?

   Answer: He thought she would be happy because she is so interested in wealth and the upper class.

8 Reading Check

Answer: He gives up the money he had been saving to buy a hunting rifle.

Differentiated Instruction for Universal Access

Vocabulary for Special-Needs Students

Help students look for context clues to understand difficult words in the selection. For example, the phrase "the poverty of her rooms" on p. 333 is followed by three examples that help readers see that *poverty* means "being poor" or "having little money."

In a passage on p. 334, the synonyms *sorry, regret, despair,* and *distress* follow a description of Madame Loisel weeping for days at a time. Explain that this suggests that the four words are all different ways to say "unhappiness."

Strategy for Less Proficient Readers

To give students a context for the selection and help them understand how to identify and interpret details of characterization, show them **Literary Analysis Graphic Organizer A** (*Graphic Organizer Transparencies,* p. 57). Review the partially completed organizer with them to make sure they see how the details lead to a logical interpretation of the character. Have students use the partically completed graphic organizer as a model for identifying other details of characterization as they continue to read the selection.

9 Literary Analysis

Characterization

1. Have students reread the last paragraph on page 335, then read the first bracketed text on page 336. **Ask** them why Madame Loisel is still dissatisfied even though she has a new dress.
   Answer: She does not have any jewels to wear.
2. **Ask** students why she rejects her husband's suggestion to wear fresh flowers.

   Answer: She feels that she would still look poverty-stricken.
3. **Ask** students the Literary Analysis question: What does Madame Loisel's comment reveal indirectly about her attitudes and values?
   Possible response: Her comment reveals that she believes she must have expensive things; she values appearances.

10 Connecting to the Big Question

1. Point out that the desire to have something often creates conflict because there may be obstacles to fulfilling this desire.
2. Have students read the second bracketed text on page 336.
   Ask: How does Madame Loisel feel about Madame Forestier's jewelry? What internal conflicts might her feelings create?

   Possible response: She wants to wear it very badly. She might feel an internal conflict between her desire for the jewelry and her desire not to seem greedy. She might also be torn between her gratitude toward her friend and her frustration that she has to ask.
3. **Ask** students: Are Madame Loisel's conflicts over the jewelry necessary? How, if at all, could she avoid them?

   Possible response: No, her conflicts are not necessary. She could avoid them by wearing fresh flowers or inexpensive jewelry, or by caring less about the status of wearing jewelry.

He suggested:

"You can wear some fresh flowers. It's considered very chic[3] at this time of year. For ten francs you can get two or three beautiful roses."

That didn't satisfy her at all.

9 "No . . . there's nothing more humiliating than to look poverty-stricken among a lot of rich women."

Literary Analysis
Characterization
What does Madame Loisel's comment reveal indirectly about her attitudes and values?

Then her husband exclaimed:

"Wait—you silly thing! Why don't you go and see Madame Forestier [fôr əs tyā̃′] and ask her to lend you some jewelry. You certainly know her well enough for that, don't you think?"

She let out a joyful cry.

"You're right. It never occurred to me."

The next day she went to see her friend and related her tale of woe.

Madame Forestier went to her mirrored wardrobe, took out a big jewel case, brought it to Madame Loisel, opened it, and said:

"Take your pick, my dear."

Her eyes wandered from some bracelets to a pearl necklace, then to a gold Venetian cross set with stones, of very fine workmanship. She tried on the jewelry before the mirror, hesitating, unable to bring herself to take them off, to give them back. And she kept asking:

"Do you have anything else, by chance?"

10 "Why yes. Here, look for yourself. I don't know which ones you'll like."

All at once, in a box lined with black satin, she came upon a superb diamond necklace, and her heart started beating with overwhelming desire. Her hands trembled as she picked it up. She fastened it around her neck over her high-necked dress and stood there gazing at herself ecstatically.

Hesitantly, filled with terrible anguish, she asked:

"Could you lend me this one—just this and nothing else?"

"Yes, of course."

She threw her arms around her friend's neck, kissed her ardently, and fled with her treasure.

Vocabulary
resplendent (ri splen′ dənt) *adj.* shining brightly

The day of the party arrived. Madame Loisel was a great success. She was the prettiest woman there—**resplendent**, graceful, beaming, and deliriously happy. All the men looked at her, asked who she was, tried to get themselves introduced to her. All the minister's aides wanted to waltz with her. The minister himself noticed her.

3. **chic** (shēk) *adj.* fashionable.

Think Aloud

Vocabulary: Using Context

Direct students' attention to the word *homage* on page 337. Using a think-aloud process, model how to use context to infer the meaning of an unknown word. Say to students:

> I'm going to show you how I would figure out the meaning of *homage* from its context.
>
> In this sentence, *homage* is used in describing one of the several feelings Madame Loisel has about her experience at the dance. In reading the entire paragraph, I see from words such as *pleasure, triumph,* and *victory* that the experience is strongly positive. In reading the words right near *homage,* I see three phrases beginning with "all this." This parallel structure is a clue that the words following "all this" might have related meanings. Those words, such as *admiration* and *desires she had stirred up* are further clues that *homage* is an attitude of respect and even awe. Yes, I think that *homage* means "respect and reverence."

11 12

▲ **Critical Viewing**
What key part of the story could this image illustrate? **[Connect]**

She danced enraptured—carried away, intoxicated with pleasure, forgetting everything in this triumph of her beauty and the glory of her success, floating in a cloud of happiness formed by all this homage, all this admiration, all the desires she had stirred up—by this victory so complete and so sweet to the heart of a woman.

When she left the party, it was almost four in the morning. Her husband had been sleeping since midnight in a small, deserted

13 
How does Madame Loisel feel at the ball?

11 Humanities

The Necklace by Richard Emile Miller (1875–1943)

Richard Miller, an American artist from St. Louis, Missouri, gained renown in the Paris art world. Only women, in pairs or singly, were the subjects of his paintings.

For discussion, ask students the following questions:

1. **Ask:** Is the woman in the painting Madame Loisel or Madame Forestier? How do you know? What might she be thinking?

   Possible response: The woman is Madame Loisel. She seems to be thinking about how lucky she is to be going to the ball and how beautiful she's going to look now that she has the necklace to wear.

2. **Ask:** What does the painting tell you about the fashion and lifestyle of the period? How does it help you understand Madame Loisel's desire for more extravagant trappings?

   Possible response: In the painting, we see the lavishness of her dress and her surroundings. The fabrics are rich and layered. The entire picture gives an impression of wealth and privilege.

12 Critical Viewing

Possible response: This image could illustrate a private moment for Madame Loisel as she prepares for the dance.

13 Reading Check

Answer: She was a great success. She looked beautiful and all of the men wanted to dance with her. She had a wonderful time.

Differentiated Instruction for Universal Access

Culturally Responsive Instruction

Culture Focus Point out how important it is to Madame Loisel to appear wealthy in front of "rich women." Note that in her world, as in many parts of America today, jewelry is a sign of wealth and status. Explain that most cultures have external signs that indicate wealth and status, such as age, clothing, titles, or cars. At different times in history, cultures have had other, more subtle indications of status, such as smooth hands, which meant the individual did not have to do any manual work. Encourage students to describe different indicators of status and/or wealth in their home culture or family's country of origin. Challenge students to consider what a culture would be like without such indicators, using questions such as these: Would people such as Madame Loisel feel less driven to prove themselves worthy? Would this be a good result or could it have negative effects?

⓮ Humanities

Emperor Franz Joseph at a Ball in Vienna by Wilhelm Gause (1853–1916)

Wilhelm Gause, a German painter, is well-known for his paintings of ballroom dancing.

Use the following questions for discussion:

1. **Ask:** From looking at this painting, who were the people who attended a ball of this type? How can you tell from the image and from the story?

   Possible response: They were clearly wealthy, based on their elaborate clothing and the very large, elegant ballroom. In addition, the story says that the Emperor was in attendance, so probably only the very wealthy and high-ranking in society would be invited.

2. **Ask:** From what you know about Madame Loisel, would she have fit in at such an event?

   Possible response: She would like to believe she would fit in, but she probably wouldn't. Since she was so beautiful, she probably would have attracted attention, but, in the end, she would have felt out of place.

⓯ Critical Viewing

Possible response: Details such as the women's elaborate gowns and the elegant ballroom, suggest the story's setting.

⓮ ⓯

▲ **Critical Viewing** What details in this painting suggest the setting of the story? **[Connect]**

sitting room, with three other gentlemen whose wives were having a wonderful time.

He brought her wraps so that they could leave and put them around her shoulders—the plain wraps from her everyday life whose shabbiness jarred with the elegance of her evening dress. She felt this and wanted to escape quickly so that the other women, who were enveloping themselves in their rich furs, wouldn't see her.

Loisel held her back.

"Wait a minute. You'll catch cold out there. I'm going to call a cab."

But she wouldn't listen to him and went hastily downstairs. Outside in the street, there was no cab to be found; they set out to look for one, calling to the drivers they saw passing in the distance.

They walked toward the Seine,[4] shivering and miserable. Finally, on the embankment, they found one of those ancient nocturnal broughams[5] which are only to be seen in Paris at night, as if they were ashamed to show their shabbiness in daylight.

4. **Seine** (sān) river flowing through Paris.
5. **broughams** (bro͞omz) *n.* horse-drawn carriages.

Think Aloud

Cause and Effect

Have students reread pages 338–339, focusing on why the characters take various actions. Use the following "think aloud" to model a way to analyze causes and effects in a series.

When I read about a character's actions or feelings, I ask myself questions to help me to explain those actions or feelings. For example, when I read that Madame Loisel went "hastily downstairs," I ask myself, *Why was she in a hurry?* Rereading shows me that she wants to avoid being seen in her plain coat. I know that actions often lead to other actions, so I ask myself if her haste had any results. If I read on, I see that she and her husband are in such a hurry that they don't wait for a cab. They start walking and end up in a shabby, old horse-drawn carriage. I see that each action the Loisels take that night causes their next action.

It took them to their door in the Rue des Martyrs, and they went sadly upstairs to their apartment. For her, it was all over. And he was thinking that he had to be at the Ministry by ten.

She took off her wraps before the mirror so that she could see herself in all her glory once more. Then she cried out. The necklace was gone; there was nothing around her neck.

Her husband, already half undressed, asked:

"What's the matter?"

She turned toward him in a frenzy:

"The . . . the . . . necklace—it's gone."

He got up, thunderstruck.

"What did you say? . . . What! . . . Impossible!"

And they searched the folds of her dress, the folds of her wrap, the pockets, everywhere. They didn't find it.

He asked:

"Are you sure you still had it when we left the ball?"

"Yes. I remember touching it in the hallway of the Ministry."

"But if you had lost it in the street, we would have heard it fall. It must be in the cab."

"Yes, most likely. Do you remember the number?"

"No. What about you—did you notice it?"

"No."

They looked at each other in utter dejection. Finally Loisel got dressed again.

"I'm going to retrace the whole distance we covered on foot," he said, "and see if I can't find it."

And he left the house. She remained in her evening dress, too weak to go to bed, sitting crushed on a chair, lifeless and blank.

Her husband returned at about seven o'clock. He had found nothing.

6 He went to the police station, to the newspapers to offer a reward, to the offices of the cab companies—in a word, wherever there seemed to be the slightest hope of tracing it.

She spent the whole day waiting, in a state of utter hopelessness before such an appalling catastrophe.

Loisel returned in the evening, his face lined and pale; he had learned nothing.

"You must write to your friend," he said, "and tell her that you've broken the clasp of the necklace and that you're getting it mended. That'll give us time to decide what to do."

> *He brought her wraps so that they could leave and put them around her shoulders—the plain wraps from her everyday life...*

Vocabulary
dejection (di jek′ shən) *n.* lowness of spirits; depression

Literary Analysis
Characterization
What do the Loisels' actions after the necklace is lost reveal about their individual characters?

17 
When does Madame Loisel discover the necklace is missing?

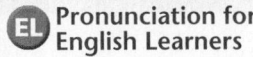

16 Literary Analysis

Characterization

1. Have students read the bracketed text which ends on page 340. Then, **ask** them what action M. Loisel takes to recover the missing necklace.

   Answer: He retraces the couple's steps, looking for the necklace. He goes to the police station and the cab company and offers a reward in the newspaper. He instructs his wife to write a letter to her friend in an attempt to buy time.

2. **Ask:** What action does Madame Loisel take?

   Answer: She sits in a chair, waiting all day while her husband looks for the necklace. She writes the letter to her friend as he dictates it.

3. Point out to students that it is M. Loisel who decides that the necklace must be replaced. Then, **ask** students the Literary Analysis question: What do the Loisels' actions after the necklace is lost reveal about their individual characters?

   Possible response: M. Loisel is a responsible person who attempts to make up for the loss. Madame Loisel is selfish and always feels that she has been wronged. In addition, she expects others to solve problems that she has created.

▶ **Monitor Progress:** Review students' graphic organizers to ensure that they are identifying and interpreting details of characterization.

▶ **Reteach:** If students have difficulty, help them identify details from pp. 338–339 that support the characterization of M. Loisel as helpful and caring, and Madame Loisel as self-centered and helpless. Have students record the information on their graphic organizers.

17 Reading Check

Answer: She noticed the necklace was missing when she looked in the mirror after she got home.

Differentiated Instruction for Universal Access

EL Pronunciation for English Learners

To help students pronounce the initial "th" sound, post these word pairs: *then, den; their, dare;* and *they, day.* Pronounce each word in turn, stressing the initial consonant digraph and emphasizing the shape of your mouth, then have students echo. Call out words at random and have volunteers circle the stated word on the board. Discuss any incorrect choices and clarify students' confusion.

Enrichment for Gifted/Talented Students

Have students create "before" and "after" portraits of Madame Loisel, using a medium of their choosing. Suggest that students include elements of body language, clothing, accessories, and background details that express a change in Madame Loisel's situation and character before the necklace is lost and after the Loisels buy the replacement necklace. Students may use pictures from this text, or other images of nineteenth-century French women, as a starting point.

18 Reading Skill

Cause and Effect

1. Read the second bracketed text aloud. Have students **summarize** Madame Forestier's attitude when Madame Loisel returns the necklace. **Ask** them how her attitude differs from when Madame Loisel borrowed the necklace.

   Answer: She is irritated and impatient when Madame Loisel returns the necklace. When Madame Loisel first borrowed the necklace, Madame Forestier seemed friendly and generous.

2. **Ask** students how Madame Forestier's attitude might have contributed to Madame Loisel's fear.

   Possible response: Madame Loisel probably worried that Madame Forestier would carefully inspect the necklace because she was so irritated by its late return.

3. **Ask** students the Reading Skill question: What fear prevents the Loisels from telling Madame Forestier the necklace was lost?

   Possible response: They are afraid that they might be accused of stealing the necklace.

Reading Skill
Cause and Effect
What fear prevents the Loisels from telling Madame Forestier the necklace was lost?

16 She wrote the letter at his dictation.

By the end of the week, they had lost all hope.

Loisel, who had aged five years, declared:

"We'll have to replace the necklace."

The next day they took the case in which it had been kept and went to the jeweler whose name appeared inside it. He looked through his ledgers:

"I didn't sell this necklace, madame. I only supplied the case."

Then they went from one jeweler to the next, trying to find a necklace like the other, racking their memories, both of them sick with worry and distress.

In a fashionable shop near the Palais Royal, they found a diamond necklace which they decided was exactly like the other. It was worth 40,000 francs. They could have it for 36,000 francs.

They asked the jeweler to hold it for them for three days, and they stipulated that he should take it back for 34,000 francs if the other necklace was found before the end of February.

Loisel possessed 18,000 francs left him by his father. He would borrow the rest.

He borrowed, asking a thousand francs from one man, five hundred from another, a hundred here, fifty there. He signed promissory notes,[6] borrowed at exorbitant rates, dealt with usurers and the entire race of moneylenders. He compromised his whole career, gave his signature even when he wasn't sure he would be able to honor it, and horrified by the anxieties with which his future would be filled, by the black misery about to descend upon him, by the prospect of physical privation and moral suffering, went to get the new necklace, placing on the jeweler's counter 36,000 francs.

18 When Madame Loisel went to return the necklace, Madame Forestier said in a faintly waspish tone:

"You could have brought it back a little sooner! I might have needed it."

She didn't open the case as her friend had feared she might. If she had noticed the substitution, what would she have thought? What would she have said? Mightn't she have taken Madame Loisel for a thief?

Madame Loisel came to know the awful life of the poverty-stricken. However, she resigned herself to it with unexpected fortitude. The crushing debt had to be paid. She would pay it. They dismissed the maid; they moved into an attic under the roof.

Vocabulary
fortitude
(fôrt´ ə to͞od´) *n.* the strength to bear misfortune and pain

She came to know all the heavy household chores, the loathsome work of the kitchen. She washed the dishes, wearing

6. **promissory** (präm´ i sôr´ ē) **notes** written promises to pay back borrowed money.

Vocabulary Development

Vocabulary Knowledge Rating

When students have completed reading and discussing "The Necklace," have them take out their **Vocabulary Knowledge Rating Chart** for this selection. Read the words aloud once more and have students rate their knowledge of the words again in the After Reading column. Clarify any words that are still problematic. Have students write their own definition and example or sentence in the appropriate column. Then have students complete the Vocabulary Practice activities at the end of the selection. Encourage students to use the words in further discussion and written work about this selection. Remind them that they will be accountable for these words on the **Selection Test, *Unit 2 Resources*,** pp. 160–162 or 163–165.

down her pink nails on greasy casseroles and the bottoms of saucepans. She did the laundry, washing shirts and dishcloths which she hung on a line to dry; she took the garbage down to the street every morning, and carried water upstairs, stopping at every floor to get her breath. Dressed like a working-class woman, she went to the fruit store, the grocer, and the butcher with her basket on her arm, bargaining, outraged, contesting each sou[7] of her pitiful funds.

Every month some notes had to be honored and more time requested on others.

Her husband worked in the evenings, putting a shopkeeper's ledgers in order, and often at night as well, doing copying at twenty-five centimes a page.

And it went on like that for ten years.

After ten years, they had made good on everything, including the usurious rates and the compound interest.

Madame Loisel looked old now. She had become the sort of strong woman, hard and coarse, that one finds in poor families. **Disheveled**, her skirts askew, with reddened hands, she spoke in a loud voice, slopping water over the floors as she washed them. But sometimes, when her husband was at the office, she would sit down by the window and muse over that party long ago when she had been so beautiful, the belle of the ball.

> *She had become the sort of strong woman, hard and coarse, that one finds in poor families.*

19 How would things have turned out if she hadn't lost that necklace? Who could tell? How strange and fickle life is! How little it takes to make or break you!

Then one Sunday when she was strolling along the Champs Elysées[8] to forget the week's chores for a while, she suddenly caught sight of a woman taking a child for a walk. It was Madame Forestier, still young, still beautiful, still charming.

Madame Loisel started to tremble. Should she speak to her? Yes, certainly she should. And now that she had paid everything back, why shouldn't she tell her the whole story?

She went up to her.

"Hello, Jeanne."

The other didn't recognize her and was surprised that this plainly dressed woman should speak to her so familiarly. She murmured:

"But . . . madame! . . . I'm sure . . . You must be mistaken."

"No, I'm not. I am Mathilde Loisel."

7. **sou** (so͞o) *n.* former French coin, worth very little; the centime (sän» tèm«), mentioned later, was also of little value.

8. **Champs Elysées** (shän zā lē zā') fashionable street in Paris.

Spiral Review

Setting How does the class-based nature of the Loisels' society influence their behavior?

Vocabulary

disheveled (di shev´ əld) *adj.* untidy

Reading Skill

Cause and Effect What causes Madame Loisel to tremble at the sight of Madame Forestier?

20 

Reading Check

How has Madame Loisel's appearance changed?

Spiral Review

Setting

1. Remind students that they studied the concept of setting in the Unit 2 Literary Analysis workshop (pp. 196–209).
2. **Ask** students the Spiral Review question.

   Possible response: The Loisels try to act like they have more money and possessions than they really do because during the time period of this story, class was largely determined by money.

19 Reading Skill

Cause and Effect

1. **Ask** students to describe how Madame Loisel has changed since she began to repay the couple's debt.

   Answer: She has dismissed her maid and resigned herself to being poor. Her looks and manners have aged and roughened.
2. Have students read the bracketed text, and then **ask** them the Reading Skill question: What causes Madame Loisel to tremble at the sight of Madame Forestier?

   Possible response: Madame Forestier has kept her grace and beauty, while Madame Loisel has become old and coarse. Perhaps Madame Loisel is overwhelmed by painful memories awakened by the sight of her former friend.
3. Point out to students that Madame Loisel wonders about how her life would have been different if it had not been for one event that set off a chain of causes and effects. Help students outline the causes and effects that have brought Madame Loisel to this point.

20 Reading Check

Answer: She looks like a woman who has struggled—old, hard, and coarse.

Concept Connector

Anticipation Guide

Have students return to their **Anticipation Guides** and respond to the statements again in the After Reading column. Then, lead a class discussion, probing for what students have learned that confirms or invalidates each statement.

Writing About the Big Question

Have students compare their responses to the sentence starters they completed before reading the story with their ideas afterward. Ask them to explain whether their thoughts have changed.

Literary Skill Graphic Organizer

Have students review the graphic organizers they completed to identify and interpret details of characterization while reading. Show them **Literary Analysis Graphic Organizer A** (*Graphic Organizer Transparencies,* p. 57) as an example. Then have students share the graphic organizers they did and the details they identified about the characters.

ASSESS

Answers

Critical Thinking

Before students respond, you may wish to have them write a brief objective summary of the selection. As they answer the questions below, remind them to support their answers with evidence from the text.

1. (a) Beautiful and charming, she believes she is ill-suited for a lower-class life. (b) Some students may think that Maupassant wants readers to empathize with Mme. Loisel. However, others will think that she is a spoiled, self-centered woman.
2. (a) He tries to find a way for her to be happy. (b) He is much less selfish and much more loving than she is.
3. (a) She loses her charm and beauty and becomes old before her time. (b) Hard, rough work and hopelessness cause her to lose her beauty and become embittered.
4. **Possible responses:** (a) There is no longer an external conflict regarding money and status, since Madame Loisel is now a common working-class woman. She no longer has to worry about dances, jewelry, or clothes. (b) Yes, if she had tried to be happy instead of always coveting other people's lifestyle and belongings, she would have been less conflicted and less likely to risk her existing status for an imagined improvement.

Her friend gave a little cry.

"Oh! Oh, my poor Mathilde, how you've changed!"

"Yes, I've been through some pretty hard times since I last saw you and I've had plenty of trouble—and all because of you!"

"Because of me? What do you mean?"

"You remember the diamond necklace you lent me to wear to the party at the Ministry?"

"Yes. What about it?"

"Well, I lost it."

"What are you talking about? You returned it to me."

"What I gave back to you was another one just like it. And it took us ten years to pay for it. You can imagine it wasn't easy for us, since we were quite poor. . . . Anyway, I'm glad it's over and done with."

Madame Forestier stopped short.

"You say you bought a diamond necklace to replace that other one?"

"Yes. You didn't even notice then? They really were exactly alike."

And she smiled, full of a proud, simple joy.

Madame Forestier, profoundly moved, took Mathilde's hands in her own.

"Oh, my poor, poor Mathilde! Mine was false. It was worth five hundred francs at the most!"

Vocabulary
profoundly (prō found′ lē) *adv.* deeply

Critical Thinking

Cite textual evidence to support your responses.

1. **Key Ideas and Details (a)** As the story begins, why is Madame Loisel unhappy with her life? **(b) Infer:** Do you think the author wants readers to sympathize with her unhappiness? Explain your response.
2. **Key Ideas and Details (a)** How does Monsieur Loisel respond to Madame Loisel's disappointment? **(b) Compare and Contrast:** How is Monsieur Loisel different from his wife? Use details from the text to explain.
3. **Integration of Knowledge and Ideas (a) Interpret:** How does the change in Madame Loisel's appearance illustrate the internal and external conflicts of the story? **(b) Draw Conclusions:** What is the effect of this change?
4. **Integration of Knowledge and Ideas (a)** What external conflict is proven unnecessary by the end of the story? **(b)** Could a change in Madame Loisel's attitude have prevented her internal conflict? *[Connect to the Big Question: Is conflict necessary?]*

Assessment Resources

Unit 2 Resources

L1 L2 EL **Selection Test A,** pp. 160–162. Administer Test A to less advanced readers.

L3 L4 EL **Selection Test B,** pp. 163–165. Administer Test B to on-level and more advanced students.

L3 L4 **Open-Book Test,** pp. 157–159. As an alternative, give the Open Book test.

All **Customizable Text Bank**

All **Self-tests**
Students may prepare for the **Selection Test** by taking the **Self-test** online.

All assessment resources are available at **www.PHLitOnline.com.**

After You Read The Necklace

Literary Analysis: Characterization

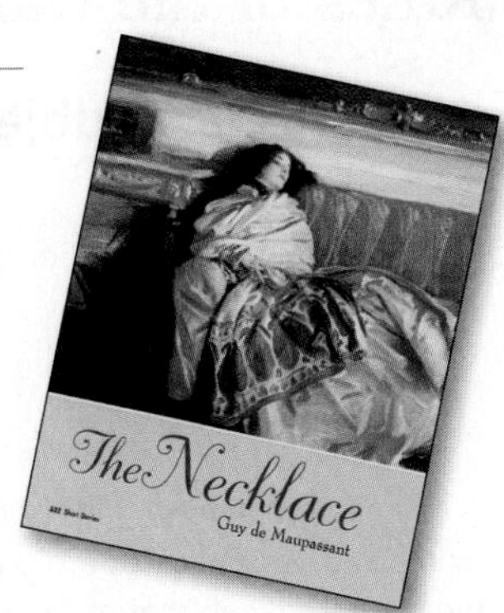

1. **Key Ideas and Details** Describe Madame Loisel's **character.** Support your answer with at least one example of each of the following methods of **indirect characterization** in the story: **(a)** Madame Loisel's actions, **(b)** her words and thoughts, and **(c)** her effect on other people.
2. **Craft and Structure** **(a)** Is the conversation on the day of the ball in which the Loisels discuss Madame's attire an example of indirect characterization or **direct characterization**? Explain your response. **(b)** What do you learn about both Monsieur and Madame Loisel's characters from this exchange?

Reading Skill: Cause and Effect

3. Use a chart like the one shown to **analyze cause and effect** in this story. Note two causes and two effects for Madame Loisel's decision to borrow the necklace from Madame Forestier.

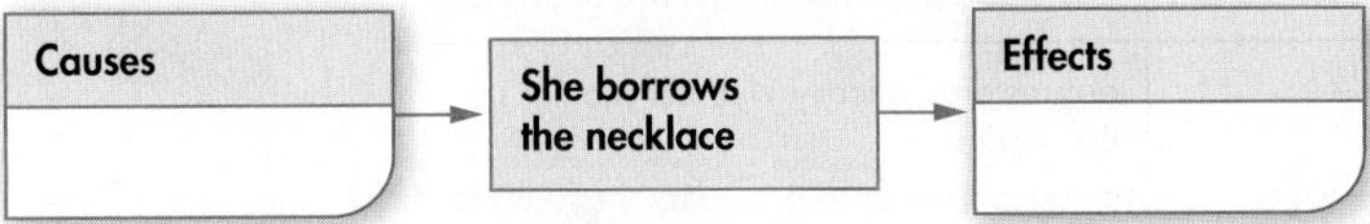

4. Does Madame Loisel cause her own suffering? Explain.

Vocabulary

Acquisition and Use Tell whether each sentence below makes sense. Use the meaning of the italicized vocabulary word to explain your answer.

1. With a *rueful* smile, she described the fun she had had at the fair.
2. The tired campers were *resplendent* as they hiked in the rain.
3. Alan went to the interview *disheveled* and wearing a new suit.
4. The class was *profoundly* moved by the story of the heroic dog.
5. One of my grandfather's greatest qualities is his *fortitude*.
6. With great *dejection*, the family celebrated the engagement.

Word Study Use the context of the sentences and what you know about the **Latin root *-jec(t)-*** to explain your answer to each question.

1. Why might a player be *ejected* from a basketball game?
2. Could you challenge an idea by raising an *objection* to it?

Word Study

The **Latin root *-jec(t)-*** means "to throw."

Apply It Explain how the root *-jec(t)-* contributes to the meanings of these words. Consult a dictionary if necessary.

project *v.*
reject *v.*
trajectory

ASSESS/EXTEND

Answers

Literary Analysis

1. Mme. Loisel is shallow, selfish, and self-centered. (a) **Actions:** She uses the money her husband has saved to buy a new dress for herself. (b) **Words and thoughts:** She dreams about all the beautiful luxuries she thinks she should have; she tells her husband that she is unhappy about the invitation to the party. (c) **Effect:** She makes her husband unhappy and finally causes him to incur a massive debt.
2. (a) It is an example of indirect characterization. The reader learns about the characters through their thoughts and what they say to each other.
(b) M. Loisel loves his wife, tries to please her, and is willing to sacrifice his own pleasure to make her happy. Madame Loisel is selfish and thoughtless; she complains about the invitation and about her clothing; she is willing to let her husband sacrifice his own pleasure for her.

Reading Skill

3. **Possible response:** (a) **Causes:** She is invited to a party; she does not want to look like she is poor. (b) **Effects:** She looks beautiful at the party; she loves the necklace; she then lives in poverty.
For other sample answers, see ***Graphic Organizer Transparencies,* Reading Skill Graphic Organizer A**, p. 60, and the **Additional Answers** section.
4. Some students will suggest that she causes her own suffering by being so discontented; others may say that she is a victim of fate.

Vocabulary

Acquisition and Use

Sample answers:

1. No, someone who had fun at a fair wouldn't have a rueful, or sorrowful, smile; he or she would be happy.
2. No, tired campers would not look resplendent, they would look dirty and wet.
3. No, Alan would look well-dressed and clean, not untidy and disheveled.

Answers Continued

4. Yes, a class would be profoundly, or deeply, moved by a story of a heroic dog.
5. Yes, fortitude, or the strength to bear misfortune, is a great quality one can have.
6. No, a family would celebrate an engagement with excitement and happiness, not dejection, or a downcast feeling.

Word Study

Sample answers:

1. A player might be *ejected*, or thrown out of a basketball game, for shoving.
2. Yes, when you raise an *objection* to an idea, you throw out a question or opposition to it.

Word Study: Apply It

Sample answers:

To *project* is to throw forward. To *reject* is to throw back. A *trajectory* is the path of an object thrown.

EXTEND/ASSESS

Answers

Conventions

Introduce the skill, using the instruction on the student page.

Think Aloud: Model the Skill

Model a way to identify subjects and predicates. Post the sentence *Blanca walks to school every day.* Say to students:

> To identify the subject in a sentence, I look for words that name someone or something that the sentence is about—here, that word is *Blanca.* To identify the predicate in a sentence, I first look for the verb that tells what the subject is or does—in this case, *walks.*

PH WRITING COACH Grade 9

Students will find instruction on and practice with subjects and predicates in Chapter 14, section 1.

Practice A

Sample answers:

1. Waverly; S: Waverly; P: watched
2. is about chess; S: book; P: is
3. grew steadily; S: interest; P: grew
4. Lau Po; S: Lau Po; P: made

Writing Application

Sample answers:

1. I have played my favorite game since I was ten.
2. We have not played my favorite game since I was ten.
3. Luckily, I have been studying my favorite game since I was ten.
4. Baseball has not been my favorite game since I was ten.

Practice B

1. S: Madame Loisel; P: felt
2. S: dreams; P: caused
3. S: necklace; P: disappeared
4. S: replacement; P: cost

Reading Application

Sample answers:

1. She had no proper wardrobe, no jewels, nothing. S: she; P: had.
2. Then one evening her husband arrived home looking triumphant and waving a large envelope. S: husband; P: arrived

PERFORMANCE TASKS

Integrated Language Skills

Rules of the Game • The Necklace

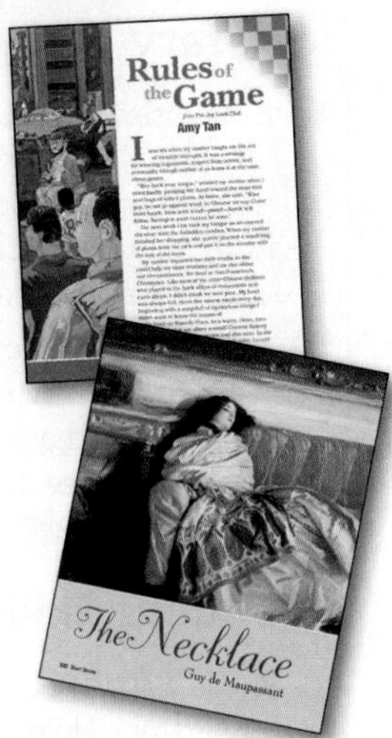

Conventions: Subjects and Predicates

The **subject** is the word or group of words that tells whom or what a sentence is about.

The **predicate** is the verb or verb phrase that tells what the subject of a sentence does or is.

A complete sentence needs both a subject and a predicate. The underlined words in these examples are the simple subject and simple predicate, or the noun and verb that make a sentence complete.

Subject	Predicate
<u>Conflict</u> between family members	<u>is</u> not unusual.
Madame Loisel's <u>desire</u> for status	<u>has created</u> a conflict with her husband.
<u>Waverly</u>	<u>argues</u> dramatically with her mother in the market.

Practice A Add a subject or predicate to complete each sentence. Identify the subject and predicate in the completed sentence.

1. __________ watched Vincent and Winston's chess games.
2. The book of rules __________.
3. Her interest in the game __________.
4. __________ soon made Waverly a skillful player.

Writing Application Create four new sentences by changing the subject and the predicate in the example sentence. *Chess has been my favorite game since I was ten.*

Practice B Identify the subject and predicate in each sentence.

1. Madame Loisel felt great dissatisfaction.
2. Her dreams of wealth and recognition caused trouble.
3. The necklace from Madame Forestier disappeared after a party.
4. Its replacement cost Madame Loisel and her husband ten years of hardship.

Reading Application Choose two sentences in "The Necklace." Identify the subject and predicate in each sentence.

PH WRITING COACH Further instruction and practice are available in *Prentice Hall Writing Coach.*

Extend the Lesson

Sentence Modeling

Choose the sentence given from the selection students have read:

My mother imparted her daily truths so she could help my older brothers and me rise above our circumstances. ("Rules of the Game")

Unable to afford jewelry, she dressed simply. ("The Necklace")

Ask students what they notice about the sentence. Elicit from them that the sentence has a subject and a predicate. Then, ask what else they notice. ("Rules of the Game": The sentence is complex and the subject is a noun; "The Necklace": The introductory phrase states a cause, and the independent clause succinctly states the effect.)

Have students imitate the sentence in a sentence on a topic of their own choosing, matching each grammatical and stylistic feature discussed. Have volunteers read their sentences aloud to the group.

Writing

Informative Text Each of these stories deals with people learning lessons. Think about a lesson that you could teach the main characters in "The Necklace" or "Rules of the Game." Create a **written presentation** that details your ideas.

- Make notes about an issue that the characters face. Consider what you might teach them and how best to convey your ideas.
- Based on your audience, purpose, and point of view as an outsider, choose an appropriate genre and text structure. For example, you might write an essay, or you might tell a story with a moral.
- As you revise, check that your presentation is organized logically. Add transitions where needed and vary your sentences for meaning, interest, and style.

Grammar Application As you write, check that subjects and predicates agree in number and tense.

Writing Workshop: *Work in Progress*

Prewriting for Exposition: Cause-and-Effect Essay It often is easier to see effects than to understand causes. For a cause-and-effect essay you may write, list ten effects for which you do not know the cause. Put this "What's the Cause?" list into your writing portfolio.

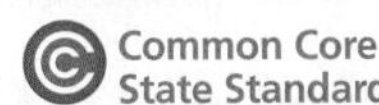

L.9-10.6; W.9-10.4; SL.9-10.2
[For the full wording of the standards, see page 312.]

Use this prewriting activity to prepare for the **Writing Workshop** on page 402.

Research and Technology

Build and Present Knowledge The characters in these stories need facts in order to succeed. With a few classmates, make an **informative brochure.**

- If you read "The Necklace," make a brochure about the qualities and uses of diamonds.
- If you read "Rules of the Game," make a brochure about the history, rules, and strategies of chess. Follow these steps.
- **Gather information** on the topic, evaluating sources as you take notes on library and authoritative Internet sources. Develop clear questions to help you gather details from a variety of sources.
- **Organize your coverage.** Plan the sections for the brochure. Decide whether illustrations should convey some of the information (for example, diagrams of chess moves).
- **Design and present your brochure.** Add visual elements but avoid a "cluttered" look. Use diverse media or formats to present your brochure to the class.

www.PHLitOnline.com
- Interactive graphic organizers
- Grammar tutorial
- Interactive journals

EXTEND/ASSESS

Writing

1. Review the assignment, using the instruction on the student page.
2. To give students guidance for writing their presentations, give them **Support for Writing,** p. 155, in ***Unit 2 Resources.***
3. To evaluate students' presentations, use the **Response to Literature** rubrics, pp. 224–225 in ***Professional Development Guidebook.*** In addition, you might evaluate students' suggestions for their practicality and creativity.

Grammar Application

Have students check their drafts to make sure the subjects and predicates of their sentences agree in number and tense.

Six Traits Focus

✓	Ideas	✓	Word Choice
✓	Organization		Sentence Fluency
	Voice		Conventions

PH WRITING COACH Grade 9

Students will find instruction on and practice with response to literature in Chapter 10.

Writing Workshop
Work in Progress

Have students save their "What's the Cause?" lists in their portfolios. They will use their lists later as they continue this Work-in-Progress assignment (see p. 373). The assignment prepares them to complete the Writing Workshop (see pp. 402–409).

Research and Technology

1. Review the assignment, using the instruction on the student page.
2. To support students' work on the assignment, have them complete the **Support for Extend Your Learning** page (***Unit 2 Resources,*** p. 156).

Teaching Resources

Unit 2 Resources

L3 L4 EL **Integrated Language Skills: Grammar,** p. 154
L3 L4 EL **Support for Writing,** p. 155
L3 L4 **Support for Extend Your Learning,** p. 156
L4 **Enrichment,** p. 135, 153

Enriched Online Student Edition
Available under After You Read for this selection:
All **Interactive Grammar Tutorial**
L3 L4 **Internet Research Activity**

Professional Development Guidebook
Rubrics for Self-Assessment: Response to Literature, pp. 224–225

PHLit Online! All print and digital resources are available at **www.PHLitOnline.com.** Online resources accessible by students are noted on the student page.

✓ Blues Ain't No Mockin Bird • ✓✓ The Invalid's Story

Lesson Pacing Guide

DAY 1 Preteach

- Administer the Reading and Vocabulary Warm-ups (*Unit 2 Resources*, pp. 166–169 or 184–187) as necessary.
- Introduce the Reading Skill: Cause and Effect.
- Introduce the Literary Analysis concept: Dialogue and Dialect.
- Distribute copies of the appropriate graphic organizer for the Reading Skill (*Graphic Organizer Transparencies*, pp. 62–64).
- Distribute copies of the appropriate graphic organizer for Literary Analysis (*Graphic Organizer Transparencies*, pp. 65–67).
- Teach the selection vocabulary.
- Introduce the Word Study skill.

DAYS 2–3 Preteach/Teach

- Build background with the Background feature.
- Develop thematic vocabulary and thematic thinking with Writing About the Big Question.
- Prepare students to read with the Activating Prior Knowledge activities (TE).
- Informally monitor comprehension while students read.
- Use the Reading Check questions to confirm comprehension.
- Develop students' ability to determine cause and effect, using the Reading Skill questions.
- Develop students' understanding of dialogue and dialect, using the Literary Analysis questions.
- Reinforce vocabulary with the Vocabulary notes.
- Reinforce unit focus standards using the Spiral Review prompts.

DAY 4 Assess

- Assess students' comprehension and mastery of the skills by having them answer the Critical Thinking, Reading Skill, and Literary Analysis questions.
- Have students complete the Vocabulary Practice activities.
- Have students complete the Word Study activities.

DAY 5 Extend/Assess

- Have students complete the Conventions lesson.
- Have students complete the Writing activity and write an informal letter. (You may assign as homework.)
- Extend learning by having students complete the Speaking and Listening, activity, a dialogue. As an alternative, assign them "Media Madness" or "Giving Back" in *Reality Central*.
- Administer Selection Test A or B (*Unit 2 Resources*, pp. 178–183 or 199–204).

Common Core State Standards

Reading Literature 3. Analyze how complex characters (e.g., those with multiple or conflicting motivations) develop over the course of a text, interact with other characters, and advance the plot or develop the theme.
4. Determine the meaning of words and phrases as they are used in the text, including figurative and connotative meanings; analyze the cumulative impact of specific word choices on meaning and tone.

Writing 3.a. Engage and orient the reader by setting out a problem, situation, or observation, establishing one or multiple point(s) of view, and introducing a narrator and/or characters; create a smooth progression of experiences or events.

Speaking and Listening 4. Present information, findings, and supporting evidence clearly, concisely, and logically, such that listeners can follow the line of reasoning and the organization, development, substance, and style are appropriate to purpose, audience, and task.

Language 1. Demonstrate command of the conventions of standard English grammar and usage when writing or speaking.
6. Acquire and use accurately grade-appropriate general academic and domain-specific words and phrases; gather vocabulary knowledge when considering a word or phrase important to comprehension or expression.

Additional Standards Practice
Common Core Companion*, *pp. 28–29; 48–49

Daily Block Scheduling
Each day in this Lesson Pacing Guide represents a 40–50 minute period. Teachers using block scheduling may combine days to revise pacing. In addition, teachers may differentiate and support core instruction by integrating components for extended and intensive support as students require. See the Guide to Selected Leveled Resources (facing page).

Guide to Selected Leveled Resources

RTI Tier 1 (students performing on level)		✓ More Accessible: Blues Ain't No Mockin Bird	✓✓ More Complex: The Invalid's Story
Warm Up	**Practice, model,** and **monitor** fluency, working **with the whole class** or **in groups**.	**Vocabulary** and **Reading Warm-ups B,** ***Unit 2 Resources,*** pp. 166–167, 169	**Vocabulary** and **Reading Warm-ups B,** ***Unit 2 Resources,*** pp. 184–185, 187
Comprehension/Skills	**Support** and **monitor** comprehension and skills development, having students complete the activities, graphic organizers, and interactive prompts **independently** or **as a class**.	• ***Reader's Notebook,*** adapted instruction and full selection EL ***Reader's Notebook: English Learner's Version,*** adapted instruction and adapted selection • **Reading Skill Graphic Organizer B,** ***Graphic Organizer Transparencies,*** p. 64 • **Literary Analysis Graphic Organizer B,** ***Graphic Organizer Transparencies,*** p. 67	• ***Reader's Notebook,*** adapted instruction and summary EL ***Reader's Notebook: English Learner's Version,*** adapted instruction and summary • **Reading Skill Graphic Organizer B,** ***Graphic Organizer Transparencies,*** p. 64 • **Literary Analysis Graphic Organizer B,** ***Graphic Organizer Transparencies,*** p. 67
Monitor Progress	**Monitor** student progress with the differentiated curriculum-based assessment in the *Unit Resources.*	• **Selection Test B,** ***Unit 2 Resources,*** pp. 181–183 • **Open-Book Test,** ***Unit 2 Resources,*** pp. 175–177	• **Selection Test B,** ***Unit 2 Resources,*** pp. 202–204 • **Open-Book Test,** ***Unit 2 Resources,*** pp. 196–198
Assess/Screen	• **Assess** student progress using Benchmark Test 4. • **Preassess** instructional needs using the Vocabulary in Context section of the test.	• **Benchmark Test 4,** ***Unit 2 Resources,*** pp. 227–235, including Vocabulary in Context diagnostic items	• **Benchmark Test 4,** ***Unit 2 Resources,*** pp. 227–235, including Vocabulary in Context diagnostic items

RTI Tier 2 (students requiring intervention)		✓ More Accessible: Blues Ain't No Mockin Bird	✓✓ More Complex: The Invalid's Story
Warm Up	**Practice, model,** and **monitor** fluency **in groups** or **with individuals.**	• **Vocabulary and Reading Warm-ups A,** ***Unit 2 Resources,*** pp. 166–168 • ***Reality Central,*** "Media Madness" • ***Hear It!*** **Audio CD (adapted text)**	• **Vocabulary and Reading Warm-ups A,** ***Unit 2 Resources,*** pp. 184–186 • ***Reality Central,*** "Giving Back" • ***Hear It!*** **Audio CD**
Comprehension/Skills	• **Support** and **monitor** comprehension and skills development, working **in small groups** or **with individuals.** • **Pair** students with more advanced peers and have them complete the writing activity in the *Real-World Writing Journal*. • As students complete the selection in the appropriate version of the *Reader's Notebook,* **monitor** comprehension frequently with group questions and individual instruction. • **Model** strategies while guiding students in completing the activities and prompts in the *Reader's Notebook,* as well as the graphic organizers. • **Practice** skills and **monitor** mastery with the *Reading Kit* worksheets.	• ***Real-World Writing Journal,*** Lesson 7, pp. 60–63 • ***Reader's Notebook: Adapted Version,*** adapted instruction and adapted selection EL ***Reader's Notebook: English Learner's Version,*** adapted instruction and adapted selection • **Reading Skill Graphic Organizer A,** ***Graphic Organizer Transparencies,*** p. 62 • **Literary Analysis Graphic Organizer A,** ***Graphic Organizer Transparencies,*** p. 65 • ***Reading Kit,*** Practice worksheets, pp. 78, 82, 86, 90, 98	• ***Real-World Writing Journal,*** Lesson 8, pp. 64–67 • ***Reader's Notebook: Adapted Version,*** adapted instruction and summary EL ***Reader's Notebook: English Learner's Version,*** adapted instruction and summary • **Reading Skill Graphic Organizer A,** ***Graphic Organizer Transparencies,*** p. 63 • **Literary Analysis Graphic Organizer A,** ***Graphic Organizer Transparencies,*** p. 66 • ***Reading Kit,*** Practice worksheets, pp. 78, 82, 86, 90, 98
Monitor Progress	**Monitor** student progress with the differentiated curriculum-based assessment in the *Unit Resources* and in the *Reading Kit.*	• **Selection Test A,** ***Unit 2 Resources,*** pp. 178–180 • ***Reading Kit,*** Assess worksheets, pp. 79, 83, 87, 91, 99	• **Selection Test A,** ***Unit 2 Resources,*** pp. 199–201 • ***Reading Kit,*** Assess worksheets, pp. 79, 83, 87, 91, 99
Assess/Screen	• **Assess** student progress using Benchmark Test 4. • **Preassess** instructional needs using the Vocabulary in Context section of the test.	• **Benchmark Test 4,** ***Unit 2 Resources,*** pp. 227–235, including Vocabulary in Context diagnostic items	• **Benchmark Test 4,** ***Unit 2 Resources,*** pp. 227–235, including Vocabulary in Context diagnostic items

TIER 3 Tier 3 intervention may require consultation with the student's special-education or dyslexia specialist. For additional support, see the Tier 2 activities and resources listed above.

One-on-one teaching | Group work | Whole class instruction | Independent work | A Assessment

For a complete guide to selection support, including support for Advanced students, see the Overview of Resources in the frontmatter.

✓Blues Ain't No Mockin Bird
✓✓The Invalid's Story

BLUES AIN'T NO MOCKIN BIRD

Toni Cade Bambara

350 Short Stories

The Invalid's Story

Mark Twain

I seem sixty and married, but these effects are due to my condition and sufferings, for I am a bachelor, and only forty-one. It will be hard for you to believe that I, who am now but a shadow, was a hale, hearty man two short years ago—a man of iron, a very athlete!—yet such is the simple truth. But stranger still than this fact is the way in which I lost my health. I lost it through helping to take care of a box of guns on a two-hundred-mile railway journey one winter's night. It is the actual truth, and I will tell you about it.

I belong in Cleveland, Ohio. One winter's night, two years ago, I reached home just after dark, in a driving snowstorm, and the first thing I heard when I entered the house was that my dearest boyhood friend and schoolmate, John B. Hackett, had died the day before, and that his last utterance had been a desire that I would take his remains home to his poor old father and mother in Wisconsin. I was greatly shocked and grieved, but there was no time to waste in emotions; I must start at once. I took the card, marked "Deacon Levi Hackett, Bethlehem, Wisconsin," and hurried off through the whistling storm to the railway station. Arrived there I found the long white-pine box which had been described to me; I fastened the card to it with some tacks, saw it put safely aboard the express car, and then ran into the eating room to provide myself with a sandwich and some cigars. When I returned, presently, there was my coffin-box back again, apparently, and a young fellow examining around it, with a card in his hands, and some tacks and

Reading Check

What was John B. Hackett's dying wish?

The Invalid's Story 363

RESOURCES FOR:

- L1 Special-Needs Students
- L2 Below-Level Students (Tier 2)
- L3 On-Level Students (Tier 1)
- L4 Advanced Students (Tier 1)
- EL English Learners
- All All Students

Vocabulary/Fluency/Prior Knowledge

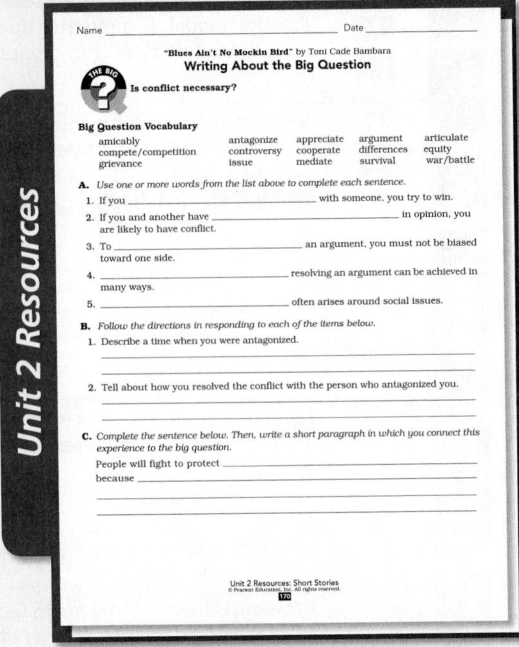

Name ______________________ Date ______________

"Blues Ain't No Mockin Bird" by Toni Cade Bambara

Writing About the Big Question

THE BIG ?

Is conflict necessary?

Big Question Vocabulary

amicably	antagonize	appreciate	argument	articulate
compete/competition	controversy	cooperate	differences	equity
grievance	issue	mediate	survival	war/battle

A. *Use one or more words from the list above to complete each sentence.*

1. If you ______________ with someone, you try to win.
2. If you and another have ______________ in opinion, you are likely to have conflict.
3. To ______________ an argument, you must not be biased toward one side.
4. ______________ resolving an argument can be achieved in many ways.
5. ______________ often arises around social issues.

B. *Follow the directions in responding to each of the items below.*

1. Describe a time when you were antagonized.
2. Tell about how you resolved the conflict with the person who antagonized you.

C. *Complete the sentence below. Then, write a short paragraph in which you connect this experience to the big question.*

People will fight to protect ______________

because ______________

Unit 2 Resources: Short Stories

170

Unit 2 Resources

All **Writing About the Big Question,** pp. 170, 188

Also available for these selections:

EL L1 L2 **Vocabulary Warm-ups A and B,** pp. 166–167, 184–185

EL L1 L2 **Reading Warm-ups A and B,** pp. 168–169, 186–187

All **Vocabulary Builder,** pp. 173, 191

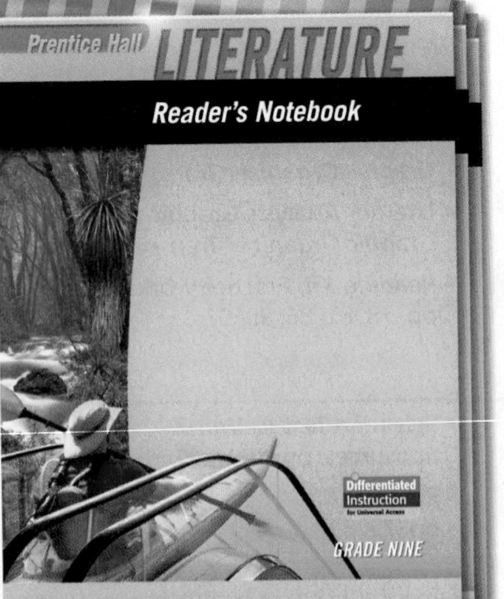

Reader's Notebooks

Pre- and postreading pages for both selections, as well as "Blues Ain't No Mockin Bird" appear in an interactive format in the *Reader's Notebooks.* Each *Notebook* is differentiated for a different group of learners. The selections in the Adapted and English Learner's versions are abridged.

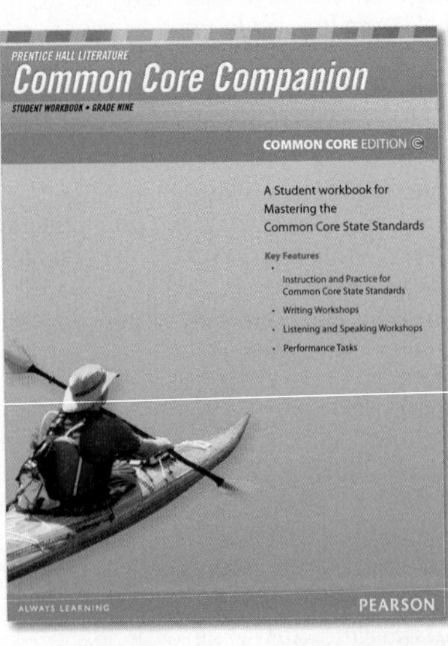

L2 L3 ***Reader's Notebook***

L1 ***Reader's Notebook: Adapted Version***

EL ***Reader's Notebook: English Learner's Version***

EL ***Reader's Notebook: Spanish Version***

Common Core Companion

Additional instruction and practice for each Common Core State Standard

Selection Support

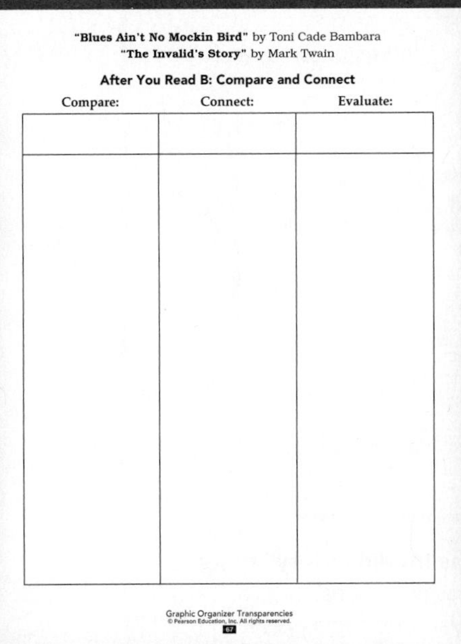

"Blues Ain't No Mockin Bird" by Toni Cade Bambara
"The Invalid's Story" by Mark Twain

After You Read B: Compare and Connect

Compare:	Connect:	Evaluate:

Graphic Organizer Transparencies
© Pearson Education, Inc. All rights reserved.
67

EL L3 **Literacy Analysis: Graphic Organizer B,** p. 67

Also available for these selections:

EL L1 L2 **Reading: Graphic Organizer A,** pp. 62, 63 (partially filled in)

EL L3 **Reading: Graphic Organizer B,** p. 64

EL L1 L2 **Literacy Analysis: Graphic Organizer A,** pp. 65, 66 (partially filled in)

Skills Development/Extension

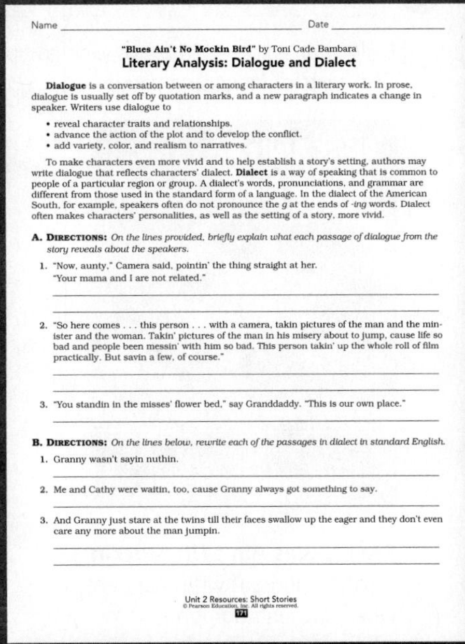

Name ______________________ Date ____________

"Blues Ain't No Mockin Bird" by Toni Cade Bambara
Literary Analysis: Dialogue and Dialect

Dialogue is a conversation between or among characters in a literary work. In prose, dialogue is usually set off by quotation marks, and a new paragraph indicates a change in speaker. Writers use dialogue to

- reveal character traits and relationships.
- advance the action of the plot and to develop the conflict.
- add variety, color, and realism to narratives.

To make characters even more vivid and to help establish a story's setting, authors may write dialogue that reflects characters' dialect. **Dialect** is a way of speaking that is common to people of a particular region or group. A dialect's words, pronunciations, and grammar are different from those used in the standard form of a language. In the dialect of the American South, for example, speakers often do not pronounce the *g* at the ends of *-ing* words. Dialect often makes characters' personalities, as well as the setting of a story, more vivid.

A. Directions: *On the lines provided, briefly explain what each passage of dialogue from the story reveals about the speakers.*

1. "Now, aunty," Camera said, pointin' the thing straight at her. "Your mama and I are not related."
2. "So here comes . . . this person . . . with a camera, takin pictures of the man and the minister and the woman. Takin' pictures of the man in his misery about to jump, cause life so bad and people been messin' with him so bad. This person takin' up the whole roll of film practically. But savin a few, of course."
3. "You standin in the misses' flower bed," say Granddaddy. "This is our own place."

B. Directions: *On the lines below, rewrite each of the passages in dialect in standard English.*

1. Granny wasn't sayin nuthin.
2. Me and Cathy were waitin, too, cause Granny always got something to say.
3. And Granny just stare at the twins till their faces swallow up the eager and they don't even care any more about the man jumpin.

Unit 2 Resources: Short Stories
© Pearson Education, Inc. All rights reserved.
171

All **Literacy Analysis: Dialogue and Dialect,** pp. 171, 189

Also available for these selections:

All **Reading: Cause and Effect,** pp. 172, 190

L4 **Enrichment,** pp. 174, 192

EL L3 L4 **Grammar,** p. 193

EL L3 L4 **Support for Writing,** p. 194

L3 L4 **Support for Extend Your Learning,** p. 195

Assessment

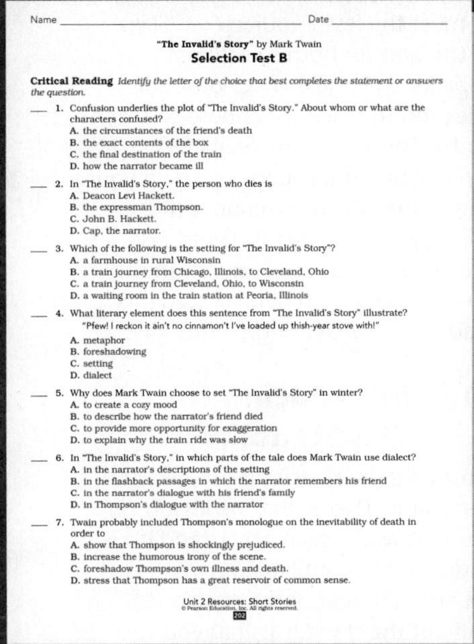

Name ______________________ Date ____________

"The Invalid's Story" by Mark Twain
Selection Test B

Critical Reading *Identify the letter of the choice that best completes the statement or answers the question.*

___ 1. Confusion underlies the plot of "The Invalid's Story." About whom or what are the characters confused?
A. the circumstances of the friend's death
B. the exact contents of the box
C. the final destination of the train
D. how the narrator became ill

___ 2. In "The Invalid's Story," the person who dies is
A. Deacon Levi Hackett.
B. the expressman Thompson.
C. John B. Hackett.
D. Cap, the narrator.

___ 3. Which of the following is the setting for "The Invalid's Story"?
A. a farmhouse in rural Wisconsin
B. a train journey from Chicago, Illinois, to Cleveland, Ohio
C. a train journey from Cleveland, Ohio, to Wisconsin
D. a waiting room in the train station at Peoria, Illinois

___ 4. What literary element does this sentence from "The Invalid's Story" illustrate?
"Pfew! I reckon it ain't no cinnamon't I've loaded up thish-year stove with!"
A. metaphor
B. foreshadowing
C. setting
D. dialect

___ 5. Why does Mark Twain choose to set "The Invalid's Story" in winter?
A. to create a cozy mood
B. to describe how the narrator's friend died
C. to provide more opportunity for exaggeration
D. to explain why the train ride was slow

___ 6. In "The Invalid's Story," in which parts of the tale does Mark Twain use dialect?
A. in the narrator's descriptions of the setting
B. in the flashback passages in which the narrator remembers his friend
C. in the narrator's dialogue with his friend's family
D. in Thompson's dialogue with the narrator

___ 7. Twain probably included Thompson's monologue on the inevitability of death in order to
A. show that Thompson is shockingly prejudiced.
B. increase the humorous irony of the scene.
C. foreshadow Thompson's own illness and death.
D. stress that Thompson has a great reservoir of common sense.

Unit 2 Resources: Short Stories
© Pearson Education, Inc. All rights reserved.
202

EL L3 L4 **Selection Test B,** pp. 181–183, 202–204

Also available for these selections:

L3 L4 **Open-Book Test,** pp. 175–177, 196–198

EL L1 L2 **Selection Test A,** pp. 178–180, 199–201

PHLit Online!
www.PHLitOnline.com

- complete narrated selection text
- a thematically related video with writing prompt
- an interactive graphic organizer
- highlighting feature
- access to all student print resources, adapted to individual student needs
- Spanish and English summaries
- adapted selection translations in Spanish

Online Resources: All print materials are also available online.

Get Connected! (thematic video with writing prompt)

Also available:

Background Video

All videos are available in Spanish.

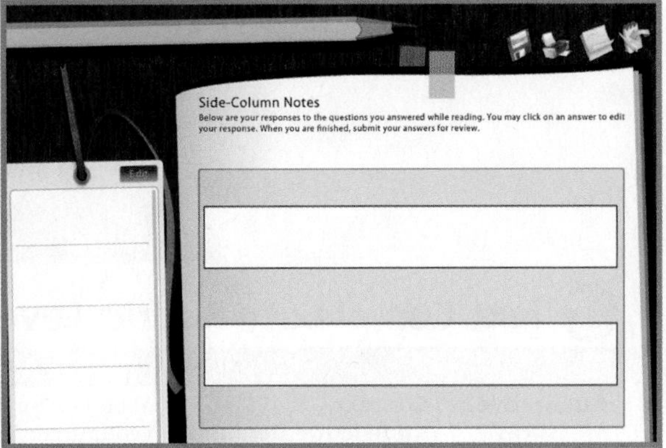

Writer's Journal (with graphics feature)

Also available:

Vocabulary Central (tools, activities, and songs for studying vocabulary)

1 Leveled Texts

You may use either "Blues Ain't No Mockin Bird" or "The Invalid's Story" to meet the lesson objectives. Skills instruction for both selections appears on page 347. Choose one selection to teach (or choose to teach both). The Text Complexity Rubric at the bottom of this page will help you determine which selection is more appropriate for your students. Use the Reader and Task Suggestions on the facing page to help all students read text of increasing complexity.

2 Introducing the CCS Standards

Introduce the standards on the student page. (Note that the lesson element with which each standard is addressed is identified in parentheses after the text of the standard.) Call out the standards that you will cover with the selections, explaining to students what each requires and how they will address it as they work through the selection you have chosen. Standards labeled "Spiral Review" are introduced in the Literary Analysis Workshop for this unit.

Before You Read

Blues Ain't No Mockin Bird • The Invalid's Story

1 Leveled Texts

Build your skills and improve your comprehension of short stories with texts of increasing complexity.

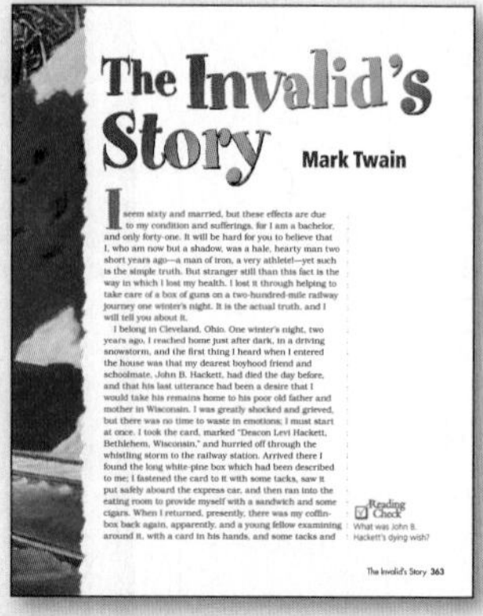

Read **"Blues Ain't No Mockin Bird"** to find out what happens when two photographers clash with a strong-willed woman.

Read **"The Invalid's Story"** to see how a master humorist takes a somber train ride and makes it comical.

2 Common Core State Standards

Meet these standards with either **"Blues Ain't No Mockin Bird"** (p. 350) or **"The Invalid's Story"** (p. 362).

Reading Literature

4. Determine the meaning of words and phrases as they are used in the text, including figurative and connotative meanings; analyze the cumulative impact of specific word choices on meaning and tone. *(Literary Analysis: Dialogue and Dialect)*

Spiral Review: RL.9-10.3

Writing

3.a. Engage and orient the reader by setting out a problem, situation, or observation, establishing one or multiple point(s) of view, and introducing a narrator and/or characters; create a smooth progression of experiences or events. *(Writing: Informal Letter)*

Speaking and Listening

4. Present information, findings, and supporting evidence clearly, concisely, and logically such that listeners can follow the line of reasoning and the organization, development, substance, and style are appropriate to purpose, audience, and task. *(Speaking and Listening: Dialogue)*

Language

1. Demonstrate command of the conventions of standard English grammar and usage when writing or speaking. *(Conventions: Active and Passive Voice)*

6. Acquire and use accurately grade-appropriate general academic and domain-specific words and phrases; gather vocabulary knowledge when considering a word or phrase important to comprehension or expression. *(Vocabulary: Analogies)*

346 Short Stories

Text Complexity Rubric: Leveled Texts

Text complexity is determined by both qualitative and quantitative measures. For this reason, the quantitative measure of a more complex selection may be lower than that of a more accessible selection.

		✓ Blues Ain't No Mockin Bird	✓✓ The Invalid's Story
Qualitative Measures	**Context/ Knowledge Demands**	Southern, rural United States in the mid-twentieth century; country life 1 (2) 3 4 5	Nineteenth-century railway car 1 (2) 3 4 5
	Structure/Language Conventionality and Clarity	Heavy use of dialect and dialogue; on-level vocabulary 1 (2) 3 4 5	Long paragraphs; lengthy sentences with embedded clauses; dialect 1 2 (3) 4 5
	Levels of Meaning/ Purpose/Concept	Accessible (family dignity and right to privacy) 1 2 (3) 4 5	Accessible (humor in a difficult situation) 1 2 (3) 4 5
Quantitative Measures	**Text Length**	Word Count: 2,629	Word Count: 2,719
	Lexile	940L	980L
Overall Complexity		✓ **More accessible**	✓✓ **More complex**

❸ Literary Analysis: Dialogue and Dialect

Dialogue is a conversation between or among characters in a literary work. In prose, dialogue is usually set off by quotation marks, and a new paragraph indicates a change in speaker. Writers use dialogue for these purposes:

- to reveal character traits and relationships
- to advance the action of the plot and develop the conflict
- to add variety, color, and realism to narratives
- to develop the **tone** of the work—the writer's attitude toward his or her subject and audience

To make characters and settings vivid, authors may write dialogue reflecting characters' **dialect.** Dialect is a way of speaking that is common to people of a region or group. The words, pronunciations, and grammar of a dialect differ from those of the standard form of a language.

As you read, notice passages of dialogue and dialect, and determine what they show about the characters and the setting. In addition, consider how they affect the tone of the story.

PHLit Online!
www.PHLitOnline.com

Hear It!
- Selection summary audio
- Selection audio

See It!
- Get Connected video
- Background video
- More about the author
- Vocabulary flashcards

Do It!
- Interactive journals
- Interactive graphic organizers
- Self-test
- Internet activity
- Grammar tutorial
- Interactive vocabulary games

❹ Reading Skill: Cause and Effect

A **cause** is an event, an action, or a feeling that produces a result. An **effect** is the result produced. When reading a story, **visualize the action to analyze cause and effect.**

- Use text details to picture the setting, characters, and action.
- Use the details of your mental picture to help you identify the relationships between actions and events.

❺ Using the Strategy: Cause-and-Effect Chart

Use a **flow chart** like this one to follow cause-and-effect relationships as you read.

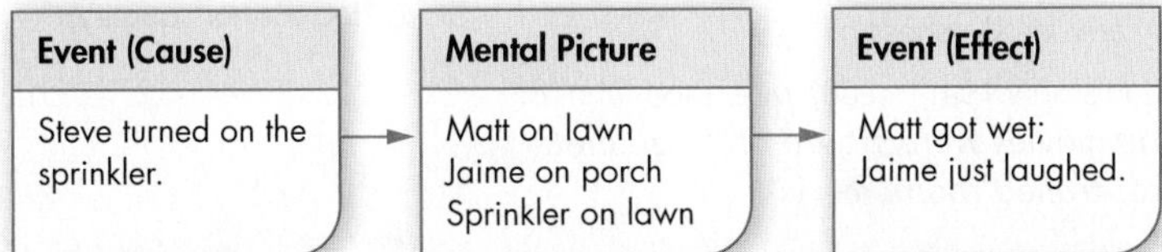

Event (Cause)
Steve turned on the sprinkler.
Mental Picture
Matt on lawn
Jaime on porch
Sprinkler on lawn
Event (Effect)
Matt got wet;
Jaime just laughed.

PRETEACH

❸ Literary Analysis

Dialogue and Dialect

1. Introduce the skill, using the instruction on the student page.
2. Tell students that they will explore dialogue and dialect as they read.

Think Aloud: Model the Skill

Model dialogue and dialect. Say to students:

> Suppose that I am listening to a conversation between two friends. Each speaks in a way that shows something about who he is and where he comes from. For example, if one friend says, "I reckon you're right," he shows that he comes from a certain part of the country—he is speaking the dialect or version of English from that region. When my other friend says, "Yeah, right," he shows something about himself, too—he can be sarcastic. When I read a story, I pay attention to clues like these in the dialogue, or words characters say, to learn more about the characters.

❹ Reading Skill

Cause and Effect

1. Introduce the skill, using the instruction on the student page.
2. Tell students that they will identify causes and effects as they read.

❺ Using the Strategy

Give students a copy of either **Reading Skill Graphic Organizer A** or **B** (*Graphic Organizer Transparencies,* pp. 62–64.) to record causes and effects. Use the examples in **Reading Skill Graphic Organizer A,** which is partially filled in, to model the process of completing the organizer.

Text Complexity: Reader and Task Suggestions

✓ Blues Ain't No Mockin Bird		✓✓ The Invalid's Story	
Preparing to Read the Text	**Leveled Tasks**	**Preparing to Read the Text**	**Leveled Tasks**
• Refer to the Background information on TE p. 349 and discuss hawks and how country people relate to their environment. • Discuss how some people may feel more strongly about privacy and family dignity than others. • Guide students to use Multidraft Reading strategies (TE p. 349).	*Levels of Meaning* If students will have difficulty with the levels of meaning, have them first read to find details showing how the family's privacy was invaded. Then, have them reread and take note on how the family responded to those invasions. *Analyzing* If students will not have difficulty with the levels of meaning, have them read and take note of ways in which Bambara uses humor to examine privacy and dignity.	• Use the Background note on TE p. 361 to discuss nineteenth-century train travel. • Review strategies for reading long, complex sentences. • Guide students to use Multidraft Reading strategies (TE p. 361).	*Structure/Language* If students will have difficulty with the language, ask them to first read the story and note details about what causes the characters' misunderstanding. Then, have them reread to identify challenging sentences. *Analyzing* If students will not have difficulty reading complex sentences, have them read and note examples of Twain's humor.

PRETEACH

❶ Writing About the Big Question

1. Review the assignment with the class.
2. **Ask** students to list things or ideas that people fight for. Then, **ask** them to list things or ideas people will fight over.
3. Have students complete the sentence starters. (**Possible responses:** People will battle to protect their families because they love them. Personal feelings and issues spark conflicts between people because when people's feelings are hurt, they may grow angry.) Review responses as a class.
4. Remind students that their answers will help them think about the Big Question, "Is conflict necessary?"

While You Read

Tell students that as they read, they should compare the responses of various characters to the situation that antagonizes Granny.

❷ Vocabulary

1. Have students preview the selection vocabulary.
2. For each word, have students say the word aloud.
3. Then, use the word in a sentence that defines the word.
4. Finally, repeat your definitional sentence or a similar sentence with the word missing and have the class "fill in the blank" chorally. Here are some examples:

   A ladle is a large, cup-like spoon used to dip out liquids. I cooked a big pot of vegetable soup and served it with a [students say "ladle"].

   Reckless means careless or rash. My brother is a very good driver and far from [students say "reckless"].

❸ Word Study

1. Introduce the skill, using the instruction in the box.
2. Ask students for another *-ity* word that names a characteristic. (**Possible answer:** *sensibility;* "the characteristic of being sensible")

Making Connections | Blues Ain't No Mockin Bird

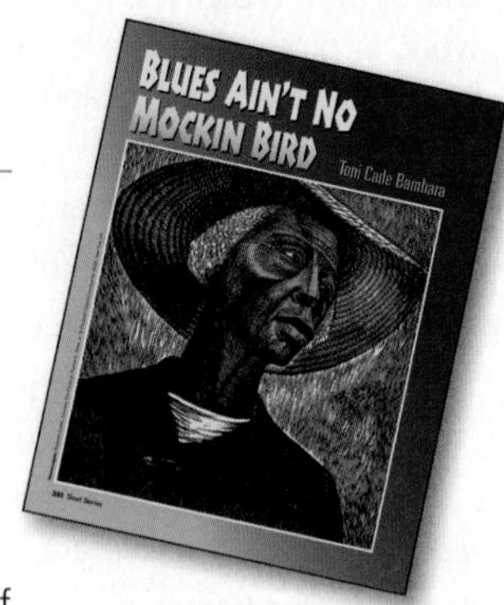

❶ Writing About the Big Question

In "Blues Ain't No Mockin Bird," an elderly woman finds it necessary to fight with people who threaten something important to her. Use these sentence starters to develop your ideas about the Big Question.

People will **battle** to protect ____________ because ____________.

Personal feelings and **issues** spark conflicts between people because ____________.

While You Read Compare the responses of the various characters to the situation that antagonizes Granny, and look for the successful resolution of the conflict.

❷ Vocabulary

Read each word and its definition. Decide whether you know the word well, know it a little bit, or do not know it at all. After you read, see how your knowledge of each word has increased.

- **ladle** (lād´ 'l) *n.* a long-handled, cuplike spoon for dipping out liquids (p. 351) ***The waiter used a ladle to put soup into my bowl.*** *ladle v.*
- **raggedy** (rag´ i dē) *adj.* torn and in bad condition (p. 354) ***I always wear raggedy old clothes to work in the garden.*** *ragged adj.*
- **stalks** (stôks) *v.* walks in a stiff, haughty, or grim manner (p. 355) ***An angry man stalks out of the room in a huff.*** *stalk n. stalker n.*
- **formality** (fôr mal´ ə tē) *n.* attention to established rules or customs (p. 356) ***His formality conveyed respect for his guests.*** *formal adj. formalize v. informal adj.*
- **reckless** (rek´ lis) *adj.* careless; rash (p. 356) ***Reckless driving is a serious offense.*** *recklessly adv. recklessness n.*
- **reels** (rēlz) *n.* frames or spools on which thread, wire, tape, film, or a net is wound (p. 357) ***The movies were stored on large metal reels in a temperature-controlled room.*** *reel v.*

❸

Word Study

The **Latin suffix *-ity*** forms nouns from adjectives. It means "the quality of showing a certain characteristic."

This story describes someone who dislikes the **formality** of the title *Miss.* She thinks it has a "too formal" quality.

Vocabulary Development

Vocabulary Knowledge Rating

Create a **Vocabulary Knowledge Rating Chart** (*Professional Development Guidebook,* p. 33) for this selection. Include the selection vocabulary and the Big Question words that appear in the Writing About the Big Question sentence starters on this page. (The Big Question vocabulary is introduced on pp. 194–195.)

Give students a copy of the chart. Read the words aloud, and have students mark their rating in the Before Reading column. Urge them to be alert to these words as they read and discuss the selection.

Tally how many students think they know a word to gauge how much instruction to provide. As students read and discuss the selection, point out the words and their context.

Vocabulary Central, featuring tools, activities, and songs for studying vocabulary, is available at **www.PHLitOnline.com.**

Meet **Toni Cade Bambara**

(1939–1995)

Author of

Blues Ain't No Mockin Bird

Toni Cade Bambara was a social activist and a writer of short stories, a novel, plays, television scripts, and documentaries. She started writing when she was in kindergarten and had her first story published when she was a senior in college.

"I write because I must," Bambara said. "If there were no more presses, no more publishing houses, I'd still be writing." She was equally devoted to social change and worked to improve the condition of African Americans. Her writing echoes that concern. Her stories are often praised for their vivid portrayals of the daily lives of African Americans in the twentieth century.

4

BACKGROUND FOR THE STORY

Hawks

Hawks are large, predatory birds. They are fiercely territorial, and they often keep the same mate for life. Usually, hawks hunt rabbits, squirrels, and other birds. However, in rural areas they may kill and eat chickens. For a poor rural family like the one in this story, defending the family's flock of chickens from hawks is a matter of survival. Sometimes, when a farmer kills a hawk that has attacked his chickens, he displays it to frighten off other hawks.

Did You Know?

Bambara was born Miltona Cade but added *Bambara* after discovering it on her great-grandmother's sketchbook. *Bambara* is also the name of an African tribe known for its textiles.

Daily Bellringer

For each class during which you will teach this selection, have students complete one of the five Research activities for Week 11 in the ***Daily Bellringer Activities*** booklet.

4 Background

Hawks

Even though most hawks are more useful to people than they are harmful, people are still sometimes intolerant of them. Hawks feed on rodents that can damage a farmer's crops. They usually find their prey while circling high above the ground. They swoop down, grab their prey with powerful talons, and kill it with their strong, pointed beaks.

Multidraft Reading

This icon ● marks natural pauses in the selection. To assist struggling readers and to deepen reading for all, assign the text in "chunks," following the icons, and apply multidraft reading protocols. For each reading, have students set the purpose indicated:

- **First reading**—identifying key ideas and details and answering any Reading Checks.
- **Second reading**—analyzing craft and structure and responding to the side-column prompts.
- **Third reading**—integrating knowledge and ideas, connecting to other texts and the world, and answering the end-of-selection questions.

For more guidance, refer to the **Classroom Strategies and Teaching Routines** card on multidraft reading.

PHLit Online!

For more about the author, practice with the selection vocabulary, or more background, go online at **www.PHLitOnline.com.**

Differentiated Instruction

Additional Instruction

EL Extended Support—English Learners

Have students complete the **Reading and Vocabulary Warm-ups, *Unit 2 Resources,*** pp. 166–169, before they read. Assign the prereading pages and the adapted selection in the ***Reader's Notebook: English Learner's Version.*** Then, have students listen to portions of the selection on the ***Hear It!* Audio CD.**

L1 L2 Extended Support—Struggling Readers

Have students complete the **Reading and Vocabulary Warm-Ups, *Unit 2 Resources,*** pp. 166–169, before they read. Assign the prereading pages and the adapted selection in the ***Reader's Notebook: Adapted Version.*** Then, have students listen to portions of the selection on the ***Hear It!* Audio CD** (adapted text).

Extended Support—Reluctant Readers

To build motivation and engagement before assigning the selection, have students read "Media Madness," a thematically related selection in ***Reality Central.*** Then, use the questions at the conclusion of the related selection to guide discussion.

❶ Activating Prior Knowledge

1. Prepare an **Anticipation Guide** (*Professional Development Guidebook*, pp. 36–38) with the following statements:
   - Every person has the right to privacy.
   - People place too high an importance on privacy.
   - Public officials have the right to collect data on people.
   - Government officials do not always treat people with respect.
2. Give students a copy of the prepared **Anticipation Guide** and have them mark their responses in the Me column. Have students discuss the statements in groups and mark the Guides again in the Group column.
3. **For further guidance, use the** ***Classroom Strategies and Teaching Routines*** **card Using an Anticipation Guide.**

Concept Connector

Students will return to the Anticipation Guide after completing "Blues Ain't No Mockin Bird."

Individual Activity

Refer students to the painting on p. 350. As students read the story, have them create a similar portrait of Granddaddy. Have them try to reveal some elements of his character.

❷ About the Selection

Bambara's story explores the issues of family dignity and the right to privacy. When photographers come to gather footage for a documentary about the county food stamp campaign, the Cains take action.

❸ Humanities

Sharecropper, Elizabeth Catlett

Elizabeth Catlett (born 1919) grew up in Washington, D.C., during the era of segregation. Many of her subjects are black women. Use this question for discussion:

What predictions can you make about the story by looking at this illustration?

Answer: An African American woman may play an important part in the story.

❶ ❷

Blues Ain't No Mockin Bird

Toni Cade Bambara

❸

Sharecropper, Elizabeth Catlett. Courtesy The Estate of Thurlow E. Tibbs, Jr., © Elizabeth Catlett/Licensed by VAGA, New York, NY

Think Aloud

Vocabulary: Using Context

Direct students' attention to the words *wagon'd* in the fourth paragraph and *tire'd* in the fifth paragraph on p. 351. Using a think-aloud process, model how to use context to infer the meaning of unfamiliar words in dialect. Say to students:

> I'm going to show you how I would figure out the meaning of *wagon'd.* In this sentence *wagon'd* is a type of contraction with *wagon* and another word. The sentence describes the men in the station wagon driving around all morning. This clue tells me that the second word in the contraction of *wagon'd* is *had*—the *wagon had* been roamin. . . .

4 **The puddle had frozen over, and me and Cathy went stompin in it. The twins from next door, Tyrone and Terry, were swingin so high out of sight we forgot we were waitin our turn on the tire.** Cathy jumped up and came down hard on her heels and started tap-dancin. And the frozen patch splinterin every which way underneath kinda spooky. "Looks like a plastic spider web," she said. "A sort of weird spider, I guess, with many mental problems." But really it looked like the crystal paperweight Granny kept in the parlor. She was on the back porch, Granny was, making the cakes drunk. The old ladle dripping rum into the Christmas tins, like it used to drip maple syrup into the pails when we lived in the Judson's woods, like it poured cider into the vats when we were on the Cooper place, like it used to scoop buttermilk and soft cheese when we lived at the dairy.

"Go tell that man we ain't a bunch of trees."

"Ma'am?"

"I said to tell that man to get away from here with that camera." Me and Cathy look over toward the meadow where the men with the station wagon'd been roamin around all mornin. The tall man with a huge camera lassoed to his shoulder was buzzin our way.

"They're makin movie pictures," yelled Tyrone, stiffenin his legs and twistin so the tire'd come down slow so they could see.

"They're makin movie pictures," sang out Terry.

"That boy don't never have anything original to say," say Cathy grown-up.

By the time the man with the camera had cut across our neighbor's yard, the twins were out of the trees swingin low and Granny was onto the steps, the screen door bammin soft and scratchy against her palms. "We thought we'd get a shot or two of the house and everything and then—"

"Good mornin," Granny cut him off. And smiled that smile.

"Good mornin," he said, head all down the way Bingo does when you yell at him about the bones on the kitchen floor. "Nice place you

6 got here, aunty. We thought we'd take a—"

"Did you?" said Granny with her eyebrows. Cathy pulled up her socks and giggled.

Literary Analysis
Dialogue and Dialect Which features of the title and opening paragraph show that this story is written in dialect?

Vocabulary
ladle (lād´ ʼl) *n.* a long-handled, cuplike spoon for dipping out liquids

5 ◀ **Critical Viewing** As you read, compare Granny with the woman in the illustration. **[Compare and Contrast]**

Reading Skill
Cause and Effect Which details in the text help you to visualize the effect that the camera crew has on Granny?

7 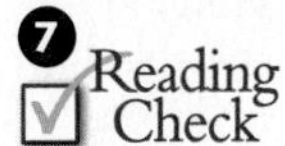

What are the men doing on Granny's property?

4 Literary Analysis
Dialogue and Dialect

1. Have students read the title and the first paragraph of the story aloud. Encourage them to pronounce the words as they are spelled.
2. **Ask** the Literary Analysis question: Which features of the title and opening paragraph show that this story is written in dialect?

   Answer: Features that show the story is written in dialect are the use of *ain't, no,* and the dropping of the final *g* in *mockin* in the title, as well as the dropping of the final *g* in several words in the first paragraph.

5 Critical Viewing

Possible response: They are both old; the woman in the picture has white hair. Granny's personality is forceful and hard; the woman's features in the picture are portrayed in strong, angular lines.

6 Reading Check
Cause and Effect

1. Refer students to the second bracketed text, which ends on p.352. **Ask** them to restate the phrase Granny talks "with her eyebrows."

   Answer: She moves her eyebrows up and down, or squeezes them together to emphasize her feelings.
2. **Ask** students the Reading Skill question: Which details in the text help you to visualize the effect that the camera crew has on Granny?

   Possible response: Students might say that the descriptions of Granny's smile, her eyebrows, and her way of saying "Good mornin" help them to visualize the camera crew's effect.

7 Reading Check

Answer: They are filming the house and property.

PHLit Online!

This selection is available in interactive format in the **Enriched Online Student Edition, www.PHLitOnline.com,** which includes a thematically related video with writing prompt and an interactive graphic organizer.

Differentiated Instruction for Universal Access

Support for Special-Needs Students
Help students understand the dialect in this story by providing them with ***Readers Notebook: Adapted Version*** and the ***Hear It!* Audio CD** (adapted text). After students have completed the story, discuss any questions they may have. You may help clarify the author's use of dialect by providing a Standard English version of some of the words and phrases.

EL Support for English Learners
To help students understand the dialect and visualize some of the unfamiliar imagery, have them use the ***Reader's Notebook: English Learner's Version.*** Then, as a group have them listen to the ***Hear It!* Audio CD.** Discuss some of the dialect with them, providing a Standard English version of a number of the words and phrases.

Spiral Review

Character

1. Remind students that they studied the concept of character in the Unit 2 Literary Analysis workshop (pp. 196–209).
2. **Ask** students the Spiral Review question.

   Possible response: Granny's words seem polite, but her eyebrow movement and movement of the screen suggest impatience. By seeming to misunderstand on purpose, Granny reveals that she is not a pushover.

8 Literary Analysis

Dialogue and Dialect

1. Have students read the second bracketed text aloud. Then, **ask** students why Granny might be annoyed with the smiling man.

   Answer: He walks on to her property without permission and begins filming.
2. **Ask** students how the camera man addresses Granny. What does she mean by her response to him?

   Answer: He calls her "aunty"; she tells him that she is not related to his mother, implying that he should not address her with such disrespectful familiarity.
3. **Ask** students to respond to the Reading Skill question.

   Answer: The film crew is condescending and assumes that they have the right to walk onto Granny's property and begin filming without asking. Granny is angry and insulted at the disrespectful way the film crew treats her, and she refuses to cooperate with them.

9 Critical Viewing

Possible response: A woman as proud and capable as Grannie would probably tend a neat and flourishing vegetable garden like the one shown here.

Spiral Review

Character What can you tell about Granny, based on her comments and behavior?

6

"Nice things here," said the man, buzzin his camera over the yard. The pecan barrels, the sled, me and Cathy, the flowers, the printed stones along the driveway, the trees, the twins, the toolshed.

"I don't know about the thing, the it, and the stuff," said Granny, still talkin with her eyebrows. "Just people here is what I tend to consider."

Camera man stopped buzzin. Cathy giggled into her collar.

"Mornin, ladies," a new man said. He had come up behind us when we weren't lookin. "And gents," discoverin the twins givin him a nasty look. "We're filmin for the county," he said with a smile. "Mind if we shoot a bit around here?"

"I do indeed," said Granny with no smile. Smilin man was smiling up a storm. So was Cathy. But he didn't seem to have another word to say, so he and the camera man backed on out the yard, but you could hear the camera buzzin still. "Suppose you just shut that machine off," said Granny real low through her teeth, and took a step down off the porch and then another.

Literary Analysis Dialogue and Dialect What does the dialogue between Granny and the film crew show about their attitudes toward each other?

"Now, aunty," Camera said, pointin the thing straight at her.

"Your mama and I are not related."

Smilin man got his notebook out and a chewed-up pencil. "Listen," he said movin back into our yard, "we'd like to have a statement from you . . . for the film. We're filmin for the county, see. Part of the food stamp campaign. You know about the food stamps?"

Granny said nuthin.

"Maybe there's somethin you want to say for the film. I see you grow your own vegetables," he smiled real nice. "If more folks did that, see, there'd be no need—"

Granny wasn't sayin nuthin. So they backed on out, buzzin at our clothesline and the twins' bicycles, then back on down to the meadow. The twins were danglin in the tire, lookin at Granny. Me and Cathy were waitin, too, cause Granny always got somethin to say. She teaches steady with no let-up. "I was on this bridge one time," she started off. "Was a crowd cause this man was goin to jump, you understand. And a minister was there and the police and some other folks. His woman was there, too."

"What was they doin?" asked Tyrone.

9 ▶ **Critical Viewing** Does this vegetable garden seem like one Granny would tend? Why or why not? **[Connect]**

10

"Tryin to talk him out of it was what they was doin. The minister talkin about how it was a mortal sin, suicide. His woman takin bites out of her own hand and not even knowin it, so nervous and cryin and talkin fast."

"So what happened?" asked Tyrone.

"So here comes . . . this person . . . with a camera, takin pictures of the man and the minister and the woman. Takin pictures of the

Vocabulary Development

CCSS Language 6

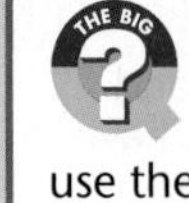

Thematic Vocabulary: The Big Question

As students are discussing "Blues Ain't No Mockin Bird," encourage them to use the thematic vocabulary presented in Introducing the Big Question, pp. 194–195. You might encourage them with sentence starters like these:

1. The film men began to *antagonize* Granny when . . .
2. Granny didn't want *controversy* but . . .
3. Rather than *cooperate,* Granny moved to . . .
4. The *differences* between Granddaddy Cain and Camera and Smilin were made apparent when . . .

man in his misery about to jump, cause life so bad and people been messin with him so bad. This person takin up the whole roll of film practically. But savin a few, of course."

10 "Of course," said Cathy, hatin the person. Me standin there wonderin how Cathy knew it was "of course" when I didn't and it was *my* grandmother.

After a while Tyrone say, "Did he jump?"

"Yeh, did he jump?" say Terry all eager. And Granny just stared at the twins till their faces swallow up the eager and they don't even care any more about the man jumpin. Then she goes back onto the porch and lets the screen door go for itself. I'm lookin to Cathy to finish the story cause she knows Granny's whole story before me even. Like she knew how come we move so much and Cathy ain't but a third cousin we picked up on the way last Thanksgivin visitin. But she knew it was on account of people drivin Granny crazy till she'd get up in the night and start packin. Mumblin and

11 
Reading Check

How does Granny respond when "Smilin" asks her to make a statement?

10 Critical Thinking

Infer

1. Read aloud the bracketed text, beginning on page 352. **Ask** students to summarize the story Granny tells in this passage.

   Answer: She sees a man about to commit suicide by jumping from a bridge; the man's wife and minister are trying to talk him out of it; meanwhile a photographer is taking photos of the event.

2. Point out that Granny says the photographer uses almost the entire roll of film, but saves a few "of course." **Ask** students why they think the photographer saved a few pictures. Why did Granny say "of course"?

   Possible response: He saved the pictures to ensure he would get a photo of the man actually jumping from the bridge. Granny says "of course" because she knows the photographer was at the scene to snap a dramatic photo of someone jumping off the bridge.

3. **Ask** students to explain Granny's attitude toward that photographer.

   Answer: She has contempt and disgust for him, because he is not interested in the welfare of the man who is suffering; he just wants to get a good picture, hoping that the man will actually jump.

11 Reading Check

Answer: She refuses to say anything.

Differentiated Instruction for Universal Access

Culturally Responsive Instruction

Culture Focus Point out to students that in some Asian cultures, people who are unknown or unrelated to older people call them "uncle" or "aunty" as a sign of respect. On the other hand, because of the history of slavery in the United States, African Americans often consider it a sign of disrespect when people other than family members call an older person "uncle" or "aunty." Such terms were used by white slave-owners addressing older enslaved African Americans and reflected attitudes of superiority. Have students discuss the light this history sheds on Granny's attitude and actions toward Camera and "Smilin Man."

⓬ Critical Thinking

Analyze

1. Have students read the bracketed text, continuing on p. 355. **Ask** students to name the common fairy tale on which Cathy is basing her story.

   Answer: She is basing her story on "Goldilocks and the Three Bears."

2. **Ask** students how Cathy's version differs from the fairy tale.

   Answer: In the fairy tale, Goldilocks is portrayed as a sweet little girl and not as someone who breaks into a house and steals and destroys things.

3. **Ask** students why they think the author includes this story, as told by Cathy.

   Possible response: The author could be pointing out that the same story can be interpreted in more than one way, depending on the viewpoint of the storyteller. The author is also pointing out that the camera crew, like Goldilocks, has no respect for people's privacy or their homes and possessions. They feel free to walk onto the property without being invited.

⓭ Literature in Context

Science Connection Even though people typically consider *carnivores* to be four-legged animals such as lions and coyotes, hawks are also carnivores because they eat mammals and small birds. Canadian scientist Dr. Louis Lefebvre recently revealed a means of measuring avian intelligence based on their inventiveness in feeding habits. According to this scale, hawks are considered one of the most intelligent birds.

Connect to the Literature Have students read the Literature in Context feature, and present the additional background information above. Point out that because some hawks mate for life, they are very protective of their mates. Then, **ask** students the Connect to the Literature question: What concerns prompt Granddaddy Cain's violence against the hawks?

Answer: Grandaddy Cain kills the first hawk to protect the family's chickens. He kills the second hawk because it flies at his family, trying to find a place to land.

Vocabulary
raggedy (rag′ i dē) *adj.* torn and in bad condition

packin and wakin everybody up sayin, "Let's get on away from here before I kill me somebody." Like people wouldn't pay her for things like they said they would. Or Mr. Judson bringin us boxes of old clothes and raggedy magazines. Or Mrs. Cooper comin in our kitchen and touchin everything and sayin how clean it all was. Granny goin crazy, and Granddaddy Cain pullin her off the people, sayin, "Now, now, Cora." But next day loadin up the truck, with rocks all in his jaw, madder than Granny in the first place.

"I read a story once," said Cathy soundin like Granny teacher. "About this lady Goldilocks who barged into a house that wasn't even hers. And not invited, you understand. Messed over the

⓭

LITERATURE IN CONTEXT

Science Connection

Hawks: Tales and Truths

A variety of hawk species, including the Northern Goshawk and the Coopers hawk, are sometimes called chickenhawks, although no such species exists. This name comes from the belief that hawks prey on chickens. While hawks do sometimes eat chickens, in reality, raccoons pose greater threats to small barnyard animals.

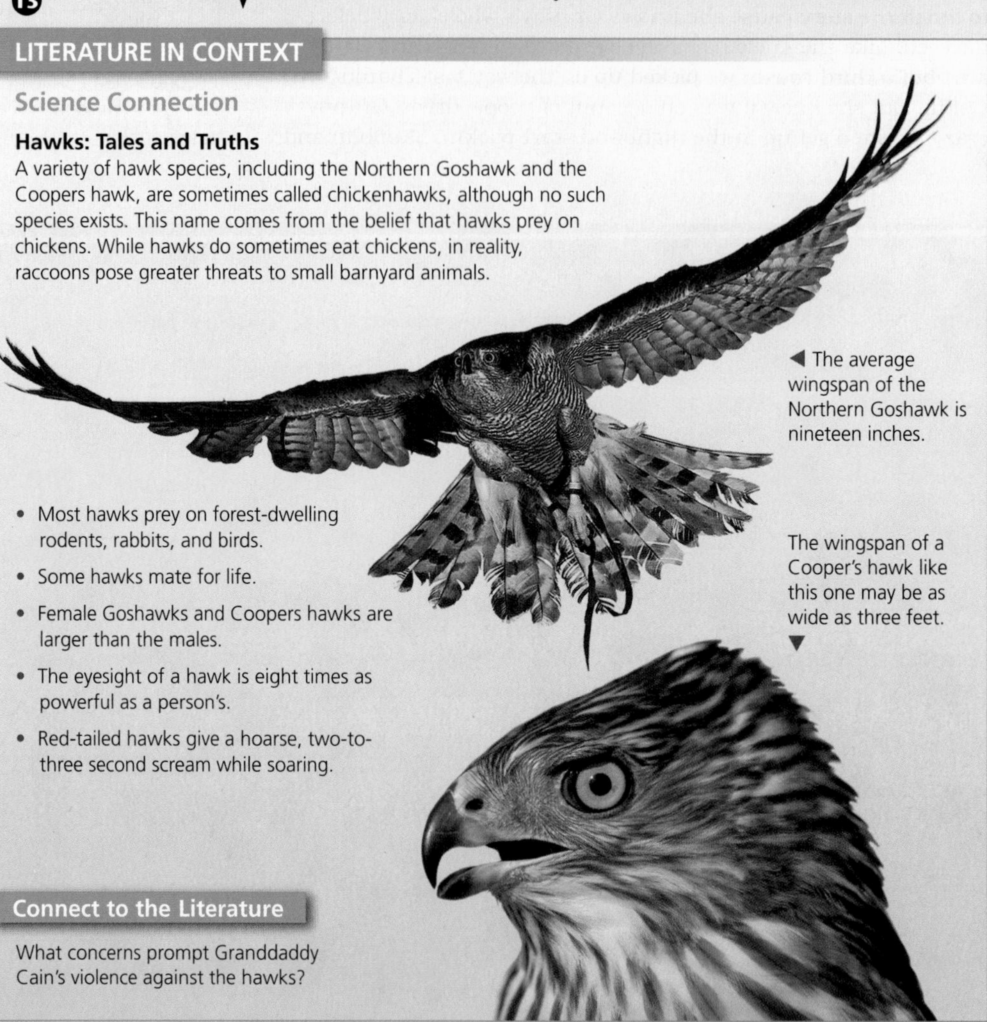

◀ The average wingspan of the Northern Goshawk is nineteen inches.

The wingspan of a Cooper's hawk like this one may be as wide as three feet. ▼

- Most hawks prey on forest-dwelling rodents, rabbits, and birds.
- Some hawks mate for life.
- Female Goshawks and Coopers hawks are larger than the males.
- The eyesight of a hawk is eight times as powerful as a person's.
- Red-tailed hawks give a hoarse, two-to-three second scream while soaring.

Connect to the Literature

What concerns prompt Granddaddy Cain's violence against the hawks?

Vocabulary Development

Ⓒ CCSS Language 6

Multiple Meanings

Direct students' attention to the word *stalks* on page 355. Have a volunteer read aloud the pertinent sentence and the glossary definition. **Ask** students to identify the part of speech *stalks* functions as in this sentence. **Answer:** It functions as a verb. Explain that *stalks* can be a verb or a noun. As a verb, it can also mean "follow or try to get close to a person, usually without being noticed" or "to walk in a steady or sinister way." As a noun, a *stalk* is the main part of a plant. It can also name a similar structure elsewhere, such as the stem of a glass or a thin supporting part of an animal's body. Challenge students to develop meaningful sentences for at least one of the noun and verb definitions for *stalks*.

2 people's groceries and broke up the people's furniture. Had the nerve to sleep in the folks' bed."

"Then what happened?" asked Tyrone. "What they do, the folks, when they come in to all this mess?"

"Did they make her pay for it?" asked Terry, makin a fist. "I'd've made her pay me."

I didn't even ask. I could see Cathy actress was very likely to just walk away and leave us in mystery about this story which I heard was about some bears.

"Did they throw her out?" asked Tyrone, like his father sounds when he's bein extra nasty-plus to the washin-machine man.

4 "Woulda," said Terry. "I woulda gone upside her head with my fist and—"

"You woulda done whatcha always do—go cry to Mama, you big baby," said Tyrone. So naturally Terry starts hittin on Tyrone, and next thing you know they tumblin out the tire and rollin on the ground. But Granny didn't say a thing or send the twins home or step out on the steps to tell us about how we can't afford to be fightin amongst ourselves. She didn't say nuthin. So I get into the tire to take my turn. And I could see her leanin up against the pantry table, staring at the cakes she was puttin up for the Christmas sale, mumblin real low and grumpy and holdin her forehead like it wanted to fall off and mess up the rum cakes.

Behind me I hear before I can see Granddaddy Cain comin through the woods in his field boots. Then I twist around to see the shiny black oilskin cuttin through what little left there was of yellows, reds, and oranges. His great white head not quite round cause of this bloody thing high on his shoulder, like he was wearin a cap on sideways. He takes the shortcut through the pecan grove, and the sound of twigs snapping overhead and underfoot travels clear and cold all the way up to us. And here comes Smilin and Camera up behind him like they was goin to do somethin. Folks like to go for him sometimes. Cathy say it's because he's so tall and quiet and like a king. And people just can't stand it. But Smilin and Camera don't hit him in the head or nuthin. They just buzz on him as he **stalks** by with the chicken hawk slung over his shoulder, squawkin, drippin red down the back of the oilskin. He passes the porch and stops a second for Granny to see he's caught the hawk at last, but she's just starin and mumblin, and not at the hawk. So he nails the bird to the toolshed door, the hammerin crackin through the eardrums. And the bird flappin himself to death and droolin down the door to paint the gravel in the driveway red, then brown, then black. And the two men movin up on tiptoe like they was invisible or we were blind, one.

Literary Analysis
Dialogue and Dialect
What does the idiom "gone upside her head" probably mean?

Vocabulary
stalks (stôks) *v.* walks in a stiff, haughty, or grim manner

15 

What does Granddaddy do with the hawk?

14 Literary Analysis

Dialogue and Dialect

1. Refer students to the second bracketed text. **Ask** them to describe Tyrone and Terry's attitude toward Goldilocks.

   Answer: They are upset that she barged into someone's house and broke their furniture.

2. **Ask** students to respond to the Literary Analysis question: What does the idiom "gone upside her head" probably mean?

   Possible response: It means he would have slapped her on the side of the head.

3. **Ask** students to identify the elements of dialect in this bracketed text.

   Answer: Elements are the dropping of the final *g* in several words, and the use of *woulda* and *whatcha*.

4. **Ask** students to read this sentence: "You woulda done whatcha always do—go cry to Mama, you big baby," said Tyrone. Then, have them rephrase the sentence in Standard English.

   Answer: The Standard English would read, "You would have done what you always do. . . . "

15 Reading Check

Answer: He nails the bird to the toolshed door.

Differentiated Instruction for Universal Access

Enrichment for Advanced Readers

Remind students that authors always have a reason for including an anecdote or a detail. Have students discuss why the author included the incident with the two hawks. What might the two hawks in this story stand for? You might have students consider the following facts about hawks:

- Hawks are birds of prey.
- Female hawks are usually larger than male hawks.
- Hawks mate for life.

Have students consider whether the two hawks stand for Granny and Granddaddy. Have them explain their thinking and support their answers. Ask whether students think the hawks might represent the photographers who prey on rural families to make their documentary. Again, have them explain their thinking and support their answers.

 Reading Skill

Cause and Effect

1. Have students read the first bracketed text. Then have them imagine the children falling to the ground. **Ask** why the children fall down on the ground when the flying hawk appears.

   Answer: They are afraid the hawk will grab their hair or try to land on their head.

2. **Ask** students what they think the children are probably doing with their hands as they lie on the gravel driveway.

   Answer: They are probably holding their hands over their heads to protect themselves from the swooping hawk.

3. **Ask** students the Reading Skill question: How does the arrival of the screaming hawk affect the film crew? How does it affect Granddaddy Cain?

   Possible response: The film crew are scared, running around, ducking, and jiggling the camera. Granddaddy stands straight, watching the hawk, not appearing to be afraid.

▶ **Monitor Progress:** Remind students that there are two types of intruders from which Granddaddy Cain is trying to protect his family.

▶ **Reteach:** If students have difficulty identifying the similarities between the second hawk and the camera man and Smilin, have them reread the bracketed passage. Tell students that this passage includes details about how the scared hawk and men seem similarly frenzied, but that Granddaddy Cain is calm and focused as he protects his family. Urge students to add these visual details to their Cause-and-Effect Charts.

Vocabulary

formality (fôr mal´ ə tē) *n.* attention to established rules or customs

reckless (rek´ lis) *adj.* careless; rash

"Get them persons out of my flower bed, Mister Cain," say Granny moanin real low like at a funeral.

"How come your grandmother calls her husband 'Mister Cain' all the time?" Tyrone whispers all loud and noisy and from the city and don't know no better. Like his mama, Miss Myrtle, tell us never mind the formality as if we had no better breeding than to call her Myrtle, plain. And then this awful thing—a giant hawk—come wailin up over the meadow, flyin low and tilted and screamin, zigzaggin through the pecan grove, breakin branches and hollerin, snappin past the clothesline, flyin every which way, flyin into things reckless with crazy.

"He's come to claim his mate," say Cathy fast, and ducks down. We all fall quick and flat into the gravel driveway, stones scrapin my face. I squinch my eyes open again at the hawk on the door, tryin to fly up out of her death like it was just a sack flown into by mistake. Her body holdin her there on that nail, though. The mate beatin the air overhead and clutchin for hair, for heads, for landin space.

16 The camera man duckin and bendin and runnin and fallin, jigglin the camera and scared. And Smilin jumpin up and down swipin at the huge bird, tryin to bring the hawk down with just his raggedy ole cap. Granddaddy Cain straight up and silent, watchin the circles of the hawk, then aimin the hammer off his wrist. The giant bird fallin, silent and slow. Then here comes Camera and Smilin all big and bad now that the awful screechin thing is on its back and broken, here they come. And Granddaddy Cain looks up at them like it was the first time noticin, but not payin them too much mind cause he's listenin, we all listenin, to that low groanin music comin from the porch. And we figure any minute, somethin in my back tells me any minute now, Granny gonna bust through that screen with somethin in her hand and murder on her mind. So Granddaddy say above the buzzin, but quiet, "Good day, gentlemen." Just like that. Like he'd invited them in to play cards and they'd stayed too long and all the sandwiches were gone and Reverend Webb was droppin by and it was time to go.

Reading Skill
Cause and Effect
How does the arrival of the screaming hawk affect the film crew? How does it affect Granddaddy Cain?

 They didn't know what to do. But like Cathy say, folks can't stand Granddaddy tall and silent and like a king. They can't neither. The smile the men smilin is pullin the mouth back and showin the teeth. Lookin like the wolf man, both of them. Then Granddaddy holds his hand out—this huge hand I used to sit in when I was a baby and he'd carry me through the house to my mother like I was a gift on a tray. Like he used to on the trains. They called the other men just waiters. But they spoke of Granddaddy separate and said, The Waiter. And said he had engines in his feet and motors in his

Vocabulary Development

Vocabulary Knowledge Rating

When students have completed reading and discussing "Blues Ain't No Mockin Bird," have them take out their **Vocabulary Knowledge Rating Chart** for this selection. Read the words aloud once more and have students rate their knowledge of the words again in the After Reading column. Clarify any words that are still problematic. Have students write their own definition and example or sentence in the appropriate column. Then have students complete the Vocabulary Practice at the end of the selection. Encourage students to use the words in further discussion and written work about this selection. Remind them that they will be accountable for these words on the **Selection Test,** ***Unit 2 Resources,*** pp. 178–180 or 181–183.

hands and couldn't no train throw him off and couldn't nobody turn him round. They were big enough for motors, his hands were. He held that one hand out all still and it gettin to be not at all a hand but a person in itself.

17 "He wants you to hand him the camera," Smilin whispers to Camera, tiltin his head to talk secret like they was in the jungle or somethin and come upon a native that don't speak the language. The men start untyin the straps, and they put the camera into that great hand speckled with the hawk's blood all black and crackly now. And the hand don't even drop with the weight, just the fingers move, curl up around the machine. But Granddaddy lookin straight at the men. They lookin at each other and everywhere but at Granddaddy's face.

"We filmin for the county, see," say Smilin. "We puttin together a movie for the food stamp program . . . filmin all around these parts. Uhh, filmin for the county."

"Can I have my camera back?" say the tall man with no machine on his shoulder, but still keepin it high like the camera was still there or needed to be. "Please, sir."

Then Granddaddy's other hand flies up like a sudden and gentle bird, slaps down fast on top of the camera and lifts off half like it was a calabash[1] cut for sharing.

"Hey," Camera jumps forward. He gathers up the parts into his chest and everything unrollin and fallin all over. "Whatcha tryin to do? You'll ruin the film." He looks down into his chest of metal **reels** and things like he's protectin a kitten from the cold.

"You standin in the misses' flower bed," say Granddaddy. "This is our own place."

The two men look at him, then at each other, then back at the mess in the camera man's chest, and they just back off. One sayin over and over all the way down to the meadow, "Watch it, Bruno. Keep ya fingers off the film." Then Granddaddy picks up the hammer and jams it into the oilskin pocket, scrapes his boots, and goes into the house. And you can hear the squish of his boots

"You standin in the misses' flower bed," say Granddaddy. "This is our own place."

1. **calabash** (kal′ ə bash′) *n.* large gourd-like fruit.

Vocabulary
reels (rēlz) *n.* frames or spools on which thread, wire, tape, film, or a net is wound

19

18

Reading Check
How does Granddaddy Cain react to the camera men's visit?

17 Connecting to the Big Question

1. **Invite** students to share different ways that people convey that they have a problem. Prompt students with examples, such as quiet requests, loud requests, and even physical actions of demand.
2. Have students read the bracketed text on pages 356–357. **Ask** students: How does Granddaddy respond to the situation that is bothering Granny? What attitude does his behavior suggest?

   Possible response: He quietly dismisses the men and holds out a hand for their camera. His behavior suggests that he expects to be respected and obeyed.
3. **Ask:** Is Granddaddy's conflict with the two men necessary? What would he have to do to avoid the conflict?

   Possible response: It is necessary because Granddaddy is protecting Granny, who doesn't want the men filming her. To avoid the conflict, Granddaddy would have to allow the man to bother Granny.

18 Reading Check

Answer: He asks the men for the camera and they give it to him. After they ask for the camera back, Granddaddy Cain uses his free hand to hit the camera with his hammer and tells the men that they're standing in his wife's flower bed.

Concept Connector

Anticipation Guide

Have students return to their **Anticipation Guides** and respond to the statements again in the After Reading column. Then, lead a class discussion, probing for what students have learned that confirms or invalidates each statement.

Writing About the Big Question

Have students compare their responses to the sentence starters they completed before they read the story with their ideas afterwards. Ask them to explain whether their thoughts have changed.

Reading Skill Graphic Organizer

Have students review the graphic organizers they completed to visualize the action to analyze cause and effect. Show them the **Reading Skill Graphic Organizer A** (*Graphic Organizer Transparencies,* p. 62) as an example. Then, have students share the graphic organizers they did and the details they visualized to help them determine cause and effect.

⑲ Reading Skill

Cause and Effect

1. Refer students to the bracketed text, which begins on p. 357. **Ask** students what expression they visualize on Granddaddy's face. What is the tone of his voice?

   Answer: He probably looks very stern and unsmiling; his voice probably sounds firm and unfriendly, maybe even threatening.
2. **Ask** students what expression they visualize on the two men's faces.

   Answer: They probably look alarmed, maybe even frightened.
3. **Ask** students the Reading Skill question: In what way does visualizing this scene help you understand the effects of Granddaddy's action?

   Possible responses: Visualizing helps one understand that Granddaddy is probably threatening to the two men, and they are probably afraid of him.

ASSESS

Answers

Critical Thinking

Before students respond, you may wish to have them write a brief objective summary of the selection. As they answer the questions below, remind them to support their answers with evidence from the text.

1. (a) They are making a documentary about the food-stamp program. (b) She is asserting her dignity and personal rights; she is expressing anger at their trespassing.
2. (a) They swoop down on people; they are frightening or threatening; they stay together. (b) He is threatening when threatened; he tries to protect his mate and drive away enemies.
3. **Possible response:** The hawks represent Granny and Granddaddy, since the intruders have threatened Granny and Granddaddy, her mate, is trying to protect her.
4. **Possible responses:** (a) The cameramen are disrespectful and ignore Granny. They try to be disrespectful to Granddaddy also, but he won't allow it. (b) Granny uses talk and Granddaddy uses force. The cameramen do not respond to words; they only respond to force.

Reading Skill
Cause and Effect
In what way does visualizing this scene help you understand the effects of Granddaddy's action?

⑲ headin through the house. And you can see the funny shadow he throws from the parlor window onto the ground by the string-bean patch. The hammer draggin the pocket of the oilskin out so Granddaddy looked even wider. Granny was hummin now—high not low and grumbly. And she was doin the cakes again, you could smell the molasses from the rum.

"There's this story I'm goin to write one day," say Cathy dreamer. "About the proper use of the hammer."

"Can I be in it?" Tyrone say with his hand up like it was a matter of first come, first served.

"Perhaps," say Cathy, climbin onto the tire to pump us up. "If you there and ready."

Critical Thinking

Cite textual evidence to support your responses.

1. **Key Ideas and Details (a)** Why are the photographers filming in the area? **(b) Infer:** What message does Granny give the men through her speech and actions?
2. **Key Ideas and Details** Make a chart like the one shown below. **(a) Compare:** In the first column, write the ways that Camera and Smilin are like the hawks. **(b) Connect:** In the second column, write the ways that Granddaddy's actions are like the actions of the male hawk.
3. **Integration of Knowledge and Ideas Discuss:** Share your chart with a partner, and discuss your responses. Then, in the third column, explain whether you think the hawks represent Granddaddy and Granny, Smilin and Camera, or both pairs.

Hawks and Camera and Smilin	Hawks and Granddaddy	What the Hawks Represent

4. **Integration of Knowledge and Ideas (a)** Why does Granddaddy become involved in the story's conflict? **(b)** Why is his way of handling the conflict successful, when Granny's is not? *[Connect to the Big Question: Is conflict necessary?]*

Assessment Resources

Unit 2 Resources

L1 L2 EL **Selection Test A,** pp. 178–180. Administer Test A to less advanced readers.

L3 L4 EL **Selection Test B,** pp. 181–183. Administer Test B to on-level and more advanced students.

L3 L4 **Open-Book Test,** pp. 175–177. As an alternative, give the Open-Book Test.

All **Customizable Test Bank**

All **Self-tests**
Students may prepare for the **Selection Test** by taking the **Self-test** online.

PHLit Online! All assessment resources are available at **www.PHLitOnline.com**.

After You Read

Blues Ain't No Mockin Bird

Literary Analysis: Dialogue and Dialect

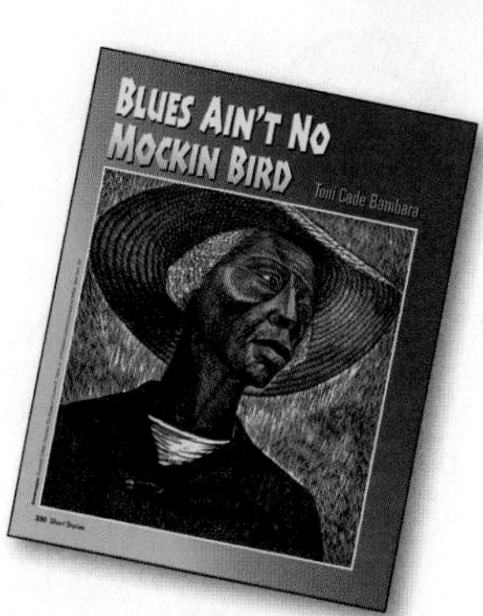

1. **Key Ideas and Details** Identify one example of **dialogue** that indicates the tension is increasing between Granny and the filmmakers.
2. **Key Ideas and Details** Identify one example of dialogue that shows Granny is tough.
3. **Craft and Structure** **(a)** Explain how the spelling and grammar used in the following passage indicate that it is an example of **dialect.** "Granny always got somethin to say. She teaches steady with no let-up." **(b)** Rewrite the passage in Standard English. **(c)** Explain how the use of dialect makes the characters and setting more vivid.

Reading Skill: Cause and Effect

4. **(a)** What is the **cause** of Granddaddy's decision to disassemble the men's camera? **(b)** What is the **effect** of Granddaddy's action on the cameramen? **(c)** What is the effect on Granny?
5. Which visual details in the story help you explain the causes and effects of Granddaddy's decision to ruin the film?

Vocabulary

Acquisition and Use In vocabulary study, **analogies** show the relationships between pairs of words. Use a word from the "Blues Ain't No Mockin Bird" vocabulary list on page 348 to complete each analogy. In each, your choice should create a word pair that matches the relationship between the first two words given. Explain the relationship that the pairs in each set share.

1. solution : intelligent :: accident : ____________
2. sportsmanship : game :: ____________ : ceremony
3. fork : meat :: ____________ : soup
4. frowns : scowls :: walks : ____________
5. powerful : weak :: unworn : ____________
6. carton : eggs :: ____________ : film

Word Study Use the context of the sentences and what you know about the **Latin suffix *-ity*** to explain your answer to each question.

1. If a plan is referred to as a *possibility,* might it be used?
2. When people take a *sensitivity* training class, what do they learn?

Word Study

The **Latin suffix *-ity*** forms nouns from adjectives. It means "the quality of showing a certain characteristic."

Apply It Explain how the suffix *-ity* contributes to the meanings of these words. You may consult a dictionary if necessary.

intensity
eccentricity
gravity

ASSESS/EXTEND

Answers

Literary Analysis

1. **Possible response:** When Granny says, "I don't know about the thing, the it, and the stuff . . . Just people here is what I tend to consider," she shows the man taking pictures that she resents his intrusion.
2. **Possible response:** When Granny says, "Your mama and I are not related," she shows that she will stand up to Camera.
3. (a) The use of "always got," instead of "always has," and "teaches steady," instead of "teaches steadily," are grammatical examples of dialect. The spelling of *something* without the *g* shows that the speaker pronounces the word according to dialect. (b) Granny always has something to say. She teaches steadily, with no pauses. (c) Dialect makes the characters seem more vivid because it makes it easier to imagine the characters as rural African Americans from the South.

Reading Skill

4. **Possible responses:** (a) The men have taken motion pictures of his family. (b) They become intimidated and leave. (c) She begins humming and seems happy.
5. The details that help to visualize the causes are the man "buzzin his camera over the yard," the smiling man with his notebook and pencil, and the men looking at each other after Granddaddy takes the camera. The effects include the cameraman clutching the film to his chest, and the men backing away.

Vocabulary

Acquisition and Use

Sample answers:

1. *reckless;* Both pairs connect a type of behavior with its result.
2. *formality;* Both pairs link a quality to an event.
3. *ladle;* Both pairs connect a tool with a food.
4. *stalks;* Both pairs are synonyms.

Answers Continued

5. *raggedy;* Both pairs are antonyms.
6. *Reels* hold *film* as a *carton* holds *eggs.*

Word Study

Sample answers:

1. Yes, the suffix *-ity* means "the quality of having a characteristic." Something that is only a *possibility* has the characteristic of being possible, but is not necessarily real.
2. They acquire *sensitivity,* or the characteristic of being aware of other people's feelings.

Word Study: Apply It

Sample answers:

Something that is felt with *intensity* has the characteristic of force. Someone who exhibits *eccentricity* shows the characteristic of oddness. A situation that has *gravity* has the characteristic of importance.

PRETEACH

Skills instruction for the ***Reading Skill*** *and* ***Literary Analysis*** *concept appears on p. 347.*

❶ Writing About the Big Question

1. Review the assignment with the class.
2. **Ask** volunteers to describe a circumstance when little or incorrect information led them to jump to a wrong conclusion.
3. Have students complete the sentence starters **(Possible response:** Lack of information can lead to a humorous conflict because it can create an entertaining misunderstanding. It can also lead to serious issues and sometimes controversy because the misunderstanding might result in negative consequences.) Review responses as a class.
4. Remind students that their answers will help them think about the Big Question, "Is conflict necessary?"

While You Read

Tell students as they read to analyze why lack of information increases the problem, and the humor.

❷ Vocabulary

1. Have students preview the selection vocabulary.
2. For each word, have students say the word aloud.
3. Then, use the word in a sentence that defines the word.
4. Repeat your definitional sentence or a similar sentence with the word missing, and have the class "fill in the blank" chorally. Here are some examples:

   Something ominous is threatening. When we heard thunder and saw bolts of lightning we knew to go inside because the weather had turned [students say "ominous"].

   Placidly means calmly or quietly. Though I was nervous about playing, I tried not to show it by facing the audience [students say "placidly"].

❸ Word Study

1. Introduce the skill, using the instruction in the box.
2. Ask students for an *-ious* word with a meaning like *judicious*. (**Answer:** *cautious*; "careful")

❶ Writing About the Big Question

In "The Invalid's Story," the two main characters try to resolve a problem but do not have all the facts. Use these sentence starters to develop your ideas about the Big Question.

Lack of information can lead to a humorous conflict because ________.
It can also lead to serious **issues** and sometimes **controversy** because ________.

While You Read Look for ways in which the lack of information makes the problem more intense—and funnier—as time passes.

❷ Vocabulary

Read each word and its definition. Decide whether you know the word well, know it a little bit, or do not know it at all. After you read, see how your knowledge of each word has increased.

- **prodigious** (prō dij′ əs) *adj.* enormous (p. 364) ***The Grand Canyon is a prodigious natural wonder.*** *prodigiously adv. prodigiousness n.*
- **deleterious** (del′ ə tir′ ē əs) *adj.* harmful to health or well-being (p. 365) ***Too much sun can be deleterious to one's skin.*** *deleteriously adv. deleteriousness n.*
- **ominous** (äm′ ə nəs) *adj.* threatening (p. 365) ***The black storm clouds coming from the West were ominous.*** *ominously adv. ominousness n. omen n.*
- **judicious** (jo͞o dish′ əs) *adj.* showing good judgment (p. 366) ***Her decision to stay indoors during the storm was judicious.*** *judiciously adv. judiciousness n. judge n. judge v.*
- **placidly** (plas′ id lē) *adv.* calmly; quietly (p. 366) ***He smiled placidly, content with his own thoughts.*** *placid adj. placidity n.*
- **desultory** (des′ əl tôr′ ē) *adj.* random (p. 367) ***They wandered through the park in a desultory way, with no clear destination.*** *desultorily adv.*

❸ Word Study

The **Latin suffix *-ous*** (or ***-ious*** or ***-uous***) forms adjectives. It means "like" or "pertaining to."

In this story, the narrator talks about "an **ominous** stillness." The stillness feels like an omen, something that foretells a future danger.

Vocabulary Development

Vocabulary Knowledge Rating

Create a **Vocabulary Knowledge Rating Chart** (***Professional Development Guidebook***, p. 33) for this selection. Include the selection vocabulary and the words that appear in the Writing About the Big Question sentence starters on this page. (The Big Question vocabulary is introduced on pp. 194–195.)

Give students a copy of the chart. Read the words aloud, and have students mark their rating in the Before Reading column. Urge them to be alert to these words as they read and discuss the selection.

Tally how many students think they know a word to gauge how much instruction to provide. As students read and discuss the selection, point out the words and their context.

Vocabulary Central, featuring tools, activities, and songs for studying vocabulary, is available at **www.PHLitOnline.com.**

Meet Mark Twain (1835–1910)

Author of The Invalid's Story

Born Samuel Clemens, Mark Twain grew up in the Mississippi River town of Hannibal, Missouri. He worked as a riverboat pilot, printer, prospector, reporter, and at many other jobs. Primarily, however, Clemens was a writer of comic stories, sketches, and novels. The most famous humorist of his day, he traveled the world entertaining people with his witty lectures.

"By the mark—twain" was a cry heard on the riverboats of Clemens's youth. It meant that the water was two fathoms deep—deep enough for a riverboat to pass unharmed. Harkening back to his youth working on those boats, Clemens took the name Mark Twain at age twenty-seven. Under that name, he wrote some of the most beloved fiction in American literature.

❹ BACKGROUND FOR THE STORY

Nineteenth-Century Train Travel

In the late nineteenth century, when this story takes place, trains were the fastest way to travel and transport cargo. Nonetheless, train cars in which people with cargo had to travel were uncomfortable. The cars were poorly ventilated boxes on wheels, and had only small windows.

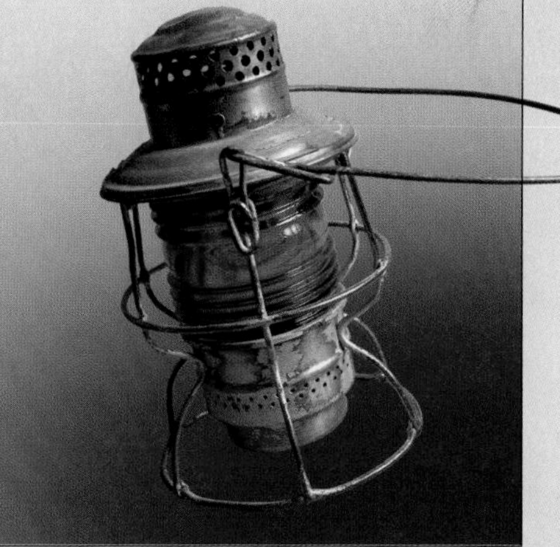

Did You Know?

Mark Twain was the first writer to turn himself into a business. He even trademarked his name!

Daily Bellringer

For each class during which you will teach this selection, have students complete one of the five Research activities for Week 11 in the *Daily Bellringer Activities* booklet.

❹ Background

Nineteenth-Century Train Travel

Mark Twain wrote this story in 1877, during the American railroad's Golden Age, when trains were the dominant form of transportation for both people and products. Twelve years earlier—on May 10, 1869—the Central Pacific and Union Pacific railroad lines had been connected in Promontory, Utah. The transcontinental railroad was a monumental achievement of engineering that changed America. It involved the laying of 1,777 miles of track through forests and mountains and across rivers and deserts. What had once been a six-month journey across the nation could now be completed in six days.

Multidraft Reading

This icon ● marks natural pauses in the selection. To assist struggling readers and to deepen reading for all, assign the text in "chunks," following the icons, and apply multidraft reading protocols. For each reading, have students set the purpose indicated:

- **First reading**—identifying key ideas and details and answering any Reading Checks.
- **Second reading**—analyzing craft and structure and responding to the side-column prompts.
- **Third reading**—integrating knowledge and ideas, connecting to other texts and the world, and answering the end-of-selection questions.

For more guidance, refer to the *Classroom Strategies and Teaching Routines* card on multidraft reading.

Differentiated Instruction — Additional Instruction

EL Extended Support—English Learners

Have students complete the **Reading and Vocabulary Warm-ups,** *Unit 2 Resources,* pp. 184–187, before they read. Assign the prereading pages in the *Reader's Notebook: English Learner's Version.* Then, have students listen to portions of the selection on the *Hear It!* **Audio CD.**

L1 L2 Extended Support—Struggling Readers

Have students complete the **Reading and Vocabulary Warm-ups,** *Unit 2 Resources,* pp. 184–187, before they read. Assign the prereading pages and the adapted selection in the *Reader's Notebook: Adapted Version.* Then, have students listen to portions of the selection on the *Hear It!* **Audio CD** (adapted text).

Extended Support—Reluctant Readers

To build motivation and engagement before assigning the selection, have students read "Giving Back," a thematically related selection in *Reality Central.* Then, use the questions at the conclusion of the related selection to guide discussion.

PHLit Online!

For more about the author, practice with the selection vocabulary, or more background, go online at **www.PHLitOnline.com.**

TEACH

❶ Activating Prior Knowledge

1. Prepare and have students complete an **Anticipation Guide** (***Professional Development Guidebook***, pp. 36–38) with the following statements:
   - It is wrong to make fun of the dead.
   - Death can be a source of humor.
   - Superstitions can be humorous.
   - Exaggeration adds to humor.
2. Give students a copy of the prepared **Anticipation Guide** and have them mark their responses in the Me column. Have students discuss the statements in groups and mark the Guides again in the Group column.
3. For further guidance, use the ***Classroom Strategies and Teaching Routines*** card **Using an Anticipation Guide.**

Concept Connector

Students will return to the Anticipation Guide after completing "The Invalid's Story."

Individual Activity

As students read, invite them to paint or draw the two men in the railroad car. Have them review the details of the time period, setting, mood, and characters to decide how they will depict the scene. Remind them to consider the personalities of the characters as well as conditions inside and outside the car.

❷ About the Selection

Death permeates Mark Twain's comic story in a very physical way. The narrator tells the story of the train trip he takes to bring the body of his newly deceased friend to his final resting place. The narrator and railway expressman suffer intolerably from what they believe is the odor of the decomposing corpse. They struggle in a foul-smelling railway express car to maintain an unbearable and, as it happens, unnecessary vigil over a dead body, according to the parameters and conventions of civilized society. The vigil is unnecessary because the coffin has been mistakenly replaced by a box of guns, and the foul smell is coming from a bag of Limburger cheese.

Vocabulary Development

Ⓒ CCSS Language 6

Thematic Vocabulary: The Big Question

As students are discussing "The Invalid's Story," encourage them to use the thematic vocabulary presented in Introducing the Big Question, pp. 194–195. You might encourage them with sentence starters like these:

1. The men began the journey *amicably* until . . .
2. They tried to ignore the *issue* of . . .
3. At first, the men couldn't *articulate* . . .
4. You wouldn't think a dead person could cause *controversy* but . . .

❶ ❷ # The Invalid's Story

Mark Twain

I seem sixty and married, but these effects are due to my condition and sufferings, for I am a bachelor, and only forty-one. It will be hard for you to believe that I, who am now but a shadow, was a hale, hearty man two short years ago—a man of iron, a very athlete!—yet such is the simple truth. But stranger still than this fact is the way in which I lost my health. I lost it through helping to take care of a box of guns on a two-hundred-mile railway journey one winter's night. It is the actual truth, and I will tell you about it.

I belong in Cleveland, Ohio. One winter's night, two years ago, I reached home just after dark, in a driving snowstorm, and the first thing I heard when I entered the house was that my dearest boyhood friend and schoolmate, John B. Hackett, had died the day before, and that his last utterance had been a desire that I would take his remains home to his poor old father and mother in Wisconsin. I was greatly shocked and grieved, but there was no time to waste in emotions; I must start at once. I took the card, marked "Deacon Levi Hackett, Bethlehem, Wisconsin," and hurried off through the whistling storm to the railway station. Arrived there I found the long white-pine box which had been described to me; I fastened the card to it with some tacks, saw it put safely aboard the express car, and then ran into the eating room to provide myself with a sandwich and some cigars. When I returned, presently, there was my coffin-box back again, apparently, and a young fellow examining around it, with a card in his hands, and some tacks and

❸ 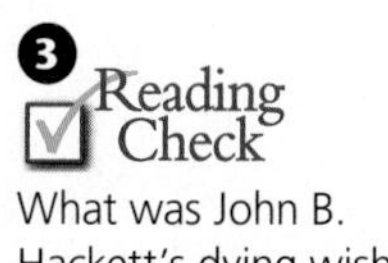

What was John B. Hackett's dying wish?

❸ Reading Check

Answer: His dying wish was that the narrator take his body back to his parents in Wisconsin.

PHLit Online!

This selection is available in interactive format in the **Enriched Online Student Edition, www.PHLitOnline.com,** which includes a thematically related video with writing prompt and an interactive graphic organizer.

Fluency

Direct students to the second paragraph on page 363, beginning "I belong in Cleveland, Ohio." Begin by reading the paragraph fluently and with expression as students track or follow along in the text by pointing to each word. Point out to students that they should use punctuation as markers that tell them when to pause and when to stop. Explain that when they see a comma, they should pause and then continue reading. When they come to a period, they should stop before continuing on to the next sentence.

After you have read the passage, have the students read it aloud together. After they have read it as a group, have students read it to themselves. Then call on a volunteer to read the passage aloud to the group.

4 Connecting to the Big Question

1. Recount an assumption you made about an item of food, perhaps from the cuisine of another culture. **Invite** students to share similar assumptions, then discuss how easy it is to make incorrect assumptions if we lack information.
2. Have students read the bracketed text on page 364. **Ask** students: What information does the narrator lack at the time he is riding the train? What funny situation appears to be arising as a result of this? **Possible response:** He doesn't know that the boxes have been switched. He doesn't know that Limburger cheese has a strong and unpleasant smell. He thinks the bad smell of the cheese is coming from his box, which he thinks contains a corpse.
3. **Ask:** Is the conflict developing in the story necessary? Why or why not? **Possible response:** In fact, the conflict is not necessary. It results from a misunderstanding of information by the narrator.

5 Critical Viewing

Possible response: Students might say that getting from place to place was not easy or comfortable in 1874. In a train heated by a stove such as the one shown, for instance, passengers near the stove would probably have been too warm, while those seated farther away might have been chilled.

a hammer! I was astonished and puzzled. He began to nail on his card, and I rushed out to the express car, in a good deal of a state of mind, to ask for an explanation. But no—there was my box, all right, in the express car; it hadn't been disturbed. [The fact is that without my suspecting it a prodigious mistake had been made. I was carrying off a box of guns which that young fellow had come to the station to ship to a rifle company in Peoria, Illinois, and he had got my corpse.] Just then the conductor sang out "All aboard," and I jumped into the express car and got a comfortable seat on a bale of buckets. The expressman was there, hard at work—a plain man of fifty, with a simple, honest, good-natured face, and a breezy, practical heartiness in his general style. As the train moved off a stranger skipped into the car and set a package of peculiarly mature and capable Limburger cheese[1] on one end of my coffin-box—I mean my box of guns. That is to say, I know now that it was Limburger cheese, but at that time I never had heard of the article in my life, and of course was wholly ignorant of its character. Well, we sped through the wild night, the bitter storm raged on, a cheerless misery stole over me, my heart went down, down, down! The old expressman made a brisk remark or two about the tempest and the arctic weather, slammed his sliding doors to, and bolted them, closed his window down tight, and then went bustling around, here and there and yonder, setting things to rights, and all the time contentedly humming "Sweet By and By" in a low tone, and flatting a good deal. Presently I began to detect a most evil and searching odor stealing about on the frozen air. This depressed my spirits still more, because of course I attributed it to my poor departed friend. There was something infinitely saddening about his calling himself to my remembrance in this dumb, pathetic way, so it was hard to

Vocabulary
prodigious (prō dij´ əs) *adj.* enormous

4

▶ **Critical Viewing**
This potbellied stove would have been found in a train car in the late 1800s. What challenges did train travel pose at that time in history? **[Analyze]**

1. **Limburger cheese** cheese with a strong odor.

Vocabulary Development

CCSS Language 6

Vocabulary Selection Reinforcement

Students will benefit from additional examples and practice with the selection vocabulary words. Reinforce their comprehension with "show-you-know" sentences. Model the strategy with this example for *deleterious:*

The effects of the medication were *deleterious*; his condition grew worse.

1. He made a *judicious* selection when he chose his vice-presidential running mate; ____________________
   Sample answer: they won the election by a landslide.
2. The waves *placidly* lapped the sandy shore; ____________________
   Sample answer: it was a quiet and peaceful scene.
3. She made a *desultory* choice of an outfit to wear to the party; ____________________
   Sample answer: she just grabbed the first thing she saw in her closet.

keep the tears back. Moreover, it distressed me on account of the old expressman, who, I was afraid, might notice it. However, he went humming tranquilly on, and gave no sign; and for this I was grateful. Grateful, yes, but still uneasy; and soon I began to feel more and more uneasy every minute, for every minute that went by that odor thickened up the more, and got to be more and more gamy and hard to stand. Presently, having got things arranged to his satisfaction, the expressman got some wood and made up a tremendous fire in his stove. This distressed me more than I can tell, for I could not but feel that it was a mistake. I was sure that the effect would be deleterious upon my poor departed friend. Thompson—the expressman's name was Thompson, as I found out in the course of the night—now went poking around his car, stopping up whatever stray cracks he could find, remarking that it didn't make any difference what kind of a night it was outside, he calculated to make us comfortable, anyway. I said nothing, but I believed he was not choosing the right way. Meantime he was humming to himself just as before; and meantime, too, the stove was getting hotter and hotter, and the place closer and closer. I felt myself growing pale and qualmish,[2] but grieved in silence and said nothing. Soon I noticed that the "Sweet By and By" was gradually fading out; next it ceased altogether, and there was an ominous stillness. After a few moments Thompson said—

"Pfew! I reckon it ain't no cinnamon't I've loaded up thish-year stove with!"

He gasped once or twice, then moved toward the cof—gun-box, stood over that Limburger cheese part of a moment, then came back and sat down near me, looking a good deal impressed. After a contemplative pause, he said, indicating the box with a gesture—

"Friend of yourn?"

"Yes," I said with a sigh.

"He's pretty ripe, ain't he!"

"Pfew! I reckon it ain't no cinnamon't I've loaded up thish-year stove with!"

Nothing further was said for perhaps a couple of minutes, each being busy with his own thoughts; then Thompson said, in a low awed voice—

"Sometimes it's uncertain whether they're really gone or not—seem gone, you know—body warm, joints limber—and so, although you think they're gone, you don't really

2. **qualmish** (kwäm´ ish) *adj.* suddenly sick.

Vocabulary
deleterious (del´ ə tir´ ē əs) *adj.* harmful to health or well-being

Vocabulary
ominous (äm´ ə nəs) *adj.* threatening

Reading Skill
Cause and Effect
When you picture this scene, what details explain the cause of Thompson's gasp?

7 

What does the narrator say depressed his spirits?

6 Reading Skill
Cause and Effect

1. Have students read the bracketed text. **Ask** why the narrator believes Thompson was not choosing the right way to make them comfortable.

   Answer: The narrator knows that the odor will get worse when the car is closed up.

2. Tell students that the tune Thompson is humming, "Sweet By and By," is a church hymn that refers to the afterlife. **Ask** students how this detail adds to the humor of the scene.

   Possible response: Students may say that the tune, which is about the afterlife, relates to the corpse in the coffin. The title of the hymn contains the word "sweet," which is the opposite of the odor in the car.

3. **Ask** students to respond to the Reading Skill question: When you picture this scene, what details explain the cause of Thompson's gasp?

   Possible response: The heat in the car makes the Limburger cheese smell worse; Thompson stops humming his tune; he makes the exclamation "pfew"; he comments that it does not smell like he has put cinnamon in the stove.

7 Reading Check

Answer: His spirits were depressed by the storm and later by the stench.

Differentiated Instruction for Universal Access

Strategy for Special-Needs Students
Students may be confused by the fact that readers know early on that the coffin has been replaced with a box of guns. They may wonder why the narrator and the expressman do not know it. Refer students to the opening paragraph that tells them that the narrator is telling the story long after it happened. Point out to students the passage at the top of page 364 that begins "The fact is that without my suspecting it. . . ."

EL Pronunciation for English Learners
To help students master the short *-i* sound, post these words: *feel, fill, sheep, ship, steel, still,* and *leap, lip.* Pronounce each word, stressing the vowel sound in each pair of contrasting words. Have students echo. Call out words at random as students write them out. Have students compare and discuss results. Discuss incorrect choices and clarify.

Spiral Review

Character

1. Remind students that they studied the concept of plot devices in the Unit 2 Literary Analysis workshop (pp. 196–209).
2. **Ask** students the Spiral Review question.

   Possible response: Thomspon's view of life is that it is uncertain. He seems to take life and death in stride. It is not easy to fluster this character.

8 Critical Thinking

Analyze

1. Refer students to the bracketed text. **Ask** them what Thompson is talking about in this passage.

   Answer: He is talking about the inevitability of death.
2. **Ask** students what the narrator means when he says that Thompson "stretched his nose out." Why did Thompson do this?

   Answer: He put his face out the window to get some fresh air. The odor in the car was unbearable.
3. **Ask** students what the men believed was causing the odor. What was actually causing the odor? What was actually in the pine box?

   Answer: The men believed a decaying corpse in the box was causing the odor. Limburger cheese was actually causing the odor. The box contained a shipment of guns.
4. **Ask** students to analyze the humor in the scene in which each of these two men alternately puts his nose out the window for fresh air.

   Possible response: Students may respond that it is humorous that the men endure the odor because they believe it is the corpse, when in fact it is foul-smelling cheese. Additionally, the coffin's actual contents of guns—instead of a corpse—is oddly comical.

Spiral Review
Character What do you learn about Thompson's view of life, based on his comments to the narrator?

know. I've had cases in my car. It's perfectly awful, becuz you don't know what minute they'll rise up and look at you!" Then, after a pause, and slightly lifting his elbow toward the box,—"But he ain't in no trance! No, sir, I go bail for him!" 

We sat some time, in meditative silence, listening to the wind and the roar of the train; then Thompson said, with a good deal of feeling:

8 "Well-a-well, we've all got to go, they ain't no getting around it. Man that is born of woman is of few days and far between, as Scriptur'[3] says. Yes, you look at it any way you want to, it's awful solemn and cur'us: they ain't nobody can get around it; all's got to go—just everybody, as you may say. One day you're hearty and strong"—here he scrambled to his feet and broke a pane and stretched his nose out at it a moment or two, then sat down again while I struggled up and thrust my nose out at the same place, and this we kept on doing every now and then—"and next day he's cut down like the grass, and the places which knowed him then knows him no more forever, as Scriptur' says. Yes'ndeedy, it's awful solemn and cur'us; but we've all got to go, one time or another; they ain't no getting around it."

There was another long pause; then—

"What did he die of?"

I said I didn't know.

"How long has he ben dead?"

It seemed judicious to enlarge the facts to fit the probabilities; so I said:

"Two or three days."

But it did no good: for Thompson received it with an injured look which plainly said, "Two or three years, you mean." Then he went right along, placidly ignoring my statement, and gave his views at considerable length upon the unwisdom of putting off burials too long. Then he lounged off toward the box, stood a moment, then came back on a sharp trot and visited the broken pane, observing:

"'Twould 'a' ben a durn sight better, all around, if they'd started him along last summer."

Thompson sat down and buried his face in his red silk handkerchief, and began to slowly sway and rock his body like one who is doing his best to endure the almost unendurable. By this

Vocabulary
judicious (jo͞o dish′ əs) *adj.* showing good judgment
placidly (plas′ id lē) *adv.* calmly; quietly

...he scrambled to his feet and broke a pane and stretched his nose out at it a moment or two...

3. **Scriptur'** scripture; the Bible.

Think Aloud

Cause and Effect

Draw students' attention to the paragraph beginning "Thompson sat down and buried his face...." Use the following "think aloud" process to model identifying cause and effect:

When I read this paragraph, in which Thompson's discomfort is described vividly, I know that I am reading the effects of something. These effects are described so vividly that I can easily visualize them and want to be sure I understand their cause. I think back on what I've read so far and remember that the narrator and Thompson both think they are accompanying a coffin. This must be the cause of the smell. But then I remember that Thompson says he later realizes that in fact the corpse is on another train and the smell comes from some Limburger cheese. That must be the cause. I'll read on to be sure.

time the fragrance—if you may call it fragrance—was just about suffocating, as near as you can come at it. Thompson's face was turning gray: I knew mine hadn't any color left in it. By and by Thompson rested his forehead in his left hand, with his elbow on his knee, and sort of waved his red handkerchief toward the box with his other hand, and said:

9 "I've carried a many a one of 'em—some of 'em considerable overdue, too—but, lordy, he just lays over 'em all!—and does it easy. Cap, they was heliotrope[4] to him!"

This recognition of my poor friend gratified me, in spite of the sad circumstances, because it had so much the sound of a compliment.

Pretty soon it was plain that something had got to be done. I suggested cigars. Thompson thought it was a good idea. He said:

"Likely it'll modify him some."

We puffed gingerly along for a while, and tried hard to imagine that things were improved. But it wasn't any use. Before very long, and without any consultation, both cigars were quietly dropped from our nerveless fingers at the same moment. Thompson said, with a sigh:

"No, Cap, it don't modify him worth a cent. Fact is, it makes him worse, becuz it appears to stir up his ambition. What do you reckon we better do, now?"

I was not able to suggest anything: indeed, I had to be swallowing and swallowing all the time, and did not like to trust myself to speak. Thompson fell to maundering, in a **desultory** and low-spirited way, about the miserable experiences of this night: and he got to referring to my poor friend by various titles—sometimes military ones, sometimes civil ones; and I noticed that as fast as my poor friend's effectiveness grew, Thompson promoted him accordingly—gave him a bigger title. Finally he said:

"I've got an idea. Suppos'n' we buckle down to it and give the Colonel a bit of a shove toward t'other end of the car?—about ten foot, say. He wouldn't have so much influence, then, don't you reckon?"

I said it was a good scheme. So we took in a good fresh breath at the broken pane, calculating to hold it till we got through: then we went there and bent over that deadly cheese and took a grip on the box. Thompson nodded "All ready," and then we threw ourselves forward with all our might: but Thompson slipped, and slumped down with his nose on the cheese, and his breath got loose. He gagged and gasped, and floundered up and made a break for the door, pawing the air and saying hoarsely, "Don't hender me!—

4. **heliotrope** (hē′ lē ə trōp′) *n.* a sweet-smelling plant.

Literary Analysis Dialogue and Dialect Which features of Thompson's speech in this passage reflect a particular dialect?

Vocabulary
desultory
(des′ əl tôr′ ē)
adj. random

10 
How do the men use the window to lessen the effect of the odor?

9 Literary Analysis
Dialogue and Dialect

1. Refer students to the bracketed text. **Ask** students what Thompson is describing in this passage.
   Answer: He is describing the odor of what he thinks is the corpse.
2. **Ask** students to respond to the Literary Analysis question: Which features of Thompson's speech in this passage reflect a particular dialect?
   Possible response: Examples of dialect include "a many a one of 'em" instead of the standard "many of them"; the abbreviated form "'em" instead of "them"; use of the word "considerable" when the standard adverb would be "considerably"; the exclamation "lordy"; the idiom "lays over 'em all!"; the term "Cap"; and the use of the singular verb "was" instead of the plural verb "were."
3. **Ask** students to explain in their own words what Thompson is saying about the corpse.
   Answer: Thompson is saying that he has transported many corpses, some of which have been dead for quite awhile, but this one is by far the smelliest. The stink of this corpse makes the others smell like a fragrant plant.

10 Reading Check

Answer: They put their faces out the window periodically to breathe fresh air.

Differentiated Instruction for Universal Access

Enrichment for Gifted/Talented Students

Students might more fully appreciate the humor of this scene if they act it out. Have students work in pairs to present the scene described on pp. 367–368. Have students write a script and stage directions based on the dialogue and descriptions from the story. Remind them to practice pronouncing Thompson's dialect.

Have students read the descriptions carefully for use as stage directions. For example, on p. 367, the narrator says he "had to be swallowing and swallowing all the time, and did not like to trust [himself] to speak." Encourage students to discuss what the author means by this. (The odor is making him nauseated.)

After students have prepared their script and practiced the scene, have them present it for the class. Then discuss which elements make the scene humorous.

⓫ Literature in Context

Cultural Connection The strong smell of Limburger cheese is said to "be able to fell trees." The name reminds many people of anything that smells potent enough to be detected for miles. One source cites a man named Limburger who had changed his name because people avoided him as if he were the cheese itself! Still, many people in various countries eat and enjoy Limburger.

Connect to the Literature Have students read the Literature in Context feature, and present the additional background information above. Then, **ask** students the Connect to the Literature question: Why do you think the narrator and Thompson are so confused about the source of the smell in the train car?

Possible response: Neither the narrator nor Thompson knows the cheese is there, nor do they know that the box contains guns instead of a body.

⓫ **LITERATURE IN CONTEXT**

Cultural Connection

Limburger Cheese

The foul stench that torments the narrator and Thompson comes from a package of Limburger cheese. This cheese was first made in Belgium and is now made in Germany and in the United States. It is notorious for its strong odor. The cheese is made from cow's milk and is "ripened" for about three months under specially controlled conditions. This ripening process gives Limburger cheese its distinctive smell and flavor. The cheese continues to ripen during shipping and its odor can become extremely intense.

Connect to the Literature

Why do you think the narrator and Thompson are so confused about the source of the smell in the train car?

gimme the road! I'm a-dying; gimme the road!" Out on the cold platform I sat down and held his head awhile, and he revived. Presently he said:

"Do you reckon we started the Gen'rul any?"

I said no: we hadn't budged him.

"Well, then, that idea's up the flume. We got to think up something else. He's suited wher' he is, I reckon; and if that's the way he feels about it, and has made up his mind that he don't wish to be disturbed, you bet he's a-going to have his own way in the business. Yes, better leave him right wher' he is, long as he wants it so; becuz he holds all the trumps, don't you know, and so it stands to reason that the man that lays out to alter his plans for him is going to get left."

But we couldn't stay out there in that mad storm; we should have frozen to death. So we went in again and shut the door, and began to suffer once more and take turns at the break in the window. By and by, as we were starting away from a station where we had stopped a moment Thompson pranced in cheerily, and exclaimed:

"We're all right, now! I reckon we've got the Commodore this time. I judge I've got the stuff here that'll take the tuck out of him."

It was carbolic acid. He had a carboy of it. He sprinkled it all around everywhere; in fact he drenched everything with it, rifle-box, cheese and all. Then we sat down, feeling pretty hopeful. But it wasn't for long. You see the two perfumes began to mix, and then—well, pretty soon we made a break for the door; and out there Thompson swabbed his face with his bandanna and said in a kind of disheartened way:

"It ain't no use. We can't buck agin him. He just utilizes everything we put up to modify him with, and gives it his own flavor and plays it back on us. Why, Cap, don't you know, it's as much as a hundred times worse in there now than it was when he first got a-going. I never did see one of 'em warm up to his work so, and take such a dumnation interest in it. No, sir, I never did, as long as I've ben on the road: and I've carried a many a one of 'em, as I was telling you."

We went in again after we were frozen pretty stiff; but my, we couldn't stay in, now. So we just waltzed back and forth, freezing, and thawing, and stifling, by turns. In about an hour we stopped at another station; and as we left it Thompson came in with a bag, and said—

Vocabulary Development

Vocabulary Knowledge Rating

When students have completed reading and discussing "The Invalid's Story," have them take out their **Vocabulary Knowledge Rating Chart** for this selection. Read the words aloud once more and have students rate their knowledge of the words again in the After Reading column. Clarify any words that are still problematic. Have students write their own definition and example or sentence in the appropriate column. Then have students complete the Vocabulary Practice activities at the end of the selection. Encourage students to use the words in further discussion and written work about this selection. Remind them that they will be accountable for these words on the **Selection Test, *Unit 2 Resources,*** pp. 199–201 or 202–204.

"Cap, I'm a-going to chance him once more—just this once; and if we don't fetch him this time, the thing for us to do, is to just throw up the sponge and withdraw from the canvass. That's the way I put it up."

He had brought a lot of chicken feathers, and dried apples, and leaf tobacco, and rags, and old shoes, and sulphur, and asafetida, and one thing or another: and he piled them on a breadth of sheet iron in the middle of the floor, and set fire to them.

12 When they got well started, I couldn't see, myself, how even the corpse could stand it. All that went before was just simply poetry to that smell—but mind you, the original smell stood up out of it just as sublime as ever—fact is, these other smells just seemed to give it a better hold: and my, how rich it was! I didn't make these reflections there—there wasn't time—made them on the platform. And breaking for the platform, Thompson got suffocated and

Reading Skill
Cause and Effect
What is the result of Thompson's final attempt to deal with the odor?

But we couldn't stay out there in that mad storm; we should have frozen to death.

12 Reading Skill

Cause and Effect

1. Have students read the bracketed text, which continues on p. 370. **Ask** students to describe how Thompson tries to get rid of the odor.

   Answer: He piled things such as rags, chicken feathers, and sulphur in the middle of the floor and set fire to the pile.

2. **Ask** students how the narrator describes the odor caused by the fire.

   Answer: He says that the odor they were trying to cover up was poetry compared to the odor caused by the fire.

3. **Ask** students to respond to the Reading Skill question: What is the result of Thompson's final attempt to deal with the odor?

   Answer: The odor of the fire is worse than the original odor; Thompson falls down suffocating, and the narrator drags him outside on the train platform.

▶ **Monitor Progress:** Using the **Reading Skill Graphic Organizer B** (*Graphic Organizer Transparencies,* p. 64), ask students to record the cause, mental image, and effect based on this question.

▶ **Reteach:** If students are having difficulty identifying details and visualizing an image, provide them with the **Reading Skill Graphic Organizer A** (*Graphic Organizer Transparencies,* p. 63). Review the graphic organizer with them, pointing out how the details of the mental picture help them understand the effects.

Concept Connector

Anticipation Guide

Have students return to their **Anticipation Guides** and respond to the statements again in the After Reading column. Then, lead a class discussion, probing for what students have learned that confirms or invalidates each statement.

Writing About the Big Question

Have students compare their responses to the sentence starters they completed before reading the story with their ideas afterwards. Ask them to explain whether their thoughts have changed.

Reading Skill Graphic Organizer

Have students review the graphic organizers they completed to identify details that helped them visualize effects while reading. Show them the **Reading Skill Graphic Organizer A** (*Graphic Organizer Transparencies,* p. 63) as an example. Then have students share the graphic organizers they did and the details they visualized to help them determine cause and effect.

⓭ Reading Skill

Cause and Effect

1. Have students read the last two paragraphs of the story aloud. **Ask** them what Thompson thinks their exposure to the odor will cause.

   Answer: Thompson is convinced that they will get typhoid fever and die.

2. **Ask** students to respond to the Reading Skill question: What effect does the experience on the train have on the narrator's health?

   Answer: He claims that his health is ruined, and that he is going to die.

ASSESS

Answers

Critical Thinking

Before students respond, you may wish to have them write a brief objective summary of the selection. As they answer the questions below, remind them to support their answers with evidence from the text.

1. (a) The men believe a decaying corpse is causing the odor. (b) Limburger cheese is causing the smell.
2. The contrast between a serious and a harmless source of the odor is humorous.
3. **Possible responses:** (a) Some sad details include the death of the narrator's friend and the grieving parents. (b) Some humorous details include the fact that Limburger cheese is causing the smell and that Thompson gasps over the box near the cheese. (c) Most students will say that the story is simply funny.
4. **Possible responses:** (a) The main character's lack of knowledge makes the story more suspenseful and thus more enjoyable. The story is very visual, and the reader can "see" the antics of the narrator and Thompson as they try to flee the stench of what they think is a dead body. (b) It would not be funny anymore and there would be no story.

⓬ fell: and before I got him dragged out, which I did by the collar, I was mighty near gone myself. When we revived, Thompson said dejectedly:

"We got to stay out here, Cap. We got to do it. They ain't no other way. The Governor wants to travel alone, and he's fixed so he can outvote us."

And presently he added:

"And don't you know, we're pisoned. It's our last trip, you can make up your mind to it. Typhoid fever is what's going to come of this. I feel it a-coming right now. Yes, sir, we're elected, just as sure as you're born."

We were taken from the platform an hour later, frozen and insensible, at the next station, and I went straight off into a virulent fever, and never knew anything again for three weeks. I found out, then, that I had spent that awful night with a harmless box of rifles and a lot of innocent cheese; but the news was too late to save me; imagination had done its work, and my health was permanently shattered; neither Bermuda nor any other land can ever bring it back to me. This is my last trip; I am on my way home to die.

Reading Skill
Cause and Effect
What effect does the experience on the train have on the narrator's health?

Critical Thinking

Cite textual evidence to support your responses.

1. **Key Ideas and Details** **(a)** What do the men believe is creating the awful smell? **(b) Connect:** What is actually creating the smell?
2. **Key Ideas and Details** **Compare and Contrast:** In what ways does the contrast between what the men think is true and what is really true contribute to the humor?
3. **Key Ideas and Details** Make a chart with three columns. **(a) Compare:** In the first column, write a list of sad details in the story. **(b) Connect:** In the second column, write the details that add humor to the story. **(c) Discuss and Evaluate:** Share your chart with a partner and discuss your responses. Then, in the third column, explain whether you think the story is sad, funny, or both.
4. **Integration of Knowledge and Ideas** **(a)** For the story to be funny, why is it critical that the narrator doesn't have all the information? **(b)** If this conflict were avoided, what would be the effect on the story? *[Connect to the Big Question: Is conflict necessary?]*

Assessment Resources

Unit 2 Resources

L1 L2 EL **Selection Test A,** pp. 199–201. Administer Test A to less advanced readers.

L3 L4 EL **Selection Test B,** pp. 202–204. Administer Test B to on-level and more advanced students.

L3 L4 **Open-Book Test,** pp. 196–198. As an alternative, give the Open-Book Test.

All **Customizable Test Bank**

All **Self-tests**
Students may prepare for the **Selection Test** by taking the **Self-test** online.

All assessment resources are available at **www.PHLitOnline.com.**

After You Read The Invalid's Story 

Literary Analysis: Dialogue and Dialect

1. **Key Ideas and Details** Identify one example of **dialogue** in the story that indicates the smell is increasing. Explain your choice.
2. **Key Ideas and Details** Identify an example of dialogue that shows that Thompson and the narrator do not know each other well. Explain your choice.
3. **Craft and Structure (a)** In what way do the spelling, grammar, and words used in this passage indicate it is an example of **dialect?**

   "No, Cap, it don't modify him worth a cent. Fact is, it makes him worse, becuz it appears to stir up his ambition. What do you reckon we better do, now?"

   (b) Rewrite the passage in Standard English. **(c)** Explain how the use of dialect makes the characters and setting more vivid.

Reading Skill: Cause and Effect

4. **(a)** What is the **cause** of the smell in the express car? **(b)** What **effect** does the smell have on Thompson and the narrator?
5. Which visual details in the story help you to explain why the characters are mistaken about the true cause of the smell?

Vocabulary

Acquisition and Use In vocabulary study, **analogies** show the relationships between pairs of words. Use a word from the vocabulary list on page 360 to complete each analogy so that the relationship in the second pair of words matches that in the first pair. Explain the relationships.

1. comedy : humorous :: measles : ____________
2. graceful : clumsy :: ____________ : foolish
3. tiny : small :: ____________ : large
4. systematic : reliable :: ____________ : unpredictable
5. violently : angry :: ____________ : content
6. praise : joyful :: warning : ____________

Word Study Use the context of the sentences and what you know about the **Latin suffix *-ous*** (or ***-ious*** or ***-uous***) to explain your answers.

1. If a sport is *hazardous,* could you be seriously hurt playing it?
2. How do most people react to *ridiculous* events?

Word Study

The **Latin suffix *-ous*** (or ***-ious*** or ***-uous***) means "like" or "pertaining to."

Apply It Explain how the suffix ***-ous*** contributes to the meanings of these words. You may consult a dictionary if necessary.

glorious
mysterious
tumultuous

ASSESS/EXTEND

Answers

Literary Analysis

1. Dialogue that reveals the increasing smell is "All that went before was just simply poetry to that smell. . . ."
2. Dialogue that reveals the unfamiliarity between Thompson and the narrator is, " 'Friend of yourn?' 'Yes,' I said with a sigh."
3. (a) Dialect in the following words and phrases includes "Cap," the use of "don't," the phrase "modify him worth a cent," the pronunciation of "becuz," the idiom "stir up his ambition," the use of "reckon," and the phrase "we better do." (b) "'No, sir, it does not change him at all. The fact is it makes him worse because it appears to make him smell even more. What do you think we should do now?'" (c) The use of dialect makes Thompson's character more specific because it provides him with a particular cultural background. His language is colorful and expressive, which makes the scene more vivid and comical.

Reading Skill

4. (a) The cause of the smell is Limburger cheese. (b) The smell forces the men to flee the car.
5. Visual details include the coffin-like box, the passenger moving through who places the Limburger cheese on the box, and Thompson leaning over the box and gasping at the odor.

Vocabulary

Acquisition and Use

Sample answers:

1. deleterious
2. judicious
3. prodigious
4. desultory
5. placidly
6. ominous

Word Study

Sample answers:

1. Yes. You could get hurt playing a sport that is *hazardous* or pertaining to hazard and danger.
2. Most people laugh at *ridiculous* events, or events that are pertaining to ridicule or absurdity.

Word Study: Apply It

Sample answers:

Glorious means something pertaining to glory or beauty. *Mysterious* means pertaining to mystery or the unexplainable. *Tumultuous* means something noisy, disorderly or pertaining to tumult.

Answers

Conventions

1. Introduce the skill, using the instruction on the student page.
2. Discuss the definitions and examples in the chart.

Think Aloud: Model the Skill

Model the skill of distinguishing verb voices. Say to students:

To distinguish between active voice and passive voice in the sentence "Hannah hugs Jill," I ask myself: Who is doing the action? Here, the verb expresses an action done by the subject, Hannah, so I know it is an active verb. In the sentence "Jill is hugged by Hannah," the verb expresses an action done to the object Jill, so I know it is a passive verb. Also, a passive verb usually includes a form of the verb *to be.*

PH WRITING COACH Grade 9

Students will find further instruction on active and passive voice in Chapter 17, Section 4.

Practice A

1. is bothered; P
2. watches; A
3. greets; A
4. are frightened; P

Writing Application

Sample answers:

1. The unwelcome visitors bother Granny.
2. They are watched in angry silence.
3. Camera and Smilin are greeted by Granddaddy Cain.
4. His size and power frighten them.

Practice B

Sample answers:

1. He had placed the cheese on the box.
2. Mark Twain wrote "The Invalid's Story."
3. Someone sent the coffin to Wisconsin by train.
4. The narrator detected a foul odor.

Speaking Application

Sample answers:

1. The train moved down the track.
2. Snow covered the tracks.
3. The train could be seen far away.
4. It was bathed in smoke.

PERFORMANCE TASKS

Integrated Language Skills

Blues Ain't No Mockin Bird • The Invalid's Story

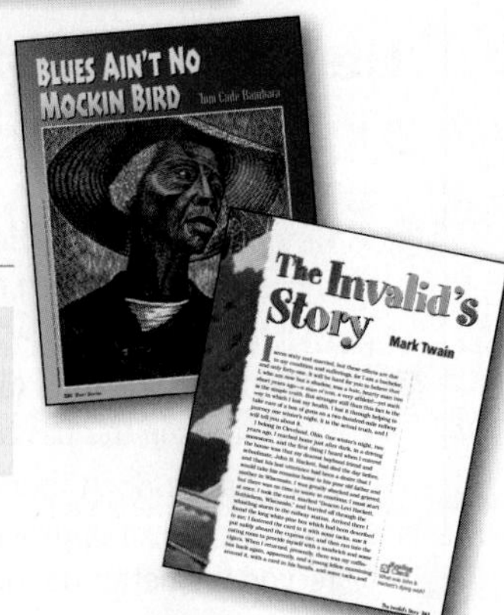

Conventions: Active and Passive Voice

A verb in the **active voice** expresses an action done ***by*** its subject.
A verb in the **passive voice** expresses an action done ***to*** its subject.

The "voice" of a verb tells whether the subject *performs* an action (active voice) or *receives* an action (passive voice).

Active Voice	Passive Voice
Bambara and Twain have written stories about memorable conflicts. (The subjects, *Bambara* and *Twain*, perform the action of the verb, *have written.*)	Stories about memorable conflicts have been written by Bambara and Twain. (The subject, *stories*, receives the action of the verb, *have been written.*)

Use the active voice for lively, direct writing. Use the passive voice to de-emphasize the performer of the action or when the performer is unknown.

Practice A Identify the verb or verb phrase in each sentence. Tell whether the writer has used the active voice or the passive voice.

1. Granny is bothered by the unwelcome visitors.
2. She watches them in angry silence.
3. Granddaddy Cain greets Camera and Smilin.
4. They are frightened by his size and power.

Writing Application Rewrite the sentences in Practice A. If the verb is in the active voice, use the passive voice. If the verb is in the passive voice, use the active voice. Explain the effect of each change.

Practice B Rewrite the following sentences using the active voice. You may need to add words to indicate who performed the action.

1. The cheese had been placed on the box.
2. "The Invalid's Story" was written by Mark Twain.
3. The coffin was sent to Wisconsin by train.
4. A foul odor was detected by the narrator.

Speaking Application Look at the image on page 369 of "The Invalid's Story." Write four sentences based on this image, using the active voice twice and the passive voice twice. With a partner, discuss which sentences are more effective and why.

PH WRITING COACH Further instruction and practice are available in *Prentice Hall Writing Coach.*

Extend the Lesson

Sentence Modeling

Choose the sentence given from the selection students have read:

Cathy jumped up and came down hard on her heels and started tap-dancin. ("Blues Ain't No Mockin Bird")

Thompson sat down and buried his face in his red silk handkerchief, and began to slowly sway and rock his body like one who is doing his best to endure the almost unendurable. ("The Invalid's Story")

Ask students what they notice about the voice in the sentence. (It is active.) Ask students what else they notice. (**Possible responses:** "Blues Ain't No Mockin Bird": Using *and* to join three verbs shows the speed and fluidity of the actions; "The Invalid's Story": *And* is used to join three simple physical actions; the final comparison shifts to exaggerated emotion.)

Have students write a sentence of their own, matching the grammatical and stylistic features discussed. Call on volunteers to act out their sentences as they read them aloud.

Writing

Narrative Text Write an **informal letter** from the point of view of a character in "Blues Ain't No Mockin Bird" or "The Invalid's Story." Choose a character who is not the narrator.

- Before writing, list the personality traits of your character.
- Write to a friend or relative, describing the story events and their significance from your character's point of view.
- Refer to your list as you write. Make sure that your details and language are consistent with the traits that you listed.

Grammar Application Check your letter to be sure that you have used active voice whenever possible.

Common Core State Standards

L.9-10.1, L.9-10.6; W.9-10.3.a.; SL.9-10.4

[For the full wording of the standards, see page 346.]

Writing Workshop: *Work in Progress*

Prewriting for Exposition: Cause-and-Effect Essay Review the "What's the Cause?" list in your writing portfolio. Highlight the effect that interests you the most. Then, list several questions to help you define the cause for this effect. Save this Highlighted Cause List.

Use this prewriting activity to prepare for the **Writing Workshop** on page 402.

Speaking and Listening

Presentation of Ideas In both of these stories, dialogue and dialect are important elements. With a partner, prepare and deliver a **dialogue.**

- If you read "Blues Ain't No Mockin Bird," have Camera and Smilin discuss their experience with Granny and Granddaddy.
- If you read "The Invalid's Story," have the narrator discuss his "shattered" health with a doctor.

Follow these steps to complete the assignment:

- Decide what the dialogue will reveal about the story events and the personalities of the speakers.
- Outline a "plot." Decide how the dialogue should begin and end. Choose at least one event for the middle of the dialogue (for example, having a character re-enact an important moment from the story). Build the dialogue around that "plot."
- Use language that is appropriate to the characters' situations and personalities, but be polite.
- After you have presented your dialogue, invite questions from the audience. If you wish, answer in character.

www.PHLitOnline.com

- Interactive graphic organizers
- Grammar tutorial
- Interactive journals

EXTEND/ASSESS

Writing

1. Review the assignment, using the instruction on the student page.
2. To give students guidance for writing their letter, give them **Support for Writing,** p. 194 in ***Unit 2 Resources.***
3. To evaluate students' letters, use the **Short Story** rubrics, pp. 226–227 in ***Professional Development Guidebook.***

Grammar Application

Have students check their drafts for active and passive voice and verb tenses.

Six Traits Focus

✓	Ideas	✓	Word Choice
	Organization		Sentence Fluency
✓	Voice		Conventions

PH WRITING COACH Grade 9

Students will find further guidance on narrative letter writing in Chapter 10.

Writing Workshop
Work in Progress

Have students save their completed questions in their portfolios. They will use their questions later as they complete the Writing Workshop (see pp. 402–409)

Speaking and Listening

1. Review the assignment, using the instruction on the student page.
2. To support students' work on the assignment, have them complete the **Support for Extend Your Learning** page (***Unit 2 Resources,*** p. 195).

Teaching Resources

Unit 2 Resources

L3 L4 EL **Integrated Language Skills: Grammar,** p. 193

L3 L4 EL **Support for Writing,** p. 194

L3 L4 **Support for Extend Your Learning,** p. 195

L4 **Enrichment,** pp. 174, 192

Enriched Online Student Edition

Available under After You Read for this selection:

All **Interactive Grammar Tutorial**

L3 L4 **Internet Research Activity**

Professional Development Guidebook

Rubrics for Self-Assessment: Short Story, pp. 226–227

PHLit Online! All print and digital resources are available at **www.PHLitOnline.com**. Online resources accessible by students are noted on the student page.

MONITORING PROGRESS

Using the Test Practice

In this two-page Test Practice, students apply the reading skill for the second half of Unit 2 to a passage of fiction and a passage of nonfiction.

Review this skill, identifying cause and effect, then administer the test. For more guidance, consult the ***Classroom Strategies and Teaching Routines*** card **Formally Assessing Students.**

ASSESS

Answers

Answers With Explanations

1. **B**—The third sentence says that Jeff kept pinching himself to stay awake. *Incorrect answers:* A—Maya pays attention to Jeff as soon as he enters the classroom. C—Jeff says he is feeling sick because he's not getting enough sleep. D—The teacher is not mentioned in the passage.
2. **A**—Nothing in the passage suggests that Jeff tried to get approval for an easier project. *Incorrect answers:* B—Jeff's frustration with his partner contributes to Jeff's lack of sleep. C—The text states that he has not been sleeping well. D—Jeff's worry about his science grade is why he's staying up late to work and sleeping little.
3. **D**—Jeff says he will tell Maya his problem because she is his best friend. *Incorrect answers:* A—Jeff already has a partner for the project. B—The passage does not discuss dating. C—Jeff does not ask to go to the nurse.
4. **C**—Jeff says he does not want his partner's laziness hurt his own grade. *Incorrect answers:* A—Jeff says his partner is not doing his share of the work, not that he will get all the credit. B—The passage does not discuss Jeff's classmates. D—The passage does not discuss summer school.

Test Practice: Reading

Cause and Effect

Fiction Selection

Directions: *Read the selection. Then, answer the questions.*

Just before the bell, Jeff stumbled into math class. Maya watched with concern as he plopped into his seat and wearily rubbed his face. Throughout the class, Jeff kept pinching himself to stay awake. Afterward, Maya confronted him, wanting to know what was wrong. Jeff sighed. "I wouldn't admit this to just anyone, Maya, but since you're my best friend . . . It's this science project. My partner isn't doing his share of the work, and I can't let his laziness hurt my grade. To make things worse, the topic we picked is a lot harder than we'd planned. I've had only three hours of sleep each night this week, and I'm feeling pretty sick."

1. Jeff pinches himself during math class in order to—

A. attract Maya's attention.
B. keep himself from falling asleep.
C. prevent himself from getting sick.
D. receive a warning from the teacher.

2. Which of the following statements is *not* a cause of Jeff's poor condition?

A. He has failed to get approval for an easier science project.
B. His science partner is not doing an equal share of work.
C. He has experienced a lack of sleep for several nights in a row.
D. He is worried about getting a good grade in science.

3. Jeff decides to explain his dilemma to Maya because he—

A. wants her help with the science project.
B. wants to ask her on a date.
C. needs her to take him to the school nurse.
D. trusts her as his closest friend.

4. Jeff believes that not spending extra time on his science project will result in which of the following effects?

A. His science partner will get all the credit for the work.
B. He will look foolish to his classmates.
C. His teacher will not give him a good grade.
D. He will have to repeat the class in summer school.

Writing for Assessment

In a paragraph, explain why Jeff is upset and having trouble sleeping. Use details from the passage to support your answer.

Writing for Assessment

Students' answers should mention Jeff's concern about his partner for the project, the difficulty of the project, and his anxiety over his grade.

Strategies for Test Taking

Very often, students will select the first answer choice that appears correct without carefully considering the other choices. Remind students that they must read all of the possible choices before they select an answer. While one choice might look like the best choice, another choice might be even more appropriate.

Nonfiction Selection

Directions: *Read the selection. Then, answer the questions.*

If you have trouble sleeping, you are in good company: About 50 million American adults suffer from sleep deprivation. Some causes, such as drinking caffeine in the evening, are avoidable. Certain medical conditions, such as asthma and depression, can interfere with sleep—and so can some medications. Sleep deprivation is something you should take seriously. It can leave you without the energy or physical strength to meet the day's demands. You may find it harder to think clearly, to solve problems, or to remember things, too. Irritability, moodiness, and anxiety often can be traced to a lack of sleep.

1. Based on the passage, what is *not* usually a cause of sleep deprivation?

A. depression
B. consuming caffeinated products
C. consuming dairy products
D. some medications

2. According to the passage, which cause-and-effect relationship is correct?

A. Irritability causes sleep problems.
B. Too much sleep may cause memory problems.
C. Asthma may interfere with sleep.
D. Sleeping less can give you more energy.

3. The passage explains that sleep deprivation may result in—

A. moodiness and an inability to solve problems.
B. asthma and emotional irritability.
C. weight loss and anxiety.
D. anxiety and an increased need for medication.

4. Which of the following statements *best* describes one way to avoid sleep deprivation?

A. Discontinue all prescription medications.
B. Take sleeping pills and high-potency vitamins.
C. Stop drinking caffeinated soda in the evening.
D. Spend time exercising just before bedtime.

Writing for Assessment

Connecting Across Texts
In the first passage, Jeff experiences sleep deprivation. Think about the causes and effects of sleep deprivation. In a short paragraph, give Jeff advice about what he might do. Use details from both passages to support your response.

www.PHLitOnline.com
- Online practice
- Instant feedback

ASSESS

Answers

Answers With Explanations

1. C—The passage does not cite dairy products as a cause of causing sleep deprivation. *Incorrect answers:* A—The passage cites depression as a cause of sleep deprivation. B—Drinking caffeine in the evening is cited as a cause of sleep deprivation. D—The passage states that some medications can cause sleep deprivation.
2. C—According to the passage, asthma can cause sleep deprivation. *Incorrect answers:* A—The reverse is true—sleep deprivation causes irritability. B—The passage says that too *little* sleep can have this effect. D—The passage says that too little sleep leaves you without energy.
3. A—The passage cites both moodiness and an inability to solve problems as results of sleep deprivation. *Incorrect answers:* B—The passage cites asthma as a cause of sleep deprivation, not an effect. C—The passage cites anxiety as a result of sleep deprivation, but does not mention weight loss. D—The passage does not mention an increased need for medication as an effect of sleep deprivation.
4. C—The passage states that avoiding caffeine in the evening is a way to prevent sleep deprivation. *Incorrect answers:* A—According to the passage, some medications can cause sleep deprivation, not all. B—The passage gives no advice about taking pills before bed. D—The passage does not mention exercise.

Writing for Assessment

Students may suggest that Jeff try to encourage his science partner to put more time into their project to relieve some of Jeff's worry about the project, limit the amount of caffeinated drinks he consumes at night, and do something relaxing before bedtime, such as watching a comedy video.

Students may take the test in interactive format with instant feedback online at **www.PHLitOnline.com.**

Differentiated Instruction for Universal Access

Strategy for Less Proficient Readers
Review the skill by walking students through item 1 on p. 374. Read the passage with students, helping them figure out what causes the effect of Jeff's pinching himself in class. Next, guide students in eliminating incorrect answer choices.

- A—The passage says that Maya is aware of Jeff as soon as he enters the room. He does not need to pinch himself to get her attention. (Eliminate.)
- B—The passage tells you that Jeff kept pinching himself to stay awake, which is the same thing as not falling asleep. (Correct.)
- C—Jeff tells Maya he is feeling sick because he has had only three hours of sleep each night this week, not because he has not pinched himself. (Eliminate.)
- D—The passage does not mention the teacher at all. (Eliminate.)

Guide students in seeing that **B** is the best choice. Have them complete the remaining items, encouraging them to apply a similar strategy to each. First, define key terms in the prompt, and then eliminate incorrect choices.

PRETEACH

Common Core State Standards

- Language 4.c, 6

Reading Skill

1. Introduce the skill, using the instruction on the student page.
2. Tell students they will analyze structure and format as they read.

Think Aloud: Model the Skill

Model the skill of analyzing structure and format. Say to students:

I can evaluate the format of a textbook by using the text and design features to help me organize the ideas it contains. For instance, I know that titles and headings tell what a section of the textbook is about. I know that textbooks often use boldface type to highlight new words, and that they use lists to make important points stand out.

Multidraft Reading

Have students follow a multidraft reading protocol.

- **First reading**—Have students read to identify key ideas and details.
- **Second reading**—Have students read to identify the structure of the text.
- **Third reading**—Have students read to integrate knowledge and ideas by connecting the text to the world, their own experiences, and other texts.

Content-Area Vocabulary

1. Have students say each word.
2. Next, use each word in a sentence that defines it.
3. Finally, repeat your definitional sentence or a similar sentence with the word missing and have the class "fill in the blank" chorally.

Reading for Information

Analyzing Functional Texts

User Guide

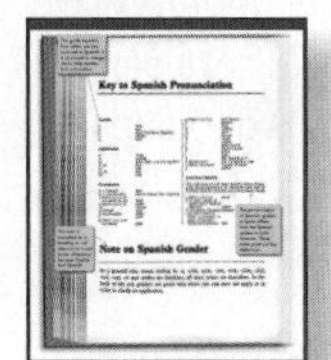
Key to Spanish Pronunciation

Note on Spanish Gender

Application

Common Core State Standards

Language

4.c. Consult general and specialized reference materials, both print and digital, to find the pronunciation of a word or determine or clarify its precise meaning, its part of speech, or its etymology.

6. Acquire and use accurately grade-appropriate general academic and domain-specific words and phrases; demonstrate independence in gathering vocabulary knowledge when considering a word or phrase important to comprehension or expression.

Reading Skills: Analyze Structure and Format

Dictionaries, applications, and other **functional** texts often use headings, labels, graphics, and other features to set off specific types of information. These documents are functional because they provide information to help people perform tasks. When working with such documents, **analyze structure and format** by identifying their text features and considering how they clarify information. The questions in this chart can help you locate and understand text features in functional documents. Think about how these features help the author convey information clearly.

Questions to Ask About Structure and Format
Are there special instructions or information?
What are the main headings on the page?
How is certain information labeled or highlighted?
What features have been pointed out? Why?

Content-Area Vocabulary

These words appear in the selections that follow. You may also encounter them in other content-area texts.

- **homographs** (hom´ ə grafs) *n.* words that are spelled the same way but have different meanings
- **idiomatic** (id´ ē ə mat´ ik) *adj.* typical of the natural way in which people using their own language speak or write
- **certifications** (sér´ tə fə kā´ shənz) *n.* official documents that state that people are qualified and allowed to do certain jobs

THE BIG ? Is conflict necessary?

Have students learn how to complete a job application and decipher a user guide for a Spanish-English dictionary. Remind students that both documents are designed to reduce the conflict in sometimes tense situations.

Differentiated Instruction for Universal Access

Reading Support

Give students reading support with the appropriate version of the *Reader's Notebooks:*

L2 L3 *Reader's Notebook*

L1 *Reader's Notebook: Adapted Version*

EL *Reader's Notebook: English Learner's Version*

Spanish-English Dictionary User Guide

User Guide

Features:

- explanations of word meanings
- a pronunciation key
- labeled features of entries
- explanations of abbreviations

In these bilingual dictionary entries, Spanish words are formatted in bold type to make them easy to find.

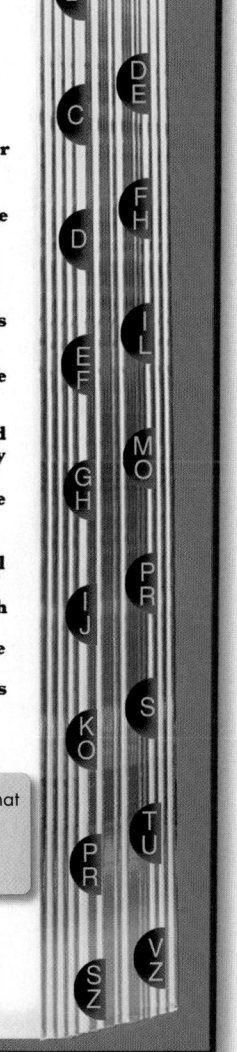

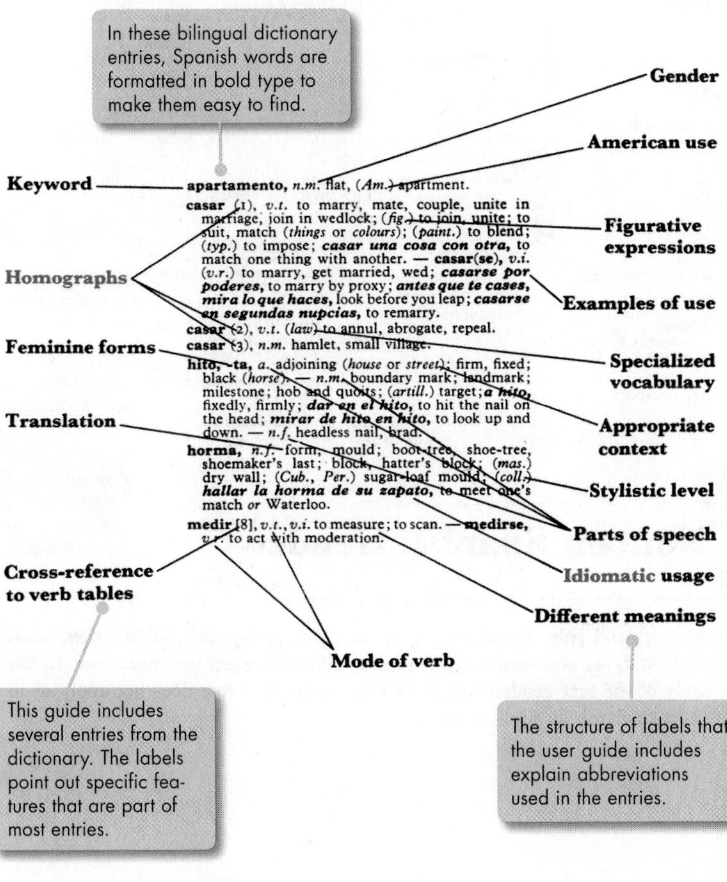

Keyword
Homographs
Feminine forms
Translation
Cross-reference to verb tables
Mode of verb
Gender
American use
Figurative expressions
Examples of use
Specialized vocabulary
Appropriate context
Stylistic level
Parts of speech
Idiomatic usage
Different meanings
apartamento, *n.m.* flat, (*Am.*) apartment.
casar (1), *v.t.* to marry, mate, couple, unite in marriage, join in wedlock; (*fig.*) to join, unite; to suit, match (*things* or *colours*); (*paint.*) to blend; (*typ.*) to impose; ***casar una cosa con otra,*** to match one thing with another. — **casar(se),** *v.i.* (*v.r.*) to marry, get married, wed; ***casarse por poderes,*** to marry by proxy; ***antes que te cases, mira lo que haces,*** look before you leap; ***casarse en segundas nupcias,*** to remarry.
casar (2), *v.t.* (*law*) to annul, abrogate, repeal.
casar (3), *n.m.* hamlet, small village.
hito, -ta, *a.* adjoining (*house* or *street*); firm, fixed; black (*horse*). — *n.m.* boundary mark; landmark; milestone; hob and quoits; (*artill.*) target; ***a hito,*** fixedly, firmly; ***dar en el hito,*** to hit the nail on the head; ***mirar de hito en hito,*** to look up and down. — *n.f.* headless nail, brad.
horma, *n.f.* form, mould; boot-tree, shoe-tree, shoemaker's last; block, hatter's block; (*mas.*) dry wall; (*Cub.*, *Per.*) sugar-loaf mould; (*coll.*) ***hallar la horma de su zapato,*** to meet one's match *or* Waterloo.
medir [8], *v.t.*, *v.i.* to measure; to scan. — **medirse,** *v.r.* to act with moderation.
C D E F G H I J K O P R S Z D E F H I L M O P R S T U V Z

This guide includes several entries from the dictionary. The labels point out specific features that are part of most entries.

The structure of labels that the user guide includes explain abbreviations used in the entries.

TEACH

About User Guides

1. Review the features listed in the User Guide box with students. **Ask** them to explain what *features* means in their own words.

   Possible response: The features of a text are the elements that are characteristic of that type of text.
2. Point out that a dictionary is meant to help people understand words and their meaning, but most dictionaries provide more information, including word origins, and so on.
3. Remind students of the basic layout of a dictionary, including the use of guidewords, alphabetizing, and the pronunciation key. Point out these familiar characteristics in the sample page from the Spanish-English dictionary user guide.

Analyze Structure and Format

1. Remind students that to analyze structure and format, they look at text and design features. Text features include headings, labels, and the structure of information. Design features include placement, images, color, and font choices.
2. Review with students the questions listed in the chart on page 376. Explain to them that writers and designers work closely together to make the information as clear as possible.
3. Divide the class into four groups. Assign each group one of the questions in the chart on page 376. Have them look at the dictionary page shown on this page and find the answers to their assigned question. Then, have each group present its findings to the class.
4. **Ask:** What are the common features between a foreign language dictionary and a standard dictionary?

   Possible response: Both have keywords, entries, parts of speech labels, definitions, idiomatic expressions, and related forms.

Differentiated Instruction for Universal Access

EL Enrichment for English Language Learners

Some students may be fluent in a second language. Draw on their experience with foreign language dictionaries as you discuss effective techniques for using these reference tools. Ask experienced students to tell the strategies they use to decipher unusual words or words that have unusual roots. Distribute foreign language dictionaries from the library and have groups of students look up the foreign words for common nouns, such as *bird, flower, game,* or *jump.* Share the foreign words with the class.

Analyze Structure and Format

1. **Ask:** What is the main purpose of a foreign language dictionary?

   Possible response: The main purpose is to help people translate words from one language to another.

2. **Ask** students why it is important to note in this dictionary the differences between pronunciations of Spanish words in Spain and in Latin America.

   Answer: A language that is used in more than one country, such as Spanish, is likely to have different dialects spoken in different places. Therefore, even though the language is essentially the same, many pronunciations might vary. In order for the dictionary to be useful to all people needing help with Spanish, the dictionary highlights the differences between the main dialects.

3. Tell students that in many languages words have a gender. When learning these languages, it is important to know the gender of nouns.

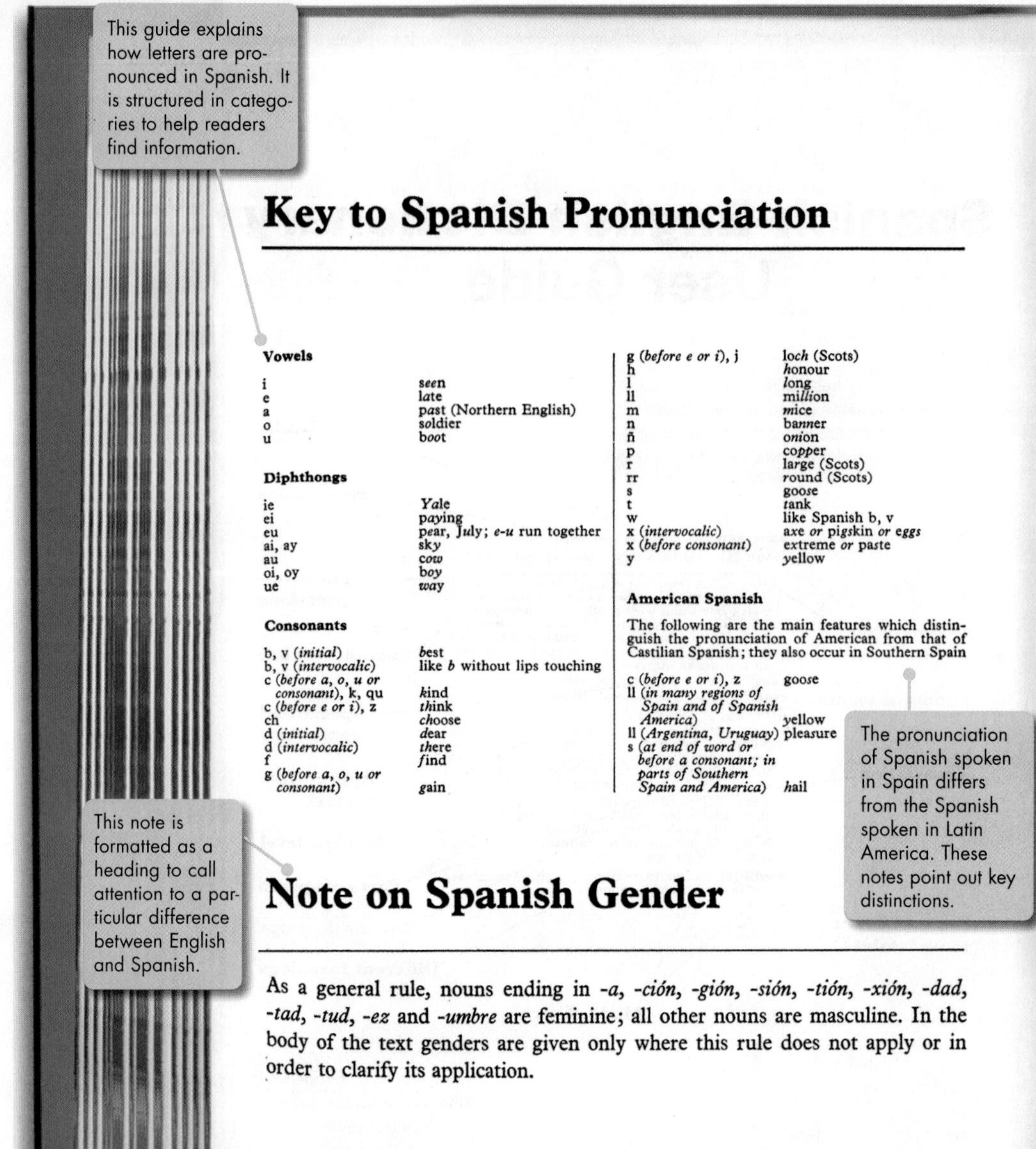
This guide explains how letters are pronounced in Spanish. It is structured in categories to help readers find information.
The pronunciation of Spanish spoken in Spain differs from the Spanish spoken in Latin America. These notes point out key distinctions.
This note is formatted as a heading to call attention to a particular difference between English and Spanish.

Key to Spanish Pronunciation

Vowels

i	seen
e	late
a	past (Northern English)
o	soldier
u	boot

Diphthongs

ie	*Y*ale
ei	paying
eu	pear, July; *e-u* run together
ai, ay	sky
au	cow
oi, oy	boy
ue	*w*ay

Consonants

b, v (*initial*)	*b*est
b, v (*intervocalic*)	like *b* without lips touching
c (*before a, o, u or consonant*), k, qu	*k*ind
c (*before e or i*), z	*th*ink
ch	*ch*oose
d (*initial*)	*d*ear
d (*intervocalic*)	*th*ere
f	*f*ind
g (*before a, o, u or consonant*)	*g*ain
g (*before e or i*), j	lo*ch* (Scots)
h	*h*onour
l	*l*ong
ll	mi*lli*on
m	*m*ice
n	ba*nn*er
ñ	o*ni*on
p	co*pp*er
r	la*r*ge (Scots)
rr	*r*ound (Scots)
s	goo*s*e
t	*t*ank
w	like Spanish b, v
x (*intervocalic*)	axe *or* pigskin *or* eggs
x (*before consonant*)	extreme *or* paste
y	*y*ellow

American Spanish

The following are the main features which distinguish the pronunciation of American from that of Castilian Spanish; they also occur in Southern Spain

c (*before e or i*), z	goo*s*e
ll (*in many regions of Spain and of Spanish America*)	*y*ellow
ll (*Argentina, Uruguay*)	plea*s*ure
s (*at end of word or before a consonant; in parts of Southern Spain and America*)	*h*ail

Note on Spanish Gender

As a general rule, nouns ending in *-a*, *-ción*, *-gión*, *-sión*, *-tión*, *-xión*, *-dad*, *-tad*, *-tud*, *-ez* and *-umbre* are feminine; all other nouns are masculine. In the body of the text genders are given only where this rule does not apply or in order to clarify its application.

Vocabulary Development

CCSS Language 6

Vocabulary from Languages

Tell students that there are some special terms that are used in dictionaries. Guide students to understand the meaning of the following words in this excerpt from the Spanish-English dictionary:

keyword: the boldface word in a dictionary entry

homograph: a word that is spelled the same as another word but that has a different meaning

cross-reference: a note directing a reader to another page with more information

figurative expression: a word or phrase that has a meaning that is different from its literal meaning

gender: indication of whether a word is feminine, masculine, or neuter

State of Georgia Job Application

Application

Features:

- spaces for providing requested information
- a line for the applicant's signature
- text written for a specific audience

STATE OF GEORGIA
APPLICATION FOR EMPLOYMENT
An Equal Opportunity Employer

Daytime Telephone Number		E-mail Address		
Last Name		First Name		Middle Initials
Street or Mailing Address				Apartment No.
City	State	Zip Code	County	

This part of the application captures contact information. Headings indicate where the applicant should fill in information.

EMPLOYMENT ELIGIBILITY: To be employed by the State of Georgia, you must meet certain State and Federal employment eligibility requirements. These include (but are not limited to) United States citizenship or authorization to work in this country, positive rehire status if previously employed by the State, and no felony convictions (for some jobs). Please answer the following questions.

1. Are you a United States citizen?	2. Are you an alien authorized to work in the Utited States?	3. Have you ever been dismissed from any State of Georgia government position?	4. Have you ever been convicted of a felony?
☐ YES ☐ NO	☐ YES ☐ NO ☐ N/A	☐ YES ☐ NO **If YES, attach an explanation.**	☐ YES ☐ NO **If YES, attach an explanation.**

TYPE OF WORK: JOB TITLE AND JOB CODE REQUIRED. If you do not know the correct job titles, information is available at the various State of Georgia agency personnel offices, the Georgia Merit System Office in Atlanta, or the Georgia Department of Labor Career Centers.

Bold and uppercase letters give the applicant important information for completing the application.

Specific Job Title Sought	Job Code	Specific Job Title Sought	Job Code
1.		2.	

EDUCATION:

High School Graduate or Equivalent (GED)? ☐Yes ☐No	Vocational/Business School:	No. of Months:	Field of Study:	Completed: Yes☐ No☐ Date: (Mo/Yr)

PLEASE LIST EXACT COLLEGE HOURS:		CREDIT RECEIVED		FIELD/AREA OF CONCENTRATION				TYPE OF DEGREE	DATE DEGREE COMPLETED
COLLEGES/UNIVERSITIES	CITY and STATE	Qtr Hrs	Sem Hrs	Major	Hrs	Minor	Hrs	(BA/BS/ MA/PhD)	(Mo./Yr.)

This section is structured as rows and columns, so that applicants can provide information in an organized way.

LANGUAGE SKILLS: ☐ **Multilingual (Specify languages)**_______________ ☐ **Sign Language**

GEORGIA LICENSES AND CERTIFICATIONS:

Type of License/Certificate	License/Certificate Number	Expiration (Mo./Yr.)	Specialization/ Endorsements
Current Valid Driver's License ☐Yes ☐No			
Current Valid Commercial Driver's License (CDL): ☐A ☐B ☐C			
Teacher Certified in Georgia: Type of Certificate Held:			
Georgia Peace Officer Standards and Training Certificate (POST)			
Other Professional License/Certificate: ________			

About Applications

1. Have students read the features of applications found in the box at the top right on page 379.
2. Tell students that applications are documents that companies and other organizations use to gather information and determine whether someone is qualified to serve in a job or to participate in a program.
3. As a group, brainstorm for situations that typically require applications. Include ideas such as getting a driver's license or applying for college.
4. **Ask:** Have you ever filled out an application? What was it for?

   Possible response: Some students may have filled out an application to participate in a sports event or to go on a school trip.

Analyze Structure and Format

1. Point out that some of the questions on the application are numbered. Tell students that the numbered items are meant to be completed in the order in which they appear.
2. Refer to the questions on page 376. Tell students to answer each question in turn. Encourage them to use the call out notes to help them with their answers.
3. Point out that the first part of the application is for basic details about the applicant's name and address. The second part is a list of yes-and-no questions. Explain that the answers to these questions may require an explanation that can be attached. **Ask:** Can you think of some situations that might need to be explained in an attachment?

   Possible response: If a person had been fired, he or she may want to explain the circumstances surrounding the incident.

Differentiated Instruction for Universal Access

Less Proficient Readers

Some questions on an application have complicated structures and will be difficult for less proficient readers to understand. Tell students to decode each sentence by looking for the main subject and the main verb. For example, question 3 asks, "Have you ever been dismissed from any State of Georgia government position?" This sentence can be reduced to a simpler sentence: "Have you ever been fired from a government job in Georgia?"

Gifted and Talented Students

To give students further practice with applications, have them make lists of their skills and qualifications. Then, have students think of positions for which they are ideally suited. Finally, have students write job descriptions for their ideal jobs.

Analyze Structure and Format

1. Have students read the instructions after the heading Work History. **Ask:** According to the instructions, which jobs should not be included on the work history list?

   Possible response: None of them. All previous jobs should be included.

2. Point out to students the line under the Work History heading that reads Reason for Leaving. **Ask:** Why might an employer want to know the reason an applicant left a former job?

   Possible response: An employer might want to know if an applicant was fired from a former job, as that may warn an employer of potential problems with an applicant.

3. **Ask:** What would an employer think if an applicant's last job lasted only 2 months?

   Possible response: The applicant may not be very reliable.

WORK HISTORY: Describe your work history below beginning with your current or most recent job. Include military and volunteer experience. If you worked for the same employer but held different jobs describe each separately. Describe in detail the specific duties beginning with your primary duties. If you need more space, print out the supplemental work history page and attach to the application. Failure to give complete and detailed information regarding each job held may result in your disqualification from employment consideration. You may submit a resume to document your work background. However, if the resume does not contain all information requested in the Work History section, please fill in that information on the application. Include additional documents as requested.

Current or Last Employer:			Your Job Title:		
Address			From (mo/yr)	To (mo/yr)	Hours per Week:
City	State	Zip Code	Check all that apply: ☐ Volunteer ☐ Intern ☐ Paid		Annual Salary
Your Supervisor's Name and Title			May We Contact Employer? ☐ YES ☐ NO	Your Supervisor's Phone Number ( )	
Reason for Leaving			# and types of employees you supervised:		
Describe in detail your job duties.					
Related Computer Skills:					

Each section asks for special information needed to complete the application. It is formatted with lines running across the page. Lines are also used to separate different parts of the application.

Current or Last Employer:			Your Job Title:		
Address			From (mo/yr)	To (mo/yr)	Hours per Week:
City	State	Zip Code	Check all that apply: ☐ Volunteer ☐ Intern ☐ Paid		Annual Salary
Your Supervisor's Name and Title			May We Contact Employer? ☐ YES ☐ NO	Your Supervisor's Phone Number ( )	
Reason for Leaving			# and types of employees you supervised:		
Describe in detail your job duties.					
Related Computer Skills:					

CERTIFICATION: Read carefully before signing and dating. Unsigned applications will not be processed. I certify that all information on this application is correct. I authorize any agent or employee of the State to verify this information and to release it to anyone who may consider me for appointment. I understand that intentionally providing false information on this form or attachments is a violation of state law. **I also understand that applications submitted electronically, via e-mail or similar media, are not valid unless I enter my name in the signature field below and such action shall constitute an electronic signature.**

Signature: **Date:**

The structure of the application includes a place for applicants to sign to show that they have been truthful in filling out the required information.

Vocabulary Development

CCSS Language 6

Vocabulary for a Job Application

Point out that job applications often use vocabulary that is specific to one particular setting. Guide students to understand the meaning of the following words that are used in the application for the State of Georgia.

supervisor: boss

résumé: a formal list of previous jobs and educational background

eligibility: ability to be employed

dismissed/terminated: fired

vocational: pertaining to a job or vocation

After You Read User Guide • Application

Comparing Functional Texts

1. **Craft and Structure** **(a)** Compare the **structures and formats** of the user guide and the job application. What elements do the texts have in common? **(b)** How do the graphics and headings help the user perform tasks efficiently?
2. **Craft and Structure** **(a)** Using the guide on pages 377 and 378, supply the precise meaning of the Spanish word *casar* and explain how it is pronounced. **(b)** Identify the text features that helped you locate this information.

Content-Area Vocabulary

3. **(a)** Identify two sets of *homographs* in English and list their meanings. **(b)** The Greek root *-phon-* means "sound." What kind of words are homophones? **(c)** Explain why *fly off the handle* is an *idiomatic,* not a literal, expression.

Timed Writing

Explanatory Text: Report

Format and Audience
The prompt directs you to write a brief report for job applicants. Include information from your source and formal language appropriate to your audience and purpose.

Write a brief report that summarizes the Georgia job application for prospective applicants. Include an explanation of how knowing this information before filling out the application might be helpful to job applicants. (20 minutes)

Academic Vocabulary
When you *summarize,* you prepare a brief statement of the most important information and details of a text.

5-Minute Planner

Complete these steps before you begin to write:

1. Review the application and take notes about its most important elements. Use the application's structure and format to guide you.
   TIP Consider questions prospective job applicants might have, and note details that address those points.
2. Consider your notes and what might be most helpful to an applicant.
3. Think about how best to structure your report, and make a quick outline. Refer to your outline and notes as you write.

ASSESS/EXTEND

Answers

Comparing Functional Texts

1. (a) **Possible response:** The Spanish-English dictionary and the job application are similar in structure because they both use headings and boldfaced type to draw attention to the most important information. The documents are structured differently since the authors' purposes are different. Call-outs and leader lines on the Spanish-English dictionary entry help the reader navigate the guide. Ruled divisions help the job applicant understand the areas in which to write on the application. (b) **Possible response:** The graphics and headings in the user guide call readers' attention to important topics and highlights certain sections, which can help readers find information easily. Graphics and headings in the application help readers stay organized and prepare them to complete sections.
2. (a) **Sample response:** **Meaning:** to marry, mate, couple, unite in marriage. **Pronunciation:** *k* (as in *kind*), *a* (as in *father*), *s* (as in *Sam*), *a* (as in *father*), *r* (as in *large*). (b) **Sample response:** The text features include keywords, explanations of word meanings, and key to Spanish pronunciation.
3. (a) *bass,* meaning freshwater fish and *bass,* meaning guitar; *dove,* meaning bird and *dove,* the past tense of *dive*. (b) **Answer:** A homophone is a word that is pronounced like another word but is spelled differently. (c) **Possible response:** *Fly off the handle* is an idiomatic expression because people don't really fly off handles when they're mad.

Timed Writing

1. Before students complete the activity, guide them in identifying and analyzing key words and phrases in the prompt, highlighted on the student page.
2. Work with students to draw up guidelines for their reports based on the key words:
   - **Focus** The report should clearly summarize the information that will be needed to complete the Georgia job application.
   - **Organization** The report should begin with a summary, followed by an explanation of how to best prepare for the process of completing the application.
   - **Elaboration** The report may include a list of items needed to complete the application, including specific documents that might be useful to reference while preparing to apply.
   - **Style** The report is intended for job applicants, so the style should be formal.
3. Have students use the 5-Minute Planner to structure their time.
4. Allow students 20 minutes to complete the assignment. Evaluate their work using the guidelines they have developed.

Common Core State Standards

- Reading Literature 4
- Writing 2

❶ Comparing Symbolism and Allegory

Symbol and Allegory

1. Introduce the skill using the instruction on the student page.
2. Give students a copy of **Comparing Symbolism and Allegory Graphic Organizer B**, *Graphic Organizer Transparencies,* p. 69. Tell them they will fill it in with symbols and meanings as they read.

Think Aloud: Model the Skill

Model a way to think about symbols. Say to students:

> To understand symbols, I think of sports team names. The names are chosen to symbolize certain qualities; a name like "the bears" symbolizes fierce strength. Character names can also carry symbolic meaning. A character named Leo, for instance, might be strong and a good leader because the name Leo is linked to lions.

Comparing Literary Works

The Scarlet Ibis • The Golden Kite, the Silver Wind

❶ Comparing Symbolism and Allegory

Works of literature can have two levels of meaning. The first level is literal—the text means exactly what it says. In some works, however, the text suggests a second, more abstract meaning. This second, deeper layer of meaning is often symbolic or allegorical.

- A **symbol** is a person or thing that represents both itself and a larger idea. For example, a dove can be a symbol of peace, and a voyage can represent the journey of life. **Symbolism** is the use of symbols to convey ideas. Writers may use traditional, or conventional, symbols that readers recognize easily, such as a rose signifying love. Writers may also create their own personal symbols within literary works. As you read, consider whether characters, objects, details, or even the setting of a story may suggest another level of meaning.
- An **allegory** is a story or poem in which every element has parallel literal and symbolic meanings. For example, in an allegory about a sailor crossing the ocean, the sailor could represent all people; storms at sea could represent life's troubles; and sails could represent the help of friends. To appreciate an allegory, consider both levels of meaning. To interpret an allegory, ask yourself what each particular element in a story might stand for. A true allegory will have a one-to-one correspondence of literal meaning to symbolic meaning throughout the narrative.

Only one of the following stories is an allegory, but both use symbols. As you read, fill out a chart like the one shown. Afterward, determine which story uses symbols to enhance the meaning and which is a true allegory.

	The Scarlet Ibis	The Golden Kite, the Silver Wind
Symbol	rotting brown petals	city wall shaped like a club
Meaning	the end of summer	a community's desire to protect itself

Common Core State Standards

Reading Literature
4. Determine the meaning of words and phrases as they are used in the text, including figurative and connotative meanings; analyze the cumulative impact of specific word choices on meaning.

Writing
2. Write informative/explanatory texts to examine and convey complex ideas, concepts, and information clearly and accurately through the effective selection, organization, and analysis of content.

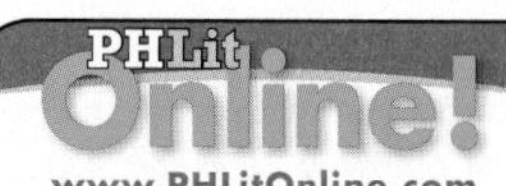

www.PHLitOnline.com

- Vocabulary flashcards
- Interactive journals
- More about the authors
- Selection audio
- Interactive graphic organizers

Vocabulary Development

Vocabulary Knowledge Rating

Create a **Vocabulary Knowledge Rating Chart** (*Professional Development Guidebook*, p. 33) featuring the words glossed in the selections:

imminent (p. 388)
infallibility (p. 390)
precariously (p. 392)
ravenous (p. 397)
spurn (p. 398)

Give students a copy of the chart, and read the words aloud. Have students mark their rating of each in the Before You Read column.

To gauge how much instruction to provide, tally the number of students who think they know each word.

Explain that the words are defined in the margin at the point where they appear in the selection. Urge students to be alert to these words as they read and discuss the selections. They will rate their knowledge again when they finish.

Vocabulary Central, featuring tools, activities, and songs for studying vocabulary, is available at **www.PHLitOnline.com.**

Is conflict necessary?

❷ Writing About the Big Question

In both of these stories, **competitiveness** leads to conflict. Complete these sentences to develop your ideas about the Big Question:

Some people like to **compete** because ________________.

To prevent a **competition** from turning into a conflict, you might ____.

Meet the Authors

James Hurst (b. 1922)

Author of "The Scarlet Ibis"

James Hurst grew up along the coast of North Carolina, a place of quiet landscapes and violent storms. After studying chemical engineering and opera and serving in the army during World War II, Hurst took a job at a New York bank. For thirty-four years, he worked as a banker and spent his evenings writing stories.

Creating Symbolism "The Scarlet Ibis," published in 1960, is Hurst's best-known story. Hurst has said that he "wanted [the ibis] to represent [the character of Doodle]—not Doodle's physical self, but his spirit."

Ray Bradbury (b. 1920)

Author of "The Golden Kite, the Silver Wind"

Born in Waukegan, Illinois, Ray Bradbury grew up in Arizona and California. He has been writing for more than sixty years and has published more than 500 stories. His work has earned him many honors, including the World Fantasy Award for lifetime achievement and the Grand Master Award from the Science Fiction Writers of America.

Writing to Entertain Bradbury is best known for his works of fantasy and science fiction. "I write for fun," Bradbury has said. "I don't see myself as a philosopher. That's awfully boring. . . . My goal is to entertain myself and others."

Teaching Resources

- All *Unit 2 Resources,* pp. 205–221
- All *Professional Development Guidebook,* pp. 33, 42
- All *Graphic Organizer Transparencies,* pp. 68–71
- All *Common Core Companion,* pp. 35–42; 190–201
- All **Enriched Online Student Edition**
- L2 EL *Hear It!* **Audio CD**
- L4 **Authors in Depth, Ray Bradbury,** pp. 33–44

All resources, including print and audio, are available at **www.PHLitOnline.com.**

Daily Bellringer

For each class during which you will teach this selection, have students complete one of the five Sentence Combining activities for Week 12 in the *Daily Bellringer Activities* booklet.

❷ Writing About the Big Question

1. Review the assignment with the class.
2. **Ask** students how a competition differs from a conflict. Discuss emotions linked to each, such as passion and tension, and explore ideas for reducing tension during competitions.
3. Have students complete the sentence starters. Review their responses as a class. (**Possible response:** Some people like to compete because they want to win. To prevent a competition from turning into a conflict, you might establish clear rules.)
4. Remind students that their answers will help them think about the Big Question, "Is conflict necessary?"

Concept Connector

Tell students that they will return to their sentence starters after they have concluded reading.

Multidraft Reading

To assist struggling readers and to deepen reading for all, apply multidraft reading protocols. For each reading, have students set the purpose indicated:

- **First reading**—identifying key ideas and details and answering any Reading Checks.
- **Second reading**—analyzing craft and structure and responding to the side-column prompts.
- **Third reading**—integrating knowledge and ideas, connecting to other texts and the world, and answering the end-of-selection questions.

For more guidance, refer to the *Classroom Strategies and Teaching Routines* card on multidraft reading.

For more about the authors and practice with the selection vocabulary, go online at **www.PHLitOnline.com.**

1 Background

The Ibis Altogether, there are about twenty species of ibis. This long-legged water bird is related to the heron, crane, and stork. Ibises eat plants, small shellfish, and mollusks. Ancient Egyptians worshiped the sacred ibis of Northern Africa, a relative of the scarlet ibis of this story.

2 Focusing Reading

Draw students into this compelling story by posting this quotation:

> *At times I was mean to Doodle. One day I took him up to the barn loft and showed him his casket, telling him how we all believed he would die.*

Ask students to predict how the relationship between the two brothers might affect the story.

Concept Connector

Students will follow up on this activity after completing "The Scarlet Ibis."

3 About the Selection

"The Scarlet Ibis" reveals that cruelty and selfishness can be entwined with love. Motivated by pride and self-interest, the narrator helps his disabled brother learn to walk and swim. Not satisfied, the narrator pushes for more. Only later does the narrator realize the depth of his feelings for his brother.

4 Critical Viewing

Answer: The person had a peaceful, quiet childhood in a pristine setting.

5 Literary Analysis

Symbolism and Allegory

1. Read aloud the first paragraph. **Ask** students to name and describe the symbol in the first sentence.

   Answer: The bleeding tree is a symbol of death, and it suggests some type of violence.

2. **Ask** the Literary Analysis question: What details about the flowers, weeds, and oriole nest symbolize death?

   Answer: Details include: rotting magnolias, "rank" weed, "graveyard flowers" that whisper names of the dead, and the "empty cradle" of a bird's nest.

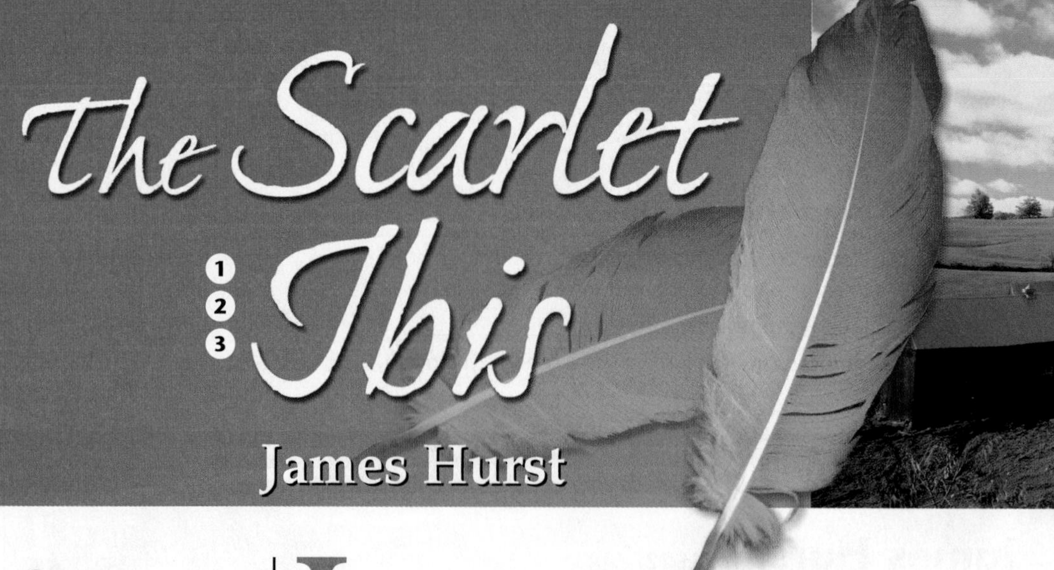

The Scarlet Ibis

1 2 3

James Hurst

4

▶ **Critical Viewing** What could you infer about the childhood of someone living in the location pictured? **[Interpret]**

Literary Analysis
Symbolism and Allegory What details about the flowers, weeds, and the oriole nest in the opening paragraph symbolize death?

It was in the clove of seasons, summer was dead but autumn had not yet been born, that the ibis lit in the bleeding tree. The flower garden was stained with rotting brown magnolia
5 petals and ironweeds grew rank amid the purple phlox. The five o'clocks by the chimney still marked time, but the oriole nest in the elm was untenanted and rocked back and forth like an empty cradle. The last graveyard flowers were blooming, and their smell drifted across the cotton field and through every room of our house, speaking softly the names of our dead.

It's strange that all this is still so clear to me, now that the summer has long since fled and time has had its way. A grindstone stands where the bleeding tree stood, just outside the kitchen door, and now if an oriole sings in the elm, its song seems to die up in the leaves, a silvery dust. The flower garden is prim, the house a gleaming white, and the pale fence across the yard stands straight and spruce. But sometimes (like right now), as I sit in the cool, green-draped parlor, the grindstone begins to turn, and time with all its changes is ground away—and I remember Doodle.

Doodle was just about the craziest brother a boy ever had. Of course, he wasn't a crazy crazy like old Miss Leedie, who was in love with President Wilson and wrote him a letter every day, but was
6 a nice crazy, like someone you meet in your dreams. He was born when I was six and was, from the outset, a disappointment. He seemed all head, with a tiny body which was red and shriveled like an old man's. Everybody thought he was going to die—everybody

Text Complexity Rubric

The Scarlet Ibis		
Qualitative Measures	**Context/ Knowledge Demands**	Conflict between two young brothers; disabled character 1 (2) 3 4 5
	Structure/ Language Clarity and Conventionality	Long sentences with embedded clauses; extensive description of setting; some regionalisms in language 1 2 (3) 4 5
	Levels of Meaning/ Purpose/Concept Level	Accessible concept (use of symbolism and allegory) 1 2 (3) 4 5
Quantitative Measures	**Text Length**	Word Count: 4,976
	Lexile	1070L

6 except Aunt Nicey, who had delivered him. She said he would live because he was born in a caul[1] and cauls were made from Jesus' nightgown. Daddy had Mr. Heath, the carpenter, build a little mahogany coffin for him. But he didn't die, and when he was three months old Mama and Daddy decided they might as well name him. They named him William Armstrong, which was like tying a big tail on a small kite. Such a name sounds good only on a tombstone.

I thought myself pretty smart at many things, like holding my breath, running, jumping, or climbing the vines in Old Woman Swamp, and I wanted more than anything else someone to race to Horsehead Landing, someone to box with, and someone to perch with in the top fork of the great pine behind the barn, where across the fields and swamps you could see the sea. I wanted a brother. But Mama, crying, told me that even if William Armstrong lived, he would never do these things with me. He might not, she sobbed, even be "all there." He might, as long as he lived, lie on the rubber sheet in the center of the bed in the front bedroom where the white marquisette curtains billowed out in the afternoon sea breeze, rustling like palmetto fronds.[2]

It was bad enough having an invalid brother, but having one who possibly was not all there was unbearable, so I began to make plans to kill him by smothering him with a pillow. However, one afternoon as I watched him, my head poked between the iron posts of the foot of the bed, he looked straight at me and grinned. I skipped through the rooms, down the echoing halls, shouting, "Mama, he smiled. He's all there! He's all there!" and he was.

1. **caul** (kôl) *n.* membrane enclosing a baby at birth.
2. **palmetto** (pal met′ ō) **fronds** (fрändz) *n.* palm leaves.

Literary Analysis
Symbolism and Allegory In what ways does the caul symbolize life and hope?

It's strange that all this is still so clear to me, now that the summer has long since fled and time has had its way.

7 

Who is Doodle?

6 Literary Analysis

Symbolism and Allegory

1. Read aloud the bracketed text, which begins on p. 384, and have students **identify** details that symbolize death.

   Answer: The baby's head is described as being "shriveled like an old man's," and the narrator says that the baby's name is fit only for being on a tombstone. In addition, most of the family members believe that the baby will die and even go so far as to build a coffin for him.

2. Tell students that the passage also contains symbols of hope and life, a pattern that readers will find throughout the story.
3. **Ask** students to respond to the Literary Analysis question: In what ways does the caul symbolize life and hope?

   Answer: A caul is a traditional symbol of good luck. Furthermore, because Aunt Nicey says the caul is made from Jesus's nightgown, it seems to symbolize that the baby is blessed or special in some way.

7 Reading Check

Answer: Doodle is the narrator's younger brother.

PHLit Online!
This selection is available in interactive format in the **Enriched Online Student Edition, www.PHLitOnline.com,** which includes an interactive graphic organizer.

Text Complexity: Reader and Task Suggestions

The Scarlet Ibis	
Preparing to Read the Text • Use the Background note on TE p. 384 to discuss the ibis. • Discuss sibling relationships in general and the issues that could arise when one sibling is disabled. • Guide students to use Multidraft Reading strategies (TE p. 383).	**Leveled Tasks** *Levels of Meaning* If students will have difficulty with levels of meaning, have them first read the story and make notes about Doodle and his health issues. Then, have them reread and note ways in which Doodle is similar to and different from the ibis. Discuss students' notes and help clarify meanings. *Analyzing* If students will not have difficulty with levels of meaning, ask them to read and note details that reveal how the narrator and Doodle feel toward each other. Tell them to look for implicit as well as explicit clues to the relationship. Encourage students to share their notes and conclusions.

❽ Literature in Context

Science Connection While known for its vibrant color, the scarlet ibis is not red when it is hatched. In fact, the young bird is brown and changes color as it grows. This interesting transformation is due to its diet, which contains a great deal of the pigment carotene. The scarlet ibis has been on the endangered species list for some time, but scientists are having limited success with breeding the birds in captivity.

Connect to the Literature Have students read the literature in context feature, and present the addtional background information above. Also point out that in the story, the appearance of the scarlet ibis seems to surprise Doodle's family. Then **ask** students the Connect to the Literature question: Why would the discovery of a scarlet ibis in coastal North Carolina, the setting of this story, be unexpected and dramatic?

Answer: The bird rarely appears north of Florida, and seeing a tropical bird in North Carolina would be quite unexpected.

❽ **LITERATURE IN CONTEXT**

Science Connection

Scarlet Ibis
Found mostly in the South American tropics, the strikingly beautiful scarlet ibis is a wading bird with long legs, a long, slender neck, black-tipped wings, and a wingspan of more than three feet. It seldom appears in the United States north of Florida.

Connect to the Literature

Why would the discovery of a scarlet ibis in coastal North Carolina, the setting of this story, be unexpected and dramatic?

When he was two, if you laid him on his stomach, he began to try to move himself, straining terribly. The doctor said that with his weak heart this strain would probably kill him, but it didn't. Trembling, he'd push himself up, turning first red, then a soft purple, and finally collapse back onto the bed like an old worn-out doll. I can still see Mama watching him, her hand pressed tight across her mouth, her eyes wide and unblinking. But he learned to crawl (it was his third winter), and we brought him out of the front bedroom, putting him on the rug before the fireplace. For the first time he became one of us.

As long as he lay all the time in bed, we called him William Armstrong, even though it was formal and sounded as if we were referring to one of our ancestors, but with his creeping around on the deerskin rug and beginning to talk, something had to be done about his name. It was I who renamed him. When he crawled, he crawled backwards, as if he were in reverse and couldn't change gears. If you called him, he'd turn around as if he were going in the other direction, then he'd back right up to you to be picked up. Crawling backward made him look like a doodle-bug, so I began to call him Doodle, and in time even Mama and Daddy thought it was a better name than William Armstrong. Only Aunt Nicey disagreed. She said caul babies should be treated with special respect since they might turn out to be saints. Renaming my brother was perhaps the kindest thing I ever did for him, because nobody expects much from someone called Doodle.

Although Doodle learned to crawl, he showed no signs of walking, but he wasn't idle. He talked so much that we all quit listening to what he said. It was about this time that Daddy built him a go-cart and I had to pull him around. At first I just paraded him up and down the piazza, but then he started crying to be taken out into the yard and it ended up by my having to lug him wherever I went. If I so much as picked up my cap, he'd start crying to go with me and Mama would call from wherever she was, "Take Doodle with you."

He was a burden in many ways. The doctor had said that he mustn't get too excited, too hot, too cold, or too tired and that he must always be treated gently. A long list of don'ts went with him, all of which I ignored once we got out of the house. To discourage his coming with me, I'd run with him across the ends of the cotton rows and careen him around corners on two wheels. Sometimes I accidentally turned him over, but he never told Mama. His skin was very sensitive, and he had to wear a big straw hat whenever he

Vocabulary Development

Ⓒ CCSS Language 6

Thematic Vocabulary: The Big Question
As students are discussing "The Scarlet Ibis," encourage them to use the thematic vocabulary presented in Introducing the Big Question, pp. 194–195. You might encourage them with sentence starters like these:

1. The narrator feels Doodle's disability is an *issue* because . . . .
2. As the narrator remembers his brother, he must *articulate* why . . .
3. Because of Doodle's *differences*, the narrator wants . . .
4. Doodle doesn't pursue an *argument* with his brother because . . .
5. The only *controversy* comes when Doodle's brother tries to . . . .

went out. When the going got rough and he had to cling to the sides of the go-cart, the hat slipped all the way down over his ears. He was a sight. Finally, I could see I was licked. Doodle was my brother and he was going to cling to me forever, no matter what I did, so I dragged him across the burning cotton field to share with him the only beauty I knew, Old Woman Swamp. I pulled the go-cart through the saw-tooth fern, down into the green dimness where the palmetto fronds whispered by the stream. I lifted him out and set him down in the soft rubber grass beside a tall pine. His eyes were round with wonder as he gazed about him, and his little hands began to stroke the rubber grass. Then he began to cry.

"For heaven's sake, what's the matter?" I asked, annoyed.

"It's so pretty," he said. "So pretty, pretty, pretty."

9 After that day Doodle and I often went down into Old Woman Swamp. I would gather wildflowers, wild violets, honeysuckle, yellow jasmine, snakeflowers, and water lilies, and with wire grass we'd weave them into necklaces and crowns. We'd bedeck ourselves with our handiwork and loll about thus beautified, beyond the touch of the everyday world. Then when the slanted rays of the sun burned orange in the tops of the pines, we'd drop our jewels into the stream and watch them float away toward the sea.

There is within me (and with sadness I have watched it in others) a knot of cruelty borne by the stream of love, much as our blood sometimes bears the seed of our destruction, and at times I was mean to Doodle. One day I took him up to the barn loft and showed him his casket, telling him how we all had believed he would die. It was covered with a film of Paris green[3] sprinkled to kill the rats, and screech owls had built a nest inside it.

Doodle studied the mahogany box for a long time, then said, "It's not mine."

"It is," I said. "And before I'll help you down from the loft, you're going to have to touch it."

"I won't touch it," he said sullenly.

"Then I'll leave you here by yourself," I threatened, and made as if I were going down.

Doodle was frightened of being left. "Don't go leave me, Brother," he cried, and he leaned toward the coffin. His hand, trembling, reached out, and when he touched the casket he screamed. A screech owl flapped out of the box into our faces, scaring us and covering us with Paris green. Doodle was paralyzed, so I put him on my shoulder and carried him down the ladder, and even when we were outside in the bright sunshine, he clung to me, crying, "Don't leave me. Don't leave me."

3. **Paris green** poisonous green powder used chiefly as an insecticide.

Literary Analysis
Symbolism and Allegory Which details in this paragraph symbolize life and beauty?

10 

Reading Check
What does the narrator force Doodle to touch?

9 Literary Analysis

Symbolism and Allegory

1. Read aloud the bracketed text, and then have students **describe** the mood.

   Answer: The mood is positive. The boys seem to be happy and enjoying their time in the swamp.
2. **Ask** the Literary Analysis question: Which details in this paragraph symbolize life and beauty?

   Answer: Symbols of life and beauty include the flowered necklaces and crowns and the image of the boys frolicking through the swamp wearing their "jewelry."
3. **Ask** students to identify the symbolic value of the final image, where the boys drop their creations in the water and watch them float away.

   Possible response: The released necklaces and crowns in the setting sun might symbolize the end of the brothers' happy times.

10 Reading Check

Answer: The narrator makes Doodle touch the coffin that was made for Doodle when he was born.

Differentiated Instruction for Universal Access

Strategy for Less Proficient Readers

Long and compound sentences like the one beginning "Doodle was my brother…" (p. 387) may prove a barrier to some students' enjoyment of the story. Have students break down long sentences like these by first identifying the three independent clauses, and reading these separately. Students should then identify the subject of each sentence (Doodle, he, I) and the rest of the sentence's phrases and clauses give further details. Once students have the sentences, they can look at the details.

 Vocabulary for English Learners

With its references to many different plants, this story's setting provides students with an opportunity to extend their vocabularies. Have students list such words as *magnolia, bleeding tree, phlox, five o'clocks,* and so on and look them up in illustrated nature guides or encyclopedias.

⓫ Literary Analysis

Symbolism and Allegory

1. Read aloud the bracketed text, and call students' attention to the narrator's reference to pride.
2. **Ask** the Literary Analysis question: How is pride like "a seed that bears two vines"?

   Answer: A single source of pride can cause both good and bad things to happen.
3. **Ask** students what other images they associate with vines and how these images might apply to the story.

   Possible response: Students might think of vines as twisting and threatening. Similarly, they might predict that the narrator's pride will eventually overtake or harm Doodle.

When Doodle was five years old, I was embarrassed at having a brother of that age who couldn't walk, so I set out to teach him. We were down in Old Woman Swamp and it was spring and the sick-sweet smell of bay flowers hung everywhere like a mournful song. "I'm going to teach you to walk, Doodle," I said.

He was sitting comfortably on the soft grass, leaning back against the pine. "Why?" he asked.

I hadn't expected such an answer. "So I won't have to haul you around all the time."

"I can't walk, Brother," he said.

"Who says so?" I demanded.

"Mama, the doctor—everybody."

"Oh, you can walk," I said, and I took him by the arms and stood him up. He collapsed onto the grass like a half-empty flour sack. It was as if he had no bones in his little legs.

"Don't hurt me, Brother," he warned.

"Shut up. I'm not going to hurt you. I'm going to teach you to walk." I heaved him up again, and again he collapsed.

This time he did not lift his face up out of the rubber grass. "I just can't do it. Let's make honeysuckle wreaths."

"Oh yes you can, Doodle," I said. "All you got to do is try. Now come on," and I hauled him up once more.

It seemed so hopeless from the beginning that it's a miracle I didn't give up. But all of us must have something or someone to be proud of, and Doodle had become mine. I did not know then that pride is a wonderful, terrible thing, a seed that bears two vines, life and death. Every day that summer we went to the pine beside the stream of Old Woman Swamp, and I put him on his feet at least a hundred times each afternoon. Occasionally I too became discouraged because it didn't seem as if he was trying, and I would say, "Doodle, don't you want to learn to walk?"

Literary Analysis
Symbolism and Allegory ⓫ How is pride like "a seed that bears two vines"?

He'd nod his head, and I'd say, "Well, if you don't keep trying, you'll never learn." Then I'd paint for him a picture of us as old men, white-haired, him with a long white beard and me still pulling him around in the go-cart. This never failed to make him try again.

Finally one day, after many weeks of practicing, he stood alone for a few seconds. When he fell, I grabbed him in my arms and hugged him, our laughter pealing through the swamp like a ringing bell. Now we knew it could be done. Hope no longer hid in the dark palmetto thicket but perched like a cardinal in the lacy toothbrush tree, brilliantly visible. "Yes, yes," I cried, and he cried it too, and the grass beneath us was soft and the smell of the swamp was sweet.

With success so **imminent**, we decided not to tell anyone until he could actually walk. Each day, barring rain, we sneaked into Old

Vocabulary
imminent (im′ ə nənt) *adj.* likely to happen soon

Vocabulary Development

Ⓒ CCSS Language 6

Selection Vocabulary Reinforcement

To reinforce and assess students' comprehension of selection vocabulary words, give them sentences in which the word may or may not be used correctly. Students must tell whether the use is correct and explain their answer. Use these sentences:

1. The brightly shining sun suggested that the forecast for severe storms was *imminent*.

   Answer: No, *imminent* is not used correctly. The shining sun does not suggest an upcoming storm.
2. Superheroes usually possess a sense of *infallibility*.

   Answer: Yes, *infallibility* is used correctly. Superheroes typically are confident that their actions are always right.
3. The picture hung *precariously* from the wall; it was safely secured with nails.

   Answer: No, *precariously* is not used correctly. It means the opposite of secure.

12

Two Boys in a Punt, 1915–Cover Illustration, *Popular Magazine,* N.C. Wyeth (1882–1945), Private Collection, Photography courtesy of Brandywine River Museum.

Woman Swamp, and by cotton-picking time Doodle was ready to show what he could do. He still wasn't able to walk far, but we could wait no longer. Keeping a nice secret is very hard to do, like holding your breath. We chose to reveal all on October eighth, Doodle's sixth birthday, and for weeks ahead we mooned around the house, promising everybody a most spectacular surprise. Aunt Nicey said that, after so much talk, if we produced anything less tremendous than the Resurrection,[4] she was going to be disappointed.

At breakfast on our chosen day, when Mama, Daddy, and Aunt Nicey were in the dining room, I brought Doodle to the door in the go-cart just as usual and had them turn their backs, making them cross their hearts and hope to die if they peeked. I helped Doodle up, and when he was standing alone I let them look. There wasn't a sound as Doodle walked slowly across the room and sat down at his place at the table. Then Mama began to cry and ran over to him, hugging him and kissing him. Daddy hugged him too, so I went to Aunt Nicey, who was thanks praying in the doorway, and began to waltz her around. We danced together quite well until she came down on my big toe with her brogans, hurting me so badly I thought I was crippled for life.

Doodle told them it was I who had taught him to walk, so everyone wanted to hug me, and I began to cry.

"What are you crying for?" asked Daddy, but I couldn't answer. They did not know that I did it for myself; that pride, whose slave I was, spoke to me louder than all their voices, and that Doodle walked only because I was ashamed of having a crippled brother.

4. **the Resurrection** (rez´ ə rek´ shən) the rising of Jesus Christ from the dead after his death and burial.

13 ◀ **Critical Viewing**
What can you tell about the brothers' relationship from the illustration and the details in the story? **[Interpret]**

"I'm going to teach you to walk, Doodle," I said.

14

Reading Check
What surprise do the boys present?

12 Humanities

Two Boys in a Punt, by N. C. Wyeth

N. C. Wyeth studied for two years at the Howard Pyle School of Art in Wilmington, Delaware. Pyle, himself a well-known illustrator and graphic artist, emphasized realism and authenticity. Wyeth became one of the school's most successful and famous graduates. His best-known works are the brilliant oil paintings with which he illustrated *Treasure Island, Robin Hood, The Last of the Mohicans,* and other novels. Use the following question for discussion:

Compare and **contrast** the boys in the painting with the brothers in "The Scarlet Ibis."

Answer: Both pairs spend time together in a rural setting. Neither boy in the painting appears dependent on the other; in the story, Doodle is dependent on the narrator.

13 Critical Viewing

Answer: The brothers in the story and in the painting share relaxed experiences in the outdoors.

14 Reading Check

Answer: The narrator has taught Doodle to walk by himself.

Differentiated Instruction for Universal Access

Strategy for Gifted/Talented Students

Ask students to rewrite the scene in which the narrator teaches Doodle to walk (p. 388) in the first person from Doodle 's point of view. Their versions should be no longer than one page and should reflect Doodle's feelings about his older brother, as well as his reactions to what happens in the scene. Have volunteers share their versions with the class in performance.

Strategy for Advanced Readers

Have students discuss how they think Doodle feels about his brother. As they read, they should watch for clues about Doodle's feelings. They should also think about how they would feel if they were in Doodle's situation. Pose the following questions to students: Does Doodle admire his brother? Is he afraid of him? Does he love him? Make sure students support their answers with details from the story and from their own experiences.

⑮ Literary Analysis

Symbolism and Allegory

1. Draw students' attention to the bracketed text. Point out that the narrator claims that Doodle's stories were much more creative than his own. Explain that Doodle's interior life (or imagination) is more developed than his brother's—a characteristic that marks Doodle as special.
2. **Ask** students to infer why all of the characters in Doodle's stories have wings.

   Possible response: Doodle's winged characters might symbolize his wish for more physical freedom and ability.
3. **Ask** students to respond to the Literary Analysis question: How might the peacock and the boy symbolize death?

   Possible response: The peacock wraps up and buries the sleeping boy in its plumage. Death (the eternal sleep) is often symbolized by sleep.

Within a few months Doodle had learned to walk well and his go-cart was put up in the barn loft (it's still there) beside his little mahogany coffin. Now, when we roamed off together, resting often, we never turned back until our destination had been reached, and to help pass the time, we took up lying. From the beginning Doodle was a terrible liar and he got me in the habit. Had anyone stopped to listen to us, we would have been sent off to Dix Hill.

Literary Analysis
Symbolism and Allegory How might the peacock and the boy symbolize death? ⑮

My lies were scary, involved, and usually pointless, but Doodle's were twice as crazy. People in his stories all had wings and flew wherever they wanted to go. His favorite lie was about a boy named Peter who had a pet peacock with a ten-foot tail. Peter wore a golden robe that glittered so brightly that when he walked through the sunflowers they turned away from the sun to face him. When Peter was ready to go to sleep, the peacock spread his magnificent tail, enfolding the boy gently like a closing go-to-sleep flower, burying him in the gloriously iridescent, rustling vortex.[5] Yes, I must admit it. Doodle could beat me lying.

Doodle and I spent lots of time thinking about our future. We decided that when we were grown we'd live in Old Woman Swamp and pick dog-tongue for a living. Beside the stream, he planned, we'd build us a house of whispering leaves and the swamp birds would be our chickens. All day long (when we weren't gathering dog-tongue) we'd swing through the cypresses on the rope vines, and if it rained we'd huddle beneath an umbrella tree and play stickfrog. Mama and Daddy could come and live with us if they wanted to. He even came up with the idea that he could marry Mama and I could marry Daddy. Of course, I was old enough to know this wouldn't work out, but the picture he painted was so beautiful and serene that all I could do was whisper Yes, yes.

Vocabulary
infallibility (in fal′ ə bil′ ə tē) *n.* condition of not being likely to fail

Once I had succeeded in teaching Doodle to walk, I began to believe in my own **infallibility** and I prepared a terrific development program for him, unknown to Mama and Daddy, of course. I would teach him to run, to swim, to climb trees, and to fight. He, too, now believed in my infallibility, so we set the deadline for these accomplishments less than a year away, when, it had been decided, Doodle could start to school.

That winter we didn't make much progress, for I was in school and Doodle suffered from one bad cold after another. But when spring came, rich and warm, we raised our sights again. Success lay at the end of summer like a pot of gold, and our campaign got off to a good start. On hot days, Doodle and I went down to Horsehead Landing and I gave him swimming lessons or showed him how to row a boat. Sometimes we descended into the cool

5. **vortex** (vôr′ teks′) *n.* rushing whirl, drawing in all that surrounds it.

Vocabulary Development

Ⓒ CCSS Language 6

Word Analysis

Write the word *infallibility* on the board, and tell students that the prefix *in-* is a variant of *un-*, which usually means "not." *Infallibility* means "not having the quality of fallibility" or "not being able to be wrong."

Next, write the following words on the board: *secure, sufficient, elegant, direct,* and *accurate.* Ask students to add the prefix *in-* to each word. They should also write a brief definition for each new word.

Answer: *insecure:* not safe; *insufficient:* not enough; *inelegant:* not elegant; crude; *indirect:* not direct or roundabout; *inaccurate:* not exact or containing mistakes.

greenness of Old Woman Swamp and climbed the rope vines or boxed scientifically beneath the pine where he had learned to walk. Promise hung about us like the leaves, and wherever we looked, ferns unfurled and birds broke into song.

That summer, the summer of 1918, was blighted. In May and June there was no rain and the crops withered, curled up, then died under the thirsty sun. One morning in July a hurricane came out of the east, tipping over the oaks in the yard and splitting the limbs of the elm trees. That afternoon it roared back out of the west, blew the fallen oaks around, snapping their roots and tearing them out of the earth like a hawk at the entrails of a chicken. Cotton bolls were wrenched from the stalks and lay like green walnuts in the valleys between the rows, while the cornfield leaned over uniformly so that the tassels touched the ground. Doodle and I followed Daddy out into the cotton field, where he stood, shoulders sagging, surveying the ruin. When his chin sank down onto his chest, we were frightened, and Doodle slipped his hand into mine. Suddenly Daddy straightened his shoulders, raised a giant knuckly fist, and with a voice that seemed to rumble out of the earth itself began cursing heaven, hell, the weather, and the Republican Party. Doodle and I, prodding each other and giggling, went back to the house, knowing that everything would be all right.

And during that summer, strange names were heard through the house: Chateau-Thierry, Amiens, Soissons, and in her blessing at the supper table, Mama once said, "And bless the Pearsons, whose boy Joe was lost at Belleau Wood."[6]

So we came to that clove of seasons. School was only a few weeks away, and Doodle was far behind schedule. He could barely clear the ground when climbing up the rope vines and his swimming was certainly not passable. We decided to double our efforts, to make that last drive and reach our pot of gold. I made him swim until he turned blue and row until he couldn't lift an oar. Wherever we went, I purposely walked fast, and although he kept up, his face turned red and his eyes became glazed. Once, he could go no further, so he collapsed on the ground and began to cry.

"Aw, come on, Doodle," I urged. "You can do it. Do you want to be different from everybody else when you start school?"

"Does it make any difference?"

"It certainly does," I said. "Now, come on," and I helped him up.

As we slipped through dog days, Doodle began to look feverish, and Mama felt his forehead, asking him if he felt ill. At night he didn't sleep well, and sometimes he had nightmares, crying out until I touched him and said, "Wake up, Doodle. Wake up."

6. **Chateau-Thierry** (sha´ tō´ tē er´ ē), **Amiens** (ȧ myan´), **Soissons** (swä sôn´), . . . **Belleau** (be lō´) **Wood** places in France where battles were fought during World War I.

Literary Analysis Symbolism and Allegory What might the "blighted" summer symbolize?

Success lay at the end of summer like a pot of gold...

17 

What plan does the narrator make for Doodle's future?

16 Literary Analysis

Symbolism and Allegory

1. After students reread the bracketed text, point out details that have negative connotations, such as the withered, dead crops; the thirsty sun; the split trees; and the chicken entrails.
2. Stress that this description of nature differs dramatically from the earlier, more serene description on p. 387.
3. **Ask** the Literary Analysis question: What might the "blighted" summer symbolize?

   Answer: The blighted summer might symbolize sickness and death.

17 Reading Check

Answer: The narrator plans to teach Doodle to run, swim, climb trees, and fight before he starts school.

Differentiated Instruction for Universal Access

EL Pronunciation for English Learners

To help students pronounce initial *t*, post these words: *time, dime; tear, dear; to, do;* and *ten, den*. Pronounce each word, stressing the initial sound. Have students echo. Call out words at random as students write them out. Have students compare and discuss results. Discuss incorrect choices and clarify.

Strategy for Advanced Readers

Have students write essays analyzing the symbolic importance of birds in this story, such as the screech owl (p. 387), the peacock (p. 390), and the ibis (pp. 392–393). Ask students to discuss the following questions: At what point in the plot does each bird appear? What actions does the bird take? How do the human characters react to the bird? Which bird seems to be given the most importance? Tell students to support their answers with details from the story.

⓲ Critical Viewing

Possible responses: Students might be excited, intrigued, or awed.

⓳ Connecting to the Big Question

1. Recall with students the earlier discussion about competition and the emotions that motivate it. Point out that people may be in competition with others or with themselves.
2. Have students read the bracketed text on page 392. **Ask** students: What is the narrator's goal in his program for Doodle? What keeps the narrator from admitting defeat in this program? **Possible response:** He wants to teach Doodle "to run, to swim, to climb trees, and to fight." The narrator's pride keeps him from admitting defeat in the program.
3. **Ask:** How is the narrator in competition with himself? Is this internal conflict necessary? Explain. **Possible response:** The narrator is in competition with himself over whether he can overcome frustration in order to reach his goals for Doodle. The conflict is necessary to keep the narrator motivated.

⓲ ▼ **Critical Viewing** How would you react if this exotic bird—an ibis—showed up in your backyard? **[Relate]**

Vocabulary
precariously (pri kerˊ ē əs lē) *adv.* insecurely

⓳ It was Saturday noon, just a few days before school was to start. I should have already admitted defeat, but my pride wouldn't let me. The excitement of our program had now been gone for weeks, but still we kept on with a tired doggedness. It was too late to turn back, for we had both wandered too far into a net of expectations and had left no crumbs behind.

Daddy, Mama, Doodle, and I were seated at the dining-room table having lunch. It was a hot day, with all the windows and doors open in case a breeze should come. In the kitchen Aunt Nicey was humming softly. After a long silence, Daddy spoke. "It's so calm, I wouldn't be surprised if we had a storm this afternoon."

"I haven't heard a rain frog," said Mama, who believed in signs, as she served the bread around the table.

"I did," declared Doodle. "Down in the swamp."

"He didn't," I said contrarily.

"You did, eh?" said Daddy, ignoring my denial.

"I certainly did," Doodle reiterated, scowling at me over the top of his iced-tea glass, and we were quiet again.

Suddenly, from out in the yard, came a strange croaking noise. Doodle stopped eating, with a piece of bread poised ready for his mouth, his eyes popped round like two blue buttons. "What's that?" he whispered.

I jumped up, knocking over my chair, and had reached the door when Mama called, "Pick up the chair, sit down again, and say excuse me."

By the time I had done this, Doodle had excused himself and had slipped out into the yard. He was looking up into the bleeding tree. "It's a great big red bird!" he called.

The bird croaked loudly again, and Mama and Daddy came out into the yard. We shaded our eyes with our hands against the hazy glare of the sun and peered up through the still leaves. On the topmost branch a bird the size of a chicken, with scarlet feathers and long legs, was perched **precariously**. Its wings hung down loosely, and as we watched, a feather dropped away and floated slowly down through the green leaves.

"It's not even frightened of us," Mama said.

"It looks tired," Daddy added. "Or maybe sick."

Doodle's hands were clasped at his throat, and I had never seen him stand still so long. "What is it?" he asked.

Daddy shook his head. "I don't know, maybe it's—"

⓴ At that moment the bird began to flutter, but the wings were uncoordinated, and amid much flapping and a spray of flying feathers, it tumbled down, bumping through the limbs of the

Vocabulary Development

Ⓒ CCSS Language 6

Word Forms

Expand students' vocabulary by helping them learn related forms of the selection vocabulary words. Three selection vocabulary words for "The Scarlet Ibis" have related forms. Give students a blank **Word Form Chart** (*Professional Development Guidebook*, p. 42), with *imminent, infallibility,* and *precariously* in the correct columns. Have students work as a class or in pairs to determine the related forms. The final chart should look like the one shown.

Noun	Verb	Adjective	Adverb
imminence		**imminent**	imminently
infallibility		infallible	infallibly
precariousness		precarious	**precariously**

20 bleeding tree and landing at our feet with a thud. Its long, graceful neck jerked twice into an S, then straightened out, and the bird was still. A white veil came over the eyes and the long white beak unhinged. Its legs were crossed and its clawlike feet were delicately curved at rest. Even death did not mar its grace, for it lay on the earth like a broken vase of red flowers, and we stood around it, awed by its exotic beauty.

"It's dead," Mama said.

"What is it?" Doodle repeated.

"Go bring me the bird book," said Daddy.

I ran into the house and brought back the bird book. As we watched, Daddy thumbed through its pages. "It's a scarlet ibis," he said, pointing to a picture. "It lives in the tropics—South America to Florida. A storm must have brought it here."

Sadly, we all looked back at the bird. A scarlet ibis! How many miles it had traveled to die like this, in our yard, beneath the bleeding tree.

"Let's finish lunch," Mama said, nudging us back toward the dining room.

"I'm not hungry," said Doodle, and he knelt down beside the ibis.

"We've got peach cobbler for dessert," Mama tempted from the doorway.

Doodle remained kneeling. "I'm going to bury him."

"Don't you dare touch him," Mama warned. "There's no telling what disease he might have had."

"All right," said Doodle. "I won't."

Daddy, Mama, and I went back to the dining-room table, but we watched Doodle through the open door. He took out a piece of string from his pocket and, without touching the ibis, looped one end around its neck. Slowly, while singing softly "Shall We Gather at the River," he carried the bird around to the front yard and dug a hole in the flower garden, next to the petunia bed. Now we were watching him through the front window, but he didn't know it. His awkwardness at digging the hole with a shovel whose handle was twice as long as he was made us laugh, and we covered our mouths with our hands so he wouldn't hear.

When Doodle came into the dining room, he found us seriously eating our cobbler. He was pale and lingered just inside the screen door. "Did you get the scarlet ibis buried?" asked Daddy.

Doodle didn't speak but nodded his head.

"Go wash your hands, and then you can have some peach cobbler," said Mama.

"I'm not hungry," he said.

Literary Analysis Symbolism and Allegory In what ways are the bird's uncoordinated movements similar to Doodle's? Explain.

On the topmost branch a bird the size of a chicken, with scarlet feathers and long legs, was perched precariously.

21 Reading Check

What does Doodle find in the bleeding tree?

20 Literary Analysis

Symbolism and Allegory

1. Remind students of James Hurst's statement that the ibis is a symbol of Doodle's spirit. Explain that the bird and Doodle also share some physical similarities
2. Have students read the bracketed text. **Ask** students the Literary Analysis question: In what ways are the bird's uncoordinated movements similar to Doodle's? Explain.

   Answer: The bird has trouble flying, just as Doodle has trouble walking.
3. **Ask** students to predict how the story will end, based on this paragraph.

   Possible response: Because the scarlet ibis is a symbol for Doodle, it seems likely that Doodle will also die.

21 Reading Check

Answer: Doodle finds a big red bird.

Differentiated Instruction for Universal Access

Strategy for Special-Needs Students

Students may have trouble identifying why the ibis serves as a symbol for Doodle. Have students create two-column charts, one column labeled "Doodle" and the other labeled "ibis." Ask students to fill the chart with descriptions of Doodle and the bird's physical characteristics. Then, have students draw lines to connect the similar traits. Finally, ask students to write a single sentence that summarizes these similarities.

EL Strategy for English Learners

To give students a context for the story and to model how to interpret elements of symbolism and allegory, show them **Comparing Symbolism and Allegory Graphic Organizer A**, p. 68 in ***Graphic Organizer Transparencies.*** The partially completed graphic organizer will give students insight into symbolism and allegory. They can use it as a model for interpreting symbols as they read.

Spiral Review

Plot Devices

1. Remind students that they studied the concept of plot devices in the Unit 2 Literary Analysis workshop (pp. 196–209).
2. **Ask** students the Spiral Review question.

   Possible response: The death of the unique bird may suggest a death or injury will happen to one of the characters.

22 Literary Analysis

Symbolism and Allegory

1. Tell students that weather sometimes serves a symbolic purpose in literature. Explain that in the last paragraphs, a dramatic storm coincides with the story's climax.
2. Have students read the bracketed text. **Ask** the Literary Analysis question: What might "black clouds" symbolize? Explain.

   Answer: Black clouds usually signal that a storm is about to come, so they might symbolize imminent trouble or danger.
3. Discuss the symbolic value of the storm. Explain that storms are often associated with tragedy. Tell students that the presence of a storm at this point of the plot heightens the drama.

Spiral Review
Plot Devices What future event might the strange episode of the scarlet ibis foreshadow?

Literary Analysis
Symbolism and Allegory What might "black clouds" symbolize? Explain.

"Dead birds is bad luck," said Aunt Nicey, poking her head from the kitchen door. "Specially red dead birds!"

As soon as I had finished eating, Doodle and I hurried off to Horsehead Landing. Time was short, and Doodle still had a long way to go if he was going to keep up with the other boys when he started school. The sun, gilded with the yellow cast of autumn, still burned fiercely, but the dark green woods through which we passed were shady and cool. When we reached the landing, Doodle said he was too tired to swim, so we got into a skiff and floated down the creek with the tide. Far off in the marsh a rail was scolding, and over on the beach locusts were singing in the myrtle trees. Doodle did not speak and kept his head turned away, letting one hand trail limply in the water.

22 After we had drifted a long way, I put the oars in place and made Doodle row back against the tide. Black clouds began to gather in the southwest, and he kept watching them, trying to pull the oars a little faster. When we reached Horsehead Landing, lightning was playing across half the sky and thunder roared out, hiding even the sound of the sea. The sun disappeared and darkness descended, almost like night. Flocks of marsh crows flew by, heading inland to their roosting trees, and two egrets, squawking, arose from the oyster-rock shallows and careened away.

Doodle was both tired and frightened, and when he stepped from the skiff he collapsed onto the mud, sending an armada of fiddler crabs rustling off into the marsh grass. I helped him up, and as he wiped the mud off his trousers, he smiled at me ashamedly. He had failed and we both knew it, so we started back home, racing the storm. We never spoke (What are the words that can solder cracked pride?), but I knew he was watching me, watching for a sign of mercy. The lightning was near now, and from fear he walked so close behind me he kept stepping on my heels. The faster I walked, the faster he walked, so I began to run. The rain was coming, roaring through the pines, and then, like a bursting Roman candle, a gum tree ahead of us was shattered by a bolt of lightning. When the deafening peal of thunder had died, and in the moment before the rain arrived, I heard Doodle, who had fallen behind, cry out, "Brother, Brother, don't leave me! Don't leave me!"

The knowledge that Doodle's and my plans had come to naught was bitter, and that streak of cruelty within me awakened. I ran as fast as I could, leaving him far behind with a wall of rain dividing us. The drops stung my face like nettles, and the wind flared the wet glistening leaves of the bordering trees. Soon I could hear his voice no more.

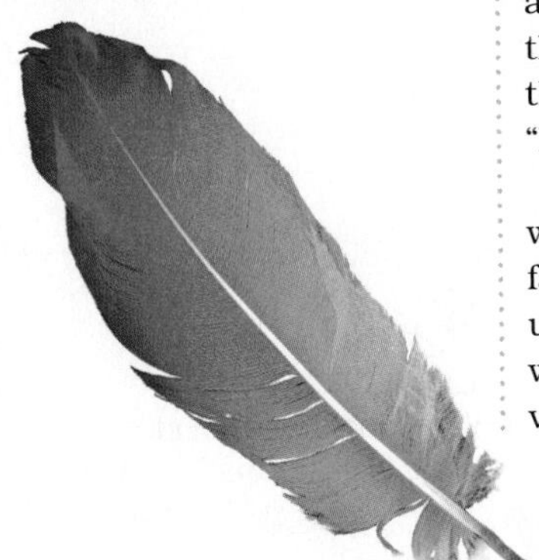

Vocabulary Development

CCSS Language 6

Selection Vocabulary Reinforcement

Students will benefit from additional examples and practice with the selection vocabulary words. Reinforce their comprehension with "show-you-know" sentences. The first part of each sentence uses the vocabulary word in an appropriate context. The second part of the sentence—the "show-you-know" part—clarifies the first part. Model this strategy with this example for *imminent:*

Her win was *imminent;* Sally could practically taste victory.

Then, give students these sentence prompts, and coach them in creating the clarification part:

1. Before he got lost, the guide had a sense of *infallibility;* ______.

   Possible response: afterward, he realized that he made mistakes like everyone else.
2. The glass was perched *precariously* on the end of the table; ______.

   Possible response: it seemed ready to fall at any moment.

I hadn't run too far before I became tired, and the flood of childish spite evanesced as well. I stopped and waited for Doodle. The sound of rain was everywhere, but the wind had died and it fell straight down in parallel paths like ropes hanging from the sky. As I waited, I peered through the downpour, but no one came. Finally I went back and found him huddled beneath a red nightshade bush beside the road. He was sitting on the ground, his face buried in his arms, which were resting on his drawn-up knees. "Let's go, Doodle," I said.

He didn't answer, so I placed my hand on his forehead and lifted his head. Limply, he fell backwards onto the earth. He had been bleeding from the mouth, and his neck and the front of his shirt were stained a brilliant red.

23 "Doodle! Doodle!" I cried, shaking him, but there was no answer but the ropy rain. He lay very awkwardly, with his head thrown far back, making his vermilion neck appear unusually long and slim. His little legs, bent sharply at the knees, had never before seemed so fragile, so thin.

I began to weep, and the tear-blurred vision in red before me looked very familiar. "Doodle!" I screamed above the pounding storm and threw my body to the earth above his. For a long long time, it seemed forever, I lay there crying, sheltering my fallen scarlet ibis from the heresy[7] of rain.

7. **heresy** (her´ ə sē) *n.* idea opposed to the beliefs of a religion or philosophy.

Literary Analysis
Symbolism and Allegory How are the details about the blood as well as Doodle's position beneath the bush similar to what happened to the scarlet ibis?

Critical Thinking

Cite textual evidence to support your responses.

1. **Key Ideas and Details** **Analyze:** Why does the narrator cry when everyone congratulates him for teaching Doodle to walk?
2. **Key Ideas and Details** **Analyze:** What do the narrator's tears reveal about his conflicted, or mixed, feelings?
3. **Key Ideas and Details** **(a)** What does Doodle do with the dead ibis? **(b) Compare and Contrast:** How does Doodle's reaction to the dead bird compare to those of his family members? Support your answer with details from the text. **(c) Infer:** What do you think motivates Doodle to treat the ibis as he does?
4. **Integration of Knowledge and Ideas** As a child, the narrator sets demanding competitive goals for Doodle. **(a)** Why do you think Doodle strives for these goals even though he does not have a competitive nature? **(b)** In what way do those goals reflect the conflict that the narrator feels about Doodle? *[Connect to the Big Question: Is conflict necessary?]*

Differentiated Instruction for Universal Access

Culturally Responsive Instruction

Culture Focus Point out to students that the central relationship in this story is between a family and one disabled member of that family. Doodle, who is physically and probably mentally disabled, lives in his family's home and is included in many of the narrator's activities. Explain that different cultures have different approaches to disabled people, and that these approaches have changed over time. Point out features of your school, such as ramps or special classes, which enable disabled students to fully participate, but explain that these were not always present in American schools. Ask students to share knowledge of ways that disabled people are included or excluded from activities in students' home culture or family's country of origin.

23 Literary Analysis
Symbolism and Allegory

1. Recall that the story draws a strong link between Doodle and the scarlet ibis.
2. Read the bracketed text aloud. **Ask** the Literary Analysis question: How are the details about the blood as well as Doodle's position beneath the bush similar to what happened to the scarlet ibis?

   Answer: Doodle's blood recalls the color of the ibis and the bleeding tree. The description of Doodle's neck and legs mirrors that of the ibis on p. 393.

Concept Connector

Have students return to their responses to Writing About the Big Question and to the Focusing Reading activity on p. 384. Revisit your discussion about the brothers' relationship and their sibiling rivalry.

ASSESS
Answers

Critical Thinking

Remind students to support their answers with evidence from the text.

1. The narrator cries because he knows that his reasons for teaching Doodle were selfish.
2. The narrator's tears reveal that he is ashamed of Doodle even though he loves him. His tears also reveal that he is ashamed of himself.
3. (a) Doodle buries the ibis.
   (b) Doodle experiences more grief about the dead bird than anyone else in his family.
   (c) Doodle is sensitive. He may have also identified with the bird's strangeness and weakness.
4. **Possible responses:** (a) Doodle wants to please his older brother and he wants his brother to take him places.
   (b) The narrator is torn between accepting Doodle as he is and wanting him to be "normal." He wants to prove to the world that he can make Doodle "normal."

TEACH

24 Background

The Cold War The Cold War is called "cold" because no direct military combat was involved. The Cold War was a standoff between the United States and the Soviet Union, which were the only great powers in the world at the end of World War II.

25 Activating Prior Knowledge

Initiate a discussion of rivalry. Include questions like these: How do rivals behave toward one another? How far will rivals go to outdo one another? What kinds of outcomes can result from a rivalry? Explain that students are about to read a story of the unexpected results of a rivalry.

Concept Connector →

Students will follow up on this activity after completing "The Golden Kite, the Silver Wind."

26 About the Selection

"The Golden Kite, the Silver Wind" is a fable that highlights the negative consequences when competition is the only form of interaction. On a literal level, the story is about two rival towns that construct ever more complex walls to empower and protect themselves. On a symbolic level, it symbolizes the behaviors of nations or groups that, from fear or arrogance, build up their defenses rather than resolve their differences.

27 Critical Viewing

Possible response: The mood of the leader in the painting is serene, while the Mandarin's mood is agitated. Both are leaders of traditional Asian societies.

24 25 26

The Golden Kite, the Silver Wind

Ray Bradbury

27 ▼ **Critical Viewing** How are the leader in this painting and the Mandarin in the story both similar and different? **[Compare and Contrast]**

Background "The Golden Kite, the Silver Wind" was written during the Cold War, a period of intense rivalry between the United States and the former Soviet Union that shaped world politics in the second half of the twentieth century. During this time, each action by one country—the creation of a weapon, the launching of a satellite—was countered by a reaction from the other country. As you read, think about the parallels between the story events and the conflicts of the Cold War.

"In the shape of a pig?" cried the Mandarin.[1]

"In the shape of a pig," said the messenger, and departed.

"Oh, what an evil day in an evil year," cried the Mandarin. "The town of Kwan-Si, beyond the hill, was very small in my childhood. Now it has grown so large that at last they are building a wall."

"But why should a wall two miles away make my good father sad and angry all within the hour?" asked his daughter quietly.

"They build their wall," said the Mandarin, "in the shape of a pig! Do you see? Our own city wall is built in the shape of an orange. That pig will devour us, greedily!"

"Ah."

They both sat thinking.

Life was full of symbols and omens. Demons lurked everywhere, Death swam in the wetness of an eye, the turn of a gull's wing meant rain, a fan held so, the tilt of a roof, and, yes, even a city wall was of immense importance. Travelers and tourists, caravans, musicians, artists, coming upon these two towns, equally judging the portents,[2] would say, "The city 28

1. **Mandarin** (man′ də rin) *n.* a high official of China; here, the ruling leader.
2. **portents** (pôr′ tents′) *n.* things that are thought to be signs of events to come; omens.

Text Complexity Rubric

The Golden Kite, the Silver Wind		
Qualitative Measures	**Context/ Knowledge Demands**	Allegorical fable parallels events of the Cold War; history of Cold War 1 2 3 (4) 5
	Structure/ Language Clarity and Conventionality	Some long sentences with embedded clauses; on-level vocabulary 1 2 (3) 4 5
	Levels of Meaning/ Purpose/Concept Level	Challenging concept (allegory of Cold War) 1 2 3 (4) 5
Quantitative Measures	**Text Length**	Word Count: 1,684
	Lexile	880L

shaped like an orange? No! I will enter the city shaped like a pig and prosper, eating all, growing fat with good luck and prosperity!"

The Mandarin wept. "All is lost! These symbols and signs terrify. Our city will come on evil days."

"Then," said the daughter, "call in your stonemasons and temple builders. I will whisper from behind the silken screen and you will know the words."

The old man clapped his hands despairingly. "Ho, stonemasons! "Ho, builders of towns and palaces!"

The men who knew marble and granite and onyx and quartz came quickly. The Mandarin faced them most uneasily, himself waiting for a whisper from the silken screen behind his throne. At last the whisper came.

"I have called you here," said the whisper.

"I have called you here," said the Mandarin aloud, "because our city is shaped like an orange, and the vile city of Kwan-Si has this day shaped theirs like a ravenous pig—"

Here the stonemasons groaned and wept. Death rattled his cane in the outer courtyard. Poverty made a sound like a wet cough in the shadows of the room.

"And so," said the whisper, said the Mandarin, "you raisers of walls must go bearing trowels and rocks and change the shape of our city!"

The architects and masons gasped. The Mandarin himself gasped at what he had said. The whisper whispered. The Mandarin went on: "And you will change our walls into a club which may beat the pig and drive it off!"

The stonemasons rose up, shouting. Even the Mandarin, delighted at the words from his mouth, applauded, stood down from his throne. "Quick!" he cried. "To work!"

When his men had gone, smiling and bustling, the Mandarin turned with great love to the silken screen. "Daughter," he whispered, "I will embrace you." There was no reply. He stepped around the screen, and she was gone.

Such modesty, he thought. She has slipped away and left me with a triumph, as if it were mine.

The news spread through the city; the Mandarin was acclaimed. Everyone carried stone to the walls. Fireworks were set off and the demons of death and poverty did not linger, as all worked together. At the end of the month the wall had been changed. It was now a mighty bludgeon with which to drive pigs, boars, even lions, far away. The Mandarin slept like a happy fox every night.

"I would like to see the Mandarin of Kwan-Si when the news is

Literary Analysis
Symbolism and Allegory What qualities do the people believe the image of a pig symbolizes?

Vocabulary
ravenous (rav´ ə nəs) *adj.* wildly hungry

Life was full of symbols and omens.

29 
Reading Check

Who whispers to the king from behind a silken screen?

28 Literary Analysis

Symbolism and Allegory

1. Read aloud the bracketed text that begins on p. 396. Point out how the Chinese people in the story place a strong value on symbols: "Life was full of symbols and omens."
2. **Ask** the Literary Analysis question: What qualities do the people believe the image of a pig symbolizes?

   Answer: The people believe that the pig symbolizes the other town's future luck and prosperity. A pig can eat, grow fat, and prosper.

29 Reading Check

Answer: The king's daughter is whispering from behind the screen.

Text Complexity: Reader and Task Suggestions

The Golden Kite, the Silver Wind	
Preparing to Read the Text • Draw upon the Background note on TE p. 396 to discuss the Cold War. • Explain that this story is an allegory. Review the meaning and uses of allegory. • Guide students to use Multidraft Reading strategies (TE p. 383).	**Leveled Tasks** *Levels of Meaning* If students will have difficulty understanding the allegory, have them read and note each time one of the towns changes its wall. Then, have students reread to look for details showing how that competition affects each town. Guide a discussion of students' notes, clarifying the parallel with the United States and Soviet Union during the Cold War. *Analyzing* If students will not have difficulty understanding the allegory, have them read and note the use of symbols in addition to those of the wall shapes. Ask them to suggest the interpretation of each symbol and share during class discussion.

30 Literary Analysis

Symbolism and Allegory

1. Have students read the bracketed text. **Ask** them to respond to the Literary Analysis question: In what ways does the "winter flower" describe the fleeting pleasure the Mandarin feels?

   Answer: The winter flower dies quickly. Similarly, the Mandarin's pleasure is short-lived.

2. Tell students that this symbol appears in the form of a simile. Remind students that similes are comparisons that use the words *like* or *as*. Point out that both similes and metaphors are often used to develop symbols.

31 Critical Thinking

Predict

1. Point out the consequences of the Mandarin's order to rebuild the walls in the shape of a club: The people have had to neglect their crops, and the whole city is impoverished.
2. **Ask** students: What do you think the consequences of this latest action will be?

   Answer: Each city will rebuild its wall in a shape superior to the shape chosen by the other city.

3. Point out to students how this chain of events was similar to the Cold War: Each action by the United States or the former Soviet Union was countered by a reaction from the other country.

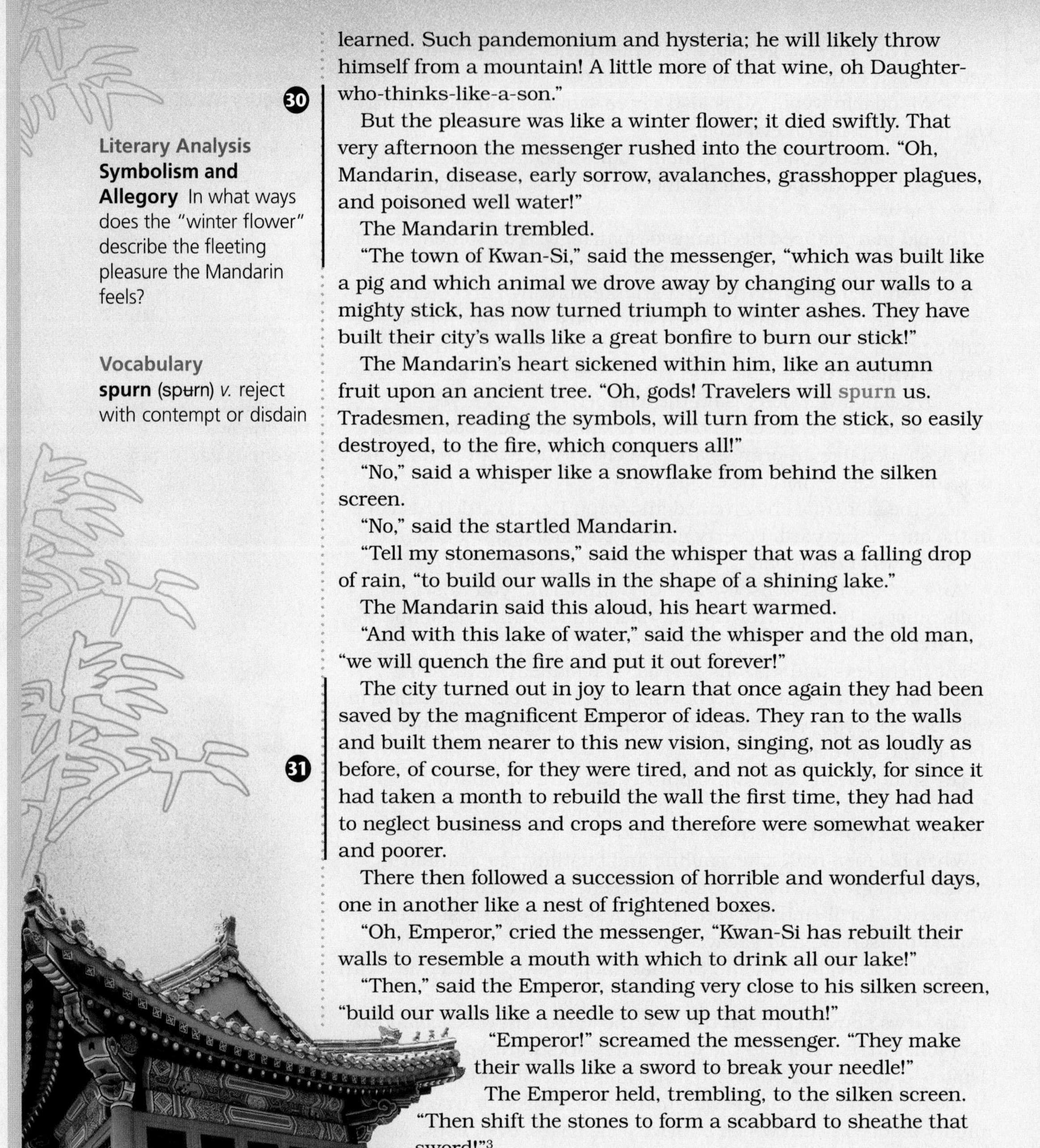

learned. Such pandemonium and hysteria; he will likely throw himself from a mountain! A little more of that wine, oh Daughter-
30 who-thinks-like-a-son."

But the pleasure was like a winter flower; it died swiftly. That very afternoon the messenger rushed into the courtroom. "Oh, Mandarin, disease, early sorrow, avalanches, grasshopper plagues, and poisoned well water!"

The Mandarin trembled.

"The town of Kwan-Si," said the messenger, "which was built like a pig and which animal we drove away by changing our walls to a mighty stick, has now turned triumph to winter ashes. They have built their city's walls like a great bonfire to burn our stick!"

The Mandarin's heart sickened within him, like an autumn fruit upon an ancient tree. "Oh, gods! Travelers will **spurn** us. Tradesmen, reading the symbols, will turn from the stick, so easily destroyed, to the fire, which conquers all!"

"No," said a whisper like a snowflake from behind the silken screen.

"No," said the startled Mandarin.

"Tell my stonemasons," said the whisper that was a falling drop of rain, "to build our walls in the shape of a shining lake."

The Mandarin said this aloud, his heart warmed.

"And with this lake of water," said the whisper and the old man, "we will quench the fire and put it out forever!"

The city turned out in joy to learn that once again they had been saved by the magnificent Emperor of ideas. They ran to the walls and built them nearer to this new vision, singing, not as loudly as
31 before, of course, for they were tired, and not as quickly, for since it had taken a month to rebuild the wall the first time, they had had to neglect business and crops and therefore were somewhat weaker and poorer.

There then followed a succession of horrible and wonderful days, one in another like a nest of frightened boxes.

"Oh, Emperor," cried the messenger, "Kwan-Si has rebuilt their walls to resemble a mouth with which to drink all our lake!"

"Then," said the Emperor, standing very close to his silken screen, "build our walls like a needle to sew up that mouth!"

"Emperor!" screamed the messenger. "They make their walls like a sword to break your needle!"

The Emperor held, trembling, to the silken screen. "Then shift the stones to form a scabbard to sheathe that sword!"[3]

Literary Analysis
Symbolism and Allegory In what ways does the "winter flower" describe the fleeting pleasure the Mandarin feels?

Vocabulary
spurn (spurn) *v.* reject with contempt or disdain

3. **scabbard** (skab´ ərd) **to sheathe** (shēth) **that sword!** case to hold the blade of the sword.

Vocabulary Development

CCSS Language 6

Thematic Vocabulary: The Big Question

As students are discussing "The Golden Kite, the Silver Wind," encourage them to use the thematic vocabulary presented in Introducing the Big Question, pp. 194–195. You might encourage them with sentence starters like these:

1. The Mandarin's *grievance* against the next town is . . .
2. The Mandarin's daughter helps him *articulate* his unhappiness by . . .
3. The two towns begin a long *competition* over . . .
4. Eventually, they learn that if they *cooperate*, . . .

"Mercy," wept the messenger the following morn, "they have worked all night and shaped their walls like lightning which will explode and destroy that sheath!"

Sickness spread in the city like a pack of evil dogs. Shops closed. The population, working now steadily for endless months upon the changing of the walls, resembled Death himself, clattering his white bones like musical instruments in the wind. Funerals began to appear in the streets, though it was the middle of summer, a time when all should be tending and harvesting. The Mandarin fell so ill that he had his bed drawn up by the silken screen and there he lay, miserably giving his architectural orders. The voice behind the screen was weak now, too, and faint, like the wind in the eaves.

"Kwan-Si is an eagle. Then our walls must be a net for that eagle. They are a sun to burn our net. Then we build a moon to eclipse their sun!"

2 Like a rusted machine, the city ground to a halt.

At last the whisper behind the screen cried out:

"In the name of the gods, send for Kwan-Si!"

Upon the last day of summer the Mandarin Kwan-Si, very ill and withered away, was carried into our Mandarin's courtroom by four starving footmen. The two mandarins were propped up, facing each other. Their breaths fluttered like winter winds in their mouths. A voice said:

"Let us put an end to this."

The old men nodded.

"This cannot go on," said the faint voice. "Our people do nothing but rebuild our cities to a different shape every day, every hour. They have no time to hunt, to fish, to love, to be good to their ancestors and their ancestors' children."

"This I admit," said the mandarins of the towns of the Cage, the Moon, the Spear, the Fire, the Sword and this, that, and other things.

"Carry us into the sunlight," said the voice.

The old men were borne out under the sun and up a little hill. In the late summer breeze a few very thin children were flying dragon kites in all the colors of the sun, and frogs and grass, the color of the sea and the color of coins and wheat.

The first Mandarin's daughter stood by his bed.

"See," she said.

"Those are nothing but kites," said the two old men.

"But what is a kite on the ground?" she said. "It is nothing. What does it need to sustain it and make it beautiful and truly spiritual?"

"The wind, of course!" said the others.

"And what do the sky and the wind need to make them beautiful?"

Spiral Review

Plot What stage of the plot does the paragraph beginning "Sickness spread..." represent? Explain your answer.

Like a rusted machine, the city ground to a halt.

33 

Reading Check

What kind of wall does the daughter suggest should be built to defeat Kwan-Si's sun?

Spiral Review

Plot

1. Remind students that they studied the concept of plot in the Unit 2 Literary Analysis workshop (pp. 196–209).
2. **Ask** students the Spiral Review question.

   Possible response: The spreading sickness is the rising action that intensifies the conflict. It brings the plot to a turning point where action must be taken to resolve the conflict.

32 Connecting to the Big Question

1. Describe the struggle of two toddlers over a toy, in which the children end up crying and exhausted, and the toy ends up broken. Discuss how people can become so focused on winning a fight that they forget what it is about.
2. Have students read the bracketed text on page 399. **Ask** students: What happens to the towns, their people, and their leaders because of the ongoing conflict?

   Possible response: The towns and their people fall into difficulties of many kinds, as do the leaders.
3. **Ask:** What command does the voice behind the screen finally utter? Why is it necessary in a conflict to know when to stop struggling? Explain.

   Possible response: The voice commands a meeting between the two Mandarins. If one doesn't know when to stop struggling in a conflict, one can end up destroying everything that was at stake in the conflict.

33 Reading Check

Answer: The daughter suggests that they build a moon to eclipse Kwan-si's sun.

Differentiated Instruction for Universal Access

Enrichment for Advanced Readers

Suggest that students read additional works by Ray Bradbury. Provide students with ***Authors In Depth,*** Gold Level, which contains the following selections:

- *The Flying Machine* (p. 33)
- *The Pedestrian* (p. 37)
- "The Other Me" (p. 42)
- "January 1999: Rocket Summer" from *The Martian Chronicles* (p. 44)

After students have read these or other works by Bradbury, have them form discussion groups in which they compare and contrast the selections. Suggest criteria for comparison, such as setting, theme, characters, and author's purpose. To extend the activity, have volunteers present to the class brief oral reports on their favorite Bradbury selections.

34 Literary Analysis

Symbolism and Allegory

1. Have students read the bracketed text. Point out that the symbols of the kite and the wind.
2. **Ask** students to respond to the Literary Analysis question: What kind of relationship do the kite and the wind symbolize? **Answer:** They represent a cooperative relationship, in which each benefits from the other.
3. Clarify that in choosing harmonious shapes, the Mandarins have ended their problems. The harmonious shapes represent the story's major theme: Cooperation is preferable to competition.

Concept Connector

Have students review their responses to Writing About the Big Question and Activating Prior Knowledge on p. 396. Revisit your discussion about rivalry and ways to resolve rivalry peacefully.

ASSESS

Answers

Critical Thinking

Remind students to support their answers with evidence from the text.

1. (a) The townspeople seem happy to rebuild in order to best the people of Kwan-Si. (b) The competition makes people tired, hungry, and sick.
2. **Possible response:** They might instead have asked the Mandarin to let them tend their crops.
3. (a) The two shapes complement one another. (b) The story suggests that excessive rivalry is destructive; it is better to work together.
4. **Possible responses:** (a) To keep one city from overpowering the other, they rebuild their cities in shapes to defeat each other. (b) They must learn that living together in peace is more important than the competition.

Literary Analysis Symbolism and Allegory What kind of relationship do the kite and the wind symbolize?

"A kite, of course—many kites, to break the monotony, the sameness of the sky. Colored kites, flying!"

"So," said the Mandarin's daughter. "You, Kwan-Si, will make a last rebuilding of your town to resemble nothing more nor less than the wind. And we shall build like a golden kite. The wind will beautify the kite and carry it to wondrous heights. And the kite will break the sameness of the wind's existence and give it purpose and meaning. One without the other is nothing. Together, all will be beauty and cooperation and a long and enduring life." 34

Whereupon the two mandarins were so overjoyed that they took their first nourishment in days, momentarily were given strength, embraced, and lavished praise upon each other, called the Mandarin's daughter a boy, a man, a stone pillar, a warrior, and a true and unforgettable son. Almost immediately they parted and hurried to their towns, calling out and singing, weakly but happily.

And so, in time, the towns became the Town of Golden Kite and the Town of the Silver Wind. And harvestings were harvested and business tended again, and the flesh returned, and disease ran off like a frightened jackal. And on every night of the year the inhabitants in the Town of the Kite could hear the good clear wind sustaining them. And those in the Town of the Wind could hear the kite singing, whispering, rising, and beautifying them.

"So be it," said the Mandarin in front of his silken screen.

Critical Thinking

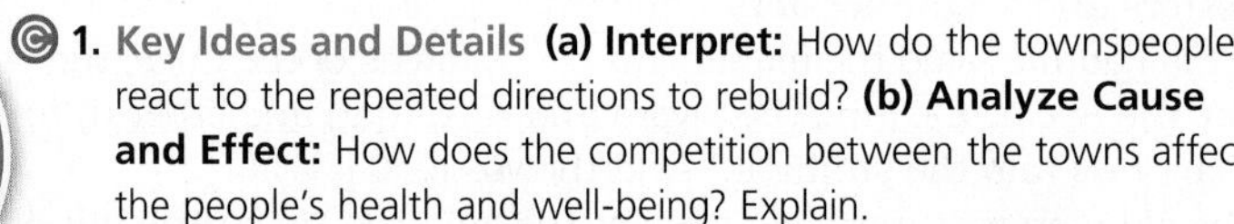

Cite textual evidence to support your responses.

1. **Key Ideas and Details (a) Interpret:** How do the townspeople react to the repeated directions to rebuild? **(b) Analyze Cause and Effect:** How does the competition between the towns affect the people's health and well-being? Explain.
2. **Integration of Knowledge and Ideas (a) Evaluate:** Should the people have continued to follow the Mandarin as a leader?
3. **Integration of Knowledge and Ideas (a) Evaluate:** Why are walls built as a kite and the wind more effective for a peaceful and harmonious relationship between the two towns? **(b) Draw Conclusions:** What lesson does this story teach for today's world?
4. **Integration of Knowledge and Ideas (a)** Why do the two Mandarins feel that their cities must compete in wall-building? **(b)** To end their conflict, what must the Mandarins realize is more important than this competition? Explain your answer. *[Connect to the Big Question: Is conflict necessary?]*

Vocabulary Development

Vocabulary Knowledge Rating

When students have competed reading and discussing "The Scarlet Ibis" and "The Golden Kite, the Silver Wind," have them take out their **Vocabulary Knowledge Rating Chart**. Read the words aloud once more and have students rate their knowledge of the words again in the After Reading column. Clarify any words that are still problematic. Have students write their own definition and example or sentence in the appropriate column. Then, have students complete the Vocabulary Practice on the next page. Encourage students to use the words in further discussion and written work about these selections. Remind them that they will be accountable for these words on the **Selection Test** (*Unit 2 Resources,* pp. 216–218 or 219–221).

After You Read

The Scarlet Ibis • The Golden Kite, the Silver Wind

Comparing Symbolism and Allegory

1. **Key Ideas and Details** Use a chart like the one shown to analyze how the characters, events, and setting in "The Golden Kite, the Silver Wind" could be **symbols** for Cold War leaders and events.

Symbol	Qualities	Meaning
Mandarin	Leader of his town; worried about losing business and reputation	Leader of a nation who wants to stay on top
Mandarin's daughter		
Walls		

2. **Key Ideas and Details (a)** In "The Scarlet Ibis," what does the ibis symbolize? **(b)** Which details support your conclusion? Explain.
3. **Craft and Structure** Based on your analysis of the **symbolism** in the stories, which of these selections is an **allegory?** Explain.
4. **Craft and Structure** Based on these stories, why do you think writers might use symbolism in their work?

Timed Writing

Explanatory Text: Essay

Write an essay in which you compare the use of symbolism in "The Scarlet Ibis" and "The Golden Kite, the Silver Wind." Use details from the texts to support your responses. **(30 minutes)**

5-Minute Planner

1. Read the prompt carefully and completely.
2. Gather your ideas. Consider these questions before you write.
   - What message or lesson does the author of each story express?
   - How do both authors use symbols to develop a message?
3. Decide on an organizational strategy.
   - Block: Discuss one story, and then another.
   - Point by Point: Discuss one aspect of each story's symbolism at a time.
4. Reread the prompt, and then draft your essay.

ASSESS

Answers

Comparing Symbolism and Allegory

1. For sample answers, see ***Graphic Organizer Transparencies,* Comparing Symbolism and Allegory Graphic Organizer A (Apply the Skills), p. 68, and the Additional Answers** section.
2. (a) The ibis symbolizes Doodle. (b) The ibis and Doodle physically and spiritually resemble one another, and they meet the same fate (death).
3. "The Golden Kite, the Silver Wind" is an allegory because almost every detail can be viewed as a symbol that contributes to the meaning of the story.
4. **Possible response:** Writers use symbolism to add depth of meaning to their work without stating the additional ideas directly.

Timed Writing

1. Review the prompt with students.
2. Have students use the 5-Minute Planner to structure their time. Guide them in answering the bulleted questions. For example, help students connect the symbols to the message by eliciting specific qualities of each symbol that support the message.
3. Allow students 30 minutes to complete the assignment.
4. As students prewrite and draft, have them refer to their completed Symbolism Graphic Organizer.

Six Traits Focus

✔	Ideas		Word Choice
✔	Organization		Sentence Fluency
	Voice		Conventions

Assessment Resources

Unit 2 Resources

L1 L2 EL **Selection Test A,** pp. 216–218
L3 L4 EL **Selection Text B,** pp. 219–221
L3 L4 **Open-Book Test,** pp. 213–215

PHLit Online! All assessment resources are available at **www.PHLitOnline.com.**

Common Core State Standards

- Writing 2, 2.a, b, c, f; 5
- Language 2.c

Introducing the Writing Assignment

Review the assignment and the criteria, using the instruction on the student page.

Wayson Choy on Cause-and-Effect Essays

Show students Segment 3 on Wayson Choy on *See It!* DVD or from this page in the **Enriched Online Student Edition** at **www.PHLitOnline.com.** Discuss what Choy says about the importance of knowing the rules of writing.

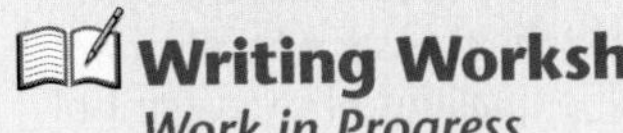

Writing Workshop *Work in Progress*

If students have completed the Work-in-Progress assignments on pp. 345 and 373, suggest that they consider developing their Work-in-Progress ideas into a cause-and-effect essay.

What Do You Notice?

1. Have a volunteer read the quotation aloud.
2. **Ask:** What do you notice about the passage? **Possible response:** It describes writings by members of her family.
3. Draw attention to the colon in the first line. **Ask** students why McCracken chose to use the colon. What does it show about the relationship between the first part of the sentence and the material that follows it? **Possible response:** The colon introduces examples of the family papers.
4. Encourage students to use examples, facts, and reasons to support their ideas as they draft.

Writing Workshop

Write Explanatory Text

Exposition: Cause-and-Effect Essay

Defining the Form Whether the subject is human nature, historical trends, or weather patterns, cause-and-effect reasoning explains why things happen. A **cause-and-effect essay** examines the relationship between or among two or more events, explaining how one causes another. You may use elements of this type of writing in science reports, history papers, and health articles, for example.

Assignment Write a cause-and-effect essay to explain an event or a condition in a subject area that interests you, such as business, the arts, technology, history, sports, or music. Include these elements:

- ✓ a clear *identification of a cause-and-effect relationship*
- ✓ an *analysis of specific aspects of the cause* or causes that produce the effects
- ✓ *facts, details, examples, and reasons that support your assertions* and *anticipate readers' questions*
- ✓ a *logical organization* clarified by smooth transitions
- ✓ error-free grammar, including correct *subject-verb agreement*

To preview the criteria on which your cause-and-effect essay may be judged, see the rubric on page 409.

Writing Workshop: *Work in Progress*

Review the work you did on pages 345 and 373.

WRITE GUY
Jeff Anderson, M.Ed.

What Do You Notice?

Sentence Structure

Read and reread this passage from Elizabeth McCracken's "Desiderata."

I could tell dozens of other stories from the pages of family papers: my aunt Blanche's pell-mell record of taking care of her favorite sister, Elizabeth, who was dying of Alzheimer's; Blanche has that disease herself now, and you can see the early signs in these notes. My great-uncles' cheery letters from Europe during World War II.

Jot down what you notice about the passage. Then, consider how you might use examples to affect the audience of your own essay.

Common Core State Standards

Writing
2. Write informative/explanatory texts to examine and convey complex ideas, concepts, and information clearly and accurately through the effective selection, organization, and analysis of content.
2.a. Introduce a topic; organize complex ideas, concepts, and information to make important connections and distinctions; include formatting, graphics, and multimedia when useful to aiding comprehension.
2.b. Develop the topic with well-chosen, relevant, and sufficient facts, extended definitions, concrete details, quotations, or other information and examples appropriate to the audience's knowledge of the topic.
5. Develop and strengthen writing as needed by planning, revising, editing, rewriting, or trying a new approach, focusing on addressing what is most significant for a specific purpose and audience.

Reading-Writing Connection

To get a feel for cause-and-effect essays, read the excerpt from *Silent Spring* by Rachel Carson on page 167.

Teaching Resources

The following resources can be used to enrich or extend the instruction.

- All *Unit 2 Resources*
  Writing Workshop, pp. 222–223
- All *Common Core Companion,* pp. 190–201; 220–221
- All *Professional Development Guidebook*
  Rubric for Self-Assessment: Cause-and-Effect Essay, pp. 238–239
- All *Graphic Organizer Transparencies*
  Rubric for Self-Assessment: Cause-and-Effect Essay, p. 72
- All *See It!* DVD
  Wayson Choy, Segments 3 and 4

All resources, including print and video, are also available online at **www.PHLitOnline.com.**

Prewriting/Planning Strategies

Examine current events. Scan newspapers or magazines for headlines that interest you. Use a three-column chart to speculate about possible causes and effects: In the middle column, write the event; in the left column, write the possible causes; in the right column, note possible effects. Notice how the event listed in the chart below—team wins championship—is an effect of the causes listed in the left column—practice, focus, and individual performance—as well as a cause of the effects listed in the right column—increased fan interest, harder to buy tickets, and revenue for city.

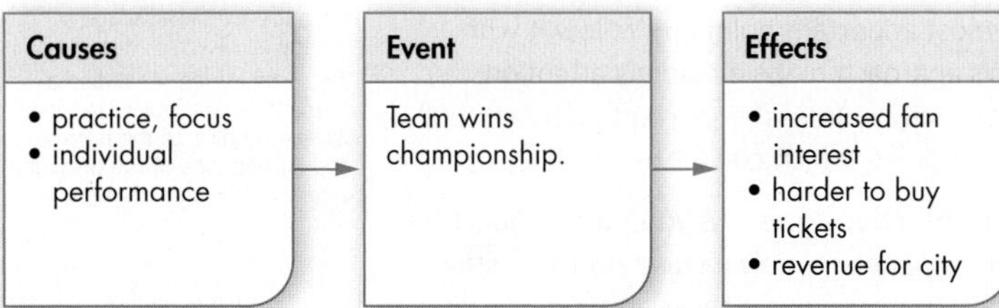

Causes
• practice, focus
• individual performance
Event
Team wins championship.
Effects
• increased fan interest
• harder to buy tickets
• revenue for city

List and freewrite. Jot down any interesting events that come to mind from the worlds of business, science, technology, the arts, nature, politics, and sports. Then, circle the item that most intrigues you. Freewrite for three minutes about that topic. As you write, note any causes and effects that come to mind. You can develop your topic from ideas you uncover in your freewriting.

Categorize to narrow your topic. You may find that your topic is too broad to manage in the scope of a single essay. Break your subject into smaller categories. For example, if your topic is about a record-breaking sports event, you might create categories such as "key player," "great coach," and "new equipment." Choose a more focused topic that interests you from your list of categories.

Chart causes and effects. Using an index card or a self-sticking note, write the central event or circumstance that is your subject. Explore the causes that produced the event and the effects the event produced. Write those factors on separate cards or notes. Write key details related to each cause and effect on the cards or notes. Then, arrange the cards or notes in a logical sequence.

PHLit Online!
www.PHLitOnline.com
- Author video: Writing Process
- Author video: Rewards of Writing

Applying Understanding by Design Principles

Clarifying Expected Outcomes: Using Rubrics

- Before students begin working on this assignment, have them preview the Rubric for Self-Assessment (p. 409) to learn what qualities their cause-and-effect essays must have. A copy of this Rubric appears in ***Graphic Organizer Transparencies,*** p. 72.
- Review the criteria in the Rubric with the class. Before students use the Rubric to assess their writing, work with them to rate the Student Model (p. 408) using the Rubric.
- If you wish to assess students' cause-and-effect essays with either a 4-point or a 6-point scoring rubric, see ***Professional Development Guidebook,*** pp. 238–239.

TEACH

Prewriting/Planning Strategies

1. Introduce the prewriting strategies, using the instruction given.
2. Have students apply the strategies.

Teaching the Strategies

1. To help students choose topics, provide them with current newspapers or magazines to scan, or schedule a visit to the library.
2. Record a class list of events on the board, including sports, politics, and current events.
3. Show how to narrow a topic by writing *Volcanoes* on the board in the center of a web. In radiating circles, write *Volcanic Eruptions* and *Types of Volcanoes.* Then, start a new web *The Olympics* and invite volunteers to make suggestions to narrow the topic.

   Possible answers: *Gymnastic competition, famous athletes*

Think Aloud: Model Categorizing

Model the strategy, using the following "think aloud":

> Let's say I've chosen *Hurricane Katrina* as my topic. I'll narrow the topic down by breaking it into smaller categories: *How a Hurricane Forms; Why the Levees Broke in New Orleans; Hurricane Katrina's Effects on New Orleans.* Then I'll choose the category that interests me most.

Six Traits Focus

✓	Ideas		Word Choice
✓	Organization		Sentence Fluency
	Voice		Conventions

Prentice Hall EssayScorer

A writing prompt for this mode of writing can be found on the ***Prentice Hall Essay Scorer*** at **www.PHLitOnline.com.**

Drafting Strategies

1. Introduce the drafting strategies, using the instruction on the student page.
2. Have students apply the strategies.

Teaching the Strategies

1. Explain that chronological order can be shown in two ways.
2. Write the following statements on the board:

   Shawna did her chores for the week.

   Shawna's parents gave her an allowance for doing her chores.

   Shawna bought a new book with her money.

   Shawna enjoyed reading her new book.

   Use a cause-and-effect flowchart to demonstrate the two ways that students can show chronological order. Refer students to the Cause-and-Effect Flowchart in **Graphic Organizer Transparencies**, p. 215.
3. Explain the different types of evidence: *details* come from observation and experience; facts are based on research; and examples can be fictional scenarios or real events.

Think Aloud: Model Evidence

Model the strategy, using the following "think aloud":

Let's say I want to show how devastating Hurricane Katrina was for pets and their owners. I'll provide *details* that show, rather than tell, what happened to pets. For example, homeless mother cats gave birth to kittens in piles of rubble. I'll include *facts* such as how many pets were injured. I'll give an *example* from a news article about groups that set up emergency animal shelters. I'll tell about a *personal experience* I had when I volunteered at a New Orleans animal shelter.

Six Traits Focus

✔	Ideas	✔	Word Choice
✔	Organization		Sentence Fluency
✔	Voice		Conventions

Drafting Strategies

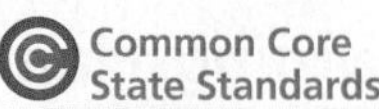

Writing

2.a. Introduce a topic; organize complex ideas, concepts, and information to make important connections and distinctions; include formatting, graphics, and multimedia when useful to aiding comprehension.

2.b. Develop the topic with well-chosen, relevant, and sufficient facts, extended definitions, concrete details, quotations, or other information and examples appropriate to the audience's knowledge of the topic.

2.e. Establish and maintain a formal style and objective tone while attending to the norms and conventions of the discipline in which they are writing.

Choose a structure. In your opening paragraph, introduce your topic and show why it is important. Here are two possibilities for organizing the body paragraphs of your essay:

- **Chronological order** is particularly valuable when describing a sequence of causes and effects. You can start with the cause and then continue by describing its effects. You can also start with the effect and then list its causes one at a time. Keep in mind, however, that a time-order relationship is not in itself proof of cause and effect.
- **Order of importance** organization can be structured in two ways. You can begin with your most important point and follow it with less important points—this approach grabs a reader's attention. Alternatively, you can begin with your least important point and build toward your most important point, which creates drama.

Use logical evidence and an objective tone. As you build support for your ideas, avoid opinions and trivial details. Rely instead on facts, statistics, and persuasive examples. Strengthen your ideas even more by using a formal writing style and an objective, serious tone.

- **Unsupported assertion:** Members of the royal family probably liked the color purple more than any other color.
- **Convincing support:** According to a primary-source historical document, members of the royal family believed the color purple symbolized power and prosperity.

Use the TRI method to develop paragraphs. Follow these steps:

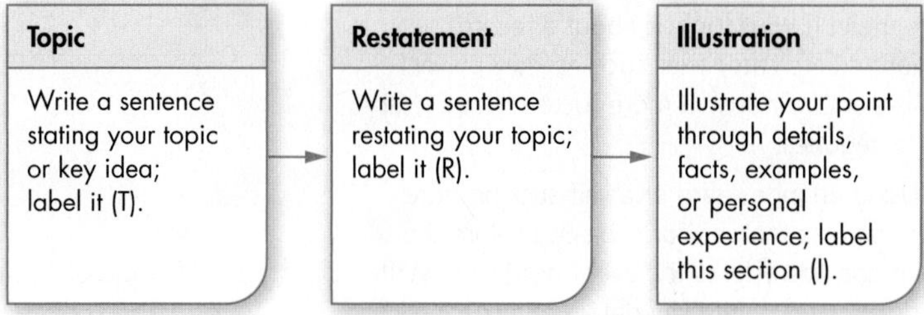

Topic
Write a sentence stating your topic or key idea; label it (T).
Restatement
Write a sentence restating your topic; label it (R).
Illustration
Illustrate your point through details, facts, examples, or personal experience; label this section (I).

You can use the TRI pattern to shift the sequence to suit the information you present and add variety to your writing.

Example: Originally, the color purple was associated with royalty. **(T)** Only kings, queens, and members of the nobility wore purple-colored clothing. **(R)** In England, Queen Elizabeth I actually made a law prohibiting anyone except herself and her relatives from wearing purple. **(I)**

Strategies for Test Taking

Students will sometimes be required to write cause-and-effect essays in testing situations. Provide these tips for writing their essays:

- Make a list of your causes and effects before you begin writing your essay.
- Decide if you are going to present your causes and effects in chronological order or in order of importance.
- Make sure that all details given support either a cause or an effect. Avoid including unnecessary details to fill space.

Writers on Writing

Wayson Choy On Showing Cause and Effect

Wayson Choy is the author of "The Jade Peony" (p. 203).

I aim for "showing, not telling."
—Wayson Choy

An origami butterfly sits on my computer to remind me that just as a butterfly must first go through various stages, my first draft will be "re-created" many times before it can take flight. During that process, I keep in mind that a sense of cause and effect is as important in fiction as in nonfiction. So, I hone the action and dialogue "to show, not tell about" the causes and effects in my characters' lives. The following draft from my novel *All That Matters* demonstrates how I do that.

Professional Model:
from *All That Matters*

I had given up a late afternoon soccer practice to do some serious studying ^for Mr. Eades's first English test. There were plenty of others like us, books opened, eyes focused. Jenny pointed to the library seat ^across from hers, and her eyes said, *No fooling around!* ~~Truth was, she took her English studies more seriously than she took me. It was frustrating. I just wanted to be with her. She was always in charge.~~

I needed to expand this account with more details to show causes and effects in the relationship between the narrator and his girlfriend, Jenny.

These two sentences tell that Jenny is an in-control girl who takes charge of the narrator. But I wanted to show it through dialogue and actions.

^As she pushed my books across the table, I thought that she and I should have, two months ago, declared ourselves an official couple, especially after our fifth double date together. But Jenny didn't want that.

^"Too showy," she had told me. "Maybe after we graduate. Next year."

^She folded both our school sweaters together and neatly draped them over one of the empty chairs.

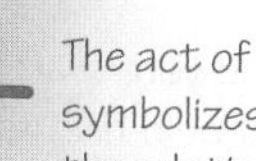

The act of folding the sweaters symbolizes Jenny's shaping of the relationship.

Wayson Choy on Showing Cause and Effect

Review the passage on the student page with the class, using Wayson Choy's comments to deepen students' understanding of the process of writing to show cause and effect.

Teaching From the Professional Model

1. Show students Segment 3 on Wayson Choy on ***See It!* DVD** or from this page in the **Enriched Online Student Edition**. Discuss how Choy uses writing as a way of discovering things about himself, his family, and his culture. Help students understand how writing helps him identify and think about the causes of events in his life and their lasting effects.
2. Point out how the changes that Choy has made to his draft replace telling with showing. Ask students to explain how each change makes the passage more engaging.
3. Call students' attention to Choy's comments about his changes. Ask what new causes and effects Choy introduces. Then, ask students how this new information changes what they know or think about the characters.
4. Have students look closely at their own essays and try to identify ways in which they can show, rather than tell about, the cause-and-effect relationships.

Enriched Online Student Edition
Show or assign the video online at **www.PHLitOnline.com.**

Strategies for Elaboration

Tell students that they can show, rather than tell, information in their writing through dialogue, sensory details, and character actions. Write the following sentence on the board: *It was hot in the house.*

Demonstrate for students how they can show, rather than tell, this information by writing the following statements on the board:

Dialogue: *"What I wouldn't do for an air-conditioner!" Juan exclaimed.*

Sensory Details: *A fan droned in the living room, nudging weak breezes through the stifling air.*

Character Actions: *Cara once again opened the freezer door and stood, letting the icy air chill the sweat on her face.*

Revising Strategies

1. Introduce the revision strategies, using the instruction on the student page.
2. Have students apply the strategies as they revise their cause-and-effect essays.

Teaching the Strategies

1. Write the following sentences on the board:

   Cause: *Devin carried the groceries into the house.*
   Effect: *The cat escaped out the door.*

   Ask students to provide details that will strengthen the connection between cause and effect.

   Possible responses: *Devin forgot to watch for the cat when he opened the kitchen door. Devin propped open the kitchen door when he went back to the car to get more groceries.*

2. Explain that a succession of short, choppy sentences can break up an essay's rhythm. Tell students that they may combine short sentences with more complex ones to add variety or to create emphasis.
3. Remind students that when they combine two simple sentences by changing one into an introductory clause, the clause should end with a comma. Write the following sentences on the board and ask students to combine them.

   A dark funnel-cloud appeared just a few miles from town.

   Then, we huddled in the basement.

   Possible response: *When a dark funnel-cloud appeared just a few miles from town, we huddled in the basement.*

   This is a complex sentence, consisting of a dependent clause and an independent clause. The newly-combined sentence helps the reader see the causal relationship between the two events.

Six Traits Focus

✓	Ideas	✓	Word Choice
✓	Organization	✓	Sentence Fluency
	Voice	✓	Conventions

Revising Strategies

Common Core State Standards

Writing

2.c. Use appropriate and varied transitions to link the major sections of the text, create cohesion, and clarify the relationships among complex ideas and concepts.

2.f. Provide a concluding statement or section that follows from and supports the information or explanation presented.

5. Develop and strengthen writing as needed by planning, revising, editing, rewriting, or trying a new approach, focusing on addressing what is most significant for a specific purpose and audience.

Clarify cause-and-effect relationships. Review your entire draft, focusing on the causes and effects you have presented. With two highlighters, use one color to mark phrases that show causes and the other to mark effects. Add details to strengthen connections, insert transitional words to make links clear, and eliminate causes or effects that do not support your main point. Provide a clear concluding statement that follows logically from the information that preceded it and that supports your main idea.

Model: Revising to Clarify Cause and Effect

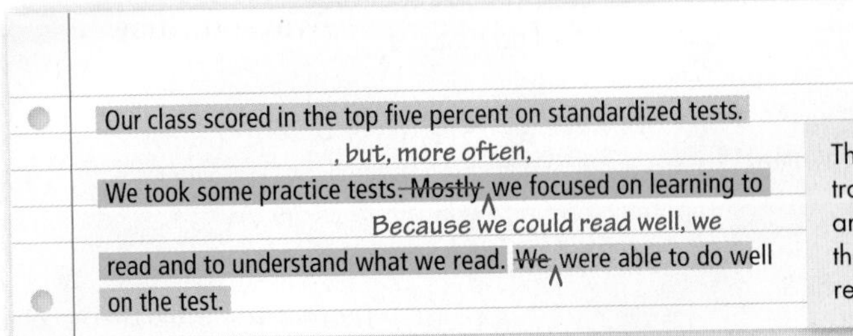

This writer adds transitional words and phrases to clarify the cause-and-effect relationships.

Combine short sentences. If you find too many short sentences, look for places to combine them using the following strategies:

- Combine two sentences using subordinating clauses that start with conjunctions such as *after, although, despite, if,* and *whenever.* Use subordinating conjunctions to show a relationship between ideas.
- Use coordinating conjunctions such as *and, but, or, nor, for, so,* and *yet* to combine ideas of equal importance.

Example: **Short Sentences:**
The team members lost hope. They found an unlikely inspiration to continue.

Combined:
The team members lost hope, but they found an unlikely inspiration to continue.

Peer Review

Ask a partner to read your draft, and then have a discussion about your work. Your reader should discuss the clarity of the cause-and-effect relationships presented throughout your essay. Consider modifying sentences, omitting or adding transitions, or reordering paragraphs to improve the logical flow of your ideas as needed.

406 Short Stories

Strategies for Improving Transitions

Emphasize that it is essential to make clear connections among ideas in a cause-and-effect essay. One way to do this is by using transitional words to indicate relationships. Explain that there are different types of transitional words that describe different relationships. Write these words on the board.

Transitions that show cause-and-effect:

because	*since*	*in order to*
consequently	*as a result*	*therefore*
once	*so*	

Transitions that show chronological or sequential order:

meanwhile	*next*	*after*
before	*first*	*now*
following	*during*	*then*

Ask students to add additional transitional words to these lists.

WRITER'S TOOLBOX

Conventions | Sentence Fluency | Voice | Organization | Word Choice | Ideas

Revising to Correct Faulty Subject-Verb Agreement

For a subject and verb to agree, they must agree in number.

Identifying Errors in Subject-Verb Agreement Agreement errors may occur with compound subjects, subjects joined by *or* or *nor,* and indefinite pronouns as subjects. Below, subjects are underlined and verbs italicized.

Compound Subject:
The coach and the captain ~~is going~~ *are going* to attend.

Subject Joined by *Or* or *Nor*:
Either Jason or his brother ~~are bringing~~ *is bringing* the snacks.

Indefinite Pronoun as Subject:
Everybody who supports our ideas ~~are helping~~ *is helping.*

If a plural subject is joined to a singular subject by *or* or *nor,* the verb should agree with the subject that is closer to it.

Correct: Either the coach or the co-captains *are going* to speak.

Correct: Either the co-captains or the coach *is going* to speak.

PH WRITING COACH
Further instruction and practice are available in *Prentice Hall Writing Coach.*

Fixing Errors To correct subject and verb agreement, follow these steps:

1. **Identify whether the subject in a sentence is singular or plural.**
2. **Select the matching form of the verb:**
   - For compound subjects joined by *and,* use plural verb forms.
   - For singular subjects joined by *or* or *nor,* use singular verb forms.
   - When the subject is an indefinite pronoun, use the appropriate verb form. Use this chart for guidance.

Indefinite Pronouns	
Always Singular	anybody, anyone, anything, each, either, every, everybody, everyone, everything, neither, nobody, no one, nothing, somebody, someone, something
Always Plural	both, few, many, others, several
Singular or Plural	all, any, more, most, none, some

Grammar in Your Writing

Scan several paragraphs in your draft and underline all compound subjects and indefinite pronouns. In each case, make sure that the verb form you have used agrees with the subject.

Differentiated Instruction for Universal Access

Strategy for Less Proficient Writers
Tell students that the key to subject-verb agreement is to correctly identify whether the subject of the sentence is singular or plural. Working with two paragraphs of their drafts, have students highlight or circle the subject of each sentence. Have them determine whether each subject is singular or plural, then check to see if the form of the verb matches.

Enrichment for Advanced Writers
Have students review their entire draft for sentences that use indefinite pronouns as subjects. Have them circle all the indefinite pronouns that can be singular or plural: *all, any, most, none, some.* Have them recheck agreement with verbs in these sentences and write a brief explanation of their choice of verb form.

Revising to Correct Faulty Subject-Verb Agreement

1. Introduce the grammar skill, using the instruction on the student page.
2. Discuss the examples and the strategies for identifying and fixing errors in subject-verb agreement.
3. Have students follow the instruction under Grammar in Your Writing to revise their drafts.

Teaching the Grammar Skill

1. Write these sentences on the board.

   There are twenty questions on the test.

   There is twenty questions on the test.

   Point out to students that *questions* is the plural subject of each sentence. **Ask** students which sentence has subject-verb agreement. **Answer:** first sentence
2. Write these sentences on the board. Have students identify the subjects and correct the verbs in each sentence:

   Almost everyone in our class want to attend the performance.
   Answer: everyone, wants

   The cities of Richmond Heights and Clayton agrees to merge.
   Answer: cities, agree

   Julie, one of the Baxters' children, babysit regularly for Ms. Alvarez.
   Answer: Julie, babysits

   There is five children in our family.
   Answer: children, are

   Neither the chairperson nor the club members likes the results.
   Answer: chairperson/members, like
3. Give students additional examples of singular subjects, such as *runner, Ms. Andrews, student,* and *athlete.* Have them create sentences in which these nouns agree with the verbs *try, forget, anticipate,* and *start.*
4. Have students work in pairs and exchange their drafts to identify errors in subject-verb agreement.

PH WRITING COACH Grade 9

Students will find practice with and guidance on subject-verb agreement in Chapter 19, Section 1.

Student Model

Review the Student Model with the class, using the annotations to analyze the writer's use of the elements of a cause-and-effect essay.

Teaching From the Student Model

1. Explain that the Student Model is a sample and that essays may be longer.
2. Tell students that they need a factual foundation to make their essay convincing to readers.
3. Give students the example of a cause-and-effect essay about how violent video games cause violent behavior. Have students think of differing opinions that could be acknowledged in the essay.

   Possible response: Violent video games do not cause violent behavior; they simply enhance violent tendencies that already exist.
4. **Ask** students why the conjunction *consequently* is useful in a cause-and-effect essay.

   Answer: The word *consequently* means "as a result of," which means that it is used to link a cause and an effect.
5. Tell students to gauge how unfamiliar their audience is going to be with the information in their essays and to write with this level of unfamiliarity in mind.
6. **Ask** students to think of a variety of processes that chronological order could be used to describe.

   Possible responses: Chronological order could be used to describe the process by which water evaporates, the process by which one attains his or her driver's license, or the process by which photographic film is developed.

Connecting to Real-Life Writing

Explain that if students feel strongly about changing situations in their communities, they can write letters to the editors of local newspapers. They can use cause-and-effect text structures to show how these issues are affecting their communities.

Student Model: Glen Milner, Charlotte, NC

Common Core State Standards

Language
2.c. Spell correctly.

Climate Effects of the North Atlantic Current

The oceans have been around since the beginning of time, yet we know relatively little about them. They are constantly moving and changing, turning up water that has been down in the depths for hundreds of years. One of these currents is the North Atlantic, also known as the Great Ocean Conveyor Belt.

The level of impact the current has on climate and the causes that change it are widely debated. The presumption held by most scientists is that we are currently experiencing global warming. Other theories state that global warming may influence the North Atlantic Current. This, consequently, may cause the exact opposite of warming— an ice age.

Models have shown that any change in speed or location of the current may well cause a rapid climate shift of great magnitude (Burroughs 17). This shift would be caused by two key changes: a decrease in salinity and an increase in the temperature of water in the North Atlantic Current. These factors would, in turn, cause the current to slow down or shut down, sending the Northern Hemisphere into an ice age.

The North Atlantic Current is a complicated system that runs for thousands of miles and combines water from all oceans. It moves heat from the tropics to the northern Atlantic. Robert Kunzig, the author of *The Restless Sea: Exploring the World Beneath the Waves* . . ., said that oceanographers call this the "global journey" of the Thermohaline Circulation, which is run by heat and salt (268). It is called a conveyor belt because warm water moves north on surface currents and then back south in deep cold-water currents, folding over itself like a conveyor belt. The heat has a drastic effect on the climate for the Northern Hemisphere. Without it, the average temperature would be much lower.

The mechanisms by which the current works are very simple. As the water moves north, it cools down. In addition, its salinity rises because winds that blow east to west across the equator transport moisture from the Atlantic to the Pacific, leaving the Atlantic more saline. The water that feeds the Atlantic from the Mediterranean is also salty because it is nearly landlocked and moisture evaporates from the Mediterranean, leaving it saltier (Mayewski 105). As the temperature decreases and salinity increases, the water becomes denser, causing it to sink. As it sinks, it spreads out deep in the ocean basin where it is pulled back toward the equator, thus creating the conveyor-like characteristics. . . .

Direct statements of fact form the basis of the essay.

Glen builds interest by acknowledging that there are differing opinions on the topic.

The coordinating conjunction *consequently* is particularly useful in a cause-and-effect essay.

The writer takes the knowledge level of his audience into account and provides explanations of scientific concepts. He supports his ideas with research.

Glen uses chronological order to explain the way the ocean currents work.

Editing and Proofreading

Check your draft for errors in spelling, grammar, and punctuation.

Focus on spelling. Double-check your spelling of words like *unnecessary* and *dissatisfied* in which a prefix is added to a base word that begins with a consonant. In most cases, the spelling of the base word does not change.

Focus on sentence clarity. Ensure that your sentences are clear by checking that the subjects agree with the verbs. In addition, read each sentence to be sure that each one expresses a complete thought.

Spiral Review

Earlier in this unit, you learned about **subjects and predicates** (p. 344) and **active and passive voice** (p. 372). Check your essay for correct subject-predicate agreement and for appropriate and effective use of active and passive voice.

Publishing and Presenting

Consider one of the following ways to share your work with others:

Present your essay. Use photographs, charts, and diagrams to help you explain the topic of your article. Include definitions of any challenging or specialized vocabulary your listeners will need to know in order to understand the information. Ask friends in the audience to provide feedback notes on your presentation.

Submit your essay for publication. If your essay focuses on a matter of local interest, send it to your school or community newspaper.

Reflecting on Your Writing

Writer's Journal Jot down your answer to this question:

How did writing about the topic help you understand it?

Rubric for Self-Assessment

Find evidence in your writing to address each category. Then, use the rating scale to grade your work.

Criteria	Rating Scale				
	not very				*very*
Focus: How clearly do you identify and explore the cause-and-effect relationship?	1	2	3	4	5
Organization: How logical is your organization?	1	2	3	4	5
Support/Elaboration: How effective are your facts, details, and reasons?	1	2	3	4	5
Style: How well do you use transitional words and phrases?	1	2	3	4	5
Conventions: How correct is your grammar, especially your use of subject-verb agreement?	1	2	3	4	5

Editing and Proofreading

1. Introduce the editing and proofreading focus, using the instruction on the student page.
2. Have students edit and proofread their essays, correcting grammar, spelling, punctuation, and word choice. Make sure they look for errors of the type noted in the lesson focus and the Spiral Review.

Teaching the Editing Focus

Have students check for subject-verb agreement by circling each subject and its verb. Also ask students to identify the subject and predicate in each sentence to help them identify incomplete sentences.

Six Traits Focus

	Ideas		Word Choice
	Organization	✓	Sentence Fluency
	Voice	✓	Conventions

ASSESS

Publishing and Presenting

1. Suggest that students consider adding flow charts to their essays to show the sequence of events.
2. If students choose to submit their essays to newspapers, tell them to rewrite their essays in letter-to-the-editor form. Tell students that they must state their topics early, and express opinions about their topics.

Reflecting on Your Writing

Encourage students to reflect on how their attitudes toward their topics changed as a result of the writing process.

Strategies for Test Taking

Tell students that one of the last things they should do during the proofreading stage is to run the spell check on their computers. Emphasize, however, that the spell check does not catch all spelling errors. For example, the spell check will not recognize whether the word *your* is incorrectly used in place of the word *you're*. After using the spell check, it is essential for students to carefully proofread for additional spelling errors.

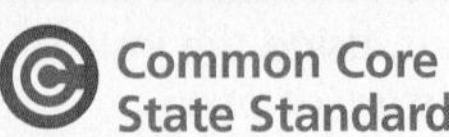

EXTEND

Common Core State Standards

- **Language 4, 4.c**
- **Speaking and Listening 3**

Etymology: Words from Mythology

1. Introduce the skill, using the instruction on the student page.
2. Review the definitions and examples in the chart.

Think Aloud: Model the Skill

Use the following "think aloud" to model the skill of using word origins to understand word meanings. Say to students:

Once I know the origins of a word, I can use that knowledge to help me better understand the word. Let's say I'm reading a historical novel about a dictator known for beheading anyone who disagrees with him. I know that the word *dictator* means "ruler," but I also know that it originates from the Latin word *dictare*, which means "to say often or to set as a rule." So a *dictator* is a ruler who exercises the power to create rules. He can make up whatever laws he likes. It is easy to imagine how a dictator like the one in my novel could abuse his power by making it illegal, on penalty of death, to disagree with him. Knowing the origin of *dictator* has helped me to better understand the word.

Practice A

Sample answers:

1. *skill:* from Old Norse *skil*, meaning "discernment, distinction"
2. *salute:* from Latin *salutare*, meaning "to wish health to"
3. *antique:* from Latin, *antiquus*, meaning "ancient, old"
4. *crisis:* from Greek, *krisis*, meaning "turning point in a disease"
5. *ship:* from Old Norse *skip*, meaning "hollowed out tree"
6. *north:* from Greek, *nerteros*, meaning "lower, infernal"

Vocabulary Workshop

Etymology: Words from Mythology

The words that make up the English language come from a variety of sources. A word's **origin,** or source, is shown in its etymology. A word's **etymology** identifies the language in which the word first appeared and tells how its spelling and meaning have changed over time. The following excerpt from a dictionary entry shows the etymology of the word *make.*

Sample Dictionary Entry

Middle English (Dictionaries usually list abbreviations at the front or back of the book.)

The Middle English source word

make (māk) ***vt.*** [ME *maken* < OE *macian*, akin to Ger *machen* < IE base **mag-*, to knead, press, stretch > MASON, Gr *magis*, kneaded mass, paste, dough, *mageus*, kneader]

This symbol means "derived from."

Many English words are derived from Greek, Roman, and Norse mythology. Having some knowledge of myths from these cultures can help you to understand the origins and meaning of new words. This chart shows some examples.

Word	Definition	Origin
narcissistic	showing excessive self-love	reference to Narcissus, a young man in Greek mythology who falls in love with his own reflection
mercurial	lively and quick-witted	reference to Mercury, a god in Roman mythology who is swift and clever
Wednesday	the fourth day of the week	Old Norse word *Othinsdagr,* which means "Odin's day," a reference to the chief god in Norse mythology

Practice A Look up each word in a print, digital, or online dictionary. Identify the original Greek, Latin, or Old Norse source word and its meaning.

1. skill
2. salute
3. antique
4. crisis
5. ship
6. north

Common Core State Standards

Language

4. Determine or clarify the meaning of unknown and multiple-meaning words and phrases based on grades 9–10 reading and content, choosing flexibly from a range of strategies.

4.c. Consult general and specialized reference materials, both print and digital, to find the pronunciation of a word or determine or clarify its precise meaning, its part of speech, or its etymology.

Teaching Resources

Unit 2 Resources

Etymology: Words from Mythology, pp. 224–225

PHLit Online! **Vocabulary Central,** featuring definitions, audio pronunciations, Word Families, and activities, is online at **www.PHLitOnline.com.**

Practice B Find each underlined word in a print, digital, or online dictionary that provides word etymologies. Write the word's definition, and then use its etymology to explain how the original source word relates to the word's use in the sentence.

1. When the ambulance sounded its siren, cars moved out of its way.
2. She seemed to be in a hypnotic state.
3. A witness came forward and told what she saw.
4. When the mouse saw the cat, he made a quick escape.
5. The club's slogan is "Do your best!"
6. We had to pay a fee before entering the park.
7. I regret that I will be unable to attend the event.
8. The Sampsons have a robot that cleans the bottom of their pool.
9. He apologized for spilling the milk.

Activity Prepare a note card like the one shown for each of these words: *derive, choice, tantalize, window,* and *curfew.* Look up each word in a dictionary and record some details about the word's origin, including notes about how older words from other languages influenced its meaning. Then, write the word's modern meaning. Finally, write a sentence using the word.

Word:

Word's origin:

Modern word's meaning:

Sentence:

Comprehension and Collaboration

Work with three classmates to research the following characters from Greek and Roman mythology. Then, use a dictionary to find an English word that is based on the character's name. Finally, write a few sentences that explain how the word's meaning relates to the character.

Mars
Vulcan
Jove

www.PHLitOnline.com

- Illustrated vocabulary words
- Interactive vocabulary games
- Vocabulary flashcards

Differentiated Instruction for Universal Access

Strategy for Special-Needs Students

Explain to students that languages change over time. New technologies and ideas, such as *robotics* and *hypnosis*, are invented and named. Languages also adopt words from other languages when the nations are in close contact. *Burrito* and *croissant* are examples of this. Some words, such as *cool*, gradually come to be used in different ways. At times, a writer uses a word in a new way, and then people start using it that way in speech. *Catch-22* is an example of this. Show students an entry in the *Oxford English Dictionary* and go over the history of the word step-by-step, showing how the meaning changed progressively over time.

Answers

Practice B

Sample answers:

1. Siren: "a device that makes a loud, wailing sound"; origin: *sereine*, "a mythical creature whose song lured sailors to their deaths." A siren warns of possible death, so cars clear the way.
2. Hypnotic: "trancelike"; origin: *hypnos*, "sleep." Her hypnotic state was similar to *sleep.*
3. Witness: "one who sees"; origin: *wit*, "knowledge." The witness *knew* what had occurred.
4. Escape: "to get away"; origin: *excappare*, "to leave a pursuer with only one's cape." The mouse escaped from the cat.
5. Slogan: "a catchword or phrase"; origin: *slaugh-ghairim*, "battle cry." The club's slogan serves as a *battle cry* for its members.
6. Pay: "to give what is due, such as money"; origin: *paiier*, "to pacify." When we paid, we *pacified* those who felt we owed something for entering the park.
7. Regret: "to feel sorry about"; origin: *gretan*, "to weep." I regretted it so much, I *wept*.
8. Robot: "a mechanical being"; origin: *robotiti*, "to work." Robots do the *work* for people.
9. Spill: "to allow to overflow"; origin: *spaltan*, "to split." When he spilled milk, he *split* some of it from the rest.

Activity

Provide dictionaries and note cards. Word origins are listed below.

Derive: Latin, *derivare*, "to lead a stream of water from its source"

Choice: French, *choisir*, "to choose"

Tantalize: Greek, *Tantalus*, "a mythological character for whom water receded whenever he bent to drink"

Window: Old Norse, *vindauga*, "wind eye"

Curfew: Old French, *covrefeu*, "cover fire"

Comprehension and Collaboration

Assign groups and provide dictionaries and books on mythology. Responses should include explanations of how words are related to the characters.

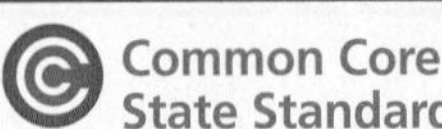

Common Core State Standards

- Speaking and Listening 3

Learn the Skills

1. Introduce the workshop, including the activity on page 413.
2. Point out that understanding the author's purpose is as important in a speech as it is in any other form of communication.
3. **Ask:** Why is evaluating arguments so important when analyzing a speech?

   Possible response: If the arguments are not well developed and well supported, the speech may misinform or encourage inappropriate action.
4. Encourage students to notice how a speaker uses language. Explain that speakers use loaded language to appeal to your feelings instead of your thoughts.
5. Encourage students to notice how a speaker uses his or her body language. **Ask:** How do hand gestures and other forms of body language help deliver a speaker's message?

   Possible response: Movement can help hold the audience's attention and emphasize a speaker's point.

SPEAKING AND LISTENING

Communications Workshop

Evaluating a Speech

When you hear a formal speech or an informal talk, strive to be an active listener. Assess the credibility of the message and the effectiveness of the speaker's techniques. Learning how to evaluate a speech will make you a critical listener, allow you to judge the value of what you hear, and give you a solid basis for improving your own oral presentations.

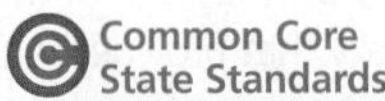

Common Core State Standards

Speaking and Listening

3. Evaluate a speaker's point of view, reasoning, and use of evidence and rhetoric, identifying any fallacious reasoning or exaggerated or distorted evidence.

Learn the Skills

Create a context. When listening to a speech or an informal talk, consider the following questions:

- What is the speaker's purpose?
- What knowledge of the subject does the speaker have?
- What traditional, cultural, or historical influences shape the message?
- As a listener, what prior knowledge do you bring to the topic?

Evaluate the development of arguments. A good speaker presents arguments that are clearly and logically stated and fully supported with evidence in the form of facts, statistics, anecdotes, and expert opinions. As you listen, ask yourself whether the speaker's information is accurate, complete, and relevant. Is important information deliberately or unintentionally excluded? Does the speaker have a point of view—the perspective from which he or she speaks—that might lead to bias, or a focus on only one side of an argument? Assess whether the speaker's use of facts is fair or biased. Try to anticipate weaknesses in certain types of arguments.

Type of Argument	Potential Flaw
Analogy: compares one situation to another	Are the two situations really alike?
Authority: cites the opinion of an expert	Is the expert knowledgeable and unbiased?
Emotion: appeals to the audience's feelings	Is the full argument balanced between logic and emotion?
Causation: shows a cause-and-effect relationship	Does the speaker oversimplify his or her arguments?

Note the speaker's choice of language. Listen for the speaker's use of words and phrases with positive or negative connotations, or associations. Note repetition of key words or stress given to certain phrases. Be alert to the fact that some speakers, as a substitute for good evidence or logical argument, may rely on emotionally "loaded" language.

Note the speaker's technique. A speech is more than words. Use the following questions to analyze nonverbal elements:

- Is the speaker's tone of voice, word choice, and rate of speaking appropriate for the audience, subject, and occasion?
- What is the effect of the speaker's nonverbal signals, such as eye contact, facial expressions, and gestures?
- When and why does the speaker pause, speak more loudly or softly, or speak more rapidly or slowly?

Strategies for Evaluating a Speech

Explain that one way a speaker may support an argument is through the use of statistics.

- Tell students that statistics provide information based on studies that may or may not be accurate. A listener must evaluate the source of the statistics and the validity of the statistics' use.
- Point out that any statistics offered without a source or with a nonspecific source should not be trusted.
- Write the following sentence on the board: *Three out of four doctors recommend brand X.*
- **Ask:** Is this statistic trustworthy? Why or why not?
- **Answer:** The statistic is only credible if the speaker provides information about who conducted the study, how they conducted it, and who the doctors were.
- Have students listen to a persuasive speech or a series of advertisements that use statistics. Then, have them list the statistics and explain whether these statistics are reliable.

Practice the Skills

Presentation of Knowledge and Ideas Use what you've learned in this workshop to perform the following task.

ACTIVITY: Evaluate a Speech

As a class, view a political speech or a televised editorial. Then, use the evaluation tools from this workshop and the following questions to write a two-paragraph evaluation of the speech or editorial. In your evaluation, assess the content (including point of view, use of supporting details, and word choice) and technique (including tone, stresses, pauses, and non-verbal gestures).

- What is the speaker's point of view?
- Does the speaker use logical reasoning? How can you tell?
- Are the speaker's points supported with facts, details, and opinions from experts?
- Was the information presented unbiased?
- Did the speaker exclude any important information?
- How do you think the speech or editorial could be improved?

Comprehension and Collaboration After you have listened to the speech or editorial and have drafted your evaluation, form groups and discuss your findings, noting what you thought were the strongest and weakest parts of the speech. As you listen to classmates, jot down notes on your classmates' views. Then, as a group, review and fill in the following Evaluation Checklist. When you have finished, share your results with the rest of the class and discuss your reasoning.

Evaluation Checklist

Speech Content

Rate the speaker's content on a scale of 1 (very poor) to 5 (excellent) for each of these items. Explain your ratings.

• met the needs of the audience	Rating: ___	• used effective main and supporting ideas	Rating: ___
• achieved its purpose	Rating: ___	• included convincing facts and expert opinions	Rating: ___
• was appropriate to the occasion	Rating: ___		

Speech Delivery

Rate the speaker's delivery on a scale of 1 (very poor) to 5 (excellentl) for each of these items. Explain your ratings.

• formal language	Rating: ___	• appropriate volume	Rating: ___
• eye contact	Rating: ___	• enunciation	Rating: ___
• effective speaking rate	Rating: ___	• appropriate gestures	Rating: ___
• pauses for effect	Rating: ___	• conventions of language	Rating: ___

EXTEND/ASSESS

Practice the Skills

1. Review the assignment with students. Make sure they understand that the first paragraph should be about content and the second paragraph should be about technique. Remind them to support their evaluations using details from the speech.
2. Explain to students that they should listen to the presentation and then write their own evaluations. In a group, they will complete the Evaluation Checklist to evaluate the presentations made by classmates.
3. Tell students to listen for the connection between the main and supporting ideas. Suggest that they ask themselves whether supporting ideas actually support the main idea or are simply additional facts or opinions about the topic.

Evaluate the Activity

1. Evaluate students' two-paragraph evaluations on the basis of the completeness of their assessment, their use of details from the speech, and their observations about the speaker's delivery.
2. When the class discusses the presentations that were easiest to follow, encourage students to make note of the features of those presentations that made them effective and to incorporate those techniques in their future presentations.

Differentiated Instruction for Universal Access

EL Strategies for English Learners

Help students distinguish English intonation patterns in presentations. Demonstrate rising voice at the end of questions. Model falling voice at the end of declarative statements. Write sample sentences on the board.

- Write *"Did you see the dog?"* Read the question and ask students to repeat it. Ask students to determine whether the voice was rising or falling. Then, explain why rising voice was used.
- Write *"Do you feel better?"* and *"Is lunch ready?"* Have pairs take turns reading the questions with proper intonation, correcting each other as needed.
- Encourage students to listen for intonation patterns in presentations.

Cumulative Review

In this Common Core Assessment Workshop (pp. 414–417), students apply and reinforce their mastery of the Common Core Standards and the skills taught in Unit 2. The practice is divided into four sections including a section of Performance Tasks addressing CCSS Reading standards.

1. Before assigning each section, review the relevant Common Core Standards and unit skills with students.
2. Set a time limit for the multiple choice items in each section, allowing a little over one minute per question. Allow twenty minutes for any timed Writing questions.
3. Administer each of the first three sections of the Cumulative Review (pp. 414–417).
4. Use the Performance Tasks on pages 418–419 to assess the depth of students' mastery of standards taught in the unit. Follow the suggestions on teacher pages 418–419 for assigning tasks and for supporting and evaluating student performance.

Reteaching Skills

1. For each practice, use the Reteach chart on the same page as the answers to determine which skills require teaching, based on which items students answered incorrectly.
2. Reteach these skills prior to assigning the **Benchmark Test** for the second half of Unit 2 (***Unit 2 Resources***, pp. 227–232).

Cumulative Review

Common Core State Standards

RL.9-10.1, RL.9-10.3, RL.9-10.4, RL.9-10.5; W.9-10.10

[For the full wording of the standards, see the standards chart in the front of your textbook.]

I. Reading Literature

Directions: *Read the passage. Then, answer each question that follows.*

It was Nicole's first year of high school. She was so nervous that her mom desperately wanted to help. To ease Nicole's transition, her mom decided that Nicole should try out for the marching band flag corps. Nicole's mom had been in the flag corps when she was young, and she had met some of her best friends there.

"I'm a total klutz," Nicole said. "I don't think I can do it." Nicole neglected to mention that she had no desire to join the flag corps. Practicing every night after school in the blazing heat did not appeal to her. Spending every weekend at football games and competitions sounded incredibly boring. Because Nicole's mom was so excited, though, Nicole couldn't bear to disappoint her.

"You'll absolutely love it," Nicole's mom said. "It is so much fun. You'll meet a whole new group of friends. It was the best thing I ever did!"

"Okay," Nicole agreed reluctantly. "I'll try it." Nicole did not have a lot of confidence about making the flag corps. She had never been coordinated—she was more of a bookworm than an athlete. Night after night, though, Nicole diligently practiced with her mom. After weeks of practice, she wasn't *so* bad.

Finally, the day of tryouts arrived. Nicole's mom was far more nervous than Nicole. Nicole, however, was apprehensive for another reason. She didn't want to join the flag corps, yet she didn't want to disappoint her mother. She felt totally and completely stuck. After weighing her options, she finally knew what she had to do.

A month later, on a Saturday afternoon, Nicole could hear her mother cheering boisterously from the audience. Nicole had just scored the winning point for the quiz bowl team. It turns out that Nicole had not tried out for the flag corps after all. She knew that finding an activity was a good idea, but the flag corps was not the one for her. Quiz bowl, though, was perfect. She made many new friends who shared her interests. Instead of being upset, Nicole's mom was happy her daughter had found a way to meet new people and do something that she enjoyed.

Differentiated Instruction for Universal Access

Strategy for Less Proficient Readers

Tell students that they will be looking for external and internal conflicts in this selection. An external conflict takes place between one character and either another character, the natural world, or society. An internal conflict takes place within a character. Use Luke in the *Star Wars* films as an example. Luke's external conflict is with the Empire. His internal conflict is within himself—between his wish to be a Jedi knight and his fear that he will not be successful in his this task.

1. What **internal conflict** does Nicole face?
   - **A.** She wants to join the flag corps but doesn't want to disappoint her mother.
   - **B.** She doesn't want to be in the flag corps or disappoint her mother.
   - **C.** She joins the flag corps but she is clumsy.
   - **D.** She doesn't know what she wants to do her first year of high school.
2. What **external conflict** does Nicole face?
   - **A.** her own clumsiness
   - **B.** her mother
   - **C.** students at high school
   - **D.** blazing heat
3. Which of the following is *not* part of this story's **setting?**
   - **A.** a quiz bowl
   - **B.** Nicole's home
   - **C.** a football game
   - **D.** the beginning of the school year
4. Which of the following is an example of **direct characterization?**
   - **A.** It was Nicole's first year of high school.
   - **B.** "You'll absolutely love it," Nicole's mom said.
   - **C.** She was more of a bookworm than an athlete.
   - **D.** Nicole had just scored the winning point for the quiz bowl team.
5. Which of the following is an example of **indirect characterization?**
   - **A.** Nicole practiced diligently with her mom.
   - **B.** But Nicole's mom was so excited, Nicole couldn't bear to disappoint her.
   - **C.** She knew she had to find something that she was interested in.
   - **D.** It was Nicole's first year of high school.
6. What does the **dialogue** reveal about Nicole's feelings?
   - **A.** She is hesitant about joining the flag corps.
   - **B.** She wants to argue with her mother.
   - **C.** She cannot express herself clearly.
   - **D.** She is angry at her mother for making her try out.
7. **Vocabulary** Which is the best definition of the underlined word *klutz?*
   - **A.** a boring person
   - **B.** a foolish person
   - **C.** a clumsy person
   - **D.** a confused person
8. How is the **conflict** in the story resolved?
   - **A.** Nicole does what her mother wants.
   - **B.** Nicole joins the quiz bowl instead of the flag corps.
   - **C.** Nicole's mother is disappointed with her.
   - **D.** Nicole doesn't make the team in tryouts.
9. Which of the following expectations creates a **surprise ending?**
   - **A.** The reader expects Nicole to join the flag corps.
   - **B.** The reader expects Nicole to fail the tryouts.
   - **C.** The reader expects Nicole to join the quiz team.
   - **D.** The reader expects Nicole's mom to be disappointed.

Timed Writing

10. Write an informative essay in which you identify and explain the **situational irony** in this story. In your essay, be sure to describe the clues that led you to expect a different story outcome.

GO ON

ASSESS/RETEACH

Answers

I. Reading Literature

Answers With Explanations

1. **B**—The statement expresses Nicole's inner dilemma. *Incorrect answers:* A—Nicole does not want to join the flag corps. C—Nicole never joins the flag corps. D—Nicole's conflict is more specific.
2. **B**—If her mother did not urge her to join the flag corps, Nicole would have no conflict. *Incorrect answers:* A—Nicole's clumsiness is internal. C—Nicole does not have problems with the other students. D—The blazing heat is only one objection among many to the flag corps.
3. **C**—No football game takes place. *Incorrect answers:* A—The story has this setting. B—same explanation as for A. D—same explanation as for A.
4. **C**—The writer directly states a character trait. *Incorrect answers:* A—This does not address Nicole's character. B—This tells you about Nicole's mother. D—This describes an action, not Nicole's character.
5. **C**—This reveals information about Nicole indirectly. *Incorrect answers:* A—This directly states Nicole's diligence. B—This directly states Nicole's feelings. D—This has nothing to do with character.
6. **A**—Nicole states her reluctance to join the flag corps twice. *Incorrect answers:* B—Nicole agrees to try out. C—She says very clearly "I don't think I can do it." D—Nicole does not express anger.
7. **C**—The passage says Nicole had never been coordinated, which supports this meaning of *klutz*. *Incorrect answers:* A—Nicole thinks that football games are boring, but she is not boring. B—Nicole is smart, not foolish. D—While Nicole is confused, that is not the meaning of *klutz*.
8. **B**—Nicole does what she wants to do and takes part in an activity, which satisfies her mother. *Incorrect answers:* A—Nicole does not join the flag corps. C—Her mother is happy for Nicole. D—Nicole does not try out for the flag corps team.

Continued from right column

9. **A**—The selection leads readers to expect that Nicole will succeed in the flag corps tryouts because of her practicing. *Incorrect answers:* B—The reader has been led to expect Nicole to win a place on the team. C—The quiz team is not mentioned until the last paragraph. D—Readers do not expect her mother to be disappointed.

Timed Writing

10. Student essays should say the situational irony in this story arises from the reader's expectation that Nicole will try out and find that she has the skills after all, when she never even tries out.

Reteach

Question	Instructional Pages to Reteach
1	211
2	211
3	200, 290
4	313
5	313
6	347
8	197, 211
9	257
10	257

II. Reading Informational Text

Answers With Explanations

1. B—The passage states that the resurgence of popularity came after the bicycle had fallen to second-class status, supporting the meaning "revival." *Incorrect answers:* A—A *decline* is the opposite of a *resurgence.* C—This choice makes no sense. D—same explanation as for C.
2. C—The four headings and subheadings introduce the passage and its three sections. *Incorrect answers:* A—There are no bulleted lists. B—The passage has no timeline. D—The passage is not in outline form.

Reteach

Question	Page to Reteach
2	376

COMMON CORE
Assessment Workshop: Short Stories

II. Reading Informational Text

Directions: *Read the passage. Then, answer each question that follows.*

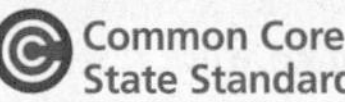

Common Core State Standards

RI.9-10.4, RI.9-10.5; L.9-10.1, L.9-10.2
[For the full wording of the standards, see the standards chart in the front of your textbook.]

History of the Bicycle

The early history of the bicycle is sparsely recorded, leading to many debates. One thing that is known for sure is that the late nineteenth century gave rise to the bicycle's popularity.

The Nineteenth Century

Bicycles were originally powered by riders who pushed against the ground with their feet to get moving. In the 1860s, inventors added pedals to bicycles. At that time, France was the home of the bicycle. The word *bicycle* comes from the French word *bicyclette.* In models at that time, the front wheel was a bit larger than the back. The iron frame and iron wheels made for an uncomfortable ride. This version of the bicycle was appropriately nicknamed the "boneshaker."

In the 1870s, interest moved to Britain and development continued there. The British introduced the "ordinary," a bicycle with solid rubber tires, a large front wheel, and a small back wheel. The ordinary proved to be hazardous. By 1885, the "safety" was invented, in which the front wheel size was reduced and the rear wheel enlarged.

In the 1890s, bicycling around the world boomed. Bicycles provided a means of transportation for men, women, and children.

The Twentieth Century

In the early 1900s, the automobile was introduced and mass transit improved, giving the bicycle a second-class status. However, a resurgence of popularity came in the 1950s and 1960s with huge sales of the banana seat bicycles. The 1970s saw the invention of the 10-speed and a huge growth in the bicycle industry. In the 1980s and 1990s, the popularity of the mountain bike grew.

Bicycling Today

Today, bicyclers can choose from a variety of bicycles. Some of the most predominant styles are the mountain bike, the racing bike, and the hybrid (a cross between the two). Bicycling has reached a new level of popularity.

1. **Vocabulary** What is the *best* definition for the underlined word *resurgence*?
   A. decline
   B. revival
   C. surprise
   D. group

2. What **text feature** does the author use in this article?
   A. bulleted lists
   B. time lines
   C. heads and subheads
   D. outlines

Strategies for Test Taking

Often the anxiety surrounding test taking causes students to bite their nails and sweat profusely. Don't worry this is normal.

Benchmark

Reteach skills as indicated by students' performance, following the Reteach charts on pp. 415–418. Then, administer the end-of-unit **Benchmark Test** (***Unit 2 Resources,*** pp. 227–235). Follow the **Interpretation Guide** for the test (***Unit 2 Resources,*** p. 239) to assign reteaching pages as necessary in the **Reading Kit.** Use **Success Tracker** online to automatically assign these pages.

III. Writing and Language Conventions

Directions: *Read the passage. Then, answer each question that follows.*

(1) Jeff's face felt hot as the redness crawled up her cheeks. (2) Every time she introduced herself, she heard, "Isn't Jeff a boy's name?" (3) It was worse when she was little. (4) Everyone thought she is a boy. (5) Now it was just embarrassing. (6) She wanted to introduce herself to him. (7) As she struggled through the crowd in the cafeteria, she noticed that Joe, the attractive boy from her English class, was there. (8) Then, his friend had to ask that question. (9) His friends chuckled, but Joe smiled kindly. (10) When lunch was over, Jeff walk away brokenhearted. (11) She knew she would never talk to Joe again. (12) Suddenly, a tap was felt on her shoulder. (13) "Jeff is a great name. It makes you special," said Joe. (14) A smile spread across Jeff's face. (15) Maybe she needed to be proud of being different.

1. Which of the following revisions *best* corrects the inconsistent **verb tense** in sentence 4?

A. Change *is* to *were.*
B. Change *is* to *was.*
C. Change *is* to *will be.*
D. Leave as is.

2. Which revision to sentence 9 helps to highlight Jeff's **internal conflict?**

A. His friends chuckled as Jeff knew they would, but Joe smiled kindly.
B. Joe smiled kindly even though his friends chuckled.
C. His friends chuckled, but Joe smiled kindly.
D. His friends chuckled and Jeff felt herself tingle with embarrassment, but Joe smiled kindly.

3. Which revision shows the *best* way to correct the use of **passive voice** in sentence 12?

A. Suddenly, she tapped on her shoulder.
B. Suddenly, on her shoulder a tap was felt by Jeff.
C. Suddenly, a tap is felt by Jeff on her shoulder.
D. Suddenly, she felt a tap on her shoulder.

4. Which revision to sentence 8 would help clarify the event being described?

A. Then his friend had to ask that question: What's your name?
B. Then his friend had to ask that same old question.
C. The question Jeff dreaded was asked by his friend.
D. Then his friend, whom Jeff didn't know, had to ask that question.

5. Which of the following revisions is the *best* way to correct the **verb tense** shift in sentence 10?

A. Change *was* to *is.*
B. Change *walk* to *walks.*
C. Change *walk* to *walked.*
D. Change *walk* to *will walk.*

6. Which revision would *best* clarify the **sequence of events** in this passage?

A. Switch sentence 12 and sentence 13.
B. Switch sentence 5 and sentence 6.
C. Switch sentence 7 and sentence 8.
D. Switch sentence 6 and sentence 7.

Reteach

Question	Pages to Reteach
1	309
2	211
3	372
4	406
5	309
6	308

Answers

III. Writing and Language Conventions

Answers With Explanations

1. B—*Was* and *thought* are both past tenses. *Incorrect answers:* A—*Were* is a plural verb, which does not go with the singular pronoun *she.* C—The future tense is inappropriate. D—With *is* in the sentence, the tenses are not consistent.
2. D—Mentioning Jeff's embarrassment reveals her inner conflict. *Incorrect answers:* A—Jeff accurately predicting the response does not show her conflict. B—This statement does not reflect Jeff's feelings. C—same explanation as for B.
3. D—The verb *felt* is in the active voice in this sentence. *Incorrect answers:* A—Jeff did not tap on her own shoulder. B—This sentence uses the passive voice and is quite awkward. C—same explanation as for B.
4. A—This clarifies the situation. *Incorrect answers:* B—This leaves the reader wondering about the question. C—This is similar to B. D—The fact that Jeff does not know Joe's friend is not important.
5. C—Both *was* and *walked* are in the past tense. *Incorrect answers:* A—The situation took place in the past, not the present. B—*Was* and *walks* are different verb tenses. D—same explanation as for B.
6. D—Jeff would have to see Joe in the crowd before she introduced herself to him. *Incorrect answers:* A—These sentences are already in the correct order. B—same explanation as for A. C—This change does not make sense.

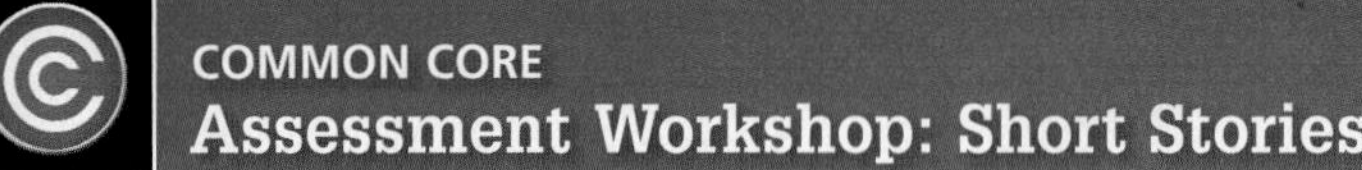

COMMON CORE
Assessment Workshop: Short Stories

Performance Tasks

Assigning Tasks/Reteaching Skills

Use the chart below to choose appropriate Performance Tasks by identifying which tasks assess lessons in the textbook that you have taught. Use the same lessons for reteaching when students' performance indicates a failure to fully master a standard. For additional instruction and practice, assign the *Common Core Companion* pages indicated for each task.

Task	Where Taught/ Pages to Reteach	*Common Core Companion* Pages
1	198, 313	28–34, 255–262
2	257	48–54, 255–262
3	211, 257	28–34, 255–262
4	197, 199, 200, 211	48–54, 255–262
5	290, 347	35–47, 293–299
6	135, 200, 313	28–34, 293–299
7	196, 200, 211	48–54, 274–281, 334–335

Assessment Pacing

In assigning the Writing Tasks on this student page, allow a class period for the completion of a task. As an alternative, assign tasks as homework. In assigning the Speaking and Listening Tasks on the facing page, consider having students do any required preparation as a homework assignment. Then, allow a class period for the presentations themselves.

Evaluating Performance Tasks

Use the rubric at the bottom of this Teacher Edition page to evaluate students' mastery of the standards as demonstrated in their Performance Task responses. Review the rubric with students before they begin work so they know the criteria by which their work will be evaluated.

Performance Tasks

Directions: *Follow the instructions to complete the tasks below as required by your teacher.*

As you work on each task, incorporate both general academic vocabulary and literary terms you learned in this unit.

Common Core State Standards

RL.9-10.1, RL.9-10.3, RL.9-10.4, RL.9-10.5; W.9-10.9.a; SL.9-10.1, SL.9-10.4; L.9-10.6
[For the full wording of the standards, see the standards chart in the front of your textbook.]

Writing

Task 1: Literature [RL.9-10.3; W.9-10.9.a]

Analyze a Complex Character

Write an essay in which you analyze the development of a complex character from a story in this unit.

- State which story and character you chose and why. Explain what qualities make the character complex. Provide a brief summary of the story's plot and your character's role in it.
- Explain how the author uses characterization—direct, indirect, or both—to develop the character. Cite details, including dialogue and descriptions of interactions between characters.
- Explain how your character changes and develops over the course of the story. Discuss how these changes help to advance the plot or develop the story's theme.
- Use proper language conventions, including correct subject and predicate agreement.

Task 2: Literature [RL.9-10.5; W.9-10.9.a]

Analyze Situational Irony in a Short Story

Analyze how an author's use of situational irony in a story from this unit creates surprise.

- State which story you chose and briefly summarize the plot.
- Explain what is ironic in the plot and show what happens that contradicts the expectations of characters or the reader.
- Explain how the story's surprise ending still makes sense and fits with details or ideas from earlier in the work.
- Provide specific examples from the text to support your analysis.
- Use active rather than passive voice whenever possible.

Task 3: Literature [RL.9-10.1; W.9-10.9.a]

Make and Support Inferences About a Main Character

Write an essay in which you explain how making inferences about a main character affected your understanding of a story from this unit.

- Introduce the story's characters, setting, and plot, and explain the main character's role in the story.
- Identify three inferences you made about the main character while reading this story. Cite specific details you used to make them.
- Show how making inferences led you to an understanding of the main character. For example, you might show how specific details suggest a character's personality traits, such as kindness, or help you predict the character's actions.

Task 4: Literature [RL.9-10.5; W.9-10.9.a]

Analyze Plot Structure

Write an essay in which you analyze how events in a story from this unit are ordered by cause-and-effect relationships.

- Identify a story from this unit in which cause-and-effect relationships play a key role. Briefly summarize the plot.
- Describe how the story's plot follows a series of causes and effects. Explain how these causes and effects are introduced and developed in the different stages of the plot—the exposition, rising action, climax, and resolution.
- Cite examples from the story that clearly show how one event causes or influences another. Explain how events lead to the story's resolution or to a character's epiphany.

Performance Task Rubric: Standards Mastery	Rating Scale (not very – very)
Critical Thinking: How clearly and consistently does the student pursue the specific mode of reasoning or discourse required by the standard, as specified in the prompt (e.g., comparing and contrasting, analyzing, explaining)?	1 2 3 4 5
Focus: How well does the student understand and apply the focus concepts of the standard, as specified in the prompt (e.g., development of theme or of complex characters, effects of structure, and so on)?	1 2 3 4 5
Support/Elaboration: How well does the student support points with textual or other evidence? How relevant, sufficient, and varied is the evidence provided?	1 2 3 4 5
Insight: How original, sophisticated, or compelling are the insights the student achieves by applying the standard to the text(s)?	1 2 3 4 5
Expression of Ideas: How well does the student organize and support ideas? How well does the student use language, including word choice and conventions, in the expression of ideas?	1 2 3 4 5

Speaking and Listening

Task 5: Literature [RL.9-10.4; SL.9-10.4]

Analyze How Language Evokes a Sense of Time and Place

Deliver an oral presentation in which you analyze how the language in a story from this unit creates a vivid picture of the setting (time and place).

- Identify the story you chose and explain the setting—where and when it takes place.
- Provide examples of words the author chose to evoke this time and place. Identify descriptive language, as well as language specific to a certain region or era. Explain how these word choices help to paint a picture of the physical setting while also building a specific mood in the story.
- Clarify the meanings of any words that might be unfamiliar to your listeners.
- Include a visual image that captures an aspect of the story's setting. It might illustrate the location or simply suggest a similar mood. Explain why you chose this image.
- Present your findings and supporting evidence clearly so your audience can follow your reasoning.

Task 6: Literature [RL.9-10.3; SL.9-10.4]

Analyze Character and Theme

Deliver an oral presentation in which you analyze how a complex character contributes to the expression of the theme in a story from this unit.

- Deliver your presentation as the character you chose. Tell the story from your point of view, describing why you, as the character, think, feel, and behave as you do.
- As the character, explain your understanding of other characters. Consider how other characters react similarly or differently to events.
- As the character, explain the insight about life or human nature your story expresses.
- Use language similar to that used by the character in the story.
- Present information clearly, concisely, and logically so that listeners can follow your reasoning.

Task 7: Literature [RL.9-10.5; SL.9-10.1; L.9-10.6]

Analyze Conflict

Deliver an oral presentation in which you analyze the conflict in a short story from this unit.

- Identify a short story from this unit that you feel has a rich and interesting conflict.
- Outline the plot points of the story and explain whether the main conflict is external, internal, or both.
- Use specific evidence from the story to show how the conflict unfolds. Explain how characters, dialogue, and setting contribute to the conflict and to its resolution.
- Use visual aids to help present your analysis to the class. For example, you might create a plot diagram on poster board to help your listeners follow your ideas.
- After your speech, invite questions from the audience. Answer questions thoughtfully, using correct academic language and literary terms.

Is conflict necessary?

At the beginning of Unit 2, you participated in a discussion of the Big Question. Now that you have completed the unit, write a response to the question. Discuss how your initial ideas have changed or been reinforced. Support your response with at least one example from literature and one example from an additional subject area or your own life. Use Big Question vocabulary words (see p. 195) in your response.

Differentiated Instruction for Universal Access

Strategy for Less Proficient Readers

Assign a Performance Task, and then have students meet in groups to review the standard assessed in that task. Remind students of the selections or independent readings to which they have previously applied the standard. Have groups summarize what they learned in applying the standard and then present their summaries. Discuss, clarifying any points of confusion. After students have completed their tasks, have groups meet again to evaluate members' work. Encourage members to revise their work based on the feedback they receive.

EL Strategy for English Learners

For each assigned Performance Task, review the instructions with students. Clarify the meaning of any unfamiliar vocabulary, emphasizing routine classroom words such as *summary*, *analysis*, and *diagram* and academic vocabulary such as *identify*. Next, have students note ideas for their responses. Pair students, and have them review each other's notes, asking questions to clarify meaning and suggested improvements. Encourage students to ask for your assistance in supplying English words or expressions they may require.

Supporting Speaking and Listening

1. Consider having students work with partners or in groups to complete Performance Tasks involving listening and speaking. For tasks that you assign for individual work, you may still wish to have students rehearse with partners, who can provide constructive feedback.
2. As students rehearse, have them keep in mind these tips:
   - Present findings and evidence clearly and concisely.
   - Observe conventions of standard English grammar and usage.
   - Be relaxed and friendly but maintain a formal tone.
   - Make eye contact with the audience, pronounce words clearly, and vary your pace.
   - When working with a group, respond thoughtfully to others' positions, modifying your own response to new evidence.

Linking Performance Tasks to Independent Reading

If you wish to cover the standards with students' independent reading, adapt Performance Tasks of your choice to the works they have selected. (Independent reading suggestions appear on the next page.)

Is conflict necessary?

1. Remind students that the unit Big Question is "Is conflict necessary?"
2. Have students complete their responses to the prompt on the student page. Point out that they have read selections in this unit about different types of conflict or responses to conflict and that they should draw on these selections in their responses. Remind them that they can also draw on their own experiences and what they have learned in other subject areas in formulating their answers.

Independent Reading

Titles featured on the Independent Reading pages at the end of each unit represent a range of reading, including stories, dramas, and poetry, as well as literary nonfiction and other types of informational text. Throughout, labels indicate the works that are CCSS Exemplar Texts. Choosing from among these featured titles will help students read works at increasing levels of text complexity in the grades 9–10 text complexity band.

Independent Reading and Pacing

See the Unit Overview and Pacing Plan, pp. 194a–194b, for suggestions on integrating independent reading with work in the Student Edition.

Using Literature Circles

A literature circle is a temporary group in which students independently discuss a book.

Use the guidance in the *Professional Development Guidebook*, pp. 47–49, as well as the teaching notes on the facing page, for additional suggestions for literature circles.

Meeting Unit 2 CCS Focus Standards

Students can use books listed on this page to apply and reinforce their mastery of the CCS Focus Standards covered in this unit. (The Focus Standards are introduced on pp. 196–199.)

Introducing Featured Titles

Have students choose a book or books for independent reading. Assist them by previewing the titles, noting their subject matter and level of difficulty. **Note:** Before recommending a work to students, preview it, taking into account the values of your community as well as the maturity of your students.

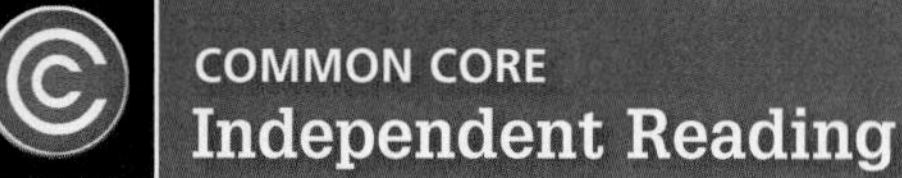

Featured Titles

In this unit, you have read a variety of short stories. Continue to read on your own. Select works that you enjoy, but challenge yourself to explore new authors and works of increasing depth and complexity. The titles suggested below will help you get started.

Literature

The Tragedy of Macbeth
by William Shakespeare
EXEMPLAR TEXT 

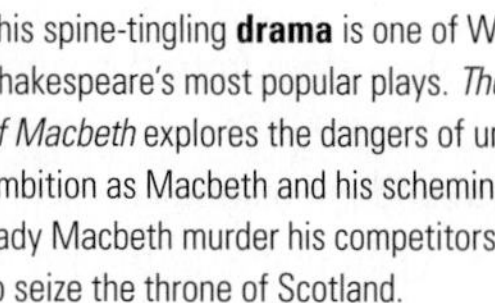

This spine-tingling **drama** is one of William Shakespeare's most popular plays. *The Tragedy of Macbeth* explores the dangers of unrestrained ambition as Macbeth and his scheming wife Lady Macbeth murder his competitors in a plot to seize the throne of Scotland.

Diary of a Madman and Other Stories
by Nikolai Gogol
Signet Classic, 2005

Written in diary form, this **novel** tells the story of a government clerk who loses his mind. At the beginning of the story, the narrator writes rationally. As the story progresses, however, the narrator descends deeper into madness. The volume also includes the author's classic story, "The Nose."

Stories by O. Henry
by O. Henry
EXEMPLAR TEXT

O. Henry is considered one of America's greatest short story writers, famous for his colorful characters and surprise endings. This collection of **short stories** includes "The Gift of the Magi" and other famous tales.

The Sea-Wolf and Selected Stories
by Jack London
Signet Classic, 2005

Captain Wolf Larsen believes the weak do not deserve to live; his crewman, Humphrey van Weyden, strongly disagrees. This tale of bitter conflict and other **short stories** in this collection whisk readers into a world of peril and adventure.

The Left Hand of Darkness
by Ursula K. Le Guin
Ace Books, 1969

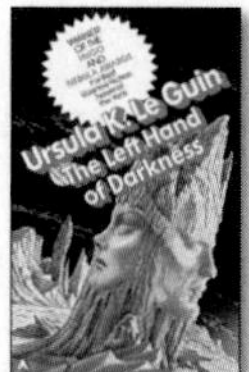

In this innovative **science-fiction novel,** Genly Ai is a government representative sent to the isolated planet of Gethen to mend relationships among an evolving galactic civilization. To do so, he must overcome his own prejudices as well as those of the people he encounters.

The Joy Luck Club
by Amy Tan
EXEMPLAR TEXT 

Amy Tan's best-selling **novel** explores the lives of Chinese American families who meet to play games and share meals. Told from the perspective of several female family members, the novel explores parent-child relationships and the dynamics of immigrant families.

Informational Texts

Literature of the Expanding Frontier

As pioneers spread across the Western frontier, they brought with them their passion for life and their hope for the future. This collection of **stories, poems, songs,** and **personal accounts** captures the spirits of everyone from Chinese immigrants building the nation's railroads to Native Americans dealing with the influx of new people as they all face the challenges of living together in the wilderness.

Text Complexity: Aligning Texts With Readers and Tasks

TEXTS	READERS AND TASKS
• *Stories by O. Henry* • *Literature of the Expanding Frontier*	**Below-Level Readers** Allow students to focus on reading for content, and challenge them to interpret multiple perspectives.
• *The Joy Luck Club* (Lexile: 930L) • *The Left Hand of Darkness* (Lexile: 970L) • *The Sea-Wolf and Selected Stories* (Lexile: 1020L)	**Below-Level Readers** Challenge students as they read for content. **On-Level Readers** Allow students to focus on reading for content, and challenge them to interpret multiple perspectives. **Advanced Readers** Allow students to focus on interpreting multiple perspectives.
• *The Tragedy of Macbeth* (NP) • *Diary of a Madman and Other Stories* (Lexile: 1060L)	**On-Level Readers** Challenge students as they read for content. **Advanced Readers** Allow students to focus on reading for content, and challenge them to interpret multiple perspectives.

Preparing to Read Complex Texts

Attentive Reading As you read literature on your own, bring your imagination and questions to the text. The questions shown below and others that you ask as you read will help you learn and enjoy literature even more.

Common Core State Standards

Reading Literature/Informational Text
10. By the end of grade 9, read and comprehend literature, including stories, dramas, poems, and literary nonfiction in the grades 9–10 text complexity band proficiently, with scaffolding as needed at the high end of the range.

When reading short stories, ask yourself...

- Who is narrating the story? Is this voice part of the story or an outside observer?
- Do I find the narrator's voice interesting and engaging? Why or why not?
- Who is the story's main character? Is he or she interesting to me? Why or why not?
- Which characters do I like or admire? Which do I dislike? How do my reactions to the characters make me feel about the story as a whole?
- Is the setting of the story—the place, time, and society—believable and interesting? Why or why not?
- What does the story mean to me? Does it convey a theme or insight that I find important and true? Why or why not?

Key Ideas and Details

- What aspects of the story grab my attention right away? Which fail to grab my attention?
- Do I find anything about the story confusing? Do my questions get answered? Why or why not?
- Is there anything different or unusual in the way the story is structured? Do I find that structure interesting or distracting?
- Are there any passages or details that I find especially strong or beautiful?
- Do I understand why characters act and feel as they do? Do their thoughts and actions seem real? Why or why not?
- What questions do I have about the characters and events?

Craft and Structure

- Does the story remind me of others I have read? If so, how?
- Have I gained new knowledge from reading this story? If so, what have I learned?
- Would I recommend this story to others? If so, to whom?
- Would I like to read other stories by this author? Why or why not?

Integration of Ideas

Text Complexity: Reader and Task Support Suggestions

INDEPENDENT READING

Increased Support Suggest that students choose a book that they feel comfortable reading and one that is a bit more challenging. Pair a more proficient reader with a less proficient reader and have them work together on the more challenging text. Partners can prepare to read the book by reviewing questions on this student page. They can also read difficult passages together, sharing questions and insights. They can use the questions on the student page to guide after-reading discussion.	*Increased Challenge* Encourage students to integrate knowledge and ideas by combining the Big Question and the Unit Focus concepts in their approach to two or more featured titles. For example, students might evaluate the positive and negative effects of conflict in *The Tragedy of Macbeth* and *The Joy Luck Club*. In addition, students can consider how conflict drives the plot in different fictional works.

Preparing to Read Complex Texts

1. Tell students they can be attentive readers by bringing their experience and imagination to the texts they read and by actively questioning those texts. Explain that the questions they see on the student page are examples of questions to ask about short stories.
2. Point out that, like writing, reading is a "multidraft" process, involving several readings of complete works or passages, revising and refining one's understanding each time.

Key Ideas and Details

3. As an example, review and amplify the fifth bulleted item. **Ask:** What key ideas and details could you cite as evidence that the story's setting is believable?

   Possible response: You might point out that the location is recognizable or that the narrator mentions real historical events in the story.

Craft and Structure

4. **Ask:** What details of craft and structure would you cite as evidence that a character acts or feels a certain way?

   Possible response: You might point to an author's skill of revealing characters' motivations through dialogue or devices like flashbacks.

Integration of Ideas

5. **Ask:** What criteria would you use to decide whether you would recommend a short story to someone else?

   Possible response: You might consider whether you agree with the story's message or how much you like the story compared to others that you've read.
6. Finally, explain to students that they should cite key ideas and details, examples of craft and structure, or instances of the integration of ideas as evidence to support their points during a book discussion. After hearing the evidence, the group might reach a consensus or might agree to disagree.

Unit 3 Features Overview

Unit Genre and Big Question

In this unit, students will analyze nonfiction. As they read they will discuss responses to the unit Big Question: Is knowledge the same as understanding?

Unit 3 Selections

Teach Selections are presented in leveled pairs. To teach the skills and meet the objectives, you need to assign only one selection in each pair.

Differentiate and Reinforce Choose the selection in a pair that is best suited for your students, based on the Text Complexity box shown on the next page. You may use the other selection to reinforce skills or provide enrichment.

Integrate Skills Each selection presents students with a reading strategy, a literary analysis concept, a vocabulary skill, and grammar instruction. Students can extend learning in the writing and extension activities.

Additional Unit Features

Literary Analysis Workshop Teach and model the Unit Focus standards. Spiral Review notes enable students to revisit these skills over the course of the unit.

Reading for Information Students analyze functional, expository, and argumentative texts and complete Timed Writing activities.

Comparing Literary Works Students study two literary works either within or across genres.

Test Practice: Reading This feature provides extra practice in utilizing reading skills to master assessments.

Writing Workshops Two writing workshops appear in each unit, along with rubrics and instruction in the writing process.

Assessment Workshop Cumulative Skill Review and Performance Tasks provide a range of assessment opportunities.

Independent Reading Students broaden their knowledge as they read longer works of increasing complexity.

THE BIG ?
Is knowledge the same as understanding?

PHLit Online!

Teaching From Technology

www.PHLitOnline.com

Log on at this address for the following:

Enriched Online Student Edition
- full narration of selections
- interactive graphic organizers
- linked **Get Connected!** and **Background** videos
- all worksheets and other student resources

Professional Development
- the ***Professional Development Guidebook*** online
- additional professional development articles by program authors

Planning, Assigning, and Monitoring
- software for online assignment of work to students, individually or to the whole class
- a system for tracking and grading student work

Types of Nonfiction

Unit 3

PHLit Online!
www.PHLitOnline.com

Hear It!
- Selection summary audio
- Selection audio
- BQ Tunes

See It!
- Author videos
- Big Question video
- Get Connected videos
- Background videos
- More about the authors
- Illustrated vocabulary words
- Vocabulary flashcards

Do It!
- Interactive journals
- Interactive graphic organizers
- Grammar tutorials
- Interactive vocabulary games
- Test practice

423

Instructional Resources

Unit 3 Resources supports unit skills with pages of the following types:

- **Benchmark Tests** assess and monitor student progress at mid-Unit and at Unit's end.
- **Vocabulary and Reading Warm-ups** provide additional vocabulary support, based on Lexile rankings of words, for each selection. "A" **Warm-ups** are for students reading two grades below level. "B" **Warm-ups** are for students reading one grade below level.
- **Selection Support** These practice pages are available for each selection:
  - Reading Skill
  - Literary Analysis
  - Writing About the Big Question
  - Vocabulary
  - Support for Writing
  - Support for Extend Your Learning
  - Enrichment

PHLit Online!

All worksheets and other student resources are also available online at **www.PHLitOnline.com.**

Text Complexity: Accessibility for Various Ability Levels

This chart gives a general text complexity rating to help you decide which selection in each leveled pair is more appropriate for your students. **Choose one selection in each pair, or choose to teach both.** You will meet the objectives for the pair when you teach either of the two selections. For additional guidance on factors that affect the complexity of each selection, see the Leveled Texts page for each selection set.

Accessibility for English Learners

This icon indicates support for English learners at point of use in this Teacher's Edition.

	✓ More Accessible	✓✓ More Complex
Pair 1	A Celebration of Grandfathers	On Summer
Pair 2	Single Room, Earth View	The News
Pair 3	Carry Your Own Skis	Libraries Face Sad Chapter
Pair 4	I Have a Dream	First Inaugural Address

COMMON CORE

UNIT 3 ▪ Overview and Pacing Plan

Common Core State Standards

Unit 3 Focus Standards

- **Reading Informational Text 3, 4, 5, 6**

Additional Activities and Assessments

- **Reading Informational Text 2, 8**
- **Writing 1, 2, 4, 8**
- **Speaking and Listening 1, 3, 4**
- **Language 1, 3, 5, 6**

	Week 1					Week 2					Week 3				
	1	2	3	4	5	1	2	3	4	5	1	2	3	4	5
Introduce the Unit Big Question (pp. 424–425).	●														
Introduce the Unit form, nonfiction, using the Literary Analysis Workshop (pp. 426–429).	●	●													
Introduce the focus CCS standards for the unit and lead students in a close reading of exemplar texts (pp. 426–427).	●	●	●												
Teach one selection from Pairing 1 (pp. 440–463).		●	●	●	●	●									
Teach one selection from Pairing 2 (pp. 464–489).						●	●	●	●						
Complete the Test Practice: Reading (pp. 490–491).									●						
Teach Reading for Information (pp. 492–497).										●					
Teach Comparing Literary Works (pp. 498–511).											●	●			
Have students complete the Writing Workshop (pp. 512–517).										●	●	●	●	●	
Administer **Benchmark Test 5** (***Unit 3 Resources***, pp. 120–125).														●	
Reteach skills, judging which skills to reteach by evaluating students' performance on **Benchmark Test 5**.															●

Independent Reading

Have students choose a full-length work from the Independent Reading feature at the end of the unit and read it while working on this unit.

Pacing Suggestions

- Have students read their chosen work for homework.
- Devote parts of class periods in each school week to Literature Circles in which students reading the same work discuss it.

	Week 4					Week 5					Week 6				
	1	2	3	4	5	1	2	3	4	5	1	2	3	4	5
Teach one selection from Pairing 3 (pp. 518–537).	●	●	●	●	●										
Teach one selection from Pairing 4 (pp. 538–563).					●	●	●	●	●						
Complete the Test-Practice: Reading (pp. 564–565).								●							
Teach Informational Texts (pp. 566–571).									●						
Teach Comparing Literary Works (pp. 572–581).										●	●				
Have students complete the Writing Workshop (pp. 582–589).									●	●	●	●	●		
Have students complete the Vocabulary Workshop (pp. 590–591).												●			
Have students complete the Communications Workshop (pp. 592–593).													●		
Have students complete the first three sections of the Assessment Workshop: Nonfiction (pp. 594–597).													●	●	●
Have students complete the selected Performance Tasks in the Assessment Workshop (pp. 598–599).														●	
Administer **Benchmark Test 6** (***Unit 3 Resources***, pp. 598 and 599).														●	
Reteach skills, judging which skills to reteach by evaluating students' performance on **Benchmark Test 6.**															●

- Cover the focus standards with independent readings, and abbreviate review of the focus standards with student-edition selections.
- Do not assign extension activities for selections (day 5 of main selection lessons), except as needed for full standards coverage.
- If students demonstrate reading proficiency, consider omitting Test Practice: Reading features in the unit.

Block and Daily Scheduling

The assignments and activities in this Unit planner are organized by week. You may adjust them to your daily or block schedule. The Time and Resource Manager for each selection set gives specific pacing suggestions, or you may use the comprehensive lesson planning support online at **www.PHLitOnline.com.**

Monitoring Progress

Diagnose Each main selection pairing in the Unit contains a more accessible and a more challenging selection. To determine which selection in each pairing to assign, refer to students' results on the **Vocabulary in Context** section of **Benchmark Test 4,** ***Unit 2 Resources***, pp. 233–235 (administered at the end of the previous Unit). Use the **Interpretation Guide** to interpret the results of the diagnostic portion of the test. **Note:** For the most accurate diagnosis of students who score in the middle range of the diagnostic portion of the test, administer the additional diagnostic questions online at **www.PHLitOnline.com**

Preteach and Prepare As indicated by the diagnostic, prepare students for reading by assigning the **Vocabulary Practice** and **Reading Warm-ups** for the selections you assign.

Teach Follow this Pacing Plan and use the resources to teach the skills and selections. For specific pacing suggestions and a list of resources, see the Time and Resource Manager and the Visual Guide to Featured Selection Resources preceding each selection pairing.

Assess After students have completed the first half of the Unit, administer **Benchmark Test 5**. Administer **Benchmark Test 6** at the end of the Unit.

Intervention and Reteach After administering each test, use the **Interpretation Guide** for the tests to determine which reteaching pages, if any, you should assign from the ***Reading Kit***. The appropriate pages are also available through the online Progress Monitoring software.

CLASSROOM STRATEGIES

Differences That Make a Difference **Arnetha Ball**

"Differentiation requires a modification of teaching routines to address a broad range of differences in students' readiness, interest, and learning styles."

Middle and high school students bring a wide range of resources and needs to the classroom. Differences in students' abilities, interests, language backgrounds, and learning preferences motivate teachers to ask questions about the effectiveness of "whole-group" approaches and "one-size-fits-all" models of teaching. Many teachers are recognizing the need to differentiate curriculum and instruction. Differentiation requires a modification of teaching routines to address a broad range of differences in students' readiness, interest, and learning styles (Tomlinson, 2001). It assumes that these differences will need to be addressed if the quality of learning is to improve for every student.

A Plan of Action for Differentiated Instruction

Teachers' acknowledgment and appreciation of student differences in learning styles, readiness, interests, cultures, and linguistic backgrounds is the first step toward helping them make significant academic gains. All differentiation of instruction should begin with an assessment of students' needs. Based on identified differences in readiness, interests, and learning needs, the teacher then proactively plans and carries out varied approaches to content, process, and product (Tomlinson, 2001, p. 7). Differentiated instruction can be carried out through a range of instructional and management strategies, including the use of literature circles, learning contracts, small-group instruction, questioning strategies, homework assignments, cooperative working groups, independent study, advanced organizers, complex instruction, and the use of supplementary materials.

The following steps can be elaborated and adapted as a plan of action for implementing differentiated instruction.

Step 1. Identify Ways to Assess Student Needs Survey records of the student's performance to determine prior and present knowledge and capabilities, past learning experiences, and family and community resources. Get to know the student's interests using a survey, an open-ended questionnaire, interest inventory, informal interview, or conference. Use various approaches to student assessment that seek to measure students' progress in a fair and equitable way. These approaches may include portfolios, rubrics, performance-based assessment, and knowledge mapping.

Step 2. Accumulate a Wide Repertoire of Teaching Strategies Create an annotated collection of engaging strategies that you find useful in meeting diverse learning needs. Four often-cited strategies in the literature on differentiated instruction include direct instruction, inquiry-based learning, cooperative learning, and questioning strategies.

Direct Instruction The most "traditional" and widely used teaching strategy, direct instruction can be used to cover a large amount of material in a limited amount of time. It is a highly structured and teacher-centered approach to instruction and is based on the assumption that students learn some materials best through a transmission model of teaching.

Inquiry-based Learning Inquiry-based learning is based on the core premise that learning should be based around student questions. Inquiry-based pedagogy and curriculum require students to work independently to solve problems. As facilitators of learning rather than dispensers of knowledge, inquiry-oriented teachers support students in the process of discovering knowledge themselves.

Cooperative Learning Cooperative learning is based on grouping small teams of students according to ability, interest, and background so they can work together to complete a task assigned to address their needs. Cooperative learning is designed explicitly to build cooperation skills by assigning roles to team members, establishing norms for conflict resolution, and providing the means for group reflection and individual self-assessment.

Questioning Strategies Questioning strategies ask students to monitor and assess their own learning and the learning of others in the classroom.

Step 3. Identify a Variety of Instructional Activities That Best Meet the Student's Needs Select varied and engaging activities that will motivate and challenge students to remain on task during the teaching learning process. Appropriately selected activities will require students to develop and apply knowledge in ways that make sense to them and that they find meaningful and relevant.

Step 4. Identify Ways to Assess and Evaluate Student Progress and Plan Next Steps In addition to using formative and summative assessments, expand opportunities for students to demonstrate authentic learning through varied tasks including portfolios, performance-based assessments, and knowledge mapping. Use the information gathered on student learning to plan future differentiated curriculum and instruction.

Modeled Strategy

See pp. 447 and 470 for point-of-use notes modeling these strategies.

Teacher Resources

- ***Professional Development Guidebook***
- ***Classroom Strategies and Teaching Routines*** **cards**

Log on as a teacher at **www.PHLitOnline.com** to access a library of all Professional Development articles by the Contributing Authors of Pearson Prentice Hall *Literature*.

Arnetha F. Ball, Ph.D.

Arnetha F. Ball, Ph.D. is a Professor in Curriculum Studies, Teacher Education, and Educational Linguistics in the School of Education at Stanford University. She was a classroom teacher for more than 25 years. Her research focuses on language and literacy studies of culturally and linguistically diverse populations.

Supporting Research

Banks, J. A. & Banks, C. A. (2001). *Multicultural education: Issues and perspectives* (4th ed.). New York: John Wiley & Sons.

Sapon-Shevin, M. (2000). Schools fit for all. *Educational Leadership*, v58, (4,) 34–39.

Thomas, E. & Robinson, H. (1972). *Improving reading in every class: A sourcebook for teachers.* Boston: Allyn & Bacon.

Tomlinson, C. A. (1999). *The Differentiated classroom: Responding to the needs of all learners.* Alexandria, VA: Association for Supervision and Curriculum Development.

Tomlinson, C. A. (2001). *How to differentiate instruction in mixed ability classrooms* (2nd ed.). Alexandria, VA: Association for Supervision and Curriculum Development.

INTRODUCE

Common Core State Standards

- Speaking and Listening 1.b
- Language 6

❶ Introducing the Big Question

1. Have a volunteer read aloud the introductory paragraph.
2. **Ask** students how knowledge might differ from understanding. (Knowledge is knowing facts. Understanding is knowing how facts fit together.) Discuss how facts can contribute to understanding.
3. **Ask** students the Big Question. (**Possible responses:** Yes, because when you know the facts about something, you understand it. No, because you might have information about a topic, but not understand it.)

❷ Exploring the Big Question

Collaboration: Group Discussion

1. Introduce the activity, using the instruction on the student page.
2. Have students work in pairs to find examples for the bulleted items, and discuss the following question:
   - Which examples do you associate more with feelings than facts? (**Sample response:** grandparents; memory)
3. Review the Big Question vocabulary on page 425, following the teaching suggestions. Have students use the vocabulary as they complete the activity on page 425.

Connecting to the Literature

Explain the Big Question strand in the unit, referring to the box at right.

Introducing the Big Question

❶ THE BIG ? Is knowledge the same as understanding?

We are constantly working to learn more about the world. We find information in a variety of sources, and we struggle to comprehend the facts. We may study books, interpret charts, and conduct further research. We may talk to others to gain insight. We may have gained knowledge, but when do we know that we truly understand? For example, does practicing soccer prepare us to play soccer? Does reading about relationships help us get along, or do we have to experience a friendship to truly understand?

❷ Exploring the Big Question

Collaboration: Group Discussion Begin thinking about the Big Question by analyzing what you know and how you know it. List topics that you have knowledge about and also understand. Describe an example from each of these categories.

- A grandparent or older adult you know well
- A concept you have learned in school
- A speech you have read over and over
- An argument you have had that still bothers you
- Something you have read about but also experienced
- The memory of an important event in your life

Share your list in a group. Talk about any differences you discover between your knowledge and your understanding of these topics.

Before you begin the discussion, set rules that will lead to a cooperative exchange. For example, consider any specific goals you want to achieve, whether to assign a mediator, and how you will handle disagreements. Capture the rules in a format everyone can use as the discussion takes place.

Connecting to the Literature Each reading in this unit will give you additional insight into the Big Question.

PHLit Online!
www.PHLitOnline.com

- Big Question video
- Illustrated vocabulary words
- Interactive vocabulary games
- BQ Tunes

Applying Understanding by Design Principles

The Big Question

Explain that students will continue to consider the Big Question as they work through the Unit 3.

- At the beginning of each selection, they will write a response to a Writing About the Big Question sentence starter.
- As they read the selection, they will look for details related to the Big Question.
- At the end of the selection, they will answer a Critical Thinking Question that is related to the Big Question.
- Tell students that their goal will be to gain a deeper understanding of literature and a more sophisticated way of discussing the Big Question.

❸ Learn Big Question Vocabulary

Acquire and Use Academic Vocabulary Academic vocabulary is the language you encounter in textbooks and on standardized tests. Review the definitions of these academic vocabulary words.

ambiguous (am big′ yo͞o əs) *adj.* having more than one meaning; able to be interpreted in different ways	**comprehend** (käm′ prē hend′) *v.* understand
clarify (klar′ ə fī) *v.* make something more clear or understandable	**concept** (kän′ sept′) *n.* idea; notion
	interpret (in tʉr′ prət) *v.* understand or explain the meaning of a concept or idea

Use these words as you complete Big Question activities that involve reading, writing, speaking, and listening.

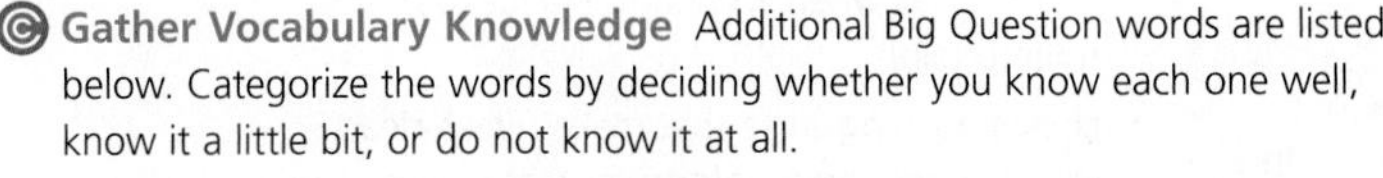

Gather Vocabulary Knowledge Additional Big Question words are listed below. Categorize the words by deciding whether you know each one well, know it a little bit, or do not know it at all.

connection	**insight**	**senses/sensory**
fact	**instinct**	**sources**
feeling	**research**	**statistics**
information		

Then, do the following:

1. Write the definitions of the words you know.
2. Consult a dictionary to confirm each word's meaning. Revise your definitions if necessary.
3. Using a print or an online dictionary, look up the meanings of the words you do not know. Then, write the meanings.
4. If a word sounds familiar but you are not sure of its meaning, consult a dictionary. Then, record the meaning.
5. Use all of the words in a brief paragraph about knowledge and understanding. Choose words and phrases that convey your ideas precisely.

Common Core State Standards

Speaking and Listening
1.b. Work with peers to set rules for collegial discussions and decision-making, clear goals and deadlines, and individual roles as needed.

Language
6. Acquire and use accurately grade-appropriate general academic and domain-specific words and phrases, sufficient for reading, writing, speaking, and listening at the college and career readiness level; demonstrate independence in gathering vocabulary knowledge when considering a word or phrase important to comprehension or expression.

❸ Learn Big Question Vocabulary

Acquire and Use Academic Vocabulary

1. Introduce the academic vocabulary words in the first word bank on the student page. Have students preview the words.
2. For each word, have students say the word aloud. Then, use the word in a sentence that defines the word.

Gather Vocabulary Knowledge

1. With the class, review the steps in the activity on the student page. Have students complete the activity independently, with partners, or in small groups.
2. Before students complete the last step, review the words and their meanings as a class. (Definitions appear below on the left.) Then, have students complete their paragraphs.

Show the Big Question video, online at **www.PHLitOnline.com.**

Gather Vocabulary Knowledge: Definitions

connection (kə nek shən) *n.* a relationship between things or ideas
fact (fakt) *n.* a piece of information that can be proven true
feeling (fēl′iŋ) *n.* an emotion
information (in′fər mā′shən) *n.* facts
insight (in′sīt′) *n.* the capacity to have a deep understanding of a person, concept, or situation
instinct (in′stiŋt) *n.* a natural way of acting or responding
research (rē′sʉrch) *n.* an investigation into a subject
senses (sens′ez) *n.* the physical means of learning about the world: sight, hearing, touch, taste, and smell
sensory (sen′sər ē) *adj.* relating to the senses
sources (sôrs′ez) *n.* people, books, or other media that supply information
statistics (stə tis′tiks) *v.* the science of analyzing and interpreting data

❶ Elements of Essays, Articles, and Speeches

1. Introduce the elements of essays, articles, and speeches, using the instruction on the student page. Referring to the chart on the student page, discuss with students the elements of nonfiction covered in the chart.
2. **Ask** students for an example of a topic that could be explored in an essay or speech.

   Sample responses: Topics for essay or speech: ending the space program, the joys of nature, teen curfew laws, why you don't like pigeons.
3. Discuss with students the three main purposes an author may have. Emphasize that a writer may have more than one purpose. For example, a humorous political writer's purpose might be both to entertain and to persuade.
4. **Ask** students to give examples of different ways articles on the following subjects might be organized: **(a)** the history of television, **(b)** how to make a great sandwich, **(c)** why people should give blood.

   Sample responses: (a) chronological order; **(b)** steps in a process; **(c)** logical order (argument).
5. **Ask** students to describe the tone of the following paragraph.

   You actually like cooking? Give me a break. Chopping, measuring, stirring—don't you have anything better to do with your time?

   Sample responses: The tone is scornful.

❶Elements of Essays, Articles, and Speeches

Essays, articles, and speeches organize factual information to present a picture of a topic—often from a particular point of view.

An essay can make you laugh. An article can make you cry. A speech can change your mind. Like all **nonfiction,** these forms of writing present facts or discuss real life.

- In an **essay,** an author supports a **thesis**—a central idea about a topic. In doing so, the author conveys his or her **point of view,** or perspective, on the topic.
- An **article** provides information about a topic. Articles are often divided into sections introduced by subheads. Each subhead names the central idea of the section it introduces. Many articles are written from an objective point of view—they give just the facts.
- A **speech** is a nonfiction text that a speaker delivers, or says, to an audience. Like the author of an essay, a speaker usually presents a thesis and expresses his or her point of view.

An author's approach to a topic depends on his or her **purpose,** or reason for writing. An author's purpose is related to the effect he or she wishes to have on readers. There are three main purposes for writing.

- **To inform,** or provide facts and explain how they relate to one another
- **To persuade,** or try to influence an audience's attitudes or actions
- **To entertain,** or engage and move the emotions of an audience

To achieve his or her purpose, a writer uses techniques such as these:

- **organizing information** in ways that make it clear (as when writing to inform) or dramatic (as when writing to persuade or to entertain)
- **choosing language** that makes ideas clear (as when writing to inform) or that creates **tone,** or conveys the writer's attitude (as when writing to persuade)

When you read nonfiction, analyze each element in the chart below.

Key Elements of Nonfiction

Element	Definition
Thesis or Central Idea	the main idea the author wants the audience to understand and remember
Purpose	the reason the author is writing about the topic
Organizational Structure	the order in which information and ideas are presented and the connections that are drawn between and among them
Tone	the author's attitude toward the topic and audience as conveyed in his or her word choices
Word Choice	the author's use of language devices, such as **figurative language,** or language that is not meant to be taken literally, and **rhetoric,** or the patterning of words

Teaching Resources

- All *Common Core Companion,* pp. 110–159
- All *Unit 3 Resources,* pp. 7–22
- All *Professional Development Guidebook,* pp. 33, 68, 69
- All *See It! DVD*
  Elizabeth McCracken, Segments 1 and 2
- All *Graphic Organizer Transparencies,* pp. 73, 74
- All *Enriched Online Student Edition*
- L2 L3 *Reader's Notebook*
- L1 *Reader's Notebook: Adapted Version*
- EL *Reader's Notebook: English Learner's Version*
- L2 EL *Hear It!* **Audio CD**
- L1 EL *Hear It!* **Audio CD (adapted text)**

All resources, including print and video, are available online at **www.PHLitOnline.com.**

❷ Types of Essays and Articles

The chart below explains five major types of essays.

Types of Essays

- **Narrative essays** tell the story of actual experiences or events.
- **Expository essays** inform readers about a topic and explain the ideas it involves.
- **Persuasive,** or **argumentative, essays** are written to convince audiences to accept an author's **claim,** or position on an issue, or to motivate audiences to take a particular course of action.
- **Descriptive essays** give vivid details about a person, place, or thing to help readers picture it.
- **Reflective essays** explore the meaning of an experience or offer the author's thoughts or feelings.

Authors may combine elements of different types of essays. For instance, in an argumentative essay persuading readers to adopt dogs from shelters, an author might include vivid descriptions of homeless dogs.

There are many types of articles. Two main types are news articles and feature articles.

Two Types of Articles

- **News articles** provide facts about current events. These articles usually answer the questions *Who? What? Where? When? Why?* and *How?* and are written from an objective, or neutral, point of view.
- **Feature articles** provide facts about topics of current interest such as fashion trends or developments in science. These articles are often written in a friendly, conversational style.

❸ Types of Speeches

What a writer says in a speech is shaped by its **occasion,** or the event at which the speech will be delivered, as well as by its **audience,** or the people to whom the speech will be addressed. The following chart gives examples of several common types of speeches, along with a possible occasion and audience for each.

Speech of Public Advocacy: a formal, prepared speech intended to persuade an audience to take action

Example: an argumentative speech that describes a community problem and proposes a possible solution

Delivered by: a citizen

Occasion: a city council meeting

Audience: the city council; fellow citizens

Talk: an informal speech presented in a conversational style

Example: a report on a science fair

Delivered by: a student

Occasion: a science club meeting

Audience: student members of the club

Impromptu Speech: a speech presented with little or no preparation, often in a conversational style

Example: a speech of celebration

Delivered by: the subject's friend

Occasion: a birthday party

Audience: the person whose birthday is being celebrated, along with the guests

❹

In This Section

Common Core State Standards

RI.9-10.3, RI.9-10.4, RI.9-10.5, RI.9-10.6

[For the full wording of the standards, see the standards chart in the front of your textbook.]

❷ Types of Essays and Articles

1. Review the first shaded box. Then, divide the class into five groups. Assign each group one of the essay types. **Ask** students to discuss their essay type and come up with a topic for that kind of essay.

   Sample responses: *Narrative essay*—story about an expedition. *Expository essay*—explanation of how a bill passes Congress. *Persuasive essay*—argument in favor of more city trees. *Descriptive essay*—description of a sunset. *Reflective essay*—exploration of what kindness is.

2. Review the second shaded box. Present students with several articles from a local newspaper and ask them to identify which are news articles and which are feature articles.

❸ Types of Speeches

1. Review the third shaded box. **Ask** students which of the speech types the following would be: **(a)** pep talk to your teammates during a time-out; **(b)** speech introducing a motion at a meeting; **(c)** a book report in class.

   Sample response:
   (a) impromptu speech;
   (b) speech of public advocacy;
   (c) talk

❹ In This Section

Explain that in the remainder of this Literary Analysis Workshop, students will analyze important nonfiction concepts such as the development and organization of ideas, word choice, and rhetoric. They will then see these applied to two Model texts. Finally, students will apply what they have learned to an Independent Practice text.

Common Core State Standards

Unit 3 Focus Standards

- **Reading Informational Text 3, 4, 5, 6**

These standards spiral through the unit.

❶ Analyzing the Development and Organization of Ideas

1. Go over the student-page material. Emphasize the importance of supporting details, and **ask** students to identify each of the following statements by type, using the definitions on the student page:

   (a) *The median age in Arizona is 35 years old, according to the U.S. Bureau of the Census.*

   (b) *A mango is a medium-sized fruit, shaped much like an egg, that is orange, yellow, and green.*

   (c) *The sun is 93 million miles away.*

   (d) *One kind of dog is an English setter.*

   (e) *The school librarian says that we need a larger budget for computer services.*

   (f) *I believe in other intelligent life in the universe because the universe is so huge.*

   Sample responses: (a) statistic; **(b)** description; **(c)** statement of fact; **(d)** example; **(e)** expert opinion; **(f)** reason

2. Go over the student-page material about Overall Organizational Structures. **Ask** students to give examples of informational text that might use each of the three types of structure defined on the student page.

   Sample responses: *Chronological order*—history of rap music. *Compare and contrast*—analysis of two different sports shoes. *Cause and effect*—explanation of why small children should ride in car seats.

❶ Analyzing the Development and Organization of Ideas

An author uses different methods to **introduce** and **develop** ideas, presenting supporting details in logical order to achieve a purpose.

Common Core State Standards

Reading Informational Text
3. Analyze how the author unfolds an analysis or series of ideas or events, including the order in which the points are made, how they are introduced and developed, and the connections that are drawn between them.
5. Analyze in detail how an author's ideas or claims are developed and refined by particular sentences, paragraphs, or larger portions of a text.

Introducing and Developing Ideas In a nonfiction work, the author will present ideas in a particular order and style. First, the author introduces the topic and key ideas. If these ideas are likely to be unfamiliar to readers, the author may introduce them with a familiar example or a simple comparison, as in this example:

> **Example: Sun Static**
> Although the sun is about 93 million miles away, solar activity can affect communications here on Earth. To understand why, picture water boiling in a pot. Bubbles on the surface burst and release steam. Similarly, solar flares on the surface of the sun can release particles that travel to the Earth.

Then, the author **develops,** or elaborates on, ideas, explaining them and showing the connections from one idea to the next. Details that illustrate, expand on, or prove the author's ideas are called **supporting details.** Here are some types of supporting details:

- **Statements of fact,** or statements that can be proved true
- **Statistics,** or numbers used to compare members of a group of people or things
- **Examples,** or specific cases
- **Descriptions,** or details that tell what something looks like, tastes like, and so on
- **Reasons,** or claims that justify a belief
- **Expert opinions,** or the judgments of people with special knowledge of a subject

Overall Organizational Structures To develop ideas and show the connections among them, an author needs to present information in a clear order. An author's purpose for writing will help her or him choose an overall **structure,** or pattern of organization, as in these examples:

- A news report about a space shuttle launch written to inform might present events in **chronological order,** or the order in which they happened. This order will aid readers in following the series of events.
- A feature article comparing the space shuttle program with older programs might use **comparison-and-contrast organization,** grouping details according to their similarities and differences.
- An editorial about the space shuttle program written to persuade readers to support the program might have a **cause-and-effect organization.** By clearly showing how the program leads to important medical discoveries, for example, this organization could help convince readers.

Each part of a work plays its role in the development of ideas. For example, the author may organize the work into **sections,** or parts. In this case, each **paragraph** in a section would elaborate on the main idea of the section. In turn, each **sentence** within a paragraph would help develop the main idea of that paragraph. In this way, the various parts of a text work together to support the author's main idea, or thesis.

❷ Analyzing Word Choice and Rhetoric

To achieve their purpose and to convey a point of view, authors use tools such as **word choice** and **rhetoric.**

Common Core State Standards

Reading Informational Text
4. Determine the meaning of words and phrases as they are used in a text, including figurative, connotative, and technical meanings; analyze the cumulative impact of specific word choices on meaning and tone.
6. Determine an author's point of view or purpose in a text and analyze how an author uses rhetoric to advance that point of view or purpose.

Whether an author's **purpose** is to inform, to persuade, or to entertain readers, the author will use words in ways designed to achieve his or her goal.

Diction An author's choice of words is called diction. By using simple diction—choosing familiar words—an author can make ideas clear. By using **technical language,** or language specific to a discipline, an author can be precise. By choosing words with strong **connotations,** or associations, an author can shape readers' views. For example, calling a situation *disastrous* creates one picture; calling it *challenging* creates another.

Tone Word choice creates tone, or conveys an attitude toward the topic and audience. An author's tone may be formal or informal, solemn or playful, joyous or annoyed, and so on. For example, this sentence has a tone of outrage: *That scoundrel will disgrace our city!*

Figurative Language Authors also convey point of view using figurative language, or language not meant to be taken literally. Here are three common figures of speech:

- A **simile** is an indirect comparison that contains the word *like* or *as: It was as tricky as skateboarding during an earthquake.*
- A **metaphor** describes one thing as if it were another, without using the words *like* or *as: Friendship is a warm place on a cold day.*
- **Personification** gives human traits to a nonhuman subject: *The winter wind slapped my face with its icy hands.*

Rhetorical Devices and Purpose Rhetorical devices are patterns of words and ideas used to emphasize points and to make them more memorable. If an author's purpose is to inform, he or she may use rhetorical devices to help readers remember key points. If an author's purpose is to persuade, he or she may use rhetorical devices that appeal to readers' emotions. Rhetorical devices include the following:

Rhetorical Devices

Repetition is the reuse of a key word, phrase, or idea:
He plays with skill. He plays with passion. He plays in a style all his own.

Parallel structure is the use of similar grammatical structures to express related ideas:
The eagle soared above the treetops, into the heavens, and beyond reach.

Restatement is the expression of the same idea in different words to strengthen a point:
Aspire to greatness. (Restatement 1:) *Aim high,* (Restatement 2:) *and dream big.*

Rhetorical questions are inquiries that have obvious answers and that are asked for effect:
Is it really so much trouble to recycle? Isn't saving our planet worth your time?

❷ Analyzing Word Choice and Rhetoric

1. Introduce the concept of diction, using the instruction on the student page. **Ask** students to give an example of **(a)** technical language and **(b)** words with strong connotations.

   Sample responses: (a) debug, programming language, vise grip **(b)** greedy, stingy, wilderness.

2. Review the concept of figurative language, using the instruction on the student page. As a class, create some examples of each of the three figurative language forms defined on the student page.

   Sample responses: (a) He's hungry as a bear in spring. **(b)** The sky was a low, gray ceiling. **(c)** The smell of cocoa spoke to me with a strong, comforting voice.

3. Introduce the rhetorical devices on the student page. Then divide the class into small groups and **ask** each group to create examples of each of the four devices, using the examples in the shaded box as models.

   Sample responses: *Repetition*—She skis with courage. She skis with strength. She skis with daring. *Parallel structure*—The squirrel darted down the tree, across the garden, and straight at my crocus bulbs. *Restatement*—Play hard. Play with heart, and give your all. *Rhetorical question*—Do you have three minutes to help the world?

4. Remind students that in this Workshop, they will read two nonfiction models and then perform their own analysis of a second text.

Differentiated Instruction for Universal Access

Support for Special-Needs Students
Have students read the **Exploring Types of Nonfiction** pages in the *Reader's Notebook: Adapted Version.* This version provides a basic-level introduction to fiction and nonfiction.

Support for Less Proficient Readers
Have students read the **Exploring Types of Nonfiction** pages in the *Reader's Notebook.* This version provides a basic-level introduction to fiction and nonfiction.

EL Support for English Learners
Have students read the **Exploring Types of Nonfiction** pages in the *Reader's Notebook: English Learner's Version.* This version provides a basic-level introduction to fiction and nonfiction.

3 Close Read: Development of Ideas

1. Review with the class the Tips for Analyzing Literary Nonfiction chart. Discuss ways in which each element might interact with the others. For example, if the author's purpose is to persuade, rhetorical devices may be used to stir strong feelings.
2. Divide students into groups. **Ask** each group to come up with a topic for an essay, article, or speech and then choose where it will be published or presented. Have them choose two of the elements in the chart and decide how they would use those elements to present their topic.

   Possible responses: *Topic*—honesty. *Published in*—a teen magazine. *Tone and word choice*—straightforward and conversational. *Point of view*—Honesty is far better than dishonesty.
3. Point out examples of highlighted text in the model on page 431. Explain that in each case, the color of the highlighting matches the color of the category in the chart. Details that illustrate a given category are highlighted in the color of that category.

3 Close Read: Development of Ideas

To understand literary nonfiction, determine the author's purpose and point of view and analyze ways in which the author develops ideas.

To paint a clear picture or to make a strong argument, authors of literary nonfiction select, organize, and make connections between details—they develop ideas. Starting from a central idea or thesis, an author provides readers with supporting information that helps them understand and accept that idea or thesis. To ensure effective development, an author uses a variety of tools, from organizational structure to tone. These tools help an author fulfill his or her purpose and convey a point of view. To guide you in analyzing an author's development of ideas, follow the tips in this chart.

Tips for Analyzing Literary Nonfiction	
Purpose and Point of View • Determine whether the author includes only details meant to inform or whether some details are meant to persuade or to entertain. • To determine the author's point of view, look for a direct statement of opinion, such as "We need year-round schools." • If there is no direct statement of opinion, infer point of view from word choices such as *good* or *unfair*.	**Rhetorical Devices** • Look for instances of repetition, parallel structure, restatement, and rhetorical questions. • Consider in each case how the device expresses the author's point of view and helps fulfill his or her purpose.
Central Idea and Support • Identify the author's central idea or thesis—the main point the work makes. • If the author does not directly state this point, infer it based on the details he or she includes. • For each new idea or detail the author presents, ask yourself, In what way does this point relate to the main idea?	**Figurative Language** • Look for similes, metaphors, and personification. • Determine in each case what the figure of speech shows about the author's point of view and purpose.
Organizational Structures Identify the overall structure of the work—chronological order, for example, or cause-and-effect. Take note of the transition words that the author uses between paragraphs, such as *First, Most important,* and *Due to,* as clues to its organization.	**Tone and Word Choice** • Notice whether the words the author chooses are formal or informal, technical or everyday, emotionally charged or objective. • Determine the reasons for the author's word choice, including the tone these choices create—what attitude toward the subject or audience they convey.

EXEMPLAR TEXT

❹ Model 1

About the Text Learned Hand (1872–1961) was a U.S. federal judge for more than half a century. On May 21, 1944, he delivered the following address in New York City's Central Park to a crowd of over one million people. His audience had gathered to attend a patriotic event called "I Am an American Day."

The annual event drew an extraordinary number of people that year because it came at a critical time in U.S. history. As World War II raged on, many Americans wanted to show support for their country. Among the Americans who attended the event that day were 150,000 newly naturalized citizens, who had come to pledge their allegiance to the United States. Hand delivered his inspirational address just before that ceremony.

"I Am an American Day" Address by Learned Hand

❺ We have gathered here to affirm a faith, a faith in a common purpose, a common conviction, a common devotion. Some of us have chosen America as the land of our adoption; the rest have come from those who did the same. For this reason we have some right to consider ourselves a picked group, a group of those who had the courage to break from the past and brave the dangers and the loneliness of a strange land. What was the object that nerved us, or those ❻ who went before us, to this choice? We sought liberty; freedom from oppression, freedom from want, freedom to be ourselves. This we then sought; this we now believe that we are by way of winning. What do we mean when we say that first of all we seek liberty? I often wonder whether we do not rest our hopes too much upon constitutions, upon laws and upon courts. These are false hopes; believe me, these are false hopes. ❼ Liberty lies in the hearts of men and women; when it dies there, no constitution, no law, no court can save it; no constitution, no law, no court can even do much to help it. While it lies there it needs no constitution, no law, no court to save it. And what is this liberty which must lie in the hearts of men and women? It is not the ruthless, the unbridled will; it is not freedom to do as one likes. That is the denial of liberty, and leads straight to its overthrow. A society in which men recognize no check upon their freedom soon becomes a society where freedom is the possession of only a savage few; as we have learned to our sorrow.

What then is the spirit of liberty? I cannot define it; I can only tell you my own faith. The spirit of liberty is the spirit which is not too sure that it is right; the spirit of liberty is the spirit which seeks to understand the minds of other men and women; the spirit of liberty is the spirit which weighs their interests alongside its own without bias; the spirit of liberty remembers that not even a

❺ **Point of View** Hand defines the occasion for the address and identifies his common bond with the audience. In doing so, he begins to reveal his beliefs about what it means to be an American.

❻ **Rhetorical Devices** Notice Hand's use of questions followed by answers stated in parallel form. With each question, Hand introduces a different aspect of his topic: liberty. With each answer, he refines his explanation of liberty, using parallelism to state the explanation in a moving, memorable way. Repeating this pattern creates clear connections between ideas.

❼ **Central Idea and Support** Here Hand states a central idea—liberty depends on the people, not on laws.

TEACH

❹ Reading the Model

1. Discuss the About the Text note. Explain that Learned Hand was one of the most respected judges in twentieth-century America.
2. Have students read the passage (pp. 431–432). Discuss, clarifying as necessary. Then, guide students in reviewing the annotations.

❺ Point of View

Read aloud the Point of View annotation.

Ask: What is Hand's point of view about who is an American?

Possible response: He says that all Americans came from somewhere else or had ancestors who came from somewhere else.

❻ Rhetorical Devices

Read aloud the bracketed passage and Rhetorical Devices annotation.

Ask students how they think these words would make a crowd of new citizens feel.

Possible response: They would probably feel very proud and moved.

❼ Central Idea and Support

Read aloud the Central Idea and Support annotation and the bracketed text.

Ask students to give one supporting detail for Hand's central idea.

Possible response: Laws cannot make people free.

Differentiated Instruction for Universal Access

Strategy for Less Proficient Readers
Guide students in making inferences and connections as they read:

- Have them reread the first paragraph. Guide them to see that the faith Hand is talking about is faith in the United States.
- Read aloud the second paragraph. Referring to the About the Text note, guide students to understand that the final statement of the paragraph refers to the war that the country was fighting at the time.

EL Strategy for English Learners
Preteach the following words from page 431, using visuals and the help of students fluent in English who share students' home language: *affirm, conviction, sought, ruthless, unbridled, overthrow, check, bias.* After students read the speech, ask them to talk about whether the context of the speech increased their understanding of the words.

8 Tone and Word Choice

Read aloud the Point of View annotation and the text highlighted in yellow. **Ask:** How would you describe the tone of this passage?

Possible response: It is serious and almost reverent.

9 Reading the Model

1. Point out that they are about to read a second nonfiction model selection. Discuss the About the Text note.
2. Have students read the passage (pp. 432–434). Discuss, clarifying as necessary. Then, guide students in reviewing the annotations.

10 Point of View

Have a volunteer read aloud the Point of View annotation and the text highlighted in green. **Ask:** How does this sentence emphasize the point of view expressed in the rest of the bracketed passage?

Possible response: The rest of the bracketed passage says that what is being decided there is very important. This sentence goes further and states that in the strongest possible terms.

Model 1 continued

8 Tone and Word Choice Hand adopts the tone of a preacher, using language that refers to the Bible as he claims a divine right to liberty and freedom. Figurative language adds a poetic quality.

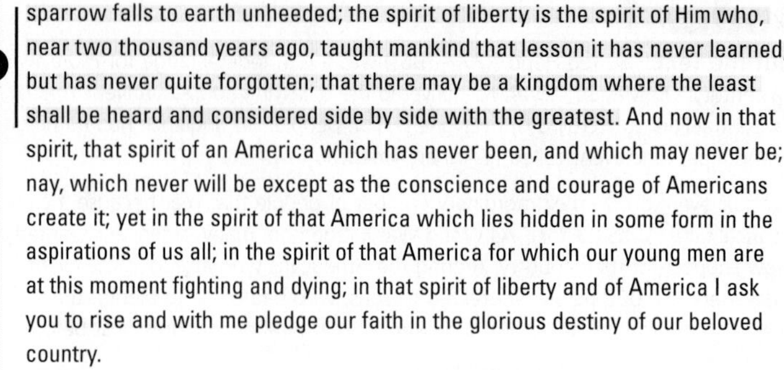

8 sparrow falls to earth unheeded; the spirit of liberty is the spirit of Him who, near two thousand years ago, taught mankind that lesson it has never learned, but has never quite forgotten; that there may be a kingdom where the least shall be heard and considered side by side with the greatest. And now in that spirit, that spirit of an America which has never been, and which may never be; nay, which never will be except as the conscience and courage of Americans create it; yet in the spirit of that America which lies hidden in some form in the aspirations of us all; in the spirit of that America for which our young men are at this moment fighting and dying; in that spirit of liberty and of America I ask you to rise and with me pledge our faith in the glorious destiny of our beloved country.

9 Model 2

About the Text In this famous speech, Patrick Henry (1736–1799) denounces the British king and urges the colonists to fight for independence. Addressing the Virginia Provincial Convention on the eve of the American Revolution, in 1775, Henry gives a fiery defense of liberty. While many of the speakers at the convention argued for a peaceful compromise with Britain, Henry called for armed resistance. His speech fanned the flames of revolution, and in 1776, the colonies declared their independence.

"Speech to the Virginia Convention" by Patrick Henry

10 Point of View In his opening, Henry begins to lay out his point of view: British rule is depriving colonists of their liberty.

Mr. President: No man thinks more highly than I do of the patriotism, as well as abilities, of the very worthy gentlemen who have just addressed the house. But different men often see the same subject in different lights; and, therefore, I hope it will not be thought disrespectful to those gentlemen, if, entertaining, as I do, opinions of a character very opposite to theirs, I shall speak forth my sentiments freely and without reserve. This is no time for ceremony. The question before the house is one of awful moment[1] to this country. For my own part, I consider it as nothing less than a question of freedom or slavery. And in proportion to the magnitude of the subject ought to be the freedom of the debate. It is only in this way that we can hope to arrive at truth, and fulfill the great responsibility which we hold to God and our country. Should I keep back my opinions at such a time, through fear of giving offense, I should consider myself as guilty of treason toward my country, and of an act of disloyalty toward the Majesty of Heaven, which I revere above all earthly kings.

Mr. President, it is natural to man to indulge in the illusions of hope. We are apt to shut our eyes against a painful truth, and listen to the song of that siren till

1. **moment** *n.* importance.

Think Aloud

Tone and Word Choice

To model the skill of analyzing tone and word choice, use the following "think aloud." Say to students:

> To figure out the tone of a speech, I imagine what it would sound like if I were listening to the speaker saying the words. Tone in a piece of writing is a lot like the "tone of voice" you use when you're talking. For example, you might use an angry tone or an enthusiastic tone. I even say written words out loud and listen to how they sound.
>
> When I read, "that there may be a kingdom where the least shall be heard and considered side by side with the greatest," I realize it's easiest to say those words in a quiet, thoughtful tone. They don't sound right if I say them angrily or loudly. That's because the words are a little bit like poetry, and they have a gentle quality to them. Also, the words refer to a religious book, which adds to this kind of tone.

11 she transforms us into beasts.[2] Is this the part of wise men, engaged in a great and arduous struggle for liberty? Are we disposed to be of the number of those who having eyes see not, and having ears hear not, the things which so nearly concern their temporal salvation? For my part, whatever anguish of spirit it may cost, I am willing to know the whole truth; to know the worst and to provide for it.

I have but one lamp by which my feet are guided, and that is the lamp of experience. I know of no way of judging of the future but by the past. And judging by the past, I wish to know what there has been in the conduct of the British ministry for the last ten years to justify those hopes with which gentlemen have been pleased to solace[3] themselves and the house? Is it that
12 insidious smile with which our petition has been lately received? Trust it not, sir; it will prove a snare to your feet. Suffer not yourselves to be betrayed with a kiss.[4] Ask yourselves how this gracious reception of our petition comports with those warlike preparations which cover our waters and darken our land. Are fleets and armies necessary to a work of love and reconciliation? Have we shown ourselves so unwilling to be reconciled that force must be called in to win back our love? Let us not deceive ourselves, sir. These are the implements of war and subjugation—the last arguments to which kings resort.

I ask gentlemen, sir, what means this martial array, if its purpose be not to force us to submission? Can gentlemen assign any other possible motive for it? Has Great Britain any enemy in this quarter of the world, to call for all this accumulation of navies and armies? No, sir, she has none. They are meant for us: they can be meant for no other. They are sent over to bind and rivet upon us those chains which the British ministry have been so long forging.

And what have we to oppose to them? Shall we try argument? Sir, we have been trying that for the last ten years. Have we anything new to offer upon the subject? Nothing. We have held the subject up in every light of which it is capable; but it has been all in vain. Shall we resort to entreaty and humble supplication?[5] What terms shall we find which have not been already exhausted? Let us not, I beseech you, sir, deceive ourselves longer. Sir, we have done everything that could be done to avert the storm which is now coming on. We have petitioned; we have remonstrated; we have supplicated; we have prostrated ourselves before the throne, and have implored its interposition[6] to

11 Rhetorical Devices Henry makes his point of view clear using rhetorical questions and charged language. His listeners will want to be counted as "wise men," not as "those who . . . see not."

12 Word Choice Henry uses the connotations, or emotional associations, of *insidious*—meaning "evil" or "treacherous"—to create a memorable image of British power.

2. **listen . . . beasts** In Homer's epic poem the *Odyssey,* the enchantress Circe transforms men into beasts after charming them with her singing.
3. **solace** (sä′ lis) *v.* comfort.
4. **betrayed with a kiss** In the Bible, in Luke 22:47–48, Judas kisses Jesus to identify Jesus to the officials who have come to arrest him.
5. **supplication** (sup′ lə kā′ shən) *n.* a plea; a humble request.
6. **interposition** (in′ tər pə zish′ ən) *n.* intervention.

11 Rhetorical Devices

Have a volunteer read aloud the bracketed passage. **Ask:** Why would it be difficult to answer the second question "No"?

Possible response: The language of the question makes anyone who answers "No" admit to being a fool.

12 Word Choice

Have a volunteer read aloud the bracketed passage. Explain to the class that the word *insidious* originally comes from a Latin word that means "ambush." It carries with it the suggestion of someone hiding in order to trap you. Most often, the person is hiding his or her true feelings and motives. **Ask:** Why would Henry say that a smile from the British ministry to the requests of the colonists was insidious?

Possible response: The British ministry's smile would hide the fact that they did not intend to give the colonists what they wanted.

⓭ Organizational Structures

Have a volunteer read aloud the bracketed passage. **Ask:** Why would Patrick Henry have to organize his speech with such a long and careful buildup to his main point?

Possible response: He is suggesting something very difficult and frightening to his listeners. The buildup leads them to the point where they are going to be more ready to hear about this terrible option.

⓮ Figurative Language

Have a volunteer read aloud the bracketed passage. **Ask:** After Henry speaks of the chains being forged, what effect does he get by adding the image of the "clanging"?

Possible response: The metaphor in "Our chains are forged" is powerful but not unusual. When Henry adds the sound of the chains clanging, he makes the chains more real to his listeners.

EXEMPLAR TEXT

Model 2 continued

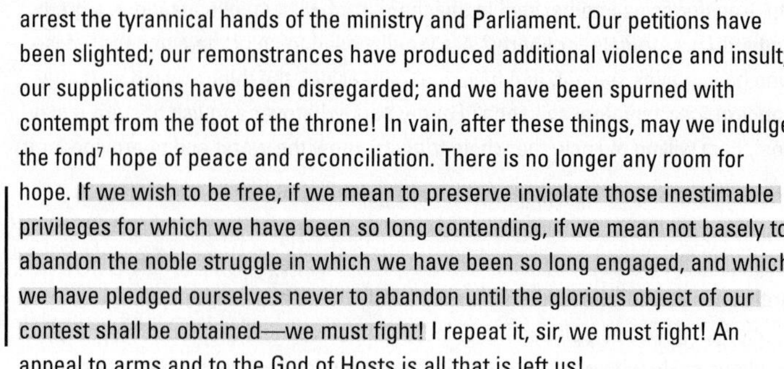

arrest the tyrannical hands of the ministry and Parliament. Our petitions have been slighted; our remonstrances have produced additional violence and insult; our supplications have been disregarded; and we have been spurned with contempt from the foot of the throne! In vain, after these things, may we indulge the fond[7] hope of peace and reconciliation. There is no longer any room for hope. ⓭ If we wish to be free, if we mean to preserve inviolate those inestimable privileges for which we have been so long contending, if we mean not basely to abandon the noble struggle in which we have been so long engaged, and which we have pledged ourselves never to abandon until the glorious object of our contest shall be obtained—we must fight! I repeat it, sir, we must fight! An appeal to arms and to the God of Hosts is all that is left us!

⓭ Organizational Structures Henry carefully builds his argument. First, he explains why he needs to speak freely and urges others not to deceive themselves. Next, he explains the motives of the British and then shows the ineffectiveness of the colonists' response. Only after carefully preparing listeners does he now speak directly of armed rebellion.

They tell us, sir, that we are weak—unable to cope with so formidable an adversary. But when shall we be stronger? Will it be the next week, or the next year? Will it be when we are totally disarmed, and when a British guard shall be stationed in every house? Shall we gather strength by irresolution and inaction? Shall we acquire the means of effectual resistance by lying supinely on our backs and hugging the delusive phantom of hope until our enemies shall have bound us hand and foot? Sir, we are not weak, if we make a proper use of those means which the God of nature hath placed in our power. Three millions of people, armed in the holy cause of liberty, and in such a country as that which we possess, are invincible by any force which our enemy can send against us. Besides, sir, we shall not fight our battles alone. There is a just God who presides over the destinies of nations and who will raise up friends to fight our battles for us. The battle, sir, is not to the strong alone; it is to the vigilant, the active, the brave. Besides, sir, we have no election;[8] if we were base enough to desire it, it is now too late to retire from the contest. There is no retreat but in submission and slavery! ⓮ Our chains are forged! Their clanging may be heard on the plains of Boston! The war is inevitable—and let it come! I repeat it, sir, let it come!

⓮ Figurative Language At the climax of his speech, Henry repeats a vivid metaphor—the British are putting the Americans in chains—to drive home his point and accomplish his purpose: persuading the colonists to revolt.

It is in vain, sir, to extenuate[9] the matter. Gentlemen may cry, "Peace, peace"—but there is no peace. The war is actually begun! The next gale that sweeps from the north[10] will bring to our ears the clash of resounding arms! Our brethren are already in the field! Why stand we here idle? What is it that gentlemen wish? What would they have? Is life so dear, or peace so sweet, as to be purchased at the price of chains and slavery? Forbid it, Almighty God! I know not what course others may take; but as for me, give me liberty or give me death!

7. **fond** *adj.* foolish.
8. **election** *n.* choice.
9. **extenuate** (ek sten´ yo͞o āt´) *v.* treat as less serious.
10. **The next gale . . . north** In Massachusetts, north of Virginia, some colonists had already shown open resistance to the British.

Vocabulary Development

Word Parts

Discuss with students some of the words that begin with the prefix *in-*, such as *inviolate, inestimable, inaction.* Remind them that *in-* is a prefix meaning "not." Explain that the meaning of a prefix will not tell exactly what a word means but will often provide important clues to meaning.

The word *inviolate*, for example means "not violated." It means "kept sacred and unbroken." Guide students in figuring out the meanings of *inestimable* and *inaction.* Then have students look up the words in the dictionary to check their definitions.

⓯ Independent Practice

About the Text Rebecca Walker's lively interest in youth culture is evident in this essay. She is a writer of magazine articles, books, and essays. At the age of twenty-five, she was named by *Time* magazine as one of fifty influential American leaders under the age of forty.

"Before Hip-Hop Was Hip-Hop" by Rebecca Walker

16 If you ask most kids today about hip-hop, they'll spit out the names of recording artists they see on TV: Eminem, P. Diddy, J. Lo, Beyonce. They'll tell you about the songs they like and the clothes they want to buy. They'll tell you about the indisputable zones of hip-hop like "EO" (East Orange, New Jersey), the "ATL" (Atlanta, Georgia), and the "West Side" (Los Angeles, California), neighborhoods they feel they know because they've seen them in all the glossiest, "flossiest" music videos. Hip-hop is natural to these kids, like air or water, just there, a part of the digital landscape that streams through their lives.

I watch this cultural sea change with fascination. It astounds me that hip-hop has grown into a global industry, a force that dominates youth culture from Paris to Prague, Tokyo to Timbuktu. I can't believe that in small, all-white towns like Lincoln, Nebraska, high school boys wear their clothes in the latest "steelo": pants sagging off their waists, sports jerseys hanging to their knees, baseball hats cocked to one side. Even in the pueblos of Mexico, where mariachi bands and old school crooners still rule, it is hip-hop that sells cars, sodas, and children's toys on TV.

17 The vast empire of hip-hop amazes me because I knew hip-hop before it was hip-hop. I was there when it all began.

Way back then, in what today's ninth graders might call the ancient eighties, there was no MTV or VH-1. We found out about music by listening to the radio, flipping through the stacks at the record store, or buying "mix tapes" from local deejays at two dollars apiece. Back then, we carried combs in our back pockets and clipped long strands of feathers to the belt loops of our designer jeans. We wore our names in cursive gold letters around our necks or in big brass letters on our belt buckles. We picked up words and inverted them, calling something that we thought was really cool, "hot," and something that had a whole lot of life, "def." 18 We didn't know a whole new language was rolling off our tongues as we flipped English upside down and pulled some Spanish and even a few words from Africa into our parlance. We didn't know that young people for years to come would recycle our fashions and sample the bass lines from our favorite tracks. We thought we were just being kids and expressing ourselves, showing the grown-ups we were different from them in a way that was safe and fun. In fact we were at the epicenter[1] of one of America's most significant cultural revolutions, making it happen. 19 Who knew?

Not me.

Tone and Word Choice Does Walker's choice of words create a formal tone or an informal tone? Explain.

Purpose What specific purpose does this statement suggest?

Central Idea and Support How do these examples help elaborate on Walker's central idea?

⓳ **Rhetorical Devices** Why does the author ask this question and then answer it?

1. **epicenter** (ep′ i sent′ ər) *n.* focal or central point.

⓯ Independent Practice

1. Discuss the About the Text note. Explain that the passage students are about to read involves the author's own experience of early hip-hop culture.
2. Have students read the passage (pp. 435–439). Discuss, clarifying as necessary. Then guide students in reviewing the annotations.

⓰ Tone and Word Choice

Have a volunteer read aloud the words and phrases highlighted in yellow. **Ask** the Tone and Word Choice question.

Possible response: Her word choice creates an informal tone because she uses a lot of slang.

⓱ Purpose

Have a volunteer read aloud the passage highlighted in green. **Ask** the Purpose question.

Possible response: It suggests that the author is going to inform the reader about early hip-hop.

⓲ Central Idea and Support

Have a volunteer read aloud the bracketed passage. **Ask** the Central Idea and Support question.

Possible response: The examples show that Walker knows what the early days of the culture were like but that she didn't know how important it would become.

⓳ Rhetorical Devices

Have a volunteer read aloud the highlighted question and answer. **Ask** the Rhetorical Devices question.

Possible response: The question and answer sum up her central idea.

PHLit Online!

Enriched Online Student Edition
To have students read the selection in interactive format, with narration and point-of-use interactive graphic organizers, go online at **www.PHLitOnline.com.**

20 Organizational Structures

Have a volunteer read aloud the bracketed passage. **Ask** the Organizational Structures question.

Possible response: It suggests a chronological structure.

21 Rhetorical Devices

Have a volunteer read aloud the bracketed passage. **Ask** the Rhetorical Devices question.

Possible response: She creates the feeling that there were all kinds of kids in the school she went to.

22 Central Idea and Support

Have a volunteer read aloud the bracketed passage. **Ask** the Central Idea and Support question.

Possible response: All the different kinds of people got together to create a mixture of cultural influences.

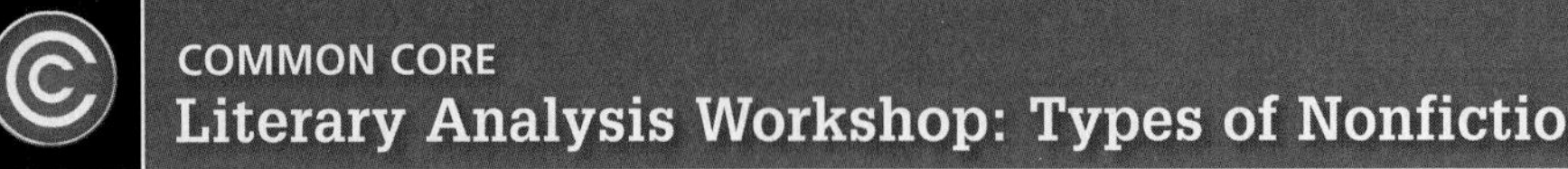

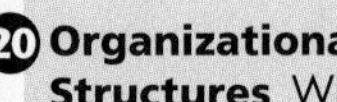

Practice continued

20 Organizational Structures What organizational structure does this statement suggest?

When I moved from Washington, D.C., to the Bronx the summer before seventh grade, I had one box of records, mostly albums I had ordered from the Columbia Record Club. In 1982, if you promised to buy a record a month for one whole year, the Club sent you eight records for a penny. I had Bruce Springsteen's "The River," REO Speedwagon's "The Letter," "Belladonna" by Stevie Nicks. I had "Stairway to Heaven," by Led Zeppelin and the soundtrack from the movie *Saturday Night Fever,* which I played so many times I thought my mother would go crazy from listening to me belt out the lyrics with those lanky, swanky Bee Gees.

Along with my albums I had loads of 45s, what today we would call singles, little records with just two songs on them, that I bought at the record store near my school for just a dollar a piece. I had Chaka Khan's "I'm Every Woman," and Luther Vandross' "Never Too Much," and Chuck Brown and Soul Searcher's big hit, "Bustin' Loose." I had Michael Jackson's "Rock with You" and even Aretha Franklin's cover of "You Make Me Feel Like a Natural Woman," which I sang along to in the mornings as I styled my hair.

If you had asked me then about rap music I would have shrugged my shoulders and looked at you like you were crazy. Rap music? What's that?

Rhetorical Devices What effect does Walker create by using repetition and parallel phrasing to list examples?

But then I started seventh grade and my whole world turned upside down. At Public School 141, I went to classes with kids from all over the Bronx. There were kids whose families came from Puerto Rico and the Dominican Republic, and kids whose families came from Russia and China. There were kids who were African-American and kids who were Irish-American, kids who were Italian-American and kids who were Greek-American. There were kids whose families were poor, kids whose families were well off, and kids whose families were somewhere in between. Some were Jewish, and others devout Catholics. Some were Muslim. Some of the Asian kids were even Buddhist.

Central Idea and Support What central idea in the paragraph do these examples support?

The charge created by so many different elements coming together was palpable.[2] The school crackled with energy, and as you can imagine, things weren't always smooth. There were some pretty entrenched[3] cliques, and a few vicious fights in the schoolyard. But there was also so much "flavor." You could hear Spanish spoken with a thick "Nuyorican" accent to a kid wearing a "yamulke." A seemingly reserved Asian-American girl would get out of her parents' car, wait for them to drive off, and then unzip her coat to reveal a fire engine red Adidas sweatsuit. A guy in a preppy, button-down shirt would "sport" gold chains with pendants of every denomination: the Jewish Star of David, the Arabic lettering for Allah, and a shiny gold cross. He was everything, that was his "steelo," and everyone gave him "props" for it.

2. **palpable** (pal′ pə bəl) *adj.* able to be touched, felt, or handled; tangible.
3. **entrenched** (en trencht′) *adj.* securely established; unmovable.

23 When I got to 141, I felt like a blank canvas. Nothing had prepared me for the dynamism, the screaming self-expression of the place and its students. For the first few weeks I secretly studied the habits of the seventh, eighth and ninth graders with whom I walked the halls and shared the cafeteria. I was transfixed by the way they infused their words with attitude and drama, moving their hands and heads as they spoke. I was captivated by the way many of them walked and ran and joked with each other with confidence and bravado.[4] I noted what they wore and how they wore it: the razor sharp creases of their Jordache jeans, the spotless sneakers with the laces left loose and untied.

Slowly, I began to add some of what I saw into my "look." I convinced my grandmother to buy me a name chain to wear around my neck, and my stepmother to buy me dark dyed designer jeans. I bought my first pair of Nike sneakers, red, white and blue Air Cortez's, with money I saved from my allowance.

One by one, I started to make friends—Diane, Loida, James, Jesus, Maya. When James and Jesus weren't making fun of me for being so "square," they took me to parties on the Grand Concourse, the big boulevard lined with old apartment buildings and department stores that ran through the Bronx. 24 The parties were incredible, filled with young people who didn't drink, smoke or fight, but who just wanted to dance and laugh and ooh and ahhh over the "scratching" sounds and funky beats the DJ's coaxed out of their turntables.

25 A lot of the kids at the parties were "breakers" or "poppers and lockers," which meant they could breakdance, a style of movement that blends the Brazilian martial art of Capoeira with a dance called the Robot, and incorporates classical dance moves as well. The "breakers" moved in "crews" that competed against each other.

Standing in a circle we watched as members of the different groups "moonwalked" into the center, and then hurled themselves to the floor, spinning on their heads, kicking their legs into the air, and making elaborate hand gestures, each more intricate and acrobatic than the last. Everyone at the party who wasn't "breaking" was a judge by default, and we registered our scores by clapping and yelling.

26 When Loida and Diane weren't "capping on" or making fun of my clothes, they were "hipping" me to Kiss 98.7 and WBLS, the radio stations that had started to slip some of the songs we liked into their rotation. Songs like "Planet Rock" by Soul Sonic Force and "Take Me Home" by Lisa Lisa and the Cult Jam. After school and on the weekends, they took me to the street vendors that sold the accessories we all coveted: the big knockoff Porsche sunglasses everybody wanted but not everybody could afford, and the heavy gold chains people collected around their necks like so many pieces of string. Loida and Diane also

4. **bravado** (brə vä′ dō) *n.* pretended courage or defiant confidence.

23 **Figurative Language** In what ways was Walker like a "blank canvas"?

24 **Point of View** What is Walker's perspective on the young people she met at the parties?

25 **Word Choice** Why does Walker define these technical, dance-related terms?

26 **Central Idea and Support** How do these examples help support Walker's central idea?

23 Figurative Language

Have a volunteer read aloud the bracketed passage.
Ask the Figurative Language question.

Possible response: She was ready to be "painted on," that is, influenced by everything around her.

24 Point of View

Have a volunteer read aloud the bracketed passage. **Ask** the Point of View question.

Possible response: She thinks they're fun and exciting. She seems to suggest that they're different from other young people she's known.

25 Word Choice

Have a volunteer read aloud the bracketed passage. **Ask** the Word Choice question.

Possible response: She defines them because they might be unfamiliar to some readers and because their definitions support her point about the various influences at work.

26 Central Idea and Support

Have a volunteer read aloud the bracketed passage. **Ask** the Central Idea and Support question.

Possible response: These examples support the central idea because they show how hip-hop was growing from the ground up.

Fluency

Distribute copies of pages 436–437, and pair students. While one partner reads, the other should mark any words with which the student reading has difficulty. Circulate to monitor the fluency of students' reading. Collect students' marked-up copies of the essay, and review difficult words and passages with the class. Look for these problem spots:

- If students have difficulty with the word *transfixed* (p. 436), remind them to use context clues to infer its meaning. For example, clues in the rest of the paragraph such as "secretly studied" and "captivated" will help them understand the word.
- If students have difficulty with the word *vendors* (p. 437), again suggest they use context clues to infer meaning. Clues such as "street" and "sold the accessories" will help them decipher meaning.

27 Central Idea and Support

Have a volunteer read aloud the bracketed passage. **Ask** the Central Idea and Support question.

Possible response: The details that support the central idea include the fact that most of her friends were from different countries and cultures and the fact that they loved the beats, the words, the dance moves, and so forth.

28 Rhetorical Devices

Have a volunteer read aloud the bracketed passage. **Ask** the Rhetorical Devices question.

Possible response: She stirs emotions and introduces a new idea that she has been building up to—that hip-hop made the kids feel free.

29 Purpose

Have a volunteer read aloud the bracketed passage. **Ask** the Purpose question.

Possible response: They support the main concept that early hip-hop was created by people who were trying to find a way to live and communicate with each other.

30 Point of View

Have a volunteer read aloud the bracketed passage. **Ask** Point of View question.

Possible response: Her point of view is that the time she spent in the Bronx taught her a great deal and was very valuable to her.

Practice continued

27 Central Idea and Support Which details support the central idea highlighted in blue?

28 Rhetorical Devices Analyze the effect Walker creates through the use of repetition and parallelism. Does she emphasize key ideas? Stir emotions? Something else? Explain.

29 Purpose How do these statements help fulfill Walker's specific purpose for writing?

30 Point of View What is Walker's point of view on the twelve months she spent in the Bronx?

took me around the city on the bus, familiarizing me with the routes of the M1 and M3 and M7, showing me all the different neighborhoods like Little Italy and Chinatown, Bed-Stuy and Harlem.

27 I remember looking out the big sliding glass windows of the bus at the lines drawn in concrete and glass and thinking that while the world outside seemed so divided, inside, in my circle, among my friends, those lines didn't seem to exist. Loida was Dominican and Diane was Puerto Rican. Our friend Mary was Irish-American, and Lisa was Italian-American. Maya's family was from Haiti. Julius was Russian-American. We were different ages, with different likes and dislikes, but we were united in our love of hip-hop. We loved the "dope"[5] beats, the ever changing and ever expanding lexicon[6], the outrageous dance moves, the cocky swagger, the feeling that we were part of something dynamic and "fresh"[7] that was bigger than any one of us. 28 That world, that other realm that we created on the streets and in our minds, that streamed from the radio in the privacy of our bedrooms and coursed between us as we talked on the phone, that was where we lived.

That was where we felt free.

29 Looking back on it now, I can see that hip-hop was born of the diversity I found at 141. Unlike the hip-hop of today, it didn't come pre-packaged from a marketing department with millions of dollars to spend. Our hip-hop was the product of a bunch of kids from a bunch of different places trying to talk to each other, trying to create a common language that could cut through the many languages people spoke at home. Intuitively, kids were making a community where there was none; we were affirming our sameness in a world that seemed to only emphasize our difference. That desire to come together irrespective of superficial differences and sometimes in celebration of them, was what gave hip-hop authenticity, that was what kept it honest and as crucial to our well being as food. It's what kept it real.

I can't say much about hip-hop today, but I can say that old hip-hop, original hip-hop, changed my life forever. I only lived in the "Boogie Down Bronx" for a year, but those twelve months gave me so much.  30 I learned that art could bring people together and make them forget their differences. I learned how good it could feel to move with a "posse," a group of friends who had my back no matter what. I learned that I could express myself and communicate with others through what I wore and how I walked and what music I liked. I learned that it doesn't take money or a special degree to transform the grit and drive and hardness of the city into something beautiful.

5. **dope** (dōp) *adj.* slang term meaning "great; irresistible."
6. **lexicon** (lek´ si kän´) *n.* the special vocabulary of a particular subject.
7. **fresh** (fresh) *adj.* slang term meaning "new."

Vocabulary Development

CCSS Language 6

Selection Vocabulary Reinforcement

Reinforce students' comprehension of selection vocabulary with "show-you-know" sentences. The first part of the sentence uses the vocabulary word in an appropriate context. The second part clarifies the first. Model the strategy with this example:

We couldn't understand most words from the presenter's *lexicon;* he was a physicist, and we were drama students.

Then, give students these sentence prompts, and coach them in creating the clarification part:

1. At the pottery class we learned a completely new *lexicon;* ________.
   Sample answer: there were more words to describe bowls than we'd ever imagined.
2. Alberto decided to boost his *lexicon* in the arts; ____________.
   Sample answer: he bought a book called *Foreign Art Terminology.*

Loyalty. Community. Self-confidence. Creativity. Hip-hop taught me more about real life than anything I learned that year in class.

31 I hope when kids today look at shiny videos by their favorite hip-hop artists, they will see through the expensive cars and exotic locations, the women in skimpy outfits and the men trying to approximate a "gangsta" lean. I hope they will remember that hip-hop was born without a formula and without a lot of expensive props or violent undertones. I hope they will marvel at the fact that in the early days of hip-hop, young people were making it up as they went along, following their hearts, following what felt good. I hope they will think about what it takes to create culture that is unique and transcendent and honest, and I hope they begin to dream about creating a new world for themselves.

I hope hip-hop inspires them to make their own revolution.

31 Rhetorical Devices How does Walker's use of repetition and parallelism help create clear connections between ideas?

After You Read "Before Hip-Hop Was Hip-Hop"

1. **Key Ideas and Details** **(a)** According to Walker, why did P.S. 141 "crackle" with energy? **(b) Analyze Cause and Effect:** In what ways did hip-hop help Walker and her friends bridge differences?
2. **Key Ideas and Details** **(a) Draw Conclusions:** Why was it so important for Walker and her friends to define themselves through dress, special language, dance, and music? **(b) Generalize:** What do teenagers use today to express themselves?
3. **Craft and Structure** **(a)** Is the **tone** of Walker's **essay** personal or impersonal? **(b)** What other adjectives appropriately describe her tone? **(c)** Which details in the first three paragraphs support your answers?
4. **Craft and Structure** What overall **organizational structure** does Walker use to organize her essay?
5. **Craft and Structure** **(a)** Use a chart like this one to analyze Walker's **style,** noting passages that support your ideas.

Level of Formality	Word Choice	Sentence Patterns

(b) Collaborate: In a small group, discuss the examples in your chart and develop a one-sentence description of Walker's writing style.

6. **Integration of Knowledge and Ideas** **(a) Compare and Contrast:** What differences does Walker find between the music of her youth and today's hip-hop? **(b) Take a Position:** Do you think Walker's judgment is fair or biased? Explain.
7. **Key Ideas and Details** Write an objective summary of "Before Hip-Hop Was Hip-Hop." Do not include your personal reaction to the essay.

Assessment Resources

The following resources can be used to assess students' knowledge and skills.

Unit 3 Resources

L1 L2 EL **Selection Test A,** pp. 17–19.

L3 L4 EL **Selection Test B,** pp. 20–22.

L3 L4 **Open-Book Test,** pp. 14–16.

Students may use the **Self-test,** online at **www.PHLitOnline.com,** to prepare for **Selection Test A** or **Selection Test B.**

31 Rhetorical Devices

Ask the Rhetorical Devices question.

Possible response: The repetition and parallelism help make the connection between hip-hop's characteristics today and its origins.

ASSESS/EXTEND

Answers

1. **Possible response: (a)** The school included students from many different cultures. **(b)** Hip-hop gave Walker and her friends common interests.
2. **Possible response: (a)** Hip-hop culture belonged to them and gave them a clear identity. **(b)** They use similar elements of popular culture.
3. **Possible response: (a)** Walker's tone is personal. **(b)** Her tone is passionate and joyous. **(c)** *Personal*—"I knew hip-hop before it was hip-hop. I was there when it all began." *Passionate*—"We were at the epicenter of one of America's most significant cultural revolutions." *Joyous*—"The parties were incredible, filled with young people who just wanted to dance."
4. **Possible response:** chronological
5. **Possible responses: (a)** *Level of formality*—informal, paragraphs 4, 15; *Word choice*—slang, paragraphs 1, 13; *Sentence patterns*—direct, short, paragraphs 11, 20. **(b)** It is direct, lively, and conversational.
6. **Possible responses: (a)** Hip-hop of her day was born from youth and diversity, but today it comes prepackaged by adults. **(b)** Her opinion is biased. She judges modern hip-hop only by what she hears on the radio.
7. **Possible response:** Walker goes to a new school, where there are many different kinds of kids. She learns that hip-hop is a form of self-expression and communication that reflects diversity, individuality, and creativity. She comes to understand herself better by developing her own identity.

✓ A Celebration of Grandfathers • ✓✓ On Summer

Lesson Pacing Guide

DAY 1 Preteach

- Administer the Reading and Vocabulary Warm-ups (*Unit 3 Resources*, pp. 23–26 or 41–44) as necessary.
- Introduce the Reading Skill: Main Idea.
- Introduce the Literary Analysis concept: Author's Style.
- Distribute copies of the appropriate graphic organizer for the Reading Skill (*Graphic Organizer Transparencies*, pp. 75–77).
- Distribute copies of the appropriate graphic organizer for Literary Analysis (*Graphic Organizer Transparencies*, pp. 78–80).
- Teach the selection vocabulary.
- Introduce the Word Study skill.

DAYS 2–3 Preteach/Teach

- Build background with the Background feature.
- Develop thematic vocabulary and thematic thinking with Writing About the Big Question.
- Prepare students to read with the Activating Prior Knowledge activities (TE).
- Informally monitor comprehension while students read.
- Use the Reading Check questions to confirm comprehension.
- Develop students' ability to determine the main idea, using the Reading Skill questions.
- Develop students' understanding of the author's style, using the Literary Analysis questions.
- Reinforce vocabulary with the Vocabulary notes.
- Reinforce unit focus standards using the Spiral Review prompts.

DAY 4 Assess

- Assess students' comprehension and mastery of the skills by having them answer the Critical Thinking, Reading Skill, and Literary Analysis questions.
- Have students complete the Vocabulary Practice activities.
- Have students complete the Word Study activities.

DAY 5 Extend/Assess

- Have students complete the Conventions lesson.
- Have students complete the Writing activity and write a book jacket copy. (You may assign as homework.)
- Extend learning by having students complete the Speaking and Listening activity, a panel discussion. As an alternative, assign them "Age in America" or "Learning Without a Break" in *Reality Central*.
- Administer Selection Test A or B (*Unit 3 Resources*, pp. 35–40 or 56–61).

Common Core State Standards

Reading Informational Text
1. Cite strong and thorough textual evidence to support analysis of what the text says explicitly as well as inferences drawn from the text.
2. Determine a central idea of a text and analyze its development over the course of the text, including how it emerges and is shaped and refined by specific details; provide an objective summary of the text.
6. Determine an author's point of view or purpose in a text and analyze how an author uses rhetoric to advance that point of view or purpose.

Writing 2. Write informative/explanatory texts to examine and convey complex ideas, concepts, and information clearly and accurately through the effective selection, organization, and analysis of content.

Speaking and Listening 1. Initiate and participate effectively in a range of collaborative discussions with diverse partners.

Language 1. Demonstrate command of the conventions of standard English grammar and usage when writing or speaking.
6. Acquire and use accurately grade-appropriate general academic and domain-specific words and phrases; gather vocabulary knowledge when considering a word or phrase important to comprehension or expression.

Additional Standards Practice
***Common Core Companion*, pp. 110–144**

Daily Block Scheduling
Each day in this Lesson Pacing Guide represents a 40–50 minute period. Teachers using block scheduling may combine days to revise pacing. In addition, teachers may differentiate and support core instruction by integrating components for extended and intensive support as students require. See the Guide to Selected Leveled Resources (facing page).

Guide to Selected Leveled Resources

RTI Tier 1 (students performing on level)		✓ More Accessible A Celebration of Grandfathers	✓✓ More Complex On Summer
Warm Up	**Practice, model,** and **monitor** fluency, working **with the whole class** or **in groups.**	**Vocabulary** and **Reading Warm-ups B,** ***Unit 3 Resources,*** pp. 23–24, 26	**Vocabulary** and **Reading Warm-ups B,** ***Unit 3 Resources,*** pp. 41–42, 44
Comprehension/Skills	**Support** and **monitor** comprehension and skills development, having students complete the activities, graphic organizers, and interactive prompts **independently** or **as a class.**	• ***Reader's Notebook,*** adapted instruction and full selection EL ***Reader's Notebook: English Learner's Version,*** adapted instruction and adapted selection • **Reading Skill Graphic Organizer B,** ***Graphic Organizer Transparencies,*** p. 77 • **Literary Analysis Graphic Organizer B,** ***Graphic Organizer Transparencies,*** p. 80	• ***Reader's Notebook,*** adapted instruction and summary EL ***Reader's Notebook: English Learner's Version,*** adapted instruction and summary • **Reading Skill Graphic Organizer B,** ***Graphic Organizer Transparencies,*** p. 77 • **Literary Analysis Graphic Organizer B,** ***Graphic Organizer Transparencies,*** p. 80
Monitor Progress	**Monitor** student progress with the differentiated curriculum-based assessment in the *Unit Resources.*	• **Selection Test B,** ***Unit 3 Resources,*** pp. 38–40 • **Open-Book Test,** ***Unit 3 Resources,*** pp. 32–34	• **Selection Test B,** ***Unit 3 Resources,*** pp. 59–61 • **Open-Book Test,** ***Unit 3 Resources,*** pp. 53–55

RTI Tier 2 (students requiring intervention)		✓ More Accessible A Celebration of Grandfathers	✓✓ More Complex On Summer
Warm Up	**Practice, model,** and **monitor** fluency **in groups** or **with individuals.**	• **Vocabulary and Reading Warm-ups A,** ***Unit 3 Resources,*** pp. 23–25 • ***Reality Central,*** "Age in America" • ***Hear It!*** **Audio CD (adapted text)**	• **Vocabulary and Reading Warm-ups A,** ***Unit 3 Resources,*** pp. 41–43 • ***Reality Central,*** "Learning Without a Break" • ***Hear It!*** **Audio CD**
Comprehension/Skills	• **Support** and **monitor** comprehension and skills development, working **in small groups** or **with individuals.** • **Pair** students with more advanced peers and have them complete the writing activity in the *Real-World Writing Journal.* • As students complete the selection in the appropriate version of the *Reader's Notebook,* **monitor** comprehension frequently with group questions and individual instruction. • **Model** strategies while guiding students in completing the activities and prompts in the *Reader's Notebook,* as well as the graphic organizers. • **Practice** skills and **monitor** mastery with the *Reading Kit* worksheets.	• ***Real-World Writing Journal,*** Lesson 1, pp. 70–73 • ***Reader's Notebook: Adapted Version,*** adapted instruction and adapted selection EL ***Reader's Notebook: English Learner's Version,*** adapted instruction and adapted selection • **Reading Skill Graphic Organizer A,** ***Graphic Organizer Transparencies,*** p. 75 • **Literary Analysis Graphic Organizer A,** ***Graphic Organizer Transparencies,*** p. 78 • ***Reading Kit,*** Practice worksheets, pp. 102, 108, 112, 114, 120	• ***Real-World Writing Journal,*** Lesson 2, pp. 74–77 • ***Reader's Notebook: Adapted Version,*** adapted instruction and summary EL ***Reader's Notebook: English Learner's Version,*** adapted instruction and summary • **Reading Skill Graphic Organizer A,** ***Graphic Organizer Transparencies,*** p. 76 • **Literary Analysis Graphic Organizer A,** ***Graphic Organizer Transparencies,*** p. 79 • ***Reading Kit,*** Practice worksheets, pp. 102, 108, 112, 114, 120
Monitor Progress	**Monitor** student progress with the differentiated curriculum-based assessment in the *Unit Resources* and in the *Reading Kit.*	• **Selection Test A,** ***Unit 3 Resources,*** pp. 35–37 • ***Reading Kit,*** Assess worksheets, pp. 103, 109, 113, 115, 121	• **Selection Test A,** ***Unit 3 Resources,*** pp. 56–58 • **Reading Kit,** Assess worksheets, pp. 103, 109, 113, 115, 121

TIER 3 Tier 3 intervention may require consultation with the student's special-education or dyslexia specialist. For additional support, see the Tier 2 activities and resources listed above.

One-on-one teaching **Group work** **Whole class instruction** **Independent work** **A Assessment**

For a complete guide to selection support, including support for Advanced students, see the Overview of Resources in the frontmatter.

A Celebration of Grandfathers
On Summer

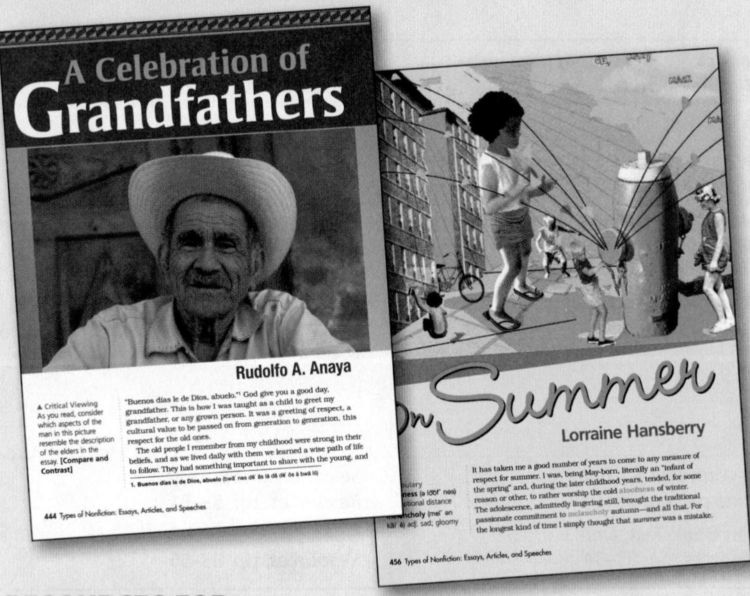

RESOURCES FOR:

- L1 Special-Needs Students
- L2 Below-Level Students (Tier 2)
- L3 On-Level Students (Tier 1)
- L4 Advanced Students (Tier 1)
- EL English Learners
- All All Students

Vocabulary/Fluency/Prior Knowledge

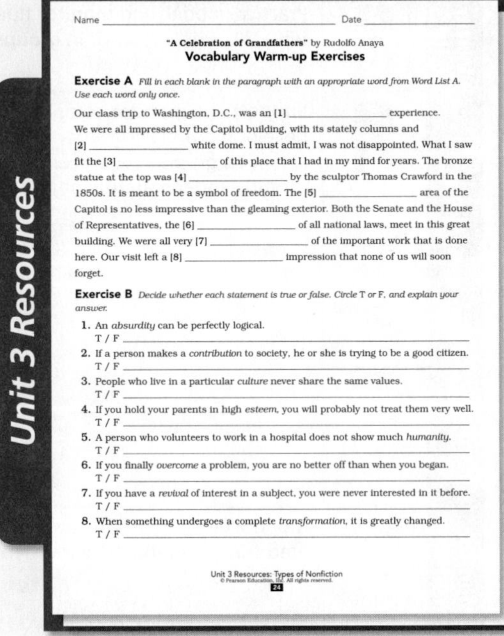

Unit 3 Resources

Name ______________________ Date ______________

"A Celebration of Grandfathers" by Rudolfo Anaya
Vocabulary Warm-up Exercises

Exercise A *Fill in each blank in the paragraph with an appropriate word from Word List A. Use each word only once.*

Our class trip to Washington, D.C., was an [1] ____________ experience. We were all impressed by the Capitol building, with its stately columns and [2] ____________ white dome. I must admit, I was not disappointed. What I saw fit the [3] ____________ of this place that I had in my mind for years. The bronze statue at the top was [4] ____________ by the sculptor Thomas Crawford in the 1850s. It is meant to be a symbol of freedom. The [5] ____________ area of the Capitol is no less impressive than the gleaming exterior. Both the Senate and the House of Representatives, the [6] ____________ of all national laws, meet in this great building. We were all very [7] ____________ of the important work that is done here. Our visit left a [8] ____________ impression that none of us will soon forget.

Exercise B *Decide whether each statement is true or false. Circle T or F, and explain your answer.*

1. An *absurdity* can be perfectly logical.
T / F ____________
2. If a person makes a *contribution* to society, he or she is trying to be a good citizen.
T / F ____________
3. People who live in a particular *culture* never share the same values.
T / F ____________
4. If you hold your parents in high *esteem*, you will probably not treat them very well.
T / F ____________
5. A person who volunteers to work in a hospital does not show much *humanity*.
T / F ____________
6. If you finally *overcome* a problem, you are no better off than when you began.
T / F ____________
7. If you have a *revival* of interest in a subject, you were never interested in it before.
T / F ____________
8. When something undergoes a complete *transformation*, it is greatly changed.
T / F ____________

Unit 3 Resources: Types of Nonfiction
24

EL L1 L2 **Vocabulary Warm-ups A and B,** pp. 23–24, 41–42

Also available for these selections:

EL L1 L2 **Reading Warm-ups A and B,** pp. 25–26, 43–44

All **Writing About the Big Question,** pp. 27, 45

All **Vocabulary Builder,** pp. 30, 48

Reader's Notebooks

Pre- and postreading pages for both selections, as well as "A Celebration of Grandfathers," appear in an interactive format in the *Reader's Notebooks.* Each *Notebook* is differentiated for a different group of learners. The selections in the Adapted and English Learner's versions are abridged.

L2 L3 ***Reader's Notebook***

L1 ***Reader's Notebook: Adapted Version***

EL ***Reader's Notebook: English Learner's Version***

EL ***Reader's Notebook: Spanish Version***

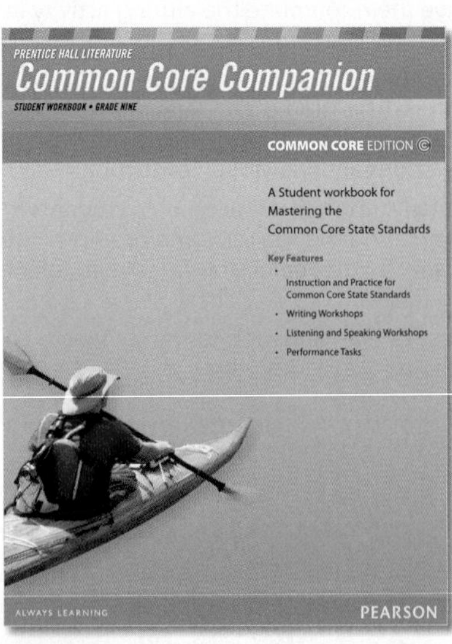

Common Core Companion

Additional instruction and practice for each Common Core State Standard

Selection Support

Graphic Organizer Transparencies

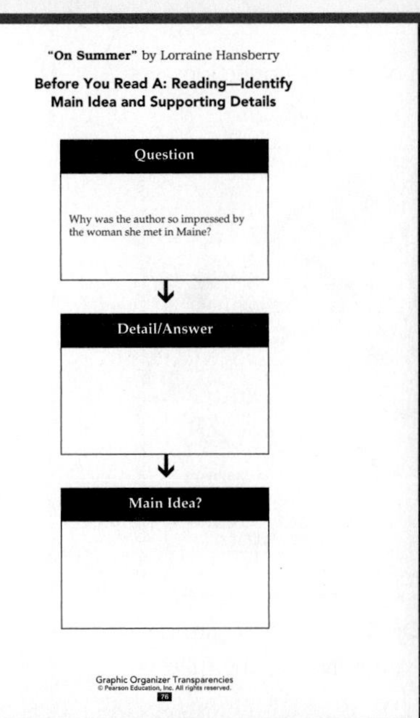

"On Summer" by Lorraine Hansberry

Before You Read A: Reading—Identify Main Idea and Supporting Details

Question

Why was the author so impressed by the woman she met in Maine?

Detail/Answer

Main Idea?

Graphic Organizer Transparencies
© Pearson Education, Inc. All rights reserved.
76

EL L1 L2 **Reading: Graphic Organizer A,** pp. 75, 76 (partially filled in)

EL L3 **Reading: Graphic Organizer B,** p. 77

Also available for these selections:

EL L1 L2 **Literary Analysis: Graphic Organizer A,** pp. 78, 79 (partially filled in)

EL L3 **Literary Analysis: Graphic Organizer B,** p. 80

Skills Development/Extension

Unit 3 Resources

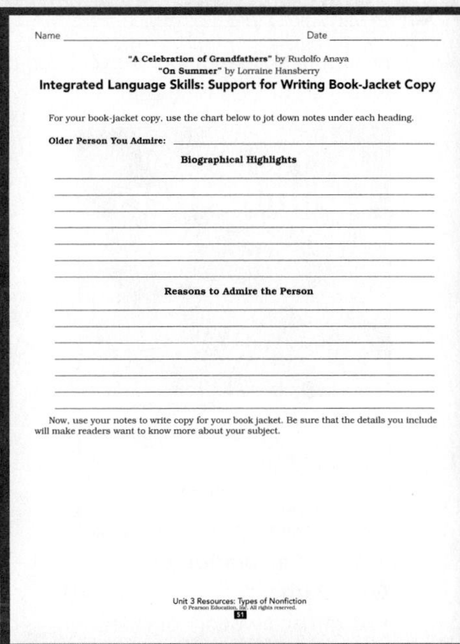

Name ______________________ Date ______________

"A Celebration of Grandfathers" by Rudolfo Anaya
"On Summer" by Lorraine Hansberry

Integrated Language Skills: Support for Writing Book-Jacket Copy

For your book-jacket copy, use the chart below to jot down notes under each heading.

Older Person You Admire: ______________________

Biographical Highlights

Reasons to Admire the Person

Now, use your notes to write copy for your book jacket. Be sure that the details you include will make readers want to know more about your subject.

Unit 3 Resources: Types of Nonfiction
© Pearson Education, Inc. All rights reserved.
51

EL L3 L4 **Support for Writing,** p. 51

Also available for these selections:

All **Literary Analysis: Author's Style,** pp. 28, 46

All **Reading: Main Idea,** pp. 29, 47

L4 **Enrichment,** pp. 31, 49

EL L3 L4 **Grammar,** p. 50

L3 L4 **Support for Extend Your Learning,** p. 52

Assessment

Name ______________________ Date ______________

"On Summer" by Lorraine Hansberry

Open-Book Test

Short Answer *Write your responses to the questions in this section on the lines provided.*

1. Based on the first three paragraphs of "On Summer," do you think the author is trying to persuade readers to like summer or dislike it? Support your opinion with two details from the essay.
2. In the first paragraph of "On Summer," Hansberry writes that when she was younger, she worshipped "the cold aloofness of winter." Is aloofness a quality that is ordinarily used to describe a season? In explaining your answer, suggest why Hansberry might have described winter as having the quality of aloofness. Base your response on the definition of *aloofness.*
3. In "On Summer," Hansberry describes many summertime activities that she engaged in as a child in Chicago. There is one that she says was the best. What was that activity, and why did she enjoy it?
4. In describing her grandmother in "On Summer," Hansberry writes that her memories of slavery "didn't sound anything like *Gone with the Wind.*" How would you describe Hansberry's tone in this passage? Is she being serious, childlike, or harsh? Explain your answer.
5. The author of an essay may support his or her main idea with facts, statistics, quotations, or anecdotes. What form of support does Hansberry use most frequently in "On Summer"? Cite two details to support your response.

Unit 3 Resources: Types of Nonfiction
© Pearson Education, Inc. All rights reserved.
53

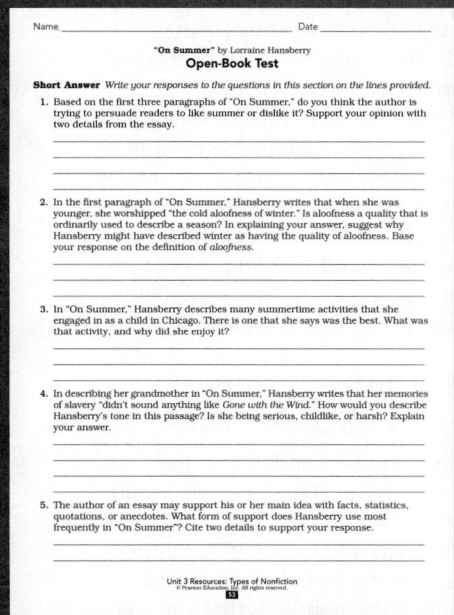

L3 L4 **Open-Book Test,** pp. 32–34, 53–55

Also available for these selections:

EL L1 L2 **Selection Test A,** pp. 35–37, 56–58

EL L3 L4 **Selection Test B,** pp. 38–40, 59–61

PHLit Online!
www.PHLitOnline.com

- complete narrated selection text
- a thematically related video with writing prompt
- an interactive graphic organizer
- highlighting feature
- access to all student print resources, adapted to individual student needs
- Spanish and English summaries
- adapted selection translations in Spanish

Online Resources: All print materials are also available online.

Background Video

Also available:

Get Connected! (thematic video with writing prompt)

All videos are available in Spanish.

Vocabulary Central (tools, activities, and songs for studying vocabulary)

Also available:

Writer's Journal (with graphics feature)

DIFFERENTIATE/PRETEACH

❶ Leveled Texts

You may use either "A Celebration of Grandfathers" or "On Summer" to teach the lesson objectives. Skills instruction for both selections appears on page 441. Choose one selection to teach (or choose to teach both). The Text Complexity Rubric at the bottom of this page will help you determine which selection is more appropriate for your students. Use the Reader and Task Suggestions on the facing page to help all students read text of increasing complexity.

❷ Introducing the CCS Standards

Introduce the standards on the student page. (Note that the lesson element with which each standard is addressed is identified in parentheses after the text of the standard.) Call out the standards that you will cover with the selections, explaining to students what each requires and how they will address it as they work through the selection you have chosen. Standards labeled "Spiral Review" are introduced in the Literary Analysis Workshop for this unit.

Before You Read

A Celebration of Grandfathers • On Summer

❶ Leveled Texts

Build your skills and improve your comprehension of literary nonfiction with texts of increasing complexity.

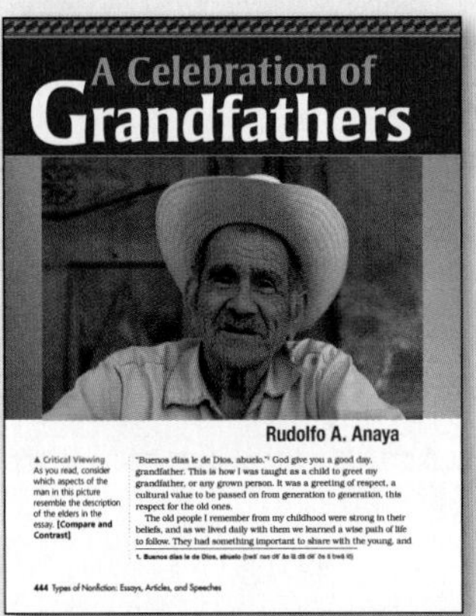

Read **"A Celebration of Grandfathers"** to know the strength and wisdom of older people.

Read **"On Summer"** to glimpse life when it is lived to the fullest.

❷ Common Core State Standards

Meet these standards with either **"A Celebration of Grandfathers"** (p. 444) or **"On Summer"** (p. 456).

Reading Informational Text

1. Cite strong and thorough textual evidence to support analysis of what the text says explicitly as well as inferences drawn from the text. *(Reading Skill: Main Idea)*

2. Determine a central idea of a text and analyze in detail its development, including how it is shaped and refined by specific details. *(Reading Skill: Main Idea)*

Spiral Review: RI.9-10.6

Writing

2. Write informative/explanatory texts to examine and convey complex ideas, concepts, and information clearly and accurately through the effective selection, organization, and analysis of content. *(Writing: Book Jacket Copy)*

Speaking and Listening

1. Initiate and participate effectively in a range of collaborative discussions with diverse partners. *(Speaking and Listening: Panel Discussion)*

Language

1. Demonstrate command of the conventions of standard English grammar and usage when writing or speaking. *(Conventions: Direct and Indirect Objects)*

6. Acquire and use accurately grade-appropriate general academic and domain-specific words and phrases; gather vocabulary knowledge when considering a word or phrase important to comprehension or expression. *(Vocabulary: Word Study)*

Text Complexity Rubric: Leveled Texts

Text complexity is determined by both qualitative and quantitative measures. For this reason, the quantitative measure of a more complex selection may be lower than that of a more accessible selection.

		✓ A Celebration of Grandfathers	✓✓ On Summer
Qualitative Measures	**Context/ Knowledge Demands**	New Mexico in the 1940s 1 2 ③ 4 5	African American life in the South in the 1930s 1 2 3 ④ 5
	Structure/Language Conventionality and Clarity	Spanish words are footnoted; relatively short sentences and clauses 1 2 ③ 4 5	Figurative language 1 2 ③ 4 5
	Levels of Meaning/ Purpose/Concept Level	Accessible concept (praising the wisdom that comes with age) 1 2 ③ 4 5	Challenging concept (attitude that changes with age) 1 2 3 ④ 5
Quantitative Measures	**Text Length**	Word Count: 2,690	Word Count: 1,438
	Lexile	960L	1180L
Overall Complexity		✓ **More accessible**	✓✓ **More complex**

3 Literary Analysis: Author's Style

An **author's style** is his or her unique way of using language. Elements that contribute to an author's style include the following:

- **Diction:** the words the author uses
- **Syntax:** the arrangement of words in sentences
- **Tone:** the author's attitude toward the audience or subject

A writer's diction and syntax might be described as *formal* or *informal, technical* or *ordinary,* or *sophisticated* or *down-to-earth.* His or her tone might be described as *serious, playful,* or *harsh.* An author's style affects the writer's ability to communicate ideas to readers.

4 Reading Skill: Main Idea

The **main, or central, idea** is the key message, insight, or opinion in a work of nonfiction. In some works, the author states his or her central idea directly. In other works the author suggests the central idea but does not state it explicitly. **Supporting details** give further information about the main idea. These details can include facts, statistics, quotations, or anecdotes. To **identify the main idea and supporting details** in a work, **generate questions prior to reading.** Before you read, ask yourself questions such as these:

- Does the author state the central idea or merely suggest it through details?
- Does the title shed light on the central idea?
- How might events in the author's life influence his or her attitude?
- What does the author want me to know?

As you read, look for details that answer these questions and point to the main idea.

5 Using the Strategy: Main Idea Chart

Record questions, details, and main ideas on a chart like this one.

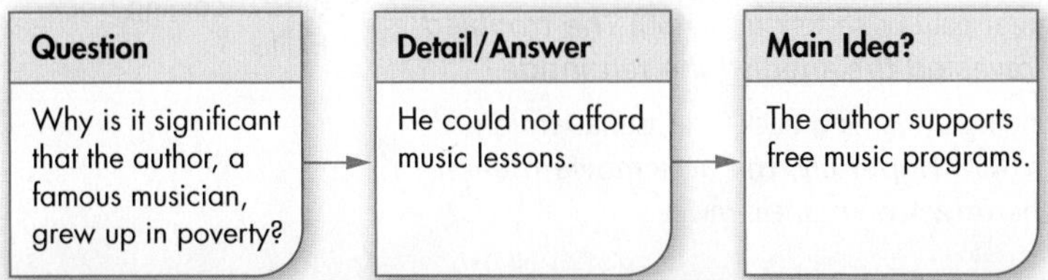

Question
Why is it significant that the author, a famous musician, grew up in poverty?
Detail/Answer
He could not afford music lessons.
Main Idea?
The author supports free music programs.

PHLit Online!
www.PHLitOnline.com

Hear It!
- Selection summary audio
- Selection audio

See It!
- Get Connected video
- Background video
- More about the author
- Vocabulary flashcards

Do It!
- Interactive journals
- Interactive graphic organizers
- Self-test
- Internet activity
- Grammar tutorial
- Interactive vocabulary games

PRETEACH

3 Literary Analysis
Author's Style

1. Introduce the skill, using instruction on the student page.
2. Tell students that they will practice analyzing the author's style as they read.

Think Aloud: Model the Skill

Model the skill of analyzing the author's style. Say to students:

As an author, the style I use depends on the message I want to convey. For example, if I am writing an educational report on global warming, I will use formal diction and syntax and a sophisticated tone. However, if I am writing a humorous essay about my family life, I will use informal diction and syntax and a comical tone.

4 Reading Skill
Main Idea

1. Introduce the skill, using instruction on the student page.
2. Tell students that they will practice identifying the main idea as they read.

5 Using the Strategy

Give students a copy of either **Reading Skill Graphic Organizer A** or **B** (*Graphic Organizer Transparencies,* pp. 75–77) to record their ideas about the main idea as they read. Use the examples in **Reading Skill Graphic Organizer A,** which is partially filled in, to model the process of completing the organizer.

Text Complexity: Reader and Task Suggestions

✓ A Celebration of Grandfathers		✓✓ On Summer	
Preparing to Read the Text	**Leveled Tasks**	**Preparing to Read the Text**	**Leveled Tasks**
• Using the Background note on TE p. 443, discuss the culture of New Mexico and describe its landscape. • Discuss how older people accumulate wisdom through life experiences. • Guide students to use Multidraft Reading strategies (TE p. 443).	*Knowledge Demands* If students will have difficulty with knowledge demands, have them read and make notes about the landscape. Then, have them reread and note how the setting affects Grandfather. *Analyzing* If students will not have difficulty with knowledge demands, have students read and take notes on how and why the grandfather changed.	• Use the Background note on TE p. 455 to discuss the Great Migration that brought many African Americans north. • Talk about how our attitudes can change as we gain experience. • Guide students to use Multidraft Reading strategies (TE p. 455).	*Levels of Meaning* If students will have difficulty with levels of meaning, have them first read and take notes about Hansberry's attitude toward summer as a child and as an adult. Explain her change in attitude. *Evaluating* If students will not have difficulty with the levels of meaning, have them read and compare the author's experiences in each of the major places she describes.

PRETEACH

❶ Writing about the Big Question

1. Review the assignment with the class.
2. Ask students what they know about their grandparents' generation. What important events did they experience growing up? Have students compare these to their own generation's experiences.
3. Have students complete the sentence starters. Review responses as a class. (**Possible response:** Knowing what people do and how they live can give insight into who they are because these experiences shape people. People of different ages often interpret ideas and events differently because their perspectives are not the same.)
4. Remind students that their answers will help them think about the Big Question, "Is knowledge the same as understanding?"

While You Read

Tell students that as they read, they should look for details that help them understand the author's grandfather.

❷ Vocabulary

1. Have students preview the selection vocabulary.
2. For each word, have students say the word aloud.
3. Then, use the word in a sentence that defines the word.
4. Finally, repeat your definitional sentence or a similar sentence with the word missing and have the class "fill in the blank" chorally. Here is an example:

   Anguish is pain or suffering. The boy could tell from the look of agony on his mother's face that she felt [students say "anguish"].

❸ Word Study

1. Introduce the skill, using the instruction in the box.
2. Have students come up with three common words with the root *-viv-*. (**Sample answers:** *vivid, vivacious, survive*)

Making Connections | A Celebration of Grandfathers

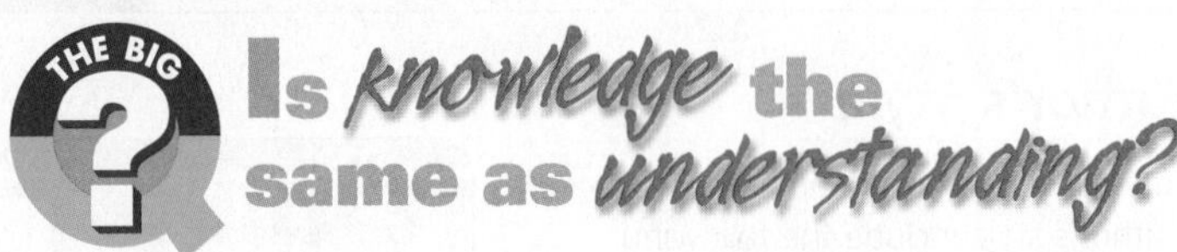

❶ Writing About the Big Question

"A Celebration of Grandfathers" explains how the author's grandfather and people of his generation lived and what they valued. Use these sentence starters to develop your ideas about the Big Question.

Knowing what people do and how they live can give **insight** into who they are because ___________.

People of different ages often **interpret** ideas and events differently because ___________.

While You Read Look for details that help you understand the author's grandfather.

❷ Vocabulary

Read each word and its definition. Decide whether you know the word well, know it a little bit, or do not know it at all. After you read, see how your knowledge of each word has increased.

- **nurturing** (nur´ chər iŋ) *n.* the raising or promoting the development of (p. 445) ***Nurturing** their children is the most important job of parents.* nurture *n.* nurture *v.*
- **perplexes** (pər pleks´ əz) *v.* confuses or puzzles (p. 445) *His odd behavior **perplexes** them.* perplex *v.* perplexing *adj.* perplexity *n.*
- **absurdity** (ab sur´ də tē) *n.* something ridiculous or nonsensical (p. 445) *To our surprise, our reasonable request was treated as an **absurdity**.* absurd *adj.* absurdly *adv.*
- **permeate** (pur´ mē āt´) *v.* spread or flow throughout (p. 446) *It didn't take long for the odor to **permeate** the entire apartment.* permeation *n.* permeable *adj.* permeating *v.*
- **anguish** (aŋ´ gwish) *n.* great pain or suffering (p. 450) *The troubled expression on her face revealed the **anguish** she felt inside.*
- **revival** (ri vī´ vəl) *n.* a bringing or coming back into use, attention, or being after a decline (p. 451) *Hopefully, the new movie theater will spark a **revival** of the downtown area.* revive *v.*

❸ Word Study

The **Latin root *-viv-*** means "to live."

In this selection, the author describes the **revival** of the valley where the author's grandfather lived. The word suggests that the area is coming back to life.

Vocabulary Development

Vocabulary Knowledge Rating

Create a **Vocabulary Knowledge Rating Chart (Professional Development Guidebook,** p. 33) for this selection. Include the selection vocabulary and the Big Question words that appear in the Writing About the Big Question sentence starters on this page. (The Big Question vocabulary is introduced on pp. 424–425.)

Give students a copy of the chart. Read the words aloud, and have students mark their rating in the Before Reading column. Urge them to be alert to these words as they read and discuss the selection.

Tally how many students think they know a word to gauge how much instruction to provide. As students read and discuss the selection, point out the words and their context.

Vocabulary Central, featuring tools, activities, and songs for studying vocabulary, is available at **www.PHLitOnline.com.**

Meet
Rudolfo A. Anaya
(b. 1937)

Author of

A Celebration of Grandfathers

Born in New Mexico, Rudolfo A. Anaya is considered the founder of modern Chicano literature. His first novel, *Bless Me, Ultima,* was praised for its depiction of the culture and history of New Mexico. Today, it is widely accepted as a classic of American literature.

A Storytelling Tradition "I am an oral storyteller," Anaya explains, "but now I do it on the printed page." Anaya's storytelling reflects his interest in the folk tales of his native Hispanic culture, which combines Spanish, Mexican, and Central American influences. Anaya has won a number of awards, including a PEN Center West Award for his 1992 novel *Albuquerque.* He is currently a professor of English at the University of New Mexico.

4 BACKGROUND FOR THE ESSAY

New Mexican Culture

Native Americans occupied present-day New Mexico thousands of years before the Spanish arrived in the late 1500s. The area remained under Spanish and then Mexican rule until 1848, when the United States gained control of it. Since then, people from all over the world have settled in New Mexico. As a result, the region has become a kind of cultural crossroads.

Did You Know?

As a teenager, Anaya was paralyzed after he dove into an irrigation ditch and fractured two vertebrae in his neck. He recovered, but the ordeal forever changed his outlook on life.

Daily Bellringer

For each class during which you will teach this selection, have students complete one of the five Quick Write activities for Week 13 in the *Daily Bellringer Activities* booklet.

4 Background

New Mexican Culture

Even though New Mexico is a cultural crossroad, the Pueblo Indians who have inhabited the region for centuries continue to follow many of their ancient traditions. Although the Pueblo people now use many modern conveniences, the basic social system remains. Their life centers on the village, and most of the people live in single-story homes just as their ancestors did. Although some Pueblo people observe certain Catholic religious practices, most continue to practice their ancient religion.

Multidraft Reading

This icon ● marks natural pauses in the selection. To assist struggling readers and to deepen reading for all, assign the text in "chunks," following the icons, and apply multidraft reading protocols. For each reading, have students set the purpose indicated:

- **First reading**—identifying key ideas and details and answering any Reading Checks.
- **Second reading**—analyzing craft and structure and responding to the side-column prompts.
- **Third reading**—integrating knowledge and ideas, connecting to other texts and the world, and answering the end-of-selection questions.

For more guidance, refer to the ***Classroom Strategies and Teaching Routines*** card on multidraft reading.

Differentiated Instruction
Additional Instruction

EL Extended Support—English Learners
Have students complete the **Reading and Vocabulary Warm-ups,** ***Unit 3 Resources,*** pp. 23–26, before they read. Assign the prereading pages and the adapted selection in the ***Reader's Notebook: English Learner's Version.*** Then, have students listen to portions of the selection on the ***Hear It!*** **Audio CD**.

L1 L2 Extended Support—Struggling Readers
Have students complete the **Reading and Vocabulary Warm-ups,** ***Unit 3 Resources,*** pp. 23–26, before they read. Assign the prereading pages and the adapted selection in the ***Reader's Notebook: Adapted Version.*** Then, have students listen to portions of the selection on the ***Hear It!*** **Audio CD** (adapted text).

Extended Support—Reluctant Readers
To build motivation and engagement before assigning the selection, have students read "Age in America," a thematically related selection in ***Reality Central.*** Then, use the questions at the conclusion of the related selection to guide discussion.

PHLit Online!
For more about the author, practice with the selection vocabulary, and more background, go online at **www.PHLitOnline.com.**

❶ Activating Prior Knowledge

1. Prepare an **Anticipation Guide** (*Professional Development Guidebook*, pp. 36–38) with the following statements:
   - It is important to share and contribute to others' welfare.
   - American media does not reflect the real lives of the elderly.
   - Older people have much that they can share with the young.
2. Give students a copy of the prepared **Anticipation Guide** and have students mark their responses in the appropriate columns.
3. For further guidance, use the ***Classroom Strategies and Teaching Routines*** card: **Using an Anticipation Guide.**

Concept Connector

Students will return to the **Anticipation Guide** after completing "A Celebration of Grandfathers."

Whole-Class Activity

As students read, have them "listen" to the silence of the old people. What effect does this silence have on the reader? How is silence sometimes more effective than speech? Have students discuss these quiet characters after reading the essay.

❷ About the Selection

In "A Celebration of Grandfathers," Rudolfo Anaya celebrates the culture of his native New Mexico, where old people were respected and honored. He describes his grandfather as a man of strength and endurance. After his grandfather's death at age ninety-four, the narrator wonders whether the values of the old man's generation are gone for good.

❸ Critical Viewing

Possible response: Like the narrator's grandfather, the man in the picture is smiling and wearing a cowboy hat. The elders in this essay are farmers who seem content with life.

❶ ❷

A Celebration of Grandfathers

Rudolfo A. Anaya

❸ ▲ **Critical Viewing** As you read, consider which aspects of the man in this picture resemble the description of the elders in the essay. **[Compare and Contrast]**

"Buenos días le de Dios, abuelo."[1] God give you a good day, grandfather. This is how I was taught as a child to greet my grandfather, or any grown person. It was a greeting of respect, a cultural value to be passed on from generation to generation, this respect for the old ones.

The old people I remember from my childhood were strong in their beliefs, and as we lived daily with them we learned a wise path of life to follow. They had something important to share with the young, and

1. **Buenos días le de Dios, abuelo** (bwā′ nəs dē′ äs lā dā dē′ ōs ä bwā lō)

Vocabulary Development

Ⓒ CCSS Language 6

Thematic Vocabulary: The Big Question

As students are discussing "A Celebration of Grandfathers," encourage them to use the thematic vocabulary presented in Introducing the Big Question, pp. 424–425. You might encourage them with sentence starters like these:

1. Anaya believes the past and the present have an important *connection* because . . .
2. Some examples of the grandfather's *insight* include . . .
3. Anaya would say that the most reliable sources of *information* about the elderly are . . .
4. Anaya's description of his grandfather evokes a *feeling* of . . .

when they spoke the young listened. These old abuelos and abuelitas[2] had worked the earth all their lives, and so they knew the value of nurturing, they knew the sensitivity of the earth. The daily struggle called for cooperation, and so every person contributed to the social fabric, and each person was respected for his contribution.

The old ones had looked deep into the web that connects all animate and inanimate forms of life, and they recognized the great design of the creation.

These *ancianos*[3] from the cultures of the Río Grande, living side by side, sharing, growing together, they knew the rhythms and cycles of time, from the preparation of the earth in the spring to the digging of the acequias[4] that brought the water to the dance of harvest in the fall. They shared good times and hard times. They helped each other through the epidemics and the personal tragedies, and they shared what little they had when the hot winds burned the land and no rain came. They learned that to survive one had to share in the process of life.

4 Hard workers all, they tilled the earth and farmed, ran the herds and spun wool, and carved their saints and their kachinas[5] from cottonwood late in the winter nights. All worked with a deep faith which perplexes the modern mind.

Their faith shone in their eyes; it was in the strength of their grip, in the creases time wove into their faces. When they spoke, they spoke plainly and with few words, and they meant what they said. When they prayed, they went straight to the source of life. When there were good times, they knew how to dance in celebration and how to prepare the foods of the fiestas.[6] All this they passed on to the young, so that a new generation would know what they had known, so the string of life would not be broken.

Today we would say that the old abuelitos lived authentic lives.

Newcomers to New Mexico often say that time seems to move slowly here. I think they mean they have come in contact with the inner strength of the people, a strength so solid it causes time itself to pause. Think of it. Think of the high, northern New Mexico villages, or the lonely ranches on the open llano.[7] Think of the Indian pueblo[8] which lies as solid as rock in the face of time. Remember the old people whose eyes seem like windows that peer into a distant past that makes absurdity of our contemporary

2. **abuelitas** (ä bwā lē´ täs) *n.* Spanish for *grandmothers.*
3. ***ancianos*** (än cē ä´ nōs) n. Spanish for *old people; ancestors.*
4. **acequias** (ä sā kē´ əs) *n.* Spanish for *irrigation ditches.*
5. **kachinas** (kə chē´ nəz) *n.* Spanish for *small wooden dolls, representing the spirit of an ancestor or a god.*
6. **fiestas** (fē es´ təz) *n.* Spanish for *celebrations; feasts.*
7. **llano** (yä´ nō) *n.* Spanish for *plain.*
8. **pueblo** (pweb´ lō) *n.* Spanish for *village or town.*

Literary Analysis
Style and Tone What is the author's tone as he discusses the *ancianos?*

Vocabulary
nurturing (nʉr´ chər iŋ) *n.* the raising or promoting the development of

perplexes (pər pleks´ əz) *v.* confuses or puzzles

absurdity (ab sʉr´ də tē) *n.* something ridiculous or nonsensical

5 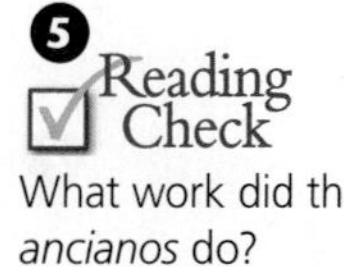

What work did the *ancianos* do?

4 Literary Analysis
Style and Tone

1. Have students note the words and phrases that the author uses to describe the old ones and their actions.

   Possible responses: Students may suggest phrases such as "recognized the great design of creation," "knew the rhythms and cycles of time," "hard workers," and "faith shone in their eyes."

2. Remind students that the diction—or words an author uses—affects the tone of the work. Then, **ask** students the Literary Analysis question: What is the author's tone as he discusses the *ancianos?*

   Possible responses: Students may suggest that the author's tone is reverent or respectful.

5 Reading Check

Answer: They farmed and raised sheep for their wool.

This selection is available in interactive format in the **Enriched Online Student Edition, www.PHLitOnline.com,** which includes a thematically related video with writing prompt and an interactive graphic organizer.

Fluency

Distribute copies of this page, and pair students. Explain that commas, periods, and other punctuation marks tell us when to pause as we read. Have partners take turns reading paragraphs aloud. While one partner reads, the other should mark any words with which the student reading has difficulty. Circulate to monitor the fluency of students' reading. Collect students' marked-up copies of the page, and review difficult words and passages with the class. Look for these problem spots:

- If students have trouble with the word *authentic*, remind them to break the word into syllables, read the syllables separately, and then blend them: *au-then-tic; authentic.*
- If students read without pausing or make pauses that distort the meaning, have students reread the sentence or section. Ask, "Does that make sense?" Point out that good readers sometimes find that what they are reading does not make sense. When that happens, they go back and reread the section. Model reading with appropriate pauses as needed.

6 Literary Analysis

Style

1. Have students identify the Spanish words *abuelos, ancianos, acequitas,* and *curanderas.*
2. Have students discuss why Anaya might have chosen to use the Spanish words rather than their English equivalents.

   Possible response: The nuances of word meanings in one language are often lost in translation to another language.
3. **Ask** the Literary Analysis question.

   Possible response: Anaya's use of Spanish words shows that he is comfortable using Spanish and takes pride in his language and culture.

Spiral Review

Author's Point of View

1. Students studied point of view in the Unit 3 Literary Analysis Workshop (pp. 426–439).
2. **Ask** students the Spiral Review question.

   Possible response: Anaya's sense of awe supports his purpose of communicating the value of his culture, and the "old ones" who represent it, by giving readers examples and illustrations that help them see his point.

7 Connecting to the Big Question

1. Read aloud the bracketed text. **Ask:** How does Anaya describe his grandfather?

   Answer: He was a plain, silent farmer with a mustache. He was short, but to Anaya he was a "giant."
2. **Ask:** How do these details help you understand the grandfather?

   Possible response: Anaya's description tells me that the grandfather's silence is important, and he seems larger than he is.
3. Tell students to look for more details about the grandfather as they continue reading.

Vocabulary
permeate (pur´ mē āt´) *v.* spread or flow throughout

Literary Analysis
Style How does Anaya's use of Spanish words add to his message of being connected to his culture?

Spiral Review
Author's Point of View In what way does the author's sense of awe about his subject relate to his purpose for writing?

world. That is what one feels when one encounters the old ones and their land, a pausing of time.

We have all felt time stand still. We have all been in the presence of power, the knowledge of the old ones, the majestic peace of a mountain stream or an aspen grove or red buttes rising into blue sky. We have all felt the light of dusk permeate the earth and cause time to pause in its flow.

6 I felt this when first touched by the spirit of Ultima, the old *curandera*[9] who appears in my first novel, *Bless Me, Ultima*. This is how the young Antonio describes what he feels:

> When she came the beauty of the llano unfolded before my eyes, and the gurgling waters of the river sang to the hum of the turning earth. The magical time of childhood stood still, and the pulse of the living earth pressed its mystery into my living blood. She took my hand, and the silent, magic powers she possessed made beauty from the raw, sun-baked llano, the green river valley, and the blue bowl which was the white sun's home. My bare feet felt the throbbing earth, and my body trembled with excitement. Time stood still . . .

At other times, in other places, when I have been privileged to be with the old ones, to learn, I have felt this inner reserve of strength upon which they draw. I have been held motionless and speechless by the power of curanderas. I have felt the same power when I hunted with Cruz, high on the Taos [tä´ ōs] mountain, where it was more than the incredible beauty of the mountain bathed in morning light, more than the shining of the quivering aspen, but a connection with life, as if a shining strand of light connected the particular and the cosmic. That feeling is an epiphany of time, a standing still of time.

7 But not all of our old ones are curanderos or hunters on the mountain. My grandfather was a plain man, a farmer from Puerto de Luna[10] on the Pecos River. He was probably a descendent of those people who spilled over the mountain from Taos, following the Pecos River in search of farmland. There in that river valley he settled and raised a large family.

Bearded and walrus-mustached, he stood five feet tall, but to me as a child he was a giant. I remember him most for his silence. In the summers my parents sent me to live with him on his farm, for I was to learn the ways of a farmer. My uncles also lived in that valley, the valley called Puerto de Luna, there where only the flow of

9. ***curandera*** (ko͞o rän dā´ rä) *n.* Spanish for *medicine woman.*
10. **Puerto de Luna** (pwer´ tō dā lo͞o´ nə) *n.* Port of the Moon, the name of a town.

Vocabulary Development

CCSS Language 6

Expressive Vocabulary

To help students broaden their expressive vocabulary, encourage them to use the following words as they discuss the selection: *appreciate, demonstrate, clarify,* and *maximize.* Have them complete these sentence starters:

1. His use of Spanish words shows that Anaya seems to *appreciate* . . .
2. Anaya uses a quotation from his novel to *demonstrate* . . .
3. To *clarify* the meaning of a Spanish word, Anaya . . .
4. Spanish words *maximize* Anaya's style by . . .

the river and the whispering of the wind marked time. For me it was a magical place.

I remember once, while out hoeing the fields, I came upon an anthill, and before I knew it I was badly bitten. After he had covered my welts with the cool mud from the irrigation ditch, my grandfather calmly said: "Know where you stand." That is the way he spoke, in short phrases, to the point.

One very dry summer, the river dried to a trickle, there was no water for the fields. The young plants withered and died. In my sadness and with the impulses of youth I said, "I wish it would rain!" My grandfather touched me, looked up into the sky and whispered, "Pray for rain." In his language there was a difference. He felt connected to the cycles that brought the rain or kept it from us. His prayer was a meaningful action, because he was a participant with the forces that filled our world, he was not a bystander.

Woodcutter and Burro ("El Lenador"), 1934, Tom Lea, on long-term loan to the New Mexico Museum of Art from the U.S. General Services Administration, Works Project Administration. Photograph by Blair Clark.

A young man died at the village one summer. A very tragic death. He was dragged by his horse. When he was found I cried, for the boy was my friend. I did not understand why death had come to one so young. My grandfather took me aside and said: "Think of the death of the trees and the fields in the fall. The leaves fall, and everything rests, as if dead. But they bloom again in the spring. Death is only this small transformation in life."

These are the things I remember, these fleeting images, few words.

I remember him driving his horse-drawn wagon into Santa Rosa in the fall when he brought his harvest produce to sell in the town. What a tower of strength seemed to come in that small man huddled on the seat of the giant wagon. One click of his tongue and the horses obeyed, stopped or turned as he wished. He never raised his whip. How unlike today when so much teaching is done with loud words and threatening hands.

9 ▲ **Critical Viewing**
How does the farmer in this painting compare with your image of the author's grandfather? **[Compare and Contrast]**

10 **Reading Check**
Why did Anaya's parents send him to stay with his grandfather in the summer?

8 Humanities

***El Leñador*, 1934, by Tom Lea**

A *leñador* is a woodcutter. This painting shows the woodcutter and his donkey with a load of wood. The woodcutter is probably using the stick to steer the animal on the uphill path. Use the following questions for discussion:

1. What can you infer about the life of the leñador in the painting?

   Possible response: He probably works hard because he is alone and has chopped a lot of wood. He isn't rich, because he does manual labor and seems to have only one donkey. His expression is tough and determined, suggesting that his tasks are difficult and strenuous.

2. What can you infer about the man's relationship with the donkey?

   Possible response: They seem to be partners; the donkey wears no halter and is being directed only by a light stick. They apparently work well together and trust each other.

9 Critical Viewing

Possible response: The man in the painting looks strong and vigorous, not old. Some students may think his face is stern. Anaya's grandfather is also tough and determined; he probably appears older.

10 Reading Check

Answer: He was sent to stay with his grandfather so that he could learn the ways of a farmer.

PROFESSIONAL DEVELOPMENT — Arnetha Ball

Questioning Strategy

One effective strategy to encourage English learners to ask and answer questions is to use a Reciprocal Questioning strategy.

Have students re-read the paragraph that begins, "These *ancianos* from the cultures..." (p. 445). Model how to ask *who, what, when, where,* and *why* questions about the text—*Who were the ancianos?* Next, ask if any students can pronounce and define the Spanish words in the text.

Then, pair students. Each pair should have a questioner and a respondent. Tell questioners to keep their books open and to ask their partners questions about the paragraph. Have respondents close their books and answer the questions, while questioners check the text for answers. Then, have students reverse roles.

For more of Arnetha Ball's strategies, see the Professional Development essay, pp. 424c–424d.

⓫ Reading Skill

Main Idea

1. Read aloud the bracketed text. **Ask** students why Anaya claims the old values are threatened.
   Answer: The sons and daughters are breaking with the past.
2. Have students explain what Anaya claims is most threatened by the break with the past.
   Answer: The break threatens the relationships with old people.
3. **Ask** what Anaya thinks is an important part of this relationship.
   Answer: It is important to understand the years of old people's final transformation.
4. **Ask** the Reading Skill question: What main idea about the loss of values does Anaya state here?
   Answer: As the young people lose the old values, a part of their humanity will be lost.

⓬ Critical Viewing

Possible response: Anaya has fond memories of his childhood in New Mexico. This landscape might remind him of the beauty, serenity, vibrant colors and majesty of his roots.

I would run to greet the wagon, and the wagon would stop. "Buenos días le de Dios, abuelo," I would say. This was the prescribed greeting of esteem and respect. Only after the greeting was given could we approach these venerable old people. "Buenos días te de Dios, mi hijo,"[11] he would answer and smile, and then I could jump up on the wagon and sit at his side. Then I, too, became a king as I rode next to the old man who smelled of earth and sweat and the other deep aromas from the orchards and fields of Puerto de Luna.

Reading Skill
Main Idea What main idea about the loss of values does Anaya state here?

We were all sons and daughters to him. But today the sons and daughters are breaking with the past, putting aside los abuelitos. The old values are threatened, and threatened most where it comes to these relationships with the old people. If we don't take the time to watch and feel the years of their final transformation, a part of our humanity will be lessened.

I grew up speaking Spanish, and oh! how difficult it was to learn English. Sometimes I would give up and cry out that I couldn't learn. Then he would say, "Ten paciencia."[12] Have patience.

▼ **Critical Viewing**
Why do you think a writer like Anaya might find this New Mexican landscape inspiring? **[Speculate]**

11. **mi hijo** (mē ē´ hō) *n.* Spanish for *my son.*
12. **Ten paciencia** (ten pä sē en´ sē ä) *n.* Spanish for *Have patience.*

Think Aloud

Author's Style
Direct students' attention to this sentence at the top of the page: "'Buenos días le de Dios, abuelo,' I would say." Point out that the essay begins with the same greeting. Use the following "think aloud" to model the process of analyzing an author's style:

> When I read this line, I think back to the beginning of the essay, when the author explains this phrase. It literally means "God give you a good day, grandfather." It is also a sign of respect for one's elders.
>
> Anaya's repetition emphasizes his feelings of admiration and respect for his grandfather. As I read on in this paragraph, I see that his grandfather replied with a similar respectful greeting. This is evidence of a mutually respectful relationship.Through his word choice and tone, Anaya conveys a warm, lyrical style.

Paciencia, a word with the strength of centuries, a word that said that someday we would overcome. *Paciencia*, how soothing a word coming from this old man who could still sling hundred-pound bags over his shoulder, chop wood for hours on end, and hitch up his own horses and ride to town and back in one day.

"You have to learn the language of the Americanos,"[13] he said. "Me, I will live my last days in my valley. You will live in a new time, the time of the gringos."[14]

13 A new time did come, a new time is here. How will we form it so it is fruitful? We need to know where we stand. We need to speak softly and respect others, and to share what we have. We need to pray not for material gain, but for rain for the fields, for the sun to nurture growth, for nights in which we can sleep in peace, and for a harvest in which everyone can share. Simple lessons from a simple man. These lessons he learned from his past which was as deep and strong as the currents of the river of life, a life which could be stronger than death. ●

13. **Americanos** (ä mer´ ē kä´ nōs) *n.* Spanish for *Americans.*
14. **gringos** (griŋ´ gōs) *n.* Spanish for *foreigners; North Americans.*

Literary Analysis
Style How does the author's repetition of the phrase "We need" add urgency to his message?

14

Why does Anaya's grandfather tell him that he must learn English?

Three Reds, Courtesy of Patrick Coffaro, Photography courtesy of Joan Cawley Licensing, Ltd.

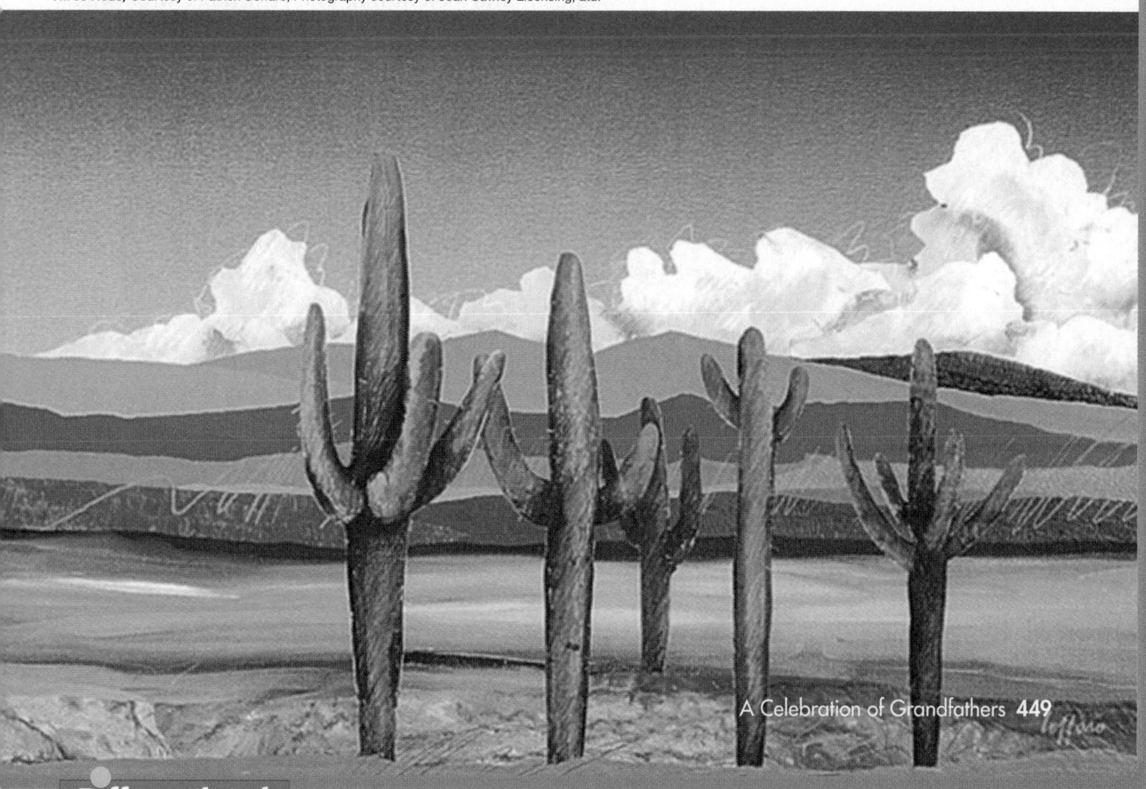

13 Literary Analysis
Style

1. Point out the repetition of "we" and "We need." Ask students to identify the tone of this paragraph.
   Answer: The tone is urgent.
2. **Ask** the Literary Analysis question: How does the author's repetition of the phrase "We need" add urgency to his message?
   Answer: The repetition of "We need" joins readers and the author as one group. His use of the word *need* emphasizes his message that these elements of life are essential to health, happiness, and community. They are not frivolous luxuries.

▶ **Monitor Progress:** Ask students how tone and choice of words are related to an author's style. Students should be able to explain that the tone, diction, and syntax—arrangement of words in a sentence—contribute to an author's style.

▶ **Reteach:** If students have difficulty identifying style, ask students to find details in the text that describe Anaya's grandfather. List the descriptive phrases on the board, and point out that such vivid language is part of Anaya's style.

14 Reading Check

Answer: He tells Anaya that Anaya must learn English because he will live in a new time.

Differentiated Instruction for Universal Access

Support for Less Proficient Readers
Arrange for small groups of less proficient readers to listen to the ***Hear It!* Audio CD**. Encourage the group to read along with the recorded version. Then, have the group generate two or three questions that they have about the material. Discuss the questions with them, and guide them to determining the answers.

Enrichment for Gifted/Talented Students
Have students draw sketches or prepare a photo collage showing grandparents or other older relatives they admire and respect. Under each sketch or photo, students should write captions that include the name and relationship of the person, as well as something about him or her that the student admires. Encourage students to display their sketches or collages in class.

15 Literature in Context

Cultural Connection In *Bless Me, Ultima,* the character of Ultima, who comes to live with Antonio's family, is a folk healer who uses folk magic in the service of others. When Antonio struggles to understand the conflicting religious beliefs of his parents and struggles with questions of good and evil, Ultima teaches him lessons of moral independence. From her, Antonio learns to choose his own destiny.

Connect to the Literature Have students review Anaya's description of the land on p. 446. Have them note the words he uses to describe the land. Then, **ask** the Connect to the Literature question: Based on what you know about Anaya's writing, how would you expect him to describe the bond between people and the land? Explain your answer.

Possible responses: Students may suggest that Anaya feels that people should be connected to the land and respect it. In the excerpt from *Bless Me, Ultima,* Anaya describes the "pulse of the living earth" and how his bare feet "felt the throbbing earth."

15 **LITERATURE IN CONTEXT**

Cultural Connection

Anaya's Best-Known Work
In this essay, Anaya quotes from his novel *Bless Me, Ultima.* First published in 1972, the novel tells the story of a young boy, Antonio, who lives with his family in Guadalupe, New Mexico. Ultima, who is respected for her healing powers and her knowledge of the uses of plants, comes to live with Antonio's family. Ultima takes the boy under her wing and teaches him about the plants and trees of the area. She also teaches him some important lessons about life.

Connect to the Literature

Based on what you know about Anaya's writing, how would you expect him to describe the bond between people and the land? Explain your answer.

He was a man; he died. Not in his valley, but nevertheless cared for by his sons and daughters and flocks of grandchildren. At the end, I would enter his room which carried the smell of medications and Vicks, the faint pungent odor of urine, and cigarette smoke. Gone were the aroma of the fields, the strength of his young manhood. Gone also was his patience in the face of crippling old age. Small things bothered him; he shouted or turned sour when his expectations were not met. It was because he could not care for himself, because he was returning to that state of childhood, and all those wishes and desires were now wrapped in a crumbling old body.

"Ten paciencia," I once said to him, and he smiled. "I didn't know I would grow this old," he said. "Now, I can't even roll my own cigarettes." I rolled a cigarette for him, placed it in his mouth and lit it. I asked him why he smoked, the doctor had said it was bad for him. "I like to see the smoke rise," he said. He would smoke and doze, and his quilt was spotted with little burns where the cigarettes dropped. One of us had to sit and watch to make sure a fire didn't start.

I would sit and look at him and remember what was said of him when he was a young man. He could mount a wild horse and break it, and he could ride as far as any man. He could dance all night at a dance, then work the acequia the following day. He helped neighbors, they helped him. He married, raised children. Small legends, the kind that make up everyman's life.

He was 94 when he died. Family, neighbors, and friends gathered; they all agreed he had led a rich life. I remembered the last years, the years he spent in bed. And as I remember now, I am reminded that it is too easy to romanticize old age. Sometimes we forget the pain of the transformation into old age, we forget the natural breaking down of the body. Not all go gentle into the last years, some go crying and cursing, forgetting the names of those they loved the most, withdrawing into an internal **anguish** few of us can know. May we be granted the patience and care to deal with our ancianos.

Vocabulary
anguish (aŋ′ gwish) *n.* great pain or suffering

For some time we haven't looked at these changes and needs of the old ones. The American image created by the mass media is an image of youth, not of old age. It is the beautiful and the young

Vocabulary Development

Vocabulary Knowledge Rating
When students have completed reading and discussing "A Celebration of Grandfathers," have them take out their **Vocabulary Knowledge Rating Chart** for this selection. Read the words aloud once more, and have students rate their knowledge of the words again in the After Reading column. Clarify any words that are still problematic. Have students write their own definition and example or sentence in the appropriate column. Then, have students complete the Vocabulary Practice activities at the end of the selection. Encourage students to use the words in further discussion and written work about this selection. Remind them that they will be accountable for these words on the **Selection Test, *Unit 3 Resources,*** pp. 35–37 or 38–40.

who are praised in this society. If analyzed carefully, we see that same damaging thought has crept into the way society views the old. In response to the old, the mass media have just created old people who act like the young. It is only the healthy, pink-cheeked, outgoing, older persons we are shown in the media. And they are
6 always selling something, as if an entire generation of old people were salesmen in their lives. Commercials show very lively old men, who must always be in excellent health according to the new myth, selling insurance policies or real estate as they are out golfing; older women selling coffee or toilet paper to those just married. That image does not illustrate the real life of the old ones.

Real life takes into account the natural cycle of growth and change. My grandfather pointed to the leaves falling from the tree. So time brings with its transformation the often painful, wearing-down process. Vision blurs, health wanes; even the act of walking carries with it the painful reminder of the autumn of life. But this process is something to be faced, not something to be hidden away by false images. Yes, the old can be young at heart, but in their own way, with their own dignity. They do not have to copy the always-young image of the Hollywood star.

> **Real life takes into account the natural cycle of growth and change.**

My grandfather wanted to return to his valley to die. But by then the families of the valley had left in search of a better future. It is only now that there seems to be a return to the valley, a revival. The new generation seeks its roots, that value of love for the land moves us to return to the place where our ancianos formed the culture.

I returned to Puerto de Luna last summer, to join the community in a celebration of the founding of the church. I drove by my grandfather's home, my uncles' ranches, the neglected adobe[15] washing down into the earth from whence it came. And I wondered, how might the values of my grandfather's generation live in our own? What can we retain to see us through these hard times? I

Vocabulary
revival (ri vī′ vəl) *n.* a bringing or coming back into use, attention, or being after a decline

17 

What happens to Anaya's grandfather?

---

15. adobe (ə dō′ bē) *n.* sun-dried clay brick.

16 Critical Thinking

Infer

1. **Ask** students what Anaya thinks about how the media portrays the elderly.

   Answer: The media portrays the elderly as lively and youthful, which the author believes is a false image.

2. **Ask** students why they think the author believes it is important to face the often painful process of aging.

   Possible response: The process of aging is part of the natural process of life. To pretend that it is otherwise is to ignore the truth.

17 Reading Check

Answer: He gets sick and returns to a childlike state. He becomes so weak that he cannot care for himself. He dies at the age of ninety-four.

Concept Connector

Anticipation Guide

Have students return to their **Anticipation Guides** and respond to the statements again in the After Reading column. They may do this individually or in their original pairs or groups. Then, lead a class discussion, probing for what students have learned that confirms or invalidates each statement. Encourage students to cite specific details, quotations, or other evidence from the text to support their responses to each statement.

Writing About the Big Question

Have students compare their responses to the sentence starters they completed before reading the essay with their ideas afterwards. Ask them to explain whether their thoughts have changed.

Reading Skill Graphic Organizer

Ask students to review the graphic organizers they completed to identify the main idea and supporting details while reading. Show them **Reading Skill Graphic Organizer A** (*Graphic Organizer Transparencies*, p. 75) as an example.

ASSESS

Answers

Critical Thinking

Before students respond, you may wish to have them write a brief objective summary of the selection. As they answer the questions below, remind them to support their answers with evidence from the text.

1. (a) Anaya remembers their wisdom, knowledge, and generosity. (b) The old ones in the essay are strong, wise, and independent. Modern mass media create misleading images of "youthful" old people—lively, healthy, and pink-cheeked.
2. Anaya's grandfather refers to the present day, when time moves faster and does not allow for patience.
3. (a) Old people should be treated with respect and care because they have wisdom and aging can be painful. (b) **Possible response:** Most students will agree with Anaya. Many may have grandparents or other elderly relatives whom they love and honor and whom they have seen suffer from aging. (c) **Possible response:** Students may say that their discussion cemented their belief that old people should receive better care.
4. (a) **Possible response:** His grandfather thought people should pay attention to their surroundings; he was spiritual and felt he had a role in his own future; he had a strong respect for family ties; and he valued patience. (b) **Possible response:** These insights help me strengthen my understanding because I can apply them to my own life and the lives of the elderly people I know.

was to become a farmer, and I became a writer. As I plow and plant my words, do I nurture as my grandfather did in his fields and orchards? The answers are not simple.

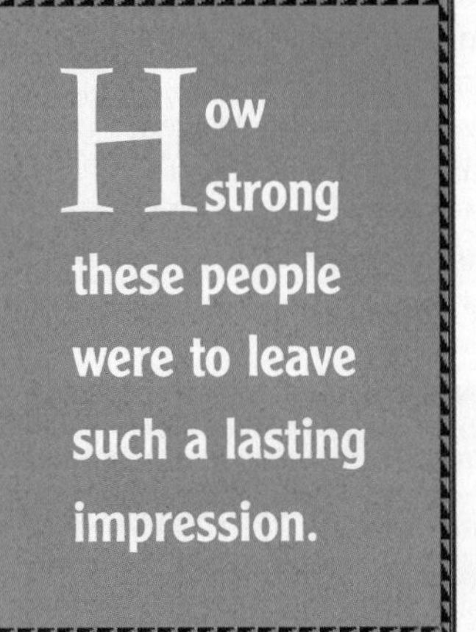
How strong these people were to leave such a lasting impression.

"They don't make men like that anymore," is a phrase we hear when one does honor to a man. I am glad I knew my grandfather. I am glad there are still times when I can see him in my dreams, hear him in my reverie. Sometimes I think I catch a whiff of that earthy aroma that was his smell, just as in lonely times sometimes I catch the fragrance of Ultima's herbs. Then I smile. How strong these people were to leave such a lasting impression.

So, as I would greet my abuelo long ago, it would help us all to greet the old ones we know with this kind and respectful greeting: "Buenos días le de Dios."

Critical Thinking

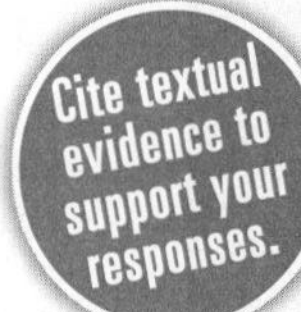
Cite textual evidence to support your responses.

1. **Key Ideas and Details (a)** What qualities of old people does Anaya remember from his childhood? **(b) Distinguish:** How are these qualities different from the images that Anaya says have been created by American mass media?
2. **Integration of Knowledge and Ideas** What does the author imply about the "new time" in which his people will live?
3. **Key Ideas and Details (a) Draw Conclusions:** What opinion does Anaya offer on the way people should be treated as they grow old? **(b) Take a Position:** Do you agree with him? Explain. **(c) Discuss:** Share your answers with a partner. Then, explain how your answer has grown or changed as a result of the discussion.
4. **Integration of Knowledge and Ideas (a)** What insights do the quotations from Anaya's grandfather give you? **(b)** How do these insights strengthen your understanding? ***[Connect to the Big Question: Is knowledge the same as understanding?]***

Assessment Resources

Unit 3 Resources

L1 L2 EL **Selection Test A,** pp. 35–37. Administer Test A to less advanced readers.

L3 L4 EL **Selection Test B,** pp. 38–40. Administer Test B to on-level and more advanced students.

L3 L4 **Open-Book Test,** pp. 32–34. As an alternative, give the Open-Book Test.

All **Customizable Test Bank**

All **Self-tests**
Students may prepare for the **Selection Test** by taking the **Self-test** online.

PHLit Online! All assessment resources are available at **www.PHLitOnline.com.**

After You Read

A Celebration of Grandfathers

Literary Analysis: Author's Style

1. **Craft and Structure** At several points in his essay, Anaya strings together sentences that have parallel structure, as in this example: "When they spoke, they spoke plainly and with few words, and they meant what they said. When they prayed, they went straight to the source of life. When there were good times, they knew how to dance in celebration. . . ." What effect does this aspect of the author's **syntax** create? Explain your response.
2. **Craft and Structure** Use a chart like the one shown to record examples of the **diction** and **tone** Anaya uses. Then, based on his diction and tone, write three adjectives in the center of the chart that describe his **style.**

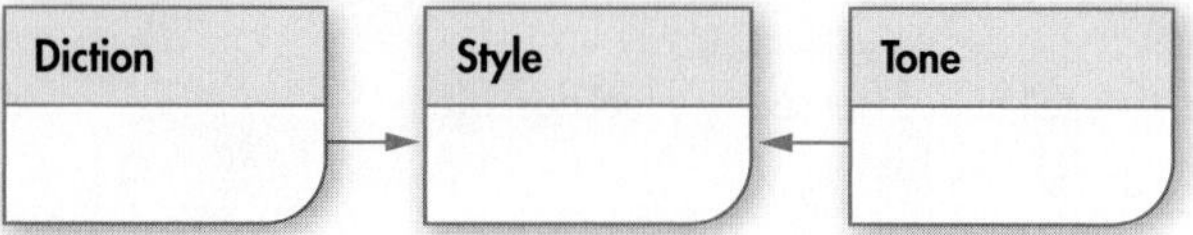

Reading Skill: Main Idea

3. State the **central idea** of Anaya's essay in your own words.
4. **(a)** List three **supporting details** that serve as evidence for the main point that Anaya makes in his essay. **(b)** Does the author adequately support his main idea with details? Why or why not?

Vocabulary

Acquisition and Use Determine whether each sentence below is true or false. Use the meaning of the italicized word to explain your reasoning.

1. A poor instruction manual is one that *perplexes* its readers.
2. It is a compliment to have a business idea labeled "an *absurdity.*"
3. To prevent a stain, allow ink to *permeate* the fabric.
4. Comforting someone in *anguish* is a kind action.
5. *Nurturing* a plant involves watering and feeding it.
6. The closing performance of a play would be a *revival.*

Word Study Use the context of the sentences and what you know about the **Latin root *-viv-*** to explain your answer to each question.

1. Do most people *survive* an embarrassing moment?
2. Is a *vivid* experience one you're likely to soon forget?

Word Study

The **Latin root *-viv-*** means "to live."

Apply It Explain how the root *-viv-* contributes to the meanings of these words. You may consult a dictionary if necessary.

convivial
vivacious
revive

Word Study

Sample answers:

1. Yes, the root *-viv-* means "to live," and *survive* means "to remain alive or live on." Most people live on after embarrassing moments.
2. No, the root *-viv-* means "to live," and *vivid* means "strong and full of life." People do not forget vivid experiences.

Word Study: Apply It

Sample answers:

Convivial means festive and full of life. *Vivacious* means animated or lively. To *revive* is to bring back to life.

ASSESS/EXTEND

Answers

Literary Analysis

1. **Possible response:** When Anaya strings together sentences that are structured in the same way, the repeated phrases place emphasis on what is being said. It draws the readers' attention to the passage and makes its importance clear.
2. **Sample answers: Diction:** words in Spanish, formal language. **Style:** enlightening, contemplative, direct. **Tone:** serious, reverent.
For other sample answers, see ***Graphic Organizer Transparencies,*** **Literary Analysis Graphic Organizer A,** p. 78, and the **Additional Answers** section.

Reading Skill

3. **Possible response:** We should honor the elderly and their wisdom.
4. **Possible response:** (a) Anaya learns from his grandfather's wisdom about death. Anaya suggests that we use a greeting similar to "Buenos días le de Dios" to respect our "old ones." He tells us to remember their values. (b) Yes, Anaya provides sufficient details to support his main idea. He provides examples involving his grandfather and how elderly people are treated today.

Vocabulary

Acquisition and Use

Sample answers:

1. True. A poor instruction manual confuses its readers.
2. False. It would be an insult to have a business idea labeled as ridiculous.
3. False. To prevent a stain you do not want ink to spread through the fabric.
4. True. It is kind to comfort someone who is suffering.
5. True. To take care of a plant you must water and feed it.
6. False. A closing performance would be at the end of a play, not at a revival, or reopening.

PRETEACH

*Skills instruction for the **Reading Skill** and the **Literary Analysis** concept appears on p. 441.*

❶ Writing about the Big Question

1. Review the assignment.
2. Ask students to think of something they either loved or hated as a child. How have their feelings or opinions changed?
3. Have students complete the sentence starters. Review responses as a class. (**Possible response:** Learning the facts of people's lives may change how we comprehend them because we gain insight into their experiences. When we make a connection with something, our feelings toward it may change because we may find more meaning in it than before.)
4. Remind students that their answers will help them think about the Big Question.

While You Read

Tell students that as they read, they should look for Hansberry's feelings about summer.

❷ Vocabulary

1. Have students preview the selection vocabulary.
2. For each word, have students say the word aloud.
3. Then, use the word in a sentence that defines the word.
4. Finally, repeat your definitional sentence or a similar sentence with the word missing, and have the class "fill in the blank" chorally. Here is an example:

   Something that is melancholy is sad or gloomy. It was clear from her depressed look and dreary mood that the girl felt [students say "melancholy"].

❸ Word Study

1. Introduce the skill, using the instruction in the box.
2. Using their knowledge of the root *-dur-*, have students define the word *durable* and use it in a sentence. (**Possible response:** Capable of holding out or lasting. Her old jeans were extremely durable.)

Making Connections | On Summer

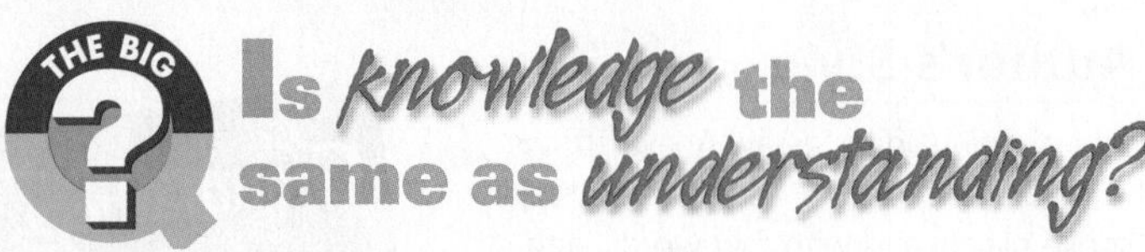

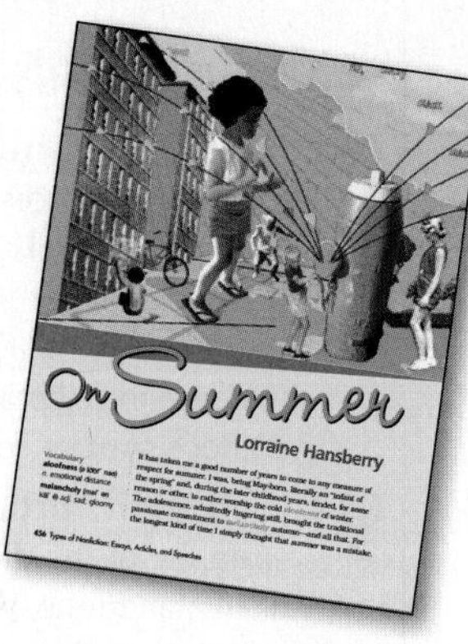

❶ Writing About the Big Question

In "On Summer," Lorraine Hansberry's growing understanding of life has changed her feelings about summer. Use these sentence starters to develop your ideas about the Big Question.

Learning the **facts** of people's lives may change how we **comprehend** them because ________.

When we make a **connection** with something, our **feelings** toward it may change because ________.

While You Read Look for details that tell about Hansberry's feelings toward summer.

❷ Vocabulary

Read each word and its definition. Decide whether you know the word well, know it a little bit, or do not know it at all. After you read, see how your knowledge of each word has increased.

- **aloofness** (ə lo͞of´ nəs) *n.* emotional distance (p. 456) ***His aloofness made him appear unfriendly.*** *aloof adj. aloofly adv.*
- **melancholy** (mel´ ən käl´ ē) *adj.* sad; gloomy (p. 456) ***The rain set a melancholy mood.*** *melancholy n. melancholic adj.*
- **bias** (bī´ əs) *n.* mental leaning or inclination; partiality (p. 457) ***For years, John has had a bias toward Italian restaurants.*** *bias v. biased adj.*
- **duration** (doo rā´ shən) *n.* the time that a thing continues or lasts (p. 457) ***To sleep better at night, decrease the duration of your afternoon nap.*** *durable adj. durability n. endure v.*
- **pretentious** (prē ten´ shəs) *adj.* grand in a showy way (p. 460) ***His pretentious manner only impressed those who had just met him.*** *pretentiousness n.*
- **apex** (ā´ peks´) *n.* highest point; peak (p. 460) ***Playing in the World Series was the apex of his baseball career.***

❸ Word Study

The **Latin root *-dur-*** means "to harden," "to hold out," or "to last."

In this story, the narrator describes the long **duration** of a summer day. She means that it seems to last for a very long time.

Vocabulary Development

Vocabulary Knowledge Rating

Create a **Vocabulary Knowledge Rating Chart** ***(Professional Development Guidebook,*** p. 33) for this selection. Include the selection vocabulary and the forms of the Big Question words that appear in the Writing About the Big Question sentence starters on this page. (The Big Question vocabulary is introduced on pp. 424–425.)

Give students a copy of the chart. Read the words aloud, and have students mark their rating in the Before Reading column. Urge them to be alert to these words as they read and discuss the selection.

Tally how many students think they know a word to gauge how much instruction to provide. As students read and discuss the selection, point out the words and their context.

Vocabulary Central, featuring tools, activities, and songs for studying vocabulary, is available at **www.PHLitOnline.com.**

Meet

Lorraine Hansberry

(1930–1965)

Author of

On Summer

Lorraine Hansberry grew up on the South Side of Chicago, where her father prospered as a real-estate broker. At the time, many white people closed their neighborhoods, refusing to sell or rent property to African Americans. Hansberry's father fought this practice, taking his case all the way to the Supreme Court, where he won.

A Pioneering Playwright As her father fought to integrate Chicago's neighborhoods, Hansberry laid claim to territories of the imagination. With the 1959 production of her play *A Raisin in the Sun*, she became the first African American woman to have a drama produced on Broadway.

4 BACKGROUND FOR THE ESSAY

The Great Migration

Beginning in the early 1900s, hundreds of thousands of African Americans left the rural South for northern cities. They fled discrimination and the floods and pests that threatened their livelihood as farmers. Many left relatives behind and, like Hansberry's Chicago family, journeyed south in summertime to visit.

Did You Know?

A Broadway revival of the play *A Raisin in the Sun* won Tony awards for Phylicia Rashad and Audra McDonald in 2004.

Daily Bellringer

For each class during which you will teach this selection, have students complete one of the five Quick Write activities for Week 13 in the *Daily Bellringer Activities* booklet.

4 Background

The Great Migration

Chicago was one of the most important destinations for African Americans migrating from the South. Between 1910 and 1920, Chicago's African American population grew from 44,000 to 110,000. An important link between Chicago and the rural African American communities of the South were the African American porters who worked on the Illinois Central Railroad. They carried the African American newspaper, the *Chicago Defender*, on their trips south. The newspaper encouraged Southern African Americans to migrate north.

Multidraft Reading

To assist struggling readers and to deepen reading for all, apply multidraft reading protocols. For each reading, have students set the purpose indicated:

- **First reading**—identifying key ideas and details and answering any Reading Checks.
- **Second reading**—analyzing craft and structure and responding to the side-column prompts.
- **Third reading**—integrating knowledge and ideas, connecting to other texts and the world, and answering the end-of-selection questions.

For more guidance, refer to the ***Classroom Strategies and Teaching Routines*** card on multidraft reading.

Differentiated Instruction Additional Instruction

EL Extended Support—English Learners

Have students complete the **Reading and Vocabulary Warm-ups, *Unit 3 Resources*,** pp. 41–44, before they read. Assign the prereading pages for the selection in the ***Reader's Notebook: English Learner's Version.*** Then, have students listen to portions of the selection on the ***Hear It!* Audio CD**.

L1 L2 Extended Support—Struggling Readers

Have students complete the **Reading and Vocabulary Warm-ups, *Unit 3 Resources*,** pp. 41–44, before they read. Assign the prereading pages for the selection in the ***Reader's Notebook: Adapted Version.*** Then, have students listen to portions of the selection on the ***Hear It!* Audio CD** (adapted text).

Extended Support—Reluctant Readers

To build motivation and engagement before assigning the selection, have students read "Learning Without a Break," a thematically related selection in ***Reality Central.*** Then, use the questions at the conclusion of the related selection to guide discussion.

PHLit Online!

For more about the author, practice with the selection vocabulary, and more background, go online at **www.PHLitOnline.com.**

TEACH

❶ Activating Prior Knowledge

1. Prepare an **Anticipation Guide** (***Professional Development Guidebook***, pp. 36–38) with the following statements:
   - Adults should pass on their childhood memories to future generations.
   - Childhood memories provide a living link to a family's past.
   - Family memories can give a clearer picture of history than books and movies can.
2. Give students a copy of the prepared **Anticipation Guide** and have students mark their responses in the appropriate columns.
3. For further guidance, use the ***Classroom Strategies and Teaching Routines*** card: **Using an Anticipation Guide**.

Concept Connector

Students will return to the **Anticipation Guide** after completing "On Summer."

Small-Group Activity

Ask students to create posters or collages that represent their favorite season. Have students form groups based on the seasons they prefer. Suggest that students show both pleasant and unpleasant aspects of the season. Display the posters in the classroom.

❷ About the Selection

In "On Summer," Hansberry recalls her childhood dislike of summers. During her eighth summer, she visits her grandmother in Tennessee. On a summer trip to Maine as an adult, she meets an elderly woman dying of cancer. Through conversations with this woman, Hansberry learns to respect and value summer as "the noblest of the seasons."

❶ ❷ On Summer

Lorraine Hansberry

Vocabulary
aloofness (ə lo͞of′ nəs) *n.* emotional distance
melancholy (mel′ ən käl′ ē) *adj.* sad; gloomy

❸ It has taken me a good number of years to come to any measure of respect for summer. I was, being May-born, literally an "infant of the spring" and, during the later childhood years, tended, for some reason or other, to rather worship the cold aloofness of winter. The adolescence, admittedly lingering still, brought the traditional passionate commitment to melancholy autumn—and all that. For the longest kind of time I simply thought that *summer* was a mistake.

Vocabulary Development

CCSS Language 6

Thematic Vocabulary: The Big Question

As students are discussing "On Summer," encourage them to use the thematic vocabulary presented in Introducing the Big Question, pp. 424–425. You might encourage them with sentence starters like these:

1. In a sense, Hansberry's ideas about summer are *ambiguous* because . . .
2. The old woman at the end of the essay provided Hansberry with *insight* about . . .
3. Hansberry shares her *sensory* experiences of summer in order to . . .
4. This essay is not based on *statistics* about summer, but rather on . . .

In fact, my earliest memory of anything at all is of waking up in a darkened room where I had been put to bed for a nap on a summer's afternoon, and feeling very, very hot. I acutely disliked the feeling then and retained the **bias** for years. It had originally been a matter of the heat but, over the years, I came actively to associate displeasure with most of the usually celebrated natural features and social by-products of the season: the too-grainy texture of sand; the too-cold coldness of the various waters we constantly try to escape into, and the icky-perspiry feeling of bathing caps.

It also seemed to me, esthetically[1] speaking, that nature had got inexcusably carried away on the summer question and let the whole thing get to be rather much. By **duration** alone, for instance, a summer's day seemed maddeningly excessive; an utter overstatement. Except for those few hours at either end of it, objects always appeared in too sharp a relief against backgrounds; shadows too pronounced and light too blinding. It always gave me the feeling of walking around in a motion picture which had been too artsily-craftsily exposed. Sound also had a way of coming to the ear without that muting influence, marvelously common to winter, across patios or beaches or through the woods. I suppose I found it too stark and yet too intimate a season.

My childhood Southside summers were the ordinary city kind, full of the street games which other rememberers have turned into fine ballets these days and rhymes that anticipated what some people insist on calling modern poetry:

Oh, Mary Mack, Mack, Mack
All dressed in black, black, black
With the silver buttons, buttons, buttons
All down her back, back, back
She asked her mother, mother, mother
For fifteen cents, cents, cents
To see the elephant, elephant, elephant
Jump the fence, fence, fence
Well, he jumped so high, high, high
'Til he touched the sky, sky, sky
And he didn't come back, back, back
'Til the Fourth of Ju-ly, ly, ly!

Evenings were spent mainly on the back porches where screen doors slammed in the darkness with those really very special summertime sounds. And, sometimes, when Chicago nights got too steamy, the whole family got into the car and went to the park and slept out in the

1. **esthetically** (es thet′ ik lē) *adv.* artistically.

Literary Analysis
Style How would you describe Hansberry's tone as she explains her childhood feelings about summer?

Vocabulary
bias (bī′ əs) *n.* mental leaning or inclination; partiality

duration (doo rā′ shən) *n.* the time that a thing continues or lasts

Literary Analysis
Style What effect does the use of the made-up word "artsily-craftsily" create?

5
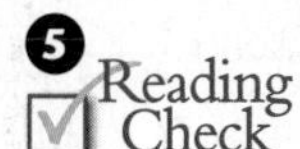
Identify one thing the author dislikes about summer.

3 Literary Analysis
Style

1. Read aloud the bracketed passage. Then, ask students to identify some of the words and phrases that the author uses to describe her feelings about summer.

   Possible responses: Some words and phrases include "very, very hot," "too-grainy texture of sand," "icky-perspiry feeling," "shadows too pronounced," and "light too blinding."

2. **Ask** the first Literary Analysis question: How would you describe Hansberry's tone as she explains her childhood feelings about summer?

   Possible response: Students may suggest that the tone is one of dislike, disdain, or disgust.

4 Literary Analysis
Style

1. **Ask** students to explain what they think *artsy-craftsy* means.

   Possible response: Students may think of something that is overdone or too elaborate.

2. **Ask** the second Literary Analysis question: What effect does the use of the made-up word "artsily-craftsily" create?

   Answer: The word adds to the author's idea that summer is overdone and too elaborate.

5 Reading Check

Possible responses: Students may mention heat, sand, cold water, and perspiration.

PHLit Online!
This selection is available in interactive format in the **Enriched Online Student Edition**, at **www.PHLitOnline.com**, which includes a thematically related video with writing prompt and an interactive graphic organizer.

Differentiated Instruction for Universal Access

Enrichment for Less Proficient Readers
Ask students to identify their own favorite season of the year and then to list special events, activities, and feelings that they think of in relation to that time of year. You may wish to have students form small groups based on their seasonal preference. Conclude by having each group create a poster that completes the statement "[Name of season] is the best because . . ." by combining favorite items of group members.

Culturally Responsive Instruction
Culture Focus Have students read the rhyme on this page aloud, clapping along with the rhythm. Explain that the purpose of the rhyme is to help the rope jumpers and turners keep a rhythm by which to play their game. Jumping rope is a popular activity in school yards throughout the United States. It is especially popular among girls in urban areas.

6 Literary Analysis

Style

1. Have a volunteer read aloud the bracketed text. Point out the repeated use of the word *and*, especially at the beginnings of sentences.
2. Then, **ask** students the Literary Analysis question.

   Answer: Use of the word *and* emphasizes the continual stream of memories that seem to flow without stopping.

Spiral Review

Author's Point of View

1. Students studied point of view in the Unit 3 Literary Analysis Workshop (pp. 426–439).
2. **Ask** students the Spiral Review question.

   Possible response: Telling the incident from the perspective of her childhood self allows her to highlight how carefree and innocent she was. She did not have the context to understand being enslaved.

7 Reading Skill

Main Idea

1. **Ask** students to summarize the author's memories of summer described on the previous pages.

   Answer: She remembers summers being hot and oppressive; she remembers playing games in the street and sleeping in the park on hot nights.
2. Then, **ask** students the Reading Skill question.

   Possible response: These anecdotes show that the author does have some pleasant memories of her childhood.

Monitor Progress: Point out that the author claims she disliked summer as a child. **Ask** students whether the memories she has described so far support that idea.

Reteach: If students have difficulty answering the above question, have them reread the selection up to this point. Help them identify the main idea in the opening paragraph.

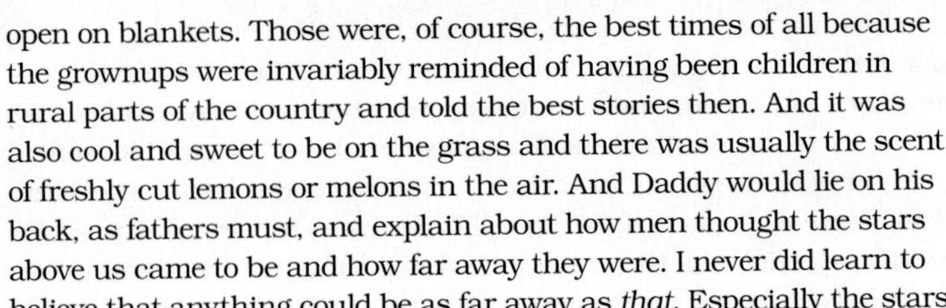

Literary Analysis 6
Style How does Hansberry's repeated use of the word *and* to begin sentences emphasize the flow and abundance of her memories?

Spiral Review
Author's Point of View Why do you think the author chose to relate this episode through her childhood perspective?

Reading Skill
Main Idea What do these anecdotes about her trips to Tennessee add to your understanding of the author's childhood summers?

open on blankets. Those were, of course, the best times of all because the grownups were invariably reminded of having been children in rural parts of the country and told the best stories then. And it was also cool and sweet to be on the grass and there was usually the scent of freshly cut lemons or melons in the air. And Daddy would lie on his back, as fathers must, and explain about how men thought the stars above us came to be and how far away they were. I never did learn to believe that anything could be as far away as *that*. Especially the stars.

My mother first took us south to visit her Tennessee birthplace one summer when I was seven or eight, I think. I woke up on the back seat of the car while we were still driving through some place called Kentucky and my mother was pointing out to the beautiful hills on both sides of the highway and telling my brothers and my sister about how her father had run away and hidden from his master in those very hills when he was a little boy. She said that his mother had wandered among the wooded slopes in the moonlight and left food for him in secret places. They were very beautiful hills and I looked out at them for miles and miles after that wondering who and what a *master* might be.

I remember being startled when I first saw my grandmother rocking away on her porch. All my life I had heard that she was a great beauty and no one had ever remarked that they meant a half century before. The woman that I met was as wrinkled as a prune and could hardly hear and barely see and always seemed to be thinking of other times. But she could still rock and talk and even make wonderful cupcakes which were like cornbread, only sweet. She was captivated by automobiles and, even though it was well into the Thirties,[2] I don't think she had ever been in one before we came down and took her driving. She was a little afraid of them and could not seem to negotiate the windows, but she loved driving. She died the next summer and that is all that I remember about her, except that she was born in slavery and had memories of it and they didn't sound anything like *Gone With the Wind*.[3]

Like everyone else, I have spent whole or bits of summers in many different kinds of places since then: camps and resorts in the Middle West and New York State; on an island; in a tiny Mexican village; Cape Cod, perched atop the Truro bluffs at Longnook Beach that Millay wrote about; or simply strolling the streets of Provincetown[4] before the hours when the parties begin.

8 And, lastly, I do not think that I will forget days spent, a few summers ago, at a beautiful lodge built right into the rocky cliffs

2. **Thirties** the 1930s.
3. ***Gone With the Wind*** novel set in the South during the Civil War period.
4. **Provincetown** resort town at the northern tip of Cape Cod, Massachusetts.

Vocabulary Development

Vocabulary Knowledge Rating

When students have completed reading and discussing "On Summer," have them take out their **Vocabulary Knowledge Rating Chart** for this selection. Read the words aloud once more and have students rate their knowledge of the words again in the After Reading column. Clarify any words that are still problematic. Have students write their own definition and example or sentence in the appropriate column. Then, have students complete the Vocabulary Practice activities at the end of the selection. Encourage students to use the words in further discussion and written work about this selection. Remind them that they will be accountable for these words on the **Selection Test, *Unit 3 Resources*,** pp. 56–58 or 59–61.

of a bay on the Maine coast. We met a woman there who had lived a purposeful and courageous life and who was then dying of cancer. She had, characteristically, just written a book and taken up painting. She had also been of radical viewpoint all her life; one of those people who energetically believe that the world *can* be changed for the better and spend their lives trying to do just that. And that was the way she thought of cancer; she absolutely refused to award it the stature of tragedy, a devastating instance of the brooding doom and inexplicability[5] of the absurdity of human destiny, etc., etc. The kind of characterization given, lately, as we all know, to far less formidable foes in life than cancer.

But for this remarkable woman it was a matter of nature in imperfection, implying, as always, work for man to do. It was an *enemy*, but a palpable one with shape and effect and source; and if it existed, it could be destroyed. She saluted it accordingly, without despondency, but with a lively, beautiful and delightfully ribald anger. There was one thing, she felt, which would prove equal to its relentless ravages and that was the genius of man. Not his mysticism, but man with tubes and slides and the stubborn human notion that the stars are very much within our reach.

5. **inexplicability** (in eks′ pli kə bil′ ə tē) *n.* condition of being unexplainable.

▼ **Critical Viewing**
How does this illustration of the Maine coast add to the description in the essay? **[Connect]**

10

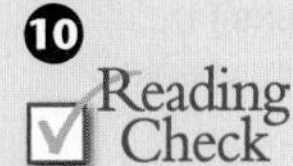

Whom does Hansberry visit in Tennessee?

8 Connecting to the Big Question

1. Point out to students that writers do not always state their feelings directly. Sometimes they show their feelings by describing particularly meaningful events.
2. Have a volunteer read aloud the bracketed text. **Ask:** What details in this passage tell about Hansberry's feelings about summer? What are those feelings?

   Answer: She talks about the beauty of the lodge and the "courageous" dying woman. These details show that Hansberry is beginning to associate summer with beauty and precious moments—time spent making life meaningful. Hansberry feels humbled and respectful toward summer.

9 Critical Viewing

Possible response: It illustrates the area that Hansberry describes and helps me understand why the old woman was determined to live long enough to see another summer.

10 Reading Check

Answer: She visits her grandmother.

Concept Connector

Anticipation Guide

Have students return to their **Anticipation Guides** and respond to the statements again in the After Reading column. They may do this individually or in their original pairs or groups. Then, lead a class discussion, probing for what students have learned that confirms or invalidates each statement.

Writing About the Big Question

Have students compare their responses to the sentence starters they completed before reading the essay with their ideas afterwards. Ask them to explain whether their thoughts have changed.

Reading Skill Graphic Organizer

Ask students to review the graphic organizers they completed to identify the main idea and supporting details while reading. Show them **Reading Skill Graphic Organizer A** ***(Graphic Organizer Transparencies,*** **p. 76)** as an example. Then, have students share the graphic organizers they did and the main ideas and supporting details they identified.

⓫ Literary Analysis
Style

Ask students the Literary Analysis question.

Possible response: Students may suggest the phrases "lively, beautiful and delightfully ribald" and "her face softened with love."

ASSESS
Answers

Critical Thinking

Before students respond, you may wish to have them write a brief objective summary of the selection. As they answer the questions below, remind them to support their answers with evidence from the text.

1. (a) Hansberry is eight at her first visit. (b) It is a memory of a specific summer; it provides a contrast to her description of the woman in Maine.
2. (a) Hansberry's attitude changes during her time in Maine with the old woman. (b) She considers summer noble because it represents life "at the apex," in its most complete form.
3. Students may suggest that she explains her change in attitude clearly, since she states her attitude about summer early in the essay and then describes how the woman in Maine affected her.
4. (a) Hansberry still thinks of summer as a time when everything is a bit overdone. (b) While Hansberry used to view summer as unpleasant, now she admires it as a symbol of life at its height. She says that the woman in Maine taught her to see summer as "life at the apex; with the gentlest nights and . . . the longest days."

Literary Analysis Style What words has Hansberry used to convey her feelings about the woman in Maine?

Vocabulary
pretentious (prē ten′ shəs) *adj.* grand in a showy way
apex (ā′ peks′) *n.* highest point; peak

The last time I saw her she was sitting surrounded by her paintings with her manuscript laid out for me to read, because, she said, she wanted to know what a *young person* would think of her thinking; one must always keep up with what *young people* thought about things because, after all, they were *change.*

Every now and then her jaw set in anger as we spoke of things people should be angry about. And then, for relief, she would look out at the lovely bay at a mellow sunset settling on the water. Her face softened with love of all that beauty and, watching her,  ⓫ I wished with all my power what I knew that she was wishing: that she might live to see at least one more *summer.* Through her eyes I finally gained the sense of what it might mean; more than the coming autumn with its pretentious melancholy; more than an austere and silent winter which must shut dying people in for precious months; more even than the frivolous spring, too full of too many false promises, would be the gift of another summer with its stark and intimate assertion of neither birth nor death but life at the apex; with the gentlest nights and, above all, the longest days.

I heard later that she did live to see another summer. And I have retained my respect for the noblest of the seasons.

Critical Thinking

Cite textual evidence to support your responses.

1. **Key Ideas and Details (a)** When does Hansberry first visit her grandmother? **(b) Infer:** Why do you think she includes the section about her grandmother in her essay? Which details led you to this idea?
2. **Integration of Knowledge and Ideas (a)** When does Hansberry's attitude toward summer begin to change? **(b) Interpret:** At the essay's end, Hansberry calls summer "the noblest of seasons." What do you think she means by this phrase?
3. **Craft and Structure Evaluate:** How clearly do you think Hansberry explains the way her feelings about summer have changed? Explain.
4. **Integration of Knowledge and Ideas (a)** In what way has Hansberry's knowledge of summer stayed the same? **(b)** How has her understanding of summer changed? Use details from the text to explain your response. ***[Connect to the Big Question: Is knowledge the same as understanding?]***

Assessment Resources

Unit 3 Resources

L1 L2 EL **Selection Test A,** pp. 56–58. Administer Test A to less advanced readers.

L3 L4 EL **Selection Test B,** pp. 59–61. Administer Test B to on-level and more advanced students.

L3 L4 **Open-Book Test,** pp. 53–55. As an alternative, give the Open-Book Test.

All **Customizable Test Bank**

All **Self-tests**
Students may prepare for the **Selection Test** by taking the **Self-test** online.

All assessment resources are available at **www.PHLitOnline.com.**

After You Read On Summer

Literary Analysis: Author's Style

1. **Craft and Structure** What one word might you use to describe the overall **tone** of "On Summer"? Explain your answer.
2. **Craft and Structure** Review the last two paragraphs of "On Summer." Use a chart like the one shown to record examples of the **diction** and **tone** Hansberry uses in describing her associations with summer. Then, based on her diction and tone in these paragraphs, write three adjectives in the center of the chart to describe Hansberry's **style.**

Reading Skill: Main Idea

3. State the **main idea** of "On Summer" in your own words.
4. **(a)** List three **supporting details** that serve as evidence for the main point that Hansberry makes in the essay. **(b)** Does the author adequately support her main idea with details? Explain.

Vocabulary

Acquisition and Use Determine whether each sentence below is true or false. Use the meaning of the italicized word to explain your reasoning.

1. Greeting a close friend with *aloofness* shows respect.
2. Cheerful songs might change someone's *melancholy* mood.
3. A *pretentious* politician is likely to be unpopular with many voters.
4. One must climb a mountain to reach its *apex*.
5. If a man has a *bias* toward cats, he feels neutral about them.
6. If we stay for the *duration* of the game, we will leave at halftime.

Word Study Use the context of sentences and what you know about the **Latin root *-dur-*** to explain your answer to each question.

1. If a manufacturer claims an item is *durable*, would you expect it to wear out quickly?
2. When a thief is caught *during* a robbery, has he or she been caught in the act?

Word Study

The **Latin root *-dur-*** means "to harden," "to hold out," or "to last."

Apply It Explain how the root *-dur-* contributes to the meanings of these words. You may consult a dictionary if necessary.

obdurate
endure
duress

ASSESS/EXTEND

Answers

Literary Analysis

1. **Possible response:** Reflective. In the essay, Hansberry reminisces about her past, reflecting upon her childhood summers and the events that led her to change her views.
2. **Sample answers: Diction:** descriptive words, figurative language; **Style:** expressive, sincere, moving; **Tone:** reflective, nostalgic

   For other sample answers, see ***Graphic Organizer Transparencies*, Literary Analysis Graphic Organizer A**, p. 79, and the **Additional Answers** section.

Reading Skill

3. **Possible response:** As we grow and gain experience, our understanding of things, such as summer, changes.
4. **Possible responses:** (a) She explains how she hated summer as a child, and how she feels differently now. She tells the reader about the old woman with cancer who made her realize that she shouldn't take her summers for granted. The last line of her essay reveals her new appreciation and respect for summer. (b) Yes, she provides sufficient details to support her main idea. She provides examples relating to her own life and experiences with summer.

Vocabulary

Acquisition and Use

Sample answers:

1. False. It does not show respect to greet a close friend with emotional distance.
2. True. Cheerful songs might make someone who is depressed happy.
3. True. Voters usually do not like politicians who are grand in a showy way.
4. True. To reach the peak of a mountain, you must climb it.
5. False. A man who feels a partiality toward cats does not feel neutral.
6. False. If you stay for the whole length of the game, you will not leave at halftime. You'll leave at the end.

Word Study

Sample answers:

1. No. The root *-dur-* means "to harden; hold out; last," and *durable* means "lasting." A durable item should last for a long time.
2. Yes. The root *-dur-* means "to harden; hold out; last," and *during* means "while something lasts." A thief caught during a robbery is caught in the act.

Word Study: Apply It

Sample answers:

To be *obdurate* is to be resistant or to hold out against outside influence. To *endure* is to hold out against. *Duress* is coercion by hard or severe treatment.

EXTEND/ASSESS

Answers

Conventions

1. Introduce the skill, using the instruction on the student page.
2. Discuss the definitions and examples.

Think Aloud: Model the Skill

Model the skill of identifying direct and indirect objects. Write the following sentence on the board: "I wrote my mother a letter." Then, say to students:

I know that a direct object answers the question, "Who or what received the action?" To identify the direct object I ask myself, "What did I write?" The answer is *a letter*, the direct object.

An indirect object answers the question, "*To* or *for whom* is the action done?" Thus, to identify the indirect object in this sentence, I ask myself, "To whom did I write?" The answer is *my mother*, the indirect object.

PH WRITING COACH Grade 9

Students will find instruction on and practice with direct and indirect objects in Chapter 14, section 3.

Practice A

1. grandfather—direct
2. him—indirect; advice—direct
3. grandfather—indirect; respect—direct
4. wagon—direct

Reading Application

Sample answer: God give you a good day, grandfather.

Practice B

Sample answers:

1. I love winter.
2. Do you like the Maine coast?
3. I mailed the author his revised manuscript.
4. My friend gave her grandmother a nice gift.

Writing Application

Sample answer: I gave the ice cream man (IO) a dollar (DO). I gave my friend (IO) a dry beach towel (DO). I gave my sister (IO) a seashell (DO).

PERFORMANCE TASKS

Integrated Language Skills

A Celebration of Grandfathers • On Summer

Conventions: Direct and Indirect Objects

A **direct object** is a noun or pronoun that *receives* the action of an action verb. An **indirect object** appears with a direct object and names the person or thing that something is *given to* or *done for.*

You can determine whether a word is a direct object by asking *Whom?* or *What?* after an action verb. You can tell whether a word is an indirect object by asking *To or for whom?* or *To or for what?* An indirect object can only appear between a subject and a direct object.

Example	Explanation
The family bought ***an old house.***	*House* is a direct object—answers the question *Bought what?*
The rain pelted ***the campers.***	*Campers* is a direct object—answers the question *Pelted whom?*
I wrote my ***brother letters.***	*Brother* is an indirect object—answers the question *Wrote to whom?* *Letters* is a direct object—answers the question *Wrote what?*

Practice A Identify the direct and indirect objects in each sentence.

1. The author greeted his grandfather.
2. His grandfather usually gave him very good advice.
3. Rudolfo Anaya always showed his grandfather respect.
4. Grandfather drove the huge wagon to market with the produce.

Reading Application In the first paragraph of "A Celebration of Grandfathers," find a sentence that uses both a direct and an indirect object.

Practice B For each item, write an original sentence using the word or phrase as directed in the information in parentheses.

1. winter (as a direct object)
2. Maine coast (as a direct object in a question)
3. author (as an indirect object), manuscript (as a direct object)
4. grandmother (as an indirect object), gift (as a direct object)

Writing Application Use this sentence starter to write three sentences about summer that each contain an indirect object (IO) and a direct object (DO): *I gave* (IO)/(DO).

PH WRITING COACH Further instruction and practice are available in *Prentice Hall Writing Coach.*

Extend the Lesson

Sentence Modeling

Choose the sentence given from the selection students have read:

My grandfather touched me, looked up into the sky and whispered, "Pray for rain." ("A Celebration of Grandfathers")

I acutely disliked the feeling then and retained the bias for years. ("On Summer")

Ask students what they notice about the sentence. Elicit from them that the sentence contains a direct object. Then, ask what else they notice. ("A Celebration of Grandfathers": Anaya's use of three main verbs gives the sentence a sing-song quality that illustrates his lyrical style. "On Summer": By putting the adverb *acutely* before the verb instead of after it, Hansberry prepares the reader for an extreme statement before she has even made it.)

Have students imitate the sentence, matching each grammatical and stylistic feature discussed. Have students share their work.

Writing

Informative Text Both of these selections describe the admiration the main characters have for someone older than they are. Think of an older person whom you admire. Write a few paragraphs of **book jacket copy** for a biography of that person.

- Include some important highlights of the person's life.
- Choose specific details that will make the reader want to know more.

Grammar Application Review your draft to identify the direct and indirect objects you have used.

Writing Workshop: *Work in Progress*

Prewriting for Business Letters For a business letter you may write, list consumer items that have not lived up to your expectations. Note what has been disappointing. Then, choose one item and consider information a company representative would need to know. Jot down three questions to be answered. Save this Questions List.

Speaking and Listening

Presentation of Ideas In a small group, hold a **panel discussion** on one of these topics.

- If you read "A Celebration of Grandfathers," discuss Anaya's claim that "the American image created by the mass media is an image of youth, not old age." To get started, think about the age of most people in television and films. Decide what images are conveyed by these actors.
- If you read "On Summer," discuss the pros and cons of each season of the year. To prepare, consider what you like about your favorite season, as well as what others might dislike about that season.

Follow these steps to complete the assignment:

- Prepare notes to use during the discussion. These will help keep you on track and remind you about what you have planned to say.
- During the discussion, clarify and defend your position. Help elaborate on the ideas of other panel members by adding useful supporting details.
- Use precise and relevant evidence such as facts, opinions, quotations, and reasoning to support your points.
- Use props, visual aids, graphs, and electronic media to make your discussion more appealing and persuasive.

Common Core State Standards

L.9-10.1; W.9-10.2; SL.9-10.1
[For the full wording of the standards, see page 440.]

Use this prewriting activity to prepare for the **Writing Workshop** on page 512.

www.PHLitOnline.com

- Interactive graphic organizers
- Grammar tutorial
- Interactive journals

Teaching Resources

All	*Unit 3 Resources*
L3 L4 EL	**Integrated Language Skills: Grammar**, p. 50
L3 L4 EL	**Support for Writing**, p. 51
L3 L4	**Support for Extend Your Learning**, p. 52
L4	**Enrichment**, pp. 31, 49
All	**Enriched Online Student Edition** Available under After You Read for this selection:
All	**Interactive Grammar Tutorial**
L3 L4	**Internet Research Activity**
	Professional Development Guidebook **Rubrics for Biography**, pp. 252–253

PHLit Online! All print and digital resources are available online at **www.PHLitOnline.com**. Online resources accessible by students are noted on the student page.

EXTEND/ASSESS

Writing

1. Review the assignment, using the instruction on the student page.
2. To guide students in writing book-jacket copy, give them **Support for Writing**, p. 51 in ***Unit 3 Resources.***
3. To evaluate students' book jacket copy, use the Biography rubrics, pp. 252–253 in ***Professional Development Guidebook.*** In addition, you might evaluate how well students choose appropriate biographical highlights and interesting details.

Grammar Application

Have students check their drafts for direct and indirect objects.

Six Traits Focus

	Ideas	✓	Word Choice
	Organization		Sentence Fluency
	Voice		Conventions

PH WRITING COACH Grade 9

Students will find instruction on and practice with response to literature in Chapter 10.

Writing Workshop
Work in Progress

Have students save their completed Questions List in their portfolios. They will use the list later as they continue this Work-in-Progress assignment (see p. 489). These assignments prepare them to complete the Writing Workshop assignment (see pp. 512–517).

Speaking and Listening

1. Review the assignment, using the instruction on the student page.
2. To support students' work on the assignment, have students complete the **Support for Extend Your Learning** page (***Unit 3 Resources***, p. 52).

✓ Single Room, Earth View • ✓✓ The News

Lesson Pacing Guide

DAY 1 Preteach

- Administer the Reading and Vocabulary Warm-ups (*Unit 3 Resources*, pp. 62–65 or 80–83) as necessary.
- Introduce the Reading Skill: Main Idea.
- Introduce the Literary Analysis concept: Expository Essay.
- Distribute copies of the appropriate graphic organizer for the Reading Skill (*Graphic Organizer Transparencies*, pp. 81–83).
- Distribute copies of the appropriate graphic organizer for Literary Analysis (*Graphic Organizer Transparencies*, pp. 84–86).
- Teach the selection vocabulary.
- Introduce the Word Study skill.

DAYS 2–3 Preteach/Teach

- Build background with the Background feature.
- Develop thematic vocabulary and thematic thinking with Writing About the Big Question.
- Prepare students to read with the Activating Prior Knowledge activities (TE).
- Informally monitor comprehension while students read.
- Use the Reading Check questions to confirm comprehension.
- Develop students' ability to determine the main idea, using the Reading Skill questions.
- Develop students' understanding of expository essays, using the Literary Analysis questions.
- Reinforce vocabulary with the Vocabulary notes.
- Reinforce unit focus standards using the Spiral Review prompts.

DAY 4 Assess

- Assess students' comprehension and mastery of the skills by having them answer the Critical Thinking, Reading Skill, and Literary Analysis questions.
- Have students complete the Vocabulary Practice activities.
- Have students complete the Word Study activities.

DAY 5 Extend/Assess

- Have students complete the Conventions lesson.
- Have students complete the Writing activity and write a script for a public service announcement. (You may assign as homework.)
- Extend learning by having students complete the Research and Technology, journal entries. (You may assign as homework.) As an alternative, assign them "One Book at a Time" or "Getting the News" in *Reality Central*.
- Administer Selection Test A or B (*Unit 3 Resources*, pp. 74–79 or 95–100).

Common Core State Standards

Reading Informational Text
1. Cite strong and thorough textual evidence to support analysis of what the text says explicitly as well as inferences drawn from the text.
2. Determine a central idea of a text and analyze its development over the course of the text.
3. Analyze how the author unfolds an analysis or series of ideas or events, including the order in which the points are made, how they are introduced and developed, and the connections that are drawn between them.

Writing 2. Write informative/explanatory texts to examine and convey complex ideas, concepts, and information clearly and accurately through the effective selection, organization, and analysis of content.
7. Conduct short as well as more sustained research projects to answer a question or solve a problem; narrow or broaden the inquiry when appropriate; synthesize multiple sources on the subject, demonstrating understanding of the subject under investigation.
8. Gather relevant information from multiple authoritative print and digital sources, using advanced searches effectively; assess the usefulness of each source in answering the research question; integrate information into the text selectively to maintain the flow of ideas.

Speaking and Listening 4. Present information, findings, and supporting evidence clearly, concisely, and logically such that listeners can follow the line of reasoning and the organization, development, substance, and style are appropriate to purpose, audience, and task.

Additional Standards Practice
***Common Core Companion*, pp. 110–144**

Daily Block Scheduling
Each day in this Lesson Pacing Guide represents a 40–50 minute period. Teachers using block scheduling may combine days to revise pacing. In addition, teachers may differentiate and support core instruction by integrating components for extended and intensive support as students require. See the Guide to Selected Leveled Resources (facing page).

Guide to Selected Leveled Resources

RTI Tier 1 (students performing on level)		✓ More Accessible Single Room, Earth View	✓✓ More Complex The News
Warm Up	**Practice, model,** and **monitor** fluency, working **with the whole class** or **in groups**.	**Vocabulary** and **Reading Warm-ups B,** ***Unit 3 Resources,*** pp. 80–81, 83	**Vocabulary** and **Reading Warm-ups B,** ***Unit 3 Resources,*** pp. 62–63, 65
Comprehension/Skills	**Support** and **monitor** comprehension and skills development, having students complete the activities, graphic organizers, and interactive prompts **independently** or **as a class**.	• ***Reader's Notebook,*** adapted instruction and full selection EL ***Reader's Notebook: English Learner's Version,*** adapted instruction and adapted selection • **Reading Skill Graphic Organizer B,** ***Graphic Organizer Transparencies,*** p. 83 • **Literary Analysis Graphic Organizer B,** ***Graphic Organizer Transparencies,*** p. 86	• ***Reader's Notebook,*** adapted instruction and summary EL ***Reader's Notebook: English Learner's Version,*** adapted instruction and summary • **Reading Skill Graphic Organizer B,** ***Graphic Organizer Transparencies,*** p. 83 • **Literary Analysis Graphic Organizer B,** ***Graphic Organizer Transparencies,*** p. 86
Monitor Progress	**Monitor** student progress with the differentiated curriculum-based assessment in the *Unit Resources.*	• **Selection Test B,** ***Unit 3 Resources,*** pp. 98–100 • **Open-Book Test,** ***Unit 3 Resources,*** pp. 92–94	• **Selection Test B,** ***Unit 3 Resources,*** pp. 77–79 • **Open-Book Test,** ***Unit 3 Resources,*** pp. 71–73
Assess/ Screen	**Assess** student progress using Benchmark Test 5.	• **Benchmark Test 5,** ***Unit 3 Resources,*** pp. 120–125	• **Benchmark Test 5,** ***Unit 3 Resources,*** pp. 120–125

RTI Tier 2 (students requiring intervention)		✓ More Accessible Single Room, Earth View	✓✓ More Complex The News
Warm Up	**Practice, model,** and **monitor** fluency **in groups** or **with individuals**.	• **Vocabulary and Reading Warm-ups A,** ***Unit 3 Resources,*** pp. 80–83 • ***Reality Central,*** "One Book at a Time" • ***Hear It!*** **Audio CD (adapted text)**	• **Vocabulary and Reading Warm-ups A,** ***Unit 3 Resources,*** pp. 62–65 • ***Reality Central,*** "Getting the News" • ***Hear It!*** **Audio CD**
Comprehension/Skills	• **Support** and **monitor** comprehension and skills development, working **in small groups** or **with individuals.** • **Pair** students with more advanced peers and have them complete the writing activity in the *Real-World Writing Journal*. • As students complete the selection in the appropriate version of the *Reader's Notebook,* **monitor** comprehension frequently with group questions and individual instruction. • **Model** strategies while guiding students in completing the activities and prompts in the *Reader's Notebook,* as well as the graphic organizers. • **Practice** skills and **monitor** mastery with the *Reading Kit* worksheets.	• ***Real-World Writing Journal,*** Lesson 3, pp. 78–81 • ***Reader's Notebook: Adapted Version,*** adapted instruction and adapted selection EL ***Reader's Notebook: English Learner's Version,*** adapted instruction and adapted selection • **Reading Skill Graphic Organizer A,** ***Graphic Organizer Transparencies,*** p. 81 • **Literary Analysis Graphic Organizer A,** ***Graphic Organizer Transparencies,*** p. 84 • ***Reading Kit,*** Practice worksheets, pp. 104, 108, 112, 116, 122	• ***Real-World Writing Journal,*** Lesson 4, pp. 62–65 • ***Reader's Notebook: Adapted Version,*** adapted instruction and summary EL ***Reader's Notebook: English Learner's Version,*** adapted instruction and summary • **Reading Skill Graphic Organizer A,** ***Graphic Organizer Transparencies,*** p. 82 • **Literary Analysis Graphic Organizer A,** ***Graphic Organizer Transparencies,*** p. 85 • ***Reading Kit,*** Practice worksheets, pp. 104, 108, 112, 116, 122
Monitor Progress	**Monitor** student progress with the differentiated curriculum-based assessment in the *Unit Resources* and in the *Reading Kit.*	• **Selection Test A,** ***Unit 3 Resources,*** pp. 95–97 • ***Reading Kit,*** Assess worksheets, pp. 105, 109, 113, 117, 123	• **Selection Test A,** ***Unit 3 Resources,*** pp. 74–76 • ***Reading Kit,*** Assess worksheets, pp. 105, 109, 113, 117, 123
Assess/ Screen	**Assess** student progress using Benchmark Test 5.	• **Benchmark Test 5,** ***Unit 3 Resources,*** pp. 120–125	• **Benchmark Test 5,** ***Unit 3 Resources,*** pp. 120–125

TIER 3 Tier 3 intervention may require consultation with the student's special-education or dyslexia specialist. For additional support, see the Tier 2 activities and resources listed above.

One-on-one teaching **Group work** **Whole class instruction** **Independent work** A **Assessment**

For a complete guide to selection support, including support for Advanced students, see the Overview of Resources in the frontmatter.

✓Single Room, Earth View
✓✓The News

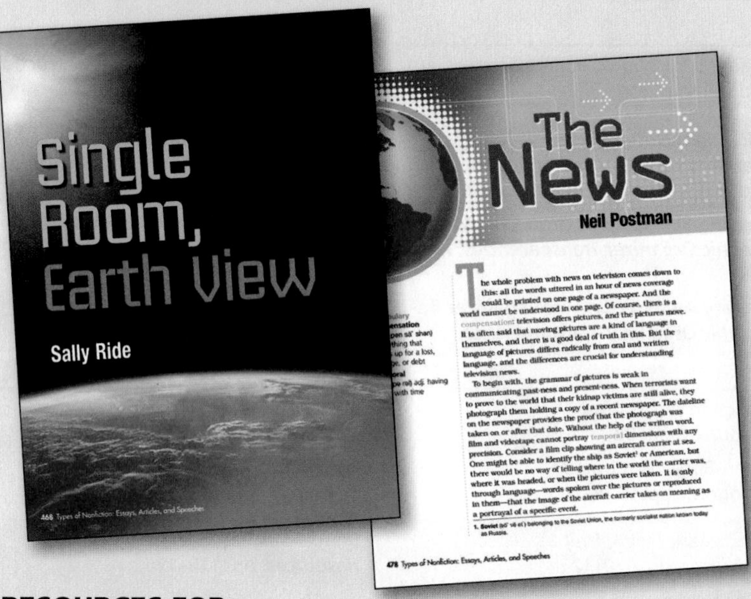

The News

Neil Postman

The whole problem with news on television comes down to this: all the words uttered in an hour of news coverage could be printed on one page of a newspaper. And the world cannot be understood in one page. Of course, there is a compensation: television offers pictures, and the pictures move. It is often said that moving pictures are a kind of language in themselves, and there is a good deal of truth in this. But the language of pictures differs radically from oral and written language, and the differences are crucial for understanding television news.

To begin with, the grammar of pictures is weak in communicating past-ness and present-ness. When terrorists want to prove to the world that their kidnap victims are still alive, they photograph them holding a copy of a recent newspaper. The dateline on the newspaper provides the proof that the photograph was taken on or after that date. Without the help of the written word, film and videotape cannot portray temporal dimensions with any precision. Consider a film clip showing an aircraft carrier at sea. One might be able to identify the ship as Soviet[1] or American, but there would be no way of telling where in the world the carrier was, where it was headed, or when the pictures were taken. It is only through language—words spoken over the pictures or reproduced in them—that the image of the aircraft carrier takes on meaning as a portrayal of a specific event.

1. Soviet belonging to the Soviet Union, the formerly socialist nation known today as Russia.

478 Types of Nonfiction: Essays, Articles, and Speeches

RESOURCES FOR:

- L1 Special-Needs Students
- L2 Below-Level Students (Tier 2)
- L3 On-Level Students (Tier 1)
- L4 Advanced Students (Tier 1)
- EL English Learners
- All All Students

Vocabulary/Fluency/Prior Knowledge

Unit 3 Resources

Name ______________________ Date ____________

"Single Room, Earth View" by Sally Ride

Reading Warm-up A

Read the following passage. Pay special attention to the underlined words. Then, read it again, and complete the activities. Use a separate sheet of paper for your written answers.

Space travel offers excitement and drama. It is a powerful experience for anyone who makes the voyage into outer space. Astronauts on the International Space Station offer another perspective on what it is like to live and work in space.

Astronaut Susan Helms spent 163 days on the International Space Station *Alpha*. She came to enjoy the quiet working environment in space. "I got very used to the peaceful life that we have up there without things like phone, mail, and cable TV and all the noise you get from daily life," she said.

The space station is a cooperative effort of the United States and other countries, including Russia, Canada, and Japan. The science facility has been inhabited continually since November 2000. There has been no break in crews since the first three-person team arrived.

The space station's circular orbit takes it around Earth sixteen times a day. Like the shuttle crews, *Alpha* astronauts study changing conditions on the planet. They make careful observations. To do so, they use expert data from scientific equipment. They add to it their own informal field notes from casual viewing. The knowledge they gain offers us information for understanding our world.

Alpha crews describe the heart-pounding sensations that come from getting a stars-eye look at Earth. They also worry about troubling developments. Astronaut Frank Culbertson piloted shuttle missions in the early 1990s. He took command of *ISS Alpha* in 2001. An immediate surprise was the change in what he could observe of Earth's face. Pollution now creates a far more cloudy view than in the decade before. "There is smoke and dust in wider-spread areas than we have seen before. . . ." he explained in an interview. He also recalled the magnificent light shows on Earth's surface at night. "It's quite amazing to see how many people actually live down there. . . ." he marveled.

1. Circle the word that is a clue to drama. Underline an adjective that can describe *drama* and explain why.
2. Circle the word that is a clue to environment. If you were concerned about the natural environment, how might you define *environment*?
3. Underline the phrase that is a clue to continually. Give a synonym for *continually*.
4. Underline words that are a clue to circular. Describe something in the classroom that is *circular*.
5. Underline two ways the passage says that astronauts make observations. Explain what *observations* are.
6. Circle the word that is a clue to informal. Explain how you would take *informal* notes.
7. Underline the clue that tells you sensations are something physical, and then explain why.
8. Explain why the lights on Earth are magnificent and what *magnificent* means here.

Unit 3 Resources: Types of Nonfiction

82

EL L1 L2 **Reading Warm-ups A and B,** pp. 64–65, 82–83

Also available for these selections:

EL L1 L2 **Vocabulary Warm-ups A and B,** pp. 62–63, 80–81

All **Writing About the Big Question,** pp. 66, 84

All **Vocabulary Builder,** pp. 69, 87

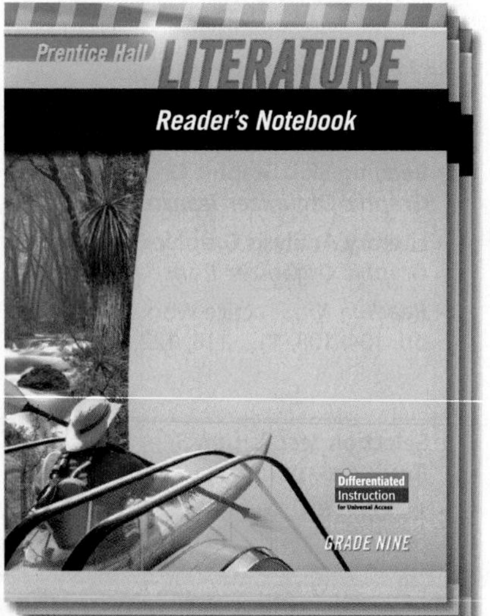

Reader's Notebooks

Pre- and postreading pages for both selections, as well as "Single Room, Earth View," appear in an interactive format in the *Reader's Notebooks.* Each *Notebook* is differentiated for a different group of learners. The selections in the Adapted and English Learner's versions are abridged.

L2 L3 ***Reader's Notebook***

L1 ***Reader's Notebook: Adapted Version***

EL ***Reader's Notebook: English Learner's Version***

EL ***Reader's Notebook: Spanish Version***

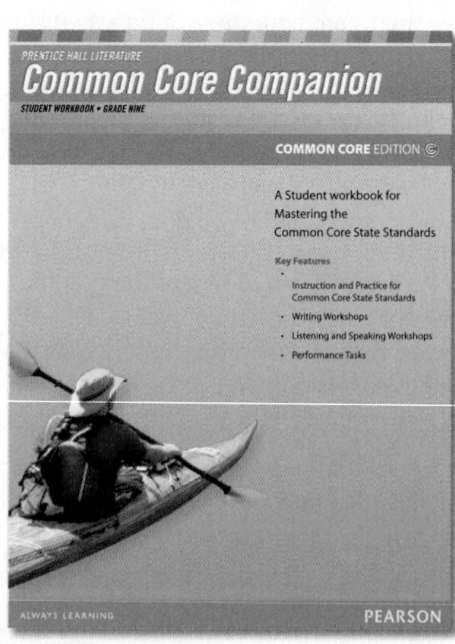

Common Core Companion

Additional instruction and practice for each Common Core State Standard

Selection Support

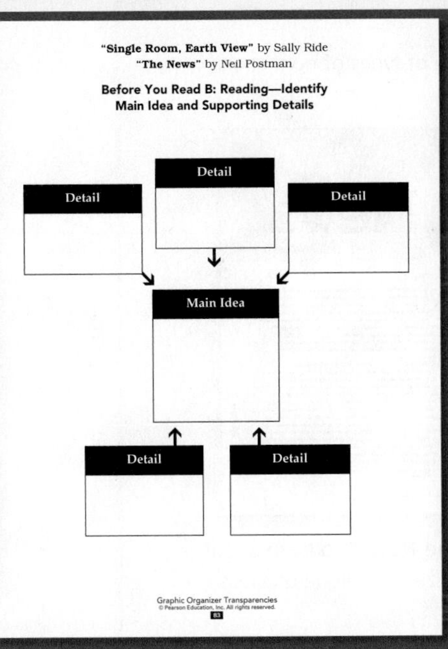

"Single Room, Earth View" by Sally Ride
"The News" by Neil Postman

Before You Read B: Reading—Identify Main Idea and Supporting Details

Graphic Organizer Transparencies
© Pearson Education, Inc. All rights reserved.
83

EL L3 **Reading: Graphic Organizer B,** p. 83

Also available for these selections:

EL L1 L2 **Literary Analysis: Graphic Organizer A,** pp. 84, 85 (partially filled in)

EL L1 L2 **Reading: Graphic Organizer A,** pp. 81, 82 (partially filled in)

EL L3 **Literary Analysis: Graphic Organizer B,** p. 86

Skills Development/Extension

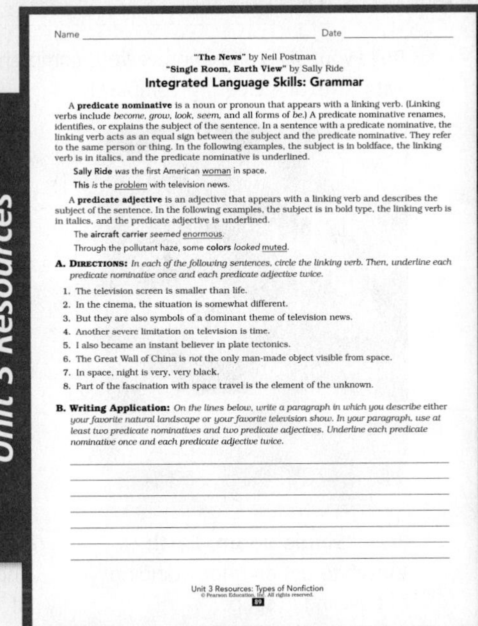

Name ____________ Date ____________

"The News" by Neil Postman
"Single Room, Earth View" by Sally Ride

Integrated Language Skills: Grammar

A **predicate nominative** is a noun or pronoun that appears with a linking verb. (Linking verbs include *become, grow, look, seem,* and all forms of *be.*) A predicate nominative renames, identifies, or explains the subject of the sentence. In a sentence with a predicate nominative, the linking verb acts as an equal sign between the subject and the predicate nominative. They refer to the same person or thing. In the following examples, the subject is in boldface, the linking verb is in italics, and the predicate nominative is underlined.

Sally Ride *was* the first American woman in space.

This *is* the problem with television news.

A **predicate adjective** is an adjective that appears with a linking verb and describes the subject of the sentence. In the following examples, the subject is in bold type, the linking verb is in italics, and the predicate adjective is underlined.

The **aircraft carrier** *seemed* enormous.

Through the pollutant haze, some **colors** *looked* muted.

A. Directions: *In each of the following sentences, circle the linking verb. Then, underline each predicate nominative once and each predicate adjective twice.*

1. The television screen is smaller than life.
2. In the cinema, the situation is somewhat different.
3. But they are also symbols of a dominant theme of television news.
4. Another severe limitation on television is time.
5. I also became an instant believer in plate tectonics.
6. The Great Wall of China is *not* the only man-made object visible from space.
7. In space, night is very, very black.
8. Part of the fascination with space travel is the element of the unknown.

B. Writing Application: *On the lines below, write a paragraph in which you describe* either *your favorite natural landscape* or *your favorite television show. In your paragraph, use at least two predicate nominatives and two predicate adjectives. Underline each predicate nominative once and each predicate adjective twice.*

Unit 3 Resources: Types of Nonfiction
© Pearson Education, Inc. All rights reserved.
89

EL L3 L4 **Grammar,** p. 89

Also available for these selections:

All **Literary Analysis: Expository Essay,** pp. 67, 85

All **Reading: Main Idea,** pp. 68, 86

L4 **Enrichment,** pp. 70, 88

EL L3 L4 **Support for Writing,** p. 90

L3 L4 **Support for Extend Your Learning,** p. 91

Assessment

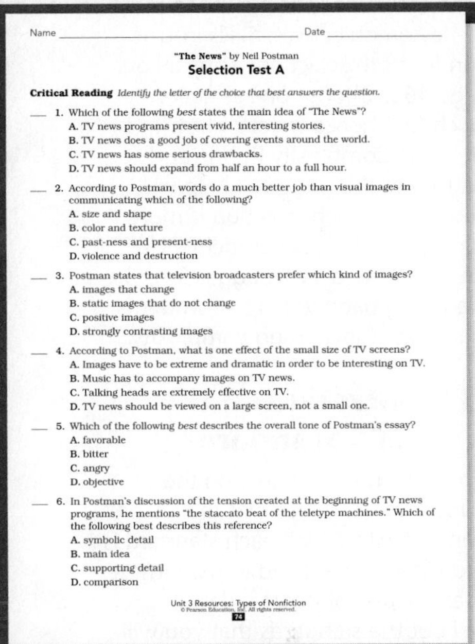

Name ____________ Date ____________

"The News" by Neil Postman

Selection Test A

Critical Reading *Identify the letter of the choice that best answers the question.*

___ 1. Which of the following *best* states the main idea of "The News"?
A. TV news programs present vivid, interesting stories.
B. TV news does a good job of covering events around the world.
C. TV news has some serious drawbacks.
D. TV news should expand from half an hour to a full hour.

___ 2. According to Postman, words do a much better job than visual images in communicating which of the following?
A. size and shape
B. color and texture
C. past-ness and present-ness
D. violence and destruction

___ 3. Postman states that television broadcasters prefer which kind of images?
A. images that change
B. static images that do not change
C. positive images
D. strongly contrasting images

___ 4. According to Postman, what is one effect of the small size of TV screens?
A. Images have to be extreme and dramatic in order to be interesting on TV.
B. Music has to accompany images on TV news.
C. Talking heads are extremely effective on TV.
D. TV news should be viewed on a large screen, not a small one.

___ 5. Which of the following *best* describes the overall tone of Postman's essay?
A. favorable
B. bitter
C. angry
D. objective

___ 6. In Postman's discussion of the tension created at the beginning of TV news programs, he mentions "the staccato beat of the teletype machines." Which of the following best describes this reference?
A. symbolic detail
B. main idea
C. supporting detail
D. comparison

Unit 3 Resources: Types of Nonfiction
© Pearson Education, Inc. All rights reserved.
74

EL L1 L2 **Selection Test A,** pp. 74–76, 95–97

Also available for these selections:

L3 L4 **Open-Book Test,** pp. 71–73, 92–94

EL L3 L4 **Selection Test B,** pp. 77–79, 98–100

PHLit Online!
www.PHLitOnline.com

Online Resources: All print materials are also available online.

- complete narrated selection text
- a thematically related video with writing prompt
- an interactive graphic organizer
- highlighting feature
- access to all student print resources, adapted to individual student needs
- Spanish and English summaries
- adapted selection translations in Spanish

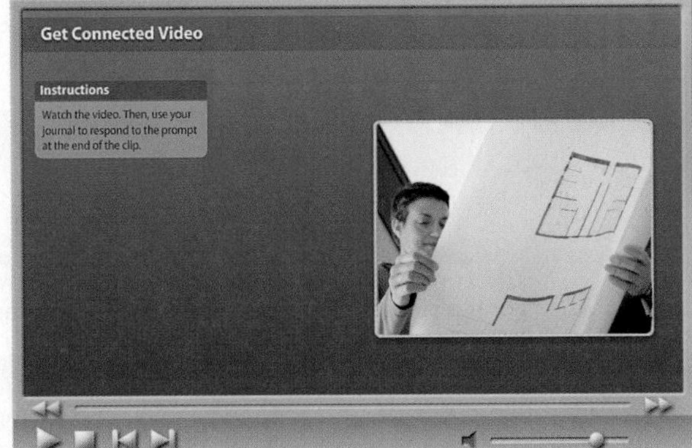

Get Connected! (thematic video with writing prompt)

Also available:

Background Video

All videos are available in Spanish.

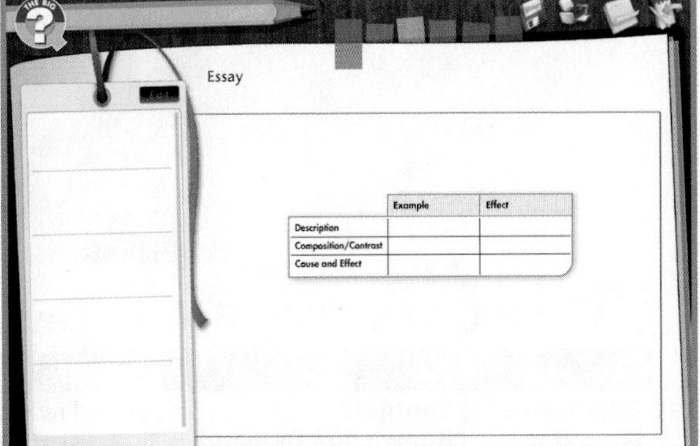

Writer's Journal (with graphics feature)

Also available:

Vocabulary Central (tools, activities, and songs for studying vocabulary)

❶ Leveled Texts

You may use either "Single Room, Earth View" or "The News" to meet the lesson objectives. Skills instruction for both selections appears on page 465. Choose one selection to teach (or choose to teach both). The Text Complexity Rubric at the bottom of this page will help you determine which selection is more appropriate for your students. Use the Reader and Task Suggestions on the facing page to help all students read text of increasing complexity.

❷ Introducing the CCS Standards

Introduce the standards on the student page. (Note that the lesson element with which each standard is addressed is identified in parentheses after the text of the standard.) Call out the standards that you will cover with the selections, explaining to students what each requires and how they will address it as they work through the selection you have chosen. Standards labeled "Spiral Review" are introduced in the Literary Analysis Workshop for this unit.

Before You Read

Single Room, Earth View • The News

❶ Leveled Texts

Build your skills and improve your comprehension of types of nonfiction with texts of increasing complexity.

Read **"Single Room, Earth View"** to get an understanding of traveling in space.

Read **"The News"** to learn about and analyze the unique qualities of TV news.

❷ Common Core State Standards

Meet these standards with either **"Single Room, Earth View"** (p. 468) or **"The News"** (p. 478).

Reading Informational Text

2. Determine a central idea of a text and analyze its development over the course of the text, including how it emerges and is shaped and refined by specific details; provide an objective summary of the text. *(Literary Analysis: Main Idea)*

3. Analyze how the author unfolds an analysis or series of ideas or events, including the order in which the points are made, how they are introduced and developed, and the connections that are drawn between them. *(Literary Analysis: Main Idea)*

Spiral Review: RI.9-10.4

Writing

2. Write informative/explanatory texts to examine and convey complex ideas, concepts, and information clearly and accurately through the effective selection, organization, and analysis of content. *(Writing: Public Service Announcement)*

7. Conduct short as well as more sustained research projects to answer a question or solve a problem; narrow or broaden the inquiry when appropriate; synthesize multiple sources on the subject, demonstrating understanding of the subject under investigation. *(Research and Technology: Journal Entries)*

8. Gather relevant information from multiple authoritative print and digital sources, using advanced searches effectively; assess the usefulness of each source in answering the research question; integrate information into the text selectively to maintain the flow of ideas. *(Research and Technology: Journal Entries)*

Speaking and Listening

4. Present information, findings, and supporting evidence clearly, concisely, and logically such that listeners can follow the line of reasoning and the organization, development, substance, and style are appropriate to purpose, audience, and task. *(Writing: Public Service Announcement)*

464 Types of Nonfiction: Essays, Articles, and Speeches

Text Complexity Rubric: Leveled Texts

Text complexity is determined by both qualitative and quantitative measures. For this reason, the quantitative measure of a more complex selection may be lower than that of a more accessible selection.

		✓ Single Room, Earth View	✓✓ The News
Qualitative Measures	**Context/ Knowledge Demands**	Personal reflections on viewing Earth from space 1 2 ③ 4 5	Commentary on contemporary television newscasts 1 2 ③ 4 5
	Structure/Language Conventionality and Clarity	On-level vocabulary; relatively short sentences 1 ② 3 4 5	Challenging vocabulary; complex sentence structure 1 2 3 ④ 5
	Levels of Meaning/ Purpose/Concept Level	Accessible concept (commentary on the beauty of Earth as seen from space) 1 2 ③ 4 5	Challenging concept (weighing the merits of broadcast journalism) 1 2 3 ④ 5
Quantitative Measures	**Text Length**	Word Count: 1,677	Word Count: 3,068
	Lexile	1320L	1170L
Overall Complexity		✓ **More accessible**	✓✓ **More complex**

❸ Literary Analysis: Expository Essay

An **expository essay** is a short piece of nonfiction that presents information, discusses ideas, or explains a process. An essay writer may use a variety of techniques to introduce and develop ideas and to draw connections between those ideas.

- **Description:** including imagery—language that appeals to the senses—and figurative language, such as simile and metaphor
- **Comparison and contrast:** showing similarities and differences between two or more ideas, people, events, or things
- **Cause and effect:** explaining the relationship between events, actions, or situations by showing how one can result from another

PHLit Online!
www.PHLitOnline.com

Hear It!
- Selection summary audio
- Selection audio

See It!
- Get Connected video
- Background video
- More about the author
- Vocabulary flashcards

Do It!
- Interactive journals
- Interactive graphic organizers
- Self-test
- Internet activity
- Grammar tutorial
- Interactive vocabulary games

❹ Reading Skill: Main Idea

The **main, or central, idea** is the key message, insight, or opinion in a work of nonfiction. The author may state the central idea explicitly, or merely suggest it. The **supporting details** are the pieces of evidence a writer uses to prove his or her point. **Reread** to help you **identify the main idea and supporting details** in a work. As you read, follow these steps:

- Note whether the author states the central idea directly. If not, note key details to decide what the main idea might be.
- If a detail does not seem to support that main idea, reread the passage to be sure that you have not misinterpreted it.
- If necessary, revise your assumptions about the main idea.

❺ Using the Strategy: Cluster Diagram

Record details and main ideas on a cluster diagram like this one.

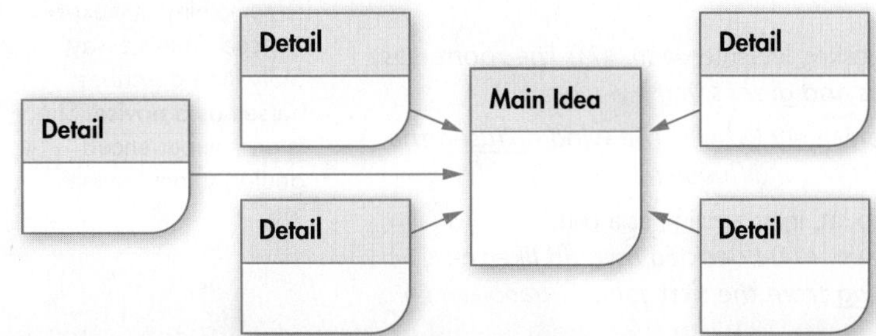

PRETEACH

❸ Literary Analysis

Expository Essay

1. Introduce the skill, using instruction on the student page.
2. Tell students that they will practice identifying aspects of expository essays as they read.

Think Aloud: Model the Skill

Model the skill of identifying expository techniques. Say to students:

Let's say I'm reading an article that explains how to stretch before exercising. The writer uses several expository techniques. First, she explains the cause-effect link between stretching and safe exercise. Then, she uses comparison and contrast to show that people who stretch get more benefits from exercise than people who don't stretch. Also, she vividly describes each step of stretching so that I can do it on my own.

❹ Reading Skill

Main Idea

1. Introduce the skill, using instruction on the student page.
2. Tell students that they will practice identifying the main idea and supporting details as they read.

❺ Using the Strategy

Give students a copy of either **Reading Skill Graphic Organizer A** or **B** (***Graphic Organizer Transparencies,*** pp. 81–83) to record main ideas and significant details as they read. Use the examples in **Reading Skill Graphic Organizer A,** which is partially filled in, to model the process of completing the organizer.

Text Complexity: Reader and Task Suggestions

✓ Single Room, Earth View		✓✓ The News	
Preparing to Read the Text	**Leveled Tasks**	**Preparing to Read the Text**	**Leveled Tasks**
• Using the Background note on TE p. 467, discuss the author's experience as an astronaut. Then, discuss early space travel and space vehicles. • Guide a discussion of what Earth looks like from space. • Guide students to use Multidraft Reading strategies (TE p. 467).	*Knowledge Demands* If students will have difficulty with knowledge demands, have them first read and make notes about what Sally Ride sees. Then, have them reread and take notes about why some of these things astonish her. *Evaluating* If students will not have difficulty with knowledge demands, have them read to note Ride's purpose in writing and whether she did or did not accomplish her purpose.	• Refer to the Background note on TE p. 477, and discuss the role of television news in reporting news. • Review strategies for clarifying the meaning of long and complex sentence structures. • Guide students to use Multidraft Reading strategies (TE p. 477).	*Structure/Language* If students will have difficulty with language, have them read first to identify diction and sentences that they find difficult. Have them reread to note pros and cons of TV news. *Evaluating* If students will not have difficulty with language, have them rate the persuasiveness of Postman's arguments and essay.

PRETEACH

❶ Writing About the Big Question

1. Read the assignment with the class.
2. Ask students how scientific explorations contribute to their knowledge and understanding of the universe.
3. Have students complete the sentence starters. Review responses as a class. (**Possible response:** Looking at Earth from space may change how we comprehend the world because we see how we fit into the entire solar system. Analyzing familiar concepts from a different perspective can help us understand them better because we approach them with a different point of view.)
4. Remind students that their answers will help them think about the Big Question, "Is knowledge the same as understanding?"

While You Read

Tell students to think about the astronauts and what it must have been like for them to travel in space.

❷ Vocabulary

1. Have students preview the selection vocabulary.
2. For each word, have students say the word aloud.
3. Then, use the word in a sentence that defines the word.
4. Finally, repeat your definitional sentence or a similar sentence with the word missing and have the class "fill in the blank" chorally. Here are some examples:

   Articulate means able to express ideas clearly. A.J. spoke clearly about his goals as student body president, so we knew that he was [students say "articulate"].

   A novice is someone who is new to a task. A runner competing in his first race is a [students say "novice"].

❸ Word Study

1. Introduce the skill, using the instruction in the box.
2. Ask students for another *-nov-* word that means "new; recent." (**Answer:** *novel*)

Making Connections | Single Room, Earth View

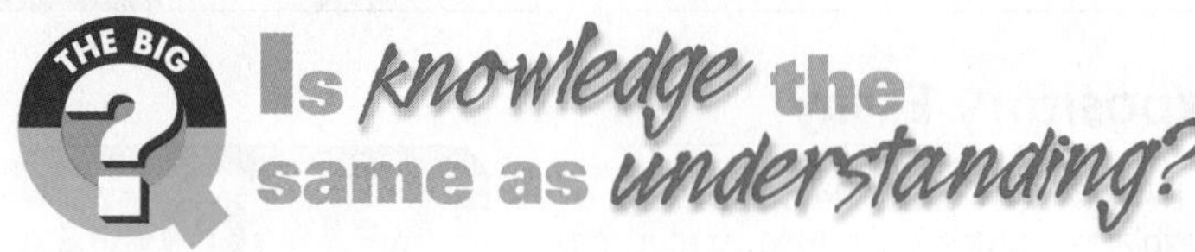

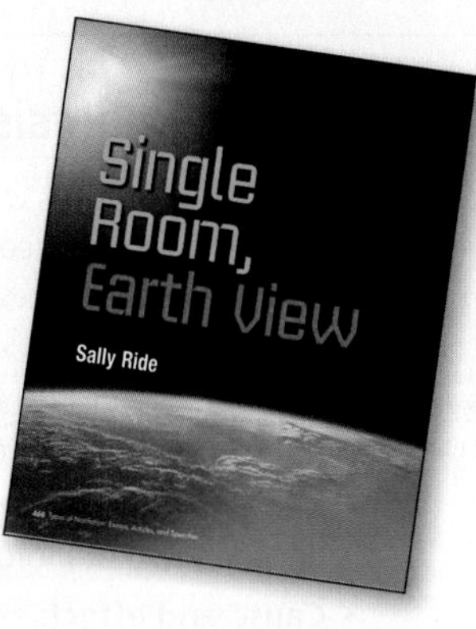

❶ Writing About the Big Question

In "Single Room, Earth View," astronaut Sally Ride explains what it is like to see Earth from the space shuttle. Use these sentence starters to develop your ideas about the Big Question.

Looking at Earth from space may change how we **comprehend** the world because _______________.

Analyzing familiar **concepts** from a different perspective can help us understand them better because _______________.

While You Read Look for a way in which the writer's knowledge grows into understanding while traveling in space for the first time.

❷ Vocabulary

Read each word and its definition. Decide whether you know the word well, know it a little bit, or do not know it at all. After you read, see how your knowledge of each word has increased.

- **articulate** (är tik′ yo͞o lit) *adj.* able to express oneself clearly and easily (p. 469) ***The candidate is an articulate public speaker.*** *articulate v. articulately adv. articulation n.*
- **surreal** (sər rē′ əl) *adj.* strange, like something from a dream (p. 470) ***The party was a surreal mixture of men in business suits and punk rockers.*** *surrealism n.*
- **novice** (näv′ is) *adj.* new to an activity; inexperienced (p. 470) ***For a novice chess player, she shows great patience and maturity.*** *nova n. novitiate n.*
- **muted** (myo͞ot′ əd) *adj.* weaker; less intense (p. 471) ***The room was furnished in muted blues and greens.*** *mute v. mute n.*
- **diffused** (di fyo͞ozd′) *v.* spread out (p. 473) ***The wind diffused the confetti over the field.*** *diffuse v. diffusion n.*
- **extrapolating** (ek strap′ ə lāt′ iŋ) *v.* arriving at a conclusion by inferring from known facts (p. 474) ***I decided I would like the whole CD by extrapolating from the first song.*** *extrapolation n.*

Word Study

The **Latin root *-nov-*** means "new" or "recent."

Someone who is new to something is inexperienced. In this essay, Sally Ride describes herself as a **novice.** She is an inexperienced geologist, new to the job.

Vocabulary Development

Vocabulary Knowledge Rating

Create a **Vocabulary Knowledge Rating Chart** ***(Professional Development Guidebook,*** p. 33) for this selection. Include the selection vocabulary and the Big Question words that appear in the Writing About the Big Question sentence starters on this page. (The Big Question vocabulary is introduced on pp. 424–425.)

Give students a copy of the chart. Read the words aloud, and have students mark their rating in the Before Reading column. Urge them to be alert to these words as they read and discuss the selection.

Tally how many students think they know a word to gauge how much instruction to provide. As students read and discuss the selection, point out the words and their context.

Vocabulary Central, featuring tools, activities, and songs for studying vocabulary, is available at **www.PHLitOnline.com.**

Meet Sally Ride

(b. 1957)

Author of Single Room, Earth View

Although best known as an astronaut, Sally Ride was also a talented athlete in her youth. She was a ranked player on the junior tennis circuit and considered turning professional before deciding to go to college instead.

The Right Stuff In 1978, Ride read a newspaper advertisement about NASA's search for astronauts. After extensive testing to be sure she had "the right stuff," NASA chose her as one of six women and twenty-five men accepted from among 8,000 applicants. Five years later, in 1983, she took her historic flight. Ride retired from NASA in 1987 and currently teaches physics at the University of California.

4

BACKGROUND FOR THE ESSAY

First American Woman in Space

On June 18, 1983, when she worked as a flight engineer and mission specialist aboard the shuttle *Challenger,* Sally Ride became the first American woman in space. Her historic mission allowed her to experience what she recounts in "Single Room, Earth View."

Did You Know?

Sally Ride holds four degrees from Stanford University, including a Master's and a Doctorate.

Daily Bellringer

For each class during which you will teach this selection, have students complete one of the five Sentence Modeling activities for Week 14 in the *Daily Bellringer Activities* booklet.

4 Background

First American Woman in Space

Sally Ride's first mission in space aboard the *Challenger* lasted six days. During that time she helped deploy several space satellites. She embarked on another space mission in October 1984. During that mission her assignment was to make scientific observations of Earth.

Multidraft Reading

This icon ● marks natural pauses in the selection. To assist struggling readers and to deepen reading for all, assign the text in "chunks," following the icons, and apply multidraft reading protocols. For each reading, have students set the purpose indicated:

- **First reading**—identifying key ideas and details and answering any Reading Checks.
- **Second reading**—analyzing craft and structure and responding to the side-column prompts.
- **Third reading**—integrating knowledge and ideas, connecting to other texts and the world, and answering the end-of-selection questions.

For more guidance, refer to the ***Classroom Strategies and Teaching Routines*** card on multidraft reading.

PHLit Online!

For more about the author, practice with the selection vocabulary, or more background, go online at **www.PHLitOnline.com.**

Differentiated Instruction Additional Instruction

EL Extended Support—English Learners

Have students complete the **Reading and Vocabulary Warm-ups, *Unit 3 Resources,*** pp. 80–83 before they read. Assign the prereading pages and the adapted selection in the ***Reader's Notebook: English Learner's Version.*** Then, have students listen to portions of the selection on the ***Hear It!* Audio CD.**

L1 L2 Extended Support—Struggling Readers

Have students complete the **Reading and Vocabulary Warm-ups, *Unit 3 Resources,*** pp. 80–83 before they read. Assign the prereading pages and the adapted selection in the ***Reader's Notebook: Adapted Version.*** Then, have students listen to portions of the selection on the ***Hear It!* Audio CD** (adapted text).

Extended Support—Reluctant Readers

To build motivation and engagement, before assigning the selection, have students read "One Book at a Time," a thematically related selection in ***Reality Central.*** Then, use the questions at the conclusion of the related selection to guide discussion.

❶ Activating Prior Knowledge

1. Form students into small groups. Give them a copy of a **KWL Chart** (see ***Professional Development Guidebook***, p. 75) with the topic identified as "Space Shuttle Travel."
2. Ask students to brainstorm together to complete the first two columns. In the Know column, they can write what they know or what they learned during the Making Connections activity. In the Want to Know column, they should write questions they have about traveling in a space shuttle.

Concept Connector

Students will assess what they have learned after completing "Single Room, Earth View."

Whole-Class Activity

This essay is about seeing the world from a new point of view. In a class discussion, have students compare the views Ride describes to their own views of geographical features such as oceans, rivers, and islands. When students go to the beach, what does the ocean look like to them? When they stand on a busy sidewalk, what does the city look like? How do these things look to Ride from 200 miles up?

❷ About the Selection

In "Single Room, Earth View," astronaut Sally Ride takes on the difficult task of describing Earth from the perspective of the space shuttle, 200 miles above the planet. She points out landmarks on Earth from a new perspective and shows how that perspective changes a space traveler's feelings about Earth.

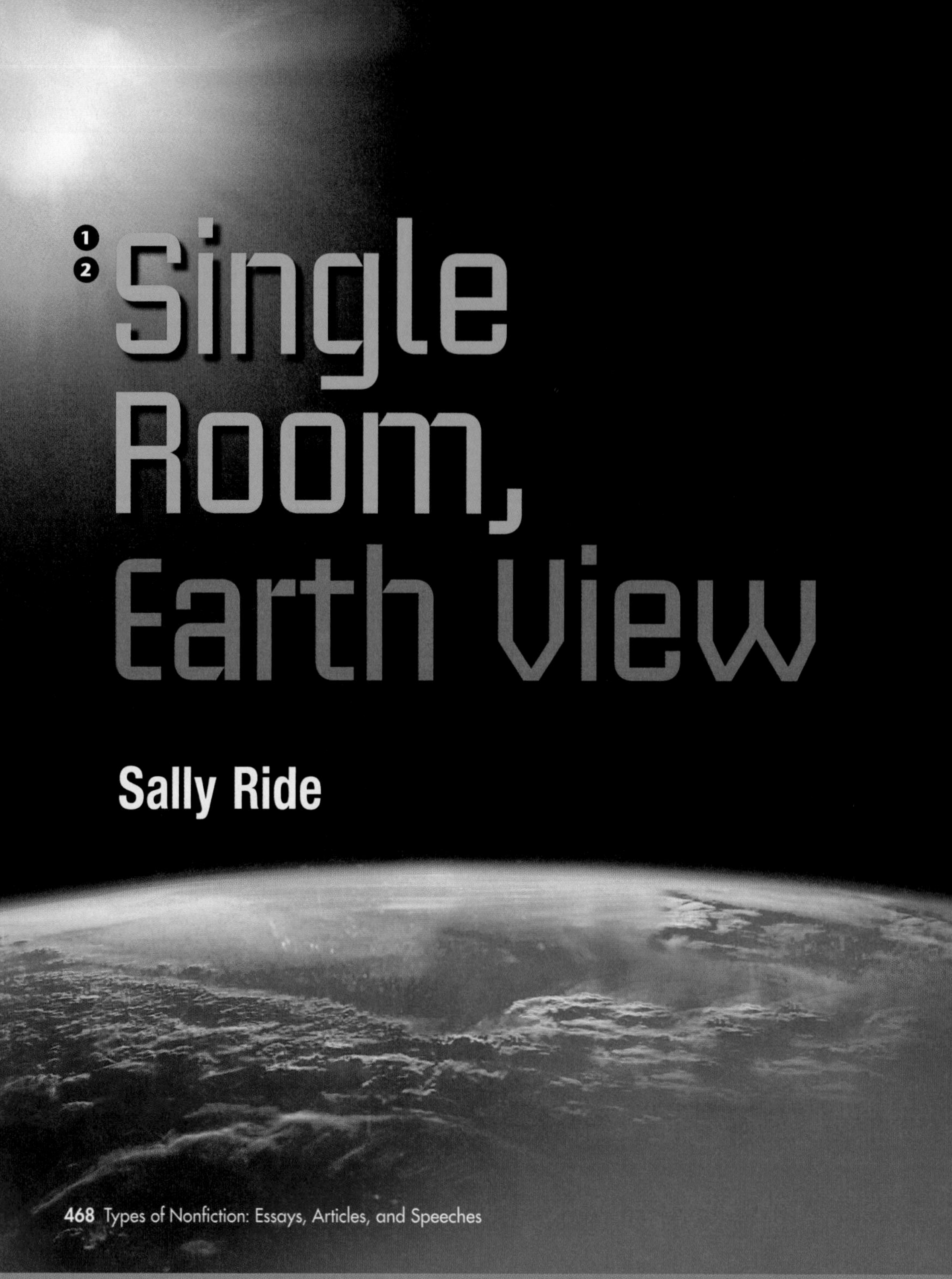

❶ ❷

Single Room, Earth View

Sally Ride

Vocabulary Development

Ⓒ CCSS Language 6

Thematic Vocabulary: The Big Question

As students are discussing "Single Room, Earth View," encourage them to use the thematic vocabulary presented in Introducing the Big Question, pp. 424–425. You might encourage them with sentence starters like these:

1. Sally Ride's essay would be an effective source for conducting *research* on . . .
2. When Ride describes what Earth looks like from the space shuttle, she uses *sensory* details such as . . .
3. Like other primary *sources,* Ride's essay provides unique insight into its topic because . . .
4. According to Ride, Earth-bound humans cannot access the *feeling* of . . .

Everyone I've met has a glittering, if vague, mental image of space travel. And naturally enough, people want to hear about it from an astronaut: "How did it feel . . . ?" "What did it look like . . . ?" "Were you scared?" Sometimes, the questions come from reporters, their pens poised and their tape recorders silently reeling in the words; sometimes, it's wide-eyed, ten-year-old girls who want answers. I find a way to answer all of them, but it's not easy.

Imagine trying to describe an airplane ride to someone who has never flown. An **articulate** traveler could describe the sights but would find it much harder to explain the difference in perspective provided by the new view from a greater distance, along with the feelings, impressions, and insights that go with that new perspective. And the difference is enormous: Spaceflight moves the traveler another giant step farther away. Eight and one-half thunderous minutes after launch, an astronaut is orbiting high above the Earth, suddenly able to watch typhoons form, volcanoes smolder, and meteors streak through the atmosphere below.

3 ◀ **Critical Viewing**
Based on this photograph, how might travel in the space shuttle defy description? **[Connect]**

Vocabulary
articulate (är tik´ yo͞o lit) *adj.* able to express oneself clearly and easily

3 Critical Viewing

Possible response: This image shows a view of Earth that can be viewed only from space. This extraordinary image—and the experience of witnessing it—cannot be compared to the Earth-bound experiences of ordinary life.

PHLit Online!

This selection is available in interactive format in the **Enriched Online Student Edition, www.PHLitOnline.com,** which includes a thematically related video with writing prompt and an interactive graphic organizer.

Fluency

Distribute copies of page 469, and pair students. Have partners take turns reading paragraphs aloud. While one partner reads, the other should mark words with which the student reading has difficulty. Circulate to monitor the fluency of students' reading. Collect the marked-up copies of the page, and review difficult words and passages with the class. Look for these problem spots:

- If students have difficulty with the word *perspective,* point out that the word has a common prefix, *per-,* and a common suffix, *-ive.* Have students cover up parts of the word with their thumbs to sound out each syllable. Then, explain that *perspective* means "point of view" or "way of looking."
- If students have difficulty with the word *orbiting,* practice oral cloze with the sentence. First, read the sentence with the word *orbiting* omitted. Then, reread the sentence and ask students to "fill in the blank" with the word that makes the most sense.

4 Reading Skill
Main Idea

1. Have students read the bracketed text.
2. **Ask** students why Ride says that the view of the Hawaiian Islands from space is surreal.

   Answer: It looks just like a page from an atlas.
3. Then, **ask** the Reading Skill question: Which details support Ride's point about the difficulties of describing space travel?

   Answer: Details include the speed at which the shuttle orbits Earth; if she turned away for a moment, she could miss an entire landmass.

5  Connecting to the Big Question

1. Have a volunteer read aloud the bracketed text. **Ask:** What is Ride describing in this passage?

   Answer: She is describing geological features of Earth, such as mountains, volcanoes, rivers, and landmasses.
2. **Ask:** How does this passage illustrate how Ride's knowledge grows into understanding as she travels in space for the first time?

   Answer: As Ride looks at familiar geological features from a completely new perspective, she begins to understand scientific explanations of how those features form and move. Her new perspective "makes theory come alive."
3. **Ask:** What does Ride's experience suggest about the relationship between knowledge and understanding?

   Possible response: It takes personal experience—and sometimes a new perspective—for knowledge to develop into true understanding.

While flying over the Hawaiian Islands, several astronauts have marveled that the islands look just like they do on a map. When people first hear that, they wonder what should be so surprising about Hawaii looking the way it does in the atlas. Yet, to the astronauts it is an absolutely startling sensation: The islands really *do* look as if that part of the world has been carpeted with a big page torn out of Rand-McNally, and all we can do is try to convey the **surreal** quality of that scene.

Vocabulary
surreal (sər rē′ əl) *adj.* strange, like something from a dream

In orbit, racing along at five miles per second, the space shuttle circles the Earth once every 90 minutes. I found that at this speed, unless I kept my nose pressed to the window, it was almost impossible to keep track of where we were at any given moment—the world below simply changes too fast. If I turned my concentration away for too long, even just to change film in a camera, I could miss an entire land mass. It's embarrassing to float up to a window, glance outside, and then have to ask a crewmate, "What continent is this?"

Reading Skill
Main Idea
Which details support Ride's point about the difficulties of describing space travel?

We could see smoke rising from fires that dotted the entire east coast of Africa, and in the same orbit only moments later, ice floes jostling for position in the Antarctic. We could see the Ganges River dumping its murky, sediment-laden water into the Indian Ocean and watch ominous hurricane clouds expanding and rising like biscuits in the oven of the Caribbean.

Mountain ranges, volcanoes, and river deltas appeared in salt-and-flour relief, all leading me to assume the role of a **novice** geologist. In such moments, it was easy to imagine the dynamic upheavals that created jutting mountain ranges and the internal wrenchings that created rifts and seas. I also became an instant believer in plate tectonics; India really *is* crashing into Asia, and Saudi Arabia and Egypt really *are* pulling apart, making the Red Sea wider. Even though their respective motion is really no more than mere inches a year, the view from overhead makes theory come alive.

Vocabulary
novice (näv′ is) *adj.* new to an activity; inexperienced

Spectacular as the view is from 200 miles up, the Earth is not the awe-inspiring "blue marble" made famous by the photos from the moon. From space shuttle height, we can't see the entire globe at a glance, but we can look down the entire boot of Italy, or up the East Coast of the United

PROFESSIONAL DEVELOPMENT **Arnetha Ball**

Apply the Strategy

Teacher's use of questioning strategies can help students formulate questions that support their own learning. To aid students in understanding "Single Room, Earth View," use a *SQ4R (Survey, Question, Read, Reflect, Recite, Review)* strategy.

First, ask students to survey the text, looking for headings or charts with italic, underlined, or bold print. Have students formulate questions about the information they found.

For example, *What does Nova Scotia look like from orbit at night?* Have students read the selection, answering their questions and reflecting on what they read. Next, have students recite their answers. Finally, ask students to review the text for any remaining questions, summarizing what they've learned.

For more of Arnetha Ball's strategies, see her Professional Development essay, pp. 424c–424d.

States from Cape Hatteras to Cape Cod. The panoramic view inspires an appreciation for the scale of some of nature's phenomena. One day, as I scanned the sandy expanse of Northern Africa, I couldn't find any of the familiar landmarks—colorful outcroppings of rock in Chad, irrigated patches of the Sahara. Then I realized they were obscured by a huge dust storm, a cloud of sand that enveloped the continent from Morocco to the Sudan.

Since the space shuttle flies fairly low (at least by orbital standards; it's more than 22,000 miles lower than a typical TV satellite), we can make out both natural and manmade features in surprising detail. Familiar geographical features like San Francisco Bay, Long Island, and Lake Michigan are easy to recognize, as are many cities, bridges, and airports. The Great Wall of China is not the only man-made object visible from space.

The signatures of civilization are usually seen in straight lines (bridges or runways) or sharp delineations (abrupt transitions from desert to irrigated land, as in California's Imperial Valley). A modern city like New York doesn't leap from the canvas of its surroundings, but its straight piers and concrete runways catch the eye—and around them, the city materializes. I found Salina, Kansas (and pleased my in-laws, who live there) by spotting its long runway amid the wheat fields near the city. Over Florida, I could see the launch pad where we had begun our trip, and the landing strip, where we would eventually land.

6 Some of civilization's more unfortunate effects on the environment are also evident from orbit. Oil slicks glisten on the surface of the Persian Gulf, patches of pollution-damaged trees dot the forests of central Europe. Some cities look out of focus, and their colors **muted**, when viewed through a pollutant haze. Not surprisingly, the effects are more noticeable now than they were a decade ago. An astronaut who has flown in both Skylab and the space shuttle reported that the horizon didn't seem quite as sharp, or the colors quite as bright, in 1983 as they had in 1973.

Of course, informal observations by individual astronauts are one thing, but more precise measurements are continually being made from space: The space shuttle has carried infrared film to document damage to citrus trees in Florida and in rain forests along the Amazon. It has carried even more sophisticated sensors in the payload bay. Here is one example: sensors used to measure atmospheric carbon monoxide levels, allowing scientists to study the environmental effects of city emissions and land-clearing fires.

Most of the Earth's surface is covered with water, and at first glance it all looks the same: blue. But with the right lighting conditions and a couple of orbits of practice, it's possible to make

Spiral Review

Word Choice and Tone Do words and phrases such as *sharp delineations, irrigated land,* and *materializes* give this paragraph a formal or informal tone? Explain.

Literary Analysis
Expository Essay
What point about environmental change does Ride support with her descriptions in this paragraph?

Vocabulary
muted (myo͞ot´ əd) *adj.* weaker; less intense

7 
What kinds of structures reveal the "signatures of civilization" from space?

Spiral Review
Word Choice and Tone

1. Remind students that they studied the concepts of word choice and tone in the Unit 3 Literary Analysis workshop (pp. 426–439).
2. Then, **ask** students the Spiral Review question.

   Possible response: The sophisticated language gives the writing a formal tone and the word choice also creates a more precise picture.

6 Literary Analysis
Expository Essay

1. Have students read the bracketed passage. **Ask** them what Ride is describing in this paragraph.

   Answer: She is describing environmental damage on Earth that she sees from the space shuttle.
2. **Ask** students to identify how Ride uses the strategy of compare and contrast to develop her point in these paragraphs.

   Answer: She compares the differences in how Earth looked in 1973 and 1983.
3. **Ask** the Literary Analysis question: What point about environmental change does Ride support with her descriptions in this paragraph?

   Answer: She makes the point that civilization has had damaging effects on the environment.

Monitor Progress:

1. **Ask** students to explain what the author is trying to do in this essay.

   Answer: She is presenting information.
2. **Ask** students what techniques the author uses in this essay.

   Answer: She uses description, comparison and contrast, and cause and effect.

7 Reading Check

Answer: Bridges, piers, fields, launch pads, and runways reveal the "signatures of civilization" from space.

Differentiated Instruction for Universal Access

EL Pronunciation for English Learners
Some students may pronounce the short *o* sound in words such as *cop* with a short *u* sound as in *cup*. Recite the following words and have students repeat after you, stressing the vowel sounds: *long, lung; off, of.* Then, write the words on the board. Finally, ask volunteers to use each word in a sentence.

Enrichment for Gifted/Talented Students
Sally Ride was able to see the "entire boot of Italy" from the space shuttle. Ask students to characterize a single geographic feature of their region in a similar way. First, have students develop a simile or metaphor that describes the feature verbally. Then, ask students to create a painting or a sketch that shows how the feature might appear when viewed from an orbiting space shuttle.

❽ Literary Analysis
Expository Essay

1. **Ask** students what characteristics of the ocean Ride describes in this paragraph.

   Answer: She describes circular and spiral eddies and standing waves.

2. **Ask** students the Literary Analysis question: What relationship between space travel and ocean study does Ride discuss in this passage?

   Answer: She explains how viewing the ocean from space reveals previously undiscovered characteristics that help scientists understand the energy balance in the oceans.

❾ Literature in Context

Science Connection A German meteorologist named Alfred Wegener proposed the theory of continental drift in 1912. He suggested that the shape and fit of the continents and the distribution of similar fossils and rock layers around the planet supported his theory. Based on his observations, Wegener proposed that all of today's modern continents were once part of a supercontinent called Pangaea, or "All-earth." As Earth's rock plates moved millions of years ago, Pangaea broke apart, and the modern continents took shape.

Connect to the Literature Have students review Ride's description of mountain ranges, volcanoes, and river deltas on p. 470. Then, **ask** the Connect to the Literature question: The theories of plate tectonics and continental drift state that the Earth's crust is made of shifting "plates." What evidence for these theories might an astronaut see from space?

Possible responses: Students might suggest that the continents seem to fit together like a jigsaw puzzle. Students may note that Ride says that she could see that "India is crashing into Asia and Saudi Arabia and Egypt are pulling apart, making the Red Sea wider," which clarified for her the theory of plate tectonics.

out the intricate patterns in the oceans—eddies and spirals become visible because of the subtle differences in water color or reflectivity.

❽ Observations and photographs by astronauts have contributed significantly to the understanding of ocean dynamics, and some of the more intriguing discoveries prompted the National Aeronautics and Space Administration to fly an oceanographic observer for the express purpose of studying the ocean from orbit. Scientists' understanding of the energy balance in the oceans has increased significantly as a result of the discoveries of circular and spiral eddies tens of kilometers in diameter, of standing waves hundreds of kilometers long, and of spiral eddies that sometimes trail into one another for thousands of kilometers. If a scientist wants to study features on this scale, it's much easier from an orbiting vehicle than from the vantage point of a boat.

Literary Analysis
Expository Essay
What relationship between space travel and ocean study does Ride discuss in this passage?

❾ Believe it or not, an astronaut can also see the wakes of large ships and the contrails of airplanes. The sun angle has to be just right, but when the lighting conditions are perfect, you can follow otherwise invisible oil tankers on the Persian Gulf and trace major shipping lanes through the Mediterranean Sea. Similarly, when atmospheric conditions allow contrail formation, the thousand-mile-long condensation trails let astronauts trace the major air routes across the northern Pacific Ocean.

LITERATURE IN CONTEXT

Science Connection

The Changing Planet: Continental Drift

350 million years ago
The continents were once part of a massive land mass.

54.8 to 33.7 million years ago
This land mass, named Pangea, started drifting apart 300 hundred million years ago.

38 to 1.6 million years ago
The continents are still moving a few inches farther apart each year.

▼ The southern hemisphere "drifting" through time

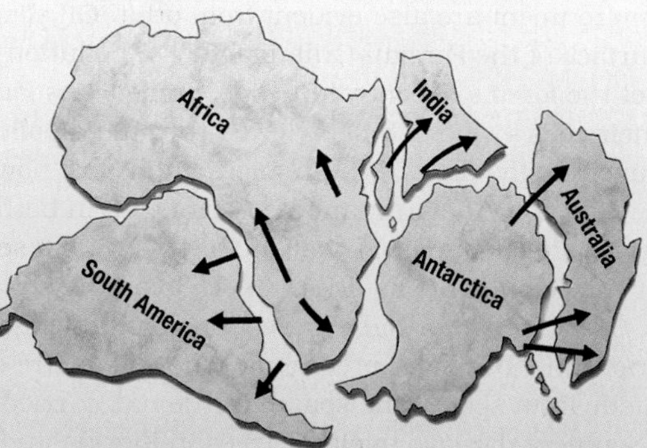

The Evidence:
Plants and animals in North America and Europe are very similar. Fossils from southern continents show that dinosaurs once roamed the entire area. In Africa and South America, 200 million-year-old matching lava has been found.

Connect to the Literature

The theories of plate tectonics and continental drift state that the Earth's crust is made of shifting "plates." What evidence for these theories might an astronaut see from space?

Vocabulary Development

Vocabulary Knowledge Rating

When students have completed reading and discussing "Single Room, Earth View," have them take out their **Vocabulary Knowledge Rating Chart** for this selection. Read the words aloud once more and have students rate their knowledge of the words again in the After Reading column. Clarify any words that are still problematic. Have students write their own definition and example or sentence in the appropriate column. Then, have students complete the Vocabulary Practice activities at the end of the selection. Encourage students to use the words in further discussion and written work about this selection. Remind them that they will be accountable for these words on the **Selection Test,** ***Unit 3 Resources,*** pp. 95–97 or 98–100.

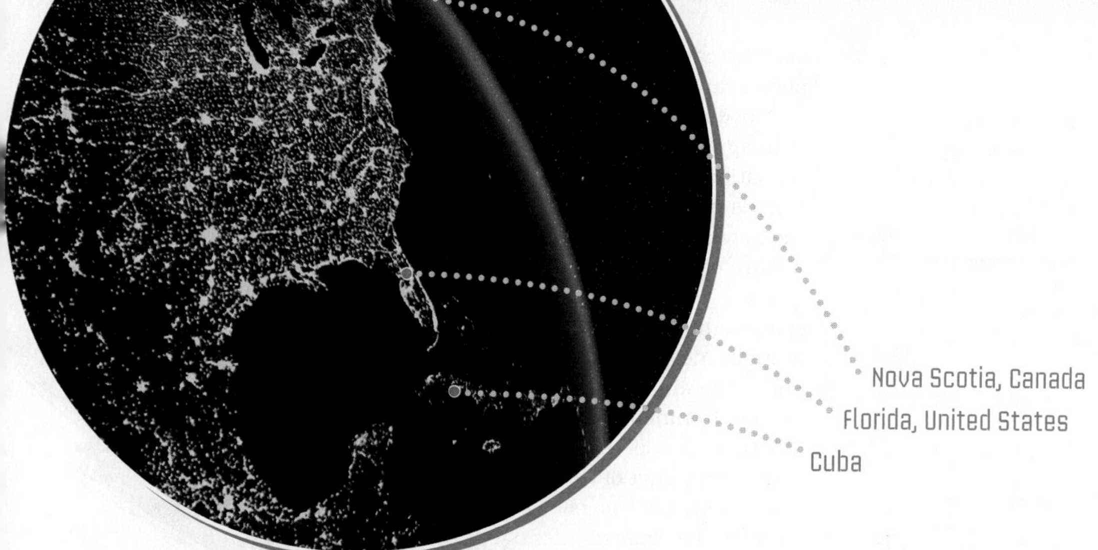

Part of every orbit takes us to the dark side of the planet. In space, night is very, very black—but that doesn't mean there's nothing to look at. The lights of cities sparkle; on nights when there was no moon, it was difficult for me to tell the Earth from the sky—the twinkling lights could be stars or they could be small cities. On one nighttime pass from Cuba to Nova Scotia, the entire East Coast of the United States appeared in twinkling outline.

When the moon is full, it casts an eerie light on the Earth. In its light, we see ghostly clouds and bright reflections on the water. One night, the Mississippi River flashed into view, and because of our viewing angle and orbital path, the reflected moonlight seemed to flow downstream—as if Huck Finn had tied a candle to his raft.

Of all the sights from orbit, the most spectacular may be the magnificent displays of lightning that ignite the clouds at night. On Earth, we see lightning from below the clouds; in orbit, we see it from above. Bolts of lightning are **diffused** by the clouds into bursting balls of light. Sometimes, when a storm extends hundreds of miles, it looks like a transcontinental brigade is tossing fireworks from cloud to cloud.

As the shuttle races the sun around the Earth, we pass from day to night and back again during a single orbit—hurtling into darkness, then bursting into daylight. The sun's appearance unleashes spectacular blue and orange bands along the horizon, a clockwork miracle that astronauts witness every 90 minutes. But I really can't describe a sunrise in orbit. The drama set against the black backdrop of space and the magic of the materializing colors

On one nighttime pass from Cuba to Nova Scotia, the entire East Coast of the United States appeared in twinkling outline.

Vocabulary
diffused (di fyo͞ozd′)
v. spread out

10 Reading Check

What can astronauts see from space when the light is right?

10 Reading Check

Answer: When the light is right, astronauts can see ghostly clouds and bright reflections on the water. Sometimes they can see reflected moonlight flowing down a river like a candle.

Concept Connector

KWL Chart

Have students complete the last column of their **KWL Charts.** Ask them to evaluate what they learned in relation to the questions they had before reading.

Writing About the Big Question

Have students compare their responses to the sentence starter they completed before reading the essay with their ideas afterwards. Ask them to explain whether their thoughts have changed.

Reading Skill Graphic Organizer

Ask students to review the graphic organizers they completed to identify the main idea and supporting details while reading. Show them **Reading Skill Graphic Organizer A** (***Graphic Organizer Transparencies,*** p. 81) as an example. Then, have students share the graphic organizers they completed and the main ideas and supporting details they identified.

ASSESS

Answers

Critical Thinking

Before students respond, you may wish to have them write a brief objective summary of the selection. As they answer the questions below, remind them to support their answers with evidence from the text.

1. (a) Ride observed ice floes, continents, mountain ranges, volcanoes, river deltas, islands, and oceans. (b) Ride felt that she could almost see geological forces working the way the theories say they work.
2. (a) Ride saw damage to the environment and the haze that obscures most big cities. (b) The dimming of colors reflects an additional ten years of pollution.
3. **Possible response:** Students may say that the essay has given them a new sense of the unity and fragility of the planet Earth.
4. **Possible response:** Yes, Ride's understanding of Earth changes because she could see so much more from space than she can see on land. She gained a renewed appreciation of the world, its geographical features, its geological processes, and its environment.

can't be captured in an astronomer's equations or an astronaut's photographs.

Vocabulary
extrapolating
(ek strap´ ə lāt´ iŋ)
v. arriving at a conclusion by inferring from known facts

I once heard someone (not an astronaut) suggest that it's possible to imagine what spaceflight is like by simply extrapolating from the sensations you experience on an airplane. All you have to do, he said, is mentally raise the airplane 200 miles, mentally eliminate the air noise and the turbulence, and you get an accurate mental picture of a trip in the space shuttle.

Part of the fascination with space travel is the element of the unknown...

Not true. And while it's natural to try to liken spaceflight to familiar experiences, it can't be brought "down to Earth"—not in the final sense. The environment is different, the perspective is different. Part of the fascination with space travel is the element of the unknown—the conviction that it's different from earthbound experiences. And it is.

Critical Thinking

Cite textual evidence to support your responses.

1. **Key Ideas and Details** **(a)** Which geological features did Ride observe from the shuttle in orbit? **(b) Interpret:** Why do you think Ride found it easier to imagine the workings of geological forces when she saw Earth from space?
2. **Key Ideas and Details** **(a)** What "unfortunate effects" does Ride say she could see as she orbited Earth? **(b) Analyze:** Why would these effects make colors seen in 1983 seem not as bright as those seen ten years earlier?
3. **Craft and Structure** **Assess:** Have Ride's descriptions of Earth changed the way you think about our planet? Explain your answer.
4. **Integration of Knowledge and Ideas** Does Ride's understanding of Earth change as a result of her experience on the space shuttle? Explain. *[Connect to the Big Question: Is knowledge the same as understanding?]*

Assessment Resources

Unit 3 Resources

L1 L2 EL **Selection Test A,** pp. 95–97. Administer Test A to less advanced readers.

L3 L4 EL **Selection Test B,** pp. 98–100. Administer Test B to on-level and more advanced students.

L3 L4 **Open-Book Test,** pp. 92–94. As an alternative, give the Open-Book Test.

All **Customizable Test Bank**

All **Self-tests**
Students may prepare for the **Selection Test** by taking the **Self-test** online.

PHLit Online! All assessment resources are available at **www.PHLitOnline.com.**

After You Read — Single Room, Earth View 

Literary Analysis: Narrative Essay

1. **Key Ideas and Details** What is the topic of Sally Ride's **expository essay?**
2. **Key Ideas and Details** **(a)** What scientific data does Ride use to make her ideas clear to readers? **(b)** Does this essay persuade you to have a certain opinion? Explain your response. **(c)** How might you extend or elaborate on Ride's ideas and share them with others?
3. **Craft and Structure** **(a)** Using a chart like the one shown, identify passages in which Ride uses **description, comparison and contrast,** or **cause and effect.** Find one example of each technique. **(b)** Explain how each example adds depth and context to the information Ride presents in that passage.

	Example	Effect
Description		
Comparison/Contrast		
Cause and Effect		

Reading Skill: Main Idea

4. Summarize the **central idea** of the essay "Single Room, Earth View" in your own words.
5. **(a)** List three **supporting details** that serve as evidence for the points that Sally Ride makes. **(b)** Do you think the author adequately supports her main idea with details? Why or why not?

Vocabulary

Acquisition and Use Review the vocabulary list on page 466. Then, identify the word in each group that does not belong and explain your response.

1. articulate, eloquent, unclear
2. novice, expert, veteran
3. diffused, scattered, withheld
4. extrapolating, concluding, donating
5. surreal, odd, normal
6. muted, intense, vibrant

Word Study Use the context of the sentences and what you know about the **Latin root *-nov-*** to explain your answer to each question.

1. Is a *novel* idea common or unusual?
2. Why might a star that suddenly becomes much brighter be called a *nova*?

Word Study

The **Latin root *-nov-*** means "new" or "recent."

Apply It Explain how the root *-nov-* contributes to the meanings of these words. Consult a dictionary if necessary.

novelty
innovation
renovate

ASSESS/EXTEND

Answers

Literary Analysis

1. The topic is space shuttle travel.
2. (a) She discusses orbital path, the speed at which the shuttle travels, the theory of plate tectonics, the sensors she uses to measure carbon monoxide levels, and the patterns of water movement in the oceans. (b) **Possible response:** It persuades me to agree that space travel is worthwhile because it advances scientific exploration. (c) **Possible response:** I might write about Ride in my blog.
3. **Possible responses: Examples: Description:** the view of the Hawaiian Islands; **Comparison/ Contrast:** comparison of the appearance of Earth from space in 1973 and 1983; **Cause and Effect:** effects of pollution on Earth's environment. **Effects:** The description conveys the sense of awe that is experienced by viewing Earth from space. The comparison and contrast emphasizes the changes that have taken place on Earth. The cause and effect example illustrates the damage that has been done to the environment.

For other sample answers, see ***Graphic Organizer Transparencies,* Literary Analysis Graphic Organizer** A, p. 84, and the **Additional Answers** section.

Reading Skill

4. **Possible response:** Space travel offers an amazing view of Earth.
5. **Possible responses:** (a) Details might include seeing the boot of Italy; seeing India crashing into Asia; and seeing the straight lines of bridges and roads. (b) She clearly supports her main idea because she uses so many vivid details and descriptions.

Vocabulary

Acquisition and Use

1. unclear; *Unclear* is the opposite of *articulate* and *eloquent.*
2. novice; *Expert* and *veteran* refer to someone who knows about a subject; a *novice* is someone new to it.

Answers Continued

3. withheld; *Diffused* and *scattered* mean "to spread out"; *withheld* means "to hold onto."
4. donating; *Extrapolating* and *concluding* mean the same thing—to reach a conclusion.
5. normal; *Surreal* and *odd* mean "strange"; *normal* is the opposite
6. muted; *Intense* and *vibrant* mean "strong"; *muted* means "subdued."

Word Study: Apply It

Sample answers:

Novelty means "something new or different."
Innovation means "a new way of doing something."
Renovate is "to make as good as new."

Word Study

Sample answers:

1. A *novel* idea is unusual because it's new.
2. A *nova* is a star that shows a sudden new light output.

PRETEACH

*Skills instruction for the **Reading Skill** and the **Literary Analysis** concept appears on p. 465.*

❶ Writing About the Big Question

1. Review the assignment with the class.
2. Ask students how the news contributes to what they know and understand.
3. Have students complete the sentence starters. Review responses as a class. (**Possible response:** We react in different ways to the presentation of news information on television and to the presentation in other media because they relate to us differently. Television news appeals to the viewers' senses by using visuals and words.)
4. Remind students that their answers will help them think about the Big Question, "Is knowledge the same as understanding?"

While You Read

Remind students to think about television newscasts that they're familiar with as they read the selection.

❷ Vocabulary

1. Have students preview the selection vocabulary.
2. For each word, have students say the word aloud.
3. Then, use the word in a sentence that defines the word.
4. Repeat your definitional sentence or a similar sentence with the word missing, and have the class "fill in the blank" chorally. Here is an example:

   If something is daunting, it is intimidating. The first time I took midterm exams, I was really worried and found the experience to be [students say "daunting"].

❸ Word Study

1. Introduce the skill, using the instruction in the box.
2. Ask students for another *-temp-* word that means "time." (**Answer:** *temporary*)

Making Connections | The News

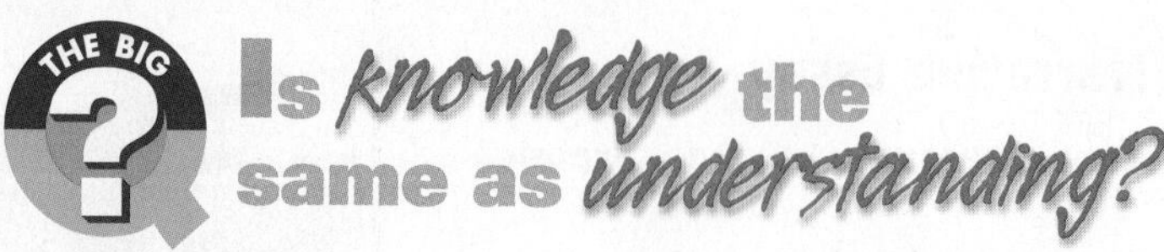

❶ Writing About the Big Question

In "The News," the author describes the pros and cons of television news. Use these sentence starters to develop your ideas about the Big Question.

We react in different ways to the presentation of news **information** on television and to the presentation in other media because __________.

Television news appeals to the viewers' **senses** by ________________ and ____________________ .

While You Read Consider the writer's ideas about television news as a source of information. Then, determine whether he believes watching television news can lead to understanding.

❷ Vocabulary

Read each word and its definition. Decide whether you know the word well, know it a little bit, or do not know it at all. After you read, see how your knowledge of each word has increased.

- **compensation** (käm´ pən sā´ shən) *n.* anything that makes up for a loss, damage, or debt (p. 478) ***They ran out of prizes, so they gave free tickets as compensation.*** *compensate v. compensatory adj.*
- **temporal** (tem´ pə rəl) *adj.* having to do with time (p. 478) ***His persistent lateness suggests that he has no temporal sense.*** *tempo n.*
- **medium** (mē´ dē əm) *n.* a particular way of communicating information and news to people, such as a newspaper or a television broadcast (p. 480) ***Politicians prefer to use the medium of television.*** *media n. pl.*
- **imposition** (im´ pə zish´ ən) *n.* the introduction of something such as a rule, tax, or punishment (p. 482) ***The imposition of the tax on tea caused many colonists to rebel.*** *imposing adj. impose v.*
- **revered** (ri vird´) *adj.* regarded with great respect and awe (p. 483) ***Many students came to the retirement party for the revered teacher.*** *revere v. reverence n.*
- **daunting** (dônt´ iŋ) *adj.* intimidating (p. 484) ***Climbing Mount Everest is a daunting task.*** *daunt v. dauntless adj.*

❸

Word Study

The **Latin root *-temp-*** means "time."

In this selection, the author comments that film alone cannot accurately show the **temporal**, or time, aspects of events.

476 Types of Nonfiction: Essays, Articles, and Speeches

Vocabulary Development

Vocabulary Knowledge Rating

Create a **Vocabulary Knowledge Rating Chart** (*Professional Development Guidebook,* p. 33) for this selection. Include the selection vocabulary and the Big Question words that appear in the Writing About the Big Question sentence starters on this page. (The Big Question vocabulary is introduced on pp. 424–425.)

Give students a copy of the chart. Read the words aloud, and have students mark their rating in the Before Reading column. Urge them to be alert to these words as they read and discuss the selection.

Tally how many students think they know a word to gauge how much instruction to provide. As students read and discuss the selection, point out the words and their context.

Vocabulary Central, featuring tools, activities, and songs for studying vocabulary, is available at **www.PHLitOnline.com.**

Meet Neil Postman (1931–2003)

Author of

The News

Neil Postman was a media critic and a revered professor of communications at New York University, where he taught for more than forty years. He called his field "media ecology," and his great concern was the effect of television on Americans.

Teachings on Television Born in New York, Postman received a doctorate in education from Columbia University. He also wrote twenty books and hundreds of articles. One of his most intense arguments is set forth in *The Disappearance of Childhood* (1982), in which he asserts that television exposes children to adult concerns far too early in their lives.

4 BACKGROUND FOR THE ESSAY

Television News

In 1948, only 400,000 American homes had a television. By 1960, more than 46 million American homes had a television, and TV began to take over as the news medium of choice. Today, television news is one of the most influential institutions in American culture.

Did You Know?

Postman once said, "You have to understand, what Americans do is watch television. I am not saying that's who they are. But that is what they do. Americans . . . watch . . . television."

Daily Bellringer

For each class during which you will teach this selection, have students complete one of the five Sentence Modeling activities for Week 14 in the *Daily Bellringer Activities* booklet.

4 Background

Television News

In 1980, Ted Turner, founder of Turner Broadcasting, created a 24-hour news station. The Cable News Network, or CNN, became the most important innovation in cable broadcasting, offering live news coverage from around the world, 24 hours a day. CNN news bureaus were opened in cities throughout the world. Today, several cable news operations compete for viewers, not only on television, but also on the Internet.

Multidraft Reading

This icon ● marks natural pauses in the selection. To assist struggling readers and to deepen reading for all, assign the text in "chunks," following the icons, and apply multidraft reading protocols. For each reading, have students set the purpose indicated:

- **First reading**—identifying key ideas and details and answering any Reading Checks.
- **Second reading**—analyzing craft and structure and responding to the side-column prompts.
- **Third reading**—integrating knowledge and ideas, connecting to other texts and the world, and answering the end-of-selection questions.

For more guidance, refer to the ***Classroom Strategies and Teaching Routines*** card on multidraft reading.

Differentiated Instruction — Additional Instruction

EL Extended Support—English Learners

Have students complete the **Reading and Vocabulary Warm-ups, *Unit 3 Resources,*** pp. 62–65, before they read. Assign the prereading pages in the ***Reader's Notebook: English Learner's Version.*** Then, have students listen to portions of the selection on the ***Hear It!* Audio CD.**

L1 L2 Extended Support—Struggling Readers

Have students complete the **Reading and Vocabulary Warm-ups, *Unit 3 Resources,*** pp. 62–65, before they read. Assign the prereading pages in the ***Reader's Notebook: Adapted Version.*** Then, have students listen to portions of the selection on the ***Hear It!* Audio CD** (adapted text).

Extended Support—Reluctant Readers

To build motivation and engagement before assigning the selection, have students read "Getting the News," a thematically related selection in ***Reality Central.*** Then, use the questions at the conclusion of the related selection to guide discussion.

PHLit Online!

For more about the author, practice with the selection vocabulary, or more background, go online at **www.PHLitOnline.com.**

TEACH

❶ Activating Prior Knowledge

1. Ask students to work in small groups. Give them a copy of a **KWL Chart** (see *Professional Development Guidebook,* p. 75) with the topic identified as "Television News Broadcasts."
2. Ask students to work together to complete the first two columns. In the Know column, they can write what they know or what they learned doing the Making Connections activity. In the Want to Know column, they should write questions they have about television news broadcasts.

Concept Connector

Students will assess what they have learned after completing "The News."

Individual Activity

Have students compare television and newspaper coverage of a news event by having them watch a local or national newscast and making notes on the details reported about one event. Then, have students find an account of the same event in their local newspaper or an online version of a newspaper. Have students list the ideas or insights given in the newspaper that were not given in the televised story. Encourage students to share their findings with the class.

❷ About the Selection

In "The News," Neil Postman discusses the limitations of television news coverage. He explains how television's reliance on visual images determines what stories are covered. Because little time can be devoted to analysis or explanation of a story, television news has become a kind of entertainment, with the news anchor as the host of the show.

❶ ❷ The News

Neil Postman

Vocabulary

compensation (käm′ pən sā′ shən) *n.* anything that makes up for a loss, damage, or debt

temporal (tem′ pə rəl) *adj.* having to do with time

The whole problem with news on television comes down to this: all the words uttered in an hour of news coverage could be printed on one page of a newspaper. And the world cannot be understood in one page. Of course, there is a compensation: television offers pictures, and the pictures move. It is often said that moving pictures are a kind of language in themselves, and there is a good deal of truth in this. But the language of pictures differs radically from oral and written language, and the differences are crucial for understanding television news.

To begin with, the grammar of pictures is weak in communicating past-ness and present-ness. When terrorists want to prove to the world that their kidnap victims are still alive, they photograph them holding a copy of a recent newspaper. The dateline on the newspaper provides the proof that the photograph was taken on or after that date. Without the help of the written word, film and videotape cannot portray temporal dimensions with any precision. Consider a film clip showing an aircraft carrier at sea. One might be able to identify the ship as Soviet[1] or American, but there would be no way of telling where in the world the carrier was, where it was headed, or when the pictures were taken. It is only through language—words spoken over the pictures or reproduced in them—that the image of the aircraft carrier takes on meaning as a portrayal of a specific event.

1. **Soviet** (sō′ vē et′) adj. belonging to the Soviet Union, the formerly socialist nation the main part of which was Russia.

Vocabulary Development

Ⓒ CCSS Language 6

Thematic Vocabulary: The Big Question

As students are discussing "The News," encourage them to use the thematic vocabulary presented in Introducing the Big Question, pp. 424–425. You might encourage them with sentence starters like these:

1. Postman argues that television news shows are not comprehensive *sources* of news because . . .
2. Without any accompanying text, a picture on television lacks crucial *information* about . . .
3. Television news relies on the *connection* between excitement and the movement of images because . . .
4. By presenting a series of disasters, the evening news taps a viewer's *instinct* to . . .

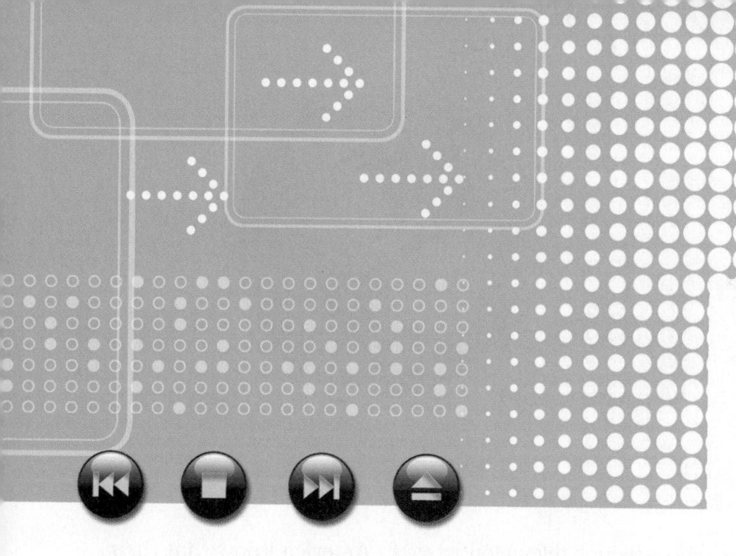

> But the language of pictures differs radically from oral and written language, and the differences are crucial for understanding television news.

Still, it is possible to enjoy the image of the carrier for its own sake. One might find the hugeness of the vessel interesting; it signifies military power on the move. There is a certain drama in watching the planes come in at high speeds and skid to a stop on the deck. Suppose the ship were burning: that would be even more interesting. This leads to a second point about
3 the language of pictures. The grammar of moving pictures favors images that change. That is why violence and destruction find their way onto television so often. When something is destroyed violently its constitution is altered in a highly visible way: hence the entrancing power of fire. Fire gives visual form to the ideas of consumption, disappearance, death—the thing which is burned is actually taken away by fire. It is at this very basic level that fires make a good subject for television news. Something was here, now it's gone, and the change is recorded on film.

Earthquakes and typhoons have the same power: before the viewer's eyes the world is taken apart. If a television viewer has relatives in Mexico City and an earthquake occurs there, then she may take an interest in the images of destruction as a report from a specific place and time. That is, she may look to television news for information about an important event. But film of an earthquake can still be interesting if the viewer cares nothing about the event itself. Which is only to say that there is another way of participating in the news—as a spectator who desires to be entertained. Actually to see buildings topple is exciting, no matter where the buildings are. The world turns to dust before our eyes.

Literary Analysis
Expository Essay
How do details about airplanes and fire support Postman's point that television favors change?

4 
Reading Check
What does Postman mean by the "grammar" of pictures?

3 Literary Analysis
Expository Essay

1. After reading the paragraph aloud, **ask** students to identify the images the author is describing here.

   Answer: The author is describing an aircraft carrier on fire with planes landing on it.

2. **Ask** the Literary Analysis question: How do details about airplanes and fire support Postman's point that television favors change?

   Answer: This image is one of airplanes skidding to a stop on the deck of the ship while fire roars, which is a dramatic scene that engages the viewer, who watches to see what will happen next.

4 Reading Check

Answer: Postman is referring to the way that pictures are presented and understood.

PHLit Online!

This selection is available in interactive format in the **Enriched Online Student Edition, www.PHLitOnline.com,** which includes a thematically related video with writing prompt and an interactive graphic organizer.

Differentiated Instruction for Universal Access

Support for Special-Needs Students

To help students with the challenging vocabulary in this essay, provide them with copies of **Vocabulary Warm-up Lists** and **Vocabulary Warm-up Practice** (*Unit 3 Resources,* pp. 62–63).

Review the lists with students. Then, have them work in pairs to complete the **Warm-up Practice** sheets.

Support for Less Proficient Readers

To give students a context for the essay and to model how to identify main idea and supporting details, show them the **Reading Skill Graphic Organizer A** (*Graphic Organizer Transparencies,* p. 82). Help them relate the main ideas and details to the text. Encourage them to use the organizer as a model for identifying the main ideas and supporting details as they read the selection.

5 Literary Analysis
Expository Essay

1. Have students read the bracketed passage.
2. **Ask** the Literary Analysis question: What topic will Postman analyze more closely in this essay?

   Answer: He will analyze the structure of a typical newscast.
3. Have students identify the technique Postman uses to support his idea.

   Answer: Postman uses description to support his idea.

Vocabulary
medium (mē′ dē əm) *n.* a particular way of communicating information and news to people, such as a newspaper or a television broadcast

Those who produce television news in America know that their medium favors images that move. That is why they despise "talking heads," people who simply appear in front of a camera and speak. When talking heads appear on television, there is nothing to record or document, no change in process. In the cinema the situation is somewhat different. On a movie screen, close-ups of a good actor speaking dramatically can sometimes be interesting to watch. When Clint Eastwood narrows his eyes and challenges his rival to shoot first, the spectator sees the cool rage of the Eastwood character take visual form, and the narrowing of the eyes is dramatic. But much of the effect of this small movement depends on the size of the movie screen and the darkness of the theater, which make Eastwood and his every action "larger than life."

The television screen is smaller than life. It occupies about 15 percent of the viewer's visual field (compared to about 70 percent for the movie screen). It is not set in a darkened theater closed off from the world but in the viewer's ordinary living space. This means that visual changes must be more extreme and more dramatic to be interesting on television. A narrowing of the eyes will not do. A car crash, an earthquake, a burning factory are much better.

Literary Analysis
Expository Essay
What topic will Postman analyze more closely in this essay? 5

With these principles in mind, let us examine more closely the structure of a typical newscast. In America, almost all news shows begin with music, the tone of which suggests important events about to unfold. (Beethoven's Fifth Symphony would be entirely appropriate.) The music is very important, for it equates the news with various forms of drama and ritual—the opera, for example, or a wedding procession—in which musical themes underscore the meaning of the event. Music takes us immediately into the realm

Vocabulary Development
CCSS Language 6

Multiple Meanings

Tell students that the vocabulary word *medium* can be used in several ways. Refer them to the word as it is used in the first paragraph on this page, and point out the definition. Tell students that in this case *medium* refers to a way of communicating information.

Explain that the word *medium* is often used to indicate a status or quality between two extremes—good or bad, large or tiny, hot or cold. For example, "His hands were an average size, so he ordered the *medium* gloves."

Medium can also be used to refer to a substance into which another substance is mixed. For example, "The painter mixed the deep green pigment into a *medium* of water to dilute the color."

Encourage students to write two sentences using *medium* in different ways. Have them share their sentences with the class.

of the symbolic, a world that is not to be taken literally. After all, when events unfold in the real world, they do so without musical accompaniment. More symbolism follows. The sound of teletype
5 machines can be heard in the studio, not because it is impossible to screen this noise out, but because the sound is a kind of music in itself. It tells us that data are pouring in from all corners of the globe, a sensation reinforced by the world map in the background (or clocks noting the time on different continents).

Already, then, before a single news item is introduced, a great deal has been communicated. We know that we are in the presence of a symbolic event, a form of theater in which the day's events are to be dramatized. This theater takes the entire globe as its subject, although it may look at the world from the perspective of a single nation. A certain tension is present, like the atmosphere in a theater just before the curtain goes up. The tension is represented
6 by the music, the staccato beat of the teletype machines, and the sight of newsworkers scurrying around typing reports and answering phones. As a technical matter, it would be no problem to build a set in which the newsroom staff remained off camera, invisible to the viewer, but an important theatrical effect would be lost. By being busy on camera, the workers help communicate urgency about the events at hand, which it is suggested are changing so rapidly that constant revision of the news is necessary.

The staff in the background also helps signal the importance of the person in the center, the anchorman (or -woman) "in command" of both the staff and the news. The anchorman plays the role of host. He welcomes us to the newscast and welcomes us back from the different locations we visit during filmed reports. His voice, appearance, and manner establish the mood of the broadcast. It would be unthinkable for the anchor to be ugly, or a nervous sort who could not complete a sentence. Viewers must be able to believe in the anchor as a person of authority and skill, a person who would not panic in a crisis—someone to trust.

This belief is based not on knowledge of the anchorman's character or achievements as a journalist, but on his presentation of self while on the air. Does he look the part of a trusted man? Does he speak firmly and clearly? Does he have a warm smile? Does he project confidence without seeming arrogant? The value the anchor must communicate above all else is control. He must be in control of himself, his voice, his emotions. He must know what is coming next in the broadcast, and he must move smoothly and

Reading Skill
Main Idea How do these descriptive details support Postman's idea that a newscast is a form of theater?

> This theater takes the entire globe as its subject, although it may look at the world from the perspective of a single nation.

7 
Reading Check
What are "talking heads" and why do television producers despise them?

6 Reading Skill
Main Idea

1. Have students use the blank **Reading Skills Organizer B** (*Graphic Organizer Transparencies,* p. 83). As you read the bracketed passage aloud, have students record details that support the idea of a newscast as a piece of theater.
2. **Ask** students the Reading Skill question: How do these descriptive details support Postman's idea that a newscast is a form of theater?

   Possible responses: These details show how a newscast is like a form of theater by describing the subject of the production, the tension at the opening, and the sounds and sights that heighten the tension.

7 Reading Check

Answer: "Talking heads" are people who simply sit and speak in front of a camera. Television producers despise them because there are no moving images on screen to keep viewers engaged.

Differentiated Instruction for Universal Access

Enrichment for Advanced Readers

Have students work in pairs to analyze a news broadcast using Postman's criteria. Have students view or videotape all or part of an evening broadcast news program, then write a report on a story from the news show. They should describe and analyze the introductory music and other introductory material, the moving images in the story, and the behavior of the anchor person. Then, have them explain whether their analysis supports Postman's claim that the news broadcast is a form of theater.

If time permits, have students present their reports to the class. If possible, have them show the video recording of the news story.

8 Connecting to the Big Question

1. Have a volunteer read aloud the bracketed text. **Ask** students to summarize Postman's point in this passage.

   Answer: Several features of a newscast help anchors—and viewers—maintain order and control over inherently disorderly events.

2. **Ask:** What does this passage suggest about Postman's ideas about television news as a source of information?

   Answer: Postman views television news as an unreliable source of information because it imposes a false orderliness on the disorder of life and events in the world.

3. **Ask:** Do you think Postman believes that watching television news can lead to understanding? Explain.

   Possible response: No, because he thinks that newscasts' presentation of information distorts reality.

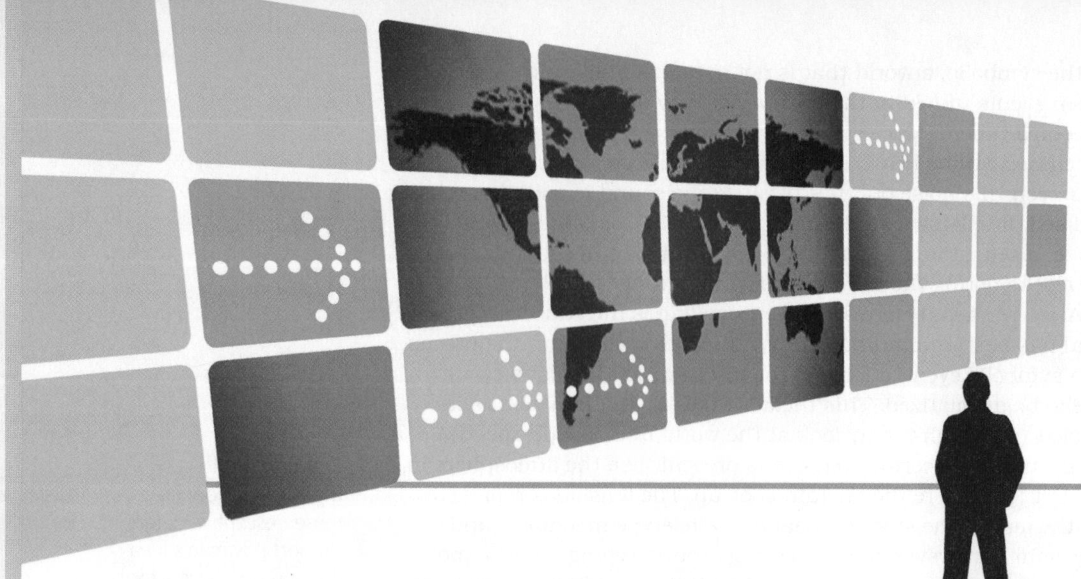

▲ **Critical Viewing** How does this image relate to the idea of people connecting to their world through the news? **[Interpret]**

confidently from segment to segment. Again, it would be unthinkable for the anchor to break down and weep over a story, or laugh uncontrollably on camera, no matter how "human" these responses may be.

Many other features of the newscast help the anchor to establish the impression of control. These are usually equated with professionalism in broadcasting. They include such things as graphics that tell the viewer what is being shown, or maps and charts that suddenly appear on the screen and disappear on cue, or the orderly progression from story to story, starting with the  most important events first. They also include the absence of gaps or "deadtime" during the broadcast, even the simple fact that the news starts and ends at a certain hour. These common features are thought of as purely technical matters, which a professional crew handles as a matter of course. But they are also symbols of a dominant theme of television news: the **imposition** of an orderly world—called "the news"—upon the disorderly flow of events.

Vocabulary
imposition (im′ pə zish′ ən) *n.* the introduction of something such as a rule, tax, or punishment

While the form of a news broadcast emphasizes tidiness and control, its content can best be described as chaotic. Because time is so precious on television, because the nature of the medium favors dynamic visual images, and because the pressures of a commercial structure require the news to hold its audience above all else, there is rarely any attempt to explain issues in depth or place events in their proper context. The news moves nervously from a warehouse fire to a court decision, from a guerrilla war to a World Cup match,

Vocabulary Development

CCSS Language 6

Word Forms

Expand students' vocabulary by helping them learn related forms of words on this page. Give students a blank **Word Form Chart** (*Professional Development Guidebook*, p. 42) with *professionalism* and *progression* in the correct columns. Work with the class, or have students work with a partner, to determine the related forms. The final chart should look like the one shown.

Noun	Verb	Adjective	Adverb
professionalism	profess	professional	professionally
progression	progress	progressive	progressively

the quality of the film often determining the length of the story. Certain stories show up only because they offer dramatic pictures. Bleachers collapse in South America: hundreds of people are crushed—a perfect television news story, for the cameras can record the face of disaster in all its anguish. Back in Washington, a new budget is approved by Congress. Here there is nothing to photograph because a budget is not a physical event; it is a document full of language and numbers. So the producers of the news will show a photo of the document itself, focusing on the cover where it says: "Budget of the United States of America." Or sometimes they will send a camera crew to the government printing plant where copies of the budget are produced. That evening, while the contents of the budget are summarized by a voice-over, the viewer sees stacks of documents being loaded into boxes at the government printing plant. Then a few of the budget's more important provisions will be flashed on the screen in written form, but this is such a time-consuming process—using television as a printed page—that the producers keep it to a minimum. In short, the budget is not televisable, and for that reason its time on the news must be brief. The bleacher collapse will get more minutes that evening.

With priorities of this sort, it is almost impossible for the news to offer an adequate account of important events. Indeed, it is the trivial event that is often best suited for television coverage. This is such a commonplace that no one even bothers to challenge it. Walter Cronkite, a revered figure in television and anchorman of the CBS Evening News for many years, has acknowledged several times that television cannot be relied on to inform the citizens of a democratic nation. Unless they also read newspapers and magazines, television viewers are helpless to understand their world, Cronkite has said. No one at CBS has ever disagreed with his conclusion, other than to say, "We do the best we can."

9 Of course, it is a tendency of journalism in general to concentrate on the surface of events rather than underlying conditions; this is as true for the newspaper as it is for the newscast. But several features of television undermine whatever efforts journalists may make to give sense to the world. One is that a television broadcast is a series of events that occur in sequence, and the sequence is the same for all viewers. This is not true for a newspaper page, which displays many items simultaneously, allowing readers to choose the order in which they read them. If a newspaper reader wants only a summary of the latest tax bill, he can read the headline and the first paragraph of an article, and if he wants more, he can keep reading. In a sense, then, everyone reads a different newspaper, for no two readers will read (or ignore) the same items.

Vocabulary
revered (ri vird′) *adj.* regarded with great respect and awe

Literary Analysis
Expository Essay
According to Postman, how are newspaper and television journalism similar and different?

10 

According to Postman, why must a news anchor-person convey *control* above all other values?

9 Literary Analysis
Expository Essay

1. Direct students' attention to the bracketed passage. **Ask** students to identify the technique that the author uses to support and develop his point.
   Answer: He is using comparison and contrast.
2. Have students identify what is being compared and contrasted in these paragraphs.
   Answer: The author is comparing and contrasting how television and newspapers present the news.
3. **Ask** the Literary Analysis question: According to Postman, how are newspaper and television journalism similar and different?
   Answer: Both television and newspapers concentrate on the surface of events. Television presents news as a series of events that is the same for all viewers. Unlike television news, a newspaper can be read in any order and to the depth of detail the reader chooses.

▶ **Monitor Progress:** Ask students what techniques the author has used so far in supporting and explaining his point. Students should be able to identify description and comparison and contrast.

▶ **Reteach:** If students have difficulty identifying the techniques, ask them to reread the passage and use a Venn diagram to chart the similarities and differences. Then, ask students whether they agree with Postman's views on television journalism.

10 Reading Check

The maintenance of control creates an impression of professionalism, prevents "deadtime" during a broadcast, and makes world events seem orderly.

Instruction for Universal Access

EL Strategy for English Learners

Arrange for English Learners to listen to the ***Hear It!* Audio CD.** Encourage students to read along with the recorded version. After students hear the CD, discuss the selection with students, eliciting and responding to questions. Point out any difficult vocabulary. Ask students to watch a news broadcast, or watch a videotape of a news broadcast together. Have them critique the program and offer suggestions on how they would improve it.

Enrichment for Gifted/Talented Students

Have students work in pairs to write a script for a television news story. Students may invent a news story or choose a current event. The script should include directions for introductory music and a description of the images to be used, as well as a script to be read by the anchor person. Tell students that the story must be limited to no more than three minutes.

⓫ Critical Thinking

Infer

1. Refer students to the bracketed passage. **Ask** them to explain the advantages that newspapers have over television news reports.

   Answer: Because not every item in a newspaper must appeal to most readers, newspapers can include items that might be of interest to only a few readers. The content of newspapers is not limited by time.

2. Point out to students that even though newspapers have many advantages over television news, millions of people rely solely on television for their news. **Ask** students why they think this is so.

   Possible responses: Students may suggest that people prefer to see moving images or to be entertained; some may suggest that people do not want to take the time to read newspapers.

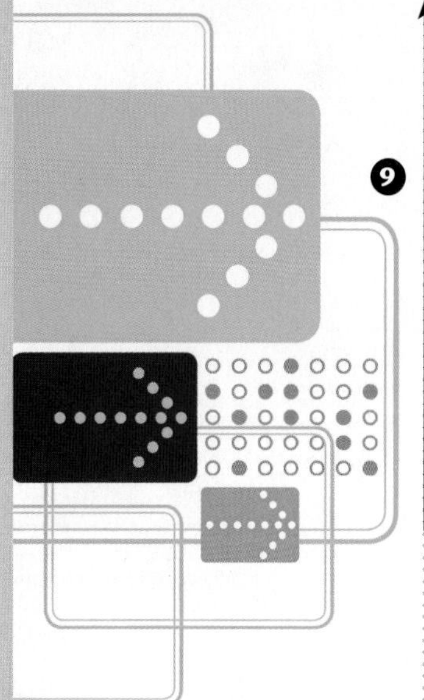

9 But all television viewers see the same broadcast. They have no choices. A report is either in the broadcast or out, which means that anything which is of narrow interest is unlikely to be included. As NBC News executive Reuven Frank once explained:

> A newspaper, for example, can easily afford to print an item of conceivable interest to only a fraction of its readers. A television news program must be put together with the assumption that each item will be of some interest to everyone that watches. Every time a newspaper includes a feature which will attract a specialized group it can assume it is adding at least a little bit to its circulation. To the degree a television news program includes an item of this sort . . . it must assume that its audience will diminish.

The need to "include everyone," an identifying feature of commercial television in all its forms, prevents journalists from offering lengthy or complex explanations, or from tracing the sequence of events leading up to today's headlines. One of the ironies of political life in modern democracies is that many problems which concern the "general welfare" are of interest only to specialized groups. Arms control, for example, is an issue that literally concerns everyone in the world, and yet the language of arms control and the complexity of the subject are so **daunting** that only a minority of people can actually follow the issue from week to week and month to month. If it wants to act responsibly, a newspaper can at least make available more information about arms control than most people want. But commercial television cannot afford to do so.

Vocabulary
daunting (dônt′ iŋ) *adj.* intimidating

11 This illustrates an important point in the psychology of television's appeal. Many of the items in newspapers and magazines are not, in a strict sense, demanded by a majority of readers. They are there because some readers might be interested or because the editors think their readers should be interested. On commercial television, "might" and "should" are not the relevant words. The producers attempt to make sure that "each item will be of some interest to everyone that watches," as Reuven Frank put it. What this means is that a newspaper or magazine can challenge its audience in a way that television cannot. Print media have the luxury of suggesting or inviting interest, whereas television must always concern itself with conforming to existing interests. In a way, television is more strictly responsive to the demands of its huge audience. But there is one demand it cannot meet: the desire to be challenged, to be told "this is worth attending to," to be surprised by what one thought would not be of interest.

Vocabulary Development

Vocabulary Knowledge Rating

When students have completed reading and discussing "The News," have them take out their **Vocabulary Knowledge Rating Chart** for this selection. Read the words aloud once more and have students rate their knowledge of the words again in the After Reading column. Clarify any words that are still problematic. Have students write their own definition and example or sentence in the appropriate column. Then, have students complete the Vocabulary Practice activities at the end of the selection. Encourage students to use the words in further discussion and written work about this selection. Remind them that they will be accountable for these words on the **Selection Test, *Unit 3 Resources*,** pp. 74–76 or 77–79.

11 Another severe limitation on television is time. There is simply not enough of it. The evening news programs at CBS, NBC, and ABC all run for thirty minutes, eight of which are taken up by commercials. No one believes that twenty-two minutes for the day's news is adequate. For years news executives at ABC, NBC, and CBS have suggested that the news be expanded to one hour. But by tradition the half-hour after the national evening news is given over to the hundreds of local affiliate stations around the country to use as they see fit. They have found it a very profitable time to broadcast game shows or half-hour situation comedies, and they are reluctant to give up the income they derive from these programs.

The evening news produced by the three networks is profitable for both the networks and the local stations. The local stations are paid a fee by the network to broadcast the network news, and they profit from this fee since the news—produced by the network—costs them nothing. It is likely that they would also make money from a one-hour newscast, but not as much, they judge, as they do from the game shows and comedies they now schedule.

> The result is that the evening news must try to do what cannot reasonably be done: give a decent account of the day's events in twenty-two minutes.

12 The result is that the evening news must try to do what cannot reasonably be done: give a decent account of the day's events in twenty-two minutes. What the viewer gets instead is a series of impressions, many of them purely visual, most of them unconnected to each other or to any sense of a history unfolding. Taken together, they suggest a world that is fundamentally ungovernable, where events do not arise out of historical conditions but rather explode from the heavens in a series of disasters that suggest a permanent state of crisis. It is this crisis—highly visual, ahistorical, and unsolvable—which the evening news presents as theater every evening.

14 The audience for this theater is offered a contradictory pair of responses. On the one hand, it is reassured by the smooth presentation of the news itself, especially the firm voice and steady gaze of the trusty anchorman. Newscasts frequently end with a "human-interest story," often with a sentimental or comic touch.

Spiral Review
Word Choice and Tone Does the use of words and phrases such as *severe limitation, by tradition, affiliates,* and *situation comedies* contribute to an appropriate tone for the author's message? Explain.

Literary Analysis
Expository Essay What sense of the world does television news cause?

13 
Reading Check

According to Postman, why are television news broadcasts so short?

Spiral Review
Word Choice and Tone

1. Remind students that they studied the concepts of word choice and tone in the Unit 3 Literary Analysis workshop (pp. 426–439).
2. Then, **ask** students the Spiral Review question.

   Possible response: The formal word choice is appropriate for the writer's message that reporting news is a significant task although content is sometimes overshadowed by images and sound bytes.

12 Literary Analysis
Expository Essay

1. Refer students to the bracketed passage. **Ask** students to identify the strategy the author uses to make the point in this paragraph.

   Answer: The author uses cause and effect.
2. **Ask** the Literary Analysis question: What sense of the world does television news cause?

   Answer: The limitations of television news cause a sense of a world that is chaotic and ungovernable.

13 Reading Check
Answer: Television news broadcasts are so short because local stations traditionally use the half-hour after national news to broadcast money-making game shows or situation comedies. Nobody in the business wants to lose income.

Concept Connector

KWL Chart
Have students complete the last column of their **KWL Charts.** Ask them to evaluate what they learned in relation to the questions they had before reading.

Writing About the Big Question
Have students compare their responses to the sentence starters they completed before reading the essay with their ideas afterwards. Ask them to explain whether their thoughts have changed.

Reading Skill Graphic Organizer
Ask students to review the graphic organizers they completed to identify the main idea and supporting details while reading. Show them **Reading Skill Graphic Organizer A** (*Graphic Organizer Transparencies,* p. 82) as an example. Then, have students share the graphic organizers they did and the main ideas and supporting details they identified.

⓮ Reading Skill

Main Idea

Ask students the Reading Skill question.

Possible response: The anecdote supports the idea that television attempts to convey the sense that no matter how chaotic the news reports seem, leaders are in control and all is well.

ASSESS

Answers

Critical Thinking

Before students respond, you may wish to have them write a brief objective summary of the selection. As they answer the questions below, remind them to support their answers with evidence from the text.

1. (a) The music in a news broadcast equates news with drama; computer monitors, maps, clocks, and workers scurrying about suggest urgency. (b) The comparison reveals that the news broadcast is an artificial medium.
2. By directly linking causes with effects, the author clearly demonstrates how the different elements of a news broadcast shape our perceptions of current events.
3. (a) The news anchor must project control. (b) The impression of control contradicts the impression of an ungovernable, chaotic world.
4. (a) They feel an evening news broadcast should last one hour. (b) Time limits mean that the viewer gets only a series of impressions, not the whole story.
5. (a) **Possible response:** Our knowledge of the news helps us determine what important events are going on in the world and how those events affect us. (b) As news outlets change, they affect how we receive news as well as who determines what is important.

Reading Skill
Main Idea What main idea does the anecdote about the little girl support? ⓮

Example: a little girl in Chicago writes Gorbachev a letter, and he answers her, saying that he and President Reagan are trying to work out their differences. This item reassures viewers that all is well, leaders are in command, we can still communicate with each other, and so on. But—and now we come to the other hand—the rest of the broadcast has told a different story. It has shown the audience a world that is out of control and incomprehensible, full of violence, disaster, and suffering. Whatever authority the anchorman may project through his steady manner is undermined by the terror inspired by the news itself.

This is where television news is at its most radical—not in giving publicity to radical causes, but in producing the impression of an ungovernable world. And it produces this impression not because the people who work in television are leftists or anarchists.[2] The anarchy in television news is a direct result of the commercial structure of broadcasting, which introduces into news judgments a single-mindedness more powerful than any ideology: the overwhelming need to keep people watching.

2. **leftists . . . anarchists** (an′ ər kists′) leftists desire to change the existing political order in the name of greater freedom for all; anarchists oppose any political authority.

Critical Thinking

Cite textual evidence to support your responses.

1. **Key Ideas and Details** **(a)** According to Postman, what elements make a news broadcast like a form of theater? **(b) Interpret:** What problem does Postman see in the similarity between television news and theater?
2. **Craft and Structure** How does the cause-and-effect text structure in the essay help you connect important ideas? Explain.
3. **Key Ideas and Details** **(a)** What type of role is an anchorperson supposed to play while presenting the news? **(b) Connect:** How does the impression created by the anchor relate to the "radical" nature of television?
4. **Key Ideas and Details** **(a)** How long do people in the news business feel the evening news broadcast should have to present the news? **(b) Cause and Effect:** What effects do time limits have on television news?
5. **Integration of Knowledge and Ideas** **(a)** How does our knowledge of the news affect our understanding of the world? **(b)** How does the changing nature of the news affect this understanding? *[Connect to the Big Question: Is knowledge the same as understanding?]*

Assessment Resources

Unit 3 Resources

L1 L2 EL **Selection Test A,** pp. 74–76. Administer Test A to less advanced readers.

L3 L4 EL **Selection Test B,** pp. 77–79. Administer Test B to on-level and more advanced students.

L3 L4 **Open-Book Test,** pp. 71–73. As an alternative, give the Open-Book Test.

All **Customizable Test Bank**

All **Self-tests**
Students may prepare for the **Selection Test** by taking the **Self-test** online.

All assessment resources are available at **www.PHLitOnline.com.**

After You Read The News

Literary Analysis: Expository Essay

1. **Key Ideas and Details** What is the purpose of Neil Postman's **expository essay?**
2. **Key Ideas and Details** **(a)** What quotations does Postman use to make his ideas clear to readers? **(b)** Does this essay persuade you to have a certain opinion? Explain your response. **(c)** How might you extend or elaborate on Postman's ideas and share them with others?
3. **Craft and Structure** **(a)** Using a chart like the one shown, identify passages in which Postman uses **description, comparison and contrast,** or **cause and effect.** Find one example of each technique. **(b)** Explain how each example adds depth and context to the information Postman presents in that passage.

	Example	Effect
Description		
Comparison/Contrast		
Cause and Effect		

Reading Skill: Main Idea

4. Summarize the **central idea** of "The News" in your own words.
5. **(a)** List three **supporting details** that serve as evidence for the points that Neil Postman makes. **(b)** Do you think the author adequately supports his main idea with details? Why or why not?

Vocabulary

Acquisition and Use Review the vocabulary list on page 476. Then, identify the word in each group that does not belong and explain your response.

1. compensation, repayment, donation
2. temporal, timed, severe
3. revered, scorned, ridiculed
4. daunting, challenging, tempting
5. medium, magazine, memory
6. law, imposition, stamp

Word Study Use the context of the sentences and what you know about the **Latin root *-temp-*** to explain your answer to each question.

1. Why is it essential for a musician to keep a *tempo*?
2. For how long might a *temporary* job last?

Word Study

The **Latin root *-temp-*** means "time."

Apply It Explain how the root *-temp-* contributes to the meanings of these words. Consult a dictionary if necessary.

temporize
extemporaneous
contemporary

Word Study

Sample answers:

1. In order for a piece of music to be played correctly, it must be played in the right rhythm.
2. A temporary job might last days or weeks.

Word Study: Apply It

Sample answers:

Temporize is to act in a way that suits the times.

Extemporaneous is done, made, or given with little advance notice.

Contemporary is modern, or pertaining to the current times.

Answers Continued

2. severe; *Temporal* and *timed* have to do with time.
3. revered; *Revered* means "held in great respect," the opposite of *scorned* and *ridiculed.*
4. tempting; *Daunting* and *challenging* mean the same thing.
5. memory; A magazine is a type of medium.
6. stamp; An *imposition* and a *law* can be the same thing.

Answers

Literary Analysis

1. The purpose is to inform.
2. (a) He uses quotations from Walter Cronkite and Reuven Frank. (b) **Possible response:** It persuades a person to view network news with a more critical eye. (c) **Possible response:** The reader might describe the commercial aspects of network news and elaborate on why the networks present their stories in a way that will keep people watching at any cost.
3. (a) **Possible responses: Examples: Description:** burning aircraft carrier with planes landing; **Comparison/Contrast:** comparison of the size of television screen to size of movie theater screen; **Cause and Effect:** need for television news stories to keep viewers watching results in brief stories. **Effects:** The description illustrates how moving images affect the audience. The comparison and contrast illustrates why moving images are more important on television. The cause and effect example shows why television news is inadequate.

For other sample answers, see *Graphic Organizer Transparencies,* **Literary Analysis Graphic Organizer A**, p. 85, and the **Additional Answers** section.

Reading Skill

4. **Possible response:** Because television news stories must appeal to everyone, they are shallow and give a false impression of the world.
5. **Possible responses:** (a) Supporting details include the length of newscasts, the Reuven Frank quote, and the description of the news broadcast as a series of visual images. (b) Students may agree that Postman provides ample support because he uses many examples.

Vocabulary

Acquisition and Use

1. donation; *Compensation* and *repayment* refer to payment for work.

Answers

Conventions

1. Introduce the skill, using the instruction on the student page.
2. Discuss the examples in the chart.

Think Aloud: Model the Skill

Model the skill of identifying predicate nominatives and predicate adjectives. On the board, write *Mr. Brooks is our teacher. His new car is black.* Say to students:

First, I ask myself, "What is the subject of the sentence?" In the first sentence, *Mr. Brooks* is the subject and *teacher* renames or refers to him. This means that *teacher* is a predicate nominative. In the second sentence, *car* is the subject and *black* is an adjective that describes the car. Therefore, *black* is a predicative adjective.

PH WRITING COACH Grade 9

Students will find instruction on and practice with predicate nominatives, predicate adjectives, and linking verbs in Chapter 13, section 2.

Practice A

1. astronaut (PN)
2. plane (PN)
3. planet (PN)
4. frontier (PN)
5. small (PA)

Reading Application

Sample answers:

Fire gives visual form to the ideas of consumption . . .

Its content can be described as chaotic.

Practice B

1. Walter Cronkite
2. stimulating
3. long and boring
4. self-important

Writing Application

Sample answers:

1. politicians and [world] leaders (PN)
2. [war-torn] cities and [angry] people (PN)
3. frightening (PA)
4. thought-provoking (PA)

PERFORMANCE TASKS

Integrated Language Skills

Single Room, Earth View • The News

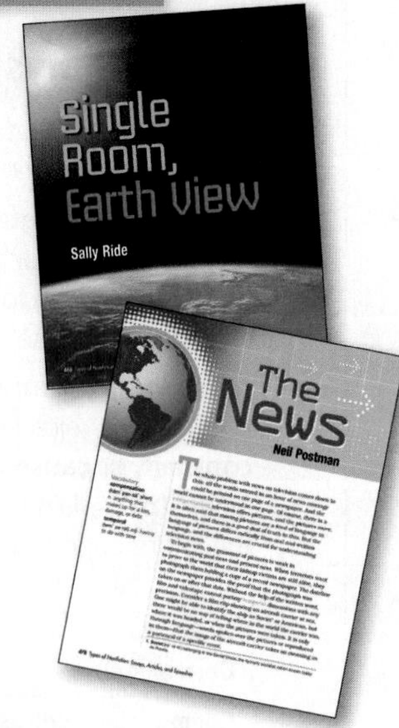

Conventions: Predicate Nominatives and Predicate Adjectives

A **predicate nominative** renames the subject of the sentence.

The predicate nominative comes after a linking verb and *renames, identifies, or explains* the subject of the sentence. In a sentence with a predicate nominative, the linking verb acts as an equals sign between the subject and the predicate nominative.

A **predicate adjective** is an adjective that appears with a linking verb and *describes* the subject of the sentence.

	Example	Explanation
Predicate Nominative	The winner of the tournament is our *team*.	*Team* renames *winner*.
	That player was the *star*.	*Star* renames *player*.
Predicate Adjective	The swimmer was *fast*.	*Fast* describes *swimmer*.
	Josh is very *clever*.	*Clever* describes *Josh*.

Practice A Identify the predicate nominatives and predicate adjectives in the following sentences.

1. Sally Ride was the first woman astronaut to join the NASA program.
2. The space shuttle is a plane capable of flying into space.
3. Earth is a beautiful, blue planet.
4. Space is a vast new frontier.
5. When viewed from space, the Earth appears small.

Reading Application In "Single Room, Earth View," find one sentence with a predicate nominative and one with a predicate adjective.

Practice B Add a predicate nominative or a predicate adjective as indicated to complete the sentence.

1. The news anchor is ________. (predicate nominative)
2. News events can be _______. (predicate adjective)
3. That film was ______. (predicate adjective)
4. Media, such as television, tend to be ______. (predicate adjective)

Writing Application Replace the underlined predicate adjective in the model sentence. Write two sentences with predicate nominatives and two with predicate adjectives. *Typical images in a TV newscast are interesting.*

PH WRITING COACH Further instruction and practice are available in *Prentice Hall Writing Coach.*

Extend the Lesson

Sentence Modeling

Choose the sentence given from the selection students have read:

And the difference is enormous: Spaceflight moves the traveler another giant step farther away. ("Single Room, Earth View")

But the language of pictures differs radically from oral and written language, and the differences are crucial for understanding television news. ("The News")

Ask students what they notice about the sentence. Elicit that the sentence contains a predicate adjective. Then, ask what else they notice. ("Single Room, Earth View": After the predicate adjective *enormous,* Ride inserts a colon and names the difference even more specifically. "The News": Postman uses the predicate adjective *crucial* to modify a plural noun—*differences.*)

Have students imitate the sentence, matching each grammatical and stylistic feature discussed. Have volunteers share their sentences.

Writing

Argument Write and present to the class a **script for a public service announcement** in which you highlight the rewards of entering a specific profession. If you read "Single Room, Earth View," write a script that NASA might use to attract candidates for astronaut training. If you read "The News," write a script that encourages people to pursue careers in journalism.

As you prepare your script for an oral presentation to the class,

- select details that will persuade people that the job is exciting.
- include visual elements that make the job seem appealing.
- structure your ideas and arguments logically.

Grammar Application Make sure to use predicate nominatives and predicate adjectives correctly as you draft your script.

Writing Workshop: *Work in Progress*

Prewriting for Business Letters From your writing portfolio, review the Questions List you generated. Answer each question using specific evidence and crafting each answer to be clear and precise. Then, save your Answers List in your writing portfolio.

Research and Technology

Build and Present Knowledge Using library and Internet resources, conduct research based on the following assignment choices and write two **journal entries.**

- If you read "Single Room, Earth View," research the training that astronauts undergo. Based on this information, write two journal entries that an astronaut might write while in training.
- If you read "The News," research the work television journalists do to prepare a news story. Then, write two journal entries a reporter might write while working on a story.

Follow these steps:

- Prepare clear research questions to guide your research.
- Use libraries, the Internet, personal interviews, and other suitable research methods to gather information.
- Use both primary and secondary sources in your research.
- Analyze and evaluate your sources to determine the usefulness, validity, and reliability of the information.
- Organize information to use in your journal entries.

Share your completed entries with the class.

Common Core State Standards

W.9-10.2, W.9-10.7, W.9-10.8; SL.9-10.4

[For the full wording of the standards, see page 464.]

Use this prewriting activity to prepare for the **Writing Workshop** on page 512.

www.PHLitOnline.com

- Interactive graphic organizers
- Grammar tutorial
- Interactive journals

EXTEND/ASSESS

Writing

1. Review the assignment, using the instruction on the student page.
2. To give students guidance for writing the script, give them **Support for Writing**, p. 90, in ***Unit 3 Resources.***
3. To evaluate students' script, use the rubrics for Persuasive Essays, pp. 230–231 in ***Professional Development Guidebook.*** In addition, you might evaluate how well students choose and describe appropriate persuasive visual images.

Grammar Application

Have students check their drafts for predicate nominatives and pedicate adjectives.

Six Traits Focus

✔	Ideas	✔	Word Choice
	Organization		Sentence Fluency
	Voice		Conventions

PH WRITING COACH Grade 9

Students will find instruction on and practice with persuasive writing in Chapter 9.

Writing Workshop
Work in Progress

Have students save their completed Questions List in their portfolios. They will use their lists to complete the Writing Workshop (see pp. 512–517).

Research and Technology

1. Review the assignment, using the instruction on the student page.
2. To support students' work on the assignment, have them complete the **Support for Extend Your Learning** page (***Unit 3 Resources,*** p. 91).

Teaching Resources

Unit 3 Resources

- L3 L4 EL **Integrated Language Skills: Grammar,** p. 89
- L3 L4 EL **Support for Writing,** p. 90
- L3 L4 **Support for Extend Your Learning,** p. 91
- L4 **Enrichment,** pp. 70, 88

Enriched Online Student Edition

Available under After You Read for this selection:

- All **Interactive Grammar Tutorial**
- L3 L4 **Internet Research Activity**

Professional Development Guidebook

Rubrics for Self-Assessment: Persuasive Essay, pp. 230–231

PHLit Online! All print and digital resources are available at **www.PHLitOnline.com.** Online resources accessible by students are noted on the student page.

MONITORING PROGRESS

Using the Test Practice

In this two-page Test Practice, students apply the reading skill for the first half of Unit 3 to a passage of fiction and a passage of nonfiction.

Review this skill, identifying the main idea, then administer the test. For more guidance, consult the ***Classroom Strategies and Teaching Routines*** card, **Formally Assessing Students.**

ASSESS

Answers

Answers With Explanations

1. C—The storm's duration would have nothing to do with its severity. *Incorrect answers:* A—Hail is a violent component of thunderstorms. B—Thunder strong enough to shake the house suggests a severe storm. D—Storms that knock out power are severe.
2. A—The passage mentions the car outside at the beginning and then describes how the storm affects it. *Incorrect answers:* B—While true, this is not the main idea. C—The passage does not mention Emily getting a job. D—This statement is a moral, not a main idea.
3. C—This sentence states exactly what happens to Emily's car in the storm. *Incorrect answers:* A—This is true but has nothing to do with the main idea. B—same explanation as for A. D—same explanation as for A.
4. D—This statement describes the increasing sound of the hailstones. *Incorrect answers:* A—This sentence does not mention the hail. B—same explanation as for A. C—same explanation as for A.

Test Practice: Reading

Main Idea

Fiction Selection

Directions: *Read the selection. Then, answer the questions.*

As the storm approached, Emily's mother urged her to bring her car into the garage. "OK, Mom," Emily replied, "as soon as I finish my history homework." She was still reading, however, when the lights went out and the first thunderclap shook the house. Then came a shower of *click* sounds, which immediately turned into *whack* sounds and then into *bam* sounds. It was hail—big hail! "My car!" cried Emily. She ran to the door, but her mother refused to let her go out into the storm. It passed as quickly as it came, leaving a broken windshield and dents in the car's roof. "How could a two-minute storm do so much damage?" Emily wailed.

1. Which detail does *not* support the idea that the thunderstorm was severe?
- **A.** The storm was accompanied by hail.
- **B.** A thunderclap shook the house.
- **C.** The storm passed quickly.
- **D.** The storm knocked out the lights.

2. What is the *best* statement of the main idea of this passage?
- **A.** A brief hailstorm damaged Emily's unprotected car.
- **B.** Hail makes a variety of very noisy sounds.
- **C.** Emily will need a job to pay for car repairs.
- **D.** Young people should always listen to their parents.

3. Which detail supports the main idea?
- **A.** "…the first thunderclap shook the house."
- **B.** "…her mother refused to let her go out into the storm."
- **C.** "…a broken windshield and dents in the car's roof."
- **D.** "Then came a shower of *click* sounds…"

4. Which detail supports the idea that the hailstorm quickly increased in strength?
- **A.** The storm arrived while Emily was finishing her homework.
- **B.** The first sign of the storm's arrival was a thunderclap and a power outage.
- **C.** Emily's mother urged Emily to put the car into the garage.
- **D.** The sound of the hail went from mild to very loud almost immediately.

Writing for Assessment

Suppose that Emily had moved the car into the garage before the storm. How would the rest of the passage change? In a detailed paragraph, state a new main idea for the passage. Then, explain how you would change or add details to support the new main idea.

Writing for Assessment

Students' essays may state this or any of their own main ideas. For instance, they could make the main idea that Emily had reason to be grateful to her mother, supported by these details: Emily was just returning from putting her car in the garage when the storm hit. As she looked at the size of the hailstones, she hugged her mother and thanked her for warning her about the storm.

Strategies for Test Taking

Remind students to look for the words that appear unimportant but that hold the clue to finding the correct answer. For example, in question 1, the question asks which detail does *not* support the idea that the thunderstorm was severe. This means that three of the four choices will provide a detail that *does* support that idea.

Nonfiction Selection

Directions: *Read the selection. Then, answer the questions.*

A hailstone usually begins in a storm cloud when a droplet of supercooled water freezes onto a snowflake or a dust particle. As the tiny hailstone falls through the cloud, more droplets freeze onto it. Still, the hailstone stays rather small—unless the winds in the storm take control. A strong updraft can carry a hailstone high into the cloud again. When the hailstone falls a second time, it collects another layer of ice. This fall-rise-fall cycle repeats until the hailstone grows too heavy for the updraft to support it; then it falls to the ground. By the time hailstones fall, they can be quite large. The largest hailstone ever recovered in the United States had a circumference of almost 19 inches.

1. Which of the following is the main idea of this passage?
  A. Storm clouds might contain strong updrafts.
  B. Storm winds directly affect the size of hailstones.
  C. Hailstones develop from tiny particles into chunks of ice during the fall-repeat-fall cycle.
  D. The biggest hailstone found in the United States had a circumference of about 19 inches, but hailstones can also be tiny.

2. Which detail gives the most effective support to the main idea?
  A. "a strong updraft can carry a hailstone high into the cloud again"
  B. "then it falls to the ground"
  C. "they can be quite large"
  D. "circumference of almost 19 inches"

3. Which of the following phrases *best* describes the author's purpose in writing about hailstones?
  A. to entertain
  B. to inform
  C. to persuade
  D. to amuse

4. Based on the main idea of this passage, which question would be the *best* guide to further reading?
  A. How do meteorologists predict storms?
  B. Which months of the year have strong storms?
  C. What damage can storm winds cause?
  D. Which types of storms produce hailstones?

Writing for Assessment

Connecting Across Texts
Emily wonders, "How could a two-minute storm do so much damage?" Write a response to her question. Make sure that your response has a main idea. Use details from the two passages to support your answer.

www.PHLitOnline.com
- Online practice
- Instant feedback

Answers With Explanations

1. **C**—This sentence states briefly the process of forming hailstones, the subject of most of the passage. *Incorrect answers:* A—This is true, but is not the main idea of the passage. B—This is true, but is only one detail of the building of a hailstone. D—This is an interesting detail, but is not a statement of the main idea.
2. **A**—This detail is related to the process of forming a hailstone. *Incorrect answers:* B—This sentence describes what happens when a hailstone reaches a certain size. C—This detail is related to the size, not the formation of hailstones. D—This detail describes one particular hailstone.
3. **B**—This passage gives scientific information about how hailstones form. *Incorrect answers:* A—Passages written to entertain are usually not about serious subjects. C—The passage does not attempt to persuade the reader to any action. D—Passages written to amuse are usually humorous.
4. **D**—This question is the most closely related to the subject of hailstones. *Incorrect answers:* A—This is an interesting question, but it does not relate to hailstones. B—same explanation as for A. C—same explanation as for A.

Writing for Assessment

Students' answers should have as a main idea that a severe storm can do great damage in just a few minutes, drawing on details from both selections to explain how and why.

Students may take the test in interactive format with instant feedback online at **www.PHLitOnline.com.**

Differentiated Instruction for Universal Access

Strategy for Less Proficient Readers
Review the skill by walking students through item 1. First, ask a volunteer to define *main idea* (the most important message the author wants to convey). Next, guide students in eliminating incorrect answer choices.

- A—This statement does reflect information in the passage, but most of the passage is about hail, not wind. (Eliminate.)
- B—While winds affect the size of hailstones, they only do so in the context of storms and in combination with certain temperature conditions. (Eliminate.)
- C—The passage, like this statement, describes the formation of hailstones. (Correct.)
- D—This is just one detail in the passage, not its main point. (Eliminate.)

Guide students in seeing that **C** is the best choice. Have them complete the remaining items, encouraging them to apply a similar strategy to each. First, define key terms in the prompt, and then eliminate incorrect choices.

PRETEACH

Common Core State Standards

- Reading Informational Text 5
- Language 6

Reading Skill

1. Introduce the skill, using the instruction on the student page.
2. Tell students they will ask relevant questions as they read.

Think Aloud: Model the Skill

Model the skill of generating relevant questions. Say to students:

> I usually know something about a subject I'm reading about, but I don't always know as much as the author. Before I begin reading, I try to form some questions in my mind. This helps me pay attention to what I'm reading by focusing on looking for the answers to my questions.

Multidraft Reading

Have students follow a multidraft reading protocol.

- **First reading**—Have students read to identify key ideas and details.
- **Second reading**—Have students read to identify the structure of the text.
- **Third reading**—Have students read to integrate knowledge and ideas by connecting the text to the world, their own experiences, and other texts.

Content-Area Vocabulary

1. Have students say each word.
2. Next, use each word in a sentence that defines it.
3. Finally, repeat your definitional sentence or a similar sentence with the word missing and have the class "fill in the blank" chorally.

Reading for Information

Analyzing Expository Texts

Technical Document

Web Article

Common Core State Standards

Reading Informational Text
5. Analyze in detail how an author's ideas or claims are developed and refined by particular sentences, paragraphs, or larger portions of a text.

Language
6. Acquire and use accurately grade-appropriate general academic and domain-specific words and phrases; demonstrate independence in gathering vocabulary knowledge when considering a word or phrase important to comprehension or expression.

Reading Skill: Generate Relevant Questions

When you read technical documents and articles, you may come across unfamiliar terms and concepts. To gain a full understanding of the text, **generate relevant questions** as you read. Use the following guidelines to help you:

- Preview how the text is structured—that is, how information is organized with headings, lists, introductory sentences, and so on. Previewing sections of text helps you predict what information each section will relate.
- Use your background knowledge of the subject to generate questions that you think each section of text can answer.
- Read each section, looking for answers to your questions. If your questions remain unanswered, generate additional questions for research.

As you read, use a chart like this one to record your prior knowledge, what you learn, and what questions to research.

What I Know	What I Learned	Relevant Questions
Part of the shuttle is destroyed when it enters Earth's atmosphere.	The external fuel tank is the part that burns up when the shuttle enters the atmosphere.	What causes the external fuel tank to burn?

Content-Area Vocabulary

These words appear in the selections that follow. You may also encounter them in other content-area texts.

- **orbit** (ôr´ bit) *n.* path used by a spacecraft around a planet or star
- **payloads** (pā´ lōdz´) *n.* things that are carried in an aircraft

THE BIG ? Is knowledge the same as understanding?

Have students consider whether their new knowledge helps them better understand space exploration.

Differentiated Instruction for Universal Access

Reading Support
Give students reading support with the appropriate version of the *Reader's Notebooks:*

L2 L3 ***Reader's Notebook***

L1 ***Reader's Notebook: Adapted Version***

EL ***Reader's Notebook: English Learner's Version***

Technical Document

Features:

- technical language
- numeric data or specifications
- diagrams or other graphics
- specific audience

These are the specifications for the shuttle. You can use this information to generate questions about elements of the shuttle's design.

NATIONAL AERONAUTICS AND SPACE ADMINISTRATION

Shuttle Statistics

Length
Space Shuttle:
56.14 meters (184.2 feet)
Orbiter:
37.23 meters (122.17 feet)

Height
Orbiter on runway:
17.27 meters (56.67 feet)

Wingspan
23.79 meters (78.06 feet)

Weight*
At liftoff: 2,041,166 kilograms (4.5 million pounds)
End of mission: 104,326 kilograms (230,000 pounds)

Maximum cargo to orbit
28,803 kilograms (63,500 pounds)

SRB Separation
Two minutes after launch

External Tank Separation
8.5 minutes after launch
Altitude: 109.26 kilometers (59 nautical miles)
Velocity: 28,067 kph (17,440 mph)

Orbit
185 to 643 kilometers (115 to 400 statute miles)
Velocity: 27,875 kph (17,321 mph)

*weight will vary depending on payloads and onboard consumables.

Space Shuttle Basics

The space shuttle is the world's first reusable spacecraft, and the first spacecraft in history that can carry large satellites both to and from orbit. The shuttle launches like a rocket, maneuvers in Earth orbit like a spacecraft and lands like an airplane. Each of the three space shuttle orbiters now in operation—*Discovery, Atlantis* and *Endeavour*—is designed to fly at least 100 missions. So far, altogether they have flown a combined total of less than one-fourth of that.

Columbia was the first space shuttle orbiter to be delivered to NASA's Kennedy Space Center, Fla., in March 1979. *Columbia* and the STS-107 crew were lost Feb. 1, 2003, during re-entry. The orbiter *Challenger* was delivered to KSC in July 1982 and was destroyed in an explosion during ascent in January 1986. *Discovery* was delivered in November 1983. *Atlantis* was delivered in April 1985. *Endeavour* was built as a replacement following the *Challenger* accident and was delivered to Florida in May 1991. An early space shuttle orbiter, the *Enterprise*, never flew in space but was used for approach and landing tests at the Dryden Flight Research Center and several launch pad studies in the late 1970s.

The space shuttle consists of three major components: the orbiter, which houses the crew; a large external fuel tank that holds fuel for the main engines; and two solid rocket boosters, which provide most of the shuttle's lift during the first two minutes of flight. All of the components are reused except for the external fuel tank, which burns up in the atmosphere after each launch.

TEACH

About Technical Documents

1. Review the features listed in the Technical Document box on page 493. **Ask** the class to define the term *numeric data* in their own words.

   Possible response: *Numeric data* refers to figures such as the size and weight of an object.

2. Invite students to share experiences they have had with technical documents. **Ask** them to tell why they needed to read the documents and whether the documents were easy to understand.

   Possible response: Students' views on the ease or difficulty of reading the documents might depend on how familiar they were with its subject.

3. Have students describe the look of the documents, including the use of charts, pictures, lists, and different font styles and sizes.

Generate Relevant Questions

1. Explain to students that they will better understand technical documents if they pose questions before they read and as they read.

2. **Ask:** What type of information do you find in "Shuttle Statistics"? Why is a list a good format for the information?

   Possible response: "Shuttle Statistics" provides numerical data about the shuttle. This information works well in a list because the information is easy to access and adds significant details to the document.

3. **Ask:** What questions do you have about the information in "Shuttle Statistics"?

   Possible responses: What is the difference between the space shuttle and the orbiter? Why does the weight change during the mission? What does the abbreviation "SRB" mean?

4. Have students read the selection, looking for answers to their questions. Have volunteers identify where in the text they found their answers.

Differentiated Instruction for Universal Access

Strategy for Special-Needs Students

Tell students that, unlike the pages of a novel, the pages in a technical document are not one block of flowing text. Point out that when they turn to a page in a novel, they start reading at the top and read to the bottom, but when they turn to a page in a technical document, they have to make choices about where to start reading.

Advise them to begin by glancing over all the different headings and features, and then to read the main text. Tell them that, while they are reading the main text, they might come to a reference to a diagram or chart. In that case, they should mark their place with a finger and look at the illustration, and then go back to reading the main text. In some cases, they might benefit by referring from the text to the figure several times if the illustration is a complex one and the text discusses it in detail. Explain that by doing so they can more easily grasp the information in the text.

Generate Relevant Questions

1. Direct students to the diagram of the shuttle. Tell them that technical documents often include diagrams to show complicated objects or processes that would be hard for readers to visualize and understand based only on a written description.
2. **Ask:** What information do you learn from the diagrams that can help you pose a relevant question?

   Possible response: The diagrams show the configuration of the shuttle at launch. The names of the components help the reader understand how the shuttle functions. The lower diagram, showing the payload bay open, shows how the shuttle functions in space. Both diagrams help the reader understand enough about how the shuttle operates to pose a relevant question.
3. Direct students' attention to the callout at the bottom of the page. **Ask** them to identify some questions they have after reading this passage.

   Possible responses: What caused the *Columbia* accident? What has been done to prevent similar problems from developing? Is NASA working on something to replace the space shuttle? What features are NASA considering for a new space vehicle, and why are they thought to be important?

You can use these diagrams to generate questions about aspects of the shuttle's design.

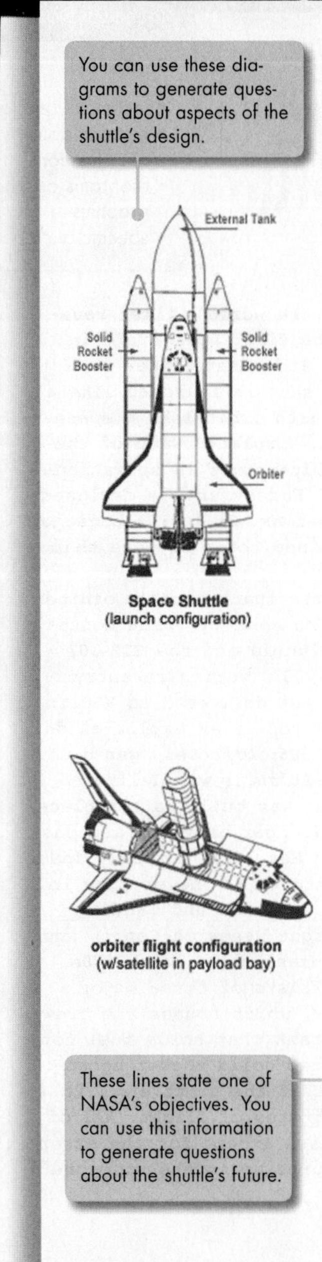

Space Shuttle (launch configuration)

orbiter flight configuration (w/satellite in payload bay)

These lines state one of NASA's objectives. You can use this information to generate questions about the shuttle's future.

The longest the shuttle has stayed in orbit on any single mission is 17.5 days on mission STS-80 in November 1996. Normally, missions may be planned for anywhere from five to 16 days in duration. The smallest crew ever to fly on the shuttle numbered two people on the first few missions. The largest crew numbered eight people. Normally, crews may range in size from five to seven people. The shuttle is designed to reach orbits ranging from about 185 kilometers to 643 kilometers (115 statute miles to 400 statute miles) high.

The shuttle has the most reliable launch record of any rocket now in operation. Since 1981, it has boosted more than 1.36 million kilograms (3 million pounds) of cargo into orbit. More than 600 crew members have flown on its missions. Although it has been in operation for almost 20 years, the shuttle has continually evolved and is significantly different today than when it first was launched. NASA has made literally thousands of major and minor modifications to the original design that have made it safer, more reliable and more capable today than ever before.

Since 1992 alone, NASA has made engine and system improvements that are estimated to have tripled the safety of flying the space shuttle, and the number of problems experienced while a space shuttle is in flight has decreased by 70 percent. During the same period, the cost of operating the shuttle has decreased by one and a quarter billion dollars annually—a reduction of more than 40 percent. At the same time, because of weight reductions and other improvements, the cargo the shuttle can carry has increased by 7.3 metric tons (8 tons).

NASA is prepared to continue flying the shuttle for at least the next decade and plans to continue to improve the shuttle during the next five years, with goals of increasing its safety by improving the highest-risk components. NASA will also be working with the Columbia Accident Investigation Board to correct any problems the board may find as it works to determine the cause of the *Columbia* accident.

In managing and operating the space shuttle, NASA holds the safety of the crew as its highest priority.

Vocabulary Development

CCSS Language 6

Vocabulary from Science

Point out that technical documents often use vocabulary that is specific to one particular setting—in this case, the space shuttle. Guide students to understand the meaning of the following words that are used in this selection:

orbit: a path of one object as it revolves around another

atmosphere: the gaseous envelope around a planet

modification: a limited change

maneuvers: methods of working that usually involve expert physical movements

satellite: an object built to circle the Earth, moon, or other planet

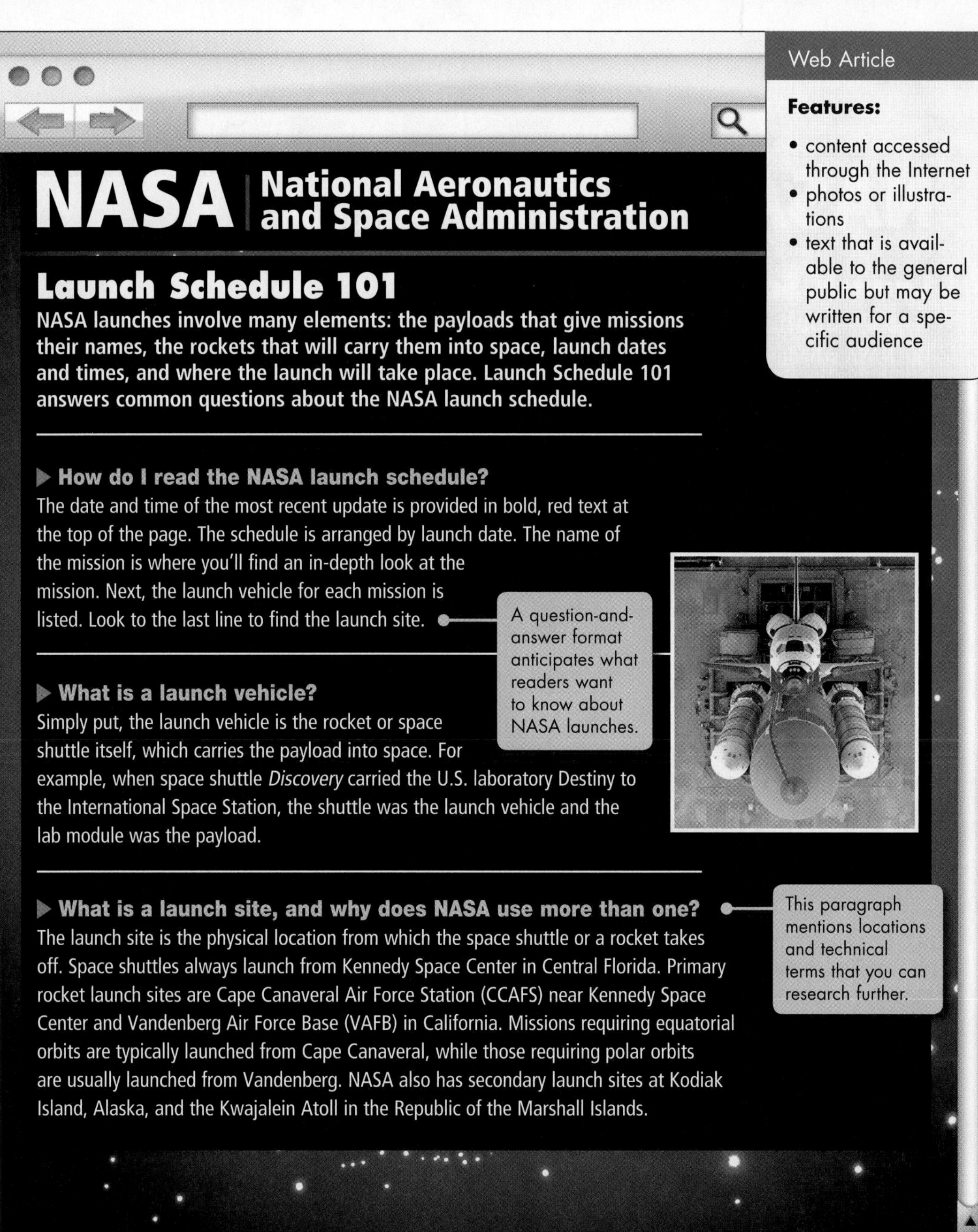

NASA | National Aeronautics and Space Administration

Launch Schedule 101

NASA launches involve many elements: the payloads that give missions their names, the rockets that will carry them into space, launch dates and times, and where the launch will take place. Launch Schedule 101 answers common questions about the NASA launch schedule.

▶ How do I read the NASA launch schedule?

The date and time of the most recent update is provided in bold, red text at the top of the page. The schedule is arranged by launch date. The name of the mission is where you'll find an in-depth look at the mission. Next, the launch vehicle for each mission is listed. Look to the last line to find the launch site.

▶ What is a launch vehicle?

Simply put, the launch vehicle is the rocket or space shuttle itself, which carries the payload into space. For example, when space shuttle *Discovery* carried the U.S. laboratory Destiny to the International Space Station, the shuttle was the launch vehicle and the lab module was the payload.

▶ What is a launch site, and why does NASA use more than one?

The launch site is the physical location from which the space shuttle or a rocket takes off. Space shuttles always launch from Kennedy Space Center in Central Florida. Primary rocket launch sites are Cape Canaveral Air Force Station (CCAFS) near Kennedy Space Center and Vandenberg Air Force Base (VAFB) in California. Missions requiring equatorial orbits are typically launched from Cape Canaveral, while those requiring polar orbits are usually launched from Vandenberg. NASA also has secondary launch sites at Kodiak Island, Alaska, and the Kwajalein Atoll in the Republic of the Marshall Islands.

A question-and-answer format anticipates what readers want to know about NASA launches.

This paragraph mentions locations and technical terms that you can research further.

Web Article

Features:

- content accessed through the Internet
- photos or illustrations
- text that is available to the general public but may be written for a specific audience

About Web Articles

1. Review with students the features listed in the Web Article box. **Ask** them to define *content* in their own words.

   Possible response: *Content* is the information that the article is about.
2. Discuss with students any experiences they have had using the Internet to search for information.
3. Explain to students that they can use the Internet to find information on almost any topic. Make sure they realize that some Web articles are written by reliable authors while others may be written by people who have less expertise or are biased.

Generate Relevant Questions

1. Remind students that to generate relevant questions, they should use what they already know and what they learn while reading. Together, this information will lead to a relevant question. **Ask** them why this Web page is called "Launch Schedule 101."

   Answer: The number "101" is similar to the course numbers that colleges assign to introductory courses, which give basic information on a subject. Using that number suggests that this Web article will have all the basic information on the subject of shuttle launches.
2. Explain to students that Web articles are often organized like books, with broad topics that contain more detailed information in subtopics.
3. Have students read the first page of the Web article about the shuttle launch schedule. Then, **ask** them to state a question they have generated after reading the article.

   Possible responses: What is the International Space Station? Why are Cape Canaveral and Vandenberg preferred as launch sites for particular types of missions?

Differentiated Instruction for Universal Access

Strategy for Special-Needs Students

Before students begin reading a Web article, suggest that they take sheets of paper and write exactly what they are looking for on the Web page. Tell them to refer to these notes before going to a different Web article or clicking on links. This will help them remember what they are looking for as they move around the page.

Enrichment for Advanced Readers

Remind students that they should not automatically believe everything they read on the Internet. Challenge students to find a reliable Web site and an unreliable Web site about the same topic. For each Web site, ask students to write an explanation of why they believe the site is reliable or not.

Generate Relevant Questions

1. **Ask:** What is the structure of this Web article? Do you think it is a good way to deliver information? Why or why not?

   Possible response: The beginning of the article is structured as a question-and-answer format. This format is useful since the questions focus on the most important points of the topic. The second section is structured as a list, which is a useful way to look up each shuttle mission because it is easy to follow.

2. **Ask:** What elements of the Web article are familiar?

   Possible response: Many students may be familiar with the hyperlinks, menu items, and the graphics that are part of most Web articles.

3. **Ask:** What questions do you have about these shuttle missions based on the descriptions? Where might you find more information?

   Possible response: Students might be unfamiliar with several of the terms used in the launch descriptions, such as "truss" and "spacecraft risk reduction." They might be able to find out more about these items by clicking on hyperlinks, if the Web site works that way, or by searching within the NASA site.

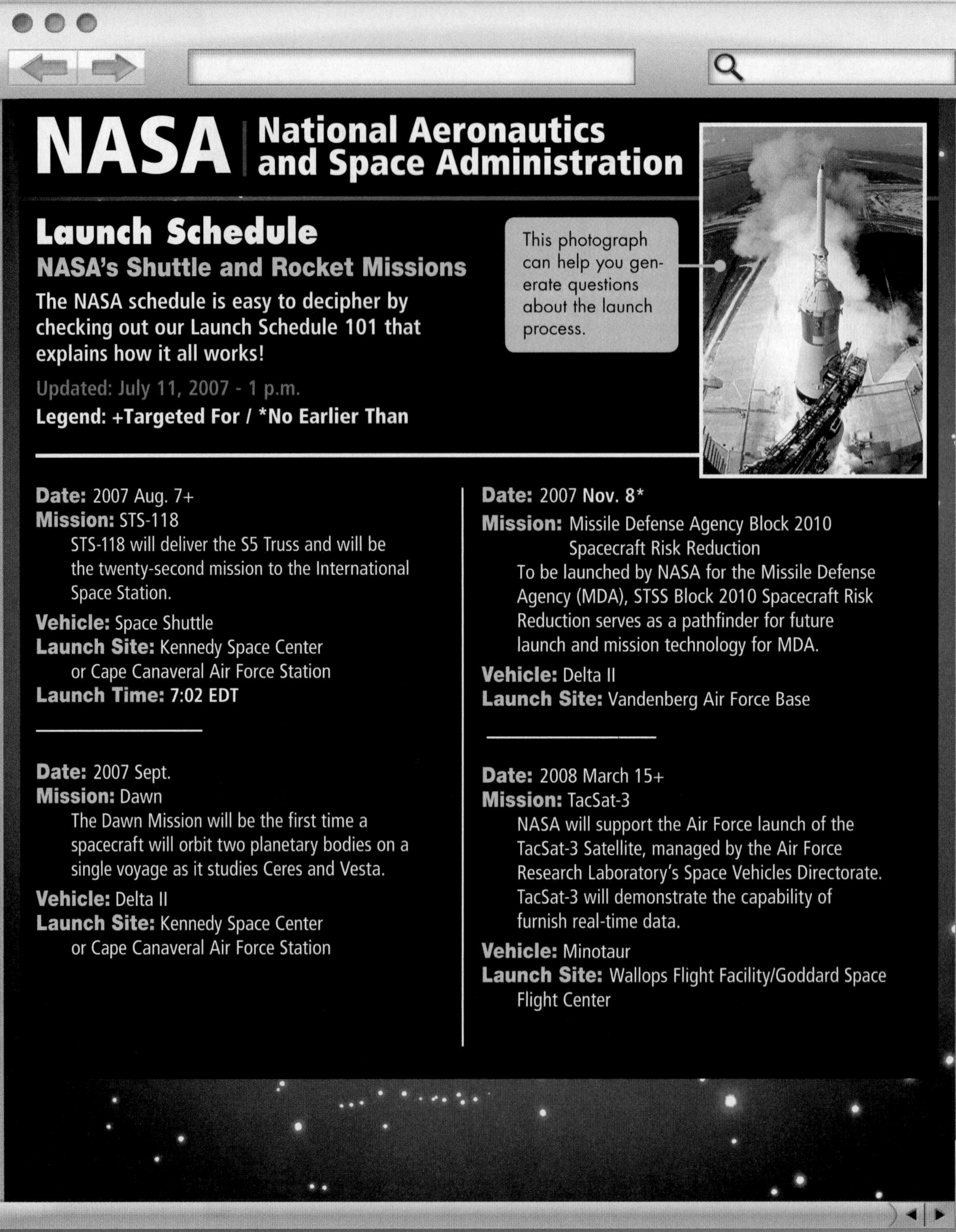

NASA National Aeronautics and Space Administration
Launch Schedule
NASA's Shuttle and Rocket Missions
The NASA schedule is easy to decipher by checking out our Launch Schedule 101 that explains how it all works!
Updated: July 11, 2007 - 1 p.m.
Legend: +Targeted For / *No Earlier Than
This photograph can help you generate questions about the launch process.
Date: 2007 Aug. 7+
Mission: STS-118
STS-118 will deliver the S5 Truss and will be the twenty-second mission to the International Space Station.
Vehicle: Space Shuttle
Launch Site: Kennedy Space Center or Cape Canaveral Air Force Station
Launch Time: 7:02 EDT
Date: 2007 Sept.
Mission: Dawn
The Dawn Mission will be the first time a spacecraft will orbit two planetary bodies on a single voyage as it studies Ceres and Vesta.
Vehicle: Delta II
Launch Site: Kennedy Space Center or Cape Canaveral Air Force Station
Date: 2007 Nov. 8*
Mission: Missile Defense Agency Block 2010 Spacecraft Risk Reduction
To be launched by NASA for the Missile Defense Agency (MDA), STSS Block 2010 Spacecraft Risk Reduction serves as a pathfinder for future launch and mission technology for MDA.
Vehicle: Delta II
Launch Site: Vandenberg Air Force Base
Date: 2008 March 15+
Mission: TacSat-3
NASA will support the Air Force launch of the TacSat-3 Satellite, managed by the Air Force Research Laboratory's Space Vehicles Directorate. TacSat-3 will demonstrate the capability of furnish real-time data.
Vehicle: Minotaur
Launch Site: Wallops Flight Facility/Goddard Space Flight Center

Think Aloud

Reading: Generating Relevant Questions

To model the skill of generating relevant questions, direct students' attention to the Web page shown on page 496. Then, use the following "think aloud." Say to students:

> The photograph on the Web site shows a rocket being launched. This makes me wonder about the process. *How often are shuttles launched? What are the missions about? What part of the government is in charge of launches?* There is equipment shown in the picture. *What is the cost of the launch in terms of labor and equipment?*

After You Read | Technical Document • Web Article

Comparing Expository Texts

1. **Key Ideas and Details** **(a)** What are two **relevant questions** for research that you can **generate** based on your reading of the technical document and the Web article? **(b)** Does either text answer any of your questions about the other text? Explain your response.

Content-Area Vocabulary

2. **(a)** Add the suffix *-al* to the base word *orbit.* Using a print or an online dictionary, explain how the suffix alters the meaning of the base word. **(b)** Do the same with the suffix *-er.* **(c)** Use each word in a sentence that shows its meaning.

Timed Writing

Informational Text: Explanation

Use information from "Space Shuttle Basics" to explain how the shuttle's solid rocket boosters and external fuel tank function during launches. Be sure to describe the tank and boosters themselves, as well as discuss the purposes they serve. Your explanation should be one paragraph long. (20 minutes)

Format
The prompt gives specific directions regarding the length of the assignment.

Academic Vocabulary
When you *describe* something, you give details that enhance your reader's understanding of the subject.

5-Minute Planner

Complete these steps before you begin to write:

1. Read the prompt carefully and completely.
2. Review the technical document, focusing on passages that discuss the shuttle's solid rocket boosters (SRBs) and external fuel tank. Make notes about their key features.
3. Decide how you will structure your explanation. For example, you might begin by describing the function of the solid rocket boosters and then describe the fuel tank's function. **TIP** Think of questions that a reader might have about the boosters and fuel tank, and then choose the clearest way to answer those questions.
4. Arrange your notes in the form of a list, based on the structure you have chosen. Refer to your list as you write your explanation.

ASSESS/EXTEND

Answers

Comparing Expository Texts

1. (a) **Possible response:** What improvements have been made over the years to the space shuttle functions on the landing pad and in space? In the future, will NASA build more shuttles for their research? (b) **Possible response:** The web page answered some parts of my questions because it helped describe how the launch pad has been specifically designed for this one ship.
2. (a) **Sample response:** orbital: the *-al* suffix makes the noun or verb orbit into an adjective that describes movement of an orbit. (b) The suffix *-er* changes *orbit* into a noun that names something that orbits. (c) The orbital path took years to complete. The small module broke and became the final orbiter.

Timed Writing

1. Before students complete the activity, guide them in identifying and analyzing key words and phrases in the prompt, highlighted on the student page.
2. Work with students to draw up guidelines for their descriptions based on the key words:
   - **Focus** The explanation should describe the appearance and purpose of the solid rocket boosters and the external fuel tank.
   - **Organization** The explanation should describe, in one paragraph, the tank and boosters themselves and discuss the purposes they serve.
   - **Support** The explanation should use details and information from the technical document in its description.
   - **Style** The writer should use descriptive words that help the reader understand how the tank and boosters look and function.
3. Have students use the 5-Minute Planner to structure their time.
4. Allow students 20 minutes to complete the assignment. Evaluate their work using the guidelines they have developed.

Common Core State Standards

- **Reading Informational Text 3**
- **Writing 2**

❶ Comparing Biographical Writing

Biographical Writing

1. Introduce the skill, using the instruction on the student page.
2. Give students a copy of the **Comparing Biographical Writing Graphic Organizer B** (***Graphic Organizer Transparencies,*** p. 88) to fill with biographical details as they read.

Think Aloud: Model the Skill

Model a way to think about biographies. Say to students:

To evaluate a biography, I first decide if the author describes the subject's life with balance. For example, a balanced biography will include both admirable and less admirable qualities. Then I examine the evidence for the author's interpretation. For example, I ask myself if the motivations given for a particular action make sense.

Comparing Literary Works

❶ Comparing Biographical Writing

Biographical writing is a form of nonfiction in which a writer tells the life story of another person. Important elements of biographical writing include the following:

- **Subject:** The subject of a biography is an important, inspiring, or fascinating figure. The subject may or may not be famous. The more important element is that the biographer presents the subject's life as compelling and worth studying.
- **Writer-Subject Connection:** The biographer usually has an intense interest in and a strong appreciation for his or her subject.
- **Research:** A biographer uses primary-source documents, other works on the subject, and, when possible, interviews with the subject or people connected to him or her.
- **Interpretation:** Biographical writing does not simply involve the telling of a subject's life story or the presentation of facts. Instead, a biographer analyzes and interprets the facts of a subject's life in order to present them in a meaningful way. The order of ideas, the details that support them, and the ways in which the writer connects different aspects of a subject's achievements or personality all contribute to this interpretation.

A biographer may openly state his or her attitude toward the subject. However, he or she may merely suggest that attitude, or **tone,** through word choice and details. As you read the biographies that follow, use an organizer like the one shown below to note details that describe specific aspects of each subject's life. Then, consider the order in which the writer presents these details, the ways in which he or she connects them, and how they support the writer's interpretation of the subject's life.

Common Core State Standards

Reading Informational Text
3. Analyze how the author unfolds an analysis or series of ideas or events, including the order in which the points are made, how they are introduced and developed, and the connections that are drawn between them.

Writing
2. Write informative/explanatory texts to examine and convey complex ideas, concepts, and information clearly and accurately through the effective selection, organization, and analysis of content.

	Lincoln	Ashe
Personality		
Upbringing		
Relationships		
Life events		
Role in major events		
Influence on others		

Vocabulary Development

Vocabulary Knowledge Rating

Create a **Vocabulary Knowledge Rating Chart** (***Professional Development Guidebook,*** p. 33) featuring the words glossed in the selections:

despotic (p. 501)
censure (p. 504)
droll (p. 506)
legacy (p. 509)
enigma (p. 509)
lithe (p. 510)

Give students a copy of the chart, and read the words aloud. Have students mark their rating of each in the Before You Read column. To gauge how much instruction to provide, tally the number of students who think they know each word.

Explain that the words are defined in the margin at the point where they appear in the selection. Urge students to be alert to these words as they read the selections. They will rate their knowledge again when they finish.

Vocabulary Central, featuring tools, activities, and songs for studying vocabulary, is available at **www.PHLitOnline.com.**

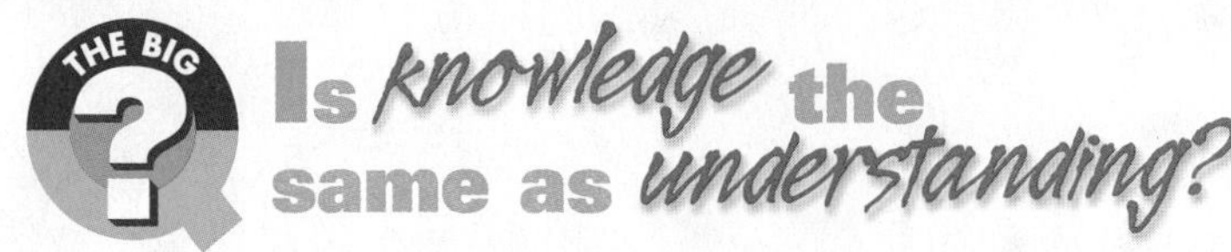

❷ Writing About the Big Question

Each of these biographers provides factual details to help readers understand the essence of his subject. Use this sentence starter to develop your ideas about the Big Question.

When I read to learn about someone, I expect to find out _______, _______, and _______.

Meet the Authors

Carl Sandburg (1878–1967)

Author of *A Lincoln Preface*

Between the ages of thirteen and twenty, Carl Sandburg worked as a porter, scene changer, truck handler, dishwasher, and farm worker. Sandburg served briefly in Puerto Rico during the Spanish-American War, which brought on the strong antiwar feelings he would hold throughout his life.

Childhood Favorite Even as a child, Sandburg was fascinated by Abraham Lincoln. For thirty years, he collected material about Lincoln, and his single-mindedness paid off. Sandburg's six-volume work about Lincoln is considered the definitive biography.

John McPhee

© Thomas Victor

Author of "Arthur Ashe Remembered"

John McPhee's big break as a writer came in 1965, when *The New Yorker* magazine published his profile of Princeton basketball star Bill Bradley. That profile, which became the basis for McPhee's first book, combined two of the author's great loves: sports and his hometown of Princeton, New Jersey, where he still lives today.

Broader Interests McPhee continues to write about sports, but he has broadened his subject matter to include the natural world, with books on Alaska, whales, and North American geology. McPhee's extraordinary prose has won many important honors, including a Pulitzer Prize.

Daily Bellringer

For each class during which you will teach this selection, have students complete one of the five Vocabulary activities for Week 15 in the ***Daily Bellringer Activities*** booklet.

❷ Writing About the Big Question

1. Review the assignment with the class.
2. To contrast knowledge and understanding, ask students what they would like to know and understand about someone famous.
3. Have students complete the sentence starter. Review responses as a class. (**Possible response:** When I read to learn about someone, I expect to find out facts, information, and insight about them.)
4. Remind students that their answers will help them think about the Big Question, "Is knowledge the same as understanding?" Tell them to read to learn about two famous men.

Concept Connector

Tell students that they will return to their sentence starter after they have concluded reading.

Multidraft Reading

To assist struggling readers and to deepen reading for all, apply multidraft reading protocols. For each reading, have students set the purpose indicated:

- **First reading**—identifying key ideas and details and answering any Reading Checks.
- **Second reading**—analyzing craft and structure and responding to the side-column prompts.
- **Third reading**—integrating knowledge and ideas, connecting to other texts and the world, and answering the end-of-selection questions.

For more guidance, see the ***Classroom Strategies and Teaching Routines*** card on multidraft reading.

For more about the authors and practice with the selection vocabulary, go online at **www.PHLitOnline.com.**

Teaching Resources

The following resources can be used to enrich, extend, or differentiate the instruction.

- All *Unit 3 Resources,* pp. 101–117
- All *Graphic Organizer Transparencies,* pp. 87–90
- All *Professional Development Guidebook,* pp. 33, 42
- All Enriched Online Student Edition
- All *Common Core Companion,* pp. 117–124, 190–201

PHLit Online! All resources, including print and audio, are available online at **www.PHLitOnline.com.**

❶ Background

Abraham Lincoln Abraham Lincoln is remembered as one of our greatest presidents, yet at the time of his election, less than half the country supported him. One reason is that Lincoln was opposed to slavery—and many landowners in the South still kept slaves. After seven southern states left the Union, the Civil War broke out in April 1861. By June 1861, a total of eleven states had left the Union and joined the Confederacy.

❷ Activating Prior Knowledge

Ask students to consider what makes a leader great. Is it wisdom, courage, luck, popularity, persuasiveness, personality, determination, success, creativity, adaptability, or something else? Work as a class to identify five key qualities of a great leader, and then rank those qualities in order of importance.

Concept Connector →

Students will follow up on this activity after completing the excerpt from *A Lincoln Preface.*

❸ About the Selection

In this excerpt from *A Lincoln Preface*—Carl Sandburg's introduction to his monumental biography of Abraham Lincoln—the author strings together a series of anecdotes that show Lincoln's humor, determination, and political skills.

❶ ❷ ❸ *from* A Lincoln Preface

Carl Sandburg

❹

Courtesy of The Lincoln Museum, Fort Wayne, Indiana, (#983) – *Lincoln Proclaiming Thanksgiving*, Dean Cornwell

Text Complexity Rubric

from **A Lincoln Preface**		
Qualitative Measures	**Context/ Knowledge Demands**	Details of President Lincoln's life and personality **1 2 ③ 4 5**
	Structure/ Language Clarity and Conventionality	Long, complex sentence structures; challenging vocabulary **1 2 ③ 4 5**
	Levels of Meaning/ Purpose/Concept Level	Challenging concept (Lincoln's challenges and the logic for his actions) **1 2 3 ④ 5**
Quantitative Measures	**Text Length**	Word Count: 2,361
	Lexile	1410L

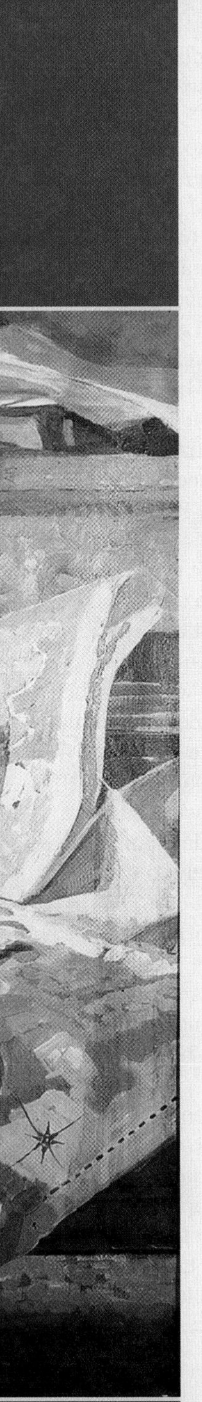

Background Ever since the birth of the United States in 1776, the issue of slavery had troubled the nation. Each time a new state entered the Union, Congress debated fiercely over whether it would be a slaveholding or free state. In 1860, when Abraham Lincoln was elected president, he refused to support any congressional proposal that would allow for new slave states. The southern slaveholding states resolved to fight to keep new states open to slavery. This conflict led to the outbreak of the Civil War in April 1861.

In the time of the April lilacs in the year 1865, a man in the City of Washington, D.C., trusted a guard to watch at a door, and the guard was careless, left the door, and the man was shot, lingered a night, passed away, was laid in a box, and carried north and west a thousand miles; bells sobbed; cities wore crepe;[1] people stood with hats off as the railroad burial car came past at midnight, dawn or noon.

During the four years of time before he gave up the ghost, this man was clothed with **despotic** power, commanding the most powerful armies till then assembled in modern warfare, enforcing drafts of soldiers, abolishing the right of habeas corpus,[2] directing politically and spiritually the wild, massive forces loosed in civil war.

Four billion dollars' worth of property was taken from those who had been legal owners of it, confiscated, wiped out as by fire, at his instigation and executive direction; a class of

1. **crepe** (krāp) *n.* thin, black cloth worn to show mourning.
2. **habeas corpus** (hā′ bē əs kôr′ pəs) *n.* right of an imprisoned person to have a court hearing.

Vocabulary
despotic (des pät′ ik) *adj.* like an absolute ruler or tyrant

6

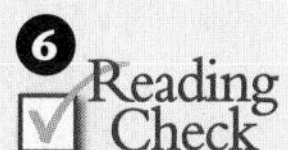

What violent event happened in April 1865?

5

◀ **Critical Viewing** Does this painting portray Lincoln as a man of great power? Explain. **[Make a Judgment]**

from A Lincoln Preface **501**

4 Humanities

Lincoln Proclaiming Thanksgiving, by Dean Cornwell

Lincoln created the national holiday of Thanksgiving by proclamation in 1863. Later, Andrew Johnson declared that Thanksgiving would always be celebrated on the last Thursday in November. In 1944, Congress ruled the day would be celebrated on the fourth Thursday of November.

American illustrator Dean Cornwell (1892–1960) was born in Lincoln's native state, Kentucky. In this oil painting, Cornwell not only presents a thoughtful man at work, but also hints at the magnitude and complexity of the president's job. Use this question for discussion:

What might Lincoln be thinking about?

Answer: He might be thinking about the proclamation he has just signed. He might be thinking about the first European immigrants who came to America in search of freedom.

5 Critical Viewing

Possible response: This painting does portray Lincoln as a man of great power because it shows a man who appears to be burdened with serious, overwhelming concerns.

6 Reading Check

Answer: Lincoln was assassinated.

This selection is available in interactive format in the **Enriched Online Student Edition,** online at **www.PHLitOnline.com,** which includes an interactive graphic organizer.

Text Complexity: Reader and Task Suggestions

***from* A Lincoln Preface**

Preparing to Read the Text	Leveled Tasks
• Using the Background notes on TE p. 500, review Lincoln's role in history. • Discuss the traits of great leaders in times of conflict. • Guide students to use Multidraft Reading strategies (TE p. 499).	*Levels of Meaning* If students will have difficulty with levels of meaning, have them first read and take note of problems that Lincoln confronted. Then, have them reread and identify his methods for solving them. Discuss student notes and offer clarification as needed. *Synthesizing* If students will not have difficulty with levels of meaning, have them read to identify qualities of Lincoln's personality and to draw conclusions about how those qualities shaped his actions. Discuss their conclusions as a class.

7 Humanities

Peculiarsome Abe, by N.C. Wyeth

Newell Convers Wyeth (1882–1945) was a native of Massachusetts. He is best remembered for the dramatic oil paintings with which he illustrated a series of children's classics such as *Robin Hood, Treasure Island,* and *Kidnapped.* Wyeth's illustrations also graced magazine covers, stories, and advertisements. Use this question for discussion:

How does this image of Lincoln contrast with the images in Sandburg's preface?

Answer: The figure is youthful and relaxed. He is a country boy who has been working in a field. Sandburg's Lincoln is mature, powerful, and faced with bigger tasks than harvesting corn.

8 Critical Viewing

Possible response: It shows that he was studious, hard working, and solitary.

7

Peculiarsome Abe, N.C. Wyeth, Courtesy of Children's Literature Research Collection, The Free Library of Philadelphia. Photography courtesy of the Brandywine River Museum

8

▲ **Critical Viewing** What impression of Lincoln does this painting convey? **[Describe]**

chattel[3] property recognized as lawful for two hundred years went to the scrap pile.

When the woman who wrote *Uncle Tom's Cabin*[4] came to see him in the White House, he greeted her, "So you're the little woman who wrote the book that made this great war," and as they seated themselves at a fireplace, "I do love an open fire: I always had one at home." As they were finishing their talk of the days of blood, he said, "I shan't last long after it's over."

An Illinois Congressman looked in on him as he had his face lathered for a shave in the White House and remarked, "If anybody had told me that in a great crisis like this the people were going out to a little one-horse town and pick out a one-horse lawyer for president, I wouldn't have believed it." The answer was, "Neither would I. But it was a time when a man with a policy would have been fatal to the country. I never had a policy. I have simply tried to do what seemed best each day, as each day came."

"I don't intend precisely to throw the Constitution overboard, but I will stick it in a hole if I can," he told a Cabinet officer. The enemy was violating the Constitution to destroy the Union, he argued, and therefore, "I will violate the Constitution, if necessary, to save the Union." He instructed a messenger to the Secretary of the Treasury, "Tell him not to bother himself about the Constitution. Say that I have that sacred instrument here at the White House, and I am guarding it with great care."

When he was renominated, it was by the device of seating delegates from Tennessee, which gave enough added votes to seat favorable delegates from Kentucky, Missouri, Louisiana, Arkansas, and from one county in Florida. Until late in that campaign of 1864, he expected to lose the November election; military victories brought the tide his way; the vote was 2,200,000 for him and 1,800,000 against him. Among those who bitterly fought him politically, and

3. **chattel** (chat′'l) *n.* a movable item of personal property.
4. **woman . . . *Cabin*** Harriet Beecher Stowe (1811–1896), whose novel stirred up opinion against slavery.

Vocabulary Development

CCSS Language 6

Word Forms

Expand students' vocabulary by helping them learn related forms of the selection vocabulary words. Three of the selection vocabulary words for the excerpt from *A Lincoln Preface* have related forms. Give students a blank **Word Form Chart** (***Professional Development Guidebook***, p. 42), with *censure, despotic,* and *droll* in the correct columns. Work with the class, or have students work with a partner, to determine the related forms. The final chart should look like the one shown.

Noun	Verb	Adjective	Adverb
censure	censure	censurable	
despot		**despotic**	despotically
drollery		**droll**	drolly

accused him of blunders or crimes, were Franklin Pierce, a former president of the United States; Horatio Seymour, the Governor of New York; Samuel F. B. Morse, inventor of the telegraph; Cyrus H. McCormick, inventor of the farm reaper; General George B. McClellan, a Democrat who had commanded the Army of the Potomac; and the *Chicago Times*, a daily newspaper. In all its essential propositions the Southern Confederacy had the moral support of powerful, respectable elements throughout the North, probably more than a million votes believing in the justice of the cause of the South as compared with the North.

While propagandas raged, and the war winds howled, he sat in the White House, the Stubborn Man of History, writing that the Mississippi was one river and could not belong to two countries, that the plans for railroad connection from coast to coast must be pushed through and the Union Pacific[5] realized.

His life, mind and heart ran in contrasts. When his white kid gloves broke into tatters while shaking hands at a White House reception, he remarked, "This looks like a general bustification." When he talked with an Ohio friend one day during the 1864 campaign, he mentioned one public man, and murmured, "He's a thistle! I don't see why God lets him live." Of a devious Senator, he said, "He's too crooked to lie still!" And of a New York editor, "In early life in the West, we used to make our shoes last a great while with much mending, and sometimes, when far gone, we found the leather so rotten the stitches would not hold. Greeley is so rotten that nothing can be done with him. He is not truthful; the stitches all tear out." As he sat in the telegraph office of the War Department, reading cipher dispatches, and came to the words, Hosanna and Husband, he would chuckle, "Jeffy D.,"[6] and at the words, Hunter and Happy, "Bobby Lee."[7]

While the luck of war wavered and broke and came again, as generals failed and campaigns were lost, he held enough forces of the Union together to raise new armies and supply them, until generals were found who made war as victorious war has always been made, with terror, frightfulness, destruction, and valor and sacrifice past words of man to tell.

A slouching, gray-headed poet,[8] haunting the hospitals at Washington, characterized him as "the grandest figure on the crowded canvas of the drama of the nineteenth century—a Hoosier Michael Angelo."[9]

5. **Union Pacific** railroad chartered by Congress in 1862 to form part of a transcontinental system.
6. **"Jeffy D."** Jefferson Davis (1808–1889), president of the Confederacy.
7. **"Bobby Lee"** Robert E. Lee (1807–1870), commander in chief of the Confederate army.
8. **slouching . . . poet** Walt Whitman (1819–1892).
9. **Michael Angelo** Michelangelo (mī′ kəl an′ jə lō′) (1475–1564), famous Italian artist.

His life, mind and heart ran in contrasts.

Literary Analysis
Biographical Writing Which details here present Lincoln's strength in the face of opposition? Explain.

10 Reading Check
Under what circumstances was Lincoln willing to violate the Constitution?

9 Literary Analysis
Biographical Writing

1. Read aloud the bracketed paragraph. Explain that Sandburg uses details about Lincoln's role in an important event, the Civil War. Tell students that he describes Lincoln as steadfast and purposeful amid the distractions of a terrible war.
2. **Ask** the Literary Analysis question: Which details here present Lincoln's strength in the face of opposition? Explain.

   Possible response: Sandburg describes Lincoln as calm and self-assured in the face of great upheaval and opposition. The stubborn president continues to advocate unification, and he pushes for a transcontinental railroad even during wartime.

10 Reading Check

Answer: He was willing to violate the Constitution to save the Union.

Differentiated Instruction for Universal Access

Strategy for Special-Needs Students
Share the background information on p. 500 of this teachers' edition with students before they begin reading. Have students also share what they already know about Lincoln. Assign peer tutors with whom students can meet to discuss the selection at intervals of one or two pages. Students should keep track of questions as they read. Tutors should help them answer the questions and make sure that they understand the information conveyed in the excerpt.

EL Strategy for English Learners
To give students a context for the selection and to model how to analyze details in biographical writing, show them **Comparing Biographical Writing Graphic Organizer A** (***Graphic Organizer Transparencies***, p. 87). The partially completed graphic organizer will give students insight into how details are used in biographical writing. They can use it as a model for recording details about the subject as they read.

11 Literary Analysis
Biographical Writing

1. Read aloud the first bracketed paragraph. Explain that it focuses on another of Lincoln's characteristics: his emotional sensitivity.
2. **Ask** the Literary Analysis question.

   Possible response: The writer's tone is respectful.

12 Connecting to the Big Question

1. Remind students of the Big Question by pointing out that the more one knows about a person, the easier it is to understand his or her actions.
2. Direct students' attention to the second bracketed passage on p. 504. **Ask:** What do you find out about Lincoln's family history in this passage?

   Answer: Lincoln lost one child to death, defended his wife against accusations, and was close to a son with a physical disability.
3. **Ask:** How does Abraham Lincoln's family history help you understand the challenges he faced in sending young men into battle?

   Possible response: Knowing that Lincoln has lost one son and has another that faces a physical disability helps readers understand that Lincoln would have known how it feels to lose a child or to have a child struggle.

Spiral Review
Organization and Structure

1. Students studied the concepts of organization and structure in the Unit 3 Literary Analysis Workshop (pp. 426–439).
2. **Ask** students the Spiral Review question.

   Possible response: The text is not organized in sequential order, but instead organized around key points illustrated by anecdotes. The dialogue within each anecdote gives an even more vivid impression of Lincoln than a sequential, objective narrative structure would.

His own speeches, letters, telegrams and official messages during that war form the most significant and enduring document from any one man on why the war began, why it went on, and the dangers beyond its end. He mentioned "the politicians," over and again "the politicians," with scorn and blame. As the platoons filed before him at a review of an army corps, he asked, "What is to become of these boys when the war is over?"

Literary Analysis
Biographical Writing What is the writer's tone as he describes Lincoln's emotional state?

He was a chosen spokesman; yet there were times he was silent; nothing but silence could at those times have fitted a chosen spokesman; in the mixed shame and blame of the immense wrongs of two crashing civilizations, with nothing to say, he said nothing, slept not at all, and wept at those times in a way that made weeping appropriate, decent, majestic. 

His hat was shot off as he rode alone one night in Washington; a son he loved died as he watched at the bed; his wife was accused of betraying information to the enemy, until denials from him were necessary; his best companion was a fine-hearted and brilliant son with a deformed palate and an impediment of speech; when a Pennsylvania Congressman told him the enemy had declared they would break into the city and hang him to a lamp-post, he said he had considered "the violent preliminaries" to such a scene; on his left thumb was a scar where an ax had nearly chopped the thumb off when he was a boy; over one eye was a scar where he had been hit with a club in the hands of a man trying to steal the cargo off a Mississippi River flatboat; he threw a cashiered[10] officer out of his room in the White House, crying, "I can bear censure, but not insult. I never wish to see your face again."

Vocabulary
censure (sen′ shər) *n.* strong disapproval

As he shook hands with the correspondent of the London *Times*, he drawled, "Well, I guess the London *Times* is about the greatest power on earth—unless perhaps it is the Mississippi River." He rebuked with anger a woman who got on her knees to thank him for a pardon that saved her son from being shot at sunrise; and when an Iowa woman said she had journeyed out of her way to Washington just for a look at him, he grinned, "Well, in the matter of looking at one another, I have altogether the advantage."

Spiral Review
Organization and Structure How does the author develop the reader's impression of Lincoln in this paragraph and in surrounding paragraphs?

He asked his Cabinet to vote on the high military command, and after the vote, told them the appointment had already been made; one Cabinet officer, who had been governor of Ohio, came away personally baffled and frustrated from an interview, to exclaim, to a private secretary, "That man is the most cunning person I ever saw in my life"; an Illinois lawyer who had been sent on errands carrying his political secrets, said, "He is a trimmer[11] and such a trimmer as the world has never seen."

10. **cashiered** (ka shird′) *adj.* dishonorably discharged.
11. **trimmer** (trim′ ər) *n.* person who changes his or her opinion to suit the circumstances.

Think Aloud

Vocabulary: Using Context

Direct students' attention to the word *impediment* on this page. Using a think-aloud process, model how to use context to infer the meaning of an unknown word. Say to students: I'm going to think aloud to show you how I would figure out the meaning of *impediment* from its context.

In this sentence, *impediment* is used to describe the way Lincoln's son talks or his speech. We see that the boy is described in the beginning of the sentence as having a *deformed palate.* I know that something deformed is out of shape. From that context, I can guess that palate has something to do with his mouth. When I put the entire sentence together, I think that an *impediment* is something that stands in the way of something. Lincoln's son's deformed palate kept him from being able to speak clearly.

He manipulated the admission of Nevada as a state in the Union, when her votes were needed for the Emancipation Proclamation, saying, "It is easier to admit Nevada than to raise another million of soldiers." At the same time he went to the office of a former New York editor, who had become Assistant Secretary of War, and said the votes of three congressmen were wanted for the required three-quarters of votes in the House of Representatives, advising, "There are three that you can deal with better than anybody else. . . . Whatever promise you make to those men, I will perform it." And in the same week, he said to a Massachusetts politician that two votes were lacking, and, "Those two votes must be procured. I leave it to you to determine how it shall be done; but remember that I am President of the United States and clothed with immense power, and I expect you to procure those votes." And while he was thus employing every last resource and device of practical politics to constitutionally abolish slavery, the abolitionist[12] Henry Ward Beecher attacked him with javelins of scorn and detestation in a series of editorials that brought from him the single comment, "Is thy servant a dog?"

When the King of Siam sent him a costly sword of exquisite embellishment, and two elephant tusks, along with letters and a photograph of the King, he acknowledged the gifts in a manner as lavish as the Orientals. Addressing the King of Siam as "Great and Good Friend," he wrote thanks for each of the gifts, including "also two elephant's tusks of length and magnitude, such as indicate they could have belonged only to an animal which was a native of Siam." After further thanks for the tokens received, he closed the letter to the King of Siam with strange grace and humor, saying, "I appreciate most highly your Majesty's tender of good offices in forwarding to this Government a stock from which a supply of elephants might be raised on our soil. . . our political jurisdiction, however, does not reach a latitude so low as to favor the multiplication of the elephant, and steam on land as well as water has been our best agent of transportation . . . . Meantime, wishing for your Majesty a long and happy life, and, for

12. **abolitionist** (ab′ ə lish′ ən ist) *n.* person in favor of doing away with slavery in the United States.

13 LITERATURE IN CONTEXT

History Connection

The Emancipation Proclamation

On January 1, 1863, Lincoln signed the Emancipation Proclamation, freeing the slaves in all Confederate states. The proclamation was largely a symbolic document because the federal government had no means to enforce it. Nevertheless, it gave Southern blacks cause to hope. Eventually, as Union armies advanced, freeing thousands of slaves, the promise of the proclamation became a reality.

Connect to the Literature

How were Lincoln's efforts to admit Nevada into the Union related to the passage of the Emancipation Proclamation?

14 

Who was Lincoln's best companion?

13 Literature in Context

History Connection Students may be surprised to learn what the Emancipation Proclamation actually says. On September 22, 1862, President Lincoln proclaimed that as of January 1, 1863, all slaves in states or territories in rebellion against the Union would be "thenceforward, and forever, free." The proclamation went on to say that states or territories would no longer be considered in rebellion against the Union if, on that date, they were represented in Congress. In other words, any Confederate state that rejoined the Union could keep its slaves. However, no state accepted this offer. On January 1, therefore, Lincoln issued a second proclamation that all slaves in these states were freed, that they would be welcomed into the Union army, and that the military and government of the United States would protect them.

Connect to the Literature Have students read the Literature in Context feature, and present the additional background information above. Then, point out that Sandburg mentions the passage of the Emancipation Proclamation. **Ask** students the Connect to the Literature question: How were Lincoln's efforts to admit Nevada into the Union related to the passage of the Emancipation Proclamation?

Answer: Lincoln needed Nevada's votes in order to pass the Proclamation, so he made sure that the state was admitted to the Union.

14 Reading Check

Answer: His best companion was his son.

Differentiated Instruction for Universal Access

Culturally Responsive Instruction

Culture Focus Point out to students that Lincoln receives gifts from another national leader, the King of Siam. The gifts are particular to the King's culture, being elephant tusks. Explain that the custom of giving and receiving gifts between guests and hosts is common, but that the type of gift varies from culture to culture. Invite students to share their own knowledge of customs in their home culture or family's country of origin, focusing on customs for gift exchange between leaders and between ordinary hosts and guests.

Also, point out the terms *Siam* and *Orientals*. These are both outdated terms. The first refers to the country now known as Thailand and the second refers to people now described as Asian. Explain that terms for countries and cultures change over time for many different reasons. Ask students to share their knowledge of different names given to their home country or citizens.

15 Literary Analysis

Biographical Writing

1. Read aloud the bracketed passage. Explain that this detail reveals yet another element of Lincoln's personality.
2. **Ask** the Literary Analysis question: What do you learn about Lincoln from the statement overheard by an Indiana man?

   Possible response: The statement demonstrates Lincoln's humor, gives a hint of his background, and reveals that he disliked violence.

▲ **Abraham Lincoln in 1863**

the generous and emulous people of Siam, the highest possible prosperity, I commend both to the blessing of Almighty God."

He sent hundreds of telegrams, "Suspend death sentence" or "Suspend execution" of So-and-So, who was to be shot at sunrise. The telegrams varied oddly at times, as in one, "If Thomas Samplogh, of the First Delaware Regiment, has been sentenced to death, and is not yet executed, suspend and report the case to me." And another, "Is it Lieut. Samuel B. Davis whose death sentence is commuted? If not done, let it be done."

While the war drums beat, he liked best of all the stories told of him, one of two Quakeresses[13] heard talking in a railway car. "I think that Jefferson will succeed." "Why does thee think so?" "Because Jefferson is a praying man." "And so is Abraham a praying man." "Yes, but the Lord will think Abraham is joking."

15 Literary Analysis Biographical Writing What do you learn about Lincoln from the statement overheard by an Indiana man?

An Indiana man at the White House heard him say, "Voorhees, don't it seem strange to you that I, who could never so much as cut off the head of a chicken, should be elected, or selected, into the midst of all this blood?"

A party of American citizens, standing in the ruins of the Forum in Rome, Italy, heard there the news of the first assassination of the first American dictator, and took it as a sign of the growing up and the aging of the civilization on the North American continent. Far out in Coles County, Illinois, a beautiful, gaunt old woman in a log cabin said, "I knowed he'd never come back."

Of men taking too fat profits out of the war, he said, "Where the carcass is there will the eagles be gathered together."

An enemy general, Longstreet, after the war, declared him to have been "the one matchless man in forty millions of people," while one of his private secretaries, Hay, declared his life to have been the most perfect in its relationships and adjustments since that of Christ.

Between the days in which he crawled as a baby on the dirt floor of a Kentucky cabin, and the time when he gave his final breath in Washington, he packed a rich life with work, thought, laughter, tears, hate, love.

Vocabulary
droll (drōl) *adj.* funny in an odd way

With vast reservoirs of the comic and the **droll**, and notwithstanding a mastery of mirth and nonsense, he delivered a volume of addresses and letters of terrible and serious appeal, with import beyond his own day, shot through here and there with

13. **Quakeresses** (kwā' kər es əz) *n.* female members of the religious group known as the Society of Friends, or Quakers.

Vocabulary Development

CCSS Language 6

Selection Vocabulary Reinforcement

Students will benefit from additional examples and practice with the selection vocabulary words. Reinforce their comprehension with "show-you-know" sentences. The first part of the sentence uses the vocabulary word in an appropriate context. The second part of the sentence—the "show-you-know" part—clarifies the first. Model the strategy with this example for *despotic:*

The *despotic* leader died at age 82; his people had suffered long under his rule.

1. She endured *censure* for forgetting to write the report; ________.

   Sample answer: her professor was angry about her absent-mindedness.
2. While the play wasn't a comedy, it was quite *droll;* ________.

   Sample answer: I caught myself laughing a few times.

far, thin ironics, with paragraphs having raillery[14] of the quality of the Book of Job,[15] and echoes as subtle as the whispers of wind in prairie grass.

Perhaps no human clay pot has held more laughter and tears.

6 The facts and myths of his life are to be an American possession, shared widely over the world, for thousands of years, as the tradition of Knute or Alfred, Lao-tse or Diogenes, Pericles or Caesar,[16] are kept. This because he was not only a genius in the science of neighborly human relationships and an artist in the personal handling of life from day to day, but a strange friend and a friendly stranger to all forms of life that he met.

He lived fifty-six years of which fifty-two were lived in the West—the prairie years.

Literary Analysis
Biographical Writing According to Sandburg, what personal qualities make Lincoln a great historical figure?

> Perhaps no human clay pot has held more laughter and tears.

14. **raillery** (rā′ lər ē) *n.* good-natured teasing.
15. **Book of Job** (jōb) *n.* book of the Old Testament in which Job is tested by God.
16. **Knute** (kno͞ot) **or Alfred, Lao-tse** (lou′ dzu′) **or Diogenes** (dī äj′ ə nēz′) **Pericles** (per′ ə klēz′) **or Caesar** (sē′ zər) well-known thinkers and leaders from different eras and places.

Critical Thinking

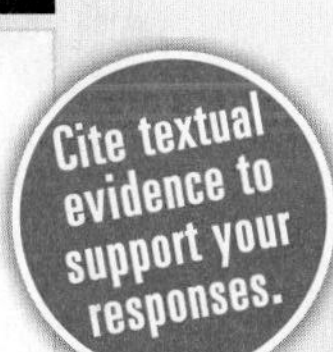
Cite textual evidence to support your responses.

1. **Key Ideas and Details (a)** To whom did Lincoln refer as "the little woman who wrote the book that made this great war"? **(b) Infer:** Why do you think Lincoln wanted to meet this woman? **(c) Draw Conclusions:** What does Lincoln's interest in meeting this woman say about his character?
2. **Key Ideas and Details (a)** How did Lincoln justify admitting Nevada to the Union? **(b) Connect:** What other examples of Lincoln's "practical" politics does the author note? **(c) Make a Judgment:** Does Sandburg seem to admire this aspect of Lincoln's character? Explain.
3. **Key Ideas and Details (a)** According to Sandburg, what aspects of Lincoln's life will be "an American possession, shared widely over the world"? **(b) Interpret:** What does Sandburg mean by this comment?
4. **Integration of Knowledge and Ideas** Sandburg says that Lincoln "packed a rich life with work, thought, laughter, tears, hate, love." Do you believe this better demonstrates Sandburg's knowledge about Lincoln or his understanding of him? Explain. *[Connect to the Big Question: Is knowledge the same as understanding?]*

Differentiated Instruction for Universal Access

Strategy for Less Proficient Readers

Most of Sandburg's sentences are long and complex. Encourage students to break down lengthy sentences to help them determine meaning. As a class, work through the last two paragraphs on p. 506, each of which is one long sentence and the second of which continues onto p. 507. You may wish to organize students in groups to discuss what is being said.

Enrichment for Advanced Readers

Encourage students who enjoyed this selection to dip into the work from which it is taken: Sandburg's classic two-volume biography of Lincoln, *The Prairie Years* and *The War Years.* Encourage students to focus on a period in Lincoln's life such as his boyhood, his law practice in Illinois, or the night of his assassination. After reading pertinent sections, have students give brief presentations of their findings about Lincoln.

16 Literary Analysis

Biographical Writing

1. Read aloud the last two paragraphs and footnote #16 to clarify historical references.
2. **Ask:** What is Sandburg saying about Lincoln by placing him in company with these figures? **Answer:** Sandburg is ranking Lincoln among the greatest civil and military leaders of all time.
3. Then, **ask** the Literary Analysis question: According to Sandburg, what personal qualities make Lincoln a great historical figure? **Answer:** Sandburg believes Lincoln's greatness lay in his ability to communicate with people of all backgrounds.

Concept Connector

Have students return to the Activating Prior Knowledge activity on p. 500 to review and revise their ideas. Then, have students compare their Writing About the Big Question responses before reading the selection with their ideas afterwards.

ASSESS

Answers

Critical Thinking

Before students respond, you may wish to have them write a brief objective summary of the selection. As they answer the questions below, remind them to support their answers with evidence from the text.

1. (a) Lincoln was referring to Harriet Beecher Stowe. (b) **Possible responses:** He was probably impressed with her presentation of the evils of slavery. (c) He valued other people's accomplishments.
2. (a) He hoped to end the war sooner and save soldiers' lives. (b) He had the Cabinet vote, despite having already appointed someone. (c) Sandburg seems to approve of Lincoln's single-minded pursuit of a worthy goal.
3. (a) Sandburg was referring to the facts and myths of Lincoln's life. (b) Lincoln is an enduring hero.
4. **Possible responses:** It takes Sandburg's understanding of Lincoln to describe these experiences as "a rich life" and to realize how these emotions influenced Lincoln's actions.

17 Background

Arthur Ashe He may have been best known as a tennis master, but Arthur Ashe (1943–1993) was also a dedicated advocate of many social causes. He spoke out angrily against South African apartheid after being denied a visa to that country because of his race. He was also a spokesman for underprivileged people who could not afford healthcare, and created the Arthur Ashe Institute for Urban Health just months before he died. This Institute is devoted to the national promotion of preventative care and health education.

18 Activating Prior Knowledge

Engage students in a discussion about their favorite athletes. Ask them to identify the traits that they admire about each one and list their answers on the board. Tell students that Arthur Ashe was admired not only for his athleticism, but also for his devotion to important social causes.

Concept Connector

Students will follow up on this activity after completing the excerpt from *Arthur Ashe Remembered.*

19 About the Selection

In this excerpt from *Arthur Ashe Remembered*, John McPhee recalls American tennis champion Arthur Ashe as a cool, self-controlled player who always took risks on the court.

17 18 19

Arthur Ashe Remembered

John McPhee

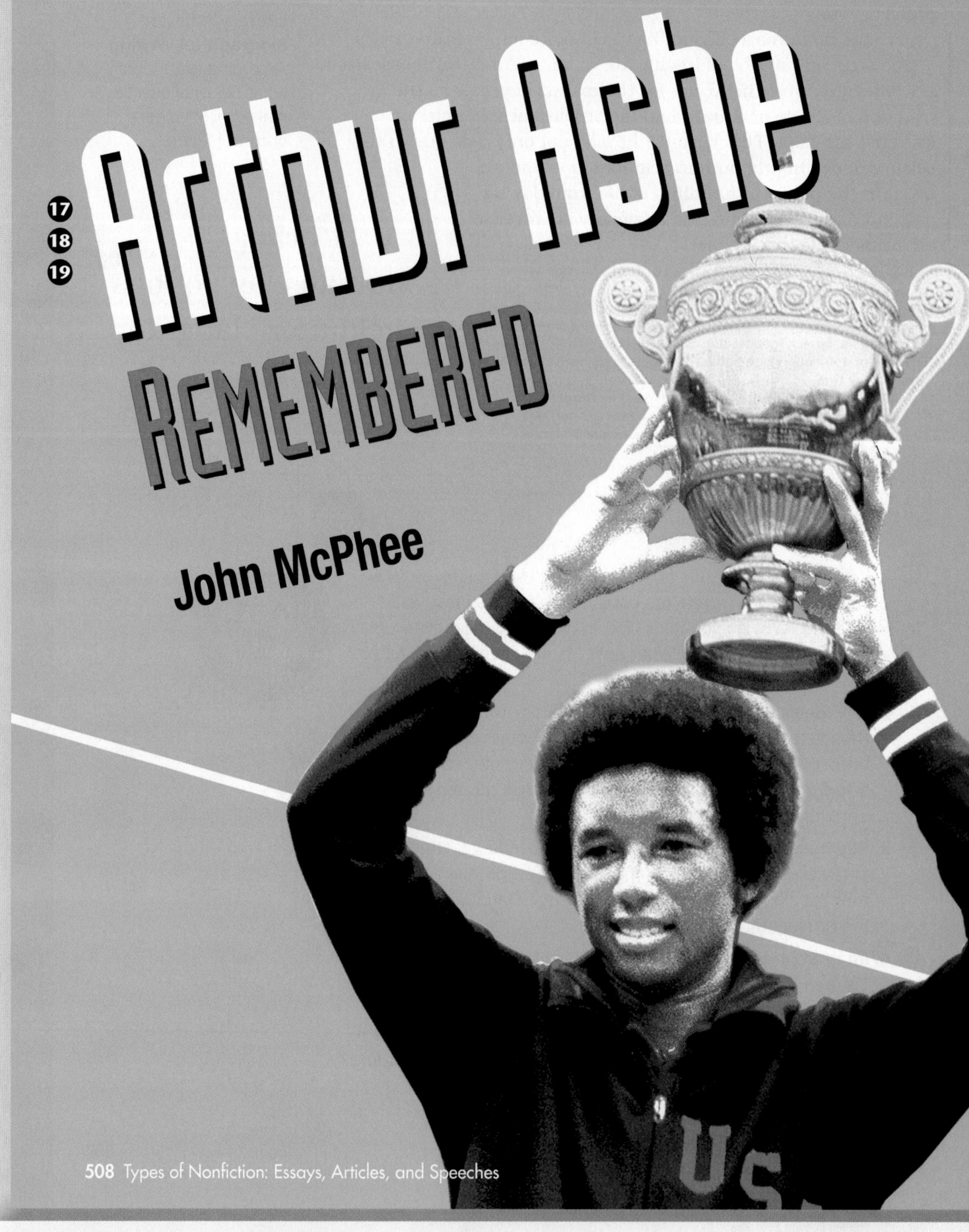

Text Complexity Rubric

Arthur Ashe Remembered		
Qualitative Measures	**Context/ Knowledge Demands**	Description of Arthur Ashe's hardships and personality 1 2 (3) 4 5
	Structure/ Language Clarity and Conventionality	Tennis vocabulary 1 2 (3) 4 5
	Levels of Meaning/ Purpose/Concept Level	Accessible concept (perseverance through hardship) 1 (2) 3 4 5
Quantitative Measures	**Text Length**	Word Count: 596
	Lexile	970L

Background Arthur Ashe was the first African American man to achieve fame in tennis. When he was six years old, his mother died of heart disease. Ashe's father worked as a caretaker in a neighborhood park, where Ashe spent hours playing on the tennis courts. Ashe went on to win numerous honors in tennis, including the 1968 U.S. Open and the 1975 Wimbledon singles championship. Throughout his life, Ashe devoted himself to issues of human rights, education, and public health. After struggling with heart problems, he contracted AIDS from a transfusion during by-pass surgery. He founded the Arthur Ashe Foundation for the Defeat of AIDS before his death in 1993.

He once described his life as "a succession of fortunate circumstances." He was in his twenties then. More than half of his life was behind him. His memory of his mother was confined to a single image: in a blue corduroy bathrobe she stood in a doorway looking out on the courts and playing fields surrounding their house, which stood in the center of a Richmond playground. Weakened by illness, she was taken to a hospital that day, and died at the age of twenty-seven. He was six.

It was to be his tragedy, as the world knows, that he would leave his own child when she was six, that his life would be trapped in a medical irony as a result of early heart disease, and death would come to him prematurely, as it had to his mother.

His mother was tall, with long soft hair and a face that was gentle and thin. She read a lot. She read a lot to him. His father said of her, "She was just like Arthur Junior. She never argued. She was quiet, easygoing, kindhearted."

If by **legacy** her son never argued, he was also schooled, instructed, coached not to argue, and as he moved alone into alien country he fashioned not-arguing into an enigma and turned the **enigma** into a weapon. When things got tough (as I noted in these pages twenty-four years ago[1]), he had control. Even in very tight moments, other players thought he was toying with them. They rarely knew what he was thinking. They could not tell if he was angry. It was maddening, sometimes, to play against him. Never less than candid, he said that what he liked best about himself on a tennis court was his demeanor: "What it is is controlled cool, in a way. Always have the situation under control, even if losing. Never betray an inward sense of defeat."

1. **twenty-four years ago** McPhee refers to an article published in 1969.

21 ◀ **Critical Viewing** Based on this photograph, what emotions did Ashe express when he won the Wimbledon Championship in 1975? **[Assess]**

Vocabulary

legacy (leg´ ə sē) *n.* something handed down from an ancestor

enigma (i nig´ mə) *n.* mystery

22 

What personality trait did Ashe share with his mother?

20 Connecting to the Big Question

1. Explain that in a biography, knowledge is communicated through the details about a person's life, while understanding is communicated through descriptions or interpretations of those details.
2. Direct students' attention to the bracketed passage. **Ask:** What qualities does John McPhee describe in Arthur Ashe? **Possible response:** He describes Ashe as strong and self-controlled.
3. **Ask** students: What details, or knowledge, does McPhee use to support his description, or understanding, of Ashe?

   Possible response: McPhee supports his understanding of Ashe with the knowledge that Ashe was brought up not to argue and that he had a maddening coolness on the court.

21 Critical Viewing

Answer: Ashe is probably excited, proud, and happy.

22 Reading Check

Answer: They were both mild-mannered.

PHLit Online!

This selection is available in interactive format in the Enriched Online Student Edition, **www.PHLitOnline.com**, which includes an interactive graphic organizer.

Text Complexity: Reader and Task Suggestions

Arthur Ashe Remembered	
Preparing to Read the Text • Use the Background information on TE p. 508 as a basis for discussing Arthur Ashe's career and his life off the court. • Review the game of tennis, identifying key terms. • Guide students to use Multidraft Reading strategies (TE p. 499).	**Leveled Tasks** *Knowledge Demands* If students will have difficulty understanding Ashe's background, have them first read and note the personal and professional obstacles he faced. Then, have them reread and identify how he dealt with these obstacles. Discuss student notes and clarify meaning. *Analyzing* If students will not have difficulty understanding Ashe's background, have them read and take notes on McPhee's techniques for sketching a brief but revealing biography of Ashe. Discuss students' notes and ideas in class.

23 Literary Analysis

Biographical Writing

1. Explain that McPhee uses details about Ashe's tennis game to make a statement about Ashe's personality.
2. **Ask** the Literary Analysis question.
   Possible response: It reveals that in tough times, Ashe was calm and determined.

ASSESS

Answers

Critical Thinking

Remind students to support their answers with evidence from the text.

1. (a) Both were quiet, easygoing, and kind-hearted; they never argued. (b) Ashe likes his self-control and optimism. (c) Ashe was self-controlled, dignified, enigmatic, and unpredictable.
2. (a) Ashe called his life "a succession of fortunate circumstances." (b) No—Ashe's life began with his mother's tragic death and ended with his own early death.
3. (a) His approach was controlled, but daring. (b) People should be daring and never give way to that "sense of defeat."
4. **Possible responses:** Details that show why Arthur Ashe kept his emotions under control and how he went all out rather than take the easy shot helped me understand him.

Vocabulary
lithe (līth) *adj.* flexible

Literary Analysis
Biographical Writing
What does this description of Ashe's tennis game reveal about his character?

And of course he never did—not in the height of his athletic power, not in the statesmanship of the years that followed, and not in the endgame of his existence. If you wished to choose a single image, you would see him standing there in his twenties, his **lithe** body a braid of cables, his energy without apparent limit, in a court situation indescribably bad, and all he does is put his index finger on the bridge of his glasses and push them back up the bridge of his nose. In the shadow of disaster, he hits out. Faced with a choice between a conservative, percentage return or a one-in-ten flat-out blast, he chooses the blast. In a signature manner, he extends his left arm to point upward at lobs as they fall toward him. His overheads, in fire bursts, put them away. His backhand is, if anything, stronger than his forehand, and his shots from either side for the most part are explosions. In motions graceful and decisive, though, and with reactions as fast as the imagination, he is a master of drop shots, of cat-and-mouse, of miscellaneous dinks and chips and (riskiest of all) the crosscourt half-volley. Other tennis players might be wondering who in his right mind would attempt something like that, but that is how Ashe plays the game: at the tensest moment, he goes for the all but impossible. He is predictably unpredictable. He is unreadable. His ballistic serves move in odd patterns and come off the court in unexpected ways. Behind his impassive face—behind the enigmatic glasses, the lifted chin, the first-mate-on-the-bridge look—there seems to be, even from this distance, a smile.

Critical Thinking

Cite textual evidence to support your responses.

1. **Key Ideas and Details (a)** According to his father, how was Ashe like his mother? **(b) Summarize:** What does Ashe say he likes best about himself on the court? **(c) Draw Conclusions:** Based on this article, how would you describe Ashe's character?
2. **Key Ideas and Details (a)** How did Ashe once describe his life? **(b) Make a Judgment:** Does this description seem accurate based on the information in this biography?
3. **Key Ideas and Details (a) Summarize:** Summarize Ashe's approach to tennis. **(b) Apply:** In what ways might Ashe's approach to tennis be seen as an approach to life?
4. **Integration of Knowledge and Ideas** Which details in the article helped you understand Ashe better than if you had read only statistics related to his tennis career? Discuss your response with a partner. ***[Connect to the Big Question: Is knowledge the same as understanding?]***

Vocabulary Development

CCSS Language 6

Vocabulary Knowledge Rating

When students have completed reading the excerpts from *A Lincoln Preface* and *Arthur Ashe Remembered,* have them take out their **Vocabulary Rating Chart.** Read the words aloud once more and have students rate their knowledge of the words again in the After Reading column. Clarify any words that are still problematic. Have students write their own definition and example or sentence in the appropriate column. Then have students complete the vocabulary practice activities on the next page. Encourage students to use the words in further discussion and written work about the selections. Remind them that they will be accountable for these words on the **Selection Test,** ***Unit 3 Resources,*** pp. 112–114 or 115–117.

After You Read

from A Lincoln Preface • Arthur Ashe Remembered

Comparing Points of View

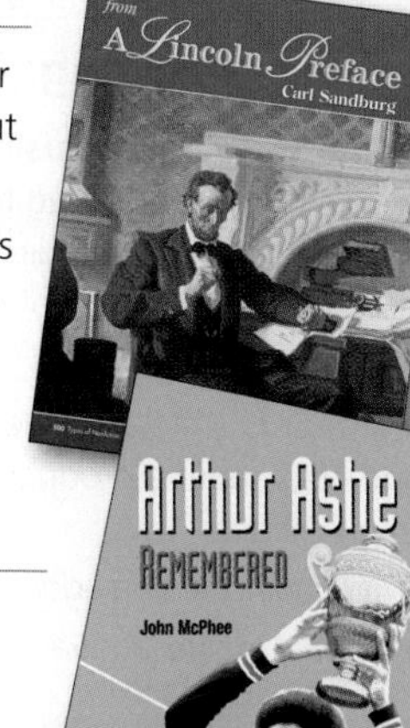

1. **Key Ideas and Details** Identify at least three facts that each author includes about his subject. Then, explain what each fact shows about the subject.
2. **Key Ideas and Details (a)** For each biography, note two statements the biographer makes that are interpretations of information about the subject. **(b)** What does each statement show about the biographer's attitude toward his subject? Explain.

Timed Writing

Explanatory Text: Essay

Write an essay in which you compare your reaction to the excerpt from *A Lincoln Preface* to your reaction to "Arthur Ashe Remembered." In your response, explain how the writer's tone affected your reaction. **(25 minutes)**

5-Minute Planner

1. Read the prompt carefully and completely.
2. Gather your ideas. Consider these questions before you write:
   - Does each writer clearly convey why his subject is important?
   - Did you respond more to the description of Abraham Lincoln or the description of Arthur Ashe? Why?
   - What main impression do you think each writer wants to convey?
   - Using a chart like the one shown, record your main impression of each author's work, as well as details that support your responses. Use these notes to build your essay.

Author	Main Impression	Details
Sandburg		
McPhee		

3. Make a quick outline of your essay, deciding which points you will cover in each section. **TIP** Consider how you will move from one point to the next. As you develop your draft, include transitions that help convey your exact meaning.
4. Reread the prompt, and then draft your essay.

Assessment Resources

The following resources can be used to assess students' knowledge and skills.

Unit 3 Resources

L1 L2 EL **Selection Test A,** pp. 112–114

L3 L4 EL **Selection Test B,** pp. 115–117

L3 L4 **Open Book Test,** pp. 109–111

All assessment resources are available at **www.PHLitOnline.com.**

ASSESS

Answers

Comparing Points of View

1. **Sample answer: Fact from** *A Lincoln Preface*—Lincoln said to Harriet Beecher Stowe, "So you're the little woman who wrote the book that made this great war." **What the fact shows:** This shows that Lincoln had a sense of humor. **Sample answer: Fact from** *Arthur Ashe Remembered*—Ashe's mother died when he was very young. **What the fact shows**—Ashe had to overcome personal loss to reach success.
2. **Sample answers:** (a) *A Lincoln Preface:* He asked his Cabinet to vote on an appointment, then revealed that the appointment had already been made; his life, mind, and heart ran in contrasts. *Arthur Ashe Remembered*: When things got tough, he had control; he is predictably unpredictable. (b) Each statement shows that the biographer respects his subject. McPhee admires Ashe for his courage, his calm demeanor, and his uncanny ability to do whatever it took to meet his goals.

Timed Writing

1. Review the prompt with students.
2. Have students use the 5-Minute Planner to structure their time. Guide them in answering the bulleted questions. For example, point out that their own cultures, backgrounds, and beliefs, as well as the writer's tone, will influence their responses to the biographical subjects.
3. Allow students 25 minutes to complete the assignment.
4. As students prewrite and draft, have them refer to their completed Comparing Biographical Writing Graphic Organizer B Graphic Organizer.

Six Traits Focus

✓	Ideas	Word Choice
✓	Organization	Sentence Fluency
	Voice	Conventions

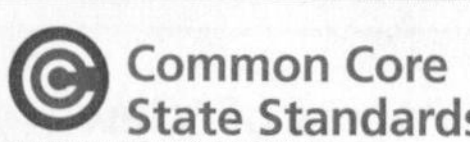

PRETEACH

Common Core State Standards

- Writing 2, 2.a, d, e, f; 4, 6

Introducing the Writing Assignment

Review the assignment and the criteria, using the instruction on the student page.

Connecting to Real-Life Writing

Explain that business letters are useful when writing cover letters for job applications and resumes.

Writing Workshop

Work in Progress

If students have completed the work in progress assignments on p. 463 and 489, suggest that they try to develop their work in progress ideas in a business letter.

TEACH

Prewriting/Planning Strategy

1. Introduce the prewriting strategy, using the instruction on the student page.
2. Have students apply the strategy to choose a topic.

Six Traits Focus

✓	Ideas	Word Choice
	Organization	Sentence Fluency
	Voice	Conventions

Writing Workshop

Write Explanatory Text

Workplace Writing: Business Letter

Defining the Form A **business letter** is a piece of correspondence that you write when conducting business or professional matters. Effective business letters are clear, direct, courteous, and well formatted. You might use elements of this type of writing in requests for information, appointments, or interviews; formal complaints or commendations; or proposals.

Assignment Write a business letter to a company in which you ask for information about a product or service you are interested in using. Include these elements:

✓ a *heading, inside address, greeting, body, closing,* and *signature*

✓ *formal, polite language*, a clear *purpose*, and relevant background information

✓ standard *formatting* with consistent spacing and indentation

✓ error-free grammar, including *correct use of compound subjects, objects, and complements*

To preview the criteria on which your business letter may be judged, see the rubric on page 517.

 **Writing Workshop:** *Work in Progress*

Review the work you did on pages 463 and 489.

Prewriting/Planning Strategy

Brainstorm and itemize. Jot down a list of products or services that interest you. Itemize each by noting what you want to learn about this product or service. Search the Internet or phone book to locate each company's address. Then, decide which details of performance, features, price, or reliability matter most to you. Choose a topic from your list.

Products and Services	Company	Interest
Bicycle	A Bicycle Shop	What kind of bike is best for me? Which has the most options for the lowest price?
Cell Phone	Air Time Cell Phones	Which phone is the cheapest and best? How reliable is the service?
Homework Help	A+ Tutors	How often is it provided? What is the improvement rate? What does it cost?

Common Core State Standards

Writing

2. Write informative/explanatory texts to examine and convey complex ideas, concepts, and information clearly and accurately through the effective selection, organization, and analysis of content.

2.a. Introduce a topic; organize complex ideas, concepts, and information to make important connections and distinctions; include formatting when useful to aiding comprehension.

2.e. Establish and maintain a formal style and objective tone while attending to the norms and conventions of the discipline in which they are writing.

4. Produce clear and coherent writing in which the development, organization, and style are appropriate to task, purpose, and audience.

Teaching Resources

The following resources can be used to enrich or extend the instruction.

All *Unit 3 Resources*
Writing Workshop, pp. 118–119

All *Common Core Companion,* pp. 190–214

All *Professional Development Guidebooks*
Rubrics for Self-Assessment: Business Letter, pp. 265–266

All *Graphic Organizer Transparencies*
Rubric for Self-Assessment: Business Letter, p. 91

All resources are also available online at **www.PHLitOnline.com**.

SIX TRAITS WRITER'S TOOLBOX SIX TRAITS

Voice | Organization | Word Choice | Ideas | Conventions | Sentence Fluency

Setting Your Tone

The **voice** of a business letter sets the stage for the response you will receive. Busy professionals respond well to concise letters that include only essential information presented in an appropriate, formal style. The voice is created by the use of formal vocabulary and tone. The **tone** is the attitude you take toward the subject of your letter.

Identifying Audience If you were writing an e-mail to a close friend, you would likely use slang, abbreviations, and a loose format, if you used a format at all. Your friend would pick up on the casual tone and likely respond in a similar manner. However, when you are writing a business letter, your tone needs to be businesslike. You are not simply chatting with a friend. You want information. You should express yourself clearly and professionally to receive the assistance you need. You might even need to do some research on your topic before you begin to write. Doing so will enable you to ask relevant questions.

Maintaining Consistency Use these steps to maintain a formal tone:

- Avoid slang and contractions.
- Replace casual language with formal expressions.
- Include only essential information the person needs to answer your questions.
- Follow formatting conventions.

These two letters request the same information, but they are quite different in tone.

Casual Letter	Formal Letter
I love riding bicycles. I have outgrown mine and want a new one really badly. Which is the best kind for me? How much does it cost?	I am planning on purchasing a new bicycle. I like riding on the street, but I mostly ride the bike trails with my parents. Would a mountain bike be best for me? Or would a hybrid better serve my needs? What is the price range for recreational bicycles like these?

Setting Your Tone

1. Introduce the writing skill, using the instruction on the student page.
2. Discuss the strategies for setting the tone of a business letter.

Teaching the Writing Skill

1. Review the use of different tones when speaking. Invite a volunteer to convey in a casual tone the information that the school is going to host a performing arts show. Invite another volunteer to convey the same information in a formal tone. Then remind the class that writing also uses casual and formal tones.
2. Write the following information on the board: *Meeting – Monday at 3 – spring sports.* Have students write two sentences, one in a casual tone and one in a formal tone, to convey that information to readers. Have volunteers read aloud their sentences.
3. Tell students that the writer of a business letter is often not acquainted with the intended recipient of the letter. Remind students that the purpose of business letters is to convey information and to ask questions, not to chat. Words and sentence structure should reflect that purpose.
4. Review the examples on the student page. Tell students that using a respectful tone in a business letter will help develop a better relationship with the letter's recipient.

Prentice Hall EssayScorer

A writing prompt for this mode of writing can be found on the ***Prentice Hall Essay Scorer*** at **www.PHLitOnline.com.**

Differentiated Instruction for Universal Access

EL Strategy for English Learners
To help English language learners distinguish between a formal and informal tone, give students the following word list: *awesome, cool, flaky, megabucks.* Review the meaning of each term and explain that these are informal, slang terms. Work with students to use an online or print thesaurus and find synonyms that are more formal in tone. *(awesome – impressive; cool – splendid; flaky – eccentric; megabucks – wealth)*

Drafting Strategies

1. Introduce the drafting strategies, using the instruction on the student page.
2. Have students apply the strategies as they draft.

Teaching the Strategies

1. Provide students with models of business letters structured in block and modified block formats.
2. Suggest that students revise the business letter elements checklist into an outline for their letters.

Six Traits Focus

	Ideas	✓	Word Choice
✓	Organization		Sentence Fluency
	Voice		Conventions

Revising Strategy

1. Introduce the revision strategy, using the instruction on the student page.
2. Have students apply the strategy as they revise their business letters.

Teaching the Strategy

1. Work with students to identify their sentences written in the passive voice.
2. Invite volunteers to share their original sentences using the passive voice and their rewritten sentences using the active voice.

Six Traits Focus

	Ideas	✓	Word Choice
	Organization		Sentence Fluency
✓	Voice		Conventions

Drafting Strategies

Select a format. Choose a standard business letter format, using a consistent font and spacing. This will contribute to the readability and impact of your letter. You may use block format, in which each part of the letter begins at the left margin. Alternatively, you may use modified block format, in which the heading, closing, and signature are indented to the center of the page. (For a sample business letter, see page R34.) Use the checklist shown here to verify that your draft includes all six elements of a business letter.

Business Letter Elements

- ❑ **Heading**—the writer's address and organization (if any) and the date
- ❑ **Inside Address**—where the letter will be sent
- ❑ **Greeting**—a salutation, always punctuated by a colon
- ❑ **Body**—a presentation of the writer's purpose
- ❑ **Closing**—an appropriate farewell
- ❑ **Signature**—a hand-signed name

Write a memo—Spread the news. If your purpose is to give information to a number of people, you might choose to send a memo instead of the more formal letter format. A memo has all the information at the top—who wrote it, whom it is to, the date, and the subject. The body of the memo contains the pertinent information. Memos do not have addresses, greetings, or closings.

E-mail—Take it to the Internet. E-mail is an efficient way to request or present information. It is less formal than a business letter, but it can be speedier and provide direct access to the source of information. When you write an e-mail, be clear in your subject line. The subject line of an e-mail is much like one in a memo. It should be short and to the point. Include a greeting, a body, a closing, and an electronic signature in your e-mail.

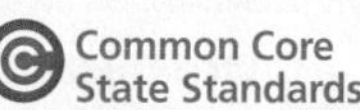

Writing

2.a. Introduce a topic; organize complex ideas, concepts, and information to make important connections and distinctions; include formatting when useful to aiding comprehension.

2.d. Use precise language and domain-specific vocabulary to manage the complexity of the topic.

2.f. Provide a concluding statement or section that follows from and supports the information or explanation presented.

6. Use technology, including the Internet, to produce, publish, and update individual or shared writing products, taking advantage of technology's capacity to link other information and to display information flexibly and dynamically.

Revising Strategy

Highlight the active voice. A verb in the active voice expresses an action done by its subject. A verb in the passive voice expresses an action done to its subject.

Passive Voice: The vacuum cleaner *was broken* by the salesman.

Active Voice: The salesman *broke* the vacuum cleaner.

The active voice is preferable because it produces a more direct and forceful sentence than the passive voice. Review your draft, highlighting verbs written in the passive voice; then, rewrite the sentences in the active voice when you can.

Applying Understanding by Design Principles

Clarifying Expected Outcomes: Using Rubrics

- Before students begin working on this assignment, have them preview the Rubric for Self-Assessment (p. 517) to learn what qualities their business letters must have. A copy of this rubric appears in ***Graphic Organizer Transparencies,*** p. 91.
- Review the criteria in the Rubric with the class. Before students use the Rubric to assess their writing, work with them to rate the Student Model (p. 516) using the Rubric.
- If you wish to assess students' business letters with either a 4-point or a 6-point scoring rubric, see ***Professional Development Guidebook,*** pp. 265–266.

SIX TRAITS WRITER'S TOOLBOX SIX TRAITS

Sentence Fluency | Voice | Organization | Word Choice | Ideas | Conventions

Revising to Combine Choppy Sentences

Revising to Combine Choppy Sentences Avoid choppy, disconnected sentences by combining two or more related ideas into a single sentence.

Methods of Sentence Combining **Compound verbs—**more than one verb linked to a single subject—can be used to combine two short sentences:

Choppy: I *disconnected* my phone. I *brought* it in for service.

Compound Verb: I *disconnected* my phone and *brought* it in for service.

Compound objects—more than one object linked to a single verb—can help combine sentences.

Choppy: I purchased *a scanner.* I purchased *a fax machine.*

Compound Object: I purchased *a scanner and a fax machine.*

A third option is the use of **compound predicate nominatives** or **predicate adjectives.**

Choppy: My newest device *is a printer.* It is also *a scanner.* It is also *a fax machine.*

Compound Predicative Nominative: My newest device *is a printer, scanner, and fax machine.*

Choppy: The fax is *automated.* It is *fast.*

Compound Predicative Adjective: The fax is *automated and fast.*

Fixing Choppy Sentences Scan your draft for sentence variety.

1. **Read your draft aloud.** Listen for overuse of short sentences.
2. **Identify sentences that can be combined.** Look for sentences that share a common subject or a common predicate element.
3. **Use a variety of sentence combining techniques.** Use compound verbs, compound direct objects, or compound predicate nominatives or predicate adjectives to create a wider variety of flowing sentences.

PH WRITING COACH

Further instruction and practice are available in *Prentice Hall Writing Coach.*

Grammar in Your Writing

Review the body paragraphs in your letter, highlighting central ideas or images. Use various types of phrases and clauses to convey specific meanings and to add interest. Be sure to use punctuation to separate items in a series.

Revising to Combine Choppy Sentences

1. Introduce the grammar skill, using the instruction on the student page.
2. Discuss the examples and methods of combining sentences and the strategies for fixing choppy sentences.
3. Have students follow the instruction under Grammar in Your Writing to correct errors in their drafts.

Teaching the Grammar Skill

1. Point out to students that choppy sentences sometimes occur when writers are overly focused on clarity or when writers fail to write with the same fluidity they use with spoken language.
2. Write the following sentences on the board and have students combine them. For enrichment, have students combine each sentence in more than one way and discuss the effects of each.
   - *Jevon sat at the table. He ate his lunch.*
   - *Fiona ordered steak. She ordered rice as well.*
   - *Taylor is a dedicated student. She is also a talented athlete.*
   - *His report is organized. It is also concise.*

Possible responses:

- *Jevon sat at the table and ate his lunch.*
- *Fiona ordered steak and rice.*
- *Taylor is a dedicated student and a talented athlete.*
- *His report is organized and concise.*

PH WRITING COACH Grade 9

Students will find practice with and guidance on combining sentences in Chapter 16.

Differentiated Instruction for Universal Access

Strategy for Advanced Readers

Point out to students that there is often more than one way to combine sentences. Also explain that some short sentences are acceptable; they add variety and interest when combined with longer sentences. Write these sentences on the board.

Jevon walked to school. Then he entered the classroom. He was early. He was also full of confidence.

Add these possible combinations to the board.

Jevon walked to school and entered the classroom. He was early and full of confidence.

Jevon walked to school. He entered the classroom early and full of confidence.

Point out that the second example demonstrates variety in writing by pairing a short sentence with a longer sentence. Have students review their drafts for a variety of sentence lengths.

Student Model

Review the Student Model with the class, using the annotations to analyze the writer's use of the elements of a business letter.

Teaching from the Student Model

1. Explain that the Student Model is a sample and that their own business letters may be longer.
2. Explain that Robin assumes the proper voice by using formal language. **Ask** students to identify instances in the letter where formal language is used.

   Possible response: Students may note *Sir or Madam, I would appreciate,* or *we are also concerned* as examples of formal language.
3. **Ask** students why the author states his purpose early in the letter and how he makes his purpose clear and concise.

   Possible response: He states the purpose early to let the reader know his intentions immediately. He makes his purpose clear and concise by avoiding chatty and unnecessary language.
4. Point out that the background information helps the reader understand why the letter has been written.
5. **Ask** students how the writer would modify this letter to use a block format.

   Answer: The writer could begin each part at the left margin.
6. Write these sentences on the board:

   I am excited to learn more about your product. Thank you for your time.

   Tell students that this is another example of a polite conclusion. Ask students to review their letters and to determine whether they have incorporated polite endings.

Connecting to Real-Life Writing

Explain to students that job applications often require cover letters. Tell students that they may need to write to a company to voice a complaint or a compliment about a product or service. Also tell students that they may be asked to write to a local official, a business owner, or another organization on behalf of a club or organization to which they belong.

Student Model: Robin Weber, St. Petersburg, FL

Intelligent Productions
220 Any Street, Suite 112
Any Town, NY 10000
December 13, 2006

G-2000 Computers
310 Infinite Loop
Any City, CA 94000

Dear Sir or Madam:

My business is currently in the market for several high-end, reliable server computers. I would like to obtain more information about your line of server products.

The computers we use are operating twenty-four hours a day, seven days a week, as servers hosting a high-traffic Internet Web site. Therefore, it would be unacceptable for my company to purchase computers that require periods of inactivity in order to remain in working condition. We are also concerned about technical support issues and costs.

I would appreciate if you could send me the exact specifications on catalog items number 1444 and 2314. In addition, there is no information on warranties in your product descriptions. Any information you can provide in this regard would be very helpful in making my purchasing decision. Also, would it be possible to obtain a high-volume discount? How would such an order affect delivery time?

Please send me any information you have on these matters. I look foward to hearing from you.

Sincerely,

Robin Weber

Robin Weber

Robin uses modified block format.

Robin's purpose is stated clearly and concisely.

In this paragraph, Robin provides important background information.

The letter includes specific questions that Robin would like answered.

In his conclusion, Robin summarizes the request using polite language.

Editing and Proofreading

Check your draft for errors in format, grammar, and punctuation.

Focus on accuracy. Make certain that the names of individuals and companies are spelled correctly and that the address is complete. Check the capitalizations and abbreviations to ensure they are correct.

Spiral Review

Earlier in the unit, you learned about **direct and indirect objects** (p. 462) and **predicate nominatives and predicate adjectives** (p. 488). Before you send your letter, check to be sure you have used these grammatical forms correctly.

Publishing and Presenting

Consider one of the following ways to share your writing:

Send your letter. If your letter is written to an existing business, mail it. When you get a response, share it with classmates.

Conduct a discussion. Use your letter to begin a class discussion about the role of communication skills in everyday life. To improve the productivity of the discussion, be open to the variety of ideas your classmates suggest. Make notes on their comments, and add your letter and notes to your writing portfolio.

Reflecting on Your Writing

Writer's Journal Jot down your answer to this question:

How is business writing different than other types of writing?

Rubric for Self-Assessment

Find evidence in your writing to address each category. Then, use the rating scale to grade your work.

Criteria	Rating Scale (not very — very)
Voice: How well have you maintained a consistently formal tone?	1 2 3 4 5
Focus: How clearly have you stated your purpose?	1 2 3 4 5
Organization: How thoroughly have you incorporated all the elements of a business letter?	1 2 3 4 5
Support/Elaboration: How comprehensive is the background information you provided?	1 2 3 4 5
Style: How formal and polite is your use of language?	1 2 3 4 5
Conventions: How correct is your grammar, especially your use of compound subjects, objects, and complements?	1 2 3 4 5

Editing and Proofreading

1. Introduce the editing and proofreading focus, using the instruction on the student page.
2. Have students edit and proofread their business letters, correcting grammar, spelling, punctuation, and word choice. Make sure they check for errors of the type noted in the lesson focus and the Spiral Review.

Teaching the Editing Focus

1. Make sure that students go beyond the heading when looking for mistakes in the names and addresses. Tell them that they should review the entire letter.
2. After they have checked names and addresses, have students exchange letters with partners. Ask partners to verify that the information is correct. Explain to students that when editing, it can be helpful to have someone else take another look for mistakes.

Six Traits Focus

	Ideas		Word Choice
	Organization		Sentence Fluency
	Voice	✓	Conventions

ASSESS

Publishing and Presenting

1. If students choose to mail their letters, review the proper format for addressing an envelope. Tell students who expect replies to enclose self-addressed, stamped envelopes as well.
2. Students can read aloud their letters to classmates and jot down any helpful feedback.

Reflecting on Your Writing

Lead a discussion on using a businesslike tone in letters. Have students compare writing a business letter to writing a letter to a friend.

Strategies for Test Taking

Tell students that when they take a test that requires them to evaluate the components of a business letter, they may have difficulty remembering all six elements (heading, inside address, greeting, body, closing, and signature). Encourage students to combine their past experiences in writing business letters with common sense and then review the letter to check whether anything appears to be missing.

✓ Carry Your Own Skis • ✓✓ Libraries Face Sad Chapter

Lesson Pacing Guide

DAY 1 Preteach

- Administer the Reading and Vocabulary Warm-ups (*Unit 3 Resources*, pp. 127–130 or 145–148) as necessary.
- Introduce the Reading Skill: Evaluate Persuasion.
- Introduce the Literary Analysis concept: Persuasive Essay.
- Distribute copies of the appropriate graphic organizer for the Reading Skill (*Graphic Organizer Transparencies*, pp. 92–94).
- Distribute copies of the appropriate graphic organizer for Literary Analysis (*Graphic Organizer Transparencies*, pp. 95–97).
- Teach the selection vocabulary.
- Introduce the Word Study skill.

DAYS 2–3 Preteach/Teach

- Build background with the Background feature.
- Develop thematic vocabulary and thematic thinking with Writing About the Big Question.
- Prepare students to read with the Activating Prior Knowledge activities (TE).
- Informally monitor comprehension while students read.
- Use the Reading Check questions to confirm comprehension.
- Develop students' ability to evaluate persuasion, using the Reading Skill questions.
- Develop students' understanding of persuasive essays, using the Literacy Analysis questions.
- Reinforce vocabulary with the Vocabulary notes.
- Reinforce unit focus standards using the Spiral Review prompts.

DAY 4 Assess

- Assess students' comprehension and mastery of the skills by having them answer the Critical Thinking, Reading Skill, and Literary Analysis questions.
- Have students complete the Vocabulary Practice activities.
- Have students complete the Word Study activities.

DAY 5 Extend/Assess

- Have students complete the Conventions lesson.
- Have students complete the Writing activity and write an abstract. (You may assign as homework.)
- Extend learning by assigning the Research and Technology, a comparative chart. (You may assign as homework.) As an alternative, assign them "Paths for Learning" or "The Community Comes to School" in *Reality Central*.
- Assign Selection Test A or B (*Unit 3 Resources*, pp. 139–144 or 160–165).

Common Core State Standards

Reading Informational Text
6. Determine an author's point of view or purpose in a text and analyze how an author uses rhetoric to advance that point of view or purpose.
8. Delineate and evaluate the argument and specific claims in a text, assessing whether the reasoning is valid and the evidence is relevant and sufficient; identify false statements and fallacious reasoning.

Writing 4. Produce clear and coherent writing in which the development, organization, and style are appropriate to task, purpose, and audience.

Speaking and Listening 4. Present information, findings, and supporting evidence clearly, concisely, and logically such that listeners can follow the line of reasoning and the organization, development, substance, and style are appropriate to purpose, audience, and task.

Language 1. Demonstrate command of the conventions of standard English grammar and usage when writing and speaking.
5. Demonstrate understanding of figurative language, word relationships, and nuances in word meanings.

Additional Standards Practice
***Common Core Companion*, pp. 110–144**

Daily Block Scheduling
Each day in this Lesson Pacing Guide represents a 40–50 minute period. Teachers using block scheduling may combine days to revise pacing. In addition, teachers may differentiate and support core instruction by integrating components for extended and intensive support as students require. See the Guide to Selected Leveled Resources (facing page).

Guide to Selected Leveled Resources

RTI Tier 1 (students performing on level)		✓ More Accessible Carry Your Own Skis	✓✓ More Complex Libraries Face Sad Chapter
Warm Up	**Practice, model,** and **monitor** fluency, working **with the whole class** or **in groups**.	**Vocabulary** and **Reading Warm-ups B,** ***Unit 3 Resources,*** pp. 127–128, 130	**Vocabulary** and **Reading Warm-ups B,** ***Unit 3 Resources,*** pp. 145–146, 148
Comprehension/Skills	**Support** and **monitor** comprehension and skills development, having students complete the activities, graphic organizers, and interactive prompts **independently** or **as a class**.	• ***Reader's Notebook,*** adapted instruction and full selection EL ***Reader's Notebook: English Learner's Version,*** adapted instruction and adapted selection • **Reading Skill Graphic Organizer B,** ***Graphic Organizer Transparencies,*** p. 94 • **Literary Analysis Graphic Organizer B,** ***Graphic Organizer Transparencies,*** p. 97	• ***Reader's Notebook,*** adapted instruction and summary EL ***Reader's Notebook: English Learner's Version,*** adapted instruction and summary • **Reading Skill Graphic Organizer B,** ***Graphic Organizer Transparencies,*** p. 94 • **Literary Analysis Graphic Organizer B,** ***Graphic Organizer Transparencies,*** p. 97
Monitor Progress	**Monitor** student progress with the differentiated curriculum-based assessment in the *Unit Resources.*	• **Selection Test B,** ***Unit 3 Resources,*** pp. 142–144 • **Open-Book Test,** ***Unit 3 Resources,*** pp. 136–138	• **Selection Test B,** ***Unit 3 Resources,*** pp. 163–165 • **Open-Book Test,** ***Unit 3 Resources,*** pp. 157–159

RTI Tier 2 (students requiring intervention)		✓ More Accessible Carry Your Own Skis	✓✓ More Complex Libraries Face Sad Chapter
Warm Up	**Practice, model,** and **monitor** fluency **in groups** or **with individuals**.	• **Vocabulary and Reading Warm-ups A,** ***Unit 3 Resources,*** pp. 127–129 • ***Reality Central,*** "Paths for Learning" • ***Hear It!*** **Audio CD (adapted text)**	• **Vocabulary and Reading Warm-ups A,** ***Unit 3 Resources,*** pp. 145–147 • ***Reality Central,*** "The Community Comes to School" • ***Hear It!*** **Audio CD**
Comprehension/Skills	• **Support** and **monitor** comprehension and skills development, working **in small groups** or **with individuals**. • **Pair** students with more advanced peers and have them complete the writing activity in the *Real-World Writing Journal*. • As students complete the selection in the appropriate version of the *Reader's Notebook,* **monitor** comprehension frequently with group questions and individual instruction. • **Model** strategies while guiding students in completing the activities and prompts in the *Reader's Notebook,* as well as the graphic organizers. • **Practice** skills and **monitor** mastery with the *Reading Kit* worksheets.	• ***Real-World Writing Journal,*** Lesson 1, pp. 86–89 • ***Reader's Notebook: Adapted Version,*** adapted instruction and adapted selection EL ***Reader's Notebook: English Learner's Version,*** adapted instruction and adapted selection • **Reading Skill Graphic Organizer A,** ***Graphic Organizer Transparencies,*** p. 92 • **Literary Analysis Graphic Organizer A,** ***Graphic Organizer Transparencies,*** p. 95 • ***Reading Kit,*** Practice worksheets, pp. 126, 132, 136, 138, 146	• ***Real-World Writing Journal,*** Lesson 2, pp. 90–93 • ***Reader's Notebook: Adapted Version,*** adapted instruction and summary EL ***Reader's Notebook: English Learner's Version,*** adapted instruction and summary • **Reading Skill Graphic Organizer A,** ***Graphic Organizer Transparencies,*** p. 93 • **Literary Analysis Graphic Organizer A,** ***Graphic Organizer Transparencies,*** p. 96 • ***Reading Kit,*** Practice worksheets, pp. 126, 132, 136, 138, 146
Monitor Progress	**Monitor** student progress with the differentiated curriculum-based assessment in the *Unit Resources* and in the *Reading Kit.*	• **Selection Test A,** ***Unit 3 Resources,*** pp. 139–141 • ***Reading Kit,*** Assess worksheets, pp. 127, 133, 137, 139, 147	• **Selection Test A,** ***Unit 3 Resources,*** pp. 160–162 • **Reading Kit,** Assess worksheets, pp. 127, 133, 137, 139, 147

TIER 3 Tier 3 intervention may require consultation with the student's special-education or dyslexia specialist. For additional support, see the Tier 2 activities and resources listed above.

One-on-one teaching **Group work** **Whole class instruction** **Independent work** **A Assessment**

For a complete guide to selection support, including support for Advanced students, see the Overview of Resources in the frontmatter.

✓Carry Your Own Skis
✓✓Libraries Face Sad Chapter

Carry Your Own Skis

Lian Dolan

When my mother was forty, she took up skiing. Or, more correctly, she and her twin sister took up skiing. They got on a bus, went to ski camp for a week, and learned to ski. After that, they'd get in the car and head up to Ladies Day at Powder Hill as often as they could to practice their stem christies.[1] Don't let the name fool you, Powder Hill (which later became the more Everest-like "Powder Ridge") was no pushover bunny slope.[2]

1. **stem christies** turns made by angling one ski and then bringing the other into alignment.
2. **bunny slope** gently sloping hill used for practice by beginning skiers.

522 Types of Nonfiction: Essays, Articles, and Speeches

Libraries Face Sad Chapter

Pete Hamill

530 Types of Nonfiction: Essays, Articles, and Speeches

RESOURCES FOR:

- L1 Special-Needs Students
- L2 Below-Level Students (Tier 2)
- L3 On-Level Students (Tier 1)
- L4 Advanced Students (Tier 1)
- EL English Learners
- All All Students

Vocabulary/Fluency/Prior Knowledge

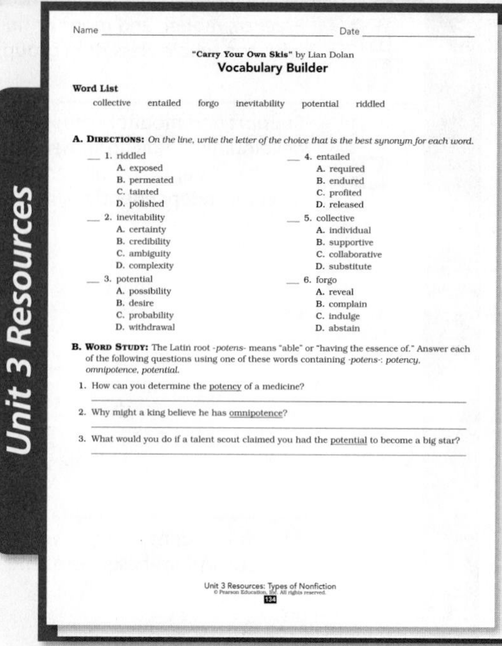
Name ______ Date ______

"Carry Your Own Skis" by Lian Dolan

Vocabulary Builder

Word List

collective entailed forgo inevitability potential riddled

A. Directions: *On the line, write the letter of the choice that is the best synonym for each word.*

___ 1. riddled
A. exposed
B. permeated
C. tainted
D. polished

___ 2. inevitability
A. certainty
B. credibility
C. ambiguity
D. complexity

___ 3. potential
A. possibility
B. desire
C. probability
D. withdrawal

___ 4. entailed
A. required
B. endured
C. profited
D. released

___ 5. collective
A. individual
B. supportive
C. collaborative
D. substitute

___ 6. forgo
A. reveal
B. complain
C. indulge
D. abstain

B. Word Study: The Latin root *-potens-* means "able" or "having the essence of." Answer each of the following questions using one of these words containing *-potens-*: *potency, omnipotence, potential.*

1. How can you determine the potency of a medicine?
2. Why might a king believe he has omnipotence?
3. What would you do if a talent scout claimed you had the potential to become a big star?

Unit 3 Resources: Types of Nonfiction

134

Unit 3 Resources

All **Vocabulary Builder,** pp. 134, 152

Also available for these selections:

EL L1 L2 **Vocabulary Warm-ups A and B,** pp. 127–128, 145–146

EL L1 L2 **Reading Warm-ups A and B,** pp. 129–130, 147–148

All **Writing About the Big Question,** pp. 131, 149

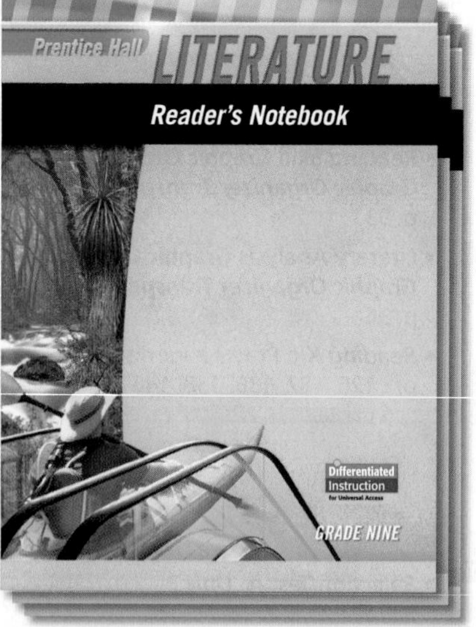

Reader's Notebooks

Pre- and postreading pages for both selections, as well as "Carry Your Own Skis," appear in an interactive format in the *Reader's Notebooks.* Each *Notebook* is differentiated for a different group of learners. The selections in the Adapted and English Learner's versions are abridged.

- L2 L3 ***Reader's Notebook***
- L1 ***Reader's Notebook: Adapted Version***
- EL ***Reader's Notebook: English Learner's Version***
- EL ***Reader's Notebook: Spanish Version***

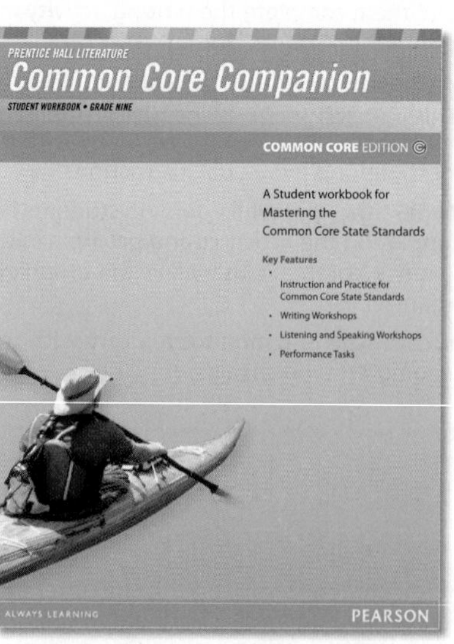

Common Core Companion

Additional instruction and practice for each Common Core State Standard

Selection Support

Graphic Organizer Transparencies

"Libraries Face Sad Chapter" by Pete Hamill

After You Read A: Literary Analysis—Persuasive Essay

Passage	Reason or Emotion
Public libraries are treasure houses.	Reason: author's favorite books and magazines

Graphic Organizer Transparencies

96

EL L1 L2 **Literary Analysis: Graphic Organizer A,** pp. 95, 96 (partially filled in)

Also available for these selections:

EL L1 L2 **Reading: Graphic Organizer A,** pp. 92, 93 (partially filled in)

EL L3 **Reading: Graphic Organizer B,** p. 94

EL L3 **Literary Analysis: Graphic Organizer B,** p. 97

Skills Development/Extension

Unit 3 Resources

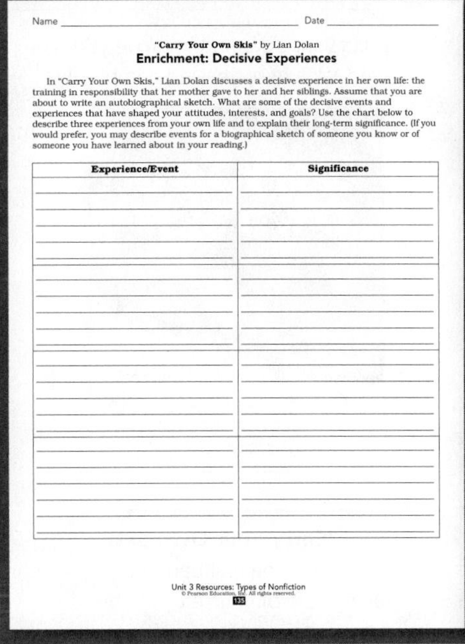

Name ______________________ Date ____________

"Carry Your Own Skis" by Lian Dolan

Enrichment: Decisive Experiences

In "Carry Your Own Skis," Lian Dolan discusses a decisive experience in her own life: the training in responsibility that her mother gave to her and her siblings. Assume that you are about to write an autobiographical sketch. What are some of the decisive events and experiences that have shaped your attitudes, interests, and goals? Use the chart below to describe three experiences from your own life and to explain their long-term significance. (If you would prefer, you may describe events for a biographical sketch of someone you know or of someone you have learned about in your reading.)

Experience/Event	Significance

Unit 3 Resources: Types of Nonfiction

135

L4 **Enrichment,** p. 135, 153

Also available for these selections:

All **Literary Analysis: Persuasove Essay,** pp. 132, 150

All **Reading: Evaluation Essay,** pp. 133, 151

EL L3 L4 **Grammar,** p. 154

EL L3 L4 **Support for Writing,** p. 155

L3 L4 **Support for Extend Your Learning,** p. 156

Assessment

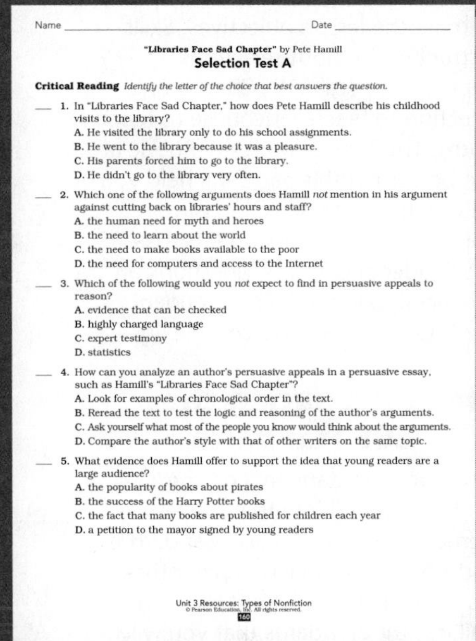

Name ______________________ Date ____________

"Libraries Face Sad Chapter" by Pete Hamill

Selection Test A

Critical Reading *Identify the letter of the choice that best answers the question.*

____ 1. In "Libraries Face Sad Chapter," how does Pete Hamill describe his childhood visits to the library?
A. He visited the library only to do his school assignments.
B. He went to the library because it was a pleasure.
C. His parents forced him to go to the library.
D. He didn't go to the library very often.

____ 2. Which one of the following arguments does Hamill *not* mention in his argument against cutting back on libraries' hours and staff?
A. the human need for myth and heroes
B. the need to learn about the world
C. the need to make books available to the poor
D. the need for computers and access to the Internet

____ 3. Which of the following would you *not* expect to find in persuasive appeals to reason?
A. evidence that can be checked
B. highly charged language
C. expert testimony
D. statistics

____ 4. How can you analyze an author's persuasive appeals in a persuasive essay, such as Hamill's "Libraries Face Sad Chapter"?
A. Look for examples of chronological order in the text.
B. Reread the text to test the logic and reasoning of the author's arguments.
C. Ask yourself what most of the people you know would think about the arguments.
D. Compare the author's style with that of other writers on the same topic.

____ 5. What evidence does Hamill offer to support the idea that young readers are a large audience?
A. the popularity of books about pirates
B. the success of the Harry Potter books
C. the fact that many books are published for children each year
D. a petition to the mayor signed by young readers

Unit 3 Resources: Types of Nonfiction

160

EL L1 L2 **Selection Test A,** pp. 139–141, 160–162

Also available for these selections:

EL L3 L4 **Selection Test B,** pp. 142–144, 163–165

L3 L4 **Open-Book Test,** pp. 136–138, 157–159

PHLit Online!
www.PHLitOnline.com

- complete narrated selection text
- a thematically related video with writing prompt
- an interactive graphic organizer
- highlighting feature
- access to all student print resources, adapted to individual student needs
- Spanish and English summaries
- adapted selection translations in Spanish

Online Resources: All print materials are also available online.

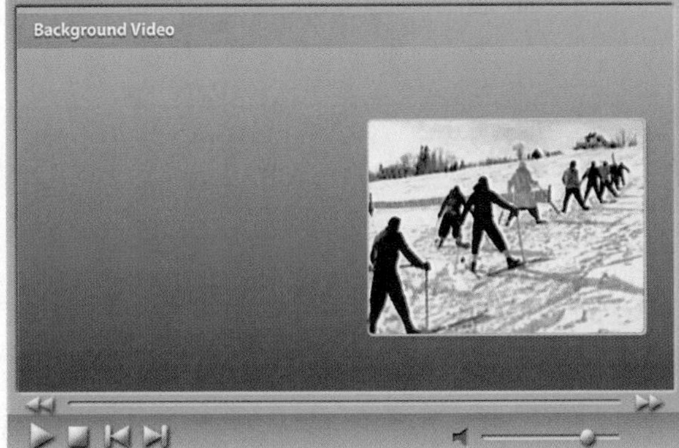

Background Video

Also available:

Get Connected! (thematic video with writing prompt)

All videos are available in Spanish.

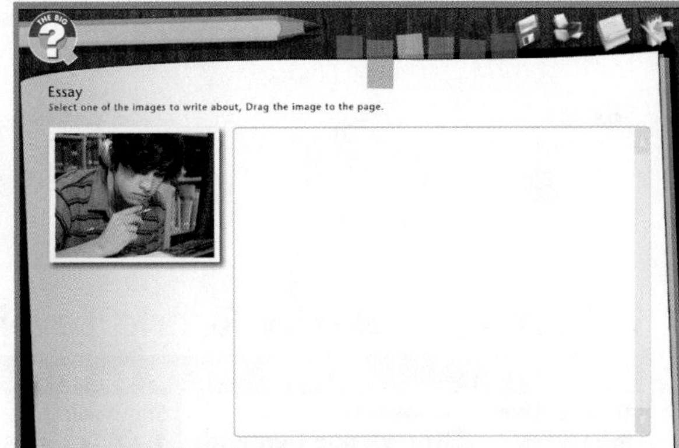

Writer's Journal (with graphics feature)

Also available:

Vocabulary Central (tools, activities, and songs for studying vocabulary)

DIFFERENTIATE/PRETEACH

❶ Leveled Texts

You may use either "Carry Your Own Skis" or "Libraries Face Sad Chapter" to meet the lesson objectives. Skills instruction for both selections appears on page 519. Choose one selection to teach (or choose to teach both). The Text Complexity Rubric at the bottom of this page will help you determine which selection is more appropriate for your students. Use the Reader and Task Suggestions on the facing page to help all students read text of increasing complexity.

❷ Introducing the CCS Standards

Introduce the standards on the student page. (Note that the lesson element with which each standard is addressed is identified in parentheses after the text of the standard.) Call out the standards that you will cover with the selections, explaining to students what each requires and how they will address it as they work through the selection you have chosen. Standards labeled "Spiral Review" are introduced in the Literary Analysis Workshop for this unit.

Before You Read

Carry Your Own Skis • Libraries Face Sad Chapter

❶ Leveled Texts

Build your skills and improve your comprehension of types of nonfiction with texts of increasing complexity.

Read **"Carry Your Own Skis"** to discover the real benefits of taking care of yourself.

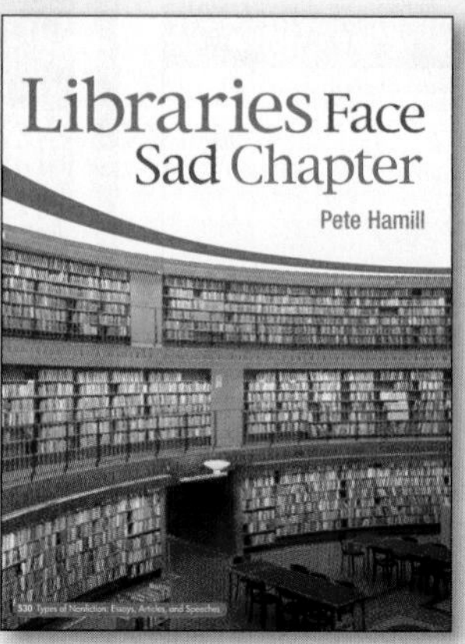

Read **"Libraries Face Sad Chapter"** to learn why libraries should be treasured and maintained.

❷ Common Core State Standards

Meet these standards with either **"Carry Your Own Skis"** (p. 522) or **"Libraries Face Sad Chapter"** (p. 530).

Reading Informational Text

6. Determine an author's point of view or purpose in a text and analyze how an author uses rhetoric to advance that point of view or purpose. *(Literary Analysis: Spiral Review)*

8. Delineate and evaluate the argument and specific claims in a text, assessing whether the reasoning is valid and the evidence is relevant and sufficient; identify false statements and fallacious reasoning. *(Reading Skill: Evaluate Persuasion)*

Writing

4. Produce clear and coherent writing in which the development, organization, and style are appropriate to task, purpose, and audience. *(Writing: Abstract)*

Speaking and Listening

4. Present information, findings, and supporting evidence clearly, concisely, and logically such that listeners can follow the line of reasoning and the organization, development, substance, and style are appropriate to purpose, audience, and task. *(Research and Technology: Persuasive Speech)*

Language

1. Demonstrate command of the conventions of standard English grammar and usage when writing and speaking. *(Conventions: Adjectives)*

5. Demonstrate understanding of figurative language, word relationships, and nuances in word meanings. *(Vocabulary: Analogies)*

Text Complexity Rubric: Leveled Texts

Text complexity is determined by both qualitative and quantitative measures. For this reason, the quantitative measure of a more complex selection may be lower than that of a more accessible selection.

		✓ Carry Your Own Skis	✓✓ Libraries Face Sad Chapter
Qualitative Measures	**Context/ Knowledge Demands**	Snow skiing 1 ② 3 4 5	Protecting America's public libraries 1 2 ③ 4 5
	Structure/Language Conventionality and Clarity	Familiar situations; simple sentences; vivid descriptions 1 ② 3 4 5	Challenging vocabulary; allusions to works of literature 1 2 ③ 4 5
	Levels of Meaning/ Purpose/Concept Level	Accessible concept (childhood memories of skiing lead to developing responsibility) 1 2 ③ 4 5	Accessible concept (childhood memories of using public libraries and a call to protect libraries) 1 2 ③ 4 5
Quantitative Measures	**Text Length**	Word Count: 1,396	Word Count: 1,160
	Lexile	980L	1070L
Overall Complexity		✓ **More accessible**	✓✓ **More complex**

❸ Literary Analysis: Persuasive Essay

A **persuasive essay** is a short nonfiction work in which the author's purpose is to convince a reader to think or act in a particular way. Persuasive essays usually include the following persuasive appeals:

- **Appeals to reason:** logical arguments based on verifiable evidence, such as facts, statistics, or expert testimony.
- **Appeals to emotion:** statements intended to affect listeners' feelings about a subject. These statements often include charged language—words with strong positive or negative associations.

As you read persuasive writing, try to identify the **author's motive,** or intent. Ask "Why does the writer include this information?"

❹ Reading Skill: Evaluate Persuasion

A persuasive argument is composed of a series of **claims.** To **analyze and evaluate an author's argument,** identify passages in which the author makes a claim in support of his or her position. Then, **reread** those passages to test the author's logic and reasoning. Ask yourself the following questions:

- Is the author's argument **credible**—supported by valid and relevant evidence—or is it based on faulty reasoning?
- Is the evidence provided **comprehensive,** or complete?
- Are the writer's **generalizations,** or broad statements, supported by evidence?

❺ Using the Strategy: Persuasion Analysis Diagram

Use a chart like the one shown to record your analysis of the author's claims. Review your analysis to decide how effectively the author has presented his or her argument.

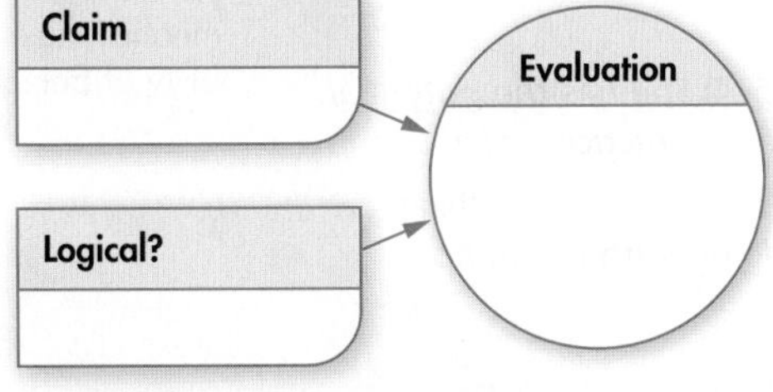

PHLit Online!
www.PHLitOnline.com

Hear It!
- Selection summary audio
- Selection audio

See It!
- Get Connected video
- Background video
- More about the author
- Vocabulary flashcards

Do It!
- Interactive journals
- Interactive graphic organizers
- Self-test
- Internet activity
- Grammar tutorial
- Interactive vocabulary games

PRETEACH

❸ Literary Analysis
Persuasive Essay

1. Introduce the skill, using instruction on the student page.
2. Tell students that they will practice identifying aspects of persuasive essays as they read.

Think Aloud: Model the Skill

Model a way to identify aspects of a persuasive essay. Say to students:

Let's say I believe that the school day is too short, and I am writing a persuasive essay. My motive is to persuade the school board to lengthen the school day.

I will appeal to reason by citing the fact that students with longer school days perform better on tests than students with a typical school day. I will appeal to emotion by telling a story about a student who joined a gang because he had nothing else to do in the afternoon.

❹ Reading Skill
Evaluate Persuasion

1. Introduce the skill, using instruction on the student page.
2. Tell students that they will practice analyzing and evaluating persuasive appeals as they read.

❺ Using the Strategy

Give students a copy of either **Reading Skill Graphic Organizer A** or **B** (***Graphic Organizer Transparencies,*** pp. 92–94) to identify the persuasive appeals used by the author. Use the examples in **Reading Skill Graphic Organizer A,** which is partially filled in, to model the process of completing the organizer.

Text Complexity: Reader and Task Suggestions

✓ Carry Your Own Skis		✓✓ Libraries Face Sad Chapter	
Preparing to Read the Text	**Leveled Tasks**	**Preparing to Read the Text**	**Leveled Tasks**
• Refer to the Background note on TE p. 521 and discuss how ski clothing has changed since the author was a child. • Discuss personal responsibility and how we learn it from parents, at school, and in other places. • Guide students to use Multidraft Reading strategies (TE p. 521).	*Levels of Meaning* If students will have difficulty with levels of meaning, ask them to first read the essay and note the advantages and disadvantages the author experienced from skiing. Then, have students reread and identify what the author says about her mother's and her own responsibility. *Analyzing* If students will not have trouble with meaning, have them read and note instances in which the author relies on emotional appeals.	• Refer to the Background information on TE p. 529 and discuss the role of libraries. • Review strategies for reading sentences containing challenging diction. • Guide students to use Multidraft Reading strategies (TE p. 529).	*Structure/Language* If students will have trouble with language, first have them read the essay and make notes about the author's main arguments for supporting libraries. Then, have them reread and identify any passages that remain unclear. *Analyzing* If students will not have difficulty with language, have them read to note examples of the author's narrative techniques.

PREATEACH

❶ Writing About the Big Question

1. Read the assignment with the class.
2. Remind students that they can know about something, like a law or an idea, but not fully understand what it means or how it works. For example, they might know that their parents encourage them to take certain subjects without understanding why those subjects are important.
3. Have students complete the sentence starters. Review responses as a class. (**Possible response:** Personal responsibility is a concept that many people do not truly understand because they don't comprehend what personal responsibility means.)
4. Remind students that their answers will help them think about the Big Question, "Is knowledge the same as understanding?"

While You Read

As they read, tell students to determine what the writer learns from her mother's edict that everyone carry his or her own skies.

❷ Vocabulary

1. Have students preview the selection vocabulary.
2. For each word, have students say the word aloud.
3. Then, use the word in a sentence that defines the word.
4. Finally, repeat your definitional sentence or a similar sentence with the word missing and have the class "fill in the blank" chorally. Here is an example:

   Riddled means full of something. The moths left my sweater [students say "riddled"] *with holes.*

❸ Word Study

1. Introduce the skill, using the instruction in the box.
2. Ask students for another *-potens-* word that means "powerful." (**Answer:** *potent*)

Making Connections | Carry Your Own Skis

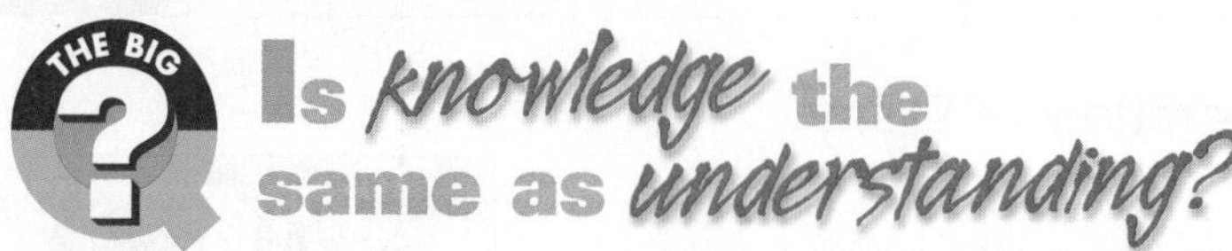

❶ Writing About the Big Question

In "Carry Your Own Skis," the author draws an analogy between carrying your own skis and taking responsibility for yourself. Use this sentence starter to develop your ideas about the Big Question.

Personal responsibility is a **concept** that many people do not truly understand because ______________ .

While You Read Look for details that illustrate the benefits of taking personal responsibility.

❷ Vocabulary

Read each word and its definition. Decide whether you know the word well, know it a little bit, or do not know it at all. After you read, see how your knowledge of each word has increased.

- **entailed** (en tāld´) *v.* caused or required as a necessary consequence; involved; necessitated (p. 523) ***The plan to repaint the house entailed a lot of work.*** *entail v. entailment n.*
- **inevitability** (in ev´ i tə bil´ ə tē) *n.* quality of being certain to happen; certainty (p. 523) ***The inevitability of losing did not keep the team from playing hard.*** *inevitable adj. inevitably adv.*
- **collective** (kə lek´ tiv) *adj.* put together as a group; gathered into a whole (p. 523) ***With our collective friends, we had enough people to get the group rate.*** *collect v. collection n. collectively adv.*
- **forgo** (fôr gō´) *v.* do without; abstain from; give up (p. 523) ***The coach said we could forgo practice tomorrow if we worked hard today.*** *forgone v.*
- **potential** (pō ten´ shəl) *n.* possibility (p. 524) ***She has the potential to be a good player, but she needs lots of practice.*** *potential adj.*
- **riddled** (rid´ 'ld) *adj.* very full of something, especially something unpleasant (p. 525) ***The old tree was riddled with worm holes.*** *riddle v.*

❸ Word Study

The **Latin root *-potens-*** means "able" or "having the essence of." The root relates to power and possibility.

When Dolan describes skiing as having the **potential** for fun, she means it has the possibility of being exciting.

Vocabulary Development

Vocabulary Knowledge Rating

Create a **Vocabulary Knowledge Rating Chart *(Professional Development Guidebook,*** p. 33) for this selection. Include the selection vocabulary and the Big Question word that appears in the Writing About the Big Question sentence starter on this page. (The Big Question vocabulary is introduced on pp. 424–425.)

Give students a copy of the chart. Read the words aloud, and have students mark their rating in the Before Reading column. Urge them to be alert to these words as they read and discuss the selection.

Tally how many students think they know a word to gauge how much instruction to provide. As students read and discuss the selection, point out the words and their context.

Vocabulary Central, featuring tools, activities, and songs for studying vocabulary, is available at **www.PHLitOnline.com.**

Meet Lian Dolan (b. 1966)

Author of Carry Your Own Skis

Lian Dolan is one of the "Satellite Sisters," a group of five sisters who host a radio show. Before helping launch the show, Dolan tried everything from working as a waitress to producing films. She also writes the column "The Chaos Chronicles" for *Working Mother* magazine.

"The Sassiest" Lian is known as the sassiest of the sisters, and she is not afraid to express her opinions on any topic. Even though Lian is the youngest of the five sisters, she directs all of their writing projects. She enjoys being the "Head Sister," giving orders to her older siblings.

4 BACKGROUND FOR THE ESSAY

Cold-Weather Clothing

Before the development of synthetic, lightweight, waterproof fabrics that "breathe" and keep the wearer dry, keeping warm on the ski slopes meant wearing heavy wool and cotton clothing. Garments made from these fabrics would become wet and cold in the snow, and they would stay wet and cold until removed.

Did You Know?

The Satellite Sisters live in four different cities on two continents. They link via satellite for their popular radio show.

Daily Bellringer

For each class during which you will teach this selection, have students complete one of the five Revision activities for Week 16 in the ***Daily Bellringer Activities*** booklet.

4 Background

Cold-Weather Clothing

Because of modern technical advances, skiers today enjoy much more comfort than did Lian Dolan and her sisters. Experienced skiers today dress in layers, and they do not use natural fibers such as cotton and wool. New fabrics such as microfleece keep heat in but allow moisture to escape. One of the most recent developments in ski clothing is a "temperature control" fabric that has been used by astronauts. It keeps skiers warm, but does not overheat them.

Multidraft Reading

This icon ● marks natural pauses in the selection. To assist struggling readers and to deepen reading for all, assign the text in "chunks," following the icons, and apply multidraft reading protocols. For each reading, have students set the purpose indicated:

- **First reading**—identifying key ideas and details and answering any Reading Checks.
- **Second reading**—analyzing craft and structure and responding to the side-column prompts.
- **Third reading**—integrating knowledge and ideas, connecting to other texts and the world, and answering the end-of-selection questions.

For more guidance, refer to the ***Classroom Strategies and Teaching Routines card*** on multidraft reading.

Differentiated Instruction — Additional Instruction

EL Extended Support—English Learners

Have students complete the **Reading and Vocabulary Warm-ups, *Unit 3 Resources*,** pp. 127–130, before they read. Assign the prereading pages and the adapted selection in the ***Reader's Notebook: English Learner's Version.*** Then, have students listen to portions of the selection on the ***Hear It!* Audio CD.**

L1 L2 Extended Support—Struggling Readers

Have students complete the **Reading and Vocabulary Warm-ups, *Unit 3 Resources*,** pp. 127–130, before they read. Assign the prereading pages and the adapted selection in the ***Reader's Notebook: Adapted Version.*** Then, have students listen to portions of the selection on the ***Hear It!* Audio CD** (adapted text).

Extended Support—Reluctant Readers

To build motivation and engagement before assigning the selection, have students read "Paths for Learning," a thematically related selection in ***Reality Central.*** Then, use the questions at the conclusion of the related selection to guide discussion.

PHLit Online!

For more about the author, practice with the selection vocabulary, or more background, go online at **www.PHLitOnline.com.**

❶ Activating Prior Knowledge

1. Prepare an **Anticipation Guide** (***Professional Development Guidebook***, pp. 36–38) with the following statements:
   - Parents should insist that their children learn a challenging sport.
   - Participating in sports helps children grow up to be responsible.
   - A person does not have to enjoy a sport to benefit from practicing it.
2. Give students a copy of the prepared **Anticipation Guide** and have students mark their responses in the appropriate columns.
3. For further guidance, use the ***Classroom Strategies and Teaching Routines*** card: **Using an Anticipation Guide.**

Concept Connector

Students will return to the **Anticipation Guide** after completing "Carry Your Own Skis."

Small-Group Activity

Have small groups act out Dolan carrying her gear from the lodge to the car. Then, have students discuss how difficult this was for her as a child, and ask them to discuss why they think she did it.

❷ About the Selection

In "Carry Your Own Skis," Lian Dolan remembers her struggles to keep up with her sisters on the ski slopes. Dolan was required to carry her skis from the lodge to the car, no matter how cold and tired she was. This became an important lesson in personal responsibility that she still practices as an adult.

❸ Critical Viewing

Possible response: Students may suggest that skiing looks like work because the skiers have to climb up the hill with heavy equipment. However, skiing also looks like recreation because the skiers are outside and enjoying the snow.

❶ ❷

Carry Your Own Skis

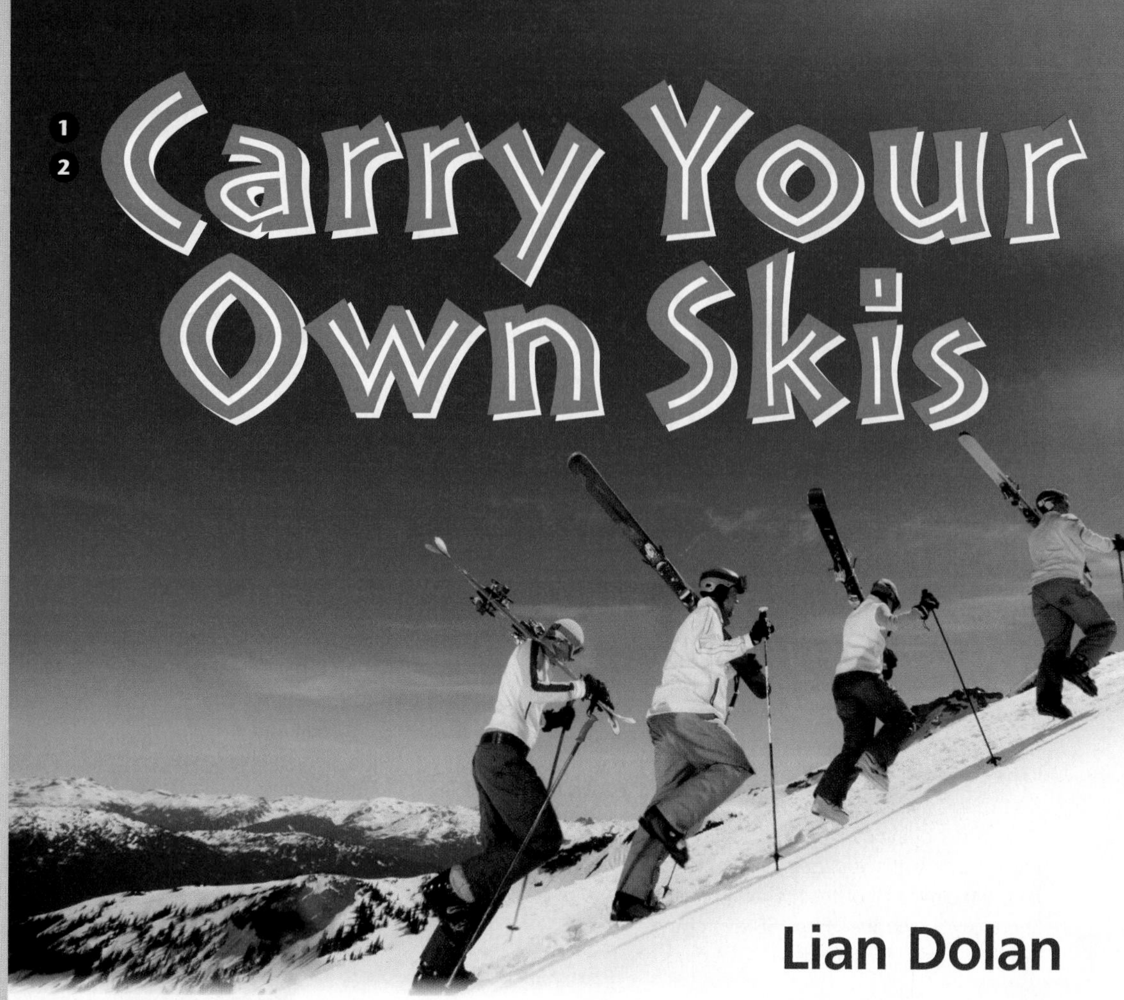

Lian Dolan

❸ ▲ **Critical Viewing** Based on this photograph, does skiing look like work or recreation? Explain. **[Analyze]**

When my mother was forty, she took up skiing. Or, more correctly, she and her twin sister took up skiing. They got on a bus, went to ski camp for a week, and learned to ski. After that, they'd get in the car and head up to Ladies Day at Powder Hill as often as they could to practice their stem christies.[1] Don't let the name fool you, Powder Hill (which later became the more Everest-like "Powder Ridge") was no pushover bunny slope.[2]

1. **stem christies** turns made by angling one ski and then bringing the other into alignment.
2. **bunny slope** gently sloping hill used for practice by beginning skiers.

Vocabulary Development

CCSS Language 6

Thematic Vocabulary: The Big Question

As students are discussing "Carry Your Own Skis," encourage them to use the thematic vocabulary presented in Introducing the Big Question, pp. 424–425. You might encourage them with sentence starters like these:

1. Dolan's mother and aunt believed in the *concept* of . . .
2. Dolan's mother and aunt felt that it was important for their children to *comprehend* . . .
3. On the ski slopes, Dolan learned through *instinct* to . . .
4. Later in life, Dolan made a *connection* between taking responsibility for her skis and . . .

This was in the mid-sixties, when skiing was work—decades before valet parking, fondue lunches, and gear that actually keeps you dry, warm, and safe. My mother and my aunt took up the kind of skiing that **entailed** wooden skis, tie boots, and rope tows[3] that could jerk your arm out of its socket. This was the kind of skiing where skiers, not the Sno-Cats, groomed the hill[4] in the morning. Ticket buyers were expected to sidestep up and down slopes and herringbone the lift lines.[5] The typical A-frame lodge had a big fireplace, a couple of bathrooms, rows of picnic tables, and maybe some hot chocolate for sale. At the end of the day, there were no hot toddies by a roaring fire in furry boots or drinks in the hot tub of a slopeside condo. Instead, my mother and her sister faced the **inevitability** of a station wagon with a dead battery and the long, dark drive back home in wet clothes.

Why did they learn to ski? It wasn't to spend some quality time outdoors together away from their responsibilities at home. They learned to ski so that they could take their **collective** children skiing, all seventeen of us. My mother's eight children and my aunt's nine. And learn to ski we did, eagerly. There was, however, one rule my mother had about skiing: Carry your own skis.

My mother didn't teach us to ski until we could carry our own skis from the car to the lodge in the morning and—this is key—from the lodge back to the car at the end of the day. Even cold, wet, and tired, we had to get our skis, poles, and boots back to that station wagon on our own. No falling behind. No dragging. And no whining. My mother had the responsibility for her gear, the giant lunch, the car, and the occasional trip to the ER for broken legs. We were in charge of our own gear and meeting at the end of the day. These were the conditions to be allowed to accompany siblings and cousins to the slopes. Carry your own skis or sit in the lodge all day.

No one wanted to get left in the lodge. A cold, wet day on the ice-blue slopes of New England, freezing in leather boots and the generation of ski clothes before microfibers was far preferable to being left out of all that fun. Miss the lunches of soggy tuna fish sandwiches and mini chocolate bars? No way! Sit in the lodge instead
4 of side-slipping your way down a sheet of ice disguised as a trail or tramping through three feet of snow to get the pole you dropped under the chair lift? Not me! **Forgo** that last run of the day in near darkness, cold and alone and crying because your siblings have skied on ahead without you? Who'd want to miss all that fun? Sitting in the

3. **rope tows** moving ropes that skiers hold to be pulled to the top of the hill.
4. **groomed the hill** packed and smoothed the snow.
5. **herringbone the lift lines** walk uphill to chair lift by stepping with skis pointed outward to avoid sliding back down the hill. The skis leave a "herringbone" pattern—a line of connected v-shapes—on the snow.

Vocabulary

entailed (en tāld′) *v.* caused or required as a necessary consequence; involved; necessitated

inevitability (in ev′ i tə bil′ ə tē) *n.* quality of being certain to happen; certainty

collective (kə lek′ tiv) *adj.* put together as a group; gathered into a whole

forgo (fôr gō′) *v.* do without; abstain from; give up

Literary Analysis
Persuasive Essay Which details in this paragraph appeal to the emotions? Explain.

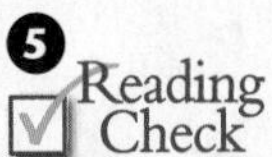

Why did Dolan's mother and aunt learn to ski?

4 Literary Analysis

Persuasive Essay

1. Ask students to think about a time when they were left out of a game, perhaps because they were sick or because they were unable to do what everyone else was doing. Then, **ask** them what emotions they felt at the time.

   Possible responses: Students may suggest that they felt emotions such as disappointment, sadness, and anger.

2. **Ask** students the Literary Analysis question: Which details in this paragraph appeal to the emotions? Explain.

   Answer: The description of the fear of being left out and of being alone and crying appeal to the emotions.

5 Reading Check

Answer: They learned to ski so that they could take their children skiing.

PHLit Online!

This selection is available in interactive format in the **Enriched Online Student Edition, www.PHLitOnline.com,** which includes a thematically related video with writing prompt and an interactive graphic organizer.

Fluency

Distribute copies of page 523, and pair students. Have partners take turns reading paragraphs aloud. While one partner reads, the other should mark any words with which the student reading has difficulty. Circulate to monitor the fluency of students' reading. Collect students' marked-up copies of the page, and review difficult words and passages with the class. Look for these problem spots:

- If students struggle to pronounce *inevitability,* divide the word into syllables and read it aloud with appropriate stress. Have students echo three times to affirm correct pronunciation.
- If students have difficulty with the word *lodge*, explain that the *d* is silent and the *ge* is pronounced like a *j*. Have students cover the *dge*, then read the word as *loj* to achieve correct pronunciation.
- If students stumble over the commas and short sentences, ask fluent readers to model the pauses indicated by commas. Then, have mixed-fluency groups read to reinforce pacing and comfort.

6 Connecting to the Big Question

1. Have a volunteer read aloud the bracketed text. **Ask:** What lesson does Dolan describe in this passage?

   Answer: If you take responsibility for yourself and your equipment, you will not miss out, and you will have fun.

2. **Ask:** How does this lesson illustrate the benefits of taking responsibility?

   Answer: One benefit of taking responsibility is that you will be part of the fun activities that are going on. On the other hand, if you do not take responsibility, you will miss out on the burden—but you will also miss out on the fun.

3. **Ask:** How does Dolan's lesson illustrate a difference between knowledge and understanding?
   Possible response: Someone might have *told* Dolan that personal responsibility was important, but she developed an *understanding* of the concept because she learned what would happen if she did not take responsibility.

7 Critical Viewing

Possible response: Students may suggest that the girl feels both excited and timid about skiing. The snow on her jacket and hat suggests that she is engaged in what she is doing, but her gaze looks a bit careful, even intimidated.

4 lodge all day just wasn't an option once we reached ski age. We were expected to participate. We learned to carry our own skis.

6 The lesson was simple, really. Be responsible for yourself and your stuff or you miss out. No one wanted to miss out. Getting across the icy parking lot and back seemed a small price to pay for the **potential** of great fun. And even if you dropped your poles or the bindings cut into your hands or you fell on your rear end, that was part of the experience. The "carry your own skis" mentality filtered into almost every area of our life as we were growing up. Doing homework, getting to practice, applying to college—be responsible for yourself and your stuff or you miss out.

Vocabulary
potential (pō ten′ shəl) *n.* possibility

8 I began to notice the people who hadn't learned to carry their own skis when I was as young as eleven. I didn't have a name for this concept yet, but I had the notion that maybe other kids operated by a different set of rules. They thought that somewhere, somebody was going to take care of things for them. I remember the girls at summer

7 ◄ **Critical Viewing**
How do you think the girl in this photograph feels about skiing? **[Speculate]**

Vocabulary Development

Vocabulary Knowledge Rating

When students have completed reading and discussing "Carry Your Own Skis," have them take out their **Vocabulary Knowledge Rating Chart** for this selection. Read the words aloud once more and have students rate their knowledge of the words again in the After Reading column. Clarify any words that are still problematic. Have students write their own definition and example or sentence in the appropriate column. Then, have students complete the Vocabulary Practice activities at the end of the selection. Encourage students to use the words in further discussion and written work about this selection. Remind them that they will be accountable for these words on the **Selection Test**, ***Unit 3 Resources***, pp. 139–141 or 142–144.

camp who never signed up to pack out or pack in for a camping trip, expecting that someone else would provide food or do all the cleanup for them. But me? I would sign up to make the PB&Js and to clean up
8 the mess. I'd load the canoes onto the truck and take 'em off again. And the tent? I'd put it up and I'd take it down. I didn't know any different. As a result, I was invited to go on a lot of camping trips. The lodge and back, baby—that was my attitude.

In high school, the kids who didn't carry their own skis called their parents to bring in assignments they'd forgotten or to ask for a ride home instead of walking or taking the late bus. In college, the no-ski carriers all had pink T-shirts—a sure sign that they had never done laundry before—and they complained about how much work they had. Isn't that what college was about—doing your own laundry and finishing your work? Then you could get to the fun stuff.

The real world is **riddled** with people who have never learned to carry their own skis—the blame-shifters, the no-RSVPers, the coworkers who never participate in those painful group birthdays except if it's their own. I admit it: I don't really get these people.

I like the folks who clear the dishes, even when they're the guests. Or the committee members who show up on time,
9 assignment completed and ready to pitch in on the next event. Or the neighbor who drives the carpool even though her kids are sick. I get these people. These people have learned to carry their own skis.

In early adulthood, carrying my own skis meant getting a job, paying off my student loans, and working hard for the company that was providing my paycheck. If I did those things, then I could enjoy the other areas of my life. Dull, yes, but freeing, too. When I wasn't responsible for myself or my stuff, I felt lousy. Sometimes I could get to the lodge, but I just couldn't get back to the station wagon at the end of the day. It was an unfamiliar feeling to let someone down by missing a deadline at work or not showing up for an early-morning run. . . . On days like that, the parking lot seemed bigger and icier than I had anticipated.

Be responsible for yourself and your stuff or you miss out.

Now I have a life that includes a husband, two children, a dog, a house, friends, schools, and a radio show that involves lots of other people, including four sisters. The "stuff" of my life may seem much heavier than two skis, two boots, and two poles, but it isn't really—just a little bit trickier to carry. I have to do more balancing and let go of the commitments that I'd probably drop anyway. If I commit to more than I can handle, I miss out. That's when I think of Powder Hill.

Reading Skill
Persuasive Appeals
How does the author support her claim that being responsible for yourself can be rewarding?

Vocabulary
riddled (rid´ 'ld) *adj.* very full of something, especially something unpleasant

Literary Analysis
Persuasive Essay
What does the paragraph beginning "I like the folks who. . . " suggest the author's motive for writing might be?

10 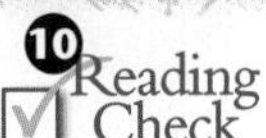
Reading Check
How did Dolan adapt the "carry your own skis" idea to other areas of her life?

8 Reading Skill
Persuasive Appeals

1. **Ask** students how the author's behavior differed from that of other children.

   Answer: She signed up to make sandwiches and to clean up; she loaded canoes and put up the tent.

2. **Ask** students the Reading Skill question.

   Answer: The author says that she was invited to go on lots of camping trips due to her responsible attitude.

9 Literary Analysis
Persuasive Essay

1. **Ask** students why they think the author approves of people who carry their own skis.

   Possible response: They take responsibility for themselves by not relying on others.

2. Then, **ask** students the Literary Analysis question.

   Possible response: She may want to persuade people to take responsibility for themselves. She may also be suggesting that those who don't take responsibility make life difficult for others.

▶ **Monitor Progress:** Provide students with **Literary Analysis Graphic Organizer B**, p. 97 in ***Graphic Organizer Transparencies,*** to complete as they read the essay.

▶ **Reteach:** If students have difficulty identifying persuasive appeals, remind them that a persuasive appeal aims to convince the reader to think or act in a certain way. Have students identify the positive aspects of "carrying your own skis" that the author identifies on p. 525. Point out that getting a job and paying off student loans have universal appeal.

10 Reading Check

Answer: Dolan took responsibility by finishing her schoolwork, doing her own laundry, getting and maintaining a job, paying off her student loans, and balancing a busy life.

Concept Connector

Anticipation Guide

Have students return to their **Anticipation Guides** and respond to the statements again in the After Reading column. They may do this individually or in their original pairs or groups. Then, lead a class discussion, probing for what students have learned that confirms or invalidates each statement. Encourage students to cite specific details, quotations, or other evidence from the text to support their responses to each statement.

Writing About the Big Question

Have students compare their responses to the sentence starter they completed before reading the essay with their ideas afterwards. Ask them to explain whether their thoughts have changed.

Reading Skill Graphic Organizer

Ask students to review the graphic organizers they completed to identify the persuasive appeals while reading. Show them **Reading Skill Graphic Organizer A** (***Graphic Organizer Transparencies,*** p. 92) as an example.

Reading Skill

Persuasive Appeals

1. **Ask** students the Reading Skill question.
2. **Possible response:** Yes. Being responsible for her skis taught her that she had to be responsible for other aspects of life in order to be happy and successful.

Spiral Review

Author's Purpose

1. Students studied author's purpose in the Unit 3 Literary Analysis Workshop (pp. 426–439).
2. **Ask** students the Spiral Review question.
   Possible response: The author shows that the negative side of her experience helped her become a responsible and self-sufficient adult.

ASSESS

Answers

Critical Thinking

Remind students to support their answers with evidence from the text.

1. (a) Her mother insisted that the children learn to carry their own skis to and from the lodge. (b) Most students will agree that her mother's expectations were reasonable, since she was unable to carry the children's skis for them.
2. (a) To participate fully in life, one has to take personal responsibility and carry one's own weight. (b) It has guided her behavior at work and at home.
3. (a) **Possible response:** Some students may agree because a considerate and responsible person will be welcome in most situations.
   (b) **Possible response:** Some students may state that they became convinced that being responsible is important to leading a happy life.
4. **Possible response:** Dolan learned about the benefits of taking responsibility through her experiences with her family on the ski slopes.

Reading Skill
Persuasive Appeals
Does the author clearly connect lessons learned from skiing with ideas about life? Explain.

Spiral Review
Author's Purpose 11
In what way does the author's presentation of the negative side of her experience help her to achieve her purpose?

The funny thing is, some of the worst moments of my childhood were spent on skis or in pursuit of skiing. The truth is, I didn't really like skiing as a kid. And I wasn't a very good skier. Most days, skiing for me was about freezing rain and constantly trying to catch up to my older, faster, more talented siblings. The hard falls on the hard ice. I can still feel the damp long underwear and the wet wool during the endless ride home. But whether I liked to ski or not didn't really matter. I was expected to learn to ski, and I did. And I also learned that in life you need to be responsible for yourself and your stuff or you miss out. The lodge and back, baby.

Critical Thinking

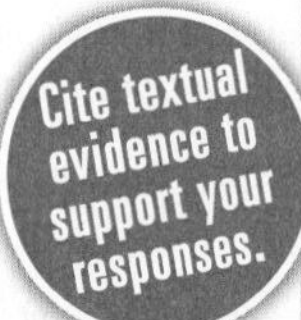
Cite textual evidence to support your responses.

1. **Key Ideas and Details (a)** What is the one rule that Dolan's mother had about skiing? **(b) Make a Judgment:** Do you think Dolan's mother's expectations of her children were reasonable? Why or why not?
2. **Key Ideas and Details (a)** What lesson does Dolan say she learned from carrying her own skis? **(b) Connect:** In what other aspects of life does the author say this lesson has guided her behavior?
3. **Integration of Knowledge and Ideas (a) Take a Position:** Do you agree or disagree with Dolan's claim that people who do not take responsibility miss out on things? Explain. **(b) Discuss:** Share your response with a partner, and then explain how the discussion has or has not changed your response to the question.
4. **Integration of Knowledge and Ideas** How do the author's family skiing experiences lead to a better understanding of her personal responsibility? *[Connect to the Big Question: Is knowledge the same as understanding?]*

Assessment Resources

Unit 3 Resources

L1 L2 EL **Selection Test A**, pp. 139–141. Administer Test A to less advanced readers.

L3 L4 EL **Selection Test B**, pp. 142–144. Administer Test B to on-level and more advanced students.

L3 L4 **Open-Book Test**, pp. 136–138. As an alternative, give the Open-Book Test.

All **Customizable Test Bank**

All **Self-tests**
Students may prepare for the **Selection Test** by taking the **Self-test** online.

All assessment resources are available at **www.PHLitOnline.com**.

ASSESS/EXTEND

After You Read

Carry Your Own Skis

Literary Analysis: Persuasive Essay

1. **Key Ideas and Details** **(a)** In this essay, what is the author trying to persuade readers to do? **(b)** What evidence does she use to support her position?
2. **Craft and Structure** **(a)** Using a chart like the one shown, identify three passages in which Dolan argues for "the 'carry your own skis' mentality." In the right-hand column, indicate whether each passage is an appeal to reason or to emotion, and explain your ideas. **(b)** Which kind of appeals does the author seem to favor—**appeals to reason** or **appeals to emotion**? Explain.

Passage	Reason or Emotion

3. **Integration of Knowledge and Ideas** What do you think is the **author's motive** for trying to persuade readers to agree with her?

Reading Skill: Evaluate Persuasion

4. Are the **claims** in this essay well-reasoned and logical? Explain.
5. Which passages are especially convincing? Explain your response.

Vocabulary

Acquisition and Use In vocabulary study, **analogies** show the relationships between pairs of words. Use a word from the vocabulary list on page 520 to complete each analogy. In each, your choice should create a word pair that matches the relationship between the first two words given.

1. conflict : agreement :: uncertainty : ______
2. idea : reality :: ______ : actual
3. soaked : water :: ______ : dents
4. hidden : revealed :: individual : ______
5. accept : attend :: ______ : decline
6. began : started :: caused : ______

Word Study Use the context of the sentences and what you know about the **Latin root -*potens*-** to explain your answers to each question.

1. Is a *potent* smell difficult to notice?
2. Is a *potentate* likely to be a weak person?

Word Study

The **Latin root -*potens*-** means "able" or "having the essence of." The root relates to power and possibility.

Apply It Explain how the root *-potens-* contributes to the meanings of these words. Consult a dictionary if necessary.

potency
potentially

Answers

Literary Analysis

1. **Possible responses:** (a) She wants to persuade people to take personal responsibility. (b) She tells anecdotes about how taking personal responsibility has improved her life.
2. **Possible responses:** (a) **Passage:** "The lesson was simple, really." **Reason or Emotion:** reason; she explains why it was necessary to learn the lesson; **Passage:** Paragraph beginning "I like the folks who clear the dishes . . ." **Reason or Emotion:** emotion; she explains that she has pleasant feelings about people who take responsibility. **Passage:** "In early adulthood. . ." **Reason or Emotion:** reason; she shows how the "carry your own skis" philosophy turned out to be a life lesson and helped her as she entered the workforce.

   (b) **Possible response:** The author seems to favor appeals to emotion. She describes feelings attached to childhood memories and her enthusiasm for the "carry your own skis" philospohy.
3. **Possible response:** She is trying to persuade readers to agree that what seemed to be a harsh rule turned out to be worthwhile. She may want people to take more responsibility for themselves.

For other sample answers, see ***Graphic Organizer Transparencies*, Literary Analysis Graphic Organizer A**, p. 95, and the **Additional Answers** section.

Reading Skill

4. **Possible response:** The author's claims are well-reasoned and logical; she gives specific examples of how taking responsibility has enriched her life.
5. **Possible response:** The most convincing passage is the one in which the author describes what would happen to her as a child if she did not carry her own skis.

Vocabulary

Acquisition and Use

Sample answers:

1. inevitability
2. potential
3. riddled
4. collective
5. forgo
6. entailed

Word Study

Sample answers:

1. No, the root *-potens-* means "able" and relates to power, and *potent* means "powerful." A *potent* smell is easy to notice.
2. No, the root *-potens-* means "able" and relates to power, and *potentate* means "a powerful person." A *potentate* is strong.

Word Study: Apply It

Sample answers:

Potency is the power or ability to achieve a particular result. *Potentially* means able to develop into actuality.

PRETEACH

Skills instruction for the ***Reading Skill*** *and the* ***Literary Analysis*** *concept appears on p. 519.*

1 Writing About the Big Question

1. Review the assignment with the class.
2. Ask volunteers to explain how knowing about library closings might help them understand a wider problem.
3. Have students complete the sentence starters. Review responses as a class. (**Possible response:** Libraries, as a source of information and a place for research, are still important because people need to be able to access information. They can help us clarify information we find on the Internet because their resources provide a way to verify Internet sources.
4. Remind students that their answers will help them think about the Big Question, "Is knowledge the same as understanding?"

While You Read

Ask students, while they read, to decide how important or unimportant library closings would be to a community.

2 Vocabulary

1. Have students preview the selection vocabulary.
2. For each word, have students say the word aloud.
3. Then, use the word in a sentence that defines the word.
4. Repeat your definitional sentence or a similar sentence with the word missing, and have the class "fill in the blank" chorally. Here is an example:

   Curtailed means "cut short or reduced." Because of the brush fires and the emergency situation, our vacation was [students say "curtailed"].

3 Word Study

1. Introduce the skill, using the instruction in the box.
2. Ask students for another *-sum-* word that means "to take." (**Answer:** *assume*)

Making Connections

Libraries Face Sad Chapter

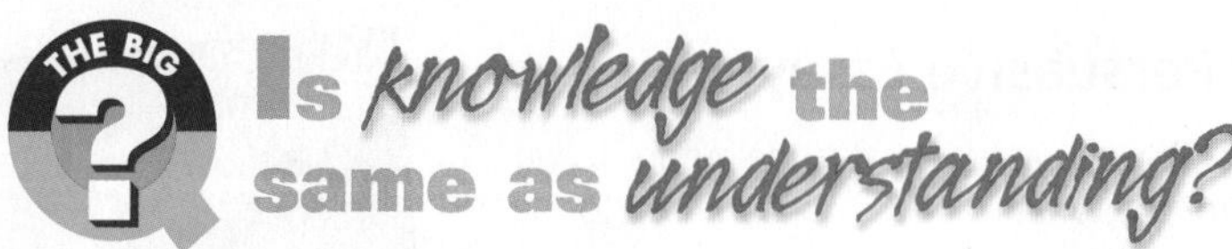

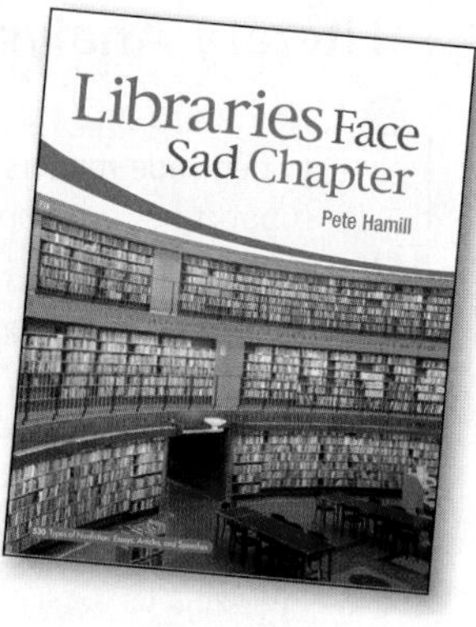

1 Writing About the Big Question

In "Libraries Face Sad Chapter," the author urges readers to contribute to a fund to support public libraries, a source of knowledge. Use these sentence starters to develop your ideas about the Big Question.

Libraries, as a **source** of **information** and a place for **research,** are still important because __________. They can help us **clarify** information we find on the Internet because __________.

While You Read Look for facts that support the author's opinion that libraries must be saved. Then, consider whether he has helped you understand the situation he describes.

2 Vocabulary

Read each word and its definition. Decide whether you know the word well, know it a little bit, or do not know it at all. After you read, see how your knowledge of each word has increased.

- **volumes** (väl′ yo͞omz) *n.* books that are either part of a set or combined into one. (p. 531) *My grandfather had random volumes of an old set of encyclopedias stored in the basement.*
- **presumed** (prē zo͞omd′) *adj.* accepted as true; supposed (p. 531) *Someone who has been arrested is presumed to be innocent until proven guilty. presume v. presumption n. presumptuous adj.*
- **curtailed** (kər tāld′) *v.* cut short; reduced (p. 532) *The game was curtailed by darkness. curtailing v.*
- **medium** (mē′ dē əm) *n.* means of communication (p. 532) *Television may be today's most popular medium. media n. pl.*
- **duration** (do͝o rā′ shən) *n.* length of time something lasts (p. 533) *The graduating class remained standing for the duration of the ceremony. durable adj. endure v.*
- **emulate** (em′ yo͞o lāt) *v.* imitate (a person or thing admired) (p. 534) *Josh tries to emulate his favorite rock star by dying his hair different colors. emulation n.*

3 Word Study

The **Latin root *-sum-*** means "to take."

Pete Hamill describes a shelf in the library that was **presumed** to be safe from children. The librarians took for granted that children would not get to the books placed there.

Vocabulary Development

Vocabulary Knowledge Rating

Create a **Vocabulary Knowledge Rating Chart** (*Professional Development Guidebook,* p. 33) for this selection. Include the selection vocabulary from this page and the words that appear in the Writing About the Big Question sentence starters on this page. (The Big Question vocabulary is introduced on pp. 424–425.)

Give students a copy of the chart. Read the words aloud, and have students mark their rating in the Before Reading column. Urge them to be alert to these words as they read and discuss the selection.

Tally how many students think they know a word to gauge how much instruction to provide. As students read and discuss the selection, point out the words and their context.

Vocabulary Central, featuring tools, activities, and songs for studying vocabulary, is available at **www.PHLitOnline.com.**

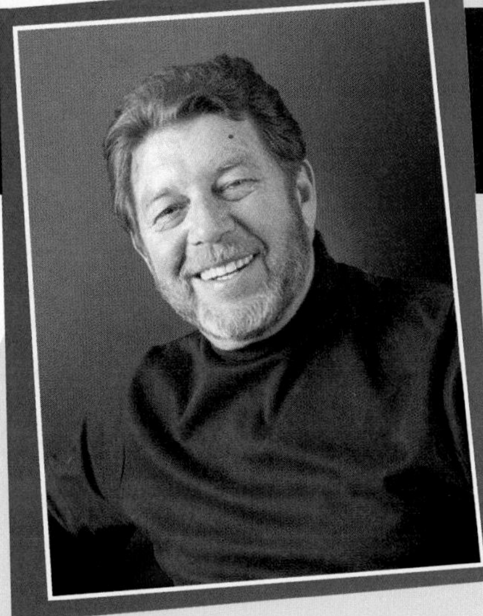

Meet Pete Hamill (b. 1935)

Author of Libraries Face Sad Chapter

Pete Hamill has had two novels on *The New York Times* Bestseller List, but he is first and foremost a journalist. After quitting school at sixteen to work in the Brooklyn Navy Yard, Hamill joined the U.S. Navy. He completed his high school education while in the navy.

"The work was everything." In 1960, Hamill went to work as a reporter for the *New York Post* newspaper. Although he would write for several other newspapers in his career, Hamill loved his job at the *Post*. He wrote, "Nothing before (or since) could compare with walking into the *New York Post* at midnight, being sent into the dark scary city on assignment and coming back to write a story."

4 **BACKGROUND FOR THE ESSAY**

Public Libraries

Although the first American library was established in 1638, it was not until the 1800s that public libraries became common in the United States. Since then, Americans have come to rely on public libraries as a free source of education, entertainment, and community.

Did You Know?

During Hamill's long career as a reporter, he covered wars in a number of countries including Vietnam, Nicaragua, Lebanon, and Northern Ireland.

Daily Bellringer

For each class during which you will teach this selection, have students complete one of the five Revision activities for Week 16 in the *Daily Bellringer Activities* booklet.

4 Background

Public Libraries

During the 1800s, large numbers of immigrants came to the United States. Public libraries played a vital role in the lives of these new immigrants. There they studied American history and government in preparation for citizenship. At the library, their children nourished their imaginations with the world's wonderful stories.

Multidraft Reading

This icon ● marks natural pauses in the selection. To assist struggling readers and to deepen reading for all, assign the text in "chunks," following the icons, and apply multidraft reading protocols. For each reading, have students set the purpose indicated:

- **First reading**—identifying key ideas and details and answering any Reading Checks.
- **Second reading**—analyzing craft and structure and responding to the side-column prompts.
- **Third reading**—integrating knowledge and ideas, connecting to other texts and the world, and answering the end-of-selection questions.

For more guidance, refer to the ***Classroom Strategies and Teaching Routines*** card on multidraft reading.

PHLit Online!

For more about the author, practice with the selection vocabulary, or more background, go online at **www.PHLitOnline.com.**

Differentiated Instruction — Additional Instruction

EL Extended Support—English Learners

Have students complete the **Reading and Vocabulary Warm-ups, *Unit 3 Resources*,** pp. 145–148, before they read. Assign the prereading pages for the selection in the ***Reader's Notebook: English Learner's Version.*** Then, have students listen to portions of the selection on the ***Hear It!* Audio CD.**

L1 L2 Extended Support—Struggling Readers

Have students complete the **Reading and Vocabulary Warm-ups, *Unit 3 Resources*,** pp. 145–148, before they read. Assign the prereading pages for the selection in the ***Reader's Notebook: Adapted Version.*** Then, have students listen to portions of the selection on the ***Hear It!* Audio CD** (adapted text).

Extended Support—Reluctant Readers

To build motivation and engagement before assigning the selection, have students read "The Community Comes to School,"a thematically related selection in ***Reality Central.*** Then, use the questions at the conclusion of the related selection to guide discussion.

❶ Activating Prior Knowledge

1. Prepare an **Anticipation Guide** (***Professional Development Guidebook***, pp. 36–38) with the following statements:
   - Public libraries enrich the lives of children.
   - Public libraries are an essential part of any community.
   - Human beings need stories and information that only books can furnish.
   - Members of a community should support their public library.
2. Give students a copy of the prepared **Anticipation Guide** and have them mark their responses in the appropriate columns.
3. For further guidance, use the ***Classroom Strategies and Teaching Routines*** card: **Using an Anticipation Guide.**

Concept Connector →

Students will return to their **Anticipation Guides** after completing "Libraries Face Sad Chapter."

Small-Group Activity

Industrialist Andrew Carnegie contributed to the building of public libraries across the United States. The buildings themselves were built on classical designs, with columns and domes. Have small groups collect photos of Carnegie libraries and create a collage. Then, have them discuss what messages the architecture seems to imply and how the architecture might affect visitors to the library.

❷ About the Selection

In "Libraries Face Sad Chapter," Pete Hamill describes his memories of using the public library as a child. He explains the importance of the public libraries to generations of new immigrants to New York, as well as to all members of the community. At the time Hamill wrote this essay, New York faced serious financial crises and forced cutbacks in service. Hamill argues that despite these problems, libraries must be protected.

❶ ❷ Libraries Face Sad Chapter

Pete Hamill

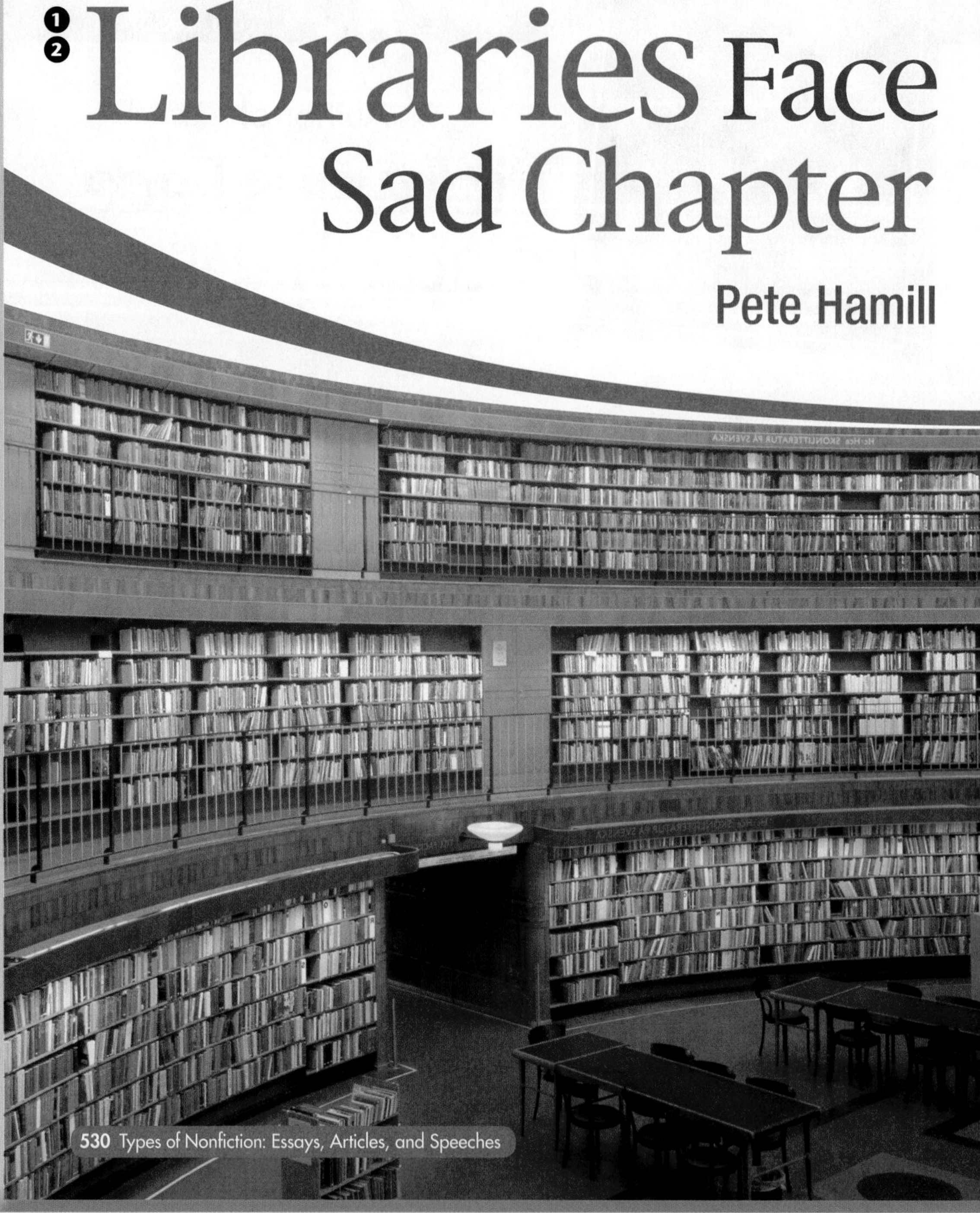

Vocabulary Development

CCSS Language 6

Thematic Vocabulary: The Big Question

As students are discussing "Libraries Face Sad Chapter," encourage them to use the thematic vocabulary presented in Introducing the Big Question, pp. 424–425. You might encourage them with sentence starters like these:

1. Pete Hamill thinks libraries are important because there is a strong *connection* between . . .
2. This article gives the reader *insight* into the role of . . .
3. Public libraries offer nearly endless *sources* of . . .
4. An interesting *fact* about Andrew Carnegie is that . . .

The library was four blocks from where we lived, on the corner of Ninth St. and Sixth Ave., and it was one of the treasure houses of our Brooklyn lives.

This was in the years before television, when we saw movies once a week at the Minerva or the Avon or the RKO Prospect, and fed our imaginations through radio and books. That is, it was in a time when *The Count of Monte Cristo* was as vivid in our minds, and talk, and dreams, as Jack Roosevelt Robinson. Dumas told the story of the count as vividly as Red Barber[1] recited the unfolding tale of No. 42.

We passed into that library between two mock-Corinthian columns that gave the building a majestic aura. For me, every visit was an astonishment. There was a children's room, first seen when I was 8, where I first read the wonderful Babar books, and then moved on to Howard Pyle's *Book of Pirates*, and all of Robert Louis Stevenson, with those rich, golden, mysterious illustrations by N.C. Wyeth.

There were bound volumes of a children's magazine called *St. Nicholas*, full of spidery drawings of animals that talked, and villains who didn't. There were picture books bursting with images of lost cities or the solar system. In that room, I learned that the world was larger than our neighborhood.

And then, at 10 or 11, I found my way into the adult stacks, to borrow books about the daily life of the Romans, the flight of Richard Hannay across Scotland, the conquests of Mexico and Peru, the cases of Sherlock Holmes. On a high shelf, presumed to be safe from the curious eyes of children, was a lavish (in memory) edition of *The Thousand and One Nights.*[2]

No teacher sent us to those leathery cliffs of books. Reading wasn't an assignment; it was a pleasure. We read for the combined thrills of villainy and heroism, along with knowledge of the vast world beyond the parish. Living in those other worlds, we could become other people: Jim Hawkins, or Edmund Dantes, or (most thrillingly) d'Artagnan, with his three musketeers.

We could live in the South Seas, or Paris, or the Rome of Caligula. It never occurred to us that we were inheriting our little share of civilization. But that's what was happening.

1. ***The Count of Monte Cristo* . . . Red Barber** *The Count of Monte Cristo* is a nineteenth-century novel by Alexandre Dumas. Jackie Robinson was the first African American major league baseball player. He joined the Brooklyn Dodgers in 1947 and wore number 42. Dodgers games were broadcast on the radio, and the action was described by announcer Red Barber.
2. ***The Thousand and One Nights*** collection of ancient tales also known as the Arabian Nights. Although many of the tales, including "Aladdin," are now retold as children's stories, the original tellings are full of violence, bloodshed, poisonings, and betrayals.

Literary Analysis
Persuasive Essay
Which words here suggest that the author appeals to positive feelings about childhood and imagination?

Vocabulary
volumes (väl′ yo͞omz) *n.* books that are either part of a set or combined into one

presumed (prē zo͞omd′) *adj.* accepted as true; supposed

◀ **Critical Viewing**
How might the young Pete Hamill have regarded this empty library? **[Speculate]**

According to Hamill, why did he read so much?

❸ Literary Analysis

Persuasive Essay

1. Read the passage aloud. Then **ask** students what the author is describing here.

   Answer: He is describing his visits to the library and the books he read as a child.

2. **Ask** the Literary Analysis question: Which words here suggest that the author appeals to positive feelings about childhood and imagination?

   Answer: Words and phrases include "majestic aura," "astonishment," "wonderful Babar books," and "rich, golden, mysterious illustrations."

▶ **Monitor Progress:** Provide students with **Literary Analysis Graphic Organizer B**, p. 97 in ***Graphic Organizer Transparencies***, to complete as they read the essay.

▶ **Reteach:** If students have difficulty identifying persuasive appeals, remind them that a persuasive appeal aims to convince the reader to think or act in a certain way. Tell students that certain words can be signals of an opinion. On the board, brainstorm for a list of these words from the essay.

❹ Critical Viewing

Possible response: Students may suggest that he would regard the library with awe, or anticipation and excitement at what its books might hold.

❺ Reading Check

Answer: Hamill read so much because books enabled him to experience the thrills of people and places that were outside his own world. He also read to gain knowledge.

Differentiated Instruction for Universal Access

Vocabulary for Special-Needs Students
Help students prepare for some of the unfamiliar vocabulary by providing them with **Vocabulary Warm-up Word Lists** and **Vocabulary Warm-up Practice,** pp. 145–146 in ***Unit 3 Resources***. Work with students in groups to complete the sheets.

Strategy for Less Proficient Readers
To give students a context for the essay and to model how to analyze the author's arguments, show them the **Reading Skill Graphic Organizer A** (***Graphic Organizer Transparencies,*** p. 93). The partially completed graphic organizer will give students insight into analyzing arguments. They can use it as a model for making their own analyses of the author's arguments as they read.

❻ Critical Viewing

Answer: The photograph shows a large, elegant room suitable for a "treasure house." The walls are lined with books, and many people are sitting at tables, engrossed in reading or working on computers. These activities require intense use of the imagination and the brain in general.

Built by Carnegie

The library of my childhood is still there, since 1975 known as the Park Slope Branch of the Brooklyn Public Library. It was built with grant money from my favorite capitalist, Andrew Carnegie, in 1906. But once again, as happened in 1992, the teeming imaginative life of libraries is in danger of being curtailed. Services might be cut. Hours trimmed. Staff reduced. The reason is the same: money, or the lack of it.

Vocabulary
curtailed (kər tāld′) *v.* cut short; reduced

Such reductions are absolutely understandable. As we all know, Mayor Bloomberg has more than a $4 billion shortfall[3] that must be made up. Unlike the spend-more tax-less leaders of the federal government, the government of New York City can't print money to keep things going. In this season of post-September 11 austerities,[4] something must give. I hope it isn't the libraries.

The reason is simple: In hard times, libraries are more important than ever. Human beings need what books give them better than any other medium. Since those ancient nights around prehistoric campfires, we have needed myth. And heroes. And moral tales. And information about the world beyond the nearest mountains or oceans.

Vocabulary
medium (mē′ dē əm) *n.* means of communication

3. **shortfall** (shôrt′ fôl′) *n.* the difference between the amount you have and the amount you need or expect.
4. **austerities** (ô ster′ ə tēz) *n.* acts of self-discipline and self-denial.

❻ ▼ **Critical Viewing**
How does this photograph support Hamill's idea that a library is a "treasure house of the imagination"? **[Connect]**

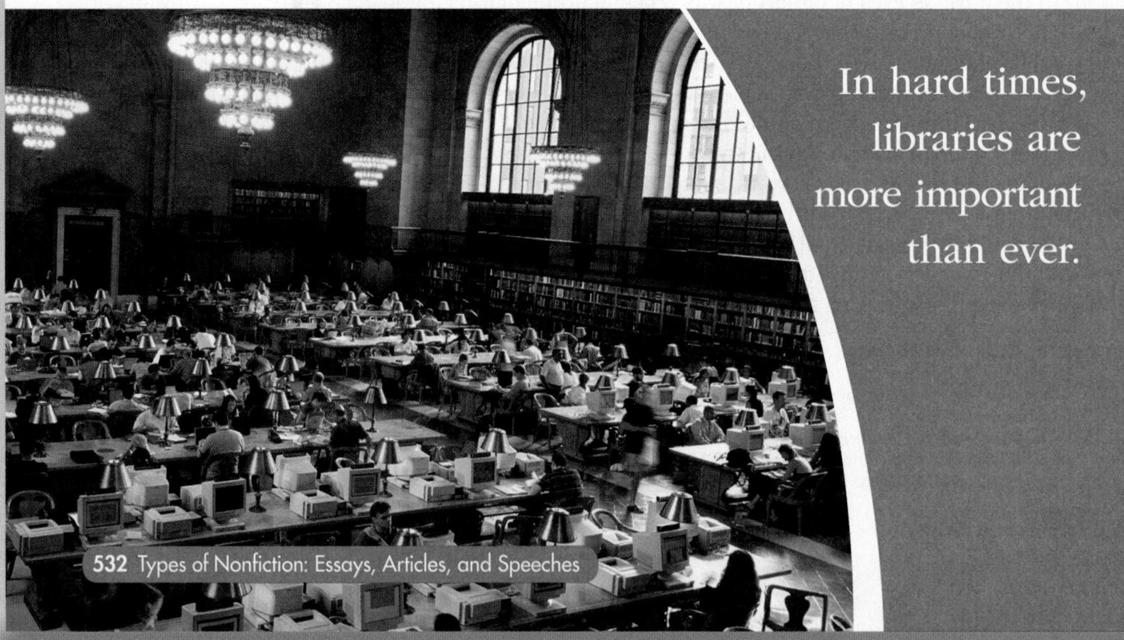

In hard times, libraries are more important than ever.

Vocabulary Development

Vocabulary Knowledge Rating

When students have completed reading and discussing "Libraries Face Sad Chapter," have them take out their **Vocabulary Knowledge Rating Chart** for this selection. Read the words aloud once more and have students rate their knowledge of the words again in the After Reading column. Clarify any words that are still problematic. Have students write their own definition and example or sentence in the appropriate column. Then, have students complete the Vocabulary Practice activities at the end of the selection. Encourage students to use the words in further discussion and written work about this selection. Remind them that they will be accountable for these words on the **Selection Test**, ***Unit 3 Resources***, pp. 160–162 or 163–165.

Today, with books and movies more expensive than ever, and television entertainment in free fall to the lowest levels of stupidity, freely circulating books are an absolute necessity. They are quite simply another kind of food. We imagine, and then we live.

Hard times are also an opportunity. Parents and teachers all moan about the refusal of the young to read. Here is the chance to revive the power of the printed page. The Harry Potter books show that the audience for young readers is potentially immense. A child who starts with Harry Potter can find his or her way to Dumas and Arthur Conan Doyle, to Mark Twain and Walt Whitman, and, yes, to Tolstoy and Joyce and Proust.

Immigrants' Appreciation

For those without money, the road to that treasure house of the imagination begins at the public library. When I was a boy, the rooms were crowded with immigrants and their children. That is, with people who came from places where there were no libraries for the poor. With their children, they built the New York in which we now live.

8 Today, the libraries of this city are still doing that work. The libraries of Brooklyn and Queens are jammed with the new immigrants and their astonishing children, the people who will build the New York of tomorrow. The older people want information about this new world, and how to get better jobs and green cards and citizenship. Their American children want to vanish into books their parents cannot afford, thus filling themselves with the endless possibilities of the future.

They are no different from the Irish, the Jews and the Italians of my childhood. My father only went to the eighth grade in Belfast. I remember my mother drilling him at our kitchen table for his citizenship test, and I know that he first read the Constitution in a book borrowed from the Prospect Branch of the Brooklyn Public Library. Lying in a darkened bed off that kitchen, I first heard the language of the Bill of Rights.

That process must go on in all the places where the poor now live. If it's impossible for the city to do it, then we must do it ourselves. Bloomberg can give us the hard numbers, explain the shortfall in the library budget and explain how much we need. Then we should try to make it up with the establishment of a private fund to maintain the libraries at full strength for the duration of the crisis.

7 **LITERATURE IN CONTEXT**

History Connection

Andrew Carnegie (1835–1919) was a Scottish immigrant who became enormously wealthy in the steel business. In 1889, Carnegie published an essay entitled "The Gospel of Wealth." In it, he argued that the rich should use their money for the public good. Under his plan, "the surplus wealth of the few will become, in the best sense, the property of the many." Unlike many other wealthy men of his time, Carnegie acted on his belief. His many charitable acts included the building of more than 2800 public libraries throughout the English-speaking world.

Connect to the Literature

How do you think Andrew Carnegie would react to the idea of cuts in library funding? Explain.

Vocabulary
duration (doo rā′ shən) *n.* length of time something lasts

7 Literature in Context

History Connection Andrew Carnegie wrote, "The man who dies rich dies disgraced." He lived by his words. An exceptional philanthropist, he gave away $350 million, which amounted to nearly 90 percent of his great fortune. In addition to the many libraries that he built, Carnegie contributed to the building of 7,000 church organs and funded the Carnegie Foundation for the Advancement of Teaching and the Carnegie Endowment for Peace.

Connect to the Literature After discussing Carnegie's contributions, **ask** the Connect to the Literature question: How do you think Andrew Carnegie would react to the idea of cuts in library funding? Explain.

Possible response: Andrew Carnegie would probably oppose cuts in library funding, since he placed great importance on public libraries. He would probably offer to help fund the libraries himself.

8 Connecting to the Big Question

1. Have a volunteer read the bracketed passage aloud. **Ask:** What point is Hamill making in this passage?

   Answer: Public libraries provide opportunities for pleasure and success for immigrants and poor people. This helps them contribute to the future of their country.

2. **Ask:** What facts does Hamill use to make his point?

   Answer: For decades, New York's public libraries have been filled with immigrants and their children. These people use the library to get better jobs, to gain citizenship, and to gather information about their new country.

3. **Ask:** How do these facts help you understand the situation that Hamill describes?

   Possible response: It shows me that public libraries help create a level playing field for Americans of different incomes and backgrounds.

Concept Connector

Anticipation Guide
Have students return to their **Anticipation Guides** and respond to the statements again in the After Reading column. They may do this individually or in their original pairs or groups. Then, lead a class discussion, probing for what students have learned that confirms or invalidates each statement. Encourage students to cite specific details, quotations, or other evidence from the text to support their responses to each statement.

Writing About the Big Question
Have students compare their responses to the sentence starters they completed before reading the essay with their ideas afterwards. Ask them to explain whether their thoughts have changed.

Reading Skill Graphic Organizer
Ask students to review the graphic organizers they completed to identify the persuasive appeals while reading. Show them **Reading Skill Graphic Organizer A** (*Graphic Organizer Transparencies*, p. 93) as an example.

Spiral Review

Author's Purpose

1. Remind students that they studied the concept of author's purpose in the Unit 3 Literary Analysis Workshop (pp. 426–439).
2. Then, **ask** students the Spiral Review question.

   Possible response: The author's purpose in suggesting a library tax is to persuade readers that we owe it to past, present, and future generations to maintain public libraries.

ASSESS

Answers

Critical Thinking

Remind students to support their answers with evidence from the text.

1. (a) He remembers *The Count of Monte Cristo*, the Babar books, the *Book of Pirates*, the Sherlock Holmes mysteries, and *St. Nicholas* magazine. (b) Hamill loved the library as a child because it gave him access to books of adventure and imagination.
2. (a) He means that books nourish the mind and the imagination. (b) Hamill considers books a necessity of life.
3. **Possible responses:** (a) Some students may agree with Hamill that public libraries are essential; others may disagree, saying that the Internet and bookstores make public libraries unnecessary. (b) Some students may say that they have changed their minds, noting the cost to taxpayers of maintaining the libraries.
4. (a) **Possible response:** Hamill wants the reader to know that literature is a wonderful diversion. When young minds are stimulated, children become much more aware of the world around them. (b) **Possible response:** Yes, I want to act because now I am aware of the importance of libraries. I want to help make sure that all people have a fair chance at happiness and success in life.

Vocabulary
emulate (em´ yōō lāt) *v.* imitate (a person or thing admired)

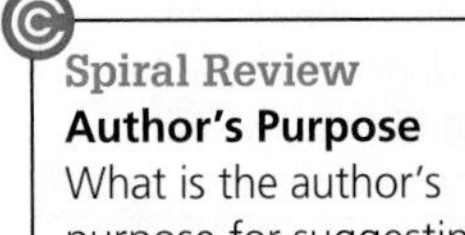

Spiral Review
Author's Purpose
What is the author's purpose for suggesting a voluntary library tax?

All of us whose lives have been affected by the treasures of public libraries could contribute. The rich could emulate Carnegie, who used his wealth to create more than 1,600 public libraries, including 65 in New York. But the middle class could also send in small amounts from $10 to $50.

This would be a kind of voluntary tax. On one level, it would be a powerful pledge to maintain the life of the mind among all classes in this city. That is obviously in our own interest. But above all, it would be a means of honoring the labor of those men and women who got us here, and who paid taxes to buy books for all New Yorkers, and first took us by the hand and walked us into the treasure houses. We who dreamed of Ebbets Field and the Chateau d'If on the same American nights owe debts to New York that we can never pay. This is one that must be honored.

Critical Thinking

Cite textual evidence to support your responses.

1. **Key Ideas and Details** **(a)** What books and magazines does Hamill remember from early visits to the library? **(b) Infer:** What do these memories suggest about how Hamill felt about the library as a child?
2. **Key Ideas and Details** **(a) Interpret:** What does Hamill mean by calling books "another kind of food"? **(b) Draw Conclusions:** What does this comparison suggest about the value he places on books?
3. **Integration of Knowledge and Ideas** **(a) Take a Position:** Do you agree with Hamill's claims about the importance of free public libraries? Explain. **(b) Discuss:** Share your response with a partner, and then explain how the discussion has or has not changed your response to the question.
4. **Integration of Knowledge and Ideas** **(a)** What does Hamill want you to know about the need for public libraries? **(b)** Do the facts he presents make you understand enough to want to act? Explain. *[Connect to the Big Question: Is knowledge the same as understanding?]*

Assessment Resources

Unit 3 Resources

L1 L2 EL **Selection Test A**, pp. 160–162. Administer Test A to less advanced readers.

L3 L4 EL **Selection Test B**, pp. 163–165. Administer Test B to on-level and more advanced students.

L3 L4 **Open-Book Test**, pp. 157–159. As an alternative, give the Open-Book Test.

All **Customizable Test Bank**

All **Self-tests**
Students may prepare for the **Selection Test** by taking the **Self-test** online.

All assessment resources are available at **www.PHLitOnline.com**.

After You Read | Libraries Face Sad Chapter

Literary Analysis: Persuasive Essay

1. **Key Ideas and Details** **(a)** In this essay, what is the author trying to persuade readers to do? **(b)** What evidence does he use to support his position?
2. **Craft and Structure** **(a)** Using a chart like the one shown, identify three passages in which Hamill asserts his position on public libraries. In the right-hand column, indicate whether each passage is an appeal to reason or to emotion and explain your ideas. **(b)** Which kind of appeals does the author seem to favor—appeals to reason or appeals to emotion? Explain.

Passage	Reason or Emotion

3. **Integration of Knowledge and Ideas** What do you think is the **author's motive** for trying to persuade readers to agree with him?

Libraries Face Sad Chapter
Pete Hamill

Reading Skill: Evaluate Persuasion

4. Are the **claims** in this essay well-reasoned and logical? Explain.
5. Which passages are especially convincing? Explain.

Vocabulary

Acquisition and Use In vocabulary study, **analogies** show the relationships between pairs of words. Use a word from the vocabulary list on page 528 to complete each analogy. In each, your choice should create a word pair that matches the relationship between the first two words.

1. sugar : sweetness :: time : ____________
2. bucket : water :: ____________ : information
3. arrived : departed :: continued : ____________
4. people : groups :: pages : ____________
5. knew : guessed :: proved : ____________
6. persuade: convince :: mimic : ____________

Word Study Use the context of the sentences and what you know about the **Latin root *-sum-*** to explain your answer to each question.

1. If you *resume* an activity, do you stop doing it?
2. Is it wise to make a *presumption* about someone else's wishes?

Word Study

The **Latin root *-sum-*** means "to take."

Apply It Explain how the root *-sum-* contributes to the meanings of these words. Consult a dictionary if necessary.

assume
sumptuous
consume

ASSESS/EXTEND

Answers

Literary Analysis

1. (a) He is trying to persuade people to support public libraries. (b) He cites his own experiences and the importance of libraries to new immigrants.
2. (a) **Possible response:** Passage: Paragraph beginning "We passed into that library . . ." **Reason or Emotion:** He appeals to emotion by recalling how important libraries were to him as a child. (b) The author seems to favor appeals to emotion. He refers to reading as a pleasure, he tells of happy childhood memories at the library, and he believes the value of maintaining libraries outweighs the cost.

   For more sample answers, see **Literary Analysis Graphic Organizer A**, p. 96, and the **Additional Answers** section in ***Graphic Organizer Transparencies***.
3. The author's motive is to persuade people how important libraries are so that they will help support libraries financially.

Reading Skill

4. **Possible response:** Most students will state that the author's claims are well reasoned and logical; he gives facts and details to support his points.
5. **Possible response:** Most students will say that the author is convincing when he describes his childhood experiences.

Vocabulary

Acquisition and Use

Sample answers:

1. duration
2. medium
3. curtailed
4. volumes
5. presumed
6. emulate

Word Study

Sample answers:

1. No, if you *resume* an activity, you take it up again.
2. No, it is unwise to make a *presumption* about someone before knowing facts.

Word Study: Apply It

To *assume* is to take for granted. Something *sumptuous* is luxurious or takes great wealth. To *consume* is to take up the attention of.

EXTEND/ASSESS

Answers

Conventions

Introduce the skill, using the instruction on the student page.

Think Aloud: Model the Skill

Model the skill of recognizing and using adjectives. On the board, write *It was a cold, wet day on the ice-blue slopes of New England.* Say to students:

Adjectives are words that describe nouns. Adjectives make a sentence come to life. In this sentence, *cold, wet*, and *ice-blue* are adjectives. *Cold* and *wet* describe day and *ice-blue* describes slopes.

PH WRITING COACH Grade 9

Students will find instruction on and practice with adjectives in Chapter 13, section 3.

Practice A

Sample Answers:

1. little, heavy; The small child carried the bulky skis.
2. wet, brown, uncomfortable; The damp, gray sweater was ugly.
3. soggy, tuna fish, tasteless; Her old, egg salad sandwich was disgusting.
4. wonderful; She smiled as she thought about her fantastic day.
5. long, icy; The ski slope is short and smooth.

Reading Application

Students should find two sentences in which the adjective comes before the noun and two sentences in which it comes after the noun.

Practice B

Sample Answers:

1. Most public libraries contain good books.
2. Small children often make cute animal drawings.
3. The head librarian is an elderly lady.
4. University and college libraries use state-of-the-art technology.
5. Public libraries need tax money.

Writing Application

Students should include at least two adjectives in each sentence. Adjectives should be placed before and after the nouns.

PERFORMANCE TASKS

Integrated Language Skills

Carry Your Own Skis • Libraries Face Sad Chapter

Conventions: Adjectives

An **adjective** is a word used to give a noun or pronoun a more specific meaning.

Adjectives modify, or change, nouns and pronouns by telling *what kind, which one, how many,* or *how much.*

Noun/Pronoun	Question	Adjective and Noun/Pronoun
school	What kind?	martial arts school
student	Which one?	involved student
cars	How many?/How much?	three cars

Usually an adjective comes before the noun it modifies. Sometimes, however, the adjective may follow the noun by coming after a linking verb.

Before The *large, yellow* dog is next door.

After The dog next door is *large and yellow.*

Practice A Identify the adjectives in the following sentences. Then, write a new sentence for each, replacing each adjective with a different adjective.

1. The little child carried the heavy skis.
2. The wet, brown sweater was uncomfortable.
3. Her soggy tuna fish sandwich was tasteless.
4. She smiled as she thought about her wonderful day.
5. The ski slope is long and icy.

Reading Application Find two sentences in "Carry Your Own Skis" in which an adjective comes before the noun it modifies. Find two sentences in which the adjective follows its noun.

Practice B Modify each noun in these sentences with one or more adjectives.

1. Most libraries contain books.
2. Children often make animal drawings.
3. The librarian is a lady.
4. Libraries use technology.
5. Libraries need money.

Writing Application Look at the image on page 532. Write four sentences describing what might be going on in this picture. Use at least two adjectives in each sentence and position them both before *and* after the noun.

PH WRITING COACH Further instruction and practice are available in *Prentice Hall Writing Coach.*

Extend the Lesson

Sentence Modeling

Choose the sentence given from the selection students have read:

A cold, wet day on the ice-blue slopes of New England, freezing in leather boots and the generation of ski clothes before microfibers was far preferable to being left out of all that fun. ("Carry Your Own Skis")

There were bound volumes of a children's magazine called St. Nicholas, *full of spidery drawings of animals that talked, and villains who didn't.* ("Libraries Face Sad Chapter")

Ask students what they notice about the sentence. Elicit that the sentence contains several adjectives. Have students circle the adjectives and underline the nouns that the adjectives modify. Then, ask what else they notice. (The writer uses sensory adjectives that help readers relate to the topic in a physical way.)

Have students imitate the sentence, matching each grammatical and stylistic feature discussed.

Writing

Informative Text Both of these essays convey an overall main idea and message for readers. Write an **abstract** of "Carry Your Own Skis" or "Libraries Face Sad Chapter." An abstract of a work is a type of summary readers consult to see if a work seems interesting or relevant to them.

- Clearly state the main point of the **essay.**
- Briefly convey important supporting details.
- Be sure your abstract will help those who have not read the essay.

Grammar Application Make sure all adjectives in your abstract are properly placed.

Writing Workshop: *Work in Progress*

Prewriting for Editorial For an editorial you may write, identify and list at least three specific elements of music, fashion, books, or movies that influence you. Put this Cultural Influences List in your writing portfolio.

Research and Technology

Build and Present Knowledge Do research and create a **comparative chart.** Use the chart in preparing and giving a **persuasive speech.**

- If you read "Carry Your Own Skis," research today's popular winter sports. Create a chart that shows which sports have the most participants and largest audience. In your speech, persuade your audience to support one of the less popular sports, making it more visible.
- If you read "Libraries Face Sad Chapter," research the services offered by libraries today. Create a chart that shows the variety of services and the average numbers of people using them. In your speech, persuade your audience to use the library more.

Follow these steps to complete the assignment:

- Follow appropriate conventions for documentation of your source material. Consult page R36 for more information.
- Organize your presentation logically and include an introduction, body, and conclusion.
- Prepare your presentation with your audience in mind, using effective verbal and nonverbal gestures in order to be persuasive.
- Include relevant media to make your chart and oral presentation effective.

Common Core State Standards

L.9-10.1; W.9-10.4; SL.9-10.4
[For the full wording of the standards, see page 518.]

Use this prewriting activity to prepare for the **Writing Workshop** on page 582.

www.PHLitOnline.com

- Interactive graphic organizers
- Grammar tutorial
- Interactive journals

EXTEND/ASSESS

Writing

1. Review the assignment, using the instruction on the student page.
2. To give students guidance for writing this abstract, give them the **Support for Writing,** p. 155 in *Unit 3 Resources.*
3. To evaluate students' abstracts, use the Summary rubrics, pp. 246–247 in *Professional Development Guidebook.* In addition, you might evaluate for how useful the abstract might be to those who have not read the selection.

Grammar Application

Have students check their drafts to make sure all of their adjectives are properly placed.

Six Traits Focus

✓	Ideas	Word Choice
✓	Organization	Sentence Fluency
	Voice	Conventions

PH WRITING COACH Grade 9

Students will find instruction on and practice with summarizing in Chapter 2.

Writing Workshop
Work in Progress

Have students save their completed Cultural Influences Lists in their portfolios. They will use their lists later as they continue this Work-in-Progress assignment (see p. 563). The assignment prepares them to complete the Writing Workshop (see pp. 582–589).

Research and Technology

1. Review the assignment, using the instruction on the student page.
2. To support students' work on the assignment, have them complete the **Support for Extend Your Learning** page (*Unit 3 Resources,* p. 156).

Teaching Resources

Unit 3 Resources
L3 L4 EL **Integrated Language Skills: Grammar,** p. 154
L3 L4 EL **Support for Writing,** p. 155
L3 L4 **Support for Extend Your Learning,** p. 156
L4 **Enrichment,** pp. 135, 153

Enriched Online Student Edition
Available under After You Read for this selection:
All **Interactive Grammar Tutorial**
L3 L4 **Internet Research Activity**

Professional Development Guidebook
Rubrics for Self-Assessment: Summary, pp. 246–247

PHLit Online! All print and digital resources are available at **www.PHLitOnline.com.** Online resources accessible by students are noted on the student page.

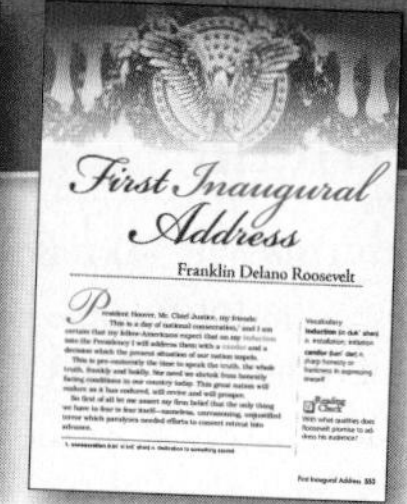

✓ "I Have a Dream" • ✓✓ First Inaugural Address

Lesson Pacing Guide

DAY 1 Preteach

- Administer the Reading and Vocabulary Warm-ups (*Unit 3 Resources*, pp. 166–169 or 184–187) as necessary.
- Introduce the Reading Skill: Evaluate Persuasion.
- Introduce the Literary Analysis concept: Persuasive Speech.
- Distribute copies of the appropriate graphic organizer for the Reading Skill (*Graphic Organizer Transparencies*, pp. 98–100).
- Distribute copies of the appropriate graphic organizer for Literary Analysis (*Graphic Organizer Transparencies*, pp. 101–103).
- Teach the selection vocabulary.
- Introduce the Word Study skill.

DAYS 2–3 Preteach/Teach

- Build background with the Background feature.
- Develop thematic vocabulary and thematic thinking with Writing About the Big Question.
- Prepare students to read with the Activating Prior Knowledge activities (TE).
- Informally monitor comprehension while students read.
- Use the Reading Check questions to confirm comprehension.
- Develop students' ability to determine the main idea, using the Reading Skill questions.
- Develop students' understanding of expository essays, using the Literary Analysis questions.
- Reinforce vocabulary with the Vocabulary notes.
- Reinforce unit focus standards using the Spiral Review prompts.

DAY 4 Assess

- Assess students' comprehension and mastery of the skills by having them answer the Critical Thinking, Reading Skill, and Literary Analysis questions.
- Have students complete the Vocabulary Practice activities.
- Have students complete the Word Study activities.

DAY 5 Extend/Assess

- Have students complete the Conventions lesson.
- Have students complete the Writing activity and write a proposal. (You may assign as homework.)
- Extend learning by having students complete the Speaking and Listening, a radio news report. (You may assign as homework.) As an alternative, assign them "Has the Dream Come True?" or "The Effect of Fear" in *Reality Central*.
- Administer Selection Test A or B (*Unit 3 Resources*, pp. 178–183 or 199–204).

Common Core State Standards

Reading Informational Text
6. Determine an author's point of view or purpose in a text and analyze how an author uses rhetoric to advance that point of view or purpose.
8. Delineate and evaluate the argument and specific claims in a text, assessing whether the reasoning is valid and the evidence is relevant and sufficient; identify false statements and fallacious reasoning.
9. Analyze seminal U.S. documents of historical and literary significance, including how they address related themes and concepts.

Writing 1. Write arguments to support claims in an analysis of substantive topics or texts, using valid reasoning and relevant and sufficient evidence.

Speaking and Listening 3. Evaluate a speaker's point of view, reasoning, and use of evidence and rhetoric, identifying any fallacious reasoning or exaggerated or distorted evidence.

Language 3. Apply knowledge of language to understand how language functions in different contexts, to make effective choices for meaning or style, and to comprehend more fully when reading or listening.
6. Acquire and use accurately grade-appropriate general academic and domain-specific words and phrases; gather vocabulary knowledge when considering a word or phrase important to comprehension or expression.

Additional Standards Practice
***Common Core Companion*, pp. 110–144**

Daily Block Scheduling
Each day in this Lesson Pacing Guide represents a 40–50 minute period. Teachers using block scheduling may combine days to revise pacing. In addition, teachers may differentiate and support core instruction by integrating components for extended and intensive support as students require. See the Guide to Selected Leveled Resources (facing page).

Guide to Selected Leveled Resources

RTI **Tier 1** (students performing on level)		✓ More Accessible "I Have a Dream"	✓✓ More Complex First Inaugural Address
Warm Up	**Practice, model,** and **monitor** fluency, working **with the whole class** or **in groups.**	**Vocabulary** and **Reading Warm-ups B,** ***Unit 3 Resources,*** pp. 166–167, 169	**Vocabulary** and **Reading Warm-ups B,** ***Unit 3 Resources,*** pp. 184–185, 187
Comprehension/Skills	**Support** and **monitor** comprehension and skills development, having students complete the activities, graphic organizers, and interactive prompts **independently** or **as a class.**	• ***Reader's Notebook,*** adapted instruction and full selection EL ***Reader's Notebook: English Learner's Version,*** adapted instruction and adapted selection • **Reading Skill Graphic Organizer B,** ***Graphic Organizer Transparencies,*** p. 100 • **Literary Analysis Graphic Organizer B,** ***Graphic Organizer Transparencies,*** p. 103	• ***Reader's Notebook,*** adapted instruction and summary EL ***Reader's Notebook: English Learner's Version,*** adapted instruction and summary • **Reading Skill Graphic Organizer B,** ***Graphic Organizer Transparencies,*** p. 100 • **Literary Analysis Graphic Organizer B,** ***Graphic Organizer Transparencies,*** p. 103
Monitor Progress	**Monitor** student progress with the differentiated curriculum-based assessment in the *Unit Resources.*	• **Selection Test B,** ***Unit 3 Resources,*** pp. 181–183 • **Open-Book Test,** ***Unit 3 Resources,*** pp. 175–177	• **Selection Test B,** ***Unit 3 Resources,*** pp. 202–204 • **Open-Book Test,** ***Unit 3 Resources,*** pp. 196–198
Assess/ Screen	• **Assess** student progress using Benchmark Test 6. • **Preassess** instructional needs using the vocabulary in Context section of the test.	• **Benchmark Test 6,** ***Unit 3 Resources,*** pp. 227–235, including Vocabulary in Context diagnostic items	• **Benchmark Test 6,** ***Unit 3 Resources,*** pp. 227–235, including Vocabulary in Context diagnostic items

RTI **Tier 2** (students requiring intervention)		✓ More Accessible "I Have a Dream"	✓✓ More Complex First Inaugural Address
Warm Up	**Practice, model,** and **monitor** fluency **in groups** or **with individuals.**	• **Vocabulary and Reading Warm-ups A,** ***Unit 3 Resources,*** pp. 166–168 • ***Reality Central,*** "Has the Dream Come True?" • ***Hear It!*** **Audio CD (adapted text)**	• **Vocabulary and Reading Warm-ups A,** ***Unit 3 Resources,*** pp. 184–186 • ***Reality Central,*** "The Effect of Fear" • ***Hear It!*** **Audio CD**
Comprehension/Skills	• **Support** and **monitor** comprehension and skills development, working **in small groups** or **with individuals.** • **Pair** students with more advanced peers and have them complete the writing activity in the *Real-World Writing Journal.* • As students complete the selection in the appropriate version of the *Reader's Notebook,* **monitor** comprehension frequently with group questions and individual instruction. • **Model** strategies while guiding students in completing the activities and prompts in the *Reader's Notebook,* as well as the graphic organizers. • **Practice** skills and **monitor** mastery with the *Reading Kit* worksheets.	• ***Real-World Writing Journal,*** Lesson 7, pp. 94–97 • ***Reader's Notebook: Adapted Version,*** adapted instruction and adapted selection EL ***Reader's Notebook: English Learner's Version,*** adapted instruction and adapted selection • **Reading Skill Graphic Organizer A,** ***Graphic Organizer Transparencies,*** p. 98 • **Literary Analysis Graphic Organizer A,** ***Graphic Organizer Transparencies,*** p. 101 • ***Reading Kit,*** Practice worksheets, pp. 128, 132, 136, 140, 148	• ***Real-World Writing Journal,*** Lesson 8, pp. 98–101 • ***Reader's Notebook: Adapted Version,*** adapted instruction and summary EL ***Reader's Notebook: English Learner's Version,*** adapted instruction and summary • **Reading Skill Graphic Organizer A,** ***Graphic Organizer Transparencies,*** p. 99 • **Literary Analysis Graphic Organizer A,** ***Graphic Organizer Transparencies,*** p. 102 • ***Reading Kit,*** Practice worksheets, pp. 128, 132, 136, 140, 148
Monitor Progress	**Monitor** student progress with the differentiated curriculum-based assessment in the *Unit Resources* and in the *Reading Kit.*	• **Selection Test A,** ***Unit 3 Resources,*** pp. 178–180 • **Reading Kit,** Assess worksheets, pp. 129, 133, 137, 141, 149	• **Selection Test A,** ***Unit 3 Resources,*** pp. 74–76 • **Reading Kit,** Assess worksheets, pp. 129, 133, 137, 141, 149
Assess/ Screen	• **Assess** student progress using Benchmark Test 6. • **Preassess** instructional needs using the Vocabulary in Context section of the test.	• **Benchmark Test 6,** ***Unit 3 Resources,*** pp. 227–235, including Vocabulary in Context diagnostic items	• **Benchmark Test 6,** ***Unit 3 Resources,*** pp. 227–235, including Vocabulary in Context diagnostic items

TIER 3 Tier 3 intervention may require consultation with the student's special-education or dyslexia specialist. For additional support, see the Tier 2 activities and resources listed above.

One-on-one teaching | Group work | Whole class instruction | Independent work | A Assessment

For a complete guide to selection support, including support for Advanced students, see the Overview of Resources in the frontmatter.

COMMON CORE
Visual Guide to Featured Selection Resources

✓"I Have a Dream"
✓✓First Inaugural Address

"I Have a Dream"

Martin Luther King, Jr.

542 Types of Nonfiction: Essays, Articles, and Speeches

First Inaugural Address

Franklin Delano Roosevelt

President Hoover, Mr. Chief Justice, my friends:

This is a day of national consecration,[1] and I am certain that my fellow-Americans expect that on my induction into the Presidency I will address them with a candor and a decision which the present situation of our nation impels.

This is pre-eminently the time to speak the truth, the whole truth, frankly and boldly. Nor need we shrink from honestly facing conditions in our country today. This great nation will endure as it has endured, will revive and will prosper.

So first of all let me assert my firm belief that the only thing we have to fear is fear itself—nameless, unreasoning, unjustified terror which paralyzes needed efforts to convert retreat into advance.

Vocabulary
induction (in duk´ shən) *n.* installation; initiation
candor (kan´ dər) *n.* sharp honesty or frankness in expressing oneself

Reading Check
With what qualities does Roosevelt promise to address his audience?

1. **consecration** (kän´ si krā´ shən) *n.* dedication to something sacred.

First Inaugural Address 553

RESOURCES FOR:

- L1 Special-Needs Students
- L2 Below-Level Students (Tier 2)
- L3 On-Level Students (Tier 1)
- L4 Advanced Students (Tier 1)
- EL English Learners
- All All Students

Vocabulary/Fluency/Prior Knowledge

Unit 3 Resources

Name ______________________ Date ____________

"I Have a Dream" by Martin Luther King, Jr.
Writing About the Big Question

THE BIG ?
Is knowledge the same as understanding?

Big Question Vocabulary

ambiguous	clarify	comprehend	concept	connection
fact	feeling	information	insight	instinct
interpret	research	senses/sensory	sources	statistics

A. *Use one or more words from the list above to complete each sentence.*

1. The ______________ helped Jill understand the civil rights movement.
2. King spoke with great ______________ that helped people understand his message.
3. He made a powerful ______________ with his audience as he gave them information on the injustices suffered by many people.
4. Andrew better understood King's appeal when he read ______________ about all the people who went to hear King speak.

B. *Follow the directions in responding to each item below.*

1. When have you heard a good speaker? Describe the occasion.
____
____
2. How did the speaker help you understand the topic? What techniques or methods did the speaker use? Use at least two of the Big Question vocabulary words.
____
____

C. In "I have a dream," Martin Luthar King makes a logical and emotional speech to help listeners understand his dream of freedom and equality. Complete the sentence below. Then, write a short paragraph in which you connect this experience to the Big Question.

The concept of equality might be ambiguous to some people because ______________
____
____
____
____
____

Unit 3 Resources: Types of Nonfiction

170

All **Writing About the Big Question,** pp. 170, 188

Also available for these selections:

EL L1 L2 **Vocabulary Warm-ups A and B,** pp. 166–167, 184–185

EL L1 L2 **Reading Warm-ups A and B,** pp. 168–169, 186–187

All **Vocabulary Builder,** pp. 173, 191

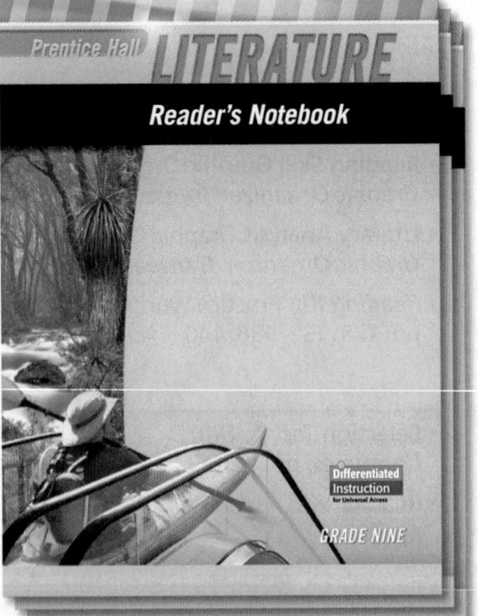

Reader's Notebooks

Pre- and postreading pages for both selections, as well as "I have a Dream," appear in an interactive format in the *Reader's Notebooks.* Each *Notebook* is differentiated for a different group of learners. The selections in the Adapted and English Learner's versions are abridged.

L2 L3 ***Reader's Notebook***

L1 ***Reader's Notebook: Adapted Version***

EL ***Reader's Notebook: English Learner's Version***

EL ***Reader's Notebook: Spanish Version***

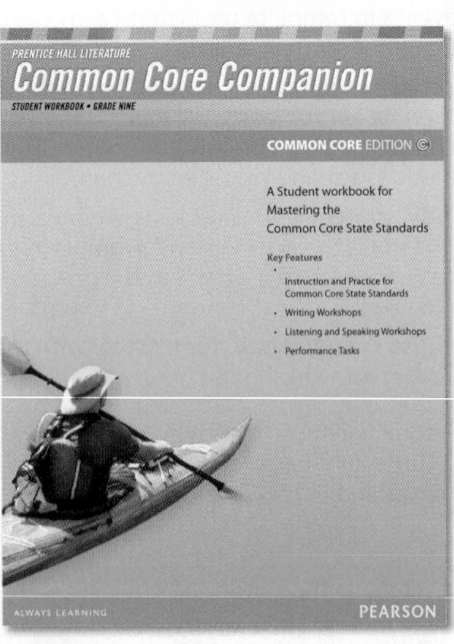

Common Core Companion

Additional instruction and practice for each Common Core State Standard

Selection Support

Graphic Organizer Transparencies

"I Have a Dream" by Martin Luther King, Jr.
"First Inaugural Address" by Franklin Delano Roosevelt

After You Read B: Literary Analysis—Persuasive Speech

	Example	Effect
Restatement		
Repetition		
Parallelism		

Graphic Organizer Transparencies

103

EL L3 **Literary Analysis: Graphic Organizer B,** p. 103

Also available for these selections:

- EL L1 L2 **Reading: Graphic Organizer A,** pp. 98, 99 (partially filled in)
- EL L3 **Reading: Graphic Organizer B,** p. 100
- EL L1 L2 **Literary Analysis: Graphic Organizer A,** pp. 101, 102 (partially filled in)

Skills Development/Extension

Unit 3 Resources

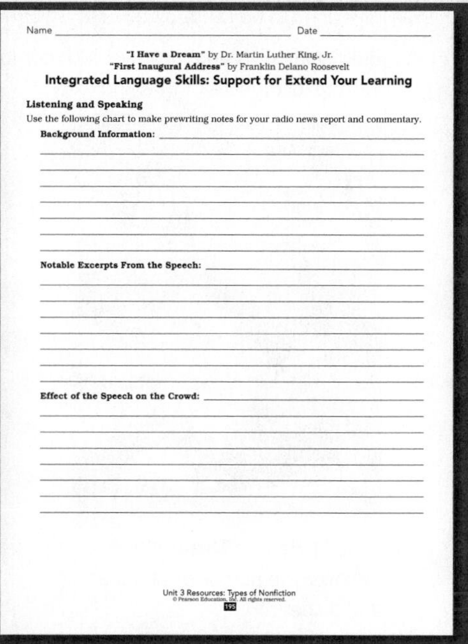
Name ______________________ Date ______________

"I Have a Dream" by Dr. Martin Luther King, Jr.
"First Inaugural Address" by Franklin Delano Roosevelt
Integrated Language Skills: Support for Extend Your Learning

Listening and Speaking
Use the following chart to make prewriting notes for your radio news report and commentary.

Background Information: ______________________

Notable Excerpts From the Speech: ______________________

Effect of the Speech on the Crowd: ______________________

Unit 3 Resources: Types of Nonfiction

195

L3 L4 **Support for Extend Your Learning,** p. 195

Also available for these selections:

- All **Literary Analysis: Persuasive Speech,** pp. 171, 189
- All **Reading: Analyze Persuasive Techniques,** pp. 172, 190
- L4 **Enrichment,** pp. 174, 192
- EL L3 L4 **Grammar,** p. 193
- EL L3 L4 **Support for Writing,** p. 194

Assessment

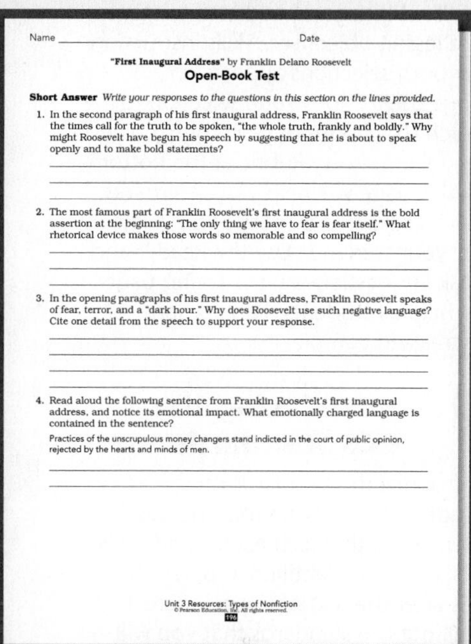
Name ______________________ Date ______________

"First Inaugural Address" by Franklin Delano Roosevelt
Open-Book Test

Short Answer *Write your responses to the questions in this section on the lines provided.*

1. In the second paragraph of his first inaugural address, Franklin Roosevelt says that the times call for the truth to be spoken, "the whole truth, frankly and boldly." Why might Roosevelt have begun his speech by suggesting that he is about to speak openly and to make bold statements?
2. The most famous part of Franklin Roosevelt's first inaugural address is the bold assertion at the beginning: "The only thing we have to fear is fear itself." What rhetorical device makes those words so memorable and so compelling?
3. In the opening paragraphs of his first inaugural address, Franklin Roosevelt speaks of fear, terror, and a "dark hour." Why does Roosevelt use such negative language? Cite one detail from the speech to support your response.
4. Read aloud the following sentence from Franklin Roosevelt's first inaugural address, and notice its emotional impact. What emotionally charged language is contained in the sentence?
Practices of the unscrupulous money changers stand indicted in the court of public opinion, rejected by the hearts and minds of men.

Unit 3 Resources: Types of Nonfiction

196

L3 L4 **Open-Book Test,** pp. 175–177, 196–198

Also available for these selections:

- EL L1 L2 **Selection Test A,** pp. 178–180, 199–201
- EL L3 L4 **Selection Test B,** pp. 181–183, 202–204

PHLit Online!
www.PHLitOnline.com

- complete narrated selection text
- a thematically related video with writing prompt
- an interactive graphic organizer
- highlighting feature
- access to all student print resources, adapted to individual student needs
- Spanish and English summaries
- adapted selection translations in Spanish

Online Resources: All print materials are also available online.

Get Connected! (thematic video with writing prompt)

Also available:

Background Video

All videos are available in Spanish.

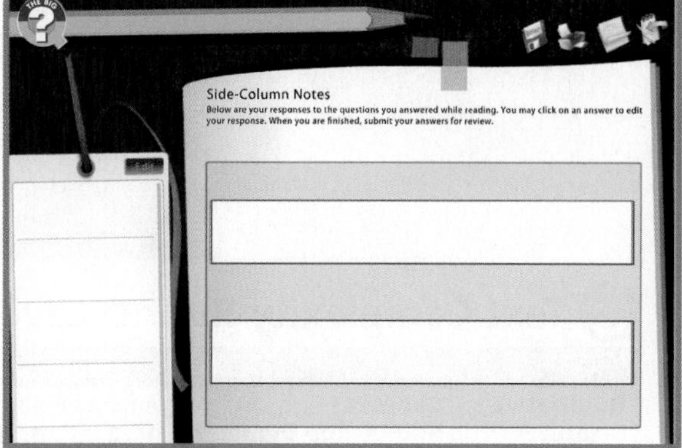

Writer's Journal (with graphics feature)

Also available:

Vocabulary Central (tools, activities, and songs for studying vocabulary)

❶ Leveled Texts

You may use either "I Have a Dream" or "First Inaugural Address" to meet the lesson objectives. Skills instruction for both selections appears on page 539. Choose one selection to teach (or choose to teach both). The Text Complexity Rubric at the bottom of this page will help you determine which selection is more appropriate for your students. Use the Reader and Task Suggestions on the facing page to help all students read text of increasing complexity.

❷ Introducing the CCS Standards

Introduce the standards on the student page. (Note that the lesson element with which each standard is addressed is identified in parentheses after the text of the standard.) Call out the standards that you will cover with the selections, explaining to students what each requires and how they will address it as they work through the selection you have chosen. Standards labeled "Spiral Review" are introduced in the Literary Analysis Workshop for this unit.

Before You Read

"I Have a Dream" • First Inaugural Address

❶ Leveled Texts

Build your skills and improve your comprehension of types of nonfiction with texts of increasing complexity.

Read **"I Have a Dream"** to discover the power of an idea and a speech.

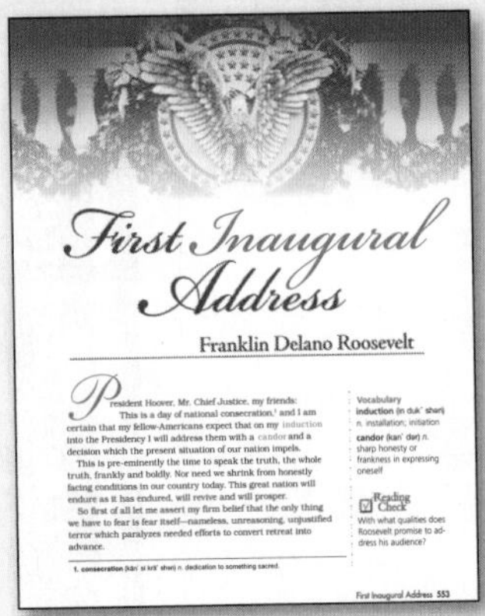

Read **"First Inaugural Address"** to learn how a president inspired hope during a challenging time.

❷ Common Core State Standards

Meet these standards with either **"I Have a Dream"** (p. 542) or **"First Inaugural Address"** (p. 552).

Reading Informational Text

6. Determine an author's point of view or purpose in a text and analyze how an author uses rhetoric to advance that point of view or purpose. *(Reading Skill: Evaluate Persuasion)*

8. Delineate and evaluate the argument and specific claims in a text, assessing whether the reasoning is valid and the evidence is relevant and sufficient; identify false statements and fallacious reasoning. *(Reading Skill: Evaluate Persuasion)*

9. Analyze seminal U.S. documents of historical and literary significance, including how they address related themes and concepts. *(Literary Analysis: Persuasive Speech)*

Writing

1. Write arguments to support claims in an analysis of substantive topics or texts, using valid reasoning and relevant and sufficient evidence. *(Writing: Proposal)*

Speaking and Listening

3. Evaluate a speaker's point of view, reasoning, and use of evidence and rhetoric, identifying any fallacious reasoning or exaggerated or distorted evidence. *(Speaking and Listening: Radio News Report)*

Language

3. Apply knowledge of language to understand how language functions in different contexts, to make effective choices for meaning or style, and to comprehend more fully when reading or listening. *(Conventions: Adverbs)*

6. Acquire and use accurately grade-appropriate general academic and domain-specific words and phrases; gather vocabulary knowledge when considering a word or phrase important to comprehension or expression. *(Vocabulary: Latin Roots)*

538 Types of Nonfiction: Essays, Articles, and Speeches

Text Complexity Rubric: Leveled Texts

Text complexity is determined by both qualitative and quantitative measures. For this reason, the quantitative measure of a more complex selection may be lower than that of a more accessible selection.

		✓ I Have a Dream	✓✓ First Inaugural Address
Qualitative Measures	**Context/ Knowledge Demands**	America in the 1960s; Civil Rights Movement 1 2 ③ 4 5	America in the 1930s; biblical references 1 2 ③ 4 5
	Structure/Language Conventionality and Clarity	Repetition reinforces concepts; challenging vocabulary 1 2 ③ 4 5	Era-specific diction; challenging vocabulary 1 2 3 ④ 5
	Levels of Meaning/ Purpose/Concept Level	Accessible concept (vision of a just America) 1 ② 3 4 5	Challenging concept (allusions to works of literature) 1 2 3 ④ 5
Quantitative Measures	**Text Length**	Word Count: 1,597	Word Count: 1,464
	Lexile	1140L	1190L
Overall Complexity		✓ **More accessible**	✓✓ **More complex**

❸ Literary Analysis: Persuasive Speech

In a **persuasive speech,** a speaker tries to convince listeners to think or act in a certain way. Good persuasive speeches present information and supporting evidence clearly, concisely, and logically so listeners can follow the reasoning. Persuasive speakers often use **rhetorical devices,** patterns of words and ideas that create emphasis and stir emotion. Common rhetorical devices include the following:

- **Parallelism:** repeating a grammatical structure or an arrangement of words to create rhythm and momentum
- **Restatement:** expressing the same idea in different words to clarify and stress key points
- **Repetition:** using the same words frequently to reinforce concepts and unify the speech
- **Analogy:** drawing a comparison that shows a similarity between two unlike things

❹ Reading Skill: Evaluate Persuasion

Persuasive techniques are devices used to influence the audience in favor of the author's argument. In addition to presenting evidence in a persuasive speech, a speaker may also use *emotionally charged language* and rhetorical devices such as those described above.

To analyze and evaluate persuasive techniques, **read aloud to hear the effect.** Notice the emotional impact of certain words and of the rhythm and momentum created by specific word patterns.

As you read, consider the purpose and effect of these techniques and then decide whether the speaker has supported his ideas with valid evidence.

❺ Using the Strategy: Techniques Chart

Use a chart like this one to analyze the effect of persuasive techniques.

Technique	
Purpose	Effect
Technique	
Purpose	Effect

PHLit Online!
www.PHLitOnline.com

Hear It!
- Selection summary audio
- Selection audio

See It!
- Get Connected video
- Background video
- More about the author
- Vocabulary flashcards

Do It!
- Interactive journals
- Interactive graphic organizers
- Self-test
- Internet activity
- Grammar tutorial
- Interactive vocabulary games

PRETEACH

❸ Literary Analysis
Persuasive Speech

1. Introduce the skill, using instruction on the student page.
2. Tell students that they will practice identifying rhetorical devices as they read.

Think Aloud: Model the Skill

Model the skill of identifying rhetorical devices in a speech. Say to students:

Suppose your football coach is giving a pep talk to inspire your team to *win.* He says, "We will keep working; we will keep fighting; and we will keep winning." He is using the rhetorical devices of parallelism ("we will keep") and repetition of the word *keep.* Then he says, "This season is a new dawn for our team. We're writing on a blank page in our history." He's used restatement to appeal to different listeners.

❹ Reading Skill
Evaluate Persuasion

1. Introduce the skill, using instruction on the student page.
2. Tell students that they will practice evaluating persuasive techniques as they read.

❺ Using the Strategy

Give students a copy of either **Reading Skill Graphic Organizer A or B** (*Graphic Organizer Transparencies,* pp. 98–100) to identify persuasive appeals. Use the examples in **Reading Skill Graphic Organizer A,** which is partially filled in, to model the process of completing the organizer.

Text Complexity: Reader and Task Suggestions

✓ I Have a Dream		✓✓ First Inaugural Address	
Preparing to Read the Text	**Leveled Tasks**	**Preparing to Read the Text**	**Leveled Tasks**
• Use the Background note on TE p. 541 to discuss the Civil Rights Movement and establish the setting. • Review strategies for deciphering unfamiliar words. • Guide students to use Multidraft Reading strategies (TE p. 541).	*Structure/Language* If students have difficulty with language, have them first read the speech and note what King is asking of his audience. Then, have them reread and cite examples of his goals. *Analyzing* If students will not have difficulty with language, have them read the speech and note ways in which King uses repetition, rhythm, and other rhetorical devices to emphasize his ideas.	• Refer to the Background information on TE p. 551 and discuss the setting for this speech. • Discuss the importance of political leadership during times of national distress. • Guide students to use Multidraft Reading strategies (TE p. 551).	*Levels of Meaning* If students will have difficulty with levels of meaning, have them first read and note details that identify the problems Roosevelt was addressing. Then, have them reread and note his solutions. *Evaluating* If students will not have difficulty with levels of meaning, have them read to identify allusions and biblical references in the speech.

PREITEACH

❶ Writing About the Big Question

1. Read the assignment with the class.
2. Point out that there is a difference between knowing what equality is and truly understanding the need for it. Ask students what experience might help a person understand the importance of equality.
3. Have students complete the sentence starters. Review responses as a class. (**Possible response:** The concept of equality might be ambiguous to some people because they already see everyone as equal. To ensure equality exists in our country, we must make connections with each other because for the good of the nation, everyone should reach his or her potential.)
4. Remind students that their answers will help them think about the Big Question, "Is knowledge the same as understanding?"

While You Read

Tell students to listen to what King says to different groups in his audience.

❷ Vocabulary

1. Have students preview the selection vocabulary.
2. For each word, have students say the word aloud.
3. Then, use the word in a sentence that defines the word.
4. Finally, repeat your definitional sentence or a similar sentence with the word missing and have the class "fill in the blank" chorally. Here is an example:

   A creed is a statement of belief. Our club adopted the statement "Everyone deserves a helping hand" as its [students say "creed"].

❸ Word Study

1. Introduce the skill, using the instruction in the box.
2. Ask students for another *-cred-* word that means "to trust, to believe." (**Answer:** *credential*)

Making Connections "I Have a Dream"

Is knowledge the same as understanding?

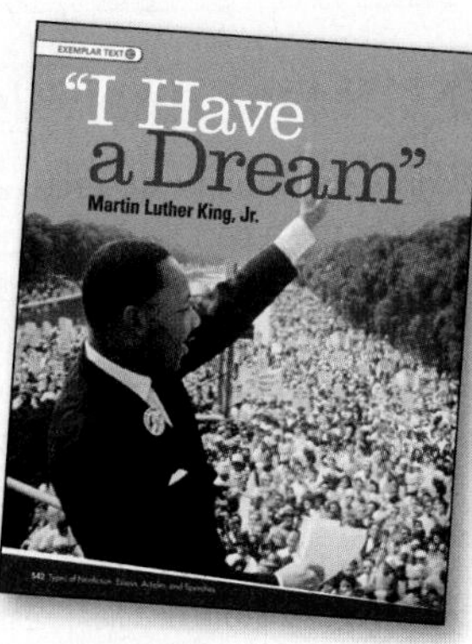

❶ Writing About the Big Question

In "I Have a Dream," Martin Luther King, Jr., makes a logical and emotional speech to help listeners understand his dream of freedom and equality. Use these sentence starters to develop your ideas about the Big Question.

The **concept** of equality might be **ambiguous** to some people because __________.

To ensure equality exists in our country, we must make **connections** with each other because __________.

While You Read Look for the arguments and evidence King uses to help his listeners understand his experience.

❷ Vocabulary

Read each word and its definition. Decide whether you know the word well, know it a little bit, or do not know it at all. After you read, see how your knowledge of each word has increased.

- **momentous** (mō men´ təs) *adj.* very important (p. 543) ***The opening of the new library was a momentous occasion in our town.*** moment *n.* momentum *n.*
- **defaulted** (dē fôlt´ əd) *v.* failed to do something or be somewhere when required or expected; failed to make payment when due (p. 543) ***The homeowners defaulted on their loan and lost their house.*** default *n.* default *v.*
- **hallowed** (hal´ ōd) *adj.* sacred (p. 544) ***The old battlefield is considered by many to be hallowed ground.*** hallow *v.*
- **degenerate** (dē jen´ ər āt´) *v.* grow worse (p. 545) ***Don't let this discussion degenerate into a shouting match.*** generate *v.*
- **creed** (krēd) *n.* statement of belief (p. 546) ***The creed of compassion is preached by many who do not practice it.*** credence *n.*
- **oppression** (ə presh´ ən) *n.* keeping others down by the unjust use of power (p. 546) ***The oppression of the poor by the rich is the theme of many novels and plays.*** oppress *v.* oppressive *adj.*

❸ Word Study

The **Latin root *-cred-*** means "to trust; to believe."

In this speech, King refers to America's **creed,** or statement of belief, that all people are created equal.

540 Types of Nonfiction: Essays, Articles, and Speeches

Vocabulary Development

Vocabulary Knowledge Rating

Create a **Vocabulary Knowledge Rating Chart** (***Professional Development Guidebook,*** p. 33) for this selection. Include the selection vocabulary and the Big Question words that appear in the Writing About the Big Question sentence starters on this page. (The Big Question vocabulary is introduced on pp. 424–425.)

Give students a copy of the chart. Read the words aloud, and have students mark their rating in the Before Reading column. Urge them to be alert to these words as they read and discuss the selection.

Tally how many students think they know a word to gauge how much instruction to provide. As students read and discuss the selection, point out the words and their context.

Vocabulary Central, featuring tools, activities, and songs for studying vocabulary, is available online at **www.PHLitOnline.com.**

Meet Dr. Martin Luther King, Jr.

(1929–1968)

Author of

"I Have a Dream"

Born in Atlanta, Georgia, Dr. Martin Luther King, Jr., was one of the most charismatic leaders of the civil rights movement. During the 1950s and 1960s, King organized nonviolent protests to bring about equal rights for all Americans.

A Voice for the Oppressed King first came to national attention in 1956 in Montgomery, Alabama, when he organized a 382-day boycott by African Americans of the city's segregated buses. He went on to lead other protests and to speak out eloquently against poverty and social injustice. He was assassinated on April 4, 1968. His birthday, January 15, has since become a national holiday.

❹ BACKGROUND FOR THE SPEECH

The Civil Rights Movement

The U.S. Constitution guarantees certain rights to all Americans. The struggle of African Americans to have their rights recognized is known as the civil rights movement. Marked by demonstrations and legal challenges, this movement began in the 1950s and was led by figures like Martin Luther King, Jr.

Did You Know?

At thirty-five, King became the youngest man and only the third black man to be awarded a Nobel Peace Prize.

Daily Bellringer

For each class during which you teach this selection, have students complete one of the five Research activities for Week 17 in the ***Daily Bellringer Activities*** booklet.

❹ Background

The Civil Rights Movement

Rosa Parks and Dr. Martin Luther King, Jr. became famous at about the same time. When Rosa Parks was arrested for refusing to give up her seat to a white person on the bus in Montgomery, Alabama, Dr. King became leader of the newly formed Montgomery Improvement Association (MIA). Dr. King led the struggle against the city's policy of segregation on the public bus system.

Multidraft Reading

This icon ● marks natural pauses in the selection. To assist struggling readers and to deepen reading for all, assign the text in "chunks," following the icons, and apply multidraft reading protocols. For each reading, have students set the purpose indicated:

- **First reading**—identifying key ideas and details and answering any Reading Checks.
- **Second reading**—analyzing craft and structure and responding to the side-column prompts.
- **Third reading**—integrating knowledge and ideas, connecting to other texts and the world, and answering the end-of-selection questions.

For more guidance, refer to the ***Classroom Strategies and Teaching Routines*** card on multidraft reading.

Differentiated Instruction — Additional Instruction

EL Extended Support—English Learners

Have students complete the **Reading and Vocabulary Warm-ups, *Unit 3 Resources*,** pp. 166–169, before they read. Assign the prereading pages and the adapted selection in the ***Reader's Notebook: English Learner's Version.*** Then, have students listen to portions of the selection on the ***Hear It!* Audio CD.**

L1 L2 Extended Support—Struggling Readers

Have students complete the **Reading and Vocabulary Warm-Ups, *Unit 3 Resources*,** pp. 166–169, before they read. Assign the prereading pages and the adapted selection in the ***Reader's Notebook: Adapted Version.*** Then, have students listen to portions of the selection on the ***Hear It!* Audio CD** (adapted text).

Extended Support—Reluctant Readers

To build motivation and engagement before assigning the selection, have students read "Has the Dream Come True" a thematically related selection in ***Reality Central.*** Then, use the questions at the conclusion of the related selection to guide discussion.

PHLit Online!

For more about the author, practice with the selection vocabulary, or more background, go online at **www.PHLitOnline.com.**

❶ Activating Prior Knowledge

1. Prepare an **Anticipation Guide** (***Professional Development Guidebook,*** pp. 36–38) with the following statements:
   - A person can change the world by the force of his or her beliefs.
   - People of all backgrounds will support a cause they believe is just.
   - A strong moral code is an important motivation for fighting for justice.
   - A powerful leader is necessary to make significant changes in the world.
2. Give students a copy of the prepared **Anticipation Guide** and have students mark their responses in the Me column. Have students discuss the statements in pairs or groups and mark the Guides again in the Group column.
3. For further guidance, use the ***Classroom Strategies and Teaching Routines*** card: **Using an Anticipation Guide.**

Concept Connector

Students will return to the **Anticipation Guide** after completing "I Have a Dream."

Whole-Class Activity

"I Have a Dream" makes a tremendous impression on listeners. If possible, show students the television broadcast of this speech. If this is not possible, have students listen to the ***Hear It!* Audio CD** that accompanies this selection. Point out the impact of hearing the speech delivered, rather than simply reading the words on a page. Have students discuss their impressions of King's delivery.

❷ About the Selection

In "I Have a Dream," King blended simple words and images with biblical and political references to urge his audience to eliminate oppression, prejudice, segregation, and injustice.

EXEMPLAR TEXT ©

❶ ❷

"I Have a Dream"

Martin Luther King, Jr.

Vocabulary Development

© CCSS Language 6

Thematic Vocabulary: The Big Question

As students are discussing "I Have a Dream," encourage them to use the thematic vocabulary presented in Introducing the Big Question, pp. 424–425. You might encourage them with sentence starters like these:

1. King built his "I Have a Dream" speech on the *concept* of . . .
2. The ideas of King's speech cannot be considered *ambiguous* because . . .
3. Listening to King's delivery helps his audience *interpret* . . .
4. King aimed to leave his listeners with a *feeling* of . . .

Background Because speeches are written to be spoken aloud, they are a more fluid form of literature than most other nonfiction. A strong speaker will react to unspoken signals from his or her listeners and adjust a speech accordingly. He or she might change words or add whole phrases. This is the case with Dr. Martin Luther King, Jr., one of the greatest speakers of the modern age. The text that appears here represents the speech exactly as it was delivered by Dr. King on the steps of the Lincoln Memorial.

Five score years ago, a great American, in whose symbolic shadow we stand today, signed the Emancipation Proclamation. This momentous decree came as a great beacon light of hope to millions of Negro slaves who had been seared in the flames of withering injustice. It came as a joyous daybreak to end the long night of their captivity.

But one hundred years later, the Negro still is not free. One hundred years later, the life of the Negro is still sadly crippled by the manacles of segregation and the chains of discrimination. One hundred years later, the Negro lives on a lonely island of poverty in the midst of a vast ocean of material prosperity. One hundred years later, the Negro is still languished in the corners of American society and finds himself an exile in his own land. So we've come here today to dramatize a shameful condition. 

In a sense we've come to our nation's Capital to cash a check. When the architects of our republic wrote the magnificent words of the Constitution and the Declaration of Independence, they were signing a promissory note[1] to which every American was to fall heir. This note was a promise that all men, yes, black men as well as white men, would be guaranteed the unalienable rights of life, liberty, and the pursuit of happiness.

It is obvious today that America has defaulted on this promissory note insofar as her citizens of color are concerned. Instead of honoring this sacred obligation, America has given the Negro people a bad check; a check which has come back marked "insufficient funds." But we refuse to believe that the bank of justice is bankrupt. We refuse to believe that there are insufficient funds in the great vaults of opportunity of this nation. And so we've come to cash this check—a check that will give us upon demand the riches of freedom and the security of justice. We have also come to

1. promissory (präm´ i sôr´ ē) **note** written promise to pay a specific amount.

Vocabulary
momentous (mō men´ təs) *adj.* very important

defaulted (dē fôlt´ əd) *v.* failed to do something or be somewhere when required or expected; failed to make payment when due

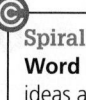

Spiral Review
Word Choice What ideas and images do King's words evoke in the paragraph beginning, "But one hundred years later..."?

Literary Analysis
Persuasive Speech Explain King's analogy between a financial transaction and the idea of justice.

5 

What injustices are King and his listeners protesting?

4 ◀ **Critical Viewing** Which details in this photograph demonstrate the importance of the event at which King gave his speech? **[Analyze]**

Spiral Review
Word Choice

1. Remind students that they studied the concept of word choice in the Unit 3 Literary Analysis workshop (pp. 426–439).
2. **Ask** students the Spiral Review question.

   Possible response: King's word choice evokes imagery related to enslaved Africans. These images and ideas highlight the injustice of discrimination.

3 Literary Analysis
Persuasive Speech

1. Read the bracketed paragraph and related footnote aloud.
2. **Ask** students to identify the financial documents King mentions and to explain how they are usually used.

   Answer: King mentions a check and a promissory note. People write checks instead of paying in cash. The check draws funds from the payer's bank account. The recipient can then go to a bank and convert the check into cash. A person gives someone else a promissory note as a pledge to pay at some future time.
3. Then, **ask** students to respond to the Literary Analysis prompt: Explain King's analogy between a financial transaction and the idea of justice.

   Answer: King is saying that the promise of freedom and justice for African Americans is like the cash payment they are owed but have not yet received.

4 Critical Viewing
Answer: The size of the crowd and the location in the nation's capital suggest the importance of the event.

5 Reading Check
Answer: They are protesting segregation and discrimination.

Differentiated Instruction for Universal Access

Support for Special-Needs Students
To help students appreciate the power of this speech, have them read the ***Reader's Notebook: Adapted Version*** as they listen to the ***Hear It!* Audio CD** (adapted text). Lead a discussion about which passages they found most effective.

Culturally Responsive Instruction
Culture Focus Point out to students that King drew on his experience as a Christian pastor to become a strong, well-spoken leader. Within many African-American communities, the pastor has enormous influence and control over his or her congregation. Black ministers were the backbone of the civil rights movement. Ask students to describe what types of leaders have power in their communities. Whom would they call upon to lead a major social movement?

6 Literary Analysis

Persuasive Speech

1. Have a volunteer read aloud the bracketed passage. **Ask** students to describe what King is talking about in these sentences beginning with *Now*.

   Answer: King is saying that now is the time to change the rules in the United States and to right the wrongs of segregation and inequality.

2. **Ask** students the Literary Analysis question: What idea does King's repetition of the word "Now" help to emphasize?

   Answer: By repeating the word *now*, King emphasizes the urgency of righting the wrongs in American society.

7 Critical Viewing

Possible responses: Students may describe King's expression as solemn, intense, or determined.

Vocabulary
hallowed (hal′ ōd) *adj.* sacred

Literary Analysis
Persuasive Speech 6
What idea does King's repetition of the word "Now" help to emphasize?

7 ▼ **Critical Viewing** 8
Describe King's expression as he delivers his speech. **[Analyze]**

this hallowed spot to remind America of the fierce urgency of *now*. This is no time to engage in the luxury of cooling off or to take the tranquilizing drug of gradualism.

Now is the time to make real the promises of Democracy.

Now is the time to rise from the dark and desolate valley of segregation to the sunlit path of racial justice.

Now is the time to lift our nation from the quicksands of racial injustice to the solid rock of brotherhood.

Now is the time to make justice a reality for all of God's children.

It would be fatal for the nation to overlook the urgency of the moment. This sweltering summer of the Negro's legitimate discontent will not pass until there is an invigorating autumn of freedom and equality. Nineteen sixty-three is not an end, but a beginning. Those who hope that the Negro needed to blow off steam and will now be content will have a rude awakening if the nation returns to business as usual. There will be neither rest nor tranquillity in America until the Negro is granted his citizenship rights. The whirlwinds of revolt will continue to shake the foundations of our nation until the bright day of justice emerges.

But there is something that I must say to my people who stand on the warm threshold which leads into the palace of justice. In the process of gaining our rightful place we must not be guilty of wrongful deeds. Let us not seek to satisfy our thirst for freedom

Vocabulary Development

© CCSS Language 6

Selection Vocabulary Reinforcement

Students will benefit from additional examples and practice with the selection vocabulary words. Reinforce their comprehension with "show-you-know" sentences. The first part of the sentence uses the vocabulary word in an appropriate context. The second part of the sentence—the "show-you-know" part—clarifies the first. Model the strategy with this example:

The orphans often wore *rueful* expressions; their loneliness showed through their big, sad eyes.

Then, give students these sentence prompts:

1. This building is a *hallowed* part of the university; ____________

   Sample answer: some of history's greatest scholars have studied and taught here.

2. Her health is beginning to *degenerate;* ____________

   Sample answer: soon she will have to be hospitalized.

8 by drinking from the cup of bitterness and hatred. We must forever conduct our struggle on the high plane of dignity and discipline. We must not allow our creative protest to **degenerate** into physical violence. Again and again we must rise to the majestic heights of meeting physical force with soul force. The marvelous new militancy which has engulfed the Negro community must not lead us to a distrust of all white people, for many of our white brothers, as evidenced by their presence here today, have come to realize that their destiny is tied up with our destiny. And they have come to realize that their freedom is inextricably bound to our freedom. We cannot walk alone.

Vocabulary
degenerate (dē jenʹ ər ātʹ) *v.* grow worse

Literary Analysis
Persuasive Speech What idea does King restate when he says, "We cannot walk alone"?

And as we walk, we must make the pledge that we shall always march ahead. We cannot turn back. There are those who are asking the devotees of civil rights, "When will you

9 be satisfied?" We can never be satisfied as long as the Negro is the victim of the unspeakable horrors of police brutality. We can never be satisfied as long as our bodies, heavy with the fatigue of travel, cannot gain lodging in the motels of the highways and the hotels of the cities. We cannot be satisfied as long as the Negro's basic mobility is from a smaller ghetto to a larger one. We cannot be satisfied as long as a Negro in Mississippi cannot vote and a Negro in New York believes he has nothing for which to vote. No, no, we are not satisfied, and we will not be satisfied until justice rolls down like waters and righteousness like a mighty stream.

I am not unmindful that some of you have come here out of great trials and tribulations. Some of you have come fresh from narrow jail cells. Some of you have come from areas where your quest for freedom left you battered by the storms of persecution and staggered by the winds of police brutality. You have been the veterans of creative suffering. Continue to work with the faith that unearned suffering is redemptive.

Go back to Mississippi, go back to Alabama, go back to South Carolina, go back to Georgia, go back to Louisiana, go back to the slums and ghettos of our northern cities, knowing that somehow this situation can and will be changed. Let us not wallow in the valley of despair.

I say to you today, my friends, so even though we face the difficulties of today and tomorrow, I still have a dream. It is a dream deeply rooted in the American dream.

10 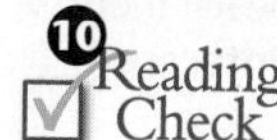
Reading Check
According to King, how should his people react to physical force?

8 Literary Analysis

Persuasive Speech

1. Read the paragraph aloud. Ask students to describe what King is cautioning against.

   Answer: He is cautioning against bitterness, hatred, violence, and distrust of all white people.

2. **Ask** students the Literary Analysis question: What idea does King restate when he says, "We cannot walk alone"?

   Answer: He restates the idea that the destinies of white people and African Americans are tied together.

9 Connecting to the Big Question

1. Have a volunteer read aloud the bracketed text. **Ask** students to summarize King's point in this passage.

   Answer: African Americans will never be satisfied unless they attain equal rights and justice in all areas of society.

2. **Ask:** What evidence does King use to help listeners understand his experience?

   Answer: He points out that African Americans face police brutality, a lack of service in the nation's hotels, and curtailed voting rights.

3. **Ask:** What do King's arguments imply about the relationship between knowledge and understanding?

   Possible response: It is easy enough to *know* that African Americans are unsatisfied and wronged, but it takes personal experience or compelling examples to *understand* the extent of the injury.

10 Reading Check

Answer: They should meet physical force with soul force (nonviolently).

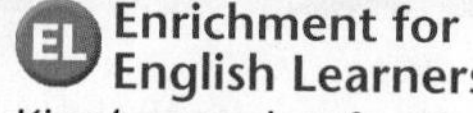

Differentiated Instruction for Universal Access

EL Enrichment for English Learners

King's speech refers to several states, such as Mississippi and Alabama, and several geographical features, such as the Allegheníes and the Colorado Rockies. Provide students with a map of the United States. Have them work in pairs to locate all the places King mentions and to practice spelling the names of the places.

Enrichment for Gifted/Talented Students

Have students research the life of Mahatma Gandhi, another advocate of nonviolence and social justice. Ask students to draw parallels between the lives of the two men, including how they battled injustice and inequality. Have them locate one of Gandhi's speeches and compare it to King's "I Have a Dream" speech.

⑪ Literary Analysis

Persuasive Speech

1. Have students read the passage aloud several times and listen for rhythm or repetition.
2. **Ask** students to respond to the Literary Analysis prompt: Identify the parallel clauses in this passage and explain how they emphasize King's ideas.

   Answer: The parallel clauses are variations of "I have a dream," which King uses to link his visions of justice, equality, and unity in the United States. By repeating *dream*, King evokes "the American dream" while making clear that his inspirational ideas are yet to be fulfilled.

▶ **Monitor Progress:** Ask students to pick out other examples of rhetorical devices on this page. King uses parallelism in "sons of former slaves . . . sons of former slaveowners" and "little black boys and black girls . . . little white boys and white girls."

▶ **Reteach:** If students have difficulty identifying rhetorical devices, have them reread this spread aloud. Point out examples of repetition.

⑫ Reading Skill

Persuasive Techniques

1. **Ask** students to read the paragraph aloud. Have them identify the repetition in the paragraph.

   Answer: The phrase "With this faith we will be able . . ." is repeated.
2. **Ask** students the Reading Skill question: What idea does King reinforce using the rhythm of repetition?

   Answer: King reinforces the idea that African Americans will be able to achieve equality "with this faith."

⑬ Critical Viewing

Answer: King's body language—raised arm, strong posture, steady eye contact, and wide-open mouth—emphasizes his points and engages the attention and emotions of his audience.

Vocabulary

creed (krēd) *n.* statement of belief

oppression (ə presh′ ən) *n.* keeping others down by the unjust use of power

I have a dream that one day this nation will rise up and live out the true meaning of its creed: "We hold these truths to be self-evident; that all men are created equal."

I have a dream that one day on the red hills of Georgia the sons of former slaves and the sons of former slaveowners will be able to sit down together at the table of brotherhood.

I have a dream that one day even the state of Mississippi, a state sweltering with the heat of injustice, sweltering with the heat of oppression, will be transformed into an oasis of freedom and justice.

I have a dream that my four little children will one day live in a nation where they will not be judged by the color of their skin but by the content of their character.

I have a dream today.

Literary Analysis
Persuasive Speech
Identify the parallel clauses in this passage and explain how they emphasize King's ideas.

I have a dream that one day down in Alabama, with its vicious racists, with its governor still having his lips dripping with the words of interposition and nullification,[2] one day right down in Alabama little black boys and black girls will be able to join hands with little white boys and white girls as sisters and brothers.

I have a dream today.

I have a dream that one day every valley shall be exalted, every hill and mountain shall be made low, the rough places will be made plains, and the crooked places will be made straight, and the glory of the Lord shall be revealed, and all flesh shall see it together.[3]

Reading Skill
Persuasive Techniques
What idea does King reinforce using the rhythm of repetition? ⑫

This is our hope. This is the faith that I go back to the South with. With this faith we will be able to hew out of the mountain of despair a stone of hope. With this faith we will be able to transform the jangling discords of our nation into a beautiful symphony of brotherhood. With this faith we will be able to work together, to pray together, to struggle together, to go to jail together, to stand up for freedom together, knowing that we will be free one day.

This will be the day when all of God's children will be able to sing with new meaning

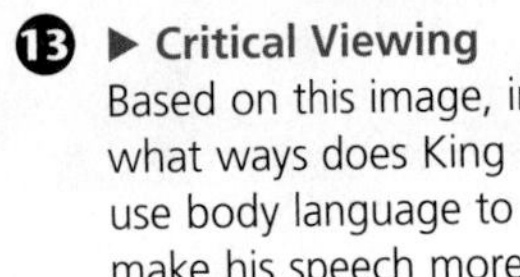

⑬ ▶ **Critical Viewing**
Based on this image, in what ways does King use body language to make his speech more effective? **[Interpret]**

My country, 'tis of thee,
Sweet land of liberty,
Of thee I sing:
Land where my fathers died,
Land of the pilgrims' pride,
From every mountainside
Let freedom ring.

2. **interposition** (in′ tər pə zish′ ən) **and nullification** (nul′ ə fi kā′ shən) disputed doctrine that a state can reject federal laws considered to be violations of its rights. Governor George C. Wallace used this doctrine to reject federal civil rights legislation.
3. **every valley . . . all flesh shall see it together** reference to a biblical passage (Isaiah 40:4–5). King is likening the struggle of African Americans to the struggle of the Israelites.

Vocabulary Development

Vocabulary Knowledge Rating

When students have completed reading and discussing "I Have a Dream," have them take out their **Vocabulary Knowledge Rating Chart** for this selection. Read the words aloud once more and have students rate their knowledge of the words again in the After Reading column. Clarify any words that are still problematic. Have students write their own definition and example or sentence in the appropriate column. Then, have students complete the Vocabulary Practice activities at the end of the selection. Encourage students to use the words in further discussion and written work about this selection. Remind them that they will be accountable for these words on the **Selection Test, *Unit 3 Resources*,** pp. 178–180 or 181–183.

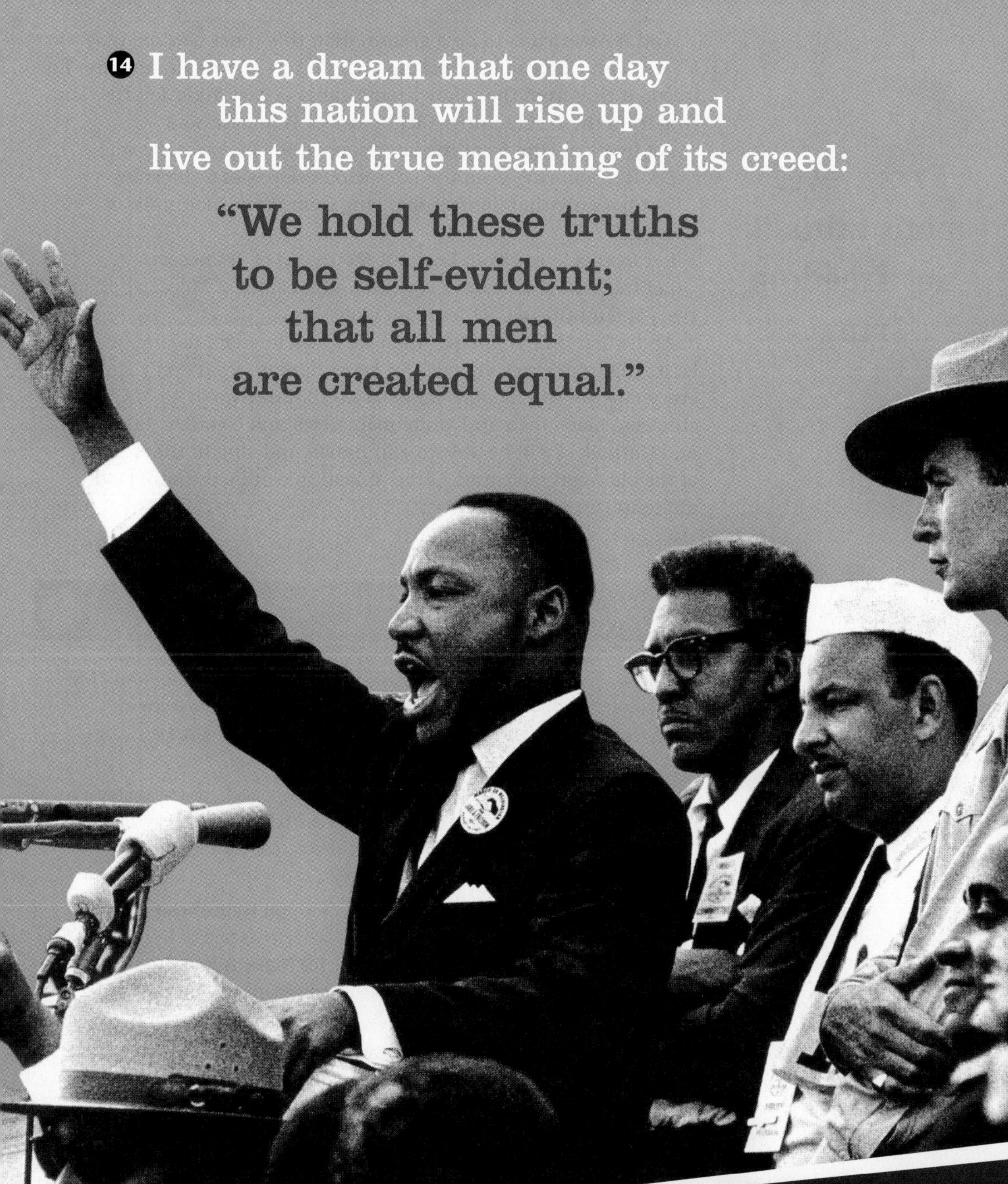

14 I have a dream that one day this nation will rise up and live out the true meaning of its creed: "We hold these truths to be self-evident; that all men are created equal."

"I Have a Dream" 547

14 Visual Connections

Whole-Class Activity

1. **Ask** students to describe what they see in the photograph.
   Possible response: I see a man speaking into several microphones. His body language is intense. There are several serious-looking men behind him, and one man is raising a fist. The people are dressed formally in the style of the 1960s.
2. Then, tell students to look at the words on the page and speculate about how the text might relate to the photograph.

   Possible response: Maybe the man is using these words to make a speech. He is appealing to people's sense of justice by quoting the Declaration of Independence.
3. Now, **ask** students what the racial mix of people in the photograph suggests about the motive of the speaker.

   Possible response: There are both black and white people in the photograph, so the speaker might be arguing for racial unity.

Small-Group Activity

1. Divide the class into small groups. Tell students to imagine themselves in the picture and discuss who they are and how they are feeling.
2. Have students share the results of their groups' discussions. To model the process of making connections to an image, choose one response and analyze how the photograph supports it.

Individual Activity

1. As a class, briefly discuss the photograph.
2. Ask students to imagine that they are in the photograph and to write a two-paragraph journal entry about their experience.
3. Have students share their journal entries.

Concept Connector

Anticipation Guide

Have students return to their **Anticipation Guides** and respond to the statements again in the After Reading column. They may do this individually or in their original pairs or groups. Then, lead a class discussion, probing for what students have learned that confirms or invalidates each statement. Encourage students to cite specific details, quotations, or other evidence from the text to support their responses to each statement.

Writing About the Big Question

Have students compare their responses to the sentence starter they completed before reading the speech with their ideas afterwards. Ask them to explain whether their thoughts have changed.

Reading Skill Graphic Organizer

Ask students to review the graphic organizers they completed to identify the persuasive appeals while reading. Show them **Reading Skill Graphic Organizer A** (*Graphic Organizer Transparencies,* p. 98) as an example. Then, have students share their graphic organizers.

ASSESS

Answers

Critical Thinking

Before students respond, you may wish to have them write a brief objective summary of the selection. As they answer the questions below, remind them to support their answers with evidence from the text.

1. (a) King quotes the first stanza. (b) He reminds everyone that the country was founded on a promise of liberty. The tone is emotional and hopeful for the future.
2. (a) He mentions states in the South; the states of New York, New Hampshire, California, and Pennsylvania; and the Rocky Mountains. (b) The mention of these places ties in with his message of equality for everyone across the nation.
3. (a) **Possible response:** The speech dramatically expressed American values at a critical point in history. (b) **Possible response:** Yes, because it articulates American values with a purity and passion that still moves listeners.
4. (a) **Possible response:** He says that the promises of the Constitution and the Declaration of Independence had not been met. Most African Americans were living in poverty, and they were still "exiles in their own land." Blacks had curtailed voting rights, were victims of unjustified police brutality, and could not stay in many hotels. (b) **Possible response:** Yes. He eloquently describes how African Americans were being treated and how the country had failed to hold true to its founding values. Due to his compelling examples, I understand why King wanted the country to change.

And if America is to be a great nation this must become true. So let freedom ring from the prodigious hilltops of New Hampshire. Let freedom ring from the mighty mountains of New York. Let freedom ring from the heightening Alleghenies of Pennsylvania!

Let freedom ring from the snowcapped Rockies of Colorado!

Let freedom ring from the curvacious slopes of California!

But not only that; let freedom ring from Stone Mountain of Georgia!

Let freedom ring from Lookout Mountain of Tennessee!

Let freedom ring from every hill and molehill of Mississippi. From every mountainside, let freedom ring.

And when this happens, when we allow freedom to ring, when we let it ring from every village and every hamlet, from every state and every city, we will be able to speed up that day when all of God's children, black men and white men, Jews and Gentiles, Protestants and Catholics, will be able to join hands and sing in the words of the old Negro spiritual, "Free at last! free at last! thank God almighty, we are free at last!"

From every mountainside, let freedom ring.

Critical Thinking

Cite textual evidence to support your responses.

1. **Craft and Structure** **(a)** Which words does King quote from "My Country 'Tis of Thee"? **(b) Interpret:** What impact are these words intended to have on the audience? What message is conveyed? What tone?
2. **Key Ideas and Details** **(a)** Which different parts of the United States does King mention in his speech? **(b) Connect:** How does the mention of all of these places help to convey King's central idea and his purpose in the speech?
3. **Integration of Knowledge and Ideas** **(a) Hypothesize:** Why do you think "I Have a Dream" has lived on as one of the best-known speeches in modern history? **(b) Make a Judgment:** Do you think it deserves this standing? Explain your response.
4. **Integration of Knowledge and Ideas** **(a)** What facts and information does King give to increase your knowledge of equality in America in the 1960s? **(b)** Do the experiences he shares help you understand the importance of his dream? Explain. *[Connect to the Big Question: Is knowledge the same as understanding?]*

Assessment Resources

Unit 3 Resources

L1 L2 EL **Selection Test A,** pp. 178–180. Administer Test A to less advanced readers.

L3 L4 EL **Selection Test B,** pp. 181–183. Administer Test B to on-level and more advanced students.

L3 L4 **Open-Book Test,** pp. 175–177. As an alternative, give the Open-Book Test.

All **Customizable Test Bank**

All **Self-tests**
Students may prepare for the **Selection Test** by taking the **Self-test** online.

PHLit Online! All assessment resources are available at **www.PHLitOnline.com.**

After You Read "I Have a Dream" 

Literary Analysis: Persuasive Speech

1. **Key Ideas and Details** In this **persuasive speech,** what is Martin Luther King, Jr.'s, purpose? Explain.
2. **Craft and Structure** What examples of figurative or connotative words appeal to the audience's emotions? To their reason? Explain.
3. **Craft and Structure** In a chart like this, list examples of **rhetorical devices** in King's speech. Then, describe the effect of each one.

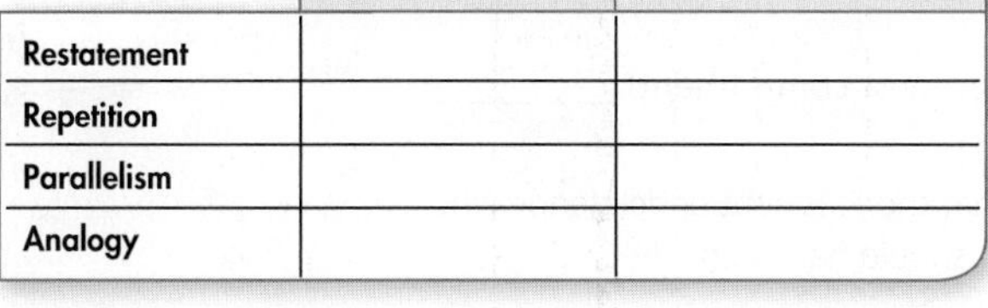

	Example	Effect
Restatement		
Repetition		
Parallelism		
Analogy		

4. **Key Ideas and Details** **(a)** What evidence does King use to support his position? **(b)** What details are most valid to his argument? Why?

Reading Skill: Evaluate Persuasion

5. **(a)** Identify a passage in which King uses emotionally charged language as a **persuasive technique. (b)** What specific purpose do you think King had in using such language? Explain.
6. Does King use rhetorical devices effectively? Explain.

Vocabulary

Acquisition and Use **Analogies** show the relationships between words. Use a word from page 540 to complete each analogy.

1. stumble : rise :: ____________ : improve
2. oath : office :: ____________ : religion
3. barren : desert :: ____________ : church
4. dull : interesting :: trivial : ____________
5. supportive : harmful :: assistance : ____________
6. broken : promise :: ____________ : agreement

Word Study Use the context of the sentences and what you know about the **Latin root *-cred-*** to explain your answer to each question.

1. Should a judge in a criminal trial have *credibility*?
2. How would you feel if someone tried to *discredit* you?

Word Study

The **Latin root *-cred-*** means "to trust; to believe."

Apply It Explain how the root *-cred-* contributes to the meanings of these words. Consult a dictionary if necessary.

credit
credential
incredible

Answers

Literary Analysis

1. He is trying to persuade the audience to continue their fight for justice and equality.
2. **Possible response:** Appeal to emotions: ". . .crippled by manacles of segregation"; "Let freedom ring." Appeal to reason: ". . . conduct our struggle on the high plane of dignity and discipline."
3. **Possible response:** (a) **Parallelism:** "This sweltering summer of the Negro's legitimate discontent . . . invigorating autumn of freedom and equality"; (b) **Effect:** This statement emphasizes the contrast between how African Americans are treated and how they should be treated.

   For other sample answers, see ***Graphic Organizer Transparencies,* Literary Analysis Graphic Organizer A**, p. 101, and the **Additional Answers** section.
4. (a) **Possible response:** He talks about the civil unrest that is already brewing. (b) **Possible response:** I think his details about discrimination are most valid because they could relate to anyone.

Reading Skill

5. **Possible response:** (a) The paragraph beginning "This is our hope. This is the faith . . ." uses emotionally charged language such as "faith," "hope," "mountain of despair," and "beautiful symphony of brotherhood." (b) By using the language of religion, King may have wanted to imply that the struggle for civil rights is a religious crusade.
6. **Possible response:** Most students will say that King is effective because the rhetorical devices and emotionally charged language emphasize his ideas.

Vocabulary

Acquisition and Use

1. degenerate
2. creed
3. hallowed
4. momentous
5. oppression
6. defaulted

Word Study

Sample answers:

1. Yes. If a judge doesn't have *credibility*, people won't feel he or she is fair.
2. I would be angry because that would mean that the person was trying to say my word didn't count.

Word Study: Apply It

Sample answers:

Credit is to believe in or trust. A *credential* is something that lets you know someone can be trusted. *Incredible* is something not to be believed.

PRETEACH

Skills instruction for the ***Reading Skill*** *and the* ***Literary Analysis*** *concept appears on p. 539.*

1 Writing About the Big Question

1. Review the assignment with the class.
2. Ask volunteers what they know about Franklin Roosevelt and what they understand about the importance of his presidency.
3. Have students complete the sentence starter. Review responses as a class. (**Possible responses:** For leaders to inspire confidence, they must comprehend people's problems because that's the only way they can create a solution.)
4. Remind students that their answers will help them think about the Big Question, "Is knowledge the same as understanding?"

While You Read

Tell students, as they read, to look for evidence that FDR understands why people are suffering and should have hope.

2 Vocabulary

1. Have students preview the selection vocabulary.
2. For each word, have students say the word aloud.
3. Then, use the word in a sentence that defines the word.
4. Repeat your definitional sentence or a similar sentence with the word missing, and have the class "fill in the blank" chorally. Here are some examples:

   Something that is arduous takes a lot of work. After a restful summer, the team was ready for athletic practices that proved [students say "arduous"].

   Something that is feasible can be accomplished realistically. We believe that our new plan has been carefully thought out, so it is practical, realistic, and [students say "feasible"].

3 Word Study

1. Introduce the skill, using the instruction in the box.
2. Ask students for another *-duct-* word that means "to lead." (**Answer:** *conduct*)

Making Connections | First Inaugural Address

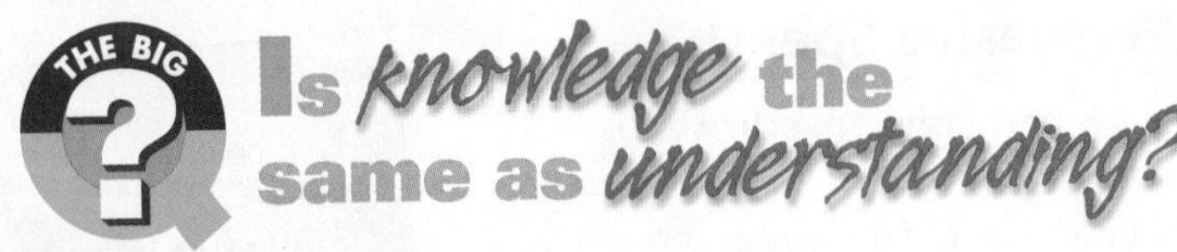
THE BIG ?
Is knowledge the same as understanding?

First Inaugural Address
Franklin Delano Roosevelt

1 Writing About the Big Question

In "First Inaugural Address," President Roosevelt acknowledges the hard realities of the Great Depression and he promises to do whatever is necessary to help the nation recover. Use this sentence starter to develop your ideas about the Big Question.

For leaders to inspire confidence, they must **comprehend** __________ because ______________.

While You Read Look for evidence that the President understands why people are suffering and also why they should have hope.

2 Vocabulary

Read each word and its definition. Decide whether you know the word well, know it a little bit, or do not know it at all. After you read, see how your knowledge of each word has increased.

- **induction** (in duk′ shən) *n.* installation; initiation (p.553) *At his official induction into the school's honor society, Pedro gave a speech.* induct *v.* inductee *n.*
- **candor** (kan′ dər) *n.* sharp honesty or frankness in expressing oneself (p. 553) *Joanna spoke with great candor about her feelings for her mother.* candid *adj.*
- **abdicated** (ab′ di kāt′ əd) *v.* gave up formally (p. 555) *The king abdicated his throne and left the country.* abdicator *n.*
- **discipline** (dis′ ə plin′) *n.* training that develops self-control, character, or efficiency (p. 557) *Working from home requires a great deal of discipline.* discipline *v.* disciplinary *adj.*
- **feasible** (fē′ zə bəl) *adj.* capable of being done or carried out; practicable; possible (p. 559) *Solar heating is both technically and economically feasible.* feasibility *n.*
- **arduous** (är′ jo͞o əs) *adj.* difficult; laborious (p. 559) *Rebuilding the house by ourselves was an arduous task.*

3 Word Study

The **Latin root *-duct-*** or ***-duc-*** means "to lead" or "to bring."

Roosevelt speaks during his **induction**—the ceremony that brought him into his role as president of the United States.

Vocabulary Development

Vocabulary Knowledge Rating

Create a **Vocabulary Knowledge Rating Chart** ***(Professional Development Guidebook***, p. 33) for this selection. Include the selection vocabulary and the word that appears in the Writing About the Big Question sentence starter on this page. (The Big Question vocabulary is introduced on pp. 424–425.)

Give students a copy of the chart. Read the words aloud, and have students mark their rating in the Before Reading column. Urge them to be alert to these words as they read and discuss the selection.

Tally how many students think they know a word to gauge how much instruction to provide. As students read and discuss the selection, point out the words and their context.

PHLit Online! **Vocabulary Central,** featuring tools, activities, and songs for studying vocabulary, is available at **www.PHLitOnline.com.**

Meet
Franklin Delano Roosevelt
(1882–1945)

Author of

First Inaugural Address

Franklin Delano Roosevelt had a relatively easy life until he was stricken with polio at age 39. Ironically, Roosevelt realized his potential as a leader only after falling victim to this illness. He was twice elected governor of New York; then, in 1932, he defeated President Herbert Hoover to become the nation's thirty-second president. Roosevelt won an unprecedented four terms as president.

A Leader in Dark Times Franklin Roosevelt led the nation through two great challenges: the Great Depression and World War II. The war was almost over when the president died of a cerebral hemorrhage in 1945.

4 BACKGROUND FOR THE SPEECH

The Great Depression

On March 4, 1933, newly elected President Franklin Delano Roosevelt delivered his inaugural address to a nation close to despair. The Great Depression had weighed down American life for more than three years. Americans sat by their radios to hear the new president's address, a speech he had written himself. In this speech, Roosevelt gave Americans hope.

Did You Know?

Roosevelt's wife, Eleanor, became one of the most active and widely admired first ladies in American history.

Daily Bellringer

For each class during which you will teach this selection, have students complete one of the five Research activities for Week 17 in the *Daily Bellringer Activities* booklet.

4 Background

The Great Depression

Throughout his presidency, Franklin Roosevelt addressed the American people directly in speeches via the radio. Families gathered around their radios to hear Roosevelt talk about a variety of topics. These talks kept the American people informed of Roosevelt's plans and offered encouragement to Americans in times of crisis. This series of speeches given by Roosevelt became known as the "Fireside Chats."

Multidraft Reading

This icon ● marks natural pauses in the selection. To assist struggling readers and to deepen reading for all, assign the text in "chunks," following the icons, and apply multidraft reading protocols. For each reading, have students set the purpose indicated:

- **First reading**—identifying key ideas and details and answering any Reading Checks.
- **Second reading**—analyzing craft and structure and responding to the side-column prompts.
- **Third reading**—integrating knowledge and ideas, connecting to other texts and the world, and answering the end-of-selection questions.

For more guidance, refer to the ***Classroom Strategies and Teaching Routines*** card on multidraft reading.

PHLit Online!

For more about the author, practice with the selection vocabulary, or more background, go online at **www.PHLitOnline.com.**

Differentiated Instruction — Additional Instruction

EL Extended Support—English Learners

Have students complete the **Reading and Vocabulary Warm-ups,** ***Unit 3 Resources,*** pp. 184–187, before they read. Assign the prereading pages for the selection in the ***Reader's Notebook: English Learner's Version.*** Then, have students listen to portions of the selection on the ***Hear It!*** **Audio CD.**

L1 L2 Extended Support—Struggling Readers

Have students complete the **Reading and Vocabulary Warm-ups,** ***Unit 3 Resources,*** pp. 184–187, before they read. Assign the prereading pages for the selection in the ***Reader's Notebook: Adapted Version.*** Then, have students listen to portions of the selection on the ***Hear It!*** **Audio CD** (adapted text).

Extended Support—Reluctant Readers

To build motivation and engagement before assigning the selection, have students read "The Effects of Fear," a thematically related selection in ***Reality Central.*** Then, use the questions at the conclusion of the related selection to guide discussion.

TEACH

❶ Activating Prior Knowledge

1. Prepare an **Anticipation Guide** (***Professional Development Guidebook***, pp. 36–38) with the following statements:
   - The best way for a president to gain the support of the people is to be absolutely truthful.
   - Material wealth is not a sign of success.
   - Citizens must be willing to sacrifice for the common good.
   - In times of crisis, the president should have extra powers.
2. Give students a copy of the prepared **Anticipation Guide** and have students mark their responses in the Me column. Have students discuss the statements in groups and mark the Guides in the Group column.
3. For further guidance, use the ***Classroom Strategies and Teaching Routines*** card: **Using an Anticipation Guide**.

Concept Connector

Students will return to the **Anticipation Guide** after completing "First Inaugural Address."

Individual Activity

In this speech, Franklin Roosevelt promises to resolve the nation's problems. Have students work individually to research some of the programs that Roosevelt instituted. Have them take notes on how these programs helped the country. Encourage students to share their findings with the class.

❷ About the Selection

In "First Inaugural Address," newly elected President Roosevelt outlines the problems facing the American people. He encourages them with the now-famous phrase, "the only thing we have to fear is fear itself." Roosevelt calls on the people to support his efforts as he works for the greater good, and he promises to work for the benefit of the nation with courage and devotion.

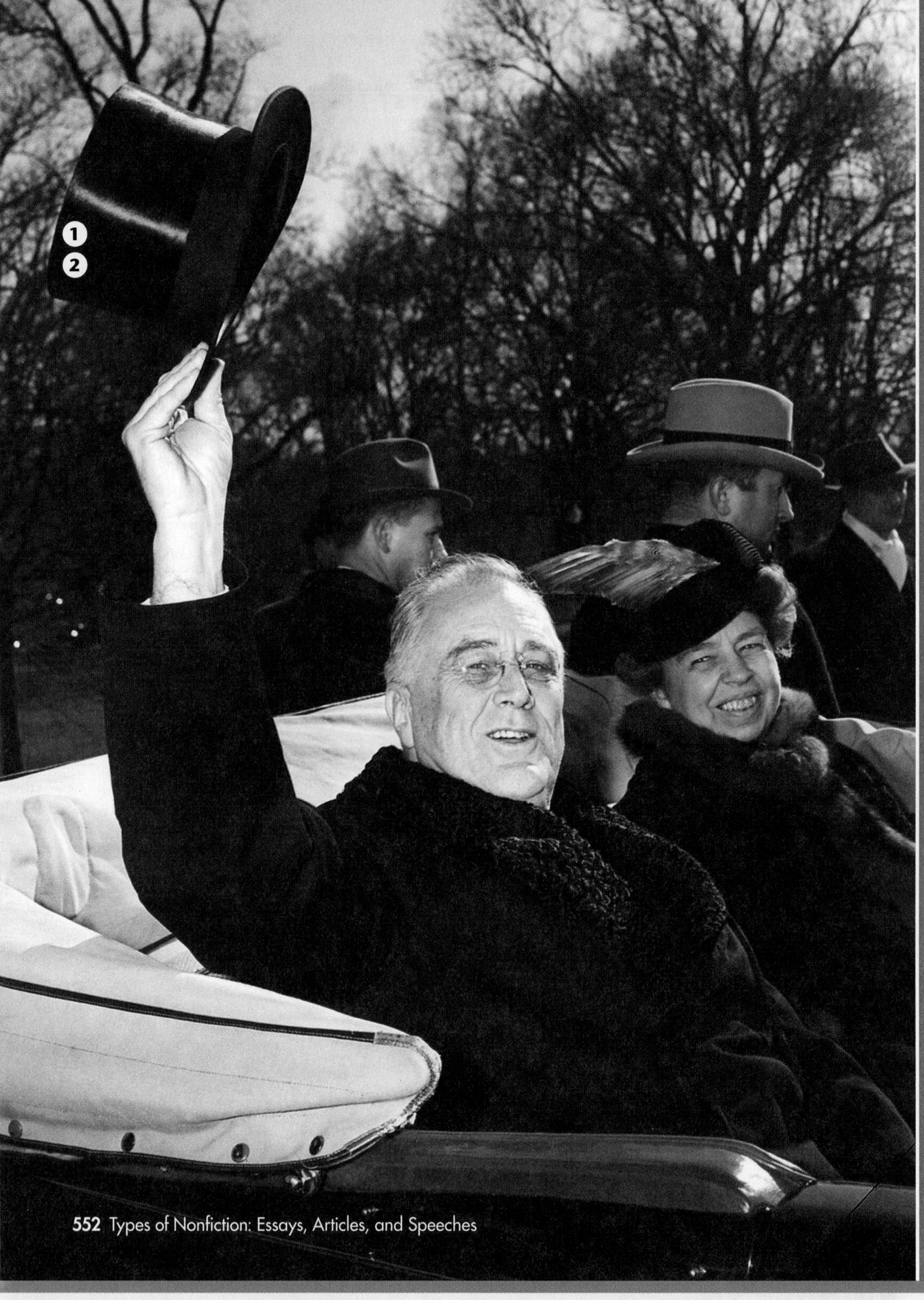

Vocabulary Development

Ⓒ CCSS Language 6

Thematic Vocabulary: The Big Question

As students are discussing "First Inaugural Address," encourage them to use the thematic vocabulary presented in Introducing the Big Question, pp. 424–425. You might encourage them with sentence starters like these:

1. During his speech, Roosevelt mentions the *fact* that . . .
2. One of the issues Roosevelt wanted to *clarify* in his speech was . . .
3. Roosevelt could have strengthened his argument by including *statistics* about . . .
4. This speech proves that Roosevelt had enormous *insight* into . . .

First Inaugural Address

Franklin Delano Roosevelt

President Hoover, Mr. Chief Justice, my friends:

This is a day of national consecration,[1] and I am certain that my fellow-Americans expect that on my **induction** into the Presidency I will address them with a **candor** and a decision which the present situation of our nation impels.

This is pre-eminently the time to speak the truth, the whole truth, frankly and boldly. Nor need we shrink from honestly facing conditions in our country today. This great nation will endure as it has endured, will revive and will prosper.

4 So first of all let me assert my firm belief that the only thing we have to fear is fear itself—nameless, unreasoning, unjustified terror which paralyzes needed efforts to convert retreat into advance.

1. **consecration** (kän′ si krā′ shən) *n.* dedication to something sacred.

Vocabulary

induction (in duk′ shən) *n.* installation; initiation

candor (kan′ dər) *n.* sharp honesty or frankness in expressing oneself

3 
Reading Check

With what qualities does Roosevelt promise to address his audience?

3 Reading Check

Answer: He promises to address his audience with candor and decisiveness.

PHLit Online!

This selection is available in interactive format in the **Enriched Online Student Edition,** at **www.PHLitOnline.com,** which includes a thematically related video with writing prompt and an interactive graphic organizer.

Differentiated Instruction for Universal Access

Vocabulary for Special-Needs Students

Much of the vocabulary in this selection will be unfamiliar to students. Have students work in pairs to read the selection, listing all of the words and phrases they do not understand. Then, have pairs work with other pairs and compare their lists. Review the lists with the group and discuss the words in context, helping them identify context clues. You may also want to provide students with the **Vocabulary Warm-up Word Lists** and **Vocabulary Warm-up Practice,** pp. 184–185 in ***Unit 3 Resources.***

EL Pronunciation for English Learners

Some students might have difficulty pronouncing the schwa sound in *address, induction,* and *candor.* Write each word on the board and point out that different letters and letter combinations can be pronounced with the schwa sound. Guide students in repeating each word after you. Then, have English learners work in pairs with fluent speakers to practice their pronunciation of each word. Encourage fluent speakers to think of additional words that share the same vowel sound and practice them with English learners.

4 Reading Skill

Persuasive Techniques

1. Ask students to read the paragraphs, and then **ask** them what Roosevelt thought the people might fear.

   Answer: They might have feared that the country would never recover its prosperity, and that they and their children would be doomed to live in poverty for the rest of their lives.

2. **Ask** students to list what words or phrases they consider emotionally charged.

   Possible responses: Students may suggest the phrases "nameless, unreasoning, unjustified terror" and "dark hour."

3. **Ask** the Reading Skill question: How do you think Roosevelt wanted listeners to respond to the emotionally charged language here?

   Possible response: He wanted them to realize that he understood the gravity of their problems and the intensity of their concerns. He wanted them to know that he saw the truth of the situation and was not attempting to pretend that things were better than they seemed.

5 Critical Viewing

Possible response: People would be fearful seeing so many people out of work and unable to feed themselves. People might be afraid that they, too, would end up in a bread line.

Reading Skill
Persuasive Techniques
How do you think Roosevelt wanted listeners to respond to the emotionally charged language here? 4

In every dark hour of our national life a leadership of frankness and vigor has met with that understanding and support of the people themselves which is essential to victory. I am convinced that you will again give that support to leadership in these critical days.

In such a spirit on my part and on yours we face our common difficulties. They concern, thank God, only material things. Values have shrunken to fantastic levels; taxes have risen; our ability to pay has fallen, government of all kinds is faced by serious curtailment of income; the means of exchange are frozen in the currents of trade; the withered leaves of industrial enterprise lie on every side; farmers find no markets for their produce; the savings of many years in thousands of families are gone.

More important, a host of unemployed citizens face the grim problem of existence, and an equally great number toil with little return. Only a foolish optimist can deny the dark realities of the moment.

5 ▼ **Critical Viewing**
This is a photograph of a bread line during the Great Depression. Why do you think conditions like this might have made Americans fearful? **[Infer]** 6

Yet our distress comes from no failure of substance. We are stricken by no plague of locusts.[2] Compared with the perils which our forefathers conquered because they believed and were not afraid, we have still much to be thankful for. Nature still offers

2. **plague of locusts** According to Exodus 10:3–20, the plague of locusts was one of ten plagues inflicted by God on the Egyptians as punishment for enslaving the Israelites.

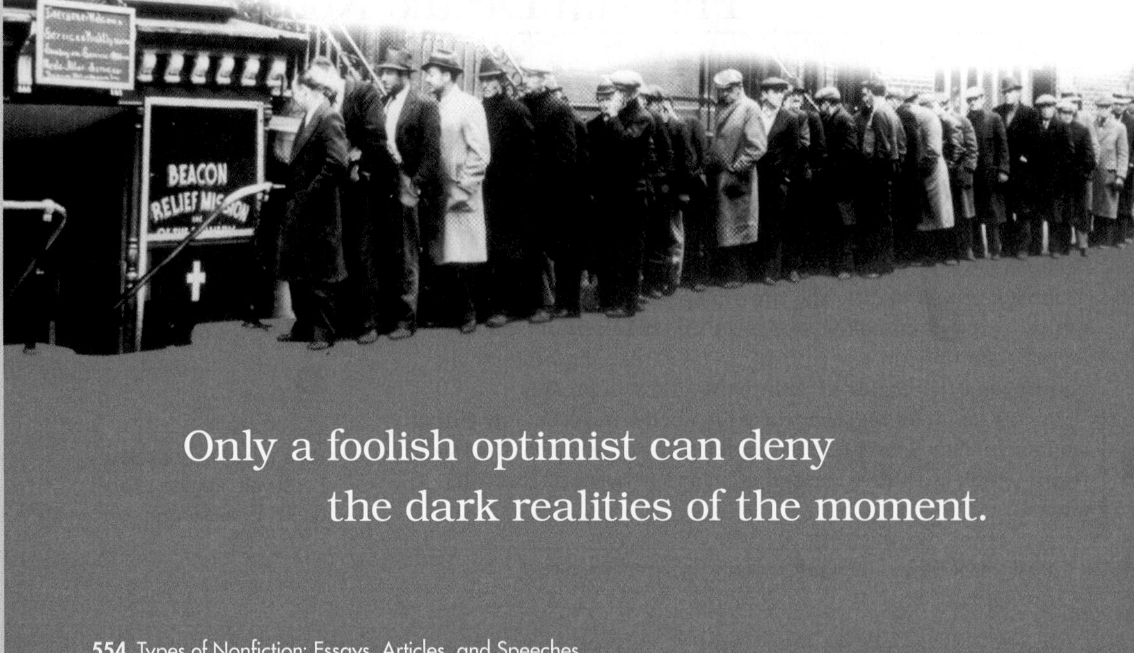

Only a foolish optimist can deny the dark realities of the moment.

Think Aloud

Persuasive Speech
Draw students' attention to this phrase in the second paragraph: "the means of exchange . . . lie on every side." Use the following "think aloud" to model the process of identifying rhetorical devices in a persuasive speech:

When I read this paragraph, I look for evidence of rhetorical devices. This phrase contains some unusual images. When I reread it, I notice that the phrase contains two examples of analogy.

Roosevelt compares the means of exchange to something frozen in the river of trade. He also compares industrial enterprise to dying leaves on a tree. These rhetorical devices help Roosevelt make his point by providing a visual way for listeners to relate to his ideas. The poetic analogies also stir the emotions of his listeners.

her bounty and human efforts have multiplied it. Plenty is at our doorstep, but a generous use of it languishes in the very sight of the supply.

Primarily, this is because the rulers of the exchange of mankind's goods have failed through their own stubbornness and their own incompetence, have admitted that failure and abdicated. Practices of the unscrupulous money changers stand indicted in the court of public opinion, rejected by the hearts and minds of men.

True, they have tried, but their efforts have been cast in the pattern of an outworn tradition. Faced by failure of credit, they have proposed only the lending of more money.

Stripped of the lure of profit by which to induce our people to follow their false leadership, they have resorted to exhortations, pleading tearfully for restored confidence. They know only the rules of a generation of self-seekers.

They have no vision, and when there is no vision the people perish.

The money changers have fled from their high seats in the temple[3] of our civilization. We may now restore that temple to the ancient truths.

Literary Analysis
Persuasive Speech How might this description of national problems have changed people's minds about their troubles?

Vocabulary
abdicated (ab′ di kāt′ əd) *v.* gave up formally

7 
Reading Check
On whom does Roosevelt place the largest blame for the Great Depression?

3. **money changers . . . temple** allusion to Matthew 21:12–13, in which Jesus overturns the money changers' tables at the temple in Jerusalem. FDR is comparing those ancient money changers to modern bankers who took great risks with depositors' money and who charged excessive interest rates for loans.

6 Literary Analysis

Persuasive Speech

1. Have students read the passage. **Ask** what positive things Roosevelt describes in this paragraph.

   Answer: He describes the nation's plentiful natural resources.

2. Then, **ask** the Literary Analysis question: How might this description of national problems have changed people's minds about their troubles?

   Answer: Roosevelt says that the problems the nation faced did not come from God or nature. Instead, human beings created the problems, which means that human beings had the power to solve them. This statement would have emboldened Roosevelt's listeners and made them turn from despair to hope.

Monitor Progress: Provide students with **Literary Analysis Graphic Organizer B,** p. 103 in ***Graphic Organizer Transparencies,*** to complete as they read the speech.

Reteach: If students have difficulty identifying persuasive appeals, point out that words with a negative connotation reinforce a persuasive appeal. Brainstorm with students for a list of words with a negative connotation that appear on p. 555, including *failed, stubbornness, money changers, lure,* and *self-seekers.* Tell students to look for ways that Roosevelt uses words with positive connotations in the remainder of the speech.

7 Reading Check

Answer: He blames the "rulers of the exchange" or "money changers."

Differentiated Instruction for Universal Access

Culturally Responsive Instruction

Culture Focus Direct students' attention to the photograph at the top of the page. Point out that President Roosevelt is shown standing, although he was the first—and only—physically challenged person elected to the presidency.

Ask students to compare the scene in the photograph to a present-day presidential inauguration. What do they notice about the crowd in the picture? Why aren't any women or minorities present?

Tell students that when Roosevelt was elected in 1932, women and people of color held few, if any, positions at the top levels of government. In fact, Franklin Roosevelt was the first president to appoint a woman—Frances Perkins—to a cabinet post as secretary of labor. This picture represents the upper echelons of the U.S. government at the time.

Challenge students to think about what the United States would be like if the political landscape were the same as it was seventy years ago. How has the country's political culture changed?

Spiral Review

Word Choice

1. Remind students that they studied the concept of word choice in the Unit 3 Literary Analysis workshop (pp. 426–439).
2. **Ask** students the Spiral Review question.

   Possible response: Roosevelt's word choice creates a formal tone; he chooses vivid words that create contrast. In addition, the multiple syllables of the words create a strong rhythm.

8 Connecting to the Big Question

1. Have students read the bracketed text and summarize the passage. **Answer:** We must work partly to feel the joy of serving others, not to become wealthy at the expense of others. In particular, public officials and bankers must remember to honor the trust put in them instead of seeking only wealth and power.
2. **Ask:** How does this passage show that the president understands why people are suffering? **Possible response:** By stating forgotten values—and by using the words *us* and *we*—he acknowledges that corruption and selfishness have impacted all Americans negatively.
3. **Ask:** How do Roosevelt's words provide a sense of hope? **Possible response:** He implies that the values of social conscience and honor once existed in American society, and therefore they may make a comeback.

9 Literary Analysis

Persuasive Speech

1. Ask students to read the two paragraphs aloud. Then, **ask** what they think Roosevelt means by the "American spirit of the pioneer."

   Possible response: He refers to the pioneer willingness to work hard and to persevere.
2. **Ask** students to respond to the Literary Analysis prompt.

   Answer: The parallel phrase is "It is the." It emphasizes the idea of the pioneer spirit.

The measure of the restoration lies in the extent to which we apply social values more noble than mere monetary profit.

Happiness lies not in the mere possession of money; it lies in the joy of achievement, in the thrill of creative effort.

Spiral Review
Word Choice How do Roosevelt's words about the moral stimulation of work create a meaning and tone suitable for the occasion? **8**

The joy and moral stimulation of work no longer must be forgotten in the mad chase of evanescent profits. These dark days will be worth all they cost us if they teach us that our true destiny is not to be ministered unto but to minister to ourselves and to our fellow-men.

Recognition of the falsity of material wealth as the standard of success goes hand in hand with the abandonment of the false belief that public office and high political position are to be valued only by the standards of pride of place and personal profit; and there must be an end to a conduct in banking and in business which too often has given to a sacred trust the likeness of callous and selfish wrongdoing.

Small wonder that confidence languishes, for it thrives only on honesty, on honor, on the sacredness of obligations, on faithful protection, on unselfish performance. Without them it cannot live.

Restoration calls, however, not for changes in ethics alone. This nation asks for action, and action now.

Our greatest primary task is to put people to work. This is no unsolvable problem if we face it wisely and courageously. . . .

> Happiness lies not in the mere possession of money; it lies in the joy of achievement, in the thrill of creative effort.

I favor as a practical policy the putting of first things first. I shall spare no effort to restore world trade by international economic readjustment, but the emergency at home cannot wait on that accomplishment.

The basic thought that guides these specific means of national recovery is not narrowly nationalistic.

It is the insistence, as a first consideration, upon the interdependence of the various elements in, and parts of, the United States—a recognition of the old and permanently important manifestation of the American spirit of the pioneer.

Literary Analysis
Persuasive Speech Identify the parallelism in the paragraph beginning "It is the way . . ." and explain what idea it emphasizes.

It is the way to recovery. It is the immediate way. It is the strongest assurance that the recovery will endure.

In the field of world policy I would dedicate this nation to the policy of the good neighbor—the neighbor who resolutely respects himself and, because he does so, respects the rights of others—the

Think Aloud

Vocabulary: Using Context
Direct students' attention to the word *languishes* on this page. Using a think-aloud process, model how to use context to infer the meaning of an unknown word. Say to students:

I'm going to think aloud to show you how I would figure out the meaning of *languishes* from its context.

In this sentence, *languishes* is used to describe what happens to confidence. In the previous sentence, Roosevelt says that people in banking and business have engaged in selfish wrongdoing. Then, he says that confidence "thrives only on honesty."

So, I think *languish* must mean "not thriving" or "not exhibiting strength and vitality."

neighbor who respects his obligations and respects the sanctity of his agreements in and with a world of neighbors.

If I read the temper of our people correctly, we now realize as we have never before, our interdependence on each other; that we cannot merely take, but we must give as well; that if we are to go forward we must move as a trained and loyal army willing to sacrifice for the good of a common discipline, because, without such discipline, no progress is made, no leadership becomes effective.

We are, I know, ready and willing to submit our lives and property to such discipline because it makes possible a leadership which aims at a larger good. •

Vocabulary
discipline (dis′ ə plin′) *n.* training that develops self-control, character, or efficiency

12 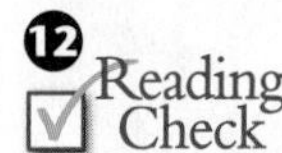
Reading Check
What does Roosevelt say is the "greatest primary task" facing the nation?

10 LITERATURE IN CONTEXT

Social Studies Connection

Getting Back to Work: FDR and the WPA
In 1935, President Roosevelt established the Works Progress Administration (WPA) to aid struggling Americans. At the height of its activity, the WPA provided jobs to one third of the unemployed, ranging from artists to construction workers.

11 

▲ This mural painted by WPA artist William Gropper shows the building of a WPA project dam.

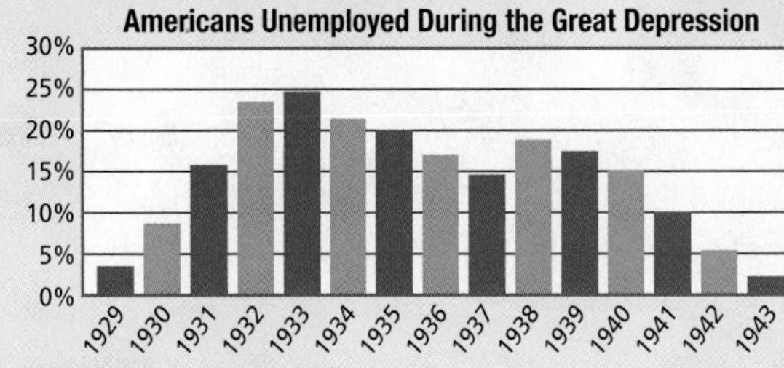

The WPA Projects

WPA workers produced:	650,000	miles of roads
	125,000	public buildings
	75,000	bridges
	8,000	parks
	800	airports
WPA artists created:	2,566	murals
	100,000	paintings
	17,700	sculptures
	300,000	fine prints

Connect to the Literature

President Roosevelt gave his First Inaugural Address in March of 1933. Basing your answer on the chart of unemployment, explain why this was a particularly hard time in American life.

10 Literature in Context

Social Studies Connection In 1935, Congress awarded the WPA (Work Progress Administration) $5 billion to underwrite public projects. President Roosevelt believed that simply giving money to people would lead to a "spiritual and moral disintegration." He thought people should work for the funds they received. The WPA decreased the national unemployment rate by putting about 8.5 million people back to work. The government hired artists and teachers as well as construction workers and engineers. Roads, dams, public buildings, bridges, parks, and airports were built, and thousands of murals and paintings were created.

Connect to the Literature **Ask** students to respond to the Connect to the Literature prompt.

Answer: In 1933, unemployment reached a new height—almost 25 percent of Americans were out of work. The unemployment of at least 13 million people had a profoundly negative effect on the economy.

11 Humanities

Construction of a Dam by William Gropper, mural, Department of Interior Museum, Washington, D.C. Gropper painted this mural in 1939, working with oil paint on canvas. Gropper's inspiration for this mural was the construction of the Grand Coulee Dam on the Columbia River and the Davis Dam on the Colorado River. **Ask** the following question for discussion: What message do you think the artist is trying to portray?

Possible response: The artist portrays the dignity of labor and the value of teamwork.

12 Reading Check

Answer: He says the "greatest primary task" is to put people to work.

Differentiated Instruction for Universal Access

Strategy for Less Proficient Readers
Have students choose partners with whom to read part of Roosevelt's speech. Students can break the speech into short sections and alternate sections as they read. Have them help one another pronounce difficult words or check a dictionary for pronunciation. At the end of each section, ask partners to summarize what they have read. Then, ask small groups to prepare choral readings of parts of the speech, such as the two full paragraphs on this page.

Enrichment for Advanced Readers
Have students research one WPA project. Ask them to find out how many people were employed in the project and what the project produced. Encourage students to share their findings with the class via a poster, written report, or multimedia presentation.

⑬ Visual Connections

Whole-Class Activity

1. **Ask** students to describe what they see in the photograph.

   Possible response: I see a formally dressed man sitting at a desk and speaking into a microphone. There are large flags and a bird behind the man, and they make him look important. He is reading from a binder on his desk.

2. Have students brainstorm for a list of words that occur to them as they look at the photograph.

   Possible response: Students may mention the words *power, important, eagle, freedom, president, formal, austere, serious,* and *speech.*

Small-Group Activity

1. Divide the class into small groups. Tell students to draw a picture that projects a message *opposite* to that of the photograph on this page. They should draw a man in a room, but the details of the man and the room should be different.
2. Have students share their drawings with the class. To model the process of making connections to an image, choose one drawing and analyze how it projects a message opposite to that of the original photograph.

Individual Activity

1. As a class, briefly discuss the photograph.
2. Ask students to imagine that they are inside this picture and having a conversation with Roosevelt. What would they say? What would he say?
3. In class or for homework, have students write a one-page dialogue between themselves and Roosevelt.
4. Have students present their work.

Vocabulary Development

Vocabulary Knowledge Rating

When students have completed reading and discussing "First Inaugural Address," have them take out their **Vocabulary Knowledge Rating Chart** for this selection. Read the words aloud once more and have students rate their knowledge of the words again in the After Reading column. Clarify any words that are still problematic. Have students write their own definition and example or sentence in the appropriate column. Then, have students complete the Vocabulary Practice activities at the end of the selection. Encourage students to use the words in further discussion and written work about this selection. Remind them that they will be accountable for these words on the **Selection Test,** ***Unit 3 Resources,*** pp. 199–201 or 202–204.

This I propose to offer, pledging that the larger purposes will bind upon us all as a sacred obligation with a unity of duty hitherto evoked only in time of armed strife.

With this pledge taken, I assume unhesitatingly the leadership of this great army of our people, dedicated to a disciplined attack upon our common problems.

Action in this image and to this end is feasible under the forms of government which we have inherited from our ancestors.

Our Constitution is so simple and practical that it is possible always to meet extraordinary needs by changes in emphasis and arrangement without loss of essential form.

That is why our constitutional system has proved itself the most superbly enduring political mechanism the modern world has produced. It has met every stress of vast expansion of territory, of foreign wars, of bitter internal strife, of world relations. . . .

I am prepared under my constitutional duty to recommend the measures that a stricken nation in the midst of a stricken world may require.

These measures, or such other measures as the Congress may build out of its experience and wisdom, I shall seek, within my constitutional authority, to bring to speedy adoption.

But in the event that the Congress shall fail to take one of these two courses, and in the event that the national emergency is still critical, I shall not evade the clear course of duty that will then confront me.

I shall ask the Congress for the one remaining instrument to meet the crisis—broad executive power to wage a war against the emergency as great as the power that would be given me if we were in fact invaded by a foreign foe.

For the trust reposed in me I will return the courage and the devotion that befit the time. I can do no less.

We face the arduous days that lie before us in the warm courage of national unity; with the clear consciousness of seeking

> Our Constitution is so simple and practical that it is possible always to meet extraordinary needs by changes . . .

Vocabulary
feasible (fē´ zə bəl) *adj.* capable of being done or carried out; practicable; possible

Literary Analysis
Persuasive Speech
What call to action does Roosevelt issue to Congress in this passage?

Vocabulary
arduous (är´ jo͞o əs) *adj.* difficult; laborious

15 ◀ **Critical Viewing**
This photograph of President Roosevelt in the Oval Office was taken on the day of his first inauguration. Do you think he projects an image of confidence? Explain. **[Analyze]**

14 Literary Analysis
Persuasive Speech

1. Have students read the bracketed passage. Then, **ask** what Roosevelt is proposing.

   Answer: He is proposing to introduce measures necessary to solve the problems of the nation.

2. **Ask** the Literary Analysis question: What call to action does Roosevelt issue to Congress in this passage?

   Answer: He calls on Congress to adopt his measures or to grant him broad executive powers so that he can act on his own.

3. **Ask** students whether they think Roosevelt was wise in suggesting that he might ask Congress for additional powers to "wage war" against the problems.

   Possible responses: Some students may say that Roosevelt was wise in demonstrating that he would do everything possible to solve the problems. Others may say that he may have given the impression of seeking to grasp too much power.

15 Critical Viewing

Answer: Most students will say that he projects an image of confidence and power, as he is surrounded by patriotic symbols, is well dressed, and has a slight smile on his face.

Concept Connector

Anticipation Guide

Have students return to their **Anticipation Guides** and respond to the statements again in the After Reading column. They may do this individually or in their original pairs or groups. Then, lead a class discussion, probing for what students have learned that confirms or invalidates each statement. Encourage students to cite specific details, quotations, or other evidence from the text to support their responses to each statement.

Writing About the Big Question

Have students compare the sentence starter they completed before reading the speech with their ideas afterwards. Ask them to explain whether their thoughts have changed.

Reading Skill Graphic Organizer

Ask students to review the graphic organizers they completed to identify the persuasive appeals while reading. Show them **Reading Skill Graphic Organizer A** (***Graphic Organizer Transparencies***, p. 99) as an example. Then, have students share their graphic organizers.

ASSESS

Answers

Critical Thinking

Before students respond, you may wish to have them write a brief objective summary of the selection. As they answer the questions below, remind them to support their answers with evidence from the text.

1. (a) He calls them unscrupulous money changers, false leaders, and self-seekers who have no vision. (b) He sends the message that the actions of these people and others like them will no longer be tolerated in the United States.
2. (a) He says they conquered perils because they were not afraid. (b) The recognition that earlier Americans had overcome adversity was probably encouraging.
3. **Possible response:** People today may approve of FDR's ideas about putting people to work and following the Constitution. References to sacrifice, discipline, and the performance of duty may be less appealing because people today are less likely to believe in sacrifice, discipline, and duty.
4. (a) **Possible response:** He outlines exactly what the problems are in detail by explaining the economic, social, and emotional status of Americans at that moment. (b) **Possible response:** He wants them to know that "they have nothing to fear but fear itself." He also wants them to know that Americans have overcome enormous obstacles in the past, and the government will help the country recover from its current obstacles.

old and precious moral values; with the clean satisfaction that comes from the stern performance of duty by old and young alike.

We aim at the assurance of a rounded and permanent national life.

We do not distrust the future of essential democracy. The people of the United States have not failed. In their need they have registered a mandate that they want direct, vigorous action.

They have asked for discipline and direction under leadership. They have made me the present instrument of their wishes. In the spirit of the gift I take it.

In this dedication of a nation we humbly ask the blessing of God. May He protect each and every one of us. May He guide me in the days to come.

Critical Thinking

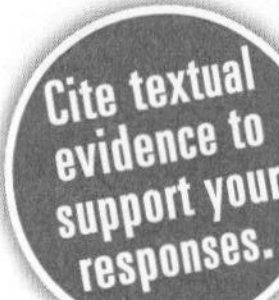
Cite textual evidence to support your responses.

1. **Craft and Structure (a)** What words does Roosevelt use to describe the leaders who caused the country's financial problems? **(b) Interpret:** What impact are these words intended have on the audience? What message is conveyed? What tone?
2. **Key Ideas and Details (a)** What does Roosevelt say about Americans from earlier periods in history? **(b) Speculate:** How do you think his listeners felt on hearing about earlier Americans?
3. **Craft and Structure Make a Judgment:** Roosevelt's speech was made more than seventy years ago to a country in economic ruin. Which parts of the speech do you think would be most appealing to Americans today? Which parts might be less appealing? Explain.
4. **Integration of Knowledge and Ideas (a)** What information in this speech lets you know that Roosevelt understands the country he is about to lead? **(b)** What is the main thing he wants his listeners to understand? *[Connect to the Big Question: Is knowledge the same as understanding?]*

Assessment Resources

Unit 3 Resources

L1 L2 EL **Selection Test A,** pp. 199–201. Administer Test A to less advanced readers.

L3 L4 EL **Selection Test B,** pp. 202–204. Administer Test B to on-level and more advanced students.

L3 L4 **Open-Book Test,** pp. 196–198. As an alternative, give the Open-Book Test.

All **Customizable Test Bank**

All **Self-tests**
Students may prepare for the **Selection Test** by taking the **Self-test** online.

PHLit Online! All assessment resources are available at **www.PHLitOnline.com.**

After You Read First Inaugural Address

Literary Analysis: Persuasive Essay

1. **Key Ideas and Details** In this **persuasive speech,** what is President Roosevelt's purpose? Explain.
2. **Craft and Structure** What examples of figurative or connotative words appeal to the audience's emotions? To their reason? Explain.
3. **Craft and Structure** In a chart like this, list examples in Roosevelt's speech of **rhetorical devices,** and describe the effect of each one.

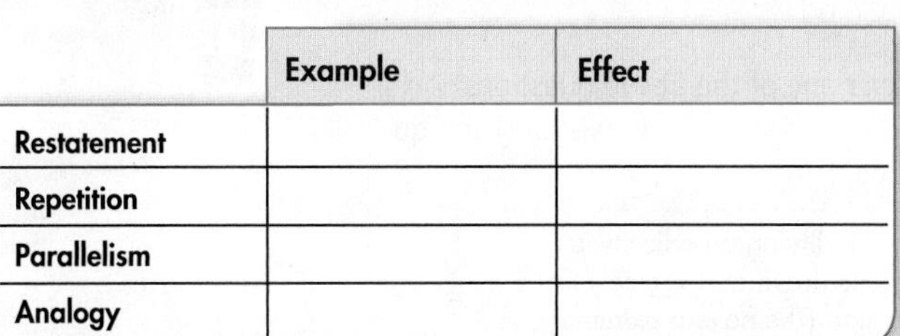

	Example	Effect
Restatement		
Repetition		
Parallelism		
Analogy		

4. **Key Ideas and Details** **(a)** What evidence does Roosevelt use to support his position? **(b)** What details are most valid? Why?

Reading Skill: Persuasive Techniques

5. **(a)** Identify a passage in which Roosevelt uses emotionally charged language as a **persuasive technique. (b)** What purpose do you think he had in using such language in the passage? Explain.
6. Does Roosevelt use rhetorical devices effectively? Explain.

Vocabulary

Acquisition and Use **Analogies** show relationships between pairs of words. Use a word from page 550 to complete each analogy.

1. coach : resigned :: ruler : ______________
2. vacation : relaxing :: labor : ______________
3. insecurity : confidence :: deception : ______________
4. vague : definite :: impossible : ______________
5. initiation : fraternity :: ______________ : military
6. left : right :: laxness : ______________

Word Study Use the context of sentences and what you know about the **Latin root *-duct-*** or ***-duc-*** to explain your answer to each question.

1. If you *introduce* someone, do you help her meet other people?
2. Is a *conductor* someone who watches an orchestra?

Word Study

The **Latin root *-duct-*** or ***-duc-*** means "to lead" or "to bring."

Apply It Explain how the root *-duct-* or *-duc-* contributes to the meanings of these words. Consult a dictionary if necessary.

conducive
deductible
conductivity

Vocabulary

Acquisition and Use

1. abdicated
2. arduous
3. candor
4. feasible
5. induction
6. discipline

Word Study

Sample answers:

1. Yes, when you *introduce* someone, you are leading him or her to someone.
2. No, a *conductor* is someone who leads an orchestra.

Word Study: Apply It

Sample answers:

Something *conductive* leads to something or is helpful.

If something is *deductible,* it can be taken or brought away.

Conductivity leads to the transmission of electricity.

EXTEND/ASSESS

Answers

Literary Analysis

1. He is trying to persuade people to have hope, to support his proposals, and to trust him to lead the nation out of its difficulties.
2. Appeals to emotions: He alludes to fear, to "money changers," and to our forefathers. Appeals to reason: He discusses the "common difficulties" that the people face and the plans he has for solving them.
3. **Sample answers: Restatement:** "Nature still offers her bounty. . . . Plenty is at our doorstep. . . ." **Effect:** Helps the listener to understand that there are solutions. **Parallelism:** "on honesty, on honor, on the sacredness of obligations, on faithful protection, on unselfish performance." **Effect:** This parallel listing of virtues creates a sense of momentum and urgency.

   For other sample answers see ***Graphic Organizer Transparencies,*** **Literary Analysis Graphic Organizer A,** p. 102, and the **Additional Answers** section.
4. (a) He talks about the unemployment rate and other current problems, and he talks about the spirit of the American people. (b) **Possible response:** The details about unemployment are most valid because they are facts.

Reading Skill

5. **Possible responses:** (a) "We are stricken by no plague of locusts. . . ." (b) He wanted to emphasize that the problems the nation faced were not insurmountable. Unlike the biblical plague of locusts, America's economic woes did not come from God.
6. **Possible response:** Some students may suggest that he made very little use of rhetorical devices, but relied primarily on emotionally charged language. Most students will agree that Roosevelt uses emotionally charged words effectively.

EXTEND/ASSESS

Answers

Conventions

1. Introduce the skill, using the instruction on the student page.
2. Discuss the definitions and the examples in the boxes.

Think Aloud: Model the Skill

Model the skill of recognizing and using adverbs. On the board write the words *terrible* and *terribly*. Say:

To identify adverbs, I ask myself what a word is describing and what question the description is answering. In the sentence *My arm hurts terribly*, the word *terribly* tells more about *hurts*, which is a verb. I know that adverbs can tell more about verbs. *Terribly* answers the question "to what extent?" It is an adverb.

PH WRITING COACH Grade 9

Students will find instruction on and practice with adverbs in Chapter 13, section 3.

Practice A

1. there; *Where?*
2. clearly, passionately; *In what way?*
3. especially; *To what extent?*
4. more forcefully; *To what extent? In what way?*

Reading Application

Sample Answers:

And as we walk, we must make the pledge that we shall always march ahead. (verb)

It is a dream deeply rooted in the American dream. (adjective)

We cannot turn back. (verb)

Practice B

1. compassionately; spoke; Roosevelt whispered softly to those sitting near him.
2. often; spoke; He sometimes talked on the radio.
3. very; clearly; He more determinedly moved to help the country.
4. calmly; resolute; He was obviously determined.

Writing Application

Students' sentences should use adverbs to modify verbs, adjectives, and adverbs.

PERFORMANCE TASKS

Integrated Language Skills

"I Have a Dream" • First Inaugural Address

Conventions: Adverbs

Adverbs are words that modify verbs, adjectives, and other adverbs. They answer the questions *Where? When? In what way?* and *To what extent?* about the words they modify.

An adverb modifying a verb can answer any of the above questions. An adverb modifying an adjective or another adverb will answer only the question *To what extent?*

Modifying a verb:
Dave drove the car smoothly. (The adverb *smoothly* modifies the verb *drove*.)

Modifying an adjective:
He drove an extremely large car. (The adverb *extremely* modifies the adjective *large*.)

Modifying another adverb:
He drove the car very smoothly. (The adverb *very* modifies the adverb *smoothly*.)

Practice A Identify the adverbs in the following sentences. Then, tell what question each adverb answers.

1. King stood there waiting to speak.
2. King spoke clearly and passionately before the large audience.
3. The audience was especially attentive to King's words.
4. King spoke more forcefully than people remembered.

Reading Application Find three sentences in "I Have a Dream" that include an adverb. Identify the word modified as a verb, an adjective, or another adverb.

Practice B In each sentence, identify each adverb and the word it modifies. Then, write a related sentence using a different adverb.

1. Roosevelt spoke compassionately to his audience.
2. Roosevelt often spoke to the nation.
3. Roosevelt very clearly understood the needs of his listeners.
4. Roosevelt was calmly resolute.

Writing Application Choose one photo from "First Inaugural Address." Write three sentences to describe the photograph. Use adverbs to modify verbs, adjectives, and adverbs.

PH WRITING COACH Further instruction and practice are available in *Prentice Hall Writing Coach*.

Extend the Lesson

Sentence Modeling

Choose the sentence given from the selection students have read:

And they have come to realize that their freedom is inextricably bound to our freedom. ("I Have a Dream")

This is no unsolvable problem if we face it wisely and courageously. . . . ("First Inaugural Address")

Ask students what they notice about the sentence. Elicit from them that the sentence contains one ("Dream") or two ("Address") adverbs. Have students circle the adverb(s) and underline the word(s) modified. Then, ask what else they notice. ("I Have a Dream": The adverb *inextricably* modifies an adjective. *Inextricably* gives the sentence more feeling. "First Inaugural Address": The adverbs *wisely* and *courageously* modify a single verb. These adverbs provide specificity and color to the verb *face*.)

Have students imitate the sentence in a sentence on a topic of their own choosing, matching each grammatical and stylistic feature discussed.

Writing

Argument Both of these speeches use persuasive techniques that inspire listeners. Write a **proposal** to persuade school leaders to invite a great speaker like Dr. King or President Roosevelt to address a school assembly.

- List some issues that concern students at your school, and list details that describe and explain the problem.
- List possible speakers and the issues that each could discuss.
- Choose one speaker, and write a proposal supporting your choice.
- Defend your idea with precise and relevant evidence and logical reasoning, including facts about the speaker and your school. Use logical reasoning to make your case.
- End with an appeal to your principal to act on the proposal.

Grammar Application Make sure to use adverbs correctly in your essay.

Common Core State Standards

L.9-10.3; W.9-10.1; SL.9-10.3
[For the full wording of the standards, see page 538.]

Writing Workshop: *Work in Progress*

Prewriting for Editorial Review your Cultural Influences List. Identify one cultural factor that you feel has the greatest effect on you. In a two-column chart, jot down three positive and three negative aspects of this influence. Save this Positive/Negative Chart in your writing portfolio.

Use this prewriting activity to prepare for the **Writing Workshop** on page 582.

Speaking and Listening

Presentation of Ideas Compose a **radio news report** that provides on-the-spot coverage of the speaker whose speech you just read. Include excerpts from the speech, a description of the crowd's reaction and appropriate background information.

- If you read "I Have a Dream," include information about the civil rights movement.
- If you read "First Inaugural Address," include information about the Great Depression.

Follow these steps to complete the assignment:

- Analyze the rhetorical devices and features that made the historical speech you read memorable.
- Consider how the language in the speech and the speaker's delivery would affect the mood and tone of the speech, and imagine how the audience would respond. Choose examples from the speech to quote.
- Add information to provide necessary background for an audience who may not be familiar with the audience or purpose of the speech.
- Broadcast your report to the class, and record it for later evaluation.

PHLit Online!
www.PHLitOnline.com

- Interactive graphic organizers
- Grammar tutorial
- Interactive journals

EXTEND/ASSESS

Writing

1. Review the assignment, using the instruction on the student page.
2. To give students guidance for writing the proposal, give them **Support for Writing**, p. 194 in ***Unit 3 Resources.***
3. To evaluate students' proposal, use the Persuasive Essay rubrics, pp. 230–231 in the ***Professional Development Guidebook.*** In addition, you might evaluate the appropriateness of issues and possible speakers chosen by the students.

Grammar Application

Have students check their drafts to make sure they are using adverbs correctly.

Six Traits Focus

✓	Ideas		Word Choice
	Organization		Sentence Fluency
	Voice		Conventions

PH WRITING COACH Grade 9

Students will find instruction on and practice with persuasive writing in Chapter 9.

Writing Workshop
Work in Progress

Have students save their completed Positive & Negative chart in their portfolios. They will use their charts later as they complete the Writing Workshop (see pp. 582–589).

Speaking and Listening

1. Review the assignment, using the instruction on the student page.
2. To support students' work on the assignment, have them complete the **Support for Extend Your Learning** page (***Unit 3 Resources,*** p. 195).

Teaching Resources

Unit 3 Resources

L3 L4 EL **Integrated Language Skills: Grammar,** p. 193
L3 L4 EL **Support for Writing,** p. 194
L3 L4 **Support for Extend Your Learning,** p. 195
L4 **Enrichment,** pp. 174 and 192

Enriched Online Student Edition
Available under After You Read for this selection:
All **Interactive Grammar Tutorial**
L3 L4 **Internet Research Activity**

Professional Development Guidebook
Rubrics for Self-Assessment: Persuasive Essay, pp. 230–231

PHLit Online! All print and digital resources are available at **www.PHLitOnline.com.** Online resources accessible by students are noted on the student page.

MONITORING PROGRESS

Using the Test Practice

In this two-page Test Practice, students apply the reading skill for the second half of Unit 3 to a passage of fiction and a passage of nonfiction.

Review this skill, evaluating persuasion, then administer the test. For more guidance, consult the ***Classroom Strategies and Teaching Routines*** card **Formally Assessing Students.**

ASSESS

Answers

Answers With Explanations

1. **B**—David cites scientists' concerns, and scientists are authorities in the areas they study. *Incorrect answers:* A—David suggests that much will be lost if we lost the rain forest, but he provides no evidence. C—David's appeal to emotion comes later in his speech, not at the beginning. D—David does not use statistics.
2. **C**—David urges those who agree with him to sign his petition. *Incorrect answers:* A—David does not mention a march. B—David does not recommend adopting rain forest animals. D—David mentions the presence of medicinal plants in the rain forest, but does not recommend buying them.
3. **A**—David does not cite the statements of anyone who opposes his viewpoint. *Incorrect answers:* B—David uses parallel construction in his sentences that begin "Do we want . . . ?" C—David cites the opinion of experts in his first statement. D—David's thesis statement is the first quoted sentence in the passage.
4. **B**—David is outraged by the loss of the rain forests. *Incorrect answers:* A—David's speech is more forceful than wishful. C—David is determined to arouse his listeners by expressing outrage. D—This may be true, but David focuses on the importance of the rain forest, not its wonder.

Test Practice: Reading

Evaluate Persuasion

Fiction Selection

Directions: *Read the selection. Then, answer the questions.*

David stepped to the front of the class and began his speech: "Scientists say that we need to protect the rain forest, and I agree. Do we want to lose the natural beauty of these areas? Do we want to be denied the medicinal plants that live there? Do we want to see the animals of the rain forest become homeless—or die?" David glanced up and saw his listeners' looks of boredom. He continued, more loudly: "I say no! It's not fair to those parts of the earth, and it's not fair to us!" David waved a sheet of paper over his head as he concluded, "So, if you agree with me, put your name on this petition. Let's get the government to care about this problem!"

1. Which type of appeal does David use to open his speech?
- **A.** appeal to evidence
- **B.** appeal to authority
- **C.** appeal to emotion
- **D.** appeal to statistics

2. What is David trying to get his listeners to do?
- **A.** join a march protesting the destruction of the rain forest
- **B.** adopt animals made homeless by rain forest destruction
- **C.** sign a petition urging greater protection of the rain forest
- **D.** buy medicines made from plants that grow in the rain forest

3. Which of the following strategies is *not* used in David's speech?
- **A.** acknowledgement of opposing viewpoints
- **B.** parallel structure
- **C.** expert opinions
- **D.** clear thesis statement

4. The questions beginning with "Do we want . . . " convey a tone of—
- **A.** wishfulness.
- **B.** outrage.
- **C.** determination.
- **D.** wonder.

Writing for Assessment

Is David's argument well reasoned and logical? Does it convince you to take the action he suggests? Write a paragraph evaluating David's speech. Use details from the passage to support your response.

Writing for Assessment

Students may say that David's speech would have been more effective had he given some statistics or suggested one or more steps the government and individuals could take to protect the rain forest.

Strategies for Test Taking

Remind students to read the directions for each item carefully. For example, question 1 asks what kind of appeal David uses to *open* his speech. Since the speech becomes very emotional, students might be tempted to choose **C** as the answer. The clue is to reread the question and see that it asks students to focus on David's approach at the *beginning* of his speech.

Nonfiction Selection

Directions: *Read the selection. Then, answer the questions.*

Perhaps the greatest environmental tragedy of our time is the destruction of the Amazon rain forest. The rain forest is home to the most diverse life on Earth. More than 2,000 of the species of rain forest plants are known to have value as medicines, but only about 10 percent of these have been studied. <u>They may disappear before scientists can study and evaluate them</u>. Some organizations, therefore, recommend that nations buy and preserve rain forest land and educate local people about living in the rain forest without destroying it. These are small first steps in saving the rain forest, but they deserve our support.

1. Which of the following is an emotionally charged phrase?
- **A.** "only about ten percent of these have been studied"
- **B.** "home to the most diverse life on earth"
- **C.** "Some organizations, therefore, recommend"
- **D.** "greatest environmental tragedy of our time"

2. What is the effect of the underlined sentence?
- **A.** It surprises listeners with an unusual analogy.
- **B.** It reminds listeners that the issue is of immediate concern.
- **C.** It comforts listeners with words about hope for the future.
- **D.** It makes listeners feel ashamed of themselves.

3. Which of the following details supports the idea that the destruction of the rain forest would be tragic for humanity?
- **A.** Some organizations recommend that nations preserve rain forest land.
- **B.** Many rain forest plants may have undiscovered medicinal value.
- **C.** Life in the rain forest is extremely diverse.
- **D.** Local people can live in harmony with the rain forest.

4. The final sentence of the passage—
- **A.** restates the author's main idea.
- **B.** includes a transition to the next idea.
- **C.** provides a call to action.
- **D.** summarizes the author's point of view.

Writing for Assessment

Connecting Across Texts
Write a comparison of the persuasive appeals in these two passages. For each passage, consider the author's motive, the use of rhetorical devices, the inclusion of evidence, and the type of appeal (emotional or logical). Use details from both passages to support your response.

www.PHLitOnline.com
- Online practice
- Instant feedback

Differentiated Instruction for Universal Access

Strategy for Special-Needs Students
Work with students to find definitions for challenging words from the nonfiction selection such as *environmental, destruction, tragedy, diverse, evaluate, recommend,* and *preserve.* Have volunteers look up and write the definitions on the board. For usage practice, ask students the following questions, adding those of your own for the remaining words if you wish: "Is the *environment* just your home, or everything that surrounds you?" "What could cause greater *destruction,* a wrecking ball or a baseball?" "Which is a *tragedy,* a lost book or a lost pet?" "Which is a *diverse* woods, one with two kinds of trees, or one with many kinds of trees?"

Answers

Answers with Explanations

1. **D**—The statement uses two words that have *emotional* impact—*greatest* and *tragedy. Incorrect answers:* A—This is an important fact but is not emotionally charged. B—same explanation as for A. C—same explanation as for A.
2. **B**—The sentence implies that time is short for studying and evaluating the Amazon rain forest. *Incorrect answers:* A—The sentence contains no analogy. C—The sentence does not contain comforting information. D—This may be the result for some listeners, but it is not the goal of the sentence.
3. **B**—The loss of medicinal sources would affect human beings. *Incorrect answers:* A—This detail recommends action to prevent the problem; it does not state the tragedy of the problem. C—This detail describes positive features of the rainforest, but not in terms of human beings' good. D—This might be a true statement but does not state a tragedy for humanity.
4. **D**—The writer takes a stand in favor of these preservation steps. *Incorrect answers:* A—The author's main idea is the tragedy that loss of the rain forest would entail. B—The statement concludes the passage; there is no next idea. C—The writer states his or her support for preservation efforts without issuing a rousing call for action.

Writing for Assessment

Students' comparisons might point out that the first writer uses rhetorical devices, such as parallel construction, asking questions, and charging the audience with a task while the second writer relies on useful evidence. They may conclude that while the first passage is more emotional, the second is more persuasive.

Students may take the test in interactive format with instant feedback online at **www.PHLitOnline.com.**

PREACHEACH

Common Core State Standards

- **Reading Informational Text 6, 8, 9**
- **Language 4.b**

Reading Skill

1. Introduce the skill, using the instruction on the student page.
2. Tell students they will evaluate the credibility of arguments.

Think Aloud: Model the Skill

Model the skill of evaluating credibility. Say to students:

Sometimes, a movie critic praises or criticizes a film and I disagree. If the critic doesn't give details to support his or her view, then I think that the critic is expressing a bias for or against the film. That makes me think that the critic has less credibility. I will tend not to put much faith in his or her reviews.

Multidraft Reading

Have students follow a multidraft reading protocol.

- **First reading**—Have students read to identify key ideas and details.
- **Second reading**—Have students read to identify the structure of the text.
- **Third reading**—Have students read to integrate knowledge and ideas by connecting the text to the world, their own experiences, and other texts.

Content-Area Vocabulary

1. Have students say each word.
2. Next, use each word in a sentence that defines it.
3. Finally, repeat your definitional sentence or a similar sentence with the word missing and have the class "fill in the blank" chorally.

Reading for Information

Analyzing Arguments

Historical Research Study

Speech

Common Core State Standards

Reading Informational Text

6. Determine an author's point of view or purpose in a text and analyze how an author uses rhetoric to advance that point of view or purpose.

8. Delineate and evaluate the argument and specific claims in a text, assessing whether the reasoning is valid and the evidence is relevant and sufficient; identify false statements and fallacious reasoning.

9. Analyze seminal U.S. documents of historical and literary significance, including how they address related themes and concepts.

Language

4.b. Identify and correctly use patterns of word changes that indicate different meanings or parts of speech.

Reading Skill: Evaluate Credibility

When an author makes an argument, his or her purpose is to convince the audience to adopt a certain position. As a reader or listener, you must **evaluate the credibility** of the argument to determine whether it is valid. Critique the argument to see if generalizations are supported by evidence, and consider the strength of that evidence.

Also note how the structure and tone of the text relate to the author's intent, or purpose. Look for words, phrases, and sentence structures that are repeated, and think about the effect that the author's use of language creates. Ask yourself whether the author is appealing to logic or to emotions. Arguments that appeal only to emotions are not credible.

Use this checklist to help you evaluate an argument's credibility.

Checklist for Evaluating an Author's Argument

- Does the author present a clear argument?
- Is the argument well-developed and supported by evidence?
- How comprehensive is the evidence?
- Is the argument structured in a logical way?
- Does the author use sound reasoning, or only emotional appeals?

Content-Area Vocabulary

These words appear in the selections that follow. You may also encounter them in other content-area texts.

- **inaugural** (in ô´ gyər əl) *adj.* marking the beginning of an activity or period in office
- **commodities** (kə mod´ ə tēz) *n.* things that are bought and sold

Is knowledge the same as understanding?

Have students consider how different people may view the same events differently.

Differentiated Instruction for Universal Access

Reading Support

Give students reading support with the appropriate version of the ***Reader's Notebooks:***

L2 L3 *Reader's Notebook*

L1 *Reader's Notebook: Adapted Version*

EL *Reader's Notebook: English Learner's Version*

Historical Research Study

Features:

- summary or excerpt of a historical document
- facts and opinions about the document
- explanations and interpretations
- text written for a specific audience

from Nothing to Fear: Lessons in Leadership from FDR

by Alan Axelrod

"This great nation will endure as it has endured, will revive and will prosper. So, first of all, let me assert my firm belief that the only thing we have to fear is fear itself—nameless, unreasoning, unjustified terror which paralyzes needed efforts to convert retreat into advance."

—First **inaugural** address, March 4, 1933

The study begins with a quotation from a speech by Franklin Delano Roosevelt. It focuses the argument on the famous line, "The only thing we have to fear is fear itself."

In *Defending Your Life*, a charmingly provocative 1991 movie written and directed by its star, Albert Brooks, we discover that the only truly unforgivable sin in life is fear. Killed in a head-on crash with a bus, yuppie Brooks finds himself transported to Judgment City, where he must "defend his life" before a pair of judges who will decide whether he is to be returned to Earth for another crack at life or be permitted to progress to the next plane of existence. His attorney (for the benevolent managers of the universe provide defense assistance) explains to him the nature of fear, which is, he says, a "fog" that obscures everything and that makes intelligent, productive action impossible.

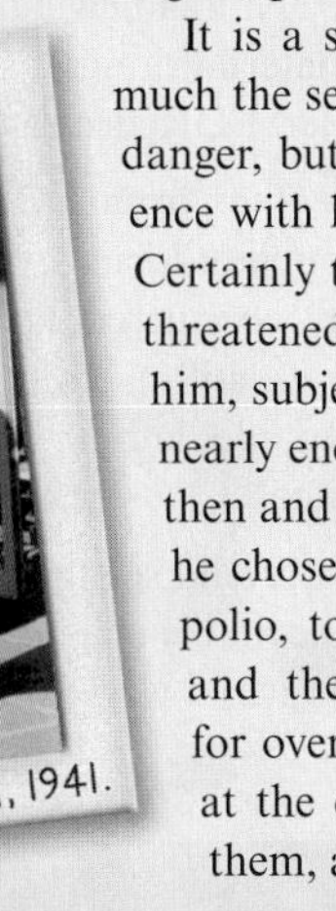

Franklin D. Roosevelt with a local child, 1941.

It is a stimulating thought—that fear is not so much the sensation accompanying the realization of danger, but a fog, an obscurer of truth, an interference with how we may productively engage reality. Certainly this is the way FDR saw it. In 1921 polio threatened first to kill him and then paralyzed him, subjected him to a life of relentless pain, and nearly ended his career in public service. He could then and there have given in to the fog of fear, but he chose not to. He chose instead to understand polio, to see clearly the extent of his disability, and then to assess—also clearly—his options for overcoming that disability. He did not blink at the odds. He looked at them, contemplated them, assessed them, and then acted on them.

TEACH

About Historical Research Studies

1. Review the features listed in the Historical Research Study box on page 567. **Ask** students to define the term *interpretation* in their own words.

   Possible response: A person's interpretation is his or her view of a person, statement, or action based on the interpreter's knowledge and values.
2. Discuss with students any experiences they have had with historical research studies. Point out that they have probably read explanations and opinions about such documents as the U.S. Constitution or famous speeches such as Abraham Lincoln's Gettysburg Address.
3. Point out that several people can have different views of why people act in certain ways based on their knowledge of those people. Explain that, similarly, historians have different interpretations of the motives that drove people to act in certain ways in the past.

Evaluate Credibility

1. Explain the importance of analyzing the reliability of the evidence that an author presents. Remind students that a fact can be proven. An opinion is a statement of belief that cannot be proven. Ensure students understand that if they are unable to verify a statement, it is an opinion, even if they agree with it. Point out that the opinions of experts on an issue carry more weight than those of a less-informed person. **Ask** why that would be the case.

   Possible response: An expert would have more facts and a better understanding of the complexities of an issue.
2. Have students read the text. **Ask:** How does FDR's experience with polio support Axelrod's thesis that FDR believed fear clouds judgment and impedes action?

   Possible response: He says FDR did not allow himself to fear polio, but studied polio and his own options and formed an action plan.

Differentiated Instruction for Universal Access

Strategy for Less Proficient Readers
Some students may find this selection difficult to read, but they should be able to understand the argument. To help them participate, pair students with more advanced readers to read the text together. Have the pairs read a paragraph and then stop to paraphrase it. If students put the text in their own words, they should be able to grasp the author's point.

Enrichment for Gifted/Talented Students
Challenge students to conduct research to learn more about polio and its prognosis in the 1920s. Allow time for students to present their findings and to discuss how they might have reacted if they had been told they had polio at that time.

Evaluate Credibility

1. Direct students to the second paragraph of page 568. **Ask:** What opinion is stated in the paragraph, and whose opinion is it?

   Possible response: The opinion is that FDR lifted the fog of fear. It is Axelrod's opinion.

2. **Ask:** How does the quotation that begins "Values have shrunken to fantastic levels" help support the author's thesis?

   Possible response: The author's thesis is that FDR believed that fear clouds judgment and impedes action. The quotation shows that FDR did not allow fear to cloud his vision of the country's problems. Instead, he focused his attention on the problems and their solutions.

3. Point out that Axelrod assumes that, true to human nature, the people at the time of the Great Depression were comforted knowing that they were not alone with their problems and that the losses they were experiencing were not unbearable because they were only material possesions.

Now, more than a decade later, assuming the office of president of the United States, he began by asking the American people to sweep aside the fog of fear, "nameless, unreasoning, unjustified terror which paralyzes needed efforts to convert retreat into advance." He didn't ask them to stop being afraid, but to stop letting fear obscure their vision of reality. He asked the people to confront what they feared, so that they could see clearly what needed to be done and thereby overcome (and the word is significant) the terror that paralyzes.

Axelrod refers back to the "fog" described in the introduction. In later paragraphs, he continues to refer to the "fog of fear." This repetition gives structure to the text.

In the second paragraph of his inaugural speech, FDR lifted the fog of fear. What did he reveal to his audience, the American people?

> Values have shrunken to fantastic levels; taxes have risen; our ability to pay has fallen; government of all kinds is faced by serious curtailment of income; the means of exchange are frozen in the currents of trade; the withered leaves of industrial enterprise lie on every side; farmers find no markets for their produce; the savings of many years in thousands of families are gone.

In this paragraph, the author makes a generalization about the speech, then supports the generalization with a direct quotation.

There is no sugarcoating of reality here! The fog has lifted, the scene is sharply etched and downright frightening: "a host of unemployed citizens face the grim problem of existence, and an equally great number toil with little return. Only a foolish optimist can deny the dark realities of the moment."

FDR did not blink at reality and he did not allow his audience to do so either. He embarked on this catalog of economic disasters by defining them as "our common difficulties," which "concern, thank God, only material things."

The fog was lifted and the president's listeners could see the reality they already knew, a reality of poverty and despair, to be sure; yet with the fog of fear lifted, they could see it in a new light: Our common difficulties "concern, thank God, only material things."

Not one to blink at disaster, FDR also saw a way out of it:

> Yet our distress comes from no failure of substance. We are stricken by no plague of locusts. Compared with the perils which our forefathers conquered because they believed and were not afraid, we have still much to be thankful for. Nature still offers her bounty and human efforts have multiplied it. Plenty is at our doorstep. . .

Lift the fog of fear and you could see that the Great Depression was not of natural, supernatural, or inevitable origin. It was not a plague of biblical proportion. Our kind has conquered worse in the past.

Vocabulary Development

CCSS Language 6

Vocabulary from Historical Speeches

Point out that historical works often use vocabulary that is more common to one particular setting—in this case, a speech made by a president. Guide students to understand the meaning of the following words that are used in the selection:

inaugural address: the speech made by a president when he or she assumes office, or is inaugurated

public service: work in government

defense: the side in a trial that argues in favor of the person charged with a crime

means of exchange: money and other financial documents used to conduct business

industrial enterprise: factories

material: relating to physical objects

from

Radio Address on Drought Conditions

by Franklin Delano Roosevelt
September 6, 1936

I have been on a journey of husbandry. I went primarily to see at first hand conditions in the drought states; to see how effectively Federal and local authorities are taking care of pressing problems of relief and also how they are to work together to defend the people of this country against the effects of future droughts.

I saw drought devastation in nine states.

I talked with families who had lost their wheat crop, lost their corn crop, lost their livestock, lost the water in their well, lost their garden and come through to the end of the summer without one dollar of cash resources, facing a winter without feed or food—facing a planting season without seed to put in the ground.

That was the extreme case, but there are thousands and thousands of families on western farms who share the same difficulties.

I saw cattlemen who because of lack of grass or lack of winter feed have been compelled to sell all but their breeding stock and will need help to carry even these through the coming winter. I saw livestock kept alive only because water had been brought to them long distances in tank cars. I saw other farm families who have not lost everything but who, because they have made only partial crops, must have some form of help if they are to continue farming next spring.

I shall never forget the fields of wheat so blasted by heat that they cannot be harvested. I shall never forget field after field of corn stunted, earless and stripped of leaves, for what the sun left the grasshoppers took. I saw brown pastures which would not keep a cow on fifty acres.

Yet I would not have you think for a single minute that there is permanent disaster in these drought regions, or that the picture I saw meant depopulating these areas. No cracked earth, no blistering sun, no burning wind, no grasshoppers, are a permanent match for the indomitable American farmers and stockmen and their wives and children who have carried on through desperate days, and inspire us with their self-reliance, their tenacity and their courage. It was their fathers' task to make homes; it is their task to keep those homes; it is our task to help them with their fight.

First let me talk for a minute about this autumn and the coming winter. We have the option, in the case of families who need actual subsistence, of putting them on the dole or putting them to work. They do not want to go on the dole and they are one thousand percent right. We agree, therefore, that we must put them to work for a decent wage, and when we reach that

Speech

Features:

- text spoken aloud to an audience
- remarks that communicate an important message
- language intended to engage listeners and support the speaker's ideas

Roosevelt repeats the word *I* to emphasize his personal experience.

Roosevelt gives examples of the hardships he saw to support the argument he is about to make.

Differentiated Instruction for Universal Access

EL Background for English Learners

Provide background about the historical context of Roosevelt's address. Make sure students realize that when he took office in 1933, the United States was in the depths of the Great Depression. During the same time, a severe drought had hit much of the Great Plains, and many people lost everything they had. Explain that this speech was focused on addressing the problems of the Great Plains farmers.

Enrichment for Advanced Readers

Challenge students to find a historical study of Roosevelt's speech. Have them evaluate the credibility of the historical study. Allow time for students to share their findings.

About Speeches

1. Review the features listed in the Speech box on page 569. **Ask** students to define the term *engage* in the context of a speech in their own words.

   Possible response: To *engage* is to capture the attention of listeners and to persuade them to favor the speaker's point of view.
2. Have students think of speeches they have heard in the past. Discuss what features made the speeches memorable.
3. **Ask:** What are some jobs that would require a person to make speeches?

   Possible response: Students might mention politicians, group leaders, or salespeople.

Evaluate Credibility

1. Remind students that to evaluate credibility, they should consider whether the author presents a clear argument, supports it with comprehensive evidence, and uses sound reasoning.
2. Explain to students that the purpose of Roosevelt's speech is to explain what he has seen and tell what he thinks should be done about it. Then, have them read the radio address. **Ask:** Do you think that the president knew what he was talking about? Explain.

   Possible response: Paragraphs 1 through 6 describe how he gathered information about the extent of the problem, so he probably knew what he was talking about.
3. **Ask:** How long does Roosevelt think the drought will last? What evidence does he give for this position?

   Answer: He says it is not permanent. He does not really offer any evidence.
4. Discuss the credibility of Roosevelt's argument. Explain that Roosevelt was reasonable to suggest that the drought would not last forever, but that his real purpose might simply have been to lift people's spirits and to give them hope.

Evaluate Credibility

1. **Ask:** What did President Roosevelt propose to do in his speech?

   Answer: He proposed having the government pay to employ the farmers, putting them to work so they can continue to buy goods and be ready to plant in the future, when the drought ends.

2. **Ask:** What is the effect of the emotional words that FDR uses in his speech, such as *spiritual, hope,* and *future*?

   Possible response: The effect of the emotional words is to give the reader a good feeling that the plan will work and that the president cares about helping to solve the problem.

3. Direct students' attention to the fourth paragraph. **Ask:** Why does Roosevelt include this passage in his speech? What is his purpose?

   Possible responses: He hopes to convince Americans who are not farmers that helping the farmers in this way is good for them, too. He does so to remove objections they might have to his plan.

decision we kill two birds with one stone, because these families will earn enough by working, not only to subsist themselves, but to buy food for their stock, and seed for next year's planting. Into this scheme of things there fit of course the government lending agencies which next year, as in the past, will help with production loans.

Every Governor with whom I have talked is in full accord with this program of doing work for these farm families, just as every Governor agrees that the individual states will take care of their unemployables but that the cost of employing those who are entirely able and willing to work must be borne by the Federal Government. . . .

Spending like this is not waste. It would spell future waste if we did not spend for such things now. These emergency work projects provide money to buy food and clothing for the winter; they keep the livestock on the farm; they provide seed for a new crop, and, best of all, they will conserve soil and water in the future in those areas most frequently hit by drought.

If, for example, in some local area the water table continues to drop and the topsoil to blow away, the land values will disappear with the water and the soil. People on the farms will drift into the nearby cities; the cities will have no farm trade and the workers in the city factories and stores will have no jobs. Property values in the cities will decline. If, on the other hand, the farms within that area remain as farms with better water supply and no erosion, the farm population will stay on the land and prosper and the nearby cities will prosper too. Property values will increase instead of disappearing. That is why it is worth our while as a nation to spend money in order to save money.

. . . The very existence of the men and women working in the clothing factories of New York, making clothes worn by farmers and their families; of the workers in the steel mills in Pittsburgh, in the automobile factories of Detroit, and in the harvester factories of Illinois, depend upon the farmers' ability to purchase the **commodities** they produce. In the same way it is the purchasing power of the workers in these factories in the cities that enables them and their wives and children to eat more beef, more pork, more wheat, more corn, more fruit and more dairy products, and to buy more clothing made from cotton, wool and leather. In a physical and a property sense, as well as in a spiritual sense, we are members one of another.

. . . We are going to have a farm policy that will serve the national welfare. That is our hope for the future.

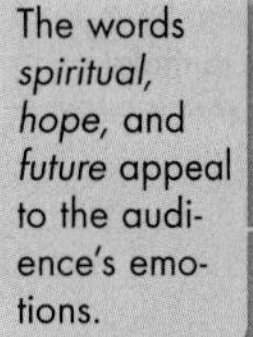
The words *spiritual, hope,* and *future* appeal to the audience's emotions.

Vocabulary Development

CCSS Language 6

Words with Multiple Meanings

Discuss that many words have multiple meanings, and that readers have to figure out the relevant meanings to make sense of their reading. Point out the given multiple meanings of these two words, and discuss which meanings are used in the speech.

table: a piece of furniture where people eat; a plateau; an arrangement of words or numbers in a chart; the level at which water stands underground

Answer: The speech discusses the level at which water stands underground, which is related to the drought suffered on the Plains.

member: one part of a whole; a person who belongs to a group or club; a beam that is part of a wall

Answer: Roosevelt says "we are members one of another," meaning that we are each a part of the whole.

After You Read | Historical Research Study • Speech

Comparing Arguments

1. **Key Ideas and Details** **(a)** In what ways are the intent, or purpose, of the historical research study and speech both similar and different? **(b)** When you evaluate the credibility of the arguments made in the two texts, do you find one more credible than the other? Explain your response.

Content-Area Vocabulary

2. **(a)** For each of the following words, explain how a change in suffix alters the meaning and part of speech of the base word *inaugural: inaugurate, inauguration.* **(b)** Use each word in a sentence that shows its meaning.

Timed Writing

Argument: Essay

Format
The prompt directs you to write a brief essay. Therefore, you will need to express your ideas in three to five paragraphs.

Write a brief essay in which you critique Alan Axelrod's interpretation of Roosevelt's first inaugural address. Analyze the historical research study and decide whether you think Axelrod's points are valid. Support your opinion with examples from the text. (25 minutes)

Academic Vocabulary
When you *analyze* a text, you closely examine its information and details.

5-Minute Planner

Complete these steps before you begin to write:

1. Read the prompt carefully and completely. Look for key words, like the ones highlighted, that help you understand the assignment.
2. Review the historical research study. Begin by rereading the quotations from Roosevelt's speech. Note your own responses to these passages before rereading Axelrod's comments about them.
3. Make notes about Axelrod's arguments and the evidence he uses to support his points. Be sure to distinguish facts from the author's opinions. Note any generalizations that are not supported by facts.
4. Based on your notes, evaluate the overall strengths and weaknesses of Axelrod's arguments. Write a sentence to sum up your evaluation.
5. Use your notes to prepare a quick outline to organize your critique.

ASSESS/EXTEND

Answers

Comparing Arguments

1. (a) **Possible response:** The purpose of the historical research study is to convince the reader that FDR had a unified position on the danger of succumbing to fear. FDR's purpose in his radio address is to convince the listener that he has a plan to help solve the national problems caused by drought. While the content is different, the purpose of both selections is the same: to persuade the reader to share the author's position. (b) **Possible response:** Since the speech by FDR was based on personal experience, it is more credible.
2. (a) **Sample response:** The suffix *-al* makes an adjective that describes something related to *inauguration*. The suffix *-ate* makes a verb that refers to the *inaugural* action. The suffix *-tion* makes a noun. (b) **Sample response:** He was worried about his inaugural speech because he wanted to start his leadership with a strong image. They will inaugurate him at a special ceremony. The inauguration was a serious and solemn event.

Timed Writing

1. Before students complete the activity, guide them in identifying and analyzing key words and phrases in the prompt, highlighted on the student page.
2. Work with students to draw up guidelines for their critique based on the key words:
   - **Focus** The essay should examine Axelrod's study and form an opinion about the validity of his argument.
   - **Organization** The essay should begin with a main impression statement, include at least three supporting paragraphs, and end with a conclusion.
   - **Support** The essay should include examples from Axelrod's study.
   - **Style** The essay is an analysis. The style should be formal and should not contain slang words or contractions.
3. Have students use the 5-Minute Planner to structure their time.
4. Allow students 25 minutes to complete the assignment. Evaluate their work using the guidelines they have developed.

Common Core State Standards

- Reading Literature 6
- Reading Informational Text 4
- Writing 2

1 Comparing Humorous Writing

Humorous Folk Tales

1. Introduce the skill, using the instruction on the student page.
2. Give students a copy of the **Comparing Humorous Writing Graphic Organizer B** (*Graphic Organizer Transparencies,* p. 105) to complete as they read.

Think Aloud: Model the Skill

Model a way of approaching humorous writing. Say to students:

We've all heard the hyperbole and understatement that add humor to writing. For example, the sentence "Her feet were as long as skis" uses hyperbole. The sentence "After 48 hours of work, he was a little fatigued" uses understatement. As I read humorous writing, I enjoy laughing but I also look for the message contained within the humor.

Cultural Context

1. Introduce the skill, using the instruction on the student page.
2. Point out that culture and background influence the colloquial language and slang a writer uses.
3. Explain that when characters seem to place special emphasis on aspects of behavior or appearances, they may be reflecting cultural perspectives.

Comparing Literary Works

The Talk • Talk

1 Comparing Humorous Writing

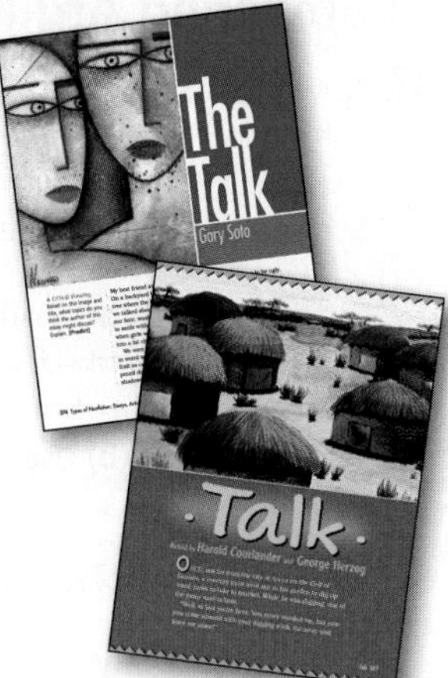

Humorous writing is intended to make the reader laugh. It can be fiction or nonfiction. One kind of nonfiction is the **humorous essay,** which seeks to entertain but may have a serious message as well.

A **folk tale** is a story passed down from generation to generation that expresses the beliefs and values of its culture. Folk tales typically present simple characters and far-fetched situations. A **humorous folk tale** is meant to entertain and instruct. In humorous writing, authors often include these figures of speech:

- **Hyperbole:** intentional, sometimes outrageous, exaggeration—for example, describing a small patch of ice as a "vast, frozen wasteland"
- **Understatement:** the presentation of an idea, a person, or an event to make it seem less than it is—for example, describing a huge loss as a "minor setback"

Besides these techniques, the writer's **comic diction,** or word choice, may include informal, colloquial language, slang, or other verbal humor.

Use a graphic organizer like the one shown to identify the serious ideas in "The Talk" and "Talk." Then, think about why the authors might have chosen to use humor to explore these issues.

Funny Detail	Serious Issue
"My gangly arms nearly touched my kneecaps."	He was young, and his body was growing in spurts.

Cultural context—the historical and social background of a literary work—can be an important element in humorous writing. This is especially true in folk tales, traditional stories that contain many cultural details. However, every story has a culture behind it. The culture of "Talk" is that of ancient Africa; the culture of "The Talk" is that of mid-century suburban America. The more readers know about the culture in which a story is set, the more they can recognize and understand humorous references. Knowledge of cultural context can also help readers appreciate serious messages contained in amusing works.

Common Core State Standards

Reading Literature
6. Analyze a particular point of view or cultural experience reflected in a work of literature from outside the United States, drawing on a wide reading of world literature.

Reading Informational Text
4. Determine the meaning of words and phrases as they are used in the text, including figurative, connotative, and technical meanings; analyze the cumulative impact of specific word choices on meaning and tone.

Writing
2. Write informative/explanatory texts to examine and convey complex ideas, concepts, and information clearly and accurately through the effective selection, organization, and analysis of content.

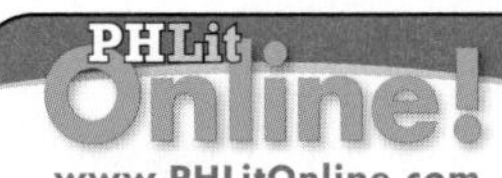

www.PHLitOnline.com

- Vocabulary flashcards
- Interactive journals
- More about the authors
- Selection audio
- Interactive graphic organizers

Vocabulary Development

Vocabulary Knowledge Rating

Create a **Vocabulary Knowledge Rating Chart** (**Professional Development Guidebook,** p. 33) featuring the words glossed in the selections:

renegade (p. 575) *bulging* (p. 580)
feisty (p. 575) *refrain* (p. 580)
wheezed (p. 579)

Give students a copy of the chart and read the words aloud. Have students mark their rating of each in the Before You Read column. To gauge how much instruction to provide, tally the students who think they know each word

Explain that the words are defined in the margin at the point where they appear in the selection. Urge students to be alert to these words as they read the selections. They will rate their knowledge again when they finish.

Vocabulary Central, featuring tools, activities, and songs for studying vocabulary, is available at **www.PHLitOnline.com.**

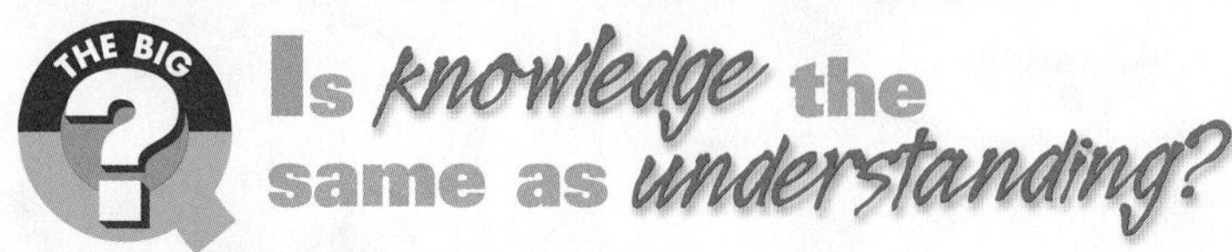

Is knowledge the same as understanding?

❷ Writing About the Big Question

In both of these selections, the writers describe serious ideas or **insights** in a humorous way. Use this sentence starter to develop your ideas about the Big Question.

Humor can help **clarify** ideas and build understanding by ________.

Meet the Authors

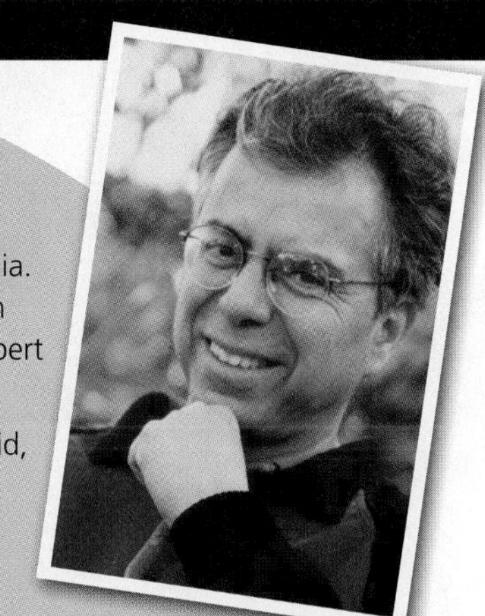

Gary Soto (b. 1952)

Author of "The Talk"

Gary Soto grew up in a Mexican American section of Fresno, California. As a child, he wanted to be either a priest or a scientist. Then, in high school, he discovered great writers, including John Steinbeck and Robert Frost. In college, Soto started writing poetry.

Living Through Books Soto's favorite pastime is reading. He has said, "It appears these days I don't have much of a life because my nose is often stuck in a book. But I discovered that reading builds a life inside the mind."

Harold Courlander (1908–1996) and George Herzog (1901–1983)

Retellers of "Talk"

"Talk" is an Ashanti folk tale. The Ashanti live in what is now the West African country of Ghana. They have a history that dates back centuries. "Talk" is retold by Harold Courlander and George Herzog.

A Distinguished Career Courlander studied the history and folklore of African and other world cultures. He wrote more than thirty-five fiction and nonfiction books inspired by these studies.

Music and Culture Born in Budapest, Hungary, Herzog pioneered the study of the cultural aspects of music. He also taught linguistics and anthropology and published books on folk music.

Teaching Resources

- All *Unit 3 Resources,* pp. 205–221
- All *Graphic Organizer Transparencies,* pp. 104–107
- All *Professional Development Guidebook,* p. 33
- All **Enriched Online Student Edition**
- All *Common Core Companion,* pp. 55–56; 117–124; 190–201

PHLit Online! All resources, including print and audio, are available at **www.PHLitOnline.com**.

Daily Bellringer

For each class during which you will teach this selection, have students complete one of the five Sentence Combining activities for Week 18 in the *Daily Bellringer Activities* booklet.

❷ Writing About the Big Question

1. Review the assignment with the class.
2. Discuss why people may use humor to talk about more serious subjects. **Ask** students how humor can make such discussions easier.
3. Have students complete the sentence starter. Review responses as a class. (**Possible response:** Humor can help clarify ideas and build understanding by showing people a way past their fears.)
4. Remind students that their answers will help them think about the Big Question. Tell them to look for insights the characters gain.

Concept Connector

Students will return to their responses to the sentence starter they completed before reading.

Multidraft Reading

To assist struggling readers and to deepen reading for all, apply multidraft reading protocols. For each reading, have students set the purpose indicated:

- **First reading**—identifying key ideas and details and answering any Reading Checks.
- **Second reading**—analyzing craft and structure and responding to the side-column prompts.
- **Third reading**—integrating knowledge and ideas, connecting to other texts and the world, and answering the end-of-selection questions.

For more guidance, see the ***Classroom Strategies and Teaching Routines*** card on multidraft reading.

For more about the authors and practice with the selection vocabulary, go to **www.PHLitOnline.com**.

1 Background

Gary Soto Gary Soto often draws upon the memories of his childhood in Fresno, California, to provide inspiration for his writing. Unlike many writers from working-class backgrounds, however, Soto does not just write about the people he grew up with; he also writes for them, using language that is common and accessible. His insistence on making his work available to a broad audience, along with his ability to write from personal experience, has made him a popular writer with many kinds of readers.

2 Activating Prior Knowledge

Ask students to list concerns or fears that adolescents commonly have about growing up. Write their ideas on the board, and then have students discuss whether such concerns are realistic, comical, or misguided. Tell them that the selection they are about to read focuses on two boys who are worried that their appearances will prevent them from being happy in the future.

Concept Connector →

Students will follow up on this activity after completing "The Talk."

3 About the Selection

In "The Talk," Gary Soto recalls a poignant conversation as he and a friend wait for a beautiful girl to appear at her window. Although they are only twelve, the two boys have planned their adult lives in detail. As they share their dreams for the future, they discuss what they see as their biggest obstacle to happiness: their appearances. While maintaining a light tone, Soto describes the feelings of being young, poor, and insecure.

4 Critical Viewing

Possible response: Based on the image and title, students might guess that the essay will involve a serious conversation about girls. The picture suggests that the conversation is somehow related to girls.

The Talk 1 2 3

Gary Soto

4 ▲ Critical Viewing Based on this image and title, what topics do you think the author of this essay might discuss? Explain. **[Predict]**

My best friend and I knew that we were going to grow up to be ugly. On a backyard lawn—the summer light failing west of the mulberry tree where the house of the most beautiful girl on the street stood—we talked about what we could do: shake the second-base dirt from our hair, wash our hands of frog smells and canal water, and learn to smile without showing our crooked teeth. We had to stop spitting when girls were looking and learn not to pile food onto a fork and into a fat cheek already churning hot grub.

We were twelve, with lean bodies that were beginning to grow in weird ways. First, our heads got large, but our necks wavered, frail as crisp tulips. The eyes stayed small as well, receding into pencil dots on each side of an unshapely nose that cast remarkable shadows when we turned sideways. It seemed that Scott's legs

Text Complexity Rubric

The Talk		
Qualitative Measures	**Context/ Knowledge Demands**	Pain, awkwardness of adolescence 1 (2) 3 4 5
	Structure/ Language Clarity and Conventionality	Conversational, informal; on-level vocabulary 1 (2) 3 4 5
	Levels of Meaning/ Purpose/Concept Level	Accessible concept (common doubts expressed by very young adults) 1 (2) 3 4 5
Quantitative Measures	**Text Length**	Word Count: 936
	Lexile	1170L

sprouted muscle and renegade veins, but his arms, blue with ink markings, stayed short and hung just below his waist. My gangly arms nearly touched my kneecaps. In this way, I was built for picking up grounders and doing cartwheels, my arms swaying just inches from the summery grass.

We sat on the lawn, with the porch light off, waiting for the beautiful girl to turn on her bedroom light and read on her stomach with one leg stirring the air. This stirred us, and our dream was a clean dream of holding hands and airing out our loneliness by walking up and down the block.

When Scott asked whom I was going to marry, I said a brown girl from the valley. He said that he was going to marry a strawberry blonde who would enjoy Millerton Lake, dirty as it was. I said mine would like cats and the sea and would think nothing of getting up at night from a warm, restless bed and sitting in the yard under the icy stars. Scott said his wife would work for the first year or so, because he would go to trade school[1] in refrigeration. Since our town was made with what was left over after God made hell, there was money in air conditioning, he reasoned.

I said that while my wife would clean the house and stir pots of nice grub, I would drive a truck to my job as a carpenter, which would allow me to use my long arms. I would need only a stepladder to hand a fellow worker on the roof a pinch of nails. I could hammer, saw, lift beams into place, and see the work I got done at the end of the day. Of course, she might like to work, and that would be okay, because then we could buy two cars and wave at each other if we should see the other drive by. In the evenings, we would drink Kool-Aid and throw a slipper at our feisty dog at least a hundred times before we went inside for a Pop-Tart and hot chocolate.

Scott said he would work hard too, but now and then he would find money on the street and the two of them could buy extra things like a second TV for the bedroom and a Doughboy swimming pool for his three kids. He planned on having three kids and a ranch house on the river, where he could dip a hand in the water, drink, and say, "Ahh, tastes good."

But that would be years later. Now we had to do something about our looks. We plucked at the grass and flung it into each other's faces.

"Rotten luck," Scott said. "My arms are too short. Look at 'em."

"Maybe we can lift weights. This would make up for our looks," I said.

"I don't think so," Scott said, depressed. "People like people with nice faces."

1. **trade school** school that specializes in teaching the skills needed to work in a particular job.

Vocabulary
renegade (ren′ ə gād′) *adj.* disloyal; traitorous

Spiral Review
Organization and Structure As the boys sit in the dark, what does the sense that this is a recurring activity add to your understanding of the story?

Literary Analysis
Humorous Writing Which details of the boys' youthful dreams might seem funny later in life?

Vocabulary
feisty (fīs′ tē) *adj.* full of spirit; energetic

6

What are the boys worried they will be like when they grow up?

Spiral Review
Organization and Structure

1. Remind students that they studied the concepts of organization and structure in the Unit 3 Literary Analysis workshop (pp. 426–439).
2. **Ask** students the Spiral Review question.

   Possible response: The recurrence of the talk adds to the understanding that the boys never take action on their wishes.

5 Literary Analysis
Humorous Writing

1. Read aloud the first bracketed text, and point out that it describes the boys' dreams of the work they will do and the women they will marry. **Ask** students to summarize the boys' current situation.

   Answer: The boys are at a particularly awkward phase of adolescence, yearning for a girl beyond their reach.
2. **Ask** the Literary Analysis question: Which details of the boys' youthful dreams might seem funny later in life?

   Possible response: Adults would probably find it funny that the boys expect to drink Kool-Aid and eat Pop Tarts when they are adults.
3. Remind students that humorous essays often deal with serious topics. **Ask** students to identify the serious issue raised in the final sentence of the bracketed text.

   Answer: The boys are worried about their looks.

6 Reading Check
Answer: The boys are worried that they will be ugly.

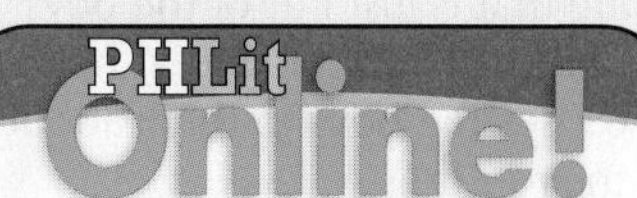

This selection is available in interactive format in the **Enriched Online Student Edition** at **www.PHLitOnline.com**, which includes an interactive graphic organizer.

Text Complexity: Reader and Task Suggestions

The Talk	
Preparing to Read the Text • Use the Background note on TE p. 574 to discuss Soto's stories and how he draws on personal experiences to craft his characters and plots. • Discuss the uncertainties most children and young adults face as they grow up and how these doubts are normal. • Guide students to use Multidraft Reading strategies (TE p. 573).	**Leveled Tasks** *Knowledge Demands* If students will have difficulty with knowledge demands, have them first read and take notes on details that describe the two boys. Then, have them reread and note what problems the boys talk about. *Synthesizing* If students will not have difficulty with knowledge demands, have them take notes as they read about the author's conversational style of writing. Have them decide how this style contributes to the development of the theme.

❼ Literary Analysis

Humorous Writing

1. Read the bracketed text. Point out that Scott's statement is both humorous and disturbing.
2. **Ask** the Literary Analysis question.
   Answer: The statement raises the issue that nice-looking people are often treated better or given more opportunities in society; people are often judged by their physical appearance alone.

Concept Connector

Have students return to the Activating Prior Knowledge activity on p. 574. Discuss the boys' fears and how they might eventually overcome the concerns. Also, have students compare their Writing About the Big Question responses before reading the selection with their ideas afterwards.

ASSESS

Answers

Critical Thinking

Before students respond, you may wish to have them write a brief objective summary of the selection. As they answer the questions below, remind them to support their answers with evidence from the text.

1. (a) Scott wants to repair air conditioners. The narrator wants to be a carpenter. (b) **Possible response:** The boys seem prepared to work hard at physical trades and to be good providers. They probably draw their strong work ethics and vocational plans from the men in their community.
2. (a) No, the boys have watched her before. They are familiar with her routine of reading on the bed. (b) The girl seems to represent beauty and the kind of life that is just out of the boys' reach. Merely looking at her causes the boys to think about their futures.
3. **Possible responses:** Everyone feels awkward when they are young and changing. They will almost certainly outgrow their current awkwardness.
4. **Possible response:** Humor helps me understand the boys' position.

Literary Analysis ❼
Humorous Writing
What serious issues do Scott's statements raise? Explain.

He was probably right. I turned onto my stomach, a stalk of grass in my mouth. "Even if I'm ugly, my wife's going to be good-looking," I said. "She'll have a lot of dresses and I'll have more shirts than I have now. Do you know how much carpenters make?"

Then I saw the bedroom light come on and the beautiful girl walk into the room drying her hair with a towel. I nudged Scott's short arm and he saw what I saw. We flicked the stalks of grass, stood up, and walked over to the fence to look at her scrub her hair dry. She plopped onto the bed and began to comb it, slowly at first because it was tangled. With a rubber band, she tied it back, and picked up a book that was thick as a good-sized sandwich.

Scott and I watched her read a book, now both legs in the air and twined together, her painted toenails like red petals. She turned the pages slowly, very carefully, and now and then lowered her face into the pillow. She looked sad but beautiful, and we didn't know what to do except nudge each other in the heart and creep away to the front yard.

"I can't stand it anymore. We have to talk about this," Scott said.

"If I try, I think I can make myself better looking," I said. "I read an article about a girl whitening her teeth with water and flour."

So we walked up the street, depressed. For every step I took, Scott took two, his short arms pumping to keep up. For every time Scott said, "I think we're ugly," I said two times, "Yeah, yeah, we're in big trouble."

"I can't stand it anymore. We have to talk about this."

Critical Thinking

Cite textual evidence to support your responses.

1. **Key Ideas and Details** **(a)** What jobs do the boys hope to have when they get older? **(b) Infer:** What do the boys' choices of future jobs suggest about their characters? Explain.
2. **Integration of Knowledge and Ideas** **(a) Infer:** Do you think this is the first time the boys have watched the beautiful girl? Why or why not? **(b) Draw Conclusions:** What do you think the girl in the window represents for the two boys?
3. **Integration of Knowledge and Ideas** **Speculate:** What advice do you think an adult might give the two boys to help them feel better about themselves?
4. **Integration of Knowledge and Ideas** Soto presents the boys' expectations of the future in a humorous way. What impact does the use of humor have on your understanding of the characters and their plight? ***[Connect to the Big Question: Is knowledge the same as understanding?]***

Vocabulary Development

CCSS Language 6

Thematic Vocabulary: The Big Question

As students are discussing "The Talk," encourage them to use the thematic vocabulary presented in Introducing the Big Question, pp. 424–425. You might encourage them with sentence starters like these:

1. The boys seemed to *comprehend* what . . .
2. In different ways, they each made a *connection* between . . .
3. As they daydreamed about their futures, they had *insight* into . . .
4. The only part of the conversation that was *ambiguous* was . . .
5. Each boy had the same *feeling* about his . . .

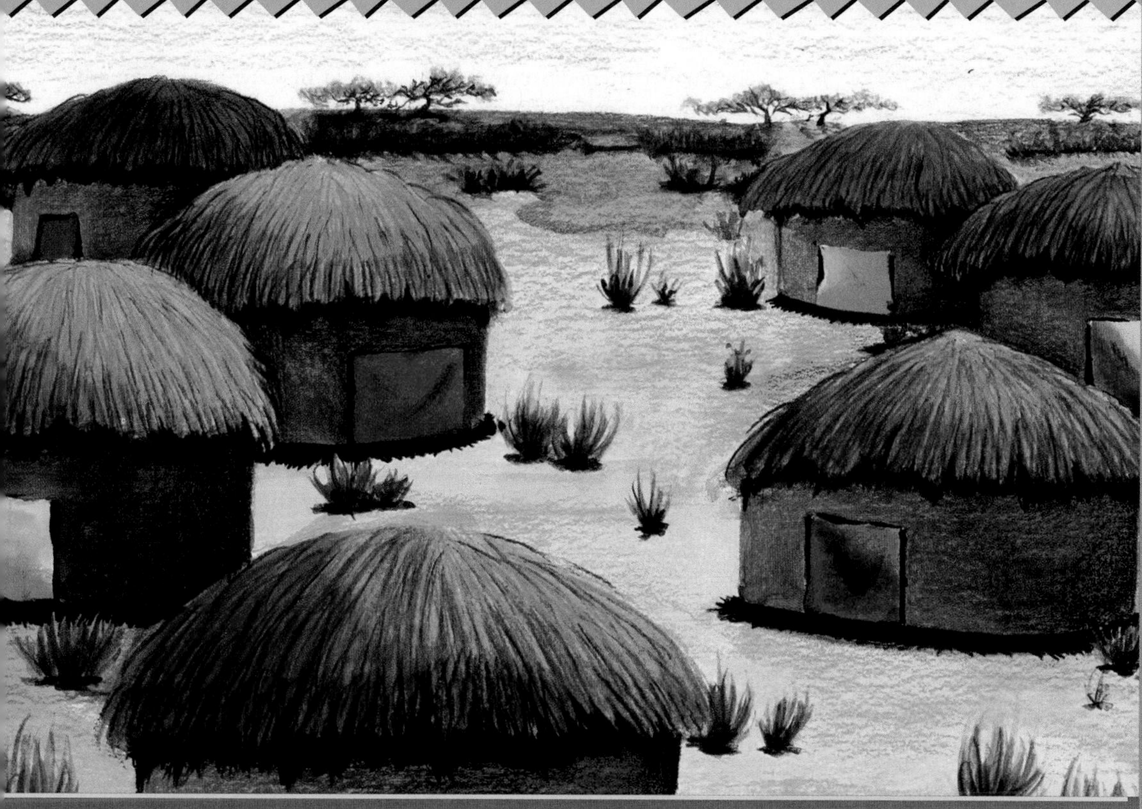

8
9
10

Talk

retold by **Harold Courlander** and **George Herzog**

ONCE, not far from the city of Accra on the Gulf of Guinea, a country man went out to his garden to dig up some yams to take to market. While he was digging, one of the yams said to him:

"Well, at last you're here. You never weeded me, but now you come around with your digging stick. Go away and leave me alone!"

8 Background

Folktales

Folktales are common to many cultures and have been passed down through the ages. The folktale "Talk" is from the Ashanti tribe of Ghana, in West Africa. The Ashanti, like other tribal cultures, passed along their folktales, songs, and legends from generation to generation as part of an oral tradition. Although the stories might differ, they usually contain many of the same elements: talking animals, repetition, humor, and a surprise ending.

9 Activating Prior Knowledge

Remind students of folktales from different countries. Ask them to list some common themes of folktales and name some typical animals featured as main characters. Tell them the folktale they are about to read features both talking animals and talking plants. Encourage volunteers to retell a familiar folktale, and to share what they enjoy about folktales.

Concept Connector

Students will follow up on this activity after completing "Talk."

10 About the Selection

When a farmer tries to pull a yam from his garden, it talks back to him and tells him to stop. The shocked farmer is admonished by his dog, a stone, and a palm branch before he runs off and tells his tale to the first person he sees. As he retells the story to every man he sees, each has an object that "talks." Finally, they reach the Chief and recount their story to him. The Chief refuses to believe them and sends them back home, but the chief's stool marvels that a yam can talk.

C Text Complexity Rubric

Talk	
Qualitative Measures	
Context/ Knowledge Demands	Folktale in which animals, plants, and inanimate objects talk 1 (2) 3 4 5
Structure/ Language Clarity	Informal; on-level vocabulary 1 (2) 3 4 5
Levels of Meaning/ Purpose	Accessible concept (the power of humor) 1 (2) 3 4 5
Quantitative Measures	
Text Length	Word Count: 823
Lexile	640L

Reader and Task Suggestions

Preparing to Read the Text

- Use the Background information on TE p. 577 to discuss folktales.
- Discuss the way in which authors use language conventions that complement their subjects.
- Guide students to use Multidraft Reading strategies (TE p. 573).

Leveled Tasks

Structure/Language If students will have difficulty with the structure, have them first read and note the plot events. Then, have them reread and note how the plot advances.

Evaluating If students will not have trouble with the structure, have them evaluate the use of dialogue in presenting the story.

11 Literary Analysis

Humorous Writing

1. Have students read the bracketed text. Then ask a volunteer to explain why the farmer is a humorous character.

   Answer: His yam, dog, stone, and palm branch have talked to him and told him what to do. He's amazed, frightened, and determined to talk about it to everyone he meets.

2. **Ask** the Literary Analysis question: How does the fisherman's response, an example of understatement, add humor to this passage?

   Answer: By asking "Is that all?," it sounds as if the fisherman is used to having his fish or equipment talk to him or that he doesn't believe the farmer, both of which make his comment funny. When the fish trap actually starts talking, the fisherman is as startled as the farmer.

PHLit Online!

This selection is available in interactive format in the **Enriched Online Student Edition, www.PHLitOnline.com,** which includes an interactive graphic organizer.

The farmer turned around and looked at his cow in amazement. The cow was chewing her cud and looking at him.

"Did you say something?" he asked.

The cow kept on chewing and said nothing, but the man's dog spoke up.

"It wasn't the cow who spoke to you," the dog said. "It was the yam. The yam says leave him alone."

The man became angry, because his dog had never talked before, and he didn't like his tone besides. So he took his knife and cut a branch from a palm tree to whip his dog. Just then the palm tree said:

"Put that branch down!"

The man was getting very upset about the way things were going, and he started to throw the palm branch away, but the palm branch said:

"Man, put me down softly!"

He put the branch down gently on a stone, and the stone said:

"Hey, take that thing off me!"

This was enough, and the frightened farmer started to run for his village. On the way he met a fisherman going the other way with a fish trap on his head.

"What's the hurry?" the fisherman asked.

"My yam said, 'Leave me alone!' Then the dog said, 'Listen to what the yam says!' When I went to whip the dog with a palm branch the tree said, 'Put that branch down!' Then the palm branch said, 'Do it softly!' Then the stone said, 'Take that thing off me!'"

Literary Analysis
Humorous Writing
How does the fisherman's response, an example of understatement, add humor to this passage?

"Is that all?" the man with the fish trap asked. "Is that so frightening?"

"Well," the man's fish trap said, "did he take it off the stone?"

"Wah!" the fisherman shouted. He threw the fish trap on the ground and began to run with the farmer, and on the trail they met a weaver with a bundle of cloth on his head.

"Where are you going in such a rush?" he asked them.

"My yam said, 'Leave me alone!'" the farmer said. "The dog said, 'Listen to what the yam says!' The tree said, 'Put that branch down!' The branch said, 'Do it softly!' And the stone said, 'Take that thing off me!'"

Vocabulary Development

CCSS Language 6

Thematic Vocabulary: The Big Question

As students are discussing "Talk," encourage them to use the thematic vocabulary presented in Introducing the Big Question, pp. 424–425. You might encourage them with sentence starters like these:

1. At first, the farmer couldn't *comprehend* . . .
2. He was surprised by the *fact* that . . .
3. When the dog began to speak, the farmer's first *instinct* was . . .
4. As he related the *information*, others along the way . . .
5. What they saw with their *senses* finally *clarified* that . . .

"And then," the fisherman continued, "the fish trap said, 'Did he take it off?'"

"That's nothing to get excited about," the weaver said, "no reason at all."

"Oh yes it is," his bundle of cloth said. "If it happened to you you'd run too!"

"Wah!" the weaver shouted. He threw his bundle on the trail and started running with the other men.

They came panting to the ford in the river and found a man bathing.

"Are you chasing a gazelle?" he asked them.

The first man said breathlessly:

"My yam talked at me, and it said, 'Leave me alone!' And my dog said, 'Listen to your yam!' And when I cut myself a branch the tree said, 'Put that branch down!' And the branch said, 'Do it softly!' And the stone said, 'Take that thing off me!'"

The fisherman panted:

"And my trap said, 'Did he?'"

The weaver **wheezed**:

"And my bundle of cloth said, 'You'd run too!'"

"Is that why you're running?" the man in the river asked.

"Well, wouldn't you run if you were in their position?" the river said.

The man jumped out of the water and began to run with the others. They ran down the main street of the village to the house of the chief. The chief's servants brought his stool out, and he came and sat on it to listen to their complaints. The men began to recite their troubles.

"I went out to my garden to dig yams," the farmer said, waving his arms. "Then everything began to talk! My yam said, 'Leave me alone!' My dog said, 'Pay attention to your yam!' The tree said, 'Put that branch down!' The branch said, 'Do it softly!' And the stone said, 'Take it off me!'"

"Wah!" the weaver shouted. He threw his bundle on the trail and started running with the other men.

Vocabulary
wheezed (wēzd′) *v.* breathed hard with a breathy sound

Spiral Review
Organization and Structure By this point in the story, what pattern have you noticed in the story's structure?

13

What prompts the man in the river to start to run with the others?

12  Connecting to the Big Question

1. Remind students of the Big Question by recalling that sometimes repetition can help us understand new information. Discuss ways that you use repetition in the classroom to build understanding.
2. Direct students' attention to the bracketed text on p. 579. **Ask:** Why do the farmer and his companions repeat what happened to them in the exact same way to everyone they meet?
   Answer: As they meet new people, they repeat the story to share how amazing it is. They hope that by telling others, they can understand what is going on.
3. **Ask:** Does the group gain understanding of the situation from the perspectives of each added person or from the addition of new objects that can talk? Explain.
   Answer: No. Each new person is equally amazed, so none of them actually achieves understanding. There is no pattern revealed by the additional talking objects, so no new understanding is gained.

Spiral Review

Organization and Structure

1. Remind students that they studied the concepts of organization and structure in the Unit 3 Literary Analysis workshop (pp. 426–439).
2. **Ask** students the Spiral Review question.
   Possible response: The pattern that is established is that each time the man expresses his fear of things talking, another thing talks, adding to his fear.

13 Reading Check

Answer: The man in the river runs with the others in shock when the river asks him a question.

Fluency

Distribute copies of page 579, and pair students. Have students take turns as readers and listeners. Have listeners mark words with which readers struggle. Circulate to monitor students' fluency, then collect the marked up pages. Review difficult words and passages, such as these:

- If students struggle to pronounce *bathing,* point out that when you add *-ing* to *bathe* the *e* is dropped. Read the word aloud again and have students echo to confirm.
- If students stumble over the different speakers, explain that they should track the text with a finger, using the quotation marks to denote a change in speaker. Ask fluent readers to model a change in their tone of voice to indicate each change in speaker. Then have mixed-fluency groups read to reinforce.
- If students have difficulty with the word *recite,* explain that the word has two long vowel sounds. Model correct pronunciation and have students echo.

⑭ Literary Analysis

Humorous Writing

1. Have students retell the story. Then reread the bracketed text.
2. **Ask** the Literary Analysis question: How would this folk tale be different if it ended with the line "Nonsense like that upsets the community"?

   Answer: The folk tale wouldn't be humorous. The humor lives in the fact that even the Chief has something that can talk and doesn't know it. Not only can it talk, but it thinks it's funny that a yam can talk.

Concept Connector

Have students revisit and expand on their ideas from Activating Prior Knowledge on p. 577. In addition, have students compare their Writing About the Big Question responses before reading the selection with their ideas afterwards.

ASSESS

Answers

Critical Thinking

Before students respond, you may wish to have them write a brief objective summary of the selection. As they answer the questions below, remind them to support their answers with evidence from the text.

1. (a) He plans to use it to beat the dog. (b) He doesn't like the dog's tone of voice.
2. (a) At first, the fisherman acts casually, as if it's not unusual that animals and things can talk. (b) He probably thinks the farmer is exaggerating. (c) He probably wonders what else can talk and what else these objects can do.
3. (a) He scoffs at their stories and tells them to get back to work. He thinks they're making it all up. (b) He probably was as startled as everyone else and ran from the stool.
4. **Possible response:** (a) The message is that the strong should not mistreat the weak because such treatment is wrong even if the weak are unable to say so. (b) People might pay more attention to a message delivered with humor rather than one delivered as a lecture.

"And my fish trap said, 'Well, did he take it off?'" the fisherman said.

"And my cloth said, 'You'd run too!'" the weaver said.

"And the river said the same," the bather said hoarsely, his eyes **bulging**.

The chief listened to them patiently, but he couldn't **refrain** from scowling.

"Now this is really a wild story," he said at last. "You'd better all go back to your work before I punish you for disturbing the peace."

So the men went away, and the chief shook his head and mumbled to himself, "Nonsense like that upsets the community."

"Fantastic, isn't it?" his stool said. "Imagine, a talking yam!"

Vocabulary
bulging (bulj iŋ) *adj.* swelling
refrain (ri frān′) *v.* hold back

Literary Analysis
Humorous Writing ⑭
How would this folk tale be different if it ended with the line "Nonsense like that upsets the community"?

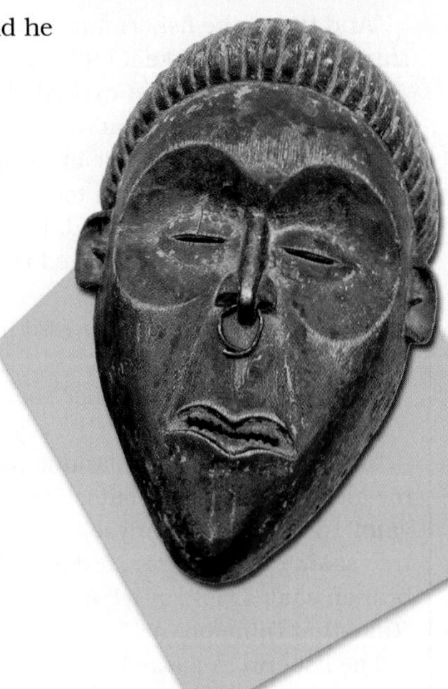

Critical Thinking

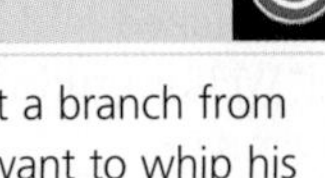

Cite textual evidence to support your responses.

1. **Key Ideas and Details** **(a)** Why does the man cut a branch from the palm tree? **(b) Interpret:** Why does the man want to whip his dog?
2. **Key Ideas and Details** **(a)** What is the fisherman's first response when he hears the farmer's story? **(b) Interpret:** Why doesn't the fisherman become frightened when he hears the farmer's story? **(c) Draw Conclusions:** Why does the fisherman become frightened only after his fish trap talks to him?
3. **Key Ideas and Details** **(a)** How does the chief react when the men tell him what happened to them? **(b) Speculate:** How do you think the chief reacted when he heard the stool talk?
4. **Integration of Knowledge and Ideas** **(a)** What serious message can you infer from the understated humor in this folktale? Explain. **(b)** What might the cultural experience reflected in this tale teach readers? *[Connect to the Big Question: Is knowledge the same as understanding?]*

Vocabulary Development

Vocabulary Knowledge Rating

When students have completed reading and discussing "The Talk" and "Talk," have them take out their **Vocabulary Knowledge Rating Chart.** Read the words aloud once more and have students rate their knowledge of the words again in the After Reading column. Clarify any words that are still problematic. Have students write their own definition and example or sentence in the appropriate column. Then, have students complete the Vocabulary Practice activities on the next page. Encourage students to use the words in further discussion and written work about these selections. Remind them that they will be accountable for these words on the **Selection Test** (*Unit 3 Resources,* pp. 216–218 or 219–221).

After You Read | The Talk • Talk

Comparing Humorous Writing

1. Craft and Structure **(a)** Use a chart like the one shown to identify at least one example of hyperbole, one example of understatement, and one example of comic diction in each piece of humorous writing. **(b)** Explain how each example adds to the humor of the writing.

Type	The Talk	Talk
Hyperbole		
Understatement		
Comic Diction		

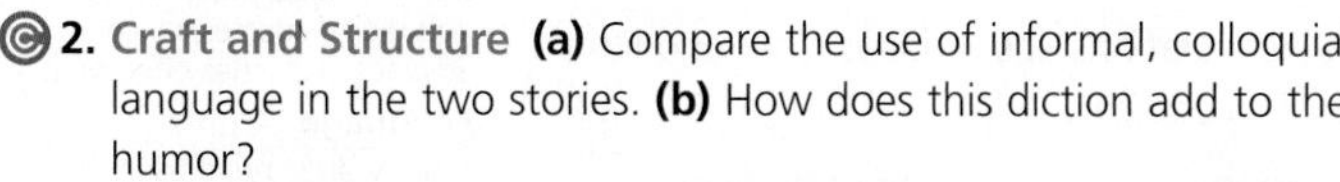

2. Craft and Structure **(a)** Compare the use of informal, colloquial language in the two stories. **(b)** How does this diction add to the humor?

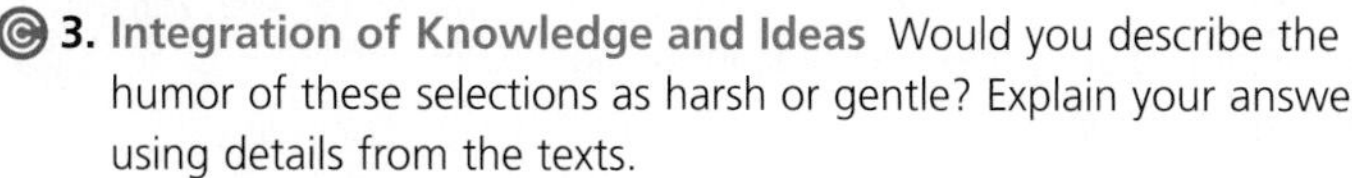

3. Integration of Knowledge and Ideas Would you describe the humor of these selections as harsh or gentle? Explain your answer using details from the texts.

Timed Writing

Explanatory Text: Essay

In an essay, discuss and compare the serious ideas expressed in each of these selections. Consider why the authors chose to present these issues through humor. Provide evidence from the text to support your response. **(25 minutes)**

5-Minute Planner

1. Read the prompt carefully and completely.
2. Gather your ideas by jotting down answers to these questions:
   - What challenges do the characters in each selection face?
   - What specific circumstances or cultural influences do you think might have added to those challenges? Note specific supporting details from each selection.
   - How are humor and seriousness featured alongside one another to convey the author's message?
   - How does the use of humor help suggest that these challenges can be overcome?
3. Reread the prompt, and then draft your essay.

ASSESS

Answers

Comparing Humorous Writing

1. (a) **Sample answer:** "The Talk": **Hyperbole**—our necks wavered, frail as crisp tulips; **Understatement**— People like people with nice faces; **Comic diction**—I think we're ugly. **"Talk": Hyperbole**—Well, wouldn't you run if you were in their position?; **Understatement**—"Now, this is really a wild story"; **Comic diction**—"Imagine, a talking yam!" (b) Students' responses should explain the humor in each example.
2. (a) The language is more colloquial and informal in "The Talk" because the boys are young teenagers. Although the characters in "Talk" are country people, they speak more formally. (b) In "The Talk," comic diction adds to the humor because of the boys' descriptions of their physical attributes. In "Talk," the repeated retelling and people's reactions add to the comic appeal of the tale.
3. The humor in both selections is gentle. The boys are sweet as they admire the girl, and the farmer's escapade is comic and non-threatening.

Timed Writing

1. Review the prompt with students.
2. Have students use the 5-Minute Planner to structure their time. Guide them in answering the bulleted questions. For example, help students identify examples where colloquial language and slang are used for humorous effect while communicating a serious message or point.
3. Allow students 25 minutes to complete the assignment.
4. As students prewrite and draft, have them refer to their completed Comparison Graphic Organizer.

Six Traits Focus

✓	Ideas		Word Choice
✓	Organization		Sentence Fluency
	Voice		Conventions

Assessment Resources

The following resources can be used to assess students' knowledge and skills.

Unit 3 Resources

L1 L2 EL **Selection Test A,** pp. 216–218.

L3 L4 EL **Selection Test B,** pp. 219–221.

L3 L4 **Open-Book Test,** pp. 213–215.

PHLit Online! All assessment resources are available at **www.PHLitOnline.com.**

Common Core State Standards

- Writing 1, 1.a, b, c, d, e; 5, 7, 8
- Language 1.a, 5.b, 2.c

Introducing the Writing Assignment

Review the assignment, using the instruction on the student page.

Rebecca Walker on Persuasive Writing

Show students Segment 3 on Rebecca Walker on *See It! DVD* or from this page in the **Enriched Online Student Edition** at **www.PHLitOnline.com.** Discuss how when writing editorials, students should research information and use Rebecca Walker's technique of combining factual information with personal opinions.

Writing Workshop *Work in Progress*

If students have done the Work-in-Progress assignments on pp. 537 and 563, suggest that they consider developing their Work-In-Progress ideas in an editorial.

What Do You Notice?

1. After students discuss their ideas with partners, have a volunteer read the passage aloud.
2. What do you notice about the title of Hamill's essay? **Possible response:** It states a main idea or thesis that libraries face difficult problems.
3. **Ask:** How do the sentences in the passage relate to Hamill's thesis? **Possible response:** They provide evidence about the value of libraries in the author's childhood.
4. As they draft, encourage students to support their theses with strong and accurate evidence.

Writing Workshop

Write an Argument

Exposition: Editorial

Defining the Form One way to take a stand is to write an **editorial.** An editorial is a brief persuasive essay that presents and defends an opinion. Examples include letters to the editor, position papers, and speeches.

Assignment Write an editorial about an issue that confronts your school or community. Include these elements:

✓ a clear *thesis statement*—a statement of your position on an issue that offers your *perspective* on the subject

✓ *evidence* that supports your position or *claim* and distinguishes it from an alternate or opposing claim

✓ *organization* of text that makes relationships of ideas clear and links sections through effective word choice

✓ *persuasive techniques* that appeal specifically to your audience

✓ a formal style and objective tone and error-free grammar, including *correct use of parallel structures*

To preview the criteria on which your editorial may be judged, see the rubric on page 589.

 **Writing Workshop:** *Work in Progress*

Review the work you did on pages 537 and 563.

WRITE GUY
Jeff Anderson, M.Ed.

What Do You Notice?

Supporting Evidence

Read the following sentences from Pete Hamill's "Libraries Face Sad Chapter" several times.

For those without money, the road to that treasure house of the imagination begins at the public library. When I was a boy, the rooms were crowded with . . . people who came from places where there were no libraries for the poor. With their children, they built the New York in which we now live.

Discuss your ideas about the passage with a partner. Then, consider how you can use evidence to support the opinions in your editorial.

Common Core State Standards

Writing
1. Write arguments to support claims in an analysis of substantive topics or texts, using valid reasoning and relevant and sufficient evidence.
1.a. Introduce precise claim(s), distinguish the claim(s) from alternate or opposing claims, and create an organization that establishes clear relationships among claim(s), counterclaims, reasons, and evidence.
7. Conduct short as well as more sustained research projects to answer a question or solve a problem; narrow or broaden the inquiry when appropriate.
8. Gather relevant information from multiple authoritative print and digital sources, using advanced searches effectively.

Language
5.b. Analyze nuances in the meaning of words with similar denotations.

Reading-Writing Connection

To get a feel for an editorial, read "Libraries Face Sad Chapter" by Pete Hamill on page 530.

Teaching Resources

The following resources can be used to enrich or extend the instruction.

- All *Unit 3 Resources* **Writing Workshop,** pp. 222–223
- All *Common Core Companion,* pp. 179–189, 234–254
- All *Professional Development Guidebook* **Rubric for Self-Assessment: Writing an Editorial,** pp. 263–264
- All *Graphic Organizer Transparencies* **Rubric for Self-Assessment: Editorial,** p. 108
- All *See It!* DVD **Rebecca Walker,** Segments 3 and 4

All resources, including print and video, are also available online at **www.PHLitOnline.com.**

Prewriting/Planning Strategies

Scan newspapers. Look for relevant information from print and digital sources. Notice articles that describe situations that strike you as unfair, foolish, or harmful. Use one of these news stories as a topic for your editorial.

Work with a partner. Pair up with a classmate, and brainstorm for topics that are important to each of you. Select an issue that has compelling arguments. Then, choose a position to support.

Write a thesis statement. After reviewing the information you have in hand, decide which part of the issue to address. Write your opinion about the topic in one sentence. That sentence is your thesis statement, an expression of your position that you must now prepare to defend.

Consider all sides of an issue. Gather evidence from a wide variety of sources. Use advanced Internet searches to narrow or broaden your topic if needed. In a chart like the one shown, record evidence on both sides of an issue. Anticipate and address readers' potential expectations, biases, and misunderstandings. Do not ignore information that contradicts or opposes your position. Plan to include summaries of opposing positions in order to refute them.

Support for School Uniforms	Opposition to School Uniforms
Reduce violence and discrimination	Take choice away from students
Create positive school image	Cause resentment among students

Appeal to logic and emotion. Effective persuasion appeals to both logic and emotion—your audience's thoughts and feelings.

- **Logic:** Make a list of ideas, facts, and details that will make people think, analyze, and reason rather than feel.
- **Emotion:** Brainstorm for relevant anecdotes, or brief stories, descriptions, case studies, analogies, and personal examples that will affect readers' emotions. Quickly jot these down. As you work, experiment with language that carries strong emotional connotations:
  - **Neutral connotation:** Megan continues to work.
  - **Strong connotation:** Megan soldiers on.

TEACH

Prewriting/Planning Strategies

1. Introduce the prewriting strategies, using the instruction on the student page.
2. Have students apply the strategies to choose a topic.

Teaching the Strategies

1. Make a list of news stories on the board. Lead students in a discussion about the stories, giving students a chance to voice and develop their opinions about the issues. Help students **choose topics** about which they have strong opinions.
2. To help students **narrow their topics** by developing thesis statements, tell them to answer this question: What is my position on this topic?
3. Tell students to **gather details** in support of their thesis statements by collecting quotations and facts. Tell students to keep track of any ideas and phrases that are not their own so that they will remember to give appropriate credit.

Think Aloud: Model Writing a Thesis Statement

Model the strategy, using the following "think aloud":

> Let's say I'm writing an editorial about a ballot question that will increase taxes. To write my thesis statement, I ask myself how I feel about the ballot question—what is my opinion of it? I think taxes should not be increased, so I write: *Voters should vote 'no' on Question 2, a proposed law that would increase taxes.* In my editorial I'll give reasons to support this thesis statement.

Six Traits Focus

✓	Ideas	Word Choice
	Organization	Sentence Fluency
	Voice	Conventions

PH WRITING COACH Grade 9

Students will find additional information on writing an editorial in Chapter 9.

Applying Understanding by Design Principles

Clarifying Expected Outcomes: Using Rubrics

- Before students begin working on this assignment, have them preview the Rubric for Self-Assessment (p. 589) to learn what qualities their editorials must have.
- Review the criteria in the Rubric with the class. Before students use the Rubric to assess their writing, work with them to rate the Student Model (p. 588) using the Rubric.
- If you wish to assess students' editorials with either a 4-point or a 6-point scoring rubric, see *Professional Development Guidebook,* pp. 263–264.

Drafting Strategies

1. Introduce the drafting strategies, using the instruction on the student page.
2. Have the students apply the strategies as they draft.

Teaching the Strategies

1. Write this example on the board and have students rank the points according to their persuasiveness:

   Thesis: Citizens should pay extra taxes to have the residential streets repaved.

   Intended Audience: Homeowners who move frequently

   Point 1: Repaving the streets would make for smoother driving.

   Point 2: Repaving the streets would raise property values.

   Point 3: Repaving the streets would make the community more presentable.

   Have students state the reasoning behind their rankings.
   Possible Answer: Ranked from the most important—Point 2, Point 3, Point 1. Financial concerns would be most important to the audience. The community's appearance would also affect resale values.
2. Have students review their supporting evidence by writing an *S* above statistical evidence, an *E* above expert opinions, a *P* above personal observations, and a *T* above testimonials.

Think Aloud: Model Distinguishing Fact from Opinion

Model the strategy, using the following "think aloud":

I know that a fact is a statement that can be proven true. I might include this fact in my editorial: *The tax increase will be $285 per household.* An opinion is a personal judgment or belief. I might also include this opinion in my editorial: *The tax increase would cause a hardship for many senior citizens.* I can base my opinion on the facts.

Six Traits Focus

✓	Ideas		Word Choice
✓	Organization		Sentence Fluency
	Voice		Conventions

Drafting Strategies

Create a structure for your draft. Plan a strategy for presenting your ideas. Be sure to structure arguments and ideas in a sustained and logical fashion.

- **Evaluate your arguments.** Review all the points that support your thesis, and consider their impact on your intended audience. Then, rank them according to their persuasiveness.
- **Use an outline.** Use your ranking to write an outline showing order-of-importance organization. Start with your least important point and build toward your most persuasive point. In addition, be sure to indicate where you will address counterarguments. The chart shown demonstrates order-of-importance organization for an editorial.

Distinguish between fact and opinion. Your thesis and arguments are statements of opinion that must be validated or supported with evidence. Facts—information that can be proved true—are the strongest evidence. Weak arguments pile opinions on top of opinions; strong arguments back opinions with relevant facts. As you draft, weave together your facts along with details that support them.

Provide evidence. For each point you make, produce convincing support. Types of effective evidence include the following:

- **Statistics:** numbers that show the impact of an issue or a proposal
  If we adopt this plan, we can save $100 every week, or $5,200 a year.
- **Expert opinions:** the viewpoints or advice of those who have relevant training and experience
  Dr. Samuel Rothman has published a checklist for those who want to start saving money—and his suggestions are easy to follow.
- **Personal observations:** your own experiences with the topic
  It happens every month—I get the paycheck from my job and the money is gone before I know it!
- **Testimonials:** statements from observers that reinforce an argument
  Dean Smolens says, "I have been tracking my spending for two weeks, and I have noticed several ways to cut back without making drastic changes."

Provide a concluding statement. Write a strong conclusion that will help readers remember your argument. For example, include a final thought or quotation that summarizes your thesis.

The use of valid and relevant quotations, as well as expressions of accepted beliefs and logical reasoning, may also help clarify your arguments. As you draft, be sure to maintain a formal style and objective tone.

Common Core State Standards

Writing

1.a. Introduce precise claim(s), distinguish the claim(s) from alternate or opposing claims, and create an organization that establishes clear relationships among claim(s), counterclaims, reasons, and evidence.

1.b. Develop claim(s) and counterclaims fairly, supplying evidence for each while pointing out the strengths and limitations of both in a manner that anticipates the audience's knowledge and concerns.

1.d. Establish and maintain a formal style and objective tone while attending to the norms and conventions of the discipline in which they are writing.

1.e. Provide a concluding statement or section that follows from and supports the argument presented.

Organizing Your Arguments

Present thesis statement.
↓
Present arguments to support thesis.
↓
Address counterarguments.
↓
Provide strongest argument in support of thesis.
↓
Provide a logical concluding statement, summarizing argument and supporting thesis.

Strategies for Using Technology in Writing

Tell students that they should always question facts obtained from Internet sources. Point out that some commercial sites—those with addresses ending in .com—feature propaganda and can be unreliable. Tell them that reputable commercial sites, such as the *New York Times,* exist as well.

Tell students that educational and government sites—those with addresses ending in .edu and .gov—are usually reliable. Point out that even these sites, however, should be critically assessed.

Encourage students to ask these questions when using information from any Web site:

- Who is the author? Why is the author qualified to write on this subject?
- Why is the author writing on this subject? Does the author have a bias?
- Who sponsors the Web site? Does this sponsor have a bias on the topic?
- How does the information compare to information from other sources?

Writers on Writing

Rebecca Walker On Choosing the Right Details

Rebecca Walker is the author of "Before Hip-Hop was Hip-Hop" (p. 435).

This excerpt is from the introductory essay to a book I edited about new perspectives on masculinity. I think about what I am going to write for a long time, maybe months, before committing my thoughts to the page. Long before I sat down to write, I knew I would prompt readers to think about masculinity in new ways by using this personal exchange between my son and me. What I didn't know was how I would finish the piece.

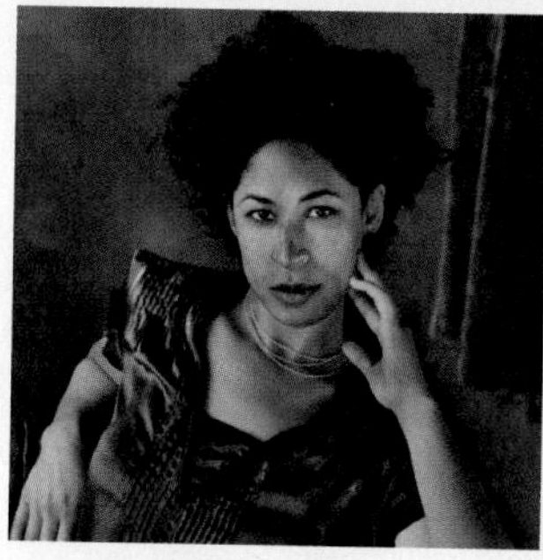

"Taking one's initial impulse to completion, that's the challenge . . ."
—Rebecca Walker

Professional Model:

from *What Makes a Man*

After a big bowl of his favorite pasta, he sat on a sofa in my study and read his science textbook as I wrote at my desk. . . . As we worked under the soft glow of paper lanterns, . . . I could feel a shift as he began to remember, deep in his body, that he was home, that he was safe, that he didn't have to brace to protect himself from the expectations of the outside world.

I wanted to convey a sense of peace and relaxation, so I added this detail to draw the reader into the tranquility of the "scene."

An hour or so passed like this before he announced that he had a question. . . . "I've been thinking that maybe I should play sports at school."

. . . I cocked my head to one side. "What brought this on?"

"I don't know," he said. "Maybe girls will like me if I play sports."

Excuse me?

I used italics here to suggest my surprise and outrage, and to reinforce a direct and intimate connection with the reader.

My boy is intuitive, smart, and creative . . . At the time he loved animals, Japanese anime, . . . and everything having to do with snowboarding. He liked to help both of his grandmothers in the garden. He read science fiction. . . . and was beginning what I thought would be a lifelong love affair with chess.

I included actual things my son enjoyed to add authenticity and texture, and to provide a strong counterpoint to sports.

Maybe girls would like him if he played sports?

Rebecca Walker on Choosing the Right Details

Review the passage on the student page with the class, using Walker's comments to deepen students' understanding of choosing details to illustrate certain points.

Teaching From the Professional Model

1. Show students Segment 3 on Rebecca Walker on ***See It! DVD*** or from this page in the **Enriched Online Student Edition.** Discuss how Walker uses details to reinforce the goal that she has for the writing.
2. Tell students that details can be used to convey the "feeling" of a setting. Give students the example of a deteriorated abandoned house as a setting. **Ask** students for a detail that could be put in the story to convey the scary "feeling" of the house.
   Possible response: The writer could use the detail of cold, biting air blowing through the broken, jagged glass of the windows.
3. **Ask** students how Walker's *"Excuse me?"* expression reinforces a connection with the reader.
   Possible response: The expression gives the reader a glance into the thought process of the narrator, showing the reader the narrator's true feelings about her son's request.
4. Write the following two sentences on the board:
   - *We walked through the unkempt yard.*
   - *We stepped over the mounds of trash and waded through the yard's knee-high grass.*

   Ask students which sentence gives more authenticity and texture. Have students explain their answers.
   Answer: Sentence 2 uses very specific details to make the description of the yard vivid and believable.

Enriched Online Student Edition
Show or assign the video online at **www.PHLitOnline.com.**

Revising Strategies

1. Introduce the revision strategies, using the instruction on the student page.
2. Have students apply the strategies as they revise their editorials.

Teaching the Strategies

1. Have students share drafts in small groups. Have them jot down questions and counterarguments that come to mind during the discussion. They can address these issues as they revise their work.
2. Suggest that students write the opposing arguments they will address on self-sticking removable notes. Tell them to stick the notes at points where it seems appropriate to address these views. Then have students write their arguments.
3. As students revise, have them replace weak verbs with strong ones and overused and non-specific nouns and adjectives with vigorous, specific ones. Provide these examples and have students choose the stronger, more exact verbs, nouns, and adjectives.
   - *The mayor needs to show* (courageous, good) *leadership.*
   - *We* (demand, want) *action on the proposal.*
   - *The park's board of directors should* (grasp, take) *this opportunity.*
   - *The* (leaders, city council) *has/have a responsibility to maintain our parks.*

   Answers: *courageous; demand; grasp; city council*

Six Traits Focus

✓	Ideas	✓	Word Choice
✓	Organization		Sentence Fluency
	Voice		Conventions

Revising Strategies

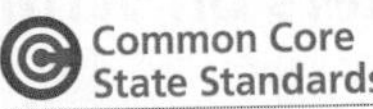

Common Core State Standards

Writing
1.c. Use words, phrases, and clauses to link the major sections of the text, create cohesion, and clarify the relationships between claim(s) and reasons, between reasons and evidence, and between claim(s) and counterclaims.
5. Develop and strengthen writing as needed by planning, revising, editing, rewriting, or trying a new approach, focusing on addressing what is most significant for a specific purpose and audience.

Language
1.a. Use parallel structure.

Revise to address readers' concerns. Not all of your readers will agree with your perspective. Show them that you are aware of their potential questions, opposing positions, and counterclaims and that you understand their concerns, biases, and expectations.

- Review your draft and highlight controversial claims that a critic of your position would oppose.
- To make sure you understand each opposing argument, write a summary that captures its main idea and line of reasoning.
- For each claim, develop strong counterarguments that you can support with explanations and evidence.
- Find a point in your editorial where you can include this information smoothly.

Choose powerful words. To be persuasive, your essay should include precise words that link major sections together, create a unified whole, and clarify relationships between ideas as they convey meaning and tone.

Neutral: Some adults *dislike* today's students' fashions.
Powerful: Some adults *deplore* today's students' fashions.

Neutral: Joanna *did not want* to wear a uniform.
Powerful: Joanna *refused* to wear a uniform.

Check a thesaurus for powerful words like the ones in this chart.

Ordinary	Powerful
Walk	Pace, trudge, scramble, shuffle
Like	Be fond of, enjoy, appreciate, adore
Nice	Pleasant, kind, gentle, thoughtful
Boring	Uninteresting, tedious, dreary, dull, mind-numbing

Peer Review

Exchange drafts with a partner. Review each other's work, highlighting weak words that could be replaced by stronger ones. Then, revise your draft, replacing neutral language with words that will encourage your readers to feel and think. After you have made your revisions, exchange drafts with your partner again. Discuss whether the new word choices are more effective.

Strategies for Test Taking

Encourage students to use online dictionaries and thesauruses to replace weak nouns, verbs, and adjectives with more vivid, precise words. Tell students that when they use online thesauruses they should check the definitions of synonyms to make sure that the words fit the context of their writing.

WRITER'S TOOLBOX

Conventions | Sentence Fluency | Voice | Organization | Word Choice | Ideas

Revising to Create Parallelism

Parallelism is the use of similar grammatical forms or patterns to express similar ideas. Effective use of parallelism adds rhythm and balance to your writing and strengthens connections among your ideas.

Identifying Nonparallel Constructions Parallel constructions place equal ideas in words, phrases, or clauses of similar types. Nonparallel constructions present equal ideas in an unnecessary mix of grammatical forms, producing awkward, distracting shifts for readers.

Nonparallel: Dress codes are less restrictive, less costly, and are not a controversial system.

Parallel: Dress codes are less restrictive, less costly, and less controversial.

Fixing Nonparallel Constructions Follow these steps:

1. Identify similar or equal ideas within a sentence.
2. Determine whether the ideas are expressed in the same form—for example, all nouns or all prepositional phrases.
3. Rewrite the sentence so that all the elements match the stronger pattern. Choose forms that produce the smoothest rhythm or require the fewest words.

Sample Parallel Forms	
Nouns	sharp eyes, strong hands, deft fingers
Verbs	to ask, to learn, to share
Phrases	under a gray sky, near an icy river
Adverb clauses	when I am happy, when I am peaceful
Adjective clauses	those who read with care, those who act with concern

Grammar in Your Writing

Review several paragraphs in your editorial, highlighting any sentences in which you present a series of ideas. Be sure your sentences contain parallel constructions as well as correct subject-verb agreement. Revise your sentences as needed.

Differentiated Instruction for Universal Access

EL Strategies for English Learners

Tell students that understanding the connotations of words is important when revising word choices. Explain that a word's connotation is the feeling and mood that the word evokes. For example, *relaxed* and *lazy* have similar meanings but different connotations. Explain that *relaxed* has a more positive connotation. Tell students that it suggests a casual, at-ease attitude, whereas the connotation of *lazy* reflects an unwillingness to make an effort or a refusal to work.

Tell students that dictionaries will help them understand the connotations of words. Explain that sometimes dictionaries explain the differences, but usually they must look up a word, study the example sentences, and infer the connotation.

Revising to Create Parallelism

1. Introduce the grammar skill, using the instruction on the student page.
2. Discuss the examples and the strategies for using parallelism.
3. Have students follow the instruction under Grammar in Your Writing to correct errors in their drafts.

Teaching the Grammar Skill

1. Read aloud the examples of nonparallel and parallel sentences.
2. Guide students in an evaluation of each of the two sentences by asking: Which is more rhythmic? Which is more memorable? Which is more effective? Lead students to understand that parallelism is more rhythmic, which makes it more memorable and effective.
3. Provide students with these additional examples of nonparallel sentences. Have them rewrite the statements in parallel form.
   - *I like riding my bike along the lake even more than I like to swim in it.*

   Answer: *I like riding my bike along the lake even more than I like swimming in it.*
   - *The helicopter hovered above the treetops and then began swooping down toward the valley.*

   Answer: *The helicopter hovered above the treetops and then swooped down toward the valley.*
   - *The audience was more ecstatic, more responsive, and it appreciated the performance more.*

   Answer: *The audience was more ecstatic, more responsive, and more appreciative of the performance.*
   - After students revise their editorials for parallel construction, have them read their revised sentences aloud, evaluating the rhythm.

Student Model

Review the Student Model with the class, using the annotations to analyze the writer's successful use of the elements of an editorial.

Teaching From the Student Model

1. Explain that the Student Model is a sample and that their own editorials may be longer.
2. Point out that the thesis statement is in the first paragraph, but it is not the first sentence. Tell students that the writer explains the situation first and places the thesis at the end, where it has greater impact.
3. Explain that including information from a published press release adds credibility to Braden's arguments.
4. **Ask** students to explain whether they think that Braden's evidence is convincing.

   Possible response: His evidence is convincing because it is factual and detailed.
5. **Ask** students to identify the additional insight the writer offers in the concluding paragraph.

   Answer: The writer suggests that dress codes will help with violence and discrimination in schools.

Connecting to Real-Life Writing

Point out to students that they will use the techniques of persuasive writing in everyday situations. For example, persuasion could be used to try and convince a friend to go hiking instead of swimming. Students could also use persuasion when writing a note requesting a teacher's permission to attend a special event instead of class. Point out to students that as they grow older, they may choose careers, such as law, sales, or business management, in which persuasion plays an important role.

Student Model: Braden Danbury, Cumming, GA

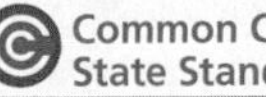
Common Core State Standards

Language
2.c. Spell correctly.

Dress Codes May Succeed Where School Uniforms Have Failed

School uniforms are becoming increasingly popular as a way to combat school violence and discrimination. Uniforms, while they may help somewhat, cause problems of their own. Students argue that it is their right to wear what they choose and uniforms violate that right. A less strict code is the answer to both of these problems, keeping appropriate attire in the school while allowing individuals to choose what they wear.

Braden offers a clear thesis statement in the form of a proposal that addresses a key problem.

Uniforms require students to wear specific shirts and pants or skirts, thus eliminating the element of choice. School uniforms may cause friction between students and school officials, which can have negative consequences. Dress codes, on the other hand, are less restrictive than school uniforms and cause less resentment among students. Students enjoy choosing what to wear to school each day, coordinating what they wear with how they feel.

While students' safety is often cited as a leading justification for requiring uniforms, safety hits the bottom of the list in a press release from the National Association of Elementary School Principals. In fact, safety ranks below such trivial things as school image. This calls into question why uniforms are touted as the answer to school safety issues.

Braden finds a way to deal with counterarguments based on safety concerns.

Dress codes make the difference where it counts. They keep students safe while forcing them to do nothing other than make sure their clothes meet acceptable standards. An added benefit of dress codes is that schools with uniform policies pay much more than schools with dress codes. Schools with uniforms have to design, order, sell, and distribute the uniforms they wish to have for their school. In addition, school officials spend time and resources making sure they receive payment for uniforms. These expenses may be hidden, but they are real. Dress codes are much less expensive to implement and follow.

Braden offers evidence that supports his position.

With the rise in school violence, students and their dress often come under suspicion and scrutiny. In addition, the wide variety of clothing in our high schools may lead students to make prejudicial judgments about each other. Dress codes address the problems of violence without causing resentment among students. They are less strict, giving the students more freedom in how they dress, while allowing school officials to set general guidelines. The amount of money it would take to implement a dress code is a fraction of the cost of school uniforms. Dress codes are not the only answer, but they are a step toward combating violence and discrimination in the schools.

Braden restates his thesis and summarizes his evidence. He also offers an additional insight.

Strategies for Test Taking

Remind students that when they take written tests, it is important to read the writing prompt carefully. A good strategy is to look for key words in the prompt. For example, if they see words such as *persuasive, opinion,* or *think* in the prompt, students should recognize them as clues about what to expect in the rest of the prompt and to determine how to respond.

Editing and Proofreading

Review your draft to correct errors in grammar, spelling, and punctuation.

Focus on spelling. An editorial that includes spelling errors loses its authority to convince. Check the spelling of each word. Look for words that you frequently misspell, and make sure they are correct. **Content-area words** come from science, history, literature, or other subject areas. While content-area words are not necessarily difficult, they may be unfamiliar to you. These words may have letters that are silent or other challenging letter patterns. Focus on the words you may spell wrong and learn their correct spellings.

Spiral Review

Earlier in this unit, you learned about **adjectives** (p. 536) and **adverbs** (p. 562). Check your essay to be sure you have used these grammatical forms correctly.

Publishing and Presenting

Consider one of the following ways to share your writing:

Deliver an oral presentation. Using technology to produce dynamic visuals, present your editorial to the class. As you speak, be sensitive to your audience. If they seem confused or doubtful, modify your word choice to clarify your ideas. After you finish, take a poll to determine whether or not you convinced your audience of your position.

Submit your editorial to a newspaper. Send your work to the school or community newspaper, condense it into a letter to the editor, or post it online.

Reflecting on Your Writing

Writer's Journal Jot down your answers to this question:
How did writing about your topic help you understand it?

Rubric for Self-Assessment

Find evidence in your writing to address each category. Then, use the rating scale to grade your work.

Criteria	Rating Scale (not very – very)
Focus: How clearly does your thesis statement express an opinion?	1 2 3 4 5
Organization: How effectively do you organize your arguments?	1 2 3 4 5
Support/Elaboration: How well do you use evidence to support your position?	1 2 3 4 5
Style: How powerful is your use of persuasive language?	1 2 3 4 5
Conventions: How correct is your grammar, especially your use of parallel structures?	1 2 3 4 5

Differentiated Instruction for Universal Access

Strategies for Special-Needs Students

Some students might be effective oral communicators, while others may communicate more effectively in writing. Help them choose methods of publishing their work that complement their strengths and promote confidence.

EL Strategies for English Learners

Students who are not yet proficient in English may need additional help with proofreading. You might work with each student to create a proofreading checklist that meets his or her specific needs. The list may include such items as verb tense, subject-verb agreement, pronoun-antecedent agreement, and homophones.

Editing and Proofreading

1. Introduce the editing and proofreading focus, using the instruction on the student page.
2. Have students edit and proofread their editorials, correcting grammar, spelling, punctuation, and word choice. Make sure they look for errors of the type noted in the lesson focus and the Spiral Review.

Teaching the Editing Focus

Using student suggestions, begin a class bank of frequently misspelled words such as *canceled, harass,* and *nickel.* Students can add to the word bank throughout the year.

Six Traits Focus

	Ideas		Word Choice
	Organization		Sentence Fluency
	Voice	✓	Conventions

ASSESS

Publishing and Presenting

1. Have listeners respond to the oral presentations with constructive criticism. **Ask:** Which point was most convincing? Were counter-arguments addressed effectively? What additional arguments could be given to support the speaker's position?
2. If students' editorials or letters are published, have them create a classroom display focusing on the theme of "Being Heard."

Reflecting on Your Writing

Lead students in discussing the reflecting question. Then ask them to respond: Do you feel that your argument is convincing? How comfortable are you with the persuasive writing process?

EXTEND/ASSESS

Answers

Common Core State Standards

- Language 4, 4.a, d

Words With Multiple Meanings

1. Introduce the skill, using the instruction on the student page.
2. Review the definitions and examples in the introduction.

Think Aloud: Model the Skill

Use the following "think aloud" to model the skill of correctly using words with multiple meanings. Say to students:

Let's say I read the sentence, "You can *mine* that report for many good ideas." First, I check which part of speech *mine* is, and I see that it's a verb. Next, I check a dictionary to see what definitions *mine* has as a verb. The first definition is "to dig in the earth for the purpose of extracting ore, coal, etc." I know this can't be the meaning I'm looking for, because my sentence is about a report and ideas, not earth and digging. I go back and find another definition, "to extract valuable materials from." Looking at my sentence, I know that an idea is a valuable thing that can be extracted from a report, so that must be the intended meaning of *mine* in this sentence.

Vocabulary Workshop

Words With Multiple Meanings

Many words in English have **multiple meanings,** or definitions that vary greatly. Look at these sentences. An identification of the word *mine* follows each sentence.

- This book is *mine,* but you are welcome to borrow it. (possessive pronoun)
- The coal *mine* has been in operation for many years. (noun describing a place where coal is dug)
- You can *mine* that report for many good ideas. (verb meaning "take from")

When it is not clear what a word means in a sentence, look for **context clues.** Context clues are in the information surrounding a word and can be used to help you determine the word's meaning. Then, refer to a dictionary and find the definition that fits the context. Notice the context clues in this sentence:

The three people made a compact to meet again in a year's time.

- "Three people" suggests that they worked together and "made" the compact.
- The people planned to do something: "meet again."

By checking a dictionary, you will find that *compact* can mean "an agreement between two or more individuals."

Common Core State Standards

Language

4. Determine or clarify the meaning of unknown and multiple-meaning words or phrases based on grades 9–10 reading and content, choosing flexibly from a range of strategies.

4.a. Use context as a clue to the meaning of a word or phrase.

4.d. Verify the preliminary determination of the meaning of a word or phrase.

Practice A Write the meaning of each italicized word in the sentences below. If necessary, consult a dictionary.

1. **(a)** Spinach is a good source of *iron.*
   (b) When using an *iron,* make sure that it is not too hot for the fabric.
2. **(a)** The truck moved slowly up the steep *grade.*
   (b) My teacher had to stay up most of the night to *grade* the essays.
3. **(a)** The hikers were able to find a *pass* through the mountain.
   (b) Were you able to *pass* the entrance exam for the university?
4. **(a)** Cook the sauce over *medium* heat until it begins to boil.
   (b) The artist's favorite *medium* is pastels.

590 Types of Nonfiction: Essays, Articles, and Speeches

Practice A

Answers:

1. (a) *iron:* a mineral important to a person's diet
   (b) *iron:* a device for smoothing wrinkles in clothes
2. (a) *grade:* a slope or incline
   (b) *grade:* give a score or mark to
3. (a) *pass:* a narrow route through a lower section in a mountainous area
   (b) *pass:* succeed by getting a certain score or mark
4. (a) *medium:* midway between low and high
   (b) *medium:* material or form used by an artist

Teaching Resources

Unit 3 Resources
Words with Multiple Meanings, pp. 224–225

Vocabulary Central, featuring definitions, audio pronunciations, Word Families, and activities, is online at **www.PHLitOnline.com.**

Practice B Using context clues, write a definition in your own words for the underlined word in each sentence. With a partner, discuss which context clues helped you to determine the meaning of the word. Then, look up the word in a dictionary and confirm or correct your definition.

1. A deeply rounded back gave the violin a rich tone.
2. The stern of the boat swung around, and we floated backward down the stream.
3. George was uncomfortable about taking the money, so he skirted the issue.
4. The kids came thundering down the stairs when they were called for dinner.
5. Which branch of the bank is located nearest to your house?
6. My sister got a ticket for peddling cosmetics door to door without a license.
7. It is important for cooks to keep their cupboards full of the staples they use every day.
8. I wouldn't hire Sue because she has base motives for wanting this job.
9. The child scrambled up the bluff through thorn bushes in pursuit of his runaway cat.
10. The movie does not warrant all the rave reviews it has been getting.

PHLit Online!
www.PHLitOnline.com
- Illustrated vocabulary words
- Interactive vocabulary games
- Vocabulary flashcards

Activity Choose five of the underlined words in Practice B. Look in a dictionary to find the multiple meanings of these words. Write each word on a separate note card like the one shown. Fill in the left column of the note card according to one of the word's meanings. Fill in the right-hand column according to another of the word's meanings. Then, trade note cards with a partner, and discuss the different meanings and uses of the words that each of you found.

Word	First Meaning	Second Meaning

Comprehension and Collaboration

Working with a partner, look up each of these words in a dictionary and talk about their multiple meanings: *scale, review, charge*. Then, write sentences using context clues that clearly show three distinct meanings for each word.

Differentiated Instruction for Universal Access

Enrichment for Gifted and Talented Students

Challenge students to write a few paragraphs in which they use as many multiple-meaning words as possible. They should use at least two meanings for each word, and they should include context clues.

ASSESS/EXTEND

Answers

Practice B

Sample answers:

1. Context clues: *rounded back, tone;* my definition: "vibrant"; dictionary definition: "resonating"
2. Context clues: *boat, backwards;* my definition: "the back of a boat"; dictionary definition: "the rear end of a boat"
3. Context clue: *uncomfortable;* my definition: "avoided"; dictionary definition: "to attempt to ignore"
4. Context clues: *came down;* my definition: "running heavily"; dictionary definition: "making a resounding, loud noise"
5. Context clues: *located, bank;* my definition: "building"; dictionary definition: "extension of a building"
6. Context clues: *cosmetics door to door;* my definition: "selling"; dictionary definition: "trying to sell by going from place to place"
7. Context clues: *cupboards;* my definition: "basic food items"; dictionary definition: "main elements of a diet"
8. Context clues: *wouldn't hire;* my definition: "dishonorable"; dictionary definition: "without principles"
9. Context clues: *scrambled up;* my definition: "high land"; dictionary definition: "steep cliff"
10. Context clues: *doesn't, rave reviews;* my definition: "deserve"; dictionary definition: "justify"

Activity

Provide dictionaries for students.

Comprehension and Collaboration

Assign partners and give each pair a dictionary. Students should write three sentences for each word, using a different meaning of the word in each. Each sentence should include context clues clearly pointing to a specific meaning of the word.

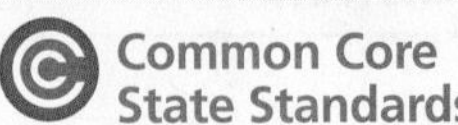

EXTEND

Common Core State Standards

- **Speaking and Listening 3, 4, 5, 6**

Learn the Skills

1. Introduce the workshop, including the activity on page 593.
2. Tell students that since listeners can't recheck ideas in your persuasive speech the way a reader can, it is necessary to organize supporting ideas logically and to connect them clearly to the main idea so that listeners can follow your line of reasoning.
3. Tell students that learning about their audience will reveal how much depth they need to go into during the speech. For example, if a speaker knows beforehand that listeners are likely to oppose the speech, the speaker can show flaws in the opposing position.
4. Explain that students should aim for a good balance of logical and emotional appeals as they craft a speech.
5. Discuss ways that speakers can use volume level, pauses, and changes in tone to hold listeners' attention.
6. Give students examples of visual aids they can use to enhance a speech:
   - Scenes from films and television shows
   - Photographs and other images
   - Bar graphs and pie charts

SPEAKING AND LISTENING

Communications Workshop

Delivering a Persuasive Speech

The ability to speak persuasively is a valuable life skill that enables you to successfully present ideas and proposals. These speaking strategies can help you refine your persuasive speaking skills.

Learn the Skills

Use these strategies to complete the activity on page 593.

Organize your evidence. Once you have determined your position on an issue or idea, gather and arrange your evidence into an introduction, body, and conclusion. Decide which method of organization will lend power to your speech. For example, you may want to use an order-of-importance organization, beginning with less-important points and leading up to your strongest argument.

Know your audience. Understanding your audience will help you present your speech effectively.

- Adjust **word choice, evidence,** and **rhetoric** to the interests, cultural perspectives, and knowledge levels of your listeners.
- **Anticipate questions** and **counterarguments.** Identify fallacious reasoning in counterarguments. You can often disarm skeptical listeners by discussing and refuting their ideas.
- **Respond to the interests of your listeners** by showing how they are affected by the issue and could benefit from your proposals.

Use rhetorical devices. Strengthen your appeals to logic and emotion by using rhetorical devices.

- **Parallel structures**—the deliberate repetition of words, sentences, and phrases—help to make your ideas clear and memorable.
- **Rhetorical questions**—questions with obvious answers that support your points—capture the attention of your audience.

Use your voice and gestures effectively. Demonstrate confidence in your ideas through your posture, bearing, and facial expression.

- Make eye contact with all your listeners, not just one or two people.
- Vary the volume, tone, and pacing of your voice to emphasize key points and to keep your audience engaged.
- Use hand gestures to support what you are saying.

Use digital media. Consider enhancing your presentation by using digital media. Visuals, such as computer-generated charts or graphs, or audio and video clips can emphasize your points and add interest to your speech.

Common Core State Standards

Speaking and Listening
3. Evaluate a speaker's point of view, reasoning, and use of evidence and rhetoric, identifying any fallacious reasoning or exaggerated or distorted evidence.
4. Present information, findings, and supporting evidence clearly, concisely, and logically such that listeners can follow the line of reasoning and the organization, development, substance, and style are appropriate to purpose, audience, and task.
5. Make strategic use of digital media in presentations to enhance understanding of findings, reasoning, and evidence and to add interest.
6. Adapt speech to a variety of contexts and tasks, demonstrating command of formal English when indicated or appropriate.

Strategies for Preparing a Persuasive Speech

Tell students that gathering reliable evidence to support their main point is a crucial part of creating a persuasive speech. Share the following suggestions:

- Look for facts, statistics, expert opinions, and eyewitness accounts as evidence to support your argument. Be sure your sources are authoritative.
- Depending on your topic, you can also use anecdotes from your own experience that have taught you something about the topic.
- Make sure your evidence is from reliable sources and can be verified. If using Internet sources, look especially for information on Web sites that end in .edu or gov.
- Keep a list of your sources so you can respond appropriately if a listener challenges something you say.

Practice the Skills

Presentation of Knowledge and Ideas Use what you've learned in this workshop to complete the following activity.

ACTIVITY: Deliver a Persuasive Speech

Develop a persuasive speech in which you take a stand on a current issue. Persuade your audience to agree with your views. Then, poll your classmates to see if your speech has altered their perspectives. Consider these questions as you prepare your speech.

- Which organization of ideas best serves my topic and argument?
- What facts and expert opinions support my claim?
- What counterarguments and questions should I anticipate and address?
- What is the knowledge level and cultural perspective of my audience?
- What rhetorical devices will strengthen my appeal to logic and emotion?

Use the Presentation Checklist to help you evaluate your classmates' presentations.

Presentation Checklist

Persuasive Speech Content

Rate the speaker's content on a scale of 1(very poor) to 5 (very good) for each of these items. Explain your ratings.

- presented ideas clearly and in a logical order Rating: ___
- included well-chosen facts and expert opinions Rating: ___
- anticipated and addressed counterarguments and claims Rating: ___
- met the knowledge level and perspective of the audience Rating: ___
- used rhetorical devices effectively Rating: ___

Persuasive Speech Delivery

Rate the speaker's delivery on a scale of 1 (very poor) to 5 (very good) for each of these items. Explain your ratings.

- formal language Rating: ___
- effective speaking rate Rating: ___
- enunciation Rating: ___
- conventions of language Rating: ___
- eye contact Rating: ___
- appropriate volume Rating: ___
- appropriate gestures Rating: ___

Comprehension and Collaboration With your classmates, discuss how you evaluated each speaker. As a group, discuss what makes a persuasive speech effective and why.

EXTEND/ASSESS

Practice the Skills

1. Review the assignment with students. Make sure that they understand that in their speech they should take a stand about something and present a convincing argument. Encourage them to consider the other side of the argument as they develop their speech.
2. Explain to students that they should use a copy of the Presentation Checklist to evaluate their own presentation and the presentations made by classmates.
3. Before students give their presentations to the class, remind listeners to ask questions if any points are unclear. To maintain order, encourage them to raise their hands and wait to be acknowledged by the presenter before stating their questions. Suggest that students making presentations scan the classroom from time to time so they will notice any students who have questions.

Evaluate the Activity

1. Evaluate students' presentations on the basis of the clarity and completeness of their ideas, the inclusion of evidence that supports their argument as well as responses to possible counterarguments, and the effective organization of the supporting evidence.
2. When the class discusses the presentations that were easiest to follow, encourage students to make note of the features of those presentations that made them effective and to incorporate those techniques in their future presentations.

Differentiated Instruction for Universal Access

EL Strategy for English Learners

Suggest that these students choose a topic with which they are familiar and for which they can find non-technical or local oral sources. If students are using oral sources, point out that they need to interview people who know the issue well and are considered experts.

Suggest that students take along a tape recorder when they interview their sources. Remind them that they should not record their sources unless they have received the interviewee's permission. Also, suggest that before they begin the interview, they record the interviewee's name, the date, and the time of the interview. Point out that during the interview they can also ask the interviewee to clarify any unclear ideas or technical vocabulary.

Once students have recorded the interview, they can listen to the recording, write words they do not understand, and look these up in a dictionary.

Cumulative Review

In this Common Core Assessment Workshop (pp. 594–597), students apply and reinforce their mastery of the Common Core State Standards and the skills taught in Unit 3. The practice is divided into four sections, including a section of Performance Tasks addressing CCS Reading standards.

1. Before assigning each section, review the relevant Common Core State Standards and unit skills with students.
2. Set a time limit for the multiple-choice items in each section, allowing a little over one minute per question. Allow twenty minutes for any Timed Writing questions.
3. Administer each of the first three sections of the Cumulative Review (pp. 594–597).
4. Use the Performance Tasks on pages 598–599 to assess the depth of students' mastery of standards taught in the unit. Follow the suggestions on teacher pages 598–599 for assigning tasks and for supporting and evaluating student performance.

Reteaching Skills

1. For each practice, use the Reteach chart on the same page as the answers to determine which skills require reteaching, based on which items students answered incorrectly.
2. Reteach these skills prior to assigning the **Benchmark Test** for the second half of Unit 3 (***Unit 3 Resources,*** pp. 227–232).

Cumulative Review

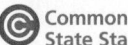

Common Core State Standards

RI.9-10.1, RI.9-10.2, RI.9-10.4, RI.9-10.5, RI.9-10.6, RI.9-10.8; L.4.a

[For the full wording of the standards, see the standards chart in the front of your textbook.]

I. Reading Literature

Directions: *Read the passage. Then, answer each question that follows.*

The statistics are in on teen smoking, and they are not good. According to the Institute of Medicine of the National Academy of Sciences, it is a fact that teens who watch movies that have characters who smoke are more likely to start the habit. Watching smoking in movies is responsible for 52 percent of young smokers. Smoking in movies is even more effective than cigarette advertising. The best way to slow the pace of teens starting is to limit their access to movies that feature characters who smoke. One way to do that is to require an R rating for movies that contain smoking. Then, teens under 17 will have to be accompanied by a parent to view the movie.

Won't there be a shortage of movies for teens? The idea behind rating smoking movies R is to encourage moviemakers to exclude smoking from PG-13 movies. It is not aimed at limiting the movie market for this audience but at convincing the movie industry to help effect positive change in the lives of young people.

Doesn't requiring an R rating restrict creativity and force censorship? The simple answer is *No.* Moviemakers who want to include smoking can opt for an R rating instead of a PG-13. They have the opportunity to exercise their creativity with few limits under the R rating. In addition, the movie industry is responsible for the rating system, not the government. Therefore, it is not censorship. However, requiring an R rating does provide incentive for moviemakers to omit the smoking scenes because PG-13 movies bring in significantly more money than R movies.

Given the outstanding statistics that prove smoking in movies contributes to teen smoking, one would think the movie industry would be eager to help. However, moviemakers and actors alike have received massive amounts of money for placing brands of cigarettes in their movies. As it stands, the movie industry makes millions from the audience and the tobacco companies, while the tobacco companies make millions from teen smokers. Teens who start smoking at a young age spend their lives addicted to a deadly substance. To give teens a better chance of avoiding the dangerous smoking trap, R ratings should be applied to any movie that includes smoking.

Strategies for Test Taking

Remind students to reread passages when necessary, in order to be sure they are answering questions correctly. Sometimes a first reading will miss an important fact or opinion.

Benchmark

Reteach skills as indicated by students' performance, following the Reteach charts on pages 595–597. Then, administer the end-of-unit **Benchmark Test** (*Unit 3 Resources,* pp. 227–232.) Follow the **Interpretation Guide** for the test (*Unit 3 Resources,* p. 239) to assign reteaching pages as necessary in the **Reading Kit.** Use **Success Tracker** online to automatically assign these pages.

1. Which word best describes the **tone** of this essay?

A. lighthearted
B. serious
C. informal
D. uncertain

2. What sentence best summarizes the **central idea** of this passage?

A. Teens should be warned that smoking is unhealthy and dangerous.
B. Smoking in movies is even more effective than cigarette advertising.
C. Teens who watch movies with smoking often begin to smoke, so movies with smoking should be rated R to cut teen viewership.
D. Movies have too great an influence on what teenagers do, and their parents should take a greater interest in what they are watching.

3. What makes the author's statement, that teens who watch movies with smoking will start the habit, more credible and valid?

A. The author's source is the National Academy of Sciences, a respectable organization.
B. The author included this information in the first paragraph, so it must be true.
C. This is a logical conclusion.
D. Movies that include smoking should be required to have an R rating.

4. Which **supporting detail** serves as evidence for the argument that an R rating would not be too restrictive?

A. Doesn't requiring an R rating restrict creativity and force censorship?
B. The simple answer is *No.*
C. Moviemakers who want to include smoking can opt for an R rating instead of a PG-13.
D. Therefore, it is not censorship.

5. The opening sentences of paragraph 2 and 3 contain which **rhetorical device?**

A. parallelism
B. restatement
C. rhetorical question
D. analogy

6. To what does this statement appeal? *Given the outstanding statistics that prove smoking in movies contributes to teen smoking . . .*

A. reason
B. sense of humor
C. emotion
D. curiosity

7. **Vocabulary** Which word is closest in meaning to the underlined word *incentive*?

A. motivation
B. regulation
C. laws
D. hope

8. What do you think is the **author's purpose?**

A. to save people money
B. to expose the movie industry
C. to decrease teen cigarette use
D. to anger the tobacco industry

9. This text is an example of what type of essay?

A. an expository essay
B. an informational essay
C. a narrative essay
D. a persuasive essay

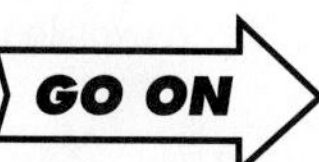

Timed Writing

10. In a multi-paragraph essay, **identify** the appeals to reason and emotion in this piece of writing. **Explain** how diction, syntax, and rhetorical devices advance the author's purpose.

GO ON

ASSESS/RETEACH

Answers

I. Reading Literature

Answers With Explanations

1. B—The subject matter and the approach are both serious. *Incorrect answers:* A—The article is not lighthearted. C—Although the article is informal, its tone is serious. D—The writer expresses no doubt.
2. C—This statement combines the most important issues. *Incorrect answers:* A—This is implied in the passage, but is not the main idea. B—This is a supporting statement for the main idea. D—The passage does not address the role of parents.
3. A—The author quotes a respected authority. *Incorrect answers:* B—Placement does not affect credibility. C—Conclusions can be logical but untrue. D—This is an opinion, not a statement of support.
4. B—This contradicts the objection, though it does not give more support. *Incorrect answers:* A—This asks a question instead of answering it. C—This merely restates the idea. D—This is a conclusion, not a supporting detail.
5. C—Both ask questions, which the paragraphs then answer. *Incorrect answers:* A—The questions are not parallel in form. B—The questions do not ask the same thing in different words. D—The questions are not analogies.
6. A—Statistics are used to appeal to readers' reasoning. *Incorrect answers:* B—The statement is not humorous. C—Authors use statistics to appeal to reason. D—same explanation as for C.
7. A—Because R-rated movies make more money than PG-13 movies, moviemakers should be motivated to act in the desired way. *Incorrect answers:* B—*Incentive* means "a benefit to be gained by acting in a certain way." C—same explanation as for B. D—same explanation as for B.
8. C—The author hopes to discourage teens from smoking. *Incorrect answers:* A—The passage does not mention the financial cost of smoking. B—The passage simply wants to change the movie industry rating system. D—The passage does not wish to provoke the tobacco industry.

Continued from right column

9. D—The essay hopes to persuade people to support a change. *Incorrect answers:* A—The passage has information, but it aims to persuade. B—same explanation as for A. C—The passage is not a narrative.

Timed Writing

10. Students' responses should cite specific examples of appeals to reason and emotion and explain how they are aided by diction, syntax, and rhetorical devices.

Reteach

Question	Instructional Pages to Reteach
1	429, 441
2	441, 465
3	519
4	465
5	539
6	519
7	—
8	519
9	519, 539

II. Reading Informational Text

Answers With Explanations

1. B—The trainer, in the dominant position, has authority over the dog. *Incorrect answers:* A—The restrictions on behavior are imposed by someone with authority. C—Dominance does not imply skill. D—This is completely unrelated.
2. D—The passage explains dog training. *Incorrect answers:* A—The passage is not written as an advertisement. B—The writer shares some personal information, but that is not his or her purpose. C—The author mentions some research early in the passage, but this is not the purpose.
3. D—The passage is written to instruct. *Incorrect answers:* A—The passage is not playful. B—The passage is not ironic. C—The passage is not bitter.
4. B—Since this phrase is used by the writer, readers would likely want to know more about it. *Incorrect answers:* A—If a reader already has a dog, he or she has already researched this question. C—This study is only mentioned briefly in the article. D—This is a good question, but is not the focus of the passage.

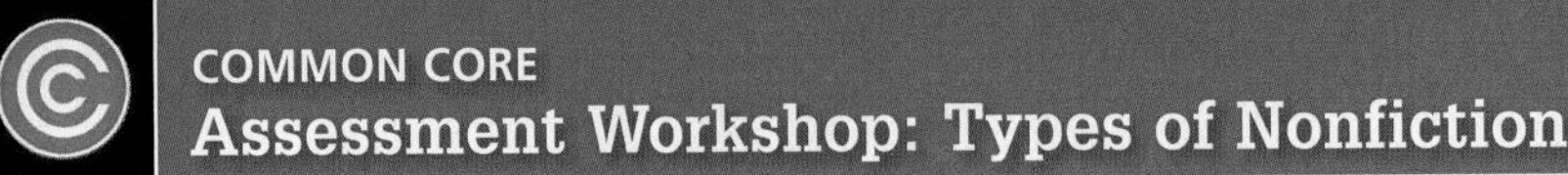

COMMON CORE
Assessment Workshop: Types of Nonfiction

II. Reading Informational Text

Directions: *Read the passage. Then, answer each question that follows.*

Common Core State Standards

RI.9-10.4, RI.9-10.6; L.3, L.4.a
[For the full wording of the standards, see the standards chart in the front of your textbook.]

Dog Training: Out With the Old, In With the New

Alpha Enforcement

Much of dog behavioral training is based on the Alpha dog mentality. This method is based on outdated information. Studies conducted in the 1940s on wolf packs led to training of housedogs in the same way we interpreted wolf behavior—training through physical force.

Alpha enforcement requires the person to handle the dog physically, rolling him or her over to force submission. Little reward is given for fear of upsetting the balance of the hierarchy. This training often results in a submissive dog, but not necessarily a well-adjusted dog. With a few changes, the Alpha dog mentality can work for both pet and human.

Alpha Mentality

Establishing one's self as the Alpha is not a matter of physical dominance. Doing so is about *mentality*—controlling the dog's access to things he needs. For example, if a dog wants to go outside, have him sit first. If a dog wants food, have him sit again. Wait until the dog performs the desired behavior, and only then reward him. He will quickly learn that to have access to things he wants, he will have to perform a specific task. No fear or aggression is involved between human and dog. Patience, however, is key.

As a dog trainer of ten years, I began my career as an Alpha enforcer and have evolved into true Alpha mentality. Thus, my human and canine clients live happy lives without the presence of fear or physical dominance.

1. **Vocabulary** What is the best definition for the underlined word *dominance*?
   A. restriction
   B. authority
   C. skill
   D. decline
2. What is the author's **purpose?**
   A. to gain business
   B. to share a personal anecdote
   C. to present research
   D. to explain dog training techniques
3. Which word best describes the author's **tone?**
   A. playful
   B. ironic
   C. bitter
   D. instructive
4. Which of the following questions would a new dog owner be most likely to research after reading this article?
   A. Is owning a dog a lot of work?
   B. Is "Alpha mentality" training effective?
   C. Why do scientists study wolf behavior?
   D. Are wolves and dogs very similar?

596 Types of Nonfiction: Essays, Articles, and Speeches

Reteach

Question	Instructional Pages to Reteach
2	487
3	426, 429, 430, 441
4	492

III. Writing and Language Conventions

Directions: *Read the passage. Then, answer each question that follows.*

(1) 57 Spruce Avenue
Brooklyn, NY 11201

(2) Call Anytime Cell Service
1000 Cellular Circle
Brooklyn, NY 11201

(3) Hello Sir or Madam:

(4) I am writing to request a termination of my one-year cellular phone contract. (5) I signed the contract three months ago. (6) The service has been sporadic. (7) I am unable to send or receive calls from my home or neighborhood. (8) In addition, when I make calls outside this area the likelihood of the call being dropped is very high.

(9) I realize that there is normally a termination fee; however, I was assured when the contract was signed by me that I would have no service problems in my area. (10) As a result of my difficulty, I would like the termination fee waived and want to receive a partial refund on the bills I have paid. (11) I need that cash! (12) Please notify me of your plan.

(13) Sincerely,
(14) *Katrina Vasquez*
(15) Katrina Vasquez

1. What should be added to the letter's **heading?**

A. the writer's name
B. the date
C. the signature
D. nothing

2. What would be the best **salutation** for this letter?

A. Dearest Friend:
B. To You:
C. Dear Sir or Madam:
D. Hello Sir or Madam:

3. Which sentences should be combined?

A. sentences 4 and 5
B. sentences 5 and 6
C. sentences 8 and 9
D. sentences 11 and 12

4. Which sentence should be removed so that the letter has formal, polite language throughout?

A. sentence 4
B. sentence 6
C. sentence 11
D. sentence 12

5. Which phrase in sentence 9 is a use of **passive voice** that should be revised?

A. *was assured*
B. *would have no service*
C. *have no service problems*
D. *was signed by me*

Differentiated Instruction for Universal Access

EL Strategy for English Learners

Review the issue of tone by walking students through item 4. Call on students to identify the features of a formal and an informal tone. Point out that, in this case, they need to find the sentence that is *not* formal. Next, guide students in eliminating incorrect answer choices.

- A—Words like *request* and *termination* and the phrase "I am writing to request" are formal rather than conversational. (Eliminate.)
- B—*Sporadic* is a formal word; more informal would be *spotty* or *sketchy*. (Eliminate.)
- C—The direct statement, the use of the informal *cash*, and the exclamation point all mark this sentence as informal. (Correct response.)
- D—The polite *please* and formal *notify me* make this sentence consistent with a formal tone. (Eliminate.)

Guide students in seeing that **C** is the best choice.

ASSESS/RETEACH

Answers

III. Writing and Language Conventions

Answers With Explanations

1. **B**—The date is always included in a letter's heading. *Incorrect answers:* A—The writer's name appears in the closing of the letter. C—same explanation as for A. D—The heading requires a date.
2. **C**—This is the correct salutation for a formal business letter. *Incorrect answers:* A—This is a salutation for an informal letter. B—This is incorrect as a salutation. D—Same explanation as B.
3. **A**—These sentences contain information that can be in one sentence. *Incorrect answers:* B—The information in these sentences does not go together. C—same explanation as for B. D—Sentence 11 should be deleted from the letter.
4. **C**—This statement is both informal and irrelevant to the arguments advanced in the letter. *Incorrect answers:* A—This sentence is written in formal language. B—same explanation as for A. D—same explanation as for A.
5. **D**—The phrase "was signed by me" is awkward. *Incorrect answers:* A—Although this is in the passive voice, it is appropriate to the meaning of the sentence. B—This phrase uses active voice. C—same explanation as for B.

Reteach

Question	Instructional Pages to Reteach
1	514
2	514
3	515
4	513
5	514

Performance Tasks

Assigning Tasks/Reteaching Skills

Use the chart below to choose appropriate Performance Tasks by identifying which tasks assess lessons in the textbook that you have taught. Use the same lessons for reteaching when students' performance indicates a failure to fully master a standard. For additional instruction and practice, assign the *Common Core Companion* pages indicated for each task.

Task	Where Taught/ Pages to Reteach	*Common Core Companion* Pages
1	426	137–149
2	428, 430	110–116
3	429, 430	117–129
4	428, 430	130–136
5	441, 465	97–109, 293–299
6	427, 430, 519, 539, 563, 566, 584, 592	137–149, 179–189, 286–292
7	430, 539, 592	117–129, 293–299

Assessment Pacing

In assigning the Writing Tasks on this student page, allow a class period for the completion of a task. As an alternative, assign tasks as homework. In assigning the Speaking and Listening Tasks on the facing page, consider having students do any required preparation as a homework assignment. Then, allow a class period for the presentations themselves.

Evaluating Performance Tasks

Use the rubric at the bottom of this Teacher Edition page to evaluate students' mastery of the standards as demonstrated in their Performance Task responses. Review the rubric with students before they begin work so they know the criteria by which their work will be evaluated.

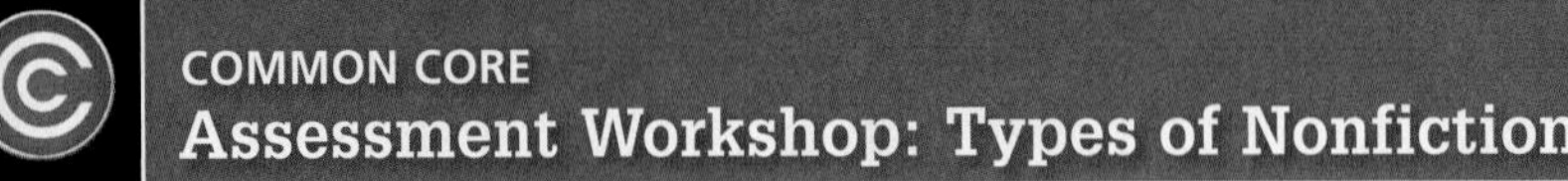

COMMON CORE
Assessment Workshop: Types of Nonfiction

Performance Tasks

Common Core State Standards

RI.9-10.3, RI.9-10.4, RI.9-10.5, RI.9-10.6; W.9-10.1, W.9-10.2; SL.9-10.1.a, SL.9-10.1.c, SL.9-10.1.d, SL.9-10.3, SL.9-10.4; L.9-10.1, L.9-10.1.a, L.9-10.3, L.9-10.5

[For the full wording of the standards, see the standards chart in the front of your textbook.]

Directions: *Follow the instructions to complete the tasks below as required by your teacher.*

As you work on each task, incorporate both general academic vocabulary and literary terms you learned in this unit.

Writing

Task 1: Informational Text [RI.9-10.6]

Determine an Author's Point of View

Write an essay in which you identify the author's purpose and point of view in a work from this unit.

- Identify the selection you will use as the focus for your essay. State the work's topic and explain the author's general and specific purposes for writing about this topic.
- Describe the author's point of view on the topic. Explain how that perspective influences his or her choice of supporting information and details.
- Evaluate how well the author uses rhetorical devices, such as parallel construction, repetition, and figurative language, to advance his or her point of view. Include examples from the text to support your evaluation.
- Edit your essay to ensure that you have used words that precisely convey your meaning.

Task 2: Informational Text [RI.9-10.3]

Analyze the Development of Ideas or Events

Write an essay in which you analyze how an author unfolds a series of ideas or events in a work of literary nonfiction in this unit.

- State which work you chose, and restate its central idea in your own words. Identify key supporting details.
- Describe how the author introduces each idea or event, and note the order in which these points are presented. Explain how this particular sequence is effective in advancing the author's ideas.
- Note any connections that are drawn between ideas or events in the work. Explain how the author makes the connections clear to the reader.
- Use parallel sentence construction as you draw connections or highlight important ideas.

Task 3: Informational Text [RI.9-10.4]

Analyze Word Choice

Write an essay in which you analyze the way the author's word choice affects the meaning and tone of a nonfiction work from this unit.

- Identify the work you will discuss and briefly summarize its main idea.
- Describe the author's tone and determine the words and phrases that help convey that tone.
- Describe the effect of unusual words, figures of speech, or technical language on the tone.
- Analyze the cumulative impact of the author's word choice on the overall meaning of the work.

Task 4: Informational Text [RL.9-10.5]

Analyze Text Structure

Write an essay in which you analyze in detail how the structure of a work in this unit helps develop and refine the author's ideas.

- State the main ideas or claims presented in the work you have chosen.
- Identify the work's organizational structure—for example, chronological order, comparison-and-contrast, or cause-and-effect.
- Analyze in detail how the text structure helps to develop and refine the author's ideas within paragraphs or sections.
- Conclude by evaluating how well the text's overall structure helps the author achieve his or her purpose.

598 Types of Nonfiction

Performance Task Rubric: Standards Mastery	Rating Scale (not very – very)
Critical Thinking: How clearly and consistently does the student pursue the specific mode of reasoning or discourse required by the standard, as specified in the prompt (e.g., comparing and contrasting, analyzing, explaining)?	1 2 3 4 5
Focus: How well does the student understand and apply the focus concepts of the standard, as specified in the prompt (e.g., development of theme or of complex characters, effects of structure, and so on)?	1 2 3 4 5
Support/Elaboration: How well does the student support points with textual or other evidence? How relevant, sufficient, and varied is the evidence provided?	1 2 3 4 5
Insight: How original, sophisticated, or compelling are insights the student achieves by applying the standard to the text(s)?	1 2 3 4 5
Expression of Ideas: How well does the student organize and support ideas? How well does the student use language, including word choice and conventions, in the expression of ideas?	1 2 3 4 5

Speaking and Listening

Task 5: Informational Text [RI.9-10.2; SL.9-10.4]

Determine the Central Idea

Write and deliver an oral report in which you determine the central idea in a nonfiction work from this unit.

- Identify the work you will discuss, explain who wrote it, and briefly summarize it.
- State your interpretation of the work's central idea.
- Show how you arrived at your interpretation by explaining how the author introduces and develops the key idea. Cite specific details from the work that support your interpretation.
- Present your information clearly, logically, and concisely. Aid your listeners' understanding by giving them an annotated copy of the work, a list of key supporting details you will discuss, or other helpful information.
- Use the conventions of standard English when presenting your report.

Task 6: Informational Text [RI.9-10.6; W.9-10.1; SL.9-10.3]

Evaluate a Speaker's Views

Deliver an oral presentation in which you evaluate the views expressed by an author of one of the speeches in this unit.

- Choose a speech from this unit. Then, plan an oral presentation in which you evaluate the writer's point of view, reasoning, supporting evidence, and use of rhetorical devices.
- Analyze the views expressed in the speech. Then, identify examples of strong or weak reasoning and evidence that the writer uses to support his or her argument.
- Evaluate the author's use of rhetorical devices, such as parallel structure, repetition, figures of speech, and other types of forceful language.
- End by expressing your overall evaluation of the speech's validity and effectiveness.

Task 7: Informational Text [RI.9-10.4; SL.9-10.4]

Analyze Word Choice, Meaning, and Tone

Write and deliver a visual presentation in which you analyze the impact of word choice on the meaning and tone of a nonfiction work from this unit.

- Choose a work that exhibits interesting word choices. Identify at least two key words and phrases from that text.
- For each word or phrase you chose, write a paragraph in which you analyze its figurative, connotative, or technical meanings. Explain how those meanings affect the meaning and tone of the work as a whole.
- Find or create visuals, such as photographs, drawings, charts, or graphs, that illustrate the ideas you expressed in words.
- Organize your written materials and visuals into a presentation that sets out a clear line of reasoning.
- Share your presentation with the class, transitioning logically between reading from your text and showing the visuals.

Is knowledge the same as understanding?

At the beginning of Unit 3, you participated in a discussion of the Big Question. Now that you have completed the unit, write a response to the question. Have you changed your mind about the relationship between knowledge and understanding after thinking about the selections in this unit? Do you still feel the same way? Support your response with at least one example from the selections you read and one from a different subject area or your own experiences. Use Big Question vocabulary words (see p. 425) in your response.

Differentiated Instruction for Universal Access

Strategy for Less Proficient Readers

Assign a Performance Task, and then have students meet in groups to review the standard assessed in that task. Remind students of the selections or independent readings to which they have previously applied the standard. Have groups summarize what they learned in applying the standard and then present their summaries. Discuss, clarifying any points of confusion. After students have completed their tasks, have groups meet again to evaluate members' work. Encourage members to revise their work based on the feedback they receive.

Strategy for English Learners

For each assigned Performance Task, review the instructions with students. Clarify the meaning of any unfamiliar vocabulary, emphasizing routine classroom words such as *rhetorical, evaluation,* and *transition* and academic vocabulary such as *illustrate.*

Next, have students note ideas for their responses. Pair students, and have them review each other's notes, asking questions to clarify meaning and suggested improvements. Encourage students to ask for your assistance in supplying English words or expressions they may require.

Supporting Speaking and Listening

1. Consider having students work with partners or in groups to complete Performance Tasks involving listening and speaking. For tasks that you assign for individual work, you may still wish to have students rehearse with partners, who can provide constructive feedback.
2. As students rehearse, have them keep in mind these tips:
   - Present findings and evidence clearly and concisely.
   - Observe conventions of standard English grammar and usage.
   - Be relaxed and friendly but maintain a formal tone.
   - Make eye contact with the audience, pronounce words clearly, and vary your pace.
   - When working with a group, respond thoughtfully to others' positions, modifying your own in response to new evidence.

Linking Performance Tasks to Independent Reading

If you wish to cover the standards with students' independent reading, adapt Performance Tasks of your choice to the works they have selected. (Independent reading suggestions appear on the next page).

Is knowledge the same as understanding?

1. Remind students that the unit Big Question is "Is knowledge the same as understanding?"
2. Have students complete their responses to the prompt on the student page. Point out that they have read selections in this unit that deal with the differences between knowledge and understanding. Certain selections may suggest that some people may have one without the other. Students should draw on these selections in their responses. Remind them that they can also draw on their own experiences and what they have learned in other subject areas in formulating their answers.

Independent Reading

Titles featured on the Independent Reading pages at the end of each unit represent a range of reading, including stories, dramas, and poetry, as well as literary nonfiction and other types of informational text. Throughout, labels indicate the works that are CCSS Exemplar Texts. Choosing from among these featured titles will help students read works at increasing levels of text complexity in the grades 9–10 text complexity band.

Independent Reading and Pacing

See the Unit Overview and Pacing Plan, pp. 424a–424b, for suggestions on integrating independent reading with work in the Student Edition.

Using Literature Circles

A literature circle is a temporary group in which students independently discuss a book.

Use the guidance in the *Professional Development Guidebook*, pp. 47-49, as well as the teaching notes on the facing page, for additional suggestions for literature circles.

Meeting Unit 3 CCS Focus Standards

Students can use books listed on this page to apply and reinforce their mastery of the CCS Focus Standards covered in this unit. (The Focus Standards are introduced on pp. 426–429.)

Introducing Featured Titles

Have students choose a book or books for independent reading. Assist them by previewing the titles, noting their subject matter and level of difficulty.

Note: Before recommending a work to students, preview it, taking into account the values of your community as well as the maturity of your students.

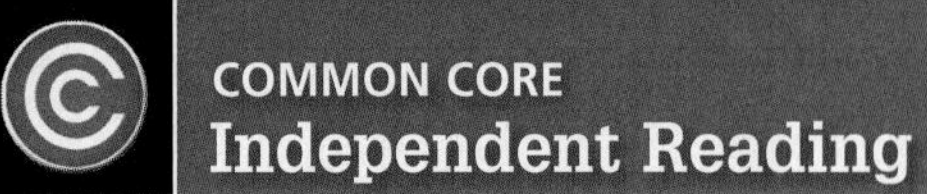

COMMON CORE
Independent Reading

Featured Titles

In this unit, you have read a variety of informational texts, including literary nonfiction. Continue to read on your own. Select works that you enjoy, but challenge yourself to explore new topics, new authors, and works of increasing depth and complexity. The titles suggested below will help you get started.

Informational Texts

Narrative of Sojourner Truth

Born a slave in New York State, Sojourner Truth became a symbol of freedom and justice for both African Americans and women. Her **autobiographical narrative,** dictated by Truth to a neighbor, reveals the transformation of an illiterate slave into a provocative, passionate speaker who paved the way for African American civil rights and feminism.

Life by the Numbers
by Keith Devlin
John Wiley & Sons, 1998 — EXEMPLAR TEXT 

This **nonfiction book** shows readers how math applies to everything: the shape of flowers, the realization of virtual reality, and the physics of sports. The author also provides interesting information about some careers in the field of mathematics.

Biography and Autobiography

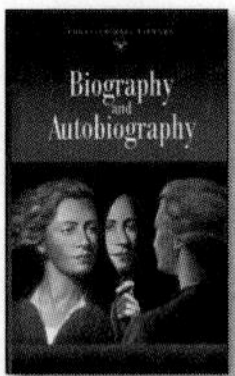

From Doris Kearns Goodwin's recollections of how television revolutionized her neighborhood to Stephen Hawking's story of how he overcame physical limitations, these **biographical** and **autobiographical narratives** give readers fresh perspectives on famous lives.

Cod: A Biography of the Fish That Changed the World
by Mark Kurlansky — EXEMPLAR TEXT

This **nonfiction book** shows how the cod, a simple fish, fed whole villages, caused several wars, and spurred European transatlantic exploration. On a darker note, Kurlansky describes the dramatic decline of this important species as a result of overfishing.

Why We Can't Wait
by Martin Luther King, Jr.
Signet, 2000 — EXEMPLAR TEXT

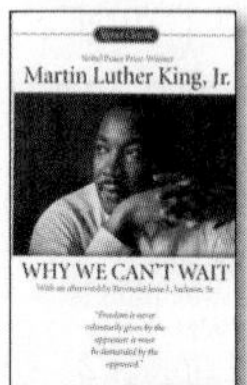

In the 1950s and 60s, Dr. King captured the minds and consciences of a country with his principled stands for justice. This **nonfiction book** is both a description of the Civil Rights movement and a poetic testament to the wisdom and courage of the man who wrote it.

Abraham Lincoln—DK Biography
by Tanya Lee Stone
Dorling Kindersley Publishing, 2005

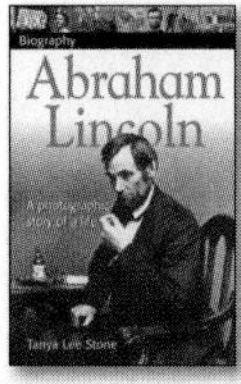

During the perilous days of the Civil War, Abraham Lincoln found himself at the center of events that would transform America as a nation. This **biography** traces Lincoln's life from his boyhood in rural Illinois to the stormy days of his presidency.

Literature

The Killer Angels
by Michael Shaara
Ballantine Books, 1974 — EXEMPLAR TEXT

This Pulitzer Prize–winning **novel** tells the story of the Battle of Gettysburg, three of the most crucial days of the Civil War. Several points of view are used to draw a complete picture of the moments before and during the battle.

Words Under the Words: Selected Poems
by Naomi Shihab Nye
Far Corner, 1995

This rich collection of **poetry** reveals how short poems can make big statements about life. Nye explores everything from her Palestinian heritage to the mysterious donor of a music box in poems that burst with imagery and questions and insights about life.

600 Types of Nonfiction

Text Complexity: Aligning Texts With Readers and Tasks

TEXTS	READERS AND TASKS
• *The Killer Angels* (Lexile: 610L) • *Narrative of Sojourner Truth*	**Below-Level Readers** Allow students to focus on reading for content, and challenge them to interpret multiple perspectives.
• *Biography and Autobiography* • *Cod: A Biography of the Fish That Changed the World* • *Abraham Lincoln—DK Biography* • *Life by the Numbers*	**Below-Level Readers** Challenge students as they read for content. **On-Level Readers** Allow students to focus on reading for content, and challenge them to interpret multiple perspectives. **Advanced Readers** Allow students to focus on interpreting multiple perspectives.
• *Words Under the Words: Selected Poems* (NP) • *Why We Can't Wait* (1200L)	**On-Level Readers** Challenge students as they read for content. **Advanced Readers** Allow students to focus on reading for content, and challenge them to interpret multiple perspectives.

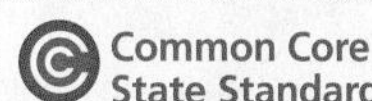

Preparing to Read Complex Texts

Attentive Reading As you read literature on your own, bring your imagination and questions to the text. The questions shown below and others that you ask as you read will help you learn and enjoy literature even more.

Common Core State Standards

Reading Literature/Informational Text
10. By the end of grade 9, read and comprehend literature, including stories, dramas, poems, and literary nonfiction in the grades 9–10 text complexity band proficiently, with scaffolding as needed at the high end of the range.

When reading literary nonfiction, ask yourself...

- Who is the author? Why did he or she write the work?
- Are the ideas the author conveys important? Do they merit my attention? If not, why?
- When did the author live and write? Do the attitudes of a particular time and place affect the ideas the author expresses? If so, how?
- Does any one idea strike me as being the most important? Why?
- How might the author's background and life experiences affect his or her views on the topic?
- How might the author's background and life experiences affect his or her use of language?
- How do my life experiences affect what I understand about this work?
- How do my life experiences affect what I feel about the work?
- What can I learn from this text?

Key Ideas and Details

- Does the author order ideas so that I can follow them? If not, what is wrong with the way the text is ordered?
- Does the author capture my interest right from the beginning, or do I have to work to get into the text? Why do I think that is?
- Does the author give me a new way of looking at a topic? If so, how? If not, why?
- Is the author an expert on the topic? How do I know?
- Has the author made me care about the subject? If so, how? If not, why?
- Does the author use strong evidence? Do I find any of the evidence unconvincing? If so, why?

Craft and Structure

- Does the work seem authentic and true? Does any aspect of the work seem exaggerated, false, or unsupported?
- Do I agree or disagree with the author's basic premise? Why?
- Have I read other works about this or a related topic? What does this work add to my knowledge of the topic?
- How would I write about a similar topic? Would I follow a similar approach as the author's, or would I handle the topic differently?

Integration of Ideas

Text Complexity: Reader and Task Support Suggestions

INDEPENDENT READING

Increased Support Suggest that students choose a book that they feel comfortable reading and one that is a bit more challenging. Pair a more proficient reader with a less proficient reader and have them work together on the more challenging text. Partners can prepare to read the book by reviewing questions on this student page. They can also read difficult passages together, sharing questions and insights. They can use the questions on the student page to guide after-reading discussion.

Increased Challenge Encourage students to integrate knowledge and ideas by combining the Big Question and the Unit Focus concepts in their approach to two or more featured titles.

For example, students might consider what the authors of *Life by the Numbers* and *Why We Can't Wait* want readers to understand about their subjects. In addition, students can focus on the ways that authors develop a central idea in literary nonfiction by using supporting details.

Preparing to Read Complex Texts

1. Tell students they can be attentive readers by bringing their experience and imagination to the texts they read and by actively questioning those texts. Explain that the questions they see on the student page are examples of questions to ask about works of literary nonfiction.
2. Point out that, like writing, reading is a "multidraft" process, involving several readings of complete works or passages, revising and refining one's understanding each time.

Key Ideas and Details

3. As an example, review and amplify the fourth bulleted item. **Ask:** What key ideas and details could you cite as evidence that one idea seems most important?

   Possible response: You might point out that an idea is repeated frequently or that the narrator provides many different kinds of supporting details to emphasize the idea's importance.

Craft and Structure

4. **Ask:** What details of craft and structure would you cite as evidence that the author is an expert on the topic?

   Possible response: You might cite an author's effective use of statistics and facts or a description of a personal experience that illustrates an important point.

Integration of Ideas

5. **Ask:** How would you evaluate the author's ideas to determine whether you agree with his or her basic premise?

   Possible response: You would analyze the author's key arguments and the supporting details that are used to back the main points.
6. Finally, explain to students that they should cite key ideas and details, examples of craft and structure, or instances of the integration of ideas as evidence to support their points during a book discussion. After hearing the evidence, the group might reach a consensus or might agree to disagree.

Unit 4 Features Overview

Unit Genre and Big Question

In this unit, students will analyze poetry. As they read they will discuss responses to the unit Big Question: How does communication change us?

Unit 4 Collections

Teach Collections are presented in leveled pairs. To teach the skills and meet the objectives, you need to assign only one selection in each pair.

Differentiate and Reinforce Choose the collection in a pair that is best suited for your students, based on the Text Complexity box shown on the next page. You may use the other collection to reinforce skills or provide enrichment.

Integrate Skills Each collection presents students with a reading strategy, a literary analysis concept, a vocabulary skill, and grammar instruction. Students can extend learning in the writing and extension activities.

Additional Unit Features

Literary Analysis Workshop Teach and model the Unit Focus standards. Spiral Review notes enable students to revisit these skills over the course of the unit.

Reading for Information Students analyze functional, expository, and argumentative texts and complete Timed Writing activities.

Comparing Literary Works Students study two literary works either within or across genres.

Test Practice: Reading This feature provides extra practice in utilizing reading skills to master assessments.

Writing Workshops Two writing workshops appear in each unit, along with rubrics and instruction in the writing process.

Assessment Workshop Cumulative Skill Review and Performance Tasks provide a range of assessment opportunities.

Independent Reading Students broaden their knowledge as they read longer works of increasing complexity.

THE BIG ?
How does
communication
change us?

PHLit Online!
www.PHLitOnline.com

Teaching From Technology

Log on at this address for the following:

Enriched Online Student Edition
- full narration of selections
- interactive graphic organizers
- linked **Get Connected!** and **Background** videos
- all worksheets and other student resources

Professional Development
- the *Professional Development Guidebook* online
- additional professional development articles by program authors

Planning, Assigning, and Monitoring
- software for online assignment of work to students, individually or to the whole class
- a system for tracking and grading student work

Unit 4 Poetry

www.PHLitOnline.com

Hear It!

- Selection summary audio
- Selection audio
- BQ Tunes

See It!

- Author videos
- Big Question video
- Get Connected videos
- Background videos
- More about the authors
- Illustrated vocabulary words
- Vocabulary flashcards

Do It!

- Interactive journals
- Interactive graphic organizers
- Grammar tutorials
- Interactive vocabulary games
- Test practice

603

Instructional Resources

Unit 4 Resources supports Unit skills with pages of the following types:

- **Diagnostic and Benchmark Tests** assess and monitor student progress at mid-Unit and at Unit's end.
- **Vocabulary and Reading Warm-ups** provide additional vocabulary support, based on Lexile rankings of words, for each selection. "A" **Warm-ups** are for students reading two grades below level. "**B**" **Warm-ups** are for students reading one grade below level.
- **Selection Support** These practice pages are available for each selection:
  - Reading Skill
  - Literary Analysis
  - Writing About the Big Question
  - Vocabulary
  - Support for Writing
  - Support for Extend Your Learning
  - Enrichment

PHLit Online!

All worksheets and other student resources are also available online at **www.PHLitOnline.com.**

Text Complexity: Accessibility for Various Ability Levels

This chart gives a general text complexity rating to help you decide which collection in each leveled pair is more appropriate for your students. **Choose one collection in each pair, or choose to teach both.** You will meet the objectives for the pair when you teach either of the two collections. For additional guidance on factors that affect the complexity of each collection, see the Leveled Texts page for each collection set.

	✓ More Accessible	✓✓ More Complex
Pair 1	Collection 1	Collection 2
Pair 2	Collection 3	Collection 4
Pair 3	Collection 5	Collection 6
Pair 4	Collection 7	Collection 8

Accessibility for English Learners

This icon indicates support for English learners at point of use in this Teacher's Edition.

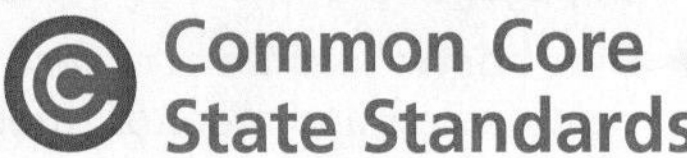

Common Core State Standards

Unit 4 Focus Standards

- Reading Literature 4

Additional Activities and Assessments

- Writing 1, 3, 4
- Speaking and Listening 1, 4, 5
- Language 1, 5
- Reading Literature 2, 5

	Week 1					Week 2					Week 3				
	1	2	3	4	5	1	2	3	4	5	1	2	3	4	5
Introduce the Unit Big Question (pp. 604–605).	●														
Introduce the unit form, poetry, using the Literary Analysis Workshop (pp. 606–609).	●														
Introduce the focus CCS standards for the unit and lead students in a close reading of exemplar texts (pp. 608–615).	●	●													
Teach one collection from Pairing 1 (pp. 616–641).		●	●	●	●	●									
Teach one collection from Pairing 2 (pp. 642–667).						●	●	●	●	●					
Complete the Test Practice: Reading (pp. 668–669).									●						
Teach Reading for Information (pp. 670–675).										●					
Teach Comparing Literary Works (pp. 676–685).											●	●			
Have students complete the Writing Workshop (pp. 686–691).										●	●	●	●	●	
Administer **Benchmark Test 7** (***Unit 4 Resources,*** pp. 120–125).														●	
Reteach skills, judging which skills to reteach by evaluating students' performance on **Benchmark Test 7.**															●

Independent Reading

Have students choose a full-length work from the Independent Reading feature at the end of the unit and read it while working on this unit.

Pacing Suggestions

- Have students read their chosen work for homework.
- Devote parts of class periods in each school week to Literature Circles in which students reading the same work discuss it.

	Week 4					Week 5					Week 6				
	1	2	3	4	5	1	2	3	4	5	1	2	3	4	5
Teach one collection from Pairing 3 (pp. 692–717).	●	●	●	●	●										
Teach one collection from Pairing 4 (pp. 718–739).					●	●	●	●	●						
Complete the Test-Practice: Reading (pp. 740–741).								●							
Teach Reading for Information (pp. 742–747).									●						
Teach Comparing Literary Works (pp. 748–755).										●	●				
Have students complete the Writing Workshop (pp. 756–763).									●	●	●	●	●		
Have students complete the Vocabulary Workshop (pp. 764–765).												●			
Have students complete the Communications Workshop (pp. 768–771).													●		
Have students complete the first three sections of the Assessment Workshop: Poetry (pp. 768–771).													●	●	●
Have students complete the selected Performance Tasks in the Assessment Workshop (pp. 772–773).														●	
Administer Benchmark Test 8 (*Unit 4 Resources,* pp. 227–235).														●	
Reteach skills, judging which skills to reteach by evaluating students' performance on **Benchmark Test 8.**															●

- Cover the focus standards with independent readings and abbreviate review of the focus standards with student-edition selections.
- Do not assign extension activities for selections (day 5 of main selection lessons), except as needed for full standards coverage.
- If students demonstrate reading proficiency, consider omitting Test Practice: Reading features in the unit.

Block and Daily Scheduling

The assignments and activities in this Unit planner are organized by week. You may adjust them to your daily or block schedule. The Time and Resource Manager for each selection set gives specific pacing suggestions, or you may use the comprehensive lesson planning support online at **www.PHLitOnline.com.**

Monitoring Progress

Diagnose Each main collection pairing in the Unit contains a more accessible and a more challenging collection. To determine which collection in each pairing to assign, refer to students' results on the **Vocabulary in Context** section of **Benchmark Test 6, *Unit 3 Resources,*** pp. 233–235 (administered at the end of the previous Unit). Use the **Interpretation Guide** to interpret the results of this diagnostic portion of the test. **Note:** For the most accurate diagnosis of students who score in the middle range of the diagnostic portion of the test, administer the additional diagnostic questions online at **www.PHLitOnline.com.**

Preteach and Prepare As indicated by the diagnostic, prepare students for reading by assigning the **Vocabulary** and **Reading Warm-ups** for the collections you assign.

Teach Follow this Pacing Plan and use the resources to teach the skills and collections. For specific pacing suggestions and a list of resources, see the Time and Resource Manager and the Visual Guide to Featured Selection Resources preceding each collection pairing.

> ***Classroom Management***
> For classroom management suggestions for using leveled texts in a mixed-ability classroom, see Harvey Daniels's professional development essay "Leveled Reading Selections," online at **www.PHLitOnline.com.**

Assess After students have completed the first half of the Unit, administer **Benchmark Test 7**. Administer **Benchmark Test 8** at the end of the Unit.

Intervention and Reteach After administering each test, use the **Interpretation Guide** for the tests to determine which reteaching pages, if any, you should assign from the ***Reading Kit***. The appropriate pages are also available through the online Progress Monitoring software.

CLASSROOM STRATEGIES

Making Connections to Real-World Texts **William G. Brozo**

"Strategic teachers recognize the value of connecting text sources from students' everyday worlds to course readings and topics."

Teachers who use sources from the everyday worlds of youth as embellishment to core textbooks do so because they know that when students find reading interesting and connected to authentic purposes, their positive attitudes toward reading increase. This lends to an increase in reading for information and enjoyment among students (Guthrie & Wigfield, 2000). Furthermore, students' reading comprehension has been shown to be greater with high-interest materials because interesting material maintains their attention more effectively (McDaniel, Waddill, & Finstad, 2000).

In most classrooms a core textbook, such as an English/language arts anthology, is the primary source for reading and learning. Anthologies are filled with enduring quality literature and emerging classics. Yet, unless students are able to relate to these texts on an engaging and meaningful level, they may not take from them as much they should. Strategic teachers recognize the value of connecting text sources from students' everyday worlds to course readings and topics (Larimer & Schleicher, 1999). They know alternative text sources, when linked to the textbook and given legitimacy in school settings, engage students in meaningful reading and learning that can lead to elevated achievement (Bushman & Haas, 2006).

Integrating Real-World and Core Texts

With the textbook as the foundation, teachers can infuse their classrooms with a range of interesting, authentic texts. These texts can be used as motivators for learning, to develop critical reading and thinking, and to expand students' appreciation of ideas and information in the textbook. Teachers who have discovered the benefits of incorporating real-world texts into their instructional practices find students are more engaged and thoughtful learners because the content is more relevant to their experiences (Brozo & Simpson, 2007).

Young Adult Literature The world of young adult literature is wonderfully rich, with countless high-quality books that cover a wide range of topics. These texts can be used as bridge books to the literature in the anthology. For example, before and during the reading of *Romeo and Juliet,* students might read *Romiette and Julio* by Sharon Draper or *Across the Barricades* by Joan Lingard, two young adult novels with parallel plots to Shakespeare's play.

Graphic Novels and Comic Books National surveys tell us that this genre is perhaps the most popular recreational reading choice of adolescents. Graphic novels come in numerous genres, and this variety makes them an enticing and useful resource for teaching and learning. Additionally, graphic novels and comic books include illustrations that serve as visual clues to the meaning of the written narrative. This is an invaluable tool for motivating reluctant readers. Shakespeare's *Romeo and Juliet* can be found in manga, a type of Japanese-styled graphic novel widely read by teens. Set in modern day Tokyo, this version of the play offers students an interesting contemporary compliment.

Primary Documents Primary documents are authentic original texts that will intrigue youths and provoke thoughtful responses. Evidence suggests that students who read primary documents on a fairly frequent basis have higher achievement scores than their peers who rarely see these sources. So there is something about primary sources that makes them attractive to students and promote meaningful and long-lasting learning. Students reading Judith Ortiz Cofer's short story "American History" might use the Internet to access the original 1963 *Time* magazine coverage of Kennedy's assassination or other newspaper accounts of that day in history.

Reality Central Virtually every issue that emerges from the study of selections in the English/language arts textbook can made more relevant with reading and discussion of linked contemporary events and issues. Prentice Hall *Reality Central* provides a linked article for every selection so teachers can routinely integrate real-world topics into their instruction. In addition, teachers can encourage students to can find articles in popular magazines or current newspapers that deal with issues and themes related to those in stories, poems, and plays. For example, as a link to a poem that stresses beauty in nature, students can locate current articles about development of government lands or about preserving wildlife refuges. Reality Central articles that link to selections in Unit 4 of this textbook address such topics as artificial intelligence (for "All Watched Over by Machines of Loving Grace"), grief support (for "The Bells"), and messages in horror movies (for "the Raven.")

Popular Media and Music Scaffolding for new understandings means working with what adolescents bring to the classroom, including their interest and knowledge of popular music. For example, a teacher might ask students to bring in lyrics from their favorite songs to analyze for figurative and symbolic expressions and idioms. Students learning about authors' use of *allusion* might be asked to use the Internet to find examples of this literary device in video clips of their favorite movies, musical groups, cartoons, and TV shows.

Modeled Strategy

See pp. 634 and 699 for point-of-use notes modeling these strategies.

Teacher Resources

- ***Professional Development Guidebook***
- ***Classroom Strategies and Teaching Routines* cards**

Log on as a teacher at **www.PHLitOnline.com** to access a library of all Professional Development articles by the Contributing Authors of Prentice Hall *Literature*.

William G. Brozo

William G. Brozo writes the "Strategic Moves" column for the journal *Thinking Classroom* and co-authors the "Content Literacy" column for *The Reading Teacher.* His work focuses on enhancing the literate lives of boys and making teaching more responsive to the needs all students.

Supporting Research

Brozo, W.G., & Simpson, M.L. (2007). *Content literacy for today's adolescents: Honoring diversity and building competence.* Upper Saddle River, NJ: Merrill/Prentice Hall.

Bushman, J. H., & Haas, K. P. (2006). *Using young adult literature in the English classroom* (4th ed.). Upper Saddle River, NJ: Prentice-Hall.

Guthrie, J., & Wigfield, A. (2000). Engagement and motivation in reading. In M. Kamil, P. Mosenthal, R. Barr, & P.D. Pearson (Eds.), *Handbook of Reading Research* (Vol. 3). Mahwah, NJ: Lawrence Erlbaum Associates.

Larimer, R., & Schleicher, L. (1999). *New ways of using authentic materials in the classroom.* Washington, DC: TESOL.

McDaniel, M., Waddill, P., & Finstad, K. (2000). The effects of text-based interest on attention and recall. *Journal of Educational Psychology,* 92, 492–502.

Common Core State Standards
- Speaking and Listening 1
- Language 6

1 Introducing the Big Question

1. Have a volunteer read aloud the introductory paragraph.
2. Guide a discussion about communication and change.
3. Provide students with an example of a situation in which communication contributes to change. (A public service announcement on the dangers of tobacco causes someone to quit smoking.)
4. **Ask** students the Big Question. (**Possible response:** It changes us by making us think differently.)
5. Tell students that the poems in this unit explore change through communication. Remind students to consider whether the poems reinforce or challenge their first answers to the Big Question.

2 Exploring the Big Question

Collaboration: Group Discussion

1. Have students work in pairs to take turns describing the examples of how people communicate Then, discuss the following questions:
   - What are some of the nonverbal ways people communicate? **Sample response:** eye contact, facial expressions, body language, art, music
   - Which forms of communication might present the biggest challenges? (**Sample response:** arguments, speech)
2. Review the Big Question vocabulary on page 605, following the teaching suggestions. Have students use the vocabulary as they complete the activity on page 605.

Connecting to the Literature

Explain the Big Question strand in the unit, referring to the box at right.

Introducing the Big Question

1 THE BIG ? **How does *communication* change us?**

Communication involves talking to other people and also listening to them and learning from them. It takes place when you discuss an issue with a friend or react to a piece of writing. Communication is the understanding you get when you read a poem. It is the empathy you feel for others after listening to a news interview with victims of a natural disaster. All of this communication may change us, but how? Does it make us smarter, wiser, kinder, angrier? Does it make us better people, or just more experienced?

2 Exploring the Big Question

Collaboration: Group Discussion Begin thinking about the Big Question by listing examples of the many ways in which you communicate. Describe an example from each of these categories.

- A discussion with a friend or parent
- A movie that moved you emotionally
- An argument you have had that still bothers you
- A speech or dramatic presentation you gave or heard
- A poem or story you will always remember
- An important conversation you have had
- A commercial or news story that moved you to take action
- A photograph, painting, or song that touched you deeply

Share your list with a small group. Talk about how these significant communications led to change.

Connecting to the Literature Each reading in this unit will give you additional insight into the Big Question.

PHLit Online!
www.PHLitOnline.com
- Big Question video
- Illustrated vocabulary words
- Interactive vocabulary games
- BQ Tunes

Applying Understanding by Design Principles

The Big Question

Explain to students that they will continue to consider the Big Question as they work through Unit 4.

- At the beginning of each selection, they will write a response to a Writing About the Big Question sentence starter.
- As they read the selection, they will look for details related to the Big Question.
- At the end of the selection, they will answer a Critical Thinking question that is related to the Big Question.
- Tell students that their goal will be to gain a deeper understanding of literature and a more sophisticated way of discussing the Big Question.

❸ Learning Big Question Vocabulary

Acquire and Use Academic Vocabulary Academic vocabulary is the language you encounter in textbooks and on standardized tests. Review the definitions of these academic vocabulary words.

comprehension (käm′ prē hen′ shən) *n.* the ability to understand something

discuss (di skus′) *v.* talk about with others

illuminate (i lo͞o′ mən āt) *v.* light up; make something clear

informed (in fôrmd′) *v.* gave someone information; *adj.* having knowledge or information

interpretation (in tur′ prə tā′ shən) *n.* a way of understanding the meaning of something

Use these words as you complete Big Question activities that involve reading, writing, speaking, and listening.

Gather Vocabulary Knowledge Additional Big Question words are listed below. Categorize the words by deciding whether you know each one well, know it a little bit, or do not know it at all.

aware	**meaning**	**resolution**
communication	**react**	**respond**
empathy	**relationship**	**understanding**
exchange		

Then, do the following:

1. Write the definitions of the words you know.
2. Consult a dictionary to confirm the word's meaning. Revise your definition if necessary.
3. Use all of the words in a brief paragraph about how communication changes us. Write in complete sentences. Avoid fragments or run-on sentences.

Common Core State Standards

Speaking and Listening
1. Initiate and participate effectively in a range of collaborative discussions with diverse partners, building on others' ideas, and expressing their own clearly and persuasively.

Language
6. Acquire and use accurately grade-appropriate general academic and domain-specific words and phrases, sufficient for reading, writing, speaking, and listening at the college and career readiness level; demonstrate independence in gathering vocabulary knowledge when considering a word or phrase important to comprehension or expression.

❸ Learning Big Question Vocabulary

Acquire and Use Academic Vocabulary

1. Introduce the academic vocabulary words in the first word bank on the student page. Have students preview the words.
2. For each word, have students say the word aloud. Then, use the word in a sentence that defines the word.

Gather Vocabulary Knowledge

1. With the class, review the steps in the activity on the student page. Have students complete the activity independently, with partners, or in small groups.
2. Before students complete the last step, review the words and their meanings as a class. (Definitions appear below on the left.) Then, have students complete their paragraphs.

Show the Big Question video, online at **www.PHLitOnline.com.**

Gather Vocabulary Knowledge: Definitions

aware [ə wer′] *adj.* having knowledge or a sense of situations, facts, or ideas

communication [kə myo͞o′ ni kā′ shən] *n.* the sharing of information or ideas

empathy [em′pə thē] *n.* the ability to understand and share someone else's feelings

exchange [eks chānj′] *v.* to trade with another; *n.* the act of trading

meaning [mē′niŋ] *n.* what is referred to or understood

react [rē′akt′] *v.* to respond in a particular way

relationship [ri lā′shən ship′] *n.* a connection between two or more people, ideas, or things

resolution [rez′ə lo͞o′shən] *n.* a decision about which way to act or not act

respond [ri spänd′] *v.* to answer in reply

understanding [un′dər stan′diŋ] *n.* the ability to perceive the meaning of something

❶ Elements of Poetry

1. Introduce the genre of poetry using the instruction on the student page.

   Discuss the three main types of poetry as they are defined on the student page. For each form, **ask** students to give an example from their own reading and explain how it fits the definition.

   Sample responses: Lyric—Example: "Success is counted sweetest" by Emily Dickinson. The poem is short and expresses one thought, that the people who think success is wonderful are the people who don't have it. Narrative—Example: "Song of Hiawatha" by Henry Wadsworth Longfellow. The poem tells a story about a young Native American man. Dramatic—The poems in *Spoon River Anthology* by Edgar Lee Masters. Each one is a dramatic monologue. Also, plays in verse, such as Shakespeare's, are dramatic poetry.

2. Have students review the quatrain in the shaded box. **Ask** students where, other than in poetry, they have seen stanzas like this used.

   Sample response: The lyrics to popular songs are often written in stanzas.

3. Have students look at the scanned lines in the second shaded box. Have a volunteer read the lines, accenting the stresses strongly. Then have another volunteer read the lines using a rhythm as near as possible to that of natural speech. Discuss with students how the two ways of reading differ.

❶ Elements of Poetry

Poetry is imaginative literature that uses precise, musical, and emotionally charged language.

Poetry is a literary form that combines the precise meanings of words with their emotional associations and musical qualities, such as rhythm and sounds. There are three main types of poetry:

- **Lyric:** a short poem that expresses the thoughts and feelings of a single speaker
- **Narrative:** a poem that tells a story
- **Dramatic:** a poem that presents the speech of one or more speakers in a dramatic situation

Poems of all types are made up of certain elements. When you read poetry, consider the poem's "voice," structure, and sound.

Speaker The speaker in a poem serves the same function as the narrator in a story: to "tell" the poem. In some poems, the speaker is an imagined character. For example, in the poem "Jabberwocky" (page 663), the speaker is not Lewis Carroll, the poet, but the Jabberwock, an imaginary character. Even in personal poems that are based on the poet's life, the speaker is not the poet. Instead, the speaker is a constructed, imagined voice.

Lines and Stanzas Most poetry is arranged in lines and **stanzas,** or groupings of lines. Stanzas are named after the number of lines they contain. For example, a couplet consists of two lines, a tercet consists of three lines, and a quatrain consists of four lines.

> **Example: Quatrain**
> Sweetest love, I do not go,
>   For weariness of thee,
> Nor in hope the world can show
>   A fitter love for me
> *(from "Song" by John Donne)*

In the quatrain, notice that each line *breaks,* or ends, before a complete thought is expressed.

Rhythm and Meter Language has its own natural rhythms, created by the stressed and unstressed syllables of words. Poets make use of this innate property of language to create **meter,** or rhythmic patterns built on the arrangement of stressed and unstressed syllables.

Readers identify the kind of meter used in a poem by counting the number and types of stresses in each line. Stressed syllables are marked with an accent symbol (´), and unstressed syllables are marked with a horseshoe symbol (˘). The stressed and unstressed syllables are then divided into units called **feet.** In the following stanza from "The Eagle" (page 647), the vertical lines (|) divide each line into four feet.

> **Example: Meter**
> Thĕ wrín | klĕd seá | ben̆eáth | him̆ cráwls,
> Hĕ wátch | ĕs fróm | his̆ moúnt | ain̆ wálls,
> An̆d liké | ă thún | dĕrbólt | hĕ fálls.

Each foot is made up of one unstressed syllable and one stressed syllable. This type of foot, called an **iamb,** mimics the rise and fall of the "wrinkled sea" described in the poem. Other types of metrical feet are as follows:

- **Trochee:** a stressed syllable followed by an unstressed syllable, as in the word *twinkle.*
- **Spondee:** two stressed syllables in a row, as in the word *schoolyard*
- **Dactyl:** a stressed syllable followed by two unstressed syllables, as in the word *beautiful*
- **Anapest:** two unstressed syllables followed by a stressed syllable, as in the word *comprehend*

Teaching Resources

- All *Common Core Companion,* pp. 35–47
- All *Unit 4 Resources,* pp. 7–22
- All *Professional Development Guidebook,* p. 33
- All *See It!* DVD **Pat Mora,** Segment 2
- All *Graphic Organizer Transparencies,* pp. 109, 110
- All **Enriched Online Student Edition**
- L2 L3 *Reader's Notebook*
- L1 *Reader's Notebook: Adapted Version*
- EL *Reader's Notebook: English Learner's Version*
- L2 EL *Hear It!* Audio CD
- L1 EL *Hear It!* Audio CD (adapted text)

All resources, including print and video, are available at **www.PHLitOnline.com.**

Rhyme In addition to meter, poets use other **sound devices,** or techniques that create musical effects. Rhyme is a sound device commonly associated with poetry, although many poems do not rhyme. Types of rhyme include the following:

- **Exact, or true, rhyme:** words that end in both the same vowel and the same consonant sounds
  Example: sun and run
- **Slant rhyme:** words that end in similar but not exact sounds
  Example: prove and love
- **End rhyme:** rhyming words that fall at the ends of two or more lines
  Example: crawls, walls, and *falls* in the passage from "The Eagle"
- **Internal rhyme:** rhyming words placed within a line
  Example: The mouse in the house woke the cat.

Rhyme Scheme A set pattern of rhyme is called a **rhyme scheme.** The rhyme scheme of a poem is identified by assigning a different letter of the alphabet to each rhyme. Notice the rhyme scheme of the following stanza from "I Wandered Lonely as a Cloud" (page 627), in which a speaker recalls a field of flowers.

Example: Rhyme Scheme

For oft, when on my couch I lie	**a**
In vacant or in pensive mood,	**b**
They flash upon that inward eye	**a**
Which is the bliss of solitude;	**b**
And then my heart with pleasure fills,	**c**
And dances with the daffodils.	**c**

Rhyme scheme helps shape the structure of a stanza and clarifies the relationships among the lines. In the example, the *abab* pattern creates a close connection among the first four lines, which describe the speaker's habit of daydreaming about the daffodils. The *cc* rhyme creates a close connection between the last two lines, which sum up the speaker's feelings as he daydreams.

Other Sound Devices A poet may use a variety of other sound devices to create musical effects. The chart below explains sound devices that are often used in poetry.

Repetition is the use of any language element more than once.
Example: *Above the town, above the lake, and high above the trees.*

Alliteration is the repetition of consonant sounds at the beginning of words.
Example: *The snake sneaked past the snail.*

Assonance is the repetition of vowel sounds followed by different consonants in two or more stressed syllables.
Example: *The green leaves fluttered in the breeze.*

Consonance is the repetition of final consonant sounds in stressed syllables with different vowel sounds.
Example: *The king sang a song.*

Onomatopoeia is the use of words to imitate sounds.
Example: *The bees buzzed, and the brook gurgled.*

In This Section

Elements of Poetry

Analyzing Poetic Language

Close Read: Poetic Language and Meaning

- Model Texts
- Practice Texts

After You Read

Common Core State Standards

RL.9-10.4

[For the full wording of the standards, see the standards chart in the front of your textbook.]

4. Introduce the sound device *rhyme* using the instruction on the student page. Discuss the four main types of rhyme as they are defined on the student page. For each form of rhyme, **ask** students to give examples.

   Sample responses: True rhyme—cool, rule; gain, cane; snoopy, droopy. Slant rhyme—game, rain; move, above. End rhyme—"An apple a day / keeps the doctor away." Internal rhyme—"Jack and Jill went up the hill / to fetch a pail of water."

5. Discuss the effects of rhyme schemes as they are described on the student page. Then change the last word in a few of the lines in the first shaded paragraph: change *lie* to *sit*, change *mood* to *dream*, change *fills* to *leaps*. Read the poem aloud. **Ask** students to discuss the difference between the two versions.

6. Introduce the other sound devices, using the instruction and the examples on the student page. Choose volunteers to share their own examples of each.

   Sample responses: Repetition—"in the rain, in the puddles, in the pavement slick streets." Alliteration—"Wicked Witch of the West"; "baby buggy bumpers." Assonance—"a few cool fools"; "low groans." Consonance—"sand on the window." Onomatopoeia—crash, croak.

2 In This Section

Explain that in the remainder of this Literary Analysis Workshop, students will analyze an important element of poetry—poetic language. After reviewing the concept, they will then see it applied in an analysis of a Model text. Finally, they will apply what they have learned to an Independent Practice text.

Common Core State Standards

Unit 4 Focus Standards

- **Reading Literature 4**

This standard spirals through the unit.

❶ Analyzing Poetic Language

1. Introduce the concept of poetic language, using the instruction on the student page.

   Emphasize that word choice in poetry is a combination of finding exactly the right meaning and exactly the right sound.
2. Introduce the concept of denotative and connotative meanings, using the instruction on the student page. Then, ask students to talk about the connotations of each of the following words: *home, snake, blossom.*

   Sample responses: Home—safety, comfort, belonging; Snake—danger, sneakiness, betrayal; Blossom—beauty, growth, fulfillment.
3. Review with students the notions of meaning and tone, defined on the student page. Have a volunteer read the lines from "I Hear America Singing" in the shaded box, and discuss the tone, or attitude, that is appropriate for the words.
4. Lead students in a discussion of the imagery in the poem in the second shaded box. **Ask:** How do the images help create the tone of the poem? How would you describe that tone?

   Sample response: The images are negative. Each one describes something that would be unpleasant to see or feel or hear. They help create a tone that could be described as unhappy or depressing.

❶ Analyzing Poetic Language

Common Core State Standards

Reading Literature 4. Determine the meaning of words and phrases as they are used in the text, including figurative and connotative meanings; analyze the cumulative impact of specific word choices on meaning and tone.

Poets use the connotations of words and figurative language to express ideas precisely and imaginatively.

Poetry relies not only on the sounds and rhythms of language but also on the precise meanings of words. Poets choose each word carefully, considering both its **denotation,** or literal definition, and its **connotation,** or emotional associations.

Denotative and Connotative Meanings
Consider the words *thrifty* and *penny-pinching.* Though both words literally mean "careful in the spending of money," their connotative meanings are quite different. *Thrifty* is associated with admirable qualities, such as economy, and therefore conveys a positive attitude. *Penny-pinching* is associated with undesirable qualities, such as stinginess, and therefore conveys a negative attitude. These types of nuances help poets express precise meaning, emotion, and attitudes.

Meaning and Tone The connotative meanings of words are especially instrumental in conveying a poem's **tone**—the poet's emotional attitude toward his or her subject. The tone of a poem can be formal, informal, lighthearted, solemn, or anything in between.

As you read the following lines from "I Hear America Singing" (page 750), try to identify the tone that the words create.

Example:
I hear America singing, the varied
carols I hear, . . .
at night the party of young fellows,
robust, friendly,
Singing with open mouths their strong
melodious songs.

The positive connotations of the words *singing, carols, robust, friendly, strong,* and *melodious* create a tone that might be described as joyous or cheerful.

Imagery Poetic language is also often rich with imagery, or descriptive language that creates word pictures. Through the use of details that appeal to the senses of sight, touch, sound, taste, and smell, poets re-create sensory experiences and emotions in words.

Notice the imagery in the following poem, and analyze the overall impression it creates.

Example:
On that long summer day,
each breath was a labor.
The air was wet wool,
Heavy and warm.

A thick, yellow haze
hung over the city,
blocking out buildings,
blinding the sun.

Not a sound could be heard.
All was sullen and silent,
save for the whir of
electric fans.

In the first stanza, the description of the heavy, warm air appeals to the sense of touch. In the second stanza, the description of the yellow haze appeals to the sense of sight. In the third stanza, the onomatopoeic word *whir* appeals to the sense of sound. The overall impression is one of exhaustion and heat.

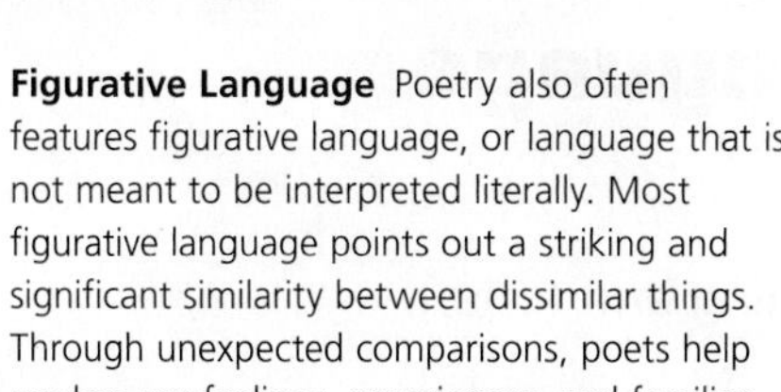

Figurative Language Poetry also often features figurative language, or language that is not meant to be interpreted literally. Most figurative language points out a striking and significant similarity between dissimilar things. Through unexpected comparisons, poets help readers see feelings, experiences, and familiar, everyday objects in a fresh new light.

Types of Figurative Language

A **simile** compares two things using the word *like* or *as*: *Her visit was as unexpected and welcome as a flower in winter.*

A **metaphor** compares two things by stating one thing in terms of something else: *Her visit was a flower in winter.*

Personification gives human qualities or abilities to nonhuman things: *The alarm clock nagged me to get out of bed.*

As you read the following poem, look for examples of each type of figurative language described above.

Example:

Tall, strong, and silent,
    the stalks of corn
    guarded the garden
    like sentries.

All ears, they listened
    for the caws of the crows.

The birds approached,
    a hungry, invading force.

In the simile "guarded the garden / like sentries," the cornstalks are compared to watchful soldiers. In a playful example of personification, the ears on the stalks of corn listen for crows. In the metaphor "The birds approached, / a hungry invading force," the crows flying to the garden are compared to an enemy force.

Free and Formal Verse The example poem on this page is **free verse**—a type of poetry that exhibits poetic language but does not follow fixed patterns. Free verse may use rhyme, sound devices, varied types of stanzas, and meter but will not do so in a set structure.

By contrast, **formal verse** follows fixed, established patterns. A pattern may require a specific rhyme scheme, meter, line structure, stanza structure, or other element. Throughout history, poets have invented lyric forms. Eventually, some of these forms, including those defined in the chart below, became part of literary tradition.

Types of Formal Poetry

Ballad	a songlike narrative poem, usually written in rhymed stanzas of four to six lines that feature repetition and strong meter
Haiku	an unrhymed three-line lyric poem, usually focused on images from nature, in which lines 1 and 3 have five syllables and line 2 has seven syllables
English Sonnet	a fourteen-line lyric poem consisting of three quatrains and a couplet, usually rhymed *abab cdcd efef gg*
Ode	a lyric poem on a serious subject, usually written in a precise structure
Concrete Poem	a poem with a shape that suggests its subject; the poet arranges letters, words, punctuation, and lines to create a picture

The process of formal invention in poetry is ongoing. Today, some poets experiment with forms based on mathematical equations, while others write hypertext poetry—poems that use electronic links online and are different for every reader.

5. Introduce the concept of figurative language, using the instruction on the student page.

   Emphasize that figurative language is a very strong tool for poets because it allows them to say a great deal in a few words and also summons up powerful images.
6. Have students look at the types of figurative language defined in the first shaded box. Lead a discussion about why a poet might sometimes use the language of a simile and sometimes the language of a metaphor.
7. Have a volunteer read the poem in the second shaded box aloud. Have students identify as many different kinds of poetic language in the poem as they can.

   Possible response: The first stanza contains a simile, several examples of alliteration (*s*, *g*), internal rhyme ("guarded the garden"). The second stanza contains personification, alliteration (*c*), onomatopoeia ("caws"), and slant rhyme or consonance ("caws of the crows"). The final stanza contains a metaphor. The students may also see examples of good word choice and other poetic language.
8. Review the types of formal poetry defined on the student page. Then, lead a discussion about why a poet might choose to use a poetic form. (Connectedness, discipline, stimulation for the imagination, etc.)
9. Remind students that in this Workshop, they will read a model analysis of the central idea of a passage and then perform their own analysis of a second passage.

Differentiated Instruction Additional Instruction

Support for Special-Needs Students
Have students read the **Exploring Poetry** pages in the ***Reader's Notebook: Adapted Version.*** This version provides a basic-level introduction to fiction and nonfiction.

Support for Less Proficient Readers
Have students read the **Exploring Poetry** pages in the ***Reader's Notebook.*** This version provides a basic-level introduction to fiction and nonfiction.

EL Support for English Learners
Have students read the **Exploring Poetry** pages in the ***Reader's Notebook: English Learner's Version.*** This version provides a basic-level introduction to fiction and nonfiction.

❷ Close Read: Poetic Language and Meaning

1. Remind students that poetic language includes word choice, imagery, and figurative language of all kinds.
2. Review with the class the Poetic Elements chart. Discuss ways in which each element might contribute to building the combination of sound and sense that make an effective poem. For example, if a poem is about a tall-grass prairie, alliteration and assonance could evoke the rustling of the grass in the prairie wind.
3. Divide students into groups. Write the following subject for a poem on the board: *Thunderstorm.* Have groups discuss which elements they think would be most important in a poem about a thunderstorm. The group should choose two elements and be prepared to explain their choice. Have groups then share their choices with the class.

   Sample responses: Sensory language and imagery would be important because you would want to capture how the storm looks and feels. Sound devices would be important because you could help the reader hear the roar and crash of the rain and thunder.
4. Point out examples of highlighted text in the model on page 611. Explain that in each case, the color of the highlighting matches the color of the category in the chart. Details that illustrate a given category are highlighted in the color of that category.

❷ Close Read: Poetic Language and Meaning

The elements of poetry combine to build meaning and tone.

Great poems synthesize the poetic elements of language, including sound, rhythms, imagery, and connotations, into works that are wonderful to read and offer profound meanings. To analyze poetry, consider all those elements and identify how they work together to build sound and sense.

Read aloud. To begin your analysis, read the poem aloud so that you can hear the language. Make note of sound devices. Consider the voice and character of the speaker. Remember that lines may break before the end of a complete thought, so let the punctuation of the poem guide your reading.

Read for imagery, figurative language, and structure. Reread the poem to identify examples of imagery and figurative language, and determine their effects and meanings. Consider any formal elements in the poem and analyze their impact on meaning and tone.

Read for connotation and tone. Read the poem again to identify words that suggest a specific tone, paying special attention to the words' connotative meanings.

To guide your analysis of poetry, refer to the chart below, which offers reminders of poetic elements and the ways in which they interact to build meaning and emotional impact in a poem.

Poetic Elements	
Word Choice and Connotation Connotative meanings that carry negative or positive associations provide clues about the ideas and emotions the poem expresses.	**Rhyme** The repetition of sounds at the ends of words creates musical effects and makes ideas memorable. A regular pattern of rhyme, or rhyme scheme, helps shape stanzas and build relationships among ideas.
Sensory Language and Imagery Word pictures that appeal to the senses express thoughts and feelings. Look for repeated or related images, as these may be clues to a poem's deeper meaning.	**Other Sound Devices** Repetition, alliteration, assonance, consonance, and onomatopoeia create musical effects and help develop meaning and tone.
Figurative Language Imaginative comparisons, such as similes, metaphors, and personification, make connections among ideas and express shades of meaning.	**Form** The form of a poem gives structure to the experiences or events it describes. Notice how formal elements in a poem emphasize certain ideas or create a specific emotional quality.

EXEMPLAR TEXT

❸ Model

About the Text Sara Teasdale (1884–1933) was born and raised in St. Louis, Missouri. The poem "Barter" is from her collection *Love Songs,* which won the first Pulitzer Prize for poetry, in 1918. A *barter* is a trade or an exchange of items.

"Barter"
by Sara Teasdale

❹
Life has loveliness to sell,
All beautiful and splendid things,
Blue waves whitened on a cliff,
Soaring fire that sways and sings, ❺
And children's faces looking up
Holding wonder like a cup.

❻ Life has loveliness to sell,
Music like a curve of gold,
Scent of pine trees in the rain,
Eyes that love you, arms that hold,
And for your spirit's still delight,
Holy thoughts that star the night.

❽
Spend all you have for loveliness,
Buy it and never count the cost; ❼
For one white singing hour of peace
Count many a year of strife well lost,
And for a breath of ecstasy
Give all you have been, or could be.

❹ **Rhyme** End rhymes add a musical dimension to the poem and help shape each stanza.

❺ **Figurative Language** The use of personification turns the fire into a living—and joyous—being.

❻ **Figurative Language** The simile allows the reader to "see" music as something tangible and as part of life's "loveliness."

❼ **Other Sound Devices** The alliteration in the repeated "l" and "c" sounds adds to the poem's music.

❽ **Word Choice and Connotation** These words connote powerfully positive emotions and convey a joyful tone.

Differentiated Instruction for Universal Access

Strategy for Less Proficient Readers
Help students comprehend the poem by reading it aloud several times, the first time as a simple read-through; the second, emphasizing sound devices and line breaks; the third, taking each line and paraphrasing what is being said. Have students work in pairs to clarify any confusing words or phrases.

EL Strategy for English Learners
Have students work in pairs, taking turns reading the different lines of the poem. If any words or phrases are not clear, provide help. Then, have each pair do an oral reading in unison, assisting one another with pronunciation, rhythm, and pacing.

TEACH

❸ Reading the Model

1. Discuss the About the Text note. Explain further that the poem students are about to read is a lyric poem about one aspect of life.
2. Have students read the poem (p. 611). Discuss, clarifying as necessary. Then, guide students in reviewing the annotations.

❹ Rhyme

Read aloud the Rhyme annotation. **Ask:** Why might rhyme be particularly effective in a poem about this subject?

Possible response: The poem is about loveliness, and the rhymes make the poem itself more lovely.

❺ Figurative Language

Read aloud the words highlighted in tan and the first Figurative Language annotation. Have students explain why this particular example of personification upholds the message of the poem.

Possible response: The fire seems to be dancing instead of burning and destroying.

❻ Figurative Language

Read aloud the second Figurative Language annotation and the words highlighted in tan. **Ask:** What might music "like a curve of gold" be like?

Sample response: A simple tune on a flute or violin.

❼ Other Sound Devices

Read aloud the words highlighted in yellow and the Other Sound Devices annotation. **Ask:** How would the line change if you replaced *cost* with *price*?

Possible response: It wouldn't be as musical.

❽ Word Choice and Connotation

Lead a class discussion about the words and phrases highlighted in aqua and what each contributes to meaning.

9 Reading the Model

1. Discuss the About the Text note. Explain further that the poem students are about to read is a lyric poem about difficult times and experiences in life.
2. Have students read the poem (p. 612). Discuss, clarifying as necessary. Then, guide students in reviewing the annotations.

10 Word Choice and Connotation

Read aloud the Word Choice and Connotation annotation and the text highlighted in aqua. **Ask:** Why might light have connotations related to seeing and understanding?

Possible response: Seeing is literally easier when it's light. When we can see a thing, literally or figuratively, it is easier to understand.

11 Figurative Language

Read aloud the first Figurative Language annotation and the text highlighted in tan. **Ask:** What do you think "Evenings of the Brain" might be?

Possible response: Times when life is difficult and hard to understand.

12 Rhyme

Read aloud the first Rhyme annotation and the text highlighted in blue. **Ask:** What is the effect of a rhyme that ends a line but not a thought?

Possible response: The rhyme stands out less.

13 Figurative Language

Read aloud the second Figurative Language annotation and the text highlighted in tan. **Ask:** What happens when your eyes adjust to darkness? What does Dickinson mean by the last line, "And Life steps almost straight."?

Possible response: You can see better. We make it through difficult times, and in the end, life is almost back to normal.

EXEMPLAR TEXT

Model

About the Text The American poet Emily Dickinson (1830–1886) wrote more than 1,700 brief poems that sparkle with wit and intelligence. She is known for a stylistic use of punctuation, especially exclamation points and dashes, and she often capitalized words within sentences to give them added emphasis.

10 Word Choice and Connotation Dickinson creates a contrast between darkness, which is associated with fear and death, and light, which is associated with seeing, or understanding.

11 Figurative Language Dickinson uses metaphors to speak of figurative darknesses. These metaphors suggest periods of great sadness.

12 Rhyme The rhyming words help shape the structure of the stanzas. They support the idea that this experience is a regular occurrence.

13 Figurative Language The metaphor continues. The "Bravest" people struggle through sadness and sometimes get hurt, but adjust and come to grips with their experiences.

"We grow accustomed to the Dark—" by Emily Dickinson

We grow accustomed to the Dark—
When Light is put away—
As when the Neighbor holds the Lamp
To witness her Goodbye—

A Moment—We uncertain step
For newness of the night—
Then—fit our Vision to the Dark—
And meet the Road—erect—

And so of larger—Darknesses—
Those Evenings of the Brain—
When not a Moon disclose a sign—
Or Star—come out—within—

The Bravest—grope a little—
And sometimes hit a Tree
Directly in the Forehead—
But as they learn to see—

Either the Darkness alters—
Or something in the sight
Adjusts itself to Midnight—
And Life steps almost straight.

Vocabulary Development

CCSS Language 6

Thematic Vocabulary: The Big Question

As students discuss the poem, encourage them to use the thematic vocabulary presented in Introducing the Big Question, pages 604–605. Help them with sentence starters such as these:

1. In the first stanza, the neighbor *illuminates* the way with . . .
2. A valid *interpretation* of the poem is that . . .
3. The speaker would probably consider being *informed* a source of . . .

14 Independent Practice

About the Text Pat Mora (b. 1942), a bilingual and bicultural Mexican American, often includes Spanish words and phrases in her poems. Her poetry is rich in imagery and feeling, and she often urges her readers to write poems and to "enjoy the word-play." This poem presents a vivid picture of a tornado.

"Uncoiling" by Pat Mora

With thorns, she scratches
15 on my window, tosses her hair dark with rain,
snares lightning, cholla,[1] hawks, butterfly
swarms in the tangles.

She sighs clouds,
16 head thrown back, eyes closed, roars
and rivers leap,
boulders retreat like crabs
17 into themselves.
She spews gusts and thunder,
spooks pale women who scurry to
lock doors, windows
when her tumbleweed skirt starts its spin.

They sing lace lullabies
so their children won't hear
her uncoiling
through her lips, howling
leaves off trees, flesh
off bones, until she becomes
18 sound, spins herself
to sleep, sand stinging her ankles,
whirring into her raw skin like stars.

15 Figurative Language What type of figurative language is introduced in the first stanza? What is the effect?

16 Imagery What emotions do the images in these lines convey?

17 Figurative Language What does this figurative language describe?

Sound Devices What sound device is used in these lines? How do the sounds emphasize the action these lines describe?

1. **cholla** (cho' yä) *n.* spiny cactus found in the southwestern United States and Mexico.

14 Independent Practice

Discuss the About the Text note. Explain further that the poem students are about to read is a free-verse poem about a tornado.

15 Figurative Language

Read aloud the text highlighted in tan. **Ask** the first Figurative Language question.

Possible response: Personification is used to make the storm seem like a dangerous person.

16 Imagery

Read aloud the text highlighted in green. **Ask** the Imagery question.

Possible response: The images convey a sense of rage.

17 Figurative Language

Read aloud the text highlighted in tan. **Ask** the second Figurative Language question.

Possible response: It describes the fury of the storm scaring women and even boulders.

18 Sound Devices

Read aloud the text highlighted in yellow. **Ask** the Sound Devices questions.

Possible response: Alliteration is used in the lines, and it emphasizes the hissing sound of sand in the wind.

PHLit Online!

Enriched Online Student Edition

To have students read the selections in interactive format, with narration and point-of-use interactive graphic organizers, go to **www.PHLitOnline.com**.

Differentiated Instruction — Additional Instruction

Support for Special-Needs Students
Have students read the adapted version of this and the next selection in the ***Reader's Notebook: Adapted Version.*** They may also listen to the adapted version on the ***Reader's Notebook: Hear It!*** **Audio CD** (adapted text).

Support for Less Proficient Readers
Have students read this and the next selection in the ***Reader's Notebook.*** After students finish the selection in the ***Reader's Notebook,*** have them complete the questions and activities in the Student Edition.

EL Support for English Learners
Have students read this and the next selection in the ***Reader's Notebook: English Learner's Version.*** English learners may also read the selection as they listen to the recorded version on the ***Hear It!*** **Audio CD.**

⓳ Introducing the Independent Practice

1. Explain to students that they will analyze the poetic language of the Independent Practice selection.
2. Discuss the About the Text note, and have students read the selection. Then, direct them to go back through and respond to the side-column prompts. As necessary, guide students in answering the prompts, using the teaching notes. Conclude by having students answer the After You Read questions on page 615.

⓴ Figurative Language

Read aloud the text highlighted in tan. **Ask** the first Figurative Language question.

Possible response: The simile used here describes the lights shining on the stage.

㉑ Word Choice and Connotation

Read aloud the text highlighted in aqua. **Ask** the Word Choice and Connotation question.

Possible response: He is very stern and judgmental.

㉒ Sound Devices

Read aloud the text highlighted in yellow. **Ask** the Sound Devices questions.

Possible response: There is alliteration (*fl, h*) and assonance (*down, house*.) They contribute to the sense of caution the speaker feels about her father.

㉓ Figurative Language

Read aloud the text highlighted in tan. **Ask** the second set of Figurative Language questions.

Possible response: The simile suggests a sense of pride in the aunt in Mexico. The personification of family stories gives a vitality and importance to family lore.

㉔ Form

Read aloud the text highlighted in pink on p. 615. **Ask** the Form questions.

Possible responses: The poet uses a four-line stanza (quatrain) throughout the poem. The shorter stanza at the end adds emphasis to the thought expressed.

⓳ Independent Practice

About the Text In this poem, the speaker describes her mother who, as a high school student, participated in a speech contest.

"A Voice" by Pat Mora

Even the lights on the stage unrelenting
as the desert sun couldn't hide the other
students, their eyes also unrelenting,
students who spoke English every night

as they ate their meat, potatoes, gravy.
Not you. In your house that smelled like
rose powder, you spoke Spanish formal
as your father, the judge without a courtroom

in the country he floated to in the dark
on a flatbed truck. He walked slow
as a hot river down the narrow hall
of your house. You never dared to race past him

to say, "Please move," in the language
you learned effortlessly, as you learned to run,
the language forbidden at home, though your mother
said you learned it to fight with the neighbors.

You like winning with words. You liked
writing speeches about patriotism and democracy.
You liked all the faces looking at you, all those eyes.
"How did I do it?" you ask me now. "How did I do it

when my parents didn't understand?"
The family story says your voice is the voice
of an aunt in Mexico, spunky[1] as a peacock.
Family stories sing of what lives in the blood.

You told me only once about the time you went
to the state capitol, your family proud as if
you'd been named governor. But when you looked
around, the only Mexican in the auditorium,

you wanted to hide from those strange faces.
Their eyes were pinpricks, and you faked
hoarseness. You, who are never at a loss
for words, felt your breath stick in your throat

⓴ **Figurative Language** What type of figurative language is used here? What does it describe?

㉑ **Word Choice and Connotation** What does this description of the father suggest about him?

㉒ **Sound Devices** What sound devices do you notice in these lines? How do the sounds contribute to the emotion of the poem?

㉓ **Figurative Language** What kinds of figurative language appear here? What does this figurative language describe, and what does it suggest?

1. **spunky** (spungʹ kē) *adj.* courageous; spirited

Vocabulary Development

Selection Vocabulary Rating

Create a **Vocabulary Knowledge Rating Chart** (***Professional Development Guidebook***, p. 33) with this word from the selections:

spunky

Give students a copy of the chart. Read the word aloud, and have students mark their rating in the Before Reading column. Urge them to be alert to this word as they read and discuss "A Voice" because they will rate their knowledge of the word again after they finish.

Tally how many students think they know the word to gauge how much instruction to provide. As students read, point out the word and its context.

like an ice cube. "I can't," you whispered.
"I can't." Yet you did. Not that day but years later.
You taught the four of us to speak up.
This is America, Mom. The undoable is done
in the next generation. Your breath moves
through the family like the wind
moves through the trees.

24

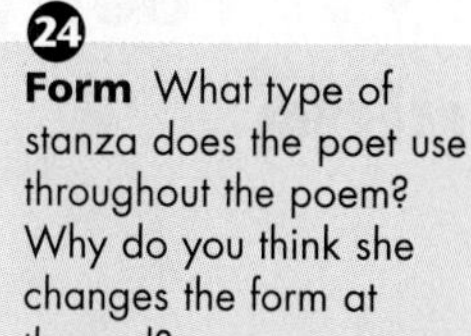

24 **Form** What type of stanza does the poet use throughout the poem? Why do you think she changes the form at the end?

After You Read Uncoiling • A Voice

1. **Key Ideas and Details (a) Infer:** In "Uncoiling," what kind of storm does the speaker describe? **(b) Interpret:** Identify three actions that the storm takes. **(c) Analyze:** How do these actions show the storm's violence?
2. **Craft and Structure (a) Analyze:** In "Uncoiling," what type of figurative language does Mora use to describe the storm? **(b)** What is the effect of this choice?
3. **Key Ideas and Details (a) Interpret:** In "A Voice," which of her mother's childhood accomplishments does the poet celebrate? **(b) Summarize:** What happens to her mother at the state capitol? **(c) Analyze:** According to the speaker, how does the mother turn the pain of that experience into triumph later in life?
4. **Craft and Structure (a)** Note one simile and one metaphor in "A Voice." **(b) Interpret:** Explain the action each example describes.
5. **Craft and Structure (a) Determine:** In "A Voice," the speaker states that family lore describes the mother's voice as being "spunky as a peacock." What type of figurative language is this? **(b) Analyze:** What meaning does this comparison suggest?
6. **Craft and Structure Compare and Contrast:** Compare and contrast the image of the wind in the last stanza of "A Voice" with the image of the wind in "Uncoiling." Explain differences in both tone and meaning.
7. **Integration of Knowledge and Ideas (a)** In the first column of a chart like the one shown, list images of breathing or speaking from the poems. In the second column, note the literal meaning of each image. In the third column, describe each image's effect—the word picture it conveys or the feeling it expresses.

What It Says	What It Means	Effect

(b) Collaborate: In a small group, discuss your findings.

ASSESS/EXTEND

Answers

1. **Possible response: (a)** The speaker is describing a desert storm. **(b)** The storm knocks against the window, brings clouds, and spews gusts and thunder. **(c)** The actions grow from clouding over to causing violent winds.
2. **Possible response: (a)** Mora uses personification to describe the storm. **(b)** The effect is to make the storm seem alive and personally threatening.
3. **Possible response: (a)** The poet celebrates her mother's speaking accomplishments. **(b)** She is too scared to speak in front of a large group. **(c)** It taught the speaker's mother that it was important to teach her children to use their voices.
4. **Possible response: (a)** "slow as a hot river," "Their eyes were pin-pricks." **(b)** The simile describes the father walking. The metaphor describes the way the eyes of the people at the state capitol felt to the speaker's mother.
5. **Possible response: (a)** The phrase is a simile. **(b)** The simile suggests that the voice is fearless and proud and probably beautiful.
6. **Possible response:** In "Uncoiling," the image of the wind is dangerous and threatening. In "A Voice," it is gentle and life-affirming. The tone of the first poem is frightening and the tone of the second is loving.
7. **Possible response: (a)** Image: What it says— "howling leaves off trees"; what it means—blowing leaves off trees; effect—suggests the sound of the wind is a monster. **(b)** Responses will vary but should convey an understanding of figurative language.

Assessment Resources

The following resources can be used to assess students' knowledge and skills.

Unit 4 Resources

L1 L2 EL **Selection Test A**, pp. 17–19.
L3 L4 EL **Selection Test B**, pp. 20–22.
L3 L4 **Open-Book Test**, pp. 14–16.

PHLit Online! Students may use the **Self-test**, online at **www.PHLitOnline.com,** to prepare for the **Selection Test A** or **Selection Test B**.

✓ **Poetry Collection 1** • ✓✓ **Poetry Collection 2**

Lesson Pacing Guide

DAY 1 Preteach

- Administer the Reading and Vocabulary Warm-ups (*Unit 4 Resources,* pp. 23–26 or 41–44) as necessary.
- Introduce the Reading Skill: Read Fluently.
- Introduce the Literary Analysis concept: Figurative Language.
- Distribute copies of the appropriate graphic organizer for the Reading Skill (*Graphic Organizer Transparencies,* pp. 114–116).
- Distribute copies of the appropriate graphic organizer for Literary Analysis (*Graphic Organizer Transparencies,* pp. 111–113).
- Teach the selection vocabulary.
- Introduce the Word Study skill.

DAYS 2–3 Preteach/Teach

- Build background with the Background feature.
- Develop thematic vocabulary and thematic thinking with Writing About the Big Question.
- Prepare students to read with the Activating Prior Knowledge activities (TE).
- Informally monitor comprehension while students read.
- Use the Reading Check questions to confirm comprehension.
- Develop students' ability to read fluently, using the Reading Skill questions.
- Develop students' understanding of figurative language, using the Literary Analysis questions.
- Reinforce vocabulary with the Vocabulary notes.
- Reinforce unit focus standards using the Spiral Review prompts.

DAY 4 Assess

- Assess students' comprehension and mastery of the skills by having them answer the Critical Thinking, Reading Skill, and Literary Analysis questions.
- Have students complete the Vocabulary Practice activities.
- Have students complete the Word Study activities.

DAY 5 Extend/Assess

- Have students complete the Conventions lesson.
- Have students complete the Writing activity and write a description of a scene. (You may assign as homework.)
- Extend learning by having students complete the Speaking and Listening activity, an impromptu speech. As an alternative, assign them "In Your Head" or "The Thinking Computer" in *Reality Central.*
- Administer Selection Test A or B (*Unit 4 Resources,* pp. 35–40 or 56–61).

Common Core State Standards

Reading Literature 4. Determine the meaning of words and phrases as they are used in the text, including figurative and connotative meanings; analyze the cumulative impact of several word choices on meaning and tone (e.g., how the language evokes a sense of time and place; how it sets a formal or informal tone).

Writing 3.d. Use precise words and phrases, telling details, and sensory language to convey a vivid picture of the experiences, events, setting, and/or characters.

Speaking and Listening 4. Present information, findings, and supporting evidence clearly, concisely, and logically such that listeners can follow the line of reasoning and the organization, development, substance, and style are appropriate to purpose, audience, and task.

Language
1. Demonstrate command of the conventions of standard English grammar and usage when writing or speaking.
5. Demonstrate understanding of figurative language, word relationships, and nuances in meanings.

Additional Standards Practice
Common Core Companion, *pp. 35–42*

Daily Block Scheduling
Each day in this Lesson Pacing Guide represents a 40–50 minute period. Teachers using block scheduling may combine days to revise pacing. In addition, teachers may differentiate and support core instruction by integrating components for extended and intensive support as students require. See the Guide to Selected Leveled Resources (facing page).

Guide to Selected Leveled Resources

RTI Tier 1 (students performing on level)		✓ More Accessible Poetry Collection 1	✓✓ More Complex Poetry Collection 2
Warm Up	**Practice, model,** and **monitor** fluency, working **with the whole class** or **in groups.**	**Vocabulary** and **Reading Warm-ups B,** ***Unit 4 Resources,*** pp. 23–24, 26	**Vocabulary** and **Reading Warm-ups B,** ***Unit 4 Resources,*** pp. 41–42, 44
Comprehension/Skills	**Support** and **monitor** comprehension and skills development, having students complete the activities, graphic organizers, and interactive prompts **independently** or **as a class.**	• ***Reader's Notebook,*** adapted instruction and full selection EL ***Reader's Notebook: English Learner's Version,*** adapted instruction and adapted selection • **Reading Skill Graphic Organizer B,** ***Graphic Organizer Transparencies,*** p. 113 • **Literary Analysis Graphic Organizer B,** ***Graphic Organizer Transparencies,*** p. 116	• ***Reader's Notebook,*** adapted instruction and summary EL ***Reader's Notebook: English Learner's Version,*** adapted instruction and summary • **Reading Skill Graphic Organizer B,** ***Graphic Organizer Transparencies,*** p. 113 • **Literary Analysis Graphic Organizer B,** ***Graphic Organizer Transparencies,*** p. 116
Monitor Progress	**Monitor** student progress with the differentiated curriculum-based assessment in the *Unit Resources.*	• **Selection Test B,** ***Unit 4 Resources,*** pp. 38–40 • **Open-Book Test,** ***Unit 4 Resources,*** pp. 32–34	• **Selection Test B,** ***Unit 4 Resources,*** pp. 59–61 • **Open-Book Test,** ***Unit 4 Resources,*** pp. 53–55

RTI Tier 2 (students requiring intervention)		✓ More Accessible Poetry Collection 1	✓✓ More Complex Poetry Collection 2
Warm Up	**Practice, model,** and **monitor** fluency **in groups** or **with individuals.**	• **Vocabulary and Reading Warm-ups A,** ***Unit 4 Resources,*** pp. 23–26 • ***Reality Central,*** "In Your Head" • ***Hear It!*** **Audio CD (adapted text)**	• **Vocabulary and Reading Warm-ups A,** ***Unit 4 Resources,*** pp. 41–44 • **Reality Central,** "The Thinking Computer" • ***Hear It!*** **Audio CD**
Comprehension/Skills	• **Support** and **monitor** comprehension and skills development, working **in small groups** or **with individuals.** • **Pair** students with more advanced peers and have them complete the writing activity in the *Real-World Writing Journal.* • As students complete the selection in the appropriate version of the *Reader's Notebook,* **monitor** comprehension frequently with group questions and individual instruction. • **Model** strategies while guiding students in completing the activities and prompts in the *Reader's Notebook,* as well as the graphic organizers. • **Practice** skills and **monitor** mastery with the *Reading Kit* worksheets.	• ***Real-World Writing Journal,*** Lesson 1, pp. 104–107 • ***Reader's Notebook: Adapted Version,*** adapted instruction and adapted selection EL ***Reader's Notebook: English Learner's Version,*** adapted instruction and adapted selection • **Reading Skill Graphic Organizer A,** ***Graphic Organizer Transparencies,*** p. 111 • **Literary Analysis Graphic Organizer A,** ***Graphic Organizer Transparencies,*** p. 114 • **Reading Kit,** Practice worksheets, pp. 152, 158, 162, 164, 170	• ***Real-World Writing Journal,*** Lesson 2, pp. 108–111 • ***Reader's Notebook: Adapted Version,*** adapted instruction and summary EL ***Reader's Notebook: English Learner's Version,*** adapted instruction and summary • **Reading Skill Graphic Organizer A,** ***Graphic Organizer Transparencies,*** p. 112 • **Literary Analysis Graphic Organizer A,** ***Graphic Organizer Transparencies,*** p. 115 • **Reading Kit,** Practice worksheets, pp. 152, 158, 162, 164, 170
Monitor Progress	**Monitor** student progress with the differentiated curriculum-based assessment in the *Unit Resources* and in the *Reading Kit.*	• **Selection Test A,** ***Unit 4 Resources,*** pp. 35–37 • **Reading Kit,** Assess worksheets, pp. 153, 159, 163, 165, 171	• **Selection Test A,** ***Unit 4 Resources,*** pp. 56–58 • **Reading Kit,** Assess worksheets, pp. 153, 159, 163, 165, 171

TIER 3 Tier 3 intervention may require consultation with the student's special-education or dyslexia specialist. For additional support, see the Tier 2 activities and resources listed above.

One-on-one teaching **Group work** **Whole class instruction** **Independent work** **A Assessment**

For a complete guide to selection support, including support for Advanced students, see the Overview of Resources in the frontmatter.

✓Poetry Collection 1
✓✓Poetry Collection 2

Dream Deferred
Langston Hughes
Dreams
Langston Hughes
Sonnet on Love XIII
Jean de Sponde
translated by David R. Slavitt
Meciendo
Gabriela Mistral
I Wandered Lonely as a Cloud
William Wordsworth
All Watched Over by Machines of Loving Grace
Richard Brautigan
"Hope" is the thing with feathers—
EMILY DICKINSON
Much Madness is divinest Sense—
EMILY DICKINSON
THE WAR AGAINST THE TREES
STANLEY KUNITZ

RESOURCES FOR:

- L1 Special-Needs Students
- L2 Below-Level Students (Tier 2)
- L3 On-Level Students (Tier 1)
- L4 Advanced Students (Tier 1)
- EL English Learners
- All All Students

Vocabulary/Fluency/Prior Knowledge

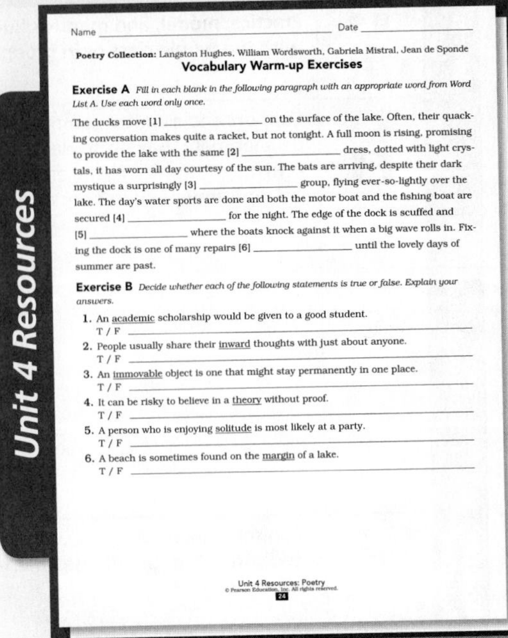

Name _______________ Date _______________

Poetry Collection: Langston Hughes, William Wordsworth, Gabriela Mistral, Jean de Sponde
Vocabulary Warm-up Exercises

Exercise A *Fill in each blank in the following paragraph with an appropriate word from Word List A. Use each word only once.*

The ducks move [1] _______________ on the surface of the lake. Often, their quacking conversation makes quite a racket, but not tonight. A full moon is rising, promising to provide the lake with the same [2] _______________ dress, dotted with light crystals, it has worn all day courtesy of the sun. The bats are arriving, despite their dark mystique a surprisingly [3] _______________ group, flying ever-so-lightly over the lake. The day's water sports are done and both the motor boat and the fishing boat are secured [4] _______________ for the night. The edge of the dock is scuffed and [5] _______________ where the boats knock against it when a big wave rolls in. Fixing the dock is one of many repairs [6] _______________ until the lovely days of summer are past.

Exercise B *Decide whether each of the following statements is true or false. Explain your answers.*

1. An academic scholarship would be given to a good student.
T / F _______________
2. People usually share their inward thoughts with just about anyone.
T / F _______________
3. An immovable object is one that might stay permanently in one place.
T / F _______________
4. It can be risky to believe in a theory without proof.
T / F _______________
5. A person who is enjoying solitude is most likely at a party.
T / F _______________
6. A beach is sometimes found on the margin of a lake.
T / F _______________

Unit 4 Resources: Poetry
© Pearson Education, Inc. All rights reserved.
24

EL L1 L2 **Vocabulary Warm-ups A and B,** pp. 23–24, 41–42

Also available for these selections:

EL L1 L2 **Reading Warm-ups A and B,** pp. 25–26, 43–44

All **Writing About the Big Question,** pp. 27, 45

All **Vocabulary Builder,** pp. 30, 48

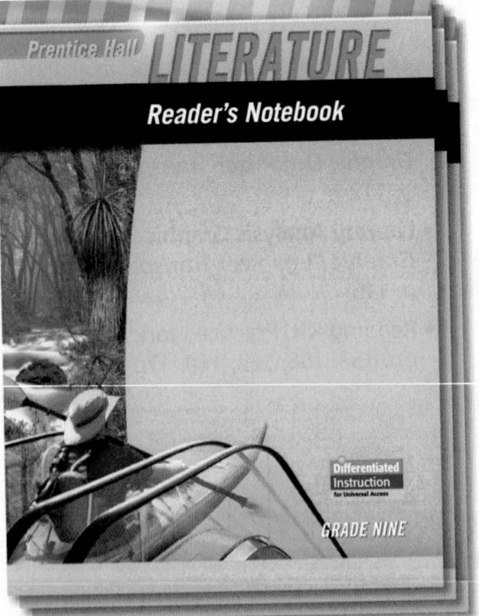

Reader's Notebooks

Pre- and postreading pages for both selections, as well as "Poetry Collection 1," appear in an interactive format in the *Reader's Notebooks.* Each *Notebook* is differentiated for a different group of learners.

The selections in the Adapted and English Learner's versions are abridged.

L2 L3 ***Reader's Notebook***

L1 ***Reader's Notebook: Adapted Version***

EL ***Reader's Notebook: English Learner's Version***

EL ***Reader's Notebook: Spanish Version***

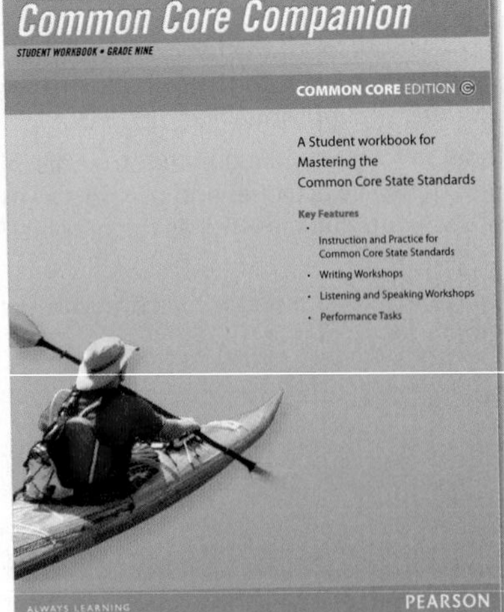

Common Core Companion

Additional instruction and practice for each Common Core State Standard

Selection Support

Graphic Organizer Transparencies

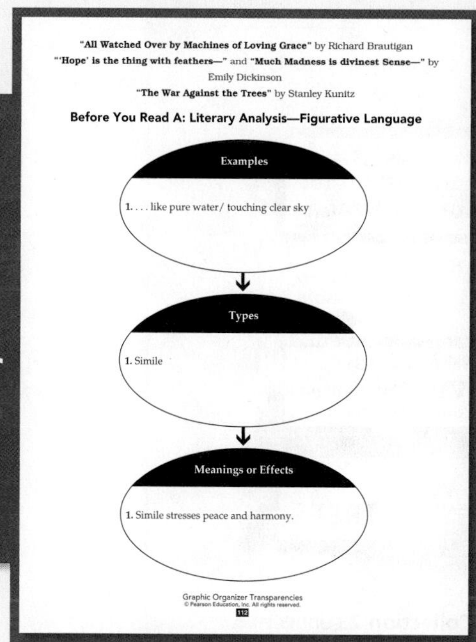
"All Watched Over by Machines of Loving Grace" by Richard Brautigan
"'Hope' is the thing with feathers—" and "Much Madness is divinest Sense—" by Emily Dickinson
"The War Against the Trees" by Stanley Kunitz

Before You Read A: Literary Analysis—Figurative Language

Examples

1. . . . like pure water/ touching clear sky

Types

1. Simile

Meanings or Effects

1. Simile stresses peace and harmony.

Graphic Organizer Transparencies
© Pearson Education, Inc. All rights reserved.
112

EL L1 L2 **Literary Analysis: Graphic Organizer A,** pp. 111–112 (partially filled in)

Also available for these selections:

EL L3 Literary Analysis: Graphic Organizer B, p. 113

EL L1 L2 Reading: Graphic Organizer A, pp. 114–115 (partially filled in)

EL L2 Reading: Graphic Organizer B, p. 116

Skills Development/Extension

Unit 4 Resources

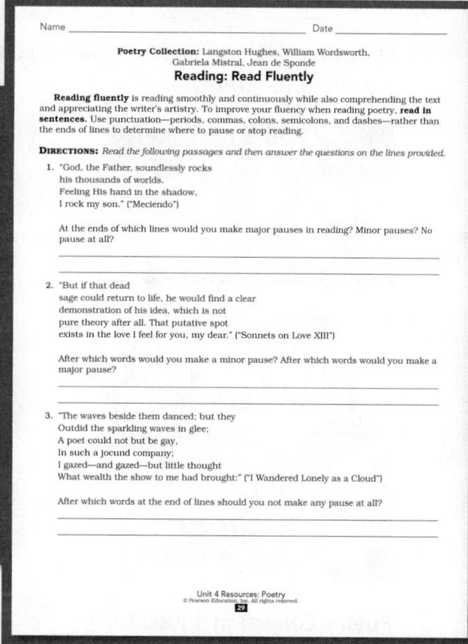
Name ______________________ Date ____________

Poetry Collection: Langston Hughes, William Wordsworth, Gabriela Mistral, Jean de Sponde

Reading: Read Fluently

Reading fluently is reading smoothly and continuously while also comprehending the text and appreciating the writer's artistry. To improve your fluency when reading poetry, **read in sentences.** Use punctuation—periods, commas, colons, semicolons, and dashes—rather than the ends of lines to determine where to pause or stop reading.

Directions: *Read the following passages and then answer the questions on the lines provided.*

1. "God, the Father, soundlessly rocks
his thousands of worlds.
Feeling His hand in the shadow,
I rock my son." ("Meciendo")

At the ends of which lines would you make major pauses in reading? Minor pauses? No pause at all?

2. "But if that dead
sage could return to life, he would find a clear
demonstration of his idea, which is not
pure theory after all. That putative spot
exists in the love I feel for you, my dear." ("Sonnets on Love XIII")

After which words would you make a minor pause? After which words would you make a major pause?

3. "The waves beside them danced; but they
Outdid the sparkling waves in glee;
A poet could not but be gay,
In such a jocund company;
I gazed—and gazed—but little thought
What wealth the show to me had brought:" ("I Wandered Lonely as a Cloud")

After which words at the end of lines should you not make any pause at all?

Unit 4 Resources: Poetry
© Pearson Education, Inc. All rights reserved.
29

All **Reading: Read Fluently,** pp. 29, 47

Also available for these selections:

All Literary Analysis: Figurative Language, pp. 28, 46

L4 Enrichment, pp. 31, 49

EL L3 L4 Grammar, p. 50

EL L3 L4 Support for Writing, p. 51

L3 L4 Support for Extend Your Learning, p. 52

Assessment

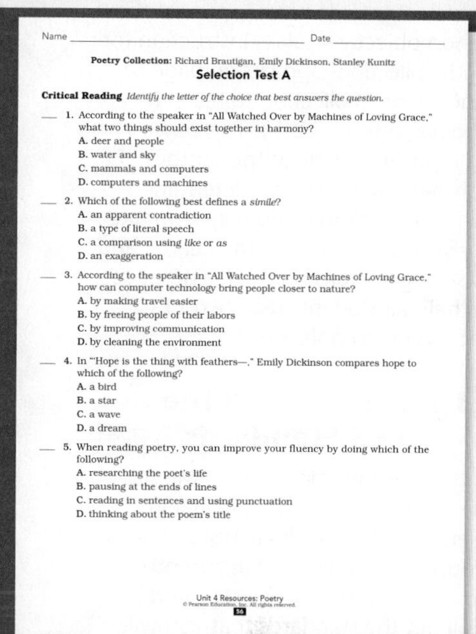
Name ______________________ Date ____________

Poetry Collection: Richard Brautigan, Emily Dickinson, Stanley Kunitz

Selection Test A

Critical Reading *Identify the letter of the choice that best answers the question.*

___ 1. According to the speaker in "All Watched Over by Machines of Loving Grace," what two things should exist together in harmony?
A. deer and people
B. water and sky
C. mammals and computers
D. computers and machines

___ 2. Which of the following best defines a *simile*?
A. an apparent contradiction
B. a type of literal speech
C. a comparison using *like* or *as*
D. an exaggeration

___ 3. According to the speaker in "All Watched Over by Machines of Loving Grace," how can computer technology bring people closer to nature?
A. by making travel easier
B. by freeing people of their labors
C. by improving communication
D. by cleaning the environment

___ 4. In "Hope is the thing with feathers—," Emily Dickinson compares hope to which of the following?
A. a bird
B. a star
C. a wave
D. a dream

___ 5. When reading poetry, you can improve your fluency by doing which of the following?
A. researching the poet's life
B. pausing at the ends of lines
C. reading in sentences and using punctuation
D. thinking about the poem's title

Unit 4 Resources: Poetry
© Pearson Education, Inc. All rights reserved.
36

EL L1 L2 **Selection Test A,** pp. 35–37, 56–58

Also available for these selections:

L3 L4 Open-Book Test, pp. 32–34, 53–55

EL L3 L4 Selection Test B, pp. 38–40, 59–61

PHLit Online!
www.PHLitOnline.com

- complete narrated selection text
- a thematically related video with writing prompt
- an interactive graphic organizer
- highlighting feature
- access to all student print resources, adapted to individual student needs
- Spanish and English summaries
- adapted selection translations in Spanish

Online Resources: All print materials are also available online.

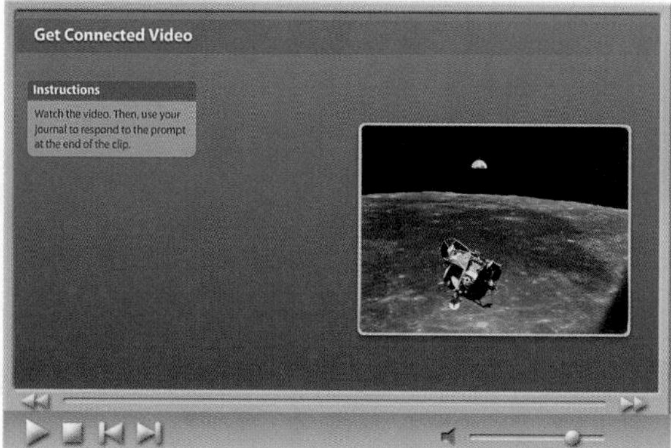

Get Connected! (thematic video with writing prompt)

Also available:

Background Video

All videos are available in Spanish.

Vocabulary Central (tools, activities, and songs for studying vocabulary)

Also available:

Writer's Journal (with graphics feature)

1 Leveled Text

You may use either Poetry Collection 1 or Poetry Collection 2 to meet the lesson objectives. Skills instruction for both collections appears on page 617. Choose one collection to teach (or choose to teach both). The Text Complexity Rubric at the bottom of this page will help you determine which collection is more appropriate for your students. Use the Reader and Task Suggestions on the facing page to help all students read text of increasing complexity.

2 Ⓒ Introducing the CCS Standards

Introduce the standards on the student page. (Note that the lesson element with which each standard is addressed is identified in parentheses after the text of the standard.) Call out the standards that you will cover with the collections, explaining to students what each requires and how they will address it as they work through the collection you have chosen. Standards labeled "Spiral Review" are introduced in the Literary Analysis Workshop for this unit.

Before You Read

Poetry Collection 1 • Poetry Collection 2

1 Ⓒ Leveled Texts

Build your skills and improve your comprehension of poetry with texts of increasing complexity.

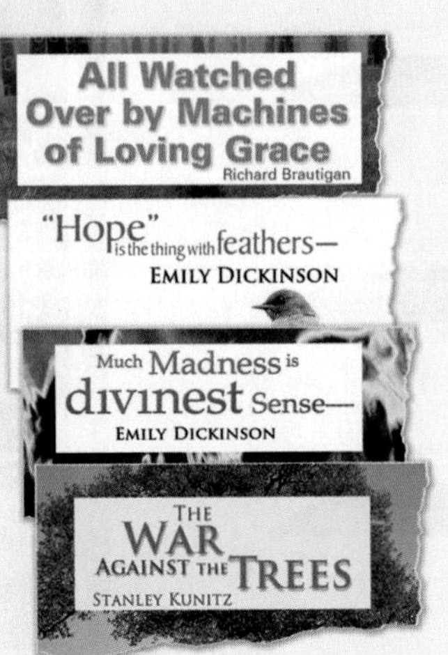

Poetry Collection 1 includes poems about dreams, the natural world, and love.

Poetry Collection 2 connects physical and emotional worlds.

2 Ⓒ Common Core State Standards

Meet these standards with either **Poetry Collection 1** (p. 618) or **Poetry Collection 2** (p. 630).

Reading Literature

4. Determine the meaning of words and phrases as they are used in a text, including figurative and connotative meanings; analyze the cumulative impact of specific word choices on meaning and tone. *(Literary Analysis: Figurative Language; Literary Analysis: Spiral Review)*

Writing

3.d. Use precise words and phrases, telling details, and sensory language to convey a vivid picture of the experiences, events, setting, and/or characters. *(Writing: Description of a Scene)*

Speaking and Listening

4. Present information, findings, and supporting evidence clearly, concisely, and logically such that listeners can follow the line of reasoning and the organization, development, substance, and style are appropriate to purpose, audience, and task. *(Speaking and Listening: Impromptu Speech)*

Language

1. Demonstrate command of the conventions of standard English grammar and usage when writing or speaking. *(Conventions: Prepositions)*

5. Demonstrate understanding of figurative language, word relationships, and nuances in meanings. *(Vocabulary: Analogies)*

616 Poetry

Ⓒ Text Complexity Rubric: Leveled Texts

Text complexity is determined by both qualitative and quantitative measures. For this reason, the quantitative measure of a more complex collection may be lower than that of a more accessible collection.

		✓ Collection 1	✓✓ Collection 2
Qualitative Measures	**Context/ Knowledge Demands**	Focus on emotions 1 (2) 3 4 5	Societal issues (technology, ecology, conformity) 1 2 (3) 4 5
	Structure/Language Conventionality and Clarity	Some challenging vocabulary: sentence structure 1 (2) 3 4 5	Challenging vocabulary and sentence structure 1 2 (3) 4 5
	Levels of Meaning/ Purpose/Concept Level	Accessible concepts (familiar subject matter: dreams, love, motherhood, nature) 1 2 (3) 4 5	Challenging concept (unexpected viewpoints) 1 2 3 (4) 5
Quantitative Measures	**Text Length**	Word Count: 52; 32; 109; 55; 54; 153	Word Count: 98; 66; 33; 192
	Lexile	NP	NP
Overall Complexity		✓ **More accessible**	✓✓ **More complex**

❸ Literary Analysis: Figurative Language

Figurative language is language that is used imaginatively rather than literally. An author's use of figurative language can significantly influence the tone, mood, and theme of a poem. Figurative language includes figures of speech, which are literary devices that make unexpected comparisons or change the usual meanings of words. The following are specific types of figures of speech:

- **Simile:** a comparison of two apparently unlike things using *like, as, than,* or *resembles:* "The morning sun is like a red rubber ball."
- **Metaphor:** a description of one thing as if it were another: "The morning sun is a red rubber ball."
- **Personification:** assignment of human characteristics to a nonhuman subject: "The sea was angry that day, my friends."
- **Paradox:** a statement, an idea, or a situation that seems contradictory but actually expresses a truth: "The more things change, the more they stay the same."

PHLit Online! www.PHLitOnline.com

Hear It!
- Selection summary audio
- Selection audio

See It!
- Get Connected video
- Background video
- More about the author
- Vocabulary flashcards

Do It!
- Interactive journals
- Interactive graphic organizers
- Self-test
- Internet activity
- Grammar tutorial
- Interactive vocabulary games

❹ Using the Strategy: Figurative Language Chart

Use a **figurative language chart** like the one shown to determine the meaning of each type of figurative language you find as you read the poems that follow.

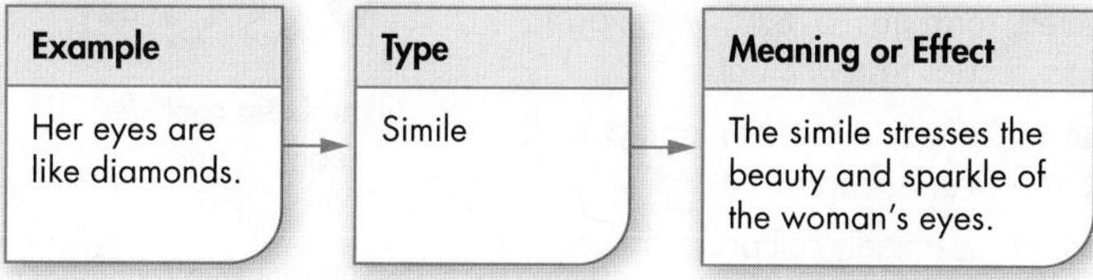

Example	Type	Meaning or Effect
Her eyes are like diamonds.	Simile	The simile stresses the beauty and sparkle of the woman's eyes.

❺ Reading Skill: Read Fluently

Reading fluently is reading continuously while also comprehending the text and appreciating the writer's artistry. Paying attention to punctuation can help you read poetry fluently. When reading poetry, **read in sentences or units of meaning.** Use punctuation rather than the ends of lines to determine where to pause or stop reading.

PRETEACH

❸ Literary Analysis

Figurative Language

1. Introduce the skill, using the instruction on the student page.
2. Tell students to identify figurative language as they read.

Think Aloud: Model the Skill

Model how to identify different figurative language. Say to students:

Figurative language adds meaning to poems, so if I know how to identify the types, I can understand poetry better. Consider this example: "The stars sparkled like diamonds." This is a simile, because the word *like* connects two different ideas, stars and diamonds. I know diamonds are considered beautiful, so the poet must be saying that the stars are beautiful, too.

❹ Using the Strategy

Give students a copy of either **Reading Skill Graphic Organizer A** or **B** (***Graphic Organizer Transparencies,*** pp. 111–113) to record examples and meanings of figurative language as they read. Use the examples in **Literary Skill Graphic Organizer A,** which is partially filled in, to model the process of completing the organizer.

❺ Reading Skill

Read Fluently

1. Introduce the skill, using instruction on the student page.
2. Tell students that they will read fluently to understand poetry.

Text Complexity: Reader and Task Suggestions

✓ Collection 1		✓✓ Collection 2	
Preparing to Read the Text	**Leveled Tasks**	**Preparing to Read the Text**	**Leveled Tasks**
• Using the Background information on TE p. 619, preview the main themes of the collection. • Review the use of imagery in poetry. • Guide students to use Multidraft Reading strategies (TE p. 619).	*Levels of Meaning* If students will have difficulty with levels of meaning, first have them read each poem and identify its main idea. Then, have them reread and discuss the poet's point of view. *Analyzing* If students will not have difficulty with levels of meaning, have them note how figurative language is used to develop the theme of each poem.	• Refer to the Background notes on TE p. 631 and preview the themes of the poems. • Review and discuss the purposes for writing poetry. • Guide students to use Multidraft Reading strategies (TE p. 631).	*Levels of Meaning* If students will have difficulty with levels of meaning, first have them read each poem and note the main idea. Then, have them reread and note details that show how the speaker's point of view is unexpected. Help students clarify their ideas. *Synthesizing* If students will not have difficulty with levels of meaning, have them take notes on the poet's purpose in each poem.

PRETEACH

❶ Writing About the Big Question

1. Review the assignment with the class.
2. Prompt students to think about speeches or presentations they have attended. Encourage volunteers to express how these experiences affected them. Then, explain that oral presentations, including poetry readings, are interactive, which helps people connect to the subject and speaker.
3. Have students complete the sentence starter. Review responses as a class. (**Possible response:** When the speaker of a poem asks the audience to respond to a question, the reader is pushed to consider the poem's meaning and his or her interpretation of it.)
4. Remind students that their answers will help them think about the Big Question, "How does communication change us?"

While You Read

Tell students that as they read each poem, they should think about the ideas the speaker wants to share.

❷ Vocabulary

1. Have students preview the collection vocabulary.
2. For each word, have students say the word aloud.
3. Then, use the word in a sentence that defines the word.
4. Finally, repeat your definitional sentence or a similar sentence with the word missing and have the class "fill in the blank" chorally. Here is an example:

   When someone deferred a task, he or she put it off until a later time. When Bill went to the movie instead of working on his project, he [students say "deferred"] *his work.*

❸ Word Study

1. Introduce the skill, using the instruction in the box.
2. **Ask** students for a *-fer-* word that means "to bring from one place to another." (**Answer:** *transfer*)

Making Connections
Poetry Collection 1

Dream Deferred • Dreams • Sonnet on Love XIII • Meciendo/Rocking • I Wandered Lonely as a Cloud

❶ Writing About the Big Question

The poets in this collection communicate ideas that help us think about the world in new ways. Use this sentence starter to develop your ideas about the Big Question.

When the speaker of a poem asks the audience to **respond** to a question, the reader is pushed to ___________ and ___________.

While You Read Think about what idea or ideas the speaker of each poem is sharing with us. Then, decide how you would respond to any questions the poetry raises.

❷ Vocabulary

Read each word and its definition. Decide whether you know the word well, know it a little bit, or do not know it at all. After you read, see how your knowledge of each word has increased.

- **deferred** (dē fu̇rd´) *adj.* put off until a future time (p. 620) *Jackie deferred her trip to Italy until she had more money.* defer *v.* deferring *v.* deferral *n.* deference *n.*
- **fester** (fes´ tər) *v.* become infected; form pus (p. 620) *The wound became infected and began to fester.* festering *adj.*
- **barren** (bar´ ən) *adj.* empty; having little or no vegetation (p. 621) *The hillside was barren after the fire.* barrenness *n.*
- **paradoxical** (par´ ə däk´ si kəl) *adj.* seemingly full of contradictions (p. 623) *I think it is paradoxical that people in cities could be lonely.* paradox *n.*
- **pensive** (pen´ siv) *adj.* deeply or seriously thoughtful (p. 628) *Everyone remembered the professor as a quiet and pensive man.* pensively *adv.* pensiveness *n.*
- **solitude** (säl´ ə to͞od´) *n.* the state of being solitary, or alone; seclusion, isolation, or remoteness (p. 628) *I enjoy a quiet moment of solitude before the guests arrive.* solitary *adj.* sole *adj.*

❸ Word Study

The **Latin root *-fer-*** means "bring" or "carry."

The first poem in Poetry Collection 1 is about a dream that has been **deferred**—the dream may have been carried away, or put off until a future time.

Vocabulary Development

Vocabulary Knowledge Rating

Create a **Vocabulary Knowledge Rating Chart** ***(Professional Development Guidebook***, p. 33) for this collection. Include the collection vocabulary and the Big Question word that appears in the Writing About the Big Question sentence starter on this page. (The Big Question vocabulary is introduced on pp. 604–605.)

Give students a copy of the chart. Read the words aloud, and have students mark their rating in the Before Reading column. Urge them to be alert to these words as they read and discuss the collection.

Tally how many students think they know a word to gauge how much instruction to provide. As students read and discuss the collection, point out the words and their context.

PHLit Online! **Vocabulary Central,** featuring tools, activities, and songs for studying vocabulary, is available online at **www.PHLitOnline.com.**

Meet the Authors

Langston Hughes

(1902–1967)

Author of "Dream Deferred" • "Dreams" (pp. 620, 621)

Born in Joplin, Missouri, Langston Hughes was the first African American to earn a living by writing literary works. As a young man, he held a variety of jobs—teacher, ranch hand, and farmer, among others. He drew on all of these experiences, but primarily on his perspective as an African American, to create his great body of work.

Jean de Sponde

(1557–1595)

Author of "Sonnet on Love XIII" (p. 622)

The French poet Jean de Sponde was a true Renaissance man who served in the court of King Henry IV, dabbled in chemistry, and published scholarly editions of ancient Greek texts. "Sonnet on Love XIII" is part of his finest work, *Sonnets of Love and Death.*

Gabriela Mistral

(1889–1957)

Author of "Meciendo/Rocking" (p. 624)

Born in Chile as Lucila Godoy y Alcayaga, this writer formed her pen name from the names of her two favorite poets, the Italian Gabriele D'Annunzio and the French Frederic Mistral. Gabriela Mistral wrote many moving poems about children and motherhood. She was awarded the Nobel Prize in Literature in 1945.

William Wordsworth

(1770–1850)

Author of "I Wandered Lonely as a Cloud" (p. 626)

William Wordsworth was born in England's rural Lake District. In 1798, he and fellow poet Samuel Taylor Coleridge published *Lyrical Ballads*—poems that use simple language to exalt everyday life. Emphasizing nature and the imagination, Wordsworth ushered in the age of Romanticism.

Daily Bellringer

For each class during which you will teach this collection, have students complete one of the five Quick Write activities for Week 19 in the **Daily Bellringer Activities** booklet.

4 Background

- **"Dream Deferred"** This poem was originally titled "Harlem: A Dream Deferred" from Langston Hughes's book *Montage of a Dream Deferred.* In this work, Hughes uses rhetorical questions and similes to ask and answer questions about life.
- **"Meciendo/Rocking"** reflects two of the central themes in many of Gabriela Mistral's poems: nature and motherhood. In this poem, she creates a feeling of calmness as she describes rocking her son and listening to the waves and the wind.
- **"I Wandered Lonely as a Cloud"** is one of William Wordsworth's most famous poems. The poem's subject, nature and memory, describes the poet's discovery of a field of daffodils by a lake, instilling in the reader a feeling of communion with nature.

Multidraft Reading

To assist struggling readers and to deepen reading for all, apply multidraft reading protocols. For each reading, have students set the purpose indicated:

- **First reading**—identifying key ideas and details and answering any Reading Checks.
- **Second reading**—analyzing craft and structure and responding to the side-column prompts.
- **Third reading**—integrating knowledge and ideas, connecting to other texts and the world, and answering the end-of-selection questions.

For more guidance, refer to the ***Classroom Strategies and Teaching Routines*** card on multidraft reading.

For more about the authors and practice with the selection vocabulary, go online at **www.PHLitOnline.com.**

Differentiated Instruction — Additional Instruction

EL Extended Support—English Learners

Have students complete the **Reading and Vocabulary Warm-ups,** ***Unit 4 Resources,*** pp. 23–26 before they read. Assign the prereading pages and the collection in the ***Reader's Notebook: English Learner's Version.*** Then, have students listen to portions of the collection on the ***Hear It!*** **Audio CD.**

L1 L2 Extended Support—Struggling Readers

Have students complete the **Reading and Vocabulary Warm-ups,** ***Unit 4 Resources,*** pp. 23–26 before they read. Assign the prereading pages and the collection in the ***Reader's Notebook: Adapted Version.*** Then, have students listen to portions of the collection on the ***Hear It!*** **Audio CD** (adapted text).

Extended Support—Reluctant Readers

To build motivation and engagement before assigning the collection, have students read "In Your Head," a thematically related selection in ***Reality Central.*** Then, use the questions at the conclusion of the related selection to guide disscussion.

TEACH

❶ Activating Prior Knowledge

Ask students to talk about dreams. Prompt them with these questions: Why do people dream about things they would like to do? How do dreams make people feel? Are they important? Why? What happens to people when their dreams are postponed or deferred?

Concept Connector →

Students will reconsider their ideas after reading the collections.

Small-Group Activity

Have students read the poems aloud as smoothly and rhythmically as they can. If they like, they can "sing" the poems. They should tap on their desks lightly with a finger or pencil to indicate stressed words.

❷ About the Selections

"Dream Deferred" uses powerful images to depict the despair of shattered dreams. In "Dreams," two vivid metaphors describe the importance of hopes and dreams. Sponde's "Sonnet on Love XIII" compares an ancient remark to the love the speaker feels for a beloved. In "Rocking," Mistral uses images of the sea, the wind, and the stars to express a mother's love. In "I Wandered Lonely as a Cloud," Wordsworth recalls a moment when he was inspired by nature's beauty.

❸ Humanities

Street Shadows by Jacob Lawrence

American painter Jacob Lawrence grew up in New York City's Harlem neighborhood, where he studied art and began to create images of African American life and history.

Use this question for discussion:

How does this image suggest the frustrating life story Hughes describes in his poem?

Possible response: The people shown might be gathering to play games because they have no jobs. Their hunched figures might suggest a weariness with life and all its burdens.

❹ Critical Viewing

Possible response: The poem's context of despair gives the image an air of hopelessness.

Street Shadows, 1959, Jacob Lawrence, © ARS, NY/ Photo courtesy of: The Jacob and Gwendolyn Lawrence Foundation / Art Resource, NY

❶❷❸ Dream Deferred

Langston Hughes

❹

▲ Critical Viewing Does the context of this poem make the image above seem hopeless or hopeful? Explain. **[Interpret]**

Harlem

What happens to a dream **deferred**?

Does it dry up
like a raisin in the sun?
Or **fester** like a sore—
And then run?
Does it stink like rotten meat?
Or crust and sugar over—
like a syrupy sweet?

Maybe it just sags
like a heavy load.

Or does it explode?

Vocabulary

deferred (dē fʉrd´) *adj.* put off until a future time

fester (fes´ tər) *v.* become infected; form pus

Vocabulary Development

Expressive Vocabulary

To help students broaden their expressive vocabulary, encourage them to use the following words as they discuss the selection: *focus, achieves, benefits,* and *maintain*. Have them complete these sentence starters.

1. The most powerful image the poems *focus* on is . . .
2. Through his images, Hughes *achieves* . . .
3. The *benefits* of dreams are shown through . . .
4. The images show that we must *maintain* our dreams or . . .

Dreams

Langston Hughes

❺ Hold fast to dreams
For if dreams die
Life is a broken-winged bird
That cannot fly.

Hold fast to dreams
For when dreams go
Life is a barren field
Frozen with snow.

Reading Skill
Read Fluently
How many sentences are in the first stanza?

Vocabulary
barren (bar´ ən) *adj.* empty; having little or no vegetation

❺ Reading Skill
Read Fluently

1. Read the poem aloud in a smooth rhythm, pausing as you would in natural speech. Point out that some pauses occur even though there are no punctuation marks. For example, a slight pause might be given at the end of the first line before continuing on to line two. Emphasize that the pause occurs not because the line ends but because there is a slight break in the ideas. "Hold fast to dreams" is a complete thought. "For if dreams die," is a dependent clause that signals a shift in ideas.
2. **Ask** students the Reading Skill question: How many sentences are in the first stanza?
Answer: The first stanza contains one sentence.

PHLit Online!
This collection is available in interactive format in the **Enriched Online Student Edition, www.PHLitOnline.com,** which includes a thematically related video with writing prompt and an interactive graphic organizer.

Differentiated Instruction for Universal Access

Strategy for Less Proficient Readers
Copy both Hughes poems on the board. Circle the questions and statements in the poems, and discuss each one. Note the opening question in "Dream Deferred" and explain that the possible answers to this question form the topic of the poem. In "Dreams," make sure that students notice that the first and second stanzas begin with the same line. The three other lines in each stanza describe in metaphors what happens when people's dreams are frustrated.

Strategy for Special-Needs Students
Help students better understand figurative language by showing them **Literary Analysis Graphic Organizer A** (***Graphic Organizer Transparencies*** p. 111). Review the types of figurative language: simile, metaphor, personification, and paradox. Ask students to look through the poems and locate the examples listed in the partially completed organizer. Use these examples to explain the characteristics of each figure of speech. Then encourage students to watch for other examples as they continue reading.

6 Humanities 6

A Learned Man by Domenico Feti

Italian painter Domenico Feti (1588/89–1623?) was one of the early baroque painters. Feti's work is characterized by his use of light and shadow and by his portrayal of ordinary people with heroic qualities. Use these questions to stimulate discussion.

1. What does the painting suggest the man is doing? Explain why you think so.
   Possible response: He is trying to solve a problem involving geography. He is looking at a map, holding his hand on a globe, and has several instruments used for geometry and geography. He appears to be deep in thought as though trying to solve a problem.
2. How does this painting reflect the image of Archimedes that is described in "Sonnet on Love XIII"?
   Possible response: It shows an intelligent, studious man pondering a problem, as Archimedes might have done while thinking about how he could "move the world."

Vocabulary Development

CCSS Language 6

Thematic Vocabulary: The Big Question

As students are discussing "Sonnet on Love XIII," encourage them to use the thematic vocabulary presented in Introducing the Big Question, pp. 604–605. You might encourage them with sentence starters like these:

1. In the poem, de Sponde uses questions as a way to *discuss*. . .
2. Each question helps describe a *relationship* between . . .
3. The reader's *interpretation* of the poem is based on . . .
4. After reading the poem, the reader may gain *understanding* of . . .

Sonnet on Love XIII

Jean de Sponde

translated by David R. Slavitt

7 **Background** Archimedes (är′ kə mē′ dēz′) (287?–212 B.C.) has been called the founder of theoretical mechanics. He was a brilliant Greek mathematician and inventor who once boasted that, given a place to stand in space and a long enough lever, he could move the Earth itself. Legend has it that when he made a great discovery, he jumped up and shouted "Eureka!" ("I have found it!").

"Give me a place to stand," Archimedes said,
"and I can move the world." **Paradoxical**, clever,
his remark which first explained the use of the lever
was an academic joke. But if that dead

sage could return to life, he would find a clear
demonstration of his idea, which is not
pure theory after all. That putative[1] spot
8 exists in the love I feel for you, my dear.

What could be more immovable or stronger?
What becomes more and more secure, the longer
it is battered by inconstancy and the stress

we find in our lives? Here is that fine fixed point
from which to move a world that is out of joint,
as he could have done, had he known a love like this.

Vocabulary
paradoxical (par′ ə däk′ si kəl) *adj.* seemingly full of contradictions

Reading Skill
Read Fluently
Where does the sentence that starts in line 10 end?

1. putative (pyo͞ot′ ə tiv) *adj.* supposed; known by reputation.

9 ◄ **Critical Viewing** Based on this depiction of Archimedes, how do you think he would have responded to de Sponde's poem? **[Speculate]**

Fluency

Distribute copies of page 623, and pair students. Have listeners mark words with which reading partners struggle. Circulate to monitor students' fluency, then collect the marked-up pages. Review difficult words and passages, such as these:

- If students struggle to syllabicate *paradoxical,* model how to cover parts of the word, pronounce each part, and then blend the parts together. Read the word aloud and have students echo to confirm.
- If students pronounce, but stumble, over the word *sage,* reinforce its meaning by pointing out the context clues *academic* and *idea*. Once students build meaning, have them reread for fluency.
- If students stop at the end of a stanza instead of continuing, point out that they should only stop if they see punctuation. Tell them to pause briefly at a comma and stop briefly at a period.

7 Background

Archimedes Archimedes was a great friend of King Hiero of Syracuse. According to one story, Hiero heard Archimedes make his claim that he could move the world if he had a place to stand. Hiero challenged him to prove it. In the harbor lay a ship that the strength of many men could not launch. Archimedes built a system of pulleys and levers and launched the ship by himself, proving his claim.

8 Reading Skill

Read Fluently

1. Remind students that when they read poetry they should read in sentences. Have students read the poem aloud. Then, **ask** students the Reading Skill question: Where does the sentence that starts in line 10 end?
   Answer: It ends line 12.
2. **Ask** a volunteer to read the sentence aloud. If necessary, coach the student in reading it fluently without pausing at the end of each line.

▶ **Monitor Progress:** Assign portions of the sonnet to different students to read. Tell them to read fluently, pausing only for natural breaks and for punctuation.

▶ **Reteach:** If students continue to have difficulty reading fluently, have them guide you in rewriting the poem in paragraph form on the board. Then have students read it as prose. Discuss how fluent reading keeps related ideas together, making the meaning clearer, and keeps the rhythm natural.

9 Critical Viewing

Possible response: Students might say that Archimedes would find the idea romantic. Some might say he would consider it nonsense for that reason. Others might say he would agree that love is a powerful human emotion that is capable of standing firm in a world of change.

⑩ Critical Viewing

Possible response: The photograph successfully illustrates the "loving sea" described in the poem. The photograph shows the vastness of the sea, verifying the poem's "thousands of waves." The photograph also shows gentle waves, which illustrates the poem's description of the sea's rocking nature.

Meciendo

Gabriela Mistral

⑩ ▲ **Critical Viewing** How well does this photograph illustrate the "loving sea" described in the poem? Explain. **[Evaluate]**

El mar sus millares de olas
mece, divino.
Oyendo a los mares amantes,
mezo a mi niño.

El viento errabundo en la noche
mece a los trigos.
Oyendo a los vientos amantes,
mezo a mi niño.

Diós Padre sus miles de mundos
mece sin ruido.
Sintiendo su mano en la sombra,
mezo a mi niño.

Think Aloud

Read Fluently

Draw students' attention to the Spanish and English versions of the poem. Use the following "think aloud" to model how to read fluently.

When I first see that this poem appears in two languages, I look for the language that I speak more fluently. I read the poem in that language first. I use the commas and periods to help me hear that rhythm, reading past the line breaks as if they were not there. I do pause briefly at the stanza breaks.

I must remember that the poet wrote the poem in Spanish first. I read the Spanish aloud to hear the rhythm of the words, even if I don't understand them. Then I study the English version and notice that the line and stanza breaks are very similar. I read the poem aloud in English, using the same fluent reading technique.

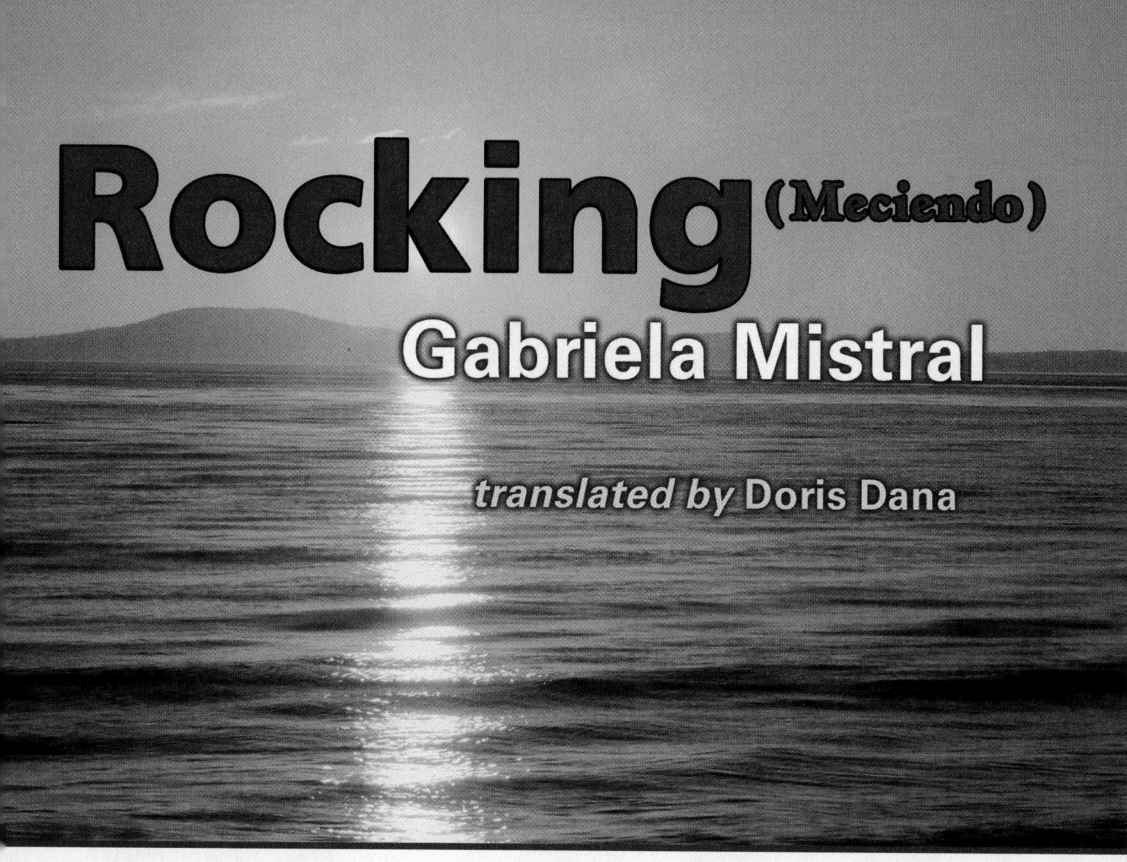

Rocking (Meciendo)

Gabriela Mistral

translated by Doris Dana

The sea rocks her thousands of waves.
The sea is divine.
Hearing the loving sea,
I rock my son.

The wind wandering by night
rocks the wheat.
Hearing the loving wind,
I rock my son.

God, the Father, soundlessly rocks
His thousands of worlds.
Feeling His hand in the shadow,
I rock my son.

Literary Analysis
Figurative Language
What human traits does the wind show in the second stanza?

Differentiated Instruction for Universal Access

EL Strategy for English Learners

Encourage students fluent in Spanish to find other poems by Gabriela Mistral that are available in both Spanish and English. Have students work in small groups to prepare and perform readings of the works in both languages for the entire class. Tell them to be prepared to discuss how the two versions of each work differ in terms of rhyme scheme and other factors.

Strategy for Advanced Readers

Explain to students that they can learn something about a poem just by looking at it in its original language—even if they don't know that language. Have students look over both poems and compare the uses of rhyme and repetition to see if they notice any differences. If students speak an addtional language, have them translate the poem into that language and compare again.

11 Literary Analysis

Figurative Language

1. Have students reread the poem silently. **Ask** the Literary Analysis question: What human traits does the wind show in the second stanza?
   Answer: The wind is "wandering" and "loving"; it "rocks the wheat."
2. Discuss the effect of the personification in this poem. Then **ask** how the personification of the sea in the first stanza and of the wind in the second stanza affects the mood of the poem.
   Possible response: It makes nature seem loving and humane.
3. Point out that the human qualities of nature in the first two stanzas lead to the third stanza where the image of God replaces that of nature. Help students see the connection: that God is a gentle, human force that cares for people.
4. Have students add the information to **Literary Analysis Graphic Organizer B** (p. 113 in *Graphic Organizer Transparencies*). Tell them to continue collecting figures of speech from the rest of the poems in the selection.

12 Connecting to the Big Question

1. Point out that poets use figurative language to communicate their ideas in a vivid manner. Discuss with students whether they find visual communication more or less effective than verbal communication and why.
2. Have students read the long bracketed passage on page 627. **Ask:** What idea do you think the speaker is trying to share? **Possible response:** The speaker shares the idea that seeing brightly colored flowers makes him or her feel less lonely.
3. **Ask** students: How does visual communication affect the reader? **Possible response:** The communication of a bright sight might change the reader's mood to a more cheerful one.

Vocabulary Development

Vocabulary Knowledge Rating

When students have completed reading and discussing this group of poems, have them take out their **Vocabulary Knowledge Rating Chart** for Poetry Collection 1. Read the words aloud once more and have students rate their knowledge of the words again in the After Reading column. Clarify any words that are still problematic. Have students write their own definition and example or sentence in the appropriate column. Then, have students complete the Vocabulary Practice activities at the end of the collection. Encourage students to use the words in further discussion and written work about these poems. Remind them that they will be accountable for these words on the **Selection Test, *Unit 4 Resources*,** pp. 35–37 or 38–40.

I Wandered Lonely as a Cloud

William Wordsworth

I wandered lonely as a cloud
That floats on high o'er vales[1] and hills,
When all at once I saw a crowd,
A host, of golden daffodils;
Beside the lake, beneath the trees,
Fluttering and dancing in the breeze.

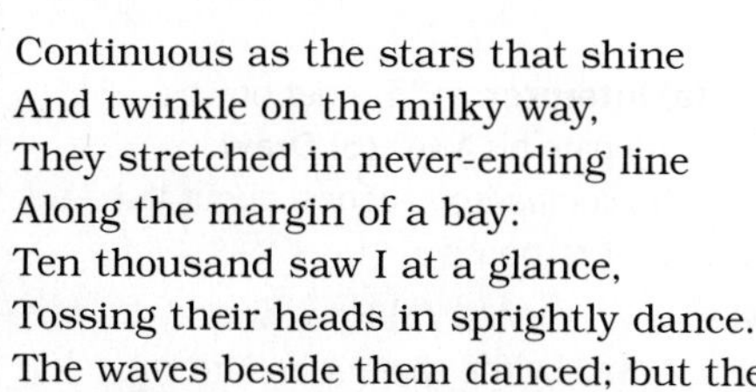

13 Continuous as the stars that shine
And twinkle on the milky way,
12 They stretched in never-ending line
Along the margin of a bay:
Ten thousand saw I at a glance,
Tossing their heads in sprightly dance.
The waves beside them danced; but they
Outdid the sparkling waves in glee;
A poet could not but be gay,
In such a jocund[2] company;

Spiral Review

Tone Compare the tone of line 1 to the tone of line 6. In what way has the tone shifted?

Literary Analysis

Figurative Language To what does the speaker compare the daffodils in the simile in lines 7–8?

1. **o'er vales** over valleys.
2. **jocund** (jak´ ənd) *adj.* cheerful.

Concept Connector

Activating Prior Knowledge
Have students reconsider their ideas about dreams. Ask them how their ideas have changed since reading the collection. Encourage them to cite specific examples from the poems.

Writing About the Big Question
Have students compare their responses to the sentence starter they completed before reading the collection with their ideas afterward. Ask them to explain whether their thoughts have changed.

Literary Analysis Graphic Organizer
Ask students to review the graphic organizers they completed to identify figurative language in the poems. Show them **Literary Analysis Graphic Organizer A** (*Graphic Organizer Transparencies,* p. 111) as an example. Then have students share the graphic organizers they did and the figurative language they identified.

Spiral Review

Tone

1. Remind students that they studied the concept of tone in the Unit 4 Literary Analysis workshop (pp. 606–614).
2. **Ask** students the Spiral Review question.
   Possible response: Line 1 conveys a sad or serious tone because of the connotations of the word *lonely*. In contrast, the words in line 6 convey a carefree tone. The words' connotations are related to things that move with joy and confidence.

13 Literary Analysis

Figurative Language

1. Bring students' attention to the first line of the poem. **Ask** students to identify the figurative language that is used in this line.
   Answer: A simile compares the speaker's loneliness to that of a cloud. The speaker also uses personification when suggesting that the cloud feels lonely.
2. Have students read lines 7–8. Then, **ask** the Literary Analysis question: To what does the speaker compare the daffodils in the simile in lines 7–8?
   Answer: The speaker compares the daffodils to stars in the Milky Way.
3. **Ask** students to explain why the speaker's daffodil comparison is a simile and not a metaphor.
   Answer: The comparison is a simile because *as* is used in "Continuous *as* the stars."
4. Point out to students that in the final lines of stanza two, the speaker describes the ten thousand daffodils as "Tossing their heads in a sprightly dance." **Ask** students to identify this figure of speech. Then, ask what characteristic helps them identify it.
   Answer: This figure of speech is personification. Students should recognize it because the speaker gives the daffodils the human characteristics of tossing their heads and dancing.

ASSESS

Answers

Critical Thinking

Before students respond, you may wish to have them write a brief objective summary of each selection. As they answer the questions below, remind them to support their answers with evidence from the text.

1. (a) The speaker compares life to an injured bird and to a barren, frozen field. (b) **Possible response:** Cherish your dreams, for without them, life is meaningless and sterile.
2. (a) "Dream Deferred" asks six questions. (b) The last question is in italics, is separated from the other questions, and comes after a statement. This treatment makes the last question the one with the most impact.
3. (a) The poem describes a field of daffodils blowing in the breeze. (b) The speaker describes the sight and sound of waves and of the wind blowing wheat. (c) **Possible response:** The sights and sounds fill the speakers with delight and comfort.
4. (a) The speaker compares his love to the spot in space on which he would stand to move the planet. (b) **Possible response:** The comparison suggests that the speaker's love is powerful and immovable, just as Archimedes' comment suggests that his thoughts and ideas were so powerful that he could change the world.
5. **Possible responses:** (a) A dream deferred may in fact be realized later on in life, if we are patient and persistent, and resist the urge to become bitter. (b) "Dreams" reaffirms the idea that dreams can be deferred but still realized if we hold on to them. Without dreams, life can dry up and become meaningless.

Vocabulary
pensive (pen´ siv) *adj.* deeply or seriously thoughtful
solitude (säl´ ə to͞od´) *n.* the state of being solitary, or alone; seclusion, isolation, or remoteness

I gazed—and gazed—but little thought
What wealth the show to me had brought:

For oft, when on my couch I lie
In vacant or in **pensive** mood,
They flash upon that inward eye
Which is the bliss of **solitude**;
And then my heart with pleasure fills,
And dances with the daffodils.

Critical Thinking

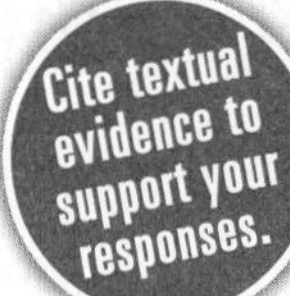
Cite textual evidence to support your responses.

1. **Key Ideas and Details (a)** To what two things does the speaker in "Dreams" compare life? **(b) Interpret:** Restate in your own words the advice that "Dreams" offers.
2. **Key Ideas and Details (a)** How many questions does "Dream Deferred" ask? Explain. **(b) Contrast:** In what way is the last question different from the others? Explain your response.
3. **Key Ideas and Details (a)** In "I Wandered Lonely as a Cloud," what natural sight does the speaker describe? **(b)** In "Meciendo/Rocking," what natural sights and sounds does the speaker describe? **(c) Compare and Contrast:** How do the natural sights and sounds affect each of the speakers? Explain how each poem reveals this.
4. **Key Ideas and Details (a) Interpret:** In "Sonnet on Love XIII," to what does the speaker compare his love? **(b) Draw Conclusions:** What does this comparison suggest about the speaker's feelings? Explain your response.
5. **Integration of Knowledge and Ideas (a)** How would you answer the main question posed by the speaker in "Dream Deferred"? Why? **(b)** How does your response to that question grow or change when you read "Dreams"? Explain. *[Connect to the Big Question: How does communication change us?]*

Assessment Resources

Unit 4 Resources

L1 L2 EL **Selection Test A,** pp. 35–37. Administer Test A to less advanced readers.

L3 L4 EL **Selection Test B,** pp. 38–40. Administer Test B to on-level and more advanced students.

L3 L4 **Open-Book Test,** pp. 32–34. As an alternative, give the Open-Book Test.

All **Customizable Test Bank**

All **Self-tests**
Students may prepare for the **Selection Test** by taking the **Self-test** online.

PHLit Online!
All assessment resources are available at **www.PHLitOnline.com.**

After You Read
Poetry Collection 1

Dream Deferred • Dreams • Sonnet on Love XIII • Meciendo/Rocking • I Wandered Lonely as a Cloud

Literary Analysis: Figurative Language

1. **Craft and Structure** **(a)** Identify one **simile** in "Dream Deferred" and one **metaphor** in "Dreams." **(b)** Explain what each **figure of speech** contributes to the overall meaning of the poem in which it appears.
2. **Craft and Structure** **(a)** Identify an example of **personification** in Poetry Collection 1. **(b)** Explain how this use of **figurative language** contributes to the overall effect of the poem in which it appears.
3. **Craft and Structure** Identify and explain the **paradox** in "Sonnet on Love XIII."

Dream Deferred — Langston Hughes
Dreams — Langston Hughes
Sonnet on Love XIII — Jean de Sponde, translated by David R. Slavitt
Meciendo — Gabriela Mistral
I Wandered Lonely as a Cloud — William Wordsworth

Reading Skill: Read Fluently

4. **(a)** Using a graphic organizer like the one shown, rewrite one stanza in Poetry Collection 1 as a prose paragraph.

Stanza	Paragraph
God, the Father, soundlessly rocks His thousands of worlds. Feeling His hand in the shadow, I rock my son.	God, the Father, soundlessly rocks His thousands of worlds. Feeling His hand in the shadow, I rock my son.

(b) Read the stanza and the paragraph aloud. How does following the punctuation help you **read fluently?**

Vocabulary

Acquisition and Use Vocabulary **analogies** show the relationships between pairs of words. Use a word from the vocabulary list on page 618 to make a word pair that matches the relationship between the first two given words.

1. active : exercise :: _______________ : ponder
2. rainy : weather :: _______________ : statement
3. empty : full :: _______________ : fruitful
4. rushed : hurried :: _______________ : delayed
5. multitude : many :: _______________ : one
6. burn : blaze :: _______________ : rot

Word Study Use the context of the sentences and what you know about the **Latin root *-fer-*** to explain your answer to each question.

1. If you *transfer* something, do you keep it in one place?
2. Does a *conference* bring people together?

Word Study

The **Latin root *-fer-*** means "bring" or "carry."

Apply It Explain how the root *-fer-* contributes to the meanings of these words. Consult a dictionary if necessary.

infer
referral
fertile

ASSESS/EXTEND

Answers

Literary Analysis

1. (a) **Possible response:** ***Simile:*** "Does it dry up like a raisin in the sun?"; ***Metaphor:*** "life is a broken-winged bird. . . " (b) **Possible response:** The simile in "Dream Deferred" makes the reader wonder if a deferred dream just wastes away. The metaphor in "Dreams" tells the reader that if dreams die, we cannot live life to its fullest extent.
2. (a) **Possible response:** One example is in "I Wandered Lonely as a Cloud": "A host, of golden daffodils . . . Fluttering and dancing in the breeze . . ." (b) **Possible response:** It makes the daffodils appear alive and playful, which adds to the joy of the poem
3. **Possible response:** The paradox is between Archimedes' place to stand and the speaker's love for his beloved. The reader realizes that the scientific impossibility reveals an emotional truth.

Reading Skill

4. (a) **Possible response:** "The wind wandering by night rocks the wheat. Hearing the loving wind, I rock my son."

   For other sample answers, see ***Graphic Organizer Transparencies,*** **Reading Skill Graphic Organizer A,** p. 114, and the **Additional Answers** section.

   (b) Following the punctuation keeps similar ideas together through sentence structure, which makes reading more fluent.

Vocabulary
Acquisition and Use
Sample answers:

1. pensive
2. paradoxical
3. barren
4. deferred
5. solitude
6. fester

Word Study
Sample answers:

1. No, the root *-fer-* means "to carry," so when you *transfer* something, you carry it to someone or someplace.
2. Yes, the root *-fer-* means "to bring," so a *conference* brings people together.

Word Study: Apply It
Sample answers: To *infer* is to come to or bring by reasoning. To give a *referral* is to "bring" a person or information to another person or place. Something *fertile* is able to bring about produce or abundance.

*Skills instruction for the **Reading Skill** and **Literary Analysis** concepts appears on p. 617.*

❶ Writing About the Big Question

1. Review the assignment with the class.
2. Prompt students to **list** advances in computer technology. (**Sample answers:** Internet, instant messaging, video capabilities, designing capabilities, etc.) Then, **ask** them how this technology has affected their lives.
3. Have students complete the sentence starter. Review responses as a class. (**Possible response:** As a result of advances in computer technology, relationships between people have become stronger because it is easier to communicate.)
4. Remind students that their answers will help them think about the Big Question, "How does communication change us?"

While You Read

Tell students that as they read, they should consider what each poem reveals about how people relate to each other and to the world around them.

❷ Vocabulary

1. Have students preview the collection vocabulary.
2. For each word, have students say the word aloud.
3. Then, use the word in a sentence that defines the word.
4. Repeat your definitional sentence or a similar sentence with the word missing, and have the class "fill in the blank" chorally. Here is an example:

   A discerning person has good judgment. When Herman carefully chooses the sneakers that fit him best, we can call him [students say "discerning"].

❸ Word Study

1. Introduce the skill, using the instruction in the box.
2. **Ask** students to identify the *-vert-* word that means "to turn into something else." (**Answer:** *convert*)

Making Connections
Poetry Collection 2

All Watched Over... • "Hope" is the thing... • Much Madness is divinest... • The War Against the Trees

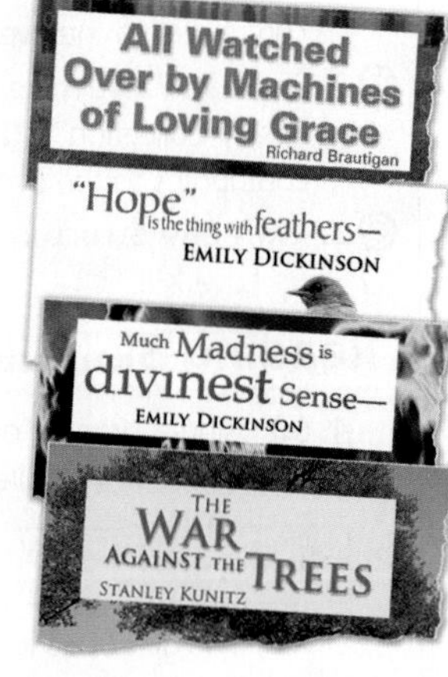

❶ Writing About the Big Question

The poets in this collection share thoughts about how technology, war, and even ideas can change both us and the way we regard the world. Use this sentence starter to develop your ideas about the Big Question:

As a result of advances in computer technology, **relationships** between people have become ____________ because ____________.

While You Read Consider what each poem has to say about how people relate to each other and to the world around them.

❷ Vocabulary

Read each word and its definition. Decide whether you know the word well, know it a little bit, or do not know it at all. After you read, see how your knowledge of each word has increased.

- **abash** (ə bash′) *v.* embarrass (p. 634) ***The bully would continuously abash his peers to make himself feel more confident.*** *abashed adj. abashedly adv. bashful adj.*
- **discerning** (di surn′ iŋ) *adj.* having good judgment or understanding (p. 635) ***The discerning viewer will realize what a bad movie this is.*** *discern v. discernment n.*
- **prevail** (prē vāl′) *v.* gain the advantage or mastery; be victorious; triumph (p. 635) ***Good prevails over evil in this holiday movie.*** *prevailing adj.*
- **preliminaries** (prē lim′ ə ner′ ēz) *n.* steps or events before the main one (p. 637) ***The preliminaries, especially the national anthem, were more exciting than the game.*** *preliminary adj.*
- **subverting** (səb vurt′ iŋ) *v.* overthrowing or destroying something established (p. 637) ***By subverting the monarchy, the revolutionaries hoped to bring freedom.*** *subvert v. subversive adj. subversion n.*
- **seizure** (sē′ zhər) *n.* a sudden and brief loss of consciousness and body control. (p. 637) ***One of the customers in the store suffered a seizure and fell to the floor.*** *seize v.*

❸ Word Study

The **Latin root *-vert-*** means "turn."

In the poem "The War Against the Trees," the speaker describes the **subverting** of trees. Bulldozers dig into the roots of the trees and *turn* the trees over from underneath.

Vocabulary Development

Vocabulary Knowledge Rating

Create a **Vocabulary Knowledge Rating Chart** (***Professional Development Guidebook***, p. 33) for this collection. Include the collection vocabulary and the Big Question word that appears in the Writing About the Big Question sentence starter on this page. (The Big Question vocabulary is introduced on pp. 604–605.)

Give students a copy of the chart. Read the words aloud, and have students mark their rating in the Before Reading column. Urge them to be alert to these words as they read and discuss the collection.

Tally how many students think they know a word to gauge how much instruction to provide. As students read and discuss the collection, point out the words and their context.

PHLit Online! **Vocabulary Central,** featuring tools, activities, and songs for studying vocabulary, is available at **www.PHLitOnline.com.**

❹ Meet the Authors

Richard Brautigan

(1935–1984)

Author of "All Watched Over by Machines of Loving Grace" (p. 632)

With his 1967 novel *Trout Fishing in America,* Richard Brautigan became a spokesperson for the hippie generation. Ironically, he was at least fifteen years older than the hippies and a product of the Beat generation that preceded them. Nevertheless, his writing demonstrates his free spirit. His books present sketches of a counterculture that resists dependence on machines, industry, and business.

Emily Dickinson

(1830–1886)

Author of "'Hope' is the thing with feathers—" • "Much Madness is divinest Sense—" (pp. 634, 635)

Despite her quiet, outward behavior, Emily Dickinson's inner life overflowed with energy. She produced at least 1,775 poems. Dickinson looked deeply into simple subjects—a fly buzzing, a bird on a walk, the changing seasons. She also made profound explorations of love, death, and the relationship between the human and the divine. She remains unquestionably one of America's finest poets.

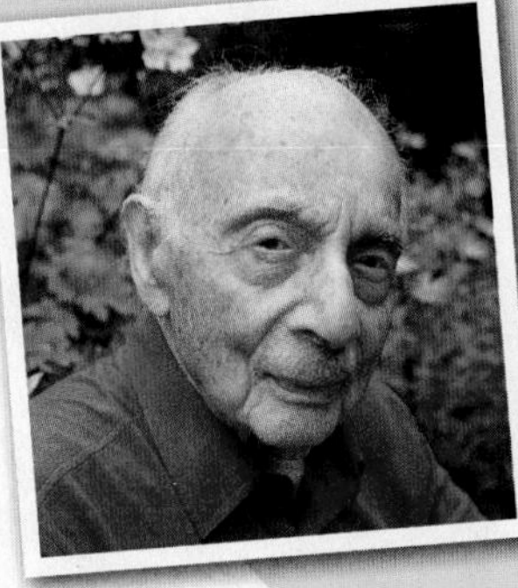

Stanley Kunitz

(1905–2006)

Author of "The War Against the Trees" (p. 636)

Stanley Kunitz was born in Worcester, Massachusetts, and published his first book of poems in 1930. Kunitz worked as an editor on many small magazines and taught countless young poets. He was named the United States Poet Laureate in 2000.

Daily Bellringer

For each class during which you will teach this collection, have students complete one of the five Quick Write activities for Week 19 in the *Daily Bellringer Activities* booklet.

❹ Background

- **"All Watched Over by Machines of Loving Grace"** In the late 1960s, when Richard Brautigan was writing, computers were fairly uncommon. Most were gigantic machines used by scientists or engineers.
- **"Much Madness is divinest Sense—"** Although Emily Dickinson composed more than 1,700 poems, few were published before her death. Those that were, however, were often heavily edited by her publisher. Her unedited poems did not become known until the 1950s.
- **"The War Against the Trees"** Elm trees once lined streets in many parts of America. These towering trees grew to nearly 100 feet tall and lived as long as 300 years. Since the late 1930s, Dutch elm disease has killed many American elms, leaving few of the giants left.

Multidraft Reading

To assist struggling readers and to deepen reading for all, apply multidraft reading protocols. For each reading, have students set the purpose indicated:

- **First reading**—identifying key ideas and details and answering any Reading Checks.
- **Second reading**—analyzing craft and structure and responding to the side-column prompts.
- **Third reading**—integrating knowledge and ideas, connecting to other texts and the world, and answering the end-of-selection questions.

For more guidance, refer to the ***Classroom Strategies and Teaching Routines*** card on multidraft reading.

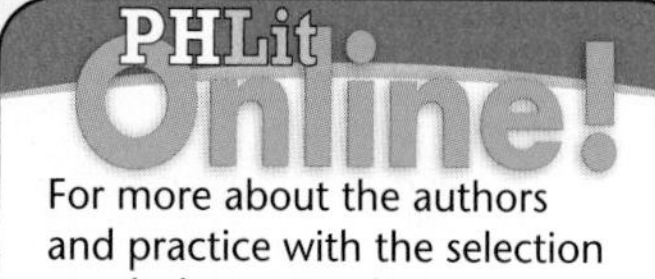

For more about the authors and practice with the selection vocabulary, go online at **www.PHLitOnline.com.**

Differentiated Instruction — Additional Instruction

EL Extended Support—English Learners
Have students complete the **Reading and Vocabulary Warm-ups, *Unit 4 Resources,*** pp. 41–44 before they read. Assign the prereading pages in the ***Reader's Notebook: English Learner's Version.*** Then, have students listen to portions of the collection on the ***Hear It!*** **Audio CD.**

L1 L2 Extended Support—Struggling Readers
Have students complete the **Reading and Vocabulary Warm-ups, *Unit 4 Resources,*** pp. 41–44 before they read. Assign the prereading pages in the ***Reader's Notebook: Adapted Version.*** Then, have students listen to portions of the collection on the ***Hear It!*** **Audio CD** (adapted text).

Extended Support—Reluctant Readers
To build motivation and engagement before assigning the collection, have students read "The Thinking Computer," a thematically related selection in ***Reality Central.*** Then, use the questions at the conclusion of the related selection to guide discussion.

TEACH

❶ Activating Prior Knowledge

Point out to students that computers are taking on more and more jobs in our society. One field of computer research involves computers that learn by themselves, so that they can adjust to unexpected changes. **Invite** students to talk about how far the capabilities of computers can go. Then **pose** this question: Will computers ever become capable of existing independently of humans?

Concept Connector

Students will reconsider their ideas after reading the collections.

Individual Activity

Have students preview the visuals that accompany the poems and make predictions about each poem based on the accompanying artwork. After reading, have them discuss in what way, if any, the artwork shaped their reactions to the poems.

❷ About the Selection

The speaker in "All Watched Over by Machines of Loving Grace" imagines a world in which people and animals live in peace, watched over by benevolent computers. In " 'Hope' is the thing with feathers—," Dickinson compares hope to a bird—small and delicate, yet constant and indomitable. "Much Madness is Divinest Sense—" examines how society defines nonconformists. "The War Against the Trees" compares the destruction of trees to war, reminding readers of ecological concerns.

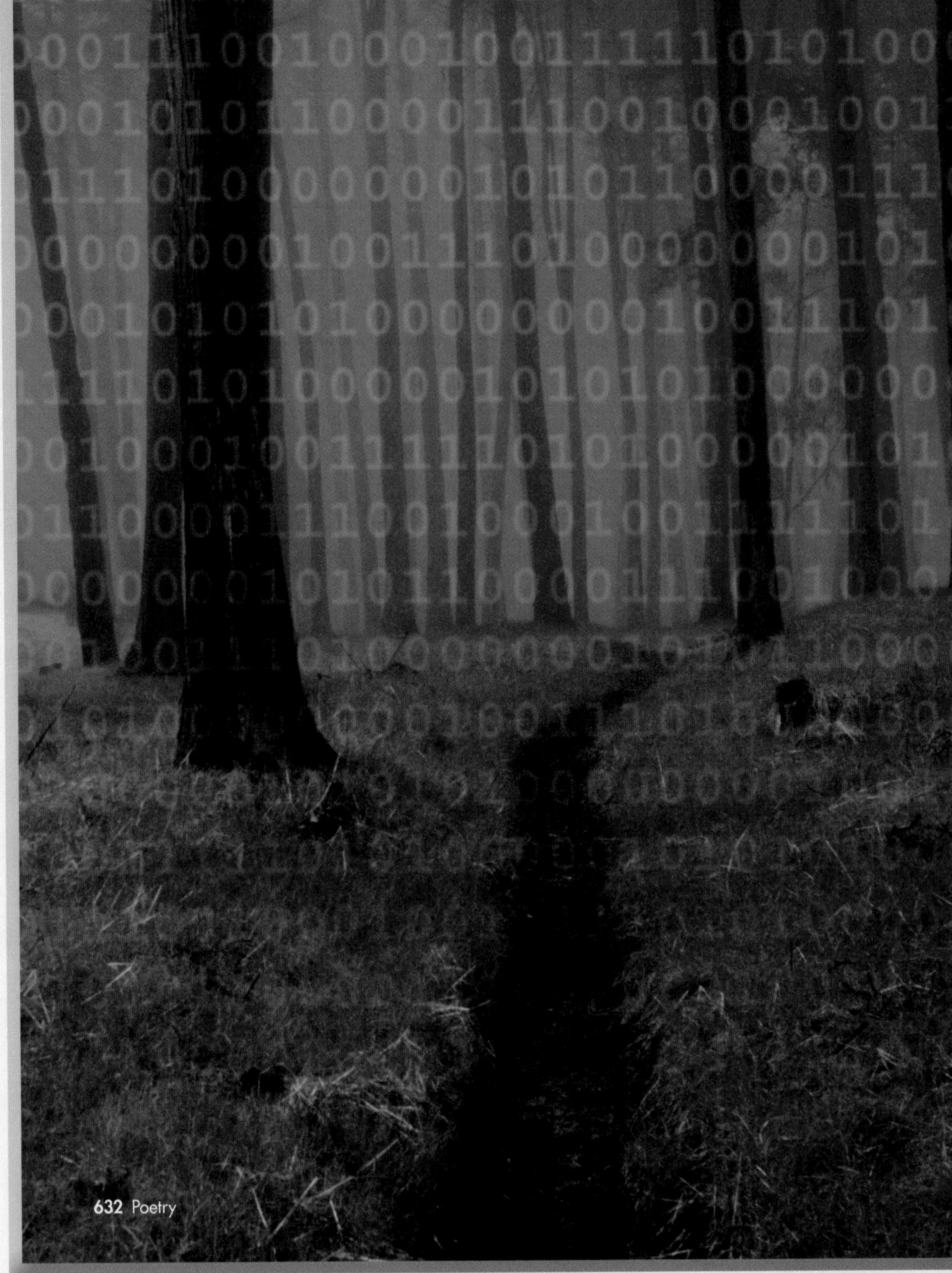

Vocabulary Development

CCSS Language 6

Thematic Vocabulary: The Big Question

As students are discussing "All Watched Over by Machines of Loving Grace," encourage them to use the thematic vocabulary presented in Introducing the Big Question, pp. 604–605.You might encourage them with sentence starters like these:

1. The poem explores the *relationship* between. . .
2. The speaker seems to feel *empathy* toward . . .
3. He also thinks that if people were more *informed* regarding . . .
4. In a perfect world, people would *exchange* . . .

1 2 # All Watched Over by Machines of Loving Grace

Richard Brautigan

I like to think (and
the sooner the better!)
of a cybernetic meadow
6 where mammals and computers
live together in mutually
programming harmony
like pure water
touching clear sky.

I like to think
(right now, please!)
of a cybernetic forest
filled with pines and electronics
where deer stroll peacefully
past computers
as if they were flowers
with spinning blossoms.

I like to think
(it has to be!)
of a cybernetic ecology
where we are free of our labors
and joined back to nature,
returned to our mammal
brothers and sisters,
and all watched over
by machines of loving grace.

Literary Analysis
Figurative Language What simile does the speaker use in lines 3–8 to describe the cybernetic meadow?

Spiral Review
Tone What tone is conveyed by the parenthetical expressions in the poem?

6 Literary Analysis

Figurative Language

1. Read the first stanza of "All Watched Over." Then, **ask** students the Literary Analysis question: What simile does the speaker use in lines 3–8 to describe the cybernetic meadow?
Answer: The speaker uses the simile "like pure water/touching clear sky."
2. Ask a volunteer to read the second stanza aloud. Then, **ask** students to identify the comparison and the type of figurative language used.
Answer: A simile compares computers to "flowers/with spinning blossoms."

For more about the author, practice with the selection vocabulary, or more background, go online at **www.PHLitOnline.com.**

Spiral Review

Tone

1. Remind students that they studied the concept of tone in the Unit 4 Literary Analysis workshop (pp. 606–614).
2. **Ask** students the Spiral Review question.
Possible response: The parenthetical words create a humorous and friendly tone by giving the impression that the speaker is sharing his impatient thoughts with readers.

Differentiated Instruction for Universal Access

Strategy for Less Proficient Readers

Help students better understand figurative language by showing them **Literary Analysis Graphic Organizer A** (*Graphic Organizer Transparencies*, p. 112). Review the types of figurative language, and then ask students to look through the poems and locate the examples listed in the partially completed organizer. Use these examples to explain the characteristics of each figure of speech. Then, encourage students to watch for other examples as they continue reading.

EL Strategy for English Learners

Before having students read "All Watched Over by Machines of Loving Grace," preview some of the nature-vocabulary used: *meadow, mammals, forest, pines, deer, blossoms, ecology,* and *nature.* Then, show students images that illustrate each term or allow more fluent speakers to find images on the Internet.

❹ Reading Skill

Read Fluently

1. Discuss with students Dickinson's use of dashes. Point out that Dickinson did not always rely so heavily on dashes. She did so during her most prolific period, which was when this poem was written. Explain that the dash calls for a strong pause, although not quite as strong as that of a period. It suggests a certain indefiniteness, as though an idea is not totally ended, but is firmly interrupted. In some ways, the dash suggests more spontaneity than periods, hinting that the writer is spinning off ideas as she thinks of them. A fluent reading of Dickinson's poem should suggest this process.
2. Demonstrate to students the skill of reading with fluency by reading the second stanza aloud slowly. Then, **ask** the Reading Skill question: Where in the second stanza could you replace a dash with a period to signify the end of a sentence?
   Answer: The final dash in the stanza could be replaced with a period.

▶ **Monitor Progress:** Have different students read stanzas from the poem. Tell them to read fluently, pausing only for natural breaks and for punctuation.

▶ **Reteach:** If students continue to have difficulty reading fluently, have them guide you in rewriting the poem in paragraph form. Replace dashes, when possible, with more familiar punctuation. Then, have students read the poem as prose. Discuss how fluent reading keeps related ideas together, thus clarifying the meaning and maintaining a natural rhythm.

❺ Critical Viewing

Possible response: Birds sing so vivaciously they seem filled with optimism and hope. Their song is especially noticeable after storms pass or in the spring, making people think of better times to come.

"Hope" is the thing with feathers—

Emily Dickinson

"Hope" is the thing with feathers—
That perches in the soul—
And sings the tune without the words—
And never stops—at all—

And sweetest—in the Gale[1]—is heard—
And sore must be the storm—
That could **abash** the little Bird
That kept so many warm—

I've heard it in the chillest land—
And on the strangest Sea—
Yet, never, in Extremity,
It asked a crumb—of Me.

Reading Skill
Read Fluently
Where in the second stanza could you replace a dash with a period to signify the end of a sentence? ❹

Vocabulary
abash (ə bash′)
v. embarrass

1. **Gale** (gāl) *n.* strong wind.

▶ **Critical Viewing**
Why might someone associate birds with hope? **[Speculate]**

PROFESSIONAL DEVELOPMENT | **William G. Brozo, Ph.D.**

Apply the Strategy

In preparation for "Hope is the thing with feathers," ask students to bring in lyrics from songs that express the theme of hope. Have your own example to share. Read the Dickinson poem aloud and discuss how hope is expressed in it. Next, have students find a partner to read and explain their song lyrics. Afterward, draw a Venn diagram on the board and ask students to copy this in their notebooks. Write ideas about hope from the poem in the left circle and ideas about hope from your lyrics in the right circle. Write ideas that the poem and song lyrics share in the area where the two circles overlap. Ask students to do the same for their song. Invite volunteers to share their findings with the class.

For more of William Brozo's strategies, see the Professional Development essay, pp. 604c–604d.

Much Madness is divinest Sense—

EMILY DICKINSON

Much Madness is divinest Sense—
To a discerning Eye—
Much Sense—the starkest Madness—
'Tis the Majority
6 In this, as All, prevail—
Assent[1]—and you are sane—
Demur[2]—you're straightway dangerous—
And handled with a Chain—

Vocabulary

discerning (di surn´ iŋ) *adj.* having good judgment or understanding

prevail (prē vāl´) *v.* gain the advantage or mastery; be victorious; triumph

1. **assent** (ə sent´) *v.* agree.
2. **demur** (dē mur´) *v.* hesitate because of doubts or objections.

6 

Connecting to the Big Question

1. Point out that one way that people relate to others is through the expression and exchange of opinions. Discuss with students how people typically react if one person expresses an unusual opinion that is not shared by the majority.
2. Have students read the poem on p. 635. **Ask** students: What does the poem say about how people must relate to others in order to be viewed as safe? **Possible response:** It says that people must agree with the majority or they will be viewed as dangerous.
3. **Ask:** If the community judges a person to be dangerous because he or she has expressed unusual ideas, has communication changed that person? Explain. **Possible response:** Yes, communicating ideas that others find threatening can have serious effects. The person expressing the views may be cast out or penalized. He or she may also be admired.

Fluency

Distribute copies of "Much Madness is divinest Sense—" on page 635, and pair students. Have listeners mark words with which reading partners struggle. Circulate to monitor students' fluency, then collect the marked up pages. Review difficult words and passages, such as these:

- If students struggle to pronounce *demur,* model the pronunciation by stressing the second syllable. Read the word aloud and have students echo to confirm.
- If students have difficulty with the rhythm of the poem, tell them to emphasize the words that are capitalized and to pause, not stop, when they come to a dash. Read aloud the entire poem, emphasizing the capitalized words and the dashes. Have students echo.
- Give pairs an opportunity to practice reading the poem. Then call on pairs to read it aloud to the class.

❼ Critical Thinking

Analyze

1. Have students read lines 1–6 of the poem on p. 637. **Ask** them to describe what happens according to the second sentence.
   Possible response: The bulldozers start the digging process by digging up a row of privet bushes.
2. **Ask** students: How might a bulldozer "drunk with gasoline" move?
   Possible response: It probably appears to move randomly, as if out of control.
3. Point out words such as *virtue* and *overthrowing*. Ask: What feelings do you associate with these words?
   Possible response: *Virtue* suggests feelings of goodness and admiration. *Overthrowing* suggests feelings of tension and combativeness.
4. **Ask** students: What relationship is the poet suggesting between the bulldozer and the soil? What mood do you think he is trying to create with this image of the bulldozers?
   Possible responses: The bulldozers are out of control and aggressive, while the soil is good and admirable. The mood is tension that overtakes peace.

Vocabulary Development

Vocabulary Knowledge Rating

When students have completed reading and discussing Poetry Collection 2, have them take out their **Vocabulary Knowledge Rating Chart** for these poems. Read the words aloud once more and have students rate their knowledge of the words again in the After Reading column. Clarify any words that are still problematic. Have students write their own definition and example or sentence in the appropriate column. Then have students complete the Vocabulary Practice activities at the end of the collection. Encourage students to use the words in further discussion and written work about these poems. Remind them that they will be accountable for these words on the **Selection Test, *Unit 4 Resources*,** pp. 56–58 or 59–61.

THE WAR AGAINST THE TREES

STANLEY KUNITZ

The man who sold his lawn to standard oil
Joked with his neighbors come to watch the show
7 While the bulldozers, drunk with gasoline,
Tested the virtue of the soil
Under the branchy sky
By overthrowing first the privet-row.

Forsythia-forays and hydrangea-raids
Were but **preliminaries** to a war
8 Against the great-grandfathers of the town,
So freshly lopped and maimed.
They struck and struck again,
And with each elm a century went down.

All day the hireling engines charged the trees,
Subverting them by hacking underground
In grub-dominions, where dark summer's mole
Rampages through his halls,
Till a northern **seizure** shook
Those crowns, forcing the giants to their knees.

Vocabulary
preliminaries (prē lim′ ə ner′ ēz) *n.* steps or events before the main one
subverting (səb vʉrt′ iŋ) *v.* overthrowing or destroying something established
seizure (sē′ zhər) *n.* a sudden and brief loss of consciousness and body control

Literary Analysis
Figurative Language What are the "giants" that are personified in line 18?

9
◀ **Critical Viewing** What does a tree like the one shown represent to the speaker of the poem? **[Connect]**

8 Literary Analysis

Figurative Language

1. Read the poem aloud for students, pausing after line 10. **Ask** students what these words mean: "war / Against the great-grandfathers."
   Answer: It refers to the destruction of the old trees in the yard.
2. Continue reading and pause again at the end of stanza three. **Ask** students the Literary Analysis question: What are the "giants" that are personified in line 18?
   Answer: The giants are the large trees.
3. Continue reading to the end of the poem. **Ask** students to identify the metaphor used in line 21.
   Answer: "The green world turned its death-foxed page. . . ."
4. Explain to students that the term "fox" is specific to books; it means a stained page.
5. **Ask:** Now that you know the meaning of the term "foxed," what is the meaning of the metaphor?
   Possible response: The trauma of the trees is likened to the turning of a "death-foxed" page by the "green world" of nature. The metaphor suggests that death is the source of the stain on the book of nature.

9 Critical Viewing

Possible response: The tree represents the treasured history of its time and also represents stability in the changing lives of people.

Concept Connector

Activating Prior Knowledge

Have students reconsider their ideas about computers and society. Discuss how their views have changed after reading the collection. Encourage students to cite examples from the poems.

Writing About the Big Question

Have students compare their responses to the sentence starter they completed before reading the collection with their ideas afterward. Ask them to explain whether their thoughts have changed.

Literary Analysis Graphic Organizer

Ask students to review the graphic organizers they completed to identify figurative language in the poems. Show them Literary Analysis Graphic Organizer A (Graphic Organizer Transparencies, p. 112) as an example. Then have students share the graphic organizers they did and the figurative language they identified.

ASSESS

Answers

Critical Thinking

Before students respond, you may wish to have them write a brief objective summary of each selection. As they answer the questions below, remind them to support their answers with evidence from the text.

1. (a) The speaker compares computers with elements in nature. (b) **Possible response:** The comparison suggests that the speaker feels comfortable and safe with computers.
2. (a) Hope sings "sweetest" in times of extremity—in storm, "chillest land," or on "the strangest Sea." (b) Hope is most needed at the worst moments of people's lives.
3. (a) People who are involved with industry and development are at war with the trees. (b) The image of war victimizes the trees, showing that the speaker is concerned about their welfare.
4. (a) Any behavior that is different from that of the majority is considered insane. (b) Students will probably agree with the speaker, arguing that different ideas and opinions often are seen unfavorably.
5. **Possible responses:** (a) The speaker envisions a world where computers do all of the work and people are free to commune with nature. (b) They might become physically and mentally lazy if computers do all the work, or they might be freed from the drudgery of work and become more innovative.

I saw the ghosts of children at their games
Racing beyond their childhood in the shade,
And while the green world turned its death-foxed page
And a red wagon wheeled,
I watched them disappear
Into the suburbs of their grievous age.

Ripped from the craters much too big for hearts
The club-roots bared their amputated coils,
Raw gorgons matted blind, whose pocks and scars
Cried Moon! on a corner lot
One witness-moment, caught
In the rear-view mirrors of the passing cars.

Critical Thinking

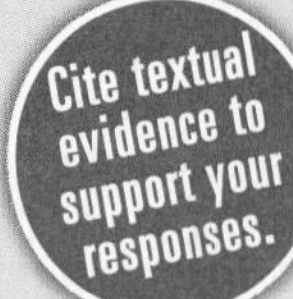
Cite textual evidence to support your responses.

1. **Key Ideas and Details (a)** To what does the speaker compare computers in the imaginary world of "All Watched Over by Machines of Loving Grace"? **(b) Interpret:** What does this comparison suggest about the speaker's feelings about computers in the real world?
2. **Key Ideas and Details (a)** In "'Hope' is the thing with feathers—," when does hope sing the sweetest? **(b) Interpret:** Why does hope sing so well at these times? Explain your response.
3. **Key Ideas and Details (a) Interpret:** In "The War Against the Trees," who or what is at war with the trees? **(b) Draw Conclusions:** What does the image of war suggest about the speaker's feelings toward the trees and what is happening to them? Explain how the poem reveals this.
4. **Integration of Knowledge and Ideas (a) Interpret:** In "Much Madness is divinest Sense—," what kind of behavior is considered insane? **(b) Evaluate:** Do you agree with the speaker's ideas? Explain your answer.
5. **Integration of Knowledge and Ideas (a)** Describe the relationship that the speaker of "All Watched Over by Machines of Loving Grace" envisions between people and computers. **(b)** How might people change as a result of this new kind of relationship with computers? Explain. *[Connect to the Big Question: How does communication change us?]*

Assessment Resources

Unit 4 Resources

L1 L2 EL **Selection Test A**, pp. 56–58. Administer Test A to less advanced students.

L3 L4 EL **Selection Test B**, pp. 59–61. Administer Test B to on-level and more advanced students.

L3 L4 **Open-Book Test**, pp. 53–55. As an alternative, give the Open-Book Test.

All **Customizable Test Bank**

All **Self-tests**
Students may prepare for the **Selection Test** by taking the **Self-test** online.

PHLit Online! All assessment resources are available at **www.PHLitOnline.com**.

After You Read
Poetry Collection 2

All Watched Over... • "Hope" is the thing... • Much Madness is divinest... • The War Against the Trees

Literary Analysis: Figurative Language

1. **Craft and Structure** **(a)** Identify a **simile** and a **metaphor** in Poetry Collection 2. **(b)** Explain what each **figure of speech** contributes to the overall meaning or effect of the poem in which it appears.
2. **Craft and Structure** **(a)** Identify one example of **personification** in Collection 2. **(b)** Explain how this use of **figurative language** contributes to the overall meaning or effect of the poem in which it appears.
3. **Craft and Structure** **(a)** Identify the **paradox** in "Much Madness is divinest Sense—." **(b)** Explain why it is a paradox.

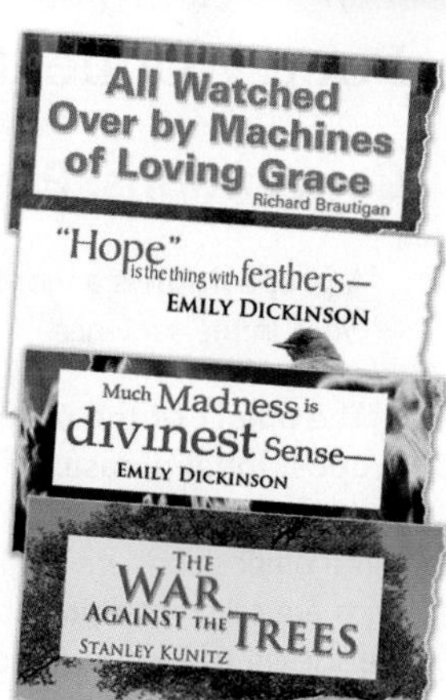

Reading Skill: Read Fluently

4. **(a)** Using a graphic organizer like the one shown, rewrite one stanza in Poetry Collection 2 as a prose paragraph.

Stanza	Paragraph
I've heard it in the chillest land— And on the strangest Sea— Yet, never, in Extremity, It asked a crumb—of Me.	I've heard it in the chillest land and on the strangest Sea, yet never, in Extremity, it asked a crumb of me.

(b) Read the stanza and the paragraph aloud. How does following punctuation help you **read fluently?**

Vocabulary

Acquisition and Use Vocabulary **analogies** show the relationships between pairs of words. Use a word from the Poetry Collection 2 list on page 630 that creates a word pair matching the relationship between the first two given words.

1. destroying : creating :: ______________ : supporting
2. forgiving : fan :: ______________ : expert
3. rehearsal : performance :: ______________ : championship
4. lose : defeat :: ______________ : victory
5. praise : confidence :: ______________ : shame
6. house : home :: ______________ : attack

Word Study Use the context of the sentences and what you know about the **Latin root *-vert-*** to explain your answer to each question.

1. Is someone who is *introverted* outgoing or shy?
2. What happens to your attention when it gets *diverted*?

Word Study

The **Latin root *-vert-*** means "turn."

Apply It Explain how the root *-vert-* contributes to the meanings of these words. Consult a dictionary if necessary.

inversion
revert
vertical

ASSESS/EXTEND

Answers

Literary Analysis

1. **Possible response:** (a) Simile: Mammals and computers that are "like pure water/touching clear sky" (from "All Watched Over"); Metaphor: "Hope is the thing with feathers" (from "Hope") (b) **Possible response:** The simile in "All Watched Over" evokes feelings of peace and harmony. The metaphor in "Hope" identifies hope with a bird, conveying both its fragility and its forcefulness in the face of great odds.
2. **Possible response:** (a) The trees in "The War Against the Trees" are described as "great-grandfathers." (b) **Possible response:** This personification humanizes the trees and gives them stature, which helps the reader sympathize with their destruction.
3. **Possible responses:** (a) The paradox is between madness and wisdom. (b) The truth of this paradox is that society can pull people into false beliefs, and individuals who look beyond the beliefs—the wisest among us—may be seen as crazy.

Reading Skill

4. (a) **Possible response: Stanza:** "Hope" is the thing with feathers—That perches in the soul—And sings the tune without the words— And never stops—at all— (from "'Hope' is the thing with feathers—"); **Paragraph:** Hope is the thing with features, that perches in the soul. It sings the tune without the words and never stops at all.

For other sample answers, see ***Graphic Organizer Transparencies,*** **Reading Skill Graphic Organizer A**, p. 115, and the **Additional Answers** section.

(b) **Possible response:** Following the punctuation allows me to see the flow of the sentence and to better grasp its meaning.

Vocabulary
Acquisition and Use
Sample answers:

1. subverting
2. discerning
3. preliminaries
4. prevail
5. abash
6. seizure

Word Study
Sample answers:

1. People who are *introverted* are shy because they turn inward.
2. When your attention is *diverted,* it turns away toward something else.

Word Study: Apply It

Sample answers: *Inversion* is something that is turned around. To *revert* is to turn back. *Vertical* is turned straight up and down.

EXTEND/ASSESS

Answers

Conventions

1. Introduce the skill, using the instruction on the student page.
2. Discuss the definitions and examples.

Think Aloud: Model the Skill

Model the skill of recognizing prepositions and their objects. Post the sentence, *I flew over the Rocky Mountains*. Then, say to students:

> I know that prepositions link nouns and pronouns to other words in the sentence. They pose questions such as *Where?* that the object of the preposition answers. For example, in the posted sentence, I see that *I* is the pronoun, and *over* is the preposition that links the pronoun to the object of the preposition, *Rocky Mountains*. Now I know *where* she flew—*over*.

PH WRITING COACH Grade 9

Students will find instruction on and practice with prepositions in Chapter 13, Section 4.

Practice A

Answers:

1. to, prep.; dreams, object of prep.
2. as, prep.; cloud, object of prep.
3. in, prep.; shadow, object of prep.
4. to, prep.; legend, object of prep.

Reading Application

Sample answers:

in the sun: in, prep.; sun, object; to a dream: to, prep.; dream, object

Practice B

Sample answers:

1. past, prep.; computers, object; Deer stroll peacefully in the forest.
2. in the chillest land: in, prep.; land, object; I've heard it on top of a mountain.
3. across the yard: across, prep.; yard, object; The bulldozers rolled up the hillside.
4. across the street: across, prep.; street, object; People stood on the wall and watched the bulldozers.

Writing Application

Students' sentences should contain a compound preposition and describe the image on p. 636.

PERFORMANCE TASKS

Integrated Language Skills

Poetry Collections 1 and 2

Poetry Collection 1

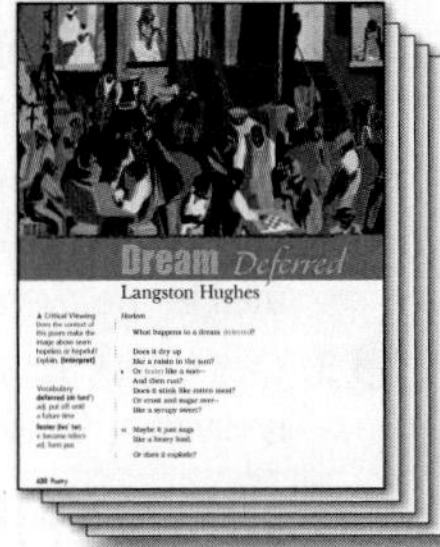

Poetry Collection 2

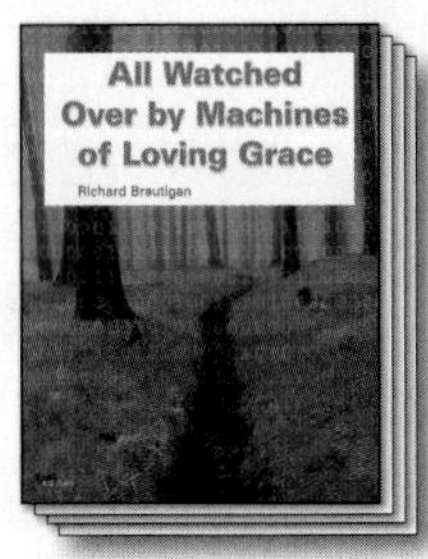

Conventions: Prepositions

A **preposition** is a word that relates a noun or pronoun to another word in the sentence.

The **object of the preposition** is the noun or pronoun at the end of a **prepositional phrase.**

Although most prepositions, such as *at* and *with,* are single words, some prepositions are made up of two or three words. These prepositions are called **compound prepositions.** Some compound prepositions are spelled as a single word, such as *into* and *throughout*. Others, such as *because of* and *in addition to,* are spelled as separate words.

Common Prepositions: about, above, across, below, beyond, by, down, except, for, from, in, of, on, over, past, through, to, under, until, up, with

Prepositional Phrase: Mr. Johnson ate at a good restaurant. (*restaurant* is the *object of the preposition at*)

Common Compound Prepositions: without, underneath, outside, according to, along with, in front of, instead of, next to

Practice A Identify the preposition and object of the preposition in each sentence.

1. Hold fast to dreams.
2. I wandered lonely as a cloud.
3. Feeling His hand in the shadow, I rock my son.
4. According to legend, Archimedes shouted "Eureka!" when he made a discovery.

Reading Application Find three sentences in "Dream Deferred" that contain a preposition. Identify both the preposition and the object of the preposition in each sentence.

Practice B Identify the preposition and object of the preposition in each sentence. Then, rewrite each sentence using a different prepositional phrase.

1. Deer stroll peacefully past computers.
2. I've heard it in the chillest land.
3. The bulldozers rolled across the yard.
4. People stood across the street and watched the bulldozers.

Writing Application Write three sentences about the image on page 636, using a compound preposition in each one.

PH WRITING COACH Further instruction and practice are available in *Prentice Hall Writing Coach.*

Extend the Lesson

Sentence Modeling

Choose the excerpt given from the collection students have read:

> *"They stretched in never-ending line/Along the margin of a bay."* ("I Wandered Lonely as a Cloud")
>
> *"I watched them disappear/Into the suburbs of their grievous age."* ("The War Against the Trees")

Ask students what they notice about the prepositions and their objects in the example. Elicit from them that the example has at least two prepositions and objects. Then, ask what else they notice. ("I Wandered Lonely as a Cloud": Prepositions *in* and *along* describe a spatial relationship, which helps reader visualize the scene; "The War Against the Trees": The prepositions are used to create a figurative relationship.)

Have students imitate the sentence on a topic of their own choosing, matching each grammatical and stylistic feature discussed. Collect the sentences, and share them with the class.

Writing

Informative Text Using one of the scenes described in either Poetry Collection 1 or Poetry Collection 2 as a model, write a **description of a scene** in nature. Using the figurative and connotative language techniques of the author you are emulating, develop your own descriptive word picture in a few paragraphs or a poem.

- Choose a scene that you know firsthand or from photographs.
- List details in the scene that appeal to one or more of the senses.
- Refer to your list of details as you draft your description, and work to establish a controlling impression.

Grammar Application Make sure you use prepositions and prepositional phrases correctly in your writing.

Writing Workshop: *Work in Progress*

Prewriting for Descriptive Essay To prepare for a descriptive essay you may write, make a Sight List of three places. For each place, write ten words that describe how the place looks. Then, choose one place and add a Sensory Word List that describes other characteristics of the place, such as smells or sounds. Save both your Sight List and your Sensory Word List.

Speaking and Listening

Comprehension and Collaboration Use one of the poems in Poetry Collection 1 or Poetry Collection 2 as the basis for an **impromptu speech** about dreams, nature, or love.

- Instead of writing a script or outline, jot down the central point you want to convey. Create concise notes to refer to during your delivery.
- Engage your audience by choosing interesting details that are appropriate to the purpose of your speech.
- As you speak, use a variety of sentence structures. Using a mix of long and short sentences as well as simple and complex sentences will help listeners follow your ideas.
- Make your ideas memorable by using figurative language.
- Use body language and eye contact to convey sincerity.
- Create a rubric so that classmates can assess your speech, and invite them to give you feedback about your performance.

Present your speech before an audience of peers. Evaluate the feedback and make notes about how you can apply it to future speeches.

Common Core State Standards

L.9-10.1, L.9-10.5; W.9-10.3.d; SL.9-10.4
[For the full wording of the standards, see page 616.]

Use this prewriting activity to prepare for the **Writing Workshop** on page 686.

www.PHLitOnline.com
- Interactive graphic organizers
- Grammar tutorial
- Interactive journals

EXTEND/ASSESS

Answers

Writing

1. Review the assignment, using the instruction on the student page.
2. To give students guidance for writing a description of a scene, give them **Support for Writing** p. 51, in ***Unit 4 Resources.***
3. To evaluate students' descriptions, use the Descriptive Essay rubrics, pp. 220–221 in ***Professional Development Guidebook.***

Grammar Application

Have students check their drafts to make sure they are using prepositions and prepositional phrases correctly.

Six Traits Focus

✓	Ideas	✓	Word Choice
✓	Organization		Sentence Fluency
	Voice		Conventions

PH WRITING COACH Grade 9

Students will find instruction on and practice with description in Chapter 7.

Writing Workshop
Work-in-Progress

Have students save their completed Sight and Sensory Word Lists in their portfolios. They will use the lists later as they continue this Work-in-Progress assignment (see p. 667). These assignments prepare them to complete the Writing Workshop assignment (see pp. 686–691).

Speaking and Listening

1. Review the assignment, using the instruction on the student page.
2. Have students complete the **Support for Extend Your Learning** page (***Unit 4 Resources,*** p. 52).

Teaching Resources

Unit 4 Resources

L3 L4 EL **Integrated Language Skills: Grammar,** p. 50

L3 L4 EL **Support for Writing,** p. 51

L3 L4 **Support for Extend Your Learning,** p. 52

L4 **Enrichment,** pp. 31, 49

Enriched Online Student Edition
Available under After You Read for this collection:

All **Interactive Grammar Tutorial**

L3 L4 **Internet Research Activity**

Professional Development Guidebook
Rubrics for Self-Assessment: Descriptive Essay, pp. 220–221

PHLit Online! All print and digital resources are available at **www.PHLitOnline.com**. Online resources accessible by students are noted on the student page.

✓ Poetry Collection 3 • ✓✓ Poetry Collection 4

Lesson Pacing Guide

DAY 1 Preteach

- Administer the Reading and Vocabulary Warm-ups (*Unit 4 Resources*, pp. 62–65 or 80–83) as necessary.
- Introduce the Reading Skill: Read Fluently.
- Introduce the Literary Analysis concept: Sound Devices.
- Distribute copies of the appropriate graphic organizer for the Reading Skill (*Graphic Organizer Transparencies*, pp. 117–119).
- Distribute copies of the appropriate graphic organizer for Literary Analysis (*Graphic Organizer Transparencies*, pp. 120–122).
- Teach the selection vocabulary.
- Introduce the Word Study skill.

DAYS 2–3 Preteach/Teach

- Build background with the Background feature.
- Develop thematic vocabulary and thematic thinking with Writing About the Big Question.
- Prepare students to read with the Activating Prior Knowledge activities (TE).
- Informally monitor comprehension while students read.
- Use the Reading Check questions to confirm comprehension.
- Develop students' ability to read fluently, using the Reading Skill questions.
- Develop students' understanding of sound devices, using the Literacy Analysis questions.
- Reinforce vocabulary with the Vocabulary notes.
- Reinforce unit focus standards using the Spiral Review prompts.

DAY 4 Assess

- Assess students' comprehension and mastery of the skills by having them answer the Critical Thinking, Reading Skill, and Literary Analysis questions.
- Have students complete the Vocabulary Practice activities.
- Have students complete the Word Study activities.

DAY 5 Extend/Assess

- Have students complete the Conventions lesson.
- Have students complete the Writing activity and write an editorial. (You may assign as homework.)
- Extend learning by having students complete the Speaking and Listening activity, an illustrated presentation. As an alternative, assign them "A Heated Debate" or "Good Words for Bad Times" in *Reality Central*.
- Administer Selection Test A or B (*Unit 4 Resources*, pp. 74–79 or 95–100).

Common Core State Standards

Reading Literature 4. Determine the meaning of words and phrases as they are used in the text, including figurative and connotative meanings; analyze the cumulative impact of specific word choices on meaning and tone (e.g., how the language evokes a sense of time and place, how it sets a formal or informal tone).

Writing 1. Write arguments to support claims in an analysis of substantive topics or texts, using valid reasoning and relevant and sufficient evidence.

Speaking and Listening
1. Initiate and participate effectively in a range of collaborative discussions with diverse partners on *grades 9–10 topics, texts, and issues,* building on others' ideas and expressing their own clearly and persuasively.
5. Make strategic use of digital media in presentations to enhance understanding of findings, reasoning, and evidence and to add interest.

Language 1. Demonstrate command of the conventions of standard English grammar and usage when writing or speaking.
5. Demonstrate understanding of figurative language, word relationships, and nuances in word meanings.

Additional Standards Practice
***Common Core Companion*, pp. 35–42**

Daily Block Scheduling
Each day in this Lesson Pacing Guide represents a 40–50 minute period. Teachers using block scheduling may combine days to revise pacing. In addition, teachers may differentiate and support core instruction by integrating components for extended and intensive support as students require. See the Guide to Selected Leveled Resources (facing page).

Guide to Selected Leveled Resources

RTI Tier 1 (students performing on level)		✓ More Accessible Poetry Collection 3	✓✓ More Complex Poetry Collection 4
Warm Up	**Practice, model,** and **monitor** fluency, working **with the whole class** or **in groups.**	**Vocabulary** and **Reading Warm-ups B,** ***Unit 4 Resources,*** pp. 62–63, 65	**Vocabulary** and **Reading Warm-ups B,** ***Unit 4 Resources,*** pp. 80–81, 83
Comprehension/Skills	**Support** and **monitor** comprehension and skills development, having students complete the activities, graphic organizers, and interactive prompts **independently** or **as a class.**	• ***Reader's Notebook,*** adapted instruction and full selection EL ***Reader's Notebook: English Learner's Version,*** adapted instruction and full selection • **Reading Skill Graphic Organizer B,** ***Graphic Organizer Transparencies,*** p. 119 • **Literary Analysis Graphic Organizer B,** ***Graphic Organizer Transparencies,*** p. 122	• ***Reader's Notebook,*** adapted instruction and summary EL ***Reader's Notebook: English Learner's Version,*** adapted instruction and summary • **Reading Skill Graphic Organizer B,** ***Graphic Organizer Transparencies,*** p. 119 • **Literary Analysis Graphic Organizer B,** ***Graphic Organizer Transparencies,*** p. 112
Monitor Progress	**Monitor** student progress with the differentiated curriculum-based assessment in the *Unit Resources.*	• **Selection Test B,** ***Unit 4 Resources,*** pp. 77–79 • **Open-Book Test,** ***Unit 4 Resources,*** pp. 71–73	• **Selection Test B,** ***Unit 4 Resources,*** pp. 98–100 • **Open-Book Test,** ***Unit 4 Resources,*** pp. 92–94
Assess/Screen	**Assess** student progress using Benchmark Test 7.	• **Benchmark Test 7,** ***Unit 4 Resources,*** pp. 120–125	• **Benchmark Test 7,** ***Unit 4 Resources,*** pp. 120–125

RTI Tier 2 (students requiring intervention)		✓ More Accessible Poetry Collection 3	✓✓ More Complex Poetry Collection 4
Warm Up	**Practice, model,** and **monitor** fluency **in groups** or **with individuals.**	• **Vocabulary and Reading Warm-ups A,** ***Unit 4 Resources,*** pp. 62–64 • ***Reality Central,*** "A Heated Debate" • ***Hear It!*** **Audio CD**	• **Vocabulary and Reading Warm-ups A,** ***Unit 4 Resources,*** pp. 80–82 • ***Reality Central,*** "Good Words for Bad Times" • ***Hear It!*** **Audio CD**
Comprehension/Skills	• **Support** and **monitor** comprehension and skills development, working **in small groups** or **with individuals.** • **Pair** students with more advanced peers and have them complete the writing activity in the *Real-World Writing Journal.* • As students complete the selection in the appropriate version of the *Reader's Notebook,* **monitor** comprehension frequently with group questions and individual instruction. • **Model** strategies while guiding students in completing the activities and prompts in the *Reader's Notebook,* as well as the graphic organizers. • **Practice** skills and **monitor** mastery with the *Reading Kit* worksheets.	• ***Real-World Writing Journal, Lesson 3,*** pp. 112–115 • ***Reader's Notebook: Adapted Version,*** adapted instruction and full selection EL ***Reader's Notebook: English Learner's Version,*** adapted instruction and full selection • **Reading Skill Graphic Organizer A,** ***Graphic Organizer Transparencies,*** p. 117 • **Literary Analysis Graphic Organizer A,** ***Graphic Organizer Transparencies,*** p. 120 • ***Reading Kit,*** Practice worksheets, pp. 154, 158, 162, 166, 172	• ***Real-World Writing Journal, Lesson 4,*** pp. 116–119 • ***Reader's Notebook: Adapted Version,*** adapted instruction and summary EL ***Reader's Notebook: English Learner's Version,*** adapted instruction and summary • **Reading Skill Graphic Organizer A,** ***Graphic Organizer Transparencies,*** p. 118 • **Literary Analysis Graphic Organizer A,** ***Graphic Organizer Transparencies,*** p. 121 • ***Reading Kit,*** Practice worksheets, pp. 154, 158, 162, 166, 172
Monitor Progress	**Monitor** student progress with the differentiated curriculum-based assessment in the *Unit Resources* and in the *Reading Kit.*	• **Selection Test A,** ***Unit 4 Resources,*** pp. 74–77 • ***Reading Kit,*** Assess worksheets, pp. 155, 159, 163, 167, 173	• **Selection Test A,** ***Unit 4 Resources,*** pp. 95–97 • **Reading Kit,** Assess worksheets, pp. 155, 159, 163, 167, 173
Assess/Screen	**Assess** student progress using Benchmark Test 7.	• **Benchmark Test 7,** ***Unit 4 Resources,*** pp. 120–125	• **Benchmark Test 7,** ***Unit 4 Resources,*** pp. 120–125

TIER 3 Tier 3 intervention may require consultation with the student's special-education or dyslexia specialist. For additional support, see the Tier 2 activities and resources listed above.

One-on-one teaching | Group work | Whole class instruction | Independent work | A Assessment

For a complete guide to selection support, including support for Advanced students, see the Overview of Resources in the frontmatter.

✓Poetry Collection 3
✓✓Poetry Collection 4

SUMMER
Walter Dean Myers
The Bells
Edgar Allan Poe
The Eagle
Alfred, Lord Tennyson
Slam, Dunk, & Hook
Yusef Komunyakaa
Analysis of Baseball
May Swenson
Jabberwocky
Lewis Carroll

RESOURCES FOR:

- **L1** Special-Needs Students
- **L2** Below-Level Students (Tier 2)
- **L3** On-Level Students (Tier 1)
- **L4** Advanced Students (Tier 1)
- **EL** English Learners
- **All** All Students

Vocabulary/Fluency/Prior Knowledge

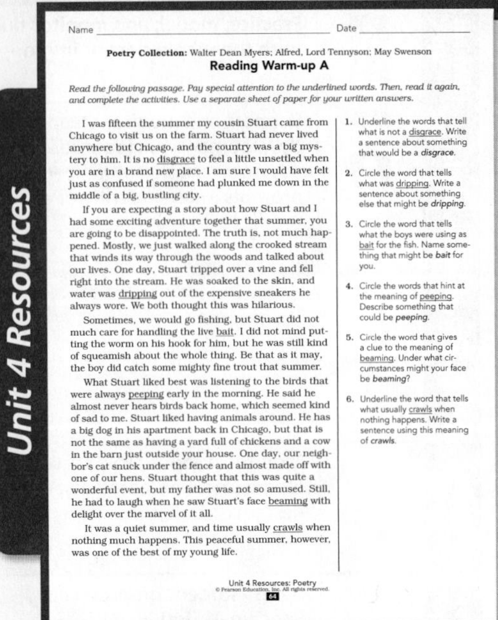

Unit 4 Resources

Name ______________________ Date ______________

Poetry Collection: Walter Dean Myers; Alfred, Lord Tennyson; May Swenson

Reading Warm-up A

Read the following passage. Pay special attention to the underlined words. Then, read it again, and complete the activities. Use a separate sheet of paper for your written answers.

I was fifteen the summer my cousin Stuart came from Chicago to visit us on the farm. Stuart had never lived anywhere but Chicago, and the country was a big mystery to him. It is no disgrace to feel a little unsettled when you are in a brand new place. I am sure I would have felt just as confused if someone had plunked me down in the middle of a big, bustling city.

If you are expecting a story about how Stuart and I had some exciting adventure together that summer, you are going to be disappointed. The truth is, not much happened. Mostly, we just walked along the crooked stream that winds its way through the woods and talked about our lives. One day, Stuart tripped over a vine and fell right into the stream. He was soaked to the skin, and water was dripping out of the expensive sneakers he always wore. We both thought this was hilarious.

Sometimes, we would go fishing, but Stuart did not much care for handling the live bait. I did not mind putting the worm on his hook for him, but he was still kind of squeamish about the whole thing. Be that as it may, the boy did catch some mighty fine trout that summer.

What Stuart liked best was listening to the birds that were always peeping early in the morning. He said he almost never hears birds back home, which seemed kind of sad to me. Stuart liked having animals around. He has a big dog in his apartment back in Chicago, but that is not the same as having a yard full of chickens and a cow in the barn just outside your house. One day, our neighbor's cat snuck under the fence and almost made off with one of our hens. Stuart thought that this was quite a wonderful event, but my father was not so amused. Still, he had to laugh when he saw Stuart's face beaming with delight over the marvel of it all.

It was a quiet summer, and time usually crawls when nothing much happens. This peaceful summer, however, was one of the best of my young life.

1. Underline the words that tell what is not a disgrace. Write a sentence about something that would be a *disgrace*.
2. Circle the word that tells what was dripping. Write a sentence about something else that might be *dripping*.
3. Circle the word that tells what the boys were using as bait for the fish. Name something that might be *bait* for you.
4. Circle the words that hint at the meaning of peeping. Describe something that could be *peeping*.
5. Circle the word that gives a clue to the meaning of beaming. Under what circumstances might your face be *beaming*?
6. Underline the word that tells what usually crawls when nothing happens. Write a sentence using this meaning of *crawls*.

Unit 4 Resources: Poetry

64

EL L1 L2 Reading Warm-ups A and B, pp. 64–65, 82–83

Also available for these selections:

EL L1 L2 Vocabulary Warm-ups A and B, pp. 62–63, 80–81

All Writing About the Big Questions, pp. 66, 84

All Vocabulary Builder, pp. 69, 87

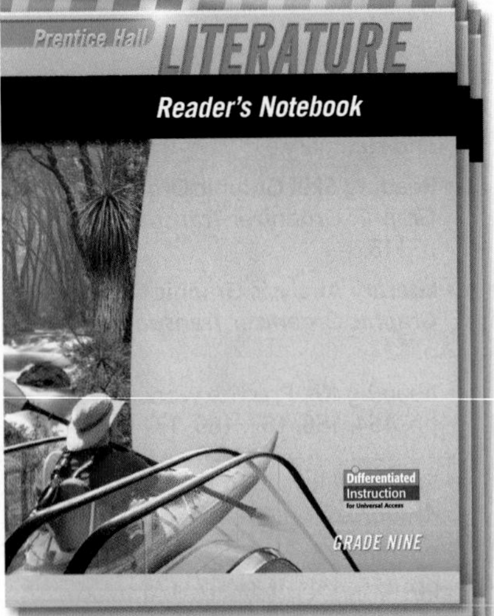

Reader's Notebooks

Pre- and postreading pages for both selections, as well as "Poetry Collection 3," appear in an interactive format in the *Reader's Notebooks.* Each *Notebook* is differentiated for a different group of learners.

The selections in the Adapted and English Learner's versions are abridged.

- **L2 L3** ***Reader's Notebook***
- **L1** ***Reader's Notebook: Adapted Version***
- **EL** ***Reader's Notebook: English Learner's Version***
- **EL** ***Reader's Notebook: Spanish Version***

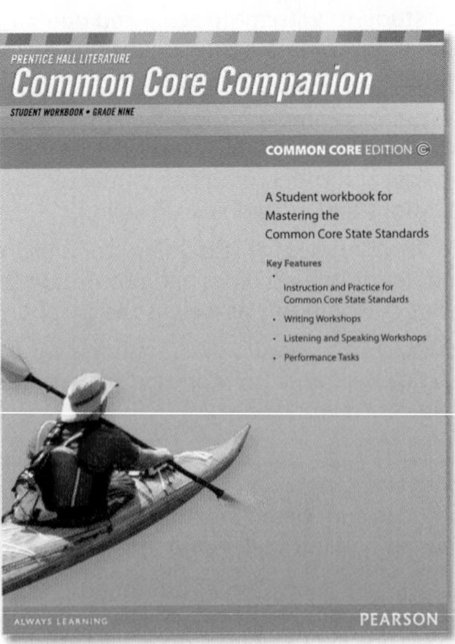

Common Core Companion

Additional instruction and practice for each Common Core State Standard

Selection Support

Graphic Organizer Transparencies

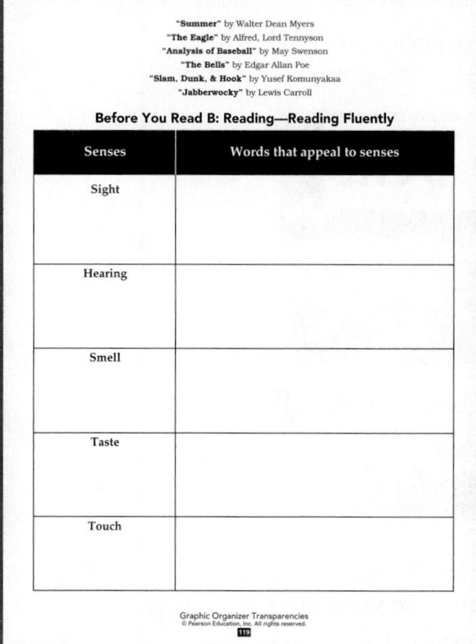

"Summer" by Walter Dean Myers
"The Eagle" by Alfred, Lord Tennyson
"Analysis of Baseball" by May Swenson
"The Bells" by Edgar Allan Poe
"Slam, Dunk, & Hook" by Yusef Komunyakaa
"Jabberwocky" by Lewis Carroll

Before You Read B: Reading—Reading Fluently

Senses	Words that appeal to senses
Sight	
Hearing	
Smell	
Taste	
Touch	

Graphic Organizer Transparencies

119

EL L3 **Reading: Graphic Organizer B,** p. 119

Also available for these selections:

EL L1 L2 **Reading: Graphic Organizer A,** pp. 117–118 (partially filled in)

EL L1 L2 **Literary Analysis: Graphic Organizer A,** pp. 120–121 (partially filled in)

EL L3 **Literary Analysis: Graphic Organizer B,** p. 122

Skills Development/Extension

Unit 4 Resources

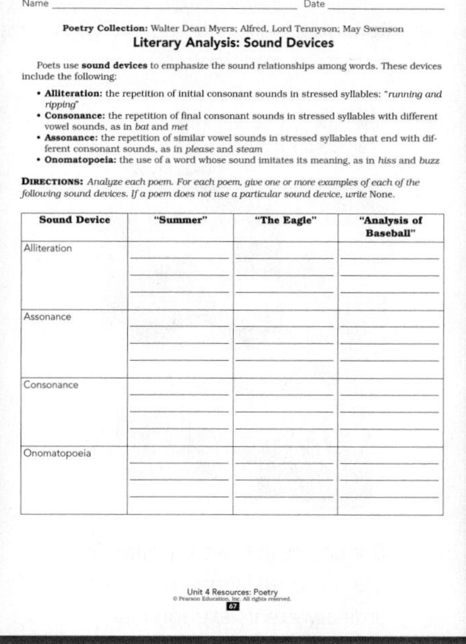

Name ______________________ Date ______________

Poetry Collection: Walter Dean Myers; Alfred, Lord Tennyson; May Swenson

Literary Analysis: Sound Devices

Poets use **sound devices** to emphasize the sound relationships among words. These devices include the following:

- **Alliteration:** the repetition of initial consonant sounds in stressed syllables: "*running and ripping*"
- **Consonance:** the repetition of final consonant sounds in stressed syllables with different vowel sounds, as in *bat* and *met*
- **Assonance:** the repetition of similar vowel sounds in stressed syllables that end with different consonant sounds, as in *please* and *steam*
- **Onomatopoeia:** the use of a word whose sound imitates its meaning, as in *hiss* and *buzz*

DIRECTIONS: *Analyze each poem. For each poem, give one or more examples of each of the following sound devices. If a poem does not use a particular sound device, write* None.

Sound Device	"Summer"	"The Eagle"	"Analysis of Baseball"
Alliteration			
Assonance			
Consonance			
Onomatopoeia			

Unit 4 Resources: Poetry

67

All **Literary Analysis: Sound Devices,** pp. 67, 85

Also available for these selections:

All **Reading: Read Fluently,** pp. 68, 86

L4 **Enrichment,** pp. 70, 88

EL L3 L4 **Grammar,** p. 89

EL L3 L4 **Support for Writing,** p. 90

L3 L4 **Support for Extend Your Learning,** p. 91

Assessment

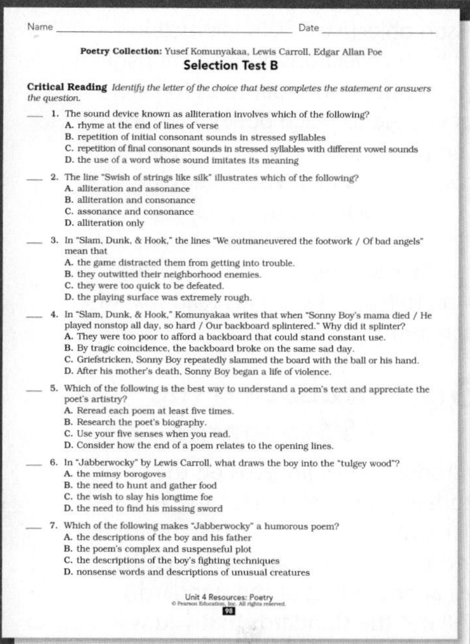

Name ______________________ Date ______________

Poetry Collection: Yusef Komunyakaa, Lewis Carroll, Edgar Allan Poe

Selection Test B

Critical Reading *Identify the letter of the choice that best completes the statement or answers the question.*

____ 1. The sound device known as alliteration involves which of the following?
A. rhyme at the end of lines of verse
B. repetition of initial consonant sounds in stressed syllables
C. repetition of final consonant sounds in stressed syllables with different vowel sounds
D. the use of a word whose sound imitates its meaning

____ 2. The line "Swish of strings like silk" illustrates which of the following?
A. alliteration and assonance
B. alliteration and consonance
C. assonance and consonance
D. alliteration only

____ 3. In "Slam, Dunk, & Hook," the lines "We outmaneuvered the footwork / Of bad angels" mean that
A. the game distracted them from getting into trouble.
B. they outwitted their neighborhood enemies.
C. they were too quick to be defeated.
D. the playing surface was extremely rough.

____ 4. In "Slam, Dunk, & Hook," Komunyakaa writes that when "Sonny Boy's mama died / He played nonstop all day, so hard / Our backboard splintered." Why did it splinter?
A. They were too poor to afford a backboard that could stand constant use.
B. By tragic coincidence, the backboard broke on the same sad day.
C. Griefstricken, Sonny Boy repeatedly slammed the board with the ball or his hand.
D. After his mother's death, Sonny Boy began a life of violence.

____ 5. Which of the following is the best way to understand a poem's text and appreciate the poet's artistry?
A. Reread each poem at least five times.
B. Research the poet's biography.
C. Use your five senses when you read.
D. Consider how the end of a poem relates to the opening lines.

____ 6. In "Jabberwocky" by Lewis Carroll, what draws the boy into the "tulgey wood"?
A. the mimsy borogoves
B. the need to hunt and gather food
C. the wish to slay his longtime foe
D. the need to find his missing sword

____ 7. Which of the following makes "Jabberwocky" a humorous poem?
A. the descriptions of the boy and his father
B. the poem's complex and suspenseful plot
C. the descriptions of the boy's fighting techniques
D. nonsense words and descriptions of unusual creatures

Unit 4 Resources: Poetry

98

EL L3 L4 **Selection Test B,** pp. 77–79, 98–100

Also available for these selections:

L3 L4 **Open-Book Test,** pp. 71–73, 92–94

EL L1 L2 **Selection Test A,** pp. 74–76, 95–97

PHLit Online!
www.PHLitOnline.com

- complete narrated selection text
- a thematically related video with writing prompt
- an interactive graphic organizer
- highlighting feature
- access to all student print resources, adapted to individual student needs
- Spanish and English summaries
- adapted selection translations in Spanish

Online Resources: All print materials are also available online.

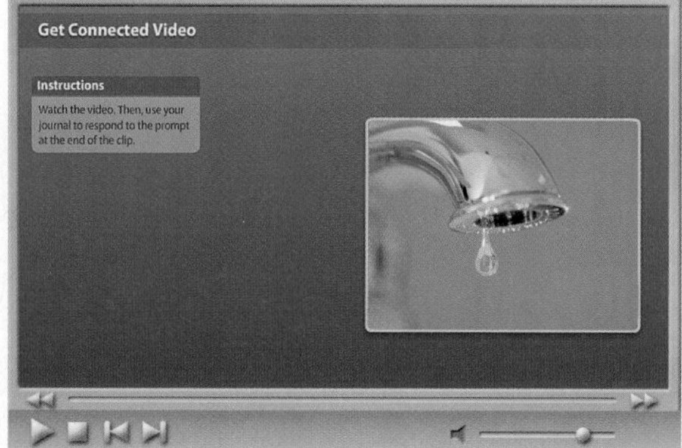

Get Connected! (thematic video with writing prompt)

Also available:

Background Video

All videos are available in Spanish.

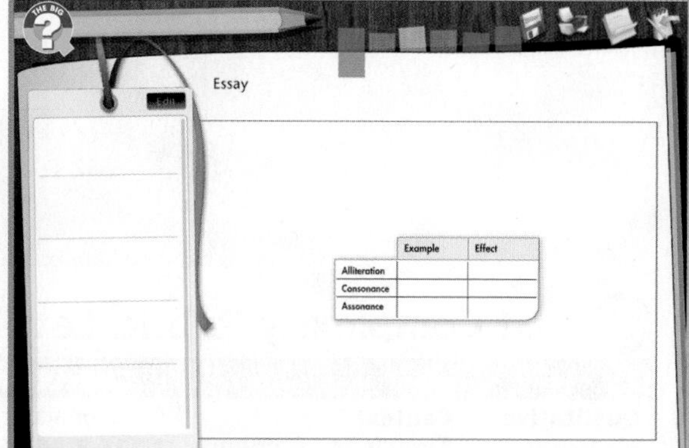

Writer's Journal (with graphics feature)

Also available:

Vocabulary Central (tools, activities, and songs for studying vocabulary)

DIFFERENTIATE/PRETEACH

❶ Leveled Texts

You may use either Poetry Collection 3 or Poetry Collection 4 to meet the lesson objectives. Skills instruction for both collections appears on page 643. Choose one collection to teach (or choose to teach both). The Text Complexity Rubric at the bottom of this page will help you determine which collection is more appropriate for your students. Use the Reader and Task Suggestions on the facing page to help all students read text of increasing complexity.

❷ Introducing the CCS Standards

Introduce the standards on the student page. (Note that the lesson element with which each standard is addressed is identified in parentheses after the text of the standard.) Call out the standards that you will cover with the collections, explaining to students what each requires and how they will address it as they work through the collection you have chosen. Standards labeled "Spiral Review" are introduced in the Literary Analysis Workshop for this unit.

Before You Read

Poetry Collection 3 • Poetry Collection 4

❶ Leveled Texts

Build your skills and improve your comprehension of poetry with texts of increasing complexity.

The poems in **Poetry Collection 3** use powerful language to make ordinary events extraordinary.

The Bells
Edgar Allan Poe
Slam, Dunk, & Hook
Yusef Komunyakaa
Jabberwocky
Lewis Carroll

The poems in **Poetry Collection 4** use sounds to add layers of meaning.

❷ Common Core State Standards

Meet these standards with either **Poetry Collection 3** (p. 646) or **Poetry Collection 4** (p. 654).

Reading Literature

4. Determine the meaning of words and phrases as they are used in the text, including figurative and connotative meanings; analyze the cumulative impact of specific word choices on meaning and tone. *(Literary Analysis: Spiral Review)*

Writing

1. Write arguments to support claims in an analysis of substantive topics or texts, using valid reasoning and relevant and sufficient evidence. *(Writing: Editorial)*

Speaking and Listening

1. Initiate and participate effectively in a range of collaborative discussions with diverse partners on *grades 9–10 topics, texts, and issues,* building on others' ideas and expressing their own clearly and persuasively.

5. Make strategic use of digital media in presentations to enhance understanding of findings, reasoning, and evidence and to add interest. *(Speaking and Listening: Illustrated Presentation)*

Language

1. Demonstrate command of the conventions of standard English grammar and usage when writing or speaking. *(Conventions: Prepositional Phrases)*

5. Demonstrate understanding of figurative language, word relationships, and nuances in word meanings. *(Vocabulary: Greek Prefixes)*

Text Complexity Rubric: Leveled Texts

Text complexity is determined by both qualitative and quantitative measures. For this reason, the quantitative measure of a more complex collection may be lower than that of a more accessible collection.

		✓ Collection 3	✓✓ Collection 4
Qualitative Measures	**Context/ Knowledge Demands**	Outdoor activities and themes 1 (2) 3 4 5	Types of bells; basketball; heroic legend 1 2 (3) 4 5
	Structure/Language and Clarity	On-level vocabulary; short sentences 1 (2) 3 4 5	Difficult diction; challenging vocabulary footnoted; invented words ("Jabberwocky") 1 2 3 (4) 5
	Levels of Meaning/ Purpose/Concept Level	Accessible concepts (descriptions of everyday things) 1 2 (3) 4 5	Challenging concepts (imagery; symbolism; parody of legends) 1 2 3 4 (5)
Quantitative Measures	**Text Length**	Word Count: 52; 39; 136	Word Count: 609; 197; 167
	Lexile	NP	NP
Overall Complexity		✓ **More accessible**	✓✓ **More complex**

❸ Literary Analysis: Sound Devices

Poets use **sound devices** to emphasize the sound relationships among words. Sound devices, such as those on the following list, also impact the meaning and tone in a poem and help bring it to life for readers.

- **Alliteration:** the repetition of initial consonant sounds in stressed syllables: *"The fair breeze blew, the white foam flew . . ."*
- **Consonance:** the repetition of final consonant sounds in stressed syllables with different vowel sounds, as in *sit* and *cat*
- **Assonance:** the repetition of similar vowel sounds in stressed syllables that end with different consonants, as in *seal* and *meet*
- **Onomatopoeia:** the use of a word whose sound imitates its meaning, such as *pop* or *hiss*

All of these sound devices work to engage the reader's senses and create musical and emotional effects.

❹ Reading Skill: Read Fluently

Reading fluently is reading smoothly and continuously while also comprehending the text. Because poetry is a condensed form of language that employs figurative language, read poems several times to unlock layers of meaning.

❺ Using the Strategy: Multiple Reading Chart

Use a multiple reading chart such as the one shown to record your understanding of the poems.

	My Understanding
1st Reading • Read for basic meaning.	
2nd Reading • Read to unlock deeper meanings.	
3rd Reading • Read to recognize and appreciate poet's craft.	

PHLit Online!
www.PHLitOnline.com

Hear It!
- Selection summary audio
- Selection audio

See It!
- Get Connected video
- Background video
- More about the author
- Vocabulary flashcards

Do It!
- Interactive journals
- Interactive graphic organizers
- Self-test
- Internet activity
- Grammar tutorial
- Interactive vocabulary games

PRETEACH

❸ Literary Analysis

Sound Devices

1. Introduce the skill, using instruction on the student page.
2. Tell students that they will analyze sound devices as they read.

Think Aloud: Model the Skill

Model the skill of analyzing sound devices. Say to students:

> I read poetry aloud to expose the writer's sound devices. For example, in the line "Stella Stevens sat still," I notice the alliteration emphasizing the initial sound *s*. In the line "roll the ball on the sill," I notice the consonance emphasizing the final consonant sound *l*. If I hear words such as *bang* or *buzz*, I recognize onomatopoeia that helps me hear the sounds that these words imitate.

❹ Reading Skill

Read Fluently

1. Introduce the skill, using instruction on the student page.
2. Tell students that they will practice using their senses as they read fluently.

❺ Using the Strategy

Give students a copy of either **Reading Skill Graphic Organizer A** or **B** (*Graphic Organizer Transparencies,* pp. 117–119) to record information from each reading. Use the examples in **Reading Skill Graphic Organizer A,** which is partially filled in, to model the process of completing the organizer.

Ⓒ Text Complexity: Reader and Task Suggestions

✓ Collection 3		✓✓ Collection 4	
Preparing to Read the Text	**Leveled Tasks**	**Preparing to Read the Text**	**Leveled Tasks**
• Refer to the Background information on TE p. 645 and discuss the poets. • Discuss how poets often help us see everyday things and activities from a fresh perspective. • Guide students to use Multidraft Reading strategies (TE p. 645).	*Levels of Meaning* If students will have difficulty with levels of meaning, have them read each poem and identify its subject. Then, have them reread and discuss the poet's attitude toward the subject. *Analyzing* If students will not have difficulty with meaning, have them read and discuss each poem for examples of lines that give everyday subjects new meanings for them.	• Using the Background information on TE p. 653, discuss the poets. • Discuss how poets use imagery to help readers extract more powerful and personal responses to their subjects. • Guide students to use Multidraft Reading strategies (TE p. 653).	*Levels of Meaning* If students will have difficulty with levels of meaning, first have them read the poems and take notes on what happens. Then, have them reread for details that suggest the purpose of each poem. *Analyzing* If students will not have difficulty with levels of meaning, have them read each poem and take notes on examples of powerful imagery.

PRETEACH

❶ Writing About the Big Question

1. Review the assignment with the class.
2. **Ask** students if they consider themselves to be highly opinionated. Then, ask students to explain if and why they have ever changed their opinion on a subject after talking about it with others.
3. Have students complete the sentence starters. Review responses as a class. (**Possible response:** Reading someone's interpretation of a common experience can illuminate one's understanding of that experience because the reader becomes more informed. When people exchange stories about the past, they become more aware of the present because they can compare.)
4. Remind students that their answers will help them think about the Big Question, "How does communication change us?"

While You Read

Tell students to determine as they read what experiences the poet is describing and if they have shared this experience.

❷ Vocabulary

1. Have students preview the selection vocabulary.
2. For each word, have students say the word aloud.
3. Then, use the word in a sentence that defines the word.
4. Finally, repeat your definitional sentence or a similar sentence with the word missing and have the class "fill in the blank" chorally. Here are some example:

   Something that is azure is blue. The poet wanted readers to imagine a vivid blue sky, so she called the sky [students say "azure"].

❸ Word Study

1. Introduce the skill, using the instruction in the box.
2. **Ask** students which of these words use the prefix *ana-*: *anagram; anaconda; anarchy.* Then **ask** them to define the words: (**Answer:** *anagram* — a word with letters that are mixed up. *anarchy*— without or against government and order.)

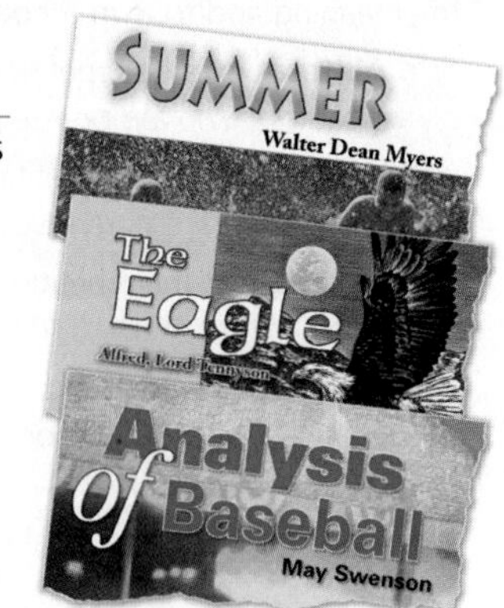

❶ Writing About the Big Question

In "Analysis of Baseball," the speaker shares her impressions of "America's pastime." Use these sentence starters to develop your ideas about the Big Question.

Reading someone's **interpretation** of a common experience can **illuminate** one's **understanding** of that experience because ______________.

When people **exchange** stories about the past, they become more **aware** of the present because ______________.

While You Read Notice when the speaker of a poem describes an experience with which you are familiar, and compare the speaker's response to your own.

❷ Vocabulary

Read each word and its definition. Decide whether you know the word well, know it a little bit, or do not know it at all. After you read, see how your knowledge of each word has increased.

- **clasps** (klasps) *v.* grips (p. 647) ***My mother clasps the steering wheel tightly whenever she approaches a sharp turn in the road.*** *clasp n.*
- **azure** (azh′ ər) *adj.* sky blue (p. 647) ***She painted the ceiling in her bedroom azure so that it would look like the sky.***
- **analysis** (ə nal′ ə sis) *n.* careful examination by studying something's elements or parts (p. 649) ***After a careful analysis of the food sample, the pathologist determined that it had been poisoned.*** *analyze v. analytical adj.*
- **disgrace** (dis grās′) *n.* loss of respect, honor, or esteem; shame (p. 649) ***After scoring on themselves and losing to their rivals as a result, the team left the field in disgrace.*** *disgraceful adj. disgraced v.*

❸ Word Study

The **Greek prefix *ana-*** means "up," "back," or "against."

Translated directly from its Greek word parts, the word **analysis** means "a loosening up." In the poem "Analysis of Baseball," the speaker "loosens up" the subject of baseball by describing its most basic parts.

Vocabulary Development

Vocabulary Knowledge Rating

Create a **Vocabulary Knowledge Rating Chart** (***Professional Development Guidebook,*** p. 33) for this collection. Include the collection vocabulary and the words that appear in the Writing About the Big Question sentence starters on this page. (The Big Question vocabulary is introduced on pp. 604–605.)

Give students a copy of the chart. Read the words aloud, and have students mark their rating in the Before Reading column. Urge them to be alert to these words as they read and discuss the selection.

Tally how many students think they know a word to gauge how much instruction to provide. As students read and discuss the selection, point out the words and their context.

Vocabulary Central, featuring tools, activities, and songs for studying vocabulary, is available at **www.PHLitOnline.com.**

4 Meet the Authors

Walter Dean Myers

(b. 1937)

Author of "Summer" (p. 646)

Growing up poor in West Virginia and New York City, Walter Dean Myers never imagined himself becoming a writer. Although he was writing poems and stories by his early teens, he believed that his dream of a literary career would never be realized. Myers's dream was fulfilled, however, when he won a writing contest sponsored by the Council on Interracial Books for Children with his book *Where Does a Day Go?*

Alfred, Lord Tennyson

(1809–1892)

Author of "The Eagle" (p. 647)

The most popular British poet during his lifetime, Alfred, Lord Tennyson rose from humble beginnings to the position of poet laureate of England. Although he was enthralled by the technological advances of the Victorian Era, Tennyson remained a poet of nature, bringing both imagination and feeling to descriptions of the landscape and its inhabitants.

May Swenson

(1919–1989)

Author of "Analysis of Baseball" (p. 648)

May Swenson has been called "one of the surest poets, clear-eyed and absolute." She was born in Logan, Utah, and attended Utah State University. After working for a while as a newspaper reporter, she moved to New York City, where she worked as an editor and as a college lecturer. Her poems were published in such magazines as *The New Yorker, Harper's,* and *The Nation.* Swenson also served as a Chancellor of The Academy of American Poets from 1980 to 1989.

Differentiated Instruction Additional Instruction

EL Extended Support—English Learners

Have students complete the **Reading and Vocabulary Warm-ups,** ***Unit 4 Resources,*** pp. 62–65, before they read. Assign the prereading pages for the collection in the ***Reader's Notebook: English Learner's Version.*** Then, have students listen to portions of the collection on the ***Hear It!*** **Audio CD.**

L1 L2 Extended Support—Struggling Readers

Have students complete the **Reading and Vocabulary Warm-ups,** ***Unit 4 Resources,*** pp. 62–65, before they read. Assign the prereading pages for the collection in the ***Reader's Notebook: Adapted Version.*** Then, have students listen to portions of the collection on the ***Hear It!*** **Audio CD** (adapted text).

Extended Support—Reluctant Readers

To build motivation and engagement before assigning the collection, have students read "A Heated Debate," a thematically related selection in ***Reality Central.*** Then, use the questions at the conclusion of the related selection to guide discussion.

Daily Bellringer

For each class during which you will teach this selection, have students complete one of the five Sentence Modeling activities for Week 20 in the ***Daily Bellringer Activities*** booklet.

4 Background

- **Walter Dean Myers** Because of a speech impediment, Walter Dean Myers often grew tense at the thought of reading in front of the class. When his teacher allowed him to read a poem he had written himself, he was fine. Walter began writing poems in the fifth grade. In those poems, he used only words he could pronounce. As he became more comfortable, his repertoire expanded to novels. Now, he mainly writes for young adults about the urban experience.
- **Alfred, Lord Tennyson** is one of the best known poets of the Victorian Age. As a boy, he was mostly home-schooled by his father before attending university. He had a successful career as a poet and outsold nearly every other poet of his generation. Tennyson's poetic themes center on sadness and mortality. At his death, Tennyson was buried in Poet's Corner in Westminster Abby in London.

Multidraft Reading

To assist struggling readers and to deepen reading for all, apply multidraft reading protocols. For each reading, have students set the purpose indicated:

- **First reading**—identifying key ideas and details and answering any Reading Checks.
- **Second reading**—analyzing craft and structure and responding to the side-column prompts.
- **Third reading**—integrating knowledge and ideas, connecting to other texts and the world, and answering the end-of-selection questions.

For more guidance, refer to the ***Classroom Strategies and Teaching Routines*** card on multidraft reading.

For more about the authors and practice with the selection vocabulary, go online at **www.PHLitOnline.com.**

TEACH

❶ Activating Prior Knowledge

Write *summer* on the board, and ask students to brainstorm for words to describe it. Tell them to think about the senses: sight, sound, touch, taste, and smell. Then have them preview the selections by looking at the titles and pictures. Invite students to add new words to the list.

Individual Activity

Have students prepare dramatic readings of one or more of the three poems accompanied by prerecorded music or music they perform live. Before they prepare their readings and choose the music, spend some time as a class discussing the feeling that each work expresses. What is the message of each poem? How do the sound devices in each poem contribute to the message?

❷ About the Selections

In "Summer," internal and terminal rhymes and a strong, irregular rhythm are as important as the literal meaning of the poet's words in creating a picture of summer. "The Eagle" is a brief, almost staccato, description of an eagle that captures the essence of the bird with its spare form, directness, and dramatic surge at the end. "Analysis of Baseball" presents the game, its strategy, and the poetry of the sport.

❸ Critical Viewing

Possible response: The poem focuses on wallowing in the heat, while the photograph shows an escape from the heat. The photograph does not capture the speaker's feelings.

❶ ❷

SUMMER

Walter Dean Myers

I like hot days, hot days
Sweat is what you got days
Bugs buzzin from cousin to cousin
Juices dripping
Running and ripping
Catch the one you love days

Birds peeping
Old men sleeping
Lazy days, daisies lay
Beaming and dreaming
Of hot days, hot days,
Sweat is what you got days

❸ ▼ **Critical Viewing** How well does this photograph illustrate the speaker's feelings about summer? Explain. **[Evaluate]**

Vocabulary Development

Ⓒ **CCSS** Language 6

Thematic Vocabulary: The Big Question

As students are discussing "Summer," "The Eagle," and "Analysis of Baseball," encourage them to use the thematic vocabulary presented in Introducing the Big Question, pp. 604–605. You might encourage them with sentence starters like these:

1. In "Summer," aspects of nature *respond* to the atmosphere of summer by . . .
2. According to Tennyson's *interpretation,* the eagle is . . .
3. In "Analysis of Baseball," Swenson portrays the *relationship* of the ball and the bat as . . .
4. "Analysis of Baseball" changed my *understanding* of baseball because . . .

The Eagle

Alfred, Lord Tennyson

He **clasps** the crag[1] with crooked hands;
Close to the sun in lonely lands,
Ring'd with the **azure** world, he stands.

❹

The wrinkled sea beneath him crawls;
He watches from his mountain walls,
And like a thunderbolt he falls.

Vocabulary

clasps (klasps) *v.* grips

azure (azh′ ər) *adj.* sky blue

1. **crag** (krag) *n.* steep, rugged rock that rises above others or projects from a rock mass.

❹ Connecting to the Big Question

1. Have a volunteer read the poem aloud. **Ask:** What experience is the speaker describing?

   Answer: The speaker is describing the experience of seeing an eagle diving from the sky, possibly to catch prey.

2. **Ask:** Have you ever seen a bird of prey dive down from the sky? Explain your experience.

   Possible response: Once I saw an osprey dive into the sea to catch a fish. It moved incredibly fast, and it barely made a splash when it entered the water.

3. **Ask:** How does the speaker's experience compare with your own?

   Possible response: Like the speaker, I was watching the osprey in "lonely lands"—I was the only human around for miles. My osprey did move "like a thunderbolt." However, my osprey did not begin its dive from a perch as the eagle of the poem does. Like the speaker, I was awed by the bird's actions and humbled by nature.

PHLit Online!

This selection is available in interactive format in the **Enriched Online Student Edition, www.PHLitOnline.com,** which includes a thematically related video with writing prompt and an interactive graphic organizer.

Differentiated Instruction for Universal Access

Strategy for Special-Needs Students

Analyze "Summer" and "The Eagle" verse by verse. Have volunteers read each verse, and then have students picture what the poet is describing. After each verse, have students write down some words that describe how that verse makes them feel. Then have students use their word lists to write a few sentences that describe the feelings they got from the verse.

Strategy for Less Proficient Readers

Help students better understand sensory language by showing them **Reading Skill Graphic Organizer A** (*Graphic Organizer Transparencies* p. 117). Ask students to look through the poems and locate the examples listed in the organizer. Use these examples to show how language can appeal to the senses. Then, encourage students to watch for other examples as they continue reading.

5 Humanities

Sliding in Yankee Stadium, by Lance Richbourg

Born in 1938 in Richmond, Virginia, artist Lance Richbourg is known for his vivid paintings of baseball scenes. Richbourg received his master of fine arts degree from the University of California, Los Angeles. He has taught extensively at the college level. Use the following questions for discussion:

1. How does this painting help you appreciate the poem?

   Possible response: It provides visual proof of the quickness required by baseball players and communicates the excitement of the game.

2. What two major visual elements from the poem are missing from this painting?

   Answer: The ball and the bat are missing from the painting.

5

Analysis of Baseball

May Swenson

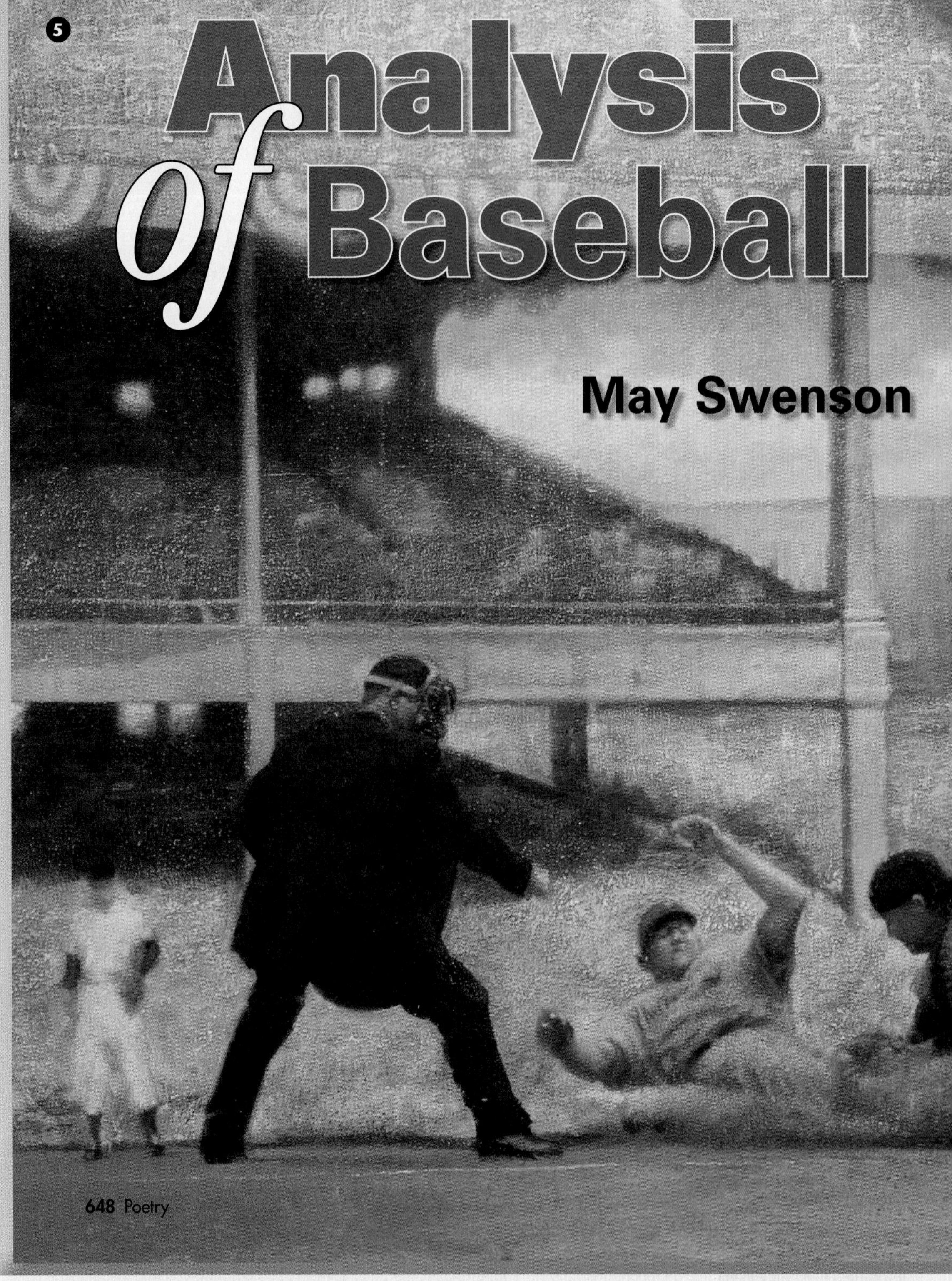

Vocabulary Development

Vocabulary Knowledge Rating

When students have completed reading and discussing Poetry Collection 3, have them take out their **Vocabulary Knowledge Rating Chart** for these poems. Read the words aloud once more and have students rate their knowledge of the words again in the After Reading column. Clarify any words that are still problematic. Have students write their own definition and example or sentence in the appropriate column. Then have students complete the Vocabulary Practice activities at the end of the collection. Encourage students to use the words in further discussion and written work about these poems. Remind them that they will be accountable for these words on the **Selection Test, *Unit 4 Resources,*** pp. 74–76 or 77–79.

It's about
the ball,
the bat,
and the mitt.
Ball hits
bat, or it
hits mitt.
6 Bat doesn't
7 hit ball, bat
meets it.
Ball bounces
off bat, flies
air, or thuds
ground (dud)
or it
fits mitt.

Bat waits
for ball
to mate.
Ball hates
to take bat's
bait. Ball
flirts, bat's
late, don't
keep the date.
Ball goes in
(thwack) to mitt,
and goes out
(thwack) back
to mitt.

Ball fits
mitt, but
not all
the time.
Sometimes
ball gets hit
(pow) when bat
meets it,
and sails
to a place
where mitt
has to quit
in disgrace.

Literary Analysis
Sound Devices What final consonant sound is repeated frequently in the first ten lines?

Reading Skill
Read Fluently After the first reading, what would you say is the basic meaning of the first stanza?

Spiral Review
Figurative Language What examples of personification can you find in the stanza that runs from lines 17 to 30?

Vocabulary
analysis (ə nal´ ə sis) *n.* careful examination by studying something's elements or parts

disgrace (dis grās´) *n.* loss of respect, honor, or esteem; shame

6 Literary Analysis
Sound Devices

1. Read the first stanza aloud, and then **ask** students the Literary Analysis question: What final consonant sound is repeated frequently in the first ten lines?
   Answer: The final consonant sound "t" is repeated frequently.
2. Point out that this poem uses onomatopoeia to help evoke the sounds of baseball. Have students **list** some examples.
   Answer: Examples include *thud, dud, thwack,* and *pow.*

Monitor Progress: **Ask** students to find an example of assonance in lines 11–16.

Answer: Assonance is found in bounces and ground.

Reteach: Review the sound devices described on p. 643. Have students review the entire poem and give examples of each device.

Possible response: Examples include the following: **alliteration:** *bat, bounce,* and *ball;* **consonance:** *bat* and *mitt;* **assonance:** *take* and *bait;* **onomatopoeia:** *dud* and *thwack.*

7 Reading Skill
Read Fluently

1. Have students reread the first stanza. **Ask** the Reading Skill question: After the first reading, what would you say is the basic meaning of the first stanza?
   Possible response: Baseball is about the moment when the ball hits the bat—or doesn't.

Spiral Review
Figurative Language

1. Remind students that they studied figurative language in the Unit 4 Literary Analysis workshop (pp. 606–614).
2. **Ask** students the Spiral Review question.
   Possible response: The bat and the ball flirt; they have feelings; they plan a date. The poet describes them as if they were people who act like they don't care about each other but are going to get together eventually.

Concept Connector

Activating Prior Knowledge
Have students review their brainstorm lists about summer. Encourage students to add new words to the list based on what they learned and discovered in the poem.

Writing About the Big Question
Have students compare their responses to the sentence starters they completed before reading the poems with their ideas afterwards. Ask them to explain whether their thoughts have changed.

Reading Skill Graphic Organizer
Ask students to review the graphic organizers they completed to list information from multiple readings. Show them **Reading Skill Graphic Organizer A** (*Graphic Organizer Transparencies,* p. 117) as an example. Then have students share the graphic organizers they did and the information they identified.

ASSESS

Answers

Critical Thinking

Before students respond, you may wish to have them write a brief objective summary of each selection. As they answer the questions below, remind them to support their answers with evidence from the text.

1. (a) Myers describes summer as so hot that people sweat. (b) Perspiration and nectar may be dripping. (c) Line 4 explains or elaborates line 2.
2. (a) The eagle is probably watching for something to eat. (b) The eagle is diving after its prey.
3. Yes, if the reader knows what a bat and a mitt are. The speaker clearly tells what is going on and how the ball, the bat, and the mitt interact.
4. (a) **Possible response:** The poem conveys the excitement of the game being played, but it is an abbreviated description of the sport. My experience includes the fans, the food, the music, and the park. (b) **Possible response:** The poem may increase students' appreciation of the basics of the sport, as it reduces baseball to interaction among ball, bat, and mitt.

▲ Critical Viewing
Which words in the poem might describe the action in this image? **[Connect]**

That's about
the bases
loaded,
about 40,000
fans exploded.

It's about
the ball,
the bat,
the mitt,
the bases
and the fans.
It's done
on a diamond,
and for fun.
It's about
home, and it's
about run.

Cite textual evidence to support your responses.

Critical Thinking

1. **Key Ideas and Details** **(a)** In lines 1–2 of "Summer," how does the speaker describe summer? **(b) Interpret:** What kind of juices might be dripping in line 4? **(c) Connect:** In what way is the image in line 4 a continuation of the one in line 2? Explain your response.
2. **Key Ideas and Details** **(a) Infer:** What is the eagle watching for in line 5 of "The Eagle"? **(b) Interpret:** What is the eagle doing when he "falls" in line 6?
3. **Integration of Knowledge and Ideas** **Make a Judgment:** Do you think the poem "Analysis of Baseball" can be appreciated by someone who is unfamiliar with the rules of baseball? Why or why not?
4. **Integration of Knowledge and Ideas** **(a)** How does "Analysis of Baseball" compare with your experience of the sport of baseball? **(b)** Does the poem change how you think about baseball? Why or why not? ***[Connect to the Big Question: How does communication change us?]***

Assessment Resources

Unit 4 Resources

L1 L2 EL **Selection Test A,** pp. 74–76. Administer Test A to less advanced readers.

L3 L4 EL **Selection Test B,** pp. 77–79. Administer Test B to on-level and more advanced students.

L3 L4 **Open-Book Test,** pp. 71–73. As an alternative, give the Open-Book Test.

All **Customizable Test Bank**

All **Self-tests**
Students may prepare for the **Selection Test** by taking the **Self-test** online.

PHLit Online! All assessment resources are available at **www.PHLitOnline.com**.

After You Read
Poetry Collection 3

Summer • The Eagle • Analysis of Baseball

Literary Analysis: Sound Devices

1. **Craft and Structure** **(a)** For each poem in Poetry Collection 3, use a chart like the one shown to list one example of each **sound device** listed. **(b)** How does each example add to the musical feeling of each poem?

	Example	Effect
Alliteration		
Consonance		
Assonance		

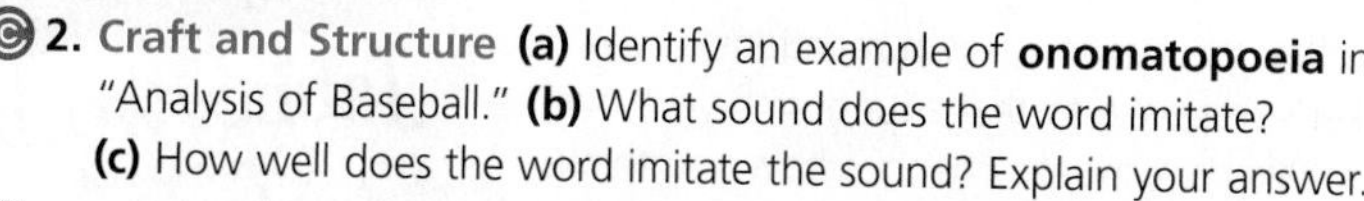

2. **Craft and Structure** **(a)** Identify an example of **onomatopoeia** in "Analysis of Baseball." **(b)** What sound does the word imitate? **(c)** How well does the word imitate the sound? Explain your answer.
3. **Craft and Structure** **(a)** Which of these poems do you think makes the most effective use of sound devices? **(b)** Discuss your choice with a small group and decide on a single response.

Reading Skill: Read Fluently

4. How did your understanding of the poems deepen with each reading? Give examples.
5. **(a)** How does **reading fluently** help you appreciate a poem's sound devices? **(b)** Which senses, other than your sense of hearing, were most engaged by each poem? Explain.

Vocabulary

Acquisition and Use Identify the word in each group that does not belong with the others. Explain your response.

1. clasps, hands, blanket
2. azure, bread, green
3. analysis, study, recording
4. disgrace, pride, approval

Word Study Use the context of the sentences and what you know about the **Greek prefix *ana-*** to explain your answer to each question.

1. If something is an *anachronism,* is it in the correct time period?
2. Why is a study of *anatomy* important for doctors?

Word Study

The **Greek prefix *ana-*** means "up," "back," or "against."

Apply It Explain how the prefix *ana-* contributes to the meanings of these words. Consult a dictionary if necessary.

anagram
analogy

ASSESS/EXTEND

Answers

Literary Analysis

1. (a) **Sample answers:** **"Summer"—alliteration:** "bugs buzzin"; **consonance:** "sweat. . . what"; **assonance:** "daisies lay." **"The Eagle"—alliteration:** "clasps. . .crag"; **consonance:** "Ring'd. . .world"; **assonance:** "clasps. . .crag." **"Analysis of Baseball"—alliteration:** "ball . . . bat"; **consonance:** "mitt. . . bat"; **assonance:** "take . . bait." (b) These devices make each poem's words sound like they fit together. Poems, like music, may have slow and fast, gentle or harsh, or loud and soft passages. Sound devices help to create these musical rhythms.

   For other sample answers, see ***Graphic Organizer Transparencies,* Literary Analysis Graphic Organizer A,** p. 120, and the **Additional Answers** section.
2. (a) Students may say "thwack." (b) The word imitates the sound of a baseball landing in a mitt. (c) "Thwack" is a good representation of the sound.
3. (a) Students may choose "Analysis of Baseball" because of its onomatopoeia. (b) Students should agree on their choices and list supporting examples.

Reading Skill

4. **Possible response:** Each reading revealed more information.
5. (a) **Possible response:** Fluent reading helps readers hear and appreciate the musical qualities that sound devices instill in the poems.
   (b) **Possible response:** Sight was the most commonly used sense in all of the poems.

Vocabulary

Acquisition and Use

1. blanket; *Hands* and *clasps* are actions that you do with your hands, while *blanket* is not.
2. bread; *Azure* and *green* are both colors; *bread* is not.
3. recording; In an *analysis* of something, one has to *study* it. *Recording* doesn't belong.
4. disgrace; *Pride* and *approval* are positive. *Disgrace* is negative.

Word Study

Sample answers:

1. No. An *anachronism* is "something that dates back to another time." Thus an anachronism is not in the correct time period.
2. *Anatomy* is the science that explains how the human body is divided up.

Word Study: Apply It

Sample answers: An *anagram* is a word that changes when the letters are mixed up. An *analogy* is a match up between two objects that are otherwise different.

PRETEACH

*Skills instruction for the **Reading Skill** and **Literary Analysis** concept appears on p. 643.*

1 Writing About the Big Question

1. Review the assignment with the class.
2. **Ask** students to name a favorite sound and explain why they like it. What ideas, people, or events do they associate with this sound?
3. Have students complete the sentence starter. Review responses as a class. (**Possible response:** By reading about the meaning that someone finds in certain sounds, a reader can learn to better appreciate the sound.)
4. Remind students that their answers will help them think about the Big Question, "How does communication change us?"

While You Read

Tell students that as they read they should notice how the speaker reacts to certain sounds and compare that with their own reaction.

2 Vocabulary

1. Have students preview the selection vocabulary.
2. For each word, have students say the word aloud.
3. Then, use the word in a sentence that defines the word.
4. Repeat your definitional sentence or a similar sentence with the word missing, and have the class "fill in the blank" chorally. Here are some examples:
   Voluminously means in great volume. When the pitcher spilled, the water flowed over the table [students say "voluminously"].
   When something is palpitating, it is beating rapidly. As Marta stepped forward to receive her award, she was so nervous that her heart was [students say "palpitating"].

3 Word Study

1. Introduce the skill, using the instruction in the box.
2. **Ask** students for a *mono-* word that means, "a word of one syllable."
   (**Answer:** *monosyllable*)

Making Connections
Poetry Collection 4

The Bells • Slam, Dunk, & Hook • Jabberwocky

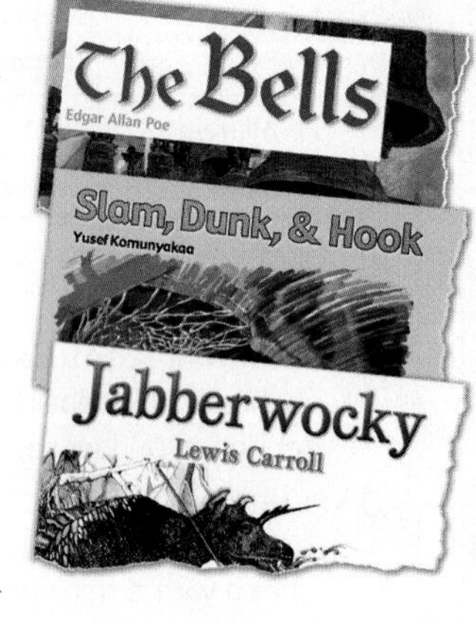

1 Writing About the Big Question

The speaker in "The Bells" describes a range of ideas associated with the sounds of different bells. Use this sentence starter to develop your ideas about the Big Question.

By reading about the **meaning** that someone finds in certain sounds, a reader can learn to ______________.

While You Read Notice when the speaker of a poem mentions a specific sound. Compare the speaker's response to that sound with your own reactions. Notice whether the speaker's response changes how you think about that sound.

2 Vocabulary

Read each word and its definition. Decide whether you know the word well, know it a little bit, or do not know it at all. After you have read the selection, see how your knowledge of each word has increased.

- **voluminously** (və lo͞o´ mə nəs lē) *adv.* fully; in great volume (p. 656) *Her coach praised her voluminously at the awards banquet.* volume *n.*
- **endeavor** (en dev´ ər) *n.* an earnest attempt or effort (p. 656) *My endeavor to stay up all night failed when I fell asleep at midnight.* endeavor *v.*
- **palpitating** (pal´ pə tāt´ iŋ) *adj.* beating rapidly; throbbing (p. 656) *The palpitating drums of the pep band excited the fans.*
- **monotone** (män´ ə tōn´) *n.* uninterrupted repetition of the same tone; utterance of successive syllables or words without change of pitch or key (p. 659) *The actor spoke in a monotone, which did nothing to keep me awake during the play.* monotonous *adj.* monotony *n.*
- **metaphysical** (met´ ə fiz´ i kəl) *adj.* spiritual; beyond the physical (p. 661) *She says that songwriting is metaphysical—the songs come to her in dreams.*
- **jibed** (jībd) *v.* changed direction (p. 661) *As the wind shifted, the crew jibed to keep the sails full.*

3 Word Study

The **Greek prefix *mono-*** means "one."

In "The Bells," the speaker describes the "muffled **monotone**" of certain bells. He refers to a kind of ringing that has only one tone, or pitch, that repeats without changing.

Vocabulary Development

Vocabulary Knowledge Rating

Create a **Vocabulary Knowledge Rating Chart** (***Professional Development Guidebook***, p. 33) for this selection. Include the selection vocabulary and the Big Question word that appears in the Writing About the Big Question sentence starter on this page. (The Big Question vocabulary is introduced on pp. 604–605.)

Give students a copy of the chart. Read the words aloud, and have students mark their rating in the Before Reading column. Urge them to be alert to these words as they read and discuss the selection.

Tally how many students think they know a word to gauge how much instruction to provide. As students read and discuss the selection, point out the words and their context.

Vocabulary Central, featuring tools, activities, and songs for studying vocabulary, is available at **www.PHLitOnline.com.**

Meet the Authors

Edgar Allan Poe

(1809–1849)

Author of "The Bells" (p. 654)

As poems like "The Bells" illustrate, Edgar Allan Poe was a master at using rhythm and sound devices to powerful effect. Many scholars believe that the idea for "The Bells" was suggested to Poe by Marie Louise Shew, a woman with medical training who treated Poe when his health began to fail.

Yusef Komunyakaa

(b. 1947)

Author of "Slam, Dunk, & Hook" (p. 660)

Yusef Komunyakaa grew up in Bogalusa, Louisiana. During the mid-1960s, he served in Vietnam as a reporter and an editor for the military newspaper *The Southern Cross.* Komunyakaa later turned his attention to poetry, winning a Pulitzer Prize for his book *Neon Vernacular: New and Selected Poems* (1993). Komunyakaa has said that he likes "connecting the abstract to the concrete."

Lewis Carroll

(1832–1898)

Author of "Jabberwocky" (p. 662)

Charles Lutwidge Dodgson was a professor of mathematics and a talented early photographer. Today, he is best remembered for two children's books he wrote under the pen name Lewis Carroll: *Alice's Adventures in Wonderland* (1865) and its sequel, *Through the Looking Glass* (1871). Huge bestsellers almost from the moment they appeared, the Alice books have been the basis of numerous stage plays and films.

Daily Bellringer

For each class during which you will teach this selection, have students complete one of the five Sentence Modeling activities for Week 20 in the *Daily Bellringer Activities* booklet.

4 Background

- **Edgar Allan Poe** was a poet, short story writer, critic, and essayist. His short story *The Fall of the House of Usher* and the poem "The Raven" are probably two of his best-known works, although he was a prolific writer of short stories as well.

  Poe had a distinguished career and is best known for his psychologically thrilling works. He is a master of suspense and many of his works have underlying themes of violence and death. Although his life was marred by tragedy, Edgar Allan Poe leaves a long list of exceptional works that readers continue to enjoy.
- **Lewis Carroll** is probably best known for his books *Alice in Wonderland* and *Alice through the Looking Glass.* Besides children's books and poems, Carroll wrote mathematical textbooks and loved to create word and logic games. Some of that originality went into producing his invented language in "Jabberwocky."

Multidraft Reading

To assist struggling readers and to deepen reading for all, apply multidraft reading protocols. For each reading, have students set the purpose indicated:

- **First reading**—identifying key ideas and details and answering any Reading Checks.
- **Second reading**—analyzing craft and structure and responding to the side-column prompts.
- **Third reading**—integrating knowledge and ideas, connecting to other texts and the world, and answering the end-of-selection questions.

For more guidance, refer to the ***Classroom Strategies and Teaching Routines*** card on multidraft reading.

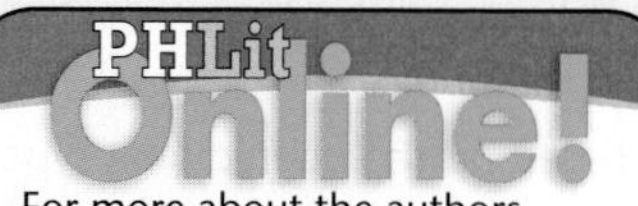

For more about the authors and practice with the selection vocabulary, go online at **www.PHLitOnline.com.**

Differentiated Instruction

Additional Instruction

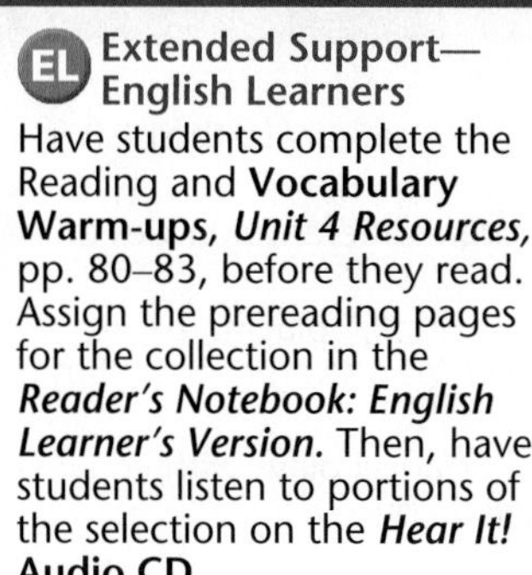

EL Extended Support—English Learners

Have students complete the Reading and **Vocabulary Warm-ups,** ***Unit 4 Resources,*** pp. 80–83, before they read. Assign the prereading pages for the collection in the ***Reader's Notebook: English Learner's Version.*** Then, have students listen to portions of the selection on the ***Hear It!*** **Audio CD.**

L1 L2 Extended Support—Struggling Readers

Have students complete the **Reading and Vocabulary Warm-ups,** ***Unit 4 Resources,*** pp. 80–83, before they read. Assign the prereading pages for the collection in the ***Reader's Notebook: Adapted Version.*** Then, have students listen to portions of the selection on the ***Hear It!*** **Audio CD** (adapted text).

Extended Support—Reluctant Readers

To build motivation and engagement before assigning the selection, have students read "Good Words for Bad Times," a thematically related selection in ***Reality Central.*** Then, use the questions at the conclusion of the related selection to guide discussion.

TEACH

❶ Activating Prior Knowledge

Write the word *bells* on the board, and then ask students to suggest words that describe how the sound of bells makes them feel. Then, have students list different kinds of bells and the purposes they serve. Ask them to draw a conclusion about bells based on these responses.

Concept Connector

Students will reconsider their ideas about bells after reading the collection.

Small-Group Activity

The poems in this collection exhibit infectious rhythms and sound words that are best appreciated when read aloud. Have small groups of students take turns reading the poems aloud and discuss their favorite parts.

❷ About the Selections

"The Bells" uses repetition and onomatopoeia to capture the sounds and symbolism of bells. In "Slam, Dunk, & Hook," the speaker rhapsodizes about the neighborhood basketball games he plays with his buddies. The intensity of the games carries one player through a grievous loss. "Jabberwocky" parodies medieval legends. The seriousness of tone contrasted with the nonsensical words has a comical effect.

❸ Humanities

The Bells of Rostov, 1983, by Sergei Chepik

Born in 1953 in Kiev, Russia, Sergei Chepik studied art at the Repin Academy of Fine Art in St. Petersburg. Due to controversy over his socially critical art, Chepik moved to Paris in 1988. Common subjects of his paintings include boxing, bullfighting, and sunflowers. Use the following questions for discussion:

1. How does this painting help you appreciate the poem?

   Possible response: It gives me a visual cue as I "hear" the bells in the poem.

2. Based on the poem, what type of bells is shown in the painting?

   Possible response: I think they are wedding bells.

❶ ❷ ❸

Vocabulary Development

© CCSS Language 6

Thematic Vocabulary: The Big Question

As students are discussing "The Bells," "Slam, Dunk, & Hook," and "Jabberwocky," encourage them to use the thematic vocabulary presented in Introducing the Big Question, pp. 604–605. You might encourage them with sentence starters like these:

1. Poe wants the reader to *react* to the bells in section III by . . .
2. Poe tries to *illuminate* different qualities of bells, such as . . .
3. In "Slam, Dunk, & Hook," playing basketball takes on a new *meaning* for Sonny Boy because . . .
4. In "Jabberwocky," Carroll plays with conventional *communication* by . . .

The Bells

Edgar Allan Poe

I

Hear the sledges[1] with the bells—
Silver bells!
What a world of merriment their melody foretells!
How they tinkle, tinkle, tinkle,
In the icy air of night!
While the stars, that oversprinkle
All the heavens, seem to twinkle
With a crystalline delight;
Keeping time, time, time,
In a sort of Runic[2] rhyme,
To the tintinnabulation[3] that so musically wells
From the bells, bells, bells, bells,
Bells, bells, bells—
From the jingling and the tinkling of the bells.

II

Hear the mellow wedding bells,
Golden bells!
What a world of happiness their harmony foretells!
Through the balmy air of night
How they ring out their delight!
From the molten golden-notes,

1. **sledges** (slej´ əz) *n.* sleighs.
2. **Runic** (ro͞o´ nik) *adj.* songlike; poetical.
3. **tintinnabulation** (tin´ ti na´ byo͞o la´ shən) *n.* ringing sound of bells.

Spiral Review
Figurative Language How does the author give the stars in lines 6–8 human qualities? What type of figurative language is this an example of?

What type of bells does section one describe?

4 Critical Thinking

Analyze

1. Read, or have a student read, section I aloud. **Ask** students to identify the mood of the verse.

   Answer: The mood is cheerful and merry.

2. Have students **identify** the words that establish this mood.

   Answer: The words include *merriment, tinkle, delight, musically,* and *jingling.*

Spiral Review

Figurative Language

1. Remind students that they studied the concept of figurative language in the Unit 4 Literary Analysis workshop (pp. 606–614).
2. **Ask** students the Spiral Review question.

   Possible response: The poet gives the stars the ability to sprinkle light the way a person sprinkles sugar. This is an example of personification.

5 Reading Check

Answer: Section I describes silver bells attached to sleighs.

PHLit Online!

This collection is available in interactive format in the **Enriched Online Student Edition, www.PHLitOnline.com,** which includes a thematically related video with writing prompt and an interactive graphic organizer.

Differentiated Instruction for Universal Access

Enrichment for Advanced Readers

Explain to students that Edgar Allan Poe was a master of using sound devices. Many words and lines in his poems combine multiple devices to create their effect. Point out that many sound devices have complex forms. For example, rhyme is typically formed from accented final syllables, but it is sometimes formed from similar sounds in unaccented syllables. Usually, it is used as end rhymes, but it can also be used as internal rhyme.

Have students choose two or three lines from "The Bells" that have memorable sound effects, and have them analyze how Poe constructs the sound. Students may want to do additional research into different sound devices and how they work. Invite volunteers to share their analyses with the class.

6 Literary Analysis

Sound Devices

1. Explain that alliteration and rhymes are prominent in Poe's poem, but it is rich in other sound devices as well. **Ask** students to identify the assonance in lines 20 to 26.

   Answer: Assonance occurs in "molten golden-notes," "liquid ditty," and "out the sounding cells."

2. Have students **identify** examples of onomatopoeia in lines 27 to 35.

   Answer: Words demonstrating onomatopoeia include *ringing* and *chiming.*

3. **Ask** students the Literary Analysis question: What quality of alarm bells might the alliteration of the *t* sound in line 38 imitate?

   Possible response: The sharp consonant sounds of the *t's* (and *d's*) suggest the urgency and attacking quality of warning or alarm bells.

Vocabulary
voluminously (və lo͞o′ mə nəs lē) *adv.* fully; in great volume

Literary Analysis
Sound Devices What quality of alarm bells might the alliteration of the *t* sound in line 38 imitate?

Vocabulary
endeavor (en dev′ ər) *n.* an earnest attempt or effort
palpitating (pal′ pə tāt′ iŋ) *v.* beating rapidly; throbbing

And all in tune,
What a liquid ditty[4] floats
To the turtle-dove[5] that listens, while she gloats
On the moon!
Oh, from out the sounding cells,
What a gush of euphony[6] **voluminously** wells!
How it swells!
How it dwells
On the future! how it tells
Of the rapture that impels
6 To the swinging and the ringing
Of the bells, bells, bells,
Of the bells, bells, bells, bells
Bells, bells, bells—
To the rhyming and the chiming of the bells!

III

Hear the loud alarum[7] bells!
Brazen[8] bells!
What a tale of terror now their turbulency tells!
In the startled ear of night
How they scream out their affright!
Too much horrified to speak,
They can only shriek, shriek,
Out of tune,
In a clamorous appealing to the mercy of the fire,
In a mad expostulation[9] with the deaf and frantic fire
Leaping higher, higher, higher,
With a desperate desire,
And a resolute **endeavor**
Now—now to sit or never,
By the side of the pale-faced moon.
Oh, the bells, bells, bells!
What a tale their terror tells
Of Despair!
How they clang, and clash, and roar!
What a horror they outpour
On the bosom of the **palpitating** air!

---

4. **ditty** (dit′ ē) *n.* short, simple song.
5. **turtle-dove** (turt′'l duv′) The turtle dove is traditionally associated with love.
6. **euphony** (yo͞o′ fə nē) *n.* pleasing sound.
7. **alarum** (ə ler′ əm) *adj.* sudden call to arms; alarm.
8. **brazen** (brā′ zən) *adj.* made of brass; having the ringing sound of brass.
9. **expostulation** (ek späs′ chə lā′ shən) *n.* objection; complaint.

Vocabulary Development

Expressive Vocabulary

To help students broaden their expressive vocabulary, encourage them to use the following words as they discuss "The Bells": *signifies, trigger, appreciate, contemplate,* and *interpret.* Have them complete these sentence starters:

1. The ringing of the bells in section III *signifies* . . .
2. The bells in section II *trigger* . . .
3. Of the different types of bells, people most *appreciate* hearing . . .
4. When I *contemplate* the bells in section IV, I feel . . .
5. The speaker wants readers to *interpret* the meaning of "The Bells" as . . .

7

Yet the ear it fully knows,
By the twanging
And the clanging,
How the danger ebbs and flows;
Yet the ear distinctly tells,
In the jangling,
And the wrangling,
How the danger sinks and swells,
By the sinking or the swelling in the anger of the bells—
8 Of the bells—
Of the bells, bells, bells, bells,
Bells, bells, bells—
In the clamor and the clangor of the bells!

IV

Hear the tolling of the bells—
Iron bells!
What a world of solemn thought their monody[10] compels!

Literary Analysis
Sound Devices What is the effect of the repetition in lines 67–68?

9 

What kind of story do the alarm bells tell?

10. monody (mä′ nə dē) *n.* poem of mourning; a steady sound; music in which one instrument or voice is dominant.

7 Humanities

The Bell! Die Glocke! by Paul Klee

Swiss artist Paul Klee (1879–1940) came from a family of musicians. He spent most of his life in Germany but drew inspiration from worldwide travel. Klee was a member of Der Blaue Reiter (the Blue Rider), a group of expressionist artists who helped shape the development of abstract art. Use the following questions for discussion:

1. How does this painting help you appreciate the poem?

   Possible response: It shows bells as part of many different human contexts.

2. How is the mood of the painting similar to the mood of the poetry on this page?

   Possible response: Like the poetry on this page, the mood of the painting is chaotic and strident.

8 Literary Analysis

Sound Devices

1. Read lines 65–69 aloud to students. **Ask** students the Literary Analysis question: What is the effect of the repetition in lines 67–68?

   Answer: The repetition of the word *bells* creates a ringing effect almost like that of real bells ringing.

2. Call students' attention to *clamor* and *clangor* in the final line of the passage, and **ask** them to analyze the sound devices represented by these two words.

   Answer: The sound effects of *clamor* and *clangor* are alliteration, onomatopoeia, and rhyme.

9 Reading Check

Answer: The wedding bells tell a story of future happiness and harmony.

Differentiated Instruction for Universal Access

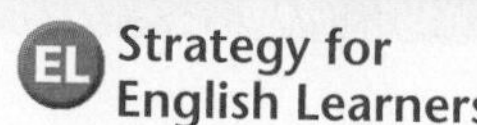

Strategy for Special-Needs Students

Have students read sections II and III aloud several times. After the first reading, discuss the difference in tone between sections II and III. Focus on the first five lines of both verses. Make sure that students realize that both verses have exactly the same structure, but the bells and their effects are completely different. Then, have the students reread the sections, using their tone of voice to express the difference in mood.

EL Strategy for English Learners

Make sure that students understand all potentially puzzling words in these verses in addition to those defined in the notes. Write some of the troublesome phrases on the board and preview them with students. For example, you might write "Harmony foretells" (line 17)—*sound predicts,* "liquid ditty" (line 22)—*smooth sound,* "monody compels" (line 72)—*song of mourning causes,* and so on. After students grasp the meaning of the verses, ask them to read the verses aloud together.

⑩ Humanities

The Bells by Edmund Dulac

Edmund Dulac (1882–1953) was a French illustrator known for the color and imagination of his work. This painting, with its somber overall mood, illustrates Part IV of "The Bells." Use these questions for discussion:

1. Using this painting as an example, explain some of the advantages of illustrating a literary work with paintings rather than photographs.

   Possible response: One advantage is a painter's ability to stray from reality in order to create a certain impression or mood. Another is the ability to use light and composition as desired for emphasis or effect.

2. How could other sections of this poem be illustrated?

   Possible response: Students might suggest that paintings or photographs of sleighs, weddings, or fires might be used to illustrate the other parts of the poem.

⑩

658 Poetry

Think Aloud

Figurative Language

Draw students' attention to lines 73–78 on page 659. Use the following "think aloud" to model the process of building meaning from figurative language.

I use my senses as I read this passage aloud to help me understand the poet's ideas. I notice sensory language that helps me place myself inside the poem. First, the word *silent* appeals to my sense of hearing and cues me to read the passage quietly. When I reach the next line, I feel a shiver of fear running through my body. Then, the phrase "melancholy menace of their tone" helps me experience the intense sound of the bells. In line 77, I can almost taste rust in my throat, and I finish the passage with the sound of a groan in my ears.

In the silence of the night,
How we shiver with affright
At the melancholy menace of their tone!
For every sound that floats
From the rust within their throats
Is a groan.
And the people—ah, the people—
They that dwell up in the steeple,
All alone,
And who tolling, tolling, tolling,
In that muffled **monotone**,
Feel a glory in so rolling
On the human heart a stone—
They are neither man nor woman—
They are neither brute nor human—
They are Ghouls:[11]
And their king it is who tolls;
And he rolls, rolls, rolls,
Rolls
A pæan from the bells!
And his merry bosom swells
With the pæan of the bells!
And he dances and he yells;
Keeping time, time, time,
In a sort of Runic rhyme,
To the pæan of the bells—
Of the bells:
Keeping time, time, time,
In a sort of Runic rhyme,
To the throbbing of the bells—
Of the bells, bells, bells—
To the sobbing of the bells;
Keeping time, time, time,
As he knells, knells, knells,
In a happy Runic rhyme,
To the rolling of the bells—
Of the bells, bells, bells—
To the tolling of the bells,
Of the bells, bells, bells, bells,
Bells, bells, bells—
To the moaning and the groaning of the bells.

11. Ghouls (go͞olz) *n.* evil spirits that rob graves.

Literary Analysis
Sound Devices What alliteration appears in lines 83–85?

Vocabulary
monotone (män′ ə tōn′) *n.* uninterrupted repetition of the same tone; utterance of successive syllables or words without change of pitch or key

Reading Skill
Read Fluently
Which repeated words in this stanza might sound like the repetitive tolling of bells?

13 Critical Viewing
Which kind of bells do you think this painting best illustrates? Why? **[Assess]**

11 Literary Analysis

Sound Devices

1. Read part IV aloud to students. Then, **ask** students the Literary Analysis question: What alliteration appears in lines 83–85?

   Answer: There are two instances of alliteration: "muffled monotone" and "human heart."

2. **Ask** students to identify the assonance in these lines.

   Answer: The assonance is developed in the /o/ sound of *so, rolling,* and *stone.*

12 Reading Skill

Read Fluently

1. Tell students that sensory language can be used to emphasize the theme of a poem.
2. **Ask** students the Reading Skill question: Which repeated words in this stanza might sound like the repetitive tolling of bells?

   Answer: Poe repeats the following words to imitate the sound of bells: *tolling* (line 82), *rolls* (lines 90–91), *time* (lines 96, 100, and 105), and *bells* (lines 102–104 and 108–113).

3. Point out to students that most literature appeals most strongly to the sense of sight. "The Bells" is an exception because sound is the primary sensory appeal.

13 Critical Viewing

Answer: The painting best illustrates the bells described in part IV because the painting captures their melancholy, frightening nature.

Fluency

Distribute copies of this page, and pair students. Have partners take turns reading paragraphs aloud. While one partner reads, the other should mark any words with which the student reading has difficulty. Circulate to monitor the fluency of students' reading. Collect students' marked-up copies of the page, and review difficult words and passages with the class. Look for these problem spots:

- If students struggle to pronounce *Ghouls,* tell students that the *h* is silent and the *ou* has the *o* sound as in *glue.* Read the word aloud clearly and have students echo to confirm correct pronunciation. Ask students to name other examples of words with a hard *g* followed by a silent *h.* (*ghost, ghastly, ghetto*)
- If students have difficulty with the word *pæan,* tell them that the *æ* has the sound long *e* and the *a* has the sound *ah* as in *ball.* Read the word aloud and have students echo. Tell them that a *pæan* is a song or hymn of joy.

⓮ Humanities

Slam Dunk, 1996, by Bill Hall

Bill Hall is best known for his images of athletes and sports. Though his works mimic oil paintings, most are in fact, digital, and done entirely with computer graphics, such as *Slam Dunk.* Hall has created digital paintings for a variety of advertising agencies. Also, his work has been seen at various sporting events, such as the New York Marathon and the 1994 World Cup of Soccer.

Ask students: How does the player in the painting compare to the representation of the players in the poem?
Answer: In the painting, the swirling movement and fierce expression on the player's face echo the intensity and energy of the players in the poem.

⓮

Slam, Dunk, & Hook

Yusef Komunyakaa

Vocabulary Development

© **CCSS** Language 6

Relevant Topical Vocabulary

Tell students that this poem contains many terms that anyone unfamiliar with basketball may find puzzling. Write the following words on the board and discuss their meaning. Encourage students with basketball knowledge to elaborate and demonstrate.

fast break: a fast attempt to score before the defense can get in place

lay up: a shot made from near the basket—usually banked off the backboard

swish: the sound the ball makes when it drops smoothly through the netting of the hoop without touching the rim

dunk balls: balls slammed through the basket from above by a leaping player

dribble: to move the ball by bouncing it repeatedly

Ask students to call out additional basketball terms from the poem. As a class, figure out the meanings.

Fast breaks. Lay ups. With Mercury's[1]
Insignia[2] on our sneakers,
We outmaneuvered the footwork
Of bad angels. Nothing but a hot
Swish of strings like silk
Ten feet out. In the roundhouse[3]
Labyrinth[4] our bodies
Created, we could almost
Last forever, poised in midair
Like storybook sea monsters.
A high note hung there
A long second. Off
The rim. We'd corkscrew
Up & dunk balls that exploded
The skullcap of hope & good
Intention. Bug-eyed, lanky,
All hands & feet . . . sprung rhythm.
16 We were **metaphysical** when girls
Cheered on the sidelines.
Tangled up in a falling,
Muscles were a bright motor
Double-flashing to the metal hoop
Nailed to our oak.
When Sonny Boy's mama died
He played nonstop all day, so hard
Our backboard splintered.
Glistening with sweat, we **jibed**
& rolled the ball off our
Fingertips. Trouble
Was there slapping a blackjack
17 Against an open palm.
Dribble, drive to the inside, feint,
& glide like a sparrow hawk.
Lay ups. Fast breaks.
We had moves we didn't know
We had. Our bodies spun
On swivels of bone & faith,
Through a lyric slipknot
Of joy, & we knew we were
Beautiful & dangerous.

1. **Mercury's** Mercury was the Roman god of travel, usually depicted with wings on his feet.
2. **insignia** (in sig′ nē ə) *n.* emblems or badges; logos.
3. **roundhouse** (round′ hous′) *n.* area on the court beneath the basket.
4. **labyrinth** (lab′ ə rinth′) *n.* maze.

15 ◀ Critical Viewing
Which details in this painting relate to lines in "Slam, Dunk, & Hook"? **[Connect]**

Vocabulary
metaphysical (met′ ə fiz′ i kəl) *adj.* spiritual; beyond the physical

jibed (jībd) *v.* changed direction

Literary Analysis
Sound Devices What sound does the poet emphasize with the use of assonance in lines 30 and 31?

15 Critical Viewing

Answer: The player at the basket illustrates lines 5, 9–10, 13–16, and 27.

16 THE BIG ? Connecting to the Big Question

1. Have a volunteer read aloud the first bracketed passage. **Ask:** What sound does the speaker mention in this passage, and how does the speaker respond to the sound? **Answer:** The speaker talks about the sound of cheerleaders cheering, which transports him or her to a spiritual place.
2. **Ask:** How does the speaker's response compare with our own?

   Possible response: I find cheerleaders' cheers exciting, but they don't transport me to a metaphysical place.
3. **Ask:** Does the speaker's response change how you think about the sound?

   Possible response: No. There are other sounds I find spiritually moving, but not cheering.

17 Literary Analysis

Sound Devices

1. Have a volunteer read the second bracketed passage. Tell students to listen for sound devices.
2. **Ask** students the Literary Analysis question: What sound does the poet emphasize with the use of assonance in lines 30 and 31?

   Answer: The poet emphasizes the /a/ sound in *slapping* and *blackjack.*

▶ **Monitor Progress:** Read aloud lines 32 and 33 and ask students to identify the sound devices used.

Answer: Sound devices used: alliteration in *Dribble* and *drive;* assonance in *drive, inside, glide,* and *like.*

▶ **Reteach:** Review the definitions of the different sound devices. Then, slowly and clearly read a few lines from the poem. Guide students in identifying each type of sound device.

Differentiated Instruction for Universal Access

Culturally Responsive Instruction

Culture Focus Point out the energy in the poem and how it depicts the action of a basketball game. Ask students to determine how the poet describes the players. Elicit that he uses the pronouns *our* and *we* throughout the poem. Encourage students to discuss the emotions people feel when they're playing a team sport like basketball.

Since basketball is now part of sports culture throughout the world, ask students why basketball, unlike some other American sports, is so popular throughout the world. Challenge students to consider what the world would be like without team sports and to discuss the pros and cons of a passionate sports culture. Use questions such as these: What are the benefits of team sports? Throughout the world, what team sports bring people together? Why are sports a good way for countries and people to come together?

18 Humanities

Illustration by Jane Breskin Zalben

Zalben illustrates and writes books for children. Her style is characterized by warm colors and friendly, gentle characters. Here, even her illustration of the Jabberwock depicts a monster that is not too threatening. Use these questions for discussion:

1. What makes the Jabberwock look threatening?

   Answer: The Jabberwock is very large compared to the knight who opposes him. Plus, the Jabberwock breathes fire.

2. If you were illustrating "Jabberwocky" for a new edition today, how would you make the pictures different from Zalben's?

   Possible response: Students' answers will vary, but some may suggest a style of art that flows from modern-day science fiction and fantasy and uses computer graphics.

Jabberwocky

Lewis Carroll

18

Vocabulary Development

Vocabulary Knowledge Rating

When students have completed reading and discussing Poetry Collection 4, have them take out their **Vocabulary Knowledge Rating Chart** for these poems. Read the words aloud once more and have students rate their knowledge of the words again in the After Reading column. Clarify any words that are still problematic. Have students write their own definition and example or sentence in the appropriate column. Then have students complete the Vocabulary Practice activities at the end of the collection. Encourage students to use the words in further discussion and written work about these poems. Remind them that they will be accountable for these words on the **Selection Test, *Unit 4 Resources,*** pp. 95–97 or 98–100.

'Twas brillig, and the slithy toves
Did gyre and gimble in the wabe;
All mimsy were the borogoves,
And the mome raths outgrabe.

"Beware the Jabberwock, my son!
The jaws that bite, the claws that catch!
Beware the Jubjub bird, and shun
The frumious Bandersnatch!"

He took his vorpal sword in hand:
Long time the manxome foe he sought—
So rested he by the Tumtum tree,
And stood awhile in thought.

And as in uffish thought he stood,
The Jabberwock, with eyes of flame,
Came whiffling through the tulgey wood,
20 And burbled as it came!

19 ◀▼ **Critical Viewing**
Which aspects of these illustrations convey the fantastical quality of "Jabberwocky"? **[Analyze]**

Literary Analysis
Sound Devices What sound or noise does the onomatopoeia *burbled* reflect?

21 **LITERATURE IN CONTEXT**

Language Connection

Carroll's Invented Language In the first chapter of *Through the Looking-Glass,* Alice encounters a creature called a Jabberwock. She cannot understand it, so Humpty Dumpty explains some of the words it uses, including these:

brillig: four o'clock in the afternoon, the time when you begin broiling things for dinner

toves: creatures that are something like badgers, something like lizards, and something like corkscrews

gyre: go round and round like a gyroscope

gimble: make holes like a gimlet (a hand tool that bores holes)

wabe: grass plot around a sundial

mome: having lost the way home

raths: something like green pigs

Connect to the Literature

What challenges do you think Carroll faced in writing a poem with invented language?

19 Critical Viewing

Answer: The fantastical aspects of "Jabberwocky" are conveyed with the burbling dragon, the egg blowing bubbles, and the calm, confident, strangely costumed child.

20 Literary Analysis

Sound Devices

1. Point out that Carroll's use of made-up language helped him play with sound devices. For example, in line 23, Carroll devised the words *callooh* and *callay* to achieve alliteration. Have students analyze other made-up words and decide how Carroll developed them as sound devices.
2. **Ask** students the Literary Analysis question: What sound or noise does the onomatopoeia *burbled* reflect?

   Answer: It reflects the sound of water bubbling and gurgling.

21 Literature in Context

Language Connection Point out that many of Carroll's words are portmanteaus or blends. These are words made up of two different words. For example, Carroll forms *slithy* by combining *slimy* and *lithe. Brillig* might combine the word *brilliant* with *broiling.* The word *galumphing* was compiled from the words *galloping* and *triumphant.*

Connect to the Literature Have students read the Literature in Context feature, and present the additional background information above. Then, explain to students that even though many of the words are nonsense words, they make sense because of the sound, their apparent part of speech, and their use in the context of the poem. **Ask** the Connect to the Literature question: What challenges do you think Carroll faced in writing a poem with invented language?

Possible response: Carroll's challenge was to make nonsense sound sensible. He accomplished this by placing his inventive words within standard grammatical patterns.

Concept Connector

Activating Prior Knowledge
Have students review and reconsider their lists about bells. Ask them to revise or add to their lists based on what they learned from the poems.

Writing About the Big Question
Have students compare their responses to the sentence starter they completed before reading the collection with their ideas afterwards. Ask them to explain whether their thoughts have changed.

Reading Skill Graphic Organizer
Have students review the graphic organizers they completed to identify information in multiple readings. Show them **Reading Skill Graphic Organizer A** (*Graphic Organizer Transparencies,* p. 118) as an example. Then, have students share the graphic organizers they did and the information they identified.

ASSESS

Answers

Critical Thinking

Before students respond, you may wish to have them write a brief objective summary of each selection. As they answer the questions below, remind them to support their answers with evidence from the text.

1. (a) The speaker describes the swish of the basketball net strings. (b) The sound is caused by the basketball dropping through the net.
2. (a) He slays the Jabberwock. (b) Students may agree that the poem makes fun of traditional heroic tales if not heroism itself.
3. Students may agree with Eliot, noting that the sounds and rhythms of "The Bells" are highly interesting in themselves.
4. **Possible response:** I am more aware of the sounds of bells and athletic movements. I am also more likely to connect everyday sounds to specific moods and atmospheres.

One, two! One, two! And through and through
  The vorpal blade went snicker-snack!
He left it dead, and with its head
  He went galumphing back.

"And hast thou slain the Jabberwock?
  Come to my arms, my beamish boy!
O frabjous day! Callooh! Callay!"
  He chortled in his joy.

'Twas brillig, and the slithy toves
  Did gyre and gimble in the wabe;
All mimsy were the borogoves,
  And the mome raths outgrabe.

Critical Thinking

Cite textual evidence to support your responses.

1. **Craft and Structure (a)** In lines 4–5 of "Slam, Dunk, & Hook," what sound does the speaker describe? **(b) Infer:** What action causes this sound?
2. **Key Ideas and Details (a)** In "Jabberwocky," what does the hero do after being warned about the Jabberwock? **(b) Evaluate:** Do you think the poem pokes fun at heroism? Explain your response.
3. **Integration of Knowledge and Ideas Take a Position:** The poet T. S. Eliot once said that poetry can be enjoyed before it is understood. Could "The Bells" be used as evidence to support this idea? Explain your answer.
4. **Integration of Knowledge and Ideas** Do any of the poems in this collection make you think differently about sounds you hear every day? Explain. ***[Connect to the Big Question: How does communication change us?]***

Assessment Resources

Unit 4 Resources

L1 L2 EL **Selection Test A**, pp. 95–97. Administer Test A to less advanced readers.

L3 L4 EL **Selection Test B**, pp. 98–100. Administer Test B to on-level and more advanced students.

L3 L4 **Open-Book Test**, pp. 92–94. As an alternative, give the Open-Book Test.

All **Customizable Test Bank**

All **Self-tests**
Students may prepare for the **Selection Test** by taking the **Self-test** online.

PHLit Online!

All assessment resources are available at **www.PHLitOnline.com**.

After You Read
Poetry Collection 4

The Bells • Slam, Dunk, & Hook • Jabberwocky

Literary Analysis: Sound Devices

1. Craft and Structure **(a)** For each poem in Poetry Collection 4, use a chart like the one shown to give one example of each **sound device** listed. **(b)** How does each example add to the musical feeling of each poem?

	Example	Effect
Alliteration		
Consonance		
Assonance		

2. Craft and Structure **(a)** Identify an example of **onomatopoeia** in "The Bells." **(b)** What sound does the word imitate? **(c)** How well does the word imitate the sound? Explain your answer.
3. Craft and Structure **(a)** Which of these poems do you think makes the most effective use of sound devices? **(b)** Discuss your idea with a small group and decide on a single response.

Reading Skill: Read Fluently

4. How did your understanding of the poems deepen with each reading? Give examples.
5. **(a)** How does **reading fluently** help you appreciate a poem's sound devices? **(b)** Which senses, other than your sense of hearing, were most engaged by each poem? Explain.

Vocabulary

Acquisition and Use Identify the word in each group that does not belong with the others. Explain your response.

1. metaphysical, concrete, bodily
2. jibed, turn, straight
3. voluminously, tiny, huge
4. palpitating, pulse, hum
5. endeavor, avoid, attempt
6. monotone, voice, flower

Word Study Use the context of the sentences and what you know about the **Greek prefix *mono-*** to explain your answer to each question.

1. If a painting is *monochromatic,* does it have one color or many?
2. If Joe is *monolingual,* how many languages does he speak?

Word Study

The **Greek prefix *mono-*** means "one."

Apply It Explain how the prefix *mono-* contributes to the meanings of these words. Consult a dictionary if necessary.

monologue
monarch
monopoly

ASSESS/EXTEND

Answers

Literary Analysis

1. (a) **Possible responses:** "The Bells" — **alliteration:** "What a tale of terror now their turbulency tells"; **consonance:** "horror they outpour"; **assonance:** "wrangling" and "danger"; **"Slam, Dunk & Hook" — alliteration:** "Swish of strings like silk"; **consonance:** "but a hot"; **assonance:** "Up & dunk". **"Jabberwocky" — alliteration:** "claws that catch"; **consonance:** "time the manxome"; **assonance:** "left it dead." (b) These devices make the words of each poem sound like they fit together. Poems, like music, have slow and fast, gentle or harsh, or loud and soft passages. Sound devices help to create these musical rhythms.

   For other sample answers, see ***Graphic Organizer Transparencies,* Literary Analysis Graphic Organizer A**, p. 121, and the **Additional Answers** section.
2. (a) One example is "jingling." (b) It imitates the sound of sleigh bells ringing. (c) The word captures the light, carefree ring of the sleigh bell.
3. (a) Students may choose "The Bells" because of its use of alliteration and onomatopoeia. (b) Students should agree on their choices and list supporting examples.

Reading Skill

4. Students may say that each reading of the poems revealed a new layer of meaning. For example, students may say that they only noticed in a second reading that the bells described in the final section of "The Bells" are most likely ringing for a funeral.
5. (a) Fluent reading helps readers hear and appreciate the poem's musical qualities. (b) Students should recognize that other than sound, sight was the most commonly used sense in all of the poems.

Vocabulary
Acquisition and Use

1. bodily; *metaphysical* and *concrete* are antonyms
2. straight; *jibed* and *turn* are synonyms
3. tiny; *voluminously* and *huge* are synonyms
4. hum; *palpitating* and *pulse* are synonyms
5. avoid; *endeavor* and *attempt* are synonyms
6. flower; a *monotone* is a way of speaking with your *voice.*

Word Study
Sample answers:

1. The prefix *mono-* means "one" and monochromatic means "one color." Thus, a *monochromatic* painting has one color.
2. The prefix *mono-* means "one" and *monolingual* means "using one language." If Joe is *monolingual*, he speaks only one language.

Word Study: Apply It
Sample answers:

A *monologue* is a speech given by one person. A *monarch* is rule by one leader. A *monopoly* is control by one company.

Conventions

1. Introduce the skill, using the instruction on the student page.
2. Discuss the definitions and examples.

Think Aloud: Model the Skill

Model the skill of using and identifying prepositional phrases. Post these sentences:

The sun in summer is hot and blazing.

Sundials work well on sunny days.

Say to students:

Prepositional phrases teach me about nouns and verbs. The first prepositional phrase is *in summer.* It tells me more about the noun, *sun*—the sun is hot and blazing "in the summer." Because it tells about a noun, the phrase functions as an adjective. The second prepositional phrase is *on sunny days.* It tells me about the verb *work*—sundials *work* well "on sunny days." Because the phrase tells me about a verb and an adverb, it functions as an adverb.

PH WRITING COACH Grade 9

Students will find instruction on and practice with prepositional phrases in Chapter 15, Section 1.

Practice A

1. of summer; adjective
2. with crooked hands; adverb
3. from his mountain walls; adverb
4. on a diamond; adverb
5. about the eagle; adjective

Reading Application

"with crooked hands"—adverb

"like a thunderbolt"—adjective

Practice B

Sample answers

1. The sound of joyful singing came from the auditorium.
2. Trees grew in the woods.
3. We sailed the boat under the bridge.
4. The ball sailed through the hoop.

Writing Application

Students' sentences should contain prepositional phrases and follow the example patterns.

PERFORMANCE TASKS

Integrated Language Skills

Poetry Collections 3 and 4

Poetry Collection 3

Poetry Collection 4

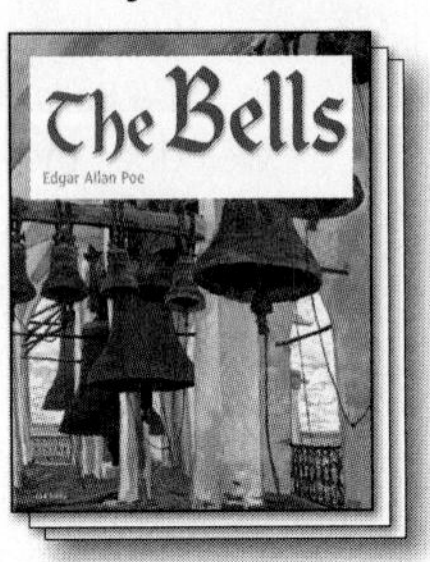

Conventions: Prepositional Phrases

A **prepositional phrase** is a group of words beginning with a preposition and ending with a noun or pronoun, called the *object* of the preposition.

A prepositional phrase may function as either an adjective or an adverb, depending on the word it modifies. An adjective phrase modifies a noun or a pronoun by telling *what kind* or *which one.* An adverb phrase modifies a verb, an adjective, or an adverb by pointing out *where, when, in what way,* or *to what extent.*

Adjective phrase: The players on their team are more experienced. (modifies the noun *players*)

Adjective phrase: The flowers with yellow petals are my favorites. (modifies the noun *flowers*)

Adverb phrase: They played with more skill. (modifies the verb *played*)

Adverb phrase: My parents walked through the door at that moment. (both phrases modify the verb *walked*)

Practice A Identify the prepositional phrase in each sentence, and tell whether it functions as an adjective or an adverb.

1. Myers's poem describes the hot days of summer.
2. He clasps the crag with crooked hands.
3. He watches from his mountain walls.
4. Baseball is played on a diamond.
5. Tennyson's poem about the eagle is very descriptive.

Reading Application In "The Eagle," find one prepositional phrase that functions as an adjective and one that functions as an adverb.

Practice B Following the instructions in parentheses, use each prepositional phrase in a sentence of your own.

1. of joyful singing (adjective phrase)
2. in the woods (adverb phrase)
3. under the bridge (adjective phrase)
4. through the hoop (adverb phrase)

Writing Application Following these models, write four sentences. Identify which phrases are used as adjectives and which are used as adverbs.

Running with a knife is not safe.

The child's book was illustrated with animals of many kinds.

PH WRITING COACH Further instruction and practice are available in *Prentice Hall Writing Coach.*

Extend the Lesson

Sentence Modeling

Choose the sentence given from the Poetry Collection students have read:

"Close to the sun in lonely lands,/ Ring'd with the azure world, he stands." ("The Eagle," Poetry Collection 3)

"So rested he by the Tumtum tree,/ And stood awhile in thought." ("Jabberwocky," Poetry Collection 4)

Ask students what they notice about the sentence. Elicit from them that the sentence contains prepositional phrases. Have students identify each prepositional phrase and label it as an adjective or adverb phrase. Then, ask what else they notice. ("The Eagle": The prepositional phrases appear in descriptions before the verb they modify, surprising the reader. "Jabberwocky": These adverb phrases help the reader visualize the poem's action.)

Have students imitate the sentence in a sentence of their own, matching each grammatical and stylistic feature discussed. Collect the sentences, and share them with the class.

Writing

Argument Write an **editorial**—a piece of writing that presents one side of an issue—related to one of the poems you read. For example, if you read Tennyson's "The Eagle," you could use it as inspiration to write an editorial about the need to preserve the North American bald eagle. If you read "Slam, Dunk, & Hook," you might use that poem as inspiration to write about the need for more funding for neighborhood sports.

- State the issue clearly and provide support for your opinion.
- Anticipate questions from those who might disagree with you.

Ask several people to respond to your editorial, including someone who disagrees with you, and refute opposing arguments.

Grammar Application Make sure to use prepositional phrases correctly in your editorial.

Writing Workshop: *Work in Progress*

Prewriting for a Descriptive Essay Using your Sight List and your Sensory Words List, list three emotions that you associate with the place you chose. Briefly, jot down clue words about the reasons for those emotions. For example, you might list some words related to meaningful events that happened there. Save this Reasons List in your writing portfolio.

Common Core State Standards

W.9-10.1; SL.9-10.1, SL.9-10.5; L.9-10.1, L.9-10.5
[For the full wording of the standards, see page 642.]

Use this prewriting activity to prepare for the **Writing Workshop** on page 686.

Speaking and Listening

Presentation of Ideas In a group, create an **illustrated presentation** of one of the poems you read. Find photographs or original artwork and, with the group, debate the merits of each choice. Negotiate to reach an agreement about which images best capture the mood of the poem. Then, choose one member of the group to present a dramatic reading of the poem. Have the speaker rehearse in front of the group, and have the group use these questions to assess the speaker's performance:

- Does the speaker maintain eye contact with the audience?
- Does the speaker use a voice register, body movements, and gestures that are appropriate for the occasion and the interests of the audience?
- Does the speaker's delivery convey the mood and tone of the poem in a way that engages the audience? Does the speaker's delivery convey the mood depicted in the images you selected?

Once you have organized your images and rehearsed your dramatic reading, present the images and the reading together to your class. Use other visual aids or electronic media to enhance your presentation.

www.PHLitOnline.com

- Interactive graphic organizers
- Grammar tutorial
- Interactive journals

EXTEND/ASSESS

Writing

1. Review the assignment, using the instruction on the student page.
2. To give students guidance for writing an editorial, give them **Support for Writing,** p. 90 in ***Unit 4 Resources.***
3. To evaluate students' editorials, use the Persuasive Essay rubrics, pp. 230–231 in ***Professional Development Guidebook.***

Grammar Application

Have students check their drafts to make sure they are using prepositional phrases correctly.

Six Traits Focus

✓	Ideas		Word Choice
✓	Organization		Sentence Fluency
	Voice		Conventions

PH WRITING COACH Grade 9

Students will find with editorials in Chapter 9.

Writing Workshop
Work in Progress

Have students save their completed Reasons lists in their portfolios. They will use their lists later as they complete the Writing Workshop (see pp. 686–691).

Speaking and Listening

1. Review the assignment, using the instruction on the student page.
2. To support students' work on the assignment, have them complete the **Support for Extend Your Learning** page (***Unit 4 Resources,*** p. 91).

Teaching Resources

Unit 4 Resources

L3 L4 EL **Integrated Language Skills: Grammar,** p. 89

L3 L4 EL **Support for Writing,** p. 90

L3 L4 **Support for Extend Your Learning,** p. 91

L4 **Enrichment,** pp. 70, 88

All **Enriched Online Student Edition**
Available under After You Read for this selection:

All **Interactive Grammar Tutorial**

L3 L4 **Internet Research Activity**

Professional Development Guidebook
Rubrics for Self-Assessment: Persuasive Essay, pp. 230–231

PHLit Online! All print and digital resources are available online at **www.PHLitOnline.com.** Online resources accessible by students are noted on the student page.

MONITORING PROGRESS

Using the Test Practice

In this two-page Test Practice, students apply the reading skill for the first half of Unit 4 to a passage of fiction and a passage of nonfiction.

Review the skill, reading fluently, then administer the test. For more guidance, consult the ***Classroom Strategies and Teaching Routines*** card, **Administering Timed Tests.**

ASSESS

Answers

Answers With Explanations

1. **B**—Each stanza is a complete sentence. *Incorrect answers:* A—The periods at the end of the fourth line of each stanza identify two sentences, not one. C—The periods identify two sentences, not three. D—The periods identify two sentences, not four.
2. **C**—When reading poetry, it is customary to pause after each punctuation mark. *Incorrect answers:* A—There is no punctuation to suggest a pause after "snow." B—There are no punctuation marks calling for pauses at the ends of lines 2 and 3. D—The comma at the end of line 1 calls for a pause.
3. **A**—The sky indicates a coming storm, and at least one flake is already falling. *Incorrect answers:* B—There is no mention of good weather in this stanza. C—The weather is not described as destructive. D—The adjective "mean" suggests that the speaker does not view the scene as beautiful.
4. **D**—These lines suggest that the natural world is not always beautiful. *Incorrect answers:* A—These lines are descriptive, but not full of deeper meaning. B—These lines continue the description in the first two lines. C—These lines describe the sound of the wind, which is a supporting detail for the deeper meaning of the poem.

Test Practice: Reading

Read Fluently

Poetry Selection

Directions: *Read the selection. Then, answer the questions.*

The Sky Is Low, the Clouds Are Mean, *by Emily Dickinson*

The sky is low, the clouds are mean,
A travelling flake of snow
Across a barn or through a rut
Debates if it will go.

A narrow wind complains all day
How some one treated him;
Nature, like us, is sometimes caught
Without her diadem.[1]

1. **diadem** (dī ə dem') *n.* crown.

1. How many sentences are in this poem?
A. one
B. two
C. three
D. four

2. At what points should a reader pause or stop in the first stanza?
A. after "mean" and after "snow"
B. at the end of each line
C. after "mean" and after "go"
D. only at the end of the stanza

3. Which sentence *best* describes the basic meaning of the first stanza?
A. The gloomy weather outside seems to indicate snow is coming.
B. Without bad weather, people would not learn to appreciate good weather.
C. Winter storms are often destructive forces in people's lives.
D. Nature is beautiful in any season.

4. Which lines most clearly point readers to one deeper meaning of this poem?
A. lines 1 and 2
B. lines 3 and 4
C. lines 5 and 6
D. lines 7 and 8

Writing for Assessment

Into how many units of meaning would you divide this poem? Write a paragraph in which you explain where you would make these divisions and why.

Writing for Assessment

Students might suggest that the units of meaning follow the punctuation, which would make line 1, lines 2–4, lines 5–6, and lines 7–8 the four units of the poem.

Strategies for Test Taking

Remind students to read the directions in each question carefully, to be sure they understand what is required in the answer. For example, in question 1, because the reading selection is a poem, the question might be read as "How many *lines* are in this poem?" A careful reading tells the reader that the question is actually about the number of *sentences* in the poem.

Nonfiction Selection

Directions: *Read the selection. Then, answer the questions.*

(1) In 1993, a relentless rain fell on the Midwest all spring and almost all summer. (2) There was no place for the water to go except into the rivers, which could not contain the water. (3) The Mississippi, Missouri, and 150 other rivers tore loose from their banks and washed over everything in their paths. (4) Thousands of people evacuated their homes. (5) The rivers destroyed 10,000 homes and put 75 towns under water. (6) Railroads shut down. (7) Airports and Interstate highways closed. (8) In some places, the flood lasted six months. (9) The cleanup, rebuilding, and pervasive moldy odor lasted even longer. (10) It was the worst flood in U.S. history up to that time.

1. To read both poetry and prose fluently, readers might do all of the following *except*—
A. group words to enhance understanding.
B. use punctuation to determine where to stop or pause.
C. reread to appreciate the writer's craft.
D. stop at the end of each line.

2. The reader should expect to read this passage—
A. slower than directions for reprogramming a computer.
B. at the same rate as a magazine article.
C. faster than a grocery list.
D. at the same rate as a medical textook.

3. At which points should a reader pause or stop in sentence 9?
A. Pause after "cleanup" and "rebuilding" and stop after "longer."
B. Stop only after "longer."
C. Pause after "cleanup," "rebuilding," and "pervasive moldy odor."
D. Stop after "rebuilding" and "longer."

4. Which sentence best describes the basic meaning of this passage?
A. People were probably frightened as they evacuated from their homes.
B. Tragedies often either tear people apart or bring them closer together.
C. Many highways closed when over 150 rivers flooding in 1993.
D. Terrible flooding caused significant damage in the Midwest in 1993.

Writing for Assessment

Connecting Across Texts

Write a two-paragraph "How-to" article for middle school students explaining how to read poetry and prose fluently. Use examples from both of these pieces to illustrate your points.

www.PHLitOnline.com
- Online practice
- Instant feedback

Differentiated Instruction for Universal Access

Strategy for Less Proficient Readers

Review the issue of pacing by walking students through item 2. Ask a volunteer to read the question and the answer options aloud. Point out that the pace of reading depends on the complexity and importance of the text. Next, guide students in eliminating incorrect answer choices.

- A—Reprogramming a computer incorrectly because of not reading the directions slowly enough could cause serious problems. Thus, you need to read them more slowly than this article. (Eliminate.)
- B—People read magazine articles to be informed, as with this article, or to be entertained. (Possible answer.)
- C—A grocery list simply itemizes things; you can read it more quickly than this article, which is full of facts and cause-and-effect relationships. (Eliminate.)
- D—Reading a medical textbook demands much more care than does reading this article. (Eliminate.)

Guide students in seeing that **B** is the best choice.

ASSESS

Answers

Answers With Explanations

1. **D**—In reading prose fluently, readers do not stop at the end of each line. *Incorrect answers:* A—Readers should group words. B—Readers should use punctuation. C—Rereading can help readers appreciate the writer's craft but not improve fluency.
2. **B**—Both this article and a magazine article could be read at about the same rate. *Incorrect answers:* A—reprogramming a computer would be read more slowly that this article. C—A grocery list would be read much faster than this article. D—A medical textbook would require more careful attention to detail than this article.
3. **A**—The punctuation indicates pauses after "cleanup" and "rebuilding," and a stop after "longer." *Incorrect answers:* B—The punctuation requires pauses only after "cleanup" and "rebuilding." C—There is no pause after "pervasive moldy odor." D—There should be a pause, not a stop, after "rebuilding" and a pause after "cleanup."
4. **D**—This sentence best summarizes the selection. *Incorrect answers:* A—This inference can be drawn from the passage but is not the basic meaning. B—The passage does not address these issues. C—This choice states a fact about the passage but not its basic meaning.

Writing for Assessment

Students may suggest reading poetry by following the punctuation and also the meaning. If an idea continues from one line to another without punctuation, the reader should not pause at the end of the line. Students may suggest reading prose by following the punctuation, pausing after commas and stopping briefly at the end of a sentence.

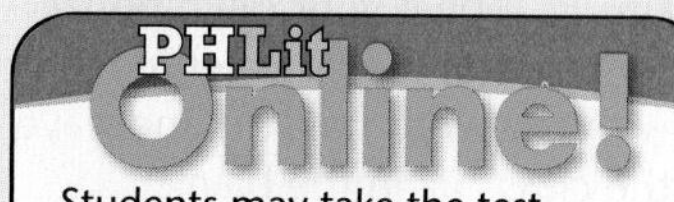

Students may take the test in interactive format with instant feedback online at **www.PHLitOnline.com.**

PRETEACH

Common Core State Standards

- **Reading Informational Text 4, 5**
- **Writing 2**
- **Language 3, 6**

Reading Skill

1. Introduce the skill, using the instruction on the student page.
2. Review the chart.
3. Tell students they will follow technical directions as they read.

Think Aloud: Model the Skill

Model the skill of following technical directions. Say to students:

When I read directions, I start at the beginning and read through the entire process before taking any action. I find that getting an overview of the process makes it easier for me to understand the individual steps and how they connect.

Multidraft Reading

Have students follow a multidraft reading protocol after they preview the selection.

- **First reading**—Have students read to identify key ideas and details.
- **Second reading**—Have students read to identify the structure of the text.
- **Third reading**—Have students read to integrate knowledge and ideas by connecting the text to the world, their own experiences, and other texts.

Content-Area Vocabulary

1. Have students say each word.
2. Next, use each word in a sentence that defines it.
3. Finally, repeat your definitional sentence or a similar sentence with the word missing and have the class "fill in the blank" chorally.

Reading for Information

Analyzing Functional and Expository Texts

Technical Directions **News Article**

Common Core State Standards

Reading Informational Text
4. Determine the meaning of words and phrases as they are used in text, including figurative, connotative, and technical meanings.
5. Analyze in detail how an author's ideas or claims are developed and refined by particular sentences, paragraphs, or larger portions of a text.

Writing
2. Write informative/explanatory texts to examine and convey complex ideas, concepts, and information clearly and accurately through the effective selection, organization, and analysis of content.

Language
3. Apply knowledge of language to understand how language functions in different contexts, to make effective choices for meaning or style, and to comprehend more fully when reading or listening.
6. Acquire and use accurately grade-appropriate general academic and domain-specific words and phrases, sufficient for reading, writing, speaking, and listening at the college and career readiness level.

Reading Skill: Follow Technical Directions

In order to properly use a mechanical or digital device, you must understand and **follow technical directions.** Technical directions provide step-by-step instructions on how to use a device correctly. To understand the directions, **analyze the structure, format,** and features of the text. Elements such as bold font, subheadings, and numbered lists can indicate important information and highlight specific sections. Use this checklist to be sure you follow technical directions correctly.

Checklist for Following Technical Directions

- Analyze the text for clues such as bold or italicized font, numbered lists, headings, and subheadings that highlight specific sections or important information.
- Read all directions carefully and completely, reviewing any sections that are complicated or unclear.
- Follow each step in the exact order given.
- Do not skip any steps.

Content-Area Vocabulary

These words appear in the selections that follow. You may also encounter them in other content-area texts.

- **blogging** (bläg′ iŋ) *n.* publishing entries on a Web site that consists of an online journal with thoughts, opinions, and links to other sites
- **download** (doun′ lōd′) *v.* transfer data from one computer system to another computer or device
- **democratizing** (di mäk′ rə tīz′ iŋ) *v.* changing a market or governing structure so that power is distributed among larger numbers of people

How does communication change us?

Students should be able to relate their own experiences communicating with newer electronic forms, such as instant messaging, text messaging, and cell phones.

Differentiated Instruction for Universal Access

Reading Support
Give students reading support with the appropriate version of the ***Reader's Notebooks:***

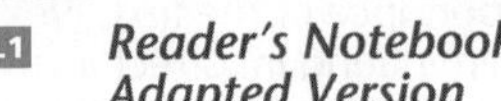

L2 L3 ***Reader's Notebook***

L1 ***Reader's Notebook: Adapted Version***

EL ***Reader's Notebook: English Learner's Version***

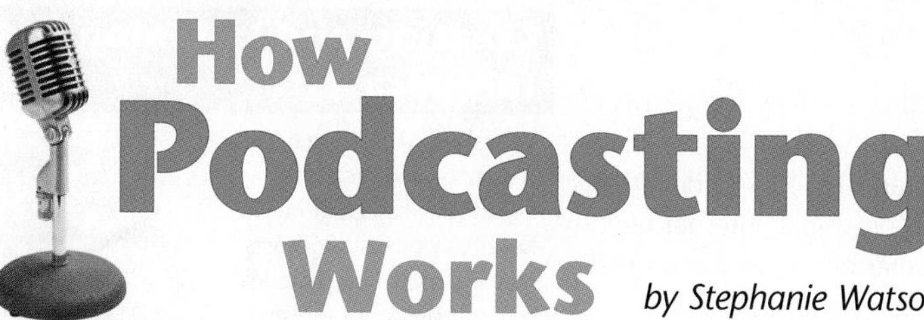

How Podcasting Works

by Stephanie Watson

Technical Directions

Features:

- some technical language
- gives background about topic
- step-by-step instructions
- text written for a general audience

This heading clearly states that this section will provide an introduction to the subject of podcasting.

Introduction to How Podcasting Works

Have you ever dreamed of having your own radio show? Are you a recording artist hoping to have your songs heard by the masses? Decades ago, you would have had to have a lot of connections—or a fortune—to get heard.

This guide gives background information about podcasting and its purposes.

But now, thanks to the Internet and its instantaneous connection to millions of people, your dreams can become reality. Just as **blogging** has enabled almost anyone with a computer to become a bona fide reporter, a new technology called podcasting is allowing virtually anyone with a computer to become a radio disc jockey, talk show host or recording artist.

If you post it, they will come. Although podcasting is still primarily used by the techie set, it's beginning to catch on with the general public. Log onto one of several podcast sites on the Web, and you can **download** content ranging from music to philosophy. . . . Podcasting combines the freedom of blogging with the technology of MP3 to create an almost endless supply of content. Some say this new technology is **democratizing** the once corporate-run world of radio.

In this article, you'll learn how podcasting works, find out what tools you need to record and receive podcasts and hear what industry analysts have to say about the future of this burgeoning technology.

Boldface text highlights key technical words.

Podcasting is a free service that allows Internet users to pull audio files (typically MP3s) from a podcasting Web site to listen to on their computer or personal digital audio player. The name comes from a combination of the words **iPod** and **broadcasting**. Even though the name is derived from the iPod, you don't need an iPod to listen to a podcast. You can use virtually any MP3 player or your computer.

Unlike with Internet radio, users don't have to "tune in" to a particular broadcast; instead, they **subscribe** to a podcast, and the audio files are automatically downloaded to their computer via **RSS feed** as often as they request. The technology is similar to that used by TiVo, a personal video recorder that lets users set which programs they'd like to record and then automatically records those programs for later viewing.

Fluency

This selection might be a good opportunity for students to develop their fluency, as the vocabulary is relatively simple and the more technical terms, such as *podcast, blogging, iPod,* and *hyperlink* may well be familiar to them. Give students an opportunity to take turns reading a paragraph aloud to practice their reading fluency. Then, ask another student to summarize the paragraph to test comprehension.

TEACH

About Technical Directions

1. Review with students the features listed in the Technical Directions box on page 671. **Ask** them to define *technical* in their own terms.

   Possible response: *Technical* means related to or using technology.
2. Have students describe their own experiences following technical directions to use a machine or piece of equipment for the first time. Invite volunteers to describe what features made the directions easy or difficult to follow.
3. Discuss with students how a set of directions should be basic enough for a beginner to use.

Follow Technical Directions

1. Explain that the text is more than a list of directions. It provides background information about how podcasting began and how it has changed radio.
2. Direct students' attention to the fourth paragraph. **Ask:** What will the reader learn in this article?

   Possible answer: The reader will learn how podcasting works, what tools are needed to use the technology, and what industry analysts have to say about its future.
3. **Ask:** How does this kind of information help the reader?

   Possible answer: The reader can use this information to determine if he or she will benefit from reading the piece.
4. **Ask:** What is the difference between Internet radio and podcasts?

   Possible answer: Users have to visit a web site to hear Internet radio, which is not the case with podcasts. They can subscribe and the programs are downloaded to a computer.
5. **Ask:** Is the background information useful in understanding how podcasting works? Explain.

   Possible answer: The background information is useful because it explains the meaning of terms, the way the technology was invented, and how it differs from other technologies.

Follow Technical Directions

1. Direct students to the first paragraph in the left column. **Ask:** Who are the people who invented podcasting, and what job experience did they probably use to create it?

   Possible answer: The inventors were Adam Curry and Dave Winer. They probably used the skills from broadcasting on MTV and programming to make the idea a reality.

2. Draw students' attention to the margin notes about the headings and lists. **Ask:** How do these features make the directions easy to read?

   Possible answer: The headings identify the subject of each set of instructions. The numbered lists help the reader follow the step-by-step process in the correct order.

3. Have students read the instructions for understanding. **Ask:** What information should the author add to make the instructions more clear?

   Possible answer: The author could add details about how to complete each step. For example, the author could give the address of a podcasting site and explain how to download the free software.

Podcasting History

Podcasting was developed in 2004 by former MTV video jockey Adam Curry and software developer Dave Winer. Curry wrote a program, called iPodder, that enabled him to automatically download Internet radio broadcasts to his iPod. Several developers improved upon his idea, and podcasting was officially born. . . .

Right now, podcasting is free from government regulation. Podcasters don't need to buy a license to broadcast their programming, as radio stations do, and they don't need to conform to the the Federal Communication Commission's (FCC) broadcast decency regulations. . . .

Although several corporations and big broadcast companies have ventured into the medium, many podcasters are amateurs broadcasting from home studios. Because podcasters don't rely on ratings as radio broadcasters do, the subject matter of podcasts can range from the refined to the silly to the excruciatingly mundane. . . .

Several companies are trying to turn podcasting into a profitable business. Podcasting aggregators. . . are including advertising on their sites. The Podcast Network, based in Australia, runs commercials and sponsorships during its audio broadcasts. Television networks have gotten into the action. National Public Radio, the Canadian Broadcasting Corporation and the BBC have begun podcasting some of their shows. Corporations. . . have created their own podcasts to attract consumers.

Some experts say podcasting still has a long way to go before it catches on with the masses. But others believe it will eventually become as popular as text blogging, which grew from a few thousand blogs in the late '90s to more than 7 million today. Some podcasts are already providing thousands of downloads a day.

Creating and Listening to Podcasts

Virtually anyone with a computer and recording capabilities can create his or her own podcast. Podcasts may include music, comedy, sports, philosophy—even people's rants and raves. Here's how the process works.

To record a podcast:

These sub-headings indicate what type of directions will follow.

1. Plug a USB headset with a microphone into your computer.
2. Install an MP3 recorder for Windows, Mac or Linux.
3. Create an audio file by making a recording (you can talk, sing or record music) and saving it as an MP3 file.
4. Finally, upload the MP3 audio file to one of the podcasting sites.

To listen to a podcast:

Numbered lists provide step-by-step instructions.

1. Go to a podcasting site and download the free software.
2. Click on the hyperlink for each podcast you want. You can listen right away on your computer (both Windows and Mac support podcasting) or download the podcast to your MP3 player.
3. You can also subscribe to one or more RSS feeds. Your podcasting software will check the RSS feeds regularly and automatically pull content that matches your playlist. When you dock your MP3 player to your computer, it automatically updates with the latest content.

Vocabulary Development

© CCSS Language 6

Vocabulary from Computer Science

Point out that technical directions often use specific vocabulary. Call on students to define the terms listed below by using context clues. Then, have them check their definitions by consulting a computer dictionary.

techie: a person who has technical knowledge, usually involving computers
download: to retrieve files posted on one computer into another computer or other storage device
MP3: a computer file format used for audio broadcasting
RSS feed: a format for delivering frequently changing files
USB: universal serial bus, a kind of interface that allows users to connect devices to a computer

News Article

Features:

- current or breaking news
- quotations from experts and other qualified sources
- text written for a general audience

This title explains the topic of the article—that podcasts are being used as sophisticated learning tools.

Georgia School Displays iPod Ingenuity

From eSchool News staff and wire service reports
March 27, 2006

The article is structured by order of importance. The broad topic is stated in the first paragraphs and is followed by details and support.

Thanks in part to an enterprising group of faculty who call themselves the iDreamers, Georgia College & State University (GSCU) is quickly becoming a leader in using Apple Computer's near-ubiquitous iPod to enhance education—and school officials say their efforts are helping to retain more students.

More than a third of the rural Georgia school's 300 staff members reportedly use the digital music and video players as an education or research tool. Rather than simply making class lectures available for downloading to iPods—a practice now routine at many colleges and even a few high schools—the school's educators are pushing to find more strategic uses of the device.

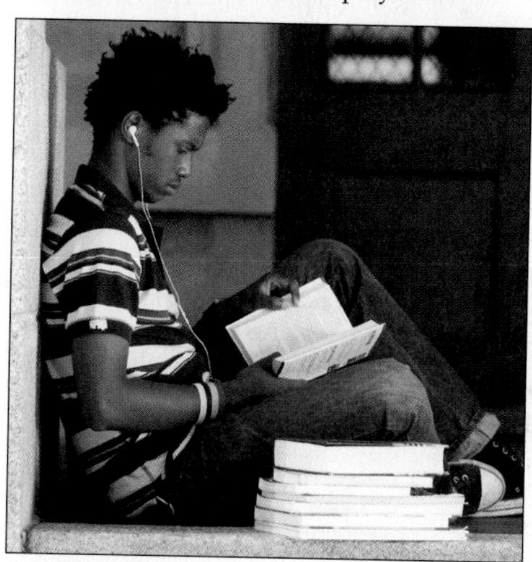

History professor Deborah Vess asks students to download 39 films to their devices so she doesn't have to spend class time screening the movies. Psychology professor Noland White has found a new-age answer to office hours: a podcast of the week's most frequently-asked questions.

And the campus has organized a group of innovative staff and faculty to conjure up other uses for the technology. Called the iDreamers, the team bats around ideas that could turn the devices into portable yearbooks and replace campus brochures with podcasts.

"The more you free up your classroom for discussion, the more efficient you are," said Dorothy Leland, the school's president.

After Leland and Jim Wolfgang, the school's chief information officer, began seeing iPods around campus in 2002, they decided to explore educational applications for the devices. They started by farming out 50 donated iPods to faculty who offered the best proposals.

Differentiated Instruction for Universal Access

Strategy for Less Proficient Readers

Some students may have trouble making the transition from a set of technical directions to a news article. To help students understand the format of the news article, walk them through the text and point out features that differ from the technical directions. As you point out features, have students ask themselves why these features are important in understanding the text. Discuss with students any features that they find to be challenging.

Enrichment for Gifted/Talented Students

Challenge students to create a podcast about an important occurrence in the community or a fellow classmate. Have students follow the directions on page 672 to create a podcast. Provide classroom time for each student to present his or her podcast.

About News Articles

1. Direct students to the features listed in the News Article box on page 673. Confirm that they understand the vocabulary used in the box.
2. Ask students which newspapers they enjoy looking at or reading. Encourage students to share the specific sections of the newspaper (sports, local news, world news, and so on).
3. **Ask** students to discuss the benefits of keeping up to date on current news.

   Possible response: Staying up to date on current news allows me to understand what is happening in the world and to build my knowledge of new ideas and discoveries.

Following Technical Directions

1. Explain that although this document does not contain technical directions, it does report on the impact of technology on college campuses.
2. Have students look at the first page of the news article. Then, **ask** them what clues allow them to determine what the article will cover.

   Answer: The boldfaced title tells me that the article will be about the use of iPods in a Georgia school.
3. Remind students that news articles typically have quotations from qualified sources in order to strengthen the article's topic.
4. **Ask:** Who are the experts and other qualified sources that the author uses to make her points?

   Possible answer: Among others, the author provides quotations from a university president about the value of this technology.
5. Have students discuss whether they find the author's sources to be convincing.

   Possible response: Students may say that the sources are convincing because they provide readers with concrete examples of how podcasts are used.

Follow Technical Directions

1. Explain to students that news articles tend to present both sides of a discussion in order to provide the reader with a complete understanding of the topic.
2. Have students think about the quotation in opposition of iPod usage that the author provides. Then, **ask** students whether they find the opposition valid.

   Possible response: Some students may say that they disagree with the director because having access to class materials will allow students to study better. Others may say that missing out on classroom discussions would be a detriment to their educational growth.

Soon Wolfgang's office was flooded with applications from educators suggesting new uses. Now, some 400 college-owned iPods are floating around campus—some loaned to students in certain classes, others available for checkout at libraries.

Hank Edmondson, a government professor known around campus as "The Podfather," was among the first to use iPods to supplement his course lectures. Edmondson makes lectures, language study programs, indigenous music, and thumbnail art sketches available for download to the iPods of students in a three-week, study-abroad program he leads.

During a recent visit to the Prado in Madrid, he recorded a 20-minute lecture on the museum's artwork. Downloading that in advance will let students spend their visit to the museum exploring, not listening to Edmondson talk.

"You want to pack everything in, but you've got a lot of travel time," he said.

Vess said having her history students screen films on their iPods allows her to dedicate class time to discussion and analysis; likewise for the weekly graduate course she teaches on historical methods.

"Now I can devote my whole three hours to Socratic dialogue," she said with a grin.

Although iPods can be useful tools for reviewing coursework, some critics argue donning a pair of earphones is not the same as actively engaging with material in a classroom setting.

Here, an objection to using iPods in an educational environment is followed by details and support that address that objection.

"Learning is through interaction, discussion, critical questioning, and challenging of assumptions," said Donna Qualters, director of the Center for Effective Teaching at Northeastern University in Boston. "Those cannot be duplicated on an iPod—you have to be there to experience that learning."

GCSU officials say the school makes sure its iPod lessons supplement classroom work—not replace it.

"We don't have any project that repeats what's going on in the classroom," Wolfgang said. "All this is value-added."

* * *

Vocabulary Development

CCSS Language 6

Vocabulary from Computer Science

Explain that articles about new technologies use language that includes types of devices, names of products, or types of files. Point out several of these terms and discuss their use.

Types of devices: digital players, laptop. A digital player may be an iPod, an MP3 player, a DVD player, or any other device that plays music or video files. A laptop is a thin, lightweight computer.

Product names: iTunes™, PowerPoint™. The author expects the reader to understand that iTunes™ is a music player. PowerPoint™ is a program that allows users to create a slide show presentation.

Types of files: video, audio, animation. Video and audio files are those that you can see and hear or just hear. Animation is illustrations that move.

After You Read | Technical Directions • News Article

Comparing Functional and Expository Texts

1. **Craft and Structure** **(a)** Compare and contrast the **structures and formats** of the **technical directions** and the news article. **(b)** Which text uses structure and format more effectively to help aid reader understanding? Explain your answer.

Content-Area Vocabulary

(a) Explain how *download* can function as either a verb or a noun, depending on the context. **(b)** What suffix could you add to change *download* into an adjective? **(c)** Use all three vocabulary words from page 670 in a paragraph that describes how blogging and podcasting can be viewed as democratizing technologies.

Timed Writing

Explanatory Text: Letter

Format and Audience
The prompt directs you to write a letter to fellow students. Therefore, be sure you properly format your response and use formal language that is appropriate for your audience.

You have just begun posting podcasts that give additional information about a topic discussed in class. Write a letter to fellow students introducing your podcast. Describe your content and explain how to download and listen to the material. Use details and information from both texts to compose your letter. (25 minutes)

Academic Vocabulary
When you *explain* something, you make it clear by providing details, examples, illustrations, and additional information.

5-Minute Planner

Complete these steps before you begin to write:

1. Read the prompt carefully and completely. Look for key words that will help you understand the assignment.
2. Choose a class subject to serve as the topic of your podcast. Make notes about what topic ideas to include in your podcast.
3. Review the technical directions and news article. Scan the texts to locate information that would be helpful in composing your letter. Make notes about details you find that should be included.
4. Consider the steps that students will need to take to access your podcast. Determine the clearest way to present the information so that students will be able to follow the technical directions you are providing. Then, create an outline of the body for your letter.
5. Refer to your outline and notes as you draft your letter.

ASSESS/EXTEND

Answers

Comparing Functional and Expository Text

1. (a) **Possible response:** Both the technical directions and the news article provided background information. The technical directions also included a list with headings of a step-by-step process to help guide the reader to perform a task. (b) **Possible response:** Some students may say that the technical directions were more effective at aiding reader understanding because they allow the reader to find out quickly how to perform the task. Others may say that the news article was more effective because of the numerous quotations from experts and qualified sources.

Content-Area Vocabulary

(a) **Sample response:** If you are writing or talking about the file, then *download* is a noun. If you are writing or talking about what you do to the file, then *download* is a verb. (b) **Sample response:** If you added *-ed* to *download* to make *downloaded,* you could use it as an adjective. The downloaded pictures took up a lot of space. (c) **Sample response:** Blogging is one way that people can share their ideas with lots of other people. Although repressive governments may make it difficult to download information from the Internet, they cannot completely stop people from sharing information. Because information can be shared widely, blogs and other social media act as a democratizing influence.

Timed Writing

1. Before students complete the activity, guide them in identifying and analyzing key words and phrases in the prompt, highlighted on the student page.
2. Work with students to draw up guidelines for their letters based on the key words:
   - **Focus** The letter should give step-by-step instructions for how to download and listen to podcasts.
   - **Organization** The letter should describe the content of the podcast and provide instructions.
   - **Style** The audience consists of fellow students, so the style should be informal.
3. Have students use the 5-Minute Planner to structure their time.
4. Allow students 25 minutes to complete the assignment. Evaluate their work using the guidelines they have developed.

PRETEACH

Common Core State Standards

- **Reading Literature 4**
- **Writing 2**

❶ Comparing Imagery

1. Introduce the skill, using the instruction on the student page.
2. Give students a copy of the **Comparing Imagery Graphic Organizer B, *Graphic Organizer Transparencies,*** p. 124. Tell them they will fill it in with sensory details as they read.

Think Aloud: Model the Skill

Model a way to think about imagery. Say to students:

To understand the images that poets use, I think about what emotions the sense words produce. An image that likens a rain to a fresh spring shower produces happy emotions. An image that compares rain to an icy winter storm makes me feel cold and uncomfortable. Once I have identified the emotions of these images, I try to see how they fit with the emotions of other images in the poem so I can gather the poet's meaning.

Cultural Perspective

1. Introduce the skill, using the instruction on the student page.
2. Point out that a writer's culture will have an influence on what kind of imagery he or she uses. Sensory details and vivid visuals that are important in a culture may be reflected in the writer's work.
3. Explain that when poets place special emphasis on themes, ideas, images, or qualities, they may be reflecting cultural perspectives.

Comparing Literary Works

There Is No Word for Goodbye • Daily • Hope • The Day of the Storm

❶ Comparing Imagery

Imagery is language that appeals to one or more of the senses—sight, hearing, touch, taste, and smell. The use of imagery allows writers to express their ideas with vividness and immediacy. Images create mental pictures for readers and help them connect their own experiences to the worlds the writers describe. The emotional responses writers evoke through the use of vivid imagery allow a poem or other work to come to life in readers' minds. Interpretations of imagery may differ as readers view a work through the lens of their own life experiences.

Comparing imagery is important in analyzing the aesthetic qualities of a variety of selections. These are the stylistic qualities that make a poem's language beautiful. Writers, for example, often include patterns of images. By recognizing these image patterns, or motifs, you can better appreciate differences and similarities among selections.

As you read, use a chart like this one to compare images and the senses they address.

Poem: "There Is No Word for Goodbye"

Sensory Language	Imagery	Effect
"wind–tanned skin"	brownish, weathered skin	The reader can see and feel Sokoya's skin.

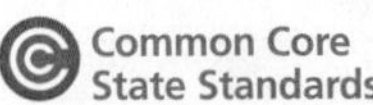

Common Core State Standards

Reading Literature
4. Determine the meaning of words and phrases as they are used in a text, including figurative and connotative meanings; analyze the cumulative impact of specific word choices on meaning and tone.

Writing
2. Write informative/explanatory texts to examine and convey complex ideas, concepts, and information clearly and accurately through the effective selection, organization, and analysis of content.

- Vocabulary flashcards
- Interactive journals
- More about the authors
- Selection audio
- Interactive graphic organizers

Vocabulary Development

Vocabulary Knowledge Rating

Create a **Vocabulary Knowledge Rating Chart** (***Professional Development Guidebook***, p. 33) featuring the vocabulary words glossed in the selections:

shriveled (p. 679) *amid* (p. 681)
scarred (p. 679) *emitting* (p. 682)
miraculously (p. 681) *succumbed* (p. 683)
awestruck (p. 681) *submerged* (p. 684)

Give students a copy of the chart, and read the words aloud. Have students mark their rating of each in the Before You Read column. To gauge how much instruction to provide, tally the number of students who think they know each word.

Explain that the words are defined in the margin where they appear in the selection. Urge students to be alert to these words as they read and discuss the selections. They will rate their knowledge again when they finish.

PHLit Online! **Vocabulary Central,** featuring tools, activities, and songs for studying vocabulary, is available at **www.PHLitOnline.com.**

THE BIG ?
How does communication change us?

2 Writing About the Big Question

In these selections, the writers want you to see an experience as clearly as they do. Use this sentence starter to develop your ideas.

Seeing the world through someone else's eyes may help a person become **aware** of ________.

Meet the Authors

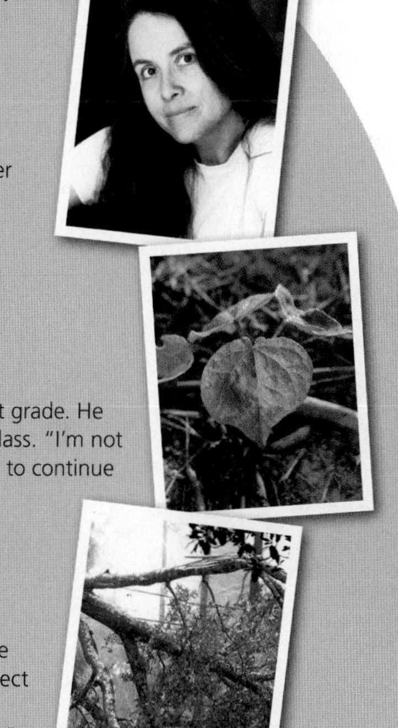

Mary Tall Mountain (1918–1991)

Author of "There Is No Word for Goodbye" (p. 678)

An Athabaskan Indian, Mary Tall Mountain was born in Alaska. When Tall Mountain was six, her mother died, and she was adopted by a family who removed her from her culture. In "There Is No Word For Goodbye," Tall Mountain reconnects with her Native American roots

Naomi Shihab Nye (b. 1952)

Author of "Daily" (p. 679)

Naomi Shihab Nye, a successful poet, was born to a Palestinian father and an American mother. Of poems, she has said, "I liked the space around them, and the way they took you to a deeper, quieter place, almost immediately."

David T. Hilbun (b. 1992)

Author of "Hope" (p. 680)

David T. Hilbun has been publishing his work since he was in the first grade. He wrote "Hope" after Hurricane Katrina for his eighth grade English class. "I'm not sure yet what I plan to do in the future," Hilbun says, "but I do want to continue writing in some fashion."

Tyroneca "Ty" Booker (b. 1987)

Author of "The Day of the Storm" (p. 682)

Tyroneca Booker resides in Louisiana. Booker's piece, "The Day of the Storm," was written in an English course when she was asked to reflect on Hurricane Katrina. She says, "I wrote from my heart, a very true account of what life was like during and after these powerful storms."

Teaching Resources

- All EL *Unit 4 Resources,* pp. 101–117
- All EL *Graphic Organizer Transparencies,* pp. 123–126
- All *Professional Development Guidebook,* pp. 33, 75
- All **Enriched Online Student Edition**
- All *Common Core Companion,* pp. 35–47; 190–201

PHLit Online! All resources, including print and audio, are available at **www.PHLitOnline.com.**

Daily Bellringer

For each class during which you will teach this selection, have students complete one of the five Vocabulary activities for Week 21 in the ***Daily Bellringer Activities*** booklet.

2 Writing About the Big Question

1. Review the assignment with the class.
2. Describe a time when you learned a lesson from someone else's experience. **Ask** volunteers to share similar stories. Discuss similarities or differences in the lessons learned.
3. Have students complete the sentence starter. Review responses as a class. (**Possible response:** Seeing the world through someone else's eyes may help a person become aware of common ground with others.)
4. Remind students that their answers will help them think about the Big Question, "How does communication change us?"

Concept Connector

Tell students that they will return to their sentence starter after they have concluded reading.

Multidraft Reading

To assist struggling readers and to deepen reading for all, apply multidraft reading protocols. For each reading, have students set the purpose indicated:

- **First reading**—identifying key ideas and details and answering any Reading Checks.
- **Second reading**—analyzing craft and structure and responding to the side-column prompts.
- **Third reading**—integrating knowledge and ideas, connecting to other texts and the world, and answering the end-of-selection questions.

For more guidance, see the ***Classroom Strategies and Teaching Routines*** card on multidraft reading.

PHLit Online!

For more about the authors and practice with the selection vocabulary, go online at **www.PHLitOnline.com.**

TEACH

1 Background

Death and the Afterlife A Shoshone legend tells of two caterpillar people who loved each other deeply. When the caterpillar man died, the caterpillar woman pulled her sorrow around her like a shawl and mourned for a year. Then the Creator clapped his hands and the caterpillar woman burst forth as a butterfly.

2 Activating Prior Knowledge

Ask students to recall and discuss a past experience that is vivid in their memory. **Ask** them to identify the sights, sounds, tastes, textures, and smells linked to the experience.

Concept Connector →

Students will follow up on this activity after completing the two poems.

3 About the Poems

"There is No Word for Goodbye" describes a meaningful exchange about the finality of death between a young adult and an elderly aunt. The busy speaker of "Daily" breathes new life into chores.

4 Literary Analysis

Imagery

1. Review that imagery is language that appeals to the senses.
2. Read the first bracketed text aloud. **Ask** the first Literary Analysis question: Which words suggest that Sokoya is an elder?

   Answer: The phrases "net of wrinkles" and "wise black pools" indicate that Sokoya is an elder.

5 Literary Analysis

Imagery

1. Read aloud the second bracketed stanza. **Ask** the second Literary Analysis question: Which image in lines 19–23 appeals to the sense of touch?
2. **Possible response:** The image of the delicate bluebell flower helps convey the idea that Sokoya touched the speaker very gently.

There is No Word for Goodbye

Mary Tall Mountain

Literary Analysis
Imagery Which words suggest that Sokoya is an elder?

Literary Analysis
Imagery Which details in lines 9–12 appeal to the sense of touch?

Sokoya, I said, looking through
the net of wrinkles into
wise black pools
of her eyes.

What do you say in Athabaskan
when you leave each other?
What is the word
for goodbye?

A shade of feeling rippled
the wind-tanned skin.
Ah, nothing, she said,
watching the river flash.

She looked at me close.
We just say, Tlaa. That means,
See you.
We never leave each other.
When does your mouth
say goodbye to your heart?

She touched me light
as a bluebell.
You forget when you leave us,
You're so small then.
We don't use that word.

We always think you're coming back,
but if you don't,
we'll see you some place else.
You understand.
There is no word for goodbye.

Sokoya: Aunt (mother's sister)

Vocabulary Development

© CCSS Language 6

Thematic Vocabulary: The Big Question

As students are discussing the poems, encourage them to use the thematic vocabulary presented in Introducing the Big Question, pp. 604–605.You might encourage them with sentence starters like these:

1. Sokoya *responds* to the narrator's question about a word for "goodbye" by . . .
2. Sokoya says the *meaning* of the word *Tiaa* is . . .
3. The Athabaskans *react to* the word "goodbye" by . . .
4. Each stanza of "Daily" *illuminates*. . .

❸ 
DAILY

Daily

Naomi Shihab Nye

These shriveled seeds we plant,
corn kernel, dried bean,
poke into loosened soil,
cover over with measured fingertips

These T-shirts we fold into
❻ perfect white squares

These tortillas we slice and fry to crisp strips
This rich egg scrambled in a gray clay bowl

This bed whose covers I straighten
smoothing edges till blue quilt fits brown blanket
and nothing hangs out

This envelope I address
so the name balances like a cloud
in the center of the sky

This page I type and retype
This table I dust till the scarred wood shines
This bundle of clothes I wash and hang and wash again
like flags we share, a country so close
no one needs to name it

The days are nouns; touch them
The hands are churches that worship the world

Vocabulary
shriveled (shriv′ əld) *adj.* shrunken and wrinkled

Literary Analysis
Imagery To which senses does the imagery of the bed covers appeal?

Vocabulary
scarred (skärd) *adj.* marked or dented

Critical Thinking

Cite textual evidence to support your responses.

1. **Key Ideas and Details** **Infer:** In "There Is No Word for Goodbye," why might the speaker want to know the word for goodbye? Support your answer.
2. **Key Ideas and Details** **(a)** Identify five tasks described in "Daily." **(b) Infer:** Does the speaker seem to take pleasure in doing these tasks? Explain.
3. **Integration of Knowledge and Ideas** **(a)** What are these writers' messages about life? **(b)** How might readers benefit from understanding these views? *[Connect to the Big Question: How does communication change us?]*

❻ Literary Analysis

Imagery

1. Read aloud the bracketed passage.
2. **Ask** students what the narrator is doing in the first four lines.
   Answer: The narrator is telling about planting seeds.
3. **Ask** the Literary Analysis question.
   Answer: The imagery appeals to the senses of sight and touch.

Concept Connector 

Have students return to the Activating Prior Knowledge activity (p. 678). Then ask them to describe how the sensory images in the poems make them seem more realistic or vivid. In addition, have students compare their Writing About the Big Question responses before reading the selection with their ideas afterwards.

ASSESS

Answers

Remind students to support their answers with evidence from the text.

1. **Possible response:** Sokoya will die soon and the speaker wants to say goodbye.
2. (a) The speaker recalls planting seeds, folding t-shirts, cooking, making a bed, addressing an envelope, typing, dusting, and washing clothes. (b) Yes, and she also finds them sacred.
3. **Possible responses:** (a) Mary Tall Mountain believes that life is a journey without end. Nye believes that life is a collection of everyday tasks worth celebrating. (b) Readers can learn to value everyday events and learn not to fear transitions.

Text Complexity Rubric

There Is No Word for Goodbye, Daily	
Qualitative Measures	
Context/Knowledge Demands	Everyday situations (saying goodbye; everyday tasks) 1 2 ③ 4 5
Structure/ Language Clarity	Complex sentences 1 2 ③ 4 5
Levels of Meaning/ Purpose	Challenging concepts (multiple levels of meaning) 1 2 3 ④ 5
Quantitative Measures	
Text Length	Word Count: 126; 133
Lexile	NP

Reader and Task Suggestions

Preparing to Read the Text	Leveled Tasks
• Refer to the Background information on TE p. 678 and discuss how many people live for the day. • Refer to the Concept Connector on TE p. 679 and discuss sensory imagery. • Guide students to use Multidraft Reading strategies (TE p. 677).	*Levels of Meaning* If students will have difficulty with levels of meaning, have them first read each poem and identify what is happening. *Synthesizing* If students will not have difficulty with levels of meaning, have them read and take notes on how the poets use vivid sensory images to help readers understand the poem.

TEACH

❼ Background

Hurricane Katrina In August of 2005, a devastating hurricane hit the Gulf Coast, including Louisiana and Mississippi. Nearly 2000 people were killed, and cities such as New Orleans had to be entirely evacuated. Property and other damage was extensive, estimated at over 100 billion dollars.

❽ Activating Prior Knowledge

Give students a **K-W-L Chart** (***Professional Development Guidebook***, p. 75). Have them list what they know about Hurricane Katrina in the first column and what they want to know in the second column.

Concept Connector →

Tell students that they will return to complete the chart after they read the selection.

❾ About the Selection

In the midst of Hurricane Katrina, Adam and his father retreat to their storm cellar for safety. Thinking that the storm's quiet center is over them, they emerge outside. After the storm, they return to total destruction except for a tiny green plant that offers hope.

❿ Literary Analysis

Imagery

1. **Ask** the Literary Analysis question: To which senses does the imagery in the first paragraph appeal?
   Answer: The paragraph addresses the senses of sound (the winds, waves, and crash of the oak tree) and sight (the tree being uprooted and falling).

❼ ❽ ❾

Hope

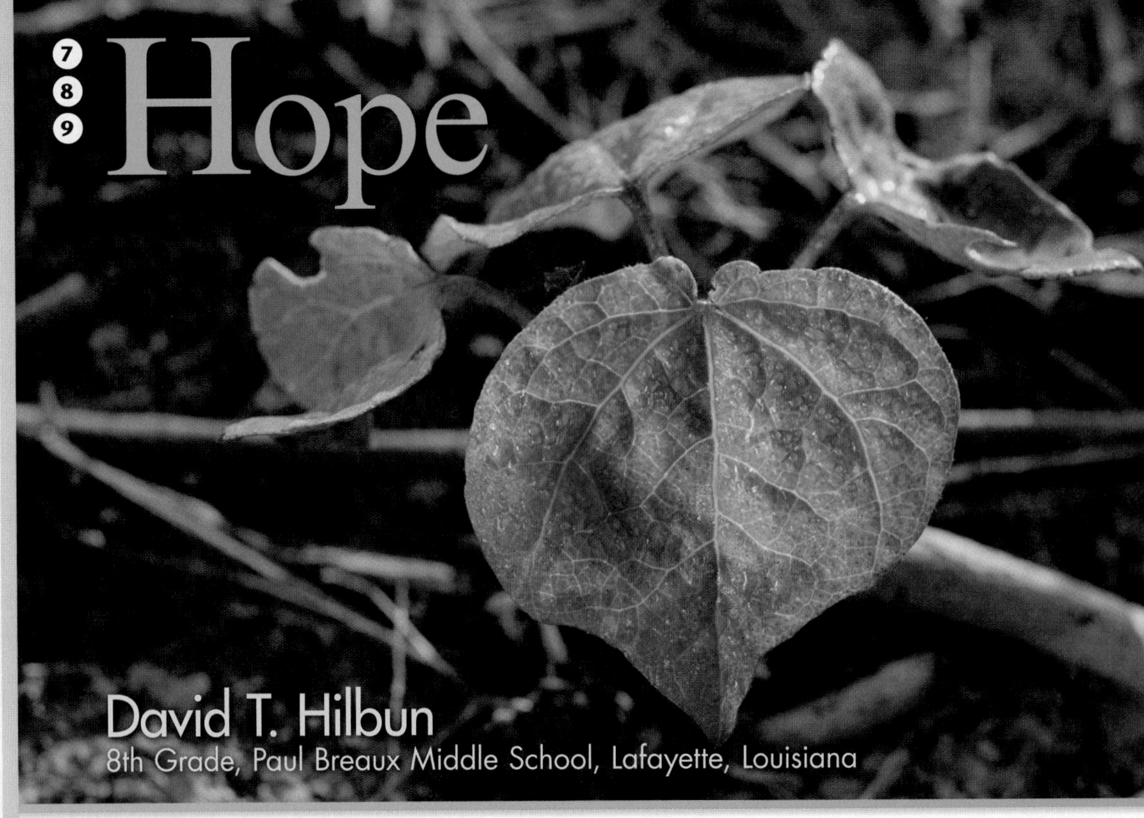

David T. Hilbun
8th Grade, Paul Breaux Middle School, Lafayette, Louisiana

Literary Analysis
Imagery To which senses does the imagery in the first paragraph appeal?

❿

"Adam, get behind me!" his dad called over the roaring winds and splashing waves. Adam's reply was cut off by the crash of a huge oak tree being ripped out of the dirt and slamming into the ground a few meters away with the force of a stick of dynamite. "Quick, into the storm cellar!" The storm cellar had been designed by Adam's dad years ago. It was made of 6-inch solid steel and had enough MRE's[1] to feed 12 hungry people for a week.

They made it to the door and were able to get inside. Fretful, cold, and frightened, they got out of the storm. In their "secret place," as Adam called it when he was littler, they felt strangely peaceful. Maybe it was the knowledge that they both were safe, maybe it was the comfort of the cellar, they didn't know, but at least they had each other.

Over time, the noise outside got worse and worse. At one point, it was so loud that it felt as if a huge gong were crashing inside their heads. Suddenly, the noise stopped.

1. **MRE's:** prepared foods; acronym for Meals Ready to Eat.

Text Complexity Rubric

Hope, The Day of the Storm	
Qualitative Measures	
Context/ Knowledge Demands	Louisiana during Hurricane Katrina, 2005 1 2 ③ 4 5
Structure/ Language Clarity	Some long sentences with embedded clauses; on-level vocabulary; idioms 1 2 ③ 4 5
Levels of Meaning/ Purpose	Accessible concept (people face natural disaster) 1 ② 3 4 5
Quantitative Measures	
Text Length	Word Count: 399; 908
Lexile	830L; 920L

Reader and Task Suggestions

Preparing to Read the Text

- Use the Background note on TE p. 680 to discuss Hurricane Katrina.
- Discuss the different ways in which people respond to unexpected disasters.
- Guide students to use Multidraft Reading strategies (TE p. 677).

Leveled Tasks

Knowledge Demands If students will have difficulty with knowledge demands, have them write notes about what happens. Have them reread and note how the characters reacted.

Analyzing If students will not have difficulty with context and knowledge demands, have them read and compare how the two writers develop their stories.

"What's going on, Dad?" Adam asked.

"I think the eyewall passed over us," he said. "We can probably go outside for a little while."

Outside was a scene of total destruction. Their house was gone, a few planks in its place.

The school was wrecked, the remains of an airliner strewn all over the football field. But worst, they saw a huge fallen tree. Sticking out from under it was a human arm.

11 Feeling sick, Adam turned to go underground when the eyewall passed over. Hundred-mile-an-hour winds lifted Adam into the air. Screaming, flipping over and over, he bid a mental farewell to his father and a mental hello to his mother. Crying, thinking all hope was lost, he was **miraculously** caught by his dad. Inch by inch, they made their way back to the cellar, where they waited out the storm.

Finally, it was over. They looked around at the scene surrounding them in **awestruck** silence. Luckily, there were no bodies this time.

Too shocked to cry, too scared to do anything but stand there, Adam and his dad looked at each other.

After a time, the shock wore off. They walked around. Adam motioned his dad over.

"Look," he said simply, smiling.

And there, **amid** all the destruction, was a single green plant.

Vocabulary

miraculously (mi rak′ yoo ləs le) *adv.* in an amazing way; as though by a miracle

awestruck (ô′ struk) *adj.* filled with wonder

amid (ə mid′) *prep.* among; in the middle of

Critical Thinking

1. **Key Ideas and Details** **(a)** Where do Adam and his father go when the storm hits? **(b) Infer:** Why do you think Adam's father had built the storm shelter?
2. **Key Ideas and Details** **(a)** What do Adam and his father find when they leave the shelter the first time? **(b) Infer:** What makes Adam feel sick?
3. **Key Ideas and Details** **(a)** What do Adam and his father find when they emerge from the shelter the last time? **(b) Interpret:** Why is the plant so meaningful to Adam?
4. **Integration of Knowledge and Ideas** **(a)** Why might readers who have experienced a tragic storm be interested in Hilbun's narrative? **(b)** Does this story change the way you regard storms? Why or why not? *[Connect to the Big Question: How does communication change us?]*

Cite textual evidence to support your responses.

Think Aloud

Vocabulary: Using Context

Direct students to the word *strewn* on page 681. Using a think-aloud process, model how to use context to infer the meaning of an unknown word. Say to students:

> I'm going to think aloud to show you how I would figure out the meaning of *strewn* from its context.
>
> In this sentence, *strewn* is used to explain where the remains of an airliner are. We know from the beginning of the selection that Adam and his father are in the middle of a very destructive storm. We also know from the beginning of the sentence that the school has been *wrecked*. These clues all suggest that the airliner is also *wrecked*. The rest of the sentence says that the airliner is "all over the field." Something that is *wrecked* and is all over the place has been scattered. I think that *strewn* means "scattered."

11 Connecting to the Big Question

1. Recall the Big Question by pointing out that communication can be verbal or visual.
2. Direct students' attention to the bracketed text. **Ask:** How does this description make you feel? **Possible response:** The description is scary and upsetting.
3. **Ask:** Does picturing Adam's experience change you? How? **Answer:** Reading a vivid description and picturing Adam's experience help me understand it.

Concept Connector

Have students return to and complete their **K-W-L** charts with information about Hurricane Katrina.

ASSESS

Answers

Critical Thinking

Have students write a brief objective summary of the selection. Remind them to support their answers with evidence from the text.

1. (a) They go into the storm shelter. (b) He wanted to be prepared for hurricanes, which were common in the area.
2. (a) They find a lot of wreckage, including their home and school. (b) He sees an arm sticking out from under a fallen tree.
3. (a) They find amidst the wreckage a single green plant. (b) It means that life will go on.
4. **Possible responses:** (a) Readers can empathize with Adam and explore a shared experience. (b) Survival stories can bring back horrible feelings survivors might not want to relive. For those who have not experienced a tragic storm, knowing a survivor's story might help them prepare for one in the future.

12 Background

Hurricane Katrina As Hurricane Katrina barreled toward New Orleans, colleges in the area worked to keep students safe. Some students left the area. Others stayed on campuses to ride out the storm. At Southeastern Louisiana University, few students were injured but many saw damage to their residence or had close friends or family missing. Many also found their educations interrupted for months.

13 Activating Prior Knowledge

Have students continue to add information to the **K-W-L Chart** (***Professional Development Guidebook***, p. 75) begun during their reading of "Hope." Have them update the chart to reflect new knowledge and new questions.

Concept Connector

Tell students that they will return to complete the chart again after they read the selection.

14 About the Selection

As Hurricane Katrina approaches the New Orleans area, student Tyroneca Booker is on the campus of Southeastern Louisiana University. After "ignoring" the storm, she realizes its strength and scrambles to collect her things and join others at the University's shelter. After the storm, she is horrified by the destruction and thankful to be alive.

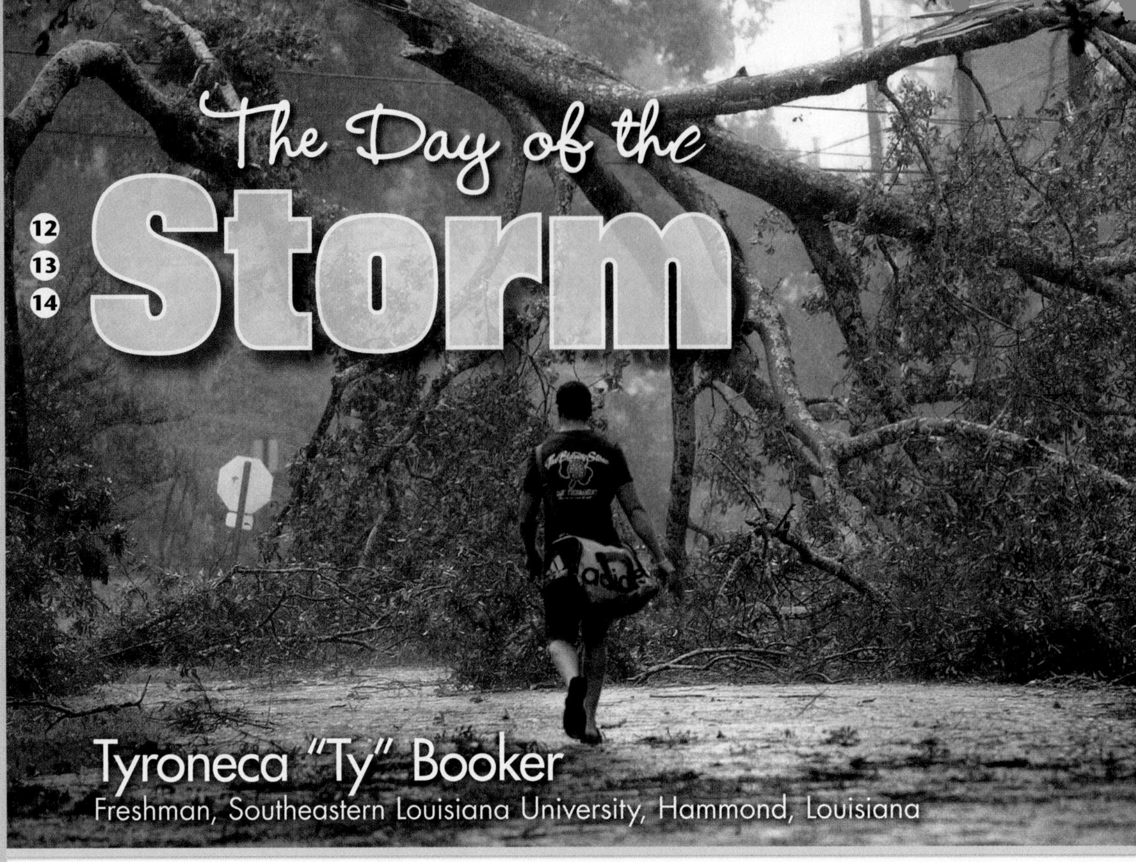

12 13 14

The Day of the Storm

Tyroneca "Ty" Booker
Freshman, Southeastern Louisiana University, Hammond, Louisiana

Vocabulary
emitting (e mit′ inj) *v.* sending out

I don't watch much T.V., so to hear a hurricane was heading for Louisiana was a scare. Earlier in the week, I was talking to my sister and she had informed me a storm was brewing in the Gulf. I paid little to no attention because every storm since Andrew in '98 was supposedly due to hit Louisiana directly and didn't. As a matter of fact, Andrew is the only "big" storm I can remember. Vivid images come to mind—pine trees, emitting their signature smells from the freshly cracked wood, lie in the street like barricades. For about a week my family survived on Cheerios and Spam; it was all we had. Since then, a hurricane only meant a day or two off from school, and Louisiana dodging the bullet one more time. Friday, August 26th, my cousin and I drove to New Orleans to pick up another relative. We took for granted the scenery and simple pleasures of the city. We never realized what lay ahead.

Vocabulary Development

Idiomatic Expressions

Point out the words *dodging the bullet* on this page. Explain that the phrase is an idiomatic expression, in which the words have a meaning other than their literal meaning. Such an expression helps writers create vivid descriptions. When Booker says Louisiana "dodged a bullet," she means that the hurricane did not hurt the state. Like a bullet that missed its target, the hurricane didn't do any damage.

Write other idiomatic expressions on the board and help students determine their meaning: *on your case, keeping an eye out, set my teeth on edge, using elbow grease.* Have students share familiar idiomatic expressions as classmates try to define them.

I have always been a hard-headed person, so this particular weekend I'd decided to stay on campus. My cousin traveled back to Baton Rouge alone to go to work, while I stayed in Hammond, ignorant of the events ahead. On Saturday, the calls flooded my cell phone. Everyone called to tell me about Katrina. I finally, after 20 phone calls, decided to turn on the T.V. There she was: coming straight for New Orleans. I was only a city or two away. Every channel and every news bulletin carried the same, yet simple message: Get out while you can! As I watched her turn like
15 a propeller, it all became grim reality—we were going to be hit and hit hard. I had nowhere to go. Here I was on the fourth floor of Livingston Hall in my room with a category five hurricane headed for a city only 52 miles away.

I knew I needed to stock up on food if I was going to be here to endure the storm. Cayman's was closed, and the Lion's Den wasn't an option. The only thing I had was my SLU ID, so I decided to make a "vending-machine run." After three trips to the electric snack havens, I'd figured that I had enough. The last time I walked across the barren, deserted parking lot, a man in Army fatigues caught my eye. Curiosity took over, and I went to inquire as to why he was on campus.

He proceeded to explain that the Kinesiology and Health Studies building was being used as shelter for ill people. As he continued to ramble on, my thoughts began to come into focus—this was serious. I pretended to listen, but only a few words stuck out in my mind: dorms closed. University Center, shelter. I thanked him,
16 walked away, and those words formed themselves into two ton bricks, each falling upon me like rain: each one came faster than the one before. I realized he had just told me we had to evacuate the dorms, and take shelter in the University Center. I panicked, packed up my belongings as if it were check-out time, and waited for the all-call.[1] At about 5:15 p.m., the clouds couldn't take the pressure as they succumbed to the rain, surrendering themselves peacefully without a fight. The wind picked up, and here I was running to the University Center on North Campus with the few belongings that I could grab. The wind began to howl like a werewolf in the night—this was the one! Katrina was here, and she was as strong as two oxen.

I made it into the University Center, soaked but safe. I looked around, found a spot and made myself at home. I drifted off into a deep sleep, the last peaceful night of rest I would get for a while. When I did awake, I heard the University President, Randy Moffett, on the loudspeaker telling us that Katrina was in fact here, and she

1. **all-call** phone system used to contact students at Southeastern Louisiana University.

Literary Analysis
Imagery To which sense does the image "turn like a propeller" appeal?

Vocabulary
succumbed (sə kumd) *v.* gave way; yielded

17 
Reading Check
What did Ty learn from the man in army fatigues?

15 Literary Analysis

Imagery

1. Read the first paragraph on p. 683 aloud as students concentrate on identifying sensory images. Then have students reread the first bracketed passage.
2. **Ask** students the Literary Analysis question: To which sense does the image "turn like a propeller" appeal?

   Answer: It appeals to the sense of sight. A propeller turns very quickly in a circle. That's the image created of the hurricane as it approached New Orleans.

16 Connecting to the Big Question

1. **Ask** students how well they communicate when they are upset or frightened.
2. Direct students' attention to the second bracketed passage. **Ask:** How does Ty respond to the soldier's information?

   Possible response: She has trouble focusing on it. She hears only a few key words. She panics.
3. **Ask:** In what ways does the soldier's communication change Ty in a positive way? In a negative way? Explain.

   Possible responses: The positive change is that Ty learns where to go for safety. The negative change is that she panics and doesn't think clearly about what to bring with her.

17 Reading Check

Answer: The man in fatigues told her that one of the campus buildings was being used as a hospital shelter, the dorms were closing, and she was to take shelter in the University Center.

PHLit Online!
This selection is available in interactive format in the **Enriched Online Student Edition, www.PHLitOnline.com,** which includes an interactive graphic organizer.

Fluency

Distribute copies of page 683, and pair students. Have listeners mark text with which readers struggle. Circulate to monitor students' fluency, then collect the marked up ages. Review difficult words and passages, such as these:

- Point out the word *hard-headed,* and explain that it is a compound adjective. Model how to read hyphenated adjectives with a very slight pause between the two words and emphasis on the second word.
- If students have difficulty with the word *fatigues,* remind them that the *u* is silent. Read the word aloud and have students echo to confirm.
- If students stumble on the word *barren,* have them cover one *r* and the final *n* to see the familiar word *bare*. Once students appreciate the word's meaning, model how to divide the word into syllables between the double *r*'s, so that both vowels are short. Have students echo.

18 Literary Analysis

Imagery

1. As students read the bracketed passage, have them concentrate on imagery.
2. **Ask:** What images does the writer use in this paragraph?

   Answer: She describes herself as "soaked but safe," she uses animal imagery to bring the storm to life, and describes a tree in pieces.
3. **Ask** the Literary Analysis question.

   Answer: Vivid images help readers understand Ty by portraying a frightening experience, which helps readers better understand that experience.

Concept Connector

Have students return to and complete their **K-W-L** charts a second time. Then, have them compare their Writing About the Big Question responses before reading the selection with their ideas afterwards.

ASSESS

Answers

Critical Thinking

Before students respond, you may wish to have them write a brief objective summary of the selection. As they answer the questions below, remind them to support their answers with evidence from the text.

1. (a) She packs everything. (b) She cannot carry any more.
2. (a) He tells them the worst is almost over. (b) She thinks it will get worse before it gets better. (c) Yes. The storm lasted at least another day, and did incredible damage.
3. (a) She realized the storm's far-reaching and horrible impact. (b) **Possible response:** She learned to take weather warnings more seriously, to be thankful for what she has, and to recognize how quickly things can change.
4. **Possible response:** (a) Before the storm, she ignored news coverage. During the storm, she had no access to news coverage. After the storm, she paid close attention to news coverage. (b) **Possible response:** The account showed me that hurricanes can be very dangerous.

Literary Analysis
Imagery How does the writer's use of imagery in this paragraph help you understand her experience? 18

was marking her territory all around us as he spoke. He told us we were in the worst two or three hours of the storm, and we had no water or lights, until the generators could be powered up. I went to the window looking out on University Avenue, and surveyed old oak trees thrown around as if they were small branches. As I took all this in, I couldn't help but think—this isn't the worst, this is only the beginning.

When we were let out of the University Center on Tuesday, August 30th, the water was on, but cold, and there was still no electricity. I came back to a dank, dark dorm room, but I was thankful to have survived and to have a place to call home to come to. Later in the day, my cousin came back to pick me up; I was relieved, and cried tears of joy. I was grateful to be back in Baton Rouge with my family, and out of harm's way. However, once I arrived, I realized the devastation Katrina's wrath caused along the Gulf Coast. When I turned on the T.V. I thought it was something unreal. I couldn't even have imagined what I saw—houses submerged to their roof, a whole city flooded. It was then that I thanked the heavens above allowing me to be fortunate, and it was then that I vowed never to take life's simple gifts for granted.

Vocabulary
submerged (səb murjd′) *adj.* covered with water or the like

Critical Thinking

Cite textual evidence to support your responses.

1. **Key Ideas and Details (a)** How does the writer prepare for evacuating the dorm? **(b) Deduce:** Why does she take so few belongings with her to the University Center?
2. **Key Ideas and Details (a)** What does the university president tell those gathered in the University Center during the height of the storm? **(b) Infer:** What does the writer think about the president's announcement? **(c) Make a Judgment:** Was she correct about the president's prediction? Explain.

Integration of Knowledge and Ideas (a) Interpret: In the final paragraph, what does the writer mean when she says she "realized the devastation of Katrina's wrath"? **(b) Draw Conclusions:** What do you think the writer learned from her experiences? Share your response with a partner.

3. **Integration of Knowledge and Ideas (a)** How does the news coverage of Katrina affect the writer's thoughts and actions before, during, and after the storm? **(b)** How does reading this account change your own understanding of hurricanes? *[Connect to the Big Question: How does communication change us?]*

Vocabulary Development

Vocabulary Knowledge Rating

When students have completed reading and discussing the selections, have them take out their **Vocabulary Knowledge Rating Chart.** Read the words aloud once more and have students rate their knowledge of the words again in the After Reading column. Clarify any words that are still problematic. Have students write their own definition and example or sentences in the appropriate column. Then, have students complete the Vocabulary Practice activities on the next page. Encourage students to use the words in further discussion and written work about the selections. Remind them that they will be accountable for these words on the **Selection Test** (*Unit 4 Resources,* pp. 112–114 or 115–117.)

After You Read

There Is No Word for Goodbye • Daily • Hope • The Day of the Storm

Comparing Imagery

1. **Craft and Structure** For each selection, find examples of imagery that appeal to as many senses as you can. Create a chart like the one below to identify and describe examples in each selection. Make a chart for each sense.

Selection	Image Appealing to Touch
"There Is No Word For Goodbye"	
"Daily"	
"Hope"	
"The Day of the Storm"	

2. **Craft and Structure** **(a)** Do any of the selections include imagery that appeals to the sense of taste? **(b)** Do any of the selections include imagery that appeals to the sense of smell? Give examples.

Timed Writing

Explanatory Text: Essay

In an essay, compare and contrast the effects of the writers' use of imagery in each selection. Provide evidence from the texts to support your response. **(35 minutes)**

5-Minute Planner

1. Read the prompt carefully and completely.
2. Consider these questions and jot down your responses.
   - In "There Is No Word For Goodbye," how do the images of Sokoya help you understand the speaker's feelings for her aunt?
   - In "Daily," how does the imagery help you understand the speaker's affection for ordinary things?
   - In "Hope," how does the sound image help convey fear?
   - In "Day of the Storm," how does the writer use images to help convey a picture of the deserted campus?
   - What effect does the imagery in these works have on the reader?
3. Reread the prompt, then reference your notes as you draft your essay.

ASSESS

Answers

Comparing Imagery

1. **Sample answers for Touch: "There Is No Word . . ."**—"shade of feeling rippled the wind-tanned skin"; **"Daily"**—"These shriv-eled seeds we plant"; **"Hope"**—"Hundred-mile-an-hour winds lifted Adam into the air"; **"The Day of the Storm"**—". . . two ton bricks, each falling upon me like rain."

   Other sample answers appear in ***Graphic Organizer Transparencies,*** **Comparing Imagery Graphic Organizer A (After You Read),** p. 125, and the **Additional Answers** section.
2. (a) "Daily" includes images of crisply fried tortillas and rich scrambled egg, both of which appeal to the sense of taste.
   (b) "The Day of the Storm" includes images of pine trees "emitting their signature smells."

Timed Writing

1. Review the prompt with students.
2. Have students use the 5-Minute Planner to structure their time. Guide them in answering the bulleted questions. For example, read the excerpts cited in bulleted items to help students recognize imagery and observe its effect.
3. Allow students 35 minutes to complete the assignment.
4. As students prewrite and draft, have them refer to the Imagery organizer.

Six Traits Focus

✓	Ideas	Word Choice
✓	Organization	Sentence Fluency
	Voice	Conventions

Assessment Resources

Unit 4 Resources

L1 L2 EL **Selection Test A,** pp. 112–114.
L3 L4 EL **Selection Test B,** pp. 115–117.
L3 L4 **Open-Book Test,** pp. 109–111.

PHLit Online! All assessment resources are available at **www.PHLitOnline.com.**

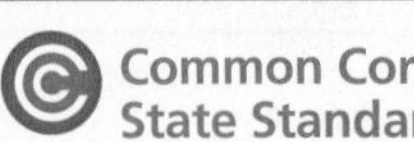

PRETEACH

Common Core State Standards

- Writing 2, 2.a, d; 4
- Language 1.b, 2.c, 5, L.6.3.a

Introducing the Writing Assignment

Review the assignment and the criteria, using the instruction on the student page.

Connecting to Real-Life Writing

Point out to students that descriptive writing is often incorporated into other types of writing. Point out these examples:

- Personal and business letters often describe places and events.
- Descriptive writing often appears in how-to articles.

Writing Workshop *Work in Progress*

If students have completed the Work-in-Progress assignments on p. 641 and 667, suggest that they try to develop their Work-in-Progress ideas in a descriptive essay.

Prentice Hall **EssayScorer**

A writing prompt for this mode of writing can be found on the *Prentice Hall Essay Scorer* at **www.PHLitOnline.com**.

Writing Workshop

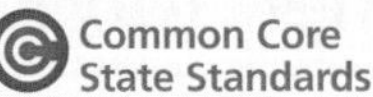

Common Core State Standards

Writing

2. Write informative/explanatory texts to examine and convey complex ideas, concepts, and information clearly and accurately through the effective selection, organization, and analysis of content.

2.a. Introduce a topic; organize complex ideas, concepts, and information to make important connections and distinctions.

2.d. Use precise language and domain-specific vocabulary to manage the complexity of the topic.

4. Produce clear and coherent writing in which the development, organization, and style are appropriate to task, purpose, and audience.

Language

5. Demonstrate understanding of figurative language, word relationships, and nuances in word meanings.

Write an Informative Text

Description: Descriptive Essay

Defining the Form Descriptive writing begins not in your imagination, but in your senses—in your ability to notice physical details. While valuable on its own, description also helps you share an experience, portray a person, and convey meaning and tone. Use descriptive elements in autobiographical writing, travel reports, and character sketches.

Assignment Write a description of a place that you enjoy or that is meaningful to you. Include these elements:

✓ *sensory details* that recreate sights, sounds, smells, tastes, and textures

✓ precise *word choice* that brings the subject into focus

✓ *figurative language*, such as metaphor, simile, and personification

✓ logical and consistent *organization*

✓ error-free grammar, especially your use of *prepositional phrases*

To preview the criteria on which your descriptive essay may be judged, see the rubric on page 691.

Writing Workshop: *Work in Progress*

Review the work you did on pages 641 and 667.

Prewriting/Planning Strategies

Keep a walking journal. Be alert to the sights, sounds, smells, tastes, and textures you encounter in your daily routine. Jot down ideas about the places you visit. Choose for your topic the location that presents the most possibilities for description.

Use trigger words. A single word or object can trigger a flood of ideas. For example, words like *friendship* or *fire* may remind you of people or places or evoke an emotion in you. Objects like a leaf or a blue ribbon may be equally suggestive. Working with a group, take turns calling out trigger words. As each person takes a turn, jot down whatever comes to mind. When the activity is finished, review your notes and choose a topic.

TEACH

Prewriting Strategies

1. Introduce the prewriting strategies.
2. Have students apply the strategies to choose a topic.

Six Traits Focus

✓	Ideas	✓	Word Choice
	Organization		Sentence Fluency
	Voice		Conventions

Teaching Resources

The following resources can be used to enrich or extend the instruction.

All *Unit 4 Resources*
Writing Workshop, pp. 118–119

All *Common Core Companion,* pp. 190–201; 213–214

All *Professional Development Guidebook*
Rubric for Self-Assessment: Descriptive Essay, pp. 220–221

All *Graphic Organizer Transparencies*
Rubric for Self-Assessment: Descriptive Essay, p. 127

All resources are available online at **www.PHLitOnline.com**.

SIX TRAITS WRITER'S TOOLBOX SIX TRAITS

Word Choice | Ideas | Conventions | Sentence Fluency | Voice | Organization

Perfecting Your Description

Word choice is the specific language a writer selects in order to create a strong impression. It has been said that you can travel the globe between the covers of a book. This is made possible by quality descriptions. Vivid detail has the ability to transport the reader to different places and times. You can affect your audience in the same way by following these tips.

Bringing the Scene to Life Descriptive writers attempt to bring a scene or subject to life by including details that appeal to as many senses as possible. Not only do the details need to be sensory, they also need to be specific. Precise and vivid description will allow you to achieve your purpose: helping your audience to imagine and experience what you are describing.

Choosing Vivid Words As you draft, you might use generic words to simply get your ideas down. However, you should review your essay, circling vague or dull word choices. Consider replacements that paint a clear and colorful picture of your subject. Also, consider adding descriptors to enhance your scene. You can use a thesaurus to help you.

PH WRITING COACH
Further instruction and practice are available in *Prentice Hall Writing Coach*.

Dull	Vivid
The air was *really* cold.	The air was *piercingly* cold.
The snow was *bright* white.	The snow was *blinding*.
The sun *came* out from behind a cloud.	The sun *peeked* out from behind a cloud.

Using Figurative Language Use similes and metaphors in your descriptions to capture your readers' interest.

A **simile** is a comparison of two unlike things using *like* or *as*.

During the storm, the wind tore through the tree branches like a power saw.

A **metaphor** compares two unlike things without using *like* or *as*.

Tree trunks were matchsticks as they snapped in the winds.

Being Precise Remember that providing a good description does not mean using a lot of words to describe one thing. Rather, it means choosing the exact words that express your perception of the subject.

Writing Workshop 687

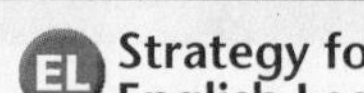

Instruction for Universal Access

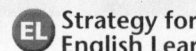

EL Strategy for English Learners

Similes and metaphors can be confusing for English learners. Point out that similes and metaphors are not meant to be taken literally. Create a list of commonly used similes for students and review their meanings. Use the following list as a starting point:

big as an elephant
blind as a bat
clear as a bell
happy as a lark
mad as a hatter
old as the hills
proud as a peacock

Strategy for Advanced Writers

Challenge students to modernize the following similes by linking each adjective to something more current. Students might consider references to modern-day technology.

smooth as silk
busy as a beaver
straight as an arrow
clean as a whistle
strong as an ox
stubborn as a mule

Perfecting Your Description

1. Introduce the writing skill, using the instruction on the student page.
2. Discuss the strategies for word choice and the examples of similes and metaphors.

Teaching the Writing Skill

1. Tell students that replacing vague, imprecise words with vivid, colorful words will help them to create more compelling descriptions in their essays. Provide an example by listing on the board the following synonyms for the word *leader: conductor, president, captain, director, ruler.* Have volunteers describe the pictures they have in their minds for each of the synonyms. Point out that carefully choosing words helps writers paint clear, colorful pictures for readers.
2. Ask students to rewrite the following sentences so that they are more descriptive.

   It was a rainy morning.

   Possible response: The morning brought hard, driving sheets of water that hurt your skin.

   The game was great.

   Possible response: Throughout the game, one sensational play followed another, culminating in an overtime shoot-out.
3. Tell students that similes and metaphors can help them create effective imagery in their descriptive writing. Point out that a simile compares two unlike things using the words *like* or *as,* while a metaphor compares two unlike things by stating that one thing is the other. Provide these additional examples of similes and metaphors:

   Simile: *My eyes were as wide as saucers.*

   Metaphor: *Suddenly, the room was a darkened theater.*

PH WRITING COACH Grade 9
Students will find additional support for descriptive essay writing in chapter 7.

Drafting Strategies

1. Introduce the drafting strategies.
2. Have students apply the strategies as they draft.

Teaching the Strategies

Help students build a word bank of spatial and time-order words, such as *next to, nearby* and *at the outset, afterward.*

Six Traits Focus

	Ideas	✓	Word Choice
✓	Organization		Sentence Fluency
	Voice		Conventions

Revising Strategies

1. Introduce the revision strategies, using the instruction on the student page.
2. Have students apply the strategies as they revise their drafts.

Teaching the Strategies

Show students how to strengthen an essay's main impression by adding and deleting details.

Think Aloud: Model Choosing Vivid Words

Model the strategy, using the following "think aloud":

Let's say that I'm describing my cat. I write, "Jack, my fat, fluffy cat, sleeps on my desk." But this doesn't really convey what Jack looks and feels like. So I'll try again: "Huge, shaggy Jack slumbers on my desk like an immense black-and-white paper weight." This puts a more vivid image into my readers' minds.

Six Traits Focus

	Ideas	✓	Word Choice
	Organization		Sentence Fluency
✓	Voice		Conventions

Drafting Strategies

Choose an effective organization. The following are two structures that work well with descriptive essays:

- **Spatial organization:** Describe your subject systematically from left to right, front to back, or top to bottom. Like a photographer, pan your "camera" over your subject, using transitional words and phrases like *above, below,* or *in the distance* that show spatial relationships.
- **Time-order organization:** Describe your subject as you first approach it and then as you move through or around it. In addition to words expressing spatial relationships, use words showing time-order relationships, such as *initially, meanwhile,* or *finally.*

Think about your audience. Consider your readers' knowledge of the place you are describing. If the place is unfamiliar, include more clarifying details that set context. If the place is familiar, draw your readers in by acknowledging shared experience.

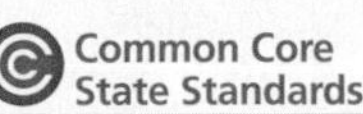
Common Core State Standards

Writing

2.a. Introduce a topic; organize complex ideas, concepts, and information to make important connections and distinctions.

2.d. Use precise language and domain-specific vocabulary to manage the complexity of the topic.

4. Produce clear and coherent writing in which the development, organization, and style are appropriate to task, purpose, and audience.

Language

1.b. Use various types of phrases and clauses to convey special meanings and add variety and interest to writing or presentations.

Revising Strategies

Strengthen your main impression. A memorable, descriptive essay conveys a single, strong impression of its subject. Review your work, adding details that support the main impression. Eliminate details that are irrelevant or distracting.

First Draft

The air was piercingly cold. The snow was blinding. The sun peeked out from behind a cloud. I sat perfectly still. I kept thinking about how hungry I was. Finally a deer walked by. It was just what I had been waiting for!

Revision

The air was piercingly cold. The snow was blinding. Then, the sun peeked out from behind a cloud. I sat perfectly still, waiting for signs of wildlife. Just then a magnificent buck meandered by in the distance. I was astounded by his strength and beauty.

Choose vivid words. Review your essay, circling vague or dull word choices. Consider replacements that paint a clear and colorful picture of your subject.

Dull: The air was *really* cold.
Vivid: The air was *shockingly* cold.

Applying Understanding by Design Principles

Clarifying Expected Outcomes: Using Rubrics

- Before students begin working on this assignment, have them preview the Rubric for Self-Assessment (p. 691) to learn what qualities their descriptive essays must have. A copy of this rubric appears in ***Graphic Organizer Transparencies,*** p.127.
- Review the criteria in the Rubric with the class. Before students use the Rubric to assess their writing, work with them to rate the Student Model (p. 690) using the Rubric.
- If you wish to assess students' essays with either a 4-point or a 6-point scoring rubric, see ***Professional Development Guidebook,*** pp. 220–221.

Revising to Vary Sentence Patterns

Overuse of the basic subject-verb pattern can make your writing stiff. To add interest, begin some sentences with prepositional phrases.

Identifying Prepositional Phrases A preposition is a word that relates a noun or pronoun to another word in the sentence. The combination of preposition and accompanying noun or pronoun—the object of the preposition—is called a prepositional phrase.

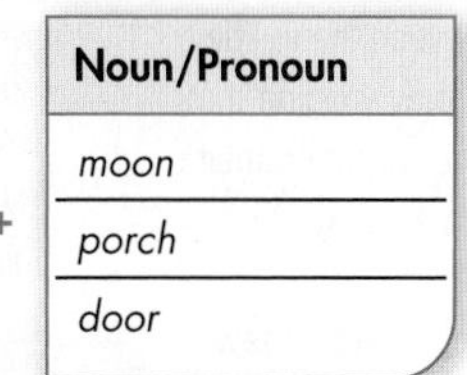

Preposition	+	Noun/Pronoun	=	Prepositional Phrase
over		*moon*		*over the moon*
under		*porch*		*under the porch*
behind		*door*		*behind the red door*

Many prepositions express spatial relationships. Appropriate use of such prepositions to begin sentences can clarify descriptive writing.

Varying Sentences In the following example, subjects are italicized, verbs are underlined, and prepositional phrases appear in parentheses.

Overuse of subject-verb pattern: The *cave* was hidden (behind the trees). The *ground* was smooth (in front of it). *I* pulled away dead branches. *I* saw large paw prints (on the cave's dirt floor).

Revision: The cave was hidden behind the trees. In front of it, the ground was smooth. I pulled away dead branches. On the cave's dirt floor, I saw large paw prints.

Follow these steps to vary your sentences in your writing.

1. Read your draft aloud, listening for places where you overuse the subject-verb sentence pattern.
2. Rewrite some sentences to begin with a prepositional phrase.
3. If an introductory prepositional phrase contains four or more words, set it off with a comma.

Grammar in Your Writing
Review the first and last paragraphs of your descriptive essay, looking for opportunities to vary a monotonous subject-verb sequence of sentences. Rewrite some sentences by beginning them with prepositional phrases.

PH WRITING COACH
Further instruction and practice are available in *Prentice Hall Writing Coach*.

Revising to Vary Sentence Patterns

1. Introduce the grammar skill, using the instruction on the student page.
2. Discuss the examples and the strategies for varying sentence patterns.
3. Have students follow the instruction under Grammar in Your Writing to correct errors in their drafts.

Teaching the Grammar Skill

1. Write the following sample paragraph on the board. Read the paragraph aloud for students, and ask them to comment on the subject-verb pattern. Is the writing interesting? Is the pattern overused?

   The house stood far back from the road. A single light shown from one high window. The light revealed a man working at a desk. My mysterious neighbor paused on the road outside. She stared upward from the shadows.

2. Ask students to work individually to revise the paragraph by moving some of the prepositional phrases to the beginning of the sentences to vary the pattern and to make the writing more engaging. Have volunteers read their revisions. Emphasize that there is more than one way to vary the sentence structures.

   Possible response: *The house stood far back from the road. From one high window, a single light shown. The light revealed a man working at a desk. On the road outside, my mysterious neighbor paused. She stared upward from the shadows.*

PH WRITING COACH Grade 9

Students will find practice with and guidance on sentence patterns in Chapter 16.

Strategies for Test Taking

Some standardized tests ask students to answer questions about sentence structure. Provide students with models to practice answering this type of question. Write the item below on the board. Ask a volunteer to select the correct response and to explain his or her reasoning.

Revise the sentence so that it begins with a prepositional phrase.

The saxophone is difficult to master for many young musicians.

A. The saxophone, for many young musicians, is difficult to master.
B. For many young musicians, the saxophone is difficult to master.
C. Many young musicians find it difficult to master the saxophone.
D. Mastering the saxophone is difficult for many young musicians.

Answer: B. *For many young musicians* is a prepositional phrase.

Student Model

Review the Student Model with the class, using the annotations to analyze the writer's use of the elements of a descriptive essay.

Teaching from the Student Model

1. Explain that the Student Model is a sample and that their own essays may be longer.
2. Ask students to identify the physical senses Zach appeals to in his first three sentences.

   Answer: Zach appeals to touch (*smooth stones, freezing winter air*), hearing (*crunch*), and sight (*lights twinkle*).

   Ask: What simile does Zach use in the second paragraph to describe the temperature in the room?

   Answer: The combination of heat lamps and outdoor air is "like a cold front passing through on a hot September day."
3. Review the final sentence with students. **Ask** them if Zach has provided sufficient details in this essay to support this conclusion.

   Possible response: Students may agree that Zach's abundance of detail enables the reader to fully understand his happiness at the end.
4. Tell students that they should include all elements of a scene to give the reader a full picture of the environment.
5. Tell students that readers can draw inspiration from powerful, meaningful statements that evolve from descriptions.

Connecting to Real-Life Writing

Tell students that they may be asked to describe scientific observations in the form of reports. Point out that scientists must describe what they see, hear, taste, touch, and smell when conducting experiments. Although figurative language may not be appropriate in a scientific setting, language that appeals to the five senses is essential. A scientist uses the descriptions gathered during a process or experiment to draw conclusions and form hypotheses.

Student Model: Zachary DeBoer, Raleigh, NC

Common Core State Standards

Language
2.c. Spell correctly.

Ziggy's Coffeehouse

As I enter the gates of the fenced-in courtyard of the humble coffeehouse, smooth stones crunch beneath my shoes and strings of Christmas lights twinkle like the stars overhead. A stranger takes my five-dollar bill and makes a mark on my hand. The freezing winter air is perfectly still while I walk up the ramp and step into the mildly dilapidated structure. Inside I am met by a sound check of guitars vibrating through speakers. I am surrounded by wood; wood floors, wood ceiling, wood walls; acoustic trampolines that make the music bounce around like mad. The guys and girls in the band tonight are good friends of mine. As they run through their set list, there is a strong sense of camaraderie between them. They dream of record deals and radio play and 25-city tours. Perhaps they imagine that their venue is not a small café, but a mammoth, sold-out arena. They put on their best performance, playing just for us and singing: "We should be dancing. We need be dancing."

The place smells like aged wood and fresh coffee, but my lack of even a few dollar bills means I'll be drinking water tonight. There are three platforms in the cafe; the lowest has a set of double doors on the stage right side that have been swung open. The heat lamps radiate warmth as the frigid air rushes in from the doors, like a cold front passing through on a hot September day. On the second tier, those who prefer to act like adults sip their skinny decaf lattes. They seem mildly interested in the music, but most are there for the lack of something better to do. Are they swaying because of the music or because they have put a bit too much sugar in their coffees? Outside in the parking lot, kids talk cars and sports and who knows what else? I'm so captivated by the band that my ears can't tell. They laugh intermittently, oblivious to the music playing inside.

On the lowest level, immediately in front of the stage, the real fans are found. We push the tables back and dance around like no one is watching us and we sing along with the songs we know at the top of our lungs. This is where we artists are, the free spirits, the *real* cool kids. I don't know most of them but I feel a connection with all of them. We are friends now, brothers and sisters, united by the music. We jump up and down, careful not to bump into each other or the tables; we are captivated by the music but respectful of those around us. We have been liberated from the bonds of everyday life. We are transported to a state of bliss. We are not escaping reality; instead, we are experiencing true reality. As the soft lights from the stage shine onto the mellow brown of the all-wood venue, I realize: On this night, at this moment, there is nowhere else I'd rather be than this place.

Zachary uses sensory details to make this introduction vivid and interesting.

Zachary does not limit himself to describing the setting; he imagines the thoughts and feelings of the people, as well.

Zachary uses details related to all the senses, including smell and taste.

Zachary pays attention to all elements of the scene.

Zachary uses description to make a meaningful point.

Differentiated Instruction for Universal Access

Strategy for Less Proficient Readers
Work as a class to identify the sensory appeals of "Ziggy's Coffeehouse." Have students create five-column charts headed *Sight, Touch, Hearing, Taste,* and *Smell.* Have students work individually on the first paragraph, then discuss their findings as a class. After students complete their charts, ask them to describe the overall effect of Zach's sensory language.

Editing and Proofreading

Check your draft for errors in spelling, grammar, and punctuation.

Focus on transitions. Make sure that you use transition words accurately and punctuate them correctly. If you begin a sentence with a transitional word or phrase, set it off with a comma.

Focus on spelling. When adding suffixes to words ending in silent *e*, drop the *e* when the suffix begins with a vowel, as in *amaze/amazing*. Keep the *e* when the suffix begins with a consonant, as in *amaze/amazement*.

Spiral Review

Prepositional Phrases Earlier in this unit you learned about **prepositions** (p. 640) and **prepositional phrases** (p. 666). Review your essay to be sure you have used prepositions and prepositional phrases correctly and effectively.

Publishing and Presenting

Consider one of the following ways to share your writing.

Prepare an oral presentation. Present your descriptive essay, making sure to establish your point of view on the subject matter as well as your relationship to the topic. Include effective and factual descriptions of appearance, concrete images, shifting perspectives, and sensory details.

Create a visitor's guide. With classmates, assemble several essays that describe places of interest in your community and create a guidebook. If possible, provide copies of the guidebook to your local library, town hall, or chamber of commerce for distribution to the public.

Reflecting on Your Writing

Writer's Journal Jot down your answer to this question:
How did describing your subject help you to understand it?

Rubric for Self-Assessment

Find evidence in your writing to address each category. Then, use the rating scale to grade your work.

Criteria	Rating Scale
Focus: How clearly do you describe your subject?	*not very* 1 2 3 4 5 *very*
Organization: How logical and consistent is your organization?	1 2 3 4 5
Support/Elaboration: How well do you use a variety of sensory details?	1 2 3 4 5
Style: How effective is your use of figurative language?	1 2 3 4 5
Conventions: How correct is your grammar, especially your use of prepositional phrases?	1 2 3 4 5
Word Choice: How precise is your word choice?	1 2 3 4 5

Editing and Proofreading

1. Introduce the editing and proofreading focus, using the instruction on the student page.
2. Have students edit and proofread their narratives, correcting grammar, spelling, punctuation, and word choice. Make sure they check for errors of the type noted in the lesson focus and the Spiral Review.

Teaching the Editing Focus

Remind students that transitional words and phrases show connections between ideas. Often transitions are set off with commas. Review the following example:

It rained during their visit to the Grand Canyon; consequently, the visit was canceled.

Six Traits Focus

	Ideas		Word Choice
	Organization		Sentence Fluency
	Voice	✓	Conventions

ASSESS

Publishing and Presenting

1. Explain how visual aids can improve an oral presentation. Tell students that many people need to see and/or touch something to help them remember information.
2. Provide copies of the visitor's guide to local libraries or the city chamber of commerce.

Reflecting on Your Writing

Ask whether students appealed to all five senses in their essays. Have them consider which senses were the easiest and most difficult to address.

Strategies for Using Technology in Writing

Whether students are giving oral presentations or preparing visitor's guides, computer programs and Internet resources provide ways to create multimedia products. The Internet provides access to photographic images that may complement oral presentations or visitor's guides. Students preparing oral presentations may also locate free music selections to incorporate into their presentations. Desktop publishing software can help students design and organize their visitor's guides.

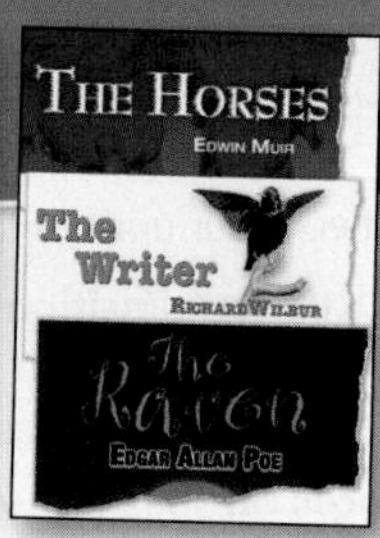

✓ Poetry Collection 5 • ✓✓ Poetry Collection 6

Lesson Pacing Guide

DAY 1 Preteach

- Administer the Reading and Vocabulary Warm-ups (*Unit 4 Resources*, pp. 127–130 or 145–148) as necessary.
- Introduce the Reading Skill: Paraphrase.
- Introduce the Literary Analysis concept: Narrative Poetry.
- Distribute copies of the appropriate graphic organizer for the Reading Skill (*Graphic Organizer Transparencies*, pp. 128–130).
- Distribute copies of the appropriate graphic organizer for Literary Analysis (*Graphic Organizer Transparencies*, pp. 131–133).
- Teach the selection vocabulary.
- Introduce the Word Study skill.

DAYS 2–3 Preteach/Teach

- Build background with the Background feature.
- Develop thematic vocabulary and thematic thinking with Writing About the Big Question.
- Prepare students to read with the Activating Prior Knowledge activities (TE).
- Informally monitor comprehension while students read.
- Use the Reading Check questions to confirm comprehension.
- Develop students' ability to evaluate persuasion, using the Reading Skill questions.
- Develop students' understanding of persuasive essays, using the Literacy Analysis questions.
- Reinforce vocabulary with the Vocabulary notes.
- Reinforce unit focus standards using the Spiral Review prompts.

DAY 4 Assess

- Assess students' comprehension and mastery of the skills by having them answer the Critical Thinking, Reading Skill, and Literary Analysis questions.
- Have students complete the Vocabulary Practice activities.
- Have students complete the Word Study activities.

DAY 5 Extend/Assess

- Have students complete the Conventions lesson.
- Have students complete the Writing activity and write a description of the scene. (You may assign as homework.)
- Extend learning by having students complete the Speaking and Listening activity, dialogue. As an alternative, assign them "Choosing the News" or "Behind the Screams" in *Reality Central*.
- Administer Selection Test A or B (*Unit 4 Resources*, pp. 139–144 or 160–165).

Common Core State Standards

Reading Literature 4. Determine the meaning of words and phrases as they are used in the text, including figurative and connotative meanings; analyze the cumulative impact of several word choices on meaning and tone (e.g., how the language evokes a sense of time and place; how it sets a formal or informal tone).
5. Analyze how an author's choices concerning how to structure a text, order events within it, and manipulate time create such effects as mystery, tension, or surprise.

Writing 4. Produce clear and coherent writing in which the development, organization, and style are appropriate to task, purpose, and audience.

Speaking and Listening 1.a. Come to discussions prepared, having read and researched material under study; explicitly draw on that preparation to stimulate a thoughtful, well-reasoned exchange of ideas.
1.b. Work with peers to set rules for collegial discussions and decision-making, clear goals and deadlines, and individual roles as needed.
1.c. Propel conversations by posing and responding to questions that relate the current discussion to broader themes or larger ideas; actively incorporate others into the discussion; and clarify, verify, or challenge ideas and conclusions.

Language 1.b. Use various types of phrases and clauses to convey specific meanings and add variety and interest to writing or presentations.

Additional Standards Practice
***Common Core Companion*, pp. 35–42**

Daily Block Scheduling
Each day in this Lesson Pacing Guide represents a 40–50 minute period. Teachers using block scheduling may combine days to revise pacing. In addition, teachers may differentiate and support core instruction by integrating components for extended and intensive support as students require. See the Guide to Selected Leveled Resources (facing page).

Guide to Selected Leveled Resources

RTI Tier 1 (students performing on level)			✓ More Accessible Poetry Collection 5	✓✓ More Complex Poetry Collection 6
Warm Up	Whole class instruction; Group work	**Practice, model,** and **monitor** fluency, working **with the whole class** or **in groups.**	**Vocabulary** and **Reading Warm-ups B,** ***Unit 4 Resources,*** pp. 127–128, 130	**Vocabulary** and **Reading Warm-ups B,** ***Unit 4 Resources,*** pp. 145–146, 148
Comprehension/Skills	Whole class instruction; Independent work	**Support** and **monitor** comprehension and skills development, having students complete the activities, graphic organizers, and interactive prompts **independently** or **as a class.**	• ***Reader's Notebook,*** adapted instruction and full selection EL ***Reader's Notebook: English Learner's Version,*** adapted instruction and full selection • **Reading Skill Graphic Organizer B,** ***Graphic Organizer Transparencies,*** p. 130 • **Literary Analysis Graphic Organizer B,** ***Graphic Organizer Transparencies,*** p. 133	• ***Reader's Notebook,*** adapted instruction and summary EL ***Reader's Notebook: English Learner's Version,*** adapted instruction and summary • **Reading Skill Graphic Organizer B,** ***Graphic Organizer Transparencies,*** p. 130 • **Literary Analysis Graphic Organizer B,** ***Graphic Organizer Transparencies,*** p. 133
Monitor Progress	Assessment	**Monitor** student progress with the differentiated curriculum-based assessment in the *Unit Resources.*	• **Selection Test B,** ***Unit 4 Resources,*** pp. 142–144 • **Open-Book Test,** ***Unit 4 Resources,*** pp. 136–138	• **Selection Test B,** ***Unit 4 Resources,*** pp. 163–165 • **Open-Book Test,** ***Unit 4 Resources,*** pp. 157–159

RTI Tier 2 (students requiring intervention)			✓ More Accessible Poetry Collection 5	✓✓ More Complex Poetry Collection 6
Warm Up	Group work; One-on-one teaching	**Practice, model,** and **monitor** fluency **in groups** or **with individuals.**	• **Vocabulary and Reading Warm-ups A,** ***Unit 4 Resources,*** pp. 127–130 • ***Reality Central,*** "Choosing the News" • ***Hear It!*** **Audio CD (adapted text)**	• **Vocabulary and Reading Warm-ups A,** ***Unit 4 Resources,*** pp. 145–148 • ***Reality Central,*** "Behind the Screams" • ***Hear It!*** **Audio CD**
Comprehension/Skills	Group work; One-on-one teaching	• **Support** and **monitor** comprehension and skills development, working **in small groups** or **with individuals.** • **Pair** students with more advanced peers and have them complete the writing activity in the *Real-World Writing Journal.* • As students complete the selection in the appropriate version of the *Reader's Notebook,* **monitor** comprehension frequently with group questions and individual instruction. • **Model** strategies while guiding students in completing the activities and prompts in the *Reader's Notebook,* as well as the graphic organizers. • **Practice** skills and **monitor** mastery with the *Reading Kit* worksheets.	• ***Real-World Writing Journal Lesson 5,*** pp. 120–123 • ***Reader's Notebook: Adapted Version,*** adapted instruction and full selection EL ***Reader's Notebook: English Learner's Version,*** adapted instruction and full selection • **Reading Skill Graphic Organizer A,** ***Graphic Organizer Transparencies,*** p. 128 • **Literary Analysis Graphic Organizer A,** ***Graphic Organizer Transparencies,*** p. 131 • ***Reading Kit,*** Practice worksheets, pp. 176, 182, 186, 188, 196	• ***Real-World Writing Journal Lesson 6,*** pp. 124–127 • ***Reader's Notebook: Adapted Version,*** adapted instruction and summary EL ***Reader's Notebook: English Learner's Version,*** adapted instruction and summary • **Reading Skill Graphic Organizer A,** ***Graphic Organizer Transparencies,*** p. 129 • **Literary Analysis Graphic Organizer A,** ***Graphic Organizer Transparencies,*** p. 132 • ***Reading Kit,*** Practice worksheets, pp. 176, 182, 186, 188, 196
Monitor Progress	Assessment	**Monitor** student progress with the differentiated curriculum-based assessment in the *Unit Resources* and in the *Reading Kit.*	• **Selection Test A,** ***Unit 4 Resources,*** pp. 139–141 • ***Reading Kit,*** Assess worksheets, pp. 177, 183, 187, 189, 197	• **Selection Test A,** ***Unit 4 Resources,*** pp. 160–162 • **Reading Kit,** Assess worksheets, pp. 177, 183, 187, 189, 197

TIER 3 Tier 3 intervention may require consultation with the student's special-education or dyslexia specialist. For additional support, see the Tier 2 activities and resources listed above.

One-on-one teaching **Group work** **Whole class instruction** **Independent work** **A Assessment**

For a complete guide to selection support, including support for Advanced students, see the Overview of Resources in the frontmatter.

Visual Guide to Featured Selection Resources

✓Poetry Collection 5
✓✓Poetry Collection 6

RESOURCES FOR:

- L1 Special-Needs Students
- L2 Below-Level Students (Tier 2)
- L3 On-Level Students (Tier 1)
- L4 Advanced Students (Tier 1)
- EL English Learners
- All All Students

Vocabulary/Fluency/Prior Knowledge

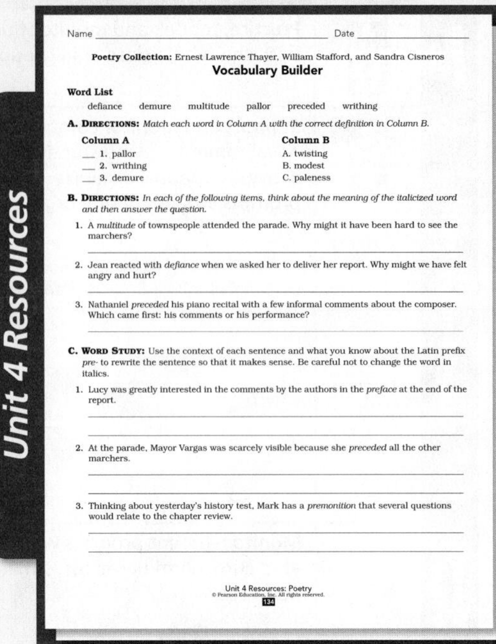

Name ______________________ Date __________

Poetry Collection: Ernest Lawrence Thayer, William Stafford, and Sandra Cisneros

Vocabulary Builder

Word List

defiance demure multitude pallor preceded writhing

A. Directions: *Match each word in Column A with the correct definition in Column B.*

Column A	Column B
___ 1. pallor	A. twisting
___ 2. writhing	B. modest
___ 3. demure	C. paleness

B. Directions: *In each of the following items, think about the meaning of the italicized word and then answer the question.*

1. A *multitude* of townspeople attended the parade. Why might it have been hard to see the marchers?
2. Jean reacted with *defiance* when we asked her to deliver her report. Why might we have felt angry and hurt?
3. Nathaniel *preceded* his piano recital with a few informal comments about the composer. Which came first: his comments or his performance?

C. Word Study: Use the context of each sentence and what you know about the Latin prefix *pre-* to rewrite the sentence so that it makes sense. Be careful not to change the word in italics.

1. Lucy was greatly interested in the comments by the authors in the *preface* at the end of the report.
2. At the parade, Mayor Vargas was scarcely visible because she *preceded* all the other marchers.
3. Thinking about yesterday's history test, Mark has a *premonition* that several questions would relate to the chapter review.

Unit 4 Resources: Poetry
© Pearson Education, Inc. All rights reserved.
134

All **Vocabulary Builder,** pp. 134, 152

Also available for these selections:

EL L1 L2 **Vocabulary Warm-ups A and B,** pp. 127–128, 145–146

EL L1 L2 **Reading Warm-ups A and B,** pp. 129–130, 147–148

All **Writing About the Big Questions,** pp. 131, 149

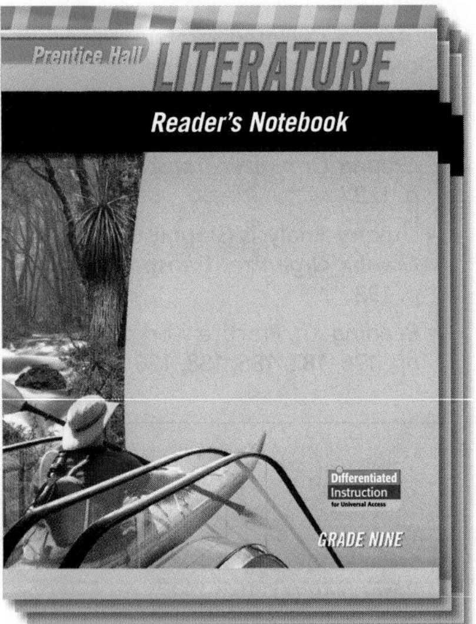

Reader's Notebooks

Pre- and postreading pages for both selections, as well as "Poetry Collection 5," appear in an interactive format in the *Reader's Notebooks.* Each *Notebook* is differentiated for a different group of learners. The selections in the Adapted and English Learner's versions are abridged.

- L2 L3 ***Reader's Notebook***
- L1 ***Reader's Notebook: Adapted Version***
- EL ***Reader's Notebook: English Learner's Version***
- EL ***Reader's Notebook: Spanish Version***

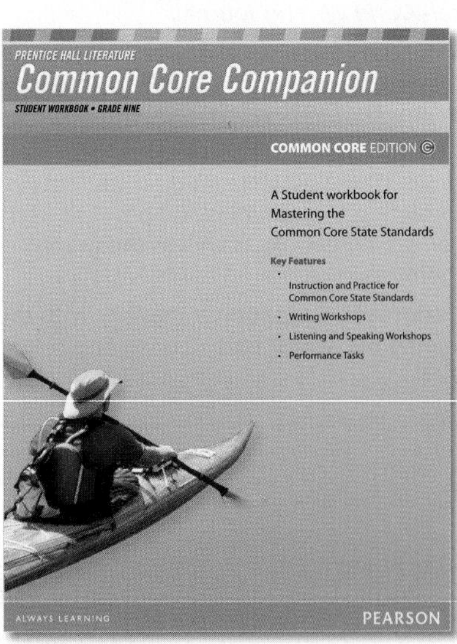

Common Core Companion

Additional instruction and practice for each Common Core State Standard

Selection Support

Graphic Organizer Transparencies

"The Horses" by Edwin Muir
"The Writer" by Richard Wilbur
"The Raven" by Edgar Allan Poe

After You Read A: Literary Analysis—Narrative Poetry

Title	Setting	Characters	Plot
"The Horses"	after a nuclear war	speaker and fellow survivors	A strange herd of horses arrive, seeming to offer the farmers hope and consolation.
"The Writer"			
"The Raven"			

Graphic Organizer Transparencies

132

EL L1 L2 **Literary Analysis: Graphic Organizer A,** pp. 131–132 (partially filled in)

Also available for these selections:

EL L1 L2 **Reading: Graphic Organizer A,** pp. 128–129 (partially filled in)

EL L3 **Reading: Graphic Organizer B,** p. 130

EL L3 **Literary Analysis: Graphic Organizer B,** p. 133

Skills Development/Extension

Unit 4 Resources

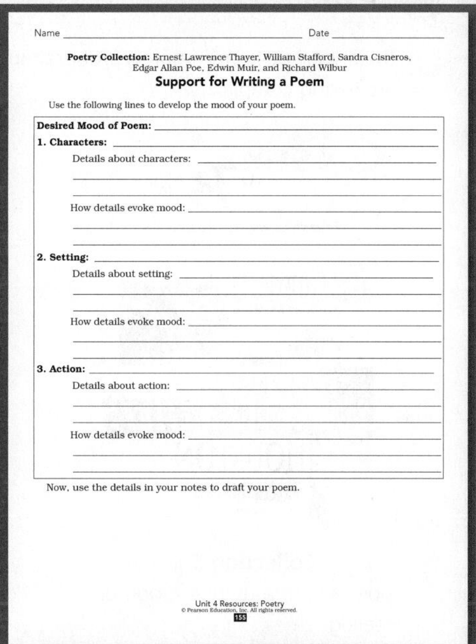

Name ______________________ Date ______________

Poetry Collection: Ernest Lawrence Thayer, William Stafford, Sandra Cisneros, Edgar Allan Poe, Edwin Muir, and Richard Wilbur

Support for Writing a Poem

Use the following lines to develop the mood of your poem.

Desired Mood of Poem: ______________________

1. Characters: ______________________

Details about characters: ______________________

How details evoke mood: ______________________

2. Setting: ______________________

Details about setting: ______________________

How details evoke mood: ______________________

3. Action: ______________________

Details about action: ______________________

How details evoke mood: ______________________

Now, use the details in your notes to draft your poem.

Unit 4 Resources: Poetry

155

EL L3 L4 **Support for Writing,** p. 155

Also available for these selections:

All **Literary Analysis: Narrative Poetry,** pp. 132, 150

All **Reading: Paraphrase,** pp. 133, 151

L4 **Enrichment,** pp. 135, 153

EL L3 L4 **Grammar,** p. 154

L3 L4 **Support for Extend Your Learning,** p. 156

Assessment

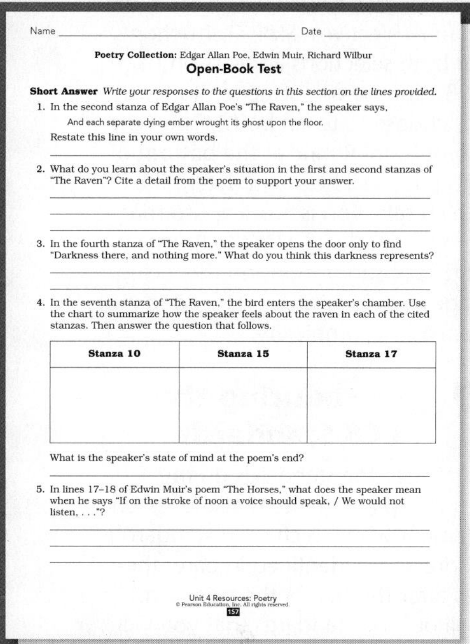

Name ______________________ Date ______________

Poetry Collection: Edgar Allan Poe, Edwin Muir, Richard Wilbur

Open-Book Test

Short Answer *Write your responses to the questions in this section on the lines provided.*

1. In the second stanza of Edgar Allan Poe's "The Raven," the speaker says,

   And each separate dying ember wrought its ghost upon the floor.

   Restate this line in your own words.

2. What do you learn about the speaker's situation in the first and second stanzas of "The Raven"? Cite a detail from the poem to support your answer.

3. In the fourth stanza of "The Raven," the speaker opens the door only to find "Darkness there, and nothing more." What do you think this darkness represents?

4. In the seventh stanza of "The Raven," the bird enters the speaker's chamber. Use the chart to summarize how the speaker feels about the raven in each of the cited stanzas. Then answer the question that follows.

Stanza 10	Stanza 15	Stanza 17

   What is the speaker's state of mind at the poem's end?

5. In lines 17–18 of Edwin Muir's poem "The Horses," what does the speaker mean when he says "If on the stroke of noon a voice should speak, / We would not listen, . . ."?

Unit 4 Resources: Poetry

157

L3 L4 **Open-Book Test,** pp. 136–138, 157–159

Also available for these selections:

EL L1 L2 **Selection Test A,** pp. 139–141, 160–162

EL L3 L4 **Selection Test B,** pp. 142–144, 163–165

PHLit Online!
www.PHLitOnline.com

- complete narrated selection text
- a thematically related video with writing prompt
- an interactive graphic organizer
- highlighting feature
- access to all student print resources, adapted to individual student needs
- Spanish and English summaries
- adapted selection translations in Spanish

Online Resources: All print materials are also available online.

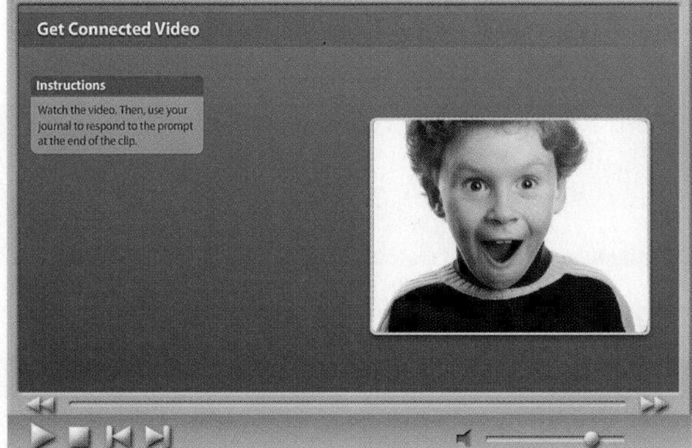

Get Connected! (thematic video with writing prompt)

Also available:

Background Video

All videos are available in Spanish.

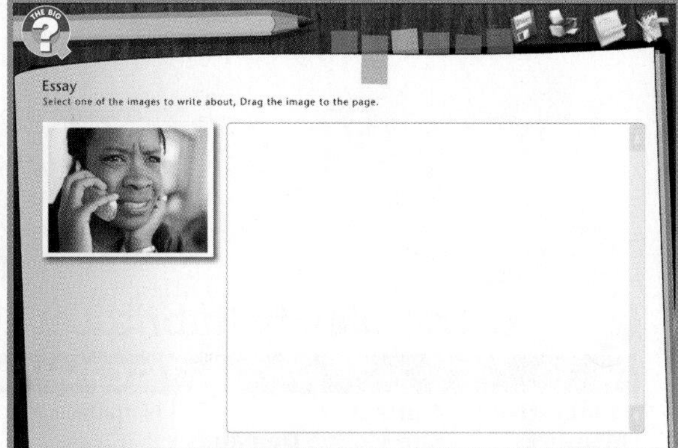

Writer's Journal (with graphics feature)

Also available:

Vocabulary Central (tools, activities, and songs for studying vocabulary)

DIFFERENTIATE/PRETEACH

❶ Leveled Texts

You may use either Poetry Collection 5 or Poetry Collection 6 to meet the lesson objectives. Skills instruction for both selections appears on page 693. Choose one selection to teach (or choose to teach both). The Text Complexity Rubric at the bottom of this page will help you determine which selection is more appropriate for your students. Use the Reader and Task Suggestions on the facing page to help all students read text of increasing complexity.

❷ Introducing the CCS Standards

Introduce the standards on the student page. (Note that the lesson element with which each standard is addressed is identified in parentheses after the text of the standard.) Call out the standards that you will cover with the selections, explaining to students what each requires and how they will address it as they work through the selection you have chosen. Standards labeled "Spiral Review" are introduced in the Literary Analysis Workshop for this unit.

Before You Read

Poetry Collection 5 • Poetry Collection 6

❶ Leveled Texts

Build your skills and improve your comprehension of poetry with texts of increasing complexity.

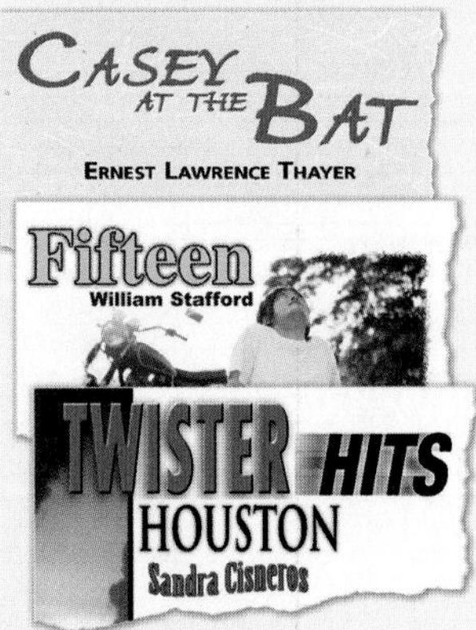

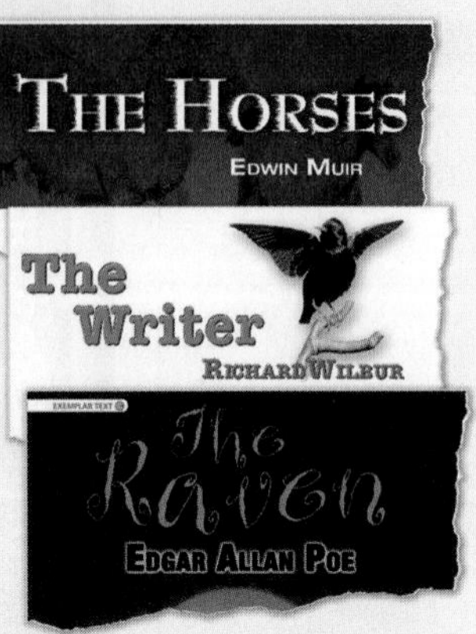

Poetry Collection 5 includes poems with a unique mood or feeling.

Poetry Collection 6 includes poems with a thought-provoking setting.

❷ Common Core State Standards

Meet these standards with either **Poetry Collection 5** (p. 696) or **Poetry Collection 6** (p. 706).

Reading Literature

4. Determine the meaning of words and phrases as they are used in the text, including figurative and connotative meanings; analyze the cumulative impact of specific word choices on meaning and tone. *(Literary Analysis: Spiral Review)*

5. Analyze how an author's choices concerning how to structure a text, order events within it, and manipulate time create such effects as mystery, tension, or surprise. *(Literary Analysis: Narrative Poetry)*

Writing

4. Produce clear and coherent writing in which the development, organization, and style are appropriate to task, purpose, and audience. *(Writing: Description of a Scene)*

Speaking and Listening

1.a. Come to discussions prepared, having read and researched material under study; explicitly draw on that preparation to stimulate a thoughtful, well-reasoned exchange of ideas. **1.b.** Work with peers to set rules for collegial discussions and decision-making, clear goals and deadlines, and individual roles as needed. **1.c.** Propel conversations by posing and responding to questions that relate the current discussion to broader themes or larger ideas; actively incorporate others into the discussion; and clarify, verify, or challenge ideas and conclusions. *(Speaking and Listening: Role-Play a Dialogue)*

Language

1.b. Use various types of phrases and clauses to convey specific meanings and add variety and interest to writing or presentations. *(Conventions: Appositive Phrases)*

Text Complexity Rubric: Leveled Texts

Text complexity is determined by both qualitative and quantitative measures. For this reason, the quantitative measure of a more complex selection may be lower than that of a more accessible selection.

		✓ Collection 5	✓✓ Collection 6
Qualitative Measures	**Context/ Knowledge Demands**	Narrative collection: baseball, motorcycles, twisters 1 2 ③ 4 5	Narrative collection: horses, writers, ravens; poems have distinct atmosphere 1 2 3 ④ 5
	Structure/Language and Clarity	On-level vocabulary; simple sentence structure 1 ② 3 4 5	Challenging vocabulary; difficult sentence structure 1 2 3 ④ 5
	Levels of Meaning/ Purpose	Accessible concept (familiar experiences) 1 2 ③ 4 5	Challenging concept (poems requiring interpretation) 1 2 3 ④ 5
Quantitative Measures	**Text Length**	Word Count: 578; 162;142	Word Count: 432; 248; 1081
	Lexile	NP	NP
Overall Complexity		✓ **More accessible**	✓✓ **More complex**

❸ Literary Analysis: Narrative Poetry

Narrative poetry tells a story and includes the same literary elements as narrative prose: a plot, or sequence of events; specific settings; and people or characters who participate in the action.

Like short stories, narrative poems convey a **mood,** or **atmosphere**—an overall feeling created by the setting, plot, specific word choices, and images. For example, a fast-paced plot may create an exciting mood. A mysterious, recurring image may create a suspenseful mood.

The choice of a speaker, or narrator, affects the meaning, tone, and mood of the poem. The speaker's point of view and personality affects how the reader responds to the poem.

PHLit Online!
www.PHLitOnline.com

Hear It!
- Selection summary audio
- Selection audio

See It!
- Get Connected video
- Background video
- More about the author
- Vocabulary flashcards

Do It!
- Interactive journals
- Interactive graphic organizers
- Self-test
- Internet activity
- Grammar tutorial
- Interactive vocabulary games

❹ Reading Skill: Paraphrase

Paraphrasing is restating in your own words what someone else has written or said. A paraphrase retains the meaning but is simpler. Paraphrasing is especially useful in comprehending poems that contain **figurative language—**words that are used imaginatively rather than literally. To paraphrase a narrative poem, picture the action.

- Based on details in the poem, form a mental image of the setting, the characters, and the characters' actions.
- To be sure that your mental picture is accurate, continue to pay attention to the poet's description of the scene.
- Then, describe your mental image of the scene.

❺ Using the Strategy: Paraphrase Chart

Use a **paraphrase chart** like the one shown to record your paraphrases.

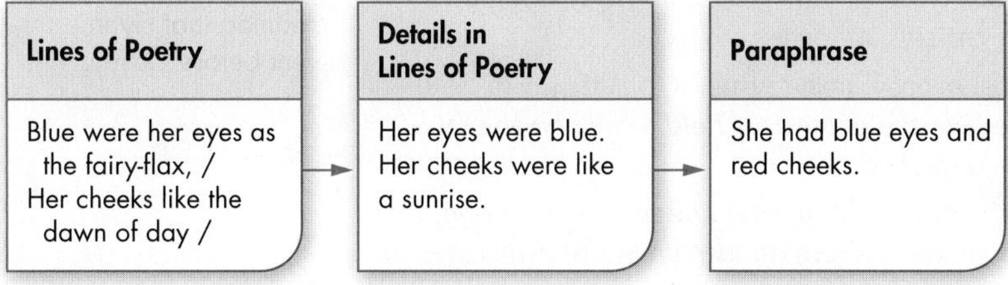

Lines of Poetry	Details in Lines of Poetry	Paraphrase
Blue were her eyes as the fairy-flax, / Her cheeks like the dawn of day /	Her eyes were blue. Her cheeks were like a sunrise.	She had blue eyes and red cheeks.

PRETEACH

❸ Literary Analysis

Narrative Poetry

1. Introduce the skill, using instruction on the student page.
2. Tell students that they will practice analyzing narrative poetry as they read.

Think Aloud: Model the Skill

Model the skill of analyzing narrative poetry. Say to students:

> While reading a narrative poem, I look for the same elements that I'd find in a narrative story.
>
> Consider the narrative poem "Paul Revere's Ride" by Henry Wadsworth Longfellow. The setting of the poem is midnight on April 18, 1775. The main character is Paul Revere. Here is the plot: Paul Revere rides his horse through towns near Boston and warns people that the British are coming. Longfellow's words create a mood of excitement, drama, and danger. This strong sense of atmosphere is essential to narrative poetry.

❹ Reading Skill

Paraphrase

1. Introduce the skill, using instruction on the student page.
2. Tell students that they will practice paraphrasing poetry as they read.

❺ Using the Strategy

Give students a copy of either **Reading Skill Graphic Organizer A** or **B** (*Graphic Organizer Transparencies,* pp. 128–130) to record details of paraphrasing as they read. Use the examples in **Reading Skill Graphic Organizer A,** which is partially filled in, to model the process of completing the organizer.

Text Complexity: Reader and Task Suggestions

✓ Collection 5		✓✓ Collection 6	
Preparing to Read the Text	**Leveled Tasks**	**Preparing to Read the Text**	**Leveled Tasks**
• Using the Background notes on TE p. 695, discuss the poets and their poems. • Discuss how narrative poems can make common experiences vivid and memorable. • Guide students to use Multidraft Reading strategies (TE p. 695).	*Levels of Meaning* If students will have difficulty with meaning, have them first read each poem and tell what happens. Then, have them reread to identify what is not expected. *Analyzing* If students will not have difficulty with meaning, have them read and take notes about how the poet makes everyday events vivid and memorable while evoking a personal response from readers.	• Using the Background notes on TE p. 705, discuss the poets. • Discuss narrative poems and how their stories can carry deeper levels of meaning. • Guide students to use Multidraft Reading strategies (TE p. 705).	*Knowledge Demands* If students will have difficulty with atmosphere, have them first read each poem, noting the events as they happen. Then, have them reread the poems and tell how the poem makes them feel. *Synthesizing* If students will not have difficulty with atmosphere, have them read each poem and take notes about how its figurative language suggests a deeper meaning.

PREACH

❶ Writing About the Big Question

1. Review the assignment with the class.
2. **Ask** students to remember a time when they were in a large audience or crowd. How does an audience or a crowd communicate their approval or disapproval at an event?
3. Have students complete the sentence starter. Review responses as a class. (**Possible response:** When a crowd communicates its support or disapproval, an athlete might <u>react</u> by performing better or worse.)
4. Remind students that their answers will help them think about the Big Question, "How does communication change us?"

While You Read

Tell students that as they read they should consider whether the crowd is a positive or negative influence on Casey.

❷ Vocabulary

1. Have students preview the selection vocabulary.
2. For each word, have students say the word aloud.
3. Then, use the word in a sentence that defines the word.
4. Finally, repeat your definitional sentence or a similar sentence with the word missing and have the class "fill in the blank" chorally. Here are some examples:

   <u>Pallor</u> means paleness of the face. When Monty came out of the hospital his skin lacked all color and had a strange [students say "pallor"].

   <u>Writhing</u> means to twist or turn in pain. When I fell, I lay on the ground, turning in pain, or [students say "writhing"].

❸ Word Study

1. Introduce the skill, using the instruction in the box.
2. **Ask** students for a word beginning with *pre-* that means "to view or show in advance." (**Answer:** *preview*)

Making Connections
Poetry Collection 5

Casey at the Bat • Fifteen • Twister Hits Houston

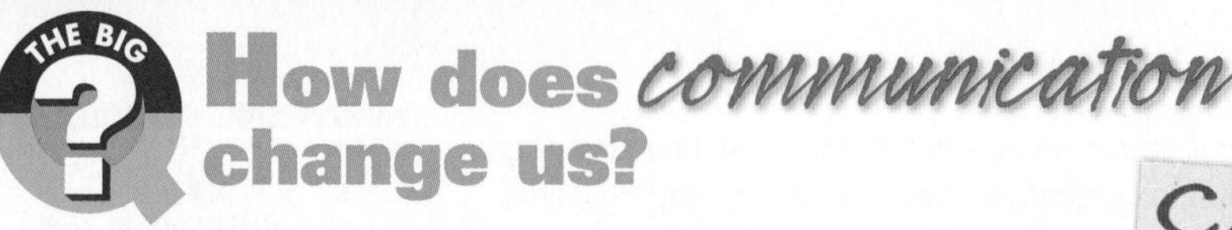

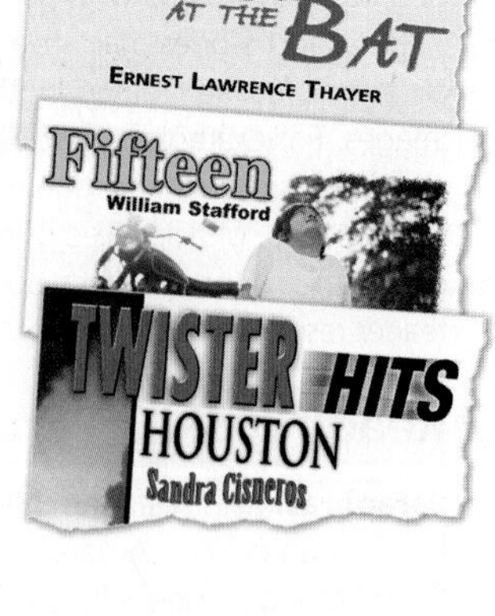

❶ Writing About the Big Question

In "Casey at the Bat," the fans of a baseball team voice their enthusiastic support for their star player. Use this sentence starter to develop your ideas about the Big Question.

When a crowd communicates its support or disapproval, an athlete might **react** by ______________.

While You Read Think about what effect the crowd's cheering has on Casey and his performance in "Casey at the Bat."

❷ Vocabulary

Read each word and its definition. Decide whether you know the word well, know it a little bit, or do not know it at all. After you read, see how your knowledge of each word has increased.

- **pallor** (pal′ ər) *n.* unnatural paleness (p. 697) ***His <u>pallor</u> made us realize just how ill he was.*** *pale adj. pallid adj.*
- **preceded** (prē cēd′ əd) *v.* came before in time, place, order, rank, or importance (p. 697) ***The police car <u>preceded</u> the floats in the annual parade.*** *precede v. preceding adj. precedence n.*
- **multitude** (mul′ tə to͞od) *n.* a large number of persons or things, especially when gathered together or considered as a unit (p. 697) ***I like to read books that have a <u>multitude</u> of characters.*** *multitudinous adj.*
- **writhing** (rīth′ iŋ) *adj.* twisting; turning (p. 698) ***He struggled to hold the <u>writhing</u> cat still.*** *writhe v.*
- **defiance** (dē fī′ əns) *n.* open, bold resistance to authority (p. 698) ***In <u>defiance</u> of the law, the protestors held a rally on the steps of city hall.*** *defy v. defiant adj.*
- **demure** (di myo͝or′) *adj.* modest (p. 699) ***The movie star's <u>demure</u> and proper behavior was refreshing.*** *demurely adv. demureness n.*

❸ Word Study

The **Latin prefix *pre-*** means "before."

In "Casey at the Bat," the speaker says that Flynn **preceded** Casey, meaning that Flynn went before Casey.

Vocabulary Development

Vocabulary Knowledge Rating

Create a **Vocabulary Knowledge Rating Chart** (*Professional Development Guidebook*, p. 33) for this collection. Include the collection vocabulary and the Big Question word that appears in the Writing About the Big Question sentence starter on this page. (The Big Question vocabulary is introduced on pp. 604–605.)

Give students a copy of the chart. Read the words aloud, and have students mark their rating in the Before Reading column. Urge them to be alert to these words as they read and discuss the selection.

Tally how many students think they know a word to gauge how much instruction to provide. As students read and discuss the selection, point out the words and their context.

Vocabulary Central, featuring tools, activities, and songs for studying vocabulary, is available at **www.PHLitOnline.com.**

❹ Meet the Authors

Ernest Lawrence Thayer

(1863–1940)

Author of "Casey at the Bat" (p. 696)

It is not surprising that "Casey at the Bat" reads like a sports story in verse. The poet, Ernest Lawrence Thayer, worked for many years as a sports reporter on the staff of newspapers in New York and California. "Casey at the Bat" first appeared in the *San Francisco Examiner* in 1888. It became so popular that in 1953 it inspired an operetta called *The Mighty Casey.*

William Stafford

(1914–1993)

Author of "Fifteen" (p. 699)

William Stafford was raised in Kansas. He did not publish his first book, *West of Your City,* until he was 46. However, he made up for lost time after that, publishing many collections, including *Traveling Through the Dark.* Fellow poet Robert Bly has said that Stafford's poems are "spoken like a friend over coffee."

Sandra Cisneros

(b. 1954)

Author of "Twister Hits Houston" (p. 700)

Sandra Cisneros was born in Chicago, but her family moved frequently between Chicago and Mexico City. She began her first novel, *The House on Mango Street,* while she was still a college student. Cisneros has worked with high-school students, serving as poet-in-residence in several schools. She has received many awards for her writing.

Differentiated Instruction — Additional Instruction

EL Extended Support—English Learners
Have students complete the **Reading and Vocabulary Warm-ups, *Unit 4 Resources,*** pp. 127–130, before they read. Assign the prereading pages and the selection in the ***Reader's Notebook: English Learner's Version.*** Then, have students listen to portions of the selection on the ***Hear It!* Audio CD.**

L1 L2 Extended Support—Struggling Readers
Have students complete the **Reading and Vocabulary Warm-ups, *Unit 4 Resources,*** pp. 127–130, before they read. Assign the prereading pages and the selection in the ***Reader's Notebook: Adapted Version.*** Then, have students listen to portions of the selection on the ***Hear It!* Audio CD** (adapted text).

Extended Support—Reluctant Readers
To build motivation and engagement before assigning the collection, have students read "Choosing the News," a thematically related selection in ***Reality Central.*** Then, use the questions at the conclusion of the related selection to guide discussion.

Daily Bellringer

For each class during which you will teach this selection, have students complete one of the five Revision activities for Week 22 in the ***Daily Bellringer Activities*** booklet.

❹ Background

- **Ernest Lawrence Thayer** As an editor of the *Harvard Lampoon,* Ernest Lawrence Thayer was used to writing comic pieces. Although Thayer worked in San Francisco, "Casey at the Bat" became popular after it was performed on Broadway by one of the leading comedy-actors of the day. Members of the New York Giants and Chicago White Stockings took part in the production.
- **Sandra Cisneros** Sandra Cisneros says that people always ask her if she writes about true experiences. She said the answer is "yes and no." She can't write about things she doesn't know about and she can't write about emotions she hasn't felt, so in some ways, every story or poem is an autobiographical experience.

Multidraft Reading

To assist struggling readers and to deepen reading for all, apply multidraft reading protocols. For each reading, have students set the purpose indicated:

- **First reading**—identifying key ideas and details and answering any Reading Checks.
- **Second reading**—analyzing craft and structure and responding to the side-column prompts.
- **Third reading**—integrating knowledge and ideas, connecting to other texts and the world, and answering the end-of-selection questions.

For more guidance, refer to the ***Classroom Strategies and Teaching Routines Card*** on multidraft reading.

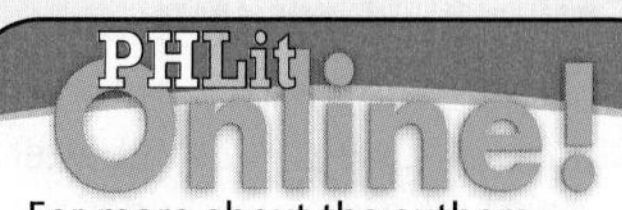

For more about the authors and practice with the selection vocabulary, go to **www.PHLitOnline.com.**

TEACH

❶ Activating Prior Knowledge

Ask student volunteers to share a thrilling or intense moment in their lives. It might be an exciting moment at a baseball or football game, or a frightening moment in a storm. Ask them to describe details of the setting in which the event occurred. Ask students whether they think the event could be the subject of a poem. Tell students that they will be reading poems about intense moments.

Concept Connector

Students will consider their ideas after reading the collection.

Small-Group Activity

The strong rhythm and regular rhyme scheme of "Casey at the Bat" have made it a favorite read-aloud for over a century. Have small groups of students collaborate on a recitation of the poem. One student can read the narration, others can take the roles of Casey and the umpire, and the rest can be the fans, cheering and booing where the poem indicates. Work with students to help them decide on sound effects. After planning and rehearsing, students can perform for the class.

❷ About the Selections

"Casey at the Bat" uses vivid words and dramatic details to create suspense. It is the ninth inning, and Mudville is down by two runs. With two men on base, the mighty Casey strides to the plate. In "Fifteen," a fifteen-year-old boy's discovery of a motorcycle leads him to an important discovery about himself. "Twister Hits Houston" retells the family story of what Papa and Mama were doing and what happened when a tornado struck their home.

❸ Critical Viewing

Possible response: The attitude and stance of Casey and the batter in the painting are similarly defiant. Unlike Casey, however, the batter in the painting looks intense in an angry way. He takes a swing and misses, whereas Casey lets the pitches go by.

❹

❸ ▲ **Critical Viewing** Compare and contrast the stance and attitude of the batter in this painting with Casey's stance and attitude in the poem. **[Compare and Contrast]**

Vocabulary Development

© CCSS Language 6

Thematic Vocabulary: The Big Question

As students are discussing "Casey at the Bat," "Fifteen," and "Twister Hits Houston," encourage them to use the thematic vocabulary presented in Introducing the Big Question, pp. 604–605. You might encourage them with sentence starters like these:

1. As the action of "Casey at the Bat" progresses, the *relationship* between Casey and the crowd becomes . . .
2. When Casey steps up to the plate, the fans *react* by . . .
3. The *resolution* of the poem "Fifteen" was different from what I'd expected because . . .
4. In "Twister Hits Houston," Papa and Mama *respond* to the tornado by . . .

1 2 # CASEY AT THE BAT

ERNEST LAWRENCE THAYER

It looked extremely rocky for the Mudville nine that day;
The score stood two to four, with but an inning left to play.
So, when Cooney died at second, and Burrows did the same,
A pallor wreathed the features of the patrons of the game.

A straggling few got up to go, leaving there the rest,
5 With that hope which springs eternal within the human breast.
For they thought: "If only Casey would get a whack at that,"
They'd put even money now, with Casey at the bat.

But Flynn preceded Casey, and likewise so did Blake,
And the former was a pudd'n, and the latter was a fake.
So on that stricken multitude a deathlike silence sat;
For there seemed but little chance of Casey's getting to the bat.

But Flynn let drive a "single," to the wonderment of all.
And the much-despised Blakey "tore the cover off the ball."
And when the dust had lifted, and they saw what had occurred,
There was Blakey safe at second, and Flynn a-huggin' third.

Then from the gladdened multitude went up a joyous yell—
It rumbled in the mountaintops, it rattled in the dell;
It struck upon the hillside and rebounded on the flat;
For Casey, mighty Casey, was advancing to the bat.

There was ease in Casey's manner as he stepped into his place,
There was pride in Casey's bearing and a smile on Casey's face;
And when responding to the cheers he lightly doffed his hat,
No stranger in the crowd could doubt 'twas Casey at the bat.

Vocabulary
pallor (pal′ ər) *n.* unnatural paleness

preceded (prē cēd′ əd) *v.* came before in time, place, order, rank, or importance

Literary Analysis
Narrative Poetry What is the setting of this narrative poem?

Vocabulary
multitude (mul′ tə to͞od) *n.* a large number of persons or things, especially when gathered together or considered as a unit

6 

Where are Blakey and Flynn when Casey comes to bat?

4 Humanities

Casey at the Bat, by Edward Wilson

This illustration often accompanies "Casey at the Bat." Use the following questions for discussion:

1. How does this illustration help you appreciate the poem?

   Possible response: It shows me what a baseball game looked like in the 1800s. I can see how intimate the crowd and the players were.

2. What does the illustration show about the continuity of baseball?

   Answer: Baseball has not changed much, though batters and catchers now wear protective equipment, and the stadiums are much larger today.

5 Literary Analysis

Narrative Poetry

1. Have students **consider** the title of the poem and the image on p. 696. **Ask** them to identify the subject of the poem.

   Answer: The subject is a baseball game.

2. **Ask:** Based on the title, who will be the main character in this narrative?

   Answer: Casey is the main character.

3. Draw students' attention to the bracketed passage. **Ask** them to respond to the Literary Analysis question: What is the setting of this narrative poem?

   Answer: The setting is a ballpark, in which a ballgame is being played.

6 Reading Check

Answer: Blakey is on second base, and Flynn is on third base.

Differentiated Instruction for Universal Access

Strategy for Special-Needs Students
To help students appreciate the narratives in these poems, have them read the ***Reader's Notebook: Adapted Version*** as they listen to the ***Hear It!* Audio CD** (adapted text). Lead a discussion about the stories told in these poems. Have students identify the main characters in the poems, and encourage them to retell the narrative in their own words.

EL Pronunciation for English Learners
Some students might have difficulty pronouncing words with the short "a" sound as in *at, bat,* and *had,* replacing it with the "ah" sound as in *hot.* To aid pronunciation write the following word pairs on the board: *hat* and *hot; sad* and *sod; map* and *mop.* Pronounce each word in turn, having students repeat each. Then, call out the words at random, having volunteers circle the correct words on the board. Discuss the results with the class, noting what might have led to incorrect choices.

PHLit Online!
This selection is available in interactive format in the **Enriched Online Student Edition, www.PHLitOnline.com,** which includes a thematically related video with writing prompt and an interactive graphic organizer.

7 Connecting to the Big Question

1. Have a volunteer read the first bracketed passage aloud. **Ask:** What happens in this passage?

   Answer: The crowd roars angrily because the umpire called a strike. Casey raises his hand to quiet the crowd, smiles, and turns toward the next pitch.

2. **Ask:** What effect does the crowd's cheering have on Casey's performance?

   Possible response: The crowd's cheering seems to remind Casey to refocus and concentrate.

3. **Ask:** How would you characterize the communication between Casey and the crowd overall?

   Possible response: Their communication is constant and mostly sympathetic, although Casey appears to find them distracting at the end of the poem.

Spiral Review

Diction and Syntax

1. Remind students that they studied the concepts of diction and syntax in the Unit 4 Literary Analysis workshop (pp. 606–614).
2. **Ask** students the Spiral Review question.

   Possible response: The diction is ordinary speech with contractions and slang. This helps the stanza reflect the sound and feeling of a crowd.

8 Literary Analysis

Narrative Poetry

1. Have students review lines 21 through 44. **Ask:** How does Casey's attitude change while he is at bat?

   Answer: When he first comes up to the plate, he is confident and at ease. After two strikes, he becomes tense and fierce.

2. Refer students to the second bracketed passage. **Ask** students to respond to the Literary Analysis question.

   Possible response: The mood of the poem parallels Casey's attitude. With two strikes against him, Casey becomes intense—as does the poem.

Vocabulary
writhing (rīth′ iŋ) *v.* twisting; turning
defiance (dē fī′ əns) *n.* open, bold resistance to authority

Ten thousand eyes were on him as he rubbed his hands with dirt,
Five thousand tongues applauded when he wiped them on his shirt;
Then when the **writhing** pitcher ground the ball into his hip,
Defiance glanced in Casey's eye, a sneer curled Casey's lip.

And now the leather-covered sphere came hurtling through the air,
And Casey stood a-watching it in haughty grandeur there.
Close by the sturdy batsman the ball unheeded sped;
"That ain't my style," said Casey. "Strike one," the umpire said.

Spiral Review
Diction and Syntax How does word choice and word arrangement in this stanza help convey the feelings of the crowd?

From the benches, black with people, there went up a muffled roar,
Like the beating of the storm waves on the stern and distant shore.
"Kill him! kill the umpire!" shouted someone on the stand;
And it's likely they'd have killed him had not Casey raised his hand.

With a smile of Christian charity great Casey's visage shone;
He stilled the rising tumult, he made the game go on;
He signaled to the pitcher, and once more the spheroid flew;
But Casey still ignored it, and the umpire said, "Strike two."

"Fraud!" cried the maddened thousands, and the echo answered "Fraud!"
But one scornful look from Casey and the audience was awed;
They saw his face grow stern and cold, they saw his muscles strain,
And they knew that Casey wouldn't let the ball go by again.

Literary Analysis
Narrative Poetry In what way does the poem's mood change in this stanza?

The sneer is gone from Casey's lips, his teeth are clenched in hate.
He pounds with cruel vengeance his bat upon the plate:
And now the pitcher holds the ball, and now he lets it go,
And now the air is shattered by the force of Casey's blow.

Oh, somewhere in this favored land the sun is shining bright,
The band is playing somewhere, and somewhere hearts are light:
And somewhere men are laughing, and somewhere children shout,
But there is no joy in Mudville: Mighty Casey has struck out.

Think Aloud

Vocabulary: Using Context

Direct students' attention to the word *haughty* in line 30. Using a think-aloud process, model how to use context to infer the meaning of an unknown word. Say to students:

> I'm going to think aloud to show you how I would figure out the meaning of *haughty* from its context.
>
> In this line *haughty* is being used to describe Casey's attitude as he comes to bat and takes the first pitch. From the previous lines, we know that Casey goes to bat with an attitude of pride and confidence. In line 28 he is described as being defiant and having a sneer. In line 32, Casey says, "That ain't my style" as he takes the first pitch.
>
> From these clues, I think that *haughty* means "having great pride and holding contempt for others."

Fifteen

William Stafford

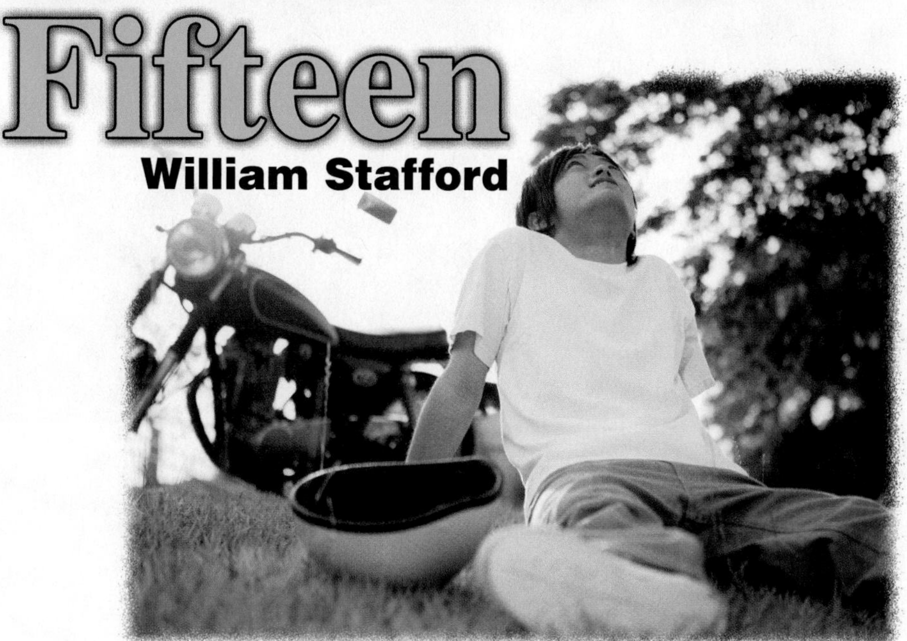

South of the bridge on Seventeenth
I found back of the willows one summer
day a motorcycle with engine running
as it lay on its side, ticking over
slowly in the high grass. I was fifteen.

I admired all that pulsing gleam, the
shiny flanks, the demure headlights
fringed where it lay; I led it gently
to the road and stood with that
companion, ready and friendly. I was fifteen.

(9) We could find the end of a road, meet
the sky on out Seventeenth. I thought about
hills, and patting the handle got back a
confident opinion. On the bridge we indulged
a forward feeling, a tremble. I was fifteen.

Thinking, back farther in the grass I found
the owner, just coming to, where he had flipped
over the rail. He had blood on his hand, was pale—
I helped him walk to his machine. He ran his hand
over it, called me a good man, roared away.

I stood there, fifteen.

Vocabulary
demure (di myoor′) *adj.* modest

Reading Skill
Paraphrase Picture the action in lines 11 and 12, and then restate the phrase "meet the sky" in your own words.

9 Reading Skill

Paraphrase

1. Have students review lines 1 through 10. **Ask** students what has happened so far in these lines.

   Answer: The speaker finds a motorcycle lying on its side in some brush off the road. He admires the motorcycle, picks it up, and pushes it back to the road.

2. Refer students to the bracketed passage. **Ask** students to explain whether this action is actually happening or is imagined.

   Answer: This action is imagined. The speaker is imagining what he could do with the motorcycle.

3. **Ask** students to respond to the Reading Skill prompt: Picture the action in lines 11 and 12, and then restate the phrase "meet the sky" in your own words.

   Possible response: Students may suggest the phrase "ride out to the open road."

▶ **Monitor Progress:** Review students' graphic organizers to ensure that they are able to paraphrase accurately.

▶ **Reteach:** If students have difficulty paraphrasing, have them reread the poem. Help them to see that paraphrasing is telling the action of the story in their own words.

PROFESSIONAL DEVELOPMENT | **William G. Brozo, Ph.D.**

Apply the Strategy

Copy pictures of advertisements for motorcycles from magazines or print them from the Internet. Before reading the poem "Fifteen," form small groups of students and give each group an ad. Instruct groups to analyze the message in their ad by answering such questions as: Who is the target of the ad? What does the motorcycle represent to potential buyers?

After reading the poem silently, ask students to compare and contrast the message in the poem with that in their motorcycle advertisement. Students should record their findings in a chart, with ideas that are similar between the two written in one column and ideas that differ in another column. Then, using these ideas, have students write their own motorcycle advertisements for the 15-year-old in the poem. Post the advertisements in the classroom.

For more of William Brozo's strategies, see the Professional Development essay, pp. 604c–604d.

⑩ Visual Connections

Whole-Class Activity

1. With the class, brainstorm for words that students associate with the photograph. Have a volunteer write the words on the board or a piece of chart paper.

   Possible responses: twister, tornado, fear, whirling, wind, cloud, Dorothy, storm, energy.

2. **Ask:** Based on this picture and the list of words we generated, what do you predict the mood of this poem will be?

   Possible response: The poem's mood will be frenetic and dramatic.

Small-Group Activity

1. Divide the class into small groups. Tell students to imagine themselves looking through the "window" and to discuss what it would be like.
2. Ask one person from each group to summarize the group's ideas.
3. Have the designated students share the results of their groups' discussions. To model the process of making connections to an image, choose one response and analyze how the photograph supports it.

Individual Activity

1. As a class, briefly discuss the photograph.
2. Ask students to imagine that this photograph is the second in a series of three photographs.
3. In class or for homework, have students draw the first and third pictures in the series.
4. Post students' drawings around the room. Invite students to present their work.

Vocabulary Development

Vocabulary Knowledge Rating

When students have completed reading and discussing this poetry collection, have them take out their **Vocabulary Knowledge Rating Chart**. Read the words aloud once more and have students rate their knowledge of the words again in the After Reading column. Clarify any words that are still problematic. Have students write their own definition and example or sentence in the appropriate column. Then have students complete the Vocabulary Practice activities at the end of the collection. Encourage students to use the words in further discussion and written work about these poems. Remind them that they will be accountable for these words on the **Selection Test**, ***Unit 4 Resources,*** pp. 139–141 or 142–144.

TWISTER HITS HOUSTON

Sandra Cisneros

Papa was on the front porch.
Mama was in the kitchen.
Mama was trying
to screw a lightbulb into a fixture.
Papa was watching the rain.
Mama, it's a cyclone for sure,
he shouted to his wife in the kitchen.
Papa who was sitting on his front porch
when the storm hit
said the twister ripped
the big black oak to splinter,

11
◀ **Critical Viewing**
How does the power of the tornado in this photograph add to your understanding of the poem? **[Connect]**

11 Critical Viewing

Possible response: The image shows the power of the storm and makes the image of a storm ripping up a tree and lifting a car more believable and vivid.

Concept Connector

Activating Prior Knowledge
Have students reconsider the settings they described before reading the collection. Lead a discussion about how their concept of an appropriate setting for a poem has changed. Encourage students to cite specific details from the text.

Writing About the Big Question
Have students compare their responses to the sentence starter they completed before reading the poems with their ideas afterwards. Ask them to explain whether their thoughts have changed.

Reading Skill Graphic Organizer
Have students review the graphic organizers they completed to paraphrase lines of poetry. Show them **Reading Skill Graphic Organizer A** (***Graphic Organizer Transparencies,*** p. 128) as an example. Then have students share the graphic organizers they did and the paraphrasing they completed.

⓬ Reading Skill

Paraphrase

Ask students the Reading Skill question.

Possible response: Students may suggest phrases such as "the back door banged loudly and continuously" or "the back door kept banging, banging, banging in the storm."

ASSESS

Answers

Critical Thinking

Before students respond, you may wish to have them write a brief objective summary of each selection. As they answer the questions below, remind them to support their answers with evidence from the text.

1. (a) The speaker uses details such as Casey's apparent pride, his defiant glance, a sneer on his lips, and his clenched teeth.
(b) Students may suggest that Casey is strong, confident or even arrogant, and a fierce competitor.
(c) He may have been overly confident in letting two pitches go by without swinging, believing that he could get a hit whenever he wanted.
2. (a) He imagines riding it out on the open road, up and down hills. (b) **Possible response:** The motorcycle represents freedom, independence, and adventure.
3. (a) He sits on the front porch.
(b) **Possible response:** No, his behavior is not appropriate, since a tornado is very dangerous. A logical response would be to take cover, not to sit calmly on the porch.
4. **Possible responses:** The crowd probably influenced Casey's performance as well as the outcome of the game. The crowd showed that they expected Casey to win the game and, at the same time, fed his ego. The crowd's high expectations, in addition to its distracting behavior, most likely compromised Casey's performance and cost him the game.

Reading Skill
Paraphrase Restate the description in line 14 of the twister banging the back door.

tossed a green sedan into his garden,
and banged the back door
like a mad cat wanting in.
Mama who was in the kitchen
said Papa saw everything,
the big oak ripped to kindling,[1]
the green sedan land out back,
the back door slam and slam.
I missed it.
Mama was in the kitchen Papa explained.
Papa was sitting on the front porch.
The light bulb is still sitting
where I left it. Don't matter now.
Got no electricity anyway.

1. **kindling** (kind′ lin) *n.* bits of dry wood used for starting fires.

Critical Thinking

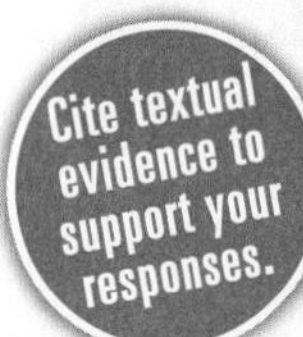
Cite textual evidence to support your responses.

1. **Key Ideas and Details** **(a)** In "Casey at the Bat," what details does the speaker use to describe Casey? **(b) Infer:** What does the description suggest about Casey's personality? **(c) Draw Conclusions:** How might his personality have affected the game's outcome?
2. **Key Ideas and Details** **(a)** In the third stanza of "Fifteen," what does the speaker imagine doing with the motorcycle? **(b) Interpret:** What does the motorcycle represent to him? Explain your response.
3. **Key Ideas and Details** **(a)** What does the speaker's father do throughout the storm in "Twister Hits Houston"? **(b) Make a Judgment:** Is his behavior appropriate for the situation? Explain your answer.
4. **Integration of Knowledge and Ideas** What role, if any, do you think the crowd played in Casey's performance in "Casey at the Bat"? Explain. *[Connect to the Big Question: How does communication change us?]*

Assessment Resources

Unit 4 Resources

L1 L2 EL **Selection Test A,** pp. 139–141. Administer Test A to less advanced readers.

L3 L4 EL **Selection Test B,** pp. 142–144. Administer Test B to on-level and more advanced students.

L3 L4 **Open-Book Test,** pp. 136–138. As an alternative, give the Open-Book Test.

All **Customizable Test Bank**

All **Self-tests**
Students may prepare for the **Selection Test** by taking the **Self-test** online.

PHLit Online! All assessment resources are available at **www.PHLitOnline.com**.

After You Read
Poetry Collection 5

Casey at the Bat • Fifteen • Twister Hits Houston

Literary Analysis: Narrative Poetry

1. **Craft and Structure** **(a)** Using a chart like the one shown, identify and describe the story elements in each **narrative poem. (b)** Explain why you think each writer chose poetry to bring these elements to life.

	Setting	Characters	Plot
"Casey at the Bat"			
"Fifteen"			
"Twister Hits Houston"			

2. **Craft and Structure** **(a)** In "Fifteen," how would you describe the speaker's personality? **(b)** Identify three phrases in "Fifteen" that contribute to the poem's **mood,** or **atmosphere,** of longing. Explain each choice.

3. **Integration of Knowledge and Ideas** **(a)** Do you think a poem is an effective way to tell a story? Why or why not? **(b)** Share your response with a partner, and then explain whether his or her response changed your own.

Reading Skill: Paraphrase

4. **(a) Paraphrase** lines 29 through 32 of "Casey at the Bat."
(b) Explain how picturing the action helped you restate the lines.

Vocabulary

Acquisition and Use In vocabulary study, **analogies** show the relationships between pairs of words. Use a word from the list on page 694 to make a word pair that matches the relationship between the first two given words.

1. flapping : bird :: ______________ : snake
2. blush : red :: ______________ : white
3. boastful : proud :: ______________ : humble
4. approval : happy :: ______________ : angry
5. club : member :: ______________ : individual
6. early : late :: ______________ : followed

Word Study Use the context of the sentences and what you know about the **Latin prefix *pre-*** to explain your answer to each question.

1. If you want to *prevent* a fire, when should you take action against it?
2. Are there any records of *prehistoric* events?

Word Study

The **Latin prefix *pre-*** means "before."

Apply It Explain how the prefix *pre-* contributes to the meanings of these words. Consult a dictionary if necessary.

predict
preview
preface

ASSESS/EXTEND

Answers

Literary Analysis

1. (a) **Sample answer:** "Casey at the Bat": **Setting**—ballpark with a game in the ninth inning; **Characters**—Cooney, Burrows, Flynn, Blakey, Casey, the umpire, the pitcher; **Plot**—The game is in the ninth inning; the opposing team leads by two runs. Casey comes to bat with two men on base, and strikes out. (b) Poetic rhythm and rhyme emphasize the excitement and suspense of a brief moment. (a) **Sample answer: "Fifteen": Setting**—an area behind some willow trees; **Characters**—a fifteen-year-old boy, a motorcyclist; **Plot**—a boy finds a turned-over motorcycle and daydreams about riding it. (b) Poetic language emphasizes the boy's wistful dream. (a) **Sample answer: "Twister Hits Houston": Setting**—a couple's kitchen; **Characters**—Mama, Papa, the narrator; **Plot**—what happened during a twister. (b) The poem describes the twister's action in vivid, economical language.

   For other sample answers, see ***Graphic Organizer Transparencies*, Literary Analysis Graphic Organizer A**, p. 131, and the **Additional Answers** section.

2. **Possible response:** (a) The speaker is a dreamer. (b) Three phrases include "I admired all that pulsing gleam," "we could find the end of the road," "we indulged a forward feeling." The phrases suggest both admiration for the machine's power and beauty and a longing to travel.

3. (a) **Possible response:** Poetry is effective in telling a brief story since it captures the main details vividly and concisely. (b) Others' responses may change students' ideas.

Reading Skill

4. **Possible responses:** (a) The baseball came flying, but Casey ignored it, saying it wasn't his style. The umpire called strike one. (b) Picturing the action makes it easier to paraphrase because then I can write down what I see in my mind's eye.

Vocabulary

Acquisition and Use

1. writhing
2. pallor
3. demure
4. defiance
5. multitude
6. preceded

Word Study

Sample answers:

1. The prefix *pre-* means "before" and *prevent* means "to keep from happening by acting before." To prevent a fire, you should take action by making your home safe before a fire is able to start.
2. No. The prefix *pre-* means "before" and *prehistoric* means "before history began." Therefore, there wouldn't be any records.

Word Study: Apply It

Sample answers:

To *predict* means to forecast or tell what is going to happen before it happens. To *preview* something means to show or view something before, like a movie. A *preface* is the introductory section that comes before a book or speech.

PRETEACH

Skills instruction for the **Reading Skill** and **Literary Analysis** concept appears on p. 693.

1 Writing About the Big Question

1. Review the assignment with the class.
2. Recall that empathy means understanding and experiencing another's feelings. **Ask** students who is the most empathetic person they know. Urge them to explain and give examples.
3. Have students complete the sentence starter. Review responses as a class. (**Possible response:** Having <u>empathy</u> for someone who is in a difficult situation might make a person realize that everyone has problems.)
4. Remind students that their answers will help them think about the Big Question, "How does communication change us?

While You Read

Tell students that as they read they should think about how the speaker in "The Writer" is affected by the sound of his daughter writing.

2 Vocabulary

1. Have students preview the selection vocabulary.
2. For each word, have students say the word aloud.
3. Then, use the word in a sentence that defines the word.
4. Repeat your definitional sentence or a similar sentence with the word missing, and have the class "fill in the blank" chorally. Here are some examples:

   <u>Beguiling</u> means charming or tricky. My younger sister's ability to get what she wants is so sneaky and charming that people describe her as [students say "beguiling"].

   A <u>respite</u> is a break or rest from a job or chore. After three hours, everyone stopped working for a brief [students say "respite"].

3 Word Study

1. Introduce the skill, using the instruction in the box.
2. **Ask** students to name and define another word with the prefix *im-*. (**Sample answer:** *Impractical* means "not practical.")

Making Connections
Poetry Collection 6
The Horses • The Writer • The Raven

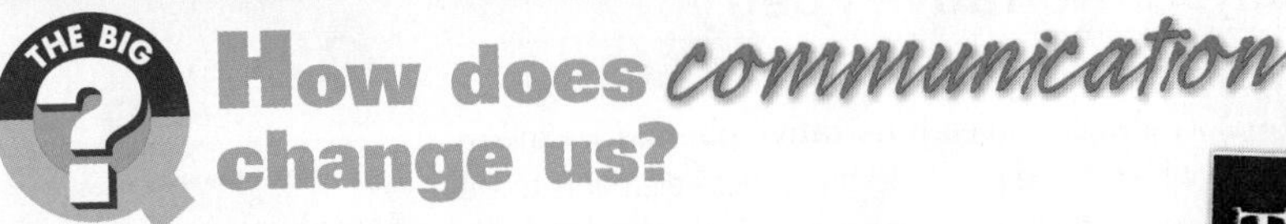

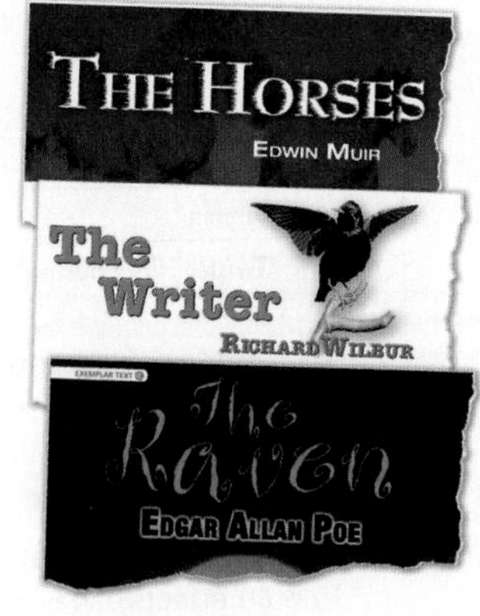

1 Writing About the Big Question

In "The Writer," a father is moved by the sound of his daughter typing a story. Use this sentence starter to develop your ideas about the Big Question.

Having **empathy** for someone who is in a difficult situation might make a person realize that ______________.

While You Read Consider how the speaker in "The Writer" is affected by his young daughter's attempt to write a story.

2 Vocabulary

Read each word and its definition. Decide whether you know the word well, know it a little bit, or do not know it at all. After you read, see how your knowledge of each word has increased.

- **impenetrable** (im pen´ i trə bəl) *adj.* that cannot be passed through; that cannot be solved or understood (p. 706) ***I could not see my hand in front of my face in the <u>impenetrable</u> darkness of the cave.*** *impenetrability n. penetrate v.*
- **archaic** (är kā´ ik) *adj.* from an earlier time; ancient (p. 707) ***Some people say the old song is timeless; others say it is <u>archaic</u>.***
- **iridescent** (ir´ i des´ ənt) *adj.* showing colors that seem to change in different lights (p. 709) ***The silvery scales of the fish were <u>iridescent</u> in the sunlight.*** *iridescence n.*
- **pondered** (pän´ dərd) *v.* thought deeply about (p. 711) ***After hearing the inspirational speaker, Ralph <u>pondered</u> the meaning of life.*** *ponder v. ponderous adj.*
- **beguiling** (bē gīl´ iŋ) *v.* tricking; charming (p. 712) ***The children's innocence was <u>beguiling</u> their parents.*** *guile n.*
- **respite** (res´ pit) *n.* rest; relief (p. 713) ***The rain provided a <u>respite</u> from the long dry spell.***

3 Word Study

The **Latin prefix *im-*** means "not."

In "The Horses," the speaker refers to an "**impenetrable** sorrow." If something is impenetrable, it cannot be penetrated, or pierced. An impenetrable sorrow is a deep sadness that cannot be relieved.

Vocabulary Development

Vocabulary Knowledge Rating

Create a **Vocabulary Knowledge Rating Chart** (***Professional Development Guidebook***, p. 33) for this collection. Include the collection vocabulary and the Big Question word that appears in the Writing About the Big Question sentence starter on this page. (The Big Question vocabulary is introduced on pp. 604–605.)

Give students a copy of the chart. Read the words aloud, and have students mark their rating in the Before Reading column. Urge them to be alert to these words as they read and discuss the selection.

Tally how many students think they know a word to gauge how much instruction to provide. As students read and discuss the selection, point out the words and their context.

Vocabulary Central, featuring tools, activities, and songs for studying vocabulary, is available at **www.PHLitOnline.com.**

❹ Meet the Authors

Edwin Muir

(1887–1959)

Author of "The Horses" (p. 706)

An author of numerous books of poetry as well as several novels, Edwin Muir had visions of the future that were rooted in his past. He spent his early years on a farm in the Orkney Islands, north of Scotland. Much of the imagery in his poetry comes from these islands.

Richard Wilbur

(b. 1921)

Author of "The Writer" (p. 708)

As a young man, Richard Wilbur planned to be a cartoonist. Instead, he became an award-winning poet. By the time he was thirty, Wilbur had published two collections of poetry and established himself as an important young writer. In 1987, Wilbur was appointed Poet Laureate of the United States.

Edgar Allan Poe

(1809–1849)

Author of "The Raven" (p. 710)

One of the first great American storytellers, Edgar Allan Poe often explored dark and bizarre events in his stories and poems. His inspiration may have come from his own life, which was often filled with sadness. He found some happiness in his marriage to Virginia Clemm, but after her death, Poe became depressed and antisocial. Many of his poems and stories focus on an ideal love that is lost.

Differentiated Instruction — Additional Instruction

EL Extended Support—English Learners

Have students complete the **Reading and Vocabulary Warm-ups, *Unit 4 Resources,*** pp. 145–148, before they read. Assign the prereading pages for the collection in the ***Reader's Notebook: English Learner's Version.*** Then, have students listen to portions of the collection on the ***Hear It!* Audio CD.**

L1 L2 Extended Support—Struggling Readers

Have students complete the **Reading and Vocabulary Warm-ups, *Unit 4 Resources,*** pp. 145–148, before they read. Assign the prereading pages for the collection in the ***Reader's Notebook: Adapted Version.*** Then, have students listen to portions of the collection on the ***Hear It!* Audio CD** (adapted text).

Extended Support—Reluctant Readers

To build motivation and engagement before assigning the collection, have students read "Behind the Screams," a thematically related selection in ***Reality Central.*** Then, use the questions at the conclusion of the related selection to guide discussion.

Daily Bellringer

For each class during which you will teach this selection, have students complete one of the five Revision activities for Week 22 in the ***Daily Bellringer Activities*** booklet.

❹ Background

- **Richard Wilbur** Besides being a writer of poetry, Richard Wilbur has translated and adapted poems and plays by other writers, notably Molière and Racine, from French, Spanish, and Russian.
- **Edwin Muir** Like Richard Wilbur, Edwin Muir was a translator as well as a writer. With his wife, Muir translated more than 40 novels from German, including those of Franz Kafka. Muir became one of the most important Scottish poets of his day and accepted a visiting professorship at Harvard University in the late 1950s.

Multidraft Reading

To assist struggling readers and to deepen reading for all, apply multidraft reading protocols. For each reading, have students set the purpose indicated:

- **First reading**—identifying key ideas and details and answering any Reading Checks.
- **Second reading**—analyzing craft and structure and responding to the side-column prompts.
- **Third reading**—integrating knowledge and ideas, connecting to other texts and the world, and answering the end-of-selection questions.

For more guidance, refer to the ***Classroom Strategies and Teaching Routines Card*** on multidraft reading.

PHLit Online!

For more about the authors and practice with the selection vocabulary, go online at **www.PHLitOnline.com.**

TEACH

❶ Activating Prior Knowledge

Have students share stories they have heard about life after a war or a world-changing crisis. Discuss how people recover after such a traumatic incident.

Concept Connector →

Students will reconsider their ideas after reading the collection.

Small-Group Activity

Organize students in small groups. Have each group create a skit portraying both the horses and the reactions of the devastated people in "The Horses." **Ask** the audience to describe the feelings evoked by each skit.

❷ About the Selections

"The Horses" is set in a rural area after a devastating war. One day, a herd of horses appears, seeming to offer solace. In "The Writer," a parent describes hopes and fears for a daughter. In "The Raven," the speaker has been shattered by the death of a woman.

❸ Literary Analysis

Narrative Poetry

1. Have students read the first stanza. Then, **ask** them to describe what has happened.
   Answer: A seven-day war has destroyed most of the world. The survivors feel numb. All the radios are silent.
2. **Ask** students the Literary Analysis question.
   Answer: Details include the mention of "the seven days war that put the world to sleep," the silent radios, and the phrase "the nations lying asleep."

❹ Critical Viewing

Possible response: No, they seem lively and eager.

①②

The Horses

Edwin Muir

Barely a twelvemonth after
The seven days war that put the world to sleep,
Late in the evening the strange horses came.
By then we had made our covenant with silence,
But in the first few days it was so still
We listened to our breathing and were afraid.
On the second day
The radios failed; we turned the knobs; no answer.
On the third day a warship passed us, heading north,
Dead bodies piled on the deck. On the sixth day
A plane plunged over us into the sea. Thereafter
Nothing. The radios dumb;
And still they stand in corners of our kitchens,
And stand, perhaps, turned on, in a million rooms
All over the world. But now if they should speak,
If on a sudden they should speak again,
If on the stroke of noon a voice should speak,
We would not listen, we would not let it bring
That old bad world that swallowed its children quick
At one great gulp. We would not have it again.
Sometimes we think of the nations lying asleep,
Curled blindly in impenetrable sorrow,
And then the thought confounds us with its strangeness.

The tractors lie about our fields; at evening
They look like dank sea-monsters couched and waiting.
We leave them where they are and let them rust:

Literary Analysis
Narrative Poetry
Which details in the first stanza reveal that the poem takes place in the future?

Vocabulary
impenetrable (im pen′ i trə bəl) *adj.* that cannot be passed through; that cannot be solved or understood

❹ ▶ **Critical Viewing** Do these horses appear "stubborn and shy" like the ones described in the poem? Explain. **[Compare and Contrast]**

Vocabulary Development

Ⓒ CCSS Language 6

Thematic Vocabulary: The Big Question

As students are discussing "The Horses," "The Writer," and "The Raven," encourage them to use the thematic vocabulary presented in Introducing the Big Question, pp. 604–605. You might encourage them with sentence starters like these:

1. In "The Horses," the horses help the devastated people find *meaning* in their lives by . . .
2. In "The Writer," the speaker's description of the starling helps *illuminate* the speaker's feelings toward his or her daughter because . . .
3. In "The Raven," the raven communicates his lack of *empathy* when . . .
4. After reading "The Raven," I believe the best *interpretation* of the raven is . . .

'They'll moulder away and be like other loam'.[1]
We make our oxen drag our rusty ploughs,
Long laid aside. We have gone back
5 Far past our fathers' land.
And then, that evening
Late in the summer the strange horses came.
We heard a distant tapping on the road,
A deepening drumming; it stopped, went on again
And at the corner changed to hollow thunder.
We saw the heads
Like a wild wave charging and were afraid.
We had sold our horses in our fathers' time
To buy new tractors. Now they were strange to us
As fabulous steeds set on an ancient shield
Or illustrations in a book of knights.
We did not dare go near them. Yet they waited,
Stubborn and shy, as if they had been sent
By an old command to find our whereabouts
And that long-lost archaic companionship.
In the first moment we had never a thought
That they were creatures to be owned and used.
Among them were some half-a-dozen colts
Dropped in some wilderness of the broken world,
Yet new as if they had come from their own Eden.[2]
Since then they have pulled our ploughs and borne our loads,
But that free servitude still can pierce our hearts.
Our life is changed; their coming our beginning.

1. **loam** (lōm) *n.* dark, rich soil.
2. **Eden** in the Bible, the garden where life began with Adam and Eve; paradise.

Reading Skill
Paraphrase Picture the scene here and paraphrase lines 31–35.

Vocabulary
archaic (är kā´ ik) *adj.* from an earlier time; ancient

5 Reading Skill

Paraphrase

1. Have students read the bracketed passage, which begins on p. 706, line 24. Ask students to focus on lines 24–27.
2. **Ask** students why they think people do not use the tractors.
   Possible response: They may not want to use things from the "old bad world," or they may not have the gasoline or spare parts to keep the tractors running.
3. **Ask** students what they picture when they read lines 24–27.
   Answer: Tractors sit unused in the fields. The tractors will eventually rust and decay and become part of the soil.
4. **Ask** students to respond to the Reading Skill prompt: Picture the scene here and paraphrase lines 31–35.
   Possible response: Late one summer evening, the horses appeared.

▶ **Monitor Progress:** Review students' graphic organizers to ensure that they are able to paraphrase accurately.

▶ **Reteach:** If students have difficulty paraphrasing, have them reread lines 33–37. Help students to paraphrase these lines, for example: "The sound of the herd grew louder, and they were afraid of the wave of horses charging toward them."

PHLit Online!
This selection is available in interactive format in the **Enriched Online Student Edition, www.PHLitOnline.com,** which includes a thematically related video with writing prompt and an interactive graphic organizer.

Differentiated Instruction for Universal Access

Strategy for Advanced Readers

Have each student choose one of the three poems in this collection and write a detailed analysis and interpretation of its meaning. Students may paraphrase lines and stanzas in their search for what the poems mean. Encourage them to notice sound devices that poets use, including rhyme and alliteration. Have them think about the use of symbols in the poems. Suggest that students do some background reading about the poets and examine other works by them as they work to interpret these poems.

❻ Literary Analysis

Narrative Poetry

1. Have students read the first stanza. **Ask** students the Literary Analysis question: What details about the characters and setting are introduced in the first stanza?

   Answer: Details include a room at the front of a house facing the east, with a window looking out over a linden tree. The characters are a daughter and the speaker, her parent.

2. **Ask:** What image is suggested by the speaker's use of "prow," "light breaks," and "windows tossed with linden"?

   Possible response: Students may suggest that the image is that of a boat sailing into morning and being tossed by winds and waves.

3. Have students read the poem through line 15. **Ask** what the image of a boat described above might suggest about the daughter.

   Possible response: The image of a boat might suggest that the daughter is at the beginning of a journey in which she might be tossed about. However, the journey may also be rewarding, since she is sailing into the sun at the beginning of the day.

❼ Connecting to the Big Question

1. Have a volunteer read aloud the second bracketed passage. **Ask:** What sound does the speaker hear in this passage?

   Answer: The speaker hears the loud "commotion" of his or her daughter's typewriter keys.

2. **Ask:** How is the speaker affected by this sound?

   Answer: The speaker is reminded that his or her daughter's life journey will have some "heavy" moments. The speaker wishes her "a lucky passage." The speaker seems to feel great affection as well as slight regret that the girl will experience pain in life.

3. Encourage students to continue monitoring how the speaker is affected by the sounds coming from upstairs.

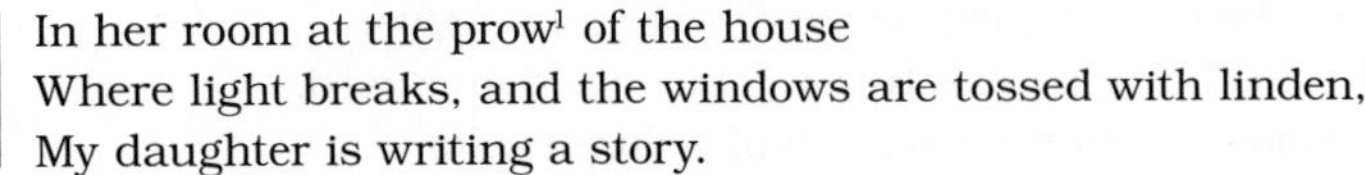

Literary Analysis
Narrative Poetry What details about the characters and setting are introduced in the first stanza? ❻

In her room at the prow[1] of the house
Where light breaks, and the windows are tossed with linden,[2]
My daughter is writing a story.

I pause in the stairwell, hearing
From her shut door a commotion of typewriter-keys
Like a chain hauled over a gunwale.[3]

❼

Young as she is, the stuff
Of her life is a great cargo, and some of it heavy:
I wish her a lucky passage.

But now it is she who pauses,
As if to reject my thought and its easy figure.
A stillness greatens, in which

The whole house seems to be thinking,
And then she is at it again with a bunched clamor
Of strokes, and again is silent.

---

1. **prow** (prou) *n.* front part of a ship or boat.
2. **linden** (lin′ dən) *n.* type of tree.
3. **gunwale** (gun′ əl) *n.* upper edge of the side of a ship or boat.

Vocabulary Development

Expressive Vocabulary

To help students broaden their expressive vocabulary, encourage them to use the following words as they discuss the selections: *evoke, respond, reinforces, suffer,* and *promote.* Have them complete these sentence starters:

1. The opening lines of "The Raven" *evoke* feelings of . . .
2. Readers might *respond* to the knocking at the door with . . .
3. The description of destruction in "The Horses" *reinforces* . . .
4. The people in "The Horses" *suffer* . . .
5. The story of a trapped bird in "The Writer" might *promote* . . .

I remember the dazed starling [4]
Which was trapped in that very room, two years ago;
How we stole in, lifted a sash

And retreated, not to affright it;
And how for a helpless hour, through the crack of the door,
We watched the sleek, wild, dark

And iridescent creature
8 Batter against the brilliance, drop like a glove
To the hard floor, or the desk-top,

And wait then, humped and bloody,
For the wits to try it again; and how our spirits
Rose when, suddenly sure,

It lifted off from a chair-back,
Beating a smooth course for the right window
And clearing the sill of the world.

It is always a matter, my darling,
Of life or death, as I had forgotten. I wish
What I wished you before, but harder.

4. starling (stär′ liŋ) *n.* bird with black feathers that shine in a greenish or purplish way.

Reading Skill
Paraphrase Picture the action here and paraphrase lines 16–30.

Vocabulary
iridescent (ir′ i des′ ənt) *adj.* showing colors that seem to change in different lights

▼ Critical Viewing
Do you think a typewriter like this would allow a writer more or less creativity than a computer? **[Speculate]**

8 Reading Skill

Paraphrase

1. Have students read the bracketed passage aloud. **Ask** what was trapped in the room and what the speaker tried to do about it.
   Answer: A bird was trapped in the room. The speaker opened a window and hoped that the bird would fly out.
2. Encourage student volunteers to describe a time when some creature, such as a bird or squirrel, became trapped in their house. Have them **explain** how the creature behaved and what they did to help it escape.
3. **Ask** students to respond to the Reading Skill prompt: Picture the action here and paraphrase lines 16–30.
   Possible response: I remember when a confused bird became trapped in that room. We sneaked in and opened a window and then left the room so we wouldn't scare it. We watched the shiny, wild bird through a crack in the door as it tried to escape. It kept flying against the window glass and falling to the floor. To our delight, the bird eventually succeeded in flying out through the open window.

9 Critical Viewing

Possible response: Some students may say that a typewriter would allow less creativity than a computer because it is very time-consuming to revise ideas once typed on paper. Other students may find no difference, asserting that creativity lies in the writer, not in the machine.

Differentiated Instruction for Universal Access

Strategy for Less Proficient Readers
To give students a model for paraphrasing, show them the **Reading Skill Graphic Organizer A** (*Graphic Organizer Transparencies,* p. 129). The partially completed graphic organizer will give students insight into the process of paraphrasing. They can use it as a model for writing their own paraphrases as they read.

Support for English Learners
Help guide these students through this set of poems by reviewing the selection vocabulary words and the footnotes with them. Then, play the ***Hear It!* Audio CD.** Give students an opportunity to explain their feelings about each poem.

⑩ Visual Connections

Whole-Class Activity

1. **Ask** students to describe what they see in the picture.

   Possible response: I see a large bird perched on a dead tree branch at night, or perhaps just after dusk. The bird lies in silhouette against a dramatically colored moon.

2. **Ask:** What word would you use to describe the atmosphere of the picture?

   Possible responses: dark, lonely, mysterious, depressing, scary, melancholy.

3. Have a few student volunteers act out how they would react upon looking out the window to see this picture.

Small-Group Activity

1. Divide the class into small groups. Have students make a list of symbols in the picture and identify what each symbol might represent.

   Possible response: The moon is a symbol representing empathy.

2. Ask one person from each group to summarize the group's ideas.
3. Have the designated students share their groups' lists. To model the process of making connections to an image, choose one symbol and analyze how the picture supports it.

Individual Activity

1. As a class, briefly discuss the picture.
2. In class or for homework, have students choose a piece of music that reflects the atmosphere of the picture.
4. Invite students to play their musical selections in class and to explain their choices.

Vocabulary Development

Word Forms

Expand students' vocabulary by helping them learn related forms of the selection vocabulary words. Give students a blank **Word Form Chart** (***Professional Development Guidebook***, p. 42) with *iridescent, pondered,* and *beguiling* in the correct columns. Work with the class, or have students work with a partner, to determine the related forms. The final chart should look like the one shown.

Noun	Verb	Adjective	Adverb
iridescence		**iridescent**	iridescently
ponderer	**pondered**	ponderous	ponderously
beguiler	**beguiling**	beguiling	beguilingly

Once upon a midnight dreary, while I **pondered**, weak and weary,
Over many a quaint and curious volume of forgotten lore,
While I nodded, nearly napping, suddenly there came a tapping,
As of someone gently rapping, rapping at my chamber door.
"Tis some visitor," I muttered, "tapping at my chamber door—
Only this, and nothing more."

11

Ah, distinctly I remember it was in the bleak December,
And each separate dying ember wrought its ghost upon the floor.
Eagerly I wished the morrow—vainly I had tried to borrow
From my books surcease[1] of sorrow—sorrow for the lost Lenore—
For the rare and radiant maiden whom the angels name Lenore—
Nameless here for evermore.

And the silken, sad, uncertain rustling of each purple curtain
Thrilled me—filled me with fantastic terrors never felt before;
So that now, to still the beating of my heart, I stood repeating
12 "'Tis some visitor entreating entrance at my chamber door—
Some late visitor entreating entrance at my chamber door—
This it is and nothing more."

Presently my soul grew stronger; hesitating then no longer,
"Sir," said I, "or Madam, truly your forgiveness I implore;
But the fact is I was napping, and so gently you came rapping,
And so faintly you came tapping, tapping at my chamber door,
That I scarce was sure I heard you"—here I opened wide the door—
Darkness there, and nothing more.

Deep into that darkness peering, long I stood there wondering, fearing,
Doubting, dreaming dreams no mortal ever dared to dream before;
But the silence was unbroken, and the darkness gave no token,
And the only word there spoken was the whispered word, "Lenore!"
This *I* whispered, and an echo murmured back the word, "Lenore!"
Merely this, and nothing more.

Then into the chamber turning, all my soul within me burning,
13 Soon I heard again a tapping somewhat louder than before.
"Surely," said I, "surely that is something at my window lattice;
Let me see, then, what thereat[2] is, and this mystery explore—

1. **surcease** (sʉr sēs´) *n.* end.
2. **thereat** (*th*er at´) *adv.* there.

Vocabulary
pondered (pän´ dərd) *v.* thought deeply about

Literary Analysis
Narrative Poetry Which details provide information about the setting and the speaker?

Reading Skill
Paraphrase Picture the action the speaker describes, and paraphrase this stanza.

Literary Analysis
Narrative Poetry How has the speaker's emotional state changed since the first stanza?

14

Reading Check
What sorrow is the speaker hoping to ease by reading?

Differentiated Instruction for Universal Access

Enrichment for Gifted/Talented Students

Have students imagine events that might have led up to this moment described in the poem, and then ask them to write a brief sketch describing the events.

Students might begin by addressing these questions:

- Who was Lenore? What was her relationship to the speaker?
- What kind of character was Lenore? What did she look like?
- How did Lenore die?
- Was Lenore a "real" person in the speaker's life, or is she just the product of his deranged mind?

Suggest that students write the sketch of Lenore and the speaker in prose or poetry form. Encourage them to share their sketches with the class.

11 Literary Analysis
Narrative Poetry

1. Have a student with a flair for the dramatic read aloud the first two stanzas of the poem.
2. **Ask** students the Literary Analysis question: Which details provide information about the setting and the speaker?

   Answer: The setting is in the speaker's room at midnight in December, and there is a dying fire in the fireplace. The speaker is reading, trying to forget his lost love.

12 Reading Skill
Paraphrase

1. Have students read the third stanza. **Ask** students what the speaker is feeling and why.

   Answer: He is feeling terror; he has heard tapping at the door and rustling of the curtains.
2. **Ask** students to respond to the Reading Skill prompt: Picture the action the speaker describes and paraphrase this stanza.

   Possible response: The rustling sound of the curtains terrifies me. To slow down my rapidly beating heart, I stand and keep telling myself that it is just some visitor knocking at the door.

13 Literary Analysis
Narrative Poetry

1. Have students review the first stanza of the poem. **Ask** them to describe the speaker's emotional state in this stanza.

   Answer: The speaker is sad and weary, thinking about his lost love.
2. Have students read lines 31–36, which end on p. 712. **Ask** the Literary Analysis question: How has the speaker's emotional state changed since the first stanza?

   Possible response: The speaker, who was sad in the first stanza, is now both terrified and hopeful at the sound of tapping. He hopes it is the spirit of his lost love.

14 Reading Check

Answer: He is hoping to ease the sorrow of losing his beloved Lenore.

15 Reading Skill

Paraphrase

1. Have students read lines 37–44. Review the footnotes to clarify difficult vocabulary in this stanza. **Ask** students to suggest what a "stately raven" might mean.

   Possible response: It might mean an elegant or dignified black bird.

2. Refer students to the phrase "saintly days of yore" in line 38. **Ask** students to define *yore.* If necessary, have them use a dictionary.

   Answer: The word *yore* means "long ago."

3. Have students **speculate** about why the speaker refers to the days of long ago as "saintly."

   Possible response: He may have considered the past a better or unspoiled time; he may have been thinking of ancient times when classical learning was valued highly.

4. **Ask** students to respond to the Reading Skill prompt: In your own words, describe how the raven behaved as it entered the chamber.

   Possible response: The raven stepped into the room while fluttering its feathers. It did not pay any attention to the speaker, but perched itself upon the bust of Athena as if it were nobility.

Spiral Review

Diction and Syntax

1. Remind students that they studied poetic language and word connotations in the Unit 4 Literary Analysis workshop (pp. 606–614).

2. **Ask** students the Spiral Review question.

   Possible response: The words *ebony, sad, grave,* and *ghastly* add to the gloomy tone with their meaning. These contribute to a dark tone because they sound heavy, ominous, and dark.

Let my heart be still a moment and this mystery explore—
'Tis the wind, and nothing more!"

Reading Skill
Paraphrase In your own words, describe how the raven behaved as it entered the chamber.

Open here I flung the shutter, when, with many a flirt[3] and flutter,
In there stepped a stately raven of the saintly days of yore;
Not the least obeisance[4] made he; not an instant stopped or stayed he;
But, with mien[5] of lord or lady, perched above my chamber door—
Perched upon a bust of Pallas just above my chamber door—
Perched, and sat, and nothing more.

Vocabulary
beguiling (bē gīl′ iŋ) *v.* tricking; charming

Then this ebony bird **beguiling** my sad fancy[6] into smiling,
By the grave and stern decorum of the countenance[7] it wore,
"Though thy crest be shorn and shaven, thou," I said, "art sure no craven,[8]
Ghastly grim and ancient raven wandering from the Nightly shore—
Tell me what thy lordly name is on the Night's Plutonian[9] shore!"
Quoth[10] the raven, "Nevermore."

Spiral Review
Diction and Syntax Which words in lines 43–48 help create a dark and gloomy tone?

Much I marveled this ungainly fowl to hear discourse so plainly,
Though its answer little meaning—little relevancy bore;
For we cannot help agreeing that no sublunary[11] being
Ever yet was blessed with seeing bird above his chamber door—
Bird or beast upon the sculptured bust above his chamber door,
With such name as "Nevermore."

But the raven, sitting lonely on the placid bust, spoke only
That one word, as if his soul in that one word he did outpour.
Nothing farther then he uttered—not a feather then he fluttered—
Till I scarcely more than muttered, "Other friends have flown before—
On the morrow *he* will leave me, as my hopes have flown before."
Quoth the raven, "Nevermore."

Wondering at the stillness broken by reply so aptly spoken,
"Doubtless," said I, "what it utters is its only stock and store,

3. **flirt** (flʉrt) *n.* quick, uneven movement.
4. **obeisance** (ō bā′ səns) *n.* bow or another sign of respect.
5. **mien** (mēn) *n.* manner.
6. **fancy** (fan′ sē) *n.* imagination.
7. **countenance** (kount′'n əns) *n.* facial appearance.
8. **craven** (krā′ vən) *n.* coward (usually an adjective).
9. **Plutonian** (plo͞o tō′ nē ən) *adj.* like the underworld, ruled by the ancient Roman god Pluto.
10. **quoth** (kwōth) *v.* said.
11. **sublunary** (sub lo͞on′ ər ē) *adj.* earthly.

Vocabulary Development

Vocabulary Knowledge Rating

When students have completed reading and discussing this poetry collection, have them take out their **Vocabulary Knowledge Rating Chart.** Read the words aloud once more and have students rate their knowledge of the words again in the After Reading column. Clarify any words that are still problematic. Have students write their own definition and example or sentence in the appropriate column. Then, have students complete the Vocabulary Practice activities at the end of the selection. Encourage students to use the words in further discussion and written work about these poems. Remind them that they will be accountable for these words on the **Selection Test,** ***Unit 4 Resources,*** pp. 160–162 or 163–165.

Caught from some unhappy master whom unmerciful Disaster
Followed fast and followed faster—so, when Hope he would
adjure,[12]
Stern Despair returned, instead of the sweet Hope he dared
adjure—
That sad answer, 'Nevermore.'"

But the raven still beguiling all my sad soul into smiling,
Straight I wheeled a cushioned seat in front of bird, and
bust, and door;
Then upon the velvet sinking, I betook myself to linking
Fancy unto fancy, thinking what this ominous bird of yore—
What this grim, ungainly, ghastly, gaunt, and ominous bird
of yore
Meant in croaking "Nevermore."

This I sat engaged in guessing, but no syllable expressing
To the fowl whose fiery eyes now burned into my bosom's core;
This and more I sat divining,[13] with my head at ease reclining
16 On the cushion's velvet lining that the lamplight gloated o'er,
But whose velvet violet lining with the lamplight gloating o'er,
She shall press, ah, nevermore!

Then, methought, the air grew denser, perfumed from
an unseen censer[14]
Swung by angels whose faint footfalls tinkled on the tufted floor.
"Wretch," I cried, "thy God hath lent thee—by these angels
he hath sent thee
Respite—respite and Nepenthe[15] from thy memories of Lenore!
Let me quaff this kind Nepenthe and forget this lost Lenore!"
Quoth the raven, "Nevermore."

"Prophet!" said I, "thing of evil!—prophet still, if bird or devil!—
Whether Tempter sent, or whether tempest tossed thee here
ashore,
Desolate, yet all undaunted, on this desert land enchanted—
On this home by Horror haunted—tell me truly, I
implore—
Is there—is there balm in Gilead?[16]—tell me—tell me, I
implore!"
Quoth the raven, "Nevermore."

12. **adjure** (ə jo͝or´) *v.* appeal to; ask earnestly.
13. **divining** (də vīn´ iŋ) *v.* guessing.
14. **censer** (sen´ sər) *n.* container for burning incense.
15. **Nepenthe** (nē pen´ *th*ē) *n.* drug believed by the ancient Greeks to cause forgetfulness of sorrow.
16. **balm** (bäm) **in Gilead** (gil´ ē əd) cure for suffering; the Bible refers to a medicinal ointment, or balm, made in a region called Gilead.

Literary Analysis
Narrative Poetry What two conflicts or problems does the speaker face in this stanza?

Vocabulary
respite (res´ pit)
n. rest; relief

17
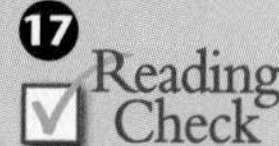

What one word does the raven repeat?

16 Literary Analysis

Narrative Poetry

1. Have students review the events in the poem up to this point. Ask what the speaker is concerned about when the poem opens.
   Answer: He is mourning his lost love Lenore and trying to forget his pain in books.
2. **Ask** students how the speaker responds when the raven begins knocking on the door.
   Answer: The speaker responds with terror when he hears the raven tapping at the door.
3. Read lines 73–78 aloud. **Ask** students the Literary Analysis question: What two conflicts or problems does the narrator face in this stanza?
   Answer: The speaker is trying to figure out what the raven means by repeating the word *nevermore.* He also is still feeling deep sadness over the loss of Lenore.

17 Reading Check

Answer: The raven repeats the word *nevermore.*

Concept Connector

Activating Prior Knowledge

Have students reconsider their ideas about how people recover from crises. Discuss how their views have changed after reading the collection. Encourage students to cite details from the poems.

Writing About the Big Question

Have students compare their responses to the sentence starter they completed before reading the poems with their ideas afterwards. Ask them to explain whether their thoughts have changed.

Reading Skill Graphic Organizer

Have students review the graphic organizers they completed to paraphrase lines of poetry. Show them **Reading Skill Graphic Organizer A** (*Graphic Organizer Transparencies,* p. 129) as an example. Then, have students share the graphic organizers they did and the paraphrasing they completed.

18 Literary Analysis

Narrative Poetry

Ask students the Literary Analysis question.

Possible response: The mood at the beginning of the poem is sad and melancholy. The mood at the end of the poem is one of gloomy despair. The speaker will never stop mourning for Lenore.

ASSESS

Answers

Critical Thinking

Before students respond, you may wish to have them write a brief objective summary of each selection. As they answer the questions below, remind them to support their answers with evidence from the text.

1. (a) The tractors have rusted in the fields. (b) **Possible response:** The tractors represent the "old bad world," while the horses represent the hope of a new world.
2. The sound of the starling beating against the window, then falling, and then trying again, reminds the speaker of his daughter's typing as she tries to set her imagination free.
3. (a) The speaker uses the adjectives *weak* and *weary*. (b) **Possible response:** The speaker's state of mind is despairing and horrified. (c) The raven's message and the speaker's interpretation of it as a statement of hopelessness change the speaker.
4. **Possible response:** The speaker experiences nostalgia, hope, love, and some bittersweet regret as he hears his daughter typing. Many images and emotions come to mind. Perhaps the sounds remind the speaker of his or her own childhood.

"Prophet!" said I, "thing of evil!—prophet still, if bird or devil!
By that Heaven that bends above us—by that God we both adore—
Tell this soul with sorrow laden if, within the distant Aidenn,[17]
It shall clasp a sainted maiden whom the angels name Lenore—
Clasp a rare and radiant maiden whom the angels name Lenore."
Quoth the raven, "Nevermore."

"Be that word our sign of parting, bird or fiend!" I shrieked, upstarting—
"Get thee back into the tempest and the Night's Plutonian shore!
Leave no black plume as a token of that lie thy soul hath spoken!
Leave my loneliness unbroken!—quit the bust above my door!
Take thy beak from out my heart, and take thy form from off my door!"
Quoth the raven, "Nevermore."

Literary Analysis
Narrative Poetry How does the mood here compare with the mood at the beginning of the poem? Explain.

And the raven, never flitting, still is sitting, still is sitting
On the pallid bust of Pallas just above my chamber door;
And his eyes have all the seeming of a demon that is dreaming,
18 And the lamplight o'er him streaming throws his shadow on the floor;
And my soul from out that shadow that lies floating on the floor
Shall be lifted—nevermore!

17. Aidenn name meant to suggest Eden, or paradise.

Critical Thinking

Cite textual evidence to support your responses.

1. **Key Ideas and Details (a)** What happens to the tractors in "The Horses"? **(b) Interpret:** Why does the poet place the tractors and the horses side by side?
2. **Key Ideas and Details Analyze:** Why does the speaker of "The Writer" recall the incident of the trapped starling? Explain your answer.
3. **Key Ideas and Details (a)** In the first line of "The Raven," which two adjectives does the speaker use to describe his state of mind? **(b) Draw Conclusions:** How would you describe the speaker's state of mind at the end of the poem? **(c) Analyze Cause and Effect:** What has caused the speaker to change?
4. **Integration of Knowledge and Ideas** How is the speaker in "The Writer" affected by his daughter's struggle to write her story? *[Connect to the Big Question: How does communication change us?]*

Assessment Resources

Unit 4 Resources

L1 L2 EL **Selection Test A**, pp. 160–162. Administer **Selection Test A** to less advanced readers.

L3 L4 EL **Selection Test B**, pp. 163–165. Administer Test B to on-level and more advanced students.

L3 L4 **Open-Book Test**, pp. 157–159. As an alternative, give the Open Book Test.

All **Customizable Test Bank**

All **Self-tests**
Students may prepare for the **Selection Test** by taking the **Self-test** online.

All assessment resources are available at **www.PHLitOnline.com**.

After You Read
Poetry Collection 6

The Horses • The Writer • The Raven

Literary Analysis: Narrative Poetry

1. **Craft and Structure** **(a)** Using a chart like the one shown, identify and describe the story elements in each **narrative poem.** **(b)** Explain why you think each writer chose poetry to bring these elements to life.

	Setting	Characters	Plot
"The Horses"			
"The Writer"			
"The Raven"			

THE HORSES
EDWIN MUIR

The Writer
RICHARD WILBUR

The Raven
EDGAR ALLAN POE

2. **Craft and Structure** **(a)** In "The Raven," how would you describe the speaker's personality? **(b)** Identify three lines or phrases in "The Raven" that contribute to the poem's mysterious and frantic **mood,** or **atmosphere.** Explain your choices.
3. **Integration of Knowledge and Ideas** **(a)** Do you think a poem is an effective way to tell a story? Why or why not? **(b)** Share your response with a partner, and then explain if his or her response changed your own.

Reading Skill: Paraphrase

4. **(a) Paraphrase** lines 37 through 39 of "The Raven." **(b)** Explain how picturing the action helped you restate the lines.

Vocabulary

Acquisition and Use In vocabulary study, **analogies** show the relationships between pairs of words. Use a word from the list on page 704 to make a word pair that matches the relationship between the first two given words.

1. stale : fresh :: _______________ : modern
2. exercise : tiredness :: _______________ : rest
3. teaching : professor :: _______________ : trickster
4. clear : glass :: _______________ : steel
5. kicked : foot :: _______________ : mind
6. spicy : bland :: _______________ : dull

Word Study Use the context of the sentences and what you know about the **Latin prefix *im-*** to explain your answer to each question.

1. Is it possible to move an *immovable* object?
2. How likely is it that an *improbable* event will occur?

Word Study

The **Latin prefix *im-*** means "not."

Apply It Explain how the prefix *im-* contributes to the meanings of these words. Consult a dictionary if necessary.

impassive
impersonal
impartial

Vocabulary

Acquisition and Use

1. archaic
2. respite
3. beguiling
4. impenetrable
5. pondered
6. iridescent

Word Study

Sample answers:

1. No. The prefix *im-* means "not" and *immovable* means "not movable." An immovable object cannot be moved.
2. The prefix *im-* means "not" and *improbable* means "not probable or likely." Something improbable will probably not happen.

Word Study: Apply It

Impassive means to not show feeling or emotion. *Impersonal* means to not refer to a particular person. *Impartial* means not partial or biased to one side or another.

ASSESS/EXTEND
Answers

Literary Analysis

1. (a) **Sample answer:** "The Horses": **Setting**—a farm; **Characters**—Speaker; **Plot**—A herd of wild horses return to a farm long after they were replaced by tractors. The speaker marvels at their beauty. **Sample answer:** "The Writer": **Setting**—outside a daughter's bedroom; **Characters**—the speaker; **Plot**—The speaker listens as the daughter types an assignment. When she stops, he or she waits in anticipation and recalls a similar incident when the two waited in anticipation of an outcome.
   Sample answer: "The Raven": **Setting**—the speaker's room on a midnight in December; **Characters**—the speaker, a man mourning for his lost love, and the raven; **Plot**—The speaker, prompted by a strange tapping, opens the window to a raven that struts into his room and sits on top of a bust of Pallas. When the speaker questions the raven, it speaks only the word "Nevermore."

For other sample answers, see ***Graphic Organizer Transparencies,*** **Literary Analysis Graphic Organizer** A, p. 132 and the **Additional Answers** section.

   (b) In all of the poems, the poet can express himself more eloquently in poetry or verse than in prose.

2. **Possible response:** (a) The speaker is a worrier. (b) Three phrases include "by then we had made our covenant with silence"; "nations lying asleep,/Curled blindly in impenetrable sorrow"; "look like dank sea-monsters couched and waiting." The phrases describe the situation's other-worldliness.
3. (a) **Possible response:** Poetry is effective telling a brief story, since it captures the main ideas vividly and concisely. (b) Others' responses may change students' ideas.

Reading Skill

4. (a) **Possible response:** When I opened the window, a raven stepped in without stopping to notice me. (b) Picturing the action makes it easier to restate because then I can describe what I imagine.

EXTEND/ASSESS

Answers

Conventions

Introduce the skill, using the instruction on the student page.

Think Aloud: Model the Skill

Model the skill of understanding appositives. Post the sentence, *Max, my best friend, lives next door.* Say to students:

I know that an appositive phrase modifies a noun that it follows and is set off by commas. In this sentence, the appositive "my best friend" describes my friend Max.

Appositives make my writing more concise. For example, I can use an appositive to rewrite these sentences, "My piano teacher will play in our orchestra. Our orchestra is the best in the county," as "My piano teacher will play in our orchestra, the best in the county." The appositive makes the writing more succinct and easier to read.

PH WRITING COACH Grade 9

Students will find instruction on and practice with appositive phrases in Chapter 15, Section 1.

Practice A

1. a fictional town
2. the best player on the team
3. a poem by William Stafford
4. the largest city in Texas

Reading Application

Sample answer:

Flynn, a pudd'n, and Blake, a fake, batted ahead of Casey.

Practice B

1. The raven perches on a bust of Pallas, an Ancient Greek goddess.
2. Muir grew up in Orkney, a group of islands north of Scotland.
3. "The Writer," one of Richard Wilbur's most famous poems, was published in 1969.
4. The speaker and his daughter watched as a bird, a starling, tried to fly through the window.

Writing Application

Sample answer:

A lone bird, a raven, sits against a silhouette of the moon.

PERFORMANCE TASKS

Integrated Language Skills

Poetry Collections 5 and 6

Poetry Collection 5

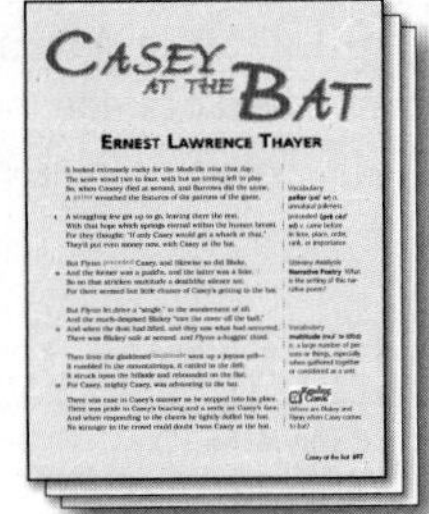

Poetry Collection 6

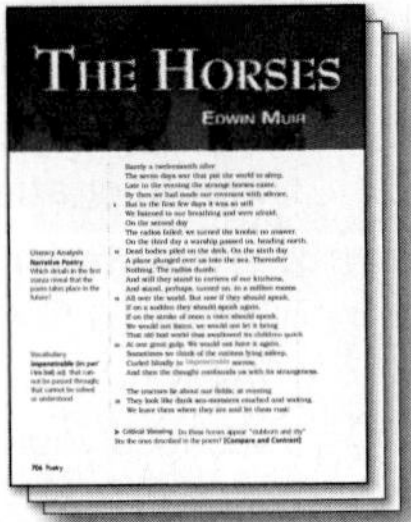

Conventions: Appositive Phrases

An **appositive phrase** is a noun or pronoun with modifiers that add information to the noun or pronoun it follows.

An appositive phrase is set off with commas and functions as a unit that identifies, renames, or explains the word that comes before it. Notice that appositive phrases do not contain any verbs.

Using appositives is a good way to make your writing more concise. Notice how combining sentences using an appositive phrase (underlined) makes the revised version more concise than the original.

Less Concise	Revision With Appositive
"The Raven" is a poem by Edgar Allan Poe. Edgar Allan Poe was one of the first great American writers.	"The Raven" is a poem by Edgar Allan Poe, <u>one of the first great American writers</u>.

Practice A Identify the appositive phrase in each sentence.

1. "Casey at the Bat" takes place in Mudville, a fictional town.
2. The crowd cheered for Casey, the best player on the team.
3. In "Fifteen," a poem by William Stafford, the speaker finds a motorcycle by the side of a road.
4. Houston, the largest city in Texas, is the setting for Cisneros's poem.

Writing Application Rewrite lines 9 and 10 of "Casey at the Bat" as two sentences. Use an appositive phrase in each one.

Practice B For each item, combine the two sentences using an appositive phrase.

1. The raven perches on a bust of Pallas. Pallas was an ancient Greek goddess.
2. Muir grew up in Orkney. Orkney is a group of islands north of Scotland.
3. "The Writer" is one of Richard Wilbur's most famous poems. "The Writer" was published in 1969.
4. The speaker and his daughter watched as the bird tried to fly through the window. The bird was a starling.

Writing Application Write two sentences about the opening image of "The Raven" on page 710. Use an appositive phrase in each one.

PH WRITING COACH Further instruction and practice are available in *Prentice Hall Writing Coach.*

Extend the Lesson

Sentence Modeling

Choose the sentence or phrase given from the Poetry Collection students have read:

On the bridge we indulged a forward feeling, a tremble. ("Fifteen," Poetry Collection 5)

Though its answer little meaning—little relevancy bore . . . ("The Raven," Poetry Collection 6)

Ask students what they notice about the sentence or phrase. Elicit from them that each example contains an appositive phrase. Then, ask what else they notice. ("Fifteen": The appositive phrase, "a tremble," gives readers a more vivid and concrete image of the "forward feeling." It appeals to our sense of touch. "The Raven": The appositive phrase, "little relevancy," provides more specificity than the word *meaning.* It both clarifies and supersedes the noun that precedes it.)

Have students imitate the sentence or phrase in a sentence on a topic of their own choosing, matching each grammatical and stylistic feature discussed. Collect the sentences, and share them with the class.

Writing

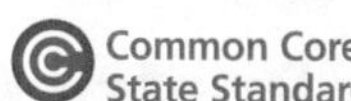

Informative Text Imagine you have been hired by a movie studio to make a short film based on one of the poems you read. Write a **description of the scene** that could be used to develop a script.

- Jot down details about the characters, setting, and action.
- Explain the mood you want to set and note how details about characters, setting, and action can evoke this mood.
- Consider the technology you might use to produce the scene. Suggest camerawork, lighting, and other elements, such as sights, sounds, movements, and gestures that should appear in the scene.

Share the poem and your proposed scene with the class, describing the technology you would use in the scene. Ask for feedback from your classmates to determine if your scene conveys the mood of the poem.

Grammar Application Make sure you correctly use appositive phrases to add variety and interest to your writing.

Common Core State Standards

L.9-10.1.b; W.9-10.4; SL.9-10.1.a, SL.9-10.1.b, SL.9-10.1.c

[For the full wording of the standards, see page 692.]

Writing Workshop: *Work in Progress*

Prewriting for a Response to Literature To prepare for a response to literature you may write, review these poems or review "Uncoiling" and "A Voice" at the beginning of Unit 4. Identify the character in each poem that makes the strongest impression on you. Jot down details that help give you that impression. Put your Character Descriptions in your writing portfolio.

Use this prewriting activity to prepare for the **Writing Workshop** on page 756.

Speaking and Listening

Presentation of Ideas With a partner, role-play a **dialogue** between either the speaker and the motorcyclist in "Fifteen" or the father and the daughter in "The Writer."

- Negotiate as partners to determine who will play each character.
- Before writing, review the poem to find relevant details.
- Analyze the situation in the poem to determine each character's concerns or interests.
- Use conventional styles, including humor, expressions, slang, or more formal words, suitable for each character.
- Decide on a voice, body movements, and language choices that are appropriate for each character.
- Use appropriate eye contact while both speaking and listening.

As you role-play your dialogue, listen carefully to what the other character says, interpreting and evaluating his or her intent.

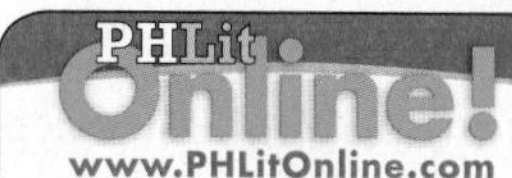

www.PHLitOnline.com

- Interactive graphic organizers
- Grammar tutorial
- Interactive journals

EXTEND/ASSESS

Answers

Writing

1. Review the assignment, using the instruction on the student page.
2. To guide students in writing a description of a scene, give them **Support for Writing**, p. 155, in ***Unit 4 Resources.***
3. To evaluate students' scenes, use the Descriptive Essay rubrics, pp. 220–221 in ***Professional Development Guidebook.*** In addition, you might evaluate for how well students use significant details in structuring their scenes.

Grammar Application

Have students check their drafts to make sure they are using appositive phrases correctly.

Six Traits Focus

✓	Ideas	✓	Word Choice
✓	Organization		Sentence Fluency
	Voice		Conventions

PH WRITING COACH Grade 9

Students will find instruction on and practice with response to literature in Chapter 10.

Writing Workshop
Work in Progress

Have students save their completed Character Descriptions in their portfolios. They will use the description later as they continue this Work-in-Progress assignment (see p. 739). These assignments prepare them to complete the Writing Workshop assignment (see pp. 756–763).

Speaking and Listening

1. Review the assignment, using the instruction on the student page.
2. To support students' work on the assignment, have students complete the **Support for Extend Your Learning** page (*Unit 4 Resources,* p. 156).

Teaching Resources

Unit 4 Resources

L3 L4 EL **Integrated Language Skills: Grammar,** p. 154

L3 L4 EL **Support for Writing,** p. 155

L3 L4 **Support for Extend Your Learning,** p. 156

L4 **Enrichment,** pp. 135, 153

Enriched Online Student Edition

Available under After You Read for this selection:

All **Interactive Grammar Tutorial**

L3 L4 **Internet Research Activity**

Professional Development Guidebook

Rubrics for Self-Assessment: Descriptive Essay, pp. 220–221

PHLit Online! All print and digital resources are available at **www.PHLitOnline.com**. Online resources accessible by students are noted on the student page.

✓ Poetry Collection 7 • ✓✓ Poetry Collection 8

Lesson Pacing Guide

DAY 1 Preteach

- Administer the Reading and Vocabulary Warm-ups (*Unit 4 Resources*, pp. 166–169 or 184–187) as necessary.
- Introduce the Reading Skill: Paraphrase.
- Introduce the Literary Analysis concept: Rhyme and Meter.
- Distribute copies of the appropriate graphic organizer for the Reading Skill (*Graphic Organizer Transparencies*, pp. 134–136).
- Distribute copies of the appropriate graphic organizer for Literary Analysis (*Graphic Organizer Transparencies*, pp. 137–139).
- Teach the selection vocabulary.
- Introduce the Word Study skill.

DAYS 2–3 Preteach/Teach

- Build background with the Background feature.
- Develop thematic vocabulary and thematic thinking with Writing About the Big Question.
- Prepare students to read with the Activating Prior Knowledge activities (TE).
- Informally monitor comprehension while students read.
- Use the Reading Check questions to confirm comprehension.
- Develop students' ability to evaluate persuasion, using the Reading Skill questions.
- Develop students' understanding of persuasive essays, using the Literacy Analysis questions.
- Reinforce vocabulary with the Vocabulary notes.
- Reinforce unit focus standards using the Spiral Review prompts.

DAY 4 Assess

- Assess students' comprehension and mastery of the skills by having them answer the Critical Thinking, Reading Skill, and Literary Analysis questions.
- Have students complete the Vocabulary Practice activities.
- Have students complete the Word Study activities.

DAY 5 Extend/Assess

- Have students complete the Conventions lesson.
- Have students complete the Writing activity and write a poem. (You may assign as homework.)
- Extend learning by having students complete the Speaking and Listening activity, a panel discussion. As an alternative, assign them "Brain Battle" or "Bridging the Generation Gap" in *Reality Central*.
- Administer Selection Test A or B (*Unit 4 Resources*, pp. 178–183 or 199–204).

Common Core State Standards

Reading Literature 4. Determine the meaning of words and phrases as they are used in the text, including figurative and connotative meanings; analyze the cumulative impact of specific word choices on meaning and tone (e.g., how the language evokes a sense of time and place; how it sets a formal or informal tone).
2. Determine a theme or central idea of a text.

Writing 4. Produce clear and coherent writing in which the development, organization, and style are appropriate to task, purpose, and audience.

Speaking and Listening 1.a. Come to discussions prepared, having read and researched material under study; explicitly draw on that preparation to stimulate a thoughtful, well-reasoned exchange of ideas.
1.c. Propel conversations by posing and responding to questions that relate the current discussion to broader themes or larger ideas; actively incorporate others into the discussion; and clarify, verify, or challenge ideas and conclusions.
1.d. Respond thoughtfully to diverse perspectives, qualify or justify their own views and understanding, and make new connections in light of the evidence and reasoning presented.

Language 1.b. Use various types of phrases and clauses to convey specific meanings and add variety and interest to writing or presentations.

Additional Standards Practice
***Common Core Companion*, pp. 35–42**

Daily Block Scheduling
Each day in this Lesson Pacing Guide represents a 40–50 minute period. Teachers using block scheduling may combine days to revise pacing. In addition, teachers may differentiate and support core instruction by integrating components for extended and intensive support as students require. See the Guide to Selected Leveled Resources (facing page).

Guide to Selected Leveled Resources

RTI Tier 1 (students performing on level)			✓ More Accessible Poetry Collection 7	✓✓ More Complex Poetry Collection 8
Warm Up	Whole class instruction; Group work	**Practice, model,** and **monitor** fluency, working **with the whole class** or **in groups.**	**Vocabulary** and **Reading Warm-ups B,** ***Unit 4 Resources,*** pp. 166–167, 169	**Vocabulary** and **Reading Warm-ups B,** ***Unit 4 Resources,*** pp. 184–185, 187
Comprehension/Skills	Whole class instruction; Independent work	**Support** and **monitor** comprehension and skills development, having students complete the activities, graphic organizers, and interactive prompts **independently** or **as a class.**	• ***Reader's Notebook,*** adapted instruction and full selection EL ***Reader's Notebook: English Learner's Version,*** adapted instruction and full selection • **Reading Skill Graphic Organizer B,** ***Graphic Organizer Transparencies,*** p. 136 • **Literary Analysis Graphic Organizer B,** ***Graphic Organizer Transparencies,*** p. 139	• ***Reader's Notebook,*** adapted instruction and summary EL ***Reader's Notebook: English Learner's Version,*** adapted instruction and summary • **Reading Skill Graphic Organizer B,** ***Graphic Organizer Transparencies,*** p. 136 • **Literary Analysis Graphic Organizer B,** ***Graphic Organizer Transparencies,*** p. 139
Monitor Progress	A	**Monitor** student progress with the differentiated curriculum-based assessment in the *Unit Resources.*	• **Selection Test B,** ***Unit 4 Resources,*** pp. 181–183 • **Open-Book Test,** ***Unit 4 Resources,*** pp. 175–177	• **Selection Test B,** ***Unit 4 Resources,*** pp. 202–204 • **Open-Book Test,** ***Unit 4 Resources,*** pp. 196–198

RTI Tier 2 (students requiring intervention)			✓ More Accessible Poetry Collection 7	✓✓ More Complex Poetry Collection 8
Warm Up	Group work; One-on-one teaching	**Practice, model,** and **monitor** fluency **in groups** or **with individuals.**	• **Vocabulary and Reading Warm-ups A,** ***Unit 4 Resources,*** pp. 166–168 • ***Reality Central,*** "Brain Battle" • ***Hear It!*** **Audio CD (adapted text)**	• **Vocabulary and Reading Warm-ups A,** ***Unit 4 Resources,*** pp. 184–186 • ***Reality Central,*** "Bridging the Generation Gap" • ***Hear It!*** **Audio CD**
Comprehension/Skills	Group work; One-on-one teaching	• **Support** and **monitor** comprehension and skills development, working **in small groups** or **with individuals.** • **Pair** students with more advanced peers and have them complete the writing activity in the *Real-World Writing Journal.* • As students complete the selection in the appropriate version of the *Reader's Notebook,* **monitor** comprehension frequently with group questions and individual instruction. • **Model** strategies while guiding students in completing the activities and prompts in the *Reader's Notebook,* as well as the graphic organizers. • **Practice** skills and **monitor** mastery with the *Reading Kit* worksheets.	• ***Real-World Writing Journal Lesson 7,*** pp. 128–131 • ***Reader's Notebook: Adapted Version,*** adapted instruction and full selection EL ***Reader's Notebook: English Learner's Version,*** adapted instruction and full selection • **Reading Skill Graphic Organizer A,** ***Graphic Organizer Transparencies,*** p. 134 • **Literary Analysis Graphic Organizer A,** ***Graphic Organizer Transparencies,*** p. 137 • ***Reading Kit,*** Practice worksheets, pp. 178, 182, 184, 190, 198	• ***Real-World Writing Journal Lesson 8,*** pp. 184–186 • ***Reader's Notebook: Adapted Version,*** adapted instruction and summary EL ***Reader's Notebook: English Learner's Version,*** adapted instruction and summary • **Reading Skill Graphic Organizer A,** ***Graphic Organizer Transparencies,*** p. 135 • **Literary Analysis Graphic Organizer A,** ***Graphic Organizer Transparencies,*** p. 138 • ***Reading Kit,*** Practice worksheets, pp. 178, 182, 184, 190, 198
Monitor Progress	A	**Monitor** student progress with the differentiated curriculum-based assessment in the *Unit Resources* and in the *Reading Kit.*	• **Selection Test A,** ***Unit 4 Resources,*** pp. 179–180 • ***Reading Kit,*** Assess worksheets, pp. 179, 183, 184, 190, 198	• **Selection Test A,** ***Unit 4 Resources,*** pp. 199–201 • **Reading Kit,** Assess worksheets, pp. 179, 183, 184, 190, 198

TIER 3 Tier 3 intervention may require consultation with the student's special-education or dyslexia specialist. For additional support, see the Tier 2 activities and resources listed above.

One-on-one teaching **Group work** **Whole class instruction** **Independent work** **A Assessment**

For a complete guide to selection support, including support for Advanced students, see the Overview of Resources in the frontmatter.

✓Poetry Collection 7
✓✓Poetry Collection 8

RESOURCES FOR:

- L1 **Special-Needs Students**
- L2 **Below-Level Students (Tier 2)**
- L3 **On-Level Students (Tier 1)**
- L4 **Advanced Students (Tier 1)**
- EL **English Learners**
- All **All Students**

Vocabulary/Fluency/Prior Knowledge

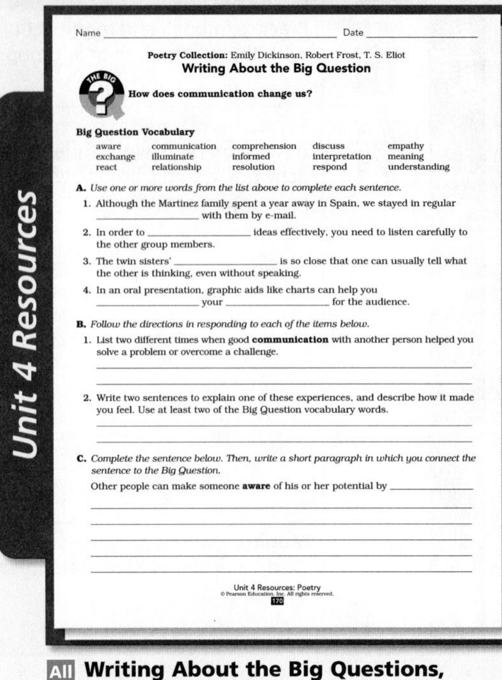
Unit 4 Resources

Name ______ Date ______

Poetry Collection: Emily Dickinson, Robert Frost, T. S. Eliot
Writing About the Big Question

THE BIG ? **How does communication change us?**

Big Question Vocabulary

aware	communication	comprehension	discuss	empathy
exchange	illuminate	informed	interpretation	meaning
react	relationship	resolution	respond	understanding

A. *Use one or more words from the list above to complete each sentence.*

1. Although the Martinez family spent a year away in Spain, we stayed in regular ______ with them by e-mail.
2. In order to ______ ideas effectively, you need to listen carefully to the other group members.
3. The twin sisters' ______ is so close that one can usually tell what the other is thinking, even without speaking.
4. In an oral presentation, graphic aids like charts can help you ______ your ______ for the audience.

B. *Follow the directions in responding to each of the items below.*

1. List two different times when good **communication** with another person helped you solve a problem or overcome a challenge.
2. Write two sentences to explain one of these experiences, and describe how it made you feel. Use at least two of the Big Question vocabulary words.

C. *Complete the sentence below. Then, write a short paragraph in which you connect the sentence to the Big Question.*

Other people can make someone **aware** of his or her potential by ______

Unit 4 Resources: Poetry
© Pearson Education, Inc. All rights reserved.
170

All **Writing About the Big Questions,** pp. 170, 188

Also available for these selections:

EL L1 L2 **Vocabulary Warm-ups A and B,** pp. 166–167, 184–185

EL L1 L2 **Reading Warm-ups A and B,** pp. 168–169, 186–187

All **Vocabulary Builder,** pp. 173, 191

Reader's Notebooks

Pre- and postreading pages for both selections, as well as "Poetry Collection 7," appear in an interactive format in the *Reader's Notebooks.* Each *Notebook* is differentiated for a different group of learners. The selections in the Adapted and English Learner's versions are abridged.

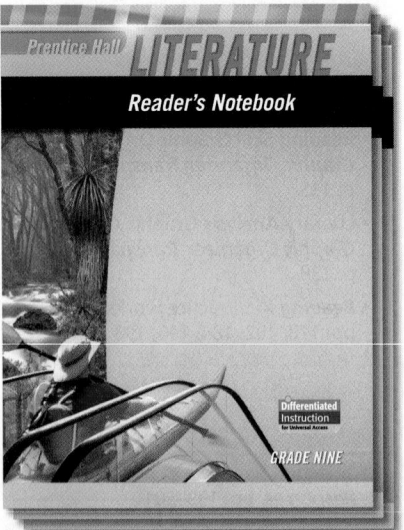

Prentice Hall LITERATURE
Reader's Notebook
Differentiated Instruction for Universal Access
GRADE NINE

L2 L3 ***Reader's Notebook***

L1 ***Reader's Notebook: Adapted Version***

EL ***Reader's Notebook: English Learner's Version***

EL ***Reader's Notebook: Spanish Version***

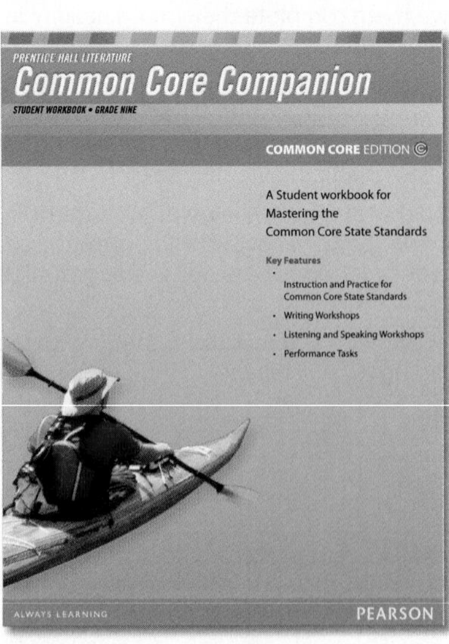

Common Core Companion

Additional instruction and practice for each Common Core State Standard

Selection Support

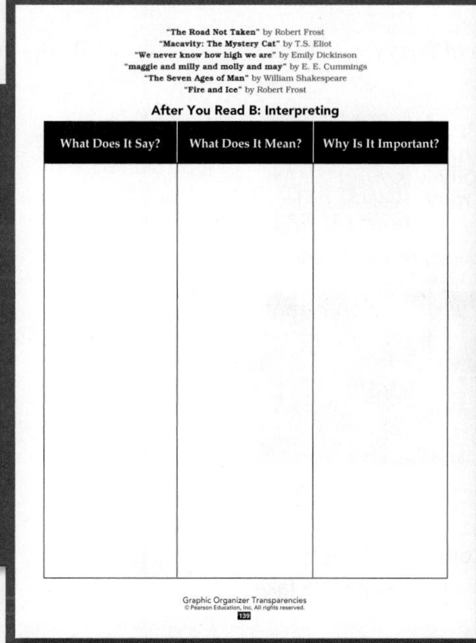
"The Road Not Taken" by Robert Frost
"Macavity: The Mystery Cat" by T.S. Eliot
"We never know how high we are" by Emily Dickinson
"maggie and milly and molly and may" by E. E. Cummings
"The Seven Ages of Man" by William Shakespeare
"Fire and Ice" by Robert Frost

After You Read B: Interpreting

What Does It Say?	What Does It Mean?	Why Is It Important?

Graphic Organizer Transparencies
© Pearson Education, Inc. All rights reserved.
139

EL L3 **Literary Analysis: Graphic Organizer B,** pp. 139

Also available for these selections:

EL L1 L2 **Reading: Graphic Organizer A,** pp. 134–135 (partially filled in)

EL L3 **Reading: Graphic Organizer B,** p. 136

EL L1 L2 **Literary Analysis: Graphic Organizer A,** p. 137, 138 (partially filled in)

Skills Development/Extension

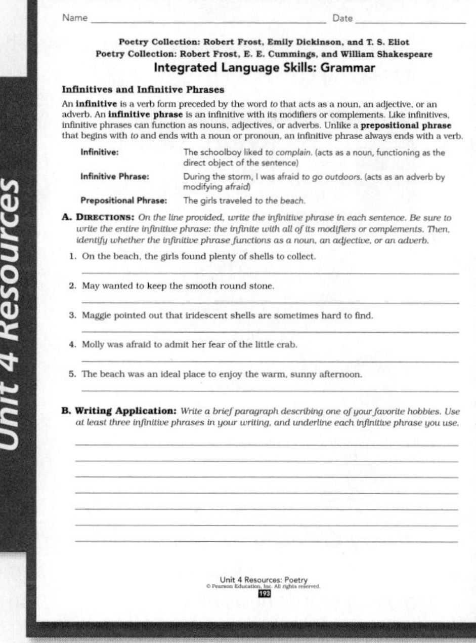
Name ______ Date ______

Poetry Collection: Robert Frost, Emily Dickinson, and T. S. Eliot
Poetry Collection: Robert Frost, E. E. Cummings, and William Shakespeare
Integrated Language Skills: Grammar

Infinitives and Infinitive Phrases

An **infinitive** is a verb form preceded by the word *to* that acts as a noun, an adjective, or an adverb. An **infinitive phrase** is an infinitive with its modifiers or complements. Like infinitives, infinitive phrases can function as nouns, adjectives, or adverbs. Unlike a **prepositional phrase** that begins with *to* and ends with a noun or pronoun, an infinitive phrase always ends with a verb.

Infinitive: The schoolboy liked *to complain.* (acts as a noun, functioning as the direct object of the sentence)

Infinitive Phrase: During the storm, I was afraid *to go outdoors.* (acts as an adverb by modifying *afraid*)

Prepositional Phrase: The girls traveled *to the beach.*

A. Directions: *On the line provided, write the infinitive phrase in each sentence. Be sure to write the entire infinitive phrase: the infinite with all of its modifiers or complements. Then, identify whether the infinitive phrase functions as a noun, an adjective, or an adverb.*

1. On the beach, the girls found plenty of shells to collect.
2. May wanted to keep the smooth round stone.
3. Maggie pointed out that iridescent shells are sometimes hard to find.
4. Molly was afraid to admit her fear of the little crab.
5. The beach was an ideal place to enjoy the warm, sunny afternoon.

B. Writing Application: *Write a brief paragraph describing one of your favorite hobbies. Use at least three infinitive phrases in your writing, and underline each infinitive phrase you use.*

Unit 4 Resources: Poetry
© Pearson Education, Inc. All rights reserved.
193

EL L3 L4 **Grammar,** p. 155

Also available for these selections:

All **Literary Analysis: Rhyme and Meter,** pp. 171, 189

All **Reading: Paraphrase,** pp. 172, 190

L4 **Enrichment,** pp. 174, 192

EL L3 L4 **Support for Writing,** p. 194

L3 L4 **Support for Extend Your Learning,** p. 195

Assessment

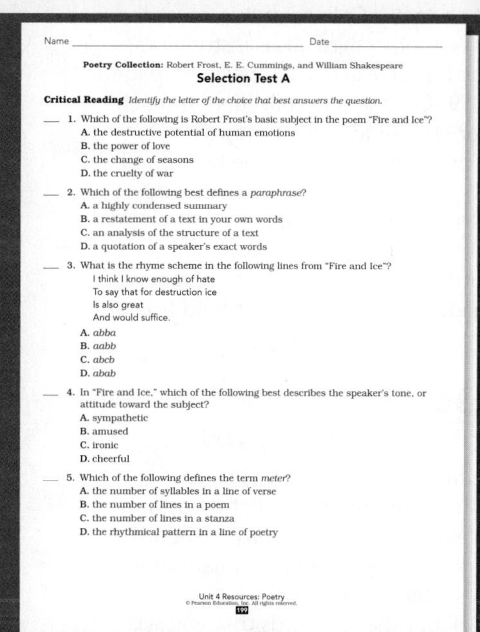
Name ______ Date ______

Poetry Collection: Robert Frost, E. E. Cummings, and William Shakespeare
Selection Test A

Critical Reading *Identify the letter of the choice that best answers the question.*

___ 1. Which of the following is Robert Frost's basic subject in the poem "Fire and Ice"?
A. the destructive potential of human emotions
B. the power of love
C. the change of seasons
D. the cruelty of war

___ 2. Which of the following best defines a *paraphrase*?
A. a highly condensed summary
B. a restatement of a text in your own words
C. an analysis of the structure of a text
D. a quotation of a speaker's exact words

___ 3. What is the rhyme scheme in the following lines from "Fire and Ice"?
I think I know enough of hate
To say that for destruction ice
Is also great
And would suffice.
A. *abba*
B. *aabb*
C. *abcb*
D. *abab*

___ 4. In "Fire and Ice," which of the following best describes the speaker's tone, or attitude toward the subject?
A. sympathetic
B. amused
C. ironic
D. cheerful

___ 5. Which of the following defines the term *meter*?
A. the number of syllables in a line of verse
B. the number of lines in a poem
C. the number of lines in a stanza
D. the rhythmical pattern in a line of poetry

Unit 4 Resources: Poetry
© Pearson Education, Inc. All rights reserved.
199

EL L1 L2 **Selection Test A,** pp. 178–180, 199–201

Also available for these selections:

L3 L4 **Open-Book Test,** pp. 175–177, 196–198

EL L3 L4 **Selection Test B,** pp. 181–183, 202–204

PHLit Online!
www.PHLitOnline.com

- complete narrated selection text
- a thematically related video with writing prompt
- an interactive graphic organizer
- highlighting feature
- access to all student print resources, adapted to individual student needs
- Spanish and English summaries
- adapted selection translations in Spanish

Online Resources: All print materials are also available online.

Get Connected! (thematic video with writing prompt)

Also available:

Background Video

All videos are available in Spanish.

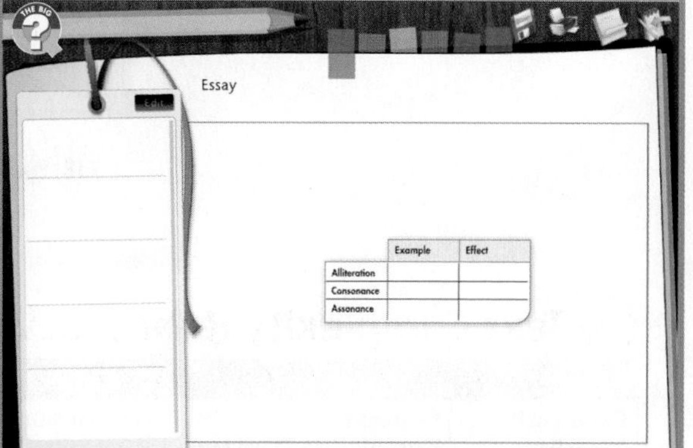

Writer's Journal (with graphics feature)

Also available:

Vocabulary Central (tools, activities, and songs for studying vocabulary)

DIFFERENTIATE/PRETEACH

1 Leveled Texts

You may use either Poetry Collection 7 or Poetry Collection 8 to meet the lesson objectives. Skills instruction for both collections appears on page 719. Choose one collection to teach (or choose to teach both). The Text Complexity Rubric at the bottom of this page will help you determine which collection is more appropriate for your students. Use the Reader and Task Suggestions on the facing page to help all students read text of increasing complexity.

2 Introducing the CCS Standards

Introduce the standards on the student page. (Note that the lesson element with which each standard is addressed is identified in parentheses after the text of the standard.) Call out the standards that you will cover with the collections, explaining to students what each requires and how they will address it as they work through the collection you have chosen. Standards labeled "Spiral Review" are introduced in the Literary Analysis Workshop for this unit.

Before You Read

Poetry Collection 7 • Poetry Collection 8

1 Leveled Texts

Build your skills and improve your comprehension of poetry with texts of increasing complexity.

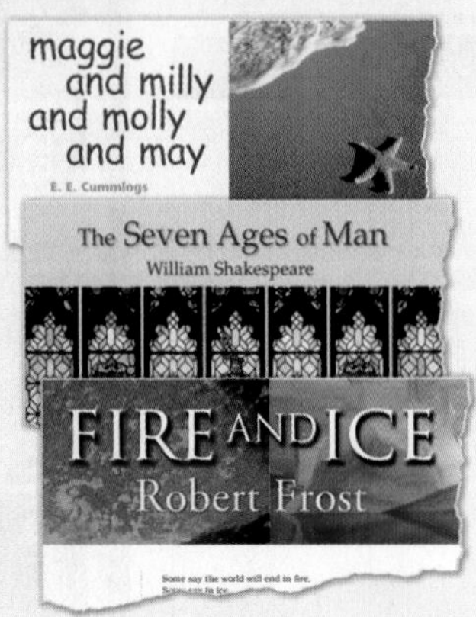

Poetry Collection 7 explores the nature of heroism and making crucial decisions.

Poetry Collection 8 explores the emotions and roles people take on in life.

2 Common Core State Standards

Meet these standards with either **Poetry Collection 7** (p. 724) or **Poetry Collection 8** (p. 732).

Reading Literature

2. Determine a theme or central idea of a text. *(Reading Skill: Paraphrasing)*

4. Determine the meaning of words and phrases as they are used in the text, including figurative and connotative meanings; analyze the cumulative impact of specific word choices on meaning and tone. *(Literary Analysis: Spiral Review)*

7. Analyze the representation of a subject or a key scene in two different artistic mediums. *(Analyze Representations)*

Writing

4. Produce clear and coherent writing in which the development, organization, and style are appropriate to task, purpose, and audience. *(Writing: Poem)*

Speaking and Listening

1.a. Come to discussions prepared, having read and researched material under study; explicitly draw on that preparation to stimulate a thoughtful, well-reasoned exchange of ideas. **1.c.** Propel conversations by posing and responding to questions that relate the current discussion to broader themes or larger ideas; actively incorporate others into the discussion; and clarify, verify, or challenge ideas and conclusions. **1.d.** Respond thoughtfully to diverse perspectives, summarize points of agreement and disagreement, and, when warranted, qualify or justify their own views and understanding, and make new connections in light of the evidence and reasoning presented. *(Speaking and Listening: Panel Discussion)*

Language

1.b. Use various types of phrases and clauses to convey specific meanings and add variety and interest to writing or presentations. *(Conventions: Infinitive Phrases)*

Text Complexity Rubric: Leveled Texts

Text complexity is determined by both qualitative and quantitative measures. For this reason, the quantitative measure of a more complex collection may be lower than that of a more accessible collection.

		✓ Collection 7	✓✓ Collection 8
Qualitative Measures	**Context/ Knowledge Demands**	Familiar situations (choices, cats, self-discovery) **1 2 ③ 4 5**	Journeys in life **1 2 3 ④ 5**
	Structure/Language Conventionality and Clarity	Difficult sentence structure; some challenging vocabulary **1 2 ③ 4 5**	Difficult sentence structure; challenging vocabulary **1 2 3 ④ 5**
	Levels of Meaning/ Purpose	Accessible concept (choices we make) **1 2 ③ 4 5**	Challenging concept (reactions to life's journey) **1 2 3 ④ 5**
Quantitative Measures	**Text Length**	Word Count: 144; 436; 47	Word Count: 93; 212; 51
	Lexile	NP	NP
Overall Complexity		✓ **More accessible**	✓✓ **More complex**

❸ Literary Analysis: Rhyme and Meter

Rhyme and meter are two literary devices often used in poetry. **Rhyme** is the repetition of sounds at the ends of words. There are several types of rhyme:

- **Exact rhyme:** the repetition of words that end with the same vowel and consonant sounds, as in *love* and *dove*
- **Slant rhyme:** the repetition of words that end with similar sounds but do not rhyme perfectly, as in *prove* and *glove*
- **End rhyme:** the rhyming of words at the ends of lines
- **Internal rhyme:** the rhyming of words within a line

A **rhyme scheme** is a regular pattern of end rhymes in a poem or stanza, in which a letter is assigned to each set of rhyming sounds. For example, in "Ring Out, Wild Bells," Alfred, Lord Tennyson uses the rhyme scheme *abba:*

Ring out, wild bells, to the wild sky, a
The flying cloud, the frosty light: b
The year is dying in the night; b
Ring out, wild bells, and let him die. a

Lewis Carroll opens "Jabberwocky" with the rhyme scheme *abab:*

'Twas brillig, and the slithy toves a
Did gyre and gimble in the wabe; b
All mimsy were the borogroves, a
And the mome raths outgrabe. b

Meter is the rhythmical pattern in a line of poetry that results from the arrangement of stressed (´) and unstressed (˘) syllables. The stress goes on the syllable that is accented in natural speech. Reading the line aloud reveals the steady rhythmic pulse of the stressed syllables:

Thĕ flýĭng clóud, thĕ fróstў líght

Hálf ă leáguĕ, hálf ă leáguĕ, / Hálf ă leáguĕ ónwărd

Each meter is named based on its length and rhythmical pattern. A common pattern uses *iambs*, beats in which the stress is on the second syllable, such as hĕlló or ălóud. In *iambic pentameter,* each line contains five iambs.

Shăll Í / cŏmpáre / thĕe tó / ă súm / mĕr's dáy?

Thŏu árt / mŏre lóve / ĭy ánd / mŏre témp / ĕr áte.

PHLit Online!
www.PHLitOnline.com

Hear It!
- Selection summary audio
- Selection audio

See It!
- Get Connected video
- Background video
- More about the author
- Vocabulary flashcards

Do It!
- Interactive journals
- Interactive graphic organizers
- Self-test
- Internet activity
- Grammar tutorial
- Interactive vocabulary games

PRETEACH

❸ Literary Analysis
Rhyme and Meter

1. Introduce the skills, using instruction on the student page.
2. Tell students that they will practice analyzing rhyme and meter as they read.

Think Aloud: Model the Skill

Write this poem on the board:

I know a man/Young and slim,/ Whose life is strife/Whose future's dim.

Model the skill of analyzing rhyme and meter. Say to students:

I read poems out loud to help bring out their rhyme scheme and meter. When I read this poem aloud, I can hear the author's use of end rhyme and exact rhyme (*slim* and *dim*), as well as internal rhyme (*life* and *strife*). Because the last words of lines 2 and 4 rhyme, this poem's rhyme scheme is abcb.

As I read aloud, I mark the stressed and unstressed syllables to identify the poem's meter. This poem has a regular meter of two stressed beats per line—for example, Ī knów ā mán.

Text Complexity: Reader and Task Suggestions

✓ Collection 7		✓✓ Collection 8	
Preparing to Read the Text	**Leveled Tasks**	**Preparing to Read the Text**	**Leveled Tasks**
• Using the Background information on TE p. 723, discuss the poets. • Discuss the kinds of choices people make in life and the intended and unintended consequences that may follow. • Guide students to use Multidraft Reading strategies (TE p. 723).	*Levels of Meaning* If students will have difficulty with levels of meaning, have them first read each poem and list the main details. Then, have them reread each poem and tell what the mystery is. *Analyzing* If students will not have difficulty with levels of meaning, have them read each poem and note why the ending follows logically from events described earlier.	• Refer to the Background note on TE p. 731 and discuss the poets. • Discuss the exalted, lofty language of poetry during Shakespeare's age as compared to less formal, modern poetic language. • Guide students to use Multidraft Reading strategies (TE p. 731).	*Levels of Meaning* If students will have difficulty with meaning, have them read each poem and identify the journey the poet describes. Then, have them reread and explain what the speaker learns. *Analyzing* If students will not have difficulty with meaning, have them note examples of figurative language in each poem. Have them relate the figurative language to the theme.

❸ Literary Analysis

(continued from p. 719)

3. Have volunteers read each of the examples given in the chart aloud. As the volunteer reads, have the class clap for each heavy stress indicated.
4. Point out to students that when the line break in a poem comes at a natural pause in the poet's sentence, it reinforces the pattern of stresses, as in the example for tetrameter. When such pauses regularly appear at the end of lines, it lends the poem a "sing-song" quality.
5. Point out by contrast the examples for dimeter and trimeter, in which the line breaks do not correspond to a natural pause. Instead, the meaning of the sentence should carry the reader smoothly from the end of one line into the beginning of the next—an effect known as enjambment.
6. Have a volunteer read the example for dimeter in a natural way, without pausing at the line break. Then, have the volunteer repeat this "natural" reading as the class claps at each strong beat. Point out that the "natural" reading of the lines as a sentence forms a counterpoint to or mutes the regular iambic beat of the lines. Note that this effect is used in many types of poetry, including contemporary hip-hop music.
7. Point out that even though free verse lacks a regular meter, poets have a variety of ways of ordering language in free verse. Discuss with students the pattern of indents Pat Mora uses in the example on the student page. Note that final line of the excerpt "looks" final because it is centered.
8. Discuss blank verse with students. Explain that poets who work in extended forms, such as Shakespeare in his plays and the English poet John Milton in his epics, may use blank verse, which frees them from the necessity of keeping up a steady rhyme scheme for pages of verse.

Before You Read

Poetry Collection 7 • Poetry Collection 8

❸ Literary Analysis: Rhyme and Meter *(continued)*

An *iambic dimeter* would consist of two iambs, a *trimeter* would consist of three iambs, a *tetrameter* would consist of four iambs, and so on. See the chart below for examples of these metric groupings.

Iambic Meter	Example
Dimeter (2 beats per line)	Ănd fór / rĕdréss Ŏf áll / mў páin,
Trimeter (3 beats per line)	Wĕ rómped / ŭntíl / thĕ páns Slĭd fróm / thĕ kítch / ĕn shélf;
Tetrameter (4 beats per line)	Ĭ thínk / thăt Í / shăll né / vĕr sée ă pó / ĕm lóve / lў ás / ă trée.

Not all poems include rhyme, a rhyme scheme, or a regular meter. Nonmetrical poetry, or poems that do not contain a regular pattern of meter, are known as **free verse.**

"Uncoiling" by Pat Mora is written as free verse:

With thorns she scratches
on my window, tosses her hair dark with rain,
snares lightning, cholla, hawks, butterfly
swarms in the tangles.

Poems that do not rhyme but consist of iambic pentameter are known as **blank verse.** William Shakespeare wrote many of his plays in blank verse as in this line from *Romeo and Juliet*:

Bŭt sóft! / Wh̆at líght / thrŏugh yón / dĕr wín / dŏw bréaks?
Ĭt ís / thĕ eást, / ănd Jú / lĭet ís / thĕ sún!

Poets often use one or more rhyming techniques to create musical effects and achieve a sense of unity in their poems.

As you read the poetry in this collection, notice their specific rhyme and meter and the effect of these poetic elements.

- Look for examples of different types of rhyme.
- Determine if the lines follow a rhyme scheme.
- Notice whether or not the lines follow a regular meter.

❹ Reading Skill: Paraphrase

Paraphrasing is restating in your own words what someone else has written or said. A paraphrase should retain the essential meaning and central ideas of the original but should be simpler to read and to understand. One way to simplify the text that you are paraphrasing is to **break down long sentences.** Follow these steps:

- Divide long sentences into parts and paraphrase those parts.
- If a sentence contains multiple subjects or verbs, see if it can be separated into smaller sentences that each contain one subject and one verb.
- If a sentence contains colons, semicolons, or dashes, create separate sentences by treating those punctuation marks as periods.
- If a sentence contains long phrases or long passages in parentheses, turn each phrase or parenthetical passage into a separate sentence.

Poets often write sentences that span several lines to give their poems fluidity. By breaking down long sentences and paraphrasing them, you can better understand how the poet gradually develops his or her central idea.

Paraphrasing can particularly help you synthesize content that comes from several works by the same author addressing a single issue. It can give you a more comprehensive picture of the author.

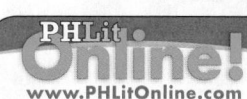

PHLit Online!
www.PHLitOnline.com

Hear It!
- Selection summary audio
- Selection audio

See It!
- Get Connected video
- Background video
- More about the author
- Vocabulary flashcards

Do It!
- Interactive journals
- Interactive graphic organizers
- Self-test
- Internet activity
- Grammar tutorial
- Interactive vocabulary games

❺ Using the Strategy: Paraphrase Chart

As you read poetry and break down long sentences, use a **paraphrase chart** like the one shown to record your work.

Original Lines	Lines in Smaller Sentences	Paraphrase
I celebrate myself and sing myself, / And what I assume you shall assume, / For every atom belonging to me as good belongs to you. —Walt Whitman	I celebrate myself. I sing myself. What I assume you shall assume. Every atom belonging to me as good belongs to you.	I celebrate myself and share my joy with you. What is mine is also yours.

❹ Reading Skill

Paraphrase

1. Introduce the skill, using instruction on the student page.
2. Tell students that they will practice paraphrasing as they read.

❺ Using the Strategy

Give students a copy of either **Reading Skill Graphic Organizer A** or **B** (*Graphic Organizer Transparencies*, pp. 134–136) to record details of paraphrasing as they read. Use the examples in **Reading Skill Graphic Organizer A,** which is partially filled in, to model the process of completing the organizer.

PRETEACH

1 Writing About the Big Question

1. Review the assignment with the class.
2. **Ask** students to think about challenges they have experienced in their life. Do they think that difficult challenges bring out the best in people? Why or why not?
3. Have students complete the sentence starter. Review responses as a class. (**Possible response:** A person can make someone else aware of his or her potential by encouraging him or her to take on a difficult task.)
4. Remind students that their answers will help them think about the Big Question, "How does communication change us?"

While You Read

Tell students that as they read they should think about whether people achieve more when more is asked of them.

2 Vocabulary

1. Have students preview the selection vocabulary.
2. For each word, have students say the word aloud.
3. Then, use the word in a sentence that defines the word.
4. Finally, repeat your definitional sentence or a similar sentence with the word missing and have the class "fill in the blank" chorally. Here are some examples:

   Disclosed means revealed or made known. The detective couldn't determine the solution to the mystery until the clues to the mystery were [students say "disclosed"].

   Diverged means branched out in different directions. As we traveled down the highway, we noticed on the map that there was an intersection where the main road [students say "diverged"].

3 Word Study

1. Introduce the skill, using the instruction in the box.
2. Ask students for a word with the suffix *-ment* that means "happiness." (**Answer:** *contentment*)

Making Connections
Poetry Collection 7

The Road Not Taken • Macavity: The Mystery Cat • We never know how high we are

How does communication change us?

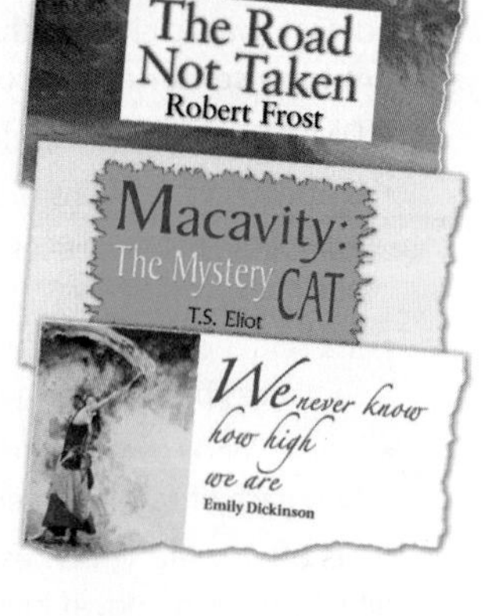

1 Writing About the Big Question

In the last poem in Collection 7, the speaker claims that "We never know how high we are / Till we are asked to rise." Use this sentence starter to develop your ideas about the Big Question.

A person can make someone else **aware** of his or her potential by _______________.

While You Read Consider whether it is true that people achieve more when more is asked of them.

2 Vocabulary

Read each word and its definition. Decide whether you know the word well, know it a little bit, or do not know it at all. After you read, see how your knowledge of each word has increased.

- **diverged** (dī vʉrjd′) *v.* branched out in different directions (p. 725) *When the highway diverged, we were not sure which way to go.* *diverge v. divergence n. diverging adj. diversity n.*
- **bafflement** (baf′ əl mənt) *n.* puzzlement; bewilderment (p. 726) *To the bafflement of many, the jet pilot was afraid of heights.* *baffle v. baffling adj.*
- **depravity** (dē prav′ ə tē) *n.* crookedness; corruption (p. 727) *The criminal's depravity was well-known, and his arrest was cheered.* *depraved adj. deprave v.*
- **rifled** (rī′ fəld) *v.* ransacked and robbed; searched quickly through a cupboard or drawer (p. 727) *My little sister rifled through my drawer and took my favorite sweater.* *rifle v.*
- **disclosed** (dis klōzd′) *v.* revealed; made known (p. 727) *John disclosed the location of his hidden treasure.* *disclose v. disclosure n.*
- **warp** (wôrp) *v.* twist; distort (p. 728) *Skilled artists can warp wood into different shapes.* *warped adj.*

3 Word Study

The **Latin suffix *-ment*** means "act" or "resulting state of."

In "Macavity: The Mystery Cat," the speaker refers to Macavity as "the **bafflement** of Scotland Yard." Bafflement is the resulting state of being baffled, or puzzled, the speaker means that Macavity is the reason Scotland Yard is puzzled.

Vocabulary Development

Vocabulary Knowledge Rating

Create a **Vocabulary Knowledge Rating Chart** (***Professional Development Guidebook***, p. 33) for this collection. Include the collection vocabulary and the word that appears in the Writing About the Big Question sentence starter on this page. (The Big Question vocabulary is introduced on pp. 604–605.)

Give students a copy of the chart. Read the words aloud, and have students mark their rating in the Before Reading column. Urge them to be alert to these words as they read and discuss the selection.

Tally how many students think they know a word to gauge how much instruction to provide. As students read and discuss the selection, point out the words and their context.

Vocabulary Central, featuring tools, activities, and songs for studying vocabulary, is available at **www.PHLitOnline.com.**

4 Meet the Authors

Robert Frost

(1874–1963)

"The Road Not Taken" (p. 724)

In January 1961, when John F. Kennedy became president of the United States, he called on fellow New Englander Robert Frost to recite two poems at the inauguration. At the time, Frost was America's most famous living poet. He became famous when *A Boy's Will* (1913) and *North of Boston* (1914) won wide praise in both the United Kingdom and the United States.

T. S. Eliot

(1888–1965)

"Macavity: The Mystery Cat" (p. 726)

A whimsical poem like "Macavity: The Mystery Cat" was a rarity in the writing of Thomas Stearns Eliot. He was better known for serious, philosophical poems. Born in the United States, Eliot settled in the United Kingdom. He became a highly influential poet and won the Nobel Prize in 1948.

Emily Dickinson

(1830–1886)

"We never know how high we are" (p. 728)

Emily Dickinson's life in Amherst, Massachusetts, seemed to be quiet and uneventful. Yet, the emotional power of her poems shows the wide range of her energy and imagination. She found profound meanings in simple subjects, and her poems still delight readers.

Differentiated Instruction — Additional Instruction

EL Extended Support—English Learners
Have students complete the **Reading and Vocabulary Warm-ups,** ***Unit 4 Resources,*** pp. 166–169, before they read. Assign the prereading pages and the collection in the ***Reader's Notebook: English Learner's Version.*** Then, have students listen to portions of the selection on the ***Hear It!*** **Audio CD.**

L1 L2 Extended Support—Struggling Readers
Have students complete the **Reading and Vocabulary Warm-ups,** ***Unit 4 Resources,*** pp. 166–169, before they read. Assign the prereading pages and the collection in the ***Reader's Notebook: Adapted Version.*** Then, have students listen to portions of the selection on the ***Hear It!*** **Audio CD** (adapted text).

Extended Support—Reluctant Readers
To build motivation and engagement before assigning the collection, have students read "Brain Battle," a thematically related selection in ***Reality Central.*** Then, use the questions at the conclusion of the related selection to guide discussion.

Daily Bellringer

For each class during which you will teach this selection, have students complete one of the five Research activities for Week 23 in the ***Daily Bellringer Activities*** booklet.

4 Background

- **Robert Frost** Although born in San Francisco, California, Robert Frost moved to New England as a child and spent many years as a young man in England. Even though his work is strongly associated with the life and beauty of New England, it is not regional and contains strong, universal themes that are common to people everywhere.

  Robert Frost, unlike most poets, became a national celebrity and is one of the most well-known American poets of the 20th century.
- **T.S. Eliot** A prolific poet, T.S. Eliot's poems were first published when he was a student at Harvard University. After moving to England, his reputation as a poet grew quite quickly. His book of poetry, *The Wasteland*, which was published in 1922, is considered to be the most influential work of poetry of the 20th century.

Multidraft Reading

To assist struggling readers and to deepen reading for all, apply multidraft reading protocols, following the pause points ● to "chunk" longer poems. For each reading, have students set the purpose indicated:

- **First reading**—identifying key ideas and details and answering any Reading Checks.
- **Second reading**—analyzing craft and structure and responding to the side-column prompts.
- **Third reading**—integrating knowledge and ideas, connecting to other texts and the world, and answering the end-of-selection questions.

For more guidance, refer to the ***Classroom Strategies and Teaching Routines*** card on multidraft reading.

For more about the authors and practice with the selection vocabulary, go online at **www.PHLitOnline.com.**

TEACH

❶ Activating Prior Knowledge

1. Prepare an **Anticipation Guide** (***Professional Development Guidebook,*** pp. 36–38) with the following statements:
   - People avoid trying to be all that they can for fear of failure.
   - Few people take the most challenging course of action.
   - Once you choose your path in life, you can never go back.
2. Give students a copy of the prepared **Anticipation Guide** and have students mark their responses in the appropriate columns.
3. For further guidance, use the ***Classroom Strategies and Teaching Routines*** card: **Using an Anticipation Guide.**

Concept Connector

Students will return to the **Anticipation Guide** after completing this poetry collection.

Whole-Class Activity

The infectious fun of "Macavity: The Mystery Cat" provides an opportunity for group reading and spontaneous discussion. With the class, conduct a choral reading and discuss the poem's humor.

❷ About the Selections

In "The Road Not Taken," the speaker must decide whether to pursue a more conventional direction or resist conformity by following his individual desires. He chooses the less conventional path.

"Macavity: The Mystery Cat" describes the mischievousness of a cat as if the characteristic were evidence of a super-criminal mind. The lively verse of T.S. Eliot enlivens the poem with humor.

In "We never know how high we are," Emily Dickinson speaks of the human fear of achieving greatness. According to the speaker, we limit ourselves to stay safe.

724 Poetry

Vocabulary Development

Ⓒ CCSS Language 6

Thematic Vocabulary: The Big Question

As students are discussing Poetry Collection 7, encourage them to use the thematic vocabulary presented in Introducing the Big Question, pp. 604–605. You might encourage them with sentence starters like these:

1. The most common *interpretation* of the fork in the road in "The Road Not Taken" is . . .
2. Macavity's *relationship* with the other characters in the poem can be described as . . .
3. Dickinson helps *illuminate* the human tendency to . . .
4. As a result of reading "We never know how high we are," we might make a *resolution* to . . .

❶ ❷ The Road Not Taken

Robert Frost

❸

Two roads diverged in a yellow wood,
And sorry I could not travel both
And be one traveler, long I stood
And looked down one as far as I could
To where it bent in the undergrowth;

Then took the other, as just as fair,
And having perhaps the better claim,
Because it was grassy and wanted wear;
Though as for that, the passing there
Had worn them really about the same,

And both that morning equally lay
In leaves no step had trodden black.
Oh, I kept the first for another day!
Yet knowing how way leads on to way,
I doubted if I should ever come back.

❹

I shall be telling this with a sigh
Somewhere ages and ages hence:
Two roads diverged in a wood, and I—
I took the one less traveled by,
And that has made all the difference.

Vocabulary
diverged (dī vʉrjd′) *v.* branched out in different directions

Reading Skill
Paraphrase In your own words, restate the decision the speaker makes in lines 6–8.

Literary Analysis
Rhyme and Meter What is the rhyme scheme of stanza four?

❺ ◀ **Analyze Representations** How is the speaker's description of the woods similar to or different from the photograph? **[Compare and Contrast]**

❸ Reading Skill
Paraphrase

1. Have students read the first two stanzas of the poem. **Ask** students to explain the situation described in the first stanza.

   Answer: A traveler is following a road in the woods and comes to a fork.
2. **Ask** students to respond to the Reading Skill prompt: In your own words, restate the decision the speaker makes in lines 6–8.

   Possible response: The speaker takes the other path, since it is just as pleasant and a little less worn.

❹ Literary Analysis
Rhyme and Meter

1. Have students read the entire poem aloud. **Ask** students what type of rhyme the poet uses.

   Answer: The poet uses exact rhyme.
2. Point out that all the stanzas in this poem are the same length. **Ask** what this suggests about the rhyme scheme.

   Answer: This suggests that the rhyme scheme is the same for all stanzas.
3. Refer students to the last stanza. **Ask** students the Literary Analysis question: What is the rhyme scheme of stanza four?

   Answer: The rhyme scheme is *abaab.*
4. **Ask:** What is the rhyme scheme of the other stanzas in the poem?

   Answer: The rhyme scheme for all the stanzas is the same: *abaab.*

❺ Critical Viewing
Possible response: People are often faced with two life choices that seem equally attractive. Taking one or the other changes the direction of their lives.

Differentiated Instruction for Universal Access

Strategy for Special-Needs Students
To help students appreciate the sound devices in these poems, have them read the ***Reader's Notebook: Adapted Version*** as they listen to the ***Hear It!* Audio CD.** Lead a discussion about the patterns of rhyme and meter in these poems. You may also discuss the humor in "Macavity: the Mystery Cat."

EL Strategy for English Learners
Students should not have much difficulty with the first and third poems in this collection, but they may have a problem understanding the humor in "Macavity: the Mystery Cat." Provide students with the ***Reader's Notebook: English Learner's Version.*** Have them work as a group to read the poems. Help them with the humor in "Macavity."

PHLit Online!
This selection is available in interactive format in the **Enriched Online Student Edition, www.PHLitOnline.com,** which includes a thematically related video with writing prompt and an interactive graphic organizer.

❻ Literary Analysis

Rhyme and Meter

1. Read the first two stanzas aloud for students. **Ask** students what fact is established about Macavity in these lines, and what is humorous about this.

   Answer: Macavity is a cat, and the speaker describes him as a master criminal, even giving him the nickname of the Hidden Paw, who defies the law and always successfully eludes law enforcement officials.

2. Refer students to the second stanza of the poem. **Ask** students the Literary Analysis question: What type of rhyme does this stanza contain?

   Answer: The stanza contains exact end rhyme.

3. Have students read two stanzas aloud, listening for the rhyme and the meter. **Ask** students to explain how the rhyme and meter of these stanzas contribute to the humor.

   Possible response: The almost sing-song, fast-moving rhythm of the lines and the repetition of the "air" sound of the end rhyme give the lines an upbeat, humorous sound.

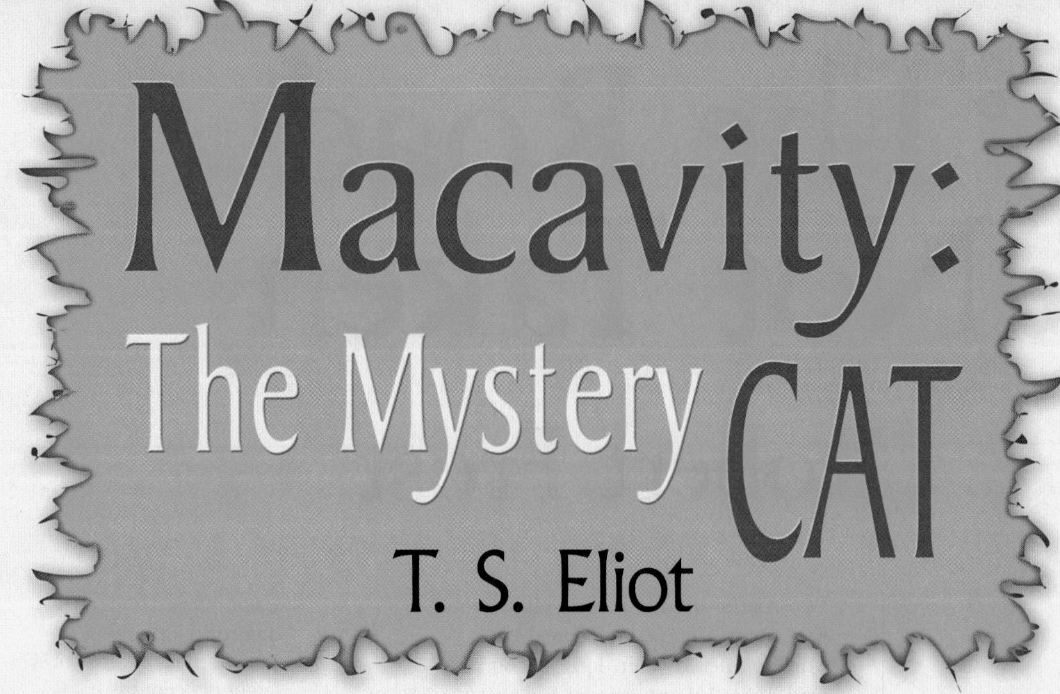

Vocabulary
bafflement (baf′ əl mənt) *n.* puzzlement; bewilderment

Macavity's a Mystery Cat: he's called the Hidden Paw—
For he's the master criminal who can defy the Law.
He's the bafflement of Scotland Yard,[1] the Flying Squad's[2] despair:
For when they reach the scene of crime—*Macavity's not there!*

❻

Macavity, Macavity, there's no one like Macavity,
He's broken every human law, he breaks the law of gravity.
His powers of levitation would make a fakir[3] stare,
And when you reach the scene of crime—*Macavity's not there!*
You may seek him in the basement, you may look up in the air—
But I tell you once and once again, *Macavity's not there!*

Literary Analysis
Rhyme and Meter
What type of rhyme does this stanza contain?

Macavity's a ginger cat, he's very tall and thin;
You would know him if you saw him, for his eyes are sunken in.

1. **Scotland Yard** London police.
2. **Flying Squad** criminal-investigation department.
3. **fakir** (fə kir′) *n.* Muslim or Hindu beggar who claims to perform miracles.

Vocabulary Development

Vocabulary Knowledge Rating

When students have completed reading and discussing this poetry collection, have them take out their **Vocabulary Knowledge Rating Chart** for these poems. Read the words aloud once more and have students rate their knowledge of the words again in the After Reading column. Clarify any words that are still problematic. Have students write their own definition and example or sentence in the appropriate column. Then have students complete the Vocabulary Practice activities at the end of the collection. Encourage students to use the words in further discussion and written work about these poems. Remind them that they will be accountable for these words on the **Selection Test, *Unit 4 Resources,*** pp. 178–180 or 181–183.

His brow is deeply lined with thought, his head is highly domed;
His coat is dusty from neglect, his whiskers are uncombed.
He sways his head from side to side, with movements like a snake;
And when you think he's half asleep, he's always wide awake.

Macavity, Macavity, there's no one like Macavity,
For he's a fiend in feline shape, a monster of depravity.
You may meet him in a by-street, you may see him in the square—
But when a crime's discovered, then *Macavity's not there!*

He's outwardly respectable. (They say he cheats at cards.)
And his footprints are not found in any file of Scotland Yard's.
And when the larder's looted, or the jewel-case is rifled,
Or when the milk is missing, or another Peke's[4] been stifled,
Or the greenhouse glass is broken, and the trellis past repair—
Ay, there's the wonder of the thing! *Macavity's not there!*

And when the Foreign Office find a Treaty's gone astray,
Or the Admiralty lose some plans and drawings by the way,
There may be a scrap of paper in the hall or on the stair—
But it's useless to investigate—*Macavity's not there!*
And when the loss has been disclosed, the Secret Service say:
'It *must* have been Macavity!'—but he's a mile away.
You'll be sure to find him resting, or a-licking of his thumbs,
Or engaged in doing complicated long division sums.

Macavity, Macavity, there's no one like Macavity,
There never was a Cat of such deceitfulness and suavity.
He always has an alibi, and one or two to spare:
7 At whatever time the deed took place—MACAVITY WASN'T THERE!
And they say that all the Cats whose wicked deeds are widely known
(I might mention Mungojerrie, I might mention Griddlebone)
Are nothing more than agents for the Cat who all the time
Just controls their operations: the Napoleon of Crime![5]

Vocabulary
depravity (dē prav′ ə tē) *n.* crookedness; corruption

rifled (rī′ fəld) *v.* ransacked and robbed; searched quickly through a cupboard or drawer

Vocabulary
disclosed (dis klōzd′) *v.* revealed; made known

Reading Skill
Paraphrase Break down the sentence in lines 43–45 into three smaller sentences. Restate each sentence in your own words.

4. **Peke** short for Pekingese, a small dog with long, silky hair and a pug nose.
5. **the Napoleon of Crime** criminal mastermind; emperor of crime—just as Napoleon Bonaparte (1769–1821) was a masterful military strategist who had himself crowned emperor.

7 Reading Check

Paraphrase

1. Have students read the balance of the poem, beginning with the third stanza. **Ask** students to describe the character of Macavity in their own words.

   Possible response: Macavity is a ginger-colored cat that is not well kept. He's a clever criminal who gets into the food, breaks things, and destroys papers. Despite his crimes, no one can catch him. When the crimes are discovered, he is always long gone from the scene.

2. **Ask** students to identify the three sentences in the sixth stanza, lines 33 through 40.

   Answer: "And when the Foreign Office . . . *Macavity's not there!*" "And when the loss . . . he's a mile away." "You'll be sure to find him . . . long division sums."

3. Refer students to lines 43–45. **Ask** students to respond to the Reading Skill prompt: Break down the sentence in lines 43–45 into three smaller sentences. Restate each sentence in your own words.

   Possible response: He always has an alibi. He has one or two to spare. At whatever time the deed took place, Macavity wasn't there! Macavity always has more than one alibi. He is never around when the crime is discovered.

Monitor Progress: Review students' graphic organizers to ensure that they are able to paraphrase accurately.

Reteach: If students have difficulty paraphrasing, have them retell a fairy tale or fable such as "Hansel and Gretel" or "The Three Little Pigs" in their own words. Paraphrasing a familiar story will provide them with practice.

Concept Connector

Anticipation Guide

Have students return to their **Anticipation Guides** and respond to the statements again in the After Reading column. They may do this individually or in their original pairs or groups. Then, lead a class discussion, probing for what students have learned that confirms or invalidates each statement. Encourage students to cite specific details, quotations, or other evidence from the poems to support their responses to each statement.

Writing About the Big Question

Have students compare their responses to the sentence starter they completed before reading the poems with their ideas afterwards. Ask them to explain whether their thoughts have changed.

Reading Skill Graphic Organizer

Have students review the graphic organizers they completed to make and verify predictions while reading. Show them **Reading Skill Graphic Organizer A** (*Graphic Organizer Transparencies,* p. 134) as an example. Then have students share their graphic organizers.

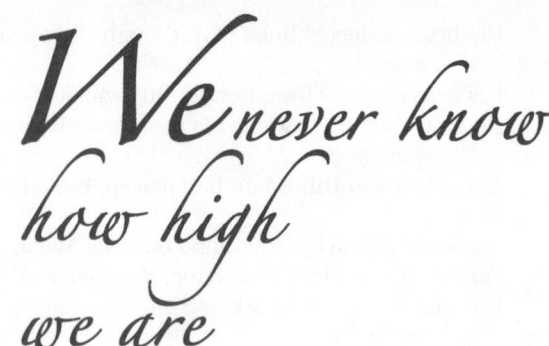

8 Connecting to the Big Question

1. Explain the expression "rise to the occasion."
2. **Ask:** Based on this poem, is it true that people achieve more when more is asked of them? Why or why not?

   Possible response: Yes. Dickinson suggests that people do rise to the occasion and achieve great things, but *only* when they are "asked to rise."

ASSESS

Answers

Critical Thinking

Before students respond, you may wish to have them write a brief objective summary of the selection. As they answer the questions below, remind them to support their answers with evidence from the text.

1. (a) The traveler chooses "the road less traveled by." (b) The final line, "And that has made all the difference," suggests that the traveler is happy with his decision.
2. Cats are mischievous and curious. They get into things, and they can move silently and quickly disappear.
3. Different types of figurative language in the poem contribute to conflicting tones. Eliot's use of personification, comparing a cat to a human criminal, creates a humorous tone, while metaphors and similes comparing Macavity to a fiend, a monster, and a snake create a sinister, dark tone. The combination of the two tones adds to the fun of the poem.
4. (a) If people are true to themselves, they rise to the occasion and "touch the skies." (b) **Possible response:** Yes, because people want to prove something to themselves, and being asked to "rise" gives them a clear opportunity to do so.

Bubbles, Watercolor, 39" x 29", by Scott Burdick, Courtesy of the artist

We never know how high we are

Emily Dickinson

We never know how high we are
Till we are asked to rise
And then if we are true to plan
Our statures touch the skies—
The Heroism we recite
Would be a normal thing
8 Did not ourselves the Cubits[1] warp
For fear to be a King—

Vocabulary
warp (wôrp) *v.* twist; distort

1. **Cubits** (kyo͞o′ bitz) *n.* ancient measure using the length of the arm from the end of the middle finger to the elbow (about 18–22 inches).

Critical Thinking

Cite textual evidence to support your responses.

1. **Key Ideas and Details (a)** In "The Road Not Taken," what does the traveler do when faced with a divide in the road? **(b) Interpret:** What details tell you he is happy with his decision?
2. **Key Ideas and Details Speculate:** Which qualities of cats might have caused T. S. Eliot to associate them with criminal activities in "Macavity: The Mystery Cat"? Explain.
3. **Craft and Structure Interpret:** How does figurative language affect the tone in "Macavity: The Mystery Cat"? Explain.
4. **Integration of Knowledge and Ideas (a)** According to "We never know how high we are," what happens when people are asked to rise to an occasion? **(b)** Do you agree with that claim? Why or why not? *[Connect to the Big Question: How does communication change us?]*

Assessment Resources

Unit 4 Resources

L1 L2 EL **Selection Test A**, pp. 178–180. Administer Test A to less advanced readers.

L3 L4 EL **Selection Test B**, pp. 181–183. Administer Test B to on-level and more advanced students.

L3 L4 **Open-Book Test**, pp. 175–177. As an alternative, give the Open-Book Test.

All **Customizable Test Bank**

All **Self-tests**
Students may prepare for the **Selection Test** by taking the **Self-test** online.

PHLit Online! All assessment resources are available at **www.PHLitOnline.com**.

After You Read Poetry Collection 7

The Road Not Taken • Macavity: The Mystery Cat • We never know how high we are

Literary Analysis: Rhyme and Meter

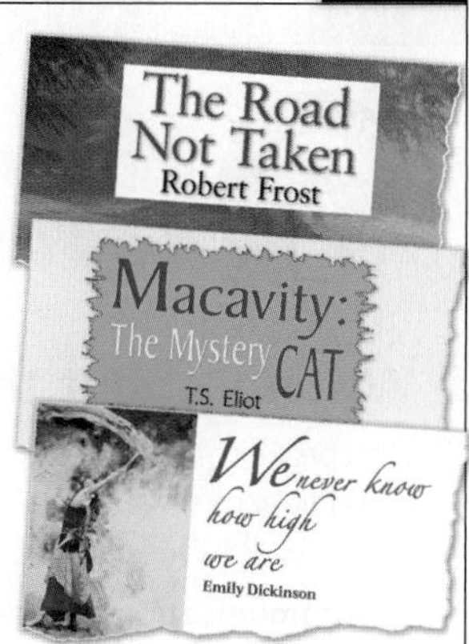

1. **Craft and Structure** Identify two lines in "The Road Not Taken" that illustrate both **exact rhyme** and **end rhyme.** Explain your choices.
2. **Craft and Structure** Which two words in line 31 of "Macavity: The Mystery Cat" illustrate both **slant rhyme** and **internal rhyme?**
3. **Craft and Structure** **(a)** Use letters to identify the **rhyme scheme** in "We never know how high we are." **(b)** In what way does the shift in rhyme scheme midway through the poem help to signal a turning point in the poem's message?
4. **Craft and Structure** **(a)** Which poem has lines with a more regular **meter:** "The Road Not Taken" or "We never know how high we are"? Explain. **(b)** Which do you find more enjoyable to read—lines with a regular meter or lines with an irregular meter? Explain.

Reading Skill: Paraphrase

5. **(a) Paraphrase** the first stanza of "The Road Not Taken" by re-writing it as a series of sentences. **(b)** In what way does **breaking down long sentences** make this poem's meaning clearer?

Vocabulary

Acquisition and Use Decide if each statement is true or false. Then, explain your answer.

1. Reporters are taught to *warp* the facts of events they cover.
2. Two people whose opinions *diverged* would be in disagreement.
3. *Bafflement* is a likely reaction to a bizarre event.
4. Laws are written to encourage *depravity* in society.
5. A closet is tidier after it has been *rifled.*
6. Information that has been *disclosed* is no longer secret.

Word Study Use the context of the sentences and what you know about the **Latin suffix *-ment*** to explain your answer to each question.

1. Would an *amusement* park entertain you?
2. When you make an *improvement,* do you make something better or worse?

Word Study

The **Latin suffix *-ment*** means "act or resulting state of."

Apply It Explain how the suffix *-ment* contributes to the meanings of these words. Consult a dictionary if necessary.

contentment
excitement
abasement

ASSESS/EXTEND

Answers

Literary Analysis

1. Lines 1–3 ("Two roads diverged in a yellow wood, /And sorry I could not travel both/And be one traveler, long I stood") have both exact rhyme and end rhyme. The words *wood* and *stood* come at the end of the lines, and they are exact rhymes.
2. The words *glass* and *past* are examples of both internal rhyme and slant rhyme.
3. (a) abcb, defe. (b) The change works as a second stanza that brings the poem's story to a conclusion.
4. (a) "We never know how high we are" has a more regular meter. Every other line has the same meter, without any variance. (b) **Possible response:** The poem with the more regular meter is more enjoyable to read because it has a predictable flowing cadence.

Reading Skill

5. (a) **Sample response:** Two roads diverged in a yellow wood. I was sorry I could not travel both and be one traveler. Long I stood and looked down one as far as I could. I saw where it bent in the undergrowth. (b) Breaking down long sentences clarifies the meaning because each new, shorter sentence contains one idea, which makes each one easier to follow.

Vocabulary

Acquisition and Use
Sample answers:

1. False. *Warp* means "to distort." Reporters are taught to report the facts as they happened, not to distort them.
2. True. *Diverged* means "to go in a different direction." Opinions that diverged would be different.
3. True. If someone expresses *bafflement,* he or she is puzzled by an event.
4. False. Laws are written to discourage *depravity,* which is corruption and crookedness.

Answers Continued

5. False. A *rifled* closet is one that has been ransacked.
6. True. If information is *disclosed,* it is revealed and everyone knows about it.

Word Study

Sample answers:

1. Yes. The suffix *-ment* means "act or resulting state of" and *amusement* means "the act of providing pleasure or amusing." The goal of an amusement park is to keep the patrons amused or entertained.
2. The suffix *-ment* means "act or resulting state of" and *improvement* means "the act of improving or progressing." An *improvement* makes something better.

Word Study: Apply It

Sample answers:

Contentment is the act of being content or happy. *Excitement* is the act of being excited. *Abasement* is the result of being humble

PRETEACH

Skills instruction for the ***Reading Skill*** *and* ***Literary Analysis*** *concept appears on pp. 719–721.*

❶ Writing About the Big Question

1. Review the assignment with the class.
2. Have students think of and describe one of their favorite characters from a play or a movie. **Ask** them to think about how the character communicates: How does the character differ from people in real life?
3. Have students complete the sentence starter. Review responses as a class. (**Possible response:** Communication between two people can seem like action in a play when they exchange and respond to dialogue.)
4. Remind students that their answers will help them think about the Big Question, "How does communication change us?"

While You Read

Tell students that as they read they should look for how people's lives and interactions can resemble actors playing roles.

❷ Vocabulary

1. Have students preview the selection vocabulary.
2. For each word, have students say the word aloud.
3. Then, use the word in a sentence that defines the word.
4. Repeat your definitional sentence or a similar sentence with the word missing, and have the class "fill in the blank" chorally. Here is an example:

   To suffice means to be enough. After budgeting the costs, I knew the $500 I had would be enough for the trip, or would [students say "suffice"].

❸ Word Study

1. Introduce the skill, using the instruction in the box.
2. **Ask** students to define the word "beautification." (**Sample answer:** The act of making something more beautiful.)

Making Connections
Poetry Collection 8

maggie and milly and molly and may • The Seven Ages of Man • Fire and Ice

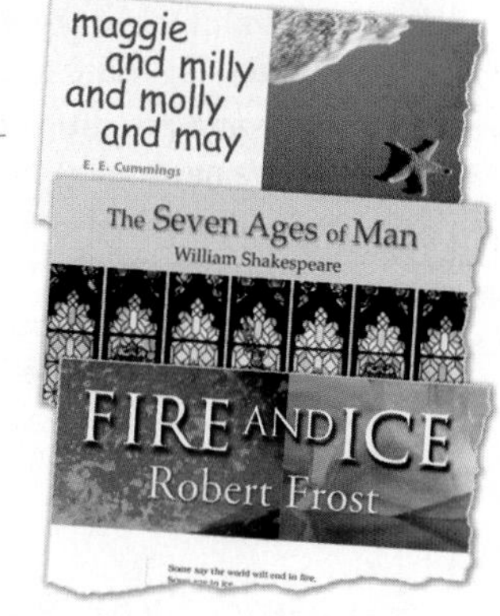

❶ Writing About the Big Question

The speaker of "The Seven Ages of Man" compares the people of the world to actors in a play. Use this sentence starter to develop your ideas about the Big Question.

Communication between two people can seem like action in a play when ________________.

While You Read Look for ways in which people's lives and interactions can resemble actors playing roles. Then, consider how this knowledge might offer a useful way to look at life.

❷ Vocabulary

Read each word and its definition. Decide whether you know the word well, know it a little bit, or do not know it at all. After you have read the selection, see how your knowledge of each word has increased.

- **stranded** (strand′ əd) *adj.* in a place or situation which one needs help to leave (p. 732) ***The stranded airline passengers had to spend the night in the terminal.*** *strand v.*
- **languid** (laŋ′ gwid) *adj.* drooping; weak (p. 732) ***The heat of the summer afternoon made us all feel languid.*** *languish v.*
- **woeful** (wō′ fəl) *adj.* full of sorrow (p. 735) ***His woeful story brought us to tears.*** *woe n. woefully adv.*
- **treble** (treb′ əl) *n.* high-pitched voice or sound (p. 735) ***The harsh treble of her alarm clock woke everyone in the house.***
- **oblivion** (ə bliv′ ē ən) *n.* forgetfulness; the state of being unconscious or unaware (p. 735) ***While sleeping, most people are in a state of total oblivion.*** *oblivious adj.*
- **suffice** (sə fīs′) *v.* be enough (p. 736) ***Five tables will suffice for a party of this size.*** *sufficient adj.*

❸ Word Study

The **Latin suffix *-ion*** means "act or condition of." It usually indicates a noun.

Someone who is oblivious is unaware. In "The Seven Ages of Man," the speaker refers to a man's final stage as "mere **oblivion**," a condition of complete unawareness.

Vocabulary Development

Vocabulary Knowledge Rating

Create a **Vocabulary Knowledge Rating Chart** (***Professional Development Guidebook***, p. 33) for this collection. Include the collection vocabulary from this page and the word that appears in the Writing About the Big Question sentence starters on this page. (The Big Question vocabulary is introduced on pp. 604–605.)

Give students a copy of the chart. Read the words aloud, and have students mark their rating in the Before Reading column. Urge them to be alert to these words as they read and discuss the selection.

Tally how many students think they know a word to gauge how much instruction to provide. As students read and discuss the selection, point out the words and their context.

Vocabulary Central, featuring tools, activities, and songs for studying vocabulary, is available at **www.PHLitOnline.com.**

Meet the Authors

❹

E. E. Cummings

(1894–1962)

"maggie and milly and molly and may" (p. 732)

Born in Cambridge, Massachusetts, Edward Estlin Cummings graduated from Harvard University. Both as poet and playwright, Cummings became notorious for his unconventional style, which reflects his individualistic outlook. Much of his work is playful and lyrical, and he often disregarded rules of grammar, spelling, and punctuation.

William Shakespeare

(1564–1616)

"The Seven Ages of Man" (p. 734)

William Shakespeare forged a perfect blend of high drama and exalted language. He wrote more than three dozen plays, and because of the timelessness of his themes and the beauty of his language, lines from his plays are quoted more often than those of any other writer. "The Seven Ages of Man" from the play *As You Like It,* is considered one of his best monologues. (For more on William Shakespeare, see p. 802.)

Robert Frost

(1874–1963)

"Fire and Ice" (p. 736)

Like the title of his poem "Fire and Ice," Robert Frost seemed warm to some people, cold to other people. All agreed, however, that poetry came first in his life. Frost produced a large body of work and became the most popular American poet of his time, winning four Pulitzer Prizes.

Daily Bellringer

For each class during which you will teach this selection, have students complete one of the five Research activities for Week 23 in the ***Daily Bellringer Activities*** booklet.

❹ Background

E. E. Cummings Like Robert Frost and T.S. Eliot, E.E. Cummings also attended Harvard and had his poems published in the university's poetry magazine. After a stint as an ambulance driver in World War I, Cummings returned to the United States and divided his time between a home in New Hampshire, one in New York's Greenwich Village, and intermittent trips to Paris. Cummings' unorthodox writing style made him extremely popular, especially among young readers. Next to Robert Frost, E. E. Cummings was the most popular and well-known poet of his day.

Multidraft Reading

To assist struggling readers and to deepen reading for all, apply multidraft reading protocols, following the pause points ● to "chunk" longer poems. For each reading, have students set the purpose indicated:

- **First reading**—identifying key ideas and details and answering any Reading Checks.
- **Second reading**—analyzing craft and structure and responding to the side-column prompts.
- **Third reading**—integrating knowledge and ideas, connecting to other texts and the world, and answering the end-of-selection questions.

For more guidance, refer to the ***Classroom Strategies and Teaching Routines*** card on multidraft reading.

For more about the authors and practice with the selection vocabulary, go online at **www.PHLitOnline.com.**

Differentiated Instruction

Additional Instruction

EL Extended Support—English Learners

Have students complete the **Reading and Vocabulary Warm-ups, *Unit 4 Resources,*** pp. 184–187, before they read. Assign the prereading pages in the ***Reader's Notebook: English Learner's Version.*** Then, have students listen to portions of the selection on the ***Hear It!* Audio CD.**

L1 L2 Extended Support—Struggling Readers

Have students complete the **Reading and Vocabulary Warm-ups, *Unit 4 Resources,*** pp. 184–187, before they read. Assign the prereading pages in the ***Reader's Notebook: Adapted Version.*** Then, have students listen to portions of the selection on the ***Hear It!* Audio CD** (adapted text).

Extended Support—Reluctant Readers

To build motivation and engagement before assigning the collection, have students read "Bridging the Generation Gap," a thematically related selection in ***Reality Central.*** Then, use the questions at the conclusion of the related selection to guide discussion.

TEACH

❶ Activating Prior Knowledge

1. Prepare an **Anticipation Guide** (*Professional Development Guidebook,* pp. 36–38) with the following statements:
   - What you play with shows what kind of person you are.
   - All human beings go through predetermined stages of life.
   - Desire is stronger than hate.
2. Give students a copy of the prepared **Anticipation Guide** and have students mark their responses in the appropriate columns.
3. For further guidance, use the ***Classroom Strategies and Teaching Routines*** card: **Using an Anticipation Guide.**

Concept Connector

Students will return to the **Anticipation Guide** after completing this poetry collection.

Small-Group Activity

Have small groups of students preview the visuals that accompany the poems and make written predictions about each poem.

❷ About the Selections

In "maggie and milly and molly and may," each character makes a self-discovery. In "The Seven Ages of Man," the speaker traces the journey from the cradle to the grave. The speaker in "Fire and Ice" considers two possible ends to the world.

❸ Literary Analysis

Rhyme and Meter

1. **Ask** students the Literary Analysis question.
2. **Answer:** He uses exact end rhyme.

❹ Critical Viewing

Possible response: This is a good illustration of the "stranded star" since it is lying out of the water, and it has extended its "five languid fingers."

---

❶ ❷

maggie and milly and molly and may

E. E. Cummings

maggie and milly and molly and may
went down to the beach (to play one day)

and maggie discovered a shell that sang
so sweetly she couldn't remember her troubles, and

milly befriended a **stranded** star
whose rays five **languid** fingers were;

❸

and molly was chased by a horrible thing
which raced sideways while blowing bubbles: and

may came home with a smooth round stone
as small as a world and as large as alone.

For whatever we lose (like a you or a me)
it's always ourselves we find in the sea

Vocabulary
stranded (strand′ əd) *adj.* in a place or situation which one needs help to leave
languid (laŋ′ gwid) *adj.* drooping; weak

Literary Analysis
Rhyme and Meter
What type of rhyme does Cummings use in the first and last stanzas?

❹ ▶ **Critical Viewing** How well does this photograph illustrate the "stranded star" in the poem? **[Evaluate]**

Vocabulary Development

CCSS Language 6

Thematic Vocabulary: The Big Question

As students are discussing Poetry Collection 8, encourage them to use the thematic vocabulary presented in Introducing the Big Question, pp. 604–605. You might encourage them with sentence starters like these:

1. As we read "maggie and milly and molly and may," we may develop *empathy* with the characters because . . .
2. In "The Seven Ages of Man," Shakespeare brings new *meaning* to the human condition through the analogy of . . .
3. In Shakespeare's poem, the speaker's *resolution* suggests that . . .
4. In "Fire and Ice," the speaker suggests that one could *exchange* fire and ice and still . . .

PHLit Online!

This selection is available in interactive format in the **Enriched Online Student Edition, www. PHLitOnline.com,** which includes a thematically related video with writing prompt and an interactive graphic organizer.

Differentiated Instruction for Universal Access

Strategy for Less Proficient Readers

To give students a model for paraphrasing, show them the **Reading Skill Graphic Organizer A** (***Graphic Organizer Transparencies,*** p. 135). The partially completed graphic organizer will give students insight into the process of paraphrasing. They can use it as a model for writing their own paraphrases as they read.

Pronunciation for English Learners

Some students might have difficulty pronouncing the short *i* sound in *milly, with,* and *in.* To aid in pronunciation, write the words *ship, sheep, lip, leap, sit,* and *seat* on the board. Pronounce each word, stressing the vowel sound, and have students echo. Call out words as students point to them. Discuss incorrect choices and clarify.

❺ Humanities

The Seven Ages of Man, stained-glass window, Folger Shakespeare Library, Washington, D.C.

Stained glass is a term used for windows or other display pieces composed of small pieces of dyed and painted glass joined with seams of lead and mounted in a metal framework. The art achieved its greatest expression in the Gothic cathedrals of the twelfth through the fourteenth centuries. Use these questions for discussion.

1. The window represents the seven ages of man described by Shakespeare. Why do you think the panels are arranged as they are?

   Answer: They were meant to rise to the fourth age, which was considered the age when a man is "in his prime," and then fall to the seventh age, when a man is back on the same level with the first.

2. Do you agree that the fourth age (the soldier) is man's prime? If not, which would you place in that position?

   Possible response: I agree that the fourth age is man's prime. A soldier is at a peak physically as well as mentally.

❺

The Seven Ages of Man, Folger Shakespeare Library, Washington, D.C.

Vocabulary Development

Vocabulary Knowledge Rating

When students have completed reading and discussing this poetry collection, have them take out their **Vocabulary Knowledge Rating Chart** for these poems. Read the words aloud once more and have students rate their knowledge of the words again in the After Reading column. Clarify any words that are still problematic. Have students write their own definition and example or sentence in the appropriate column. Then have students complete the Vocabulary Practice activities at the end of the collection. Encourage students to use the words in further discussion and written work about these poems. Remind them that they will be accountable for these words on the **Selection Test, *Unit 4 Resources,*** pp. 199–201 or 202–204.

The Seven Ages of Man

William Shakespeare

All the world's a stage,
6 And all the men and women merely players:[1]
They have their exits and their entrances;
And one man in his time plays many parts,
His acts being seven ages. At first the infant,
Mewling[2] and puking in the nurse's arms.
And then the whining schoolboy, with his satchel,
And shining morning face, creeping like snail
Unwillingly to school. And then the lover,
Sighing like furnace, with a woeful ballad
Made to his mistress' eyebrow. Then a soldier,
Full of strange oaths, and bearded like the pard,[3]
Jealous in honor,[4] sudden and quick in quarrel,
Seeking the bubble reputation
7 Even in the cannon's mouth. And then the justice,[5]
In fair round belly with good capon[6] lined,
With eyes severe and beard of formal cut,
Full of wise saws and modern instances;[7]
And so he plays his part. The sixth age shifts
Into the lean and slippered pantaloon,[8]
With spectacles on nose and pouch on side,
His youthful hose[9] well saved, a world too wide
For his shrunk shank;[10] and his big manly voice,
Turning again toward childish treble, pipes
And whistles in his sound. Last scene of all,
That ends this strange eventful history,
Is second childishness, and mere oblivion,
Sans[11] teeth, sans eyes, sans taste, sans everything.

1. **players** actors.
2. **Mewling** (myo͞ol´ iŋ) *v.* whimpering; crying weakly.
3. **pard** (pärd) *n.* leopard or panther.
4. **Jealous in honor** very concerned about his honor.
5. **justice** judge.
6. **capon** (kā´ pän´) *n.* roasted chicken.
7. **wise saws and modern instances** sayings, and examples that show the truth of the sayings.
8. **pantaloon** (pan´ tə lo͞on´) *n.* thin, foolish old man who is a character in old comedies.
9. **hose** (hōz) *n.* stockings.
10. **shank** (shaŋk) *n.* leg.
11. **sans** (sanz) *prep.* without; lacking.

Literary Analysis
Rhyme and Meter
What is the pattern of stressed and unstressed syllables in lines 2–4?

Vocabulary
woeful (wō´ fəl) *adj.* full of sorrow

Spiral Review
Figurative Language
Why might a person's reputation be like a bubble?

Vocabulary
treble (treb´ əl) *n.* high-pitched voice or sound

oblivion (ə bliv´ ē ən) *n.* forgetfulness; the state of being unconscious or unaware

8 ◀ **Analyze Representations**
How do the images in this stained-glass window add to your understanding of the poem? **[Relate]**

6 Literary Analysis
Rhyme and Meter

1. Read the poem aloud.
2. **Ask** students how many stressed syllables they hear in each line.
   Answer: There are five stressed syllables in each line.
3. Refer students to lines 2–4. **Ask** the Literary Analysis question: What is the pattern of stressed and unstressed syllables in lines 2–4?
   Answer: Each of these lines has five sets of unstressed/stressed syllables.

▶ **Monitor Progress:** Ask students to identify the pattern of stressed and unstressed syllables in lines 21 and 22.

▶ **Reteach:** If students have difficulty identifying the pattern, have them read the poem aloud and clap when they hear a stressed syllable.

Spiral Review
Figurative Language

1. Remind students that they studied the concept of figurative language in the Unit 4 Literary Analysis workshop (pp. 606–614).
2. **Ask** students the Spiral Review question.
   Possible response: A reputation can grow and seem better as it gets bigger, but like a bubble, the bigger it gets, the more vulnerable it is. Eventually, it becomes impossible to keep up—it is too blown up.

7 Connecting to the Big Question

1. Read aloud the second bracketed passage.
2. **Ask:** How does this passage illustrate ways in which people's lives and interactions resemble actors playing roles?
   Answer: It talks about how judges wear their expected costumes and play the role of wise arbiter.

8 Critical Viewing
Possible response: The images help me visualize the life stages the poem describes.

Concept Connector

Anticipation Guide
Have students return to their **Anticipation Guides** and respond to the statements again in the After Reading column. They may do this individually or in their original pairs or groups. Then, lead a class discussion, probing for what students have learned that confirms or invalidates each statement. Encourage students to cite specific details, quotations, or other evidence from the poems to support their responses to each statement.

Writing About the Big Question
Have students compare their responses to the sentence starter they completed before reading the poems with their ideas afterwards. Ask them to explain whether their thoughts have changed.

Reading Skill Graphic Organizer
Have students review the graphic organizers they completed to make and verify predictions while reading. Show them **Reading Skill Graphic Organizer A** (*Graphic Organizer Transparencies,* p. 135) as an example. Then have students share their graphic organizers.

9 Critical Thinking

Interpret

1. Have students reread lines 3–4 and 6–9.
2. **Ask** students what the speaker is suggesting by linking desire and hate to fire and ice.

   Possible response: The world will die from either too much warm feeling—desire—or too much cold feeling—hate.

ASSESS

Answers

Critical Thinking

Before students respond, you may wish to have them write a brief objective summary of the selection. As they answer the questions below, remind them to support their answers with evidence from the text.

1. (a) maggie discovers a sweetly singing sea shell; milly finds a stranded starfish; molly is chased by a crab; may finds a smooth round stone. (b) Each character is drawn to something that reflects her inner wishes or fears.
2. (a) The speaker associates fire with passion or desire and ice with hatred. (b) Fire is a fitting metaphor for desire because desire "burns." Ice is a fitting metaphor for hate because hate is a "cold" emotion. (c) **Possible response:** People my age often have to deal with desires and with feelings of hatred.
3. **Possible responses:** Some students may suggest that their perspective is changed, since the stages seem to make sense; others may say that the stages seem to be artificial.

FIRE AND ICE

Robert Frost

Some say the world will end in fire,
Some say in ice.
From what I've tasted of desire
I hold with those who favor fire.
But if it had to perish twice,
9 I think I know enough of hate
To say that for destruction ice
Is also great
And would suffice.

Vocabulary
suffice (sə fīs′)
v. be enough

Critical Thinking

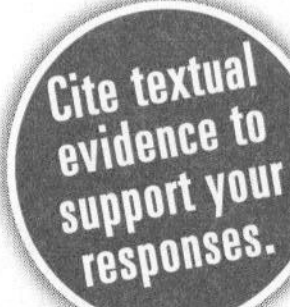
Cite textual evidence to support your responses.

1. **Key Ideas and Details** **(a)** In "maggie and milly and molly and may," what experience does each character have? **(b) Connect:** How does each character's experience support the conclusion in the poem's final line?
2. **Key Ideas and Details** **(a)** In "Fire and Ice," which emotions does the speaker associate with fire and ice? **(b) Interpret:** Why are fire and ice fitting metaphors for these emotions? **(c) Discuss:** Share your answers with a partner or group, and explain how the poem's message applies to teenagers.
3. **Integration of Knowledge and Ideas** Does "The Seven Ages of Man" in any way change your perspective on the stages of life and the "roles" people play? Explain your response. *[Connect to the Big Question: How does communication change us?]*

Assessment Resources

Unit 4 Resources

L1 L2 EL **Selection Test A**, pp. 199–201. Administer Test A to less advanced readers.

L3 L4 EL **Selection Test B**, pp. 202–204. Administer Test B to on-level and more advanced students.

L3 L4 **Open-Book Test**, pp. 196–198. As an alternative, administer the Open-Book Test.

All **Customizable Test Bank**

All **Self-tests**
Students may prepare for the **Selection Test** by taking the **Self-test** online.

PHLit Online!

All assessment resources are available at **www.PHLitOnline.com**.

After You Read
Poetry Collection 8

maggie and milly and molly and may • The Seven Ages of Man • Fire and Ice

Literary Analysis: Rhyme and Meter

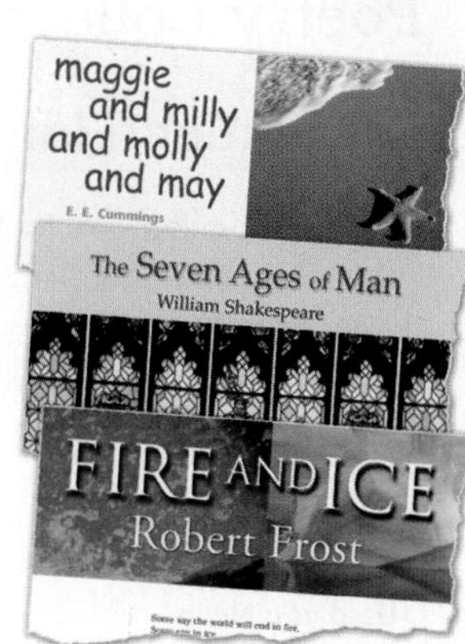

1. **Craft and Structure** Identify two lines in "maggie and milly and molly and may" that illustrate both **exact rhyme** and **end rhyme.** Explain your choices.
2. **Craft and Structure** Which two words in line 17 of "The Seven Ages of Man" illustrate both **slant rhyme** and **internal rhyme?**
3. **Craft and Structure (a)** Use letters to identify the **rhyme scheme** in "Fire and Ice." **(b)** In what way does the shift in rhyme scheme midway through the poem help signal a turning point in the poem's message?
4. **Craft and Structure (a)** Which poem has lines with a more regular **meter:** "Fire and Ice" or "The Seven Ages of Man"? Explain. **(b)** Which do you find more enjoyable to read—lines with a regular meter or lines with an irregular meter? Explain.

Reading Skill: Paraphrase

5. **(a) Paraphrase** the first ten lines of "maggie and milly and molly and may" by rewriting them as a series of sentences. **(b)** In what way does **breaking down long sentences** make this poem's meaning more clear?

Vocabulary

Acquisition and Use Decide if each statement is true or false. Then, explain your answer.

1. If something will *suffice,* it will be satisfactory.
2. A captain should avoid letting his ship become *stranded.*
3. Coaches hope their players will be *languid* during a game.
4. A *woeful* sight is likely to inspire pity.
5. A *treble* is a deep sound like a foghorn.
6. Sleep is a kind of *oblivion.*

Word Study Use the context of the sentences and what you know about the **Latin suffix *-ion*** to explain your answer to each question.

1. Could complicated directions lead to *confusion*?
2. Is *precision* a good quality for a surgeon to possess?

Word Study

The **Latin suffix *-ion*** means "act or condition of." It usually indicates a noun.

Apply It Explain how the suffix *-ion* contributes to the meanings of these words. Consult a dictionary if necessary.

derision
opinion
illusion

ASSESS/EXTEND

Answers

Literary Analysis

1. Lines 9 – 10 represent exact rhyme and end rhyme. The words *stone* and *alone* come at the end of the lines, and they are exact rhymes.
2. The words *severe* and *beard* represent internal rhyme and slant rhyme.
3. (a) The rhyme scheme is abaabcbcb. (b) In the first four lines, the speaker states how he thinks the world will end; in the last five lines, he presents an alternative ending.
4. (a) "Fire and Ice" has a more regular meter, since it follows the pattern of unstressed/stressed syllables throughout. (b) **Possible response:** The poem with the more regular meter is more enjoyable to read because it has a predictable rhythm.

Reading Skill

5. (a) Maggie, Milly, Molly, and May went down to the beach to play one day. Maggie discovered a shell that sang so sweetly she couldn't remember her troubles. Milly befriended a stranded star. Its rays were five languid fingers. Molly was chased by a horrible thing. It raced sideways while blowing bubbles. May came home with a smooth round stone. It was as small as a world and as large as alone. (b) Breaking down long sentences clarifies the meaning because each new, shorter sentence contains one idea, which makes each one easier to follow.

Vocabulary
Acquisition and Use
Sample answers:

1. True. If something will *suffice,* it is enough.
2. True. A captain doesn't want his ship to be *stranded* in a place so that it cannot leave.
3. False. Coaches want their players to be strong, not *languid* or weak during a game.
4. True. A *woeful* sight is sorrowful and would inspire pity.

Answers Continued

5. False. A *treble* is a high-pitched sound, not a deep sound.
6. True. When you sleep, you enter a state where you are unaware or in *oblivion.*

Word Study
Sample answers:

1. Yes. The suffix *-ion* means "act or condition of" and *confusion* means "the condition of being confused." Complicated directions could lead to confusion because the driver wouldn't know where to go.
2. Yes. The suffix *-ion* means "act or condition of" and *precision* means "the act of being exact or precise." A surgeon must be precise or follow exact instructions.

Word Study: Apply It
Sample answers:

Derision is the act of deriding, or mocking. An *opinion* is the act or condition of believing something to be true. An *illusion* is something that has the condition of being false or untrue.

Conventions

1. Introduce the skill, using the instruction on the student page.
2. Discuss the definitions and the examples in the chart.

Think Aloud: Model the Skill

Model the skill of using infinitives. Post these sentences:
To sing requires passion.
To sing well requires devotion.
Say to students:

To determine how an infinitive functions, I look at the role the infinitive plays in the sentence. In the sentences above, the infinitive "to sing" and the infinitive phrase "to sing well" are each the subject of their sentence. Thus, they must function as nouns.

PH WRITING COACH Grade 9

Students will find instruction on and practice with infinitives in Chapter 15, Section 1.

Practice A

1. to learn; adverb
2. to be a king; adjective
3. to take the more difficult path; noun
4. to catch Macavity; noun

Reading Application
Sample answer:

Adverb—But it's useless to investigate—*Macavity's not there*!
Adjective—He always has an alibi, and one or two to spare. . .

Practice B
Sample answers:

1. to play; Maggie went down to the beach to dance.
2. to represent hate; Frost uses ice to create an image for readers.
3. to pass; To grow in seven ages is man's destiny.
4. to be quoted by other writers; "The "Seven Ages of Man' is not the only speech to capture the thoughts of other writers.

Writing Application
Sample answer:

The waves are beginning to wash up. The starfish is about to be splashed.

PERFORMANCE TASKS

Integrated Language Skills

Poetry Collections 7 and 8

Poetry Collection 7

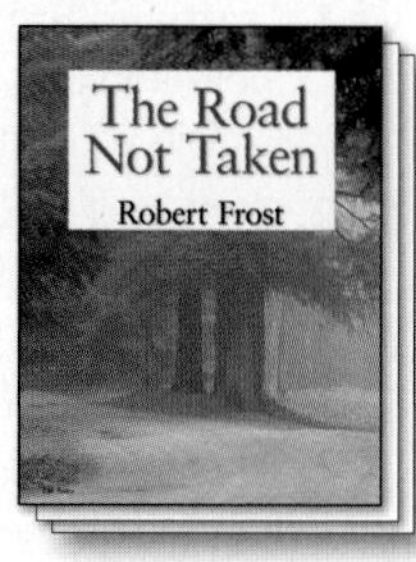

Poetry Collection 8

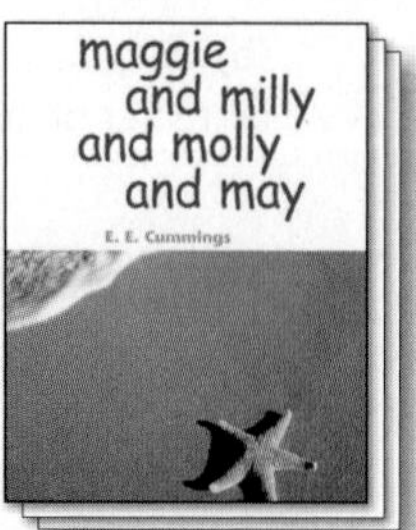

Conventions: Infinitives

An **infinitive** is a verb form that generally appears with the word *to* and acts as a noun, adjective, or adverb.

An **infinitive phrase** is an infinitive with modifiers, complements, or a subject. Like infinitives, infinitive phrases can function as nouns, adjectives, or adverbs.

Infinitive	Infinitive Phrase
Used as a Noun *To write* requires dedication.	**Used as a Noun** *To win a Pulitzer Prize* is an honor.
Used as an Adjective E. E. Cummings is a good poet *to study.*	**Used as an Adjective** Cummings had a desire *to write unconventional poetry.*
Used as an Adverb When Shakespeare sat down *to work,* he used a quill dipped in ink.	**Used as an Adverb** Shakespeare wrote his plays *to be performed on a stage.*

Infinitives include *to* and a verb, as in *to hear*; prepositional phrases include *to* and a noun or pronoun, as in *to the house*.

Practice A Identify the infinitive or infinitive phrase and its function in each sentence.

1. It is important to learn about these poets.
2. One needs confidence to be a king.
3. The speaker of "The Road Not Taken" chose to take the more difficult path.
4. The police have failed to catch Macavity.

Reading Application Find two infinitives or infinitive phrases in "Macavity: The Mystery Cat" and identify each one's function.

Practice B Identify the infinitive or infinitive phrase in each sentence. Then, rewrite the sentence using a different infinitive or infinitive phrase.

1. Maggie went down to the beach to play.
2. Frost uses ice to represent hate.
3. To pass through seven ages is man's destiny.
4. "The Seven Ages of Man" is not the only speech to be quoted by other writers.

Writing Application Write two sentences about the beach image on page 733. Use an infinitive or an infinitive phrase in each one.

PH WRITING COACH Further instruction and practice are available in *Prentice Hall Writing Coach*.

Extend the Lesson

Sentence Modeling

Choose the sentence given from the poetry collection students have read:

"We never know how high we are/Till we are asked to rise." ("We never know how high we are," Poetry Collection 7)

"I think I know enough of hate/To say that for destruction ice/Is also great/And would suffice." ("Fire and Ice," Poetry Collection 8)

Ask students what they notice about the sentence. Elicit that the sentence contains an infinitive. Have students identify the infinitive and its function as a noun, adjective, or adverb. Then, ask what else they notice. ("We never know…": Dickinson emphasizes the action in the infinitive by putting it at the end of a line. "Fire and Ice": Frost stresses the importance of certain ideas by changing traditional word order.)

Have students imitate the sentence in a sentence on a topic of their own choosing, matching each grammatical and stylistic feature discussed.

Writing

Poetry Each poem in both collections has a specific rhyme scheme. Write a **poem** using the same rhyme scheme and format as a poem in Collection 7 or Collection 8.

- Choose a poem and identify its rhyme scheme.
- Decide on a topic, an event, an experience, or an emotion to use as the subject of your poem.
- Brainstorm for a list of images, precise details, phrases, or vivid words.
- Draft your lines, making them rhyme only after you have expressed your ideas and feelings.

Share your poem with a classmate. Ask him or her to identify the poem's rhyme scheme and discuss the way the rhythm and word choice affect the mood of the poem.

Grammar Application Make sure you correctly use infinitives and infinitive phrases in your writing.

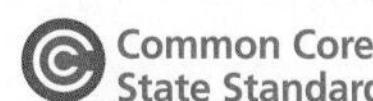

Common Core State Standards

L.9-10.1.b; W.9-10.4; SL.9-10.1.a, SL.9-10.1.c, SL.9-10.1.d

[For the full wording of the standards, see page 718.]

Writing Workshop: *Work in Progress*

Prewriting for a Response to Literature Review your Character Descriptions, and write a one-sentence conclusion about each character. Save this Draft Thesis in your writing portfolio.

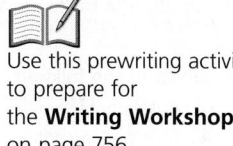

Use this prewriting activity to prepare for the **Writing Workshop** on page 756.

Speaking and Listening

Presentation of Ideas With classmates, hold a **panel discussion** about possible interpretations of a poem by Robert Frost.

Conduct research about the poet's extensive works. Assemble an electronic database of texts by and about Robert Frost. Identify primary and secondary sources about Frost's poetry. Consider these questions:

- What topics and themes does Frost's work often address?
- What style does he most frequently use?
- What have others said about his works?

Write concise notes for use during the discussion. Be sure to convey your sources' information accurately and coherently.

When you are ready to hold your discussion, follow these steps:

- Begin by stating the purpose of the discussion.
- Use listening strategies to interpret and summarize others' comments.
- Then, look for connections between the ideas expressed by other panel members. Use these connections to develop a position statement that is acceptable to most panelists.

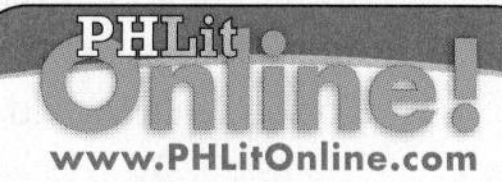

www.PHLitOnline.com

- Interactive graphic organizers
- Grammar tutorial
- Interactive journals

EXTEND/ASSESS

Writing

1. Review the assignment, using the instruction on the student page.
2. To guide students in writing a poem, give them **Support for Writing,** p. 194 in ***Unit 4 Resources.***
3. To evaluate students' poems, use the Poem rubrics, pp. 248–249 ***Professional Development Guidebook.*** In addition, you might evaluate for how well students develop original ideas and imagery.

Grammar Application

Have students check their drafts to make sure they are using infinitives and infinitive phrases correctly.

Six Traits Focus

✓	Ideas	✓	Word Choice
	Organization		Sentence Fluency
	Voice		Conventions

PH WRITING COACH Grade 9

Students will find instruction on and practice with poetry in Chapter 7.

Writing Workshop
Work-in-Progress

Have students save their Draft Thesis in their portfolios. They will use their sentence later as they complete the Writing Workshop (see pp. 756–763).

Speaking and Listening

1. Review the assignment, using the instruction on the student page.
2. To support students' work on the assignment, have them complete the **Support for Extend Your Learning** page (***Unit 4 Resources,*** p. 195).

Teaching Resources

Unit 4 Resources

L3 L4 EL **Integrated Language Skills: Grammar,** p. 193

L3 L4 EL **Support for Writing,** p. 194

L3 L4 **Support for Extend Your Learning,** p. 195

L4 **Enrichment,** pp. 174, 192

All **Enriched Online Student Edition**
Available under After You Read for this selection:

All **Interactive Grammar Tutorial**

L3 L4 **Internet Research Activity**

Professional Development Guidebook

Rubrics for Self-Assessment: Poem, pp. 248–249

PHLit Online! All print and digital resources are available at **www.PHLitOnline.com.** Online resources accessible by students are noted on the student page.

MONITORING PROGRESS

Using the Test Practice

In this two-page Test Practice, students apply the reading skill for the second half of Unit 4 to a passage of fiction and a passage of nonfiction.

Review the skill, paraphrasing, then administer the test. For more guidance, consult the ***Classroom Strategies and Teaching Routines*** card, **Administering Timed Tests.**

ASSESS

Answers

Answers With Explanations

1. **A**—Tom is surprised because he had given up on the return of the bottle. *Incorrect answers:* B—Tom's disbelief is about seeing the bottle, not about the bottle being real. C—Tom is awake. D—We have no idea what Tom was thinking beforehand.
2. **C**—This sentence restates sentence 5. *Incorrect answers:* A—This sentence restates information in sentences 3 through 5. B—This statement is probably true, but is not part of the passage. D—Sentence 5 says only that the two had written a note, not what the note said.
3. **B**—Sentence 5 states what the grandfather's idea was. *Incorrect answers:* A—The passage does not support this choice. C—Tom's grandfather did not plan this. D—Tom's grandfather sent him a postcard, not the bottle.
4. **D**—Paraphrasing generally uses simpler words, not harder words. *Incorrect answers:* A—Picturing the action can help a reader paraphrase a passage. B—Breaking down long sentences helps a reader understand the meaning clearly enough to restate it in simpler words. C—Paraphrasing must say the same thing in different words.

Test Practice: Reading

Paraphrase

Fiction Selection

Directions: *Read the selection. Then, answer the questions.*

(1) Tom stared in disbelief at the bottle. (2) He remembered the day six months ago. (3) It was his birthday, and the last day before his grandfather moved to Florida. (4) It had been his grandfather's idea. (5) They had written a note and sealed it in the bottle, and Tom had thrown it into the surf. (6) "The world is small," his grandfather had said with a wink, "your bottle will be back." (7) Tom had wanted to hear from someone far away, but as weeks passed he gave up hope. (7) Like his grandfather, the bottle seemed to be gone forever. (8) Tom was wrong. (9) Today's mail had brought a package, and inside was the bottle. (10) It had been found by strangers an ocean away. (11) Tom grinned as he noticed a second piece of mail—a postcard from his grandfather.

1. Which of the following is the *best* paraphrase of sentence 1?
A. Tom was surprised to see the bottle.
B. Tom didn't believe it was a bottle.
C. Tom was dreaming about a bottle.
D. Tom was thinking of something else.

2. Which of the following is the *best* paraphrase of sentence 5?
A. Tom's grandfather had the brilliant idea to throw a bottle into the ocean on Tom's birthday.
B. Tom and his grandfather did many enjoyable activities together.
C. Tom and his grandfather put a bottle with a message inside into the ocean.
D. Tom's grandfather wrote a detailed note including an address, and then Tom and his grandfather sent the bottle into the ocean to see what would happen.

3. In sentence 4, Tom's grandfather had an idea to—
A. celebrate Tom's birthday with a trip to the beach.
B. put a note in a bottle and throw it in the sea.
C. send the bottle back to the sender.
D. mail the bottle to Tom as a souvenir.

4. If you were paraphrasing this passage, you might do all of the following *except*—
A. picture the action.
B. break down long sentences.
C. make sure your paraphrase has the same essential meaning.
D. replace simple words with more difficult words.

Writing for Assessment

Use details from this passage to write a one-sentence paraphrase describing what Tom received in the mail and why it was significant.

Writing for Assessment

Students' responses should include Tom's receipt of the bottle in the mail and his surprise that it had reached someone across the ocean.

Strategies for Test Taking

Remind students to pay attention to words in italics when they read questions. For example, question 4 says that in paraphrasing the passage, readers might do all of the following *except* . . . This means that students will look for the answer choice that describes something they would *not* do when paraphrasing. All the other choices name something they *would* do.

Nonfiction Selection

Directions: *Read the selection. Then, answer the questions.*

(1) In 1977, the National Aeronautics and Space Administration (NASA) launched two spacecraft, *Voyagers 1* and *2.* (2) Their mission was to analyze Jupiter and Saturn, but scientists knew they could go beyond and enter deep space, where they might be found by extraterrestrials. (3) Therefore, NASA packed a record with images, natural sounds, greetings from Earth, and other data and sealed it inside the *Voyagers.* (4) It was like putting a message in a bottle and casting it into the sea of space. (5) In 2007, *Voyagers 1* and *2* were still traveling. (6) *Voyager 1* was 9.5 billion miles from Earth. (7) Will they be found? (8) Will our message ever be read?

1. Which sentence best states the main idea of the passage?
A. NASA sent *Voyagers 1* and *2* to collect data and to send a "message in a bottle" to space.
B. The primary mission of *Voyagers 1* and *2* was to study Jupiter and Saturn.
C. NASA is an organization that focuses on space exploration.
D. *Voyagers 1* and *2* have traveled billions of miles into deep space, where they might be found by extraterrestrials.

2. The pronoun *they* in sentence 7 refers to—
A. scientists.
B. NASA.
C. aliens.
D. *Voyagers 1* and *2.*

3. Which of the following is the *best* paraphrase of sentence 2?
A. NASA built the spacecraft to study Jupiter and Saturn but scientists hoped the spacecraft would be found by aliens.
B. The spacecraft could go into deep space and be found by aliens.
C. NASA scientists knew the spacecraft could enter deep space.
D. The mission was to find life on other planets.

4. For a paraphrase of sentence 3 which word is the best replacement for *data?*
A. material
B. sounds
C. information
D. messages

Writing for Assessment

Connecting Across Texts
Write a brief essay in which you describe how the *Voyager* spacecraft and Tom's bottle are alike. Use details from both passages, restated in your own words, to support your response.

www.PHLitOnline.com
- Online practice
- Instant feedback

ASSESS

Answers

Answers With Explanations

1. **A**—This answer choice combines the two missions of the *Voyagers. Incorrect answers:* B—This answer choice states only one part of the main idea. C—While true, this is not the main idea of the passage. D—This explains what the *Voyagers* have done and suggests a possible result of their voyages, but it does not state the main idea.
2. **D**—The pronoun "They" refers to the two space vehicles. *Incorrect answers:* A—The scientists were not launched into space, so they could not be found. B—The correct pronoun for NASA would be *it.* C—The aliens will, perhaps, be doing the finding; it is the space vehicles that might be found. Thus, "they" refers to *Voyagers 1* and *2.*
3. **A**—This paraphrase addresses both the original mission and the additional possibility. *Incorrect answers:* B—This paraphrase neglects the missions to Jupiter and Saturn. C—same explanation as for A. D—This is not stated anywhere in the selection.
4. **C**—*Information* is another word for "data." *Incorrect answers:* A—This word does not mean the same thing as "data." B—same explanation as for A. D—same explanation as for A.

Writing for Assessment

Students might suggest that both Tom's bottle and the *Voyagers* contained messages and were sent far away with no specific destination. Tom learns that his bottle has reached someone across the ocean. Scientists have yet to learn if the messages in *Voyagers 1* and *2* have been received.

PHLit Online!
Students may take the test in interactive format with instant feedback online at **www.PHLitOnline.com.**

Differentiated Instruction for Universal Access

Strategy for Special-Needs Students
Some students may have trouble seeing the similarities between the *Voyagers* and Tom's bottle. They may be focusing on the concrete facts: Tom is not a scientist, his bottle is not a spacecraft, the ocean and deep space are very different, etc. To help students focus on general ideas instead of concrete details, rephrase the information about Tom and his bottle, replacing all specific details with general words: "A person put a message in a container and sent it far away without knowing if anyone would receive it. Someone did receive it and sent it back." Guide students to rephrase the information about the scientists and the *Voyagers* in a similar way. (People put messages in pieces of equipment and sent them to study far away places. The people do not know if their messages will be received.) Guide students to see the similarities between the two general phrasings.

PREACH

Common Core State Standards

Reading Informational Text 2
Language 6

Reading Skill

1. Introduce the skill, using the instruction on the student page.
2. Tell students to think about which ideas will remain when they paraphrase what they read.

Think Aloud: Model the Skill

Model the skill of paraphrasing a text. Say to students:

When I read, I focus on the most important ideas. I look for topic sentences, and then I put the ideas stated in my own words. Using this step helps me to remember the ideas and connect them in my mind.

Multidraft Reading

Have students follow a multidraft reading protocol after they preview the selection.

- **First reading**—Have students read to identify key ideas and details.
- **Second reading**—Have students read to identify the structure of the text.
- **Third reading**—Have students read to integrate knowledge and ideas by connecting the text to the world, their own experiences, and other texts.

Content-Area Vocabulary

1. Have students say each word.
2. Next, use each word in a sentence that defines it.
3. Finally, repeat your definitional sentence or a similar sentence with the word missing and have the class "fill in the blank" chorally.

Reading for Information

Analyzing Expository Texts

Case Study

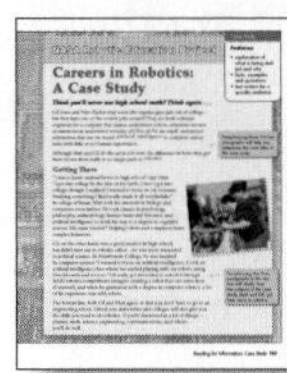

News Article

Common Core State Standards

Reading Informational Text
2. Determine a central idea of a text and analyze its development over the course of the text, including how it emerges and is shaped and refined by specific details; provide an objective summary of the text.

Language
6. Acquire and use accurately general academic and domain-specific words and phrases, sufficient for reading, writing, speaking, and listening at the college and career readiness level; demonstrate independence in gathering vocabulary knowledge when considering a word or phrase important to comprehension or expression.

Reading Skill: Paraphrase a Text: Main Idea

Paraphrasing a text—putting the ideas into your own words—helps you determine the **central idea.** Clearly stating information allows you to judge the significance of ideas in order to decide which are most important. Paraphrasing ideas will also enable you to more easily **find connections** between those ideas and ideas in other sources that deal with related topics. Use this checklist to find connections.

To Paraphrase and Connect Ideas:

- Paraphrase the ideas in the first source.
- Use your paraphrase to determine the central ideas.
- Find similar or related ideas in the second source.
- Connect ideas from the two sources by drawing conclusions based on your paraphrases of the central ideas.

Content-Area Vocabulary

These words appear in the selections that follow. You may also encounter them in other content-area texts.

- **artificial intelligence** (ärt´ ə fish´ əl in tel´ ə jəns) *n.* the ability of a computer to complete tasks that require intelligence when done by humans
- **robotics** (rō bät´ iks) *n.* the study, design, manufacture, and use of robots
- **stimuli** (stim´ yə lī´) *n.* things that provoke responses

How does communication change us?

Direct students to consider how new methods of communication have brought people closer by allowing them to communicate over large distances. In addition, have them consider whether these technologies have made people more distant. They may explain how communicating would be different without the devices.

Differentiated Instruction for Universal Access

Reading Support
Give students reading support with the appropriate version of the ***Reader's Notebooks:***

- L2 L3 *Reader's Notebook*
- L1 *Reader's Notebook: Adapted Version*
- EL *Reader's Notebook: English Learner's Version*

NASA Robotic Education Project

Careers in Robotics: A Case Study

Case Study

Features:

- explanation of what is being studied and why
- facts, examples, and quotations
- text written for a specific audience

Think you'll never use high school math? Think again . . .

Gil Jones and Matt Zucker may seem like regular guys just out of college—but they have one of the coolest jobs around! They are both software engineers for a company that makes underwater robots, otherwise known as autonomous underwater vehicles (AUVs). AUVs are small, unmanned submarines that use on-board **artificial intelligence** to complete survey tasks with little or no human supervision.

Although Matt and Gil do the same job now, the difference in how they got there shows there really is no single path to **robotics**.

Paraphrasing these first two paragraphs will help you determine the main idea of the case study.

Getting There

"I was a classic underachiever in high school," says Matt. "I got into college by the skin of my teeth. Once I got into college, though, I realized I wanted to focus on my interests. Studying something I liked really made it all worthwhile." In college at Vassar, Matt took his interests in biology and computers even further. He took classes in psychology, philosophy, anthropology, human brain and behavior, and artificial intelligence to work his way to a degree in cognitive science. His main interest? Helping robots and computers learn complex behaviors.

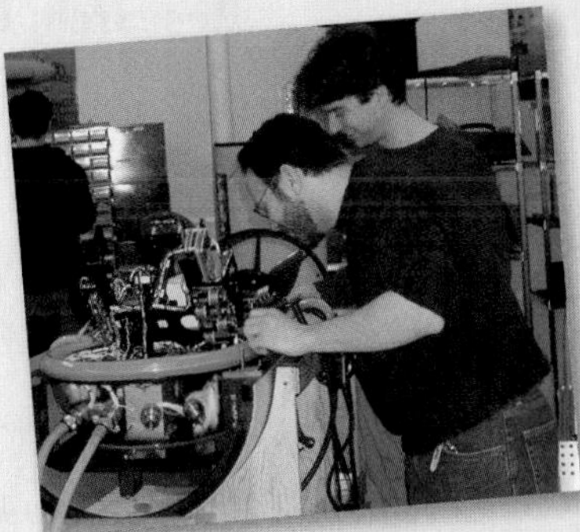

Gil, on the other hand, was a good student in high school, but didn't start out in robotics either—he was more interested in political science. At Swarthmore College, he was inspired by computer science. "I wanted to focus on artificial intelligence. I took an artificial intelligence class where we started playing with toy robots, using Handyboards and sensors." Gil really got interested in robotics through AAAI robotics competitions (imagine creating a robot that can serve hors d'oeuvres!), and when he graduated with a degree in computer science, a lot of his experience was with robots.

Paraphrasing the three paragraphs in this section will clarify how the subjects of the case study, Matt and Gil, got their starts in robotics.

The bottom line, both Gil and Matt agree, is that you don't have to go to an engineering school. Liberal arts universities and colleges will also give you the skills you need to do robotics. If you're interested in a lot of things—physics, math, science, engineering, communications, and others—you'll do well.

TEACH

About Case Studies

1. Review with students the features listed in the Case Study box. Ask them to define the term *case study* in their own words.

   Possible response: A *case study* presents a real-life example of how a person or group handled a particular situation, which can be used as a tool for teaching.
2. Have students discuss whether they think people can learn from the experiences of others.
3. Explain that teachers use case studies to teach some subjects. Students read how someone approached a particular problem or situation and then analyze and critique the person's response.

Paraphrase a Text: Main Idea

1. Remind students that readers often paraphrase the text when they explain what they read.
2. Explain that case studies usually include an introduction, a detailed description of the situation, an analysis, and a conclusion.
3. Explain that introductions to case studies typically explain what is being studied and why. **Ask:** What does this case study present?

   Possible response: This case study examines careers in robotics to show that there are different paths for getting involved in the field.
4. Remind students that a paraphrase presents the main idea in your own language. **Ask:** How would you paraphrase the paragraph about Matt?

   Possible response: Matt barely got into college, but he did well by taking courses related to computers and biology, his main interests.
5. Then, **ask** them to paraphrase the paragraph about Gil.

   Possible response: Gil started out studying political science in college, but he was inspired by computer science and then became interested in robotics.

Differentiated Instruction for Universal Access

Strategy for Less Proficient Readers

Students might have difficulty understanding what an AUV is. Encourage them to understand the term by analyzing each of the words that the acronym represents. Explain that *autonomous* means that the device acts alone, without humans inside. Then, have them decipher the other two parts of the name to define the vehicle.

After they have defined *AUV,* direct their attention to the second paragraph under the heading "Getting There." Challenge them to identify what the last two letters in "AAAI" stand for. Explain that there is a clue within that paragraph. (The letters stand for "artificial intelligence"; the clue is Gil's statement about his interest in that field.)

Paraphrase a Text: Main Idea

1. Remind students that case studies provide details to help readers get a clear picture of the situation being studied. Point out that readers should paraphrase what they read to be sure to understand the overriding concepts.
2. Invite volunteers to paraphrase the section titled "Landing the Job." (Real, hands-on experience is often the best way to get a job in a chosen career.) **Ask:** Which details support this statement?

   Possible answer: Both Gil and Matt had summer internships that gave them work experience and an idea of how to get a job in the field.
3. Direct students to "Next Steps," the conclusion of the case study. **Ask:** How would you paraphrase the conclusion?

   Possible response: Robotics is a large, constantly changing field with many different possibilities.

Landing the Job

Both Gil and Matt did summer internships during college that provided them with work experience and an idea of how to get a job in robotics. During one summer, Gil worked for the Naval Research Laboratory doing software artificial intelligence research and then, after graduating, spent the summer preparing for another AAAI competition. When one of his friends got a job at a robotics company, Gil learned about the company and then applied to be a software engineer. Matt got an internship at the same company during the summer between his junior and senior years and was then offered a job following graduation. What's their best advice for getting internships and jobs? Perseverance! "Just find someone who works in robotics and ask them for advice," says Matt. Gil adds, "Sometimes it's difficult to get in, but keep trying. Think about doing an internship for free. Often internships are the first step through the door."

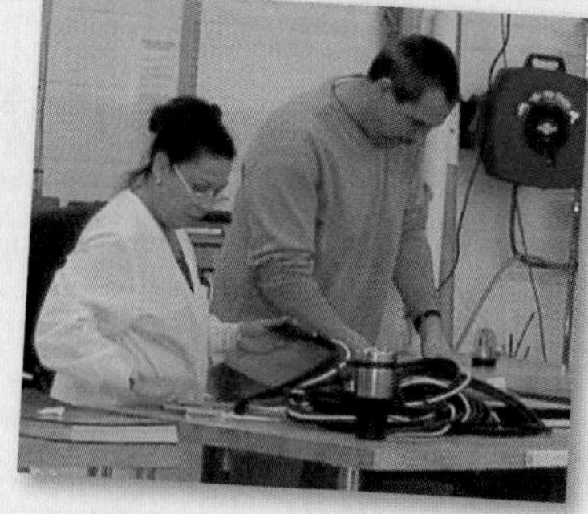

Research, Programming, and . . . Cruising(?)

One of the great things about this job is the variety. Sometimes they spend all day reading up on robotics research, sometimes they spend all day in front of a computer . . . and sometimes they spend all day hanging out on a boat testing the robot in the ocean! "You're making something that has a purpose, something that's part of a bigger project," says Gil. "You get to see if what you did worked. Of course, that means you're entirely responsible." Another perk, according to Matt, is that "you usually get to learn something big and new every few weeks." One warning: Pay attention in high school math classes. "You'll use trigonometry like crazy!"

The final paragraph of the text often contains key details. Paraphrasing will ensure you understand these points.

Next Steps

Both Matt and Gil plan on going back to school sometime to do graduate work. Matt wants to study computer science, focusing on computer graphics and computer-human interfaces. Eventually, he wants to be a professor. Gil plans to go back to school specifically in robotics. He finds underwater robotics exciting because it requires autonomy, but there are a lot of other cool areas of robotics he'd like to explore. The draw for both of them is that robotics is a quickly changing and very open field. As they point out, "You can do new stuff in any of the related areas and that's exciting!"

Vocabulary Development

CCSS Language 6

Vocabulary from Science

Point out that case studies often use vocabulary that is specific to a particular subject, in this case the field of robotics. Guide students to understand the meaning of the following words that are used in this selection:

autonomous: done without outside control

artificial intelligence: the capability of machines to imitate intelligent human behavior

cognitive science: an interdisciplinary course of study to develop theories about human thought, learning, and perception

handyboard: a controller chip used to operate robots

TEAM BUILDS 'SOCIABLE' ROBOT

Elizabeth A. Thompson, News Office

February 14, 2001

"Hello, Kismet," said Cynthia Breazeal in a singsong voice. Leaning closer to the object of her attention, she asked, "Are you going to talk to me?"

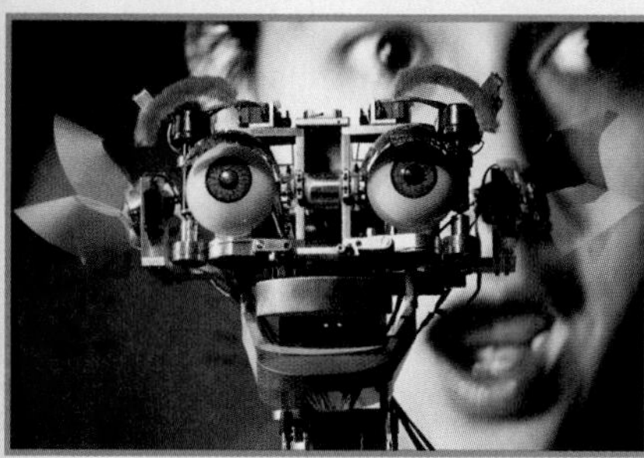

The exchange could be familiar to any parent, but Kismet is not a child. It's a robotic head that can interact with humans in a human-like way via myriad facial expressions, head positions, and tones of voice. "The goal is to build a socially intelligent machine that learns things as we learn them, through social interactions," said Dr. Breazeal, a postdoctoral associate at MIT's Artificial Intelligence Laboratory and leader of the Kismet team.

Paraphrase the doctor's quote to be sure you understand it fully.

Building a sociable machine, she believes, is also key to building a smarter machine. Most current robots are programmed to be very good at a specific task—say, navigating a room—but they can't do much more. "Can we build a much more open-ended learning system?" asks Dr. Breazeal.

"I'm building a robot that can leverage off the social structure that people already use to help each other learn. If we can build a robot that can tap into that system, then we might not have to program in every piece of its behavior."

INSPIRED BY KIDS

The work, which began in 1997, is heavily inspired by child developmental psychology. "The robot starts off in a rather helpless and primitive condition, and requires the help of a sophisticated and benevolent caretaker to learn and develop," Dr. Breazeal said. Even Kismet's physical features—which include big blue eyes, lips, ears and eyebrows—are patterned after features known to elicit a caregiving response from human adults.

Paraphrase complex sentences and ideas like the ones in this paragraph to clarify the information.

The eyes, in particular, are actually sensors that allow the robot to glean information from its environment, such as whether something is being jiggled next to its face. Kismet can then respond to such **stimuli**—by moving its head back if an object gets too close, for example—and communicate a number of emotion-like processes (such as happiness, fear and disgust).

A human wears a microphone to talk to the robot, which also has microphones in its ears. The latter will eventually be used for sound localization.

The robot's features, behavior and "emotions" work together so it can "interact with humans in an intuitive, natural way,"

News Article

Features:

- information on current events
- descriptions, examples, and quotations
- text written for a general or specific audience

About News Articles

1. Review with students the features listed in the News Article box. **Ask** them to define the term *quotations* in their own words.

   Answer: A *quotation* is the accurate reproduction of words spoken by a person.
2. Remind students about the text features used in the news article about podcasting in college courses.
3. **Ask:** How do such features as headings and pictures make a news article easier to understand?

   Possible responses: The headings break up the article into specific subtopics. The photographs offer good examples of the content.

Paraphrase a Text: Main Idea

1. Explain that main ideas often appear in the first sentence of a paragraph. Have students look at the first paragraph under the heading "Inspired by Kids." **Ask:** What is the main idea of the paragraph?

   Answer: The work is heavily inspired by child developmental psychology.
2. Tell students that section headings should identify the main idea of all the paragraphs that follow. Each paragraph should support the heading. **Ask:** What details in the paragraphs under the heading "Inspired by Kids" support the main idea?

   Possible answer: The following paragraphs mention facial expressions, emotional responses, social cues, and fear responses.
3. **Ask:** How would you paraphrase the same section using the details that support the main idea?

   Possible response: The scientists made the robot childlike in its expressions and reactions so that it would seem more approachable to most users.

Differentiated Instruction for Universal Access

Strategy for Special-Needs Students
Some students may have trouble identifying a main idea statement in a paragraph where it is not directly stated. Point out the second paragraph of the article. Discuss the information in the paragraph. Separate the parts of the paragraph that identify the speaker. Then, ask students to use the details to determine the paragaph's main idea. (Dr. Breazeal has invented a robot that uses facial expressions and voice to develop a social character.)

Enrichment for Gifted/Talented Students
Explain that body language—posture, arm and hand movements, and facial expressions—can communicate people's emotions as effectively as words. Challenge students to demonstrate different movements and expressions and call on the class to identify the emotion they represent.

Paraphrase a Text: Main Idea

1. The first paragraph under the heading "Making It Lifelike" contains the main idea of the section. **Ask:** How would you paraphrase this main idea?

   Possible response: Dr. Breazeal has used information from psychology and cartoon animators to make her robot seem lifelike.

2. Point out the paragraph that begins "Results to date are encouraging." Explain that this short sentence is the main idea of the paragraph. **Ask:** What details are offered to support the main idea?

   Possible responses: People feel that Kismet has a real presence. Others feel jarred when Kismet is turned off.

3. **Ask** students how paraphrasing the article can help them remember its content.

   Possible response: Paraphrasing something requires one to know its meaning. This helps one to remember the material.

Dr. Breazeal said. For example, if an object is too close for the robot's cameras to see well, Kismet backs away. "This behavior, by itself, aids the cameras somewhat by increasing the distance between Kismet and the human," Dr. Breazeal said. "But the behavior can have a secondary and greater effect through social amplification. A withdrawal response is a strong social cue for the human to back away."

Kismet, she noted, is the exact opposite of HAL, the menacing robot in the movie *2001: A Space Odyssey*. "HAL is simply a glowing red light with no feedback as to what the machine is thinking. That's why it's so eerie. Kismet, on the other hand, both gives and takes feedback to communicate."

"I think people are often afraid that technology is making us less human. Kismet is a counterpoint to that; it really celebrates our humanity. This is a robot that thrives on social interactions."

MAKING IT LIFELIKE

To make Kismet as lifelike as possible, Dr. Breazeal and colleagues have not only incorporated findings from developmental psychology, but have also invited the comments of cartoon animators. "How do you make something that's not alive appear lifelike? That's what animators do so well," Dr. Breazeal explained.

> The first paragraph under a subheading often contains the main ideas of that paragraph. Paraphrasing will make these ideas clear.

The proverbial wizard behind the curtain (or in this case, wall) is a bank of some 15 computers. These process software programs that allow the robot to perceive its environment, analyze what it finds and react.

In experiments over the last year or so, the researchers have been exploring how the

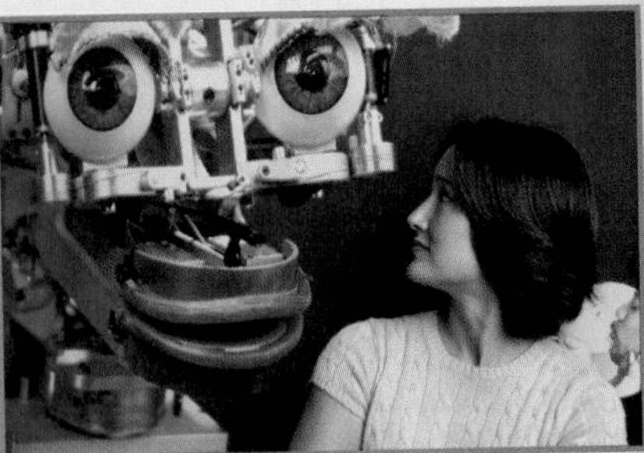

robot interacts with people who aren't familiar with it. Are Kismet's actions and emotions understandable? Do people use those actions as feedback to adjust their own responses? Conversely, is the robot correctly "reading" its visitors?

Results to date are encouraging. For example, many of the people who've met Kismet have told Dr. Breazeal that the robot has a real presence. "It seems to really impact them on an emotional level, to the point where they tell me that when I turn Kismet off, it's really jarring. That's powerful. It means that I've really captured something in this robot that's special. That kind of reaction is also critical to the robot's design and purpose."

Once Kismet's social skills are optimized, "we can move on to other forms of learning," Dr. Breazeal said. In early work to that end, the researchers are teaching Kismet how to use its voice to negotiate the social world. "We want it to be able to get people to do things for it, much like a very young child."

The algorithms that are crucial to this will allow the robot to "learn" by trial and error. When it first attempts a task, it won't be very good. The robot will "remember" its mistakes, however, and make incremental improvements as it goes along. It can then apply what it's learned to completing the same task under different conditions.

Vocabulary Development

CCSS Language 6

Vocabulary from Science

Explain that the author of the article sometimes uses difficult and technical vocabulary. Call on students to define these terms from the selection.

open-ended—able to accept and use new information

stimuli—sounds, sights, or actions outside the observer that can provoke a response

sound localization—the finding of the source of a sound

optimized—the best they can be

algorithms—decision-making rules programmed into a computer

After You Read | Case Study • News Article

Comparing Expository Texts

1. **Key Ideas and Details** **(a) Paraphrase** the second paragraphs of the case study and the news article. **(b)** Determine the **central idea** in each paraphrase. **(c)** Connect the texts by comparing and contrasting the central ideas.

Content-Area Vocabulary

2. **(a)** Remove the *s* from the word *robotics.* Using a print or an online dictionary, explain how removing the letter *s* reveals a different word with a different part of speech. **(b)** Then, use the words *robotics* and *robotic* in sentences that show their meaning.

Timed Writing

Argument: Persuasive Essay

Format
The prompt directs you to write a persuasive essay. Therefore, be sure your response includes an introduction, body paragraphs with strong supporting details, and a conclusion.

Robert Collier said, "Success is the sum of small efforts, repeated day in and day out." Write a persuasive essay in response to this quote. Support or refute it using details from both texts. (30 minutes)

Academic Vocabulary
When you *support* a quote, you show that it is true. When you *refute* a quote, you show that it is not true.

5-Minute Planner

Complete these steps before you begin to write:

1. Read the prompt carefully and completely. Look at the highlighted words to help you understand the assignment.
2. Determine whether you agree or disagree with the quote.
3. Review the case study and the news article to find support for your opinion. Identify and make notes about connections between the ideas in the texts to build a strong, convincing argument.
   TIP Paraphrasing short sections of texts can help you connect ideas.
4. Decide in what order you will present your supporting details. Then, create a brief outline for your essay.
5. Refer to your notes and outline as you draft your persuasive essay.

Answers

Comparing Expository Texts

1. (a) **Possible response:** *Case Study:* Matt and Gil got jobs in robotics in different ways. *News article:* Kismet is a robotic head that uses facial expressions to interact with humans. Dr. Breazeal's goal is to build a machine that learns from social interactions. (b) **Possible response:** *Case Study:* There are a variety of routes that a person can take to obtain a job in robotics. *News Article:* Kismet is a socially intelligent machine developed by Dr. Breazeal. (c) **Possible response:** Both main ideas focus on pursuing a career in robotics.

Content-Area Vocabulary

2. (a) **Sample response:** When the word has an *-s,* it is a plural noun that names the study or group of activities related to using robot technology. When you take the -*s* away, the word becomes an adjective that describes robot-like characteristics, such as being stiff and mechanical. (b) **Sample responses:** I think a career in robotics would be very exciting. Some people do their work in an almost robotic way.

Timed Writing

1. Before students complete the activity, guide them in identifying and analyzing key words and phrases in the prompt, highlighted on the student page.
2. Work with students to draw up guidelines for their essays based on the key words:
   - **Focus** The essay should present a position on the quote provided.
   - **Organization** The essay should offer a position statement and support it with details from the text.
   - **Support** The essay should provide details from the text to support the response.
   - **Style** The audience is not specified, so an informal style is suitable.
3. Have students use the 5-Minute Planner to structure their time.
4. Allow students 30 minutes to complete the assignment. Evaluate their work using the guidelines they have developed.

PRETEACH

Common Core State Standards

Reading Literature 5
Writing 2.a

❶ Comparing Forms of Lyric Poetry

Lyric Poetry

1. Introduce the skill, using the instruction on the student page.
2. Give students a copy of the **Comparing Forms of Lyric Poetry Graphic Organizer B, *Graphic Organizer Transparencies,*** p. 141 to complete as they read.

Think Aloud: Model the Skill

Model a way to think about lyric poetry. Say to students:

We hear lyric poetry in real life all the time, such as in the words, or lyrics, of songs. Lyrics may be written in free verse, without regular rhythm or rhyme, or feature other traditional patterns. I listen for the rhythm and rhyme in lyric poems as I would in songs. These elements help me "hear" the poem's music.

Cultural Perspective

1. Introduce the skill, using the instruction on the student page.
2. Point out that some poetic forms, such as haiku, have their roots in specific cultures.
3. Explain that the images and ideas that poets focus on can be a reflection of cultural background.

Comparing Literary Works

I Hear America Singing • Three Haiku • Women • Sonnet 30

❶

Comparing Forms of Lyric Poetry

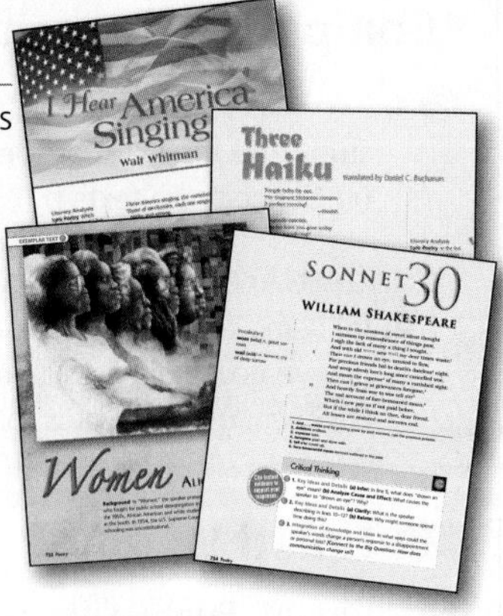

Lyric poetry has a musical quality that expresses the thoughts and feelings of a speaker. It does not tell a complete story, but it does describe an emotion or a mood, often by using vivid imagery. A lyric poem is relatively short and produces a single effect. Poets can use a variety of **lyric forms** or structures to explore topics and themes, and create different effects.

- A **sonnet** is a fourteen-line poem that is usually written in iambic pentameter and often rhymes. Two common sonnet types are the Italian, or Petrarchan, and the English, or Shakespearean, sonnet.
- A **haiku** is a classical Japanese form of poetry. Haiku is an unrhymed verse form arranged into three lines of five, seven, and five syllables. The author of a haiku often uses a striking image from nature to convey a strong emotion.
- A **free verse** poem does not follow a regular pattern of rhythm or rhyme. The poet may use sound and rhythmic devices and even rhyme—but not in a regular pattern.

Each of the following poems depicts one speaker's thoughts. As you read, consider how the poet's choice of a particular lyric form adds to the poem's meaning. Use this chart and the other information on this page to help you understand how each poem's structure enhances its message.

Shakespearean Sonnet	
Formatting: usually presented with no spaces between the stanzas, which are unified by their distinct ideas and rhyme schemes	**Three quatrains (four-line stanzas):** each explores a different aspect of the poem's theme
Final couplet: the two lines at the end of a sonnet, which present a concluding comment	**Rhyme scheme:** the lines in each quatrain follow a regular pattern of *abab cdcd efef gg*

Common Core State Standards

Reading Literature
5. Analyze how an author's choices concerning how to structure a text, order events within it, and manipulate time create such effects as mystery, tension, or surprise.

Writing
2.a. Introduce a topic; organize complex ideas, concepts, and information to make important connections and distinctions; include formatting, graphics, and multimedia when useful to aiding comprehension.

- Vocabulary flashcards
- Interactive journals
- More about the authors
- Selection audio
- Interactive graphic organizers

Vocabulary Development

Vocabulary Knowledge Rating

Create a **Vocabulary Knowledge Rating Chart** (***Professional Development Guidebook,*** p. 33) featuring the vocabulary words glossed in the selections:

intermission (p. 750) *woes* (p. 754)
stout (p. 753) *wail* (p. 754)

Give students a copy of the chart, and read the words aloud. Have students mark their rating of each in the Before You Read column.

To gauge how much instruction to provide, tally the number of students who think they know each word.

Explain that the words are defined in the margin where they appear in the selection. Urge students to be alert to these words as they read and discuss selections. They will rate their knowledge again when they finish.

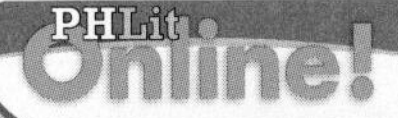

Vocabulary Central, featuring tools, activities, and songs for studying vocabulary, is available at **www.PHLitOnline.com.**

2 ## Writing About the Big Question

In few words, the speakers in these poems communicate intense thoughts and feelings. Use this sentence starter to develop your ideas.

A powerful piece of writing can make readers **aware** of ___________.

Meet the Authors

Walt Whitman (1819–1892)

Author of "I Hear America Singing" (p. 750)

American poet Walt Whitman celebrated individual freedom. He published his first book of poetry, *Leaves of Grass*, at his own expense. Now, *Leaves of Grass* is known as a very influential volume in American literature.

Bashō and Chiyojo

(1644–1694) (1703–1775)

Authors of "Three Haiku" (p. 751)

One of the greatest Japanese poets, Bashō raised the haiku from a comic form to a high art. In his youth, he lived in luxury, but he later devoted himself to haiku. Chiyojo was the wife of a samurai's servant. After her husband died, she became a nun and studied poetry.

◀ Bashō

Alice Walker (b. 1944)

Author of "Women" (p. 752)

From the age of eight, Alice Walker kept a journal and wrote poems. Today, Walker is an acclaimed novelist, essayist, and poet. Her works include the novel *The Color Purple*, which was made into a movie and a Broadway show.

William Shakespeare (1564–1616)

Author of "Sonnet 30" (p. 754)

English poet and playwright William Shakespeare is one of the most beloved writers of all time. Experts believe Shakespeare possessed the largest vocabulary of any writer in history. His many plays, including *Romeo and Juliet*, are still performed around the world.

Teaching Resources

- All EL *Unit 4 Resources,* pp. 205–221
- All EL *Graphic Organizer Transparencies,* pp. 140–143
- All *Professional Development Guidebook,* pp. 33
- All *Enriched Online Student Edition*
- All *Common Core Companion,* pp. 48–54; 190–201

PHLit Online! All resources, including print and audio, are available at **www.PHLitOnline.com.**

Daily Bellringer

For each class during which you will teach this selection, have students complete one of the five Sentence Combining activities for Week 24 in the *Daily Bellringer Activities* booklet.

2 Writing About the Big Question

1. Read the assignment with the class.
2. **Ask** students what communication with different people from different backgrounds has taught them.
3. Have students complete the sentence starter. Review responses as a class. (**Possible response:** A powerful piece of writing can make readers aware of different points of view.)
4. Remind students that their answers will help them think about the Big Question, "How does communication change us?" Tell them to look for the ideas and emotions these poets convey.

Concept Connector

Tell students that they will return to their sentence starter after they have concluded reading.

Multidraft Reading

To assist struggling readers and to deepen reading for all, apply multidraft reading protocols. For each reading, have students set the purpose indicated:

- **First reading**—identifying key ideas and details and answering any Reading Checks.
- **Second reading**—analyzing craft and structure and responding to the side-column prompts.
- **Third reading**—integrating knowledge and ideas, connecting to other texts and the world, and answering the end-of-selection questions.

For more guidance, refer to the *Classroom Strategies and Teaching Routines* card on multidraft reading.

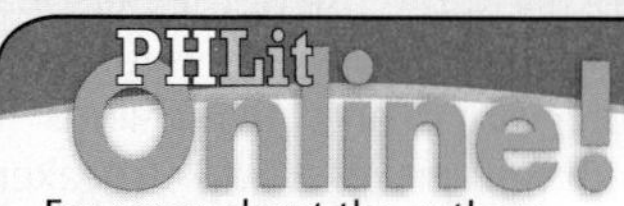

For more about the authors and practice with the selection vocabulary, go to **www.PHLitOnline.com**.

TEACH

❶ Background

- "Leaves of Grass" When it was first published, this collection was widely criticized because, among other things, it was written in free verse. Ironically, Whitman's work went on to inspire countless poets who eventually popularized free verse.
- "Haiku" The haiku form has endured across many centuries. It was first used by Buddhist monks in the 1400s. More recently, haiku has influenced Western literary movements such as Imagism, a group of early twentieth-century poets led by Ezra Pound.

❷ Activating Prior Knowledge

Provide students with templates for a haiku and a line of lyric poetry modeled on "I Hear America Singing"

Remind students that haiku uses imagery from nature to convey emotion while Whitman's poem celebrates Americans and their daily lives. Ask students to think of aspects of nature and daily life that evoke joy, surprise, or wonder. Have students write poetic lines or haiku about one of these emotions.

Concept Connector →

Students will follow up on this activity after completing the poems.

❸ About the Selection

"I Hear America Singing" celebrates the common working men and women of America. The haiku by Bashō and Chiyojo create dominant impressions for readers with one or two striking images from nature.

❹ Literary Analysis

Lyric Poetry

1. Read aloud the bracketed text. Review features of lyric poetry.
2. **Ask** the Literary Analysis question: Which word in the opening line helps identify this as a lyric poem?

   Answer: The use of the personal pronoun "I" suggests that this poem will express the feelings and thoughts of a single speaker. The concept of "singing" further relates the poem to lyric poetry.

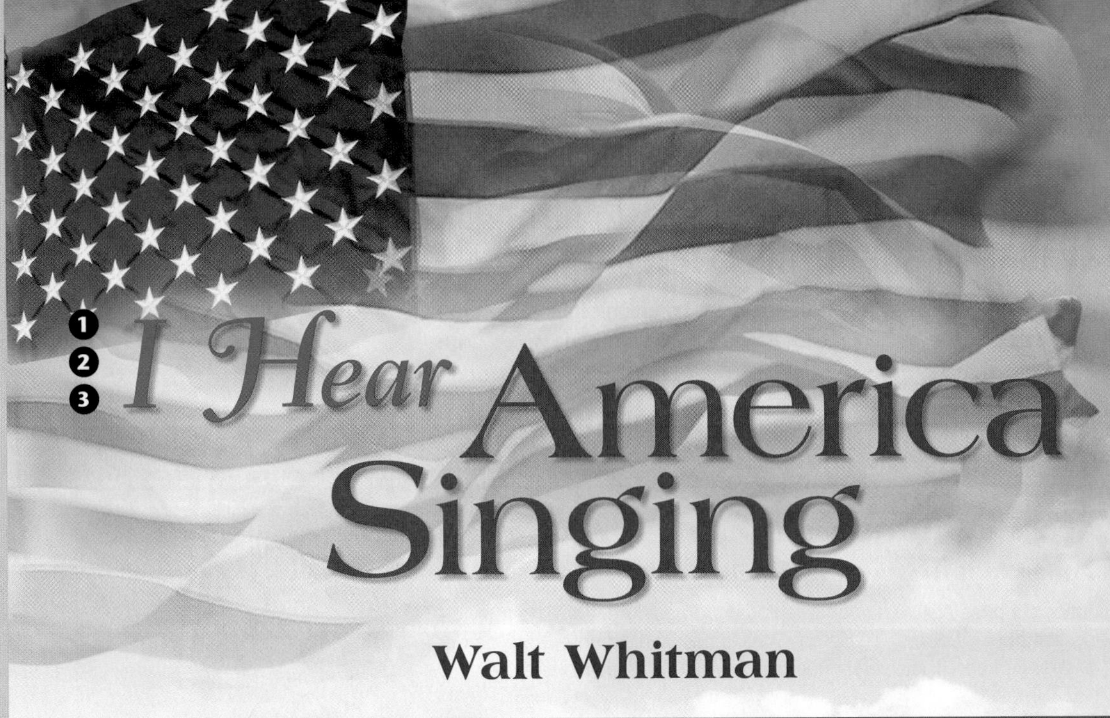

❶❷❸ I Hear America Singing

Walt Whitman

Literary Analysis
Lyric Poetry Which word in the opening line helps identify this as a lyric poem?

Vocabulary
intermission (in′ tər mish′ ən) *n.* any kind of break; more specifically, a break during a performance

❹ I hear America singing, the varied carols I hear,
Those of mechanics, each one singing his as it should be blithe and strong,
The carpenter singing his as he measures his plank or beam,
The mason singing his as he makes ready for work, or leaves off work,
The boatman singing what belongs to him in his boat, the deckhand singing on the steamboat deck,
The shoemaker singing as he sits on his bench, the hatter singing as he stands,
The wood-cutter's song, the ploughboy's on his way in the morning, or at noon intermission or at sundown,
The delicious singing of the mother, or of the young wife at work, or of the girl sewing or washing,
Each singing what belongs to him or her and to none else,
The day what belongs to the day—at night the party of young fellows, robust, friendly,
Singing with open mouths their strong melodious songs.

Ⓒ Text Complexity Rubric

I Hear America Singing and Three Haiku		
Qualitative Measures	**Context/ Knowledge Demands**	America's workers and friendships; the natural world 1 2 ③ 4 5
	Structure/ Language Clarity and Conventionality	Complex sentences; long lines; free verse; concise images; some historical vocabulary 1 2 ③ 4 5
	Levels of Meaning/ Purpose/Concept Level	Accessible concept (feelings of national pride); challenging concept (the timelessness of nature) 1 2 ③ 4 5
Quantitative Measures	**Text Length**	Word Count: 156; 38
	Lexile	NP

Three Haiku

translated by Daniel C. Buchanan

Temple bells die out.
The fragrant blossoms remain.
A perfect evening!
—Bashō

Dragonfly catcher,
How far have you gone today
In your wandering?
—Chiyojo

5 Bearing no flowers,
I am free to toss madly
Like the willow tree.
—Chiyojo

Literary Analysis
Lyric Poetry What impression does the speaker convey by comparing herself to a willow tree?

Critical Thinking

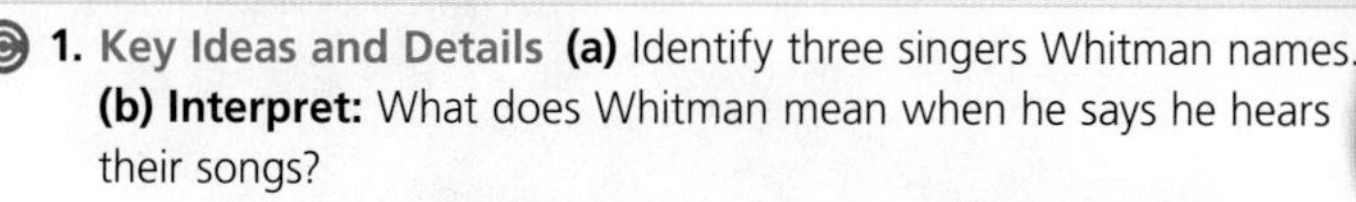

Cite textual evidence to support your responses.

1. **Key Ideas and Details (a)** Identify three singers Whitman names. **(b) Interpret:** What does Whitman mean when he says he hears their songs?
2. **Integration of Knowledge and Ideas Generalize:** How does the language of haiku, works from a non–English-speaking literary tradition, differ from the language in poems you have read from English-speaking literary traditions?
3. **Key Ideas and Details (a)** In Bashō's haiku, what dies out and what remains? **(b) Interpret:** To which senses does Bashō's haiku appeal? **(c) Analyze:** Why are these senses most appropriate in a poem about evening?
4. **Craft and Structure Assess:** Would the first haiku by Chiyojo be as effective if it had been written as a statement rather than as a question? Explain.
5. **Integration of Knowledge and Ideas** Which of these poems causes you to see something from a different or more intense point of view? Use details from the poem you select to explain your response. *[Connect to the Big Question: How does communication change us?]*

5 Literary Analysis

Lyric Poetry

Read aloud the bracketed haiku and point out imagery from nature. **Ask** the Literary Analysis question.
Answer: She gives the impression that she is flexible and can freely move about.

PHLit Online!

This selection is available in interactive format in the **Enriched Online Student Edition, www.PHLitOnline.com,** which includes an interactive graphic organizer.

Concept Connector

Allow students to revisit their haiku or poetic line and revise. Also have students compare their Writing About the Big Question responses before reading the selection with their ideas afterwards.

ASSESS

Answers

Critical Thinking

Remind students to support their answers with evidence from the text.

1. (a) "Singers" include mechanics, carpenters, or masons. (b) He means that he is aware of the pleasure they take in being alive and working.
2. Language from haiku is very concise and primarily concerned with the natural world. English-language poems address a variety of topics and may have complicated syntax as well as higher word counts.
3. (a) The bells die out and the fragrant blossoms remain. (b) The bells appeal to hearing and the blossoms appeal to smell. (c) In night's darkness, it is more appropriate to appeal to these senses.
4. The question form is more effective as it suggests a wanderer's journey.
5. **Possible response:** The first haiku was so intense that I could hear the bells fading, smell the blossoms, and visualize a perfect evening.

Text Complexity: Reader and Task Suggestions

I Hear America Singing and Three Haiku

Preparing to Read the Text	Leveled Tasks
• Use the Background notes on TE p. 750 to provide support for the poems. • Review the structure and subject matter of haiku. • Guide students to use Multidraft Reading strategies (TE p. 749).	*Levels of Meaning* If students will have difficulty with the meaning and purpose, have them first read each poem and note the main ideas or image(s). Then, have them reread and summarize how each poem makes them feel or what it makes them think about. Discuss student notes and clarify meaning. *Synthesizing* If students will not have difficulty with meaning and purpose, have them read each poem and jot down notes about its form and structure. Have them note how the poem's structure contributes to its meaning. Discuss student findings.

❻ Background

Desegregation In 1954, when the Supreme Court ruled against segregation, there were 17 states in which segregation was mandated. Three years later, only nine states had even started the process of desegregation. Segregation remained a problem in the South well into the 1960s.

❼ Activating Prior Knowledge

Provide students with a list of collective noun, such as *women, men, teachers, dogs,* or *singers*. Tell students that "Women" uses such a noun as the starting point for a poem about a particular group of women and their achievements. Have students write one line of a poem about a collective group they admire.

Concept Connector →

Tell students that they will follow up on this activity after they read the selection.

❽ About the Selection

In "Women," the speaker recognizes that her way has been paved by African American women of previous generations.

EXEMPLAR TEXT

The Quiltmakers 22 11/16" x 24", Paul Goodnight, Color Circle Art Publishing Inc.

❻ ❼ ❽

Women

ALICE WALKER

Background In "Women," the speaker praises African American women who fought for public school desegregation in the American South. Until the 1950s, African American and white students attended different schools in the South. In 1954, the U.S. Supreme Court ruled that segregated public schooling was unconstitutional.

Text Complexity Rubric

Women and Sonnet 30		
Qualitative Measures	**Context/ Knowledge Demands**	"Women" is about African Americans in the twentieth century; "Sonnet 30" reflects on personal loss 1 2 3 ④ 5
	Structure/ Language Clarity and Conventionality	Conversational tone; long lines; free verse; some challenging vocabulary 1 2 3 ④ 5
	Levels of Meaning/ Purpose/Concept Level	Accessible concept (struggles of African Americans); challenging concepts (death and the power of love) 1 2 3 ④ 5
Quantitative Measures	**Text Length**	Word Count: 61; 117
	Lexile	NP

They were women then
My mama's generation
Husky of voice—Stout of
Step
With fists as well as
Hands
How they battered down
Doors
And ironed
Starched white
Shirts
How they led
Armies
Headragged Generals
Across mined
Fields
Booby-trapped
Kitchens
To discover books
Desks
A place for us
How they knew what we
Must know
Without knowing a page
Of it
Themselves.

Vocabulary
stout (stout) *adj.* sturdy

Literary Analysis
Lyric Poetry What emotion or feeling does the phrase "Headragged Generals" evoke?

◀ **Critical Viewing**
Is the artist's attitude toward these women similar to the one expressed by the poet? **[Compare]**

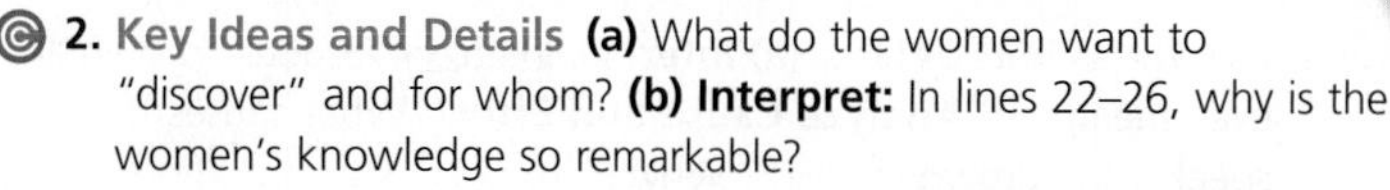

Critical Thinking

Cite textual evidence to support your responses.

1. **Craft and Structure** **(a)** List three images in the poem that convey the women's determination to help their children. **(b) Assess:** Which image did you find the most powerful? Why?
2. **Key Ideas and Details** **(a)** What do the women want to "discover" and for whom? **(b) Interpret:** In lines 22–26, why is the women's knowledge so remarkable?
3. **Integration of Knowledge and Ideas** **(a)** What message about education do the women communicate with their actions? Use details to support your answer. **(b)** What impact do you think this message had on their children? Explain your answer. ***[Connect to the Big Question: How does communication change us?]***

9 Literary Analysis
Symbolism and Allegory

1. Read the bracketed text aloud. **Ask** students to describe the image and tell who it describes.
   Answer: The image is of generals wearing headscarves, leading armies across fields. It describes African American women working for desegregation.
2. **Ask** the Literary Analysis question: What emotion or feeling does the phrase "Headragged Generals" evoke?
   Answer: It evokes a feeling of the power of everyday people.

Concept Connector

Allow students to revisit their poetic line and revise. Invite volunteers to share. In addition, have students compare their Writing About the Big Question responses before reading the selection with their ideas afterwards.

10 Critical Viewing

Answer: No, the women in the painting seem calm and complacent, but the poet depicts the women as strong, aggressive and relentless.

ASSESS
Answers

Critical Thinking

Remind students to support their answers with evidence from the text.

1. (a) **Possible response:** Images include: "battered down Doors," "led armies," "Headragged Generals." (b) **Possible response:** The image of women heading an army to ensure a child's education is most powerful.
2. (a) The women want to discover books—that is, education—for their children. (b) It is remarkable that the women knew that education was the key to their children's success even though they lacked it themselves.
3. **Possible responses:** (a) They communicate the message that an education is worth a fight. War images support the message. (b) It probably made the children admire their mothers and value education.

Text Complexity: Reader and Task Suggestions

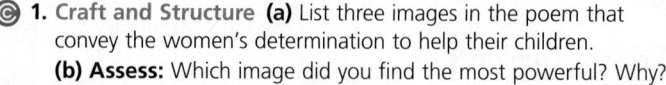

Women and Sonnet 30	
Preparing to Read the Text • Refer to the Background information on TE p. 752 and discuss desegregation and the role of women in supporting their families during times of strife and injustice. • Review strategies for reading long sentences by first identifying the main action and then breaking the rest of the sentence down into smaller parts. • Guide students to use Multidraft Reading strategies (TE p. 749).	**Leveled Tasks** *Levels of Meaning* If students will have difficulty with levels of meaning, have them first read each poem and note the main idea of the poem. Then, have them reread and note details that suggest how the speaker thinks or feels about the subject. Discuss student notes and clarify understanding. *Analyzing* If students will not have difficulty with levels of meaning, have them read and note how the poet uses imagery to make the theme vivid and memorable. Have students contribute their notes and ideas in class discussion.

TEACH

⓫ Background

Shakespeare wrote 154 sonnets. More than 120 of his (including "Sonnet 30") are addressed to an unidentified man.

⓬ Activating Prior Knowledge

Provide students with a list of emotions. Explain that "Sonnet 30" explores emotions. Have students write one line of a poem about an emotion.

Concept Connector

Tell students that they will follow up on this activity after they read the selection.

⓭ About the Selection

In "Sonnet 30," Shakespeare describes memories and friendship.

Concept Connector

Allow students to revise their poetic line and share. Then, have students compare their Writing About the Big Question responses before reading the selection with their ideas afterwards.

ASSESS

Answers

Critical Thinking

Remind students to support their answers with evidence from the text.

1. (a) It means "to cry." (b) The speaker cries over past sad times.
2. (a) The speaker is reviewing the "costs" of past woes. (b) It is part of the grieving process.
3. **Possible response:** The words can reassure readers of compensations in life that balance loss.

⓫ ⓬ ⓭

SONNET 30

WILLIAM SHAKESPEARE

Vocabulary

woes (wōz) *n.* great sorrows

wail (wāl) *n.* lament; cry of deep sorrow

When to the sessions of sweet silent thought
I summon up remembrance of things past,
I sigh the lack of many a thing I sought,
And with old woes new wail my dear times waste:[1]
Then can I drown an eye, unused to flow,
For precious friends hid in death's dateless[2] night,
And weep afresh love's long since cancelled woe,
And moan the expense[3] of many a vanished sight:
Then can I grieve at grievances foregone,[4]
And heavily from woe to woe tell o'er[5]
The sad account of fore-bemoanèd moan,[6]
Which I new pay as if not paid before.
But if the while I think on thee, dear friend,
All losses are restored and sorrows end.

1. **And . . . waste** and by grieving anew for past sorrows, ruin the precious present.
2. **dateless** endless.
3. **expense** loss.
4. **foregone** past and done with.
5. **tell o'er** count up.
6. **fore-bemoanèd moan** sorrows suffered in the past.

Critical Thinking

Cite textual evidence to support your responses.

1. **Key Ideas and Details (a) Infer:** In line 5, what does "drown an eye" mean? **(b) Analyze Cause and Effect:** What causes the speaker to "drown an eye"? Why?
2. **Key Ideas and Details (a) Clarify:** What is the speaker describing in lines 10–12? **(b) Relate:** Why might someone spend time doing this?
3. **Integration of Knowledge and Ideas** In what ways could the speaker's words change a person's response to a disappointment or personal loss? *[Connect to the Big Question: How does communication change us?]*

Vocabulary Development

Vocabulary Knowledge Rating

When students have completed reading and discussing the selections, have them take out their **Vocabulary Rating Chart.** Read the words aloud once more and have students rate their knowledge of the words again in the After Reading column. Clarify any words that are still problematic. Have students write their own definition and example or sentence in the appropriate column. Then, have students complete the Vocabulary Practice activities on the next page. Encourage students to use the words in further discussion and written work about the poems. Remind them that they will be accountable for these words on the **Selection Test** (*Unit 4 Resources,* pp. 216–218 or 219–221).

After You Read

I Hear America Singing • Three Haiku • Women • Sonnet 30

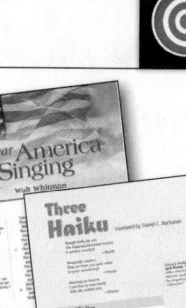

Comparing Forms of Lyric Poetry

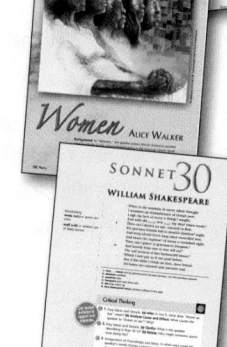

1. **Craft and Structure** Both "I Hear America Singing" and "Women" are **free verse,** with a form imposed by the poet. **(a)** Compare the emotions conveyed in these poems. **(b)** Which poem follows more of a pattern? Explain.
2. **Craft and Structure** Compare and contrast the subjects and structure of the three **haiku** to the three poems from English-speaking traditions.
3. **Craft and Structure** In his **sonnet,** Shakespeare presents an idea or a question in the first quatrain (four lines), explores the idea in the next two quatrains, and reaches a conclusion in the final couplet. Use a chart like the one shown to analyze the content of "Sonnet 30."

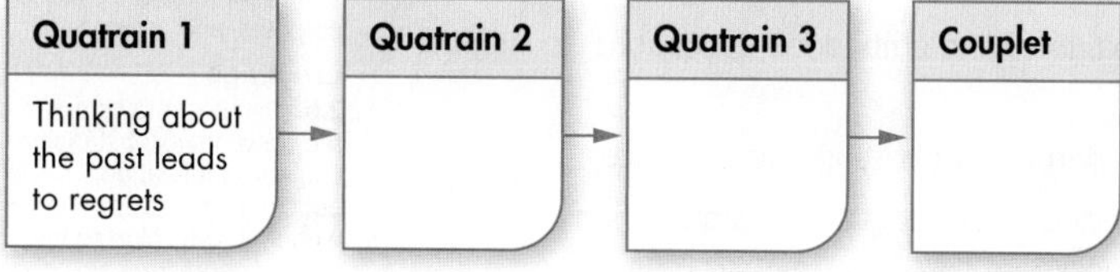

Timed Writing

Explanatory Text: Essay

In an essay, compare the ways the structure of the different lyric forms affect the meanings of these poems. Choose two poems and structures to discuss. Cite textual evidence to support your response. **(30 minutes)**

5-Minute Planner

1. Read the prompt carefully and completely.
2. Gather your ideas by jotting down answers to these questions:
   - How does the free verse structure of Whitman's and Walker's poems help the strength of each poem's message?
   - How does the strict form of the haiku help to capture the feeling of a brief moment in time?
   - How would the meaning of "Sonnet 30" be different without the final two lines?
3. Reread the prompt. Then, refer to your notes as you draft your essay.

Assessment Resources

Unit 4 Resources

L1 L2 EL **Selection Test A,** pp. 216–218.
L3 L4 EL **Selection Test B,** pp. 219–221.
L3 L4 **Open Book Test,** pp. 213–215.

PHLit Online! All assessment resources are available at **www.PHLitOnline.com.**

ASSESS

Answers

Comparing Forms of Lyric Poetry

1. (a) Both poems sing the praises of people who believe in America and the idea of success. (b) "I Hear America Singing" follows more of a pattern because of its extensive use of repetition.
2. A haiku has three unrhymed lines. The first and last lines have five syllables; the middle line has seven. "Three Haiku" follow these formal requirements.
3. **Quatrain 2:** Thinking about the past can cause tears. **Quatrain 3:** The sadness of things that have happened in the past does not necessarily fade with time. **Couplet:** Friendship can help overcome sadness.

   For other sample answers, see ***Graphic Organizer Transparencies,* Comparing Forms of Lyric Poetry Graphic Organizer A (After You Read),** p. 142, and the **Additional Answers** section.

Timed Writing

1. Review the prompt with students.
2. Have students use the 5-Minute Planner to structure their time. Guide them in answering the bulleted questions. For example, guide students to identify the key characteristics of sonnet, haiku, and free verse so they can respond to the effect of structure.
3. Allow students 30 minutes to complete the assignment.
4. As students prewrite and draft, have them refer to their completed Quatrain Graphic Organizer.

Six Traits Focus

✓	Ideas	✓	Word Choice
✓	Organization		Sentence Fluency
	Voice		Conventions

Common Core State Standards

- Writing 2, 2.b, d; 4, 5, 9.a, 10
- Language 2.b; 4.3.a, b; 6.3.b

Introducing the Writing Assignment

Review the assignment and the criteria, using the instruction on the student page.

Pat Mora on Responding to Literature

Show students Segment 3 on Pat Mora on *See It!* DVD or from this page in the **Enriched Online Student Edition,** at **www.PHLitOnline.com.** Discuss how Mora creates a mood for writing and how she finds ideas. Ask students to respond to Mora's methods of revising to find just the right words and rhythms.

Writing Workshop *Work in Progress*

If students have completed the Work-in-Progress assignments on pp. 717 and 739, suggest that they consider developing their Work-In-Progress in a response to literature.

What Do You Notice?

1. Have a volunteer read the passage aloud.
2. **Ask** students what do you notice about the passage? (**Possible response:** It contains a direct quotation from FDR.)
3. Point out that Axelrod introduces the quotation with an interpretive statement. **Ask** students: How does he interpret FDR's writing? **Possible response:** He interprets FDR's writing as being realistic and honest.)
4. **Ask** how the quotation supports that interpretation. (**Possible response:** The quotation describes grim problems in the world.)

Writing Workshop

Write Explanatory Texts

Exposition: Response to Literature

Defining the Form A formal **response to literature** gives you an opportunity to analyze and reflect on a specific work. You might use elements of this type of writing in journals, critical reviews, literary analyses, and annotated bibliographies.

Assignment Write a response to a work of literature that engages you as a reader. Include these elements:

- ✓ an *analysis* of the work's content, its related ideas, and its effect on you
- ✓ a *thesis statement* that characterizes your response
- ✓ a *focus* on a single aspect or an overall view of the work
- ✓ *evidence from the text,* including embedded quotations, to support your opinions
- ✓ a *tone* that suits your purpose for writing and audience
- ✓ error-free grammar, including correct use of colons when introducing lists or quotations

To preview the criteria on which your response to literature may be judged, see the rubric on page 763.

Writing Workshop: *Work in Progress*

If you have completed the Work-in-Progress assignments on pages 717 and 739, use these ideas as you complete the Writing Workshop.

WRITE GUY
Jeff Anderson, M.Ed.

What Do You Notice?

Direct Quotations

The following excerpt is from *Nothing to Fear: Lessons in Leadership from FDR* by Alan Axelrod. Read the excerpt several times.

There is no sugarcoating of reality here! The fog has lifted, the scene is sharply etched and downright frightening: "a host of unemployed citizens face the grim problem of existence, and an equally great number toil with little return."

Jot down what you find effective about the use of a quotation in this excerpt. As you work on your response to literature, think of ways you can best use direct quotations to support your ideas.

Common Core State Standards

Writing

2. Write informative/explanatory texts to examine and convey complex ideas, concepts, and information clearly and accurately through the effective selection, organization, and analysis of content.

4. Produce clear and coherent writing in which the development, organization, and style are appropriate to task, purpose, and audience.

9.a. Draw evidence from literary or informational texts to support analysis, reflection and research. Apply grades 9-10 reading standards to literature.

10. Write routinely over extended time frames and shorter time frames for a range of tasks, purposes, and audiences.

Language

2.b. Demonstrate command of the conventions of standard English capitalization, punctuation, and spelling when writing. Use a colon to introduce a list or quotation.

Reading-Writing Connection

To get a feel for responses to literature, read the excerpt from *Nothing to Fear: Lessons in Leadership from FDR* by Alan Axelrod on page 567.

Teaching Resources

The following resources can be used to enrich or extend the instruction.

- All *Unit 4 Resources* **Writing Workshop,** pp. 222–223
- All *Common Core Companion,* pp. 190–201
- All *Professional Development Guidebook* **Rubric for Self-Assessment: Response to Literature,** pp. 224–225
- All *Graphic Organizer Transparencies* **Rubric for Self-Assessment: Response to Literature,** p. 144
- All *See It!* DVD **Pat Mora,** Segments 3 and 4

All resources, including video, are also available online at **www.PHLitOnline.com.**

Prewriting/Planning Strategies

Make a top-ten list. Think of stories, poems, or other works of literature that you found memorable. Create a top-ten list of these titles and authors. Next to each entry, briefly note your initial reactions to the work and any ideas you might want to share about it. Review your list and choose one work as your topic.

Clarify your purpose. Determine the specific purpose, or goal, of your essay. For example, you may want to share your enthusiasm for a new writer, find fresh insights into a well-known poem, or analyze the meaning of a short story. Write a statement of purpose for your essay. Use both the title and the author's name in your statement:

- **Example of statement of purpose:** *In this essay, I will analyze the character of General Zaroff in Richard Connell's short story "The Most Dangerous Game."*

Identify types of details you will need. The purpose or goal of your essay determines the kinds of details you need to include. Consider these tips:

- **To praise,** include concrete details about what you liked.
- **To analyze,** support your ideas with evidence from the selection as well as other outside resources.
- **To explain a personal response,** show how the work connects to your own experiences and ideas.

Find supporting evidence. Return to the work of literature you have selected to find examples, excerpts, and direct quotations that relate to your topic. Consider how well your research supports your own responses. Prepare a series of index cards, with one card for every idea you want to prove. Write your main point or idea across the top of the card. Underneath, write your notes on the details you gathered from the text to support that point or idea.

By breaking down the details and referring them back to your purpose, you will be able to present complex ideas in a sustained and compelling manner.

PHLit Online!
www.PHLitOnline.com
- Author video: Writing Process
- Author video: Rewards of Writing

Identifying Supporting Evidence

Thesis: What I want to prove:
General Zaroff's civilized exterior conceals a ruthless, heartless murderer.

How I can prove it:
His elegant castle is also a prison.

Explain in detail:
Zaroff makes Rainsford comfortable in the castle in order to make him healthy and, therefore, the hunt more intriguing.

TEACH

Prewriting Strategies

1. Introduce the prewriting strategies, using the instruction on the student page.
2. Have students apply the strategies to choose a topic.

Teaching the Strategies

1. Encourage media literacy by allowing students to include films in their lists.
2. Tell students that they can clarify their purposes by beginning with a question, such as *Why is General Zaroff an important character in Richard Connell's short story "The Most Dangerous Game"?*
3. Have students create three note cards, each listing a character trait for General Zaroff, to help them gather examples.

Think Aloud: Model Identifying Types of Details

Model the strategy, using the following "think aloud":

Let's say I'm writing an essay that analyzes Robert Frost's poem, "The Road Not Taken." I might write that the poem is about deciding which path in life to follow. I'll give evidence to support this analysis by including a quote from the poem: "Two roads diverged in a wood, and I—I took the one less traveled by, and that has made all the difference." Using the quote shows details that help support my ideas about the poem.

Six Traits Focus

✓	Ideas		Word Choice
✓	Organization		Sentence Fluency
	Voice		Conventions

Prentice Hall EssayScorer

A writing prompt for this mode of writing can be found in the *Prentice Hall Essay Scorer* at www.PHLitOnline.com.

Applying Understanding by Design Principles

Clarifying Expected Outcomes: Using Rubrics

- Before students begin working on this assignment, have them preview the Rubric for Self-Assessment (p. 763) to learn what qualities their essays must have.
- Review the criteria in the Rubric with the class. Before students use the Rubric to assess their writing, work with them to rate the Student Model (p. 762) using the Rubric.
- If you wish to assess students' essays with either a 4-point or a 6-point scoring rubric, see *Professional Development Guidebook*, pp. 224–225.

Drafting Strategies

1. Introduce the drafting strategies, using the instruction on the student page.
2. Have students apply the strategies as they draft.

Teaching the Strategies

1. In creating their organizational charts, tell students to eliminate any details on their note cards that do not relate directly to their thesis statements. Now that they have working thesis statements, encourage students to go back to the stories and locate additional supporting details.
2. With students, determine the audience for these responses and help students understand the difference between summarizing a literary work and providing supporting evidence for a thesis statement.
3. Review how to punctuate quotations, and clarify the difference between summarizing and paraphrasing.
4. *For more on elaboration, see Pat Mora's comments on p. 759.*

Think Aloud: Model Identifying Your Thesis

Model the strategy, using the following "think aloud":

Let's say the story I'm writing about involves a character who is a thief and whom I strongly dislike. As I look over my notes on the story, I'm able to figure out *why* this character is so disturbing to me. He acts in a gentlemanly, refined, and polite manner in public, but he is actually a crook. I can use this contrast between how he appears and the type of person he really is as the basis for my thesis statement.

Six Traits Focus

✔	Ideas		Word Choice
✔	Organization		Sentence Fluency
	Voice	✔	Conventions

Drafting Strategies

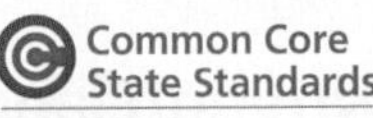

Writing

2.b. Develop the topic with well-chosen, relevant, and sufficient facts, extended definitions, concrete details, quotations, or other information and examples appropriate to the audience's knowledge of the topic.

5. Develop and strengthen writing as needed by planning, revising, editing, rewriting, or trying a new approach, focusing on addressing what is most significant for a specific purpose and audience.

Identify your thesis. Your draft should have a clear thesis statement that you will develop and support throughout your essay. Review your notes to draft a single sentence that combines the statement of purpose you wrote earlier with the ideas and evidence you have accumulated. Use the following thesis statement to direct the writing of your essay.

Example of thesis statement: *In Richard Connell's short story "The Most Dangerous Game," the character of General Zaroff reveals the murderous mind lurking behind an illusion of refinement.*

Organize your ideas. Create an organizational chart like the one shown to present your ideas in a logical way. Your introduction should include your thesis, and every body paragraph should provide its support.

Organize Your Ideas

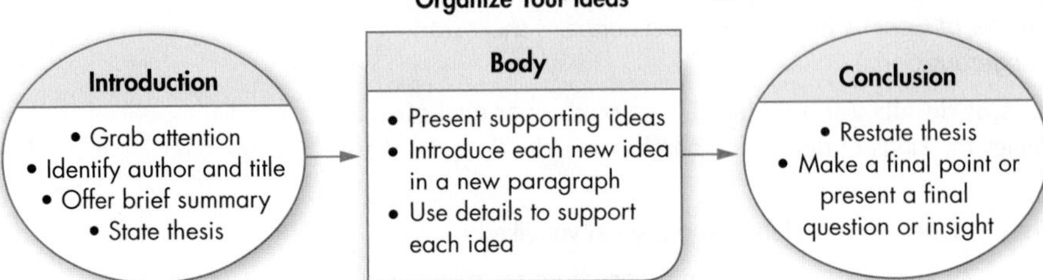

Introduction
• Grab attention
• Identify author and title
• Offer brief summary
• State thesis
Body
• Present supporting ideas
• Introduce each new idea in a new paragraph
• Use details to support each idea
Conclusion
• Restate thesis
• Make a final point or present a final question or insight

Consider your audience. The nature of your audience—who they are and what they know—influences the amount and kind of information you include in your response to literature. For example, if your audience already knows the work, limit the background information and proceed to your core ideas. If your audience is unfamiliar with the work, give more context and explanation.

Provide supporting details. Include evidence from the literary work for every claim you make in your essay. Consider these suggestions:

- **Quotations** can illustrate a character's attitude, a writer's word choice, or an essayist's opinion. Be sure that quotations are exact and enclosed in quotation marks.
- **Examples** of a character's actions or of a specific literary element can enhance your analysis.
- **Paraphrases,** or restatements in your own words, can help you explain a writer's theme, discuss the conflict, analyze a character, or clarify key ideas. Paraphrases must accurately reflect the original text.

Avoid padding your draft with irrelevant passages or unnecessary summaries of the plot. Focus on conveying the point of your essay.

Strategies for Using Technology in Writing

Encourage students to compose their drafts on computers. As students write, they will find that they may need to clarify or reword their thesis statements. They may also need to delete or add supporting details as they flesh out their thesis statements. Computers facilitate the process of adding and deleting material.

Also encourage students to save multiple drafts of their responses. Writers often find the need to go back to previous versions of a draft as they revise. By saving multiple drafts, students provide themselves with this option.

In some cases, students may find that they need to change the order in which they present their main points and supporting details to make their arguments more logical. The cut-and-paste feature in most word processing programs enables students to reorder ideas and entire paragraphs as they revise and refine their drafts.

Writers on Writing

Pat Mora On Responding to Literature

Pat Mora is the author of "Uncoiling" (p. 613) and "A Voice" (p. 614).

Many of my best teachers are authors I will never meet. In the essay "Unseen Teachers," I explore how authors help me experience the world more intensely. Literature and all forms of art can make us more human.

This passage from the essay was inspired by a quotation from Southwest artist Georgia O'Keeffe saying that she was trying to prompt the viewer to notice. As I tried to show, writers who see their work as part of a group's struggle for justice do the same

"I love words and their interweavings."
—Pat Mora

Professional Model:

from "Unseen Teachers," from *Nepantla*

I still smile at her [Georgia O'Keeffe's] laughing confession that by painting huge flowers, she forced us to notice. . . .

I love art and often get ideas in museums. Many readers know O'Keeffe's paintings of flowers. Here, they make my thesis colorful and concrete.

We too seek to force a society to notice the bitter and the sweet. Often we both participate in our communities and are solitary writers, a tension. The mere cover of Denise Levertov's *The Poet in the World* reminds me of her firm conviction: "Both life and poetry fade, wilt, shrink when they are divorced." Lorna Dee Cervantes, Sandra Cisneros, Alice Walker, Lucille Clifton, Amy Tan, Joy Harjo, and Linda Hogan are thick in the struggle of their people, and their writing is part of that struggle. Though the daily realities—high dropout rates, low per capita income, high unemployment—continue, these women teach me that the arrangement and rearrangement of work on the page is neither elitist nor irrelevant. It is the appropriate task of the person who weaves words for people's use.

I debated what names to include and what realities to list. These authors support the diversity that's a theme for the book.

Braids or weaves, I wondered? Both, like writing, are hand activities. I chose weaves because weavers create both basic items of clothing and beautiful art pieces.

Pat Mora on Responding to Literature

Review the passage on the student page with the class, using Mora's comments to deepen students' understanding of the process of writing about literature.

Teaching From the Professional Model

1. Show students Segment 3 on Pat Mora on ***See It!* DVD.** Discuss how Pablo Neruda is another unseen teacher for Pat Mora and how he fits into Mora's group of writers who "are thick in the struggle of their people." Ask students to volunteer examples of unseen teachers in their own lives.
2. Point out how Pat Mora uses the image of O'Keeffe's flower paintings to further her thesis. Have students brainstorm for images they can use to further ideas in their literary responses. Ask volunteers to share ideas for imagery with the class.
3. **Ask** students how Mora's citing of names and daily realities helps further her thesis.

   Possible answer: The names give readers examples of writers who are using their writing for good causes, and the daily realities show readers the importance of these writers' works.
4. Explain to students how, like Pat Mora, they must be careful with their word choice. Ask students to review their drafts to identify words that are used incorrectly.

Show or assign the video online at **www.PHLitOnline.com.**

Differentiated Instruction for Universal Access

Enrichment for Advanced Writers

Pat Mora says that writers who see their work as part of a group's struggle for social justice prompt viewers to notice. Lead students in a discussion about what she means by this statement. Who are the groups who struggle for social justice? How can art and literature serve as a voice for the people who belong to these groups? Who is the intended audience for these artistic works? What does Mora hope that the audience will notice?

Revising Strategies

1. Introduce the revision strategies, using the instruction on the student page.
2. Have students apply the strategies as they revise their essays.

Teaching the Strategies

1. If students have difficulty working with whole drafts, suggest that they print copies of their drafts to cut apart. Tell them to cut out their thesis statements, main points, and supporting details. Using a desktop or table to arrange their paper strips, students can examine each main point and detail for its relevance.
2. Have students work with partners to eliminate unnecessary information.
3. Provide these examples that show students how to replace dull, vague words with colorful, precise words:

   The character was happy.
   The character was ecstatic.

   Darkness fell fast.
   Darkness fell abruptly.

   Tomas came into the room slowly.
   Tomas entered the room cautiously.
4. Help students identify words that convey approval or criticism. Compare *Her honest portrayal of her life captures the reader's attention* with *Her inaccurate portrayal of her life leaves the reader confused.* Encourage students to create separate word banks for words of approval and words of criticism.

Six Traits Focus

	Ideas	✔	Word Choice
✔	Organization	✔	Sentence Fluency
	Voice		Conventions

Revising Strategies

Revise to eliminate unnecessary information. Use words and phrases to convey ideas precisely by reviewing your draft to eliminate extra details. Identify instances in which the information you provide may not support your main idea, but may actually distract from it. Follow these steps:

- Underline your thesis and the main ideas of each paragraph.
- Highlight sentences that do not support your thesis.
- Consider revising details to make a tighter connection to your main idea.
- Eliminate any paragraphs or details that do not clearly contribute to your analysis.

Check words of praise or criticism. Review your response to literature, making sure your word choices are precise and that they accurately reflect your purpose, your audience, and your attitude toward the literary work.

Vague: This *factual* account of the author's life is *interesting.*

Precise: This *honest* account of the author's life *captures* the reader's attention.

In addition, pay close attention to the degree, or form, of the adjectives you use, especially when making comparisons. Use the degree that accurately reflects your meaning. The **comparative** degree, which is usually formed by adding *-er* to the adjective or by using the word *more,* is used to compare two items. The **superlative** degree, which is usually formed by adding *-est* to the adjective or by using the word *most,* is used to compare more than two items.

Comparative degree: Zaroff is a *more disagreeable* character than Rainsford. (*Compares two items*)

Superlative degree: Zaroff is the *most disagreeable* character in the story. (*Compares more than two items*)

Peer Review

Exchange drafts with a partner. Review each other's work, circling words that convey approval or criticism. Underline words that express degrees of comparison. Determine whether you have used these words correctly and whether they are precise or vague. Then, revise your draft, replacing vague, dull, or incorrect language with choices that pinpoint your meaning. As you revise, be sure to maintain a consistency in style and tone throughout your work.

Common Core State Standards

Writing
2.d. Use precise language and domain-specific vocabulary to manage the complexity of the topic.
5. Develop and strengthen writing as needed by planning, revising, editing, rewriting, or trying a new approach, focusing on addressing what is most significant for a specific purpose and audience.

Language
2.b. Use a colon to introduce a list or quotation.

Strategies for Using Precise Words

Tell students that a question-and-answer strategy can help them identify vague words and choose more precise ones. Write this example on the board, and use the following questions to demonstrate.

In this mystery story, a newspaper reported an incident in which a man broke into a house. A neighbor heard a big noise and called the authorities, who found the man in the house cooking a meal.

Question nouns: *What is the incident?* (A *robbery* rather than an *incident*)

Question people: *Who are the man and the authorities?* (A *robber* rather than a *man; police* rather than *authorities*)

Question adjectives: *What kind of noise?* (A *crashing* noise rather than a *big* noise)

Question location: *Whose house? What part of the house?* (The *Myers' house* rather than *house; in the kitchen* rather than *in the house*)

WRITER'S TOOLBOX

Conventions | Sentence Fluency | Voice | Organization | Word Choice | Ideas

Using Quotations

Direct quotations are passages from a work of literature taken word for word. Indirect quotations are paraphrases of the words from literature.

Punctuating Direct Quotations All direct quotations in the running text must be enclosed in quotation marks. A direct quotation is usually preceded by a comma and sometimes by a colon. It is followed by its corresponding page number enclosed in parentheses. The period or comma from the quotation follows the page number. See the example below.

Example of direct quotations in running text:

Rainsford is horrified when he realizes the truth of his situation: "The Cossack was the cat; he was the mouse" (232).

When you quote a passage from the text that runs more than four lines, set it off from the text by indenting it ten spaces. In this case, do not use quotation marks. This type of quotation is often preceded by a colon. Also, the end punctuation comes before the page number citation.

PH WRITING COACH

Further instruction and practice are available in *Prentice Hall Writing Coach.*

Example of block indented quotations:

As Rainsford awaits Zaroff's discovery of him, he breathes a sigh of relief when Zaroff leaves. Then the horror of the situation hits him:

> *Rainsford did not want to believe what his reason told him was true, but the truth was as evident as the sun that had by now pushed through the morning mists. The general was playing with him! The general was saving him for another day's sport! (231)*

Zaroff's true character becomes apparent to Rainsford in this moment.

Punctuating Indirect Quotations Because indirect quotations are paraphrases of the text, you do not need to put them in quotation marks.

Example of indirect quotation in running text:

When Rainsford realizes that Zaroff is playing a game of cat and mouse, he is horrified.

Grammar in Your Writing

Scan your essay to identify any direct quotations. Make sure they have quotation marks at the beginning and end of the quotation. Check whether your end punctuation is inside or outside of the quotation marks. Most periods and commas should be inside. Revise punctuation that is incorrect.

Using Quotations

1. Introduce the grammar skill, using the instruction on the student page.
2. Discuss the examples and the strategies for using quotations.
3. Have students follow the instruction under Grammar in Your Writing to correct errors in their drafts.

Teaching the Grammar Skill

1. Tell students that a direct quotation represents a person's exact speech or thoughts. Explain that direct quotations are enclosed in quotation marks. Provide these examples:

   "Steven, let's hurry or we'll miss the train."

   "Please pass the salt and pepper."
2. Remind students that when they include a direct quotation in their essay, they must reference the page number in the text where the quotation is found. Point out that the page number is enclosed in parentheses and is placed immediately following the quotation.
3. **Ask** students why they think that passages longer than four lines are indented.

   Answer: It makes it easier for readers to distinguish the quotation from other text.
4. Remind students that paraphrasing text means restating the information using their own words.

PH WRITING COACH Grade 9

Students will find practice with and guidance on quotations in chapter 23, Section 4.

Differentiated Instruction for Universal Access

Strategy for Less Proficient Writers
Students may benefit from a discussion about plagiarism. Explain that plagiarism is using someone else's writing and claiming it as your own. Some students may believe that if they change one or two words of a quotation, they have paraphrased the quotation. Caution students against this practice. Tell them that if they change only a word or two and then use the sentence as if it were their own, it may be considered plagiarism.

Student Model

Review the Student Model with the class, using the annotations to analyze the writer's use of the elements of a critical essay.

Teaching From the Student Model

1. Explain that the Student Model is a sample and that students' own essays may be longer.
2. Ask students to make sure that their titles convey an accurate impression of what is to come in their essays.
3. **Ask** students to give examples of the strong language that the writer uses in his thesis statement.

   Possible answers: *civilized, murderous, illusion, charming, charismatic*
4. Ask students whether they have used quotations to support their thesis statements. If not, have students review their literary selections to identify quotations that will help them to support their thesis statements.
5. **Ask** students why the writer's conclusion leaves a lasting impression on the reader.

   Possible Answer: The writer relates his thesis to a universal and vivid image.

Connecting to Real-Life Writing

Discuss some of the situations in real life in which students will be challenged to present a solid, convincing explanation of their response to a work of art. For example, students may be called on by friends to tell why they liked a movie or theatrical performance. They may feel compelled to write a letter to the editor challenging a reviewer's comments about a favorite musician.

Student Model: Jeff Rutherford, Broken Arrow, OK

Characterization of General Zaroff

What lies at the heart of a refined man? In Richard Connell's short story "The Most Dangerous Game," the deranged, yet cunning and elegant General Zaroff shares his taste for hunting with an unsuspecting visitor. Although he is civilized in his dress and habits, Zaroff's beliefs reveal a murderous mind behind the illusion of a charming, charismatic man.

When we first encounter General Zaroff, our initial reaction is one of delight and admiration for his wealth and charm. Zaroff lives in a massive castle, feasts on the finest delicacies, and wears expensive clothes. His luxurious surroundings and lifestyle reflect a highly civilized, eloquent, and proper gentleman. As readers soon learn, however, there is more to Zaroff than food and elegance.

Beneath Zaroff's fine qualities lies an overwhelming attitude of arrogance. This attitude comes from his firm belief that his way of thinking is superior to that of the average person. Zaroff also fancies himself a phenomenal hunter: "My hand was made for the trigger," he claims. It is this deadly mixture of arrogance, superior hunting skills, and belief that it is natural for the strong to prevail over the weak that makes him disregard the value of human life.

Zaroff's extreme beliefs lead him to conclude that only the intelligent mind of a human being can provide him with the dangerous game he desires. Rationalizing that "the weak were created to please the strong," he chooses to hunt humans instead of animals. Unfortunately, Rainsford steps into this situation. The major conflicts in "The Most Dangerous Game" demonstrate what happens during such an inhumane hunt.

However, the general's arrogance and disregard for human life blind him to the fear and desperation of his prey. His attitude leads to his own demise at the hands of Rainsford, his prey. The characterization of Zaroff as a murderer hiding behind a mask of civility shows that beneath even the most beautiful rose can lie a sharp and deadly thorn.

The title indicates that the essay will focus on a single character.

Jeff uses vivid language to state his thesis clearly.

Direct quotations provide evidence for this understanding of Zaroff.

Jeff concludes his response with an illuminating analogy that neatly summarizes his analysis.

Strategies for Test Taking

On many tests, students may be asked to respond to literature. Explain that this is an opportunity for students to draw on their prior knowledge and personal experience. For instance, students can use events out of their own lives, stories they have already read, and even family anecdotes as resources to connect personal responses to almost any literary work.

Students also need to remember how to structure responses to literature. Tell them to memorize these features of a literary response:

- an analysis of a work's content, its ideas, or its effect on the reader
- a focused thesis statement
- evidence to support the thesis statement

Editing and Proofreading

Review your draft to correct errors in spelling, grammar, and punctuation.

Correcting Common Usage Problems *Among* and *between* are not interchangeable. *Among* always implies three or more elements, whereas *between* is generally used with only two elements. *Like, as, as if,* and *as though* are not interchangeable. *Like* is a preposition meaning "similar to" or "such as." It should not be used in place of *as, as if,* or *as though,* which are conjunctions that introduce clauses.

Spiral Review

Earlier in this unit, you learned about **appositive phrases** (p. 716) and **infinitives and infinitive phrases** (p. 738). Check your response to literature to be sure you have used these correctly.

Publishing and Presenting

Consider one of the following ways to share your writing:

Deliver an oral presentation. Read your response to literature aloud. Have a copy of the literary work on hand in the event that your classmates wish to read or review it.

Publish a collection of responses to literature. Gather the essays of several of your classmates. Organize them in a binder and make the collection available in the school library.

Reflecting on Your Writing

Writer's Journal Jot down your answer to this question:
How did writing about the work help you to understand it?

Rubric for Self-Assessment

Find evidence in your writing to address each category. Then, use the rating scale to grade your work.

Criteria	Rating Scale (*not very* – *very*)				
Focus: How clearly have you stated your purpose?	1	2	3	4	5
Organization: How well have you crafted a thesis statement and a clear analysis of the literary work?	1	2	3	4	5
Support/Elaboration: How comprehensive is the background information you provided?	1	2	3	4	5
Style: How formal is your use of language?	1	2	3	4	5
Conventions: Have you accurately quoted from the literary work and correctly punctuated your quotations?	1	2	3	4	5

Differentiated Instruction for Universal Access

Strategy for Special-Needs Students
If students are having difficulty understanding the correct usage of *like, as, as if,* and *as though,* you may want to review these adverbs with them. For each use of these words in their papers, suggest that students read the sentence with each construction to identify the correct usage: *Rainsford fled, just like Zaroff planned. Rainsford fled, just as Zaroff planned. Rainsford fled, just as if Zaroff planned.* Tell students that when *as* or *as if* makes sense in a sentence in place of *like,* they should substitute *as* or *as if.*

Enrichment for Gifted/Talented Students
Challenge students to write humorous paragraphs or poems about the use of troublesome words such as *between* and *among* and *like, as, as if,* and *as though.* Have them use as many of these words as possible in their writing. Invite them to share their compositions with the class.

Editing and Proofreading

1. Introduce the editing and proofreading focus, using the instruction on the student page.
2. Have students edit and proofread their essays, correcting grammar, spelling, punctuation, and word choice. Make sure they look for errors of the type noted in the lesson focus and the Spiral Review.

Teaching the Editing Focus

Remind students that *like* is used as a preposition and that prepositions precede nouns. Provide this example: *The dog howled like* (preposition) *a wolf* (noun). Explain that the words *as, as if,* and *as though* are conjunctions that introduce clauses with a subject and a verb. Give this example: *The dog howled as if* (conjunction) *it* (subject) *were* (verb) *a wolf.*

Six Traits Focus

	Ideas		Word Choice
	Organization	✓	Sentence Fluency
	Voice		Conventions

ASSESS

Publishing and Presenting

1. Suggest that students complement the oral presentations of their papers with oral interpretations of excerpts from the literary works that they are analyzing.
2. Have students talk with the librarian in advance about placing their collection in the library. They might also volunteer to create a display in the library that includes copies of the literature they have reviewed.

Reflecting on Your Writing

Ask students to relate the experience of responding to literature to the experience of responding to a film or CD.

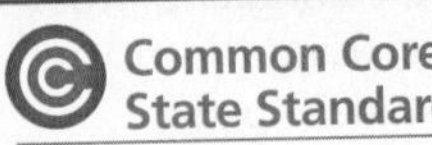

EXTEND

Common Core State Standards

- Language 3, 5.b

Connotation and Denotation

1. Introduce the skill, using the instruction on the student page.
2. Review the examples in the chart.

Think Aloud: Model the Skill

Use the following "think aloud" to model connotations and denotations. Say to students:

If I already know the denotation, or dictionary meaning, of a word, I can use this knowledge to help me understand the word's connotation. For example, my associations with the word *house* seem neutral. A *house* is a building in which people live; the word doesn't tell you if the house is nice or not. Now I imagine how people describe *homes*: they are cozy and safe. When people feel comfortable, they feel *at home.* I see that *home* has positive associations. Now I'll try *shack.* I imagine someplace small and rundown. *Shack* has a negative connotation.

Practice A

Sample answers:

1. defeated
2. untidy
3. silent
4. dirty
5. leader
6. surprised

Vocabulary Workshop

Connotation and Denotation

The **denotation** of a word is its direct, dictionary meaning. Its **connotations** include the ideas, images, and feelings that are associated with the word. Consider the words *fragrance, smell,* and *stench.* These words are synonyms, which means they share a similar denotation—having a scent or odor. However, their connotations are very different.

The connotation of *smell* is about the same as its denotation. It has a neutral connotation and can be defined as "the quality that you recognize by using your nose." The connotation of *fragrance* is positive, suggesting a pleasant, sweet smell or scent. *Stench* has negative connotations, suggesting a foul, unpleasant odor. The following graphic shows the positive, neutral, and negative connotations of some synonyms.

Positive →	Neutral →	Negative
fragrance	smell	stench
modest	shy	mousy
inquisitive	curious	nosy
home	house	shack

Common Core State Standards

Language

3. Apply knowledge of language to understand how language functions in different contexts, to make effective choices for meaning and style, and to comprehend more fully when reading or listening.

5.b. Analyze nuances in the meaning of words with similar denotations.

Practice A Choose the word that has the more neutral connotation.

1. On Friday, the Bridgeport Wolves (defeated, crushed) the North Point Beacons.
2. Helen was embarrassed by her (sloppy, untidy) appearance.
3. Julian remained (silent, sullen) as I told him the news.
4. Because of the weekend-long festival, the street was (filthy, dirty).
5. The (tyrant, leader) signed the new legislation into law.
6. She seemed (surprised, staggered) by the question.

Teaching Resources

Unit 4 Resources
Connotation and Denotation, pp. 224–225

PHLit Online! **Vocabulary Central,** featuring definitions, audio pronunciations, Word Families, and activities, is online at **www.PHLitOnline.com.**

Practice B Rewrite each sentence, replacing the italicized word with a word that has a more positive connotation. Use a dictionary or thesaurus if necessary.

1. Adrian is too *cheap* to spend money on a ticket to the play.
2. I've been around Elena long enough to appreciate her *cunning*.
3. Jevon's *arrogance* makes him a natural leader.
4. When I told him the joke, Marcus *cackled* uncontrollably.
5. Michelle was *lazy* and spent the day reading.
6. The boy and his *cronies* are playing ball.
7. I would never forgive him for his *treachery*.
8. Ana was *stubborn* and kept practicing to make the team.
9. Janine was *disgusted* when her friend moved out of town.
10. The *old* man walked slowly across the street.

www.PHLitOnline.com
- Illustrated vocabulary words
- Interactive vocabulary games
- Vocabulary flashcards

Activity Prepare four note cards with the headings as shown below. Then, write a sentence for each of these words: *argue, fashionable, rumpled, chuckle*. Using a dictionary and thesaurus, write four synonyms for each word. Then, circle the synonym whose connotation best matches the meaning of the word used in your sentence. Compare cards with a partner. See if you chose the same synonyms. Talk about the differences in connotations of the words.

Word:

Sentence:

Synonyms:

Comprehension and Collaboration

Write sentences to show how the connotations of the words in each pair differ: *visionary, dreamer; investigate, snoop; clumsy, awkward*. Use a dictionary and thesaurus if you need to. Meet with a group and compare your sentences and talk about the connotations of the words.

ASSESS/EXTEND

Answers

Practice B

Sample answers:

1. Adrian is too thrifty to spend money on a ticket to the play.
2. I've been around Elena long enough to appreciate her resourcefulness.
3. Jevon's confidence makes him a natural leader.
4. When I told him the joke, Marcus giggled uncontrollably.
5. Michelle was idle and spent the day reading.
6. The boy and his friends are playing ball.
7. I would never forgive him for his disloyalty.
8. Ana was persistent and kept practicing to make the team.
9. Janine was unhappy when her friend moved out of town.
10. The elderly man walked slowly across the street.

Activity

Provide each student with a dictionary and four note cards. Give students a time limit, and then have them compare their synonyms with partners. Ask them to discuss the connotations of each synonym and to explain their choices to each other.

Comprehension and Collaboration

Provide dictionaries for students. Have them imagine a person or situation for each word. Suggest that they also try to remember when they have heard or seen these words before, and whether the words were used in a positive or negative way. Have groups discuss what they imagined or remembered for each word.

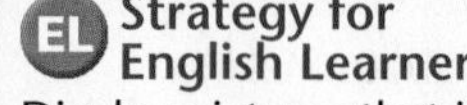

Differentiated Instruction for Universal Access

EL Strategy for English Learners

Display pictures that illustrate words with similar denotations, but with different connotations. For example, show students pictures of a flower, a plant, and a weed. Explain that the pictures show the different connotations of words with similar meanings.

Have students create and maintain connotation dictionaries, listing synonyms and their connotations. Students can use pictures or notes to explain the subtle differences between the meanings of the words.

Strategy for Less Proficient Students

Assign small groups and ask each group to choose three words with the same denotation but different connotations. Have each group make a poster with three panels, one showing each word. Illustrations should clearly show the different connotations of the words. Have groups share their posters with the class.

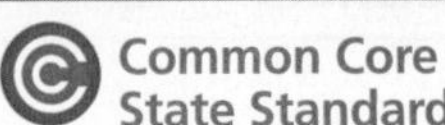

Common Core State Standards

- Speaking and Listening 6

Learn the Skills

1. Introduce the workshop, including the activity on page 767.
2. Explain that students must be sure to understand the selection—including the tone, mood, sound devices, and theme—before they begin to prepare their interpretation.
3. Suggest that students make an audio or video recording of their presentation as they practice. This will allow them to analyze their interpretation for pronunciation and tone of voice.
4. Point out that the purpose of providing a brief introduction is to give the audience a context so they can more easily understand a literary work that is unfamiliar, long, or abstract.
5. If students are struggling with a poem's punctuation, suggest that they write the poem in prose format to eliminate the distraction of the line breaks.
6. Remind students that each character should have a unique voice.

   Ask students to consider how they would give voice to a talking turtle in a fable.

   Possible response: Students might say that they would speak slowly with long pauses.

SPEAKING AND LISTENING

Communications Workshop

Oral Interpretation of Literature

An oral interpretation of literature can be fun: sharing stories, poems, or plays aloud is an activity that is enjoyable for people of all ages. An oral interpretation of literature is also challenging: in order to present one well, you must have a strong comprehension of the work and its meaning. As you prepare your interpretation and engage with the work in a detailed, specific way, you will increase your understanding of the literary work. In presenting the interpretation, you will share your appreciation with others. The following strategies can help you prepare and deliver your oral interpretation.

Common Core State Standards

Speaking and Listening
6. Adapt speech to a variety of contexts and tasks, demonstrating command of formal English when indicated or appropriate.

Learn the Skills

Understand the literature. Your interpretation should demonstrate an accurate understanding of the literary work's content and meaning. Make sure you are thoroughly familiar with your selection.

Rehearse the interpretation. Make a copy of the literary work to mark performance notes as you practice. Plan and practice appropriate gestures, facial expressions, intonations, and timing until they feel natural. If certain words or phrases become stumbling points, memorize them to assure confidence and poise. Always practice aloud. Use the checklist shown here to help you prepare.

Consider your audience. Provide context to help your audience better understand the literary work you are presenting. Write an introduction to help your readers visualize the situation and characters. You may also include information about the author, including his or her style and the circumstances in which he or she wrote the selection.

Your familiarity with the selection should give you the freedom to maintain eye contact with your audience as you read.

Practice reading poetry. Use the poem's punctuation, not the ends of lines, as cues to pause when reading. Avoid lapsing into sing-song rhythms; instead, maintain a flow that sounds like natural speech. Vary your volume and pace to create emphasis.

Practice reading stories and plays. When expressing a character's quoted words, use a change in intonation to distinguish speech from narration. Modulate your vocal inflections, facial expressions, and posture to indicate whether a speaker is male or female, adult or child.

Oral Interpretation Tips

- Read the text multiple times.
- Mark performance notes and cues on your reading copy.
- Choose appropriate gestures, costumes, and props to suggest characters or situations.
- Vary your pace and tone of voice to create emphasis.

Strategies for Reading Out Loud

Give students these additional strategies for reading out loud.

- Explain that students should change their voices as they read. Tell them to vary their volume, tone, and inflection to hold their listeners' attention.
- Caution students to take their time as they read. Explain that rushing will make it difficult for the audience to follow along.
- Tell students not to worry about making mistakes. Everyone mispronounces a word or loses their place occasionally.
- Remind students to think about punctuation as they read. Tell them to use commas and periods as cues to pause.

Practice the Skills

Presentation of Knowledge and Ideas Use what you've learned in this workshop to complete the following activity.

ACTIVITY: Prepare and Deliver an Oral Presentation

Choose a favorite poem, story, or dramatic speech and prepare an oral interpretation using the strategies outlined in this workshop. Remember that your interpretation should enhance the literature's meaning for your audience. Consider these questions as you prepare and rehearse your presentation:

- What is the knowledge level and cultural perspective of my audience? What context best sets up my presentation?
- How will I organize and present ideas in my introduction?
- What props or costume will best enhance my presentation?
- What gestures are most appropriate for this work of literature?
- What pace and tone of voice best enhance this particular piece?

Use the Presentation Checklist below to analyze your classmates' presentations.

Presentation Checklist

Presentation Content

Determine whether or not the speaker provided support for the audience's understanding.

- ❑ considered audience and provided context
- ❑ provided organized and informative introduction
- ❑ included props and costumes effectively

Presentation Delivery

Determine whether or not the speaker engaged with the audience.

- ❑ appropriate eye contact
- ❑ effective speaking rate and volume
- ❑ effective tone of voice
- ❑ appropriate gestures

Comments on most effective elements of presentation: ____________________

Comprehension and Collaboration With your classmates, discuss how you evaluated each presenter. As a group, discuss what makes an oral presentation effective and why.

EXTEND/ASSESS

Practice the Skills

1. Review the assignment with students. Make sure that they understand the difference between reading and interpreting a text. Explain that their oral interpretation should help listeners better understand the poem, story, or speech.
2. Explain to students that they should use a copy of the Presentation Checklist to evaluate their own presentation and the presentations made by classmates.
3. Before students give their presentations to the class, remind listeners to ask questions if any points are unclear. To maintain order, encourage them to raise their hands and wait to be acknowledged by the presenter before stating their questions. Suggest that students making presentations scan the classroom from time to time so they will notice any students who have questions.

Evaluate the Activity

1. Evaluate students' presentations on the basis of appropriate pace and tone, effective use of nonverbal communication, and the student's level of engagement with the audience.
2. When the class discusses the presentations that were easiest to follow, encourage students to make note of the features of those presentations that made them effective and to incorporate those techniques in their future presentations.

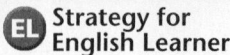

Differentiated Instruction for Universal Access

EL Strategy for English Learners

In order for students to feel comfortable and to present an oral interpretation successfully, they need to select a literary work that has accessible language.

Help students choose a short selection that is not too complex. Then, have students go through the selection, underlining any vocabulary that they do not understand. Have them use a dictionary to define the words, and clarify for them any words that they still do not understand.

Once students understand their selection, **ask:** What feeling is the speaker showing, and how can you display this feeling in your presentation?

Possible responses: Students will indicate a variety of responses based on their selection. Guide them to use appropriate gestures and intonation based on their responses.

To help students with punctuation, tape record the problem words or the entire selection so that students can hear the words. You may also wish to provide additional instruction on the use of punctuation to guide reading.

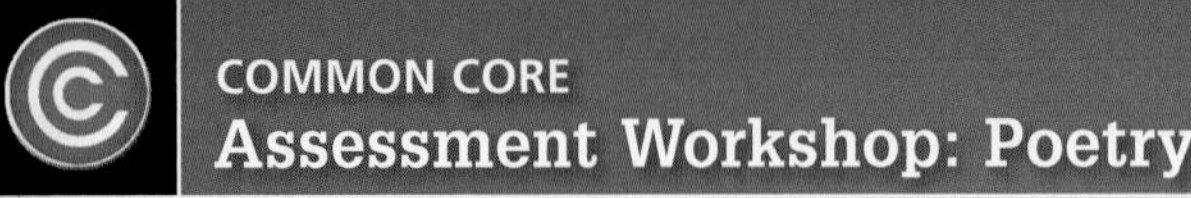

Cumulative Review

In this Test Practice workshop (pp. 768–773), students apply the skills in Unit 4. The practice is divided into four sections.

1. Before assigning each section, review the relevant Unit skills with students.
2. Set a time limit for the multiple choice items in each section, allowing a little over one minute per question. Allow ten to fifteen minutes for any Writing for Assessment questions.
3. Administer each section. Have students write the starting time at the top of their papers. When half the time for the multiple choice items has run out, ask students to write the time next to the answer on which they are working. Have them do the same when the time is three quarters through and again when time is up. Have them note the start and end times for any Writing for Assessment questions as well.
4. Review with students the pacing reflected in their notes.

Reteaching Skills

1. For each practice, use the Reteach chart on the same page as the answers to determine which skills require reteaching, based on which items students answered incorrectly.
2. Reteach these skills prior to assigning the **Benchmark Test** for the second half of Unit 4 (***Unit 4 Resources,*** pp. 267–231).

Cumulative Review

Common Core State Standards

RL.9-10.4; L.9-10.5, L.9-10.6
[For the full wording of the standards, see the standards chart in the front of your textbook.]

I. Reading Literature

Directions: *Read the passage. Then, answer each question that follows.*

Early in the morning, Samantha and her father drove to the trailhead. She and her father had been planning this trip for two years, and they could not wait. They began the hike soon after dawn.

The uphill climb was a challenge as Samantha walked with pounds of gear on her back. She was barely aware of it by the time they reached the top of the hill because of the beauty of the surrounding woods. She saw a flock of turkeys to start. "Gobble, gobble," the jakes called to the hens. The birds had their own special language. They chatted like old married couples.

As Samantha and her father continued, her father motioned for her to stop as he pointed to the right. Just within sight, Samantha could see a black bear with two cubs. She knew she had to be very quiet. She heard the pounding of the drum of her heart in her ears. The cubs rolled around and frolicked happily as they followed their mother into the distance. Samantha could hardly believe her luck to see a bear on the first day.

The wind whipped through the trees, their new leaves singing a beautiful song to Samantha. The branches and dead leaves crackled under her feet. She imagined being an explorer in the 1600s, before there were trails and markers to guide the way. At lunch she returned from her daydream and was thankful to have the convenience and comforts of the twenty-first century. She loved her energy bars.

They climbed higher and hiked farther. The woods became denser and darker. The sun was setting in the west when Samantha's father suggested they set up camp for the night. They gathered firewood and stones to make a circle for the fire. After starting the fire, they set up their tents and prepared their provisions for dinner. The tight blanket of night covered the surrounding forest. All Samantha could see was a small circle of light cast by the campfire. She didn't want to admit it, but she was a little scared. She and her father had been planning this trip for two years. Now they were resting for the night after hiking for eight hours. Her legs felt like rubber because she was so exhausted, but she was so pleased to be on the hike.

Samantha was satisfied with a fine day of adventure. Though she was nervous to sleep deep in the woods, she was excited to see what the next day held in store for her and her father. Maybe she would see a coyote, she thought, as she heard distant howls echo through the forest.

Differentiated Instruction for Universal Access

Strategy for Less Proficient Readers

Help students review some forms of figurative language. Tell them that *onomatopoeia* is a form of figurative language in which a word imitates the sound it describes. Examples are *splash, hiss,* and *sob.* Ask students to find an example of onomatopoeia in paragraph 4, and to explain why the word is an example. (Sentence 2 has the word *crackled,* which sounds like the sound dead leaves make when you have stepped on them.)

Then, ask students to define *metaphor.* (A metaphor is a form of figurative language which compares two unlike things without using the words *like* or *as.*) Have students identify the metaphor in paragraph 5 and explain what two unlike things the metaphor compares. (The metaphor is "The tight blanket of night," which compares the night with a tight blanket.)

1. The author of this story most likely uses **figurative language** in order to—
   A. explain a complicated concept.
   B. add suspense to the plot of the story.
   C. characterize Samantha and her father.
   D. describe the hike in an original way.

2. Which is an example of a **simile?**
   A. They began the hike soon after dawn.
   B. The birds had their own special language.
   C. Now they were resting for the night after hiking for eight hours.
   D. Her legs felt like rubber because she was so exhausted.

3. Which **sound device** is used in the phrase *barely aware?*
   A. alliteration
   B. assonance
   C. rhyme
   D. onomatopoeia

4. Which sentence contains an example of a **metaphor?**
   A. Just within sight, Samantha could see a black bear with her two cubs.
   B. She knew she had to be very quiet.
   C. She could hear the pounding of the drum of her heart in her ears.
   D. Samantha was satisfied with a fine day of adventure.

5. Which sentence contains an example of **onomatopoeia?**
   A. She saw a flock of turkeys to start.
   B. "Gobble, gobble," the jakes called to the hens.
   C. She and her father stopped and stared at the big birds' stepping and strutting.
   D. They chatted like old married couples.

6. Which sentence contains an example of **personification?**
   A. The wind whipped through the trees, their new leaves singing a beautiful song to Samantha.
   B. The branches and dead leaves crackled under her feet.
   C. She imagined being an explorer in the 1600s, before there were trails and markers to guide the way.
   D. Samantha could hardly believe her luck to see a bear on the first day.

7. **Vocabulary** Which word is closest in meaning to the underlined word *frolicked?*
   A. cried
   B. hunted
   C. played
   D. studied

8. Which phrase is an example of **alliteration?**
   A. climbed higher
   B. denser and darker
   C. setting in the west
   D. circle for the fire

9. Which phrase is an example of **consonance?**
   A. gathered firewood
   B. tight blanket of night
   C. held in store
   D. distant howls

Timed Writing

10. **Identify** three examples of figurative language in this passage. In a paragraph, **explain** how the use of figurative language impacts meaning and tone.

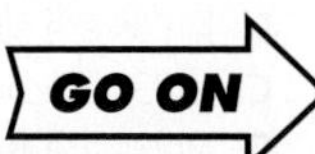

Reteach

Question	Instructional Pages to Reteach
1	617
2	617
3	643
4	617
5	643
6	617
8	643
9	643
10	617

ASSESS/RETEACH

Answers

I. Reading Literature

Answers With Explanations

1. D—Figurative language adds originality and color to the narrative. *Incorrect answers:* A—The narrative has no complicated concepts. B—The passage is not suspenseful. C—The figurative language primarily describes the setting, not the characters.
2. D—The sentence compares legs to rubber and uses the word *like*. *Incorrect answers:* A—There is no comparison here. B—This example is personification. C—same explanation as for A.
3. B—Assonance is the repetition of vowel sounds within words. *Incorrect answers:* A—Alliteration is the repetition of sounds, usually consonants, at the beginning of words. C—*Barely* and *aware* do not rhyme. D—This example does not mimic sounds.
4. C—The example compares Samantha's heart with a pounding drum. *Incorrect answers:* A—There is no comparison in this sentence. B—same explanation as for A. D—same explanation as for A.
5. B—"Gobble, Gobble" mimics the sounds turkeys make. *Incorrect answers:* A—There are no sound words in this sentence. C— same explanation as for A. D—This is an example of personification.
6. A—The leaves are given the human ability of singing. *Incorrect answers:* B—This is an example of onomatopoeia. C—There is no figurative language in this choice. D—same explanation as for C.
7. C—*Played* is very similar to *frolicked. Incorrect answers:* A—*Cried* suggests sadness; *frolicked* connotes pleasure. B—same explanation as for A. D—same explanation as for A.
8. B—Both *denser* and *darker* begin with the same consonant sound. *Incorrect answers:* A—These words do not begin with the same consonant sound. C—same explanation as for A. D—same explanation as for A.
9. B—The repeated -*t* sound in "tight blanket of night" is consonance. *Incorrect answers:* A—This is not an example of consonance.

Answers continued

C—same explanation as for A.
D—same explanation as for A.

Timed Writing

10. Students may use any three examples from the selection, including those used on the test, and explain why each one helped them visualize the events.

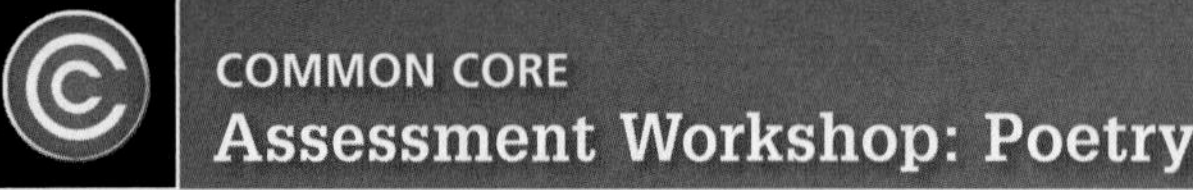

COMMON CORE
Assessment Workshop: Poetry

II. Reading Informational Text

Answers With Explanations

1. A—The paragraph is about how different the MP3 format is. *Incorrect answers:* B—The passage does not discuss cost. C—The passage suggests that everyone should be happy with the new technology. D—Revolutions always have consequences.
2. A—Both articles emphasize the superiority of MP3s to other formats. *Incorrect answers:* B—The articles do not mention that MP3s are easy to find. C—The articles state just the opposite. D—The MP3s are undoubtedly fun to share with friends, but the articles do not say so.
3. B—This is the first step. *Incorrect answers:* A—This is Step 3 in the instructions. C—This is Step 2 of the instructions. D—This is Step 4 of the instructions.
4. B—The articles give examples of how convenient the technology is. *Incorrect answers:* A—The articles do not mention cost. C—The articles say the technology is easy. D—The technology does involve computers, but the articles do not say that this is why MP3s are desirable.

Reteach

Question	Instructional Pages to Reteach
2	742
3	670
4	742

II. Reading Informational Text

Common Core State Standards

RI.9-10.2; L.9-10.3, L.9-10.4.a, L.9-10.5
[For the full wording of the standards, see the standards chart in the front of your textbook.]

Directions: *Read the passages. Then, answer each question that follows.*

MP3 Mania!

The new wave in technology is the MP3 format for music files. Long gone are the days of vinyl records, cassettes, and even CDs. What was once considered new technology is now overshadowed by MP3 files. Who needs to carry around bulky CDs when your whole music collection can be stored on a palm-sized MP3 player? With this revolutionary, new technology, you can not only carry around your entire CD collection but you can also purchase files on the Internet, totally bypassing the need for storage space outside of the computer and player. MP3s provide hours of entertainment without the hassles of bulky players and the need for excess storage.

Simple Instructions for MP3 Players

MP3 files have brought music into the computer age. With this technology, you can carry your entire music library in a tiny player. All you need is a computer, an MP3 player, and a USB cord. Follow these directions to start rocking.

Step 1. Download the music from your CDs onto your computer. Your computer should come equipped with a program to store and access music. Insert the CD, choose Download, and let the computer do the work.

Step 2. Connect your MP3 player to your computer with the USB cord. Your computer will update your MP3 player, loading all your music onto it.

Step 3. Allow the battery of your MP3 player to charge as it is connected to the computer. Your player will alert you when the battery is charged.

Step 4. Disconnect your player and follow the manual to play your music.

1. **Vocabulary** What is the *best* definition for the underlined word *revolutionary?*
   A. causing a change
   B. more affordable
   C. upsetting
   D. without consequences

2. What **central idea** do these texts share?
   A. MP3s are better than old music formats.
   B. MP3s are simple to use and easy to find.
   C. MP3s are overrated and difficult.
   D. MP3s are fun to share with friends.

3. To convert to MP3 format, you must first—
   A. allow your MP3 player battery to charge.
   B. download your CDs onto your computer.
   C. use the USB cord to connect your player.
   D. disconnect your player from the computer.

4. According to these texts, why is the MP3 format so good?
   A. It is inexpensive.
   B. It is convenient.
   C. It is complex.
   D. It involves computers.

Strategies for Test Taking

Remind students to read each step in sequential order, so as not to miss important steps. For example, in Step 2 you connect your MP3 player to the computer in order to load music onto it. However, you cannot load any music onto your player if you did not complete Step 1, which is when you download the music from your CDs onto your computer.

Benchmark

Reteach skills as indicated by students' performance, following the Reteach charts on pages 768–773. Then, administer the end-of-unit **Benchmark Test** (*Unit 4 Resources,* pp. 226–231.Follow the **Interpretation Guide** for the test (*Unit 4 Resources,* pp. 235–240) to assign reteaching pages as necessary in the **Reading Kit**. Use **Success Tracker** online to assign the pages automatically.

III. Writing and Language Conventions

Directions: *Read the passage. Then, answer each question that follows.*

(1) The smell of turkey filled my room, and before my eyes even opened, my mouth widened to a smile. (2) This was Thanksgiving, my favorite holiday, and all the members of my huge family had already arrived. (3) I heard the soft murmur of voices bubbling up from the kitchen. (4) I ran downstairs to greet my aunts, uncles, and cousins. (5) Later, dinner was ready. (6) I loved the steaming turkey. (7) I loved the seasoned stuffing, too. (8) I loved the conversation, my favorite part of Thanksgiving. (9) My cousin Ana talked about her surfing lessons in Florida. (10) My uncle Charlie told a funny story about his New Orleans jazz band. (11) When my family described their lives all over the country, I felt like I got to visit each place without leaving my home. (12) My grandpa Joe explained how he dug himself out of his house when three feet of snow fell on his home in Buffalo.

1. Which choppy sentences should be combined?

A. Sentences 1 and 2
B. Sentences 2 and 3
C. Sentences 3 and 4
D. Sentences 4 and 5

2. In what way should sentences 6, 7, and 8 be combined to vary the **sentence patterns?**

A. I loved the steaming turkey and seasoned stuffing, but my favorite part of Thanksgiving was the conversation.
B. I loved the steaming turkey, seasoned stuffing, and the conversation.
C. I loved the steaming turkey, and I loved the seasoned stuffing, but also the conversation.
D. Although I loved the Thanksgiving conversation, I loved the turkey and stuffing as well.

3. How could you improve the organization?

A. Combine sentence 10 with sentence 11.
B. Delete sentence 5.
C. Switch sentence 1 with sentence 2.
D. Move sentence 12 before sentence 11.

4. To incorporate **figurative language** into sentence 1, add—

A. "as wide as the sea" after "smile."
B. "delicious" before "smell."
C. "bed" before "room,"
D. "that morning" after "opened."

5. Which sentence contains an example of **sensory language?**

A. Sentence 2
B. Sentence 3
C. Sentence 5
D. Sentence 10

6. Which transition word or phrase should replace "Later" in sentence 5 to be more precise?

A. Sometime on Thanksgiving,
B. That day,
C. Now,
D. Within three hours,

Differentiated Instruction for Universal Access

Strategy for Less Proficient Readers

Review the issue of tone by walking students through item 1. Remind them that choppy sentences are brief and follow a similar structural pattern. Next, guide students in eliminating incorrect answer choices.

- A—Both these sentences are long and full of information. (Eliminate)
- B—These two longish sentences are not really about the same topic, and probably would not work well together. (Eliminate)
- C—It makes sense that, when the narrator hears the voices, he would go downstairs, so combining these sentences would be logical. (Correct response)
- D—These two sentences are short and somewhat choppy, but they are about different subjects. (Eliminate)

Guide students in seeing that **C** is the best choice.

ASSESS/RETEACH

Answers

III. Writing and Language Conventions

Answers With Explanations

1. C—These sentences, connected by *and,* would read better as a single sentence. *Incorrect answers:* A—These are not choppy sentences. B—These sentences discuss separate topics and do not belong together. D—same explanation as for B.

2. D—This sentence combines all the information and has a different pattern. *Incorrect answers:* A—This sentence follows the same pattern as the originals. B—same explanation as for A. C—This statement is a run-on, not a sentence.

3. D—Sentence 11 is a concluding sentence to the paragraph, and sentence 12 is a detail sentence. *Incorrect answers:* A—Sentence 10 is a detail sentence, whereas sentence 11 is summary in nature. B—This sentence provides a transition. C—These two sentences work better in the original order.

4. A—Writing ". . . a smile as wide as the sea" provides a simile. *Incorrect answers:* B—*Delicious* is not figurative language. C—Adding *bed* simply makes the description more precise. D—The phrase would add a detail, but would not be figurative language.

5. B—The phrase "soft murmur of voices bubbling up" is an example of onomatopoeia. *Incorrect answers:* A—This sentence does not contain sensory language. C—same explanation as for A. D—same explanation as for A.

6. D—The phrase "within three hours" is a precise time. *Incorrect answers:* A—This phrase is not precise. B—same explanation as for A. C—This word is not precise.

Reteach

Question	Instructional Pages to Reteach
1	689
2	689
3	688
4	617
5	676
6	691

Performance Tasks

Assigning Tasks/Reteaching Skills

Use the chart below to choose appropriate Performance Tasks by identifying which tasks assess lessons in the textbook that you have taught. Use the same lessons for reteaching when students' performance indicates a failure to fully master a standard. For additional instruction and practice, assign the *Common Core Companion* pages indicated for each task.

Task	Where Taught/ Pages to Reteach	*Common Core Companion* Pages
1	607, 608–609, 601–611, 617	35–47, 255–262
2	693	48–54, 255–262
3	606, 748	35–54
4	608–609, 610–611, 643	35–47, 293–299
5	742–743	84–96, 110–116, 293–299
6	196	15–27, 234–254, 282–285

Assessment Pacing

In assigning the Writing Tasks on this student page, allow a class period for the completion of a task. As an alternative, assign tasks as homework. In assigning the Speaking and Listening Tasks on the facing page, consider having students do any required preparation as a homework assignment. Then, allow a class period for the presentations themselves.

Evaluating Performance Tasks

Use the rubric at the bottom of this Teacher Edition page to evaluate students' mastery of the standards as demonstrated in their Performance Task responses. Review the rubric with students before they begin work so they know the criteria by which their work will be evaluated.

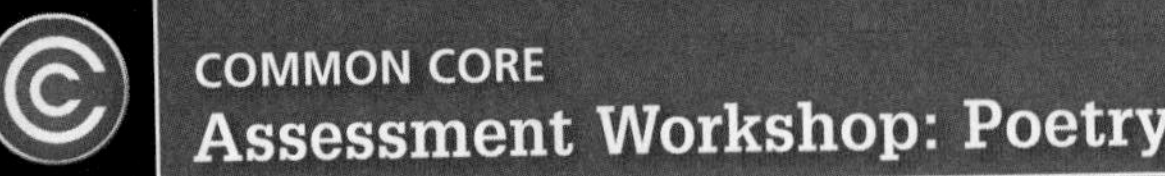

COMMON CORE
Assessment Workshop: Poetry

Performance Tasks

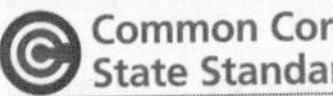

Common Core State Standards

RL.9-10.4, RL.9-10.5; RI.9-10.3; W.9-10.2.b, W.9-10.2.e, W.9-10.2.f, W.9-10.7, W.9-10.9.a; SL.9-10.2, SL.9-10.4

[For the full wording of the standards, see the standards chart in the front of your textbook.]

Directions: *Follow the instructions to complete the tasks below as required by your teacher.*

As you work on each task, incorporate both general academic vocabulary and literary terms you learned in this unit.

Writing

Task 1: Literature [RL.9-10.4; W.9-10.9.a]

Analyze Figurative Language in a Poem

Write an essay in which you analyze the figurative language in a poem from this unit.

- State which poem you chose, and explain why you chose it.
- Identify a key metaphor, simile, or other example of figurative language in the poem. Explain why this figurative language is important to the poem's meaning.
- Analyze the meaning of the figurative language. Explain your analysis clearly.
- Explain how the figurative language contributes to the tone of the poem. For example, explain how the poet's word choices build or maintain a sense of formality or informality. Cite details to support your ideas.
- Edit your essay for correct punctuation and spelling.

Task 2: Literature [RL.9-10.5; W.9-10.9.a]

Analyze the Structure in a Narrative Poem

Analyze how a poet uses structure to present events in a narrative poem from this unit. Consider how the order of events creates an effect such as mystery or suspense.

- Give a brief summary of the plot.
- Describe how the poem is structured, or arranged in lines and stanzas.
- Explain how the poet uses the structure to organize information and tell the story. For example, consider how the poet uses the structure to introduce characters, describe the setting, or show action.
- Explain how other structural elements, such as rhyme scheme, add to the poem.
- Consider whether the poet uses any devices to manipulate time. For example, explain whether the poet uses a flashback or alters the pacing. Explain the effects of these choices.
- Cite specific details from the poem to support your analysis.

Task 3: Literature [RL.9-10.5; W.9-10.2.b]

Compare Forms of Lyric Poetry

Compare two different forms of lyric poetry from this unit, and show how the form of each helps to express the speaker's thoughts and feelings.

- Review the different forms of lyric poetry from this unit—sonnet, haiku, and free verse. Choose two poems, each with a different structure, as the basis for your comparison.
- Analyze each poem, explaining its structure and form.
- Show how each poem's structure aids the speaker in conveying important thoughts and feelings. Provide specific examples from each poem.
- Compare and contrast the structures of the two poems, explaining how the patterns of rhythm or rhyme affect the overall mood and feeling each expresses.
- Finally, evaluate the two poems, explaining which poem, in your opinion, better uses its structure to convey the speaker's ideas. Use text evidence to support your judgments.

Performance Task Rubric: Standards Mastery	Rating Scale (*not very* – *very*)
Critical Thinking: How clearly and consistently does the student pursue the specific mode of reasoning or discourse required by the standard, as specified in the prompt (e.g., comparing and contrasting, analyzing, explaining)?	1 2 3 4 5
Focus: How well does the student understand and apply the focus concepts of the standard, as specified in the prompt (e.g., development of theme or of complex characters, effects of structure, and so on)?	1 2 3 4 5
Support/Elaboration: How well does the student support points with textual or other evidence? How relevant, sufficient, and varied is the evidence provided?	1 2 3 4 5
Insight: How original, sophisticated, or compelling are the insights the student achieves by applying the standard to the text(s)?	1 2 3 4 5
Expression of Ideas: How well does the student organize and support ideas? How well does the student use language, including word choice and conventions, in the expression of ideas?	1 2 3 4 5

Speaking and Listening

Task 4: Literature [RL.9-10.4; SL.9-10.4]
Analyze How Word Choice Affects the Tone of a Poem

Write and deliver an oral presentation in which you analyze how the poet's word choice in a poem affects its tone.

- Introduce the poem and briefly summarize it. If the poem is short, read it aloud.
- Describe the tone of the poem. Cite specific words that help to develop this tone. Be sure to explain how a variety of different words combine to create an overall effect.
- Provide a concluding statement that follows from and supports the information you presented earlier.
- Organize your findings and supporting evidence logically so your audience can follow your reasoning.
- As you speak, maintain consistency in your style and tone.

Task 5: Informational Text [RI.9-10.3; SL.9-10.4]
Deliver a Speech Analyzing a Central Idea

Deliver a speech in which you analyze the central idea expressed in a nonfiction work from this unit.

- State which work you will discuss and provide an objective summary of the piece. Then, explain the central idea and analyze how the details in the text develop and support the central idea. Include details from the beginning, middle, and end of the work.
- Cite strong and thorough textual evidence to support your analysis.
- Use appropriate and varied transitions to link the major ideas in your speech.
- Present information clearly, concisely, and logically so that listeners can follow your reasoning.
- Conclude with a statement that supports the information you have presented.

Task 6: Literature [RL.9-10.2; W.9-10.7; SL.9-10.2]
Deliver a Multimedia Presentation on Your Research of a Poet

Deliver a multimedia presentation in which you explain how the theme expressed in a poem from this unit reflects the poet's life experiences.

- To gather materials for your presentation, conduct research on the poet's life and literary influences. Find texts, images, and, if possible, audio or video clips that you can use in your presentation.
- Identify the poet and poem you will discuss. State the poem's theme and cite details that support your interpretation.
- Explain how the theme expressed in this poem relates to aspects of the poet's life or work. Use evidence from your research and from the poem to support your ideas.
- If possible, use digital media such as digital images, audio, or even video to provide evidence and to add interest to your presentation.
- End with a conclusion that supports the information you presented.

How does communication change us?
At the beginning of Unit 4, you participated in a discussion about the Big Question. Now that you have completed the unit, write a response to the question. Discuss how your initial ideas have either changed or been reinforced. Cite specific examples from the literature in this unit, from other subject areas, and from your own life to support your ideas. Use Big Question vocabulary words (see p. 605) in your response.

Differentiated Instruction for Universal Access

Strategy for Less Proficient Readers
Assign a Performance Task, and then have students meet in groups to review the standard assessed in that task. Remind students of the selections or independent readings to which they have previously applied the standard. Have groups summarize what they learned in applying the standard and then present their summaries. Discuss, clarifying any points of confusion. After students have completed their tasks, have groups meet again to evaluate members' work. Encourage members to revise their work based on the feedback they receive.

EL Strategy for English Learners
For each assigned Performance Task, review the instructions with students. Clarify the meaning of any unfamiliar vocabulary, emphasizing routine classroom words such as *review, research,* and *details* and academic vocabulary such as *organize.* Next, have students note ideas for their responses. Pair students and have them review each other's notes, asking questions to clarify meaning and suggesting improvements. Encourage students to ask for your assistance in supplying English words or expressions they may require.

Supporting Speaking and Listening

1. Consider having students work with partners or in groups to complete Performance Tasks involving listening and speaking. For tasks that you assign for individual work, you may still wish to have students rehearse with partners, who can provide constructive feedback.
2. As students rehearse, have them keep in mind these tips:
   - Present findings and evidence clearly and concisely.
   - Observe conventions of standard English grammar and usage.
   - Be relaxed and friendly but maintain a formal tone.
   - Make eye contact with the audience, pronounce words clearly, and vary your pace.
   - When working with a group, respond thoughtfully to others' positions, modifying your own in response to new evidence.

Linking Performance Tasks to Independent Reading

If you wish to cover the standards with students' independent reading, adapt Performance Tasks of your choice to the works they have selected. (Independent reading suggestions appear on the next page).

How does communication change us?

1. Remind students that the unit Big Question is "How does communication change us?"
2. Have students complete their responses to the prompt on the student page. Point out that they have read selections in this unit that deal with the effects that different types of communication (or a lack of communication) can have on people, and that students should draw on these selections in their responses. Remind them that they can also draw on their own experiences and what they have learned in other subject areas in formulating their answers.

EXTEND

Independent Reading

Titles featured on the Independent Reading pages at the end of each unit represent a range of reading, including stories, dramas, and poetry, as well as literary nonfiction and other types of informational text. Throughout, labels indicate the works that are CCSS Exemplar Texts. Choosing from among these featured titles will help students read works at increasing levels of text complexity in the grades 9–10 text complexity band.

Independent Reading and Pacing

See the Unit Overview and Pacing Plan, pp. 604a–604b, for suggestions on integrating independent reading with work in the Student Edition.

Using Literature Circles

A literature circle is a temporary group in which students independently discuss a book.

Use the guidance in the *Professional Development Guidebook*, pp. 47–49, as well as the teaching notes on the facing page, for additional suggestions for literature circles.

Meeting Unit 4 CCS Focus Standards

Students can use books listed on this page to apply and to reinforce their mastery of the CCS Focus Standards covered in this unit. (The Focus Standards are introduced on pp. 606–609.)

Introducing Featured Titles

Have students choose a book or books for independent reading. Assist them by previewing the titles, noting their subject matter and level of difficulty. **Note:** Before recommending a work to students, preview it, taking into account the values of your community as well as the maturity of your students.

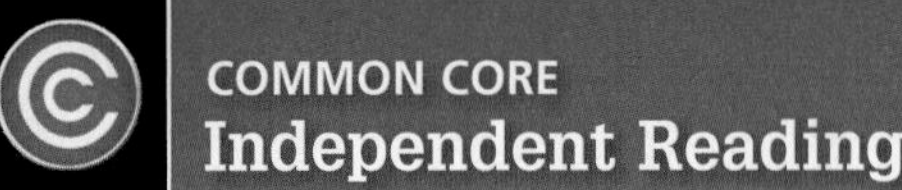

Featured Titles

In this unit, you have read a wide variety of poems by many different poets. Continue to read on your own. Select works that you enjoy, but challenge yourself to explore new poets and works of increasing depth and complexity. The titles suggested below will help you get started.

Literature

The Sonnets
by William Shakespeare
Signet Classic, 1999 EXEMPLAR TEXT 

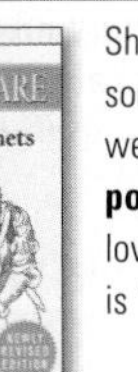

Shakespeare wrote and published about 150 sonnets, which became some of the most well-known verse in literature. In these **poems,** he offers his observations about love, time, and beauty. Included in this volume is "Sonnet 73."

The Collected Poetry of W. H. Auden EXEMPLAR TEXT 

Often referred to as one of the twentieth century's most influential poets, Auden is renowned for his range and depth. He wrote **poems** that describe countless aspects of life, from the ordinary to the profound.

The Collected Poems of Emily Dickinson EXEMPLAR TEXT

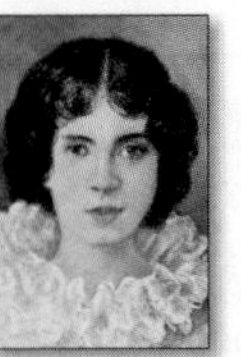

In contrast to her current reputation as an important poet, Emily Dickinson was little known during her lifetime. Shy, Dickinson spent most of her time at home, reading and writing. In one of the best-known **poems** in this collection, the now-famous recluse wrote: "I'm nobody! Who are you?"

Reflections on a Gift of Watermelon Pickle

Voices from a variety of backgrounds and cultures blend in the second edition of this collection of modern **poems.** Skilled poets such as Sandra Cisneros and Li-Young Lee capture the world around us in their verses.

Trouble the Water: 250 Years of African-American Poetry
Edited by Jerry W. Ward, Jr. EXEMPLAR TEXT 

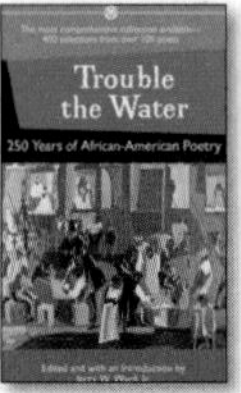

African American heritage comes alive in this collection of **poems** covering 300 years. From the spirituals sung in the days of slavery to vibrant poems from the 1990s, this volume spans many aspects of the African American experience. This collection contains poems by Countee Cullen and Alice Walker.

The Book Thief
by Markus Zusak EXEMPLAR TEXT

Death is the narrator of this **novel** about a nine-year-old girl who goes to live in a tough German neighborhood in the late 1930s. The fast-paced action of this book complements the poetic language.

Informational Texts

House of Houses
by Pat Mora
Beacon Press, 1997

In this **memoir,** five generations of Pat Mora's Mexican American family come alive to retell their stories and weave in and out of each others' lives. In the retelling, history is shared and their understanding of one another is changed.

The Hot Zone: A Terrifying True Story
by Richard Preston EXEMPLAR TEXT

This **nonfiction thriller** dramatizes a real-life outbreak of the Ebola virus in an animal laboratory located in a Washington, D.C., suburb. Known for its chilling suspense, this "bio-thriller" was a best-seller when it first appeared and has fascinated readers ever since.

Text Complexity: Aligning Texts with Readers and Tasks

TEXTS	READERS AND TASKS
• *The Book Thief* (Lexile: 730L) • *Trouble the Water: 250 Years of African-American Poetry*	**Below-Level Readers** Allow students to focus on reading for content, and challenge them to interpret multiple perspectives.
• *The Collected Poetry of W. H. Auden* • *The Collected Poems of Emily Dickinson* • *Reflections on a Gift of a Watermelon Pickle*	**Below-Level Readers** Challenge students as they read for content. **On-Level Readers** Allow students to focus on reading for content, and challenge them to interpret multiple perspectives. **Advanced Readers** Allow students to focus on interpreting multiple perspectives.
• *House of Houses* • *The Sonnets* • *The Hot Zone: A Terrifying True Story* (Lexile: 1030L)	**On-Level Readers** Challenge students as they read for content. **Advanced Readers** Allow students to focus on reading for content, and challenge them to interpret multiple perspectives.

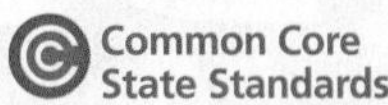

Preparing to Read Complex Texts

Attentive Reading As you read literature on your own, bring your imagination and questions to the text. The questions shown below and others that you ask as you read will help you learn and enjoy literature even more.

Common Core State Standards

Reading Literature/Informational Text
10. By the end of grade 9, read and comprehend literature, including stories, dramas, poems, and literary nonfiction in the grades 9–10 text complexity band proficiently, with scaffolding as needed at the high end of the range.

When reading poetry, ask yourself...

- What, if anything, do I understand about the poem from its title?
- Who is the speaker of the poem? What is the speaker telling me?
- What subject matter does the poem address?
- Is the poem telling a story? If so, who are the characters, and what are they doing?
- What theme, meaning, or insight does the poem express? Are there any lines or sections that simply state that theme? If so, which ones? If not, which details help me understand the poem's deeper meaning?

Key Ideas and Details

- How does the poem look on the page? How does the poem's appearance affect the way I read it?
- Is the poem an example of a particular form, such as sonnet, ballad, or haiku? If so, what do I expect from the poem based on its form?
- Is the poem an example of free verse? If so, does it have any formal elements?
- How does the form affect what I understand and feel about the poem?
- What do I notice about the stanzas? Are they always a set number of lines, or do they vary in length? What new idea or piece of information does each stanza give me?
- What do I notice about the way the poem sounds? Does the poet use repetition? Does the poet use rhyme, and, if so, what kind? Does the poet use other sound devices?
- How do sound devices affect my enjoyment of the poem? How do they emphasize the meaning?
- What do I notice about any symbols or images? Does any one symbol or image repeat? What connections do I see between the symbol or image and the poem's deeper meaning?

Craft and Structure

- Even if I do not understand every word, do I like this poem? Why or why not?
- Has the poem helped me understand something in a new way? If so, how?
- In what ways is this poem similar to others I have read? In what ways is it different from others I have read?
- What insights have I gained from reading this poem?
- Would I like to read more poems by this poet? Why or why not?
- Could this poem serve as an inspiration to other writers, artists, or musicians? Why or why not?

Integration of Ideas

Text Complexity: Reader and Task Support Suggestions

INDEPENDENT READING

Increased Support Suggest that students choose a book that they feel comfortable reading and one that is a bit more challenging. Pair a more proficient reader with a less proficient reader and have them work together on the more challenging text. Partners can prepare to read the book by reviewing questions on this student page. They can also read difficult passages together, sharing questions and insights. They can use the questions on the student page to guide after-reading discussion.

Increased Challenge Encourage students to integrate knowledge and ideas by combining the Big Question and the Unit Focus concepts in their approach to two or more featured titles.

For example, students might consider new insights they gain from reading the ideas and feelings communicated in *The Collected Poems of Emily Dickinson* or *Trouble the Water: 250 Years of African-American Poetry.* In addition, students can focus on similarities and differences in the ways poets use elements such as word choice and sound devices.

Preparing to Read Complex Texts

1. Tell students they can be attentive readers by bringing their experience and imagination to the texts they read and by actively questioning those texts. Explain that the questions they see on the student page are examples of questions to ask about poetry.
2. Point out that, like writing, reading is a "multidraft" process, involving several readings of complete works or passages, revising and refining one's understanding each time.

Key Ideas and Details

3. As an example, review and amplify the fifth bulleted item. **Ask:** What poetic devices could help you identify a poem's deeper meaning?

   Possible response: You might consider the overall tone or look for sensory language that contributes to the poem's meaning.

Craft and Structure

4. **Ask:** What details of craft and structure would you cite as evidence that a poem is an example of free verse?

   Possible response: You might point to a poet's use of irregular meter or the absence of a rhyme scheme.

Integration of Ideas

5. **Ask:** How would you compare and contrast a poem with others you have read?

   Possible response: You would consider elements like the poem's topic, form, imagery, and language to describe how it is similar to and different from other poems.
6. Finally, explain to students that they should cite key ideas and details, examples of craft and structure, or instances of the integration of ideas as evidence to support their points during a book discussion. After hearing the evidence, the group might reach a consensus or might agree to disagree.

Unit 5 Features Overview

Unit Genre and Big Question

In this unit, students will analyze works of drama. As they read they will discuss responses to the unit Big Question: Do our differences define us?

Unit 5 Selections

Teach Use the selections in this unit to teach the unit skills and meet the unit objectives.

Differentiate and Reinforce Use the information in the Text Complexity box on the next page to guide your teaching of the selections.

Integrate Skills Each selection presents students with a reading strategy, a literary analysis concept, a vocabulary skill, and grammar instruction. Students can extend learning in the writing and extension activities.

Additional Unit Features

Literary Analysis Workshop Teach and model the Unit Focus standards. Spiral Review notes enable students to revisit these skills over the course of the unit.

Reading for Information Students analyze functional, expository, and argumentative texts and complete Timed Writing activities.

Comparing Literary Works Students study two literary works either within or across genres.

Test Practice: Reading This feature provides extra practice in utilizing reading skills to master assessments.

Writing Workshops Two writing workshops appear in each unit, along with rubrics and instruction in the writing process.

Assessment Workshop Cumulative Skill Review and Performance Tasks provide a range of assessment opportunities.

Independent Reading Students broaden their knowledge as they read longer works of increasing complexity.

THE BIG ?
Do our
differences
define us?

PHLit Online! www.PHLitOnline.com

Teaching From Technology

Log on at this address for the following:

Enriched Online Student Edition

- full narration of selections
- interactive graphic organizers
- linked **Get Connected!** and **Background** videos
- All worksheets and other student resources

Professional Development

- the *Professional Development Guidebook* online
- additional professional development articles by program authors

Planning, Assigning, and Monitoring

- software for online assignment of work to students, individually or to the whole class
- a system for tracking and grading student work

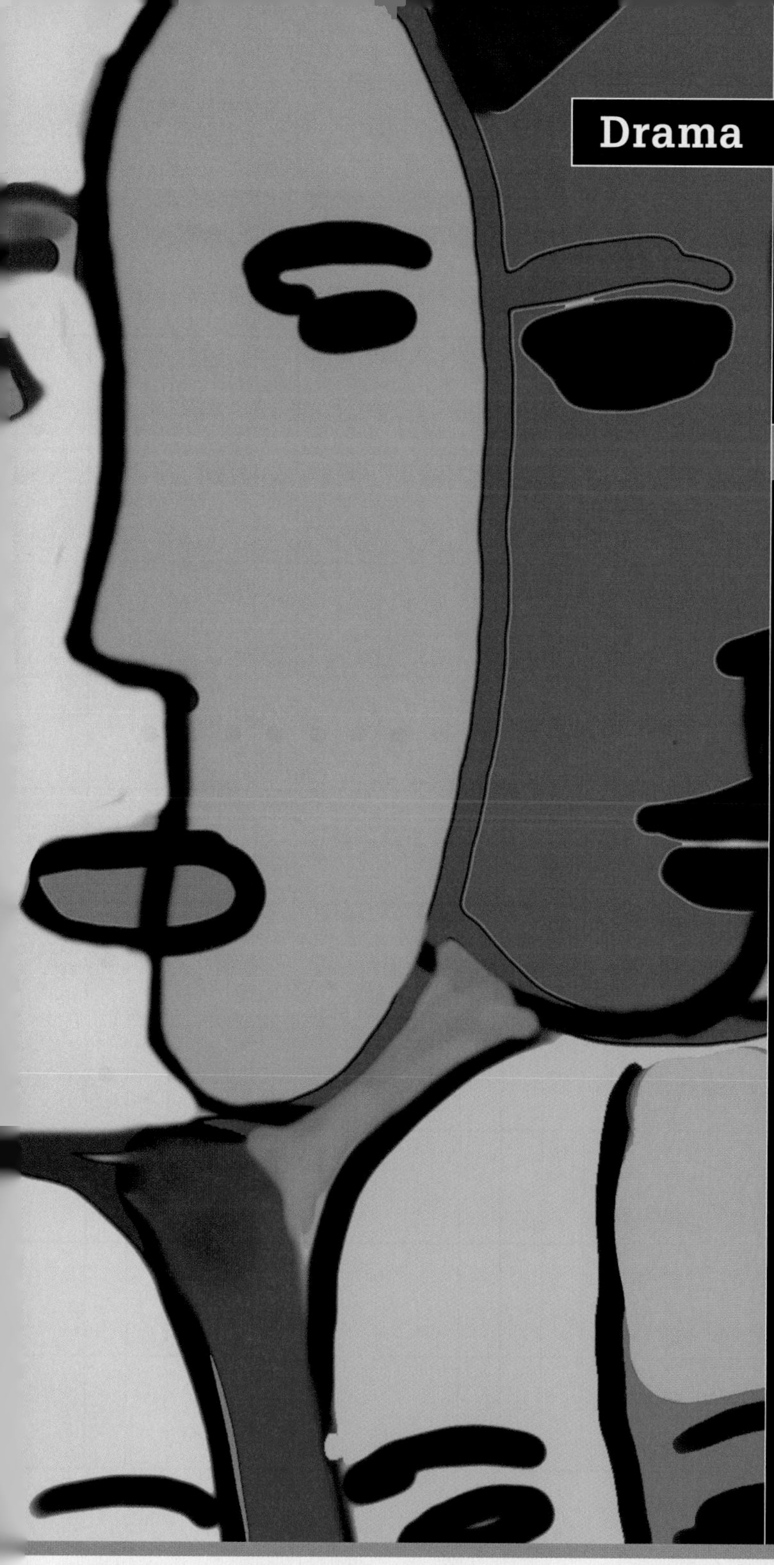

Unit 5

Drama

PHLit Online!
www.PHLitOnline.com

Hear It!
- Selection summary audio
- Selection audio
- BQ Tunes

See It!
- Author videos
- Big Question video
- Get Connected videos
- Background videos
- More about the authors
- Illustrated vocabulary words
- Vocabulary flashcards

Do It!
- Interactive journals
- Interactive graphic organizers
- Grammar tutorials
- Interactive vocabulary games
- Test practice

777

Instructional Resources

Unit 5 Resources supports Unit skills with pages of the following types:

- **Benchmark Tests** assess and monitor student progress at mid-Unit and at Unit's end.
- **Vocabulary and Reading Warm-ups** provide additional vocabulary support, based on Lexile rankings of words, for each selection. "A" **Warm-ups** are for students reading two grades below level. "B" **Warm-ups** are for students reading one grade below level.
- **Selection Support** These practice pages are available for each selection:
  - Reading Skill
  - Literary Analysis
  - Writing About the Big Question
  - Vocabulary
  - Support for Writing
  - Support for Extend Your Learning
  - Enrichment

All worksheets and other student resources are also available online at **www.PHLitOnline.com.**

Text Complexity: Accessibility for Various Ability Levels

This chart gives a general text complexity rating to help you determine the depth of the prereading and reading support you will need to provide students for each selection. For additional guidance on factors that affect accessibility of each selection, see the Before You Read page for each.

	✓ Accessible	✓✓ Complex
Play 1		Romeo and Juliet
Play 2	The Inspector-General	

Accessibility for English Learners

This icon indicates support for English learners at point of use in this Teacher's Edition.

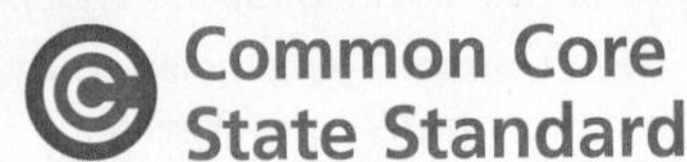

Common Core State Standards

Unit 5 Focus Standards

- Reading Literature 3

Additional Activities and Assessments

- Reading Literature 1, 2, 5, 7
- Writing 1, 3, 4, 7
- Speaking and Listening 1, 4
- Language 1, 5, 6

	Week 1					Week 2					Week 3				
	1	2	3	4	5	1	2	3	4	5	1	2	3	4	5
Introduce the Unit Big Question (pp. 778–779).	●														
Introduce the unit forms, fiction and nonfiction, using the Literary Analysis Workshop (pp. 782–797).		●													
Introduce the focus CCS standards for the unit and lead students in a close reading of exemplar texts. (p. 800a).		●	●												
Teach *The Tragedy of Romeo and Juliet* (pp. 784–797).			●	●	●	●	●	●	●	●	●	●	●	●	
Complete the Test Practice: Reading (pp. 936–937).														●	
Teach Reading for Information (pp. 938–943).															●
Teach Comparing Literary Works (pp. 944–959).															●
Have students complete the Writing Workshop (pp. 960–965).															
Administer **Benchmark Test 9** (***Unit 5 Resources,*** pp. 136–141).															
Reteach skills, judging which skills to reteach by evaluating students' performance on **Benchmark Test 9.**															

Independent Reading

Have students choose a full-length work from the Independent Reading feature at the end of the unit and read it while working on this unit.

Pacing Suggestions

- Have students read their chosen work for homework.
- Devote parts of class periods in each school week to Literature Circles in which students reading the same work discuss it.

Week 4						Week 5					Week 6				
1	2	3	4	5		1	2	3	4	5	1	2	3	4	5
					Teach *The Inspector-General* (pp. 966–977).	●	●	●							
					Complete the Test-Practice: Reading (pp. 978–979).			●							
					Teach Reading for Information (pp. 980–985).				●						
					Teach Comparing Literary Works (pp. 986–1001).					●	●				
					Have students complete the Writing Workshop (pp. 1002–1013).				●	●	●	●	●		
					Have students complete the Vocabulary Workshop (pp. 1014–1015).							●			
●					Have students complete the Communications Workshop (pp. 1016–1017, 1018).								●		
●	●	●	●	●	Have students complete the first three sections of the Assessment Workshop: Fiction and Nonfiction (pp. 1019–1021).								●	●	●
			●		Have students complete the selected Performance Tasks in the Assessment Workshop (pp. 1022–1023).									●	
				●	Administer Benchmark Test 10 (***Unit 5 Resources,*** pp. 186–194).									●	
					Reteach skills, judging which skills to reteach by evaluating students' performance on **Benchmark Test 10.**										●

- Cover the focus standards with independent readings and abbreviate review of the focus standards with student-edition selections.
- Do not assign extension activities for selections (day 5 of main selection lessons), except as needed for full standards coverage.
- If students demonstrate reading proficiency, consider omitting Test Practice: Reading features in the unit.

Block and Daily Scheduling

The assignments and activities in this Unit planner are organized by week. You may adjust them to your daily or block schedule. The Time and Resource Managers for the selection set gives specific pacing suggestions, or you may use the comprehensive lesson planning support online at **www.PHLitOnline.com.**

Monitoring Progress

Diagnose Refer to students' results on **Benchmark Test 8, *Unit 4 Resources,*** pp. 227–235 (administered at the end of the previous Unit). Use the **Interpretation Guide** to interpret the results of the diagnostic portion of the test. **Note:** For the most accurate diagnosis of students who score in the middle range, administer the additional diagnostic questions online at **www.PHLitOnline.come.**

Preteach and Prepare As indicated by the diagnostic, prepare students for reading by assigning the **Vocabulary** and **Reading Warm-ups** for the selections you assign.

Teach Follow this Pacing Plan and use the resources to teach the skills and selections. For specific pacing suggestions and a list of resources, see the Time and Resource Manager and the Visual Guide to Selection Resources preceding each selection.

Classroom Management
For classroom management suggestions for using leveled texts in a mixed-ability classroom, see Harvey Daniels's professional development essay "Leveled Reading Selections," online at **www.PHLitOnline.com.**

Assess After students have completed the first half of the Unit, administer **Benchmark Test 9**. Administer **Benchmark Test 10** at the end of the Unit.

Intervention and Reteach After administering each test, use the **Interpretation Guide** for the tests to determine which reteaching pages, if any, you should assign from the ***Reading Kit.*** The appropriate pages are also available through the online Progress Monitoring software.

CLASSROOM STRATEGIES

Bringing Literature to Life **Sheridan Blau**

> Every text is a lazy machine asking the reader to do some of its work. (Umberto Eco; novelist, literary critic, philosopher)

Texts are dead on the page, until a reader brings them to life. Students often fail to realize how vital their own imaginative activity is to creating meaning from the marks on the page. Readers of stories fill in gaps in a text, visualizing details that the writer never provided—details that fill in an imaginative picture. Nowhere is this more evident than in dramatic texts, texts that are written to be performed in costume, movement, sound, and spectacle, yet often without detailed instructions from the playwright about how the text should be performed.

Helping Students Read and Interpret

When we invite students to transform words from a play to sounds and movements on stage, we provide an opportunity for them to practice literary interpretation. For example, when students decide how to act out a line or scene, they realize how every action they take to dramatize the lines of the play must be supported by the words spoken by or about the character whose actions they are performing.

Reaching Reluctant Readers

Reluctant readers typically find little or no meaning in text because they read without imaginatively hearing a voice or seeing action. When a reluctant reader is forced to decide how he should speak a line and how he should move or gesture in speaking it, that reader discovers—sometimes for the first time—how words on a page are human utterances, spoken to express a meaning to an auditor who is expected to find them meaningful.

Bringing Shakespeare from the Page to the Stage

Group Students in Acting Companies An excellent strategy for helping students become active interpreters of texts is to organize them into small acting "companies" of two or three students each. Students might select names for their company, following the practice of Shakespeare's time. Share with students that Shakespeare belonged to two acting companies: first, the Lord Chamberlain's Men, and later, the King's Men. Require each small "classroom company" to rehearse and (possibly) perform an important or interesting micro-scene from the play being studied.

Select Micro-Scenes A micro-scene is about six lines from the play or, as a general rule, no fewer than four and no more than twelve. The segment of text assigned (or selected by students) must be quite small so that students can study the words closely enough to determine how to perform them, and so that students can memorize their lines. Make sure the selected scenes are important to the action of the play or to the revelation of one or more of its characters. Ideally a micro-scene will provide speaking lines for every member of the company, or for two members, with the third taking the director's role. Don't worry if two groups of students select the same lines to perform. It can be a learning opportunity if they are later given the chance to discuss how they came to interpret their lines differently or similarly.

The Process: Rehearsal as Learning Time Each company must figure out how their scene should be played on the stage. This means determining the following:

1. How the actors should move (blocking)
2. How they should speak their lines (attitude, volume, facial expressions, accents, etc)
3. What the lighting should be like
4. What background or focal music, if any, might be playing.

Students will accomplish this task mainly by rehearsing the scene. But they can also do whatever research may be needed to understand their lines. They must also discuss the scene and take notes on their discussion and experiments in rehearsing it. Rehearsals may require more than one class hour, but the rewards in learning are worth the investment. The most important learning takes place in the give-and-take of the rehearsal process.

The Product Ideally, students will be asked to perform their scene in front of the entire class. But even without such a performance, they can write about their scene or report on it based on their rehearsal experience. For performances, students may be encouraged to supply props or improvise costumes to give their scene dramatic appeal.

Follow-up Writing and Discussion

- Students should be asked to explain (in writing or discussion or both) their choices—the bases for their decisions and the debates that may have transpired about how to perform their lines.
- Advanced students should be asked to create two versions of their scene, representing two different possibilities for imagining and realizing it on the stage.
- Any lines that are difficult to interpret can be explored productively by asking students in small groups to take them into rehearsal and work on them as if preparing for a performance.

Modeled Strategy

See p. 991 for a point-of-use note modeling these strategies.

Teacher Resources

- ***Professional Development Guidebook***
- ***Classroom Strategies and Teaching Routines* cards**

Log on as a teacher at **www.PHLitOnline.com** to access a library of all Professional Development articles by the Contributing Authors of Pearson Prentice Hall *Literature.*

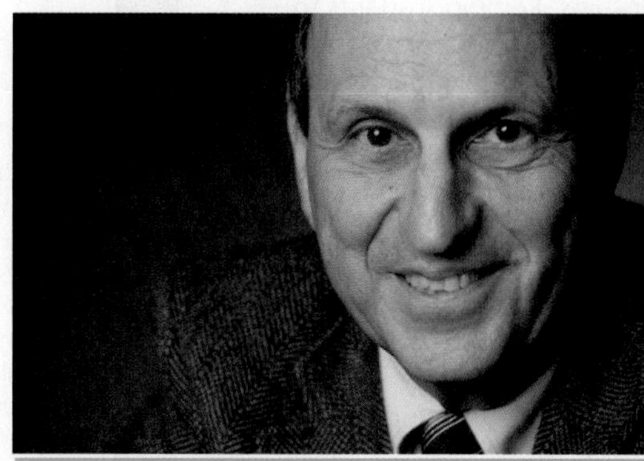

Sheridan Blau

Sheridan Blau is Professor of English and Education at the University of California, Santa Barbara, where he directs the South Coast Writing Project and the Literature Institute for Teachers. A former President of the National Council of Teachers of English, he has published widely on the teaching of English.

Supporting Research

Flachmann, M. (2007). *Shakespeare: From page to stage.* Upper Saddle River, NJ: Prentice Hall.

Loehlin, J. (2007). Teaching through performance. In B. Hodgdon & W. Worthen (Eds.), *Companion to Shakespeare and performance.* Oxford, England: Blackwell Publishing.

Wilhelm, J. D. (2002). *Action strategies for deepening comprehension: Using drama strategies to assist improved reading performance.* New York: Scholastic.

Wilhelm, J. D. & Edmiston, B. (1998). *Imagining to learn: Inquiry, ethics and integration through drama.* Portsmouth, NH: Heinemann.

Common Core State Standards

- Speaking and Listening 1
- Language 6

1 Introducing the Big Question

1. Have a volunteer read aloud the introductory paragraph.
2. Discuss the ways that differences may stem from genetics, culture, or geography.
3. **Ask** students why differences may result in conflict among people. (**Possible responses:** People may want others to be like themselves.)
4. **Ask** students the Big Question. (**Possible responses:** Yes, because they show the uniqueness of each individual. No, because we are all human.)
5. Tell students that the dramatic selections in this unit explore differences between people and how they affect people's relationships. Remind students to consider whether the selections reinforce or challenge their first answers to the Big Question.

2 Exploring the Big Question

Collaboration: One-on-One Discussion

1. Introduce the activity, using the instruction on the student page.
2. Have students work individually to make their lists. Then, discuss the following questions:
   - What kinds of differences have the biggest impact on how people interact? (**Sample response:** ability to accept others; values, opinions; interests and hobbies)
   - Which differences might lead people to learn from one another? (**Sample response:** cultural; opinions)
3. Have students use the Big Question vocabulary on page 779 as they complete the activity on page 778.

Connecting to the Literature

Explain the Big Question strand in the unit, referring to the box at right.

Introducing the Big Question

1

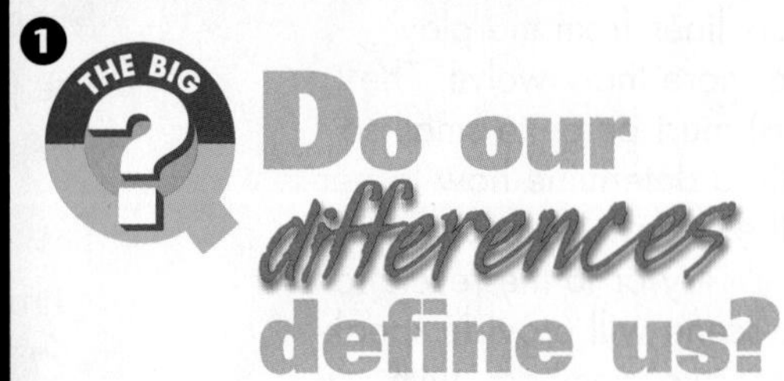
THE BIG
Do our differences define us?

The **differences** among human beings can certainly be obvious, like hair color, height, or the accents that mark our speech. Other, more subtle differences may be noticed only when we get to know each other. These differences might show up in our values and in the mannerisms and traditions that are rooted in our individual culture. While differences make us unique, they may also put us at odds with each other. Do our differences define who we are?

2 Exploring the Big Question

Collaboration: One-on-One Discussion Start thinking about the Big Question by listing examples of ways in which people may differ. List differences that you have observed or read about among people. Describe one specific example of each of these differences.

- physical appearance
- culture or family traditions
- personal style, such as the way people dress and talk
- values
- personal opinions
- personality traits
- interests, sports, or hobbies

Share your list with a partner. Talk about whether these differences help to define the people around us or whether people are more than just the sum of their individual attributes and interests. Use the Big Question Vocabulary in your discussion.

Connecting to the Literature Each reading in this unit will give you additional insight into the Big Question.

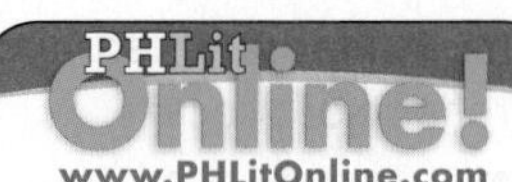
PHLit Online!

www.PHLitOnline.com

- Big Question video
- Illustrated vocabulary words
- Interactive vocabulary games
- BQ Tunes

Applying Understanding by Design Principles

The Big Question

Explain to students that they will continue to consider the Big Question as they work through the Unit.

- At the beginning of each selection, they will write a response to a Writing About the Big Question sentence.
- As they read the selection, they will look for details related to the Big Question.
- At the end of the selection, they will answer a Critical Thinking Question that is related to the Big Question.
- Tell students that their goal will be to gain a deeper understanding of literature and a more sophisticated way of discussing the Big Question.

❸ Learning Big Question Vocabulary

Acquire and Use Academic Vocabulary Academic vocabulary is the language you encounter in textbooks and on standardized tests. Review the definitions of these academic vocabulary words.

defend (dē fend′) *v.* protect against attack

determine (dē tür′ mən) *v.* cause something to happen in a certain way

differentiate (dif′ ər en′ shē āt′) *v.* distinguish between items or ideas

discriminate (di skrim′i nāt′) *v.* recognize differences; act because of prejudice

unique (yo͞o nēk′) *adj.* one of a kind

Use these words as you complete Big Question activities in this unit that involve reading, writing, speaking, and listening.

Common Core State Standards

Speaking and Listening
1. Initiate and participate effectively in a range of collaborative discussions (one-on-one, in groups, and teacher-led) with diverse partners, building on others' ideas and expressing their own clearly and persuasively.

Language
6. Acquire and use accurately grade-appropriate general academic and domain-specific words and phrases, sufficient for reading, writing, speaking, and listening at the college and career readiness level; demonstrate independence in gathering vocabulary knowledge when considering a word or phrase important to comprehension or expression.

Gather Vocabulary Knowledge Additional Big Question words are listed below. Categorize the words by deciding whether you know each one well, know it a little bit, or do not know it at all.

accept	**assimilated**	**background**
conformity	**culture**	**differences**
individuality	**similarity**	**understanding**
values		

Then, do the following:

1. Write the definitions of the words you know.
2. Consult a dictionary to confirm the meanings of the words whose definitions you wrote down. Revise your definitions if necessary.
3. Using a print or an online dictionary, look up the meanings of the words you are unsure of or do not know. Then, write definitions for those words.
4. Use all of the words in a brief paragraph about how strongly our differences define us.

❸ Learning Big Question Vocabulary

Acquire and Use Academic Vocabulary

1. Introduce the academic vocabulary words in the first word bank on the student page. Have students preview the words.
2. For each word, have students say the word aloud. Then, use the word in a sentence that defines the word.

Gather Vocabulary Knowledge

1. With the class, review the steps in the activity on the student page. Have students complete the activity independently, with partners, or in small groups.
2. Before students complete the last step, review the words and their meanings as a class. (Definitions appear below on the left.) Then, have students complete their paragraphs.

Show the Big Question video, online at **www.PHLitOnline.com.**

Gather Vocabulary Knowledge: Definitions

accept [ak sept′] *v.* to regard with approval or to recognize as valid

assimilated [ə sim′ə lāt′ed] *v.* taken in or absorbed; *adj.* having been taken in and become part of a wider group

background [bak′ground′] *n.* a person's history, education, and experience

conformity [kən fôr′mə tē] *n.* thinking or behavior that is in agreement with customs or social standards

culture [kul′chər] *n.* the ideas, customs, skills, and arts of a group of people during a specific time period

differences [dif′ər ən′ sez] *n.* ways in which things or people are not the same

individuality [in′də vij′o͞o al′ə tē] *n.* qualities that make a person unique

similarity [sim′ə ler′ə tē] *n.* state of being alike

understanding [un′dər stan′diŋ] *n.* recognition and acknowledgement of other people or their situations

values [val′yo͞oz] *n.* beliefs or standards held by a group or an individual

❶ Elements of Drama

1. Introduce the form, drama, using the instruction on the student page.

   Discuss the four basic elements of drama as they are defined on the student page. Explain that, in reading a play, they will have available to them only the first two elements: the dialogue that makes up the scenes and acts, and the stage directions. They will need to imagine the sets and props, and the stage directions will help them do that. They may also want to imagine the actors of the play. Sometimes it is helpful to "cast" the play in your mind with actors you have seen on television or in movies.

2. Divide the class into small groups. Have each group choose a story they are familiar with and imagine that it has been turned into a play. **Ask** students to cast the play with actors they know of and to describe the kind of sets and props they would use in a production of the play.

   Sample response: *Story:* "Beauty and the Beast." *Cast:* Erica Hubbard (Beauty), Jesse Williams (Beast), Courtney B. Vance (Beauty's father). *Set:* Beast's castle, represented by long drapes in beautiful colors and fabrics. *Props:* The rose, a sword, dishes and glasses.

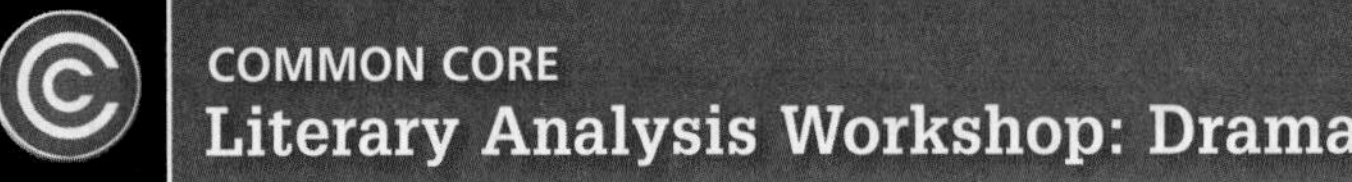

❶Elements of Drama

Drama is narrative, or storytelling, written for performance.

A **drama** is a play, a story written to be performed by actors on a stage or in a film. Sometimes, people use the word *drama* to refer to a work about a serious subject. However, the broad genre of drama includes every type of performed narrative work, whether lighthearted or serious.

Like other works of narrative literature, dramatic works feature **characters,** or personalities who take part in the action of the story. The main characters face a **conflict,** a struggle or problem that propels the sequence of events called the **plot.** The highest point of interest in the plot, the **climax,** occurs during the point of greatest tension between characters. As the story winds down, the **resolution** of the conflict leads to the conclusion of the play.

Acts are the basic units of organization in a drama. Acts are often further divided into **scenes.** A scene may move the action to a new setting or time of day, it may introduce new characters, or it may shift a play's mood. For example, an evening scene may follow a daytime scene, or a comic scene may lighten the mood of a serious play.

The author of a play, called a **playwright** or **dramatist,** writes the **script,** or text of the story. The script contains **dialogue,** or the characters' spoken words. It also contains **stage directions,** which are instructions about how the play should be performed. In some plays, the playwright gives detailed stage directions, while in others he or she provides few or none at all.

All the elements of drama combine in performance to produce an illusion of reality known as **dramatic effect.** Dramatic effect allows viewers to believe in the events of the story, even though they know the play is artificial. Through this effect, the dramatist explores a **theme**—a deeper meaning or insight about life.

The Elements of Drama	
Acts and Scenes	Acts and scenes are the basic sections of drama. A drama may consist of one or more acts, each of which may contain any number of scenes.
Stage Directions	Stage directions are the playwright's instructions about how a play should be performed. They are usually set in italics and/or set off by brackets. They may include the following information: • Background about the setting or characters • Abbreviations for where actors should move or say their lines—for example, *D.S.* means downstage, or closer to the audience, while *U.S.* means upstage, or farther from the audience • Details about physical elements of the performance, such as sets, lighting, and costumes
Sets	Sets are constructions that define the area in which the play's action occurs. Sets may be realistic and look like actual places. They may also be abstract or minimalist and merely suggest real places.
Props	Props are movable objects, like swords or pens, that actors use on stage.

Teaching Resources

- All *Common Core Companion,* pp. 28–34
- All *Unit 5 Resources,* pp. 7–22
  Professional Development Guidebook, pp. 33, 39–40, 42
- All *See It!* DVD Gary L. Blackwood, Segments 1 and 2
- All *Graphic Organizer Transparencies,* pp. 145, 146
- All Enriched Online Student Edition
- L2 L3 *Reader's Notebook*
- L1 *Reader's Notebook: Adapted Version*
- EL *Reader's Notebook: English Learner's Version*
- L2 EL *Hear It!* Audio CD
- L1 EL *Hear It!* Audio CD (adapted text)

All resources, including print and audio, are available at **www.PHLitOnline.com.**

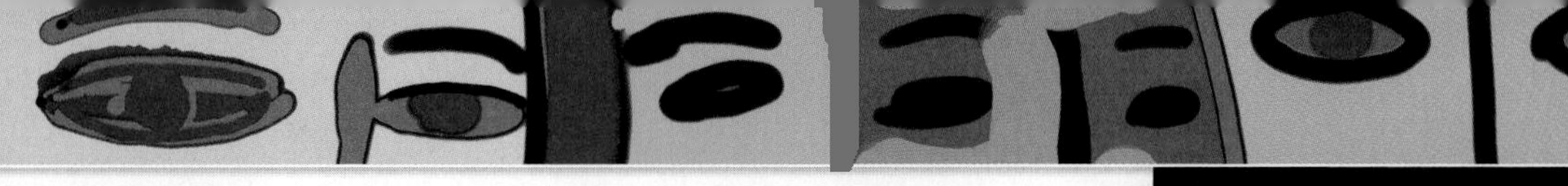

❷ Forms of Drama

The ancient Greeks, who developed drama as an organized literary form, created two basic types of plays. We still use these two categories to define dramatic forms.

- A **tragedy** traces the downfall of the main character, often called the **tragic hero.** In classical drama, the tragic hero is always an important person, such as a general or a king. The hero is admirable but is defeated by a **tragic flaw**—a mistake or a character defect.
- A **comedy** has a happy ending. Comedies usually feature a series of events in which the order or balance of the world is disrupted. A comic ending restores order and harmony.

Comedies are often funny, but humor is not their defining trait. The main distinction between tragedy and comedy is how the story ends: tragedies end in death, defeat, or exile, while comedies end in weddings, births, reunions, or other positive, joyful events.

Dramatic Structures Classical dramas, such as most works written by the ancient Greeks and by Shakespeare, take place in five acts and are called **five-act plays.** The acts follow the structure of most narrative works: **Act 1** = introduction/exposition; **Act 2** = rising action; **Act 3** = climax; **Act 4** = falling action; **Act 5** = resolution.

In some dramatic works, the five segments of plot are compressed into fewer acts. For example, many **screenplays,** or scripts written for films, occur in three acts. Act 1 introduces the main characters and the basic situation. Act 2 sets up a problem. Act 3 provides the resolution.

One-act plays are dramatic works that are organized in a single act. The one act may still contain multiple scenes.

❸ Types of Dramatic Speeches

In most dramatic works, dialogue is the playwright's main tool for developing characters and furthering the plot. Ancient Greek playwrights also used the convention of the **chorus,** a group of observers who were part of the play but not part of the story. The chorus provided background information and reacted to the events that unfolded on stage.

In some modern dramas, a **narrator** replaces the chorus. The narrator is a personality or voice that comments on but does not participate in the story. In some films, for example, an unseen narrator may introduce the story as a whole, set up a scene, or tell viewers about a character.

Playwrights use other types of dramatic speeches to supplement dialogue and reveal the thoughts, feelings, and motivations of the characters. The main types of dramatic speeches are explained in the chart below.

❹

In This Section

Elements of Drama

Analyzing Character Development

Close Read: Character, Plot, and Theme
- Model Text
- Practice Text

After You Read

Common Core State Standards

RL.9-10.3

[For the full wording of the standards, see the standards chart in the front of your textbook.]

Types of Dramatic Speeches

Type of Speech	Definition	Examples from *The Tragedy of Romeo and Juliet*
Monologue	A long, uninterrupted speech delivered by a character to other characters on stage	Romeo speaks about love to Benvolio. *(p. 813, line 171)*
Soliloquy	A speech in which a character, alone on stage, reveals private thoughts that the audience is allowed to overhear	Juliet reveals her private thoughts. *(p. 871, line 17)*
Aside	A brief remark a character makes to the audience rather than to other characters	Juliet tells the audience that Romeo is no villain. *(p. 885, line 83)*

❷ Forms of Drama

Introduce dramatic forms and conventions using the material on the student page. Emphasize that drama no longer fits neatly into the categories of tragedy and comedy. Many serious plays do not involve the destruction of the main character. They are called simply "dramas." Present students with these summaries and ask them to identify each one as tragedy, comedy, or drama.

Screenplay: *A girl has a crush on her next-door neighbor and does silly things to get his attention. She gets the attention of his younger brother and they end up going to prom together.*

Teleplay: *A family struggles with their feelings when one of the sons gets lost while camping. He returns unharmed, but the family is changed.*

Play: *A good, strong candidate accepts a campaign contribution from a crook because she feels so strongly she is the right person for the office. Her crime is exposed and her political career is over.*

Answers: Screenplay: comedy. Teleplay: drama. Play: tragedy.

❸ Types of Dramatic Speeches

Review the types of dramatic speeches in the passage and the chart. Discuss with students how effective they think each of these types of speech would be.

❹ In This Section

Explain that in the remainder of this Literary Analysis Workshop, students will analyze important elements of drama. After reviewing the concepts, they will then see them applied in an analysis of a Model text. Finally, they will apply what they have learned to an Independent Practice text.

Unit 5 Focus Standards

- **Reading Literature 3**

These standards spiral through the unit.

❶ Analyzing Character Development

1. Introduce the concept of complex characters in drama, using the material on the student page. Emphasize the importance of complex characters to the overall effect of a play.
2. Discuss types of characters, using the chart on the student page. Then **ask** students for an example of a complex character from a movie they have seen and an example of a flat, static character. They should also explain why each character fits the definition.

   Sample response: Complex character: Scout in *To Kill a Mockingbird*; she is strong, smart, and brave, but innocent. During the movie, she loses a lot of her innocence, but remains a good person. Flat character: Bart Simpson; because he is highly predictable in his behavior and never learns or changes.

❶Analyzing Character Development

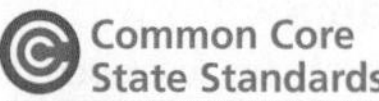

Reading Literature
3. Analyze how complex characters develop over the course of a text, interact with other characters, and advance the plot or develop the theme.

Characters' reactions to conflict propel the plot and point to thematic meanings.

Characters and Conflict

In both tragedies and comedies, characters face **conflicts,** or struggles between opposing forces. There are two main types of conflict: external and internal.

- **External Conflict:** a struggle against an outside force, such as an enemy, nature, or the pressures of society

Example:
Romeo and Juliet struggle against pressures from their feuding families.

- **Internal Conflict:** a struggle posed by a character's own beliefs, thoughts, or feelings

Example:
As she enacts the plan that will allow her to join Romeo, Juliet struggles with her fears.

The most interesting dramatic works feature important conflicts that engage the audience. For tragic characters, the conflict is often literally life threatening. For comic characters, the conflict is often symbolically life threatening. For example, the hero in a romantic comedy may not win the woman of his dreams. The quality of his life, if not its substance, is at risk.

Protagonist and Antagonist Most plays focus on a single main character—the protagonist. The character who opposes the main character and either creates or adds to the conflict is called the antagonist.

Complex Characters Great dramas present interesting characters, both protagonists and antagonists, whose stories are compelling to audiences. Such characters are complex, which means they have strengths and weaknesses and experience mixed emotions. Complex characters have multiple motivations, or a variety of reasons for feeling and behaving as they do. In literary terms, complex characters are round, rather than flat, and dynamic, rather than static.

Character Types

Flat One-dimensional; have only one quality	**Round** Multi-dimensional; have many qualities
Static Unchanging; remain the same	**Dynamic** Change and grow

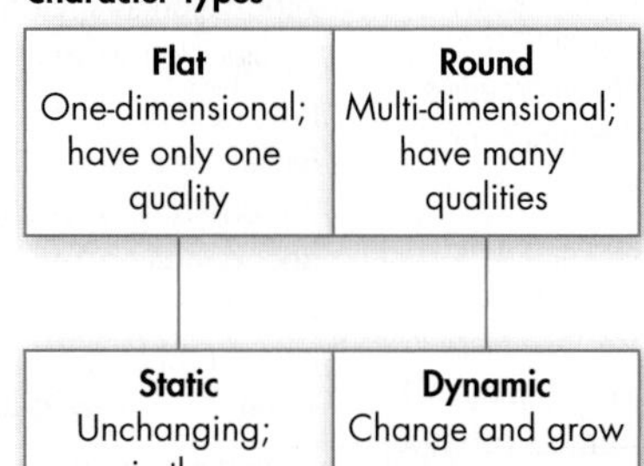

*Flat, static characters are often **stock figures,** or stereotypes, such as the villain or the damsel in distress.*

A play is, in part, an exploration of a round, dynamic character's journey from one state of being to another. By dramatizing that journey, a playwright also explores insights into the human condition, or thematic meaning.

Vocabulary Development

CCSS Language 6

Thematic Vocabulary: The Big Question

As students discuss understanding characters in drama, encourage them to use the thematic vocabulary presented in Introducing the Big Question, pages 778–779. Help them with sentence starters such as these:

1. One way to determine what a character is like is . . .
   (**Sample response:** to read the dialogue.)
2. When you're reading, you should be able to differentiate easily . . .
   (**Sample response:** between the characters.)
3. A character feels like a unique, complex character when . . .
   Sample response: he or she has many different traits and changes during the play.)

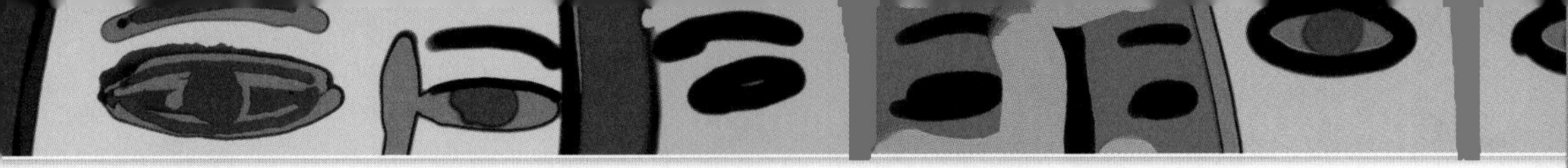

Character Development

In any work of literature, a writer uses the tools of character development, or **characterization,** to show what characters are like. There are two general approaches available to a writer: direct and indirect characterization.

2 In **direct characterization,** a writer simply tells the audience about a character. In dramatic works, direct characterization may appear in stage directions. Alternatively, the chorus, a narrator, or another character might tell the audience what a character is like. For example, in Shakespeare's *The Tragedy of Julius Caesar,* Caesar describes the suspicious character of Cassius:

He is a great observer, and he looks
Quite through the deeds of men.

In **indirect characterization,** the writer shows the audience what a character is like in any of the following ways:

- Descriptions of a character's physical appearance
- The character's own words
- The character's actions and behavior
- Other characters' reactions to the character

An actor brings a character to life on the stage or in a movie by using his or her voice, facial expressions, gestures, and body language, as well as the pitch and phrasing of his or her speech. Costumes and sets then help to emphasize elements of a character's personality. However, when you read a drama, you must use textual clues to understand characters' motivations, feelings, actions, and thoughts.

Clues to Characterization When Reading Drama Playwrights help readers understand complex characters by using dialogue, stage directions, punctuation, and word choice to show emotions, relationships, and differences in characters' status, education, and environment. As you read drama, look for these clues to complex characters.

Examples: Characterization in Drama

Punctuation Showing Emotion: That's unbelievable! You mean—the bank will give us the loan?

Stage Directions Showing Attitude: *[Stanley runs to Anna, arms outstretched.]*

Dialogue Suggesting Social Class: Really, Madam. I don't see why we can't just enjoy our tea!

Word Choice Showing Relationships: You're fantastic, sweet pea! You rustled up my favorite meal!

Dramatic Speeches The different types of dramatic speeches, described on page 781, also provide critical clues to characters' motivations and actions. For example, in a monologue or soliloquy, a character can explain what he or she thinks and feels. The audience learns about the character's conflicts and even his or her secrets. Such speeches help propel the plot because they explain why characters do what they do. Often, these types of speeches also express ideas that are key to the play's theme.

Characters and Theme There are many ways in which characters provide clues to a play's theme. To determine and analyze the theme of a drama, pay attention to characters' words, motivations, actions, and reactions. Ask yourself questions such as the following:

- How do the characters respond to conflicts?
- What are their reasons for responding as they do?
- What change or growth do characters undergo as a result of their experiences?
- What central ideas are emphasized throughout the drama through the words and actions of the characters?
- What insights about life or the human condition do these ideas convey?

2 Character Development

1. Introduce the Character Development passage and the Characterization in Drama chart on the student page. Emphasize that, just as in reading a short story or novel, most of what an audience knows about a character comes from his or her words and actions. These will be revealed in dialogue and stage directions. Even many of a character's thoughts can be found in dialogue. Also, other characters will describe or react to a character, revealing a great deal about him or her. Have students read the following **monologue** in the voice of a character called Lulu.

   "I hate it that I have detention! I'm going to miss volleyball practice. But at least Jill will be there. We need to talk about dyeing my hair again. I'm getting really tired of purple. (She walks more quickly.) *And now I'm going to be late to detention! Just because I stopped to explain quadratic equations to Ned, who is unbelievably cute. It's too bad Jill already likes him."*

2. **Ask** students to tell what they learned about Lulu from this **monologue.** Have them explain whether Lulu is a complex character.

   Sample response: Lulu is a complex character. She is an athlete and she also knows enough about math to explain quadratic equations. She is going to detention, so she is not always well-behaved. She cares about how she looks and is open to experimentation. She seems energetic, confident, and loyal.

❸ Close Read: Characters, Plot, and Theme

1. Review with the class the Clues chart. Discuss ways in which each element might interact with the others. For example, if the setting is a single room, the actions of the characters may be limited. In the same setting, if the characters are in serious conflict, being enclosed may bring that out.
2. Divide students into six groups. Assign each group one of the shaded boxes in the Clues chart. Have them read and discuss the questions. Then **ask** each of the groups to come up with a simple example of the aspect of drama they have discussed, with regard to a modern play based on "Beauty and the Beast." Then, have the groups share their examples with the class.

   Sample responses: *Characters:* At first, Beast is the antagonist, but he later redeems himself. *Stage Directions:* Enter the Beast's courtyard. *Actions and Events:* Father takes a rose. *Conflicts:* Beast threatens father's death. *Dialogue and Dramatic Speeches:* "Is this how you repay my generosity?" *Characterization:* Beauty grows to love Beast but longs for home.
3. Point out examples of highlighted text in the model on page 785. Explain that, in each case, the color of the highlighting matches the color of the category in the chart. Details that illustrate a given category are highlighted in the color of that category.

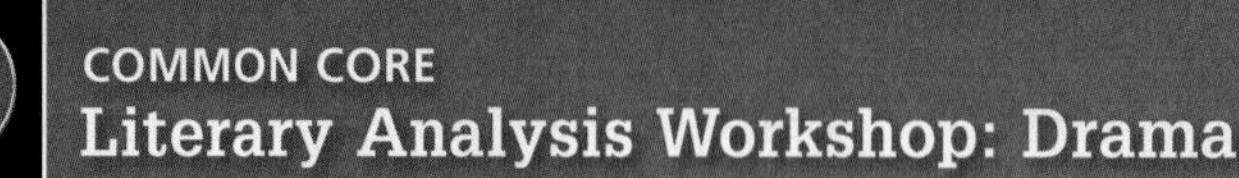

❸ Close Read: Character, Plot, and Theme

Complex characters advance the plot and develop the theme in drama.

Audiences have been entertained by dramatic works for thousands of years. However, powerful dramas offer more than just entertainment; they provide thematic insights into life and human nature. When you read or watch drama, look for relationships among the characters and events to arrive at your interpretation of a play's deeper meaning. The questions shown below can help you find thematic connections among the characters and events of a play.

Clues to Analyzing Character, Plot, and Theme in Drama	
Characters • Who is the protagonist? What qualities make this character special or important? • Who is the antagonist? How is he or she similar to or different from the protagonist? • What do characters want? What do they do to achieve their goals? • Are all characters round and dynamic, or are some characters flat or static?	**Characterization** • Do you find any examples of direct characterization? If so, what do they tell you about characters? • Do you notice examples of indirect characterization, such as descriptions of characters' appearance; characters' actions; characters' statements; other characters' words and reactions? • What do details of indirect characterization tell you about characters' feelings, thoughts, motivations, behaviors, and actions?
Actions and Events • What do characters do? • How do characters' actions cause other events? • How do characters react to events or others' actions?	**Stage Directions** • Does the playwright offer direct statements about the setting, characters, or conflicts? • Does the playwright include explanatory details about how characters speak, move, or feel? • Do stage directions suggest characters' emotions through specific word choices or punctuation?
Conflicts • What is the main conflict? • Are there any other conflicts? • Are the conflicts primarily external or internal? • How do different characters react to the conflicts? • What bigger ideas do these conflicts suggest?	**Dialogue and Dramatic Speeches** • What do the characters say to each other? What do they hide from each other? • What do characters' word choices tell you about them? • Do characters share information with the audience but not with one another? If so, what do you learn about them?

TEACH

EXEMPLAR TEXT

4 Model

About the Text *The Glass Menagerie* helped open the door to fame and fortune for its playwright, Tennessee Williams. The drama, which was first produced in Chicago in 1944, tells the story of the struggling Wingfield family. Years earlier, the family was abandoned by the father. The mother, Amanda, is now a desperate, fading Southern belle. Her son, Tom, wants to be a poet instead of an ambitious businessman who could support the family. Amanda's daughter, Laura, is so painfully shy she can barely leave the house and spends her time arranging her collection of glass animals.

In the following scene, Tom and Amanda discuss the friend from work whom Tom has invited for dinner.

from *The Glass Menagerie* by Tennessee Williams

Tom: What are you doing?

5 **Amanda:** I'm brushing that cowlick down! *[She attacks his hair with the brush.]* What is this young man's position at the warehouse?

Tom: *[submitting grimly to the brush and the interrogation]:* This young man's position is that of a shipping clerk, Mother.

Amanda: Sounds to me like a fairly responsible job, the sort of a job *you* would be in if you just had more *get-up.* What is his salary? Have you any idea?

6 **Tom:** I would judge it to be approximately eighty-five dollars a month.

Amanda: Well—not princely, but—

Tom: Twenty more than I make.

Amanda: Yes, how well I know! But for a family man, eighty-five dollars a month is not much more than you can just get by on. . . .

Tom: Yes, but Mr. O'Connor is not a family man.

Amanda: He might be mightn't he? Some time in the future?

Tom: I see. Plans and provisions.

5 **Stage Directions** The word *attack* provides a clue to Amanda's feelings of anger toward Tom. The word *grimly* suggests Tom's response to his mother.

6 **Dialogue** Amanda reveals the source of her irritation—she believes her son lacks ambition. The quick pace of the dialogue suggests that Amanda and Tom have discussed this topic many times before.

4 Reading the Model

1. Discuss the About the Text note. Explain further that *The Glass Menagerie* was written by Tennessee Williams, one of America's greatest playwrights.
2. Have students read the passage (pp. 785–786). Discuss, clarifying as necessary. Then, guide students in reviewing the annotations.

5 Stage Directions

Read aloud the Stage Directions annotation and bracketed text. **Ask:** How do you think Amanda feels about Tom at this point?

Possible response: She seems to be annoyed at Tom.

6 Dialogue

Read aloud the Dialogue annotation and the bracketed passage. Remind them of the information about Tom's sister, Laura, in the About the Text note. **Ask:** What do you think Amanda has in mind about Mr. O'Connor?

Possible response: She is hoping he will be interested in Laura.

Differentiated Instruction for Universal Access

Strategy for Less Proficient Readers

Guide students in making inferences and connections as they read:

- Have students reread the first three exchanges of dialogue between Tom and Amanda. Guide them to see that there is tension between mother and son.
- Have students reread the rest of the dialogue on this page. By referring to the About the Text note, guide students to understand that Amanda is accustomed to managing her children's lives.

EL Strategy for English Learners

Preteach the following words from page 785, using visuals and the help of students fluent in English who share students' home language: *cowlick, grimly, interrogation, position, princely.* After students read the passage, ask them to talk about whether the context of the dialogue increased their understanding of the words.

7 Conflict

1. Read aloud the Conflict annotation and the bracketed text. Explain to students that dialogue tells you a lot more than what is on the surface.
2. Tell students that, when you're reading drama, you need to use your prior information to fill in what is sometimes called the subtext of the words. In this case, you know that Tom is a young man who wants to be a poet but is working in a warehouse. There is no mention of his mother working, and his sister is too shy to leave the house, so he is probably sacrificing his dreams to support the family. Now, **ask:** How would you describe the main conflict between Tom and his mother? Do you think it's entirely about his job?

   Possible response: The main conflict seems to be about his job, but it probably also has to do with her attempts to manage his life for him.

8 Characterization

1. Remind students that, in plays, there is usually no narrator. Most of the information about characters and events is conveyed through dialogue. In the dialogue between Tom and Amanda so far, we have learned who Tom's friend is and something about him. We have learned that there is a conflict between Tom and his mother. All of this has come out in the dialogue.
2. Have a volunteer read aloud the bracketed text. **Ask:** What does the dialogue here tell you about an event that has helped shape Amanda's emotions and motivations?

   Possible response: Amanda fell in love with a charming, handsome man, and it was a terrible mistake.

EXEMPLAR TEXT

Model continued

7 Conflict Amanda fears for her family. Tom longs to pursue his own life. The conflict between Amanda and Tom drives both this scene and the events of the play as a whole.

8 Characterization Amanda's memories of her girlhood are romantic and idealized. Tom's understanding of her "tragic mistake" shows his sense of painful truths she chooses to ignore.

Amanda: You are the only young man that I know of who ignores the fact that the future becomes the present, the present the past, and the past turns into everlasting regret if you don't plan for it!

Tom: I will think that over and see what I can make of it.

Amanda: Don't be supercilious with your mother! Tell me some more about this—what do you call him?

Tom: James D. O'Connor. The D. is for Delaney.

Amanda: Irish on *both* sides! *Gracious!* And doesn't drink?

Tom: Shall I call him up and ask him right this minute?

Amanda: The only way to find out about those things is to make discreet inquiries at the proper moment. When I was a girl in Blue Mountain and it was suspected that a young man drank, the girl whose attentions he had been receiving, if any girl *was,* would sometimes speak to the minister of his church, or rather her father would if her father was living, and sort of feel him out on the young man's character. That is the way such things are discreetly handled to keep a young woman from making a tragic mistake!

Tom: Then how did you happen to make a tragic mistake?

Amanda: That innocent look of your father's had everyone fooled! He *smiled*—the world was *enchanted!* No girl can do worse than put herself at the mercy of a handsome appearance! I hope that Mr. O'Connor is not too good-looking.

Think Aloud

Theme

To model the skill of dialogue, use the following "think aloud." Say to students:

To figure out what dialogue really means, I imagine what it would sound like if I were listening to an actor saying those words. Sometimes I read the words out loud to see how they sound to me. When I read Amanda's line that starts "You are the only young man that I know. . .," it doesn't sound right in a kind, gentle tone of voice. It only sounds right to me when I say it as though I'm angry with Tom and scolding him.

When I read Tom's line, "I will think that over and see what I can make of it," I realize I could say those words in a couple of different ways. I could say them in a quiet, thoughtful tone. Or I could say them in a sarcastic way. The second way fits better with the way Tom has talked to his mother so far. Amanda's next line tells me I'm right. She tells him not to be rude to his mother. I know that means he's being sneering and superior.

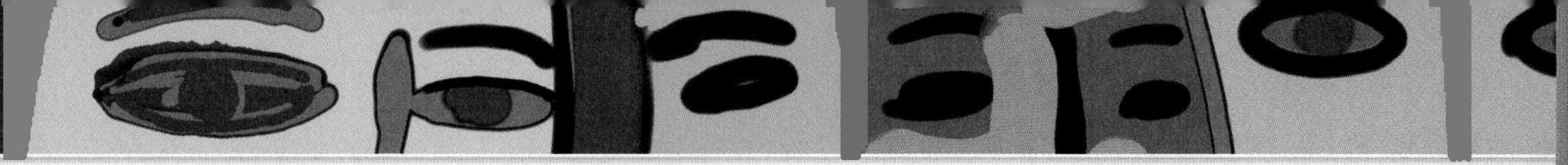

9 Independent Practice

About the Text Gary Blackwood's novel *The Shakespeare Stealer,* which he adapted into this play, is set in England in 1601, during the period when playwright William Shakespeare was writing his most famous works. In this opening scene from the play, Widge, an orphan who knows a method for writing quickly, is given a task that will lead him into Shakespeare's world.

from *The Shakespeare Stealer* by Gary Blackwood

Prologue

SANDER. I bid you welcome. For an hour or so
I ask you to imagine, if you will,
10 That this poor stage is not a stage at all
But England, some four hundred years ago.
That the actors who—I hope—will soon appear
Are something more than they appear to be,
That they are not mere shadows on a stage
But men and women of another age.

Act I

At the rear of the playing area is a shallow, two-story set with a narrow flight of steps leading to the upper story. In the center of the upper story is a single wide doorway draped with a curtain. The lower story has two smaller openings, one at Left and one at Right, also covered by curtains. At various times, this set will represent DR. TIMOTHY BRIGHT's apothecary, with WIDGE's living quarters upstairs; SIMON BASS's house; and the backstage area at the Globe Theatre. At Lights Up, it is Dr. BRIGHT's apothecary in Berwick-in-Elmet, Yorkshire, c. 1601. A table at Center contains glass and earthenware jars and beakers. One of the containers bubbles over a pot filled with burning pitch. WIDGE sits on a stool at the table, copying something from a small bound notebook onto loose sheets of paper, using a plumbago pencil—a stick of graphite wrapped in paper, similar to a grease pencil or charcoal pencil. WIDGE is a slight boy of fourteen with a "pudding basin," or bowl, haircut. He wears a working-class tunic. All is quiet and peaceful for a long moment. Then the audience is startled by the entrance of DR. TIMOTHY BRIGHT, a florid, overweight man in his forties or fifties, who is slightly deaf. He strides on brandishing a walking stick, and roaring—but he is nearly as comical as he is menacing.

11 (margin marker beside stage directions) · 12 (margin marker beside Bright's entrance)

10 Dramatic Speeches
How does Sander's speech emphasize the artificiality of a play? What deeper meanings might this suggest?

11 Stage Directions
What do you learn about Widge in these stage directions?

12 Characterization
In what ways is the description of Bright's entrance an example of both direct and indirect characterization?

9 Independent Practice

1. Discuss the About the Text note. Explain further that many people have written plays, movies, and stories that imagine Shakespeare and his time. In this play, the writer imagines a boy named Widge, who is an apprentice.
2. Have students read the passage (pp. 787–796). Discuss, clarifying as necessary. Then, guide students in reviewing the annotations.

10 Dramatic Speeches

Have a volunteer read aloud the bracketed text. **Ask** the Dramatic Speeches questions.

Possible response: The speaker is asking the audience to believe for a little while that what is happening on the stage is real. No play or movie can make people believe something is real unless they want to.

11 Stage Directions

Have a volunteer read aloud the bracketed text. **Ask** the Stage Directions question.

Possible response: There can be different furniture and props on different parts of the stage. These stage directions tell us where Widge lives.

12 Characterization

Have a volunteer read aloud the bracketed text. **Ask** the Characterization question.

Possible response: Direct: describes his physical appearance, age, and disability; indirect: implies his attitude.

Enriched Online Student Edition
To have students read the selection in interactive format, with narration and point-of-use interactive graphic organizers, go to **www.PHLitOnline.com**.

⓭ Dialogue

Have a volunteer read aloud the bracketed text. **Ask** the Dialogue question.

Possible response: Dr. Bright is Widge's boss, and Widge is afraid of him.

⓮ Action and Events

Have a volunteer read aloud the bracketed text. **Ask** the Action and Events questions.

Possible response: He's accused of copying sermons for Dr. Bright. This is probably going to be important in the plot.

Practice continued

13 Dialogue What do Bright's word choices and actions tell you about him?

Bright. You! . . . clod-pated drivel! *(WIDGE reacts, knocking a beaker to the floor, where it shatters, enraging BRIGHT even more)* You . . . halfwitted hoddypeak! Do you know what you've done?!

Widge. *(Puts the table between himself and BRIGHT)* I—I didn't mean to! I'll clean it up at once!

Bright. Not *that,* you simpleton! This! *(He waves a paper about)* It's from the bishop's secretary. I've been accused of stealing sermons from my fellow rectors! How in heaven's name did the bishop get wind of this? Have you let a hint drop to anyone of what you were up to? Anyone at all?

Widge. Nay, I never! So help me God and halidom!

Bright. Has anyone shown any signs of suspecting you?

Widge. Nay, no one.

14 Actions and Events What has Widge been accused of doing? Why do you think this information is included in the first scene of the play?

Bright. You're lying. No, don't bother to deny it. I've the proof here. The rector at Leeds caught you red-handed. Isn't that so? Isn't that so?

Widge. *(murmurs)* Aye.

Bright. What's that? Speak up, boy!

Widge. Aye! It was a fortnight ago. 'A spotted me scribbling away, and afore I could make me escape, 'a collared me and snatched away me table-book!

Bright. Why did you not tell me this sooner?

Widge. I was afeared. I kenned you'd be angry.

Bright. You were right. But . . . if he took away your transcription of his sermon, then . . . then whose sermon was it that I . . . *(he doesn't want to say "stole")* . . . used as my model last Sunday?

Widge. Well . . . I—I wrote it all out as best I could remember . . .

Bright. *You?* I delivered a sermon composed by my idle-headed apprentice? You deceitful little whelp! When will you learn not to lie to me? Well, by St. Pintle, I'll teach you right from wrong! Come here! *(WIDGE dodges the man's grasp, circling the table, but then he slips on the contents of the broken beaker,*

Vocabulary Development

CCSS Language 6

Thematic Vocabulary: The Big Question

As students are discussing *The Shakespeare Stealer,* encourage them to use the thematic vocabulary presented in Introducing the Big Question, pp. 778–779. You might encourage them with sentence starters like these:

1. Falconer shows an *understanding* of Widge's feelings when . . .
2. Falconer tries to *defend* Widge when . . .
3. Widge shows his *individuality* by . . .
4. Dr. Bright demonstrates that one of his *values* is . . .

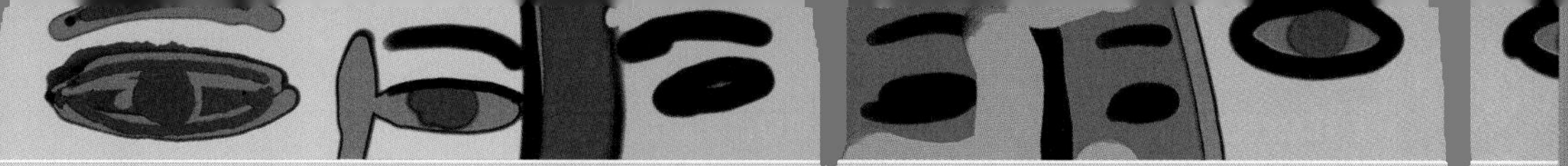

15 *and is caught. BRIGHT raises the stick as if to strike; WIDGE cowers and flinches. But then BRIGHT tosses him aside and, puffing with the exertion, plops down on the stool)* Ahh, what's the use of it? If I haven't beaten some sense into you by now, I never will. *(shakes his head)* When I think of all I've done for you, all the years I've invested in you. When I took you in five years ago—

WIDGE: Seven.

BRIGHT. Eh? What's that?

WIDGE. It's been seven years, sir.

BRIGHT. That's beside the point. When I took you in, you were a feckless illiterate orphan with no prospects whatever in the world. I taught you to read and cipher, taught you about medicine, even taught you my system of swift writing, and this is what I get in return? *(waves the paper)* If someone were to offer it, I'd sell your services for a farthing; it's far more than you're worth. Yes, and I expect you'd jump at the chance to change masters, wouldn't you? Eh? *(The way WIDGE hangs his head makes it clear that he would)* Well, all I can say is, be careful what you wish for, boy. There are far worse places than this, believe me, and far worse masters than me.

16 **WIDGE.** *(aside)* Aye, the Devil, for one.

BRIGHT. What's that?

WIDGE. Nothing. *(He sets about cleaning up the broken beaker, while BRIGHT checks his boiling potion. The silence is broken by the sound of an iron door knocker pounding O.S. Right)*

BRIGHT. Yes, yes, coming. Bloody patients. Why can't they be sick in the daytime? *(He crosses to Left, reaches O.S. to open a door, then backs up as*
17 *FALCONER enters, a tall figure in a hooded cloak, looking as grim as Death. Beneath the cloak he carries a rapier. We seldom see his face, but when he does reveal a glimpse of it, we see that he has a bushy, dark beard and a hooked nose. A nasty scar disfigures one side of his face)* G-good evening, sir. How may I serve you?

FALCONER. *(seems to reach for his rapier, but instead takes a leatherbound book from beneath his cloak. In a deep, almost spectral voice)* This is yours, is it not?

15 **Conflict** What do these stage directions and dialogue add to your understanding of Dr. Bright and Widge? How does this interaction reveal at least one of the play's conflicts?

16 **Dramatic Speeches** Why does Widge speak this line in confidence to the audience?

17 **Characterization** How is this passage about Falconer an example of indirect characterization? What does it tell you about Falconer's character?

15 Conflict

Have a volunteer read aloud the bracketed text. **Ask** the Conflict questions.

Possible response: Dr. Bright often beats Widge, and Widge is afraid of him. It highlights how the characters see things differently.

16 Dramatic Speeches

Have a volunteer read aloud the bracketed text. **Ask** the Dramatic Speeches question.

Possible response: He doesn't want Bright to hear and get angry.

17 Characterization

Have a volunteer read aloud the bracketed text. **Ask** the Characterization question.

Possible response: He's a scary character, probably in disguise. It uses his appearance to represent his character.

18 Dialogue

Have a volunteer read aloud the bracketed text. **Ask** the Dialogue questions.

Possible response: Dr. Bright has probably never praised him before. Widge may not know how good he is.

Practice continued

Bright. *(moves hesitantly closer to the man)* Why, yes. Yes, it is. It's a copy of my book on charactery.

Falconer. Does it work?

Bright. I beg your pardon?

Falconer. Your system of charactery. Does it work?

Bright. Of course it works. Using my system of swift writing, one may without effort transcribe the written or the spoken word—

Falconer. How long does it take?

Bright. As I was about to say, one may set down speech as rapidly as it is spoken—

Falconer. *(impatient)* Yes, yes, but how long to learn it?

Bright. Well, that depends upon the aptitude of the—

Falconer. How *long*?

Bright. *(nervously, stretching the truth)* Oh, two months, perhaps three. Well, let's say four. Five, at the outside.

Falconer. *(tosses the book rather contemptuously onto the table)* To how many have you taught this system of yours?

Bright. Let me see . . . There's my apprentice, here, and then . . .

Falconer. How many?

Bright. Well . . . one, actually.

Falconer. And how proficient is he?

18 **Bright.** Oh, quite proficient. Extremely. *(WIDGE is surprised to hear this)*

Falconer. Show me.

Bright. *(to WIDGE)* Are you deaf, boy? The gentleman wishes a demonstration of your skill.

Widge. *(picks up notebook and pencil)* What must I write?

Falconer. Write this: "I hereby convey to the bearer of this paper the services of my former apprentice—"

18 Dialogue Why is Widge surprised at Bright's words? What does his reaction tell you about his relationship with Bright?

Fluency

Distribute copies of page 790, and pair students. While one partner reads, the other should mark any words with which the student reading has difficulty. Circulate to monitor the fluency of students' reading. Collect students' marked-up copies of the essay, and review difficult words and passages with the class. Look for these problem spots:

- If students have difficulty with the word *transcribe* (p. 790), remind them to use context clues to infer its meaning. If they read the rest of the paragraph containing the word, clues such as "writing" and "spoken" will help them understand the word.
- If students have difficulty with the word *aptitude* (p. 790), remind them to use context clues to infer its meaning. If they read the rest of the sentence containing the word, clues such as "learn" and "how long" will help them understand the word.

19 **WIDGE.** Go on. I've kept up wi' you.

FALCONER. Your name.

WIDGE. Pardon?

FALCONER. What is your *name*?

BRIGHT. Widge. It's Widge. *(laughs as if to show that he realizes how odd it sounds)*

FALCONER. "—my former apprentice, Widge, in consideration of which I have accepted the amount of ten pounds sterling."

BRIGHT. *(staggered)* Ten p—?!

WIDGE. Is that all, then?

FALCONER. Let me see it. *(WIDGE hands him the notebook. Skeptical)* You've copied down every word?

WIDGE. Aye.

FALCONER. Read it back.

20 **WIDGE.** *(takes notebook)* "I hereby convey to the bearer of this paper the services of my former apprentice, Widge, in consideration—" *(the meaning of the words finally sinks in)* Do you—does this mean—?

FALCONER. Copy it out, now, in a normal hand.

BRIGHT. *(when WIDGE hesitates)* Go on. Do as he says! *(While WIDGE copies it out, FALCONER takes out a purse and counts out ten sovereigns onto the table, with BRIGHT watching greedily)*

FALCONER. If there's anything you want to take along, you'd best fetch it now, boy. I'll be outside. *(to BRIGHT)* Where can I water my horse?

BRIGHT. On the north side of the house, there's a trough. *(to WIDGE)* Go on, lad. *(through the following WIDGE goes upstairs, collects his meager belongings, including a leather wallet on a strap. To FALCONER)* I hope you'll keep a close eye on the boy. *(The concern this implies is belied by BRIGHT's next line)* He can be sluggish if you don't stir him from time to time with a stick. *(FALCONER exits)* Move your bones, boy, before he changes his mind. *(WIDGE descends the stairs reluctantly)*

Dialogue What does Widge's noticeably different way of speaking tell you about his character? How does his speech distinguish him from Bright and Falconer?

Actions and Events How does this demonstration of Widge's writing advance the plot? What is the importance of his writing ability?

19 Dialogue

Have a volunteer read aloud the bracketed passage. **Ask** the Dialogue questions.

Possible response: It shows he is not educated. It's important that even though Dr. Bright taught him some things, he's not an educated person.

20 Actions and Events

Have a volunteer read aloud the bracketed passage. **Ask** the Actions and Events questions.

Possible response: Widge's writing shows that he's going to be of value to Falconer in some way. It seems that Falconer needs him for his writing.

21 Characterization

Have a volunteer read aloud the bracketed text. **Ask** the Characterization questions.

Possible response: Bright's place is the only home he's known since he was seven. He has a very human desire to feel that he made some kind of impression on Bright.

22 Stage Directions

Have a volunteer read aloud the bracketed text. **Ask** the Stage Directions questions.

Possible response: They tell us where he and Falconer are. They are alone in a forest.

23 Conflict

Have a volunteer read aloud the bracketed text. **Ask** the Conflict questions.

Possible response: Falconer answers quite pleasantly, showing he's not afraid of the thieves, even though they have weapons. It tells you he is probably able to take care of himself.

Practice continued

21 Characterization Why does Widge ask this question? What does the request reveal about his character?

22 Stage Directions What do the stage directions suggest about Falconer's and Widge's journey up to this point? What do they suggest about their current situation?

23 Conflict How does Falconer react to the thief's challenge? What does his reaction show about his character?

WIDGE. Must I go with him, then?

BRIGHT. *(busy fondling the sovereigns)* Eh? Of course you must. He's paid for you, and far more handsomely than I would have dreamed.

WIDGE. Will you not bid me farewell, at least, sir?

BRIGHT. *(perfunctorily)* Of course, of course. Fair 'chieve you, boy, fair 'chieve you.

Transition

(FALCONER enters at Down Right, looking about warily, trailed by WIDGE, who is rubbing his backside)

WIDGE. Gog's blood, I'm glad to be off that horse.

FALCONER. It won't be for long. Here. *(Hands WIDGE a journey cake, nibbles at one himself, still looking about alertly. They pass a flask of something back and forth)*

WIDGE. When will we be at our destination?

FALCONER. When we get there.

WIDGE. These woods are much more . . . wild than around Berwick, and more dense. It feels almost as though they're closing in on us. *(shivers)*

FALCONER. Stop your wagging tongue. You'll have every cutpurse within a league down upon us.

WIDGE. Cutpurse? *(looks about even more fearfully)* You mean . . . there are thieves in these woods? *(realizes he's still talking)* Sorry.

(Horse whinnies O.S. Right. FALCONER reacts, abruptly puts away the flask and loosens his rapier in its sheath, looking about and listening intently. THREE THIEVES enter at Left, one armed with a pistol, two with swords)

THIEF #1. Don't move, if you value your life.

FALCONER. *(unexpectedly amiable)* God rest you, gentlemen.

THIEF #1. God, is it? Don't tell me you're a parson.

FALCONER. No, no. Far from it.

THIEF #1. Good. I don't like doing business with parsons. They're too parsimonious. *(Laughs)* All right, let's have it, then.

Vocabulary Development

Expressive Vocabulary

To help students broaden their expressive vocabulary, encourage them to use the following words as they discuss the selection: *illuminates, confirmed, episode,* and *aspect*. Have them complete these sentence starters:

1. The scene between Widge and Libby *illuminates* Widge's character by . . .
2. My opinion of Falconer's motivation was *confirmed* when he . . .
3. The *episode* in which Bright sells Widge made me think . . .
4. One *aspect* of drama that I notice in this play is . . .

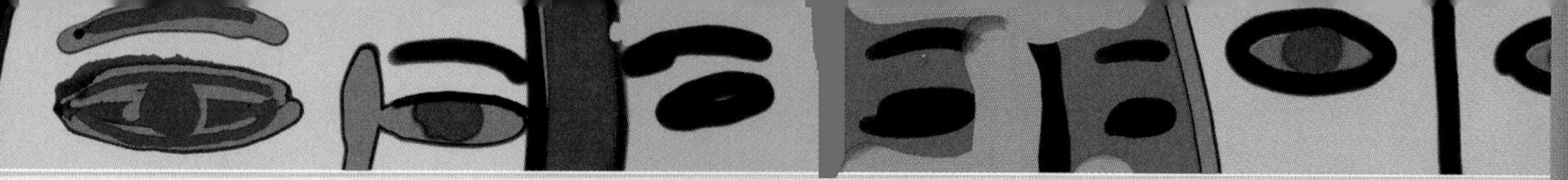

FALCONER. Have what?

THIEF #1. *(Laughs again)* Have what, 'a says! Have what? Why, have a pot of ale wi' us, of course. *(More soberly)* Come now, enough pleasantries. Let's have your purse, man.

FALCONER. *(Pulls out his hefty purse. Still amiable)* Ah. Forgive me for not taking your meaning.

THIEF #1. Oh, aye, an you forgive *me* for taking your purse.

24 *(FALCONER steps to the man, who holds out a hand for the purse. Instead of handing it over, FALCONER swings it swiftly upward, catching THIEF #1 alongside the head. The man cries out, crumples to the ground; his pistol goes off wildly. The other thieves spring forward. FALCONER draws his rapier, parries an ineffectual blow, kicks the man in the groin. WIDGE picks up a rock, but has no chance to use it. FALCONER grasps the third man's blade in his cloak-wrapped hand, yanks it away, and slices the man's ribs with his own sword. With the thieves lying about groaning, FALCONER lifts his purse with the point of his sword, flips it in the air, catches it, then shakes a single coin from it and throws it at the men's feet)*

FALCONER. If this is a toll road, you might simply have tolled me.

THIEF #1. *(laughs, then groans in pain)* Would that you had been a parson after all.

FALCONER. *(to WIDGE)* Come. *(starts Off Right)*

WIDGE. What you did back there—I've never seen the like of it.

FALCONER. Yes, well, you haven't seen much, have you?

Transition

(A bed has been brought on upstairs, and a writing desk and two chairs downstairs. FALCONER and WIDGE enter at Right. WIDGE is walking stiffly, wincing)

WIDGE. Are we in London, then?

FALCONER. *(scoffing)* Hardly. This is Leicester.

25 *(LIBBY, a sympathetic, plain woman in a maid's garb, emerges from one of the downstairs doorways)*

LIBBY. Welcome back, sir.

24 **Actions and Events** What does the action described here show about Falconer? How does this action affect Widge?

Character What new character is introduced in this scene? Why might it be important that she is described as "sympathetic"?

24 Actions and Events

Have a volunteer read aloud the bracketed text. **Ask** the Actions and Events questions.

Possible response: It shows that he is a very good fighter. It amazes Widge.

25 Character

Have a volunteer read aloud the bracketed text. **Ask** the Characterization questions.

Possible response: Libby; the characters could use a rest.

Fluency

Distribute copes of pages 792–793, and put students in groups of five. Have students take parts and read the text aloud. (One student can read the stage directions.) While one student reads, the others should mark any words with which the student reading has difficulty. Circulate to monitor the fluency of students' reading. Collect students' marked-up copies of the pages, and review difficult words and passages with the class. Look for these problem spots:

- If students struggle with the text as they sound out words one syllable at a time or read in a laborious manner, have the class read the speeches chorally. Encourage students to read with emotion.
- If students have difficulty recognizing roots, prefixes, and suffixes in the words *ineffectual* (p. 792), *exhausted* (p. 793), *unfamiliar* (p. 793), *approachable* (p. 793), or *prickliness* (p. 795), help students use their thumbs to cover up parts of the words to recognize their components.

26 Dialogue

Have a volunteer read aloud the highlighted text. **Ask** the Dialogue questions.

Possible response: The line reveals that Falconer is unpredictable. It also shows that he is her boss.

27 Stage Directions

Have a volunteer read aloud the bracketed text. **Ask** the Stage Directions question.

Possible response: The lines tell us where the characters are. Falconer's tone shows how he feels about Widge's innocence.

28 Characterization

Have a volunteer read aloud the bracketed text. **Ask** the Characterization question.

Possible response: Widge's reaction helps the audience understand how impressive the room is. It reinforces that Widge has little experience of the world. Furthermore, the way Bass responds to Widge's reaction shows that he is quite different from Falconer.

Practice continued

FALCONER. The boy will be staying the night. Show him to the garret. *(Exits upstage)*

LIBBY. Yes, sir. *(looking WIDGE over)* Where you from, then?

WIDGE. Berwick-in-Elmet.

LIBBY. Where's *that*?

WIDGE. Up Yorkshire way. Near Leeds.

LIBBY. I see. Well, come. We'd best get you to your room. *(Leads him up the steps)* I'll bring you some food up in a bit. Here you are. It's not much.

WIDGE. More than I'm used to. Mind you, it could be a pit of snakes for all I care, I'm that exhausted. *(sinks down on the bed)* You didn't seem surprised at all, that 'a came back wi' me in tow.

Dialogue What does Libby's line reveal about Falconer? What does it show about her relationship with him?

 **LIBBY.** Nothing the master does surprises me. Have a good rest.

Transition

(WIDGE wakes up, rubs eyes, looks around at the unfamiliar surroundings then hobbles downstairs. LIBBY is at the bottom of the steps)

Stage Directions What critical information about Bass and Falconer do you learn from these stage directions?

LIBBY. I was just coming to wake you. The master said to bring you to him as soon as you were up. I don't think he expected you to sleep so late. *(They cross to where SIMON BASS sits at the writing desk. He is played by the same actor who plays FALCONER, minus the hooded cloak, the curly black wig, the hooked nose, the swarthy skin, the beard, the scar, and the high boots that make him several inches taller. BASS is much more approachable and genial, but a prickliness lurks beneath the surface)*

WIDGE. Will 'a be cross wi' me, do you wis?

LIBBY. I can't say. He's a queer one, the master is. *(sotto voce)* Not to tell him I said so, now. *(Leaning into desk area)* I've brought the boy, sir.

BASS. *(without turning; we still assume it's FALCONER sitting there)* Come in, Widge. *(WIDGE enters the "room," clearly awed by the furnishings)* Sit down.

Characterization How does Widge's reaction to the setting show his inexperience and reveal important information about Bass?

WIDGE. Eh? Oh. *(sits)* Sorry. It's just that I've never seen such a grand room, with so many books, not even at Squire Cheyney's.

BASS. Wait until you see the houses in London. *(He turns, rises. We and WIDGE get our first good look at him. WIDGE is obviously bewildered)*

Widge. Who—who are you?

Bass. My name is Simon Bass. I'm your new master.

Widge. But—but I thought—

Bass. You thought the one who brought you here was to be your master.

Widge. Aye.

Bass. *(shrugs)* Falconer is not the most communicative of men, I warrant, nor the most genial. But he is reliable and effective. I could not go to Yorkshire myself . . . for various reasons. He got you here safe and sound, it appears.

Widge. *(squirming on his sore rear end)* Well, *safe,* at any rate.

Bass. Let's get down to business. You'll want to know what's expected of you.

Widge. Aye.

29 **Bass.** Very well. The first thing I expect is for you to say "yes," rather than "*aye.*" I'd just as soon you did not sound like a complete rustic. Understood?

Widge. Aye—I mean, yes.

Bass. Excellent. Now, when you go to London—

Widge. London?

Bass. Yes. It's a large city to the south.

Widge. I ken that, but—

Bass. Let me finish, then ask questions. You will be attending a play called *The Tragedy of Hamlet, Prince of Denmark.* You will copy down the play, every word of it, in Dr. Bright's charactery, and then you will deliver it to me. *(WIDGE looks uncomfortable)* Do you have some objection to that?

Widge. Nay, not especially. It's only words, after all. It's just that— Well, when a wight back home caught me copying his sermons, 'a got very upset wi' me.

Bass. Then you'll have to make certain you don't get caught, won't you? You will use a small tablebook, easily concealed . . . *(rummages through his desk)* You see how easily it's concealed? Even I can't find it. Ah, here it is. *(hands it to WIDGE)* Keep it in your wallet. You have a plumbago pencil?

29 **Dialogue** What do Bass's words indicate about his attitude toward Widge? What might this attitude mean for their relationship?

29 Dialogue

Have a volunteer read aloud the bracketed text. **Ask** the Dialogue questions.

Possible response: Bass's words show that he is planning to help Widge sound more sophisticated. It might mean that Bass will give Widge more responsibility or expect more from him than people have in the past.

Think Aloud

Drama

Draw students' attention to page 795. Use the following "think aloud" to model the skill of evaluating the requirements for set and props:

As I read this page, I pretend that I am the stage manager of *The Shakespeare Stealer* and I have to make a list of props and set requirements. To make this list, I have to read the entire text, not just the stage directions.

The first evidence of props occurs in Libby's first line on the page. The stage directions say that she is "leaning into desk area," which means I need to put a desk in the room. One line later, I notice that Bass is sitting down, so I will need a chair.

When Widge enters the room, he is "clearly awed by the furnishings," so the furniture in the room should be fancy. Then, Widge sits down, which indicates that I will need another chair. Widge's comment about "so many books" means that I'll need to find lots of books. I continue to read the text carefully and take note of more set and prop requirements.

30 Character

Have a volunteer read aloud the bracketed text. **Ask** the Character questions.

Possible response: Answers will vary, but students should demonstrate knowledge of complex characters.

31 Conflict

Have a volunteer read aloud the bracketed text. **Ask** the Conflict question.

Possible response: Widge is not sure he wants to do something dishonest.

32 Theme

Ask the Theme question.

Possible response: The theme of the play may have something to do with honesty.

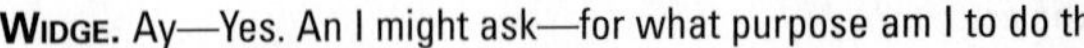

Practice continued

30 **Character** Is Bass a round, or complex, character? Is WIdge a round character? Explain your answers.

31 **Conflict** What is Widge's new conflict?

WIDGE. Ay—Yes. An I might ask—for what purpose am I to do this?

BASS. Does it matter?

WIDGE. Nay; I was only curious. The only plays I've ever seen are the ones the church does at Easter and Yuletide, and those certainly didn't seem worth stealing.

BASS. *(being prickly now)* I would prefer it if you did not use that term. I am not a thief. I am a man of business, and one of my more profitable ventures is a company of players. They are not so successful as the Lord Chamberlain's Men or the Admiral's Men, of course, but they draw a sizable audience here in the Midlands. If we could stage a current work, by a well-known poet, we could double our profits. Now, sooner or later someone will pry this *Tragedy of Hamlet* from the grasp of its author, Mr. Shakespeare, just as they have his earlier plays. I would like that someone to be me. If I wait for others to do it, they will do a botched job, cobbled together from various sources, none of them very reliable. Mr. Shakespeare deserves better. He is a poet of quality, perhaps of genius, and if his work is to be borrowed, it should be done properly. That is your mission. If you fulfill it satisfactorily, the reward will be considerable.

WIDGE. And . . . what an I do not?

BASS. Falconer will make certain that you do.

WIDGE. Oh. I didn't ken that 'a would go wi' me.

BASS. Did you suppose I would send you off to London on your own? I might as well send you to Guiana. Go and rest now, or soak your haunches, or whatever you will. You'll be leaving for London early in the morning. *(He exits. WIDGE shuffles downstage as LIBBY enters at Left)*

32 **Theme** Considering Widge's inexperience and his treatment thus far by his masters, what might be one theme of this play?

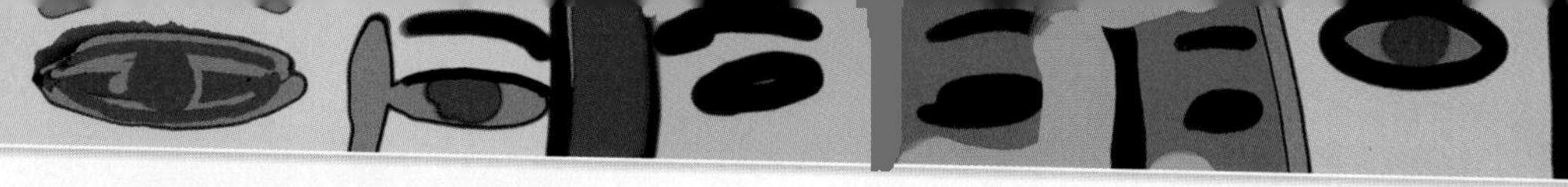

After You Read — The Shakespeare Stealer

1. **Key Ideas and Details (a)** Which details in the stage directions show that the play is set in Shakespearean England? **(b) Identify:** Which lines of dialogue establish the play's setting?
2. **Key Ideas and Details (a)** What does the opening scene tell you about Widge, Dr. Bright, and their relationship? **(b) Infer:** Which details indicate that Widge is a complex character?
3. **Craft and Structure Generalize:** Based on this excerpt, how do you think this play differs from Blackwood's novel?
4. **Craft and Structure (a)** What is the climax of this excerpt? **(b) Analyze:** How do plot events and character development lead up to this climax?
5. **Integration of Knowledge and Ideas (a) Speculate:** The excerpt ends with uncertainty about whether Widge will comply with Falconer's request. What do you think Widge will do? **(b) Infer:** What theme is suggested by Widge's conflict? Use details from the text to support your answer.
6. **Integration of Knowledge and Ideas Compare and Contrast:** Do you see any similarities between Bass's plan and modern-day practices involving music or movies? Explain.
7. **Integration of Knowledge and Ideas (a)** Use a chart like the one shown to explore how characters use props to reveal their personalities. **(b)** In the first column, list props that are used by Dr. Bright, Widge, and Falconer. In the second column, record how the characters use each prop. In the third column, describe what their actions show about their personalities.

Prop	How It Is Used	What It Shows

(c) Collaborate: Compare charts with a partner. How do the other students' details add to your understanding of the characters?

ASSESS/EXTEND

Answers

1. **Possible response: (a)** The first scene takes place in an apothecary. Widge uses an old-fashioned pencil. Falconer carries a rapier. **(b)** "So help me God and halidom"; "halfwitted hoddypeak"
2. **Possible response: (a)** It tells you that Dr. Bright is Widge's boss and that Widge is afraid of him. **(b)** The way Widge does whatever Bright commands of him shows that he is obedient. But Widge's aside to the audience reveals that, despite his obedience, he is resentful.
3. **Sample response:** It doesn't have a narrator. It probably has less description.
4. **Possible response: (a)** The climax is when Bass reveals what Widge is to do. **(b)** Answers will vary but should show that students understand the plot and how characters develop over the course of the play.
5. **Possible response: (a)** Answers will vary, but students should support their answers with textual evidence. **(b)** The world can be a very dishonest place. This theme can be inferred from what Bass is asking Widge to do.
6. **Possible response:** Yes. Bass's plan is like piracy of songs and movies.
7. **Sample response: (b)** *Prop:* Dr. Bright—walking stick. *How It Is Used:* He uses it to intimidate Widge. *What It Shows:* He likes to be in control of others. **(c)** They point out things I didn't notice.

Assessment Resources

The following resources can be used to assess students' knowledge and skills.

Unit 5 Resources

L1 L2 EL **Selection Test A,** pp. 17–19
L3 L4 EL **Selection Test B,** pp. 20–22
L3 L4 **Open Book Test,** pp. 14–16

PHLit Online! Students may use the **Self-test,** at **www.PHLitOnline.com,** to prepare for the **Selection Test A** or **Selection Test B.**

❶ Preparing to Read

The purpose of the Extended Study section is to introduce background information that might help students when reading *The Tragedy of Romeo and Juliet.*

❷ The Rebirth of Learning

1. Draw students' attention to how developments in science and exploration during the Renaissance upset the religious and political order of the day.
2. **Ask:** What are some ways new ideas and philosophies might have an unsettling effect upon society today?

   Sample responses: The recent calls for democracy in many countries throughout the world are a threat to some existing political establishments. The possibility that distant solar systems might support life challenges some people's religious convictions. The idea that human activity may be responsible for climate change has the potential for upsetting the world economic order.

❸ The Renaissance in England

1. Help students understand the irony of Elizabeth's birth and subsequent political power. Point out that Queen Elizabeth is not the only woman to have exercised great authority in a traditionally male role.
2. **Ask:** What other women can you think of who have become national leaders?

   Sample responses: *In history:* Cleopatra, Queen of Egypt; Isabella I, Queen of Spain; Joan of Arc, French military leader; Catherine the Great, Empress of Russia; Queen Victoria of England; Tzu-his, Empress of China. *In recent times:* Indira Gandhi, Prime Minister of India; Margaret Thatcher, Prime Minister of England; Golda Meir, Prime Minister of Israel; Hillary Rodham Clinton, presidential candidate and Secretary of State.

❶ Preparing to Read
The Tragedy of Romeo and Juliet

The works of William Shakespeare are among the greatest achievements of the Renaissance.

Historical Background: Elizabethan England

The Rebirth of Learning Sometime around the year 1350, at the end of the Middle Ages, Italian city-states, such as Venice and Genoa, began to trade extensively with the East. With trade came more knowledge and growing curiosity about the world. Soon, Italy was leading the way in a flowering of European learning known as the Renaissance (ren′ ə sans′). Commerce, science, and the arts blossomed as people shifted their focus ❷ to the interests and pursuits of human life here on earth. The astronomers Copernicus and Galileo questioned long-held beliefs to prove that the world was round and that it circled the sun, not vice versa. Navigators, including Christopher Columbus and Ferdinand Magellan, braved the seas in tiny boats to explore new lands and seek new trade routes. Religious thinkers, such as Martin Luther and John Calvin, challenged the authority of the Roman Catholic Church and spurred the Protestant Reformation. Artists, including Michelangelo and Leonardo da Vinci, painted and sculpted lifelike human beings. Writers, such as Miguel de Cervantes and William Shakespeare, wrote insightfully about complex human personalities in fiction and drama.

▲ Elizabeth ruled from 1558 to 1603, but her reign was so successful that the entire Renaissance in England is often called the Elizabethan Age.

The Renaissance in England The Renaissance was slow to come to England. The delay was caused mainly by civil war between two great families, or houses, claiming the English throne—the House of York and the House of Lancaster. The conflict ended in 1485 when Henry Tudor of the House of Lancaster took the throne as King Henry VII. After a successful rule in which English commerce expanded, he was succeeded by his son Henry VIII, whose reign was filled with turmoil. Henry sought a divorce from the Spanish princess Catherine of Aragon so that he could remarry and possibly have a son. He was convinced that only a male would be strong enough to hold the throne. When the Pope refused to grant the divorce, Henry renounced the Roman Catholic Church and made England a Protestant ❸ nation. Ironically, his remarriage, to a woman named Anne Boleyn, produced not a son but a daughter, Elizabeth. Even more ironically, when Elizabeth took the throne, she proved to be one of the strongest monarchs that England has ever known.

The symbol of the House of York was a white rose, while the symbol of the House of Lancaster was a red rose. For that reason, the civil wars fought between the two houses were called the Wars of the Roses. Shakespeare wrote several plays about English monarchs involved in these conflicts.

Enrichment: Investigating Science

Galileo and the Solar System

The discovery that the Earth and its fellow planets revolve around the sun was one of the revolutionary achievements of the Renaissance. First described by the Polish astronomer Nicolaus Copernicus, the concept of a heliocentric solar system was refined by the Italian genius Galileo Galilei (1564–1642), who employed the newly invented telescope to collect evidence. The idea met with angry resistance from religious leaders of the day, who were convinced that the Earth was the center of the universe.

Activity: Draw Conclusions Have students research the astronomical observations of Galileo and the conclusions to which his revolutionary evidence led him. Encourage students to develop a monologue in which they play the role of Galileo, describing what he saw through his telescope and drawing conclusions regarding the solar system based on these observations. Alternatively, have pairs of students stage a TV-style interview in which Galileo is invited to air his controversial conclusions.

The Elizabethan World The reign of Elizabeth I is often seen as a golden age in English history. Treading a moderate and frugal path, Elizabeth brought economic and political stability to the nation, thus allowing commerce and culture to thrive. Advances in mapmaking helped English explorers sail the Old World and claim lands in the New. Practical inventions improved transportation at home. Craft workers created lovely wares for the homes of the wealthy. Musicians composed fine works for the royal court, and literature thrived, peaking with the plays of William Shakespeare.

London became a bustling capital on the busy River Thames (**temz**), where ships from all over the world sailed into port. The city attracted newcomers from the countryside and immigrants from foreign lands. Streets were narrow, dirty, and crowded, but they were also lined with shops where vendors sold merchandise from near and far. English women enjoyed more freedoms than did women elsewhere in Europe, and the class system was more fluid as well. To be sure, those of different ranks led very different lives. Yet even the lowborn were able to attend one of the city's most popular new amusements: the theater.

▼ In 1796, more than 200 years after the defeat of the Spanish Armada, English artist Philippe-Jacques de Loutherbourg painted this image of those dramatic events.

Elizabeth I and the Spanish Armada

In 1588, King Phillip of Spain sent an armada, or fleet of military ships, to invade England. At the time, Spain was the most powerful nation on earth. Nevertheless, the English soundly defeated the invading forces. The victory cemented Elizabeth's popularity with her people. Prior to the battle, the Queen visited her troops to inspire them to fight. Here is a portion of the speech she delivered:

. . . And therefore I am come amongst you at this time, not as for my recreation or sport, but being resolved, in the midst and heat of the battle, to live or die amongst you all; to lay down, for my God, and for my kingdom, and for my people, my honor and my blood, even the dust. I know I have but the body of a weak and feeble woman; but I have the heart of a king, and of a king of England too. . . .

4 The Elizabethan World

1. Introduce the description of life in London during Shakespeare's time.
2. Have two volunteers read the bracketed paragraphs aloud, alternating sentences. Help students visualize the bustling activity in the growing city and the changes that developments in transportation, commerce, and the arts contributed to the city's environment.

5 Connect to History

1. Explain that England was in a desperate state when the huge Spanish Armada approached her shores in 1588. Heavily outnumbered and outgunned by Spain, the English navy did not appear to stand a chance in open battle. Point out that in such circumstances, a powerful leader can change the course of history with inspirational rhetoric. Invite a volunteer to read the excerpt from Queen Elizabeth's address to her troops.
2. **Ask:** What makes this an effective political speech?

   Sample response: Elizabeth shows resolve, passion, and courage. She indicates how important this moment is by expressing her willingness to die with her soldiers. She uses emotionally charged words like *God, kingdom, England, honor, blood,* and *heart*. By implying that the spirit is more important than physical strength, she suggests that England is capable of victory, despite being heavily outnumbered.

1 Theater in Elizabethan England

1. Point out that in the Middle Ages, acting was not a prestigious occupation. Acting companies had no permanent theaters, and actors received little compensation for their performances. Discuss with students how economic and social changes during the English Renaissance might have helped elevate the acting profession.
2. **Ask:** From what you know about the Renaissance, why might the theater have become a popular form of entertainment in England?
   Sample responses: People were becoming curious about new ideas and foreign lands. They found excitement and escape in the theater. Increasing prosperity gave the public more leisure time and money to spend. Political stability allowed the theater to flourish.

3. Ask students to imagine watching a play in which a twelve-year-old boy plays the romantic female role. Introduce the term "suspension of disbelief," explaining that playgoers have to enter a theater prepared to believe what they see.
4. **Ask:** How are playgoers today asked to suspend their disbelief?
   Sample responses: The sets may be plywood facades. Food and drink are often artificial. Actors fly on wires and fight with blunt swords and blank ammunition. "Daylight" is electric. In simple productions, the audience has to imagine that two chairs represent a car or a sofa suggests a living room. In student productions, children and teens play the roles of adults.

1 Theater in Elizabethan England

Elizabethan audiences included all levels of society, from the "groundlings," who paid a penny entrance fee, to the nobility.

During the Middle Ages, simple religious plays were performed at inns, in castle halls, and on large wagons at pageants. In early Elizabethan times, acting companies still traveled the countryside to perform their plays. However, the best companies acquired noble patrons, or sponsors, who then invited the troupes to perform in their homes. At the same time, Elizabethan dramatists began to use the tragedies and comedies of ancient Greece and Rome as models for their plays. By the end of the sixteenth century, many talented playwrights had emerged, including Christopher Marlowe, Ben Jonson, and, of course, William Shakespeare.

Audience members ate and drank while they watched the plays and apparently made a lot of noise. In 1990, archaeologists found the remains of the foundation of the original Globe Theatre. They also found the discarded shells of the many hazelnuts audiences munched on while watching performances.

England's First Theater England's first successful public theater opened in 1576. Known simply as the Theatre, it was built by an actor named James Burbage. Since officials had banned the performance of plays in London, Burbage built his theater in an area called Shoreditch, just outside the London city walls. Some of Shakespeare's earliest plays were first performed here, including *The Tragedy of Romeo and Juliet*, which probably starred James Burbage's son, Richard, as Romeo. 2

When the lease on the Theatre expired, Richard Burbage, in charge of the company after his father died, decided to move the company to Southwark (suth′ərk), just across the River Thames from London proper. The Shoreditch landlord had been causing problems, and Southwark was emerging as a popular theater district. Using timbers from the old theater building, Burbage had a new theater built, bigger and better than the one before. It opened in 1599 and was called the Globe. Under that name it would become the most famous theater in the history of the English stage, for many more of Shakespeare's plays were first performed there.

During Shakespeare's day, acting companies were entirely male. Women did not perform because it was considered improper. The roles of women were usually played by boys of about eleven or twelve—that is, before their voices changed.

3 ◀ This photograph of the reconstructed Globe Theatre was made with a special lens. It shows the pit, where the groundlings stood to watch the show, as well as the sheltered galleries.

Differentiated Instruction for Universal Access

Culturally Responsive Instruction

Culture Focus Point out to students that the writing and performance of drama involve culturally based traditions. Discuss with students various dramatic traditions with which they are familiar. Begin by comparing and contrasting the elements of Shakespearean drama with those of plays performed in North America today. Then, elicit students' prior knowledge about different dramatic traditions from around the world. Ask the following questions:

- What do the stage, sets, and lighting look like?
- Is live music traditionally played?
- What are the costumes like?
- Do the actors use many props?
- How long do performances last?
- What are the actors' age ranges and genders?
- What are some common dramatic themes?
- What is the audience's role in the performance? How does the audience show its appreciation?
- Do plays serve a ritual purpose? If so, what?

Theater Layout No floor plans of the Theatre or the Globe survive, but people's descriptions and sketches of similar buildings suggest what they were like. They were either round or octagonal, with a central stage open to the sky. This stage stretched out into an area called the pit, where theatergoers called groundlings paid just a penny to stand and watch the play. The enclosure surrounding this open area consisted of two or three galleries, or tiers. The galleries accommodated audience members who paid more to watch the play while under shelter from the elements, and with some distance from the groundlings. The galleries probably also included a few elegant box seats where members of the nobility could both watch the play and be seen by the masses.

Staging the Play The enclosure directly behind the stage was used not for seating but for staging the play. Actors entered and left the stage from doors at stage level. The stage also had a trap door through which mysterious characters, such as ghosts or witches, could disappear suddenly. Some space above the backstage area was used for storage or dressing rooms. The first gallery, however, was visible to the audience and used as a second stage. It would have been on a second stage like this that the famous balcony scene in *Romeo and Juliet* was performed.

These open-air theaters did not use artificial light. Instead, performances took place in the afternoon, when it was still light outside. There was also no scenery in the theaters of Shakespeare's day. Instead, the setting for each scene was communicated through dialogue. With no need for set changes, scenes could follow one another in rapid succession. Special effects were simple—smoke might billow at the disappearance of a ghost, for example. By contrast, costumes were often elaborate. The result was a fast-paced, colorful production that lasted about two hours.

The Blackfriars In 1609, Shakespeare's acting company began staging plays in the Blackfriars Theatre as well as the Globe. Located in London proper, the Blackfriars was different from the earlier theaters in which Shakespeare's plays were performed. It was an indoor space with no open area for groundlings. Instead, it relied entirely on a wealthier clientele. It was also one of the first English theaters to use artificial lighting, an innovation that allowed for nighttime performances.

The Globe Theatre ❹

The three-story structure, open to the air, could house as many as 3,000 people in the pit and surrounding galleries.

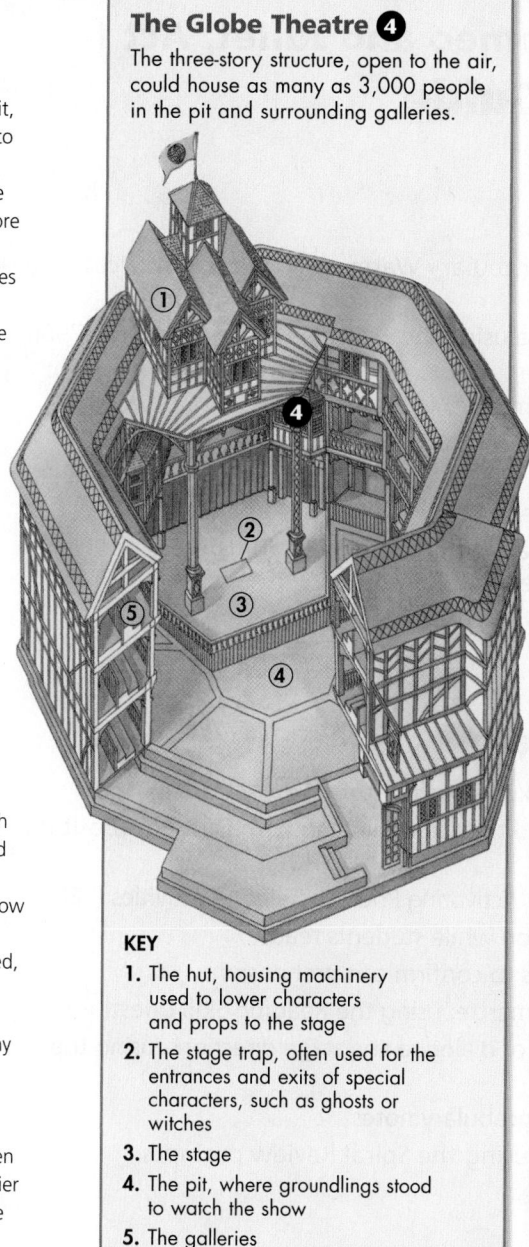

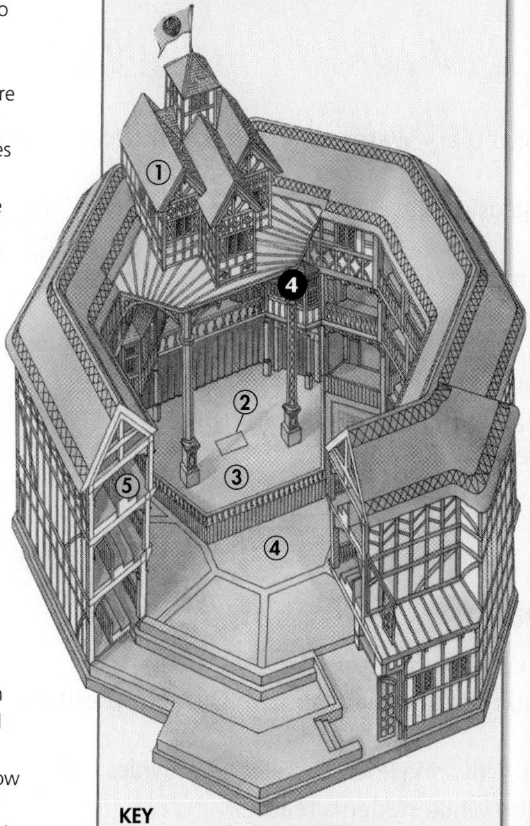

KEY

1. The hut, housing machinery used to lower characters and props to the stage
2. The stage trap, often used for the entrances and exits of special characters, such as ghosts or witches
3. The stage
4. The pit, where groundlings stood to watch the show
5. The galleries

Critical Viewing

❸ Viewing the Photograph

1. Draw students' attention to the photograph at the bottom of page 798. Explain that this reconstruction of the Globe Theatre is in London, near the site of the original building, and was completed in 1993.
2. **Ask:** How do you imagine going to a play in the modern Globe Theatre would be different from attending a performance in 1600?

   Sample responses: Elizabethan performances would have been crowded, noisy, and smelly. A modern audience would have been cleaner, quieter, and generally more respectful. Unlike modern audiences, Elizabethans ate and drank during a production. You might hear the actors better during a production today, but an Elizabethan performance would likely have been a more vivid experience.

❹ Viewing the Diagram

3. Ask students to study the diagram of the Globe Theatre. Invite them to point out major differences between this Elizabethan theater and a typical theater of today.
4. **Ask:** What might be the pros of attending a play by Shakespeare in a theater like the Globe? What might be the cons?

   Sample responses: *Pros:* Shakespeare intended his plays to be performed in this type of theater. The audience is always close to the action. As a groundling, you can move around to see the performance from several angles. The Globe is less formal and stuffy than a modern theater. *Cons:* You sit on hard benches or stand. Groundlings get wet in the rain. There is no heating or air conditioning. Special effects are limited.

Vocabulary Development

CCSS Language 6

Vocabulary of the Theater

Ask students to examine the items in the Key under the diagram of the Globe Theatre. Invite them to list words that have specific theatrical meanings (*hut, props, trap, pit, groundlings*). Point out that people involved in the theater today have a vocabulary of their own. Some of the terms are relevant to Shakespeare's theater; others are more modern. Write the following words on the board. Ask pairs of students to look up their theatrical definitions. Challenge students to identify which words might apply to productions in Shakespeare's Globe Theatre.

- arena: a stage surrounded by seats (no)
- black box: a small black room used as a theater (no)
- downstage: the part of the stage nearest the audience (yes)
- flat: a wall used for scenery (no)
- house: part of the theater used by the audience (yes)
- proscenium: a stage framed by an arch with the audience on one side (no)
- wings: offstage areas to the sides of the stage (no)

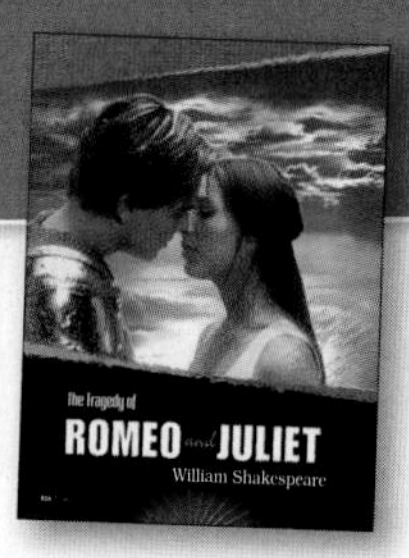

✓ The Tragedy of Romeo and Juliet, Act I
Lesson Pacing Guide

DAY 1 Preteach

- Administer the Reading and Vocabulary Warm-ups (*Unit 5 Resources*, pp. 23–26) as necessary.
- Build background and knowledge using the Extended Study (pp. 798A–798B, 798–799, 800–805).
- Introduce the Reading Skill: Summarize.
- Introduce the Literary Analysis concept: Dialogue and Stage Directions.
- Distribute copies of the appropriate graphic organizer for the Reading Skill (*Graphic Organizer Transparencies*, pp. 147–148).
- Distribute copies of the appropriate graphic organizer for Literary Analysis (*Graphic Organizer Transparencies*, pp. 149–150).
- Teach the selection vocabulary.
- Introduce the Word Study skill.

DAYS 2–3 Preteach/Teach

- Build background with the Background feature.
- Develop thematic vocabulary and thematic thinking with Writing About the Big Question.
- Prepare students to read with the Activating Prior Knowledge activities (TE).
- Informally monitor comprehension while students read.
- Use the Reading Check questions to confirm comprehension.
- Develop students' ability to summarize, using the Reading Skill questions.
- Develop students' understanding of dialogue and stage directions, using the Literary Analysis questions.
- Reinforce vocabulary with the Vocabulary notes.
- Reinforce unit focus standards using the Spiral Review prompts.

DAY 4 Assess

- Assess students' comprehension and mastery of the skills by having them answer the Critical Thinking, Reading Skill, and Literary Analysis questions.
- Have students complete the Vocabulary Practice activities.
- Have students complete the Word Study activities.

DAY 5 Extend/Assess

- Extend learning by having students complete the Speaking and Listening activity, a staged performance, p. 934. As an alternative, assign them "What Is Love?" in *Reality Central*.
- Administer Selection Test A or B (*Unit 5 Resources*, pp. 35–40).

Common Core State Standards

Reading Literature 2. Provide an objective summary of the text.
3. Analyze how complex characters (e.g., those with multiple or conflicting motivations) develop over the course of a text, interact with other characters, and advance the plot or develop the theme.
5. Analyze how an author's choices concerning how to structure a text, order events within it, and manipulate time create such effects as mystery, tension, or surprise.

Writing 1. Write arguments to support claims in an analysis of substantive topics or texts, using valid reasoning and relevant and sufficient evidence.
4. Produce clear and coherent writing in which the development, organization, and style are appropriate to task, purpose, and audience.
7. Conduct short as well as more sustained research projects to answer a question or solve a problem.

Speaking and Listening 1. Initiate and participate effectively in a range of collaborative discussions.
4. Present information, findings, and supporting evidence clearly, concisely, and logically such that listeners can follow the line of reasoning.

Language 1. Demonstrate command of the conventions of standard English grammar and usage when writing or speaking.

Additional Standards Practice
***Common Core Companion*, pp. 28–29**

Daily Block Scheduling
Each day in this Lesson Pacing Guide represents a 40–50 minute period. Teachers using block scheduling may combine days to revise pacing. In addition, teachers may differentiate and support core instruction by integrating components for extended and intensive support as students require. See the Guide to Selected Leveled Resources (facing page).

Guide to Selected Leveled Resources

RTI Tier 1 (students performing on level)			The Tragedy of Romeo and Juliet, Act I
Warm Up	Whole class instruction; Group work	**Practice, model,** and **monitor** fluency, working **with the whole class** or **in groups.**	**Vocabulary** and **Reading Warm-ups B,** ***Unit 5 Resources,*** pp. 23–24, 26
Comprehension/Skills	Whole class instruction; Independent work	**Support** and **monitor** comprehension and skills development, having students complete the activities, graphic organizers, and interactive prompts **independently** or **as a class.**	• ***Reader's Notebook,*** adapted instruction and full selection EL ***Reader's Notebook: English Learner's Version,*** adapted instruction and adapted selection • **Reading Skill Graphic Organizer B,** ***Graphic Organizer Transparencies,*** p. 148 • **Literary Analysis Graphic Organizer B,** ***Graphic Organizer Transparencies,*** p. 150
Monitor Progress	A	**Monitor** student progress with the differentiated curriculum-based assessment in the *Unit Resources.*	• **Selection Test B,** ***Unit 5 Resources,*** pp. 38–40 • **Open-Book Test,** ***Unit 5 Resources,*** pp. 32–34

RTI Tier 2 (students requiring intervention)			The Tragedy of Romeo and Juliet, Act I
Warm Up	Whole class instruction; Group work	**Practice, model,** and **monitor** fluency **in groups** or **with individuals.**	• **Vocabulary and Reading Warm-ups A,** ***Unit 5 Resources,*** pp. 23–26 • ***Reality Central,*** "What Is Love?" • ***Hear It!*** **Audio CD (adapted text)**
Comprehension/Skills	Whole class instruction; Independent work	• **Support** and **monitor** comprehension and skills development, working **in small groups** or **with individuals.** • **Pair** students with more advanced peers and have them complete the writing activity in the *Real-World Writing Journal.* • As students complete the selection in the appropriate version of the *Reader's Notebook,* **monitor** comprehension frequently with group questions and individual instruction. • **Model** strategies while guiding students in completing the activities and prompts in the *Reader's Notebook,* as well as the graphic organizers. • **Practice** skills and **monitor** mastery with the *Reading Kit* worksheets.	• ***Real-World Writing Journal,*** Lesson 1, pp. 138–141 • ***Reader's Notebook: Adapted Version,*** adapted instruction and adapted selection EL ***Reader's Notebook: English Learner's Version,*** adapted instruction and adapted selection • **Reading Skill Graphic Organizer A,** ***Graphic Organizer Transparencies,*** p. 147 • **Literary Analysis Graphic Organizer A,** ***Graphic Organizer Transparencies,*** p. 149 • **Reading Kit,** Practice worksheets, pp. 202, 214, 218
Monitor Progress	A	**Monitor** student progress with the differentiated curriculum-based assessment in the *Unit Resources* and in the *Reading Kit.*	• **Selection Test A,** ***Unit 5 Resources,*** pp. 35–37 • **Reading Kit,** Assess worksheets pp. 203, 215, 219

TIER 3 Tier 3 intervention may require consultation with the student's special-education or dyslexia specialist. For additional support, see the Tier 2 activities and resources listed above.

One-on-one teaching **Group work** **Whole class instruction** **Independent work** **A Assessment**

For a complete guide to selection support, including support for Advanced students, see the Overview of Resources in the frontmatter.

✓ The Tragedy of Romeo and Juliet, Act I

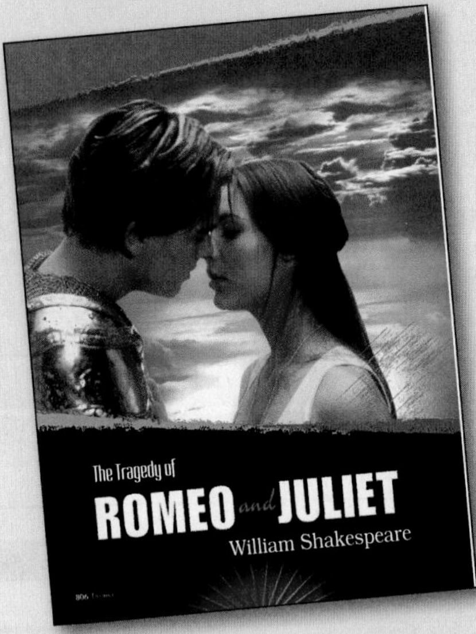

RESOURCES FOR:

- L1 Special-Needs Students
- L2 Below-Level Students (Tier 2)
- L3 On-Level Students (Tier 1)
- L4 Advanced Students (Tier 1)
- EL English Learners
- All All Students

Vocabulary/Fluency/Prior Knowledge

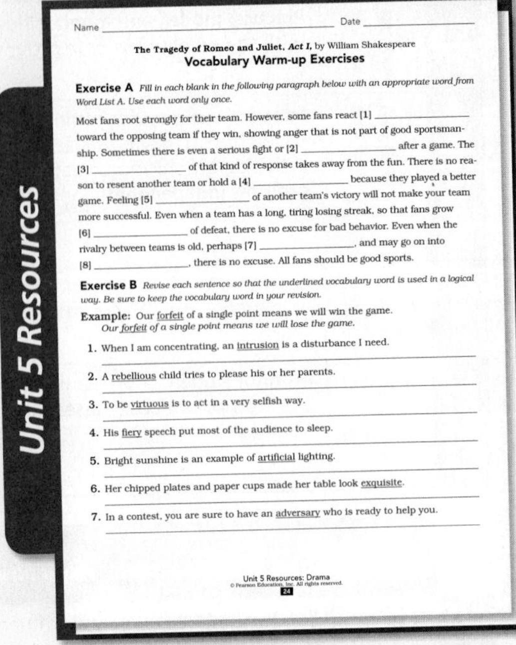

Name ____________________ Date ____________

The Tragedy of Romeo and Juliet, *Act I,* by William Shakespeare
Vocabulary Warm-up Exercises

Exercise A *Fill in each blank in the following paragraph below with an appropriate word from Word List A. Use each word only once.*

Most fans root strongly for their team. However, some fans react [1] ____________ toward the opposing team if they win, showing anger that is not part of good sportsmanship. Sometimes there is even a serious fight or [2] ____________ after a game. The [3] ____________ of that kind of response takes away from the fun. There is no reason to resent another team or hold a [4] ____________ because they played a better game. Feeling [5] ____________ of another team's victory will not make your team more successful. Even when a team has a long, tiring losing streak, so that fans grow [6] ____________ of defeat, there is no excuse for bad behavior. Even when the rivalry between teams is old, perhaps [7] ____________, and may go on into [8] ____________, there is no excuse. All fans should be good sports.

Exercise B *Revise each sentence so that the underlined vocabulary word is used in a logical way. Be sure to keep the vocabulary word in your revision.*

Example: Our forfeit of a single point means we will win the game.
Our forfeit of a single point means we will lose the game.

1. When I am concentrating, an intrusion is a disturbance I need.
2. A rebellious child tries to please his or her parents.
3. To be virtuous is to act in a very selfish way.
4. His fiery speech put most of the audience to sleep.
5. Bright sunshine is an example of artificial lighting.
6. Her chipped plates and paper cups made her table look exquisite.
7. In a contest, you are sure to have an adversary who is ready to help you.

Unit 5 Resources: Drama
© Pearson Education, Inc. All rights reserved.
24

EL L1 L2 **Vocabulary Warm-ups A and B,** pp. 23–24

Also available for this selection:

EL L1 L2 **Reading Warm-ups A and B,** pp. 25–26

All **Writing About the Big Question,** p. 27

All **Vocabulary Builder,** p. 30

L2 L3 ***Reader's Notebook***

L1 ***Reader's Notebook: Adapted Version***

EL ***Reader's Notebook: English Learner's Version***

EL ***Reader's Notebook: Spanish Version***

Reader's Notebooks

Pre- and postreading pages, as well as the selection *The Tragedy of Romeo and Juliet,* Act I, appear in an interactive format in the *Reader's Notebooks*. Each *Notebook* is differentiated for a different group of learners. The selections in the Adapted and English Learner's versions are abridged.

Common Core Companion

Additional instruction and practice for each Common Core State Standard

Selection Support

The Tragedy of Romeo and Juliet, **Act I** by William Shakespeare

Before You Read A: Reading—Summarizing

Act I

Scene	Summary of Action
Prologue	Chorus gives overview of play.
i	Servants of Montagues and Capulets fight. Prince warns families. Romeo is lovesick.
ii	
iii	
iv	
v	

Graphic Organizer Transparencies

147

Graphic Organizer Transparencies

EL L1 L2 Reading: Graphic Organizer A, p. 147 (partially filled in)

Also available for this selection:

- **EL L3 Reading: Graphic Organizer B,** p. 148
- **EL L1 L2 Literary Analysis: Graphic Organizer A,** p. 149 (partially filled in)
- **EL L3 Literary Analysis: Graphic Organizer B,** p. 150

Skills Development/Extension

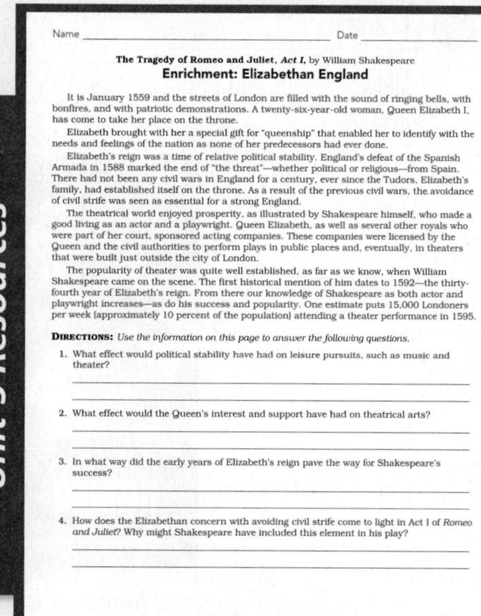
Name ______________________ Date ____________

The Tragedy of Romeo and Juliet, *Act I,* by William Shakespeare

Enrichment: Elizabethan England

It is January 1559 and the streets of London are filled with the sound of ringing bells, with bonfires, and with patriotic demonstrations. A twenty-six-year-old woman, Queen Elizabeth I, has come to take her place on the throne.

Elizabeth brought with her a special gift for "queenship" that enabled her to identify with the needs and feelings of the nation as none of her predecessors had ever done.

Elizabeth's reign was a time of relative political stability. England's defeat of the Spanish Armada in 1588 marked the end of "the threat"—whether political or religious—from Spain. There had not been any civil wars in England for a century, ever since the Tudors, Elizabeth's family, had established itself on the throne. As a result of the previous civil wars, the avoidance of civil strife was seen as essential for a strong England.

The theatrical world enjoyed prosperity, as illustrated by Shakespeare himself, who made a good living as an actor and a playwright. Queen Elizabeth, as well as several other royals who were part of her court, sponsored acting companies. These companies were licensed by the Queen and the civil authorities to perform plays in public places and, eventually, in theaters that were built just outside the city of London.

The popularity of theater was quite well established, as far as we know, when William Shakespeare came on the scene. The first historical mention of him dates to 1592—the thirty-fourth year of Elizabeth's reign. From there our knowledge of Shakespeare as both actor and playwright increases—as do his success and popularity. One estimate puts 15,000 Londoners per week (approximately 10 percent of the population) attending a theater performance in 1595.

Directions: *Use the information on this page to answer the following questions.*

1. What effect would political stability have had on leisure pursuits, such as music and theater?
2. What effect would the Queen's interest and support have had on theatrical arts?
3. In what way did the early years of Elizabeth's reign pave the way for Shakespeare's success?
4. How does the Elizabethan concern with avoiding civil strife come to light in Act I of *Romeo and Juliet*? Why might Shakespeare have included this element in his play?

Unit 5 Resources: Drama

31

Unit 5 Resources

All Enrichment, p. 31

Also available for this selection:

- **All Reading: Summarize,** p. 29
- **L4 Literary Analysis: Dialogue and Stage Directions,** p. 28
- **EL L3 L4 Grammar,** p. 104
- **EL L3 L4 Support for Writing,** p. 105
- **L3 L4 Support for Extend Your Learning,** pp. 106, 107

Assessment

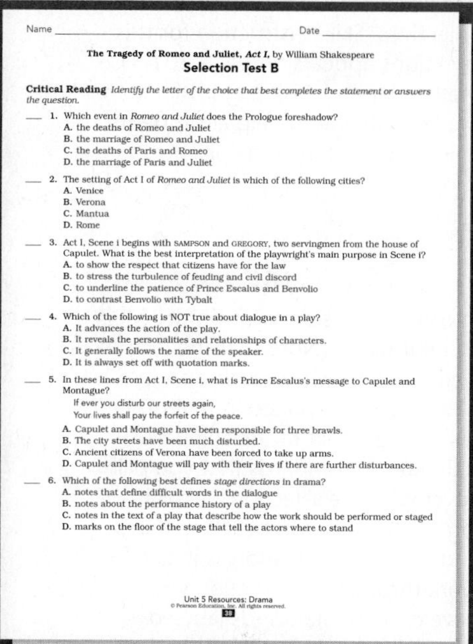
Name ______________________ Date ____________

The Tragedy of Romeo and Juliet, *Act I,* by William Shakespeare

Selection Test B

Critical Reading *Identify the letter of the choice that best completes the statement or answers the question.*

___ 1. Which event in *Romeo and Juliet* does the Prologue foreshadow?
A. the deaths of Romeo and Juliet
B. the marriage of Romeo and Juliet
C. the deaths of Paris and Romeo
D. the marriage of Paris and Juliet

___ 2. The setting of Act I of *Romeo and Juliet* is which of the following cities?
A. Venice
B. Verona
C. Mantua
D. Rome

___ 3. Act I, Scene i begins with SAMPSON and GREGORY, two servingmen from the house of Capulet. What is the best interpretation of the playwright's main purpose in Scene i?
A. to show the respect that citizens have for the law
B. to stress the turbulence of feuding and civil discord
C. to underline the patience of Prince Escalus and Benvolio
D. to contrast Benvolio with Tybalt

___ 4. Which of the following is NOT true about dialogue in a play?
A. It advances the action of the play.
B. It reveals the personalities and relationships of characters.
C. It generally follows the name of the speaker.
D. It is always set off with quotation marks.

___ 5. In these lines from Act I, Scene i, what is Prince Escalus's message to Capulet and Montague?
If ever you disturb our streets again,
Your lives shall pay the forfeit of the peace.
A. Capulet and Montague have been responsible for three brawls.
B. The city streets have been much disturbed.
C. Ancient citizens of Verona have been forced to take up arms.
D. Capulet and Montague will pay with their lives if there are further disturbances.

___ 6. Which of the following best defines *stage directions* in drama?
A. notes that define difficult words in the dialogue
B. notes about the performance history of a play
C. notes in the text of a play that describe how the work should be performed or staged
D. marks on the floor of the stage that tell the actors where to stand

Unit 5 Resources: Drama

38

EL L3 L4 Selection Test B, pp. 38–40

Also available for this selection:

- **L3 L4 Open-Book Test,** pp. 32–34
- **EL L3 L4 Selection Test A,** pp. 35–37

PHLit Online!
www.PHLitOnline.com

- complete narrated selection text
- a thematically related video with writing prompt
- an interactive graphic organizer
- highlighting feature
- access to all student print resources, adapted to individual student needs
- Spanish and English summaries
- adapted selection translations in Spanish

Online Resources: All print materials are also available online.

Background Video

Also available:

Get Connected! (thematic video with writing prompt)

All videos are available in Spanish.

Vocabulary Central (tools, activities, and songs for studying vocabulary)

Also available:

Writer's Journal (with graphics feature)

Drama

You may use *The Tragedy of Romeo and Juliet,* Act I to meet the lesson objectives. Skills instruction for this selections appears on page 801. Use the Reader and Task Suggestions on the facing page to help all students read text of increasing complexity.

1 Introducing the CCS Standards

Introduce the standards on the student page. (Note that the lesson element with which each standard is addressed is identified in parentheses after the text of the standard.) Call out the standards that you will cover with the selections, explaining to students what each requires and how they will address it as they work through the selection you have chosen. Standards labeled "Spiral Review" are introduced in the Literary Analysis Workshop for this unit.

Before You Read — The Tragedy of Romeo and Juliet, Act I

Drama

Build your skills and improve your comprehension of drama with this selection.

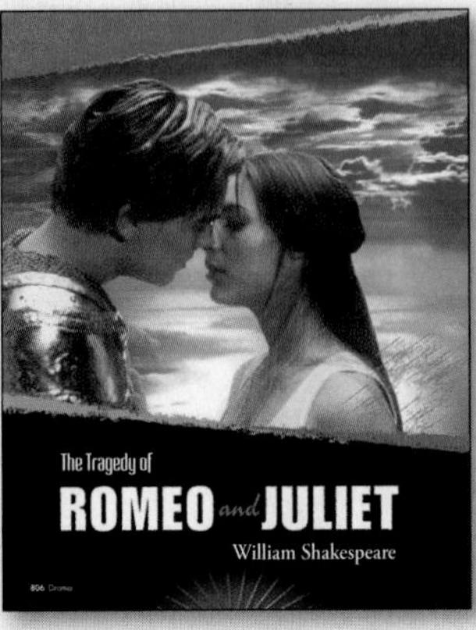

Read ***Romeo and Juliet*** to learn about the tragedy of a passionate love torn apart by conflict.

1 Common Core State Standards

Meet these standards with ***The Tragedy of Romeo and Juliet,* Act I** (p. 806).

Reading Literature

2. Provide an objective summary of the text. *(Reading: Summarize)*

3. Analyze how complex characters develop over the course of a text. *(Literary Analysis: Spiral Review)*

5. Analyze how an author's choices concerning how to structure a text, order events within it, and manipulate time create such effects as mystery, tension, or surprise. *(Literary Analysis: Dialogue and Stage Directions)*

Writing

1. Write arguments to support claims in an analysis of substantive topics or texts, using valid reasoning and relevant and sufficient evidence. *(Writing: Persuasive Letter)*

4. Produce clear and coherent writing in which the development, organization, and style are appropriate to task, purpose, and audience. *(Writing: Editorial)*

7. Conduct short as well as more sustained research projects to answer a question or solve a problem. *(Research and Technology: Annotated Flowchart; Multimedia Presentation)*

Speaking and Listening

1. Initiate and participate effectively in a range of collaborative discussions.

4. Present information, findings, and supporting evidence clearly, concisely, and logically such that listeners can follow the line of reasoning. *(Research and Technology: Annotated Flowchart; Multimedia Presentation)*

Language

1. Demonstrate command of the conventions of standard English grammar and usage when writing or speaking. *(Conventions: Participles and Participial Phrases, Gerunds and Gerund Phrases)*

Text Complexity Rubric

The Tragedy of Romeo and Juliet, Act I		
Qualitative Measures	**Context/ Knowledge Demands**	Historical: Verona, Italy 1 2 3 4 (5)
	Structure/ Language Clarity and Conventionality	Challenging vocabulary; Elizabethan terms 1 2 3 4 (5)
	Levels of Meaning/ Purpose/Concept Level	Accessible concept (classic tale of star-crossed lovers) 1 2 (3) 4 5
Quantitative Measures	**Text Length**	Word Count: 6,105
	Lexile	NP
Overall Complexity		**Complex**

2 Literary Analysis: Dialogue and Stage Directions

Dialogue is conversation between characters. In prose, dialogue is usually set off with quotation marks. In drama, it generally follows the name of the speaker, as in this example:

> **BENVOLIO.** My noble uncle, do you know the cause?
> **MONTAGUE.** I neither know it nor can learn of him.

Dialogue reveals the personalities and relationships of the characters and advances the action of the play. Dialogue captures the language of the time in which a play is set. As you read, note the words characters use to express themselves.

Stage directions are notes in a play that describe how the work should be performed, or staged. They describe scenes, lighting, sound effects, and character actions. They are usually set in italics and are sometimes set off in brackets or parentheses, as in this example:

> ***Scene iii.*** FRIAR LAWRENCE's cell.
> [*Enter* FRIAR LAWRENCE *alone, with a basket.*]

As you read, notice how the dialogue and stage directions work together to help you "see" and "hear" the play in your mind.

3 Reading Skill: Summarize

Summarizing is briefly stating the main ideas in a piece of writing. Pausing to summarize as you read helps you check your comprehension before you read further. To be sure that you understand Shakespeare's language before you summarize, **use text aids**—the numbered explanations that appear with the text.

- If you are confused by a passage, check to see if there is a footnote or side note and read the corresponding explanation.
- **Reread** the passage, using the information from the note to be sure you grasp the meaning of the passage.

4 Using the Strategy: Summarizing Chart

As you read, use a chart like this one to summarize each scene.

Act I	
Scene	Summary of Action

PREteach

2 Literary Analysis

Dialogue and Stage Directions

1. Introduce the skill, using instruction on the student page.
2. Tell students that they will practice analyzing dialogue and stage directions as they read.

Think Aloud: Model the Skill

Write the following on the board:

> **Benvolio.** My noble uncle, do you know the cause?
> **Montague.** I neither know it nor can learn of him.

Model the skill of analyzing dialogue and stage directions. Say to students:

> In this dialogue, I first notice that the characters speak in antiquated English. The play must take place a century ago or more.

3 Reading Skill

Summarize

1. Introduce the skill, using instruction on the student page.
2. Tell students that they will practice summarizing as they read.

4 Using the Strategy

Give students a copy of either **Reading Skill Graphic Organizer A** or **B** (*Graphic Organizer Transparencies,* pp. 147–148) to record details as they read. Use the examples in **Reading Skill Graphic Organizer A,** which is partially filled in, to model completing the organizer.

Text Complexity: Reader and Task Suggestions

The Tragedy of Romeo and Juliet, Act I

Preparing to Read the Text	Leveled Tasks
• Use the Background information on TE pp. 802–803 to discuss Shakespearean drama. • Discuss the basic plot of the play and other stories of star-crossed lovers that students may have read or seen. Explain that this play has been retold in different forms, including cartoons *(Lady and the Tramp)* and Broadway musicals *(West Side Story).* • Guide students to use Multidraft Reading strategies (TE p. 805).	***Structure/Language*** If students will have trouble with Shakespeare's complex sentences, have them first read the act and jot down notes on the main events. Then, have them reread and identify sentences and passages that continue to cause them difficulty. Discuss these confusing passages. ***Synthesizing*** If students will not have difficulty with Shakespeare's complex sentences, have them read and note details about the characters, the situation, and the setting. Have them use their notes to contribute to class discussion.

❶ Discuss the Author

1. Point out that political and social power in Shakespeare's day was largely in the hands of a hereditary aristocracy—nobles and knights whose titles had been in their families for generations. Review the bracketed passage with students. Lead them to understand that Shakespeare was not a member of the ruling class.
2. **Ask:** How would you explain the fact that so little was written about Shakespeare during his lifetime?

   Sample response: Farmers, merchants, and playwrights were not considered socially important people during Shakespeare's day.
3. Discuss with students whether a class system can exist without a hereditary aristocracy. Ask them to consider the role of class in American society today.

1. Point out that while little was written about Shakespeare during his lifetime, his professional and financial paper trail allows us to construct a character portrait of him.
2. **Ask:** What adjectives could you use to describe William Shakespeare based on this brief biography?

   Sample responses: energetic; ambitious; gifted; successful; restless; curious; materialistic; shrewd; sociable

William Shakespeare (1564–1616)

SHAKESPEARE'S PLAYS AND POETRY ARE REGARDED AS THE FINEST WORKS EVER WRITTEN IN ENGLISH.

William Shakespeare is revered as England's greatest writer. Four centuries after his death, his plays are still read and performed every single day. Who was this remarkable author of so many masterpieces? In actual fact, we know very little about him.

❶ **From Stratford to London** Shakespeare grew up in Stratford-upon-Avon, a busy market town on the Avon River about seventy-five miles northwest of London. Church and town records indicate that his mother, Mary Arden, was the daughter of a wealthy farmer who owned the land on which Shakespeare's grandfather lived. Shakespeare's father, John, was a prosperous merchant who also served for a time as Stratford's mayor. Shakespeare most likely went to the local grammar school, where he would have studied Latin and Greek as well as English and world history. He would eventually put all those lessons to use in plays about historical figures, such as Julius Caesar and King Henry IV.

In 1582, when he was eighteen, Shakespeare married a woman named Anne Hathaway and with her had three children, including a set of twins. The next decade of his life is shrouded in mystery, but by 1592 he had moved to London, where he gravitated to the theater. Starting off as an actor, he soon began writing plays as well. By 1594 he had become the principal playwright of the Lord Chamberlain's Men, the Burbages' acting company. Some of the early plays Shakespeare wrote at this time include the romantic comedy *The Taming of the Shrew* and the romantic tragedy *The Tragedy of Romeo and Juliet.*

❷ Shakespeare was not just a performer and a playwright, however; he was also part owner of the theater company. This meant that he earned money in three ways—from fees for his plays, from his acting salary, and from his share of the company's profits. Those profits rose substantially after the Lord Chamberlain's Men moved to the Globe Theatre, where as many as 3,000 people might attend a single performance. It was at the Globe that many of Shakespeare's later masterpieces premiered, probably beginning with *The Tragedy of Julius Caesar* in 1599.

Enrichment: Investigating a Literary Biography

The Shakespeare Identity Mystery

There is no doubt that a man named William Shakespeare was born and died in Stratford-upon-Avon, married Anne Hathaway, and had three children. These and other facts about his life are well established. Yet a group of literary scholars and amateur detectives are convinced that this William Shakespeare did not write the famous plays with which his name has long been associated. Their evidence differs, but their central question remains the same: How could a middle-class son of a merchant have been the author of such masterpieces?

Activity: Weighing Evidence Have students conduct research on the possibility that another author was responsible for writing Shakespeare's plays. Invite a panel of students to present the evidence in favor of other authors. Encourage the class to discuss this controversy and to reach some understanding as to why Shakespeare's biography still exerts a fascination.

3 **The King's Players** In 1603 Queen Elizabeth I died, and her Scottish cousin took the throne as James I. Partial to the theater, James was particularly supportive of the Lord Chamberlain's Men, which had emerged as one of the two best acting companies in the land. Not only did it have a brilliant playwright in William Shakespeare, but it also had a fine actor in Richard Burbage, who starred in most of Shakespeare's plays. In 1606, flattered by the king's patronage, the company changed its name to the King's Men. It is believed that Shakespeare wrote his great Scottish play, *The Tragedy of Macbeth*, to appeal particularly to James I.

Three years later, the King's Men began performing at the Blackfriars Theatre, using the Globe only in summer months. By utilizing this indoor theater in winter, the King's Men further increased profits. The company did so well that Shakespeare was soon able to retire. In 1610, he moved back to Stratford-upon-Avon, buying one of the finest homes in town. He died of unknown causes in 1616.

4 Shakespeare Says . . .

Shakespeare's impact on the English language has been enormous. Not only did he coin new words and new meanings for old words, but he also used many expressions that have become part of our everyday speech. Here are just a few examples:

Expression and Source	Meaning
Eat out of house and home *(Henry VI, Part II)*	Eat so much that it makes the provider poor
For ever and a day *(The Taming of the Shrew)*	Indefinitely; with no end in sight
Give the devil his due *(Henry IV, Part I)*	Recognize an opponent's achievement
Greek to me *(Julius Caesar)*	Completely unintelligible to me
Green-eyed monster *(Othello)*	Jealousy
In a pickle *(The Tempest)*	In trouble
In stitches *(Twelfth Night)*	Laughing so hard it hurts
Lay it on with a trowel *(As You Like It)*	Flatter excessively
Makes your hair stand on end *(Hamlet)*	Really frightens you
The milk of human kindness *(Macbeth)*	Compassion
A plague on both your houses *(Romeo and Juliet)*	I'm fed up with both sides (in an argument)
Salad days *(Anthony and Cleopatra)*	Green, or naïve, youth
Star-crossed lovers *(Romeo and Juliet)*	Ill-fated lovers
Wear your heart upon your sleeve *(Othello)*	Show your love to all
Won't budge an inch *(The Taming of the Shrew)*	Will not give in; stands firm

3 The King's Players

Read the bracketed text with students. **Ask:** What caused the King's Men acting company to become so profitable?

Sample responses: King James I became a patron, the company had a brilliant actor and playwright, and they were able to use an indoor theater in winter, increasing attendance.

4 Connect to Language

1. Have the class read through the list of expressions in the table. Point out that while the meanings of these phrases are perfectly ordinary, their power and beauty stem from Shakespeare's use of figurative language. As an example, explain that in the expression "forever and a day" Shakespeare has created a memorable expression by using overstatement to emphasize a period of time that seems to have no end.
2. **Ask:** Why is the expression "green-eyed monster" such a fitting description of jealousy?

   Sample response: Anyone who has experienced jealousy knows that it can become a monstrous obsession. The green eyes serve to emphasize its dangerous and terrifying nature.
3. Model for students a phrase from the table in context. (Example: I tried to persuade her to change her mind, but she wouldn't budge an inch.) Invite students to use other phrases from the table in context.
4. Explain that Shakespeare is more than a phrase maker. Many of the words we still use first appeared in his plays. The *Oxford English Dictionary* credits Shakespeare as the inventor of *bedazzle, fashionable, go-between, lustrous, outbreak, pander, unearthly, vulnerable, well-bred,* and many others.

Vocabulary Development

Shakespeare's Elizabethan Vocabulary

Explain that some of the words common in English 400 years ago are no longer current. Prepare students for reading by introducing these words.

against: for; in preparation for
alack: alas (an exclamation of sorrow)
an, and: if
anon: soon
aye: yes
but: only; except
e'en: even
e'er: ever
haply: perhaps
happy: fortunate
hence: away; from here
hie: hurry
hither: here
marry: indeed
whence: where
wilt: will
withal: in addition; notwithstanding
would: wish

PREETEACH

❶ Writing About the Big Question

1. Review assignment with the class.
2. Have volunteers name reasons why families might engage in a feud.
3. Have students complete the sentence starter. Review responses as a class. (**Possible response:** When family differences stand between two people, it can be destructive because they often make unwise choices.)
4. Remind students that their answers will help them think about the Big Question, "Do our differences define us?"

While You Read

Tell students, as they read, to determine how Romeo and Juliet's family background influences their love.

❷ Vocabulary

1. Have students preview the selection vocabulary.
2. For each word, have students say the word aloud.
3. Then, use the word in a sentence that defines the word.
4. Finally, repeat your definitional sentence or a similar sentence with the word missing and have the class "fill in the blank" chorally. Here are some examples:

   Something pernicious is "extremely harmful." The new student's reputation was ruined because of gossip that was [students say "pernicious"].

   A grievance is a real or imagined wrong. Although the employee returned to work, the union decided to investigate and make a determination regarding his reported [students say "grievance"].

❸ Word Study

1. Introduce the skill, using the instruction in the box.
2. Ask students for a *trans-* word that means "to carry or move across, over, or through." (**Answer:** *transport*)

Making Connections

The Tragedy of Romeo and Juliet, Act 1

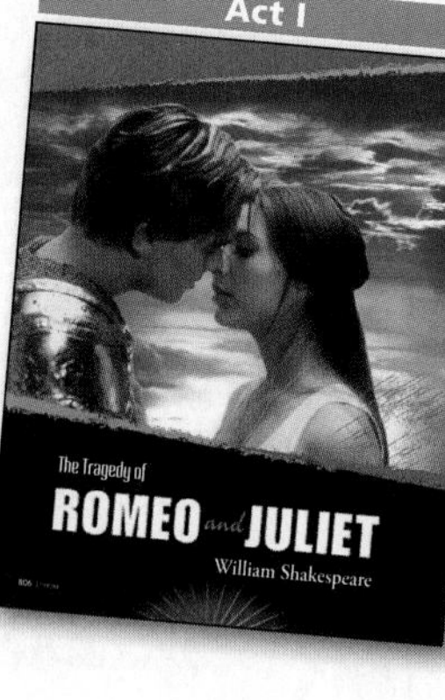

❶ Writing About the Big Question

In *The Tragedy of Romeo and Juliet,* two young people from families locked in a deadly feud fall in love. That difference defines their relationship and forces the plot toward tragic consequences. Use this sentence starter to develop your ideas about the Big Question.

When family **differences** stand between two people, it can be destructive because ______________.

While You Read Look for ways in which family background influences the love between Romeo and Juliet.

❷ Vocabulary

Read each word and its definition. Decide whether you know the word well, know it a little bit, or do not know it at all. After you read, see how your knowledge of each word has increased.

- **pernicious** (pər nish′ əs) *adj.* causing great injury or ruin (p. 811) ***The spy's activities had a pernicious effect on the top-secret project.*** *perniciously adv.*
- **adversary** (ad′ vər ser′ ē) *n.* a person who opposes or fights against another (p. 811) ***Standing tall and trying to look brave, Pam faced her adversary in fencing.*** *adverse adj. adversarial adj.*
- **augmenting** (ôg ment′ iŋ) *v.* increasing; enlarging (p. 812) ***With small deposits each week, our family is augmenting its savings.*** *augmentable adj. augmentation n.*
- **grievance** (grēv′ əns) *n.* injustice; complaint (p. 813) ***The board investigated the worker's grievance against his supervisor.***
- **oppression** (ə presh′ ən) *n.* feeling of being weighed down with worries or problems (p. 813) ***He could not pay all of his bills, and this caused a feeling of oppression.*** *oppress v. oppressive adj.*
- **transgression** (trans gresh′ ən) *n.* wrong-doing; sin (p. 813) ***Stealing from the poor is a transgression against humanity.*** *transgress v. transgressor n.*

❸

Word Study

The **Latin prefix *trans-*** means "across," "over," or "through."

In the play, Romeo describes his friend's sympathy for him as love's **transgression.** The word suggests that love has crossed a boundary and unfairly involved his friend.

Vocabulary Development

Vocabulary Knowledge Rating

Create a **Vocabulary Knowledge Rating Chart** (***Professional Development Guidebook,*** p. 33) for this selection. Include the selection vocabulary and the Big Question word that appears in the Writing About the Big Question sentence starter on this page. (The Big Question vocabulary is introduced on pp. 778–779.)

Give students a copy of the chart. Read the words aloud, and have students mark their rating in the Before Reading column. Urge them to be alert to these words as they read and discuss the selection.

Tally how many students think they know a word to gauge how much instruction to provide. As students read and discuss the selection, point out the words and their context.

Vocabulary Central, featuring tools, activities, and songs for studying vocabulary, is available at **www.PHLitOnline.com.**

❹ Background for the Play

Star-Crossed Lovers

Written in 1594 or 1595, when Shakespeare was still a fairly young man, *The Tragedy of Romeo and Juliet* is a play about young love. The basic plot is simple: Two teenagers from feuding families fall in love and marry against their families' wishes, with tragic results. The story is set in Verona, Italy, and is based on an Italian legend that was fairly well known in England at the time.

Shakespeare's Sources Elizabethan writers deeply respected Italy as the birthplace of the Renaissance and often drew on Italian sources for inspiration. In 1562, an English poet named Arthur Brooke wrote *The Tragicall History of Romeus and Juliet*, a long narrative poem based on the Romeo and Juliet legend. Three years later, a prose version of the legend also appeared in England. Scholars believe, however, that Brooke's poem was Shakespeare's chief source.

That poem contains a great deal of moralizing, stressing the disobedience of the young lovers, along with fate, as the cause of their doom. Shakespeare's portrayal of the young lovers is more sympathetic, but he does stress the strong role that fate plays in their tragedy. In fact, at the very start of the play, the Chorus describes Romeo and Juliet as "star-crossed lovers," indicating that their tragic ending is written in the stars, or fated by forces beyond their control.

The Play Through the Centuries Of all the love stories ever written, *The Tragedy of Romeo and Juliet* may well be the most famous. Acting celebrities down through the centuries have played the leading roles—Edwin Booth and Ellen Terry in the nineteenth century, for example, and John Gielgud and Judi Dench in the twentieth. There have been dozens of film versions of the play, numerous works of art depicting its scenes, over twenty operatic versions, a famous ballet version by Prokofiev, and an equally famous musical overture by Tchaikovsky. The play is often adapted to reflect the concerns of different eras: *West Side Story*, for example, adapts the story as a musical set amid the ethnic rivalries of 1950s New York City; *Romanoff and Juliet* is a comedy of the Cold War set during the 1960s. One of the most recent popular adaptations was the 1996 film *Romeo + Juliet* starring Leonardo di Caprio and Claire Danes, which sets the play in Verona Beach, California.

Elizabethan Language

English has changed a great deal since Shakespeare's time. Some of the words he uses are now archaic, or outdated. For instance, Shakespeare uses *anon* for "soon" and *haply* for "perhaps." He also uses outdated grammatical forms, such as the pronouns *thou, thee, thy*, and *thine* instead of *you, your*, and *yours*. In addition, Shakespeare's verbs often have archaic endings: *cometh* for "come," for example, and *dost* for "do." Word order, too, is sometimes different from modern English, especially in questions. For instance, instead of "What do you say?" Shakespeare writes, "What say you?" The numbered marginal notes that accompany the text of the play will help you with the unfamiliar language.

Daily Bellringer

For each class during which you will teach this selection, have students complete one of the activities for Weeks 25–27 in the ***Daily Bellringer Activities*** booklet.

❹ Background

The Tragedy of Romeo and Juliet has been made into a film many times, but teenagers do not often play the two young lovers. Franco Zeffirelli's 1968 film version, which stars Olivia Hussey and Leonard Whiting—fifteen and seventeen years old respectively—is said by critics to come closest to the characters as Shakespeare envisioned them.

Multidraft Reading

This icon ● marks natural pauses in the selection. To assist struggling readers and to deepen reading for all, assign the text in "chunks," following the icons, and apply multidraft reading protocols. For each reading, have students set the purpose indicated:

- **First reading**—identifying key ideas and details and answering any Reading Checks.
- **Second reading**—analyzing craft and structure and responding to the side-column prompts.
- **Third reading**—integrating knowledge and ideas, connecting to other texts and the world, and answering the end-of-selection questions.

For more guidance, refer to the ***Classroom Strategies and Teaching Routines*** card on multidraft reading.

For more about the author, practice with the selection vocabulary, and more background, go to **www.PHLitOnline.com**.

Differentiated Instruction Additional Instruction

EL Extended Support—English Learners
Have students complete the **Reading and Vocabulary Warm-ups, *Unit 5 Resources*,** pp. 23–26, before they read. Assign the prereading pages for the selection in the ***Reader's Notebook: English Learner's Version***. Then, have students listen to portions of the selection on the ***Hear It!* Audio CD**.

L1 L2 Extended Support—Struggling Readers
Have students complete the **Reading and Vocabulary Warm-ups, *Unit 5 Resources*,** pp. 23–26, before they read. Assign the prereading pages for the selection in the ***Reader's Notebook: English Learner's Version***. Then, have students listen to portions of the selection on the ***Hear It!* Audio CD** (adapted text).

Extended Support—Reluctant Readers
To build motivation and engagement before assigning the selection, have students read "What Is Love?" a thematically related selection in ***Reality Central***. Then, use the questions at the conclusion of the related selection to guide discussion.

TEACH

❶ Activating Prior Knowledge

The Tragedy of Romeo and Juliet is probably Shakespeare's most famous play, and possibly the most famous play in all of English literature. Build students' interest by inviting them to share what they know—or think they know—about Romeo and Juliet. After they have read Act I, they can ask themselves: In what ways does the play match my expectations? In what ways does it surprise me?

Concept Connector →

Students will reconsider their ideas after reading the selection.

Small-Group Activity

Have students work in small groups to analyze the Prologue and the conflict that it describes. Then, have them work together to write a news broadcast about the conflict. Have each group work as "co-anchors" for the broadcast.

❷ About the Selection

In *The Tragedy of Romeo and Juliet,* "A pair of star-crossed lovers . . . Doth with their death bury their parents' strife." The Prologue that opens the play tells briefly of the terrible events that mark a tender but tragic love, while the five scenes that follow set these events in motion. We first meet Romeo just after a bitter and long-standing feud between members of his family, the Montagues, and their foes, the Capulets, has erupted into a street brawl. Romeo's kinsman, Benvolio, suggests that they secretly attend a feast being given that night by the Capulets. There, Romeo and Juliet meet for the first time.

❸ Background

Film

The photos that illustrate this play are stills from Australian director Baz Luhrmann's film *Romeo + Juliet,* which was released in 1996. The updated story takes place in Verona Beach—a contemporary city that resembles a cross between Miami and Mexico City—rather than sixteenth-century Verona, Italy. Shakespeare's plot is intact, however. The movie stars Leonardo DiCaprio and Claire Danes.

❶ ❷ ❸

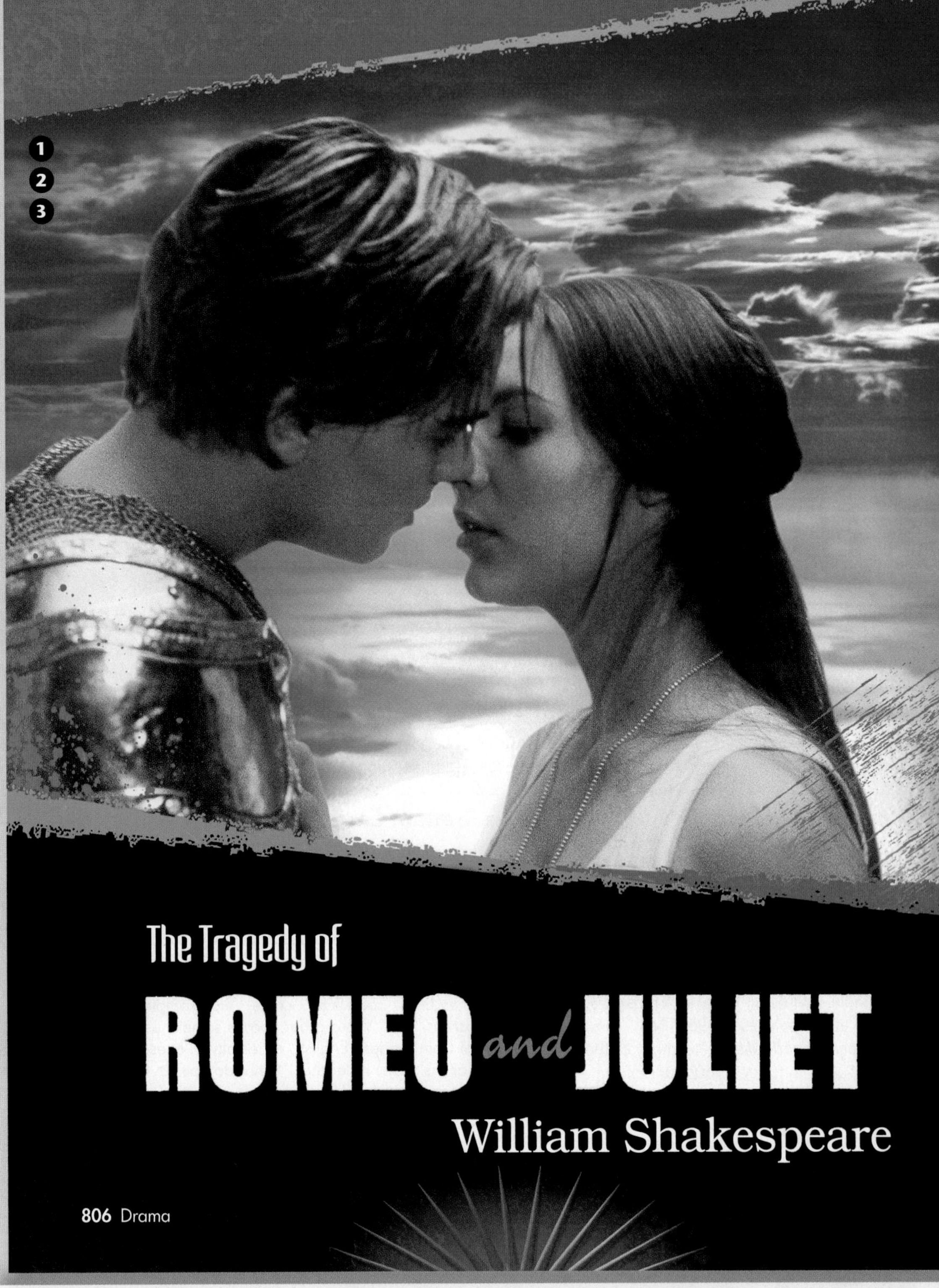

The Tragedy of ROMEO *and* JULIET

William Shakespeare

Vocabulary Development

CCSS Language 6

Thematic Vocabulary: The Big Question

As students are discussing *The Tragedy of Romeo and Juliet,* Act I, encourage them to use the thematic vocabulary presented in Introducing the Big Question, pp. 778–779. You might encourage them with sentence starters like these:

1. The Capulets and the Montagues show their *differences* by . . .
2. In the Prologue, the Chorus provides *background* for . . .
3. Ironically, Capulet and Montague seem to share the *values* of . . .
4. Juliet's attitude toward marriage illustrates her desire to assert her *individuality* because . . .

Characters

CHORUS
ESCALUS, Prince of Verona
PARIS, a young count, kinsman to the Prince
MONTAGUE
CAPULET
AN OLD MAN, of the Capulet family
ROMEO, son to Montague
MERCUTIO, kinsman to the Prince and friend to Romeo
BENVOLIO, nephew to Montague and friend to Romeo
TYBALT, nephew to Lady Capulet
FRIAR LAWRENCE, Franciscan
FRIAR JOHN, Franciscan
BALTHASAR, servant to Romeo
SAMPSON, servant to Capulet
GREGORY, servant to Capulet
PETER, servant to Juliet's nurse
ABRAM, servant to Montague
AN APOTHECARY
THREE MUSICIANS
AN OFFICER
LADY MONTAGUE, wife to Montague
LADY CAPULET, wife to Capulet
JULIET, daughter to Capulet
NURSE TO JULIET
CITIZENS OF VERONA, Gentlemen and Gentlewomen of both houses, Maskers, Torchbearers, Pages, Guards, Watchmen, Servants, and Attendants

Scene: Verona; Mantua

[Enter CHORUS.*]*

CHORUS. Two households, both alike in dignity,[1]
In fair Verona, where we lay our scene,
From ancient grudge break to new mutiny,[2]
Where civil blood makes civil hands unclean.[3]
From forth the fatal loins of these two foes
A pair of star-crossed[4] lovers take their life;
4 Whose misadventured piteous overthrows[5]
Doth with their death bury their parents' strife.
The fearful passage of their death-marked love,
And the continuance of their parents' rage,
Which, but[6] their children's end, naught could remove,
Is now the two hours' traffic[7] of our stage;
The which if you with patient ears attend,
What here shall miss, our toil shall strive to mend.[8] *[Exit.]*

1. **dignity** high social rank.
2. **mutiny** violence.
3. **Where . . . unclean** in which the blood of citizens stains citizens' hands.
4. **star-crossed** ill-fated by the unfavorable positions of the stars.
5. **Whose . . . overthrows** whose unfortunate, sorrowful destruction.
6. **but** except.
7. **two hours' traffic** two hours' business.
8. **What . . . mend** What is not clear in this prologue we actors shall try to clarify in the course of the play.

4 Background

Greek Chorus

The use of a *chorus*—a figure or group of figures who comment on a play's action—goes back to ancient Greek and Roman drama. In Shakespeare's time, it was common for a chorus to deliver a *prologue*—an opening speech that introduces the play's main characters, plot, and setting.

PHLit Online!

This selection is available in interactive format in the **Enriched Online Student Edition, www.PHLitOnline.com,** which includes a thematically related video with writing prompt and an interactive graphic organizer.

Differentiated Instruction for Universal Access

Strategy for Special-Needs Students

To give students a context for the play and to model how to summarize, show them **Reading Skill Graphic Organizer A** (*Graphic Organizer Transparencies,* p. 147). The partially completed graphic organizer will give students insight into the process of summarizing. They can use it as a model for summarizing scenes as they read.

Strategy for Less Proficient Readers

Advise students to use the character list on this page. They may check it whenever they are unsure of a character's identity. As an example, ask them to use the list to find Sampson, Gregory, Juliet, and Capulet. Discuss with students how Gregory and Sampson are connected to Juliet. Point out that Juliet is Capulet's daughter, and the two men are servants who work for Capulet.

5 Critical Thinking

Analyze

1. Have students use the side notes to look up the meanings of footnoted terms in the bracketed passage.
2. **Ask** students what two meanings of the phrase "to carry coals" are used in the exchange between Sampson and Gregory. As a hint, tell them that one usage is literal and one is figurative.

   Answer: Literally, the phrase "carry coals" means "to sell coal," while figuratively the phrase means "to endure insults."
3. **Ask** students what effect this wordplay has on the scene.

   Answer: Students may describe the effect as playful and humorous.

6 Literary Analysis

Dialogue and Stage Directions

1. Remind students that Sampson and Gregory are servants of the Capulets. Have them describe what they learn about Sampson and Gregory in this scene.

   Possible response: Sampson and Gregory are boastful, flippant, insulting, and apparently eager to do battle with Montague's men.
2. **Ask** students the Literary Analysis question: What does this conversation among servants reveal about the Montagues?

   Answer: The conversation reveals that there is great hostility between the Capulets and the Montagues and that both households are large, with numerous servants.

Scene i. Verona. A public place.

[Enter SAMPSON *and* GREGORY, *with swords and bucklers,*[1] *of the house of Capulet.]*

SAMPSON. Gregory, on my word, we'll not carry coals.[2]

GREGORY. No, for then we should be colliers.[3]

SAMPSON. I mean, an we be in choler, we'll draw.[4]

GREGORY. Ay, while you live, draw your neck out of collar.[5]

SAMPSON. I strike quickly, being moved.

GREGORY. But thou art not quickly moved to strike.

SAMPSON. A dog of the house of Montague moves me.

GREGORY. To move is to stir, and to be valiant is to stand. Therefore, if thou art moved, thou run'st away.

SAMPSON. A dog of that house shall move me to stand. I will take the wall[6] of any man or maid of Montague's.

GREGORY. That shows thee a weak slave; for the weakest goes to the wall.

SAMPSON. 'Tis true; and therefore women, being the weaker vessels, are ever thrust to the wall. Therefore I will push Montague's men from the wall and thrust his maids to the wall.

GREGORY. The quarrel is between our masters and us their men.

SAMPSON. Tis all one. I will show myself a tyrant. When I have fought with the men, I will be civil with the maids—I will cut off their heads.

GREGORY. The heads of the maids?

SAMPSON. Ay, the heads of the maids or their maidenheads. Take it in what sense thou wilt.

GREGORY. They must take it in sense that feel it.

1. **bucklers** small shields.
2. **carry coals** endure insults.
3. **colliers** sellers of coal.
4. **an . . . draw** If we are angered, we'll draw our swords.
5. **collar** hangman's noose.
6. **take the wall** assert superiority by walking nearer the houses and therefore farther from the gutter.

Literary Analysis
Dialogue and Stage Directions What does this conversation among servants reveal about the Montagues?

Vocabulary Development

CCSS Language 6

Expressive Vocabulary

To help students broaden their expressive vocabulary, encourage them to use the following words as they discuss the selection: *illustrates, contrast, emphasizes, reinforces,* and *adapt*. Have them complete these sentence starters:

1. The deliberate attempt of Sampson and Gregory to start a fight with the Montagues *illustrates* . . .
2. The main *contrast* between Sampson and Gregory and Abram and Balthasar is . . .
3. The fight between Sampson and Gregory and Abram and Balthasar *emphasizes* . . .
4. The entrance of Benvolio *reinforces* . . .
5. Benvolio would like to *adapt* . . .

Challenge students to use these words as you continue to discuss the play.

SAMPSON. Me they shall feel while I am able to stand; and 'tis known I am a pretty piece of flesh.

GREGORY. Tis well thou art not fish; if thou hadst, thou hadst been Poor John. Draw thy tool![7] Here comes two of the house of Montagues.

[Enter two other Servingmen, ABRAM *and* BALTHASAR.*]*

SAMPSON. My naked weapon is out. Quarrel! I will back thee.

GREGORY. How? Turn thy back and run?

7 **SAMPSON.** Fear me not.

GREGORY. No, marry. I fear thee!

SAMPSON. Let us take the law of our sides;[8] let them begin.

GREGORY. I will frown as I pass by, and let them take it as they list.[9]

SAMPSON. Nay, as they dare. I will bite my thumb[10] at them, which is disgrace to them if they bear it.

ABRAM. Do you bite your thumb at us, sir?

SAMPSON. I do bite my thumb, sir.

ABRAM. Do you bite your thumb at us, sir?

8 **SAMPSON.** *[Aside to* GREGORY*]* Is the law of our side if I say ay?

GREGORY. *[Aside to* SAMPSON*]* No.

SAMPSON. No, sir, I do not bite my thumb at you, sir; but I bite my thumb, sir.

GREGORY. Do you quarrel, sir?

ABRAM. Quarrel, sir? No, sir.

SAMPSON. But if you do, sir, I am for you. I serve as good a man as you.

ABRAM. No better.

SAMPSON. Well, sir.

[Enter BENVOLIO.*]*

GREGORY. *[Aside* to SAMPSON.*]* Say "better." Here comes one of my master's kinsmen.

SAMPSON. Yes, better, sir.

ABRAM. You lie.

7. **tool** weapon.

Reading Skill
Summarize How does footnote 8 help you understand Sampson's logic in line 36?

8. **take . . . sides** make sure the law is on our side.
9. **list** please.
10. **bite . . . thumb** make an insulting gesture.

Literary Analysis
Dialogue and Stage Directions Which words in the stage directions in line 44 clarify that Sampson is not speaking to Abram?

9
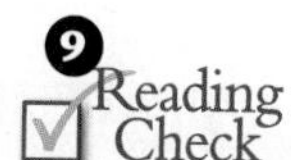
Reading Check
With which family are the quarreling servants affiliated?

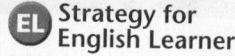

Differentiated Instruction for Universal Access

EL Strategy for English Learners

Students may have difficulty identifying the various factions in this scene.

Students might better understand this scene as they read by making a chart to show the different affiliations as the stage fills up with characters. Column 1 of the chart should be labeled *Capulet,* Column 2 labeled *Montague,* and Column 3, *Other.* As each character enters the stage, have students write the name in the correct column. If students have trouble identifying the affiliation of a character, have them refer to the characters list on p. 807.

Make sure students understand the function or role of each character.

7 Reading Skill
Summarize

1. **Ask** students to identify the play on words used in the first two lines of the bracketed passage.

   Possible response: *Back* is used to mean "back you up" or "support you," as well as the back of a person who is running away in cowardice.

2. **Ask** students the Reading Skill question: How does footnote 8 help you understand Sampson's logic in line 36?

   Answer: The footnote says that the phrase "take the law of our sides" means "make sure the law is on our side." Sampson's logic is to let the other side begin the fight because that will keep the law on Sampson and Gregory's side. When officials come to break up the fight, they will be harsher on those who actually started it.

8 Literary Analysis
Dialogue and Stage Directions

1. Have students review lines 32 through 43. **Ask** who is present on the stage at line 43.

   Answer: Abram and Balthasar and Sampson and Gregory are present.

2. Invite three students to read the bracketed passage aloud.

3. **Ask** students to review the stage directions and then to explain who is fighting in these lines.

   Answer: Sampson and Gregory fight Abram and Balthasar.

4. **Ask** students the Literary Analysis question: Which words in the stage directions in line 44 clarify that Sampson is not speaking to Abram?

   Answer: The words "Aside to Gregory" clarify that Sampson is not speaking to Abram.

9 Reading Check

Answer: The servants are from the Montague and Capulet families.

⑩ Critical Thinking

Analyze

1. Choose students to take each of the five parts in the bracketed passage. Have them read the lines aloud.
2. **Ask:** What does Lady Capulet tell her husband he needs?

   Answer: She tells him he needs a crutch, not a sword.
3. **Ask** students to describe the attitude of the two wives.

   Possible response: They do not want their husbands to fight.
4. **Ask** students what the men's attitude says about the feud between their two families.

   Answer: They must have carried the hostility for a long time; they still want to fight, even though they are too old.

⑪ Literature in Context

History Connection

Shakespeare set several of his plays in Verona, an important city located in northern Italy between the cities of Milan and Venice. Today Verona remains an important trading center that exports textiles, machinery, shoes, and other products throughout Europe.

Verona has several architectural landmarks that were built between the twelfth and sixteenth centuries, notably the Basilica of San Zeno Maggiore, the Church of Sant'Anastasia, and the palaces of Bevilacqua, Canossa, and Pompeii. Its Roman amphitheater from the first century CE is still used for open-air concerts.

Connect to the Literature

Remind students that people loyal to the Capulets and Montagues have begun to fight. Then, **ask** the Connect to the Literature question: Which part of his authority is Prince Escalus exercising in this scene—mayor, police chief, or head of the army? Explain.

Answer: He is acting as police chief. He is breaking up a fight and threatening to punish the feuding families.

SAMPSON. Draw, if you be men. Gregory, remember thy
swashing[11] blow. *[They fight.]*

BENVOLIO. Part, fools!
Put up your swords. You know not what you do.

[*Enter* TYBALT.]

TYBALT. What art thou drawn among these heartless hinds?[12]
Turn thee, Benvolio; look upon thy death.

BENVOLIO. I do but keep the peace. Put up thy sword,
Or manage it to part these men with me.

TYBALT. What, drawn, and talk of peace? I hate the word
As I hate hell, all Montagues, and thee.
Have at thee, coward! *[They fight.]*

[*Enter an* OFFICER, *and three or four* CITIZENS *with clubs or partisans.*[13]]

OFFICER. Clubs, bills,[14] and partisans! Strike! Beat them down!
Down with the Capulets! Down with the Montagues!

[*Enter old* CAPULET *in his gown, and his* WIFE.]

CAPULET. What noise is this? Give me my long sword, ho!

LADY CAPULET. A crutch, a crutch! Why call you for a sword?

CAPULET. My sword, I say! Old Montague is come
And flourishes his blade in spite[15] of me.

[*Enter old* MONTAGUE *and his* WIFE.]

11. **swashing** hard downward swordstroke.
12. **heartless hinds** cowardly servants. *Hind* also means "a female deer."
13. **partisans** spearlike weapons with broad blades.
14. **bills** weapons consisting of hook-shaped blades with long handles.
15. **spite** defiance.

⑪

LITERATURE IN CONTEXT

History Connection

Prince of Verona

When Prince Escalus intervenes in the fight between the Capulets and the Montagues, he does so under his authority as the podesta, or "chief magistrate," of Verona. The powers and duties of the podesta combined those of a modern mayor, chief of police, and head of the local militia. Scholars believe that Shakespeare based the character of Prince Escalus on Bartolomeo della Scala, who ruled the northern Italian city of Verona during the early fourteenth century.

Connect to the Literature

Which part of his authority is Prince Escalus exercising in this scene—mayor, police chief, or head of the army? Explain.

Think Aloud

Vocabulary: Using Context

Direct students' attention to the word *flourishes* in line 74. Using a think-aloud process, model how to use context to infer the meaning of an unknown word. Say to students:

> I'm going to think aloud to show you how I would figure out the meaning of *flourishes* based on its context.
>
> In this sentence, *flourishes* is a verb identifying an action of Montague. I know from earlier in the act that the servants of Capulet and Montague are fighting each other with swords. The "blade" to which Capulet refers must be Montague's sword—or the swords of his servants. Since I know that the servants' blades have been drawn and used in battle, *flourishes* must mean something like "draws and gestures with."

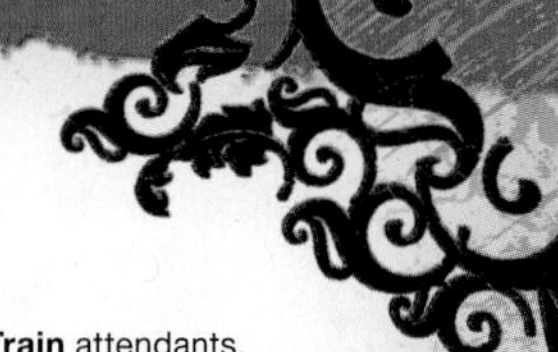

MONTAGUE. Thou villain Capulet!—Hold me not; let me go.

LADY MONTAGUE. Thou shalt not stir one foot to seek a foe.

[*Enter* PRINCE ESCALUS, *with his Train.*[16]]

PRINCE. Rebellious subjects, enemies to peace,
Profaners[17] of this neighbor-stainèd steel—
Will they not hear? What, ho! You men, you beasts,
That quench the fire of your pernicious rage
With purple fountains issuing from your veins!
On pain of torture, from those bloody hands
Throw your mistempered[18] weapons to the ground
And hear the sentence of your movèd prince.
Three civil brawls, bred of an airy word
By thee, old Capulet, and Montague,
Have thrice disturbed the quiet of our streets
And made Verona's ancient citizens
Cast by their grave beseeming ornaments[19]
To wield old partisans, in hands as old,
Cank'red with peace, to part your cank'red hate.[20]
(12) If ever you disturb our streets again,
Your lives shall pay the forfeit of the peace.
For this time all the rest depart away.
You, Capulet, shall go along with me;
And, Montague, come you this afternoon,
To know our farther pleasure in this case,
To old Freetown, our common judgment place.
Once more, on pain of death, all men depart.

[*Exit all but* MONTAGUE, *his* WIFE, *and* BENVOLIO.]

MONTAGUE. Who set this ancient quarrel new abroach?[21]
Speak, nephew, were you by when it began?

BENVOLIO. Here were the servants of your adversary
And yours, close fighting ere I did approach.
I drew to part them. In the instant came
The fiery Tybalt, with his sword prepared;
Which, as he breathed defiance to my ears,
He swung about his head and cut the winds,
Who, nothing hurt withal, hissed him in scorn.
While we were interchanging thrusts and blows,
Came more and more, and fought on part and part,[22]
Till the Prince came, who parted either part.

LADY MONTAGUE. O, where is Romeo? Saw you him today?
Right glad I am he was not at this fray.

16. Train attendants.

17. Profaners those who show disrespect or contempt.

Vocabulary
pernicious (pər nish′ əs) *adj.* causing great injury or ruin

18. mistempered hardened for a wrong purpose; bad-tempered.

19. Cast . . . ornaments put aside their dignified and appropriate clothing.

20. Cank'red . . . hate rusted from lack of use, to put an end to your malignant feuding.

Reading Skill
Summarize Summarize the warning that the Prince issues to the Montagues and Capulets in this speech.

21. Who . . . abroach? Who reopened this old fight?

Vocabulary
adversary (ad′ vər ser′ ē) *n.* a person who opposes or fights against another

22. on . . . part on one side and the other.

(13)

Reading Check

Who stops the brawl between the Montagues and the Capulets?

(12) Reading Skill
Summarize

1. Read aloud lines 85 through 91. Have students read side notes 19 and 20. Then, **ask** students what the Prince accuses the families of doing to the citizens of Verona in these lines.

   Answer: The Prince accuses the families of having three public brawls that have forced the citizens of the city to take up arms to stop the violence.

2. Read aloud lines 92 through 99. **Ask** students to respond to the Reading Skill prompt: Summarize the warning that the Prince issues to the Montagues and Capulets in this speech.

   Answer: The Prince tells them that if they ever disturb the peace again, they will pay for it with their lives.

(13) Reading Check

Answer: Prince Escalus stops the brawl.

Differentiated Instruction for Universal Access

Strategy for Less Proficient Readers
Point out to students that Shakespearean language often inverts the subject and the verb, or puts the object before the subject and verb. Point out examples in lines 82–83 ("from those bloody hands/Throw your mistempered weapons to the ground"); line 96 ("And, Montague, come you this afternoon"); lines 104–105 ("In the instant came/The fiery Tybalt"); line 112 ("O, where is Romeo? Saw you him today?"); and line 113 ("Right glad I am he was not at this fray.")

Review these lines with students. Demonstrate the customary syntax for the first of these lines. Then, guide students to restate each of these lines in more ordinary syntax. Encourage students to watch for inverted syntax and to restate the lines, which will help them understand the meaning and summarize passages.

⓮ Critical Thinking

Infer

1. Have students read the bracketed passage. **Ask** students what information is exchanged between Benvolio and Montague in these lines.

   Answer: Montague tells Benvolio that Romeo is often out in the sycamore grove in the night, and as soon as dawn comes, he locks himself in his room and covers the windows to keep out the sunlight.

2. **Ask** students what they can infer about Benvolio based on his interaction with Montague.

   Answer: Benvolio is polite; he addresses Montague as "my noble uncle." He is concerned about Romeo's welfare.

BENVOLIO. Madam, an hour before the worshiped sun
Peered forth the golden window of the East,
A troubled mind drave me to walk abroad:
Where, underneath the grove of sycamore
That westward rooteth from this city side,
So early walking did I see your son.
Towards him I made, but he was ware[23] of me
And stole into the covert[24] of the wood.
I, measuring his affections[25] by my own,
Which then most sought where most might not be found,[26]
Being one too many by my weary self,
Pursued my humor not pursuing his,[27]
And gladly shunned who gladly fled from me.

⓮ **MONTAGUE.** Many a morning hath he there been seen,
With tears **augmenting** the fresh morning's dew,
Adding to clouds more clouds with his deep sighs;
But all so soon as the all-cheering sun
Should in the farthest East begin to draw
The shady curtains from Aurora's bed,
Away from light steals home my heavy[28] son
And private in his chamber pens himself,
Shuts up his windows, locks fair daylight out,
And makes himself an artificial night.
Black and portentous[29] must this humor prove
Unless good counsel may the cause remove.

BENVOLIO. My noble uncle, do you know the cause?

MONTAGUE. I neither know it nor can learn of him.

BENVOLIO. Have you importuned[30] him by any means?

MONTAGUE. Both by myself and many other friends;
But he, his own affections' counselor,
Is to himself—I will not say how true—
But to himself so secret and so close,
So far from sounding[31] and discovery,
As is the bud bit with an envious worm
Ere he can spread his sweet leaves to the air
Or dedicate his beauty to the sun.
Could we but learn from whence his sorrows grow,
We would as willingly give cure as know.

[*Enter* ROMEO.]

23. **ware** aware; wary.
24. **covert** hidden place.
25. **measuring . . . affections** judging his feelings.
26. **Which . . . found** which wanted to be where there was no one else.
27. **Pursued . . . his** followed my own mind by not following after Romeo.

Vocabulary
augmenting (ôg ment′ iŋ) *v.* increasing; enlarging

28. **heavy** sad; moody.
29. **portentous** promising bad fortune.
30. **importuned** questioned deeply.
31. **sounding** understanding.

Vocabulary Development

Ⓒ CCSS Language 6

Word Forms

Help students learn related forms of selection vocabulary words. Give students a blank **Word Form Chart** (***Professional Development Guidebook,*** p. 42) with the original vocabulary words in the correct columns. Work with the class to determine the related forms. The final chart should look like this:

Noun	Verb	Adjective	Adverb
grievance	grieve	grievous	grievously
oppression	oppress	oppressive	oppressively
transgression	transgress	transgressive	transgressively

BENVOLIO. See, where he comes. So please you step aside;
I'll know his grievance, or be much denied.

MONTAGUE. I would thou wert so happy by thy stay
To hear true shrift.[32] Come, madam, let's away.

[*Exit* MONTAGUE *and* WIFE.]

BENVOLIO. Good morrow, cousin.

ROMEO. Is the day so young?

BENVOLIO. But new struck nine.

ROMEO. Ay me! Sad hours seem long.
Was that my father that went hence so fast?

BENVOLIO. It was. What sadness lengthens Romeo's hours?

ROMEO. Not having that which having makes them short.

BENVOLIO. In love?

ROMEO. Out—

BENVOLIO. Of love?

ROMEO. Out of her favor where I am in love.

BENVOLIO. Alas that love, so gentle in his view,[33]
Should be so tyrannous and rough in proof![34]

ROMEO. Alas that love, whose view is muffled still,[35]
Should without eyes see pathways to his will!
Where shall we dine? O me! What fray was here?
Yet tell me not, for I have heard it all.
Here's much to do with hate, but more with love.[36]
Why then, O brawling love, O loving hate,
O anything, of nothing first created!
O heavy lightness, serious vanity,
Misshapen chaos of well-seeming forms,
Feather of lead, bright smoke, cold fire, sick health,
15 Still-waking sleep, that is not what it is!
This love feel I, that feel no love in this.
Dost thou not laugh?

BENVOLIO. No, coz,[37] I rather weep.

ROMEO. Good heart, at what?

BENVOLIO. At thy good heart's oppression.

ROMEO. Why, such is love's transgression.
Griefs of mine own lie heavy in my breast,

Vocabulary
grievance (grēv′ əns) *n.* injustice; complaint

32. **I . . . shrift** I hope you are lucky enough to hear him confess the truth.

Literary Analysis
Dialogue What does this conversation reveal about Romeo's state of mind?

33. **view** appearance.
34. **in proof** when experienced.
35. **whose . . . still** Cupid is traditionally represented as blindfolded.
36. **but . . . love** loyalty to family and love of fighting. In the following lines, Romeo speaks of love as a series of contradictions—a union of opposites.
37. **coz** cousin.

Vocabulary
oppression (ə presh′ ən) *n.* feeling of being weighed down with worries or problems
transgression (trans gresh′ ən) *n.* wrongdoing; sin

16 **Reading Check**
What reason for his sadness does Romeo give to Benvolio?

15 Literary Analysis

Dialogue

1. Refer students to lines 167–179. **Ask** them what Romeo's words reveal about his personality.
   Answer: Romeo's words show him to be a sensitive person with emotions that are very close to the surface.
2. **Ask** students the Literary Analysis question: What does this conversation reveal about Romeo's state of mind?
   Answer: The speech shows that Romeo is in a state of confusion. He makes many statements that contain opposites, such as "O brawling love," "O loving hate," and "O heavy lightness," to show that he is in terrible conflict about his feelings.

16 Reading Check

Answer: Romeo tells Benvolio that he is sad because he is in love but is not loved in return.

Differentiated Instruction for Universal Access

Background for Advanced Readers

Tell students that this play contains many examples of a literary figure of speech called an *oxymoron,* from the Greek *oxys,* meaning "sharp," and *moros,* meaning "stupid." The oxymoron is a seemingly contradictory statement, such as "cold fire." An oxymoron can show the contradictory elements of life, or the degree to which each element of a pair can generate its own opposite—love and hate, pleasure and pain.

Have students list the oxymoronic expressions found in Romeo's speech on this page, showing how conflicted he is about his feelings of love.

When students have completed their lists, have them write some more oxymorons of their own to express a feeling of conflict. Common oxymorons include "accidentally on purpose," "clearly confused," "awfully good," and "a definite maybe."

17 Reading Skill

Summarize

1. Based on footnotes 43–45, **ask** students to describe the kind of person Romeo loves.

   Answer: She is chaste and has the good sense to avoid love. She is not charmed by the spell of love, and she does not put up with words and looks of love.

2. **Ask:** Based on footnotes 46–47, what does Romeo claim will be her fate?

   Answer: If she dies chaste, her beauty will die with her, since she will have no children.

▶ **Monitor Progress:** Review students' graphic organizers to ensure that they are accurately summarizing passages.

▶ **Reteach:** If students are having difficulty summarizing, have them reread the play to this point and review the footnotes.

18 Background

Danae and Zeus

Line 210, "Nor ope her lap to saint-seducing gold," is an allusion to Danae and Zeus, characters from Greek mythology. Danae was the daughter of King Acrisius. When Acrisius received a prophecy that Danae's son would kill him, Acrisius wanted to make sure Danae had no children, so he locked her in a tower of bronze. But the god Zeus came to Danae in the form of a shower of gold. Soon afterward, Danae's son Perseus was born, and Perseus eventually fulfilled the prophecy and killed the king.

19 Critical Viewing

Possible response: Based on his expression and body language, Romeo appears troubled and deep in thought; he's love-sick and not feeling like himself.

---

38. Which . . . thine which griefs you will increase by adding your own sorrow to them.

39. discreet intelligently sensitive.

40. gall a bitter liquid.

41. Soft! Wait!

42. in sadness seriously.

43. Dian's wit the mind of Diana, goddess of chastity.

44. proof armor.

45. stay endure; put up with.

46. That . . . store in that her beauty will die with her if she does not marry and have children.

Which thou wilt propagate, to have it prest
With more of thine.[38] This love that thou hast shown
Doth add more grief to too much of mine own.
Love is a smoke made with the fume of sighs;
Being purged, a fire sparkling in lovers' eyes;
Being vexed, a sea nourished with loving tears.
What is it else? A madness most discreet,[39]
A choking gall,[40] and a preserving sweet.
Farewell, my coz.

BENVOLIO. Soft![41] I will go along.
And if you leave me so, you do me wrong.

ROMEO. Tut! I have lost myself; I am not here;
This is not Romeo, he's some other where.

BENVOLIO. Tell me in sadness,[42] who is that you love?

ROMEO. What, shall I groan and tell thee?

BENVOLIO. Groan? Why, no;
But sadly tell me who.

ROMEO. Bid a sick man in sadness make his will.
Ah, word ill urged to one that is so ill!
In sadness, cousin, I do love a woman.

BENVOLIO. I aimed so near when I supposed you loved.

ROMEO. A right good markman. And she's fair I love.

BENVOLIO. A right fair mark, fair coz, is soonest hit.

ROMEO. Well, in that hit you miss. She'll not be hit
With Cupid's arrow. She hath Dian's wit,[43]
And, in strong proof[44] of chastity well armed,
From Love's weak childish bow she lives uncharmed.
She will not stay[45] the siege of loving terms,
Nor bide th' encounter of assailing eyes,
Nor ope her lap to saint-seducing gold.
O, she is rich in beauty; only poor
That, when she dies, with beauty dies her store.[46]

BENVOLIO. Then she hath sworn that she will still live chaste?

ROMEO. She hath, and in that sparing make huge waste;
For beauty, starved with her severity,

19 ◀ **Critical Viewing** What does this photograph reveal about Romeo's feelings? **[Analyze]**

Vocabulary Development

CCSS Language 6

Selection Vocabulary Reinforcement

Reinforce students' comprehension with "show-you-know" sentences. The first part of the sentence uses the vocabulary word in an appropriate context. The second part clarifies the first. Model the strategy with this example:

> It was obvious that the two-year-old was guilty of a *transgression;* all of the cookies had disappeared from the cookie jar.

Then, give students these sentence prompts, and coach them in creating the clarification part:

1. I decided to make up for my *transgression* against my hockey team; ________.

   Sample answer: I skated a hundred extra laps and apologized.

2. At summer camp, we weren't allowed even one *transgression;* ____________.

   Sample answer: if we broke a rule, we were sent home immediately.

Cuts beauty off from all posterity.[47]
She is too fair, too wise, wisely too fair
To merit bliss by making me despair.[48]
She hath forsworn to[49] love, and in that vow
Do I live dead that live to tell it now.

BENVOLIO. Be ruled by me; forget to think of her.

ROMEO. O, teach me how I should forget to think!

BENVOLIO. By giving liberty unto thine eyes.
Examine other beauties.

ROMEO. 'Tis the way
To call hers, exquisite, in question more.[50]
These happy masks that kiss fair ladies' brows,
Being black puts us in mind they hide the fair.
He that is strucken blind cannot forget
The precious treasure of his eyesight lost.
Show me a mistress that is passing fair:
What doth her beauty serve but as a note
Where I may read who passed that passing fair?[51]
Farewell. Thou canst not teach me to forget.

BENVOLIO. I'll pay that doctrine, or else die in debt.[52] [*Exit all.*]

Scene ii. A street.

[*Enter* CAPULET, COUNTY PARIS, *and the* CLOWN, *his servant.*]

CAPULET. But Montague is bound as well as I,
In penalty alike; and 'tis not hard, I think,
For men so old as we to keep the peace.

PARIS. Of honorable reckoning[1] are you both,
And pity 'tis you lived at odds so long.
But now, my lord, what say you to my suit?

CAPULET. But saying o'er what I have said before:
My child is yet a stranger in the world,
She hath not seen the change of fourteen years;
Let two more summers wither in their pride
Ere we may think her ripe to be a bride.

PARIS. Younger than she are happy mothers made.

CAPULET. And too soon marred are those so early made.
Earth hath swallowed all my hopes[2] but she;
She is the hopeful lady of my earth.[3]
But woo her, gentle Paris, get her heart;
My will to her consent is but a part.

47. **in . . . posterity** By denying herself love and marriage, she wastes her beauty, which will not live on in future generations.
48. **She . . . despair** She is being too good—she will earn happiness in heaven by dooming me to live without her love.
49. **forsworn to** sworn not to.
50. **'Tis . . . more** That way will only make her beauty more strongly present in my mind.
51. **who . . . fair** who surpassed in beauty that very beautiful woman.
52. **I'll . . . debt** I will teach you to forget, or else die trying.

1. **reckoning** reputation.
2. **hopes** children.
3. **She . . . earth** My hopes for the future rest in her; she will inherit all that is mine.

21

What advice does Benvolio give to Romeo about the woman he loves?

20 Literary Analysis

Dialogue

1. Have students read lines 221 through 234. **Ask** what Benvolio is urging Romeo to do.

   Answer: He is urging Romeo to forget about his love and look around for other girls.
2. **Ask:** How does Romeo respond to Benvolio's suggestion?

   Answer: Romeo says he cannot forget his love. Looking at other beautiful girls will just remind him of her.
3. **Ask** students what contrasting attitudes are revealed in this exchange between Romeo and Benvolio.

   Possible response: Benvolio is more realistic and believes that if one loves someone who does not reciprocate, one should find someone else. Romeo believes the opposite: Once having committed to love, he can see no alternative.

21 Reading Check

Answer: He advises Romeo to forget her.

Differentiated Instruction for Universal Access

Enrichment for Gifted/Talented Students

Tell students that the situation in which Romeo and Benvolio find themselves is a common human condition. Young men fall in love with girls who do not love them in return, and the young men's friends urge them to find somebody else.

Have students review the conversation between Benvolio and Romeo in lines 156–234. Then, have them rewrite the dialogue in modern language. Urge students to think about the language that they and their friends use every day to convey the same ideas. What words would a young man say to his lovelorn friend? Tell students they should not paraphrase each line, but simply condense the ideas into modern language.

After they have produced a script, have them present the scene to the class.

22 Reading Skill
Summarize

1. **Ask** students what the servant has been requested to do in lines 34–37.

   Answer: He has been requested to find the people on the list that Lord Capulet hands him and to invite those people to Lord Capulet's home for a feast.

2. **Ask** students to respond to the Reading Skill prompt: Use footnote 8 to help you summarize the servant's remarks here.

   Possible response: The servant wonders why he is asked to find the people who are on the list. He thinks people should stick with what they know, and he can't read. He has to find someone who can read the list for him.

An she agree, within her scope of choice
Lies my consent and fair according voice.[4]
This night I hold an old accustomed feast,
Whereto I have invited many a guest,
Such as I love; and you among the store,
One more, most welcome, makes my number more.
At my poor house look to behold this night
Earth-treading stars[5] that make dark heaven light.
Such comfort as do lusty young men feel
When well-appareled April on the heel
Of limping Winter treads, even such delight
Among fresh fennel buds shall you this night
Inherit at my house. Hear all, all see,
And like her most whose merit most shall be;
Which, on more view of many, mine, being one,
May stand in number, though in reck'ning none.[6]
Come, go with me. [*To* SERVANT, *giving him a paper*]
Go, sirrah, trudge about
Through fair Verona; find those persons out
Whose names are written there, and to them say
My house and welcome on their pleasure stay.[7]

[*Exit with* PARIS.]

SERVANT. Find them out whose names are written here? It is written that the shoemaker should meddle with his yard and the tailor with his last, the fisher with his pencil and the painter with his nets;[8] but I am sent to find those persons whose names are here writ, and can never find what names the writing person hath here writ. I must to the learned. In good time![9]

[*Enter* BENVOLIO *and* ROMEO.]

BENVOLIO. Tut, man, one fire burns out another's burning;
One pain is less'ned by another's anguish;
Turn giddy, and be holp by backward turning;[10]
One desperate grief cures with another's languish.
Take thou some new infection to thy eye,
And the rank poison of the old will die.

ROMEO. Your plantain leaf[11] is excellent for that.

BENVOLIO. For what, I pray thee?

ROMEO. For your broken shin.

BENVOLIO. Why, Romeo, art thou mad?

4. **an . . . voice** If she agrees, I will consent to and agree with her choice.
5. **Earth-treading stars** young ladies.
6. **Which . . . none** If you look at all the young girls, you may see her as merely one among many, and not worth special admiration.
7. **stay** await.

Reading Skill
Summarize Use footnote 8 to help you summarize the servant's remarks here.

8. **shoemaker . . . nets** The servant is confusing workers and their tools. He intends to say that people should stick with what they know.
9. **In good time!** Just in time! The servant has seen Benvolio and Romeo, who can read.
10. **Turn . . . turning** If you are dizzy from turning one way, turn the other way.
11. **plantain leaf** leaf used to stop bleeding.

Vocabulary Development

Graphic Organizers

To help students explore the meaning of the word *languish* (line 48), create a Frayer model map. First, write *languish* in the central circle. Then, elicit a definition and guide students in brainstorming for characteristics, examples, and non-examples. The finished map should look like this:

Definition: depression; weakness; grief	**Characteristics:** teary, low, upset, rejected, sighing, down, lacking energy
Examples: loss of a loved one, getting a low grade, breaking up with someone, being rejected	**Non-examples:** winning an award, getting invited to a party, receiving a compliment, getting a high grade

languish

ROMEO. Not mad, but bound more than a madman is;
Shut up in prison, kept without my food,
Whipped and tormented and—God-den,[12] good fellow.

SERVANT. God gi' go-den. I pray, sir, can you read?

ROMEO. Ay, mine own fortune in my misery.

SERVANT. Perhaps you have learned it without book.
But, I pray, can you read anything you see?

ROMEO. Ay, if I know the letters and the language.

SERVANT. Ye say honestly. Rest you merry.[13]

ROMEO. Stay, fellow; I can read. [*He reads the letter.*]
"Signior Martino and his wife and daughters;
County Anselm and his beauteous sisters;
The lady widow of Vitruvio;
Signior Placentio and his lovely nieces;
23 Mercutio and his brother Valentine;
Mine uncle Capulet, his wife and daughters;
My fair niece Rosaline; Livia;
Signior Valentio and his cousin Tybalt;
Lucio and the lively Helena."
A fair assembly. Whither should they come?

SERVANT. Up.

ROMEO. Whither? To supper?

SERVANT. To our house.

ROMEO. Whose house?

SERVANT. My master's.

ROMEO. Indeed I should have asked you that before.

SERVANT. Now I'll tell you without asking. My master is the great rich Capulet; and if you be not of the house of Montagues, I pray come and crush a cup of wine. Rest you merry. [*Exit.*]

BENVOLIO. At this same ancient[14] feast of Capulet's
Sups the fair Rosaline whom thou so loves;
With all the admirèd beauties of Verona.
Go thither, and with unattainted[15] eye
Compare her face with some that I shall show,
And I will make thee think thy swan a crow.

ROMEO. When the devout religion of mine eye
Maintains such falsehood, then turn tears to fires:

12. **God-den** good afternoon; good evening.

13. **Rest you merry** May God keep you happy—a way of saying farewell.

Literary Analysis
Dialogue and Stage Directions What important information in the stage directions clarifies Romeo's speech here?

14. **ancient** long-established; traditional.
15. **unattainted** unprejudiced.

24

Why does Capulet's servant talk to Romeo and Benvolio?

23 Literary Analysis

Dialogue and Stage Directions

1. **Ask** students why the servant approaches Romeo and Benvolio.
   Answer: The servant cannot read the list of people who are being invited to Capulet's feast. When the servant sees Romeo and Benvolio, he knows by their bearing that they are able to read.
2. **Ask** students the Literary Analysis question: What important information in the stage directions clarifies Romeo's speech here?
   Answer: The stage directions state that he is reading the letter.
3. **Ask** students what is in the letter that Romeo is reading.
   Answer: He is reading the list of people who are to be invited to Capulet's feast.

24 Reading Check

Answer: The servant wants them to read the letter.

Differentiated Instruction for Universal Access

Strategy for Special-Needs Students

Since there is little action in Scene ii, students might struggle with its difficult language. Hearing the language spoken aloud may help them better understand the conversations. Encourage them to reread the scene, reading aloud along with them or providing them with the ***Hear It!* Audio CD** and having them read along with it.

Before having students reread and listen to the CD, review all the footnotes in the scene. Ask students to place sticky notes next to the difficult passages that are causing them trouble as they read along with the CD. After students hear Scene ii, review the material and respond to any questions they have.

㉕ Critical Thinking

Analyze

1. Have students read lines 90–101.

   Ask: What does Romeo imply his love for Rosaline is like? What will happen if he withdraws his love for her?

   Answer: He implies that his love is like a religious devotion, and he will be a heretic if he turns from her.

2. **Ask:** Under what condition does Romeo agree to go to the feast?

   Answer: He agrees to go with the understanding that he is not going to look at other beauties, but to enjoy the beauty of his own love, Rosaline.

And these, who, often drowned, could never die,
Transparent heretics, be burnt for liars![16]
One fairer than my love? The all-seeing sun
Ne'er saw her match since first the world begun.

BENVOLIO. Tut! you saw her fair, none else being by,
Herself poised with herself in either eye;[17]
But in that crystal scales[18] let there be weighed
Your lady's love against some other maid
That I will show you shining at this feast,
And she shall scant show well that now seems best.

ROMEO. I'll go along, no such sight to be shown,
But to rejoice in splendor of mine own.[19] [*Exit all.*]

16. **When . . . liars!** When I see Rosaline as just a plain-looking girl, may my tears turn to fire and burn my eyes out!
17. **Herself . . . eye** Rosaline compared with no one else.
18. **crystal scales** your eyes.
19. **mine own** my own love, Rosaline.

Scene iii. A room in Capulet's house.

[*Enter* CAPULET'S WIFE, *and* NURSE.]

LADY CAPULET. Nurse, where's my daughter? Call her forth to me.

NURSE. Now, by my maidenhead at twelve year old,
I bade her come. What, lamb! What, ladybird!
God forbid, where's this girl? What, Juliet!

[*Enter* JULIET.]

JULIET. How now? Who calls?

NURSE. Your mother.

JULIET. Madam, I am here.
What is your will?

LADY CAPULET. This is the matter—Nurse, give leave[1] awhile;
We must talk in secret. Nurse, come back again.
I have remembr'd me; thou's hear our counsel.[2]
Thou knowest my daughter's of a pretty age.

NURSE. Faith, I can tell her age unto an hour.

㉕

LADY CAPULET. She's not fourteen.

NURSE. I'll lay fourteen of my teeth—
And yet, to my teen[3] be it spoken, I have but four—
She's not fourteen. How long is it now
To Lammastide?[4]

LADY CAPULET. A fortnight and odd days.[5]

NURSE. Even or odd, of all days in the year,
Come Lammas Eve at night shall she be fourteen.

1. **give leave** Leave us alone.
2. **thou's . . . counsel** You shall hear our conference.
3. **teen** sorrow.
4. **Lammastide** August 1, a holiday celebrating the summer harvest.
5. **A fortnight and odd days** two weeks plus a few days.

Think Aloud

Dialogue

Draw students' attention to lines 1–14 in Scene iii. Use the following "think aloud" to model the skill of analyzing dialogue:

As I read these lines, I pay close attention to the dialogue in order to learn more about the characters and their relationships. Here, I can glean a few details about the relationships among the Nurse, Lady Capulet, and Juliet. First, I notice that the Nurse and Lady Capulet discuss Juliet's age at length. I interpret this to mean that both women assume a care-giving role with Juliet. Also, when Lady Capulet changes her mind and asks the Nurse to stay for her conversation with Juliet, it suggests that Lady Capulet respects the Nurse's love for Juliet and seeks her counsel.

The dialogue on this page also reveals cultural details about mother-daughter relationships. By calling her mother "Madam" and asking "What is your will?" Juliet shows both respect and obedience. I get the impression that this kind of respect was expected in Juliet's culture and time period.

Susan and she (God rest all Christian souls!)
Were of an age.[6] Well, Susan is with God;
She was too good for me. But, as I said,
On Lammas Eve at night shall she be fourteen;
That shall she, marry; I remember it well.
'Tis since the earthquake now eleven years.
And she was weaned (I never shall forget it),
Of all the days of the year, upon that day;
For I had then laid wormwood to my dug,
Sitting in the sun under the dovehouse wall.
My lord and you were then at Mantua.
Nay, I do bear a brain. But, as I said,
When it did taste the wormwood on the nipple
Of my dug and felt it bitter, pretty fool,
To see it tetchy and fall out with the dug!
26 Shake, quoth the dovehouse! 'Twas no need, I trow,
To bid me trudge.
And since that time it is eleven years,
For then she could stand high-lone; nay, by th' rood,
She could have run and waddled all about;
For even the day before, she broke her brow;
And then my husband (God be with his soul!
'A was a merry man) took up the child.
"Yea," quoth he, "dost thou fall upon thy face?
Thou wilt fall backward when thou hast more wit;
Wilt thou not, Jule?" and, by my holidam,
The pretty wretch left crying and said, "Ay."
To see now how a jest shall come about!
I warrant, and I should live a thousand years,
I never should forget it. "Wilt thou not, Jule?" quoth he,
And, pretty fool, it stinted and said, "Ay."

LADY CAPULET. Enough of this. I pray thee hold thy peace.

NURSE. Yes, madam. Yet I cannot choose but laugh
To think it should leave crying and say, "Ay."
27 And yet, I warrant, it had upon it brow
A bump as big as a young cock'rel's stone;
A perilous knock; and it cried bitterly.
"Yea," quoth my husband, "fall'st upon thy face?
Thou wilt fall backward when thou comest to age,
Wilt thou not, Jule?" It stinted and said, "Ay."

JULIET. And stint thou too, I pray thee, nurse, say I.

NURSE. Peace, I have done. God mark thee to His grace!

6. **Susan . . . age** Susan, the Nurse's child, and Juliet were the same age.

Literary Analysis
Dialogue and Stage Directions What do the Nurse's words here reveal about her devotion to Juliet?

Literary Analysis
Dialogue and Stage Directions What does this conversation reveal about the Nurse's personality?

28

How old is Juliet?

26 Literary Analysis

Dialogue and Stage Directions

1. Have students read the Nurse's speech, lines 16–48. Have them speculate about who Susan is.

   Answer: Susan was the Nurse's daughter.

2. **Ask:** What does the Nurse mean when she says that Susan and Juliet "were of an age"?

   Answer: She means that Susan and Juliet were the same age.

3. **Ask** students the Literary Analysis question: What do the Nurse's words here reveal about her devotion to Juliet?

   Answer: Because Susan and Juliet were the same age, the Nurse became even more devoted to Juliet after Susan died.

27 Literary Analysis

Dialogue and Stage Directions

1. Have students read lines 50–62. **Ask** what the Nurse is discussing here. What is "it" to which she refers?

   Answer: The Nurse is telling a story about when Juliet was little and fell and bumped her head. *It* refers to Juliet.

2. Tell students that the word *stinted* in line 57 means "ceased," meaning in this case that the child ceased crying. **Ask** students what Juliet means by her response to the Nurse in line 58.

   Answer: She is asking the Nurse to stop talking about when she was small.

3. **Ask** students the Literary Analysis question: What does this conversation reveal about the Nurse's personality?

   Answer: The Nurse can be talkative to the point of being annoying; however, she is genuinely devoted to Juliet and has her best interests at heart.

28 Reading Check

Answer: Juliet is fourteen.

Fluency

Distribute copies of p. 819, and pair students. Have partners take turns reading paragraphs aloud. While one partner reads, the other should mark any words with which the student reading has difficulty. Circulate to monitor the fluency of students' reading. Collect students' marked-up copies of the page, and review difficult words and passages with the class. Look for these problem spots:

- If students read a line or passage in a choppy, repetitious, or slow way, practice repeated reading. Pair struggling students and English learners with fluent readers. Have the fluent reader read the passage aloud. Then, have the struggling reader or English learner repeat until his or her fluency improves.
- If students have difficulty recognizing roots, prefixes, and suffixes in the words *perilous, bitterly,* or *backward,* help students use their thumbs to cover up parts of the words to recognize their components.
- If English learners have difficulty with the concept of waddling (line 37) or the phrase "comest to age," (line 56), tell stories to help students grasp the meaning.

29 Reading Skill

Summarize

1. Have students read lines 75–78. **Ask** who the subject of this discussion is and what opinion the Nurse and Lady Capulet seem to have of this person.

   Answer: They are discussing Paris, and both the Nurse and Lady Capulet seem to have a high opinion of him.

2. **Ask** students to respond to the Reading Skill prompt: Use the information in footnote 8 and the dialogue to help you summarize the Nurse's opinion of Paris.

   Answer: The Nurse believes there is not an equal to Paris in all the world; he is the very model of a man.

Thou wast the prettiest babe that e'er I nursed.
(27) And I might live to see thee married once,
I have my wish.

LADY CAPULET. Marry, that "marry" is the very theme
I came to talk of. Tell me, daughter Juliet,
How stands your dispositions to be married?

JULIET. It is an honor that I dream not of.

NURSE. An honor? Were not I thine only nurse,
I would say thou hadst sucked wisdom from thy teat.

LADY CAPULET. Well, think of marriage now. Younger than you,
Here in Verona, ladies of esteem,
Are made already mothers. By my count,
I was your mother much upon these years
That you are now a maid.[7] Thus then in brief;
The valiant Paris seeks you for his love.

NURSE. A man, young lady! Lady, such a man
As all the world—Why, he's a man of wax.[8]

(29)

LADY CAPULET. Verona's summer hath not such a flower.

NURSE. Nay, he's a flower, in faith—a very flower.

LADY CAPULET. What say you? Can you love the gentleman?
This night you shall behold him at our feast.
Read o'er the volume of young Paris' face,
And find delight writ there with beauty's pen;
Examine every married lineament,
And see how one another lends content;[9]
And what obscured in this fair volume lies
Find written in the margent[10] of his eyes.
This precious book of love, this unbound lover,
To beautify him only lacks a cover.[11]
(30) The fish lives in the sea, and 'tis much pride
For fair without the fair within to hide.
That book in many's eyes doth share the glory,
That in gold clasps locks in the golden story;
So shall you share all that he doth possess,
By having him making yourself no less.

NURSE. No less? Nay, bigger! Women grow by men.

LADY CAPULET. Speak briefly, can you like of Paris' love?

JULIET. I'll look to like, if looking liking move;[12]
But no more deep will I endart mine eye

7. **I . . . maid** I was your mother when I was as old as you are now.
8. **he's . . . wax** He's a model of a man.

Reading Skill
Summarize Use the information in footnote 8 and the dialogue to help you summarize the Nurse's opinion of Paris.

9. **Examine . . . content** Examine every harmonious feature of his face, and see how each one enhances every other. Throughout this speech, Lady Capulet compares Paris to a book.
10. **margent** margin. Paris's eyes are compared to the margin of a book, where whatever is not clear in the text (the rest of his face) can be explained by notes.
11. **cover** metaphor for wife.
12. **I'll . . . move** If looking favorably at someone leads to liking him, I will look at Paris in a way that will lead to liking him.

Vocabulary Development

Dictionary Use

Point out the word *volume* in line 81 on this page. Using a think-aloud process, model how to use context to infer the appropriate definition of the word. Say to students:

> I'm going to think aloud to show you how I would figure out the correct dictionary definition of *volume* by using context clues. The dictionary says that *volume* can mean: 1. the amount of space occupied by a three-dimensional object; 2. a large amount; 3. a book.
>
> In this speech, Lady Capulet is encouraging Juliet to "read o'er the *volume* of young Paris' face." The first definition simply doesn't make sense; how would you "read over" an amount of space? The second definition doesn't make sense either. However, Juliet is being asked to "read" young Paris' face for his fitness as a husband. Definition 3 fits well in the line: "Read o'er the book of young Paris' face." In this context, *volume* means "book."

Than your consent gives strength to make it fly.[13]

[*Enter* SERVINGMAN.]

SERVINGMAN. Madam, the guests are come, supper served up, you called, my young lady asked for, the nurse cursed in the pantry, and everything in extremity. I must hence to wait. I beseech you follow straight. [*Exit.*]

LADY CAPULET. We follow thee. Juliet, the County stays.[14]

NURSE. Go, girl, seek happy nights to happy days. [*Exit all.*]

Scene iv. A street.

[*Enter* ROMEO, MERCUTIO, BENVOLIO, *with five or six other* MASKERS; TORCHBEARERS.]

ROMEO. What, shall this speech[1] be spoke for our excuse?
Or shall we on without apology?

BENVOLIO. The date is out of such prolixity.[2]
We'll have no Cupid hoodwinked with a scarf,
Bearing a Tartar's painted bow of lath,
Scaring the ladies like a crowkeeper,
Nor no without-book prologue, faintly spoke
After the prompter, for our entrance;
But, let them measure us by what they will,
We'll measure them a measure and be gone.

ROMEO. Give me a torch. I am not for this ambling.
Being but heavy,[3] I will bear the light.

MERCUTIO. Nay, gentle Romeo, we must have you dance.

ROMEO. Not I, believe me. You have dancing shoes
With nimble soles; I have a soul of lead
So stakes me to the ground I cannot move.

MERCUTIO. You are a lover. Borrow Cupid's wings
And soar with them above a common bound.

ROMEO. I am too sore enpiercèd with his shaft
To soar with his light feathers; and so bound
I cannot bound a pitch above dull woe.
Under love's heavy burden do I sink.

MERCUTIO. And, to sink in it, should you burden love—
Too great oppression for a tender thing.

Literary Analysis
Dialogue and Stage Directions What does the dialogue reveal about Juliet's attitude toward marriage and Paris?

13. **But . . . fly** But I will not look harder than you want me to.
14. **the County stays** The Count, Paris, is waiting.

1. **this speech** Romeo asks whether he and his companions, being uninvited guests, should follow custom by announcing their arrival in a speech.
2. **The . . . prolixity** Such wordiness is outdated. In the following lines, Benvolio says, in sum, "Let us forget about announcing our entrance with a show. The other guests can look over as they see fit. We will dance a while, then leave."
3. **heavy** weighed down with sadness.

31 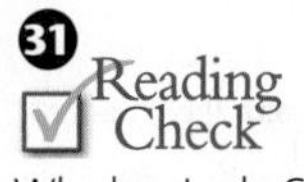

Why has Lady Capulet come to talk to Juliet?

30 Literary Analysis

Dialogue and Stage Directions

1. Have students recall Lord Capulet's dialogue with Paris on pp. 815–816 and compare his views of Juliet and marriage with Lady Capulet's views.

   Answer: Lord Capulet thinks Juliet is too young to be married. Lady Capulet, who was already married and a mother when she was fourteen, apparently does not think Juliet is too young.

2. **Ask** students the Literary Analysis question: What does the dialogue reveal about Juliet's attitude toward marriage and Paris?

   Possible response: Juliet has not really thought about it, but she seems hesitant. She is willing to meet Paris and see whether she can like him, but only so far as her mother approves.

31 Reading Check

Answer: She wants to discuss whether Juliet would be interested in marrying Paris.

Differentiated Instruction for Universal Access

EL Pronunciation for English Learners

Students might have difficulty pronouncing the "sh" sound, as in *shall, shoes,* and *shaft.* They might replace it with the "ch" sound, as in *child.* The following strategies can help students to pronounce the "sh" sound.

- Write the following word pairs on the board: *chip* and *ship, cheat* and *sheet,* and *chair* and *share.* Pronounce each word pair in turn, having students repeat each. Then, call out the words at random, having volunteers circle the correct words on the board. Discuss the results with the class, noting what might have led to incorrect choices.
- Pair English learners with fluent speakers. Ask each pair to pronounce the word pairs: *chip* and *ship, cheat* and *sheet,* and *chair* and *share.* Encourage fluent speakers to assist English learners. In any case in which the English learner errs, his or her "peer tutor" should pronounce each word carefully, guiding the English learner to correct the answer.

32 Literary Analysis

Dialogue and Stage Directions

1. Have students review footnotes 4 through 13.
2. **Ask** students the Literary Analysis question: What contrast between Mercutio and Romeo does the dialogue reveal?

   Answer: Mercutio is fun-loving, good-natured, and outgoing. He is able to enjoy life and poke fun at himself and others, in contrast to Romeo, who is moody and too serious.

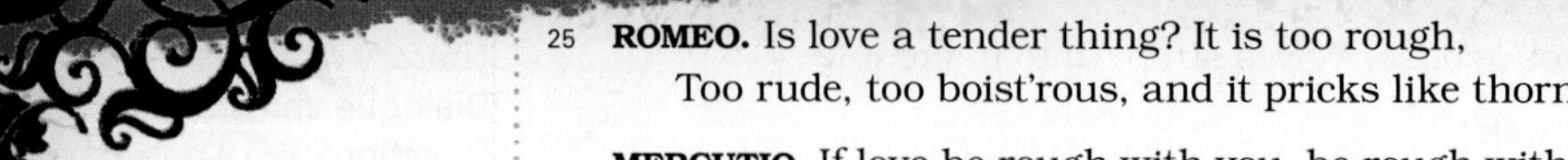

ROMEO. Is love a tender thing? It is too rough,
Too rude, too boist'rous, and it pricks like thorn.

MERCUTIO. If love be rough with you, be rough with love.
Prick love for pricking, and you beat love down.
Give me a case to put my visage[4] in.
A visor for a visor![5] What care I
What curious eye doth quote deformities?[6]
Here are the beetle brows shall blush for me.

BENVOLIO. Come, knock and enter; and no sooner in
But every man betake him to his legs.[7]

ROMEO. A torch for me! Let wantons light of heart
Tickle the senseless rushes[8] with their heels;
For I am proverbed with a grandsire phrase,[9]
I'll be a candleholder and look on;
The game was ne'er so fair, and I am done.[10]

MERCUTIO. Tut! Dun's the mouse, the constable's own word![11]
If thou art Dun,[12] we'll draw thee from the mire
Of this sir-reverence love, wherein thou stickest
Up to the ears. Come, we burn daylight, ho!

ROMEO. Nay, that's not so.

MERCUTIO. I mean, sir, in delay
We waste our lights in vain, like lights by day.
Take our good meaning, for our judgment sits
Five times in that ere once in our five wits.[13]

ROMEO. And we mean well in going to this masque,
But 'tis no wit to go.

MERCUTIO. Why, may one ask?

ROMEO. I dreamt a dream tonight.

MERCUTIO. And so did I.

ROMEO. Well, what was yours?

MERCUTIO. That dreamers often lie.

ROMEO. In bed asleep, while they do dream things true.

MERCUTIO. O, then I see Queen Mab[14] hath been with you.
She is the fairies' midwife, and she comes
In shape no bigger than an agate stone
On the forefinger of an alderman,
Drawn with a team of little atomies[15]
Over men's noses as they lie asleep;

4. **visage** mask.
5. **A visor . . . visor!** A mask for a mask—which is what my real face is like!
6. **quote deformities** notice my ugly features.
7. **betake . . . legs** start dancing.
8. **Let . . . rushes** Let fun-loving people dance on the floor coverings.
9. **proverbed . . . phrase** directed by an old saying.
10. **The game . . . done** No matter how much enjoyment may be had, I will not have any.
11. **Dun's . . . word!** Lie low like a mouse—that is what a constable waiting to make an arrest might say.
12. **Dun** proverbial name for a horse.

32 Literary Analysis Dialogue and Stage Directions What contrast between Mercutio and Romeo does the dialogue reveal?

13. **Take . . . wits** Understand my intended meaning. That shows more intelligence than merely following what your senses perceive.
14. **Queen Mab** the queen of fairyland.
15. **atomies** creatures.

Vocabulary Development

CCSS Language 6

Selection Vocabulary Reinforcement

To reinforce and assess students' comprehension of selection vocabulary words, give them sentences using the words in which the word may or may not be used correctly. Students must tell whether the use is correct and explain their answers. Use these sentences:

1. The *pernicious* rumor that he was a thief ruined his entire career.

   Answer: Yes, *pernicious* is used correctly here, because it means "causing great injury," and the destruction of a career is a great injury.
2. His *transgression* made his parents very proud.

   Answer: No, *transgression* is not used correctly. A *transgression* is a wrongdoing, and parents would probably not be very proud if their son committed a wrongdoing.

Her wagon spokes made of long spinners'[16] legs,
The cover, of the wings of grasshoppers;
Her traces, of the smallest spider web;
Her collars, of the moonshine's wat'ry beams;
Her whip, of cricket's bone; the lash, of film;[17]
Her wagoner, a small gray-coated gnat,
Not half so big as a round little worm
Pricked from the lazy finger of a maid;
Her chariot is an empty hazelnut,
Made by the joiner squirrel or old grub,[18]
Time out o' mind the fairies' coachmakers.
And in this state she gallops night by night
Through lovers' brains, and then they dream of love;
34 On courtiers' knees, that dream on curtsies straight;
O'er lawyers' fingers, who straight dream on fees;
O'er ladies' lips, who straight on kisses dream,
Which oft the angry Mab with blisters plagues,
Because their breath with sweetmeats[19] tainted are.
Sometimes she gallops o'er a courtier's nose,
And then dreams he of smelling out a suit;[20]
And sometime comes she with a tithe pig's[21] tail
Tickling a parson's nose as 'a lies asleep,
Then he dreams of another benefice.[22]
Sometime she driveth o'er a soldier's neck,
And then dream he of cutting foreign throats,
Of breaches, ambuscadoes,[23] Spanish blades,
Of healths[24] five fathom deep; and then anon

16. **spinners** spiders.
17. **film** spider's thread.
18. **old grub** insect that bores holes in nuts.
19. **sweetmeats** candy.
20. **smelling . . . suit** finding someone who has a petition (suit) for the king and who will pay the courtier to gain the king's favor for the petition.
21. **tithe pig** pig donated to a parson.
22. **benefice** church appointment that included a guaranteed income.
23. **ambuscadoes** ambushes.
24. **healths** toasts ("To your health!").

33 

How does Romeo feel about going to the Capulets' feast?

33 Reading Check

Answer: Romeo does not want to go to the feast. He is too sad and heavy-hearted about his love to enjoy himself.

Differentiated Instruction for Universal Access

Enrichment for Gifted/Talented Students

Mercutio's Queen Mab speech is one of the finest and most famous passages of poetry in Shakespeare's early works. Artistically talented students may enjoy creating an illustration of the speech. Based on the descriptions in lines 53–94, have them draw an illustration of Queen Mab, who is "no bigger than an agate stone . . . " and pulled by a team of small creatures across men's noses at night, and so on.

Encourage students to write lines from the play as captions or call-outs next to elements in the illustration. For example, they might use the line "Her wagon spokes made of long spinners' legs" next to the spokes of the wagon. Have students display their work in the classroom.

34 Reading Skill
Summarize

1. Have students read lines 53–94, paying special attention to the footnotes.
2. **Ask** students to respond to the Reading Skill prompt: Review Mercutio's speech and summarize his ideas about Queen Mab.

   Possible response: Queen Mab is a tiny fairy who rides a coach drawn by tiny little creatures. She gallops every night through people's brains, bringing dreams to people according to their position in life. To lovers she brings dreams of love; to lawyers she brings dreams of fees; to soldiers she brings dreams of war; and so on.

35 Literary Analysis
Dialogue and Stage Directions

1. Have students read the bracketed text. **Ask** students the Literary Analysis question: What do Mercutio's comments about dreams reveal about his character?

   Possible response: Mercutio likes to indulge his sense of poetry, and he likes to hear the sound of his own voice.
2. **Ask** students how this contrasts with Romeo's character.

   Answer: Romeo is more down-to-earth and practical. He wants to proceed with whatever they are going to do.

36 Reading Skill
Summarize

Ask students to respond to the Reading Skill prompt: Use footnote 28 to help you summarize Romeo's response to Benvolio.

Possible response: Romeo says that he is afraid that something he can't control will begin tonight, and the result will be his early death—but they should go on.

---

25. plats tangles.
26. elflocks tangled hair.

27. carriage posture.

Reading Skill
Summarize Review Mercutio's speech and summarize his ideas about Queen Mab.

Literary Analysis
Dialogue and Stage Directions What do Mercutio's comments about dreams reveal about his character?

Reading Skill
Summarize Use footnote 28 to help you summarize Romeo's response to Benvolio.

28. my mind . . . death My mind is fearful that some future event, fated by the stars, shall start to run its course tonight and cut my life short.

1. trencher wooden platter.

Drums in his ear, at which he starts and wakes,
And being thus frighted, swears a prayer or two
And sleeps again. This is that very Mab
That plats[25] the manes of horses in the night
And bakes the elflocks[26] in foul sluttish hairs,
34 Which once untangled much misfortune bodes.
This is the hag, when maids lie on their backs,
That presses them and learns them first to bear,
Making them women of good carriage.[27]
This is she—

ROMEO. Peace, peace, Mercutio, peace!
Thou talk'st of nothing.

MERCUTIO. True, I talk of dreams;
Which are the children of an idle brain,
35 Begot of nothing but vain fantasy;
Which is as thin of substance as the air,
And more inconstant than the wind, who woos
Even now the frozen bosom of the North
And, being angered, puffs away from thence,
Turning his side to the dew-dropping South.

BENVOLIO. This wind you talk of blows us from ourselves.
Supper is done, and we shall come too late.

ROMEO. I fear, too early; for my mind misgives
Some consequence yet hanging in the stars
36 Shall bitterly begin his fearful date
With this night's revels and expire the term
Of a despisèd life, closed in my breast,
By some vile forfeit of untimely death.[28]
But he that hath the steerage of my course
Direct my sail! On, lusty gentlemen!

BENVOLIO. Strike, drum.

[They march about the stage, and retire to one side.]

Scene v. A hall in Capulet's house.

[SERVINGMEN *come forth with napkins.*]

FIRST SERVINGMAN. Where's Potpan, that he helps not to take away? He shift a trencher![1] He scrape a trencher!

37 **SECOND SERVINGMAN.** When good manners shall lie all in one or two men's hands, and they unwashed too, 'tis a foul thing.

Think Aloud

Vocabulary: Using Context
Direct students' attention to the word *idle* in line 97. Using a think-aloud process, model how to use context to infer the meaning of an unknown word. Say to students:

> I'm going to think aloud to show you how I would figure out the meaning of *idle* based on its context.
>
> In this sentence, *idle* is an adjective that Mercutio uses to describe the brain of children. Mercutio has created a metaphor here: dreams are the "children of an idle brain." In the next line, Mercutio says that the idle brains of these children are filled with nothing but "vain fantasy." I know that the human brain is capable of processing many ideas and sensations at the same time—not just fantasies and dreams. Therefore, I would guess that an *idle* brain is one that doesn't have very much inside it; the brain is slow and inactive. Based on the context, I think *idle* means "inactive."

FIRST SERVINGMAN. Away with the joint-stools, remove the
court cupboard, look to the plate. Good thou, save me a
piece of marchpane,[2] and, as thou loves me, let the porter
let in Susan Grindstone and Nell. Anthony and Potpan!

37 **SECOND SERVINGMAN.** Ay, boy, ready.

FIRST SERVINGMAN. You are looked for and called for,
asked for and sought for, in the great chamber.

THIRD SERVINGMAN. We cannot be here and there too.
Cheerly, boys! Be brisk awhile, and the longest liver
take all. [*Exit.*]

[*Enter* CAPULET, *his* WIFE, JULIET, TYBALT, NURSE, *and all the* GUESTS *and* GENTLEWOMEN *to the* MASKERS.]

CAPULET. Welcome, gentlemen! Ladies that have their toes
Unplagued with corns will walk a bout[3] with you.
Ah, my mistresses, which of you all
Will now deny to dance? She that makes dainty,[4]
She I'll swear hath corns. Am I come near ye now?
Welcome, gentlemen! I have seen the day
That I have worn a visor and could tell
A whispering tale in a fair lady's ear,
Such as would please. 'Tis gone, 'tis gone, 'tis gone.
You are welcome, gentlemen! Come, musicians,
play.
[*Music plays, and they dance.*]
A hall,[5] a hall! Give room! And foot it, girls.
More light, you knaves, and turn the tables up,
And quench the fire; the room is grown too hot.
Ah, sirrah, this unlooked-for sport comes well.
Nay, sit; nay, sit, good cousin Capulet;
For you and I are past our dancing days.
How long is't now since last yourself and I
Were in a mask?

SECOND CAPULET. By'r Lady, thirty years.

CAPULET. What, man? 'Tis not so much, 'tis not so
much;
'Tis since the nuptial of Lucentio,
Come Pentecost as quickly as it will,
Some five-and-twenty years, and then we masked.

SECOND CAPULET. 'Tis more, 'tis more. His son is elder, sir;
His son is thirty.

2. **marchpane** marzipan, a confection made of sugar and almonds.

3. **walk a bout** dance a turn.

4. **makes dainty** hesitates; acts shy.

5. **A hall** clear the floor, make room for dancing.

Spiral Review

Character What do lines 15 through 32 reveal about Capulet?

38

Reading Check

What does Romeo fear might happen in the near future?

37 Critical Thinking

Interpret

1. Tell students that Shakespeare often uses humor based on characters from London's lower social classes of the time to break or interrupt the tension. Point out that the exchange among the servants is meant to be funny.
2. **Ask** students what is meant to be humorous about the words of the second servingman in lines 3–4.

   Possible response: Griping about Potpan, the servingman says it's a foul thing when everything is left to those whose hands are dirty. The play on words is "'tis a foul thing," meaning both "it's too bad" and "dirty hands are foul."
3. **Ask** students how minor characters like the servingmen add to the play.

   Answer: They add humor and help set up new scenes.

Spiral Review

Character

1. Remind students that they studied the concept of character in the Unit 5 Literary Analysis Workshop (pp. 780–797).
2. **Ask** students the Spiral Review question.

   Possible response: His words reveal that he is irreverent and merry, with a mischievous sense of humor. He is important because he can get away with teasing people.

38 Reading Check

Answer: Romeo fears he will die young.

Differentiated Instruction for Universal Access

Strategy for Less Proficient Readers

Help students visualize the action in this scene by displaying the **Series-of-Events Chain Graphic Organizer** (*Graphic Organizer Transparencies,* p. 221). Begin with line 15, when Capulet welcomes his guests, urges them to dance, and then engages in a conversation with a relative. Meanwhile, Romeo sees a beautiful woman and asks a servant her name. Tybalt overhears him, recognizes his voice, and calls for his weapon.

Point out to students that at this point, Romeo has not exchanged words with Capulet or with Tybalt. Romeo hasn't even noticed Tybalt.

In the next event, Tybalt approaches his uncle, who tells Tybalt to just ignore Romeo, since he's not causing any trouble. When Tybalt continues his ranting, Capulet becomes angry. Remind students that meanwhile Romeo, unaware of the exchange between Tybalt and Capulet, is making his way toward the beautiful girl.

39 Critical Viewing

Possible response: Romeo and Juliet are quickly falling in love. They seem transfixed and lost in their own world as they gaze at each other.

40 Literary Analysis

Dialogue and Stage Directions

1. Have students read lines 40–52.

   Ask what Romeo is describing in these lines.

   Answer: He is describing a beautiful woman he has just seen.

2. **Ask** students the Literary Analysis question: What do the stage direction in line 40 and the dialogue that follows reveal about Romeo?

   Possible response: The stage direction reveals that Romeo has seen a beautiful woman whom he does not know, and he asks the servingman who she is. The dialogue that follows reveals that Romeo has fallen in love at first sight.

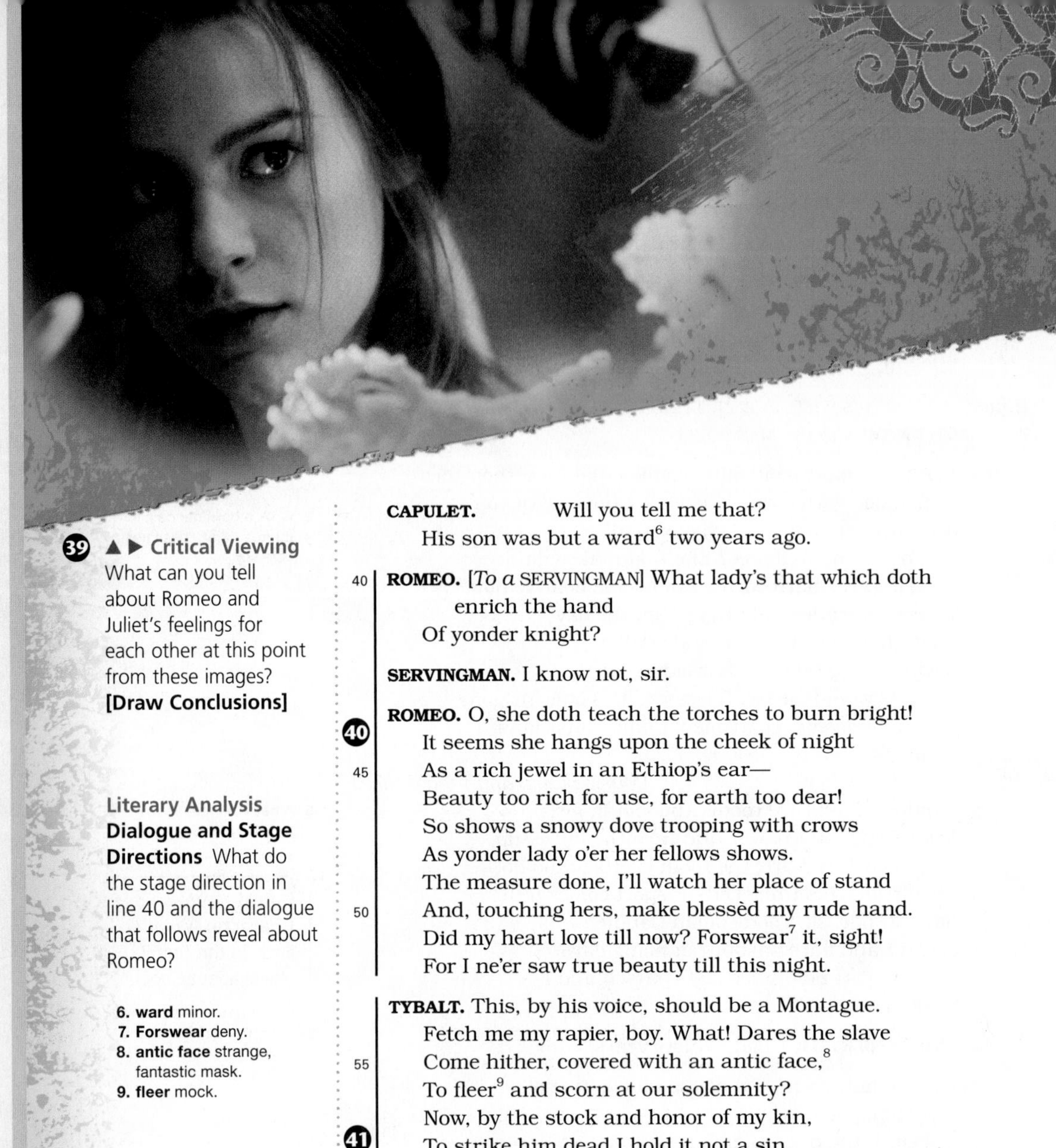

39 ▲ ▶ **Critical Viewing** What can you tell about Romeo and Juliet's feelings for each other at this point from these images? **[Draw Conclusions]**

CAPULET. Will you tell me that?
His son was but a ward[6] two years ago.

ROMEO. [*To a* SERVINGMAN] What lady's that which doth enrich the hand
Of yonder knight?

SERVINGMAN. I know not, sir.

ROMEO. O, she doth teach the torches to burn bright!
It seems she hangs upon the cheek of night
As a rich jewel in an Ethiop's ear—
Beauty too rich for use, for earth too dear!
So shows a snowy dove trooping with crows
As yonder lady o'er her fellows shows.
The measure done, I'll watch her place of stand
And, touching hers, make blessèd my rude hand.
Did my heart love till now? Forswear[7] it, sight!
For I ne'er saw true beauty till this night.

40 Literary Analysis **Dialogue and Stage Directions** What do the stage direction in line 40 and the dialogue that follows reveal about Romeo?

TYBALT. This, by his voice, should be a Montague.
Fetch me my rapier, boy. What! Dares the slave
Come hither, covered with an antic face,[8]
To fleer[9] and scorn at our solemnity?
Now, by the stock and honor of my kin,
To strike him dead I hold it not a sin.

41

CAPULET. Why, how now, kinsman? Wherefore storm you so?

TYBALT. Uncle, this is a Montague, our foe,
A villain, that is hither come in spite

6. **ward** minor.
7. **Forswear** deny.
8. **antic face** strange, fantastic mask.
9. **fleer** mock.

Vocabulary Development

CCSS Language 6

Selection Vocabulary Reinforcement

Students will benefit from additional examples and practice with the selection vocabulary words. Reinforce their comprehension with "show-you-know" sentences. The first part of the sentence uses the vocabulary word in an appropriate context. The second part of the sentence—the "show-you-know" part—clarifies the first. Model the strategy with this example for *pernicious:*

The effects of the medication were *pernicious;* she nearly died from the side effects.

Then, give students these sentence prompts, and coach them in creating the clarification part:

1. The company had received a *grievance* about one of its products; __________.

   Sample answer: it was investigating the basis for the complaint.

2. He is planning on *augmenting* his income; __________.

   Sample answer: he is currently looking for a part-time job in the evening.

To scorn at our solemnity this night.

CAPULET. Young Romeo is it?

TYBALT. 'Tis he, that villain Romeo.

CAPULET. Content thee, gentle coz,[10] let him alone.
'A bears him like a portly gentleman,[11]
And, to say truth, Verona brags of him
To be a virtuous and well-governed youth.
I would not for the wealth of all this town
Here in my house do him disparagement.[12]
Therefore be patient; take no note of him.
It is my will, the which if thou respect,
Show a fair presence and put off these frowns,
An ill-beseeming semblance[13] for a feast.

41 **TYBALT.** It fits when such a villain is a guest.
I'll not endure him.

CAPULET. He shall be endured.
What, goodman[14] boy! I say he shall. Go to![15]
Am I the master here, or you? Go to!
You'll not endure him, God shall mend my soul![16]
You'll make a mutiny among my guests!
You will set cock-a-hoop.[17] You'll be the man!

TYBALT. Why, uncle, 'tis a shame.

CAPULET. Go to, go to!
You are a saucy boy. Is't so, indeed?
This trick may chance to scathe you.[18] I know what.
You must contrary me! Marry, 'tis time—
Well said, my hearts!—You are a princox[19]—go!
Be quiet, or—more light, more light!—For shame!
I'll make you quiet. What!—Cheerly, my hearts!

10. **coz** Here, "coz" is used as a term of address for a relative.
11. **'A . . . gentleman** He behaves like a dignified gentleman.
12. **disparagement** insult.
13. **ill-beseeming semblance** inappropriate appearance.
14. **goodman** term of address for someone below the rank of gentleman.
15. **Go to!** expression of angry impatience.
16. **God . . . soul!** expression of impatience, equivalent to "God save me!"
17. **You will set cock-a-hoop** You want to swagger like a barnyard rooster.

Literary Analysis
Dialogue What does the dialogue between Capulet and Tybalt show about their relationship?

18. **This . . . you** This trait of yours may turn out to hurt you.
19. **princox** rude youngster; wise guy.

42 
Reading Check
How does Capulet respond when Tybalt says he will not tolerate Romeo's presence at the party?

Differentiated Instruction for Universal Access

EL Pronunciation for English Learners
Students may have difficulty pronouncing the "v" sound as in *villain, Verona,* and *virtuous.* They may replace it with the "b" sound as in *ball.* To aid with pronunciation, write the following word pairs on the board: *bat* and *vat, best* and *vest,* and *buy* and *vie.* Pronounce each word in turn, having students repeat each. Then, call out the words at random, having students write down each word. Compare and discuss the results with the class, noting what might have led to incorrect choices.

Culturally Responsive Instruction
Culture Focus On this page, Capulet insists that Romeo be treated respectfully, even though Romeo is an enemy. Point out to students that the treatment of guests involves culturally based traditions and norms. Discuss students' cultural traditions. Use the following questions to prompt discussion:

- How do you greet houseguests?
- What food, drink, or other items do you offer your guests?
- Where do overnight guests stay?

41 Literary Analysis
Dialogue

1. Have students read lines 53–87. Have students recall Tybalt's first appearance in the play (p. 810) and compare it with the dialogue in lines 53–58. Are the two scenes similar or different?
   Answer: Here, as earlier, Tybalt is instantly ready to fight and kill anyone he sees as a threat to the Capulets. He is hotheaded and dangerous.
2. **Ask** students what Tybalt means by his first line of dialogue.
   Answer: He means that he can tell who Romeo is by his voice. Since Romeo and his friends have put on masks, they cannot be recognized by their appearances.
3. **Ask** what Tybalt means by saying that Romeo has come with an "antic face,/To fleer and scorn at our solemnity"?
   Answer: He means that Romeo has come wearing a mask to mock the Capulets in their important celebration.
4. **Ask** how Capulet responds in lines 64–73 when he learns that Romeo is at his feast.
   Answer: He does not seem disturbed by Romeo's presence. He says that Romeo is behaving like a gentleman, and besides, he has heard good things about Romeo. He does not want Romeo to be insulted in his house, so he advises Tybalt to ignore his presence.
5. Have students review lines 60–87. Then, **ask** the Literary Analysis question: What does the dialogue between Capulet and Tybalt show about their relationship?
   Possible response: The dialogue shows that Capulet has authority over Tybalt, and that he thinks Tybalt is rude, arrogant, and a troublemaker.

42 Reading Check

Answer: Capulet rebukes Tybalt's contrariness and tells him to leave Romeo alone.

43 Literary Analysis

Dialogue and Stage Directions

1. Have students read lines 92–109. **Ask** students why Romeo apologizes in lines 92–93.

   Answer: He has taken Juliet's hand in his.

2. **Ask** students what Romeo means when he asks Juliet if saints have lips. What is Juliet's answer?

   Answer: Romeo suggests that saints, if they have lips, can kiss with lips rather than touch hands. Juliet deftly responds that saints' lips are used for prayer.

3. **Ask** students the Literary Analysis question: What do the dialogue and stage directions in this passage reveal about Romeo's and Juliet's feelings?

   Answer: The dialogue and stage directions reveal that Romeo and Juliet are strongly attracted to each other.

4. **Ask** what character traits Romeo and Juliet reveal in their words to each other.

   Answer: Romeo and Juliet are both clever and playful; they also show a mixture of modesty and frankness.

44 Background

Sonnet

Point out that lines 92–105 form a Shakespearean sonnet. The original form of the sonnet, known as the Italian or Petrarchan sonnet, was created by the Italian poet Petrarch in the fourteenth century and consists of two stanzas—an octave with the rhyme scheme *abba abba* and a sestet with the rhyme scheme *cdecde* or *cdcdcd*. Shakespeare adapted a variant, which consists of three quatrains and a terminal couplet, and has the rhyme scheme *abab cdcd efef gg*.

Shakespeare, the acknowledged master of the sonnet, demonstrated his talent by working sonnets into *The Tragedy of Romeo and Juliet*.

TYBALT. Patience perforce with willful choler meeting[20]
Makes my flesh tremble in their different greeting.
I will withdraw; but this intrusion shall,
Now seeming sweet, convert to bitt'rest gall. [*Exit.*]

ROMEO. If I profane with my unworthiest hand
This holy shrine,[21] the gentle sin is this:
My lips, two blushing pilgrims, ready stand
To smooth that rough touch with a tender kiss.

JULIET. Good pilgrim, you do wrong your hand too much,
Which mannerly devotion shows in this;
For saints have hands that pilgrims' hands do touch
And palm to palm is holy palmers'[22] kiss.

ROMEO. Have not saints lips, and holy palmers too?

JULIET. Ay, pilgrim, lips that they must use in prayer.

ROMEO. O, then, dear saint, let lips do what hands do!
They pray; grant thou, lest faith turn to despair.

JULIET. Saints do not move,[23] though grant for prayers' sake.

ROMEO. Then move not while my prayer's effect I take.
Thus from my lips, by thine my sin is purged. [*Kisses her.*]

JULIET. Then have my lips the sin that they have took.

ROMEO. Sin from my lips? O trespass sweetly urged![24]
Give me my sin again. [*Kisses her.*]

JULIET. You kiss by th' book.[25]

NURSE. Madam, your mother craves a word with you.

ROMEO. What is her mother?

NURSE. Marry, bachelor,
Her mother is the lady of the house,
And a good lady, and a wise and virtuous.
I nursed her daughter that you talked withal.
I tell you, he that can lay hold of her
Shall have the chinks.[26]

ROMEO. Is she a Capulet?
O dear account! My life is my foe's debt.[27]

BENVOLIO. Away, be gone; the sport is at the best.

ROMEO. Ay, so I fear; the more is my unrest.

20. **Patience . . . meeting** enforced self-control mixing with strong anger.
21. **shrine** Juliet's hand.
22. **palmers** pilgrims who at one time carried palm branches from the Holy Land.
23. **move** initiate involvement in earthly affairs.
24. **O . . . urged!** Romeo is saying, in substance, that he is happy. Juliet calls his kiss a sin, for now he can take it back—by another kiss.
25. **by th' book** as if you were following a manual of courtly love.
26. **chinks** cash.
27. **My life . . . debt** Since Juliet is a Capulet, Romeo's life is at the mercy of the enemies of his family.

Literary Analysis
Dialogue and Stage Directions What do the dialogue and stage directions in this passage reveal about Romeo's and Juliet's feelings?

Vocabulary Development

Vocabulary Knowledge Rating

When students have completed reading and discussing Act I of *The Tragedy of Romeo and Juliet,* have them take out their **Vocabulary Knowledge Rating Chart** for this selection. Read the words aloud once more and have students rate their knowledge of the words again in the After Reading column. Clarify any words that are still problematic. Have students write their own definition and example or sentence in the appropriate column. Then, have students complete the Vocabulary Practice activities at the end of the selection. Encourage students to use the words in further discussion and written work about this selection. Remind them that they will be accountable for these words on the **Selection Test, *Unit 5 Resources*,** pp. 35–37 or 38–40.

CAPULET. Nay, gentlemen, prepare not to be gone;
We have a trifling foolish banquet towards.[28]
Is it e'en so?[29] Why then, I thank you all.
I thank you, honest gentlemen. Good night.
More torches here! Come on then; let's to bed.
Ah, sirrah, by my fay,[30] it waxes late;
I'll to my rest. [*Exit all but* JULIET *and* NURSE.]

45 **JULIET.** Come hither, nurse. What is yond gentleman?

NURSE. The son and heir of old Tiberio.

JULIET. What's he that now is going out of door?

NURSE. Marry, that, I think, be young Petruchio.

JULIET. What's he that follows here, that would not dance?

NURSE. I know not.

JULIET. Go ask his name—If he is married,

28. **towards** being prepared.
29. **Is . . . so?** Is it the case that you really must leave?
30. **fay** faith.

Literary Analysis
Dialogue and Stage Directions How can you tell that the dialogue that follows line 126 is a private conversation?

46 
Reading Check
How does Romeo get Juliet to kiss him?

45 Literary Analysis

Dialogue and Stage Directions

1. **Ask** students what is happening in lines 117–126.

   Answer: When Romeo realizes Juliet is a Capulet, he starts to leave. Capulet, seeing Romeo and his friends leaving, urges them to stay and have some food, but they rush out.

2. Refer students to lines 125–126. **Ask** the Literary Analysis question: How can you tell that the dialogue that follows line 126 is a private conversation?

   Answer: The stage directions indicate that everyone but Juliet and the Nurse leave.

3. **Ask** students what Juliet wants to know about Romeo after he leaves the feast.

   Answer: Juliet asks the Nurse who Romeo is and whether he is married.

46 Reading Check

Answer: He asks her to purge his sin and answer his prayer by kissing him with her saintly lips.

Concept Connector

Activating Prior Knowledge

Have students return to the ideas they generated before reading this act. Discuss in what ways the play met their expectations and in what ways it surprised them.

Writing About the Big Question

Have students compare their responses to the sentence starter they completed before reading this act with their ideas afterwards. Ask them to explain whether their thoughts have changed.

Reading Skill Graphic Organizer

Have students review the graphic organizers they completed to summarize scenes. Show them **Reading Skill Graphic Organizer A** (*Graphic Organizer Transparencies*, p. 147) as an example. Then, have students share the graphic organizers they did and the summaries they completed.

47 Connecting to the Big Question

1. Read the bracketed text.
2. **Ask:** Based on this passage, how does family background influence the young couple's love?

   Possible response: Juliet laments the fact that she has fallen in love with her only enemy, and she has found out too late. Their family backgrounds cast a shadow over the love between Romeo and Juliet.

ASSESS

Answers

Critical Thinking

Remind students to support their answers with evidence from the text.

1. (a) Both Romeo and Juliet are children of privilege with authoritative parents. (b) Romeo is moody, impulsive, and romantic. Juliet, by contrast, is a dutiful young girl who, before meeting Romeo, does not seem to have given much thought to love. When they meet, they are so in tune with each other that their words create a sonnet.
2. (a) Both families are of high social rank and carry an ancient grudge. (b) Juliet realizes that she is in love with a family enemy.
3. The practical Benvolio and the joking Mercutio create a contrast to the moody Romeo.
4. (a) The families are feuding, and Juliet's parents are considering marrying her to Paris. (b) **Possible response:** They may attempt to meet in secret.
5. **Possible response:** Romeo's brief passion for Rosaline and his instant love for Juliet show a teen's intense emotions.
6. **Possible response:** Since they come from feuding families, their differences set up their relationship as betrayal. However, their differences may make them even more attracted to each other, since their love is forbidden.

My grave is like to be my wedding bed.

NURSE. His name is Romeo, and a Montague,
The only son of your great enemy.

45

47 **JULIET.** My only love, sprung from my only hate!
Too early seen unknown, and known too late!
Prodigious[31] birth of love it is to me
That I must love a loathèd enemy.

NURSE. What's this? What's this?

JULIET. A rhyme I learnt even now.
Of one I danced withal. [*One calls within, "JULIET."*]

NURSE. Anon, anon!
Come, let's away; the strangers all are gone. [*Exit all.*]

31. Prodigious monstrous; foretelling misfortune.

Critical Thinking

Cite textual evidence to support your responses.

1. **Key Ideas and Details** **(a)** Based on Act I, what do you know about Romeo's life and Juliet's life? **(b) Compare and Contrast:** Use details from the text to show how their personalities are similar and different.
2. **Key Ideas and Details** **(a)** What information about the two households is presented in the Prologue? **(b) Connect:** How does Juliet's comment in Act I, Scene v, lines 137–138, echo the Prologue? Explain your response.
3. **Key Ideas and Details** **Analyze:** How do the comments of Mercutio and Benvolio add to your understanding of Romeo's character? Explain your answer.
4. **Key Ideas and Details** **(a) Analyze:** What threats to Romeo and Juliet's love already exist in Act I? **(b) Speculate:** How do you think Romeo and Juliet will react to these threats? Explain your response.
5. **Integration of Knowledge and Ideas** **Evaluate:** Based on Romeo's behavior in Act I, do you think Shakespeare accurately portrays a teenager in love? Explain.
6. **Integration of Knowledge and Ideas** How do the differences between Romeo and Juliet define their relationship? Explain. *[Connect to the Big Question: Do our differences define us?]*

Assessment Resources

Unit 5 Resources

L1 L2 EL **Selection Test A,** pp. 35–37. Administer Test A to less advanced students.

L3 L4 EL **Selection Test B,** pp. 38–40. Administer Test B to on-level and more advanced students.

L3 L4 **Open-Book Test,** pp. 32–34. As an alternative, give the Open-Book Test.

All **Customizable Test Bank**

All **Self-tests**
Students may prepare for the **Selection Test** by taking the **Self-test** online.

PHLit Online! All assessment resources are available at **www.PHLitOnline.com.**

After You Read The Tragedy of Romeo and Juliet, Act I

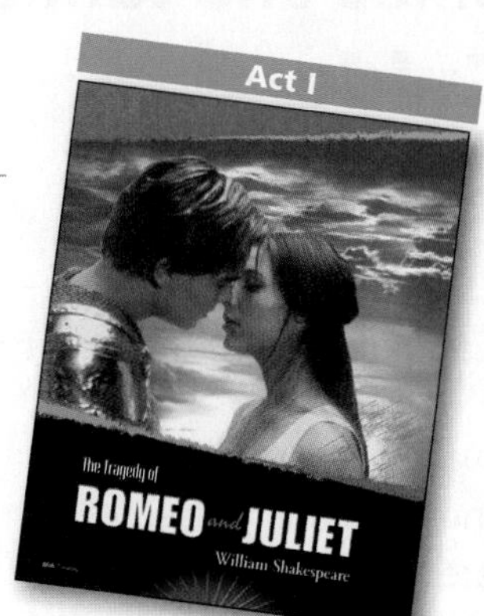

Literary Analysis: Dialogue and Stage Directions

1. **Key Ideas and Details** Using a chart like the one shown, explain what the **dialogue** involving the Nurse, Juliet, and Lady Capulet in Act I, Scene iii, reveals about each character.

Character	Dialogue	→	Reveals
		→	

2. **Craft and Structure (a)** Identify three examples of **stage directions** that do more than simply dictate characters' movements on and off stage. **(b)** Explain what each direction tells about the characters and the action.

Reading Skill: Summarize

3. Use **text aids** to restate Capulet's scolding of Tybalt in Act I, Scene v, lines 77–87, in your own words.
4. **(a)** Using text aids to clarify her meaning, explain the play on words in Juliet's speech in Act I, Scene v, lines 96–99.
   (b) Summarize her speech in a few sentences.

Vocabulary

Acquisition and Use An **oxymoron** is a phrase combining contradictory or opposing ideas, often used as a figure of speech for poetic effect. Review the vocabulary list on page 804. Then, explain the meaning of each phrase and tell why each one is an oxymoron.

1. pernicious blessing
2. augmenting scarcity
3. flattering grievance
4. honorable transgression
5. cooperative adversary
6. cheerful oppression

Word Study Use the context of the sentences and what you know about the **Latin prefix *trans-*** to explain your answer to each question.

1. Can you *transfer* information from the Internet to a computer?
2. If the operation of a government office is *transparent,* will people know what is going on?

Word Study

The **Latin prefix *trans-*** means "across," "over," or "through."

Apply It Explain how the prefix *trans-* contributes to the meanings of these words. You may consult a dictionary if necessary.

transport
translucent
transition

ASSESS/EXTEND

Answers

Literary Analysis

1. **Character**: Nurse; **Dialogue:** lines 59–62. **Reveals:** She is very talkative; she is very fond of Juliet.

   For other sample answers, see ***Graphic Organizer Transparencies,*** **Literary Analysis Graphic Organizer A,** p. 149, and the **Additional Answers** section.

2. (a) and (b) In Scene i, "Aide to Gregory" tells the reader that Sampson is whispering to Gregory so that Abram does not hear; in Scene i, "They fight" indicates that Gregory and Sampson are fighting Abram and Balthasar. In Scene v, "Music plays" indicates that guests at Capulet's feast begin to dance.

Reading Skill

3. **Possible response:** "Leave him alone. Who's in charge here, me or you? If you don't leave him alone, my guests will riot. But you want to act macho. That's going to hurt you."
4. (a) Juliet is playing on the words *palm* and *palmer,* implying that she and Romeo have kissed by touching hands. (b) **Possible response:** "Don't be concerned about your hand touching mine. Pilgrims placed their palms against a saint's palms, which is the same as a kiss."

Vocabulary

Acquisition and Use

1. *Pernicious* means "causing great injury," and it's the opposite of a *blessing,* which is something good.
2. *Augmenting* means "increasing" and *scarcity* means the opposite, "lacking" or a "shortage".
3. Something *flattering* is pleasing. A *grievance* is an injury or an injustice, so these words are opposites.
4. A *transgression* is a wrongdoing, so it would not be something that would be considered *honorable.*
5. An *adversary* is someone you oppose, so you wouldn't feel *cooperative* or helpful toward him or her.

Continued from right column

6. Someone who is feeling *oppression* is weighed down with worry and wouldn't be *cheerful.*

Word Study

Sample answers:

1. Yes, the prefix *trans-* means "over," so *transfer* means "to move from one place over to another." Information in the Internet can be downloaded—transferred onto a computer.
2. Yes, the prefix *trans-* means "through," *so transparent* means "easily seen through." If a government office is *transparent,* it is operating out in the open so everyone knows what is going on.

Word Study: Apply It

Sample answers:

To *transport* is to move across or through. If something is *translucent,* you can see through it. A *transition* is a change from one condition over to another.

The Tragedy of Romeo and Juliet, Act II
Lesson Pacing Guide

DAY 1 Preteach

- Administer the Reading and Vocabulary Warm-ups (*Unit 5 Resources*, pp. 41–44) as necessary.
- Introduce the Reading Skill: Summarize.
- Introduce the Literary Analysis concept: Blank Verse.
- Distribute copies of the appropriate graphic organizer for the Reading Skill (*Graphic Organizer Transparencies*, pp. 151–152).
- Distribute copies of the appropriate graphic organizer for Literary Analysis (*Graphic Organizer Transparencies*, pp. 153–154).
- Teach the selection vocabulary.
- Introduce the Word Study skill.

DAYS 2–3 Preteach/Teach

- Build background with the Background feature.
- Develop thematic vocabulary and thematic thinking with Writing About the Big Question.
- Prepare students to read with the Activating Prior Knowledge activities (TE).
- Informally monitor comprehension while students read.
- Use the Reading Check questions to confirm comprehension.
- Develop students' ability to summarize, using the Reading Skill questions.
- Develop students' understanding of blank verse, using the Literary Analysis questions.
- Reinforce vocabulary with the Vocabulary notes.
- Reinforce unit focus standards using the Spiral Review prompts.

DAY 4 Assess

- Assess students' comprehension and mastery of the skills by having them answer the Critical Thinking, Reading Skill, and Literary Analysis questions.
- Have students complete the Vocabulary Practice activities.
- Have students complete the Word Study activities.

DAY 5 Extend/Assess

- Have students complete the Conventions lesson.
- Extend learning by having students complete the Research and Technology activity, an annotated flowchart, p. 935. (You may assign as homework.) As an alternative, assign them "What Is Love?" in *Reality Central*.
- Administer Selection Test A or B (*Unit 5 Resources*, pp. 53–58).

Common Core State Standards

Reading Literature

2. Determine a theme or central idea of a text; provide an objective summary of the text.

3. Analyze how complex characters (e.g., those with multiple or conflicting motivations) develop over the course of a text, interact with other characters, and advance the plot or develop the theme.

5. Analyze how an author's choices concerning how to structure a text, order events within it, and manipulate time create such effects as mystery, tension, or surprise.

Additional Standards Practice
***Common Core Companion*, pp. 28–29**

Daily Block Scheduling
Each day in this Lesson Pacing Guide represents a 40–50 minute period. Teachers using block scheduling may combine days to revise pacing. In addition, teachers may differentiate and support core instruction by integrating components for extended and intensive support as students require. See the Guide to Selected Leveled Resources (facing page).

Guide to Selected Leveled Resources

RTI Tier 1 (students performing on level)			The Tragedy of Romeo and Juliet, Act II
Warm Up	Whole class instruction; Group work	**Practice, model,** and **monitor** fluency, working **with the whole class** or **in groups.**	**Vocabulary** and **Reading Warm-ups B,** ***Unit 5 Resources,*** pp. 41–42, 44
Comprehension/Skills	Whole class instruction; Independent work	**Support** and **monitor** comprehension and skills development, having students complete the activities, graphic organizers, and interactive prompts **independently** or **as a class.**	• ***Reader's Notebook,*** adapted instruction and full selection EL ***Reader's Notebook: English Learner's Version,*** adapted instruction and adapted selection • **Reading Skill Graphic Organizer B,** ***Graphic Organizer Transparencies,*** p. 152 • **Literary Analysis Graphic Organizer B,** ***Graphic Organizer Transparencies,*** p. 154
Monitor Progress	A	**Monitor** student progress with the differentiated curriculum-based assessment in the *Unit Resources.*	• **Selection Test B,** ***Unit 5 Resources,*** pp. 56–58 • **Open-Book Test,** ***Unit 5 Resources,*** pp. 50–52

RTI Tier 2 (students requiring intervention)			The Tragedy of Romeo and Juliet, Act II
Warm Up	Whole class instruction; Group work	**Practice, model,** and **monitor** fluency **in groups** or **with individuals.**	• **Vocabulary and Reading Warm-ups A,** ***Unit 5 Resources,*** pp. 41–44 • ***Reality Central,*** "What Is Love?" • ***Hear It!*** **Audio CD (adapted text)**
Comprehension/Skills	Whole class instruction; Independent work	• **Support** and **monitor** comprehension and skills development, working **in small groups** or **with individuals.** • **Pair** students with more advanced peers and have them complete the writing activity in the *Real-World Writing Journal.* • As students complete the selection in the appropriate version of the *Reader's Notebook,* **monitor** comprehension frequently with group questions and individual instruction. • **Model** strategies while guiding students in completing the activities and prompts in the *Reader's Notebook,* as well as the graphic organizers. • **Practice** skills and **monitor** mastery with the *Reading Kit* worksheets.	• ***Real-World Writing Journal,*** Lesson 1, pp. 138–141 • ***Reader's Notebook: Adapted Version,*** adapted instruction and adapted selection EL ***Reader's Notebook: English Learner's Version,*** adapted instruction and adapted selection • **Reading Skill Graphic Organizer A,** ***Graphic Organizer Transparencies,*** p. 151 • **Literary Analysis Graphic Organizer A,** ***Graphic Organizer Transparencies,*** p. 153 • **Reading Kit,** Practice worksheets, pp. 204, 214, 218
Monitor Progress	A	**Monitor** student progress with the differentiated curriculum-based assessment in the *Unit Resources* and in the *Reading Kit.*	• **Selection Test A,** ***Unit 5 Resources,*** pp. 53–55 • **Reading Kit,** Assess worksheets pp. 205, 215, 219

TIER 3 Tier 3 intervention may require consultation with the student's special-education or dyslexia specialist. For additional support, see the Tier 2 activities and resources listed above.

One-on-one teaching **Group work** **Whole class instruction** **Independent work** **A Assessment**

For a complete guide to selection support, including support for Advanced students, see the Overview of Resources in the frontmatter.

Visual Guide to Featured Selection Resources

✓ The Tragedy of Romeo and Juliet, Act II

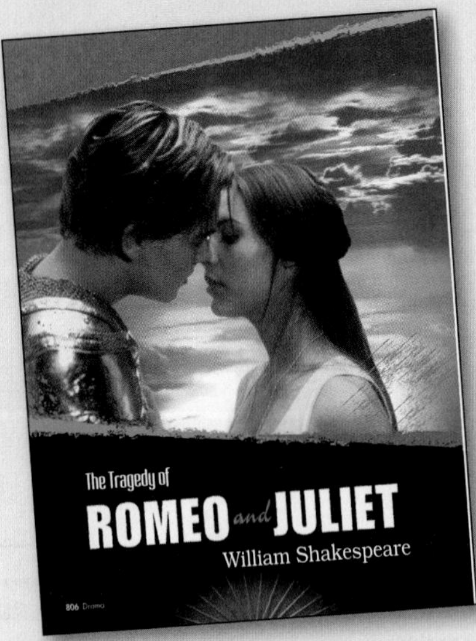

RESOURCES FOR:

- **L1 Special-Needs Students**
- **L2 Below-Level Students (Tier 2)**
- **L3 On-Level Students (Tier 1)**
- **L4 Advanced Students (Tier 1)**
- **EL English Learners**
- **All All Students**

Vocabulary/Fluency/Prior Knowledge

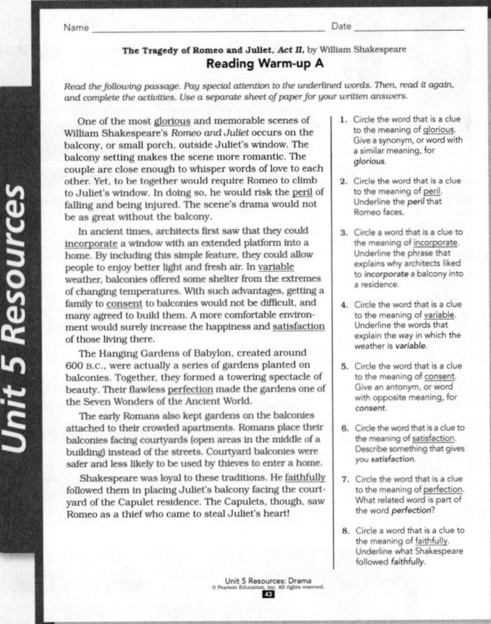

Unit 5 Resources

Name ____________________ Date ____________

The Tragedy of Romeo and Juliet, *Act II*, by William Shakespeare

Reading Warm-up A

Read the following passage. Pay special attention to the underlined words. Then, read it again, and complete the activities. Use a separate sheet of paper for your written answers.

One of the most glorious and memorable scenes of William Shakespeare's *Romeo and Juliet* occurs on the balcony, or small porch, outside Juliet's window. The balcony setting makes the scene more romantic. The couple are close enough to whisper words of love to each other. Yet, to be together would require Romeo to climb to Juliet's window. In doing so, he would risk the peril of falling and being injured. The scene's drama would not be as great without the balcony.

In ancient times, architects first saw that they could incorporate a window with an extended platform into a home. By including this simple feature, they could allow people to enjoy better light and fresh air. In variable weather, balconies offered some shelter from the extremes of changing temperatures. With such advantages, getting a family to consent to balconies would not be difficult, and many agreed to build them. A more comfortable environment would surely increase the happiness and satisfaction of those living there.

The Hanging Gardens of Babylon, created around 600 B.C., were actually a series of gardens planted on balconies. Together, they formed a towering spectacle of beauty. Their flawless perfection made the gardens one of the Seven Wonders of the Ancient World.

The early Romans also kept gardens on the balconies attached to their crowded apartments. Romans place their balconies facing courtyards (open areas in the middle of a building) instead of the streets. Courtyard balconies were safer and less likely to be used by thieves to enter a home.

Shakespeare was loyal to these traditions. He faithfully followed them in placing Juliet's balcony facing the courtyard of the Capulet residence. The Capulets, though, saw Romeo as a thief who came to steal Juliet's heart!

1. Circle the word that is a clue to the meaning of glorious. Give a synonym, or word with a similar meaning, for *glorious*.
2. Circle the word that is a clue to the meaning of peril. Underline the *peril* that Romeo faces.
3. Circle a word that is a clue to the meaning of incorporate. Underline the phrase that explains why architects liked to *incorporate* a balcony into a residence.
4. Circle the word that is a clue to the meaning of variable. Underline the words that explain the way in which the weather is *variable*.
5. Circle the word that is a clue to the meaning of consent. Give an antonym, or word with opposite meaning, for *consent*.
6. Circle the word that is a clue to the meaning of satisfaction. Describe something that gives you *satisfaction*.
7. Circle the word that is a clue to the meaning of perfection. What related word is part of the word *perfection*?
8. Circle a word that is a clue to the meaning of faithfully. Underline what Shakespeare followed *faithfully*.

Unit 5 Resources: Drama

43

EL L1 L2 **Reading Warm-ups A and B,** pp. 43–44

Also available for this selection:

EL L1 L2 **Vocabulary Warm-ups A and B,** pp. 41–42

All **Writing About the Big Question,** p. 45

All **Vocabulary Builder,** p. 48

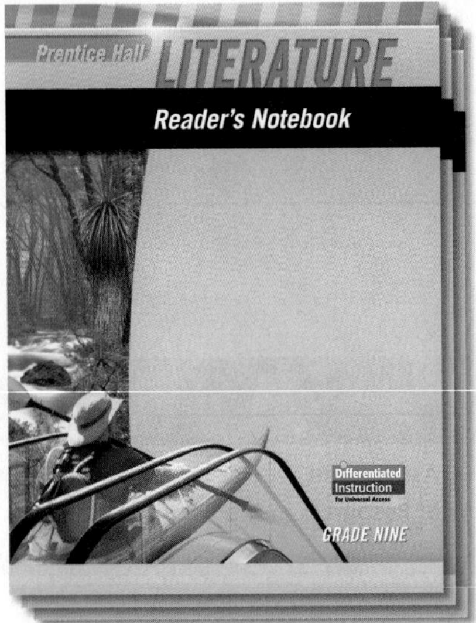

Reader's Notebooks

Pre- and postreading pages, as well as the selection *The Tragedy of Romeo and Juliet,* Act II, appear in an interactive format in the *Reader's Notebooks*. Each *Notebook* is differentiated for a different group of learners. The selections in the Adapted and English Learner's versions are abridged.

L2 L3 ***Reader's Notebook***

L1 ***Reader's Notebook: Adapted Version***

EL ***Reader's Notebook: English Learner's Version***

EL ***Reader's Notebook: Spanish Version***

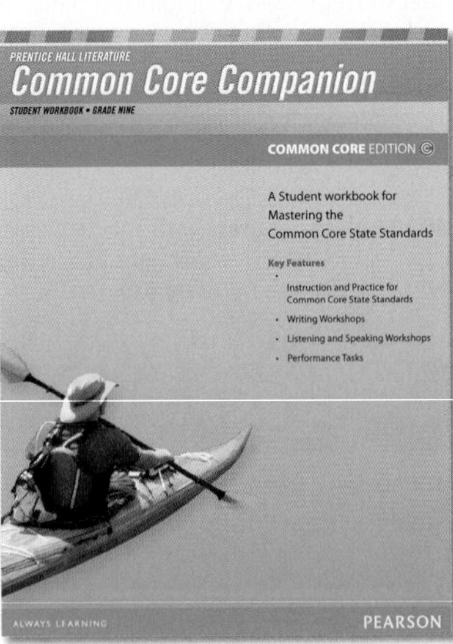

Common Core Companion

Additional instruction and practice for each Common Core State Standard

Selection Support

Graphic Organizer Transparencies

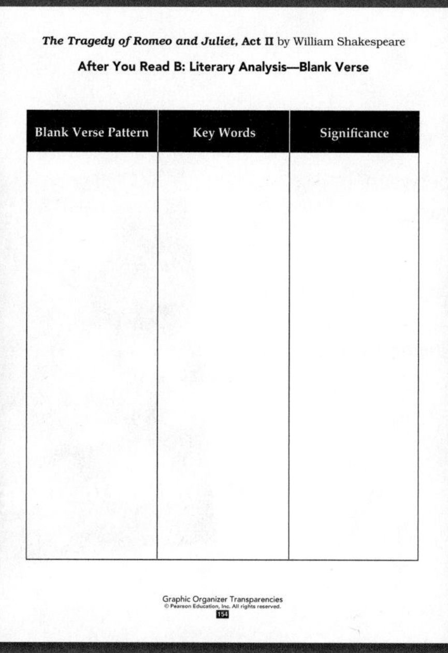

The Tragedy of Romeo and Juliet, **Act II** by William Shakespeare

After You Read B: Literary Analysis—Blank Verse

Blank Verse Pattern	Key Words	Significance

Graphic Organizer Transparencies

154

EL L3 Literary Analysis: Graphic Organizer B, p. 154

Also available for this selection:

- **EL L1 L2 Reading: Graphic Organizer A,** p. 151 (partially filled in)
- **EL L3 Reading: Graphic Organizer B,** p. 152
- **EL L1 L2 Literary Analysis: Graphic Organizer A,** p. 153 (partially filled in)

Skills Development/Extension

Unit 5 Resources

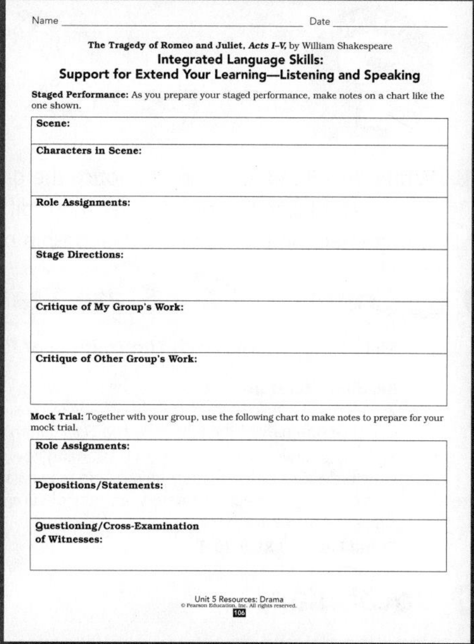

Name ______________________ Date __________

The Tragedy of Romeo and Juliet, *Acts I–V,* by William Shakespeare
Integrated Language Skills:
Support for Extend Your Learning—Listening and Speaking

Staged Performance: As you prepare your staged performance, make notes on a chart like the one shown.

Scene:
Characters in Scene:
Role Assignments:
Stage Directions:
Critique of My Group's Work:
Critique of Other Group's Work:

Mock Trial: Together with your group, use the following chart to make notes to prepare for your mock trial.

Role Assignments:
Depositions/Statements:
Questioning/Cross-Examination of Witnesses:

Unit 5 Resources: Drama

106

All Support for Extend Your Learning, p. 106

Also available for this selection:

- **All Reading: Summarize,** p. 47
- **All Literary Analysis: Blank Verse,** p. 46
- **L4 Enrichment,** p. 49
- **EL L3 L4 Grammar,** p. 104
- **EL L3 L4 Support for Writing,** p. 105

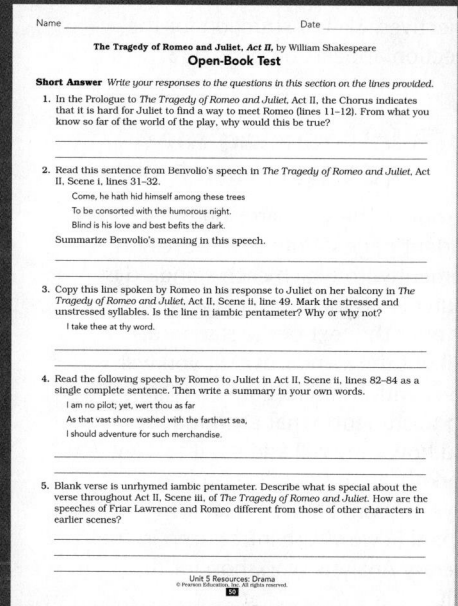

Assessment

Name ______________________ Date __________

The Tragedy of Romeo and Juliet, *Act II,* by William Shakespeare
Open-Book Test

Short Answer *Write your responses to the questions in this section on the lines provided.*

1. In the Prologue to *The Tragedy of Romeo and Juliet*, Act II, the Chorus indicates that it is hard for Juliet to find a way to meet Romeo (lines 11–12). From what you know so far of the world of the play, why would this be true?
2. Read this sentence from Benvolio's speech in *The Tragedy of Romeo and Juliet*, Act II, Scene i, lines 31–32.
   Come, he hath hid himself among these trees
   To be consorted with the humorous night.
   Blind is his love and best befits the dark.
   Summarize Benvolio's meaning in this speech.
3. Copy this line spoken by Romeo in his response to Juliet on her balcony in *The Tragedy of Romeo and Juliet*, Act II, Scene ii, line 49. Mark the stressed and unstressed syllables. Is the line in iambic pentameter? Why or why not?
   I take thee at thy word.
4. Read the following speech by Romeo to Juliet in Act II, Scene ii, lines 82–84 as a single complete sentence. Then write a summary in your own words.
   I am no pilot; yet, wert thou as far
   As that vast shore washed with the farthest sea,
   I should adventure for such merchandise.
5. Blank verse is unrhymed iambic pentameter. Describe what is special about the verse throughout Act II, Scene iii, of *The Tragedy of Romeo and Juliet*. How are the speeches of Friar Lawrence and Romeo different from those of other characters in earlier scenes?

Unit 5 Resources: Drama

50

L3 L4 Open-Book Test, pp. 50–52

Also available for this selection:

- **EL L1 L2 Selection Test A,** pp. 53–55
- **EL L3 L4 Selection Test B,** pp. 56–58

PHLit Online!
www.PHLitOnline.com

- complete narrated selection text
- a thematically related video with writing prompt
- an interactive graphic organizer
- highlighting feature
- access to all student print resources, adapted to individual student needs
- Spanish and English summaries
- adapted selection translations in Spanish

Online Resources: All print materials are also available online.

Get Connected! (thematic video with writing prompt)

Also available:

Background Video

All videos are available in Spanish.

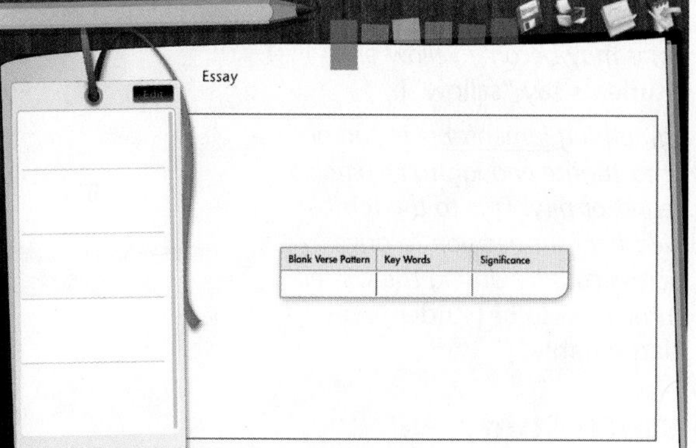

Writer's Journal (with graphics feature)

Also available:

Vocabulary Central (tools, activities, and songs for studying vocabulary)

DIFFERENTIATE/PRETEACH

Leveled Text

You may use "The Tragedy of Romeo and Juliet, Act II" to meet the lesson objectives. Skills instruction for the selection appears on page 833.

1 Introducing the CCS Standards

Introduce the standards on the student page. (Note that the lesson element with which each standard is addressed is identified in parentheses after the text of the standard.) Call out the standards that you will cover with the selections, explaining to students what each requires and how they will address it as they work through the selection you have chosen. Standards labeled "Spiral Review" are introduced in the Literary Analysis Workshop for this unit.

2 Vocabulary

1. Have students preview the selection vocabulary.
2. For each word, have students say the word aloud.
3. Then, use the word in a sentence that defines the word.
4. Finally, repeat your definitional sentence or a similar sentence with the word missing and have the class "fill in the blank" chorally. Here are some examples:

   Something sallow is of an unhealthy, yellowish color. When illness affects the skin, the skin's color may become yellow or [students say "sallow"].

   Something lamentable is bad or unfortunate enough to inspire regret or pity. Due to the terrible weather, our decision to drive across country during the winter turned out to be [students say "lamentable"].

3 Word Study

1. Introduce the skill, using the instruction in the box.
2. Using their knowledge of the Latin prefix, ask students for a *pro-* word that means "before" or "forward." *(project, provide)*

Before You Read

The Tragedy of Romeo and Juliet, Act II

THE BIG ?
Do our differences define us?

While You Read Continue to notice the differences between Romeo and Juliet. Decide whether these differences have a strong effect on the way their relationship develops.

1 Common Core State Standards

Meet these standards with ***The Tragedy of Romeo and Juliet*, Act II** (p. 834).

Reading Literature

2. Determine a theme or central idea of a text; provide an objective summary of the text. *(Reading Skill: Summarize)*

5. Analyze how an author's choices concerning how to structure a text, order events within it, and manipulate time create such effects as mystery, tension, or surprise. *(Literary Analysis: Blank Verse)*

Spiral Review: RL.9-10.3

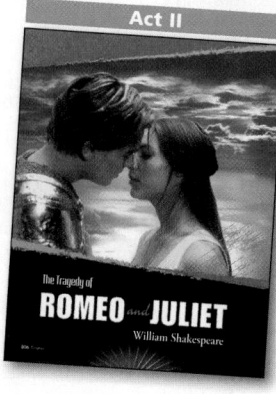

2 Vocabulary

Read each word and its definition. Decide whether you know the word well, know it a little bit, or do not know it at all. After you read, see how your knowledge of each word has increased.

- **procure** (prō kyoor′) *v.* get; obtain (p. 843) *The hungry man tried to procure food.* procurement *n.* procurable *adj.*
- **predominant** (prē däm′ ə nənt) *adj.* of or having stronger influence (p. 845) *Despite some disagreement, the predominant tone of the meeting was one of unity.* predominantly *adv.* dominant *adv.* dominate *v.*
- **intercession** (in′ tər sesh′ ən) *n.* act of pleading on another's behalf (p. 846) *Thanks to the intercession by Andy and Paula, Jim was allowed into the concert without a ticket.* intercede *v.*
- **sallow** (sal′ ō) *adj.* of a sickly, pale-yellowish hue (p. 846) *When her sickness passed, her face no longer looked sallow.* sallowness *n.*
- **lamentable** (lam′ ən tə bəl) *adj.* distressing; sad (p. 848) *His lack of concern about his health is lamentable.* lament *v.* lamentably *adv.*
- **unwieldy** (un wēl′ dē) *adj.* awkward; clumsy (p. 854) *Joe's sprained ankle made him unwieldy on the dance floor.* wield *v.*

3 Word Study

The **Latin prefix *pro-*** means "before," "forward."

In this play, Juliet promises to **procure** the opportunity to come to Romeo, if his intentions are to marry her. She means she will take steps beforehand so that she can see him.

❹ Literary Analysis: Blank Verse

Blank verse is unrhymed poetry written in a meter called iambic pentameter. A line of iambic pentameter has five stressed syllables, each preceded by an unstressed syllable, as in the following example:

- Bŭt sóft! Whăt líght thrŏugh yóndĕr wíndŏw bréaks?
- Ĭt ís thĕ eást, ănd Júlĭĕt ís thĕ sún!

Much of *The Tragedy of Romeo and Juliet* is written in blank verse. Shakespeare uses its formal meter to reinforce character rank. Important or aristocratic characters typically speak in blank verse. Minor or comic characters often do not speak in verse. This deliberate change in style has an impact on the tone and mood of the character's interactions.

❺ Reading Skill: Summarize

Summarizing is briefly stating the main ideas in a piece of writing. Stopping periodically to summarize what you have read helps you to check your comprehension before you read further.

Summarizing is especially useful when reading a play that has long passages of blank verse. When you encounter one of these passages, **read in sentences**—just as if you were reading a poem. Pause according to the punctuation instead of at the end of each line. As you become more accustomed to the form, you will be able to increase your speed.

Once you have grasped the meanings of individual sentences in blank verse, you can more easily and accurately summarize long passages.

❻ Using the Strategy: Summarizing Chart

Use a chart like this one to summarize passages in this act of the drama.

Passage	Sentences	Summary
What's Montague? It is nor hand, nor foot, / Nor arm, nor face, nor any other part / Belonging to a man. O, be some other name! / What's in a name? That which we call a rose / By any other name would smell as sweet.	❶ What's Montague? ❷ It is nor hand, nor foot, Nor arm, nor face, nor any other part Belonging to a man. ❸ O, be some other name! ❹ What's in a name? ❺ That which we call a rose By any other name would smell as sweet.	Montague is just a name; it's not who Romeo physically is, but Juliet wishes he had another name because of what she knows it represents.

PHLit Online!
www.PHLitOnline.com

Hear It!
- Selection summary audio
- Selection audio

See It!
- Get Connected video
- Background video
- More about the author
- Vocabulary flashcards

Do It!
- Interactive journals
- Interactive graphic organizers
- Self-test
- Internet activity
- Grammar tutorial
- Interactive vocabulary games

❹ Literary Analysis

Blank Verse

1. Introduce the skill, using instruction on the student page.
2. Tell students that they will practice analyzing blank verse as they read.

Think Aloud: Model the Skill

Write the following line on the board: *She tramped among the tiger lilies fair.* Model a way to analyze blank verse. Say to students:

As I read this line of poetry, I notice that it is in blank verse and contains five stressed syllables, each preceded by an unstressed syllable. The stressed syllables are *tramp-, -mong, ti-, lil-,* and *fair.*

Because this line comes from a play during Shakespeare's time, I conclude that the character delivering the line is of high social rank. The meter lends formality and distinction to both the writing and the character.

❺ Reading Skill

Summarize

1. Introduce the skill, using instruction on the student page.
2. Tell students that they will practice summarizing as they read.

❻ Using the Strategy

Give students a copy of either **Literary Analysis Graphic Organizer A** or **B** (*Graphic Organizer Transparencies,* pp. 153–154) to record details about blank verse. Use the examples in **Literary Analysis Graphic Organizer A,** which is partially filled in, to model completing the organizer.

Differentiated Instruction — Additional Instruction

EL Extended Support—English Learners
Have students complete the **Reading and Vocabulary Warm-Ups, *Unit 5 Resources,*** pp. 41–44, before they read. Assign the prereading pages for the selection in the ***Reader's Notebook: English Learner's Version.*** Then, have students listen to portions of the selection on the ***Hear It!*** **Audio CD.**

L1 L2 Extended Support—Struggling Readers
Have students complete the **Reading and Vocabulary Warm-Ups, *Unit 5 Resources,*** pp. 41–44, before they read. Assign the prereading pages for the selection in the ***Reader's Notebook: Adapted Version.*** Then, have students listen to portions of the selection on the ***Hear It!*** **Audio CD** (adapted text).

Extended Support—Reluctant Readers
To build motivation and engagement before assigning the selection, have students read "What Is Love?," a thematically related selection in ***Reality Central.*** Then, use the questions at the conclusion of the related selection to guide discussion.

TEACH

❶ Activating Prior Knowledge

1. Read aloud the paragraphs under **Review and Anticipate** on p. 835.
2. Lead a discussion on the two questions posed in these paragraphs: How will Romeo and Juliet respond to their love and its problems? How will their families react?
3. Write the two questions on the board. Then, have students offer responses. Instruct students to record their responses in their notebooks. They will return to these after reading Act II.

Concept Connector

Students will return to this activity once they have read the selection.

Individual Activity

Tell students that some critics contend that Juliet is more mature than Romeo and teaches him the meaning of true love. Invite students to compare the two characters as they read this act to see whether they agree or disagree with this assessment. Have students take notes as they read and identify specific evidence supporting their viewpoint.

❷ About the Selection

You may wish to have students summarize the main plot points of Act I before they begin to read Act II. The main action of *The Tragedy of Romeo and Juliet*, Act II, is the young couple's betrothal, which occurs the night they meet, and their marriage, which occurs the day after. The act invites the audience to speculate about Romeo and Juliet's love for each other. On the one hand, they are the archetypal teenage lovers—reckless, impulsive, passionate, and head over heels in love. On the other hand, they are growing toward an adult version of love—marriage, devotion, and a willingness to make sacrifices and to take risks. As the play progresses, their love will continue to be tested.

834 Drama

Text Complexity Rubric

The Tragedy of Romeo and Juliet, Act II		
Qualitative Measures	**Context/ Knowledge Demands**	Historical: Verona, Italy 1 2 3 4 (5)
	Structure/ Language Clarity and Conventionality	Challenging vocabulary; Elizabethan terms 1 2 3 4 (5)
	Levels of Meaning/ Purpose/Concept Level	Accessible concept (classic tale of star-crossed lovers) 1 2 (3) 4 5
Quantitative Measures	**Text Length**	Word Count: 5,650
	Lexile	NP
Overall Complexity		**Complex**

❶ Review and Anticipate

❷ Act I reveals a bitter, long-standing feud between the Montagues and the Capulets. It also introduces the play's title characters, who meet at a feast and immediately fall in love, only to discover that they come from opposing sides of the feud.

Based on what you have learned about the personalities of Romeo and Juliet, how do you expect them to respond to their love for each other and to the problems it poses? How do you think their families will react?

Prologue

[*Enter* CHORUS.]

❸ **CHORUS.** Now old desire[1] doth in his deathbed lie,
And young affection gapes to be his heir;[2]
That fair[3] for which love groaned for and would die,
With tender Juliet matched, is now not fair.
Now Romeo is beloved and loves again,
Alike bewitchèd[4] by the charm of looks;
But to his foe supposed he must complain,[5]
And she steal love's sweet bait from fearful hooks.

1. **old desire** Romeo's love for Rosaline.
2. **young . . . heir** Romeo's new love for Juliet is eager to replace his love for Rosaline.
3. **fair** beautiful woman (Rosaline).
4. **Alike bewitchèd** Both Romeo and Juliet are enchanted.
5. **complain** address his words of love.

❸ Critical Thinking

Relate

1. Have a volunteer read the bracketed text aloud.
2. **Ask:** What is the Chorus announcing in this passage?

   Answer: Romeo has fallen out of love with Rosaline, and now he is in love with Juliet.
3. **Ask:** Based on what we learn in Act I, how do you think Rosaline would react if she found out that she has been replaced?

   Possible responses: Some students may say that Rosaline wouldn't care, since she didn't return Romeo's love. Other students may suggest that Rosaline would become jealous of Juliet because she enjoyed being the object of Romeo's affection.
4. **Ask:** How does this situation relate to your own life?

   Possible response: Students may cite examples of falling in and out of love with peers quickly and in succession.

PHLit Online!

This selection is available in interactive format in the **Enriched Online Student Edition,** at **www.PHLitOnline.com,** which includes a thematically related video with writing prompt and an interactive graphic organizer.

© Text Complexity: Reader and Task Suggestions

The Tragedy of Romeo and Juliet, Act II	
Preparing to Read the Text	**Leveled Tasks**
• Refer to the Background information on TE p. 836 and discuss Shakespeare's use of verse in the drama, explaining and pointing out examples of blank verse, iambic pentameter, and rhymed couplets. • Remind students to look for footnotes that explain unfamiliar vocabulary and Elizabethan terms. Review the use of context clues to figure out the meaning of words. • Guide students to use Multidraft Reading strategies (TE p. 805).	***Structure/Language*** If students will have trouble with the challenging vocabulary and Elizabethan terms, have them first read the act and take notes on unfamiliar words or phrases. Ask them to cite clues in the play that may help define the language. Then, have them reread and note language that remains unclear. ***Evaluating*** If students will not have trouble with challenging vocabulary and Elizabethan terms, have them read and note examples of especially powerful figurative language. Have them contribute their examples during class discussion.

❹ Background

Rhymed Couplets

Tell students that lines in iambic pentameter can also be rhymed. The rhyming of two successive lines creates a rhymed couplet. This form gives extra emphasis to the words a character speaks and creates a sense of completeness or finality. The exits of major characters and the ends of scenes are often marked by a rhymed couplet. Have students compare the rhyme scheme in the first twelve lines of the Chorus, beginning on p. 835, with the rhyme scheme in the final two lines.

❺ Literary Analysis

Blank Verse

1. Refer students to Mercutio's speech, lines 7–21. Have students read lines 15–16 aloud, listening to the meter. **Ask** students to identify the meter in these two lines.

   Answer: These two lines are in iambic pentameter.

2. **Ask** students the Literary Analysis question: Based on the meter of this speech, how can you tell that Mercutio is an aristocratic character?

   Answer: The speech is in iambic pentameter. This is the meter used for blank verse, and blank verse indicates that an important or aristocratic character is speaking.

Being held a foe, he may not have access
To breathe such vows as lovers use to swear,
And she as much in love, her means much less
To meet her new belovèd anywhere;
But passion lends them power, time means to meet,
Temp'ring extremities with extreme sweet.[6]
[*Exit.*]

6. Temp'ring . . . sweet easing their difficulties with great delights.

Scene i. Near Capulet's orchard.

[*Enter* ROMEO *alone.*]

ROMEO. Can I go forward when my heart is here?
Turn back, dull earth,[1] and find thy center[2] out.

[*Enter* BENVOLIO *with* MERCUTIO. ROMEO *retires.*]

1. dull earth lifeless body.
2. center heart, or possibly soul (Juliet).

BENVOLIO. Romeo! My cousin Romeo! Romeo!

MERCUTIO. He is wise.
And, on my life, hath stol'n him home to bed.

BENVOLIO. He ran this way and leapt this orchard wall.
Call, good Mercutio.

MERCUTIO. Nay, I'll conjure[3] too.
Romeo! Humors! Madman! Passion! Lover!
Appear thou in the likeness of a sigh;
Speak but one rhyme, and I am satisfied!
Cry but "Ay me!" Pronounce but "love" and "dove";
Speak to my gossip[4] Venus one fair word,
One nickname for her purblind son and heir,
Young Abraham Cupid, he that shot so true
When King Cophetua loved the beggar maid!
He heareth not, he stirreth not, he moveth not;
The ape is dead,[5] and I must conjure him.
I conjure thee by Rosaline's bright eyes,
By her high forehead and her scarlet lip,
By her fine foot, straight leg, and quivering thigh,
And the demesnes that there adjacent lie,
That in thy likeness thou appear to us!

3. conjure recite a spell to make Romeo appear.

4. gossip merry old lady.
5. The ape is dead Romeo, like a trained monkey, seems to be playing.

Literary Analysis
Blank Verse Based on the meter of this speech, how can you tell that Mercutio is an aristocratic character?

BENVOLIO. And if he hear thee, thou wilt anger him.

MERCUTIO. This cannot anger him. 'Twould anger him
To raise a spirit in his mistress' circle
Of some strange nature, letting it there stand
Till she had laid it and conjured it down.

Vocabulary Development

Ⓒ CCSS Language 6

Thematic Vocabulary: The Big Question

As students are discussing *The Tragedy of Romeo and Juliet*, Act II, encourage them to use the thematic vocabulary presented in Introducing the Big Question, pp. 778–779. You might encourage them with sentence starters like these:

1. Romeo and Juliet, unlike many of their friends, express *individuality* by . . .
2. Because of Juliet's *background*, at first, she denies . . .
3. After the balcony scene, Juliet reaches an *understanding* with Romeo and . . .
4. Romeo and Juliet decide that their *unique* bond is worth . . .

That were some spite; my invocation
Is fair and honest; in his mistress' name,
I conjure only but to raise up him.

BENVOLIO. Come, he hath hid himself among these trees
To be consorted[6] with the humorous[7] night.
Blind is his love and best befits the dark.

MERCUTIO. If love be blind, love cannot hit the mark.
Now will he sit under a medlar[8] tree
And wish his mistress were that kind of fruit
As maids call medlars when they laugh alone.
O, Romeo, that she were, O that she were
An open *et cetera*, thou a pop'rin pear!
Romeo, good night. I'll to my truckle bed;[9]
This field bed is too cold for me to sleep.
Come, shall we go?

BENVOLIO. Go then, for 'tis in vain
To seek him here that means not to be found.

[*Exit with others.*]

6. **consorted** associated.
7. **humorous** humid; moody, like a lover.
8. **medlar** applelike fruit.
9. **truckle bed** trundlebed, placed under a larger bed when not in use.

Scene ii. Capulet's orchard.

6 **ROMEO.** [*Coming forward*] He jests at scars that never felt a wound.

[*Enter* JULIET *at a window.*]

But soft! What light through yonder window breaks?
It is the East, and Juliet is the sun!
Arise, fair sun, and kill the envious moon,
Who is already sick and pale with grief
That thou her maid art far more fair than she.
Be not her maid, since she is envious.
Her vestal livery[1] is but sick and green,
7 And none but fools do wear it. Cast it off.
It is my lady! O, it is my love!
O, that she knew she were!
She speaks, yet she says nothing. What of that?
Her eye discourses; I will answer it.
I am too bold; 'tis not to me she speaks.
Two of the fairest stars in all the heaven,
Having some business, do entreat her eyes
To twinkle in their spheres[2] till they return.
What if her eyes were there, they in her head?

Literary Analysis
Blank Verse Which line in Romeo's speech breaks the pattern of five stressed syllables per line?

1. **livery** clothing or costume worn by a servant.
2. **spheres** orbits.

8 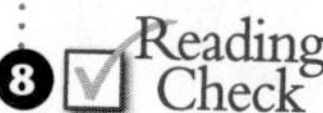

Reading Check

Whom does Romeo see at the window?

6 Background

This is the beginning of the famous "balcony scene" in *The Tragedy of Romeo and Juliet*—one of the most famous scenes in all of Shakespeare's plays. In these lines Romeo is making an extended comparison that reveals his strong feelings for Juliet. First, he says that Juliet's beauty is so great that she lights up the world, as the sun does when it rises. Then, he says that even the moon is envious of her, the way the moon might be envious of the brighter, "more fair" sun.

7 Literary Analysis

Blank Verse

1. Read lines 4–14 aloud as students follow along in their text. Have students listen closely to the meter.
2. **Ask** students the Literary Analysis question: Which line in Romeo's speech breaks the pattern of five stressed syllables per line?

   Answer: Line 11 breaks the pattern of five stressed syllables per line. It has only three stressed syllables.

8 Reading Check

Answer: Romeo sees Juliet at the window.

Fluency

Distribute copies of p. 837, and pair students. Have partners take turns reading paragraphs aloud. While one partner reads, the other should mark any words with which the student reading has difficulty. Circulate to monitor the fluency of students' reading. Collect students' marked-up copies of the page, and review difficult words and passages with the class. Look for these problem spots:

- If students struggle with the rhyme and meter, read several lines aloud and have students echo. Remind students to use the punctuation to remind them where to stop and start. Have them pause slightly at commas or semicolons and stop at exclamation points, question marks, or periods. Remind them not to pause at the end of a line if there is no punctuation mark.
- If students have difficulty with the word *envious*, read the word aloud syllable by syllable. Have students echo. Point out that the suffix *-ous* indicates that a word is an adjective.
- If students have difficulty comprehending the beginning of Romeo's speech, have them reread lines 2–17 and guide them in paraphrasing each sentence.

9 Critical Viewing

Possible response: "The brightness of her cheek would shame those stars/As daylight doth a lamp. . . ."

10 Connecting to the Big Question

1. Have a volunteer read the bracketed text aloud.
2. **Ask:** What suggestion is Juliet making in this passage?

   Possible response: She is suggesting that either Romeo reject the name Montague or Juliet reject the name Capulet.
3. **Ask:** Based on Juliet's feelings and words at this point, does she believe that her and Romeo's differences define them? Explain.

   Answer: Juliet does seem to believe that her and Romeo's differences define them. More specifically, their last names define them. She is implying that if she or Romeo were to take different names, they would change their identities and thus be allowed to love each other in peace.

The brightness of her cheek would shame those stars
As daylight doth a lamp; her eyes in heaven
Would through the airy region stream so bright
That birds would sing and think it were not night.
See how she leans her cheek upon that hand,
O, that I were a glove upon that hand,
That I might touch that cheek!

JULIET. Ay me!

ROMEO. She speaks.
O, speak again, bright angel, for thou art
As glorious to this night, being o'er my head,
As is a wingèd messenger of heaven
Unto the white-upturnèd wond'ring eyes
Of mortals that fall back to gaze on him
When he bestrides the lazy puffing clouds
And sails upon the bosom of the air.

JULIET. O Romeo, Romeo! Wherefore art thou Romeo?[3]
Deny thy father and refuse thy name;
Or, if thou wilt not, be but sworn my love,
And I'll no longer be a Capulet.

9 ▼ **Critical Viewing** Which line of dialogue in this scene might this photograph capture? **[Connect]**

3. Wherefore . . . Romeo? Why are you Romeo—a Montague?

Vocabulary Development

CCSS Language 6

Expressive Vocabulary

To help students broaden their expressive vocabulary, encourage them to use the following words as they discuss the selection: *anticipate, circumstance, reluctant,* and *mutual.* Have them complete these sentence starters:

1. Romeo cannot *anticipate* . . .
2. The two lovers' *circumstance* . . .
3. Juliet is *reluctant* to . . .
4. Romeo and Juliet share a *mutual* . . .

Challenge students to use these words as you continue to discuss the play.

ROMEO. [*Aside*] Shall I hear more, or shall I speak at this?

JULIET. Tis but thy name that is my enemy.
Thou art thyself, though not[4] a Montague.
What's Montague? It is nor hand, nor foot,
Nor arm, nor face, nor any other part
Belonging to a man. O, be some other name!
11 What's in a name? That which we call a rose
By any other name would smell as sweet.
So Romeo would, were he not Romeo called,
Retain that dear perfection which he owes[5]
Without that title. Romeo, doff[6] thy name;
And for thy name, which is no part of thee,
Take all myself.

ROMEO. I take thee at thy word.
Call me but love, and I'll be new baptized;
Henceforth I never will be Romeo.

JULIET. What man art thou, thus bescreened in night,
12 So stumblest on my counsel?[7]

ROMEO. By a name
I know not how to tell thee who I am.
My name, dear saint, is hateful to myself
Because it is an enemy to thee.
Had I it written, I would tear the word.

JULIET. My ears have yet not drunk a hundred words
Of thy tongue's uttering, yet I know the sound.
Art thou not Romeo, and a Montague?

ROMEO. Neither, fair maid, if either thee dislike.

JULIET. How camest thou hither, tell me, and wherefore?
The orchard walls are high and hard to climb,
And the place death, considering who thou art,
If any of my kinsmen find thee here.

ROMEO. With love's light wings did I o'erperch[8] these walls;
For stony limits cannot hold love out,
And what love can do, that dares love attempt.
Therefore thy kinsmen are no stop to me.

JULIET. If they do see thee, they will murder thee.

ROMEO. Alack, there lies more peril in thine eye
Than twenty of their swords! Look thou but sweet,
And I am proof[9] against their enmity.

4. **though not** even if you were not.

Reading Skill
Summarize Briefly summarize Juliet's speech about Romeo's name.

5. **owes** owns; possesses.
6. **doff** remove.

7. **counsel** secret thoughts.

Literary Analysis
Blank Verse How do the stressed syllables in line 57 reinforce Romeo's meaning?

8. **o'erperch** fly over.

9. **proof** protected, as by armor.

13 

Why does Romeo say his name is hateful to him?

11 Reading Skill
Summarize

1. Have students read the bracketed text.
2. **Ask** students what Juliet is wishing for in this speech.
   Answer: She is wishing that Romeo had another name—that he was not a Montague, her family's enemy.
3. **Ask** students to respond to the Reading Skill prompt: Briefly summarize Juliet's speech about Romeo's name.
   Answer: Juliet says that it is Romeo's name that is the enemy. Why is a name important, anyway? If he had a different name, he would still be the same person. So Romeo should get rid of his name, which is not really part of him, and then he could have Juliet.

12 Literary Analysis
Blank Verse

1. Have students read lines 49–57. **Ask** students who speaks line 49.
   Answer: Juliet speaks the first part of the line, and Romeo speaks the second part.
2. **Ask** students what strong feeling Romeo is expressing in lines 53–57.
   Answer: He is saying that he hates his name because his name is Juliet's enemy.
3. **Ask** students the Literary Analysis question: How do the stressed syllables in line 57 reinforce Romeo's meaning?
   Answer: The stressed syllables—*I, writ-, I, tear,* and *word*—reinforce Romeo's intense feeling about how hateful his name is to him.

13 Reading Check

Answer: Romeo's name is hateful to him because it is an enemy to Juliet, whose family is feuding with Romeo's family.

Differentiated Instruction for Universal Access

EL Support for English Learners
Have students use the ***Reader's Notebook: English Learner's Version*** for Scene ii of this act. After students have completed the exercises, have them work in pairs to listen to the ***Hear It!* Audio CD** and read along in the Student Edition.

Enrichment for Gifted/Talented Students
Have students look on this page for sections of dialogue between Romeo and Juliet that they would use as the basis for a song in a musical version of the play. Have students establish criteria and then explain how their choices meet the criteria. Students should also identify the musical style of the song.

14 Critical Thinking

Interpret

1. **Ask** students why a person might blush.

   Possible responses: A person might blush because he or she is embarrassed, overheated, or angry.

2. Have a volunteer read the bracketed text aloud. **Ask:** What is Juliet saying in this passage?

   Answer: She says that she is blushing, but Romeo can't see it because it is nighttime.

3. **Ask:** What is Juliet's specific meaning in lines 85–87?

   Answer: She means that her loving and bold comments to Romeo should make her embarrassed or ashamed, but the excitement of the night—along with the depth of her emotion—excuses her behavior. Juliet is unashamed.

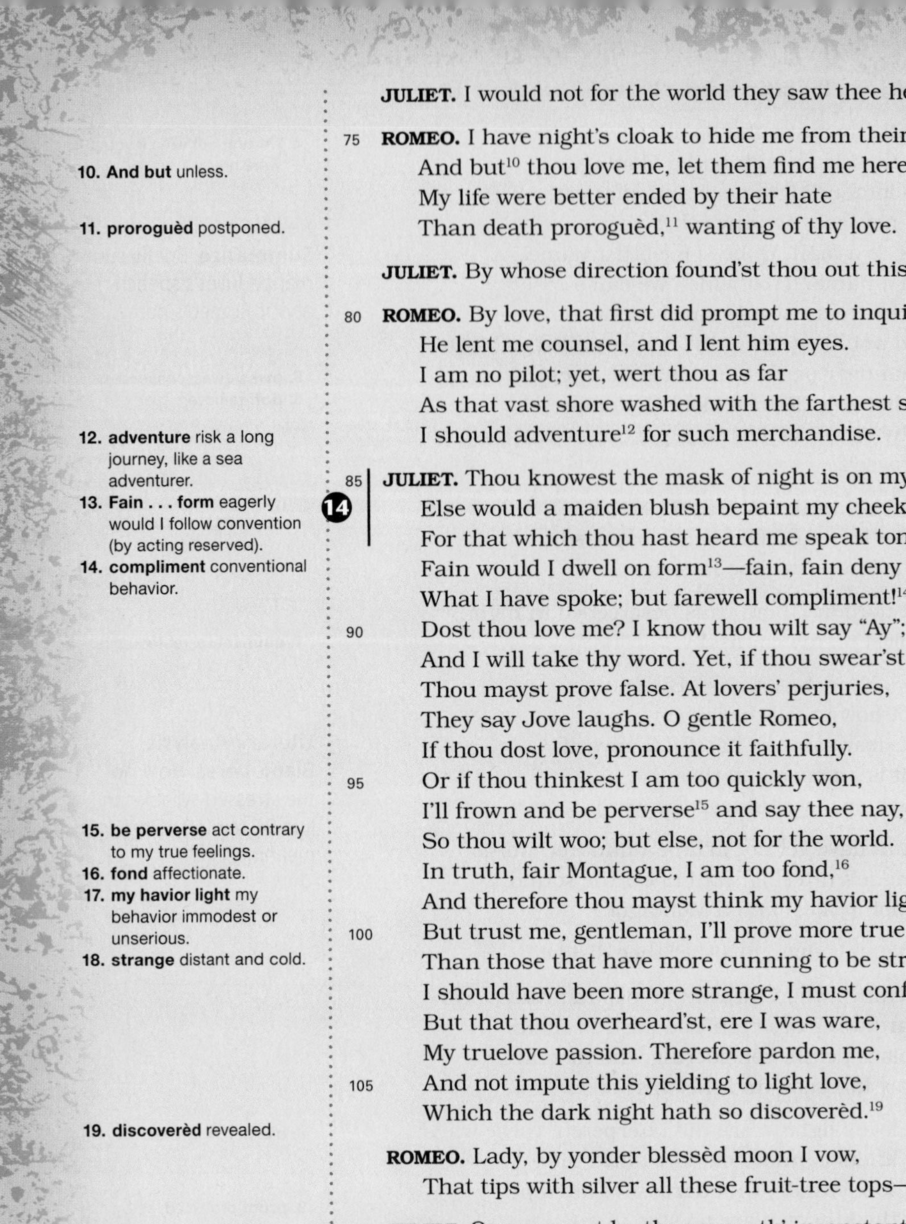

JULIET. I would not for the world they saw thee here.

ROMEO. I have night's cloak to hide me from their eyes;
And but[10] thou love me, let them find me here.
My life were better ended by their hate
Than death proroguèd,[11] wanting of thy love.

JULIET. By whose direction found'st thou out this place?

ROMEO. By love, that first did prompt me to inquire.
He lent me counsel, and I lent him eyes.
I am no pilot; yet, wert thou as far
As that vast shore washed with the farthest sea,
I should adventure[12] for such merchandise.

JULIET. Thou knowest the mask of night is on my face;
14 Else would a maiden blush bepaint my cheek
For that which thou hast heard me speak tonight.
Fain would I dwell on form[13]—fain, fain deny
What I have spoke; but farewell compliment![14]
Dost thou love me? I know thou wilt say "Ay";
And I will take thy word. Yet, if thou swear'st,
Thou mayst prove false. At lovers' perjuries,
They say Jove laughs. O gentle Romeo,
If thou dost love, pronounce it faithfully.
Or if thou thinkest I am too quickly won,
I'll frown and be perverse[15] and say thee nay,
So thou wilt woo; but else, not for the world.
In truth, fair Montague, I am too fond,[16]
And therefore thou mayst think my havior light;[17]
But trust me, gentleman, I'll prove more true
Than those that have more cunning to be strange.[18]
I should have been more strange, I must confess,
But that thou overheard'st, ere I was ware,
My truelove passion. Therefore pardon me,
And not impute this yielding to light love,
Which the dark night hath so discoverèd.[19]

ROMEO. Lady, by yonder blessèd moon I vow,
That tips with silver all these fruit-tree tops—

JULIET. O, swear not by the moon, th' inconstant moon,
That monthly changes in her circle orb,
Lest that thy love prove likewise variable.

10. **And but** unless.
11. **proroguèd** postponed.
12. **adventure** risk a long journey, like a sea adventurer.
13. **Fain . . . form** eagerly would I follow convention (by acting reserved).
14. **compliment** conventional behavior.
15. **be perverse** act contrary to my true feelings.
16. **fond** affectionate.
17. **my havior light** my behavior immodest or unserious.
18. **strange** distant and cold.
19. **discoverèd** revealed.

840 Drama

Vocabulary Development

CCSS Language 6

Selection Vocabulary Reinforcement

Students will benefit from additional examples and practice with the selection vocabulary words. Reinforce their comprehension with "show-you-know" sentences. The first part of the sentence uses the vocabulary word in an appropriate context. The second part of the sentence—the "show-you-know" part—clarifies the first. Model the strategy with *procure*:

> We need to *procure* art supplies; we're almost out and need to get more to finish the project.

Then, give students these sentence prompts and coach them in creating the clarification part.

1. We need to identify the *predominant* problem; ____________

   Sample answer: we should solve that before we address lesser problems.

2. The coach's *intercession* on behalf of the team was successful; ____________

   Sample answer: they were able to get new uniforms.

ROMEO. What shall I swear by?

JULIET. Do not swear at all;
Or if thou wilt, swear by thy gracious self,
Which is the god of my idolatry,
And I'll believe thee.

ROMEO. If my heart's dear love—

JULIET. Well, do not swear. Although I joy in thee,
I have no joy of this contract[20] tonight.
It is too rash, too unadvised, too sudden;
Too like the lightning, which doth cease to be
Ere one can say it lightens. Sweet, good night!
This bud of love, by summer's ripening breath,
May prove a beauteous flow'r when next we meet.
Good night, good night! As sweet repose and rest
Come to thy heart as that within my breast!

ROMEO. O, wilt thou leave me so unsatisfied?

JULIET. What satisfaction canst thou have tonight?

ROMEO. Th'exchange of thy love's faithful vow for mine.

Literary Analysis
Blank Verse The five stressed syllables of lines 112 and 115 are split between the two speakers. What does this weaving together of dialogue suggest about the speakers' relationship?

20. contract betrothal.

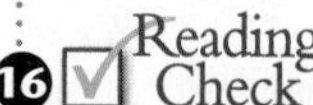

Why does Juliet tell Romeo not to swear his love by the moon?

Differentiated Instruction for Universal Access

Enrichment for Gifted/Talented Students

Tell students that the timeless story of *The Tragedy of Romeo and Juliet* has been set to film and stage using many different settings, from the classical setting of the 1968 Zeffirelli film to a 1996 film starring Leonardo DiCaprio. The latter film is set in modern-day California in the fictional city of Verona Beach. This scene (Act II, Scene ii) is the best known in the play and perhaps the most famous scene in all of Shakespeare's plays.

Have students listen to the scene in the ***Hear It!* Audio CD** as they read along. Then, have them sketch this "balcony scene," Scene ii. Encourage them to think about whether they want the sketch to reflect the classical medieval setting, a modern-day setting, or some other time and place. Remind them that the costumes and architecture should reflect the setting.

Have students display their sketches in the classroom.

15 Literary Analysis

Blank Verse

1. Remind students that although blank verse has five feet per line, a line can be split between two speakers.
2. **Ask** students to speculate about why a poet might split a blank verse line between two speakers.

   Possible response: Students may suggest that a poet might want to indicate fast-moving dialogue; the poet might also want to show a connection between two characters.
3. **Ask** students the Literary Analysis question: The five stressed syllables of lines 112 and 115 are split between the two speakers. What does this weaving together of dialogue suggest about the speakers' relationship?

   Possible response: Students may suggest that two lovers would likely finish each other's sentences. They also may say that people in love "speak with one voice."

16 Reading Check

Answer: The moon changes throughout the month, and if he swears by the moon his love might also prove to be changeable.

⑰ Literature in Context

Culture Connection Falconers begin training birds by placing a soft leather hood over their heads and attaching leather thongs to their legs. The falconer wears a heavy glove to protect his hand from the bird's sharp claws as he carries the bird on his fist for several hours a day. Then, the bird is taught to feed by flying after and catching a lure. The lure is a padded weight attached to a long cord. The wings of a pigeon or other bird are attached to the lure, along with a piece of meat. The falconer twirls the lure while the bird flies after it, catches it, and feeds on the meat attached to the lure. Eventually the bird learns to kill for itself and return to the fist of the falconer.

Connect to the Literature
Have students read lines 158–159 on p. 843. Remind them that Juliet has been called away by her Nurse and has just returned to the balcony. Then, **ask** the Connect to the Literature question: Why do you think Juliet wishes Romeo would respond to her voice as a falcon does the falconer's commands?

Answer: Juliet wishes she could call softly, like a falconer to his bird, and Romeo would come back to her as willingly.

JULIET. I gave thee mine before thou didst request it;
And yet I would it were to give again.

ROMEO. Wouldst thou withdraw it? For what purpose, love?

JULIET. But to be frank[21] and give it thee again.
And yet I wish but for the thing I have.
My bounty[22] is as boundless as the sea,
My love as deep; the more I give to thee,
The more I have, for both are infinite,
I hear some noise within. Dear love, adieu!

[NURSE *calls within.*]

Anon, good nurse! Sweet Montague, be true.
Stay but a little, I will come again. [*Exit.*]

21. frank generous.

22. bounty what I have to give.

LITERATURE IN CONTEXT

Culture Connection

Falconry
When Juliet longs for "a falc'ners voice," she is referring to someone who practices falconry, the sport of hunting with falcons. Falcons are swift, hawk-like birds of prey. The falconer trains the bird to respond to a combination of physical and vocal commands.

During Shakespeare's time, one's rank in society determined the kind of bird one could own:

Rank	Type of Bird
King	Gyr falcon
Prince	Peregrine falcon (male)
Knight	Saker falcon
Squire	Lanner falcon
Lady	Merlin (female)
Yeoman (landowner)	Goshawk
Servants, children	Kestrel

◀ Falconry began as a way to obtain food but gradually evolved into the "sport of kings."

Thick leather gloves protected the falconer from the bird's talons. ▶

Connect to the Literature

Why do you think Juliet wishes Romeo would respond to her voice as a falcon does to the falconer's commands?

Vocabulary Development

Dictionary Use
Point out the word *true* in line 137 on this page. Using a "think-aloud" process, model how to use context to infer the appropriate definition of the word. Say to students:

> I'm going to think aloud to show you how I would figure out the correct dictionary definition of *true* by using context clues. The dictionary says that *true* can mean: 1. consistent; 2. accurate; 3. loyal and steadfast.
>
> In this sentence, Juliet is asking Romeo to be "true." The first definition makes some sense; Juliet probably would want Romeo to be consistent in his love for her. I'm going to consider the other definitions before I make a decision, though. Does Juliet want Romeo to be accurate? This doesn't really make sense, because a person can't be accurate. The third definition, however, has promise. Juliet and Romeo have been declaring their newfound love for each other, and Juliet has every reason to ask for Romeo's loyalty. Definition 3 fits best in this context.

ROMEO. O blessèd, blessèd night! I am afeard,
Being in night, all this is but a dream,
Too flattering-sweet to be substantial.[23]

[*Enter* JULIET *again.*]

JULIET. Three words, dear Romeo, and good night indeed.
If that thy bent[24] of love be honorable,
Thy purpose marriage, send me word tomorrow,
By one that I'll procure to come to thee,
Where and what time thou wilt perform the rite;
And all my fortunes at thy foot I'll lay
And follow thee my lord throughout the world.

NURSE. [*Within*] Madam!

JULIET. I come anon.—But if thou meanest not well,
I do beseech thee—

NURSE. [*Within*] Madam!

JULIET. By and by[25] I come.—
To cease thy strife[26] and leave me to my grief.
Tomorrow will I send.

ROMEO. So thrive my soul—

JULIET. A thousand times good night! [*Exit.*]

18 ROMEO. A thousand times the worse, to want thy light!
Love goes toward love as schoolboys from their books;
But love from love, toward school with heavy looks.

[*Enter* JULIET *again.*]

JULIET. Hist! Romeo, hist! O for a falc'ner's voice
To lure this tassel gentle[27] back again!
Bondage is hoarse[28] and may not speak aloud,
Else would I tear the cave where Echo[29] lies
And make her airy tongue more hoarse than mine
With repetition of "My Romeo!"

ROMEO. It is my soul that calls upon my name.
How silver-sweet sound lovers' tongues by night,
Like softest music to attending ears!

19 JULIET. Romeo!

ROMEO. My sweet?

JULIET. What o'clock tomorrow
Shall I send to thee?

23. **substantial** real.
24. **bent** purpose; intention.

Vocabulary
procure (prō kyoor′)
v. get; obtain

25. **By and by** at once.
26. **strife** efforts.

Literary Analysis
Blank Verse Based on the fact that Romeo and Juliet speak in blank verse, what can you conclude about their character rank?

27. **tassel gentle** male falcon.
28. **Bondage is hoarse** Being bound in by my family restricts my speech.
29. **Echo** In classical mythology, the nymph Echo, unable to win the love of Narcissus, wasted away in a cave until nothing was left of her but her voice.

20 **Reading Check**
Why can't Juliet speak loudly to Romeo?

18 Background

When Romeo compares love with schoolboys leaving school and the absence of love with boys going to school in lines 156–157, he is expressing the common dislike of men of Shakespeare's time of their formal schooling. In Stratford, boys—and only boys—were expected to start school as soon as they could read and write. Most of their learning was in Latin.

19 Literary Analysis

Blank Verse

1. **Ask** students what Romeo and Juliet are doing in lines 169–175.
   Answer: They are trying to find reasons to keep from having to say good night.
2. **Ask** students the Literary Analysis question: Based on the fact that Romeo and Juliet speak in blank verse, what can you conclude about their character rank?
   Answer: In Shakespeare's plays, characters who speak in blank verse are important or aristocratic. Romeo and Juliet are both.

20 Reading Check

Answer: She is afraid someone in the household will overhear her.

Differentiated Instruction for Universal Access

EL Pronunciation for English Learners

Students may have difficulty pronouncing the initial "r" sound as in *Romeo, rite,* and *repetition.* They may roll or trill the *r.* The following strategies can help students to pronounce the "r" sound.

- Pronounce *Romeo, rite,* and *repetition* in turn, and have students repeat each. Correct students' pronunciation as necessary.
- Using a sentence that repeats the initial "r" sound—such as "Romeo really likes rats and rocks"—play a game of telephone with students. Whisper the sentence to one student, who passes it to another, and so on. At the end, reveal the correct sentence and review its pronunciation.

21 Reading Skill

Summarize

1. Have students read the bracketed text. Have them note the stage directions as the scene opens.
2. **Ask** students to use the footnotes and context clues to determine what the Friar is doing in lines 7 and 8.

   Answer: The Friar is collecting plants of different kinds, both poisonous and beneficial.
3. **Ask** students to read lines 15–22 and summarize what the Friar believes about the natural world.

   Possible response: The Friar believes that things found in the natural world can be used for either good or evil.
4. **Ask** students to respond to the Reading Skill prompt: Briefly state the main points of the Friar's speech in lines 1–30.

   Answer: The sun is rising. I must gather herbs, both poisonous and beneficial. Even the most poisonous herbs have some virtue, and even the most beneficial herbs, if overused, are harmful. Some plants contain both good and ill. It is the same in man; and if the worse is predominant, then it eats up the soul.

ROMEO. By the hour of nine.

JULIET. I will not fail. 'Tis twenty year till then.
I have forgot why I did call thee back.

19

ROMEO. Let me stand here till thou remember it.

JULIET. I shall forget, to have thee still stand there,
Rememb'ring how I love thy company.

ROMEO. And I'll stay, to have thee still forget,
Forgetting any other home but this.

JULIET. 'Tis almost morning. I would have thee gone—
And yet no farther than a wanton's[30] bird,
That lets it hop a little from his hand,
Like a poor prisoner in his twisted gyves,[31]
And with a silken thread plucks it back again,
So loving-jealous of his liberty.

ROMEO. I would I were thy bird.

JULIET. Sweet, so would I.
Yet I should kill thee with much cherishing.
Good night, good night! Parting is such sweet sorrow
That I shall say good night till it be morrow. [*Exit.*]

ROMEO. Sleep dwell upon thine eyes, peace in thy breast!
Would I were sleep and peace, so sweet to rest!
Hence will I to my ghostly friar's[32] close cell,[33]
His help to crave and my dear hap[34] to tell. [*Exit.*]

30. **wanton's** spoiled, playful child's.
31. **gyves** (jīvz) chains.
32. **ghostly friar's** spiritual father's.
33. **close cell** small room.
34. **dear hap** good fortune.

Scene iii. Friar Lawrence's cell.

[*Enter* FRIAR LAWRENCE *alone, with a basket.*]

FRIAR. The gray-eyed morn smiles on the frowning night,
Check'ring the eastern clouds with streaks of light;
And fleckèd[1] darkness like a drunkard reels
From forth day's path and Titan's burning wheels.[2]
Now, ere the sun advance his burning eye
The day to cheer and night's dank dew to dry,
I must upfill this osier cage[3] of ours
With baleful[4] weeds and precious-juicèd flowers.
The earth that's nature's mother is her tomb.
What is her burying grave, that is her womb;
And from her womb children of divers kind[5]
We sucking on her natural bosom find,
Many for many virtues excellent,

Reading Skill
Summarize Briefly state the main points of the Friar's speech in lines 1–30.

21

1. **fleckèd** spotted.
2. **Titan's burning wheels** wheels of the sun god's chariot.
3. **osier cage** willow basket.
4. **baleful** poisonous.
5. **divers kind** different kinds.

Vocabulary Development

CCSS Language 6

Selection Vocabulary Reinforcement

To reinforce and assess students' comprehension of selection vocabulary words, give them sentences using the words in which the word may or may not be used correctly. Students must tell whether the use is correct and explain their answers. Use these sentences:

1. The model had a lovely, *sallow* complexion.

   Answer: No, *sallow* is not used correctly. *Sallow* means "sickly and pale-yellowish," which would not make someone "lovely."
2. This backpack is so *unwieldy* that I can barely get it under my desk.

   Answer: Yes, *unwieldy* is used correctly, since it means "awkward" or "not easy to handle."

None but for some, and yet all different.
O, mickle[6] is the powerful grace[7] that lies
In plants, herbs, stones, and their true qualities;
For naught so vile that on the earth doth live
But to the earth some special good doth give;
Nor aught so good but, strained[8] from that fair use,
Revolts from true birth,[9] stumbling on abuse.
Virtue itself turns vice, being misapplied,
And vice sometime by action dignified.

[*Enter* ROMEO.]

Within the infant rind[10] of this weak flower
Poison hath residence and medicine power;[11]
For this, being smelt, with that part cheers each part;[12]
Being tasted, stays all senses with the heart.[13]
Two such opposèd kings encamp them still[14]
In man as well as herbs—grace and rude will;
And where the worser is **predominant**,
Full soon the canker[15] death eats up that plant.

ROMEO. Good morrow, father.

FRIAR. *Benedicite!*[16]
What early tongue so sweet saluteth me?
Young son, it argues a distemperèd head[17]
So soon to bid good morrow to thy bed.
Care keeps his watch in every old man's eye,
And where care lodges, sleep will never lie;
But where unbruisèd youth with unstuffed[18] brain
Doth couch his limbs, there golden sleep doth reign,
Therefore thy earliness doth me assure
Thou art uproused with some distemp'rature;[19]
Or if not so, then here I hit it right—
Our Romeo hath not been in bed tonight.

ROMEO. That last is true. The sweeter rest was mine.

FRIAR. God pardon sin! Wast thou with Rosaline?

ROMEO. With Rosaline, my ghostly father? No.
I have forgot that name and that name's woe.

FRIAR. That's my good son! But where hast thou been then?

ROMEO. I'll tell thee ere thou ask it me again.
I have been feasting with mine enemy,
Where on a sudden one hath wounded me
That's by me wounded. Both our remedies

6. **mickle** great.
7. **grace** divine power.
8. **strained** turned away.
9. **Revolts . . . birth** conflicts with its real purpose.
10. **infant rind** tender skin.
11. **and medicine power** and medicinal quality has power.
12. **with . . . part** with that quality—odor—revives each part of the body.
13. **stays . . . heart** kills (stops the working of the five senses along with the heart).
14. **still** always.
15. **canker** destructive caterpillar.

Vocabulary
predominant (prē däm′ ə nənt) *adj.* of or having stronger influence

16. ***Benedicite!*** God bless you!
17. **distemperèd head** troubled mind.

18. **unstuffed** not filled with cares.
19. **distemp'rature** illness.

Literary Analysis
Blank Verse What sets the Friar's lines apart from normal blank verse?

What plan do Romeo and Juliet make for the following day?

22 Literary Analysis

Blank Verse

1. Have students read all of Scene iii, pp. 844–847.
2. Then, **ask** students the Literary Analysis question: What sets the Friar's lines apart from normal blank verse?

   Answer: The Friar's verse rhymes.
3. Tell students that all of Scene iii is written in rhymed couplets. However, Friar Lawrence does not speak in rhymed couplets in other scenes. **Ask** students why they think Shakespeare chose to write this scene in rhyme.

   Possible response: Students may suggest that the rhymed lines set the Friar apart as a holy person, who apparently has special powers to deal with good and bad herbs, as well as to join two people in marriage.

23 Reading Check

Answer: They plan to meet again and find a way to marry.

Differentiated Instruction for Universal Access

Enrichment for Advanced Readers

Suggest that students read additional works by William Shakespeare. You may wish to use **Authors in Depth**, Gold Level, which contains the following selections:

- from *The Tragedy of King Lear* from Act I, Scene i
- from *A Midsummer Night's Dream* from Act III, Scene i
- Sonnet 23
- Sonnet 27
- Sonnet 60
- Sonnet 98

After students have read these or other works by Shakespeare, have them form discussion groups in which they compare and contrast the selections they have read. Suggest criteria for comparison, such as imagery, style of verse, and rhyme scheme. To extend the activity, have volunteers present to the class brief oral reports or readings of their favorite Shakespeare selections.

24 Critical Viewing

Analyze

1. **Ask** students to describe Romeo's relationship with Friar Lawrence.

   Answer: Romeo apparently has a close relationship with the Friar. The Friar knows about Rosaline and Romeo's feelings for her. Romeo is willing to tell the Friar about his change of heart from loving Rosaline to loving Juliet and to ask the Friar to marry them.

2. **Ask** students what they can tell about the meaning of the Friar's speech in lines 65–68, based on emphasized words and/or syllables.

   Answer: The stressed words in lines 65–68 give readers the sense that Friar Lawrence is concerned about the *change* in Romeo's feelings and about *Rosaline*, whom Romeo apparently did *love so dear*, but who is now *forsaken*.

25 Background

The Good Friar

Friar, which comes from the Latin word for *brother*, is a general term for a member of a religious order. Friars had no worldly possessions or fixed place to live, which allowed them to devote themselves exclusively to preaching, missionary work, and other charitable undertakings. Friars wore robes called *habits* that were gray, black, or white.

Students should understand the difference between a friar, such as Friar Lawrence, and a monk. A monk is a man who has taken religious vows of poverty, chastity, and obedience and has retired from worldly life to live with other monks, study the Scriptures, pray, and meditate. A friar lives among ordinary people and helps them, as Friar Lawrence tries to help the two star-crossed lovers.

Vocabulary
intercession (in′ tər sesh′ ən) *n.* the act of pleading on another's behalf

20. **physic** (fiz′ ik) medicine.
21. **My . . . foe** my plea also helps my enemy (Juliet, a Capulet).
22. **and . . . drift** and simple in your speech.
23. **Riddling . . . shrift** A confusing confession will get you uncertain forgiveness. The Friar means that unless Romeo speaks clearly, he will not get clear and direct advice.
24. **And . . . save** and we are united in every way, except for (save).
25. **brine** salt water (tears).

Vocabulary
sallow (sal′ ō) *adj.* of a sickly, pale-yellowish hue

Within thy help and holy physic[20] lies.
I bear no hatred, blessèd man, for, lo,
My **intercession** likewise steads my foe.[21]

FRIAR. Be plain, good son, and homely in thy drift.[22]
Riddling confession finds but riddling shrift.[23]

ROMEO. Then plainly know my heart's dear love is set
On the fair daughter of rich Capulet;
As mine on hers, so hers is set on mine,
And all combined, save[24] what thou must combine
By holy marriage. When and where and how
We met, we wooed, and made exchange of vow,
I'll tell thee as we pass; but this I pray,
That thou consent to marry us today.

FRIAR. Holy Saint Francis! What a change is here!
Is Rosaline, that thou didst love so dear,
So soon forsaken? Young men's love then lies
Not truly in their hearts, but in their eyes.
Jesu Maria! What a deal of brine[25]
Hath washed thy **sallow** cheeks for Rosaline!
How much salt water thrown away in waste
To season love, that of it doth not taste!
The sun not yet thy sighs from heaven clears,
Thy old groans ring yet in mine ancient ears.
Lo, here upon thy cheek the stain doth sit
Of an old tear that is not washed off yet.
If e'er thou wast thyself, and these woes thine,
Thou and these woes were all for Rosaline.
And art thou changed? Pronounce this sentence then:
Women may fall[26] when there's no strength[27] in men.

26. **fall** be weak or inconstant.
27. **strength** constancy; stability.
28. **doting** being infatuated.
29. **badst** urged.

ROMEO. Thou chidst me oft for loving Rosaline.

FRIAR. For doting,[28] not for loving, pupil mine.

ROMEO. And badst[29] me bury love.

FRIAR. Not in a grave
To lay one in, another out to have.

ROMEO. I pray thee chide me not. Her I love now
Doth grace[30] for grace and love for love allow.[31]
The other did not so.

FRIAR. O, she knew well
Thy love did read by rote, that could not spell.[32]

30. **grace** favor.
31. **allow** give.
32. **Thy . . . spell** your love recited words from memory with no understanding of them.

Vocabulary Development

CCSS Language 6

Word Analysis

Call students' attention to the word *intercession* in line 54 on this page. Have students read the word's definition in the side note. Tell students that the prefix *inter-* means "between or among." The root word is based on the Latin word for "go."

Tell students that based on the prefix, another way to define *intercession* is "the act of going between two people or groups in an effort to resolve a dispute or to obtain a favor."

Ask students to suggest other words containing the prefix *inter-*. Students may suggest words such as *interact, intercept, interrupt, interchange,* and *international.*

But come, young waverer, come go with me.
In one respect I'll thy assistant be;
For this alliance may so happy prove
To turn your households' rancor[33] to pure love.

ROMEO. O, let us hence! I stand on[34] sudden haste.

FRIAR. Wisely and slow. They stumble that run fast. [*Exit all.*]

Scene iv. A street.

[*Enter* BENVOLIO *and* MERCUTIO.]

MERCUTIO. Where the devil should this Romeo be? Came he not home tonight?

BENVOLIO. Not to his father's. I spoke with his man.

MERCUTIO. Why, that same pale hardhearted wench, that
Rosaline,
torments him so that he will sure run mad.

BENVOLIO. Tybalt, the kinsman to old Capulet,
Hath sent a letter to his father's house.

MERCUTIO. A challenge, on my life.

BENVOLIO. Romeo will answer it.

MERCUTIO. Any man that can write may answer a letter.

BENVOLIO. Nay, he will answer the letter's master, how he dares, being dared.

MERCUTIO. Alas, poor Romeo, he is already dead: stabbed with a white wench's black eye; run through the ear with a love song; the very pin of his heart cleft with the blind bow-boy's butt-shaft;[1] and is he a man to encounter Tybalt?

BENVOLIO. Why, what is Tybalt?

MERCUTIO. More than Prince of Cats.[2] O, he's the courageous captain of compliments.[3] He fights as you sing pricksong[4]—keeps time, distance, and proportion; he rests his minim rests,[5] one, two, and the third in your bosom! The very butcher of a silk button,[6] a duelist, a duelist! A gentleman of the very first house,[7] of the first and second cause.[8] Ah, the immortal *passado*! The *punto reverso*! The hay![9]

BENVOLIO. The what?

MERCUTIO. The pox of such antic, lisping, affecting

33. **rancor** hatred.
34. **stand on** insist on.

Literary Analysis
Blank Verse In what way is Mercutio's and Benvolio's speech in this scene different from what it was earlier in Act II?

1. **blind bow-boy's butt-shaft** Cupid's blunt arrow.
2. **Prince of Cats** Tybalt, or a variation of it, is the name of the cat in medieval stories of Reynard the Fox.
3. **captain of compliments** master of formal behavior.
4. **as you sing pricksong** with attention to precision.
5. **rests . . . rests** observes all formalities.
6. **button** exact spot on his opponent's shirt.
7. **first house** finest school of fencing.
8. **the first and second cause** reasons that would cause a gentleman to challenge another to a duel.
9. ***passado*! . . . *punto reverso*! . . . hay!** lunge . . . backhanded stroke . . . home thrust.

Reading Check

What does the Friar think Romeo and Juliet's love will do for the Capulets and Montagues?

26 Literary Analysis

Blank Verse

1. Have students read lines 1–36. **Ask** students what they learn in this exchange between Benvolio and Mercutio.
   Answer: Benvolio says that Tybalt has sent a letter to Romeo at the Montague's house, and Mercutio says that the letter probably challenges Romeo to a duel.
2. **Ask** students how Mercutio seems to feel about the challenge.
   Answer: Mercutio seems to think that Tybalt is an accomplished swordsman, and Romeo, in his lovelorn condition, will be no match for him.
3. **Ask** students the Literary Analysis question: In what way is Mercutio's and Benvolio's speech in this scene different from what it was earlier in Act II?
   Answer: Their speech is not in blank verse, as it is in earlier scenes.
4. Then, **ask** how students can tell that Mercutio's speech is not in blank verse.
   Answer: It does not have five stressed syllables per line.

27 Reading Check

Answer: He thinks Romeo and Juliet's love might end the feud between the two families.

Differentiated Instruction for Universal Access

Strategy for Special-Needs Students

For students who are still struggling with identifying characters' ranks based on blank verse, show them the **Literary Analysis Graphic Organizer A** (*Graphic Organizer Transparencies*, p. 151). Review the partially completed graphic organizer.

You may wish to point out that in Scene iv, Mercutio and Benvolio do not speak in blank verse. However, this scene is an exception, and they usually speak in blank verse in other scenes.

EL Enrichment for English Learners

Students might enjoy determining whether the meaning of a character's name reflects his or her personality. Tell students that the name *Benvolio* comes from the Latin words *bene*, meaning "well," and *volo*, meaning "I wish." Mercutio's name comes from the Latin name for Mercury, the messenger of the gods, who was known for his quickness, skill, wit, and eloquence. Ask students whether they think the characters are well named.

Literature in Context

History Connection Shakespeare would have been very familiar with Petrarch and Laura. Petrarch developed Italian (also called Petrarchan) sonnets to a high form. He wrote more than 300 sonnets to his beloved Laura over a period of twenty years.

Traditionally, Laura was believed to be Laura de Noves of Avignon, which is in modern France. Supposedly, Petrarch saw Laura for the first time in St. Claire Church in Avignon on April 6, 1327. He fell in love with her and loved her for the rest of his life, even though she was a married woman and a mother. Laura died during a terrible pandemic called the Black Death, which killed as much as a third of Europe's population. Even after her death, however, Petrarch continued writing sonnets expressing his love for her.

Petrarch's sonnets were the inspiration for English poets, among them William Shakespeare, who developed the Elizabethan (Shakespearean) sonnet to a splendid form. He wrote some of the most beautiful sonnets in the English language.

Connect to the Literature Remind students how Romeo behaves over his unrequited love for Rosaline in Act I. Then, **ask** the Connect to the Literature question: Why is Mercutio's use of grand references and exaggerated language a fitting way to tease Romeo?

Answer: Mercutio's teasing is fitting because Romeo had so exaggerated his sadness and pain over Rosaline, who did not return his love.

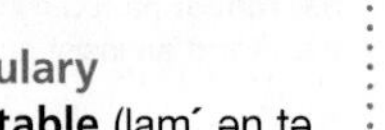

10. The pox . . . accent May the plague strike these absurd characters with their phony manners.

Vocabulary
lamentable (lam´ ən tə bəl) *adj.* distressing; sad

11. these pardon-me's these men who are always saying "Pardon me."
12. Without . . . herring worn out.
13. numbers verses of love poems.

14. slip escape. *Slip* is also a term for a counterfeit coin.

fantasticoes—these new tuners of accent![10] "By Jesu, a very good blade! A very tall man! A very good whore!" Why, is not this a lamentable thing, grandsir, that we should be thus afflicted with these strange flies, these fashionmongers, these pardon-me's,[11] who stand so much on the new form that they cannot sit at ease on the old bench? O, their bones, their bones!

[*Enter* ROMEO.]

BENVOLIO. Here comes Romeo! Here comes Romeo!

MERCUTIO. Without his roe, like a dried herring.[12] O flesh, flesh, how art thou fishified! Now is he for the numbers[13] that Petrarch flowed in. Laura, to his lady, was a kitchen wench (marry, she had a better love to berhyme her), Dido a dowdy, Cleopatra a gypsy, Helen and Hero hildings and harlots, Thisbe a gray eye or so, but not to the purpose. Signior Romeo, *bonjour*! There's a French salutation to your French slop. You gave us the counterfeit fairly last night.

ROMEO. Good morrow to you both. What counterfeit did I give you?

MERCUTIO. The slip,[14] sir, the slip. Can you not conceive?

28 **LITERATURE IN CONTEXT**

History Connection

Mercutio's Allusions

The women Mercutio names as he taunts Romeo are famous figures in European literature and history. Laura was the name of a woman to whom the Italian poet Petrarch addressed much of his love poetry. Dido, according to Roman mythology, was the queen of Carthage and love interest of Aeneas, the founder of Rome. Cleopatra was the famed Egyptian queen with whom Julius Caesar and later Mark Antony fell in love. Helen, Hero, and Thisbe are all legendary beauties in Greek mythology. Mercutio mocks Romeo by saying that Romeo thinks none of them compare with Rosaline.

Connect to the Literature

Why is Mercutio's use of grand references and exaggerated language a fitting way to tease Romeo?

Think Aloud

Vocabulary: Using Context

Direct students' attention to the word *bonjour* in line 44. Using a think-aloud process, model how to use context to infer the meaning of an unknown word. Say to students:

> I'm going to think aloud to show you how I would figure out the meaning of *bonjour* based on its context.
>
> In line 44, Mercutio says "*bonjour!*" to Romeo soon after Romeo enters the scene. Immediately afterward, in line 45, Mercutio says, "There's a French salutation to your French slop." Since Romeo has just entered the scene, it would make sense for Mercutio to greet Romeo. In addition, the word *salutation* means "greeting." Other examples of salutations are "Hello," "Greetings," and "Hi." Based on the context, I think *bonjour* is a French word meaning "hello."

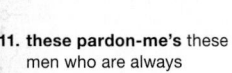

ROMEO. Pardon, good Mercutio. My business was great, and in such a case as mine a man may strain courtesy.

MERCUTIO. That's as much as to say, such a case as yours constrains a man to bow in the hams.[15]

ROMEO. Meaning, to curtsy.

MERCUTIO. Thou hast most kindly hit it.

ROMEO. A most courteous exposition.

MERCUTIO. Nay, I am the very pink of courtesy.

ROMEO. Pink for flower.

MERCUTIO. Right.

ROMEO. Why, then is my pump[16] well-flowered.

MERCUTIO. Sure wit, follow me this jest now till thou hast worn out thy pump, that, when the single sole of it is worn, the jest may remain, after the wearing, solely singular.[17]

ROMEO. O single-soled jest, solely singular for the singleness![18]

(29) **MERCUTIO.** Come between us, good Benvolio! My wits faints.

ROMEO. Swits and spurs, swits and spurs; or I'll cry a match.[19]

MERCUTIO. Nay, if our wits run the wild-goose chase, I am done; for thou hast more of the wild goose in one of thy wits than, I am sure, I have in my whole five. Was I with you there for the goose?

ROMEO. Thou wast never with me for anything when thou wast not there for the goose.

MERCUTIO. I will bite thee by the ear for that jest.

ROMEO. Nay, good goose, bite not!

MERCUTIO. Thy wit is a very bitter sweeting;[20] it is a most sharp sauce.

ROMEO. And is it not, then, well served in to a sweet goose?

MERCUTIO. O, here's a wit of cheveril,[21] that stretches from an inch narrow to an ell broad!

ROMEO. I stretch it out for that word "broad," which added to the goose, proves thee far and wide a broad goose.

15. **hams** hips.

16. **pump** shoe.

17. **when . . . singular** the jest will outwear the shoe and will then be all alone.

18. **O . . . singleness!** O thin joke, unique for only one thing—weakness!

19. **Swits . . . match** Drive your wit harder to beat me or else I will claim victory in this match of word play.

Literary Analysis
Blank Verse Why do you think Romeo does not speak in blank verse in this conversation with his friends?

20. **sweeting** kind of apple.

21. **cheveril** easily stretched kid leather.

(30) 

How does Romeo respond when Mercutio says that Romeo gave his friends "the slip" the night before?

(29) Literary Analysis

Blank Verse

1. Have students read lines 37–90. **Ask** students why Romeo's friends are teasing him. Where do they believe Romeo spent the night?

   Answer: They believe he spent the night with Rosaline, and they are teasing him about her.

2. **Ask** students how Romeo's verbal exchanges with Mercutio in this scene are different from what they are in Scenes i–iv in Act I.

   Answer: Here, Romeo exchanges lively jokes with his friend. In Act I, Romeo is sad and mournful and does not appear to be having much fun.

3. Tell students that this conversation between Romeo and Mercutio is one long battle of wits, in which each man is making puns out of the other man's words. Understanding the exact logic of the puns is less important than understanding the spirit of the game, which you might compare to ways that teenage boys today playfully trade insults.

4. **Ask** students the Literary Analysis question: Why do you think Romeo does not speak in blank verse in this conversation with his friends?

   Possible response: Students may say that Shakespeare chose prose for this conversation because he wanted to capture the kinds of rude remarks and jokes that teenage boys might use to mock a lovesick friend.

(30) Reading Check

Answer: Romeo says that his business was so important that it warranted poor manners.

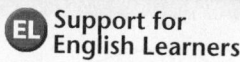

Differentiated Instruction for Universal Access

EL Support for English Learners

The punning and joking that goes on in Scene iv between Romeo and Mercutio may be especially difficult for English learners to follow.

Review the footnotes for lines 38–87. Remind English learners that they don't have to understand every pun to get the spirit of the jokes. Then, play the ***Hear It!* Audio CD** for this passage. Students should be able to grasp the spirit of this passage by hearing the tone and inflections in the voices of the actors.

After students have listened to the CD, discuss how they might have experienced or overheard these kinds of joking insults and teasing among teenage boys in their peer group or in their school.

31 Literary Analysis

Blank Verse

1. Have students read the bracketed text. **Ask** students what kind of language they would expect Mercutio and Romeo to use, given that they are members of the upper class.

   Answer: Mercutio and Romeo would be expected to speak in blank verse, the verse of the upper class.

2. **Ask** students the Literary Analysis question: How does Shakespeare reveal Romeo and Mercutio's intelligence even when they are not speaking in blank verse?

   Answer: Shakespeare reveals their intelligence through their quick and imaginative wit.

▶ Monitor Progress:

1. **Ask** students whether the characters on this page are speaking in blank verse.

   Answer: The characters are not speaking in blank verse.

2. **Ask** students which characters on this page might normally be expected to speak in blank verse. Why?

   Answer: Mercutio, Romeo, and Benvolio would normally be expected to speak in blank verse because they are members of the upper class.

▶ Reteach: If students have problems answering these questions, review the discussion of blank verse on p. 833. Guide students in scanning some lines of blank verse in this act.

MERCUTIO. Why, is not this better now than groaning for love? Now art thou sociable, now art thou Romeo; now art thou what thou art, by art as well as by nature. For this driveling love is like a great natural[22] that runs lolling[23] up and down to hide his bauble[24] in a hole.

29

BENVOLIO. Stop there, stop there!

MERCUTIO. Thou desirest me to stop in my tale against the hair.[25]

BENVOLIO. Thou wouldst else have made thy tale large.

MERCUTIO. O, thou art deceived! I would have made it short; for I was come to the whole depth of my tale, and meant indeed to occupy the argument[26] no longer.

ROMEO. Here's goodly gear![27]

[*Enter* NURSE *and her Man,* PETER.]

A sail, a sail!

MERCUTIO. Two, two! A shirt and a smock.[28]

NURSE. Peter!

PETER. Anon.

NURSE. My fan, Peter.

MERCUTIO. Good Peter, to hide her face; for her fan's the fairer face.

NURSE. God ye good morrow, gentlemen.

MERCUTIO. God ye good-den, fair gentlewoman.

NURSE. Is it good-den?

MERCUTIO. 'Tis no less, I tell ye; for the bawdy hand of the dial is now upon the prick of noon.

31

NURSE. Out upon you! What a man are you!

ROMEO. One, gentlewoman, that God hath made, himself to mar.

NURSE. By my troth, it is well said. "For himself to mar," quoth 'a? Gentlemen, can any of you tell me where I may find the young Romeo?

ROMEO. I can tell you; but young Romeo will be older when you have found him than he was when you sought him. I am the youngest of that name, for fault[29] of a worse.

22. natural idiot.
23. lolling with tongue hanging out.
24. bauble toy.
25. the hair natural inclination.
26. occupy the argument talk about the matter.
27. goodly gear good stuff for joking (Romeo sees Nurse approaching).
28. A shirt and a smock a man and a woman.
29. fault lack.

Literary Analysis
Blank Verse How does Shakespeare reveal Romeo and Mercutio's intelligence even when they are not speaking in blank verse?

Vocabulary Development

Graphic Organizers

1. To help students explore the concepts of *art* and *nature* (line 85), create a Venn diagram.
2. Draw two overlapping circles with the headings ART, BOTH, and NATURE.
3. Elicit definitions of *art* and *nature* as Mercutio means them in line 85. Then, guide students in brainstorming for differences and similarities between the two words. The finished diagram should look like this:

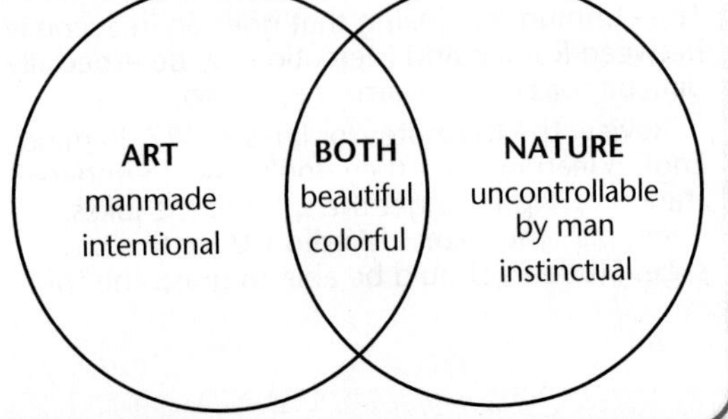

NURSE. You say well.

MERCUTIO. Yea, is the worst well? Very well took,[30] i' faith! Wisely, wisely.

NURSE. If you be he, sir, I desire some confidence[31] with you.

BENVOLIO. She will endite him to some supper.

MERCUTIO. A bawd, a bawd, a bawd! So ho!

ROMEO. What hast thou found?

MERCUTIO. No hare, sir; unless a hare, sir, in a lenten pie, that is something stale and hoar ere it be spent.

[*He walks by them and sings.*]

An old hare hoar,
And an old hare hoar,
Is very good meat in Lent;
But a hare that is hoar
Is too much for a score
When it hoars ere it be spent.

30. **took** understood.

31. **confidence** Nurse means "conference."

33 

Who interrupts Romeo and his friends to ask about Romeo?

32

32 Humanities

Film

This picture from the movie *Romeo + Juliet*, directed by Baz Luhrmann, shows Romeo played by Leonardo DiCaprio. Use the following questions for discussion.

- Based on this image from the movie, what idea about Romeo do you think the director is trying to communicate?

  Possible response: Romeo is smiling and seems relaxed and content. His mood has transformed between Acts I and II.

- What details in the picture help you understand the events that have occurred so far in Act II?

  Answer: Romeo's wistful and relaxed expression suggests that he is pleased with what has transpired. He has a plan and is ready to carry it out.

33 Reading Check

Answer: The Nurse interrupts Romeo.

Differentiated Instruction for Universal Access

Enrichment for Advanced Readers

Recommend that students watch the video of the musical *West Side Story*, which has a similar theme as *The Tragedy of Romeo and Juliet*.

Tell students the story is set in New York City in the late 1950s and concerns Tony, a founding member of a street gang, and Maria, the sister of the leader of a rival gang.

Encourage students to make a comparison/contrast chart as they watch, noting similarities and differences in the two works. Students should compare and contrast setting, characters, pivotal scenes (such as the first meeting of the lovers, the "balcony scene," and the marriage), and the ending.

Have students share their charts with the class.

34 Critical Thinking

Analyze

1. Review with students the Nurse's role in the play thus far.
2. **Ask** students to describe how the Nurse and Friar Lawrence have similar roles in the play, given what students know about the two characters so far.

   Answer: The Nurse and Friar Lawrence are both willing—perhaps too willing—to help Romeo and Juliet be together.

Spiral Review

Character

1. Remind students that they learned about the concept of character in the Unit 5 Literary Analysis Workshop (pp. 780–797).
2. **Ask** students the Spiral Review question.

   Possible response: The way she speaks reveals that she is not a sophisticated speaker and might be nervous talking to Romeo because of the class difference between them. The meaning of her comments reveals her strong sense of what is proper and her protectiveness of Juliet.

Romeo, will you come to your father's? We'll to dinner thither.

ROMEO. I will follow you.

MERCUTIO. Farewell, ancient lady. Farewell, [*singing*] "Lady, lady, lady."[32] [*Exit* MERCUTIO, BENVOLIO.]

NURSE. I pray you, sir, what saucy merchant was this that was so full of his ropery?[33]

ROMEO. A gentleman, nurse, that loves to hear himself talk and will speak more in a minute than he will stand to in a month.

NURSE. And 'a[34] speak anything against me, I'll take him down, and 'a were lustier than he is, and twenty such Jacks; and if I cannot, I'll find those that shall. Scurvy knave! I am none of his flirt-gills;[35] I am none of his skainsmates.[36] And thou must stand by too, and suffer every knave to use me at his pleasure!

PETER. I saw no man use you at his pleasure. If I had, my weapon should quickly have been out, I warrant you. I dare draw as soon as another man, if I see occasion in a good quarrel, and the law on my side.

NURSE. Now, afore God, I am so vexed that every part about me quivers. Scurvy knave! Pray you, sir, a word; and, as I told you, my young lady bid me inquire you out. What she bid me say, I will keep to myself; but first let me tell ye, if ye should lead her in a fool's paradise, as they say, it were a very gross kind of behavior, as they say; for the gentlewoman is young; and therefore, if you should deal double with her, truly it were an ill thing to be off'red to any gentlewoman, and very weak[37] dealing.

ROMEO. Nurse, commend[38] me to thy lady and mistress. I protest unto thee—

NURSE. Good heart, and i' faith I will tell her as much. Lord, Lord, she will be a joyful woman.

ROMEO. What wilt thou tell her, nurse? Thou dost not mark me.

NURSE. I will tell her, sir, that you do protest, which, as I take it, is a gentlemanlike offer.

32. **"Lady . . . lady"** line from an old ballad, "Chaste Susanna."
33. **ropery** Nurse means "roguery," the talk and conduct of a rascal.
34. **'a** he.
35. **flirt-gills** common girls.
36. **skainsmates** criminals; cutthroats.
37. **weak** unmanly.
38. **commend** convey my respect and best wishes.

Spiral Review
Character What do Nurse's comments to Romeo reveal about her feelings for Juliet?

Vocabulary Development

CCSS Language 6

Multiple Meanings

Draw students' attention to the word *minute* in line 138 on this page. Point out that Romeo is using the most common definition of *minute*—"one-sixtieth of an hour"—to make a point about how much Mercutio speaks.

Minute has some less common definitions, however. The word is also used as a fraction of a degree of longitude or latitude. In this context, a *minute* equals one-sixtieth of a degree.

Used as a plural noun, *minutes* means "official record of the proceedings of a meeting." For example, to remind ourselves what happened last week, we read the *minutes* of the previous meeting.

Finally, *minute* is also an adjective meaning "very small." For example, an editor pays attention to the *minute* details of a manuscript.

Have students write an original sentence using each meaning of the word *minute*.

ROMEO. Bid her devise
Some means to come to shrift[39] this afternoon;
And there she shall at Friar Lawrence' cell
Be shrived and married. Here is for thy pains.

NURSE. No, truly, sir; not a penny.

ROMEO. Go to! I say you shall.

NURSE. This afternoon, sir? Well, she shall be there.

ROMEO. And stay, good nurse, behind the abbey wall.
Within this hour my man shall be with thee
And bring thee cords made like a tackled stair.[40]
35 Which to the high topgallant[41] of my joy
Must be my convoy[42] in the secret night.
Farewell. Be trusty, and I'll quit[43] thy pains.
Farewell. Commend me to thy mistress.

NURSE. Now God in heaven bless thee! Hark you, sir.

ROMEO. What say'st thou, my dear nurse?

NURSE. Is your man secret? Did you ne'er hear say,
Two may keep counsel, putting one away?[44]

ROMEO. Warrant thee my man's as true as steel.

NURSE. Well, sir, my mistress is the sweetest lady. Lord, Lord! When 'twas a little prating[45] thing—O, there is a nobleman in town, one Paris, that would fain lay knife aboard;[46] but she, good soul, had as lieve[47] see a toad, a very toad, as see him. I anger her sometimes, and tell her that Paris is the properer man; but I'll warrant you, when I say so, she looks as pale as any clout[48] in the versal world.[49] Doth not rosemary and Romeo begin both with a letter?

ROMEO. Ay, nurse; what of that? Both with an R.

NURSE. Ah, mocker! That's the dog's name.[50] R is for the— No; I know it begins with some other letter; and she hath the prettiest sententious[51] of it, of you and rosemary, that it would do you good to hear it.

36 **ROMEO.** Commend me to thy lady.

NURSE. Ay, a thousand times. [*Exit* ROMEO.] Peter!

PETER. Anon.

NURSE. Before, and apace.[52] [*Exit, after* PETER.]

39. **shrift** confession.

Reading Skill
Summarize Read in sentences to summarize Romeo's instructions to the Nurse in lines 175–181.

40. **tackled stair** rope ladder.
41. **topgallant** summit.
42. **convoy** conveyance.
43. **quit** reward; pay you back for.

44. **Two . . . away** Two can keep a secret if one is ignorant, or out of the way.
45. **prating** babbling.
46. **fain . . . aboard** eagerly seize Juliet for himself.
47. **had as lieve** would as willingly.
48. **clout** cloth.
49. **versal world** universe.
50. **dog's name** *R* sounds like a growl.
51. **sententious** Nurse means "sentences"—clever, wise sayings.
52. **Before, and apace** Go ahead of me, and quickly.

Literary Analysis
Blank Verse What is the effect of hearing Romeo's blank verse after long passages of prose?

37 
Reading Check
What does Romeo ask the Nurse to tell Juliet?

35 Reading Skill
Summarize

1. Have two volunteers read aloud lines 164–181.
2. **Ask** students to respond to the Reading Skill prompt: Read in sentences to summarize Romeo's instructions to the Nurse in lines 175–181.

   Answer: Stay behind the abbey wall. Within the hour my servant will bring you a rope ladder. This will be my means of reaching the peak of happiness at night. Be reliable and I'll reward you. Greet your mistress for me.

36 Literary Analysis
Blank Verse

1. Have students review Romeo's lines, starting with line 161. **Ask** them if they notice any change in Romeo's speech.

   Answer: Romeo is now speaking in blank verse.
2. **Ask** students the Literary Analysis question: What is the effect of hearing Romeo's blank verse after long passages of prose?

   Possible response: Students may suggest that the change in the means of expression emphasizes the change in emotional state. After the boyish and boisterous exchange with his friends, he is now turning to serious concerns, and this is reflected in his speech.

37 Reading Check

Answer: Romeo asks the Nurse to tell Juliet to meet him at Friar Lawrence's that afternoon, after saying to her family that she is going to confession.

Differentiated Instruction for Universal Access

Culturally Responsive Instruction

Culture Focus On this page, Romeo asks the Nurse to have Juliet pretend to go to shrift (confession) so that she can marry him in Friar Lawrence's room. Point out to students that confession is a ritual of the Roman Catholic faith. When a person goes to confession, he or she enters a special area of a church and confesses sins—wrongdoings—to a religious leader called a priest. The priest has the power to absolve a person from his sins, meaning to free the person from guilt or responsibility.

Discuss with students various cultural and religious traditions for seeking forgiveness and atoning for wrongdoing. These traditions can involve words, actions, and rituals such as confession. Encourage students to show sensitivity toward their classmates as they talk about their beliefs and practices.

38 Critical Thinking

Analyze

1. **Ask** students what problem Juliet is having with her Nurse.

   Answer: Juliet is complaining that her Nurse is late.

2. **Ask** students why Juliet is so impatient.

   Answer: Juliet knows the Nurse will have word of Romeo and his plans for their marriage.

Scene v. Capulet's orchard.

[*Enter* JULIET.]

JULIET. The clock struck nine when I did send the nurse;
In half an hour she promised to return.
Perchance she cannot meet him. That's not so.
O, she is lame! Love's heralds should be thoughts,
Which ten times faster glides than the sun's beams
Driving back shadows over low'ring[1] hills.
Therefore do nimble-pinioned doves draw Love,[2]
And therefore hath the wind-swift Cupid wings.
Now is the sun upon the highmost hill
Of this day's journey, and from nine till twelve
Is three long hours; yet she is not come.
Had she affections and warm youthful blood,
She would be as swift in motion as a ball;
My words would bandy her[3] to my sweet love,
And his to me.
But old folks, many feign[4] as they were dead—
Unwieldy, slow, heavy and pale as lead.

[*Enter* NURSE *and* PETER.]

O God, she comes! O honey nurse, what news?
Hast thou met with him? Send thy man away.

NURSE. Peter, stay at the gate. [*Exit* PETER.]

JULIET. Now, good sweet nurse—O Lord, why lookest thou sad?
Though news be sad, yet tell them merrily;
If good, thou shamest the music of sweet news
By playing it to me with so sour a face.

NURSE. I am aweary, give me leave[5] awhile.
Fie, how my bones ache! What a jaunce[6] have I!

JULIET. I would thou hadst my bones, and I thy news.
Nay, come, I pray thee speak. Good, good nurse, speak.

NURSE. Jesu, what haste? Can you not stay a while?
Do you not see that I am out of breath?

JULIET. How art thou out of breath when thou hast breath
To say to me that thou art out of breath?
The excuse that thou dost make in this delay
Is longer than the tale thou dost excuse.
Is thy news good or bad? Answer to that.

1. **low'ring** darkening.
2. **Therefore . . . Love** therefore, doves with quick wings pull the chariot of Venus, goddess of love.
3. **bandy her** send her rapidly.
4. **feign** act.
5. **give me leave** excuse me; give me a moment's rest.
6. **jaunce** rough trip.

Vocabulary
unwieldy (un wēl′ dē) *adj.* awkward; clumsy

Vocabulary Development

CCSS Language 6

Word Analysis

Draw student's attention to the word *unwieldy* in line 17 on this page. Point out that this word contains the prefix *un-*, meaning "not." Tell students that *non-* is another prefix that generally means "not," and that these two prefixes can be used with the same word, with each prefix giving a slightly different meaning.

The prefix *un-* is used to indicate the opposite of something, as in *unwieldy*, meaning "not able to be wielded." The prefix *non-* is used to give a negative meaning to something.

These two prefixes can be attached to the same word to convey slightly different meanings. For example, a *non-American* is a person who is not an American citizen. To be *un-American* is to act in a way opposite to American values.

Have students brainstorm for other words that can be used with either *un-* or *non-* to give different meanings.

Possible responses: Students might suggest words such as *conventional* and *responsive*.

Say either, and I'll stay the circumstance.[7]
Let me be satisfied, is't good or bad?

NURSE. Well, you have made a simple[8] choice; you know not how to choose a man. Romeo? No, not he. Though his face be better than any man's, yet his leg excels all men's; and for a hand and a foot, and a body, though they be not to be talked on, yet they are past compare. He is not the flower of courtesy, but, I'll warrant him, as gentle as a lamb. Go thy ways, wench; serve God. What, have you dined at home?

JULIET. No, no. But all this I did know before.
What says he of our marriage? What of that?

NURSE. Lord, how my head aches! What a head have I!
It beats as it would fall in twenty pieces.
My back a[9] t'other side—ah, my back, my back!
Beshrew[10] your heart for sending me about
39 To catch my death with jauncing up and down!

JULIET. I' faith, I am sorry that thou art not well.
Sweet, sweet, sweet nurse, tell me, what says my love?

NURSE. Your love says, like an honest gentleman, and a courteous, and a kind, and a handsome, and, I warrant, a virtuous—Where is your mother?

JULIET. Where is my mother? Why, she is within.
Where should she be? How oddly thou repliest!
"Your love says, like an honest gentleman,
'Where is your mother?'"

NURSE. O God's Lady dear!
Are you so hot?[11] Marry come up, I trow.[12]
Is this the poultice[13] for my aching bones?
Henceforward do your messages yourself.

JULIET. Here's such a coil![14] Come, what says Romeo?

NURSE. Have you got leave to go to shrift today?

JULIET. I have.

NURSE. Then hie you hence to Friar Lawrence' cell;
There stays a husband to make you a wife.
Now comes the wanton[15] blood up in your cheeks:
They'll be in scarlet straight at any news.
Hie you to church: I must another way,

7. **stay the circumstance** wait for the details.
8. **simple** foolish; simpleminded.
9. **a** on.
10. **Beshrew** shame on.

Literary Analysis
Blank Verse What might Shakespeare be indicating about the Nurse's character by having her switch between prose and blank verse?

11. **hot** impatient; hot-tempered.
12. **Marry . . . trow** Indeed, cool down, I say.
13. **poultice** remedy.
14. **coil** disturbance.
15. **wanton** excited.

40 
Reading Check
How does the Nurse describe Romeo?

39 Literary Analysis
Blank Verse

1. Have students read the bracketed text aloud. **Ask:** How would you identify the form of writing?
   Answer: Some of the lines are blank verse, and some are not.
2. **Ask** students the Literary Analysis question: What might Shakespeare be indicating about the Nurse's character by having her switch between prose and blank verse?
   Possible response: Shakespeare might be indicating that the Nurse is trying to match Juliet's mood and method of speech in this emotionally charged scene, but because it is not her normal way of speaking, she does not quite carry it off. It also suggests that she is both an honorable character with deep feelings and serious intentions and something of a busybody.

40 Reading Check
Answer: The Nurse says that Romeo is handsome and gentle but does not have good manners.

Differentiated Instruction for Universal Access

Background for Gifted/Talented Students
Tell students that various actresses who have played Juliet have brought their own interpretations of the character to the role. One famous actress was Sarah Siddons (1755–1831), who critics claimed was the greatest Shakespearean actress of her time. One theatergoer wrote this of her performance in Act II, Scene v: "The pouting scene with the old Nurse was the cleverest thing I ever saw—so pretty, so babyish, so charming. . . ."

Have students work in groups of three or four to perform dramatic interpretations of Scene v. Students should take turns playing Juliet and the Nurse. Encourage students to use their own imaginations in interpreting how Juliet might speak and behave. Point out that as long as they have a basic understanding of the scene and of Juliet's character, there is no "right" way to deliver the lines. Encourage students to perform the scene for the class.

⓫ Literary Analysis

Blank Verse

1. **Ask** students to interpret the phrase "hie you to the cell" in line 77.

   Possible responses: Students should say that the phrase means something like "Get yourself to the cell" or "Go to the cell."

2. **Ask** students the Literary Analysis question: What effect is created by making Juliet's last line rhyme with the Nurse's last line?

   Answer: The lines create a rhyming couplet, which Shakespeare often used to close a scene. It also shows that the Nurse and Juliet are in agreement about Juliet's wedding plans.

42 Critical Viewing

Possible response: They are walking arm in arm, smiling, and gazing into each other's eyes. They are wearing wedding attire, which suggests that they have been unified in marriage. They seem happy and in love.

Literary Analysis
Blank Verse What effect is created by making Juliet's last line rhyme with the Nurse's last line?

To fetch a ladder, by the which your love
Must climb a bird's nest soon when it is dark.
I am the drudge, and toil in your delight:
But you shall bear the burden soon at night.
Go; I'll to dinner; hie you to the cell.

JULIET. Hie to high fortune! Honest nurse, farewell.

[*Exit all.*]

Scene vi. Friar Lawrence's cell.

[*Enter* FRIAR LAWRENCE *and* ROMEO.]

FRIAR. So smile the heavens upon this holy act
That afterhours with sorrow chide us not![1]

ROMEO. Amen, amen! But come what sorrow can,
It cannot countervail[2] the exchange of joy
That one short minute gives me in her sight.
Do thou but close our hands with holy words,
Then love-devouring death do what he dare—
It is enough I may but call her mine.

FRIAR. These violent delights have violent ends
And in their triumph die, like fire and powder,[3]
Which, as they kiss, consume. The sweetest honey

1. **That . . . not!** that the future does not punish us with sorrow.
2. **countervail** equal.
3. **powder** gunpowder.

42 ▶ **Critical Viewing** Which details in this picture reflect the feelings Romeo and Juliet have for each other? **[Interpret]**

Vocabulary Development

Vocabulary Knowledge Rating

When students have completed reading and discussing Act II of *The Tragedy of Romeo and Juliet*, have them take out their **Vocabulary Knowledge Rating Chart** for this selection. Read the words aloud once more and have students rate their knowledge of the words again in the After Reading column. Clarify any words that are still problematic. Have students write their own definition and example or sentence in the appropriate column. Then, have students complete the Vocabulary Practice activities at the end of the selection. Encourage students to use the words in further discussion and written work about this selection. Remind them that they will be accountable for these words on the **Selection Test**, ***Unit 5 Resources***, pp. 53–55 or 56–58.

Is loathsome in his own deliciousness
And in the taste confounds[4] the appetite.
Therefore love moderately: long love doth so;
Too swift arrives as tardy as too slow.

[*Enter* JULIET.]

Here comes the lady. O, so light a foot
Will ne'er wear out the everlasting flint.[5]
A lover may bestride the gossamers[6]
That idles in the wanton summer air,
And yet not fall; so light is vanity.[7]

JULIET. Good even to my ghostly confessor.

FRIAR. Romeo shall thank thee, daughter, for us both.

4. **confounds** destroys.

5. **flint** stone.
6. **gossamers** spider webs.
7. **vanity** foolish things that cannot last.

43 Critical Thinking

Make a Judgment

1. Have a volunteer read aloud the bracketed text. **Ask:** What is happening in Scene vi?

   Answer: Romeo and Juliet are meeting with Friar Lawrence, and they are about to be married.

2. **Ask:** What does Friar Lawrence notice about Juliet in lines 16–20?

   Answer: He notices that she is treading lightly as if she were a spider on a web.

3. **Ask:** Why do you think Juliet is behaving this way?

   Possible response: She is deeply in love and excited about marrying Romeo.

4. Have students make a judgment. **Ask:** Is Juliet committing an act of betrayal by marrying Romeo, or are her actions justified?

   Possible responses: Some students might say that Juliet's actions are justified because people should be able to love whomever they wish, and Romeo never harmed her family in any specific way. Other students might say that Juliet is showing disloyalty to her family, and she is lying to them by marrying Romeo in secret.

Concept Connector

Activating Prior Knowledge

Have students compare their responses to the activity they completed before reading this act with their ideas afterwards. Ask them to explain whether their thoughts have changed.

Literary Analysis Graphic Organizer

Have students review the graphic organizers they completed while reading to identify characters' rank based on their understanding of blank verse. Show them the partially completed **Literary Analysis Graphic Organizer A** (*Graphic Organizer Transparencies*, p. 151) as an example. Then, have students share the graphic organizers they did and how they identified characters' ranks.

ASSESS

Answers

Critical Thinking

Before students respond, you may wish to have them write a brief objective summary of the selection. As they answer the questions below, remind them to support their answers with evidence from the text.

1. (a) Romeo and Juliet declare their love for each other in the balcony scene. (b) The darkness conceals Romeo from Juliet's relatives. It also provides an illusion of privacy so that Juliet feels she can speak her thoughts aloud.
2. (a) The Friar says that Romeo is fickle. Romeo argues that Rosaline did not return his love and Juliet does. (b) The Friar wants to end the feud between the families, while the couple wants to be together because they are in love.
3. (a) Juliet awaits the Nurse. (b) Juliet is highly impatient, and her exasperation increases as she tries to extract news from the breathless Nurse.
4. **Possible response:** Students may say that the romantic words and images, the danger of discovery, the vivid descriptions, and the expressions of devotion are extremely powerful.
5. **Possible response:** If anything, the differences between Romeo and Juliet have made their love more intense and have strengthened their determination to be together. If it were not for the family feud, they would be able to meet out in the open rather than in hiding. The idea of meeting in secret and enlisting the aid of the Friar and the Nurse makes the situation more dramatic. On the other hand, Romeo and Juliet do not let their differences dissuade them from pursuing marriage.

JULIET. As much to him,[8] else is his thanks too much.

ROMEO. Ah, Juliet, if the measure of thy joy
Be heaped like mine, and that thy skill be more
To blazon it,[9] then sweeten with thy breath
This neighbor air, and let rich music's tongue
Unfold the imagined happiness that both
Receive in either by this dear encounter.

JULIET. Conceit, more rich in matter than in words,
Brags of his substance, not of ornament.[10]
They are but beggars that can count their worth;
But my true love is grown to such excess
I cannot sum up sum of half my wealth.

FRIAR. Come, come with me, and we will make short work;
For, by your leaves, you shall not stay alone
Till Holy Church incorporate two in one. *[Exit all.]*

8. **As . . . him** the same greeting to him.
9. **and . . . it** and if you are better able to proclaim it.
10. **Conceit . . . ornament** Understanding does not need to be dressed up in words.

Critical Thinking

Cite textual evidence to support your responses.

1. **Key Ideas and Details (a)** Where do Romeo and Juliet first mutually declare their love? **(b) Interpret:** What role does darkness play in the scene?
2. **Key Ideas and Details (a)** What weakness in Romeo does the Friar point out before agreeing to help? **(b) Compare and Contrast:** How do the Friar's motives differ from the couple's motives? Explain your response.
3. **Key Ideas and Details (a)** For whom does Juliet wait in Act II, Scene v? **(b) Analyze:** What are her feelings as she waits? Explain your answer.
4. **Integration of Knowledge and Ideas Evaluate:** Why do you think the love scene in Capulet's garden is one of the most famous dramatic scenes in all literature? Explain.
5. **Integration of Knowledge and Ideas** Have the differences between Romeo and Juliet affected their relationship? Use details from the text to support your response. ***[Connect to the Big Question: Do our differences define us?]***

Assessment Resources

Unit 5 Resources

L1 L2 EL **Selection Test A,** pp. 53–55. Administer Test A to less advanced readers.

L3 L4 EL **Selection Test B,** pp. 56–58. Administer Test B to on-level and more advanced students.

L3 L4 **Open-Book Test,** pp. 50–52. As an alternative, give the Open-Book Test.

All **Customizable Test Bank**

All **Self-tests**
Students may prepare for the **Selection Test** by taking the **Self-test** online.

All assessment resources are available at **www.PHLitOnline.com.**

After You Read
The Tragedy of Romeo and Juliet, Act II

Literary Analysis: Blank Verse

1. **Craft and Structure** Copy the following passages of **blank verse.** Then, indicate the pattern of accented (´) and unaccented (˘) syllables in each line. **(a)** Act II, Scene ii, lines 43–51 **(b)** Act II, Scene vi, lines 3–8
2. **Craft and Structure** Using a chart like the one shown, rewrite the following two lines, marking stressed and unstressed syllables. Then, identify the key words stressed in each line, and explain what meaning is conveyed. **(a) ROMEO.** Can I go forward when my heart is here? **(b) JULIET.** But my true love is grown to such excess.

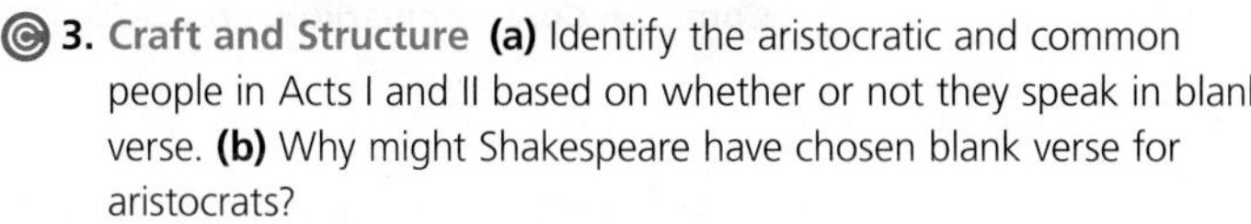

Blank Verse Pattern	Key Words	Significance

3. **Craft and Structure (a)** Identify the aristocratic and common people in Acts I and II based on whether or not they speak in blank verse. **(b)** Why might Shakespeare have chosen blank verse for aristocrats?

Reading Skill: Summarize

4. **(a)** How many sentences are in lines 1–8 of Act II, Scene v? **(b)** Write a **summary** of these lines.

Vocabulary

Acquisition and Use Answer each question. Then, explain your answer.

1. Where would you go to <u>procure</u> groceries?
2. What is the <u>predominant</u> feeling at a celebration?
3. How many people are needed for an <u>intercession</u> to occur?
4. Is a <u>sallow</u> complexion a sign of good health?
5. If a situation is <u>lamentable</u>, are people likely to be happy about it?
6. Is an <u>unwieldy</u> package something you would want to carry far?

Word Study Use the context of the sentences and what you know about the **Latin prefix *pro-*** to explain your answer to each question.

1. If you make a *proposal,* have you suggested a course of action?
2. If you are *proactive,* are you waiting for something to occur?

Word Study

The **Latin prefix *pro-*** means "before," "forward."

Apply It Explain how the prefix *pro-* contributes to the meanings of these words. Consult a dictionary if necessary.

program
project
prorate

Continued from right column

Word Study
Sample answers:
1. Yes. The prefix *pro-* means "before, forward," and *proposal* means "a plan offered before an action." If you make a *proposal,* you have suggested a plan to carry out an action.
2. No. The prefix *pro-* means "before, forward," and *proactive* means "acting in advance or before in order to deal with a difficulty." If you are *proactive,* you initiate action, not wait for it to occur.

Word Study: Apply It
Sample answers: To *program* is to schedule or plan <u>before</u>hand. To *project* means to move <u>forward</u>. To *prorate* means to determine a rate proportionately <u>before</u>hand.

ASSESS/EXTEND

Answers

Literary Analysis

1. Use an overhead projector to mark the unaccented and accented syllables in these passages as a class.
2. **Blank Verse Pattern:** (a) Căn Í gŏ fórwărd whén mȳ héart ĭs hére? (b) Bŭt mý trŭe lóve ĭs grówn tŏ súch ĕxcéss. **Key Words:** *I, forward, heart, here, my, love, grown, such, excess* **Significance:** The words help communicate key ideas.

   For other sample answers, see ***Graphic Organizer Transparencies,*** **Literary Analysis Graphic Organizer A,** p. 153, and the **Additional Answers** section.
3. (a) The Capulets and the Montagues, their friends, the Prince, and the Friar speak in blank verse. The servants and the Nurse are common people and, for the most part, speak in prose. (b) **Possible response:** Blank verse signals seriousness and status. Shifts from verse to prose also emphasize changes in mood and tone.

Reading Skill

4. (a) There are six sentences in these lines. (b) It was nine o'clock when Juliet sent the Nurse, who promised to return in half an hour. Juliet worries that perhaps the Nurse cannot meet Romeo and frets that she is so slow.

Vocabulary
Acquisition and Use
Sample answers:

1. I'd go to a market. *Procure* means "to obtain."
2. The feeling is happiness or joy; *predominant* means "having main influence."
3. At least one other person is needed. An *intercession* is the act of pleading on one's behalf.
4. No, it is a sign of bad health. *Sallow* means "of a sickly complexion."
5. No. If a situation is *lamentable,* it is sad or distressing, so people wouldn't be happy about it.
6. No. Something *unwieldy* is difficult, not easy, to carry.

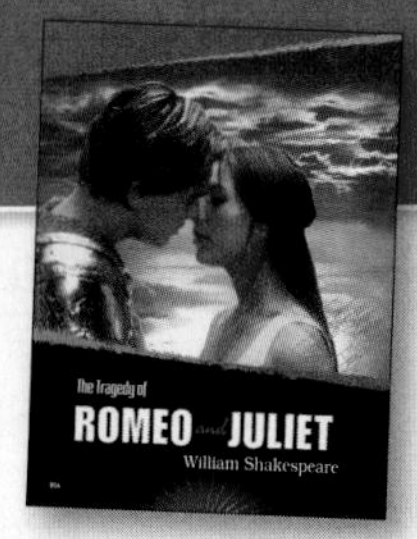

✓ The Tragedy of Romeo and Juliet, Act III

Lesson Pacing Guide

DAY 1 Preteach

- Administer the Reading and Vocabulary Warm-ups (*Unit 5 Resources*, pp. 59–62) as necessary.
- Introduce the Reading Skill: Summarize.
- Introduce the Literary Analysis concept: Dramatic Speeches
- Distribute copies of the appropriate graphic organizer for the Reading Skill (*Graphic Organizer Transparencies*, pp. 157–158).
- Distribute copies of the appropriate graphic organizer for Literary Analysis (*Graphic Organizer Transparencies*, pp. 155–156).
- Teach the selection vocabulary.
- Introduce the Word Study skill.

DAYS 2–3 Preteach/Teach

- Build background with the Background feature.
- Develop thematic vocabulary and thematic thinking with Writing About the Big Question.
- Prepare students to read with the Activating Prior Knowledge activities (TE).
- Informally monitor comprehension while students read.
- Use the Reading Check questions to confirm comprehension.
- Develop students' ability to summarize, using the Reading Skill questions.
- Develop students' understanding of dramatic speech, using the Literary Analysis questions.
- Reinforce vocabulary with the Vocabulary notes.
- Reinforce unit focus standards using the Spiral Review prompts.

DAY 4 Assess

- Assess students' comprehension and mastery of the skills by having them answer the Critical Thinking, Reading Skill, and Literary Analysis questions.
- Have students complete the Vocabulary Practice activities.
- Have students complete the Word Study activities.

DAY 5 Extend/Assess

- Have students complete the Conventions lesson.
- Have students complete the Writing activity and write an editorial, p. 933. (You may assign as homework.)
- Assign students "What Is Love?" in *Reality Central*.
- Administer Selection Test A or B (*Unit 5 Resources*, pp. 71–76).

Common Core State Standards

Reading Literature 2. Determine a theme or central idea of a text; provide an objective summary of the text.
5. Analyze how an author's choices concerning how to structure a text, order events within it, and manipulate time create such effects as mystery, tension, or surprise.

Additional Standards Practice
***Common Core Companion**, pp. 28–29*

Daily Block Scheduling
Each day in this Lesson Pacing Guide represents a 40–50 minute period. Teachers using block scheduling may combine days to revise pacing. In addition, teachers may differentiate and support core instruction by integrating components for extended and intensive support as students require. See the Guide to Selected Leveled Resources (facing page).

Guide to Selected Leveled Resources

RTI **Tier 1** (students performing on level)		The Tragedy of Romeo and Juliet, Act III
Warm Up	**Practice, model,** and **monitor** fluency, working **with the whole class** or **in groups.**	**Vocabulary** and **Reading Warm-ups B,** ***Unit 5 Resources,*** pp. 77–78, 80
Comprehension/Skills	**Support** and **monitor** comprehension and skills development, having students complete the activities, graphic organizers, and interactive prompts **independently** or **as a class.**	• ***Reader's Notebook,*** adapted instruction and full selection EL ***Reader's Notebook: English Learner's Version,*** adapted instruction and adapted selection • **Reading Skill Graphic Organizer B,** ***Graphic Organizer Transparencies,*** p. 156 • **Literary Analysis Graphic Organizer B,** ***Graphic Organizer Transparencies,*** p. 158
Monitor Progress	**Monitor** student progress with the differentiated curriculum-based assessment in the *Unit Resources.*	• **Selection Test B,** ***Unit 5 Resources,*** pp. 74–76 • **Open-Book Test,** ***Unit 5 Resources,*** pp. 68–70

RTI **Tier 2** (students requiring intervention)		The Tragedy of Romeo and Juliet, Act III
Warm Up	**Practice, model,** and **monitor** fluency **in groups** or **with individuals.**	• **Vocabulary and Reading Warm-ups A,** ***Unit 5 Resources,*** pp. 77–80 • ***Reality Central,*** "What Is Love?" • ***Hear It!*** **Audio CD (adapted text)**
Comprehension/Skills	• **Support** and **monitor** comprehension and skills development, working **in small groups** or **with individuals.** • **Pair** students with more advanced peers and have them complete the writing activity in the *Real-World Writing Journal.* • As students complete the selection in the appropriate version of the *Reader's Notebook,* **monitor** comprehension frequently with group questions and individual instruction. • **Model** strategies while guiding students in completing the activities and prompts in the *Reader's Notebook,* as well as the graphic organizers. • **Practice** skills and **monitor** mastery with the *Reading Kit* worksheets.	• ***Real-World Writing Journal,*** Lesson 1, pp. 138–141 • ***Reader's Notebook: Adapted Version,*** adapted instruction and adapted selection EL ***Reader's Notebook: English Learner's Version,*** adapted instruction and adapted selection • **Reading Skill Graphic Organizer A,** ***Graphic Organizer Transparencies,*** p. 155 • **Literary Analysis Graphic Organizer A,** ***Graphic Organizer Transparencies,*** p. 157 • **Reading Kit,** Practice worksheets, pp. 206, 214, 218, 230
Monitor Progress	**Monitor** student progress with the differentiated curriculum-based assessment in the *Unit Resources* and in the *Reading Kit.*	• **Selection Test A,** ***Unit 5 Resources,*** pp. 71–73 • **Reading Kit,** Assess worksheets pp. 207, 215, 219, 231

TIER 3 Tier 3 intervention may require consultation with the student's special-education or dyslexia specialist. For additional support, see the Tier 2 activities and resources listed above.

One-on-one teaching **Group work** **Whole class instruction** **Independent work** A **Assessment**

For a complete guide to selection support, including support for Advanced students, see the Overview of Resources in the frontmatter.

✓ The Tragedy of Romeo and Juliet, Act III

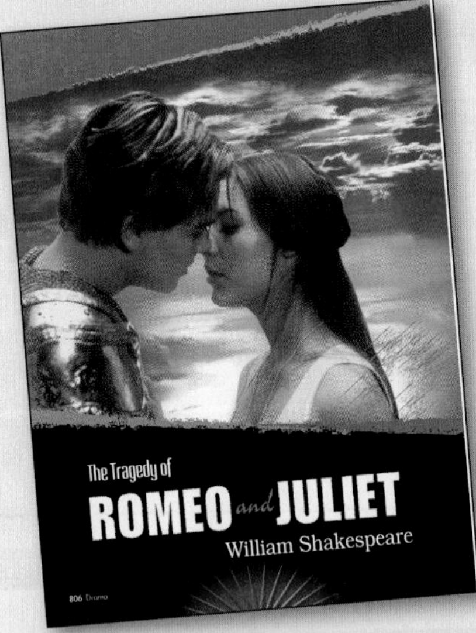

RESOURCES FOR:

- L1 Special-Needs Students
- L2 Below-Level Students (Tier 2)
- L3 On-Level Students (Tier 1)
- L4 Advanced Students (Tier 1)
- EL English Learners
- All All Students

Vocabulary/Fluency/Prior Knowledge

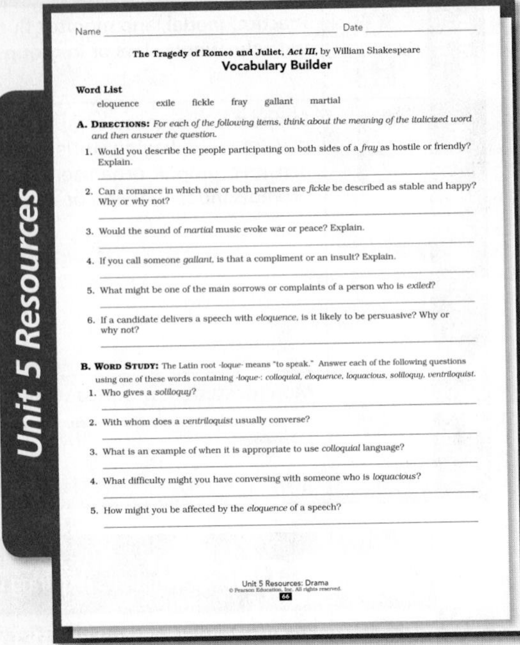

Name ______ Date ______

The Tragedy of Romeo and Juliet, *Act III*, by William Shakespeare
Vocabulary Builder

Word List
eloquence exile fickle fray gallant martial

A. Directions: *For each of the following items, think about the meaning of the italicized word and then answer the question.*

1. Would you describe the people participating on both sides of a *fray* as hostile or friendly? Explain.
2. Can a romance in which one or both partners are *fickle* be described as stable and happy? Why or why not?
3. Would the sound of *martial* music evoke war or peace? Explain.
4. If you call someone *gallant*, is that a compliment or an insult? Explain.
5. What might be one of the main sorrows or complaints of a person who is *exiled*?
6. If a candidate delivers a speech with *eloquence*, is it likely to be persuasive? Why or why not?

B. Word Study: The Latin root *-loque-* means "to speak." Answer each of the following questions using one of these words containing *-loque-*: *colloquial, eloquence, loquacious, soliloquy, ventriloquist.*

1. Who gives a *soliloquy*?
2. With whom does a *ventriloquist* usually converse?
3. What is an example of when it is appropriate to use *colloquial* language?
4. What difficulty might you have conversing with someone who is *loquacious*?
5. How might you be affected by the *eloquence* of a speech?

Unit 5 Resources: Drama
© Pearson Education, Inc. All rights reserved.
66

All **Vocabulary Builder,** p. 66

Also available for this selection:

EL L1 L2 **Vocabulary Warm-ups A and B,** pp. 59–60

EL L1 L2 **Reading Warm-ups A and B,** pp. 61–62

All **Writing About the Big Question,** p. 63

Reader's Notebooks

Pre- and postreading pages, as well as the selection *The Tragedy of Romeo and Juliet*, Act III, appear in an interactive format in the *Reader's Notebooks*. Each *Notebook* is differentiated for a different group of learners. The selections in the Adapted and English Learner's versions are abridged.

L2 L3 ***Reader's Notebook***

L1 ***Reader's Notebook: Adapted Version***

EL ***Reader's Notebook: English Learner's Version***

EL ***Reader's Notebook: Spanish Version***

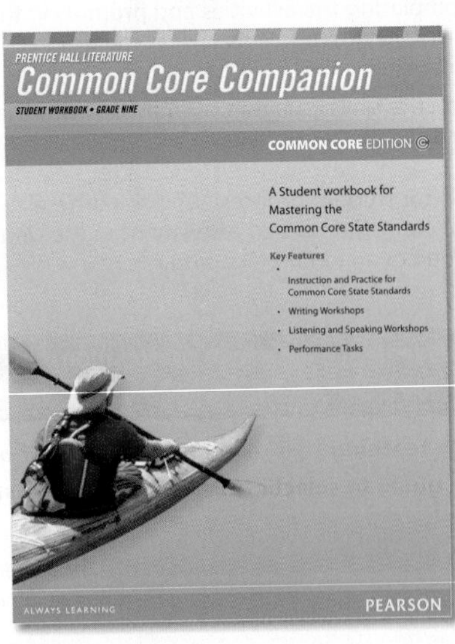

Common Core Companion

Additional instruction and practice for each Common Core State Standard

Selection Support

Graphic Organizer Transparencies

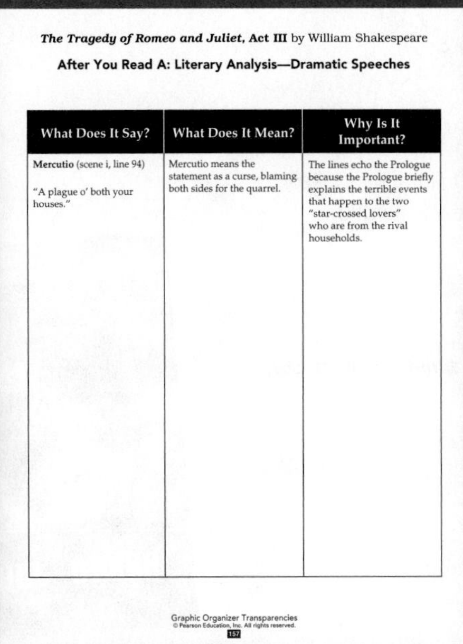

The Tragedy of Romeo and Juliet, **Act III** by William Shakespeare

After You Read A: Literary Analysis—Dramatic Speeches

What Does It Say?	What Does It Mean?	Why Is It Important?
Mercutio (scene i, line 94) "A plague o' both your houses."	Mercutio means the statement as a curse, blaming both sides for the quarrel.	The lines echo the Prologue because the Prologue briefly explains the terrible events that happen to the two "star-crossed lovers" who are from the rival households.

Graphic Organizer Transparencies
© Pearson Education, Inc. All rights reserved.
157

EL L1 L2 **Graphic Organizer A,** p. 157 (partially filled in)

Also available for this selection:

EL L1 L2 **Reading Skill: Graphic Organizer A,** p. 155 (partially filled in)

EL L3 **Reading Skill: Graphic Organizer B,** p. 156

EL L3 **Literary Analysis: Graphic Organizer B,** p. 158

Skills Development/Extension

Unit 5 Resources

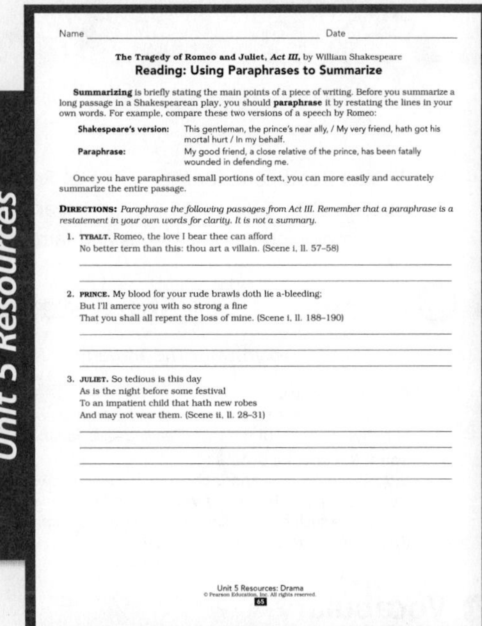

Name ______________________ Date ____________

The Tragedy of Romeo and Juliet, *Act III*, by William Shakespeare

Reading: Using Paraphrases to Summarize

Summarizing is briefly stating the main points of a piece of writing. Before you summarize a long passage in a Shakespearean play, you should **paraphrase** it by restating the lines in your own words. For example, compare these two versions of a speech by Romeo:

Shakespeare's version: This gentleman, the prince's near ally, / My very friend, hath got his mortal hurt / In my behalf.

Paraphrase: My good friend, a close relative of the prince, has been fatally wounded in defending me.

Once you have paraphrased small portions of text, you can more easily and accurately summarize the entire passage.

DIRECTIONS: *Paraphrase the following passages from Act III. Remember that a paraphrase is a restatement in your own words for clarity. It is not a summary.*

1. **TYBALT.** Romeo, the love I bear thee can afford
No better term than this: thou art a villain. (Scene i, ll. 57–58)

2. **PRINCE.** My blood for your rude brawls doth lie a-bleeding;
But I'll amerce you with so strong a fine
That you shall all repent the loss of mine. (Scene i, ll. 188–190)

3. **JULIET.** So tedious is this day
As is the night before some festival
To an impatient child that hath new robes
And may not wear them. (Scene ii, ll. 28–31)

Unit 5 Resources: Drama
© Pearson Education, Inc. All rights reserved.
65

All **Reading: Summarize,** p. 65

Also available for this selection:

All **Literary Analysis: Dramatic Speeches,** p. 64

L4 **Enrichment,** p. 67

EL L3 L4 **Grammar,** p. 104

EL L3 L4 **Support for Writing,** p. 105

L3 L4 **Support for Extend Your Learning,** p. 106

Assessment

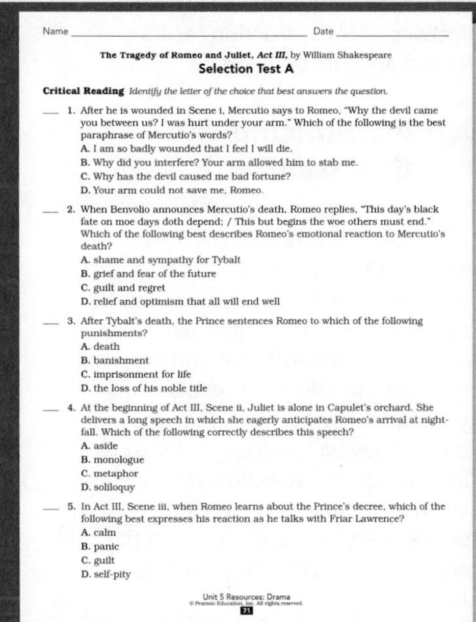

Name ______________________ Date ____________

The Tragedy of Romeo and Juliet, *Act III*, by William Shakespeare

Selection Test A

Critical Reading *Identify the letter of the choice that best answers the question.*

___ 1. After he is wounded in Scene i, Mercutio says to Romeo, "Why the devil came you between us? I was hurt under your arm." Which of the following is the best paraphrase of Mercutio's words?
A. I am so badly wounded that I feel I will die.
B. Why did you interfere? Your arm allowed him to stab me.
C. Why has the devil caused me bad fortune?
D. Your arm could not save me, Romeo.

___ 2. When Benvolio announces Mercutio's death, Romeo replies, "This day's black fate on moe days doth depend; / This but begins the woe others must end." Which of the following best describes Romeo's emotional reaction to Mercutio's death?
A. shame and sympathy for Tybalt
B. grief and fear of the future
C. guilt and regret
D. relief and optimism that all will end well

___ 3. After Tybalt's death, the Prince sentences Romeo to which of the following punishments?
A. death
B. banishment
C. imprisonment for life
D. the loss of his noble title

___ 4. At the beginning of Act III, Scene ii, Juliet is alone in Capulet's orchard. She delivers a long speech in which she eagerly anticipates Romeo's arrival at nightfall. Which of the following correctly describes this speech?
A. aside
B. monologue
C. metaphor
D. soliloquy

___ 5. In Act III, Scene iii, when Romeo learns about the Prince's decree, which of the following best expresses his reaction as he talks with Friar Lawrence?
A. calm
B. panic
C. guilt
D. self-pity

Unit 5 Resources: Drama
© Pearson Education, Inc. All rights reserved.
71

EL L1 L2 **Selection Test A,** pp. 71–73

Also available for this selection:

EL L3 L4 **Open-Book Test,** pp. 68–70

EL L3 L4 **Selection Test B,** pp. 74–76

PHLit Online!
www.PHLitOnline.com

- complete narrated selection text
- a thematically related video with writing prompt
- an interactive graphic organizer
- highlighting feature
- access to all student print resources, adapted to individual student needs
- Spanish and English summaries
- adapted selection translations in Spanish

Online Resources: All print materials are also available online.

Background Video

Also available:

Get Connected! (thematic video with writing prompt)

All videos are available in Spanish.

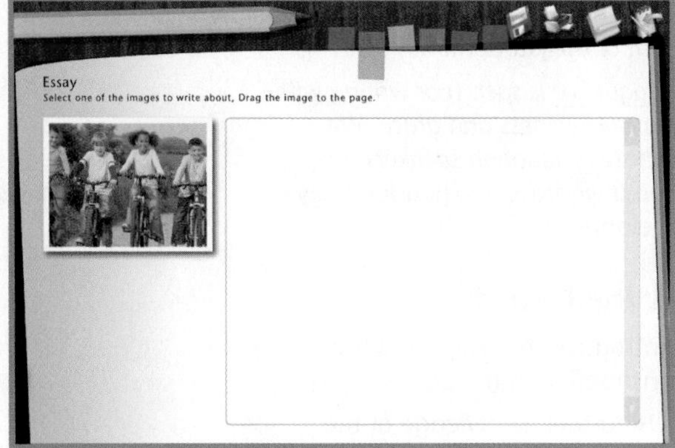

Writer's Journal (with graphics feature)

Also available:

Vocabulary Central (tools, activities, and songs for studying vocabulary)

Leveled Texts

You may use *The Tragedy of Romeo and Juliet,* Act III to meet the lesson objectives. Skills instruction for the selection appears on page 861.

1 Introducing the CCS Standards

Introduce the standards on the student page. (Note that the lesson element with which each standard is addressed is identified in parentheses after the text of the standard.) Call out the standards that you will cover with the selections, explaining to students what each requires and how they will address it as they work through the selection you have chosen. Standards labeled "Spiral Review" are introduced in the Literary Analysis Workshop for this unit.

2 Vocabulary

1. Have students preview the selection vocabulary.
2. For each word, have students say the word aloud.
3. Then, use the word in a sentence that defines the word.
4. Finally, repeat your definitional sentence or a similar sentence with the word missing and have the class "fill in the blank" chorally. Here are some examples:

   A fray is a noisy fight. The two children fought loudly, but their parents just watched and stayed out of the [students say "fray"].

   Eloquence is speech or writing with persuasiveness and grace. We chose graduation speakers based on their grace and [students say "eloquence"].

3 Word Study

1. Introduce the skill, using the instruction in the box.
2. Using their knowledge of the Latin root, ask students for a *-loque-* word that means "able to speak well." (*eloquent*)

Before You Read The Tragedy of Romeo and Juliet, Act III

While You Read Look for the steps that Romeo and Juliet try to take to overcome their differences—and think about the new separations they are developing among friends and family.

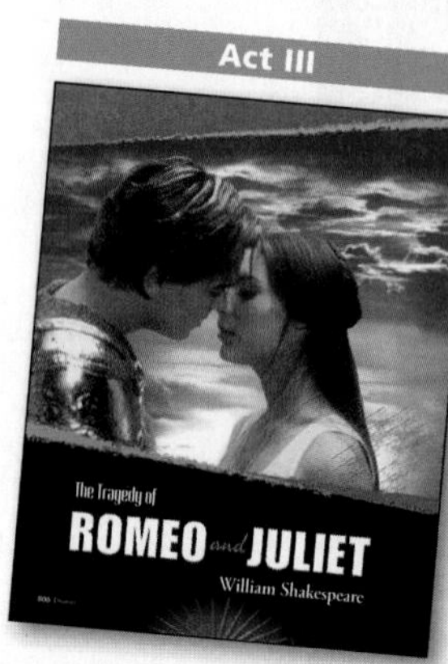

1 Common Core State Standards

Meet these standards with ***The Tragedy of Romeo and Juliet,* Act III** (p. 862).

Reading Literature
2. Determine a theme or central idea of a text; provide an objective summary of the text. *(Reading Skill: Summarize)*

Spiral Review: RL.9–10.3
5. Analyze how an author's choices concerning how to structure a text, order events within it, and manipulate time create such effects as mystery, tension, or surprise. *(Literary Analysis: Dramatic Speeches)*

2 Vocabulary

Read each word and its definition. Decide whether you know the word well, know it a little bit, or do not know it at all. After you read, see how your knowledge of each word has increased.

- **gallant** (gal′ ənt) *adj.* brave and noble (p. 868) ***We called the firefighters gallant, but they said they were just doing their job.*** *gallantly adv. gallantry n.*
- **fray** (frā) *n.* noisy fight (p. 869) ***The crew argued, but the captain stayed above the fray.*** *fray v. frayed adj.*
- **martial** (mär′ shəl) *adj.* military; warlike (p. 869) ***The band played martial music to honor the soldiers.*** *martialist n.*
- **exile** (eks′ īl′) *v.* banish (p. 870) ***Years ago, rulers would exile criminals to faraway places.*** *exiler n.*
- **eloquence** (el′ ə kwəns) *n.* speech that is graceful and persuasive (p. 871) ***The eloquence of her speech moved the audience.*** *eloquent adj. eloquently adv.*
- **fickle** (fik′ əl) *adj.* changeable (p. 884) ***His fickle sense of style made buying clothes for him difficult.*** *fickleness n.*

3 Word Study

The **Latin root *-loque-*** means "talk," "speak," or "say."

In Act III, Juliet says that everyone who speaks Romeo's name speaks **eloquence.** She means that the name itself is a graceful, vivid expression.

4 Literary Analysis: Dramatic Speeches

In most plays, the dramatic action takes place through **dialogue**—the conversations between characters. Some playwrights, however, make use of specialized dialogue in the form of **dramatic speeches.**

- **Soliloquy:** a lengthy speech in which a character—usually alone on stage—expresses his or her true thoughts or feelings. Soliloquies are unheard by other characters.
- **Aside:** a character revealing his or her true thoughts or feelings in a remark that is unheard by other characters.
- **Monologue:** a lengthy speech by one character. Unlike a soliloquy or an aside, a monologue is addressed to other characters.

Characters' speeches reflect their individual character traits, and Shakespeare often uses dialogue and action to emphasize differences between characters. As you read, look for **foils,** or characters whose words and actions show you clear personality contrasts.

5 Reading Skill: Summarize

Summarizing is briefly stating the main points in a piece of writing. Before you summarize a passage of a play by Shakespeare, **paraphrase** it, or restate the lines in your own words. Compare these two versions of a speech by Romeo:

Shakespeare's version: "This gentleman, the Prince's near ally, / My very friend, hath got his mortal hurt / In my behalf. . . ."
Paraphrase: My good friend, a close relative of the prince, has been fatally wounded in defending me.

Once you have paraphrased small portions of text, you can more easily and accurately summarize an entire passage.

6 Using the Strategy: Summarizing Chart

Use a chart like this one to paraphrase and summarize the text.

Text	Paraphrase	Summary
"I pray thee, good Mercutio, let's retire. The day is hot, the Capulets abroad, And, if we meet, we shall not 'scape a brawl, For now, these hot days, is the mad blood stirring."	Please, Mercutio, let's leave. It's hot out, and the Capulets are around. And if we meet up with them, we will most likely fight, because on these hot days we have fight in us.	Benvolio is trying to convince Mercutio to leave the public place they are meeting in, because he is afraid a brawl with the Capulets is inevitable.

4 Literary Analysis

Dramatic Speeches

1. Introduce the skill, using the instruction on the student page.
2. Tell students that they will analyze dramatic speeches as they read.

Think Aloud: Model the Skill

Model a way to analyze dramatic speeches. Say to students:

Each kind of dramatic speech reminds me of speech in real life. A *soliloquy,* in which only the audience can hear what the character says, reminds me of talking to myself to practice a lesson. An *aside,* in which the audience hears what the character is thinking, reminds me of someone talking under his or her breath. A *monologue,* in which a character speaks at length to another character, reminds me of the long stories my friends tell. When I read plays, I watch for these different kinds of speeches.

5 Reading Skill

Summarize

1. Introduce the skill, using the instruction on the student page.
2. Tell students that they will practice summarizing by paraphrasing as they read.

6 Using the Strategy

Give students a copy of either **Reading Skill Graphic Organizer A** or **B** (*Graphic Organizer Transparencies,* pp. 155–156) to summarize lines of dialogue as they read. Use the examples in **Reading Skill Graphic Organizer A,** which is partially filled in, to model the process of completing the organizer.

Differentiated Instruction Additional Instruction

EL Extended Support—English Learners

Have students complete the **Reading and Vocabulary Warm-ups, *Unit 5 Resources,*** pp. 59–62, before they read. Assign the prereading pages for the selection in the ***Reader's Notebook: English Learner's Version.*** Then, have students listen to portions of the selection on the ***Hear It!* Audio CD.**

L1 L2 Extended Support—Struggling Readers

Have students complete the **Reading and Vocabulary Warm-ups, *Unit 5 Resources,*** pp. 59–62 before they read. Assign the prereading pages for the selection in the ***Reader's Notebook: Adapted Version.*** Then, have students listen to portions of the selection on the ***Hear It!* Audio CD** (adapted text).

Extended Support—Reluctant Readers

To build motivation and engagement before assigning the selection, have students read "What Is Love?," a thematically related selection in *Reality Central.* Then, use the questions at the conclusion of the related selection to guide discussion.

❶ Activating Prior Knowledge

1. Remind students that at the end of Act II, Romeo and Juliet seem to be on the way to happiness. They have married. Now they must inform their families and hope that their marriage will finally resolve the old feud. While this is a problem, it does not seem insurmountable at this point.
2. Ask students to imagine how they might act if they were Romeo or Juliet. Would they inform their parents immediately of their marriage? How would they inform their families? How would their parents react? Ask students to respond to these questions and to record their responses.

Concept Connector

Students will reconsider their ideas after reading *The Tragedy of Romeo and Juliet,* Act III.

Individual Activity

Have students review the images in Act III. Ask them what they can predict from the images. Have them record their responses and then confirm or revise their ideas as they read Act III.

❷ About the Selection

In this act of *The Tragedy of Romeo and Juliet*, circumstances and Romeo's impulsive, passionate nature conspire to wreck Romeo and Juliet's happiness in the wake of their secret wedding. Events move toward the tragic outcome that follows from Romeo's killing of Tybalt and banishment from Verona, and the Capulets' plan to marry Juliet to Paris.

Text Complexity Rubric

The Tragedy of Romeo and Juliet, Act III		
Qualitative Measures	**Context/ Knowledge Demands**	Historical: Verona, Italy 1 2 3 4 ⑤
	Structure/ Language Clarity and Conventionality	Challenging vocabulary; Elizabethan terms 1 2 3 4 ⑤
	Levels of Meaning/ Purpose/Concept Level	Accessible concept (classic tale of star-crossed lovers) 1 2 ③ 4 5
Quantitative Measures	**Text Length**	Word Count: 6,413
	Lexile	NP
Overall Complexity		**Complex**

Review and Anticipate

In Act II, Romeo and Juliet express their mutual love and enlist the aid of Juliet's nurse and Friar Lawrence to arrange a secret marriage ceremony. As the act closes, the young couple is about to be married. Before performing the ceremony, the Friar warns, "These violent delights have violent ends. . . ." How might this statement hint at events that will occur in Act III or later in the play?

Scene i. A public place.
[*Enter* MERCUTIO, BENVOLIO, *and* MEN.]

BENVOLIO. I pray thee, good Mercutio, let's retire.
The day is hot, the Capulets abroad,
And, if we meet, we shall not 'scape a brawl,
For now, these hot days, is the mad blood stirring.

MERCUTIO. Thou art like one of these fellows that, when he enters the confines of a tavern, claps me his sword upon the table and says, "God send me no need of thee!" and by the operation of the second cup draws him on the drawer,[1] when indeed there is no need.

BENVOLIO. Am I like such a fellow?

MERCUTIO. Come, come, thou art as hot a Jack in thy mood as any in Italy; and as soon moved to be moody, and as soon moody to be moved.[2]

1. **and . . . drawer** and by the effect of the second drink, draws his sword against the waiter.
2. **and . . . moved** and as quickly stirred to anger as you are eager to be so stirred.

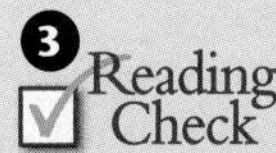

❸ Why does Benvolio want to get off the street?

❸ Reading Check

Answer: He wants to avoid the street because conditions are ripe for a violent encounter with the Capulets.

PHLit Online!

This selection is available in interactive format in the **Enriched Online Student Edition,** at **www.PHLitOnline.com,** which includes a thematically related video with writing prompt and an interactive graphic organizer.

© Text Complexity: Reader and Task Suggestions

The Tragedy of Romeo and Juliet, Act III	
Preparing to Read the Text • Read the Review and Anticipate note (SE p. 863) with students and discuss the concept of foreshadowing with students. Explain how foreshadowing helps build suspense. • Point out that the play is realistically set in the city of Verona, a place of narrow streets, broad plazas, and homes with striking balconies. Discuss the value of the setting in building a believable story. • Guide students to use Multidraft Reading strategies (TE p. 805).	**Leveled Tasks** ***Levels of Meaning*** If students will have difficulty with levels of meaning, have them first read the text and note details showing how Romeo's actions shape events in Act III. Then, have them reread and list questions they have about the setting and events. Review student notes and help clarify their understanding. ***Analyzing*** If students will not have difficulty with levels of meaning, have them read the text and note the sequence of cause-and-effect events building through the act. Have them share their notes in class discussion.

❹ Literary Analysis

Dramatic Speeches

1. Have students recall from earlier acts the kind of character Benvolio exhibits. **Answer:** Benvolio attempted to break up a fight in Act I. He is cool-headed.
2. **Ask** students the Literary Analysis question: Which details of Mercutio's speech indicate that it is a monologue and not a soliloquy?

   Answer: Mercutio speaks directly to Benvolio, and other characters are listening.

❺ Reading Skill

Summarize

Ask the Reading Skill question: How would you paraphrase the exchange between Tybalt and Mercutio?

Possible response: TYBALT: Hello, gentlemen. I'd like a word with one of you. MERCUTIO: Just a word? You can do better than that. Make it a word and a punch. TYBALT: I might just do that if you give me a reason. MERCUTIO: Can't you find a reason of your own? TYBALT: Mercutio, you consort with Romeo. MERCUTIO: Consort? What do you think we are—musicians? If you're going to call us musicians, you'll be hearing some sour notes. Here's my sword—this will make you dance. Let's fight!

❻ Literary Analysis

Dramatic Speeches

Ask students the Literary Analysis question.

Answer: The dialogue reveals Mercutio's aggressive and confrontational nature and in contrast, Benvolio's desire to avoid conflict.

Literary Analysis
Dramatic Speeches Which details of Mercutio's speech indicate that it is a monologue and not a soliloquy?

3. **addle** scrambled; crazy.

4. **doublet** jacket.
5. **riband** ribbon.
6. **tutor . . . quarreling** instruct me not to quarrel.
7. **fee simple** complete possession.
8. **an hour and a quarter** length of time that a man with Mercutio's fondness for quarreling may be expected to live.
9. **O simple!** O stupid!

Reading Skill
Summarize How would you paraphrase the exchange between Tybalt and Mercutio?

10. **occasion** cause; reason.
11. **consortest** associate with.
12. **Consort** associate with; "consort" also meant a group of musicians.
13. **discords** harsh sounds.
14. **Zounds** exclamation of surprise or anger ("By God's wounds").

Literary Analysis
Dramatic Speeches How does the dialogue here set Mercutio and Benvolio as foils?

BENVOLIO. And what to?

MERCUTIO. Nay, and there were two such, we should have none shortly, for one would kill the other. Thou! Why, thou wilt quarrel with a man that hath a hair more or a hair less in his beard than thou hast. Thou wilt quarrel with a man for cracking nuts, having no other reason but because thou hast hazel eyes. What eye but such an eye would spy out such a quarrel? Thy head is as full of quarrels as an egg is ❹ full of meat; and yet thy head hath been beaten as addle[3] as an egg for quarreling. Thou hast quarreled with a man for coughing in the street, because he hath wakened thy dog that hath lain asleep in the sun. Didst thou not fall out with a tailor for wearing his new doublet[4] before Easter? With another for tying his new shoes with old riband?[5] And yet thou wilt tutor me from quarreling![6]

BENVOLIO. And I were so apt to quarrel as thou art, any man should buy the fee simple[7] of my life for an hour and a quarter.[8]

MERCUTIO. The fee simple? O simple![9] ❻

[*Enter* TYBALT, PETRUCHIO, *and* OTHERS.]

BENVOLIO. By my head, here comes the Capulets.

MERCUTIO. By my heel, I care not.

TYBALT. Follow me close, for I will speak to them.
Gentlemen, good-den. A word with one of you.

MERCUTIO. And but one word with one of us? Couple it with something; make it a word and a blow.

❺ **TYBALT.** You shall find me apt enough to that, sir, and you will give me occasion.[10]

MERCUTIO. Could you not take some occasion without giving?

TYBALT. Mercutio, thou consortest[11] with Romeo.

MERCUTIO. Consort?[12] What, dost thou make us minstrels? And thou make minstrels of us, look to hear nothing but discords.[13] Here's my fiddlestick; here's that shall make you dance. Zounds,[14] consort!

BENVOLIO. We talk here in the public haunt of men.
Either withdraw unto some private place,
Or reason coldly of your grievances,
Or else depart. Here all eyes gaze on us.

Vocabulary Development

Ⓒ CCSS Language 6

Selection Vocabulary Reinforcement

Students will benefit from additional examples and practice with the selection vocabulary words. Reinforce their comprehension with "show-you-know" sentences. The first part of the sentence uses the vocabulary word in an appropriate context. The second part of the sentence—the "show-you-know" part—clarifies the first. Model the strategy with this example for *gallant*:

He was a *gallant* soldier; he risked his life to save his buddy.

Then, give students these sentence prompts and coach them in creating the clarification part:

1. Jimmy was always in the *fray*; ____________

   Sample answer: he was constantly fighting with his brothers.
2. He was a master of *martial* arts; ____________

   Sample answer: he could defeat anyone in hand-to-hand combat.

MERCUTIO. Men's eyes were made to look, and let them gaze.
I will not budge for no man's pleasure, I.

[*Enter* ROMEO.]

TYBALT. Well, peace be with you, sir. Here comes my man.[15]

MERCUTIO. But I'll be hanged, sir, if he wear your livery.[16]
Marry, go before to field,[17] he'll be your follower!
Your worship in that sense may call him man.

7

TYBALT. Romeo, the love I bear thee can afford
No better term than this: thou art a villain.[18]

ROMEO. Tybalt, the reason that I have to love thee
Doth much excuse the appertaining[19] rage
To such a greeting. Villain am I none.
Therefore farewell. I see thou knowest me not.

15. **man** man I am looking for; "man" also meant "manservant."
16. **livery** servant's uniform.
17. **field** dueling place.
18. **villain** low, vulgar person.
19. **appertaining** appropriate.

8

What are Mercutio and Benvolio arguing about?

7 Critical Thinking

Analyze Cause and Effect

1. Have students reread the bracketed text, which continues onto p. 866. Point out to students that the confrontation involving Tybalt, Romeo, and Mercutio is made worse because all three characters are acting on incomplete knowledge and false assumptions. **Ask** students what Tybalt thinks Romeo's motive was for coming to the Capulets' party, and what Romeo's real motive was.

   Answer: Tybalt thinks Romeo came to the party to mock the Capulets, but Romeo came only to see Rosaline.

2. Point out to students that both Tybalt and Mercutio believe that Romeo is a foe of the Capulets. **Ask** students whether this is still true.

   Answer: Romeo is now married to Juliet; Tybalt is his wife's cousin. Romeo wants no more quarreling with the Capulets.

8 Reading Check

Answer: Mercutio and Benvolio are arguing about Mercutio's fondness for starting fights.

Differentiated Instruction for Universal Access

Strategy for Special-Needs Students
Act III is long, with several intense scenes. Students may benefit from using the ***Reader's Notebook: Adapted Version*** along with the ***Hear It!* Audio CD** (adapted text) in small groups. Encourage students to read along as they listen to the CD and to discuss each scene with their group.

Strategy for Less Proficient Readers
Have students use the ***Reader's Notebook: Adapted Version*** along with the ***Hear It!* Audio CD** (adapted text). Suggest that students read along as they listen to the CD. Students may wish to use the ***Reader's Notebook: Adapted Version*** as an introduction to the act. After they have completed the ***Reader's Notebook***, have them choose one or two scenes to read in the Student Edition text.

9 Connecting to the Big Question

1. Remind students of the Big Question by recalling that our opinions are an important difference that can define us. Offer your opinion about an appropriate, but controversial local issue, and invite students to share theirs. Discuss how different views help define us.
2. Have students read the bracketed passage. **Ask:** What creates the gulf that divides Tybalt, Romeo, and Mercutio here?

   Possible response: Misinformation creates the gulf.
3. **Ask** students: Is what we think about others a difference, if what we think is inaccurate or is based on inaccurate information? Explain.

   Possible response: Yes, our perceptions of others can divide us even if they are flawed.

10 Critical Viewing

Answer: The two young men look tense and worried. The men in black look angry and threatening.

TYBALT. Boy, this shall not excuse the injuries
That thou hast done me; therefore turn and draw.

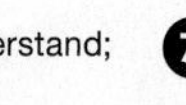

ROMEO. I do protest I never injured thee,
But love thee better than thou canst devise[20]
Till thou shalt know the reason of my love;
And so, good Capulet, which name I tender[21]
As dearly as mine own, be satisfied.

MERCUTIO. O calm, dishonorable, vile submission!
Alla stoccata[22] carries it away. [*Draws.*]
Tybalt, you ratcatcher, will you walk?

TYBALT. What wouldst thou have with me?

MERCUTIO. Good King of Cats, nothing but one of your
nine lives. That I mean to make bold withal,[23] and, as
you shall use me here-after, dry-beat[24] the rest of the
eight. Will you pluck your sword out of his pilcher[25]
by the ears? Make haste, lest mine be about your
ears ere it be out.

TYBALT. I am for you. [*Draws.*]

ROMEO. Gentle Mercutio, put thy rapier up.

MERCUTIO. Come, sir, your *passado*! [*They fight.*]

ROMEO. Draw, Benvolio; beat down their weapons.
Gentlemen, for shame! Forbear this outrage!
Tybalt, Mercutio, the Prince expressly hath

20. **devise** understand; imagine.
21. **tender** value.
22. ***Alla stoccata*** at the thrust—an Italian fencing term that Mercutio uses as a nickname for Tybalt.
23. **make bold withal** make bold with; take.
24. **dry-beat** thrash.
25. **pilcher** scabbard.

Critical Viewing Which details in these photographs suggest that a duel is about to take place? **[Analyze]**

Vocabulary Development

CCSS Language 6

Thematic Vocabulary: The Big Question

As students are discussing *The Tragedy of Romeo and Juliet*, Act III, encourage them to use the thematic vocabulary presented in Introducing the Big Question, pp. 778–779. You might encourage them with sentence starters like these:

1. Trouble comes because Romeo is unable to *accept* . . .
2. The sword fight with Tybalt and Mercutio reflects the *culture* of . . .
3. Over and over, Romeo encounters *differences* with . . .
4. Romeo finds himself needing to *defend* . . .

Forbid this bandying in Verona streets.
Hold, Tybalt! Good Mercutio!

[TYBALT *under* ROMEO'S *arm thrusts* MERCUTIO *in, and flies.*]

11 **MERCUTIO.** I am hurt.
A plague a[26] both houses! I am sped.[27]
Is he gone and hath nothing?

BENVOLIO. What, art thou hurt?

MERCUTIO. Ay, ay, a scratch, a scratch. Marry, 'tis enough.
Where is my page? Go, villain, fetch a surgeon. [*Exit* PAGE.]

ROMEO. Courage, man. The hurt cannot be much.

MERCUTIO. No, 'tis not so deep as a well, nor so wide as
13 a church door; but 'tis enough, 'twill serve. Ask for
me tomorrow, and you shall find me a grave man. I
am peppered,[28] I warrant, for this world. A plague a
both your houses! Zounds, a dog, a rat, a mouse, a

26. a on.
27. sped wounded; done for.

28. peppered finished off.

12 
Reading Check
What is the outcome of the duel between Tybalt and Mercutio?

11 Background

Fencing

When Tybalt, Mercutio, and Romeo fence, they fight to kill. Fencing became a sport only in the late 1700s; today fencers compete at the Olympic Games.

The object of fencing is to touch the opponent with a sword and to avoid being touched. Three different weapons may be used: the *foil*, the *epee*, and the *saber*. These differ in size, weight, and appearance, but all include devices to blunt their points for safety. Fencers wear a strong wire-mesh mask and protective clothing to avoid injury. They must develop precision, speed, timing, and tactical judgment. Many professional actors study and practice fencing for use on the stage.

Have students discuss what a dueling scene adds to a performance. Have them compare and contrast the dueling scenes in *The Tragedy of Romeo and Juliet* with action scenes in contemporary movies, including car chases, shoot-outs, and martial-arts sequences.

12 Reading Check

Answer: When Romeo attempts to come between Tybalt and Mercutio, Tybalt strikes Mercutio under Romeo's arm and kills Mercutio.

Differentiated Instruction for Universal Access

EL Support for English Learners

To help students through this long and intense act, lead a quick "selection tour" before they read. Focus their attention on the pictures, the questions in the side margins, and Reading Check questions. Pay special attention to the footnotes, making sure that students understand the explanations.

Reassure students that it is not necessary to understand every word or every line to understand and appreciate the play. Advise them that if they get stuck on a line or a passage they can't understand even with the footnotes, they should flag it with a sticky note and keep reading. After they complete reading the act, review the questions they have marked with the sticky notes.

13 Reading Skill

Summarize

1. **Ask** students to read lines 93–106 beginning on p. 867. Have them summarize what has happened since Tybalt injured Mercutio.

   Answer: Tybalt flees; Mercutio says he is dying and blames Romeo for coming between him and Tybalt; Romeo says he was just trying to help; Mercutio curses the Montagues and Capulets several times; Benvolio carries Mercutio offstage.

2. Have students read line 104. **Ask** students to respond to the Reading Skill prompt: Paraphrase Mercutio's line "A plague a both your houses!" and summarize his reasons for uttering this curse.

   Possible answer: "Curse the Capulets and the Montagues both." Mercutio is cursing both families because their feuding has led to his death.

---

29. **by . . . arithmetic** by formal rules.

Reading Skill 13
Summarize
Paraphrase Mercutio's line "A plague a both your houses!" and summarize his reasons for uttering this curse.

30. **I have it** I have got my deathblow.
31. **ally** relative.

Vocabulary
gallant (gal′ ənt) *adj.* brave and noble

32. **aspired** climbed to.
33. **moe** more.
34. **depend** hang over.

35. **respective lenity** thoughtful mercy.
36. **conduct** guide.

cat, to scratch a man to death! A braggart, a rogue,
a villain, that fights by the book of arithmetic![29] Why
the devil came you between us? I was hurt under
your arm.

ROMEO. I thought all for the best.

MERCUTIO. Help me into some house, Benvolio,
Or I shall faint. A plague a both your houses!
They have made worms' meat of me. I have it,[30]
And soundly too. Your houses! [*Exit* MERCUTIO *and* BENVOLIO.]

ROMEO. This gentleman, the Prince's near ally,[31]
My very friend, hath got his mortal hurt
In my behalf—my reputation stained
With Tybalt's slander—Tybalt, that an hour
Hath been my cousin. O sweet Juliet,
Thy beauty hath made me effeminate
And in my temper soft'ned valor's steel!

[*Enter* BENVOLIO.]

BENVOLIO. O Romeo, Romeo, brave Mercutio is dead!
That **gallant** spirit hath aspired[32] the clouds,
Which too untimely here did scorn the earth.

ROMEO. This day's black fate on moe[33] days doth depend;[34]
This but begins the woe others must end.

[*Enter* TYBALT.]

BENVOLIO. Here comes the furious Tybalt back again.

ROMEO. Alive in triumph, and Mercutio slain?
Away to heaven respective lenity,[35]
And fire-eyed fury be my conduct[36] now!
Now, Tybalt, take the "villain" back again
That late thou gavest me; for Mercutio's soul
Is but a little way above our heads,
Staying for thine to keep him company.
Either thou or I, or both, must go with him.

TYBALT. Thou, wretched boy, that didst consort him here,
Shalt with him hence.

ROMEO. This shall determine that.
[*They fight.* TYBALT *falls.*]

14 **BENVOLIO.** Romeo, away, be gone!

Vocabulary Development

CCSS Language 6

Expressive Vocabulary

To help students broaden their expressive vocabulary, encourage them to use the following words as they discuss this scene in which Mercutio and Tybalt are killed: *complies*, *eloquent*, *drastic*, and *tolerate*. Have them complete these sentence starters:

1. Despite the threat of death, neither Mercutio nor Tybalt *complies* . . .
2. Romeo's *eloquent* words fail . . .
3. Romeo wants to avoid the *drastic* . . .
4. Mercutio cannot *tolerate* . . .

Challenge students to use these words as you continue to discuss the play.

The citizens are up, and Tybalt slain.
Stand not amazed. The Prince will doom thee death
If thou art taken. Hence, be gone, away!

ROMEO. O, I am fortune's fool![37]

37. **fool** plaything.

BENVOLIO. Why dost thou stay?

[*Exit* ROMEO.]

[*Enter* CITIZENS.]

CITIZEN. Which way ran he that killed Mercutio?
Tybalt, that murderer, which way ran he?

BENVOLIO. There lies that Tybalt.

CITIZEN. Up, sir, go with me.
I charge thee in the Prince's name obey.

[*Enter* PRINCE, OLD MONTAGUE, CAPULET, *their* WIVES, *and all.*]

PRINCE. Where are the vile beginners of this fray?

Vocabulary
fray (frā) *n.* noisy fight

BENVOLIO. O noble Prince, I can discover[38] all
The unlucky manage[39] of this fatal brawl.
There lies the man, slain by young Romeo,
That slew thy kinsman, brave Mercutio.

38. **discover** reveal.
39. **manage** course.

LADY CAPULET. Tybalt, my cousin! O my brother's child!
O Prince! O cousin! Husband! O, the blood is spilled
Of my dear kinsman! Prince, as thou art true,
For blood of ours shed blood of Montague.
O cousin, cousin!

PRINCE. Benvolio, who began this bloody fray?

BENVOLIO. Tybalt, here slain, whom Romeo's hand did slay.
Romeo, that spoke him fair, bid him bethink
How nice[40] the quarrel was, and urged withal
Your high displeasure. All this—utterèd
With gentle breath, calm look, knees humbly bowed—
Could not take truce with the unruly spleen[41]
Of Tybalt deaf to peace, but that he tilts[42]
With piercing steel at bold Mercutio's breast;
Who, all as hot, turns deadly point to point,
And, with a martial scorn, with one hand beats
Cold death aside and with the other sends
It back to Tybalt, whose dexterity
Retorts it. Romeo he cries aloud,
"Hold, friends! Friends, part!" and swifter than his tongue,
His agile arm beats down their fatal points,

40. **nice** trivial.

41. **spleen** angry nature.
42. **tilts** thrusts.

Vocabulary
martial (mär′ shəl) *adj.* military

15 Reading Check
Who does Benvolio say started the brawl?

14 Critical Thinking

Interpret

1. Have students read lines 130–134, which begin on p. 868. **Ask** students what urgent warning Benvolio is giving to Romeo in these lines.

   Answer: Benvolio is telling Romeo to stop standing around staring. He wants Romeo to flee.

2. Ask students why Benvolio is so concerned.

   Answer: If Romeo is present when the Prince arrives, Romeo will be condemned to death for fighting, according to the Prince's earlier order.

15 Reading Check

Answer: He says that Tybalt was hot-headed and, although Romeo tried to stop the fight, Tybalt was "deaf to peace" and continued fighting.

Differentiated Instruction for Universal Access

Enrichment for Advanced Readers

Tell students that some critics have argued that Shakespeare kills off Mercutio so early in the play because the lively, exuberant character of Mercutio makes Romeo pale in comparison.

Another critic argues that Mercutio becomes irrelevant once Juliet and Romeo fall profoundly in love. Mercutio has no place in the play once it becomes dominated by the love between Romeo and Juliet.

Have students form small groups to discuss these questions: Was Mercutio killed off because he was more interesting than Romeo? If Shakespeare had not killed him off early in the drama, what role might he have continued to play? If Mercutio had not been killed by Tybalt, would Romeo have killed Tybalt?

By discussing these questions, students may more clearly appreciate the genius of Shakespeare in destroying one of the most interesting and vibrant characters in the play.

16 Literary Analysis

Dramatic Speeches

1. **Ask** students whether Benvolio's speech on pp. 869–870 is a soliloquy or a monologue. Why?

   Answer: Benvolio's speech is a monologue. He delivers it to the Prince, and other characters listen.

2. **Ask** students whether Benvolio's monologue describing the fight is factual or biased. How do you know?

   Answer: His description is basically factual, though his adjectives slyly favor Mercutio, the Prince's relative.

3. **Ask** the Literary Analysis question: Which details of Benvolio's speech suggest that he is trying to portray Romeo favorably?

   Possible response: Benvolio says that Romeo was reasonable and tried to avoid the fight. When Tybalt and Mercutio began to fight, Romeo attempted to stop it. After Tybalt killed Mercutio he fled, but came back to fight Romeo, who was by then angry about his friend's death.

17 Critical Thinking

Interpret

1. Have students read lines 180–196. Remind students what the Prince decreed earlier about street fighting. **Ask** students what "the price of his dear blood" might be.

   Answer: The price might be Romeo's life.

2. **Ask** why Montague pleads for Romeo's life.

   Answer: Montague is Romeo's father.

3. **Ask** what sentence the Prince pronounces for Romeo and what warning he gives Montague.

   Answer: He exiles Romeo and warns Montague that no pleading will make him change his mind; if Romeo is found in the city, he will pay with his life.

Literary Analysis
Dramatic Speeches Which details of Benvolio's speech suggest that he is trying to portray Romeo favorably? 16

43. **envious** full of hatred.
44. **entertained** considered.

And 'twixt them rushes; underneath whose arm
An envious[43] thrust from Tybalt hit the life
Of stout Mercutio, and then Tybalt fled;
But by and by comes back to Romeo,
Who had but newly entertained[44] revenge,
And to't they go like lightning; for, ere I
Could draw to part them, was stout Tybalt slain;
And, as he fell, did Romeo turn and fly.
This is the truth, or let Benvolio die.

LADY CAPULET. He is a kinsman to the Montague;
Affection makes him false, he speaks not true.
Some twenty of them fought in this black strife,
And all those twenty could but kill one life.
I beg for justice, which thou, Prince, must give.
Romeo slew Tybalt; Romeo must not live.

PRINCE. Romeo slew him; he slew Mercutio.
Who now the price of his dear blood doth owe?

MONTAGUE. Not Romeo, Prince; he was Mercutio's friend;
His fault concludes but what the law should end,
The life of Tybalt.[45]

45. **His fault . . . Tybalt** by killing Tybalt, he did what the law would have done.

Vocabulary
exile (eks´ īl´) *v.* banish

PRINCE. And for that offense
Immediately we do exile him hence.
I have an interest in your hate's proceeding.
My blood[46] for your rude brawls doth lie a-bleeding;
But I'll amerce[47] you with so strong a fine
That you shall all repent the loss of mine.
I will be deaf to pleading and excuses;
Nor tears nor prayers shall purchase out abuses.
Therefore use none. Let Romeo hence in haste,
Else, when he is found, that hour is his last.
Bear hence this body and attend our will.[48]
Mercy but murders, pardoning those that kill.

[Exit with others.]

46. **My blood** Mercutio was related to the Prince. 17
47. **amerce** punish.
48. **attend our will** await my decision.

Scene ii. Capulet's orchard.
[*Enter* JULIET *alone.*]

JULIET. Gallop apace, you fiery-footed steeds,[1]
Towards Phoebus' lodging![2] Such a wagoner
As Phaëton[3] would whip you to the west
And bring in cloudy night immediately.

1. **fiery-footed steeds** horses of the sun god, Phoebus.
2. **Phoebus' lodging** below the horizon.
3. **Phaëton** Phoebus' son, who tried to drive his father's horses but was unable to control them. 18

Vocabulary Development

CCSS Language 6

Multiple Meanings

Refer students to the word *civil* in Scene ii, line 10 (p. 871). Tell students that in this line the word *civil* is used in its obsolete sense of "somber; not gaudy or showy," a definition that was usually applied to clothing. Today, one use of the word *civil* reflects a related older meaning: "refraining from being rude," as in "keep a civil tongue."

Tell students that today, however, the most common use of the word *civil* is in its meanings related to citizens, cities, law, and government, and it is used in many common phrases. Write the following phrases on the board:

civil rights, civil servant, civil engineer, civil war, civil defense, civil disobedience, civil marriage

Ask students to choose two of these phrases and use the dictionary to find their definitions. Then, explain what meaning of the word *civil* is reflected in each phrase.

Spread thy close curtain, love-performing night,
That runaways' eyes may wink,[4] and Romeo
Leap to these arms untalked of and unseen.
Lovers can see to do their amorous rites,
And by their own beauties; or, if love be blind,
It best agrees with night. Come, civil night,
Thou sober-suited matron all in black,
And learn me how to lose a winning match,
Played for a pair of stainless maidenhoods.
Hood my unmanned blood, bating in my cheeks,[5]
With thy black mantle till strange[6] love grow bold,
Think true love acted simple modesty,
Come, night; come, Romeo; come, thou day in night;
For thou wilt lie upon the wings of night
Whiter than new snow upon a raven's back.
18 Come, gentle night; come, loving, black-browed night;
Give me my Romeo; and when I shall die,
Take him and cut him out in little stars,
And he will make the face of heaven so fine
That all the world will be in love with night
And pay no worship to the garish sun.
O, I have bought the mansion of a love,
But not possessed it; and though I am sold,
Not yet enjoyed. So tedious is this day
As is the night before some festival
To an impatient child that hath new robes
And may not wear them. O, here comes my nurse,

[*Enter* NURSE, *with cords.*]

And she brings news; and every tongue that speaks
But Romeo's name speaks heavenly **eloquence**.
Now, nurse, what news? What hast thou there, the cords
That Romeo bid thee fetch?

NURSE. Ay, ay, the cords.

JULIET. Ay me! What news? Why dost thou wring thy hands?

NURSE. Ah, weraday![7] He's dead, he's dead, he's dead!
We are undone, lady, we are undone!
Alack the day! He's gone, he's killed, he's dead!

JULIET. Can heaven be so envious?

NURSE. Romeo can,
Though heaven cannot. O Romeo, Romeo!
Who ever would have thought it? Romeo!

Literary Analysis
Dramatic Speeches How can you tell that Juliet's speech is a soliloquy?

4. **That runaways' eyes may wink** so that the eyes of busybodies may not see.
5. **Hood . . . cheeks** hide the untamed blood that makes me blush.
6. **strange** unfamiliar.

Spiral Review
Character What does Juliet reveal about herself in this soliloquy?

Vocabulary
eloquence (el′ ə kwəns) *n.* speech that is graceful and persuasive

7. **Ah, weraday!** alas!

19

Reading Check
What punishment does the Prince order for Romeo?

Differentiated Instruction for Universal Access

Enrichment for Gifted/Talented Students

Help students appreciate the beauty of Shakespeare's poetry by referring them to Scene ii, lines 17–25. Have them write out the lines on a separate sheet, and read the lines aloud. **Ask** them to explain the metaphor in lines 17–19.

Answer: Romeo is the brightness in the night; the night is as black as a raven, and Romeo is the brightness in it, as white as snow against the black of night.

Have students notice the repetition of the word *night*. **Ask** them to point out other words with the "i" sound in this passage and explain the effect of these "i" sounds.

Answer: Other *i* words include *lie, whiter, I, die,* and *fine*. These words help create a smooth, flowing sound.

Point out the jarring effect line 25 has on the ear after the previous smooth, flowing lines. **Ask** students how this jarring sound is in keeping with the sense or meaning of the line.

Answer: The jarring sound reflects the unfavorable comparison of the "garish sun" to the "loving" night.

18 Literary Analysis

Dramatic Speeches

1. Direct students to read the stage directions for Scene ii on 870. **Ask** what information the stage directions provide.
   Answer: Scene ii is set in Capulet's orchard. Juliet enters alone.
2. Have students reread the bracketed passage, which begins on p. 870. **Ask** the Literary Analysis question: How can you tell that Juliet's speech is a soliloquy?
   Answer: The speech is a soliloquy because Juliet is alone on stage and expresses her thoughts in a lengthy speech to the audience. Even though an aside is also spoken directly to the audience, it is very short.
3. **Ask** students what the audience learns from this soliloquy about what Juliet wants to happen and about her feelings.
   Answer: The audience learns that Juliet is impatient for the night to come, so that she can be with her husband on their wedding night. The audience learns that Juliet is both passionate and modest.

Spiral Review

Character

1. Remind students that they learned about the concept of character in the Unit 5 Literary Analysis Workshop (pp. 780–797).
2. **Ask** students the Spiral Review question.
   Possible response: Juliet reveals that she has a poetic nature; she is a romantic; she is impatient and impulsive.

19 Reading Check

Answer: The Prince orders exile as a punishment for Romeo.

⑳ Literature in Context

History Connection According to legend, the cockatrice is hatched from the egg of a rooster brooded by a toad or a serpent. A similar creature is the basilisk, which also possessed a lethal glance—and therefore also had a deadly fear of mirrors. Both creatures appear as literary allusions in Shakespeare's plays and other classic literature.

Connect to the Literature

1. Remind students that Juliet is beside herself with anguish. The Nurse has said only Romeo's name, and has not mentioned Tybalt.
2. Have students read the Literature in Context feature, and present the additional background information above. Then, **ask** the Connect to the Literature question: How does Juliet's allusion to a cockatrice reinforce the nature of her conversation with the Nurse?

Answer: Juliet's reference to the deadly creature intensifies the frantic grief that she is expressing.

⑳ LITERATURE IN CONTEXT

History Connection

Cockatrice

In a play on words, Juliet links "Ay" with the dangerous "eye" of a cockatrice (Act III, scene ii, line 47). The cockatrice is a serpent that, according to myth, could kill with a look or transform people into stone. The creature resembles a snake with the head and yellow feathers of a rooster. It feared the song of the rooster and its own reflection in a mirror.

Connect to the Literature

How does Juliet's allusion to a cockatrice reinforce the nature of her conversation with the Nurse?

JULIET. What devil art thou that dost torment me thus?
This torture should be roared in dismal hell.
Hath Romeo slain himself? Say thou but "Ay,"
And that bare vowel "I" shall poison more
Than the death-darting eye of cockatrice.
I am not I, if there be such an "Ay,"[8]
Or those eyes' shot[9] that makes thee answer "Ay."
If he be slain, say "Ay"; or if not, "No."
Brief sounds determine of my weal or woe.

NURSE. I saw the wound, I saw it with mine eyes,
(God save the mark![10]) here on his manly breast.
A piteous corse,[11] a bloody piteous corse;
Pale, pale as ashes, all bedaubed in blood,
All in gore-blood. I sounded[12] at the sight.

JULIET. O, break, my heart! Poor bankrout,[13] break at once!
To prison, eyes; ne'er look on liberty!
Vile earth, to earth resign;[14] end motion here,
And thou and Romeo press one heavy bier![15]

NURSE. O Tybalt, Tybalt, the best friend I had!
O courteous Tybalt! Honest gentleman!
That ever I should live to see thee dead!

JULIET. What storm is this that blows so contrary?[16]
Is Romeo slaught'red, and is Tybalt dead?
My dearest cousin, and my dearer lord?
Then, dreadful trumpet, sound the general doom![17]

8. **"Ay"** yes.
9. **eyes' shot** the Nurse's glance.
10. **God save the mark!** May God save us from evil!
11. **corse** corpse.
12. **sounded** swooned; fainted.
13. **bankrout** bankrupt.
14. **Vile . . . resign** let my body return to the earth.
15. **bier** platform on which a corpse is displayed before burial.
16. **contrary** in opposite directions.
17. **dreadful . . . doom** let the trumpet that announces doomsday be sounded.

Vocabulary Development

Ⓒ CCSS Language 6

Selection Vocabulary Reinforcement

To reinforce and assess students' comprehension of selection vocabulary words, give them sentences using the words in which the word may or may not be used correctly. Students must tell whether the use is correct and explain their answers. Use these sentences:

1. He was hoping that the judge would *exile* him so he would not have to leave.
   Answer: No. To be *exiled* means a person is banished from a place and must leave it.
2. Her *eloquence* was so remarkable that the audience got up and left.
   Answer: No. *Eloquence* is graceful and persuasive speech, which would hold an audience's interest.
3. Her *fickle* behavior toward her friends made everyone love her.
   Answer: No. If a person is *fickle*, she is changeable, which would make it difficult for her to keep friends.

For who is living, if those two are gone?

NURSE. Tybalt is gone, and Romeo banishèd;
Romeo that killed him, he is banishèd.

JULIET. O God! Did Romeo's hand shed Tybalt's blood?

NURSE. It did, it did! Alas the day, it did!

JULIET. O serpent heart, hid with a flow'ring face!
Did ever dragon keep so fair a cave?
Beautiful tyrant! Fiend angelical!
Dove-feathered raven! Wolvish-ravening lamb!
Despisèd substance of divinest show!
Just opposite to what thou justly seem'st—
A damnèd saint, an honorable villain!
O nature, what hadst thou to do in hell
When thou didst bower the spirit of a fiend
In mortal paradise of such sweet flesh?
Was ever book containing such vile matter
So fairly bound? O, that deceit should dwell
In such a gorgeous palace!

NURSE. There's no trust,
No faith, no honesty in men; all perjured,
All forsworn,[18] all naught, all dissemblers.[19]
Ah, where's my man? Give me some aqua vitae.[20]
These griefs, these woes, these sorrows make me old.
Shame come to Romeo!

JULIET. Blistered be thy tongue
For such a wish! He was not born to shame.
Upon his brow shame is ashamed to sit;
For 'tis a throne where honor may be crowned
Sole monarch of the universal earth.
O, what a beast was I to chide at him!

NURSE. Will you speak well of him that killed your cousin?

JULIET. Shall I speak ill of him that is my husband?
Ah, poor my lord, what tongue shall smooth thy name
When I, thy three-hours wife, have mangled it?
But wherefore, villain, didst thou kill my cousin?
That villain cousin would have killed my husband.
Back, foolish tears, back to your native spring!
Your tributary[21] drops belong to woe,
Which you, mistaking, offer up to joy.
My husband lives, that Tybalt would have slain;

Reading Skill
Summarize Briefly summarize Juliet's remarks about Romeo in lines 73–84.

18. **forsworn** are liars.
19. **dissemblers** hypocrites.
20. **aqua vitae** brandy.

21. **tributary** in tribute.

22
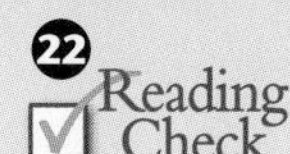

What is Juliet's initial reaction to Romeo's involvement in Tybalt's death?

21 Reading Skill

Summarize

1. Have students read lines 73–84. **Ask** how Juliet's attitude changes abruptly in line 73.

   Answer: She goes from being in anguish, believing that Romeo is dead, to being angry and even hateful toward Romeo when she learns that he has killed her dear cousin Tybalt.

2. Have students **identify** some of the opposites Juliet uses to demonstrate her conflicted feelings about Romeo.

   Possible response: Opposites include the following: "Beautiful tyrant!" "Fiend angelical!" "Dove-feathered raven!" and "Wolvish-ravening lamb."

3. **Ask** students to respond to the Reading Skill prompt: Briefly summarize Juliet's remarks about Romeo in lines 73–84.

   Answer: Juliet says that Romeo is the opposite of what he appears. He seems to be beautiful, kind, and honorable, but he is truly hateful and deceitful.

22 Reading Check

Answer: Juliet is angry and reviles Romeo for killing Tybalt. She calls Romeo a beautiful deceiver.

Differentiated Instruction for Universal Access

Support for Special-Needs Students

Point out the soliloquy (lines 1–33) and monologue (lines 97–127) in this act. Review definitions. Offer clues to distinguish the two speech types. Note the stage direction on p. 870, "Enter Juliet alone," which makes her speech a soliloquy until line 31 when "Nurse enters." Next, note line 96, when the Nurse asks Juliet a question. Juliet's response is a monologue, as she is not alone on stage.

Pronunciation for English Learners

To help students differentiate short *i* and the "ee" sound in *seem*, post these words: *hid, heed; lip, leap; bit, beet;* and *sit, seat*. Pronounce each word in turn, stressing the vowel sound, and then have students echo. Call out words at random and have volunteers circle the stated word on the board. Discuss any incorrect choices and clarify.

23 Literary Analysis

Dramatic Speeches

1. Have a volunteer read the bracketed text aloud. **Ask** students why they think Juliet first condemns Romeo for killing Tybalt and then changes her mind.

   Possible response: Juliet responds to the news first in terms of thinking about her family. Tybalt is her cousin, and she condemns Romeo for killing him. Then, she realizes that she is Romeo's family now, and that Tybalt would have killed Romeo if he had had the chance.

2. **Ask** students the Literary Analysis question: What makes this speech a monologue but not a soliloquy?

   Answer: Juliet's speech is not a soliloquy because she is not alone and does not deliver her words to the audience, but to her Nurse.

3. Point out that although Juliet is delivering her words to her Nurse, she is really addressing someone else. **Ask** students whom she is addressing. How can they tell?

   Answer: Beginning in line 98, Juliet is addressing Romeo. She says "thy name," "thy three-hours wife," and "thou kill my cousin." She is also addressing herself. In line 102 she speaks to her tears: "Back, foolish tears." In line 118, Juliet refers to the Nurse as "she"—"when she said"—indicating that she is addressing someone other than the Nurse—that is, herself.

▶ **Monitor Progress:** Use students' responses to these questions to monitor their understanding of dramatic speeches.

▶ **Reteach:** If students have difficulty identifying dramatic speeches, review the discussion on p. 861. In addition, have them read aloud Juliet's speech, beginning at line 90. By hearing the speech, they may be better able to understand with whom Juliet is speaking.

Literary Analysis
Dramatic Speeches
What makes this speech a monologue but not a soliloquy?

And Tybalt's dead, that would have slain my husband.
All this is comfort; wherefore weep I then?
Some word there was, worser than Tybalt's death,
That murd'red me. I would forget it fain;
But O, it presses to my memory
Like damnèd guilty deeds to sinners' minds!
"Tybalt is dead, and Romeo—banishèd."
That "banishèd," that one word "banishèd,"
Hath slain ten thousand Tybalts. Tybalt's death
Was woe enough, if it had ended there;
Or, if sour woe delights in fellowship
And needly will be ranked with[22] other griefs,
Why followed not, when she said "Tybalt's dead,"
Thy father, or thy mother, nay, or both,
Which modern[23] lamentation might have moved?
But with a rearward[24] following Tybalt's death,
"Romeo is banishèd"—to speak that word
Is father, mother, Tybalt, Romeo, Juliet,
All slain, all dead. "Romeo is banishèd"—
There is no end, no limit, measure, bound,
In that word's death; no words can that woe sound.
Where is my father and my mother, nurse?

NURSE. Weeping and wailing over Tybalt's corse.
Will you go to them? I will bring you thither.

JULIET. Wash they his wounds with tears? Mine shall be spent,
When theirs are dry, for Romeo's banishment.
Take up those cords. Poor ropes, you are beguiled,
Both you and I, for Romeo is exiled.
He made you for a highway to my bed;
But I, a maid, die maiden-widowèd.
Come, cords; come, nurse. I'll to my wedding bed;
And death, not Romeo, take my maidenhead!

NURSE. Hie to your chamber. I'll find Romeo
To comfort you. I wot[25] well where he is.
Hark ye, your Romeo will be here at night.
I'll to him; he is hid at Lawrence' cell.

JULIET. O, find him! Give this ring to my true knight
And bid him come to take his last farewell. [*Exit with* NURSE]

22. **needly . . . with** must be accompanied by.
23. **modern** ordinary.
24. **rearward** follow up; literally, a rear guard.
25. **wot** know.

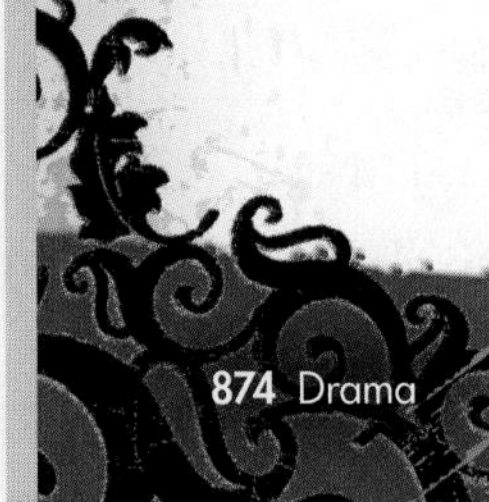

Think Aloud

Summarize

Draw students' attention to lines 97–127 on pages 873–874. Use the following "think aloud" to model the process of paraphrasing in order to summarize.

In order to understand Juliet's lengthy speech on pages 873–874, I can paraphrase or restate what she is saying in my own words. For example, I rephrase lines 106–108 as "And Tybalt, who wanted to kill my husband, is dead. So why am I crying?" As I continue to read, I rephrase lines 113–114 as "That word 'banished'... Romeo's banishment is worse than the murder of ten thousand Tybalts." I continue to paraphrase the speech until I fully understand what Juliet is saying.

Then, I can summarize some of the speech's main ideas. I realize that although the death of her cousin Tybalt is upsetting, Juliet is more upset that Romeo has been exiled.

Scene iii. Friar Lawrence's cell.
[*Enter* FRIAR LAWRENCE.]

FRIAR. Romeo, come forth; come forth, thou fearful man.
Affliction is enamored of thy parts,[1]
And thou art wedded to calamity.

[*Enter* ROMEO.]

ROMEO. Father, what news? What is the Prince's doom?[2]
What sorrow craves acquaintance at my hand
That I yet know not?

FRIAR. Too familiar
Is my dear son with such sour company.
I bring thee tidings of the Prince's doom.

ROMEO. What less than doomsday[3] is the Prince's doom?

FRIAR. A gentler judgment vanished[4] from his lips—
Not body's death, but body's banishment.

ROMEO. Ha, banishment? Be merciful, say "death";
For exile hath more terror in his look,
Much more than death. Do not say "banishment."

FRIAR. Here from Verona art thou banishèd.
Be patient, for the world is broad and wide.

ROMEO. There is no world without[5] Verona walls,
But purgatory, torture, hell itself.
Hence banishèd is banished from the world,
And world's exile is death. Then "banishèd"
Is death mistermed. Calling death "banishèd,"
Thou cut'st my head off with a golden ax
And smilest upon the stroke that murders me.

FRIAR. O deadly sin! O rude unthankfulness!
Thy fault our law calls death;[6] but the kind Prince,
Taking thy part, hath rushed[7] aside the law,
And turned that black word "death" to "banishment."
This is dear mercy, and thou seest it not.

ROMEO. 'Tis torture, and not mercy. Heaven is here,
Where Juliet lives; and every cat and dog
And little mouse, every unworthy thing,
Live here in heaven and may look on her;
But Romeo may not. More validity,[8]
More honorable state, more courtship lives
In carrion flies than Romeo. They may seize

1. **Affliction . . . parts** misery is in love with your attractive qualities.
2. **doom** final decision.
3. **doomsday** my death.
4. **vanished** escaped; came forth.
5. **without** outside.
6. **Thy fault . . . death** for what you did our law demands the death penalty.
7. **rushed** pushed.
8. **validity** value.

Reading Skill
Summarize
Paraphrase Romeo's complaint in lines 29–33, and then summarize his reaction to his banishment.

25 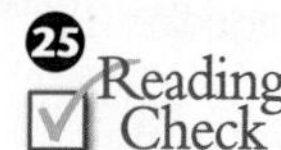

What punishment does the Friar say Romeo could have received for his crime?

24 Reading Skill
Summarize

1. Have students read the bracketed passage, which continues onto p. 876. **Ask** how Romeo describes banishment to the Friar.
   Answer: Romeo compares banishment to death.
2. Have students explain how the Friar attempts in lines 10–11, 15–16, and 27–28 to comfort Romeo in the face of his banishment.
   Answer: The Friar tells Romeo that he is not being put to death but only banished from Verona. He tells Romeo that the Prince has shown mercy, though Romeo cannot see this.
3. **Ask** students to respond to the Reading Skill prompt: Paraphrase Romeo's complaint in lines 29–33, and then summarize his reaction to his banishment.
   Answer: "It is not merciful to send me away. My only heaven is here with Juliet. Here everything that lives and moves can be in Juliet's presence, whether it is worthy or not. But I cannot see her." **Summary:** Banishment is not merciful because I cannot be with Juliet.

25 Reading Check

Answer: The Friar reminds Romeo that the Prince could have put Romeo to death.

Fluency

Distribute copies of Romeo's speech (lines 29–51, pp. 875–876) and pair students. Have listeners mark words with which readers struggle. Circulate to monitor students' fluency, and collect the marked-up pages. Review difficult words and passages, such as these:

- If students struggle to pronounce "banishèd and "damnèd" (p. 876), point out the accent marks and read the words aloud. Have students echo. Clarify that you are emphasizing the accented letter and pronouncing the *ed* as a separate syllable.
- If students stumble on *carrion* (p. 875), point out the VCCV pattern and model how to divide the word accordingly. Ask volunteers to reread the word aloud to show fluency.
- If students have difficulty with rhythm and meter, tell them to use the punctuation to determine when to stop and to pause. They are to stop at periods and pause at commas and semicolons. Tell them to continue reading where there is no punctuation.

26 Background

Foreshadowing

Remind students of earlier passages in the play in which readers are given suggestions as to what will ultimately happen—for example, Romeo and Juliet mutually sense that something will doom their love. Then, point out the foreshadowing in lines 44–45, in which Romeo asks the Friar to give him some way to kill himself rather than leave Juliet.

Ask students to keep this scene in mind as they complete the play. The references to *poison* and to *knife* in line 44 are significant.

Background

Romeo and Juliet Through the Years

Over the years, *Romeo and Juliet*, Shakespeare's most famous play, has been performed and adapted countless times. Over forty films of this play have been made; there is even a ballet of the play. The story of *Romeo and Juliet* is continuously adapted to fit new generations and has inspired films such as Jet Li's *Romeo Must Die* and the musical *West Side Story*.

Ask students to think of other modern adaptations or interpretations of *Romeo and Juliet*.

On the white wonder of dear Juliet's hand
And steal immortal blessing from her lips,
Who, even in pure and vestal modesty,
Still blush, as thinking their own kisses sin;
But Romeo may not, he is banishèd.
Flies may do this but I from this must fly;
They are freemen, but I am banishèd.
(24) And sayest thou yet that exile is not death?
(26) Hadst thou no poison mixed, no sharp-ground knife,
No sudden mean[9] of death, though ne'er so mean,[10]
But "banishèd" to kill me—"banishèd"?
O friar, the damnèd use that word in hell;
Howling attends it! How hast thou the heart,
Being a divine, a ghostly confessor,
A sin-absolver, and my friend professed,
To mangle me with that word "banishèd"?

FRIAR. Thou fond mad man, hear me a little speak.

ROMEO. O, thou wilt speak again of banishment.

FRIAR. I'll give thee armor to keep off that word;
Adversity's sweet milk, philosophy,
To comfort thee, though thou art banishèd.

9. **mean** method.
10. **mean** humiliating.

Romeo and Juliet Through the Years

These illustrations and images from various productions of *Romeo and Juliet* mark the timelessness of Shakespeare's most dramatized piece. The core qualities of the play, including its theme and language, have moved forward into the present with updated costumes and props, diverse casts, and new technology.

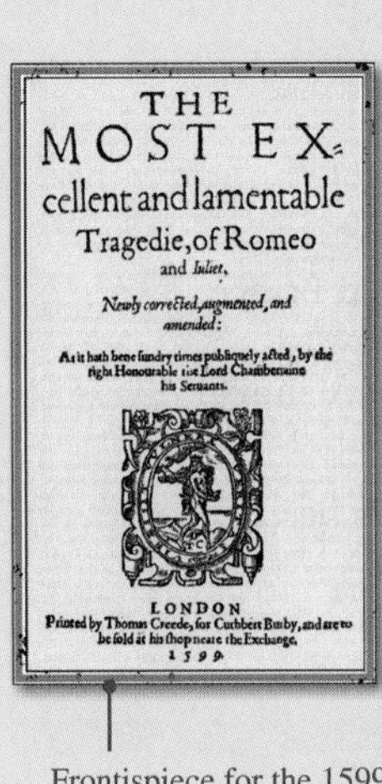

THE MOST EX-cellent and lamentable Tragedie, of Romeo and Iuliet.

Newly corrected, augmented, and amended:

As it hath bene sundry times publiquely acted, by the right Honourable the Lord Chamberlaine his Seruants.

LONDON

Printed by Thomas Creede, for Cuthbert Burby, and are to be sold at his shop neare the Exchange.

1599.

Frontispiece for the 1599 edition

Movie – 1916 Romeo and Juliet

Book illustration – 1905

Vocabulary Development

CCSS Language 6

Expressive Vocabulary

To help students broaden their expressive vocabulary, encourage them to use the following words as they discuss the scene between Romeo and the Friar: *comply*, *drastic*, *eloquent*, and *tolerate*. Have them complete these sentence starters:

1. Although he hates the thought, Romeo will be forced to *comply* . . .
2. Romeo suggests a *drastic* plan to . . .
3. Romeo makes an *eloquent* . . .
4. Romeo cannot *tolerate* . . .

ROMEO. Yet "banishèd"? Hang up philosophy!
Unless philosophy can make a Juliet,
Displant a town, reverse a prince's doom,
It helps not, it prevails not. Talk no more.

FRIAR. O, then I see that madmen have no ears.

ROMEO. How should they, when that wise men have no eyes?

FRIAR. Let me dispute[11] with thee of thy estate.[12]

ROMEO. Thou canst not speak of that thou dost not feel.
Wert thou as young as I, Juliet thy love,
An hour but married, Tybalt murderèd,
Doting like me, and like me banishèd,
Then mightst thou speak, then mightst thou tear thy hair,
And fall upon the ground, as I do now,
Taking the measure of an unmade grave.

[*Knock.*]

FRIAR. Arise, one knocks. Good Romeo, hide thyself.

ROMEO. Not I; unless the breath of heartsick groans
Mistlike infold me from the search of eyes. [*Knock.*]

Reading Skill
Summarize
Summarize Romeo's ideas in lines 57–60. What do they suggest about his state of mind?

11. **dispute** discuss.
12. **estate** condition; situation.

28

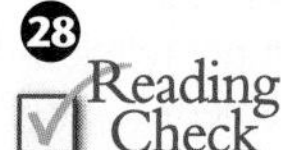

How does Romeo view his banishment?

Movie – 1936
Poster and balcony scene.
(Director: George Cukor
Actors: Norma Shearer and Leslie Howard)

Movie – 1968
Balcony scene.
(Director: Franco Zeffirelli
Actors: Leonard Whiting and Olivia Hussey)

27 Reading Skill

Summarize

1. **Ask** students what the Friar suggests to Romeo as a possible comfort to the young man.

   Answer: The Friar suggests that philosophy is an armor for Romeo to use against the hated idea of banishment.

2. Have students reread lines 57–60. **Ask** them to respond to the Reading Skill prompt: Summarize Romeo's ideas in lines 57–60. What do they suggest about his state of mind?

   Answer: Romeo says that philosophy is useless unless it can make a Juliet, move a town, and reverse a Prince's order. It is no help, and he doesn't want to hear any more about it. These words suggest that Romeo is overcome by emotion and cannot listen to reason.

28 Reading Check

Answer: Romeo is upset and depressed. He falls on the floor crying. He views banishment as a fate equal to or worse than death.

Differentiated Instruction for Universal Access

Strategy for Advanced Readers

Help students understand Scene iii and Friar Lawrence's role in this tragedy. Point out that the Friar may be a minor character, yet he enables the tragedy to occur. Have students form small groups to discuss the character and the role of the Friar by addressing these questions:

- Why does the Friar marry Romeo and Juliet in secret, knowing their parents would disapprove?
- The Friar is a man of the Church. Why hasn't he chided Romeo for murdering Tybalt or offered to hear Romeo's confession? (Remind students that Romeo was not simply defending himself as the Friar implies; Romeo attacked Tybalt in a rage.)
- Why does the Friar arrange for Romeo to spend the night in Verona, knowing that the Prince decreed exile and that Romeo would be killed if found?

Tell students the Friar will also play a pivotal role in the final tragedy later on in the play.

29 Literary Analysis

Dramatic Speeches

1. Have students read the bracketed text. **Ask** students what the Nurse is scolding Romeo about.

   Answer: She is scolding him for weeping and crying, saying he should stand up like a man for Juliet's sake.

2. **Ask** students the Literary Analysis question: What does this brief speech by the Nurse reveal about her relationship with Romeo?

   Possible response: It reveals that she thinks of him as a child, just as she does Juliet, and she feels sympathy for him even though she scolds him.

FRIAR. Hark, how they knock! Who's there? Romeo, arise;
Thou wilt be taken.—Stay awhile!—Stand up; [*Knock.*]
Run to my study.—By and by![13]—God's will,
What simpleness[14] is this.—I come, I come! [*Knock.*]
Who knocks so hard? Whence come you? What's your will?

[*Enter* NURSE.]

NURSE. Let me come in, and you shall know my errand.
I come from Lady Juliet.

FRIAR. Welcome then.

NURSE. O holy friar, O, tell me, holy friar,
Where is my lady's lord, where's Romeo?

FRIAR. There on the ground, with his own tears made drunk.

NURSE. O, he is even in my mistress' case,
Just in her case! O woeful sympathy!
Piteous predicament! Even so lies she,
Blubb'ring and weeping, weeping and blubb'ring.
Stand up, stand up! Stand, and you be a man.
For Juliet's sake, for her sake, rise and stand!
Why should you fall into so deep an O?[15]

Literary Analysis
Dramatic Speeches What does this brief speech by the Nurse reveal about her relationship with Romeo? 29

13. **By and by!** In a minute! (said to the person knocking).
14. **simpleness** silly behavior (Romeo does not move).
15. **O** cry of grief.

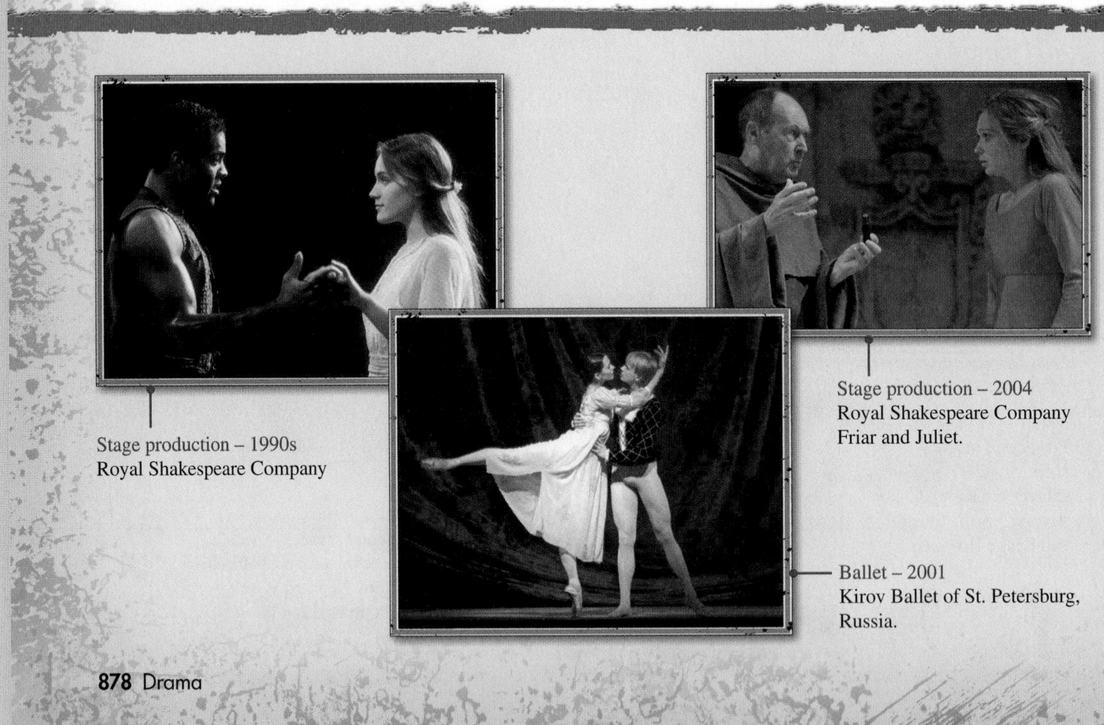

Stage production – 1990s
Royal Shakespeare Company

Ballet – 2001
Kirov Ballet of St. Petersburg, Russia.

Stage production – 2004
Royal Shakespeare Company
Friar and Juliet.

ROMEO. [*Rises.*] Nurse—

NURSE. Ah sir, ah sir! Death's the end of all.

ROMEO. Spakest thou of Juliet? How is it with her?
Doth not she think me an old murderer,
Now I have stained the childhood of our joy
With blood removed but little from her own?
Where is she? And how doth she? And what says
My concealed lady[16] to our canceled love?

NURSE. O, she says nothing, sir, but weeps and weeps;
And now falls on her bed, and then starts up,
And Tybalt calls; and then on Romeo cries,
And then down falls again.

ROMEO. As if that name,
Shot from the deadly level[17] of a gun,
Did murder her; as that name's cursèd hand
Murdered her kinsman. O, tell me, friar, tell me,
In what vile part of this anatomy
Doth my name lodge? Tell me, that I may sack[18]
The hateful mansion.

[*He offers to stab himself, and* NURSE *snatches the dagger away.*]

16. **concealed lady** secret bride.

17. **level** aim.

18. **sack** plunder.

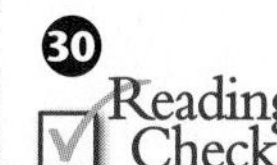

30 Reading Check

What does Romeo nearly do before the Nurse stops him?

Stage production – 2004 Royal Shakespeare Company Fight scene.

Verona, Italy Balcony and Juliet

Illustration – 2006

30 Reading Check

Answer: Romeo nearly stabs himself.

Differentiated Instruction for Universal Access

Strategy for Special-Needs Students

To model how to summarize, show students the **Reading Skill Graphic Organizer A** (*Graphic Organizer Transparencies*, p. 155). The partially completed graphic organizer will give students insight into how to summarize dialogue. They can use it as a model for summarizing as they read.

Strategy for Less Proficient Readers

Show students the **Reading Skill Graphic Organizer A** (*Graphic Organizer Transparencies*, p. 155). The partially completed graphic organizer will give students insight into how to summarize dialogue. Students can use the organizer as a model for summarizing as they read.

(31) Connecting to the Big Question

1. Have a volunteer read aloud the bracketed text.
2. **Ask** students what reasons the Friar gives Romeo for being happy in his situation.

   Answer: He tells Romeo that he should be happy because Juliet is alive, he killed Tybalt before Tybalt killed him, and he received a sentence of exile instead of death.
3. **Ask:** How do the Friar and Romeo differ in their view of the current predicament? How does this difference help to define them as characters?

   Possible response: Romeo is gloomy under the circumstances, thinking the situation to be dire. The Friar says that Romeo is "like a misbehaved and sullen wench" who "puts up," or pouts over, the turn of events. The Friar is essentially optimistic in his outlook and focuses on the positive, such as Juliet's being alive, Tybalt's death, and Romeo's having been given the lesser sentence of exile. The difference can also be linked to age: Romeo is young and given to emotion, and the Friar is older and able to draw upon more life experience, which may be part of what helps him view the situation differently.

FRIAR. Hold thy desperate hand.
Art thou a man? Thy form cries out thou art;
Thy tears are womanish, thy wild acts denote
The unreasonable fury of a beast.
Unseemly[19] woman in a seeming man!
And ill-beseeming beast in seeming both![20]
Thou hast amazed me. By my holy order,
I thought thy disposition better tempered.
Hast thou slain Tybalt? Wilt thou slay thyself?
And slay thy lady that in thy life lives,
By doing damnèd hate upon thyself?
Why railest thou on thy birth, the heaven, and earth?
Since birth and heaven and earth, all three do meet
In thee at once; which thou at once wouldst lose.
Fie, fie, thou shamest thy shape, thy love, thy wit,[21]
Which, like a usurer,[22] abound'st in all,
And usest none in that true use indeed
Which should bedeck[23] thy shape, thy love, thy wit.
Thy noble shape is but a form of wax,
Digressing from the valor of a man;
Thy dear love sworn but hollow perjury,
Killing that love which thou hast vowed to cherish;
(32)
Thy wit, that ornament to shape and love,
Misshapen in the conduct[24] of them both,
Like powder in a skilless soldier's flask,[25]
Is set afire by thine own ignorance,
And thou dismemb'red with thine own defense.[26]
What, rouse thee, man! Thy Juliet is alive,
For whose dear sake thou wast but lately dead.[27]
There art thou happy.[28] Tybalt would kill thee,
But thou slewest Tybalt. There art thou happy.
The law, that threat'ned death, becomes thy friend
And turns it to exile. There art thou happy.
A pack of blessings light upon thy back;
Happiness courts thee in her best array;
But, like a misbehaved and sullen wench,[29]
Thou puts up[30] thy fortune and thy love.
Take heed, take heed, for such die miserable.
(31)
Go get thee to thy love, as was decreed,
Ascend her chamber, hence and comfort her.
But look thou stay not till the watch be set,[31]
For then thou canst not pass to Mantua,
Where thou shalt live till we can find a time
To blaze[32] your marriage, reconcile your friends,

19. **Unseemly** inappropriate (because unnatural).
20. **And . . . both!** Romeo has inappropriately lost his human nature because he seems like a man and woman combined.
21. **wit** mind; intellect.
22. **Which, like a usurer** who, like a rich money-lender.
23. **bedeck** do honor to.
24. **conduct** management.
25. **flask** powder flask.
26. **And thou . . . defense** the friar is saying that Romeo's mind, which is now irrational, is destroying rather than aiding him.
27. **but lately dead** only recently declaring yourself dead.
28. **happy** fortunate.
29. **wench** low, common girl.
30. **puts up** pouts over.
31. **watch be set** watchmen go on duty.
32. **blaze** announce publicly.

Vocabulary Development

CCSS Language 6

Word Analysis

Draw student's attention to the word *misbehaved* in line 143 on this page. Point out that this word contains the prefix *mis-*, which can mean "wrong" or can mean "bad."

Have students explain whether the prefix *mis-* in each sentence means "wrong" or whether it means "bad."

1. The Mayor has been accused of *misgoverning* this city for the past four years.

   Answer: *Mis-* means "bad"; *misgoverning* means "governing badly."
2. He often *mispronounces* my last name.

   Answer: *Mis-* means "wrong." To *mispronounce* a word is to pronounce it wrongly.
3. She has had a series of *misfortunes*.

   Answer: *Mis-* means "bad"; *misfortune* means "bad luck."
4. He was frantically looking for the keys he had *misplaced*.

   Answer: *Mis-* means "wrong." To misplace something is to put it in the wrong place.

Beg pardon of the Prince, and call thee back
With twenty hundred thousand times more joy
Than thou went'st forth in lamentation.
Go before, nurse. Commend me to thy lady,
And bid her hasten all the house to bed,
Which heavy sorrow makes them apt unto.[33]
Romeo is coming.

NURSE. O Lord, I could have stayed here all the night
To hear good counsel. O, what learning is!
My lord, I'll tell my lady you will come.

ROMEO. Do so, and bid my sweet prepare to chide.[34]
[NURSE *offers to go in and turns again.*]

NURSE. Here, sir, a ring she bid me give you, sir.
Hie you, make haste, for it grows very late. [*Exit.*]

ROMEO. How well my comfort is revived by this!

FRIAR. Go hence; good night; and here stands all your state:[35]
Either be gone before the watch be set,
Or by the break of day disguised from hence.
Sojourn[36] in Mantua. I'll find out your man,
And he shall signify[37] from time to time
Every good hap to you that chances here.
Give me thy hand. 'Tis late. Farewell; good night.

ROMEO. But that a joy past joy calls out on me,
It were a grief so brief to part with thee.
Farewell. [*Exit all.*]

Scene iv. A room in Capulet's house.
[*Enter old* CAPULET, *his* WIFE, *and* PARIS.]

CAPULET. Things have fall'n out, sir, so unluckily
That we have had no time to move[1] our daughter.
Look you, she loved her kinsman Tybalt dearly,
And so did I. Well, we were born to die.
'Tis very late; she'll not come down tonight.
I promise you, but for your company,
I would have been abed an hour ago.

PARIS. These times of woe afford no times to woo.
Madam, good night. Commend me to your daughter.

LADY. I will, and know her mind early tomorrow;
Tonight she's mewed up to her heaviness.[2]

Reading Skill
Summarize Briefly state the main points of the Friar's speech to Romeo.

33. apt unto likely to do.

34. chide rebuke me (for slaying Tybalt).

35. here . . . state this is your situation.

36. Sojourn remain.
37. signify let you know.

1. move discuss your proposal with.
2. mewed . . . heaviness locked up with her sorrow.

34 Reading Check
What reason do the Capulets give Paris to explain why Juliet cannot see him?

32 Reading Skill
Summarize

1. Have students read the Friar's monologue, beginning at line 108 on p. 879.
2. **Ask** students what plan the Friar puts forward in lines 146–154 to resolve Romeo's unhappiness.
   Answer: He tells Romeo to go to Juliet, but to leave her before dawn so that he can leave the city without being seen. He is to go to the city of Mantua, where he should stay until the Friar informs his family of the marriage and gains a pardon from the Prince, at which time he will return to Verona with joy much greater than was his sorrow at leaving.
3. **Ask** students the Reading Skill question.
   Answer: The Friar says that Romeo is acting womanish and like a beast in trying to kill himself. He is being irrational, and he should pull himself together and think of the things he has to be thankful for. He should go to Juliet for the night and then leave for Mantua, and meanwhile the Friar will announce their wedding and reconcile his family and the Prince, and he can then return to Verona.

33 Literary Analysis
Dramatic Speeches

1. Have students summarize the exchange between Lord Capulet and Paris in lines 1–9.
   Sample answer: Lord Capulet says that Tybalt's death has made it impossible to discuss Paris's proposal of marriage with Juliet. Paris responds that sad times are not good for wooing and asks Lady Capulet to remember him to Juliet.
2. **Ask** students: Is Paris's brief remark in line 8 an aside? Explain.
   Answer: Paris's remark is not an aside. An aside is delivered to the audience; Paris's remark is addressed to Lord and Lady Capulet.

34 Reading Check

Answer: Lord Capulet tells Paris that it is very late, and she cannot come down.

Differentiated Instruction for Universal Access

EL Support for English Learners

Help students understand and appreciate Shakespearean language by working with them on Scene iv on pp. 881–882. First, have students use the ***Reader's Notebook: English Learner's Version*** and the ***Hear It!* Audio CD.** Review the footnotes with students. Then **ask** students to summarize this scene.

Sample answer: Capulet tells Paris that it is late, and he cannot see Juliet. Capulet says he has not had a chance to talk to Juliet about their marriage because of the situation with Tybalt. However, he believes Juliet will do as he asks. He sets the wedding between Paris and Juliet for the following Thursday.

Then, have students work in groups of three to read the scene aloud, with each taking turns playing one of the three parts. Remind them to read in sentences, not lines. Monitor their reading and help them with pronunciation, emphasis, and tone.

35 Reading Skill
Summarize

1. Have students read the bracketed text. **Ask:** What is ironic about this scene involving Lord and Lady Capulet and Paris? What do readers and the audience know that the Capulets and Paris do not know?

   Answer: It's ironic that the three are discussing the marriage of Juliet to Paris; the reader knows that Juliet is already married to Romeo.

2. Have students contrast Capulet's words in this scene with his previous talk with Paris, in which he says that Juliet's consent to marriage is important to him.

   Answer: In this scene, Capulet thinks Juliet will do as he asks.

3. **Ask** students to respond to the Reading Skill prompt: Summarize Lord Capulet's remarks about the timing of Juliet's marriage to Paris.

   Answer: Capulet says at first that the wedding should be the following Wednesday, and then, realizing that it is Monday, he says Wednesday is too soon and it should be set for Thursday.

CAPULET. Sir, Paris, I will make a desperate tender[3]
Of my child's love. I think she will be ruled
In all respects by me; nay more, I doubt it not.
Wife, go you to her ere you go to bed;
Acquaint her here of my son[4] Paris' love
And bid her (mark you me?) on Wednesday next—
But soft! What day is this?

PARIS. Monday, my lord.

CAPULET. Monday! Ha, ha! Well, Wednesday is too soon.
A[5] Thursday let it be—a Thursday, tell her,
She shall be married to this noble earl.
Will you be ready? Do you like this haste?
We'll keep no great ado[6]—a friend or two;
For hark you, Tybalt being slain so late,
It may be thought we held him carelessly,[7]
Being our kinsman, if we revel much.
Therefore we'll have some half a dozen friends,
And there an end. But what say you to Thursday?

PARIS. My lord, I would that Thursday were tomorrow.

CAPULET. Well, get you gone. A Thursday be it then.
Go you to Juliet ere you go to bed;
Prepare her, wife, against[8] this wedding day.
Farewell, my lord.—Light to my chamber, ho!
Afore me,[9] it is so very late
That we may call it early by and by.
Good night. *[Exit all.]*

3. **desperate tender** risky offer.
4. **son** son-in-law.
5. **A** on.
6. **We'll . . . ado** We will not make a great fuss.
7. **held him carelessly** did not respect him enough.
8. **against** for.
9. **Afore me** indeed (a mild oath).

Reading Skill
Summarize
Summarize Lord Capulet's remarks about the timing of Juliet's marriage to Paris.

Scene v. Capulet's orchard.
[*Enter* ROMEO *and* JULIET *aloft.*]

JULIET. Wilt thou be gone? It is not yet near day.
It was the nightingale, and not the lark,
That pierced the fearful hollow of thine ear.
Nightly she sings on yond pomegranate tree.
Believe me, love, it was the nightingale.

ROMEO. It was the lark, the herald of the morn;
No nightingale. Look, love, what envious streaks
Do lace the severing[1] clouds in yonder East.
Night's candles[2] are burnt out, and jocund day
Stands tiptoe on the misty mountaintops.
I must be gone and live, or stay and die.

1. **severing** parting.
2. **Night's candles** stars.

Think Aloud

Vocabulary: Using Context

Direct students' attention to the word *revel* in line 26 on this page. Using a think-aloud process, model how to use context to infer the meaning of an unknown word. Say to students:

> I'm going to think aloud to show you how I would figure out the meaning of *revel* from its context.
>
> In this sentence, *revel* is used as a verb. The speaker, Lord Capulet, is talking about the upcoming marriage of Juliet and Paris. Capulet says that people may think that they are not concerned about Tybalt's death if they *revel* too much. Apparently, one would not want to *revel* during a sad time.
>
> Capulet goes on to say that they will only have a half dozen friends at the wedding. This means that the celebration is being limited, so I think that *revel* refers to celebrating with a large gathering at a feast or a party—or, in this case, a wedding.

36 LITERATURE IN CONTEXT

Literature Connection

The Nightingale and the Lark

The nightingale and the lark are two birds that appear frequently in literature, particularly in poetry. Both birds are admired for their beautiful singing, and they also have symbolic associations. The nightingale and its song are traditionally associated with night; the lark and its song with dawn. Shakespeare draws on these associations in this exchange between Romeo and Juliet.

Connect to the Literature

Why do Romeo and Juliet have negative associations with the lark at this point in the play?

JULIET. Yond light is not daylight; I know it, I.
It is some meteor that the sun exhales[3]
To be to thee this night a torchbearer
And light thee on thy way to Mantua.
Therefore stay yet; thou need'st not to be gone.

ROMEO. Let me be ta'en, let me be put to death.
I am content, so thou wilt have it so.
I'll say yon gray is not the morning's eye,
'Tis but the pale reflex of Cynthia's brow;[4]
Nor that is not the lark whose notes do beat
The vaulty heaven so high above our heads.
I have more care to stay than will to go.
Come, death, and welcome! Juliet wills it so.
How is't, my soul? Let's talk; it is not day.

JULIET. It is, it is! Hie hence, be gone, away!
It is the lark that sings so out of tune,
Straining harsh discords and unpleasing sharps.[5]
Some say the lark makes sweet division;[6]
This doth not so, for she divideth us.
Some say the lark and loathèd toad change eyes;[7]
O, now I would they had changed voices too,
Since arm from arm that voice doth us affray,[8]
Hunting thee hence with hunt's-up[9] to the day.
O, now be gone! More light and light it grows.

ROMEO. More light and light—more dark and dark our woes.

3. **exhales** sends out.

4. **reflex . . . brow** reflection of the moon (Cynthia was a name for the moon goddess).

5. **sharps** shrill high notes.
6. **division** melody.
7. **change eyes** exchange eyes (because the lark has a beautiful body with ugly eyes and the toad has an ugly body with beautiful eyes).
8. **affray** frighten.
9. **hunt's-up** morning song for hunters.

37
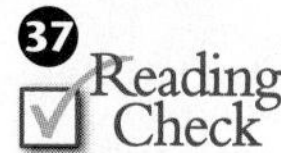

What do the Capulets plan for Juliet on Thursday?

36 Literature in Context

Literature Connection More than fifty different species of birds appear in Shakespeare's plays. Students may recall Benvolio, earlier in the play, telling Romeo that there are more attractive women than Rosaline:

> "Compare her face with some that I shall show,/And I will make thee think thy swan a crow."

Shakespeare was particularly fond of the skylark and used it in fifteen of his plays, including *Richard III, Love's Labor's Lost, A Midsummer Night's Dream, Titus Andronicus, Cymbeline,* and *King Lear*, as well as in two poems. But the most famous of the lark imagery occurs in *The Tragedy of Romeo and Juliet* in Act III, Scene v.

Connect to the Literature Have students read the Literature in Context feature, and present the additional background information above. Point out that Romeo and Juliet both dread their parting. Then, **ask** the Connect to the Literature question: Why do Romeo and Juliet have negative associations with the lark at this point in the play?

Answer: The lark signals morning; Romeo must leave Juliet in the morning.

37 Reading Check

Answer: The Capulets plan Juliet's wedding to Paris on Thursday.

Differentiated Instruction for Universal Access

Culturally Responsive Instruction

Culture Focus Point out the discussion and reference to birds in lines 1–25, and the Literature in Context feature on this page. Explain that many cultures assign special meaning or significance to different birds. Many have birds as representative symbols, such as the American bald eagle. Others feature birds in popular folklore. Encourage students to describe different common birds of their home culture or family's country of origin, and to explain the meaning of these birds to the culture. Challenge students to compare and contrast the significance of the same bird in different cultures or the same ideas symbolized by different birds in different cultures: Do people associate any common ideas with birds in general, or do they associate specific ideas with specific birds? If the latter, why?

38 Reading Check

Summarize

1. Have students reread the bracketed passage. **Ask** students how Juliet uses figurative language to show Romeo how she will age while he is absent.

   Answer: Juliet says that when Romeo is away from her, every minute will appear to be many days long, so that she will be much older when she sees him again.

2. Have students **translate** Romeo and Juliet's conversation in lines 48–53 into modern English.

   Possible response: ROMEO: Good-bye! I won't miss any chance to be in touch with you, Juliet. JULIET: Do you think we'll ever see each other again? ROMEO: I'm sure of it. And later on we'll laugh about all of the problems we're having right now.

3. **Ask** students to respond to the Reading Skill prompt: Identify the key points of the farewell conversation between Romeo and Juliet.

   Answer: Juliet tells Romeo that every minute he is gone will seem like an age to her. Romeo tells her that he will be in touch at every opportunity. When Juliet asks if he thinks they will meet again, Romeo tells her that they will laugh about these troubles someday. They both note that they look pale, and Romeo says it is the sadness that makes them look so pale.

[*Enter* NURSE.]

NURSE. Madam!

JULIET. Nurse?

NURSE. Your lady mother is coming to your chamber.
The day is broke; be wary, look about. [*Exit.*]

JULIET. Then, window, let day in, and let life out.

ROMEO. Farewell, farewell! One kiss, and I'll descend. [*He goeth down.*]

JULIET. Art thou gone so, love-lord, ay husband-friend?
I must hear from thee every day in the hour,
For in a minute there are many days.
O, by this count I shall be much in years[10]
Ere I again behold my Romeo!

ROMEO. Farewell!
I will omit no opportunity
That may convey my greetings, love, to thee.

JULIET. O, think'st thou we shall ever meet again?

ROMEO. I doubt it not; and all these woes shall serve
For sweet discourses[11] in our times to come.

JULIET. O God, I have an ill-divining[12] soul!
Methinks I see thee, now thou art so low,
As one dead in the bottom of a tomb.
Either my eyesight fails, or thou lookest pale.

ROMEO. And trust me, love, in my eye so do you.
Dry sorrow drinks our blood.[13] Adieu, adieu! [*Exit.*]

JULIET. O Fortune, Fortune! All men call thee fickle.
If thou art fickle, what dost thou[14] with him
That is renowned for faith? Be fickle, Fortune,
For then I hope thou wilt not keep him long
But send him back.

[*Enter* MOTHER.]

LADY CAPULET. Ho, daughter! Are you up?

JULIET. Who is't that calls? It is my lady mother.
Is she not down so late,[15] or up so early?
What unaccustomed cause procures her hither?[16]

LADY CAPULET. Why, how now, Juliet?

Reading Skill
Summarize Identify the key points of the farewell conversation between Romeo and Juliet.

10. **much in years** much older.

11. **discourses** conversations.
12. **ill-divining** predicting evil.
13. **Dry sorrow . . . blood** It was once believed that sorrow drained away the blood.
14. **dost thou** do you have to do.

Vocabulary
fickle (fik´ əl) *adj.* changeable

15. **Is she . . . late** Has she stayed up so late?
16. **What . . . hither?** What unusual reason brings her here?

Vocabulary Development

CCSS Language 6

Multiple Meanings

Refer students to the word *Fortune* in line 60 on this page. Tell students that the word *Fortune* in this line refers to the Greek goddess of chance. In medieval and Renaissance times, Fortune was used as a personification of fate and was considered a force or power that would bring good or bad luck.

Today, people use the word *fortune* to mean luck, as in, "He had the good *fortune* to get the job, even though he was not the most qualified candidate." In this case, the idea of fate is usually not associated with the word.

Fortune is also used to refer to what is going to happen to someone in the future, such as in the phrase "fortune teller," meaning "someone who predicts what will happen to another in the future."

Finally, *fortune* can mean "great wealth," such as "He inherited his *fortune* from his father."

Ask students to write a sentence for each of these meanings of the word *fortune*.

JULIET. Madam, I am not well.

LADY CAPULET. Evermore weeping for your cousin's death?
What, wilt thou wash him from his grave with tears?
And if thou couldst, thou couldst not make him live.
Therefore have done. Some grief shows much of love;
But much of grief shows still some want of wit.

JULIET. Yet let me weep for such a feeling[17] loss.

LADY CAPULET. So shall you feel the loss, but not the friend
Which you weep for.

JULIET. Feeling so the loss,
I cannot choose but ever weep the friend.

LADY CAPULET. Well, girl, thou weep'st not so much for his death
As that the villain lives which slaughtered him.

JULIET. What villain, madam?

LADY CAPULET. That same villain Romeo.

JULIET. [*Aside*] Villain and he be many miles asunder.[18]—
God pardon him! I do, with all my heart;
And yet no man like he doth grieve my heart.

LADY CAPULET. That is because the traitor murderer lives.

JULIET. Ay, madam, from the reach of these my hands.
Would none but I might venge my cousin's death!

LADY CAPULET. We will have vengeance for it, fear thou not.
Then weep no more. I'll send to one in Mantua,
Where that same banished runagate[19] doth live,
Shall give him such an unaccustomed dram[20]
That he shall soon keep Tybalt company;
And then I hope thou wilt be satisfied.

JULIET. Indeed I never shall be satisfied
With Romeo till I behold him—dead[21]—
Is my poor heart so for a kinsman vexed.
Madam, if you could find out but a man
To bear a poison, I would temper[22] it;
That Romeo should, upon receipt thereof,
Soon sleep in quiet. O, how my heart abhors
To hear him named and cannot come to him,
To wreak[23] the love I bore my cousin
Upon his body that hath slaughtered him!

17. feeling deeply felt.

18. asunder apart.

Literary Analysis
Dramatic Speeches What qualities of an aside do you find in line 82?

19. runagate renegade; runaway.

20. unaccustomed dram unexpected dose of poison.

21. dead Juliet is deliberately ambiguous here. Her mother thinks *dead* refers to Romeo. But Juliet is using the word with the following line, in reference to her heart.

22. temper mix; weaken.

23. wreak (rēk) avenge; express.

What are Lady Capulet's plans for Romeo?

39 Literary Analysis
Dramatic Speeches

1. **Ask** students what is ironic about Lady Capulet's words to Juliet in lines 70–74.

   Answer: Lady Capulet thinks Juliet is mourning Tybalt's death, but Juliet is sad because of Romeo's absence and their situation in general.

2. Have students read the bracketed text. **Ask** the Literary Analysis question: What qualities of an aside do you find in line 82?

   Answer: Juliet speaks her words about Romeo to the audience because she does not want her mother to hear them.

3. **Ask** students to state the meaning of lines 82–84 in their own words.

   Possible response: He is not at all like a villain. I hope God forgives him! I do, and yet he makes me very sad.

4. **Ask** students to explain the double meanings in line 84—the one that Juliet's mother understands and the one Juliet really means.

   Answer: Juliet's mother understands her to mean that Romeo has grieved Juliet because he has taken Tybalt's life; Juliet really means that she grieves for Romeo because she has to be parted from him.

40 Reading Check

Answer: Lady Capulet plans to have Romeo poisoned.

Differentiated Instruction for Universal Access

Enrichment for Gifted/Talented Students

Point out that on this page Lady Capulet mentions murdering Romeo with poison. Tell students that during the late 1400s, poisoning was a common method of homicide, especially in Italy. The art of poison reached its height under the powerful Borgia family, whose most notable member was Pope Alexander VI. The Borgias poisoned their political enemies with such frequency that the phrase "tasting the cup of the Borgias" became a euphemism for death. The Borgias developed a potent poison known as *cantarelle*.

Apothecaries and so-called sorcerers of the time were adept at mixing deadly poisons for use by anyone who would pay.

Ask students to think about the Friar's special knowledge about poisonous herbs. Have them be alert as they read for the role that poison will play in the next acts.

⓸⓵ Literary Analysis

Dramatic Speeches

Ask students the Literary Analysis question: How does Lady Capulet's dialogue here show Paris as a foil to Romeo?

Answer: Lady Capulet previously described Romeo as a "villain" and a "traitor," but she describes Paris as the opposite— a "gallant" and "noble" man who will make Juliet very happy.

⓸⓶ Reading Skill

Summarize

1. Have students read the bracketed text. Have them **determine** whether Lady Capulet's words about telling Juliet joyful tidings are ironic. Why or why not?

   Answer: Her words are ironic because readers and audience members know that her news will be a dreadful shock to Juliet.

2. **Ask** students to respond to the Reading Skill prompt: Summarize the comparison Lord Capulet makes in lines 130–138.

   Answer: Lord Capulet compares Juliet's body to a little boat tossed on a sea of her tears, with her sighs as the wind.

LADY CAPULET. Find thou the means, and I'll find such a man.
But now I'll tell thee joyful tidings, girl.

JULIET. And joy comes well in such a needy time.
What are they, I beseech your ladyship?

LADY CAPULET. Well, well, thou hast a careful[24] father, child;
One who, to put thee from thy heaviness,
Hath sorted out[25] a sudden day of joy
That thou expects not nor I looked not for.

JULIET. Madam, in happy time![26] What day is that?

LADY CAPULET. Marry, my child, early next Thursday morn
The gallant, young, and noble gentleman,
The County Paris, at Saint Peter's Church,
Shall happily make thee there a joyful bride.

JULIET. Now by Saint Peter's Church, and Peter too,
He shall not make me there a joyful bride!
I wonder at this haste, that I must wed
Ere he that should be husband comes to woo.
I pray you tell my lord and father, madam,
I will not marry yet; and when I do, I swear
It shall be Romeo, whom you know I hate,
Rather than Paris. These are news indeed!

LADY CAPULET. Here comes your father. Tell him so yourself,
And see how he will take it at your hands.

[*Enter* CAPULET *and* NURSE.]

CAPULET. When the sun sets the earth doth drizzle dew,
But for the sunset of my brother's son
It rains downright.
How now? A conduit,[27] girl? What, still in tears?
Evermore show'ring? In one little body
Thou counterfeits a bark,[28] a sea, a wind:
For still thy eyes, which I may call the sea,
Do ebb and flow with tears; the bark thy body is,
Sailing in this salt flood; the winds, thy sighs,
Who, raging with thy tears and they with them,
Without a sudden calm will overset
Thy tempest-tossèd body. How now, wife?
Have you delivered to her our decree?

LADY CAPULET. Ay, sir; but she will none, she gives you thanks.[29]
I would the fool were married to her grave!

24. **careful** considerate.
25. **sorted out** selected.
26. **in happy time** just in time.
27. **conduit** water pipe.
28. **bark** boat.
29. **she will none . . . thanks** she will have nothing to do with it, thank you.

Literary Analysis
Dramatic Speeches
How does Lady Capulet's dialogue here show Paris as a foil to Romeo?

Reading Skill
Summarize
Summarize the comparison Lord Capulet makes in lines 130–138.

Vocabulary Development

CCSS Language 6

Expressive Vocabulary

To help students broaden their expressive vocabulary, encourage them to use the following words as they discuss the rest of the scene in which Lord and Lady Capulet confront Juliet about marrying Paris: *comply, drastic, eloquent,* and *tolerate.* Have them complete these sentence starters:

1. Juliet does not want to *comply* . . .
2. Capulet threatens *drastic* . . .
3. Juliet makes an *eloquent* plea to . . .
4. Capulet refuses to *tolerate* . . .

CAPULET. Soft! Take me with you,[30] take me with you, wife.
How? Will she none? Doth she not give us thanks?
Is she not proud?[31] Doth she not count her blest,
Unworthy as she is, that we have wrought[32]
So worthy a gentleman to be her bride?

JULIET. Not proud you have, but thankful that you have.
Proud can I never be of what I hate,
But thankful even for hate that is meant love.

CAPULET. How, how, how, how, chopped-logic?[33] What is this?
"Proud"—and "I thank you"—and "I thank you not"—
And yet "not proud"? Mistress minion[34] you,
Thank me no thankings, nor proud me no prouds,
But fettle[35] your fine joints 'gainst Thursday next
To go with Paris to Saint Peter's Church,
Or I will drag thee on a hurdle[36] thither.
Out, you greensickness carrion![37] Out, you baggage![38]
You tallow-face![39]

LADY CAPULET. Fie, fie! What, are you mad?

JULIET. Good father, I beseech you on my knees,
Hear me with patience but to speak a word.

CAPULET. Hang thee, young baggage! Disobedient wretch!
I tell thee what—get thee to church a Thursday
Or never after look me in the face.
Speak not, reply not, do not answer me!
My fingers itch. Wife, we scarce thought us blest
That God had lent us but this only child;
But now I see this one is one too much,
And that we have a curse in having her.
Out on her, hilding![40]

NURSE. God in heaven bless her!
You are to blame, my lord, to rate[41] her so.

CAPULET. And why, my Lady Wisdom? Hold your tongue,
Good Prudence. Smatter with your gossips, go![42]

NURSE. I speak no treason.

CAPULET. O, God-i-god-en!

NURSE. May not one speak?

CAPULET. Peace, you mumbling fool!
Utter your gravity[43] o'er a gossip's bowl,
For here we need it not.

30. **Soft! Take . . . you** Wait a minute. Let me understand you.
31. **proud** pleased.
32. **wrought** arranged.
33. **chopped-logic** contradictory, unsound thought and speech.
34. **Mistress minion** Miss Uppity; overly proud.
35. **fettle** prepare.
36. **hurdle** sled on which prisoners were taken to their execution.
37. **greensickness carrion** anemic lump of flesh.
38. **baggage** naughty girl.
39. **tallow-face** wax-pale face.
40. **hilding** worthless person.
41. **rate** scold; berate.
42. **Smatter . . . go!** Go chatter with the other old women.
43. **gravity** wisdom.

Literary Analysis
Dramatic Speeches What feelings and personality traits does Lord Capulet reveal in this brief speech?

44 

Rather than Paris, whom does Juliet threaten to marry?

43 Literary Analysis

Dramatic Speeches

1. **Ask** students what Capulet means in lines 150–154.

   Answer: He means that he thinks Juliet is talking in circles and making no sense.

2. **Ask** students why Capulet is so angry.

   Answer: He is angry because he thinks he has made a good match for Juliet, and she is resisting marrying Paris; he thinks she is being ungrateful.

3. Have students read lines 161–169. Then, **ask** the Literary Analysis question: What feelings and personality traits does Lord Capulet reveal in this brief speech?

   Answer: Capulet reveals intense anger and disgust at Juliet; he reveals a bad temper and an unkind nature.

44 Reading Check

Answer: Juliet threatens to marry Romeo.

Differentiated Instruction for Universal Access

Strategy for Less Proficient Readers
As students read Act III, help them summarize by using the **Series-of-Events Chain Graphic Organizer** in *Graphic Organizer Transparencies*, p. 221. Have students recall key events from each scene. List them on a posted copy of the organizer.

After completing the organizer with students, have them discuss the details of each scene.

Strategy for Advanced Readers
Point out the word *marry*, the first word in line 113 of Lady Capulet's speech on p. 886. **Ask** students whether the word is a pun as it is used here, and suggest that they use the glossary of Elizabethan words on p. 803 for assistance.

Answer: The word is used to mean "indeed," as in "Indeed, my child, early next Thursday morn." It is also used in the conventional way, meaning "to wed," in which case Lady Capulet's words mean "You will be married, my child, early next Thursday morn."

45 Reading Skill

Summarize

1. **Ask** students what Capulet's main criticism of Juliet seems to be in lines 177–197.

   Answer: Capulet says in different ways that Juliet is ungrateful for the wonderful marriage contract he has arranged for her.

2. Have students read lines 177–197. Then, **ask** students to respond to the Reading Skill prompt: Summarize the threat that Lord Capulet makes to Juliet in this monologue.

   Answer: Capulet tells Juliet that if she does not marry Paris, he will disown her and throw her out of his house.

3. **Ask** students what Juliet does when she cannot convince her father to change his mind.

   Answer: Juliet turns her attention to her mother.

4. Have students read lines 200–204. Then, **ask** what options Juliet offers her mother.

   Answer: Juliet asks her mother not to turn her back on her, but to delay the marriage for a month or even a week. Juliet says that if her mother won't help her, Juliet will end up dead like Tybalt.

▶ **Monitor Progress:** Use students' responses to assess their understanding of summarizing.

▶ **Reteach:** If students have difficulty identifying the main ideas in a passage, have them work in pairs to summarize lines 214–219 on p. 889.

LADY CAPULET. You are too hot.

CAPULET. God's bread![44] It makes me mad.
Day, night; hour, tide, time; work, play;
Alone, in company; still my care hath been
To have her matched; and having now provided
A gentleman of noble parentage,
Of fair demesnes,[45] youthful, and nobly trained,
Stuffed, as they say, with honorable parts,[46]
Proportioned as one's thought would wish a man—
And then to have a wretched puling[47] fool,
A whining mammet,[48] in her fortune's tender,[49]
To answer "I'll not wed, I cannot love;
I am too young, I pray you pardon me"!
But, and you will not wed, I'll pardon you!
Graze where you will, you shall not house with me.
Look to't, think on't; I do not use to jest.
Thursday is near; lay hand on heart, advise:[50]
And you be mine, I'll give you to my friend;
And you be not, hang, beg, starve, die in the streets,
For, by my soul, I'll ne'er acknowledge thee,
Nor what is mine shall never do thee good.
Trust to't. Bethink you. I'll not be forsworn.[51] *[Exit.]*

JULIET. Is there no pity sitting in the clouds
That sees into the bottom of my grief?
O sweet my mother, cast me not away!
Delay this marriage for a month, a week;
Or if you do not, make the bridal bed
In that dim monument where Tybalt lies.

LADY CAPULET. Talk not to me, for I'll not speak a word.
Do as thou wilt, for I have done with thee. *[Exit.]*

JULIET. O God!—O nurse, how shall this be prevented?
My husband is on earth, my faith in heaven.[52]
How shall that faith return again to earth
Unless that husband send it me from heaven
By leaving earth?[53] Comfort me, counsel me.

44. **God's bread!** By the holy Eucharist!
45. **demesnes** property.
46. **parts** qualities.
47. **puling** whining.
48. **mammet** doll.
49. **in . . . tender** when good fortune is offered her.
50. **advise** consider.
51. **forsworn** made to violate my promise.
52. **my faith in heaven** my marriage vow is recorded in heaven.
53. **leaving earth** dying.

Reading Skill
Summarize
Summarize the threat that Lord Capulet makes to Juliet in this monologue.

Vocabulary Development

Vocabulary Knowledge Rating

When students have completed reading and discussing Act III of *The Tragedy of Romeo and Juliet,* have them take out their **Vocabulary Knowledge Rating Chart** for this selection. Read the words aloud once more and have students rate their knowledge of the words again in the After Reading column. Clarify any words that are still problematic. Have students write their own definition and example or sentence in the appropriate column. Then, have students complete the Vocabulary Practice activities at the end of the selection. Encourage students to use the words in further discussion and written work about this selection. Remind them that they will be accountable for these words on the **Selection Test, *Unit 5 Resources,*** pp. 71–73 or 74–76.

Alack, alack, that heaven should practice stratagems[54]
Upon so soft a subject as myself!
What say'st thou? Hast thou not a word of joy?
Some comfort, nurse.

NURSE. Faith, here it is.
Romeo is banished; and all the world to nothing[55]
That he dares ne'er come back to challenge[56] you;
Or if he do, it needs must be by stealth.
Then, since the case so stands as now it doth,
I think it best you married with the County.
O, he's a lovely gentleman!
Romeo's a dishclout to him.[57] An eagle, madam,
Hath not so green, so quick, so fair an eye
As Paris hath. Beshrew my very heart,
I think you are happy in this second match,
For it excels your first; or if it did not,
Your first is dead—or 'twere as good he were
As living here and you no use of him.

JULIET. Speak'st thou from thy heart?

NURSE. And from my soul too; else beshrew them both.

JULIET. Amen!

54. stratagems tricks; plots.

55. all . . . nothing the odds are overwhelming.

56. challenge claim.

57. a dishclout to him a dishcloth compared with him.

47 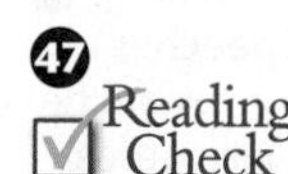

How do the Capulets respond to the Nurse's attempts to defend Juliet?

46 ▶ **Critical Viewing** In what ways does this picture suggest Juliet's vulnerability? Explain. **[Interpret]**

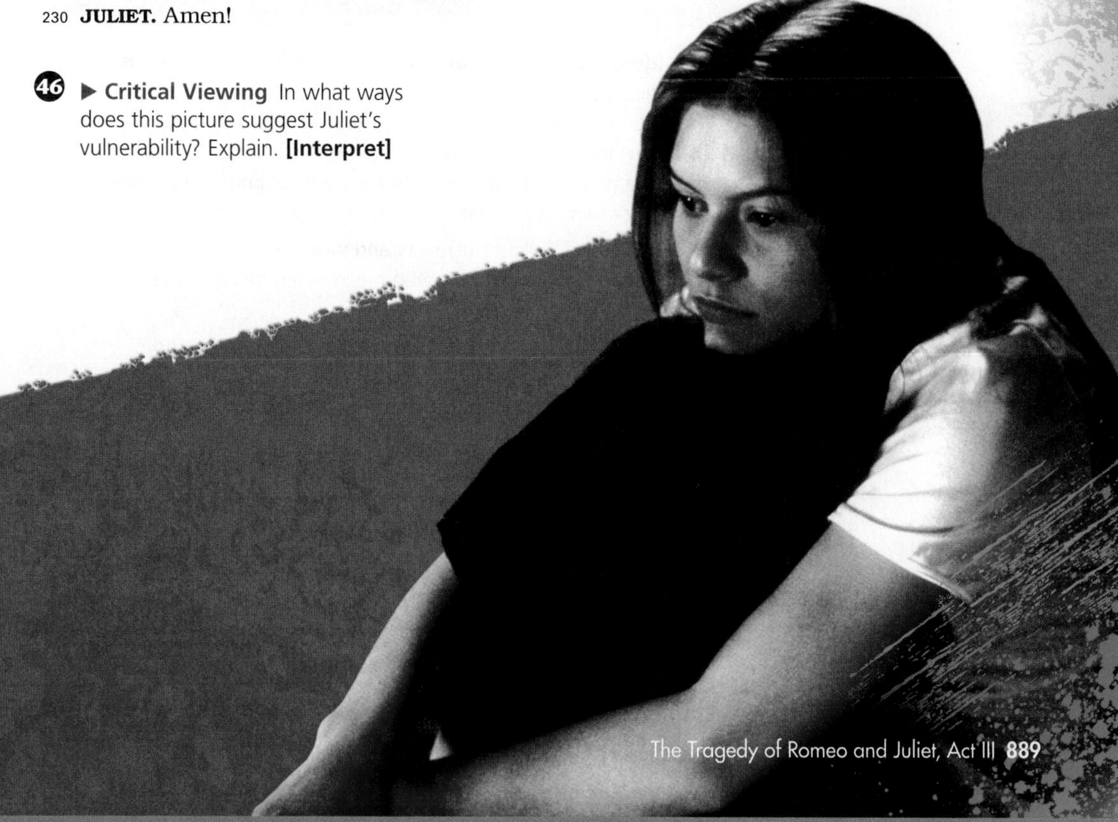

46 Critical Viewing

Possible response: The picture shows Juliet alone, looking sad and lonely.

47 Reading Check

Answer: The Capulets tell the Nurse to be quiet.

Concept Connector

Activating Prior Knowledge

Have students return to the ideas they generated in Activating Prior Knowledge on p. 862. Ask students if their ideas have changed.

Reading Skill Graphic Organizer

Have students review the graphic organizers they completed while reading to summarize lines of dialogue. Show them **Reading Skill Graphic Organizer A** (*Graphic Organizer Transparencies*, p. 155) as an example. Then, have students share the graphic organizers they did and how they identified characters' rank.

48 Literary Analysis

Dramatic Speeches

Ask the Literary Analysis question: What feelings toward her Nurse does Juliet reveal in this soliloquy?

Answer: Juliet feels anger and disgust toward her Nurse. She feels that she has been betrayed by the "wicked fiend" who has advised her to forget her husband.

ASSESS

Answers

Critical Thinking

Before students respond, you may wish to have them write a brief objective summary of the selection. As they answer the questions below, remind them to support their answers with evidence from the text.

1. (a) "A plague on both your houses." (b) Mercutio means the statement as a curse, blaming both sides for the quarrel. (c) The lines echo the Prologue because the Prologue briefly explains the terrible events that happen to the two "star-crossed lovers" who are from the rival households.
2. (a) Romeo kills Tybalt in a sword fight to avenge Mercutio's death. (b) Romeo feels he is a victim of fate.
3. (a) Juliet's vacillation between rage and love is expressed in a series of oxymorons ("Fiend angelical"). Her tumultuous emotions subside into grief at Romeo's banishment. (b) Both Romeo and Juliet react drastically to his banishment. Juliet alludes to suicide in Scene ii, and Romeo asserts that separation from Juliet will be far worse than death.
4. **Possible response:** Students may say that Romeo could have held his temper or revealed his secret marriage.
5. **Possible response:** After the deaths of Mercutio and Tybalt, the differences between Romeo and Juliet become even more apparent. As people die and Romeo is banished, the consequences of the lovers' differences begin to escalate.

NURSE. What?

JULIET. Well, thou hast comforted me marvelous much.
Go in; and tell my lady I am gone,
Having displeased my father, to Lawrence' cell,
To make confession and to be absolved.[58]

NURSE. Marry, I will; and this is wisely done. [*Exit.*]

JULIET. Ancient damnation![59] O most wicked fiend!
Is it more sin to wish me thus forsworn,
Or to dispraise my lord with that same tongue
Which she hath praised him with above compare
So many thousand times? Go, counselor!
Thou and my bosom henceforth shall be twain.[60]
I'll to the friar to know his remedy.
If all else fail, myself have power to die. [*Exit.*]

58. **be absolved** receive forgiveness for my sins.
59. **Ancient damnation!** Old devil!
60. **Thou . . . twain** You will from now on be separated from my trust.

Literary Analysis 48
Dramatic Speeches
What feelings toward her Nurse does Juliet reveal in this soliloquy?

Critical Thinking

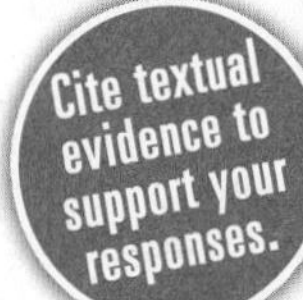
Cite textual evidence to support your responses.

1. **Key Ideas and Details** **(a)** Make a three-column chart. In the first column, write the remark regarding the Montagues and Capulets that Mercutio makes three times as he is dying. **(b) Infer:** In the second column, explain what Mercutio means by this exclamation. **(c) Interpret:** In the third column, explain how his remark reinforces ideas set forth in the play's Prologue.
2. **Key Ideas and Details** **(a)** How and why does Romeo kill Tybalt? **(b) Interpret:** What does Romeo mean when he says, after killing Tybalt, "I am fortune's fool"?
3. **Key Ideas and Details** **(a) Analyze:** Describe the clashing emotions Juliet feels when the Nurse reports Tybalt's death and Romeo's punishment. **(b) Compare and Contrast:** In what ways are Romeo's and Juliet's reactions to Romeo's banishment similar and different? Explain.
4. **Integration of Knowledge and Ideas** **Draw Conclusions:** How might Tybalt's death have been avoided?
5. **Integration of Knowledge and Ideas** How have the differences between Romeo and Juliet returned to threaten their future together? Explain. ***[Connect to the Big Question: Do our differences define us?]***

Assessment Resources

Unit 5 Resources

L1 L2 EL **Selection Test A,** pp. 71–73. Administer Test A to less advanced students.

L3 L4 EL **Selection Test B,** pp. 74–76. Administer Test B to on-level and more advanced students.

L3 L4 **Open-Book Test,** pp. 68–70. As an alternative, give the Open-Book Test.

All **Customizable Test Bank**

All **Self-tests**
Students may prepare for the **Selection Test** by taking the **Self-test** online.

PHLit Online!

All assessment resources are available at **www.PHLitOnline.com**.

After You Read The Tragedy of Romeo and Juliet, Act III

Literary Analysis: Dramatic Speeches

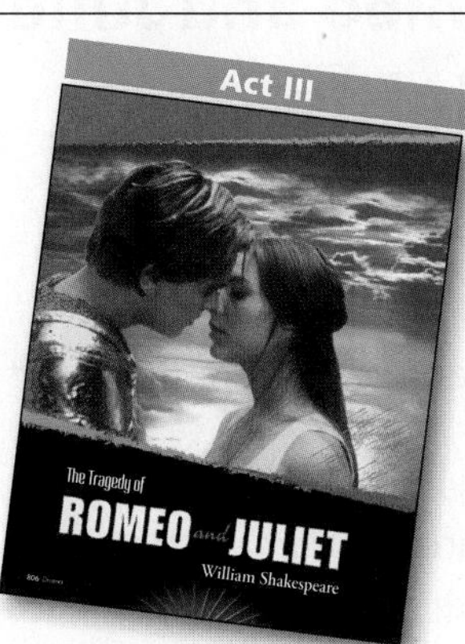

Act III
The Tragedy of
ROMEO and JULIET
William Shakespeare

1. **Key Ideas and Details** **(a)** What thoughts and feelings does Juliet express in the **soliloquy** that opens Scene ii of Act III? **(b)** When Juliet makes an **allusion** to Phoebus and Phaëton, what is she hoping will happen?
2. **Key Ideas and Details** What criticisms of Romeo does the Friar address in his Scene iii **monologue** beginning, "Hold thy desperate hand"?
3. **Key Ideas and Details** In Act III, Scene v, when her mother refers to Romeo as a villain, Juliet utters the **aside,** "Villain and he be many miles asunder." What has happened? Why does Juliet speak only to the audience?
4. **Key Ideas and Details** **(a)** How would you describe the personalities of each of the following characters: Romeo, Tybalt, Benvolio, Mercutio. **(b)** Which of these men are **foils** to each other? Explain.

Reading Skill: Summarize

5. **(a) Paraphrase** lines 29–51 in Act III, Scene iii. **(b)** Write a few sentences that **summarize** what Romeo says to the Friar. Then summarize the events of Act III.

Vocabulary

Acquisition and Use Identify which two words in each group are **synonyms** and which one is an **antonym** of the other two. Explain your response.

1. gallant, courageous, cowardly
2. fray, truce, brawl
3. exile, banishment, welcome
4. martial, peaceful, warlike
5. eloquence, expressiveness, inarticulateness
6. fickle, unpredictable, constant

Word Study Use the context of the sentences and what you know about the **Latin root *-loque-*** to explain your answer to each question.

1. Would a *colloquialism* be out of place when used among friends?
2. What would you expect to happen at a *colloquium* on William Shakespeare?

Word Study

The **Latin root *-loque-*** means "talk," "speak," or "say."

Apply It Explain how the root *-loque-* contributes to the meanings of these words. Consult a dictionary if necessary.

ventriloquist
soliloquy
loquacious

ASSESS/EXTEND

Answers

Literary Analysis

1. (a) Juliet is impatient for the night to arrive so she can be with her new husband. (b) She is hoping the sun will set quickly, so that Romeo will come.
2. The Friar calls Romeo "womanish" and "beastly" for attempting to kill himself, and claims that Romeo will kill Juliet by killing himself.
3. Juliet means that there is a vast distance between Romeo and a villain; in other words, Romeo is not a villain. It is important that Lady Capulet not hear how Juliet feels, but also that the audience knows Juliet's true feelings.
4. (a) Romeo is idealistic and passionate. Tybalt is aggressive, violent, and extremely proud. Benvolio is nonconfrontational. Mercutio is rash and aggressive. (b) Mercutio and Benvolio are foils to each other. Benvolio's passivity directly contrasts Mercutio's aggression.

Reading Skill

5. (a) Banishment is torture, not mercy, for heaven is where Juliet lives. While every little creature may look upon Juliet, I cannot. I must go. Even flies have it better than I, for they can hear Juliet speak. But I cannot hear Juliet's voice because I am banished. You say that exile is not death, but it is. The damned howl the word *banished* in hell. How can you torture me with the word *banished?* (b) **Possible response:** Banishment is not mercy, because I am separated from Juliet. Every other living creature can see her, but not me, and that is torture. Students' summaries will vary but should convey an understanding of the events.

Vocabulary

Acquisition and Use

Sample answers:

1. *Gallant* and *courageous* both mean "brave." *Cowardly* means "not brave."
2. *Fray* and *brawl* both mean "a fight." *Truce* is an agreement or treaty.
3. *Exile* and *banishment* both mean "being expelled from a country." *Welcome* means "a kind reception."
4. *Martial* and *warlike* both mean "military." *Peaceful* has the opposite meaning.
5. *Expressiveness* and *eloquence* both mean "grace, as in speech." *Inarticulateness* is the inability to express oneself coherently.
6. *Fickle* and *unpredictable* both mean "changeable." *Constant* means "unchanging."

Word Study

Sample answers:

1. No, *-loque-* means "talk, speak, or say," so *colloquialism* means "informal speech." Friends would use colloquialisms with each other.
2. The root *-loque-* means "talk," so *colloquium* means "a talk in which experts discuss a topic." At a colloquium on Shakespeare, experts would discuss his work.

Word Study: Apply It

Sample answers:

A *ventriloquist* can project his or her voice as if someone else is speaking. A *soliloquy* is a speech in which a lone character reveals personal thoughts. A *loquacious* person is talkative.

✓ The Tragedy of Romeo and Juliet, Act IV

Lesson Pacing Guide

DAY 1 Preteach

- Administer the Reading and Vocabulary Warm-ups (*Unit 5 Resources*, pp. 77–80) as necessary.
- Introduce the Reading Skill: Summarize.
- Introduce the Literary Analysis concept: Dramatic Irony.
- Distribute copies of the appropriate graphic organizer for the Reading Skill (*Graphic Organizer Transparencies*, pp. 159–160).
- Distribute copies of the appropriate graphic organizer for Literary Analysis (*Graphic Organizer Transparencies*, pp. 161–162).
- Teach the selection vocabulary.
- Introduce the Word Study skill.

DAYS 2–3 Preteach/Teach

- Build background with the Background feature.
- Develop thematic vocabulary and thematic thinking with Writing About the Big Question.
- Prepare students to read with the Activating Prior Knowledge activities (TE).
- Informally monitor comprehension while students read.
- Use the Reading Check questions to confirm comprehension.
- Develop students' ability to summarize, using the Reading Skill questions.
- Develop students' understanding of dramatic irony, using the Literary Analysis questions.
- Reinforce vocabulary with the Vocabulary notes.
- Reinforce unit focus standards using the Spiral Review prompts.

DAY 4 Assess

- Assess students' comprehension and mastery of the skills by having them answer the Critical Thinking, Reading Skill, and Literary Analysis questions.
- Have students complete the Vocabulary Practice activities.
- Have students complete the Word Study activities.

DAY 5 Extend/Assess

- Have students complete the Writing activity and write a persuasive letter, p. 933. (You may assign as homework.)
- Extend learning by having students complete the Research and Technology activity, a multimedia presentation, p. 935. (You may assign as homework.) As an alternative, assign them "Staying Connected" in *Reality Central*.
- Administer Selection Test A or B (*Unit 5 Resources*, pp. 89–94).

Common Core State Standards

Reading Literature
2. Determine a theme or central idea of a text; provide an objective summary of the text.
3. Analyze how complex characters (e.g., those with multiple or conflicting motivations) develop over the course of a text, interact with other characters, and advance the plot or develop the theme.
5. Analyze how an author's choices concerning how to structure a text, order events within it, and manipulate time create such effects as mystery, tension, or surprise.

Language 5.a. Interpret figures of speech in context and analyze their role in the text.

Additional Standards Practice
Common Core Companion, pp. 28–29

Daily Block Scheduling
Each day in this Lesson Pacing Guide represents a 40–50 minute period. Teachers using block scheduling may combine days to revise pacing. In addition, teachers may differentiate and support core instruction by integrating components for extended and intensive support as students require. See the Guide to Selected Leveled Resources (facing page).

Guide to Selected Leveled Resources

RTI **Tier 1** (students performing on level)			The Tragedy of Romeo and Juliet, Act IV
Warm Up	Whole class instruction; Group work	**Practice, model,** and **monitor** fluency, working **with the whole class** or **in groups.**	**Vocabulary** and **Reading Warm-ups B,** ***Unit 5 Resources,*** pp. 77–78, 80
Comprehension/Skills	Whole class instruction; Independent work	**Support** and **monitor** comprehension and skills development, having students complete the activities, graphic organizers, and interactive prompts **independently** or **as a class.**	• ***Reader's Notebook,*** adapted instruction and full selection EL ***Reader's Notebook: English Learner's Version,*** adapted instruction and adapted selection • **Reading Skill Graphic Organizer B,** ***Graphic Organizer Transparencies,*** p. 160 • **Literary Analysis Graphic Organizer B,** ***Graphic Organizer Transparencies,*** p. 162
Monitor Progress	A	**Monitor** student progress with the differentiated curriculum-based assessment in the *Unit Resources.*	• **Selection Test B,** ***Unit 5 Resources,*** pp. 92–94 • **Open-Book Test,** ***Unit 5 Resources,*** pp. 86–88

RTI **Tier 2** (students requiring intervention)			The Tragedy of Romeo and Juliet, Act IV
Warm Up	Whole class instruction; Group work	**Practice, model,** and **monitor** fluency **in groups** or **with individuals.**	• **Vocabulary and Reading Warm-ups A,** ***Unit 5 Resources,*** pp. 77–80 • ***Reality Central,*** "Staying Connected" • ***Hear It!*** **Audio CD (adapted text)**
Comprehension/Skills	Whole class instruction; Independent work	• **Support** and **monitor** comprehension and skills development, working **in small groups** or **with individuals.** • **Pair** students with more advanced peers and have them complete the writing activity in the *Real-World Writing Journal.* • As students complete the selection in the appropriate version of the *Reader's Notebook,* **monitor** comprehension frequently with group questions and individual instruction. • **Model** strategies while guiding students in completing the activities and prompts in the *Reader's Notebook,* as well as the graphic organizers. • **Practice** skills and **monitor** mastery with the *Reading Kit* worksheets.	• ***Real-World Writing Journal,*** Lesson 2, pp. 142–145 • ***Reader's Notebook: Adapted Version,*** adapted instruction and adapted selection EL ***Reader's Notebook: English Learner's Version,*** adapted instruction and adapted selection • **Reading Skill Graphic Organizer A,** ***Graphic Organizer Transparencies,*** p. 159 • **Literary Analysis Graphic Organizer A,** ***Graphic Organizer Transparencies,*** p. 161 • **Reading Kit,** Practice worksheets, pp. 208, 214, 218, 234
Monitor Progress	A	**Monitor** student progress with the differentiated curriculum-based assessment in the *Unit Resources* and in the *Reading Kit.*	• **Selection Test A,** ***Unit 5 Resources,*** pp. 89–91 • **Reading Kit,** Assess worksheets pp. 209, 215, 219, 235

TIER 3 Tier 3 intervention may require consultation with the student's special-education or dyslexia specialist. For additional support, see the Tier 2 activities and resources listed above.

One-on-one teaching **Group work** **Whole class instruction** **Independent work** **A Assessment**

For a complete guide to selection support, including support for Advanced students, see the Overview of Resources in the frontmatter.

✓ The Tragedy of Romeo and Juliet, Act IV

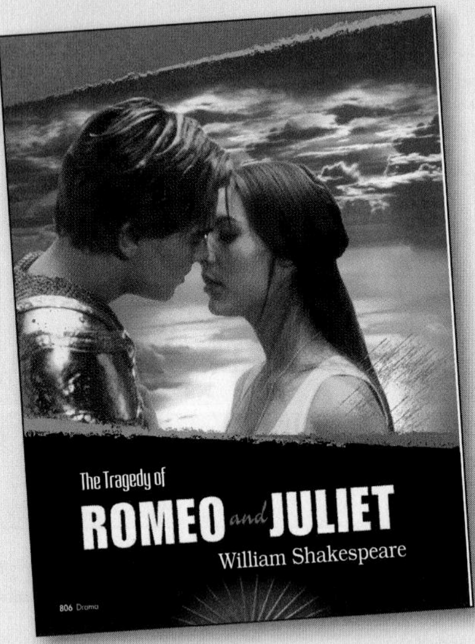

RESOURCES FOR:

- L1 Special-Needs Students
- L2 Below-Level Students (Tier 2)
- L3 On-Level Students (Tier 1)
- L4 Advanced Students (Tier 1)
- EL English Learners
- All All Students

Vocabulary/Fluency/Prior Knowledge

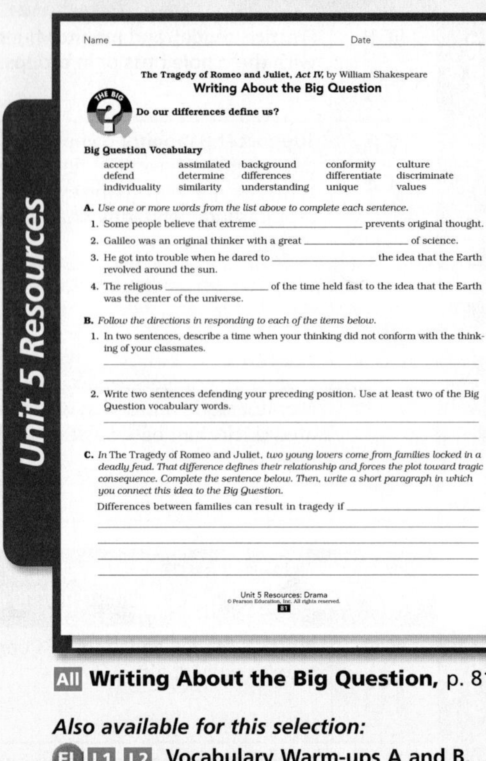

Unit 5 Resources

Name ______________________ Date ______________

The Tragedy of Romeo and Juliet, ***Act IV,*** by William Shakespeare

Writing About the Big Question

THE BIG ? **Do our differences define us?**

Big Question Vocabulary

accept	assimilated	background	conformity	culture
defend	determine	differences	differentiate	discriminate
individuality	similarity	understanding	unique	values

A. *Use one or more words from the list above to complete each sentence.*

1. Some people believe that extreme ________________ prevents original thought.
2. Galileo was an original thinker with a great ________________ of science.
3. He got into trouble when he dared to ________________ the idea that the Earth revolved around the sun.
4. The religious ________________ of the time held fast to the idea that the Earth was the center of the universe.

B. *Follow the directions in responding to each of the items below.*

1. In two sentences, describe a time when your thinking did not conform with the thinking of your classmates.

____

____

2. Write two sentences defending your preceding position. Use at least two of the Big Question vocabulary words.

____

____

C. *In* The Tragedy of Romeo and Juliet, *two young lovers come from families locked in a deadly feud. That difference defines their relationship and forces the plot toward tragic consequence. Complete the sentence below. Then, write a short paragraph in which you connect this idea to the Big Question.*

Differences between families can result in tragedy if ________________

____

____

____

____

Unit 5 Resources: Drama

81

All **Writing About the Big Question,** p. 81

Also available for this selection:

EL L1 L2 **Vocabulary Warm-ups A and B,** pp. 77–78

EL L1 L2 **Reading Warm-ups A and B,** pp. 79–80

All **Vocabulary Builder,** p. 84

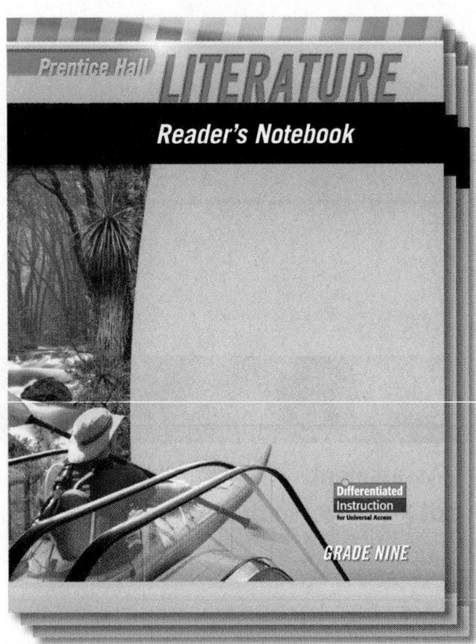

Reader's Notebooks

Pre- and postreading pages, as well as the selection *The Tragedy of Romeo and Juliet,* Act IV, appear in an interactive format in the *Reader's Notebooks*. Each *Notebook* is differentiated for a different group of learners. The selections in the Adapted and English Learner's versions are abridged.

L2 L3 ***Reader's Notebook***

L1 ***Reader's Notebook: Adapted Version***

EL ***Reader's Notebook: English Learner's Version***

EL ***Reader's Notebook: Spanish Version***

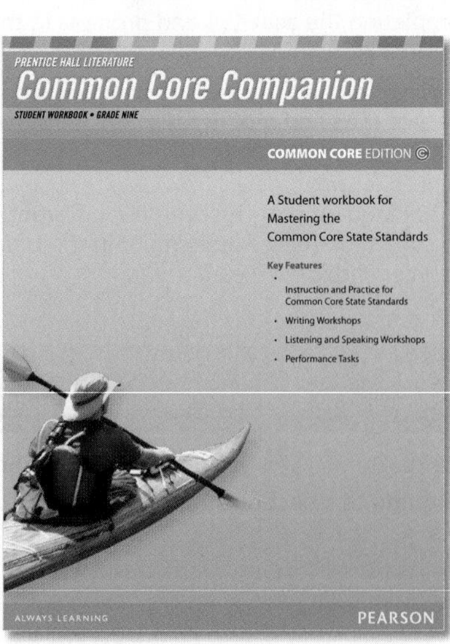

Common Core Companion

Additional instruction and practice for each Common Core State Standard

Selection Support

Graphic Organizer Transparencies

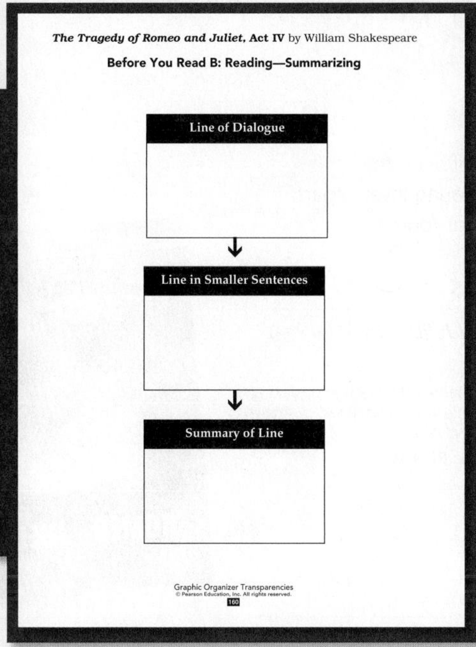

***The Tragedy of Romeo and Juliet*, Act IV** by William Shakespeare

Before You Read B: Reading—Summarizing

Line of Dialogue

↓

Line in Smaller Sentences

↓

Summary of Line

Graphic Organizer Transparencies

160

EL L3 **Reading: Graphic Organizer B,** p. 160

Also available for this selection:

- EL L1 L2 **Reading: Graphic Organizer A,** p. 159 (partially filled in)
- EL L1 L2 **Literary Analysis: Graphic Organizer A,** p. 161 (partially filled in)
- EL L3 **Literary Analysis: Graphic Organizer B,** p. 162

Skills Development/Extension

Unit 5 Resources

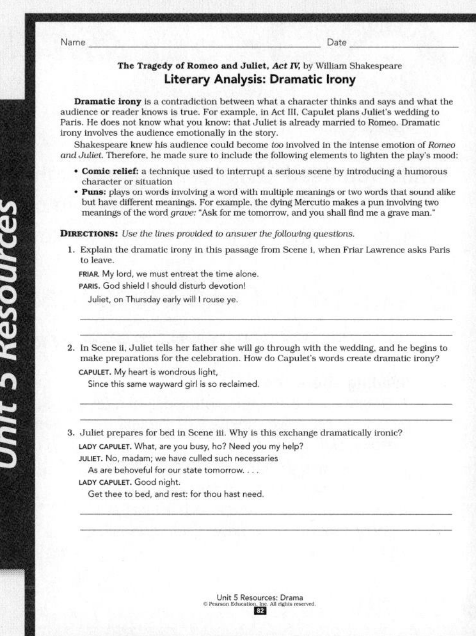

Name ______________________ Date ____________

The Tragedy of Romeo and Juliet, ***Act IV,*** by William Shakespeare

Literary Analysis: Dramatic Irony

Dramatic irony is a contradiction between what a character thinks and says and what the audience or reader knows is true. For example, in Act III, Capulet plans Juliet's wedding to Paris. He does not know what you know: that Juliet is already married to Romeo. Dramatic irony involves the audience emotionally in the story.

Shakespeare knew his audience could become *too* involved in the intense emotion of *Romeo and Juliet.* Therefore, he made sure to include the following elements to lighten the play's mood:

- **Comic relief:** a technique used to interrupt a serious scene by introducing a humorous character or situation
- **Puns:** plays on words involving a word with multiple meanings or two words that sound alike but have different meanings. For example, the dying Mercutio makes a pun involving two meanings of the word *grave:* "Ask for me tomorrow, and you shall find me a grave man."

DIRECTIONS: *Use the lines provided to answer the following questions.*

1. Explain the dramatic irony in this passage from Scene i, when Friar Lawrence asks Paris to leave.

   FRIAR. My lord, we must entreat the time alone.
   PARIS. God shield I should disturb devotion!
   Juliet, on Thursday early will I rouse ye.

   ____

   ____

2. In Scene ii, Juliet tells her father she will go through with the wedding, and he begins to make preparations for the celebration. How do Capulet's words create dramatic irony?

   CAPULET. My heart is wondrous light,
   Since this same wayward girl is so reclaimed.

   ____

   ____

3. Juliet prepares for bed in Scene iii. Why is this exchange dramatically ironic?

   LADY CAPULET. What, are you busy, ho? Need you my help?
   JULIET. No, madam; we have culled such necessaries
   As are behoveful for our state tomorrow. . . .
   LADY CAPULET. Good night.
   Get thee to bed, and rest: for thou hast need.

   ____

   ____

Unit 5 Resources: Drama

82

All **Literary Analysis: Dramatic Irony,** p. 82

Also available for this selection:

- All **Reading: Summarize,** p. 83
- L4 **Enrichment,** p. 85
- EL L3 L4 **Grammar,** p. 104
- EL L3 L4 **Support for Writing,** p. 105
- L3 L4 **Support for Extend Your Learning,** p. 106

Assessment

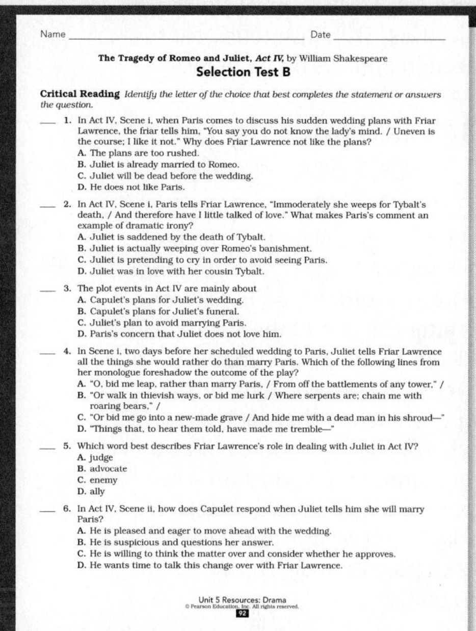

Name ______________________ Date ____________

The Tragedy of Romeo and Juliet, ***Act IV,*** by William Shakespeare

Selection Test B

Critical Reading *Identify the letter of the choice that best completes the statement or answers the question.*

____ 1. In Act IV, Scene i, when Paris comes to discuss his sudden wedding plans with Friar Lawrence, the friar tells him, "You say you do not know the lady's mind. / Uneven is the course; I like it not." Why does Friar Lawrence not like the plans?
A. The plans are too rushed.
B. Juliet is already married to Romeo.
C. Juliet will be dead before the wedding.
D. He does not like Paris.

____ 2. In Act IV, Scene i, Paris tells Friar Lawrence, "Immoderately she weeps for Tybalt's death, / And therefore have I little talked of love." What makes Paris's comment an example of dramatic irony?
A. Juliet is saddened by the death of Tybalt.
B. Juliet is actually weeping over Romeo's banishment.
C. Juliet is pretending to cry in order to avoid seeing Paris.
D. Juliet was in love with her cousin Tybalt.

____ 3. The plot events in Act IV are mainly about
A. Capulet's plans for Juliet's wedding.
B. Capulet's plans for Juliet's funeral.
C. Juliet's plan to avoid marrying Paris.
D. Paris's concern that Juliet does not love him.

____ 4. In Scene i, two days before her scheduled wedding to Paris, Juliet tells Friar Lawrence all the things she would rather do than marry Paris. Which of the following lines from her monologue foreshadow the outcome of the play?
A. "O, bid me leap, rather than marry Paris, / From off the battlements of any tower," /
B. "Or walk in thievish ways, or bid me lurk / Where serpents are; chain me with roaring bears," /
C. "Or bid me go into a new-made grave / And hide me with a dead man in his shroud—"
D. "Things that, to hear them told, have made me tremble—"

____ 5. Which word best describes Friar Lawrence's role in dealing with Juliet in Act IV?
A. judge
B. advocate
C. enemy
D. ally

____ 6. In Act IV, Scene ii, how does Capulet respond when Juliet tells him she will marry Paris?
A. He is pleased and eager to move ahead with the wedding.
B. He is suspicious and questions her answer.
C. He is willing to think the matter over and consider whether he approves.
D. He wants time to talk this change over with Friar Lawrence.

Unit 5 Resources: Drama

92

EL L3 L4 **Selection Test B,** pp. 92–94

Also available for this selection:

- L3 L4 **Open-Book Test,** pp. 86–88
- EL L1 L2 **Selection Test A,** pp. 89–91

PHLit Online!
www.PHLitOnline.com

- complete narrated selection text
- a thematically related video with writing prompt
- an interactive graphic organizer
- highlighting feature
- access to all student print resources, adapted to individual student needs
- Spanish and English summaries
- adapted selection translations in Spanish

Online Resources: All print materials are also available online.

Get Connected! (thematic video with writing prompt)

Also available:

Background Video

All videos are available in Spanish.

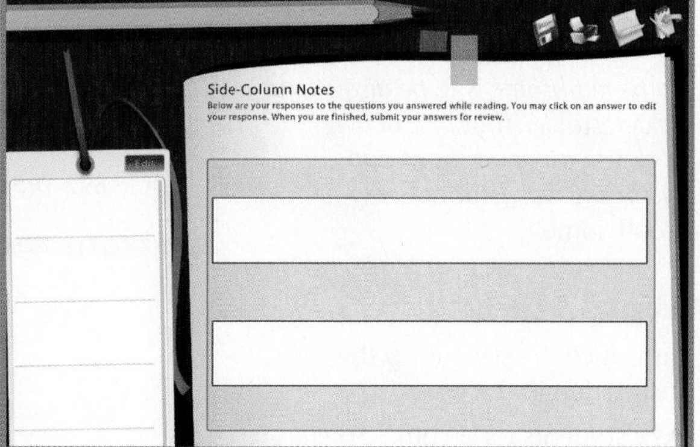

Writer's Journal (with graphics feature)

Also available:

Vocabulary Central (tools, activities, and songs for studying vocabulary)

Leveled Texts

You may use *The Tragedy of Romeo and Juliet,* Act IV to meet the lesson objectives. Skills instruction for the selection appears on page 893.

1 Introducing the CCS Standards

Introduce the standards on the student page. (Note that the lesson element with which each standard is addressed is identified in parentheses after the text of the standard.) Call out the standards that you will cover with the selections, explaining to students what each requires and how they will address it as they work through the selection you have chosen. Standards labeled "Spiral Review" are introduced in the Literary Analysis Workshop for this unit.

2 Vocabulary

1. Have students preview the selection vocabulary.
2. For each word, have students say the word aloud.
3. Then, use the word in a sentence that defines the word.
4. Finally, repeat your definitional sentence or a similar sentence with the word missing and have the class "fill in the blank" chorally. Here are some examples:

   Someone who is wayward is headstrong. Because my brother always refuses to listen to our parents' advice, they say he is [students say "wayward"].

   To be loathsome is to be disgusting or detestable. The sight of overflowing garbage cans at our picnic site was [students say "loathsome"].

3 Word Study

1. Introduce the skill, using the instruction in the box.
2. **Ask** students for a common *en-* word that means "to go into." (**Answer:** *enter*)

Before You Read The Tragedy of Romeo and Juliet, Act IV

While You Read Look for the ways that the feud between the Montagues and the Capulets continues to drive the young lovers apart. Then, decide whether the actions they take are wise or foolish.

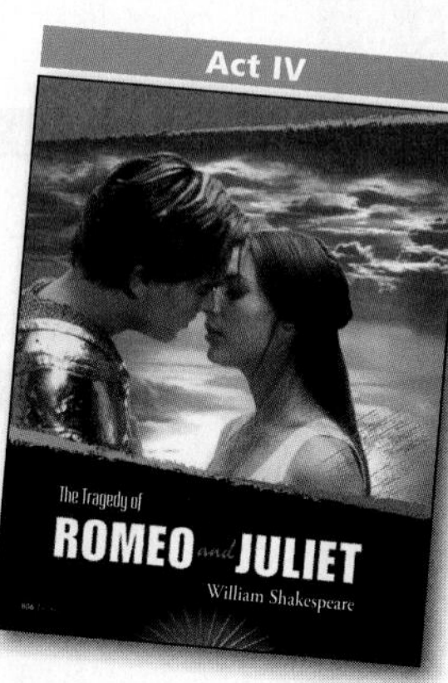

1 Common Core State Standards

Meet these standards with ***The Tragedy of Romeo and Juliet,* Act IV** (p. 894).

Reading Literature

2. Determine a theme or central idea of a text; provide an objective summary of the text. *(Reading Skill: Summarize)*

5. Analyze how an author's choices concerning how to structure a text, order events within it, and manipulate time create such effects as mystery, tension, or surprise. *(Literary Analysis: Dramatic Irony)*

Language

5.a. Interpret figures of speech in context and analyze their role in the text. *(Literary Analysis: Comic Relief and Puns)*

Spiral Review: RL.9-10.3

2 Vocabulary

Read each word and its definition. Decide whether you know the word well, know it a little bit, or do not know it at all. After you read, see how your knowledge of each word has increased.

- **pensive** (pen′ siv) *adj.* deeply thoughtful (p. 896) ***She listened intently, looking pensive.*** *pensively adv. pensiveness n.*
- **vial** (vī′ əl) *n.* small bottle containing medicine or other liquids (p. 898) ***The vial was filled with expensive perfume.***
- **enjoined** (en joind′) *v.* ordered (p. 900) ***The jurors were enjoined not to discuss the case.*** *enjoin v. enjoinment n.*
- **wayward** (wā′ wərd) *adj.* headstrong (p. 900) ***The wayward boy did not listen to anyone and insisted on working alone.*** *waywardly adv. waywardness n.*
- **dismal** (diz′ məl) *adj.* causing gloom or misery (p. 901) ***The dismal sight of his abandoned house made the old man sad.*** *dismally adv.*
- **loathsome** (lōth′ səm) *adj.* disgusting; detestable (p. 903) ***The loathsome smell of rotten eggs filled the laboratory.*** *loathe v. loathing n.*

3 Word Study

The **Latin prefix *en-*** means "in," "into," or "within."

In Act IV, Juliet says she is **enjoined** by Friar Lawrence to be ruled by her father. She means that Friar Lawrence wants her to join with her father by obeying his wishes.

❹ Literary Analysis: Dramatic Irony

Dramatic irony is a contradiction between what a character thinks and what the audience knows to be true. Dramatic irony engages the audience emotionally; tension and suspense build as the audience waits for the truth to be revealed to the characters.

Shakespeare understood the importance of providing a balance of tragic and comic elements in his plays. Injecting humor into an otherwise tragic plot allows the audience to experience a range of reactions to the events unfolding onstage. These comic elements are used thoughout the play:

- **Comic relief:** the introduction of a humorous character or situation into an otherwise tragic scene.
- **Puns:** plays on words using a word with multiple meanings or two words that sound alike but have different meanings. For example, the dying Mercutio makes a pun using the word *grave:* "Ask for me tomorrow, and you shall find me a grave man."

As you read, notice how Shakespeare uses dramatic irony, comic relief, and puns to balance strong emotion with humor and wit.

PHLit Online!
www.PHLitOnline.com

Hear It!
- Selection summary audio
- Selection audio

See It!
- Get Connected video
- Background video
- More about the author
- Vocabulary flashcards

Do It!
- Interactive journals
- Interactive graphic organizers
- Self-test
- Internet activity
- Grammar tutorial
- Interactive vocabulary games

❺ Reading Skill: Summarize

To summarize long passages of Shakespearean dialogue, you should **break down long sentences** into shorter units of meaning.

- If a sentence contains multiple subjects or verbs, separate it into smaller sentences with one subject and one verb.
- If a sentence contains colons, semicolons, or dashes, treat these marks as periods in order to make shorter sentences.

❻ Using the Strategy: Summarizing Chart

Use a chart like this one to help you break down long sentences.

Line of Dialogue	Line in Smaller Sentences	Summary
Immoderately she weeps for Tybalt's death, / And therefore have I little talked of love; / For Venus smiles not in a house of tears.	1. Immoderately she weeps for Tybalt's death. 2. Therefore have I little talked of love. 3. Venus smiles not in a house of tears.	Paris has not talked of love with Juliet because she is crying over Tybalt's death.

❹ Literary Analysis

Dramatic Irony

1. Introduce the skill, using the instruction on the student page.
2. Tell students that they will analyze dramatic irony as they read.

Think Aloud: Model the Skill

Model a way to understand dramatic irony. Say to students:

> Suppose a play features three characters in a lifeboat—a well-known executive, an Olympic athlete, and a frail young woman. Who will save the day? The audience is surprised when the young woman turns out to be the hero. The outcome is ironic because it is not what the audience expects.

❺ Reading Skill

Summarize

1. Introduce the skill, using the instruction on the student page.
2. Tell students that they will break down long sentences in order to summarize as they read.

❻ Using the Strategy

Give students a copy of either **Reading Skill Graphic Organizer A** or **B** (*Graphic Organizer Transparencies,* pp. 159–160) to break down sentences as they read. Use the examples in **Reading Skill Graphic Organizer A,** which is partially filled in, to model the process of completing the organizer.

Differentiated Instruction — Additional Instruction

EL Extended Support—English Learners
Have students complete the **Reading and Vocabulary Warm-ups,** ***Unit 5 Resources,*** pp. 77–80, before they read. Assign the prereading pages for this selection in the ***Reader's Notebook: English Learner's Version.*** Then, have students listen to portions of the selection on the ***Hear It!*** **Audio CD.**

L1 L2 Extended Support—Struggling Readers
Have students complete the **Reading and Vocabulary Warm-ups,** ***Unit 5 Resources,*** pp. 77–80, before they read. Assign the prereading pages for this selection in the ***Reader's Notebook: Adapted Version.*** Then, have students listen to portions of the selection on the ***Hear It!*** **Audio CD** (adapted text).

Extended Support—Reluctant Readers
To build motivation and engagement before assigning the selection, have students read "Staying Connected," a thematically related selection in ***Reality Central.*** Then, use the questions at the conclusion of the related selection to guide discussion.

❶ Activating Prior Knowledge

1. As this act opens, plans for Juliet's marriage to Paris are moving ahead. Romeo is exiled in Mantua, and Juliet alone must decide what to do about marrying Paris.
2. Have students imagine themselves in Juliet's place. Remind them that only the Nurse and the Friar know of her marriage to Romeo. The Nurse has already betrayed her by advising her to forget Romeo, pretend she never married him, and go ahead and marry Paris.
3. Have students brainstorm for solutions to Juliet's problem. Write the possible solutions on the chalkboard. Then, next to each, have students write the possible consequences of the solution.

Concept Connector

Students will follow up on this activity after completing *The Tragedy of Romeo and Juliet,* Act IV.

Whole-Class Activity

Tell students that this act alternates scenes of high emotion with scenes of humor. As students read this act, have them note how the act is structured—which scenes are emotionally charged and which scenes provide the comic relief. Then, have students discuss how the comic scenes and their placement in the story affect the act. Ask what would happen if the comic scenes were left out. How do the comic scenes further the action of the play?

❷ About the Selection

Act IV belongs to Juliet as she interacts with the Friar, Paris, her parents, and the Nurse. Using witty wordplay and misleading statements, Juliet avoids suspicion about her true intent. Her unwillingness to confront her parents and her trust in the Friar lead her further along the road to tragedy. Act IV illustrates a paradox at work within Juliet: She is brave enough to follow the Friar's risky plan, but she is at the same time afraid to tell her parents the truth.

Text Complexity Rubric

The Tragedy of Romeo and Juliet, Act IV		
Qualitative Measures	**Context/ Knowledge Demands**	Historical: Verona, Italy 1 2 3 4 ⑤
	Structure/ Language Clarity and Conventionality	Challenging vocabulary; Elizabethan terms 1 2 3 4 ⑤
	Levels of Meaning/ Purpose/Concept Level	Accessible concept (classic tale of star-crossed lovers) 1 2 ③ 4 5
Quantitative Measures	**Text Length**	Word Count: 3,319
	Lexile	NP
Overall Complexity		**Complex**

3 Reading Check

Answer: The Friar complains about the hastiness of the planned wedding.

This selection is available in interactive format in the **Enriched Online Student Edition,** at **www.PHLitOnline.com,** which includes a thematically related video with writing prompt and an interactive graphic organizer.

Review and Anticipate

Romeo and Juliet are married for only a few hours when disaster strikes. In Act III, Juliet's cousin Tybalt kills Mercutio, and then Romeo kills Tybalt. This leads to Romeo's banishment from Verona. To make matters worse, Juliet's parents are determined to marry her to Paris. Will Romeo and Juliet ever be able to live together as husband and wife? What, if anything, can the lovers now do to preserve their relationship?

Scene i. Friar Lawrence's cell.

[*Enter* FRIAR LAWRENCE *and* COUNTY PARIS.]

FRIAR. On Thursday, sir? The time is very short.

PARIS. My father[1] Capulet will have it so,
And I am nothing slow to slack his haste.[2]

FRIAR. You say you do not know the lady's mind.
Uneven is the course;[3] I like it not.

4

PARIS. Immoderately she weeps for Tybalt's death,
And therefore have I little talked of love;
For Venus smiles not in a house of tears.
Now, sir, her father counts it dangerous

1. **father** future father-in-law.
2. **I . . . haste** I will not slow him down by being slow myself.
3. **Uneven . . . course** irregular is the plan.

3 

What is the Friar's complaint to Paris about the impending wedding?

C Text Complexity: Reader and Task Suggestions

The Tragedy of Romeo and Juliet, Act IV

Preparing to Read the Text	Leveled Tasks
• Using the Background notes on TE pp. 898 and 903, discuss the Friar's potion and how it could have been a realistic though risky strategy during the time in which the play is set as well as in Shakespeare's own time. • Discuss the use of soliloquies in Shakespeare's play, noting how they were meant to reveal the speaker's thoughts and plans to the audience. • Guide students to use Multidraft Reading strategies (TE p. 805).	*Levels of Meaning* If students will have difficulty with levels of meaning, have them first read and note the motivations behind each character's actions. Then, have them reread and take notes on events and actions that seem fantastic or unrealistic to them. *Synthesizing* If students will not have difficulty with levels of meaning, have them read and note details that describe the Friar's personality and actions and then draw conclusions about his character.

4 Literary Analysis

Dramatic Irony

1. Have students read lines 6–15, which begin on p. 895. **Ask** students what Paris is trying to explain to the Friar in his speech.

   Answer: Paris is explaining why his marriage to Juliet must occur as quickly as possible.
2. Remind students that dramatic irony is a contradiction between what a character thinks is true and what the reader or audience knows is true.
3. **Ask** students what the reader and the audience know about Juliet's crying.

   Answer: Juliet is crying because her parents are trying to marry her to Paris when she and Romeo are already married.
4. **Ask** students to respond to the Literary Analysis question: In what way does Paris' comment show that he does not understand the real reason that Juliet is crying?

   Answer: Paris says that Juliet is crying over Tybalt's death.

5 Critical Thinking

Predict

1. Have volunteers read lines 18–36 aloud. **Ask** whether Juliet actually lies to Paris at any time in this exchange. What does she do?

   Answer: Juliet does not lie to Paris, but she keeps him off balance with her clever wordplay.
2. Have students interpret the exchange in lines 35–36.

   Answer: Paris says that Juliet's face belongs to him. Juliet seems to agree with him, but readers know that Juliet means that her face belongs to Romeo.
3. **Ask** students whether Juliet will consider Paris an ally based on this dialogue. Why or why not?

   Answer: Juliet will not consider Paris an ally because she doesn't want to marry him. Also, she plays word games with him instead of answering him truthfully.

---

4. **inundation** flood.

5. **minded** thought about.

Literary Analysis
Dramatic Irony In what way does Paris' comment show that he does not understand the real reason that Juliet is crying?

6. **That's . . . text** That is a certain truth.

7. **price** value.

8. **before their spite** before the harm that the tears did.

Vocabulary
pensive (pen´ siv) *adj.* deeply thoughtful

9. **entreat . . . alone** ask to have this time to ourselves.

That she do give her sorrow so much sway,
And in his wisdom hastes our marriage
4 To stop the inundation[4] of her tears,
Which, too much minded[5] by herself alone,
May be put from her by society.
Now do you know the reason of this haste.

FRIAR. [*Aside*] I would I knew not why it should be slowed.—
Look, sir, here comes the lady toward my cell.

[*Enter* JULIET.]

PARIS. Happily met, my lady and my wife!

JULIET. That may be, sir, when I may be a wife.

PARIS. That "may be" must be, love, on Thursday next.

JULIET. What must be shall be.

FRIAR. That's a certain text.[6]

PARIS. Come you to make confession to this father?

JULIET. To answer that, I should confess to you.

PARIS. Do not deny to him that you love me.

JULIET. I will confess to you that I love him.

5 **PARIS.** So will ye, I am sure, that you love me.

JULIET. If I do so, it will be of more price,[7]
Being spoke behind your back, than to your face.

PARIS. Poor soul, thy face is much abused with tears.

JULIET. The tears have got small victory by that,
For it was bad enough before their spite.[8]

PARIS. Thou wrong'st it more than tears with that report.

JULIET. That is no slander, sir, which is a truth;
And what I spake, I spake it to my face.

PARIS. Thy face is mine, and thou hast sland'red it.

JULIET. It may be so, for it is not mine own.
Are you at leisure, holy father, now,
Or shall I come to you at evening mass?

FRIAR. My leisure serves me, pensive daughter, now.
My lord, we must entreat the time alone.[9]

Vocabulary Development

CCSS Language 6

Thematic Vocabulary: The Big Question

As students are discussing *The Tragedy of Romeo and Juliet,* Act IV, encourage them to use the thematic vocabulary presented in Introducing the Big Question, pp. 778–779. You might encourage them with sentence starters like these:

1. Up to this point, Romeo and Juliet's family *differences* have led to . . .
2. Juliet abandons her family's *values* when she . . .
3. She enlists the aid of her nurse and persuades her to *accept* . . .
4. Romeo and Juliet put the Friar in a *unique* position when he . . .

PARIS. God shield[10] I should disturb devotion!
Juliet, on Thursday early will I rouse ye.
Till then, adieu, and keep this holy kiss. *[Exit.]*

JULIET. O, shut the door, and when thou hast done so,
Come weep with me—past hope, past care, past help!

FRIAR. O Juliet, I already know thy grief;
It strains me past the compass of my wits.[11]
I hear thou must, and nothing may prorogue[12] it,
On Thursday next be married to this County.

JULIET. Tell me not, friar, that thou hearest of this,
Unless thou tell me how I may prevent it.
If in thy wisdom thou canst give no help,
Do thou but call my resolution wise
And with this knife I'll help it presently.[13]
God joined my heart and Romeo's, thou our hands;
❻ And ere this hand, by thee to Romeo's sealed,
Shall be the label to another deed,[14]
Or my true heart with treacherous revolt
Turn to another, this shall slay them both.
Therefore, out of thy long-experienced time,
Give me some present counsel; or, behold,
'Twixt my extremes and me[15] this bloody knife
Shall play the umpire, arbitrating[16] that
Which the commission of thy years and art
Could to no issue of true honor bring.[17]
Be not so long to speak. I long to die
If what thou speak'st speak not of remedy.

FRIAR. Hold, daughter. I do spy a kind of hope,
Which craves[18] as desperate an execution
As that is desperate which we would prevent.
If, rather than to marry County Paris,
❼ Thou hast the strength of will to slay thyself,
Then is it likely thou wilt undertake
A thing like death to chide away this shame,
That cop'st with death himself to scape from it;[19]
And, if thou darest, I'll give thee remedy.

JULIET. O, bid me leap, rather than marry Paris,
From off the battlements of any tower,
Or walk in thievish ways,[20] or bid me lurk

10. **shield** forbid.

11. **past . . . wits** beyond the ability of my mind to find a remedy.

12. **prorogue** delay.

13. **presently** at once.

14. **Shall . . . deed** shall give the seal of approval to another marriage contract.

15. **'Twixt . . me** between my misfortunes and me.

16. **arbitrating** deciding.

17. **Which . . . bring** which the authority that derives from your age and ability could not solve honorably.

18. **craves** requires.

19. **That cop'st . . . it** that bargains with death itself to escape from it.

20. **thievish ways** roads where criminals lurk.

Literary Analysis
Dramatic Irony Which two meanings of the word "long" does Juliet use to make a pun in line 66?

❽ 

What does Juliet threaten to do to avoid marrying Paris?

❻ Literary Analysis

Dramatic Irony

1. Have students read lines 46–49. Ask them to identify the Friar's message to Juliet in these lines.

   Answer: The Friar has no more ideas about what to do for the two lovers. He says that nothing will delay the marriage and Juliet should accept the inevitable.

2. Have students read lines 50–67. **Ask** how Juliet responds to the Friar's suggestion.

   Answer: Juliet tells him not to speak of the wedding unless he can tell her how to prevent it. Otherwise she will die.

3. **Ask** students in which two ways Juliet uses the word *speak* in line 67.

   Answer: She uses *speak'st* to mean "say," and she uses *speak* to mean "inform."

4. **Ask** students the Literary Analysis question: Which two meanings of the word *long* does Juliet use to make a pun in line 66?

   Answer: In the first sentence, she uses *long* to mean "do not take a long time." In the second sentence, she uses it to mean "I wish."

❼ Critical Thinking

Analyze

Have students think about how the Friar has involved himself with Romeo and Juliet. Then, **ask** students whether they think the Friar has acted responsibly so far. Why or why not?

Possible response: Students may suggest that the Friar has helped Romeo and Juliet deceive their parents, and now he is going to suggest a dangerous solution to Juliet's problems rather than advising her to tell the truth to her parents. He does not seem to be acting responsibly.

❽ Reading Check

Answer: Juliet threatens to kill herself with a knife rather than marry Paris.

Differentiated Instruction for Universal Access

Strategy for Special-Needs Students
Tell students that the mood swings back and forth in Act IV between Juliet's sadness, the joy of the Capulets' preparing for the wedding, the humor of the serving men, Juliet's terror, and the profound sorrow of the Capulets when they believe Juliet is dead. Students may best understand the variety of emotions in this act by listening to the ***Hear It!* Audio CD** (adapted text). Have students listen in small groups, pausing to discuss each scene.

Strategy for Less Proficient Readers
To give students a context for Act IV and to model how to summarize, show them **Reading Skill Graphic Organizer A** (*Graphic Organizer Transparencies*, p. 159). The partially completed graphic organizer will give students insight into the process of breaking lines into smaller sentences before summarizing. They can use it as a model for summarizing scenes as they read.

9 Critical Thinking

Predict

1. Have students read lines 89–103. **Ask** what the Friar tells Juliet to do.

   Answer: He tells her to go home, be cheerful, and inform her parents that she will marry Paris. He tells her to then drink a "distilling liquor" that will make her appear to have died.

2. **Ask** students to predict what the Friar's complete plan will turn out to be.

   Possible response: The Friar plans to put Juliet into a deep sleep so that she appears to be dead, thereby avoiding marriage to Paris.

10 Background

Medicine

In these lines, the Friar gives Juliet a potion that will make her appear dead when she drinks it. It may be difficult to believe that someone could be thought dead when he or she is not. However, the technology for determining death was very primitive in the times in which these events took place. Medieval doctors did not use a stethoscope, which was invented in 1816. Doctors at this time determined death by putting their ear next to the patient's body to hear the sounds of the body's organs.

---

21. charnel house vault for bones removed from graves to be reused.
22. reeky foul-smelling.
23. chapless jawless.

Vocabulary
vial (vī´ əl) *n.* small bottle containing medicine or other liquids

24. humor fluid; liquid.
25. native natural.
26. surcease stop.
27. wanny ashes to the color of pale ashes.
28. eyes' windows eyelids.
29. supple government ability for maintaining motion.

30. uncovered on the bier displayed on the funeral platform.
31. against before.
32. drift purpose; plan.

Where serpents are; chain me with roaring bears,
Or hide me nightly in a charnel house,[21]
O'ercovered quite with dead men's rattling bones,
With reeky[22] shanks and yellow chapless[23] skulls;
Or bid me go into a new-made grave
And hide me with a dead man in his shroud—
Things that, to hear them told, have made me tremble—
And I will do it without fear or doubt,
To live an unstained wife to my sweet love.

FRIAR. Hold, then. Go home, be merry, give consent
To marry Paris. Wednesday is tomorrow.
Tomorrow night look that thou lie alone;
Let not the nurse lie with thee in thy chamber.
Take thou this vial, being then in bed,
And this distilling liquor drink thou off;
When presently through all thy veins shall run
A cold and drowsy humor;[24] for no pulse
Shall keep his native[25] progress, but surcease;[26]
No warmth, no breath, shall testify thou livest;
The roses in thy lips and cheeks shall fade
To wanny ashes,[27] thy eyes' windows[28] fall
Like death when he shuts up the day of life;
Each part, deprived of supple government,[29]
Shall, stiff and stark and cold, appear like death;
And in this borrowed likeness of shrunk death
Thou shalt continue two-and-forty hours,
And then awake as from a pleasant sleep.
Now, when the bridegroom in the morning comes
To rouse thee from thy bed, there art thou dead.
Then, as the manner of our country is,
In thy best robes uncovered on the bier[30]
Thou shalt be borne to that same ancient vault
Where all the kindred of the Capulets lie.
In the meantime, against[31] thou shalt awake,
Shall Romeo by my letters know our drift;[32]
And hither shall he come; and he and I

Vocabulary Development

CCSS Language 6

Expressive Vocabulary

To help students broaden their expressive vocabulary, encourage them to use the following words as they discuss Juliet's predicament and the remedy that Friar Lawrence suggests: *intense, potential, liberate, sacrifice,* and *assess.* Have them complete these sentence starters:

1. Juliet's *intense* sorrow leads her to . . .
2. The potion Friar Lawrence offers has the *potential* to . . .
3. Juliet hopes to *liberate* . . .
4. Juliet is willing to make any *sacrifice* to . . .
5. The Friar does not *assess* . . .

Challenge students to use these words as you continue to discuss the play.

Will watch thy waking, and that very night
Shall Romeo bear thee hence to Mantua.
And this shall free thee from this present shame,
If no inconstant toy[33] nor womanish fear
Abate thy valor[34] in the acting it.

JULIET. Give me, give me! O, tell not me of fear!

FRIAR. Hold! Get you gone, be strong and prosperous
In this resolve. I'll send a friar with speed
To Mantua, with my letters to thy lord.

JULIET. Love give me strength, and strength shall help afford.
Farewell, dear father. *[Exit with* FRIAR.]

33. **inconstant toy** passing whim.

34. **Abate thy valor** Lessen your courage.

Literary Analysis
Dramatic Irony What information does Juliet now have that Romeo does not?

Scene ii. Hall in Capulet's house.

[*Enter* FATHER CAPULET, MOTHER, NURSE, *and* SERVINGMEN, *two or three.*]

CAPULET. So many guests invite as here are writ.
[Exit a SERVINGMAN.]

Sirrah, go hire me twenty cunning[1] cooks.

SERVINGMAN. You shall have none ill, sir; for I'll try[2] if they can lick their fingers.

CAPULET. How canst thou try them so?

SERVINGMAN. Marry, sir, 'tis an ill cook that cannot lick his own fingers.[3] Therefore he that cannot lick his fingers goes not with me.

CAPULET. Go, begone.
[Exit SERVINGMAN.]

We shall be much unfurnished[4] for this time.
What, is my daughter gone to Friar Lawrence?

NURSE. Ay, forsooth.[5]

CAPULET. Well, he may chance to do some good on her.
A peevish self-willed harlotry it is.[6]

[*Enter* JULIET.]

NURSE. See where she comes from shrift with merry look.

CAPULET. How now, my headstrong? Where have you been gadding?

1. **cunning** skillful.
2. **try** test.
3. **'tis . . . fingers** It is a bad cook who will not taste his own cooking.

4. **unfurnished** unprepared.
5. **forsooth** in truth.
6. **A peevish . . . it is** It is the ill-tempered, selfish behavior of a woman without good breeding.

12

According to the Friar, how will Romeo learn of Juliet's plan to meet him?

11 Literary Analysis

Dramatic Irony

1. Read the bracketed lines aloud. **Ask** students what Juliet says to the Friar when he says that the plan will only work if she has courage.

   Answer: She says she does not want to hear from him about fear and that her love gives her strength.

2. **Ask** students to respond to the Literary Analysis question: What information does Juliet now have that Romeo does not?

   Answer: Juliet now has a plan for escaping marriage to Paris by feigning death.

12 Reading Check

Answer: Friar Lawrence will send another friar to Mantua with letters to Romeo explaining the plan.

Differentiated Instruction for Universal Access

Enrichment for Gifted/Talented Students
The plan that the Friar outlines for saving Juliet and reuniting the two lovers is ingenious. However, many things could go wrong.

Have students work in small groups to analyze the potential flaws in the Friar's plan. Tell students they should identify at least three problems that could spell disaster for Romeo and Juliet.

After identifying the flaws in the Friar's plan, have students develop a "Plan B"—a better strategy to prevent Juliet's marriage to Paris and to reunite her safely with Romeo. They should keep in mind the flaws of the Friar's plan.

Tell students that they must use only the resources of the time (no helicopter rescues, for example). Furthermore, their plan must preserve the secret of Juliet's marriage to Romeo.

Have groups present their completed plans to the class, and have the class critique the plans and choose the one they believe to be the most likely to succeed.

13 Background

Names

Students may find the word *County* a strange one as a title for Paris. The word was an English form for the Italian *conte,* meaning "count" or "earl."

14 Literary Analysis

Dramatic Irony

1. Have students read lines 24–31. **Ask** students to explain what Juliet tells her father in lines 24–26 and what he takes it to mean.

   Answer: She tells her father that she has met Paris and has professed as much love as she modestly could. He takes it to mean that she is now happy to be marrying Paris.
2. **Ask** students what change in schedule is revealed in this conversation.

   Answer: Lord Capulet says they will not wait until Thursday; the wedding will occur "tomorrow morning."
3. **Ask** students how this change of the wedding date might affect the outcome of the Friar's plan.

   Answer: The Friar has less time to notify Romeo, so Romeo might not be at the tomb when Juliet awakens.
4. **Ask** students to respond to the Literary Analysis question: What is ironic about Lord Capulet's relief in this scene?

   Answer: Capulet is relieved because he believes Juliet and Paris will be married tomorrow according to his wishes. In fact, the change of the date and haste of the marriage will bring tragedy to his family.

Vocabulary
enjoined (en jɔind′)
v. ordered

7. **behests** requests.
8. **fall prostrate** lie face down in humble submission.

9. **becomèd** suitable; proper.

Literary Analysis
Dramatic Irony What is ironic about Lord Capulet's relief in this scene?

10. **bound** indebted.
11. **closet** private room.
12. **ornaments** clothes.

13. **short . . . provision** lacking time for preparation.

14. **deck up her** dress her; get her ready.
15. **What, ho!** Capulet is calling for his servants.

Vocabulary
wayward (wā′ wərd)
adj. headstrong

JULIET. Where I have learnt me to repent the sin
Of disobedient opposition
To you and your behests,[7] and am **enjoined**
By holy Lawrence to fall prostrate[8] here
To beg your pardon. Pardon, I beseech you!
Henceforward I am ever ruled by you.

13 **CAPULET.** Send for the County. Go tell him of this.
I'll have this knot knit up tomorrow morning.

JULIET. I met the youthful lord at Lawrence' cell
And gave him what becomèd[9] love I might,
Not stepping o'er the bounds of modesty.

14 **CAPULET.** Why, I am glad on't. This is well. Stand up.
This is as't should be. Let me see the County.
Ay, marry, go, I say, and fetch him hither.
Now, afore God, this reverend holy friar,
All our whole city is much bound[10] to him.

JULIET. Nurse, will you go with me into my closet[11]
To help me sort such needful ornaments[12]
As you think fit to furnish me tomorrow?

LADY CAPULET. No, not till Thursday. There is time enough.

CAPULET. Go, nurse, go with her. We'll to church tomorrow.
[*Exit* JULIET *and* NURSE.]

LADY CAPULET. We shall be short in our provision.[13]
'Tis now near night.

CAPULET. Tush, I will stir about,
And all things shall be well, I warrant thee, wife.
Go thou to Juliet, help to deck up her.[14]
I'll not to bed tonight; let me alone.
I'll play the housewife for this once. What, ho![15]
They are all forth; well, I will walk myself
To County Paris, to prepare up him
Against tomorrow. My heart is wondrous light,
Since this same **wayward** girl is so reclaimed.
[*Exit with* MOTHER.]

Vocabulary Development

© CCSS Language 6

Word Analysis

Refer students to the selection vocabulary word *wayward* in line 46. Tell students that the suffix *-ward* means "in a direction." This suffix appears in the word *wayward,* which means "headstrong" or "insistent upon going in one's own direction."

Write the following words on the chalkboard: *forward, skyward,* and *outward.*

Ask students to use the meaning of the suffix *-ward*—"in a direction"—to define each of these words.

Answer: *Forward* means "in the direction of the front or head." *Skyward* means "in the direction of the sky." *Outward* means "to or toward the outside."

Scene iii. Juliet's chamber.

[*Enter* JULIET *and* NURSE.]

JULIET. Ay, those attires are best; but, gentle nurse,
I pray thee leave me to myself tonight;
For I have need of many orisons[1]
To move the heavens to smile upon my state,[2]
Which, well thou knowest, is cross[3] and full of sin.

[*Enter* MOTHER.]

15 **LADY CAPULET.** What, are you busy, ho? Need you my help?

JULIET. No, madam; we have culled[4] such necessaries
As are behoveful[5] for our state tomorrow.
So please you, let me now be left alone,
And let the nurse this night sit up with you:
For I am sure you have your hands full all
In this so sudden business.

LADY CAPULET. Good night.
Get thee to bed, and rest: for thou hast need.

[*Exit* MOTHER *and* NURSE.]

JULIET. Farewell! God knows when we shall meet again.
I have a faint cold fear thrills through my veins
That almost freezes up the heat of life.
I'll call them back again to comfort me.
Nurse!—What should she do here?
My dismal scene I needs must act alone.
Come, vial.
What if this mixture do not work at all?
Shall I be married then tomorrow morning?
No, no! This shall forbid it. Lie thou there.

[*Lays down a dagger.*]

What if it be a poison which the friar
Subtly hath minist'red[6] to have me dead,
16 Lest in this marriage he should be dishonored
Because he married me before to Romeo?
I fear it is; and yet methinks it should not,
For he hath still been tried[7] a holy man.
How if, when I am laid into the tomb,
19 I wake before the time that Romeo
Come to redeem me? There's a fearful point!

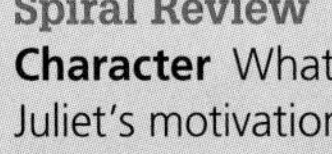

Spiral Review
Character What is Juliet's motivation for deceiving the Nurse?

1. **orisons** prayers.
2. **state** condition.
3. **cross** selfish; disobedient.

Reading Skill
Summarize Briefly state the reasons Juliet gives her Nurse and Lady Capulet for why she should be alone.

4. **culled** chosen.
5. **behoveful** desirable; appropriate.

Vocabulary
dismal (diz′ məl) *adj.* causing gloom or misery

6. **minist'red** given me.

7. **tried** proved.

17 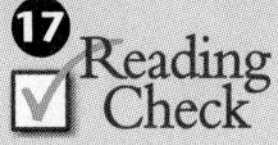

How does Juliet regain her parents' favor?

Differentiated Instruction for Universal Access

Culturally Responsive Instruction

Culture Connection Discuss with students Father Capulet's desire to choose his daughter's husband. Point out that in Shakespeare's time, arranged marriages were the rule and love matches the exception. This custom continues in modern times in some cultures, such as in parts of Asia and the Middle East. Immigrants from such cultures may also continue the custom when living in the United States. Invite students to share marriage customs from their home culture or family's country of origin.
If time allows, have students briefly research marriage customs in a culture of interest. Then, have students discuss the different customs: What may be the positive and negative aspects of different marriage customs?

Spiral Review

Character

Ask the Spiral Review question.

Answer: Juliet is planning to fake her death so she can run away with Romeo. Juliet deceives the nurse so that she can carry out her plan.

15 Reading Skill

Summarize

1. Have students read lines 1–12. Then, **ask** students to identify the setting of this scene and which characters are present.
   Answer: The scene is Juliet's bedroom. She and the Nurse are present as the scene opens, and her mother enters.
2. **Ask** why Lady Capulet and the Nurse come to Juliet's room.
   Answer: They want to help her get ready for the wedding the next day.
3. **Ask** students to respond to the Reading Skill prompt.
   Answer: She says she has many prayers to say; she and the Nurse have chosen all her things for the next day.

16 Critical Thinking

Interpret

Have students read lines 24–27. **Ask** students why Juliet might wonder whether the Friar has given her a drink that really will kill her.

Answer: Juliet recognizes that the Friar has put himself in a difficult position. He has married Romeo and Juliet secretly, and he has encouraged Juliet to go along with the plans for marriage to Paris. If the marriage takes place, the Friar has made Juliet a bigamist. However, if Juliet really dies, his scheme will not be revealed. Other students might argue that Friar Lawrence is, after all, a member of the Church, and he would not knowingly kill a person.

17 Reading Check

Answer: She tells her father that she has seen Paris and has pledged as much love to him as she modestly could.

18 Humanities

Film

Juliet contemplates drinking the fateful potion in this scene from Baz Luhrmann's *Romeo and Juliet.* Use the following questions for discussion:

- Look at Juliet's expression. What emotion or emotions is she experiencing?

  Possible responses: Students may say that Juliet's expression reflects her desperation or fear, her love for Romeo, or her determination to act.

- What elements of the setting help to reinforce these emotions?

  Answer: Students may say the dimly lit background emphasizes the impending tragedy, and the candlelight emphasizes the solemnity of the moment.

902 Drama

Vocabulary Development

CCSS Language 6

Multiple Meanings

Call students' attention to the word *spit* on p. 903, line 56. Tell students that the word has two different sets of meanings with two different origins.

The first set of meanings of *spit* comes from a Middle English word meaning "a point." Here the word can mean: 1. (noun) "a thin pointed rod on which meat is placed to be roasted"; 2. (noun) "a point of land that extends into the water"; 3. (verb) "to thrust a pointed rod through."

The second set of meanings is related to the Latin word *sputum.* In this sense, *spit* can mean 1. (verb) "to eject saliva from the mouth"; 2. (verb) "to rain or snow slightly"; 3. (noun) "saliva."

After reading these two sets of definitions to students, ask students to read lines 55–57 and explain which definition of *spit* they think applies in this context.

Answer: Juliet means "to thrust a pointed rod through," from the first set of meanings.

19 Shall I not then be stifled in the vault,
To whose foul mouth no healthsome air breathes in,
And there die strangled ere my Romeo comes?
Or, if I live, is it not very like
The horrible conceit[8] of death and night,
Together with the terror of the place—
As in a vault, an ancient receptacle
Where for this many hundred years the bones
Of all my buried ancestors are packed;
Where bloody Tybalt, yet but green in earth,[9]
Lies fest'ring in his shroud; where, as they say,
At some hours in the night spirits resort—
Alack, alack, is it not like[10] that I,
So early waking—what with **loathsome** smells,
And shrieks like mandrakes[11] torn out of the earth,
20 That living mortals, hearing them, run mad—
O, if I wake, shall I not be distraught,[12]
Environèd[13] with all these hideous fears,
And madly play with my forefathers' joints,
And pluck the mangled Tybalt from his shroud,
And, in this rage, with some great kinsman's bone
As with a club dash out my desp'rate brains?
O, look! Methinks I see my cousin's ghost
Seeking out Romeo, that did spit his body
Upon a rapier's point. Stay, Tybalt, stay!
Romeo, Romeo, Romeo, I drink to thee.
[She falls upon her bed within the curtains.]

8. **conceit** idea; thought.
9. **green in earth** newly entombed.
10. **like** likely.

Vocabulary
loathsome (lōth′ səm) *adj.* disgusting; detestable

11. **mandrakes** plants with forked roots that resemble human legs. The mandrake was believed to shriek when uprooted and cause the hearer to go mad.
12. **distraught** insane.
13. **Environèd** surrounded.

Reading Skill
Summarize Summarize the fears that Juliet expresses in this soliloquy.

22
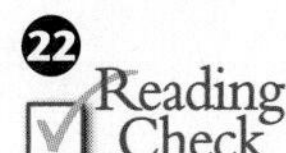
What does Juliet do after her mother and the Nurse leave her chambers?

21
◀ **Critical Viewing** In what way do the colors in this photograph enhance the mood of the scene? **[Analyze]**

19 Background

Direct students to lines 30–35, which begin on p. 901. Juliet's fears of being buried alive in the tomb, or of dying from the potion, were well founded. During the period in which the play is set, people's fear of being buried alive was legitimate, as comas and other physiological states could mimic death for a time. Although the play never says what the Friar's potion is, it is likely to be a very strong tranquilizer made from a local plant. Taking such a drug would be an enormous risk.

20 Reading Skill

Summarize

1. Have students review Juliet's entire soliloquy, beginning on p. 901, line 14.
2. **Ask** students to respond to the Reading Skill prompt: Summarize the fears that Juliet expresses in this soliloquy.

   Answer: She wonders what will happen if the potion doesn't work, and then she will have to go through with the wedding. What will happen if the Friar has deliberately made the potion strong enough to kill her and save himself? What if she wakes before Romeo arrives? That would be the worst. She would have to lie there in the tomb among the dead bodies. Tybalt lies there, his body still decaying. What if the spirits of the dead rise up, or she goes mad in the hideous place?

21 Critical Viewing

Possible response: The muted colors add to the sense of mystery and the dark possibilities of Juliet's plan.

22 Reading Check

Answer: Juliet faces her anxieties about taking the potion, and then she drinks it.

Fluency

Distribute copies of Juliet's soliloquy from pp. 901 and 903 to partners. Have listeners mark words with which readers struggle. Circulate to monitor students' fluency, then collect the marked-up pages. Review difficult words and passages, such as these:

- If students struggle to pronounce *subtly* in line 25 (p. 901), point out that the *b* is silent. Say the word aloud and have students echo.
- If students stumble over *methinks* in line 28 (p. 901), suggest that they read it as two words: *me* and *thinks*. When they can fluently pronounce the words separately, students can read the words as one.
- Encourage students to list any Shakespearean language they find difficult, such as *ere* in line 35 (p. 903), *fest'ring* in line 43 (p. 903), *alack* in line 45 (p. 903), *environèd* in line 50 (p. 903), and so on. Review each word to demonstrate correct pronunciation, and clarify meaning if necessary. Have students reread the lines with the correct pronunciation.

㉓ Critical Thinking

Interpret

1. Have students read Scene iv, which continues on p. 905. **Ask** what kinds of activities are taking place in this scene. What is the general mood?

   Answer: The Capulets are making food preparations for the wedding; servants who have been on watch are now ordered to bed; Lord and Lady Capulet are insulting each other; Capulet calls to the Nurse to wake Juliet. The general mood is one of excitement and good cheer.

2. **Ask** students to predict how the activities and mood in this household will change shortly.

   Possible response: When the Capulets find Juliet and believe she is dead, the preparations will begin for a funeral rather than a wedding. The mood will change from joy to sorrow.

㉔ Literary Analysis

Dramatic Irony

1. Have students read lines 16–21. **Ask** what the fellows who enter here are carrying.

   Answer: They are carrying spits and logs for the fire, and baskets.

2. **Ask** students what Capulet asks them to fetch. Why does Capulet tell them to ask Peter for help?

   Answer: He asks them to fetch drier logs. He tells them to ask Peter because he does not think they can figure out where to find drier logs.

3. **Ask** students the Literary Analysis question: Re-read lines 16–21. In what way does Capulet's pun in line 21 contribute to the mood of Scene iv?

   Possible response: Students may say that the pun adds to the general mood of good humor as the household prepares for the coming wedding feast.

Scene iv. Hall in Capulet's house.

[*Enter* LADY OF THE HOUSE *and* NURSE.]

LADY CAPULET. Hold, take these keys and fetch more spices,
nurse.

NURSE. They call for dates and quinces[1] in the pastry.[2]

[*Enter old* CAPULET.]

CAPULET. Come, stir, stir, stir! The second cock hath crowed,
The curfew bell hath rung, 'tis three o'clock.
Look to the baked meats, good Angelica;[3]
Spare not for cost.

NURSE. Go, you cotquean,[4] go,
Get you to bed! Faith, you'll be sick tomorrow
For this night's watching.[5]

CAPULET. No, not a whit. What, I have watched ere now
All night for lesser cause, and ne'er been sick.

LADY CAPULET. Ay, you have been a mouse hunt[6] in your time;
But I will watch you from such watching now.
[*Exit* LADY *and* NURSE.]

㉓

CAPULET. A jealous hood,[7] a jealous hood!

[*Enter three or four* FELLOWS *with spits and logs and baskets.*]

Now, fellow,
What is there?

FIRST FELLOW. Things for the cook, sir; but I know not what.

CAPULET. Make haste, make haste. [*Exit* FIRST FELLOW.] Sirrah,
fetch drier logs.
Call Peter; he will show thee where they are.

㉔

SECOND FELLOW. I have a head, sir, that will find out logs
And never trouble Peter for the matter.

CAPULET. Mass,[8] and well said; a merry whoreson, ha!
Thou shalt be loggerhead.[9]
[*Exit* SECOND FELLOW, *with the others.*]
Good faith, 'tis day.
The County will be here with music straight,
For so he said he would. [*Play music.*]
I hear him near.
Nurse! Wife! What, ho! What, nurse, I say!

1. **quinces** golden, apple-shaped fruits.
2. **pastry** baking room.
3. **Angelica** This is probably the Nurse's name.
4. **cotquean** (kat′ kwēn′) man who does housework.
5. **watching** staying awake.
6. **mouse hunt** woman chaser.
7. **jealous hood** jealousy.
8. **Mass** by the Mass (an oath).
9. **loggerhead** blockhead.

Literary Analysis
Dramatic Irony Reread lines 16–21. In what way does Capulet's pun in line 21 contribute to the mood of Scene iv?

Think Aloud

Vocabulary: Using Context
Direct students' attention to the word *lamentable* on p. 905, line 17. Using a think-aloud process, model how to use context to infer the meaning of an unknown word. Say to students:

> In this line, the word *lamentable* is used to describe the day as the Nurse views it. We know from Scene iii that Juliet has drunk a potion that makes her appear dead. Lines 14–16 suggest that her appearance of death is convincing, and that the Nurse is upset. This suggests that *lamentable* means "sad" in some way, as Juliet's death would create a sad day. Lady Capulet's response in lines 19–21 further confirms this, as she is clearly also very upset. I think that *lamentable* means "sad and upsetting."

[*Enter* NURSE.]

23 Go waken Juliet; go and trim her up.
I'll go and chat with Paris. Hie, make haste,
Make haste! The bridegroom he is come already:
Make haste, I say. [*Exit.*]

Scene v. Juliet's chamber.

NURSE. Mistress! What, mistress! Juliet! Fast,[1] I warrant her, she.
Why, lamb! Why, lady! Fie, you slugabed.[2]
Why, love, I say! Madam; Sweetheart! Why, bride!
What, not a word? You take your pennyworths now;
Sleep for a week; for the next night, I warrant,
The County Paris hath set up his rest
That you shall rest but little. God forgive me!
25 Marry, and amen. How sound is she asleep!
I needs must wake her. Madam, madam, madam!
Ay, let the County take you in your bed;
He'll fright you up, i' faith. Will it not be?
[*Draws aside the curtains.*]
What, dressed, and in your clothes, and down again?[3]
I must needs wake you. Lady! Lady! Lady!
Alas, alas! Help, help! My lady's dead!
O weraday that ever I was born!
Some aqua vitae, ho! My lord! My lady!

[*Enter* MOTHER.]

LADY CAPULET. What noise is here?

NURSE. O lamentable day!

LADY CAPULET. What is the matter?

NURSE. Look, look! O heavy day!

LADY CAPULET. O me, O me! My child, my only life!
Revive, look up, or I will die with thee!
Help, help! Call help.

[*Enter* FATHER.]

CAPULET. For shame, bring Juliet forth; her lord is come.

NURSE. She's dead, deceased; she's dead, alack the day!

LADY CAPULET. Alack the day, she's dead, she's dead, she's dead!

1. **Fast** fast asleep.
2. **slugabed** sleepyhead.
3. **down again** back in bed.

Literary Analysis
Dramatic Irony In what way does the Nurse's carefree chatter add to the irony of the scene?

26 What does the Nurse find when she draws aside the curtains in Juliet's chamber?

25 Literary Analysis

Dramatic Irony

1. Read lines 1–16 aloud. **Ask** students why the Nurse is not immediately concerned when she cannot wake Juliet.

   Answer: The Nurse thinks Juliet is too deeply asleep to awaken easily.

2. **Ask** students to respond to the Literary Analysis question: In what way does the Nurse's carefree chatter add to the irony of the scene?

   Possible response: The audience knows that Juliet is not going to wake up and that the Nurse's teasing banter will soon turn to shock and grief.

3. **Ask** students to describe how Lady Capulet reacts when she first sees Juliet.

   Answer: She calls for help to revive Juliet.

4. **Ask** students what is ironic about the Capulets' behavior in this scene.

   Answer: Readers and audience know that Juliet is not actually dead.

26 Reading Check

Answer: She finds Juliet in bed, presumably dead.

Differentiated Instruction for Universal Access

Strategy for Less Proficient Readers

Have students refer to the silly conversation in lines 13–25 (p. 904), which is an example of *comic relief.* Note that this scene follows Juliet's intense soliloquy in Scene iii, and precedes the discovery of Juliet's apparently lifeless body in Scene v. Review the events and emotions of Scene iii, and have students visualize Juliet's anxieties. Then, explain that lines 13–25 in Scene iv offer a chance to recover. Scene iv also creates an air of suspense about what will happen when Juliet is discovered.

Support for English Learners

Students may be confused by the Nurse's repeated use of the word *why* in the opening of this scene. Point out that the repetition of the word *why* emphasizes the number of times the Nurse struggles to wake Juliet. Read Scene v, lines 1–10, aloud for students, modeling how the Nurse uses the word. Point out that the word itself suggests the meaning, "Why won't you wake up, girl?!" or words to that effect.

27 Literary Analysis

Dramatic Irony

1. Refer students to the bracketed passage. **Ask** students why the Friar has come to the Capulets' home.

   Answer: He has come to marry Juliet and Paris.

2. Have students read line 38. **Ask** the Literary Analysis question: In what way does the Friar's question add to the dramatic irony of the scene?

   Possible response: The Friar knows that everyone will believe that Juliet is dead, and he will be escorting her to the church for burial, not for a wedding.

3. **Ask** students to what Lord Capulet compares death in lines 36–39.

   Answer: Capulet compares Death to Juliet's bridegroom, Capulet's son-in-law, and Capulet's heir. He says that Death will be left with everything when Capulet dies.

4. **Ask** students how Paris' words in lines 41–42 contribute to the dramatic irony.

   Answer: Paris has come to the Capulets looking forward to seeing Juliet on their wedding day. Now he sees her dead, or so he thinks.

28 Literary Analysis

Dramatic Irony

1. Read lines 43–64 aloud. Point out that in the first and second lines of each of the speeches by Lady Capulet, Paris, and Capulet in this passage, the character uses a long series of adjectives to describe the day or the event. Nurse also uses a series of laments, although her vocabulary is more limited than the other three characters.

2. **Ask** students how these series of adjectives affect the reader or audience.

   Answer: The adjectives reinforce the sense of lamenting and the grief that the characters have for Juliet.

CAPULET. Ha! Let me see her. Out alas! She's cold,
Her blood is settled, and her joints are stiff;
Life and these lips have long been separated.
Death lies on her like an untimely frost
Upon the sweetest flower of all the field.

NURSE. O lamentable day!

LADY CAPULET. O woeful time!

CAPULET. Death, that hath ta'en her hence to make me wail,
Ties up my tongue and will not let me speak.

[*Enter* FRIAR LAWRENCE *and the* COUNTY PARIS, *with* MUSICIANS.]

27 Literary Analysis
Dramatic Irony In what way does the Friar's question add to the dramatic irony of the scene?

FRIAR. Come, is the bride ready to go to church?

CAPULET. Ready to go, but never to return.
O son, the night before thy wedding day
Hath Death lain with thy wife. There she lies,
Flower as she was, deflowerèd by him.
Death is my son-in-law, Death is my heir;
My daughter he hath wedded. I will die
And leave him all. Life, living, all is Death's.

PARIS. Have I thought, love, to see this morning's face,
And doth it give me such a sight as this?

LADY CAPULET. Accursed, unhappy, wretched, hateful day!
Most miserable hour that e'er time saw
In lasting labor of his pilgrimage!
But one, poor one, one poor and loving child,
But one thing to rejoice and solace[4] in,
And cruel Death hath catched it from my sight.

NURSE. O woe! O woeful, woeful, woeful day!
Most lamentable day, most woeful day
That ever ever I did yet behold!
O day, O day, O day! O hateful day!
Never was seen so black a day as this.
O woeful day! O woeful day!

28

PARIS. Beguiled,[5] divorcèd, wrongèd, spited, slain!
Most detestable Death, by thee beguiled,
By cruel, cruel thee quite overthrown.
O love! O life!—not life, but love in death!

CAPULET. Despised, distressèd, hated, martyred, killed!
Uncomfortable[6] time, why cam'st thou now
To murder, murder our solemnity?[7]

4. **solace** find comfort.
5. **Beguiled** cheated.
6. **Uncomfortable** painful, upsetting.
7. **solemnity** solemn rites.

Vocabulary Development

CCSS Language 6

Synonyms

Refer students to lines 49–64 on pp. 906–907. Point out the many adjectives that the characters use to describe their grief at what they believe is Juliet's death.

Have students use a dictionary or thesaurus to find a synonym for three of these adjectives. Then, have them imagine they are one of the characters in this passage and use these synonyms in three sentences describing their grief for Juliet.

Help students get started by giving them this example:

A synonym for *woeful* is *sorrowful*. This is the most *sorrowful* day of my life; my dear child is dead.

LITERATURE IN CONTEXT

Culture Connection

Rosemary

When the Capulets discover Juliet apparently dead, the Friar advises, "Dry up your tears and stick your rosemary / On this fair corse." Rosemary is an evergreen herb that traditionally signifies remembrance, loyalty, and love. Shakespeare often included references to herbs in his plays for symbolic purposes, and rosemary is one herb that turned up often in his works. *Hamlet, King Lear, The Winter's Tale,* and *Pericles* all include references to rosemary as a symbol of remembrance.

Connect to the Literature

Why do you think the Friar tells the Capulets to lay a sprig of rosemary on Juliet's body?

O child, O child! My soul, and not my child!
Dead art thou—alack, my child is dead,
And with my child my joys are burièd!

FRIAR. Peace, ho, for shame! Confusion's cure lives not
In these confusions.[8] Heaven and yourself
Had part in this fair maid—now heaven hath all,
And all the better is it for the maid.
Your part in her you could not keep from death,
But heaven keeps his part in eternal life.
The most you sought was her promotion,
For 'twas your heaven she should be advanced;
And weep ye now, seeing she is advanced
Above the clouds, as high as heaven itself?
O, in this love, you love your child so ill
That you run mad, seeing that she is well.[9]
She's not well married that lives married long,
But she's best married that dies married young.
Dry up your tears and stick your rosemary[10]
On this fair corse, and, as the custom is,
And in her best array bear her to church:
For though fond nature[11] bids us all lament,
Yet nature's tears are reason's merriment.[12]

8. **Confusion's . . . confusions** The remedy for this calamity is not to be found in these outcries.
9. **well** blessed in heaven.
10. **rosemary** evergreen herb signifying love and remembrance.
11. **fond nature** mistake-prone human nature.
12. **Yet . . . merriment** While human nature causes us to weep for Juliet, reason should cause us to be happy (since she is in heaven).

30 Reading Check

What does the Friar recommend that the Capulets do when they discover Juliet and believe she is dead?

29 Literature in Context

Culture Connection

Rosemary is popular today for its many uses. It is still considered an emblem of remembrance. Its fragrant stems are used in floral arrangements. Dried branches of rosemary are made into fragrant wreaths at Christmastime. The oil of the plant is used in toiletries and in aromatherapy products.

Rosemary is also a popular herb in cooking. The leaves—dried or fresh—are used in soups, stews, tomatoes and tomato sauces, and in a variety of recipes for meats and vegetables.

Connect to the Literature Have students read the Literature in Context feature, and present the additional background information above. Remind students of rosemary's fragrance. Then, **ask** the Connect to the Literature question: Why do you think the Friar tells the Capulets to lay a sprig of rosemary on Juliet's body?

Possible response: The Friar suggests rosemary as an emblem of remembrance and love for Juliet. The Friar may also be thinking of the fragrant properties of rosemary, which would be comforting to Juliet when she awoke in the damp, dark tomb.

30 Reading Check

Answer: He tells them to dry their tears, place rosemary on her body, and carry her to church.

Differentiated Instruction for Universal Access

Strategy for Advanced Readers

Discuss with students Friar Lawrence's role in *The Tragedy of Romeo and Juliet*. Point out that literary critics see Friar Lawrence in basically two opposing ways. In one view, the Friar is a surrogate father figure to Romeo because he aids and counsels the young man. In the other view, the Friar is a well-meaning but incompetent counselor who leads Romeo and Juliet to their deaths.

Have students work in small groups to discuss these characterizations of Friar Lawrence:

- a busybody who knows nothing about life or love
- a well-meaning but incompetent counselor
- a wise and sage counselor whose plans go awry because of circumstances beyond his control

Have students report the results of their discussion to the class.

31 Connecting to the Big Question

1. Point out that major life rituals can be more similar to one another than different. Discuss aspects of weddings and funerals that are the same or different.
2. Have students read lines 84–90. **Ask:** What comparison and contrast is Capulet making?
   Answer: He's comparing and contrasting the planned wedding between Juliet and Paris with the funeral for Juliet.
3. **Ask:** In what way do the differences between these events define the events and those attending? In what way are the differences unimportant?
   Possible response: The differences define the mood of the events and the emotional state of those attending. However, many of the same people would attend both events, so in some ways the differences are unimportant.

32 Literary Analysis

Dramatic Irony

Ask students the Literary Analysis question: In what way does the dramatic irony of the Friar's words heighten the play's suspense?

Possible response: The Friar wants to hurry them to the burial while Juliet is still in her coma-like state, but he claims he does not want them to cross the fates again. This heightens the suspense, as the audience sees that the plan has worked so far and wonders how everything will work once Juliet awakes.

- **Monitor Progress:** Use students' answers to these questions to assess their understanding of dramatic irony.
- **Reteach:** If students are having difficulty with the concept of dramatic irony, review p. 893. In this scene, everyone but the Friar believes Juliet is dead. Only the reader and the Friar know the true cause of her death-like state.

CAPULET. All things that we ordainèd festival[13]
Turn from their office to black funeral—
Our instruments to melancholy bells,
31 Our wedding cheer to a sad burial feast;
Our solemn hymns to sullen dirges[14] change;
Our bridal flowers serve for a buried corse;
And all things change them to the contrary.

FRIAR. Sir, go you in; and, madam, go with him;
And go, Sir Paris. Everyone prepare
32 To follow this fair corse unto her grave.
The heavens do low'r[15] upon you for some ill;
Move them no more by crossing their high will.

[*Exit, casting rosemary on her and shutting the curtains. The* NURSE *and* MUSICIANS *remain.*]

FIRST MUSICIAN. Faith, we may put up our pipes and be gone.

NURSE. Honest good fellows, ah, put up, put up!
For well you know this is a pitiful case.[16] [*Exit.*]

FIRST MUSICIAN. Ay, by my troth, the case may be amended.

[*Enter* PETER.]

PETER. Musicians, O, musicians, "Heart's ease," "Heart's ease"!
O, and you will have me live, play "Heart's ease."

FIRST MUSICIAN. Why "Heart's ease"?

33 **PETER.** O, musicians, because my heart itself plays "My heart is full."
O, play me some merry dump[17] to comfort me.

FIRST MUSICIAN. Not a dump we! 'Tis no time to play now.

PETER. You will not then?

FIRST MUSICIAN. No.

PETER. I will then give it you soundly.

FIRST MUSICIAN. What will you give us?

PETER. No money, on my faith, but the gleek.[18] I will give you[19] the minstrel.[20]

Literary Analysis
Dramatic Irony In what way does the dramatic irony of the Friar's words heighten the play's suspense?

13. **ordainèd festival** planned to be part of a celebration.
14. **dirges** funeral hymns.
15. **low'r** frown.
16. **case** situation; instrument case.
17. **dump** sad tune.
18. **gleek** scornful speech.
19. **give you** call you.
20. **minstrel** a contemptuous term (as opposed to "musician").

Vocabulary Development

Vocabulary Knowledge Rating

When students have completed reading and discussing Act IV of *The Tragedy of Romeo and Juliet*, have them take out their **Vocabulary Knowledge Rating Chart** for this act. Read the words aloud once more and have students rate their knowledge of the words again in the After Reading column. Clarify any words that are still problematic. Have students write their own definition and example or sentence in the appropriate column. Then, have students complete the Vocabulary Practice activities at the end of the selection. Encourage students to use the words in further discussion and written work about this selection. Remind them that they will be accountable for these words on the **Selection Test, *Unit 5 Resources*,** pp. 89–91 or 92–94.

FIRST MUSICIAN. Then will I give you the serving-creature.

PETER. Then will I lay the serving-creature's dagger on your pate.
I will carry no crotchets.[21] I'll *re* you, I'll *fa* you. Do you note me?
33

FIRST MUSICIAN. And you *re* us and *fa* us, you note us.

SECOND MUSICIAN. Pray you put up your dagger, and put out your wit.
Then have at you with my wit!

PETER. I will dry-beat you with an iron wit, and put up my iron dagger. Answer me like men.
"When griping grief the heart doth wound,
And doleful dumps the mind oppress,
34 Then music with her silver sound"—
35 Why "silver sound"? Why "music with her silver sound"?
What say you, Simon Catling?

FIRST MUSICIAN. Marry, sir, because silver hath a sweet sound.

PETER. Pretty! What say you, Hugh Rebeck?

21. **crotchets** whims; quarter notes.

33 Critical Thinking

Make Judgments

1. Have students read lines 96–117, which begin on p. 908. **Ask** students which characters are left on stage when the Capulets, the Friar, Paris, and the Nurse exit.
   Answer: The musicians remain, and Peter enters immediately.
2. **Ask** students why they think Shakespeare chose to end Scene v with the bantering of the musicians.
   Possible response: The banter of the musicians provides comic relief from the high drama of Juliet's actions and her family's grief.

34 Background

Names

Shakespeare is having fun with the names of the musicians. The three musicians' names are based on musical terms. A *catling* is a lute string. A *rebeck* is a kind of violin. A *soundpost* is part of a violin.

Concept Connector

Activating Prior Knowledge

Have students return to the ideas they generated in Activating Prior Knowledge on p. 894. Ask students if their ideas have changed.

Reading Skill Graphic Organizer

Have students review the graphic organizers they completed to summarize lines of dialogue. Show students **Reading Skill Graphic Organizer A** (*Graphic Organizer Transparencies,* p.159) as an example. Then, have students share the graphic organizers they did and the summaries they completed.

㉟ Literary Analysis

Dramatic Irony

1. **Ask** students the Literary Analysis question: What kind of mood does the pun in line 127 help to create in this scene?
2. **Answer:** The pun helps to create a lighthearted mood, in contrast to the somber mood earlier in the scene.

ASSESS

Answers

Critical Thinking

Before students respond, you may wish to have them write a brief objective summary of the selection. As they answer the questions below, remind them to support their answers with evidence from the text.

1. (a) Friar Lawrence will give Juliet a potion to make her comatose. She will be placed in the tomb. Friar Lawrence will bring Romeo to the tomb, and they will be there when Juliet wakes. Romeo will then take Juliet to Mantua. (b) **Possible response:** Juliet trusts the Friar because he is older and a clergyman.
2. (a) The potion may not work; it may kill her; she may wake up before Romeo comes. (b) The soliloquy reveals that Juliet is fully aware of the grave risks she is undertaking, yet is brave enough to proceed.
3. (a) **Possible responses:** It is a courageous act because it is her only way to be with Romeo again. It is a foolish act because she is relying on an unknown potion and the actions of others to save her. (b) Juliet has developed; she is no longer a girl, but a woman willing to risk danger for her love.
4. (a) Juliet believes love only occurs with the right person, while her parents believe love should develop between people of the same social status. (b) **Possible response:** They reveal that she is willing to act on her principles.

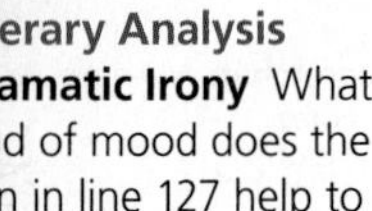

Literary Analysis Dramatic Irony What kind of mood does the pun in line 127 help to create in this scene?

22. cry you mercy beg your pardon.

SECOND MUSICIAN. I say "silver sound" because musicians sound for silver.

PETER. Pretty too! What say you, James Soundpost?

THIRD MUSICIAN. Faith, I know not what to say.

PETER. O, I cry you mercy,[22] you are the singer. I will say for you. It is "music with her silver sound" because musicians have no gold for sounding.

"Then music with her silver sound
With speedy help doth lend redress." [*Exit.*]

FIRST MUSICIAN. What a pestilent knave is this same!

SECOND MUSICIAN. Hang him, Jack! Come, we'll in here, tarry for the mourners, and stay dinner. [*Exit with others.*]

Critical Thinking

Cite textual evidence to support your responses.

1. **Key Ideas and Details (a)** What is Friar Lawrence's plan for Juliet? **(b) Analyze:** Why do you think Juliet trusts the Friar? Explain using details from the text.
2. **Key Ideas and Details (a)** What three fears does Juliet reveal in her Act IV, Scene iii, soliloquy? **(b) Interpret:** What does the soliloquy reveal about her personality? Explain your response.
3. **Integration of Knowledge and Ideas (a) Evaluate:** Do you think drinking the potion is a brave act or a foolish act? Explain. **(b) Draw Conclusions:** How has Juliet changed in the course of the play? Give details to explain.
4. **Integration of Knowledge and Ideas (a)** In what way do Juliet's ideas about love differ from her parents' ideas? **(b)** What do Juliet's rebellious actions reveal about her? ***[Connect to the Big Question: Do our differences define us?]***

Assessment Resources

Unit 5 Resources

L1 L2 EL **Selection Test A**, pp. 89–91. Administer Test A to less advanced readers.

L3 L4 EL **Selection Test B**, pp. 92–94. Administer Test B to on-level and more advanced students.

L3 L4 **Open-Book Test**, pp. 86–88. As an alternative, give the Open-Book Test.

All **Customizable Test Bank**

All **Self-tests**
Students may prepare for the **Selection Test** by taking the **Self-test** online.

All assessment resources are available at **www.PHLitOnline.com.**

After You Read

The Tragedy of Romeo and Juliet, Act IV

Literary Analysis: Dramatic Irony

1. **Craft and Structure** In what way is Juliet's encounter with Paris in Friar Lawrence's cell an instance of **dramatic irony?**
2. **Craft and Structure** Complete a chart like the one shown to demonstrate why Capulet's statement in Act IV, Scene iv, line 25, is dramatic irony.

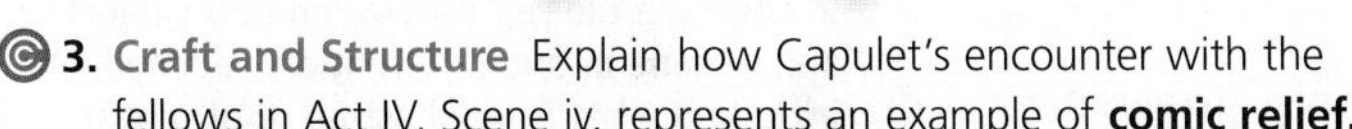

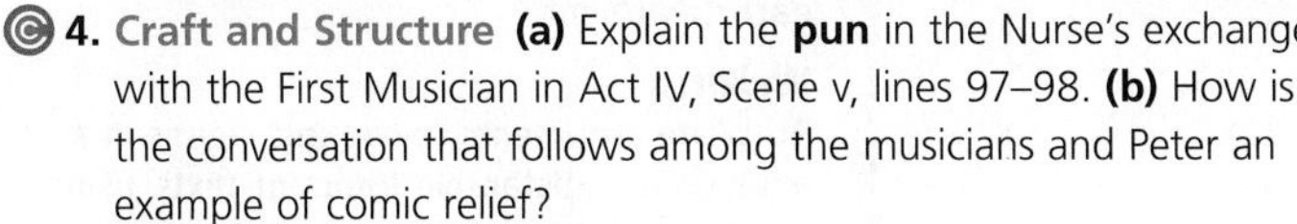

3. **Craft and Structure** Explain how Capulet's encounter with the fellows in Act IV, Scene iv, represents an example of **comic relief.**
4. **Craft and Structure** **(a)** Explain the **pun** in the Nurse's exchange with the First Musician in Act IV, Scene v, lines 97–98. **(b)** How is the conversation that follows among the musicians and Peter an example of comic relief?

Reading Skill: Summarize

5. **(a) Summarize** lines 50–59 of Juliet's monologue to Friar Lawrence in Act IV, Scene i. **(b)** Then, summarize all of Act IV. Break long sentences into smaller ones to clarify speakers' thoughts.

Vocabulary

Acquisition and Use Indicate whether each of the following statements is *True* or *False*. Revise the sentences that are false to make them true.

1. Clowns make children laugh by appearing *pensive*.
2. If you have been *enjoined* to attend an event, you should not go.
3. A *wayward* person would probably dislike orders.
4. If you were in a *dismal* mood, you would be good company.
5. A *loathsome* meal is not likely to be eaten quickly.
6. A *vial* would be a good container for a cough syrup.

Word Study Use the context of the sentences and what you know about the **Latin prefix *en-*** to explain your answer to each question.

1. Would a terrible insult *enrage* you?
2. What happens when someone *enlists* in the armed forces?

Word Study

The **Latin prefix *en-*** means "in," "into," "within."

Apply It Explain how the prefix *en-* contributes to the meanings of these words. Consult a dictionary if necessary.

encage
entrap
entreat

ASSESS/EXTEND

Answers

Literary Analysis

1. She leads him to believe that she is looking forward to their wedding. She and the audience know that she is already married and has no intention of marrying him.
2. **What Character Thinks:** Capulet thinks that Juliet is in her bed asleep. **What Audience Knows:** The audience knows that Juliet is in a comatose state and cannot be awakened.

   For other sample answers, see ***Graphic Organizer Transparencies*, Literary Analysis Graphic Organizer A**, p. 161, and the **Additional Answers** section.
3. The humorous scene breaks the intensity of the act because it follows Juliet's intense soliloquy and precedes the discovery of her body.
4. (a) The pun is on the word *case*, in which the Nurse tells the musician that this is a pitiful case, meaning a sad situation, and the word also refers to the musician's instrument case. (b) The scene relieves the intensity of the previous scene in which Juliet is believed dead, and it sets up the suspense for Act V.

Reading Skill

5. (a) Juliet tells the Friar that if he cannot help her, then she will kill herself. Therefore, he must tell her something immediately or she will die. (b) **Possible response:** Friar Lawrence speaks with Paris about his marriage to Juliet; Juliet expresses again that she does not want to marry Paris; the Friar gives Juliet a sleeping potion to drink before her wedding to Paris and says once she appears to be dead, he will bring her to Romeo; the Capulets prepare for the wedding; Juliet "agrees" to wed Paris; Juliet drinks the sleeping potion; Juliet is found "dead"; the Nurse, Paris, and the Capulets mourn.

Vocabulary

Acquisition and Use

Sample answers:

1. False. Clowns make children laugh by appearing happy, not pensive.
2. False. If you have been enjoined to attend an event, you've been ordered to go.
3. True.
4. False. If you were in a dismal mood, you'd be bad company.
5. True.
6. True.

Word Study

Sample answers:

1. Yes, the prefix *en-* means "in, into, within," and *enrage* means "put into a rage." A terrible insult would put me into a rage.
2. The prefix *en-* means "in, into, within," and *enlist* means "to enroll or enter into." When someone *enlists* in the armed forces, he or she joins, or enters into, a branch of the military.

Word Study: Apply It

Sample answers: To *encage* is to "keep in a cage." To *entrap* is "to catch or put something in a trap." To *entreat* means to "beg or ask with seriousness in your manner."

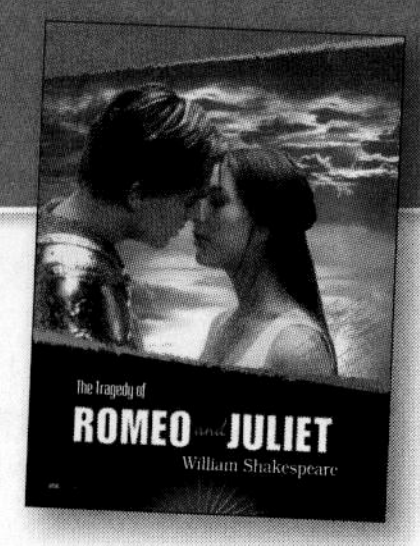

✓ The Tragedy of Romeo and Juliet, Act V
Lesson Pacing Guide

DAY 1 Preteach

- Administer the Reading and Vocabulary Warm-ups (*Unit 5 Resources*, pp. 95–98) as necessary.
- Introduce the Reading Skill: Summarize.
- Introduce the Literary Analysis concept: Tragedy and Motive.
- Distribute copies of the appropriate graphic organizer for the Reading Skill (*Graphic Organizer Transparencies*, pp. 163–164).
- Distribute copies of the appropriate graphic organizer for Literary Analysis (*Graphic Organizer Transparencies*, pp. 165–166).
- Teach the selection vocabulary.
- Introduce the Word Study skill.

DAYS 2–3 Preteach/Teach

- Build background with the Background feature.
- Develop thematic vocabulary and thematic thinking with Writing About the Big Question.
- Prepare students to read with the Activating Prior Knowledge activities (TE).
- Informally monitor comprehension while students read.
- Use the Reading Check questions to confirm comprehension.
- Develop students' ability to summarize, using the Reading Skill questions.
- Develop students' understanding of tragedy and motive, using the Literary Analysis questions.
- Reinforce vocabulary with the Vocabulary notes.
- Reinforce unit focus standards using the Spiral Review prompts.

DAY 4 Assess

- Assess students' comprehension and mastery of the skills by having them answer the Critical Thinking, Reading Skill, and Literary Analysis questions.
- Have students complete the Vocabulary Practice activities.
- Have students complete the Word Study activities.

DAY 5 Extend/Assess

- Have students complete the Conventions lesson.
- Have students complete the Research and Technology activity, a film review, p. 935. (You may assign as homework.)
- Extend learning by having students complete the Listening and Speaking activity, a mock trial, p. 934. As an alternative, assign them "Staying Connected" in *Reality Central*.
- Administer Selection Test A or B (*Unit 5 Resources*, pp. 111–116).

Common Core State Standards

Reading Literature
2. Determine a theme or central idea of a text; provide an objective summary of the text.
7. Analyze the representation of a subject or a key scene in two different artistic mediums, including what is emphasized or absent in each treatment.

Writing
1. Write arguments to support claims in an analysis of substantive topics or texts, using valid reasoning and relevant and sufficient evidence.
1.c. Use words, phrases, and clauses to link the major sections of the text, create cohesion, and clarify the relationships between claim(s) and reasons, between reasons and evidence, and between claim(s) and counterclaims.
4. Produce clear and coherent writing in which the development, organization, and style are appropriate to task, purpose, and audience.

Speaking and Listening
1. Initiate and participate effectively in a range of collaborative discussions.
4. Present information, findings, and supporting evidence clearly, concisely, and logically such that listeners can follow the line of reasoning.

Language 1.b. Use various types of phrases and clauses to convey specific meanings and add variety and interest to writing or presentations.

Additional Standards Practice
***Common Core Companion**, pp. 28–29*

Daily Block Scheduling
Each day in this Lesson Pacing Guide represents a 40–50 minute period. Teachers using block scheduling may combine days to revise pacing. In addition, teachers may differentiate and support core instruction by integrating components for extended and intensive support as students require. See the Guide to Selected Leveled Resources (facing page).

Guide to Selected Leveled Resources

RTI Tier 1 (students performing on level)			The Tragedy of Romeo and Juliet, Act V
Warm Up	Whole class instruction; Group work	**Practice, model,** and **monitor** fluency, working **with the whole class** or **in groups.**	**Vocabulary** and **Reading Warm-ups B,** ***Unit 5 Resources,*** pp. 95–96, 98
Comprehension/Skills	Whole class instruction; Independent work	**Support** and **monitor** comprehension and skills development, having students complete the activities, graphic organizers, and interactive prompts **independently** or **as a class.**	• ***Reader's Notebook,*** adapted instruction and full selection EL ***Reader's Notebook: English Learner's Version,*** adapted instruction and adapted selection • **Reading Skill Graphic Organizer B,** ***Graphic Organizer Transparencies,*** p. 164 • **Literary Analysis Graphic Organizer B,** ***Graphic Organizer Transparencies,*** p. 166
Monitor Progress	A	**Monitor** student progress with the differentiated curriculum-based assessment in the *Unit Resources.*	• **Selection Test B,** ***Unit 5 Resources,*** pp. 114–116 • **Open-Book Test,** ***Unit 5 Resources,*** pp. 108–110
Assess/ Screen	A	**Assess** student progress using Benchmark Test 9.	• **Benchmark Test 9,** ***Unit 5 Resources,*** pp. 136–141

RTI Tier 2 (students requiring intervention)			The Tragedy of Romeo and Juliet, Act V
Warm Up	Whole class instruction; Group work	**Practice, model,** and **monitor** fluency **in groups** or **with individuals.**	• **Vocabulary and Reading Warm-ups A,** ***Unit 5 Resources,*** pp. 95–98 • ***Reality Central,*** "Staying Connected" • ***Hear It!*** **Audio CD (adapted text)**
Comprehension/Skills	Whole class instruction; Independent work	• **Support** and **monitor** comprehension and skills development, working **in small groups** or **with individuals.** • **Pair** students with more advanced peers and have them complete the writing activity in the *Real-World Writing Journal.* • As students complete the selection in the appropriate version of the *Reader's Notebook,* **monitor** comprehension frequently with group questions and individual instruction. • **Model** strategies while guiding students in completing the activities and prompts in the *Reader's Notebook,* as well as the graphic organizers. • **Practice** skills and **monitor** mastery with the *Reading Kit* worksheets.	• ***Real-World Writing Journal,*** Lesson 2, pp. 142–145 • ***Reader's Notebook: Adapted Version,*** adapted instruction and adapted selection EL ***Reader's Notebook: English Learner's Version,*** adapted instruction and adapted selection • **Reading Skill Graphic Organizer A,** ***Graphic Organizer Transparencies,*** p. 163 • **Literary Analysis Graphic Organizer A,** ***Graphic Organizer Transparencies,*** p. 165 • **Reading Kit,** Practice worksheets, pp. 210, 214, 218, 220, 222
Monitor Progress	A	**Monitor** student progress with the differentiated curriculum-based assessment in the *Unit Resources* and in the *Reading Kit.*	• **Selection Test A,** ***Unit 5 Resources,*** pp. 111–113 • **Reading Kit,** Assess worksheets pp. 211, 215, 219, 221, 223
Assess/ Screen	A	**Assess** student progress using Benchmark Test 9.	• **Benchmark Test 9,** ***Unit 5 Resources,*** pp. 136–141

TIER 3 Tier 3 intervention may require consultation with the student's special-education or dyslexia specialist. For additional support, see the Tier 2 activities and resources listed above.

One-on-one teaching **Group work** **Whole class instruction** **Independent work** **A Assessment**

For a complete guide to selection support, including support for Advanced students, see the Overview of Resources in the frontmatter.

The Tragedy of Romeo and Juliet, Act V

RESOURCES FOR:

- L1 Special-Needs Students
- L2 Below-Level Students (Tier 2)
- L3 On-Level Students (Tier 1)
- L4 Advanced Students (Tier 1)
- EL English Learners
- All All Students

Vocabulary/Fluency/Prior Knowledge

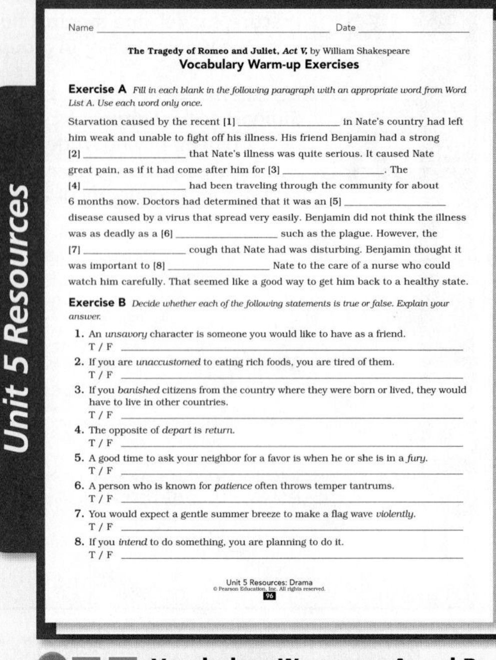

Unit 5 Resources

Name ______________________ Date ______________

The Tragedy of Romeo and Juliet, ***Act V,*** by William Shakespeare
Vocabulary Warm-up Exercises

Exercise A *Fill in each blank in the following paragraph with an appropriate word from Word List A. Use each word only once.*

Starvation caused by the recent [1] ______________ in Nate's country had left him weak and unable to fight off his illness. His friend Benjamin had a strong [2] ______________ that Nate's illness was quite serious. It caused Nate great pain, as if it had come after him for [3] ______________. The [4] ______________ had been traveling through the community for about 6 months now. Doctors had determined that it was an [5] ______________ disease caused by a virus that spread very easily. Benjamin did not think the illness was as deadly as a [6] ______________ such as the plague. However, the [7] ______________ cough that Nate had was disturbing. Benjamin thought it was important to [8] ______________ Nate to the care of a nurse who could watch him carefully. That seemed like a good way to get him back to a healthy state.

Exercise B *Decide whether each of the following statements is true or false. Explain your answer.*

1. An *unsavory* character is someone you would like to have as a friend.
   T / F ______________________
2. If you are *unaccustomed* to eating rich foods, you are tired of them.
   T / F ______________________
3. If you *banished* citizens from the country where they were born or lived, they would have to live in other countries.
   T / F ______________________
4. The opposite of *depart* is *return.*
   T / F ______________________
5. A good time to ask your neighbor for a favor is when he or she is in a *fury.*
   T / F ______________________
6. A person who is known for *patience* often throws temper tantrums.
   T / F ______________________
7. You would expect a gentle summer breeze to make a flag wave *violently.*
   T / F ______________________
8. If you *intend* to do something, you are planning to do it.
   T / F ______________________

Unit 5 Resources: Drama

96

EL L1 L2 **Vocabulary Warm-ups A and B,** pp. 95–96

Also available for this selection:

EL L1 L2 **Reading Warm-ups A and B,** pp. 97–98

All **Writing About the Big Question,** p. 99

All **Vocabulary Builder,** p. 102

Reader's Notebooks

Pre- and postreading pages, as well as the selection *The Tragedy of Romeo and Juliet,* Act V, appear in an interactive format in the *Reader's Notebooks.* Each *Notebook* is differentiated for a different group of learners. The selections in the Adapted and English Learner's versions are abridged.

L2 L3 ***Reader's Notebook***

L1 ***Reader's Notebook: Adapted Version***

EL ***Reader's Notebook: English Learner's Version***

EL ***Reader's Notebook: Spanish Version***

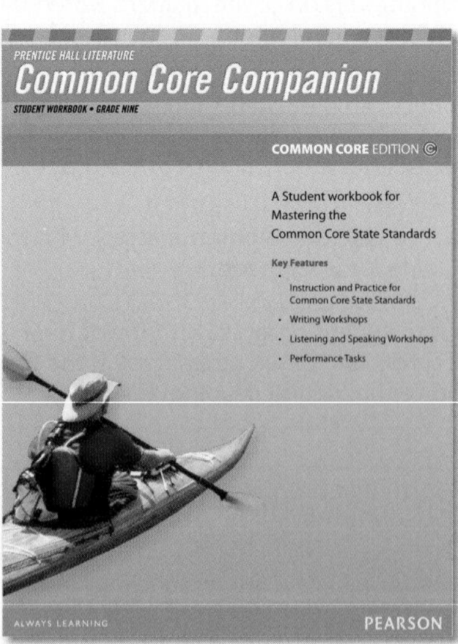

Common Core Companion

Additional instruction and practice for each Common Core State Standard

Selection Support

Graphic Organizer Transparencies

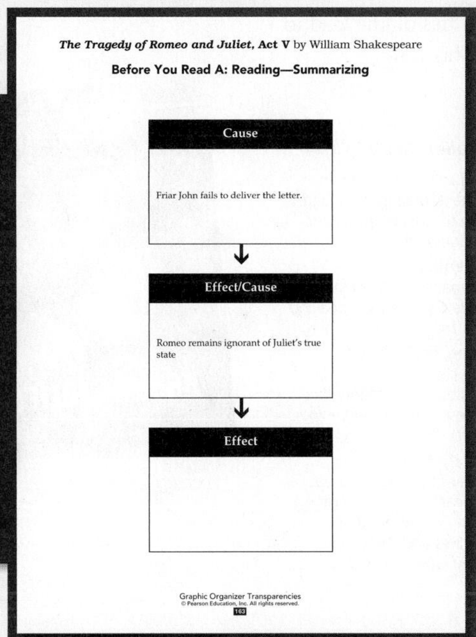

The Tragedy of Romeo and Juliet, **Act V** by William Shakespeare

Before You Read A: Reading—Summarizing

Cause
Friar John fails to deliver the letter.

↓

Effect/Cause
Romeo remains ignorant of Juliet's true state

↓

Effect

Graphic Organizer Transparencies
© Pearson Education, Inc. All rights reserved.
163

EL L1 L2 **Reading: Graphic Organizer A,** p. 163 (partially filled in)

Also available for this selection:

EL L3 **Reading: Graphic Organizer B,** p. 164

EL L1 L2 **Literary Analysis: Graphic Organizer A,** p. 165 (partially filled in)

EL L3 **Literary Analysis: Graphic Organizer B,** p. 166

Skills Development/Extension

Unit 5 Resources

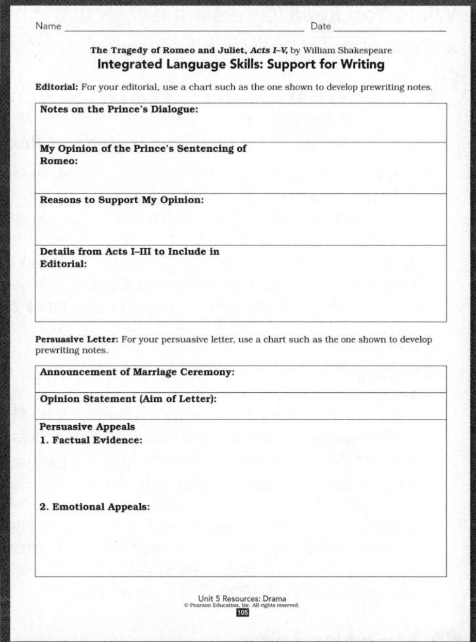

Name ____________ Date ____________

The Tragedy of Romeo and Juliet, *Acts I–V*, by William Shakespeare

Integrated Language Skills: Support for Writing

Editorial: For your editorial, use a chart such as the one shown to develop prewriting notes.

Notes on the Prince's Dialogue:
My Opinion of the Prince's Sentencing of Romeo:
Reasons to Support My Opinion:
Details from Acts I–III to Include in Editorial:

Persuasive Letter: For your persuasive letter, use a chart such as the one shown to develop prewriting notes.

Announcement of Marriage Ceremony:
Opinion Statement (Aim of Letter):
Persuasive Appeals **1. Factual Evidence:** **2. Emotional Appeals:**

Unit 5 Resources: Drama
© Pearson Education, Inc. All rights reserved.
105

EL L3 L4 **Support for Writing,** p. 105

Also available for this selection:

All **Reading: Summarize,** p. 101

All **Literary Analysis: Tragedy and Motive,** p. 100

L4 **Enrichment,** p. 103

EL L3 L4 **Grammar,** p. 104

L3 L4 **Support for Extend Your Learning,** p. 106

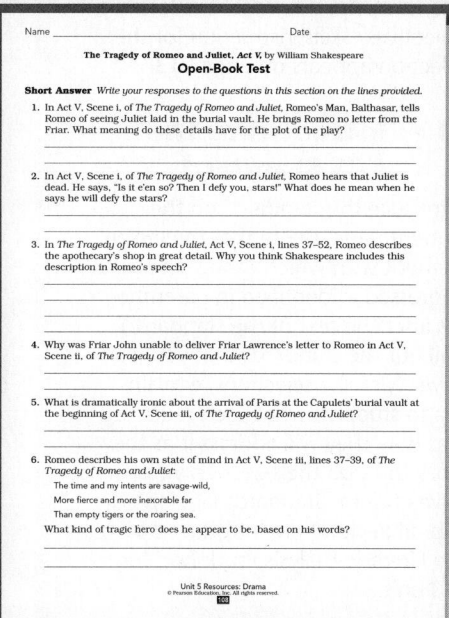

Assessment

Name ____________ Date ____________

The Tragedy of Romeo and Juliet, *Act V*, by William Shakespeare

Open-Book Test

Short Answer *Write your responses to the questions in this section on the lines provided.*

1. In Act V, Scene i, of *The Tragedy of Romeo and Juliet*, Romeo's Man, Balthasar, tells Romeo of seeing Juliet laid in the burial vault. He brings Romeo no letter from the Friar. What meaning do these details have for the plot of the play?
2. In Act V, Scene i, of *The Tragedy of Romeo and Juliet*, Romeo hears that Juliet is dead. He says, "Is it e'en so? Then I defy you, stars!" What does he mean when he says he will defy the stars?
3. In *The Tragedy of Romeo and Juliet*, Act V, Scene i, lines 37–52, Romeo describes the apothecary's shop in great detail. Why you think Shakespeare includes this description in Romeo's speech?
4. Why was Friar John unable to deliver Friar Lawrence's letter to Romeo in Act V, Scene ii, of *The Tragedy of Romeo and Juliet?*
5. What is dramatically ironic about the arrival of Paris at the Capulets' burial vault at the beginning of Act V, Scene iii, of *The Tragedy of Romeo and Juliet?*
6. Romeo describes his own state of mind in Act V, Scene iii, lines 37–39, of *The Tragedy of Romeo and Juliet:*

   The time and my intents are savage-wild,
   More fierce and more inexorable far
   Than empty tigers or the roaring sea.

   What kind of tragic hero does he appear to be, based on his words?

Unit 5 Resources: Drama
© Pearson Education, Inc. All rights reserved.
108

L3 L4 **Open-Book Test,** pp. 108–110

Also available for this selection:

EL L1 L2 **Selection Test A,** pp. 111–113

EL L3 L4 **Selection Test B,** pp. 114–116

PHLit Online!
www.PHLitOnline.com

- complete narrated selection text
- a thematically related video with writing prompt
- an interactive graphic organizer
- highlighting feature
- access to all student print resources, adapted to individual student needs
- Spanish and English summaries
- adapted selection translations in Spanish

Online Resources: All print materials are also available online.

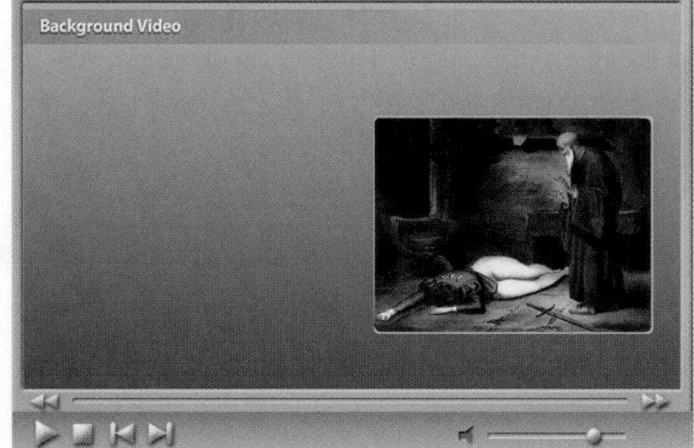

Background Video

Also available:

Get Connected! (thematic video with writing prompt)

All videos are available in Spanish.

Vocabulary Central (tools, activities, and songs for studying vocabulary)

Also available:

Writer's Journal (with graphics feature)

DIFFERENTIATE/PRETEACH

Leveled Texts

You may use *The Tragedy of Romeo and Juliet,* Act V to meet the lesson objectives. Skills instruction for the selection appears on page 913.

❶ Introducing the CCS Standards

Introduce the standards on the student page. (Note that the lesson element with which each standard is addressed is identified in parentheses after the text of the standard.) Call out the standards that you will cover with the selections, explaining to students what each requires and how they will address it as they work through the selection you have chosen. Standards labeled "Spiral Review" are introduced in the Literary Analysis Workshop for this unit.

❷ Vocabulary

1. Have students preview the selection vocabulary.
2. For each word, have students say the word aloud.
3. Then, use the word in a sentence that defines the word.
4. Finally, repeat your definitional sentence or a similar sentence with the word missing and have the class "fill in the blank" chorally. Here are some examples:

    To be haughty is to be arrogant. From her egotistical attitude and overconfident way of talking, it was clear that the woman was [students say "haughty"].

    A scourge is an instrument for inflicting punishment. When children are misbehaving, often parents take away privileges as a [students say "scourge"].

❸ Word Study

1. Introduce the skill, using the instruction in the box.
2. Using their knowledge of the Latin prefix, ask students for a *ambi-* word that means "both." *(ambidextrous)*

Before You Read The Tragedy of Romeo and Juliet, Act V

While You Read Consider the ways that differences in this drama lead to a tragic end. Then, decide if the events had to happen this way.

❶ Common Core State Standards

Meet these standards with ***The Tragedy of Romeo and Juliet,* Act V** (p. 914).

Reading Literature

2. Determine a theme or central idea of a text; provide an objective summary of the text. *(Reading Skill: Summarize)*

7. Analyze the representation of a subject or a key scene in two different artistic mediums, including what is emphasized or absent in each treatment. *(Research and Technology: Film Review)*

Writing

1. Write arguments to support claims in an analysis of substantive topics or texts, using valid reasoning and relevant and sufficient evidence. *(Writing: Persuasive Letter)*

1.c. Use words, phrases, and clauses to link the major sections of the text, create cohesion, and clarify the relationships between claim(s) and reasons, between reasons and evidence, and between claim(s) and counterclaims. *(Writing: Persuasive Letter)*

4. Produce clear and coherent writing in which the development, organization, and style are appropriate to task, purpose, and audience. *(Writing: Editorial)*

Speaking and Listening

1. Initiate and participate effectively in a range of collaborative discussions. *(Speaking and Listening: Mock Trial)*

4. Present information, findings, and supporting evidence clearly, concisely, and logically such that listeners can follow the line of reasoning. *(Research and Technology: Annotated Flowchart)*

Language

1.b. Use various types of phrases and clauses to convey specific meanings and add variety and interest to writing or presentations. *(Conventions: Participles and Participial Phrases; Gerunds and Gerund Phrases)*

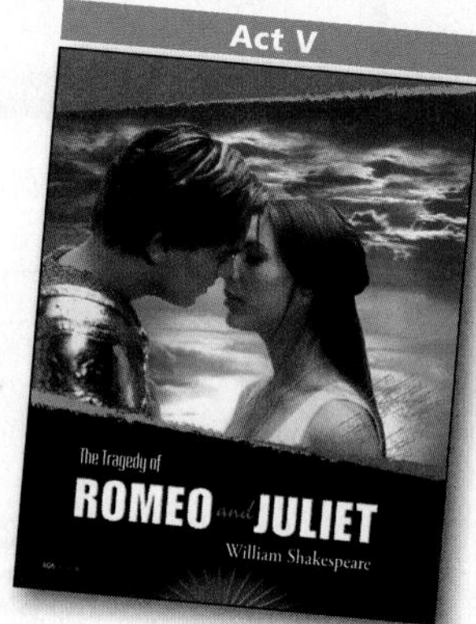

❷ Vocabulary

Read each word and its definition. Decide whether you know the word well, know it a little bit, or do not know it at all. After you read, see how your knowledge of each word has increased.

- **remnants** (rem′ nənts) *n.* what is left over; remainders (p. 917) ***The remnants of the house still stood after the fire.***
- **penury** (pen′ yo͞o rē) *n.* extreme poverty (p. 917) ***His choice was either to find work or to live in penury.*** penurious *adj.*
- **disperse** (di spʉrs′) *v.* to break up and scatter in all directions; spread about; distribute widely (p. 918) ***Our group will disperse flyers about the fundraiser in the mall.*** dispersal *n.* dispersion *n.* dispersible *adj.*
- **haughty** (hôt′ ē) *adj.* arrogant (p. 921) ***He acts haughty onstage but humble offstage.*** haughtily *adv.* haughtiness *n.*
- **ambiguities** (am′ bə gyo͞o′ ə tēz) *n.* statements or events whose meanings are unclear (p. 927) ***Voters were confused by the ambiguities in the candidate's speech.*** ambiguous *adj.* ambiguously *adv.*
- **scourge** (skʉrj) *n.* instrument for inflicting punishment (p. 929) ***Longer practices were the scourge that the coach used to punish the players for their laziness.***

❸ Word Study

The **Latin prefix *ambi-*** means "both."

In this drama, the Prince says he wants to clear up the **ambiguities** and learn the truth. He means that the facts are uncertain and can be understood from two or more points of view.

❹ Literary Analysis: Tragedy and Motive

A **tragedy** is a drama in which the major character, who is of noble stature, meets with disaster or great misfortune. The tragic hero's downfall is usually the result of one of the following:

- *fate,* or the idea of a pre-planned destiny
- a serious character flaw
- some combination of both

Motive is an important element of a tragic hero's character. A character's motives guide his or her thoughts or actions. Often, the hero's motives are basically good but misguided. As a result, the hero suffers a tragic fate that may seem undeserved.

Although tragedies are sad, they can also be uplifting and instructive. They can teach us about ourselves. They can show the greatness and nobility of the human spirit when faced with grave challenges. As you read the final act of *Romeo and Juliet,* consider what positive message the tragic events ultimately convey.

PHLit Online!
www.PHLitOnline.com

Hear It!
- Selection summary audio
- Selection audio

See It!
- Get Connected video
- Background video
- More about the author
- Vocabulary flashcards

Do It!
- Interactive journals
- Interactive graphic organizers
- Self-test
- Internet activity
- Grammar tutorial
- Interactive vocabulary games

❺ Reading Skill: Summarize

Summarizing is briefly stating the central ideas in a piece of writing. In summarizing the action, it is useful to first **identify causes and effects.**

- A *cause* is an event, action, or emotion that produces a result.
- An *effect* is the result produced by the cause.

Tragedies often involve a chain of causes and effects that advance the plot and lead to the tragic outcome. Recognizing the sequence will help you summarize plots like the one in this play.

❻ Using the Strategy: Cause-and-Effect Chart

As you read Act V, use a chart like this one to record causes and effects.

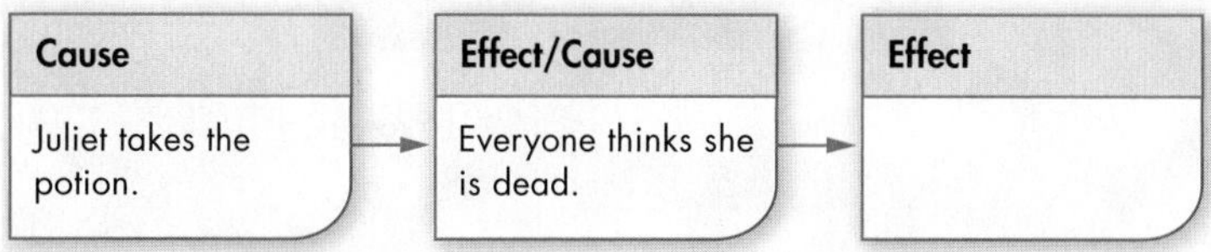

❹ Literary Analysis

Tragedy and Motive

1. Introduce the skill, using instruction on the student page.
2. Tell students that they will practice analyzing tragedy and motive as they read.

Think Aloud: Model the Skill

Model the skill of analyzing tragedy and motive. Say to students:

> Let's say I'm analyzing tragedy and motive in *Romeo and Juliet*. Romeo and Juliet qualify as tragic heroes because they are central characters of noble stature and suffer a tragic fate.
>
> Romeo and Juliet's motives are good—they are in love and want to heal their families—but are perhaps misguided, as they try to solve problems secretly.

❺ Reading Skill

Summarize

1. Introduce the skill, using instruction on the student page.
2. Tell students that they will practice identifying causes and effects as they read.

❻ Using the Strategy

Give students a copy of either **Reading Skill Graphic Organizer** A or B (*Graphic Organizer Transparencies,* pp. 163–164) to record causes and effects as they read. Use the examples in **Reading Skill Graphic Organizer A,** which is partially filled in, to model completing the organizer.

Differentiated Instruction — Additional Instruction

EL Extended Support—English Learners
Have students complete the **Reading and Vocabulary Warm-ups,** ***Unit 5 Resources,*** pp. 95–98, before they read. Assign the prereading pages for the ***Reader's Notebook: English Learner's Version.*** Then, have students listen to portions of the selection on the ***Hear It!*** **Audio CD.**

L1 L2 Extended Support—Struggling Readers
Have students complete the **Reading and Vocabulary Warm-ups,** ***Unit 5 Resources,*** pp. 95–98, before they read. Assign the prereading pages for the selection in the ***Reader's Notebook: Adapted Version.*** Then, have students listen to portions of the selection on the ***Hear It!*** **Audio CD** (adapted text).

Extended Support—Reluctant Readers
To build motivation and engagement before assigning the selection, have students read "Staying Connected," a thematically related selection in ***Reality Central.*** Then, use the questions at the conclusion of the related selection to guide discussion.

TEACH

❶ Activating Prior Knowledge

1. Prepare an **Anticipation Guide** (***Professional Development Guidebook***, pp. 36–38) with the following statements:
   - Teenagers may not be mature enough to experience true love.
   - People should be willing to risk everything for true love.
   - A person can have only one true love in his or her lifetime.
   - It is noble to die for love.
2. Give students a copy of the prepared **Anticipation Guide** and have students mark their responses in the appropriate columns.
3. For further guidance, use the ***Classroom Strategies and Teaching Routines*** card: **Using an Anticipation Guide.**

Concept Connector

Students will return to the **Anticipation Guide** after completing *The Tragedy of Romeo and Juliet,* Act V.

Individual Activity

Have students preview the visuals for this last act. Based on the visuals and what students already know, have students write answers to the following questions:

- Will Juliet awake from her sleep, or will the potion kill her?
- Will Romeo arrive at the tomb to find Juliet awake?
- How will the two lovers die?

❷ About the Selection

As *The Tragedy of Romeo and Juliet* draws to a close, circumstances conspire to exact a terrible penalty from the two lovers as the price for their families' feud. Others pay as well—Tybalt and Mercutio, earlier in the play, and now Lady Montague and Paris.

Text Complexity Rubric

The Tragedy of Romeo and Juliet, Act V		
Qualitative Measures	**Context/ Knowledge Demands**	Historical: Verona, Italy 1 2 3 4 (5)
	Structure/ Language Clarity and Conventionality	Challenging vocabulary; Elizabethan terms 1 2 3 4 (5)
	Levels of Meaning/ Purpose/Concept Level	Accessible concept (classic tale of star-crossed lovers) 1 2 (3) 4 5
Quantitative Measures	**Text Length**	Word Count: 3,474
	Lexile	NP
Overall Complexity		**Complex**

3 Reading Check

Answer: Romeo has had a wonderfully propitious dream: Juliet finds him dead and awakens him with kisses.

PHLit Online!

This selection is available in interactive format in the **Enriched Online Student Edition**, at **www.PHLitOnline.com**, which includes a thematically related video with writing prompt and an interactive graphic organizer.

Act V

Review and Anticipate

To prevent her marriage to Paris, Juliet has taken the Friar's potion and, as Act V begins, is in a temporary deathlike sleep. Her unsuspecting family plans her funeral. Meanwhile, the Friar has sent a messenger to Mantua to tell Romeo of the ruse, so that he may return and rescue Juliet from her family tomb. What do you think might go wrong with the Friar's plan?

Scene i. MANTUA. A STREET.

[*Enter* ROMEO.]

ROMEO. If I may trust the flattering truth of sleep,[1]
My dreams presage[2] some joyful news at hand.
My bosom's lord[3] sits lightly in his throne,
And all this day an unaccustomed spirit
Lifts me above the ground with cheerful thoughts.
I dreamt my lady came and found me dead
(Strange dream that gives a dead man leave to think!)
And breathed such life with kisses in my lips
That I revived and was an emperor.
Ah me! How sweet is love itself possessed,
When but love's shadows[4] are so rich in joy!

[*Enter* ROMEO'S MAN, BALTHASAR, *booted.*]

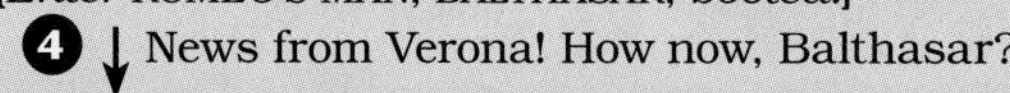

4 News from Verona! How now, Balthasar?

1. **flattering . . . sleep** pleasing illusions of dreams.
2. **presage** foretell.
3. **bosom's lord** heart.

4. **shadows** dreams; unreal images.

3

Why is Romeo in a good mood?

Text Complexity: Reader and Task Suggestions

The Tragedy of Romeo and Juliet, Act V

Preparing to Read the Text	Leveled Tasks
• Refer to the Literature in Context note on TE p. 918 and discuss the history of the plague in Europe. Make the connection to the play. • Discuss how dialogue is used to develop characters, plot, and setting in dramas. Compare it to the use of dialogue in short stories and other literary forms. • Guide students to use Multidraft Reading strategies (TE p. 805).	*Structure/Language* If students will have difficulty with dialogue in the play, have them first read to note what goes wrong in this last act that leads to the tragedy. Then, have students reread and note pieces of dialogue that reveal the mistakes. Help students clarify their understanding. *Evaluating* If students will not have difficulty with dialogue, have them read the act and jot down notes about the causes of the final tragedy. Ask them to draw conclusions from the entire play about the single most important cause of the tragedy.

❹ Literary Analysis

Tragedy and Motive

1. Have students read lines 12–16.
2. Have students determine the reason for Romeo's second question to Balthasar.

   Answer: Romeo has been expecting to hear from the Friar and wonders why Balthasar does not have letters for him.
3. **Ask:** Which person is Romeo most concerned about in his questions to Balthasar?

   Answer: Romeo is most concerned about Juliet.
4. **Ask:** What motivates Romeo's questions?

   Answer: Romeo has been away from Juliet, not by choice, and is eager to know how she is.

❺ Literary Analysis

Tragedy and Motive

1. Have students speculate on Balthasar's meaning in line 17.

   Answer: Balthasar means that although she is dead, Juliet is well because she is in heaven.
2. **Ask** students the Literary Analysis question: In what way does Romeo's remark in line 24 reinforce fate's role in the tragedy?

   Answer: When Romeo says "Then I defy you, stars!" he means that the stars (representing fate) have been responsible for Juliet's death, and Romeo is now their enemy. He will now defy fate by setting in motion a series of events that will culminate in tragedy.

❹
Dost thou not bring me letters from the friar?
How doth my lady? Is my father well?
How fares my Juliet? That I ask again,
For nothing can be ill if she be well.

MAN. Then she is well, and nothing can be ill.
Her body sleeps in Capels' monument,[5]
And her immortal part with angels lives.
I saw her laid low in her kindred's vault
And presently took post[6] to tell it you.
❺
O, pardon me for bringing these ill news,
Since you did leave it for my office,[7] sir.

ROMEO. Is it e'en so? Then I defy you, stars!
Thou knowest my lodging. Get me ink and paper
And hire post horses. I will hence tonight.

5. **Capels' monument** the Capulets' burial vault.
6. **presently took post** immediately set out on horseback.
7. **office** duty.

Literary Analysis
Tragedy and Motive In what way does Romeo's remark in line 24 reinforce fate's role in the tragedy?

916 Drama

Vocabulary Development

CCSS Language 6

Thematic Vocabulary: The Big Question

As students are discussing *The Tragedy of Romeo and Juliet,* Act V, encourage them to use the thematic vocabulary presented in Introducing the Big Question, pp. 778–779. You might encourage them with sentence starters like these:

1. Romeo and Juliet have shown a resistance to *conformity* to their families' priorities by . . .
2. It is difficult to *differentiate* the reasons for the characters' deaths in Act V because . . .
3. At the end of the play, we find out that a person's family *background* can . . .
4. The Prince's last speech implies that time will *determine* the fate of . . .

MAN. I do beseech you, sir, have patience.
Your looks are pale and wild and do import
Some misadventure.[8]

ROMEO. Tush, thou art deceived.
Leave me and do the thing I bid thee do.
Hast thou no letters to me from the friar?

MAN. No, my good lord.

ROMEO. No matter. Get thee gone.
And hire those horses. I'll be with thee straight.

[*Exit* BALTHASAR.]

Well, Juliet, I will lie with thee tonight.
Let's see for means. O mischief, thou art swift
To enter in the thoughts of desperate men!
I do remember an apothecary,[9]
And hereabouts 'a dwells, which late I noted
In tatt'red weeds, with overwhelming brows,
Culling of simples.[10] Meager were his looks,
Sharp misery had worn him to the bones;
And in his needy shop a tortoise hung,
An alligator stuffed, and other skins
Of ill-shaped fishes; and about his shelves
A beggarly account[11] of empty boxes,
Green earthen pots, bladders, and musty seeds,
Remnants of packthread, and old cakes of roses[12]
Were thinly scatterèd, to make up a show.
Noting this **penury** to myself I said,

8. **import / Some misadventure** suggest some misfortune.

9. **apothecary** one who prepares and sells drugs and medicines.

10. **In tatt'red . . . simples** in torn clothing, with overhanging eyebrows, sorting out herbs.

11. **beggarly account** small number.

12. **cakes of roses** pressed rose petals (used for perfume).

Vocabulary

remnants (rem′ nənts) *n.* what is left over; remainders

penury (pen′ yo͞o rē) *n.* extreme poverty

7

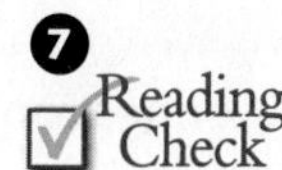

What does Romeo learn from Balthasar?

6 Critical Thinking

Infer

1. Ask students to read Romeo's soliloquy beginning at line 34. **Ask** them to infer what kind of reputation an apothecary had in these times.

   Possible response: The apothecary was not a highly respected person, judging from Romeo's descriptions of him and his shop.

2. **Ask** students what causes Romeo to buy poison from an apothecary.

   Answer: Romeo intends to kill himself because he believes Juliet is dead.

7 Reading Check

Answer: Romeo learns that Juliet is believed dead.

Differentiated Instruction for Universal Access

EL Pronunciation for English Learners

Students may have difficulty pronouncing the "st" sound in *straight* and *stuffed;* they may add an "eh" sound before *st*. For example, students may say "eh-straight." The following strategies can help students to pronounce the "st" sound.

- Write the words *straight, stuffed,* and *stare* on the board. Pronounce the words in turn, having students repeat each. Correct students' pronunciation as necessary.
- Using a sentence that repeats the initial "st" sound—such as "Stew always steals stuff"—play a game of telephone with the students. Whisper the sentence to one student, who passes it to another, and so on. At the end, reveal the correct sentence and review its pronunciation.

8 Literature in Context

History Connection

Italy—the setting for *The Tragedy of Romeo and Juliet*—was especially hard hit by the Black Death. Italian merchants were the first to bring the Black Death to Europe. In 1347 a fleet of their ships arrived in a port town on Sicily, an island just off the tip of the Italian mainland. Other Italian merchant ships carrying the plague docked in the major port cities of Genoa and Venice—not far from Verona—as well as other ports along Italy's Mediterranean coast. Within several months, all of Italy was overwhelmed with the plague. By the time the Black Death had run its course, between 40 and 50 percent of Italy's total population had died.

Connect to the Literature

Remind students of why Friar John was unable to deliver Friar Lawrence's letter. Then, **ask** the Connect to the Literature question: In what way does the Black Death contribute to the tragedy in *Romeo and Juliet?*

Answer: Because of the Black Death, Friar John is quarantined and unable to deliver Friar Lawrence's letter. Romeo receives news that Juliet is dead, but he never receives the letter from Friar Lawrence explaining that she is merely drugged.

Vocabulary
disperse (di spurs′) v. to break up and scatter in all directions; spread about; distribute widely

6

"And if a man did need a poison now
Whose sale is present death in Mantua,
Here lives a caitiff[13] wretch would sell it him."
O, this same thought did but forerun my need,
And this same needy man must sell it me.
As I remember, this should be the house.
Being holiday, the beggar's shop is shut.
What, ho! Apothecary!

[*Enter* APOTHECARY.]

APOTHECARY. Who calls so loud?

ROMEO. Come hither, man. I see that thou art poor.
Hold, there is forty ducats.[14] Let me have
A dram of poison, such soon-speeding gear[15]
As will **disperse** itself through all the veins
That the life-weary taker may fall dead,
And that the trunk[16] may be discharged of breath
As violently as hasty powder fired
Doth hurry from the fatal cannon's womb.

9

APOTHECARY. Such mortal drugs I have; but Mantua's law
Is death to any he that utters[17] them.

13. **caitiff** miserable.

14. **ducats** (duk′ əts) gold coins.
15. **soon-speeding gear** fast-working stuff.

16. **trunk** body.
17. **utters** sells.

8

LITERATURE IN CONTEXT

History Connection

Plague Searchers
The Black Plague, or Black Death, was a disease that swept through Europe, Asia, and the Middle East during the 1300s, with outbreaks continuing until 1400. It is thought that as much as a third of Europe's population died of the disease between 1347 and 1351. During an outbreak of plague, officials would appoint plague searchers to quarantine people infected with the disease and dispose of victims' remains. In *Romeo and Juliet*, Friar John is quarantined by plague searchers who fear he has been infected. As a result, he is unable to deliver Friar Lawrence's letter to Romeo.

Connect to the Literature

In what way does the Black Death contribute to the tragedy in *Romeo and Juliet?*

Vocabulary Development

Ⓒ CCSS Language 6

Word Forms

Expand students' vocabulary by helping them learn related forms of the selection vocabulary words. Give students a blank **Word Form Chart** (***Professional Development Guidebook***, p. 42) with the original vocabulary words in the correct columns. Have partners determine the related forms. The final chart should look like this:

Noun	Verb	Adjective	Adverb
penury		penurious	penuriously
dispersal	**disperse**	dispersible	dispersedly
haughtiness		**haughty**	haughtily
ambiguities		ambiguous	ambiguously

ROMEO. Art thou so bare and full of wretchedness
And fearest to die? Famine is in thy cheeks,
Need and oppression starveth in thy eyes,
Contempt and beggary hangs upon thy back:
The world is not thy friend, nor the world's law;
The world affords no law to make thee rich;
Then be not poor, but break it and take this.

APOTHECARY. My poverty but not my will consents.

ROMEO. I pay thy poverty and not thy will.

APOTHECARY. Put this in any liquid thing you will
And drink it off, and if you had the strength
Of twenty men, it would dispatch you straight.

ROMEO. There is thy gold—worse poison to men's souls,
Doing more murder in this loathsome world,
Than these poor compounds[18] that thou mayst not sell.
I sell thee poison; thou hast sold me none.
Farewell. Buy food and get thyself in flesh.
Come, cordial[19] and not poison, go with me
To Juliet's grave; for there must I use thee. [*Exit all.*]

Scene ii. Friar Lawrence's cell.

[*Enter* FRIAR JOHN, *calling* FRIAR LAWRENCE.]

JOHN. Holy Franciscan friar, brother, ho!

[*Enter* FRIAR LAWRENCE.]

LAWRENCE. This same should be the voice of Friar John.
Welcome from Mantua. What says Romeo?
Or, if his mind be writ, give me his letter.

JOHN. Going to find a barefoot brother out,
One of our order, to associate[1] me
Here in this city visiting the sick,
And finding him, the searchers of the town,
Suspecting that we both were in a house
Where the infectious pestilence did reign,
Sealed up the doors, and would not let us forth,
So that my speed to Mantua there was stayed.

LAWRENCE. Who bare my letter, then, to Romeo?

JOHN. I could not send it—here it is again—
Nor get a messenger to bring it thee,
So fearful were they of infection.

Spiral Review
Conflict What conflicting motivations does the Apothecary face?

Literary Analysis
Tragedy and Motive What is the apothecary's motive for selling Romeo the poison?

18. **compounds** mixtures.
19. **cordial** health-giving drink.

Reading Skill
Summarize Briefly state the causes and effects of Friar John's failure to deliver Friar Lawrence's letter.

1. **associate** accompany.

What does Romeo plan to do with the apothecary's help?

Fluency

Distribute copies of p. 919, and pair students. Have partners take turns reading paragraphs aloud. While one partner reads, the other should mark any words with which the student reading has difficulty. Circulate to monitor the fluency of students' reading. Collect students' marked-up copies of the page, and review difficult words and passages with the class. Look for these problem spots:

- If students have difficulty with the word *infectious* (line 10), point out that the word features a common prefix, *in-*, and a common suffix, *-ous*. Have students cover up parts of the word with their thumbs to sound out each syllable in turn. Then, explain that *infectious* means "able to be passed on to someone else."
- If students have difficulty with the word *affords* (line 73), practice oral cloze with the sentence. First, read the sentence with the word *affords* omitted. Then, reread the sentence and ask students to "fill in the blank" with the word that makes the most sense.

Spiral Review

Conflict

1. Remind students that they studied the concept of conflict in the Unit 5 Literary Analysis Workshop (pp. 780–797).
2. **Ask** students the Spiral Review question.
   Answer: The conflicting motivations the Apothecary faces are poverty and the knowledge that selling the poison is wrong.

9 Literary Analysis

Tragedy and Motive

1. Remind students that in a tragedy, the main character is partially brought down by a character flaw. **Ask** them what character flaw motivates Romeo to act so quickly.
   Answer: Romeo acts without thinking. He does not pause to verify Balthasar's news or to consider waiting to speak with the Friar.
2. **Ask** students the Literary Analysis question.
   Answer: The apothecary is poor and starving; he needs money.

10 Reading Skill

Summarize

1. Have students explain how the letter fit into Friar Lawrence's plan for uniting Romeo and Juliet.
   Answer: Friar Lawrence gave Juliet the potion to make her appear dead and thus avoid marriage to Paris. She was to be buried in the family tomb. Meanwhile, Friar Lawrence would send a letter to Romeo explaining the plan. Romeo would be told to arrive at the tomb when Juliet awoke and would then take her to Mantua.
2. **Ask** students to respond to the Reading Skill prompt.
   Answer: Friar John cannot deliver the letter because he is quarantined by authorities who fear he has the plague. Romeo hears that Juliet is dead, but he does not receive the letter from Friar Lawrence explaining the true situation. Romeo buys poison and prepares to kill himself.

11 Reading Check

Answer: He plans to go to Juliet's grave and kill himself.

12 Literary Analysis

Tragedy and Motive

1. **Ask** students why they think Friar Lawrence asks Friar John to get him a crow in lines 21–22.

   Answer: Students should infer that a crow is a crowbar and that Friar Lawrence will need the tool to force his way into the Capulet tomb, where Juliet is lying.

2. **Ask** students the Literary Analysis question: What motivates Friar Lawrence's decision to go to the monument?

   Answer: The Friar wants to be at the monument to ease Juliet's shock at awakening in a tomb and to explain why Romeo is not yet there.

Literary Analysis
Tragedy and Motive
What motivates Friar Lawrence's decision to go to the monument?

2. nice trivial.
3. full of charge, / Of dear import urgent and important.

4. beshrew blame.
5. accidents happenings.

LAWRENCE. Unhappy fortune! By my brotherhood,
The letter was not nice,[2] but full of charge,
Of dear import;[3] and the neglecting it
May do much danger. Friar John, go hence,
Get me an iron crow and bring it straight
Unto my cell.

JOHN. Brother, I'll go and bring it thee. [*Exit.*]

LAWRENCE. Now must I to the monument alone.
Within this three hours will fair Juliet wake.
She will beshrew[4] me much that Romeo
Hath had no notice of these accidents;[5]
But I will write again to Mantua,
And keep her at my cell till Romeo come—
Poor living corse, closed in a dead man's tomb! [*Exit.*]

Scene iii. A churchyard; in it a monument belonging to the Capulets.

[*Enter* PARIS *and his* PAGE *with flowers and sweet water.*]

1. aloof apart.

2. lay . . . along lie down flat.

PARIS. Give me thy torch, boy. Hence, and stand aloof.[1]
Yet put it out, for I would not be seen.
Under yond yew trees lay thee all along,[2]
Holding thy ear close to the hollow ground.
So shall no foot upon the churchyard tread
(Being loose, unfirm, with digging up of graves)
But thou shalt hear it. Whistle then to me,
As signal that thou hearest something approach.
Give me those flowers. Do as I bid thee, go.

3. adventure chance it.

PAGE. [*Aside*] I am almost afraid to stand alone
Here in the churchyard; yet I will adventure.[3] [*Retires.*]

4. sweet perfumed.

5. obsequies memorial ceremonies.
6. cross interrupt.

PARIS. Sweet flower, with flowers thy bridal bed I strew
(O woe! thy canopy is dust and stones)
Which with sweet[4] water nightly I will dew;
Or, wanting that, with tears distilled by moans.
The obsequies[5] that I for thee will keep
Nightly shall be to strew thy grave and weep. [**BOY** *whistles.*]
The boy gives warning something doth approach.
What cursèd foot wanders this way tonight
To cross[6] my obsequies and true love's rite?
What, with a torch? Muffle me, night, awhile. [*Retires.*]

[*Enter* ROMEO, *and* BALTHASAR *with a torch, a mattock, and a crow of iron.*]

Vocabulary Development

CCSS Language 6

Selection Vocabulary Reinforcement

Reinforce students' comprehension with "show-you-know" sentences. The first part of the sentence uses the vocabulary word in an appropriate context. The second part of the sentence—the "show-you-know" part—clarifies the first. Model the strategy with this example:

Remnants of the party filled the room; used napkins, empty glasses and cans, and half-eaten plates of food were all that were left of the celebration.

Then, give students these sentence prompts, and coach them in creating the clarification part.

1. He feared that he might soon be living in *penury;* ____________

   Sample answer: he couldn't find a job, and all his savings were nearly gone.

2. He is known for his *haughty* attitude; ____________

   Sample answer: his arrogance has cost him many friends.

ROMEO. Give me that mattock and the wrenching iron.
Hold, take this letter. Early in the morning
See thou deliver it to my lord and father.
Give me the light. Upon thy life I charge thee,
Whate'er thou hearest or seest, stand all aloof
And do not interrupt me in my course.
Why I descend into this bed of death
Is partly to behold my lady's face,
But chiefly to take thence from her dead finger
A precious ring—a ring that I must use
In dear employment.[7] Therefore hence, be gone.
But if thou, jealous,[8] dost return to pry
In what I farther shall intend to do,
By heaven, I will tear thee joint by joint
And strew this hungry churchyard with thy limbs.
The time and my intents are savage-wild,
More fierce and more inexorable[9] far
Than empty[10] tigers or the roaring sea.

BALTHASAR. I will be gone, sir, and not trouble ye.

ROMEO. So shalt thou show me friendship. Take thou that.
Live, and be prosperous; and farewell, good fellow.

BALTHASAR. [*Aside*] For all this same, I'll hide me hereabout.
His looks I fear, and his intents I doubt. [*Retires.*]

ROMEO. Thou detestable maw,[11] thou womb of death,
Gorged with the dearest morsel of the earth,
Thus I enforce thy rotten jaws to open,
And in despite[12] I'll cram thee with more food.

[ROMEO *opens the tomb.*]

PARIS. This is that banished **haughty** Montague
That murd'red my love's cousin—with which grief
It is supposed the fair creature died—
And here is come to do some villainous shame
To the dead bodies. I will apprehend[13] him.
Stop thy unhallowèd toil, vile Montague!
Can vengeance be pursued further than death?
Condemnèd villain, I do apprehend thee.
Obey, and go with me; for thou must die.

ROMEO. I must indeed; and therefore came I hither.
Good gentle youth, tempt not a desp'rate man.

Literary Analysis Tragedy and Motive What different motives do Paris and Romeo have for visiting Juliet's tomb? (13)

7. **dear employment** important business.
8. **jealous** curious.
9. **inexorable** uncontrollable.
10. **empty** hungry.
11. **maw** stomach.
12. **despite** scorn.
13. **apprehend** seize; arrest.

Vocabulary
haughty (hôt´ ē) *adj.* arrogant

(14) 
How does Paris react to seeing Romeo at Juliet's tomb?

(15)

Differentiated Instruction for Universal Access

Enrichment for Gifted/Talented Students

This final scene of the play is long and complicated, with many characters coming and going and with limited stage directions, which may make the action difficult to follow.

Ask students to rewrite this last scene in prose, with a narrator filling in the action and summarizing much of the dialogue. For example, in lines 7–11, a prose version might read as follows:

"Paris took the flowers from the page, telling him to leave. 'If you hear someone coming, whistle as a signal,' he told the page. The page left, muttering to himself about being afraid to be alone in the churchyard."

Encourage students to visualize the scene and to give a fuller description of the setting. Have students write dialogue that will add to the story, using Shakespeare's words where suitable, or recasting the language into modern English.

Have students share their completed scenes with a classmate.

(13) Literary Analysis

Tragedy and Motive

1. **Ask** what Paris and Romeo bring to the tomb.

   Answer: Paris brings flowers and perfume, and Romeo brings tools to help him get into the tomb.
2. Have students note the stage direction in line 21. Tell them that "retires" means that Paris steps out of sight to see who is approaching. He watches, unseen by Romeo and Balthasar.
3. **Ask** students the Literary Analysis question: What different motives do Paris and Romeo have for visiting Juliet's tomb?

   Answer: Paris visits the tomb to bring Juliet flowers; Romeo visits the tomb to kill himself.
4. **Ask** students what reason Romeo gives Balthasar for entering the tomb. What does Romeo say will happen if Balthasar tries to spy on him?

   Answer: Romeo tells Balthasar he is going to get a ring from Juliet's finger. He says that he will kill Balthasar if he does not obey him.
5. **Ask** students whether Balthasar believes Romeo has come to get a ring. **Ask** whether students believe Romeo will really kill Balthasar.

   Possible response: Balthasar says in an aside that he does not believe Romeo's story. Students may say that Romeo is exaggerating about killing Balthasar to show him how serious he is about not being disturbed.

(14) Reading Check

Answer: Paris curses Romeo and insists that Juliet is dead because of Romeo. Paris then starts a fight with Romeo.

⓯ Reading Skill

Summarize

Ask students to respond to the Reading Skill prompt: Summarize the causes that you think will produce a tragic effect in the confrontation between Romeo and Paris.

Possible response: Ignorance causes the fatal confrontation. Paris is unaware that Romeo and Juliet are married; he blames Romeo for the deaths of Tybalt and Juliet. Seeing Romeo trying to break into the Capulet family tomb is triply offensive to Paris. Romeo is unaware of Paris's love for Juliet. He is not even aware that it is Paris whom he is killing.

⓰ Literary Analysis

Tragedy and Motive

1. Have students read lines 74–87. **Ask** how Romeo feels about killing Paris. How can you tell?

   Answer: Romeo is sorry that he had to kill Paris. He speaks of him as a "slaught'red youth" and places him in the tomb by Juliet.

2. Have students recall another important scene in which someone wants to fight Romeo and Romeo tries to avoid it.

   Answer: In Act III, Scene i, Romeo tries to avoid dueling with Tybalt.

3. **Ask** students the Literary Analysis question: What tragic mistake does Romeo make regarding Juliet's appearance?

   Answer: Romeo believes that Juliet is dead despite the signs of life and health in her appearance.

Reading Skill
Summarize Summarize the causes that you think will produce a tragic effect in the confrontation between Romeo and Paris.

14. conjurations solemn appeals.
15. felon criminal.

Fly hence and leave me. Think upon these gone;
Let them affright thee. I beseech thee, youth,
Put not another sin upon my head
By urging me to fury. O, be gone!
By heaven, I love thee better than myself,
For I come hither armed against myself.
Stay not, be gone. Live, and hereafter say
A madman's mercy bid thee run away. ⓯

PARIS. I do defy thy conjurations.[14]
And apprehend thee for a felon[15] here.

ROMEO. Wilt thou provoke me? Then have at thee, boy!
[*They fight.*]

PAGE. O Lord, they fight! I will go call the watch.
[*Exit.* PARIS *falls.*]

PARIS. O, I am slain! If thou be merciful,
Open the tomb, lay me with Juliet. [*Dies.*]

16. peruse look over.
17. betossèd upset.
18. attend give attention to.

ROMEO. In faith, I will. Let me peruse[16] this face.
Mercutio's kinsman, noble County Paris!
What said my man when my betossèd[17] soul
Did not attend[18] him as we rode? I think
He told me Paris should have married Juliet.
Said he not so, or did I dream it so?
Or am I mad, hearing him talk of Juliet,
To think it was so? O, give me thy hand,
One writ with me in sour misfortune's book!
I'll bury thee in a triumphant grave.
A grave? O, no, a lanthorn,[19] slaught'red youth,
For here lies Juliet, and her beauty makes
This vault a feasting presence[20] full of light.
Death, lie thou there, by a dead man interred.
[*Lays him in the tomb.*]
How oft when men are at the point of death
Have they been merry! Which their keepers[21] call
A lightning before death. O, how may I
Call this a lightning? O my love, my wife!
Death, that hath sucked the honey of thy breath,
Hath had no power yet upon thy beauty.
Thou art not conquered. Beauty's ensign[22] yet ⓰
Is crimson in thy lips and in thy cheeks,
And death's pale flag is not advancèd there.

19. lanthorn windowed structure on top of a room to admit light; also, a lantern.
20. feasting presence chamber fit for celebration.
21. keepers jailers.
22. ensign banner.

Literary Analysis
Tragedy and Motive What tragic mistake does Romeo make regarding Juliet's appearance?

Vocabulary Development

Ⓒ CCSS Language 6

Expressive Vocabulary

To help students broaden their expressive vocabulary, encourage them to use the following words as they discuss the selection: *react, circumstance, assess,* and *significant*. Have them complete these sentence starters:

1. Paris is quick to *react* when he sees . . .
2. Juliet is horrified at the *circumstance* that greets her when she awakes: . . .
3. Friar Lawrence does not take the time to *assess* . . .
4. Friar Lawrence does not recognize that Romeo and Juliet face *significant* risks, such as . . .

Tybalt, liest thou there in thy bloody sheet?
O, what more favor can I do to thee
Than with that hand that cut thy youth in twain
To sunder[23] his that was thine enemy?
Forgive me, cousin! Ah, dear Juliet,
Why art thou yet so fair? Shall I believe
That unsubstantial Death is amorous,[24]
And that the lean abhorrèd monster keeps
Thee here in dark to be his paramour?
For fear of that I still will stay with thee
And never from this pallet[25] of dim night
Depart again. Here, here will I remain
With worms that are thy chambermaids. O, here
Will I set up my everlasting rest
And shake the yoke of inauspicious[26] stars
From this world-wearied flesh. Eyes, look your last!

23. **sunder** cut off.

24. **amorous** full of love.

25. **pallet** bed.

26. **inauspicious** promising misfortune.

17 

What happens to Paris at Juliet's tomb?

17 Reading Check

Answer: Paris is killed in a fight with Romeo.

Differentiated Instruction for Universal Access

Culturally Responsive Instruction

Culture Focus Discuss with students burial practices. Point out that different religions and cultures have unique burial customs. In the United States, people's remains are usually entombed in a family crypt or mausoleum, buried underground in a grave, or cremated.

Tell students that throughout history, the time period between death and burial has depended on custom, culture, and religion. Some traditions demand that a person be buried within 24 hours, while others allow for weeks of mourning before burial.

The type of burial also varies depending on the social status of the departed. In ancient Egypt, pharaohs were buried in pyramids with their favorite objects so that they would have everything they needed in the afterlife. The ancient Norsemen placed their fallen warriors on a funeral boat, set it ablaze, and sent it out to sea. While cremation was common for those who fell in battle, with time, entombment became popular.

Ask volunteers to talk about unique burial practices with which they are familiar.

⓲ Critical Viewing

Possible responses: The image conveys grief, heartbreak, and love. Some students may say that Romeo looks relieved to be dead alongside his beloved.

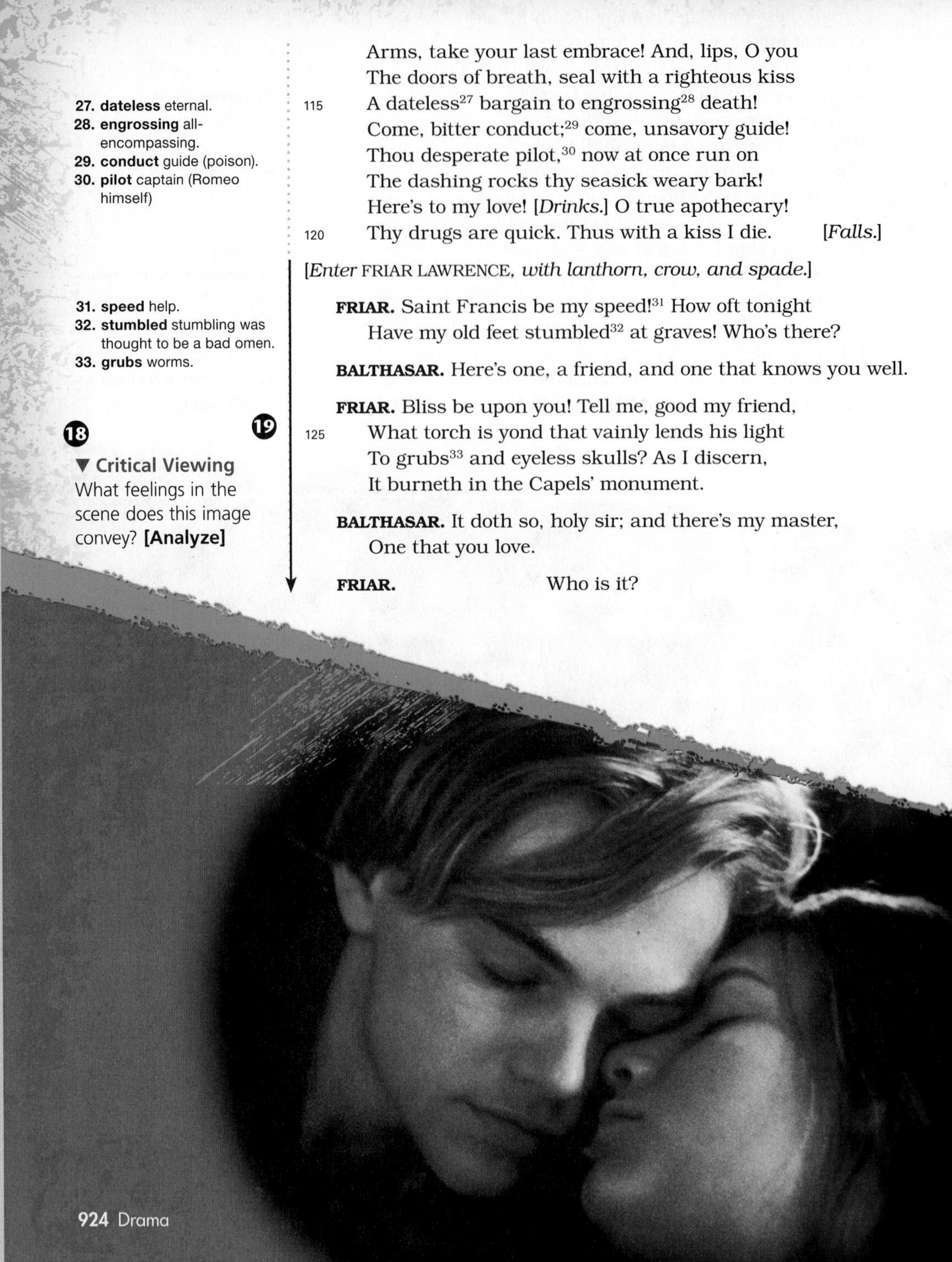

27. **dateless** eternal.
28. **engrossing** all-encompassing.
29. **conduct** guide (poison).
30. **pilot** captain (Romeo himself)

Arms, take your last embrace! And, lips, O you
The doors of breath, seal with a righteous kiss
A dateless[27] bargain to engrossing[28] death!
Come, bitter conduct;[29] come, unsavory guide!
Thou desperate pilot,[30] now at once run on
The dashing rocks thy seasick weary bark!
Here's to my love! [*Drinks.*] O true apothecary!
Thy drugs are quick. Thus with a kiss I die. [*Falls.*]

[*Enter* FRIAR LAWRENCE, *with lanthorn, crow, and spade.*]

31. **speed** help.
32. **stumbled** stumbling was thought to be a bad omen.
33. **grubs** worms.

FRIAR. Saint Francis be my speed![31] How oft tonight
Have my old feet stumbled[32] at graves! Who's there?

BALTHASAR. Here's one, a friend, and one that knows you well.

FRIAR. Bliss be upon you! Tell me, good my friend,
What torch is yond that vainly lends his light
To grubs[33] and eyeless skulls? As I discern,
It burneth in the Capels' monument.

BALTHASAR. It doth so, holy sir; and there's my master,
One that you love.

FRIAR. Who is it?

⓲ ⓳

▼ **Critical Viewing**
What feelings in the scene does this image convey? **[Analyze]**

Think Aloud

Vocabulary: Using Context

Direct students' attention to the word *bark* in line 118. Using a think-aloud process, model how to use context to infer the meaning of an unknown word. Say to students:

> I'm going to think aloud to show you how I would figure out the meaning of *bark* based on its context.
>
> In this sentence, Romeo refers to himself as a captain whose "seasick weary bark" has crashed against the rocks. The image that springs to my mind is of a ship that runs into rocks at high speed and capsizes at sea. I know that *bark* means "the outer layer of a tree" in most contexts, but that meaning doesn't make sense here. The outer layer of a tree would not crash against rocks and thus make a captain desperate. Based on the context, I think that a *bark* is a particular kind of boat. It's the only meaning that truly makes sense.

BALTHASAR. Romeo.

FRIAR. How long hath he been there?

BALTHASAR. Full half an hour.

FRIAR. Go with me to the vault.

BALTHASAR. I dare not, sir.
My master knows not but I am gone hence,
And fearfully did menace me with death
If I did stay to look on his intents.

FRIAR. Stay then; I'll go alone. Fear comes upon me.
19 O, much I fear some ill unthrifty[34] thing.

BALTHASAR. As I did sleep under this yew tree here,
I dreamt my master and another fought,
And that my master slew him.

FRIAR. Romeo!
Alack, alack, what blood is this which stains
The stony entrance of this sepulcher?
What mean these masterless[35] and gory swords
To lie discolored by this place of peace? [*Enters the tomb.*]
Romeo! O, pale! Who else? What, Paris too?
And steeped in blood? Ah, what an unkind[36] hour
Is guilty of this lamentable chance!
The lady stirs. [JULIET *rises.*]

JULIET. O comfortable[37] friar! Where is my lord?
I do remember well where I should be,
And there I am. Where is my Romeo?

FRIAR. I hear some noise. Lady, come from that nest
Of death, contagion, and unnatural sleep.
A greater power than we can contradict
20 Hath thwarted our intents. Come, come away.
Thy husband in thy bosom there lies dead;
And Paris too. Come, I'll dispose of thee
Among a sisterhood of holy nuns.
Stay not to question, for the watch is coming.
Come, go, good Juliet. I dare no longer stay.

JULIET. Go, get thee hence, for I will not away. [*Exit* FRIAR.]
What's here? A cup, closed in my truelove's hand?
Poison, I see, hath been his timeless[38] end.
O churl![39] Drunk all, and left no friendly drop
To help me after? I will kiss thy lips.

Literary Analysis Tragedy and Motive In what way is Friar Lawrence's late arrival another example of chance contributing to this tragedy?

34. **unthrifty** unlucky.

35. **masterless** discarded (without masters).

36. **unkind** unnatural.

37. **comfortable** comforting.

38. **timeless** untimely; too soon.

39. **churl** rude fellow.

Literary Analysis Tragedy and Motive Why do you think Friar Lawrence wants to "dispose of Juliet" in a sisterhood of nuns?

21

How does Juliet react when she wakes up?

19 Literary Analysis

Tragedy and Motive

1. **Ask** students what Romeo suggests in lines 109–112 (pp. 923–924) will be accomplished by his death.

   Answer: Romeo believes that when he dies, the fate that has plagued him ("yoke of inauspicious stars") will come to an end.

2. **Ask** students the first Literary Analysis question: In what way is Friar Lawrence's late arrival another example of chance contributing to this tragedy?

   Answer: If Friar Lawrence had arrived minutes earlier, he could have prevented the deaths of Paris and Romeo.

20 Literary Analysis

Tragedy and Motive

1. **Ask:** How does the Friar explain to Juliet what has happened?

   Answer: The Friar lays the blame for the events on a greater power—the gods, chance, or fate.

2. **Ask** students the second Literary Analysis question: Why do you think Friar Lawrence wants to "dispose of Juliet" in a sisterhood of nuns?

   Possible response: The Friar may feel that a convent would be the best place for Juliet to recover from her grief and live out her ruined life. A less charitable interpretation is that the Friar hopes to prevent Juliet from revealing the full scope of the tragedy, thus exposing his own culpability.

21 Reading Check

Answer: She finds the Friar's presence comforting, but she immediately looks for Romeo.

Differentiated Instruction for Universal Access

Enrichment for Advanced Readers

In the eighteenth century, a writer and director staged *The Tragedy of Romeo and Juliet* and rewrote the "death scene" of Romeo and Juliet as follows:

ROMEO: . . . Arms take your last embrace; and lips do you/the doors of breath seal with a righteous kiss./Soft! soft! She breathes and stirs! [*Juliet wakes*]

JULIET: Where am I? Defend me, powers!

ROMEO: She speaks, she lives! And we shall still be blessed!/My kind propitious stars o'erpay me now/For all my sorrows past. Rise, rise, my Juliet,/And from this cave of death, this house of horror,/Quick let me snatch thee to Romeo's arms,/There breathe a vital spirit in the lips,/And call thee back to life and love! [*Takes her hand.*]

Have students discuss this ending by answering the following questions:

- Would the play be a tragedy with this ending? Why or why not?

22 Literary Analysis

Tragedy and Motive

1. **Ask** students why the Chief Watchman is demanding that everyone in the vicinity be arrested.

   Answer: The Chief Watchman is acting as a modern police officer would; he is securing the scene of the crime and rounding up the suspects.

2. **Ask** students the Literary Analysis question: How might the tragic ending have been averted if Paris, Romeo, and the Friar had come to Juliet's tomb in a different order?

   Answer: If the Friar had arrived first, he could have explained the circumstances to Romeo; if Paris had arrived after Romeo, Romeo and Juliet might already have fled to Mantua, and so forth.

---

40. restorative medicine.

41. happy convenient; opportune.

42. attach arrest.

43. ground cause.

44. without circumstance descry see clearly without details.

Haply some poison yet doth hang on them
To make me die with a restorative.[40] [*Kisses him.*]
Thy lips are warm!

CHIEF WATCHMAN. [*Within*] Lead, boy. Which way?

JULIET. Yea, noise? Then I'll be brief. O happy[41] dagger!
[*Snatches* ROMEO'S *dagger.*]
This is thy sheath; there rust, and let me die.
[*She stabs herself and falls.*]

[*Enter* PARIS' BOY *and* WATCH.]

BOY. This is the place. There, where the torch doth burn.

CHIEF WATCHMAN. The ground is bloody. Search about the churchyard.
Go, some of you; whoe'er you find attach.[42]
[*Exit some of the* WATCH.]
Pitiful sight! Here lies the County slain;
And Juliet bleeding, warm, and newly dead,
Who here hath lain this two days buriè d.
Go, tell the Prince; run to the Capulets;
Raise up the Montagues; some others search.
[*Exit others of the* WATCH.]
22
We see the ground whereon these woes do lie,
But the true ground[43] of all these piteous woes
We cannot without circumstance descry.[44]

[*Enter some of the* WATCH, *with* ROMEO'S MAN, BALTHASAR.]

SECOND WATCHMAN. Here's Romeo's man. We found him in the churchyard.

CHIEF WATCHMAN. Hold him in safety till the Prince come hither.

[*Enter* FRIAR LAWRENCE *and another* WATCHMAN.]

THIRD WATCHMAN. Here is a friar that trembles, sighs and weeps.
We took this mattock and this spade from him
As he was coming from this churchyard's side.

CHIEF WATCHMAN. A great suspicion! Stay the friar too.

[*Enter the* PRINCE *and* ATTENDANTS.]

Literary Analysis
Tragedy and Motive How might the tragic ending have been averted if Paris, Romeo, and the Friar had come to Juliet's tomb in a different order?

Vocabulary Development

CCSS Language 6

Selection Vocabulary Reinforcement

To reinforce and assess students' comprehension of selection vocabulary words, give them sentences using the words in which the word may or may not be used correctly. Students must tell whether the use is correct and explain their answers. Use these sentences.

1. There were many *ambiguities* in the situation; it was clear exactly what happened.

   Answer: No, *ambiguities* is not used correctly. *Ambiguities* refers to things that are not clear.

2. During the Middle Ages, disease was the common *scourge* of human beings.

   Answer: Yes, *scourge* is used correctly, since it refers to something that causes pain or inflicts punishment.

PRINCE. What misadventure is so early up,
That calls our person from our morning rest?

[*Enter* CAPULET *and his* WIFE *with others.*]

CAPULET. What should it be, that is so shrieked abroad?

LADY CAPULET. O, the people in the street cry "Romeo,"
Some "Juliet," and some "Paris"; and all run
With open outcry toward our monument.

PRINCE. What fear is this which startles in your ears?

CHIEF WATCHMAN. Sovereign, here lies the County Paris slain;
And Romeo dead; and Juliet, dead before,
Warm and new killed.

PRINCE. Search, seek, and know how this foul murder comes.

CHIEF WATCHMAN. Here is a friar, and slaughtered Romeo's man,
With instruments upon them fit to open
These dead men's tombs.

CAPULET. O heavens! O wife, look how our daughter bleeds!
This dagger hath mista'en, for, lo, his house[45]
Is empty on the back of Montague,
And it missheathèd in my daughter's bosom!

LADY CAPULET. O me, this sight of death is as a bell
That warns my old age to a sepulcher.

[*Enter* MONTAGUE *and others.*]

PRINCE. Come, Montague; for thou art early up
To see thy son and heir more early down.

MONTAGUE. Alas, my liege,[46] my wife is dead tonight!
Grief of my son's exile hath stopped her breath.
What further woe conspires against mine age?

23 **PRINCE.** Look, and thou shalt see.

MONTAGUE. O thou untaught! What manners is in this,
To press before thy father to a grave?

PRINCE. Seal up the mouth of outrage[47] for a while,
Till we can clear these **ambiguities**
And know their spring, their head, their true descent;
And then will I be general of your woes[48]
And lead you even to death. Meantime forbear,
And let mischance be slave to patience.[49]
Bring forth the parties of suspicion.

Reading Skill
Summarize
Summarize the losses that the families have experienced as a result of Romeo and Juliet's relationship.

45. house sheath.
46. liege (lēj) lord.
47. mouth of outrage violent cries.
48. general . . . woes leader in your sorrow.
49. let . . . patience be patient in the face of misfortune.

Vocabulary
ambiguities (am′ bə gyōō′ ə tēz) *n.* statements or events whose meanings are unclear

What effect did Romeo's exile have on his mother?

23 Reading Skill
Summarize

1. **Ask** students what the Prince means by telling Montague that his son is "early down."

   Answer: The Prince means that Romeo has met an untimely death.

2. **Ask** students to respond to the Reading Skill prompt: Summarize the losses that the families have experienced as a result of Romeo and Juliet's relationship.

   Answer: Those who died as a result of Romeo and Juliet's relationship are Paris, Romeo, Juliet, and Lady Montague.

▶ **Monitor Progress:** Review students' graphic organizers to ensure that they are able to identify causes and effects.

▶ **Reteach:** If students have difficulty identifying cause and effect, provide them with **Reading Skill Graphic Organizer** (*Graphic Organizer Transparencies,* p. 163) as a model.

24 Reading Check

Answer: Romeo's mother died of grief at Romeo's exile.

Differentiated Instruction for Universal Access

Enrichment for Advanced Readers

Tell students that many critics consider *The Tragedy of King Lear* to be Shakespeare's greatest tragedy.

Remind students that in a tragedy, the central character meets with great misfortune, often because of a serious character flaw. Remind students that in *The Tragedy of Romeo and Juliet,* Romeo's serious flaw is his impatience. If he had waited for a letter from the Friar, or if he had not been so hasty to kill himself, he and Juliet could have been united.

Suggest that students form a small group to read and discuss Act I, Scene i, of *The Tragedy of King Lear* in **Authors in Depth,** Gold Level. Encourage students to address the following questions in their discussion:

- Who is the tragic hero of the play?
- What will prove to be Lear's serious character flaw?
- Which of the three sisters will prove to be loyal, and which will prove to be treacherous? Explain.

25 Literary Analysis

Tragedy and Motive

1. **Ask** students to interpret the Friar's words in lines 231–235.

   Possible response: The Friar is admitting that his actions played a part in the deaths of Romeo, Juliet, and Paris, but that he did not actually kill anyone.

2. **Ask** students the Literary Analysis question: What examples of fate or character flaws do you find in the tragic events that the Friar recounts?

   Answer: Examples of character flaws include the following: Romeo and Juliet's haste in marrying secretly; Romeo's vengeful response to Mercutio's slaying in killing Tybalt; the Capulets' haste in arranging for a marriage that Juliet did not consent to; and Romeo's rash decision to die upon learning of Juliet's supposed death. Examples of fate involve messages—the true message that Romeo never receives and the false report that he does receive. Multiple instances of bad timing on the fatal night are also fateful.

FRIAR. I am the greatest, able to do least,
Yet most suspected, as the time and place
Doth make against me, of this direful[50] murder;
And here I stand, both to impeach and purge[51]
Myself condemnèd and myself excused.

PRINCE. Then say at once what thou dost know in this.

FRIAR. I will be brief, for my short date of breath[52]
Is not so long as is a tedious tale.
Romeo, there dead, was husband to that Juliet;
And she, there dead, that's Romeo's faithful wife.
I married them; and their stol'n marriage day
Was Tybalt's doomsday, whose untimely death
Banished the new-made bridegroom from this city;
For whom, and not for Tybalt, Juliet pined.
You, to remove that siege of grief from her,
Betrothed and would have married her perforce
To County Paris. Then comes she to me
And with wild looks bid me devise some mean
To rid her from this second marriage,
Or in my cell there would she kill herself.
Then gave I her (so tutored by my art)
A sleeping potion; which so took effect
As I intended, for it wrought on her
The form of death. Meantime I writ to Romeo
That he should hither come as[53] this dire night
To help to take her from her borrowed grave,
Being the time the potion's force should cease,
But he which bore my letter, Friar John,
Was stayed by accident, and yesternight
Returned my letter back. Then all alone
At the prefixèd hour of her waking
Came I to take her from her kindred's vault;
Meaning to keep her closely[54] at my cell
Till I conveniently could send to Romeo.
But when I came, some minute ere the time
Of her awakening, here untimely lay
The noble Paris and true Romeo dead.
She wakes; and I entreated her come forth
And bear this work of heaven with patience;
But then a noise did scare me from the tomb,
And she, too desperate, would not go with me,
But, as it seems, did violence on herself.
All this I know, and to the marriage

50. **direful** terrible.
51. **impeach and purge** accuse and declare blameless.
52. **date of breath** term of life.

Literary Analysis Tragedy and Motive What examples of fate or character flaws do you find in the tragic events that the Friar recounts?

53. **as** on.
54. **closely** hidden; secretly.

Vocabulary Development

Vocabulary Knowledge Rating

When students have completed reading and discussing Act V of *The Tragedy of Romeo and Juliet,* have them take out their **Vocabulary Knowledge Rating Chart** for Act V. Read the words aloud once more and have students rate their knowledge of the words again in the After Reading column. Clarify any words that are still problematic. Have students write their own definition and example or sentence in the appropriate column. Then, have students complete the Vocabulary Practice at the end of the selection. Encourage students to use the words in further discussion and written work about this selection. Remind them that they will be accountable for these words on the **Selection Test, *Unit 5 Resources,*** pp. 111–113 or 114–116.

25 Her nurse is privy;[55] and if aught in this
Miscarried by my fault, let my old life
Be sacrificed some hour before his time
Unto the rigor[56] of severest law.

PRINCE. We still have known thee for a holy man.
Where's Romeo's man? What can he say to this?

BALTHASAR. I brought my master news of Juliet's death;
And then in post he came from Mantua
To this same place, to this same monument.
This letter he early bid me give his father,
And threat'ned me with death, going in the vault,
If I departed not and left him there.

PRINCE. Give me the letter. I will look on it.
Where is the County's page that raised the watch?
Sirrah, what made your master[57] in this place?

BOY. He came with flowers to strew his lady's grave;
And bid me stand aloof, and so I did.
Anon comes one with light to ope the tomb;
And by and by my master drew on him;
And then I ran away to call the watch.

PRINCE. This letter doth make good the friar's words,
Their course of love, the tidings of her death;
And here he writes that he did buy a poison
Of a poor 'pothecary and therewithal
Came to this vault to die and lie with Juliet.
Where be these enemies? Capulet, Montague,
See what a scourge is laid upon your hate,
That heaven finds means to kill your joys with love.
And I, for winking at[58] your discords too,
Have lost a brace[59] of kinsmen. All are punished.

CAPULET. O brother Montague, give me thy hand.
This is my daughter's jointure,[60] for no more
Can I demand.

MONTAGUE. But I can give thee more;
For I will raise her statue in pure gold,
That whiles Verona by that name is known,
There shall no figure at such rate[61] be set
28 As that of true and faithful Juliet.

CAPULET. As rich shall Romeo's by his lady's lie—
Poor sacrifices of our enmity![62]

55. privy secretly informed about.

56. rigor strictness.

57. made your master was your master doing.

Vocabulary
scourge (skurj) *n.* instrument for inflicting punishment

58. winking at closing my eyes to.
59. brace pair (Mercutio and Paris).
60. jointure wedding gift; marriage settlement.
61. rate value.
62. enmity hostility.

27 
Reading Check
How does the Friar explain his role in the fate of Romeo and Juliet?

26 Connecting to the Big Question

1. Tell students that one type of difference among people is that of social status.
2. Have a volunteer read the bracketed passage aloud.
3. **Ask:** What is the Friar doing in lines 266–269?

   Answer: He is claiming some responsibility for the recent deaths and asking for appropriate punishment.
4. **Ask:** What is the Prince's main point in line 270?

   Answer: He still sees the Friar as holy and not worthy of being condemned for wrongdoing.
5. **Ask:** What does this passage imply about how people's differences define them?

   Possible response: In the Prince's mind, the Friar's position of authority makes him different—holier—than a "regular" person. The Friar's social status defines him in a way that makes the Prince somewhat blind to the Friar's questionable actions.

27 Reading Check

Answer: The Friar explains everything that happened—how he married Romeo and Juliet; how he gave Juliet a sleeping potion to keep her from marrying Paris; and how he wrote to Romeo to explain what he did, but the letter didn't arrive in time. He says that he should receive the severest punishment, but only if he is judged to be at fault.

Concept Connector

Anticipation Guide

Have students return to their **Anticipation Guides** and respond to the statements again in the After Reading column. They may do this individually or in their original pairs or groups. Then, lead a class discussion, probing for what students have learned that confirms or invalidates each statement. Encourage students to cite specific details, quotations, or other evidence from the text to support their responses to each statement.

Writing About the Big Question

Have students compare their responses to the sentence starter they completed before reading Act V with their ideas afterwards. Ask them to explain whether their thoughts have changed.

Reading Skill Graphic Organizer

Ask students to review the graphic organizers they completed to identify causes and effects. Show them **Reading Skill Graphic Organizer A** (*Graphic Organizer Transparencies*, p. 163) as an example.

28 Literary Analysis

Tragedy and Motive

Ask students the Literary Analysis question.

Possible response: Montague may wish to honor Juliet's faithfulness to his son. He may also want a reminder of the cost of the feud between the Montagues and the Capulets, so that the feud will never be renewed.

ASSESS

Answers

Critical Thinking

Before students respond, you may wish to have them write a brief objective summary of the selection. As they answer the questions below, remind them to support their answers with evidence from the text.

1. (a) Romeo is challenging fate. (b) This is consistent with his rash, dramatic character.
2. (a) The Friar's message goes astray; the Capulets rush Juliet's wedding; Romeo arrives at the tomb before the Friar. (b) The Friar's plan relies too much on perfect timing.
3. (a) The fathers shake hands and promise to build monuments to the other's child. (b) **Possible response:** Some students may say that the marriage by itself might have ended the feud. (c) **Possible response:** Most students will say that it is not a fair exchange.
4. **Possible responses:** Some students will say that Romeo and Juliet didn't have control over their differences because they couldn't change who their parents were or what caused their families to fight. Other students will say that Romeo and Juliet could have reasoned with their families to end the feud rather than acting in secret.

63. glooming cloudy; gloomy.

Literary Analysis
Tragedy and Motive What might be Lord Montague's motive for the promise he makes to Lord Capulet?

PRINCE. A glooming[63] peace this morning with it brings.
The sun for sorrow will not show his head.
Go hence, to have more talk of these sad things;
Some shall be pardoned, and some punishèd;
For never was a story of more woe
Than this of Juliet and her Romeo. *[Exit all.]*

Critical Thinking

Cite textual evidence to support your responses.

1. **Key Ideas and Details (a)** In Act V, Scene i, what causes Romeo to exclaim, "Then I defy you, stars"? **(b) Interpret:** In what way are Romeo's words consistent with what you know of his character?
2. **Key Ideas and Details (a)** Identify at least three events that cause the Friar's scheme to fail. **(b) Analyze:** Why is it not surprising that the scheme fails?
3. **Integration of Knowledge and Ideas (a)** How does the relationship between the feuding families change at the end of the play? **(b) Draw Conclusions:** Were the deaths of Romeo and Juliet necessary for this change to occur? Explain. **(c) Make a Judgment:** Is the end of long-term violence between their families a fair exchange for the deaths of Romeo and Juliet? Explain your response.
4. **Integration of Knowledge and Ideas** Did Romeo and Juliet have any control over the differences that separated them and led to their tragic end? Explain. *[Connect to the Big Question: Do our differences define us?]*

Assessment Resources

Unit 5 Resources

L1 L2 EL **Selection Test A,** pp. 111–113. Administer Test A to less advanced readers.

L3 L4 EL **Selection Test B,** pp. 114–116. Administer Test B to on-level and more advanced students.

L3 L4 **Open-Book Test,** pp. 108–109. As an alternative, give the Open-Book Test.

All **Customizable Test Bank**

All **Self-tests**
Students may prepare for the **Selection Test** by taking the **Self-test** online.

PHLit Online! All assessment resources are available at **www.PHLitOnline.com.**

After You Read The Tragedy of Romeo and Juliet, Act V

Literary Analysis: Tragedy and Motive

1. **Key Ideas and Details** **(a)** Use a chart like the one shown to identify details of the elements that contribute to the **tragedy** in the play. **(b)** Explain which element you think is most responsible for the tragic events.

Romeo and Juliet's Personalities	Fate or Chance	Other Causes

2. **Key Ideas and Details** **(a)** What is the Friar's **motive** for helping Romeo and Juliet? **(b)** To what extent is he responsible for their tragedy? Explain.
3. **Integration of Knowledge and Skills** What theme or message does Shakespeare convey through the tragic events in the play?
4. **Integration of Knowledge and Ideas** What positive message about the human spirit, if any, does this tragic play offer? Explain.

Reading Skill: Summarize

5. **(a)** What events cause Romeo and Paris to arrive at Juliet's tomb at the same time? **(b)** What is the effect of this? Explain your answer.
6. **(a)** Analyze the chain of causes and effects that leads to the tragic ending. **(b)** **Summarize** the events that occur at the tomb.

Vocabulary

Acquisition and Use Identify the word in each group that does not belong with the others. Explain your response.

1. remnants, future, past
2. penury, poor, wealthy
3. haughty, proud, insecure
4. ambiguities, absolute, uncertain
5. scourge, pleasure, happiness
6. disperse, scatter, collect

Word Study Use the context of the sentences and what you know about the **Latin prefix *ambi-*** to explain your answer to each question.

1. Would you know how to respond if someone asked an *ambiguous* question?
2. Is an *ambivalent* person unsure of what he or she wants in life?

Word Study

The **Latin prefix *ambi-*** means "both."

Apply It Explain how the prefix *ambi-* contributes to the meanings of these words. Consult a dictionary if necessary.

ambivalent
ambient
ambidextrous
ambition

ASSESS/EXTEND

Answers

Literary Analysis

1. **Possible responses:** (a) **Romeo's and Juliet's Personalities**—Romeo: impulsive, hotheaded; Juliet: strong-willed, disobedient; **Fate or Chance**—the accidental meeting; Tybalt's misunderstanding of Romeo; the Friar's luckless plan. **Other Causes**—The feud between the Montagues and the Capulets. (b) Fate is most responsible for the tragic events because it took a long series of mischances to produce the final outcome.
   For other sample answers, see ***Graphic Organizer Transparencies,*** **Literary Analysis Graphic Organizer A,** p. 165, and the **Additional Answers** section.
2. (a) The Friar wants to end the feud between the families. (b) He is responsible to some extent because his plan is too elaborate and time-sensitive.
3. **Possible response:** Shakespeare appears to be saying that old anger can destroy new love.
4. Shakespeare affirms that love—even in death—can triumph over dissension and enmity.

Reading Skill

5. (a) Paris comes to mourn Juliet. Romeo arrives to die beside her. (b) Paris believes Romeo is vandalizing the tomb and provokes him into a combat fatal to Paris.
6. (a) Romeo hears of Juliet's death and hastens to her tomb to die, missing the Friar's letter but meeting and killing Paris. Juliet awakens to find Romeo dead; she stabs herself. (b) Families, servants, lawmen, and the Prince gather at the tomb; the Friar explains everything. The Prince, Capulet, and Montague meet at the tomb, and the two families end their feud.

Vocabulary

Acquisition and Use

1. *Future* and *past* are antonyms; *remnants* means "what is left over," so it doesn't belong.
2. *Penury* and *poor* are synonyms meaning "poverty"; *wealthy* doesn't belong.

Answers Continued

3. *Haughty* and *proud* are similar in meaning; *insecure* doesn't belong.
4. *Ambiguities* and *uncertain* both mean "unclear"; *absolute* doesn't belong.
5. *Pleasure* and *happiness* both mean "a pleased feeling"; *scourge* doesn't belong.
6. *Disperse* and *scatter* both mean "to spread about"; *collect* doesn't belong.

Word Study
Sample answers:

1. No, the prefix *ambi-* means "both," and *ambiguous* means "capable of being understood in both or many ways." An *ambiguous* question is unclear, so it is difficult to answer.
2. Yes, *ambivalent* means "having conflicting feelings," so an *ambivalent* person would be unsure about what he or she wants.

Word Study: Apply It
Sample answers:

To be *ambivalent* is to be both sure and unsure. *Ambient* is encompassing or on both or all sides. To be *ambidextrous* is to be both right-handed and left-handed. *Ambition* implies wanting both success and power.

Conventions

Introduce the skill, using the instruction on the student page.

Think Aloud: Model the Skill

Model the skill of using participles and gerunds. Say to students:

> In the sentence "Smiling relatives greeted their guests," *smiling* is a participle because it describes the noun *relatives*. In the sentence "Smiling enthusiastically, the relatives greeted their guests," "smiling enthusiastically" is a participial phrase, describing the noun *relatives*.

PH WRITING COACH Grade 9

Students will find instruction on and practice with participial and gerund phrases in Chapter 15, Section 1.

Practice A

1. suffering
2. fighting
3. doomed
4. weeping

Reading Application

Sample answer:

Participle: ". . .he should hither come as this dire night/To help to take her from her borrowed grave . . ."

Gerund: ". . . and the neglecting it/ May do much danger."

Practice B

1. Killing Romeo was Tybalt's only thought.
2. Feeling great sorrow, Juliet held the knife.
3. Wanting his daughter married, Capulet gave her to Paris.
4. Thinking of Juliet was his greatest joy.

Writing Application

Sample answer:

The killing of Tybalt was a pivotal moment. Romeo's drinking the contents of the vial sealed his fate.

PERFORMANCE TASKS

Integrated Language Skills

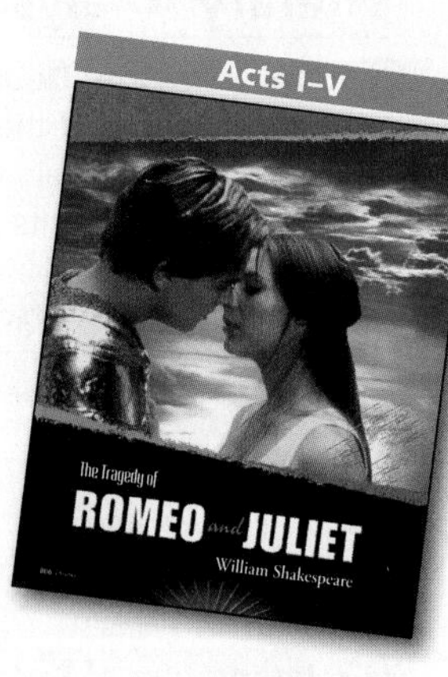

Acts I–V
The Tragedy of
ROMEO and JULIET
William Shakespeare

The Tragedy of Romeo and Juliet

Conventions: Participles and Participial Phrases, Gerunds and Gerund Phrases

A **participle** is a verb form that is used as an adjective.

A **present participle** ends in *-ing.* The past participle of a regular verb ends in *-ed.* A **participial phrase** is a group of words that functions as an adjective in the sentence and contains a participle.

Present Participle	*growing* child
Past Participle	*troubled* child
Participial Phrase	*Focusing intently,* the driver stopped in time.

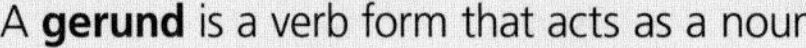

A **gerund** is a verb form that acts as a noun.

It can function as a subject, an object, a predicate noun, or the object of a preposition. A **gerund phrase** is a gerund and its modifiers. A gerund phrase, also called a **noun phrase,** also acts as a noun.

Subject	*Remodeling* the building's style was a good idea.
Direct Object	Michael enjoys *painting.*
Predicate Noun	His favorite sport is *fishing.*
Object of the Preposition	Lucille never gets tired of *singing.*
Gerund Phrase	The *loud, shrill howling* continued all morning.

Practice A Identify the participle or gerund in each sentence.

1. Suffering greatly, Romeo emptied the vial.
2. The young men seemed to enjoy fighting.
3. The doomed lovers yearned for each other.
4. Loud weeping spread through Verona.

Reading Application In *The Tragedy of Romeo and Juliet,* find one sentence that uses a participle or participle phrase and one that uses a gerund or gerund phrase.

Practice B In each sentence, change one of the verbs to a participle or a gerund. Then, use that word or phrase to combine the two sentences.

1. Tybalt wanted to kill Romeo. It was his only thought.
2. Juliet felt great sorrow. She held the knife.
3. Capulet wanted his daughter married. He gave her to Paris.
4. He thought of Juliet. It was his greatest joy.

Writing Application Write two sentences following the models in the second chart above.

PH WRITING COACH Further instruction and practice are available in *Prentice Hall Writing Coach.*

Extend the Lesson

Sentence Modeling

Draw students' attention to the following sentence from *The Tragedy of Romeo and Juliet,* Act V:

> *A glooming peace this morning with it brings./ The sun for sorrow will not show his head.*

Ask students what they notice about the sentence. Elicit from them that in the sentence, the word *glooming* is a participle. Then, ask what else they notice. (By using the participle *glooming* instead of a normal adjective to describe *peace,* Shakespeare provides the reader with a vivid image of the atmosphere and infuses the moment with a sense of movement.)

Have students imitate the sentence in a sentence on a topic of their own choosing, matching each grammatical and stylistic feature discussed. Have volunteers read their sentences aloud to the class.

Writing

Argumentative Text Imagine that you are the editor of a newspaper in Verona at the time of the play. Write an **editorial** addressing the Prince's response to the deaths of Tybalt and Mercutio.

- Reread the Prince's dialogue in Act III, Scene i.
- Decide whether Romeo's sentence was appropriate, and explain whether you agree or disagree with the Prince's order.
- Write the editorial, supporting your ideas with details from Act III, Scenes i–iii.

Share your editorial with classmates, and encourage them to write letters to the editor in support of or in opposition to your editorial.

Argumentative Text As Friar Lawrence, write a **persuasive letter** to both Lord Capulet and Lord Montague. Urge them to end their feud.

- Make a list of factual evidence and emotional pleas that support your argument. Consider appealing to the families' sense of logic and ethical beliefs.
- Begin your draft by explaining the benefits of marriage and the benefits of becoming allies rather than enemies.
- Use persuasive techniques, such as powerful word choice, repetition, and rhetorical questions, to strengthen your argument.

Grammar Application Make sure to use participles, participial phrases, gerunds, and gerund phrases correctly in your editorial and persuasive letter.

Common Core State Standards

L.9-10.1.b; W.9-10.1, W.9-10.4

[For the full wording of the standards, see page 912.]

Writing Workshop: *Work in Progress*

Prewriting for How-to Essay For a how-to essay you may write, record five tasks that you do well. Choose one and complete each of these steps:

1. Make a list of steps necessary to complete your task.
2. Visualize performing the task step by step. After you have finished visualizing, go back and add any missed steps to your list.
3. Use stick figures to make a "cartoon frame" for each step on your list. Add dialogue bubbles to each frame and write a sentence in which you explain the step.

Save your work in your writing portfolio.

Use this prewriting activity to prepare for the **Writing Workshop** on page 1002.

EXTEND/ASSESS

Answers

Writing

1. Review the assignments, using the instruction on the student page.
2. Guide students to select one of the Writing activities to complete.
3. To support students in writing an editorial or a persuasive letter, give them **Support for Writing,** p. 105 in ***Unit 5 Resources.***
4. To evaluate students' editorials, use the Writing an Editorial rubric, pp. 263–264 in ***Professional Development Guidebook.*** To evaluate students' letters, use the Persuasive Essay rubric, pp. 230–231 in ***Professional Development Guidebook.***
5. ***Provide the following tips for students:***
   - When writing an editorial, there is no wrong opinion, as long as it can be supported with details from the text.
   - A successful persuasive letter should include both factual evidence and emotional pleas, and it should use techniques such as powerful word choice and rhetorical questions to strengthen the argument.

Grammar Application

Have students check their drafts to make sure they have used participles and gerunds correctly.

Six Traits Focus

	Ideas		Word Choice
✓	Organization	✓	Sentence Fluency
	Voice	✓	Conventions

PH WRITING COACH Grade 9

Students will find instruction on and practice with editorials in Chapter 9.

Writing Workshop
Work in Progress

Have students save their completed lists of task steps in their portfolios. They will use them later as they complete the Writing Workshop assignment (see pp. 960–965).

Speaking and Listening

1. Review the assignments, using the instruction on the student page.
2. Guide students to select one of the Listening and Speaking activities to complete.
3. To support students' work on the assignments, have students complete the **Support for Extend Your Learning** page (***Unit 5 Resources,*** p. 106).
4. Provide the following tips for students:
   - When preparing for a staged performance, highlight and practice challenging vocabulary to improve reading fluency during the performance.
   - In a mock trial, in addition to considering the clarity, quality, and effectiveness of the speakers' arguments, the jury must evaluate the validity of the speakers' claims.

PERFORMANCE TASKS

Integrated Language Skills

Speaking and Listening

Comprehension and Collaboration Select a scene from *The Tragedy of Romeo and Juliet* and plan a **staged performance** with classmates. Choose a scene with at least three characters. Then, plan and rehearse the scene. Follow these steps:

- Decide who will play each role.
- As you rehearse, use appropriate gestures, body movements, and eye contact that convey the qualities of your character. Adjust your tone of voice and speed of delivery to dramatize the performance.
- Pause periodically during your rehearsal to assess the group's work. Take turns critiquing the performance. Express your thoughts clearly and convey your criticism in a respectful way. As others present criticism, listen carefully and ask questions to clarify comments. Discuss ways to respond to comments and to improve the performance.

When you are ready, perform the scene for the class, and invite comments and feedback from the audience.

Comprehension and Collaboration As a class, conduct a **mock trial** to investigate the causes of the tragedy in *The Tragedy of Romeo and Juliet.* Follow these steps:

- Assign roles for the main characters of the play, the lawyers, and the judge. The rest of the class should serve as the jury.
- Take depositions, or statements in which each character tells the story from his or her perspective. Lawyers should follow up the statements of witnesses with questions to clarify and expand on the witnesses' stories.
- All participants should use appropriate gestures, eye contact, and a speaking voice that projects the correct tone and mood.
- Choose language—formal, informal, slang, or jargon—that fits the social, cultural, and professional status of each character.

Jury members should listen carefully to distinguish between valid claims and *propaganda*—arguments that twist or ignore facts to present a biased and distorted picture of events. Listeners should also evaluate the clarity, quality, effectiveness, and coherence of each speaker's arguments, evidence, and delivery.

When the trial is completed, the jury members should present their verdict, explaining which characters bear the most blame for the tragedy.

Research and Technology

Presentation of Knowledge and Ideas Conduct research to create an **annotated flowchart** that accurately displays and explains the structure of the nobility in sixteenth-century Verona. Your flowchart should show the relative positions of the Prince, Count Paris, the Montagues, and the Capulets.

- Use both primary and secondary sources as you learn more about the time period in which the story unfolds.
- Evaluate the validity and reliability of the information you research and the sources you use.
- Organize your text and images logically.
- Remember to document sources for both ideas and images, using standard citation style. (For more on citing sources, see page R36.)

Present your flowchart to the class, explaining where you located information.

Presentation of Knowledge and Ideas With a small group, view a filmed version of *Romeo and Juliet,* and then write a **film review**. It might be a movie version, a filmed stage production, or a filmed version of the ballet. Take notes as you view, using the following questions to guide your note taking:

- What specific effects contribute to the beauty or artistry of the film?
- How do the movements of the actors or dancers communicate the play's ideas?
- How does the film use music, stage sets, and camerawork to convey mood?
- How do key scenes in the film compare to those in the written version? If scenes are changed or omitted in the filmed version, how does the change affect meaning?

After viewing, use your notes to draft your review. Be sure to highlight the key differences between the filmed version and the written version, and explain which version you thought was more effective. Finally, present your review to the class.

Presentation of Knowledge and Ideas With a partner, create a **multimedia presentation** on Renaissance music. Use library or Internet resources to collect examples of music that would have been played by the musicians in Act IV, Scene v. Find pictures of instruments from the period as well. Record accurate bibliographic information about your sources, using correct citation style.

Present your findings in class using available props, visual aids, and electronic media. Then, lead a discussion about the music and its effects on listeners.

Common Core State Standards

SL.9-10.1, SL.9-10.4; RL9-10.7
[For the full wording of the standards, see page 912.]

www.PHLitOnline.com
- Interactive graphic organizers
- Grammar tutorial
- Interactive journals

EXTEND/ASSESS

Research and Technology

1. Review the assignments, using the instruction on the student page.
2. Guide students to select one of the Research and Technology choices.
3. To support students' work on the assignments, have students complete the **Support for Extend Your Learning** page (***Unit 5 Resources,*** p. 107).
4. Provide the following tips for students:
   - When conducting research, remember to organize your research logically, to evaluate the validity and reliability of your sources, and to document your sources correctly.
   - When reviewing the film, be sure to consider multiple aspects of the film, such as the camera work, dance, music, and lighting.
   - Remember that in a multimedia presentation, the visual aids are meant to *accompany* the oral presentation. Including too much text on the visual aids will overwhelm the audience and draw attention away from the presenter.

Teaching Resources

Unit 5 Resources

L3 L4 EL **Integrated Language Skills: Grammar,** p. 104

L3 L4 EL **Support for Writing,** p. 105

L3 L4 **Support for Extend Your Learning,** pp. 106 and 107

L4 **Enrichment,** pp. 31, 49, 67, 85, and 103

Enriched Online Student Edition
Available under After You Read for this selection:

L4 **Interactive Grammar Tutorial**

L3 L4 **Internet Research Activity**

Professional Development Guidebook
Rubrics for Self-Assessment: How-to Essay, pp. 228–229

All print and digital resources are available at **www.PHLitOnline.com.** Online resources accessible by students are noted on the student page.

MONITORING PROGRESS

Using the Test Practice

In this two-page Test Practice, students apply the reading skill for the first half of Unit 5 to a passage of fiction and a passage of nonfiction.

Review the skill, summarizing, then administer the test. For more guidance, consult the ***Classroom Strategies and Teaching Routines*** card, **Administering Timed Tests.**

ASSESS

Answers

Answers With Explanations

1. **B**—This sentence includes all key details in the stage directions. *Incorrect answers:* A—This sentence leaves out the two women, their costumes, and their posture. C—This sentence omits the lighting and the dress and posture of the women. D—This sentence omits the lighting and is not specific enough in describing the women.
2. **A**—This sentence summarizes the important information in the scene. *Incorrect answers:* B—This sentence ignores the interaction between the characters. C—The focus of the scene is not on Sojourner Truth, but the two women. D—This sentence does not mention Sarah or Sojourner Truth.
3. **A**—Sarah tells Abigail that Sojourner Truth's words inspired her. *Incorrect answers:* B—Sarah states no desire to speak at a convention. C—On the contrary, Sarah was moved by the speakers. D—Sarah does not express an opinion about the length of the convention.
4. **D**—The women's attire is too insignificant to include in a summary. *Incorrect answers:* A—This sentence is important and sets up the scene. B—same explanation as for A. C—same explanation as for A.

Test Practice: Reading

Summarize

Drama Selection

Directions: *Read the selection. Then, answer the questions.*

The stage is dark. A spotlight shines on two young women sitting on a bench. Both wear plain, long dresses in a 19th-century style. It is evident from their posture and position that the two women are strangers.

SARAH. *(turning shyly to the other woman on the bench)* Did you attend the Women's Rights Convention today? Did you hear Sojourner Truth?

ABIGAIL. *(looking startled and then annoyed)* I would never get mixed up with that nonsense!

SARAH. *(gaining confidence)* I also felt that way before I went to the convention. The struggle for women's rights may seem impossible, but it is not. Some women have overcome so much already. Don't you believe that you deserve equal rights? *(Abigail nods and leans towards Sarah, appearing interested.)* Let me tell you about Sojourner Truth's speech. Her words may inspire you just as they inspired me.

1. Which sentence best summarizes the first set of stage directions?

A. The stage is mostly dark, with one blindingly bright spotlight shining.
B. A spotlight shines on two women in 19th-century dresses seated on a bench.
C. There are two young women.
D. One woman in a long, plain dress sits next to another woman in a long, plain dress.

2. Which statement best summarizes the action in the scene?

A. Sarah meets Abigail and begins to tell her about Sojourner Truth's speech.
B. Sarah witnesses Sojourner Truth's speech at a convention.
C. Sojourner Truth attends a Women's Rights Convention and gives a speech that many women find inspirational.
D. Abigail is originally not interested in women's rights, but becomes curious.

3. How does Sarah feel about the Women's Rights Convention?

A. She is inspired by the convention.
B. She wants to speak at a convention.
C. The convention speakers annoy her.
D. The convention was too short for her.

4. Which sentence should be left out of a summary of this scene?

A. Sarah attended a convention.
B. Sarah was excited about equal rights.
C. Sojourner Truth's speech inspired Sarah.
D. Sarah and Abigail wore plain dresses.

Writing for Assessment

Write a three-sentence summary of the scene. Be sure to use your own words and include only the main ideas in your summary.

Writing for Assessment

Students' summaries should contain these main ideas: Sarah attended the Women's Rights Convention, she was inspired by Sojourner Truth's speech there, and she tries to persuade Abigail of the importance of women's rights.

Strategies for Test Taking

Remind students to read each question carefully. The questions test students' understanding of summarizing statements. A summary is different from a main idea and a restatement. A summary shortens the information but uses many of the same words. A main idea states only one important idea. A restatement gives the same information using different words. Urge students to keep these differences in mind as they read the answer choices.

Nonfiction Selection

Directions: *Read the selection. Then, answer the questions.*

Women's rights activist and abolitionist Sojourner Truth was born in 1797 in New York State. She was born into slavery and spent the early years of her life enslaved, Suffering brutalities too numerous to mention. When she escaped slavery in 1827, she retrieved her son who had been sold to a plantation owner in Alabama at age five. As a free woman, Sojourner Truth took it upon herself to fight for the rights of slaves and women and to help those freed after the Civil War. Sojourner Truth's best-known speech "Ain't I a Woman?" was given at the Women's Rights Convention in Akron, Ohio. Over the years, Sojourner Truth traveled the country preaching and speaking out for women's rights and the abolition of slavery. She was a powerful force in both movements.

1. Into how many basic units of thought can sentence 2 be broken?

A. one
B. two
C. three
D. four

2. Which sentence *best* summarizes the first three sentences of the selection?

A. Sojourner Truth suffered greatly when she was enslaved from 1797 to 1827.
B. Sojourner Truth, women's rights activist, abolitionist, and former slave, was born in 1797 in New York.
C. Sojourner Truth was a women's rights activist who lived through and fought against slavery.
D. Abolitionist and former slave Sojourner Truth was born in New York in 1797.

3. What did Sojourner Truth make her life's work after she escaped slavery?

A. teaching other freed slaves
B. fighting for the rights of the oppressed
C. keeping public speaking engagements
D. writing speeches to deliver at conventions

4. Which sentence *best* summarizes the selection?

A. Born in 1797, Sojourner Truth was enslaved; she rescued her son from slavery after she herself escaped.
B. Sojourner Truth was born in 1797 in New York and lived as a slave until 1827, when she escaped.
C. Sojourner Truth gave a famous speech at a convention for women's rights.
D. Sojourner Truth escaped slavery to become a powerful force in the women's rights and abolitionist movements.

Writing for Assessment

Connecting Across Texts
How does reading the biography of Sojourner Truth help you understand Sarah's reaction to her speech? Give your response in a paragraph. Use details from both passages.

www.PHLitOnline.com
- Online practice
- Instant feedback

Differentiated Instruction for Universal Access

Strategy for Special-Needs Students
To help students prepare for the Writing for Assessment assignment, review the dialogue on p. 936 with them. Ask them how Sarah was affected by attending the convention. (She was inspired by Sojourner Truth's speech.) Then, read the nonfiction selection with students. Tell them to listen for important facts about Sojourner Truth. After they have finished rereading the selection, work with them to create a list of facts they remember. Then, ask them to identify facts that would make a person admire Sojourner Truth. (Possible responses: Students might cite such matters as her escape from slavery, which might have involved danger, and her dedication to the cause of equal rights.) Encourage them to use these ideas in writing their responses.

ASSESS

Answers

Answers With Explanations

1. C—The sentence has three units of thought: she was born in slavery, she lived her early years in slavery, and that life was marked by suffering. *Incorrect answers:* A—While the three ideas are all about slavery, they are distinct. B—There are three units of thought. D—same explanation as for B.
2. C—This sentence includes the key facts in the first three sentences. *Incorrect answers:* A—This sentence leaves out the fact that Truth was a women's rights activist and an abolitionist. B—This summary mostly focuses on the information in sentence 1. D—This sentence omits Truth's work as a women's rights activist.
3. B—The passage says she fought for the rights of both slaves and women. *Incorrect answers:* A—The passage never says that she taught former freed slaves, and this answer ignores her work for women's rights. C—Her public speaking was part of her fight for the oppressed. D—same explanation as for C.
4. D—This summary states the importance of Sojourner Truth's life in a few words. *Incorrect answers:* A—This sentence focuses only on the first part of the selection. B—same explanation as for A. C—This is only one important fact from the selection.

Writing for Assessment

Students' essays should give details about Truth's life and explain how someone like Sarah, hearing Truth speak at the Women's Rights Convention, could be inspired to work for equal rights for women.

Students may take the test in interactive format with instant feedback online at **www.PHLitOnline.com.**

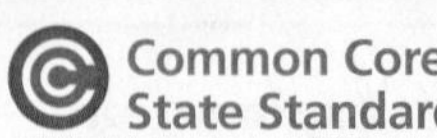

PRETEACH

Common Core State Standards

- Reading Informational Text 3
- Writing 2
- Language 4.c, 6

Reading Skill

1. Introduce the skill, using the instruction on the student page.
2. Review the chart.
3. Tell students that they will read for understanding as they explore the atlas entry in this section.

Think Aloud: Model the Skill

Model the skill of analyzing text information. Say to students:

When I try to analyze the information in a text, I start by looking at the headings. I sometimes flip through several pages to see what is coming up. Then I read each section carefully. After I read, I think about how each part fits together logically.

Multidraft Reading

Have students follow a multidraft reading protocol after they preview the selection.

- **First reading**— Have students read to identify key ideas and details.
- **Second reading**— Have students read to identify the structure of the text.
- **Third reading**— Have students read to integrate knowledge and ideas by connecting the text to the world, their own experiences, and other texts.

Content-Area Vocabulary

1. Have students say each word.
2. Next, use each word in a sentence that defines it.
3. Finally, repeat your definitional sentence or a similar sentence with the word missing and have the class "fill in the blank" chorally.

Reading for Information

Analyzing Functional and Expository Texts

Atlas Entry

Travel Brochure

Common Core State Standards

Reading Informational Text

3. Analyze how the author unfolds an analysis or series of ideas or events, including the order in which the points are made, how they are introduced and developed, and the connections that are drawn between them.

Writing

2. Write informative/explanatory texts to examine and convey complex ideas, concepts, and information clearly and accurately through the effective selection, organization, and analysis of content. *(Timed Writing)*

Language

4.c. Consult general and specialized reference materials, both print and digital, to find the pronunciation of a word or determine or clarify its precise meaning, its part of speech, or its etymology.

6. Acquire and use accurately grade-appropriate general academic and domain-specific words and phrases; demonstrate independence in gathering vocabulary knowledge when considering a word or phrase important to comprehension or expression.

Reading Skill: Analyze Text Information

Reading about the same subject across different types of informational documents provides a more complete understanding of that subject. Here the subject is Italy. **Examine the sequence** in which information is presented in each document and critique its logic. To do this, **analyze** which details are emphasized and whether that information is in a logical order. Text features, such as maps and headings, can give clues about the sequence of information and can also aid understanding of the text.

Feature	How the Feature Aids Understanding
title or heading	states a broad topic
subheading	organizes details and support by subtopic
bold print	draws readers' attention to key words or details
map	provides broad overview of a particular place (geography, location, distance)
image	illustrates and clarifies details mentioned in the text

Content-Area Vocabulary

These words appear in the selections that follow. You may also encounter them in other content-area texts.

- **peninsula** (pə nin´ sə lə) *n.* land mass almost completely surrounded by water
- **temperate** (tem´ pər it) *adj.* not very hot and not very cold
- **Renaissance** (ren´ə säns´) *n.* term meaning "rebirth"; period in Europe (14th-17th centuries) when the arts and sciences flourished after a long period of inactivity

Do our differences define us?

Suggest that climate is an easy basis for comparison of places. Encourage students to think of other aspects of geography, both physical and cultural, that they can use as the basis of analyzing the similarities and differences between places.

Differentiated Instruction for Universal Access

Reading Support

Give students reading support with the appropriate version of the *Reader's Notebooks:*

- L2 L3 *Reader's Notebook*
- L1 *Reader's Notebook: Adapted Version*
- EL *Reader's Notebook: English Learner's Version*

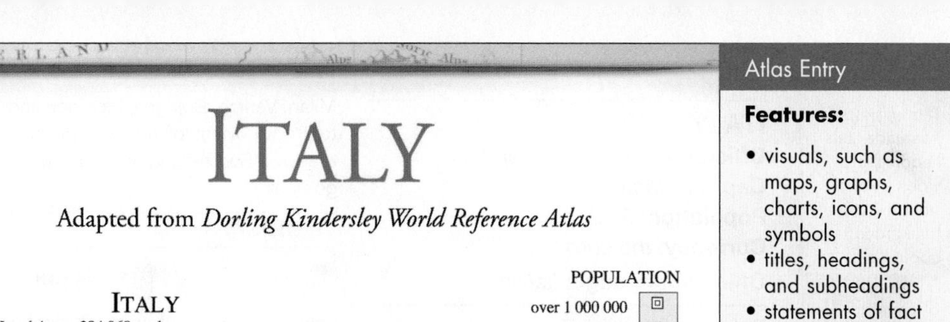

ITALY

Adapted from *Dorling Kindersley World Reference Atlas*

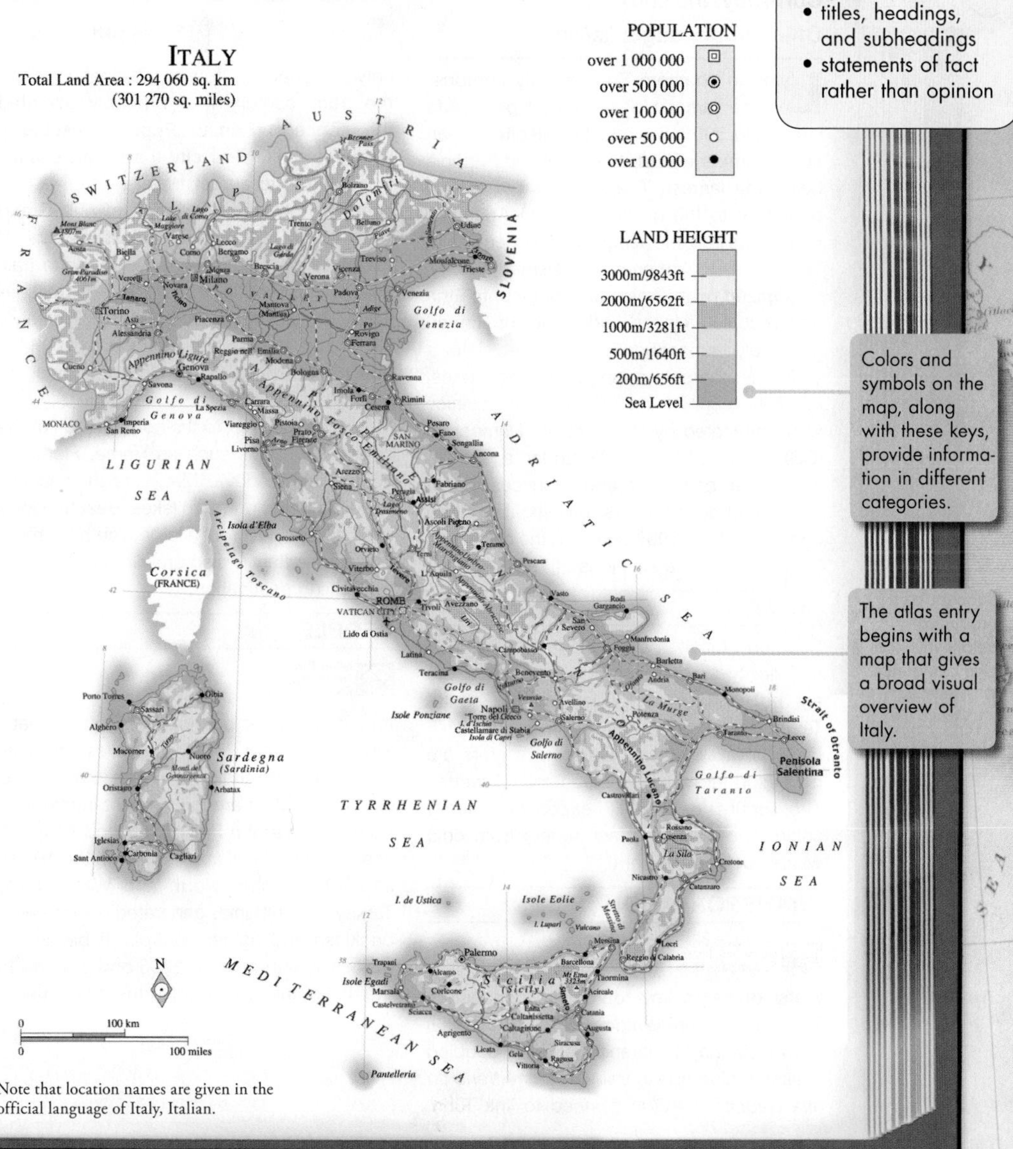

Note that location names are given in the official language of Italy, Italian.

Atlas Entry

Features:

- visuals, such as maps, graphs, charts, icons, and symbols
- titles, headings, and subheadings
- statements of fact rather than opinion

Colors and symbols on the map, along with these keys, provide information in different categories.

The atlas entry begins with a map that gives a broad visual overview of Italy.

Differentiated Instruction for Universal Access

Culturally Responsive Instruction

Give students the opportunity to develop their own atlas page about one of the nations that reflects their own ethnic heritage. Suggest that they download a map and consult authoritative, reliable sources for the information in the text accompanying it. Encourage them to describe the people, customs, traditions, and festivals of their chosen nation. They might also post recipes of traditional dishes from the nation's cuisine. If students know the language of the country, they could include some common sayings or proverbs both in the native language and translated into English. Display students' completed work in the classroom to celebrate the diverse backgrounds represented in the class.

TEACH

About Atlas Entries

1. Review with students the features listed in the Atlas Entry box on page 939. **Ask** them to define the term *icons* in their own words.

   Possible response: Icons are small pictures used to stand for a concept or action.

2. Discuss with students any experiences they have had using an atlas for information. Ask what information they were looking for and how easy it was to find in an atlas.
3. Explain to students that atlases are valuable tools to consult when searching for information about a geographic location.

Analyze Text Information

1. Remind students that atlases use both text and graphics to present information. Explain that in this atlas, each nation is profiled by a map and a written description. **Ask:** What information can you gather from the map?

   Possible response: The map shows the shape and landforms of Italy. In addition, different types of symbols for cities show the number of people living in them.

2. Direct students' attention to the two keys on the right side of the atlas page. **Ask:** How are these keys necessary for understanding some aspects of the map?

   Answer: The population key explains what size population is represented by each symbol. Without this information, someone using the atlas would not know how large cities are and how they compare in size. The land height key explains how high above sea level different areas of Italy are. Without this information, the colors on the map would not make sense.

3. Direct their attention to the scale in the lower left corner of the atlas page. **Ask:** How does this information help someone use the atlas map?

   Answer: The scale helps someone using the map translate the distance between two points on the map into actual distance in Italy.

Analyze Text Information

1. Remind students that atlases use headings and graphics to help users locate information quickly.
2. Tell students to look at the subheadings of the document. **Ask:** Under which section would you find information about a high speed train?

   Answer: That information would appear under the subheading "Transportation."
3. **Ask:** What kind of information is found under the heading "Climate"?

   Answer: The section under the heading "Climate" describes temperature and precipitation in different parts of Italy.
4. Have students look at the icons found under four of the section subheadings. **Ask:** What purpose do these icons serve?

   Possible response: The icons represent specific bits of information that are called out from the text within each heading.
5. Call on the students to discuss how useful they think the icons are, and whether they highlight truly important information. Challenge them to give reasons to support their judgments.

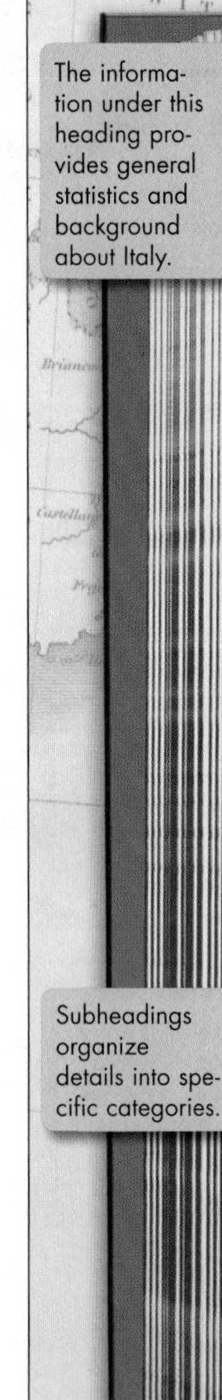

The information under this heading provides general statistics and background about Italy.

ITALY

Official Name: *Italian Republic*
Capital: *Rome*
Population: *57.2 million*
Currency: *the euro*
Official Language: *Italian*

Lying in southern Europe, Italy comprises the famous boot-shaped **peninsula** stretching 500 miles into the Mediterranean and a number of islands—Sicily and Sardinia being the largest. The Alps form a natural boundary to the north, while the Apennine Mountains run the length of the peninsula. The south is an area of seismic activity, epitomized by the volcanoes of Mounts Etna and Vesuvius. United under ancient Roman rule, Italy subsequently developed into a series of competing kingdoms and states, not fully reunited until 1870. Italian politics was dominated by the Christian Democrats (CD) from 1945 to 1992 under a system of political patronage and a succession of short-lived governments. Investigations into corruption from 1992 on led to the demise of this system in the elections of 1994.

Subheadings organize details into specific categories.

CLIMATE

Southern Italy has a Mediterranean climate; the north is more **temperate**. Summers are hot and dry, especially in the south. Temperatures range from 75°F to over 81°F in Sardinia and Sicily. Southern winters are mild; northern ones are cooler and wetter. The mountains usually experience heavy snow. The Adriatic coast suffers from cold winds such as the bora.

TRANSPORTATION

Many of Italy's key routes are congested. The trans-Apennine *autostrada* (expressway) from Bologna to Florence is being doubled in size. A high-speed train program (*treno ad alta velocità*—TAV) is planned to link Turin, Milan, Venice, Bologna, Florence and Naples to Rome. Most of Italy's exports travel by road, via Switzerland and Austria. Only 16% goes by sea.

TOURISM

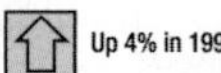

Italy has been a tourist destination since the 16th century and probably invented the concept. Roman Popes consciously aimed to make their city the most beautiful in the world to attract travelers. In the 18th century, Italy was the focus of any Grand Tour. Today, its many unspoilt centers of Renaissance culture continue to make Italy one of the world's major tourism destinations. The industry accounts for 3% of Italy's GDP, and hotels and restaurants employ one million out of a working population of 21 million.

Most visitors travel to the northern half of the country, to cities such as Rome, Florence, Venice and Padova. Many are increasingly traveling to the northern lakes. Beach resorts such as Rimini attract a large, youthful crowd in summer. Italy is also growing in popularity as a skiing destination.

PEOPLE

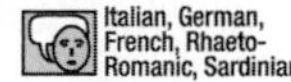

Italy is a remarkably homogeneous society. Most Italians are Roman Catholics, and Italy has far fewer ethnic minorities than its EU neighbors. Most are fairly recent immigrants from Ethiopia, the Philippines and Egypt. A sharp rise in illegal immigration in the 1980's and 1990's, from North and West Africa, Turkey and Albania, generated a right-wing backlash and tighter controls. It became a major election issue in 1993 and a factor in the rise of the federalist Northern League.

Think Aloud

Reading Skill
Model the skill of analyzing text information using the following "think aloud." Say to students:

I'll think out loud to show you how I might analyze text information. If I wanted to go to Italy for a trip, I would start by looking at the atlas entry. I might start by reading the information on this page, particularly the material on tourism. While reading this text, I might look now and then at the map to see how near different cities are to each other. I would also read the section on transportation to try to learn the easiest way to get into Italy and to travel within it once I was there. After I learned all I could from the atlas, I would be ready to look at some tourist brochures to figure out what things I could do in Italy.

Italy

from *Liberty Travel: Europe*

Italy's illustrious history is evident everywhere you go and each city treasures its own collection of cultural masterpieces.

The picturesque qualities of its cityscape and its rich cultural history give Rome an air of romance. Begin your exploration at the Spanish Steps or the Piazza St. Maria Maggiore, popular meeting places where visitors mix easily with locals. In the Holy See, you can spend days perusing the vast collections of the Vatican Museum & Gallery. Michelangelo's frescoes in the Sistine Chapel continue to mesmerize tourists and pilgrims alike.

Florence is Europe's capital of beauty and the birthplace of the **Renaissance**. Must-sees here include the Academy and Uffizi galleries, which house some of the world's finest collections of paintings and sculptures. The Duomo boasts sculptures by Michelangelo, and the Palazzo Vecchio is a splendid palace dating back to 1299.

Venice lives up to its reputation. Every bit as beautiful as you imagine, it is built on 120 tiny islands networked by canals, an elegant feat of engineering. A ride in a romantic gondola and a walk through the quaint streets are quintessential ways to tour the city. In St. Mark's Square, watch the figures in the Clock Tower signal the end of the day as you sip a rich coffee blend at Florian's historic botega de caffè.

A visit to Milan is an encounter with the height of Italian fashion and sophistication. The spired cathedral in the central Piazza del Duomo is aptly inspiring. You can easily find a table at one of Milan's many fine restaurants, but you'll have to make reservations to view da Vinci's Last Supper in the church of Santa Maria delle Grazie.

Each of the old Mediterranean seaside towns of the Amalfi Coast has its own distinct character. Highlights include the church of Santa Maria Assunta in Positano, Villa Cimbrone and Villa Rufolo in Ravello, and the views from the "Amalfi Drive," a narrow cliff-top route to Sorrento.

String together the jewel cities of Italy and create one unforgettable vacation.

This first paragraph gives a general statement about visiting the country of Italy. Following paragraphs discuss specific Italian cities.

Travel Brochure

Features:

- descriptions of travel services
- specific tour dates and times
- photos of destinations and landmarks
- text written for a general audience

About Travel Brochures

1. Review with students the features listed in the Travel Brochure box on page 941. **Ask** them to define the term *tour* in their own words.

   Possible response: A tour is a planned visit to another nation.

2. Call on students to describe vacations they have taken or would like to take with their families. Encourage them to discuss what kinds of sights they enjoyed, or would enjoy, seeing.

3. Remind students that the purpose of the travel brochure is to inform the reader about the background and the important attractions of a place. Point out the features of the travel brochure, including the pictures, the tour schedules, and the descriptive language about the destination.

Analyze Text Information

1. Direct students' attention to the callout pointing to the opening paragraph. Have students analyze the structure of the brochure. **Ask:** What cities does the brochure focus on?

   Answer: The brochure describes Rome, Florence, Venice, Milan, and seaside towns of the Amalfi Coast.

2. Point out that the author uses descriptive language to help the reader picture each city.

   Ask: What descriptive language does the author use to describe the attractions in Florence?

   Possible response: The descriptive language includes the words *beauty, must-sees, world's finest, boasts,* and *splendid*.

3. Draw attention to the photograph on the brochure. **Ask:** How does the photograph relate to the text?

   Possible responses: It helps the reader visualize the buildings and flowers that may be typical in Italy. It shows the visual beauty of Italy, making the text descriptions more believable.

Differentiated Instruction for Universal Access

Strategy for Less Proficient Readers

Use the text of the travel brochure to review proper nouns. Point out that the paragraphs mention the names of famous people and places, as well as the names of the cities themselves. Make a list on the board of the proper nouns. Call on students to supply a description that explains the category to which each proper noun belongs. You can use the following list to start:
Rome: city
Spanish Steps: famous location
Michelangelo: artist

Enrichment for Advanced Readers

Challenge students to apply what they have learned about analyzing text information in a travel brochure to virtual travel brochures that they find on the Internet. Have them investigate the informative and persuasive language of these brochures as well as the photographs that entice the reader to learn more. Call on them to write a brief evaluation of one travel-related Web site, explaining how it uses different features to communicate its message.

Analyze Text Information

1. Explain that travel brochures typically contain descriptions of different organized tours. Then, point out the headings on the page. **Ask:** How is the text on this page different from the first page of the travel brochure?

   Possible response: On the first page, the author gives an overview of the major cities and attractions. On this page, the author describes specific trips in Italy.

2. Have students read the descriptions of the tours. **Ask:** What information is contained in each description?

   Possible response: Each description tells where the tour will go and what the tourist will see. It tells how long the trip is, and where it will end.

3. **Ask** students to explain how the two parts of the brochure complement each other.

   Possible response: The first part gives general information about Italy and specific attractions of several cities. The second part identifies which specific sites a person can see on some actual tours.

4. **Ask:** What additional information would a tourist want to know about each trip?

   Possible response: A tourist would want to know the price of these tours.

Rome Sightseeing

Monumental Rome

Marvel at the glory of Rome via guided bus tour • View the Piazza della Repubblica Fontana di Trevi. Castel Sant'Angelo, and St. Peter's Basilica, home of Michelangelo's Pietà • Tour stops at the Pantheon, Piazza Navona and St. Peter's • Half day, mornings

Subheadings direct the reader to specific information about the different tours available.

Naples & Pompeii

Ride via deluxe motorcoach along the toll road A1, nicknamed Autostrada del Sole (Sun Highway) to Naples • In Naples, see the Mergellina, Lungomare Caracciolo, the Royal Palace, and the San Carlo Theatre • Continue to ancient Pompeii for lunch • Visit the beautifully restored ruins of Pompeii where, in AD 79, the eruption of Mt. Vesuvius buried portions of the city and some of its inhabitants in volcanic ash and pumice • Take in panoramic views of the Tyrrhenian Sea • Return to Rome • Full day

Florence

Ride via deluxe motorcoach along the Autostrada del Sole superhighway to Florence for a day of art and architecture • Visit the Cathedral of Santa Maria del Fiore, Giotto's Bell Tower and Baptistry, and the Academy Gallery, where Michelangelo's David resides • Lunch in a Florentine restaurant • Proceed to the Piazza Santa Croce for free time and shopping • End the day with a stop at the Piazzale Michelangelo for a panoramic view of Florence and the scenic Ponte Vecchio • Return to Rome • Full day

Illuminated Rome

Tour begins on the elegant Via Veneto • See the Aurelian Walls. Triton Fountain, and Quirinal Square with the Presidential Palace • Stop at the famous Trevi Fountain • Pass through Piazza Venezia and see the Colosseum and Theatre of Marcellus • After a visit to Piazza Navona, it's on to Castel Sant' Angelo and St. Peter's Basilica in Vatican City • Departs 8pm • Daily

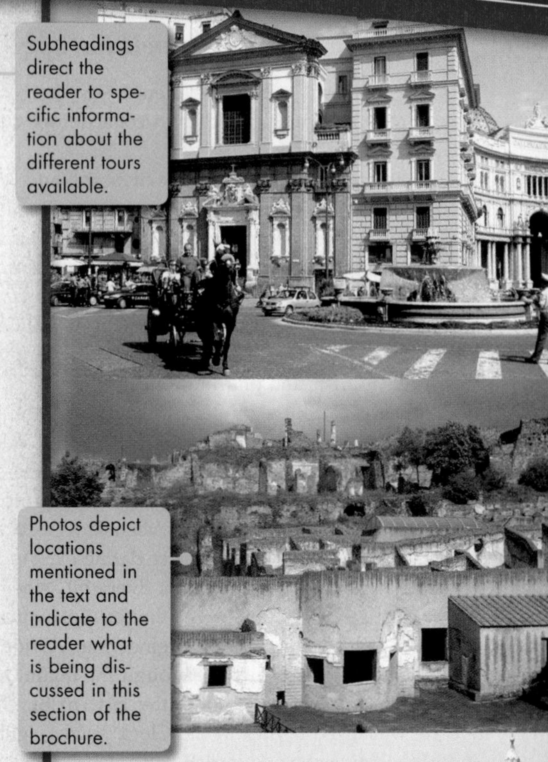

Photos depict locations mentioned in the text and indicate to the reader what is being discussed in this section of the brochure.

942 Drama

Think Aloud

Vocabulary: Using Context

Show students how to determine the meaning of an unfamiliar word by using context with this "think aloud." Direct their attention to the word *via,* which appears in the first lines of the first three entries on page 942:

> I'm going to show you how I can determine the meaning of the unfamiliar word *via* by using context clues. I see in the first line of the description of the first tour that you visit "via guided bus tour." I know that "guided bus tour" means that a bus will carry people around the city and a tour guide will describe the sights they see. I see that the rest of the entry identifies particular places that the tour will visit. From these clues, I conclude that *via* means "by" or "through the mechanism of."

After You Read | Atlas Entry • Travel Brochure 

Comparing Functional and Expository Texts

1. **Craft and Structure** **(a) Analyze text information** by comparing and contrasting the types and **sequences of information** in the atlas entry and the travel brochure. **(b)** How does the sequence of information in each text aid the reader's understanding? **(c)** What idea connects the first and second pages of the travel brochure?

Content-Area Vocabulary

2. **(a)** Use a dictionary to explain how the meanings of *temperature* and *intemperately* are related to *temperate.* **(b)** Name another *temperate peninsula* in the world, besides Italy. **(c)** List two works of art that are associated with the *Renaissance.* **(d)** What era, in your opinion, represents a *renaissance* in popular music? Explain.

Timed Writing

Explanatory Text: Essay

Format
The prompt directs you to write a brief explanatory essay. Therefore, your response should be three to five paragraphs in length and should provide facts and explanations.

Using information from the atlas entry, write a brief explanatory essay that gives an overview of Italy as a tourist destination. Use information from both the graphics and text to describe the country's size and location, its land and climate, and its people. Also note any key facts that would help tourists make the most of their visit. (35 minutes)

Academic Vocabulary
When you *describe* something, you use details, examples, and vivid language to form a picture in your reader's mind.

5-Minute Planner

Complete these steps before you begin to write:

1. Read the prompt carefully and completely.
2. Review both documents, including graphics and text. Take notes about key facts and details that you will include in your essay.
3. Decide in what order you will present your information. Choose an order that is logical. Then, create an outline for your essay.
TIP Review the sequences of information in the atlas entry and travel brochure. Consider the best sequence to use in your essay.
4. Refer to your notes and use your outline as you draft your essay.

ASSESS/EXTEND

Answers

Comparing Functional and Expository Texts

1. (a) **Possible response:** The atlas entry begins with a map. It follows with detailed data about Italy that is separated by a heading and subheadings. The travel brochure begins with a description of prominent tourist destinations in Italy. It is followed by subheadings, text, and photographs that describe sightseeing tours that are available in Italy. (b) **Possible response:** The sequence of information in the atlas helps the reader visualize the nation as a whole before analyzing the data. The travel brochure piques the reader's interest before offering specifics about the tours. (c) **Possible response:** The connecting concept between the first and second pages is that Italy's major cities have many sites to visit.
2. (a) **Sample response:** The words come from the root *temper*: *temperature* is a noun that names the measurement for how hot or cold the air is; *temperate* is an adjective that can mean "not too hot or too cold," literally and figuratively; *intemperately* is the adverb formed with *-ly* that means "not acting in a moderate way." (b) **Sample response:** Greece. (c) Sample response: Leonardo da Vinci's Mona Lisa; Michelangelo's Sistine Chapel ceiling. (d) Answers will vary but should convey an understanding of the term *renaissance.*

Timed Writing

1. Before students complete the activity, guide them in identifying and analyzing key words and phrases in the prompt, highlighted on the student page.
2. Work with students to draw up guidelines for their essays based on the key words:
   - **Focus** The essay should provide an overview of Italy as a tourist destination.
   - **Organization** The essay should begin with a general statement about Italy as a tourist destination. It should be followed by details from the atlas entry that describe the country and support the general statement.
   - **Support** The essay should provide information from the text that supports students' ideas and describes the country.
   - **Style** The essay should be written in a formal style.
3. Have students use the 5-Minute Planner to structure their time.
4. Allow students 35 minutes to complete the assignment. Evaluate their work using the guidelines they have developed.

Common Core State Standards
- **Reading Literature 3, 9**
- **Writing 2**

❶ Comparing Archetypal Themes

Satire

1. Introduce the skill, using the instruction on the student page.
2. Give students a copy of **Comparing Archetypal Themes Graphic Organizer B,** ***Graphic Organizer Transparencies,*** p. 168. Tell them they will record aspects of theme as they read.

Think Aloud: Model the Skill

Model a way of approaching archetypal themes. Say to students:

> As I approach stories, I think about their theme, or message about life. For example, in a superhero movie like *Spiderman,* good will likely triumph and the main character is a hero who protect innocents from evil. This story features a universal theme—one people everywhere recognize—and an archetypal hero—one with familiar heroic qualities. When I read, I look for these universal themes and archetypal characters.

Cultural Perspective

1. Introduce the skill, using the instruction on the student page.
2. Point out that literature from different cultures may use different characters and settings, but still express similar themes.
3. Explain that when authors place special emphasis on certain aspects of themes, they may be reflecting cultural perspectives.

Comparing Literary Works

Pyramus and Thisbe • *from* A Midsummer Night's Dream

❶ Comparing Archetypal Themes

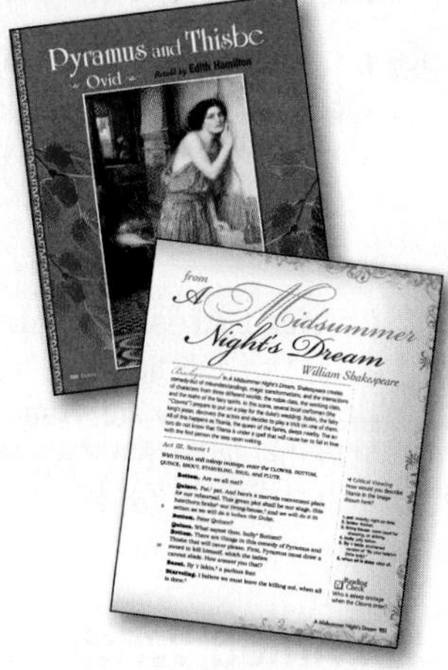

An **archetype** is a plot, character, image, or setting that appears in literature, mythology, and folklore from around the world and throughout history. Archetypes represent universal themes and truths about life and are said to mirror the working of the human mind. The following are some common archetypes:

- Characters: the hero; the outcast; the fool
- Plot types: the quest, or search; the task
- Symbols: water as a symbol of life; fire as a symbol of power

A **theme** is the central idea, message, or insight of a literary work. **Archetypal stories** can be thought of as original models on which other versions are based.

Archetypal themes develop or explore fundamental or universal ideas. Ill-fated love is one archetypal theme that appears in literature from all over the world. A complex character's fall from grace is another archetypal theme. Works of literature can differ for a variety of reasons in their presentations of the same archetypal theme. For example, the values of the work's era, the author's purpose, and the author's culture and language may affect how a writer presents a universal theme.

As you read Ovid's "Pyramus and Thisbe," a classic tale from ancient Rome, make comparisons to Shakespeare's treatment of a similar tale in two of his works: *The Tragedy of Romeo and Juliet* and the comedy *A Midsummer Night's Dream.* Consider how Shakespeare draws on the original source to develop his story and theme in both the full-length tragedy and the subplot of the comedy. Use a chart like the one shown to organize your observations.

	Similarities	Differences
Characters		
Events		

Common Core State Standards

Reading Literature
3. Analyze how complex characters develop over the course of a text, interact with other characters, and advance the plot or develop the theme.
9. Analyze how an author draws on and transforms source material in a specific work (e.g., how Shakespeare treats a theme or topic from Ovid or the Bible or how a later author draws on a play by Shakespeare).

Writing
2. Write informative/explanatory texts to examine and convey complex ideas, concepts, and information clearly and accurately through the effective selection, organization, and analysis of content.

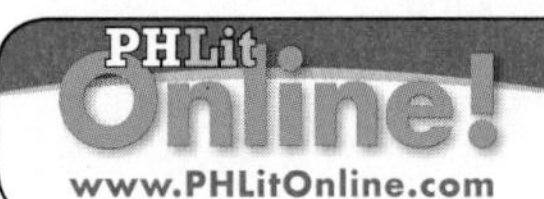

- Vocabulary flashcards
- Interactive journals
- More about the authors
- Selection audio
- Interactive graphic organizers

Vocabulary Development

Vocabulary Knowledge Rating

Create a **Vocabulary Knowledge Rating Chart** (***Professional Development Guidebook,*** p. 33) featuring the words glossed in the selections:

lament (p. 947) *enamored* (p. 955)
inevitable (p. 948) *enthralled* (p. 955)

Give students a copy of the chart, and read the words aloud. Have students mark their rating of each in the Before You Read column.

To gauge how much instruction to provide, tally the students who think they know each word.

Explain that the words are defined in the margin at the point where they appear in the selection. Urge students to be alert to these words as they read the selections. They will rate their knowledge again when they finish.

Vocabulary Central, featuring tools, activities, and songs for studying vocabulary, is available online at **www.PHLitOnline.com.**

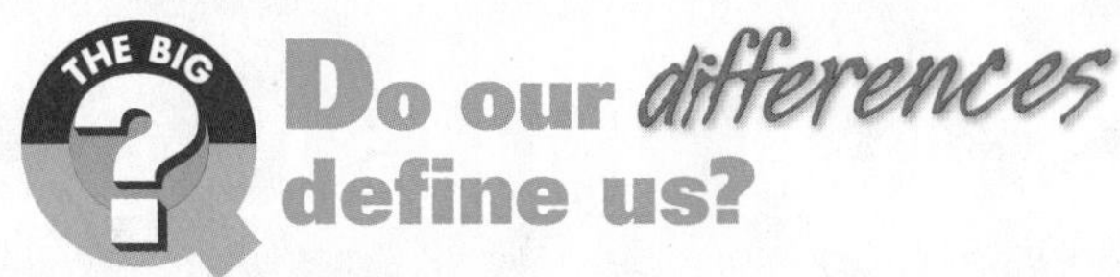

Do our differences define us?

❷ Writing About the Big Question

In these selections, the main characters fall in love despite the differences that separate them. Use this sentence starter to develop your ideas about the Big Question:

The **differences** between two people can be less important than ____.

Meet the Authors

Ovid (43 B.C.–A.D. 17)

Author of "Pyramus and Thisbe"

Educated in Rome, Ovid began his career writing poems about love and pleasure. However, the emperor Augustus wanted citizens to focus on morality and work toward an ideal Roman state. In response, Ovid decided to write about myths and traditional stories, such as "Pyramus and Thisbe."

Achievement and Exile After completing his masterpiece, *Metamorphoses,* in A.D. 8, Ovid was banished to a remote village. The reasons for his banishment are not entirely clear, but the emperor might have felt that Ovid's work endangered public morals. Although he continued to write, he was never allowed to return to Rome.

William Shakespeare (1564–1616)

Author of *A Midsummer Night's Dream*

Perhaps the greatest of all playwrights, William Shakespeare was born in the town of Stratford-on-Avon and gained his successes in the flourishing theatrical world of London. He worked as an actor, a playwright, and part owner of a theater company, earning enough to retire to Stratford in 1610.

Kings and Clowns, Lovers and Villains Shakespeare's 37 plays are populated with a wide range of characters who embody the depth and variety of human experience. No writer has played a more significant role in shaping the English language and English literature.

Teaching Resources

- All EL *Unit 5 Resources,* pp. 117–133
- All *Common Core Companion,* pp. 28–29, 69–70; 190–201
- All EL *Graphic Organizer Transparencies,* pp. 167–170
- All *Professional Development Guidebook,* pp. 33, 36–38
- All Enriched Online Student Edition
- L2 EL *Hear It!* Audio CD

All resources, including print and audio, are available at **www.PHLitOnline.com**.

Daily Bellringer

For each class during which you will teach this selection, have students complete one of the five Revision activities for Week 28 in the *Daily Bellringer Activities* booklet.

❷ Writing About the Big Question

1. Review the assignment with the class.
2. **Ask** students why people think that differences between themselves and others are important. Discuss ways that people can connect despite differences.
3. Have students complete the sentence starter. Review responses as a class. (**Possible response:** The differences between two people can be less important than what they can share with each other.)
4. Remind students that their answers will help them think about the Big Question, "Do our differences define us?"

Concept Connector

Tell students that they will return to their sentence starter after they have concluded reading.

Multidraft Reading

To assist struggling readers and to deepen reading for all, apply multidraft reading protocols. For each reading, have students set the purpose indicated:

- **First reading**—identifying key ideas and details and answering any Reading Checks.
- **Second reading**—analyzing craft and structure and responding to the side-column prompts.
- **Third reading**—integrating knowledge and ideas, connecting to other texts and the world, and answering the end-of-selection questions.

For more guidance, see the *Classroom Strategies and Teaching Routines* card on multidraft reading.

For more about the authors and practice with the selection vocabulary, go to **www.PHLitOnline.com.**

1 Background

Metamorphoses Stories of gods or people being transformed into plants, animals, or inanimate objects were popular long before Ovid, and almost certainly grew out of the folk tradition. Ovid's collection (a poem, not prose, as in Edith Hamilton's version) includes examples of a variety of natural creatures. Metamorphosis is itself an archetypal theme, just like ill-fated love.

2 Activating Prior Knowledge

1. Prepare an **Anticipation Guide** (***Professional Development Guidebook***, pp. 36–38) with the following statements:
   - A crisis can make a person change shockingly fast.
   - The most important changes are those that take place slowly.
   - Love is the greatest cause of change in people's lives.
   - Important changes are caused by the decisions people make.
2. Give students a copy of the prepared **Anticipation Guide** and have students mark their responses in the Me column. Have students discuss the statements in pairs or groups and mark the guides again in the group column.
3. For further guidance, use the ***Classroom Strategies and Teaching Routines*** card **Using an Anticipation Guide.**

Concept Connector

Students will return to the **Anticipation Guide** after completing the selection.

3 About the Selection

Edith Hamilton's retelling of Ovid's "Pyramus and Thisbe" reads like a fairy tale, even beginning with "Once upon a time." Pyramus and Thisbe, children of neighboring families in Babylon, love each other but are forbidden to marry. Through a chink in the wall that joins their houses, they express their love and plan their escape. They agree to run away and meet at a tomb under a mulberry tree, but their plans miscarry through a tragic misunderstanding.

1 2 3 4

Pyramus and Thisbe

Ovid

retold by **Edith Hamilton**

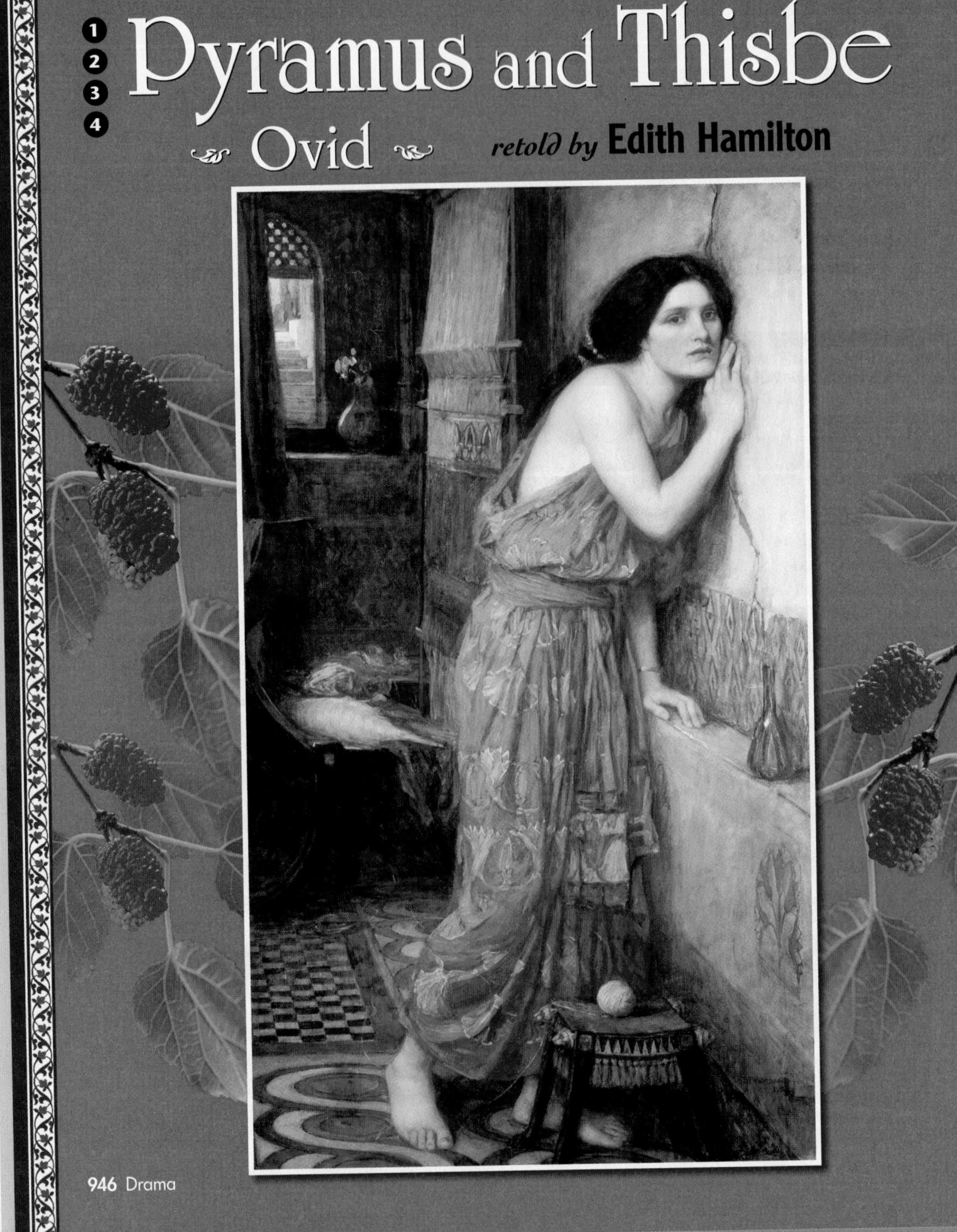

Text Complexity Rubric

Pyramus and Thisbe		
Qualitative Measures	**Context/ Knowledge Demands**	Babylon in ancient times; mythology 1 2 (3) 4 5
	Structure/ Language Clarity and Conventionality	Short sentences; a few archaic expressions and constructions 1 2 (3) 4 5
	Levels of Meaning/ Purpose/Concept Level	Accessible concept (tragic love story) 1 (2) 3 4 5
Quantitative Measures	**Text Length**	Word Count: 902
	Lexile	870L

Background The tale of Pyramus and Thisbe appears in Book IV of *Metamorphoses,* Ovid's greatest achievement. A poem of nearly 12,000 lines, it tells a series of stories beginning with the creation of the world and ending with the death of Julius Caesar. In each story, someone or something undergoes a change. Divided into fifteen books, the stories are linked by clever transitions, so that the entire work reads as one long, uninterrupted tale.

Once upon a time the deep red berries of the mulberry tree[1] were white as snow. The change in color came about strangely and sadly. The death of two young lovers was the cause.

Pyramus and Thisbe, he the most beautiful youth and she the loveliest maiden of all the East, lived in Babylon, the city of Queen Semiramis, in houses so close together that one wall was common to both. Growing up thus side by side they learned to love each other. They longed to marry, but their parents forbade. Love, however, cannot be forbidden. The more that flame is covered up, the hotter it burns. Also love can always find a way. It was impossible that these two whose hearts were on fire should be kept apart.

In the wall both houses shared there was a little chink.[2] No one before had noticed it, but there is nothing a lover does not notice. Our two young people discovered it and through it they were able to whisper sweetly back and forth. Thisbe on one side, Pyramus on the other. The hateful wall that separated them had become their means of reaching each other. "But for you we could touch, kiss," they would say. "But at least you let us speak together. You give a passage for loving words to reach loving ears. We are not ungrateful." So they would talk, and as night came on and they must part, each would press on the wall kisses that could not go through to the lips on the other side.

Every morning when the dawn had put out the stars, and the sun's rays had dried the hoarfrost on the grass, they would steal to the crack and, standing there, now utter words of burning love and now lament their hard fate, but always in softest whispers. Finally a day came when they could endure no longer. They decided that that very night they would try to slip away and steal out through the city into the open country where at last they could be together in freedom. They agreed to meet at a well-known place, the Tomb of Ninus, under a tree there, a tall mulberry full of snow-white berries, near which a cool spring bubbled up. The plan pleased them and it seemed to them the day would never end.

1. **mulberry** (mul′ ber′ rē) **tree** *n.* tree with an edible, purplish-red fruit.
2. **chink** (chiŋk) *n.* narrow opening; crack.

❺ ◀ **Critical Viewing** What do you think the girl is feeling as she listens through the crack in the wall? **[Speculate]**

Literary Analysis
Archetypal Theme What is the main obstacle the lovers face?

Vocabulary
lament (lə ment′) *v.* express deep sorrow; mourn

❼ 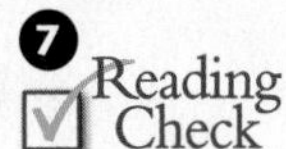

How do Pyramus and Thisbe communicate with each other?

❹ Humanities

Thisbe, by John William Waterhouse

John William Waterhouse (1849–1917) was an English Pre-Raphaelite painter who loved Greek mythology and classical history. He often painted strong or tragic female characters, such as Shakespeare's Ophelia and Homer's Penelope. Use the following question for discussion:

Ask students why Waterhouse painted Thisbe in a red gown.

Answer: The color of her gown suggests the mulberry that turns red in her memory.

❺ Critical Viewing

Possible responses: The girl may be feeling love, longing, frustration, disappointment, fear, doubt, or resentment.

❻ Literary Analysis

Archetypal Theme

1. Remind students that an archetypal theme addresses a basic, common, or universal aspect of human experience. **Ask** students to identify some of the most common issues that teenagers have always faced.
   Possible responses: Teenagers face restrictions by parents, demands of society, peer pressure, and anxieties about the future.
2. Read the bracketed passage aloud. **Ask** the Literary Analysis question: What is the main obstacle the lovers face?
   Answer: The lovers' main obstacle is restriction from their parents.
3. Have students **speculate** about possible solutions for the lovers.
   Possible responses: The lovers might run away together. They might talk to their parents.

❼ Reading Check

Answer: Pyramus and Thisbe whisper through a chink in the wall that joins their houses.

This selection is available in interactive format in the **Enriched Online Student Edition,** online at **www.PHLitOnline.com,** which includes an interactive graphic organizer.

Text Complexity: Reader and Task Suggestions

Pyramus and Thisbe

Preparing to Read the Text	Leveled Tasks
• Using the Background information on TE p. 946, discuss the origin of the myth and the enduring qualities of myths due to their universal themes. • Discuss the theme of love and why it appeals so strongly to readers whether it is love fulfilled or love lost. • Guide students to use Multidraft Reading strategies (TE p. 945).	*Knowledge Demands* If students will have difficulty with the setting of the story, have them first read and note events in the story and their causes. Then, have them reread and take notes about the setting and how it affects events. Discuss students' notes and provide clarification. *Evaluating* If students will not have difficulty with the setting of the story, have them read and note details about the main characters. Have them evaluate the characters and decide whether the final outcome is or is not true to their characters.

8 Literary Analysis

Archetypal Theme

1. **Ask** students what personality traits they think Thisbe probably has, based on her actions so far.

   Possible responses: She is obedient to her parents, based on her endurance of their restrictions. She is sensitive and romantic, based on her whispering through the wall.

2. Have students read the bracketed passage. Then, **ask** the Literary Analysis question: What does Thisbe's "bold" behavior suggest about the power of love?

   Answer: Her behavior suggests that love can give people courage, make them forceful and practical, or even make them desperate and willing to break rules.

3. Discuss with students the different kinds of metamorphoses that people can experience—including physical, intellectual, spiritual, and emotional. **Ask** students how they think love can affect all the different kinds of metamorphosis.

   Possible responses: Love can cause people to try to make themselves more physically attractive and more intellectually and financially successful. Love can foster spiritual growth and lead to self-discipline, self-sacrifice, and emotional maturity.

9 Critical Viewing

In the story, the lioness is bloody from a recent kill; this lioness is clean. Both lionesses are fierce and powerful hunters.

Literary Analysis
Archetypal Theme
What does Thisbe's "bold" behavior suggest about the power of love? 8

At last the sun sank into the sea and night arose. In the darkness Thisbe crept out and made her way in all secrecy to the tomb. Pyramus had not come; still she waited for him, her love making her bold. But of a sudden she saw by the light of the moon a lioness. The fierce beast had made a kill; her jaws were bloody and she was coming to slake her thirst in the spring. She was still far enough away for Thisbe to escape, but as she fled she dropped her cloak. The lioness came upon it on her way back to her lair and she mouthed it and tore it before disappearing into the woods. That is what Pyramus saw when he appeared a few minutes later. Before him lay the bloodstained shreds of the cloak and clear in the dust were the tracks of the lioness. The conclusion was **inevitable**. He never doubted that he knew all. Thisbe was dead. He had let his love, a tender maiden, come alone to a place full of danger, and not been there first to protect her. "It is I who killed you," he said. He lifted up from the trampled dust what was left of the cloak and kissing it again and again carried it to the mulberry tree. "Now," he said, "you shall drink my blood too." He drew his sword and plunged it into his side. The blood spurted up over the berries and dyed them a dark red.

Vocabulary
inevitable (in ev´ i tə bəl) *adj.* unavoidable; certain

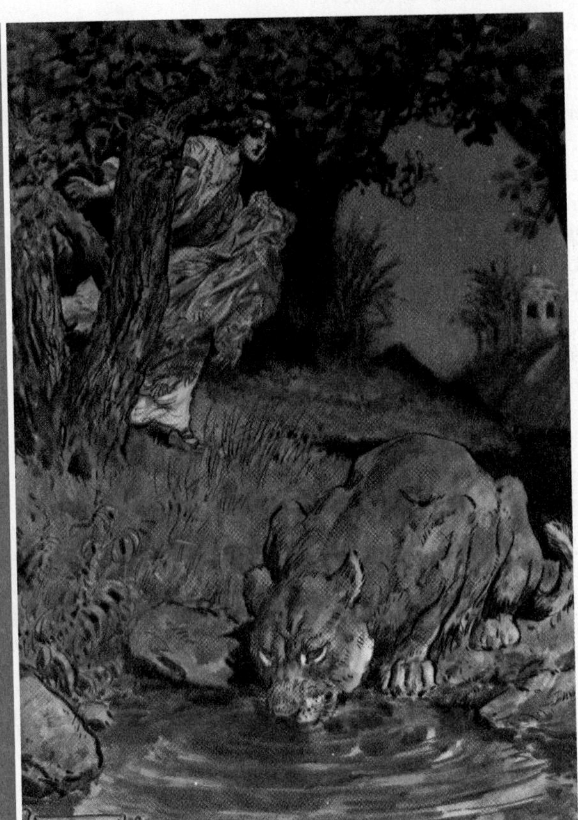

Thisbe, although terrified of the lioness, was still more afraid to fail her lover. She ventured to go back to the tree of the tryst, the mulberry with the shining white fruit. She could not find it. A tree was there, but not one gleam of white was on the branches. As she stared at it, something moved on the ground beneath. She started back shuddering. But in a moment, peering through the shadows, she 10

9
◀ **Critical Viewing**
Explain the similarities and differences between this lioness and the one Thisbe sees. **[Compare and Contrast]**

Think Aloud

Make Inferences
Draw students' attention to the bracketed passage at the top of this page. Use the following "think aloud" to model the process of making an inference.

When I read that Thisbe "crept out and made her way in all secrecy to the tomb," I can use my prior knowledge to make an inference about her actions. I know that people creep secretly when they don't want to be caught. This tells me that Thisbe was risking a lot to leave her home alone and in the dark. Since she has up until now only spoken with Pyramus through a wall, I can also infer that she hadn't before disobeyed her parents and wasn't in the habit of sneaking away to meet him. The two inferences help me decide that her behavior is highly unusual for her and show me how much she must love Pyramus. I will read on to see how else her love affects her actions.

saw what was there. It was Pyramus, bathed in blood and dying. She flew to him and threw her arms around him. She kissed his cold lips and begged him to look at her, to speak to her. "It is I, your Thisbe, your dearest," she cried to him. At the sound of her name he opened his heavy eyes for one look. Then death closed them.

She saw his sword fallen from his hand and beside it her cloak stained and torn. She understood all. "Your own hand killed you," she said, "and your love for me. I too can be brave. I too can love. Only death would have had the power to separate us. It shall not have that power now." She plunged into her heart the sword that was still wet with his life's blood.

The gods were pitiful at the end, and the lovers' parents too. The deep red fruit of the mulberry is the everlasting memorial of these true lovers, and one urn holds the ashes of the two whom not even death could part.

Literary Analysis
Archetypal Theme In deciding to return to the tree, is Thisbe guided more by love or by reason? Explain.

Critical Thinking

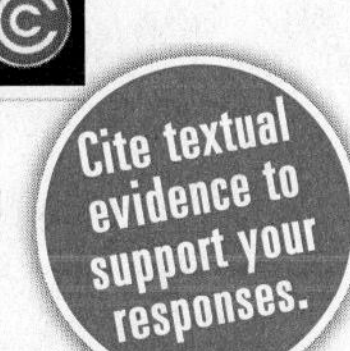
Cite textual evidence to support your responses.

1. **Key Ideas and Details** **(a)** How do the parents feel about the romance between Pyramus and Thisbe? **(b) Analyze Cause and Effect:** What actions do Pyramus and Thisbe take as a result of their parents' feelings? **(c) Make a Judgment:** Do you think Pyramus and Thisbe or their parents are more responsible for the tragic outcome?
2. **Key Ideas and Details** **(a)** What does the chink in the wall enable the couple to do? **(b) Speculate:** How might the story be different if the chink did not exist?
3. **Integration of Knowledge and Ideas** **(a) Draw Conclusions:** What does the mulberry tree symbolize in this story? **(b) Analyze:** In what way does this symbol reinforce the story's theme?
4. **Integration of Knowledge and Ideas** **Speculate:** Do you think this story will continue to appeal to readers in the future? Why or why not?
5. **Integration of Knowledge and Ideas** **(a)** How do Pyramus and Thisbe's wishes differ from that of their families? **(b)** In what way did those differences lead to tragedy? *[Connect to the Big Question: Do our differences define us?]*

10 Literary Analysis

Archetypal Theme

1. Have students read the final paragraphs of the story.
2. **Ask** the Literary Analysis question: In deciding to return to the tree, is Thisbe guided more by love or by reason? Explain.

   Answer: Thisbe is guided more by love than by reason; she did not want to fail her lover.

Concept Connector

Have students return to their **Anticipation Guides** and respond to the statements again in the After Reading column, working individually or in their original pairs or groups. Explore what students have learned that confirms or invalidates each statement. In addition, have students compare their Writing About the Big Question responses before reading the selection with their ideas afterwards.

ASSESS

Answers

Critical Thinking

Remind students to support their answers with evidence from the text.

1. (a) The parents forbid the romance. (b) They whisper through the wall, plan an escape, and run away. (c) Some students will blame the parents; others will blame the lovers.
2. (a) It enables the couple to whisper and express their feelings. (b) **Possible response:** The lovers would have had to find another way to communicate, or their love may have faded.
3. (a) The mulberry symbolizes the true love of Pyramus and Thisbe. (b) The fruit of the mulberry, dyed red by blood, represents the sacrifice the lovers make for each other.
4. **Possible response:** The story will endure as long as people experience frustration and encounter restrictions to their love.
5. **Possible responses:** (a) Pyramus and Thisbe wish to be married, which is forbidden by their families. (b) Since Pyramus and Thisbe were forbidden to be together, they had to see each other in secret. It is during this secret tryst that a tragedy occurs.

Differentiated Instruction for Universal Access

Strategy for Less Proficient Readers
To help students grasp the sequence of events leading to the tragedy of Pyramus and Thisbe, have them create a storyboard of the plot. Tell students to review the story and list what happens. Then, have them put the events in order with a simple drawing to illustrate each event.

Enrichment for Advanced Readers
Have students read and report on another story from Ovid's *Metamorphoses.* They might consider the stories of Actaeon, Daphne, Arachne, Phaethon, or Narcissus. Ask students to tell how the story is like, or unlike, the tale of Pyramus and Thisbe.

⑪ Visual Connections

Whole-Class Activity

1. Have students study the picture. **Ask:** What does the picture show?

   Answer: It shows a queen, wearing elaborate and golden garments.

2. Then, tell students to read the title on p. 951, and **ask** what the inclusion of the word *dream* suggests about the play.

   Possible response: It suggests that the play may have some elements of fantasy or at least distorted reality in it.

3. Now **ask** students what the picture and title suggest about the setting and characters of this play.

   Possible response: The play will take place in the summer. It will feature a queen or other royal characters. It may have some fantasy elements.

Small-Group Activity

1. Have small groups study the picture and discuss the character it shows. Have them make predictions about the play and character based on their discussion.
2. Ask one member of each group to summarize the group's ideas.
3. Record students' predictions on the board. To model the process of making connections to an image, choose one of the ideas and analyze how that idea is supported by the picture.

Individual Activity

1. As a class, briefly discuss the picture.
2. Ask students to write a one-paragraph description of the character, based on the picture.
3. Post the descriptions for students to reference as they read the play.

⑪

Ⓒ Text Complexity Rubric

from A Midsummer Night's Dream		
Qualitative Measures	**Context/ Knowledge Demands**	Elizabethan comedy; mix of social classes 1 2 3 4 ⑤
	Structure/ Language Clarity and Conventionality	Difficult sentence structure; Shakespearean word usage 1 2 3 4 ⑤
	Levels of Meaning/ Purpose/Concept Level	Challenging concept (play within play) 1 2 3 ④ 5
Quantitative Measures	**Text Length**	Word Count: 1,594
	Lexile	NP

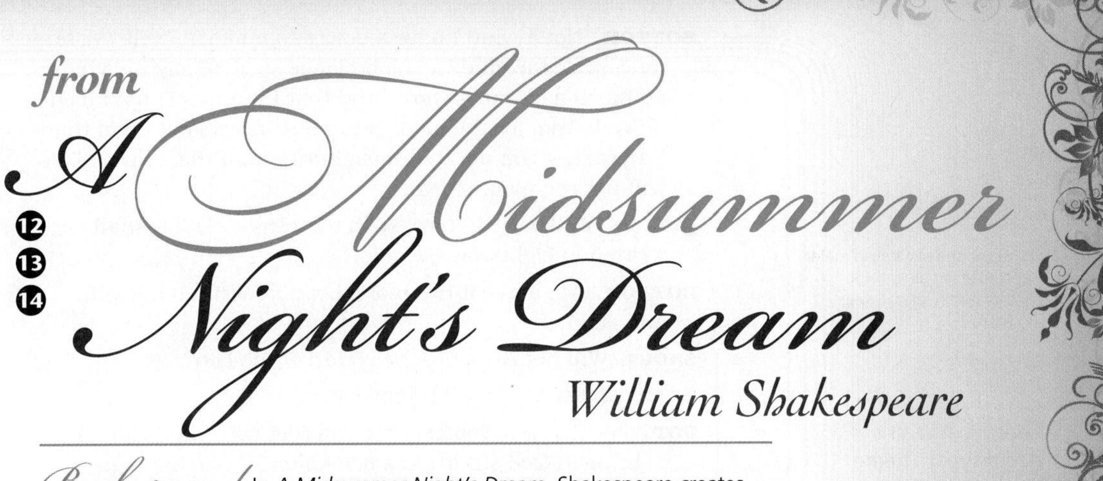

from A Midsummer Night's Dream

12 13 14

William Shakespeare

Background In *A Midsummer Night's Dream,* Shakespeare creates comedy out of misunderstandings, magic transformations, and the interactions of characters from three different worlds: the noble class, the working class, and the realm of the fairy spirits. In this scene, several local craftsmen (the "Clowns") prepare to put on a play for the duke's wedding. Robin, the fairy king's jester, discovers the actors and decides to play a trick on one of them. All of this happens as Titania, the queen of the fairies, sleeps nearby. The actors do not know that Titania is under a spell that will cause her to fall in love with the first person she sees upon waking.

Act III, Scene i

With TITANIA *still asleep onstage, enter the* CLOWNS, BOTTOM, QUINCE, SNOUT, STARVELING, SNUG, *and* FLUTE.

BOTTOM. Are we all met?

QUINCE. Pat,[1] pat. And here's a marvels convenient place for our rehearsal. This green plot shall be our stage, this hawthorn brake[2] our tiring-house,[3] and we will do it in action as we will do it before the Duke.

BOTTOM. Peter Quince?

QUINCE. What sayest thou, bully[4] Bottom?

BOTTOM. There are things in this comedy of Pyramus and Thisbe that will never please. First, Pyramus must draw a sword to kill himself, which the ladies cannot abide. How answer you that?

SNOUT. By 'r lakin,[5] a parlous fear.

STARVELING. I believe we must leave the killing out, when all is done.[6]

15

◀ **Critical Viewing** How would you describe Titania in the image shown here?

1. **pat** exactly; right on time.
2. **brake** thicket.
3. **tiring house** room used for dressing, or attiring.
4. **bully** jolly fellow.
5. **By 'r lakin** shortened version of "By your ladykin (little lady)."
6. **when all is done** after all.

16

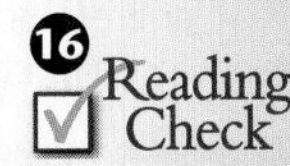

Reading Check Who is asleep onstage when the Clowns enter?

12 Background

A Midsummer Night's Dream

Shakespeare's version of "Pyramus and Thisbe" is original. He uses unprofessional "actors" to play out the exaggerated story, making the main plot of the play more comic.

13 Activating Prior Knowledge

1. Prepare an **Anticipation Guide** (***Professional Development Guidebook,*** pp. 36–38) with the following statements:
   - Love at first sight is possible.
   - People who fall in love quickly are doomed to regret it.
2. Give students a copy of the prepared **Anticipation Guide** and have them mark responses in the Me column. Have students discuss the statements in pairs or groups and mark the guides again in the group column.
3. For further guidance, use the ***Classroom Strategies and Teaching Routines*** card: **Using an Anticipation Guide.**

Concept Connector →

Students will revisit the **Anticipation Guide** after reading the selection.

14 About the Selection

The performance of "Pyramus and Thisbe" as a play within a play provides a parody of the lovers' actions in the outer main plot. The actors make special efforts to explain that they are not really Pyramus and a lion. This tells the audience that similiar tricks appear in the outer play.

15 Critical Viewing

Possible responses: Titania may be described as wealthy, commanding, severe, or frightening.

16 Reading Check

Answer: Titania is asleep onstage.

PHLit Online!

This selection is available in interactive format in the **Enriched Online Student Edition,** online at **www.PHLitOnline.com,** which includes an interactive graphic organizer.

© Text Complexity: Reader and Task Suggestions

from **A Midsummer Night's Dream**	
Preparing to Read the Text • Refer to the Background information on TE p. 951 and discuss the myth of Pyramus and Thisbe, pointing out that there are many different versions. • Discuss Shakespearean language with students and remind them to look for footnotes for explanations of difficult expressions. • Guide students to use Multidraft Reading strategies (TE p. 945).	**Leveled Tasks** *Levels of Meaning* If students will have difficulty with levels of meaning, have them first read the play and identify the main characters and describe their traits. Then, have them reread the play and note details showing their roles in the plot. Discuss students' notes and offer clarification. *Analyzing* If students will not have difficulty with levels of meaning, have them read the play and compare the plot and characters in "Pyramus and Thisbe" to the plot and characters in *A Midsummer Night's Dream.*

⑰ Literary Analysis

Archetypal Theme

1. Have students read the bracketed passage. **Ask** them what Bottom and the other Clowns are afraid of doing when they present their play.
2. **Answer:** They are afraid of frightening and offending the audience.
3. **Ask** students the Literary Analysis question: How do the Clowns plan to soften their presentation of the lion?

   Answer: Bottom instructs the actor to identify himself, peek out of the neck of the lion costume, and assure the ladies that he is not a real lion.
4. **Ask** students why the concerns of the Clowns are comical.

   Answer: Their concerns are comical because the audience knows that the people who will be watching the play could not possibly think that the lion is real.

⑱ Literature in Context

Almanacs The best known of American almanacs is the one published by Benjamin Franklin in Philadelphia during the years 1732–1757—*Poor Richard's Almanack.* Franklin followed English models, but he made his almanac more literary by having characters deliver comic comments and useful proverbs.

Connecting to the Literature
Have students read the Literature in Context feature. Then, present the additional background information above. Point out that almanacs cannot predict whether or not the moon will be hidden by clouds on any given night. **Ask** students the Connect to the Literature question: Do you think the "Clowns" are wise to rely on the accuracy of the almanac with regard to moonlight? Why or why not?

Answer: The Clowns are foolish to rely on the accuracy of an almanac for moonlight; an almanac cannot predict a cloudless night.

BOTTOM. Not a whit! I have a device to make all well. Write me a prologue, and let the prologue seem to say we will do no harm with our swords, and that Pyramus is not killed indeed. And, for the more better assurance, tell them that I, Pyramus, am not Pyramus, but Bottom the weaver. This will put them out of fear.

QUINCE. Well, we will have such a prologue, and it shall be written in eight and six.[7]

BOTTOM. No, make it two more. Let it be written in eight and eight.

SNOUT. Will not the ladies be afeard of the lion?

STARVELING. I fear it, I promise you.

BOTTOM. Masters, you ought to consider with yourself, to bring in God shield us! a lion among ladies is a most dreadful thing. For there is not a more fearful wildfowl than your lion living, and we ought to look to it.

SNOUT. Therefore another prologue must tell he is not a lion.

⑰ **BOTTOM.** Nay, you must name his name, and half his face must be seen through the lion's neck, and he himself must speak through, saying thus, or to the same defect: "Ladies," or "Fair ladies, I would wish you," or "I would request you," or "I would entreat you not to fear, not to tremble! My life for yours. If you think I come hither as a lion, it were pity of my life.[8] No, I am no such thing. I am a man as other men are." And there indeed let him name his name and tell them plainly he is Snug the joiner.

7. **eight and six** ballad meter containing alternating eight- and six-syllable lines.

8. **it were . . . my life** risky for me.

Literary Analysis
Archetypal Theme
How do the Clowns plan to soften their presentation of the lion?

LITERATURE IN CONTEXT

Science Connection

Almanacs
When Bottom calls for an almanac, he is referring to a type of book that was very popular in Elizabethan times. The almanac was essentially a calendar, but it also provided lists of upcoming natural events, such as tides, full moons, and eclipses. The book was especially useful to farmers because it included gardening tips and weather predictions. Almanacs of various kinds are still published and consulted today.

Connect to the Literature

Do you think the "Clowns" are wise to rely on the accuracy of the almanac with regard to moonlight? Why or why not?

Vocabulary Development

CCSS Language 6

Word Analysis

Bottom suggests adding a prologue to the play—a speech that would be given before, or ahead of, the rest of the play. The prefix *pro-* means "forward or ahead of." Bottom wants to speak before the events of the play begin so that the audience will not be frightened by the violent actions that will follow.

Have students identify the meaning of each of the following words with the prefix *pro-*, using a dictionary if necessary.

proceed – move forward
proclaim – announce or put forward
produce – bring out or bring forward
progress – move forward
project – throw forward
promote – move forward
propel – push or drive forward
protrude – thrust forward or stick out

QUINCE. Well, it shall be so. But there is two hard things: that is, to bring the moonlight into a chamber, for you know Pyramus and Thisbe meet by moonlight.

SNOUT. Doth the moon shine that night we play our play?

BOTTOM. A calendar, a calendar! Look in the almanac. Find out moonshine, find out moonshine.

QUINCE *takes out a book.*

QUINCE. Yes, it doth shine that night.

BOTTOM. Why, then, may you leave a casement of the great chamber window, where we play, open, and the moon may shine in at the casement.

QUINCE. Ay, or else one must come in with a bush of thorns[9] and a lantern and say he comes to disfigure[10] or to present the person of Moonshine. Then there is another thing: we must have a wall in the great chamber, for Pyramus and Thisbe, says the story, did talk through the chink of a wall.

SNOUT. You can never bring in a wall. What say you, Bottom?

BOTTOM. Some man or other must present Wall. And let him have some plaster, or some loam, or some roughcast[11] about him to signify wall, or let him hold his fingers thus, and through that cranny shall Pyramus and Thisbe whisper.

(19) **QUINCE.** If that may be, then all is well. Come, sit down, every mother's son, and rehearse your parts. Pyramus, you begin. When you have spoken your speech, enter into that brake, and so every one according to his cue.

Enter ROBIN *invisible to those onstage.*

ROBIN. *(aside)*

What hempen homespuns[12] have we swaggring
here
So near the cradle[13] of the Fairy Queen?
What, a play toward?[14] I'll be an auditor—
An actor too perhaps, if I see cause.

QUINCE. Speak, Pyramus.—Thisbe, stand forth.

BOTTOM. *(as Pyramus)*

Thisbe, the flowers of odious savors sweet—

QUINCE. Odors, odors!

BOTTOM. *(as Pyramus)*

. . . odors savors sweet.
So hath thy breath, my dearest Thisbe dear—

9. **a bush of thorns** according to legend, the man in the moon collected firewood on Sundays and was thus banished to the sky.

10. **disfigure** Quince means figure, as in "symbolize" or "stand for."

11. **plaster . . . roughcast** three different blended materials, each used for plastering walls.

12. **hempen homespuns** characters wearing clothing homemade from hemp, probably from the country.

13. **cradle** bower where Titania sleeps.

14. **toward** being rehearsed.

(20) **Reading Check**

How do the Clowns plan to present the wall that separates Pyramus and Thisbe?

(19) Critical Thinking

Evaluate

1. Have students reread the play's beginning and evaluate the planning and decision-making of the Clowns. First, **ask** students to list the criteria for a good rehearsal.

   Possible responses: A good rehearsal might be described as organized, practical, imaginative, creative, intelligent, and efficient.

2. Then, **ask** students to identify the problems and issues that the actors face and how they decide to solve them.

   Answer: The actors will not scare the audience by including a prologue and having the lion talk. They will show moonshine by opening a window or having a man carry a lantern. They will represent a wall by having a man wear plaster and hold his fingers apart for the chink in the wall.

3. Next, have students read the bracketed text and **apply** the criteria to the rehearsal about to begin. Have students **evaluate** the rehearsal as a whole.

   Possible response: Students might say that the rehearsal seems unorganized and inefficient but that the actors are imaginative and creative in their attempts to solve problems.

(20) Reading Check

Answer: The Clowns plan to have a man dressed in plaster who will hold his fingers apart to represent the chink in the wall.

Differentiated Instruction for Universal Access

Strategy for Less Proficient Readers

List the names of all the Clowns on the board—Quince, Bottom, Snout, Starveling, Snug, and Flute. Have students listen to the rehearsal portion of the scene on the ***Hear It!* Audio CD**. As they listen, point to the name of each speaker so that students can recognize the characters and the characteristics of Bottom and Quince.

Enrichment for Gifted/Talented Students

Suggest that students give a performance of the rehearsal portion of this scene from *A Midsummer Night's Dream* (the first 95 lines). Assign roles and encourage students to create their own costumes and props. Remind them that the Clowns are funny because they act so seriously. Have them rehearse their performance and present it to the class.

21 Critical Viewing

Answer: Bottom would probably be angry and insulted.

22 Critical Thinking

Make Inferences

1. Have students read the first bracketed passage. Point out that Shakespeare sometimes names his characters according to their personal qualities and that this adds to the comic effect.
2. **Ask** students what they can infer about Flute from his name.

   Answer: Flute, apparently the youngest of the group, has a very high voice, appropriate for playing Thisbe.
3. Recall other characters' names and **ask** students what they can infer about Snout and Starveling from their names.

   Answer: Snout's name suggests that he has a big or distinctive nose, and Starveling's name suggests that he is very thin and gaunt from having little to eat.

23 Connecting to the Big Question

1. Remind students of the Big Question by pointing out that differences are often visually apparent.
2. Direct students' attention to the second bracketed passage. **Ask:** What is different about Bottom's appearance as he enters the scene?

   Answer: He has the head of an ass, or donkey.
3. **Ask:** How does Bottom's different appearance define him and those around him?

   Possible response: He looks different, so others react to him differently. In this case, they run away frightened and conclude that they are haunted.

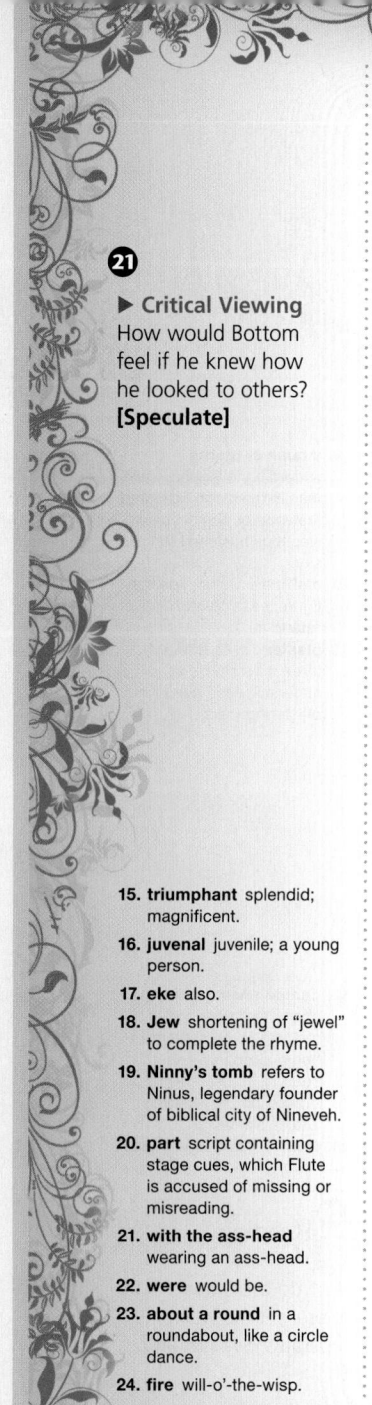

But hark, a voice! Stay thou but here awhile.
And by and by I will to thee appear. *(He exits.)*

ROBIN. *(aside)*
A stranger Pyramus than e'er played here.

(He exits.)

FLUTE. Must I speak now?

QUINCE. Ay, marry, must you, for you must understand he goes but to see a noise that he heard and is to come again.

Flute. *(as Thisbe)*
Most radiant Pyramus, most lily-white of hue,
Of color like the red rose on triumphant[15] brier,
Most brisky juvenal[16] and eke[17] most lovely Jew,[18]
As true as truest horse, that yet would never tire.
I'll meet thee, Pyramus, at Ninny's tomb.[19]

21 ▶ **Critical Viewing** How would Bottom feel if he knew how he looked to others? **[Speculate]**

22

QUINCE. "Ninus tomb," man! Why, you must not speak that yet. That you answer to Pyramus. You speak all your part[20] at once, cues and all.— Pyramus, enter. Your cue is past. It is "never tire."

FLUTE. O!
(As Thisbe) As true as truest horse, that yet would never tire.

Enter ROBIN, *and* BOTTOM *as Pyramus with the ass-head.*[21]

23

BOTTOM. *(as Pyramus)*
If I were fair, fair Thisbe, I were[22] only thine.

QUINCE. O monstrous! O strange! We are haunted. Pray, masters, fly, masters! Help!

24

QUINCE, FLUTE, SNOUT, SNUG, *and* STARVELING *exit.*

ROBIN. I'll follow you. I'll lead you about a round,[23]
Through bog, through bush, through brake, through brier.
Sometime a horse I'll be, sometime a hound,
A hog, a headless bear, sometime a fire.[24]

15. **triumphant** splendid; magnificent.
16. **juvenal** juvenile; a young person.
17. **eke** also.
18. **Jew** shortening of "jewel" to complete the rhyme.
19. **Ninny's tomb** refers to Ninus, legendary founder of biblical city of Nineveh.
20. **part** script containing stage cues, which Flute is accused of missing or misreading.
21. **with the ass-head** wearing an ass-head.
22. **were** would be.
23. **about a round** in a roundabout, like a circle dance.
24. **fire** will-o'-the-wisp.

Vocabulary Development

CCSS Language 6

Malapropisms

Malapropisms are vocabulary mistakes, blunders in which people say words that do not mean what they think they do. Shakespeare uses malapropisms in the Clown scenes in *A Midsummer Night's Dream,* and these mistakes are funny because the word used often has a meaning wildly different from the one intended.

1. Have students identify the malapropism in line 71 on p. 953 (*odious* instead of *odors*).
2. Have them look up *odious* in a dictionary and state its meaning.
3. Then, have them explain why this vocabulary mistake would be funny when it is spoken by a lover to his beloved.

And neigh, and bark, and grunt, and roar, and burn,
Like horse, hound, hog, bear, fire, at every turn.

(He exits.)

BOTTOM. Why do they run away? This is a knavery of them to make me afeard.

24 *Enter* SNOUT.

SNOUT. O Bottom, thou art changed! What do I see on thee?

BOTTOM. What do you see? You see an ass-head of your own, do you? *(SNOUT exits.)*

Enter QUINCE.

QUINCE. Bless thee, Bottom, bless thee! Thou art translated![25] *(He exits.)*

BOTTOM. I see their knavery. This is to make an ass of me, to fright me, if they could. But I will not stir from this place, do what they can. I will walk up and down here, and I will sing, that they shall hear I am not afraid.

(He sings.) The ouzel cock,[26] so black of hue,
With orange-tawny bill,
The throstle[27] with his note so true,
The wren with little quill—[28]

TITANIA. *(waking up)*
What angel wakes me from my flow'ry bed?

BOTTOM. *(sings)*
The finch, the sparrow, and the lark,
The plainsong cuckoo[29] gray,
Whose note full many a man doth mark
And dares not answer "nay"—[30]

for, indeed, who would set his wit to so foolish a bird? Who would give a bird the lie[31] though he cry "cuckoo" never so?[32]

TITANIA.
I pray thee, gentle mortal, sing again.
Mine ear is much enamored of thy note,
So is mine eye enthralled to thy shape,
And thy fair virtue's force perforce doth move me[33]
On the first view to say, to swear, I love thee.

BOTTOM. Methinks, mistress, you should have little reason for that. And yet, to say the truth, reason and love keep little company together nowadays. The more the pity that some

Literary Analysis
Archetypal Theme How does Bottom's transformation make fun of the character of Pyramus?

25. **translated** changed; transformed.
26. **ouzel cock** male blackbird.
27. **throstle** thrush; a bird.
28. **quill** literally, a small reed pipe, but here meaning a tiny piping song.
29. **plainsong cuckoo** bird whose song is likened to church music called plainsong.
30. **Whose . . . "nay"** whose song married men listen to as a sign that their wives may be unfaithful, and who cannot deny that this may be so.
31. **Who would . . .the lie** who would use his intelligence to answer a foolish bird, yet who would dare to contradict the cuckoo's taunt?
32. **never so** over and over; ever so much.
33. **thy . . . move me** your beauty is so powerful it moves me whether I want it to or not.

Vocabulary

enamored (en am´ ərd) *v.* filled with love and desire; charmed

enthralled (en *thrôld*´) *v.* held as in a spell; captivated

25 Reading Check

What physical change happens to Bottom?

24 Literary Analysis

Archetypal Theme

1. **Ask** students how love determined the fate of Pyramus.

   Answer: Love drove Pyramus to run away with Thisbe and then to kill himself when he thought she was dead.

2. **Ask** students in what sense Pyramus was "transformed" by his love.

   Answer: Love robbed Pyramus of his reason and he became completely ruled by passion.

3. Have students reread the bracketed text passage, beginning on p. 954. **Ask** students to answer the Literary Analysis question: How does Bottom's transformation make fun of the character of Pyramus?

   Possible response: Bottom is a foolish fellow playing the role of a romantic hero with great exaggeration. His transformation into an ass mirrors Pyramus' transformation by love into a rash and foolish man. Bottom's transformation is a parody of Pyramus' loss of self-control. Both characters are enchanted, one tragically, one comically.

25 Reading Check

Answer: Bottom is transformed into an ass, or donkey.

Differentiated Instruction for Universal Access

Culturally Responsive Instruction

Culture Focus Bottom experiences metamorphosis. Explain that such transformations feature in the stories of many cultures. For example, students might know the transforming American superhero Spiderman. Have students describe such characters from the literature of their home culture. Discuss what these characters gain and lose by their metamorphoses.

26 Critical Viewing

Answer: Titania and Bottom seem to be madly in love and completely mesmerized with each other.

▲ **Critical Viewing** How do Titania and Bottom seem to feel about each other in this image? **[Describe]**

honest neighbors will not make them friends. Nay, I can gleek[34] upon occasion.

TITANIA.
Thou art as wise as thou art beautiful.

BOTTOM. Not so neither; but if I had wit enough to get out of this wood, I have enough to serve mine own turn.

TITANIA.
Out of this wood do not desire to go.
Thou shalt remain here whether thou wilt or no.
I am a spirit of no common rate.[35]
The summer still doth tend[36] upon my state,
And I do love thee. Therefore go with me.
I'll give thee fairies to attend on thee,
And they shall fetch thee jewels from the deep
And sing while thou on pressed flowers dost sleep.

34. gleek jest; joke.
35. rate value; rank.
36. still doth tend still serves.

Think Aloud

Vocabulary: Using Context

Direct students' attention to the word *gambol* in line 155 on p. 957. Using the following "think aloud," model how to use context to infer the meaning of an unknown word. Say the following to students:

> I'm going to think aloud to show you how I would figure out the meaning of *gambol* from its context.
>
> Titania tells the Fairies to *gambol* in Bottom's eyes. She has previously told them to be "kind and courteous," so *gambol* must be something positive. In the same line, she tells the Fairies to "hop in his walks," that is, dance around him wherever he goes. So *gambol* probably means "dance and skip around, to frolic."

And I will purge thy mortal grossness[37] so
That thou shalt like an airy spirit go.—
Peaseblossom, Cobweb, Mote,[38] and Mustardseed!

Enter four Fairies: PEASEBLOSSOM, COBWEB, MOTE, *and* MUSTARDSEED.

PEASEBLOSSOM. Ready.

COBWEB. And I.

MOTE. And I.

MUSTARDSEED. And I.

ALL. Where shall we go?

TITANIA.
Be kind and courteous to this gentleman.
Hop in his walks and gambol in his eyes;
Feed him with apricocks and dewberries.[39]
With purple grapes, green figs, and mulberries;
The honey-bags steal from the humble-bees,
And for night-tapers crop their waxen thighs
And light them at the fiery glowworms' eyes
To have my love to bed and to arise;
And pluck the wings from painted butterflies
To fan the moonbeams from his sleeping eyes.
Nod to him, elves, and do him courtesies.

27

PEASEBLOSSOM. Hail, mortal!

COBWEB. Hail!

MOTE. Hail!

MUSTARDSEED. Hail!

BOTTOM. I cry your Worships mercy,[40] heartily.—I beseech your Worship's name.

COBWEB. Cobweb.

BOTTOM. I shall desire you of more acquaintance, good Master Cobweb. If I cut my finger, I shall make bold with you.[41]—Your name, honest gentleman?

PEASEBLOSSOM. Peaseblossom.

BOTTOM. I pray you, commend me to Mistress Squash,[42] your mother, and to Master Peascod,[43] your father. Good Master Peaseblossom, I shall desire you of more acquaintance, too.—Your name, I beseech you, sir?

MUSTARDSEED. Mustardseed.

37. **mortal grossness** the physical, mortal state of human beings.

38. **Mote** a speck, but also moth, as this word was pronounced similarly.

39. **apricocks and dewberries** apricots and blackberries.

Literary Analysis
Archetypal Theme
How do Titania's commands emphasize the absurdity of her feelings toward Bottom?

40. **cry. . . mercy** beg your pardon.

41. **Master . . . you** cobwebs were used to stop bleeding.

42. **squash** an unripe pea pod.

43. **peascod** a ripe pea pod.

28

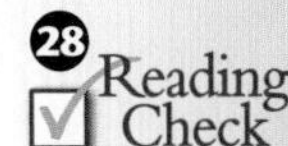

How does Titania want the fairies to treat Bottom?

27 Literary Analysis

Archetypal Theme

1. **Ask** students to summarize what Titania wants the fairies to do for Bottom.

   Answer: Titania wants the fairies to dance around Bottom, feed him fruits and honey, light his way to bed, and fan him when he is sleeping.

2. **Ask** students to answer the Literary Analysis question: How do Titania's commands emphasize the absurdity of her feelings toward Bottom?

   Answer: Titania's commands are appropriate to give honor to a king, not a donkey. A donkey would not appreciate such courtesies or sleep in a bed.

3. **Ask** students why Titania's love is ill-fated.

   Answer: Titania is made to love a donkey.

4. Point out that the archetypal theme of ill-fated love can be treated tragically, as it is in the tale of Pyramus and Thisbe, or comically, as it is in *A Midsummer Night's Dream.*

28 Literary Analysis

Answer: Titania wants the fairies to treat Bottom with kindness and courtesy.

Fluency

Distribute copies of page 957, and pair students. Have listeners mark words with which readers struggle. Circulate to monitor students' fluency, then collect the marked up pages. Review difficult words and passages, such as these:

- If students struggle to syllabicate *courteous,* model how to cover parts of the word, pronounce each part, and then blend the parts together. Read the word aloud and have students echo to confirm.
- If students have difficulty with Titania's long speech, invite fluent students to read the speech aloud as others listen and repeat to achieve fluency.
- If students pronounce, but stumble on the meaning of the word *night-tapers,* point out context clues such as *bees, waxen,* and *light.* Stress that students should try to figure out meaning separately from learning how to pronounce a word.

Concept Connector

Have students return to their **Anticipation Guides** and respond to the statements again in the After Reading column, working alone or in their original pairs or groups. Then probe for what students have learned that confirms or invalidates each statement. Also, have students compare their Writing About the Big Question responses before reading the selection with their ideas afterwards.

ASSESS

Answers

Critical Thinking

Before students respond, you may wish to have them write a brief objective summary of the selection. As they answer the questions below, remind them to support their answers with evidence from the text.

1. (a) The Clowns are preparing a play about Pyramus and Thisbe. (b) Bottom is magically transformed into an ass; the rehearsal ends with the actors fleeing.
2. (a) Robin, a fairy, changes Bottom as a joke. (b) Bottom is unaware of the change; he cannot understand his friends' reactions. (c) Bottom's personality is unchanged; he retains his usual self-confidence.
3. (a) Titania is the fairy queen. (b) The match between a queen and a donkey-head mocks the idea that love unites opposites.
4. Bottom's transformation emphasizes the truth that he is an affable buffoon (or ass) who has an exaggerated idea of himself.
5. (a) The Clowns plan to explain that Pyramus is only an actor who will not actually die; they will change the lion costume to show the actor within. (b) **Possible response:** Students may agree that the audience will find the Clowns' intended tragedy to be hilarious.
6. **Possible response:** (a) Titania is a fairy queen and Bottom is a clown who is turned into a donkey. (b) They are both victims of magic and, because of the magic, are attracted to one another and love each other's company. (c) Students' responses will vary.

BOTTOM. Good Master Mustardseed, I know your patience[44] well. That same cowardly, giantlike ox-beef hath devoured many a gentleman of your house. I promise you, your kindred hath made my eyes water ere now. I desire you of more acquaintance, good Master Mustardseed.

TITANIA. Come, wait upon him. Lead him to my bower.
The moon, methinks, looks with a watery eye,
And when she weeps, weeps every little flower,
Lamenting some enforcèd chastity.[45]
Tie up my lover's tongue. Bring him silently.

They exit.

44. your patience your story; your experience.

45. enforcèd chastity violation; requirement.

Critical Thinking

Cite textual evidence to support your responses.

1. **Key Ideas and Details (a)** What are the Clowns trying to accomplish in this scene? **(b) Analyze Cause and Effect:** What events prevent their success? Explain.
2. **Key Ideas and Details (a)** How is Bottom transformed? **(b) Infer:** Is Bottom aware of his transformation? Explain. **(c) Analyze:** Does the transformation alter Bottom's personality as well as his appearance? Why or why not?
3. **Key Ideas and Details (a)** Who is Titania? **(b) Analyze:** In what ways does the match between Titania and Bottom mock typical portrayals of romantic love?
4. **Integration of Knowledge and Ideas Analyze:** Does Bottom's transformation actually reveal a truth about his character? Explain.
5. **Key Ideas and Details (a) Summarize:** What alterations to script and costumes do the Clowns plan in order to minimize the frightening aspects of their play? **(b) Speculate:** Do you think the Clowns' eventual audience will enjoy their production of "Pyramus and Thisbe"? Explain.
6. **Integration of Knowledge and Ideas (a)** What are the major differences between Titania and Bottom? **(b)** What similarities help them overcome their differences? **(c)** Do you think their differences or their similarities will matter more in the end? Explain. *[Connect to the Big Question: Do our differences define us?]*

Vocabulary Development

Vocabulary Knowledge Rating

When students have completed reading and discussing "Pyramus and Thisbe" and the excerpt from *A Midsummer Night's Dream,* have them take out their **Vocabulary Knowledge Rating Chart.** Read the words aloud once more and have students rate their knowledge of the words again in the After Reading column. Clarify any words that are still problematic. Have students write their own definition and example or sentence in the appropriate column. Then, have students complete the Vocabulary Practice activities on the next page. Encourage students to use the words in further discussion and written work about the selections. Remind them that they will be accountable for these words on the **Selection Test, *Unit 5 Resources,*** pp. 128–130 or 131–133.

After You Read

Pyramus and Thisbe • *from* A Midsummer Night's Dream

Comparing Archetypal Themes

1. Key Ideas and Details Use a chart like the one shown to identify the characters, obstacles, and main events depicted in the scene Bottom and his friends rehearse in *A Midsummer Night's Dream,* the full version of *The Tragedy of Romeo and Juliet,* and Ovid's "Pyramus and Thisbe."

Selection	Characters	Obstacles	Main Events
A Midsummer Night's Dream			
The Tragedy of Romeo and Juliet			
Pyramus and Thisbe			

2. Craft and Structure (a) Using your chart, explain how Shakespeare draws on and transforms Ovid's story in both *A Midsummer Night's Dream* and *Romeo and Juliet.* **(b)** What are the differences in the ways the three selections present this theme?

3. Integration of Knowledge and Ideas (a) Why is Titania and Bottom's love ill-fated? **(b)** How do these reasons compare to the obstacles faced by Romeo and Juliet or Pyramus and Thisbe?

Timed Writing

Explanatory Text: Essay

In an essay, compare the way Shakespeare uses the characters and events from "Pyramus and Thisbe" in *The Tragedy of Romeo and Juliet* with the way he uses them in *A Midsummer Night's Dream.* Discuss why Shakespeare might explore the same story in both a tragedy and a comedy. **(40 minutes)**

5-Minute Planner

1. Read the prompt carefully and completely.
2. Gather your ideas by jotting down answers to these questions:
   - How do the different settings and characters in each of Shakespeare's plays affect the two presentations of the archetypal theme?
   - How do you think Shakespeare wanted audiences to feel about the ill-fated love in each play?
3. Reread the prompt, and then draft your essay.

Assessment Resources

The following resources can be used to assess students' knowledge and skills.

Unit 5 Resources

L1 L2 EL **Selection Test A,** pp. 128–130

L3 L4 EL **Selection Test B,** pp. 131–133

L3 L4 **Open-Book Test,** pp. 125–127

All assessment resources are available at **www.PHLitOnline.com.**

ASSESS

Answers

Comparing Archetypal Themes

1. **Possible responses:** ***Romeo and Juliet*—Characters:** Romeo, Juliet, Mercutio, Tybalt, Friar Lawrence; **Obstacles:** feud, ages of the lovers, arranged marriage; **Events:** lovers meeting, secret wedding, banishment, error by Romeo, deaths of lovers.

   "Pyramus and Thisbe"—Characters: Pyramus, Thisbe, lion; **Obstacles:** parents' restrictions, ages of the lovers, lion; **Events:** running away, lion, error by Pyramus, deaths of the lovers.

   Other sample answers appear in ***Graphic Organizer Transparencies,* Comparing Archetypal Themes (After You Read) Graphic Organizer Transparency A,** p. 169 and in the **Additional Answers** section.
2. (a) In both plays, lovers are destroyed through chance and fatal misunderstanding. (b) *Romeo and Juliet* presents the theme with greater length, complexity, and realism. The characters are more emotionally involving. Pyramus and Thisbe meet their fate alone; the fate of Romeo and Juliet involves many people.
3. (a) Titania and Bottom belong to different worlds. (b) Titania and Bottom are entangled by magic. The humans face real-world obstacles.

Timed Writing

1. Review the prompt with students.
2. Have students use the 5-Minute Planner to structure their time. Guide them in answering the bulleted questions. For example, have them recall specific details of the settings and characters in the two works.
3. Allow students 40 minutes to complete the assignment.
4. As students prewrite and draft, have them refer to the selection comparison organizer.

Six Traits Focus

✓	Ideas		Word Choice
✓	Organization		Sentence Fluency
	Voice		Conventions

PRETEACH

Common Core State Standards

- **Writing 2, 2.a, b, c, d, f; 4, 5**
- **Language 1.b**

Introducing the Writing Assignment

Review the assignment and the criteria, using the instruction on the student page.

Connecting to Real-Life Writing

Point out that elements of a how-to essay are often incorporated into other types of writing: Scientific papers often explain how experiments were done, and presentations in social studies often explain how problems were solved.

Writing Workshop

Work in Progress

If students have completed the Work-in-Progress assignments on p. 933, suggest that they try to develop their Work-in-Progress ideas in a how-to essay.

TEACH

Prewriting Strategy

1. Introduce the prewriting strategy, using the instruction on the student page.
2. Have students apply the strategy to choose a topic.

Six Traits Focus

✓	Ideas		Word Choice
✓	Organization		Sentence Fluency
	Voice		Conventions

Writing Workshop

Write an Explanatory Text

Exposition: How-to Essay

Defining the Form A **how-to essay** provides step-by step instructions for completing a specific task. The best how-to essays are clearly written so readers can avoid mistakes and follow the best path to a desired outcome. You might use elements of the how-to essay in repair instructions, travel directions, recipes, training manuals, and problem solving.

Assignment Write a how-to essay about an activity or a process that you know well. Include these elements:

- ✓ *specific, well-chosen, and sufficient information* presented in logical sequence
- ✓ *step-by-step directions* for each stage in the process
- ✓ *examples* and *concrete definitions* that demonstrate key concepts
- ✓ *instructions* that anticipate readers' questions
- ✓ error-free grammar, including use of *modifying phrases*

To preview the criteria on which your how-to essay may be judged, see the rubric on page 965.

Writing Workshop: *Work in Progress*

Review the work you did on page 933.

Common Core State Standards

Writing

2. Write informative/explanatory texts to examine and convey complex ideas, concepts and information clearly and accurately through the effective selection, organization, and analysis of content.

2.a. Introduce a topic; organize complex ideas, concepts, and information to make important connections and distinctions; include formatting when useful to aiding comprehension.

2.b. Develop the topic with well-chosen, relevant, and sufficient facts, extended definitions, concrete details, quotations, or other information and examples appropriate to the audience's knowledge of the topic.

2.d. Use precise language and domain-specific vocabulary to manage the complexity of the topic.

2.f. Provide a concluding statement or section that follows from and supports the information or explanation presented.

4. Produce clear and coherent writing in which the development, organization, and style are appropriate to task, purpose, and audience.

Prewriting/Planning Strategy

Choose a topic by thinking about some of your daily activities. Select as a topic an activity that involves several steps you feel confident about explaining.

List the materials. Write down all the materials, tools, and information your readers will need to accomplish the activity you plan to describe. First, make a list of items needed. Then, note all of the steps involved, in the order in which they occur. Take time to identify basic rules of behavior—for example, about safety, care of equipment, or working with others. Be sure to list all technical terms and notations accurately.

Items or Tools Needed	Steps in Process	Rules to Follow

Teaching Resources

The following resources can be used to enrich or extend the instruction.

All *Unit 5 Resources*
Writing Workshop, pp. 134,135

All *Common Core Companion,*
pp. 190–201, 213–221

All *Professional Development Guidebook*
Rubrics for Self-Assessment: How-to Essay, pp. 228–229

All *Graphic Organizer Transparencies*
Rubric for Self-Assessment: How-to Essay, p. 171

All resources are available online at **www.PHLitOnline.com.**

WRITER'S TOOLBOX

Organization | Word Choice | Ideas | Conventions | Sentence Fluency | Voice

Getting Organized

The **organization** of an essay is the order in which the information is put together. Organization is especially important in a how-to essay because readers have to understand completely in order to do the task. There are two kinds of organization to think about as you plan your essay:

- The order of steps in the task you are describing
- The order of information in your essay

Organizing the Steps How-to essays are usually organized in chronological order. Often, the easiest way to start is to list things that need to be done as you think of them. When you finish listing, number them in the order they need to be completed. Include preparation as one of the steps. Think about what materials you need to have on hand. For example, in preparing for a part in a play, your steps might include the following:

1. Get a copy of the play you can mark up.
2. Read the play thoroughly.
3. Read it a second time while underlining the lines you will read.
4. Reread your lines and think about your character.

Organizing the Essay An effective how-to essay has three main parts: introduction, body, and conclusion. In your introduction, identify your task and give readers a reason to read your essay. In the body, explain the process in step-by-step order. Finally, write a conclusion that emphasizes the importance of the process you have explained. Use the chart shown to help you organize your essay.

Organizing Information

1. State the purpose of your how-to-essay.
2. List the materials and conditions necessary to complete the activity.
3. Provide examples to demonstrate the activity.
4. List steps to complete in consecutive order.
5. Suggest solutions to common problems when performing the activity.
6. Present your final thoughts in a conclusion.

PH WRITING COACH

Further instruction and practice are available in *Prentice Hall Writing Coach*.

Getting Organized

1. Introduce the writing skill, using the instruction on the student page.
2. Discuss the ways of organizing a how-to essay and the information in the chart.

Teaching the Writing Skill

1. Tell students to make lists of the steps that readers must go through in order to perform the tasks that they will describe in their how-to essays. Suggest that students write each step on a separate note card so that they can rearrange the steps as needed.
2. Ask students to determine if their tasks require materials such as ingredients or tools, or if they require advance preparation. If materials or preparation are necessary, tell students to include these in their essays before the steps of the task itself.
3. Direct students' attention to the box. Remind students that the essay's introduction should define what task the reader will perform, how long the task will take, and the materials that are needed to complete the task.
4. Tell students that if their essays explained how to build an item, the essay's conclusion may also contain suggestions on how to use the item described.

PH WRITING COACH Grade 9

Students will find additional support for writing a how-to essay in chapter 8.

Prentice Hall EssayScorer

A writing prompt for this mode of writing can be found in the ***Prentice Hall Essay Scorer*** at **www.PHLitOnline.com.**

Differentiated Instruction for Universal Access

EL Strategy for English Learners

English Learners may have difficulty with technical terms or vocabulary that is specific to a task. Prior to writing their how-to essays, help students make lists of the English words that are specific to their tasks or processes. Suggest that students use dictionaries or online translation programs as needed.

Strategy for Less Proficient Writers

Before writing their how-to essays, help students make a list of transitional words and phrases that are often used in how-to essays. The list might include words such as *before, next, additionally, however, last, specifically,* and *afterwards.* Tell students that using transitional words and phrases will help them smoothly link the steps in a task.

Drafting Strategies

1. Introduce the drafting strategies, using the instruction on the student page.
2. Have students apply the strategies as they draft.

Teaching the Strategies

Caution students against overusing graphics; too many pictures can create clutter. Have students read their drafts to find the places that would benefit from graphics.

Six Traits Focus

	Ideas		Word Choice
✔	Organization		Sentence Fluency
	Voice		Conventions

Revising Strategies

1. Introduce the revision strategies, using the instruction on the student page.
2. Have students apply the strategies as they revise their drafts.

Teaching the Strategies

Tell students that when they revise for clarity, they should keep in mind their audience's knowledge.

Think Aloud: Model Revising for Transitions

Model the strategy, using the following "think aloud":

My essay is about making a braided rug from T-shirts. I write: "Collect some cotton T-shirts. Choose colors that go well together. Cut the T-shirts into strips." I'll add some transitional words to make the steps clearer: "First, collect some T-shirts. Then pick a few shirts whose colors go well together. Finally, cut the T-shirts into strips." Now readers will understand better what to do.

Six Traits Focus

	Ideas	✔	Word Choice
✔	Organization		Sentence Fluency
✔	Voice		Conventions

Drafting Strategies

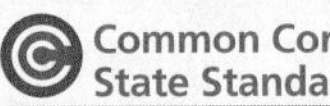

Common Core State Standards

Writing

2.a. Introduce a topic; organize complex ideas, concepts, and information to make important connections and distinctions; include formatting, graphics, and multimedia when useful to aiding comprehension.

2.c. Use appropriate and varied transitions to link the major sections of the text, create cohesion, and clarify the relationships among complex ideas and concepts.

2.d. Use precise language and domain-specific vocabulary to manage the complexity of the topic.

5. Develop and strengthen writing as needed by planning, revising, editing, rewriting, or trying a new approach, focusing on addressing what is most significant for a specific purpose and audience.

Language

1.b. Use various types of phrases and clauses to convey specific meanings and add variety and interest to writing or presentations.

Begin writing. Once you have planned your how-to essay, begin your first draft. Refer to your notes, and present your directions simply and clearly.

Use formatting. To present information that must be followed in a specific order, use numbered lists. Use bulleted lists to present items that do not have to be followed step by step. For example, use a bulleted list to present materials that are needed or to list precautions.

Use graphic devices. Locate or create graphics to reinforce your instructions, and place them at appropriate points in your essay. If you have access to a computer, use graphics features to create helpful diagrams and drawings.

Define unfamiliar terms. How-to essays often require the inclusion of specialized language that may be unfamiliar to your readers. To avoid confusion, be sure to explain any terms that you think your readers might not know—especially when describing complex tasks.

Revising Strategies

Revise for clarity. Look over your draft to identify instructions, steps, or information that may be unclear to your reader. Mark these sections, and then go back to them, rewriting or adding language that better explains your points. If the order in which you have explained the steps is confusing, rearrange paragraphs to create a better flow of information.

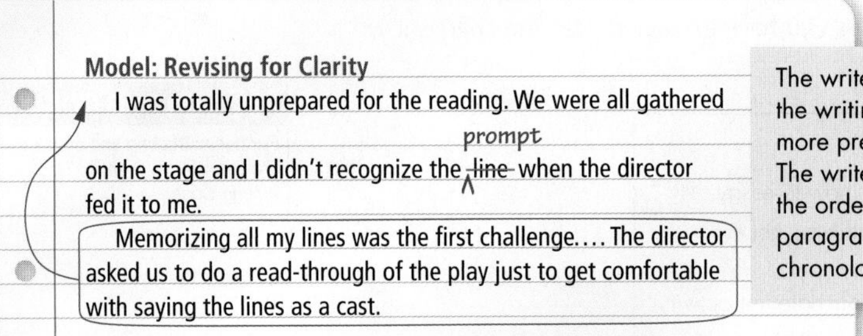

Model: Revising for Clarity
I was totally unprepared for the reading. We were all gathered
on the stage and I didn't recognize the ~~line~~ prompt when the director
fed it to me.
Memorizing all my lines was the first challenge.... The director asked us to do a read-through of the play just to get comfortable with saying the lines as a cast.
The writer clarifies the writing by using a more precise term. The writer changes the order of the paragraphs to follow chronological order.

Revise for transitions. Look for sections in your draft that need transitional language to connect the steps. In this example, the words *first* and *then* would make the instruction easier to understand.

First study the character and *then* think how you can express the character's personality.

Applying Understanding by Design Principles

Clarifying Expected Outcomes: Using Rubrics

- Before students begin working on this assignment, have them preview the Rubric for Self-Assessment (p. 965) to learn what qualities their how-to essays must have. A copy of this rubric appears in ***Graphic Organizer Transparencies,*** p.171.
- Review the criteria in the rubric with the class. Before students use the rubric to assess their writing, work with them to rate the Student Model (p. 964) using the rubric.
- If you wish to assess students' essays with either a 4-point or a 6-point scoring rubric, see ***Professional Development Guidebook,*** pp. 228–229.

WRITER'S TOOLBOX

Sentence Fluency | Voice | Organization | Word Choice | Ideas | Conventions

Revising to Combine Sentences With Phrases

To avoid a series of too many simple sentences, combine some sentences by converting the idea in one sentence into a modifying phrase in another.

Identifying Modifying Phrases An **appositive phrase** is a group of words that clarifies the meaning of a noun or pronoun. The following sentences can be combined using an appositive phrase.

Original: Sophia is a talented actress. She has appeared in more than twenty productions.

Combined: Sophia, *a talented actress,* has appeared in more than twenty productions. (appositive phrase)

Verbal phrases, which use verbs as nouns, adjectives, or adverbs, can also be used to combine sentences. Verbal phrases may be classified as participial, gerund, and infinitive, depending on their function.

Participle	Gerund	Infinitive
Finding himself alone onstage, Aaron paced nervously.	*Meeting with new people* is difficult for some people.	The director's advice was *to focus first on learning the lines.*
Adjective modifies *Aaron*	Noun acts as subject of sentence	Noun acts as complement of verb *was*

When adding a modifying phrase to a sentence, place the phrase close to the word it modifies. A misplaced modifier can confuse readers.

Misplaced: *Hanging from a silken thread,* Jeremy noticed a spider. (Participial phrase seems to modify *Jeremy.*)

Correct: Jeremy noticed a spider *hanging from a silken thread.*

Combining With Phrases Follow these steps to revise a series of short sentences by using phrases to combine them.

1. Express the information from one sentence as an appositive or a verbal phrase.
2. Insert the phrase in a new sentence, locating it near the word or words being modified.
3. Make sure that the revised sentence is punctuated correctly.

Grammar in Your Writing

Review your draft, looking for short sentences that might be combined using appositive, participial, gerund, or infinitive phrases. Consider combining these sentences.

PH WRITING COACH

Further instruction and practice are available in *Prentice Hall Writing Coach.*

Strategies for Using Technology in Writing

If students are using word processing software, suggest that they use the *cut, copy,* and *paste* features to combine sentences. After they have combined choppy sentences, advise students to check each new sentence they have created to make sure it reads properly and has appropriate punctuation, including additional commas as needed, and a period.

Revising to Combine Sentences With Phrases

1. Introduce the grammar skill, using the instruction on the student page.
2. Discuss the examples and the strategies for correct use of modifying phrases.
3. Have students follow the instruction under Grammar in Your Writing to correct errors in their drafts.

Teaching the Grammar Skill

1. Tell students that too many short sentences make writing sound stilted and unnatural.
2. Have students combine these sentences by creating an appositive phrase.

   Gerard enjoys eating fruit and granola. He is a strict vegetarian.
   Answer: Gerard, a strict vegetarian, enjoys eating fruit and granola.
3. Give student pairs the following sets of sentences. Have them combine each set by converting one sentence into a verbal phrase. Have students identify the types of verbal phrases they create.

   Mya walked across the balance beam. She held her arms out to her sides.
   Possible response: *Holding her arms out to her sides, Mya walked across the balance beam.* (participial)

   It is fulfilling for me to volunteer at the women's shelter. It is also beneficial for the women.
   Possible response: *Volunteering at the women's shelter is fulfilling for me and beneficial for the women.* (gerund)
4. Ask which of the following sentences has a misplaced modifier. Have students correct the sentence.

   Sucking the pacifier, Colette smiled at the baby.

   Closing his ears, Mikah scolded the screeching bird.
   Answer: The first sentence should be rewritten as follows: *Colette smiled at the baby sucking the pacifier.*

PH WRITING COACH Grade 9

Students will find practice with and guidance on combining sentences in Chapter 16.

Student Model

Review the Student Model with the class, using the annotations to analyze the writer's use of the elements of a how-to essay.

Teaching From the Student Model

1. Explain that the Student Model is a sample and that students' own essays may be longer.
2. **Ask** students why Carmen's numbering system is effective.

   Answer: It separates the steps, making it easier for the reader to follow the process. It also helps the reader to focus on the steps one at a time, rather than all together.
3. Give students the example of a student who is writing an essay about how to stay healthy. Write the following sentences on the chalkboard:

   You should avoid certain foods. You should take vitamins every day.

   Ask students what questions or concerns about these sentences the writer should address in his or her essay.

   Possible response: *What kinds of foods should I avoid? What kind of vitamins should I take?*
4. Draw students' attention to the way in which Carmen offers suggestions to help the reader better perform the process, as well as explanations to reinforce the importance of the information she has chosen to include in her essay.

Connecting to Real-Life Writing

Point out that people must often explain to others the steps in a process. At work, for example, people might be required to provide information to coworkers about using computer programs. At home, they might have to explain how to use a DVR to record a television program.

Student Model: Carmen Rose Viviano-Crafts Syracuse, NY

Preparing for a Dramatic Role

One of the first challenges of a new dramatic role is the task of memorizing lines. Use the following guidelines to memorize lines more efficiently:

1. Read the entire play at least twice to familiarize yourself with the setting and situations. When performing, it is essential to know what is going on around you in order to provide the appropriate reactions.

   The numbering system allows Carmen to present information logically.
2. Highlight or underline all your lines to identify when your character speaks.
3. Begin to concentrate solely on your parts. Look at the script scene by scene, memorizing one or two scenes a day, depending on how much time you have. Reading the lines out loud speeds up the process by making the lines more memorable.

   By offering time suggestions, Carmen anticipates readers' questions and concerns.
4. Once you feel confident enough, begin to "run" your lines. Read them aloud, with another person reading the other characters' lines. This prepares you for being onstage with other actors.
5. When you begin rehearsing with fellow cast members, you will be able to try out different ways of saying things, and you'll start to develop your character. Here are the steps to use when developing a character:
   - If your role is based on a real person, research that person or observe someone in a similar situation. Try to find out as much information as you can so that you can play the part realistically.

     Advice about conducting research elaborates on Carmen's earlier suggestions.
   - If you are playing a fictional character, study the script closely. The character's words can tell you about his or her feelings, likes, and dislikes.
   - Once you have learned some aspects of your character, begin to delve into the mind and soul of the person. Make up an entire life story for your character. The more you know about the person, the easier it is to put yourself in his or her place. Think of a past experience to relate to something your character is going through. Bring the emotions you felt in that situation to your character's situation.
   - Finally, conduct general conversations with other cast members, with each of you speaking from your own character's point of view. Ask things like "How do you feel about me?" and "How do you think I feel about you?" This lets you know how you are perceived by the other actors/characters in the play and allows you to react more realistically.

     These ideas explain the value of each strategy.
6. After each rehearsal, consider what worked well and what felt wrong to you. Use your after-rehearsal notes as feedback to improve your next performance.

Strategies for Test Taking

When students are taking a test that requires them to explain the steps in a process, they should pay careful attention to the use of transitional words and phrases. Remind students that these words and phrases tell readers where they are in the process and explain how one step relates to the next.

Editing and Proofreading

Check your draft for errors in spelling, grammar, and punctuation.

Focus on formatting. If you include bullets or numbered lists in your essay, be sure that you use these elements consistently in your final draft. Check that numbers are consecutive and that bullets are the same size and shape. In addition, check that spacing is consistent and appropriate.

Spiral Review

Earlier in this unit, you learned about **participles and participial phrases** and **gerunds and gerund phrases** (p. 932). Check your essay to be sure you have used these forms correctly.

Publishing and Presenting

Consider one of the following ways to share your writing:

Deliver an oral presentation. Share your essay with classmates and give an instructional presentation in which you accurately utilize technical terms and notations. If the process you describe can be done in a classroom, have a classmate demonstrate the steps as you describe them. Ask for feedback about the clarity of your presentation.

Prepare a how-to manual. With a group of classmates, compile several how-to essays into a booklet. Add step-by-step photographs or illustrations to your instructions. Make the collection available to the class.

Reflecting on Your Writing

Jot down your answers to this question:

How did writing a how-to essay help you understand the process you outlined?

Rubric for Self-Assessment

Find evidence in your writing to address each category. Then, use the rating scale to grade your work.

Criteria	Rating Scale (not very — very)
Focus: How specific is your focus?	1 2 3 4 5
Organization: How logical is your organization of the process into steps?	1 2 3 4 5
Support/Elaboration: How effective are your examples in demonstrating key concepts?	1 2 3 4 5
Style: How well do your instructions anticipate readers' questions?	1 2 3 4 5
Conventions: How correct is your grammar, especially your use of modifying phrases?	1 2 3 4 5
Sentence Fluency: How well have you combined sentences to eliminate a series of too many simple sentences?	1 2 3 4 5

Editing and Proofreading

1. Introduce the editing and proofreading focus, using the instruction on the student page.
2. Have students edit and proofread their narratives, correcting grammar, spelling, punctuation, and word choice. Make sure they check for errors of the type noted in the lesson focus and the Spiral Review.

Teaching the Editing Focus

Stress to students the importance of consistency in their lists. Tell students that if readers see inconsistencies, they are liable to focus on these rather than on the information presented.

Six Traits Focus

	Ideas		Word Choice
	Organization	✔	Sentence Fluency
	Voice	✔	Conventions

ASSESS

Publishing and Presenting

1. For any processes that can be demonstrated in class, have students give the oral presentation while a partner demonstrates the steps.
2. As students create a collection of how-to essays, encourage them to organize the essays logically, perhaps by dividing them into categories.

Reflecting on Your Writing

Ask if how-to writing seems more natural to them than other forms of writing. Ask if they would be comfortable writing such an essay in a test situation.

Differentiated Instruction for Universal Access

Strategy for Less Proficient Writers
Organize students into small groups. Have students attach blank sheets of paper to their essays and share their essays among their groups. Every student should have a chance to silently read each essay. Tell students to notice any places in the essays that are confusing. Have students write their feedback for each essay on its blank sheet of paper. Students can then use the comments to revise their essays.

Strategy for Advanced Writers
Ask students to write their how-to essays without numbers. They should rely on transition words to communicate the sequence of steps. Challenge them to organize the steps into logical paragraphs. Have students work in pairs to determine whether their essays are clear and complete.

✓ The Inspector-General
Lesson Pacing Guide

DAY 1 Preteach

- Administer the Reading and Vocabulary Warm-ups (*Unit 5 Resources*, pp. 143–146) as necessary.
- Introduce the Reading Skill: Draw Conclusions.
- Introduce the Literary Analysis concept: Comedy.
- Distribute copies of the appropriate graphic organizer for the Reading Skill (*Graphic Organizer Transparencies*, pp. 172–173).
- Distribute copies of the appropriate graphic organizer for Literary Analysis (*Graphic Organizer Transparencies*, pp. 174–175).
- Teach the selection vocabulary.
- Introduce the Word Study skill.

DAYS 2–3 Preteach/Teach

- Build background with the Background feature.
- Develop thematic vocabulary and thematic thinking with Writing About the Big Question.
- Prepare students to read with the Activating Prior Knowledge activities (TE).
- Informally monitor comprehension while students read.
- Use the Reading Check questions to confirm comprehension.
- Develop students' ability to draw conclusions, using the Reading Skill questions.
- Develop students' understanding of comedy, using the Literary Analysis questions.
- Reinforce vocabulary with the Vocabulary notes.
- Reinforce unit focus standards using the Spiral Review prompts.

DAY 4 Assess

- Assess students' comprehension and mastery of the skills by having them answer the Critical Thinking, Reading Skill, and Literary Analysis questions.
- Have students complete the Vocabulary Practice activities.
- Have students complete the Word Study activities.

DAY 5 Extend/Assess

- Have students complete the Conventions lesson.
- Have students complete the Writing activity and write a play. (You may assign as homework.)
- Extend learning by having students complete the Research and Technology activity, informational chart. (You may assign as homework.) As an alternative, assign them "In Your Name" and "On Patrol" in *Reality Central*.
- Administer Selection Test A or B (*Unit 5 Resources*, pp. 158–163).

Common Core State Standards

Reading Literature 1. Cite strong and thorough textual evidence to support inferences drawn from the text.
3. Analyze how complex characters (e.g., those with multiple or conflicting motivations) develop over the course of a text, interact with other characters, and advance the plot or develop the theme.
5. Analyze how an author's choices concerning how to structure a text, order events within it, and manipulate time create such effects as mystery, tension, or surprise.

Writing 3. Write narratives to develop real or imagined experiences or events using effective technique, well-chosen details, and well-structured event sequences.
3.a. Engage and orient a reader by setting out a problem, situation, or observation, establishing one or multiple point(s) of view, and introducing a narrator and/or characters; create a smooth progression of experiences or events.
3.b. Use narrative techniques.
3.c. Use a variety of techniques to sequence events.
7. Conduct short as well as more sustained research projects to answer a question or solve a problem.

Language 1. Demonstrate command of the conventions of standard English grammar and usage when writing or speaking.
1.b. Use various types of phrases and clauses to convey specific meanings and add variety and interest to writing or presentations.

Additional Standards Practice
***Common Core Companion*, pp. 28–29**

Daily Block Scheduling
Each day in this Lesson Pacing Guide represents a 40–50 minute period. Teachers using block scheduling may combine days to revise pacing. In addition, teachers may differentiate and support core instruction by integrating components for extended and intensive support as students require. See the Guide to Selected Leveled Resources (facing page).

Guide to Selected Leveled Resources

RTI Tier 1 (students performing on level)			The Inspector-General
Warm Up	Whole class instruction; Group work	**Practice, model,** and **monitor** fluency, working **with the whole class** or **in groups.**	**Vocabulary** and **Reading Warm-ups B,** ***Unit 5 Resources,*** pp. 143–144, 146
Comprehension/Skills	Whole class instruction; Independent work	**Support** and **monitor** comprehension and skills development, having students complete the activities, graphic organizers, and interactive prompts **independently** or **as a class.**	• ***Reader's Notebook,*** adapted instruction and full selection EL ***Reader's Notebook: English Learner's Version,*** adapted instruction and adapted selection • **Reading Skill Graphic Organizer B,** ***Graphic Organizer Transparencies,*** p. 173 • **Literary Analysis Graphic Organizer B,** ***Graphic Organizer Transparencies,*** p. 175
Monitor Progress	A	**Monitor** student progress with the differentiated curriculum-based assessment in the *Unit Resources.*	• **Selection Test B,** ***Unit 5 Resources,*** pp. 161–163 • **Open-Book Test,** ***Unit 5 Resources,*** pp. 155–157
Assess/Screen	A	• **Assess** student progress using Benchmark Test 10. • **Preassess** instructional needs using the Vocabulary in Context section of the test.	• **Benchmark Test 10,** ***Unit 5 Resources,*** pp. 186–194, including Vocabulary in Context diagnostic items

RTI Tier 2 (students requiring intervention)			The Inspector-General
Warm Up	Whole class instruction; Group work	**Practice, model,** and **monitor** fluency **in groups** or **with individuals.**	• **Vocabulary and Reading Warm-ups A,** ***Unit 5 Resources,*** pp. 143–146 • ***Reality Central,*** "In Your Name" and "On Patrol" • ***Hear It!*** **Audio CD (adapted text)**
Comprehension/Skills	Whole class instruction; Independent work	• **Support** and **monitor** comprehension and skills development, working **in small groups** or **with individuals.** • **Pair** students with more advanced peers and have them complete the writing activity in the *Real-World Writing Journal.* • As students complete the selection in the appropriate version of the *Reader's Notebook,* **monitor** comprehension frequently with group questions and individual instruction. • **Model** strategies while guiding students in completing the activities and prompts in the *Reader's Notebook,* as well as the graphic organizers. • **Practice** skills and **monitor** mastery with the *Reading Kit* worksheets.	• ***Real-World Writing Journal,*** Lessons 3–4, pp. 146–153 • ***Reader's Notebook: Adapted Version,*** adapted instruction and adapted selection EL ***Reader's Notebook: English Learner's Version,*** adapted instruction and adapted selection • **Reading Skill Graphic Organizer A,** ***Graphic Organizer Transparencies,*** p. 172 • **Literary Analysis Graphic Organizer A,** ***Graphic Organizer Transparencies,*** p. 174 • **Reading Kit,** Practice worksheets, pp. 238, 242, 246, 248, 254
Monitor Progress	A	**Monitor** student progress with the differentiated curriculum-based assessment in the *Unit Resources* and in the *Reading Kit.*	• **Selection Test A,** ***Unit 5 Resources,*** pp. 158–160 • **Reading Kit,** Assess worksheets pp. 239, 243, 247, 249, 255
Assess/Screen	A	• **Assess** student progress using Benchmark Test 10. • **Preassess** instructional needs using the Vocabulary in Context section of the test.	• **Benchmark Test 10,** ***Unit 5 Resources,*** pp. 186–194, including Vocabulary in Context diagnositc items

TIER 3 Tier 3 intervention may require consultation with the student's special-education or dyslexia specialist. For additional support, see the Tier 2 activities and resources listed above.

One-on-one teaching **Group work** **Whole class instruction** **Independent work** **A Assessment**

For a complete guide to selection support, including support for Advanced students, see the Overview of Resources in the frontmatter.

The Inspector-General

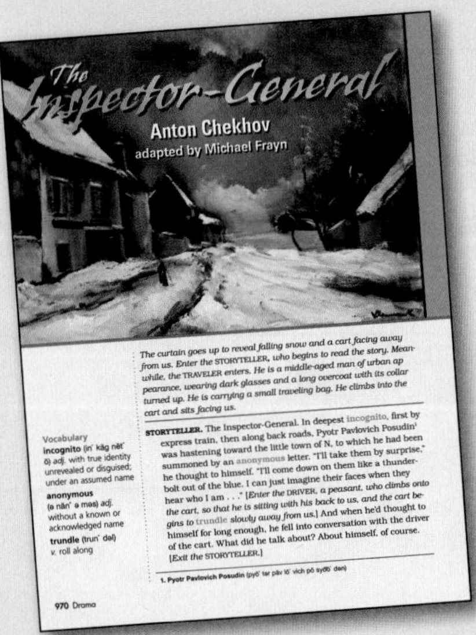

The Inspector-General
Anton Chekhov
adapted by Michael Frayn

The curtain goes up to reveal falling snow and a cart facing away from us. Enter the STORYTELLER, *who begins to read the story. Mean-while, the* TRAVELER *enters. He is a middle-aged man of urban ap pearance, wearing dark glasses and a long overcoat with its collar turned up. He is carrying a small traveling bag. He climbs into the cart and sits facing us.*

STORYTELLER. The Inspector-General. In deepest incognito, first by express train, then along back roads, Pyotr Pavlovich Posudin[1] was hastening toward the little town of N, to which he had been summoned by an anonymous letter. "I'll take them by surprise," he thought to himself. "I'll come down on them like a thunder-bolt out of the blue. I can just imagine their faces when they hear who I am . . ." [*Enter the* DRIVER, *a peasant, who climbs onto the cart, so that he is sitting with his back to us, and the cart be-gins to trundle slowly away from us.*] And when he'd thought to himself for long enough, he fell into conversation with the driver of the cart. What did he talk about? About himself, of course. [*Exit the* STORYTELLER.]

Vocabulary
incognito (in' käg nēt' ō) *adj.* with true identity unrevealed or disguised; under an assumed name
anonymous (ə nän' ə məs) *adj.* without a known or acknowledged name
trundle (trun' dəl) *v.* roll along

1. Pyotr Pavlovich Posudin (pyō' tər päv lō' vich pō sydō' dən)

970 Drama

RESOURCES FOR:

- L1 Special-Needs Students
- L2 Below-Level Students (Tier 2)
- L3 On-Level Students (Tier 1)
- L4 Advanced Students (Tier 1)
- EL English Learners
- All All Students

Vocabulary/Fluency/Prior Knowledge

Unit 5 Resources

"The Inspector-General" by Anton Chekhov
Vocabulary Warm-up Word Lists

Study these words from "The Inspector-General." Then, apply your knowledge to the activities that follow.

Word List A

conversation [kahn vuhr SAY shuhn] *n.* talk between two or more people
We had an interesting conversation about our summer plans.

creeps [KREEPS] *v.* moves quietly with the body held low so that no one will notice
Sometimes, the dog creeps into my room late at night.

express [ek SPRES] *adj.* direct and rapid; not making many stops
We rode the express elevator straight to the top floor of the skyscraper.

gestures [JES chuhrz] *v.* moves a hand, an arm, or the head to communicate
Cross the street when the police officer gestures toward you.

pounces [POWNS ez] *v.* jumps suddenly on someone or something
The lion pounces on the fleeing antelope.

stamps [STAMPS] *v.* brings a foot down hard
To get attention, my baby brother pounds his fists and stamps his feet.

swig [SWIG] *n.* large amount drunk in one gulp
If you are thirsty, have a swig of juice.

wheezes [WEEZ ez] *v.* breathes with difficulty, making a whistling sound in the chest
Because of her chest cold, she wheezes when she runs.

Word List B

carriage [KA rij] *n.* four-wheeled, horse-drawn vehicle for carrying passengers
They enjoyed the ride through the park in the black-and-gold carriage.

cunning [KUHN ing] *adj.* smart in a dishonest or clever way
The jewel thieves devised a cunning plan to break into the museum.

discreetly [di SKREET lee] *adv.* in a way that is not noticeable
When the bullies arrived at the playground, I left discreetly.

hastening [HAYS uhn ing] *v.* moving or acting quickly
The general and his troops were hastening toward the battle.

housekeeper [HOWS keep uhr] *n.* someone hired to do chores in a house or hotel
The housekeeper at the hotel brought us fresh towels each morning.

offended [uh FEND id] *adj.* hurt or angry because of rudeness or an insult
The offended man demanded an apology.

storyteller [STAWR ee tel uhr] *n.* one who tells stories (sometimes a character in a story)
Many children came to hear the storyteller at the library.

urban [UR buhn] *adj.* relating to a city
They sold the farm and moved to an urban community.

Unit 5 Resources: Drama
© Pearson Education, Inc. All rights reserved.
143

EL L1 L2 **Vocabulary Warm-ups A and B,** pp. 143–144

Also available for this selection:

EL L1 L2 **Reading Warm-ups A and B,** pp. 145–146

All **Vocabulary Builder,** p. 150

All **Writing About the Big Question,** p. 147

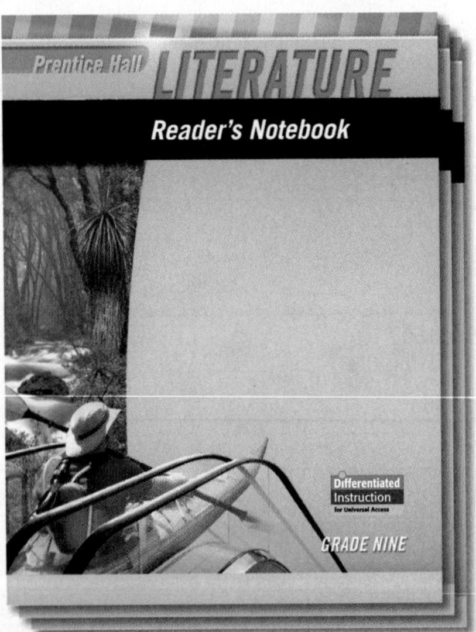

Reader's Notebooks

Pre- and postreading pages, as well as *The Inspector-General*, appear in an interactive format in the *Reader's Notebooks*. Each *Notebook* is differentiated for a different group of learners. The selections in the Adapted and English Learner's versions are abridged

L2 L3 ***Reader's Notebook***

L1 ***Reader's Notebook: Adapted Version***

EL ***Reader's Notebook: English Learner's Version***

EL ***Reader's Notebook: Spanish Version***

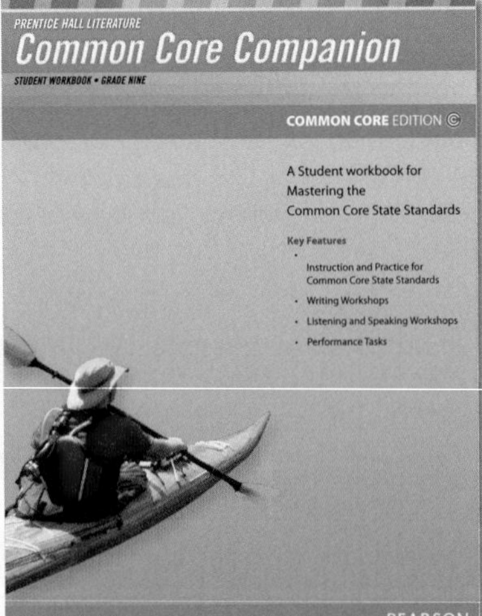

Common Core Companion

Additional instruction and practice for each Common Core State Standard

Selection Support

Graphic Organizer Transparencies

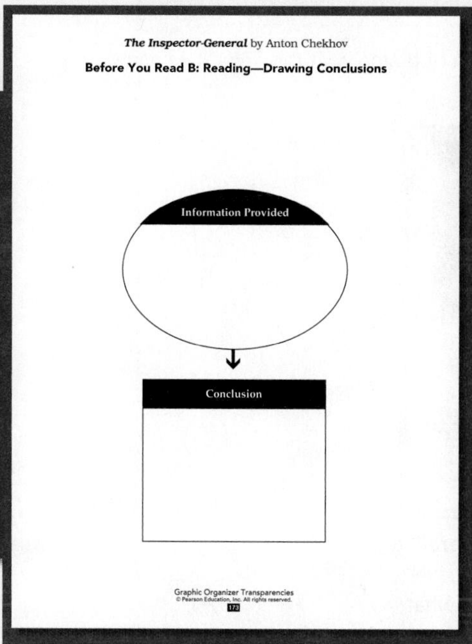

The Inspector-General by Anton Chekhov

Before You Read B: Reading—Drawing Conclusions

Information Provided

Conclusion

Graphic Organizer Transparencies

173

EL L3 **Reading: Graphic Organizer B,** p. 173

Also available for this selection:

- EL L1 L2 **Reading: Graphic Organizer A,** p. 172 (partially filled in)
- EL L1 L2 **Literary Analysis: Graphic Organizer A,** p. 174 (partially filled in)
- EL L3 **Literary Analysis: Graphic Organizer B,** p. 175

Skills Development/Extension

Unit 5 Resources

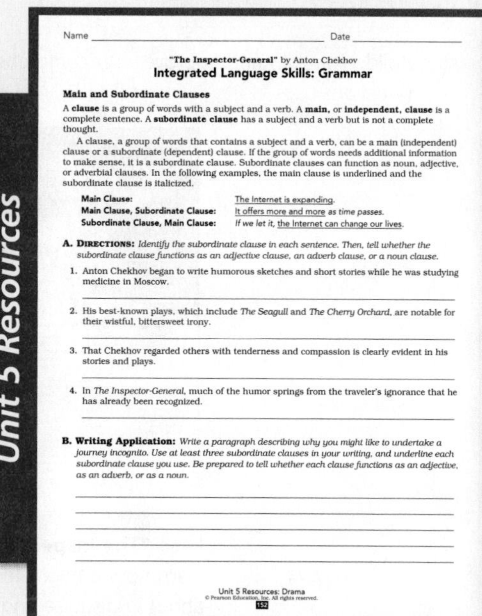

Name ______________________ Date ____________

"The Inspector-General" by Anton Chekhov

Integrated Language Skills: Grammar

Main and Subordinate Clauses

A **clause** is a group of words with a subject and a verb. A **main,** or **independent, clause** is a complete sentence. A **subordinate clause** has a subject and a verb but is not a complete thought.

A clause, a group of words that contains a subject and a verb, can be a main (independent) clause or a subordinate (dependent) clause. If the group of words needs additional information to make sense, it is a subordinate clause. Subordinate clauses can function as noun, adjective, or adverbial clauses. In the following examples, the main clause is underlined and the subordinate clause is italicized.

Main Clause: The Internet is expanding.
Main Clause, Subordinate Clause: It offers more and more *as time passes.*
Subordinate Clause, Main Clause: *If we let it,* the Internet can change our lives.

A. Directions: *Identify the subordinate clause in each sentence. Then, tell whether the subordinate clause functions as an adjective clause, an adverb clause, or a noun clause.*

1. Anton Chekhov began to write humorous sketches and short stories while he was studying medicine in Moscow.
2. His best-known plays, which include *The Seagull* and *The Cherry Orchard,* are notable for their wistful, bittersweet irony.
3. That Chekhov regarded others with tenderness and compassion is clearly evident in his stories and plays.
4. In *The Inspector-General,* much of the humor springs from the traveler's ignorance that he has already been recognized.

B. Writing Application: *Write a paragraph describing why you might like to undertake a journey incognito. Use at least three subordinate clauses in your writing, and underline each subordinate clause you use. Be prepared to tell whether each clause functions as an adjective, as an adverb, or as a noun.*

Unit 5 Resources: Drama

152

EL L3 L4 **Grammar,** p. 152

Also available for this selection:

- All **Reading: Draw Conclusions,** p. 149
- All **Literary Analysis: Comedy,** p. 148
- L4 **Enrichment,** p. 151
- EL L3 L4 **Support for Writing,** p. 153
- L3 L4 **Support for Extend Your Learning,** p. 154

Assessment

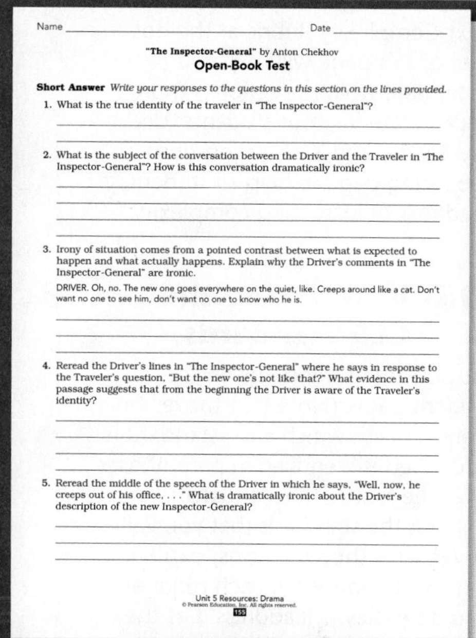

Name ______________________ Date ____________

"The Inspector-General" by Anton Chekhov

Open-Book Test

Short Answer *Write your responses to the questions in this section on the lines provided.*

1. What is the true identity of the traveler in "The Inspector-General"?
2. What is the subject of the conversation between the Driver and the Traveler in "The Inspector-General"? How is this conversation dramatically ironic?
3. Irony of situation comes from a pointed contrast between what is expected to happen and what actually happens. Explain why the Driver's comments in "The Inspector-General" are ironic.

   DRIVER. Oh, no. The new one goes everywhere on the quiet, like. Creeps around like a cat. Don't want no one to see him, don't want no one to know who he is.
4. Reread the Driver's lines in "The Inspector-General" where he says in response to the Traveler's question, "But the new one's not like that?" What evidence in this passage suggests that from the beginning the Driver is aware of the Traveler's identity?
5. Reread the middle of the speech of the Driver in which he says, "Well, now, he creeps out of his office, . . ." What is dramatically ironic about the Driver's description of the new Inspector-General?

Unit 5 Resources: Drama

155

L3 L4 **Open-Book Test,** pp. 155–157

Also available for this selection:

- EL L1 L2 **Selection Test A,** pp. 158–160
- EL L3 L4 **Selection Test B,** pp. 161–163

PHLit Online!
www.PHLitOnline.com

Online Resources: All print materials are also available online.

- complete narrated selection text
- a thematically related video with writing prompt
- an interactive graphic organizer
- highlighting feature
- access to all student print resources, adapted to individual student needs
- Spanish and English summaries
- adapted selection translations in Spanish

Get Connected! (thematic video with writing prompt)

Also available:

Background Video

All videos are available in Spanish.

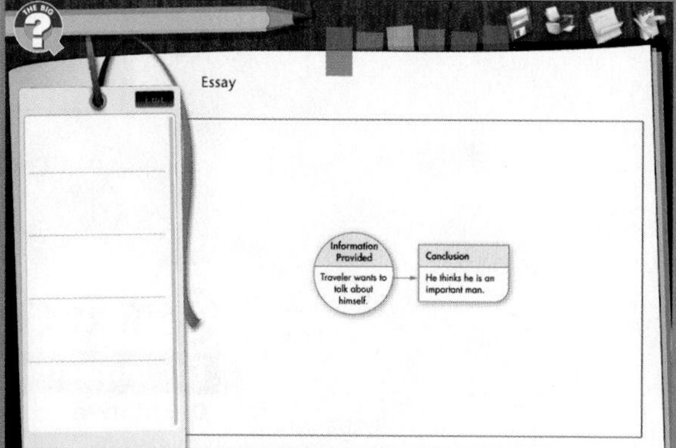

Writer's Journal (with graphics feature)

Also available:

Vocabulary Central (tools, activities, and songs for studying vocabulary)

PRETEACH

❶ Leveled Texts

You may use "The Inspector-General" to meet the lesson objectives. The Text Complexity Rubric at the bottom of this page will help you determine which selection is more appropriate for your students. Use the Reader and Task Suggestions on the facing page to help all students read text of increasing complexity.

❷ Introducing the CCS Standards

Introduce the standards on the student page. (Note that the lesson element with which each standard is addressed is identified in parentheses after the text of the standard.) Call out the standards that you will cover with the selections, explaining to students what each requires and how they will address it as they work through the selection you have chosen. Standards labeled "Spiral Review" are introduced in the Literary Analysis Workshop for this unit

Before You Read

The Inspector-General

❶ Drama

Build your skills and improve your comprehension of drama with this selection.

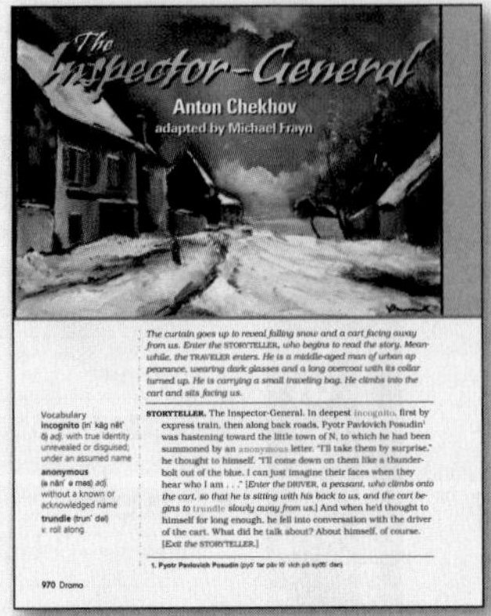

Read **"The Inspector-General"** to learn how it might feel to travel about in disguise and hear what people have to say about you.

❷ Common Core State Standards

Meet these standards with **"The Inspector General"** (p. 968).

Reading Literature

1. Cite strong and thorough textual evidence to support analysis of what the text says explicitly as well as inferences drawn from the text. *(Reading Skill: Draw Conclusions)*

5. Analyze how an author's choices concerning how to structure a text, order events within it, and manipulate time create such effects as mystery, tension, or surprise. *(Literary Analysis: Comedy)*

Spiral Review RL.9-10.3

Writing

3. Write narratives to develop real or imagined experiences or events using effective technique, well-chosen details, and well-structured event sequences. **3.a.** Engage and orient the reader by setting out a problem, situation, or observation, establishing one or multiple point(s) of view, and introducing a narrator and/or characters; create a smooth progression of experiences or events. **3.b.** Use narrative techniques, such as dialogue, pacing, description, reflection, and multiple plot lines, to develop experiences, events, and/or characters. **3.c.** Use a variety of techniques to sequence events so that they build on one another to create a coherent whole. *(Writing: Play)*

7. Conduct short as well as more sustained research projects to answer a question or solve a problem. *(Research and Technology: Informational Chart)*

Language

1. Demonstrate command of the conventions of standard English grammar and usage when writing or speaking. **1.b.** Use various types of phrases and clauses to convey specific meanings and add variety and interest to writing or presentations. *(Conventions: Main and Subordinate Clauses)*

966 Drama

Text Complexity Rubric

The Inspector-General		
Qualitative Measures	**Context/ Knowledge Demands**	Rural, Czarist Russia 1 2 3 ④ 5
	Structure/ Language Clarity and Conventionality	On-level vocabulary; idiomatic expressions footnoted; Dialogue 1 2 ③ 4 5
	Levels of Meaning/ Purpose/Concept Level	Accessible concept (peasant outsmarts government official) 1 2 ③ 4 5
Quantitative Measures	**Text Length**	Word Count: 1,160
	Lexile	NP
Overall Complexity		**Accessible**

3 Literary Analysis: Comedy

Comedy is a form of drama that is lighter in mood than tragedy, ends happily, and aims primarily to amuse. The humor in comic plays may arise from one or more of the following elements:

- Funny character names and fast-paced, witty dialogue
- **Incongruous situations,** such as a woman in high heels stomping grapes or a clown conducting a meeting
- Character misunderstandings and mistaken identities

Humor is often created by **dramatic irony,** a form of irony that occurs when the audience knows or understands something that the character does not. As a result, the characters' statements and behavior are often misguided or inappropriate, provoking laughter from the knowing audience. As you read, look for ways in which the author creates dramatic irony by providing information to the audience while withholding it from the characters.

4 Reading Skill: Draw Conclusions

A **conclusion** is an inference based on a number of details in a text. In drawing conclusions about a play, consider stated and implied information. The following strategies can help you draw conclusions about characters in a play:

- Consider what the **dialogue** reveals about characters' personalities and circumstances.
- Read **stage directions** closely for details about the scene and about characters' appearances and behavior.
- Note other details that could prove essential to the plot or ideas.

5 Using the Strategy: Conclusion Chart

As you read, use a chart like the one shown to record conclusions you draw about characters.

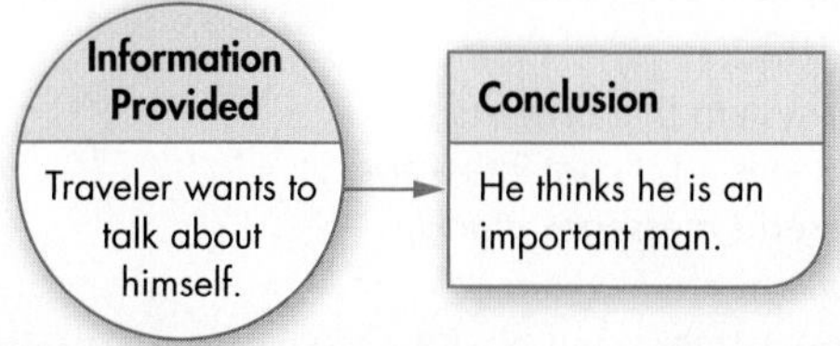

PHLit Online!
www.PHLitOnline.com

Hear It!
- Selection summary audio
- Selection audio

See It!
- Get Connected video
- Background video
- More about the author
- Vocabulary flashcards

Do It!
- Interactive journals
- Interactive graphic organizers
- Self-test
- Internet activity
- Grammar tutorial
- Interactive vocabulary games

PRETEACH

3 Literary Analysis

Comedy

1. Introduce the skill, using the instruction on the student page.
2. Tell students that they will note elements of comedy as they read.

Think Aloud: Model the Skill

Model a way to identify comedy and dramatic irony. Say to students:

We read and view different kinds of comedy all the time. For example, TV comedies often feature an awkward and clumsy man, usually with an odd name such as *Kramer* or *Mr. Bean.* Somehow, he gets himself in sticky situations and ends up making more trouble for himself. Often, the audience knows the trouble he is in, even if he does not. This contradiction between what a character knows and what the audience knows is known as dramatic irony.

4 Reading Skill

Draw Conclusions

1. Introduce the skill, using the instruction on the student page.
2. Tell students that they will draw conclusions as they read.

5 Using the Strategy

Give students a copy of either **Reading Skill Graphic Organizer A** or **B** (*Graphic Organizer Transparencies,* pp. 172–173) to record conclusions. Use the examples in **Reading Skill Graphic Organizer A,** which is partially filled in, to model the process of completing the organizer.

Text Complexity: Reader and Task Suggestions

The Inspector-General	
Preparing to Read the Text • Using the Background information on TE p. 969, discuss Czarist Russia and the role of officials like inspectors-general in enforcing the Czar's rule. • Review the use of dialogue in developing characterization. Remind students to think about what characters say as well as what they leave unsaid. • Guide students to use Multidraft Reading strategies (TE p. 969).	**Leveled Tasks** *Levels of Meaning* If students will have difficulty with the meaning and concept levels, have them first read the play and jot down notes describing the characters of the Inspector-General and the Driver. Then, have them reread the play and identify when the Inspector-General realized that the Driver knew who he was. Discuss student notes and provide clarification. *Analyzing* If students will not have difficulty with meaning and concept levels, have them read the play and note examples of irony in the dialogue. Have them share their examples during class discussion.

PRETEACH

❶ Writing About the Big Question

1. Review the assignment with the class.
2. Have volunteers list elements of background that can be different among people, such as their language or where they were born.
3. Have students complete the sentence starter. Review responses as a class. (**Possible response:** A person's background may be difficult to conceal because his or her mannerisms and speech will reveal it.)
4. Remind students that their answers will help them think about the Big Question, "Do our differences define us?"

While You Read

Tell students that as they read, they should look for clues that give away Inspector-General's identity.

❷ Vocabulary

1. Have students preview the selection vocabulary.
2. For each word, have students say the word aloud.
3. Then, use the word in a sentence that defines the word.
4. Finally, repeat your definitional sentence or a similar sentence with the word missing and have the class "fill in the blank" chorally. Here are some examples:

   To be anonymous is to be unknown. People who give away a million dollars may not want anyone to know about it, so they choose to remain [students say "anonymous"].

   If you do something discreetly, you do it without drawing attention to yourself. When you step away from a meeting to take a private phone call, you are behaving [students say "discreetly"].

❸ Word Study

1. Introduce the skill, using the instruction in the box.
2. Ask students for a *-nym-* or *-nom-* word that means "to name someone for an office." (**Answer:** *nominate*)

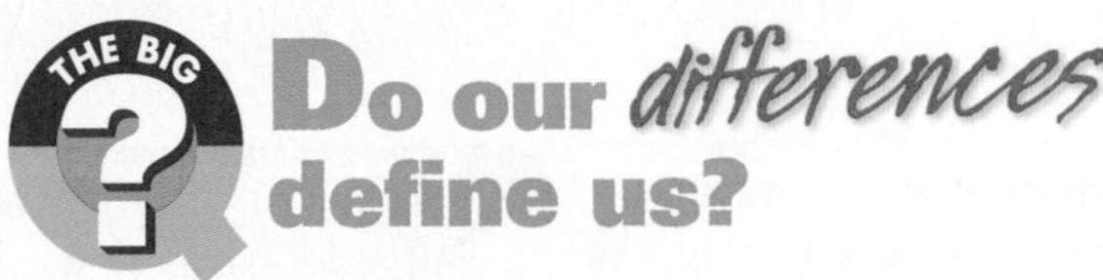

❶ Writing About the Big Question

In "The Inspector-General," the Inspector-General dresses in disguise so people won't know he's on official business. He is different from those around him, though, and the truth is hard to conceal. Use this sentence starter to develop your ideas about the Big Question.

A person's **background** may be difficult to conceal because ________.

While You Read Look for clues about the Inspector-General's identity.

❷ Vocabulary

Read each word and its definition. Decide whether you know the word well, know it a little bit, or do not know it at all. After you read, see how your knowledge of each word has increased.

- **incognito** (in´ käg nēt´ ō) *adj.* with true identity unrevealed or disguised; under an assumed name (p. 970) ***The movie star was incognito because she hoped to have some privacy.***
- **anonymous** (ə nän´ ə məs) *adj.* without a known or acknowledged name (p. 970) ***Wishing to remain anonymous, the writer sent an unsigned letter.*** *anonymously adv.*
- **trundle** (trun´ dəl) *v.* roll along (p. 970) ***While we were chatting, the shopping cart began to trundle down the aisle.*** *trundling v.*
- **discreetly** (di skrēt´ lē) *adv.* without drawing attention (p. 972) ***The candidate avoided embarrassment by discreetly straightening his crooked tie during the debate.*** *discreet adj. discreetness n.*
- **cunning** (kun´ iŋ) *adj.* skilled in deception (p. 972) ***The small but cunning animal is usually able to outwit and escape its predators.*** *cunningly adv.*
- **telegraph** (tel´ ə graf´) *n.* an apparatus or system that converts a coded message into electric impulses and sends it to a distant receiver (p. 974) ***The telegraph was invented to send messages quickly.*** *telegraph v. telegraphic adj. telegraphically adv.*

❸ Word Study

The **Latin root *-nym-*** or ***-nom-*** means "name."

In this selection, the Inspector-General receives an **anonymous** letter, summoning him to a small town. The letter was *anonymous* because there was no name on it.

Vocabulary Development

Vocabulary Knowledge Rating

Create a **Vocabulary Knowledge Rating Chart** (***Professional Development Guidebook***, p. 33) for this selection. Include the selection vocabulary and the Big Question word that appears in the Writing About the Big Question sentence starter on this page. (The Big Question vocabulary is introduced on pp. 778–779.)

Give students a copy of the chart. Read the words aloud, and have students mark their rating in the Before Reading column. Urge them to be alert to these words as they read and discuss the selection.

Tally how many students think they know a word to gauge how much instruction to provide. As students read and discuss the selection, point out the words and their context.

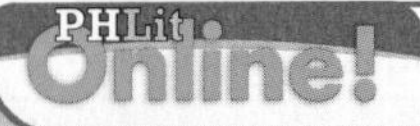

Vocabulary Central, featuring tools activities, and songs for studying vocabulary, is available at **www.PHLitOnline.com**.

Meet Anton Chekhov
(1860–1904)

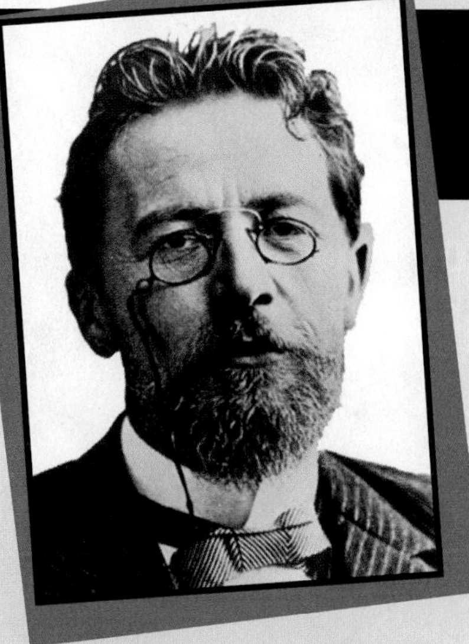

Author of *The Inspector-General*

The grandson of a former serf who had purchased his freedom, Anton Chekhov grew up in a small Russian coastal town. He later attended medical school in Moscow, where he began writing humorous stories. Writing soon became his major focus.

Passion and Compassion Chekhov wrote many short stories as well as several acclaimed plays, including *The Seagull* (1896), *Uncle Vanya* (1897), and *The Three Sisters* (1901). His characters range from old peasants to young society women, from those whom life has treated kindly, to those who are disappointed. Chekhov treats them all with respect and sympathy. His humor and ability to portray characters of great depth and authenticity have helped make Chekhov a beloved author.

❹

BACKGROUND FOR THE PLAY

Inspectors General

"The Inspector-General" is set in imperial Russia, when the country was ruled by an emperor, or czar. To oversee the many officials in Russia's vast expanse, the czars employed inspectors-general. They observed how local schools, courts, and hospitals were functioning. Many citizens resented the czar's authority, however, and inspectors-general were often unwelcome.

Did You Know?

Chekhov married a famous actress, Olga Knipper.

Daily Bellringer

For each class during which you teach this selection, have students complete one of the activities for Week 29 in the ***Daily Bellringer Activities*** booklet.

❹ Background

Inspectors General

Although inspectors general were unpopular wherever they went, these officials of the Czarist government were intended to provide some stability and accountability in local governments. Because of the vast size of the empire in an era of slow transportation, local government officials sometimes set up their own fiefdoms, running the towns as they wished, often in highly corrupt ways. The job of the inspectors general was to rein in the corruption and make the local officials accountable to the czar.

Multidraft Reading

This icon ● marks natural pauses in the selection. To assist struggling readers and to deepen reading for all, assign the text in "chunks," following the icons, and apply multidraft reading protocols. For each reading, have students set the purpose indicated:

- **First reading**—identifying key ideas and details and answering any Reading Checks.
- **Second reading**—analyzing craft and structure and responding to the side-column prompts.
- **Third reading**—integrating knowledge and ideas, connecting to other texts and the world, and answering the end-of-selection questions.

For more guidance, refer to the ***Classroom Strategies and Teaching Routines*** card on multidraft reading.

Differentiated Instruction — Additional Instruction

EL Extended Support—English Learners
Have students complete the **Reading and Vocabulary Warm-ups, *Unit 5 Resources*,** pp. 143–146 before they read. Assign the prereading pages and the adapted selection in the ***Reader's Notebook: English Learner's Version.*** Then, have students listen to portions of the selection on the ***Hear It!* Audio CD.**

L1 L2 Extended Support—Struggling Readers
Have students complete the **Reading and Vocabulary Warm-ups, *Unit 5 Resources*,** pp. 143–146 before they read. Assign prereading pages and the adapted selection in the ***Reader's Notebook: Adapted Version.*** Then, have students listen to portions of the selection on the ***Hear It!* Audio CD** (adapted text).

Extended Support—Reluctant Readers
To build motivation and engagement before assigning the selection, have students read "In Your Name" and "On Patrol," thematically related selections in ***Reality Central.*** Then, use the questions at the conclusion of the related selection to guide discussion.

PHLit Online!
For more about the author, practice with the selection vocabulary, or more background, go online at **www.PHLitOnline.com**.

❶ Activating Prior Knowledge

1. Prepare an **Anticipation Guide** (see ***Professional Development Guidebook***, pp. 36–38) with the following statements:
   - People in small communities cannot outsmart the central government.
   - No one likes to be made a fool of.
   - If you want to know what the rich and powerful are up to, talk to their servants.
2. Give students a copy of the prepared **Anticipation Guide** and have students mark their responses in the Me column. Have students discuss the statements in pairs or groups and mark the guides again in the Group column.
3. For further guidance, use the ***Classroom Strategies and Teaching Routines*** card: **Using an Anticipation Guide.**

Concept Connector →

Students will return to the **Anticipation Guide** after completing *The Inspector-General.*

Whole-Class Activity

The stage directions in *The Inspector-General* include gestures and facial expressions that help reveal the characters' feelings and motives. Students can enhance this aspect of the comedy by performing a version that captures these important nonverbal details.

❷ About the Selection

Brimming with ironies, *The Inspector-General* shows what happens when the tables are turned on a self-satisfied fellow who is proud of his craftiness. Pyotr Pavlovich Posudin discovers that the joke is on him.

❸ Humanities

Valmondois Sous La Neige, by Maurice de Vlaminck

Maurice de Vlaminck was born in Paris in 1876. He belonged to a group of artists known for their bold use of color. Use the following question for discussion:

Ask: What might life be like in a setting such as the one depicted?

Answer: Students may say life would be dreary and uneventful.

The Inspector-General

Anton Chekhov

adapted by Michael Frayn

The curtain goes up to reveal falling snow and a cart facing away from us. Enter the STORYTELLER, *who begins to read the story. Meanwhile, the* TRAVELER *enters. He is a middle-aged man of urban appearance, wearing dark glasses and a long overcoat with its collar turned up. He is carrying a small traveling bag. He climbs into the cart and sits facing us.*

Vocabulary

incognito (in′ käg nēt′ ō) *adj.* with true identity unrevealed or disguised; under an assumed name

anonymous (ə nän′ ə məs) *adj.* without a known or acknowledged name

trundle (trun′ dəl) *v.* roll along

STORYTELLER. The Inspector-General. In deepest incognito, first by express train, then along back roads, Pyotr Pavlovich Posudin[1] was hastening toward the little town of N, to which he had been summoned by an anonymous letter. "I'll take them by surprise," he thought to himself. "I'll come down on them like a thunderbolt out of the blue. I can just imagine their faces when they hear who I am . . ." [*Enter the* DRIVER, *a peasant, who climbs onto the cart, so that he is sitting with his back to us, and the cart begins to trundle slowly away from us.*] And when he'd thought to himself for long enough, he fell into conversation with the driver of the cart. What did he talk about? About himself, of course. [*Exit the* STORYTELLER.]

1. **Pyotr Pavlovich Posudin** (pyō′ tər päv lō′ vich pō syo͞o′ dən)

Vocabulary Development

Ⓒ **CCSS** Language 6

Thematic Vocabulary: The Big Question

As students are discussing *The Inspector-General,* encourage them to use the thematic vocabulary presented in Introducing the Big Question, pp. 778–779. You might encourage them with sentence starters such as these:

1. When the driver looks at many inspector-generals, he sees a *similarity* in . . .
2. However, the driver may not have a true *understanding* of . . .
3. The travelers may want to *defend* the Inspector-General by . . .
4. The driver may want to *discriminate* against the Inspector-General because . . .

TRAVELER. I gather you've got a new Inspector-General in these parts.

DRIVER. True enough.

TRAVELER. Know anything about him? [*The driver turns and looks at the* TRAVELER, *who turns his coat collar up a little higher.*]

DRIVER. Know anything about him? Of course we do! We know everything about all of them up there! Every last little clerk—we know the color of his hair and the size of his boots! [*He turns back to the front, and the* TRAVELER *permits himself a slight smile.*]

TRAVELER. So, what do you reckon? Any good, is he? [*The* DRIVER *turns around.*]

DRIVER. Oh, yes, he's a good one, this one.

TRAVELER. Really?

DRIVER. Did one good thing straight off.

TRAVELER. What was that?

DRIVER. He got rid of the last one. Holy terror he was! Hear him coming five miles off! Say he's going to this little town. Somewhere like we're going, say. He'd let all the world know about it a month before. So now he's on his way, say, and it's like thunder and lightning coming down the road. And when he gets where he's going he has a good sleep, he has a good eat and drink—and then he starts. Stamps his feet, shouts his head off. Then he has another good sleep, and off he goes.

TRAVELER. But the new one's not like that?

DRIVER. Oh, no, the new one goes everywhere on the quiet, like. Creeps around like a cat. Don't want no one to see him, don't want no one to know who he is. Say he's going to this town down the road here. Someone there sent him a letter on the sly, let's say. "Things going on here you should know about." Something of that kind. Well, now, he creeps out of his office, so none of them up there see him go. He hops on a train just like anyone else, just like you or me. Then when he gets off he don't go jumping into a cab or nothing fancy. Oh, no. He wraps himself up from head to toe so you can't see his face, and he wheezes away like an old dog so no one can recognize his voice.

TRAVELER. Wheezes? That's not wheezing! That's the way he talks! So I gather.

4 **Crtical Viewing**
How might the people of a small town like this react to the arrival of an inspector? **[Speculate]**

Reading Skill
Draw Conclusions
What conclusion about the Inspector-General can you draw from the stage direction that he "permits himself a slight smile"?

6

Why is the Inspector-General traveling to the town?

4 Critical Viewing

Answer: They would be suspicious. They would be conscious of his every move and talk about him among themselves, comparing experiences and trading information.

5 Reading Skill

Draw Conclusions

1. Have students take roles and read from the opening dialogue to the end of the bracketed passage.
2. **Ask** students the Reading Skill question: What conclusion about the Inspector-General can you draw from the stage direction that he "permits himself a slight smile"?
Answer: Students may conclude that the Inspector-General is confident that the villagers are exceptionally naive and know nothing about him. The smile represents his desire to appear amused and at ease when he is really nothing of the sort.
3. **Ask** students what clues led them to form their conclusion.
Possible response: In the storyteller's comments, he says the Inspector-General is pleased with himself and the deception he is executing. "I'll come down on them like a thunderbolt," he thinks to himself. His smile confirms that he is pleased and confident the townspeople know nothing.

6 Reading Check

Answer: The Inspector-General is traveling to the town to check on its management. He does so in response to an anonymous letter.

PHLit Online!

This selection is available in interactive format in the **Enriched Online Student Edition, www.PHLitOnline.com,** which includes a thematically related video with writing prompt and an interactive graphic organizer.

Differentiated Instruction for Universal Access

Strategy for Less Proficient Readers

To help students better apply the skill of drawing conclusions, show them **Reading Skill Graphic Organizer A** (*Graphic Organizer Transparencies*, p. 172). Review the process of drawing conclusions, and then discuss the partial answers provided in the organizer. Encourage students to think about the process demonstrated on the organizer and to draw their own conclusions about the play and characters as they continue reading.

EL Support for English Learners

Point out to students that dialogue is a basic way for writers to develop characterization. However, speakers of dialogue in plays and stories are not required to use correct grammar. Have students note the driver's use of incomplete sentences, double negatives, and other examples of nonstandard grammar. Work as a class to create correct versions of these inconsistencies.

7 Literary Analysis

Comedy

1. Have two students perform the bracketed text of dialogue.
2. Then, **ask** the Literary Analysis question: How does your knowledge of the Traveler's true identity make this dialogue humorous?

   Possible response: It is humorous because the audience knows that the Traveler is the Inspector-General, exactly the person whom the Driver is insulting.
3. **Ask** students if the Driver is also in on the joke.

   Answer: Students should realize that the Driver knows exactly whom he is talking to.

▶ **Monitor Progress: Ask** students how the Driver's awareness of who his passenger is contributes to the humor.

Answer: The Driver's knowledge that he is carrying the Inspector-General means that he, too, is in on the joke. Only the Inspector-General is in the dark.

▶ **Reteach:** Have students turn back to p. 967 and name the three elements that help make comedies humorous. Then, ask them to explain *dramatic irony*. Finally, have students work in pairs and find examples of at least two of each of these elements in the play.

8 Connecting to the Big Question

1. Point out to students that sometimes people's differences are made even more apparent when they try to hide them.
2. Have students read the bracketed text. **Ask:** How do the Traveler's remarks and actions suggest his real identity?

   Possible response: He is upset that people are telling tales about the Inspector-General. He is startled and offended that people think the Inspector-General drinks, which suggests that he is the Inspector-General because he reacts personally to the comments.
3. **Ask:** Has the Inspector-General's disguise hidden his differences from the town's people?

   Possible response: No, being a stranger is enough to make him stand out in a small town.

Literary Analysis
Comedy How does your knowledge of the Traveler's true identity make this dialogue humorous?

Vocabulary
discreetly (di skrēt′ lē) *adv.* without drawing attention
cunning (kun′ iŋ) *adj.* skilled in deception

DRIVER. Oh, is it? But the tales they tell about him. You'd laugh till you burst your tripes![2]

TRAVELER. [*sourly*]. I'm sure I would.

DRIVER. He drinks, mind!

TRAVELER. [*startled*]. Drinks?

DRIVER. Oh, like a hole in the ground. Famous for it.

TRAVELER. He's never touched a drop! I mean, from what I've heard.

7 8 **DRIVER.** Oh, not in public, no. Goes to some great ball—"No thank you, not for me." Oh, no, he puts it away at home! Wakes up in the morning, rubs his eyes, and the first thing he does, he shouts, "Vodka!" So in runs his valet with a glass. Fixed himself up a tube behind his desk, he has. Leans down, takes a pull on it, no one the wiser.

TRAVELER. [*offended*]. How do you know all this, may I ask?

DRIVER. Can't hide it from the servants, can you? The valet and the coachman have got tongues in their heads. Then again, he's on the road, say, going about his business, and he keeps the bottle in his little bag. [*The* TRAVELER *discreetly pushes the traveling bag out of the* DRIVER'S *sight.*] And his housekeeper . . .

TRAVELER. What about her?

DRIVER. Runs circles around him, she does, like a fox round his tail. She's the one who wears the trousers.[3] The people aren't half so frightened of him as they are of her.

TRAVELER. But at least he's good at his job, you say?

DRIVER. Oh, he's a blessing from heaven, I'll grant him that.

TRAVELER. Very cunning—you were saying.

DRIVER. Oh, he creeps around all right.

TRAVELER. And then he pounces, yes? I should think some people must get the surprise of their life, mustn't they?

DRIVER. No, no—let's be fair, now. Give him his due. He don't make no trouble.

TRAVELER. No, I mean, if no one knows he's coming . . .

DRIVER. Oh, that's what he thinks, but we all know.

---

2. **tripes** (trīps) *n.* parts of the stomach, usually of an ox or a sheep, when used as food.
3. **wears the trousers** has the greatest authority; is really in charge.

Vocabulary Development

Vocabulary Knowledge Rating

When students have completed reading and discussing *The Inspector-General,* have them take out their **Vocabulary Knowledge Rating Chart** for this selection. Read the words aloud once more and have students rate their knowledge of the words again in the After Reading column. Clarify any words that are still problematic. Have students write their own definition and example or sentence in the appropriate column. Then, have students complete the Vocabulary Practice at the end of the selection. Encourage students to use the words in further discussion and written work about this selection. Remind them that they will be accountable for these words on the **Selection Test,** ***Unit 5 Resources,*** pp. 158–160 or 161–163.

9

White Night, 1901, Edvard Munch, Photo: J. Lathion ©Nasjonalgalleriet 1997, ©2003 The Munch Museum/The Munch-Ellingsen Group/Artists Rights Society (ARS), NY

TRAVELER. You know?

DRIVER. Oh, some gentleman gets off the train at the station back there with his greatcoat up to his eyebrows and says, "No, I don't want a cab, thank you, just an ordinary horse and cart for me." Well, we'd put two and two together, wouldn't we! Say it was you, now, creeping along down the road here. The lads would be down there in a cab by now! By the time you got there the whole town would be as regular as clockwork! And you'd think to yourself, "Oh, look at that! As clean as a whistle! And they didn't know I was coming!" No, that's why he's such a blessing after the other one. This one believes it!

TRAVELER. Oh, I see.

 ▲ **Critical Viewing** How does the countryside depicted in this painting compare to the setting of the play? **[Compare and Contrast]**

Spiral Review
Character What does the dialogue reveal about the Inspector-General's character?

9 Humanities

White Nights, 1901, by Edvard Munch

Edvard Munch (1863–1944) was one of the early leaders of the Expressionist movement. He is best known for his paintings from the 1890s, which include *The Scream* (1893), his most famous painting. Use these questions for discussion:

- What does the setting in the painting suggest about the remote location of this house in comparison to the central government?

  Answer: The setting appears remote and isolated from the government.

- Why would the government want to send an inspector-general into such an area?

  Possible responses: The place is so remote, it could easily ignore government regulations. An inspector-general may be needed to keep control of such an area.

10 Critical Viewing

Answer: Students may say that the countryside of both the painting and the play is quiet and calm.

Spiral Review

Character

1. Remind students that they learned about the concept of character in the Unit 5 Literary Analysis Workshop (pp. 780–797).
2. **Ask** students the Spiral Review question.

   Possible response: The dialogue reveals that the Inspector-General is not as clever or as upstanding as he wants people to think. The people are aware of his bad habits, and he does not fool anyone.

Concept Connector

Anticipation Guide

Have students return to the **Anticipation Guide** they began before they read *The Inspector-General.* You may wish to have them work individually or in pairs to complete the After Reading column. Then, guide a class discussion about whether this information confirmed or invalidated any of their responses to the questions.

Writing About the Big Question

Have students compare their responses to the sentence starter they completed before reading the play with their ideas afterwards. Ask them to explain whether their thoughts have changed.

Reading Skill Graphic Organizer

Have students review the graphic organizers they prepared while reading to draw conclusions. Show them **Reading Skill Graphic Organizer A** (p. 172, ***Graphic Organizer Transparencies***) as an example. Have students share their graphic organizers.

⓫ Reading Skill

Draw Conclusions

Give students a copy of **Reading Skill Graphic Organizer B,** p. 173, in ***Graphic Organizer Transparencies.*** Have them complete the organizer. Then, **ask** the Reading Skill question.

Possible response: The Traveler has realized that the townspeople know who he is. Not only will proceeding with his mission be useless because they are prepared for him, but the entire situation could be embarrassing.

ASSESS

Answers

Critical Thinking

Before students respond, you may wish to have them write a brief objective summary of the selection. As they answer the questions below, remind them to support their answers with evidence from the text.

1. (a) The Traveler pushes the bag containing his flask out of view of the Driver. (b) The Traveler is embarrassed by his drinking habits.
2. (a) The town gets everything in order so the Inspector-General will find nothing wrong. (b) The Traveler realizes he is wasting his time trying to find anything amiss, and he is embarrassed to realize that all his cleverness has been so transparent.
3. (a), (b) Answers will vary. Accept all reasonable responses.
4. **Possible response:** (a) He wanted to take the townspeople by surprise so they wouldn't have time to put the place in order. (b) The townspeople had sent him an anonymous letter, so they were expecting someone. Then, the stranger gave himself away by wearing an overcoat and asking for a horse and car instead of a cab.

Vocabulary
telegraph (tel′ ə graf′) *n.* an apparatus or system that converts a coded message into electric impulses and sends it to a distant receiver

DRIVER. What, you thought we wouldn't know him? Why, we've got the electric telegraph these days! Take today, now. I'm going past the station back there this morning, and the fellow who runs the buffet comes out like a bolt of lightning. Arms full of baskets and bottles. "Where are you off to?" I say. "Doing drinks and refreshments for the Inspector-General!" he says, and he jumps into a carriage and goes flying off down the road here. So there's the old Inspector-General, all muffled up like a roll of carpet, going secretly along in a cart somewhere—and when he gets there, nothing to be seen but vodka and cold salmon!

Reading Skill
Drawing Conclusions
What conclusion can you draw based on the Traveler's sudden order to turn around? ⓫

TRAVELER. [*shouts*]. Right—turn around, then . . . !

DRIVER. [*to the horse*]. Whoa, boy! Whoa! [*To the* TRAVELER.] Oh, so what's this, then? Don't want to go running into the Inspector-General, is that it? [*The* TRAVELER *gestures impatiently for the* DRIVER *to turn the cart around.* DRIVER *to the horse.*] Back we go, then, boy. Home we go. [*He turns the cart around, and the* TRAVELER *takes a swig from his traveling bag.*] Though if I know the old devil, he's like as not turned around and gone home again himself. [*Blackout.*]

Critical Thinking

Cite textual evidence to support your responses.

1. **Key Ideas and Details (a)** What does the Traveler do when the Driver mentions that the Inspector-General keeps a flask of vodka? **(b) Infer:** What does this action tell you about the Traveler?
2. **Key Ideas and Details (a)** According to the Driver, what preparations does the town make for the Inspector-General's arrival? **(b) Interpret:** Why does the Driver's account provoke the Traveler's demand to turn around?
3. **Craft and Structure (a)** How does the dramatic irony in the story work to create humor? **(b) Analyze:** How might the story be considered an incongruous situation?
4. **Integration of Knowledge and Ideas (a)** Why did the Inspector-General want to hide his background? **(b)** How was the driver able to determine the Inspector-General's identity? *[Connect to the Big Question: Do our differences define us?]*

Assessment Resources

Unit 5 Resources

L1 L2 EL **Selection Test A,** pp. 158–160. Administer Test A to less advanced readers.

L3 L4 EL **Selection Test B,** pp. 161–163. Administer Test B to on-level and more advanced students.

L3 L4 **Open-Book Test,** pp. 155–157. As an alternative, give the Open-Book Test.

All **Customizable Test Bank**

All **Self-tests**
Students may prepare for the **Selection Test** by taking the **Self-test** online.

PHLit Online!

All assessment resources are available at **www.PHLitOnline.com.**

After You Read The Inspector-General

Literary Analysis: Comedy

1. **Craft and Structure** Note specific ways in which "The Inspector-General" does or does not meet these criteria for **comedy:** It ends happily; it uses witty dialogue; it presents an incongruous or comic situation; it seeks to amuse.
2. **Craft and Structure** **(a)** What information, conveyed by the Storyteller, sets up the **dramatic irony** in "The Inspector-General"? **(b)** Identify an exchange between the Driver and the Traveler that highlights the dramatic irony of the situation.

Reading Skill: Draw Conclusions

3. What **conclusions** can you draw about the character of the Traveler based on the stage directions *sourly, startled,* and *offended* that precede three of his lines?
4. What conclusions can you draw about the character of the Driver based on his dialogue with the Traveler? Explain your answer.
5. Who do you think is the wiser and cleverer man, the Driver or the Traveler? Explain.

Vocabulary

Acquisition and Use Indicate whether each statement is *True* or *False.* Explain your answers. Then, revise false sentences to make them true.

1. Someone making an *anonymous* donation wants recognition.
2. A tricycle is something that might *trundle.*
3. The best way to send a message *discreetly* is to shout.
4. If a man is *cunning,* he may not always tell the truth.
5. Movie stars sometimes travel *incognito* so they can escape notice.
6. People once used the *telegraph* to send packages and letters.

Word Study Use the context of the sentences and what you know about the **Latin root -*nym*- or -*nom*-** to explain your answer to each question.

1. Is scientific *nomenclature* for different animals hard to remember?
2. Do you think someone who is only the *nominal* Inspector-General would fulfill the responsibilities of the job?

Word Study

The **Latin root -*nym*- or -*nom*-** means "name."

Apply It Explain how the root *-nym-* or *-nom-* contributes to the meanings of these words. Consult a dictionary if necessary.

synonym
nominate
misnomer

ASSESS/EXTEND

Answers

Literary Analysis

1. **Possible response:** The play ends happily, or at least humorously, as the Inspector-General leaves town with no harm done except to his pride; the Driver's dialogue is witty, and he cleverly insults the Inspector-General, who is forced to bear the barbs in silence in order to keep his identity secret; the situation of the Inspector-General sneaking into town in disguise while everyone around town knows his identity is humorous; Chekhov amuses the audience by letting them in on all the secrets.
2. (a) The storyteller sets up the dramatic irony by letting the audience in on the secret, first by explaining that the traveler is incognito and then by explaining that the Inspector-General thinks he will surprise the townspeople. (b) **Possible response:** The Driver comments that "He drinks, mind!" to which the traveler responds "[startled] Drinks?" The driver then says, "Oh, like a hole in the ground. Famous for it."

Reading Skill

3. **Possible response:** Students may conclude that the Traveler, or Inspector-General, is foolish, arrogant, and self-deluded.
4. The Driver is clever and has a sense of humor. All of the dialogue supports this conclusion. Any example will suffice.

   For other sample answers, see ***Graphic Organizer Transparencies,* Literary Analysis Graphic Organizer A**, p. 174 and the **Additional Answers** section.
5. **Possible response:** The cleverer man is the Driver. He knows all about the Traveler and has used his wit both to insult the Inspector-General and to get him to leave town.

Vocabulary

Acquisition and Use

1. False. Someone making an anonymous donation does not want recognition.
2. True. A tricycle can trundle, or roll along, because it has wheels.

Continued from right column

3. False. The best way to send a message discreetly is to whisper.
4. True. A cunning person is skilled in deception, so he or she may lie.
5. True. Movie stars might wear disguises, or travel incognito, in order to escape attention.
6. False. People once used the telegraph to send short messages over wires, not packages and letters.

Word Study
Sample answers:

1. Yes, the root *-nym-* means "name" and *nomenclature* means "system of names." The scientific *nomenclature* of different animals may be difficult to remember.
2. No, the root *-nom-* means "name" and *nominal* means "having the name of." A *nominal* Inspector-General would not fulfill the job's responsibilities.

Word Study: Apply It
Sample answers:

A *synonym* is a word, or name, with the same meaning as another word. To *nominate* is to put someone's name forward for elective office. A *misnomer* is a wrong name.

Conventions

Introduce the skill, using the instruction on the student page.

Think Aloud: Model the Skill

To model the skill of identifying main and subordinate clauses, post this sentence: *When we left for town, we were already late.* Say:

To tell the difference between a main and subordinate clause, I ask myself this question: *Does the clause make sense by itself?* If the answer is *yes,* then the clause is a main clause. *We were already late* makes sense by itself. *When we left* does not, so it is a subordinate clause.

PH WRITING COACH Grade 9

Students will find instruction on and practice with main and subordinate clauses in Chapter 15, Section 2.

Practice A

Sample answers:

1. subordinate; When the train stopped, some passengers got off.
2. subordinate; After the Inspector-General climbed into the cart, the driver began the journey.
3. main
4. main

Reading Application

Sample answers: Main: We know everything about all of them up there! Subordinate: And when he'd thought to himself for long enough . . .

Practice B

Sample answers:

1. Because the Inspector-General was a clever man, he dressed in disguise.
2. He thought to himself that he would surprise the townspeople.
3. When he came to town, everyone knew.
4. As the driver smiled to himself, the Inspector-General got back on the train.

Writing Application

Check that students have written two sentences made only of main clauses and two sentences that include at least one subordinate clause.

PERFORMANCE TASKS

Integrated Language Skills

The Inspector-General

Conventions: Main and Subordinate Clauses

A **clause** is a group of words that contains a subject and a verb. It can be a **main** (independent) **clause** or a **subordinate** (dependent) **clause.**

A main clause can stand by itself as a complete sentence. It may be used by itself, be connected to another independent clause, or be connected to a subordinate clause. In contrast, a subordinate clause cannot stand by itself. It needs additional information to make sense. Subordinate clauses can function as noun, adjective, or adverbial clauses. Subordinate clauses include subordinating conjunctions such as however, although, when, if, after, or because.

Main Clause	Subordinate Clause
The Inspector-General hoped	that someone would speak up.
A man got off the train	which was stopped at the station.
The cart raced down the road	as fast as the horse could run.

Practice A Identify each of the following as a main or subordinate clause. Then, add to each subordinate clause to make it a complete sentence.

1. when the train stopped
2. after the Inspector-General climbed into the cart
3. the driver turned the cart around
4. he shoved the satchel out of sight

Reading Application In "The Inspector-General," find one example of a main clause that stands alone and one example of a subordinate clause.

Practice B Combine each of the following pairs of sentences into one sentence by changing one main clause into a subordinate clause.

1. The Inspector-General was a clever man. He dressed in disguise.
2. He thought to himself. He would surprise the townspeople.
3. He came to town. Everyone knew.
4. The driver smiled to himself. The Inspector-General got back on the train.

Writing Application Write two sentences about "The Inspector-General" that are made up only of main clauses. Then, write two sentences that include at least one subordinate clause.

PH WRITING COACH Further instruction and practice are available in *Prentice Hall Writing Coach.*

Extend the Lesson

Sentence Modeling

Have the students consider the following sentence from the selection:

"And when he gets where he's going he has a good sleep, he has a good eat and drink—and then he starts."

Ask students what they notice about the sentence. Elicit from them that the sentence contains two subordinate clauses and two main clauses. Then, ask what else they notice. (The sentence uses the parallel structure of "he has a good _____" for emphasis.)

Have students imitate the sentence in a sentence on a topic of their own choosing, matching each grammatical and stylistic feature discussed. Have volunteers read their sentences aloud to the group.

Writing

Narrative Text Write a brief **play** in which students outwit a bully. Create *dramatic irony* by including scenes in which the audience knows something the bully does not know.

- Use a realistic school setting and dialogue that sounds true to life.
- Write to entertain and teach without being cruel.
- Make sure that your play includes narrative elements including a conflict and its resolution.

Rehearse your play with classmates and perform it for your class. Use any available props within the classroom to bring your setting to life. Also deliver your dialogue convincingly to convey a true-to-life feeling.

Grammar Application Make sure to use main and subordinate clauses correctly as you write your play.

Writing Workshop: *Work in Progress*

Prewriting for Research Report For a research report you may be asked to write, discuss details in "The Inspector-General" drawn from historical research—for example, note details about language, dress, writing, or theatrical practices of the day. Keep these in your portfolio.

Common Core State Standards

L.9-10.1.b; W.9-10.3, W.9-10.3.a, W.9-10.3.b, W.9-10.3.c ,W.9-10.7

[For the wording of the standards, see page 966.]

Use this prewriting activity to prepare for the Writing Workshop on page 1002.

Research and Technology

Build and Present Knowledge Use library and Internet resources to research what life was like in Russia during the rule of the czars, including the role of inspectors-general at that time. Organize your findings in an **informational chart**. Follow these steps:

- Take careful notes and observe which key terms, research tools, and processes help you locate the best information.
- Identify topics to include in your report, such as typical jobs; freedoms; and role of government.
- As you gather details, identify the distinctions between the relative value and significance of the data, facts, and ideas you find. Decide what information is most important and which details may support these larger ideas. Eliminate irrelevant information.
- Make sure the formatting of your chart enhances your information.
- To finalize your work, write an introductory paragraph that explains the purpose of your chart. Then, list your sources. Use a style manual, such as an MLA handbook, for assistance.

www.PHLitOnline.com

- Interactive graphic organizers
- Grammar tutorial
- Interactive journals

EXTEND/ASSESS

Writing

1. Review the assignment, using the instruction on the student page.
2. To give students guidance for writing a short play, give them **Support for Writing**, p. 153 in ***Unit 5 Resources.***
3. To evaluate students' plays, use the General (Holistic) writing rubrics, pp. 256–257 in ***Professional Development Guidebook.***

Grammar Application

Have students check their drafts to ensure that they have used main and subordinate clauses correctly.

Six Traits Focus

✓	Ideas	✓	Word Choice
✓	Organization		Sentence Fluency
	Voice		Conventions

PH WRITING COACH Grade 9

Students will find instruction on and practice with narrative elements in Chapters 5 and 6.

Writing Workshop
Work in Progress

Have students save their Historical Research Notes on details in "The Inspector-General" in their portfolios. They will use their notes later as they complete the Writing Workshop assignment (see pp. 1002–1013).

Research and Technology

1. Review the assignment, using the instruction on the student page.
2. Have students complete the **Support for Extend Your Learning** page (*Unit 5 Resources,* p. 154).

Teaching Resources

Unit 3 Resources

L3 L4 EL **Integrated Language Skills: Grammar,** p. 152

L3 L4 EL **Support for Writing,** p. 153

L3 L4 **Support for Extend Your Learning,** p. 154

L4 **Enrichment,** p. 151

Enriched Online Student Edition
Available under After You Read for this selection:

All **Interactive Grammar Tutorial**

L3 L4 **Internet Research Activity**

Professional Development Guidebook
Rubrics for Self-Assesment: Research Report, pp. 242–243

All print and digital resources are available at **www.PHLitOnline.com.** Online resources accessible by students are noted on the student page.

MONITORING PROGRESS

Using the Test Practice

In this two-page Test Practice, students apply the reading skill for the second half of Unit 5 to a passage of fiction and a passage of nonfiction.

Review the skill, drawing conclusions, then administer the test. For more guidance, consult the ***Classroom Strategies and Teaching Routines*** card, **Administering Timed Tests.**

ASSESS

Answers

Answers With Explanations

1. A—If the Tigers have already defeated the Eagles, they are probably capable of defeating them again. *Incorrect answers:* B—If anything, the reverse is true. C—The passage does not say this. D—Victory does not always reflect desire.
2. A—Since Jack had played four games with the high school team, he must be a student at the school. *Incorrect answers:* B—Jack is sidelined because of an injury, not because he has quit the game. C—The passage does not say who Jack believes will win. D—Hockey is never mentioned.
3. C—Jack's behavior shows that he wants the Eagles to win. *Incorrect answers:* A—The passage does not say Jack is angry. B—Jack clearly enjoys cheering for his team. D—Jack is on the team, so he probably knows the rules of baseball.
4. A—The fans cheered wildly after the Eagles won the championship game. *Incorrect answers:* B—The selection does not say that Jack caught the ball. C—Tony's home run comes earlier in the game than the cheering. D—They were cheering for the Eagles.

Test Practice: Reading

Draw Conclusions

Fiction Selection

Directions: *Read the selection. Then, answer the questions.*

It was the summer of 2006, and the Clark High School baseball team was playing in the state championship. Their rivals, the Morristown Tigers, had defeated the Clark Eagles earlier in the season. Jack was going to see the championship game, and he was ecstatic. Although he had played in the first four games of the season with the Eagles, an ankle injury had put him on the sideline for the rest of the season. Now, he couldn't wait to cheer his team on to victory.

Jack made it to his seats just before the game began. The Eagles were the first to score. Then, the Tigers took the lead. Jack was on the edge of his seat. He kept cheering with all his might. His classmate Tony, an outfielder, tied the score in the sixth inning with a home run. With two runs in the ninth inning, the Eagles won the game and the championship. Jack was surrounded by fans cheering wildly. Jack jumped out of his seat and hurried to the field to congratulate his friends. He could not wait until next year when he would again join his team on the field.

1. What can you conclude based on the fact that the Tigers defeated the Eagles earlier in the season?

A. The Eagles could lose to the Tigers.
B. The Eagles are better than the Tigers.
C. The Tigers are an undefeated team.
D. The Tigers want to win more than the Eagles.

2. Based on the details in the selection, one can conclude that Jack—

A. is a student at Clark High School.
B. has decided to quit baseball.
C. believes that the Tigers are an unbeatable team.
D. prefers hockey to baseball.

3. What can you conclude about Jack's feelings about the game?

A. He was angry he could not play.
B. His injury prevented him from enjoying the game.
C. He hoped the Eagles would win.
D. He wanted to learn the rules of baseball.

4. The fans near Jack cheered wildly because—

A. they were excited their team had won.
B. Jack had caught a home run ball.
C. Tony had just hit a home run.
D. they were proud of the Tigers.

Writing for Assessment

What can you conclude were the high and low points for Jack in the game? Write a paragraph in which you support your answer with details.

Writing for Assessment

Students' essays should note the following high points for Jack: going to the championship game (he was ecstatic); the Eagles' championship win (Jack jumped from his seat and ran down to the field to congratulate his friends). The low point is the taking of the lead by the Tigers (Jack was on the edge of his seat, anxious).

Strategies for Test Taking

Remind students to start by eliminating obviously incorrect answers. Direct their attention to question 2. Call on a volunteer to read the question and the answer choices. Ask them if they think answer D could be correct. Guide students to see that the passage says absolutely nothing about hockey; it is strictly about baseball. Based on this analysis, answer D is clearly incorrect. By eliminating this answer, students have fewer options to consider.

Nonfiction Selection

Directions: *Read the selection. Then, answer the questions.*

The National Baseball Hall of Fame and Museum, located in Cooperstown, New York, draws many fans of baseball each year. First opened on June 12, 1939, the museum includes artifacts from baseball's past, exhibits on famous players and coaches, and plaques for every member of the hall of fame. Over the years, the museum has changed a great deal. Visits to the museum now begin with "The Baseball Experience," a digitally-enhanced, multimedia experience designed to appeal to baseball fans of all ages. The museum offers more than just entertainment, though; it also includes a research library, utilized by baseball scholars as they study what is often called "America's Favorite Pastime." Whether you want to study baseball or just experience the joy of the sport, a visit to Cooperstown will have a lot to offer you.

1. What can you conclude about the author's perspective on the National Baseball Hall of Fame and Museum?

A. The author believes it is not worth visiting.
B. The author is arguing that the museum should close its doors.
C. The author wants the museum to raise its prices.
D. The author thinks the museum may appeal to a variety of people.

2. Based on this passage, what conclusion can you draw about the museum?

A. The museum is not very successful.
B. Only older people visit the museum.
C. The hall of fame plaques are the best part of the museum.
D. The museum highlights different aspects of baseball.

3. Based on the details of the selection, "America's Favorite Pastime" is a nickname for—

A. museums.
B. baseball.
C. research.
D. multimedia presentations.

4. Based on this selection, what conclusion can you draw about Cooperstown?

A. Many people visit Cooperstown in order to go to the National Baseball Museum.
B. Cooperstown should open a new art museum.
C. People who live in Cooperstown get annoyed with the large number of tourists.
D. Cooperstown is the capital city of New York State.

Writing for Assessment

Connecting Across Texts
Would Jack enjoy visiting the National Baseball Museum? Explain your answer in a paragraph. Use details from both passages.

www.PHLitOnline.com
- Online practice
- Instant feedback

Differentiated Instruction for Universal Access

Strategy for Less Proficient Readers
Help students practice the skill of drawing conclusions by working through question 2 with them. Remind them that they will make a logical guess based on information they have read.

- A—The first sentence says that the museum draws many fans each year, suggesting it is quite successful. (Eliminate.)
- B—The selection states that the multimedia experience appeals to fans of all ages, suggesting that people of all ages come to the museum. (Eliminate.)
- C—The author does not state what he or she thinks is the best part of the museum, but suggests that each person might have a different view, based on personal interests. (Eliminate.)
- D—In describing a variety of displays and features, the selection suggests that the museum does address a variety of aspects of baseball. This is a logical conclusion.

Help students to see that choice **D** states the only conclusion that can be drawn from the selection.

ASSESS

Answers

Answers With Explanations

1. **D**—The author describes visitors with several different interests who would enjoy the museum. *Incorrect answers:* A—The author says that the institution has a lot to offer. B—same explanation as for A. C—The author does not mention entrance prices.
2. **D**—The selection describes several different aspects of baseball that are addressed in exhibits. *Incorrect answers:* A—The first sentence says that the museum draws many fans each year. B—The selection says that the multimedia presentation appeals to fans of all ages. C—The author does not state which exhibit is the best part of the museum.
3. **B**—Context makes clear that baseball has been called "America's Favorite Pastime." *Incorrect answers:* A—The selection focuses on only one museum, and the nickname refers to baseball, not the museum. C—The nickname refers to the sport, not one aspect of the museum's presentations on it. D—same explanation as for C.
4. **A**—The opening sentence states that the National Baseball Museum in Cooperstown draws many fans each year. *Incorrect answers:* B—The selection does not mention art museums. C—This might be true, but the selection does not mention it. D—The selection does not say this.

Writing for Assessment
Students' paragraphs should note that Jack's interest and excitement about playing baseball suggest that he would be interested in learning about the great players of the game. The Museum has displays that appeal to a variety of people interested in baseball, so Jack would probably enjoy it.

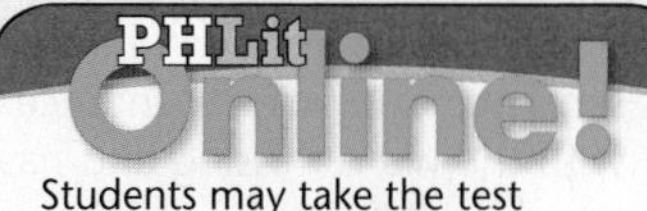

Students may take the test in interactive format with instant feedback online at **www.PHLitOnline.com.**

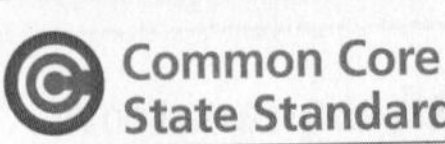

PRETEACH

Common Core State Standards

- Reading Informational Text 3
- Language 6

Reading Skill

1. Introduce the skill, using the instruction on the student page.
2. Tell students that they will evaluate the sources for a Web site and a Web encyclopedia entry in this section.

Think Aloud: Model the Skill

Model the skill of evaluating sources. Say to students:

When I'm researching a topic, I want the most reliable source I can find. Many pages on the Web are written by people who are not experts. When I'm not sure if a source is reliable, I compare it to several other sources. If other sources say the same things, I'm more confident that the source is reliable.

Multidraft Reading

Have students follow a multidraft reading protocol after they preview the selection.

- **First reading**—Have students read to identify key ideas and details.
- **Second reading**—Have students read to identify the structure of the text.
- **Third reading**—Have students read to integrate knowledge and ideas by connecting the text to the world, their own experiences, and other texts.

Content-Area Vocabulary

1. Have students say each word.
2. Next, use each word in a sentence that defines it.
3. Finally, repeat your definitional sentence or a similar sentence with the word missing and have the class "fill in the blank" chorally.

Reading for Information

Analyzing Expository Texts

Web Site

Web Encyclopedia Entry

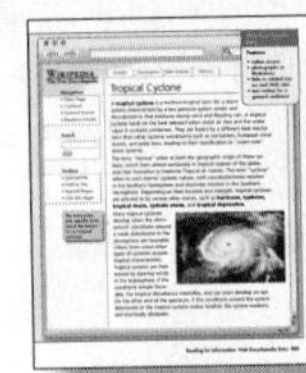

Common Core State Standards

Reading Informational Text
3. Analyze how the author unfolds an analysis or series of ideas or events, including the order in which the points are made, how they are introduced and developed, and the connections that are drawn between them.

Language
6. Acquire and use accurately grade-appropriate general academic and domain-specific words and phrases.

Reading Skill: Evaluate Sources

When you **extend the ideas** presented in a text, you consider and build on those ideas. One way to do this is through **evaluating the source**—judging the validity and reliability of the information presented. Extending the ideas in a source will allow you to connect those ideas to other sources on similar issues and draw general conclusions about your topic. Use this checklist to help you evaluate sources.

Evaluating Sources

- Is the main idea fully supported by the evidence?
- Are the author's arguments logical and valid?
- Does support consist of specific facts?
- Can the evidence presented be verified?
- Is the material presented in an impartial way?
- Who is the author or sponsor of the site?
  - For Web sites, what is the URL ending? (e.g., ".edu" and ".gov" tend to be the most reliable sites)
  - Is the source current?

Content-Area Vocabulary

These words appear in the selections that follow. You may also encounter them in other content-area texts.

- **meteorological** (mē′ tē ər ə loj′ ə kəl) *adj.* related to the science and study of atmosphere and weather
- **atmospheric** (at′ mə sfir′ ik) *adj.* referring to the air that surrounds Earth

Do our differences define us?

Have students think about how living in areas that experience extreme heat or cold could affect the clothing, transportation, employment, and food choices in a region.

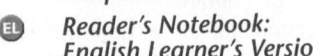

Differentiated Instruction for Universal Access

Reading Support
Give students reading support with the appropriate version of the ***Reader's Notebooks:***

L2 L3 *Reader's Notebook*

L1 *Reader's Notebook: Adapted Version*

EL *Reader's Notebook: English Learner's Version*

Web Site

Features:

- home page with links to other pages
- informative text for research or leisure reading
- photos or other images

Weather Page
Fujita Tornado Damage Scale

Category F0: Light Damage (<73 mph); Some damage to chimneys and sign boards, branches broken off trees, shallow-rooted trees pushed over.

Category F1: Moderate Damage (73–112 mph); Peels surface off roofs; mobile homes pushed off foundations or overturned; moving autos blown off road.

Category F2: Considerable Damage (113–157 mph); Roofs torn off frame houses; mobile homes demolished; boxcars over-turned; large trees snapped or uprooted; light-object missiles generated; cars lifted off ground.

Category F3: Severe Damage (158–206 mph); Roofs and some walls torn off well-constructed houses, trains overturned; most trees in forest uprooted; heavy cars lifted off ground and thrown.

Category F4: Devastating Damage (207–260 mph); Well-constructed houses leveled; structure with weak foundations blown off some distance; cars thrown and large missiles generated.

Category F5: Incredible Damage (261–318 mph); Strong frame houses lifted off foundations and swept away; automobile sized missiles fly through the air in excess of 100 meters (109 yards); trees debarked.

Tornadoes

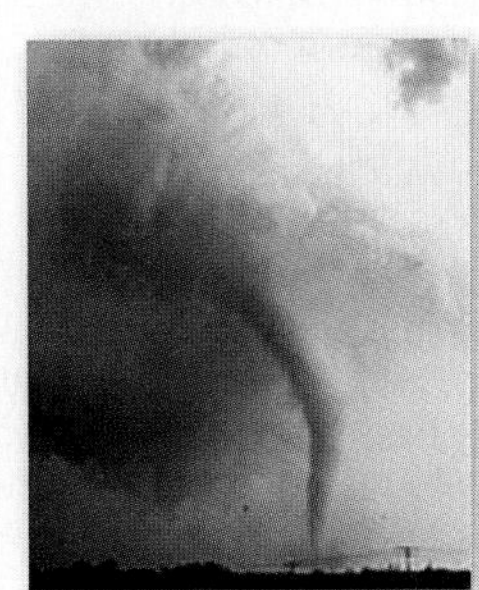

Tornadoes are one of nature's most violent storms. In an average year, about 1,000 tornadoes are reported across the United States, resulting in 80 deaths and over 1,500 injuries. A tornado is a violently rotating column of air extending from a thunderstorm to the ground. The most violent tornadoes are capable of tremendous destruction with wind speeds of 250 mph or more. Damage paths can be in excess of one mile wide and 50 miles long.

Tornadoes come in all shapes and sizes and can occur anywhere in the U.S. at any time of the year. In the southern states, peak tornado season is March through May, while peak months in the northern states are during the summer.

Preparedness Guides

- Are you prepared for Nature's Most Violent Storms? A preparedness guide including safety information for schools prepared by the National Weather Service, FEMA and the American Red Cross.
- Thunderstorms and Camping Safety
- Weather Safety for Kids - Owlie Skywarn's Weather Book about Tornadoes

You can extend ideas presented on this text by following links to other Web pages.

More Info

- Weather Glossary for Storm Spotters
- Storm Reports - includes monthly tornado statistics, deadly tornadoes, current severe weather reports and more from the National Weather Service's Storm Prediction Center.
- Tornadoes of the 20th Century - a list of the more notable tornado out-breaks that occurred in the U.S. during the 20th century.

TEACH

About Web Sites

1. Review with students the features listed in the Web Site box on page 981. **Ask** them to define the term *leisure* in their own terms.

   Possible response: Leisure means "for fun" or "activities unrelated to schooling or work."
2. Talk with students about Web sites they have visited in the past. Have them describe what was helpful about the information, menus, links, and images on the site.
3. **Ask:** Why might people use Web sites for research? **Possible response:** People could use Web sites to do research for school, to comparison shop for something, or to learn more about a place.

Evaluate Sources

1. Have students read the Web page about tornadoes. Remind them that the heading and URL give information about the source. **Ask:** What is the source of this Web site?

   Answer: The source is NOAA, the National Oceanic and Atmospheric Administration, which is a government agency.
2. Define the word *impartial* and have students consider whether the NOAA Web site is impartial. **Ask:** What features of the page convince you that the material is impartially presented?

   Possible responses: The material presents statistics on the number of deaths due to different tornadoes, and it has links to preparedness guides. It includes the Fujita Tornado Damage Scale that categorizes tornadoes.
3. **Ask:** What information on the page helps the reader understand the different types of tornadoes?

   Possible response: The Fujita Tornado Damage Scale tells how tornadoes differ in strength.

Differentiated Instruction for Universal Access

Support for Special-Needs Students

Review the chart for evaluating sources. Have students answer each question for both the NOAA Web site and for Owlie Skywarn's Weather Book page on page 982. Encourage students to make a Venn diagram to record how the pages are similar and how they are different. Have them consider the difference in the images, the writing style, and the authority of the source.

Enrichment for Gifted/Talented Students

Challenge students to write a sample Web page about a type of weather. Like Owlie Skywarn's page, the audience for the students' work should be children and should use data from a reliable source. Encourage them to write in easily understandable language and to include details that would be useful to children.

Evaluate Sources

1. Point out to students that the Web site on page 981 has a link to the page shown here. **Ask:** How is the audience for this page different from the one for the NOAA home page?

   Possible response: The audience for this page is children. It is geared toward a younger audience.
2. Direct students' attention to the header of this page. **Ask** them to identify the name of the Web site and the group that publishes it.

   Answer: The name of the site is "Owlie Skywarn's Weather Book." The group publishing the site is the National Weather Service, which, like NOAA, is an agency of the government.
3. **Ask:** Based on the name, would you think the Web site was reliable? Why or why not?

   Possible response: The name does not suggest that the Web site is reliable because it is so informal.
4. **Ask:** Based on the group that publishes the site, would you expect the information to be reliable? Why or why not?

   Answer: Since the publisher is a government agency, like NOAA, the information in it is probably reliable.
5. **Ask:** When was the page most recently updated, assuming it has been updated in the current year or the last one?

   Answer: Students should cite the date on the Web page and tell how long ago it is from now.
6. Discuss the importance of recent updates to Web pages. Have students consider what new information or scientific studies might make the page inaccurate.

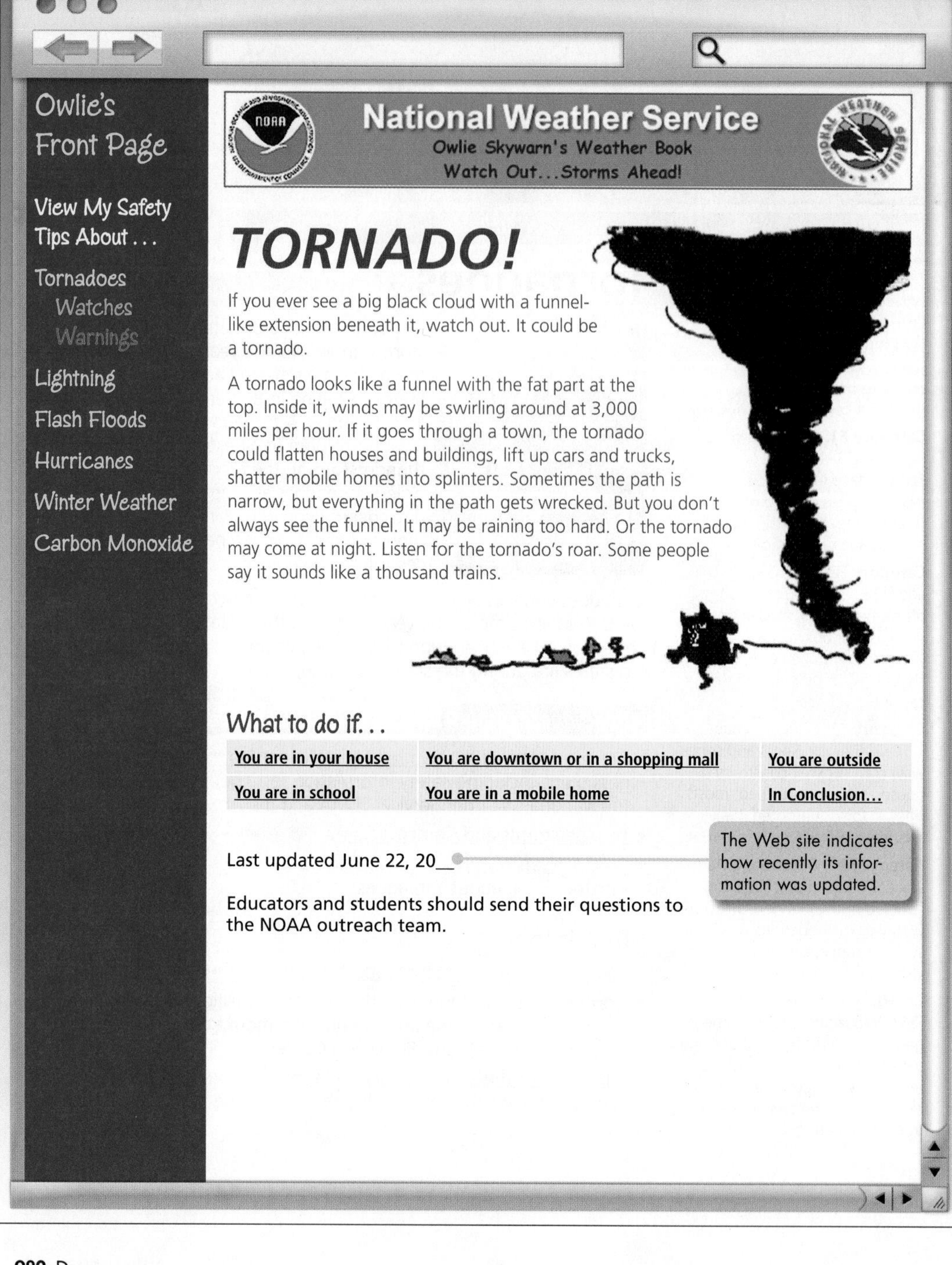

982 Drama

Vocabulary Development

CCSS Language 6

Vocabulary for Web Sites

Tell students that discussion of Web sites often involves using specialized terms. Guide them to understand the meaning of the following words on the "Tornadoes" Web site.

navigation bar: A collection of links grouped together to help readers find information within a Web site.

Web site: A group of Web pages generally hyperlinked together.

Web page: An electronic document posted online.

hyperlink: An electronic link providing direct access from one location in a document to another document or another location within the same document.

WIKIPEDIA
The Free Encyclopedia

Navigation
- Main Page
- Contents
- Current Events
- Random Article

Search

GO

Toolbox
- Upload File
- Add to File
- Special Pages
- Cite this Page

Article | Discussion | Edit Article | History

Tropical Cyclone

A **tropical cyclone** is a **meteorological** term for a storm system characterized by a low pressure system center and thunderstorms that produces strong wind and flooding rain. A tropical cyclone feeds on the heat released when moist air rises and the water vapor it contains condenses. They are fueled by a different heat mechanism than other cyclonic windstorms such as nor'easters, European windstorms, and polar lows, leading to their classification as "warm core" storm systems.

The term "tropical" refers to both the geographic origin of these systems, which form almost exclusively in tropical regions of the globe, and their formation in Maritime Tropical air masses. The term "cyclone" refers to such storms' cyclonic nature, with counterclockwise rotation in the Northern Hemisphere and clockwise rotation in the Southern Hemisphere. Depending on their location and strength, tropical cyclones are referred to by various other names, such as **hurricane, typhoon, tropical storm, cyclonic storm,** and **tropical depression.**

Many tropical cyclones develop when the **atmospheric** conditions around a weak disturbance in the atmosphere are favorable. Others form when other types of cyclones acquire tropical characteristics. Tropical systems are then moved by steering winds in the troposphere; if the conditions remain favorable, the tropical disturbance intensifies, and can even develop an eye. On the other end of the spectrum, if the conditions around the system deteriorate or the tropical cyclone makes landfall, the system weakens and eventually dissipates.

The entry presents specific facts about the behavior of tropical cyclones.

Web Encyclopedia Entry

Features:
- online access
- photographs or illustrations
- links to related topics and Web sites
- text written for a general audience

About Web Encyclopedia Entries

1. Review with students the features listed in the Web Encyclopedia Entry box on page 983. **Ask** them to define the term *access* in terms of research, using their own words.

   Possible response: In terms of research, access means "to have a source available."
2. Talk with students about encyclopedia entries they have used. Have them describe what was helpful about the style and organization of the encyclopedia entries.
3. Explain to students that they are likely to encounter encyclopedia entries when researching a topic for school or out of curiosity.

Evaluate Sources

1. Have students review the features of the entry including the top and side navigation tabs and the boldface terms. **Ask:** If you wanted to discuss the article or make a change to it, where would you go on the page?

   Possible response: The tabs at the top of the page allow a reader to discuss and edit the entry.
2. Point out that when readers can change the content of an encyclopedia entry, the information may not be accurate or verifiable. **Ask:** How can you make sure the information in a Web encyclopedia entry is accurate?

   Possible response: You can check it in another reliable printed source, such as a print encyclopedia or other reference book.

Differentiated Instruction for Universal Access

EL Vocabulary for English Learners

Use the encyclopedia entry as an opportunity to review terms for different weather conditions. Point out that synonyms for *cyclone* are *hurricane, typhoon, tropical storm.* Ask students to offer synonyms for other weather words, such as *snowstorm* (*blizzard*), *rain* (*sprinkles, shower, thunderstorm*), and *atmosphere* (*air, wind*).

Strategy for Advanced Readers

To give students further practice with encyclopedia entries, have them each choose a topic of interest. Tell them to each find at least three encyclopedia articles about the topic and write a report explaining how the encyclopedia entries are alike and how they are different. Have them conclude by saying which encyclopedia they think is most reliable and why.

Evaluate Sources

1. Direct students' attention to the callout at the top of the page. Make sure they understand the purpose of this particular page from the online encyclopedia.
2. Point out the headings on the page. **Ask:** What rules does Wikipedia have for editing its entries?

   Possible answer: Changes to entries must be verifiable using reliable sources.
3. **Ask:** Why do you think Wikipedia is concerned with making sure its information is verifiable?

   Possible response: The Web site would not be useful to most people doing research if the information were not verifiable.
4. Point to the last paragraph, which identifies the most reliable sources. **Ask:** How has the discussion of evaluating sources helped you understand why this list is important?

   Possible response: These sources are checked for accuracy and have reputations for reliability. They are print materials, not Web sources.

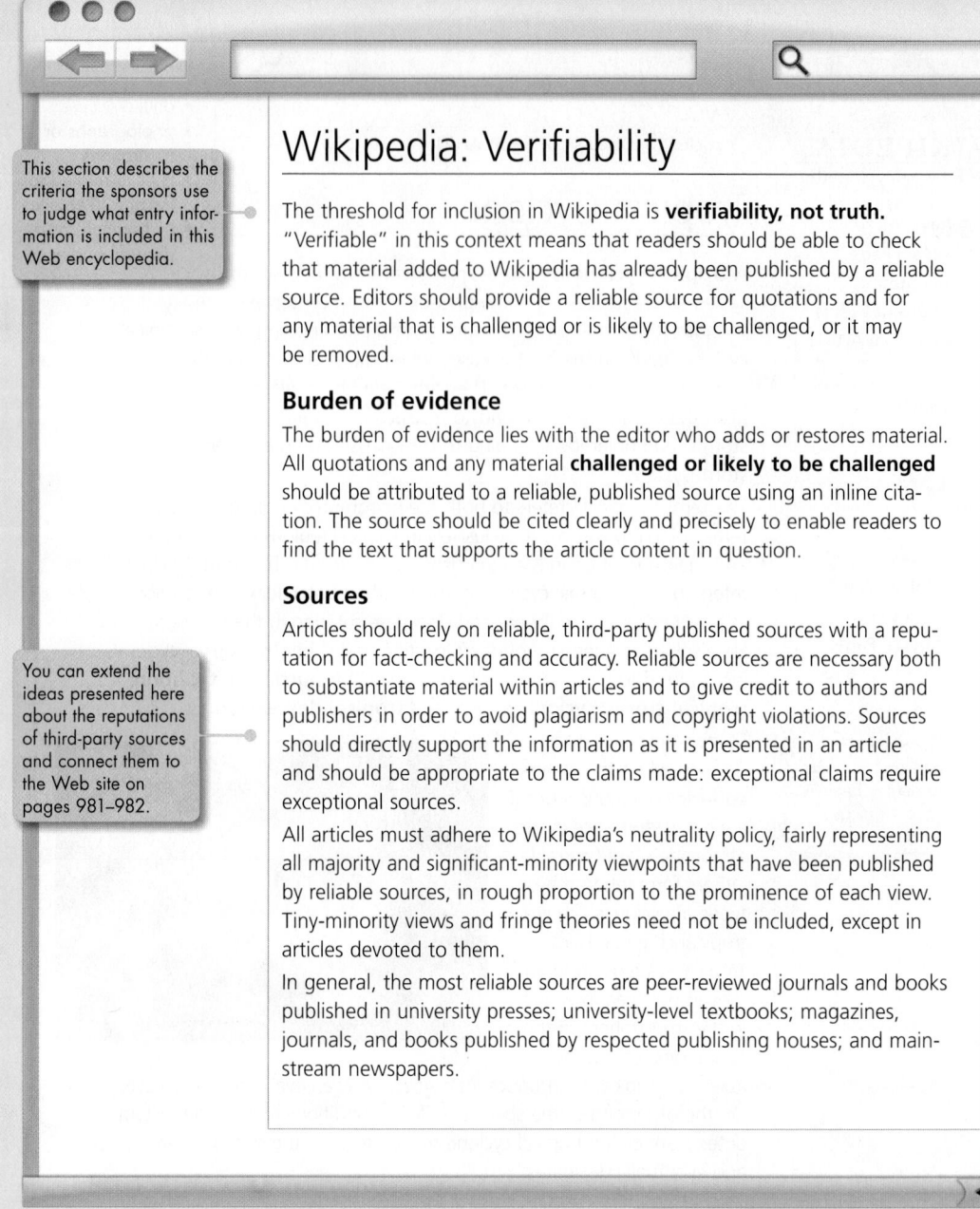

This section describes the criteria the sponsors use to judge what entry information is included in this Web encyclopedia.

Wikipedia: Verifiability

The threshold for inclusion in Wikipedia is **verifiability, not truth.** "Verifiable" in this context means that readers should be able to check that material added to Wikipedia has already been published by a reliable source. Editors should provide a reliable source for quotations and for any material that is challenged or is likely to be challenged, or it may be removed.

Burden of evidence

The burden of evidence lies with the editor who adds or restores material. All quotations and any material **challenged or likely to be challenged** should be attributed to a reliable, published source using an inline citation. The source should be cited clearly and precisely to enable readers to find the text that supports the article content in question.

Sources

You can extend the ideas presented here about the reputations of third-party sources and connect them to the Web site on pages 981–982.

Articles should rely on reliable, third-party published sources with a reputation for fact-checking and accuracy. Reliable sources are necessary both to substantiate material within articles and to give credit to authors and publishers in order to avoid plagiarism and copyright violations. Sources should directly support the information as it is presented in an article and should be appropriate to the claims made: exceptional claims require exceptional sources.

All articles must adhere to Wikipedia's neutrality policy, fairly representing all majority and significant-minority viewpoints that have been published by reliable sources, in rough proportion to the prominence of each view. Tiny-minority views and fringe theories need not be included, except in articles devoted to them.

In general, the most reliable sources are peer-reviewed journals and books published in university presses; university-level textbooks; magazines, journals, and books published by respected publishing houses; and mainstream newspapers.

Vocabulary Development

CCSS Language 6

Vocabulary from Science

Explain that the author of the article uses some difficult and technical vocabulary. List examples on the board and offer synonyms that can be used in context.

tropical: occurring in the tropics (regions close to the equator, known for warm temperatures and seasons of heavy rain)

windstorms: violent weather with high winds

nor'easters: winds or storms from the northeast

atmospheric: pertaining to the atmosphere or air

troposphere: the lowest level of the atmosphere, containing breathable air and clouds

After You Read | Web Site • Web Encyclopedia Entry

Comparing Expository Texts

1. **Integration of Knowledge and Ideas** **(a) Evaluate** the Web site and the Web encyclopedia entry by comparing and contrasting their reliability as sources on types of extreme weather. **(b)** Which source do you judge to be more reliable? Explain.

Content-Area Vocabulary

2. **(a)** Explain the parts of speech and meanings of the following words: *meteorology, meteorologically, meteoric, meteoroid.* **(b)** Use each word in a sentence that shows its meaning.

Timed Writing

Argument: Evaluation

Format
The prompt directs you to write an evaluation. Therefore, your response should include observations and judgments about the elements mentioned in the prompt.

Write an evaluation of the Web encyclopedia entry as a source for research about tropical cyclones. Assess the usefulness of the information presented, and draw conclusions about its validity and reliability. Use details and examples from the text to support your evaluations and conclusions. (30 minutes)

Academic Vocabulary
When you *assess,* you make a determination about something's value.

5-Minute Planner

Complete these steps before you begin to write:

1. Read the prompt carefully and completely. Look at the highlighted words to help you understand the assignment.
2. Review the Web encyclopedia entry on tropical cyclones. Note details that help you understand the subject. Decide how useful the information in the entry would be if you were researching tropical cyclones.
3. Review the Web encyclopedia's statement regarding the verifiability of information on the site. Based on that statement, decide whether you think the information in the entry is completely reliable. **TIP Extend ideas** presented in the statement on verifiability by considering whether information in the entry could be verified using another reliable source.
4. Make notes and create a rough outline for your evaluation. Then, refer to your outline as you draft your response.

ASSESS/EXTEND

Answers

Comparing Expository Texts

1. (a) **Possible response:** The Web site is based on official information and is written by scientists who are affiliated with a credible government organization. The Web encyclopedia entry contains information that is verifiable. A scientist may write it, but anyone can change it. The experts from the Web site do not review the material instantly. (b) **Possible response:** The Web site is more reliable because it is written and edited by government scientists. Readers can change the Web encyclopedia entry, so it may not be as reliable as the Web site.
2. (a) **Sample response:** All the words come from the root *meteor*. The suffix *-ology* indicates the study of something. Meteorology is the study of the atmosphere and weather. The suffix *-ally* makes an adverb that describes actions related to weather study. The suffix *-ic* usually creates an adjective. Here, the adjective means "like a meteor"—quickly shooting. The word *meteoroid* adds *-oid* to the root to create a different noun that names the particle that creates the visible stream of light we call a shooting star or meteor. (b) **Sample response:** Meteorology is not an exact science. Meteorologically, it looked like a good day for a picnic. Her rise in popularity was meteoric. The meteoroid was tiny but it created a spectacular meteor.

Timed Writing

1. Before students complete the activity, guide them in identifying and analyzing key words and phrases in the prompt, highlighted on the student page.
2. Work with students to draw up guidelines for their evaluation based on the key words:
   - **Focus** The essay should evaluate the Web encyclopedia entry as a source.
   - **Organization** The essay should assess the usefulness of the information and draw a conclusion about its credibility.
   - **Support** The essay should use details and examples from the text to support evaluations and conclusions.
   - **Style** The assignment is an evaluation, so it should be formal in tone. Writers should avoid using slang words and contractions.
3. Have students use the 5-Minute Planner to structure their time.
4. Allow students 30 minutes to complete the assignment. Evaluate their work using the guidelines they have developed.

PRETEACH

Common Core State Standards

- **Reading Literature 4**
- **Writing 2, 2.a, 2.b**

❶ Comparing Satire

Archetype and Theme

1. Introduce the skill, using the instruction on the student page.
2. Give students a copy of **Comparing Satire Graphic Organizer B, *Graphic Organizer Transparencies,*** p. 177. Tell them to answer its questions about the two selections as they read.

Think Aloud: Model the Skill

Model ways to identify satire. Say to students:

I know that satire ridicules someone or something. For example, consider the high school basketball player who expects to get a college scholarship. To show off, he often challenges friends to pick-up games. One day, a short, out-of-shape guy wearing glasses joins the game and beats him easily. Asked to explain, the guy says he used to play regularly but that to make sure he got into college, he had to spend his free time studying. The story has all the elements: ridicule, humor, and a lesson. I look for these same elements in satire that I read.

Comparing Literary Works

from **The Importance of Being Earnest** • *from* **Big Kiss**

❶ Comparing Satire

Satire is writing that exposes and makes fun of the foolishness and faults of an individual, an institution, a society, or a situation. Although a satire may make readers laugh, it may also aim to correct the flaws that it criticizes. Some satires address serious social problems, while others explore less important subjects. Satirical writings vary in style and tone, level of *subtlety,* and the writer's attitude toward the subject and the audience. A satire may have the following characteristics:

- It may be gentle and sympathetic or angry and bitter in tone.
- It might use *sarcasm* or *irony*—language that means the opposite of what it says.
- It may exaggerate faults to make them both funny and obvious.

In addition, the perspective of the satirist plays a key role. Some satirists write as outside onlookers, while others include themselves as objects of the satire. Skilled satirists reveal their targets with subtleties in the text rather than elements that are overly obvious.

As you read these selections, answer questions like those in the chart to better understand and evaluate the satire in each one.

Questions About Satire
Subject • What or whom is ridiculed? • Is the topic serious or trivial? • Does the writer include him- or herself as an object of the satire?
Tone • Is the tone gentle or harsh? • Does the writer use sarcasm or irony?
Purpose • Is the satire funny? • Does the satirist want to correct the flaws he/she exposes?

Common Core State Standards

Reading Literature

4. Determine the meaning of words and phrases as they are used in the text, including figurative and connotative meanings; analyze the cumulative impact of specific word choices on meaning and tone.

Writing

2. Write informative/explanatory texts to examine and convey complex ideas, concepts, and information clearly and accurately through the effective selection, organization, and analysis of content.

2.a. Intoduce a topic; organize complex ideas, concepts, and information to make important connections and distinctions.

2.b. Develop the topic with well-chosen, relevant, and sufficient facts, extended definitions, concrete details, quotations, or other information and examples appropriate to the audience's knowledge of the topic.

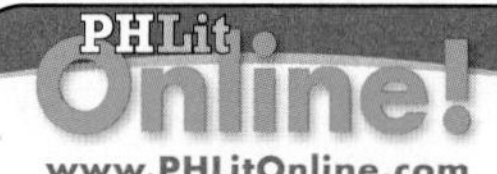

- Vocabulary flashcards
- Interactive journals
- More about the authors
- Selection audio
- Interactive graphic organizers

Vocabulary Development

Vocabulary Knowledge Rating

Create a **Vocabulary Knowledge Rating Chart** (***Professional Development Guidebook,*** p. 33) featuring the words glossed in the selections:

ignorance (p. 992) *assiduous* (p. 999)

Give students a copy of the chart, and read the words aloud. Have students mark their rating of each in the Before You Read column. To gauge how much instruction to provide, tally the students who think they know each word.

Explain that the words are defined in the margin at the point where they appear in the selection. Urge students to be alert to these words as they read the selections. They will rate their knowledge again when they finish.

Vocabulary Central, featuring tools, activities, and songs for studying vocabulary, is available online at **www.PHLitOnline.com.**

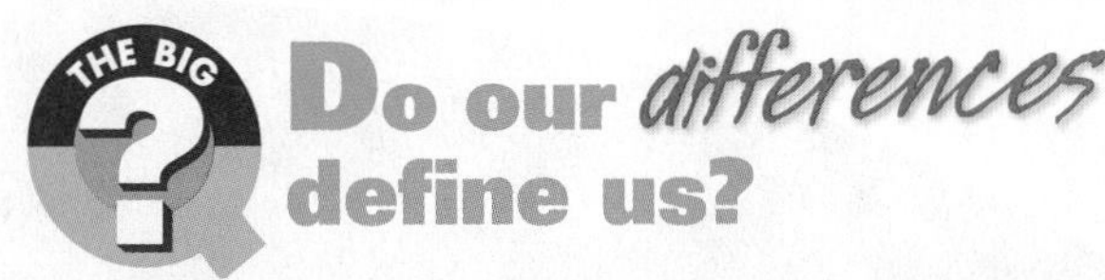
THE BIG
?
Do our differences define us?

❷ Writing About the Big Question

Both these selections use people's differences to satirize an element of life or society. Use this sentence starter to develop your ideas about the Big Question.

When writers expose what is foolish in society, we can learn that our **differences** ____.

Meet the Authors

Oscar Wilde (1854–1900)

Author of *The Importance of Being Earnest*

Oscar Wilde was educated in Dublin and at Oxford University, where he became notorious for his wit. While he wrote poems and celebrated works of fiction, it was in his plays that Wilde's genius found its voice.

The Importance of Being Funny In a series of brilliant comedies, including *A Woman of No Importance* and *An Ideal Husband*, Wilde targeted the strait-laced manners and hypocrisy of English society in the 1890s. His masterpiece is *The Importance of Being Earnest*, a drama about Victorian values that still entertains audiences today.

Henry Alford (b. 1962)

Author of *Big Kiss*

Henry Alford calls himself an "investigative humorist," a comic journalist who unearths humor wherever it hides. Armed with dry wit and charm, he uncovers what makes popular culture funny, amazing, or outrageous.

Comic Escapades *Big Kiss: One Actor's Desperate Attempt to Claw His Way to the Middle* chronicles Alford's adventures as he tries to become an actor. He faces humiliation at the hands of acting teachers and directors, but he relishes his minor victory as an extra in *Godzilla*.

Teaching Resources

- All EL *Unit 5 Resources,* pp. 164–180
- All *Common Core Companion,* 35–42; 190–201
- All EL *Graphic Organizer Transparencies,* pp. 176–179
- All *Professional Development Guidebook,* pp. 33, 42
- All **Enriched Online Student Edition**
- L2 ***Hear It!* Audio CD (adapted text)**

PHLit Online! All resources, including print and audio, are available at **www.PHLitOnline.com.**

Daily Bellringer

For each class during which you will teach this selection, have students complete one of the five Sentence Combining activities for Week 30 in the *Daily Bellringer Activities* booklet.

❷ Writing About the Big Question

1. Review the assignment with the class.
2. Discuss with students the ways that humor allows people to criticize without being insulting.
3. Have students complete the sentence starter. Review responses as a class. (**Possible response:** When writers expose what is foolish in society, we can learn that our differences aren't that important.)
4. Remind students that their answers will help them think about the Big Question. Tell students to look for ways that differences are identified as they read.

Concept Connector

Tell students that they will return to their sentence starters after they have concluded reading.

Multidraft Reading

To assist struggling readers and to deepen reading for all, apply multidraft reading protocols. For each reading, have students set the purpose indicated:

- **First reading**—identifying key ideas and details and answering any Reading Checks.
- **Second reading**—analyzing craft and structure and responding to the side-column prompts.
- **Third reading**—integrating knowledge and ideas, connecting to other texts and the world, and answering the end-of-selection questions.

For more guidance, refer to the *Classroom Strategies and Teaching Routines* card on multidraft reading.

PHLit Online!

For more about the authors and practice with the selection vocabulary, go to **www.PHLitOnline.com.**

❶ Background

The Importance of Being Earnest The subtitle of Wilde's 1895 play is "A Trivial Comedy for Serious People," stressing the vital link between the humorous and the serious. One of Wilde's techniques for achieving this link is to reverse common expressions. *Earnest* is full of lines that are not only funny but also cause readers to think about how they might be true. Wilde believed that the purpose of art was a kind of useful lying: "Lying, the telling of beautiful untrue things, is the proper aim of art." Wilde's "lies" do satirize Victorian society, but their main purpose is to be purely delightful. As Wilde said, *Earnest* is "exquisitely trivial, a delicate bubble of fancy, and it has its philosophy. . . . That we should treat all the trivial things of life seriously, and all the serious things of life with sincere and studied triviality."

❷ Activating Prior Knowledge

Have students share what they know about Victorian society, including class differences and social expectations. Allow students to preview the images in the selection for ideas. Ask students to predict which aspects of Victorian society would make good topics for satirical writing.

Concept Connector →

Students will return to this activity after completing the excerpt from *The Importance of Being Earnest.*

❸ About the Selection

In this excerpt from *The Importance of Being Earnest,* Jack finally gets a chance to propose to Gwendolen. Jack is astounded that Gwendolen loves him, thinking his name Ernest, and he begins his awkward proposal. Lady Bracknell interrupts, sends Gwendolen out, and interviews Jack to determine his suitability for marriage. Her questions satirize Victorian values, and Jack's answers do not satisfy her snobbish requirements. To Lady Bracknell, being found in a handbag does not constitute being of a good family, and she storms out.

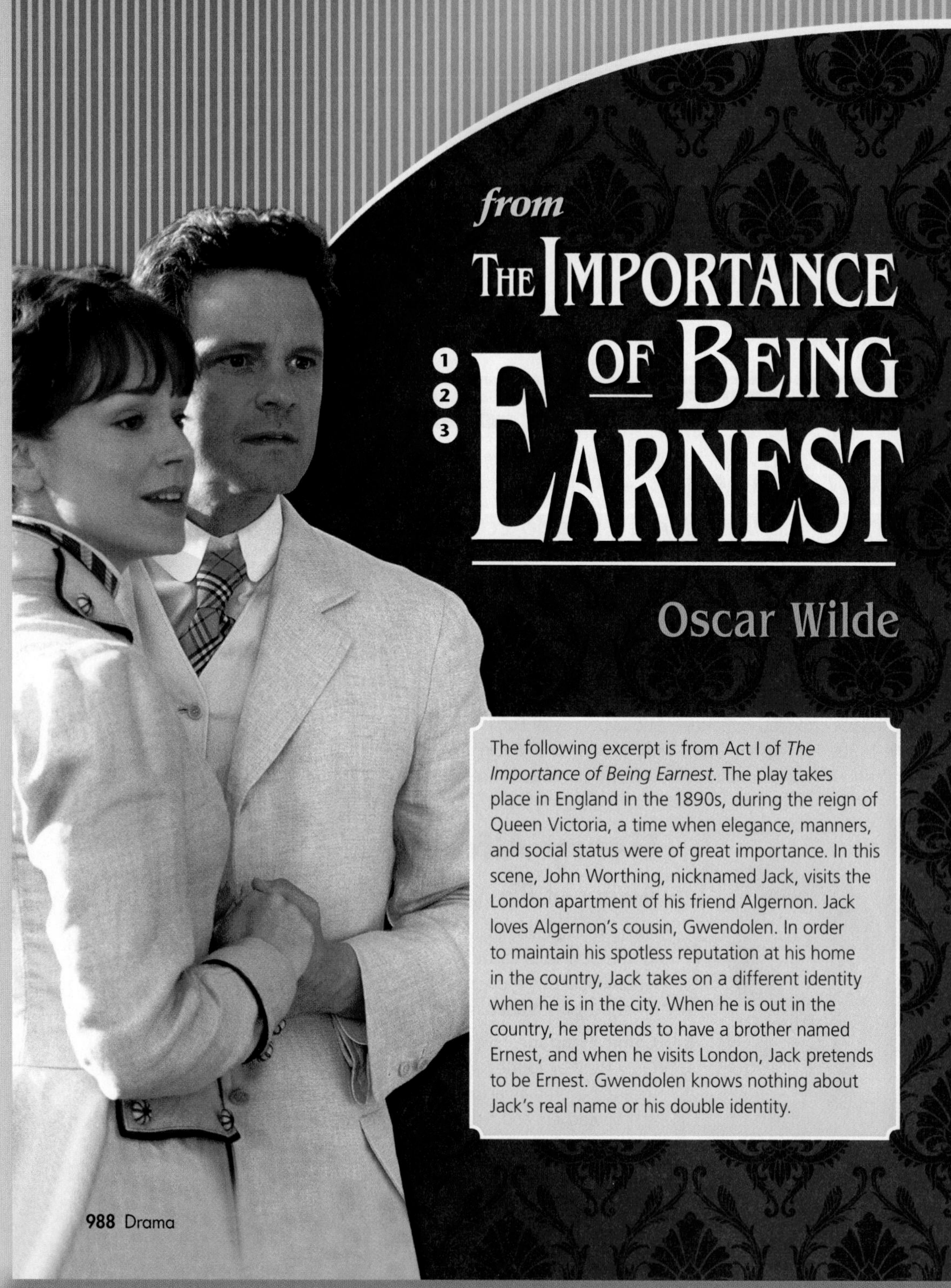

from The Importance of Being Earnest

❶ ❷ ❸

Oscar Wilde

The following excerpt is from Act I of *The Importance of Being Earnest.* The play takes place in England in the 1890s, during the reign of Queen Victoria, a time when elegance, manners, and social status were of great importance. In this scene, John Worthing, nicknamed Jack, visits the London apartment of his friend Algernon. Jack loves Algernon's cousin, Gwendolen. In order to maintain his spotless reputation at his home in the country, Jack takes on a different identity when he is in the city. When he is out in the country, he pretends to have a brother named Ernest, and when he visits London, Jack pretends to be Ernest. Gwendolen knows nothing about Jack's real name or his double identity.

Ⓒ Text Complexity Rubric

from The Importance of Being Earnest		
Qualitative Measures	**Context/ Knowledge Demands**	Victorian England; comedy of manners 1 2 3 ④ 5
	Structure/ Language Clarity and Conventionality	Elegant, upper-class speech; satiric quips; witty exchanges; challenging vocabulary 1 2 3 ④ 5
	Levels of Meaning/ Purpose/Concept Level	Challenging concept (satire of Victorian society) 1 2 3 ④ 5
Quantitative Measures	**Text Length**	Word Count: 2,031
	Lexile	710L

CHARACTERS
John Worthing, JP
Lady Bracknell
Hon. Gwendolen Fairfax
Algernon

LADY BRACKNELL *and* ALGERNON *go into the music room,* GWENDOLEN *remains behind.*

JACK. Charming day it has been, Miss Fairfax.

GWENDOLEN. Pray don't talk to me about the weather, Mr Worthing. Whenever people talk to me about the weather, I always feel quite certain that they mean something else. And that makes me so nervous.

JACK. I do mean something else.

GWENDOLEN. I thought so. In fact, I am never wrong.

JACK. And I would like to be allowed to take advantage of Lady Bracknell's temporary absence. . . .

GWENDOLEN. I would certainly advise you to do so. Mamma has a way of coming back suddenly into a room that I have often had to speak to her about.

JACK. *(nervously)* Miss Fairfax, ever since I met you I have admired you more than any girl . . . I have ever met since . . . I met you.

GWENDOLEN. Yes, I am quite aware of the fact. And I often wish that in public, at any rate, you had been more demonstrative. For me you have always had an irresistible fascination. Even before I met you I was far from indifferent to you. *(Jack looks at her in amazement)* We live, as I hope you know, Mr Worthing, in an age of ideals. The fact is constantly mentioned in the more expensive monthly magazines, and has reached the provincial pulpits I am told; and my ideal has always been to love someone of the name of Ernest. There is something in that name that inspires absolute confidence. The moment Algernon first mentioned to me that he had a friend called Ernest, I knew I was destined to love you.

JACK. You really love me, Gwendolen?

GWENDOLEN. Passionately!

JACK. Darling! You don't know how happy you've made me.

Literary Analysis
Satire Which words here make fun of Gwendolen's haughtiness?

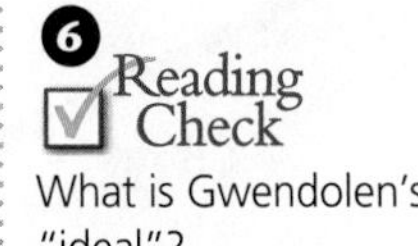

6 **Reading Check**
What is Gwendolen's "ideal"?

5 ◀ **Critical Viewing** Judging from the actor playing Jack in this photograph, what do you think Jack will be like? **[Predict]**

4 Literary Analysis

Satire

1. Have students read the bracketed text. Then, **ask** them how Gwendolen manipulates the conversation with Jack from the start.

   Answer: Gwendolen tells Jack that she does not want to talk about the weather.

2. **Ask** students the Literary Analysis question: Which words here make fun of Gwendolen's haughtiness?

   Answer: Gwendolen says, "I am never wrong," and she says that she is "quite aware of the fact" that Jack admires her. In fact, she is wrong about Jack's name. She also says that she has admonished her mother about barging into rooms, although that seems unlikely.

3. **Ask** students in what sense both lovers might be called "enchanted."

   Answer: Jack is so in love with Gwendolen that he ignores her haughtiness and foolishness. Gwendolen, although in love with Jack, seems equally in love with her idea of herself, social forms, and her comical "ideal" to love someone named Ernest.

5 Critical Viewing

Possible response: Some students may expect Jack to be serious; others may think he will be mischevous.

6 Reading Check

Answer: Her "ideal" is to love a man named Ernest.

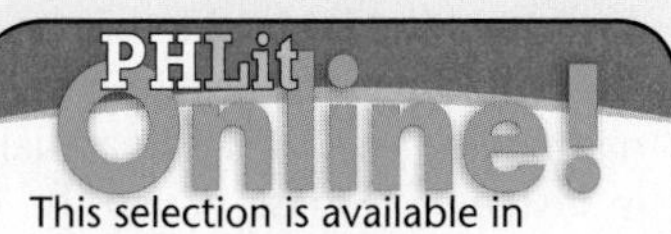

This selection is available in interactive format in the **Enriched Online Student Edition, www.PHLitOnline.com,** which includes an interactive graphic organizer.

Ⓒ Text Complexity: Reader and Task Suggestions

from The Importance of Being Earnest	
Preparing to Read the Text	**Leveled Tasks**
• Refer to the Background information on TE p. 988 and discuss Wilde's statement that the aim of art is "the telling of beautiful untrue things . . ." • Discuss Victorian society, particularly the pretentions and expectations of the upper and middle classes and the strict class distinctions they recognized. • Guide students to use Multidraft Reading strategies (TE p. 987).	*Levels of Meaning* If students will have difficulty with satire in this play, have them first read the play and identify the goals of the main characters. Then, have them reread the play and note specific elements of satire in the characters' dialogue. Discuss student notes and offer clarification. *Analyzing* If students will not have difficulty with satire in this play, have them read and take notes about which characters learned something, what they learned, and how it changed their actions. Have students contribute their ideas during class discussion.

7 Literary Analysis

Satire

1. Remind students that, although the speaker indicator reads "JACK," Gwendolen believes that she is in love with a man named Ernest.
2. **Ask** the Literary Analysis question: What is ironic about Gwendolen's fascination with the name Ernest and her feelings for Jack?

   Answer: Gwendolen's fascination with Jack is ironic because it is based on a name that is not his. Her passion is founded on an illusion.
3. **Ask** students why Gwendolen's fascination with the name Ernest is an example of satire.

   Possible responses: Wilde is making fun of a person who is so shallow that she will fall in love with a man and marry him merely because of his name.
4. **Ask** students why Wilde's choice of the name Ernest adds to the satire.

   Answer: Wilde adds to the satire by making the name itself a homonym for *earnest,* a synonym for *sincere.*

8 Connecting to the Big Question

1. Remind students of the Big Question by recalling that superficial differences are often viewed as very important.
2. Direct students' attention to the bracketed text. **Ask:** What difference about Jack is Gwendolen considering?

   Answer: She is considering how she would feel about him if his name were Jack, which it actually is, instead of Ernest, which she thinks it to be.
3. **Ask:** In Gwendolen's eyes, how would a different name define Ernest/Jack?

   Possible response: As Ernest, she finds him fascinating. As Jack, she thinks he would be ordinary.

9 Critical Viewing

Possible response: Jack's expression might be described as showing astonishment, uncertainty, or anxiety.

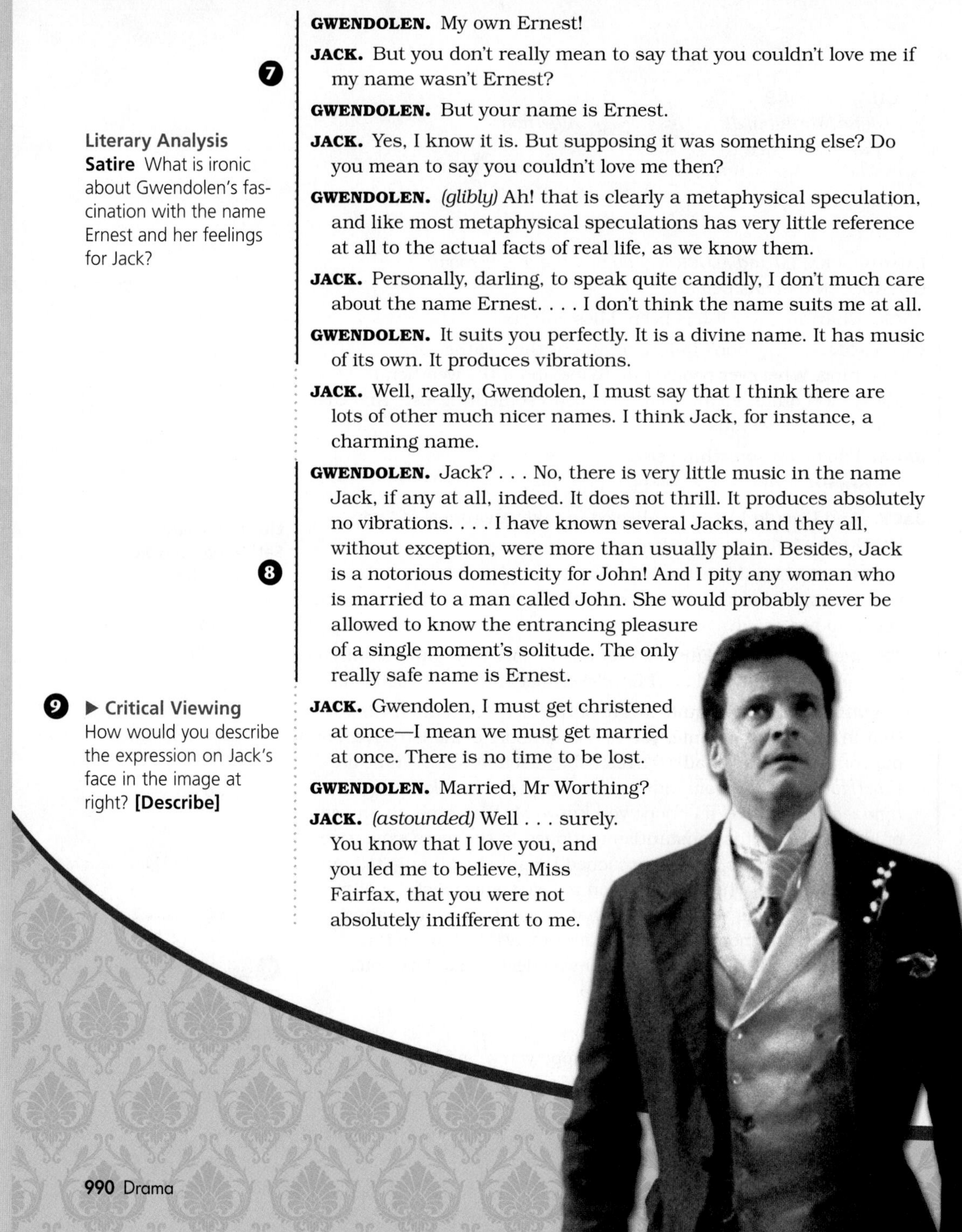

GWENDOLEN. My own Ernest!

7 **JACK.** But you don't really mean to say that you couldn't love me if my name wasn't Ernest?

GWENDOLEN. But your name is Ernest.

JACK. Yes, I know it is. But supposing it was something else? Do you mean to say you couldn't love me then?

GWENDOLEN. *(glibly)* Ah! that is clearly a metaphysical speculation, and like most metaphysical speculations has very little reference at all to the actual facts of real life, as we know them.

JACK. Personally, darling, to speak quite candidly, I don't much care about the name Ernest. . . . I don't think the name suits me at all.

GWENDOLEN. It suits you perfectly. It is a divine name. It has music of its own. It produces vibrations.

JACK. Well, really, Gwendolen, I must say that I think there are lots of other much nicer names. I think Jack, for instance, a charming name.

8 **GWENDOLEN.** Jack? . . . No, there is very little music in the name Jack, if any at all, indeed. It does not thrill. It produces absolutely no vibrations. . . . I have known several Jacks, and they all, without exception, were more than usually plain. Besides, Jack is a notorious domesticity for John! And I pity any woman who is married to a man called John. She would probably never be allowed to know the entrancing pleasure of a single moment's solitude. The only really safe name is Ernest.

JACK. Gwendolen, I must get christened at once—I mean we must get married at once. There is no time to be lost.

GWENDOLEN. Married, Mr Worthing?

JACK. *(astounded)* Well . . . surely. You know that I love you, and you led me to believe, Miss Fairfax, that you were not absolutely indifferent to me.

Literary Analysis
Satire What is ironic about Gwendolen's fascination with the name Ernest and her feelings for Jack?

9 ▶ **Critical Viewing** How would you describe the expression on Jack's face in the image at right? **[Describe]**

Vocabulary Development

CCSS Language 6

Selection Vocabulary Reinforcement

Students will benefit from additional examples and practice with the selection vocabulary words. Reinforce their comprehension with "show-you-know" sentences. The first part of the sentence uses the vocabulary word in an appropriate context. The second part of the sentence—the "show-you-know" part—clarifies the first. Model the strategy with this example:

When he read the questions on the test, he realized his ignorance; there were so many facts he simply did not know.

Then, give students these sentence prompts, and coach them in creating the clarification part:

1. She knew that a formal dinner was not a place to be *demonstrative;* __________.

   Sample answer: she would have to keep her feelings to herself.
2. The professor admitted his *ignorance;* __________.

   Sample answer: he planned to research the topic later.

GWENDOLEN. I adore you. But you haven't proposed to me yet. Nothing has been said at all about marriage. The subject has not even been touched on.

JACK. Well . . . may I propose to you now?

GWENDOLEN. I think it would be an admirable opportunity. And to spare you any possible disappointment, Mr Worthing, I think it only fair to tell you quite frankly beforehand that I am fully determined to accept you.

JACK. Gwendolen!

GWENDOLEN. Yes, Mr Worthing, what have you got to say to me?

JACK. You know what I have got to say to you.

GWENDOLEN. Yes, but you don't say it.

JACK. Gwendolen, will you marry me? *(Goes on his knees)*

GWENDOLEN. Of course I will, darling. How long you have been about it! I am afraid you have had very little experience in how to propose.

JACK. My own one, I have never loved anyone in the world but you.

GWENDOLEN. Yes, but men often propose for practice. I know my brother Gerald does. All my girlfriends tell me so. What wonderfully blue eyes you have, Ernest! They are quite, quite blue. I hope you will always look at me just like that, especially when there are other people present.

(Enter LADY BRACKNELL*)*

LADY BRACKNELL. Mr Worthing! Rise, sir, from this semi-recumbent posture. It is most indecorous.

GWENDOLEN. Mamma! *(He tries to rise; she restrains him)* I must beg you to retire. This is no place for you. Besides, Mr Worthing has not quite finished yet.

LADY BRACKNELL. Finished what, may I ask?

GWENDOLEN. I am engaged to Mr Worthing, mamma.

(They rise together)

LADY BRACKNELL. Pardon me, you are not engaged to anyone. When you do become engaged to someone, I, or your father, should his health permit him, will inform you of the fact. An engagement should come on a young girl as a surprise, pleasant or unpleasant, as the case may be. It is hardly a matter that she could be allowed to arrange for herself. . . . And now I have a few questions to put to you, Mr Worthing. While I am making these inquiries, you, Gwendolen, will wait for me below in the carriage.

GWENDOLEN. *(reproachfully)* Mamma!

Literary Analysis

Satire What does Lady Bracknell's use of elaborate expressions suggest about her character?

11

What is Gwendolen's response to Jack's proposal?

10 Literary Analysis

Satire

1. Read the bracketed text aloud. Tell students that *recumbent* means "lying-down." Remind them that Jack is proposing to Gwendolen, and **ask** what they think "semi-recumbent posture" means.

   Answer: The expression means "kneeling."

2. **Ask** students to respond to the Literary Analysis question: What does Lady Bracknell's use of elaborate expressions suggest about her character?

   Answer: Lady Bracknell is devoted to the forms of society and its elegant speech, including euphemisms—words that are considered less offensive than clear and direct speech. Lady Bracknell is pompous and a slave to social conventions.

3. **Ask** students to explain why Lady Bracknell's use of such expressions is an example of satire.

   Answer: Such expressions reveal that Lady Bracknell is domineering, foolish, and prudish. By exaggerating her speech with such expressions, Wilde enables us to laugh at her and recognize that she and the society she represents are overly restrictive, blinded by social convention, and hypocritical.

11 Reading Check

Answer: Gwendolen accepts Jack's proposal.

PROFESSIONAL DEVELOPMENT | **Sheridan Blau**

Apply the Strategy

After students have read pages 989–991, put students in groups of three. Have them reread the scene from *The Importance of Being Earnest*. Encourage them to ask for clarification when they do not understand a line or the action or motive of a character.

Then, ask students to select a segment of 6-10 lines and rehearse it in their groups. Students should elect one member of their group to be director. As they rehearse, they should note what problems arise in deciding how to interpret a character or say the lines. Students may have questions about whether Gwendolyn really loves Jack, for example. Finally, share and discuss students' questions as a class.

For more of Sheridan Blau's strategies, see his Professional Development essay, pp. 778c–778d.

⓬ Literary Analysis

Satire

1. **Ask** students what questions they think parents should ask a young man who wants to marry their daughter.

   Possible response: The main questions should be "Do you love her?" and "Does she love you?" Other questions might involve where and how the young people plan to live.

2. Have students read the bracketed text, and then **ask** them the Literary Analysis question: Is Lady Bracknell truly "a really affectionate mother"? Explain.

   Answer: Lady Bracknell is not "really affectionate" because she cares more about money and social position than about her daughter's emotional happiness.

3. Have students **explain** why Lady Bracknell's description of herself as "really affectionate" is satirical.

   Answer: Her description is satiric because she thinks that "affection" is shown by a concern for money and social position instead of kindness and understanding. Wilde is satirizing her triviality, her mercenary values, and her self-serving attitudes.

⓭ Critical Viewing

Possible response: Lady Bracknell looks exactly as I thought she would—overdressed, bossy, and loud. Gwendolen also looks like I imagined she would—pretty, snippy, and stiff.

LADY BRACKNELL. In the carriage, Gwendolen!

GWENDOLEN *goes to the door. She and* JACK *blow kisses to each other behind* LADY BRACKNELL'S *back.* LADY BRACKNELL *looks vaguely about as if she could not understand what the noise was. Finally turns round*

Gwendolen, the carriage!

GWENDOLEN. Yes, mamma.

Goes out, looking back at JACK

LADY BRACKNELL. *(sitting down)* You can take a seat, Mr Worthing. *(Looks in her pocket for note-book and pencil)*

JACK. Thank you, Lady Bracknell, I prefer standing.

⓬ **LADY BRACKNELL.** *(pencil and note-book in hand)* I feel bound to tell you that you are not down on my list of eligible young men, although I have the same list as the dear Duchess of Bolton has. We work together, in fact. However, I am quite ready to enter your name, should your answers be what a really affectionate mother requires. How old are you?

> **Literary Analysis**
> **Satire** Is Lady Bracknell truly "a really affectionate mother"? Explain.

JACK. Twenty-nine.

LADY BRACKNELL. A very good age to be married at. I have always been of opinion that a man who desires to get married should know either everything or nothing. Which do you know?

JACK. *(after some hesitation)* I know nothing, Lady Bracknell.

LADY BRACKNELL. I am pleased to hear it. I do not approve of anything that tampers with natural ignorance. **Ignorance** is like a delicate exotic fruit; touch it and the bloom is gone. The whole theory of modern education is radically unsound. Fortunately in England, at any rate, education produces no effect whatsoever. If it did, it would prove a serious danger to the upper classes, and probably lead to acts of violence in Grosvenor Square. What is your income?

> **Vocabulary**
> **ignorance** (ig′ nə rəns) *n.* lack of knowledge

JACK. Between seven and eight thousand a year.

LADY BRACKNELL. *(makes a note in her book)* In land, or in investments?

JACK. In investments, chiefly.

LADY BRACKNELL. That is satisfactory. What between the duties expected of one during one's lifetime, and the duties exacted from one after one's death, land has ceased to be either a profit or a pleasure. It gives one position, and prevents one from keeping it up. That's all that can be said about land.

> ⓭ ▶ **Critical Viewing** How do these actresses' portrayals of Lady Bracknell and Gwendolen compare to your mental image of the characters? **[Compare and Contrast]**

JACK. I have a country house with some land, of course, attached to it, about fifteen hundred acres, I believe; but I don't depend

Think Aloud

Vocabulary: Using Context

Direct students' attention to the word *reproachfully* at the bottom of page 991. Using a think-aloud process, model how to use context to infer the meaning of an unknown word. Say the following to students:

I'm going to think aloud to show you how I would figure out the meaning of *reproachfully* from its context.

The stage direction tells how Gwendolen says "Mamma!" Her expression is "full of reproach." Her mother is telling her to leave the room and wait in the carriage, which Gwendolen does not want to do. Gwendolen disapproves, but in the Victorian era, she would never dare show real anger toward her mother. So *reproachfully* must mean "expressing disapproval or blame."

on that for my real income. In fact, as far as I can make out, the poachers are the only people who make anything out of it.

14 **LADY BRACKNELL.** A country house! How many bedrooms? Well, that point can be cleared up afterwards. You have a town house, I hope? A girl with a simple, unspoiled nature, like Gwendolen, could hardly be expected to reside in the country.

JACK. Well, I own a house in Belgrave Square, but it is let by the year to Lady Bloxham. Of course, I can get it back whenever I like, at six months' notice.

LADY BRACKNELL. Lady Bloxham? I don't know her.

JACK. Oh, she goes about very little. She is a lady considerably advanced in years.

LADY BRACKNELL. Ah, nowadays that is no guarantee of respectability of character. What number in Belgrave Square?

JACK. 149.

LADY BRACKNELL. *(shaking her head)* The unfashionable side. I thought there was something. However, that could easily be altered.

JACK. Do you mean the fashion, or the side?

LADY BRACKNELL. *(sternly)* Both, if necessary, I presume. What are your politics?

JACK. Well, I am afraid I really have none. I am a Liberal Unionist.

LADY BRACKNELL. Oh, they count as Tories. They dine with us. Or come in the evening, at any rate. Now to minor matters. Are your parents living?

JACK. I have lost both my parents.

LADY BRACKNELL. Both? . . . That seems like carelessness. Who was your father?

Literary Analysis
Satire Does Gwendolen really have a "simple, unspoiled, nature"? Explain.

Spiral Review
Character What do you learn about Lady Bracknell's character from her comments about the house in Belgrave Square?

15

What kind of list does Lady Bracknell keep?

Differentiated Instruction for Universal Access

Strategy for Less Proficient Readers
Write the following questions on the board: *What does Jack try to do? What does Gwendolen expect Jack to do? Why is Lady Bracknell outraged?* Have students listen to the scene on the ***Hear It!* Audio CD (adapted text).** Pause the CD several times to allow students to answer the questions aloud.

Strategy for Gifted/Talented Students
Have students perform the excerpt or part of the excerpt. Encourage them to convey the comedy of manners with precise pronunciation and articulation. Remind them that the satire is effective because the characters are serious: Money, marriage, respectability, and social position are vital to them.

14 Literary Analysis

Satire

1. Read aloud the bracketed text, and point out that Lady Bracknell's comment about the country house is another of Wilde's humorous contradictions. Living in the country is usually associated with having a "simple, unspoiled nature."
2. **Ask** students the Literary Analysis question: Does Gwendolen really have a "simple, unspoiled nature"? Explain.

   Answer: No. Gwendolen is a more manipulative and calculating person than she says she is. She is wealthy, snobbish, and pampered, and she knows how to get Jack to do whatever she wants.
3. **Ask** students why Lady Bracknell's comment about Gwendolen is satiric.

   Answer: Gwendolen is far from simple. Wilde is satirizing the values and attitudes of Gwendolen and her mother. As representatives of their class, both are superficial and manipulative.

Spiral Review

Character

1. Remind students that they studied the concept of character in the Unit 5 Literary Analysis Workshop (pp. 780–797).
2. **Ask** students the Spiral Review question.

   Possible response: Her comments reveal that she is a snob who thinks she is very reasonable.

15 Reading Check

Answer: Lady Bracknell keeps a list of young men eligible to marry Gwendolen.

16 Literary Analysis
Satire

1. Have students read the first bracketed text. **Ask** the first Literary Analysis question: How does Jack's explanation of being "found" make fun of the Victorian value of proper lineage and family ties?

   Answer: Jack's "lineage" is unknown, and his very name is the result of chance, violating the established social order. Wilde reduces "lineage" to an absurd reliance on something ultimately arbitrary and irrelevant.

2. **Ask** students why Lady Bracknell is so disturbed by the handbag story.

   Answer: The appearance of social impropriety is what most disturbs Lady Bracknell.

3. **Ask:** What quality more important than lineage does Jack have?

   Answer: He has a strong and selfless love for Gwendolen.

17 Literary Analysis
Satire

1. Read the second bracketed text aloud. **Ask** students what Lady Bracknell's mention of the French Revolution reveals about her values.

   Answer: Lady Bracknell compares Jack's personal history to the overthrow of aristocratic values that accompanied the French Revolution. The exaggeration satirizes her lack of proportion in anything that has to do with manners and morals.

2. **Ask** students to respond to the second Literary Analysis prompt: Explain how Lady Bracknell's use of exaggeration adds to the satire.

   Answer: Her exaggerated concern for "ordinary decencies" and her elaborate, socially acceptable ways of talking about unacceptable matters satirize her society's fears and hypocrisies. Her words are as out of proportion as her values.

3. **Ask** students what Lady Bracknell most fears.

   Answer: She is terrified that society may think she is related in any way with a "social indiscretion."

He was evidently a man of some wealth. Was he born in what the Radical papers call the purple of commerce, or did he rise from the ranks of the aristocracy?

16

JACK. I am afraid I really don't know. The fact is, Lady Bracknell, I said I had lost my parents. It would be nearer the truth to say that my parents seem to have lost me. . . . I don't actually know who I am by birth. I was . . . well, I was found.

LADY BRACKNELL. Found!

Literary Analysis
Satire How does Jack's explanation of being "found" make fun of the Victorian value of proper lineage and family ties?

JACK. The late Mr Thomas Cardew, an old gentleman of a very charitable and kindly disposition, found me, and gave me the name of Worthing, because he happened to have a first-class ticket for Worthing in his pocket at the time. Worthing is a place in Sussex. It is a seaside resort.

LADY BRACKNELL. Where did the charitable gentleman who had a first-class ticket for this seaside resort find you?

JACK. *(gravely)* In a hand-bag.

LADY BRACKNELL. A hand-bag?

JACK. *(very seriously)* Yes, Lady Bracknell. I was in a hand-bag—a somewhat large, black leather handbag, with handles to it—an ordinary hand-bag in fact.

LADY BRACKNELL. In what locality did this Mr James, or Thomas, Cardew come across this ordinary hand-bag?

JACK. In the cloak-room at Victoria Station. It was given to him in mistake for his own.

LADY BRACKNELL. The cloak-room at Victoria Station?

JACK. Yes. The Brighton line.

Literary Analysis
Satire Explain how Lady Bracknell's use of exaggeration adds to the satire.

LADY BRACKNELL. The line is immaterial. Mr Worthing, I confess I feel somewhat bewildered by what you have just told me. To be born, or at any rate bred, in a hand-bag, whether it had handles or not, seems to me to display a contempt for the ordinary decencies of family life that reminds one of the worst excesses of the French Revolution. And I presume you know what that unfortunate movement led to? As for the particular locality in which the hand-bag was found, a cloak-room at a railway station might serve to conceal a social indiscretion—has probably, indeed, been used for that purpose before now—but it could hardly be regarded as an assured basis for a recognized position in good society.

JACK. May I ask you then what you would advise me to do? I need hardly say I would do anything in the world to ensure Gwendolen's happiness.

Vocabulary Development

CCSS Language 6

Word Forms

Expand students' vocabulary by helping them learn related forms of the selection vocabulary words. Give students a blank **Word Form Chart** (***Professional Development Guidebook***, p. 42), with *demonstrative* and *ignorance* in the correct columns. Work with the class, or have students work with a partner, to determine the related forms. The final chart should look like the one shown. Hold students accountable for integrating the related forms of the words into their speaking and writing.

Noun	Verb	Adjective	Adverb
demonstration	demonstrate	**demonstrative**	demonstratively
ignorance	ignore	ignorant	ignorantly

LADY BRACKNELL. I would strongly advise you, Mr Worthing, to try and acquire some relations as soon as possible, and to make a definite effort to produce at any rate one parent, of either sex, before the season is quite over.

JACK. Well, I don't see how I could possibly manage to do that. I can produce the hand-bag at any moment. It is in my dressing-room at home. I really think that should satisfy you, Lady Bracknell.

LADY BRACKNELL. Me, sir! What has it to do with me? You can hardly imagine that I and Lord Bracknell would dream of allowing our only daughter—a girl brought up with the utmost care—to marry into a cloak-room, and form an alliance with a parcel? Good morning, Mr Worthing!

Lady Bracknell sweeps out in majestic indignation

JACK. Good morning! (ALGERNON, *from the other room, strikes up the Wedding March.* JACK *looks perfectly furious, and goes to the door*) For goodness' sake don't play that ghastly tune, Algy! How idiotic you are!

Literary Analysis
Satire How does Lady Bracknell's final demand add to the satire?

Critical Thinking

Cite textual evidence to support your responses.

1. **Key Ideas and Details** **(a)** How does Gwendolen respond to Jack's proposal? **(b) Infer:** How would you describe Gwendolen's feelings for Jack?
2. **Key Ideas and Details** **(a)** According to Lady Bracknell, how should a young girl learn she is engaged? **(b) Infer:** What do Lady Bracknell's remarks suggest about Victorian attitudes toward marriage and family?
3. **Key Ideas and Details** **(a) Summarize:** Write a summary of the personal information that Lady Bracknell needs from Jack. **(b) Interpret:** In what ways does Lady Bracknell find Jack both acceptable and unacceptable as a possible husband? **(c) Assess:** Based on her judgment of Jack, describe Lady Bracknell's character.
4. **Integration of Knowledge and Ideas** **(a) Interpret:** What values does Lady Bracknell hold dear? Explain. **(b) Compare and Contrast:** How do you think Lady Bracknell's values compare to the values of most people today?
5. **Integration of Knowledge and Ideas** **(a)** Which qualities in Jack are most important to Gwendolen and her mother? **(b)** What do you think the author suggests is more important than these differences? Support your answer. *[Connect to the Big Question: Do our differences define us?]*

Differentiated Instruction for Universal Access

Culturally Responsive Instruction
Culture Focus Lady Bracknell will not accept Jack for her daughter without knowing his parents. Customs about parental roles in approving marriages vary from culture to culture. Have students describe these roles in their home culture or family's country of origin. Discuss ways in which these roles have changed over time, as they have in America and England.

18 Literary Analysis

Satire

Ask the Literary Analysis question.

Answer: Lady Bracknell's demand emphasizes her belief that appearances matter most.

Concept Connector

Have students return to the Activating Prior Knowledge activity and revise or verify their predictions. Then, have them compare their Writing About the Big Question responses before reading with their ideas afterwards.

ASSESS

Answers

Critical Thinking

Before students respond, you may wish to have them write a brief objective summary of the selection. As they answer the questions below, remind them to support their answers with evidence from the text.

1. (a) Gwendolen accepts Jack even before he proposes. (b) She seems to like Jack, although her feelings are clearly colored by her odd infatuation with his false name and presumed money.
2. (a) Her mother or father should inform her. (b) **Possible response:** The remarks indicate the fierce Victorian faith in marriage and family.
3. (a) She wants to know his age, what he knows, his income, property, politics, and parents. (b) Jack's answers are acceptable, except the tale of his parentage. (c) Her rejection of Jack shows her dependence on rules of propriety.
4. (a) She values money, property, propriety, and appearance. (b) **Possible response:** Today, social class has less significance, but money's influence is still great.
5. **Possible responses:** (a) Gwendolen values Jack's confidence. Her mother values Jack's social status. (b) Wilde suggests that a person's character is most important.

19 Background

Big Kiss The title of Alford's book comes from an adventure in self-promotion. To get publicity as an aspiring actor, he tries to persuade owners of Manhattan delicatessens to hang his photo among all the other celebrity photos. He offers to write the words "Big Kiss!" on it, suggesting a personal relationship that does not exist. His plan fails. He is more successful working as an extra in *Godzilla,* the 1998 remake of the Japanese classic, directed by Roland Emmerich and starring Matthew Broderick.

20 Activating Prior Knowledge

Ask students whether they would like to appear in a Hollywood movie. Have them describe ways to break into the movie business. **Ask:** What kind of movie would you like to be in? Why? What kinds of characters would you like to play? What training might you need?

Concept Connector →

Students will follow up on this activity after reading the selection.

21 About the Selection

In this excerpt from *Big Kiss,* Alford, a young actor, takes a job as an extra in the remake of *Godzilla.* Working on location, he waits with hundreds of other extras and longs for a line of dialogue. Although this doesn't happen, he enjoys the long, arduous day of shooting the same scene twenty times, pretending to run from the monster, and watching the outrageous performances of all the other extras—who just as desperately try to expand their tiny roles.

22 Literary Analysis

Satire

1. Point out that Alford says that he is "no stranger to adverse meteorological conditions" and can "play wet." **Ask** students why such language has a satiric effect.

   Answer: Alford's high-flown, flowery language makes fun of extras who inflate their roles.

2. **Ask** the Literary Analysis question: Which details make Alford's role as an extra sound important?

   Answer: He mentions the "prodigious" rain, his ability to "play wet," and needing to "be available all day and night."

19 20 21

In the acting profession, as in life, you must make the most of your tiny allotment. He who waits until he has been cast as Othello to pull out all the stops is setting himself up for disappointment—it will be Othello, not Desdemona,[1] who is strangled in this production. So when a classmate told me she was helping to cast extras for the remake of *Godzilla,* I quickly recommended myself for duty. I clearly had not slayed them at improv camp in Wisconsin; here was an opportunity to channel my feelings of disappointment into bravura acting. And perhaps, in so doing, to achieve every extra's dream: to be awarded a line of dialogue.

Literary Analysis
Satire Which details make Alford's role as an extra sound important?

22 My classmate called me two days later and said that the filming, to be done that Sunday, would involve prodigious amounts of stage rain. I assured her that I was no stranger to adverse meteorological conditions, natural and man-made, and, as such, could "play wet." The pay for non-Screen Actors Guild[2] talent was seventy-five dollars; I needed to be available all day and night. I was to wear a raincoat and carry a black umbrella.

The harbinger[3] of location shooting in a metropolitan area is a table on the sidewalk, heaped high with haggard bagels. When

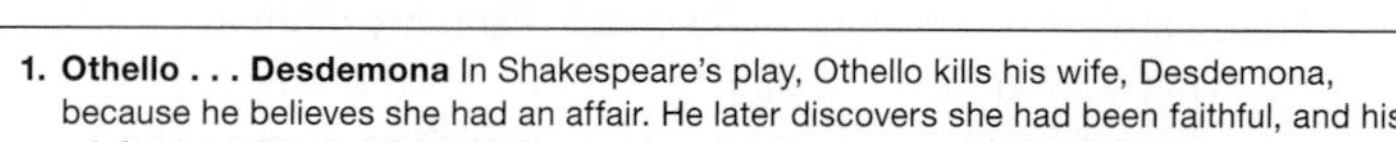

1. **Othello . . . Desdemona** In Shakespeare's play, Othello kills his wife, Desdemona, because he believes she had an affair. He later discovers she had been faithful, and his grief causes him to kill himself.
2. **Screen Actors Guild** (SAG) labor union for performers.
3. **harbinger** (här′ bin jər) *n.* something that comes before to give an indication of what follows.

Text Complexity Rubric

from The Big Kiss		
Qualitative Measures	**Context/ Knowledge Demands**	First-person report on being a movie extra 1 (2) 3 4 5
	Structure/ Language Clarity and Conventionality	Contemporary language; some comically pretentious vocabulary 1 2 (3) 4 5
	Levels of Meaning/ Purpose/Concept Level	Accessible concept (fun and frustration of trying to be a movie actor) 1 2 (3) 4 5
Quantitative Measures	**Text Length**	Word Count: 1,469
	Lexile	1090L

I arrived at the appointed location in the Financial District that Sunday morning at six-thirty, although the chaos I found there—Teamsters[4] bickering over sports scores, thick black cables veining the streets as if to depict the late stages of arteriosclerosis—had all the earmarks of filmmaking, I did not see the telltale breadstuffs and so was moved to ask the first walkie-talkie-wielding individual I saw, "Where are the bagels?"

"Are you SAG or non-SAG?" she asked.

"Non."

"You're in the tent."

She pointed to a huge, dun-colored tent around which loitered hundreds of men and women, many of whom were also wearing raincoats and carrying umbrellas. "My people," I exclaimed. I walked over to the tent and, seeing a line formed at one of the twenty or so tables thereunder, queued up. Four minutes later the casting people had checked my name off on a list and I had been given a voucher, the form by which I would be paid.

All was actor-clogged; I could barely find an empty seat at a table. I was glad I finally did—we proceeded to wait for two hours. During this time, small groups of us were presented to a young, unshaven man from Wardrobe who was, by turns, exhausted and sniffy. He looked at the camouflage cap that the fortysomething gentleman ahead of me in line was wearing and said, "I don't know anyone who would wear that cap." Then he scanned me—that is to say, my tan raincoat, my black umbrella, and my wingtips encased in black rubbers—and yawned, "You're fine."

23 Shortly thereafter we were herded down to the set in groups of thirty or forty. The set was Federal Hall, the majestic site of George Washington's inauguration, rich in Corinthian columns and impressive stairways, which dead-ends Broad Street in the manner of a lion's gaping jaws. Halfway up its main stairs was a podium, festooned with red, white, and blue bunting and a sign reading RE-ELECT MAYOR EBERT. I wondered aloud, "Where's the reptile?"

The self-appointed expert in my group explained, "They're gonna blue-screen[5] him in later."

We lined up on the sidewalk and then, one by one, walked through a small, cordoned-off area where a sweet, pale, bespectacled man was handing out props. It looked like about a third of the extras were being given still cameras and two thirds were being given placards reading RE-ELECT EBERT.

"I hope I get a camera," the woman standing behind me in line said.

4. **Teamsters** (tēm′ stərz) *n.* members of a large labor union for truck drivers and other occupations.

5. **blue-screen** *v.* film against a blue background, in order to apply special effects later.

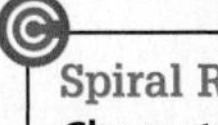

Spiral Review

Character What do the details in this paragraph reveal about the narrator?

Literary Analysis

Satire What does the word "herded" convey about the experience of extras?

24 Reading Check

What instructions does Alford's friend give him?

Spiral Review

Character

1. Remind students that they studied the concept of character in the Unit 5 Literary Analysis Workshop (pp. 780–797).
2. **Ask** students the Spiral Review question.

   Possible response: The details the narrator includes indicate he thinks he is above the other people working on the set. His attitude about the other extras and the man from wardrobe are dismissive and condescending.

23 Literary Analysis

Satire

1. Read the bracketed text aloud. Point out that hundreds of people are waiting in the tent with Alford. Then, **ask** the Literary Analysis question: What does the word "herded" convey about the experience of extras?

   Answer: "Herded" conveys the impression that the extras are a mass of undifferentiated animals, not the individual actors they want to be.
2. **Ask** students what the word "herded" adds to the satire.

   Answer: The word is a way in which Alford deflates both his own pretensions of stardom and those of the other extras.

24 Reading Check

Answer: He needed to be available all day and night and was to wear a raincoat and carry a black umbrella.

PHLit Online!

This selection is available in interactive format in the **Enriched Online Student Edition, www.PHLitOnline.com,** which includes an interactive graphic organizer.

Text Complexity: Reader and Task Suggestions

***from* The Big Kiss**

Preparing to Read the Text	Leveled Tasks
• Refer to the Background information on TE p. 996 and discuss the difficult process of becoming an actor. Clarify the work of an extra and discuss why people compete to get these jobs. • Review the use of context clues to figure out the meaning of unfamiliar words. • Guide students to use Multidraft Reading strategies (TE p. 987).	*Levels of Meaning* If students will have difficulty with the meaning, have them first read and note the sequence of events the author reports on. Then, have students reread the text and take notes on the author's attitude as he tells the story. *Analyzing* If students will not have difficulty with the meaning, have them read and note examples of the author's use of language to evoke humor. Encourage them to share examples of humorous language.

㉕ Critical Viewing

Answer: The extras in this scene help to provide a sense of physical scale, an atmosphere of terror, and the drama of human lives in jeopardy.

㉖ Literary Analysis

Satire

1. Have students read the bracketed text. **Ask** why the camera is taken away from Alford.

   Answer: The assistant director needs the prop for another extra in the front of the crowd.
2. Point out that the prop might have been taken away from someone else. Alford happened to be chosen, probably because of where he was standing. Chance—not talent or character—determined his role.
3. **Ask** students to respond to the Literary Analysis prompt: Explain the satire in Alford's reaction when the assistant director takes his camera.

   Answer: Alford says that he based his "character interpretation" on the presence of the camera, but he really does not have a character to interpret. The satire again pokes fun at the pretensions of an aspiring actor.

㉗ Connecting to the Big Question

1. Remind students of the Big Question by asking if their birthdays are in spring or fall. Point out there is always a way to divide people.
2. Direct students' attention to the bracketed text. **Ask:** How are those with January–April birthdays different from those with May–August birthdays?

   Answer: Each group responds to Godzilla differently.
3. **Ask:** Is birth date an acceptable way to define differences? Explain.

   Possible response: Yes; The director needs to make groups. This division is practical, but never values one group over another.

25

▼ **Critical Viewing** How do the "extras" in this image from the movie *Godzilla* help increase the impact of the scene? **[Analyze]**

Eager to be filmed shooting at Godzilla, I responded, "I hope I get a Taser."

Moments later I was handed three props—a fake 35-millimeter camera, a fanny pack, and a press badge. I looked at the badge. The first thing I noticed was that the photo on it was of the man who had just handed it to me. Hovering over the photo was the name Sean Haworth and the call letters WAQR. These call letters sounded more like radio than TV to me; but then why was I carrying a still camera?

Rather than let this seeming contradiction bother me, I decided to base my character interpretation on it. What if Sean Haworth labored under the impression that if he took a good enough photograph it would be aired on the radio? Wouldn't this, character-wise, raise the stakes, and imbue him with the driven quality that makes for an interesting dramatic character? Poor Sean, you can almost hear the editorial staff at WAQR whispering over the water cooler. If only he understood that ours is an aural medium.

Literary Analysis
Satire Explain the satire in Alford's reaction when the assistant director takes his camera.

26

But five minutes later an assistant director who had assembled about a hundred of us in front of Federal Hall took away my camera.

"I based my character interpretation on that!" I exclaimed, hoping that this would translate to him as "Serious actor. Could handle a line of dialogue."

"I need it for up front," he reported tersely, then walked to the front of the crowd.

One of my fellow colleagues—a vivacious English as a Second Language tutor and sometime actress in her early thirties with whom I had fallen into conversation back in the tent—witnessed my loss of camera and counseled, "You were probably overpropped anyway."

"Yes," I responded, "my work was getting proppy."

27

We proceeded to work for almost eleven hours, lunch break included, on variations of a single shot. In it, about four hundred of us New Yorkers are standing in the rain, listening to Mayor Ebert (Michael Lerner) give a speech. All of a sudden, we hear a thump. Some of the crowd—those born between January and April, to be precise—look behind them, down Broad Street, whence the sound originates. The mayor continues to netter on when thump! May through August now look down the street, too, expressing restlessness, a sense of discomfort, the vague possibility that this little piece of earth they call their own will soon be rent asunder.

Vocabulary Development

CCSS Language 6

Thematic Vocabulary: The Big Question

As students are discussing the excerpt from *Big Kiss,* encourage them to use the thematic vocabulary presented in Introducing the Big Question, pp. 778–779. You might encourage them with sentence starters like these:

1. The author is part of the film *culture* that . . .
2. Henry Alford doesn't try to *defend* his . . .
3. Instead, he thinks of his desire to be an "extra" as a *unique* . . .
4. At the movie shoot, Henry notices the *similarity* between . . .
5. Each movie extra strives to *differentiate* him- or herself from . . .

28 LITERATURE IN CONTEXT

Take 1
Tyrannosaurus
skeleton
Add 1
Chinese dragon
Mix in a pinch
of crocodile
Raise the heat.
Serve with a heaping
portion of special effects.

Media Connection

Recipe for a Monster

He's big, he's green, he's mean, and his breath is radioactive. Godzilla—named "Gojira" in his native Japan—has been stomping on Tokyo since 1954, when he made his movie debut. A dinosaur transformed into a giant monster as the result of atomic testing, Godzilla's appearance was created by scientists and sculptors using the ingredients below.

Connect to the Literature How do you think Alford's performance might have changed if Godzilla had been played by an actor instead of being a special effect?

Then seconds later a third THUMP!: Godzilla appears, causing the crowd, regardless of natal season, to shriek with abandon, perhaps to drop umbrellas or placards, and to run off in a prescribed direction.

Since I was born in February, my prescribed direction was straight ahead, up the thirty or so stairs of Federal Hall. So, hearing my thump, I would look behind me down Broad Street in highly nuanced, ever-burgeoning panic; erupt into a despair-tinged, Edvard Munch-calibre scream[6] on hearing the third thump; run northward, negotiating my way through what was, by now, a very festival of bad acting; ascend the stairs two at a time; look behind me again while closing my umbrella (note the elegant adherence to decorum, even in the face of apocalypse); and then hurl my body against Federal Hall's massive stone doors in an attempt to gain entry.

I loved this work. I would be hard-pressed to recount any event from my personal or professional life that more accurately typified the phrase crazy fun. Yes, my colleagues and I encountered much wetness; the rain machines were **assiduous** in their ministrations. Moreover, no lines of dialogue were being doled out by the director

6. **Edvard Munch-calibre scream** an outcry with the intensity of *The Scream*, a famous painting by Norwegian artist Edvard Munch [munk] (1863–1944), which shows a person screaming.

Vocabulary
assiduous (ə sij′ o͞o əs) *adj.* done with constant and careful attention

29 
Reading Check

How do the film-makers divide the crowd of extras into groups?

28 Literature in Context

Media Connection In *Big Kiss*, Alford's task is to respond to an invisible monster and the filmmakers will "blue-screen him in later." However, blue-screen acting takes skill and practice, and film schools offer courses in how to do it. To improve their believability, acting students learn to focus their eyes and concentrate on simulated objects and actions. They learn to make their imagined perceptions more physically evident to the audience. With the recent growth in computer-generated imagery, some movies—such as *Sky Captain and the World of Tomorrow* (2004)—now combine actors and *entirely* computer-generated backgrounds. As a result, skilled blue-screen actors are more and more in demand.

Connect to the Literature Have students read the Literature in Context feature, and present the additional background information above. Discuss the pros and cons of having an actor in a costume play Godzilla versus using a special effect. Then, **ask** the Connect to the Literature question: How do you think Alford's performance might have changed if Godzilla had been played by an actor instead of being a special effect?

Possible responses: Alford's performance might have been more realistic if he had been able to respond to a physically present monster. However, it may have been more difficult for him to portray genuine terror in the face of a man in a rubber suit.

29 Reading Check

Answer: The people in the crowd are divided according to when they were born.

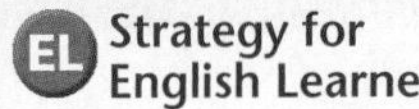

Differentiated Instruction for Universal Access

EL Strategy for English Learners

Model the movements of the crowd of extras, according to Alford's description, then have students repeat. Explain that they will react to the thumping sound according to when they were born. Then, have them form a group and turn, look, exclaim, and run from the monster in different directions—according to when they were born.

Strategy for Less Proficient Readers

Students may have some difficulty picking up on the humorous tone and satiric intent of some of Alford's lines. Focus on the following lines to help them hear Alford's self-mocking tone and recognize the satire:

"My people," I exclaimed.
"I hope I get a Taser."
"My work was getting proppy."
"Zilla monster ate me baby!"

30 Literary Analysis

Satire

1. Read the bracketed text aloud. **Ask** the Literary Analysis question: How do the extras' hopes to be noticed compare to their actual experiences? Explain.
   Answer: The extras hope they will be picked out of the crowd, but they are all reduced to anonymous figures in the rain.

Concept Connector

Ask students to revisit their answers to the questions posed in the Activating Prior Knowledge activity. Discuss whether students' opinions about appearing in a movie have changed since reading the excerpt. In addition, have students compare their Writing About the Big Question responses before reading the selection with their ideas afterwards.

ASSESS

Answers

Critical Thinking

Before students respond, you may wish to have them write a brief objective summary of the selection. As they answer the questions below, remind them to support their answers with evidence from the text.

1. (a) Every extra's dream is to be awarded a line of dialogue. (b) **Possible response:** Alford seems to feel his experience was worthwhile because at least he worked in a movie and learned something about himself and the people who work as extras.
2. (a) Alford and the other extras are supposed to look around, shriek, and run away. (b) Many engage in "scenery chewing," some run directly at the camera, and one repeatedly drops and retrieves her prop. (c) They want to be noticed.
3. **Possible responses:** (a) Some extras drop their props, scream loudly, or look directly at the camera. (b) Someone in charge takes away a prop or puts the extras in a place where they aren't as visible. (c) He's making fun of everyone, including himself, for their desperate wish to be in a film, even as an extra.

or assistant directors. But the acting task at hand wedded blitzkrieg-strength drama with stuntman-strength athleticism and, as such, was wholly engaging. Screaming at full force in the canyons of Wall Street on a Sunday morning was particularly liberating. On the first few takes (by the end of the day we would do more than twenty) I would yell, "There he is!" By the eighth take I was screaming, "Here comes trouble!" By the late afternoon, punchy, I was shrieking, in an accent vaguely Caribbean, vaguely Cockney, "'Zilla monster ate me baby!" causing the self-appointed expert to glare at me and say, "Let's keep it real, huh?"

Literary Analysis
Satire How do the extras' hopes to be noticed compare to their actual experiences? Explain.

30 This statement might have chastened were it not for the other extras. Seldom have I seen such a preponderance of scenery-chewing; my colleagues' every utterance and movement seemed to offer ready proof that vaudeville[7] is not dead. Several of the extras, in an attempt to make themselves noticed, would run directly at the camera. Another one, a tall, fiftysomething woman who appeared to be a recent graduate of the Lucille Ball School of Clown Makeup, made such a spectacle of repeatedly dropping and then retrieving her umbrella that an assistant director was forced to take the umbrella away from her; the woman, divested of her gimmick, then devoted her energies to shrieking.

"That woman just screamed right in my eardrum," the ESL tutor told me between takes, motioning with her head toward the offender.

"Yes," I acknowledged, "her work is particularly broad."

7. **vaudeville** (vôd´ vil) old-fashioned stage shows of mixed specialty acts, including songs, dances, and comic skits.

Critical Thinking

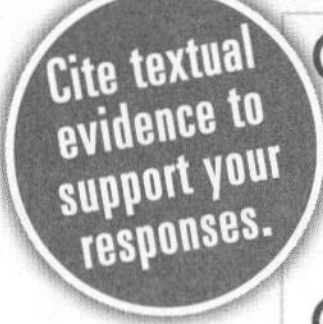

Cite textual evidence to support your responses.

1. **Key Ideas and Details** **(a)** According to Alford's opening paragraph, what is every extra's dream? **(b) Analyze:** Even though his dream does not come true, does he still feel his experience was worthwhile? Explain.
2. **Key Ideas and Details** **(a)** What are Alford and the other extras required to do during the scene? **(b) Generalize:** What do they actually do? **(c) Analyze:** Why do they do so much more than required?
3. **Integration of Knowledge and Ideas** **(a)** What tricks do the extras try to make themselves "different" for the camera? **(b)** How do these tricks backfire? **(c)** What or whom do you think the author is mocking, or making fun of? Explain. *[Connect to the Big Question: Do our differences define us?]*

Vocabulary Development

Vocabulary Knowledge Rating

When students have completed reading and discussing the excerpts from *The Importance of Being Earnest* and *Big Kiss,* have them take out their **Vocabulary Knowledge Rating Chart.** Read the words aloud once more and have students rate their knowledge of the words again in the After Reading column. Clarify any words that are still problematic. Have students write their own definition and example or sentence in the appropriate column. Then, have students complete the Vocabulary Practice activities on the next page. Encourage students to use the words in further discussion and written work about the selections. Remind them that they will be accountable for these words on the **Selection Test** (*Unit 5 Resources,* pp. 175–177 or 178–180).

After You Read

from The Importance of Being Earnest • *from* Big Kiss

Comparing Satire

1. **Craft and Structure** **(a)** Use a chart like the one shown to identify elements of satire in both *The Importance of Being Earnest* and *Big Kiss*. **(b)** Explain specific ways in which both selections use humor to expose people's foolishness or flaws.

Selection	Subject of the Satire	Foolishness or Faults Exposed	Author's Tone or Attitude
The Importance of Being Earnest			
Big Kiss			

2. **Integration of Knowledge and Ideas** **(a)** Which selection satirizes serious social issues, and which one satirizes trivial or light-hearted issues? **(b)** Which selection is harsher toward the people it satirizes? Explain.

Timed Writing

Explanatory Text: Essay

The perspective, or vantage point, of the writer helps shape the satire. In *The Importance of Being Earnest,* Wilde is not part of the events he satirizes. In the excerpt from *The Big Kiss,* Alford is a participant in the action. In an essay, discuss how these different perspectives affect the satire. **(35 minutes)**

5-Minute Planner

1. Read the prompt carefully and completely.
2. Note your answers to the following questions:
   - What purpose do you think Wilde had in writing this play about Victorian society?
   - What subtle hints in the text reveal Wilde's view of his characters?
   - Does Alford's point of view make him more or less sympathetic to the other actors he satirizes?
   - How do Alford's inner thoughts add to the humor of the satire?
   - Which text clues suggest Alford's level of seriousness about his topic?
   - Which satire do you think is more successful? Why?
3. Reread the prompt. Then, refer to your notes and draft your essay.

Assessment Resources

Unit 5 Resources

L1 L2 EL **Selection Test A,** pp. 175–177.

L3 L4 EL **Selection Test B,** pp. 178–180.

L3 L4 **Open Book Test,** pp. 172–174.

All assessment resources are available at **www.PHLitOnline.com.**

ASSESS

Answers

Comparing Satire

1. (a) ***The Importance of Being Earnest*—Subject:** Victorian high society. **Faults:** Excessive value of manners and status. **Tone:** Humorous with a serious undertone. ***Big Kiss*—Subject:** Hollywood extras. **Faults:** Self-importance and self-promotion. **Tone:** Humorous and sympathetic.

   Other sample answers appear in ***Graphic Organizer Transparencies,* Comparing Satire Graphic Organizer A** (After You Read), p. 178, and in the **Additional Answers** section.

   (b) Wilde's humor includes Gwendolen's fixation with the name "Ernest," Jack's handbag "lineage," and Lady Bracknell's ridiculous questions. Alford's humor includes the extras' scenery chewing and the absurdity of his developing a character when he is one of many anonymous figures.
2. (a) *Earnest* targets the Victorians' restrictive values. Alford's target is more trivial—the excesses of movie extras. (b) *Earnest* is harsher in its satire, exposing the folly of judging people based on wealth, status, and lineage.

Timed Writing

1. Review the prompt with students.
2. Have students use the 5-Minute Planner to structure their time. Guide them in answering the bulleted questions. For example, have them recall specific details of the settings and characters in the two works.
3. Allow students 35 minutes to complete the assignment.
4. As students prewrite and draft, have them refer to the selection comparison organizer.

Six Traits Focus

✓	Ideas		Word Choice
✓	Organization		Sentence Fluency
	Voice		Conventions

PREACH

Common Core State Standards

- Writing 5, 6, 7, 8
- Language 1.b; 3.a

Introducing the Writing Assignment

Review the assignment and the criteria, using the instruction on the student page.

Gary L. Blackwood on Research

Show students Segment 3 on Gary L. Blackwood on the ***See It!*** **DVD** or from this page in the **Enriched Online Student Edition**, at **www.PHLitOnline.com.** Discuss the value of primary and secondary sources in research writing.

Writing Workshop
Work in Progress

If students have done the Work-in-Progress assignment on p. 977, suggest that they examine their recorded ideas as they begin prewriting. They may wish to consider developing their Work-In-Progress ideas in a research report.

What Do You Notice?

1. Read the passage aloud.
2. **Ask:** What do you notice? **Possible response:** The passage describes FDR's reaction to polio.
3. Point out that Axelrod uses examples to support his thesis that FDR faced polio with courage.
4. **Ask:** What example does Axelrod provide when he repeats *chose*? **Possible response:** FDR could have chosen to give in, but chose instead a more courageous path.
5. Urge students to use strong examples to support their research report theses.

Writing Workshop

Write an Informative Text

Research Writing: Research Report

Defining the Form A **research report** presents and interprets information gathered through the extensive study of a subject. You might use elements of a research report in writing lab reports, documentaries, annotated bibliographies, histories, and persuasive essays.

Assignment Write a research report on a subject that is both interesting and worth exploring in depth. Include these elements:

✓ a *thesis statement* that is clearly expressed

✓ *factual support* from a variety of reliable, credited sources

✓ a *clear organization* that includes an *introduction, a body,* and a *conclusion*

✓ a *bibliography* or *works-cited list* that provides a complete listing of research sources formatted in an approved style.

✓ error-free grammar, including use of *adverb clauses*

To preview the criteria on which your report may be judged, see the rubric on page 1013.

Writing Workshop: *Work in Progress*

Review the work you did on page 977.

WRITE GUY
Jeff Anderson, M.Ed.

What Do You Notice?

Examples that Build an Argument

This excerpt is from Alan Axelrod's historical research study *Nothing To Fear: Lessons in Leadership from FDR.* Read it several times.

He could then and there have given in to the fog of fear, but he chose not to. He chose instead to understand polio, to see clearly the extent of his disability, and then to assess—also clearly—his options for overcoming that disability.

What do you notice about these sentences? Discuss your observations with a partner. Consider how you can use examples to build an argument in your research report.

Common Core State Standards

Writing

5. Develop and strengthen writing as needed by planning, revising, editing, rewriting, or trying a new approach, focusing on addressing what is most significant for a specific purpose and audience.

7. Conduct short as well as more sustained research projects to answer a question (including a self-generated question) or solve a problem; narrow or broaden the inquiry when appropriate.

8. Gather relevant information from multiple authoritative print and digital sources, using advanced searches effectively; assess the usefulness of each source in answering the research question.

Reading-Writing Connection

To get a feel for research writing, read the selection from *Nothing To Fear* by Alan Axelrod on page 567.

Teaching Resources

The following resources can be used to enrich or extend the instruction.

All *Unit 5 Resources*
Writing Workshop, pp. 181, 182

All *Common Core Companion,*
pp. 220–254

All *Professional Development Guidebook*
Rubrics for Self-Assessment: Research Report, pp. 242–243

All *Graphic Organizer Transparencies*
Rubric for Self-Assessment: Research Report, p. 180

All *See It!* DVD
Gary L. Blackwood, Segments 3 and 4

All resources, including print and video, are also available at **www.PHLitOnline.com.**

Prewriting/Planning Strategies

Brainstorm for categories. Identify an area of general interest and list specific related categories. For example, from the area of art, you might list sculpture, painting, and ceramics. Repeat the process: from painting, you might list Impressionism, Cubism, and Pop Art. Continue listing categories until you find a topic to research.

Review notebooks. Flip through the notebooks you keep for each class in school to find subjects or ideas that spark your interest. Choose one of these as the topic of your research paper.

Identify an open-ended research question. Before you begin, compose a question about your topic. This question may become your thesis statement, or it may lead up to it. The question will also help focus your research into a comprehensive but flexible search plan, as well as prevent you from gathering details that are too broad for your purpose. As you continue to learn more about your topic as you research, you may find it necessary to change, refocus, or adapt your original question.

Question: *How did the Impressionist school of painting begin?*

PHLit Online!
www.PHLitOnline.com
- Author video: Writing Process
- Author video: Rewards of Writing

Gathering Details Through Research

Use a variety of primary and secondary sources. To get a full view of your topic, use *primary sources* (firsthand or original accounts, such as interview transcripts and newspaper articles) and *secondary sources* (accounts that are not original, such as encyclopedia entries).

Find appropriate sources. Analyze and apply evaluative criteria to assess that your sources are appropriate to the purpose of your report and your audience. You may find the information you need to answer your research question in specialized and authoritative resources, such as almanacs (for social, cultural, and natural statistics), government publications (for law, government programs, and subjects such as agriculture), and information services. Also, consider consumer, workplace, and public documents. Consult your librarian on the best sources to use. You can find sources of specific information through an online search, a card catalog, or by using more advanced tools:

- **Databases:** Access databases of information to find appropriate sources. For example, the Modern Language Association (MLA) database indexes articles on topics within the humanities.
- **Indexes:** Locate magazine or newspaper articles by consulting the *Readers' Guide to Periodical Literature.*

TEACH

Prewriting Strategies

1. Introduce the prewriting strategies, using the instruction on the student page.
2. Have students apply the strategies to choose a topic.

Teaching the Strategies

1. Help students choose a topic for their reports by suggesting they choose something from a list of things that interest them, such as people, careers, conflicts, historical events, and so on.
2. Provide students with a copy of a KWL chart in ***Professional Development Guidebook***, p. 75. Tell students to identify a research question to narrow their topics by filling out the first two columns of the KWL chart. In the first column, have them list topics that they know something about. In the second column, have them write several questions they have about the topics. For instance, if they are interested in NASCAR, one of their questions might be, "How and when did NASCAR get started?" Tell students to choose the question that they are most interested in. Students may wish to complete the KWL chart after they write.

Gathering Details Through Research

1. Introduce the strategies, using the instruction on the student page.
2. Have students apply the strategies as they conduct research.

Prentice Hall EssayScorer

A writing prompt for this mode of writing can be found on the ***Prentice Hall Essay Scorer*** at **www.PHLitOnline.com.**

Applying Understanding by Design Principles

Clarifying Expected Outcomes: Using Rubrics

- Before students begin working on this assignment, have them preview the Rubric for Self-Assessment (p. 1013) to learn what qualities their reports must have. A copy of this rubric appears in ***Graphic Organizer Transparencies,*** p. 180.
- Review the criteria in the Rubric with the class. Before students use the Rubric to assess their writing, work with them to rate the Student Model (pp. 1010–1012) using the Rubric.
- If you wish to assess students' reports with either a 4-point or a 6-point scoring rubric, see ***Professional Development Guidebook,*** pp. 242–243.

Gathering Details Through Research *(cont.)*

Teaching the Strategies

1. As students are gathering details, remind them that some Internet sites provide unreliable and undocumented information. Tell students that *.gov, .edu* and *.org* websites are generally more reliable than *.com* websites.
2. Contact a librarian and arrange for students to go on a guided library tour. Have the librarian point out to students where and how they can find information, such as how to gain access to database indexes and where they can find periodicals. Make sure that the librarian shows students the types of information that each source presents. Encourage students to ask the librarian questions.

Think Aloud: Model Questioning Your Sources

Model the strategy, using the following "think aloud":

I want to be sure that the information I find is valid, so I'm going to be careful about the Web sites I select. I know that Web addresses ending with *.edu* are college or university sites and those ending with *.gov* are government sites. Web addresses ending with *.org* are usually nonprofit organizations' Web sites. I know I can trust these three types of Web sites to provide reliable information. I'll also trust my instincts. If a Web site has a lot of flashy ads, seems poorly written, or contains information that I suspect is inaccurate, I'll steer clear of that site.

Six Traits Focus

✔	Ideas		Word Choice
	Organization		Sentence Fluency
	Voice		Conventions

Writing and Grammar Interactive Textbook Online

Students can use the following tools at **www.pearsonsuccessnet.com** as they complete their research reports:

- Considering Your Audience and Purpose (Section 12.2)
- Write an Outline (Section 12.3)
- Revision Checkers: Language Variety (Drop-down Menu)

Gathering Details Through Research *(continued)*

Question your sources. As you locate information, choose sources representing a variety of viewpoints. If you find information you do not trust, consult a second source to verify its validity.

Record and organize information. Take notes as you locate and connect pertinent information from multiple sources, and keep a reference list of every source you use. This will help you to make distinctions between the relative value and significance of specific data, facts, and ideas.

- **Source Cards:** Create a card that identifies the author, title, publisher, city, date of publication, and page number of each source you consult. For Internet sources, record the name and Web address of the site, and the date you accessed the information.
- **Note cards:** For each item of information, create a separate note card that includes both the fact or idea and its source.

Quote accurately. Responsible research begins with the first note you take. Be sure to quote and paraphrase your sources accurately so you can identify these sources later. In your notes, circle all quotations and paraphrases to distinguish them from your own comments. When photocopying from a source, include the copyright information. Also, remember to include the Web addresses of printouts from online sources.

Sample *Readers' Guide* Entry

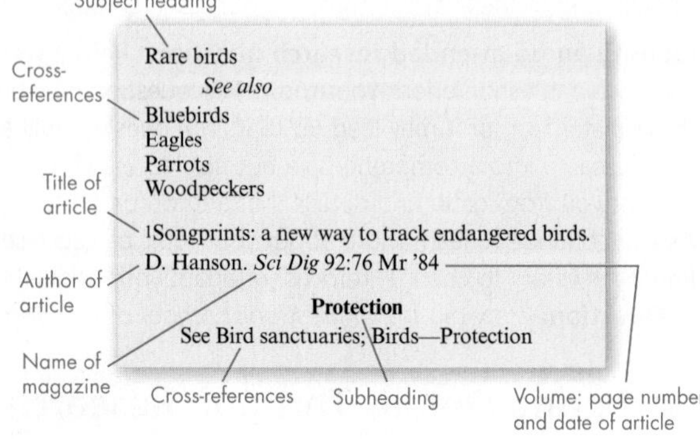

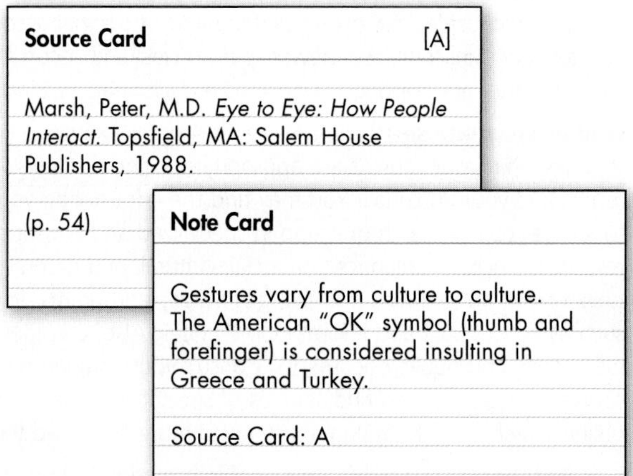

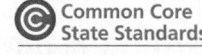

Common Core State Standards

Writing

7. Synthesize multiple sources on the subject, demonstrating understanding of the subject under investigation.

8. Gather relevant information from multiple authoritative print and digital sources; integrate information into the text selectively, avoiding plagiarism and following a standard format for citation.

Drafting Strategies

Propose a thesis statement. Write a sentence that takes a position and can be supported by most of your research. A thesis statement is a controlling idea that gives your essay coherence.

- **Sample Thesis Statement:** *Claude Monet's use of light in his water lily paintings typifies Impressionist techniques.*

Choose a text structure. Use your thesis statement and knowledge of your audience to choose an organizational structure. Consider these options:

- **Chronological order:** Present events in the order in which they occur. This is ideal for reporting a subject's history.
- **Order of importance:** Present details in order of increasing or decreasing significance. This is ideal for building an argument.
- **Comparison and contrast:** Present similarities and differences. This is ideal for addressing two or more subjects.

Write an outline. Review your note cards and build a road map that shows your plan for integrating and presenting key information. In an outline, use headings to identify the main idea in each section, and order these ideas so they flow logically. Use this outline to develop your draft.

Make direct references to sources. Use these methods to incorporate the facts, examples, and quotations you have found:

- **Direct Quotation:** Enclose a writer's exact words in quotation marks. Omissions should not alter the intent of the passage. Indicate omitted words with **ellipses,** or dots.
- **Paraphrase:** Restate a writer's specific ideas in your own words, accurately reflecting the writer's meaning.
- **Summary:** Condense an extended idea into a brief statement in your own words to introduce background information or review key ideas.

Credit your sources. To avoid **plagiarism**—presenting another's work as your own—include documentation every time you use another writer's ideas. Note the author's last name and the page numbers of material used. Later, use these notes to create formal citations in a bibliography or works-cited list at the end of your paper.

Plan for visuals. You may include visual aids, such as charts, maps, and graphs, to organize and display information in your report. Whenever you include additional information—whether it is visuals or quotations—be sure to make a clear link from your thesis to the data you include and reference.

Drafting Strategies

1. Introduce the drafting strategies, using the instruction on the student page.
2. Have students apply the strategies as they draft.

Teaching the Strategies

1. Remind students that a thesis statement clearly communicates the main idea or purpose of an essay.
2. Explain that drafting an essay is easier once an organizational system has been chosen.
3. Give students a copy of the Outline in ***Graphic Organizer Transparencies,*** p. 219, and have them use it to outline their ideas. Show how to paraphrase by writing this example on the board:

   Direct Quotation: *"Eleanor of Aquitaine was a medieval woman who leaped over the barriers of proper behavior set for her sex."*

   Paraphrase: *Eleanor of Aquitaine did not conform to the expectations for women during the Middle Ages.*

Think Aloud: Model Choosing a Text Structure

Model the strategy, using the following "think aloud." Say to students:

> Suppose that I am writing about events that occurred in New Orleans leading up to and following Hurricane Katrina. I'll write about these events in the order they happened—in chronological order. This text structure makes the most sense for my report because I am writing about the history of what happened before and after the hurricane.

Six Traits Focus

✔	Ideas		Word Choice
✔	Organization		Sentence Fluency
	Voice		Conventions

Differentiated Instruction for Universal Access

Strategy for Less Proficient Readers

Help students identify gaps in their research by analyzing their topics in terms of *who? what? when? where? why?* and *how?* Have students create questions using these words, such as the following: *Who was Jackie Robinson? What did he do to become a good ballplayer? When was he recognized for his achievements? Where did he play before he joined the major leagues? Why was he ostracized by fans? How did he overcome taunts and cruelties?* Answers to these questions can help students identify areas that need further research and give students ideas for their outlines.

Revising Strategies

1. Introduce the revision strategies, using the instruction on the student page.
2. Have students apply the strategies as they revise their drafts.

Teaching the Strategies

1. Students may have difficulty determining whether their sources are reliable. Have students work in pairs to evaluate each other's work and find additional sources to confirm information.
2. Tell students that when they replace overused words with synonyms, they should make sure that the new word fits into the context of the sentence.
3. Remind students of your criteria for length, format, and documentation of sources.
4. Emphasize to students that when they document sources they must follow the standard format exactly. Tell students to pay attention to the order of the information, the punctuation marks used, and the use of italics. Tell students that even the smallest details of formatting are important.

Think Aloud: Model Varying Word Choice

Model the strategy, using the following "think aloud":

> Let's say I've written these two sentences: *Olivia noticed a change in her friend. She couldn't decide if the change was mental or physical.* I've repeated the word *change* in the second sentence, so I want to replace it. I'll revise my sentences like this: *Olivia noticed a change in her friend. She couldn't decide if the difference was mental or physical.* Replacing the word *change* with the word *difference* fits the context of the sentence.

Six Traits Focus

	Ideas	✓	Word Choice
✓	Organization		Sentence Fluency
	Voice		Conventions

Revising Strategies

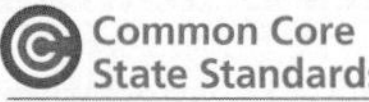

Writing

5. Develop and strengthen writing as needed by planning, revising, editing, rewriting, or trying a new approach, focusing on addressing what is most significant for a specific purpose and audience.

6. Use technology, including the Internet, to produce, publish, and update individual or shared writing products, taking advantage of technology's capacity to link to other information and to display information flexibly and dynamically.

Language

3.a. Write and edit work so that it conforms to the guidelines in a style manual appropriate for the discipline and writing type.

Evaluate your sources. Underline any fact in your draft that may not have a trustworthy source. For example, you may have found information from a newspaper or a Web site known for sensationalizing or exaggerating events. Confirm this information through a more reliable source, such as an established encyclopedia, a scholarly Web site, or a reputable newspaper.

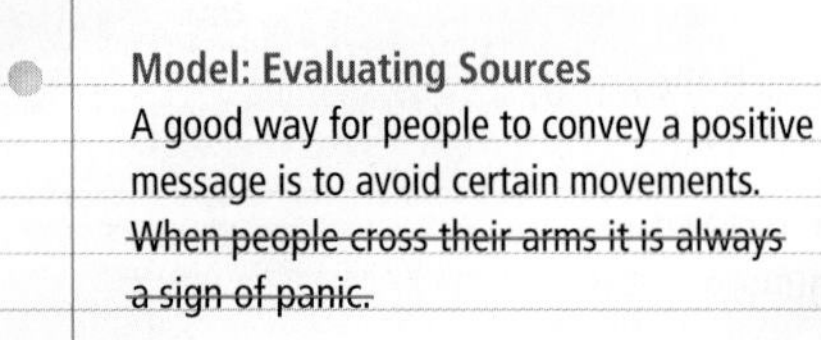
Model: Evaluating Sources

A good way for people to convey a positive message is to avoid certain movements. ~~When people cross their arms it is always a sign of panic.~~

The writer found that this claim was supported by only one source. Since it was not important to her basic argument, she chose to delete it.

Revise to vary word choice. Except for specific terminology required by your topic, avoid overuse of particular words and expressions. Review your draft to identify words that you may have overused. For each, use a dictionary and thesaurus to generate a list of possible synonyms, and substitute them as appropriate.

Example Synonym Banks

invention: innovation, development, contrivance, device

theory: belief, policy, system, position, idea, supposition

Peer Review

Exchange drafts with a partner. As you read each other's reports, circle or highlight words that recur repeatedly. Working together, identify replacements to improve word variety in the writing.

Revise to follow a consistent research format. As you finalize your report, be sure that it meets your teacher's criteria for length, format, and documentation of sources. The Modern Language Association (MLA) requires standardized parenthetical citations of sources and a works-cited list that includes only the sources used in the report.

To credit sources within a research paper, include direct documentation in the form of footnotes, endnotes, or parenthetical citations. At the end of your paper, provide a reference list giving complete bibliographic information. If possible, use the footnoting function in a word processing program to aid your efforts.

Strategies for Using Technology in Writing

If students who are using word processors decide to order their information differently, suggest that they use the cut-and-paste function to quickly move their sentences and paragraphs to different places in the report.

Remind students that they should save their document frequently during their revisions to prevent any loss of work.

Writers on Writing

Gary L. Blackwood On Showing, Not Telling

Gary L. Blackwood is the author of the excerpt from *The Shakespeare Stealer* (p. 787).

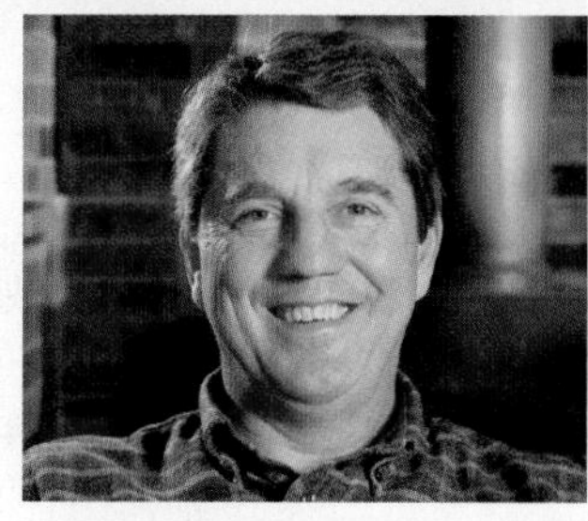

"It helps to read sentences aloud."
—Gary L. Blackwood

To me, research is as much fun as beachcombing: You never know what fascinating items you're going to find. Since books are generally more reliable than the Internet, I do most of my beachcombing in libraries. I know that some people consider nonfiction dull, but I find good nonfiction more compelling than a novel, because I know the events really happened. Who could invent a story as singular and mysterious as that of Kaspar Hauser, which I came upon while researching my four-volume work *Unsolved History*?

Professional Model:

from *Perplexing People,*

a volume in the *Unsolved History* series published by Benchmark Books (Marshall Cavendish), Sept. 2005

~~Sometime in the afternoon of~~ *On* May 26, 1828, a peculiar boy of about sixteen appeared, seemingly from nowhere, on a street in the German city of Nuremberg. His clothing was shabby and ill-fitting and he walked with a ~~peculiar~~ *strange* waddling gait, as though intoxicated. His face wore a vacant expression; he spoke and understood only a few words. Within a year he would become one of the ~~best known and most discussed~~ *most celebrated and controversial* people in Europe. . . .

The police questioned the boy, but his replies consisted of two phrases in ungrammatical German: "Don't know" and "I want to be a horseman as my father is." When they gave him paper and a pen ~~and asked to write his name and address,~~ he produced a series of scribbles, of which only two were intelligible: "cavalryman" and "Kaspar Hauser."

Writing can be factual without also being sleep-inducing. I try to liven things up by using vivid adjectives.

To add interest and a feeling of authenticity, I use a lot of quotes from primary sources—people who actually witnessed or participated in the events or chroniclers of the time.

Good prose—whether it's fiction or nonfiction—is clear and concise. I do a lot of cutting of superfluous words and phrases, and I may reword a sentence half a dozen times before I'm satisfied with it.

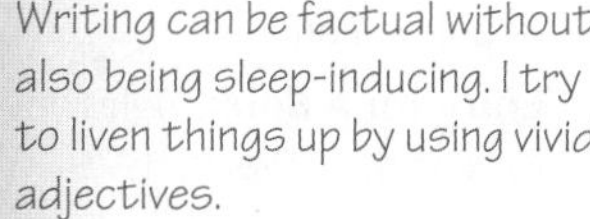

Gary L. Blackwood On Showing, Not Telling

Review the passage on the student page with the class, using Blackwood's comments to deepen students' understanding of the process of showing, not telling, when writing a research report.

Teaching From the Professional Model

1. Show students Segment 3 on Gary L. Blackwood on the *See It!* **DVD** or from this page in the **Enriched Online Student Edition** at **www.PHLitOnline.com.** Discuss how Blackwood uses primary sources to give authenticity to his writing.
2. Have students go through their reports and identify weak adjectives. Have students replace them with stronger, more vivid adjectives. Give students the following example to model the process. Before revision: *The strong tornado tore across the empty landscape.* After revision: *The raging tornado tore across the barren landscape.*
3. Tell students that they can keep their writing clear and concise by eliminating any unnecessary words or phrases.
4. Draw students' attention to Blackwood's use of direct quotes from primary sources. Encourage students to search for quotes from people who witnessed or participated in the events that they are researching.

Enriched Online Student Edition
Show or assign the video online at **www.PHLitOnline.com.**

Strategies for Improving Word Choice

Give students these suggestions for revising for word choice.

1. Look for places in your writing that are awkward or clumsy.
2. Manipulate the sentence by breaking it into two sentences, cutting words to simplify it, or adding a clarification.
3. Read the revised paragraph aloud, listening for clumsy language.
4. Revise it until the sentences sound smooth and natural when read aloud.

Documenting Sources

Teaching the Strategies

1. Tell students that it is important that they give credit to others for any ideas and words that students use in their reports. Remind students that they must indicate this by placing citations after sentences or passages that should be credited to a source.
2. Review with students the required information for citing print works and Web sources within the body of a research report.
3. Tell students that their research reports must also contain a Works Cited list, or bibliography, at the end of their reports. Review the MLA style requirements, including the alphabetical order of entries and the specific details for citing books, periodical articles, and Web sites.
4. Tell students that they can refer to the section on MLA style on page R40 of their student books for more information.

Six Traits Focus

	Ideas		Word Choice
✓	Organization		Sentence Fluency
	Voice	✓	Conventions

Documenting Sources

You must give proper credit to the people whose ideas and words you have borrowed. Failing to do this raises legal and ethical issues. Libel, slander, copyright infringement, and plagiarism are serious accusations. Good writers are thorough and accurate in citing all of their sources.

When citing sources, follow a specific format. Modern Language Association (MLA) style calls for citations in parentheses directly following the material being cited.

- For print works, provide the author's or editor's name followed by a page number. If the work does not have an author, use a keyword or phrase from the title.

  Citing a Print Work: . . . body language makes up approximately 65 percent of human communication (Aylesworth 3).

- For Web sources, give the author's name and the title of the article, if any, or title of the site.

  Citing a Web Source: Unsolvedmysteries.com describes a lottery winner whose dreams reveal a winning ticket ("Winning the Lottery").

At the end of your report, give information for each source you cite. MLA style calls for an alphabetical *Works Cited* list.

- For books, give the author's name (last name first), the title of the work, the city of publication, the name of the publisher, and the year of publication.

  Entry for a Book: Aylesworth, Thomas G. *Understanding Body Talk*. New York: F. Watts, 1979.

- For articles in periodicals, give the author's last name, first name, title of the article, the name of the magazine, the date of the issue, the volume and issue number, and the pages of the article. For any month with more than four letters, abbreviate the month by using the first three letters followed by a period.

  Entry for a Periodical Article: Kreisler, Kristin V. "Why We Dream What We Dream." *Reader's Digest*. Feb. 1995: 28.

- For Web sites, give any of the following information that is available, in this order: author's name, title of the page, title of the site, date of last update, and name of the sponsoring organization. Give the date you consulted the site and its full URL, or Web address.

  Entry for a Web Site: "Winning the Lottery in Your Dreams." *Unsolved Mysteries*. 11 March 2000. http://unsolvedmysteries.com/usm397.html

For more information on citing sources using MLA style, see page R36.

Common Core State Standards

Writing

8. Gather relevant information from multiple authoritative print and digital sources, avoiding plagiarism and following a standard format for citation.

Language

1.b. Use various types of phrases and clauses to convey specific meanings and add variety and interest to writing or presentations.

3.a. Write and edit work so that it conforms to the guidelines in a style manual appropriate for the discipline and writing type.

WRITER'S TOOLBOX

Sentence Fluency | Voice | Organization | Word Choice | Ideas | Conventions

Revising to Combine Sentences Using Adverb Clauses

Adverb clauses can be used to combine information from two sentences into one sentence. Often, the revised sentence will make the intended meaning more obvious.

Two sentences: I joined the panel. Jay is the leader.

Combined: I joined the panel because Jay is the leader.

Identifying Adverb Clauses A clause is any group of words with a subject and a verb. An *independent clause* can stand by itself as a complete sentence; a *subordinate clause* is not complete because it does not express a full idea. An *adverb clause* is a subordinate clause that modifies a verb, an adjective, or another adverb in a sentence. It begins with a subordinating conjunction that tells *where, when, in what way, to what extent, under what condition,* or *why.*

When: *After I read the report,* I agreed with the mayor.

Condition: Dan will ask for a refund *if you will go with him.*

In what way: The bulldog yawned *as if he were utterly bored.*

Why: I drew a map *so that they would not get lost.*

PH WRITING COACH

Further instruction and practice are available in *Prentice Hall Writing Coach.*

Combining Sentences When combining two short sentences using adverb clauses, follow these steps:

1. Look for a relationship between the ideas of the two clauses.
2. Select the appropriate subordinate conjunction to show that relationship. Place the adverb clause at the beginning or end of the combined sentence—wherever it conveys your intent more clearly.
3. Use a comma to separate a subordinate clause only when it begins a sentence.

Grammar in Your Writing

Review several paragraphs of your report and highlight any consecutive short sentences that you find. Look for a possible adverbial relationship (*where, when, in what way,* and so on) in two of the sentences. Following the steps outlined here, combine the sentences using an appropriate subordinating conjunction.

Common Subordinate Conjunctions

after	because	since	when
although	before	so that	whenever
as	even though	unless	whether
as soon as	if	until	while

Revising to Combine Sentences Using Adverb Clauses

1. Introduce the grammar skill, using the instruction on the student page.
2. Discuss the examples and the strategies for combining sentences.
3. Have students follow the instruction under Grammar in Your Writing to make improvements in their drafts.

Teaching the Grammar Skill

1. Write the words *even if, in order that, once, although, before, while,* and *when* on the board and explain that these are additional subordinate conjunctions students might use to introduce an adverb clause in their reports.
2. Ask students to practice identifying the adverb clauses in the following sentences. Then, have them identify the verb or adjective that the clause modifies:

   New York City is interesting *because it is home to so many ethnic groups.*

   Answer: The clause modifies "interesting."

   When she arrived at the airport, Rachel phoned.

   Answer: The clause modifies "phoned."

   As the Earth's population grows, a greater supply of food will become necessary.

   Answer: The clause modifies "will become."

PH WRITING COACH Grade 9

Students will find practice with and guidance on combining sentences in Chapter 16.

Differentiated Instruction for Universal Access

Strategy for Special-Needs Students

Review the major parts of speech with students using the following example sentences.

- The *fans* cheer. (noun, subject)
- *Run* home! (verb)
- Robinson hits the *ball.* (noun, direct object)
- The players run *fast.* (adverb)
- What a *noisy* crowd! (adjective)
- I want to go *to the game.* (prepositional phrase)

Write each sentence on the board and underline the italicized words. Ask students to identify the parts of speech. Provide help and additional examples if necessary.

Student Model

Review the Student Model with the class, using the annotations to analyze the writer's use of the elements of a research report.

Teaching From the Student Model

1. Explain that the Student Model is a sample and that their own research reports may be longer.
2. Tell students that it is important to grab the reader's attention immediately so that readers become engaged in the report and are interested in reading on.
3. Point out to students that the second sentence immediately uses a paraphrase from a source to back up the first sentence. **Ask** students why that is an effective technique.

   Possible responses: By quoting an expert stating that 65 percent of human communication is nonverbal, Lyndsey immediately lends credibility to her argument. The reader now is ready to accept the premise of the paper and the examples and details that follow.
4. Write the following sample thesis statement on the board and model how to clarify it.

   Jackie Robinson joined the Major Leagues against the wishes of many white players even though he had an outstanding record.

   Revised: *Despite Jackie Robinson's outstanding record, many white players opposed his addition into the Major Leagues.*

Student Model: Lyndsey Regan, Canyon Country, CA

Body Language

When we speak to other people, they are not only listening to our actual words, but sensing our facial expression, tone of voice, gestures, level of eye contact, posture, and movements as well. Nonverbal communication, or body language, makes up approximately 65 percent of human communication (Aylesworth 3). Body language has a major impact on how others perceive what we say. It can also be a tool for miscommunication when the speaker and listener are from different cultures or are communicating through technology that deprives them of visual cues. In fact, we often realize the importance of body language only when we cannot interpret someone else's body language correctly.

In *Eye to Eye: How People Interact*, Dr. Peter Marsh explains that before we speak, our gestures, posture, and facial expressions are already broadcasting messages to those around us. While we are speaking, these gestures continue to communicate messages—usually clarifying what we are saying, but sometimes contradicting us in telltale ways (Marsh 116–119).

Often, body language is an unconscious act that triggers the most developed senses in other people—hearing and sight (Aylesworth 18). That is why body language is such a great way to emphasize words and ideas. Many people take advantage of this. Advertisers, for example, cast actors in their commercials who use body language that appeals to viewers.

Studies have shown that people's body language changes when they are not telling the truth (Vrij, Edward, Roberts, and Bull 239–263). If someone's body language is inconsistent with what he or she is saying, people tend to believe what the body is telling them. A good way for people to convey a positive message is to avoid certain movements, like fidgeting or letting your eyes wander. Instead, good communicators maintain steady eye contact, nod in agreement, and smile. You may notice that people on television, like hosts of infomercials and talk-shows, generally display this positive body language when speaking.

The opening line captures the reader's attention by presenting a surprising perspective.

Lyndsey expresses her thesis statement clearly and concisely.

Lyndsey smoothly introduces a research source and explains the ideas it provided.

Differentiated Instruction for Universal Access

Strategy for English Learners

Have students work in pairs to read through the Student Model, noting any words or phrases they need to look up for better understanding. After students have looked up these words and phrases, have a class discussion in which each pair takes a turn identifying and describing a troublesome word or phrase. Continue until students have touched on every troublesome word or phrase.

Body language is usually learned, but it can also be inherited. It is affected by age, gender, background, and situation. The meaning of body language can change depending on cultural context. According to Dr. Marsh, each culture has developed its own repertoire of symbolic gestures, many with original associations that have now long been forgotten (Marsh 53–54). This sometimes causes people to be alarmed by foreign visitors or nervous around people when they visit new countries.

In the United States, people have a wide variety of regional influences because the country is a melting pot of diverse cultures. A gesture that means the same thing throughout the Unite States is the "OK" sign made with the thumb and forefinger. This gesture is interpreted similarly in some European countries, but if you were to perform this sign in Greece or Turkey, it would be considered very insulting (Marsh 54).

There are other cultural differences in body language within Europe. In Germany, body language often reflects social status, and Germans often use body language for emphasis. Italian gestures are often passionate, emotional expressions communicated with the face, arms, and shoulders. Italians often use body language to clarify themselves or to express urgency. In France, people tend to use more formal gestures. They are generally not as expressive or insistent as Italians. The body language of the French is not nearly as casual as we are used to in America (Ruesch and Kees 23–25). As you can see by exploring a few examples from different cultures, there are many differences in body language. Therefore, when you communicate with people from other countries, take special care in your use of body language.

Technological advancements in our society affect the way we communicate. For example, when we speak on the telephone, we are unable to see the person on the other end of the line. The message that a person may be trying to convey may be misinterpreted without the additional visual information provided by his or her body language. With electronic mail, there is no visual or verbal communication whatsoever. As a result, people cannot completely understand the meaning of what is being communicated. Therefore, people using e-mail should be careful about what they write. To avoid miscommunication, communicating the old-fashioned way—in person—may be the best approach.

Whenever Lyndsey presents a specific piece of evidence that is not her own idea or common knowledge, she cites it using the appropriate format.

Lyndsey's organizational structure is logical and clear. First, she discusses how body language is used in a variety of cultures. Next, she gives examples of what happens when we do not have body language to guide us.

Student Model *(cont.)*

Teaching From the Student Model

1. Point out the internal citations Lyndsey uses in her report. Remind students to refer to their note cards when making citations in their reports.
2. Explain to students that the parenthetical citation and the accompanying Works Cited page of this sample model are the most frequently used method of citing source information.
3. Explain that Lyndsey addresses many different topics under the main subject of body language. **Ask** students to identify some of the specific topics she explores.

   Answer: Under the overall subject of body language, Lyndsey addresses cultural differences and the effects of technology.

Student Model *(cont.)*

Teaching From the Student Model

1. Point out how Lyndsey uses her conclusion to summarize and tie together all the topics she covered in her report.
2. **Ask** students what other purposes a conclusion can serve.

   Possible response: A conclusion can end a paper with a memorable feature, like a quote, or it can provide a strong restatement of the paper's main ideas.
3. Point out that the first two works on Lyndsey's Works-Cited List are both books with one author. The third is a book with two authors, and the fourth is a journal article with four authors.
4. Encourage students to use these citations as models for their own Works-Cited Lists.
5. Provide students with a Works-Cited Style Sheet copied from a style manual, such as *The Chicago Manual of Style,* since many sources will not fit into the form of the citations shown here.
6. Establish an acceptable format for Internet sources in your classroom. Clarify the format for students.

Connecting to Real-Life Writing

Explain that students will most likely be required to write research papers for many college classes. Also, tell students that many careers require research writing, including attorney, business manager, Web site writer, and graphic designer.

In conclusion, body language is a significant component of communication, even though we are often not aware of it. Body language, like facial expression and gestures, frequently enables people to clearly understand one another, but we must remember that people cannot always be read like a book. With cultural differences, body language can take on different meanings, and this allows for potential miscommunication. Changes in technology present a different kind of problem, but with a similar result. When body language cannot be seen, people may misinterpret the meaning of the communicator, making them angry or confused. As you can see, the additional information we provide with our body language plays a major role in how we communicate our thoughts and ideas.

Works-Cited List

Aylesworth, Thomas G. *Understanding Body Talk.* New York: F. Watts, 1979.

Marsh, Peter, M.D. *Eye to Eye: How People Interact.* Topsfield, MA: Salem House Publishers, 1988.

Ruesch, Jurgen, and Weldon Kees. *Nonverbal Communication: Notes on the Visual Perception of Human Relations.* Berkeley, CA: University of California Press, 1969.

Vrij, Aldert, Katherine Edward, Kim P. Roberts, and Ray Bull. "Detecting Deceit via Analysis of Verbal and Nonverbal Behavior." *Journal of Nonverbal Behavior,* Winter 2000: 239–263.

Common Core State Standards

Language
3.a. Write and edit work so that it conforms to the guidelines in a style manual appropriate for the discipline and writing type.

After her conclusion, Lyndsey presents the complete information for the works cited in her report using MLA format, a common style for citation.

Strategies for Using Technology in Writing

Remind students that the Internet is a haven of inaccurate information, and that sites with *.gov, .edu,* and *.org* endings are generally the most reliable sites. Tell students that they can also use the Internet to obtain bibliographies containing the names and authors of books and articles on their topic. These bibliographies may help students rely less on Internet sources and focus more on reliable print sources.

Editing and Proofreading

Review your draft to correct errors in format, grammar, and spelling.

Focus on format. Follow the manuscript requirements by including an appropriate title page, pagination, spacing and margins, and citations. Make sure you have used the preferred system for crediting sources in your paper and for bibliographical sources at the end. Double-check all punctuation and capitalization.

Notice unusual consonant groupings. Some words are difficult to spell because they contain unusual letter combinations. Certain consonant groupings, such as the *rh* in *rhythm*, don't occur in many words. Other consonant groups are hard to hear (ex<u>hi</u>larating) or contain a silent letter (sil<u>h</u>ouette). Be sure to double-check these problematic words.

Spiral Review

Earlier in the unit, you learned about **main and subordinate clauses** (p. 976). Review your research report to be sure that no subordinate clause stands by itself.

Publishing and Presenting

Consider one of the following ways to share your writing:

Deliver an oral presentation. Read your research report aloud to your classmates, or consider recreating the report as a multimedia presentation using presentation software. Add appropriate visual aids as needed, such as charts, maps, and graphs.

Organize a panel discussion. If several of your classmates have written on a similar topic, plan a discussion to compare and contrast your findings. Speakers can summarize their research before opening the panel to questions from the class.

PH WRITING COACH

Further instruction and practice are available in *Prentice Hall Writing Coach.*

Reflecting on Your Writing

Jot down your answers to this question:

How did writing a research report affect your understanding of your topic?

Rubric for Self-Assessment

Find evidence in your writing to address each category. Then, use the rating scale to grade your work.

Criteria	Rating Scale (not very → very)
Focus: How clear is your thesis statement?	1 2 3 4 5
Organization: How logical and consistent is your organization?	1 2 3 4 5
Support/Elaboration: How effective and varied is your support?	1 2 3 4 5
Style: How well do you summarize background information?	1 2 3 4 5
Conventions: According to an accepted format, how complete and accurate are your citations?	1 2 3 4 5

Editing and Proofreading

1. Introduce the editing and proofreading focus, using the instruction on the student page.
2. Have students edit and proofread their narratives, correcting grammar, spelling, punctuation, and word choice. Make sure they check for errors of the type noted in the lesson focus and the Spiral Review.

Teaching the Editing Focus

1. Tell students to go through their reports and make sure that they have credited every source. Emphasize the serious nature of plagiarism and the importance of giving a writer credit for his or her work.
2. After students have thoroughly examined their parenthetical and bibliographical information, have them exchange papers and examine each other's citations. Tell students that because of the precise formatting it can be easy to miss small errors.

Six Traits Focus

	Ideas		Word Choice
	Organization		Sentence Fluency
	Voice	✔	Conventions

ASSESS

Publishing and Presenting

1. If students are preparing to deliver their reports as speeches, have them practice in pairs. Partners should offer suggestions about delivery and should ask questions about each other's topics, as an audience might.
2. If several students have researched related topics, suggest that they combine their work into a compilation of chapters on a particular subject.

Reflecting on Your Writing

To help students evaluate how the research changed their view of the topic, have them write three facts that they learned through the research. They can add these facts to the last column of their KWL charts.

Strategies for Test Taking

When students are taking a test that requires them to respond to an expository writing prompt, they should spend time organizing the order of the information in their responses. After students have brainstormed for the details that they will use, encourage them to use an outline to organize that information. A few minutes spent organizing will make the drafting and revising stages much easier.

PH WRITING COACH Grade 9

Students will find more information on the writing process in Chapter 3.

EXTEND/ASSESS

Answers

Common Core State Standards

- Language 3, 4.c, d

Borrowed and Foreign Words

1. Introduce the skill, using the instruction on the student page.
2. Review the definitions and the examples in the charts.

Think Aloud: Model the Skill

Use this "think aloud" to model how to proceed when encountering a borrowed or foreign word. Say to students:

> When I come across a borrowed or foreign word that I don't know, I check for context clues before looking in a dictionary. Maybe I can determine the general meaning of the word without interrupting my reading. Let's say I read the sentence, "Three women in kayaks moved silently through the icy water." I don't know what *kayak* means, so I look for context clues: the kayaks are carrying people through water. I can infer that a *kayak* is a type of boat. If I look up *kayak* in a dictionary, I can see that it is a type of boat made by Eskimos. Looking up the word has enriched my understanding of my reading, but I didn't need to interrupt my reading to do it.

Vocabulary Workshop

Borrowed and Foreign Words

English has more words than any other language. Many of these words are taken directly from other languages. At first, these new words are treated as **foreign words.**

Over time, as the words become common in everyday speech, most of them are accepted into the language and are considered to be English. Words that enter the languages in this way are called **borrowed words.** You use them every day. The first chart shows some common borrowed words that are now part of the English language.

Borrowed Words	Original Language
ballet, cavalry, infantry, bigot	French
cargo, canyon, ranch, tornado	Spanish
chipmunk (Algonquian), pecan (Illinois), raccoon (Virginia Algonquian), moccasin (Algonquian)	Native American
bandanna, pajamas, thug, shampoo	Hindi
kindergarten, hamburger, dollar, vandal	German

Some words are not fully adopted into the language and are always treated as foreign words. Some of these words are written in italics. Dictionaries often indicate those that should be italicized. See how many of these words you know.

au courant	up-to-date, informed on current affairs	French
mot juste	the exact, appropriate word	French
carpe diem	seize the day, or live for the day	Latin
nom de plume	a pen name	French
caveat emptor	let the buyer beware	Latin

Practice A Look up each of these foreign words in a dictionary. Identify the original language and write the definition.

1. ad infinitum
2. *cause célèbre*
3. pro bono
4. ex post facto
5. *bon mot*
6. *mea culpa*

Common Core State Standards

Language

3. Apply knowledge of language to understand how language functions in different contexts, to make effective choices for meaning or style, and to comprehend more fully when reading or listening.

4.c. Consult general and specialized reference materials, both print and digital, to find the pronunciation of a word or determine or clarify its precise meaning, its part of speech, or its etymology.

4.d. Verify the preliminary determination of the meaning of a word or phrase.

Practice A

Sample answers:

1. Latin; "endlessly, forever, without limit"
2. French; "a famous law case, trial, or controversy"
3. Latin; "involving professional services provided free of charge for charitable organizations or poor persons"
4. Latin; "done or made afterward, especially when having retroactive effect"
5. French; "a clever or witty remark"
6. Latin; "(by) my fault; I am to blame"

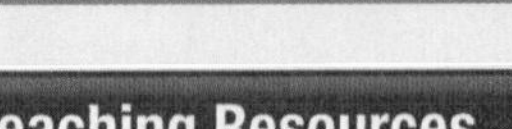

Teaching Resources

Unit 5 Resources
Borrowed and Foreign Words, pp. 183, 184

PHLit Online! **Vocabulary Central,** featuring definitions, audio pronunciations, word families, and activities, is online at **www.PHLitOnline.com.**

Practice B Complete each sentence with the correct borrowed or foreign word from the box. Identify the original language. Then, use a print or online dictionary to verify the accuracy of each choice.

embargo	status quo	desperado	mesa	*mano a mano*
algebra	RSVP	onslaught	sushi	*fait accompli*

PHLit Online!
www.PHLitOnline.com
- Illustrated vocabulary words
- Interactive vocabulary games
- Vocabulary flashcards

1. After turning in his report, Alexis declared it a ________________ .
2. Joshua really enjoyed eating the ________________ until someone told him it was raw fish.
3. It was a steep climb to the top of the ________________ , but then the ground became level.
4. I usually do well in ________________ , but that one equation puzzled me.
5. "Tyler," said the smaller boy, "I challenge you to a game of basketball ________________ ."
6. The card said ________________ , so I immediately called Megan and accepted the invitation.
7. He was not a common thief, but a dangerous ________________ wanted in ten states.
8. The United States declared an ________________ on all goods from the country until hostilities ended.
9. The fort quickly fell before the ________________ of the invaders.
10. Helena hated the ________________ so she began working to make changes.

Comprehension and Collaboration

Use these words in a paragraph: *persona non grata, voilà, coup de grace, per se.* Then, meet with a partner and critique each other's word usage. Read the paragraphs aloud, being careful to pronounce the words correctly. Verify your definitions and pronunciations in a dictionary.

Activity Prepare four notecards like the one shown. Then, write one of these foreign words on each card: *hoi polloi, savoir faire, vis-à-vis, ad hoc.* Look up each word in a print or online dictionary. Write the definition, the pronunciation, and a sentence that clearly shows each meaning.

Word:

Definition:

Sentence:

ASSESS/EXTEND

Answers

Practice B

Answers:

1. *fait accompli;* French
2. sushi; Japanese
3. mesa; Spanish
4. algebra; Arabic
5. *mano a mano;* Spanish
6. RSVP; French
7. desperado; Spanish
8. embargo; Latin
9. onslaught; Dutch
10. status quo; Latin

Activity

Give each student a dictionary and four notecards. Set a time limit for them to complete the activity. When students are finished, have volunteers pronounce each word correctly and share their definitions and sentences. Then have the entire class pronounce each word aloud together.

Comprehension and Collaboration

Provide dictionaries and assign partners. Have students write their paragraphs independently, and then read them aloud to their partners. Partners should listen for mistakes in pronunciation and word usage. Have a few volunteers share their revised paragraphs with the class.

Differentiated Instruction for Universal Access

Strategy for English Learners

Ask students to brainstorm words that originated in their native languages but that they have heard in English, and words from English that are spoken and understood in their native languages. Students may also think of words that originated in other languages and were borrowed by both their native languages and by English. Have students work together to make a poster illustrating these words, and then ask them to share their poster with the class.

Strategy for Gifted/Talented Students

Have students use the Internet to find foreign words and phrases that are commonly used in conversation and writing. Suggest that students work together to create a classroom dictionary of such words and phrases, providing the correct pronunciation of the words, their languages of origin, and their literal and idiomatic meanings.

Common Core State Standards

- Speaking and Listening 1.d, 5

Learn the Skills

1. Introduce the workshop, including the activity on page 1017.
2. Share the following tips for organizing content:
   - Point out that students must consider what equipment is available when they plan their presentations.
   - Remind students that planning their content and their media simultaneously makes more sense than planning each element separately. Explain that they should shape their presentations according to the available media.
   - Caution students against overwhelming their audience with too much media.
3. Share these strategies to help students plan their presentations:
   - Tell students to establish a certain length of time for their presentations.
   - Remind them that their presentations should be smooth and continuous. If gaps exist, they could lose their audience.
   - Encourage students to make sure they feel comfortable with the technology they are using as they rehearse their presentations.

SPEAKING AND LISTENING

Communications Workshop

Multimedia Presentation of a Research Report

Modern classrooms offer students several ways to add sound and visuals to a verbal report. Students may choose from an array of equipment to make multimedia presentations. The following strategies will help you develop and deliver a multimedia presentation of a research report.

Learn the Skills

Organizing Content Your choice of media depends on the equipment and software available to you, your topic, and your target audience. Use the following tips:

- Use a two-column format for your outline. Arrange the content of your report in the left column; plan media elements in the right column. Use this same pattern in your final script: Run your speaking text in the left column and your media cues in the right.
- Use media strategically. Incorporate audio, video, and graphic elements where they will be the most effective. Media should enhance your audience's understanding of material in a presentation.
- Choose media appropriate to your content. Dry recitation of statistics can be replaced with colorful graphs and charts to enhance the appeal and accuracy of your presentation. If your report is historical, incorporate music from the time period. Photographs or video images may clarify complex procedures.
- Distribute media use evenly throughout your report to make it easier for you to manage the equipment and to maintain audience interest.

Preparing the Presentation An effective multimedia presentation is the result of planning and practice. These tips may help you prepare:

- If possible, rehearse your presentation in the room where it will take place. Check sight lines to make sure that your visual materials will be seen by all of your audience. Do a sound check as well.
- Make sure that words on your slides are readable; do not put too much content on any one slide.
- Practice shifting from spoken content to media elements. Plan what you will do and say if any piece of equipment fails.

Common Core State Standards

Speaking and Listening
1.d. Respond thoughtfully to diverse perspectives, summarize points of agreement and disagreement, and, when warranted, qualify or justify their own views and understanding and make new connections in light of the evidence and reasoning presented.
5. Make strategic use of digital media in presentations to enhance understanding of findings, reasoning, and evidence and to add interest.

1016 Drama

Strategies for Preparing a Multimedia Presentation

Give students these additional strategies for preparing a multimedia presentation:

- Tell students to spend extra time rehearsing with equipment that is unfamiliar. Explain they might need to learn how to operate unfamiliar equipment.
- Ask students to double-check that their media elements are ready to share. For example, students playing an audio recording should make sure that it will begin in the correct place.
- Encourage students to think about how media is used throughout their presentations. Remind them that media should be used to support the content. It should not be the focus.
- Explain that students must make sure their presentations can move forward if equipment fails.

Practice the Skills

Presentation of Knowledge and Ideas Use what you've learned in this workshop to perform the following task.

ACTIVITY: Give a Multimedia Presentation

Use a research report from your portfolio as the basis of a multimedia presentation. Plan and practice your presentation using the guidelines from page 1016. Remember the following important points:

- Create a script based on your research report that includes media elements.
- Choose media relating to your content.
- Use media evenly throughout the report.
- Media should enhance your key points.

As your classmates make their presentations, use the Presentation Checklist below to offer them some feedback. Your classmates will also use the checklist to analyze your presentation.

Presentation Checklist

Presentation Content
Does the presentation meet the requirements of the activity? Check all that apply.

- ❑ The media related to the content.
- ❑ Media was used evenly throughout the report.
- ❑ Media helped listeners to understand key points.

Presentation Delivery
Did the speaker use the media successfully?

- ❑ Equipment functioned properly.
- ❑ Media was visible and audible.
- ❑ Transitions between media uses were smooth.

Comprehension and Collaboration With a small group, discuss the presentations you have viewed. Consider the ways in which media added to your understanding of information in each presentation. Ask what group members learned from multimedia presentations that they could not have learned from reading research reports. Determine which presentations used media most effectively, and why. If there are multiple perspectives, summarize points of agreement and disagreement.

EXTEND/ASSESS

Practice the Skills

1. Review the assignment with students. Make sure that they understand that media should be used strategically to support or elaborate on important points in their research report and to help hold the audience's interest. Encourage them to practice the transitions between spoken passages and multimedia elements to ensure a smooth, even presentation.
2. Explain to students that they should use a copy of the Presentation Checklist to evaluate their own presentation and the presentations made by classmates.
3. Before students give their presentations to the class, remind listeners to ask questions if any points are unclear. To maintain order, encourage them to raise their hands and wait to be acknowledged by the presenter before stating their questions. Suggest that students making presentations scan the classroom from time to time so they will notice any students who have questions.

Evaluate the Activity

1. Evaluate students' presentations on the basis of the relevance of media, even pacing, and the student's skill with handling the equipment.
2. When the class discusses the presentations that were easiest to follow, encourage students to make note of the features of those presentations that made them effective and to incorporate those techniques in their future presentations.

Differentiated Instruction for Universal Access

EL Strategy for English Learners

Before students begin organizing their presentations, they may need clarification on both the assignment and the rubric. Have students take their research report and review it. Then, help them to work through each of the steps for organizing the content.

Depending on their familiarity with the equipment, you may need to have someone walk them through the equipment use or provide them with a diagram. Have students look at the Feedback Form. **Ask** students what each of the content and organization points means.
Answers: The first point means that they have chosen a type of media that works with the topic. The second means that they have used media throughout their presentation, not just in certain parts. The third means that the media makes their report clearer or more interesting.

Then have students discuss the points under "Presentation Delivery," making sure they understand how each point is reflected in their delivery.

Cumulative Review

In this Common Core Assessment Workshop (pp. 1018–1023), students apply and reinforce their mastery of the Common Core Standards and the skills taught in Unit 5. The practice is divided into four sections including a section of Performance Tasks addressing CCSS Reading standards.

1. Before assigning each section, review the relevant Common Core Standards and unit skills with students.
2. Set a time limit for the multiple choice items in each section, allowing a little over one minute per question. Allow twenty minutes for any Timed Writing questions.
3. Administer each of the first three sections of the Cumulative Review (pp. 1018–1021).
4. Use the Performance Tasks on pages 1022–1023 to assess the depth of students' mastery of standards taught in the unit. Follow the suggestions on teacher pages 1022–1023 for assigning tasks and for supporting and evaluating student performance

Reteaching Skills

1. For each practice, use the Reteach chart on the same page as the answers to determine which skills require reteaching, based on which items students answered incorrectly.
2. Reteach these skills prior to assigning the **Benchmark Test** for the second half of Unit 5 (***Unit 5 Resources,*** pp. 189–194).

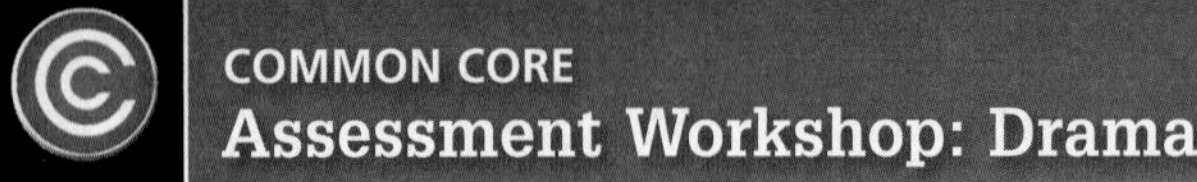

Cumulative Review

Common Core State Standards

RL.9-10.3, RL.9-10.4; W.9-10.3.b; L.9-10.4.a

[For the full wording of the standards, see the standards chart in the front of your textbook.]

I. Reading Literature

Directions: *Read the passage. Then, answer each question that follows.*

The stage is dark. Bill, a somewhat scrawny, brainy-looking teenager, stands center stage. A spotlight shines on him as he begins his speech.

BILL. *(dramatically)* To be or not to be: that is the question. At least that's what Hamlet said. Of course, this is not life and death, but it could be social suicide. I don't want to be a tattletale. But I also don't want to be an <u>accomplice</u> to cheating—I don't want to help break the rules. What to do? *(with a sigh)* Jack—the football team captain—knows that I know he cheated. He caught me looking his way as he glanced at the cheat sheet he had on his arm. After Mrs. Lundy's class, he confronted me. "I have to pass this test to stay on the team. I can count on you not to rat me out, right?" he said menacingly. I said I wouldn't. But why should he get away with cheating? It's not right. If I tell, he will know it's me. I'll lose my social life—the little I have. I will be an outcast. What do I do? I need help.

The curtain falls. It opens to show a guidance counselor's office stage right. The older guidance counselor sits behind a desk. Bill walks in to see the guidance counselor, Mr. Peters. Bill has a look of concern on his face.

MR. PETERS. *(in a friendly tone as Bill enters)* So you wanted to talk to me about something, Bill? You making plans for college already? *(pauses and looks at Bill)* Don't look so worried. *(smiles and offers Bill a seat)*

BILL. *(nervously)* Actually, I need a different kind of help, Mr. Peters. I don't know what to do. If I just tell you the basics, will you help me decide?

MR. PETERS. Let's give it a shot. I will certainly try to help.

BILL. *(looks around to make sure no one is listening)* I caught someone cheating. He knows I saw it and told me not to rat him out. I don't want people to think I am a rat, but I also don't want to be an accomplice to cheating. We both have a lot to lose if I tell. I don't know what to do.

MR. PETERS. *(smiling knowingly)* I think you know what you need to do.

BILL. *(resigned)* I guess you are right. I will talk to Mrs. Lundy at lunch. *The curtain falls.*

Differentiated Instruction for Universal Access

Strategy for Less Proficient Readers

Review with students how plays look on the printed page, with stage directions set in italic type and labels identifying the name of each character who speaks. Then, draw students' attention to the stage directions in the dialogue. Explain that these directions tell the actors how to read the lines and how to move. Direct students' attention to the first speech by Mr. Peters. Then, write the following on the board:

> "So you wanted to talk to me about something, Bill?" said Mr. Peters in a friendly tone. "You making plans for college already?" He paused and looked at Bill. "Don't look so worried," he said, as he smiled and offered Bill a seat.

Explain that, if it appeared in a prose narrative, the passage in the play would look the way you wrote it on the board.

As students read the play to themselves, encourage them to hear the words of the characters as the stage directions describe them.

1. What do you learn from the first set of **stage directions?**
   A. how Bill acts
   B. how Bill feels
   C. how the stage looks
   D. how Mr. Peters' office is set up

2. What **allusion** does Bill make in his first speech?
   A. to a speech he gave
   B. to a news report
   C. to the play *Hamlet*
   D. to a TV show

3. Which of Bill's speaking parts is a **soliloquy?**
   A. first
   B. second
   C. third
   D. fourth

4. What makes Bill's speech a **soliloquy** instead of a **monologue?**
   A. He addresses another character.
   B. He makes a brief remark to the audience.
   C. He is thinking aloud alone on the stage.
   D. He is talking about another character.

5. Based on the **dialogue** and **stage directions,** how would you best describe Mr. Peters?
   A. harsh
   B. smug
   C. funny
   D. caring

6. Which element of **drama** is missing from this selection?
   A. aside
   B. dialogue
   C. stage directions
   D. conflict

7. **Vocabulary** Which word is closest in meaning to the underlined word *accomplice?*
   A. friend
   B. accessory
   C. tattletale
   D. teacher

8. The set of **stage directions** beginning "The curtain falls. It opens…" describes everything *except—*
   A. Bill's expression.
   B. where Mr. Peters is in his office.
   C. Mr. Peters' physical appearance.
   D. why Bill enters the office.

9. Bill's **dialogue** with Mr. Peters reveals—
   A. Bill and Mr. Peters will remain friendly for years.
   B. Mr. Peters believes that Bill cheated on his test and will not confess.
   C. Mr. Peters has advised Bill previously.
   D. Bill trusts Mr. Peters' opinion very much.

Timed Writing

10. **Write** a ten-sentence **monologue** that Bill might deliver to Mrs. Lundy. Be sure he directly addresses the teacher. **Explain** the situation and **describe** his fears in the monologue.

GO ON

Answers

I. Literary Skills

Answers With Explanations

1. C—The directions tell how the stage is lighted and where Bill is positioned. *Incorrect answers:* A—The stage directions do not describe this. B—same explanation as for A. D—The first scene does not take place in Mr. Peters's office.
2. C—Bill refers to Shakespeare's character Hamlet, who also had to make an important decision. *Incorrect answers:* A—Bill does not make this reference. B—same explanation as for A. D—same explanation as for A.
3. A—A soliloquy is a speech made by an actor when onstage alone. *Incorrect answers:* B—In this speech, Bill is talking to another character. C—same explanation as for B. D—same explanation as for B.
4. C—An actor giving a soliloquy is alone on stage. *Incorrect answers:* A—Bill is not addressing another character. B—Bill talks at length and to himself. D—Speaking about another character does not characterize a soliloquy.
5. D—Mr. Peters wants to help Bill. *Incorrect answers:* A—Mr. Peters is concerned about Bill. B—There is nothing self-satisfied about Mr. Peters's manner. C—Mr. Peters smiles but is not being funny.
6. A—An aside is a statement made by an actor that the audience hears but other actors are not meant to hear. *Incorrect answers:* B—The selection has this element. C—same explanation as for B. D—Bill has an internal conflict.
7. B—An accessory, like an accomplice, helps someone else break rules or commit a crime. *Incorrect answers:* A—An accomplice may be a friend, but this is not the closest meaning. C—A tattletale is not an accomplice. D—A teacher is someone who helps another person learn.
8. D—The stage directions do not say why Bill enters. *Incorrect answers:* A—They do describe Bill's expression. B—They say Mr. Peters is sitting behind his desk. C—They describe Mr. Peters as "older."

Reteach

Question	Pages to Reteach
1	801
2	891
3	861
4	861
5	801, 861
6	861
7	—
8	801
9	801

Continued from right column

9. D—Bill would not seek Mr. Peters's advice if he did not trust the counselor. *Incorrect answers:* A—The dialogue does not imply this. B—Mr. Peters does not seem suspicious of Bill. C—This may be true, but option D is a better answer.

Timed Writing

10. Students' monologues should have Bill describe the cheating by Jack and express his own feelings about the situation.

Answers

II. Informational Reading Skills

Answers With Explanations

1. A—This definition best fits a word that describes a task as difficult as improving the environment. *Incorrect answers:* B—A task cannot be intelligent. C—A task cannot be attentive. D—Individuals might be extremely responsible, but a task cannot be.
2. D—As a government agency, the EPA is a respectable organization. *Incorrect answers:* A—Many Web sites are full of inaccuracies. B—Coverage of current events can be inaccurate. C—Media outlets can publish inaccurate information.
3. C—One would scan to find out a specific piece of information, such as the meaning of *EPA*. *Incorrect answers:* A—One would not scan an article to find out its general focus. B—The article does not reveal everything about the EPA. D—The causes of climate change are not discussed in the article.
4. A—The passage says that scientists are working on proving theories about climate change in order to determine its effects. *Incorrect answers:* B—The passage does not say that scientists are somewhat sure. C—The passage does not say that there is certainty about the effects of climate change. D—same explanation as for C.

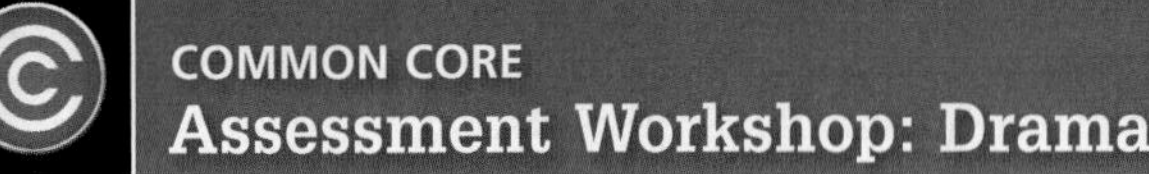

COMMON CORE
Assessment Workshop: Drama

II. Reading Informational Text

Directions: *Read the passage. Then, answer each question that follows.*

Common Core State Standards

RI.9-10.1; W.9-10.5; L.9-10.3, L.9-10.4.a.

[For the full wording of the standards, see the standards chart in the front of your textbook.]

Planet Protection: The EPA

Taking care of the environment is an issue that seems to be constantly reported by the media. Although it may seem that protecting the climate has just become an issue recently, helping the environment is nothing new. One organization devoted to this purpose is the Environmental Protection Agency.

The Environmental Protection Agency (EPA) was founded in 1970 to limit pollution, monitor pesticide use, and ensure clean air and water for all. Since that time, the EPA has been involved in everything from cleaning up oil spills to enforcing laws that make sure drinking water in the United States is safe.

The EPA has recently established the U.S. Climate Change Site in order to provide information to the public about the state of global warming, what is known, and what is still questionable. According to the EPA, we know that the earth's temperature has increased over 1 degree in the last century. Their sources suggest that the temperature will continue to increase. However, scientists are unsure of how quickly and drastically the increase will occur. Scientists are working on proving theories about climate change, thus allowing them to make more accurate predictions about events to come.

The EPA Web site states, "Climate change may be a big problem, but there are many little things we can do to make a difference." The site suggests a variety of ways that people, old and young, can make small changes to take better care of the environment. Although improving the environment may seem to be a daunting task that is too much for one person, these tips can help guide people to small daily changes that do make a difference.

1. **Vocabulary** What is the best definition for *daunting?*
   - **A.** incredibly difficult
   - **B.** oddly intelligent
   - **C.** kindly attentive
   - **D.** extremely responsible
2. How do you know the quotation in the last paragraph is from a reliable source?
   - **A.** It comes from a Web site.
   - **B.** It is from the coverage of a current event.
   - **C.** It comes from a media outlet.
   - **D.** It is from a respected organization.
3. You might scan this article to learn—
   - **A.** its general focus.
   - **B.** everything about the EPA.
   - **C.** what the letters "EPA" represent.
   - **D.** all the causes of climate change.
4. According to the article, how sure are scientists about the effects to come from global warming?
   - **A.** They are not sure at all.
   - **B.** They are somewhat sure.
   - **C.** They are extremely sure.
   - **D.** They have no doubt.

Reteach

Question	Instructional Pages to Reteach
1	—
2	1008
3	—
4	1002

Differentiated Instruction for Universal Access

Strategy for Special-Needs Students

Help students review different types of organization by having them identify these examples:

Inside the store, the produce section was on the right, the dairy counter on the left, and the grocery aisles in the middle. (spatial order)

When Alex was three, she loved to paint. By age five, she was creating clay sculptures. (chronological order)

On Monday a commuter train derailed, injuring 40 people. This halted rail traffic for a full day. (cause and effect)

III. Writing and Language Conventions

Exposition: How-to Essay

Directions: *Read the passage. Then, answer each question that follows.*

(1) One of the easiest and most basic commands to teach your dog is *Sit.* (2) With a little practice, the right technique, and a few treats, you will have a dog that knows how to sit on command. (3) The dog will pick it up within a few brief training sessions. (4) Use the following procedure:

(5) • Gather small training treats.
(6) • Next, stand in front of your dog.
(7) • Then, hold the treat in your hand. (8) Place your hand in front of the dog's nose. (9) Then, move the treat over its head toward the tail as you say your dog's name and "Sit." (10) The dog's head and nose should follow the treat and the rear end should hit the ground. (11) Be sure not to hold the treat too high or the dog will jump up to get it.
(12) • When the dog's hindquarters hit the ground, say "Good sit" and immediately give the dog the treat. (13) Do not give the dog the treat if it doesn't sit. (14) Start over again.
(15) • Repeat.

1. How is the how-to essay **organized?**
- **A.** in step-by-step order
- **B.** in spatial order
- **C.** in chronological order
- **D.** in order of importance

2. How should sentences 7 and 8 be **combined?**
- **A.** Before you hold your hand in front of the dog's nose, hold the treat there.
- **B.** When holding the treat with your hand.
- **C.** Then, holding the treat in your hand, place it in front of the dog's nose.
- **D.** Then, hold the treat in your hand.

3. What **word choice** in sentence 1 establishes the level of difficulty of the task?
- **A.** easiest, most basic
- **B.** One, easiest
- **C.** commands, teach
- **D.** teach, *Sit*

4. Which best describes the **structure** of the instruction?
- **A.** paragraphs
- **B.** list
- **C.** anecdotes
- **D.** charts

5. What would clarify the step in sentence 15?
- **A.** Replace "Repeat" with "Do again."
- **B.** Move sentence 15 earlier in the passage.
- **C.** Explain how many times you should repeat.
- **D.** Describe why this technique works.

6. Which **transition word** belongs in sentence 5?
- **A.** Then
- **B.** Later
- **C.** First
- **D.** Next

III. Writing and Language Conventions

Answers With Explanations

1. A—The writer explains the technique in bulleted steps. *Incorrect answers:* B—There is no use of spatial order. C—The steps include possibilities of what may occur; thus, they are not in chronological order. D—Each step is equally important.
2. C—This eliminates choppy sentences and puts the information in the correct order. *Incorrect answers:* A—It is not possible to hold the treat in front of the dog's nose before holding your hand in that spot. B—This statement is a sentence fragment and does not contain all the information in the original. D—This uses the information in only one sentence.
3. A—The words *easiest* and *basic* explain that the task is not difficult. *Incorrect answers:* B—*One* does not suggest a level of difficulty. C—These words do not suggest a level of difficulty. D—same explanation as for C.
4. B—The instruction is given as a bulleted list. *Incorrect answers:* A—There is only one paragraph. C—The writer does not tell any illustrative stories. D—There are no charts.
5. C—Explaining that one should repeat until the dog learns the lesson clarifies how long to repeat the training. *Incorrect answers:* A—This means the same thing as the original sentence. B—This shift in location would confuse rather than clarify. D—The step-by-step passage already explains why the technique works.
6. C—The word *first* would signal that what follows is a step-by-step process. *Incorrect answers:* A—*Then* should not be used before any steps have been explained. B—*Later* would not make sense to start a process. D—*Next* should be used in the middle of the process.

Reteach

Question	Pages to Reteach
1	960
2	963
3	962
4	960
5	962
6	962

Benchmark

Reteach skills as indicated by students' performance, following the Reteach charts on pages 1019–1021. Then, administer the end-of-unit **Benchmark Test** (***Unit 2 Resources,*** pp. 189–194.) Follow the **Interpretation Guide** for the test **(*Unit 5 Resources,*** pp. 201–206) to assign reteaching pages as necessary in the **Reading Kit**. Use **Success Tracker** online to automatically assign these pages.

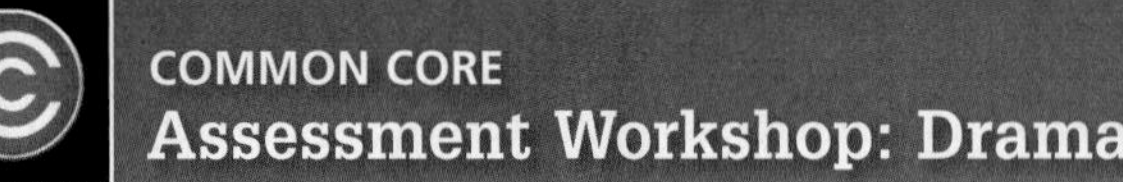

Performance Tasks

Assigning Tasks/Reteaching Skills

Use the chart below to choose appropriate Performance Tasks by identifying which tasks assess lessons in the textbook that you have taught. Use the same lessons for reteaching when students' performance indicates a failure to fully master a standard. For additional instruction and practice, assign the *Common Core Companion* pages indicated for each task.

Task	Where Taught/ Pages to Reteach	*Common Core Companion* Pages
1	944–945, 951	69–75, 190–201, 255–262
2	782	28–34, 255–262
3	861	48–54
4	782–783, 913	28–34, 293–299
5	784, 944	15–27, 302–306
6	608, 681	35–47, 293–299

Assessment Pacing

In assigning the Writing Tasks on this student page, allow a class period for the completion of a task. As an alternative, assign tasks as homework. In assigning the Speaking and Listening Tasks on the facing page, consider having students do any required preparation as a homework assignment. Then, allow a class period for the presentations themselves.

Evaluating Performance Tasks

Use the rubric at the bottom of this Teacher Edition page to evaluate students' mastery of the standards as demonstrated in their Performance Task responses. Review the rubric with students before they begin work so they know the criteria by which their work will be evaluated.

Performance Tasks

Directions: *Follow the instructions to complete the tasks below as required by your teacher.*

As you work on each task, incorporate both general academic vocabulary and literary terms you learned in this unit.

Common Core State Standards

RL.9-10.3, RL.9-10.4, RL.9-10.5; W.9-10.2, W.9-10.9.a; SL.9-10.1; SL.9-10.4
[For the complete wording of the standards, see the standards chart in the front of your textbook.]

Writing

Task 1: Literature [RL.9-10.9; W.9-10.2, W.9-10.9.a]

Analyze Theme in Related Works

Write an essay in which you analyze how Shakespeare draws on the work of Ovid to convey a theme.

- Explain that you will discuss similarities and differences between Ovid's "Pyramus and Thisbe" and Shakespeare's *Romeo and Juliet.*
- Identify specific ways in which the story and the play are similar and different. Consider main characters, minor characters, settings, and events. For each work, describe the reasons that characters act as they do. Finally, explain the themes each work expresses.
- Choose an organizational style that allows you to express ideas clearly and logically. Use a variety of transitional words and phrases to clarify the relationships among ideas.
- Include a clear thesis statement, explaining what you believe to be the theme of both works. Use well-chosen details and quotations to support your interpretation.
- Provide a clear and concise conclusion that summarizes your analysis.

Task 2: Literature [RL.9-10.3; W.9-10.9.a]

Analyze a Complex Character

Write an essay in which you analyze a complex character in a literary work from this unit.

- Explain which work and character you will discuss. Summarize the plot and describe the character's role in the story.
- Present a well-reasoned analysis of the character's actions and motivations. Explain whether the character has multiple or conflicting motivations.
- Explain how the character interacts with other characters. Discuss whether the character changes over the course of the work, and describe the nature of any changes.
- Explain specific ways in which the character's behavior, thoughts, statements, and actions advance the plot and help to express the theme.
- Cite specific details and use quotations from the work to support your ideas.

Task 3: Literature [RL.9-10.5; W.9-10.2]

Analyze Structural Choices

Write an essay in which you analyze the role of a dramatic speech or section of dialogue in a work from this unit.

- State which play and which soliloquy, monologue, or section of dialogue you will discuss.
- Explain why the example you chose is important to the plot and theme of the work as a whole.
- Summarize the circumstances in which the speech or dialogue is delivered. Explain why you think the playwright chose to include this speech or dialogue at this point in the play.
- Interpret the message conveyed in the speech or dialogue. Consider both explicit and implicit meanings.
- Cite specific details to support your ideas.

Performance Task Rubric: Standards Mastery	Rating Scale (*not very* – *very*)
Critical Thinking: How clearly and consistently does the student pursue the specific mode of reasoning or discourse required by the standard, as specified in the prompt (e.g., comparing and contrasting, analyzing, explaining)?	1 2 3 4 5
Focus: How well does the student understand and apply the focus concepts of the standard, as specified in the prompt (e.g., development of theme or of complex characters, effects of structure, and so on)?	1 2 3 4 5
Support/Elaboration: How well does the student support points with textual or other evidence? How relevant, sufficient, and varied is the evidence provided?	1 2 3 4 5
Insight: How original, sophisticated, or compelling are the insights the student achieves by applying the standard to the text(s)?	1 2 3 4 5
Expression of Ideas: How well does the student organize and support ideas? How well does the student use language, including word choice and conventions, in the expression of ideas?	1 2 3 4 5

Speaking and Listening

Task 4: Literature [RL.9-10.3; SL.9-10.4]

Present a Tragic Character

Deliver a speech in which you discuss how a complex character from a play in this unit qualifies as a tragic figure.

- Begin your speech by presenting background for the play—its setting and plot. Then, introduce the character and describe him or her in detail, including his or her role in the plot.
- Consider your audience, purpose, and task as you compose and deliver your presentation. Include information your audience needs in order to understand the general concept of a tragic figure as well as details about your character's choices, motivations, thoughts, and feelings.
- Present your information and supporting evidence clearly, concisely, and logically so that your audience can understand your ideas. Use relevant examples and quotations from the drama to support your analysis.
- End with a memorable conclusion that restates the key elements of your analysis.

Task 5: Literature [RL.9-10.2; SL.9-10.1]

Analyze the Development of a Theme

Lead a small-group discussion about the theme expressed in a literary work from this unit.

- Conduct your own analysis of the text and prepare handouts in which you state your interpretation of the theme. Cite specific details from the beginning, middle, and end of the work that support your point of view.
- Write down three questions you have about the theme and its development throughout the play.
- Share your handouts with the group. Then, ask the first of your questions to start the discussion. Pose your remaining questions as the discussion continues.
- As you lead the discussion, respond thoughtfully to group members' ideas. Work with your group to arrive at a shared understanding of the theme.

Task 6: Literature [RL.9-10.4; SL.9-10.4]

Analyze Word Choice and Tone

Deliver a visual presentation in which you analyze the cumulative impact of word choice on tone in a literary work from this unit.

- State which work you chose and summarize its key elements—setting, character, events, and insight, or theme.
- Define the tone of the work. Cite at least three specific word choices that contribute to this tone.
- Discuss the denotative and connotative meanings of each word you chose. Explain how the connotations of the words contribute to the overall tone of the work.
- Incorporate visuals, such as drawings or photographs, that illustrate specific word choices and the overall tone of the work you chose.
- Present your information clearly, concisely, and logically so that listeners can follow your line of reasoning.

Do our differences define us?
At the beginning of Unit 5, you participated in a discussion about the Big Question. Now that you have completed the unit, write a response to the question. Discuss how your initial ideas have either changed or been reinforced. Cite specific examples from the literature in this unit, from other subject areas, and from your own life to support your ideas. Use Big Question vocabulary words (see p. 779) in your response.

Differentiated Instruction for Universal Access

Strategy for Less Proficient Readers
Assign a Performance Task, and then have students meet in groups to review the standard assessed in that task. Remind students of the selections or independent readings to which they have previously applied the standard. Have groups summarize what they learned in applying the standard and then present their summaries. Discuss, clarifying any points of confusion. After students have completed their tasks, have groups meet again to evaluate members' work. Encourage members to revise their work based on the feedback they receive.

EL Strategy for English Learners
For each assigned Performance Task, review the instructions with students. Clarify the meaning of any unfamiliar vocabulary, emphasizing routine classroom words such as *background, concept,* and *section* and academic vocabulary such as *interpret.* Next, have students note ideas for their responses. Pair students, and have them review each other's notes, asking questions to clarify meaning and suggesting improvements. Encourage students to ask for your assistance in supplying English words or expressions they may require.

Supporting Speaking and Listening

1. Consider having students work with partners or in groups to complete Performance Tasks involving listening and speaking. For tasks that you assign for individual work, you may still wish to have students rehearse with partners, who can provide constructive feedback.
2. As students rehearse, have them keep in mind these tips:
   - Present findings and evidence clearly and concisely.
   - Observe conventions of standard English grammar and usage.
   - Be relaxed and friendly but maintain a formal tone.
   - Make eye contact with the audience, pronounce words clearly, and vary your pace.
   - When working with a group, respond thoughtfully to others' positions, modifying your own in response to new evidence.

Linking Performance Tasks to Independent Reading

If you wish to cover the standards with students' independent reading, adapt Performance Tasks of your choice to the works they have selected. (Independent reading suggestions appear on the next page).

Do our differences define us?

1. Remind students that the unit Big Question is "Do our differences define us?"
2. Have students complete their responses to the prompt on the student page. Point out that they have read selections in this unit about how people are sometimes defined by the ways in which they are different, and that students should draw on these selections in their responses. Remind them that they can also draw on their own experiences and what they have learned in other subject areas in formulating their answers.

EXTEND

Independent Reading

Titles featured on the Independent Reading pages at the end of each unit represent a range of reading, including stories, dramas, and poetry, as well as literary nonfiction and other types of informational text. Throughout, labels indicate the works that are CCSS Exemplar Texts. Choosing from among these featured titles will help students read works at increasing levels of text complexity in the grades 9–10 text complexity band.

Independent Reading and Pacing

See the Unit Overview and Pacing Plan, pp. 778a–778b, for suggestions on integrating independent reading with work in the Student Edition.

Using Literature Circles

A literature circle is a temporary group in which students independently discuss a book.

Use the guidance in the *Professional Development Guidebook*, pp. 47–49, as well as the teaching notes on the facing page, for additional suggestions for literature circles.

Meeting Unit 5 CCS Focus Standards

Students can use books listed on this page to apply and to reinforce their mastery of the CCS Focus Standards covered in this unit. (The Focus Standards are introduced on pp. 780–783.)

Introducing Featured Titles

Have students choose a book or books for independent reading. Assist them by previewing the titles, noting their subject matter and level of difficulty. **Note:** Before recommending a work to students, preview it, taking into account the values of your community as well as the maturity of your students.

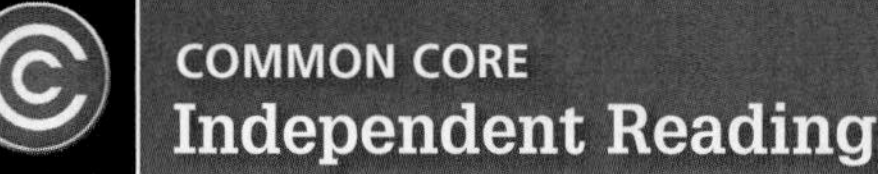

Featured Titles

In this unit, you have read a variety of dramatic works. Continue to read on your own. Select works that you enjoy, but challenge yourself to explore new playwrights and works of increasing depth and complexity. The titles suggested below will help you get started.

Literature

Our Town
by Thornton Wilder
Harper Collins, 2003 — EXEMPLAR TEXT

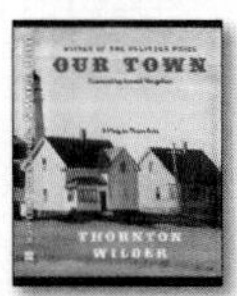

This Pulitzer Prize–winning **drama** explores the daily lives of the citizens of Grover's Corners, a typical American small town. Through everyday events and conversations, the play's characters reveal the impermanence of life and the desperate need to value every moment, no matter how ordinary.

The Glass Menagerie
by Tennessee Williams — EXEMPLAR TEXT

In his first major **drama,** Williams shows what happens when the lid is lifted off lives of quiet desperation. The situation appears simple. Tom Wingfield, a man frustrated with his dead-end life, invites a friend to meet his sister Laura. However, when Tom's fragile sister and overprotective mother meet his friend, the consequences prove complicated—and devastating.

A Pocket Full of Rye
by Agatha Christie
Signet, 2004

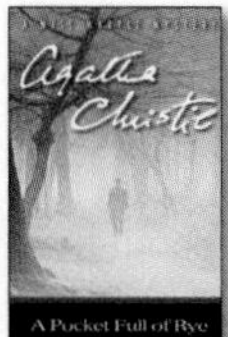

Agatha Christie is a famous name in the world of **mystery fiction.** Her brilliant amateur detective Miss Marple solves crimes that appear unsolvable to everyone else. In this case, the crimes are murders that leave behind clues referring to childhood nursery rhymes that baffle the police.

The Giant's House
by Elizabeth McCracken
The Dial Press, 1996

An unlikely romance blossoms in this **novel** when a lonely librarian falls for a gigantic young man researching his height problems. As the two fall in love, they start to see the world through one another's eyes.

The Shakespeare Stealer
by Gary Blackwood
Dutton, 1998

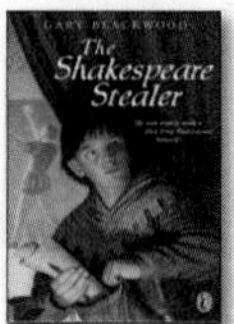

In this **novel,** the young orphan Widge is ordered by his greedy master to steal Shakespeare's new play, *Hamlet.* Welcomed in the theater by Shakespeare's actors, Widge must betray his new friends or risk everything.

Twentieth-Century American Drama — EXEMPLAR TEXT

The **plays** in this volume speak powerfully about the American mind and spirit during the twentieth century, capturing the experiences that define us as Americans and as people. Through these pages, get acquainted with some giants of the American theater—Lorraine Hansberry, Arthur Miller, Thornton Wilder, and Tennessee Williams.

Informational Texts

American Speeches — EXEMPLAR TEXT

This collection of famous American **speeches** features works from some of the country's most memorable speakers, including Martin Luther King, Jr., and Patrick Henry.

Reaching Out
by Francisco Jiménez

In this award-winning **autobiography,** the son of Mexican immigrants shares his experiences as the first member of his family to attend university. As Jiménez adjusts to university life, his family's traditions of hard work and determination help him overcome the challenges of poverty and prejudice.

1024 Drama

Text Complexity: Aligning Texts With Readers and Tasks

TEXTS	READERS AND TASKS
• *The Shakespeare Stealer* (Lexile: 840L) • *Our Town*	**Below-Level Readers** Allow students to focus on reading for content, and challenge them to interpret multiple perspectives.
• *The Giant's House* • *Reaching Out* (Lexile: 910L) • *A Pocket Full of Rye*	**Below-Level Readers** Challenge students as they read for content. **On-Level Readers** Allow students to focus on reading for content, and challenge them to interpret multiple perspectives. **Advanced Readers** Allow students to focus on interpreting multiple perspectives.
• *American Speeches* • *The Glass Menagerie* • *Twentieth-Century American Drama*	**On-Level Readers** Challenge students as they read for content. **Advanced Readers** Allow students to focus on reading for content, and challenge them to interpret multiple perspectives.

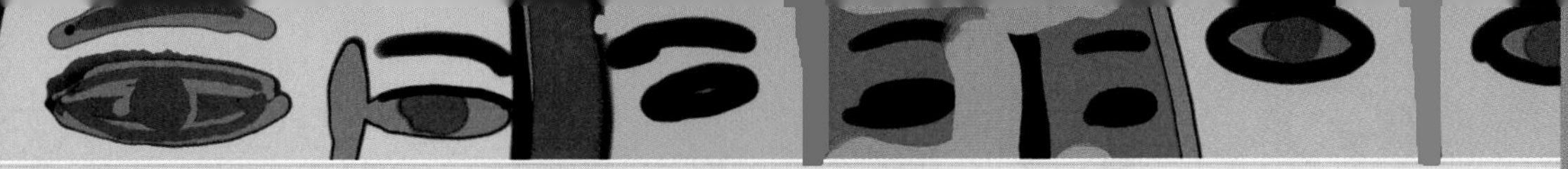

Preparing to Read Complex Texts

Attentive Reading As you read literature on your own, bring your imagination and questions to the text. The questions shown below and others that you ask as you read will help you learn and enjoy literature even more.

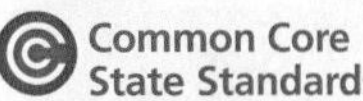 Common Core State Standards

Reading Literature/Informational Text

10. By the end of grade 9, read and comprehend literature, including stories, dramas, poems, and literary nonfiction in the grades 9–10 text complexity band proficiently, with scaffolding as needed at the high end of the range.

When reading drama, ask yourself...

- Who is the main character? What struggles does this character face?
- What other characters are important? How do these characters relate to the main character?
- Is there more than one conflict? If so, how do they connect?
- What is the setting of the play? Does the setting cause conflicts or affect the characters' actions? Why or why not?
- Is there more than one setting? If so, do the settings create different moods or conflicts?
- Are the characters, setting, and events believable? Why or why not?
- Does the play end happily, sadly, or somewhere in between? How does the ending make me feel?
- What theme or insight do I think the play conveys? Is that theme or insight important and true?

Key Ideas and Details

- How is the play structured? How many acts does it have? What events unfold in each act?
- Are there multiple plots—a main plot and a subplot? If so, how do the different plots relate to each other?
- Does the dialogue sound authentic and believable? Why or why not?
- What do the stage directions tell me about the characters and situations? In what other ways do I learn about the characters?
- At what point in the play do I feel the most concern for the characters? Why?
- What point of view does the main character express? Do other characters express similar points of view? If not, is this difference a point of conflict?
- If characters express different points of view, which one do I think the playwright shares? Why? Which point of view do I share? Why?

Craft and Structure

- What do I find most interesting, unusual, or powerful about this play?
- In what ways is the play similar to or different from others I have read or seen?
- What insights have I gained from reading this play?
- What actors would I choose to play the roles in this play?
- If I were to be cast in this play, which role would I want? Why?
- If I were directing this play, how might I stage it?
- After reading this play, do I want to read others by this playwright? Why or why not?

Integration of Ideas

 Text Complexity: Reader and Task Support Suggestions

INDEPENDENT READING

Increased Support Suggest that students choose a book that they feel comfortable reading and one that is a bit more challenging. Pair a more proficient reader with a less proficient reader and have them work together on the more challenging text. Partners can prepare to read the book by reviewing questions on this student page. They can also read difficult passages together, sharing questions and insights. They can use the questions on the student page to guide after-reading discussion.	*Increased Challenge* Encourage students to integrate knowledge and ideas by combining the Big Question and the Unit Focus concepts in their approach to two or more featured titles. For example, students might consider how differences define the characters in *Our Town* and *The Glass Menagerie*. In addition, students can focus on similarities and differences in the values held by different characters.

Preparing to Read Complex Texts

1. Tell students they can be attentive readers by bringing their experience and imagination to the texts they read and by actively questioning those texts. Explain that the questions they see on the student page are examples of questions to ask about works of drama.
2. Point out that, like writing, reading is a "multidraft" process, involving several readings of complete works or passages, revising and refining one's understanding each time.

Key Ideas and Details

3. As an example, review and amplify the last bulleted item in the first section. **Ask:** What key actions, dialogue, and other details could you use to identify a play's theme?

   Possible response: You might point to a particular scene or to details like the opinions that characters express through dialogue.

Craft and Structure

4. **Ask:** What details of craft and structure would you cite as evidence that the dialogue sounds authentic?

   Possible response: You might point to an author's effective use of dialect or word choice.

Integration of Ideas

5. **Ask:** How would you decide which actors to cast in the play?

   Possible response: You might study the physical descriptions of characters in the play or consider actors' work in other plays and films.
6. Finally, explain to students that they should cite key ideas and details, examples of craft and structure, or instances of the integration of ideas as evidence to support their points during a book discussion. After hearing the evidence, the group might reach a consensus or might agree to disagree.

Unit 6 Features Overview

Unit Genre and Big Question

In this unit, students will analyze themes in literature. As they read they will discuss responses to the unit Big Question: Do heroes have responsibilities?

Unit 6 Selections

Teach Selections are presented in leveled pairs. To teach the skills and meet the objectives, you need to assign only one selection in each pair.

Differentiate and Reinforce Choose the selection in a pair that is best suited for your students, based on the Text Complexity box shown on the next page. You may use the other selection to reinforce skills or provide enrichment.

Integrate Skills Each selection presents students with a reading strategy, a literary analysis concept, a vocabulary skill, and grammar instruction. Students can extend learning in the writing and extension activities.

Additional Unit Features

Literary Analysis Workshop Teach and model the Unit Focus standards. Spiral Review notes enable students to revisit these skills over the course of the unit.

Reading for Information Students analyze functional, expository, and argumentative texts and complete Timed Writing activities.

Comparing Literary Works Students study two literary works either within or across genres.

Test Practice: Reading This feature provides extra practice in utilizing reading skills to master assessments.

Writing Workshops Two writing workshops appear in each unit, along with rubrics and instruction in the writing process.

Assessment Workshop Cumulative Skill Review and Performance Tasks provide a range of assessment opportunities.

Independent Reading Students broaden their knowledge as they read longer works of increasing complexity.

THE BIG Q
Do heroes have responsibilities?
W

PHLit Online! www.PHLitOnline.com

Teaching From Technology

Log on at this address for the following:

Enriched Online Student Edition
- full narration of selections
- interactive graphic organizers
- linked **Get Connected!** and **Background** videos
- all worksheets and other student resources

Professional Development
- the *Professional Development Guidebook* online
- additional professional development articles by program authors

Planning, Assigning, and Monitoring
- software for online assignment of work to students, individually or to the whole class
- a system for tracking and grading student work

Themes in Literature: Heroism

Unit 6

PHLit Online!
www.PHLitOnline.com

Hear It!
- Selection summary audio
- Selection audio
- BQ Tunes

See It!
- Author videos
- Big Question video
- Get Connected videos
- Background videos
- More about the authors
- Illustrated vocabulary words
- Vocabulary flashcards

Do It!
- Interactive journals
- Interactive graphic organizers
- Grammar tutorials
- Interactive vocabulary games
- Test practice

1027

Instructional Resources

Unit 6 Resources supports Unit skills with pages of the following types:

- **Benchmark Tests** assess and monitor student progress at mid-Unit and at Unit's end.
- **Vocabulary and Reading Warm-ups** provide additional vocabulary support, based on Lexile rankings of words, for each selection. "A" **Warm-ups** are for students reading two grades below level. "B" **Warm-ups** are for students reading one grade below level.
- **Selection Support** These practice pages are available for each selection:
  - Reading Skill
  - Literary Analysis
  - Writing About the Big Question
  - Vocabulary
  - Support for Writing
  - Support for Extend Your Learning
  - Enrichment

PHLit Online!

All worksheets and other student resources are also available online at **www.PHLitOnline.com.**

Text Complexity: Accessibility for Various Ability Levels

This chart gives a general text complexity rating to help you determine the depth of the prereading and reading support you will need to provide students for each selection. For additional guidance on factors that affect accessibility of each selection, see the Before You Read page for each.

Accessibility for English Learners

This icon indicates support for English learners at point of use in this Teacher's Edition.

	✓ More Accessible	✓✓ More Complex
Text 1		*from* the Odyssey, Part 1
Text 2		*from* the Odyssey, Part 2
Pair 1	Three Skeleton Key	The Red-headed League
Pair 2	There Is a Longing	Glory and Hope

COMMON CORE
UNIT 6 ▪ Overview and Pacing Plan

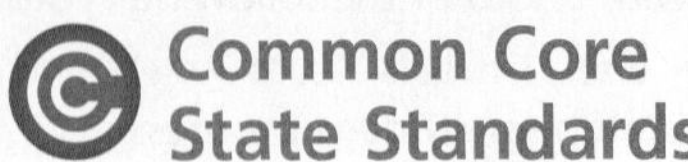

Common Core State Standards

Unit 6 Focus Standards
- **Reading Literature 2, 6**

Additional Activities and Assessments
- **Reading Literature 3, 4, 6**
- **Writing 2, 3, 4, 7**
- **Speaking and Listening 1, 2, 3**
- **Language 1, 2, 6**
- **Reading Informational Text 3, 6**

	Week 1					Week 2					Week 3				
	1	2	3	4	5	1	2	3	4	5	1	2	3	4	5
Introduce the Unit Big Question (pp. 1028–1029).	●														
Introduce the unit forms, themes in literature, using the Literary Analysis Workshop (pp. 1030–1033).	●														
Introduce the focus CCS standards for the unit and lead students in a close reading of exemplar texts. (pp. 1032–1039).	●	●													
Teach one selection from Pairing 1 (pp. 1040–1085).		●	●	●	●	●									
Teach one selection from Pairing 2 (pp. 1086–1117).						●	●	●	●	●					
Complete the Test Practice: Reading (pp. 1118–1119).									●						
Teach Reading for Information (pp. 1120–1125).										●					
Teach Comparing Literary Works (pp. 1126–1137).											●	●			
Have students complete the Writing Workshop (pp. 1138–1143).										●	●	●	●	●	
Administer **Benchmark Test 11** (***Unit 6 Resources,*** pp. 84–90).														●	
Reteach skills, judging which skills to reteach by evaluating students' performance on **Benchmark Test 11.**															●

Independent Reading

Have students choose a full-length work from the Independent Reading feature at the end of the unit and read it while working on this unit.

Pacing Suggestions
- Have students read their chosen work for homework.
- Devote parts of class periods in each school week to Literature Circles in which students reading the same work discuss it.

	Week 4					Week 5					Week 6				
	1	2	3	4	5	1	2	3	4	5	1	2	3	4	5
Teach one selection from Pairing 3 (pp. 1144–1191).	●	●	●	●	●										
Teach one selection from Pairing 4 (pp. 1192–1207).					●	●	●	●	●						
Complete the Test-Practice: Reading (pp. 1208–1209).								●							
Teach Reading for Information (pp. 1210–1215).									●						
Teach Comparing Literary Works (pp. 1216–1233).										●	●				
Have students complete the Writing Workshop (pp. 1234–1241).									●	●	●	●	●		
Have students complete the Vocabulary Workshop (pp. 1242–1243).												●			
Have students complete the Communications Workshop (pp. 1244–1245).													●		
Have students complete the first three sections of the Assessment Workshop: Fiction and Nonfiction (pp. 1246–1249).													●	●	●
Have students complete the selected Performance Tasks in the Assessment Workshop (pp. 1250–1251).														●	
Administer **Benchmark Test** 12 (***Unit 6 Resources,*** pp. 188–193).														●	
Reteach skills, judging which skills to reteach by evaluating students' performance on **Benchmark Test 12.**															●

- Cover the focus standards with independent readings and abbreviate review of the focus standards with student-edition selections.
- Do not assign extension activities for selections (day 5 of main selection lessons), except as needed for full standards coverage.
- If students demonstrate reading proficiency, consider omitting Test Practice: Reading features in the unit.

Block and Daily Scheduling

The assignments and activities in this Unit planner are organized by week. You may adjust them to your daily or block schedule. The Time and Resource Manager for each selection or set gives specific pacing suggestions, or you may use the comprehensive lesson planning support online at **www.PHLitOnline.com.**

Monitoring Progress

Diagnose The last two selection pairings in the Unit contain a more accessible and a more complex selection. To determine which selection in each pairing to assign, refer to students' results on the **Vocabulary in Context** section of **Benchmark Test 10, *Unit 5 Resources,*** pp. 192–194 (administered at the end of the previous Unit). Use the **Interpretation Guide** to interpret the results of this diagnostic portion of the test. **Note:** For the most accurate diagnosis of students who score in the middle range of the diagnostic portion of the test, administer the additional diagnostic questions online at **www.PHLitOnline.com**.

Preteach and Prepare As indicated by the diagnostic, prepare students for reading by assigning the **Vocabulary** and **Reading Warm-ups** for the selections you assign.

Teach Follow this Pacing Plan and use the resources to teach the skills and selections. For specific suggestions and resources, see the Time and Resource Manager and the Visual Guide to Featured Selection Resources preceding each selection pairing.

> ***Classroom Management***
> For classroom management suggestions for using leveled texts in a mixed-ability classroom, see Harvey Daniels's professional development essay "Leveled Reading Selections," online at **www.PHLitOnline.com.**

Assess After students have completed the first half of the Unit, administer **Benchmark Test 11**. Administer **Benchmark Test 12** at the end of the Unit.

Intervention and Reteach After administering each test, use the **Interpretation Guide** for the tests to determine which reteaching pages, if any, you should assign from the ***Reading Kit.*** The appropriate pages are also available through the online Progress Monitoring software.

CLASSROOM STRATEGIES

Write Now **Kelly Gallagher**

> Our richest thinking about what we read occurs when we write.

When considering how to deepen our students' reading comprehension, let us not forget the important role that writing plays in the process. Thinking about the reading-writing connection, I am reminded of the words of E.M. Forster: "How can I know what I think until I see what I say?" Forster is right—our deepest thinking occurs when we write. Therefore, when our students read we want them to stretch their thinking by having them write as much as possible. In short, writing is the tool that enables adolescents to get to the deepest level of reading comprehension. Our richest thinking about what we read occurs when we write.

Why Write

1. **Writing helps students to draw on relevant knowledge and experience as preparation for new activities.** Often, having students write *before* they read deepens their comprehension. Before reading about the Holocaust, for example, having students reflect through writing what they know about concentration camps helps them to begin thinking in the direction of the upcoming reading. By "framing" the text through writing, students warm up for the reading at hand.
2. **Writing helps students to consolidate and review ideas and experiences.** When reading extended difficult text, students' comprehension increases when they take periodic breaks to capture their thinking via writing. When reading *The Odyssey,* for example, students might stop occasionally to write about key lines or to make written connections between the text and the modern world. Doing so enables students to better follow the narrative and allows them to consider some of the "big" ideas on a deeper level.
3. **Writing helps students to reformulate and extend knowledge.** Many times in class I have paused at an intense section of text and asked students what they thought, only to be confronted by a sea of blank faces. I don't do that anymore. Instead, I now pause during the reading and ask my students to explore what they are thinking for a few minutes in their Writers' Notebooks. I have learned that writing is not simply a tool for having students repeat what they already know. Writing is often generative—that is, it *can create new thinking.* Allowing five minutes of writing reflection often turns dumbfounded students into thinkers. Sometimes students have to think before they can think, and writing short reflections enables them to discover what they think.

Strategies for Deepening Reading Comprehension Through Writing

A recent study on the importance of the reading-writing connection ends with a key point: "Writing is not simply a way for students to demonstrate what they know. It is to help them understand what they know. At its best, writing is learning." With this in mind, here are some strategies proven to help students deepen their reading comprehension via writing:

Focus Questions To help students get in the proper frame of mind to read, I often begin class by asking students to write in response to a focus question. There are two types of focus questions: text-dependent and text-independent. Text-dependent questions are used when students are in the middle of a multi-day reading. They are often designed to bring students' minds back to yesterday's reading (e.g., "In yesterday's scene, was Romeo wise to flee to Mantua?"). These questions are text "dependent" because they depend on the students having read the text prior to answering. I also ask text-independent questions–questions that can be answered without having read the passage (e.g., "Can long-term feuds ever be buried?"). Text-independent questions are often used to frame a big idea that will soon be found in that day's reading.

Exit Slips To help students consolidate and review their thinking I often employ the Exit Slip strategy. With five minutes left in the period, I have students take out a half sheet of paper and ask them to reflect on the most interesting idea found in their reading. They write their thinking via a quick writing blast and hand it to me as they leave. This piece of writing is their ticket out the door.

Write Before Talk A simple, but critical strategy. When grappling with difficult passages, I will often ask students challenging questions. Very rarely will I get thoughtful response off the top of their heads. If I want deeper responses, I have to provide them time to explore their thinking. If I am aiming for rich discussion, my students are required to explore their thinking in writing before the discussion. A post-writing discussion is always richer.

Pass-the-Reflection If time permits, students exchange their free responses. When a student receives another's paper, she responds through writing. She can continue the thread, argue against what is being said, or take the conversation in a new direction. Every few minutes the papers are rotated so that students react to a number of views.

Modeled Strategy

See pp. 1047 and 1158 for point-of-use notes modeling these strategies.

Teacher Resources

- ***Professional Development Guidebook***
- ***Classroom Strategies and Teaching Routines* cards**

Log on as a teacher at **www.PHLitOnline.com** to access a library of all Professional Development articles by the Contributing Authors of Pearson Prentice Hall *Literature.*

Kelly Gallagher

Kelly Gallagher is a full-time English teacher at Magnolia High School in Anaheim, California, where he has taught for twenty-two years. He is a former co-director of the South Basin Writing Project and is the author of *Deeper Reading: Comprehending Challenging Texts.*

Supporting Research

Langer, J.A. and Applebee, A.N. (1978). *How writing shapes thinking: A study of teaching and learning.* Urbana, IL: National Council of Teachers of English.

National Commission on Writing For America's Families, Schools, and Colleges. (2003). *The neglected 'R': The need for a writing revolution.* New York: The College. www.writingcommission.org/prod_downloads/writingcom/neglectedr.pdf.

Common Core State Standards
- Speaking and Listening 1
- Language 6

1 Introducing the Big Question

1. Have a volunteer read aloud the introductory paragraph.
2. Guide students in a discussion of heroes. **Ask:** What makes someone a hero? (**Possible response:** A hero goes beyond ordinary expectations to help others.) **Ask** students the Big Question. (**Possible responses:** Yes, because heroes are thinking of others and feel responsible for others; no, because heroes act on their own.)
3. Point out that different heroes feel responsibility to different people or things.

2 Exploring the Big Question

Collaboration: One-on-One Discussion

1. Introduce the activity, using the instruction on the student page.
2. Discuss the following questions:
   - How have the examples changed or reinforced your ideas about heroes? **Sample response:** Students who associate heroes with fame may say they have realized that heroes may be "unsung."
   - Why do you think each person does what they do? **Sample response:** Firefighters save people because it is their job, but they might have become firefighters because they wanted to help people.
3. Review the Big Question vocabulary on page 1029, following the teaching suggestions. Have students use the vocabulary as they complete the activity on page 1028.

Connecting to the Literature

Explain the Big Question strand in the unit, referring to the box at right.

1 Do heroes have responsibilities?

Heroes are all around us. We find them in literature and in the real world. Heroes sometimes show strength of character and an unusual depth of wisdom. They make important choices and selflessly get involved when others might stand back. Heroes may serve others and fight for justice. Often, they exhibit outstanding courage, honesty, and leadership, but sometimes they do not have any of these qualities. They can be ordinary, unassuming people who somehow stand up in a crisis and act in heroic ways. Think about who heroes are and what makes them take action. Is it character? Is it a sense of responsibility?

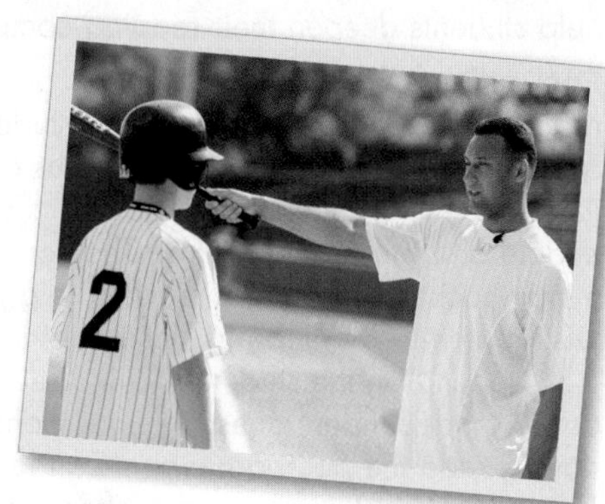

2 Exploring the Big Question

Collaboration: One-on-One Discussion Start thinking about the Big Question by listing heroes whom you know about. They might be people you know personally or have read about in works of nonfiction, such as biographies, history books, or newspapers. They might be characters you have watched on TV shows or in movies or read about in works of fiction. To help identify heroes you already know about, describe a hero from each of these categories:

- A person whose courageous act saves or protects those who are in danger
- Someone who chooses honesty or integrity over self-interest
- A leader who guides others to success
- A person who sacrifices himself or herself to help others
- Someone who acts to help others without a desire for reward or recognition

After you have completed your list, share it with a partner. As you describe each person on your list, provide details that show why he or she is a hero. As your partner reads from his or her list, listen carefully and ask questions if the description or the qualities of a hero that your partner has chosen are not clear to you. Then, use the Big Question vocabulary as you discuss whether a sense of responsibility motivated the heroes on your lists. Work actively to clarify, challenge, and enrich each other's ideas. Finally, come to an agreement on the qualities that make up a hero, select one or two examples of a hero who has such qualities, and present your findings to the class.

Connecting to the Literature Each reading in this unit will give you additional insight into the Big Question.

PHLit Online!
www.PHLitOnline.com
- Big Question video
- Illustrated vocabulary words
- Interactive vocabulary games
- BQ Tunes

Applying Understanding by Design Principles

The Big Question

Explain to students that they will continue to consider the Big Question as they work through Unit 6.
- At the beginning of each selection, they will write a response to a Writing About the Big Question sentence starter.
- As they read the selection, they will look for details related to the Big Question.
- At the end of the selection, they will answer a Critical Thinking question that is related to the Big Question.
- Tell students that their goal will be to gain a deeper understanding of literature and a more sophisticated way of discussing the Big Question.

3 Learning Big Question Vocabulary

Acquire and Use Academic Vocabulary Academic vocabulary is the language you encounter in textbooks and on standardized tests. Review the definitions of these academic vocabulary words.

choices (choí sez) *n.* a variety of possibilities that a person can select from

hero (hir′ o) *n.* a person who is admired for brave or noble actions

identify (i den′ tə fí) *v.* define who someone is or what something is

intentions (in ten′ shənz) *n.* aims or purposes that a person has in mind

serve (surv) *v.* perform duties for another person or be useful to him or her

Use these words as you complete Big Question activities in this unit that involve reading, writing, speaking, and listening.

Gather Vocabulary Knowledge Additional Big Question words are listed below. Categorize the words by deciding whether you know each one well, know it a little bit, or do not know it at all.

character	justice	standard
honesty	morality	wisdom
imitate	obligation	
involvement	responsibility	

Then, do the following:

1. Work with a partner to write each word on one side of an index card and its definition on the other side.
2. Verify each definition by looking the word up in a print or online dictionary. Revise your definitions as needed.
3. Place the cards with the words facing up in a pile.
4. Take turns drawing a word card, pronouncing the word, and making a true or false statement that uses the word and is related to ideas of heroism and responsibility. Here is an example: *Thoughtlessness is typical of a heroic character.* Invite your partner to determine whether the statement is true or false.

Common Core State Standards

Speaking and Listening
1. Initiate and participate effectively in a range of collaborative discussions with diverse partners on *grades 9–10 topics, texts, and issues,* building on others' ideas and expressing their own clearly and persuasively.
1.c. Propel conversations by posing and responding to questions that relate to broader themes or larger ideas; actively incorporate others into the discussion; and clarify, verify, or challenge ideas and conclusions.

Language
6. Acquire and use accurately general academic and domain-specific words and phrases, sufficient for reading, writing, speaking, and listening at the college and career readiness level; demonstrate independence in gathering vocabulary knowledge when considering a word or phrase important to comprehension or expression.

3 Learning Big Question Vocabulary

Acquire and Use Academic Vocabulary

1. Introduce the academic vocabulary words in the first word bank on the student page. Have students preview the words.
2. For each word, have students say the word aloud. Then, use the word in a sentence that defines the word.

Gather Vocabulary Knowledge

1. With the class, review the steps in the activity on the student page.
2. Before students complete the last step, review the words and their meanings as a class. (Definitions appear below on the left.)

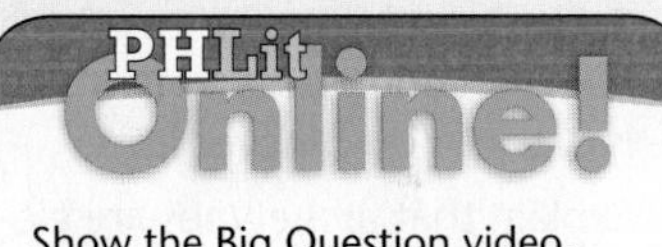

Show the Big Question video, online at www.PHLitOnline.com.

Gather Vocabulary Knowledge: Definitions

character [kar′ək tər] *n.* intellectual or moral qualities that make a person unique

honesty [än′is tē] *n.* the quality of being truthful

imitate [im′i tāt′] *v.* to copy the actions of another person

involvement [in välv′mənt] *n.* the state of participating in, or being associated with, something

justice [jus′tis] *n.* fair and impartial behavior

morality [mə ral′i tē] *n.* principles that a person uses to determine whether behavior is right or wrong

obligation [äb′li gā′shən] *n.* duty or commitment

responsibility [ri spän′sə bil′ə tē] *n.* a sense of duty in dealing with a person or situation

standard [stan′dərd] *n.* a value or a way of conduct that directs people's behavior

wisdom [wiz′dəm] *n.* the ability to make good judgments based on knowledge and experience

TEACH

❶ Theme and the Oral Tradition

1. Introduce the concepts of theme and oral tradition, using the instruction on the student page.
2. **Ask** students to list types of oral literature they have read.

   Sample responses: folk tales, fairy tales, fables, tall tales, legends, myths, ballads, proverbs, or parables.

   Choose a specific example that most students know, and discuss how it reflects the cultural experiences of its first tellers. For example, the legend of King Arthur reflects a culture in which knights followed a strict code of honor.
3. Challenge students to identify other universal themes.

   Sample responses: Loss is painful. Everyone wants to fit in. Love is grand. Youth never lasts.
4. Explain that archetypes are elements that recur throughout history and literature. Common archetypes include three wishes, the journey of discovery, the wise elder, and magical transformation. Discuss with students how these archetypes are used in stories they know.
5. Refer to the chart on the student page and discuss the concept of quest. Challenge students to identify examples of quests they have read in stories or books or seen in films.

❶Theme and the Oral Tradition

Stories from the oral tradition teach a culture's central values and beliefs. They also convey universal themes.

Oral Tradition Storytellers and poets of long ago did not write down the tales they told. Instead, they learned the stories and poems of their culture from others and recited them from memory. The term **oral tradition** refers to the literature they passed down through the ages by word of mouth. Eventually, these spoken stories and poems were retold in writing.

The tales of love, ambition, and friendship in the oral tradition do more than entertain. They record the history, customs, beliefs, and values of the cultures from which they sprang. The **points of view,** or perspectives on life, expressed in this literature reflect the **cultural experiences** of the tellers—the basic experiences that shaped life in their society. For example, the stories of a warrior culture tell of battle and adventure, heroism and sacrifice. Experiences of war along with the emphasis placed on bravery and loyalty form the **social and cultural context** for such tales—the values, beliefs, and experiences the tales reflect and affirm.

Themes Like much literature, works in the oral tradition convey **themes—**deeper meanings or insights. A **universal theme** is an insight into life and human nature that appears in the literature of many different times and cultures.

Universal themes concern fundamental ideas such as the importance of heroism, the strength of loyalty, the power of love, the responsibilities of leadership, the struggle between good and evil, and the dangers of greed.

Storytellers in the oral tradition often explore universal themes, and they frequently do so using archetypes. An **archetype** is an element that recurs throughout the literature of different cultures. Character types, plot patterns, images, and symbols all may be archetypes, as in the examples shown below.

Example: Archetypes
- The **trickster** is a clever person or animal who can fool others but often gets into trouble through curiosity.
- In the **hero's quest,** a clever or brave person undergoes a series of tests or trials while on a search for something of great importance.
- The character of the hero is often called the **protagonist,** and his **antagonist** is the character or force that opposes him. Often, the opposing force is a **monster,** a nonhuman or semi-human figure that menaces society and must be destroyed by the hero.

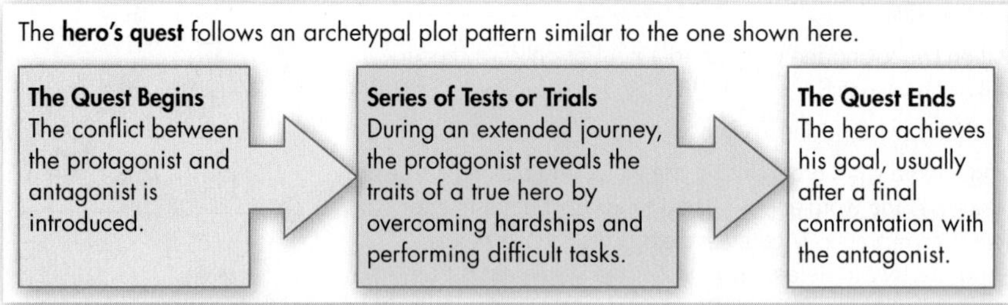

The Quest Begins
The conflict between the protagonist and antagonist is introduced.
Series of Tests or Trials
During an extended journey, the protagonist reveals the traits of a true hero by overcoming hardships and performing difficult tasks.
The Quest Ends
The hero achieves his goal, usually after a final confrontation with the antagonist.

The **hero's quest** follows an archetypal plot pattern similar to the one shown here.

Teaching Resources

- All *Common Core Companion,* pp.15–27, 55–61
- All *Unit 6 Resources,* pp. 7–22
  Professional Development Guidebook, p. 33
- All *See It!* DVD **Dean Smith and John Kilgo,** Segments 2 and 4
- All *Graphic Organizer Transparencies,* pp. 181–182
- All **Enriched Online Student Edition**
- L2 L3 *Reader's Notebook*
- L1 *Reader's Notebook: Adapted Version*
- EL *Reader's Notebook: English Learners Version*
- L2 EL *Hear It!* Audio CD
- L1 EL *Hear It!* Audio CD (adapted text)

PHLit Online! All resources, including print and video, are available online at **www.PHLitOnline.com.**

❷ Forms from the Oral Tradition

Across cultures, storytellers in the oral tradition developed specific narrative forms. Among these forms are myths, folk tales, legends, and epics.

Narratives in each of these forms express the values, ideals, and behaviors held important by the culture from which they came. They also reflect the oral nature of the tradition. For example, epics may feature *epithets,* or descriptive phrases that are repeated when a character is named. These epithets may have helped storytellers memorize the story. They might also have helped listeners recognize and remember the characters.

Literary Forms in the Oral Tradition

Form	Characteristics	Example
Myth	• describes the actions of gods or heroes or explains the origins of elements of nature • is present in the literature of every ancient culture. Ancient Greek and Roman myths are known as **classical mythology.**	Prometheus, son of the Greek god Zeus, defies his father and the other gods by giving fire to humans.
Folk Tale	• follows a simple formula • deals with heroics, adventure, magic, or romance • frequently contains animal characters with human traits, such as the trickster coyote • includes fables and fairy tales	A poor fisherman catches a golden fish. The fish and the man strike a deal: in exchange for its freedom, the fish will grant the man a wish. The man agrees, but he and his wife become greedy and demand more wishes. The fish vanishes, leaving the fisherman in poverty once more.
Legend	• recounts the adventures of a hero from the past • relates events that may or may not be based on a historical truth • includes tall tales, which feature exaggeration	Stories of Davy Crockett portray this real-life hero as a superhero who frees the sun, uses lightning to fly, and defeats the entire British navy.
Epic	• is a long narrative poem • describes the deeds of a larger-than-life hero • combines features of myths and legends • depicts a hero who usually goes on a dangerous journey or quest; the hero is helped or hindered by supernatural creatures or gods • gives a detailed portrait of a culture	The ancient Mesopotamian king Gilgamesh, who is part human and part god, displays wisdom and strength as he struggles against the gods, nature, and his own human weaknesses.

❸ In This Section

Theme and the Oral Tradition

Determining Themes

Analyzing Point of View and Cultural Experience

Close Read: Theme and Point of View
- Model Text
- Practice Text

After You Read

Common Core State Standards

RL.9-10.2, RL.9-10.6
[For the full wording of the standards, see the standards chart in the front of your textbook.]

❷ Forms of Oral Tradition

1. Introduce the forms of oral tradition, using the instruction and chart on the student page.
2. Explain that myths were early attempts at explaining natural phenomena. Unable to provide scientific explanations for natural phenomena, early people ascribed them to a supernatural force, such as a god or goddess.
3. Explore students' knowledge of the literary forms of oral tradition. Challenge students to list additional examples of the literary forms in the chart.

   Possible responses: Students may mention the myth of Icarus flying too close to the sun, the folk tale of the girl who danced herself to death while wearing enchanted red shoes, the legend of King Arthur, or the epic of Aeneas, founder of Rome.
4. **Ask:** How are myths and legends similar and different?

   Sample response: Both may be very old, and both were often used to explain a natural or historical occurrence. Myths focus on gods and goddesses, while legends focus on people who once lived.

❸ In This Section

Explain that in the remainder of this Literary Analysis Workshop, students will learn to determine theme in the oral tradition and analyze point of view and cultural experience. After reviewing the concepts, students will then see them applied in an analysis of a Model text. Finally, they will apply what they have learned to an Independent Practice text.

Differentiated Instruction for Universal Access

Strategy for Less Proficient Readers

Even less proficient readers are likely to be familiar with stories from the oral tradition, especially fairy tales. They will also likely know about popular fiction, movies, and television series that draw on elements of oral tradition.

On the board, list some popular stories, films, and television series that contain elements of oral literary forms. Then, place students in small groups. Ask each group to select one of the titles from the board. Students should then reread the Characteristics column in the chart on page 1031 and ascertain which characteristics apply to their chosen title. Students may discover that the work contains characteristics of more than one literary form.

Ask each group to share its findings with the class. Afterward, as a class, formulate a generalization about the influence of oral tradition on modern storytelling.

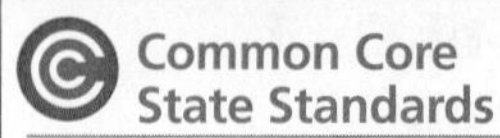

Common Core State Standards

Unit 6 Focus Standards

- **Reading Literature 2**
- **Reading Literature 6**

These standards spiral through the unit.

❶ Determining Themes

1. Introduce the concept of theme, using the instruction on the student page.
2. Emphasize that most literary works imply, or suggest, their themes rather than state them directly. For example, a story may suggest a theme about the power of love through the actions and fates of characters or through plot events.
3. Review with students the concept of universal themes and archetypes, defined on the student page. Make sure students understand that not every theme is universal.
4. Lead students in a discussion of the development and determination of theme in a story. **Ask:** How does a pattern of events in a story support the theme?

   Sample response: Each time a similar event happens, it reinforces an important idea or theme.
5. **Ask:** How are archetypes and patterns similar?

   Sample response: They both recur across stories and cultures. They both help express a theme.

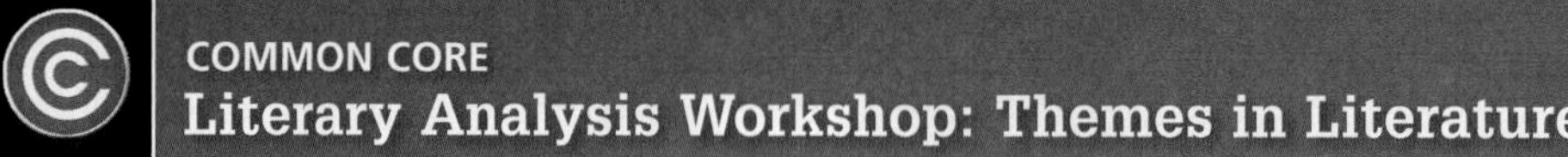

COMMON CORE

Literary Analysis Workshop: Themes in Literature

❶ Determining Themes

At the center of a literary work is its **theme**—the insight or message that its details combine to convey.

Common Core State Standards

Reading Literature

2. Determine a theme or central idea of a text and analyze in detail its development over the course of the text, including how it emerges and is shaped and refined by specific details; provide an objective summary of the text.

6. Analyze a particular point of view or cultural experience reflected in a work of literature from outside the United States, drawing on a wide reading of world literature.

The **theme,** or central insight or message of a literary work, may be stated directly. For example, a fable ends with a statement of the moral of the story, such as "He who hesitates is lost." Frequently, however, the theme of a work is **implied,** or suggested, by story details. Readers can determine an implied theme by analyzing the way storytellers pattern details.

Development of Themes To introduce and develop a theme, writers create patterns of events and actions or of contrasts between characters and their fates. As the story unfolds, new events may reinforce these patterns or alter them, suggesting new ideas to readers.

By identifying such patterns as you read, you will gain clues to the implied theme. Restating the patterns in general terms will help you reach a conclusion about an implied theme, as shown in the following example:

Title	"Midas and the Golden Touch"
Pattern	Everything King Midas touches turns to gold, including his beloved daughter.
Generalized Restatement	Driven by greed, a person destroys what he loves.
Theme	Greed can destroy all that is good in a person's life.

Determining Universal Themes In the oral tradition, universal themes—themes found in the literature of many cultures—are often conveyed through the use of **archetypes,** or recurring elements common to many stories. Your ability to recognize these archetypes as the story develops and to interpret their meanings can help you determine a story's universal themes, as in the following example:

Story	**The Tortoise and the Hare** A tortoise and a hare compete in a race. The hare assumes he will win and stops for a nap. The tortoise keeps going and wins.
Archetypes	• Overconfident, boastful character (hare) • Quiet, confident character (tortoise) • Plot pattern: Competition in which a weaker character succeeds because of the pride of a stronger character
Universal Themes	• Slow and steady wins the race. • Too much pride can have bad results.

Culturally Specific Themes Not all themes in the oral tradition are universal. Some are specific to the time and the culture in which the story originated. These themes reflect the specific social and cultural backgrounds of their authors. Generally, they do not apply to people in modern cultures. Still, they provide an interesting window into the values, beliefs, and customs of bygone eras.

Think Aloud

Theme

To model determining theme in the story of King Midas, say to students:

First, I recall that a god grants Midas the power to turn things into gold by touching them. The god warns of problems, but Midas thinks of how rich he will become. Midas is pleased, until he turns his beloved daughter into gold. At that point, he wishes to be rid of the power.

Now I consider the pattern of events. Each time Midas turns ordinary objects into gold, he is happy because he feels rich. When he turns his daughter into gold, he is sad. So I can make a generalized statement "Driven by greed, Midas destroys what he truly loves."

Next, I turn the generalization into a universal theme: "Greed can destroy all that is good in a person's life." That theme applies not only to this story and ancient Greek culture but also to other cultures, including our own.

❷ Analyzing Point of View and Cultural Experience

Authors' cultural backgrounds influence their points of view.

Point of View An author's **point of view,** or perspective, consists of his or her attitudes toward, and beliefs about, a subject. Point of view determines how the writer approaches a subject. An author's point of view is influenced in part by his or her cultural experiences—the basic experiences, beliefs, and values that shape life in his or her society.

Literature in the oral tradition usually expresses a cultural—rather than an individual—point of view. By contrast, works of modern literature usually express an author's unique and individual point of view. This point of view may even be critical of the author's own culture. In both cases, it is important for readers to recognize the point of view and cultural experiences that shape a literary text.

Examples

Author's Cultural Experiences
The history, beliefs, values, and behavior of a specific group

↓

Author's Point of View, or Perspective
The author's attitude—feelings, opinions, and ideas—about a subject; the author's view of the world

Cultural Experience and Purpose The author's **purpose** is his or her main reason for writing. Writers usually write **to entertain, to inform or explain,** or **to persuade.** Although entertainment was a means for getting the attention of listeners, storytellers in the oral tradition also felt responsible for preserving the identity of their culture. Through stories and poems, they reminded people of their history; they communicated values to younger members of their group; and they shared religious beliefs. Storytellers were more than just entertainers; they served as historians, teachers, and advisors.

Modern writers may also create literature with more than one purpose in mind. For example, an author might write a story that includes information about a serious problem in the world, and at the same time provide readers with a satisfying narrative that entertains.

Changing Points of View As stories were passed among generations and cultures, details changed to reflect different values and attitudes. Consider this example of a story that has been retold in numerous cultures.

Example: Cinderella
After Cinderella's mother dies, her father remarries and leaves Cinderella with his new wife and her two daughters. Cinderella is enslaved by the unreasonable demands of her cruel stepmother and stepsisters. She attends the King's ball and she meets the Prince. Eventually, Cinderella and the Prince marry and live happily ever after.

Culture/ Version	Cultural Viewpoint	Specific Details
German tale retold by the Brothers Grimm in 1812	Medieval view: Cruelty and violence are part of the world.	At the end, birds peck out the eyes of the stepsisters.
American version, based on a retelling by the French writer Charles Perrault in 1697	Modern view: Violence and cruelty should be hidden from children's view.	At the end, Cinderella forgives her stepsisters and invites them to live in the castle.

❷ Analyzing Point of View and Cultural Experience

1. Introduce the concepts of point of view and cultural experience, using the instruction on the student page.
2. Make sure students understand the distinction between individual and cultural points of view. Give an example of an individual point of view that clashes with a cultural point of view. (A writer thinks that following a vegetarian lifestyle is important, but the culture in which that person lives thinks that eating meat is good for one's health.) Emphasize to students that knowing how a writer's individual point of view relates to the cultural point of view can help them understand what they read.
3. Review the different purposes for storytelling. Challenge students to identify examples of writing for each purpose.
4. Have students read the "Cinderella" summary and the information in the second column of this page. **Ask:** How did the cultural viewpoint change over time?

   Sample response: Violence became less acceptable, especially in entertainment meant for children.
5. Remind students that in this Workshop they will read a model analysis of a passage and then perform their own analysis of a second passage.

3 Close Read: Theme and Point of View

1. Remind students that a theme of a work is its central insight about life. A point of view is the storyteller's perspective.
2. Review the Clues to Identifying Theme and Point of View chart. Discuss how each element helps readers determine theme or point of view. For example, if a character fails in a quest, the element of character contributes to a theme about the whims of fate.
3. Select a work, such as a fairy tale, that all students know. Place students in groups. Assign each group a category from the chart (except Word Choice and Sentence Patterns, if students do not have the text in front of them). Tell students to meet with group members and apply the statements in their category to the work. For "Cinderella," students might suggest the following:

   Theme: good and evil

   Social and Cultural Context: practice of remarriage and shunning of stepchildren

   Setting: long ago, in Europe; a world hostile to children

   Characters: Cinderella is good but wears rags; marrying the prince rewards her goodness
4. Point out examples of highlighted text in the model on pages 1035–1036. Explain how the color of the highlighting matches the category.

3 Close Read: Theme and Point of View

Recognizing theme and point of view in literature will enrich your reading experience and broaden your appreciation of the written word.

From the oral tradition to works of modern literature, stories and poems teach us about life, other cultures, and ourselves. They also express distinctive points of view of the world. To convey themes and express point of view, storytellers use a variety of literary elements as well as details that reflect their cultural experiences. Note that nonfiction writers, too, may incorporate literary elements into their works. For example, a work of literary nonfiction may express its writer's point of view as it conveys a central idea, or theme. Analyze literary elements as you read to draw conclusions about theme and point of view. Use the tips in the chart to guide you.

Clues to Theme and Point of View

Archetype As you read, look for • essential opposites, such as good and evil, or dark and light; • character types, such as the hero, the trickster, the warrior, or the mysterious guide; • patterns of events, such as a sequence of obstacles, or a series of riddles.	**Characters** As you read, notice • what you learn about characters from their appearances, thoughts, actions, and words; • ways in which characters' values, beliefs, and struggles reflect the cultural context of the work; • what insight into life characters' actions and ultimate fates suggest.
Social and Cultural Context As you read, think about • cultural practices described in the text; • values and beliefs suggested by characters' actions, thoughts, and statements; • the writer's background, including his or her culture, geographic location, and beliefs.	**Direct Statements or Observations** As you read, notice • any direct statements or observations characters make about themselves or their situations; • any direct statements the author makes about his or her values, background, or beliefs.
Setting The time and place in which a work takes place may shed light on the theme and cultural point of view. As you read, consider • the **setting**—when and where the story occurs; • what insights about the world the setting suggests—for example, whether the setting is hostile or friendly, fertile or arid, unforgiving or welcoming.	**Word Choice and Sentence Patterns** As you read, look for • descriptive details that help express the writer's point of view; • words with strong positive or negative connotations, or associations, suggesting a point of view; • repeated sentence patterns that emphasize particular ideas.

Vocabulary Development

CCSS Language 6

Domain-Specific Words: Literature

Reinforce comprehension of the literary terms on this page by having students complete these "show-you-know" sentences. The second part of each provides a definition of the term.

Example: The character of the noble prince is an *archetype*; it recurs in many stories from different time periods and cultures.

1. The *setting* of most versions of "Cinderella" is Europe during the eighteenth century; ______

   Sample response: that is the time and place in which the story occurs.
2. Cinderella is the main *character*; ______

   Sample response: she is the person at the center of the story.
3. The *point of view* of the author of "Cinderella" is that modest, hardworking people deserve to be rewarded; ______

   Sample response: the point of view is the writer's perspective.

❹ Model

About the Text The *Ramayana* is one of the famous epic poems of India. The poet Valmiki wrote the earliest surviving version in the ancient Indian language of Sanskrit some time after 300 B.C. Grounded in Hindu culture, the poem tells the life story of Rama, who embodies the spirit of the Hindu god Vishnu.

from the *Ramayana* retold by R. K. Narayan

Background: *As an adult, Rama is about to inherit the throne from his father when evil plots result in his banishment from the kingdom. For fourteen years, he wanders in exile with his wife, Sita, and his brother, Lakshmana. During this time, Sita is kidnapped by the evil giant Ravana, chief of a group of rakshasas, or demons. His name means "He who makes the universe scream." Rama sets out to rescue Sita with the help of Hanuman, the monkey god, and a huge battle ensues. This selection opens as the battle is reaching its climax.* ❺

Rama and Ravana in Battle

Every moment, news came to Ravana of fresh disasters in his camp. One by one, most of his commanders were lost. No one who went forth with battle cries was heard of again. Cries and shouts and the wailings of the widows of warriors came over the chants and songs of triumph that his courtiers arranged to keep up at a loud pitch in his assembly hall. Ravana became restless and abruptly left the hall and went up on a tower, from which he could obtain a full view of the city. He surveyed the scene below but could not stand it. One who had spent a lifetime in destruction, now found the gory spectacle intolerable. Groans and wailings reached his ears with deadly clarity. . . . This was too much for him. He felt a terrific rage rising within him, mixed with some admiration for Rama's valor. He told himself, "The time has come for me to act by myself again." ❻

❼ He hurried down the steps of the tower, returned to his chamber, and prepared himself for the battle. He had a ritual bath and performed special prayers to gain the benediction of Shiva; donned his battle dress, matchless armor, armlets, and crowns. He had on a protective armor for every inch of his body. . . .

When he emerged from his chamber, his heroic appearance was breathtaking. He summoned his chariot, which could be drawn by horses or move on its own if the horses were hurt or killed. People stood aside when he came out of the palace and entered his chariot. "This is my resolve," he said to himself: "Either that woman Sita, or my wife Mandodari, will soon have cause to cry and roll in the dust in grief. Surely, before this day is done, one of them will be a widow."

❽ The gods in heaven noticed Ravana's determined move and felt that Rama would need all the support they could muster. They requested Indra to send down his special chariot for Rama's use. When the chariot appeared at his camp, Rama was deeply impressed with the magnitude and brilliance of the vehicle. . . .

Rama fastened his sword, slung two quivers full of rare arrows over his shoulders, and climbed into the chariot.

❺ **Archetype** Sita's kidnapping sets up the conflict between Rama and Ravana. This struggle is an archetype that expresses an important universal theme—the question of whether good or evil ultimately triumphs.

❻ **Characters** The narrator reveals Ravana's disturbed state of mind as Ravana prepares to face Rama. These details develop one important theme—evil is associated with a lack of self-control.

❼ **Social and Cultural Context** Shiva is the Hindu god of destruction. This reference would have special meaning for members of the Hindu religion.

❽ **Social and Cultural Context** The gods' support for Rama reflects Hindu belief in a moral universe and is key to the story's cultural point of view.

TEACH

❹ Reading the Model

Discuss the About the Text note. Then have students read the passage (pp. 1035–1036).

❺ Archetype

Have a volunteer read aloud the Background paragraph and the Archetype annotation. Challenge students to predict how the epic will end.

❻ Characters

Read aloud the bracketed sentences and the Characters annotation. **Ask:** How would you describe Ravana?

Sample response: He is restless and angry. He is used to violence and is ready for a fight.

❼ Social and Cultural Context

Tell students to read the bracketed sentences and the Social and Cultural Context annotation. **Ask:** What do you learn here about Ravana's culture?

Sample response: In his culture, warriors prepare for battle with special rituals and prayers.

❽ Social and Cultural Context

Have a volunteer read aloud the bracketed sentences and the Social and Cultural Context annotation. Remind students that epics, like myths, often feature gods.

Fluency

Have students work in pairs. Distribute copies of page 1035. Direct partners to take turns reading aloud, starting with "He hurried down the steps . . ." and ending with the last paragraph on the page. Have the partner who is listening mark any words or phrases with which the reader has difficulty. (Students should not mark unfamiliar names, such as Shiva, Sita, or Mandodari.) Collect and review students' copies. Look for these problem spots:

- If students have difficulty with the phrase "matchless armor, armlets, and crowns," explain that here *matchless* means "better than all others." Explain that armlets are protective armor that fit around the wrist and forearm.
- If students have difficulty with the phrase "slung two quivers full of rare arrows," tell them that a quiver is a special holder for arrows. Explain that "rare arrows" most likely means the arrows were special or even magical. If necessary, demonstrate the movement of slinging a quiver onto your back to illustrate the movement described in the paragraph.

9 Word Choice

Read aloud the bracketed text and the Word Choice annotation. **Ask:** Which words and phrases evoke the excitement of the approaching battle? Why?

Sample responses: The words and phrases *beat, drums, cries, trumpets, rolling chariots,* and *deafening* all suggest the noise of soldiers readying for battle.

10 Characters

Have a volunteer read aloud the bracketed text and the Characters annotation. Help students compare Rama and Ravana by drawing a T-chart on the board. Have students list the qualities of each character in the appropriate column.

11 Social and Cultural Context

Read aloud the bracketed text and the Social and Cultural Context annotation. **Ask:** What were the ominous signs?

Sample response: snapping bow-strings, shaking mountains, thunder, weeping horses, and sad elephants

12 Word Choice

Ask a volunteer to read aloud the bracketed text and the Word Choice annotation. **Ask:** Why is *doom* an appropriate word here?

Sample response: *Doom* is a serious word that suggests Ravana's fate is one of total annihilation or destruction.

Model continued

9 Word Choice The use of descriptive phrases creates a vivid picture of the scene. The mood of excitement and chaos reflects the author's perspective—the battle will be exciting.

10 Characters In the heat of battle, Rama is calm, wise, and rational. The contrast between Rama's and Ravana's states of mind helps refine an important theme—good is associated with rational thought and action, evil with disorder.

11 Social and Cultural Context Omens, or events regarded as signs of the future, were often taken quite seriously in ancient cultures.

12 Word Choice The phrase "his own doom" reveals that Rama will triumph over Ravana. This outcome develops the universal theme that good triumphs over evil.

9 The beat of war drums, the challenging cries of soldiers, the trumpets, and the rolling chariots speeding along to confront each other, created a deafening mixture of noise. While Ravana had instructed his charioteer to speed ahead, 10 Rama very gently ordered his chariot driver, "Ravana is in a rage; let him perform all the antics he desires and exhaust himself. Until then be calm; we don't have to hurry forward. Move slowly and calmly, and you must strictly follow my instructions; I will tell you when to drive faster."

Ravana's assistant and one of his staunchest supporters, Mahodara—the giant among giants in his physical appearance—begged Ravana, "Let me not be a mere spectator when you confront Rama. Let me have the honor of grappling with him. Permit me to attack Rama."

"Rama is my sole concern," Ravana replied. "If you wish to engage yourself in a fight, you may fight his brother Lakshmana."

Noticing Mahodara's purpose, Rama steered his chariot across his path in order to prevent Mahodara from reaching Lakshmana. Whereupon Mahodara ordered his chariot driver, "Now dash straight ahead, directly into Rama's chariot."

The charioteer, more practical-minded, advised him, "I would not go near Rama. Let us keep away." But Mahodara, obstinate and intoxicated with war fever, made straight for Rama. He wanted to have the honor of a direct encounter with Rama himself in spite of Ravana's advice; and for this honor he paid a heavy price, as it was a moment's work for Rama to destroy him, and leave him lifeless and shapeless on the field. Noticing this, Ravana's anger mounted further. He commanded his driver, "You will not slacken now. Go." Many ominous signs were seen now—his bowstrings suddenly snapped; the mountains shook; thunders rumbled in the skies; tears flowed from the horses' eyes; elephants with decorated foreheads moved along dejectedly. 11 Ravana, noticing them, hesitated only for a second, saying, "I don't care. This mere mortal Rama is of no account, and these omens do not concern me at all." Meanwhile, Rama 12 paused for a moment to consider his next step; and suddenly turned towards the armies supporting Ravana, which stretched away to the horizon, and destroyed them. He felt that this might be one way of saving Ravana. With his armies gone, it was possible that Ravana might have a change of heart. But it had only the effect of spurring Ravana on; he plunged forward and kept coming nearer Rama and his own doom.

⓭ Independent Practice

About the Text In this excerpt from *The Carolina Way,* Coach Dean Smith, who describes himself as an "open-minded dictator," offers his perspectives on how to build and maintain a winning team, whether in sports, business, or any other area of life.

"Play Hard; Play Together; Play Smart" from *The Carolina Way* by Dean Smith with John Kilgo

⓮ I never went into a season as North Carolina's head coach thinking we'd just plug things into the previous year's plan and duplicate ourselves. As I said, we never had the same team return, and there were any number of other variables from one year to the next. We couldn't have had the long run of success that we enjoyed if we'd been too stubborn to change and come up with new ideas and different ways to play the game.

I will repeat this several times in this book: Don't fear change. Sometimes change can refresh a stale team; sometimes it's mandated by changing personnel; sometimes the rules of the game change. We adapted each year to hide our weaknesses and accentuate our strengths.

Although we didn't have a system at North Carolina, we certainly had a philosophy. We believed in it strongly and didn't stray very far from it. It pretty much stayed the same from my first year as head coach. It was our mission statement; our strategic plan, our entire approach in a nutshell: Play hard; play smart; play together.

Hard meant with effort, determination, and courage; *together* meant unselfishly, trusting your teammates, and doing everything possible not to let them down; *smart* meant with good execution and poise, treating each possession as if it were the only one in the game.

⓯ That was our philosophy; we believed that if we kept our focus on those tenets, success would follow. Our North Carolina players seldom heard me or my assistants talk about winning. Winning would be the by-product of the process. There could be no shortcuts.

Making winning the ultimate goal usually isn't good teaching. Tom Osborne, the great former football coach of the University of Nebraska, said that making winning the goal can actually get in the way of winning. I agree. So many things happened in games that were beyond our control: the talent and experience of the teams; bad calls by officials; injuries; bad luck.

By sticking to our philosophy, we asked realistic things from our players. A player could play hard. He could play unselfishly and do things to help his teammates succeed. He could play intelligently if we did the job in practice as coaches. We measured our success by how we did in those areas.

⓮ **Setting** Dean Smith coached basketball at the University of North Carolina from 1961 through 1997. In what way, if any, might this setting be important to the development of his theme?

⓯ **Direct Statements and Observations** Smith explains each of the beliefs that make up his philosophy. What do these direct statements tell you about his point of view on basketball?

⓭ Introducing the Independent Practice

1. Explain to students that they will analyze the theme and point of view of the Independent Practice selection.
2. Discuss the About the Text note, and have students read the selection. Then, direct them to respond to the prompts, guiding them as necessary. Finally, have students answer the After You Read questions on page 1039.

⓮ Setting

1. Review that setting involves both time and place. Invite volunteers to share what they already know about college sports, particularly basketball. Guide students in understanding that college sports are competitive; teams at big state universities are typically expected to play and win tournaments.
2. Read aloud the bracketed text. Then **ask** the Setting question.

   Possible response: The university setting might contribute to a theme about what young people learn from playing sports. The fact that Smith coached at the same place for more than 35 years might contribute to a theme about how to be successful.

⓯ Direct Statements and Observations

1. Read aloud the two sections of text highlighted in green. Then ask the Direct Statements and Observations question.

   Possible response: The author's statements tell readers that he believes in hard work, teamwork, and intelligence.

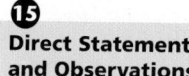

Differentiated Instruction for Universal Access

Support for Special-Needs Students
Have students read the adapted version of *The Carolina Way* in the ***Reader's Notebook: Adapted Version.*** They may also listen to the adapted version on the ***Hear It!* Audio CD** (adapted text).

Support for Less Proficient Readers
Have students read *The Carolina Way* in the ***Reader's Notebook.*** After students finish the selection in the ***Reader's Notebook,*** have them complete the questions and activities in the Student Edition.

EL Support for English Learners
Have students read the adapted version of *The Carolina Way* in the ***Reader's Notebook: English Learner's Version.*** English learners may also read the selection as they listen to the recorded version on the ***Hear It!* Audio CD.**

PHLit Online!

Enriched Online Student Edition
To have students read the selection in interactive format, with narration and point-of-use interactive graphic organizers, go to **www.PHLitOnline.com.**

16 Social and Cultural Context

1. Read aloud the first part of the Social and Cultural Context annotation. Challenge students to draw on their knowledge of other cultures to confirm or refute the annotation. Students may suggest that the ancient and modern Olympics, as well as the excerpt from the *Ramayana*, show that many cultures enjoy competition.
2. **Ask** the Social and Cultural Context question. **Possible response:** Smith's reaction shows that he doesn't believe in competing to show superiority; he values teamwork and respect for others.

17 Sentence Patterns

Read aloud the bracketed text and **ask** the Sentence Patterns question.

Possible response: The sentences emphasize a theme about the importance of working hard and as a team, in order to build character, not to win the game.

18 Social and Cultural Context

Have a volunteer read aloud the bracketed text. Then **ask** the Social and Cultural Context questions.

Possible responses: Words and phrases include "set screens," "play team defense," "box out," "open man." The words and phrases show that Smith is a credible expert on basketball.

Practice continued

16 Social and Cultural Context American culture is not the only one that values fierce competition. The oral tradition shows that many ancient cultures engaged in competitions as a means of proving superiority. What does Smith's reaction to the player at the Air Force Academy show about the difference between his values and those commonly held in his culture?

17 Sentence Patterns In what way does the repetition of sentences help emphasize and develop Smith's theme?

18 Social and Cultural Context What words and phrases in this sentence are specific to the culture of basketball? Why does Smith include them here?

When we put these elements together, the players had fun, one of my goals as their coach. I wanted our players to enjoy the experience of playing basketball for North Carolina. Each player on our team knew he was important. Each did a terrific job of sharing the ball, which also made the game enjoyable for more players. All won and lost as a team.

16 Of course it is easier to talk about playing hard, playing smart, and playing together than it is to do all three. It begins by the recruiting of unselfish players, who subscribe to the philosophy of team over individual. In a summer physical education class I once taught at the Air Force Academy there was one young man who shot every time he touched the ball. Exasperated from watching him, I pulled his four teammates off the court. He asked who would throw the ball inbounds to him. "You understand that it takes at least one more player," I said to him.

Playing Hard

Maybe a player wasn't the fastest, the tallest, or the most athletic person on the court. In the course of any given game that was out of his control. But each of them could control the effort with which he played. "Never let anyone play harder than you," I told them. "That is part of the game you can control." If another team played harder than we did, we had no excuse for it. None. We worked on it in every practice. If a player didn't give maximum effort, we dealt with it right then. We stopped practice and had the entire team run sprints for the offending player. We played a style of basketball that was physically exhausting and made it impossible for a player to go full throttle for forty minutes. 17 When he got tired, he flashed the tired signal, a raised fist, and we substituted for him. He could put himself back in the game once he had rested. We didn't want tired players on the court because they usually tried to rest on defense. That wouldn't work in our plan. Therefore we watched closely in practice and in games to make sure players played hard. If they slacked off, it was important to catch them and get them out of the game, or if it occurred in practice, to have the entire team run.

Playing Together

One of the first things I did at the beginning of preseason practice was to spell out for our players the importance of team play. Basketball is a game that counts on togetherness. I pointed out that seldom, if ever, did the nation's leading scorer play on a ranked team. He certainly didn't play on a championship team. I made them understand that our plan would fall apart if they didn't take care of one another: set screens; play team defense; box out; pass to the open man. 18 One man who failed to do his job unselfishly could undermine the efforts of the four other players on the court.

Playing Smart

We taught and drilled until we made the things we wanted to see become habits. The only way to have a smart team is to have one that is fundamentally

Vocabulary Development

Multiple-Meaning Words

Remind students that a word may have more than one meaning when used in different contexts. A word may also be more than one part of speech, which affects the way it is used in a sentence. Have students meet with a partner and scan the passage "Play Hard; Play Together; Play Smart" from *The Carolina Way* for at least five words that have more than one meaning or may be used as more than one part of speech. If students need help, provide them with this list: *game, mission, smart, goal, elements, practice, screens, box, pass, plan.*

Allow students to use a dictionary to check the meanings and parts of speech of their words. If time allows, have students write original sentences that use the words to show their different meanings and parts of speech. Ask each pair to share a couple of their original sentences with the class.

sound. We didn't skimp on fundamentals. We worked on them hard in practice and repeated them until they were down cold. We didn't introduce something and then move away from it before we had nailed it. Our entire program was built around practice, which we will talk more about in a later chapter. Practice, competitive games, late-game situations, and my relationship with our players are what I've missed most since I retired from coaching. We expected our team to execute well and with precision. If we practiced well and learned, we could play smart. It was another thing we could control. . . .

19 I stay in touch with many members of my extended family, former Carolina basketball players. These men have brought great happiness to my life. Ninety-six percent of them earned their college degrees, and one-third of those continued their studies at graduate and professional schools. It's the way a teacher's career should be judged. Our former players are doing great things for people in all walks of life.

The Carolina Way isn't the only way, that's for certain. But playing hard, playing smart, playing together certainly worked well for us.

Our trophy case is full, but far more important, our Museum of Good Memories runneth over.

19 **Point of View** How does Smith measure his success? How does his attitude reinforce the theme of the selection?

After You Read

Play Hard; Play Together; Play Smart *from* The Carolina Way

1. **Key Ideas and Details** Write an **objective summary** of "Play Hard; Play Together; Play Smart." Remember that an objective summary should not include your personal reaction to the selection and should include just the most important ideas and details.
2. **Key Ideas and Details Infer:** What is Dean Smith's main purpose for writing "Play Hard; Play Together; Play Smart"? Explain.
3. **Key Ideas and Details (a) Cite:** Name two factors in sports that, according to Smith, are beyond a team's control. **(b) Drawing Conclusions:** In what way might Smith's point of view on coaching help a team deal with the unexpected?
4. **Key Ideas and Details Cite:** According to Smith, how should a teacher's career be judged?
5. **Craft and Structure Analyze:** How does Smith's point of view influence the organization of main ideas in the text?
6. **Integration of Knowledge and Ideas (a) Analyze:** Using a chart like the one shown, analyze the values that Smith emphasized as a basketball coach. In the first column, list the three values that Smith taught. In the second column, give an example of how Smith promoted each value among his players. In the third column, suggest ways that Smith's values could apply to other areas of life.

Value	Specific Examples	Application to Life

(b) Collaborate: In a small group, discuss your findings, and add new insights to your chart.

Assessment Resources

The following resources can be used to assess students' knowledge and skills.

Unit 6 Resources

L1 L2 EL **Selection Test A,** pp. 17–19.
L3 L4 EL **Selection Test B,** pp. 20–22.
L3 L4 **Open-Book Test,** pp. 14–16.

PHLit Online! Students may use the Self-test, at **www.PHLitOnline.com** to prepare for **Selection Test A** or **Selection Test B.**

19 Point of View

Read aloud the bracketed text and **ask** the Point of View questions.

Possible responses: He measures his success by the graduation rate and post-basketball careers of his players. His attitude reinforces the theme that working hard and intelligently as a team is more important than winning.

ASSESS/EXTEND

Answers

1. **Possible response:** Coach Smith says not to fear change because it makes a team stronger. He teaches his players the philosophy "Play hard; play together; play smart" and does not focus on winning. Smith measures his own success by his students' accomplishments in life.
2. **Possible response:** His purpose is to inform about the philosophy behind his team's success.
3. **Answers: (a)** Students should mention two of these factors: the talent of the opposing team, injuries, bad calls by officials, and bad luck. **Possible responses: (b)** If each player plays hard, plays smart, and plays together, the team will be able to respond to unexpected events.
4. **Possible responses:** A teacher's career should be judged by his or her students' success in the world.
5. **Possible response:** In the text, Smith devotes a section of text to each part of his philosophy.
6. **Sample response: (a) Value—** Play hard. **Specific Examples—** Give maximum effort. Admit to being tired. Take a break. **Application to Life—**Be the best that you can be. Do not be afraid to ask for help. **(b)** After discussion, students should present their ideas.

❶ Preparing to Read

The purpose of the Extended Study section is to introduce background information that might help students when reading the *Odyssey*.

❷ The Minoans and Mycenaeans

1. Draw students' attention to the fact that two major civilizations preceded what is known today as Ancient Greece. Point out that the Minoans dominated the area for nearly 600 years before giving way to the Mycenaeans. Explain that the rise and fall of civilizations is a continuing pattern in human history.
2. **Ask:** What other civilizations do you know of that have exerted great influence and then faded from power?

   Sample responses: Students may suggest Ancient Egypt; Ancient Greece and Rome; the Mayan, Aztec, and Inca civilizations; Ancient China; and Britain's nineteenth-century empire.
3. Invite students to consider the civilizations of the contemporary world. Discuss with the class how this balance of power may alter during the next century.

❸

4. Point out that most great civilizations have had their own systems of writing. Learning to decipher these written records is an important step in understanding an ancient culture.
5. **Ask:** Why might Linear A, the Minoan writing system, remain undeciphered?

   Sample responses: It may be that the collapse of Minoan civilization was so rapid that there was a sudden break between its writing system and that of the Mycenaeans. As a result, archaeologists have had few clues to assist them.

❶ Preparing to Read the *Odyssey*

Homer's epic poems celebrate the legendary heroes and heritage of a great culture.

Historical Background: Ancient Greece

The world of ancient Greece included the Greek mainland, dipping down from continental Europe, and western Asia Minor, the Asian part of present-day Turkey. It also included hundreds of islands in the Aegean (ē jē´ ən) Sea, the arm of the Mediterranean Sea between mainland Greece and Asia Minor, and in the Ionian (ī ō´ nē ən) Sea, the arm of the Mediterranean to the west of mainland Greece. Odysseus, the legendary hero of Homer's *Odyssey*, was said to be the ruler of Ithaca, one of the western islands.

❷ **The Minoans and Mycenaeans** Nearly a thousand years before Odysseus would have lived, Greek civilization rose to greatness on Crete, another island south of the mainland. By about 2000 B.C., a sophisticated society called the Minoan (mi nō´ ən) civilization had developed on Crete. Judging by the archaeological evidence, the Minoans produced elegant stone palaces and fine carvings and ❸ metalwork. They also developed a writing system, preserved on a few hundred of the clay tablets on which they wrote. Scholars call that writing system Linear A and have yet to decipher it.

❷ For several centuries, Minoan civilization dominated the Greek world. Then, in about 1450 B.C., it collapsed rather suddenly, perhaps due to earthquakes and invasion. With the weakening of Minoan culture, the Mycenaeans (mī´sə nē´ ənz) became the dominant force in the Greek world. Originating on mainland Greece, the Mycenaeans had swept south and into Crete. Strongly influenced by Minoan civilization, the Mycenaeans too had a palace culture, an economy based on trade, and a writing system that mostly used clay tablets. Evidence of their writing is found in Knossos and Chania on Crete as well as in Mycenae, Pylos, and Thebes, three of ❸ their mainland strongholds. Because the Mycenaeans spoke an archaic, or older, form of Greek, scholars have been able to decipher their writing, known as Linear B. It was used primarily to keep palace records.

Sir Arthur Evans, the British archaeologist who worked extensively on Crete, named Minoan civilization for King Minos (mī´ näs), a ruler of Crete in Greek mythology.

◀ ▲ The photograph above shows a reconstruction of one wall of The Palace of Minos at Knossos, Crete. The photo at left shows a fresco, or wall painting, from the palace's interior.

Enrichment: Investigating Archaeology

Ancient Writing Systems

Point out that Linear A, the writing system of the Minoan civilization, is still a mystery to archaeologists. Explain that Egyptian hieroglyphics once presented a similar problem. The key to its deciphering came in dramatic fashion with the discovery, in 1799, of a tablet known as the Rosetta Stone, on which the same text appeared in two languages and three scripts. This allowed archaeologists to interpret the hieroglyphics by working from Greek, a language they knew.

Activity: Create Posters Have students read an overview of ancient writing systems and choose one system that they wish to investigate further. Invite students to design a poster for their chosen script, explaining its basic rules and giving examples of a simple translation into English. Invite students to present their research to the class.

4

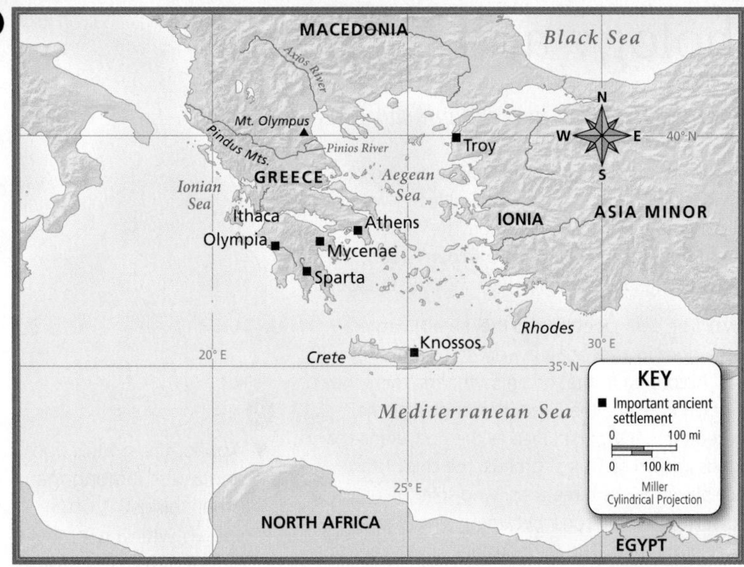

◀ Ancient Greece included mainland territories and hundreds of islands clustered in the the Aegean and Ionian Seas. Odysseus' kingdom of Ithaca is a small island in the Ionian Sea.

Legendary Conflicts The writing and archaeological remains suggest early cities with large central palaces and thick protective walls, each ruled by a wanax, or king. Others in society included priests, slaves, workers in trades or crafts, administrative officials, and a warrior class. The Mycenaens wore armor in battle, in which they engaged with apparent frequency. Their warfare with Troy, on the northwest coast of Asia Minor, has become one of the most famous military ventures of all time—the Trojan War. If there really was a King Odysseus, he would have been a key player in that conflict.

Scholars date the Trojan War to somewhere around 1200 B.C. Shortly thereafter, Mycenaean civilization collapsed as the Greek world fell into chaos and confusion. For some three hundred years, writing seems to have disappeared in what is often called the Greek Dark Ages. Then, in about 850 B.C., Greece began emerging from this darkness, spurred by flourishing trade throughout the Mediterranean region. Along with the economic boom came a resurgence of the arts and learning that peaked with the epic poems of Homer. These poems—the *Iliad* and the *Odyssey*—chronicle the Trojan War and the subsequent adventures of the hero Odysseus.

The Rise of City-States After Homer's time, Greek civilization grew more organized and sophisticated. Smaller communities organized as city-states—cities that functioned independently, as countries do. Among them were Sparta, known for its military prowess, and Athens, the birthplace of democracy. Though rivalries sometimes led to warfare among city-states, the Greeks still recognized their common heritage as Hellenes, as they by then usually called themselves. They coordinated efforts to fight common enemies, such as the Persians. They participated in the Olympic games, which records indicate began in 776 B.C. Together, too, they saw the works of Homer as pillars of their heritage, two great epics that celebrated their common past and its heroes.

The Greek word for "city-state" is *polis*, the origin of our words *metropolis* and *politics*.

4 Critical Viewing

1. Ask students what they notice about the geography of Greece. Help them appreciate the enormous length of coastline relative to Greece's land mass.
2. **Ask:** How do you suppose the geography of Greece might have influenced the way civilization developed? How might the proximity of the sea have been an advantage? A disadvantage?

   Sample response: The Greeks must have been a seafaring people, depending on ships for access to coastal cities and for travel from island to island. The sea would have encouraged trade and maritime technology. It would also have served to separate the many small island kingdoms.
3. Have students find Troy and Ithaca on the map. Point out that according to legend, the Greek siege of Troy lasted for ten years. Odysseus, the hero of the *Odyssey*, was among the Greek generals. His return journey from Troy to his kingdom of Ithaca is the stage for Homer's narrative.
4. **Ask:** What can you infer about the journey that Odysseus had to make when returning from Troy to Ithaca?

   Sample response: Odysseus must have had a challenging journey because Ithaca is on the west coast of Greece, a long way from Asia Minor. Odysseus would have had to navigate three seas and thread his way through hundreds of islands.

Differentiated Instruction for Universal Access

Strategy for Special-Needs Students

Help students understand the chronology of Ancient Greek civilization by creating a time line. List the following dates on the board: 2000 B.C., 1450 B.C., 1200 B.C., 850 B.C., 776 B.C. Ask students to review the text on pages 1040A and 1040B to identify what occurred at these moments in history. Write the information on the board beside the dates as students give it to you (respectively, Minoan civilization, Mycenaean civilization, Trojan War, end of Greek Dark Ages, first Olympic Games.)

Create a timeline on the board, divided up into 100-year intervals, from 2000 B.C. to the beginning of the modern era. Have pairs of students copy the timeline and enter the dates and events listed on the board in the correct locations on their papers. Then, invite volunteers to fill in the timeline on the board. Check students' understanding by reviewing the events recorded on the timeline.

❶ Greek Mythology and Customs

1. Introduce the terms *monotheism* and *polytheism*. Explain that whereas the major religions of North America are monotheistic—that is, acknowledging the existence of only one god—the Ancient Greeks, with their many gods, were polytheistic. Discuss with students how a belief in several gods might influence an individual's view of the world.
2. **Ask:** How might belonging to a polytheistic religion affect your behavior?

   Sample responses: I might have a favorite god to whom I prayed, while believing that other gods were out to get me. I might explain bad things that happened as a result of quarrels between the gods.
3. Point out that the plot of the *Odyssey* hinges on the behavior and prejudices of the gods. Remind students to look out for the effects of polytheism on Odysseus's adventures.

❷ Celebrating the Gods

1. Help students understand the difference between myth and legend. Explain that myths are frequently religious stories that serve to explain the origin of the world and its living things. Myths generally feature gods and other supernatural beings. Legends, on the other hand, tell about historical people, often exaggerating their qualities and achievements.
2. **Ask:** How would you classify two North American stories with the following titles: "How Skywoman Brought Light to the Earth" and "George Washington and the Cherry Tree"? Explain your reasoning.

   Sample responses: "How Skywoman Brought Light to the Earth" is a myth because it tells of the origin of light. "George Washington and the Cherry Tree" is a legend because it refers to a real person, although the story may not be true.

❶ Greek Mythology and Customs

All aspects of Greek culture reflected belief in the Olympian gods.

Ancient Greek religion was based on a belief in many gods. Zeus was king of the gods; Hera, his beautiful and powerful wife. Other gods and goddesses were associated with different aspects of nature or human behavior. The most important ones were said to dwell on Mount Olympus, the tallest mountain in Greece, where Zeus sat on a throne of gold. These Olympians, however, were not the first gods.

The Titans are Overthrown The early poet Hesiod (hē′ sē əd) wrote a mythic account of the origin of the gods in *Theogony*, a work the Greeks revered almost as much as Homer's epics. According to that origin myth, first there was Chaos, a dark, empty void. Out of Chaos came the Earth, personified as the goddess Gaea. The Earth generated the skies, personified as the god Uranus, who with Gaea produced the giant gods known as Titans. Cronus, the chief Titan, ruled the universe until he was displaced by his three sons, who split the universe among them. Zeus, the most powerful of these sons, became ruler of the heavens. His brother Poseidon became ruler of the seas. The third brother, Hades, became ruler of the underworld, a dark region also called Hades, which was inhabited by shades of the dead.

❹

▼ Apollo, the god of light and music (among many other things), is often shown with a lyre, the stringed instrument from which the English word *lyric* derives.

The Greek gods were powerful, but they were not all-powerful: even Zeus had to bow to fate. The gods displayed many human qualities and were often vengeful and quarrelsome. They were also quick to slap down human beings guilty of hubris (hyo͞o′ or ho͞o′ bris), or excessive pride. To appease the gods, human beings performed sacrifices, which often involved the killing of animals. In the *Odyssey*, Odysseus makes several sacrifices to plead for divine aid on his journey home.

Celebrating the Gods The Greeks worshipped the gods in temples dedicated to many gods or just one. The Parthenon in Athens, for instance, was a temple dedicated to the goddess Athena. The Greeks also celebrated their gods at great festivals such as the Olympic games, which were dedicated to Zeus.

The Greeks believed in prophecy, which they associated with the god Apollo. In the *Odyssey*, Odysseus journeys all the way to the underworld to consult the blind prophet Tiresias (tī rē′ sē əs), who continues to have the gift of prophecy

❷ even though he has died. The Greeks also believed in myths, stories about gods and heroes that they used to explain the world around them. The *Iliad* and the *Odyssey* drew on these myths; however, for future generations of ancient Greeks, Homer's two epics—like Hesiod's *Theogony*—took on the aura of myths themselves.

3 Gods in Greek Mythology

You may be more familiar with the Roman names for the Greek gods. The ancient Romans accepted Greek mythology, but they had their own names for its gods and heroes. For example, they called Odysseus *Ulysses*. For each Greek god listed below, the Roman equivalent is also given.

Zeus (zo͞os) king of the gods and ruler of the heavens; Roman *Jupiter*, sometimes called *Jove*
Hera (her´ ə) wife of Zeus and goddess of married women; Roman *Juno*
Poseidon (pō sī´dən) god of the seas; Roman *Neptune*
Hades (hā´dēz) god of the underworld; Roman *Pluto*
Aphrodite (af´ rə dītē) goddess of love and beauty; Roman *Venus*
Ares (er´ ēz) god of war; Roman *Mars*
Apollo (əp ol´ ō) god of prophecy and music; also called Phoebus (fē´ bəs); Roman *Apollo*
Artemis (är´ tə mis) goddess of the hunt and the moon; Roman *Diana*
Athena (ə thē´ nə) goddess of wisdom, skills, and war; Roman *Minerva*
Hephaestus (hē fes´ təs) god of fire and metalwork; Roman *Vulcan*
Hermes (hur´ mēz) god of commerce and cunning; messenger of the gods; Roman *Mercury*
Demeter (di mē´ tər) goddess of the harvest; Roman *Ceres* (sir´ ez)
Dionysus (dī´ ən ī´səs) god of wine and revelry, also called Bacchus (bak´ əs); Roman *Dionysus* or *Bacchus*
Hestia (hes´ tē ə) goddess of home and hearth; Roman *Vesta*
Helios (hē´ lē os´) sun god; Roman *Sol*
Uranus (yo͞o rə´ nəs) sky god supplanted by his son Cronus; Roman *Uranus*
Gaea (jē´ ə) earth goddess and mother of the Titans and Cyclopes; Roman *Tellus* or *Terra*
Cronus (krō´ nəs) Titan who ruled the universe before his son Zeus dethroned him; Roman *Saturn*
Rhea (rē´ ə) wife of Cronus and mother of Zeus; Roman *Cybele* (sib´ ə lē)
Cyclops (sī´ klops) any one of three Titans who forged thunderbolts for Zeus; plural, Cyclopes (sī´ klō pēs)
The Fates three goddesses who wove the threads of each person's life: Clotho (klō´ thō) spun the thread; Lachesis (lak´ i sis) measured out the amount of thread; Atropos (a´ trə pis) snipped the thread
The Muses (myo͞o´ ziz) nine goddesses who presided over the arts and sciences, including Calliope (kə lī´ ə pē´), the Muse of epic poetry

4

▼ Poseidon, god of the sea, was also the god of earthquakes and horses. His symbols include the trident, a three-pronged spear.

Extended Study: The Odyssey 1040D

3 Connect to Mythology

1. Ask students to review the descriptions of the gods listed in the table. Point out that while some gods had great powers and assumed many roles, others had very specific areas of authority. Explain that people would appeal to the god who was in the best position to assist them.
2. **Ask:** Why might a person appeal to Demeter? Why to Poseidon?

   Sample response: A farmer might appeal to Demeter for good weather when harvesting the crops. A wife might pray to Poseidon for a calm voyage if her husband was at sea.
3. Invite volunteers to select a god from the table and to give a specific reason why someone might ask that god for a favor.
4. Have the class vote on the six gods from the table that they would select for protection and assistance in today's world. Encourage them to explain their selections.

4 Critical Viewing

1. Direct students' attention to the images of the statues of Apollo and Poseidon on pages 1040C and 1040D, respectively.
2. **Ask:** Based on these statues, how would you describe the Greeks' view of their gods? How are Apollo and Poseidon alike? How are they different?

   Sample response: The Greeks probably thought of these gods as powerful beings, possessing qualities way beyond those of humans. They are both strong and powerful. Apollo seems more peaceful and thoughtful and Poseidon more assertive, active.

Fluency

The Names of the Greek Gods

Help students gain fluency in saying the gods' names by having them examine the pronunciation keys to the right of each listing. Review the meaning of the long and short vowel markings and point out how the accented syllables are indicated. Then read each god's name on the list and have students repeat it after you in unison.

When students are comfortable saying the names chorally, ask them to stand up and form a circle. Choose a student at random to read the first name on the list (Zeus). The student next to him or her should read the second name (Hera). Continue around the circle several times, reading the names in order until each student has had a chance to pronounce most of the names.

❶ Discuss the Author

1. Draw students' attention to the fact that Homer may never even have existed. At best, he is a legend; at worst, he is a complete fiction. Yet his name is forever associated with two great epics, the *Iliad* and the *Odyssey*.
2. **Ask:** Why do you suppose people continue to associate Homer's name with the *Odyssey* when there is no proof that a poet named Homer ever lived?

   Sample responses: People naturally want to put a name to a great creation. A work as important as the *Odyssey* must have had an author.

❷

1. Have a volunteer read the bracketed text. Explain that oral poetry is a tradition that has existed in many pre-literate civilizations. A poet, or bard, might be employed at a court or castle to recite adventures, myths, and legends. Because the poems were passed down from generation to generation, the epics would evolve, their details altering slightly over the years.
2. **Ask:** What effect would writing down an oral poem such as the *Odyssey* have upon the work?

   Sample responses: Writing down a piece of oral poetry would tend to stop its natural evolution. The poem would remain fixed in its written form forever.

❸

1. Have a volunteer read the bracketed text, beginning with "They recited the poems...." Point out that even today the *Odyssey* is part of the high-school curriculum in much of the United States. Works that are read widely throughout a society are said to be part of a "core curriculum."
2. **Ask:** Why might an education system have certain books that everybody reads?

   Sample responses: Reading the same book gives everyone a common experience and helps build a cultural community.

HOMER *epic poet*

THE POEMS ATTRIBUTED TO HOMER STILL INFLUENCE LITERATURE AND CULTURE TODAY.

Homer is the legendary poet credited with writing the Iliad *and the* Odyssey. *These epics, known for their sweeping scope, gripping stories, and vivid style, have captured readers' imaginations for almost 3,000 years.*

❶ **Was there really a Homer?** No one can prove his existence with any certainty, for no authentic record of Homer's life exists. Tradition has it that he was born in Ionia in western Asia Minor, perhaps on the island of Chios, and that he was blind. The location is not unreasonable, for Ionia was a center of poetry and learning, where eastern and western cultures met and new intellectual currents were born. Descriptions of Asia Minor in the *Iliad* show in-depth knowledge of the landscape; moreover, both the *Iliad* and the *Odyssey* contain plot elements found in the world's first known epic, *Gilgamesh*, which by Homer's era had traveled from Mesopotamia (present-day Iraq) to become familiar in Asia Minor. For example, the hero Gilgamesh visits the underworld, just like the hero of the *Odyssey*; he also has a very good friend who is killed, just like Achilles has in the *Iliad*.

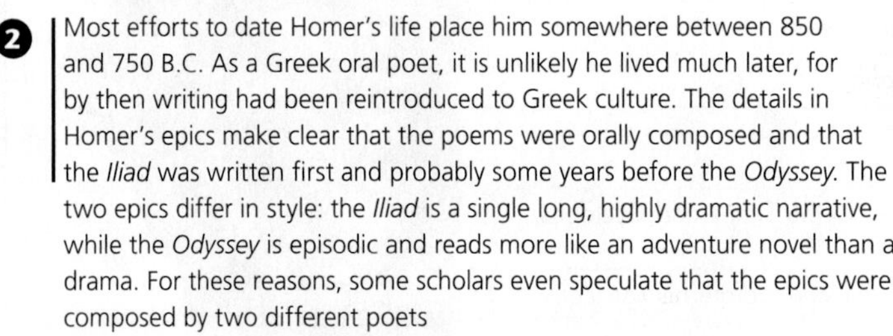

❷ Most efforts to date Homer's life place him somewhere between 850 and 750 B.C. As a Greek oral poet, it is unlikely he lived much later, for by then writing had been reintroduced to Greek culture. The details in Homer's epics make clear that the poems were orally composed and that the *Iliad* was written first and probably some years before the *Odyssey*. The two epics differ in style: the *Iliad* is a single long, highly dramatic narrative, while the *Odyssey* is episodic and reads more like an adventure novel than a drama. For these reasons, some scholars even speculate that the epics were composed by two different poets

Inspiring Poems Whatever the truth about Homer may be, no one disputes the quality of the two epics with which he is credited. The ancient ❸ Greeks revered the *Iliad* and the *Odyssey*. They recited the poems at religious festivals and had children memorize them in school. All the Greek writers and philosophers who came after Homer drew on the two epics. Their influence spread to Rome and beyond, and they became foundational works of western literature. Even in modern times, great works from James Joyce's *Ulysses* to Derek Walcott's *Omeros* have been directly inspired by Homer's verse.

Differentiated Instruction for Universal Access

Preparing Students for the Challenging Selection

If you wish to prepare lower-level readers to read the selection from the *Odyssey*, Part I, follow these steps:

- Have students read the list of characters on p. 1046 as you give background information about some of the Greek gods and goddesses. Allow students to share their own knowledge of the myths, and correct any misunderstandings as needed.
- Help students take notes and summarize as they read "Sailing from Troy" (pp. 1047–1048). Have a student read a section of the text. Then, ask volunteers to summarize what was read. Take notes on the board. Have another volunteer continue reading, and then pause to summarize and take notes again. Tell students to use these skills as they read the rest of the selection.
- Students may have difficulty with the formal and archaic vocabulary in the selection. Have students look for the definition of unfamiliar words in the side notes. Also, as many words do not appear in the side notes, review strategies to define words from the sentence's context.

❹ The Epic Form

An **epic** is a long narrative poem that relates important events in the history or folklore of the culture that produced it. Its central character, or **epic hero,** is a larger-than-life figure who embodies traits that the culture values. Typical among those characteristics are physical strength, bravery, high birth, fame, and effective skills as a leader and in battle.

❺ The *Iliad* and the *Odyssey* influenced virtually all the great western epics that followed them. From the *Aeneid*, the great epic of ancient Rome, to *Beowulf*, the foundational epic of Old English; from *The Divine Comedy*, the masterful epic by the Italian poet Dante, to *Paradise Lost*, the brilliant epic by Britain's John Milton—all had Homer's epics as models. Literary devices in Homer's epics are often imitated in these later works, even though many of the later epics were not orally composed. Influential literary devices found in Homer's epics include the following:

- **Opening invocation to the Muse:** The speaker of the poem asks the Muse for inspiration.
- **Starting the story in medias res,** or "in the middle of things": Beginning (after the invocation) with action instead of background information helps capture audience attention.
- **Lofty style:** Elegant language stresses the nobility of the subject.
- **Objective tone:** By keeping an emotional distance, the poet focuses attention on the story.
- **Meter,** or a fixed rhythmic pattern: A strong meter helps the oral poet remember the lines. In the original Greek, the *Odyssey* uses hexameter, or six beats to a line, which helps create a fast pace.
- **Epithet,** a characterizing phrase for a person, place, or thing: Recurring epithets are easy to remember and can help fill out the meter. Some examples of Homer's epithets include "rosy-fingered dawn" and "son of Laertes" for Odysseus.
- **Epic simile,** a long comparison over many lines: Such similes were another way to fill out the meter and aid the poet's memory.

Ionia, from where Homer may have come, was on the west coast of Asia Minor. The Ionian Sea, where Odysseus's island of Ithaca lies, is off the west coast of Greece. The duplicated names are likely no coincidence; Greek speakers from Ionia probably migrated to the west of Greece and brought the name with them (just as British settlers often brought British place names to America).

▼ The island of Ionia, Homer's possible birthplace, as it appears today

❹ Connect to Literature

1. Point out that the epic hero is still current in popular culture. Invite students to think about the popular *Star Wars* film series, especially its central character, Luke Skywalker.
2. **Ask:** How could you argue that Luke Skywalker is a classic epic hero?

   Sample responses: Luke is brave, just, and nobly born (even if his father has gone to the dark side). He shows enormous skill as a leader in battle.
3. Encourage students to suggest other figures in popular culture that might qualify as epic heroes. Ask them to explain their reasoning.

❺

1. Explain that epics often tell truly exciting stories but that their style also gives them a sense of importance and formality. Point out that many of the literary devices used by Homer and listed on this page have the result of ennobling the author's subject. Creators of modern epics often seek the same effect.
2. **Ask:** Think about *Star Wars* again. How does George Lucas convince the viewer that his epic narrative is important?

   Sample response: The characters are noble and their mission is extremely important—defeating the evil empire that threatens to destroy virtue. They do battle with their lightsabers like knights in the legends of King Arthur.

Enrichment: Understanding Epic Meter

Homer's Hexameter

Help students understand Homer's hexameter—his six-beat line. Point out that the American poet Longfellow wrote a narrative poem in Homer's epic meter. Write the first line on the board, marked as follows: *This´ is the for´ est prim e´ val. The mur´ mur ing pines´ and the hem´ locks. . .* Invite volunteers to read the line, making sure that they emphasize the marked syllables. Point out that this six-beat line is typical of Homer's verse in the original Greek, but that some translations into English and other languages may not follow the original meter.

Activity: Identifying Stress Have pairs of students mark the six accented syllables in each of the following lines:

Bearded with moss, and in garments green, indistinct in the twilight,
Stand like Druids of eld, with voices sad and prophetic,
Stand like harpers hoar, with beards that rest on their bosoms.

Discuss students' answers and write their marked verses on the board.

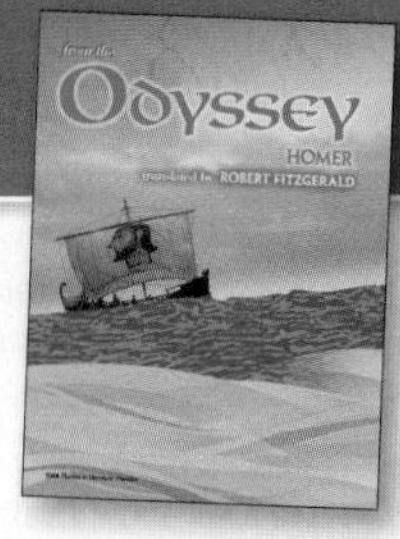

✓ *from the* Odyssey, Part 1
Lesson Pacing Guide

DAY 1 Preteach

- Administer the Reading and Vocabulary Warm-ups (*Unit 6 Resources*, pp. 23–26) as necessary.
- Build background and knowledge using the Extended Study (pp. 1040A–1040F, 1040–1043).
- Introduce the Reading Skill: Historical and Cultural Context.
- Introduce the Literary Analysis concept: Epic Hero.
- Distribute copies of the appropriate graphic organizer for the Reading Skill (*Graphic Organizer Transparencies*, pp. 183–184).
- Distribute copies of the appropriate graphic organizer for Literary Analysis (*Graphic Organizer Transparencies*, pp. 185–186).
- Teach the selection vocabulary.
- Introduce the Word Study skill.

DAYS 2–3 Preteach/Teach

- Build background with the Background feature.
- Develop thematic vocabulary and thematic thinking with Writing About the Big Question.
- Prepare students to read with the Activating Prior Knowledge activities (TE).
- Informally monitor comprehension while students read.
- Use the Reading Check questions to confirm comprehension.
- Develop students' ability comprehend historical and cultural context, using the Reading Skill questions.
- Develop students' understanding of epic heroes, using the Literary Analysis questions.
- Reinforce vocabulary with the Vocabulary notes.
- Reinforce unit focus standards using the Spiral Review prompts.

DAY 4 Assess

- Assess students' comprehension and mastery of the skills by having them answer the Critical Thinking, Reading Skill, and Literary Analysis questions.
- Have students complete the Vocabulary Practice activities.
- Have students complete the Word Study activities.

DAY 5 Extend/Assess

- Have students complete the Conventions lesson.
- Have students complete the Writing activity and write an everyday epic. (You may assign as homework.)
- Extend learning by having students complete the Speaking and Listening activity, a conversation. As an alternative, assign them "In the Path of Danger" and "The Borders of Giving" in *Reality Central*.
- Administer Selection Test A or B (*Unit 6 Resources*, pp. 38–43).

Common Core State Standards

Reading Literature 2. Determine a theme or central idea of a text and analyze in detail its development over the course of the text.
3. Analyze how complex characters develop over the course of a text.
5. Analyze how an author's choices concerning how to structure a text, order events within it, and manipulate time create such effects as mystery, tension, or surprise.
6. Analyze a particular point of view or cultural experience reflected in a work of literature from outside the United States.

Writing 3. Write narratives to develop real or imagined experiences or events using effective technique, well-chosen details, and well-structured event sequences. **3.a.** Engage and orient the reader by setting out a problem, situation, or observation, establishing one or multiple point(s) of view, and introducing a narrator and/or characters. **3.b.** Use narrative techniques, such as dialogue, pacing, description, reflection, and multiple plot lines. **3.c.** Use a variety of techniques to sequence events so that they build on one another to create a coherent whole. **3.d.** Use precise words and phrases, telling details, and sensory language to convey a vivid picture of the experiences, events, setting, and/or characters.

Speaking and Listening
1. Initiate and participate effectively in a range of collaborative discussions. **1.a.** Come to discussions prepared, having read and researched material under study. **1.b.** Work with peers to set individual roles as needed.

Language 1. Demonstrate command of the conventions of standard English grammar and usage when writing or speaking.

Additional Standards Practice
***Common Core Companion*, pp. 15–22, 55–56**

Daily Block Scheduling
Each day in this Lesson Pacing Guide represents a 40–50 minute period. Teachers using block scheduling may combine days to revise pacing. In addition, teachers may differentiate and support core instruction by integrating components for extended and intensive support as students require. See the Guide to Selected Leveled Resources (facing page).

Guide to Selected Leveled Resources

RTI Tier 1 (students performing on level)			*from the* Odyssey, Part 1
Warm Up	[Whole class instruction] [Group work]	**Practice, model,** and **monitor** fluency, working **with the whole class** or **in groups.**	**Vocabulary and Reading Warm-ups B,** ***Unit 6 Resources,*** pp. 23–24, 26
Comprehension/Skills	[Whole class instruction] [Independent work]	**Support** and **monitor** comprehension and skills development, having students complete the activities, graphic organizers, and interactive prompts **independently** or **as a class.**	• ***Reader's Notebook,*** adapted instruction and full selection EL ***Reader's Notebook: English Learner's Version,*** adapted instruction and adapted selection • **Reading Skill Graphic Organizer B,** ***Graphic Organizer Transparencies,*** p. 184 • **Literary Analysis Graphic Organizer B,** ***Graphic Organizer Transparencies,*** p. 186
Monitor Progress	A	**Monitor** student progress with the differentiated curriculum-based assessment in the *Unit Resources.*	• **Selection Test B,** ***Unit 6 Resources,*** pp. 41–43 • **Open-Book Test,** ***Unit 6 Resources,*** pp. 35–37

RTI Tier 2 (students requiring intervention)			*from the* Odyssey, Part 1
Warm Up	[Group work] [One-on-one teaching]	**Practice, model,** and **monitor** fluency **in groups** or **with individuals.**	• **Vocabulary and Reading Warm-ups A,** ***Unit 6 Resources,*** pp. 23–26 • ***Reality Central,*** "In the Path of Danger" and "The Borders of Giving" • ***Hear It!*** **Audio CD (adapted text)**
Comprehension/Skills	[Group work] [One-on-one teaching]	• **Support** and **monitor** comprehension and skills development, working **in small groups** or **with individuals.** • **Pair** students with more advanced peers and have them complete the writing activity in the *Real-World Writing Journal.* • As students complete the selection in the appropriate version of the *Reader's Notebook,* **monitor** comprehension frequently with group questions and individual instruction. • **Model** strategies while guiding students in completing the activities and prompts in the *Reader's Notebook,* as well as the graphic organizers. • **Practice** skills and **monitor** mastery with the *Reading Kit* worksheets.	• ***Real-World Writing Journal,*** Lessons 1–2, pp. 156–163 • ***Reader's Notebook: Adapted Version,*** adapted instruction and adapted selection EL ***Reader's Notebook: English Learner's Version,*** adapted instruction and adapted selection • **Reading Skill Graphic Organizer A,** ***Graphic Organizer Transparencies,*** p. 183 • **Literary Analysis Graphic Organizer A,** ***Graphic Organizer Transparencies,*** p. 185 • **Reading Kit,** Practice worksheets, pp. 264, 258, 268, 270, 276
Monitor Progress	A	**Monitor** student progress with the differentiated curriculum-based assessment in the *Unit Resources* and in the *Reading Kit.*	• **Selection Test A,** ***Unit 6 Resources,*** pp. 38–40 • **Reading Kit,** Assess worksheets pp. 265, 259, 269, 271, 277

TIER 3 Tier 3 intervention may require consultation with the student's special-education or dyslexia specialist. For additional support, see the Tier 2 activities and resources listed above.

One-on-one teaching **Group work** **Whole class instruction** **Independent work** **A Assessment**

For a complete guide to selection support, including support for Advanced students, see the Overview of Resources in the frontmatter.

✓*from the* Odyssey, Part 1

RESOURCES FOR:

- **L1 Special-Needs Students**
- **L2 Below-Level Students (Tier 2)**
- **L3 On-Level Students (Tier 1)**
- **L4 Advanced Students (Tier 1)**
- **EL English Learners**
- **All All Students**

Vocabulary/Fluency/Prior Knowledge

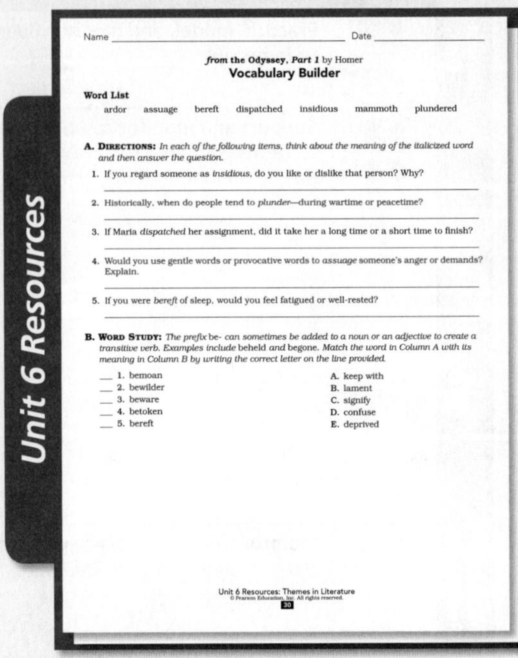

Unit 6 Resources

Name ______ Date ______

from the* Odyssey, *Part 1 by Homer
Vocabulary Builder

Word List

ardor assuage bereft dispatched insidious mammoth plundered

A. Directions: *In each of the following items, think about the meaning of the italicized word and then answer the question.*

1. If you regard someone as *insidious*, do you like or dislike that person? Why?
2. Historically, when do people tend to *plunder*—during wartime or peacetime?
3. If Maria *dispatched* her assignment, did it take her a long time or a short time to finish?
4. Would you use gentle words or provocative words to *assuage* someone's anger or demands? Explain.
5. If you were *bereft* of sleep, would you feel fatigued or well-rested?

B. Word Study: *The prefix* be- *can sometimes be added to a noun or an adjective to create a transitive verb. Examples include* beheld *and* begone. *Match the word in Column A with its meaning in Column B by writing the correct letter on the line provided.*

___ 1. bemoan	A. keep with
___ 2. bewilder	B. lament
___ 3. beware	C. signify
___ 4. betoken	D. confuse
___ 5. bereft	E. deprived

Unit 6 Resources: Themes in Literature
© Pearson Education, Inc. All rights reserved.
30

All Vocabulary Builder, p. 30

Also available for this selection:

EL L1 L2 Vocabulary Warm-ups A and B, pp. 23–24

All Reading Warm-ups A and B, pp. 25–26

All Writing About the Big Question, p. 27

Reader's Notebooks

Pre- and postreading pages, as well as the selection from the *Odyssey*, Part 1, appear in an interactive format in the *Reader's Notebooks*. Each *Notebook* is differentiated for a different group of learners. The selections in the Adapted and English Learner's versions are abridged.

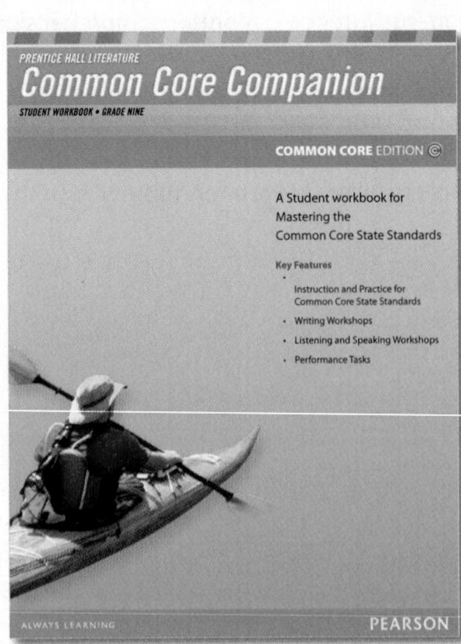

L2 L3 *Reader's Notebook*

L1 *Reader's Notebook: Adapted Version*

EL *Reader's Notebook: English Learner's Version*

EL *Reader's Notebook: Spanish Version*

Common Core Companion

Additional instruction and practice for each Common Core State Standard

Selection Support

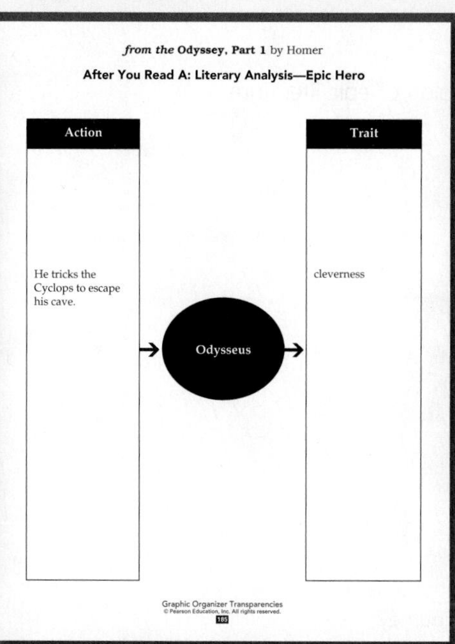

from the **Odyssey, Part 1** by Homer

After You Read A: Literary Analysis—Epic Hero

Action		Trait
He tricks the Cyclops to escape his cave.	→ Odysseus →	cleverness

Graphic Organizer Transparencies
© Pearson Education, Inc. All rights reserved.
185

EL L1 L2 Literary Analysis: Graphic Organizer A, p. 185 (partially filled in)

Also available for this selection:

- **EL L1 L2 Reading: Graphic Organizer A,** p. 183 (partially filled in)
- **EL L3 Reading: Graphic Organizer B,** p. 184
- **EL L3 Literary Analysis: Graphic Organizer B,** p. 186

Skills Development/Extension

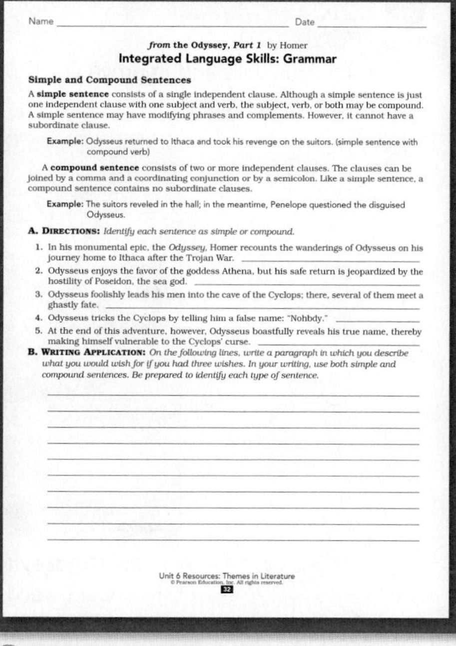

Name ______________________ Date ______________

from the **Odyssey, Part 1** by Homer

Integrated Language Skills: Grammar

Simple and Compound Sentences

A **simple sentence** consists of a single independent clause. Although a simple sentence is just one independent clause with one subject and verb, the subject, verb, or both may be compound. A simple sentence may have modifying phrases and complements. However, it cannot have a subordinate clause.

Example: Odysseus returned to Ithaca and took his revenge on the suitors. (simple sentence with compound verb)

A **compound sentence** consists of two or more independent clauses. The clauses can be joined by a comma and a coordinating conjunction or by a semicolon. Like a simple sentence, a compound sentence contains no subordinate clauses.

Example: The suitors reveled in the hall; in the meantime, Penelope questioned the disguised Odysseus.

A. Directions: *Identify each sentence as simple or compound.*

1. In his monumental epic, the *Odyssey*, Homer recounts the wanderings of Odysseus on his journey home to Ithaca after the Trojan War. ______
2. Odysseus enjoys the favor of the goddess Athena, but his safe return is jeopardized by the hostility of Poseidon, the sea god. ______
3. Odysseus foolishly leads his men into the cave of the Cyclops; there, several of them meet a ghastly fate. ______
4. Odysseus tricks the Cyclops by telling him a false name: "Nohbdy." ______
5. At the end of this adventure, however, Odysseus boastfully reveals his true name, thereby making himself vulnerable to the Cyclops' curse. ______

B. Writing Application: *On the following lines, write a paragraph in which you describe what you would wish for if you had three wishes. In your writing, use both simple and compound sentences. Be prepared to identify each type of sentence.*

Unit 6 Resources: Themes in Literature
© Pearson Education, Inc. All rights reserved.
32

EL L3 L4 Grammar, p. 32

Also available for this selection:

- **All Reading: Historical and Cultural Context,** p. 29
- **All Literary Analysis: Epic Hero,** p. 28
- **L4 Enrichment,** p. 31
- **EL L3 L4 Support for Writing,** p. 33
- **L3 L4 Support for Extend Your Learning,** p. 34

Assessment

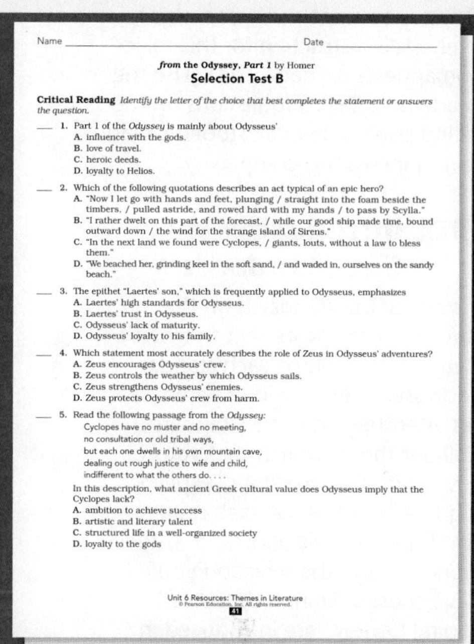

Name ______________________ Date ______________

from the **Odyssey, Part 1** by Homer

Selection Test B

Critical Reading *Identify the letter of the choice that best completes the statement or answers the question.*

___ 1. Part 1 of the *Odyssey* is mainly about Odysseus'
A. influence with the gods.
B. love of travel.
C. heroic deeds.
D. loyalty to Helios.

___ 2. Which of the following quotations describes an act typical of an epic hero?
A. "Now I let go with hands and feet, plunging / straight into the foam beside the timbers, / pulled astride, and rowed hard with my hands / to pass by Scylla."
B. "I rather dwelt on this part of the forecast, / while our good ship made time, bound outward down / the wind for the strange island of Sirens."
C. "In the next land we found were Cyclopes, / giants, louts, without a law to bless them."
D. "We beached her, grinding keel in the soft sand, / and waded in, ourselves on the sandy beach."

___ 3. The epithet "Laertes' son," which is frequently applied to Odysseus, emphasizes
A. Laertes' high standards for Odysseus.
B. Laertes' trust in Odysseus.
C. Odysseus' lack of maturity.
D. Odysseus' loyalty to his family.

___ 4. Which statement most accurately describes the role of Zeus in Odysseus' adventures?
A. Zeus encourages Odysseus' crew.
B. Zeus controls the weather by which Odysseus sails.
C. Zeus strengthens Odysseus' enemies.
D. Zeus protects Odysseus' crew from harm.

___ 5. Read the following passage from the *Odyssey*:
Cyclopes have no muster and no meeting,
no consultation or old tribal ways,
but each one dwells in his own mountain cave,
dealing out rough justice to wife and child,
indifferent to what the others do. . . .
In this description, what ancient Greek cultural value does Odysseus imply that the Cyclopes lack?
A. ambition to achieve success
B. artistic and literary talent
C. structured life in a well-organized society
D. loyalty to the gods

Unit 6 Resources: Themes in Literature
© Pearson Education, Inc. All rights reserved.
41

EL L3 L4 Selection Test B, pp. 41–43

Also available for this selection:

- **L3 L4 Open-Book Test,** pp. 35–37
- **EL L1 L2 Selection Test A,** pp. 38–40

PHLit Online!
www.PHLitOnline.com

- complete narrated selection text
- a thematically related video with writing prompt
- an interactive graphic organizer
- highlighting feature
- access to all student print resources, adapted to individual student needs
- Spanish and English summaries
- adapted selection translations in Spanish

Online Resources: All print materials are also available online.

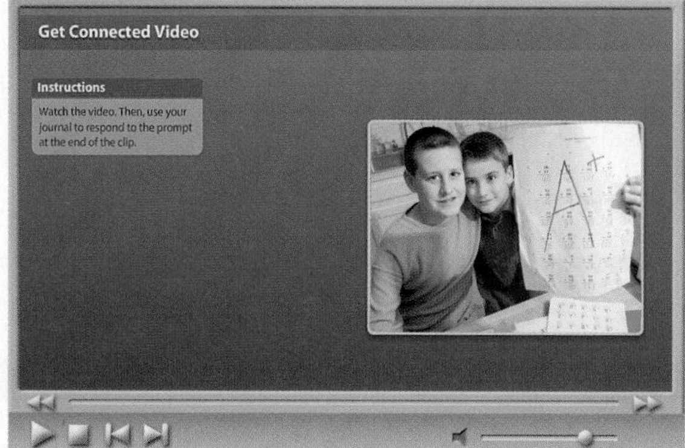

Get Connected! (thematic video with writing prompt)

Also available:

Background Video

All videos are available in Spanish.

Vocabulary Central (tools, activities, and songs for studying vocabulary)

Also available:

Writer's Journal (with graphics feature)

Epic

You may use the excerpt from the Odyssey to meet the lesson objectives. Skills instruction for this selection appears on page 1041. Use the Reader and Task Suggestions on the facing page to help all students read text of increasing complexity.

1 Introducing the CCS Standards

Introduce the standards on the student page. (Note that the lesson element with which each standard is addressed is identified in parentheses after the text of the standard.) Call out the standards that you will cover with the selections, explaining to students what each requires and how they will address it as they work through the selection you have chosen. Standards labeled "Spiral Review" are introduced in the Literary Analysis Workshop for this unit.

Before You Read *from the* Odyssey, Part 1

Epic

Build your skills and improve your comprehension of epic literature with this selection.

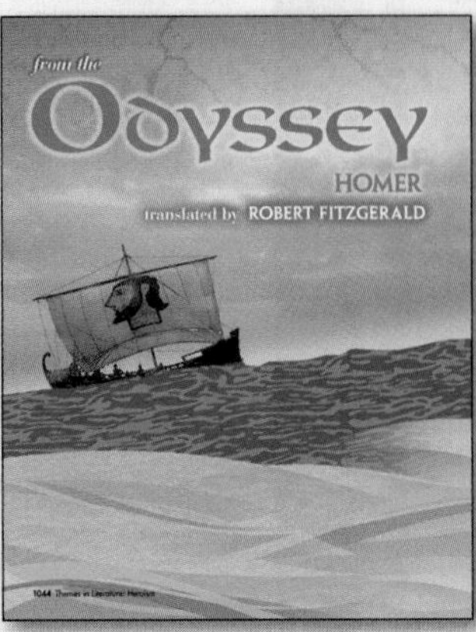

Read the ***Odyssey*** to learn about a hero of the ancient world, his long journey home, and the choices he makes.

1 Common Core State Standards

Meet these standards with Part 1 of the ***Odyssey*** (p. 1044).

Reading Literature

3. Analyze how complex characters develop over the course of a text, interact with other characters, and advance the plot or develop the theme. *(Literary Analysis: Epic Hero)*

Spiral Review: RL.9-10.2

5. Analyze how an author's choices concerning how to structure a text, order events within it, and manipulate time create such effects as mystery, tension, or surprise. *(Literary Analysis: Epic Hero)*

6. Analyze a particular point of view or cultural experience reflected in a work of literature from outside the United States, drawing on a wide reading of world literature. *(Reading Skill: Historical and Cultural Context)*

Writing

3. Write narratives to develop real or imagined experiences or events using effective technique, well-chosen details, and well-structured event sequences. **3.a.** Engage and orient the reader by setting out a problem, situation, or observation, establishing one or multiple point(s) of view, and introducing a narrator and/or characters. **3.b.** Use narrative techniques, such as dialogue, pacing, description, reflection, and multiple plot lines. **3.c.** Use a variety of techniques to sequence events so that they build on one another to create a coherent whole. **3.d.** Use precise words and phrases, telling details, and sensory language to convey a vivid picture of the experiences, events, setting, and/or characters. *(Writing: Everyday Epic)*

Speaking and Listening

1. Initiate and participate effectively in a range of collaborative discussions. **1.a.** Come to discussions prepared, having read and researched material under study. **1.b.** Work with peers to set individual roles as needed. *(Speaking and Listening: Conversation)*

Language

1. Demonstrate command of the conventions of standard English grammar and usage when writing or speaking. *(Conventions: Simple and Compound Sentences)*

Text Complexity Rubric

from the Odyssey, Part 1		
Qualitative Measures	**Context/ Knowledge Demands**	Ancient Greece and Trojan War; allusions to Greek mythology 1 2 3 (4) 5
	Structure/ Language Clarity	Narrative poem; symbolic language; challenging vocabulary 1 2 3 4 (5)
	Levels of Meaning	Challenging concept (journey of epic hero) 1 2 3 4 (5)
Quantitative Measures	**Text Length**	Word Count: 8,471
	Lexile	NP
Overall Complexity		**Complex**

❷ Literary Analysis: Epic Hero

An **epic hero** is the larger-than-life character in an **epic**—a long narrative poem about important events in the history or folklore of a culture. The epic hero demonstrates traits that are valued by the society. The character's traits can be communicated in narration as well as through dialogue. Here, Odysseus speaks about his own courage and leadership:

Now, by the gods, I drove my big hand spike
deep in the embers, charring it again,
and cheered my men along with battle talk
to keep their courage up; no quitting now.

Traditional epics like the *Odyssey* use specific plot devices, or structures, that both provide background information and allow the story to unfold in an exciting way. For example, many epics begin *in medias res* ("in the middle of things"), meaning that major events occurred before events in the poem begin. The audience is, thus, thrust into the middle of the action. In addition, the hero's adventures are often recounted in a **flashback,** a scene that interrupts a narrative to relate earlier events. Consider how these structural elements added excitement and tension to the story for Homer's original audiences and continue to affect readers today.

PHLit Online!
www.PHLitOnline.com

Hear It!
- Selection summary audio
- Selection audio

See It!
- Get Connected video
- Background video
- More about the author
- Vocabulary flashcards

Do It!
- Interactive journals
- Interactive graphic organizers
- Self-test
- Internet activity
- Grammar tutorial
- Interactive vocabulary games

❸ Reading Skill: Historical and Cultural Context

The **historical and cultural context** of a work is the backdrop of details of the time and place in which the work is set or in which it was written. These details include specific events, beliefs, and customs. When you read a work from another time and culture, **use background and prior knowledge** to analyze the influence of the historical and cultural context—the themes and issues important at that time and place.

- Read the author biography, footnotes, and other text aids.
- Note how characters' behavior and attitudes reflect the historical and cultural context.

❹ Using the Strategy: Context Chart

As you read, use a chart like the one shown to note the influences of ancient Greek culture in Homer's *Odyssey.*

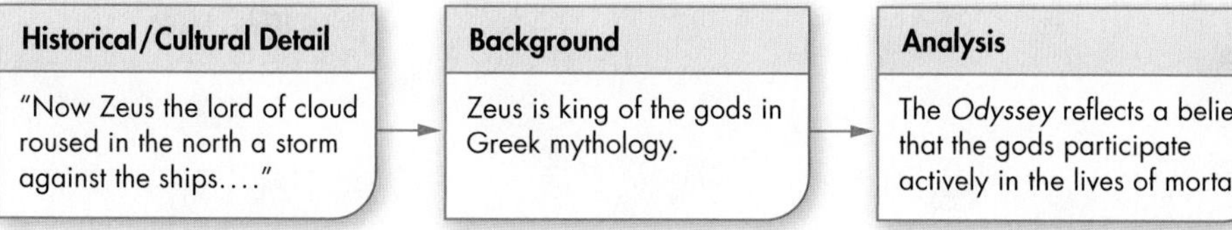

Historical/Cultural Detail
"Now Zeus the lord of cloud roused in the north a storm against the ships...."
Background
Zeus is king of the gods in Greek mythology.
Analysis
The *Odyssey* reflects a belief that the gods participate actively in the lives of mortals.

❷ Literary Analysis

Epic Hero

1. Introduce the skill, using instruction on the student page.
2. Tell students that they will practice analyzing epic heroes as they read.

Think Aloud: Model the Skill

Model the skill of analyzing an epic hero. Say to students:

Consider the original three movies in the *Star Wars* series. Luke Skywalker is an epic hero; he is brave, just, and connected to the Force. When Luke says "I want to learn the ways of the Force and become a Jedi like my father," he demonstrates bravery and a sense of duty. *Star Wars* is an epic that begins *in medias res.* It took three prequels to fill in the background events of Luke's life!

❸ Reading Skill

Historical and Cultural Context

1. Introduce the skill, using instruction on the student page.
2. Tell students that they will practice identifying historical and cultural details as they read.

❹ Using the Strategy

Give students a copy of either **Reading Skill Graphic Organizer** A or B (*Graphic Organizer Transparencies,* pp. 183–184) to record their ideas about historical and cultural context as they read. Use the examples in the **Reading Skill Graphic Organizer A,** which is partially filled in, to model the process of completing the organizer.

Ⓒ Text Complexity: Reader and Task Suggestions

from the Odyssey, Part 1	
Preparing to Read the Text	**Leveled Tasks**
• Refer to the Background information on TE p. 1043 and discuss the Greek city states and the Trojan War. • Discuss the role of epic heroes to a nation or culture. • Guide students to use Multidraft Reading strategies (TE p. 1043).	*Levels of Meaning* If students will have difficulty with meaning and concepts, have them first read Part 1 and note the main events in the plot. Then, have them reread and note why Odysseus makes the decisions he does. *Evaluating* If students will not have difficulty with meaning and concepts, have them read Part 1 and take notes on the roles of the Greek gods in the epic. Have students contribute their ideas during class discussion.

❶ Writing About the Big Question

1. Review the assignment with the class.
2. Remind students that certain positions have certain responsibilities and expectations. Have students think of a popular hero. What are his or her responsibilities? What expectations do people have of him or her?
3. Have students complete the sentence starters. Review responses as a class. (**Possible response:** A hero has an obligation to act selflessly because this shows that he or she is concerned about the greater good. The choices he or she makes are looked at closely and even scrutinized because a hero is held to a higher standard than is the general public.)
4. Remind students that their answers will help them think about the Big Question, "Do heroes have responsibilities?"

While You Read

Tell students that as they read they should look for characteristics of an epic hero and look for how Odysseus looks after his men.

❷ Vocabulary

1. Have students preview the selection vocabulary.
2. For each word, have students say the word aloud.
3. Then, use the word in a sentence that defines the word.
4. Finally, repeat your definitional sentence or a similar sentence with the word missing and have the class "fill in the blank" chorally. Here is an example:

   Something that is mammoth, is extremely large. One way to describe the size of an elephant is to say that it is [students say "mammoth"].

❸ Word Study

1. Introduce the skill, using the instruction in the box.
2. Ask students for a word with the prefix *be-* that means "to make friends with." (**Answer:** *befriend*)

Making Connections *from the* Odyssey, Part 1

Do *heroes* have responsibilities?

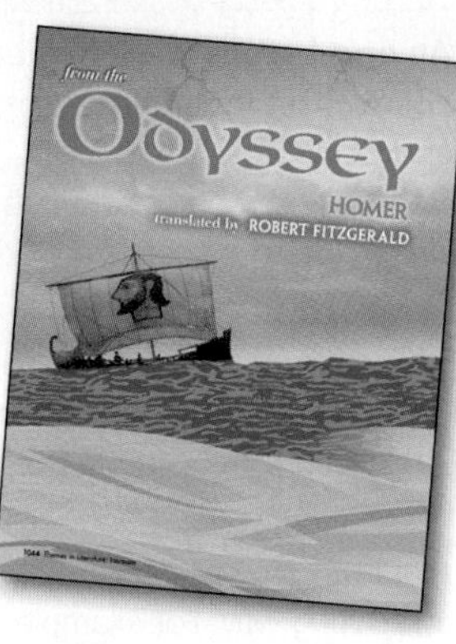

❶ Writing About the Big Question

In Part 1 of the *Odyssey,* Homer describes the hero Odysseus' long and dangerous journey home. Use these sentence starters to develop your ideas about the Big Question.

A **hero** has an **obligation** to ____________ because ____________.

The **choices** he or she makes are looked at closely and even scrutinized because ____________.

While You Read Look for characteristics that define the epic hero and take note of the ways in which Odysseus looks after his men.

❷ Vocabulary

Read each word and its definition. Decide whether you know the word well, know it a little bit, or do not know it at all. After you read, see how your knowledge of each word has increased.

- **plundered** (plun′ dərd) *v.* took goods by force; looted (p. 1045) *The fierce pirates captured the merchant ship and plundered it.* *plunderous adj. plunderer n.*
- **dispatched** (di spacht′) *v.* finished quickly (p. 1053) *Remarkably, she dispatched the assignment an hour before anyone else did.*
- **assuage** (ə swāj′) *v.* calm; pacify (p. 1065) *Gentle words may assuage their anger.* *assuaged v. assuagement n.*
- **bereft** (bē reft′) *adj.* deprived (p. 1068) *Bereft of sleep, she struggled to stay awake during the movie.* *bereavement n.*
- **ardor** (är′ dər) *n.* passion; enthusiasm (p. 1073) *The audience cheered their favorite characters with ardor.* *ardent adj.*
- **insidious** (in sid′ ē əs) *adj.* characterized by craftiness and betrayal (p. 1077) *The traitor's insidious actions led to the city's downfall.* *insidiously adv. insidiousness n.*

❸ Word Study

The **Old English prefix *be-*** means "around," "make," or "covered with."

In this selection, Tiresias warns Odysseus that he will be **bereft** of his companions. Tiresias means that Odysseus will lose his companions. **Bereft** is a form of **bereave,** which means "made to suffer a loss."

Vocabulary Development

Vocabulary Knowledge Rating

Create a **Vocabulary Knowledge Rating Chart** (***Professional Development Guidebook,*** p. 33) for this selection. Include the selection vocabulary and the Big Question words that appear in the Writing About the Big Question sentence starters on this page. (The Big Question vocabulary is introduced on pp. 1028–1029.)

Give students a copy of the chart. Read the words aloud, and have students mark their rating in the Before Reading column. Urge them to be alert to these words as they read and discuss the selection.

Tally how many students think they know a word to gauge how much instruction to provide. As students read and discuss the selection, point out the words and their context.

Vocabulary Central, featuring tools, activities, and songs for studying vocabulary, is available at **www.PHLitOnline.com.**

Background for the Story

The Trojan War

In the Iliad, *Homer focuses on the final year of the Trojan War; in the* Odyssey, *he tells what happened to one of the key warriors afterward.*

It Begins with Strife According to legend, the Trojan War began when Eris, goddess of strife, brought among the gods a golden apple inscribed "To the fairest." Hera, Athena, and Aphrodite all wanted that apple. They asked Paris, son of the king of Troy, to decide which of them deserved it. Each tried to bribe him: Hera offered power; Athena, wisdom; and Aphrodite, the world's most beautiful woman. The famous Judgment of Paris was that Aphrodite was the fairest. Soon, on a diplomatic mission to Sparta, Paris met Helen, the world's most beautiful woman and Sparta's queen. With Aphrodite's help, the two fell in love and eloped. When Menelaus (men′ ə lā′ əs), king of Sparta, could not persuade the Trojans to send his wife, Helen, back, he went to his brother Agamemnon (ag′ ə mem′ nän), king of Mycenae and the most powerful Greek leader. Agamemnon called on all the Greek rulers to honor a pact and go to Troy to fight to bring Helen home. The Greeks agreed and sailed to Troy. They laid siege to the city but for ten long years could not breach its impregnable walls.

"Trojan" is the adjective form of the ancient city of Troy. It is also the name for a person from Troy.

War Crimes and Punishment Agamemnon might have been a more powerful king and Achilles (ə kil′ ēz) a superior warrior, but Odysseus, king of Ithaca, was cleverest of them all. He devised a scheme in which the Greeks left a great wooden horse outside the walls of Troy and tricked the Trojans into taking it inside. That night, the Greeks hiding inside the horse—Odysseus among them—slipped out, unlocked the gates of the city, and allowed their fellow warriors to come swarming in to defeat the Trojans and sack the city. The fighting was brutal and destructive. King Priam (prī′ əm), Paris's father, for example, was killed while he was praying. The Greeks' behavior angered many of the gods, who made their voyages home very difficult.

Named for Odysseus, the *Odyssey* gave rise to our English word *odyssey*, meaning "an extended journey."

Odysseus was no exception. Following the Greek victory, he set sail for Ithaca but encountered a series of perilous misadventures that made his journey last ten years. It is this difficult, adventure-filled journey that Homer's *Odyssey* recounts.

▼ The Trojan horse, as depicted in the film *Troy* (Warner Brothers, 2004)

Differentiated Instruction — Additional Instruction

EL Extended Support—English Learners
Have students complete the **Reading and Vocabulary Warm-ups,** ***Unit 6 Resources,*** pp. 23–26 before they read. Assign the prereading pages and the adapted selection in the ***Reader's Notebook: English Learner's Version.*** Then, have students listen to portions of the selection on the ***Hear It!*** **Audio CD.**

L1 L2 Extended Support—Struggling Readers
Have students complete the **Reading and Vocabulary Warm-ups,** ***Unit 6 Resources,*** pp. 23–26 before they read. Assign the prereading pages and the adapted selection in the ***Reader's Notebook: Adapted Version.*** Then, have students listen to portions of the selection on the ***Hear It!*** **Audio CD** (adapted text).

Extended Support—Reluctant Readers
To build motivation and engagement before assigning the selection, have students read "In the Path of Danger," a thematically related selection in ***Reality Central.*** Then, use the questions at the conclusion of the related selection to guide discussion.

Daily Bellringer

For each class during which you will teach this selection, have students complete one of the five Quick Write activities for Week 31 in the ***Daily Bellringer Activities*** booklet.

Background

The Trojan War

The siege of Troy finally ended when the Greeks pretended to depart, leaving a giant wooden horse behind. Thinking that they had won the war, the Trojans dragged the horse inside the walls of their city. That night, Greek warriors who had hidden within the hollow horse crept out and opened the city gates to their waiting comrades, who then conquered the city.

Multidraft Reading

This icon ● marks natural pauses in the selection. To assist struggling readers and to deepen reading for all, assign the text in "chunks," following the icons, and apply multidraft reading protocols. For each reading, have students set the purpose indicated:

- **First reading**—identifying key ideas and details and answering any Reading Checks.
- **Second reading**—analyzing craft and structure and responding to the side-column prompts.
- **Third reading**—integrating knowledge and ideas, connecting to other texts and the world, and answering the end-of-selection questions.

For more guidance, refer to the ***Classroom Strategies and Teaching Routines*** card on multidraft reading.

PHLit Online!
For more about the author, practice with the selection vocabulary, and more background, go to **www.PHLitOnline.com.**

❶ Activating Prior Knowledge

1. Prepare an **Anticipation Guide** (see ***Professional Development Guidebook,*** pp. 36–38) with the following statements:
   - *The best travel is well planned and has no surprises.*
   - *Good leaders are people who can think on their feet.*
   - *Fear is an excellent motivator.*
   - *It is important to be able to adapt to changes.*
2. Give students a copy of the prepared **Anticipation Guide** and have students mark their responses in the appropriate columns.
3. For further guidance, use the ***Classroom Strategies and Teaching Routines*** card: **Using an Anticipation Guide.**

Concept Connector

Students will return to the **Anticipation Guide** after completing Part 1 of the *Odyssey.*

Whole-Class Activity

As students read the selection, lead them in a discussion about the similarities and differences between Odysseus and other superheroes in literature and film. On the board, create a chart, Venn diagram, or other graphic organizer to record students' responses.

❷ About the Selection

The *Odyssey* is a classic adventure story. It combines realistic elements of historical events with wildly imagined scenes of fantastic places and creatures. The epic also includes skillful characterizations. Odysseus, for example, represents the model epic hero. A leader of courage, daring, and wit, he pursues his goal—to return home after many years of war—in the face of many setbacks. However, he is also overly curious, foolishly cocky, and clever to the point of being tricky.

EXEMPLAR TEXT ©

from the Odyssey

❶
❷

HOMER

translated by **ROBERT FITZGERALD**

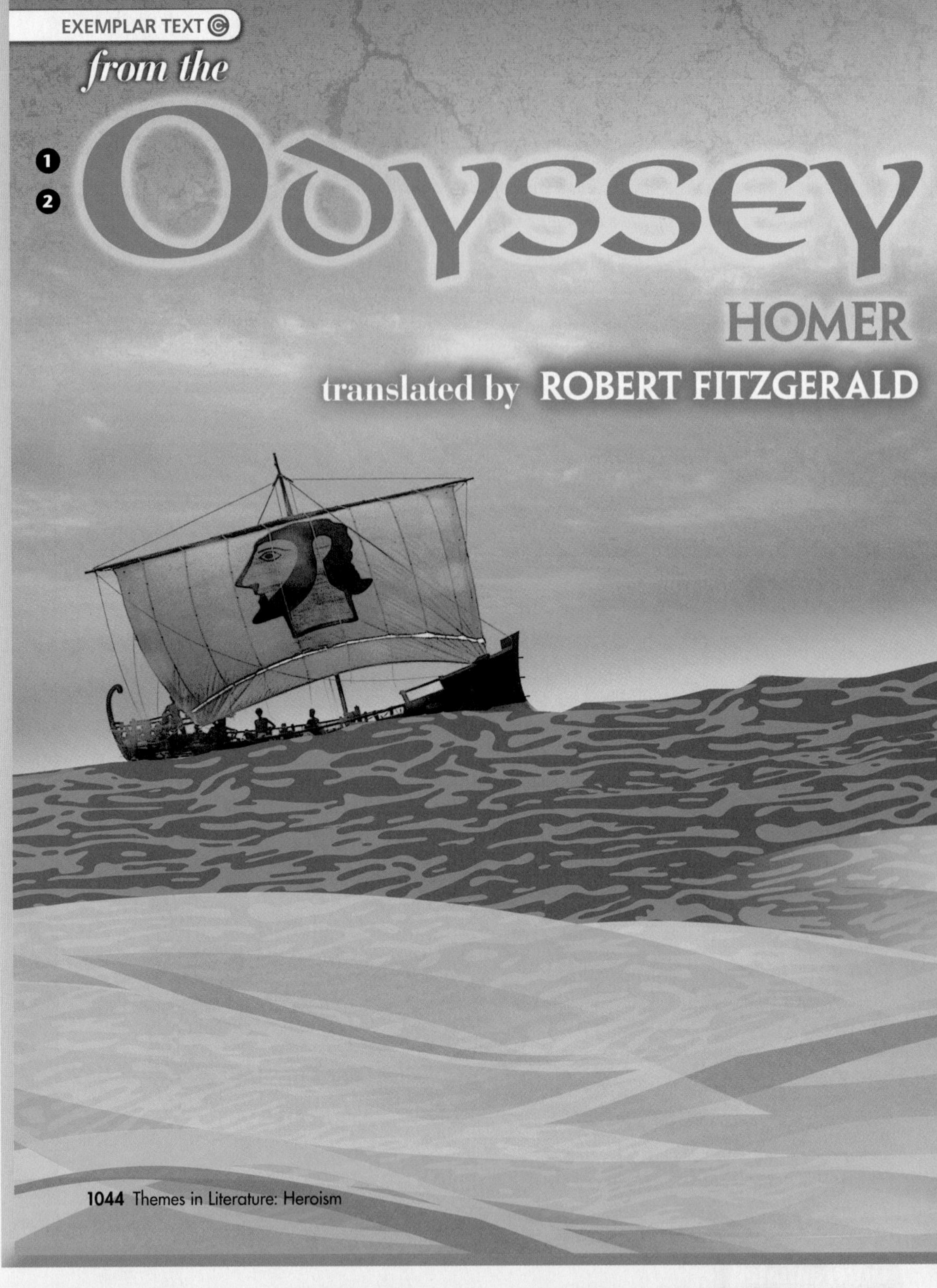

Vocabulary Development

© CCSS Language 6

Thematic Vocabulary: The Big Question

As students are discussing the *Odyssey, Part 1,* encourage them to use the thematic vocabulary presented in Introducing the Big Question, pp. 1028–1029. You might encourage them with sentence starters like these:

1. While the men are on their journey, Odysseus has an *obligation* to . . .
2. One way that Odysseus shows *wisdom* is . . .
3. Odysseus' men look to him to make *choices* about . . .
4. It is important for Odysseus to determine the *intentions* of the Cyclops because . . .

PART 1

The Adventures of Odysseus

In the opening verses, Homer addresses the muse of epic poetry. He asks her help in telling the tale of Odysseus.

Sing in me, Muse,[1] and through me tell the story
of that man skilled in all ways of contending,
the wanderer, harried for years on end,
after he plundered the stronghold
on the proud height of Troy.[2]
He saw the townlands
and learned the minds of many distant men,
and weathered many bitter nights and days
in his deep heart at sea, while he fought only
to save his life, to bring his shipmates home.
But not by will nor valor could he save them,
for their own recklessness destroyed them all—
children and fools, they killed and feasted on
the cattle of Lord Helios,[3] the Sun,
and he who moves all day through heaven
took from their eyes the dawn of their return.
Of these adventures, Muse, daughter of Zeus,[4]
tell us in our time, lift the great song again.

Note: In translating the *Odyssey*, Fitzgerald spelled Greek names to suggest the sound of the original Greek. In these excerpts, more familiar spellings have been used. For example, Fitzgerald's "Kirkê," "Kyklops," and "Seirênês" are spelled here as "Circe," "Cyclops," and "Sirens."

1. **Muse** (myo͞oz) any one of the nine goddesses of the arts, literature, and sciences; the spirit that is thought to inspire a poet or other artist.
2. **Troy** (troi) city in northwest Asia Minor; site of the Trojan War.

Vocabulary
plundered (plun′ dərd) *v.* took goods by force; looted

3. **Helios** (hē′ lē äs′) sun god.
4. **Zeus** (zo͞os) king of the gods.

3 Literary Analysis

Epic Hero

1. Remind students of other heroes they have encountered in their reading. Have the class discuss what makes characters appear especially heroic. Then, **ask** students what qualities mark Odysseus as a hero.

   Answer: Odysseus has a "deep heart," and he bravely fights to bring his shipmates home.

2. Have students review the description of epic heroes on p. 1041. Discuss the phrase "skilled in all ways of contending" in line 2, on this page, which means, in essence, "versatile." **Ask** students to explain how being skilled in many ways can be a heroic quality.

   Possible response: A person who is skilled in many ways can solve many problems and serve society in many different capacities. This increases his or her heroic potential.

PHLit Online!

This selection is available in interactive format in the **Enriched Online Student Edition, www.PHLitOnline.com,** which includes a thematically related video and writing prompt and an interactive graphic organizer.

Differentiated Instruction for Universal Access

Support for Less Proficient Readers
Point out that this page describes events that will be recounted during the telling of the epic. Ask students to summarize the page and then tell what they can infer from it.

Enrichment for Advanced Readers
Point out to students that reading the legends, epics, myths, and folk literature of a culture will help them understand a culture. The *Odyssey* provides historical background as well as cultural insights. Discuss students' growing knowledge of Greek culture at the end of each day's reading.

4 Critical Thinking

Classify

1. Have students read the list of characters on this page.
2. **Ask** students to classify the characters' relationships to Odysseus based on the descriptions. Students should use a chart with the headings **Helpful to Odysseus, Harmful to Odysseus,** and **Unclear**.

   Possible response:

Helpful to Odysseus	Harmful to Odysseus	Unclear
Calypso	Polyphemus	Alcinous
Circe	Sirens	Zeus
Laertes	Scylla	Apollo
Perimedes	Charybdis	Agamemnon
Eurylochus		Poseidon
Tiresias		Athena
Telemachus		Cronus
Eumaeus		Persephone
Penelope		Lampetia
		Hermes
		Antinous
		Eurynome
		Eurymachus
		Amphinomus

3. Remind students that their current classifications are predictions, and they should revise their charts as they read. **Ask:** Based on your chart, do you think Odysseus will be successful or unsuccessful in this story?

   Possible response: I think he will be successful because many of the characters seem to be on his side.

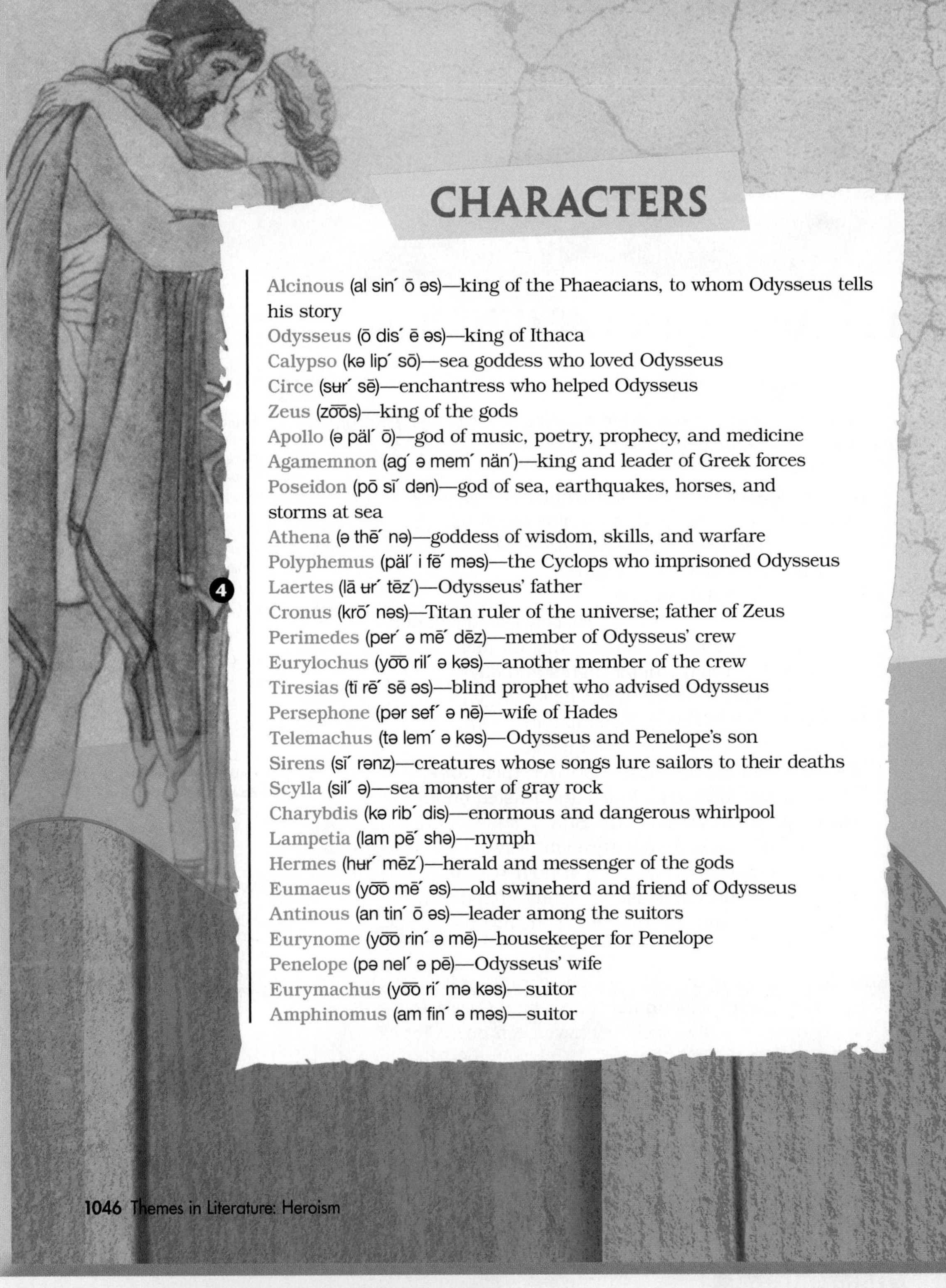

CHARACTERS

4 Alcinous (al sin´ ō əs)—king of the Phaeacians, to whom Odysseus tells his story
Odysseus (ō dis´ ē əs)—king of Ithaca
Calypso (kə lip´ sō)—sea goddess who loved Odysseus
Circe (sʉr´ sē)—enchantress who helped Odysseus
Zeus (zo͞os)—king of the gods
Apollo (ə päl´ ō)—god of music, poetry, prophecy, and medicine
Agamemnon (ag´ ə mem´ nän´)—king and leader of Greek forces
Poseidon (pō sī´ dən)—god of sea, earthquakes, horses, and storms at sea
Athena (ə thē´ nə)—goddess of wisdom, skills, and warfare
Polyphemus (päl´ i fē´ məs)—the Cyclops who imprisoned Odysseus
Laertes (lā ʉr´ tēz´)—Odysseus' father
Cronus (krō´ nəs)—Titan ruler of the universe; father of Zeus
Perimedes (per´ ə mē´ dēz)—member of Odysseus' crew
Eurylochus (yo͞o ril´ ə kəs)—another member of the crew
Tiresias (tī rē´ sē əs)—blind prophet who advised Odysseus
Persephone (pər sef´ ə nē)—wife of Hades
Telemachus (tə lem´ ə kəs)—Odysseus and Penelope's son
Sirens (sī´ rənz)—creatures whose songs lure sailors to their deaths
Scylla (sil´ ə)—sea monster of gray rock
Charybdis (kə rib´ dis)—enormous and dangerous whirlpool
Lampetia (lam pē´ shə)—nymph
Hermes (hʉr´ mēz´)—herald and messenger of the gods
Eumaeus (yo͞o mē´ əs)—old swineherd and friend of Odysseus
Antinous (an tin´ ō əs)—leader among the suitors
Eurynome (yo͞o rin´ ə mē)—housekeeper for Penelope
Penelope (pə nel´ ə pē)—Odysseus' wife
Eurymachus (yo͞o ri´ mə kəs)—suitor
Amphinomus (am fin´ ə məs)—suitor

Vocabulary Development ⓒ CCSS Language 6

Words from Greek Mythology

The names and actions of the characters listed may be more meaningful to students if they are familiar with examples that have entered English usage. Have students look up the words *odyssey* and *siren* and use these words in sentences that show their general meaning. Challenge students to find the derivation of other words from mythology, including *atlas, echo, mentor,* and *morphine.*

Sailing from Troy

Ten years after the Trojan War, Odysseus departs from the goddess Calypso's island. He arrives in Phaeacia, ruled by Alcinous. Alcinous offers a ship to Odysseus and asks him to tell of his adventures.

"I am Laertes'[5] son, Odysseus.
Men hold me
formidable for guile[6] in peace and war:
this fame has gone abroad to the sky's rim.

My home is on the peaked sea-mark of Ithaca[7]
under Mount Neion's wind-blown robe of leaves,
in sight of other islands—Dulichium,
Same, wooded Zacynthus—Ithaca
being most lofty in that coastal sea,
and northwest, while the rest lie east and south.
A rocky isle, but good for a boy's training;
I shall not see on earth a place more dear,
though I have been detained long by Calypso,[8]
loveliest among goddesses, who held me
in her smooth caves, to be her heart's delight,
as Circe of Aeaea,[9] the enchantress,
desired me, and detained me in her hall.
But in my heart I never gave consent.
Where shall a man find sweetness to surpass
his own home and his parents? In far lands
he shall not, though he find a house of gold.

What of my sailing, then, from Troy?
What of those years
of rough adventure, weathered under Zeus?
The wind that carried west from Ilium[10]
brought me to Ismarus, on the far shore,
a strongpoint on the coast of Cicones.[11]
I stormed that place and killed the men who fought.
Plunder we took, and we enslaved the women,
to make division, equal shares to all—
but on the spot I told them: 'Back, and quickly!
Out to sea again!' My men were mutinous,[12]
fools, on stores of wine. Sheep after sheep

5. Laertes (lā ur′ tēz′)
6. guile (gīl) *n.* craftiness; cunning.
7. Ithaca (*ith′* ə kə) island off the west coast of Greece.

Literary Analysis
Epic Hero For what quality does Odysseus say he is famous?

8. Calypso (kə lip′ sō) sea goddess who loved Odysseus.
9. Circe (sur′ sē) **of Aeaea** (ē′ ē ə)
10. Ilium (il′ ē əm) Troy.

11. Cicones (si kō′ nēz)
12. mutinous (myo͞ot′'n əs) *adj.* rebellious.

6

Reading Check
Who has asked Odysseus to tell his tale?

5 Literary Analysis

Epic Hero

1. Discuss with students how Odysseus' speech serves to introduce him and to illustrate his character. Point out that he gives details about his background and childhood in this opening speech.
2. **Ask** students where Odysseus' home is and why he holds it dear.

   Answer: His home is Ithaca, which has a view of other islands. He says that it is rocky but good for a boy's training.
3. **Ask** students to name qualities they associate with heroism.

   Possible response: Students may say that bravery or determination is a heroic quality.
4. **Ask** students the Literary Analysis question: For what quality does Odysseus say he is famous?

   Answer: Odysseus is famous for his guile, which makes him effective in both war and peace.

6 Reading Check

Answer: Alcinous, king of the Phaeacians, has asked Odysseus to tell his story.

PROFESSIONAL DEVELOPMENT | **Kelly Gallagher**

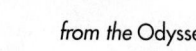

Apply the Strategy

Exit Slips: While students are reading the *Odyssey,* Exit Slips can be used for the following purposes:

- **To monitor confusion:** After reading "Sailing from Troy," have students write what they find confusing on slips of paper. Collect these when they exit the room. Use them at the beginning of the next class and discuss confusion. Have students first work in small groups; clarify any remaining confusion as a class.
- **To extend thinking:** Have students write about "hot spots" on exit slips. For example, after reading a segment, say, "What is the most important word in this passage? Write the word and defend your answer." Collect these when students leave; share them the next day as a warm-up.

For more of Kelly Gallagher's strategies, see his Professional Development essay, pp. 1028c–1028d.

7 Reading Skill

Historical and Cultural Context

1. **Ask** students what mistakes Odysseus and his men made on Ismarus.

   Possible response: Odysseus' men were greedy and mutinous. They drank wine and feasted on sheep and cattle but paid little attention to people who went inland. The crew's behavior exposed them to the Cicone army.

2. **Ask** students what the empty benches in line 63 reveal about the outcome of the battle, as well as the type of ship Odysseus sailed in.

   Possible response: The empty benches show the number of men killed in battle. The benches also show how the sailors sat on the boat, possibly to row with oars.

3. **Ask** students the Reading Skill question: What beliefs and values are reflected in lines 65–69?

   Possible response: The sailors' grief indicates how close they are to one another and how much they honor the men with whom they fight.

8 Literary Analysis

Epic Hero

1. Remind students that Odysseus is explaining to his listener why it has taken him so long to return home.

   Ask students to mark the words that show the passage of time in the first ten lines of "The Lotus-Eaters."

   Answer: The words and phrases *now, two long days and nights, until,* and *then* show the passage of time.

2. **Ask** students the Literary Analysis question: What words in line 82 remind you that this part is a flashback?

   Answer: The phrase "that time" indicates that Odysseus is retelling one of the many incidents that happened on his journey.

they butchered by the surf, and shambling cattle,
feasting,—while fugitives went inland, running
to call to arms the main force of Cicones.
This was an army, trained to fight on horseback
or, where the ground required, on foot. They came
with dawn over that terrain like the leaves
and blades of spring. So doom appeared to us,
dark word of Zeus for us, our evil days.
My men stood up and made a fight of it—
backed on the ships, with lances kept in play,
from bright morning through the blaze of noon
holding our beach, although so far outnumbered;
but when the sun passed toward unyoking time,
then the Achaeans,[13] one by one, gave way.
Six benches were left empty in every ship
that evening when we pulled away from death.
And this new grief we bore with us to sea:
our precious lives we had, but not our friends.
No ship made sail next day until some shipmate
had raised a cry, three times, for each poor ghost
unfleshed by the Cicones on that field.

13. **Achaeans** (ə kē´ ənz) *n.* Greeks; here, Odysseus' men.

Reading Skill
Historical and Cultural Context What beliefs and values are reflected in lines 65–69?

The Lotus-Eaters

Now Zeus the lord of cloud roused in the north
a storm against the ships, and driving veils
of squall moved down like night on land and sea.
The bows went plunging at the gust; sails
cracked and lashed out strips in the big wind.
We saw death in that fury, dropped the yards,
unshipped the oars, and pulled for the nearest lee:[14]
then two long days and nights we lay offshore
worn out and sick at heart, tasting our grief,
until a third Dawn came with ringlets shining.
Then we put up our masts, hauled sail, and rested,
letting the steersmen and the breeze take over.

I might have made it safely home, that time,
but as I came round Malea the current
took me out to sea, and from the north
a fresh gale drove me on, past Cythera.
Nine days I drifted on the teeming sea
before dangerous high winds. Upon the tenth

14. **lee** (lē) *n.* area sheltered from the wind.

Literary Analysis
Epic Hero What words in line 82 remind you that this part is a flashback?

Vocabulary Development

CCSS Language 6

Expressive Vocabulary

Ask students to think about Odysseus' travels with his men. Were they more terrified by their battles with the seas or by their encounters with monsters? Did they ever lose hope of returning home? Which of their delays are avoidable, and which are unavoidable? To help students broaden their expressive vocabulary, encourage them to use the following words as they discuss the questions above: *encounter, interact, highlight,* and *eliminate.* Have them complete these sentence starters:

1. The Greeks' *encounter* with the Cicones could have been avoided if . . .
2. The sailors *interact* with people who forget their memories when . . .
3. Odysseus takes the time to *highlight* his men's grief at the death of their comrades after . . .
4. Odysseus cannot *eliminate* his men's errors when . . .

we came to the coastline of the Lotus-Eaters,
who live upon that flower. We landed there
to take on water. All ships' companies
mustered alongside for the mid-day meal.
Then I sent out two picked men and a runner
to learn what race of men that land sustained.
They fell in, soon enough, with Lotus-Eaters,
who showed no will to do us harm, only
offering the sweet Lotus to our friends—
but those who ate this honeyed plant, the Lotus,
never cared to report, nor to return:
they longed to stay forever, browsing on
that native bloom, forgetful of their homeland.
I drove them, all three wailing, to the ships,
tied them down under their rowing benches,
and called the rest: 'All hands aboard;
(9) come, clear the beach and no one taste
the Lotus, or you lose your hope of home.'
Filing in to their places by the rowlocks
my oarsmen dipped their long oars in the surf,
and we moved out again on our sea faring.

Literary Analysis
Epic Hero Which characteristics of an epic hero does Odysseus show in this episode?

Critical Thinking

Cite textual evidence to support your responses.

1. **Key Ideas and Details** **(a)** While on Ismarus, in what ways do Odysseus' men disobey orders? **(b) Analyze Cause and Effect:** What is the result of this disobedience? **(c) Speculate:** What lesson might Odysseus take away from this experience?
2. **Key Ideas and Details** **(a)** What happens to the men who eat the Lotus? **(b) Infer:** What does this episode suggest about the main problem that Odysseus has with his men? **(c) Evaluate:** Do you think Odysseus responds appropriately to the three men who long to stay with the Lotus-Eaters? Why or why not?
3. **Key Ideas and Details** **(a)** Note two points at which Odysseus mentions a desire to return home. **(b) Infer:** What significant role might his longing for home play in Odysseus' epic journey?
4. **Integration of Knowledge and Ideas** **(a)** In this episode, does Odysseus prove himself to be a hero? **(b)** What responsibilities does he demonstrate, if any? *[Connect to the Big Question: Do heroes have responsibilities?]*

(9) Literary Analysis

Epic Hero

1. Read aloud lines 101–105.
2. **Ask** the Literary Analysis question: Which characteristics of an epic hero does Odysseus show in this episode?

   Possible response: Odysseus displays wisdom and leadership.

ASSESS

Answers

Critical Thinking

Before students respond, you may wish to have them write a brief objective summary of the selection. As they answer the questions below, remind them to support their answers with evidence from the text.

1. (a) The Greeks mutiny, drink wine, and refuse to come back to the ship. (b) They are attacked by the Cicones, and many Greeks are killed. (c) Odysseus might learn that he needs to exercise discipline over his men.
2. (a) The men are lulled into a state of calm forgetfulness and no longer want to return home. (b) The men lack self-control and discipline. (c) **Possible response:** Odysseus has no choice but to force the men back on the ship; their skills are needed on board to help everyone get home safely.
3. (a) He mentions a desire to return home as he describes being held by Circe (line 35) and when he describes his escape from the Lotus-Eaters (line 105).

   (b) **Possible response:** His longing for home might give Odysseus extra strength or drive to escape from difficulties.
4. (a) **Possible response:** Students are likely to say that Odysseus proves himself to be a hero because he shows leadership and determination. (b) **Possible response:** He takes responsibility for his men. He forces them onto the ship because he does not want to leave them behind.

Fluency

Distribute copies of p. 1049, and pair students. Have partners take turns reading paragraphs aloud. While one partner reads, the other should mark any words with which the student reading has difficulty. Circulate to monitor the fluency of students' reading. Collect students' marked-up copies of the page, and review difficult words and passages with the class. Look for these problem spots:

- If students struggle to pronounce *browsing* (line 99), tell students that it rhymes with the word *now*. Read the word aloud clearly and have students echo to confirm correct pronunciation. Ask students to name other examples of words that contain the letters *ow* and rhyme with *now*. *(allow, sow, prow, how)*.
- If students read the lines of text in a hesitant, uneven way, remind them that the punctuation—not the line breaks—should guide their reading. Model reading lines 94–100 by keeping the sentence flowing. Pause slightly after each comma, and pause markedly after the dash, the colon, and the period. Have a volunteer read lines 101–105 aloud and pause appropriately at each punctuation mark.

⑩ Reading Skill

Historical and Cultural Context

1. Point out to students that conflicts in the *Odyssey* are signaled before they actually occur. **Ask** students to point out some of the warnings of conflict in this passage.

   Answer: Odysseus finds fault with the Cyclopes' uncivilized ways. The Cyclopes do not farm, and they have no laws. They deal out rough justice to women and children.

2. **Ask** students the first Reading Skill question: Based on Odysseus' criticism of the Cyclopes, what kind of society do you think the Greeks valued?

   Possible response: The Greeks must have valued an ordered society that practiced agriculture and abided by rules of law.

⑪ Reading Skill

Historical and Cultural Context

1. Read the bracketed passage with students and point out the words *alone, remote,* and *solitude,* which describe how the Cyclopes live separate from others.

2. **Ask** students the second Reading Skill question: What does this passage reveal about ancient Greek attitudes toward the importance of community?

   Possible response: The Greeks placed a high value on living in community with others and participating in society. Community living was an indication of advanced civilization.

The Cyclops

In the next land we found were Cyclopes,[15]
giants, louts, without a law to bless them.
In ignorance leaving the fruitage of the earth in mystery
to the immortal gods, they neither plow
nor sow by hand, nor till the ground, though grain—
⑩ wild wheat and barley—grows untended, and
wine-grapes, in clusters, ripen in heaven's rains.
Cyclopes have no muster and no meeting,
no consultation or old tribal ways,
but each one dwells in his own mountain cave
dealing out rough justice to wife and child,
indifferent to what the others do. . . .

As we rowed on, and nearer to the mainland,
at one end of the bay, we saw a cavern
yawning above the water, screened with laurel,
and many rams and goats about the place
inside a sheepfold—made from slabs of stone
earthfast between tall trunks of pine and rugged
towering oak trees.
A prodigious[16] man
slept in this cave alone, and took his flocks
to graze afield—remote from all companions,
knowing none but savage ways, a brute
⑪ so huge, he seemed no man at all of those
who eat good wheaten bread; but he seemed rather
a shaggy mountain reared in solitude.
We beached there, and I told the crew
to stand by and keep watch over the ship:
as for myself I took my twelve best fighters
and went ahead. I had a goatskin full
of that sweet liquor that Euanthes' son,
Maron, had given me. He kept Apollo's[17]
holy grove at Ismarus; for kindness
we showed him there, and showed his wife and child,
he gave me seven shining golden talents[18]
perfectly formed, a solid silver winebowl,
and then this liquor—twelve two-handled jars
of brandy, pure and fiery. Not a slave
in Maron's household knew this drink; only
he, his wife and the storeroom mistress knew;

15. Cyclopes (sī klō′ pēz′) *n.* plural form of Cyclops (sī′ kläps′), race of giants with one eye in the middle of the forehead.

Reading Skill Historical and Cultural Context Based on Odysseus' criticism of the Cyclopes, what kind of society do you think the Greeks valued?

16. prodigious (prō dij′ əs) *adj.* enormous.

Reading Skill Historical and Cultural Context What does this passage reveal about ancient Greek attitudes toward the importance of community?

17. Apollo (ə päl′ ō) god of music, poetry, prophecy, and medicine.

18. talents units of money in ancient Greece.

and they would put one cupful—ruby-colored,
honey-smooth—in twenty more of water,
but still the sweet scent hovered like a fume
over the winebowl. No man turned away
when cups of this came round.
A wineskin full
I brought along, and victuals[19] in a bag,
for in my bones I knew some towering brute
would be upon us soon—all outward power,
a wild man, ignorant of civility.

We climbed, then, briskly to the cave. But Cyclops
had gone afield, to pasture his fat sheep,
so we looked round at everything inside:
a drying rack that sagged with cheeses, pens
crowded with lambs and kids,[20] each in its class:
firstlings apart from middlings, and the 'dewdrops,'
or newborn lambkins, penned apart from both.
And vessels full of whey[21] were brimming there—
bowls of earthenware and pails for milking.
My men came pressing round me, pleading:
'Why not
take these cheeses, get them stowed, come back,
throw open all the pens, and make a run for it?
We'll drive the kids and lambs aboard. We say
put out again on good salt water!'

Ah,
12 how sound that was! Yet I refused. I wished
to see the cave man, what he had to offer—
no pretty sight, it turned out, for my friends.
We lit a fire, burnt an offering,
and took some cheese to eat; then sat in silence
around the embers, waiting. When he came
he had a load of dry boughs[22] on his shoulder
to stoke his fire at suppertime. He dumped it
with a great crash into that hollow cave,
and we all scattered fast to the far wall.
Then over the broad cavern floor he ushered
the ewes he meant to milk. He left his rams
and he-goats in the yard outside, and swung
high overhead a slab of solid rock

19. **victuals** (vit´ əlz) *n.* food or other provisions.

20. **kids** young goats.

21. **whey** (hwā) *n.* thin, watery part of milk separated from the thicker curds.

22. **boughs** (bouz) *n.* tree branches.

Literary Analysis
Epic Hero What character flaw does the hero Odysseus reveal by refusing to leave the cave?

13

Where is Cyclops when Odysseus and his men enter the cave?

12 Literary Analysis

Epic Hero

1. Point out that in this passage, Odysseus reveals one of the qualities that get him into trouble: he doesn't listen to his men.
2. **Ask** students if they think that Odysseus should stay and get more information or leave and avoid trouble.

   Possible response: Students may say that they think Odysseus should leave now unless he is sure he can find an escape route.
3. **Ask** students the Literary Analysis question: What character flaw does the hero Odysseus reveal by refusing to leave the cave?

   Possible response: Odysseus' curiosity leads him to disregard good advice. He knows it would be wise to seize the food and leave, but he is too curious to see the "cave man."

13 Reading Check

Answer: Cyclops is in the field taking care of his sheep.

Differentiated Instruction for Universal Access

Support for Less Proficient Readers

Point out that this page describes the food that the Greeks find in the Cyclops cave. Ask a volunteer to read lines 159–165. List the food items on the board. Then, ask students to draw the scene in the Cyclops' cave.

EL Support for English Learners

Reread lines 160–165. Point out the terms that describe the animals, such as *firstlings, middlings,* and *dewdrops*. Ask students why those animals would have to be separated. Finally, have students find other words to describe animal offspring, such as *nestling, fawn, duckling, eaglet, cub, gosling, joey, piglet,* and *cygnet*. Have students identify the parent of each of these offspring.

⓮ Literary Analysis

Epic Hero

1. Have students read aloud lines 204–215. Discuss what verbal inflection they might use in the phrases "We served under Agamemnon," "the whole world knows," and "have a care."
2. **Ask** students what earlier events would give Odysseus reason to be proud of his men and his own behavior.

   Possible response: The Greeks have defeated the Trojans at war; Odysseus and his men have sailed through many storms and have escaped the Cicones and the Lotus-Eaters.

⓯ Reading Skill

Historical and Cultural Context

1. Point out to students Odysseus' use of the word *courtesy* in line 215. Explain to students that *courtesy* meant more than just "politeness" in Greek society. Ancient Greek custom held that any guest must be offered hospitality in one's home. All guests were treated with courtesy, in part because the gods could assume human form and appear at one's doorstep.
2. Now **ask** students the Reading Skill question: What ancient Greek beliefs regarding the gods, military might, and respect for strangers does Odysseus express in his words to the Cyclops?

   Possible response: Odysseus' answer shows that the Greek custom of hospitality is well established. The rules of hospitality are part of the Greeks' religious beliefs and are thought to be enforced by the gods.

to close the cave. Two dozen four-wheeled wagons,
with heaving wagon teams, could not have stirred
the tonnage of that rock from where he wedged it
over the doorsill. Next he took his seat
and milked his bleating ewes. A practiced job
he made of it, giving each ewe her suckling;
thickened his milk, then, into curds and whey,
sieved out the curds to drip in withy[23] baskets,
and poured the whey to stand in bowls
cooling until he drank it for his supper.
When all these chores were done, he poked the fire,
heaping on brushwood. In the glare he saw us.

'Strangers,' he said, 'who are you? And where from?
What brings you here by seaways—a fair traffic?
Or are you wandering rogues, who cast your lives
like dice, and ravage other folk by sea?'

We felt a pressure on our hearts, in dread
of that deep rumble and that mighty man.
But all the same I spoke up in reply:
'We are from Troy, Achaeans, blown off course
by shifting gales on the Great South Sea;
homeward bound, but taking routes and ways
uncommon; so the will of Zeus would have it.
We served under Agamemnon,[24] son of Atreus—
the whole world knows what city
he laid waste, what armies he destroyed.
⓮ It was our luck to come here; here we stand,
beholden for your help, or any gifts
⓯ you give—as custom is to honor strangers.
We would entreat you, great Sir, have a care
for the gods' courtesy; Zeus will avenge
the unoffending guest.'
He answered this
from his brute chest, unmoved:

'You are a ninny,
or else you come from the other end of nowhere,
telling me, mind the gods! We Cyclopes
care not a whistle for your thundering Zeus
or all the gods in bliss; we have more force by far.

23. **withy** (with´ ē) *adj.* made from tough, flexible twigs.

24. **Agamemnon** (ag´ ə mem´ nän´) king who led the Greek army during the Trojan War.

Reading Skill
Historical and Cultural Context What ancient Greek beliefs regarding the gods, military might, and respect for strangers does Odysseus express in his words to the Cyclops?

Think Aloud

Vocabulary: Using Context

Direct students' attention to the word *rogues* on this page, line 199. Using a think-aloud process, model how to use context to infer the meaning of an unknown word. Say to students:

> I'm going to think aloud to show you how I would figure out the meaning of *rogue* from its context.
>
> In this sentence, *rogue* is used by the Cyclops to describe people who "ravage other folk by sea." We know that earlier in the passage the Greeks have stolen into the Cyclops' cave, and, from his point of view, they could be robbers. The word *ravage,* meaning "ruin," is a clue that a *rogue* is a person who does no good. Since the Greeks have broken into the Cyclops' cave, I think *rogue* refers to some kind of a scoundrel.

I would not let you go for fear of Zeus—
you or your friends—unless I had a whim[25] to.
Tell me, where was it, now, you left your ship—
around the point, or down the shore, I wonder?'

He thought he'd find out, but I saw through this,
and answered with a ready lie:

16 'My ship?
Poseidon[26] Lord, who sets the earth a-tremble,
broke it up on the rocks at your land's end.
A wind from seaward served him, drove us there.
We are survivors, these good men and I.'

Neither reply nor pity came from him,
but in one stride he clutched at my companions
and caught two in his hands like squirming puppies
to beat their brains out, spattering the floor.
Then he dismembered them and made his meal,
gaping and crunching like a mountain lion—
everything: innards, flesh, and marrow bones.
We cried aloud, lifting our hands to Zeus,
powerless, looking on at this, appalled;
but Cyclops went on filling up his belly
with manflesh and great gulps of whey,
then lay down like a mast among his sheep.
My heart beat high now at the chance of action,
and drawing the sharp sword from my hip I went
along his flank to stab him where the midriff
17 holds the liver. I had touched the spot
when sudden fear stayed me: if I killed him
we perished there as well, for we could never
move his ponderous doorway slab aside.
So we were left to groan and wait for morning.

When the young Dawn with fingertips of rose
lit up the world, the Cyclops built a fire
and milked his handsome ewes, all in due order,
putting the sucklings to the mothers. Then,
his chores being all dispatched, he caught
another brace[27] of men to make his breakfast,
and whisked away his great door slab

25. **whim** (hwim) *n.* sudden thought or wish to do something.

26. **Poseidon** (pō sī´ dən) god of the sea, earthquakes, horses, and storms at sea.

Literary Analysis
Epic Hero In what way does Odysseus' response show that he is "formidable for guile"?

Literary Analysis
Epic Hero How do lines 244–250 show Odysseus' ability to think ahead?

Vocabulary
dispatched (di spacht´) *v.* finished quickly

27. **brace** (brās) *n.* pair.

18 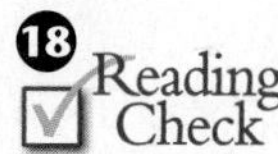

What does Odysseus tell the Cyclops happened to his ship?

Differentiated Instruction for Universal Access

Strategy for Special-Needs Students
Remind students that Odysseus is a complex character who can respond to difficulties in surprising ways. Have students keep track of Odysseus' surprising responses with a **Character Wheel** ***(Graphic Organizer Transparencies,*** p. 216) by jotting down quotations from the selection and analyzing what the quotations reveal about Odysseus. Help students get started by pointing them to quotations such as "I saw through this and answered with a ready lie."

Strategy for Advanced Readers
Have students profile Odysseus' character by discussing both his strengths and weaknesses. Have them write brief essays in which they identify the most striking parts of his personality and explain which of these qualities—his bravery, his leadership, or his brains, for example—are most important to his survival and success.

16 Literary Analysis

Epic Hero

1. **Ask** students why the Cyclops would want to know the location of the Greeks' ship.

   Possible response: He might want to rob the ship of goods, or he might want to kill any other sailors left on board.

2. **Ask** students the first Literary Analysis question: In what way does Odysseus' response show that he is "formidable for guile"?

   Possible response: Odysseus is clever enough to see through his opponent's trickery and to outwit him in return.

17 Literary Analysis

Epic Hero

1. Point out that Odysseus is prepared to kill Cyclops by stabbing him in the liver. **Ask:** What factors complicate the Greeks' attempts at escaping?

   Possible response: The Cyclops has sealed the entrance to the cave with a stone too big for humans to move. The Cyclops continues to eat Odysseus' men as long as they are trapped in the cave.

2. Then, **ask** the second Literary Analysis question: How do lines 244–250 show Odysseus' ability to think ahead?

   Possible response: Odysseus realizes that, although he could successfully kill the Cyclops, he would doom himself to imprisonment in the cave. He knows his escape must involve the Cyclops' removing the stone blocking the entry to the cave.

18 Reading Check

Answer: Odysseus says that his ship has broken up on the rocks. He lies because he thinks that Cyclops may want to destroy the Greek ship.

19 Literary Analysis

Epic Hero

1. Review with students the plans that Odysseus makes to attempt his escape. **Ask** students how long it took them to figure out what Odysseus is doing with the olive tree.

   Possible response: Students may say they did not see Odysseus' intention until he declares that he will "grind that spike" into the Cyclops' eye.

2. **Ask** students the first Literary Analysis question: What heroic qualities does Odysseus reveal as he plots against the Cyclops?

   Possible response: Odysseus shows the ability to construct a detailed plan. He has the discipline to carry out each step of the plan, without rushing in a way that would tip off the Cyclops that he is about to be tricked.

3. Point out how Odysseus combines the bravery and strength of an epic hero with intelligence and cunning. Have students give examples of more one-dimensional heroes and compare them with the depth of Odysseus' character.

20 Literary Analysis

Epic Hero

1. Review with students Odysseus' earlier discussion of this wine and its potency. Remind students that humans enjoyed the drink when it was diluted considerably with water.

2. **Ask** students the second Literary Analysis question: What plan do you think Odysseus has in mind by offering the Cyclops the wine?

   Possible responses: Odysseus hopes to slow the Cyclops' reaction time or perhaps put him to sleep.

---

28. cap a quiver (kwiv´ ər) close a case holding arrows.
29. din (din) *n.* loud, continuous noise; uproar.
30. Athena (ə thē´ nə) goddess of wisdom, skills, and warfare.
31. felled green and left to season chopped down and exposed to the weather to age the wood.
32. lugger (lug´ ər) *n.* small sailing vessel.

Literary Analysis
Epic Hero What heroic qualities does Odysseus reveal as he plots against the Cyclops?

to let his sheep go through—but he, behind,
reset the stone as one would cap a quiver.[28]
There was a din[29] of whistling as the Cyclops
rounded his flock to higher ground, then stillness.
And now I pondered how to hurt him worst,
if but Athena[30] granted what I prayed for.
Here are the means I thought would serve my turn:

a club, or staff, lay there along the fold—
an olive tree, felled green and left to season[31]
for Cyclops' hand. And it was like a mast
a lugger[32] of twenty oars, broad in the beam—
a deep-sea-going craft—might carry:
so long, so big around, it seemed. Now I
chopped out a six foot section of this pole
and set it down before my men, who scraped it;
and when they had it smooth, I hewed again
to make a stake with pointed end. I held this
in the fire's heart and turned it, toughening it,
then hid it, well back in the cavern, under
(19) one of the dung piles in profusion there.
Now came the time to toss for it: who ventured
along with me? whose hand could bear to thrust
and grind that spike in Cyclops' eye, when mild
sleep had mastered him? As luck would have it,
the men I would have chosen won the toss—
four strong men, and I made five as captain.

At evening came the shepherd with his flock,
his woolly flock. The rams as well, this time,
entered the cave: by some sheepherding whim—
or a god's bidding—none were left outside.
He hefted his great boulder into place
and sat him down to milk the bleating ewes
in proper order, put the lambs to suck,
and swiftly ran through all his evening chores.
Then he caught two more men and feasted on them.
My moment was at hand, and I went forward
holding an ivy bowl of my dark drink,
looking up, saying:

'Cyclops, try some wine.
(20) Here's liquor to wash down your scraps of men.
Taste it, and see the kind of drink we carried

Literary Analysis
Epic Hero What plan do you think Odysseus has in mind by offering the Cyclops the wine?

Vocabulary Development

CCSS Language 6

Word Forms

Expand students' vocabulary by helping them learn related forms of the selection vocabulary words. Some selection vocabulary words for the *Odyssey*, Part 1, have related forms. Give students a blank **Word Form Chart** (*Professional Development Guidebook*, p. 42) with the original vocabulary words in the correct columns. Work with the class, or have students work with a partner, to determine the related forms. The final chart should look like the one shown.

Noun	Verb	Adjective	Adverb
plunder	**plundered**		
bereavement	bereave	**bereft**	
insidiousness		**insidious**	insidiously

under our planks. I meant it for an offering
if you would help us home. But you are mad,
unbearable, a bloody monster! After this,
will any other traveler come to see you?'

He seized and drained the bowl, and it went down
so fiery and smooth he called for more:

'Give me another, thank you kindly. Tell me,
how are you called? I'll make a gift will please you.
Even Cyclopes know the wine grapes grow
out of grassland and loam in heaven's rain,
22 but here's a bit of nectar and ambrosia!'[33]

Three bowls I brought him, and he poured them down.
I saw the fuddle and flush come over him,
then I sang out in cordial tones:

21 ▲ Critical Viewing
What traits does this image of the Cyclops illustrate? **[Interpret]**

33. **nectar** (nek´ tər) **and ambrosia** (am brō´ zhə) drink and food of the gods.

23 Reading Check
What does Odysseus plan to do with the stake that he and his men make?

21 Critical Viewing

Answer: The Cyclops is gigantic compared to the men. He is extremely muscular, and he has only one eye.

22 THE BIG ? Connecting to the Big Question

1. Remind students of the characteristics of a hero. Specifically discuss the heroic traits of bravery and wisdom.
2. Read the bracketed passage aloud. **Ask:** What do you think Odysseus' men think of him when they see how the Cyclops responds to the "gift" of wine?

   Possible response: The men are impressed with Odysseus' wise and crafty plan.
3. **Ask:** Do you think Odysseus has a responsibility to help his men even in the midst of grave danger? Explain.

   Possible response: Yes. He is their leader, and leaders have a responsibility to take care of their followers.
4. As students continue reading, have them look for examples of Odysseus' heroic actions and his men's responses to those actions.

23 Reading Check

Answer: Odysseus plans to blind the Cyclops by ramming the stake into the creature's eye.

Differentiated Instruction for Universal Access

EL Pronunciation for English Learners

Some students might have difficulty with the pronunciation of the short *i* in *gift, bit* and *him,* replacing it with a long "e" sound, as in *beat.* The following strategy will help students pronounce the short *i.*

- Write the following word pairs on the board: *bit/beat, pill/peel,* and *sin/seen.* Pronounce each word pair aloud, having students repeat each. Then, call out each word at random and have volunteers circle the correct word on the board. As a class, discuss results and what might have led to incorrect choices.

Enrichment for Advanced Readers

Advanced readers may be interested in finding more information about mythical monsters. Assign students to do research about the portrayal of monsters in different cultures. Ask them to do a multicultural literature search for examples of giants, one-eyed monsters, trolls, and other kinds of monsters. Discuss their findings and compare their examples with the Cyclops of Homer's *Odyssey.*

24 Reading Skill

Historical and Cultural Context

1. Have students review the text to find instances in which Odysseus evokes the gods. Remind them that Zeus was thought to "avenge" guests who were treated improperly.
2. **Ask** students the Reading Skill question: What cultural values are represented in Odysseus' reference to "the gods" in line 323?

   Possible response: Odysseus' response shows that he is a man who respects the authority of the gods. The reference to "the gods" shows that he asks for help from a greater power in his time of need.

'Cyclops,
you ask my honorable name? Remember
the gift you promised me, and I shall tell you.
My name is Nohbdy: mother, father, and friends,
everyone calls me Nohbdy.'
And he said:
'Nohbdy's my meat, then, after I eat his friends.
Others come first. There's a noble gift, now.'

Even as he spoke, he reeled and tumbled backward,
his great head lolling to one side; and sleep
took him like any creature. Drunk, hiccuping,
he dribbled streams of liquor and bits of men.

Reading Skill
Historical and Cultural Context What cultural values are represented in Odysseus' reference to "the gods" in line 323?

24 Now, by the gods, I drove my big hand spike
deep in the embers, charring it again,
and cheered my men along with battle talk
to keep their courage up: no quitting now.
The pike of olive, green though it had been,
reddened and glowed as if about to catch.
I drew it from the coals and my four fellows
gave me a hand, lugging it near the Cyclops
as more than natural force nerved them; straight
forward they sprinted, lifted it, and rammed it
deep in his crater eye, and leaned on it
turning it as a shipwright turns a drill
in planking, having men below to swing
the two-handled strap that spins it in the groove.
So with our brand we bored[34] that great eye socket
while blood ran out around the red-hot bar.
Eyelid and lash were seared; the pierced ball
hissed broiling, and the roots popped.

In a smithy
one sees a white-hot axehead or an adze
plunged and wrung in a cold tub, screeching steam—
the way they make soft iron hale and hard—:
just so that eyeball hissed around the spike.
The Cyclops bellowed and the rock roared round him,
and we fell back in fear. Clawing his face
he tugged the bloody spike out of his eye,
threw it away, and his wild hands went groping;

34. **bored** (bôrd) *v.* made a hole in.

Vocabulary Development — CCSS Language 6

Word Analysis

In line 353, Odysseus reveals that the Cyclops' name is Polyphemus. The name means "much or many" (*poly*) and "telling" (*phemus*). In other words, Polyphemus—"much telling"—is a braggart. Have students use the dictionary to find other words with the prefix *poly-* and use their knowledge of this Greek word part to help figure out the definition. Sample vocabulary words could include *polymath* (much learning), *polyglot* (many tongues), and *polychrome* (many colors).

then he set up a howl for Cyclopes
who lived in caves on windy peaks nearby.
Some heard him; and they came by divers[35] ways
to clump around outside and call:
'What ails you,
Polyphemus?[36] Why do you cry so sore
in the starry night? You will not let us sleep.
Sure no man's driving off your flock? No man
has tricked you, ruined you?'
Out of the cave
the mammoth Polyphemus roared in answer:

'Nohbdy, Nohbdy's tricked me, Nohbdy's ruined me!'

To this rough shout they made a sage[37] reply:

'Ah well, if nobody has played you foul
there in your lonely bed, we are no use in pain
given by great Zeus. Let it be your father,
Poseidon Lord, to whom you pray.'

So saying
(25) they trailed away. And I was filled with laughter
to see how like a charm the name deceived them.
Now Cyclops, wheezing as the pain came on him,
fumbled to wrench away the great doorstone
and squatted in the breach with arms thrown wide
for any silly beast or man who bolted—
hoping somehow I might be such a fool.
But I kept thinking how to win the game:
death sat there huge; how could we slip away?
I drew on all my wits, and ran through tactics,
reasoning as a man will for dear life,
until a trick came—and it pleased me well.
The Cyclops' rams were handsome, fat, with heavy
fleeces, a dark violet.
Three abreast
I tied them silently together, twining
cords of willow from the ogre's bed;
then slung a man under each middle one
to ride there safely, shielded left and right.

35. divers (dī′ vərz) *adj.* several; various.

36. Polyphemus (päl′ i fē′ məs)

37. sage (sāj) *adj.* wise.

Literary Analysis
Epic Hero What does Odysseus' gleeful response to his successful trick reveal about his character?

(26) 

What do the other Cyclopes think Polyphemus is saying when he says, "Nohbdy's tricked me"?

(25) Literary Analysis

Epic Hero

1. Remind students of the Greeks' dire circumstances. **Ask** students how many of Odysseus' men the Cyclops has eaten.

   Answer: The Cyclops has eaten six men.

2. Have students describe Odysseus' wordplay, in which he claims that his name is "Nohbdy," meaning "Nobody." **Ask** students why his game turns out to be important to his survival.

   Possible response: Odysseus' claim that he is "Nohbdy" is important because it keeps the other Cyclopes from coming to Polyphemus' rescue.

3. **Ask** students the Literary Analysis question: What does Odysseus' gleeful response to his successful trick reveal about his character?

   Possible response: Odysseus' laughter shows his great love of life. He takes enormous pleasure in his trick and is able to set aside the suffering he has endured to appreciate how thoroughly his wordplay fooled the Cyclopes.

4. Have students discuss Odysseus' laughter and compare it with other heroes they have encountered in their reading. **Ask** them whether a hero with a sense of humor is ordinary or unusual.

   Possible response: Students may say that most heroes are more serious than Odysseus.

(26) Reading Check

Answer: The other Cyclopes think that Polyphemus is saying, "I am in pain, but no one has tricked me." They believe that there is nothing they can do to help Polyphemus.

Differentiated Instruction for Universal Access

Strategy for Special-Needs Students

The Greeks' encounter with the Cyclops involves many plot turns and setbacks. Have students mark pages with different colored self-stick adhesive notes, using one color for instances in which the Cyclops overpowers the Greeks and another color for instances in which Odysseus outwits the Cyclops. Once students have found the instances and marked them, have them jot down the most important details of the encounter on the note.

EL Support for English Learners

Provide English learners with an oral synopsis of key content areas before reading the Cyclops section of the *Odyssey.* A synopsis could include: the Greeks' landing on the Cyclops' island; the Greeks' discovery of the Cyclops' cave; their entrapment in the cave; Odysseus' daring plot to blind the Cyclops; and the Greeks' escape using the Cyclops' sheep. Also, discuss how Odysseus' curiosity, cunning, and trickery play a role in the Greeks' capture and escape.

 Humanities

"Cyclops and Ram," by C. E. Brock

Born in Holloway, England, artist and illustrator Charles Edmund Brock (1870–1938) is known for his vivid illustrations of books by famous authors such as Jane Austen and Jonathan Swift. In this picture, the blinded Polyphemus struggles to find Odysseus. Use the following questions for discussion:

1. How do Odysseus' actions in the illustration reflect what happens in the text?

   Answer: Odysseus is escaping from Polyphemus' cave by clinging to the belly of a ram.

2. Based on the appearance of the ram, how can you tell who its owner is?

   Answer: The ram must belong to the Cyclops because it is several times larger than a ram that a human would own. The ram dwarfs Odysseus.

27

Vocabulary Development © CCSS Language 6

Animal Terms

The description of the Greeks' escape includes a number of words relating to animals, especially sheep: *rams, dams, udders, pasture, milking, fleece, wool, graze, fold,* and *herd.* Ask students to indicate which words they can figure out by the context of the passage. Students may need to look up some multiple-meaning words in the dictionary, such as *fold* and *dams,* to learn the definition used in the selection. Ask students to show their understanding of the animal words by using them in sentences.

So three sheep could convey each man. I took
the woolliest ram, the choicest of the flock,
and hung myself under his kinky belly,
pulled up tight, with fingers twisted deep
in sheepskin ringlets for an iron grip.
So, breathing hard, we waited until morning.

When Dawn spread out her fingertips of rose
the rams began to stir, moving for pasture,
and peals of bleating echoed round the pens
where dams with udders full called for a milking.
Blinded, and sick with pain from his head wound,
the master stroked each ram, then let it pass,
but my men riding on the pectoral[38] fleece
the giant's blind hands blundering never found.
Last of them all my ram, the leader, came,
weighted by wool and me with my meditations.
The Cyclops patted him, and then he said:

'Sweet cousin ram, why lag behind the rest
in the night cave? You never linger so,
but graze before them all, and go afar
to crop sweet grass, and take your stately way
leading along the streams, until at evening
you run to be the first one in the fold.
Why, now, so far behind? Can you be grieving
over your Master's eye? That carrion rogue[39]
(28) and his accurst companions burnt it out
when he had conquered all my wits with wine.
Nohbdy will not get out alive, I swear.
Oh, had you brain and voice to tell
where he may be now, dodging all my fury!
Bashed by this hand and bashed on this rock wall
his brains would strew the floor, and I should have
rest from the outrage Nohbdy worked upon me.'

He sent us into the open, then. Close by,
I dropped and rolled clear of the ram's belly,
going this way and that to untie the men.
With many glances back, we rounded up
his fat, stiff-legged sheep to take aboard,
and drove them down to where the good ship lay.

38. **pectoral** (pek´ tə rəl) *adj.* located in or on the chest.

39. **carrion** (kar´ ē ən) **rogue** (rōg) repulsive scoundrel.

Literary Analysis
Epic Hero What details of this speech show that Polyphemus is far less clever than Odysseus?

(29) ◄ **Critical Viewing**
How does this image compare with your mental picture of the Cyclops? **[Analyze]**

(30)

How do the men escape from the Cyclops' cave?

(28) Literary Analysis

Epic Hero

1. Have students describe the Cyclops and the type of life he leads. **Ask** them what the Cyclops' greatest assets or weapons are.

   Possible response: The Cyclops is a herder, but he lives in solitude. His greatest assets are his size and strength.

2. Review with students the Cyclops' conversations with Odysseus. **Ask** what the conversations reveal about the Cyclops' personality.

   Possible response: The Cyclops is a creature of action and can be tricked, such as the time when Odysseus claims that his name is "Nohbdy."

3. Remind students that the Cyclops must know that the Greeks are still in his cave, because the stone has blocked its entrance. **Ask** students the Literary Analysis question: What details of this speech show that Polyphemus is far less clever than Odysseus?

   Possible response: Polyphemus knows the ram is acting in an unusual manner. The change in the ram's behavior, however, does not make the Cyclops suspicious. He does not seem to expect that the Greeks might try to escape.

(29) Critical Viewing

Possible response: The Cyclops looks angry and fierce, just as I picture him. However, I pictured the Cyclops as more of a monster. Here, he looks like a gigantic man.

(30) Reading Check

Answer: Odysseus smuggles his men out by tying the Cyclops' sheep together in sets of three and binding one man under the middle sheep of each set. The men escape when the Cyclops releases his sheep to graze.

Differentiated Instruction for Universal Access

Strategy for Less Proficient Readers

As students read the Cyclops section of the *Odyssey,* have them note each time the Greeks find themselves in a different location. Their note paper should have different headings, such as "Arrive on the Beach," "Trapped in the Cyclops' Cave," and "Escaping in Their Ships." Ask students to write two sentences for each location: one that explains how the Greeks get there, and one that explains how they leave.

Strategy for Gifted/Talented Students

Odysseus' escape from the Cyclops shows the hero's flair for drama. Have students perform a dramatic interpretation of Odysseus' taunts to the Cyclops, his men's pleas for him to stop, and Polyphemus' sobbing prayer for revenge. Ask students to provide different interpretations: Can Polyphemus be portrayed as a sympathetic victim in this scene? Or can Odysseus, an epic hero, be interpreted as a bully? Ask students to explain the different readings that they provide.

31 Critical Viewing

Possible response: The illustration depicts the moment after Odysseus taunts the Cyclops while his men sail furiously away from the island. In the image, the giant has broken off the top of a hill and is preparing to hurl it at Odysseus' ship. The artist has added some details not evident in the poem, including the swirling steam around the giant. Also, for emphasis, he adds a glow around the ship.

Spiral Review

Universal Theme

1. Remind students that they studied the concept of universal theme in the Unit 6 Literary Analysis workshop (pp. 1030–1039).
2. Then, **ask** students the Spiral Review question.

   Possible response: The conflict reflects a universal theme of clever resourcefulness being more useful than brute strength. Some students may point out the story of David and Goliath as an example of this universal "underdog" theme.

32 Literary Analysis

Epic Hero

1. Recall with students Odysseus' earlier behavior, in which he exalts in tricking the Cyclops. **Ask** students how this example is similar to or different from the earlier one.

   Possible response: Earlier, Odysseus gloats silently over his victory. Here, he shouts his victory to the Cyclops.
2. Point out to students the prudence of leaving the island silently. **Ask** them what the Greeks have to gain by taunting the Cyclops.

   Possible response: The Greeks have nothing to gain. They can only enrage their enemy.
3. **Ask** the Literary Analysis question: Despite his heroism, what human weaknesses does Odysseus reveal as he sails away?

   Possible response: Odysseus allows his anger and arrogance to get the best of him. It would have been much wiser to be quiet. He is acting in a boastful and vindictive manner.

31

▶ Critical Viewing Odysseus and his surviving men escape in their ship as the blinded Cyclops hurls boulders and curses. How does this illustration compare to your mental image of the scene? **[Analyze]**

Spiral Review

Universal Theme What universal theme does the fight between Odysseus and the Cyclops suggest?

Literary Analysis

Epic Hero Despite his heroism, what human weaknesses does Odysseus reveal as he sails away?

We saw, as we came near, our fellows' faces
shining; then we saw them turn to grief
tallying those who had not fled from death.
I hushed them, jerking head and eyebrows up,
and in a low voice told them: 'Load this herd;
move fast, and put the ship's head toward the breakers.'
They all pitched in at loading, then embarked
and struck their oars into the sea. Far out,
as far off shore as shouted words would carry,
I sent a few back to the adversary:
'O Cyclops! Would you feast on my companions?
Puny, am I, in a cave man's hands?
How do you like the beating that we gave you,
you damned cannibal? Eater of guests
under your roof! Zeus and the gods have paid you!'

The blind thing in his doubled fury broke
a hilltop in his hands and heaved it after us.
Ahead of our black prow it struck and sank
whelmed in a spuming geyser, a giant wave
that washed the ship stern foremost back to shore.
I got the longest boathook out and stood
32 fending us off, with furious nods to all
to put their backs into a racing stroke—
row, row, or perish. So the long oars bent
kicking the foam sternward, making head
until we drew away, and twice as far.
Now when I cupped my hands I heard the crew
in low voices protesting:

'Godsake, Captain!
Why bait the beast again? Let him alone!'

'That tidal wave he made on the first throw
all but beached us.'

'All but stove us in!'
'Give him our bearing with your trumpeting,
he'll get the range and lob a boulder.'

'Aye
He'll smash our timbers and our heads together!'
I would not heed them in my glorying spirit,

Vocabulary Development

CCSS Language 6

Expressive Vocabulary

To help students broaden their expressive vocabulary, encourage them to use the following words as they discuss Odysseus' escape from the Cyclops: *coincides, encounter, highlights,* and *eliminate*. Have them complete these sentence starters:

1. The Greeks' escape from the Cyclops *coincides* with . . .
2. Odysseus could have avoided another *encounter* with the Cyclops if . . .
3. The Cyclops' prayer to his father *highlights* . . .
4. The Cyclops wanted to *eliminate* Odysseus' hope of . . .

Polyphemus, The Cyclops N. C. Wyeth, Brandywine River Museum

33 Humanities

Polyphemus, The Cyclops,
by N. C. Wyeth

N. C. Wyeth (1882–1945) was an American artist whose enchanting illustrations of children's classics made him popular and successful. He illustrated several novels by Robert Louis Stevenson and James Fenimore Cooper.

Polyphemus was commissioned for a luxury edition of the *Odyssey* published in 1929. The illustration demonstrates the skill with which Wyeth was able to depict fantastic creatures. Use the following questions for discussion.

1. Which lines in the *Odyssey* match the moment portrayed by Wyeth in this painting?

   Answer: The picture illustrates the lines "The blind thing in his doubled fury broke/a hilltop in his hands and heaved it after us," lines 436–437.

2. How does the mood of the illustration reflect that of the story?

   Possible response: The gloomy, stormy skies and seas suggest the danger and tension surrounding the event.

Differentiated Instruction for Universal Access

Enrichment for Advanced Readers
Have students do research to find out the Cyclops' family tree. Have them learn more about Poseidon, his relationships to other Greek gods, and his other children, both mortal and immortal. Ask students to speculate about the positive and negative aspects of being so closely related to a deity.

Enrichment for Gifted/Talented Students
Have students draw a "before" and "after" portrait of the Cyclops and his island. Suggest that the portraits illustrate the Cyclops' animals, his daily labor, and his relationship with the other Cyclopes on his island. Challenge students to try to illustrate many of the changes brought by the Greeks, including the Cyclops' blindness and the binding together of the sheep.

34 Reading Skill

Historical and Cultural Context

1. Refer students to their copies of **Reading Skill Graphic Organizer B** (p. 184 in ***Graphic Organizer Transparencies***). Have students put relevant quotations in the Historical/Cultural Detail box. Quotations might include "I'll treat you well, praying the god of earthquake to befriend you" or "The god of earthquake could not heal you there!"
2. Have students review the bracketed passage to see what they can learn about the god Poseidon from the text. **Ask** what the passage reveals about the Cyclops' father.

   Possible response: Poseidon must be a god of the ocean, because he is "girdler of the islands." He also can cause earthquakes.
3. **Ask** students the Reading Skill question: What do lines 472–493 suggest about ancient Greek beliefs about the gods' involvement in the mortal world?

   Possible responses: The Greeks believed that the gods had control over specific elements of human life and could be asked to intervene in human affairs.

▶**Monitor Progress:** Review students' graphic organizers to ensure that they are making reasonable inferences.

▶**Reteach:** Work with students to make a chart showing the Greek gods and goddesses who have been mentioned to this point: Zeus, Athena, Apollo, and Poseidon. Discuss with students the qualities of these deities and their connections with human beings and other creatures on Earth.

but let my anger flare and yelled:
'Cyclops,
32 if ever mortal man inquire
how you were put to shame and blinded, tell him
Odysseus, raider of cities, took your eye:
Laertes' son, whose home's on Ithaca!'

At this he gave a mighty sob and rumbled:
'Now comes the weird[40] upon me, spoken of old.
A wizard, grand and wondrous, lived here—Telemus,[41]
a son of Eurymus;[42] great length of days
he had in wizardry among the Cyclopes,
and these things he foretold for time to come:
my great eye lost, and at Odysseus' hands.
Always I had in mind some giant, armed
in giant force, would come against me here.
But this, but you—small, pitiful and twiggy—
you put me down with wine, you blinded me.
Come back, Odysseus, and I'll treat you well,
praying the god of earthquake[43] to befriend you—
his son I am, for he by his avowal
fathered me, and, if he will, he may
heal me of this black wound—he and no other
34 of all the happy gods or mortal men.'

Few words I shouted in reply to him:

'If I could take your life I would and take
your time away, and hurl you down to hell!
The god of earthquake could not heal you there!'

At this he stretched his hands out in his darkness
toward the sky of stars, and prayed Poseidon:

'O hear me, lord, blue girdler of the islands,
if I am thine indeed, and thou art father:
grant that Odysseus, raider of cities, never
see his home: Laertes' son, I mean,
who kept his hall on Ithaca. Should destiny
intend that he shall see his roof again
among his family in his father land,
far be that day, and dark the years between.

40. **weird** (wird) *n.* fate or destiny.
41. **Telemus** (tel e′ məs)
42. **Eurymus** (yo͞o rim′ əs)
43. **god of earthquake** Poseidon.

Reading Skill Historical and Cultural Context What do lines 472–493 suggest about ancient Greek beliefs about the gods' involvement in the mortal world?

Think Aloud

Vocabulary: Using Context
Direct students' attention to the word *disdained* in line 512. Using a think-aloud process, model how to use context to infer the meaning of an unknown word. Say to students:

> I'm going to think aloud to show you how I would figure out the meaning of *disdained* from its context.
>
> In this sentence, *disdained* describes Zeus' reaction to Odysseus' offering. Odysseus says that he burned the ram's thighbones as an offering to the god. Zeus' response, though, is "destruction for my ships" and "death for those who sailed them." The words *destruction* and *death* indicate Zeus' displeasure. I think *disdained* must mean that Zeus disliked the gift or rejected it.

Let him lose all companions, and return
under strange sail to bitter days at home.'
In these words he prayed, and the god heard him.
Now he laid hands upon a bigger stone
and wheeled around, titanic for the cast,
to let it fly in the black-prowed vessel's track.
But it fell short, just aft the steering oar,
and whelming seas rose giant above the stone
to bear us onward toward the island.
There
as we ran in we saw the squadron waiting,
the trim ships drawn up side by side, and all
our troubled friends who waited, looking seaward.
We beached her, grinding keel in the soft sand,
and waded in, ourselves, on the sandy beach.
Then we unloaded all the Cyclops' flock
to make division, share and share alike,
only my fighters voted that my ram,
the prize of all, should go to me. I slew him
by the seaside and burnt his long thighbones
to Zeus beyond the stormcloud, Cronus'[44] son,
who rules the world. But Zeus disdained my offering:
destruction for my ships he had in store
and death for those who sailed them, my companions.
Now all day long until the sun went down
we made our feast on mutton and sweet wine,
till after sunset in the gathering dark
we went to sleep above the wash of ripples.

When the young Dawn with fingertips of rose
touched the world, I roused the men, gave orders
to man the ships, cast off the mooring lines;
and filing in to sit beside the rowlocks
oarsmen in line dipped oars in the gray sea.
So we moved out, sad in the vast offing,[45]
having our precious lives, but not our friends.

Literary Analysis
Epic Hero What admirable quality does Odysseus show by dividing the sheep among his men?

44. **Cronus** (krō′ nəs) Titan who was ruler of the universe until he was overthrown by his son Zeus.

45. **offing** (ôf′ iŋ) *n.* distant part of the sea visible from the shore.

What does the Cyclops ask for in his prayer to Poseidon?

35 Literary Analysis

Epic Hero

1. Remind students that spoils, such as the sheep, often were divided among soldiers by rank in ancient Greece. Odysseus could have taken the larger part for himself.
2. **Ask** students why Odysseus might want to be generous with his men. **Possible responses:** He might want to keep their loyalty. He might want to thank them for their good work in escaping from the Cyclops.
3. Then, **ask** the Literary Analysis question: What admirable quality does Odysseus show by dividing the sheep among his men?
   Possible response: Odysseus shows a sense of fairness by dividing the sheep equally among his men—"share and share alike."

36 Reading Check

Answer: The Cyclops prays that Odysseus will lose all his men and, if he returns at all, that he may arrive home only after many "dark" years of hardship. The Cyclops' prayer amounts to a precise prophecy.

Differentiated Instruction for Universal Access

EL Pronunciation for English Learners

Students may have difficulty pronouncing the final *k* in words such as *track, flock,* and *alike,* replacing it with a "d" sound. The following strategies will help students pronounce the final "k" sound.

- Write these word pairs on the board: *sock/sod, rock/rod, deck/dead,* and *tack/tad.* Read each pair aloud, emphasizing the "k" and "d" sounds at the end of each word. Have students pronounce each word pair. Then, call out a word aloud at random and have a volunteer come to the board and circle the word.
- Pair English learners with fluent speakers and have students pronounce the word pairs together. Fluent speakers should assist English learners in successfully discriminating and pronouncing the words given. If the English learner errs, encourage "peer tutors" to pronounce each word carefully and guide the English learner to the correct answer.

37 Reading Skill

Historical and Cultural Context

1. Remind students of the number of gods and goddesses in Odysseus' tale and their powers. For example, Poseidon can cause earthquakes. Zeus can send storms that can harm Odysseus' men.
2. Have students **describe** the wind that controls the Greeks' ships.

   Possible response: It is a strong wind that comes from the land and fills their sails. The wind originates from a nymph.
3. **Ask** the Reading Skill question: What details here suggest that the source of wind was mysterious to ancient Greeks?

   Answer: Odysseus claims that Circe, a nymph, creates the wind.

The Land of the Dead

Odysseus and his men sail to Aeolia, where Aeolus,[46] king of the winds, sends Odysseus on his way with a gift: a sack containing all the winds except the favorable west wind. When they are near home, Odysseus' men open the sack, letting loose a storm that drives them back to Aeolia. Aeolus casts them out, having decided that they are detested by the gods. They sail for seven days and arrive in the land of the Laestrygonians,[47] a race of cannibals. These creatures destroy all of Odysseus' ships except the one he is sailing in. Odysseus and his reduced crew escape and reach Aeaea, the island ruled by the sorceress-goddess Circe. She transforms half of the men into swine. Protected by a magic herb, Odysseus demands that Circe change his men back into human form. Before Odysseus departs from the island a year later, Circe informs him that in order to reach home he must journey to the land of the dead, Hades, and consult the blind prophet Tiresias.

We bore down on the ship at the sea's edge
and launched her on the salt immortal sea,
stepping our mast and spar in the black ship;
embarked the ram and ewe and went aboard
in tears, with bitter and sore dread upon us.
But now a breeze came up for us astern—
a canvas-bellying landbreeze, hale shipmate
sent by the singing nymph with sunbright hair;[48]
so we made fast the braces, took our thwarts,
and let the wind and steersman work the ship
with full sail spread all day above our coursing,
till the sun dipped, and all the ways grew dark
upon the fathomless unresting sea.

By night
our ship ran onward toward the Ocean's bourne,
the realm and region of the Men of Winter,
hidden in mist and cloud. Never the flaming
eye of Helios lights on those men
at morning, when he climbs the sky of stars,
nor in descending earthward out of heaven;
ruinous night being rove over those wretches.
We made the land, put ram and ewe ashore,

46. Aeolia (ē ō′ lē ə) . . . **Aeolus** (ē′ ə ləs)

47. Laestrygonians (les tri gō′ nē ənz)

48. singing nymph . . . hair Circe.

Reading Skill Historical and Cultural Context What details here suggest that the source of wind was mysterious to ancient Greeks?

and took our way along the Ocean stream
to find the place foretold for us by Circe.
There Perimedes and Eulylochus[49]
pinioned[50] the sacred beasts. With my drawn blade
I spaded up the votive[51] pit, and poured
libations[52] round it to the unnumbered dead:
sweet milk and honey, then sweet wine, and last
clear water; and I scattered barley down.
Then I addressed the blurred and breathless dead,
vowing to slaughter my best heifer for them
before she calved, at home in Ithaca,
and burn the choice bits on the altar fire;
as for Tiresias, I swore to sacrifice
a black lamb, handsomest of all our flock.
Thus to **assuage** the nations of the dead
I pledged these rites, then slashed the lamb and ewe,
letting their black blood stream into the wellpit.
Now the souls gathered, stirring out of Erebus,[53]
brides and young men, and men grown old in pain,
and tender girls whose hearts were new to grief;
many were there, too, torn by brazen lanceheads,
battle-slain, bearing still their bloody gear.
From every side they came and sought the pit
with rustling cries; and I grew sick with fear.
But presently I gave command to my officers
to flay those sheep the bronze cut down, and make
burnt offerings of flesh to the gods below—
to sovereign Death, to pale Persephone.[54]
Meanwhile I crouched with my drawn sword to keep
the surging phantoms from the bloody pit
till I should know the presence of Tiresias.[55]

One shade came first—Elpenor, of our company,
who lay unburied still on the wide earth
as we had left him—dead in Circe's hall,
untouched, unmourned, when other cares compelled us.
Now when I saw him there I wept for pity
and called out to him:
'How is this, Elpenor,
how could you journey to the western gloom
swifter afoot than I in the black lugger?'
He sighed, and answered:

49. Perimedes (per′ ə mē′ dēz) and Eurylochus (yo͞o ril′ ə kəs)

50. pinioned (pin′ yənd) *v.* confined or shackled.

51. votive (vōt′ iv) *adj.* done to fulfill a vow or express thanks.

52. libations (lī bā′ shənz) *n.* wine or other liquids poured upon the ground as a sacrifice or offering.

Vocabulary
assuage (ə swāj′)
v. calm; pacify

53. Erebus (er′ ə bəs) dark region under the earth through which the dead pass before entering the realm of Hades.

54. Persephone (pər sef′ ə nē) wife of Hades.

55. Tiresias (tī rē′ sē əs)

What does Circe say that Odysseus must do in order to reach home?

38 Reading Check

Answer: Circe says that Odysseus must go to Hades, the land of the dead, in order to reach home. In Hades, Odysseus must consult the blind prophet Tiresias.

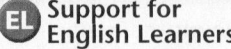

Differentiated Instruction for Universal Access

Strategy for Special-Needs Students
To help students begin the new section, direct them to the italicized summary and review with them the parts of the story that have been omitted. Help students make the transition to the new section and answer any questions they may have about Circe's role in Odysseus' next adventure.

EL Support for English Learners
Some of the vocabulary that relates to sailing and oceans may prove unfamiliar to students. Preview and teach the sea-faring jargon before students read the story: *mast* (a tall pole that holds a sail), *spar* (another pole that holds a sail), *canvas-bellying landbreeze* (a wind that fills a sail), and *Ocean's bourne* (the boundary of the ocean).

 Humanities

Odysseus in the Land of the Dead, by N. C. Wyeth

This painting was commissioned for a 1929 limited edition of the *Odyssey.* The 500 copies of this edition included sixteen full-color illustrations signed by N. C. Wyeth. Use these questions for discussion:

1. Which lines in Homer's *Odyssey* are illustrated by this picture?

   Answer: The painting illustrates lines 564–578.

2. Do you think the artist portrayed Odysseus as Homer pictured him at this moment?

   Possible response: The artist has captured Homer's image of Odysseus crouching by the "bloody pit" with his drawn sword. He is sick with fear but determined to achieve his goal of consulting Tiresias.

3. Do you think that Wyeth has portrayed the dead accurately?

   Possible responses: Yes, because Homer says that the dead appear in "their bloody gear," or as they were when they died. No, because the dead look skeletal and long dead, rather than recently deceased.

Odysseus in the Land of the Dead* from Homer's *The Odyssey, N.C. Wyeth, Brandywine River Museum

Vocabulary Development

CCSS Language 6

Selection Vocabulary Reinforcement

To reinforce and assess students' comprehension of selection vocabulary words, give them sentences using the words in which the word may or may not be used correctly. Students must tell whether the use is correct.

1. The furious customers were *assuaged* by the store's refusal to take back the shoddy merchandise.

   Answer: No, *assuaged* is not used correctly. It means "to calm or pacify," and the customers are not calmed by the store's policy.

2. After the waiter apologized for his error and brought the correct dessert, the diners were *assuaged* and promised to return to the restaurant soon.

   Answer: Yes, *assuaged* is used correctly here. The diners are pleased and calmed after the waiter's apology.

'Son of great Laertes,
Odysseus, master mariner and soldier,
bad luck shadowed me, and no kindly power;
ignoble death I drank with so much wine.
I slept on Circe's roof, then could not see
the long steep backward ladder, coming down,
and fell that height. My neckbone, buckled under,
snapped, and my spirit found this well of dark.
Now hear the grace I pray for, in the name
of those back in the world, not here—your wife
and father, he who gave you bread in childhood,
and your own child, your only son, Telemachus,[56]
long ago left at home.

When you make sail
and put these lodgings of dim Death behind,
you will moor ship, I know, upon Aeaea Island;
there, O my lord, remember me, I pray,
do not abandon me unwept, unburied,
(41) to tempt the gods' wrath, while you sail for home;
but fire my corpse, and all the gear I had,
and build a cairn[57] for me above the breakers—
an unknown sailor's mark for men to come.
Heap up the mound there, and implant upon it
the oar I pulled in life with my companions.'

He ceased, and I replied:

'Unhappy spirit,
I promise you the barrow and the burial.'

So we conversed, and grimly, at a distance,
with my long sword between, guarding the blood,
while the faint image of the lad spoke on.
Now came the soul of Anticlea, dead,
my mother, daughter of Autolycus,[58]
dead now, though living still when I took ship
for holy Troy. Seeing this ghost I grieved,
but held her off, through pang on pang of tears,
till I should know the presence of Tiresias.
Soon from the dark that prince of Thebes[59] came forward
bearing a golden staff; and he addressed me:

(40) ◀ **Critical Viewing** What can you infer about ancient Greek beliefs concerning death and the afterlife from lines 555–577 on page 1065 and from this illustration? **[Infer]**

56. Telemachus (tə lem′ ə kəs)

57. cairn (kern) *n.* conical heap of stones built as a monument.

58. Autolycus (ô täl′ i kəs)

59. Thebes (thēbz)

Reading Skill Historical and Cultural Context What ancient Greek values and beliefs are suggested by Elpenor's requests?

(42) 

Reading Check

What does Elpenor's spirit ask of Odysseus?

(40) Critical Viewing

Answer: From the illustration, we can infer that the Greeks believed that a person's spirit continued to exist after death. The spirit had to make a long journey to the underworld and could not complete its journey unless the proper rites were observed. The spirits that had not yet reached the underworld were frightening, restless, and hungry.

(41) Reading Skill

Historical and Cultural Context

1. Discuss with students the kinds of requests people might make in their wills to be carried out after they die. Discuss how people use wills to dispose of their property and personal effects.
2. **Ask** students the Reading Skill question: What ancient Greek values and beliefs are suggested by Elpenor's requests?

   Possible responses: He describes a burial that involves heaping stones over his corpse and putting a personal artifact—his oar—among the stones. Elpenor's request suggests that his spirit will be able to find peace after his corpse is treated according to ancient Greek ritual.

(42) Reading Check

Answer: Elpenor's spirit asks Odysseus to burn Elpenor's body and to build a memorial for him on the shore of Aeaea Island.

Differentiated Instruction for Universal Access

Culturally Responsive Instruction

Culture Focus After students have read the description of the Greeks' offerings to the dead, ask them to research the customs surrounding death in a culture other than their own. Cite, for example, the funeral pyre of the Hindus, the Jewish custom of sitting shiva, and the Mandan Indian tradition of leaving the dead body on an elevated platform to decay naturally. Have students share their findings with the class. Then, discuss death and burial customs in students' own cultures.

⓸③ Reading Skill

Historical and Cultural Context

1. Have students recall some of the incidents that led to trouble in Odysseus' voyage, such as his men's mutiny, or his refusal to leave the Cyclops' cave when he could have escaped easily.
2. **Ask** students if they see any patterns in the events that have caused Odysseus trouble.

   Possible response: Odysseus' men have not obeyed him, and Odysseus himself has not shown self-discipline.
3. **Ask** the Reading Skill question: What ancient Greek value is reflected in the "narrow strait" that Tiresias describes (lines 637–638)?

   Possible responses: Tiresias indicates that Odysseus can overcome Poseidon's wrath if Odysseus focuses on his task and disciplines both himself and his crew. Odysseus will be able to return home only if he can practice self-restraint.
4. Point out that the "narrow strait" also refers to a real place—the Straits of Gibraltar.

'Son of Laertes and the gods of old,
Odysseus, master of landways and seaways,
why leave the blazing sun, O man of woe,
to see the cold dead and the joyless region?
Stand clear, put up your sword;
let me but taste of blood, I shall speak true.'

At this I stepped aside, and in the scabbard
let my long sword ring home to the pommel silver,
as he bent down to the somber blood. Then spoke
the prince of those with gift of speech:

'Great captain,
a fair wind and the honey lights of home
are all you seek. But anguish lies ahead;
the god who thunders on the land prepares it,
not to be shaken from your track, implacable,
in rancor for the son whose eye you blinded.
One narrow strait may take you through his blows:
denial of yourself, restraint of shipmates.
When you make landfall on Thrinacia first
and quit the violet sea, dark on the land
you'll find the grazing herds of Helios
by whom all things are seen, all speech is known.
Avoid those kine,[60] hold fast to your intent,
and hard seafaring brings you all to Ithaca.
But if you raid the beeves, I see destruction
for ship and crew. Though you survive alone,
bereft of all companions, lost for years,
under strange sail shall you come home, to find
your own house filled with trouble: insolent men
eating your livestock as they court your lady.
Aye, you shall make those men atone in blood!
But after you have dealt out death—in open
combat or by stealth—to all the suitors,
go overland on foot, and take an oar,
until one day you come where men have lived
with meat unsalted, never known the sea,
nor seen seagoing ships, with crimson bows
and oars that fledge light hulls for dipping flight.
The spot will soon be plain to you, and I
can tell you how: some passerby will say,
"What winnowing fan is that upon your shoulder?"

Reading Skill
Historical and Cultural Context What ancient Greek value is reflected in the "narrow strait" that Tiresias describes (lines 637–638)?

60. **kine** (kīn) *n.* cattle.

Vocabulary
bereft (bē reft′) *adj.* deprived

Vocabulary Development

© CCSS Language 6

Vocabulary Reinforcement

Students will benefit from additional examples and practice with the Vocabulary words. Reinforce their comprehension with "show-you-know" sentences. The first part of the sentence uses the vocabulary word in an appropriate context. The second part of the sentence—the "show-you-know" part—clarifies the first. Model the strategy with this example for *bereft*:

The sailors' deaths left Odysseus lonely and *bereft* of his friends.

Then give students these sentence prompts and coach them in creating the clarification part:

1. The toddler was *bereft* when her sister went to school; ____________

   Sample answer: her constant companion was gone until 3 P.M.
2. The business's bankruptcy left many small investors *bereft;* ____________

   Sample answer: many of them lost their life savings.

Halt, and implant your smooth oar in the turf
and make fair sacrifice to Lord Poseidon:
a ram, a bull, a great buck boar; turn back,
and carry out pure hecatombs[61] at home
to all wide heaven's lords, the undying gods,
to each in order. Then a seaborne death
soft as this hand of mist will come upon you
when you are wearied out with rich old age,
your country folk in blessed peace around you.
And all this shall be just as I foretell.'

61. **hecatombs** (hek′ ə tōmz′) *n.* large-scale sacrifices to the gods in ancient Greece; often, the slaughter of 100 cattle at one time.

Critical Thinking

Cite textual evidence to support your responses.

1. **Key Ideas and Details** **(a)** Before the meeting with the Cyclops, what had Odysseus received from Maron at Ismarus? **(b) Generalize:** What does the encounter with Maron reveal about ancient Greek attitudes regarding hospitality?
2. **Key Ideas and Details** **(a)** How do Odysseus and his companions expect to be treated by the Cyclops? **(b) Infer:** What "laws" of behavior and attitude does Polyphemus violate?
3. **Key Ideas and Details** **(a) Summarize:** How do Odysseus and his crew escape from the Cyclops? **(b) Evaluate:** What positive and negative character traits does Odysseus demonstrate in his adventure with the Cyclops?
4. **Integration of Knowledge and Ideas** **(a) Compare and Contrast:** Compare and contrast Odysseus' reactions to the three ghosts he meets in the Land of the Dead—Elpenor, Anticlea, and Tiresias. **(b) Analyze:** What character trait does Odysseus display in the Land of the Dead that he did not reveal earlier?
5. **Key Ideas and Details** **(a) Summarize:** What difficulty does Tiresias predict for the journey to come? **(b) Speculate:** Why would Odysseus continue, despite the grim prophecies?
6. **Integration of Knowledge and Ideas** **Assess:** Judging from Tiresias' prediction, which heroic qualities will Odysseus need to rely upon as he continues his journey? Explain.
7. **Integration of Knowledge and Ideas** **(a)** What are Odysseus' responsibilities as he reaches the land of the Cyclopes? **(b)** How well does he fulfill these responsibilities? *[Connect to the Big Question: Do heroes have responsibilities?]*

ASSESS

Answers

Critical Thinking

Remind students to support their answers with evidence from the text.

1. (a) Gold, a silver winebowl, and twelve jars of brandy. (b) Hospitality is highly valued; hosts are judged by their courteousness and the richness of their gifts.
2. (a) They expect to be honored. (b) He violates the laws of hospitality, of honoring the gods, and the taboo against cannibalism.
3. (a) They attach themselves to the underside of the Cyclops' sheep and escape when Polyphemus lets his flocks out to graze. (b) Odysseus displays curiosity, boastfulness, cleverness, leadership, and bravery.
4. (a) He weeps when he encounters Elpenor and Anticlea, but does not let Anticlea approach. He allows Tiresias to approach and listens to his prophecy. (b) Odysseus shows compassion and determination.
5. (a) He predicts Odysseus will lose his ship and crew, struggle alone, and arrive home to trouble. (b) **Possible response:** He may think he can avoid the cattle of Helias.
6. Odysseus will need courage, resourcefulness, and leadership.
7. (a) **Possible response:** He must keep his crew safe and solve problems. (b) **Possible response:** He fails because the Cyclops ends up eating several of the men.

Differentiated Instruction for Universal Access

Strategy for Less Proficient Readers
Have students prepare a two-column chart. In one column, they should write the events Tiresias foretells. As they read on, have them fill in the adventures to which the prophecies refer. Students will discover that line 637 refers to Scylla and Charybdis; line 638 refers to the Sirens; lines 639–646 refer to " . . . Twenty years gone, and I am home again" [Part 2]; and line 651 refers to Odysseus' Revenge [Part 2].

Strategy for Gifted/Talented Students
Suggest that students draw or paint a scene from the *Odyssey.* Encourage students to research examples of Greek art to gather specific details they might include, such as the patterns and borders used to frame the images.

44 Humanities

***Circe Meanwhile Had Gone Her Ways . . .*, (1924) by William Russell Flint**

The Scottish painter and illustrator William Russell Flint (1880–1969) became interested in watercolor at a young age. For many years, this was his favorite medium, and his works were exhibited in Europe to much acclaim. He added another dimension to his work when he began to create illustrations for various literary works. Flint was elected a full member of the Royal Academy in 1933 and was knighted in 1947. Use these questions for discussion.

1. What special abilities does Circe seem to have?

   Answer: She seems to command the attention and obedience of animals, such as the sheep.

2. What elements in the painting give a sense of the setting of the *Odyssey?*

   Possible response: The time and place are suggested in Circe's clothes and pose, the carved marble pedestal, the stylized spirals of the rams' horns and wool and of the blue-and-purple decorations on the ship, and the form of the ship in the background.

44

Circe Meanwhile Had Gone Her Ways . . ., 1924, William Russell Flint Collection of the New York Public Library, Special Collections/ Art Resources

The Sirens

Odysseus returns to Circe's island. The goddess reveals his course to him and gives advice on how to avoid the dangers he will face: the Sirens, who lure sailors to their destruction; the Wandering Rocks, sea rocks that destroy even birds in flight; the perils of the sea monster Scylla and, nearby, the whirlpool Charybdis;[62] *and the cattle of the sun god, which Tiresias has warned Odysseus not to harm.*

As Circe spoke, Dawn mounted her golden throne,
and on the first rays Circe left me, taking
her way like a great goddess up the island.
I made straight for the ship, roused up the men
to get aboard and cast off at the stern.
They scrambled to their places by the rowlocks
and all in line dipped oars in the gray sea.
But soon an offshore breeze blew to our liking—
a canvas-bellying breeze, a lusty shipmate
sent by the singing nymph with sunbright hair.
So we made fast the braces, and we rested,
letting the wind and steersman work the ship.
The crew being now silent before me, I
addressed them, sore at heart:

'Dear friends,
more than one man, or two, should know those things
Circe foresaw for us and shared with me,
so let me tell her forecast: then we die
with our eyes open, if we are going to die,
or know what death we baffle if we can. Sirens
weaving a haunting song over the sea
we are to shun, she said, and their green shore
all sweet with clover; yet she urged that I
alone should listen to their song. Therefore
you are to tie me up, tight as a splint,
erect along the mast, lashed to the mast,
and if I shout and beg to be untied,
take more turns of the rope to muffle me.'

I rather dwelt on this part of the forecast,
while our good ship made time, bound outward down
the wind for the strange island of Sirens.

62. **Charybdis** (kə rib′ dis)

45 ◀ Critical Viewing The sorceress Circe both helps and hinders Odysseus on his journey home. What can you tell about Circe from this illustration? **[Deduce]**

Literary Analysis
Epic Hero What does Odysseus reveal about his character by sharing information with his men?

47 

Reading Check

What instructions does Odysseus give his shipmates as they prepare to deal with the Sirens?

45 Critical Viewing

Possible response: Circe looks seductive, confident of her power, mysterious, and a bit mischievous.

46 Literary Analysis

Epic Hero

1. Discuss with students how good leaders give responsibilities to their followers and trust them to do their work well.
2. **Ask** students how Odysseus' men might respond if asked to do a task that has not been explained to them.

   Possible response: Odysseus' men have mutinied before. If asked to do something that does not make sense to them, they might refuse.
3. **Ask** the Literary Analysis question: What does Odysseus reveal about his character by sharing information with his men?

   Possible response: Odysseus shows that he trusts his men to follow his orders. He also shows that he is not a leader who must keep all knowledge and power to himself.

47 Reading Check

Answer: Odysseus asks his men to tie him to the mast.

Differentiated Instruction for Universal Access

Support for Special-Needs Students
Provide students with additional support by having them read along with a recorded version of the *Odyssey*. Provide students with the ***Hear It!* Audio CD,** and have them follow the text for a section or two. Tell students that many epics were recited by storytellers, and discuss the difference between reading a text silently and hearing the story read aloud.

Strategy for Less Proficient Readers
Tell students that the Sirens were half bird, half woman. Discuss with students what kind of bird would be appropriate for a tempting Siren. Remind students that some birds are symbolic. The dove, for example, often is a symbol of peace; a peacock often symbolizes pride; and a raven often represents death. Ask students to sketch a Siren based on their discussions.

48 Reading Skill

Historical and Cultural Context

1. **Ask** students how the sun appeared to early peoples.

   Possible response: The sun might appear to be a ball of fire.

2. **Ask** the Reading Skill question: What does Odysseus' mention of Helios reveal about ancient Greek beliefs regarding astronomical events?

   Possible response: Greeks believed that gods controlled the sun and the planets. Helios controlled the sun.

▶ **Monitor Progress:** Review students' graphic organizers to ensure that they are making reasonable inferences.

▶ **Reteach:** Point out to students that the Greeks did not understand the science behind the rising and setting of the sun. The Greeks explained daylight as a god driving a chariot across the sky. Ask students to use research tools to find other examples of how Greeks explained natural phenomena.

49 Literary Analysis

Epic Hero

1. Point out the Sirens' strategy with students. Explain that they offer men the opportunity to escape from their homesickness and enjoy themselves. The men who are lured in by the Sirens then die at sea.

2. **Ask** the Literary Analysis question: Which details in the Sirens' song are designed to flatter the epic hero?

   Possible response: The description of the Greeks' victory over Troy is designed to flatter Odysseus.

Then all at once the wind fell, and a calm
came over all the sea, as though some power
lulled the swell.
The crew were on their feet
briskly, to furl the sail, and stow it; then,
each in place, they poised the smooth oar blades
and sent the white foam scudding by. I carved
a massive cake of beeswax into bits
and rolled them in my hands until they softened—
no long task, for a burning heat came down
from Helios, lord of high noon. Going forward
I carried wax along the line, and laid it
thick on their ears. They tied me up, then, plumb
amidships, back to the mast, lashed to the mast,
and took themselves again to rowing. Soon,
as we came smartly within hailing distance,
the two Sirens, noting our fast ship
off their point, made ready, and they sang:

This way, oh turn your bows,
Achaea's glory,
As all the world allows—
Moor and be merry.

Sweet coupled airs we sing.
No lonely seafarer
Holds clear of entering
Our green mirror.

Pleased by each purling note
Like honey twining
From her throat and my throat,
Who lies a-pining?

Sea rovers here take joy
Voyaging onward,
As from our song of Troy
Graybeard and rower-boy
Goeth more learnèd.

All feats on that great field
In the long warfare,
Dark days the bright gods willed,
Wounds you bore there,

Reading Skill
Historical and Cultural Context What does Odysseus' mention of Helios reveal about ancient Greek beliefs regarding astronomical events?

Literary Analysis
Epic Hero Which details in the Sirens' song are designed to flatter the epic hero?

Vocabulary Development — CCSS Language 6

Word Analysis
Tell students that the root word of *ardor* comes from a Latin word meaning "to burn." It can be a literal burning, as in a flame, or a metaphorical burning, as in enthusiasm (*His ardor for soccer was intense*) or passion (*His ardor for his wife pushed him to impress her with his bravery*). Have students look at the context of the Sirens' song and describe the type of "burning" they convey in their song.

49

Argos' old soldiery[63]
On Troy beach teeming,
Charmed out of time we see.
No life on earth can be
Hid from our dreaming.

The lovely voices in **ardor** appealing over the water
made me crave to listen, and I tried to say
'Untie me!' to the crew, jerking my brows;
but they bent steady to the oars. Then Perimedes
got to his feet, he and Eurylochus,
and passed more line about, to hold me still.
So all rowed on, until the Sirens
dropped under the sea rim, and their singing
dwindled away.
My faithful company
rested on their oars now, peeling off
the wax that I had laid thick on their ears;
then set me free.

Scylla and Charybdis

But scarcely had that island
faded in blue air than I saw smoke
and white water, with sound of waves in tumult—
a sound the men heard, and it terrified them.
Oars flew from their hands; the blades went knocking
wild alongside till the ship lost way,
with no oar blades to drive her through the water.
Well, I walked up and down from bow to stern,
trying to put heart into them, standing over
every oarsman, saying gently,

51

'Friends,
have we never been in danger before this?
More fearsome, is it now, than when the Cyclops
penned us in his cave? What power he had!
Did I not keep my nerve, and use my wits
to find a way out for us?

63. Argos' old soldiery soldiers from Argos, a city in ancient Greece.

Vocabulary
ardor (är′ dər) *n.* passion; enthusiasm

Spiral Review
Universal Theme What details in this scene suggest the importance of having loyal friends and companions?

50 **Reading Check** How does Odysseus keep his shipmates from hearing the Sirens sing?

Spiral Review
Universal Theme

1. Remind students that they studied the concept of universal theme in the Unit 6 Literary Analysis workshop (pp. 1030–1039).
2. **Ask** students the Spiral Review question.

Possible response: The details that reinforce Odysseus' inability to control himself and the description of the men peacefully but firmly ignoring his requests suggest that loyal friends and companions are important because they are the ones who will oppose us when necessary.

50 Reading Check
Answer: Odysseus puts wax in his men's ears so they cannot hear the Sirens.

Differentiated Instruction for Universal Access

Strategy for Advanced Readers
Challenge students to update the Sirens' song for the present day. What new temptations or needs would they insert in the song? What types of words would the Sirens use today? Suggest that students rewrite the song or compose a new version of their own.

Strategy for Gifted/Talented Students
Ask students to set the Sirens' song to music. They can select existing instrumental music or compose their own accompaniment. Students also may want to chant the words in a rap. Offer opportunities for students to perform the song for the class.

51 Literary Analysis

Epic Hero

1. Ask volunteers to read the bracketed passage aloud. **Ask** the volunteers where they put the emphasis in their reading and why.

   Possible response: Students may say that they emphasized the positive statement "What power he had!" because it would be encouraging to listeners.

2. Review with students how Odysseus' audience might have responded to his speech. **Ask** what they might say to the question, "Have we never been in danger before this?"

   Possible response: Odysseus' sailors might say, "Of course we've been in danger before. We can probably get out of this situation, too."

3. **Ask** the Literary Analysis question: What parts of Odysseus' speech demonstrate his strength as a leader?

   Possible response: Odysseus addresses his men as "Friends," which shows that he considers them his equals. His reminders that the men have endured hardships before show that he is able to encourage and motivate his crew.

52 The Big Question: Connecting to the Big Question

1. Have a volunteer read aloud the bracketed passage.

2. **Ask:** How does Odysseus try to motivate his men in this passage?

   Answer: He gives them clear orders and asks for help from Zeus.

3. **Ask:** How do the men react, and what does their reaction suggest about Odysseus' heroic qualities?

   Possible response: The men spring to action. This reaction suggests that Odysseus knows exactly what to do to motivate his men. He can think on his feet.

Literary Analysis
Epic Hero What parts of Odysseus' speech demonstrate his strength as a leader?

Now I say
by hook or crook this peril too shall be
something that we remember.

Heads up, lads!
We must obey the orders as I give them.
Get the oar shafts in your hands, and lay back
hard on your benches; hit these breaking seas.
Zeus help us pull away before we founder.
You at the tiller, listen, and take in
all that I say—the rudders are your duty;
keep her out of the combers and the smoke;[64]
steer for that headland; watch the drift, or we
fetch up in the smother, and you drown us.'

That was all, and it brought them round to action.
But as I sent them on toward Scylla,[65] I
told them nothing, as they could do nothing.
They would have dropped their oars again, in panic,
to roll for cover under the decking. Circe's
bidding against arms had slipped my mind,
so I tied on my cuirass[66] and took up
two heavy spears, then made my way along
to the foredeck—thinking to see her first from there,
the monster of the gray rock, harboring
torment for my friends. I strained my eyes
upon the cliffside veiled in cloud, but nowhere
could I catch sight of her.

And all this time,
in travail,[67] sobbing, gaining on the current,
we rowed into the strait—Scylla to port
and on our starboard beam Charybdis, dire
gorge[68] of the salt seatide. By heaven! when she
vomited, all the sea was like a cauldron
seething over intense fire, when the mixture
suddenly heaves and rises.

The shot spume
soared to the landside heights, and fell like rain.
But when she swallowed the sea water down
we saw the funnel of the maelstrom,[69] heard
the rock bellowing all around, and dark
sand raged on the bottom far below.
My men all blanched against the gloom, our eyes

64. **the combers** (kōm´ ərs) **and the smoke** the large waves that break on the beach and the ocean spray.

65. **Scylla** (sil´ ə)

66. **cuirass** (kwi ras´) *n.* armor for the upper body.

67. **travail** (trə vāl´) *n.* very hard work.

68. **gorge** (gôrj) *n.* throat or gullet.

69. **maelstrom** (māl´ strəm) *n.* large, violent whirlpool.

Vocabulary Development

CCSS Language 6

Selection Vocabulary Reinforcement

To reinforce and assess students' comprehension of selection vocabulary words, give them sentences using the words in which the word may or may not be used correctly. Students must tell whether the use is correct and explain their answers. Use these sentences:

1. One of the disloyal men made an *insidious* argument that tempted others to make dangerous choices.

   Answer: Yes, *insidious* is used correctly here. Insidious means "crafty," and the disloyal man tempts others.

2. The faithful servant made an *insidious* choice that proved to be safe and reasonable.

   Answer: No, *insidious* is not used correctly. It means "crafty" or "disloyal," and the servant is loyal and makes a reasonable choice.

were fixed upon that yawning mouth in fear
of being devoured.
Then Scylla made her strike,
whisking six of my best men from the ship.
I happened to glance aft at ship and oarsmen
and caught sight of their arms and legs, dangling
high overhead. Voices came down to me
in anguish, calling my name for the last time.

A man surfcasting on a point of rock
for bass or mackerel, whipping his long rod
to drop the sinker and the bait far out,

53

◀ **Critical Viewing**
How does this image compare with the description of Scylla in the scene? **[Compare and Contrast]**

54

What demand does Odysseus make of his men as they approach the rough waters?

53 Critical Viewing

Possible response: The image shows the men dangling in the air, just as they are described in the text. Homer doesn't describe Scylla's physical appearance in detail, but the picture, like the text, portrays her as a horrible monster.

54 Reading Check

Answer: Odysseus orders his shipmates to row hard and set a course.

Differentiated Instruction for Universal Access

Culturally Responsive Instruction

Culture Focus Discuss with students examples of how boats are used in various cultures and time periods. For example, different cultures use boats for war, pleasure, athletics, procurement of food, and trade. Have students give examples of different types of boats and their uses. In addition to being useful objects, what do boats symbolize for the people and cultures that build them?

Enrichment for Advanced Readers

Have students learn more about creatures, such as Scylla, that once were thought to lure sailors into dangerous waters. Ask them to search research tools to find further descriptions for creatures such as Sirens, mermaids, and water nymphs. Have them find out what made these creatures so attractive, and then share their findings with the class.

55 Literary Analysis

Epic Hero

1. **Ask:** How have Odysseus and his men responded to the deaths of their crewmates?

   Answer: They have grieved deeply.

2. **Ask** the Literary Analysis question: What quality of heroic leadership does Odysseus show in lines 823–825?

   Possible response: He shows compassion and care for his men.

56 Reading Skill

Historical and Cultural Context

1. Review with students some of the specific gods that Odysseus has encountered and the elements that these gods controlled.
2. **Ask** the first Reading Skill question: Which details here suggest that ancient Greeks believed the gods controlled the weather?

   Possible response: Odysseus claims that Zeus creates storms and can manipulate winds and clouds.

57 Reading Skill

Historical and Cultural Context

1. Have students recall Odysseus' argument with Poseidon. **Ask** how Poseidon felt toward Odysseus.

   Answer: Poseidon was angry with Odysseus because he had blinded Poseidon's son, the Cyclops.

2. **Ask** the second Reading Skill question: How does this passage show that ancient Greeks believed their gods had human-like emotions?

   Possible response: Helios loves his sheep and would be angry if they were hurt.

Literary Analysis
Epic Hero What quality of heroic leadership does Odysseus show in lines 823–825?

Reading Skill
Historical and Cultural Context Which details here suggest that ancient Greeks believed the gods controlled the weather?

Reading Skill
Historical and Cultural Context How does this passage show that ancient Greeks believed their gods had human-like emotions?

will hook a fish and rip it from the surface
to dangle wriggling through the air:
so these
were borne aloft in spasms toward the cliff.

She ate them as they shrieked there, in her den,
in the dire grapple, reaching still for me—
and deathly pity ran me through
55 at that sight—far the worst I ever suffered,
questing the passes of the strange sea.
We rowed on.
The Rocks were now behind; Charybdis, too,
and Scylla dropped astern.

The Cattle of the Sun God

In the small hours of the third watch, when stars
that shone out in the first dusk of evening
had gone down to their setting, a giant wind
56 blew from heaven, and clouds driven by Zeus
shrouded land and sea in a night of storm;
so, just as Dawn with fingertips of rose
touched the windy world, we dragged our ship
to cover in a grotto, a sea cave
where nymphs had chairs of rock and sanded floors.
I mustered all the crew and said:

'Old shipmates,
our stores are in the ship's hold, food and drink;
the cattle here are not for our provision,
or we pay dearly for it.
Fierce the god is
57 who cherishes these heifers and these sheep:
Helios; and no man avoids his eye.'

To this my fighters nodded. Yes. But now
we had a month of onshore gales, blowing
day in, day out—south winds, or south by east.
As long as bread and good red wine remained
to keep the men up, and appease their craving,
they would not touch the cattle. But in the end,
when all the barley in the ship was gone,

hunger drove them to scour the wild shore
with angling hooks, for fishes and seafowl,
whatever fell into their hands; and lean days
wore their bellies thin.
The storms continued.
So one day I withdrew to the interior
to pray the gods in solitude, for hope
that one might show me some way of salvation.
Slipping away, I struck across the island
to a sheltered spot, out of the driving gale.
I washed my hands there, and made supplication
to the gods who own Olympus,[70] all the gods—
but they, for answer, only closed my eyes
under slow drops of sleep.
Now on the shore Eurylochus
made his insidious plea:
'Comrades,' he said,
'You've gone through everything; listen to what I say.
All deaths are hateful to us, mortal wretches,
but famine is the most pitiful, the worst
end that a man can come to.
Will you fight it?
Come, we'll cut out the noblest of these cattle
for sacrifice to the gods who own the sky;
and once at home, in the old country of Ithaca,
if ever that day comes—
we'll build a costly temple and adorn it
with every beauty for the Lord of Noon.[71]
But if he flares up over his heifers lost,
wishing our ship destroyed, and if the gods
make cause with him, why, then I say: Better
open your lungs to a big sea once for all
than waste to skin and bones on a lonely island!'

Thus Eurylochus; and they murmured 'Aye!'
trooping away at once to round up heifers.
Now, that day tranquil cattle with broad brows
were gazing near, and soon the men drew up
around their chosen beasts in ceremony.
They plucked the leaves that shone on a tall oak—
having no barley meal—to strew the victims,
performed the prayers and ritual, knifed the kine

70. Olympus (ō lim′ pəs) Mount Olympus, home of the gods.

Vocabulary
insidious (in sid′ ē əs) *adj.* characterized by craftiness and betrayal

71. Lord of Noon Helios.

Literary Analysis
Epic Hero How are the values of Eurylochus different from those of Odysseus?

59 
Reading Check

Who owns the heifers and sheep on the island?

58 Literary Analysis

Epic Hero

1. Discuss with students Odysseus' response to the shortage of food. **Ask** them why they think Odysseus is able to resist the temptation of eating the cows he sees before him.

   Possible response: Odysseus received Circe's warning and clearly knows that he and his men will suffer if the cows are harmed. Perhaps Odysseus has more self-discipline then his men have.

2. Then, **ask** why students think Eurylochus was able to convince the sailors that they should eat the cattle.

   Possible response: The sailors were all hungry, and Odysseus was not there to remind them of the punishment they would receive for harming the cattle.

3. **Ask** the Literary Analysis question: How are the values of Eurylochus different from those of Odysseus?

   Possible response: Eurylochus believes it is better to tempt the wrath of the gods and sacrifice the cattle than to risk starvation on the island. Odysseus believes that the warning to avoid eating the cattle must be observed at all costs.

59 Reading Check

Answer: The sun god Helios owns the heifers and sheep on the island.

Differentiated Instruction for Universal Access

Strategy for Advanced Readers
Most sea captains keep a log, a record of events and sailing data for each day of a voyage. Ask students to write three to five entries in a ship's log that Odysseus might have kept on his journey. Entries should be based on events from Part 1 of the *Odyssey*.

Strategy for Gifted/Talented Students
Ask students to draw their own map tracing Odysseus' route. Encourage them to add photographs or illustrations to depict the Mediterranean setting and specific episodes and figures from the *Odyssey*.

60 Literature in Context

Geography Connection Odysseus sailed throughout the Mediterranean, leaving from Troy in modern day Turkey, past Crete, to several small islands off the coasts of Sicily, Tunisia, Sardinia, Italy, and Corsica. Scholars speculate that the "narrow strait" mentioned in line 637 might be the Straits of Gibraltar.

Connect to the Literature You may wish to compare the places on the map on p. 1078 with a current map of the Mediterranean. Point out the locations of Troy, Ithaca, and the Straits of Gibraltar. **Ask** students the Connect to the Literature question: How does the inclusion of real places make the story's imaginary events more believable?

Answer: Real places lend credibility to Homer's tale. By mentioning them, he also helps the readers of his time connect to the story.

60

LITERATURE IN CONTEXT

Geography Connection

Real Places and Imaginary Events in the *Odyssey*

Odysseus' journey carries him to real places, including Troy, Sparta, and the Strait of Gibraltar. However, in the story, many of these real places are populated by imaginary creatures, such as the Cyclops and the Sirens. The combination of real places and fantastic events is part of the story's appeal.

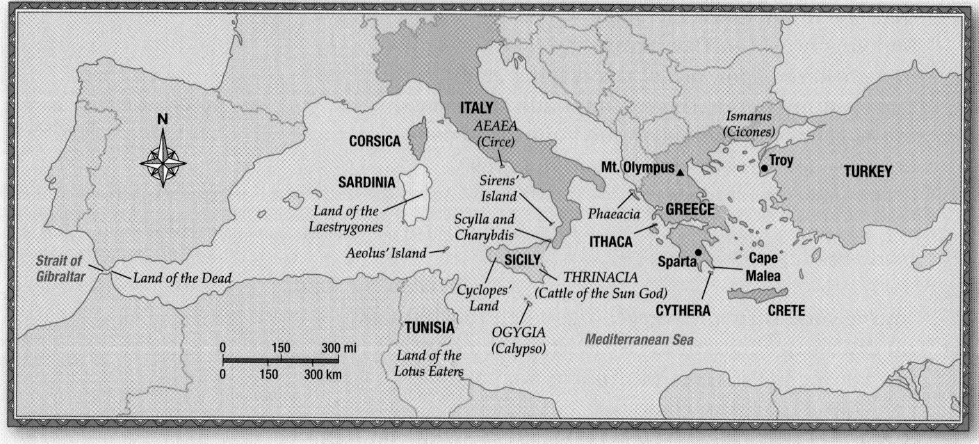

Connect to the Literature How does the inclusion of real places make the story's imaginary events more believable?

and flayed each carcass, cutting thighbones free
to wrap in double folds of fat. These offerings,
with strips of meat, were laid upon the fire.
Then, as they had no wine, they made libation
with clear spring water, broiling the entrails first;
and when the bones were burnt and tripes shared,
they spitted the carved meat.
Just then my slumber
left me in a rush, my eyes opened,
and I went down the seaward path. No sooner
had I caught sight of our black hull, than savory
odors of burnt fat eddied around me;
grief took hold of me, and I cried aloud:

'O Father Zeus and gods in bliss forever,
you made me sleep away this day of mischief!
O cruel drowsing, in the evil hour!
Here they sat, and a great work they contrived.'[72]

72. contrived (kən trīvd′) *v.* thought up; devised.

Vocabulary Development

CCSS Language 6

Ocean and Sailing Terms

You may wish to clarify with students the terms related to the ocean that are used in this section of the *Odyssey*. With a clearer sense of what these terms mean, students should get a better picture of this crucial scene in the story.

Gales: winds
Astern: behind a ship
Thunderhead: storm cloud
Squall: storm
Bilge: the bottommost, interior part of a ship
Stepping the mast and sail: setting up a mast and sail by securing it into the hull of a ship, usually on the ship's keel

Lampetia[73] in her long gown meanwhile
had borne swift word to the Overlord of Noon:
'They have killed your kine.'
And the Lord Helios
burst into angry speech amid the immortals:

'O Father Zeus and gods in bliss forever,
punish Odysseus' men! So overweening,
now they have killed my peaceful kine, my joy
at morning when I climbed the sky of stars,
and evening, when I bore westward from heaven.
Restitution or penalty they shall pay—
and pay in full—or I go down forever
to light the dead men in the underworld.'

Then Zeus who drives the stormcloud made reply:
'Peace, Helios: shine on among the gods,
shine over mortals in the fields of grain.
Let me throw down one white-hot bolt, and make
splinters of their ship in the winedark sea.'

—Calypso later told me of this exchange,
as she declared that Hermes[74] had told her.
Well, when I reached the sea cave and the ship,
I faced each man, and had it out; but where
could any remedy be found? There was none.
The silken beeves[75] of Helios were dead.
The gods, moreover, made queer signs appear:
cowhides began to crawl, and beef, both raw
and roasted, lowed like kine upon the spits.

Now six full days my gallant crew could feast
upon the prime beef they had marked for slaughter
from Helios' herd; and Zeus, the son of Cronus,
added one fine morning.
All the gales
had ceased, blown out, and with an offshore breeze
we launched again, stepping the mast and sail,
to make for the open sea. Astern of us
the island coastline faded, and no land
showed anywhere, but only sea and heaven,
when Zeus Cronion piled a thunderhead
above the ship, while gloom spread on the ocean.

73. Lampetia (lam pē′ shə) a nymph.

74. Hermes (hur′ mēz′) *n.* god who serves as herald and messenger of the other gods.

75. beeves (bēvz) *n.* alternate plural form of "beef."

Literary Analysis
Epic Hero What details in lines 920–921 clarify the flashback presented here?

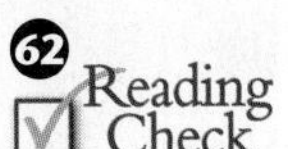

What do Odysseus' shipmates do while he is sleeping?

61 Literary Analysis

Epic Hero

1. Read aloud Helios' complaint to Zeus in lines 907–914. Then, discuss with students Odysseus' unusual perspective. **Ask** students how Odysseus could have information about a conversation between two gods.

   Possible response: Odysseus was not present, so someone who was there must have given him the information.

2. Discuss whether Odysseus could have known about Helios' conversation with Zeus at the time that it happened. **Ask** students whether Odysseus might have made different decisions if he had known about Zeus' promise to hit his ship with a "bolt."

   Possible response: Odysseus could not have known of the conversation until later. He shows no indication that he is threatened by Zeus when he tries to sail away.

3. **Ask** the Literary Analysis question: What details in lines 920–921 clarify the flashback presented here?

   Answer: Odysseus indicates that he learns this information later from Calypso, who heard the story from the god Hermes.

62 Reading Check

Answer: While Odysseus is sleeping, his men sacrifice some of the cattle belonging to Helios.

63 Humanities

La Nef de Telemachus *(The Ship of Telemachus)*

This is an illustration for the *Odyssey*. It was inspired by statues, pottery, and frescoes from ancient Greece. The rich blue of the ocean, echoed in the duller blue of the cloudy sky, forms a striking frame for the massive black ship. Powered by sail and oar, this craft is the kind on which Odysseus and his men would have sailed to and from Troy. Use the following questions for discussion.

1. How do you think this ship compares in size with Columbus' vessels or with a modern ocean liner?

   Possible response: This ship is smaller than a fifteen-century wooden ship, and it is much smaller than a hotel-sized ocean liner.

2. How do you think this ship would fare in a storm?

   Possible response: As a relatively small ship, it would be buffeted by a storm and might be damaged or even sunk.

63

La Nef de Telemachus (The Ship of Telemachus), New York Public Library Picture Collection

Vocabulary Development

Vocabulary Knowledge Rating

When students have completed reading and discussing the *Odyssey*, Part 1, have them take out their **Vocabulary Knowledge Rating Chart** for this selection. Read the words aloud once more and have students rate their knowledge of the words again in the After Reading column. Clarify any words that are still problematic. Have students write their own definition and example or sentence in the appropriate column. Then have students complete the Vocabulary Practice activities at the end of the selection. Encourage students to use the words in further discussion and written work about this selection. Remind them that they will be accountable for these words on the **Selection Test, *Unit 6 Resources,*** pp. 38–40 or 41–43.

We held our course, but briefly. Then the squall
struck whining from the west, with gale force, breaking
both forestays, and the mast came toppling aft
along the ship's length, so the running rigging
showered into the bilge.
On the afterdeck
the mast had hit the steersman a slant blow
bashing the skull in, knocking him overside,
as the brave soul fled the body, like a diver.
With crack on crack of thunder, Zeus let fly
a bolt against the ship, a direct hit,
so that she bucked, in reeking fumes of sulphur,
and all the men were flung into the sea.
They came up 'round the wreck, bobbing awhile
like petrels[76] on the waves.
No more seafaring
homeward for these, no sweet day of return;
the god had turned his face from them.
I clambered
fore and aft my hulk until a comber
split her, keel from ribs, and the big timber
floated free; the mast, too, broke away.
A backstay floated dangling from it, stout
rawhide rope, and I used this for lashing
mast and keel together. These I straddled,
riding the frightful storm.

Nor had I yet
seen the worst of it: for now the west wind
dropped, and a southeast gale came on—one more
twist of the knife—taking me north again,
straight for Charybdis. All that night I drifted,
and in the sunrise, sure enough, I lay
off Scylla mountain and Charybdis deep.
There, as the whirlpool drank the tide, a billow
tossed me, and I sprang for the great fig tree,
catching on like a bat under a bough.
Nowhere had I to stand, no way of climbing,
the root and bole[77] being far below, and far
above my head the branches and their leaves,
massed, overshadowing Charybdis pool.
But I clung grimly, thinking my mast and keel
would come back to the surface when she spouted.

64 ◀ **Critical Viewing**
In the *Odyssey*, Odysseus' son Telemachus searches for his father in a ship like this one. From what you observe in the painting, how does this ship compare with modern ships? **[Compare and Contrast]**

76. petrels (pe´ trəlz) *n.* small, dark sea birds.

Literary Analysis
Epic Hero Which of Odysseus' heroic qualities does he demonstrate in this passage?

77. bole (bōl) *n.* tree trunk.

66 

How is Odysseus' ship destroyed?

64 Critical Viewing

Possible response: Most ships today are powered by engines and propellers rather than by the wind and oars. Today's ships make use of highly advanced technology both to navigate and to communicate with other ships.

65 Literary Analysis

Epic Hero

1. Recount with students the calamity that has befallen Odysseus' men, including the destruction of the ship and the death of his crew. **Ask** students if there are any other survivors from the wreck.

   Answer: Odysseus does not mention any survivors.

2. Read aloud lines 948–955. Then, **ask** students what hope they see for Odysseus to return home.

   Possible responses: Students may say that Odysseus has escaped from disasters before. Or they may say that he no longer has men to assist him, and that he has powerful gods angry at him, so his chances for survival do not look promising.

3. **Ask** the Literary Analysis question: Which of Odysseus' heroic qualities does he demonstrate in this passage?

   Possible response: Odysseus is brave, resourceful, and skillful at seafaring. He also is determined. Even though it would seem that he is destined for certain death, he refuses to give up.

66 Reading Check

Answer: Zeus destroys the ship with a "bolt."

Concept Connector

Anticipation Guide

Have students return to their **Anticipation Guides** and respond to the statements again in the After Reading column. They may do this individually or in groups. Then, lead a class discussion, probing for what students have learned that confirms or invalidates each statement. Encourage students to cite specific evidence from the text to support their responses.

Writing About the Big Question

Have students compare their responses to the sentence starters they completed before reading the selection with their ideas afterwards. Ask them to explain whether their thoughts have changed.

Reading Skill Graphic Organizer

Ask students to review the graphic organizers they completed to chart historical/cultural details. Show them **Reading Skill Graphic Organizer A** (p. 183 in ***Graphic Organizer Transparencies***) as an example. Then, have students share their graphic organizers.

67 Literary Analysis

Epic Hero

1. **Ask** students the Literary Analysis question.
2. **Possible response:** Odysseus breaks off his narrative and speaks directly to his host.

ASSESS

Answers

Critical Thinking

Before students respond, you may wish to have them write a brief objective summary of the selection. As they answer the questions below, remind them to support their answers with evidence from the text.

1. (a) Odysseus drags the men back onto the ship. (b) Odysseus understands that his men will be glad they went with him once the lotus' effects wear off.
2. (a) The crew kills the cattle because they are hungry. (b) Odysseus yells at the men. (c) Odysseus takes the commands of the gods seriously.
3. (a) **Possible response:** People enjoy stories about dangerous moments, journeys, monsters, and heroes. (b) **Possible response:** Some students may have developed a greater appreciation for the story after listening to their classmates.
4. **Possible response:** I don't think Odysseus could have saved his men. There is no way he can watch his men constantly. Also, Odysseus says that the gods make him sleep soundly through the sacrifice of the cattle. This suggests that fate had a role in the men's deaths.

And ah! how long, with what desire, I waited!
till, at the twilight hour, when one who hears
and judges pleas in the marketplace all day
between contentious men, goes home to supper,
the long poles at last reared from the sea.

Now I let go with hands and feet, plunging
straight into the foam beside the timbers,
pulled astride, and rowed hard with my hands
to pass by Scylla. Never could I have passed her
had not the Father of gods and men,[78] this time,
kept me from her eyes. Once through the strait,
nine days I drifted in the open sea
before I made shore, buoyed up by the gods,
upon Ogygia[79] Isle. The dangerous nymph
Calypso lives and sings there, in her beauty,
and she received me, loved me.

67 But why tell
the same tale that I told last night in hall
to you and to your lady? Those adventures
made a long evening, and I do not hold
with tiresome repetition of a story."

78. Father . . . men Zeus.

79. Ogygia (o jij′ ī ə)

Literary Analysis
Epic Hero In what way do lines 994–997 remind you that Odysseus is telling his story to an audience?

Critical Thinking

Cite textual evidence to support your responses.

1. **Key Ideas and Details (a)** In the episode of the Lotus-Eaters, how does Odysseus handle the men who ate the lotus? **(b) Interpret:** What does Odysseus understand that his men do not?
2. **Key Ideas and Details (a)** In the episode of the Cattle of the Sun God, why does the crew kill the cattle? **(b) Interpret:** How does Odysseus react to this action? **(c) Analyze:** What does Odysseus' reaction show about the importance of the gods to him?
3. **Integration of Knowledge and Ideas (a) Evaluate:** The *Odyssey* has entertained people for thousands of years. Why do you think it has remained such an enduring work of literature? **(b) Discuss:** In a small group, share your ideas. As a group, choose one response to share with the class.
4. **Integration of Knowledge and Ideas** Could Odysseus have prevented his men from eating the cattle of Helios and so saved their lives? Explain. *[Connect to the Big Question: Do heroes have responsibilities?]*

Assessment Resources

Unit 6 Resources

L1 L2 EL **Selection Test A,** pp. 38–40. Administer Test A to less advanced students.

L3 L4 EL **Selection Test B,** pp. 41–43. Administer Test B to on-level or more advanced students.

L3 L4 **Open-Book Test,** pp. 35–37. As an alternative, give the Open-Book Test.

All **Customizable Test Bank**

All **Self-tests**
Students may prepare for the **Selection Test** by taking the **Self-test** online.

PHLit Online! All assessment resources are available at **www.PHLitOnline.com.**

After You Read *from the* Odyssey, Part 1

Literary Analysis: Epic Hero

1. **Key Ideas and Details (a)** Using a chart like the one shown, identify three other actions that the **epic hero** Odysseus performs. **(b)** For each action, identify the character trait that it reveals. **(c)** Then, explain which character traits the ancient Greeks admired most.

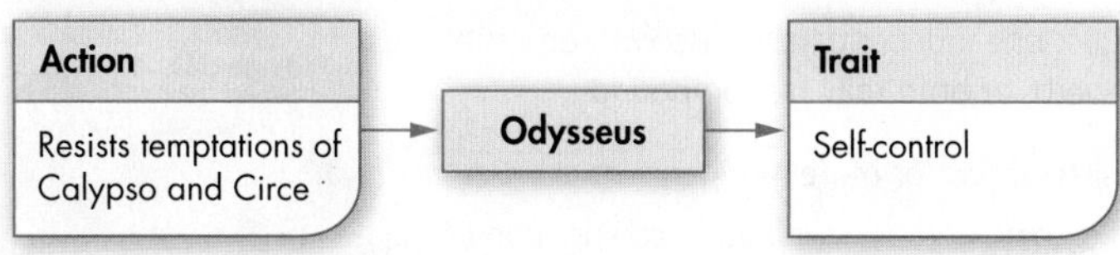

2. **Craft and Structure** Odysseus recounts most of the action in Part 1 in the form of a **flashback.** List the events of Part 1 in chronological sequence, beginning with the end of the Trojan War.
3. **Key Ideas and Details** The epic hero recounts his own adventures. In what way does this affect your reaction to the events he describes? Explain.

Reading Skill: Historical and Cultural Context

4. Consider the **historical and cultural context** of Homer's *Odyssey.* What role do ancient Greek religious beliefs play in the epic?
5. What abilities or features of modern technology could have helped Odysseus on his journey had they been available in ancient times?

Vocabulary

Acquisition and Use Identify the word in each group that does not belong.

1. plundered, robbed, donated
2. dispatched, hesitated, completed
3. assuage, soothe, increase
4. bereft, after, without
5. ardor, spirit, fear
6. insidious, traitorous, friendly

Word Study Use the context of the sentences and what you know about the **Old English prefix *be-*** to explain your answer to each question.

1. If people *begrudge* your success, are they happy for you?
2. What might happen if a sailing ship were *becalmed*?

Word Study

The **Old English prefix *be-*** means "around," "make," or "covered with."

Apply It Explain how the prefix *be-* contributes to the meanings of these words. Consult a dictionary if necessary.

bemuse
belittle
befriend

ASSESS

Answers

Literary Analysis

1. (a) **Action:** Odysseus tricks the Cyclops to escape his cave; he taunts the Cyclops and receives Poseidon's wrath; he urges men not to lose heart in rough seas. (b) **Trait:** cleverness; pride or boldness; fellowship (c) The Greeks admired wit, cleverness, and boldness.
   For other sample answers, see ***Graphic Organizer Transparencies,* Literary Analysis Graphic Organizer A**, p. 185, and the **Additional Answers** section.
2. The Trojan War ends; the winds carry Odysseus to Ismarus where his men battle the Cicones; he escapes from the Lotus-Eaters, the land of forgetfulness; he is captured by and escapes from the Cyclops; he sails to Aeolia and to Laestrygonia and later reaches Aeaea, where he is held by the sorceress Circe; he visits the Land of the Dead to get information from Tiresias; he escapes from the Sirens by lashing himself to a mast; he loses men to the sea monster Scylla; his men anger the sun god Helios when they eat his cattle; and Zeus punishes the men by destroying Odysseus' ship.
3. Odysseus makes himself a sympathetic character and the focal point of the tale.

Reading Skill

4. Greek religious beliefs are illustrated in the way the Greeks speak directly to the gods, offer them sacrifices, and suffer their anger.
5. Odysseus would have benefited from a navigation system and a communication system.

Vocabulary

Acquisition and Use
Sample answers:

1. Donated; Plundered and *robbed* are synonyms.
2. Hesitated; Dispatched and *completed* are synonyms.
3. Increase; Assuage and *soothe* are synonyms.

Answers continued

4. After; Bereft and *without* are synonyms.
5. Fear; Ardor and *spirit* both refer to passion.
6. Friendly; Insidious and *traitorous* are synonyms.

Word Study
Sample answers:

1. No, the prefix *be-* means "around," "make," or "covered with," and *begrudge* means "to resent or have a grudge around something." If someone begrudges your happiness, he or she will resent you.
2. The prefix *be-* means "around," "make," or "covered with," and *becalmed* means "made calm." If a sailing ship were *becalmed*, it would be made calm and would stop moving.

Word Study: Apply It

Sample answers: To *bemuse* is to make someone confused or bewildered. To *belittle* someone is to make him or her feel or seem little or unimportant. To *befriend* someone is to make friends with him or her

Answers

Conventions

Introduce the skill, using the instruction on the student page.

Think Aloud: Model the Skill

Post the following sentences:

"I went to the store."

"I went to the store, and I bought some milk."

"My mother and I went to the store."

Model the skill of identifying simple and compound sentences. Say:

> To identify whether a sentence is simple or compound I look up its clauses. The first sentence has one independent clause and is a simple sentence. The second sentence has two independent connected by the *and*. Thus, it is a compound sentence. The third sentence is a simple sentence with a *compound subject*—"my mother and I."

PH WRITING COACH Grade 9

Students will find instruction on and practice with simple and compound sentences in Chapter 14, Section 1. and Chapter 15, Section 3.

Practice A

1. Simple
2. Compound; and
3. Compound; but
4. Simple

Reading Application

Sample answer: All ships' companies mustered alongside for the midday mean. We beached there, and I told the crew to stand by and keep watch over the ship . . .

Practice B

Sample answers:

1. Odysseus yelled insults at Polyphemus, and the Cyclopes hurled a rock at the ship.
2. The Sirens sang; the ship sailed on.
3. Scylla swooped down on the ship; she grabbed six men.
4. The men screamed for help, but Odysseus stood by helplessly.

Writing Application

Each simple sentence should contain one independent clause; each compound sentence should contain two or more independent clauses.

Integrated Language Skills

from the Odyssey, Part 1

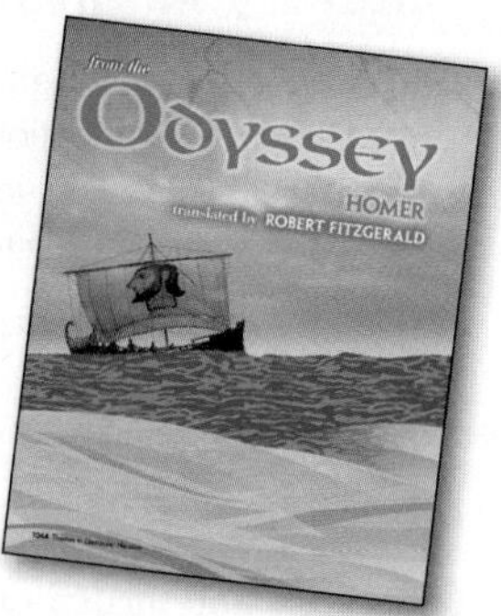

Conventions: Simple and Compound Sentences

A **simple sentence** consists of a single independent clause.

Although a simple sentence is just one independent clause with one subject and one verb, the subject, verb, or both may be compound.

A **compound sentence** consists of two or more independent clauses.

The clauses can be joined by a comma and a coordinating conjunction or by a semicolon. The coordinating conjunctions are *and, but, or, nor, for, yet,* and *so.*

Simple sentence	He remembered an old story.
Simple sentence with compound subject	He and she remembered an old story.
Compound sentence	They laughed together, and they remembered an old story.

Practice A Identify each of the following sentences as simple or compound. For compound sentences, identify the coordinating conjunction.

1. Odysseus led his ship through the perils of Scylla and Charybdis.
2. The Cyclops captured the Greeks, and he ate some of them.
3. The men were starving, but Odysseus commanded them not to eat Helios' cattle.
4. Calypso and Circe both helped and hindered Odysseus.

Reading Application In the *Odyssey,* find one simple sentence and one compound sentence.

Practice B Combine each pair of simple sentences to form a compound sentence. Use a comma and coordinating conjunction or a semicolon to separate the clauses.

1. Odysseus yelled insults at Polyphemus. The Cyclopes hurled a rock at the ship.
2. The Sirens sang. The ship sailed on.
3. Scylla swooped down on the ship. She grabbed six men.
4. The men screamed for help. Odysseus stood by helplessly.

Writing Application Write four sentences about your response to the *Odyssey.* Use two simple sentences and two compound sentences.

PH WRITING COACH Further instruction and practice are available in *Prentice Hall Writing Coach.*

Extend the Lesson

Sentence Modeling

Draw students' attention to the following sentences from the *Odyssey,* Part 1:

> *"Then he caught two more men and feasted on them."*
>
> *"My neckbone, buckled under, snapped, and my spirit found this well of dark."*

Ask students what they notice about the sentences. Elicit from them that the first is a simple sentence and the second is a compound sentence. Then, ask what else they notice. (The first sentence contains two action verbs: *caught* and *feasted.* The second sentence contains two action verbs: *snapped* and *found.* However, it also contains a verb participle, *buckled,* which is used as an adjective to modify *neckbone.*)

Have students imitate the sentences in sentences on topics of their own choosing, matching each grammatical and stylistic feature discussed. Have volunteers read their sentences aloud to the class.

Writing

Narrative Text Write an **everyday epic.** Choose an ordinary daily event, and write an account that makes it seem larger than life. Recite your work for the class.

- Outline the plot of your story, adding points in the action where you can demonstrate your hero's traits, such as generosity and bravery. Include extreme challenges and plan appearances by gods and monsters.
- Use multiple points of view. Begin with the voice of a speaker outside the story, and then have one of the characters tell the tale.
- Use the models you find in the *Odyssey* to help you incorporate figurative language to accurately describe scenes for your reader.
- Reveal the emotions of your characters through dialogue.

Grammar Application As you write your epic, use a variety of sentence types, including both simple and compound.

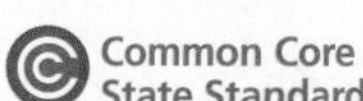

L.9-10.1; W.9-10.3, W.9-10.3.a, W.9-10.3.b, W.9-10.3.c; SL.9-10.1, SL.9-10.1.a, SL.9-10.1.b
[For the full wording of the standards, see page 1040.]

Writing Workshop: *Work in Progress*

Prewriting for Technical Document To choose a topic for a Technical Document you may write, list tasks that you do well. For example, you might be good at using a computer program, or you might know how to use an outdated tool that not many people can work anymore. You might be a skilled party planner. Save this Task List in your writing portfolio.

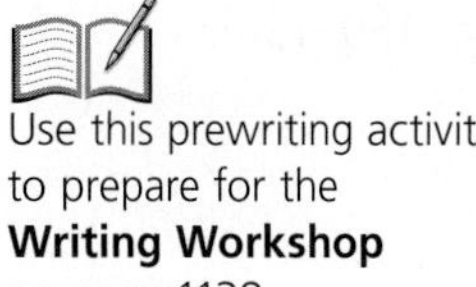

Use this prewriting activity to prepare for the **Writing Workshop** on page 1138.

Speaking and Listening

Presentation of Ideas With two classmates, improvise a **conversation** among ordinary Greeks discussing Odysseus' exploits. Each character's statements should reflect the ancient Greek values shown in the *Odyssey.*

- Plan your conversation for an audience of contemporaries—imagine that they, like your characters, also live in Greece during the time the *Odyssey* takes place.
- Work together to assign specific roles for each participant.
- As a group, sketch out the general direction the conversation will take. Leave room for improvisation, but agree about a broad plan.
- As you speak, use verbal techniques such as tone, volume, and change of pace to add realism and interest to your conversation.
- In addition, use nonverbal techniques, such as gestures, facial expressions, and eye contact to help convey your message.

Practice your conversation, including the verbal and nonverbal presentation techniques. Then, present the conversation to your class, using the techniques you rehearsed with your group.

www.PHLitOnline.com

- Interactive graphic organizers
- Grammar tutorial
- Interactive journals

EXTEND/ASSESS

Writing

1. Review the assignment, using the instruction on the student page.
2. To guide students in writing an everyday epic, give them **Support for Writing**, p. 33 in *Unit 6 Resources.*
3. To evaluate students' narrative texts, give them the Short Story rubrics, pp. 226–227 in *Professional Development Guidebook.*

Grammar Application

Have students check to see that they have formed simple and compound sentences correctly.

Six Traits Focus

✓	Ideas	✓	Word Choice
✓	Organization		Sentence Fluency
✓	Voice		Conventions

PH WRITING COACH Grade 9

Students will find instruction on and practice with fictional narratives in Chapter 6.

Writing Workshop
Work in Progress

Have students save their completed Task Lists in their portfolios. They will use the lists later as they continue this Work-in-Progress assignment (see p. 1117). These assignments prepare them to complete the Writing Workshop assignment (see pp. 1138–1143).

Speaking and Listening

1. Review the assignment, using the instruction on the student page.
2. To support students' work on the assignment, have students complete the **Support for Extend Your Learning** page (*Unit 6 Resources,* p. 34).

Teaching Resources

All *Unit 6 Resources*

L3 L4 EL **Integrated Language Skills: Grammar,** p. 32

L3 L4 EL **Support for Writing,** p. 33

L3 L4 **Support for Extend Your Learning,** p. 34

L4 **Enrichment,** p. 31

All **Enriched Online Student Edition**
Available under After You Read for this selection:

All **Interactive Grammar Tutorial**

L3 L4 **Internet Research Activity**

Professional Development Guidebook

Rubrics for Self-Assessment: Short Story, pp. 226–227

PHLit Online! All print and digital resources are available at **www.PHLitOnline.com.** Online resources accessible by students are noted on the student page.

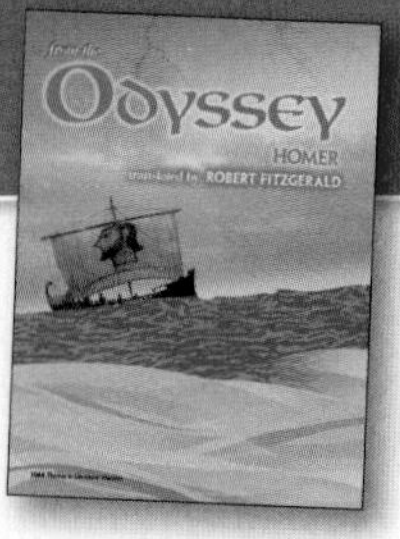

✓ *from the* Odyssey, Part 2
Lesson Pacing Guide

DAY 1 Preteach

- Administer the Reading and Vocabulary Warm-ups (*Unit 6 Resources*, pp. 44–47) as necessary.
- Introduce the Reading Skill: Historical and Cultural Context.
- Introduce the Literary Analysis concept: Epic Simile.
- Distribute copies of the appropriate graphic organizer for the Reading Skill (*Graphic Organizer Transparencies*, pp. 187–188).
- Distribute copies of the appropriate graphic organizer for Literary Analysis (*Graphic Organizer Transparencies*, pp. 189–190).
- Teach the selection vocabulary.
- Introduce the Word Study skill.

DAYS 2–3 Preteach/Teach

- Build background with the Background feature.
- Develop thematic vocabulary and thematic thinking with Writing About the Big Question.
- Prepare students to read with the Activating Prior Knowledge activities (TE).
- Informally monitor comprehension while students read.
- Use the Reading Check questions to confirm comprehension.
- Develop students' ability to comprehend historical and cultural context, using the Reading Skill questions.
- Develop students' understanding of epic similes, using the Literary Analysis questions.
- Reinforce vocabulary with the Vocabulary notes.
- Reinforce unit focus standards using the Spiral Review prompts.

DAY 4 Assess

- Assess students' comprehension and mastery of the skills by having them answer the Critical Thinking, Reading Skill, and Literary Analysis questions.
- Have students complete the Vocabulary Practice activities.
- Have students complete the Word Study activities.

DAY 5 Extend/Assess

- Have students complete the Conventions lesson.
- Have students complete the Writing activity, a biography. (You may assign as homework.)
- Extend learning by having students complete the Speaking and Listening activity, a debate. As an alternative, assign them "Making Things Better" and "Supporting the Troops" in *Reality Central*.
- Administer Selection Test A or B (*Unit 6 Resources*, pp. 59–64).

Common Core State Standards

Reading Literature 2. Determine a theme or central idea of a text and analyze in detail its development over the course of the text, including how it emerges and is shaped and refined by specific details; provide a specific summary of the text.
4. Determine the meaning of words and phrases as they are used in the text, including figurative and connotative meanings; analyze the cumulative impact of specific word choices on meaning and tone.
6. Analyze a particular point of view or cultural experience reflected in a work of literature from outside the United States, drawing on a wide reading of world literature.

Writing 4. Produce clear and coherent writing in which the development, organization, and style are appropriate to task, purpose, and audience.

Speaking and Listening 1. Initiate and participate effectively in a range of collaborative discussions with diverse partners, building on others' ideas and expressing their own clearly and persuasively.
3. Evaluate a speaker's point of view, reasoning, and use of evidence and rhetoric, identifying any fallacious reasoning or exaggerated or distorted evidence.

Language 1. Demonstrate command of the conventions of standard English grammar and usage when writing or speaking.
6. Acquire and use accurately general academic and domain-specific words and phrases.

Additional Standards Practice
Common Core Companion,
pp. 15–22; 55–56

Daily Block Scheduling
Each day in this Lesson Pacing Guide represents a 40–50 minute period. Teachers using block scheduling may combine days to revise pacing. In addition, teachers may differentiate and support core instruction by integrating components for extended and intensive support as students require. See the Guide to Selected Leveled Resources (facing page).

Guide to Selected Leveled Resources

RTI Tier 1 (students performing on level)

			from the Odyssey, Part 2
Warm Up	Whole class instruction; Group work	**Practice, model,** and **monitor** fluency, working **with the whole class** or **in groups.**	**Vocabulary and Reading Warm-ups B,** ***Unit 6 Resources,*** pp. 23–24, 26
Comprehension/Skills	Whole class instruction; Independent work	**Support** and **monitor** comprehension and skills development, having students complete the activities, graphic organizers, and interactive prompts **independently** or **as a class.**	• ***Reader's Notebook,*** adapted instruction and full selection EL ***Reader's Notebook: English Learner's Version,*** adapted instruction and adapted selection • **Reading Skill Graphic Organizer B,** ***Graphic Organizer Transparencies,*** p. 184 • **Literary Analysis Graphic Organizer B,** ***Graphic Organizer Transparencies,*** p. 186
Monitor Progress	A	**Monitor** student progress with the differentiated curriculum-based assessment in the *Unit Resources.*	• **Selection Test B,** ***Unit 6 Resources,*** pp. 62–64 • **Open-Book Test,** ***Unit 6 Resources,*** pp. 56–58
Assess/ Screen	A	**Assess** student progress using Benchmark Test 11.	• **Benchmark Test 11,** ***Unit 6 Resources,*** pp. 84–90

RTI Tier 2 (students requiring intervention)

			from the Odyssey, Part 2
Warm Up	Group work; One-on-one teaching	**Practice, model,** and **monitor** fluency **in groups** or **with individuals.**	• **Vocabulary and Reading Warm-ups A,** ***Unit 6 Resources,*** pp. 44–47 • ***Reality Central,*** "Making Things Better" and "Supporting the Troops" • ***Hear It!*** **Audio CD (adapted text)**
Comprehension/Skills	Group work; One-on-one teaching	• **Support** and **monitor** comprehension and skills development, working **in small groups** or **with individuals.** • **Pair** students with more advanced peers and have them complete the writing activity in the *Real-World Writing Journal.* • As students complete the selection in the appropriate version of the *Reader's Notebook,* **monitor** comprehension frequently with group questions and individual instruction. • **Model** strategies while guiding students in completing the activities and prompts in the *Reader's Notebook,* as well as the graphic organizers. • **Practice** skills and **monitor** mastery with the *Reading Kit* worksheets.	• ***Real-World Writing Journal,*** Lessons 3–4, pp. 164–171 • ***Reader's Notebook: Adapted Version,*** adapted instruction and adapted selection EL ***Reader's Notebook: English Learner's Version,*** adapted instruction and adapted selection • **Reading Skill Graphic Organizer A,** ***Graphic Organizer Transparencies,*** p. 187 • **Literary Analysis Graphic Organizer A,** ***Graphic Organizer Transparencies,*** p. 189 • **Reading Kit,** Practice worksheets, pp. 264, 260, 268, 272, 278
Monitor Progress	A	**Monitor** student progress with the differentiated curriculum-based assessment in the *Unit Resources* and in the *Reading Kit.*	• **Selection Test A,** ***Unit 6 Resources,*** pp. 59–61 • **Reading Kit,** Assess worksheets pp. 265, 261, 269, 273, 279
Assess/ Screen	A	**Assess** student progress using Benchmark Test 11.	• **Benchmark Test 11,** ***Unit 6 Resources,*** pp. 84–90

TIER 3 Tier 3 intervention may require consultation with the student's special-education or dyslexia specialist. For additional support, see the Tier 2 activities and resources listed above.

One-on-one teaching | Group work | Whole class instruction | Independent work | A Assessment

For a complete guide to selection support, including support for Advanced students, see the Overview of Resources in the frontmatter.

from the Odyssey, Part 2

RESOURCES FOR:

- L1 Special-Needs Students
- L2 Below-Level Students (Tier 2)
- L3 On-Level Students (Tier 1)
- L4 Advanced Students (Tier 1)
- EL English Learners
- All All Students

Vocabulary/Fluency/Prior Knowledge

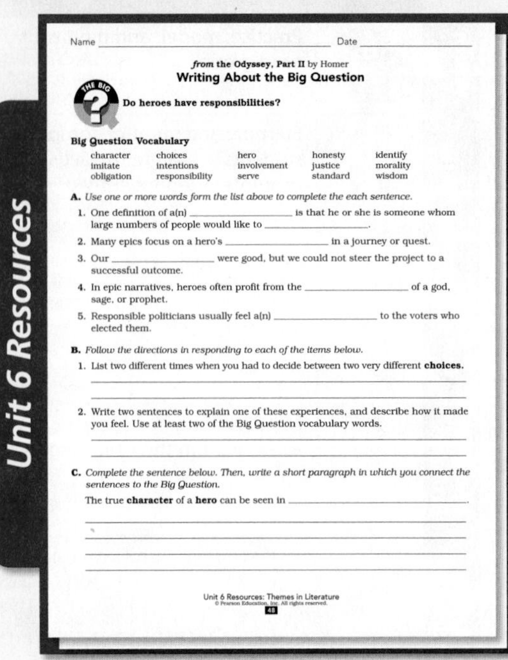

Name ______________ Date ______________

from the Odyssey, Part II by Homer
Writing About the Big Question

Do heroes have responsibilities?

Big Question Vocabulary

character	choices	hero	honesty	identify
imitate	intentions	involvement	justice	morality
obligation	responsibility	serve	standard	wisdom

A. *Use one or more words form the list above to complete the each sentence.*

1. One definition of a(n) ______________ is that he or she is someone whom large numbers of people would like to ______________.
2. Many epics focus on a hero's ______________ in a journey or quest.
3. Our ______________ were good, but we could not steer the project to a successful outcome.
4. In epic narratives, heroes often profit from the ______________ of a god, sage, or prophet.
5. Responsible politicians usually feel a(n) ______________ to the voters who elected them.

B. *Follow the directions in responding to each of the items below.*

1. List two different times when you had to decide between two very different **choices.**
2. Write two sentences to explain one of these experiences, and describe how it made you feel. Use at least two of the Big Question vocabulary words.

C. *Complete the sentence below. Then, write a short paragraph in which you connect the sentences to the Big Question.*

The true **character** of a **hero** can be seen in ______________.

Unit 6 Resources: Themes in Literature
© Pearson Education, Inc. All rights reserved.
48

Unit 6 Resources

All **Writing About the Big Question,** p. 48

Also available for this selection:

EL L1 L2 **Vocabulary Warm-ups A and B,** pp. 44–45

EL L1 L2 **Reading Warm-ups A and B,** pp. 46–47

All **Vocabulary Builder,** p. 51

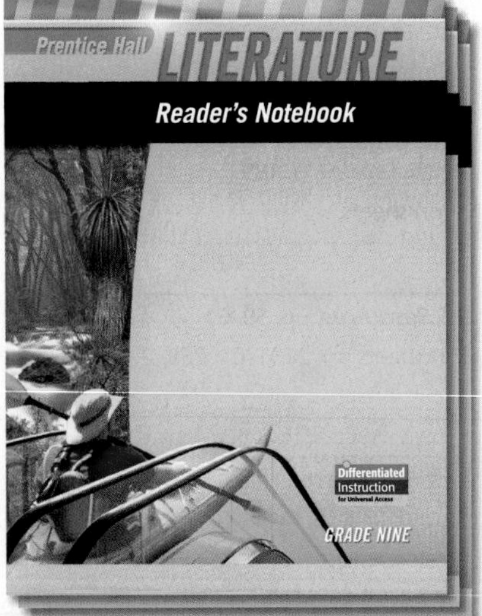

Reader's Notebooks

Pre- and postreading pages, as well as the selection from the *Odyssey*, Part 2, appear in an interactive format in the *Reader's Notebooks*. Each *Notebook* is differentiated for a different group of learners. The selections in the Adapted and English Learner's versions are abridged.

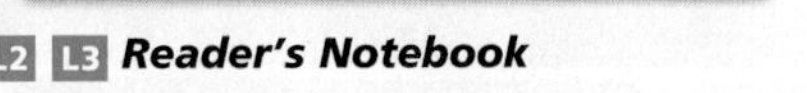

L2 L3 ***Reader's Notebook***

L1 ***Reader's Notebook: Adapted Version***

EL ***Reader's Notebook: English Learner's Version***

EL ***Reader's Notebook: Spanish Version***

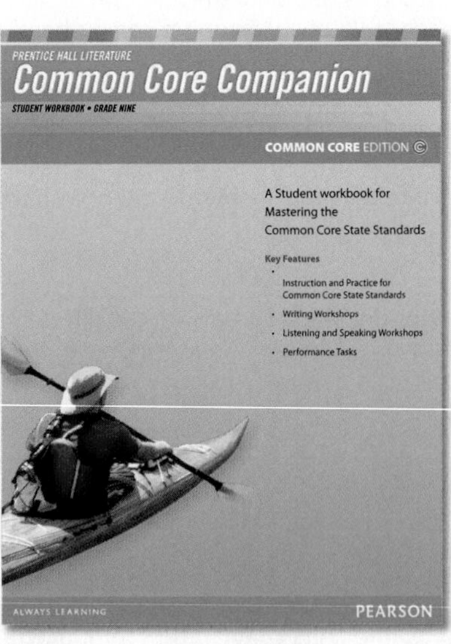

Common Core Companion

Additional instruction and practice for each Common Core State Standard

Selection Support

Graphic Organizer Transparencies

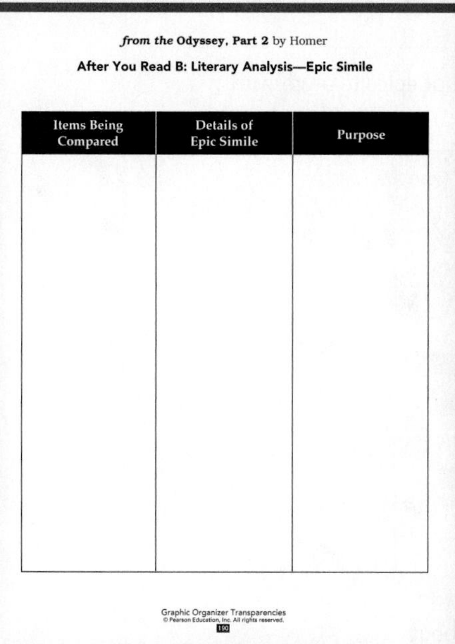

from the **Odyssey, Part 2** by Homer

After You Read B: Literary Analysis—Epic Simile

Items Being Compared	Details of Epic Simile	Purpose

Graphic Organizer Transparencies
© Pearson Education, Inc. All rights reserved.
190

EL L3 **Literary Analysis: Graphic Organizer B,** p. 190

Also available for this selection:

EL L1 L2 **Reading: Graphic Organizer A,** p. 187 (partially filled in)

EL L3 **Reading: Graphic Organizer B,** p. 188

EL L1 L2 **Literary Analysis: Graphic Organizer A,** p. 189 (partially filled in)

Skills Development/Extension

Unit 6 Resources

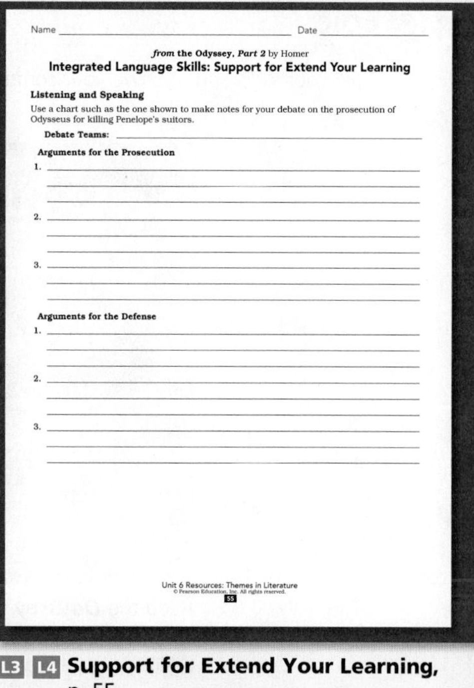

Name ______________________ Date __________

from the **Odyssey, *Part 2*** by Homer

Integrated Language Skills: Support for Extend Your Learning

Listening and Speaking

Use a chart such as the one shown to make notes for your debate on the prosecution of Odysseus for killing Penelope's suitors.

Debate Teams: ______________________

Arguments for the Prosecution

1. ______________________
2. ______________________
3. ______________________

Arguments for the Defense

1. ______________________
2. ______________________
3. ______________________

Unit 6 Resources: Themes in Literature
© Pearson Education, Inc. All rights reserved.
55

L3 L4 **Support for Extend Your Learning,** p. 55

Also available for this selection:

All **Literary Analysis: Epic Simile,** p. 49

All **Reading: Historical and Cultural Context,** p. 50

L4 **Enrichment,** p. 52

EL L3 L4 **Grammar,** p. 53

EL L3 L4 **Support for Writing,** p. 54

Assessment

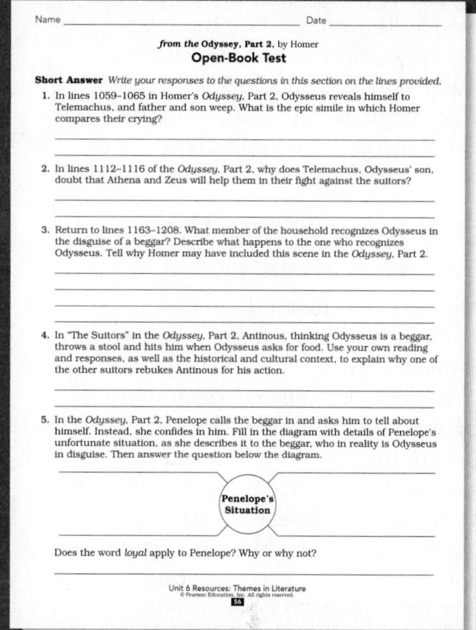

Name ______________________ Date __________

from the **Odyssey, Part 2,** by Homer

Open-Book Test

Short Answer *Write your responses to the questions in this section on the lines provided.*

1. In lines 1059–1065 in Homer's *Odyssey*, Part 2, Odysseus reveals himself to Telemachus, and father and son weep. What is the epic simile in which Homer compares their crying?
2. In lines 1112–1116 of the *Odyssey*, Part 2, why does Telemachus, Odysseus' son, doubt that Athena and Zeus will help them in their fight against the suitors?
3. Return to lines 1163–1208. What member of the household recognizes Odysseus in the disguise of a beggar? Describe what happens to the one who recognizes Odysseus. Tell why Homer may have included this scene in the *Odyssey*, Part 2.
4. In "The Suitors" in the *Odyssey*, Part 2, Antinous, thinking Odysseus is a beggar, throws a stool and hits him when Odysseus asks for food. Use your own reading and responses, as well as the historical and cultural context, to explain why one of the other suitors rebukes Antinous for his action.
5. In the *Odyssey*, Part 2, Penelope calls the beggar in and asks him to tell about himself. Instead, she confides in him. Fill in the diagram with details of Penelope's unfortunate situation, as she describes it to the beggar, who in reality is Odysseus in disguise. Then answer the question below the diagram.

Does the word *loyal* apply to Penelope? Why or why not?

Unit 6 Resources: Themes in Literature
© Pearson Education, Inc. All rights reserved.
56

L3 L4 **Open-Book Test,** pp. 56–58

Also available for this selection:

EL L1 L2 **Selection Test A,** pp. 59–61

EL L3 L4 **Selection Test B,** pp. 62–64

PHLit Online!
www.PHLitOnline.com

Online Resources: All print materials are also available online.

- complete narrated selection text
- a thematically related video with writing prompt
- an interactive graphic organizer
- highlighting feature
- access to all student print resources, adapted to individual student needs
- Spanish and English summaries
- adapted selection translations in Spanish

Get Connected! (thematic video with writing prompt)

Also available:

Background Video

All videos are available in Spanish.

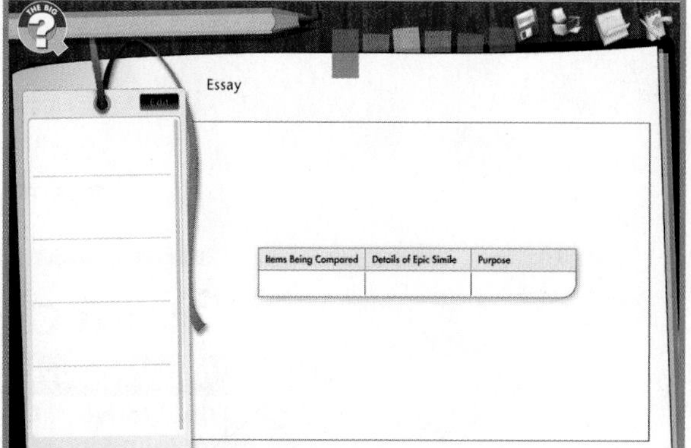

Writer's Journal (with graphics feature)

Also available:

Vocabulary Central (tools, activities, and songs for studying vocabulary)

❶ Epic

You may use the excerpt from the *Odyssey* to meet the lesson objectives. Skills instruction for the selection appears on page 1087. Use the Reader and Task Suggestions on the facing page to help all students read text of increasing complexity.

❷ Introducing the CCS Standards

Introduce the standards on the student page. (Note that the lesson element with which each standard is addressed is identified in parentheses after the text of the standard.) Call out the standards that you will cover with the selections, explaining to students what each requires and how they will address it as they work through the selection you have chosen. Standards labeled "Spiral Review" are introduced in the Literary Analysis Workshop for this unit.

Before You Read *from the* Odyssey, Part 2

❶ Epic

Build your skills and improve your comprehension of epic literature with this selection.

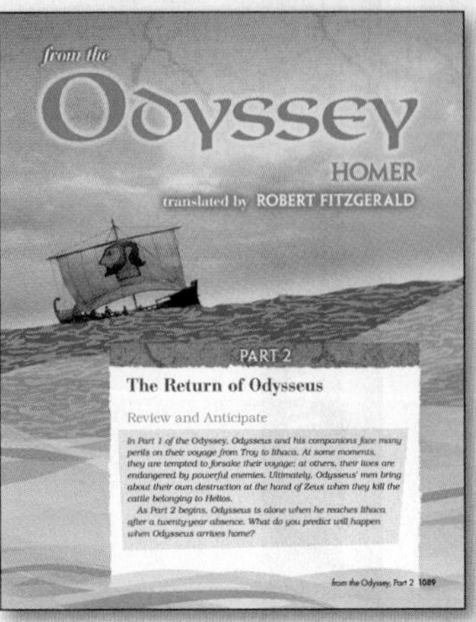

Read the ***Odyssey*** to learn about Odysseus' return to Ithaca and the battle he must wage to regain his home.

❷ Common Core State Standards

Meet these standards with Part 2 of the ***Odyssey*** (p. 1089).

Reading Literature

4. Determine the meaning of words and phrases as they are used in the text, including figurative and connotative meanings; analyze the cumulative impact of specific word choices on meaning and tone. *(Literary Analysis: Epic Simile)*

6. Analyze a particular point of view or cultural experience reflected in a work of literature from outside the United States, drawing on a wide reading of world literature. *(Reading Skill: Historical and Cultural Context)*

Writing

4. Produce clear and coherent writing in which the development, organization, and style are appropriate to task, purpose, and audience. *(Writing: Biography)*

Speaking and Listening

1. Initiate and participate effectively in a range of collaborative discussions with diverse partners, building on others' ideas and expressing their own clearly and persuasively. **3.** Evaluate a speaker's point of view, reasoning, and use of evidence and rhetoric, identifying any fallacious reasoning or exaggerated or distorted evidence. *(Speaking and Listening: Debate)*

Language

1. Demonstrate command of the conventions of standard English grammar and usage when writing or speaking. *(Conventions: Complex and Compound-Complex Sentences)*

6. Acquire and use accurately general academic and domain-specific words and phrases. *(Vocabulary: Word Study)*

1086 Themes in Literature: Heroism

Text Complexity Rubric

***from the* Odyssey, Part 2**		
Qualitative Measures	**Context/ Knowledge Demands**	Ancient Greece; allusions to Greek mythology **1 2 3 ④ 5**
	Structure/ Language Clarity	Narrative poem; formal and symbolic language; challenging vocabulary **1 2 3 4 ⑤**
	Levels of Meaning	Challenging concept (journey of epic hero) **1 2 3 4 ⑤**
Quantitative Measures	**Text Length**	Word Count: 5,610
	Lexile	930L
Overall Complexity		**Complex**

❷ Literary Analysis: Epic Simile

An **epic simile** is an elaborate comparison that may extend for several lines and that may use the words *like, as, just as,* or *so.* Unlike a normal simile, which draws a comparison to a single image, an epic simile might recall an entire place or story. In Part 1, lines 268–271, Odysseus uses an epic simile to describe the size of the tree from which he creates a weapon.

> And it was like a mast / a lugger of twenty oars, broad in the beam— / a deep-sea-going craft—might carry: / so long so big around, it seemed.

As you read, notice how Homer uses epic similes—sometimes called Homeric similes—to bring descriptions to life.

❸ Reading Skill: Historical and Cultural Context

The **historical and cultural context** of a work is the time and place in which it is set or was written. Details in a work reflect the beliefs and customs of that time and place. When you **identify influences on your own reading and responses,** you become aware of your own cultural context and how it affects your understanding of literature. Follow these steps:

- Keep your own beliefs and customs in mind.
- Notice the ways in which your reactions to ideas and situations in the work differ from the reactions of the characters.
- Consider whether your reactions reflect your cultural values.

❹ Using the Strategy: Cultural Influences Chart

As you read, use a chart like this one to note the differences between your own beliefs and values and those reflected in the *Odyssey.*

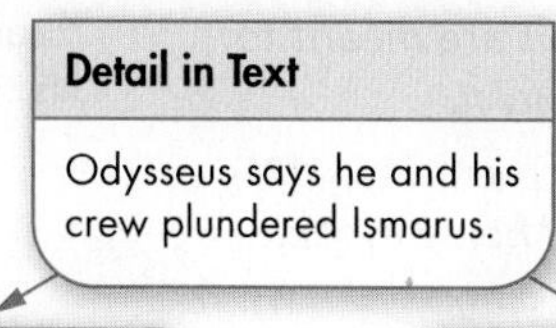

Detail in Text
Odysseus says he and his crew plundered Ismarus.

Meaning for Characters
Winners can take valuables from the defeated.

Meaning in My Culture
Looting is shameful.

PHLit Online!
www.PHLitOnline.com

Hear It!
- Selection summary audio
- Selection audio

See It!
- Get Connected video
- Background video
- More about the author
- Vocabulary flashcards

Do It!
- Interactive journals
- Interactive graphic organizers
- Self-test
- Internet activity
- Grammar tutorial
- Interactive vocabulary games

PRETEACH

❷ Literary Analysis

Epic Simile

1. Introduce the skill, using instruction on the student page.
2. Tell students that they will practice analyzing epic similes as they read.

Think Aloud: Model the Skill

Model the skill of analyzing epic similes. Say to students:

> Epic similes are larger than life. Let's say I come across this simple simile: "The man was as tall as a house." The simile does not become epic until the author extends it over several lines. For example, the author might compare the man's legs to the house's foundation, his arms to the ceiling beams, and his eyes to the windows.

❸ Reading Skill

Historical and Cultural Context

1. Introduce the skill, using instruction on the student page.
2. Tell students that they will practice analyzing historical and cultural context as they read.

❹ Using the Strategy

Give students a copy of either **Reading Skill Graphic Organizer** A or B (*Graphic Organizer Transparencies,* pp. 187–188) to record their ideas about cultural influences as they read. Use the examples in **Reading Skill Graphic Organizer A,** which is partially filled in, to model the process of completing the organizer.

Text Complexity: Reader and Task Suggestions

***from the* Odyssey, Part 2**

Preparing to Read the Text	Leveled Tasks
• Refer to the Activating Prior Knowledge information on TE p. 1089 and discuss the importance of home life. • Discuss the language structure and characteristics of epic poems, especially Greek epics. • Guide students to use Multidraft Reading strategies (TE p. 1043).	***Structure/Language*** If students will have difficulty with structure and clarity, have them first read Part 2 and note what has happened in Ithaca since Odysseus has been gone. Then, have them reread and identify any language that is not clear. ***Analyzing*** If students will not have difficulty with structure and clarity, have them read Part 2 and note examples of similes and symbols.

Making Connections *from the* Odyssey, Part 2

❶ Writing About the Big Question

In Part 2 of the *Odyssey,* Homer describes Odysseus' arrival home and the confrontation with suitors who are there to marry his wife and steal his lands. Use this sentence starter to develop your ideas about the Big Question.

The true **character** of a **hero** can be seen when ______________.

While You Read Look for Odysseus' reactions to the challenges he faces. Also, note examples of the responsibilities Odysseus may have and what he does to fulfill them.

❷ Vocabulary

Read each word and its definition. Decide whether you know the word well, know it a little bit, or do not know it at all. After you read, see how your knowledge of each word has increased.

- **dissemble** (di sem′ bəl) *v.* conceal under a false appearance; disguise (p. 1090) ***The spy was able to dissemble and seem like a patriot.*** *dissemblance n. resemble v.*
- **incredulity** (in′ krə do͞o′ lə tē) *n.* unwillingness or inability to believe (p. 1092) ***During the eclipse, they were silent with incredulity.*** *incredulous adj. incredible adj.*
- **bemusing** (bē myo͞oz′ iŋ) *v.* stupefying or muddling (p. 1095) ***After bemusing the audience, the speaker received little applause.*** *bemusement n. amuse v.*
- **equity** (ek′ wit ē) *n.* fairness; justice (p. 1100) ***Laws are meant to treat everyone with equity.*** *equitable adj. inequity n.*
- **maudlin** (môd′ lin) *adj.* tearfully and foolishly sentimental (p. 1101) ***The scene in which the lost dog finally returned home evoked maudlin responses from the audience.*** *maudlinly adv. maudlinness n.*
- **contempt** (kən tempt′) *n.* disdain or scorn (p. 1108) ***A good athlete shows respect, not contempt, for an opponent.*** *contemptible adj.*

❸

Word Study

The **Latin prefix *dis-*** means "away," "apart," or "not."

In this selection, the goddess Athene tells Odysseus not to **dissemble,** or not disguise himself, from his son Telemachus.

1088 Themes in Literature: Heroism

PRETEACH

❶ Writing About the Big Question

1. Review the assignment with the class.
2. Have students think about the heroes in our culture today. Who are our heroes? Ask students what they think makes someone a hero.
3. Have students complete the sentence starter. Review responses as a class. (**Possible response:** The true <u>character</u> of a <u>hero</u> can be seen when he or she responds to a difficult situation.)
4. Remind students that their answers will help them think about the Big Question, "Do heroes have responsibilities?"

While You Read

Tell students that as they read, they should look for the ways that Odysseus reacts to challenges and for examples of how he fulfills his responsibilities.

❷ Vocabulary

1. Have students preview the selection vocabulary.
2. For each word, have students say the word aloud.
3. Then, use the word in a sentence that defines the word.
4. Finally, repeat your definitional sentence or a similar sentence with the word missing and have the class "fill in the blank" chorally. Here are some examples:

   <u>Equity</u> is fairness or justice. The students hate their teacher because she always favors the same individuals and never treats the class with [students say "equity"].

   To hold something in <u>contempt</u> is to show no respect for it. Sometimes in court, a judge will warn a person to follow the rules or else they will be held on charges of [students say "contempt"].

❸ Word Study

1. Introduce the skill, using the instruction in the box.
2. Ask students for three other commonly used words with the prefix *dis-*. (**Sample answer:** *dispute, dishevel,* and *disembark*)

Vocabulary Development

Vocabulary Knowledge Rating

Create a **Vocabulary Knowledge Rating Chart** (***Professional Development Guidebook***, p. 33) for this selection. Include the selection vocabulary and the Big Question words that appear in the Writing About the Big Question sentence starter on this page. (The Big Question vocabulary is introduced on pp. 1028–1029.)

Give students a copy of the chart. Read the words aloud, and have students mark their rating in the Before Reading column. Urge them to be alert to these words as they read and discuss the selection.

Tally how many students think they know a word to gauge how much instruction to provide. As students read and discuss the selection, point out the words and their context.

Vocabulary Central, featuring tools, activities, and songs for studying vocabulary, is available at **www.PHLitOnline.com.**

EXEMPLAR TEXT

HOMER

translated by ROBERT FITZGERALD

PART 2

The Return of Odysseus

Review and Anticipate

In Part 1 of the Odyssey, *Odysseus and his companions face many perils on their voyage from Troy to Ithaca. At some moments, they are tempted to forsake their voyage; at others, their lives are endangered by powerful enemies. Ultimately, Odysseus' men bring about their own destruction at the hand of Zeus when they kill the cattle belonging to Helios.*

As Part 2 begins, Odysseus is alone when he reaches Ithaca after a twenty-year absence. What do you predict will happen when Odysseus arrives home?

Differentiated Instruction Additional Daily Instruction

EL Extended Support for English Learners
Have students complete the **Reading and Vocabulary Warm-ups,** ***Unit 6 Resources,*** pp. 44–47, before they read. Assign the prereading pages and the adapted selection in the ***Reader's Notebook: English Learner's Version.*** Then, have students listen to portions of the selection on the ***Hear It!*** **Audio CD.**

L1 L2 30 Minutes for Struggling Readers
Have students complete the **Reading and Vocabulary Warm-ups,** ***Unit 6 Resources,*** pp. 44–47, before they read. Assign the prereading pages and the adapted selection in the ***Reader's Notebook: Adapted Version.*** Then, have students listen to portions of the selection on the ***Hear It!*** **Audio CD** (adapted text).

Extended Support—Reluctant Readers
To build motivation and engagement before assigning the selection, have students read "Making Things Better," a thematically related selection in ***Reality Central.*** Then, use the questions at the conclusion of the related selection to guide discussion.

TEACH

1 Activating Prior Knowledge

1. Prepare an Anticipation Guide (***Professional Development Guidebook,*** pp. 36–38) with the following statements:
   - The important things in your home will never change, no matter how long you stay away.
   - People won't remain faithful to your memory if you have been gone for a long time.
   - You can never go home again.
2. Give students copies of the prepared **Anticipation Guide.** Have students mark their responses in the appropriate columns.
3. For further guidance, use the ***Classroom Strategies and Teaching Routines*** card: **Using an Anticipation Guide.**

Concept Connector
Students will return to the **Anticipation Guide** after completing the *Odyssey,* Part 2.

Whole-Class Activity

Key scenes in the *Odyssey,* Part 2, focus on tests—Odysseus tests people to see whether they have remained faithful to him. Ask students to discuss the unstated rules that govern interactions between people in relationships that require trust. Have students describe an encounter in which people have tested one another.

2 About the Selection

Of the two great epic poems attributed to Homer, the *Iliad* has been called a war poem, and the *Odyssey* has been called a postwar poem. The wanderings of Odysseus after his victory at Troy and the difficulties of readjusting to a civil society upon his return home have made the themes of the *Odyssey* relevant to many generations of readers. Discuss with students the difficulties and emotions that Odysseus is likely to face after twenty years away.

❸ Critical Viewing

Possible response: Eumaeus appears to be patient, loyal, and practical. The pigs in the sty behind him are a clue to his profession.

This selection is available in interactive format in the **Enriched Online Student Edition, www.PHLitOnline.com,** which includes a thematically related video with writing prompt and an interactive graphic organizer.

"Twenty years gone, and I am back again . . ."

Odysseus has finished telling his story to the Phaeacians. The next day, young Phaeacian noblemen conduct him home by ship. He arrives in Ithaca after an absence of twenty years. The goddess Athena appears and informs him of the situation at home. Numerous suitors, believing Odysseus to be dead, have been continually seeking the hand of his wife, Penelope, in marriage, while overrunning Odysseus' palace and enjoying themselves at Penelope's expense. Moreover, they are plotting to murder Odysseus' son, Telemachus, before he can inherit his father's lands. Telemachus, who, like Penelope, still hopes for his father's return, has journeyed to Pylos and Sparta to learn what he can about his father's fate. Athena disguises Odysseus as a beggar and directs him to the hut of Eumaeus,[1] his old and faithful swineherd. While Odysseus and Eumaeus are eating breakfast, Telemachus arrives. Athena then appears to Odysseus.

1. **Eumaeus** (yo͞o mē´ əs)

. . . From the air
she walked, taking the form of a tall woman,
handsome and clever at her craft, and stood
beyond the gate in plain sight of Odysseus,
unseen, though, by Telemachus, unguessed,
for not to everyone will gods appear.
Odysseus noticed her; so did the dogs,
who cowered whimpering away from her. She only
nodded, signing to him with her brows,
a sign he recognized. Crossing the yard,
he passed out through the gate in the stockade
to face the goddess. There she said to him:
"Son of Laertes and the gods of old,
Odysseus, master of landways and seaways,
dissemble to your son no longer now.
The time has come: tell him how you together
will bring doom on the suitors in the town.
I shall not be far distant then, for I
myself desire battle."
Saying no more,
she tipped her golden wand upon the man,
making his cloak pure white, and the knit tunic
fresh around him. Lithe and young she made him,
ruddy with sun, his jawline clean, the beard

❸ ▶ **Critical Viewing** What can you tell about Eumaeus from this illustration? **[Infer]**

Vocabulary
dissemble (di sem´ bəl) *v.* conceal under a false appearance; disguise

Vocabulary Development

© **CCSS** Language 6

Thematic Vocabulary: The Big Question

As students are discussing the *Odyssey,* Part 2, encourage them to use the thematic vocabulary presented in Introducing the Big Question, pp. 1028–1029. You might encourage them with sentence starters like these:

1. The various suitors' *intentions* for Penelope's son are . . .
2. Some of the characters in this selection show questionable *morality* when . . .
3. According to the customs of the day, Penelope has an *obligation* to . . .
4. Telemachus shows that he will *serve* his father by . . .

4

4 Humanities

Eumaeus, the Swineherd,
by N. C. Wyeth

This illustration, like many for this selection, was among the sixteen paintings that N. C. Wyeth, the foremost American illustrator of children's books and classics, painted for a 1929 edition of the *Odyssey*. Use the following questions for discussion:

1. In the *Odyssey*, Eumaeus is characterized as loyal and noble. How does Wyeth's painting convey these traits?

   Possible response: Eumaeus is pictured as tall, straight, and sturdy. He looks like a man who will not be moved easily. The firmness of his stance makes him look trustworthy.

2. Which dog in the illustration might be Argus?

   Possible response: Argus is described in line 1164 as "an old hound, lying near." Argus would be the dog lying down on the left.

Differentiated Instruction for Universal Access

Strategy for Less Proficient Readers

Have partners paraphrase the opening passage that describes the entrance of Athena. A possible paraphrase might be as follows: "The goddess Athena, looking like a beautiful, intelligent woman, appeared to Odysseus. Telemachus, however, could not see her."

EL Support for English Learners

Students may find the appearance of a goddess in this scene challenging. Explain that gods and goddesses often appear in human form in Greek literature. Tell them that readers would be familiar with this convention, as well as with Telemachus' inability to see the goddess, although his father sees her plainly. Ask students to identify details that emphasize Athena's godlike qualities—for example, her height and the dogs' fear of her—and the details that make her seem more like a human being.

5 Reading Skill

Historical and Cultural Context

1. Tell students that the Greeks believed their gods often intervened in the affairs of human beings. They took an interest in humans' welfare and helped or hindered them. Remind students of the gods who have made Odysseus' journey back to Ithaca so difficult.
2. **Ask** students the Reading Skill question: What do lines 1021–1029 suggest about the way ancient Greeks responded to the presence of a god?

   Possible response: Taking the transformed Odysseus for a god, Telemachus shows awe, fear, and reverence. However, he also speaks freely to the "god" and makes requests. These lines suggest that Greeks responded to the gods as higher, but approachable, beings.

Spiral Review

Archetype

1. Remind students that they studied the concept of archetype in the Unit 6 Literary Analysis workshop (pp. 1030–1039).
2. **Ask** students the Spiral Review question.

   Possible response: The meeting is an archetype. The archetype of the hero is a quest or journey that involves either a literal or symbolic death and resurrection. His unexpectedly youthful appearance, thanks to Athena's charm, represents a resurrection.

Reading Skill Historical and Cultural Context What do lines 1021–1029 suggest about the way ancient Greeks responded to the presence of a god?

2. **oblation** (äb lā′ shən) *n.* offering to a god.

Spiral Review Archetypes Is the encounter described in lines 1034–1035 an example of an archetype? Why or why not?

Vocabulary
incredulity (in′ krə do͞o′ lə tē) *n.* unwillingness or inability to believe

no longer gray upon his chin. And she
withdrew when she had done.
Then Lord Odysseus
reappeared—and his son was thunderstruck.
Fear in his eyes, he looked down and away
as though it were a god, and whispered:

5

"Stranger,
you are no longer what you were just now!
Your cloak is new; even your skin! You are
one of the gods who rule the sweep of heaven!
Be kind to us, we'll make you fair oblation[2]
and gifts of hammered gold. Have mercy on us!"

The noble and enduring man replied:

"No god. Why take me for a god? No, no.
I am that father whom your boyhood lacked
and suffered pain for lack of. I am he."

Held back too long, the tears ran down his cheeks
as he embraced his son.
Only Telemachus,
uncomprehending, wild
with **incredulity**, cried out:
"You cannot
be my father Odysseus! Meddling spirits
conceived this trick to twist the knife in me!
No man of woman born could work these wonders
by his own craft, unless a god came into it
with ease to turn him young or old at will.
I swear you were in rags and old,
and here you stand like one of the immortals!"

Odysseus brought his ranging mind to bear
and said:
"This is not princely, to be swept
away by wonder at your father's presence.
No other Odysseus will ever come,
for he and I are one, the same; his bitter
fortune and his wanderings are mine.
Twenty years gone, and I am back again
on my own island.

Vocabulary Development

CCSS Language 6

Word Forms

Two of the Vocabulary Builder words for the *Odyssey* can form other parts of speech by adding suffixes. Give students a blank **Word Form Chart** (***Professional Development Guidebook***, p. 42) with *dissemble* and *incredulity* in the correct columns. Work with the class, or have students work with a partner, to determine the related forms. The final chart should look like the one shown.

Hold students accountable for integrating the related forms of the words into their speaking and writing.

Noun	Verb	Adjective	Adverb
dissembler	**dissemble**	dissembling	dissemblingly
incredulity		incredulous	incredulously

As for my change of skin,
that is a charm Athena, Hope of Soldiers,
uses as she will; she has the knack
to make me seem a beggar man sometimes
and sometimes young, with finer clothes about me.
It is no hard thing for the gods of heaven
to glorify a man or bring him low."

When he had spoken, down he sat.
Then, throwing
his arms around this marvel of a father
Telemachus began to weep. Salt tears
rose from the wells of longing in both men,
6 and cries burst from both as keen and fluttering
as those of the great taloned hawk,
whose nestlings farmers take before they fly.
So helplessly they cried, pouring out tears,
and might have gone on weeping so till sundown,
had not Telemachus said:

"Dear father! Tell me
what kind of vessel put you here ashore
on Ithaca? Your sailors, who were they?
I doubt you made it, walking on the sea!"

Then said Odysseus, who had borne the barren sea:

"Only plain truth shall I tell you, child.
Great seafarers, the Phaeacians, gave me passage
as they give other wanderers. By night
over the open ocean, while I slept,
they brought me in their cutter,[3] set me down
on Ithaca, with gifts of bronze and gold
and stores of woven things. By the gods' will
these lie all hidden in a cave. I came
to this wild place, directed by Athena,
so that we might lay plans to kill our enemies.
Count up the suitors for me, let me know
what men at arms are there, how many men.
I must put all my mind to it, to see
if we two by ourselves can take them on
or if we should look round for help."

Literary Analysis
Epic Simile To what are Odysseus' and Telemachus' cries compared in the epic simile in lines 1063–1065?

3. **cutter** (kut′ər) *n.* small, swift ship or boat carried aboard a large ship to transport personnel or supplies.

7 

Why is Telemachus initially doubtful that the man before him is Odysseus, his father?

6 Literary Analysis

Epic Simile

1. Remind students that an *epic simile* is a device that helps describe what is happening in the *Odyssey*. Beyond that, however, an epic simile underscores the drama of the action and paints vivid images in the reader's mind.
2. **Ask** students the Literary Analysis question: To what are Odysseus' and Telemachus' cries compared in the epic simile in lines 1063–1065?

   Answer: The cries of Odysseus and Telemachus are compared to those of a hawk that has lost its nestlings to a farmer.

7 Reading Check

Answer: Telemachus is initially doubtful because of the change in Odysseus' appearance, which leads Telemachus to assume he is a god.

Differentiated Instruction for Universal Access

Strategies for Less Proficient Readers

Some students may need help following the time span covered by Odysseus' lengthy journey. Display the **Timeline** (***Graphic Organizer Transparencies***, p. 224) and have students chart some of the important events that occur in the *Odyssey* in the twenty years between the end of the Trojan War and Odysseus' return to Ithaca. Remind students to plot events that Odysseus tells about long after they happen, such as the arrival of the suitors

8 Reading Skill

Historical and Cultural Context

1. Remind students that Athena was the goddess of wisdom. Then **ask** students why she might be particularly interested in helping Odysseus.

   Possible response: Odysseus is known for his wit and cleverness. Athena, the goddess of wisdom, may admire his intelligence.

2. Then, **ask** students the Reading Skill question: What does Odysseus' statement in lines 1109–1111 suggest about ancient Greek beliefs about the gods' interest in human affairs?

   Possible response: Odysseus' response indicates that the Greeks believed they could depend on the gods to help them in very specific ways in time of need.

3. Discuss with students how Homer's story shows the Greek gods responding to humans' material needs in very active ways. In this section, for example, Athena has disguised Odysseus and then restored him to his youthful appearance.

Telemachus
replied:
"O Father, all my life your fame
as a fighting man has echoed in my ears—
your skill with weapons and the tricks of war—
but what you speak of is a staggering thing,
beyond imagining, for me. How can two men
do battle with a houseful in their prime?[4]
For I must tell you this is no affair
of ten or even twice ten men, but scores,
throngs of them. You shall see, here and now.
The number from Dulichium alone
is fifty-two picked men, with armorers,
a half dozen; twenty-four came from Same,
twenty from Zacynthus; our own island
accounts for twelve, high-ranked, and their retainers,
Medon the crier, and the Master Harper,
besides a pair of handymen at feasts.
If we go in against all these
I fear we pay in salt blood for your vengeance.
You must think hard if you would conjure up
the fighting strength to take us through."
Odysseus
who had endured the long war and the sea
answered:
"I'll tell you now.
8 Suppose Athena's arm is over us, and Zeus
her father's, must I rack my brains for more?"

Clearheaded Telemachus looked hard and said:

"Those two are great defenders, no one doubts it,
but throned in the serene clouds overhead;
other affairs of men and gods they have
to rule over."

And the hero answered:
"Before long they will stand to right and left of us
in combat, in the shouting, when the test comes—
our nerve against the suitors' in my hall.
Here is your part: at break of day tomorrow
home with you, go mingle with our princes.
The swineherd later on will take me down

4. **in their prime** in the best or most vigorous stage of their lives.

Reading Skill
Historical and Cultural Context What does Odysseus' statement in lines 1109–1111 suggest about ancient Greek beliefs about the gods' interest in human affairs?

Vocabulary Development

CCSS Language 6

Selection Vocabulary Reinforcement

Students will benefit from additional examples and practice with the selection vocabulary words. Reinforce their comprehension with "show-you-know" sentences. The first part of the sentence uses the vocabulary word in an appropriate context. The second part of the sentence—the "show-you-know" part—clarifies the first. Model the strategy with this example for *bemusing*:

He ended up *bemusing* the crowd with his monotonous defense of public trash cans.

Then, give students these sentence prompts and coach them in creating the clarification part.

1. She reacted with *incredulity* __________

   Sample answer: after hearing that the team had won the championship.

2. We questioned the *equity* of the law; __________

   Sample answer: it seemed to favor one group of people over another.

the port-side trail—a beggar, by my looks,
hangdog and old. If they make fun of me
in my own courtyard, let your ribs cage up
your springing heart, no matter what I suffer,
no matter if they pull me by the heels
or practice shots at me, to drive me out.
Look on, hold down your anger. You may even
plead with them, by heaven! in gentle terms
to quit their horseplay—not that they will heed you,
rash as they are, facing their day of wrath.
Now fix the next step in your mind.

Athena,
counseling me, will give me word, and I
shall signal to you, nodding: at that point
round up all armor, lances, gear of war
left in our hall, and stow the lot away
back in the vaulted storeroom. When the suitors
miss those arms and question you, be soft
in what you say: answer:

'I thought I'd move them
out of the smoke. They seemed no longer those
bright arms Odysseus left us years ago
when he went off to Troy. Here where the fire's
hot breath came, they had grown black and drear.
One better reason, too, I had from Zeus:
suppose a brawl starts up when you are drunk,
you might be crazed and bloody one another,
and that would stain your feast, your courtship.
Tempered
iron can magnetize a man.'

Say that.
But put aside two broadswords and two spears
for our own use, two oxhide shields nearby
when we go into action. Pallas Athena
and Zeus All-Provident will see you through,
bemusing our young friends.

Now one thing more.
If son of mine you are and blood of mine,
let no one hear Odysseus is about.
Neither Laertes, nor the swineherd here,
nor any slave, nor even Penelope.

9

LITERATURE IN CONTEXT

Cultural Connection

Athena
Athena was the goddess of wisdom, skills, and warfare. When she helps Odysseus in this epic, it is not the first time that she offers assistance to a Greek hero. In Homer's *Iliad,* Athena helps the Greek hero Achilles defeat the Trojan warrior Hector. Athena favored Achilles for his unmatched skill in battle, but Odysseus was her favorite among the Greeks. He displayed not only skill in warfare, but also ingenuity and cunning.

Connect to the Literature

Which of Odysseus' deeds in the *Odyssey* might have helped him to earn Athena's favor? Explain.

Vocabulary
bemusing (bē myo͞oz′ iŋ) *v.* stupefying or muddling

10 

How does Odysseus tell his son to respond if the suitors "practice shots" on Odysseus?

9 Literature in Context:

Cultural Connection The Greeks had more than one god whom they believed was assigned to war. The god Ares represented the spirit of battle—a grimmer, bloodier side of war than that associated with Athena. Her association was more with the intellectual and civilized side of war, which she combined with the values of justice and skill. Athena was associated with war, but she was also a keeper of civilization, as shown by her namesake city, Athens, the birthplace of democracy.

Connect to the Literature Remind students of Odysseus' early claim that he is "formidable for guile in peace and war" (line 19). Then **ask** the Connect to the Literature question: Which of Odysseus' deeds in the *Odyssey* might have helped him to earn Athena's favor? Explain.

Possible response: Athena may have been impressed by Odysseus' clever thinking as he escaped from the Cyclops. She may have appreciated how his escape required both intelligence and physical strength.

10 Reading Check

Answer: If the suitors "practice shots" on Odysseus, who is pretending to be a beggar, Telemachus is to hold his anger and to refrain from acknowledging his father.

Differentiated Instruction for Universal Access

Strategy for Special-Needs Students

Students may need additional support and practice with the Reading Skill, Historical and Cultural Context. Explain that many details within the text offer insight into the way Greeks lived at the time of Homer. For example, Odysseus' instructions to hide weapons from the suitors (lines 1135–1138) reveal how much "gear of war" was stored in a house at any given time.

To model how to analyze the historical and cultural context, show students **Reading Skill Graphic Organizer A** (***Graphic Organizer Transparencies,*** p. 187). The partially completed chart will give students insight into the process of analyzing a story's context. They can use it as a model for their own analysis as they read.

⓫ Critical Viewing

Possible response: Students may say that the Greeks incorporated worship of their gods into everyday events. The scenes on the pottery show the importance to the Greeks of honoring and commemorating significant events in Greek history and mythology.

⓬ Humanities

Greek vessel

This vessel is one of several being used to illustrate this edition of the *Odyssey*. The Greeks used such vessels to store or transport liquids such as oil or wine. Greek artists used several methods to decorate these vessels. In the "black figure" technique, color is applied to the figures, and the background takes the natural color of the clay. The vessel on this page is an example of this style. In the "red figure" technique, the process is reversed; the background is painted black.

These artifacts have survived for thousands of years—evidence of a durable art form that not only is intrinsically beautiful, but also presents a detailed picture of the life and culture of ancient Greeks. Use the following question for discussion:

In 1,000 years, what objects from our own culture might reveal our values to the people who find them?

Possible response: Our televisions, computers, and musical equipment might indicate our culture's interest in entertainment.

But you and I alone must learn how far
the women are corrupted; we should know
how to locate good men among our hands,
the loyal and respectful, and the shirkers[5]
who take you lightly, as alone and young."

5. **shirkers** (shurk′ ərz) *n.* people who get out of doing what needs to be done.

Argus

Odysseus heads for town with Eumaeus. Outside the palace, Odysseus' old dog, Argus, is lying at rest as his long-absent master approaches.

While he spoke
an old hound, lying near, pricked up his ears
and lifted up his muzzle. This was Argus,
trained as a puppy by Odysseus,
but never taken on a hunt before
his master sailed for Troy. The young men, afterward,
hunted wild goats with him, and hare, and deer,
but he had grown old in his master's absence.
Treated as rubbish now, he lay at last
upon a mass of dung before the gates—
manure of mules and cows, piled there until
fieldhands could spread it on the king's estate.
Abandoned there, and half destroyed with flies,
old Argus lay.
But when he knew he heard
Odysseus' voice nearby, he did his best
to wag his tail, nose down, with flattened ears,
having no strength to move nearer his master.
And the man looked away,
wiping a salt tear from his cheek; but he
hid this from Eumaeus. Then he said:

"I marvel that they leave this hound to lie
here on the dung pile;
he would have been a fine dog, from the look of him,
though I can't say as to his power and speed
when he was young. You find the same good build
in house dogs, table dogs landowners keep
all for style."

▼ **Critical Viewing** What can you infer about the ancient Greeks based on the fact that they depicted their gods on everyday objects like this urn? **[Infer]**

⓬

And you replied, Eumaeus:

"A hunter owned him—but the man is dead
in some far place. If this old hound could show
the form he had when Lord Odysseus left him,
going to Troy, you'd see him swift and strong.
He never shrank from any savage thing
he'd brought to bay in the deep woods; on the scent
no other dog kept up with him. Now misery
has him in leash. His owner died abroad,
and here the women slaves will take no care of him.
You know how servants are: without a master
they have no will to labor, or excel.
(13) For Zeus who views the wide world takes away
half the manhood of a man, that day
he goes into captivity and slavery."

Eumaeus crossed the court and went straight forward
into the megaron[6] among the suitors:
but death and darkness in that instant closed
the eyes of Argus, who had seen his master,
Odysseus, after twenty years.

Reading Skill
Historical and Cultural Context How do Eumaeus' beliefs about servitude and slavery compare with those of your own culture?

6. **megaron** (meg′ ə rön) *n.* great, central hall of the house, usually containing a center hearth.

The Suitors

Still disguised as a beggar, Odysseus enters his home. He is confronted by the haughty[7] suitor Antinous.[8]

7. **haughty** (hôt′ ē) *adj.* arrogant.
8. **Antinous** (an tin′ ō əs)

But here Antinous broke in, shouting:

"God!
What evil wind blew in this pest?
Get over,
stand in the passage! Nudge my table, will you?
Egyptian whips are sweet
to what you'll come to here, you nosing rat,
making your pitch to everyone!
These men have bread to throw away on you
because it is not theirs. Who cares? Who spares
another's food, when he has more than plenty?"

(14) 

How does Antinous react to Odysseus, who is disguised as a beggar?

(13) Reading Skill

Historical and Cultural Context

1. Discuss with students how many cultures have practiced slavery, often by enslaving people who were captured in war. Slavery based on race was practiced in American colonies and in the United States until the Civil War.
2. Then, **ask** the Reading Skill question: How do Eumaeus' beliefs about servitude and slavery compare with those of your own culture?
   Possible response: Eumaeus believes that slaves will not do good work if they are not supervised. My culture believes that enslaving people is morally wrong and that no one should be subjected to slavery, even if it is under a "good" master such as Odysseus.

(14) Reading Check

Answer: Antinous berates Odysseus and calls him a pest and a rat.

Differentiated Instruction for Universal Access

Culturally Responsive Instruction

Culture Focus Ask students why they think dogs are often called "man's best friend." Point out that the bond between dogs and people may go back as far as 14,000 years, as shown in Paleolithic cave drawings of dogs.

Have students find out more about how dogs are viewed in different cultures. Assign students to research the roles that dogs have played, such as the hunting dog, the farm dog, the sled dog, and the dog god in ancient Egypt. Have students share their findings with the class.

Strategy for Gifted/Talented Students

Challenge students to draw a portrait of Odysseus in his disguise as a beggar. Tell students that their portraits should not only reflect Odysseus' humble appearance, but also suggest his hidden qualities as a hero. Students may want to contrast his appearance with that of the swineherd Eumaeus or with one of the proud suitors, such as Antinous.

⓯ Reading Skill

Historical and Cultural Context

1. Remind students of Greek culture's emphasis on hospitality. Point out also that Antinous is an unwanted guest in another person's home, and that he has been treated with courtesy.
2. **Ask** students the first Reading Skill question: What conflicting values does this exchange between Antinous and Odysseus reveal?

   Possible response: Odysseus practices the values of the gods and treats strangers with courtesy. Antinous is only rude, and he also violates his culture's rules regarding hospitality.

⓰ Reading Skill

Historical and Cultural Context

1. Review the exchange between Antinous and Odysseus, beginning with the suitor's insult of the disguised Odysseus.
2. **Ask** students why Antinous becomes so angry with the beggar.

   Answer: The disguised Odysseus points out Antinous' selfish and inappropriate behavior.
3. **Ask** the second Reading Skill question: What values regarding the use of physical force are evident in this speech?

   Possible response: Odysseus' speech indicates that physical force is appropriate when defending one's property. Antinous, however, uses force for an inappropriate reason.
4. Discuss with students the difference in power between Antinous (a suitor) and a beggar, who is Odysseus in disguise. Tell them that Antinous takes advantage of someone who is in a lower social and economic class, and who is not in a position to defend himself.

Reading Skill Historical and Cultural Context What conflicting values does this exchange between Antinous and Odysseus reveal?

9. impudence (im΄ pyo͞o dəns) *n.* quality of being shamelessly bold; disrespectful.

Reading Skill Historical and Cultural Context What values regarding the use of physical force are evident in this speech?

10. Furies (fyo͝or΄ ēz) *n.* three terrible female spirits who punish the doers of unavenged crimes.

With guile Odysseus drew away, then said:

"A pity that you have more looks than heart.
You'd grudge a pinch of salt from your own larder
to your own handyman. You sit here, fat
on others' meat, and cannot bring yourself
to rummage out a crust of bread for me!"

Then anger made Antinous' heart beat hard,
and, glowering under his brows, he answered:
"Now!
You think you'll shuffle off and get away
after that impudence?[9] Oh, no you don't!"

The stool he let fly hit the man's right shoulder
on the packed muscle under the shoulder blade—
like solid rock, for all the effect one saw.
Odysseus only shook his head, containing
⓯ thoughts of bloody work, as he walked on,
then sat, and dropped his loaded bag again
upon the door sill. Facing the whole crowd
he said, and eyed them all:

"One word only,
my lords, and suitors of the famous queen.
One thing I have to say.
There is no pain, no burden for the heart
⓰ when blows come to a man, and he defending
his own cattle—his own cows and lambs.
Here it was otherwise. Antinous
hit me for being driven on by hunger—
how many bitter seas men cross for hunger!
If beggars interest the gods, if there are Furies[10]
pent in the dark to avenge a poor man's wrong, then may
Antinous meet his death before his wedding day!"

Then said Eupeithes' son, Antinous:

"Enough.
Eat and be quiet where you are, or shamble elsewhere,
unless you want these lads to stop your mouth
pulling you by the heels, or hands and feet,
over the whole floor, till your back is peeled!"

Vocabulary Development

Ⓒ CCSS Language 6

Expressive Vocabulary

To help students broaden their expressive vocabulary, encourage them to use the following words as they discuss Odysseus' encounter with the suitors: *deception, furious,* and *courtesy*. Have them complete these sentence starters:

1. Odysseus practices *deception* when he . . .
2. The suitors' behavior makes Odysseus *furious* because . . .
3. Greek culture required that hosts extend *courtesy* to . . .

But now the rest were mortified, and someone
spoke from the crowd of young bucks to rebuke him:

(17) "A poor show, that—hitting this famished tramp—
bad business, if he happened to be a god.
You know they go in foreign guise, the gods do,
looking like strangers, turning up
in towns and settlements to keep an eye
on manners, good or bad."
But at this notion
Antinous only shrugged.
Telemachus,
after the blow his father bore, sat still
without a tear, though his heart felt the blow.
Slowly he shook his head from side to side,
containing murderous thoughts.
Penelope
on the higher level of her room had heard
the blow, and knew who gave it. Now she murmured:

"Would god you could be hit yourself, Antinous—
hit by Apollo's bowshot!"

Reading Skill
Historical and Cultural Context What ancient Greek belief is conveyed in this suitor's speech?

(18) 

How does Penelope regard Antinous?

(17) Reading Skill
Historical and Cultural Context

1. Recall with students Odysseus' speech to the Cyclops. **Ask** them to recall why Odysseus hoped the Cyclops would welcome the Greeks he found in his cave.

   Possible response: Odysseus hoped that the Cyclops would observe the rules of hospitality. He also hoped that the Cyclops might fear angering the gods if he was not courteous to strangers.

2. **Ask** students how Odysseus' position in relation to hospitality is similar to or different from what it was in Cyclops' cave.

   Possible response: Students may say that Odysseus was thinking of robbing the Cyclops, and perhaps was not so deserving of hospitality. A penniless beggar, however, is certainly worthy of hospitality.

3. Now **ask** students the Reading Skill question: What ancient Greek belief is conveyed in this suitor's speech?

   Possible response: The suitor's speech reflects the belief that gods can travel in human form and punish those who do not treat them well.

(18) Reading Check

Answer: Penelope wishes that Antinous could be shot with an arrow by the gods; she does not like him.

Differentiated Instruction for Universal Access

Strategy for Advanced Readers
On his arrival, Odysseus is greeted with insults: "pest," "nosing rat," and "famished tramp." Have students record the insults on a **Cluster Diagram** (***Graphic Organizer Transparencies***, p. 217) and see whether they can find any common elements in these insults. Suggest that students begin by looking for references to animals and to poverty. Ask students to write an essay analyzing the insults by showing how they reveal what Greeks despised—and, by implication, what they valued and esteemed.

Spiral Review
Archetype

1. Remind students that they studied the concept of archetype in the Unit 6 Literary Analysis workshop (pp. 1030–1039).
2. **Ask** students the Spiral Review question.

   Possible response: Tricksters often use disguises to gather information, to surprise their enemies, and to gain advantage. By hiding his identity, Odysseus will learn Penelope's true feelings and intentions.

19 Literary Analysis
Epic Simile

1. Read aloud lines 1290–1297 and tell students it is an example of an epic simile.
2. Ask students to draw the Literary Analysis graphic organizer on p. 1115, or give them a copy of **Literary Analysis Graphic Organizer B** (***Graphic Organizer Transparencies***, p. 190). Have students write down the two items that are being compared in this epic simile and the details that are included in the comparison.
3. Discuss with students Odysseus' reasons for drawing this extended comparison and point out that he is avoiding Penelope's question about his homeland. Then, **ask** what they think Odysseus' comparison reveals about his feelings toward his wife.

   Possible response: The epic simile indicates that Odysseus believes that Penelope has been faithful to him.
4. After students have discussed Odysseus' comparison, ask them to fill out the "Purpose" section of their graphic organizers.

▶ **Monitor Progress:** Review students' graphic organizers to ensure that they understand the items being compared in the epic simile and the purpose of the comparison.

▶ **Reteach:** Explain to students that Odysseus is comparing Penelope's name to the honor of a good king. In other words, he believes she has been faithful to him.

And Eurynome[11]
her housekeeper, put in:

"He and no other?
If all we pray for came to pass, not one
would live till dawn!"

Her gentle mistress said:

"Oh, Nan, they are a bad lot; they intend
ruin for all of us; but Antinous
appears a blacker-hearted hound than any.
Here is a poor man come, a wanderer,
driven by want to beg his bread, and everyone
in hall gave bits, to cram his bag—only
Antinous threw a stool, and banged his shoulder!"

So she described it, sitting in her chamber
among her maids—while her true lord was eating.
Then she called in the forester and said:

"Go to that man on my behalf, Eumaeus,
and send him here, so I can greet and question him.
Abroad in the great world, he may have heard
rumors about Odysseus—may have known him!"

Penelope

In the evening, Penelope interrogates the old beggar.

"Friend, let me ask you first of all:
who are you, where do you come from, of what nation
and parents were you born?"

And he replied:

"My lady, never a man in the wide world
should have a fault to find with you. Your name
has gone out under heaven like the sweet
honor of some god-fearing king, who rules
in equity over the strong: his black lands bear
both wheat and barley, fruit trees laden bright,
new lambs at lambing time—and the deep sea
gives great hauls of fish by his good strategy,
so that his folk fare well.

Spiral Review
Archetype
Odysseus hides his true identity from Penelope. How does this behavior suggest the trickster archetype?

Vocabulary
equity (ek′ wit ē) *n.* fairness; justice

11. **Eurynome** (yo͞o rin′ əm ē)

Vocabulary Development

CCSS Language 6

Word Analysis

Call students' attention to the word *equity* and its definition. Tell students that the Latin root *-equi-* means "same" or "equal." Ask students to think of other words that contain this root, and ask a volunteer to list them on the board. Possibilities include *equidistant, equilateral,* and *equivalent.*

Have students look up the listed words in a dictionary to clarify the definitions. Then, have students use each word in a sentence that illustrates its meaning.

O my dear lady,
this being so, let it suffice to ask me
of other matters—not my blood, my homeland.
Do not enforce me to recall my pain.
My heart is sore; but I must not be found
sitting in tears here, in another's house:
it is not well forever to be grieving.
One of the maids might say—or you might think—
I had got maudlin over cups of wine."

And Penelope replied:

"Stranger, my looks,
my face, my carriage,[12] were soon lost or faded
when the Achaeans crossed the sea to Troy,
Odysseus my lord among the rest.
If he returned, if he were here to care for me,
I might be happily renowned!
But grief instead heaven sent me—years of pain.
Sons of the noblest families on the islands,
Dulichium, Same, wooded Zacynthus,[13]
with native Ithacans, are here to court me,
against my wish; and they consume this house.
Can I give proper heed to guest or suppliant
or herald on the realm's affairs?
How could I?
wasted with longing for Odysseus, while here
they press for marriage.
Ruses[14] served my turn
to draw the time out—first a close-grained web
I had the happy thought to set up weaving
on my big loom in hall. I said, that day:
'Young men—my suitors, now my lord is dead,
let me finish my weaving before I marry,
or else my thread will have been spun in vain.
It is a shroud I weave for Lord Laertes
when cold Death comes to lay him on his bier.
(20) The country wives would hold me in dishonor
if he, with all his fortune, lay unshrouded.'
I reached their hearts that way, and they agreed.
So every day I wove on the great loom,
but every night by torchlight I unwove it;
and so for three years I deceived the Achaeans.

Vocabulary
maudlin (môd′ lin) *adj.* tearfully and foolishly sentimental

12. **carriage** (kar′ ij) *n.* posture.

13. **Zacynthus** (za sin′ *th*us)

14. **ruses** (ro͞oz′ iz) *n.* tricks.

Reading Skill
Historical and Cultural Context How do the ancient Greek ideas in Penelope's speech about honoring the dead compare to modern ideas?

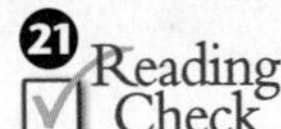

How was Penelope able to delay marriage for three years?

(20) Reading Skill

Historical and Cultural Context

1. Read aloud Penelope's description of making her husband a shroud. Then, discuss with students how a shroud would represent Penelope's respect for her dead husband. **Ask** how weaving a shroud could honor the person who had died.

   Possible response: Weaving a shroud is an established custom that has evolved to show respect. The Greeks may have believed that they should clothe a dead person in a fine garment before they send him or her into the underworld.

2. Discuss with the class ways that people today honor their dead. You may want to mention the custom of traffic stopping to let a funeral procession pass, the playing of taps at military funerals, or holidays such as All Saints' Day or Dia de los Muertos in honor of loved ones who have passed away. Have volunteers offer examples of people showing respect for the dead.

3. **Ask** students the Reading Skill question: How do the ancient Greek ideas in Penelope's speech about honoring the dead compare to modern ideas?

   Possible response: Students may say that both the Greeks and people in modern times have rituals that honor the dead. They may observe that modern society does not always follow a strict set of burial customs as people did in ancient Greece.

(21) Reading Check

Answer: Penelope said that she could not marry until she completed weaving her dead husband's shroud. She wove the shroud by day and unraveled it each night.

Differentiated Instruction for Universal Access

Culturally Responsive Instruction

Culture Focus Discuss with students the cultural aspects of homecomings. Elicit examples of reasons why young people today leave home for extended periods of time. For example, young people go to college or boarding school, serve in the armed forces, do volunteer work or student exchanges abroad, and take long trips to see the world. Ask students about current cultural traditions and practices for greeting people when they return home after a long time away. Use the following questions for discussion:

- How do people keep in touch with their loved ones while they are gone?
- What major changes might a person face upon returning home?
- How might it be difficult to adjust to being home again?
- How do we usually greet people when they return from a long trip? Do we throw a party, have a parade, or engage in a religious ritual?
- Do we tend to treat people differently when they return home after a long time? If so, how?

22 Humanities

The Trial of the Bow,
by N. C. Wyeth

N. C. Wyeth studied with Howard Pyle, an illustrator famous for his work on children's classics such as the tales of Robin Hood. Pyle encouraged Wyeth to make his paintings dramatic and to paint from his own experience.

In *The Trial of the Bow*, Penelope promises that she will marry the man who can string Odysseus' bow and shoot an arrow through twelve ax handle sockets. In this painting, Odysseus, disguised as a beggar, has succeeded in the first part of this challenge. Use these questions for discussion:

1. Why do you think Wyeth chose to illustrate this particular moment in the story?

   Possible response: This is an especially dramatic moment because Odysseus is about to win the contest, reveal his true identity to the suitors, and then take his revenge.

2. Why didn't the artist illustrate the scene a few moments later, when the arrow goes through the ax handles?

   Possible response: At that point, Odysseus would no longer be focusing on the target, but would be giving instructions to Telemachus. This moment shows Odysseus at his best—muscles flexed and attention fixed on his target.

22

The Trial of the Bow from Homer's ***The Odyssey,*** N.C. Wyeth, Brandywine River Museum

But when the seasons brought a fourth year on,
as long months waned, and the long days were spent,
through impudent folly in the slinking maids
they caught me—clamored up to me at night;
I had no choice then but to finish it.
And now, as matters stand at last,
I have no strength left to evade a marriage,
cannot find any further way; my parents
urge it upon me, and my son
will not stand by while they eat up his property.
He comprehends it, being a man full-grown,
able to oversee the kind of house
Zeus would endow with honor.
But you too
confide in me, tell me your ancestry.
You were not born of mythic oak or stone."

Penelope again asks the beggar to tell about himself. He makes up a tale in which Odysseus is mentioned and declares that Penelope's husband will soon be home.

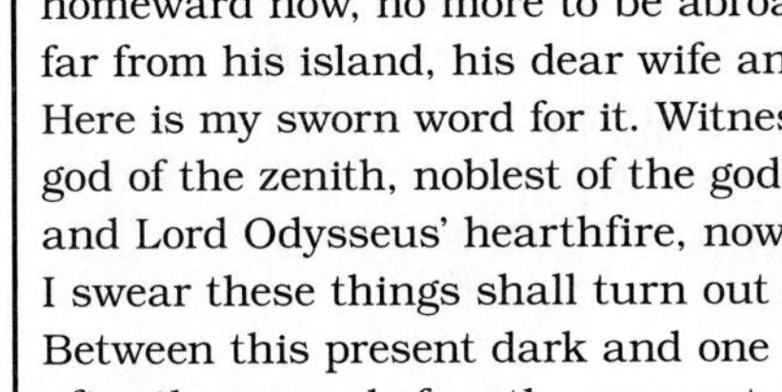

"You see, then, he is alive and well, and headed
homeward now, no more to be abroad
far from his island, his dear wife and son.
Here is my sworn word for it. Witness this,
god of the zenith, noblest of the gods,[15]
and Lord Odysseus' hearthfire, now before me:
I swear these things shall turn out as I say.
Between this present dark and one day's ebb,
after the wane, before the crescent moon,
Odysseus will come."

The Challenge

Pressed by the suitors to choose a husband from among them, Penelope says she will marry the man who can string Odysseus' bow and shoot an arrow through twelve axhandle sockets. The suitors try and fail. Still in disguise, Odysseus asks for a turn and gets it.

And Odysseus took his time,
turning the bow, tapping it, every inch,
for borings that termites might have made

◀ **Critical Viewing** The winner of the archery contest will win Penelope's hand in marriage. What details or artistic techniques capture the tension in this scene? **[Interpret]**

15. god of the zenith, noblest of the gods Zeus.

Reading Check

What means does Penelope decide she will use to choose a husband?

23 Critical Viewing

Answer: The emotional tension is captured in the physical tension of Odysseus' arm and leg muscles and the taut bowstring. In addition, everyone else is focused on the targets. Additional suspense comes from the point in time the picture captures: The arrow has not been released, and the viewers, like the people in the painting, wait in expectation.

24 Connecting to the Big Question

1. Discuss with students how our emotions can make it difficult to carry out a responsibility or to face a challenge. **Ask:** Do you think heroes have a responsibility to control their emotions? Explain.

   Possible response: I don't think heroes should have to control their emotions more than any other person would. Emotions can actually help guide us through difficult situations.

2. Read the bracketed passage aloud. **Ask:** Why do you think Odysseus decides to hide his identity from Penelope even though he probably wants to reveal it?

   Possible response: He chooses not to reveal his identity because he wants to keep Penelope safe. He feels responsible for protecting her.

3. As students continue reading, have them look for other ways in which Odysseus takes responsibility.

25 Reading Check

Answer: Penelope says that she will marry whoever can string Odysseus' bow and shoot an arrow through twelve ax handle sockets.

Differentiated Instruction for Universal Access

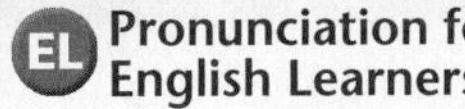

Pronunciation for English Learners

Students may have difficulty pronouncing the *-ng* sound that appears in *long, things,* and *string,* replacing it with an *n* sound. The following strategies can help students to pronounce the *-ng* sound.

- Write the following word pairs on the board: *thing* and *thin*; *sing* and *sin*; and *rang* and *rain*. Pronounce each word pair in turn and then have students pronounce each. Then, call out each word at random and have students write down the word they hear. Compare and discuss results and what might have led to any discrepancies.
- Using a sentence that contains both *-n* and *-ng* sounds—such as, "Vin has a thin ring that sings"—play a game of telephone with the students. Whisper the sentence to one student, who passes it to another, and so on. At the end, reveal the correct sentence and review its pronunciation.

26 Critical Viewing

Possible response: Students may find the hunter's posture on the pottery to be somewhat stylized and artificial in contrast to the easy grace that Odysseus displays.

while the master of the weapon was abroad.
The suitors were now watching him, and some
jested among themselves:

"A bow lover!"

"Dealer in old bows!"

"Maybe he has one like it
at home!"

"Or has an itch to make one for himself."

"See how he handles it, the sly old buzzard!"

And one disdainful suitor added this:
"May his fortune grow an inch for every inch he bends it!"

But the man skilled in all ways of contending,
satisfied by the great bow's look and heft,
like a musician, like a harper, when
with quiet hand upon his instrument
he draws between his thumb and forefinger
a sweet new string upon a peg: so effortlessly
Odysseus in one motion strung the bow.
Then slid his right hand down the cord and plucked it,
so the taut gut vibrating hummed and sang
a swallow's note.

In the hushed hall it smote the suitors
and all their faces changed. Then Zeus thundered
overhead, one loud crack for a sign.
And Odysseus laughed within him that the son
of crooked-minded Cronus had flung that omen down.
He picked one ready arrow from his table
where it lay bare: the rest were waiting still
in the quiver for the young men's turn to come.
He nocked[16] it, let it rest across the handgrip,
and drew the string and grooved butt of the arrow,
aiming from where he sat upon the stool.

26 ▲ **Critical Viewing** Does the hunter pictured here show the same grace as does Odysseus in lines 1370–1392? Explain. **[Compare and Contrast]**

16. **nocked** (näkt) set an arrow into the bowstring.

Vocabulary Development

CCSS Language 6

Archery Terms

Have students identify the words used to describe Odysseus' bow. Ask them to fill in a **Web** (***Graphic Organizer Transparencies***, p. 227) with the archery terms used in the selection. Students can write the words used to describe the bow, the arrow, or the act of shooting. Examples of this special vocabulary would include *arrow, quiver, nocked, handgrip, string,* and *twanging*. Have students use the web to show the relationships between the words and how they explain the act of shooting an arrow.

Now flashed
arrow from twanging bow clean as a whistle
through every socket ring, and grazed not one,
to thud with heavy brazen head beyond.
Then quietly
Odysseus said:

"Telemachus, the stranger
you welcomed in your hall has not disgraced you.
I did not miss, neither did I take all day
stringing the bow. My hand and eye are sound,
not so contemptible as the young men say.
The hour has come to cook their lordships' mutton—
supper by daylight. Other amusements later,
with song and harping that adorn a feast."

He dropped his eyes and nodded, and the prince
Telemachus, true son of King Odysseus,
belted his sword on, clapped hand to his spear,
and with a clink and glitter of keen bronze
stood by his chair, in the forefront near his father.

Critical Thinking

Cite textual evidence to support your responses.

1. **Key Ideas and Details (a)** Who does Telemachus think Odysseus is when they first reunite? **(b) Compare and Contrast:** Compare Odysseus' emotions with those of Telemachus at their reunion.
2. **Key Ideas and Details (a)** Describe Antinous' treatment of Odysseus. **(b) Analyze Cause and Effect:** Why do you think Antinous treats Odysseus as he does?
3. **Integration of Knowledge and Ideas (a)** What does Odysseus tell Penelope about himself? **(b) Infer:** Why do you think Odysseus chooses not to reveal his identity to his wife? **(c) Take a Position:** Is it wrong for Odysseus to deceive Penelope? Explain your response.
4. **Integration of Knowledge and Ideas (a)** Which of Odysseus' responsibilities are revealed in this section? **(b)** Do you think he manages them heroically? Explain your response. *[Connect to the Big Question: Do heroes have responsibilities?]*

ASSESS

Answers

Critical Thinking

Before students respond, you may wish to have them write a brief objective summary of the selection. As they answer the questions below, remind them to support their answers with evidence from the text.

1. (a) Telemachus first thinks Odysseus is a beggar. Then, after Athena changes his appearance, Telemachus thinks he is a god. (b) Telemachus is at first confused and skeptical, then throws his arms around his father and begins to cry. Tears run down Odysseus' face as he reveals himself to his son.
2. (a) Antinous insults the apparent beggar and flings a stool at him. (b) **Possible response:** Antinous may despise people he regards as his inferiors.
3. (a) Odysseus initially tells Penelope that he is a wanderer with a past too painful to reveal. (b) **Possible response:** Students may suggest that Odysseus feels that he is not yet ready to trust that his wife has been loyal to him. Or, he may not want to reveal too much until he has executed his plan. (c) **Possible response:** Some students may say that it is always wrong to deceive a loved one. Others may say he is acting in their mutual best interest—that to execute his planned revenge successfully, it is best not to involve his wife.
4. (a) This section reveals Odysseus' responsibilities to keep his family safe and to defend his wife's honor. (b) **Possible response:** Yes, because he keeps his identity a secret, even from his wife. He probably wants to tell her, but he takes personal responsibility for her safety and decides to keep his plan secret.

Fluency

Distribute copies of pp. 1104–1105, and pair students. Have partners take turns reading paragraphs aloud. While one partner reads, the other should mark any words with which the student reading has difficulty. Circulate to monitor the fluency of students' reading. Collect students' marked-up copies of the page, and review difficult words and passages with the class. Look for these problem spots:

- If students have difficulty with multi-syllabic words, such as *disdainful* (line 1368), *effortlessly* (line 1375), or *contemptible* (line 1397), show them how to read the word parts one at a time and then blend the sounds.
- If students struggle with new sounds in Greek names such as Zeus, Cronus, and Telemachus, tell students not to worry too much about pronunciation as long as they know the identities of the characters.
- If students have difficulty with the word *clapped* (line 1403), practice oral cloze with the sentence. First, read the sentence with the word *clapped* omitted. Then, reread the sentence and ask students to "fill in the blank" with the word that makes the most sense.

27 Humanities

The Slaughter of the Suitors,
by N. C. Wyeth

In this painting of Odysseus' revenge, Wyeth adds drama and animation to an already exciting story. His depiction includes several pieces of Greek armor; the fighters' helmets and armor would likely have been made of bronze. Use the following questions for discussion.

1. Which lines from the *Odyssey* does this painting illustrate?

   Answer: It illustrates lines 1521–1530.

2. Who are the four figures on the right side of the painting? How do you know?

   Answer: They are Odysseus, Telemachus, Eumaeus, and the cowherd. They are wearing armor, have weapons, and are obviously winning the battle.

3. What details make the painting exciting?

   Possible responses: The flung spear, the spears about to be thrown, the positions of the men's bodies, and the dust of battle make the painting exciting. The giant columns in the background create a heroic mood for the scene.

27

The Slaughter of the Suitors from Homer's ***The Odyssey,*** N.C. Wyeth, Licensed by ASAP Worldwide.
Photo courtesy of the Archives of the American Illustrators Gallery, NYC.

Odysseus' Revenge

Now shrugging off his rags the wiliest[17] fighter of the islands
leapt and stood on the broad doorsill, his own bow in his hand.
He poured out at his feet a rain of arrows from the quiver
and spoke to the crowd:

"So much for that. Your clean-cut game is over.
Now watch me hit a target that no man has hit before,
if I can make this shot. Help me, Apollo."

He drew to his fist the cruel head of an arrow for Antinous
just as the young man leaned to lift his beautiful drinking cup,
embossed, two-handled, golden: the cup was in his fingers:
the wine was even at his lips: and did he dream of death?
How could he? In that revelry[18] amid his throng of friends
who would imagine a single foe—though a strong foe indeed—
29 could dare to bring death's pain on him and darkness on his eyes?
Odysseus' arrow hit him under the chin
and punched up to the feathers through his throat.

Backward and down he went, letting the winecup fall
from his shocked hand. Like pipes his nostrils jetted
crimson runnels, a river of mortal red,
and one last kick upset his table
knocking the bread and meat to soak in dusty blood.
Now as they craned to see their champion where he lay
the suitors jostled in uproar down the hall,
everyone on his feet. Wildly they turned and scanned
the walls in the long room for arms; but not a shield,
not a good ashen spear was there for a man to take and throw.
All they could do was yell in outrage at Odysseus:

"Foul! to shoot at a man! That was your last shot!"
"Your own throat will be slit for this!"
"Our finest lad is down!
You killed the best on Ithaca."
"Buzzards will tear your eyes out!"

17. **wiliest** (wīl´ ē əst) *adj.* craftiest; slyest.

◀ **Critical Viewing** Do you think this illustration presents the slaughter of the suitors accurately? Explain. **[Evaluate]**

18. **revelry** (rev´ əl rē) *n.* noisy festivity.

Reading Skill
Historical and Cultural Context
Does the manner in which Odysseus kills Antinous agree with your idea of a "fair fight"? Explain.

Whom does Odysseus kill first?

28 Critical Viewing

Possible response: Students may say that the suitors were sitting at tables. Others may say that Odysseus' bow and arrows should have been represented.

29 Reading Skill

Historical and Cultural Context

1. Remind students that Antinous is the most obnoxious suitor and the first to insult Odysseus. Penelope thinks he is the worst of the lot.
2. Tell students that there are different cultural responses to insults. **Ask** students to give examples of cultural responses to anger or insults that they have found in their reading.

   Possible response: Students may say that in some cultures, people fight duels in response to insults. In other cultures, insults may be forgiven with apologies or gifts.
3. **Ask** the Reading Skill question: Does the manner in which Odysseus kills Antinous agree with your idea of a "fair fight"? Explain.

   Possible responses: Students may say that the fight was not fair because Antinous did not get a chance to fight back. Other students may say that Odysseus acts fairly because Antinous insulted him and took advantage of his family and their hospitality.

30 Reading Check

Answer: Odysseus kills the suitor Antinous first.

Differentiated Instruction for Universal Access

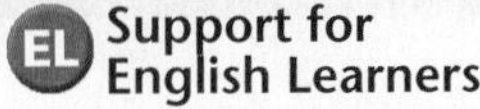

Support for English Learners

Students may need help reading and understanding Odysseus' battle with the suitors. Before addressing the Reading Skill question, preview the bracketed passage with ***Hear It!* Audio CD**. Have students read along as they listen. They may need particular help understanding how the descriptions break into the action. For example, explain that lines 1415–1418 break to show that Antinous does not dream that he has a deadly enemy in Odysseus' house.

Enrichment for Advanced Readers

To enrich the Reading Skill exercise, encourage students to research rules of warfare. For example, students might find information about ancient Greek customs that were observed during wartime, the various customs that once applied to dueling, or the Geneva Convention guidelines that apply to the treatment of prisoners today. Have students share their research with the rest of the class.

31 Reading Skill

Historical and Cultural Context

1. Review with students the indignities that Odysseus has suffered at the hands of the suitors. Remind them that they have abused his home, his wife, his child, and his hospitality.
2. **Ask** students to recall the Greeks' beliefs about the rules of hospitality and how the gods figure into those beliefs.

   Answer: Strangers to one's home should be treated with courtesy. The Greeks believed that gods could visit homes in disguise and would punish humans who did not treat them well.
3. **Ask** the Reading Skill question: What cultural values are revealed by Odysseus' explanation for his anger in lines 1441–1444?

   Possible responses: Odysseus is angry because the suitors have plundered his house and tried to claim his wife while he was gone. He also is angry because the suitors have dishonored the Greeks' religious laws regarding hospitality and the authority of the gods.

Vocabulary
contempt (kən tempt′) *n.* disdain or scorn

Reading Skill
Historical and Cultural Context What cultural values are revealed by Odysseus' explanation for his anger in lines 1441–1444?

19. **Eurymachus** (yōō ri′ mə kəs)

For they imagined as they wished—that it was a wild shot,
an unintended killing—fools, not to comprehend
they were already in the grip of death.
But glaring under his brows Odysseus answered:

"You yellow dogs, you thought I'd never make it
home from the land of Troy. You took my house to
plunder. . .
You dared bid for my wife while I was still alive.
31 Contempt was all you had for the gods who rule wide
heaven,
contempt for what men say of you hereafter.
Your last hour has come. You die in blood."

As they all took this in, sickly green fear
pulled at their entrails, and their eyes flickered
looking for some hatch or hideaway from death.
Eurymachus[19] alone could speak. He said:

"If you are Odysseus of Ithaca come back,
all that you say these men have done is true.
Rash actions, many here, more in the countryside.
But here he lies, the man who caused them all.
Antinous was the ringleader, he whipped us on
to do these things. He cared less for a marriage
than for the power Cronion has denied him
as king of Ithaca. For that
he tried to trap your son and would have killed him.
He is dead now and has his portion. Spare
your own people. As for ourselves, we'll make
restitution of wine and meat consumed,
and add, each one, a tithe of twenty oxen
with gifts of bronze and gold to warm your heart.
Meanwhile we cannot blame you for your anger."

Odysseus glowered under his black brows
and said:
"Not for the whole treasure of your fathers,
all you enjoy, lands, flocks, or any gold
put up by others, would I hold my hand.
There will be killing till the score is paid.
You forced yourselves upon this house. Fight your way out,
or run for it, if you think you'll escape death.

Vocabulary Development

CCSS Language 6

Dictionary Use

Point out the word *rash* in line 1451. Using a think-aloud process, model how to use context to infer the appropriate definition of the word. Say to students:

> I'm going to think aloud to show you how I would figure out the correct dictionary definition of *rash* by using context clues. The dictionary says that *rash* can mean: 1. (n) an eruption on the body; 2. (n) several instances of something in a short period of time; 3. (adj) hasty.
>
> First, I will look at the phrase in which *rash* appears to determine the word's part of speech. Based on the context, *rash* appears to be an adjective modifying the word *actions*. Eurymachus is discussing the immoral actions of the suitors while Odysseus was away from home. Definition 3, "hasty," fits because the suitors wasted no time before taking advantage of Odysseus's absence. Definitions 1 and 2 are the wrong part of speech, and they do not make sense in the original phrase.

I doubt one man of you skins by."

They felt their knees fail, and their hearts—but heard
Eurymachus for the last time rallying them.
"Friends," he said, "the man is implacable.
Now that he's got his hands on bow and quiver
he'll shoot from the big doorstone there
until he kills us to the last man.
Fight, I say,
let's remember the joy of it. Swords out!
Hold up your tables to deflect his arrows.
After me, everyone: rush him where he stands.
If we can budge him from the door, if we can pass
into the town, we'll call out men to chase him.
This fellow with his bow will shoot no more."

32 He drew his own sword as he spoke, a broadsword of fine bronze,
honed like a razor on either edge. Then crying hoarse and loud
he hurled himself at Odysseus. But the kingly man let fly
an arrow at that instant, and the quivering feathered butt
sprang to the nipple of his breast as the barb stuck in his liver.
The bright broadsword clanged down. He lurched and fell aside,
pitching across his table. His cup, his bread and meat,
were spilt and scattered far and wide, and his head slammed on the ground.
Revulsion, anguish in his heart, with both feet kicking out,
he downed his chair, while the shrouding wave of mist closed on his eyes.

Amphinomus now came running at Odysseus,
broadsword naked in his hand. He thought to make
the great soldier give way at the door.
But with a spear throw from behind Telemachus hit him
between the shoulders, and the lancehead drove
clear through his chest. He left his feet and fell
forward, thudding, forehead against the ground.
Telemachus swerved around him, leaving the long dark spear
planted in Amphinomus. If he paused to yank it out

Literary Analysis
Epic Simile Why is the comparison of Eurymachus' sharp sword to a razor only a simile and not an epic simile?

33 

What does Eurymachus offer Odysseus to try to calm his anger?

32 Literary Analysis

Epic Simile

1. Have students review the Literary Analysis section on p. 1087. **Ask** them to compare a typical simile with an epic simile and to give an example of each.

   Possible response: A typical simile makes a comparison to one thing. For example, "The arrow flew like a hawk." An epic simile is longer and more complex. A possible example is, "The arrow flew like a hawk. Its feathers glinted in the sun, and its point bit like a hawk's beak. It attacked its victim as a hawk clutches its prey."
2. Stress to students that not all similes in the *Odyssey* are epic similes.
3. Then, **ask** students the Literary Analysis question: Why is the comparison of Eurymachus' sharp sword to a razor only a simile and not an epic simile?
4. **Possible response:** This is a simile because it compares a sword to a razor. An epic simile, however, would run across several lines.

▶ **Monitor Progress:** Review students' graphic organizers to ensure that they understand the comparison and why it is not an epic simile.

▶ **Reteach:** Work with students to expand this simile into an epic simile. Brainstorm for words that might be used to extend the simile, including *blade, slice,* and *cut*.

33 Reading Check

Answer: He offers to make restitution of all the meat and wine consumed, plus gifts of oxen, bronze, and gold.

Differentiated Instruction for Universal Access

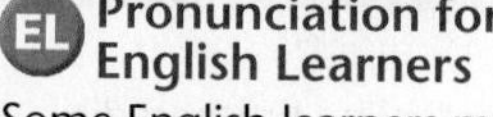

EL Pronunciation for English Learners

Some English learners may have difficulty pronouncing the initial "h" consonants. Instead of saying *hearts, hands,* and *heard*, for example, they might drop the "h" and say *'earts, 'ands* and *'eard.* The following strategies will help students with the pronunciation of the initial *h* sound.

- Write the following words on the board: *heart, hands, heard,* and *his*. Pronounce each word, emphasizing the *h* sound. Then, point to each word and have students pronounce each. Make sure they correctly pronounce the *h*.
- Direct students' attention to lines 1484–1486 on p.1109. Have students work with partners to read aloud these lines from the selection, making sure to pronounce the initial *h* sound correctly, when it appears. Circulate and listen to students, and provide corrective feedback as needed.

34 Reading Skill

Historical and Cultural Context

1. Discuss with students the ways that different cultures emphasize that children should honor their parents. You may want to cite the example of ancestor worship in Chinese culture or the biblical commandment to "honor thy father and mother."
2. Have students **describe** how Telemachus responds to his father's return and what those actions reveal about him.

   Possible response: Telemachus weeps with joy when his father reveals himself, and he has obeyed his father's commands to prepare for battling the suitors. Telemachus' response shows his love and respect for his father.
3. **Ask** the Reading Skill question: What cultural values are reflected in Telemachus' behavior toward his father?

   Possible response: Telemachus shows respect for his father as he fights beside him in battle and hurries to bring him the weapons that he needs for the fight.

someone might jump him from behind or cut him down with a sword
at the moment he bent over. So he ran—ran from the tables
to his father's side and halted, panting, saying:

"Father let me bring you a shield and spear,
a pair of spears, a helmet.
I can arm on the run myself; I'll give
outfits to Eumaeus and this cowherd.
Better to have equipment."

Said Odysseus:
"Run then, while I hold them off with arrows
as long as the arrows last. When all are gone
if I'm alone they can dislodge me."

34 Quick
upon his father's word Telemachus
ran to the room where spears and armor lay.
He caught up four light shields, four pairs of spears,
four helms of war high-plumed with flowing manes,
and ran back, loaded down, to his father's side.
He was the first to pull a helmet on
and slide his bare arm in a buckler strap.
The servants armed themselves, and all three took their stand
beside the master of battle.

While he had arrows
he aimed and shot, and every shot brought down
one of his huddling enemies.
But when all barbs had flown from the bowman's fist,
he leaned his bow in the bright entryway
beside the door, and armed: a four-ply shield
hard on his shoulder, and a crested helm,
horsetailed, nodding stormy upon his head,
then took his tough and bronze-shod spears. . . .

Reading Skill Historical and Cultural Context What cultural values are reflected in Telemachus' behavior toward his father?

Aided by Athena, Odysseus, Telemachus, Eumaeus, and other faithful herdsmen kill all the suitors.

And Odysseus looked around him, narrow-eyed,
for any others who had lain hidden
while death's black fury passed.

Vocabulary Development

CCSS Language 6

Graphic Organizers

1. To help students explore the differences and similarities of a *sword* and a *spear*, create a Venn diagram.
2. First, draw two overlapping circles on the board or on a piece of chart paper. Write *sword* at the top of the left-hand circle; write *spear* at the top of the right-hand circle; and write *both* at the top of the intersecting portion.
3. Elicit definitions of *sword* and *spear* as they are used on this page. Then, guide students in brainstorming for differences and similarities between the two objects. The finished diagram should look like this:

sword
handle
used against other swords
kept in hand when used
sharp along entire shaft

both
pointy end
weapons
used in warfare

spear
used for fishing and hunting
only sharp at end
sometimes thrown when used

In blood and dust
he saw that crowd all fallen, many and many slain.

Think of a catch that fishermen haul in to a half-moon bay
in a fine-meshed net from the whitecaps of the sea:
how all are poured out on the sand, in throes for the salt sea,
twitching their cold lives away in Helios' fiery air:
so lay the suitors heaped on one another.

Penelope's Test

Penelope tests Odysseus to prove he really is her husband.

Greathearted Odysseus, home at last,
was being bathed now by Eurynome
and rubbed with golden oil, and clothed again
in a fresh tunic and a cloak. Athena
lent him beauty, head to foot. She made him
taller, and massive, too, with crisping hair
in curls like petals of wild hyacinth
but all red-golden. Think of gold infused
on silver by a craftsman, whose fine art
Hephaestus[20] taught him, or Athena: one
whose work moves to delight: just so she lavished
beauty over Odysseus' head and shoulders.
He sat then in the same chair by the pillar,
facing his silent wife, and said:

"Strange woman,
the immortals of Olympus made you hard,
harder than any. Who else in the world
would keep aloof as you do from her husband
if he returned to her from years of trouble,
cast on his own land in the twentieth year?

Nurse, make up a bed for me to sleep on.
Her heart is iron in her breast."

Penelope
spoke to Odysseus now. She said:

"Strange man,
if man you are . . . This is no pride on my part

Literary Analysis
Epic Simile Which aspects of the slain suitors' appearance does the epic simile in lines 1535–1539 emphasize?

Literary Analysis
Epic Simile Which details in the epic simile in lines 1547–1551 compare Odysseus' hair to a work of art?

20. **Hephaestus** (hē fes´ təs) god of fire and metalworking.

Who helps Odysseus defeat the suitors?

35 Literary Analysis

Epic Simile

1. **Ask** the Literary Analysis question: Which aspects of the slain suitors' appearance does the epic simile in lines 1535–1539 emphasize?

   Possible response: The image of the fish flopping on the deck of a ship emphasizes the suitors' struggling and writhing in their final moments.
2. Point out to students that the comparison of the suitors to dying fish does not serve to make their deaths glorious. Homer does not try to immortalize the suitors.

36 Literary Analysis

Epic Simile

1. Discuss the contrast between Odysseus' appearance and his earlier appearance as a beggar. Ask students why they think Homer emphasizes Odysseus' physical attractiveness as this point.

   Possible response: Homer is drawing a sharp contrast to Odysseus' previous guise as a beggar. Odysseus is being prepared almost as a new bridegroom, an appropriate comparison as he approaches Penelope to renew their marriage.
2. **Ask** the second Literary Analysis question: Which details in the epic simile in lines 1547–1551 compare Odysseus' hair to a work of art?

   Possible responses: The comparison to gold and silver, as well as the term *craftsman* and the references to Hephaestus and Athena, all compare Odysseus' hair to artwork.

37 Reading Check

Answer: Athena, Telemachus, Eumaeus, and herdsmen help Odysseus defeat the suitors.

Differentiated Instruction for Universal Access

Strategy for Less Proficient Readers
Review with students some of the critical details that take place in Odysseus' slaughter of the suitors, beginning with the death of Antinous. Have students use a **Series-of-Events Chain** (***Graphic Organizer Transparencies***, p. 221) to plot important moments in the story, including Odysseus' use of his bow and arrows, Eurymachus' offer of reparations, and Telemachus' coming to his father's aid.

EL Support for English Learners
Preview with English Learners some of the vocabulary that relates to Odysseus' battle with the suitors. The specific vocabulary can include words that relate to weapons, such as *broadsword, spear, armor, shields,* and *helms.* It also can include poetic phrases such as "bowman's fist" and the "master of battle."

38 Literary Analysis

Epic Simile

1. Read aloud the bracketed passage. Then, **ask** students to identify the items that are being compared.

   Answer: The trunk of the olive tree is compared to a pillar.

2. **Ask** students to list any supporting details about the appearance or other qualities of the pillar.

   Answer: No other details are included.

3. **Ask** students to respond to the Literary Analysis prompt: Explain why the simile comparing the olive trunk to a pillar is not an epic simile.

   Answer: The text compares the two items but does not draw out the explanation by including other details. The comparison is mentioned only once and is not extended.

nor scorn for you—not even wonder, merely.
I know so well how you—how he—appeared
boarding the ship for Troy. But all the same . . .

Make up his bed for him, Eurycleia.
Place it outside the bedchamber my lord
built with his own hands. Pile the big bed
with fleeces, rugs, and sheets of purest linen."

With this she tried him to the breaking point,
and he turned on her in a flash raging:

"Woman, by heaven you've stung me now!
Who dared to move my bed?
No builder had the skill for that—unless
a god came down to turn the trick. No mortal
in his best days could budge it with a crowbar.
There is our pact and pledge, our secret sign,
built into that bed—my handiwork
and no one else's!

Literary Analysis
Epic Simile Explain why the simile comparing the olive trunk to a pillar is not an epic simile.

38 An old trunk of olive
grew like a pillar on the building plot,
and I laid out our bedroom round that tree,
lined up the stone walls, built the walls and roof,
gave it a doorway and smooth-fitting doors.
Then I lopped off the silvery leaves and branches,
hewed and shaped that stump from the roots up
into a bedpost, drilled it, let it serve
as model for the rest. I planed them all,
inlaid them all with silver, gold and ivory,
and stretched a bed between—a pliant web
of oxhide thongs dyed crimson.
There's our sign!
I know no more. Could someone else's hand
have sawn that trunk and dragged the frame away?"

Their secret! as she heard it told, her knees
grew tremulous and weak, her heart failed her.
With eyes brimming tears she ran to him,
throwing her arms around his neck, and kissed him,
murmuring:
"Do not rage at me, Odysseus!

Vocabulary Development

Vocabulary Knowledge Rating

When students have completed reading and discussing the *Odyssey*, Part 2, have them take out their **Vocabulary Knowledge Rating Chart** for this selection. Read the words aloud once more and have students rate their knowledge of the words again in the After Reading column. Clarify any words that are still problematic. Have students write their own definition and example or sentence in the appropriate column. Then have students complete the Vocabulary Practice activities at the end of the selection. Encourage students to use the words in further discussion and written work about the *Odyssey*. Remind them that they will be accountable for these words on the **Selection Test, *Unit 6 Resources***, pp. 59–61 or 62–64.

◀ **Critical Viewing** How does this image convey the events in text? **[Connect]**

No one ever matched your caution! Think
what difficulty the gods gave: they denied us
life together in our prime and flowering years,
kept us from crossing into age together.
Forgive me, don't be angry. I could not
welcome you with love on sight! I armed myself
long ago against the frauds of men,
impostors who might come—and all those many
whose underhanded ways bring evil on! . . .
But here and now, what sign could be so clear
as this of our own bed?
No other man has ever laid eyes on it—
only my own slave, Actoris, that my father
sent with me as a gift—she kept our door.
You make my stiff heart know that I am yours."

How does Odysseus react to Penelope's attitude toward him?

39 Critical Viewing

Possible response: The picture shows a woman weaving while a man mistreats a beggar. The woman appears to be Penelope; the beggar is Odysseus in disguise; and the man appears to be a bully like Antinous.

40 Reading Check

Answer: Odysseus describes Penelope as hard and aloof.

Concept Connector

Anticipation Guide

Have students return to their Anticipation Guides and respond to the statements again in the After Reading column. They may do this individually or in groups. Then, lead a class discussion, probing for what students have learned that confirms or invalidates each statement. Encourage students to cite specific evidence from the text to support their responses.

Writing About the Big Question

Have students compare their responses to the sentence starter they completed before reading the selection with their ideas afterwards. Ask them to explain whether their thoughts have changed.

Reading Skill Graphic Organizer

Ask students to review the graphic organizers they completed to chart historical/cultural details. Show them **Reading Skill Graphic Organizer A** (***Graphic Organizer Transparencies***, p. 187) as an example. Then, have students share their graphic organizers.

41 Literary Analysis

Epic Simile

1. **Ask** students the Literary Analysis question.
2. **Answer:** The comparison to "rough water," "gale winds," and "tons of sea" recalls the many tough times that Odysseus faced—and his near drowning—before he returned home.

ASSESS

Answers

Critical Thinking

Remind students to support their answers with evidence from the text.

1. (a) Odysseus is helped by Athena, Eumaeus, Telemachus, and a cowherd. (b) Odysseus is comfortable with both goddesses and swineherds.
2. (a) Odysseus asks Telemachus to move the armor so the suitors will not have access to it. (b) When the suitors begin to fight, they have no weapons.
3. (a) Penelope lets Odysseus think that she has moved his bed. Odysseus passes her test when he reveals that the bedpost was hewn from a live olive tree and could not be moved. (b) She has grown cautious and must be sure. (c) The happiness of the reunited couple is shadowed by the trials of the past.
4. Odysseus' planning of his revenge is consistent with the cunning and guile he has shown elsewhere. His success in battle is not surprising. The harshness of his revenge recalls his treatment of Cyclops.
5. (a) **Possible response:** Odysseus kills the suitors in part because he has a responsibility to protect his family. However, it also seems that Odysseus kills the men for his own pleasure, or to appease his anger. (b) **Possible response:** Students are likely to feel that Odysseus's revenge is justified because the men clearly were unconcerned about his wife. They just wanted money and power. In addition, the suitors were going to kill Odysseus' son.

Literary Analysis
Epic Simile In what way does this epic simile recall the dangers Odysseus faced on his journey home?

Now from his breast into his eyes the ache
of longing mounted, and he wept at last,
his dear wife, clear and faithful, in his arms,
longed for as the sunwarmed earth is longed for by a swimmer
41 spent in rough water where his ship went down
under Poseidon's blows, gale winds and tons of sea.
Few men can keep alive through a big surf
to crawl, clotted with brine, on kindly beaches
in joy, in joy, knowing the abyss[21] behind:
and so she too rejoiced, her gaze upon her husband,
her white arms round him pressed as though forever.

21. **abyss** (ə bis′) *n.* ocean depths.

The Ending

Odysseus is reunited with his father. Athena commands that peace prevail between Odysseus and the relatives of the slain suitors. Odysseus has regained his family and his kingdom.

Critical Thinking

Cite textual evidence to support your responses.

1. **Key Ideas and Details (a)** When Odysseus returns to his home, who helps him? **(b) Interpret:** What does the varying social status of Odysseus' helpers suggest about his character?
2. **Key Ideas and Details (a)** What planning does Odysseus do before he battles the suitors? **(b) Analyze:** How does his planning help him defeat his opponents?
3. **Key Ideas and Details (a)** What is Penelope's test, and how does Odysseus pass it? **(b) Infer:** Why does Penelope feel the need to test Odysseus even though he has abandoned his disguise? **(c) Interpret:** Is the mood after the test altogether happy? Explain.
4. **Integration of Knowledge and Ideas** Are Odysseus' actions in dealing with the suitors consistent with his actions in earlier episodes of the epic? Support your response.
5. **Integration of Knowledge and Ideas (a)** Do you think Odysseus kills the suitors to fulfill his responsibilities? Explain. **(b)** Is Odysseus' revenge justified? Why or why not? ***[Connect to the Big Question: Do heroes have responsibilities?]***

Assessment Resources

Unit 6 Resources

- L1 L2 EL **Selection Test A,** pp. 59–61. Administer Test A to less advanced readers.
- L3 L4 EL **Selection Test B,** pp. 62–64. Administer Test B to on-level and more advanced students.
- L3 L4 **Open-Book Test,** pp. 56–58. As an alternative, give the Open-Book Test.
- All **Customizable Test Bank**
- All **Self-tests** Students may prepare for the **Selection Test** by taking the **Self-test** online.

All assessment resources are available at **www.PHLitOnline.com.**

After You Read *from the* Odyssey, Part 2

Literary Analysis: Epic Simile

1. Craft and Structure (a) Using a chart like the one shown, analyze the **epic simile** in lines 1613–1624.

Items Being Compared	Details of Epic Simile	Purpose

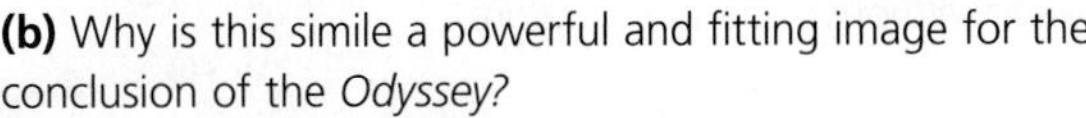

(b) Why is this simile a powerful and fitting image for the conclusion of the *Odyssey?*

Reading Skill: Historical and Cultural Context

2. (a) What attitudes and values are reflected in Odysseus' actions toward the suitors? **(b)** What do his actions suggest about the **cultural and historical context** of Homer's *Odyssey* and the attitudes and values of ancient Greeks? Explain your answer.

3. (a) Name one of Odysseus' cultural beliefs, attitudes, or practices that is similar to an idea or a tradition in your own culture. **(b)** Name one that is significantly different. **(c)** Are Odysseus' values unique to his culture, or are they universal? Explain.

Vocabulary

Acquisition and Use Indicate whether each statement is *True* or *False*. Explain your answers. Then, revise false sentences to make them true.

1. People sometimes *dissemble* in order to hide their true feelings.
2. An event that is common and predictable evokes *incredulity.*
3. If road signs are *bemusing* drivers, the signs are working well.
4. A good judge is one with a strong sense of *equity.*
5. A pep band should play *maudlin* songs if it wants to excite fans.
6. Successful salespeople always show *contempt* for customers.

Word Study Use the context of the sentences and what you know about the **Latin prefix *dis-*** to explain your answer to each question.

1. If a reporter *discloses* the source of information, does she tell where she got the information?
2. If you are *disheartened* by some news, do you feel better?

Word Study

The **Latin prefix *dis-*** means "away," "apart," or "not."

Apply It Explain how the prefix *dis-* contributes to the meanings of these words. Consult a dictionary if necessary.

dispute
dishevel
disembark

ASSESS

Answers

Literary Analysis

1. (a) **Sample response: Items Being Compared:** Odysseus' longing for his wife compared to a swimmer's longing for the shore. **Details of Epic Simile:** "rough water," "Poseidon's blows," "gale winds and tons of sea," "big surf," "clotted with brine," "kindly beaches." **Purpose:** to show the intensity of Odysseus' feelings as he returns to Penelope. (b) The image indicates that being with Penelope is another life-saving rescue.

For other sample answers, see ***Graphic Organizer Transparencies,* Literary Analysis Graphic Organizer A**, p. 189, and the **Additional Answers** section.

Reading Skill

2. (a) His actions show that he values honor—his and Penelope's—above all; he will not accept apologies, but requires that the suitors battle to the death. (b) Greeks honored battle, especially to defend or uphold one's family, home, or honor. The Greeks did not appear to value negotiation or reparation for wrongs that had been done.
3. **Possible responses:** (a) Odysseus believed in the practice of hospitality. (b) The practice of settling disputes through violence is not accepted today. (c) Many of Odysseus' values are universal, such as that of hospitality and his longing for home. His belief that the gods participate in human affairs may be unique to his culture.

Vocabulary

Acquisition and Use

Sample answers:

1. True; If people do not want their true feelings known, they dissemble, or disguise, them.
2. False; a usual event does not provoke attention. An event that is uncommon evokes incredulity.
3. False; bemused drivers will not drive well. If road signs are bemusing, they will distract drivers.
4. True; a judge with a sense of equity would treat people fairly.

Continued from right column

5. False; maudlin songs would make people feel sad. A band should play maudlin songs if it wants a crowd to be depressed.
6. False; people who treat customers with contempt would not succeed. Salespeople who show contempt for customers will lose business.

Word Study

Sample answers:

1. Yes, the prefix *dis-* can mean "not" and *disclose* means "reveal or not keep secret." When someone *discloses* something, he or she reveals it.
2. No, the prefix *dis-* can mean "not" and *disheartened* means "without or not with spirit or morale." If something causes you to feel *disheartened,* you are upset by it.

Word Study: Apply It

Sample answers: A *dispute* is an argument in which people's views are apart or different. When something is *disheveled* it is away from where it belongs, or messy. When you *disembark,* you leave, or go away from, a ship or airplane.

EXTEND/ASSESS

Answers

Conventions

Introduce the skill, using the instruction on the student page.

Think Aloud: Model the Skill

Post the sentence: "When he arrived, the crowd applauded." Model the skill of identifying complex and complex-compound sentences. Say:

> This sentence is complex. It has a dependent clause—"When he arrived"—and an independent clause—"the crowd applauded."
>
> To make this a compound-complex sentence, I need to add another independent clause. For example, I write, "When he arrived, the crowd applauded and the girls screamed."

PH WRITING COACH Grade 9

Students will find instruction on and practice with complex and compound-complex sentences in Chapter 15, Section 3.

Practice A

1. complex; IC: Penelope . . . husband; SC: Because . . . disguised
2. compound-complex; IC: (1) the suitors were amazed (2) they stopped laughing; SC: When . . . the bow
3. compound-complex; IC: (1) Telemachus . . . sword; (2) he stood . . . father; SC: while they fought
4. complex; IC: Odysseus . . . of them; SC: Although . . . suitors

Reading Application

C: Held back too long, . . . as he embraced his son. CC: I marvel that they leave this hound . . . when he was young.

Practice B

1. Argus recognized Odysseus before he died.
2. Odysseus strung the bow while Telemachus looked on.
3. After Odysseus tested the bow, the suitors mocked him and they called him names.
4. The suitors were awed when he shot the arrow and it passed through each ring.

Writing Application

Complex sentences must have only one independent clause. Compound-complex sentences must have at least two independent clauses.

PERFORMANCE TASKS

Integrated Language Skills

from the Odyssey, Part 2

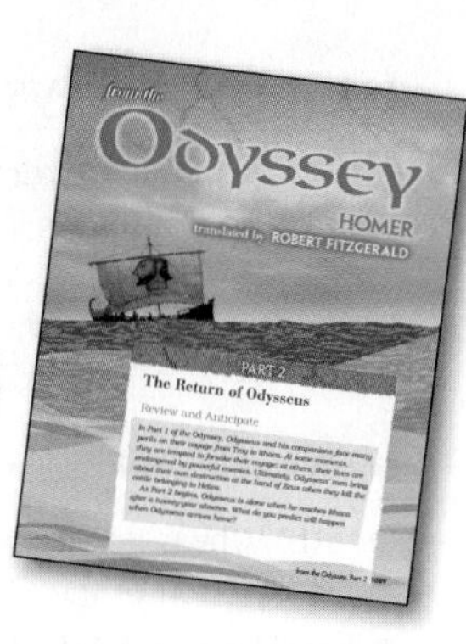

Conventions: Complex and Compound-Complex Sentences

Sentences can be classified by the number of dependent and independent clauses they contain. An *independent clause* contains a subject and a verb and can stand alone as a sentence. A *dependent* or *subordinate clause* contains a subject and a verb but cannot stand as a sentence. It begins with a subordinate conjunction such as *when, although, because, before, since,* or *while.*

A **complex sentence** consists of one independent clause and one or more subordinate clauses.
A **compound-complex sentence** consists of two or more independent clauses and one or more subordinate clauses.

As with compound sentences, the independent clauses in compound-complex sentences are connected by a comma and a coordinating conjunction.

Complex sentence	Compound-complex sentence
When the lights came on, he saw the audience.	When the lights came on, he saw the audience, and he waved to his parents.

Practice A Identify each sentence as complex or compound-complex. Identify the independent clauses and the subordinate clauses.

1. Because Odysseus was disguised, Penelope did not recognize her husband.
2. When Odysseus strung the bow, the suitors were amazed, and they stopped laughing.
3. Telemachus grabbed a sword, and he stood by his father while they fought.
4. Although there were many suitors, Odysseus killed every one of them.

Reading Application In the *Odyssey,* find one complex sentence and one compound-complex sentence.

Practice B Combine the simple sentences to form one new sentence, as directed by the sentence type indicated in parentheses.

1. Argus recognized Odysseus. He died. (complex)
2. Odysseus strung the bow. Telemachus looked on. (complex)
3. Odysseus tested the bow. The suitors mocked him. They called him names. (compound-complex)
4. He shot the arrow. It passed through each ring. The suitors were awed. (compound-complex)

Writing Application Write six simple sentences about the *Odyssey.* Choose from among these sentences to build two complex sentences and two compound-complex sentences.

PH WRITING COACH Further instruction and practice are available in *Prentice Hall Writing Coach.*

Extend the Lesson

Sentence Modeling

Draw students' attention to the following sentence from the *Odyssey*, Part 2:

> *"When he had spoken, down he sat."*

Ask students what they notice about the sentence. Elicit from them that the sentence is a complex sentence. Have students identify the independent and dependent clauses. Then, ask what else they notice. (Here the word order of the independent clause is unusual; the adverb comes before the subject and verb instead of after the verb. This gives the sentence a poetic feel, appropriate to the style of the epic poem.)

Have students imitate the sentence in sentences on topics of their own choosing, matching each grammatical and stylistic feature discussed. Have volunteers read their sentences aloud to the class.

Writing

Informative Text Write a short **biography** of Odysseus based on details in the *Odyssey.* Present the basic facts of his life and adventures, and hold your reader's attention by describing the dramatic situations in detail.

- List events in the *Odyssey* that are suitable for your biography. Focus on events that reveal the character of Odysseus.
- Include quotations from the epic to add detail and depth.
- Share your biography with classmates, and compare the events you each chose to include. In your discussion, consider what makes some events more significant than others.

Grammar Application As you write your biography, use a variety of sentence types, including complex and compound-complex sentences.

Common Core State Standards

L.9-10.1; W.9-10.4; SL.9-10.1, SL.9-10.3
[For the full wording of the standards, see page 1086.]

Writing Workshop: *Work in Progress*

Prewriting for Technical Document From your Task List, choose a topic for your Technical Document. Think about the steps in the task and the order in which the instructions should be presented. Make an outline to plan your document. Save this Organizational Outline in your portfolio.

Use this prewriting activity to prepare for the **Writing Workshop** on page 1138.

Speaking and Listening

Comprehension and Collaboration Conduct a **debate** to decide whether Odysseus should be prosecuted for the murders of Penelope's suitors. Follow these steps to effectively practice the art of persuasion and debate:

- Divide into two opposing teams.
- With teammates, prepare a rational argument expressing your position. Be sure to support this logical assertion with details from the *Odyssey.*
- Plan an introduction to your remarks, a body that includes your arguments, and a conclusion that summarizes your position.
- Consider techniques to enhance your arguments. For example, you might use changes in tone and rhythm, gestures, and eye contact.
- During the debate, listen carefully and evaluate the opposing team's facts and reasoning so you can respond effectively.

Present your argument before the class, and ask your audience to decide which team was more persuasive.

PHLit Online!
www.PHLitOnline.com
- Interactive graphic organizers
- Grammar tutorial
- Interactive journals

EXTEND/ASSESS

Writing

1. Review the assignment, using the instruction on the student page.
2. To guide students in writing a biography, give them **Support for Writing,** p. 54 in ***Unit 6 Resources.***
3. To evaluate students' informative texts, use the Biography rubric, pp. 252–253 in ***Professional Development Guidebook.***

Grammar Application

Have students check to see that they have used complex and compound-complex sentences correctly.

Writing Workshop
Work in Progress

Have students save their completed Organizational Outline in their portfolios. They will use the outline later as they complete the Writing Workshop assignment (see pp. 1138–1143).

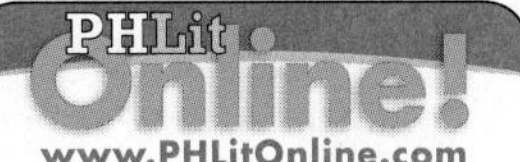

Students will find instruction and practice for nonfiction narrative writing in Chapters 2 and 5.

Six Traits Focus

✓	Ideas	✓	Word Choice
	Organization		Sentence Fluency
✓	Voice		Conventions

Speaking and Listening

1. Review the assignment, using the instruction on the student page.
2. To support students' work on the assignment, have them complete the **Support for Extend Your Learning** page (***Unit 6 Resources,*** p. 55).

Teaching Resources

Unit 6 Resources
- L3 L4 EL **Integrated Language Skills: Grammar,** p. 53
- L3 L4 EL **Support for Writing,** p. 54
- L3 L4 **Support for Extend Your Learning,** p. 55
- L4 **Enrichment,** p. 52

Enriched Online Student Edition
Available under After You Read for this selection:
- All **Interactive Grammar Tutorial**
- L3 L4 **Internet Research Activity**

Professional Development Guidebook
Rubrics for Self-Assessment: Biography, pp. 252–253

PHLit Online! All print and digital resources are available at **www.PHLitOnline.com.** Online resources accessible by students are noted on the student page.

MONITORING PROGRESS

Using the Test Practice

In this two-page Test Practice, students apply the reading skill for the first half of Unit 6 to a passage of fiction and a passage of nonfiction.

Review the skill, understanding cultural and historical context, then administer the test. For more guidance, consult the ***Classroom Strategies and Teaching Routines*** card, **Administering Timed Tests.**

ASSESS

Answers

Answers With Explanations

1. **D**—The references to the Web, laser eye surgery, and e-mail imply that this passage is set in the present. ***Incorrect answers:*** A—A future setting would be likely include more advanced technology. B—Since Sue is using the family laptop, she is probably at home. C—The Web and e-mail were not in use in the 1950s.
2. **A**—These two activities are dependent on technology. ***Incorrect answers:*** B—Only the laptop is a form of technology. C—Only e-mail is a form of technology. D—By comparing treatment of mononucleosis to laser-eye surgery, Sue shows an interest in technology, but understanding the need for rest does not show interest in technology.
3. **B**—The passage says that Sue found that everything required extra effort, which implies inconvenience. ***Incorrect answers:*** A—The passage does not mention punishment. C—Sue is not afraid, merely bored. D—This option suggests enjoyment, which Sue does not seem to be experiencing.
4. **B**—The fact that Sue did research shows that she is willing to question doctors' advice. ***Incorrect answers:*** A—Sue does not imply this. C—same explanation as for A. D—Sue would not be doing research on the Web if she held this belief.

Test Practice: Reading

Cultural and Historical Context

Fiction Selection

Directions: *Read the selection. Then, answer the questions.*

Sue rolled out of bed and crept over to the family laptop. Since she had been diagnosed with mononucleosis—the "kissing disease" as her best friend Lisa kept teasing her—everything required extra effort. Updating her weblog was the only thing she could find energy to do.

"Mono, Day 9," she typed. "I cannot believe that I've missed so much school. I'm so glad it is almost summer vacation. The doctor tells me to rest and drink fluids; these days, when people can get laser eye surgery, you would think they would be able to do more for this. The Web says the same thing, though, so I guess the doctor's right. My doctor is usually correct, but doing extra research cannot hurt. At least I have the computer to keep me busy. E-mail me if you want. I want to know what is going on with everyone at school." With that, Sue slid back into bed for a nap.

1. Based on the cultural and historical context of this passage, a reader can infer that Sue probably lives—

A. in the future.
B. at a boarding school.
C. in the 1950s.
D. in the present day.

2. Which details suggest that Sue values technology?

A. She keeps a weblog and she researches her illness online.
B. She knows what a laptop is and she is glad it is almost summer vacation.
C. She enjoys e-mail and she follows her doctor's advice.
D. She questions the lack of available treatments and she knows she should rest.

3. Based on the details in this passage, one can infer that Sue believes her illness is—

A. punishment for a poor decision.
B. an inconvenience.
C. a terrifying ordeal.
D. an exciting adventure.

4. Based on the details in this passage, one can conclude Sue believes that a doctor's advice—

A. never leads to a quick recovery.
B. can and should be questioned.
C. is usually confusing.
D. should be trusted in all cases.

Writing for Assessment

Imagine that Sue lived in ancient times. Write a paragraph describing how the experience of having mononucleosis might be different. Use details from this passage as a guide.

Writing for Assessment

Students' paragraphs should note that the treatment for mononucleosis in ancient times might have been the same, but the patient with the illness might have had more direct care from family members. Also, the patient would not use a computer for entertainment.

Strategies for Test Taking

Remind students that to infer means to guess about a fact based on the information given in a passage, without having the fact stated directly. For example, in question 1, the passage never states the time frame for the story, but the references to modern-day technology such as the Web, e-mail, and laser surgery allow readers to infer that the selection is set in modern times.

Nonfiction Selection

Directions: *Read the selection. Then, answer the questions.*

Between 1347 and 1353, the Black Death, or bubonic plague, killed one out of every three people in Europe. The disease was first spread by fleas on rats. Rats were common in Europe at the time and few people paid attention to them. People threw garbage into the streets, and the rats thrived in these unsanitary conditions. The plague could also be spread from person to person through the air. Therefore, most doctors would not treat people who were infected. The few who did treat people wore a leather mask with a beak filled with herbs. They believed the herbs would keep them from being infected. Doctors often treated patients by "bleeding" them. They thought that draining excess blood would balance bodily fluids and make the patient better. This practice made the problem worse. In all, over 25 million people died from the Black Death in Europe alone—more than in any war in history.

1. Which of the following details help you infer that people at the time did not know the source of the plague?

A. People allowed conditions in which rats could thrive.
B. The plague could be spread from person to person through the air.
C. Doctors would not treat infected people.
D. The plague was called the Black Death.

2. Which detail suggests that people at the time did not understand the connection between filth and disease?

A. The plague was first spread by fleas.
B. People threw garbage into the streets.
C. Doctors thought spices prevented infection.
D. Doctors wore masks to treat patients.

3. Which of the following is *not* a logical assumption about Europe in the 1300s, based on details in the passage?

A. People were not prepared for a plague like the Black Death.
B. Antibiotic medicines were not available.
C. People did not fully understand how diseases spread.
D. People did not trust doctors.

4. Based on the passage, what can you conclude about medical science during the plague?

A. It was less advanced than medical science today.
B. It was the same as medical science today.
C. Doctors only used herbs to treat illness.
D. Doctors did not believe that herbs had any use in medicine.

Writing for Assessment

Connecting Across Texts
The Black Death was especially terrible because people misunderstood its causes and treatments. How is people's understanding of illness related to the time and place in which they live? Support your answer using details from both passages and your own knowledge.

www.PHLitOnline.com

- Online practice
- Instant feedback

Strategies for Special-Needs Students
Suggest that students use charts to take notes for the writing question. They should use one column to note knowledge and beliefs about the origin and course of disease in one column and corresponding details about medicine in another column. Or, they could use a chart to list facts about medical care in the 1300s in one column and facts about medical care today in another. This method of prewriting gives them examples they can use in their writing.

EL Strategies for English Learners
Remind students to reject answer options that do not relate to the question. Have them read the four options for question 1. Then, ask them to state whether each answer option logically addresses the source of the plague. (A: yes; B: in part, but not the original cause; C: no; D: no.) Explain that in this way, they can narrow their choices to only two possible answers.

ASSESS

Answers

Answers with Explanations

1. A—If people had known that rats played a part in the plague, they would have paid more attention to them. ***Incorrect answers:*** B—This is true but it is not the source of the plague. C—This statement does not address the source of the plague. D—same explanation as for C.
2. B—If people had known that filth is a breeding ground for disease, they probably would not have done this. ***Incorrect answers:*** A—While true, this statement does not address the connection between filth and disease. C—same explanation as for A. D—same explanation as for A.
3. D—The passage does not suggest that people mistrusted doctors, only that doctors were helpless in the face of the plague. ***Incorrect answers:*** A—The passage clearly shows that people were not ready for such a plague. B—Since doctors treated people by bleeding them, rather than by giving medicines, this is a logical assumption. C—If people had understood how diseases spread, doctors would have known that herbs would not prevent them from becoming infected.
4. A—The lack of understanding of the causes of disease and the lack of medicines suggest this conclusion. B—The passage implies the opposite. C—Doctors used herbs and bleeding. D—Doctors did use herbs.

Writing for Assessment

Students' responses might draw on examples from the 1300s to show how the limits of knowledge can prevent effective treatment, contrasting that with advances known today based on deeper knowledge of physical processes.

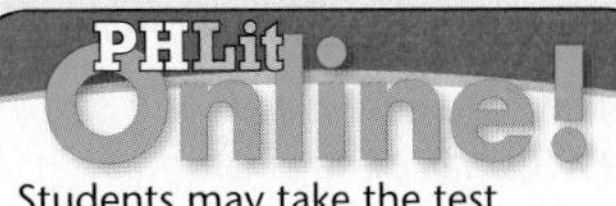

Students may take the test in interactive format with instant feedback online at **www.PHLitOnline.com.**

PREACH

Common Core State Standards

- Reading Informational Text 6
- Writing 1.a
- Language 4.b, 6

Reading Skill

1. Introduce the skill, using the instruction on the student page.
2. Review the chart.
3. Tell students that they will identify the characteristics of various types of texts, including a commentary and a movie review.

Think Aloud: Model the Skill

Model the skill of identifying characteristics of various types of texts. Say to students:

When I read a text, I ask myself what it is about. Does it give a firsthand account? Does it report about an event using accounts of witnesses? Does it give an opinion about an event? Answering these questions helps me evaluate what I am reading.

Multidraft Reading

Have students follow a multidraft reading protocol.

- **First reading**—Have students read to identify key ideas and details.
- **Second reading**—Have students read to identify the structure of the text.
- **Third reading**—Have students read to integrate knowledge and ideas by connecting the text to the world, their own experiences, and other texts.

Content-Area Vocabulary

1. Have students say each word.
2. Next, use each word in a sentence that defines it.
3. Finally, repeat your definitional sentence or a similar sentence with the word missing and have the class "fill in the blank" chorally.

Reading for Information

Analyzing Argumentative Texts

Commentary

Movie Review

Reading Skill: Identify Characteristics of Various Types of Texts

To analyze an informational text, begin by **identifying characteristics of the text.** For example, if you read a text about a historical event, first determine the author's purpose for writing and his or her central, or main, idea. Then, examine the sources used as support for the main idea, including whether they are primary sources—firsthand accounts—or secondary sources—accounts by those who did not see the event. Next, evaluate the sources to decide if they are trustworthy and effective as support. Finally, extend the ideas presented in a text by identifying questions you have that are left unanswered and by researching to find out more about the topic. As you read, consider these questions:

Extending Ideas	Questions to Ask
Analysis	• What is the text about? What details are presented? • What are the characteristics or features of the text?
Evaluation	• How well are the main ideas presented and supported? • Does the text achieve its purpose?
Elaboration	• What connections can I make with the text? • What additional ideas and questions do I have?

Content-Area Vocabulary

These words appear in the selections that follow. You may also encounter them in other content-area texts.

- **conventional** (kən ven′ shə nəl) *adj.* following custom and traditional models
- **footage** (fo͝ot′ ij) *n.* any length of film that has been shot

Common Core State Standards

Reading Informational Text
6. Determine an author's point of view or purpose in a text and analyze how an author uses rhetoric to advance that point of view or purpose.

Writing
1.a. Introduce precise claim(s), distinguish the claim(s) from alternate or opposing claims, and create an organization that establishes clear relationships among claim(s), counterclaims, reasons, and evidence.

Language
4.b. Identify and correctly use patterns of word changes that indicate different meanings or parts of speech.
6. Acquire and use accurately general academic and domain-specific words and phrases, sufficient for reading, writing, speaking, and listening at the college and career readiness level.

THE BIG ?

Do heroes have responsibilities?

Have students consider how people might not think of themselves as heroes with responsibilities.

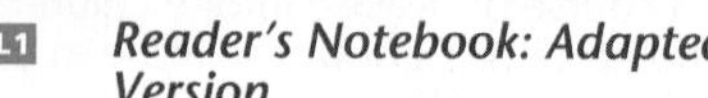

Differentiated Instruction for Universal Access

Reading Support
Give students reading support with the appropriate version of the ***Reader's Notebooks:***

L2 L3 ***Reader's Notebook***

L1 ***Reader's Notebook: Adapted Version***

EL ***Reader's Notebook: English Learner's Version***

A Hero in Our Midst

by Justice Paul E. Pfeifer

Sept. 13, 2006

This week marks the fifth anniversary of the Sept. 11 terrorist attacks on the United States. The news that day was nothing but grim; horror unleashed on a large scale. But recently, those of us who work at the Supreme Court of Ohio discovered an unexpected ray of light that emerged from the darkness of that day, and in the process learned a lesson about bravery and humility, and that greatness can be right before your eyes without you even knowing it.

Analyzing this paragraph reveals that the author discusses events he was not personally involved in, indicating that this commentary is a secondary source.

Last month Paramount Pictures released a movie about the attack in New York City. The film, entitled *World Trade Center*, was directed by Oliver Stone—the man who makes movies that sometimes raise almost as much controversy as they do cash. This time, Stone has made a pretty **conventional** film that tells the true story of two New York City Port Authority police officers who were trapped under the crumbled towers.

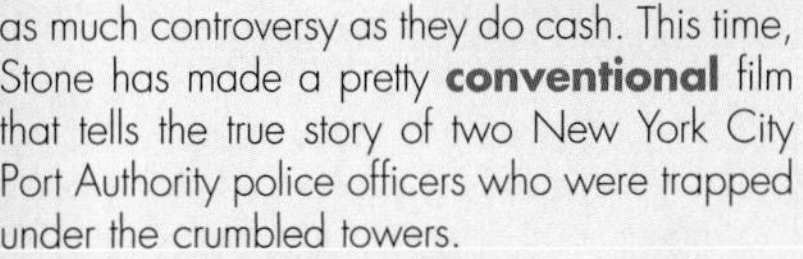

While the movie focuses primarily on the police officers—John McLoughlin and Will Jimeno—there are two other characters vital to the story: the two Marines who found the trapped men and led others to their rescue.

One of the Marines, Staff Sergeant David Karnes, was actually two years out of the Corps and working as an accountant in Connecticut at the time. When he heard about the attacks that morning, Karnes put on his old uniform and headed into the city to help with rescue efforts. In the days following Sept. 11, Karnes spoke with the press and his story is well chronicled in the movie.

The other man, known only as Sergeant Thomas, remained something of a mystery. Karnes encountered Thomas in the chaos surrounding the collapsed towers, teamed up with him to search the wreckage, and then, after the rescue, never saw him again. Like a mythic figure of old, Thomas had seemingly just appeared where people were in peril, performed his heroics, then vanished into the mist and confusion.

Extending the ideas in this paragraph might lead you to research how filmmakers were able to depict a character they knew so little about.

For five years no one knew who he was, though the police and other authorities searched for him. The filmmakers sought him as well. When they came up empty, the movie was made without knowing any more about Sergeant Thomas.

But when commercials for the film began appearing on television, the movie, you might say, found Sergeant Thomas. When he saw the previews he recognized his character on the screen. After nearly five years of silence, Sergeant Thomas finally decided to come forward.

Sergeant Thomas is actually Jason Thomas. And, as it turns out, Jason is now a security officer here at the Supreme Court of Ohio, in Columbus. For more than two years Jason has kept a watchful eye over all of us, and no one at the court—not his close friends or his casual acquaintances—had ever heard about his role on Sept. 11.

Commentary

Features:

- details that show the author's point of view
- personal information about the author
- the author's feelings and opinions
- text written for a general or specific audience

Differentiated Instruction for Universal Access

Strategy for Special-Needs Students

To help students understand the sequence of events in the text, draw a timeline on the board from September 11, 2001 through September 13, 2006. Explain that some texts do not relate events in chronological order. Tell students that they can figure out the order of events by reading carefully. Read through the article with students and write these events on the appropriate places in the timeline: *World Trade Center attack,* World Trade Center *movie released, Jason Thomas comes forward.*

Enrichment for Gifted/Talented Students

Challenge students to write a letter to Sergeant Jason Thomas, the subject of the commentary. Have students write in a formal style. Suggest that they offer Sergeant Thomas their own views of his actions. Have volunteers share their letters with the class.

TEACH

About Commentaries

1. Review the list of features of Commentaries shown in the box at the upper right on page 1121.
2. Make sure students understand that the root word of *commentary* is *comment*. Explain that the author of a commentary is making his or her own personal comments on a situation or event.
3. **Ask** students where they have read commentaries.

   Possible response: Students may say they have read commentaries in the features section of a newspaper.
4. Talk with students about the kinds of writing that contain opinions. Point out that persuasive writing contains opinions. Explain that in commentaries, however, authors offer opinions to share with readers rather than to persuade them.

Identify Characteristics of Texts

1. Have students read the commentary. **Ask** them to describe what it is about.

   Answer: The text tells about a man in an Ohio town who stepped forward after the release of an Oliver Stone movie about the World Trade Center attack.
2. Point out that the author of the text has a title before his name, *Justice*, indicating that he is a judge. Explain that understanding who an author is helps readers evaluate a text. **Ask** students how the author knows Sergeant Thomas.

   Answer: The author and Sergeant Thomas both work at the Supreme Court of Ohio.
3. **Ask** students what opinion the author holds about Jason Thomas. Have volunteers give details to support their answers.

   Possible response: The author holds a favorable opinion of Jason Thomas. The author states that Jason has kept a watchful eye over the people at the Ohio Supreme Court for more than two years.

Identify Characteristics of Texts

1. Point out that the author reinforces his opinion about Sergeant Jason Thomas in the commentary on this page. **Ask** students what they learn about Sergeant Thomas on this page.

   Possible response: Students may say that they learn that Sergeant Thomas walked into danger to rescue people.

2. Discuss how the author includes details in the commentary to support his opinion that Jason Thomas is a brave man who deserves our respect.

3. Remind students that they can make connections to their own lives when they evaluate a text. **Ask** students what connections they made from the commentary to their own lives or to other texts they have read.

   Possible response: Students may say that they made a connection between Sergeant Thomas's role as a father and their knowledge about fathers bearing a sense of responsibility toward others. Students may also make a connection between Sergeant Thomas's bravery and other stories they have read about soldiers heading into danger.

And it's not as if Jason is easy to miss. He is a mountain of a man, a broad-shouldered former football player who exudes—and inspires—confidence. If you didn't know Jason had been a Marine, you would think he ought to become one. They should use him for the recruitment posters.

One characteristic of a commentary is that the author offers his own opinions and feelings about his subject.

But until the movie came out, this quiet man never felt the need to speak of what he'd done. . . .

That morning, Jason was dropping off his newborn daughter at his mother's house on Long Island before heading off to class. His mother met him on the porch and told him that a plane had hit one of the twin towers. Sensing this wasn't a freak accident, Jason's first words to her were: "They got us."

Although Jason had been out of the Marine Corps for a year, his uniform was in the trunk of his car. Why was it there? Because he was in the middle of moving, and he didn't want his most valued possession—his Marine uniform—getting lost among the boxes.

Donning his uniform, he told his mother to contact his wife, Kirsti, who worked in midtown Manhattan, to tell her that he was headed to the crash site. "I had all this military training," he said. "That's my city. I felt compelled to help out." His mother didn't try to stop him. "She knew it would be a waste of words. . . ."

As he got out of his car, the smoke and ash engulfed him. Sticking his head into his shirt for air, he crouched down as the world went dark around him. Then, while dozens ran for safety away from the buildings, Jason Thomas bowed his back and ran toward the fallen towers.

What makes a man run into danger rather than from it? Part of it, Jason said, is his upbringing. His parents taught him—and his ten brothers and six sisters—to never leave someone behind. "You go together, you come back together," their mother always told them.

It is characteristic of a commentary to pose questions and then answer them. You can extend these ideas by analyzing the text and forming your own questions for research.

And then there's the Marine training. Robert Kaplan, a journalist who was embedded with the Marines in Fallujah, has written that running into gunfire "rather than seeking cover from it goes counter to every human survival instinct—trust me." But in Fallujah, Kaplan saw Marines—without being ordered—running straight into the direction of fire time and again.

Although they didn't know it, John McLoughlin and Will Jimeno—trapped and dying beneath a mountain of concrete and steel—were about to reap the benefits of Jason Thomas's Marine training, and the sense of duty, instilled by his parents, to help those in need.

Sergeant Jason Thomas

1122 Themes in Literature: Heroism

Vocabulary Development — CCSS Language 6

Vocabulary from Social Studies

Students may benefit from additional instruction for words used in the commentary that relate to social studies. Review with students the meaning of the following words and phrases:

chronicled: told an historical account
mythic: legendary, larger than life
peril: great danger
exudes: exhibits in abundance
engulfed: swallowed up or overwhelmed

Sign In/Register | Search by Movie | Search by Actor

MENU | EDITORIAL REVIEW | NEWS | TRAILERS

Movie Review

Features:

- a reviewer's opinion of the movie
- a summary of the plot
- names of the actors and the roles they play
- general information about the film and its makers

World Trade Center

Movie Review *by Rebecca Murray*

After the Twin Towers fell on September 11, 2001, only 20 people were pulled from the rubble alive. *20 people.* Port Authority Police Sergeant John McLoughlin and Officer Will Jimeno were numbers 18 and 19. *World Trade Center* is their story, told through the eyes of Jimeno, McLoughlin and their families. There's no political agenda or finger-pointing. *World Trade Center* is very simply a tale of hope, courage and survival on one of America's darkest days.

One characteristic of a movie review is that the reviewer summarizes the plot of the film.

The film begins with the central characters going through the mundane motions of preparing for work, lining up for duty, and then heading out on patrol. From there the events of 9/11 unfold with the officers racing to the Twin Towers. Focus shifts from outside the Towers to inside, swiftly narrowing the story to spotlight a small group of Port Authority officers led by Sergeant McLoughlin (played by Nicolas Cage).

Of course the officers don't have a grasp on the full picture and, without knowing just how bad things will ultimately become, set out gathering equipment for a rescue operation that never has time to materialize. They get no further than the concourse level when the Tower falls. McLoughlin and Jimeno (Michael Pena) become pinned 20 feet below the surface under piles of twisted metal and burning rubble. Critically injured, the men spend hours keeping each other awake as their families cling to the hope they'll somehow make it out alive.

If you didn't know this was an Oliver Stone movie going in, chances are you won't know it as you leave the theater unless you stay for the credits. Stone refrained from inserting his own view of the events into this story and tonally, visually, and substance-wise, *World Trade Center* is nothing like any of his previous films. Stone not only didn't include his own politics in the movie, but also chose not to include **footage** of the planes hitting the buildings, the Towers actually collapsing, or other all-too-familiar scenes from that horrific day. None of that sort of footage would have benefited the story and Stone, to his credit, manages to show the scope of the devastation just by focusing on the specific area surrounding Jimeno and McLoughlin.

It is typical of a movie review to include comparisons to the filmmaker's other works. You can extend these ideas by connecting the information given here to what you may know about other films.

Movie Photos

About Movie Reviews

1. Have students read the features of Movie Reviews shown in the box at the top right on page 1123.
2. Ask volunteers to describe reviews they have read. Have them share how the reviews made them feel about the works being reviewed. **Ask** students whether the reviews influenced their decision to see, read, or listen to the works.

   Possible response: Students may say that they learned something interesting about a movie or a book that made them want to see it or read it.
3. **Ask** students who have read reviews and then seen, read, or listened to the works reviewed whether they agreed with the reviews after having experienced the works for themselves.

   Possible response: Students may say they held a different opinion from the reviewers and disagreed with a review.

Identify Characteristics of Texts

1. Have students read the movie review of *World Trade Center.*
2. Remind students that it is important to consider whether the author of a review is reliable before making judgments or decisions based on the information a reviewer provides.
3. Explain that reviews represent the author's opinion about a work and that a review should include examples that support the author's opinions. Discuss how readers can evaluate the information an author uses to support his or her opinion.
4. **Ask:** What is the focus of Rebecca Murray's review?

   Possible response: Murray focuses on the movie *World Trade Center.*
5. Point out that the review begins with background information about the events of September 11, 2001, and follows with an overview of the film. **Ask** students what opinion Murray holds about Oliver Stone's direction of the film.

   Possible response: Murray thinks Stone did a good job of keeping his own politics out of the film.

Fluency

To improve students' reading fluency, pair nonfluent readers with fluent readers. Have the nonfluent reader read aloud while the fluent reader follows along silently. If the nonfluent reader mispronounces a word or hesitates for several seconds, have the fluent reader provide the difficult word. Then have the first student repeat the word. Encourage students to repeat the exercise until all the words in the selection are familiar.

Identify Characteristics of Texts

1. **Ask** students what details the author providès to support her opinion that Nicolas Cage gives a powerful movie performance.

   Answer: Murray gives details in the second paragraph about how Cage uses his voice and facial expressions to hold the audience's attention.

2. Point out that the final paragraph of the review offers a counterbalance to the author's overall opinion of the movie.

Sign In/Register | Search by Movie | Search by Actor

MENU | EDITORIAL REVIEW | NEWS | TRAILERS

More Photos

World Trade Center is only the second major feature film to focus on the horrible events of 9/11 so comparisons to Paul Greengrass' *United 93* are inevitable. Unfortunately for Stone's film, *United 93* not only made it to theaters first but also did a better job of capturing the extreme anxiety of the day - and even did a far better job of involving the audience emotionally. Because Stone's *World Trade Center* is not just the story of the two men trapped in the ruins of the Towers but also the story of their wives and families, Stone's film is forced to devote time away from the rescue operation of Jimeno and McLoughlin. Not to take anything away from the suffering the real Donna McLoughlin and Allison Jimeno went through waiting for word on their husbands, screenwriter Andrea Berloff's script and Stone's direction fail to adequately capture what must have been the most difficult day in the lives of both women. Instead of furthering the film's heart wrenching story, when the focus shifts to the homes of Jimeno and McLoughlin, the movie bogs down and loses intensity.

As for the performances in *World Trade Center,* Stone has to be commended for casting against type and getting the best out of his eclectic group of actors. Cage in particular gives a powerful performance as Sergeant McLoughlin. At least half of Cage's time onscreen is spent trapped in rubble, leaving only his voice and facial expressions to hold our attention. Cage pulls it off, giving one of the most tightly controlled performances of his career. . . .

Shot in New York with the cooperation of the Port Authority Police Department and the brave men and women involved in Jimeno and McLoughlin's rescue, *World Trade Center* tries hard to get the story right. The filmmakers should be applauded for doing their research and keeping the politics out of this particular story.

World Trade Center moves a little too slow—the pacing's not quite right—but otherwise it's a decent film and one that's a fitting tribute to the best in people during the worst of times.

Characteristically, the movie review ends with a summary of the reviewer's opinions about the film.

Vocabulary Development

CCSS Language 6

Vocabulary from Filmmaking

Tell students that this movie review uses terms that are specific to the filmmaking industry. Guide them to understand the meaning of the following words that are used in "*World Trade Center* Movie Review":

characters: the people in a movie or story
spotlight: to draw attention to
credits: the list of people who worked on a film
footage: a scene or series of scenes
feature film: a movie about a particular event
screenwriter: the person who writes the movie's script
casting: selecting actors for roles in a film
pacing: speed of the action in a film

After You Read Commentary • Movie Review

Comparing Argumentative Texts

1. **Craft and Structure** **(a)** In what ways are the **characteristics** and features of the commentary and the movie review similar and different? **(b)** Analyze the characteristics of each text to determine how the authors use them to advance their purposes for writing and to introduce and develop their central ideas.

Content-Area Vocabulary

2. **(a)** Remove the suffix *-al* from the word *conventional.* Using a print or an online dictionary, explain how removing the suffix alters the meaning of the word and its part of speech. **(b)** Then, use the words *conventional* and *convention* in a sentence that shows their meanings.

Timed Writing

Argumentative Text: Critique

Format
The prompt directs you to write a critique. Therefore, your response should offer judgments and opinions about the review, supported by evidence and examples.

Write a critique of the movie review. Analyze the types of details presented and evaluate the strength of those details as support for the reviewer's claims. Consider whether the review leaves important questions unanswered and whether the text reveals too much of the plot. Use details from the text to support your critique. (40 minutes)

Academic Vocabulary
When you *analyze* a text, you examine it in detail. When you *evaluate* a text, you judge its value or worth.

5-Minute Planner

Complete these steps before you begin to write:

1. Read the prompt carefully, noting highlighted key words.
2. Skim the movie review. Make notes about whether the reviewer's claims are sufficiently supported by the details provided. **TIP** Make a two-column chart, noting claims in one column and supporting details or evidence in the other. Then, consult your chart to make your evaluation.
3. Consider whether the reviewer reveals too much or too little about the plot of the film. Support your judgment with specific details. Note any additional questions you have about the movie.
4. Sketch a rough outline for your critique. Then, refer to your notes and outline as you write.

ASSESS/EXTEND

Answers

Comparing Argumentative Texts

1. (a) **Possible response:** Both the commentary and the movie review offer the authors' opinions about the film. The movie review discusses the presentation of the film. The commentary discusses the content of the film and tells background information that is not part of the film.

   (b) **Possible response:** Features of the commentary that help the reader understand the topic are the third person narrative—its inviting and approachable style—and the ample background information that helps the reader understand the significance of the action. As for the movie review, the reviewer presents an opinion and backs it up with details from the movie. She cites characters and film techniques to help the reader understand her position.
2. (a) **Sample response:** Removing *-al* from *conventional* changes it from an adjective describing something usual or generally done to the noun *convention,* which names a thing that is a standard or normal practice.
   (b) **Sample response:** The conventional way to make past-tense verbs is to add *-ed*. She understood the convention for writing past-tense verbs.

Timed Writing

1. Before students complete the activity, guide them in identifying and analyzing key words and phrases in the prompt, highlighted on the student page.
2. Work with students to draw up guidelines for their critique based on the key words:
   - **Focus** The critique should analyze and evaluate the movie review.
   - **Organization** The critique should offer an opinion statement about the movie review, followed by an analysis of the details provided.
   - **Support** The critique should offer details from the text to support the position.
   - **Style** The critique should include persuasive language. Writers should base their opinions on facts and details, but may also include personal opinion statements.
3. Have students use the 5-Minute Planner to structure their time.
4. Allow students 40 minutes to complete the assignment. Evaluate their work using the guidelines they have developed.

PRETEACH

Common Core State Standards

- Reading Literature 7, 9
- Writing 2, 2.a, 9

❶ Comparing Contemporary Interpretations

Contemporary Interpretation

1. Introduce the skill, using the instruction on the student page.
2. Give students a copy of the **Comparing Contemporary Interpretations Graphic Organizer B, *Graphic Organizer Transparencies,*** p. 192, to complete as they read.

Think Aloud: Model the Skill

Model a way to approach contemporary interpretations. Say to students:

An *allusion* is a reference to a well-known person, place, event, or work of art. For example, a story that calls a character "a Romeo" alludes to Shakespeare's famous play *Romeo and Juliet*. To understand such an allusion, I might recall or research the original work. This would tell me that "a Romeo" is a lover devoted against all odds. This approach helps me understand allusions in contemporary interpretations.

Comparing Literary Works

An Ancient Gesture • Siren Song • *from* The Odyssey • Ithaca

❶ Comparing Contemporary Interpretations

A **contemporary interpretation** of a literary work is a new piece of writing that a modern-day author bases on an older work. Even when they are based on the same work, contemporary interpretations can differ widely in purpose and theme. Each writer's cultural and historical backgrounds, attitudes, and beliefs profoundly affect his or her perceptions of the older work and influence the creation of the new work.

Writers draw from classic, traditional, or simply well-known source material for a variety of reasons, such as the following:

- Timeless or universal themes that are relevant to modern-day life
- Recognizable characters, settings, and conflicts
- Established meaning and importance
- Quick introduction of complex ideas
- Basis for additional interpretation and new layers of meaning

The characters and events of Homer's *Odyssey* are timeless and universal in their appeal. They have inspired many contemporary interpretations, including the poems you are about to read. By reinventing and transforming Homer's tales, modern-day writers shed new light on Homer's ancient words.

Contemporary interpretations of literature from ages past can be viewed as extended allusions to the ancient or traditional texts. An **allusion** is a reference to a well-known person, place, event, or work of literature or art. As you read, use a chart like the one shown to note the extended allusion each poet makes to Homer's *Odyssey*. Then, think about the ways in which the allusion helps each poet express a new, modern meaning.

Poem	Allusion to the *Odyssey*	Meaning

Common Core State Standards

Reading Literature

7. Analyze the representation of a subject or a key scene in two different artistic mediums.

9. Analyze how an author draws on and transforms source material in a specific work.

Writing

2. Write informative/explanatory texts to examine and convey complex ideas, concepts, and information clearly and accurately through the effective selection, organization, and analysis of content.

2.a. Introduce a topic; organize complex ideas, concepts, and information to make important connections and distinctions.

9. Draw evidence from literary or informational texts to support analysis, reflection, and research.

www.PHLitOnline.com

- Vocabulary flashcards
- Interactive journals
- More about the authors
- Selection audio
- Interactive graphic organizers

Vocabulary Development

Vocabulary Knowledge Rating

Create a **Vocabulary Knowledge Rating Chart** (***Professional Development Guidebook,*** p. 33) for this selection. Include the selection vocabulary and the forms of the Big Question words that appear in the Writing About the Big Question sentence starters on the next page. (The Big Question vocabulary is introduced on pp. 1028–1029.)

Give students a copy of the chart. Read the words aloud, and have students mark their rating in the Before Reading column. Urge them to be alert to these words as they read and discuss the selection.

Tally how many students think they know a word to gauge how much instruction to provide. As students read and discuss the selection, point out the words and their context.

Vocabulary Central, featuring tools, activities, and songs for studying vocabulary, is available at **www.PHLitOnline.com.**

❷ Writing About the Big Question

In these selections, characters have different ways of living up to their responsibilities. Use these sentence starters to develop your ideas about the Big Question.

In my own life, I know I am **responsible** for ________.
If I do not live up to this **obligation,** one consequence might be ________.
When I make **responsible choices,** one positive result is ________.

Meet the Authors

Edna St. Vincent Millay (1892–1950)

Author of "An Ancient Gesture" (p. 1128)

Edna St. Vincent Millay is remembered for her artistic experimentation and her rebelliousness. Her poetry collection *The Harp Weaver and Other Poems* (1923) earned her a Pulitzer Prize.

Margaret Atwood (b. 1939)

Author of "Siren Song" (p. 1130)

Much of Margaret Atwood's writing is about what it means to be a woman in a period of social change. In "Siren Song," Atwood presents another of her themes—the role of mythology in people's lives.

Derek Walcott (b. 1930)

Author of *The Odyssey* (p. 1132)

Born in St. Lucia, an island in the Caribbean Sea, Walcott writes poems that reflect his background. In 1992, he won the Nobel Prize in Literature. "Prologue" and "Epilogue" are from his stage version of *The Odyssey.*

Constantine Cavafy (1863–1933)

Author of "Ithaca" (p. 1135)

Constantine Cavafy was born to Greek parents in Alexandria, Egypt. "Ithaca" showcases his creative method: using Greek mythology to speak to the modern reader.

Teaching Resources

- All *Unit 6 Resources,* pp. 65–81
- All *Graphic Organizer Transparencies,* pp. 191–194
- All *Professional Development Guidebook,* pp. 33
- All **Enriched Online Student Edition**
- L2 EL *Hear It!* Audio CD
- All *Common Core Companion,* pp. 62–63, 69–70; 190–201, 255–262

PHLit Online! All print and digital resources are available at **www.PHLitOnline.com.**

Daily Bellringer

For each class during which you will teach this selection, have students complete one of the five Vocabulary activities for Week 33 in the *Daily Bellringer Activities* booklet.

❷ Writing About the Big Question

1. Review the assignment with the class.
2. Discuss different ideas about what it means to be a hero.
3. Have students complete the sentence starters. Review responses as a class. (**Possible response:** In my own life, I know I am responsible for my school effort. If I do not live up to this obligation, one consequence might be my parents' disappointment. When I make responsible choices, one positive result is school success.)
4. Remind students that their answers will help them think about the Big Question, "Do heroes have responsibilities?"

Concept Connector →

Tell students that they will return to their sentence starters after they have concluded reading.

Multidraft Reading

To assist struggling readers and to deepen reading for all, apply multidraft reading protocols. For each reading, have students set the purpose indicated:

- **First reading**—identifying key ideas and details and answering any Reading Checks.
- **Second reading**—analyzing craft and structure and responding to the side-column prompts.
- **Third reading**—integrating knowledge and ideas, connecting to other texts and the world, and answering the end-of-selection questions.

For more guidance, see the ***Classroom Strategies and Teaching Routines*** card on multidraft reading.

For more about the authors and practice with the selection vocabulary, go online at **www.PHLitOnline.com.**

TEACH

❶ Background

Heroism Old and New Just as the heroic character of Odysseus can be revisited today to reveal the qualities that the ancient Greeks valued in a man, Penelope's character can reveal the qualities valued in a woman. Odysseus' courage, adventurous spirit, and guile are celebrated in the *Odyssey,* while Penelope is most notable for her loyalty and patience. She also shares some of her husband's gift for cleverness in holding off the suitors and testing Odysseus' identity. In "An Ancient Gesture," Millay uses Odysseus and Penelope to ask what both characters reveal about the heroism of suffering.

❷ Activating Prior Knowledge

Draw a cluster diagram on the board and in the center write *hero.* Ask students what they associate with being a hero, based on prior knowledge and experience. Then ask how the meaning of *hero* has changed from ancient times to today. Tell students that the poems they are going to read look at the *Odyssey* with a fresh perspective and offer contemporary interpretations of what it means to be a hero.

Concept Connector →

Students will follow up on this activity after completing the poems.

❸ About the Selection

In "An Ancient Gesture," a gesture by Penelope is echoed by a modern woman, suggesting that enduring grief and loneliness is itself heroic.

❶ ❷ ❸

An Ancient Gesture

Edna St. Vincent Millay

Text Complexity Rubric

An Ancient Gesture, Siren Song, Odyssey, and Ithaca		
Qualitative Measures	**Context/ Knowledge Demands**	Modern perspectives on ancient Greek characters 1 2 3 (4) 5
	Structure/ Language Clarity and Conventionality	Contemporary language; some challenging vocabulary 1 2 (3) 4 5
	Levels of Meaning/ Purpose/Concept Level	Challenging concepts (allusions to ancient Greek literature) 1 2 3 (4) 5
Quantitative Measures	**Text Length**	Word Count: 143; 139; 260; 260
	Lexile	NP

I thought, as I wiped my eyes on the corner of my apron:
Penelope did this too.
And more than once: you can't keep weaving all day
And undoing it all through the night;
Your arms get tired, and the back of your neck gets tight;
And along towards morning, when you think it will never
be light,
And your husband has been gone, and you don't know
where, for years,
Suddenly you burst into tears;
There is simply nothing else to do.

And I thought, as I wiped my eyes on the corner of my apron:
This is an ancient gesture, authentic, antique,
In the very best tradition, classic, Greek;
Ulysses[1] did this too.
But only as a gesture,—a gesture which implied
To the assembled throng that he was much too moved
to speak.
He learned it from Penelope . . .
Penelope, who really cried.

1. **Ulysses** Latin name for Odysseus.

Literary Analysis Contemporary Interpretations What connection does the speaker make between herself and Penelope?

Vocabulary
authentic (ô then´ tik) *adj.* genuine

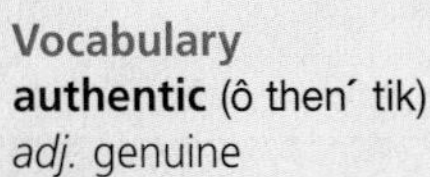

◀ Analyze Representations How does the representation of Penelope in this painting compare to her portrayal in the poem? **[Interpret]**

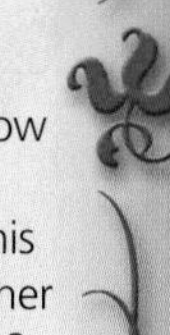

Critical Thinking

Cite textual evidence to support your responses.

1. **Key Ideas and Details (a)** What is the "ancient gesture"? **(b) Summarize:** According to the speaker, what caused Penelope to employ this gesture? **(c) Infer:** Why might the speaker have made a similar gesture?

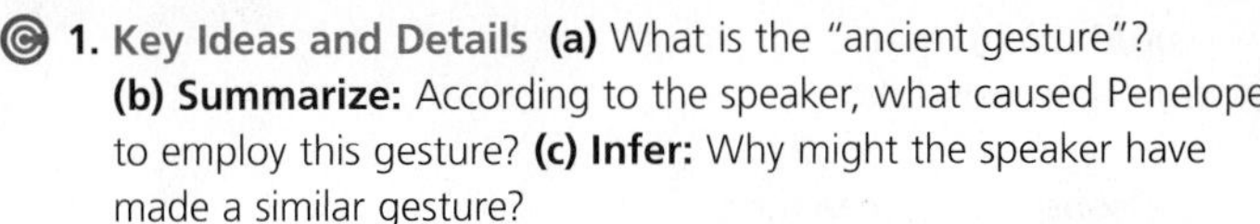

2. **Key Ideas and Details (a)** According to the speaker, who else made this ancient gesture? **(b) Compare and Contrast:** How did this gesture differ from Penelope's? **(c) Analyze:** What do the different qualities of their gestures show about these characters?

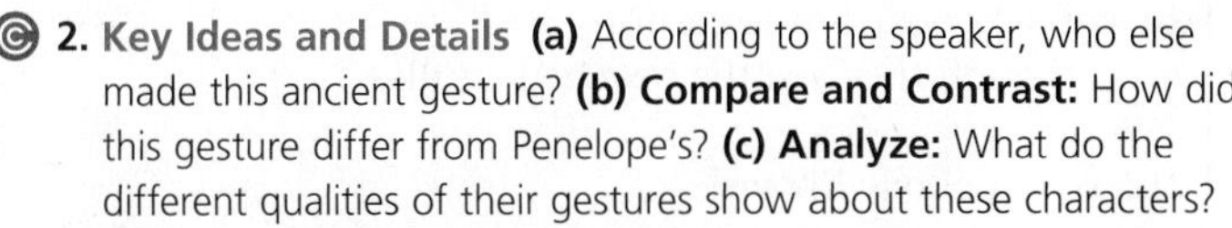

3. **Integration of Knowledge and Ideas (a) Assess:** What questions about the speaker are left unanswered? **(b) Analyze Cause and Effect:** What effect do these unanswered questions create?
4. **Integration of Knowledge and Ideas (a)** According to this interpretation, does Odysseus live up to his responsibility as a husband? Explain. **(b)** Who do you think the author felt was the hero in the *Odyssey*—Penelope or Odysseus? *[Connect to the Big Question: Do heroes have responsibilities?]*

4 Literary Analysis

Contemporary Interpretations

Read the poem aloud. **Ask** the Literary Analysis question.

Possible response: Both women know the great sadness of lost husbands; both cry and wipe their eyes on their aprons.

5 Analyze Representations

Possible response: In the painting, Penelope's posture and facial expression show her focus and dedication. The poem portrays Penelope as distracted from her weaving out of grief for her husband.

PHLit Online!

This selection is available in interactive format in the Enriched Online Student Edition, **www.PHLitOnline.com**, which includes an interactive graphic organizer.

Concept Connector

Have students add to the cluster diagram they began before reading. Then, have them compare their Writing About the Big Question responses before reading the selection with their ideas afterwards.

ASSESS

Answers

Critical Thinking

Remind students to support their answers with evidence from the text.

1. (a) The ancient gesture is wiping tears with an apron. (b) Penelope thought her husband was probably dead. (c) Her husband has also been gone for years.
2. (a) Ulysses made this gesture. (b) He wanted to sway a crowd. (c) Penelope and the speaker are truly sad. Ulysses is faking.
3. (a) The reader does not know why the husband left, where he is, or if he is alive. (b) **Possible responses:** The questions create a sense of sad mystery.
4. **Possible responses:** (a) Odysseus does not live up to his responsibility because he pretends to care but his tears are not genuine. (b) The author thinks Penelope is the hero because she really cried.

Text Complexity: Reader and Task Suggestions

An Ancient Gesture, Siren Song, Odyssey, and Ithaca

Preparing to Read the Text	Leveled Tasks
• Using the Background information on TE pp. 1128, 1130, 1132, and 1135, discuss the universal qualities exhibited by Greek heroes. • Discuss the use of allusions in poetry, pointing out that allusions allow poets to expand their meaning beyond the explicit meaning of their poems. • Guide students to use Multidraft Reading strategies (TE p. 1127).	***Levels of Meaning*** If students will have difficulty with levels of meaning, have them first read the poems and identify each character's situation. Then, have them reread and note ideas, expressions, or other details that reflect a modern perspective. ***Analyzing*** If students will not have difficulty with levels of meaning, have them read and identify the theme of each poem and note what details support those themes. Have students contribute their ideas during class discussion.

6 Background

Sirens The Sirens were mythological beings said to live on an island and lure sailors with their singing. Odysseus plugged his sailors' ears with wax. In this way they couldn't hear the song and would keep the ship on course. They tied him to a mast so that he could listen but wouldn't put the ship in danger.

7 Activating Prior Knowledge

Have students suggest more ideas about what it means to be a hero.

Concept Connector

Tell students that they will return to the diagram again after they read the selection.

8 About the Selection

In "Siren Song," a Siren admits that her song is a cry for help that continues to lure and destroy men.

9 Literary Analysis

Contemporary Interpretations

1. Remind students that the Sirens are creatures—each half-bird and half-woman—whose song lures men to destruction.
2. Have students read aloud the poem. Then **ask:** What do the men see on the beach?

   Answer: They see skulls.
3. **Ask** students what the men should infer from the skulls.

   Answer: They should infer that they will die among the Sirens.
4. Have students reread the bracketed lines. **Ask** students the Literary Analysis question: What allusion do lines 4–9 make to the *Odyssey?*

   Answer: The lines allude to the episode in which Odysseus and his men row past the Sirens. Odysseus puts wax in his men's ears but has himself tied to the mast so that he can hear the song.
5. Point out that the men meet their deaths because they go "overboard." **Ask** students what double meaning "go overboard" has for those who pursue the Sirens.

   Answer: The men leap out of their ship, but they also "go overboard" with passion, and abandon both the boat and reason.

6 7 8

Siren Song

Margaret Atwood

This is the one song everyone
would like to learn: the song
that is irresistible:

the song that forces men
to leap overboard in squadrons
even though they see the beached skulls

9

the song nobody knows
because anyone who has heard it
is dead, and the others can't remember.

Shall I tell you the secret
and if I do, will you get me
out of this bird suit?[1]

Literary Analysis Contemporary Interpretations What allusion do lines 4–9 make to the *Odyssey?*

1. **bird suit** Sirens are usually represented as half bird and half woman.

Vocabulary Development

CCSS Language 6

Thematic Vocabulary: The Big Question

As students are discussing the poems, encourage them to use the thematic vocabulary presented in Introducing the Big Question, pp. 1028–1029. You might encourage them with sentence starters like these:

1. Penelope shows her *honesty* when she . . .
2. The Sirens reveal a sense of *responsibility* by . . .
3. The Prologue and Epilogue from the *Odyssey* show how the *character* has . . .
4. "Ithaca" suggests that modern people *imitate* . . .

I don't enjoy it here
squatting on this island
looking **picturesque** and mythical

with these two feathery maniacs,
I don't enjoy singing
this trio, fatal and valuable.

I will tell the secret to you,
to you, only to you.
Come closer. This song

(10) is a cry for help: Help me!
Only you, only you can,
you are unique

at last. Alas
it is a boring song
but it works every time.

Vocabulary
picturesque (pik´ chər esk´) *adj.* attractive and interesting

Literary Analysis
Contemporary Interpretations What does the contemporary Siren say to flatter and lure the listener?

Critical Thinking 

Cite textual evidence to support your responses.

1. **Key Ideas and Details** **(a)** In the first stanza, what song does the speaker say everyone wants to learn? **(b) Analyze Cause and Effect:** What does this song have the power to do?
2. **Key Ideas and Details** **(a)** What does the speaker want in exchange for revealing the song's secret? **(b) Interpret:** Why does the speaker want to make this deal?
3. **Integration of Knowledge and Ideas** **(a) Analyze:** Why do you think the speaker's compliment in lines 23 and 24 is so effective? **(b) Make Generalizations:** What might the speaker be saying about the relationships between men and women?
4. **Key Ideas and Details** **(a) Summarize:** How does the speaker feel about her song and its secret? **(b) Support:** Which details in the poem support your answer?
5. **Integration of Knowledge and Ideas** **(a)** How does the Siren affect heroes? Explain. **(b)** Do you think the Siren should be held responsible for her effect on heroes? Why or why not? *[Connect to the Big Question: Do heroes have responsibilities?]*

Differentiated Instruction for Universal Access

Strategy for Gifted/Talented Students
Suggest that students create a picture or a sculpture of a Siren. They may research a Siren's appearance in works of art or rely purely on their own imaginations. Challenge some students to create an image of Margaret Atwood's modern Siren. Some students may wish to accompany their images with music or sound effects that convey the Siren's song.

Strategy for Advanced Readers
Margaret Atwood uses an allusion from classic literature to create a contemporary interpretation of some relationships between men and women. Ask students to write brief essays in which they use another character from literature (Romeo or Juliet, for example) to make their own contemporary interpretation of some relationships between men and women.

(10) Literary Analysis

Contemporary Interpretations
Read the bracketed lines aloud. **Ask** the Literary Analysis question: What does the contemporary Siren say to flatter and lure the listener?

Answer: She says that she needs help and that only the listener can help her.

This selection is available in interactive format in the **Enriched Online Student Edition, www.PHLitOnline.com,** which includes an interactive graphic organizer.

Concept Connector
Have students add ideas about heroism to the cluster diagram. Then, have them compare their Writing About the Big Question responses before reading the selection with their ideas afterwards.

ASSESS

Answers

Critical Thinking
Remind students to support their answers with evidence from the text.

1. (a) Everyone wants to learn the irresistible song. (b) The song can drive men crazy and destroy them.
2. (a) The speaker wants the listener to get her out of her bird suit. (b) The speaker wants to be freed from her role as a Siren.
3. (a) The compliment works because the man is vain. (b) The speaker suggests that sometimes men and women use each other.
4. (a) The speaker feels her song is boring but effective. (b) In the final lines, she sighs "Alas," admits it is "boring," and notes, "it works every time."
5. **Possible responses:** (a) The heroes are either killed or lose their memories. (b) Students are likely to say that the Siren should be held responsible because she knows what will happen.

11 Background

Story Structure A prologue appears before the main part of a story. An epilogue appears after the main story. In Homer's *Odyssey*, the poem begins in the middle of the journey. Homer then returns to the beginning of Odysseus' journey to explain how his hero has arrived at the point where the poem began.

12 Activating Prior Knowledge

Have students suggest more ideas about what it means to be a hero.

Concept Connector

Tell students that they will return to the diagram again after they read the selection.

13 About the Selection

"Prologue and Epilogue from the *Odyssey*" retells the opening and closing of Homer's poem in a modern idiom.

14 Literary Analysis

Contemporary Interpretations

1. Read the bracketed lines aloud. **Ask** the Literary Analysis question: What actions in lines 6–8 reflect the *Odyssey?* Explain.
   Answer: The lines reflect the unending waves of the sea on which Odysseus travels and the tireless weaving of Penelope as she makes and unmakes the shroud.
2. **Ask** students: What point about his story is the contemporary singer communicating with these lines?
   Possible response: The singer communicates the point that his song, his story, and his theme are universal and timeless.

PHLit Online!

This selection is available in interactive format in the **Enriched Online Student Edition, www.PHLitOnline.com,** which includes an interactive graphic organizer.

11 12 13 Prologue and Epilogue from the
Odyssey
Derek Walcott

PROLOGUE

Sound of surf.

BILLY BLUE *(Sings)*
Gone sing 'bout that man because his stories please us,
Who saw trials and tempests for ten years after Troy.

I'm Blind Billy Blue, my main man's sea-smart Odysseus,
Who the God of the Sea drove crazy and tried to destroy.

Andra moi ennepe mousa polutropon hos mala polla . . .[1]
The shuttle of the sea moves back and forth on this line,

All night, like the surf, she shuttles and doesn't fall
Asleep, then her rosy fingers at dawn unstitch the design.

When you hear this chord
(Chord)
Look for a swallow's wings
A swallow arrowing seaward like a messenger

Passing smoke-blue islands, happy that the kings
Of Troy are going home and its ten years' siege is over.

So my blues drifts like smoke from the fire of that war,
Cause once Achilles was ashes, things sure fell apart.

Slow-striding Achilles, who put the hex on Hector
A swallow twitters in Troy. That's where we start.
(Exit.)

Literary Analysis
Contemporary Interpretations What actions in lines 6–8 reflect the *Odyssey*? Explain.

Vocabulary
siege (sēj) *n.* encirclement of a fortified place by an opposing armed force intending to take it

1. **Andra moi. . .** the first line of Homer's *Odyssey* in Greek.

Vocabulary Development

CCSS Language 6

Compound Adjectives

Like Homer, Walcott's singer uses compound adjectives to add a concrete vividness to his descriptions: *sea-smart* Odysseus, *smoke-blue* islands, *rock-steady* woman. Point out to students that each of these compound adjectives consists of a noun and a related adjective that, together, increase the descriptive power of the expression.

Have students tell in their own words what they think each of the following compound adjectives means: *rosy-fingered* dawn, *wine-dark* sea, *ivory-wristed* goddess. Then ask students to combine modern nouns and adjectives to create some contemporary compound adjectives of their own—for example, *computer-savvy* student or *fashion-conscious* model.

EPILOGUE

BILLY BLUE *(Sings)*

I sang of that man against whom the sea still rages,
Who escaped its terrors, that despair could not destroy,

Since that first blind singer, others will sing down the ages
Of the heart in its harbour, then long years after Troy,
after Troy.

And a house, happy for good, from a swallow's omen,
Let the trees clap their hands, and the surf whisper amen.

For a rock, a rock, a rock, a rock-steady woman
Let the waves clap their hands and the surf whisper amen.

For that peace which, in their mercy, the gods allow men.
(Fade. Sound of surf.)

Literary Analysis Contemporary Interpretations Which words suggest that the story of the *Odyssey* will always be meaningful?

Spiral Review
Cultural Context
What aspect of Derek Walcott's Caribbean background might these lines suggest?

Critical Thinking

Cite textual evidence to support your responses.

1. **Key Ideas and Details** **(a)** Who is the speaker's "main man"? **(b) Interpret:** What is the speaker's attitude toward this "main man"?
2. **Key Ideas and Details** **(a) Infer:** What type of music does the speaker sing? **(b) Analyze:** Considering the loneliness, death, and defeat that occur in Homer's *Odyssey*, why is the speaker's musical style appropriate?
3. **Key Ideas and Details** **(a)** How is Penelope described in the Epilogue? **(b) Infer:** What seems to be the speaker's attitude toward Penelope?
4. **Integration of Knowledge and Ideas** **Generalize:** Overall, which elements from Homer's *Odyssey* seem most interesting to Walcott?
5. **Integration of Knowledge and Ideas** **(a)** Which details suggest that the poet felt a responsibility to show respect for Homer's *Odyssey?* **(b)** Do you think Billy Blue feels responsible for sharing Odysseus' story? Why or why not? ***[Connect to the Big Question: Do heroes have responsibilities?]***

Differentiated Instruction for Universal Access

Strategy for Less Proficient Readers
Students may need to hear Walcott's poem read aloud to grasp the connection between Homer and Blind Billy Blue. Remind them that Homer (or the long line of poet/performers he represents) was a blind singer and entertainer. Have students read along as they listen to the recording on the ***Hear It!*** **Audio CD**.

Strategy for Gifted/Talented Students
Billy Blue sings the blues in these passages. Suggest that students prepare a performance of the Prologue and Epilogue as a blues song. Ask students to find instrumental music or recordings to accompany the text. The performer might read or sing the passages to the blues rhythms.

15 Literary Analysis

Contemporary Interpretations

1. Have students reread the bracketed lines. **Ask** the Literary Analysis question.
   Answer: "Others will sing down the ages" suggests that the story will always be meaningful.
2. **Ask** students: What do you think is the meaning of the story?
   Possible responses: One should never give up; resourcefulness is a hero's most valuable quality; it is possible to be a hero in every age and culture.

Spiral Review

Cultural Context

Ask students the Spiral Review question.

Possible response: The imagery of waves, rocks, and surf reflects the ocean, an important aspect of Walcott's Caribbean island background.

ASSESS

Answers

Critical Thinking

Remind students to support their answers with evidence from the text.

1. (a) Odysseus is the speaker's "main man." (b) He admires Odysseus for his courage, intelligence, and resourcefulness.
2. (a) The speaker sings blues. (b) The blues often focus on loss, loneliness, and suffering.
3. (a) Penelope is described as "rock-steady." (b) The speaker admires Penelope for her endurance and steadfastness.
4. Walcott seems most interested in the personal elements of the tale, the ability of Odysseus and Penelope to endure, and their relationship with each other.
5. **Possible responses:** (a) The poet describes Odysseus as "sea-smart" and talks of the happiness that came when he finally returned home. (b) Yes, he wants to share this story to please people and hopes others will do the same to keep the story alive.

16 Visual Connections

Whole-Class Activity

1. Have students study the picture and read the title of the poem. **Ask:** What does the picture suggest about the city of Ithaca?

   Answer: It is a lush area. The boats suggest this is a port town or a fishing community.
2. Have students think about the mood suggested by this image. **Ask:** What feelings does this picture evoke? **Answer:** The setting is serene and seems like a small community where someone might quickly feel "at home."
3. Remind students that Odysseus was away from his home of Ithaca for many years. **Ask:** What does this picture suggest the poem will say about Ithaca?

   Possible response: The poem may describe Odysseus's feelings while away. It may deal with his feelings on returning.

Small-Group Activity

1. Have small groups study the picture and discuss the feelings it evokes.
2. Ask one member of each group to summarize the group's ideas.
3. After all groups have given their summaries, allow students to identify any common themes, or unique ideas, that arose.

Individual Activity

1. Remind students that Odysseus was away from his home of Ithaca for many years. Have students think about the mood of this picture, then write a few sentences to identify the emotions the picture evokes in them as viewers.
2. Have students expand their initial response into a short paragraph discussing what they expect the poem to say about Odysseus and his feelings for his hometown.
3. Ask volunteers to read their paragraphs aloud before reading the poem "Ithaca" together.

16

Think Aloud

Setting

Recall that setting is where and when a story takes place. Have students view the picture on this page and read the title of the poem. Use the following "think aloud" to model the process of analyzing setting (introduced on p. 290):

> When I read the title of a work and see that it is a place name, I immediately expect the setting to have special importance. In this case, I remember that Ithaca was Odysseus's home town—the place he left behind and to which he longs to return.
>
> As I read the poem, I will think about how I feel about my "home town." For example, I might consider how I feel when I remember it, since I moved away a long time ago. Some readers have never gone far from home. They might think about how they might feel about leaving in the future.

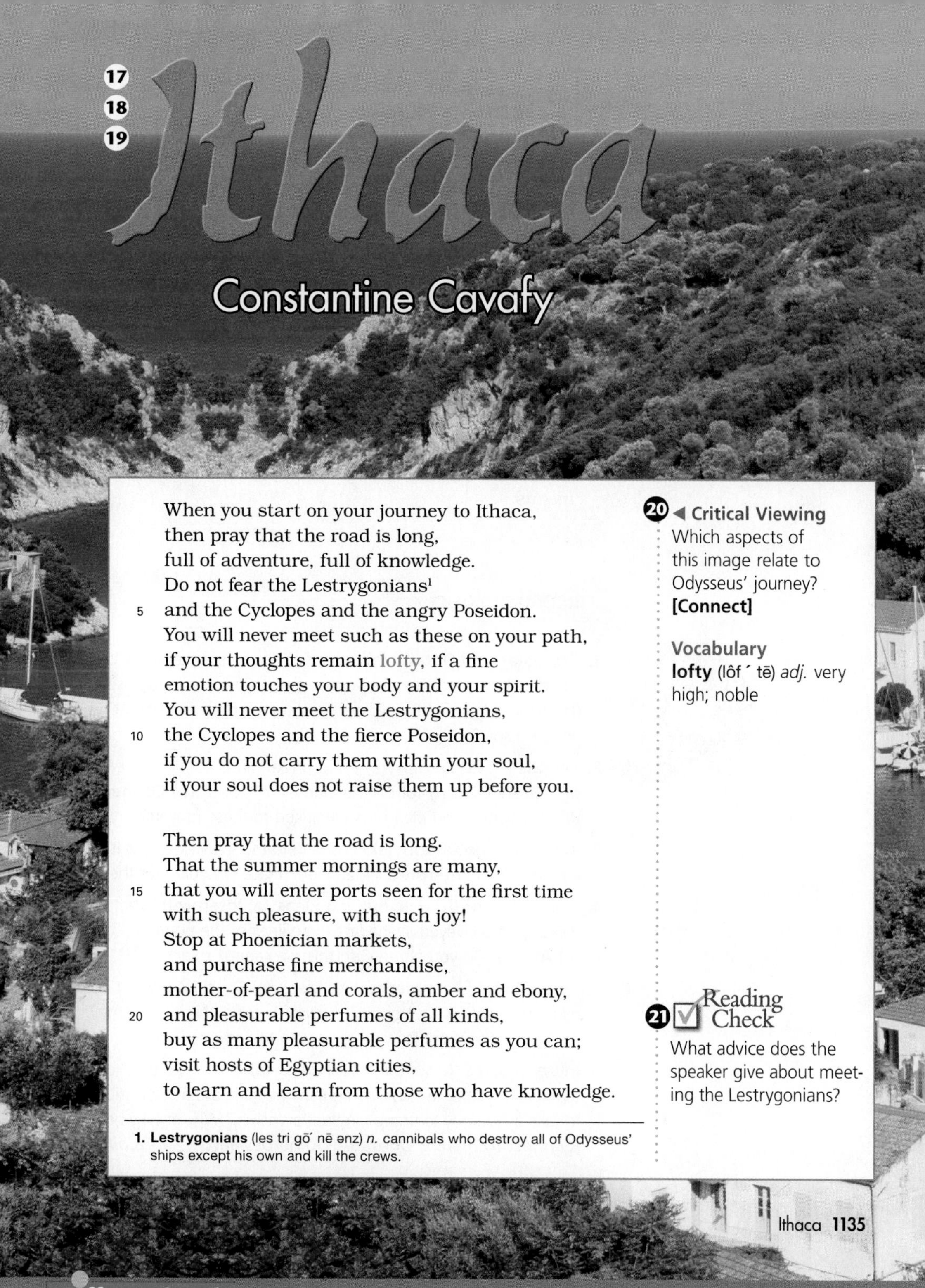

17 18 19

Ithaca

Constantine Cavafy

When you start on your journey to Ithaca,
then pray that the road is long,
full of adventure, full of knowledge.
Do not fear the Lestrygonians[1]
and the Cyclopes and the angry Poseidon.
You will never meet such as these on your path,
if your thoughts remain lofty, if a fine
emotion touches your body and your spirit.
You will never meet the Lestrygonians,
the Cyclopes and the fierce Poseidon,
if you do not carry them within your soul,
if your soul does not raise them up before you.

Then pray that the road is long.
That the summer mornings are many,
that you will enter ports seen for the first time
with such pleasure, with such joy!
Stop at Phoenician markets,
and purchase fine merchandise,
mother-of-pearl and corals, amber and ebony,
and pleasurable perfumes of all kinds,
buy as many pleasurable perfumes as you can;
visit hosts of Egyptian cities,
to learn and learn from those who have knowledge.

1. **Lestrygonians** (les tri gō´ nē ənz) *n.* cannibals who destroy all of Odysseus' ships except his own and kill the crews.

20 ◀ **Critical Viewing**
Which aspects of this image relate to Odysseus' journey? **[Connect]**

Vocabulary
lofty (lôf ´ tē) *adj.* very high; noble

21 **Reading Check**
What advice does the speaker give about meeting the Lestrygonians?

17 Background

Ithaca One of the Ionian Islands, Ithaca is part of Greece. During the time of Odysseus, Ithaca and the other Ionian Islands were important social and political centers. The islands are hilly and very green. People grow olives and grapes along with grains, and tourism brings many visitors to the warm waters.

18 Activating Prior Knowledge

Have students continue to suggest ideas about what it means to be a hero.

Concept Connector

Tell students that they will return to the diagram again after they read the selection.

19 About the Selection

"Ithaca" applies the image of the epic journey to everyone's modern life.

20 Critical Viewing

Possible response: The sea plays a big part of Odysseus's journey and this image shows a city on the sea.

21 Reading Check

Answer: If your "thoughts remain lofty," you will never meet the Lestrygonians.

Differentiated Instruction for Universal Access

Strategy for Less Proficient Readers
This poem will become easier for students once they recognize the possible meanings of Ithaca. Tell them that Ithaca represents not only home, an end to struggle, and reunion with loved ones; it can also be any major goal in life, something to be accomplished or discovered. Point out that the speaker is an experienced person who is trying to teach a lesson to a younger person.

Strategy for Advanced Readers
Have students deepen their understanding of "Ithaca" by applying Cavafy's concept of Ithaca to another work of literature that they have read. For example, what would Romeo and Juliet's Ithaca be? Have students choose a story, poem, or play, and write an essay in which they describe what Ithaca—the goal or final destination—would mean to one of the characters.

22 Literary Analysis

Contemporary Interpretations

1. Read the bracketed lines aloud. **Ask** the Literary Analysis question.

   Answer: Odysseus wants to reach home as soon as possible. Cavafy says not to hurry.

Concept Connector

Have students complete their cluster diagrams to any final insights into heroism. Then, have them compare their Writing About the Big Question responses before reading the selection with their ideas afterwards.

ASSESS

Answers

Critical Thinking

Remind students to support their answers with evidence from the text.

1. (a) If people maintain lofty thoughts and fine emotions, they will not meet the Lestrygonians, the Cyclopes, and Poseidon. (b) People often create their own opportunities or difficulties.
2. (a) Pray for a long road, many summer mornings, and entrance into new ports. (b) These prayers are linked to stopping at markets, buying fine things, and learning.
3. (a) Ithaca marks the end of the journey. (b) Ithaca might symbolize old age or death.
4. (a) **Possible response:** Even if the destination is disappointing, the experience is what matters. (b) Students may agree with the emphasis on the journey.
5. (a) The speaker might have advised Odysseus to travel slowly and learn all he could. (b) Students should explain why they agree or disagree with the advice.
6. (a) The journey symbolizes a person's life, and the way that we learn and grow along the way. (b) **Possible response:** Yes, people should try to learn and make an effort to grow and develop themselves.

Literary Analysis Contemporary Interpretations
How does Odysseus' desire for an end to his journey differ from the contemporary poet's attitude toward the journey?

Vocabulary
defrauded (dē frôd′ əd) *v.* cheated

Always keep Ithaca fixed in your mind.
To arrive there is your ultimate goal.
But do not hurry the voyage at all.
It is better to let it last for long years;
and even to anchor at the isle when you are old,
rich with all that you have gained on the way,
not expecting that Ithaca will offer you riches.

Ithaca has given you the beautiful voyage.
Without her you would never have taken the road.
But she has nothing more to give you.

And if you find her poor, Ithaca has not **defrauded** you.
With the great wisdom you have gained, with so much
  experience,
You must surely have understood by then what Ithaca
  means.

Critical Thinking

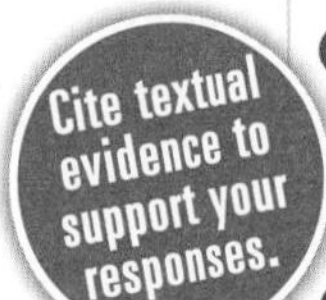
Cite textual evidence to support your responses.

1. **Key Ideas and Details (a)** According to the speaker, how can you avoid meeting the Lestrygonians, the Cyclopes, and Poseidon? **(b) Infer:** Why might a person carry such terrors as these in his or her own soul?
2. **Key Ideas and Details (a)** What three things does the speaker say you should pray for on the journey to Ithaca? **(b) Connect:** What activities and pleasures are linked to these prayers?
3. **Key Ideas and Details (a)** According to the speaker, why is Ithaca important? **(b) Interpret:** What might Ithaca symbolize for the poet?
4. **Integration of Knowledge and Ideas (a) Interpret:** What message is conveyed in the last three lines of the poem? **(b) Assess:** Do you agree with this message? Explain.
5. **Integration of Knowledge and Ideas (a) Speculate:** What advice might the speaker have given to Odysseus during his long journey? **(b) Take a Position:** Do you agree with this advice? Explain.
6. **Integration of Knowledge and Ideas (a)** What does the "journey to Ithaca" symbolize? **(b)** Do you think people have a responsibility to take a "journey to Ithaca" in their own lives? Why or why not? *[Connect to the Big Question: Do heroes have responsibilities?]*

Vocabulary Development

Vocabulary Knowledge Rating

When students have completed reading and discussing "An Ancient Gesture," "Siren Song," "Prologue and Epilogue," and "Ithaca," have them take out their **Vocabulary Knowledge Rating Chart**. Read the words aloud once more and have students rate their knowledge of the words again in the After Reading column. Clarify any words that are still problematic. Have students write their own definition and example or sentence in the appropriate column. Then have students complete the Vocabulary Practice activities on the next page. Encourage students to use the words in further discussion and written work about the poems. Remind them that they will be accountable for these words on the **Selection Test** ***Unit 6 Resources*** (pp. 76–78 or 79–81).

After You Read

An Ancient Gesture • Siren Song • *from* The Odyssey • Ithaca

Comparing Contemporary Interpretations

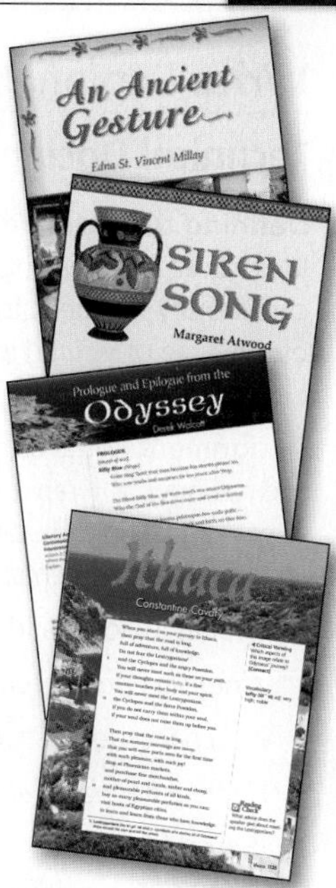

1. Craft and Structure The author of each contemporary interpretation in this section uses Homer's work as inspiration for new ideas. Use a chart like the one shown to explain how each poem is like and unlike Homer's *Odyssey*.

2. Key Ideas and Details Select one poem in this section, and identify the comment the poet is making about modern life. Support your explanation with details from your completed chart.

3. Craft and Structure **(a)** Identify an allusion in at least two of the poems. **(b)** Explain what the reference adds to the meaning of the poem. **(c)** Tell which allusion you think is more (or most) effective, and why.

Timed Writing

Explanatory Text: Essay

Each writer in this section draws on Homer's epic to communicate a message suited to today's world. In an essay, compare how each poet uses classical allusions in combination with his or her own perspective. Support your ideas with evidence from the text. **(40 minutes)**

5-Minute Planner

1. Read the prompt carefully and completely.
2. Think about these questions and jot down ideas for your essay:
   - What is each poet's main message?
   - What makes each poet's allusion appropriate for his or her message?
   - In what ways does each poem shed new light on the events or characters of the *Odyssey*?
3. Choose and plan an organizational strategy for your essay.
4. Reread the prompt. Then, refer to your notes as you draft your essay.

ASSESS

Answers

Comparing Contemporary Interpretations

1. **Sample responses:** "An Ancient Gesture": reflects Penelope's sorrow and endurance, but portrays Odysseus as less heroic. **"Siren Song"**: uses mythological creature; but portrays Siren as a reluctant destroyer. **"Prologue and Epilogue"**: tells the tale of heroic adventure; but uses modern idiom and emphasizes Penelope. **"Ithaca"**: uses image of journey; but uses journey as symbol of discovery and growth.

   Other sample answers appear in ***Graphic Organizer Transparencies*, Comparing Contemporary Interpretations Graphic Organizer A (After You Read)**, p. 193, and in the **Additional Answers** section.
2. **Possible response:** In "An Ancient Gesture," the poet says that both modern life and ancient life are full of sorrow and loneliness.
3. (a) In "Ithaca," the poet alludes to the Lestrygonians. In "Prologue and Epilogue," the poet alludes to Penelope as the "rock-steady woman." (b) The allusions give new ideas about the characters. (c) **Possible response:** The allusion to the Lestrygonians in "Ithaca" is more effective because it relates an ancient tale to a modern viewpoint: People create their own monsters.

Timed Writing

1. Review the prompt with students.
2. Have students use the 5-Minute Planner to structure their time. Guide them in answering the bulleted questions. For example, have them identify the allusions and clarify meaning before making comparisons.
3. Allow students 40 minutes to complete the assignment.
4. As students prewrite and draft, have them refer to the selection comparison organizer.

Assessment Resources

The following resources can be used to assess students' knowledge and skills.

Unit 6 Resources

L1 L2 EL **Selection Test A,** pp. 76–78

L3 L4 EL **Selection Test B,** pp. 79–81

L3 L4 **Open Book Test,** pp. 73–75

PHLit Online! All assessment resources are available at **www.PHLitOnline.com.**

Six Traits Focus

✓	Ideas	✓	Word Choice
✓	Organization		Sentence Fluency
	Voice		Conventions

PRETEACH

Common Core State Standards

- Writing 2, 2.a, b, d, e; 5
- Language 1, 2, 2.c

Introducing the Writing Assignment

Review the assignment, using the instruction on the student page.

Connecting to Real-Life Writing

Point out that technical documents explain how to use consumer products, such as appliances, vehicles, or computer software. They are often included with the product's packaging.

Writing Workshop
Work in Progress

If students have completed the work-in-progress assignments on p. 1085 and 1117, suggest that they try to develop their work-in-progress ideas in a technical document.

TEACH

Prewriting Strategy

1. Introduce the prewriting strategy.
2. Have students apply the strategy.

Six Traits Focus

✓	Ideas	Word Choice
	Organization	Sentence Fluency
	Voice	Conventions

Writing Workshop

Write Explanatory Text

Technical Document

Defining the Form Technical writing conveys information and ideas logically while providing details and specifications. A technical manual can identify the steps to take to complete a task. You might use elements of this type of writing in instruction manuals, rule books, and assembly directions.

Assignment Write a manual for others to use when completing a task, such as how to wrap a gift, how to establish an exercise routine, how to take meeting minutes, or how to work together to resolve conflicts. Include these elements:

✓ *ideas* logically and correctly conveyed

✓ *detailed and accurate specifications*

✓ *scenarios, definitions*, and *examples* to aid comprehension

✓ *understandable abbreviations* and *legible writing*

✓ error-free grammar, especially correct use of *sentence fragments and run-ons*

To preview the criteria on which your manual may be judged, see the rubric on page 1143.

 **Writing Workshop:** *Work in Progress*

Review the work you did on pages 1085 and 1117.

Prewriting/Planning Strategy

Identify the information you will need to share. Before you write, think about how someone would successfully complete the task you will explain. Consider your audience and what they need to learn the task you have chosen. List the necessary materials, and any specific skills you may need to detail. Complete a chart like the one shown to help you prepare to write your manual. If necessary, conduct research to learn more about your topic.

Task:		
Materials:	Steps:	Special Skills:

Common Core State Standards

Writing

2. Write informative/explanatory texts to examine and convey complex ideas, concepts, and information clearly and accurately through the effective selection, organization, and analysis of content.

2.a. Introduce a topic; organize complex ideas, concepts, and information to make important connections and distinctions; include formatting, graphics, and multimedia when useful to aiding comprehension.

2.b. Develop the topic with well-chosen, relevant, and sufficient facts, extended definitions, concrete details, quotations, or other information and examples appropriate to the audience's knowledge of the topic.

2.d. Use precise language and domain-specific vocabulary to manage the complexity of the topic.

5. Develop and strengthen writing as needed by planning, revising, editing, rewriting, or trying a new approach, focusing on addressing what is most significant for a specific purpose and audience.

Teaching Resources

The following resources can be used to enrich or extend the instruction.

All *Unit 6 Resources*
Writing Workshop, pp. 82–83

All *Common Core Companion,*
pp. 190–201; 220–221

All *Professional Development Guidebook*
Rubrics for Self-Assessment: Technical Document, pp. 261–262

All *Graphic Organizer Transparencies*
Rubric for Self-Assessment: Technical Document, p. 195

All *See It!* **DVD**
Gary L. Blackwood, Segments 3 and 4

All resources are available online at **www.PHLitOnline.com.**

SIX TRAITS WRITER'S TOOLBOX SIX TRAITS

Ideas | Conventions | Sentence Fluency | Voice | Organization | Word Choice

Expressing Your Ideas

Ideas are the basis for any form of writing, even technical writing. To provide instruction on how to accomplish a task, you must express your ideas clearly and organize them logically. Think about the obvious steps you take to complete the process, record them logically, and then review them to make sure you didn't miss anything.

Teach your audience. The main purpose of constructing a manual is to teach your audience how to accomplish a task. Begin by laying the groundwork for the task you will explain. You may need to define any new vocabulary. Provide a sufficient number of examples, scenarios, and clarifications related to your purpose to help your audience learn a new skill and complete the task in a variety of situations.

Use visual aids. Remember that visual aids can be helpful tools to convey basic information. It may be helpful to provide diagrams, charts, or maps. Alternatively, you might prepare a demonstration using presentation software. A labeled illustration like the one shown would be very helpful in a manual on bicycle repair.

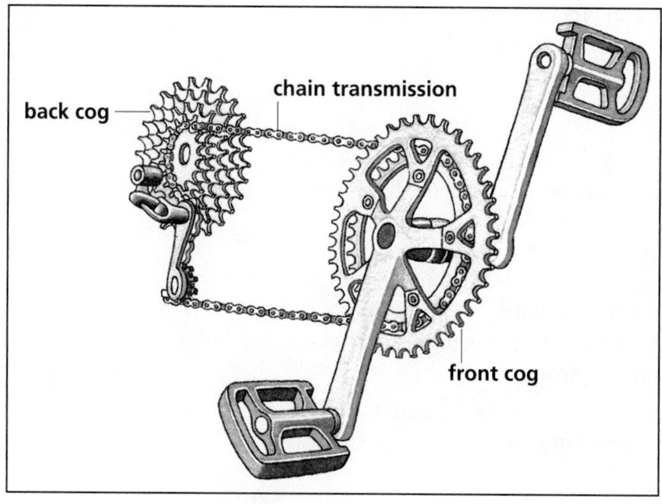

Expressing Your Ideas

1. Introduce the writing skill, using the instruction on the student page.
2. Discuss the strategies for expressing ideas and the example of a visual aid.

Teaching the Writing Skill

1. Remind students that the purpose of a technical document is to convey information clearly and precisely. Tell students that it is important to carefully think through the steps needed to accomplish the task.
2. Have students brainstorm a wide variety of possible tasks and list some of their answers on the board.
3. For each task, ask students who might be the audience for the manual. Write the audience beside each task.
4. Discuss the importance of graphics in explaining how to accomplish a task. For each task, ask students what visual aids might be helpful. List them on the board beside the task. Remind students that illustrations, diagrams, and examples help readers better understand the process.

Prentice Hall EssayScorer

A writing prompt for this mode of writing can be found on the *Prentice Hall Essay Scorer* at **www.PHLitOnline.com.**

Differentiated Instruction for Universal Access

EL Strategy for English Learners

Tell students that technical documents explaining how to do things are similar to instructions. Review prepositions and their role in instructions. Write these prepositions on the board: *across, after, around, beside, before, during, following, from, in, inside, near, on, opposite, to, towards, under, with.* Provide an example by discussing how the prepositions *to* and *from* change the meaning of these two sentences: *I am walking to the house. I am walking from the house.*

Strategy for Advanced Writers

Challenge students to write succinctly. Tell students that their manuals should contain a maximum of 750 words. Remind them that they should eliminate any irrelevant or redundant wording. If computers are available, have students compose their manuals using word-processing programs so that they can use the automatic word count function.

Drafting Strategies

1. Introduce the drafting strategies, using the instruction on the student page.
2. Have students apply the strategies as they draft.

Teaching the Strategies

1. Review with students how to organize the instructions in their manuals. Suggest that students sketch possible formats, experimenting with the placement of numbered steps, boxes, and illustrations.
2. Have students review one another's papers as though they are considering completing the task outlined, then trade papers and review again as each of the other types of reader. Have them provide feedback on how easily they found the information they needed as each reader.

Six Traits Focus

✔	Ideas		Word Choice
✔	Organization		Sentence Fluency
	Voice		Conventions

Revising Strategies

1. Introduce the revision strategies, using the instruction on the student page.
2. Have students apply the strategies as they revise their drafts.

Teaching the Strategies

Have students use thesauruses to find synonyms for repeated words. Remind them to check dictionaries to make sure that they are using words with the desired connotations.

Think Aloud: Model Reviewing Word Choice

Model the strategy, using the following "think aloud":

> I have the sentence, "Even if the rain is just tickling your face, the road may be slippery." Figurative language is inappropriate here, so I'll revise to use precise, vivid words instead: "Even a drizzle can make the road slippery."

Six Traits Focus

✔	Ideas	✔	Word Choice
✔	Organization		Sentence Fluency
✔	Voice		Conventions

Drafting Strategies

Organize details in step-by-step order. Because most manuals describe a process that takes place over time, chronological order is often the most effective organization.

Choose the best format. Paragraphs are not always the best way to present information meant to instruct or explain. Your readers will have different needs at different times:

- A reader who is considering doing the activity outlined in your manual will want a quick overview of materials and steps.
- A reader who is in the middle of following your instructions will need to locate a step quickly.
- A reader who is looking for special tips or background information will want additional information.

To meet the needs of each of these readers, consider these formatting possibilities as you draft:

- Present essential steps as a series of numbered points or in a bulleted list for ease of reading.
- Organize information below specific headings.
- Provide additional information in separate sections, such as boxes inset alongside your main instructions. You may decide to build a troubleshooting chart to help with problems your reader may encounter.

Revising Strategies

Evaluate repeated words. A manual or how-to guide should be written in a formal style with straightforward language, but that does not mean it has to be boring. As you revise, incorporate more precise language or technical vocabulary that would help to explain the topic of your manual to the reader. Avoid overuse of words that may dull your writing. Go back through your draft to find and circle words you have used several times. Review the words you have circled to decide whether you should replace a word with a synonym or even rephrase the sentence.

Draft: Dry each part of your dog by squeezing the fur dry with towels. When the dog is mostly dry, have it sit on a dry towel until its fur completely dries.

Revision: Dry each part of your dog by squeezing the water from the fur with towels. When the dog is barely damp, have it sit on a fresh towel until its fur completely dries.

Common Core State Standards

Writing

2.a. Organize complex ideas, concepts, and information to make important connections and distinctions; include formatting, graphics, and multimedia when useful to aiding comprehension.

2.d. Use precise language and domain-specific vocabulary to manage the complexity of the topic.

2.e. Establish and maintain a formal style and objective tone while attending to the norms and conventions of the discipline in which they are writing.

Language

1. Demonstrate command of the conventions of standard English grammar and usage when writing or speaking.

2. Demonstrate command of the conventions of standard English punctuation when writing.

Applying Understanding by Design Principles

Clarifying Expected Outcomes: Using Rubrics

- Before students begin working on this assignment, have them preview the Rubric for Self-Assessment (p. 1143) to learn what qualities their manuals must have. A copy of this rubric appears in *Graphic Organizer Transparencies,* p. 195.
- Review the criteria in the rubric with the class. Before students use the rubric to assess their writing, work with them to rate the Student Model (p. 1142) using the rubric.
- If you wish to assess students' essays with either a 4-point or a 6-point scoring rubric, see ***Professional Development Guidebook,*** pp. 261–262.

WRITER'S TOOLBOX

Conventions | Sentence Fluency | Voice | Organization | Word Choice | Ideas

Revising to Correct Fragments and Run-ons

A **fragment** is a group of words that does not express a complete thought but is punctuated as if it were a sentence. A **run-on** is two or more complete sentences that are not properly joined or separated.

Identifying and Correcting Fragments Fragments express incomplete thoughts. Often, they offer information that belongs to a nearby sentence. Correct fragments by attaching them to sentences.

Fragment: They waited at the bus stop. *Huddled under an umbrella.*

Revised: They waited at the bus stop, huddled under an umbrella.

Other fragments can be corrected through expansion—adding the words needed to make a complete sentence.

Fragment: *As long as you agree to help.*

Expanded: I will wash the car as long as you agree to help.

Identifying and Correcting Run-ons Run-ons include sentences that are fused with no punctuation at all or that are linked by only a comma.

Fused: She speaks Spanish fluently she does not speak Italian at all.

Comma splice: She speaks Spanish fluently, she does not speak Italian at all.

Three Ways to Correct a Run-on Sentence

Use an appropriate end mark to separate a run-on into two sentences. Begin the second sentence with a capital letter.	She speaks Spanish fluently. She does not speak Italian at all.
Use a comma and a coordinating conjunction, such as *and, but, or, for,* and *nor,* to combine two related independent clauses.	She speaks Spanish fluently, but she does not speak Italian at all.
Use a semicolon to connect two closely related ideas.	She speaks Spanish fluently; she does not speak Italian at all.

Grammar in Your Writing

Scan your technical document for fragments and run-ons by looking for sentences that seem too short or too long. Neatly correct any sentence problems you find using the strategies that have been presented.

PH WRITING COACH

Further instruction and practice are available in *Prentice Hall Writing Coach*.

Revising to Correct Fragments and Run-ons

1. Introduce the grammar skill, using the instruction on the student page.
2. Discuss the examples and the strategies for correcting run-on sentences.
3. Have students follow the instruction under Grammar in Your Writing to correct errors in their drafts.

Teaching the Grammar Skill

1. Tell students that fragments are unfinished ideas. Explain that fragments are confusing to readers and should be either eliminated or expanded to make complete sentences.
2. Review how to identify fragments. Tell students that fragments are odd-sounding phrases that do not quite make sense.
3. Write the following fragments on the board. **Ask** students to expand them so that they are complete sentences.
   - *Listened carefully and attentively.*

   Possible response: The group of campers listened carefully and attentively.
   - *While we hiked up the steep path.*

   Possible response: The wind was howling while we hiked up the steep path.
4. Use the chart on the student page to review ways to correct run-on sentences.

PH WRITING COACH Grade 9

Students will find practice with and guidance on fragments and run-ons in Chapter 16, Section 4.

Strategies for Using Technology in Writing

If students are using word-processing software to draft and revise their manuals, suggest that they use the Spelling and Grammar feature to locate fragments. When students find a fragment, have them examine the sentences surrounding it and determine how to correct the fragment by incorporating it into another sentence. Point out that Spelling and Grammar features are not always accurate and cannot replace careful proofreading.

Student Model

Review the Student Model with the class, using the annotations to analyze the writer's use of the elements of a technical document.

Teaching From the Student Model

1. Point out to students that the steps for taking minutes of a meeting are formatted with numbers. Explain that using a numbered format makes it easier for a reader to follow chronological order.
2. Note that the writer assumes that a reader has no familiarity at all with the process of taking meeting minutes and therefore the writer provides even the most basic details.
3. Have students determine whether the writer has thought about mistakes that a reader might make in the process of taking meeting minutes. **Ask** students to point out where in the student model the writer has addressed this issue.

   Answer: Step 3, first sentence

Connecting to Real-Life Writing

Tell students that most jobs require explanations of processes or tasks. The ability to break a task into its separate steps and explain them clearly to others is an important skill in the workplace.

Student Model: C.J. Geeza, San Juan Capistrano, CA

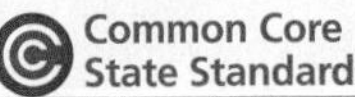

Language
2.c. Spell correctly.

Taking Meeting Minutes

One day, you just might get asked to take meeting notes for a meeting you are attending. Whether it is a business, sports, or student council meeting, taking meeting notes is important because notes capture discussion and decisions. It's easy to understand meeting notes if you break it down into five simple steps.

In the opening paragraph, C.J. explains what meeting minutes are before instructing how to take them.

1. **Get Yourself Ready**—This first step in writing meaningful meeting minutes takes place before the meeting has started. Make sure you go to the meeting ready to listen objectively. Meeting minutes are usually the official record of what happened, so it is important to be accurate. Decide how you are going to record information. This could be a computer or pen and paper. If you're using your computer, you might want to consider sitting next to an outlet. A great hint is to use the meeting agenda, or an organized layout of the topics that are going to be discussed, to create an outline for your note taking. This will make it easier to move between topics as the meeting progresses. Make a map of the seating arrangement and write down names so you can make sure you know who said what.
2. **Just the Facts**—This next part is the most important part of taking meeting minutes. Start by writing down the date, time the meeting starts and ends, and who is and is not in attendance for the meeting. Listen to who is speaking and what is said. It's better to summarize what is said rather than to go into great detail. Do not make the mistake of recording every single comment. Be objective—your opinion is not needed.
3. **Make a Draft**—You should not wait too long before you write a draft of the meeting minutes using your notes. Use complete sentences and provide detail on the items discussed, major points raised, and decisions made. Be sure not to take sides in any arguments in your writing, as your job is only to record the meeting, not to cause more conflict. After you are finished with your draft, go back and revise it. You can organize your minutes by adding bullet points or numbers. Cut out any unimportant information not related to the meeting. Also, make sure the reader can point out important topics and comments by underlining, boldfacing, color coding, etc.
4. **Get it Right**—Compare your notes and final copy in order to make sure that you have covered all the content you wanted to include. Make sure that you only use one system of bullets and numbering. Check the spelling of names and words, grammar, and punctuation.
5. **Get it Out**—Making copies of your meeting minutes is a great idea. This way, you can give a copy to the people who were not at the meeting so they know what happened and a copy to those in attendance as a friendly reminder about any follow-up needed.

Providing organizational tips teaches the reader how to effectively note what is said in the meeting.

The numbering system and headings allow C.J. to present information logically for the reader.

Meeting notes are an effective way to document the details and action items of a meeting. Learning to listen objectively and record notes accurately is a skill that will be used in the workplace. Like any other skill, the more you do it the better you become at it.

C.J. uses a conclusion to tie the steps together as an essay.

Editing and Proofreading

Check your draft for errors in spelling, grammar, and punctuation.

Review basic spelling skills. When you edit and proofread your writing, make sure you spell everything correctly. Review common errors in usage and check words you often confuse. Confirm word formation rules, such as adding prefixes, suffixes, and changing spellings.

Focus on legibility. Make sure revisions are clear and readable. Draw a single line through a word to delete it. Use a caret (^) to show where words or letters need to be added. Underline letters three times to show that they need to be capitalized.

Spiral Review

Earlier in the unit, you learned about **simple and compound sentences** (p. 1084) and **complex and compound-complex sentences** (p. 1116). Make sure you have properly constructed these sentence types in your instructions.

Publishing and Presenting

Consider one of the following ways to share your writing:

Print a manual. Make a clean copy of your final draft. Enter your instructions into a word-processing program and print out a manual for others to consult.

Create a podcast. Use your manual as the basis for a podcast script. Record your podcast, making sure you express your organization clearly.

Reflecting on Your Writing

Writer's Journal Jot down your answers to this question:

How did writing directions for the process you chose help you understand it better?

Rubric for Self-Assessment

Find evidence in your writing to address each category. Then, use the rating scale to grade your work.

Criteria	Rating Scale (not very – very)
Focus: How clearly does your manual focus on the task at hand?	1 2 3 4 5
Organization: How logical is your organization?	1 2 3 4 5
Support/Elaboration: How effectively do you include specific details, examples, and descriptions to support your instruction?	1 2 3 4 5
Style: How well does your style match your audience's needs?	1 2 3 4 5
Conventions: How correct is your grammar, especially avoiding fragments and run-ons?	1 2 3 4 5
Ideas: How clearly do you express your ideas through instruction?	1 2 3 4 5

Editing and Proofreading

1. Introduce the editing and proofreading focus, using the instruction on the student page.
2. Have students edit and proofread their narratives, correcting grammar, spelling, punctuation, and word choice. Make sure they check for errors of the type noted in the lesson focus and the Spiral Review.

Teaching the Editing Focus

Have students proofread their manuals, focusing on correcting spelling, grammar and punctuation errors.

Six Traits Focus

	Ideas		Word Choice
	Organization	✔	Sentence Fluency
	Voice	✔	Conventions

ASSESS

Publishing and Presenting

1. Discuss with students the size requirements for the pages of their manuals. Point out that pages that are too small are not easy to read and pages that are too large are difficult to handle.
2. Suggest that before recording their podcasts, students practice reading their manuals aloud to partners, using appropriate emphasis and expression. Have partners suggest areas for improvement.

Reflecting on Your Writing

Ask students whether writing about the process of taking meeting minutes helped them recognize steps in the process that they were previously unaware of.

✓ Three Skeleton Key • ✓✓ The Red-headed League

Lesson Pacing Guide

DAY 1 Preteach

- Administer the Reading and Vocabulary Warm-ups (*Unit 6 Resources*, pp. 92–95 or 110–113) as necessary.
- Introduce the Reading Skill: Comparing and Contrasting Characters.
- Introduce the Literary Analysis concept: Protagonist and Antagonist.
- Distribute copies of the appropriate graphic organizer for the Reading Skill (*Graphic Organizer Transparencies*, pp. 199–201).
- Distribute copies of the appropriate graphic organizer for Literary Analysis (*Graphic Organizer Transparencies*, pp. 196–198).
- Teach the selection vocabulary.
- Introduce the Word Study skill.

DAYS 2–3 Preteach/Teach

- Build background with the Background feature.
- Develop thematic vocabulary and thematic thinking with Writing About the Big Question.
- Prepare students to read with the Activating Prior Knowledge activities (TE).
- Informally monitor comprehension while students read.
- Use the Reading Check questions to confirm comprehension.
- Develop students' ability to compare and contrast characters, using the Reading Skill questions.
- Develop students' understanding of a protagonist and antagonist, using the Literary Analysis questions.
- Reinforce vocabulary with the Vocabulary notes.
- Reinforce unit focus standards using the Spiral Review prompts.

DAY 4 Assess

- Assess students' comprehension and mastery of the skills by having them answer the Critical Thinking, Reading Skill, and Literary Analysis questions.
- Have students complete the Vocabulary Practice activities.
- Have students complete the Word Study activities.

DAY 5 Extend/Assess

- Have students complete the Conventions lesson.
- Have students complete the Writing activity and write three journal entries. (You may assign as homework.)
- Extend learning by having students complete the Research and Technology activity, an oral report. (You may assign as homework.) As an alternative, assign them "Facing Danger at Sea" or "Inner Circles" in *Reality Central*.
- Administer Selection Test A or B (*Unit 6 Resources*, pp. 104–109 or 125–130).

Common Core State Standards

Reading Literature 3. Analyze how complex characters develop over the course of a text, interact with other characters, and advance the plot or develop the theme.

Writing
3.d. Use precise words and phrases, telling details, and sensory language to convey a vivid picture of the experiences, events, setting, and/or characters.
7. Conduct short as well as more sustained research projects to answer a question or solve a problem; synthesize multiple sources on the subject, demonstrating understanding of the subject under investigation.

Speaking and Listening 2. Integrate multiple sources of information presented in diverse media or formats evaluating the credibility and accuracy of each source.
5. Make strategic use of digital media in presentations to enhance understanding of findings, reasoning, and evidence and to add interest.

Language
2. Demonstrate command of the conventions of standard English capitalization, punctuation, and spelling when writing.
5. Demonstrate understanding of figurative language, word relationships, and nuances in word meanings.

Additional Standards Practice
Common Core Companion,* *pp.15–22; 55–56

Daily Block Scheduling
Each day in this Lesson Pacing Guide represents a 40–50 minute period. Teachers using block scheduling may combine days to revise pacing. In addition, teachers may differentiate and support core instruction by integrating components for extended and intensive support as students require. See the Guide to Selected Leveled Resources (facing page).

Guide to Selected Leveled Resources

RTI Tier 1 (students performing on level)			✓ More Accessible Three Skeleton Key	✓✓ More Complex The Red-headed League
Warm Up	Whole class instruction; Group work	**Practice, model,** and **monitor** fluency, working **with the whole class** or **in groups.**	**Vocabulary** and **Reading Warm-ups B,** ***Unit 6 Resources,*** pp. 92–93, 95	**Vocabulary** and **Reading Warm-ups B,** ***Unit 6 Resources,*** pp. 110–111, 113
Comprehension/Skills	Whole class instruction; Independent work	**Support** and **monitor** comprehension and skills development, having students complete the activities, graphic organizers, and interactive prompts **independently** or **as a class.**	• ***Reader's Notebook,*** adapted instruction and full selection EL ***Reader's Notebook: English Learner's Version,*** adapted instruction and adapted selection • **Reading Skill Graphic Organizer B,** ***Graphic Organizer Transparencies,*** p. 198 • **Literary Analysis Graphic Organizer B,** ***Graphic Organizer Transparencies,*** p. 201	• ***Reader's Notebook,*** adapted instruction and summary EL ***Reader's Notebook: English Learner's Version,*** adapted instruction and summary • **Reading Skill Graphic Organizer B,** ***Graphic Organizer Transparencies,*** p. 198 • **Literary Analysis Graphic Organizer B,** ***Graphic Organizer Transparencies,*** p. 201
Monitor Progress	A	**Monitor** student progress with the differentiated curriculum-based assessment in the *Unit Resources.*	• **Selection Test B,** ***Unit 6 Resources,*** pp. 107–109 • **Open-Book Test,** ***Unit 6 Resources,*** pp. 101–103	• **Selection Test B,** ***Unit 6 Resources,*** pp. 128–130 • **Open-Book Test,** ***Unit 1 Resources,*** pp. 122–124

RTI Tier 2 (students requiring intervention)			✓ More Accessible Three Skeleton Key	✓✓ More Complex The Red-headed League
Warm Up	Group work; One-on-one teaching	**Practice, model,** and **monitor** fluency **in groups** or **with individuals.**	• **Vocabulary and Reading Warm-ups A,** ***Unit 6 Resources,*** pp. 92–95 • ***Reality Central,*** "Facing Danger at Sea" • ***Hear It!*** **Audio CD (adapted text)**	• **Vocabulary and Reading Warm-ups A,** ***Unit 6 Resources,*** pp. 110–113 • ***Reality Central,*** "Inner Circle" • ***Hear It!*** **Audio CD**
Comprehension/Skills	Group work; One-on-one teaching	• **Support** and **monitor** comprehension and skills development, working **in small groups** or **with individuals.** • **Pair** students with more advanced peers and have them complete the writing activity in the *Real-World Writing Journal.* • As students complete the selection in the appropriate version of the *Reader's Notebook,* **monitor** comprehension frequently with group questions and individual instruction. • **Model** strategies while guiding students in completing the activities and prompts in the *Reader's Notebook,* as well as the graphic organizers. • **Practice** skills and **monitor** mastery with the *Reading Kit* worksheets.	• ***Real-World Writing Journal,*** Lesson 5, pp. 172–175 • ***Reader's Notebook: Adapted Version,*** adapted instruction and adapted selection EL ***Reader's Notebook: English Learner's Version,*** adapted instruction and adapted selection • **Reading Skill Graphic Organizer A,** ***Graphic Organizer Transparencies,*** p. 196 • **Literary Analysis Graphic Organizer A,** ***Graphic Organizer Transparencies,*** p. 199 • **Reading Kit,** Practice worksheets, pp. 288, 282, 292, 294, 302	• ***Real-World Writing Journal,*** Lesson 6, pp. 176–179 • ***Reader's Notebook: Adapted Version,*** adapted instruction and summary EL ***Reader's Notebook: English Learner's Version,*** adapted instruction and summary • **Reading Skill Graphic Organizer A,** ***Graphic Organizer Transparencies,*** p. 197 • **Literary Analysis Graphic Organizer A,** ***Graphic Organizer Transparencies,*** p. 200 • **Reading Kit,** Practice worksheets, pp. 288, 282, 292, 294, 302
Monitor Progress	A	**Monitor** student progress with the differentiated curriculum-based assessment in the *Unit Resources* and in the *Reading Kit.*	• **Selection Test A,** ***Unit 6 Resources,*** pp. 104–106 • **Reading Kit,** Assess worksheets, pp. 289, 283, 293, 295, 303	• **Selection Test A,** ***Unit 6 Resources,*** pp. 125–127 • **Reading Kit,** Assess worksheets, pp. 289, 283, 293, 295, 303

TIER 3 Tier 3 intervention may require consultation with the student's special-education or dyslexia specialist. For additional support, see the Tier 2 activities and resources listed above.

One-on-one teaching **Group work** **Whole class instruction** **Independent work** **A Assessment**

For a complete guide to selection support, including support for Advanced students, see the Overview of Resources in the frontmatter.

✓Three Skeleton Key
✓✓The Red-headed League

Three Skeleton Key

George G. Toudouze

Vocabulary
monotonous (mə nät′ ′n əs) *adj.* having little or no variation

My most terrifying experience? Well, one does have a few in thirty-five years of service in the Lights, although it's mostly monotonous routine work—keeping the light in order, making out the reports.

When I was a young man, not very long in the service, there was an opening in a lighthouse newly built off the coast of Guiana,[1] on a small rock twenty miles or so from the mainland. The pay was high, so in order to reach the sum I had set out to save before I married, I volunteered for service in the new light.

1. **Guiana** (gē an′ ə) region on the northern coast of South America.

1148 Themes in Literature: Heroism

The Red-headed League

Sir Arthur Conan Doyle

I had called upon my friend, Mr. Sherlock Holmes, one day in the autumn of last year and found him in deep conversation with a very stout, florid-faced, elderly gentleman with fiery red hair. With an apology for my intrusion, I was about to withdraw when Holmes pulled me abruptly into the room and closed the door behind me.

1166 Themes in Literature: Heroism

RESOURCES FOR:

- L1 Special-Needs Students
- L2 Below-Level Students (Tier 2)
- L3 On-Level Students (Tier 1)
- L4 Advanced Students (Tier 1)
- EL English Learners
- All All Students

Vocabulary/Fluency/Prior Knowledge

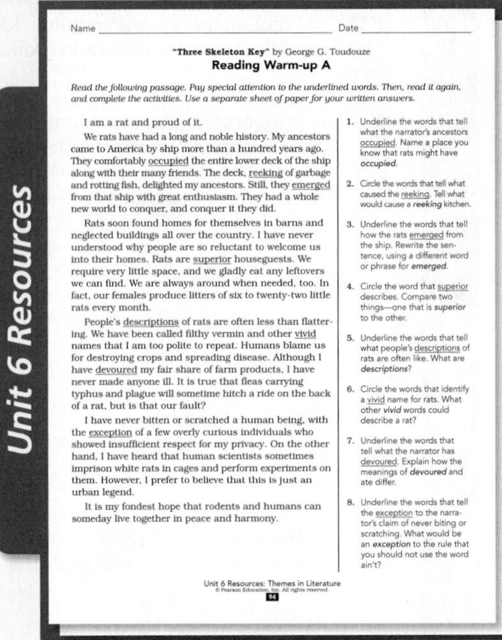
Unit 6 Resources

Name ______________________ Date ______________

"Three Skeleton Key" by George G. Toudouze
Reading Warm-up A

Read the following passage. Pay special attention to the underlined words. Then, read it again, and complete the activities. Use a separate sheet of paper for your written answers.

I am a rat and proud of it.

We rats have had a long and noble history. My ancestors came to America by ship more than a hundred years ago. They comfortably occupied the entire lower deck of the ship along with their many friends. The deck, reeking of garbage and rotting fish, delighted my ancestors. Still, they emerged from that ship with great enthusiasm. They had a whole new world to conquer, and conquer it they did.

Rats soon found homes for themselves in barns and neglected buildings all over the country. I have never understood why people are so reluctant to welcome us into their homes. Rats are superior houseguests. We require very little space, and we gladly eat any leftovers we can find. We are always around when needed, too. In fact, our females produce litters of six to twenty-two little rats every month.

People's descriptions of rats are often less than flattering. We have been called filthy vermin and other vivid names that I am too polite to repeat. Humans blame us for destroying crops and spreading disease. Although I have devoured my fair share of farm products, I have never made anyone ill. It is true that fleas carrying typhus and plague will sometime hitch a ride on the back of a rat, but is that our fault?

I have never bitten or scratched a human being, with the exception of a few overly curious individuals who showed insufficient respect for my privacy. On the other hand, I have heard that human scientists sometimes imprison white rats in cages and perform experiments on them. However, I prefer to believe that this is just an urban legend.

It is my fondest hope that rodents and humans can someday live together in peace and harmony.

1. Underline the words that tell what the narrator's ancestors occupied. Name a place you know that rats might have *occupied*.
2. Circle the words that tell what caused the reeking. Tell what would cause a *reeking* kitchen.
3. Underline the words that tell how the rats emerged from the ship. Rewrite the sentence, using a different word or phrase for *emerged*.
4. Circle the word that superior describes. Compare two things—one that is *superior* to the other.
5. Underline the words that tell what people's descriptions of rats are often like. What are *descriptions*?
6. Circle the words that identify a vivid name for rats. What other *vivid* words could describe a rat?
7. Underline the words that tell what the narrator has devoured. Explain how the meanings of *devoured* and ate differ.
8. Underline the words that tell the exception to the narrator's claim of never biting or scratching. What would be an *exception* to the rule that you should not use the word ain't?

Unit 6 Resources: Themes in Literature
© Pearson Education, Inc. All rights reserved.
94

EL L1 L2 **Reading Warm-ups A and B,** pp. 94–95, 112–113

Also available for this selection:

EL L1 L2 **Vocabulary Warm-ups A and B,** pp. 92–93, 110–111

All **Writing About the Big Question,** pp. 96, 114

All **Vocabulary Builder,** pp. 99, 117

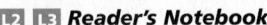

Reader's Notebooks

Pre- and postreading pages for both selections, as well as "Three Skeleton Key," appear in an interactive format in the *Reader's Notebooks.* Each *Notebook* is differentiated for a different group of learners. The selections in the Adapted and English Learner's versions are abridged.

L2 L3 ***Reader's Notebook***

L1 ***Reader's Notebook: Adapted Version***

EL ***Reader's Notebook: English Learner's Version***

EL ***Reader's Notebook: Spanish Version***

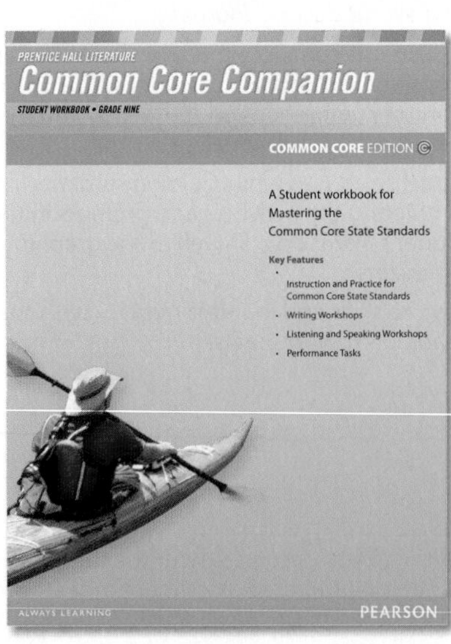

Common Core Companion

Additional instruction and practice for each Common Core State Standard

Selection Support

Graphic Organizer Transparencies

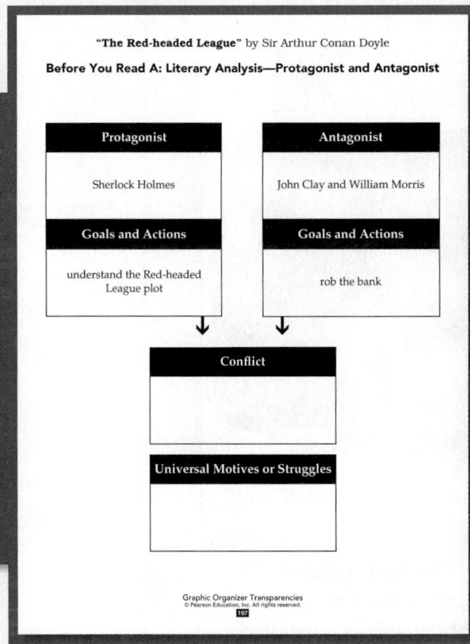

"The Red-headed League" by Sir Arthur Conan Doyle

Before You Read A: Literary Analysis—Protagonist and Antagonist

Protagonist	Antagonist
Sherlock Holmes	John Clay and William Morris
Goals and Actions	**Goals and Actions**
understand the Red-headed League plot	rob the bank

Conflict

Universal Motives or Struggles

Graphic Organizer Transparencies
© Pearson Education, Inc. All rights reserved.
197

EL L1 L2 **Literary Analysis: Graphic Organizer A,** pp. 196–197 (partially filled in)

Also available for this selection:

EL L3 **Literary Analysis: Graphic Organizer B,** p. 198

EL L1 L2 **Reading: Graphic Organizer A,** pp. 199–200 (partially filled in)

EL L3 **Reading: Graphic Organizer B,** p. 201

Skills Development/Extension

Unit 6 Resources

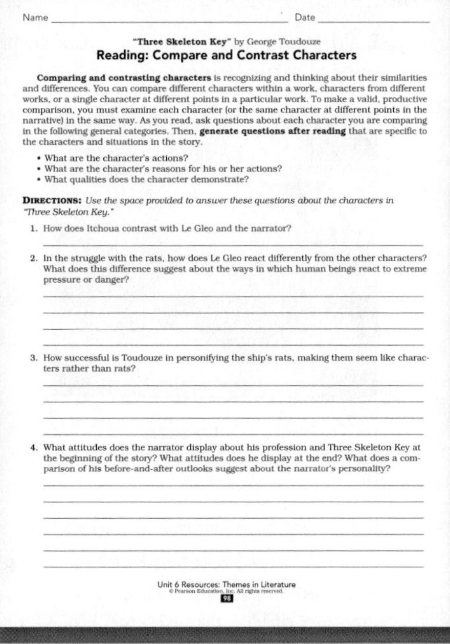

Name ______________________ Date ____________

"Three Skeleton Key" by George Toudouze

Reading: Compare and Contrast Characters

Comparing and contrasting characters is recognizing and thinking about their similarities and differences. You can compare different characters within a work, characters from different works, or a single character at different points in a particular work. To make a valid, productive comparison, you must examine each character (or the same character at different points in the narrative) in the same way. As you read, ask questions about each character you are comparing in the following general categories. Then, **generate questions after reading** that are specific to the characters and situations in the story.

- What are the character's actions?
- What are the character's reasons for his or her actions?
- What qualities does the character demonstrate?

Directions: *Use the space provided to answer these questions about the characters in "Three Skeleton Key."*

1. How does Itchoua contrast with Le Gleo and the narrator?
2. In the struggle with the rats, how does Le Gleo react differently from the other characters? What does this difference suggest about the ways in which human beings react to extreme pressure or danger?
3. How successful is Toudouze in personifying the ship's rats, making them seem like characters rather than rats?
4. What attitudes does the narrator display about his profession and Three Skeleton Key at the beginning of the story? What attitudes does he display at the end? What does a comparison of his before-and-after outlooks suggest about the narrator's personality?

Unit 6 Resources: Themes in Literature
© Pearson Education, Inc. All rights reserved.
98

All **Reading: Compare and Contrast,** pp. 98, 116

Also available for this selection:

All **Literary Analysis: Protagonist and Antagonist,** pp. 97, 115

L4 **Enrichment,** pp. 100, 118

EL L3 L4 **Grammar,** p. 119

EL L3 L4 **Support for Writing,** p. 126

L3 L4 **Support for Extend Your Learning,** p. 121

Assessment

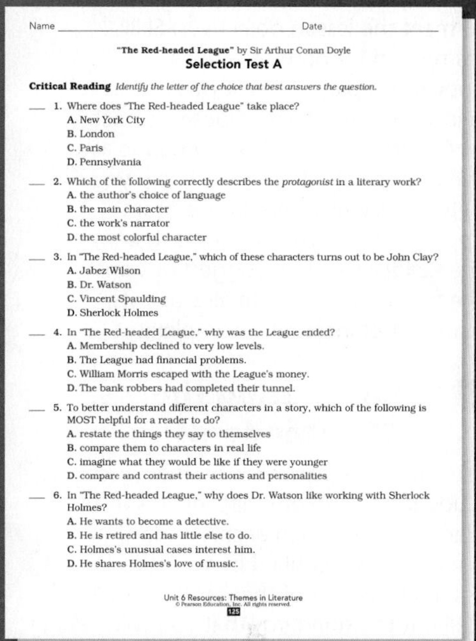

Name ______________________ Date ____________

"The Red-headed League" by Sir Arthur Conan Doyle

Selection Test A

Critical Reading *Identify the letter of the choice that best answers the question.*

___ 1. Where does "The Red-headed League" take place?
A. New York City
B. London
C. Paris
D. Pennsylvania

___ 2. Which of the following correctly describes the *protagonist* in a literary work?
A. the author's choice of language
B. the main character
C. the work's narrator
D. the most colorful character

___ 3. In "The Red-headed League," which of these characters turns out to be John Clay?
A. Jabez Wilson
B. Dr. Watson
C. Vincent Spaulding
D. Sherlock Holmes

___ 4. In "The Red-headed League," why was the League ended?
A. Membership declined to very low levels.
B. The League had financial problems.
C. William Morris escaped with the League's money.
D. The bank robbers had completed their tunnel.

___ 5. To better understand different characters in a story, which of the following is MOST helpful for a reader to do?
A. restate the things they say to themselves
B. compare them to characters in real life
C. imagine what they would be like if they were younger
D. compare and contrast their actions and personalities

___ 6. In "The Red-headed League," why does Dr. Watson like working with Sherlock Holmes?
A. He wants to become a detective.
B. He is retired and has little else to do.
C. Holmes's unusual cases interest him.
D. He shares Holmes's love of music.

Unit 6 Resources: Themes in Literature
© Pearson Education, Inc. All rights reserved.
123

EL L1 L2 **Selection Test A,** pp. 104–106, 125–127

Also available for this selection:

L3 L4 **Open-Book Test,** pp. 101–103, 122–123

EL L3 L4 **Selection Test B,** 107–109, 128–130

PHLit Online!
www.PHLitOnline.com

- complete narrated selection text
- a thematically related video with writing prompt
- an interactive graphic organizer
- highlighting feature
- access to all student print resources, adapted to individual student needs
- Spanish and English summaries
- adapted selection translations in Spanish

Online Resources: All print materials are also available online.

Background Video

Also available:

Get Connected! (thematic video with writing prompt)

All videos are available in Spanish.

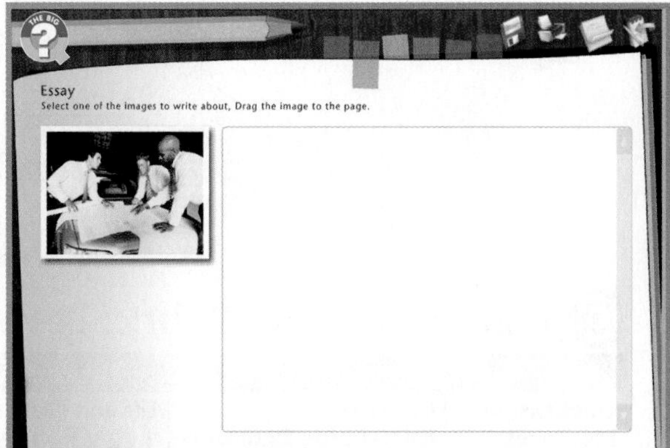

Writer's Journal (with graphics feature)

Also available:

Vocabulary Central (tools, activities, and songs for studying vocabulary)

DIFFERENTIATE/PRETEACH

❶ Leveled Texts

You may use either "Three Skeleton Key" or "The Red-headed League" to meet the lesson objectives. Skills instruction for both selections appears on page 1145. Choose one selection to teach (or choose to teach both). The Text Complexity Rubric at the bottom of this page will help you determine which selection is more appropriate for your students. Use the Reader and Task Suggestions on the facing page to help all students read text of increasing complexity.

❷ Introducing the CCS Standards

Introduce the standards on the student page. (Note that the lesson element with which each standard is addressed is identified in parentheses after the text of the standard.) Call out the standards that you will cover with the selections, explaining to students what each requires and how they will address it as they work through the selection you have chosen. Standards labeled "Spiral Review" are introduced in the Literary Analysis Workshop for this unit.

Before You Read

Three Skeleton Key • The Red-headed League

❶ Leveled Texts

Build your skills and improve your comprehension of short stories with texts of increasing complexity.

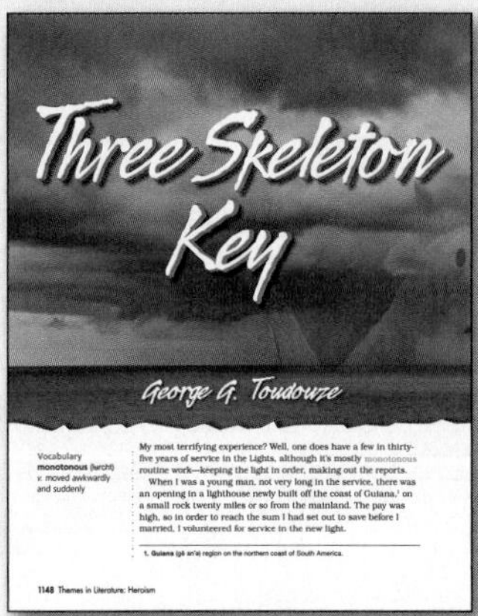

Read **"Three Skeleton Key"** to experience the unexpected dangers of life at an isolated lighthouse.

Read **"The Red-headed League"** to learn how a brilliant detective's mind works as he tracks a thief.

❷ Common Core State Standards

Meet these standards with either **"Three Skeleton Key"** (p. 1148) or **"The Red-headed League"** (p. 1166).

Reading Literature
3. Analyze how complex characters develop over the course of a text, interact with other characters, and advance the plot or develop the theme. *(Literary Analysis: Protagonist and Antagonist; Reading Skill: Comparing and Contrasting Characters)*

Writing
3.d. Use precise words and phrases, telling details, and sensory language to convey a vivid picture of the experiences, events, setting, and/or characters. *(Writing: Journal Entries)*
7. Conduct short as well as more sustained research projects to answer a question or solve a problem; synthesize multiple sources on the subject, demonstrating understanding of the subject under investigation. *(Research and Technology: Report)*

Speaking and Listening
2. Integrate multiple sources of information presented in diverse media or formats evaluating the credibility and accuracy of each source. *(Research and Technology: Report)*
5. Make strategic use of digital media in presentations to enhance understanding of findings, reasoning, and evidence and to add interest. *(Research and Technology: Report)*

Language
2. Demonstrate command of the conventions of standard English capitalization, punctuation, and spelling when writing. *(Conventions: Commas and Dashes)*
5. Demonstrate understanding of figurative language, word relationships, and nuances in word meanings. *(Vocabulary: Analogies)*

Text Complexity Rubric: Leveled Texts

Text complexity is determined by both qualitative and quantitative measures. For this reason, the quantitative measure of a more complex selection may be lower than that of a more accessible selection.

		✓ Three Skeleton Key	✓✓ The Red-headed League
Qualitative Measures	**Context/ Knowledge Demands**	Life and death struggle with a pack of rats 1 2 (3) 4 5	Sherlock Holmes mystery story 1 2 3 (4) 5
	Structure/Language Conventionality and Clarity	Subject-specific vocabulary; long sentences with conversational tone 1 2 3 (4) 5	Challenging vocabulary; extensive dialogue; regionalisms 1 2 3 4 (5)
	Levels of Meaning/ Purpose/Concept Level	Accessible concept (struggle for survival) 1 2 (3) 4 5	Challenging concept (complex mystery) 1 2 3 (4) 5
Quantitative Measures	**Text Length**	Word Count: 4,438	Word Count: 9,105
	Lexile	1190L	1070L
Overall Complexity		✓ **More accessible**	✓✓ **More complex**

❸ Literary Analysis: Protagonist and Antagonist

The **protagonist** is the chief character in a literary work. Some literary works also have an **antagonist**—a character or force that opposes the protagonist. The antagonist is often another character, but may also be an external force, such as nature. The conflict between the protagonist and antagonist is essential to the story. It usually drives the plot and may also be a key to the story's deeper meaning, or theme.

- The protagonist's motives may be universally understood feelings and goals, such as curiosity or the search for love.
- The protagonist's conflict with the antagonist may represent a universal struggle, such as the conflict between good and evil.

PHLit Online!
www.PHLitOnline.com

Hear It!
- Selection summary audio
- Selection audio

See It!
- Get Connected video
- Background video
- More about the author
- Vocabulary flashcards

Do It!
- Interactive journals
- Interactive graphic organizers
- Self-test
- Internet activity
- Grammar tutorial
- Interactive vocabulary games

❹ Using the Strategy: Protagonist and Antagonist Chart

As you read, fill in a chart like the one shown.

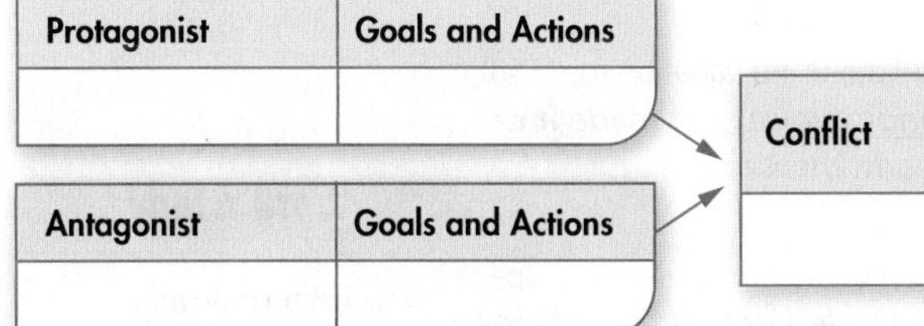

❺ Reading Skill: Compare and Contrast Characters

Comparing and contrasting characters is recognizing and thinking about their similarities and differences. You can compare different characters in a work, characters from different works, or a single character at different points. As you read, **generate questions** about each character. Your answers will show you important differences and similarities.

- What are the character's actions?
- What are the character's reasons for his or her actions?
- What qualities does the character demonstrate?

PRETEACH

❸ Literary Analysis

Protagonist and Antagonist

1. Introduce the skill, using the instruction on the student page.
2. Tell students that they will examine protagonists and antagonists as they read.

Think Aloud: Model the Skill

Model a way to analyze the relationship between protagonists and antagonists. Say to students:

> When I think of protagonists and antagonists, I think of a friend—the protagonist—and his exercise buddy—the antagonist. While my friend wishes to sleep late or skip rainy days—feelings that I can easily understand—his buddy forces him to exercise harder. When they compete, each is motivated by the universal desire to win, and each competes fiercely. When I read, I identify the protagonist and the antagonist and try to understand the struggle between them.

❹ Using the Strategy

Give students a copy of either **Literary Analysis Graphic Organizer A** or **B** (*Graphic Organizer Transparencies,* pp. 196–198) to record their ideas about protagonists and antagonists. Use the examples in the **Literary Analysis Graphic Organizer A**, which is partially filled in, to model the process of completing the organizer.

❺ Reading Skill

Compare and Contrast Characters

1. Introduce the skill, using the instruction on the student page.
2. Tell students they will compare and contrast characters as they read.

Ⓒ Text Complexity: Reader and Task Suggestions

✓ Three Skeleton Key		✓✓ The Red-headed League	
Preparing to Read the Text	**Leveled Tasks**	**Preparing to Read the Text**	**Leveled Tasks**
• Use the Background note on TE p. 1147 to discuss lighthouses. • Review strategies for reading long sentences by first identifying the main action and then breaking down the rest of the sentence into smaller parts. • Guide students to use Multidraft Reading strategies (TE p. 1147).	*Structure/Language* If students will have difficulty with language, have them first read the story and note main events in the plot. Then, have them reread and identify long sentences or passages that continue to cause them difficulty on the second reading. *Analyzing* If students will not have difficulty with language, have them read and note how the author builds suspense in the story.	• Using the Background information on TE p. 1165, discuss the Sherlock Holmes mysteries with students. • Discuss the characteristics of a mystery story. • Guide students to use Multidraft Reading strategies (TE p. 1165).	*Structure/Language* If students will have difficulty with archaic language, have them first read the story and note details that help describe the characters of Holmes and Watson. Then, have them reread and note confusing expressions. *Synthesizing* If students will not have difficulty with archaic language, have them read and note details that explain the logic of Holmes's solution.

PRETEACH

❶ Writing About the Big Question

1. Review the assignment with the class.
2. Have students think about people who become heroes suddenly, for example as a result of their actions in an emergency. **Ask** them if they think the people acted from a sense of responsibility or a sense of instinct or some other motivation.
3. Have students complete the sentence starter. Review responses as a class. (**Possible response:** Some people often choose to take on the responsibility that can come with the role of hero because they believe in solving problems rather than waiting for others to act.)
4. Remind students that their answers will help them think about the Big Question, "Do heroes have responsibilities?"

While You Read

Tell students that as they read they should look for the choices the protagonist faces and think about reasons he makes choices.

❷ Vocabulary

1. Have students preview the selection vocabulary.
2. For each word, have students say the word aloud.
3. Then, use the word in a sentence that defines the word.
4. Finally, repeat your definitional sentence or a similar sentence with the word missing and have the class "fill in the blank" chorally. Here is an example: *Monotonous means sounding the same over and over without variety. When a song contains the same chords over and over, it sounds* [students say "monotonous"].

❸ Word Study

1. Introduce the skill, using the instruction in the box.
2. **Ask** students for a *-min-* word that means "the smallest amount allowed or required." (**Answer:** *minimum*).

Making Connections | Three Skeleton Key

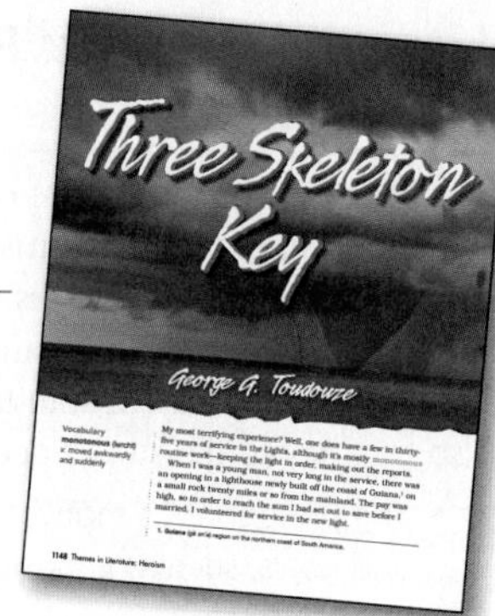

❶ Writing About the Big Question

In "Three Skeleton Key," three men who are staying on a tiny island confront an unexpected and dangerous enemy. Use this sentence starter to develop your ideas about the Big Question.

Some people often **choose** to take on the **responsibility** that can come with the role of **hero** because ______________.

While You Read Look for choices the protagonist makes for his group and think about his responsibility for their situation.

❷ Vocabulary

Read each word and its definition. Decide whether you know the word well, know it a little bit, or do not know it at all. After you read, see how your knowledge of each word has increased.

- **monotonous** (mə nät´ 'n əs) *adj.* having little or no variation (p. 1148) *The speaker lectured with a monotonous voice that made it difficult to pay attention.* *monotonously adv. monotony n. monotone n.*
- **provisions** (prə vizh´ ənz) *n.* something provided, prepared, or supplied for the future (p. 1150) *The scouts carried enough provisions to last them the entire hike.* *provisioned v. provide v.*
- **lurched** (lurcht) *v.* moved awkwardly and suddenly (p. 1152) *The newborn calf lurched forward as it tried to stand.*
- **diminution** (dim´ ə nōō´ shən) *n.* lessening (p. 1156) *The players' diminution of enthusiasm caused them to play poorly.* *diminutive adj.*
- **incessantly** (in ses´ ənt lē) *adv.* continuing in a way that seems endless; continually; unceasingly (p. 1156) *The wind blew so incessantly during the storm that the streets were covered with toppled garbage cans when it was over.* *incessant adj. cease v.*
- **derisive** (di rī´ siv) *adj.* mocking (p. 1159) *The critic's derisive laugh offended the artist.* *derisively adv. derisiveness n.*

Word Study

The **Latin root *-min-*** means "small," "little," or "less."

In this selection, the narrator says there were so many rats, they could not see any **diminution,** or lessening, of their numbers when some were eaten by sharks.

Vocabulary Development

Vocabulary Knowledge Rating

Create a **Vocabulary Knowledge Rating Chart** (***Professional Development Guidebook***, p. 33) for this selection. Include the selection vocabulary and the forms of the Big Question words that appear in the Writing About the Big Question sentence starter on this page. (The Big Question vocabulary is introduced on pp. 1028–1029.)

Give students a copy of the chart. Read the words aloud, and have students mark their rating in the Before Reading column. Urge them to be alert to these words as they read and discuss the selection.

Tally how many students think they know a word to gauge how much instruction to provide. As students read and discuss the selection, point out the words and their context.

Vocabulary Central, featuring tools, activities, and songs for recording and studying vocabulary, is available at **www.PHLitOnline.com.**

Meet George G. Toudouze

(1877–1971)

Author of *Three Skeleton Key*

The award-winning writer, editor, and scholar George Gustave Toudouze was born in Paris, France.

Writer of the Sea A maritime expert, Toudouze wrote nineteen books about the ocean and served as chief editor of *The French Maritime and Colonial League.* He also earned a doctorate of letters at the Sorbonne, one of the oldest and most distinguished universities in the world. He went on to become a professor of history and dramatic literature at the Paris Conservatory. His claim to fame, however, rests entirely upon one story, "Three Skeleton Key," which was published in 1937 in *Esquire* magazine.

4 BACKGROUND FOR THE STORY

Lighthouses

A lighthouse, or "light," is a tower built on an island or other prominent point to warn ships away from treacherous areas near a coast. The tower is usually several stories high, with a large, bright, movable light at the top. Most lighthouses are now automated, but they used to be occupied by people who maintained and operated the light, moving the beam across the water when a ship approached. A lighthouse is often located on a key, which is a small island or a reef near a larger land mass.

DID YOU KNOW?

"Three Skeleton Key" is the only one of Toudouze's stories to appear in English.

Daily Bellringer

For each class during which you will teach this selection, have students complete one of the five Revision activities for Week 34 in the ***Daily Bellringer Activities*** booklet.

4 Background

Lighthouses

Lighthouses provide an unusual setting for short stories. A writer may select a lighthouse as the setting for a story in order to create a mood of loneliness or of contemplation. Traditionally, lighthouse operators were left alone for long periods of time. They tended to be independent souls who were reliable workers and content to spend time alone. When using this setting in a story, writers must be inventive to find a source of conflict to drive the story and help the characters develop.

Multidraft Reading

This icon ● marks natural pauses in the selection. To assist struggling readers and to deepen reading for all, assign the text in "chunks," following the icons, and apply multidraft reading protocols. For each reading, have students set the purpose indicated:

- **First reading**—identifying key ideas and details and answering any Reading Checks.
- **Second reading**—analyzing craft and structure and responding to the side-column prompts.
- **Third reading**—integrating knowledge and ideas, connecting to other texts and the world, and answering the end-of-selection questions.

For more guidance, refer to the ***Classroom Strategies and Teaching Routines*** card on multidraft reading.

PHLit Online!

For more about the author, practice with the selection vocabulary, and more background, go online at **www.PHLitOnline.com.**

Differentiated Instruction — Additional Instruction

EL Extended Support—English Learners

Have students complete the **Reading and Vocabulary Warm-ups, *Unit 6 Resources,*** pp. 92–95, before they read. Assign the prereading pages and the adapted selection in the ***Reader's Notebook: English Learner's Version.*** Then, have students listen to portions of the selection on the ***Hear It!* Audio CD.**

L1 L2 Extended Support—Struggling Readers

Have students complete the **Reading and Vocabulary Warm-ups, *Unit 6 Resources,*** pp. 92–95, before they read. Assign prereading pages and the adapted selection in the ***Reader's Notebook: Adapted Version.*** Then, have students listen to portions of the selection on the ***Hear It!* Audio CD** (adapted text).

Extended Support—Reluctant Readers

To build motivation and engagement before assigning the selection, have students read "Facing Danger at Sea," a thematically related selection in ***Reality Central.*** Then, use the questions at the conclusion of the related selection to guide discussion.

❶ Activating Prior Knowledge

1. Prepare an **Anticipation Guide** (see ***Professional Development Guidebook***, pp. 36–38) with the following statements:
   - "Every man for himself" is a good strategy to follow during a crisis.
   - Perseverance can lead to success.
   - Dire situations can cause people to behave erratically.
   - People always act similarly in a crisis.
2. Give students a copy of the prepared **Anticipation Guide** and have students mark their responses in the Me column. Have students discuss the statements in pairs or groups and mark the Guides again in the Group column.
3. For further guidance, use the ***Classroom Strategies and Teaching Routines*** card: **Using an Anticipation Guide.**

Concept Connector

Students will return to the **Anticipation Guide** after completing "Three Skeleton Key."

Individual Activity

Have students list words Toudouze uses on pp. 1153–1156 and later in the story to describe the rats. Have students use the details about the rats' appearance, sound, smell, and movement as the basis for a series of illustrations. Have students use story details to write captions.

❷ About the Selection

In "Three Skeleton Key," the narrator has just returned to his lighthouse after a short break. He is prepared for another monotonous period of service with his fellow lighthouse keepers, Le Gleo and Itchoua. Nine days after his return, however, Itchoua wakes the other two men in the middle of the night to watch the unusual movements of a large ship that is drifting toward the lighthouse. In daylight, the men realize, to their horror, that the ship has been overrun by a vicious swarm of rats that have killed the ship's crew. The ship runs aground at the lighthouse and the starving rats swarm over the lighthouse.

1
2
3

Vocabulary
monotonous (mə nät´ 'n əs) *adj.* having little or no variation

My most terrifying experience? Well, one does have a few in thirty-five years of service in the Lights, although it's mostly monotonous routine work—keeping the light in order, making out the reports.

When I was a young man, not very long in the service, there was an opening in a lighthouse newly built off the coast of Guiana,[1] on a small rock twenty miles or so from the mainland. The pay was high, so in order to reach the sum I had set out to save before I married, I volunteered for service in the new light.

1. **Guiana** (gē an´ ə) region on the northern coast of South America.

Vocabulary Development

CCSS Language 6

Thematic Vocabulary: The Big Question

As students are discussing "Three Skeleton Key," have them use the thematic vocabulary presented in Introducing the Big Question, pp. 1028–1029. You might encourage them with sentence starters like these:

1. The men *identify* the problem with the ship as . . .
2. This story presents the mice as *characters* by . . .
3. The men make a choice not to fulfill their main *obligation*, which is to . . .
4. The narrator acts like a *hero* when he . . .

3

Three Skeleton Key, the small rock on which the light stood, bore a bad reputation. It earned its name from the story of the three convicts who, escaping from Cayenne[2] in a stolen dugout canoe, were wrecked on the rock during the night, managed to escape the sea but eventually died of hunger and thirst. When they were discovered, nothing remained but three heaps of bones, picked clean by the birds. The story was that the three skeletons, gleaming with phosphorescent light,[3] danced over the small rock, screaming. . . .

4 

How did Three Skeleton Key get its name?

2. **Cayenne** (kī en´) capital city of French Guiana.
3. **phosphorescent** (fäs´ fə res´ ənt) **light** a glowing light produced by certain natural chemical reactions.

3 Critical Thinking

Analyze

1. Invite students to look at the illustration and the title on pp. 1148–1149 for clues to the story.
2. **Ask** students to identify what clues the illustration provides and to make predictions based on them.

   Possible response: The illustration suggests that the story involves a lighthouse. The darkness of the illustration and the lettering of the title both suggest that the story will be scary or eerie.
3. Have students return to their predictions as they read the story to confirm or update them.

4 Reading Check

Answer: Huge sharks swarm the waters around the lighthouse.

PHLit Online!

This selection is available in interactive format in the **Enriched Online Student Edition**, at **www.PHLitOnline.com,** which includes a thematically related video with writing prompt and an interactive graphic organizer.

Differentiated Instruction for Universal Access

Strategy for Less Proficient Readers

To give students a context for the story and to help them identify the characteristics of protagonists and antagonists, show them **Literary Analysis Graphic Organizer A** (*Graphic Organizer Transparencies*, p. 196). The partially completed graphic organizer will give students insight into the goals, motives, and actions of protagonists and antagonists. They can use it as a model for identifying the traits of the protagonist and antagonist in the story.

EL Support for English Learners

Help students grasp pronunciation by allowing them to listen to "Three Skeleton Key" on the ***Hear It!*** **Audio CD**. Have students follow along in the story and mark down on a separate sheet of paper any words whose pronunciation surprised them. Make a class list of these words, and review these words with students.

5 Literary Analysis

Protagonist and Antagonist

1. Remind students that the protagonist of a story is its central and most compelling character. Then read aloud the first bracketed passage, which runs from p. 1148 to p. 1150.
2. **Ask** the Literary Analysis question: Which details in the story's first four paragraphs suggest that the narrator is the central character in this story?

   Possible response: The narrator tells the story using the first person, so he is probably important to the story. Also, the narrator is focusing on details about his own life, rather than details about someone else's life.
3. **Ask** students what they know about the narrator/ protagonist after reading the first four paragraphs.

   Answer: The narrator is no longer a young man. He became a lighthouse operator in Guiana in order to make money. The narrator was not frightened by scary stories about the island.
4. Discuss with students whether they think the narrator is trustworthy and will tell a story that they can believe. Elicit from students that the narrator seems honest and not easily frightened or upset.

6 Reading Skill

Contrasting Characters

1. Have students read the second bracketed passage. **Ask** students the Reading Skill question: What difference in the characters' ages does the narrator point out?

   Answer: Itchoua is twelve or so years older than the other two men.
2. **Ask** students what else they learn about the two characters, Le Gleo and Itchoua.

   Answer: Le Gleo is a Breton. Itchoua is a Basque.
3. Point out that the narrator does not say much about the other two characters at this point. Tell students that the other two men will distinguish themselves as the story progresses. Have students pay attention to the differences in the three men's actions and reactions during the story.

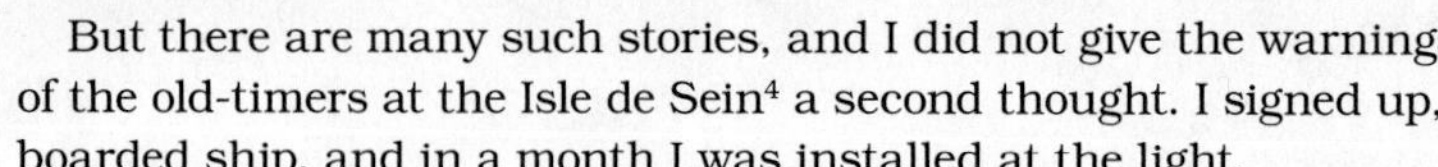

Literary Analysis
Protagonist and Antagonist 5 Which details in the story's first four paragraphs suggest that the narrator is the central character in this story?

But there are many such stories, and I did not give the warnings of the old-timers at the Isle de Sein[4] a second thought. I signed up, boarded ship, and in a month I was installed at the light.

Picture a gray, tapering cylinder, welded to the solid black rock by iron rods and concrete, rising from a small island twenty odd miles from land. It lay in the midst of the sea, this island, a small, bare piece of stone, about one hundred fifty feet long, perhaps forty wide. Small, barely large enough for a man to walk about and stretch his legs at low tide.

This is an advantage one doesn't find in all lights, however, for some of them rise sheer from the waves, with no room for one to move save within the light itself. Still, on our island, one must be careful, for the rocks were treacherously smooth. One misstep and down you would fall into the sea—not that the risk of drowning was so great, but the waters about our island swarmed with huge sharks who kept an eternal patrol around the base of the light.

Vocabulary
provisions (prə vizh′ ənz) *n.* something provided, prepared, or supplied for the future

Still, it was a nice life there. We had enough **provisions** to last for months, in the event that the sea should become too rough for the supply ship to reach us on schedule. During the day we would work about the light, cleaning the rooms, polishing the metalwork and the lens and reflector of the light itself, and at night we would sit on the gallery and watch our light, a twenty thousand candle-power lantern, swinging its strong, white bar of light over the sea from the top of its hundred-twenty-foot tower. Some days, when the air would be very clear, we could see the land, a thread-like line to the west. To the east, north and south stretched the ocean. Landsmen, perhaps, would soon have tired of that kind of life, perched on a small island off the coast of South America for eighteen weeks, until one's turn for leave ashore came around. But we liked it there, my two fellow-tenders and myself—so much so that, for twenty-two months on end with the exception of shore leaves, I was greatly satisfied with the life on Three Skeleton Key.

Reading Skill
Contrasting Characters What difference in the characters' ages does the narrator point out? 6

I had just returned from my leave at the end of June, that is to say mid-winter in that latitude, and had settled down to the routine with my two fellow-keepers, a Breton[5] by the name of Le Gleo and the head-keeper, Itchoua, a Basque[6] some dozen years or so older than either of us.

Eight days went by as usual, then on the ninth night after my return, Itchoua, who was on night duty, called Le

4. **Isle de Sein** (ēl′ də sen′) island off the northwestern coast of France.
5. **Breton** (bret′ ′n) person born or living in Brittany, a region on the northwestern coast of France.
6. **Basque** (bask) member of a people who inhabit a region between Spain and France on the Bay of Biscay.

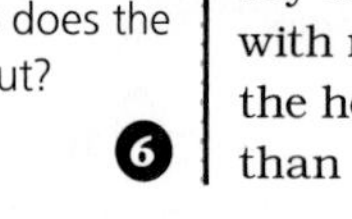

Vocabulary Development

CCSS Language 6

Words from an Earlier Time
The lighthouse operators in "Three Skeleton Key" lived in an earlier time. In the story, they use now-obscure language and unusual technical terms to describe the world they live in. You might wish to clarify with students terms related to nineteenth-century lighthouses, sailing, and the sea.

fellow-tenders: co-workers, or fellow lighthouse tenders

three-master: a ship with three main masts

dugout canoe: a canoe made from a hollowed out log

candle-power: the intensity of a light source

landsmen: a person who has lived always on land, as opposed to sailors, who live at sea

derelict: a ship that has been abandoned on the open sea

Gleo and me, sleeping in our rooms in the middle of the tower, at two in the morning. We rose immediately and, climbing the thirty or so steps that led to the gallery, stood beside our chief.

Itchoua pointed, and following his finger, we saw a big three-master, with all sail set, heading straight for the light. A queer course, for the vessel must have seen us, our light lit her with the glare of day each time it passed over her.

Now, ships were a rare sight in our waters, for our light was a warning of treacherous reefs, barely hidden under the surface and running far out to sea. Consequently we were always given a wide berth, especially by sailing vessels, which cannot maneuver as readily as steamers.

No wonder that we were surprised at seeing this three-master heading dead for us in the gloom of early morning. I had immediately recognized her lines, for she stood out plainly, even at the distance of a mile, when our light shone on her.

She was a beautiful ship of some four thousand tons, a fast sailor that had carried cargoes to every part of the world, plowing the seas unceasingly. By her lines she was identified as Dutch-built, which was understandable as Paramaribo and Dutch Guiana are very close to Cayenne.

Watching her sailing dead for us, a white wave boiling under her bows, Le Gleo cried out:

"What's wrong with her crew ? Are they all drunk or insane? Can't they see us?"

Itchoua nodded soberly, looked at us sharply as he remarked: "See us? No doubt—if there is a crew aboard!"

8 "What do you mean, chief?" Le Gleo had started, turned to the Basque, "Are you saying that she's the Flying Dutchman?"[7]

His sudden fright had been so evident that the older man laughed:

"No, old man, that's not what I meant. If I say that no one's aboard, I mean she's a derelict."

Then we understood his queer behavior. Itchoua was right. For some reason, believing her doomed, her crew had abandoned her.

One misstep and down you would fall into the sea...

7

▲ **Critical Viewing**

How does this photograph of a Dutch sailing ship help establish the time period of the story? **[Connect]**

9

Reading Check

In the middle of the night, what surprising sight does Itchoua show his companions?

7. **Flying Dutchmwan** fabled ghost ship doomed to sail forever

7 Critical Viewing

Possible response: The boat in this image is small and clearly of an earlier time.

8 Critical Thinking

1. Have students reread the bracketed text, focusing on Itchoua's reaction to Le Gleo's fear. **Ask** what Le Gleo's fear suggests about his character.

   Answer: Le Gleo is superstitious and easily frightened.

2. Then **ask** what Itchoua's response to Le Gleo tells the reader about Itchoua.

   Possible response: Itchoua is observant, not superstitious. He is not easily upset by what he sees.

3. Point out that the narrator does not participate in the conversation between Le Gleo and Itchoua. **Ask** students what they can infer about the narrator's character here.

   Possible response: The narrator is observant and patient. He is waiting to learn more about the situation before formulating an opinion.

9 Reading Check

Answer: Itchoua shows his companions a ship adrift in dangerously shallow waters.

Differentiated Instruction for Universal Access

Strategy for Special-Needs Students

Have students create graphic organizers on which to outline the story's basic plot, characters, setting, and theme. Have partners compare organizers to see whether they agree on the main points. If they disagree, have them go back to the story to resolve the difference of opinion. Ask students which of these four elements is most important to the story's overall effect. Then, have them explain why they think so.

Strategy for Less Proficient Readers

Ask each student to find a descriptive passage that seems particularly effective, or one that gave them a special reading challenge. Make sure that they choose lengthy paragraphs. Have each student summarize his or her paragraph in a couple of sentences. Then ask students to reread their paragraphs slowly and carefully, making sure that they read each detail. Ask students to explain why they thought the paragraph was effective or difficult.

⑩ Reading Skill

Contrasting Characters

1. Have students reread the bracketed section in which the three characters watch the ship crash and sink.
2. **Ask** students the Reading Skill question: In what ways are Le Gleo's and the narrator's reactions to the doomed ship similar and different?

   Possible response: Le Gleo is excited to see the ship crash, while the narrator is unhappy to see the beautiful ship demolished. They are both having an emotional reaction; Le Gleo is shouting and excited, while the narrator is shedding tears.
3. **Ask** students to compare their own reactions to those of the characters. Ask students if the sinking ship inspires any particular feelings.

   Possible response: Students may suggest that the image of a sinking ship fills them with dread or with interest.

Vocabulary
lurched (lurcht) *v.* moved awkwardly and suddenly

Then she had righted herself and sailed on, wandering with the wind.

The three of us grew tense as the ship seemed about to crash on one of our numerous reefs, but she suddenly lurched with some change of the wind, the yards swung around, and the derelict came clumsily about and sailed dead away from us.

In the light of our lantern she seemed so sound, so strong, that Itchoua exclaimed impatiently:

"But why the devil was she abandoned? Nothing is smashed, no sign of fire—and she doesn't sail as if she were taking water."

Le Gleo waved to the departing ship:

"Bon voyage!"[8] he smiled at Itchoua and went on. "She's leaving us, chief, and now we'll never know what—"

"No she's not!" cried the Basque. "Look! She's turning!"

As if obeying his words, the derelict three-master stopped, came about and headed for us once more. And for the next four hours the vessel played around us—zigzagging, coming about,[9] stopping, then suddenly lurching forward. No doubt some freak of current and wind, of which our island was the center, kept her near us.

Then suddenly, the tropic dawn broke, the sun rose and it was day, and the ship was plainly visible as she sailed past us. Our light extinguished, we returned to the gallery with our glasses and inspected her.

Reading Skill
Contrasting Characters ⑩ In what ways are Le Gleo's and the narrator's reactions to the doomed ship similar and different?

The three of us focused our glasses on her poop,[10] saw standing out sharply, black letters on the white background of a life-ring, the stenciled name:

"*Cornelius-de-Witt*, Rotterdam."

We had read her lines correctly, she was Dutch. Just then the wind rose and the *Cornelius-de-Witt* changed course, leaned to port and headed straight for us once more. But this time she was so close that we knew she would not turn in time.

"Thunder!" cried Le Gleo, his Breton soul aching to see a fine ship doomed to smash upon a reef, "She's going to pile up! She's gone!"

I shook my head:

"Yes, and a shame to see that beautiful ship wreck herself. And we're helpless."

There was nothing we could do but watch. A ship sailing with all sail spread, creaming the sea with her forefoot as she runs before the wind, is one of the most beautiful sights in the world—but this time I could feel the tears stinging my eyes as I saw this fine ship headed for her doom.

8. **Bon voyage** (bän′ vwä äzh′) French for "pleasant journey;" a farewell to a traveler.
9. **coming about** changing direction according to the direction of the wind.
10. **poop** (po͞op) *n.* raised deck at the rear of a sailing ship.

Vocabulary Development

Ⓒ CCSS Language 6

Selection Vocabulary Reinforcement

Students will benefit from additional examples and practice with the selection vocabulary words. Reinforce their comprehension with "show-you-know" sentences. The first part of the sentence uses the vocabulary word in an appropriate context. The second part of the sentence—the "show-you-know" part—clarifies the first. Model the strategy with this example for *lurched*:

1. When she stepped on the wrong pedal, the car *lurched* forward; it moved suddenly out of the parking space.

Then give students these sentence prompts, and coach them in creating the clarification part:

1. The *diminution* of the rain meant that the team could go outside and practice; ________.

   Sample answer: the rain had slowed to a barely recognizable drizzle.
2. The audience's *derisive* laughter embarrassed the play's cast; ________.

   Sample answer: the play was a serious drama, but the audience was mocking it.

All this time our glasses were riveted on her, and we suddenly cried out together:

"The rats!"

Now we knew why this ship, in perfect condition, was sailing without her crew aboard. They had been driven out by the rats. Not those poor specimens of rats you see ashore, barely reaching the length of one foot from their trembling noses to the tip of their skinny tails, wretched creatures that dodge and hide at the mere sound of a footfall.

No, these were ships' rats, huge, wise creatures, born on the sea, sailing all over the world on ships, transferring to other, larger ships as they multiply. There is as much difference between the rats of the land and these maritime rats as between a fishing smack and an armored cruiser.

The rats of the sea are fierce, bold animals. Large, strong and intelligent, clannish and seawise, able to put the best of mariners
1 to shame with their knowledge of the sea, their uncanny ability to foretell the weather.

And they are brave, these rats, and vengeful. If you so much as harm one, his sharp cry will bring hordes of his fellows to swarm over you, tear you and not cease until your flesh has been stripped from the bones.

The ones on this ship, the rats of Holland, are the worst, superior to other rats of the sea as their brethren are to the land rats. There is a well-known tale about these animals.

A Dutch captain, thinking to protect his cargo, brought aboard his ship—not cats—but two terriers, dogs trained in the hunting,

Reading Skill
Contrasting Characters In what way are the rats on the *Cornelius-de-Witt* different from other rats in the world?

12 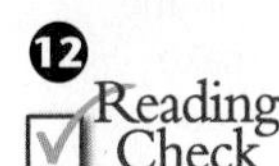
Reading Check

What detail do the men notice that shows that the crew of the *Cornelius-de-Witt* did not abandon ship?

The rats of the sea are fierce, bold animals.

11 Reading Skill

Contrasting Characters

1. Read the bracketed text aloud. Remind students that animals may be characters in a story. Suggest that the swarm of rats is a character in the story, the way a force of nature, such as a snowstorm, might be in a Jack London story. Tell students that, as characters, the rats will shape the story in an important way.
2. **Ask** students how the rats probably contributed to the state of the ship.

   Answer: The rats overpowered and killed the crew of the ship.
3. **Ask** students the Reading Skill question: In what way are the rats on the *Cornelius-de-Witt* different from other rats in the world?

   Possible response: Unlike rats that are skinny, wretched, and meek, the rats on the ship are huge, wise, sea-faring creatures that are strong, brave, clannish, and quick to defend themselves. They are vicious rats.

12 Reading Check

Answer: The small boats are still on the ship, which tells the narrator that the crew did not abandon the ship.

Differentiated Instruction for Universal Access

Culturally Responsive Instruction

Culture Focus Point out that on p. 1151, the men decide that the ship is Dutch. They have studied the ship's lines, or its shape, to help them form this conclusion. When they see the name and home port, they know that their assumption was correct. Discuss how and why names might be associated with particular cultures, such as through language. Invite students to share a selection of names from their home culture or family's country of origin. Point out that in today's world, names may be less accurate as indicators of a person's country of origin than in the time of the story. Discuss reasons for this, such as that people move around the world more often and that marriage across ethnic and cultural boundaries is now common.

13 Literary Analysis

Protagonist and Antagonist

1. Have students refer to **Literary Analysis Graphic Organizer B** (*Graphic Organizer Transparencies,* p. 198). Review what students know about the protagonist's goals and actions so far in the story.

   Answer: Students should remember that the protagonist has taken the job of lighthouse keeper in order to make money to get married.

2. Point out that until this point in the story, the protagonist has not had any conflicts. **Ask** students to predict what conflict the protagonist may experience after the *Cornelius-de-Witt* sinks.

   Possible response: If the rats on the ship make it to the lighthouse, the narrator will have to fight for his life.

3. Have students reread the bracketed text. **Ask** the Literary Analysis question: What details here might make readers sympathetic toward the narrator? Why?

   Possible response: The narrator explains that the ship is isolated and that the chances of the ship actually hitting the island were slight, but it happened anyway. Readers will feel sympathetic because of the narrator's dire situation and his bad luck.

4. As students continue to read the story, have them fill in the rest of the **Literary Analysis Graphic Organizer B.**

14 Critical Viewing

Possible response: Their sharp claws and attack stance make them appear fearsome.

---

fighting and killing of vicious rats. By the time the ship, sailing from Rotterdam, had passed the Ostend light, the dogs were gone and never seen again. In twenty-four hours they had been overwhelmed, killed and eaten by the rats.

At times, when the cargo does not suffice, the rats attack the crew, either driving them from the ship or eating them alive. And studying the *Cornelius-de-Witt,* I turned sick, for her small boats were all in place. She had not been abandoned.

Over her bridge, on her deck, in the rigging, on every visible spot, the ship was a writhing mass—a starving army coming towards us aboard a vessel gone mad!

Literary Analysis Protagonist and Antagonist What details here might make readers sympathetic toward the narrator? Why?

Our island was a small spot in that immense stretch of sea. The ship could have grazed us, passed to port or starboard with its ravening cargo—but no, she came for us at full speed, as if she were leading the regatta at a race, and impaled herself on a sharp point of rock.

There was a dull shock as her bottom stove in, then a horrible crackling as the three masts went overboard at once, as if cut down with one blow of some gigantic sickle. A sighing groan came as the water rushed into the ship, then she split in two and sank like a stone.

14 **▼ Critical Viewing** Which details in the photograph make these rats appear fearsome, like the ones in "Three Skeleton Key"? **[Analyze]**

But the rats did not drown. Not these fellows! As much at home in the sea as any fish, they formed ranks in the water, heads lifted, tails stretched out, paws paddling. And half of them, those from the forepart of the ship, sprang along the masts and onto the rocks in the instant before she sank. Before we had time even to move, nothing remained of the three-master save some pieces of wreckage floating on the surface and an army of rats covering the rocks left bare by the receding tide. 13

Thousands of heads rose, felt the wind and we were scented, seen! To them we were fresh meat, after possible weeks of starving. There came a scream, composed of innumerable screams, sharper than the howl of a saw attacking a bar of iron, and in the one motion, every rat leaped to attack the tower!

We barely had time to leap back, close the door leading onto the gallery, descend the stairs and shut every window tightly. Luckily the door at the base of the light, which we never could have reached in time, was of bronze set in granite and was tightly closed.

Vocabulary Development

© CCSS Language 6

Expressive Vocabulary

To help students broaden their expressive vocabulary, encourage them to use the following words as they discuss the unusual events in the story: *isolate, access, forgo, induces*. Have them complete these sentence starters:

1. To *isolate* themselves from the rats, the men . . .
2. The rats cannot gain *access* . . .
3. When the ship comes close, the men *forgo* . . .
4. The fear that something is not right with the ship *induces* the characters to . . .

The horrible band, in no measurable time, had swarmed up and over the tower as if it had been a tree, piled on the embrasures of the windows, scraped at the glass with thousands of claws, covered the lighthouse with a furry mantle and reached the top of the tower, filling the gallery and piling atop the lantern.

15 Their teeth grated as they pressed against the glass of the lantern-room, where they could plainly see us, though they could not reach us. A few millimeters of glass, luckily very strong, separated our faces from their gleaming, beady eyes, their sharp claws and teeth. Their odor filled the tower, poisoned our lungs and rasped our nostrils with a pestilential, nauseating smell. And there we were, sealed alive in our own light, prisoners of a horde of starving rats.

That first night, the tension was so great that we could not sleep. Every moment, we felt that some opening had been made, some window given away, and that our horrible besiegers were pouring through the breach. The rising tide, chasing those of the rats which had stayed on the bare rocks, increased the numbers clinging to the walls, piled on the balcony—so much so that clusters of rats clinging to one another hung from the lantern and the gallery.

With the coming of darkness we lit the light, and the turning beam completely maddened the beasts. As the light turned, it successively blinded thousands of rats crowded against the glass, while the dark side of the lantern-room gleamed with thousands of points of light, burning like the eyes of jungle beasts in the night.

16 All the while we could hear the enraged scraping of claws against the stone and glass, while the chorus of cries was so loud that we had to shout to hear one another. From time to time, some of the rats fought among themselves and a dark cluster would detach itself, falling into the sea like a ripe fruit from a tree. Then we would see phosphorescent streaks as triangular fins slashed the water—sharks, permanent guardians of our rock, feasting on our jailors.

The next day we were calmer, and amused ourselves by teasing the rats, placing our faces against the glass which separated us. They could not fathom the invisible barrier which separated them from us, and we laughed as we watched them leaping against the heavy glass.

But the day after that, we realized how serious our position was. The air was foul; even the heavy smell of oil within our stronghold could not dominate the fetid odor of the beasts massed around us, and there was no way of admitting fresh air without also admitting the rats.

The morning of the fourth day, at early dawn, I saw the wooden framework of my window, eaten away from the outside, sagging

Literary Analysis
Protagonist and Antagonist With what external force are the narrator, Le Gleo, and Itchoua now in conflict?

Reading Skill
Comparing Characters In what way do the sharks and the rats behave similarly?

17 

What do the rats do almost immediately after landing on the island?

15 Literary Analysis

Protagonist and Antagonist

1. Read the first bracketed passage aloud. **Ask** the Literary Analysis question: With what external force are the narrator, Le Gleo, and Itchoua now in conflict?

   Answer: The rats are the force with which the men are now in conflict.

2. Review the definitions of protagonist and antagonist with students. **Ask** students to explain how the rats now fit the definition of antagonist.

   Possible response: The rats are a force that opposes the protagonist and his friends. The protagonist must struggle for survival against the rats.

3. **Ask** students to identify the conflict between the men and the rats.

   Answer: The rats want to attack and kill the men. The men want to survive the attack of the rats.

16 Reading Skill

Comparing Characters

1. Remind students that, like the rats, the sharks are also characters in the story. Have students reread the second bracketed passage.
2. **Ask** the Reading Skill question: In what way do the sharks and the rats behave similarly?

   Possible response: Like the rats, the sharks are wild animals that travel in swarms and attack their food fiercely.

17 Reading Check

Answer: Upon landing, the rats immediately swarm the lighthouse tower, covering it from top to bottom.

Differentiated Instruction for Universal Access

Strategy for Special-Needs Students
Students may benefit from using a timeline to plot out the events in the story. Give students copies of the **Timeline Graphic Organizer Transparency** in *Graphic Organizer Transparencies,* p. 224. Have students work in pairs or small groups to review the story and identify when events happened. Tell students that the story takes place over the course of about ten days. Have students label the timeline with days that are mentioned in the story and the significant events that happened on these days.

Strategy for Advanced Readers
Students should understand that the characters' feelings about their predicament change over the course of the story. Have students write a daily journal entry for each of the men that covers the time the men are trapped in the lighthouse. Remind students to choose words that match the voice and feelings of each character. After students complete the story and complete their entries, ask them to sum up how each of the characters changed during the crisis.

18 Critical Thinking

Analyze and Predict

1. Have students reread the bracketed text on p. 1156, paying attention to how the men respond to the emergency.
2. **Ask** students to identify the strategies the men use to pass the time and to stay calm while they are under siege from the rats.

   Answer: They entertain themselves by watching the rats fall, counting the rats, and studying the leader rats.
3. **Ask** students what the men's activities say about them.

   Possible response: The men stay calm at first and try to make the best of their situation. The narrator and Itchoua seem to be people who are not prone to getting excited or upset.
4. Remind students to think about what they already know about the characters. **Ask** students to predict how the men's situation might change and how the men will react.

   Possible response: The rats could find a way in, and the men will have to react quickly to save their lives. Le Gleo is easily frightened and therefore, will probably falter. Itchoua and the narrator will probably be stronger in the situation because of their calmer natures.

19 Critical Viewing

Answer: Sharks are much bigger than rats and have much sharper teeth. The rats can't swim away from a school of hungry sharks.

inwards. I called my comrades and the three of us fastened a sheet of tin in the opening, sealing it tightly. When we had completed the task, Itchoua turned to us and said dully:

"Well—the supply boat came thirteen days ago, and she won't be back for twenty-nine." He pointed at the white metal plate sealing the opening through the granite—"If that gives way—" he shrugged—"they can change the name of this place to Six Skeletons Key."

18 The next six days and seven nights, our only distraction was watching the rats whose holds were insecure fall a hundred and twenty feet into the maws of the sharks—but they were so many that we could not see any diminution in their numbers.

Thinking to calm ourselves and pass the time, we attempted to count them, but we soon gave up. They moved incessantly, never still. Then we tried identifying them, naming them.

One of them, larger than the others, who seemed to lead them in their rushes against the glass separating us, we named "Nero";[11] and there were several others whom we had learned to distinguish through various peculiarities.

But the thought of our bones joining those of the convicts was always in the back of our minds. And the gloom of our prison fed these thoughts, for the interior of the light was almost completely

Vocabulary
diminution (dim′ ə nōō′ shən) *n.* lessening
incessantly (in ses′ ənt lē) *adv.* continuing in a way that seems endless; continually; unceasingly

19 ▼ **Critical Viewing**
Why are even the fierce ship rats no match for a school of sharks like these? **[Assess]**

11. **Nero** (nir′ ō) (A.D. 37–68) Roman emperor who was notoriously cruel.

—"they can change the name of this place to Six Skeletons Key."

Think Aloud

Vocabulary: Using Context

Direct students' attention to the word *maniacal* in the first full paragraph on p. 1157. Using a think-aloud process, model how to use context to infer the meaning of an unknown word. Say to students:

> I'm going to think aloud to show you how I would figure out the meaning of *maniacal* from its context.
>
> The paragraph in which *maniacal* appears gives me three clues. First, I read that Le Gleo has had nightmares. The nightmares are full of crazy things like dancing skeletons. Then, I learn that Le Gleo's descriptions of these nightmares are not only *maniacal* but also *raving*. I know that you rave when you act crazy or insane. Finally, I recognize the word *maniac* in the word *maniacal*. A maniac is someone who acts crazy or insane. So most likely *maniacal* means "like a crazy or insane person."

dark, as we had to seal every window in the same fashion as mine, and the only space that still admitted daylight was the glassed-in lantern-room at the very top of the tower.

20 Then Le Gleo became morose and had nightmares in which he would see the three skeletons dancing around him, gleaming coldly, seeking to grasp him. His maniacal, raving descriptions were so vivid that Itchoua and I began seeing them also.

It was a living nightmare, the raging cries of the rats as they swarmed over the light, mad with hunger; the sickening, strangling odor of their bodies—

True, there is a way of signaling from light-houses. But to reach the mast on which to hang the signal we would have to go out on the gallery where the rats were.

21 There was only one thing left to do. After debating all of the ninth day, we decided not to light the lantern that night. This is the greatest breach of our service, never committed as long as the tenders of the light are alive; for the light is something sacred, warning ships of danger in the night. Either the light gleams, a quarter hour after sundown, or no one is left alive to light it.

Well, that night, Three Skeleton Light was dark, and all the men were alive. At the risk of causing ships to crash on our reefs, we left it unlit, for we were worn out—going mad!

Literary Analysis
Protagonist and Antagonist In addition to the rats, what other problems do the men face?

22 

What happens in Le Gleo's nightmares?

Differentiated Instruction for Universal Access

Pronunciation for English Learners

To help students correctly pronounce initial *s*, post these words: *supply, sealing, six, seven, so, see, soon, still*. Read the words aloud, stressing the initial /s/. Have students echo. Then direct students to point to these words on page 1156 as you read the first three paragraphs aloud. Have students echo again.

Enrichment for Gifted/Talented Students

Have students work in pairs or small groups to talk about how to turn the story into an effective movie script. Students should work together to identify key dialogue, images, and scenes from the story to incorporate into a script. Have students create a five-to-ten-page script and ask them to read their scripts aloud to the class. Ask the class to evaluate if the scripts are as suspenseful and interesting as the original story.

20 Literary Analysis

Protagonist and Antagonist

1. Remind students that conflict is part of what makes a protagonist interesting to a reader. Readers want to know how the protagonist overcomes obstacles and resolves problems.
2. Also, remind students that conflict may be external or internal. For example, the lighthouse keepers' struggle with the rats is an external conflict. An internal struggle is one that a character has within his or her own mind.
3. Have students reread the first bracketed passage. Then, **ask** the Literary Analysis question.

   Possible response: The men struggle with their own fears.
4. **Ask** students to identify these other conflicts as internal or external.

   Answer: The men's struggle with their own fears is an internal struggle because it takes place in their minds.

21  Connecting to the Big Question

1. Remind students of the Big Question by **asking** them what kinds of decisions mark a hero.

   Possible response: A hero makes decisions based on the greater good or values such as right and wrong, rather than on convenience or personal gain.
2. Then direct students to read the second bracketed passage. **Ask:** Why would this be such a difficult decision for the men?

   Answer: On one hand, the men would be breaking their trust as light-keepers and thus risking the lives of others at sea. On the other hand, not lighting the light may serve a greater good.
3. **Ask:** Do you think that making a decision like this makes the narrator heroic or cowardly?

   Possible Response: It is a heroic decision because it shows bravery, and a willingness to look for an unusual solution to a difficult problem.

22 Reading Check

Answer: Three skeletons dance around Le Gleo and try to grab him.

㉓ Literary Analysis
Protagonist and Antagonist

1. Review that a motive is a reason for taking action. For example, the rats' motive for attacking the lighthouse is to get food. The narrator's motive for taking the lighthouse job is to earn money so that he can get married.
2. Have students read the first bracketed passage. **Ask** students the Literary Analysis question: What do you think motivates the narrator and Le Gleo to risk their own lives to help Itchoua?

   Possible response: They want to save him because he is their friend and colleague. Also, they have a better chance of surviving if all three men stay together.
3. Have students refer to their **Literary Analysis Graphic Organizer B**. Turn their attention to the box labeled *Universal Motives or Struggles*.
4. Have students discuss the motives and struggles that the men share in this story. **Elicit** that all three men have the same motive—to survive the invasion of the rats.

㉔ Reading Skill
Contrasting Characters

1. Point out that although the men have a common enemy and conflict in the rats, their different reactions to their situation puts them in conflict with one another. Have students **summarize** how the men have reacted since the rats broke through the lighthouse wall.

   Answer: Le Gleo stares vacantly, laughs and shouts hysterically, and then cries after the narrator hits him. The narrator tries to stay calm, but yells at Le Gleo and hits him. Itchoua sits and stares at his wounds before taking action.
2. Read the second bracketed text aloud. **Ask** the Reading Skill question: What differences between the narrator and Le Gleo do their reactions make clear?

   Possible response: Le Gleo's hysterical laughing, shouting, and crying show that he cannot handle a crisis, while the narrator's handling of Le Gleo shows that he wants to get a grip on the situation and will not be distracted by Le Gleo's insanity. The narrator clearly can function in a crisis.

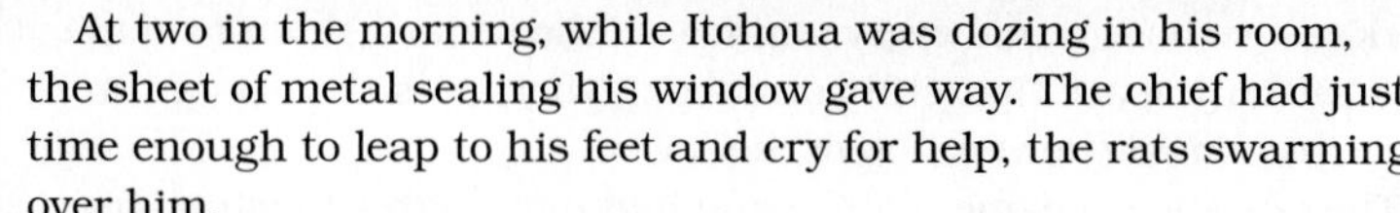

Literary Analysis Protagonist and Antagonist What do you think motivates the narrator and Le Gleo to risk their own lives to help Itchoua?

At two in the morning, while Itchoua was dozing in his room, the sheet of metal sealing his window gave way. The chief had just time enough to leap to his feet and cry for help, the rats swarming over him.

㉓ But Le Gleo and I, who had been watching from the lantern-room, got to him immediately, and the three of us battled with the horde of maddened rats which flowed through the gaping window. They bit, we struck them down with our knives—and retreated.

We locked the door of the room on them, but before we had time to bind our wounds, the door was eaten through and gave way, and we retreated up the stairs, fighting off the rats that leaped on us from the knee-deep swarm.

I do not remember, to this day, how we ever managed to escape. All I can remember is wading through them up the stairs, striking them off as they swarmed over us; and then we found ourselves, bleeding from innumerable bites, our clothes shredded, sprawled across the trapdoor in the floor of the lantern-room—without food or drink. Luckily, the trapdoor was metal set into the granite with iron bolts.

The rats occupied the entire light beneath us, and on the floor of our retreat lay some twenty of their fellows, who had gotten in with us before the trapdoor closed, and whom we had killed with our knives. Below us, in the tower, we could hear the screams of the rats as they devoured everything edible that they found. Those on the outside squealed in reply, and writhed in a horrible curtain as they stared at us through the glass of the lantern-room.

Itchoua sat up, stared silently at his blood trickling from the wounds on his limbs and body, and running in thin streams on the floor around him. Le Gleo, who was in as bad a state (and so was I, for that matter) stared at the chief and me vacantly, started as his gaze swung to the multitude of rats against the glass, then suddenly began laughing horribly:

"Hee! Hee! The Three Skeletons! Hee! Hee! The Three Skeletons are now six skeletons! Six skeletons!"

㉔ He threw his head back and howled, his eyes glazed, a trickle of saliva running from the corners of his mouth and thinning the blood flowing over his chest. I shouted to him to shut up, but he did not hear me, so I did the only thing I could to quiet him—I swung the back of my hand across his face.

Reading Skill Contrasting Characters What differences between the narrator and Le Gleo do their reactions make clear?

The howling stopped suddenly, his eyes swung around the room, then he bowed his head and began weeping softly, like a child.

Our darkened light had been noticed from the mainland, and as dawn was breaking, the patrol was there to investigate the failure of our light. Looking through my binoculars, I could see the horrified

PROFESSIONAL DEVELOPMENT | **Kelly Gallagher**

Apply the Strategy

Write Before Talking: Students' deepest thinking does not come immediately; often it occurs after they have some time to reflect. To encourage reflective thinking, direct students' attention to the line, "There was only one thing left to do" (p. 1157). Then, ask, "What is left to do? What would you do in this situation?" Have them reflect their thoughts in a written response; give them 5–7 minutes to write.

Then, to explore students' reflections and build anticipation for completing the story, share and discuss responses as a class.

To finish the story, say something like, "Thanks for sharing your thinking. Now let's read the rest of the story to see how it really ends."

For more of Kelly Gallagher's strategies, see his Professional Development essay, pp. 1028c–1028d.

expression on the faces of the officers and crew when, the daylight strengthening, they saw the light completely covered by a seething mass of rats. They thought, as I afterwards found out, that we had been eaten alive.

But the rats had also seen the ship, or had scented the crew. As the ship drew nearer, a solid phalanx[12] left the light, plunged into the water and, swimming out, attempted to board her. They would have succeeded, as the ship was hove to, but the engineer connected his steam to a hose on the deck and scalded the head of the attacking column, which slowed them up long enough for the ship to get under way and leave the rats behind.

Then the sharks took part. Belly up, mouths gaping, they arrived in swarms and scooped up the rats, sweeping through them like a sickle through wheat. That was one day that sharks really served a useful purpose.

25 The remaining rats turned tail, swam to the shore, and emerged dripping. As they neared the light, their comrades greeted them with shrill cries, with what sounded like a derisive note predominating. They answered angrily and mingled with their fellows. From the several tussles that broke out, they resented being ridiculed for their failure to capture the ship.

But all this did nothing to get us out of our jail. The small ship could not approach, but steamed around the light at a safe distance, and the tower must have seemed fantastic, some weird, many-mouthed beast hurling defiance at them.

Finally, seeing the rats running in and out of the tower through the door and the windows, those on the ship decided that we had perished and were about to leave when Itchoua, regaining his senses, thought of using the light as a signal. He lit it and, using a plank placed and withdrawn before the beam to form the dots and dashes, quickly sent out our story to those on the vessel.

Our reply came quickly. When they understood our position—how we could not get rid of the rats, Le Gleo's mind going fast, Itchoua and myself covered with bites, cornered in the lantern-room without food or water—they had a signalman send us their reply.

12. **phalanx** (fā′ laŋks′) *n.* group of individuals advancing in a close, compact formation.

Vocabulary
derisive (di rī′ siv) *adj.* mocking

26 
Reading Check
What do the men do that results in the arrival of a patrol ship?

25 Critical Thinking

Compare and Contrast

1. Draw students' attention to the reaction of the rats to those that had failed to reach the ship and had returned to the lighthouse. Tell students that the rats on the lighthouse seemed to greet their failed "comrades" with derisive scorn.
2. **Ask** students to compare the rats' reactions to their "comrades'" failures to the men's responses to each other.

   Possible response: The rats on the lighthouse taunt the rats that failed to reach the ship. The men are more supportive of each other. Even though the narrator hits Le Gleo, he does not deride him. The men stick together.

26 Reading Check

Answer: The men choose not to light the lighthouse. A boat patrols to find out why the light was not lit.

Fluency

Distribute copies of pages 1158–1159 to partners. Have listeners mark sections with which readers struggle. Circulate to monitor the fluency of students' reading. Then collect the papers and review fluency issues, such as this one:

Students may replace difficult words with other words, either real or nonsensical, such as *occupied* with *occur*, or *investigate* with *invite*. Have students reread the sentence with the incorrect word. Ask students whether the text made sense. Point out that when text does not make sense, students should stop and reread, carefully pronouncing each word part until they understand the words and the text meaning is clear. Students can then ask a partner for help to confirm understanding. Partners may be able to read the word and that sentence correctly, further guiding the first student toward understanding.

27 Reading Skill

Comparing Characters

1. Ask a volunteer to read aloud the last sentence on p. 1160. "They were true rats of Holland, fearing no man, fighting for the right to live!"
2. **Ask** students the Reading Skill question: What similarity between the rats and the men does the narrator's remark about the rats reveal?

   Answer: Both the men and the rats have strong survival instincts.
3. Challenge students to **make a generalization** about the difference between the way the rats and the men fight for survival.

   Possible response: The men stick together and every rat fights for itself.

28 Critical Viewing

Answer: The sharks are much bigger than rats and swim fast, so they ought to be able to attack immediately.

His arms swinging like those of a windmill, he quickly spelled out: "Don't give up. Hang on a little longer! We'll get you out of this!"

Then she turned and steamed at top speed for the coast, leaving us little reassured.

She was back at noon, accompanied by the supply ship, two small coast guard boats, and the fire boat—a small squadron. At twelve-thirty the battle was on.

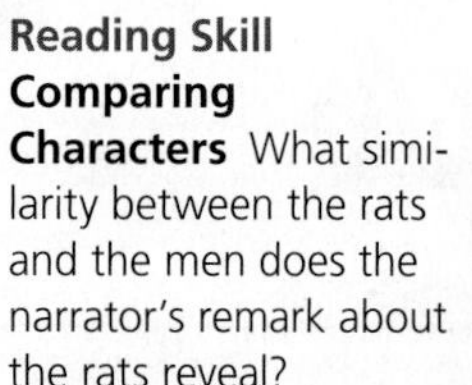

Reading Skill Comparing Characters What similarity between the rats and the men does the narrator's remark about the rats reveal?

After a short reconnaissance,[13] the fire boat picked her way slowly through the reefs until she was close to us, then turned her powerful jet of water on the rats. The heavy stream tore the rats from their places, hurled them screaming into the water where the sharks gulped them down. But for every ten that were dislodged, seven swam ashore, and the stream could do nothing to the rats within the tower. Furthermore, some of them, instead of returning to the rocks, boarded the fire boat, and the men were forced to battle them hand to hand. 27 They were true rats of Holland, fearing no man, fighting for the right to live!

13. **reconnaissance** (ri kän′ ə səns) *n.* exploratory survey or examination.

28 ▼ **Critical Viewing** Based on this photograph, how easily do you think the sharks could attack the rats? Explain. **[Evaluate]**

Vocabulary Development

Vocabulary Knowledge Rating

When students have completed reading and discussing "Three Skeleton Key," have them take out their **Vocabulary Knowledge Rating Chart** for this selection. Read the words aloud once more and have students rate their knowledge of the words again in the After Reading column. Clarify any words that are still problematic. Have students write their own definition and example or sentence in the appropriate column. Then have students complete the Vocabulary Practice activities at the end of the selection. Encourage students to use the words in further discussion and written work about this selection. Remind them that they will be accountable for these words on the **Selection Test, *Unit 6 Resources,*** pp. 104–106 or 107–109.

Nightfall came, and it was as if nothing had been done, the rats were still in possession. One of the patrol boats stayed by the island; the rest of the flotilla[14] departed for the coast. We had to spend another night in our prison. Le Gleo was sitting on the floor, babbling about skeletons, and as I turned to Itchoua, he fell unconscious from his wounds. I was in no better shape and could feel my blood flaming with fever.

Somehow the night dragged by, and the next afternoon I saw a tug, accompanied by the fire boat, coming from the mainland with a huge barge in tow. Through my glasses, I saw that the barge was filled with meat.

29 Risking the treacherous reefs, the tug dragged the barge as close to the island as possible. To the last rat, our besiegers deserted the rock, swam out and boarded the barge reeking with the scent of freshly cut meat. The tug dragged the barge about a mile from shore, where the fire boat drenched the barge with gasoline. A well placed incendiary shell from the patrol boat set her on fire.

The barge was covered with flames immediately, and the rats took to the water in swarms, but the patrol boat bombarded them with shrapnel from a safe distance, and the sharks finished off the survivors.

A whaleboat from the patrol boat took us off the island and left three men to replace us. By nightfall we were in the hospital in Cayenne.

14. **flotilla** (flō til′ ə) *n.* small fleet.

Spiral Review
Archetypes How is the narrator different from the typical hero?

Literary Analysis
Protagonist and Antagonist In what way does human intelligence ultimately overcome the rats' brutality?

30 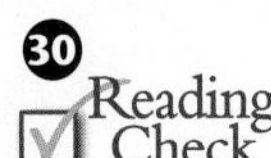

Reading Check

What does the fire boat do to attack the rats? What is the result?

They were true rats of Holland, fearing no man, fighting for the right to live!

Spiral Review

Archetypes

1. Remind students that they studied the concept of archetypes in the Unit 6 Literary Analysis workshop (pp. 1030–1039).
2. **Ask** students the Spiral Review question.

   Possible response: The archetype of a hero is an active participant in rescue or change. The narrator is passive in his own rescue; others must come to save him. However, he can be considered a hero because he is resourceful and takes action that allows him and his companions to survive until help arrives.

29 Literary Analysis

Protagonist and Antagonist

Have students read the bracketed passage. Make sure that students understand how well the men in the boats worked together to save the men in the lighthouse.

Ask the Literary Analysis question: In what way does human intelligence ultimately overcome the rats' brutality?

Possible response: The men on the boats work together to outwit the rats, luring them into a trap.

30 Reading Check

Answer: The fire boat covers the barge with gasoline and then shoots a shell, or cannon, at the barge to light it on fire. The fire kills many rats immediately. Those rats that get off of the barge are killed by sharks. No rats survive.

Concept Connector

Anticipation Guide

Have students return to their **Anticipation Guides** and respond to the statements again in the After Reading column. They may do this individually or in groups. Then, lead a class discussion, probing for what students have learned that confirms or invalidates each statement. Encourage students to cite specific evidence from the text to support their responses.

Writing About the Big Question

Have students compare their responses to the sentence starter they completed before reading the story with their ideas afterwards. Ask them to explain whether their thoughts have changed.

Literary Analysis Graphic Organizer

Ask students to review the graphic organizers they completed while reading. Then have students share their graphic organizers. Show them **Literary Analysis Graphic Organizer A** (p. 196 in ***Graphic Organizer Transparencies***) as an example. Then, have students share their graphic organizers.

31 Reading Skill

Contrasting Characters

Read the bracketed text aloud. **Ask** the Reading Skill question: How is Le Gleo changed by the attack?

Answer: He is now insane and living in an asylum.

▶ **Monitor Progress:** Ask students to define how each character was changed by the event.

Possible response: Itchoua is dead. The narrator seems little changed. Le Gleo has gone insane.

▶ **Reteach:** If students have trouble comparing characters before and after the story, have them create a two-column chart labeled "Beginning" and "End." Have students review the story for details about each character and fill in the chart.

ASSESS

Answers

Critical Thinking

Remind students to support their answers with evidence from the text.

1. (a) The rats arrive at the lighthouse when their ship sinks. (b) **Possible response:** The rats are dangerous and destructive. (c) The rescuers lure the rats to a barge, set it on fire, and force the rats into shark-infested water.
2. (a) Itchoua says that if the window breaks, they can call it Six Skeletons Key. (b) Itchoua means that the three would die. (c) The remark emphasizes how dire the situation is and adds new meaning to the title.
3. (a) Intelligent: The rats have knowledge of the sea, are able to foretell the weather, and work together. Vicious: The rats attack in a frenzy, and fight amongst themselves. (b) **Possible response:** Describing the rats' size, strength, and intelligence makes them seem deadly.
4. **Possible responses:** (a) Yes, the narrator is a hero because he keeps his head in a trying situation. He helps his fellow workers, and he defeats the rats. (b) Yes, he helps Itchoua when he is injured. He tries to keep Le Gleo from going insane.

Reading Skill Contrasting Characters How is Le Gleo changed by the attack?

What became of my friends? Well, Le Gleo's mind had cracked and he was raving mad. They sent him back to France and locked him up in an asylum,[15] the poor devil; Itchoua died within a week; a rat's bite is dangerous in that hot, humid climate, and infection sets in rapidly.

As for me—when they fumigated[16] the light and repaired the damage done by the rats, I resumed my service there. Why not? No reason why such an incident should keep me from finishing out my service there, is there?

Besides—I told you I liked the place—to be truthful, I've never had a post as pleasant as that one, and when my time came to leave it forever, I tell you that I almost wept as Three Skeleton Key disappeared below the horizon.

15. **asylum** (ə sī´ ləm) *n.* institution for the care of the mentally ill.
16. **fumigated** (fyo͞o´ mə gāt´ id) *v.* disinfected with fumes.

Critical Thinking

Cite textual evidence to support your responses.

1. **Key Ideas and Details** **(a)** How do the rats come to the lighthouse? **(b) Infer:** What impression of the rats does this method of arrival create? **(c) Summarize:** Explain how the rescuers defeat the rats.
2. **Integration of Knowledge and Ideas** **(a)** What does Itchoua say about the name of the island and what will happen if the window seal gives way? **(b) Infer:** What does he mean by this remark? **(c) Interpret:** How does this remark create suspense and add meaning to the story's title?
3. **Key Ideas and Details** **(a) Categorize:** Which details portray the rats as intelligent and organized and which portray them as mindlessly vicious? **(b) Evaluate:** Does Toudouze make you believe that actual rats would be capable of the actions he describes? Explain.
4. **Integration of Knowledge and Ideas** **(a)** Is the narrator a hero? Explain. **(b)** Do the narrator's actions reflect a sense of responsibility toward the other characters? Why or why not? *[Connect to the Big Question: Do heroes have responsibilities?]*

Assessment Resources

Unit 6 Resources

L1 L2 EL **Selection Test A,** pp. 105–107. Administer Test A to less advanced students.

L3 L4 EL **Selection Test B,** pp. 108–110. Administer Test B to on-level and more advanced students.

L3 L4 **Open-Book Test,** pp. 102–104. As an alternative, give the Open-Book Test.

All **Customizable Test Bank**

All **Self-tests**
Students may prepare for the **Selection Test** by taking the **Self-test** online.

All assessment resources are available at **www.PHLitOnline.com**.

After You Read Three Skeleton Key

Literary Analysis: Protagonist and Antagonist

1. Craft and Structure **(a)** Identify the **protagonist** in the narrative. **(b)** What is the protagonist's goal? **(c)** Why are readers interested in whether the protagonist achieves his goal?

2. Craft and Structure **(a)** Identify the **antagonist.** **(b)** What is the antagonist's goal?

3. Integration of Knowledge and Ideas **(a)** Why is the story's conflict interesting? **(b)** What universal struggle does this conflict represent?

Reading Skill: Comparing and Contrasting Characters

4. **(a)** Complete a Venn diagram to **compare and contrast** the narrator's outlook at the beginning of the story with his outlook at the end of the story. **(b)** Explain whether the narrator has or has not changed as a result of his experience.

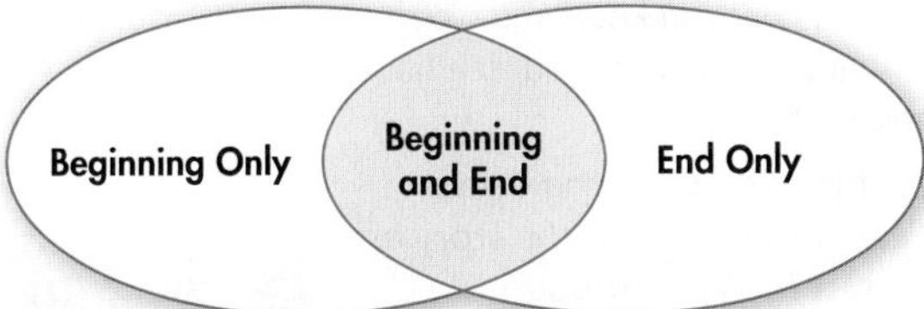

Vocabulary

Acquisition and Use **Analogies** show the relationships between pairs of words. Use a word from the list on page 1146 to complete each analogy.

1. enlargement : increase :: ______________ : decrease
2. glided : graceful :: ______________ : clumsy
3. complimentary : praise :: ______________ : ridicule
4. infrequently : rarely :: ______________ : constantly
5. gasoline : automobile :: ______________ : people
6. exciting : exhilarating :: ______________ : boring

Word Study Use the context of the sentences and what you know about the **Latin root *-min-*** to explain your answer to each question.

1. Would a very hungry man want a *diminutive* sandwich?
2. Does exercise *minimize* the risk of heart attacks?

Word Study

The **Latin root *-min-*** means "small," "little," or "less."

Apply It Explain how the root *-min-* contributes to the meanings of these words. Consult a dictionary if necessary.

minimum
minority
diminish

ASSESS/EXTEND

Answers

Literary Analysis

1. (a) The narrator is the protagonist. (b) The protagonist's goal is to survive the rats. (c) Readers are invested in the character and want him to live.
2. (a) The rats are the antagonists. (b) The antagonists' goal is to devour the men.
3. (a) The conflict is interesting because each side's goal is very basic—survival. (b) The conflict represents the universal struggle to survive.

Reading Skill

4. (a) **Sample answers: Beginning Only**—The narrator is young and inexperienced. He enjoys life. He is not superstitious; **End Only**—The narrator has barely survived the attack, and he has lost two friends; **Beginning and End**—He still enjoys the island and his work on it, and he still doesn't believe the superstitions. (b) The narrator is wiser but basically unchanged.

   For other sample answers, see ***Graphic Organizer Transparencies*, Reading Skill Graphic Organizer A**, p. 199, and the **Additional Answers** section.

Vocabulary

Acquisition and Use

Sample answers:

1. diminution
2. lurched
3. derisive
4. incessantly
5. provisions
6. monotonous

Word Study

Sample answers:

1. No, the root *-min-* means "small, little, less" and *diminutive* means "small." A hungry man would want a large sandwich, not a small one.
2. Yes, the root *-min-* means "small, little, less" and *minimize* means "to reduce to the smallest possible amount." Exercise reduces the risk of heart attacks.

Word Study: Apply It

Sample answers: The *minimum* amount is the smallest amount. A *minority* is a small group of people. When you *diminish* something, you make less of it.

PRETEACH

*Skills instruction for the **Reading Skill** and **Literary Analysis** concept for this selection appears on p. 1145.*

❶ Writing About the Big Question

1. Review the assignment with the class.
2. Remind students of the Big Question by noting that we choose our leaders. Have students describe criteria for these choices and then contrast the criteria with those for a hero.
3. Have students complete the sentence starters. Review responses as a class. (**Possible response:** When a crime is being committed, a hero will take action by calling the police. The hero's involvement may show his or her character because the hero may have to stand up to the criminal.)
4. Remind students that their answers will help them think about the Big Question, "Do heroes have responsibilities?"

While You Read

Tell students that as they read, they should look at Sherlock Holmes's reasons for solving the mystery.

❷ Vocabulary

1. Have students preview the selection vocabulary.
2. For each word, have students say the word aloud.
3. Then, use the word in a sentence that defines the word.
4. Finally, repeat your definitional sentence or a similar sentence with the word missing and have the class "fill in the blank" chorally. Here is an example:

   Something formidable is amazing and awe-inspiring. The team, undefeated for five seasons, has several amazing players and can be described as [students say "formidable"].

❸ Word Study

1. Introduce the skill, using the instruction in the box.
2. **Ask** students for a *-spect-* word that describes how students should treat each other. (**Answer:** *respectfully*)

Making Connections | The Red-headed League

❶ Writing About the Big Question

In "The Red-headed League," Sherlock Holmes sets out to solve a peculiar mystery involving men with brilliant red hair. Use these sentence starters to develop your ideas about the Big Question.

When a crime is being committed, a **hero** will _______________.

The hero's **involvement** may show his or her **character** because _______________.

While You Read Look for Sherlock Holmes's motivations for solving the mystery and decide whether his actions make him a hero.

❷ Vocabulary

Read each word and its definition. Decide whether you know the word well, know it a little bit, or do not know it at all. After you read, see how your knowledge of each word has increased.

- **embellish** (em bel′ ish) *v.* decorate or improve by adding details; ornament; adorn (p. 1167) ***Max decided to embellish the story as he noticed his listeners losing interest halfway through.*** *embellishment n.*
- **endeavored** (en dev′ ərd) *v.* made an earnest attempt to achieve or succeed; tried (p. 1168) ***Jennifer endeavored to rank among the top ten students in her class.*** *endeavor n/v.*
- **introspective** (in′ trə spek′ tiv) *adj.* having to do with looking into one's own thoughts and feelings (p. 1178) ***The touching movie put me in an introspective mood.*** *introspection n. introspectively adv.*
- **vex** (veks) *v.* annoy (p. 1180) ***My allergies continued to vex me throughout the spring.*** *vexing adj. vexation n. vexatiously adv.*
- **formidable** (fôr′ mə də bəl) *adj.* awe-inspiring (p. 1180) ***Mt. Everest is a formidable sight.*** *formidably adv. formidability n.*
- **tenacious** (tə nā′ shəs) *adj.* holding firmly to your point or beliefs; persistent; stubborn (p. 1183) ***The tenacious man could not admit that he was wrong.*** *tenacity n. tenaciousness n. tenaciously adv.*

❸ Word Study

The **Latin root *-spect-*** means "see," "look," or "examine."

In this selection, Sherlock Holmes describes a German music program as **introspective** because it helps him look into his own thoughts.

Vocabulary Development

Vocabulary Knowledge Rating

Create a **Vocabulary Knowledge Rating Chart** (*Professional Development Guidebook*, p. 33) for this selection. Include the selection vocabulary and the Big Question words that appear in the Writing About the Big Question sentence starters on this page. (The Big Question vocabulary is introduced on pp. 1028–1029.)

Give students a copy of the chart. Read the words aloud, and have students mark their rating in the Before Reading column. Urge them to be alert to these words as they read and discuss the selection.

Tally how many students think they know a word to gauge how much instruction to provide. As students read and discuss the selection, point out the words and their context.

Vocabulary Central, featuring tools, activities, and songs for recording and studying vocabulary, is available at **www.PHLitOnline.com.**

Meet
Sir Arthur Conan Doyle
(1859–1930)

Author of
The Red-headed League

Sir Arthur Conan Doyle began his career as a doctor. He also pursued a career in writing. In a few years, he sold his first novel, *A Study in Scarlet,* which introduced Sherlock Holmes to the world.

The World's Favorite Detective It is likely that Conan Doyle modeled Sherlock Holmes on Dr. Joseph Bell, a professor of his who could diagnose illnesses from clues that other physicians had missed. Conan Doyle made the narrator of the Holmes mysteries Dr. John Watson. In the stories, Watson greatly admires Holmes but can never match his friend's powers of observation and reasoning.

Readers grew to love Sherlock Holmes. When Conan Doyle killed him off in a story in 1893, readers protested so strongly that the author was forced to bring back the beloved detective.

DID YOU KNOW?
Although Holmes is often depicted in a plaid cape and a deerstalker hat, the stories never mention such clothing.

4 BACKGROUND FOR THE STORY
Sherlock Holmes

This story is one of many tales about the exploits of one of the world's most famous fictional detectives, Sherlock Holmes. Often depicted wearing a plaid cape and a deerstalker cap, Sherlock Holmes is widely recognized by people around the world.

Daily Bellringer
For each class during which you will teach this selection, have students complete one of the five Revision activities for Week 34 in the *Daily Bellringer Activities* booklet.

4 Background
Sherlock Holmes

London's popular *Strand* magazine commissioned a series of six Sherlock Holmes stories from writer Arthur Conan Doyle in 1891. Readers went wild for Holmes after the first story appeared, and Doyle was able to nearly double his fee. Doyle's final Holmes story appeared in 1927, but the detective is as popular today as he was when his creator was alive. Holmes has been the subject of scholarly biographies, fans have founded numerous societies and reading clubs, and writers such as Laurie King continue to publish new Holmes adventures. Doyle created one of the most beloved literary characters of all time in his keen-eyed, sharp-witted consulting detective.

Multidraft Reading
This icon ● marks natural pauses in the selection. To assist struggling readers and to deepen reading for all, assign the text in "chunks," following the icons, and apply multidraft reading protocols. For each reading, have students set the purpose indicated:

- **First reading**—identifying key ideas and details and answering any Reading Checks.
- **Second reading**—analyzing craft and structure and responding to the side-column prompts.
- **Third reading**—integrating knowledge and ideas, connecting to other texts and the world, and answering the end-of-selection questions.

For more guidance, refer to the *Classroom Strategies and Teaching Routines* card on multidraft reading.

PHLit Online!
For more about the author, practice with the selection vocabulary, and more background, go online at **www.PHLitOnline.com.**

Differentiated Instruction — Additional Instruction

EL Extended Support—English Learners
Have students complete the **Reading and Vocabulary Warm-ups,** ***Unit 6 Resources,*** pp. 110–113 before they read. Assign the prereading pages for the selection in the ***Reader's Notebook: English Learner's Version.*** Then, have students listen to portions of the selection on the ***Hear It!*** **Audio CD.**

L1 L2 Extended Support—Struggling Readers
Have students complete the **Reading and Vocabulary Warm-ups,** ***Unit 6 Resources,*** pp. 110–113 before they read. Assign the prereading pages for the selection in the ***Reader's Notebook: Adapted Version.*** Then, have students listen to portions of the selection on the ***Hear It!*** **Audio CD** (adapted text).

Extended Support—Reluctant Readers
To build motivation and engagement before assigning the selection, have students read "Inner Circles," a thematically related selection in ***Reality Central.*** Then, use the questions at the conclusion of the related selection to guide discussion.

TEACH

❶ Activating Prior Knowledge

1. Prepare an **Anticipation Guide** (*Professional Development Guidebook*, pp. 36–38) with the following statements:
   - It is important to pay attention to the small details in life.
   - Being observant is a skill that is not very useful.
   - When two people observe the same thing, they always interpret it the same way.
   - You should be wary of things that are too good to be true.
2. Give students a copy of the prepared **Anticipation Guide** and have students mark their responses in the Me column. Have students discuss the statements in pairs or groups and mark the Guides again in the Group column.
3. For further guidance, use the ***Classroom Strategies and Teaching Routines*** card **Using an Anticipation Guide.**

Concept Connector
Students will return to the **Anticipation Guide** after completing "The Red-headed League."

Whole-Class Activity
Have students discuss books they have read or movies they have seen that are mysteries or involve crimes. **Ask** students to identify the protagonist and antagonist in the book or movie and give a brief summary of how the characters behaved. On the board, create a simple chart listing the characters and stories.

❷ About the Selection

In "The Red-headed League," pawnbroker Jabez Wilson consults detective Sherlock Holmes about the mysterious "Red-headed League" that offered him employment for several weeks and then disappeared. Holmes soon discovers that master criminals invented the League to lure Wilson from his pawnshop so that they could dig a tunnel from his cellar into the vaults of a nearby bank.

❶ ❷

The Red-headed League

Sir Arthur Conan Doyle

I had called upon my friend, Mr. Sherlock Holmes, one day in the autumn of last year and found him in deep conversation with a very stout, florid-faced, elderly gentleman with fiery red hair. With an apology for my intrusion, I was about to withdraw when Holmes pulled me abruptly into the room and closed the door behind me.

Vocabulary Development — CCSS Language 6

Thematic Vocabulary: The Big Question
As students are discussing "The Red-headed League," have them use the thematic vocabulary presented in Introducing the Big Question, pp. 1028–1029. You might encourage them with sentence starters like these:

1. Sherlock Holmes's *wisdom* is shown through . . .
2. Dr. Watson's *character* could be described as . . .
3. When Holmes goes to the pawnshop the first time, his *intentions* are to . . .
4. Mr. Clay's *involvement* in the crime begins with . . .

"You could not possibly have come at a better time, my dear Watson," he said cordially.

"I was afraid that you were engaged."

"So I am. Very much so."

"Then I can wait in the next room."

"Not at all. This gentleman, Mr. Wilson, has been my partner and helper in many of my most successful cases, and I have no doubt that he will be of the utmost use to me in yours also."

The stout gentleman half rose from his chair and gave a bob of greeting, with a quick little questioning glance from his small, fat-encircled eyes.

3 "Try the settee,"[1] said Holmes, relapsing into his armchair and putting his finger tips together, as was his custom when in judicial moods. "I know, my dear Watson, that you share my love of all that is bizarre and outside the conventions and humdrum routine of everyday life. You have shown your relish for it by the enthusiasm which has prompted you to chronicle, and, if you will excuse my saying so, somewhat to **embellish** so many of my own little adventures."

"Your cases have indeed been of the greatest interest to me," I observed.

"You will remember that I remarked the other day, just before we went into the very simple problem presented by Miss Mary Sutherland, that for strange effects and extraordinary combinations we must go to life itself, which is always far more daring than any effort of the imagination."

"A proposition which I took the liberty of doubting."

4 "You did, Doctor, but none the less you must come round to my view, for otherwise I shall keep on piling fact upon fact on you until your reason breaks down under them and acknowledges me to be right. Now, Mr. Jabez Wilson here has been good enough to call upon me this morning, and to begin a narrative which promises to be one of the most singular which I have listened to for some time. You have heard me remark that the strangest and most unique things are very often connected not with the larger but with the smaller crimes, and occasionally, indeed, where there is room for doubt whether any positive crime has been committed. As far as I have heard it is impossible for me to say whether the present case is an instance of crime or not, but the course of events is certainly among the most singular that I have ever listened to. Perhaps, Mr. Wilson, you would have the great kindness to recommence your

Reading Skill
Comparing Characters According to Holmes, what do he and Watson have in common?

Vocabulary
embellish (em bel′ ish) *v.* decorate or improve by adding details; ornament; adorn

Literary Analysis
Protagonist and Antagonist What details in Holmes's speech here help present him as a protagonist?

5
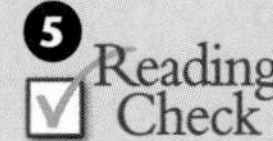
Reading Check
What interest do Watson and Holmes share?

1. **settee** (se tē′) *n.* small sofa.

3 Reading Skill

Comparing Characters

1. Have students read the first bracketed passage. Explain to students that, like the reader, Watson often misses clues and is confused. His job is to ask Holmes questions and make him explain his deductions.
2. **Ask** the Reading Skill question: According to Holmes, what do he and Watson have in common?

   Answer: Both Holmes and Watson have a love of bizarre events and mysteries.

4 Literary Analysis

Protagonist and Antagonist

1. Review the characteristics of a protagonist. Remind students that a protagonist is a character who may have flaws but who always interests the reader. Then read the second bracketed passage aloud.
2. **Ask** the Literary Analysis question: What details in Holmes's speech here help present him as a protagonist?

   Answer: Holmes is clearly an interesting character who is in charge of what happens in the story.
3. Have students write their ideas on copies of **Literary Analysis Graphic Organizer B *(Graphic Organizer Transparencies,*** p. 198). Remind students as they read to write down information about the protagonist's goals, actions, and conflicts.

5 Reading Check

Answer: Watson and Holmes are both interested in bizarre and unusual events.

Differentiated Instruction for Universal Access

Strategy for Special-Needs Students

To give students a context for the story and to help them identify the characteristics of protagonists and antagonists, show them **Literary Analysis Graphic Organizer A** (***Graphic Organizer Transparencies,*** p. 197). The completed graphic organizer will give students insight into the goals, motives, and actions of protagonists and antagonists. They can use it as a model for identifying the motives and goals of the protagonist and antagonist in the story.

EL Support for English Learners

"The Red-headed League" is a good story to hear as well as read. Play the ***Hear It!* Audio CD** for students. Play the CD to the point in the story when Mr. Wilson leaves Mr. Holmes. Ask students to review what has happened so far in the story and to make predictions about what will happen next. Continue playing the CD as students progress through the selection. Stop the CD at key points in the narrative to ask students to summarize and make predictions.

PHLit Online!

This selection is available in interactive format in the **Enriched Online Student Edition, www.PHLitOnline.com**, which includes a thematically related video with writing prompt and an interactive graphic organizer.

6 Reading Skill

Contrasting Characters

1. Point out that it is standard in a Sherlock Holmes story for Holmes and Watson to come to very different conclusions about an event or a person.
2. Have students reread the last two paragraphs on this page. **Ask** students how the two men's conclusions are different.

   Possible response: Watson decides that Mr. Wilson is unremarkable. Holmes reaches some very specific conclusions about Mr. Wilson's life and work.
3. **Ask** students the Reading Skill question: How are Watson and Holmes different in terms of their powers of observation?

   Answer: Both Watson and Holmes observe many small details about Mr. Wilson, but only Holmes is able to use the details to draw specific conclusions about the man's life.

narrative. I ask you not merely because my friend Dr. Watson has not heard the opening part but also because the peculiar nature of the story makes me anxious to have every possible detail from your lips. As a rule, when I have heard some slight indication of the course of events, I am able to guide myself by the thousands of other similar cases which occur to my memory. In the present instance I am forced to admit that the facts are, to the best of my belief, unique."

The portly client puffed out his chest with an appearance of some little pride and pulled a dirty and wrinkled newspaper from the inside pocket of his great coat. As he glanced down the advertisement column, with his head thrust forward and the paper flattened out upon his knee, I took a good look at the man and **endeavored**, after the fashion of my companion, to read the indications which might be presented by his dress or appearance.

Vocabulary
endeavored (en dev´ ərd) *v.* made an earnest attempt to achieve or succeed; tried

I did not gain very much, however, by my inspection. Our visitor bore every mark of being an average commonplace British tradesman, obese, pompous, and slow. He wore rather baggy gray shepherd's check trousers, a not over-clean black frock coat, unbuttoned in the front, and a drab waistcoat with a heavy brassy Albert chain, and a square pierced bit of metal dangling down as an ornament. A frayed top hat and a faded brown overcoat with a wrinkled velvet collar lay upon a chair beside him. Altogether, look as I would, there was nothing remarkable about the man save his blazing red head, and the expression of extreme chagrin and discontent upon his features.

Reading Skill
Contrasting Characters How are Watson and Holmes different in terms of their powers of observation?

Sherlock Holmes's quick eye took in my occupation, and he shook his head with a smile as he noticed my questioning glances. "Beyond the obvious facts that he has at some time done manual labor, that he takes snuff,[2] that he is a Freemason,[3] that he has been in China, and that he has done a considerable amount of writing lately, I can deduce nothing else."

---

2. **snuff** (snuf) *n.* powdered tobacco.
3. **Freemason** member of a secret society.

Vocabulary Development

CCSS Language 6

Multiple Meanings

Point out the word *vacancy* at the bottom of p. 1169 and ask students to think about the word's meaning. Tell students that *vacancy* has several meanings. Write the following sentences on the board, and guide students in developing definitions for each use of the word *vacancy*.

1. The beach's *vacancy* during the winter makes me feel lonely.
2. The look on her face reflected the *vacancy* of her mind.
3. The post office has a *vacancy* in the sorting department.

Ask students to write additional sentences showing the different meanings of *vacancy*. Review the meanings of the word and decide which definition best fits the use of the word *vacancy* on this page.

Answers: 1. emptiness or blankness; 2. the state of being free of thought; 3. an unfilled position or job. Definition 3 best fits the meaning of the word as it is used on p. 1169.

Mr. Jabez Wilson started up in his chair, with his forefinger upon the paper, but his eyes upon my companion.

"How, in the name of good fortune, did you know all that, Mr. Holmes?" he asked. "How did you know, for example, that I did manual labor? It's as true as gospel, for I began as a ship's carpenter."

"Your hands, my dear sir. Your right hand is quite a size larger than your left. You have worked with it, and the muscles are more developed."

"Well, the snuff, then, and the Freemasonry?"

"I won't insult your intelligence by telling you how I read that, especially as, rather against the strict rules of your order, you use an arc-and-compass breastpin."

"Ah, of course, I forgot that. But the writing?"

"What else can be indicated by that right cuff so very shiny for five inches, and the left one with the smooth patch near the elbow where you rest it upon the desk?"

"Well, but China?"

"The fish that you have tattooed immediately above your right wrist could only have been done in China. I have made a small study of tattoo marks and have even contributed to the literature of the subject. That trick of staining the fishes' scales of a delicate pink is quite peculiar to China. When, in addition, I see a Chinese coin hanging from your watch-chain, the matter becomes even more simple."

Mr. Jabez Wilson laughed heavily. "Well, I never!" said he. "I thought at first that you had done something clever, but I see that there was nothing in it, after all."

7 "I begin to think, Watson," said Holmes, "that I make a mistake in explaining. '*Omne ignotum pro magnifico*,'[4] you know, and my poor little reputation, such as it is, will suffer shipwreck if I am so candid. Can you not find the advertisement, Mr. Wilson?"

"Yes, I have got it now," he answered with his thick red finger planted halfway down the column. "Here it is. This is what began it all. You just read it for yourself, sir."

I took the paper from him and read as follows:

To THE RED-HEADED LEAGUE:

On account of the bequest of the late Ezekiah Hopkins, of Lebanon, Pennsylvania, U. S. A., there is now another vacancy open

4. ***Omne ignotum pro magnifico*** (äm′ nā ig nō′ təm prō mag nē′ fē kō) Latin for "Whatever is unknown is magnified."

8 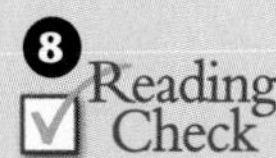

What facts about Mr. Wilson does Holmes deduce based on Wilson's appearance?

7 Connecting to the Big Question

1. Remind students of the Big Question by **asking** them for ideas about why heroes take the actions that make them so admirable.
2. Have students read the bracketed text on p. 1169. **Ask:** When Mr. Jabez Wilson laughs at him, why does Holmes think it may have been a mistake to explain his reasoning?

   Answer: When people understand how Mr. Holmes thinks, they are less impressed by his work. He wants people to think he is amazing.
3. **Ask:** What does this statement suggest about one of Holmes's motivations for solving crimes?

   Answer: It suggests that Holmes enjoys the praise and recognition that he gets. It also suggests that Holmes enjoys the mental challenge, and solving crimes affirms his own view of himself as a very smart man.

8 Reading Check

Answer: Holmes deduces that Mr. Wilson has worked with his hands, uses tobacco, is a member of a secret society, has visited China, and has been writing a great deal.

Differentiated Instruction for Universal Access

Culturally Responsive Instruction

Culture Focus Point out the reference to Freemasonry. Explain that the freemasons are a secret society. In most, if not all, cultures, people join groups or clubs. Some groups are more exclusive than others, and some are secretive, like the freemasons. Have students share the different types of groups that they are familiar with from their home culture or family's country of origin. Examples include religious organizations, scouting groups, hobby clubs, the Rotary Club, and professional organizations. Finally, ask students why they think a group might want to be secretive. Students can discuss the advantages and disadvantages of this type of organization.

9 Literature in Context

Math Connection When this story was written, British money was divided into pounds, shillings, and pence. Twelve pence (pennies) made a shilling, and twenty shillings made a pound. Other coins included the crown (worth 5 shillings), the sovereign (worth one pound), the half-crown, the half sovereign, and the florin (worth 2 shillings). Late in the twentieth century, England shifted to a decimal monetary system in which 100 pence made one pound.

Connect to the Literature Have students read the Literature in Context feature, and present the additional background information above. Before students answer the question, ask them to share and respond to get-rich-quick schemes they have heard about. Elicit that even though many schemes are suspect, some people are always interested because getting a lot of money for little work always sounds appealing. **Ask** students the Connect to the Literature question: Why might an offer of a large sum of money "for purely nominal services" be cause for suspicion?

Answer: The promise of receiving a lot of money for little work is almost always too good to be true.

10 Literary Analysis

Protagonist and Antagonist

1. Remind students that the antagonist provides obstacles and conflicts to the protagonist. Tell students that, at this point in the story, the protagonist Holmes does not yet have an antagonist. Read the bracketed text aloud.
2. Challenge students to **predict** who Holmes's antagonist will be. Have students **consider** the likely candidates based on the reading so far.

   Answer: Students may suggest that whoever set up Mr. Wilson will be Holmes's antagonist. Mr. Wilson himself is another candidate.
3. **Ask** students the Literary Analysis question: Which details in the description of Vincent Spaulding attract Holmes's notice?

   Answer: The detail that catches Holmes's attention is that Spaulding works for half the wages he could get elsewhere.

9

LITERATURE IN CONTEXT

Math Connection

Pound Conversions
The advertisement that concerns Mr. Wilson announces a salary of four pounds a week. The pound is the monetary unit of Great Britain. Its equivalency in American dollars fluctuates depending on current economic conditions. At the time Doyle wrote the story, one British pound equaled about $4.85, so four pounds would have equaled about $19.40. This was considered a large amount at the time in which the story is set, particularly for easy work.

Connect to the Literature

Why might an offer of a large sum of money "for purely nominal services" be cause for suspicion?

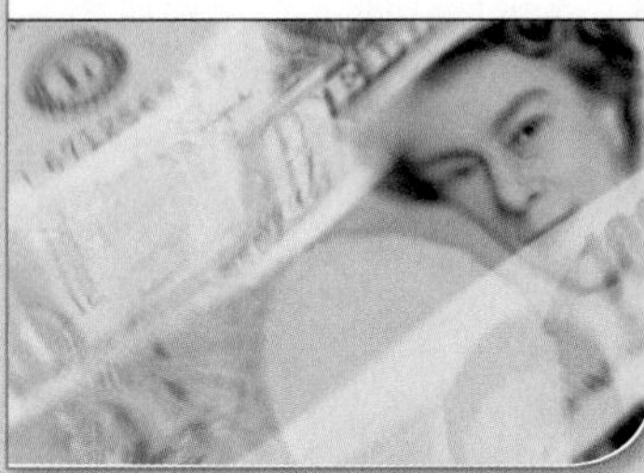

which entitles a member of the League to a salary of £4 a week for purely nominal services. All red-headed men who are sound in body and mind, and above the age of twenty-one years, are eligible. Apply in person on Monday, at eleven o'clock, to Duncan Ross, at the offices of the League, 7 Pope's Court, Fleet Street.

"What on earth does this mean?" I ejaculated after I had twice read over the extraordinary announcement.

Holmes chuckled and wriggled in his chair, as was his habit when in high spirits. "It is a little off the beaten track, isn't it?" said he. "And now, Mr. Wilson, off you go at scratch and tell us all about yourself, your household, and the effect which this advertisement had upon your fortunes. You will first make a note, Doctor, of the paper and the date."

"It is *The Morning Chronicle* of April 27, 1890. Just two months ago."

"Very good. Now, Mr. Wilson?"

"Well, it is just as I have been telling you, Mr. Sherlock Holmes," said Jabez Wilson, mopping his forehead; "I have a small pawnbroker's business at Coburg Square, near the City. It's not a very large affair, and of late years it has not done more than just give me a living. I used to be able to keep two assistants, but now I only keep one; and I would have a job to pay him but that he is willing to come for half wages so as to learn the business."

"What is the name of this obliging youth?" asked Sherlock Holmes.

"His name is Vincent Spaulding, and he's not such a youth, either. It's hard to say his age. I should not wish a smarter assistant, Mr. Holmes; and I know very well that he could better himself and earn twice what I am able to give him. But, after all, if he is satisfied, why should I put ideas in his head?" 10

"Why, indeed? You seem most fortunate in having an employee who comes under the full market price. It is not a common experience among employers in this age. I don't know that your assistant is not as remarkable as your advertisement."

Literary Analysis Protagonist and Antagonist Which details in the description of Vincent Spaulding attract Holmes's notice?

"Oh, he has his faults, too," said Mr. Wilson. "Never was such a fellow for photography. Snapping away with a camera when he ought to be improving his mind, and then diving down into the cellar like a rabbit into its hole to develop his pictures. That is his main fault, but on the whole he's a good worker. There's no vice in him."

"He is still with you, I presume?"

Vocabulary Development CCSS Language 6

Expressive Vocabulary
To help students broaden their expressive vocabulary, encourage them to use the following words as they discuss the selection: *perceive, observe, differentiate,* and *reveals*. Have them complete these sentence starters:

1. Holmes and Watson *perceive* . . .
2. Watson likes to *observe* . . .
3. The reader can *differentiate* Watson from Holmes by . . .
4. Holmes *reveals* to Watson . . .

Accept all of students' answers. Ask the class to determine if words are used properly in context. Point out to students sentences that use the words correctly.

"Yes, sir. He and a girl of fourteen, who does a bit of simple cooking and keeps the place clean—that's all I have in the house, for I am a widower and never had any family. We live very quietly, sir, the three of us; and we keep a roof over our heads and pay our debts, if we do nothing more.

"The first thing that put us out was that advertisement. Spaulding, he came down into the office just this day eight weeks, with this very paper in his hand, and he says:

"'I wish to the Lord, Mr. Wilson, that I was a red-headed man.'

"'Why that?' I asks.

"'Why,' says he, 'here's another vacancy on the League of the Red-headed Men. It's worth quite a little fortune to any man who gets it, and I understand that there are more vacancies than there are men, so that the trustees are at their wits' end what to do with the money. If my hair would only change color, here's a nice little crib all ready for me to step into.'

Reading Skill Contrasting Characters In what ways does Wilson's lack of awareness of the outside world present a contrast to Holmes and Watson?

12

"'Why, what is it, then?' I asked. You see, Mr. Holmes, I am a very stay-at-home man, and as my business came to me instead of my having to go to it, I was
11 often weeks on end without putting my foot over the doormat. In that way I didn't know much of what was going on outside, and I was always glad of a bit of news.

"'Have you never heard of the League of the Red-headed Men?' he asked with his eyes open.

"'Never.'

"'Why, I wonder at that, for you are eligible yourself for one of the vacancies.'

"'And what are they worth?' I asked.

"'Oh, merely a couple of hundred a year, but the work is slight, and it need not interfere very much with one's other occupations.'

"Well, you can easily think that that made me prick up my ears, for the business has not been over-good for some years, and an extra couple of hundred would have been very handy.

"'Tell me all about it,' said I.

"'Well,' said he, showing me the advertisement, 'you can see for

13 **Reading Check**

Who is eligible for the position in the advertisement?

11 Reading Skill

Contrasting Characters

1. **Ask** students to sum up what they know about Mr. Wilson and to make a generalization about him.

   Answer: Mr. Wilson works hard but does not make a lot of money. He is a pawnbroker who does not go out very much. He would like to make more money.

2. Have students reread the bracketed text. **Ask** students the Reading Skill question: In what ways does Wilson's lack of awareness of the outside world present a contrast to Holmes and Watson?

   Answer: Holmes and Watson are the opposite; they are detectives who must have knowledge about the world around them.

3. Invite students to think of labels for each of the characters they have met so far. For example, they might label Holmes "Mr. Know-It-All." Discuss students' labels and encourage them to think of new labels for characters as they meet them or as they learn more about characters they have already labeled.

12 Humanities

Illustrations for "The Red-headed League," by Sidney Paget

Englishman Sidney Paget (1860–1908) had a successful career as a painter and illustrator. He is best remembered for his original illustrations for the Holmes stories, which first appeared in the popular *Strand* magazine. Use the following question for discussion:

How do Paget's illustrations help you appreciate the story?

Possible response: They show the styles of hair and clothing worn at the time. They depict dramatic moments in the story.

13 Reading Check

Answer: Any red-headed man who is over the age of 21 and in good physical and mental health is eligible.

Differentiated Instruction for Universal Access

Strategy for Less Proficient Readers

As students read, they can fill out graphic organizers that identify details about the plot, characters, setting, and theme of the story. Afterwards, they can use their notes to briefly retell the story to a partner. Listeners should be sure students' retellings are accurate in detail.

Enrichment for Advanced Readers

Have students gather in a small group to debate which of the four short-story elements (plot, character, setting, theme) is most important to "The Red-headed League." In discussing each element, students should consider questions such as "Would the story have worked in a different setting or with different characters?" and "What is the message at the heart of the story?" Ask students to summarize their discussion for the class.

 Reading Skill

Contrasting Characters

1. Remind students that Sherlock Holmes is gathering information as he listens to Mr. Wilson's story. Tell students to think like Sherlock Holmes as they read or listen to the story themselves.
2. **Ask** students what they have learned so far about the character of Spaulding.

   Possible response: He works cheaply for Mr. Wilson, enjoys photography, spends a lot of time in the basement, and seems eager for Mr. Wilson to get the position with the Red-headed League.
3. Read the bracketed passage aloud. Then, **ask** the Reading Skill question: Who seems more invested in Wilson's joining the Red-headed League—Wilson or Spaulding? Explain.

   Possible response: Students should suggest that although Mr. Wilson would like to make more money, Mr. Spaulding seems very enthusiastic. He promotes the League heavily, and when they arrive at the League's offices, he pushes Mr. Wilson to the front of the crowd.
4. **Ask** students to speculate why Spaulding would want Mr. Wilson to take the job.

   Answer: Students may suggest that Spaulding wants Mr. Wilson to get the money so that Mr. Wilson can pay him better wages. Some students may suggest that Spaulding is up to no good.

yourself that the League has a vacancy, and there is the address where you should apply for particulars. As far as I can make out, the League was founded by an American millionaire, Ezekiah Hopkins, who was very peculiar in his ways. He was himself red-headed, and he had a great sympathy for all red-headed men; so when he died it was found that he had left his enormous fortune in the hands of trustees, with instructions to apply the interest to the providing of easy berths to men whose hair is of that color. From all I hear it is splendid pay and very little to do.

Reading Skill Contrasting Characters Who seems more invested in Wilson's joining the Red-headed League—Wilson or Spaulding? Explain.

"'But,' said I, 'there would be millions of red-headed men who would apply.'

"'Not so many as you might think,' he answered. 'You see it is really confined to Londoners, and to grown men. This American had started from London when he was young, and he wanted to do the old town a good turn. Then, again, I have heard it is no use your applying if your hair is light red, or dark red, or anything but real bright, blazing, fiery red. Now, if you cared to apply, Mr. Wilson, you would just walk in; but perhaps it would hardly be worth your while to put yourself out of the way for the sake of a few hundred pounds.'

"Now, it is a fact, gentlemen, as you may see for yourselves, that my hair is of a very full and rich tint, so that it seemed to me that if there was to be any competition in the matter I stood as good a chance as any man that I had ever met. Vincent Spaulding seemed to know so much about it that I thought he might prove useful so I just ordered him to put up the shutters for the day and to come right away with me. He was very willing to have a holiday,[5] so we shut the business up and started off for the address that was given us in the advertisement.

"I never hope to see such a sight as that again, Mr. Holmes. From north, south, east, and west every man who had a shade of red in his hair had tramped into the city to answer the advertisement. Fleet Street was choked with red-headed folk, and Pope's Court looked like a coster's orange barrow.[6] I should not have thought there were so many in the whole country as were brought together by that single advertisement. Every shade of color they were—straw, lemon, orange, brick, Irish-setter, liver, clay; but, as Spaulding said, there were not many who had the real vivid flame-colored tint. When I saw how many were waiting, I would have given it up in despair; but Spaulding would not hear of it. How he did it I could not imagine, but he pushed and pulled and butted until he got me through the crowd, and right up to the steps which led to the office. There was a double stream upon the stair, some going up in hope, and some coming back dejected; but we wedged in as well as we could and soon found ourselves in the office."

5. **holiday** day off from work; vacation.
6. **coster's orange barrow** pushcart of a seller of oranges.

Think Aloud

Vocabulary: Using Context

Direct students' attention to the word *benefactor* on p. 1173. Using a think-aloud process, model how to use context to infer the meaning of an unknown word. Say to students:

I'm going to think aloud to show you how I can figure out the meaning of *benefactor* from its context.

In this sentence, Mr. Ross uses the word *benefactor* to refer to the man who left money for the Red-headed League. The word *noble* suggests that *benefactor* has a positive connotation. Also, *benefactor* reminds me of *benefit* and *beneficial*, which also have positive connotations.

It is a positive thing to leave money to help out strangers, so I think that a benefactor refers to someone who gives money or who donates to charitable causes.

"Your experience has been a most entertaining one," remarked Holmes as his client paused and refreshed his memory with a huge pinch of snuff. "Pray continue your very interesting statement."

"There was nothing in the office but a couple of wooden chairs and a deal table, behind which sat a small man with a head that was even redder than mine. He said a few words to each candidate as he came up, and then he always managed to find some fault in them which would disqualify them. Getting a vacancy did not seem to be such a very easy matter, after all. However, when our turn came the little man was much more favorable to me than to any of the others, and he closed the door as we entered, so that he might have a private word with us.

15 "'This is Mr. Jabez Wilson,' said my assistant, 'and he is willing to fill a vacancy in the League.'

"'And he is admirably suited for it,' the other answered. 'He has every requirement. I cannot recall when I have seen anything so fine.' He took a step backward, cocked his head on one side, and gazed at my hair until I felt quite bashful. Then suddenly he plunged forward, wrung my hand, and congratulated me warmly on my success.

"'It would be injustice to hesitate,' said he. 'You will, however, I am sure, excuse me for taking an obvious precaution.' With that he seized my hair in both his hands, and tugged until I yelled with the pain. 'There is water in your eyes,' said he as he released me. 'I perceive that all is as it should be. But we have to be careful, for we have twice been deceived by wigs and once by paint. I could tell you tales of cobbler's wax which would disgust you with human nature.' He stepped over to the window and shouted through it at the top of his voice that the vacancy was filled. A groan of disappointment came up from below, and the folk all trooped away in different directions until there was not a red head to be seen except my own and that of the manager.

"'My name,' said he, 'is Mr. Duncan Ross, and I am myself one of the pensioners upon the fund left by our noble benefactor. Are you a married man, Mr. Wilson? Have you a family?'

"I answered that I had not.

"His face fell immediately.

"'Dear me!' he said gravely, 'that is very serious indeed! I am sorry to hear you say that. The fund was, of course, for the propagation and spread of the red-heads as well as for their maintenance. It is exceedingly unfortunate that you should be a bachelor.'

"My face lengthened at this, Mr. Holmes, for I thought that I was not to have the vacancy after all; but after thinking it over for a few minutes he said that it would be all right.

Reading Skill Contrasting Characters In what way is the man's behavior toward Mr. Wilson different from his behavior toward the other candidates?

16 
Who helps Wilson push through the crowd of men applying for the Red-headed League?

15 Reading Skill

Contrasting Characters

1. **Ask** students to think about the conventions of murder mysteries or thrillers they have read or seen. For example, most television crime shows start with a murder or other serious crime and the police spend the rest of the show trying to solve it.
2. **Ask** students how this story is different from these other mysteries.

   Possible response: In other mysteries, the crime takes place at the beginning of the story, and the detective has to figure out who has committed it. Here, it is not clear what the crime is, let alone who did it. Holmes has to figure out both things.
3. Remind students that when reading a Sherlock Holmes mystery, they should be suspicious of every character they meet—except for Holmes and Watson, of course. Then have them reread the bracketed text.
4. **Ask** the Reading Skill question: In what way is the man's behavior toward Mr. Wilson different from his behavior toward the other candidates?

   Possible response: The man has been easily finding reasons to disqualify the other men, but he is immediately favorable to Mr. Wilson.
5. **Ask** students if they are suspicious of the way that the position at the Red-headed League was filled. Have students explain their answers.

   Possible response: Students may suggest that they are suspicious because the position seemed to be filled arbitrarily. Students may also be wary of how the interviewer warmed so easily to Mr. Wilson.

16 Reading Check

Answer: Spaulding pushes Mr. Wilson through the crowd of red-headed men.

Fluency

Distribute copies of pages 1172–1173 to partners. Have listeners circle words with which readers struggle. Circulate to monitor the fluency of students' reading. Collect students' lists of words. Use these techniques to address problems:

- If students have difficulty with the word *dejected* (p. 1172), point out the word parts. Then model reading each syllable (*de-ject-ed*) and combining the syllables into one word (*dejected*).
- If students have difficulty with the word *experience* (p. 1173), write the word on the board. Cover up the word with your hand. Uncover the *ex* and say "*ex*." Continue to uncover letters or groups of letters as you pronounce the word. Show students how to gradually pronounce, correcting as you go. For example, you might say *ekspa* (for *expe*), and then change that to *exper* (*exper*), and then, as you uncover more letters, pronounce the word correctly.

17 Literary Analysis

Protagonist and Antagonist

1. After students read the bracketed text about Mr. Wilson's duties at the Red-headed League, **ask** them the Literary Analysis question: Which details in the description of Wilson's responsibilities make Ross seem like a suspicious character?

   Possible response: Ross seems suspicious because of his insistence on staying in the room, the odd job of encyclopedia writing, and the lack of a supply of writing materials.

2. **Ask** students to predict what Sherlock Holmes may think about this episode of Mr. Wilson's story.

   Possible response: Sherlock Holmes will know what Ross is up to and will identify the crime that Ross is probably committing.

"'In the case of another,' said he, 'the objection might be fatal, but we must stretch a point in favor of a man with such a head of hair as yours. When shall you be able to enter upon your new duties?'

"'Well, it is a little awkward, for I have a business already,' said I.

"'Oh, never mind about that, Mr. Wilson!' said Vincent Spaulding. 'I should be able to look after that for you.'

"'What would be the hours?' I asked.

"'Ten to two.'

"Now a pawnbroker's business is mostly done of an evening, Mr. Holmes, especially Thursday and Friday evening, which is just before pay-day; so it would suit me very well to earn a little in the mornings. Besides, I knew that my assistant was a good man, and that he would see to anything that turned up.

"'That would suit me very well,' said I. 'And the pay?'

"'Is £4 a week.'

"And the work?'

"'Is purely nominal.'

"What do you call purely nominal?'

"'Well, you have to be in the office, or at least in the building, the whole time. If you leave, you forfeit your whole position forever. The will is very clear upon that point. You don't comply with the conditions if you budge from the office during that time.'

"'It's only four hours a day, and I should not think of leaving,' said I.

17 "'No excuse will avail,' said Mr. Duncan Ross; 'neither sickness nor business nor anything else. There you must stay, or you lose your billet.'[7]

"'And the work?'

"'Is to copy out the Encyclopedia Britannica. There is the first volume of it in that press. You must find your own ink, pens, and blotting-paper, but we provide this table and chair. Will you be ready tomorrow?'

"'Certainly,' I answered.

"'Then, good-bye, Mr. Jabez Wilson, and let me congratulate you

Literary Analysis
Protagonist and Antagonist Which details in the description of Wilson's responsibilities make Ross seem like a suspicious character?

7. **billet** (bil′ it) *n.* position; job.

Vocabulary Development

CCSS Language 6

Word Forms

Give students a blank **Word Forms Chart** (***Professional Development Guidebook***, p. 42) with *introspective, vex,* and *formidable* in the correct columns. Work with the class, or have students work with a partner, to determine the related forms.

Hold students accountable for integrating the related forms of the words into their speaking and writing.

Noun	Verb	Adjective	Adverb
introspection	introspect	**introspective**	introspectively
vexation	**vex**	vexatious	vexatiously
formidability		**formidable**	formidably

once more on the important position which you have been fortunate enough to gain.' He bowed me out of the room, and I went home with my assistant, hardly knowing what to say or do, I was so pleased at my own good fortune.

"Well, I thought over the matter all day, and by evening I was in low spirits again; for I had quite persuaded myself that the whole affair must be some great hoax or fraud, though what its object might be I could not imagine. It seemed altogether past belief that anyone could make such a will, or that they would pay such a sum for doing anything so simple as copying out the Encyclopedia Britannica. Vincent Spaulding did what he could to cheer me up, but by bedtime I had reasoned myself out of the whole thing. However, in the morning I determined to have a look at it anyhow, so I bought a penny bottle of ink, and with a quill-pen, and seven sheets of foolscap paper, I started off for Pope's Court.

"Well, to my surprise and delight, everything was as right as possible. The table was set out ready for me, and Mr. Duncan Ross was there to see that I got fairly to work. He started me off upon the letter A, and then he left me; but he would drop in from time to time to see that all was right with me. At two o'clock he bade me good-day, complimented me upon the amount that I had written, and locked the door of the office after me.

18 "This went on day after day, Mr. Holmes, and on Saturday the manager came in and planked down four golden sovereigns for my week's work. It was the same next week, and the same the week after. Every morning I was there at ten, and every afternoon I left at two. By degrees Mr. Duncan Ross took to coming in only once of a morning, and then, after a time, he did not come in at all. Still, of course, I never dared to leave the room for an instant, for I was not sure when he might come, and the billet was such a good one, and suited me so well, that I would not risk the loss of it.

"Eight weeks passed away like this, and I had written about Abbots and Archery and Armor and Architecture and Attica, and hoped with diligence that I might get on to the B's before very long. It cost me something in foolscap, and I had pretty nearly filled a shelf with my writings. And then suddenly the whole business came to an end."

"To an end?"

"Yes, sir. And no later than this morning. I went to my work as

19 
Reading Check

Who offers to look after Wilson's pawnbroker business while he is at his other job?

18 Critical Thinking

Summarize

1. **Ask** students to read the bracketed text, then to **summarize** the routine that Mr. Wilson and Mr. Ross develop over the course of the eight weeks.

   Possible response: Mr. Wilson goes to the office at 10 o'clock every morning, copies the encyclopedia, and leaves at 2 o'clock every afternoon. Mr. Ross meets Mr. Wilson at the door and checks on him periodically throughout the day. Over time, Mr. Ross checks in less frequently.

2. **Ask** students to explain why Mr. Ross checks in less frequently.

   Possible response: Mr. Ross probably realized that he could trust Mr. Wilson to stay in the office.

19 Reading Check

Answer: Spaulding offers to look after Mr. Wilson's business while Wilson does his duties for the League.

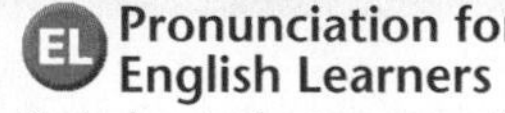

Differentiated Instruction for Universal Access

EL Pronunciation for English Learners

To help students correctly pronounce initial *h*, post these words: *head, hair, he, Holmes, hoax, however, had, hoped.* Read the words aloud, stressing the initial /h/. Have students echo. Then point to a word and ask students to say it aloud. Have students read the pertinent sentence aloud to reinforce.

Enrichment for Gifted/Talented Students

Have students pretend that they are editors to whom this story has been submitted for publication. Have them write reviews discussing the plot, characters, setting, and theme. Students should use details from the story to make a strong case for or against publication.

20 Reading Skill

Contrasting Characters

1. Have students read the first bracketed passage aloud. **Ask** students the Reading Skill question: How do the reactions of Watson and Holmes to the announcement compare with Mr. Wilson's? Explain.

   Possible response: Watson and Holmes think the announcement is funny because Mr. Wilson is so disappointed. They must have known from the beginning that the Red-headed League position was a fraud, and they think it is funny that Mr. Wilson should have expected it to continue. Mr. Wilson, on the other hand, had gotten over his doubts about the League and was disappointed not to receive any more money.

2. Based on what they have read so far in the story, **ask** students to **make some generalizations** about the differences between Wilson and the two detectives.

   Possible response: Watson and Holmes have more education and more money than Wilson. They are also more suspicious than Wilson and more observant of details.

21 Literary Analysis

Protagonist and Antagonist

1. Read the second bracketed passage aloud. Remind students that in a mystery, characters are not always what they appear to be or who they say they are. Make sure that students realize that Duncan Ross was really a man named William Morris.

2. **Ask** the Literary Analysis question: What does William Morris's dishonesty about his identity suggest about his character?

   Answer: By posing as another person, Morris suggests that he is not a person to be trusted.

usual at ten o'clock, but the door was shut and locked, with a little square of cardboard hammered on to the middle of the panel with a tack. Here it is, and you can read for yourself."

He held up a piece of white cardboard about the size of a sheet of notepaper. It read in this fashion:

THE RED-HEADED LEAGUE IS DISSOLVED.
October 9, 1890.

Reading Skill
Contrasting Characters How do the reactions of Watson and Holmes to the announcement compare with Mr. Wilson's? Explain. 20

Sherlock Holmes and I surveyed this curt announcement and the rueful face behind it, until the comical side of the affair so completely overtopped every other consideration that we both burst out into a roar of laughter.

"I cannot see that there is anything very funny," cried our client, flushing up to the roots of his flaming head. "If you can do nothing better than laugh at me, I can go elsewhere."

"No, no," cried Holmes, shoving him back into the chair from which he had half risen. "I really wouldn't miss your case for the world. It is most refreshingly unusual. But there is, if you will excuse my saying so, something just a little funny about it. Pray what steps did you take when you found the card upon the door?"

"I was staggered, sir. I did not know what to do. Then I called at the offices round, but none of them seemed to know anything about it. Finally, I went to the landlord, who is an accountant living on the ground floor, and I asked him if he could tell me what had become of the Red-headed League. He said that he had never heard of any such body. Then I asked him who Mr. Duncan Ross was. He answered that the name was new to him.

"'Well,' said I, 'the gentleman at No. 4.'

"'What, the red-headed man?'

"'Yes.'

"'Oh,' said he, 'his name was William Morris. He was a solicitor[8] and was using my room as a temporary convenience until his new premises were ready. He moved out yesterday.'

21 **Literary Analysis**
Protagonist and Antagonist What does William Morris's dishonesty about his identity suggest about his character?

"'Where could I find him?'

"'Oh, at his new offices. He did tell me the address. Yes, 17 King Edward Street, near St. Paul's.'

"I started off, Mr. Holmes, but when I got to that address it was a manufactory of artificial kneecaps, and no one in it had ever heard of either Mr. William Morris or Mr. Duncan Ross."

"And what did you do then?" asked Holmes.

"I went home to Saxe-Coburg Square, and I took the advice of my assistant. But he could not help me in any way. He could only say

8. **solicitor** (sə lis′ it ər) *n.* member of the legal profession.

Vocabulary Development

CCSS Language 6

Selection Vocabulary Reinforcement

Give students sentences using the selection vocabulary words, in which the word may or may not be used correctly. Students must tell whether the use is correct and explain their answer. Use these sentences:

1. Juan was feeling *introspective*, so he went to the festival and met new people. **Answer:** No, *introspective* is not used correctly. It means "having to do with looking into one's own thoughts." A social activity would prevent this.
2. The child was *vexed* by all of the gifts she was receiving at her birthday party. **Answer:** No, *vexed* is not used correctly. It is not likely that gifts would annoy a child on her birthday.
3. Providing food for the massive wedding was a *formidable* task for the caterer. **Answer:** Yes, *formidable* is used correctly. *Formidable* means "overwhelming," and catering a large wedding would be overwhelming.

that if I waited I should hear by post. But that was not quite good enough, Mr. Holmes. I did not wish to lose such a place without a struggle, so, as I had heard that you were good enough to give advice to poor folk who were in need of it, I came right away to you."

"And you did very wisely," said Holmes. "Your case is an exceedingly remarkable one, and I shall be happy to look into it. From what you have told me I think that it is possible that graver issues hang from it than might at first sight appear."

"Grave enough!" said Mr. Jabez Wilson. "Why, I have lost four pound a week."

"As far as you are personally concerned," remarked Holmes, "I do not see that you have any grievance against this extraordinary league. On the contrary, you are, as I understand, richer by some £30, to say nothing of the minute knowledge which you have gained on every subject which comes under the letter A. You have lost nothing by them."

"No, sir. But I want to find out about them, and who they are, and what their object was in playing this prank—if it was a prank—upon me. It was a pretty expensive joke for them, for it cost them two and thirty pounds."

"We shall endeavor to clear up these points for you. And, first, one or two questions, Mr. Wilson. This assistant of yours who first called your attention to the advertisement—how long had he been with you?"

"About a month then."

"How did he come?"

"In answer to an advertisement."

22 "Was he the only applicant?"

"No, I had a dozen."

"Why did you pick him?"

"Because he was handy and would come cheap."

"At half-wages, in fact."

"Yes."

"What is he like, this Vincent Spaulding?"

Literary Analysis
Protagonist and Antagonist What reason might Holmes have for being suspicious of Vincent Spaulding?

23 

What reasons does Mr. Wilson give for hiring Vincent Spaulding?

22 Literary Analysis

Protagonist and Antagonist

1. At this point in the story, have students **list** characters who might be considered suspects. Students' lists should contain Spaulding and Ross/Morris.
2. Then, have students **identify** reasons why these characters might be suspects. Elicit from students that the men have acted suspiciously—Spaulding has been enthusiastic about Wilson getting the position at the league. Ross has lied about his identity.
3. Have students read the bracketed text, which continues on to p. 1178. **Ask** the Literary Analysis question: What reason might Holmes have for being suspicious of Vincent Spaulding?

   Possible response: Spaulding's willingness to work at half wages interests Holmes, but the detail about the white mark on Spaulding's forehead seems to interest him more.
4. Challenge students to **explain** Holmes's excitement after hearing the description of Spaulding.

   Answer: Holmes probably knows about a criminal who has a white mark on his forehead.

23 Reading Check

Answer: Mr. Spaulding was handy and willing to work for half-wages.

Differentiated Instruction for Universal Access

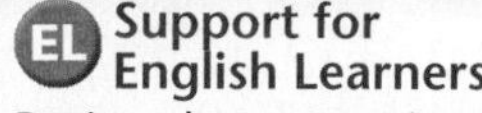

Support for English Learners

Review the conventions of dialogue with students: the use of quotation marks to mark the beginning and ending of a quotation and the starting of a new paragraph to indicate a change in speaker. Then, have students look over the dialogue on this page and figure out which character is saying each line of dialogue.

Strategy for Advanced Readers

After students complete the story, challenge them to retell it from Holmes's point of view. Their versions will be much shorter than the original; they need not repeat Wilson's story, for instance. Have students consider the tone Holmes would use and how he would reveal his solution to the crime.

24 Literary Analysis

Protagonist and Antagonist

1. Read the second bracketed passage aloud. Point out that once Mr. Wilson has finished speaking, Holmes returns to the center of the story. **Ask** students what qualities Holmes demonstrates that continue to qualify him as the protagonist of the story. For example, is he still the most interesting character? Does he seem in charge of the story?

   Possible response: Students should agree that Holmes is the protagonist. Readers are interested in seeing how he solves the mystery of the Red-headed League.

2. **Ask** students the Literary Analysis question: What does Holmes's expectation of reaching a conclusion in two days reveal about his character?

   Answer: Holmes is confident that he can solve the mystery.

"Small, stout-built, very quick in his ways. No hair on his face, though he's not short of thirty. Has a white splash of acid upon his forehead."

22 Holmes sat up in his chair in considerable excitement. "I thought as much," said he. "Have you ever observed that his ears are pierced for earrings?"

"Yes, sir. He told me that a gypsy had done it for him when he was a lad."

"Hum!" said Holmes, sinking back in deep thought. "He is still with you?"

"Oh, yes, sir; I have only just left him."

"And has your business been attended to in your absence?"

"Nothing to complain of, sir. There's never very much to do of a morning."

24 "That will do, Mr. Wilson. I shall be happy to give you an opinion upon the subject in the course of a day or two. Today is Saturday, and I hope that by Monday we may come to a conclusion."

Literary Analysis Protagonist and Antagonist What does Holmes's expectation of reaching a conclusion in two days reveal about his character?

"Well, Watson," said Holmes when our visitor had left us, "what do you make of it all?"

"I make nothing of it," I answered frankly. "It is a most mysterious business."

"As a rule," said Holmes, "the more bizarre a thing is the less mysterious it proves to be. It is your commonplace, featureless crimes which are really puzzling, just as a commonplace face is the most difficult to identify. But I must be prompt over this matter."

"What are you going to do, then?" I asked.

"To smoke," he answered. "It is quite a three pipe problem, and I beg that you won't speak to me for fifty minutes." He curled himself up in his chair, with his thin knees drawn up to his hawk-like nose, and there he sat with his eyes closed and his black clay pipe thrusting out like the bill of some strange bird. I had come to the conclusion that he had dropped asleep, and indeed was nodding myself, when he suddenly sprang out of his chair with the gesture of a man who has made up his mind and put his pipe down upon the mantelpiece.

"Sarasate[9] plays at the St. James's Hall this afternoon," he remarked. "What do you think, Watson? Could your patients spare you for a few hours?"

"I have nothing to do today. My practice is never very absorbing."

"Then put on your hat and come. I am going through the City first, and we can have some lunch on the way. I observe that there is a good deal of German music on the program, which is rather more to my taste than Italian or French. It is **introspective**, and I want to introspect. Come along!"

Vocabulary
introspective (in′ trə spek′ tiv) *adj.* having to do with looking into one's own thoughts and feelings

9. **Sarasate** (sä rä sä′ tä) Spanish violinist and composer.

Vocabulary Development

CCSS Language 6

Word Analysis

Read aloud the last paragraph on this page. Point out the definition of the word *introspective* in the margin. Write the word on the board and break it up into its prefix, root, and suffix. Students should easily understand that *intro-* means "into, inside, inward." If you or any students in the class wear eyeglasses, point them out and tell the class that eyeglasses are also called *spectacles*. This clue will help students remember that *-spec-* has to do with looking or seeing.

Challenge students to put the pieces of the word together to understand that *introspective* means "able to look inward at one's own thoughts." Encourage students to think of other words based on the root *-spec-*.

Possible responses: *respect, prospect, aspect, inspect, spectator, spectacular, spectrum,* and other forms of these words.

We traveled by the Underground as far as Aldersgate; and a short walk took us to Saxe-Coburg Square, the scene of the singular story which we had listened to in the morning. It was a poky, little, shabby-genteel place, where four lines of dingy two-storied brick houses looked out into a small railed-in enclosure, where a lawn of weedy grass and a few clumps of faded laurel bushes made a hard fight against a smoke-laden and uncongenial atmosphere. Three gilt balls and a brown board with "JABEZ WILSON" in white letters, upon a corner house, announced the place where our red-headed client carried on his business. Sherlock Holmes stopped in front of it with his head on one side and looked it all over, with his eyes shining brightly between puckered lids. Then he walked slowly up the street, and then down again to the corner, still looking keenly at the houses. Finally he returned to the pawnbroker's, and, having thumped vigorously upon the pavement with his stick two or three times, he went up to the door and knocked. It was instantly opened by a bright-looking, clean-shaven young fellow, who asked him to step in.

"Thank you," said Holmes, "I only wished to ask you how you would go from here to the Strand."

"Third right, fourth left," answered the assistant promptly, closing the door.

"Smart fellow, that," observed Holmes as we walked away. "He is, in my judgment, the fourth smartest man in London, and for daring I am not sure that he has not a claim to be third. I have known something of him before."

"Evidently," said I, "Mr. Wilson's assistant counts for a good deal in this mystery of the Red-headed League. I am sure that you inquired your way merely in order that you might see him."

"Not him."

"What then?"

"The knees of his trousers."

"And what did you see?"

"What I expected to see."

"Why did you beat the pavement?"

"My dear doctor, this is a time for observation, not for talk. We are spies in an enemy's country. We know something of Saxe-Coburg Square. Let us now explore the parts which lie behind it."

The road in which we found ourselves as we turned round the corner from the retired Saxe-Coburg Square presented as great a contrast to it as the front of a picture does to the back. It was one

Reading Skill Comparing Characters Based on Holmes's remark about Spaulding, what trait do the two men share? Explain.

27 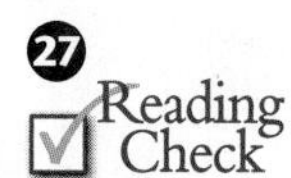

Which aspect of Spaulding's appearance does Holmes want to observe?

25 Critical Thinking

Draw Conclusions

1. Direct students to the long bracketed passage. **Ask** them identify the actions taken by Holmes and the details that he has noticed during his visit to Mr. Wilson's shop.

   Answer: Holmes has studied the houses on the street, met Spaulding and looked at the knees of his trousers, and tapped on the pavement.

2. **Ask** students to use their own powers of deduction to guess at what Holmes has discovered.

   Possible response: Holmes has discovered a secret passage under the house by tapping on the stones, and the passage leads to another building. Mr. Spaulding is a suspect because of the evidence on his trousers.

26 Reading Skill

Comparing Characters

1. Point out that Holmes has started his search for answers in earnest at this point in the story. After students finish reading p. 1179, focusing on the shorter bracketed passage, **ask** them to think of adjectives that describe Holmes during this part of the crime-solving process.

   Possible response: Holmes is observant, focused, thorough, introspective, and unwilling to share information.

2. **Ask** students the Reading Skill question: Based on Holmes's remark about Spaulding, what trait do the two men share? Explain.

   Answer: Both men are very intelligent. Holmes is impressed by Spaulding's intelligence and by his daring nature.

27 Reading Check

Answer: Holmes wants to look at the knees of Spaulding's trousers.

Differentiated Instruction for Universal Access

Strategy for Less Proficient Readers

Have students consider this story as a series of causes and effects. They should note each interesting or surprising detail, such as Spaulding's willingness to work for half wages, in one column of a chart. In the other column, they can note possible causes of this effect.

EL Support for English Learners

Invite students to identify capitalized proper nouns and adjectives on pp. 1178–1179. Students should identify character names, place names, and the names of languages. Remind students that in English, specific names of persons, places, and things are capitalized.

28 Critical Thinking

Analyze

1. Explain to students that one of the reasons Holmes is such a well-loved character is that he is unpredictable. Point out that, instead of charging out to find the criminal, Holmes goes to a concert to enjoy himself.
2. Ask students to reread the last paragraph on p. 1180 and to use the information in it to learn more about Holmes's character. **Ask** students to **make a generalization** about the two sides of Holmes's nature.

   Possible response: Holmes is either dreaming and contemplative or energetic and searching. He can swing from one personality to the other without warning.
3. Have students return to **Literary Analysis Graphic Organizer B** ***(Graphic Organizer Transparencies,*** p. 198). Have students use the information on p. 1180 to provide insight into Holmes's actions and goals. Students should understand that one of Holmes's goals is to solve puzzles and thwart criminals. Another is to enjoy the simple pleasures of food and entertainment.

of the main arteries which conveyed the traffic of the City to the north and west. The roadway was blocked with the immense stream of commerce flowing in a double tide inward and outward, while the footpaths were black with the hurrying swarm of pedestrians. It was difficult to realize as we looked at the line of fine shops and stately business premises that they really abutted on the other side upon the faded and stagnant square which we had just quitted.

"Let me see," said Holmes, standing at the corner and glancing along the line, "I should like just to remember the order of the houses here. It is a hobby of mine to have an exact knowledge of London. There is Mortimer's, the tobacconist, the little newspaper shop, the Coburg branch of the City and Suburban Bank, the Vegetarian Restaurant, and McFarlane's carriage-building depot. That carries us right on to the other block. And now, Doctor, we've done our work, so it's time we had some play. A sandwich and a cup of coffee, and then off to violin land, where all is sweetness and delicacy and harmony, and there are no red-headed clients to vex us with their conundrums."

Vocabulary
vex (veks) *v.* annoy
formidable (fôr´ mə də bəl) *adj.* awe-inspiring

My friend was an enthusiastic musician, being himself not only a very capable performer but a composer of no ordinary merit. All the afternoon he sat in the stalls wrapped in the most perfect happiness, gently waving his long, thin fingers in time to the music, while his gently smiling face and his languid, dreamy eyes were as unlike those of Holmes, the sleuthhound, Holmes the relentless, keen-witted, ready-handed criminal agent, as it was possible to conceive. In his singular character the dual nature alternately asserted itself, and his extreme exactness and astuteness represented, as I have often thought, the reaction against the poetic and contemplative mood which occasionally predominated
28 in him. The swing of his nature took him from extreme languor to devouring energy; and, as I knew well, he was never so truly formidable as when, for days on end, he had been lounging in his armchair amid his improvisations and his black-letter editions. Then it was that the lust of the chase would suddenly come upon him, and that his brilliant reasoning power would rise to the level of intuition, until those who were unacquainted with his methods would look askance at him as on a man whose knowledge was not that of other mortals. When I saw him that afternoon so enwrapped in the music at St. James's Hall I felt that an evil time might be coming upon those whom he had set himself to hunt down.

"You want to go home, no doubt, Doctor," he remarked as we emerged.

Think Aloud

Vocabulary: Using Context

Direct students' attention to the word *ominous* in the long paragraph on p. 1181. Using a think-aloud process, model how to use context to infer the meaning of an unknown word. Say to students:

> I'm going to think aloud to show you how I would figure out the meaning of *ominous* from its context.
>
> The sentence in which *ominous* appears gives me a clue. Watson uses the word to describe Holmes's parting remark. I look back at the previous paragraph and reread Holmes's words: "And, I say, Doctor, there may be some little danger, so kindly put your army revolver in your pocket." To me, Holmes's words seem like a warning of danger. I look again at the word *ominous*. What does it sound or look like? It kind of reminds me of the word *omen*. An *omen* is also a kind of warning. My guess, then, is that *ominous* is used to describe something that "warns of future danger or threats."

"Yes, it would be as well."

"And I have some business to do which will take some hours. This business at Coburg Square is serious."

"Why serious?"

"A considerable crime is in contemplation. I have every reason to believe that we shall be in time to stop it. But today being Saturday rather complicates matters. I shall want your help tonight."

"At what time?"

"Ten will be early enough."

"I shall be at Baker Street at ten."

"Very well. And, I say, Doctor, there may be some little danger, so kindly put your army revolver in your pocket." He waved his hand, turned on his heel, and disappeared in an instant among the crowd.

I trust that I am not more dense than my neighbors, but I was always oppressed with a sense of my own stupidity in my dealings with Sherlock Holmes. Here I had heard what he had heard, I had seen what he had seen, and yet from his words it was evident that he saw clearly not only what had happened but what was about to happen, while to me the whole business was still confused and grotesque. As I drove home to my house in Kensington I thought over it all, from the extraordinary story of the red-headed copier of the Encyclopedia down to the visit to Saxe-Coburg Square, and the ominous words with which he had parted from me. What was this nocturnal expedition, and why should I go armed? Where were we going, and what were we to do? I had the hint from Holmes that this smooth-faced pawnbroker's assistant was a formidable man—a man who might play a deep game. I tried to puzzle it out, but gave it up in despair and set the matter aside until night should bring an explanation.

It was a quarter past nine when I started from home and made my way across the Park, and so through Oxford Street to Baker Street. Two hansoms were standing at the door, and as I entered the passage I heard the sound of voices from above. On entering his room I found Holmes in animated conversation with two men, one of whom I recognized as Peter Jones, the official police agent, while the other was a long, thin, sadfaced man, with a very shiny hat and oppressively respectable frock coat.

"Ha! our party is complete," said Holmes, buttoning up his

30 **LITERATURE IN CONTEXT**

Culture Connection

Hansoms

The hansom, also known as the hansom cab, is a two-wheeled covered carriage for two passengers that is pulled by one horse. The cab was named for its inventor, Joseph Hansom (1803–1882), a London architect. By the late 1850s, the hansom was popular in New York and Boston as well as in London. Customers could enjoy a scenic and romantic ride in private with an unobstructed view because the driver sat above and behind the passengers' cab. Today, updated hansom cabs are a popular tourist attraction in New York's Central Park. However, in this story, they are a common form of transportation.

Connect to the Literature

What problems would traveling by hansom pose for someone rushing to stop a crime?

Reading Check

Where do the men plan to go in the evening?

29 Critical Thinking

Deduce

1. Remind students that in a mystery, the conflict is between the detective and the criminal. Then have students read the bracketed text.
2. Challenge students to **explain** what they know about the crime at this point in the story.

   Answer: The crime has not yet happened. Holmes hopes to prevent it. The crime is serious enough to require Watson's gun and a police officer.
3. Then **ask** them to guess at the identity of the criminal, or the antagonist in the story.

   Possible response: Based on Holmes's inquiries, the criminal is probably Spaulding.

30 Literature in Context

Culture Connection Hansoms were not the only form of transportation in Holmes's London. The London Underground is one of the world's oldest subway systems; trains began running in 1863. The Metropolitan Line, the oldest in the system, was completed in 1884. By 1900, three separate companies had constructed individual train lines. Holmes and Watson take a Metropolitan Line train from Baker Street station, which is across the street from Holmes's flat.

Connect to the Literature Have students read the Literature in Context feature, and present the additional background provided above. Then, have students study the illustration of the hansom cab on p. 1181 and think about the advantages and disadvantages of using a horse-powered vehicle rather than a motorized vehicle. **Ask** the Connect to the Literature question: What problems would traveling by hansom pose for someone rushing to stop a crime?

Answer: A hansom would be slow and difficult to maneuver.

31 Reading Check

Answer: The men plan to meet each other at Baker Street. Holmes has not given Watson any more information than this, except to say he should bring a gun.

Differentiated Instruction for Universal Access

Strategy for Special-Needs Students

Have students think of questions that they asked while reading the story that they were not able to answer on their own. They can discuss their questions with a partner. Have students work together to look back at the story to try and find the answers. Remind them that not all questions readers have are answered in a story; sometimes readers have to answer questions for themselves. For example, "The Red-headed League" does not explain how Holmes knew the criminal at the center of the story.

After this exercise, students can gather in groups, introduce their questions, and discuss their attempts to find answers. Have students share ideas about their answers to each other's questions. Remind students to support all answers with details from the story.

32 Reading Skill

Comparing Characters

1. Explain that one way writers build tension in a story is to give their protagonist and antagonist equal but opposite strengths. Give students the example of the cartoon characters Wiley E. Coyote and Roadrunner. Wiley is sly and grumpy, but Roadrunner is equally cheerful and quick. Challenge students to think of examples of other protagonists and antagonists whose qualities are well matched.
2. Have students reread the bracketed text. **Ask** students the Reading Skill question: Despite their differences, in what ways are Sherlock Holmes and John Clay similar?

   Answer: Both Holmes and Clay are remarkable, intelligent, unpredictable, and cultured men.
3. Then, **ask** how the two men are different.

   Answer: Holmes is a detective and Clay is a criminal. Holmes helps citizens, while Clay robs citizens.

peajacket and taking his heavy hunting crop from the rack. "Watson, I think you know Mr. Jones, of Scotland Yard? Let me introduce you to Mr. Merryweather, who is to be our companion in tonight's adventure."

"We're hunting in couples again, Doctor, you see," said Jones in his consequential way. "Our friend here is a wonderful man for starting a chase. All he wants is an old dog to help him to do the running down."

"I hope a wild goose may not prove to be the end of our chase," observed Mr. Merryweather gloomily.

"You may place considerable confidence in Mr. Holmes, sir," said the police agent loftily. "He has his own little methods, which are, if he won't mind my saying so, just a little too theoretical and fantastic, but he has the makings of a detective in him. It is not too much to say that once or twice, as in that business of the Sholto murder and the Agra treasure, he has been more nearly correct than the official force."

"Oh, if you say so, Mr. Jones, it is all right," said the stranger with deference. "Still, I confess that I miss my rubber.[10] It is the first Saturday night for seven-and-twenty years that I have not had my rubber."

"I think you will find," said Sherlock Holmes, "that you will play for a higher stake tonight than you have ever done yet, and that the play will be more exciting. For you, Mr. Merryweather, the stake will be some £30,000; and for you, Jones, it will be the man upon whom you wish to lay your hands."

Reading Skill
Comparing Characters Despite their differences, in what ways are Sherlock Holmes and John Clay similar?

32

"John Clay, the murderer, thief, smasher, and forger. He's a young man, Mr. Merryweather, but he is at the head of his profession, and I would rather have my bracelets on him than on any criminal in London. He's a remarkable man, is young John Clay. His grandfather was a royal duke, and he himself has been to Eton[11] and Oxford.[12] His brain is as cunning as his fingers, and though we meet signs of him at every turn, we never know where to find the man himself. He'll crack a crib[13] in Scotland one week, and be raising money to build an orphanage in Cornwall the next. I've been on his track for years and have never set eyes on him yet."

"I hope that I may have the pleasure of introducing you tonight. I've had one or two little turns also with Mr. John Clay, and I agree with you that he is at the head of his profession. It is past ten, however, and quite time that we started. If you two will take the first hansom, Watson and I will follow in the second."

Sherlock Holmes was not very communicative during the long

10. **rubber** a term for a type of card game.
11. **Eton** famous British secondary school for boys.
12. **Oxford** oldest university in Great Britain.
13. **crack a crib** commit burglary.

Think Aloud

Vocabulary: Dictionary Use

Using a think-aloud process, model how to use a dictionary to identify the meaning of *labyrinth*, which appears at the top of p. 1183. Say to students:

> I'm going to think aloud to show you how I would find the correct meaning of *labyrinth* in the dictionary.
>
> There are three definitions. The first definition is "a maze or network of twisting passages." That fits. The men have just traveled on winding streets.
>
> The second definition is "a confusing arrangement or state of affairs." This definition is more abstract than the first.
>
> The third definition is a medical one—"the inner ear." This definition is obviously incorrect.
>
> Let's insert the first definition into the sentence. "We rattled through an endless maze or network of gas-lit streets until we emerged into Farrington Street." The first definition works best.

drive and lay back in the cab humming the tunes which he had heard in the afternoon. We rattled through an endless labyrinth of gas-lit streets until we emerged into Farrington Street.

"We are close there now," my friend remarked. "This fellow Merryweather is a bank director, and personally interested in the matter. I thought it as well to have Jones with us also. He is not a bad fellow, though an absolute imbecile in his profession. He has one positive virtue. He is as brave as a bulldog and as tenacious as a lobster if he gets his claws upon anyone. Here we are, and they are waiting for us."

We had reached the same crowded thoroughfare in which we had found ourselves in the morning. Our cabs were dismissed, and, following the guidance of Mr. Merryweather, we passed down a narrow passage and through a side door, which he opened for us. Within there was a small corridor, which ended in a very massive iron gate. This also was opened, and led down a flight of winding stone steps, which terminated at another formidable gate. Mr. Merryweather stopped to light a lantern, and then conducted us down a dark, earth-smelling passage, and so, after opening a third door, into a huge vault or cellar, which was piled all round with crates and massive boxes.

"You are not very vulnerable from above," Holmes remarked as he held up the lantern and gazed about him.

"Nor from below," said Mr. Merryweather, striking his stick upon the flags which lined the floor. "Why, dear me, it sounds quite hollow!" he remarked, looking up in surprise.

"I must really ask you to be a little more quiet!" said Holmes severely. "You have already imperiled the whole success of our expedition. Might I beg that you would have the goodness to sit down upon one of those boxes, and not to interfere?"

The solemn Mr. Merryweather perched himself upon a crate, with a very injured expression upon his face, while Holmes fell upon his knees upon the floor and, with the lantern and a magnifying lens, began to examine minutely the cracks between the stones. A few seconds sufficed to satisfy him, for he sprang to his feet again and put his glass in his pocket.

"We have at least an hour before us," he remarked, "for they can hardly take any steps until the good pawnbroker is safely in bed. Then they will not lose a minute, for the sooner they do their work

Vocabulary
tenacious (tə nā´ shəs) *adj.* holding firmly to your point or beliefs; persistent; stubborn

34

Reading Check
Where does Mr. Merryweather lead Holmes and his companions?

33 Critical Thinking
Infer

1. Tell students that one way to make inferences about characters is to analyze their actions and dialogue. Have them read the bracketed passage.
2. **Ask** students how Holmes reacts on p. 1183 when Mr. Merryweather makes an unnecessary noise.

   Answer: Holmes becomes irritated with him.
3. **Challenge** students to analyze Holmes's response to Mr. Merryweather and make an inference about Holmes's character based on his response.

   Possible response: Holmes reprimands Mr. Merryweather severely and treats him like a child. This response shows that Holmes's biggest concern is solving the case; he is not concerned with hurting Mr. Merryweather's feelings. His response also shows that he has full faith in his theories, revealing that he is a very confident man.

34 Reading Check
Answer: Mr. Merryweather leads the men to the cellar of his bank where French gold is being stored.

Differentiated Instruction for Universal Access

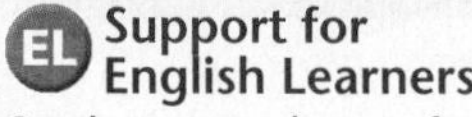

EL Support for English Learners
Students may be confused by the dialogue and the unfolding of events in the last part of the story. It may help them to listen to the last part of the story on ***Hear It!* Audio CD**. Ask students to read along as they listen. At the end of each page, stop the CD and ask students to summarize what has happened. If students are still confused, play the CD again and talk about the specific words or pieces of information that confuse them.

Strategy for Advanced Readers
Ask students to think of modern mysteries or thrillers they have read and to compare them to "The Red-headed League." Students should identify similarities and differences in the plots and characters, and in the authors' writing styles. Ask students to comment on which type of story—modern or traditional—they prefer and to explain why.

35 Literary Analysis

Protagonist and Antagonist

1. Have students read the bracketed text. **Ask** students the Literary Analysis question: What kind of enemy does Holmes anticipate he and his companions will face?

   Possible response: The criminals are smart enough to wait until the pawnbroker is safely in bed, yet daring enough to attempt to rob a major London bank.

2. Point out that Holmes has created a picture of his antagonist as a daring, reckless man. **Ask** students how Holmes compares, particularly in the bracketed paragraph.

   Possible response: Holmes is not reckless but calm. He calmly gives instructions. He shows his thoughtful and civilized side, too. He brings playing cards for Mr. Merryweather.

Spiral Review

Archetypes

1. Remind students that they studied the concept of archetypes in the Unit 6 Literary Analysis workshop (pp. 1030–1039).

2. **Ask** students the Spiral Review question.

   Possible response: The red-headed man's visit is the call to adventure; heroes gather companions and guides; Holmes gathers the police officer, bank manager, and Watson; the night journey (like the hansom ride to the bank) is a feature of a hero's quest; catching the bank thief who has been troubling society is Holmes's "gift" or "boon" to the world. Watson's description of Holmes's "trances" and his extra effectiveness after such spells represent the hero's death and resurrection or rescue during a quest.

Literary Analysis Protagonist and Antagonist What kind of enemy does Holmes anticipate he and his companions will face?

the longer time they will have for their escape. We are at present, Doctor—as no doubt you have divined—in the cellar of the City branch of one of the principal London banks. Mr. Merryweather is the chairman of directors, and he will explain to you that there are reasons why the more daring criminals of London should take a considerable interest in this cellar at present."

"It is our French gold," whispered the director. "We have had several warnings that an attempt might be made upon it."

"Your French gold?"

"Yes. We had occasion some months ago to strengthen our resources and borrowed for that purpose 30,000 napoleons from the Bank of France. It has become known that we have never had occasion to unpack the money, and that it is still lying in our cellar. The crate upon which I sit contains 2,000 napoleons packed between layers of lead foil. Our reserve of bullion is much larger at present than is usually kept in a single branch office, and the directors have had misgivings upon the subject."

"Which were very well justified," observed Holmes.

Spiral Review

Archetypes In what ways is Holmes's case a type of hero's quest?

"And now it is time that we arranged our little plans. I expect that within an hour matters will come to a head. In the meantime, Mr. Merryweather, we must put the screen over that dark lantern."

"And sit in the dark?"

35 "I am afraid so. I had brought a pack of cards in my pocket, and I thought that, as we were a *partie carrée*,[14] you might have your rubber after all. But I see that the enemy's preparations have gone so far that we cannot risk the presence of a light. And, first of all, we must choose our positions. These are daring men, and though we shall take them at a disadvantage, they may do us some harm unless we are careful. I shall stand behind this crate, and do you conceal yourselves behind those. Then, when I flash a light upon them, close in swiftly. If they fire, Watson, have no compunction about shooting them down."

I placed my revolver, cocked, upon the top of the wooden case behind which I crouched. Holmes shot the slide across the front of his lantern and left us in pitch darkness—such an absolute darkness as I have never before experienced. The smell of hot metal remained to assure us that the light was still there, ready to flash out at a moment's notice. To me, with my nerves worked up to a pitch of expectancy, there was something depressing and subduing in the sudden gloom, and in the cold dank air of the vault.

"They have but one retreat," whispered Holmes. "That is back through the house into Saxe-Coburg Square. I hope that you have done what I asked you, Jones?"

"I have an inspector and two officers waiting at the front door."

14. ***partie carrée*** (pär tē′ cä rā′) French for "group of four."

Vocabulary Development

CCSS Language 6

Word Analysis

Point out the word *expectancy* at the bottom of p. 1184. Write the word on the board and challenge students to define it. Students should understand that the word *expectancy* means "state of waiting or looking forward to a probable event."

Explain that *ex-* is a Latin prefix meaning "out" or "out of." When *ex-* is combined with the root *-spec-*, the s is dropped, because its sound is already made by the letter *x*. Knowing the prefix and the root should help students figure out that *ex* + *spec* means "looking out" or "looking forward."

Have students apply the same process to define the word *inspector*. Students should explain that because the prefix *in-* means "in" or "into," an inspector is a person who looks into, or investigates, things.

"Then we have stopped all the holes. And now we must be silent and wait."

36 What a time it seemed! From comparing notes afterwards it was but an hour and a quarter, yet it appeared to me that the night must have almost gone, and the dawn be breaking above us. My limbs were weary and stiff, for I feared to change my position; yet my nerves were worked up to the highest pitch of tension, and my hearing was so acute that I could not only hear the gentle breathing of my companions, but I could distinguish the deeper, heavier in-breath of the bulky Jones from the thin, sighing note of the bank director. From my position I could look over the case in the direction of the floor. Suddenly my eyes caught the glint of a light.

Literary Analysis Protagonist and Antagonist What details of Watson's account help build the suspense of the conflict?

At first it was but a lurid spark upon the stone pavement. Then it lengthened out until it became a yellow line, and then, without any warning or sound, a gash seemed to open and a hand appeared; a white, almost womanly hand, which felt about in the center of the little area of light. For a minute or more the hand, with its writhing fingers, protruded out of the floor. Then it was withdrawn as suddenly as it appeared, and all was dark again save the single lurid spark which marked a chink between the stones.

37 Its disappearance, however, was but momentary. With a rending, tearing sound, one of the broad, white stones turned over upon its side and left a square, gaping hole, through which streamed the light of a lantern. Over the edge there peeped a clean-cut, boyish face, which looked keenly about it, and then, with a hand on either side of the aperture, drew itself shoulder-high and waist-high, until one knee rested upon the edge. In another instant he stood at the side of the hole and was hauling after him a companion, lithe and small like himself, with a pale face and a shock of very red hair.

Reading Skill Comparing Characters In what ways is the first burglar's appearance similar to that of Vincent Spaulding?

"It's all clear," he whispered. "Have you the chisel and the bags? Great Scott! Jump, Archie, jump, and I'll swing for it."

Sherlock Holmes had sprung out and seized the intruder by the collar. The other dived down the hole, and I heard the sound of rending cloth as Jones clutched at his skirts. The light flashed upon the barrel of a revolver, but Holmes's hunting crop came down on the man's wrist, and the pistol clinked upon the stone floor.

"It's no use, John Clay," said Holmes blandly. "You have no chance at all."

"So I see," the other answered with the utmost coolness. "I fancy that my pal is all right, though I see you have got his coattails."

"There are three men waiting for him at the door," said Holmes.

"Oh, indeed! You seem to have done the thing very completely. I must compliment you."

"And I you," Holmes answered. "Your red-headed idea was very

38 

What color is Clay's accomplice's hair?

36 Literary Analysis

Protagonist and Antagonist

1. Remind students that Watson's job is to stand in for the readers in the story. Like them, he observes Holmes in action and asks questions the reader probably has. His emotional state should reflect what the reader should be feeling.
2. Have students reread the first bracketed passage on p. 1185 where Watson describes how time has passed.
3. **Ask** students the Literary Analysis question: What details of Watson's account help build the suspense of the conflict?

   Possible response: Watson tells of his watchfulness, tension, and fear. His comment about being afraid to move and feeling nervous should make readers feel the suspense. When Watson sees the gleam of light, the readers should be very curious about what is going to happen next.

37 Reading Skill

Comparing Characters

1. Students should understand that the story is approaching its climax. Now they will begin to see the pieces of the story come together. Have them read the second bracketed passage.
2. **Ask** the Reading Skill question: In what ways is the first burglar's appearance similar to that of Vincent Spaulding?

   Answer: Like Vincent Spaulding, the first burglar is quick, slender, and boyish looking.
3. **Ask** students how the second burglar is similar in appearance to William Morris (Duncan Ross).

   Answer: Like Morris, the second burglar has red hair.

38 Reading Check

Answer: Clay's accomplice has red hair.

Differentiated Instruction for Universal Access

Enrichment for Gifted/Talented Students

Have students plan and perform a dramatic version of "The Red-headed League." Seven students could play the roles of the detectives, the police officer, the banker, Mr. Wilson, and the criminals. Others in the group could direct rehearsals, collaborate on a script, decide on a type of presentation (dramatic reading, radio play, video, and so on). One team of students might work on developing sets. What props or sound would make an audience think of nineteenth-century London? Allow time for rehearsals, and then have students perform for the class. Afterwards, have the audience compare the performance with the story, comment on any differences, and discuss the effect on the overall impact of the piece.

39 Reading Skill

Contrasting Characters

Have students read the bracketed text. **Ask** students the Reading Skill question: What difference between Holmes and Clay is revealed by Holmes's refusal to accept a reward?

Answer: Unlike Clay, Holmes uses his intellect to help others, not to make money.

Monitor Progress: Ask students to summarize how Holmes and Clay are similar and different.

Answer: Both Holmes and Clay are daring, intelligent, and cultured. Unlike Holmes, Clay is a criminal.

Reteach: If students have trouble identifying similarities and differences, give them a copy of **Reading Skill Transparency A** (*Graphic Organizer Transparencies*, p. 200). Show students the partially completed graphic organizer and point out the details that show similarities in the characters and the details that show differences in the characters.

new and effective."

"You'll see your pal again presently," said Jones. "He's quicker at climbing down holes than I am. Just hold out while I fix the derbies."[15]

"I beg that you will not touch me with your filthy hands," remarked our prisoner as the handcuffs clattered upon his wrists. "You may not be aware that I have royal blood in my veins. Have the goodness, also, when you address me always to say 'sir' and 'please.'"

"All right," said Jones with a stare and a snigger. "Well, would you please, sir, march upstairs, where we can get a cab to carry your Highness to the police station?"

"That is better," said John Clay serenely. He made a sweeping bow to the three of us and walked quietly off in the custody of the detective.

"Really, Mr. Holmes," said Mr. Merryweather as we followed them from the cellar, "I do not know how the bank can thank you or repay you. There is no doubt that you have detected and defeated in the most complete manner one of the most determined attempts at bank robbery that have ever come within my experience."

"I have had one or two little scores of my own to settle with Mr. John Clay," said Holmes. "I have been at some small expense over this matter, which I shall expect the bank to refund, but beyond that I am amply repaid by having had an experience which is in many ways unique, and by hearing the very remarkable narrative of the Red-headed League."

Reading Skill Contrasting Characters 39 What difference between Holmes and Clay is revealed by Holmes's refusal to accept a reward?

"You see, Watson," he explained in the early hours of the morning as we sat over a glass of whisky and soda in Baker Street, "it was perfectly obvious from the first that the only possible object of this rather fantastic business of the advertisement of the League, and the copying of the Encyclopedia, must be to get this not over-bright pawnbroker out of the way for a number of hours every day. It was a curious way of managing it, but, really, it would be difficult to

15. **derbies** handcuffs.

Vocabulary Development

Vocabulary Knowledge Rating

When students have completed reading and discussing "The Red-headed League," have them take out their **Vocabulary Knowledge Rating Chart** for this selection. Read the words aloud once more and have students rate their knowledge of the words again in the After Reading column. Clarify any words that are still problematic. Have students write their own definition and example or sentence in the appropriate column. Then have students complete the Vocabulary Practice activities at the end of the selection. Encourage students to use the words in further discussion and written work about this selection. Remind them that they will be accountable for these words on the **Selection Test, *Unit 6 Resources,*** pp. 125–127 or 128–130.

suggest a better. The method was no doubt suggested to Clay's ingenious mind by the color of his accomplice's hair. The £4 a week was a lure which must draw him, and what was it to them, who were playing for thousands? They put in the advertisement, one rogue has the temporary office, the other rogue incites the man to apply for it, and together they manage to secure his absence every morning in the week. From the time that I heard of the assistant having come for half wages, it was obvious to me that he had some strong motive for securing the situation."

"But how could you guess what the motive was?"

"Had there been women in the house, I should have suspected a mere vulgar intrigue. That, however, was out of the question. The man's business was a small one, and there was nothing in his house which could account for such elaborate preparations, and such an expenditure as they were at. It must, then, be something out of the house. What could it be? I thought of the assistant's fondness for photography, and his trick of vanishing into the cellar. The cellar! There was the end of this tangled clue. Then I made inquiries as to this mysterious assistant and found that I had to deal with one of the coolest and most daring criminals in London. He was doing something in the cellar—something which took many hours a day for months on end. What could it be, once more? I could think of nothing save that he was running a tunnel to some other building.

"So far I had got when we went to visit the scene of action. I surprised you by beating upon the pavement with my stick. I was ascertaining whether the cellar stretched out in front or behind. It was not in front. Then I rang the bell, and, as I hoped, the assistant answered it. We have had some skirmishes, but we had never set eyes upon each other before. I hardly looked at his face. His knees were what I wished to see. You must yourself have remarked how worn, wrinkled, and stained they were. They spoke of those hours of burrowing. The only remaining point was what they were burrowing for. I walked round the corner, saw that the City and Suburban Bank abutted on our friend's premises, and felt that I had solved my problem. When you drove home after the concert I called upon Scotland Yard and upon the chairman of the bank directors, with the result that you have seen."

"And how could you tell that they would make their attempt tonight?" I asked.

"Well, when they closed their League offices that was a sign that they cared no longer about Mr. Jabez Wilson's presence—in other words, that they had completed their tunnel. But it was essential

Literary Analysis
Protagonist and Antagonist What was Clay's (Spaulding's) motivation in arranging for Wilson to be out of the house?

41

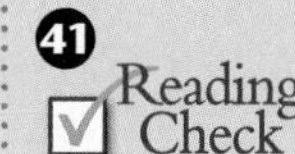

What was the motive behind the Red-headed League?

40 Literary Analysis

Protagonist and Antagonist

1. Remind students that a character's motivation is his or her reason for doing something. For example, Watson's motivation for working with Holmes is his enjoyment in watching Holmes work or his desire to learn how to solve crimes.
2. Read the bracketed passage aloud. **Ask** students the Literary Analysis question: What was Clay's (Spaulding's) motivation in arranging for Wilson to be out of the house?

   Possible response: His motivation was to get Wilson out of the house while he and Duncan Ross dug a tunnel from the pawnshop cellar to the basement of a nearby bank.

41 Reading Check

Answer: The Red-Headed League was a way of getting Mr. Wilson out of the shop so that the men could dig a tunnel to the bank. They did not want Mr. Wilson to hear them digging and realize their plan.

Concept Connector

Anticipation Guide

Have students return to their **Anticipation Guides** and respond to the statements again in the After Reading column. They may do this individually or in groups. Then, lead a class discussion, probing for what students have learned that confirms or invalidates each statement. Encourage students to cite specific evidence from the text to support their responses.

Writing About the Big Question

Have students compare their responses to the sentence starters they completed before reading the story with their ideas afterwards. Ask them to explain whether their thoughts have changed.

Literary Analysis Graphic Organizer

Ask students to review the graphic organizers they completed while reading. Then have students share their graphic organizers. Show them **Literary Analysis Graphic Organizer A** (p. 197 in ***Graphic Organizer Transparencies***) as an example. Then, have students share their graphic organizers.

㊷ Literary Analysis

Protagonist and Antagonist

1. Have students reread the last page of the story. Make sure that they understand the meaning of the word *ennui.*
2. **Ask** students the Literary Analysis question: What does Holmes claim is his reason for solving crimes?

   Answer: Holmes suggests that solving crimes keeps him from getting bored. Crime solving lets him escape from the ordinariness of life.

ASSESS

Answers

Critical Thinking

Before students respond, you may wish to have them write a brief objective summary of the selection. As they answer the questions below, remind them to support their answers with evidence from the text.

1. (a) Wilson wants to know about the Red-headed League. (b) Holmes enjoys it because it is unique.
2. (a) Holmes and his friends hide in the cellar and catch the criminals when they return to steal the gold. (b) Spaulding's trousers showed that he had been digging in the cellar. The bank's property bordered Wilson's shop. (c) **Possible response:** Spaulding's trousers might have gotten dirty because he was on the floor looking for something. The other details might have been coincidences.
3. (a) "It is your commonplace, featureless crimes which are really puzzling, just as a commonplace face is the most difficult to identify." (b) He means that adept criminals make their crimes unremarkable, making them difficult to solve. (c) The remark suggests that great detectives know that crimes are not as they seem.
4. **Possible responses:** Yes, Holmes is a hero because he solves the mystery and prevents the crime from being committed. Holmes also captures a very dangerous criminal.

that they should use it soon, as it might be discovered, or the bullion might be removed. Saturday would suit them better than any other day, as it would give them two days for their escape. For all these reasons I expected them to come tonight."

"You reasoned it out beautifully," I exclaimed in unfeigned admiration. "It is so long a chain, and yet every link rings true."

Literary Analysis
Protagonist and Antagonist What does Holmes claim is his reason for solving crimes?

"It saved me from ennui,"[16] he answered, yawning. "Alas! I already feel it closing in upon me. My life is spent in one long effort to escape from the commonplaces of existence. These little problems help me to do so."

"And you are a benefactor of the race," said I.

He shrugged his shoulders. "Well, perhaps, after all, it is of some little use," he remarked. "'*L'homme c'est rien—l'oeuvre c'est tout,*'[17] as Gustave Flaubert wrote to George Sand."[18]

---

16. **ennui** (än′ wē′) *n.* boredom.
17. ***L'homme c'est rien—l'oeuvre c'est tout*** (lum sä rē en′ lʉvr sä to͞o) French for "Man is nothing—the work is everything."
18. **Gustave Flaubert** (go͞os täv′ flō ber′) **. . . George Sand** notable French novelists of the nineteenth century.

Critical Thinking

Cite textual evidence to support your responses.

1. **Key Ideas and Details** **(a)** Why does Jabez Wilson visit Sherlock Holmes? **(b) Infer:** Why does Holmes find Wilson's story interesting?
2. **Key Ideas and Details** **(a)** What happens the night of the attempted burglary? **(b) Analyze Cause and Effect:** Which clues found at Saxe-Coburg Square lead to Holmes's solution of the mystery? **(c) Speculate:** What details could have been misinterpreted, leading to an incorrect conclusion? Explain your response.
3. **Integration of Knowledge and Ideas** **(a)** What remark does Holmes make about commonplace crimes? **(b) Infer:** What does Holmes mean? **(c) Interpret:** What does his remark suggest about the qualities that make a great detective?
4. **Integration of Knowledge and Ideas** Would you call Holmes a hero? Why or why not? *[Connect to the Big Question: Do heroes have responsibilities?]*

Assessment Resources

Unit 6 Resources

L1 L2 EL **Selection Test A**, pp. 125–127. Administer Test A to less advanced readers.

L3 L4 EL **Selection Test B**, pp. 128–130. Administer Test B to on-level and more advanced students.

L3 L4 **Open-Book Test**, pp. 124–126. As an alternative, give the Open-Book Test.

All **Customizable Test Bank**

All **Self-tests**
Students may prepare for the **Selection Test** by taking the **Self-test** online.

All assessment resources are available at **www.PHLitOnline.com**.

After You Read: The Red-headed League

Literary Analysis: Protagonist and Antagonist

1. **Craft and Structure** **(a)** Identify the **protagonist** in the narrative. **(b)** What is the protagonist's goal? **(c)** Why are readers interested in whether the protagonist achieves his goal?
2. **Craft and Structure** **(a)** Identify the **antagonist.** **(b)** What is the antagonist's goal?
3. **Integration of Knowledge and Ideas** **(a)** Why is the story's conflict interesting? **(b)** What universal struggle does this conflict represent?

Reading Skill: Comparing and Contrasting Characters

4. Use a Venn diagram to compare and contrast Holmes's character at the beginning and end of the story. Does he change? Explain.

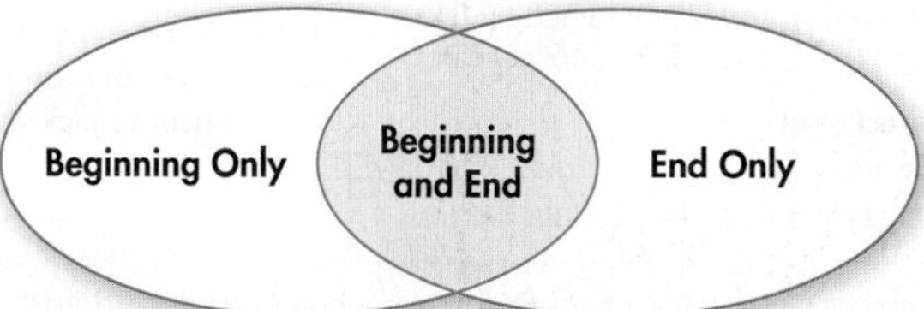

Vocabulary

Acquisition and Use **Analogies** show the relationship between pairs of words. Use a word from the list on page 1164 to complete each analogy.

1. kind : gentle :: ______________ : fearsome
2. burn : candle :: ______________ : problem
3. descending : downward :: ______________ : inward
4. lose : misplace :: ______________ : exaggerate
5. brutal : kind :: ______________ : indecisive
6. inquire : ask :: ______________ : attempt

Word Study Use the context of the sentences and what you know about the **Latin root *-spec-*** to explain your answer to each question.

1. Might a *prospector* hope to find gold or silver?
2. If you take a new *perspective*, might you have new ideas?

Word Study

The **Latin root *-spec-*** means "see," "look," or "examine."

Apply It Explain how the root *-spec-* contributes to the meanings of these words. Consult a dictionary if necessary.

spectacle
inspector
spectator

Literary Analysis

1. (a) Holmes is the protagonist. (b) His goal is to understand the Red-headed League plot. (c) Readers too are curious about the odd league.
2. (a) John Clay and William Morris are the antagonists. (b) Their goal is to rob the bank.
3. (a) Readers will want to know who will prevail. (b) The conflict represents the universal struggle between good and evil.

Reading Skill

4. **Sample answers: Beginning Only**—Holmes is intrigued by Wilson's story; **End Only**—Holmes can take pride in capturing a known criminal; **Beginning and End**—Holmes uses deduction to solve crimes. He solves crimes to escape boredom. He awaits the next new crime. Holmes is basically unchanged. He is neither wiser nor richer after the story.

For other sample answers, see ***Graphic Organizer Transparencies*, Reading Skill Graphic Organizer A,** p. 200, and the **Additional Answers** section.

Vocabulary

Acquisition and Use

Sample answers:

1. formidable
2. vex
3. introspective
4. embellish
5. tenacious
6. endeavor

Word Study

Sample answers:

1. Yes, the root *spec* means "see, look, examine," and *prospector* means "someone who looks for mineral deposits." A prospector may hope to find gold or silver.
2. Yes, the root *spec* means "see, look, examine," and *perspective* means "one's ideas and the way one looks at things." When you take a new perspective, you should have new ideas.

Continued from right column

Word Study: Apply It

Sample answers: A *spectacle* is something that is so extravagant people stare or look at it. An *inspector* is someone who examines something carefully. A *spectator* is someone who watches an event.

EXTEND/ASSESS

Answers

Conventions

1. Introduce the skill, using the instruction on the student page.
2. Discuss the definitions and examples in the chart.

Think Aloud: Model the Skill

Model the skill of using commas correctly. Post the sentence: *Sadly when we were in Chicago Illinois I broke my favorite necklace which was very expensive.* Say to students:

> When I am writing, I insert a comma wherever I feel there is a short pause, such as after *Sadly*, *Illinois*, and *necklace*. Then, I double check usage rules. I remember that commas separate parts of places, so I insert a comma after *Chicago* as well.

PH WRITING COACH Grade 9

Students will find instruction on and practice with commas and dashes in Chapter 23, Section 2.

Practice A

1. direct quotations
2. introductory word
3. parenthetical or nonessential expression
4. three or more words, phrases, or clauses in a series
5. to set off an interrupting idea

Reading Application

Sample answers:

1) Now we knew why this ship, in perfect condition, was sailing with her crew abroad. 2) But the day after that, we realized how serious our position was. 3) I shouted to him to shut up, but he did not hear me . . .

Practice B

1. The man was stout, elderly, and red-headed.
2. Mr. Watson opened the door, but he saw that Holmes was not alone.
3. Blonde or red-headed—which is preferable?
4. After he had thought for some minutes, Holmes leaped to his feet.
5. "Stop," the constable called out.

Writing Application

Sample answer:

"The Red-headed League" was an interesting, suspenseful, and well-written story.

PERFORMANCE TASKS

Integrated Language Skills

Three Skeleton Key • The Red-headed League

Conventions: Using Commas and Dashes

Use **commas** when you need to indicate a short pause in your writing. Two basic principles guide all comma usage.

Use a **dash** to indicate an abrupt change of thought, a dramatic interruption, or a summary statement.

Use Commas to Separate…	Use Commas to Set Off…	Use Dashes to Indicate…
Two independent clauses in a compound sentence I turned the ignition key, but the car did not start.	**An introductory word, phrase, or clause** Coincidentally, we all ended up at the same beach.	**An abrupt change of thought** That man stole all that money—I don't even want to think about it.
Three or more words, phrases, or clauses in a series He spoke with passion, with gravity, and with sorrow.	**Parenthetical or nonessential expressions** The magazine, which I unfortunately misplaced, had some great articles.	**To set off an interrupting idea** John—his mom calls him Sweetie Pie—has a great sense of humor.
Parts of dates, places, or certain titles We went to Sonoma, California, for the weekend.	**Direct quotations** President Roosevelt declared, "The only thing we have to fear is fear itself."	**To set off a summary statement** Lemon, lime, or orange—deciding which flavor to pick was difficult.

Practice A Identify the rule that the commas or dashes in each of these sentences follow.

1. The men called out, "Rats!"
2. Incredibly, the ship was covered with rats.
3. The rats, which were on the ship, leaped to the island.
4. The rats climbed, squealed, and chewed.
5. The lighthouse —if you could believe it—was under seige.

Reading Application In "Three Skeleton Key," find three sentences with commas that follow three different rules.

Practice B Copy each sentence, and add commas or dashes where they are necessary. Indicate which rule(s) you are following.

1. The man was stout elderly and red-headed.
2. Mr. Watson opened the door but he saw that Holmes was not alone.
3. Blonde or red-headed which is preferable?
4. After he had thought for some minutes Holmes leaped to his feet.
5. "Stop" the constable called out.

Writing Application Write four sentences about stories of suspense. Use commas in each sentence. Demonstrate correct usage of at least three rules.

PH WRITING COACH Further instruction and practice are available in *Prentice Hall Writing Coach.*

Extend the Lesson

Sentence Modeling

Choose the sentence given from the selection students have read:

> *"Large, strong, and intelligent, clannish and seawise, . . . their uncanny ability to foretell the weather." ("Three Skeleton Key")*

> *"All the afternoon he sat in the stalls wrapped in the most perfect happiness, gently waving his long, thin fingers in time to the music, while his gently smiling face and his languid, dreamy eyes were as unlike those of Holmes . . ." ("The Red-headed League")*

Discuss the commas used. Then, ask what else students notice. (Toudouze breaks grammar rules to list the rats' many capabilities, giving them a powerful, superhuman quality. Doyle's repeated use of commas echoes the description of Holmes as relaxed.)

Have students create a sentence that matches each grammatical and stylistic feature discussed.

Writing

Narrative Text Imagine that you are one of the characters in the story you read. Choose a character other than the narrator in "Three Skeleton Key," or write as Dr. Watson in "The Red-headed League." Write three **journal entries** describing the events in the story as they unfold.

- Review the story and create a timeline for the major events.
- Decide which days you will record in your journal.
- As the character, write your thoughts about what happens each day.
- Use descriptive words and phrases to capture the events, setting, and characters memorably.

As you write, stay in character, making sure that your journal reflects any changes that the character experiences in the story.

Grammar Application Use commas and dashes correctly as you write your entries, especially in nonrestrictive phrases, contrasting expressions, and parenthetical information.

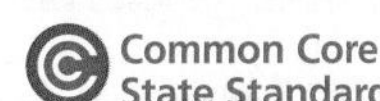

Common Core State Standards

L.9-10.2; W.9-10.3.d, W.9-10.7; SL.9-10.2, SL.9-10.5.

[For the full wording of the standards, see page 1144.]

Writing Workshop: *Work in Progress*

Prewriting for Comparison and Contrast For a comparison-and-contrast essay you may write, choose two places that you know well. For each, note the purpose, sound, and look of the place. Save your list.

Use this prewriting activity to prepare for the **Writing Workshop** on page 1234.

Research and Technology

Build and Present Knowledge Prepare an **oral report** about a topic from the story you read.

- If you read "Three Skeleton Key," conduct research about ship's rats and how these rats differ from other rats.
- If you read "The Red-headed League," research criminology. Find information on fingerprinting, lie detectors, and police sketches.

Follow these steps to complete the assignment.

- Before you begin, generate research questions about your topic. Use the questions to direct and focus your research.
- Consult multiple sources, such as the Internet, encyclopedias, and other reference books. Make sure to verify information from one source with another.
- Then, compare what you learn to details presented in the story.
- To help you organize and present the information you find, develop visual aids using computer software or other technology.

Present your report to your class and invite questions. As others give reports, evaluate their information and techniques and ask questions.

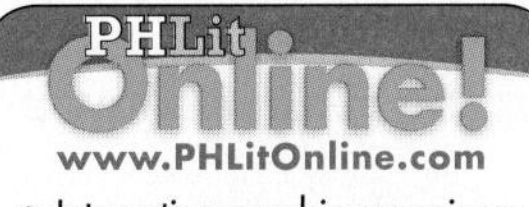

www.PHLitOnline.com

- Interactive graphic organizers
- Grammar tutorial
- Interactive journals

EXTEND/ASSESS

Writing

1. Review the assignment, using the instruction on the student page.
2. To guide students in writing narrative texts, give them **Support for Writing**, p. 120, in ***Unit 6 Resources***.
3. To evaluate students' narrative texts, use the **Short Story** rubrics, pp. 226–227 in ***Professional Development Guidebook***.

Grammar Application

Have students check their drafts for correct use of commas and dashes.

Six Traits Focus

✓	Ideas		Word Choice
	Organization		Sentence Fluency
✓	Voice		Conventions

PH WRITING COACH Grade 9

Students will find guidance on narrative writing in Chapters 5 and 6.

Writing Workshop
Work in Progress

Have students save their completed Comparison List in their portfolios. They will use the list later as they continue this Work-in-Progress assignment (see p. 1207). These assignments prepare them to complete the Writing Workshop assignment (see pp. 1234–1241).

Research and Technology

1. Review the assignment, using the instruction on the student page.
2. To support students' work on the assignment, have students complete the **Support for Extend Your Learning** page (***Unit 6 Resources***, p. 121).

Teaching Resources

All *Unit 6 Resources*

L3 L4 EL **Integrated Language Skills: Grammar,** p. 119

L3 L4 EL **Support for Writing,** p. 120

L3 L4 **Support for Extend Your Learning,** p. 121

L4 **Enrichment,** pp. 100, 118

All **Enriched Online Student Edition**
Available under After You Read for this selection:

All **Interactive Grammar Tutorial**

L3 L4 **Internet Research Activity**

Professional Development Guidebook
Rubrics for Self-Assessment: Short Story
pp. 226–227

PHLit Online! All print and digital resources are available at **www.PHLitOnline.com**. Online resources accessible by students are noted on the student page.

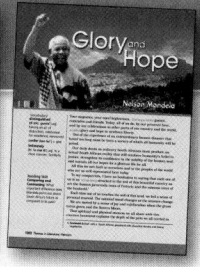

✓ There Is a Longing • ✓✓ Glory and Hope
Lesson Pacing Guide

DAY 1 Preteach

- Administer the Reading and Vocabulary Warm-ups (*Unit 6 Resources*, pp. 131–134 or 147–150) as necessary.
- Introduce the Reading Skill: Compare and Contrast
- Introduce the Literary Analysis concept: Philosophical Assumptions.
- Distribute copies of the appropriate graphic organizer for the Reading Skill (*Graphic Organizer Transparencies*, pp. 205–207).
- Distribute copies of the appropriate graphic organizer for Literary Analysis (*Graphic Organizer Transparencies*, pp. 202–204).
- Teach the selection vocabulary.
- Introduce the Word Study skill.

DAYS 2–3 Preteach/Teach

- Build background with the Background feature.
- Develop thematic vocabulary and thematic thinking with Writing About the Big Question.
- Prepare students to read with the Activating Prior Knowledge activities (TE).
- Informally monitor comprehension while students read.
- Use the Reading Check questions to confirm comprehension.
- Develop students' ability to compare and contrast, using the Reading Skill questions.
- Develop students' understanding of philosophical assumptions, using the Literary Analysis questions.
- Reinforce vocabulary with the Vocabulary notes.
- Reinforce unit focus standards using the Spiral Review prompts.

DAY 4 Assess

- Assess students' comprehension and mastery of the skills by having them answer the Critical Thinking, Reading Skill, and Literary Analysis questions.
- Have students complete the Vocabulary Practice activities.
- Have students complete the Word Study activities.

DAY 5 Extend/Assess

- Have students complete the Conventions lesson.
- Have students complete the Writing activity, a letter. (You may assign as homework.)
- Extend learning by having students complete the Speaking and Listening activity, a panel discussion. As an alternative, assign them "The Choice to Lead" or "A Time to Protest" in *Reality Central*.
- Administer Selection Test A or B (*Unit 6 Resources*, pp. 143–146 or 162–165).

Common Core State Standards

Reading Informational Text
3. Analyze how the author unfolds an analysis or series of ideas or events, including the order in which the points are made, how they are introduced and developed, and the connections that are drawn between them.
6. Determine an author's point of view or purpose in a text and analyze how an author uses rhetoric to advance that point of view or purpose.

Writing 2. Write informative/explanatory texts. **2.b.** Develop the topic with well-chosen, relevant, and sufficient facts, extended definitions, concrete details, quotations, or other information and examples appropriate to the audience's knowledge of the topic. **2.e.** Establish and maintain a formal style and objective tone while attending to the norms and conventions of the discipline in which they are writing.

Speaking and Listening 1.a. Come to discussions prepared, having read and researched material under study.
1.c. Propel conversations by posing and responding to questions; actively incorporate others into the discussion; clarify conclusions.

Language 2. Demonstrate command of the conventions of standard English capitalization, punctuation, and spelling when writing.
6. Acquire and use accurately grade-appropriate general academic and domain-specific words and phrases.

Additional Standards Practice
Common Core Companion,
pp. 15–22; 55–56

Daily Block Scheduling
Each day in this Lesson Pacing Guide represents a 40–50 minute period. Teachers using block scheduling may combine days to revise pacing. In addition, teachers may differentiate and support core instruction by integrating components for extended and intensive support as students require. See the Guide to Selected Leveled Resources (facing page).

Guide to Selected Leveled Resources

RTI Tier 1 (students performing on level)		✓ More Accessible There Is a Longing	✓✓ More Complex Glory and Hope
Warm Up	Practice, model, and monitor fluency, working with the whole class or in groups.	Vocabulary and Reading Warm-ups B, *Unit 6 Resources,* pp. 131–132, 134	Vocabulary and Reading Warm-ups B, *Unit 6 Resources,* pp. 147–148, 150
Comprehension/Skills	**Support** and **monitor** comprehension and skills development, having students complete the activities, graphic organizers, and interactive prompts **independently** or **as a class.**	• *Reader's Notebook,* adapted instruction and full selection EL *Reader's Notebook: English Learner's Version,* adapted instruction and adapted selection • Reading Skill Graphic Organizer B, *Graphic Organizer Transparencies,* p. 204 • Literary Analysis Graphic Organizer B, *Graphic Organizer Transparencies,* p. 207	• *Reader's Notebook,* adapted instruction and summary EL *Reader's Notebook: English Learner's Version,* adapted instruction and summary • Reading Skill Graphic Organizer B, *Graphic Organizer Transparencies,* p. 204 • Literary Analysis Graphic Organizer B, *Graphic Organizer Transparencies,* p. 207
Monitor Progress	**Monitor** student progress with the differentiated curriculum-based assessment in the *Unit Resources.*	• Selection Test B, *Unit 6 Resources,* pp. 145–146 • Open-Book Test, *Unit 6 Resources,* pp. 140–142	• Selection Test B, *Unit 6 Resources,* pp. 164–165 • Open-Book Test, *Unit 6 Resources,* pp. 159–161
Assess/ Screen	• **Assess** student progress using Benchmark Test 12. • **Preassess** instructional needs using the Vocabulary in Context section of the test.	• Benchmark Test 12, *Unit 6 Resources,* pp. 188–193, including Vocabulary in Context diagnostic items	• Benchmark Test 12, *Unit 6 Resources,* pp. 188–193, including Vocabulary in Context diagnostic items

RTI Tier 2 (students requiring intervention)		✓ More Accessible There Is a Longing	✓✓ More Complex Glory and Hope
Warm Up	Practice, model, and monitor fluency **in groups** or **with individuals.**	• Vocabulary and Reading Warm-ups A, *Unit 6 Resources,* pp. 131–134 • *Reality Central,* "The Choice to Lead" • *Hear It!* Audio CD (adapted text)	• Vocabulary and Reading Warm-ups A, *Unit 6 Resources,* pp. 147–150 • *Reality Central,* "A Time to Protest" • *Hear It!* Audio CD
Comprehension/Skills	• **Support** and **monitor** comprehension and skills development, working **in small groups** or **with individuals.** • **Pair** students with more advanced peers and have them complete the writing activity in the *Real-World Writing Journal*. • As students complete the selection in the appropriate version of the *Reader's Notebook,* **monitor** comprehension frequently with group questions and individual instruction. • **Model** strategies while guiding students in completing the activities and prompts in the *Reader's Notebook,* as well as the graphic organizers. • **Practice** skills and **monitor** mastery with the *Reading Kit* worksheets.	• *Real-World Writing Journal,* Lesson 7, pp. 180–183 • *Reader's Notebook: Adapted Version,* adapted instruction and adapted selection EL *Reader's Notebook: English Learner's Version,* adapted instruction and adapted selection • Reading Skill Graphic Organizer A, *Graphic Organizer Transparencies,* p. 202 • Literary Analysis Graphic Organizer A, *Graphic Organizer Transparencies,* p. 205 • Reading Kit, Practice worksheets, pp. 288, 284, 292, 296, 304	• *Real-World Writing Journal,* Lesson 8, pp. 184–189 • *Reader's Notebook: Adapted Version,* adapted instruction and summary EL *Reader's Notebook: English Learner's Version,* adapted instruction and summary • Reading Skill Graphic Organizer A, *Graphic Organizer Transparencies,* p. 203 • Literary Analysis Graphic Organizer A, *Graphic Organizer Transparencies,* p. 206 • Reading Kit, Practice worksheets, pp. 288, 284, 292, 296, 304
Monitor Progress	**Monitor** student progress with the differentiated curriculum-based assessment in the *Unit Resources* and in the *Reading Kit.*	• Selection Test A, *Unit 6 Resources,* pp. 143–144 • Reading Kit, Assess worksheets, pp. 289, 285, 293, 297, 305	• Selection Test A, *Unit 6 Resources,* pp. 162–163 • Reading Kit, Assess worksheets, pp. 289, 285, 293, 297, 305
Assess/ Screen	• **Assess** student progress using Benchmark Test 12. • **Preassess** instructional needs using the Vocabulary in Context section of the test.	• Benchmark Test 12, *Unit 6 Resources,* pp. 188–193, including Vocabulary in Context diagnostic items	• Benchmark Test 12, *Unit 6 Resources,* pp. 188–193, including Vocabulary in Context diagnostic items

TIER 3 Tier 3 intervention may require consultation with the student's special-education or dyslexia specialist. For additional support, see the Tier 2 activities and resources listed above.

One-on-one teaching | Group work | Whole class instruction | Independent work | A Assessment

For a complete guide to selection support, including support for Advanced students, see the Overview of Resources in the frontmatter.

✓There Is a Longing
✓✓Glory and Hope

RESOURCES FOR:

- L1 Special-Needs Students
- L2 Below-Level Students (Tier 2)
- L3 On-Level Students (Tier 1)
- L4 Advanced Students (Tier 1)
- EL English Learners
- All All Students

Vocabulary/Fluency/Prior Knowledge

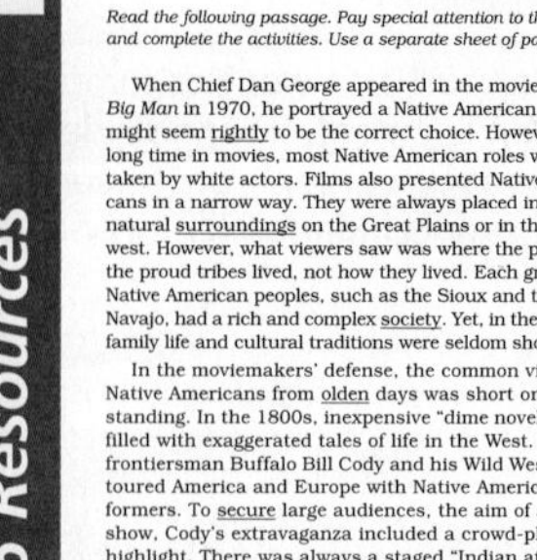

Unit 6 Resources

Name ____________ Date ____________

"There Is a Longing" by Chief Dan George
Reading Warm-up B

Read the following passage. Pay special attention to the underlined words. Then, read it again, and complete the activities. Use a separate sheet of paper for your written answers.

When Chief Dan George appeared in the movie *Little Big Man* in 1970, he portrayed a Native American. That might seem rightly to be the correct choice. However, for a long time in movies, most Native American roles were taken by white actors. Films also presented Native Americans in a narrow way. They were always placed in their natural surroundings on the Great Plains or in the Southwest. However, what viewers saw was where the people of the proud tribes lived, not how they lived. Each group of Native American peoples, such as the Sioux and the Navajo, had a rich and complex society. Yet, in the movies, family life and cultural traditions were seldom shown.

In the moviemakers' defense, the common view of Native Americans from olden days was short on understanding. In the 1800s, inexpensive "dime novels" were filled with exaggerated tales of life in the West. The frontiersman Buffalo Bill Cody and his Wild West Show toured America and Europe with Native American performers. To secure large audiences, the aim of any show, Cody's extravaganza included a crowd-pleasing highlight. There was always a staged "Indian attack."

However, over time, different images began to emerge. Native American performers came out of the experience of working in entertainment with the determination to improve the portrayal of their people. One example is Jay Silverheels. He played the native character Tonto in the popular 1950s series "The Lone Ranger." Silverheels was a Mohawk from Canada who formed the Indian Actors Workshop. It encouraged Native American performers and pushed for more accurate roles. It was the tools and instruments of the acting craft, such as strong training that created powerful performances, that helped audiences enjoy seeing Native Americans onscreen.

The endurance of actors like Silverheels and George paid off. Their ability to weather the hardships of earlier times produced breakthroughs in film. Today, movies show a deeper view of Native American life and history.

1. Circle the word clue for rightly. Give a synonym for *rightly*.
2. Circle a word that describes a type of surroundings and two places with different *surroundings*. Underline a phrase that helps explain the meaning of *surroundings*.
3. Underline features that are part of a society. Circle a word that explains who makes up a *society*.
4. Underline a phrase that is a clue to the meaning of olden. Give an antonym for *olden*.
5. Underline one way Cody managed to secure a large audience. Describe an aim you hope to *secure* in life.
6. Circle the phrase with a clue to the meaning of emerge. Explain what helped a different portrayal of Native Americans to *emerge*.
7. Circle the word clue for instruments. Underline an example of the *instruments* of acting.
8. Underline the phrase with a clue to the meaning of endurance. Give a synonym for *endurance*.

Unit 6 Resources: Themes in Literature

134

EL L1 L2 **Reading Warm-ups A and B,** pp. 133–134, 149–150

Also available for this selection:

- EL L1 L2 **Vocabulary Warm-ups A and B,** pp. 131–132, 147–148
- All **Writing About the Big Question,** pp. 135, 151
- All **Vocabulary Builder,** pp. 138, 154

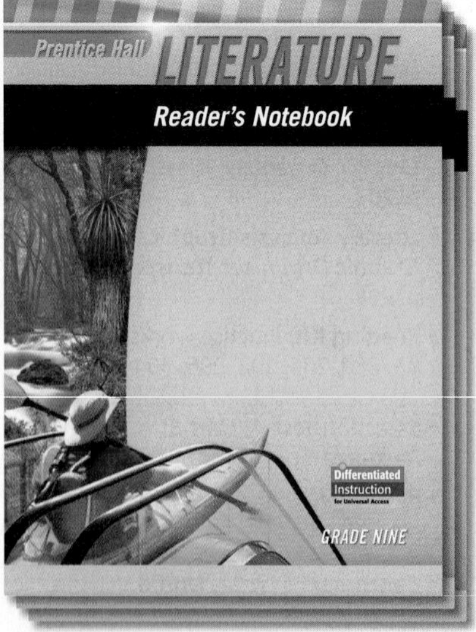

Reader's Notebooks

Pre- and postreading pages for both selections, as well as "There Is a Longing," appear in an interactive format in the *Reader's Notebooks*. Each *Notebook* is differentiated for a different group of learners. The selections in the Adapted and English Learner's versions are abridged.

- L2 L3 ***Reader's Notebook***
- L1 ***Reader's Notebook: Adapted Version***
- EL ***Reader's Notebook: English Learner's Version***
- EL ***Reader's Notebook: Spanish Version***

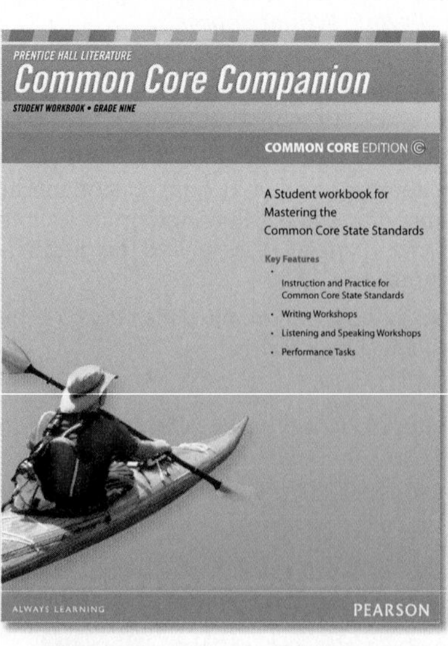

Common Core Companion

Additional instruction and practice for each Common Core State Standard

Selection Support

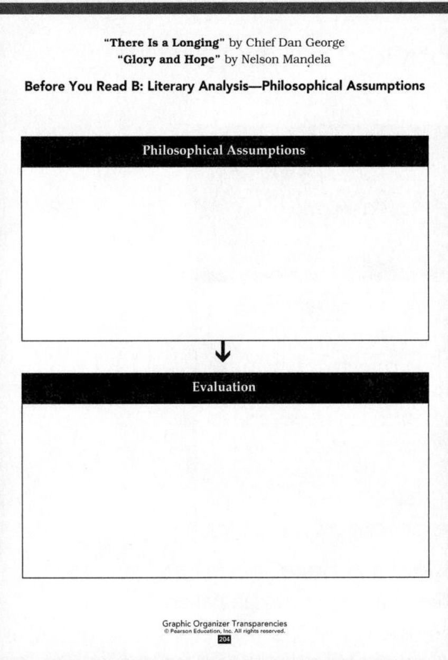

"There Is a Longing" by Chief Dan George
"Glory and Hope" by Nelson Mandela

Before You Read B: Literary Analysis—Philosophical Assumptions

Philosophical Assumptions

Evaluation

Graphic Organizer Transparencies

204

EL L3 **Literary Analysis: Graphic Organizer B,** p. 204

Also available for this selection:

EL L1 L2 **Literary Analysis: Graphic Organizer A,** pp. 202–203 (partially filled in)

EL L1 L2 **Reading: Graphic Organizer A,** pp. 205–206 (partially filled in)

EL L3 **Reading: Graphic Organizer B,** p. 207

Skills Development/Extension

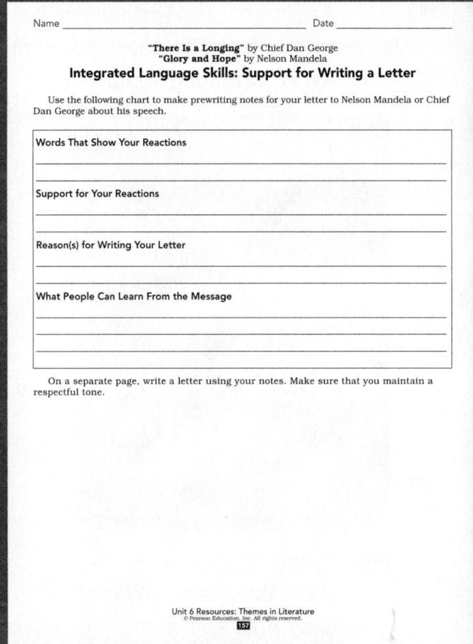

Name ______________________ Date ____________

"There Is a Longing" by Chief Dan George
"Glory and Hope" by Nelson Mandela

Integrated Language Skills: Support for Writing a Letter

Use the following chart to make prewriting notes for your letter to Nelson Mandela or Chief Dan George about his speech.

Words That Show Your Reactions
Support for Your Reactions
Reason(s) for Writing Your Letter
What People Can Learn From the Message

On a separate page, write a letter using your notes. Make sure that you maintain a respectful tone.

Unit 6 Resources: Themes in Literature

157

EL L3 L4 **Support for Writing,** p. 157

Also available for this selection:

All **Literary Analysis: Philosophical Assumptions,** pp. 136, 152

All **Reading: Compare and Contrast** pp. 137, 153

L4 **Enrichment,** pp. 139, 155

EL L3 L4 **Grammar,** p. 156

L3 L4 **Support for Extend Your Learning,** p. 158

Assessment

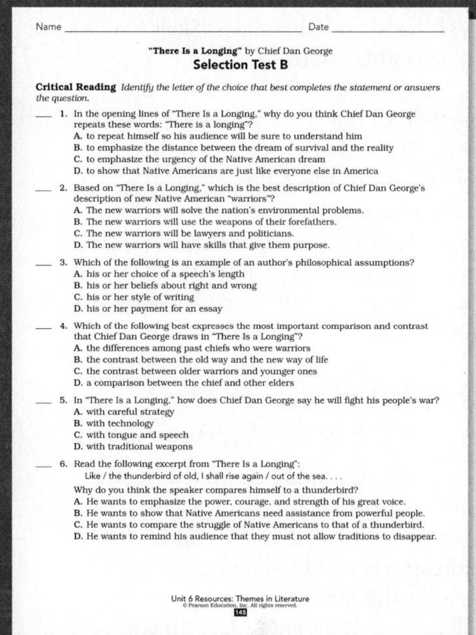

Name ______________________ Date ____________

"There Is a Longing" by Chief Dan George

Selection Test B

Critical Reading *Identify the letter of the choice that best completes the statement or answers the question.*

___ 1. In the opening lines of "There Is a Longing," why do you think Chief Dan George repeats these words: "There is a longing"?
A. to repeat himself so his audience will be sure to understand him
B. to emphasize the distance between the dream of survival and the reality
C. to emphasize the urgency of the Native American dream
D. to show that Native Americans are just like everyone else in America

___ 2. Based on "There Is a Longing," which is the best description of Chief Dan George's description of new Native American "warriors"?
A. The new warriors will solve the nation's environmental problems.
B. The new warriors will use the weapons of their forefathers.
C. The new warriors will be lawyers and politicians.
D. The new warriors will have skills that give them purpose.

___ 3. Which of the following is an example of an author's philosophical assumptions?
A. his or her choice of a speech's length
B. his or her beliefs about right and wrong
C. his or her style of writing
D. his or her payment for an essay

___ 4. Which of the following best expresses the most important comparison and contrast that Chief Dan George draws in "There Is a Longing"?
A. the differences among past chiefs who were warriors
B. the contrast between the old way and the new way of life
C. the contrast between older warriors and younger ones
D. a comparison between the chief and other elders

___ 5. In "There Is a Longing," how does Chief Dan George say he will fight his people's war?
A. with careful strategy
B. with technology
C. with tongue and speech
D. with traditional weapons

___ 6. Read the following excerpt from "There Is a Longing":
Like / the thunderbird of old, I shall rise again / out of the sea. . . .
Why do you think the speaker compares himself to a thunderbird?
A. He wants to emphasize the power, courage, and strength of his great voice.
B. He wants to show that Native Americans need assistance from powerful people.
C. He wants to compare the struggle of Native Americans to that of a thunderbird.
D. He wants to remind his audience that they must not allow traditions to disappear.

Unit 6 Resources: Themes in Literature

145

EL L3 L4 **Selection Test B,** pp. 145–146, 164–165

Also available for this selection:

L3 L4 **Open-Book Test,** pp. 140–142, 159–161

EL L1 L2 **Selection Test A,** pp. 143–144, 162–163

www.PHLitOnline.com

- complete narrated selection text
- a thematically related video with writing prompt
- an interactive graphic organizer
- highlighting feature
- access to all student print resources, adapted to individual student needs
- Spanish and English summaries
- adapted selection translations in Spanish

Online Resources: All print materials are also available online.

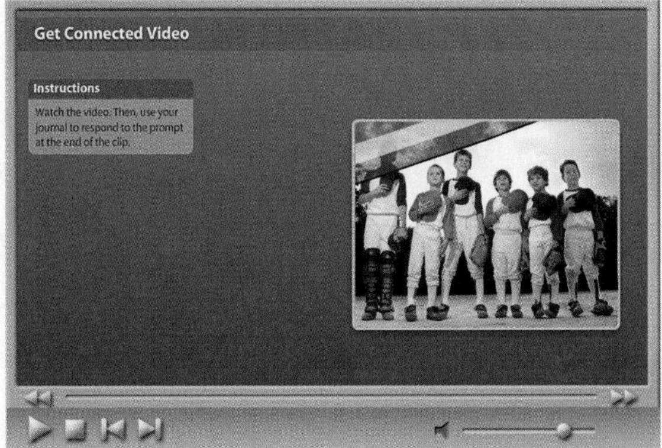

Get Connected! (thematic video with writing prompt)

Also available:

Background Video
All videos are available in Spanish.

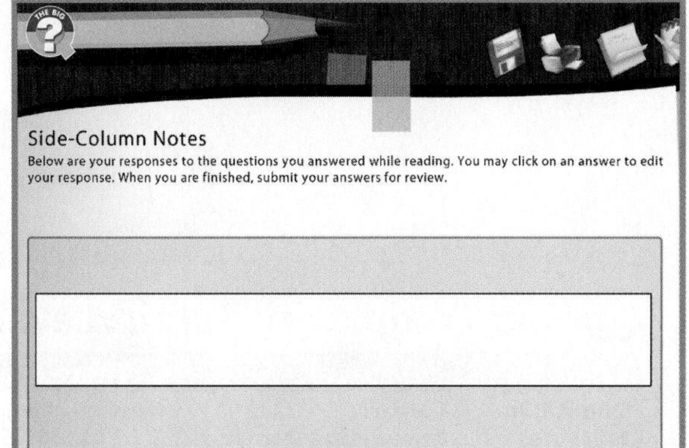

Writer's Journal (with graphics feature)

Also available:

Vocabulary Central (tools, activities, and songs for studying vocabulary)

DIFFERENTIATE/PRETEACH

1 Leveled Texts

You may use either "There Is a Longing" or "Glory and Hope" to meet the lesson objectives. Skills instruction for both selections appears on page 1193. Choose one selection to teach (or choose to teach both). The Text Complexity Rubric at the bottom of this page will help you determine which selection is more appropriate for your students. Use the Reader and Task Suggestions on the facing page to help all students read text of increasing complexity.

2 Introducing the CCS Standards

Introduce the standards on the student page. (Note that the lesson element with which each standard is addressed is identified in parentheses after the text of the standard.) Call out the standards that you will cover with the selections, explaining to students what each requires and how they will address it as they work through the selection you have chosen. Standards labeled "Spiral Review" are introduced in the Literary Analysis Workshop for this unit.

Before You Read

There Is a Longing • Glory and Hope

1 Leveled Texts

Build your skills and improve your comprehension of types of nonfiction with texts of increasing complexity.

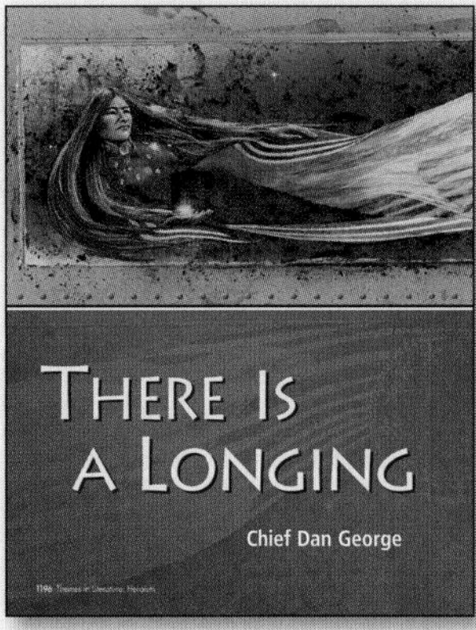

Read **"There Is a Longing"** to learn about the dreams and goals of a Native American leader.

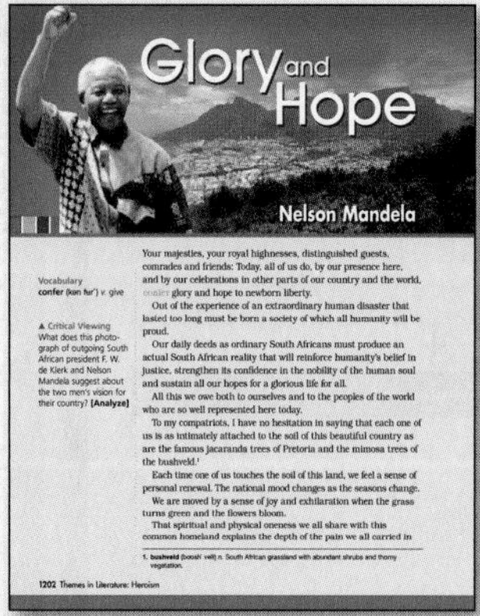

Read **"Glory and Hope"** to see how the leader of a reborn African nation celebrates liberty.

2 Common Core State Standards

Meet these standards with either **"There is a Longing"** (p. 1196) or **"Glory and Hope"** (p. 1202).

Reading Informational Text
3. Analyze how the author unfolds an analysis or series of ideas or events, including the order in which the points are made, how they are introduced and developed, and the connections that are drawn between them. *(Reading Skill: Compare and Contrast)*
6. Determine an author's point of view or purpose in a text and analyze how an author uses rhetoric to advance that point of view or purpose. *(Literary Analysis: Philosophical Assumptions)*

Writing
2. Write informative/explanatory texts. **2.b.** Develop the topic with well-chosen, relevant, and sufficient facts, extended definitions, concrete details, quotations, or other information and examples appropriate to the audience's knowledge of the topic. **2.e.** Establish and maintain a formal style and objective tone while attending to the norms and conventions of the discipline in which they are writing. *(Writing: Letter)*

Speaking and Listening
1.a. Come to discussions prepared, having read and researched material under study; explicitly draw on that preparation to stimulate a thoughtful well-reasoned exchange of ideas. **1.c.** Propel conversations by posing and responding to questions; actively incorporate others into the discussion; clarify conclusions. *(Speaking and Listening: Panel Discussion)*

Language
2. Demonstrate command of the conventions of standard English capitalization, punctuation, and spelling when writing. *(Conventions: Colons, Semicolons, and Ellipsis Points)*
6. Acquire and use accurately grade-appropriate general academic and domain-specific words and phrases; gather vocabulary knowledge when considering a word or phrase important to comprehension or expression. *(Vocabulary: Word Study)*

1192 Themes in Literature: Heroism

Text Complexity Rubric: Leveled Texts

Text complexity is determined by both qualitative and quantitative measures. For this reason, the quantitative measure of a more complex selection may be lower than that of a more accessible selection.

		✓ There Is a Longing	✓✓ Glory and Hope
Qualitative Measures	**Context/ Knowledge Demands**	Message of empowerment for Native Americans 1 2 (3) 4 5	Nelson Mandela; apartheid in South Africa 1 2 3 (4) 5
	Structure/Language Conventionality and Clarity	Poetic language with vivid imagery; on-level vocabulary 1 2 3 (4) 5	Long, complicated sentences; challenging vocabulary 1 2 3 (4) 5
	Levels of Meaning/ Purpose/Concept Level	Accessible concept (hope for the future) 1 2 (3) 4 5	Accessible concept (hope for the future) 1 2 (3) 4 5
Quantitative Measures	**Text Length**	Word Count: 264	Word Count: 889
	Lexile	900L	1390L
Overall Complexity		✓ **More accessible**	✓✓ **More complex**

❸ Literary Analysis: Philosophical Assumptions

An **author's purpose,** or goal, is shaped by his or her **philosophical assumptions,** or basic beliefs. Philosophical assumptions can be based on many factors, such as political beliefs, moral or ethical values, and cultural influences. In some cases, the author may use these basic beliefs to support his or her argument. The response of the **audience,** or readers, may depend on whether they share the author's basic beliefs.

To read critically, identify the author's basic beliefs and assumptions in the work. The author may state such beliefs directly or may suggest them in details and varied types of language, such as words that carry positive or negative associations. As you read, decide whether you accept these beliefs and whether the audience would be likely to accept them. Then, evaluate whether these assumptions help the author achieve his or her purpose.

❹ Using the Strategy: Assumptions Chart

As you read, use a chart like the one shown to record your ideas.

Philosophical Assumptions		Evaluation
The basic beliefs included in the author's work	→	How basic beliefs do or do not support the author's purpose

❺ Reading Skill: Compare and Contrast

When you **compare and contrast,** you recognize similarities and differences. In persuasive writing, authors often use a compare-and-contrast organization to help readers see the similarities and differences between one point of view and another. As you read, **use self-monitoring techniques** like these to make sure you understand the comparisons and contrasts:

- Identify the things or ideas being compared.
- Restate the similarities and differences in your own words.
- Explain the significance of the similarities and differences.

If you cannot identify, restate, or explain the author's points, reread to clarify and to find words or phrases that were unclear.

PHLit Online!
www.PHLitOnline.com

Hear It!
- Selection summary audio
- Selection audio

See It!
- Get Connected video
- Background video
- More about the author
- Vocabulary flashcards

Do It!
- Interactive journals
- Interactive graphic organizers
- Self-test
- Internet activity
- Grammar tutorial
- Interactive vocabulary games

PRETEACH

❸ Literary Analysis

Philosophical Assumptions

1. Introduce the skill, using the instruction on the student page.
2. Tell students that they will evaluate author's assumptions as they read.

Think Aloud: Model the Skill

Model the skill of evaluating author's assumptions. Say to students:

We reveal our basic beliefs when we speak, even if we don't state them directly. For example, if I tell a friend that my weekend plans are to work in my yard and clean out my closet, I have shown a basic belief in caring for my home. If my friend suggests a trip to the gym instead, she is showing a basic belief in the value of exercise. When I read, I look for similar basic beliefs, then decide if I agree with them.

❹ Using the Strategy

Give students a copy of either **Literary Analysis Graphic Organizer A** or **B** (***Graphic Organizer Transparencies***, pp. 202–204) to record their ideas about assumptions. Use the examples in the **Literary Analysis Graphic Organizer A,** which is partially filled in, to model the process of completing the organizer.

❺ Reading Skill

Compare and Contrast

1. Introduce the skill, using the instruction on the student page.
2. Tell students that they will compare and contrast as they read.

Text Complexity: Reader and Task Suggestions

✓ There Is a Longing		✓✓ Glory and Hope	
Preparing to Read the Text	**Leveled Tasks**	**Preparing to Read the Text**	**Leveled Tasks**
• Refer to the Background information on TE p. 1195 and discuss the struggles of Native Americans to maintain their culture. • Review the use and purposes of poetic language and imagery. • Guide students to use Multidraft Reading strategies (TE p. 1195).	***Structure/Language*** If students will have difficulty with language, have them first read the selection and note details about George's purpose. Then, have them reread and identify lines in which poetic language obscures their understanding. ***Evaluating*** If students will not have difficulty with language, have them read and take notes on the author's purpose for writing.	• Using the Background note on TE p. 1201, discuss Nelson Mandela's role in fighting apartheid. • Review strategies for reading long sentences and using context clues. • Guide students to use Multidraft Reading strategies (TE p. 1201).	***Structure/Language*** If students will have difficulty with language, have students first read and note Mandela's main ideas. Then have them reread and note those sentences that remain unclear to them. ***Analyzing*** If students will not have difficulty with language, have them read and note Mandela's use of rhetorical techniques.

❶ Writing About the Big Question

1. Review the assignment with the class.
2. Talk with students about what makes a leader a hero. **Ask** students to name people they view as heroes, and to **speculate** if these people feel extra responsibility for their actions.
3. Have students complete the sentence starters. Review responses as a class. (**Possible response:** Not all heroes know they are heroes because they just do what they think is right. A leader can be a true <u>hero</u> when he or she stands up for others.)
4. Remind students that their answers will help them think about the Big Question, "Do heroes have responsibilities?"

While You Read

Tell students that as they read they should look for ways in which Chief Dan George accepts responsibilities, and decide whether or not he is a hero.

❷ Vocabulary

1. Have students preview the selection vocabulary.
2. For each word, have students say the word aloud.
3. Then, use the word in a sentence that defines the word.
4. Finally, repeat your definitional sentence or a similar sentence with the word missing and have the class "fill in the blank" chorally. Here are some examples:

   A <u>longing</u> is a strong desire or hope for something. All my life, I have dreamed of traveling to Antarctica, so this wish is a [students say "longing"].

   To <u>emerge</u> is to come into view. When children jump out of their hiding place into view, they [students say "emerge"].

❸ Word Study

1. Introduce the skill, using the instruction in the box.
2. **Ask** students for a *-merg-* word that they might see on a street sign telling cars to join the traffic. (**Answer:** *merge*).

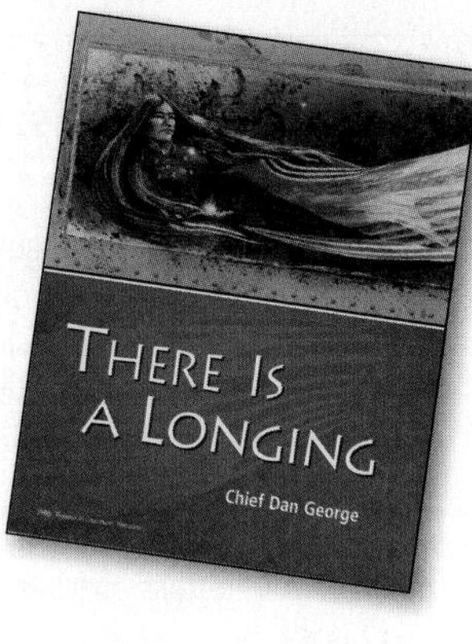

❶ Writing About the Big Question

In his speech, Chief Dan George says his power to make war is gone, but he longs to serve his people. Use these sentence starters to develop your ideas about the Big Question.

Not all **heroes** know they are heroes because ______________.

A leader can be a true **hero** when he or she ______________.

While You Read Look for ways in which Chief Dan George accepts the responsibilities of leadership. Consider whether he is a hero.

❷ Vocabulary

Read each word and its definition. Decide whether you know the word well, know it a little bit, or do not know it at all. After you read, see how your knowledge of each word has increased.

- **longing** (lôŋ´ iŋ) *n.* a yearning, especially for something unattainable (p. 1197) ***The passing dessert cart left the child <u>longing</u> for a piece of cake during the whole dinner.*** *long v. longingly adv.*
- **determination** (dē tʉr´ mi nā´ shən) *n.* firm intention (p. 1197) ***The runner's <u>determination</u> enabled him to win the race.*** *determined adj.*
- **endurance** (en do͝or´ əns) *n.* ability to withstand hardship over time (p. 1197) ***Surviving the hurricane required courage and <u>endurance</u>.*** *endure v. enduring adj.*
- **emerge** (ē mʉrj´) *v.* come into existence; become visible or known (p. 1197) ***Joe's parents hoped that after college he would <u>emerge</u> as a strong candidate for the business world.*** *emerging adj. emergent adj.*
- **humbly** (hum´ blē) *adv.* in a manner that is not proud or arrogant; modestly (p. 1198) ***Shannon accepted her award <u>humbly</u>, thanking everyone who helped her achieve it.*** *humble adj. humbled v.*
- **segment** (seg´ mənt) *n.* a division or section (p. 1198) ***Claire approached each <u>segment</u> of the test cautiously because the directions seemed to change with every one.*** *segmented adj.*

❸ Word Study

The **Latin root *-merg-*** means "dip" or "plunge."

In this selection, Chief Dan George says the young of his nation will **emerge** from years of study, as if rising up from the waters. They will take their place in society.

Vocabulary Development

Vocabulary Knowledge Rating

Create a **Vocabulary Knowledge Rating Chart** (***Professional Development Guidebook***, p. 33) for the selection vocabulary words and for the thematic words in the Writing About the Big Question sentence starters on this page.

Give each student a copy of the chart with the words on it. Read the words aloud, and have students mark their rating of each in the Before Reading column. When students have completed reading and discussing "There Is a Longing," have them take out their **Vocabulary Knowledge Rating** charts for the speech. Read the words aloud and have students rate their knowledge again in the After Reading column. Clarify any words that are still problematic. Then, have students complete the Vocabulary Practice at the end of the selection.

Vocabulary Central, featuring tools, activities, and songs for studying vocabulary, is available at **www.PHLitOnline.com**.

Meet
Chief Dan George
(1899–1981)

Author of
THERE IS A LONGING

Chief Dan George had many careers, including actor and writer. Chief of a Salish Band of Native Americans in British Columbia, Canada, he was deeply concerned about improving the relationships between Native Americans and other North Americans.

Celebrity Activist Chief Dan George used the prominence he gained from his film and television roles to raise public awareness about the plight of Canada's native peoples. By the 1960s, he had become an unofficial spokesman for Native Americans and the environment. Throughout all of his endeavors against injustice, he always advocated peace over violence.

4

BACKGROUND FOR THE SPEECH

The Struggle of Native Americans

When Europeans settled in the Americas, they encountered tribal peoples who had lived on the land for thousands of years. Their initial fear and prejudice led to violence, and many native tribes were destroyed. Nevertheless, Native American culture survived. Today, Native Americans continue to discover ways to succeed in the twenty-first century while maintaining their own cultural identity.

DID YOU KNOW?

Chief Dan George was nominated for an Academy Award as Best Supporting Actor for his role in the movie *Little Big Man.*

Daily Bellringer

For each class during which you will teach this selection, have students complete one of the five Research activities for Week 35 in the ***Daily Bellringer Activities*** booklet.

4 Background

The Struggle of Native Americans

Indian Nations are sovereign governments, which leads to a special relationship with the United States federal government. Despite this special relationship, interactions between the Indian Nations and the United States have often been troubled. After years of conflict and unresolved treaty issues, the National Congress of American Indians was founded in 1944. Its goal was to provide representation of the different American Indian tribes at the national level. Since then, the NCAI has helped federal lawmakers create legislation that recognizes the needs of the Indian Nations.

Multidraft Reading

This icon ● marks natural pauses in the selection. To assist struggling readers and to deepen reading for all, assign the text in "chunks," following the icons, and apply multidraft reading protocols. For each reading, have students set the purpose indicated:

- **First reading**—identifying key ideas and details and answering any Reading Checks.
- **Second reading**—analyzing craft and structure and responding to the side-column prompts.
- **Third reading**—integrating knowledge and ideas, connecting to other texts and the world, and answering the end-of-selection questions.

For more guidance, refer to the ***Classroom Strategies and Teaching Routines*** card on multidraft reading.

For more about the author, practice with the selection vocabulary, and more background, go online at **www.PHLitOnline.com.**

Differentiated Instruction — Additional Instruction

EL Extended Support—English Learners

Have students complete the **Reading and Vocabulary Warm-ups, *Unit 6 Resources,*** pp. 131–134, before they read. Assign the prereading pages and the adapted selection in the ***Reader's Notebook: English Learner's Version.*** Then, have students listen to portions of the selection on the ***Hear It!* Audio CD.**

L1 L2 Extended Support—Struggling Readers

Have students complete the **Reading and Vocabulary Warm-ups, *Unit 6 Resources,*** pp. 131–134, before they read. Assign prereading pages and the adapted selection in the ***Reader's Notebook: Adapted Version.*** Then, have students listen to portions of the selection on the ***Hear It!* Audio CD** (adapted text).

Extended Support—Reluctant Readers

To build motivation and engagement before assigning the selection, have students read "The Choice to Lead," a thematically related selection in ***Reality Central.*** Then, use the questions at the conclusion of the related selection to guide discussion.

TEACH

❶ Activating Prior Knowledge

Initiate a discussion of civil rights. Include questions like these: How can a group demand its rights? What obstacles is that group likely to meet? Why is it important for a group to lobby for its rights? Students may answer these questions based on their knowledge of civil rights movements they have studied.

Concept Connector

Students will follow up on this activity after completing "There Is a Longing."

Whole-Class Activity

Lead students in a discussion about their hopes for the future. Encourage students to think about their hopes for their families, communities, the state or country, and the world at large. Have a few students record the class's ideas on the board.

❷ About the Selection

In "There Is a Longing," Chief Dan George believes that Native Americans must ensure their survival and their standing in today's world by acknowledging their ancient heritage and pride in traditional values as they also work to embrace what is best of "the white man's success."

❸ Humanities

We the People, by Kathy Morrow

Artist Kathy Morrow grew up on Apache and Sioux reservations, where her father trained Native American police forces. Her title is taken from the preamble to the United States Constitution: "We, the people of the United States of America . . ." Use this question for discussion:

How does this artwork convey a sense of longing and determination?

Possible response: Students may observe that the outstretched hands convey a sense of reaching out. The movement of the eagle seems focused and follows the direction of the reaching.

3

1 2

There Is a Longing

Chief Dan George

Vocabulary Development

CCSS Language 6

Thematic Vocabulary: The Big Question

As students are discussing "There Is a Longing," have them use the thematic vocabulary presented in Introducing the Big Question, pp. 1028–1029. You might encourage them with sentence starters like these:

1. Chief Dan George says that young people have a *responsibility* to . . .
2. Chief Dan George asks the Great Spirit for *wisdom* because . . .
3. Some new *choices* open to the people of Chief Dan George's nation are . . .
4. Chief Dan George states that he will *serve* his people by . . .

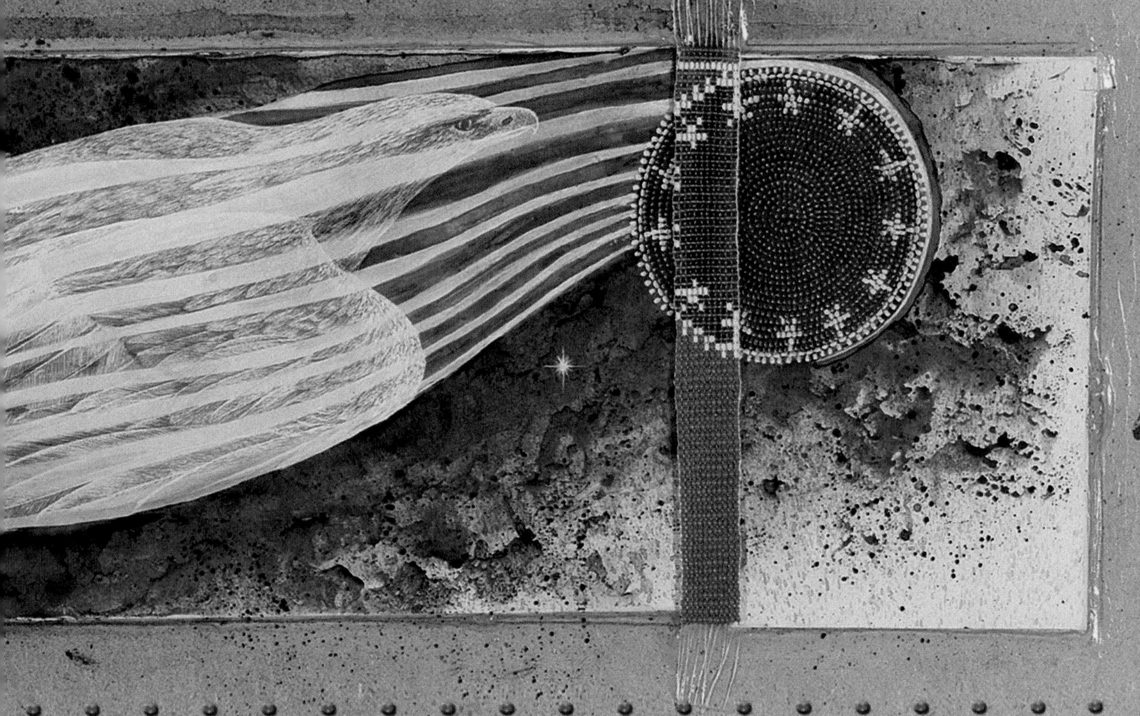

We the People, Kathy Morrow, Original scratchboard painting with hand-loomed beadwork. Courtesy of the artist.

There is a **longing** in the heart of my people to reach out and grasp that which is needed for our survival. There is a longing among the young of my nation to secure for themselves and their people the skills that will provide them with a sense of worth and (5) purpose. They will be our new warriors. Their training will be much longer and more demanding than it was in olden days. The long years of study will demand more **determination**; separation from home and family will demand **endurance**. But they will **emerge** with their hand held forward, not to receive welfare, but to grasp the place in society that is rightly ours. I am a chief, but my power to make war is gone, and the only weapon left to me is speech. It is only with tongue and speech that I can fight my people's war.

4 ▲ Critical Viewing
Which images in this painting reflect ideas found in the speech? **[Analyze]**

Vocabulary

longing (lôŋ´ iŋ) *n.* a yearning, especially for something unattainable

determination (dē tʉr´ mi nā´ shən) *n.* firm intention

endurance (en dʊ͝or´ əns) *n.* ability to withstand hardship over time

emerge (ē mʉrj´) *v.* come into existence; become visible or known

4 Critical Viewing

Answer: The painting illustrates the blending of old and new traditions. It illustrates the chief's wish that his people be "the proudest segment of your society... ruling and being ruled by the knowledge and freedoms of our great land."

5 Writing About the Big Question

1. To remind students of the Big Question, **ask** them to name a few responsibilities a young Native American might have had in the 1600s. Then **ask** them to name a few daily responsibilities they have today.
2. Then direct students to read the bracketed text on p. 1197. **Ask:** Why do you think Chief Dan George calls young educated Native Americans "our new warriors"? What kind of battle will they fight?

   Answer: They will be his people's leaders. They will fight with ideas to help Native Americans solve problems and succeed.
3. **Ask:** What responsibility does Chief Dan George expect his people to take upon themselves?

   Answer: He wants them to get an education and become leaders.

PHLit Online!

This selection is available in interactive format in the **Enriched Online Student Edition, www.PHLitOnline.com,** which includes a thematically related video with writing prompt and an interactive graphic organizer.

Concept Connector

Activating Prior Knowledge

Have students reconsider their discussion of civil rights. Then, lead a class discussion, probing for what students have learned that confirms or invalidates their original ideas. Encourage students to cite specific details, quotations, or other evidence from the text to support their statements.

Writing About the Big Question

Have students compare their responses to the sentence starters they completed before reading the speech with their ideas afterwards. Ask them to explain whether their thoughts have changed.

Literary Analysis Graphic Organizer Ask students to review the graphic organizers they completed. Show them **Literary Analysis Graphic Organizer A** (*Graphic Organizer Transparencies,* p. 202) as an example. Then have students share their graphic organizers.

6 Literary Analysis

Philosophical Assumptions

1. **Ask:** What does Chief Dan George ask of the Great Spirit?

   Answer: He wants courage, he wants to live in harmony with the environment, and he wants to accept the new culture around him.

2. **Ask** the Literary Analysis question: What belief about the keys to success in the "new culture" does this passage reflect?

   Answer: The keys to success—education and government—are good because they lead to pride in and responsibility for one's society.

▶ **Monitor Progress: Ask** students to articulate Chief Dan George's ideas about American culture.

▶ **Reteach:** If students have trouble identifying the writer's philosophical assumptions, help students skim the selection for what is important to Chief Dan George. Explain that these answers show Chief Dan George's basic beliefs, or his philosophical assumptions.

ASSESS

Answers

Critical Thinking

Before students respond, you may wish to have them write a brief objective summary of the selection. As they answer the questions below, remind them to support their answers with evidence from the text.

1. (a) His people long to take their place in society. (b) He fears that he may not have the courage and wisdom of former chiefs.
2. (a) They will need many years of school. (b) He wants his people to be able to grasp opportunity.
3. (a) He can only fight with words. (b) He can make speeches and use logic as his weapon.
4. If his people follow his suggestions, their lives will be improved; they will be able to help their families and communities.
5. **Possible response:** Yes, a great leader uses words to convince others to take actions or change beliefs, which is often heroic.

Literary Analysis Philosophical Assumptions What belief about the keys to success in the "new culture" does this passage reflect?

Vocabulary

humbly (hum′ blē) *adj.* in a manner that is not proud or arrogant; modestly

segment (seg′ mənt) *n.* a division or section

Oh, Great Spirit![1] Give me back the courage
of the olden Chiefs. Let me wrestle with
my surroundings. Let me once again,
live in harmony with my environment.
Let me humbly accept this new culture
and through it rise up and go on. Like
the thunderbird[2] of old, I shall rise again
out of the sea; I shall grab the instruments
of the white man's success—his
education, his skills. With these new tools
I shall build my race into the proudest
segment of your society. I shall see our
young braves and our chiefs sitting in
the houses of law and government, ruling
and being ruled by the knowledge and
freedoms of our great land.

1. **Great Spirit** for many Native Americans, the greatest power or god.
2. **thunderbird** powerful supernatural creature that was thought to produce thunder by flapping its wings and to produce lightning by opening and closing its eyes. In the folklore of some Native American nations, the thunderbird is in constant warfare with the powers beneath the waters.

Critical Thinking

Cite textual evidence to support your responses.

1. **Key Ideas and Details (a)** What does Chief Dan George say is his community's longing? **(b) Infer:** What is his greatest fear?
2. **Key Ideas and Details (a)** What training will the new warriors have to endure? **(b) Analyze:** Why does Chief Dan George believe that this training is necessary?
3. **Key Ideas and Details (a) Infer:** In what way is Chief Dan George different from the "olden" chiefs? **(b) Interpret:** What does the chief mean when he refers to fighting a war "with tongue and speech"?
4. **Integration of Knowledge and Ideas Assess:** Do you think the chief's goal of achieving success through education and skills is the best means for improving his people's lives? Explain your response.
5. **Integration of Knowledge and Ideas** Chief Dan George talks about fighting his people's war with "tongue and speech." Can someone who fights only with such weapons be a hero? *[Connect to the Big Question: Do heroes have responsibilities?]*

Assessment Resources

Unit 6 Resources

L1 L2 EL **Selection Test A,** pp. 143–144. Administer Test A to less advanced readers.

L3 L4 EL **Selection Test B,** pp. 145–146. Administer Test B to on-level and more advanced students.

L3 L4 **Open-Book Test,** pp. 141–142. As an alternative, give the Open-Book Test.

All **Customizable Test Bank**

All **Self-tests**
Students may prepare for the **Selection Test** by taking the **Self-test** online.

PHLit Online! All assessment resources are available at **www.PHLitOnline.com.**

After You Read | There Is a Longing

Literary Analysis: Philosophical Assumptions

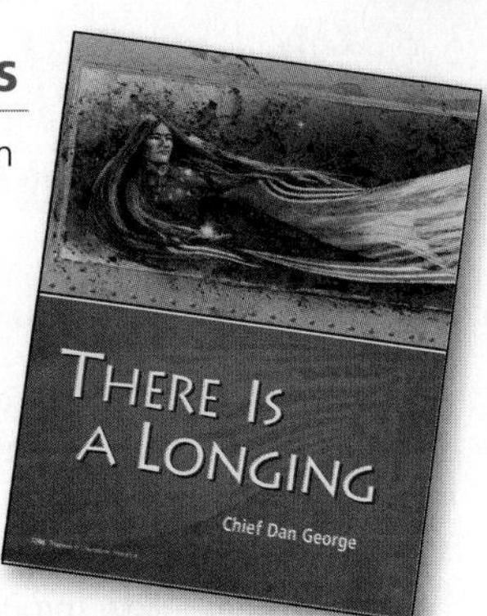

1. **Key Ideas and Details** **(a)** What is Chief Dan George's **purpose** in writing? **(b)** What are the **philosophical assumptions,** or beliefs, that shape his purpose?
2. **Key Ideas and Details** **(a)** For what **audience** did Chief Dan George originally write? **(b)** What details in the text indicate his intended audience? **(c)** Do you think his intended audience shared his basic beliefs? Support your answer with details from the text.
3. **Integration of Knowledge and Ideas** Using Chief Dan George's speech as an example, explain how the audience for a speech can change over time.

Reading Skill: Compare and Contrast

4. **(a)** Use a chart like the one shown to record the ideas Chief Dan George presents about the past, present, and future.

Past	Present	Future

(b) Explain the point Chief Dan George makes by **comparing and contrasting** his ideas about the past, present, and future.

Vocabulary

Acquisition and Use Indicate whether each statement is *True* or *False*. Explain your answers. Then, revise any sentences that are false to make them true.

1. Difficult tasks require *determination* to be completed.
2. Rock climbing requires less *endurance* than television watching.
3. When a winner responds *humbly* to a victory, he or she claims to be the world's greatest champion.
4. No one really wants to *emerge* from a time of pain or unpleasantness.
5. Only fortunate people have a *longing* to improve their lives.
6. Students are one *segment* of our society.

Word Study Use the context of the sentences and what you know about the **Latin root *-merg-*** to explain your answer to each question.

1. In an *emergency,* is someone in serious, unexpected trouble?
2. Is a *submersible* a ship built to float on the surface of the water?

Word Study

The **Latin root *-merg-*** means "dip" or "plunge."

Apply It Explain how the root *-merg-* contributes to the meanings of these words. Consult a dictionary if necessary.

immerge
submerge
merger

ASSESS/EXTEND

Answers

Literary Analysis

1. (a) His purpose is to empower Native Americans so that they can re-emerge as a proud and strong people. (b) He assumes that his people wish to survive and prosper, their greatness is in the future as well as the past, and the road will be difficult.
2. (a) The audience originally was Native Americans. (b) The speaker refers to his people; he addresses the Great Spirit directly; he refers at the end of the speech to "our young braves and our chiefs." (c) Students should suggest that the audience shares his belief in the potential of Native Americans.
3. **Sample answer:** Though the speech was intended for Native Americans, it now has a broader appeal to many groups.

Reading Skill

4. (a) **Sample answers:** **Past**—His people were once great. They fought war with weapons. Training was easier in the past. The olden Chiefs had courage. **Present**—The people are filled with longing. They are faced with hard work, isolation, and study. The Chief has only the power to make speeches. **Future**—The people can be great again. They can be leaders. They can be educated. They can be free. (b) By comparing the past, present, and future, the writer shows how the former greatness of his people can be reestablished.

For other sample answers, see ***Graphic Organizer Transparencies,* Reading Skill Graphic Organizer A**, p. 205, and the **Additional Answers** section.

Vocabulary

Acquisition and Use

Sample answers:

1. True. Difficult tasks require determination because you must solve problems.
2. False. Rock climbing requires more endurance than television watching because it requires more effort and ability to withstand hardship.

Continued from right column

3. False. When someone responds humbly to a victory, he or she takes little credit and so does not claim greatness.
4. False. People want to emerge from, or escape, a time of pain.
5. False. All people, regardless of their situation, have a longing, or wish, to improve their lives.
6. True. Students are one segment, or part, of society.

Word Study

Sample answers:

1. Yes, the root *-merg-* means "dip or plunge" and *emergency* means "an unplanned event that one is plunged into." Emergencies are always serious and unexpected.
2. No, the root *-merg-* means "dip or plunge," and *submersible* means "a ship that is capable of plunging under water." A *submersible* does not float on the surface.

Word Study: Apply It

To *immerge* is to plunge into something completely. To *submerge* is to plunge something under water. A *merger* occurs when two entities combine and plunge into business together.

PRETEACH

*Skills instruction for the **Reading Skill** and **Literary Analysis** concept for this selection appears on p. 1193.*

1 Writing About the Big Question

1. Review the assignment with the class.
2. Discuss with students responsibilities that they believe every leader has.
3. Have students complete the sentence starters. Review responses as a class. (**Possible response:** When a leader promises to serve his or her nation, he or she has an obligation to follow through because this promise creates a sacred trust between leader and people. The leader may become a heroic figure to many because of his or her deeds.)
4. Remind students that their answers will help them think about the Big Question.

While You Read

Tell students that as they read they should look for Mandela's values and goals and decide if Mandela is a hero.

2 Vocabulary

1. Have students preview the selection vocabulary.
2. For each word, have students say the word aloud.
3. Then, use the word in a sentence that defines the word.
4. Finally, repeat your definitional sentence or a similar sentence with the word missing and have the class "fill in the blank" chorally. Here is an example:

   Something pernicious is very destructive. A virus that kills animals can be called [students say "pernicious"].

3 Word Study

1. Introduce the skill, using the instruction in the box.
2. **Ask** students for a *-fer-* word that means "to carry back." (**Answer:** *refer*)

Do heroes have responsibilities?

1 Writing About the Big Question

In his speech, Nelson Mandela celebrates the liberty newly gained by his country and pleads for national reconciliation and liberty. Use these sentence starters to develop your ideas about the Big Question.

When a leader promises to **serve** his or her nation, he or she has an **obligation** to follow through because _______________. The leader may become a **heroic** figure to many because _____________.

While You Read Look for the values that Mandela celebrates and the goals that he has set. Consider whether you believe he is a hero.

2 Vocabulary

Read each word and its definition. Decide whether you know the word well, know it a little bit, or do not know it at all. After you read, see how your knowledge of each word has increased.

- **distinguished** (di stiŋ´ gwisht) *adj.* having an air of distinction; celebrated for excellence; renowned (p. 1202) *The distinguished gentleman stood and bowed to the crowd that acknowledged him.* distinguish *v.* distinct *adj.*
- **confer** (kən fʉr´) *v.* give (p. 1202) *The school will confer an honorary degree on the singer.* conferable *adj.*
- **intimately** (in´ tə mət lē) *adv.* in a close manner; familiarly (p. 1202). *Because they had worked together for years, Sandy and her colleagues knew each other intimately.* intimate *adj.* intimacy *n.*
- **pernicious** (pər nish´ əs) *adj.* destructive (p. 1203) *A pernicious insect destroyed the tree.* perniciously *adv.* perniciousness *n.*
- **covenant** (kuv´ ə nənt) *n.* agreement or contract, especially a sacred one (p. 1203) *They made a covenant to be friends forever.*
- **reconciliation** (rek´ ən sil´ ē ā´ shən) *n.* the settling of a conflict or argument; agreement; compromise (p. 1204) *Maryanne hoped she would come to some sort of reconciliation with her daughter after their terrible fight.* reconcile *v.* reconcilable *adj.*

3 Word Study

The **Latin root *-fer-*** means "carry" or "produce."

In this selection, Mandela says that by celebrating the change in South Africa, they will **confer,** or carry, glory and hope on their new liberty.

Vocabulary Development

Vocabulary Knowledge Rating

Create a **Vocabulary Knowledge Rating Chart** (***Professional Development Guidebook,*** p. 33) for the selection vocabulary words and for the thematic words in the Writing About the Big Question sentence starters on this page.

Give each student a copy of the chart with the words on it. Read the words aloud, and have students mark their rating of each in the Before Reading column. When students have completed reading and discussing "Glory and Hope," have them take out their **Vocabulary Knowledge Rating** charts for the speech. Read the words aloud and have students rate their knowledge again in the After Reading column. Clarify any words that are still problematic. Then, have students complete the Vocabulary practice at the end of the selection.

Vocabulary Central, featuring tools, activities, and songs for recording and studying vocabulary, is available at **www.PHLitOnline.com.**

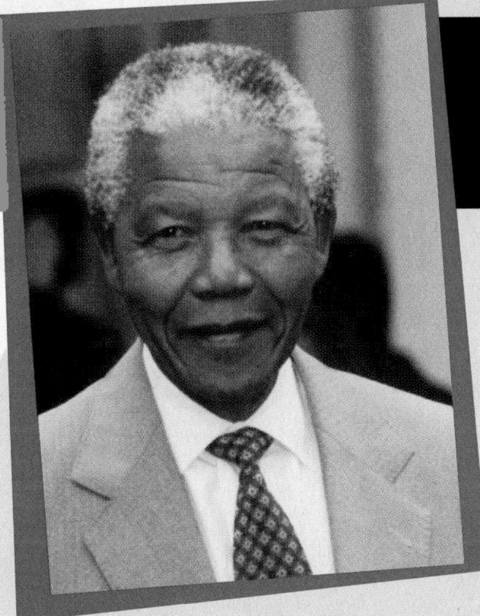

Meet Nelson Mandela

(b. 1918)

Author of Glory and Hope

Nelson Rolihlahla Mandela was born in South Africa, a nation whose white government maintained a strict policy of apartheid, or legal discrimination against blacks. In 1944, Mandela began protesting apartheid. Twenty years later, after several arrests, he was sentenced to life in prison for acts of protest.

Freedom for a Man and a Nation In 1990, after long years of imprisonment, Mandela was released. He continued to fight for equal rights for all South Africans. In 1991, apartheid was finally abolished and, in 1993, Mandela and South African president F. W. de Klerk shared the Nobel Prize for Peace. The next year, Mandela became the first black man to be elected president of South Africa. He retired from public life in 1999, and he currently lives in his birthplace, Qunu, Transkei.

Did You Know?

Robben Island, Mandela's prison for so many years, has now been turned into a learning center.

4 BACKGROUND FOR THE SPEECH

Apartheid

In Afrikaans, one of the languages of South Africa, *apartheid* means "apartness." Apartheid is the policy of segregation and discrimination that was once practiced against nonwhites by the South African government. When apartheid became law in 1948, it affected housing, education, and transportation. In order to help end apartheid, many nations reduced trade with South Africa. Apartheid was finally abolished in 1991.

Daily Bellringer

For each class during which you will teach this selection, have students complete one of the five Research activities for Week 35 in the ***Daily Bellringer Activities*** booklet.

4 Background

Apartheid

Apartheid laws categorized all South Africans as either white, black, Asian, or "colored" (meaning "of mixed ancestry"). These groups were to live apart in defined areas and have their own separate political institutions. Intermarriage between races was illegal. Black South Africans were the least privileged of the four groups. The 1991 repeal of apartheid did not solve South Africa's problems overnight, and some painful legacies remain to be overcome.

Multidraft Reading

This icon ● marks natural pauses in the selection. To assist struggling readers and to deepen reading for all, assign the text in "chunks," following the icons, and apply multidraft reading protocols. For each reading, have students set the purpose indicated:

- **First reading**—identifying key ideas and details and answering any Reading Checks.
- **Second reading**—analyzing craft and structure and responding to the side-column prompts.
- **Third reading**—integrating knowledge and ideas, connecting to other texts and the world, and answering the end-of-selection questions.

For more guidance, refer to the ***Classroom Strategies and Teaching Routines Card*** on multidraft reading.

PHLit Online!

For more about the author, practice with the selection vocabulary, and more background, go to **www.PHLitOnline.com.**

Differentiated Instruction — Additional Instruction

EL Extended Support—English Learners

Have students complete the **Reading and Vocabulary Warm-ups, *Unit 6 Resources,*** pp. 147–150, before they read. Assign the prereading pages for the selection in the ***Reader's Notebook: English Learner's Version.*** Then, have students listen to portions of the selection on the ***Hear It!* Audio CD**.

L1 L2 Extended Support—Struggling Readers

Have students complete the **Reading and Vocabulary Warm-ups, *Unit 6 Resources,*** pp. 147–150, before they read. Assign the prereading pages for the selection in the ***Reader's Notebook: Adapted Version.*** Then, have students listen to portions of the selection on the ***Hear It!* Audio CD** (adapted text).

Extended Support—Reluctant Readers

To build motivation and engagement before assigning the selection, have students read "A Time to Protest," a thematically related selection in ***Reality Central.*** Then, use the questions at the conclusion of the related selection to guide discussion.

❶ Activating Prior Knowledge

Read the Background feature on p. 1201 aloud. Then lead a discussion about the efforts of groups to obtain civil rights. Have students draw on their knowledge of civil rights movements in the United States and elsewhere to explore what deprivation of civil rights can lead to and what options exist to correct the problem.

Concept Connector

Students will follow up on this activity after completing "Glory and Hope."

Individual Activity

Have students pay attention to the effect of repetition in the selection. For example, Mandela begins several paragraphs with the word *we* followed by a verb. Later he repeats the phrase "Let there be . . ." As he closes, Mandela repeats the word *never* three times. Have students write a paragraph that analyzes the effect of this technique on Mandela's message.

❷ About the Selection

In "Glory and Hope," the inaugural address given the day he took office, President Nelson Mandela of South Africa leads his listeners from a divided past toward a united future. He urges listeners to face the challenges ahead with hope and determination.

❸ Reading Skill

Comparing and Contrasting

1. Read the bracketed text, which ends on p. 1203, aloud. Point out the description of the "country tearing itself apart in terrible conflict." **Ask:** What happened to South Africa as a direct result of that conflict?

   Answer: South Africa was isolated, as other nations boycotted and avoided South Africa.

2. **Ask** the Reading Skill question: What important difference does Mandela point out about South Africa's future as compared to its past?

   Answer: In the past, the country was marked by racism and oppression. The future is going to be one of peace, prosperity, equality, and democracy.

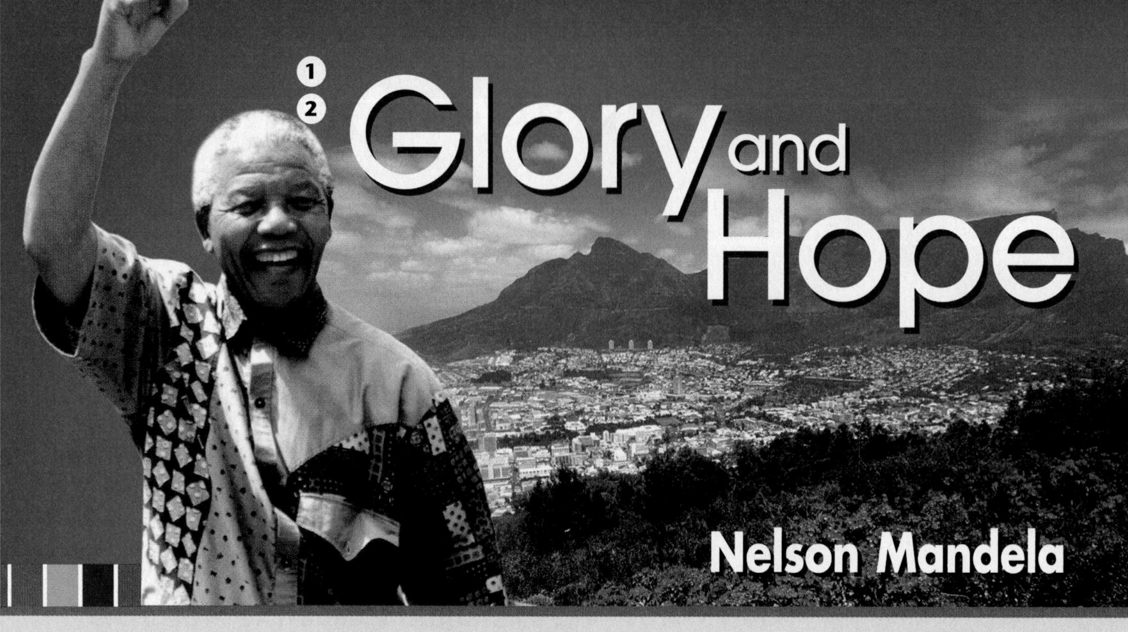

❶ ❷ Glory and Hope

Nelson Mandela

Vocabulary

distinguished (di stiŋ′ gwisht′) *adj.* having an air of distinction; celebrated for excellence; renowned

confer (kən fʉr′) *v.* give

intimately (in′ tə mət lē) *adj.* In a close manner; familiarly

Reading Skill

Comparing and Contrasting What important difference does Mandela point out about South Africa's future as compared to its past?

Your majesties, your royal highnesses, **distinguished** guests, comrades and friends: Today, all of us do, by our presence here, and by our celebrations in other parts of our country and the world, **confer** glory and hope to newborn liberty.

Out of the experience of an extraordinary human disaster that lasted too long must be born a society of which all humanity will be proud.

Our daily deeds as ordinary South Africans must produce an actual South African reality that will reinforce humanity's belief in justice, strengthen its confidence in the nobility of the human soul and sustain all our hopes for a glorious life for all.

All this we owe both to ourselves and to the peoples of the world who are so well represented here today.

To my compatriots, I have no hesitation in saying that each one of us is as **intimately** attached to the soil of this beautiful country as are the famous jacaranda trees of Pretoria and the mimosa trees of the bushveld.[1]

Each time one of us touches the soil of this land, we feel a sense of personal renewal. The national mood changes as the seasons change.

We are moved by a sense of joy and exhilaration when the grass turns green and the flowers bloom.

That spiritual and physical oneness we all share with this common homeland explains the depth of the pain we all carried in

1. **bushveld** (boosh′ velt) *n.* South African grassland with abundant shrubs and thorny vegetation.

Vocabulary Development

CCSS Language 6

Thematic Vocabulary: The Big Question

As students are discussing "Glory and Hope," have them use the thematic vocabulary presented in Introducing the Big Question, pp. 1028–1029. You might encourage them with sentence starters like these:

1. Mandela welcomes the *involvement* of people around the world because . . .
2. Mandela describes the *morality* of his new government as one in which . . .
3. Mandela shows that he intends to *serve* the people of the country by . . .
4. Mandela would describe a *hero* or heroine as someone who . . .

our hearts as we saw our country tear itself apart in terrible conflict, and as we saw it spurned, outlawed and isolated by the peoples of the world, precisely because it has become the universal base of the pernicious ideology and practice of racism and racial oppression.

3 We, the people of South Africa, feel fulfilled that humanity has taken us back into its bosom, that we, who were outlaws not so long ago, have today been given the rare privilege to be host to the nations of the world on our own soil.

We thank all our distinguished international guests for having come to take possession with the people of our country of what is, after all, a common victory for justice, for peace, for human dignity.

We trust that you will continue to stand by us as we tackle the challenges of building peace, prosperity, nonsexism, nonracialism and democracy.

We deeply appreciate the role that the masses of our people and their democratic, religious, women, youth, business, traditional and other leaders have played to bring about this conclusion. Not least among them is my Second Deputy President, the Honorable F. W. de Klerk.

We would also like to pay tribute to our security forces, in all their ranks, for the distinguished role they have played in securing our first democratic elections and the transition to democracy, from bloodthirsty forces which still refuse to see the light.

The time for the healing of the wounds has come.

4 The moment to bridge the chasms that divide us has come.

The time to build is upon us.

We have, at last, achieved our political emancipation. We pledge ourselves to liberate all our people from the continuing bondage of poverty, deprivation, suffering, gender and other discrimination.

We succeeded to take our last steps to freedom in conditions of relative peace. We commit ourselves to the construction of a complete, just and lasting peace.

We have triumphed in the effort to implant hope in the breasts of the millions of our people. We enter into a covenant that we shall build the society in which all South Africans, both black and white, will be able to walk tall, without any fear in their hearts, assured of their inalienable right to human dignity—a rainbow nation at peace with itself and the world.

As a token of its commitment to the renewal of our country, the new Interim Government of National Unity will, as a matter of urgency, address the issue of amnesty for various categories of our people who are currently serving terms of imprisonment.

We dedicate this day to all the heroes and heroines in this country and the rest of the world who sacrificed in many ways and surrendered their lives so that we could be free.

Vocabulary
pernicious (pər nishʹ əs) *adj.* destructive

Spiral Review
Universal Theme
How do Mandela's words in the three short paragraphs that begin with "The time for the healing of the wounds has come" evoke a possible theme of hope and rebirth?

Vocabulary
covenant (kuvʹ ə nənt) *n.* agreement or contract, especially a sacred one

5 

What does Mandela say must be born "out of the experience of an extraordinary human disaster"?

Spiral Review
Universal Theme
1. Remind students that they studied the concept of universal theme in the Unit 6 Literary Analysis workshop (pp. 1030–1039).
2. **Ask** students the Spiral Review question.

Possible response: Mandela's words *bridging, healing,* and *building* evoke hope and rebirth through figurative language that is generally understood to represent positive change and reconciliation.

4 Connecting to the Big Question
1. Remind students of the Big Question by asking them to list some responsibilities they think all citizens have to resolve conflicts.
2. Have students read the second bracketed passage on p. 1203. **Ask:** What actions does Mandela call for here? **Answer:** He calls wounds to be healed, differences to be resolved, and constructive actions to be taken.
3. **Ask:** Does a leader have particular responsibilities to bring divided groups together? Explain.

Possible Response: Yes. Because a divided society is less productive, leaders have an added responsibility to heal divisions and redirect people's efforts toward productive behavior.

5 Reading Check
Answer: A "society of which all humanity will be proud" is what must be born out of the experience.

Concept Connector
Activating Prior Knowledge
Have students reconsider their discussion of groups seeking civil rights. Then, lead a class discussion, probing for what students have learned that confirms or invalidates their original ideas. Encourage students to cite specific details, quotations, or other evidence from the text to support their statements.

Writing About the Big Question
Have students compare their responses to the sentence starters they completed before they read the story to their ideas afterwards. Ask them to explain whether their thoughts have changed and, if so, how.

Literary Analysis Graphic Organizer
Ask students to review the graphic organizers they completed. Then have students share the graphic organizers. Show them **Literary Analysis Graphic Organizer A** (*Graphic Organizer Transparencies,* p. 203) as an example. Then, have students share their graphic organizers.

PHLit Online!
This selection is available in interactive format in the **Enriched Online Student Edition, www.PHLitOnline.com,** which includes a thematically related video with writing prompt and an interactive graphic organizer.

ASSESS

Answers

Critical Thinking

Before students respond, you may wish to have them write a brief objective summary of the selection. As they answer the questions below, remind them to support their answers with evidence from the text.

1. (a) Liberty is newborn. (b) "Newborn" creates a sense of excitement and freshness.
2. (a) The covenant is to create a "rainbow nation at peace with itself and the world." (b) Students may cite such ideas as equality, dignity, and peace.
3. (a) "Glory" is the triumph of actual results, while "hope" is optimism about future results. (b) Mandela feels that the present moment is glorious and that the future is hopeful.
4. **Possible response:** Perhaps Mandela's greatest challenge is overcoming racism.
5. **Possible response:** Yes, Mandela led people to take actions that would help heal the wounds of the past. He drew on his own experiences with suffering to set an example of how to move forward.

Vocabulary
reconciliation (rek´ ən sil´ ē ā´ shən) *n.* the settling of a conflict or argument; agreement; compromise

Their dreams have become reality. Freedom is their reward.

We are both humbled and elevated by the honor and privilege that you, the people of South Africa, have bestowed on us, as the first President of a united, democratic, nonracial and nonsexist South Africa, to lead our country out of the valley of darkness.

We understand it still that there is no easy road to freedom.

We know it well that none of us acting alone can achieve success.

We must therefore act together as a united people, for national **reconciliation**, for nation building, for the birth of a new world.

Let there be justice for all.

Let there be peace for all.

Let there be work, bread, water and salt for all.

Let each know that for each the body, the mind and the soul have been freed to fulfill themselves.

Never, never and never again shall it be that this beautiful land will again experience the oppression of one by another and suffer the indignity of being the skunk of the world.

The sun shall never set on so glorious a human achievement!

Let freedom reign. God bless Africa!

Critical Thinking

Cite textual evidence to support your responses.

1. **Key Ideas and Details (a)** What does Nelson Mandela say is "newborn" in his country? **(b) Interpret:** What emotion does the word "newborn" add to his remarks?
2. **Key Ideas and Details (a)** Into what "covenant" does Mandela say the South African people are now entering? **(b) Generalize:** Which ideas in the speech are especially important for safeguarding the human rights of all people throughout today's world?
3. **Key Ideas and Details (a) Interpret:** What do the words "glory" and "hope" mean? **(b) Connect:** How does the title of the speech connect with the ideas that Mandela conveys? Explain your response.
4. **Integration of Knowledge and Ideas Take a Position:** Basing your answer on Mandela's speech, what do you think was the new leader's greatest challenge? Explain.
5. **Integration of Knowledge and Ideas** Based on what you know about Nelson Mandela from his speech, would you call him a hero? Explain. ***[Connect to the Big Question: Do heroes have responsibilities?]***

Assessment Resources

Unit 6 Resources

L1 L2 EL **Selection Test A,** pp. 162–163. Administer **Selection Test A** to less advanced readers.

L3 L4 EL **Selection Test B,** pp. 164–165. Administer Test B to on-level and more advanced students.

L3 L4 **Open-Book Test,** pp. 160–161. As an alternative, give the Open-Book Test.

All **Customizable Test Bank**

All **Self-tests**
Students may prepare for the **Selection Test** by taking the **Self-test** online.

PHLit Online!

All assessment resources are available at **www.PHLitOnline.com.**

After You Read Glory and Hope

Literary Analysis: Philosophical Assumptions

1. **Key Ideas and Details** **(a)** What is Nelson Mandela's **purpose** in his speech? **(b)** What are the **philosophical assumptions,** or beliefs, that shape his purpose?
2. **Key Ideas and Details** **(a)** For what **audience** did Nelson Mandela originally speak? **(b)** What details in the text indicate his intended audience? **(c)** Do you think his intended audience shared his basic beliefs? Support your answer with details from the text.
3. **Integration of Knowledge and Ideas** Using Nelson Mandela's speech as an example, explain how the audience for a speech can change over time.

Reading Skill: Compare and Contrast

4. **(a)** Use a chart like the one shown to record the ideas Nelson Mandela presents about the past, present, and future.

Past	Present	Future

(b) Explain the point that Nelson Mandela makes by **comparing and contrasting** his ideas about the past, present, and future.

Vocabulary

Acquisition and Use Indicate whether each statement is *True* or *False.* Explain your answers. Then, revise any sentences that are false to make them true.

1. A signature serves to *confer* authenticity to a document.
2. A *pernicious* idea is always welcome at a team meeting.
3. Each party in a *covenant* hopes that the other party will break it.
4. A *distinguished* guest is well-known to many people.
5. If you're *intimately* involved in an event, you know little about it.
6. If you make a *reconciliation* with a friend with whom you've quarreled, you might sit down together and talk things through.

Word Study Use the context of the sentences and what you know about the **Latin root -*fer*-** to explain your answer to each question.

1. Does an unhappy and *vociferous* shopper complain quietly?
2. Why might an employer ask for a *referral* from a teacher?

Word Study

The **Latin root -*fer*-** means "carry" or "produce."

Apply It Explain how the root *-fer-* contributes to the meanings of these words. Consult a dictionary if necessary.

ferry
fertile
transfer

ASSESS/EXTEND

Answers

Literary Analysis

1. (a) His purpose is to let people know that he is hopeful about South Africa's future. (b) He assumes that apartheid was wrong and that democracy is a good form of government. Also, Mandela believes that South Africa is a beautiful land with people who deserve freedom.
2. (a) Mandela's audience was the citizens of South Africa primarily, but also dignitaries from other countries. (b) Mandela begins by addressing "distinguished guests, comrades, and friends." (c) **Possible response:** Most citizens share his beliefs because these beliefs target justice, peace, and work "for all."
3. **Sample answer:** Though the speech was intended for South Africans, it now speaks of justice to an international audience.

Reading Skill

4. (a) **Sample answers: Past**—South Africa was oppressed by the apartheid system. **Present**—South Africa is experiencing "newborn liberty." **Future**—South Africa faces many challenges to becoming a full-fledged democracy. (b) Mandela shows that the country has already come a long way, and it will find its way to peace.

For other sample answers, see ***Graphic Organizer Transparencies,* Reading Skill Graphic Organizer A,** p. 206, and the **Additional Answers** section.

Vocabulary

Acquisition and Use

Sample answers:

1. True. A signature confers, or gives, authenticity to a document.
2. False. A pernicious, or destructive, idea would not be welcome at a team meeting.
3. False. Each party in a covenant, or sacred agreement, hopes that the other party will honor it.
4. True. A distinguished guest is someone of great honor and is often well-known.

Continued from right column

5. False. If you are intimately involved in something, you know a great deal about it.
6. True. A reconciliation between friends that have quarreled would include talking things through.

Word Study

Sample answers:

1. No, the root *-fer-* means "carry or produce," and *vociferous* means "producing loud cries." A *vociferous* person would have a loud voice and would complain loudly.
2. The root *-fer-* means "carry or produce" and *referral* means "a recommendation, usually for the work one produces." An employer might want a referral to learn whether a potential employee is a good worker.

Word Study: Apply It

Sample answers: A *ferry* is a boat that carries people a relatively short distance. If something is *fertile*, it is able to produce offspring. When you *transfer* something, you move, or carry, it to another place.

EXTEND/ASSESS

Answers

Conventions

1. Introduce the skill, using the instruction on the student page.
2. Discuss the definitions and the examples in the chart.

Think Aloud: Model the Skill

Model a way to choose the correct punctuation. Say to students:

Correct punctuation keeps my meaning clear. When listing items that come after a main clause, I should use a colon after the main clause. When connecting two independent clauses, or sentences, that focus on related ideas, I use a semicolon. When replacing words or text that I have removed or will leave out, I use ellipsis points.

PH WRITING COACH Grade 9

Students will find instruction on and practice with colons, semicolons, and ellipsis points in Chapter 23, Section 3 and Chapter 23, Section 8.

Practice A

1. A semicolon is used to connect the two related independent clauses.
2. Ellipsis points are used to show that text has been omitted from the quotation.
3. A colon is used after the main clause to introduce a list.
4. Ellipsis points are used to show time passing in a narrative.

Writing Application

Sentences should relate to the image on pp. 1196–1197 and should include the listed punctuation types.

Practice B

1. Nelson Mandela talked of the past, talked of the celebration in the past, and talked of . . .
2. Mandela spent years working for liberty; the years had brought him to this moment.
3. He wanted many things for his country: justice, peace, work, and food for all.
4. The work was long; the goal was liberty; they celebrated the achievement.

Writing Application

Sentences should relate to the image on p. 1202 and should include the listed punctuation types.

PERFORMANCE TASKS

Integrated Language Skills

There Is a Longing • Glory and Hope

Conventions: Colons, Semicolons, and Ellipsis Points

Punctuation helps a writer clarify the meaning of a sentence.

A **colon** is used mainly to list items following an independent clause. A **semicolon** is used to join independent clauses that are closely related. A semicolon is also used to separate independent clauses or items in a series that already contain several commas.

Ellipsis points (. . .) are punctuation marks that show that something has not been expressed. Ellipsis points usually indicate one of the following:

- words that have been left out of a quotation
- a series that continues beyond the items mentioned
- time passing or action occurring in a narrative

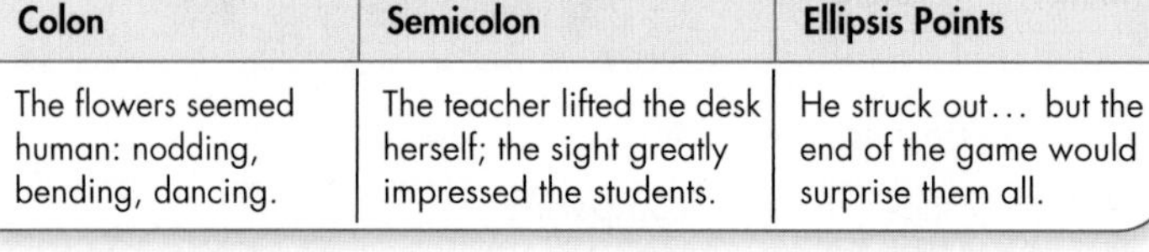

Colon	Semicolon	Ellipsis Points
The flowers seemed human: nodding, bending, dancing.	The teacher lifted the desk herself; the sight greatly impressed the students.	He struck out… but the end of the game would surprise them all.

Practice A Explain the use of the colon, semicolon, or ellipsis points in each sentence.

1. Chief Dan George was a chief; he wanted to lead his people to a better future.
2. "I am a chief," he said, "but . . . the only weapon left to me is speech."
3. Chief Dan George expected great things for his people: education, participation in government, and freedom.
4. He spoke softly . . . and quietly sat down.

Writing Application Write three sentences about the opening image of "There Is a Longing." Use a colon, semicolon, and ellipsis points in your sentences.

Practice B Copy these sentences, adding colons, semicolons, or ellipsis points wherever necessary.

1. Nelson Mandela talked of the past, talked of the celebration in the present, and talked of.
2. Mandela had spent years working for liberty the years had brought him to this moment.
3. He wanted many things for his country justice, peace, work, and food for all.
4. The work was long the goal was liberty they celebrated the achievement.

Writing Application Write three sentences about Nelson Mandela's facial and bodily expressions in the opening image of "Glory and Hope." Use a colon, semicolon, and ellipsis points in your writing.

PH WRITING COACH Further instruction and practice are available in *Prentice Hall Writing Coach.*

Extend the Lesson

Sentence Modeling

Choose the sentence given from the selection students have read:

"The long years of study will demand more determination; separation from home and family will demand endurance." ("There Is a Longing")

"Your majesties, your royal highnesses, distinguished guests, comrades and friends: Today, all of us do, by our presence here, and by our celebrations in other parts of our country and the world, confer glory and hope to newborn liberty." ("Glory and Hope")

Ask what students notice about the sentence. Elicit that the sentence contains a colon or semicolon. Then, ask what else they notice. ("There Is a Longing": The two clauses have parallel structure, using the verb *will demand* to link two pairs of ideas. "Glory and Hope": The colon is used as it would be used in a business letter greeting.)

Have students write their own sentence, matching each grammatical and stylistic feature discussed. Have volunteers read their sentences aloud to the group.

Writing

Informative Text Write a **letter** to the author of the speech you read expressing what you found most inspiring.

- List words that describe how the speech makes you feel. Next to each word, write the line or lines that evoke that emotion.
- Tell the author why you are writing and why you think the speech has a message for *all* readers.
- As you draft, use a friendly yet respectful tone, and maintain focus throughout your letter.
- Use formal business letter format. *(For an example, see page R34.)*

Grammar Application Make sure you have used colons, semicolons, and ellipsis points properly in your letter.

Writing Workshop: *Work in Progress*

Prewriting for Comparison and Contrast Review the Comparison List in your writing portfolio. Think about the two places you have listed. Next, jot down emotions you connect with each one. Then, use a Venn diagram to compare and contrast the two places. Save your Comparison work.

Speaking and Listening

Comprehension and Collaboration In a group, hold a **panel discussion** to talk about the kind of world you hope future generations will enjoy. Keep in mind the issues that the speech you read addresses. Consider these tips:

- In order to discuss the issues in greater depth with other panel members, review the speech you read and note the key points the author makes.
- Using note cards, jot down the key ideas and important details from the speech you read.
- Use your note cards to help you respond to questions and convey details that you wish to share, such as key points from the speech or memorable lines.
- During the discussion, show respect for everyone's opinions and speak in turn.

When the discussion ends, analyze the process to decide how to improve future discussions.

Common Core State Standards

L.9-10.2; W.9-10.2, W.9-10.2.b, W.9-10.2.e; SL.9-10.1.a, SL.9-10.1.c
[For the full wording of the standards, see page 1192.]

Use this prewriting activity to prepare for the **Writing Workshop** on page 1234.

www.PHLitOnline.com
- Interactive graphic organizers
- Grammar tutorial
- Interactive journals

EXTEND/ASSESS

Answers

Writing

1. Review the assignment, using the instruction on the student page.
2. To guide students in writing a letter, give them **Support for Writing,** p. 157 in ***Unit 6 Resources.***
3. To evaluate students' informative texts, adapt the Letter rubrics, pp. 236–237 in ***Professional Development Guidebook.*** Make sure that students express their response to the speaker's message while respecting the conventions of a formal letter.

Grammar Application

Have students check their drafts for correct use of colons, semicolons, and ellipsis points.

Six Traits Focus

✓	Ideas		Word Choice
✓	Organization		Sentence Fluency
✓	Voice	✓	Conventions

PH WRITING COACH Grade 9

Students will find guidance on letter writing in Chapters 10 and 12.

Writing Workshop *Work in Progress*

Have students save their Venn diagrams in their portfolios. They will use their diagrams later as they complete the Writing Workshop assignment (see pp. 1234–1241).

Speaking and Listening

1. Review the assignment, using the instruction on the student page.
2. To support students' work on the assignment, have them complete the **Support for Extend Your Learning** page (*Unit 6 Resources,* p. 158).

Teaching Resources

All *Unit 6 Resources*
L3 L4 EL **Integrated Language Skills: Grammar,** p. 156
L3 L4 EL **Support for Writing,** p. 157
L3 L4 **Support for Extend Your Learning,** p. 158
L4 **Enrichment,** pp. 139, 155

Enriched Online Student Edition
Available under After You Read for this selection:
All **Interactive Grammar Tutorial**
L3 L4 **Internet Research Activity**

Professional Development Guidebook
Rubrics for Self-Assessment: Letter, pp. 236–237

PHLit Online! All print and digital resources are available at **www.PHLitOnline.com**. Online resources accessible by students are noted on the student page.

MONITORING PROGRESS

Using the Test Practice

In this two-page Test Practice, students apply the reading skill for the second half of Unit 6 to a passage of fiction and a passage of nonfiction.

Review the skill, comparing and contrasting, then administer the test. For more guidance, consult the ***Classroom Strategies and Teaching Routines*** card, **Administering Timed Tests.**

ASSESS

Answers

Answers With Explanations

1. A—Each boy is sure he has the best idea for the school's charity fundraiser. *Incorrect answers:* B—Only Chris wants to organize a luau. C—Only Ron wants to organize a basketball game. D—Both boys come up with the same name for the event, but this happens at the end of the passage.
2. A—The passage states that Chris is a guitarist for the school's most popular band, and Ron is the captain of the basketball team. *Incorrect answers:* B—Both boys want to hold a fundraiser. C—Both boys are on the student council. D—This cannot be determined from the passage.
3. C—Both boys come up with fundraising ideas connected to their main interests. *Incorrect answers:* A—The passage does not address this issue. B—Both activities suggested for the fundraiser will require organization. D—The passage does not address this issue.
4. D—Ron says Chris's idea sounds like fun, and both boys combine their ideas into one event. *Incorrect answers:* A—This statement is true. B—same explanation as for A. C—same explanation as for A.

Test Practice: Reading

Compare and Contrast

Fiction Selection

Directions: ***Read the selection. Then, answer the questions.***

Ron and Chris both smiled as they entered the student council meeting. Each one was sure he had the best idea for the school's charity fundraiser. Chris, guitarist for the school's most popular band, spoke first. "We should have a Hawaiian-style luau! We can have food and hula dancing, and I can play Hawaiian music on my guitar. It will be great!"

Ron, the captain of the basketball team, spoke next. "That sounds like fun, but everyone knows that people in this town love basketball more than anything else. We should challenge the other school in town to a basketball game for charity."

"Maybe we can do both," Chris replied. "We can have the basketball game, and then invite people to stay afterward for the luau. We can even give a preview of the music and dancing at halftime during the game."

"Great idea! I have a perfect name for the event," said Ron, grinning. Then they both said together, "Hula Hoops for Charity!"

1. What common goal do Chris and Ron have at the beginning of the passage?

A. They both want to raise money for charity.
B. They both want to organize a luau.
C. They both want to organize a basketball game.
D. They both want the same name for the charity event.

2. In which of the following ways are Chris and Ron *different*?

A. Chris is a musician and Ron is a basketball player.
B. Chris wants to hold a charity fundraiser and Ron does not.
C. Chris is a member of the student council and Ron is not.
D. Chris cares more than Ron about the charity fundraiser.

3. Based on the details in this passage, one way that Chris and Ron are *similar* is that their—

A. schoolwork is not difficult for them.
B. plans will not require any organization.
C. interests influence their fundraising ideas.
D. popularity is very important to them.

4. Which of the following statements about Chris and Ron's original ideas is *not* true?

A. Chris wants to organize a luau.
B. Ron wants to organize a basketball game.
C. Both boys think that a luau would be fun.
D. Both boys dislike each other's ideas.

Writing for Assessment

In a paragraph, explain why you think Chris and Ron started out with different ideas but were able to agree in the end. Support your answer with details from the passage.

Writing for Assessment

Students should note that each boy's original idea is based on his specific interest; they may say that the boys combined the ideas so that each would be able to realize his vision for the fundraiser.

Strategies for Test Taking

Tell students to pay close attention to italicized words in questions. These words are usually important hints that help readers find the correct answer choice. For example, in question 2, students are asked how Chris and Ron are *different.* Ask students what they have to do in such a question: compare the boys, contrast the boys, find a cause-and-effect relationship, or something else? (Readers must contrast the boys.) Follow a similar exercise with questions 3 and 4.

Nonfiction Selection

Directions: *Read the selection. Then, answer the questions.*

In 1796, the United States faced a challenge. George Washington had been the clear choice to be the first president of the young nation. Now, after two terms in office, the popular president was retiring. America had to elect a new president. The two leading candidates were Thomas Jefferson and John Adams. Jefferson was tall, thin, and soft-spoken. Adams was short and stocky, and loved to argue. The two men had worked closely together in the cause for American independence. They had formed a strong friendship, but it had been strained in recent years by political differences. Adams was from the North and favored industry and a strong central government. Jefferson was from the South and favored farming and strong state governments. The vote between the two candidates was close, but Adams was elected president. According to the Constitution at that time, Jefferson—who received the second highest number of votes—was to be made vice president. Although Adams and Jefferson had different visions for the country, they knew they would have to put aside their differences and work together for the good of the nation they had helped to found.

1. Which of the following statements about Adams and Jefferson is *true*?

A. They had the same views on government.
B. They wanted America to be successful.
C. They were both tall.
D. They were both from the North.

2. Which detail conveys Adams's and Jefferson's different visions for the United States?

A. Adams craved power and Jefferson did not.
B. Jefferson wanted to carry out Washington's vision; Adams did not.
C. Adams favored strong central government; Jefferson favored state government.
D. Adams believed in a strong military; Jefferson supported farming.

3. Why was it especially important for the two men to look beyond their differences?

A. Both men ran for president.
B. The nation had just been created.
C. Both men were friends with Washington.
D. Jefferson had to be Adams's vice president.

4. Which statement *contrasts* the two men?

A. Adams favored industry, while Jefferson favored farming.
B. Both were for strong central government.
C. Jefferson and Adams worked together for American independence.
D. Adams and Jefferson served as president and vice president, respectively.

Writing for Assessment

Connecting Across Texts
How is the relationship between Adams and Jefferson similar to the relationship between Chris and Ron? Which one is more complex? Write an essay in which you explain your answer using details from both passages.

- Online practice
- Instant feedback

Differentiated Instruction for Universal Access

Strategy for Special-Needs Students
After students have read the passage, encourage them to use a chart to show the differences between Adams and Jefferson. They can head the left-hand part of the chart *John Adams* and the right-hand side *Thomas Jefferson.* Have them use the text to match each description on the left with the contrasting description on the right. The beginning of the chart might look like this:

John Adams	Thomas Jefferson
short, stocky	

Ask students what description of Jefferson's appearance they should write in the same row as this description of Adams's appearance. (Students should say "tall, thin.") Have them fill in more details about the two men, covering such elements as their manners with other people, the sections of the country they were from, their philosophical positions, and their eventual offices.

ASSESS

Answers

Answers With Explanations

1. **B**—The final sentence says the two men put aside their differences for the good of the nation. *Incorrect answers:* A—The passage clearly says they had political differences. C—The passage states that Adams was short. D—The passage states that Jefferson was from the South.
2. **C**—The passage gives this information about their differences. *Incorrect answers:* A—The passage does not address the issue of the desire for power. B—The passage does not compare their ideas with Washington's. D—The passage does not give Adams's ideas on the military.
3. **D**—The men would have to work together as president and vice president. *Incorrect answers:* A—This would not require that the men look beyond their differences. B—same explanation as for A. C—The passage does not describe their relationship with Washington, nor would this be an important factor.
4. **A**—This statement shows a difference between the two men and uses the signal word *while.* *Incorrect answers:* B –This claims, falsely, that the two men were similar. C—This statement reveals an activity that they shared, not a difference between them. D—This statement describes the offices they held but does not contrast their characters.

Writing for Assessment

Connecting Across Texts
Students should note that both Chris and Ron are leaders in their school and have strong ideas about the fundraiser. Adams and Jefferson were both leaders of political parties and had strong ideas about how the country should be run. The relationship between Adams and Jefferson is more complex because it is based on philosophical and geographic differences as well as on common core beliefs.

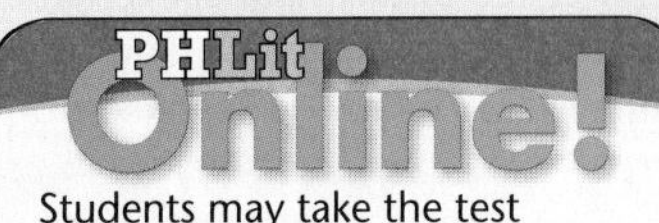

Students may take the test in interactive format with instant feedback online at **www.PHLitOnline.com.**

Common Core State Standards

- **Reading Informational Text 6**
- **Writing 2.b**
- **Language 4.b, c**

Reading Skill

1. Introduce the skill, using the instruction on the student page.
2. Tell students that they will evaluate two primary sources, a news article and an online posting.

Think Aloud: Model the Skill

Model the skill of analyzing primary sources. Say to students:

> A primary source explains a personal experience. For example, if I read "My heart swelled with pride as the band played the national anthem," I know the author was in the scene. To analyze the source, I might think about the occasion for which the band played. I continue reading to see if these details are included.

Multidraft Reading

Have students follow a multidraft reading protocol.

- **First reading**—Have students read to identify key ideas and details.
- **Second reading**—Have students read to identify the structure of the text.
- **Third reading**—Have students read to integrate knowledge and ideas by connecting the text to the world, their own experiences, and other texts.

Content-Area Vocabulary

1. Have students say each word.
2. Next, use each word in a sentence that defines it.
3. Finally, repeat your definitional sentence or a similar sentence with the word missing and have the class "fill in the blank" chorally.

Reading for Information

Analyzing Expository Texts

News Article

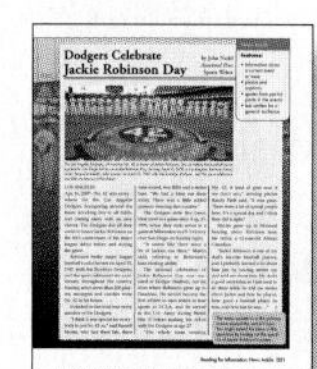
Dodgers Celebrate Jackie Robinson Day

Online Posting

The Academy of American Poets
Emily Dickinson Poetfans: Sharyn Moore and her students

Reading Skill: Analyze Primary Sources

A **primary source** is a firsthand account of events or experiences. Unlike a secondary source, in which a person describes events from an outside perspective, a primary source presents information from the perspective of someone with immediate knowledge of the events. The writer's beliefs and attitudes—his or her point of view—will usually inform the ideas, emotions, and reactions he or she describes.

Use these questions to help you **analyze** each author's point of view or perspective and extend the ideas they present:

Questions for Analyzing Primary Sources

- How was the writer or speaker involved in the events he or she describes?
- Is the account biased or neutral?
- What is the writer or speaker's tone, or attitude, toward the topic?
- What details are included, and what details may have been left out?
- What additional information about this topic might be available from other sources?

Content-Area Vocabulary

These words appear in the selections that follow. You may also encounter them in other content-area texts.

- **debut** (dā byo͞o) *n.* first appearance before the public as a performer or player
- **pedagogical** (ped´ ə goj´ ə kəl, ped´ ə gō´ jə kəl) *adj.* relating to teaching or educational methods
- **contemporary** (kən tem´ pə rer´ ē) *adj.* belonging to or living in the same period of time

Common Core State Standards

Reading Informational Text
6. Determine an author's point of view or purpose in a text and analyze how an author uses rhetoric to advance that point of view or purpose.

Writing
2.b. Develop the topic with well-chosen, relevant, and sufficient facts, extended definitions, concrete details, quotations, or other information and examples appropriate to the audience's knowledge of the topic. *(Timed Writing)*

Language
4.b. Identify and correctly use patterns of word changes that indicate different meanings or parts of speech.
4.c. Consult general and specialized reference materials, both print and digital, to find the pronunciation of a word or determine or clarify its precise meaning, its part of speech, or its etymology.

Do heroes have responsibilities?

Remind students that famous people may be heroes to people they have never met.

Differentiated Instruction for Universal Access

Reading Support
Give students reading support with the appropriate version of the ***Reader's Notebooks:***

L2 L3 *Reader's Notebook*

L1 *Reader's Notebook: Adapted Version*

EL *Reader's Notebook: English Learner's Version*

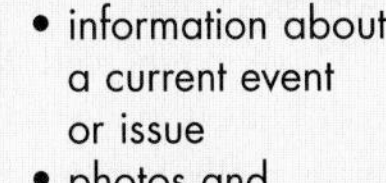

News Article

Features:

- information about a current event or issue
- photos and captions
- quotes from participants in the events
- text written for a general audience

Dodgers Celebrate Jackie Robinson Day

by John Nadel
Associated Press
Sports Writer

The Los Angeles Dodgers, all wearing No. 42 in honor of Jackie Robinson, line up before the baseball game against the San Diego Padres on Jackie Robinson Day, Sunday, April 15, 2007, in Los Angeles. Robinson broke major league baseball's color barrier on April 15, 1947, with the Brooklyn Dodgers, and the sport celebrated the 60th anniversary of his debut.

LOS ANGELES

Apr. 16, 2007—No. 42 was everywhere for the Los Angeles Dodgers. Scampering around the bases, knocking hits to all fields, and coming away with an easy victory. The Dodgers did all they could to honor Jackie Robinson on the 60th anniversary of his major league debut before and during the game.

Robinson broke major league baseball's color barrier on April 15, 1947, with the Brooklyn Dodgers, and the sport celebrated the anniversary throughout the country Sunday, when more than 200 players, managers and coaches wore No. 42 in his honor.

Included in that total was every member of the Dodgers.

"I think it was special for everybody to put No. 42 on," said Russell Martin, who had three hits, three runs scored, two RBIs and a stolen base. "We had a blast out there today. There was a little added pressure wearing that number."

The Dodgers stole five bases, their most in a game since Aug. 23, 1999, when they stole seven in a game at Milwaukee in a 9–3 victory over San Diego on Sunday night.

"It seems like there were a lot of Jackies out there," Martin said, referring to Robinson's base-stealing ability.

The national celebration of Jackie Robinson Day was centered at Dodger Stadium, not far from where Robinson grew up in Pasadena. He would become the first athlete to earn letters in four sports at UCLA, and he served in the U.S. Army during World War II before making his **debut** with the Dodgers at age 27.

"The whole team wearing No. 42, it kind of goes sour if we don't win," winning pitcher Randy Wolf said. "It was great. There were a lot of special people here. It's a special day and I think they did it right."

Martin grew up in Montreal hearing about Robinson from his father, a 62-year-old African Canadian.

"Jackie Robinson is one of my dad's favorite baseball players, and I probably learned a lot about him just by hearing stories my dad told me about him. My dad's a good storyteller, so I just used to sit there while he told me stories about Jackie and how he played, how good a baseball player he was, and how fast he was...."

The many quotations in this primary source support the author's topic. You might extend the ideas in this quotation by finding out the specifics of Jackie Robinson's career.

TEACH

About News Articles

1. Have students read the features of News Articles shown in the box on page 1211.
2. **Ask** students to name news articles they have recently read.

   Possible response: Students may say they have read an article about a musical concert or a new technology product.
3. Remind students that news articles are sources of information for the general public. Discuss how news articles may be found in print or displayed in electronic form on the Internet.

Analyze Primary Sources

1. Have students read the news article. **Ask** them to tell what the article is about.

   Answer: The article is about a baseball game celebrating the 60-year anniversary of Jackie Robinson's Major League baseball debut.
2. Point out that the author of the text uses quotations from players who were present that day. **Ask:** How do the quotations help the reader understand the event?

   Possible response: The quotations help explain how the players feel about Jackie Robinson and how devoted they are to honoring him. The quotations give the article authenticity.
3. **Ask:** What details are included in the news article that portray the events of the day?

   Possible response: The article includes a photo of all the players wearing number 42, Robinson's number. It tells how many bases were stolen in the game, as Robinson was known for base-stealing. It includes personal stories about how Jackie Robinson affected some of the players.

Fluency

For students who are struggling to read the text, encourage improved fluency by using the technique of echo reading. Divide students into small groups. Read the passage aloud to students fluently and with expression. Have students track the words in the article while you read. Then have volunteers read the passage back. Have all students in the group take turns reading at least one paragraph aloud.

Analyze Primary Sources

1. **Ask:** Why do you think the author includes the names and details about famous visitors at the ballgame?

   Possible response: Telling which famous people were at the event conveys its importance.

2. **Ask** students whether they can determine the author's attitude toward Mrs. Robinson from reading the article.

   Possible response: Yes, the author's attitude toward Mrs. Robinson is respectful. He gives details about the scholarship program she runs, along with a quotation by her.

3. **Ask:** What other source could you use to find out more about the celebration of the 60th anniversary of Jackie Robinson's debut?

   Possible response: There may have been television coverage of the event with videos created to commemorate the occasion. There may be photographs and eyewitness accounts published in sports magazines.

Before the game, commissioner Bud Selig called Robinson an American hero.

"I've often said that baseball's most powerful moment in its really terrific history was Jackie Robinson's coming into baseball," Selig said. "It's an incredible story not just for baseball, but for society."

This primary source includes facts, statistics, and detailed information.

Hank Aaron and Frank Robinson threw out ceremonial first pitches, and fellow Hall of Famers Joe Morgan and Dave Winfield were on hand, joined by actors Courtney B. Vance and Marlon Wayans. Academy Award winner Jennifer Hudson sang "The Star-Spangled Banner."

Adding a personal touch were Robinson's widow, Rachel, and two Dodgers who knew him. Broadcaster Vin Scully paid tribute to Rachel Robinson, and Don Newcombe, Robinson's former teammate and a longtime Dodgers executive, looked on.

San Diego's Mike Cameron, who also wore No. 42, said this was a day he'd never forget.

"It was a pretty special moment to have all of the household names here, all of the Hall of Famers, and to get a chance to go out and play in probably one of the biggest games that I'll play in this year besides going to the playoffs," he said.

Padres pitcher Chris Young (1-1), making his first start since signing a four-year, $14.5 million contract, allowed five runs in two-plus innings, and it would have been worse had Kevin Cameron not worked out of a bases-loaded, no-out jam in the third.

"I was terrible," Young said. "I just never found my rhythm and never found my groove. I put the guys in a hole early in the game and it was just too much to overcome."

Young wrote about Robinson for his 2002 Princeton thesis, and said that in doing the work, he learned a tremendous respect and appreciation for the former Dodgers' star.

"I can't imagine, having to go through that, the courage it took, the discipline, and just how successful he was," said Young, a 27-year-old right-hander from Dallas. "I mean, he wasn't just successful integrating the game. He was a great baseball player. He's a Hall of Fame baseball player. He wouldn't allow himself to fail, and that's tremendous."

Selig presented Mrs. Robinson with the Commissioner's Historic Achievement Award for her work with the Jackie Robinson Foundation, formed in 1973 to raise scholarship money for qualified minorities. Robinson died in October 1972 at age 53.

Rachel Robinson, Jackie's widow, works with the Jackie Robinson Foundation. You might extend the ideas presented here by visiting the Jackie Robinson Foundation Web site.

"She's made an enormous impact on our sport," Selig said. "We are an institution with enormous social responsibilities. She keeps us focused on that."

Robinson retired following the 1956 season after the Dodgers traded him to the rival Giants and was elected to the Hall of Fame in 1962.

His impact has been lasting. Mrs. Robinson said 1,100 scholarship students have graduated from college and 266 are presently in school.

"We needed to find a way to hold onto him," Mrs. Robinson said of her late husband. "Jack's legacy is all over the place."

Vocabulary Development

CCSS Language 6

Vocabulary for Sports: Baseball

Point out that news articles often use vocabulary that is specific to a particular sport, in this case, baseball. Guide students to understand the meaning of the following sports- and baseball-related words:

commissioner: an official chosen by a sports club to perform certain duties

ceremonial: formal, having to do with a ceremony

Hall of Famers: people who have been inducted into the Hall of Fame

right-hander: a baseball pitcher who throws with the right hand

legacy: something handed down from the past

The Academy of American Poets

Emily Dickinson Poetfans: Sharyn Moore and her students

Online Posting

Features:

- the personal experiences of the author
- information about events presented from the perspective of the author
- informal text written for an audience with a specific interest

The author gives a first-hand account of her experiences as a teacher, indicating that this text is a primary source.

Finding poetry and a poet for college-bound international students is a **pedagogical** puzzle. Do I want someone funny, someone simple? Do I want symbolism, metaphor, rhythm, or clarity? Do I need someone **contemporary**; someone who will relate to these young adults from Japan, Brazil, Italy, or Saudi Arabia?

Emily Dickinson. Her verses are short; use symbolism; present idioms and vocabulary that can be guessed in context; set an obtainable challenge to meaning and contemporary application; and, surprisingly enough, are accessible to our multi-national student body.

For an elective course entitled "Here's Hollywood," ("Fame is a fickle food / Upon a shifting plate…") idiom, metaphor and new vocabulary lead to discussion, contemporary analogies and the realization, "I can understand poetry, in English!"

About Primary Source

1. Have students read the features of Primary Sources in the box on page 1213.
2. Point out that a primary source is a first-person account by an author. **Ask:** What other primary sources have you read or are you familiar with?

   Possible response: Students may say they have read published diaries, such as *The Diary of Anne Frank.*
3. Point out that anyone can write a primary source. **Ask** students what topics they would write primary sources about.

   Possible response: Students may say they would write about their opinions on school uniforms or the latest hit music.

Analyze Primary Sources

1. Have students read the primary source article.
2. Point out that the author begins by describing a challenge from her own professional experience. **Ask:** Why is a personal memory an effective start to the essay?

   Possible response: The discussion of the qualities of Emily Dickinson's poetry becomes less abstract because they are related to a problem the writer needs to solve.
3. Remind students that primary sources often reveal a writer's perspective on events—his or her thoughts about and reactions to events. **Ask:** What does the essay reveal so far about the writer's perspective on education?

   Possible response: The writer feels it is important to provide international students with readings to which they can relate. She also wants readings that provide opportunities to learn new words and that promote discussion. Finally, she thinks it is important to give English learners poems that they can understand more or less easily, to ensure that students build confidence.

Differentiated Instruction for Universal Access

Culturally Responsive Instruction

Culture Connection Encourage students to draw from their own culture to write a primary source essay about a favorite artist or poem. Encourage students to express themselves in the most comfortable language of their own culture. Have them begin with a personal memory of their subject, such as when they first learned about the person or work. Essays should include some details about their favorite pieces by the artist or poet, quotations or photographs, and a personal opinion statement about why the art or poetry is relevant to their own life and culture. Have student volunteers share their essays with the class, reading them aloud in their language or dialect of their own culture.

Analyze Primary Sources

1. Point out to students that in the first paragraph on this page, the writer makes a connection between teaching Emily Dickinson and teaching world events. **Ask** students: What lesson about world politics does she find in Emily Dickinson's poetry? Have them explain their answers.

   Possible response: The writer gives students a magazine article on war and hopes that the article will lead them to "a commitment . . . to practice peace and hold hope." She ties this commitment to a line of Dickinson's poetry.

2. **Ask:** What does this primary source reveal about the writer's view of contemporary events?

   Possible response: She believes in making a stand for peace and probably opposes war.

Analyzing this section reveals that the author's tone is one of respect for Dickinson's poetry and for her students' ability to find meaning in it.

An advanced level reading of a news magazine article on war and its victims ("Hope is the thing with feathers / That perches in the soul…") leads to a commitment on the part of the students to practice peace and hold hope….

Miss Dickinson's poetry has been used for dictation, vocabulary, grammar analysis, discussion, debate, journal entries, essays, film tie-ins, and, most of all, has made amazing contributions to cross-cultural understanding and global connections. Take an American woman of letters, apply her verse to issues in current culture, and global youth begin to talk about fame, hope, and death. What educator could help but be an ardent fan?

Sharyn Moore
Santa Monica, California

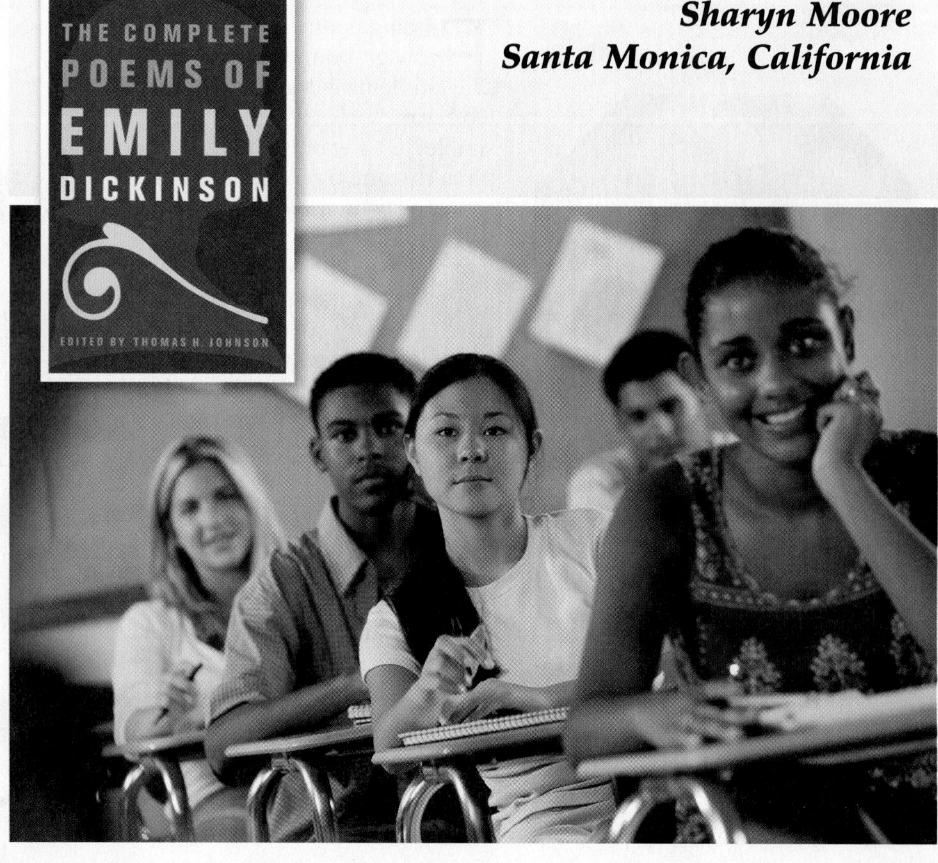

Vocabulary Development

CCSS Language 6

Vocabulary for Teaching

Tell students that this essay uses terms that are specific to the writer's profession—teaching. Guide them to understand the meaning of the following words that are used in the essay:

pedagogical: having to do with the theory or technique of teaching

elective: for the individual's choice; referring to classes that are not required

dictation: an exercise in which the teacher reads a passage in a given language aloud for students learning the language to copy down

After You Read | News Article • Online Posting

Comparing Expository Texts

1. **Key Ideas and Details** **(a) Analyze primary sources** by describing how the authors of the article and the posting were involved in the events they describe. **(b)** What underlying attitudes and values, or points of view, does each author bring to the writing? **(c)** Which specific words and phrases best reflect the authors' points of view toward their subjects? Explain your choices.

Content-Area Vocabulary

2. **(a)** Consider the words *pedagogic* and *pedagogical*. Explain how a change in suffix alters the meaning and part of speech of the base word *pedagogy*. If necessary, consult a dictionary for help. **(b)** Use each word in a sentence that shows its meaning.

Timed Writing

Explanatory Text: Expository Essay

Format
The prompt directs you to write an expository essay. Therefore, your writing should present information or discuss ideas.

Using information from the news article, write an expository essay in which you discuss the significance of Jackie Robinson's contributions to baseball and to the lives of his fans. Support your ideas with details and examples from the text. (40 minutes)

Academic Vocabulary
When you *discuss* a subject in an essay, you write about various aspects of that subject in detail.

5-Minute Planner

Complete these steps before you begin to write:

1. Read the prompt carefully and completely.
2. Develop the topic by reviewing the news article to find details and make notes about Jackie Robinson's accomplishments and their impact on baseball and on people's lives. Organize your supporting details cohesively, using transitions to link the facts and examples you choose to include.
   TIP Look for firsthand testimonies in which people describe how Jackie Robinson's achievements affected them personally.
3. Extend ideas presented in the news article by considering how Jackie Robinson's accomplishments might have affected the lives of people beyond those mentioned in the news article. Provide a concluding statement that supports the ideas in your essay. Make a quick list of your ideas.
4. Use your notes and your list to create a rough outline. Then, use your outline to help you organize and write your essay.

ASSESS/EXTEND

Answers

Comparing Expository Texts

1. (a) **Possible response:** The author of the news article attended the celebration as a reporter. He was not an invitee or a player on the team. The author of the primary source teaches a class in which she uses Dickinson's poetry for her students. (b) **Possible response:** As a sports writer, John Nadel has limited involvement in the stories he covers. His writing tone is unbiased and factual. Sharyn Moore has only her own interpretation of the poet. This affects the tone of Moore's writing through the use of quotations and opinion statements about the power of the poetry in class. (c) Responses will vary but should convey an understanding of the texts.
2. (a) *Pedagogy* is the science or art of teaching. *Pedagogic* is an adjective meaning "of or relating to a teacher"; *pedagogical* is an adjective also meaning "of or relating to a teacher"; and a *pedagogue* is a noun meaning "a teacher, especially one that is dull or formal." (b) My boss's leadership style is very *pedagogic*; The presentation was too *pedagogical* for my taste; The professor is a *pedagogue* whose lessons focus too much on reading directly from a textbook.

Timed Writing

1. Before students complete the activity, guide them in identifying and analyzing key words and phrases in the prompt, highlighted on the student page.
2. Work with students to draw up guidelines for their expository essays based on the key words:
   - **Focus** The essay should clearly explain how Jackie Robinson contributed to baseball and to the lives of his fans.
   - **Organization** The essay should introduce the explanation and then provide examples from the text.
   - **Support** The essay should provide details and information from the text to support the explanation.
   - **Style** The audience is not specified, so a formal style is appropriate.
3. Have students use the 5-Minute Planner to structure their time.
4. Allow students 40 minutes to complete the assignment. Evaluate their work using the guidelines they have developed.

PRETEACH

Common Core State Standards

- Reading Literature 7, 9
- Writing 2, 2.a

❶ Literary Analysis

Comparing Tall Tale and Myth

1. Introduce the skill, using the instruction on the student page.
2. Give students a copy of **Comparing Tall Tales and Myths Graphic Organizer B,** ***Graphic Organizer Transparencies,*** p. 209, to complete as they read.

Think Aloud: Model the Skill

Model a way of understanding tall tales and myths. Say to students:

> We often make statements that belong in tall tales. For example, the statement "She reads 1000 books a day" is hyperbole. Real humans can't read 1000 books a day, but we enjoy the image of this amazing feat. We also create new myths, such as stories of soldiers who win impossible battles against the odds. When I read tall tales and myths, I look for hyperbole and amazing heroes.

Comparing Literary Works

Pecos Bill: The Cyclone • Perseus

❶ Comparing Tall Tale and Myth

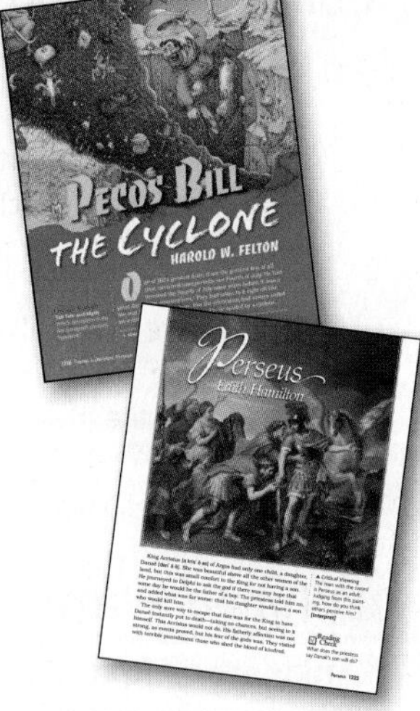

A **tall tale** is a type of folk tale that is characterized by *hyperbole*, or overstatement. Tall tales usually contain larger-than-life heroes, far-fetched situations, amazing feats, and a great deal of humor. Tall tales are a kind of legend, a traditional story about the past that is often based on historical fact. Many tall tales come from the American frontier and reflect the ideas of that period. The purpose of a tall tale is to entertain readers and audiences.

A **myth** is an ancient story that is intended to explain the actions of gods or human heroes, the reasons for certain traditions, or the causes of natural features and events. Every culture has its own collection of myths, or mythology. Originally religious in nature, myths often express the central values of the people who created them.

In general, tall tales describe how humans make things happen on their own, while myths tell how gods shape human life. These qualities are reflected in the types of **heroes** featured in the two forms. Mythic heroes have the following attributes:

- Divine parents and supernatural aid
- Special knowledge or weapons
- Ability to achieve impossible tasks

By contrast, the heroes in tall tales are outsized, but nevertheless human. They are able to perform amazing feats because of their great size, strength, cleverness, or sheer force of will.

Cultural Values Both forms are deeply rooted in the oral tradition and express the values of the cultures in which they developed. Modern authors Harold W. Felton and Edith Hamilton honor these origins as they draw upon source material and make it their own. "Pecos Bill and the Cyclone" is told in the energetic American tall-tale tradition, full of bold, unexplained impossibility. "Perseus" is told in the classic tradition of the Greek myths. As you read, use a chart like the one shown to compare and contrast the heroes in these selections.

	Human or partly divine?	Performs amazing feats?	Receives divine aid?	Story has humor and exaggeration?
Pecos Bill				
Perseus				

Common Core State Standards

Reading Literature

7. Analyze the representation of a subject or a key scene in two different artistic mediums.

9. Analyze how an author draws on and transforms source material in a specific work.

Writing

2. Write informative/explanatory texts to examine and convey complex ideas, concepts, and information clearly and accurately.

2.a. Introduce a topic; organize complex ideas, concepts, and information to make important connections and distinctions.

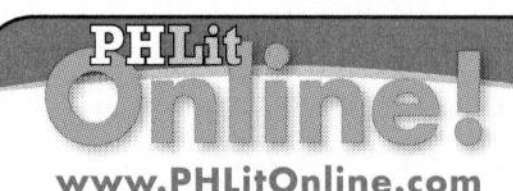

www.PHLitOnline.com

- Vocabulary flashcards
- Interactive journals
- More about the authors
- Selection audio
- Interactive graphic organizers

Vocabulary Development

Vocabulary Knowledge Rating

Create a **Vocabulary Knowledge Rating Chart (Professional Development Guidebook,** p. 33) featuring the words glossed in the selections:

usurped (p. 1221) *mortified* (p. 1227)
skeptics (p. 1223) *revelry* (p. 1229)

Give students a copy of the chart, and read the words aloud. Have students mark their rating of each in the Before You Read column.

To gauge how much instruction to provide, tally the students who think they know each word. Explain that the words are defined in the margin at the point where they appear in the selection. Urge students to be alert to these words as they read the selections. They will rate their knowledge again when they finish.

Vocabulary Central, featuring tools, activities, and songs for studying vocabulary, is available at **www.PHLitOnline.com.**

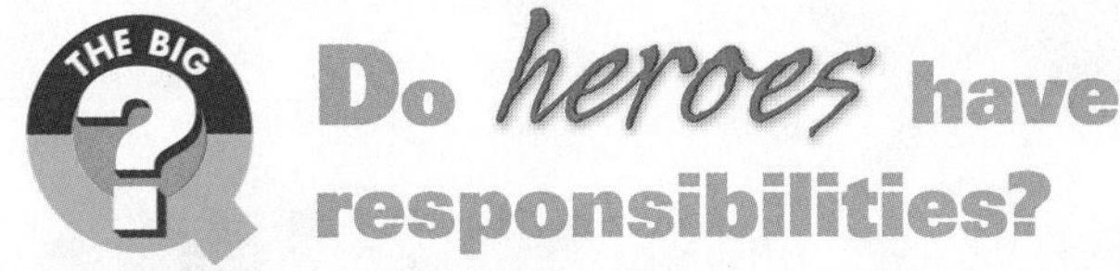

❷ Writing About the Big Question

Both these selections present larger-than-life heroes who must face certain danger. Use this sentence starter to develop your ideas about the Big Question.

The level of danger in a situation is/is not important when assessing heroism because ________

For someone to be heroic, his or her intentions must be ________.

Meet the Authors

Harold W. Felton (1902–1991)

Author of "Pecos Bill: The Cyclone"

Harold William Felton practiced law and worked for the Internal Revenue Service, but over the years, he became increasingly interested in the legends and folklore of the United States.

Collector and Reteller Felton published collections of stories about folk heroes and the cowboys of the West. His book *Legends of Paul Bunyan* contains more than one hundred folk tales about the great logger.

Edith Hamilton (1867–1963)

Author of "Perseus"

Edith Hamilton was a groundbreaking educator who helped found the Bryn Mawr School in Baltimore, the first college preparatory school for women. She taught a generation of young women not to limit their goals simply because they were not men.

Modern Woman, Ancient Tales After leaving Bryn Mawr, Hamilton began writing articles about ancient Greece, which she later turned into a book entitled *The Greek Way* (1930). Her other books include *The Roman Way* (1932) and *Mythology* (1942), which are both beautifully crafted retellings of the Greek myths.

Daily Bellringer

For each class during which you will teach this selection, have students complete one of the five Sentence Combining activities for Week 36 in the ***Daily Bellringer Activities*** booklet.

❷ Writing About the Big Question

1. Review the assignment with the class.
2. Review students' ideas about heroes and their qualities.
3. Have students complete the sentence starters. Review responses as a class. (**Possible response:** The level of danger in a situation is important when assessing heroism because it measures the hero's bravery. For someone to be heroic, her intentions must be heroic.)
4. Remind students that their answers will help them think about the Big Question, "Do heroes have responsibilities?"

Concept Connector

Tell students that they will return to their sentence starters after they read.

Multidraft Reading

To assist struggling readers and to deepen reading for all, apply multidraft reading protocols. For each reading, have students set the purpose indicated:

- **First reading**—identifying key ideas and details and answering any Reading Checks.
- **Second reading**—analyzing craft and structure and responding to the side-column prompts.
- **Third reading**—integrating knowledge and ideas, connecting to other texts and the world, and answering the end-of-selection questions.

For more guidance, see the ***Classroom Strategies and Teaching Routines*** card on multidraft reading.

For more about the authors and practice with the selection vocabulary, go online at **www.PHLitOnline.com.**

Teaching Resources

- All *Unit 6 Resources,* pp. 166–182
- All *Graphic Organizer Transparencies,* pp. 208–211
- All *Professional Development Guidebook,* pp. 33, 36–38, 42
- All **Enriched Online Student Edition**
- All *Common Core Companion,* pp. 62–63, 69–70, 190–201

PHLit Online! All resources, including print and video, are available at **www.PHLitOnline.com.**

❶ Background

Pecos Bill Pecos Bill is a fictional character invented in 1923 by Edward O'Reilly, a magazine writer. O'Reilly describes Bill as a cowboy, train robber, and western fighter who traveled the southwest.

❷ Activating Prior Knowledge

1. Prepare an **Anticipation Guide** (*Professional Development Guidebook*, pp. 36–38) with the following statements:
   - Mythological heroes are not at all like modern-day heroes.
   - Women can be heroes too.
   - Courage is the most important quality of a hero.
   - No one tells tall tales.
2. Give students a copy of the prepared **Anticipation Guide** and have students mark their responses in the Me column. Have students discuss the statements in pairs or groups and mark the Guides again in the group column.
3. For further guidance, use the ***Classroom Strategies and Teaching Rountines*** card: **Using an Anticipation Guide.**

Concept Connector →

Students will return to the **Anticipation Guide** after completing "Pecos Bill: The Cyclone."

❸ About the Selection

"Pecos Bill: The Cyclone" is a tall tale about a fictional cowboy who tames an angry cyclone. Bill rides the cyclone like a bucking bronco (using a common Western skill) until it loses its strength. Bill's encounter with the cyclone creates some of the West's natural wonders, such as the Grand Canyon and Death Valley.

❹ Tall Tale and Myth

Read the bracketed passage aloud. **Ask** the Literary Analysis question.

Answer: The hyperboles in this passage include the "greatest" feat of all time, Bill "invented" the Fourth of July, and a cyclone "always" ended the day.

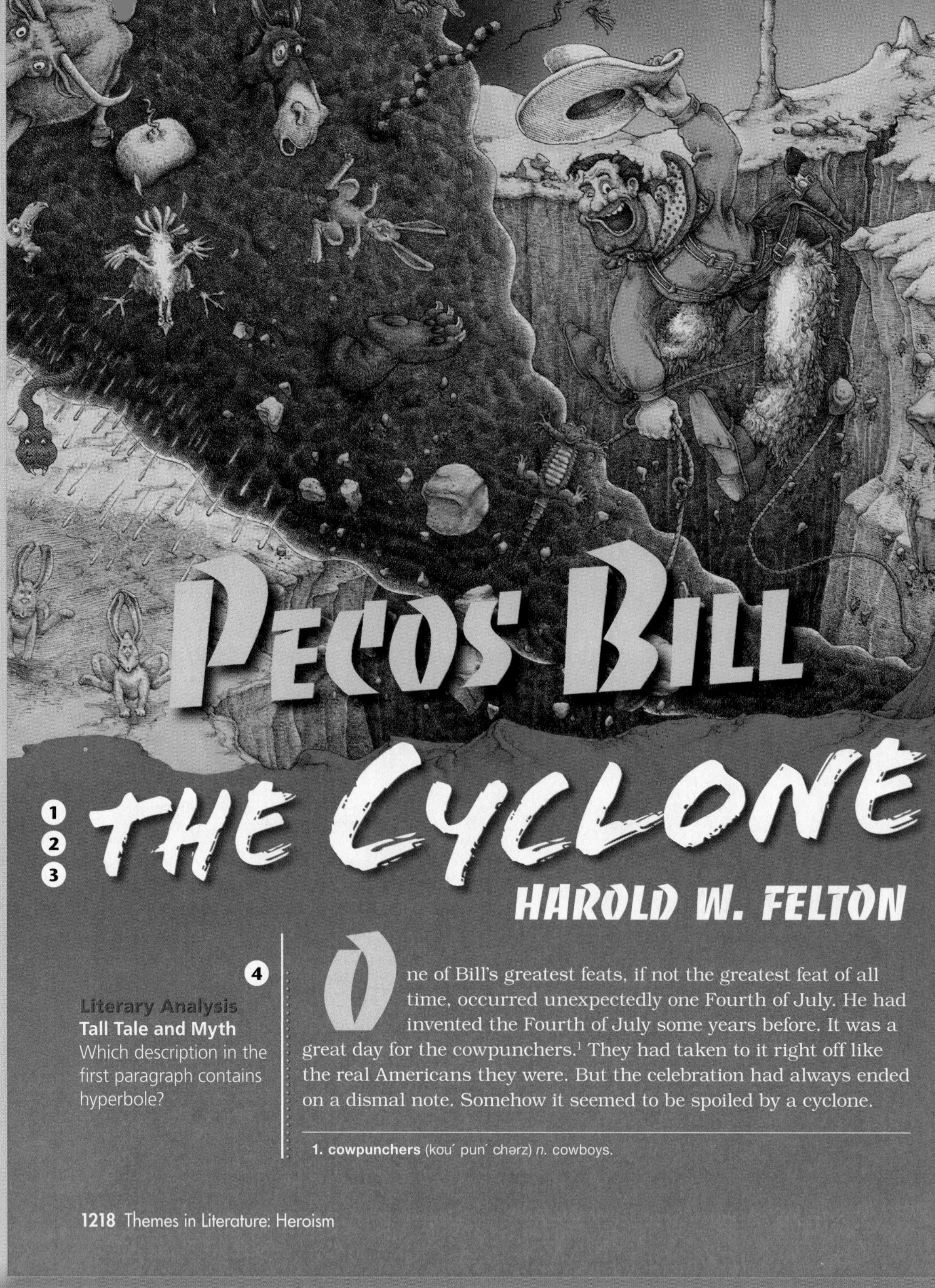

1 2 3

Pecos Bill The Cyclone

Harold W. Felton

4

Literary Analysis
Tall Tale and Myth
Which description in the first paragraph contains hyperbole?

One of Bill's greatest feats, if not the greatest feat of all time, occurred unexpectedly one Fourth of July. He had invented the Fourth of July some years before. It was a great day for the cowpunchers.[1] They had taken to it right off like the real Americans they were. But the celebration had always ended on a dismal note. Somehow it seemed to be spoiled by a cyclone.

1. **cowpunchers** (kou′ pun′ chərz) *n.* cowboys.

1218 Themes in Literature: Heroism

Think Aloud

Persuasive Speech

Draw students' attention to the first paragraph of the story. Remind them that writers use a character's actions and words, narrative description, and the reactions of other characters to create characterizations. Then use the following "think aloud" to model the process of analyzing character and characterization (introduced on p. 125). Say to students:

> As I read the story, I will look at how the writer portrays the title character of Pecos Bill. The first sentence implies that Bill achieved many great feats. Then I read that Bill "invented" the Fourth of July. This action suggests he has amazing abilities. It also seems that the people around him really like him—the "cowpunchers" really enjoyed the holiday that he created.
>
> This first paragraph uses a narrative description of Pecos Bill, description of Bill's actions, and the reactions of other characters. As I read on, I will look for other techniques the writer uses to characterize Pecos Bill, such as Bill's dialogue.

Bill had never minded the cyclone much. The truth is he rather liked it. But the other celebrants ran into caves for safety. He invented cyclone cellars for them. He even named the cellars. He called them "'fraid holes." Pecos wouldn't even say the word "afraid." The cyclone was something like he was. It was big and strong too. He always stood by musing pleasantly as he watched it.

The cyclone caused Bill some trouble, though. Usually it would destroy a few hundred miles of fence by blowing the postholes away. But it wasn't much trouble for him to fix it. All he had to do was to go and get the postholes and then take them back and put the fence posts in them. The holes were rarely ever blown more than twenty or thirty miles.

In one respect Bill even welcomed the cyclone, for it blew so hard it blew the earth away from his wells. The first time this happened, he thought the wells would be a total loss. There they were, sticking up several hundred feet out of the ground. As wells they were useless. But he found he could cut them up into lengths and sell them for postholes to farmers in Iowa and Nebraska. It was very profitable, especially after he invented a special posthole saw to cut them with. He didn't use that type of posthole himself. He got the prairie dogs to dig his for him. He simply caught a few gross[2] of prairie dogs and set them down at proper intervals. The prairie dog would dig a hole. Then Bill would put a post in it. The prairie dog would get disgusted and go down the row ahead of the others and dig another hole. Bill fenced all of Texas and parts of New Mexico and Arizona in this manner. He took a few contracts and fenced most of the Southern Pacific right of way too. That's the reason it is so crooked. He had trouble getting the prairie dogs to run a straight fence.

6 As for his wells, the badgers dug them. The system was the same as with the prairie dogs. The labor was cheap so it didn't make much difference if the cyclone did spoil some of the wells. The badgers were digging all of the time anyway. They didn't seem to care whether they dug wells or just badger holes.

One year he tried shipping the prairie dog holes up north, too, for postholes. It was not successful. They didn't keep in storage and they couldn't stand the handling in shipping. After they were installed they seemed to wear out quickly. Bill always thought the difference in climate had something to do with it.

2. **gross** (grōs) *n.* twelve dozen.

5

◀ **Critical Viewing** Which details in this image suggest that this selection is a tall tale? Explain. **[Analyze]**

Literary Analysis
Tall Tale and Myth Which realistic details here add humor?

7

Where does Pecos Bill get the postholes he sells to farmers in Iowa and Nebraska?

5 Critical Viewing

Answer: The picture shows a cowboy with a rope around a tornado, or cyclone. The image is far-fetched and whimsical.

6 Literary Analysis

Tall Tale and Myth

1. Have students read the bracketed paragraph.
2. **Ask** the Literary Analysis question: Which realistic details here add humor?

   Possible response: Bill fenced all of Texas and parts of New Mexico and Arizona; he took contracts for fencing; prairie dog holes didn't keep in storage, couldn't stand handling, and wore out quickly. Giving specific geographic and financial details about the imaginary work adds humor because of the contrast it creates between the serious and the fanciful. Applying practical consequences to inanimate holes is absurd and therefore amusing.

7 Reading Check

Answer: When the cyclone blew the earth away from his wells, Bill cut the wells into lengths and sold them as postholes.

PHLit Online!
This selection is available in interactive format in the **Enriched Online Student Edition,** which includes an interactive graphic organizer.

Text Complexity Rubric

Pecos Bill: The Cyclone	
Qualitative Measures	
Context/ Knowledge Demands	American West in frontier times 1 2 ③ 4 5
Structure/ Language Clarity	American vernacular and idioms 1 2 ③ 4 5
Levels of Meaning	Accessible concept (tale of unbelievable events) 1 2 ③ 4 5
Quantitative Measures	
Text Length	Word Count: 2,644
Lexile	790L

Reader and Task Suggestions

Preparing to Read the Text
- Refer to the Background information on TE p. 1218 and discuss the history of the Pecos Bill character.
- Discuss setting and how it may or may not be important in plot development.
- Guide students to use Multidraft Reading strategies (TE p. 1217).

Leveled Tasks

Levels of Meaning If students will have difficulty with levels of meaning, have them first read the story and take notes on why Pecos Bill takes on the cyclone. Then have them reread and note each unbelievable event.

Analyzing If students will not have difficulty with meaning, have them read the text and note how the author uses American vernacular language and idioms to develop the tale.

8 Literary Analysis

Tall Tale and Myth

1. Remind students that a story is given its flavor by specific, concrete details of time and place. Have them read the bracketed text.
2. **Ask** the Literary Analysis question: Which details give this tall tale a particularly American flavor?

   Answer: The culture of this tale is clearly American. It celebrates the Fourth of July; it features cowboys, cyclones, fences, and prairie dogs; and it specifically mentions several American states.
3. **Ask** students why they think the writer decided to set the tale on the Fourth of July.

   Possible response: The Fourth of July is the definitive American holiday, the day that most directly celebrates the American character.

Literary Analysis
Tall Tale and Myth Which details give this tall tale a particularly American flavor?

It should be said that in those days there was only one cyclone. It was the first and original cyclone, bigger and more terrible by far than the small cyclones of today. It usually stayed by itself up north around Kansas and Oklahoma and didn't bother anyone much. But it was attracted by the noise of the Fourth of July celebration and without fail managed to put in an appearance before the close of the day.

On this particular Fourth of July, the celebration had gone off fine. The speeches were loud and long. The contests and games were hard fought. The high point of the day was Bill's exhibition with Widow Maker, which came right after he showed off Scat and Rat.[3] People seemed never to tire of seeing them in action. The mountain lion was almost useless as a work animal after his accident, and the snake had grown old and somewhat infirm, and was troubled with rheumatism in his rattles. But they too enjoyed the Fourth of July and liked to make a public appearance. They relived the old days.

Widow Maker had put on a good show, bucking as no ordinary horse could ever buck. Then Bill undertook to show the gaits[4] he had taught the palomino.[5] Other mustangs at that time had only two gaits. Walking and running. Only Widow Maker could pace. But now Bill had developed and taught him other gaits. Twenty-seven in all. Twenty-three forward and three reverse. He was very proud of the achievement. He showed off the slow gaits and the crowd was eager for more.

He showed the walk, trot, canter, lope, jog, slow rack, fast rack, single foot, pace, stepping pace, fox trot, running walk and the others now known. Both men and horses confuse the various gaits nowadays. Some of the gaits are now thought to be the same, such as the rack and the single foot. But with Widow Maker and Pecos Bill, each one was different. Each was precise and to be distinguished from the others. No one had ever imagined such a thing.

Then the cyclone came! All of the people except Bill ran into the 'fraid holes. Bill was annoyed. He stopped the performance. The remaining gaits were not shown. From that day to this horses have used no more than the gaits Widow Maker exhibited that day. It is unfortunate that the really fast gaits were not shown. If they were, horses might be much faster today than they are.

Bill glanced up at the cyclone and the quiet smile on his face faded into a frown. He saw the cyclone was angry. Very, very angry indeed.

3. **Widow Maker . . . Scat and Rat.** Widow Maker is a mustang, a type of wild horse. Scat is Bill's mountain lion, and Rat is Bill's pet rattlesnake.
4. **gaits** (gāts) *n.* foot movements of a horse.
5. **palomino** (pal´ ə mē´ nō) *n.* golden-tan or cream-colored horse that has a white, silver, or ivory tail and, often, white spots on the face and legs.

Vocabulary Development

CCSS Language 6

Selection Vocabulary Reinforcement

Students will benefit from additional examples and practice with the selection vocabulary words. Reinforce their comprehension with "show-you-know" sentences. The first part of the sentence uses the vocabulary word in an appropriate context. The second part of the sentence—the "show-you-know" part—clarifies the first. Model the strategy with this example for *usurped:*

The new leader clearly *usurped* his authority; he gave orders he had no right to give.

Then give students this sentence prompt, and coach them in creating the clarification part:

The crowd was amazed but full of *skeptics;* ________.

Sample answer: most of the people did not believe what they had just seen.

The cyclone had always been the center of attention. Everywhere it went people would look up in wonder, fear and amazement. It had been the undisputed master of the country. It had observed Bill's rapid climb to fame and had seen the Fourth of July celebration grow. It had been keeping an eye on things all right.

In the beginning, the Fourth of July crowd had aroused its curiosity. It liked nothing more than to show its superiority and power by breaking the crowd up sometime during the day. But every year the crowd was larger. This preyed on the cyclone's mind. This year it did not come to watch. It deliberately came to spoil the celebration. Jealous of Bill and of his success, it resolved to do away with the whole institution of the Fourth of July once and for all. So much havoc and destruction would be wrought that there would never be another Independence Day Celebration. On that day, in future years, it would circle around the horizon leering and gloating. At least, so it thought.

The cyclone was resolved, also, to do away with this bold fellow who did not hold it in awe and run for the 'fraid hole at its approach. For untold years it had been the most powerful thing in the land. And now, here was a mere man who threatened its position. More! Who had usurped its position!

When Bill looked at the horizon and saw the cyclone coming, he recognized the anger and rage. While a cyclone does not often smile, Bill had felt from the beginning that it was just a grouchy fellow who never had a pleasant word for anyone. But now, instead of merely an unpleasant character, Bill saw all the viciousness of which an angry cyclone is capable. He had no way of knowing that the cyclone saw its kingship tottering and was determined to stop this man who threatened its supremacy.

But Bill understood the violence of the onslaught even as the monster came into view. He knew he must meet it. The center of the cyclone was larger than ever before. The fact is, the cyclone had been training for this fight all winter and spring. It was in best form and at top weight. It headed straight for Bill intent on his destruction. In an instant it was upon him. Bill had sat quietly and silently on the great pacing mustang. But his mind was working rapidly. In the split second between his first sight of the monster and the time for action he had made his plans. Pecos Bill was ready! Ready and waiting!

Green clouds were dripping from the cyclone's jaws. Lightning flashed from its eyes as it swept down upon him. Its plan was to envelop Bill in one mighty grasp. Just as it was upon him, Bill turned Widow Maker to its left. This was a clever move for the cyclone was right-handed, and while it had been training hard to

Vocabulary
usurped (yo͞o sʉrpt′) *v.* took power without right

Spiral Review
Universal Theme Why do you think that the cyclone is given human characteristics in this tale?

10 Reading Check
Why is the cyclone angry with Bill?

9 Connecting to the Big Question

1. Remind students of the Big Question by asking what responsibilities people have to protect those weaker than themselves.
2. Direct students' attention to the bracketed passage on p. 1219. **Ask:** How does Bill feel when he sees the cyclone?
   Answer: He knows he must meet it.
3. **Ask:** Do you agree that Bill has a responsibility to battle the cyclone and protect the celebration? Explain.
   Possible response: Yes; He appears to be the only person who can battle the cyclone. Since he invented the holiday, he has a responsibility to protect it. No; A cyclone is a natural event and Bill need not try to fight nature.

Spiral Review
Universal Theme

1. Remind students that they studied the concept of universal theme in the Unit 6 Literary Analysis workshop (pp. 1030–1039).
2. **Ask** students the Spiral Review question.
   Possible response: Giving the cyclone human characteristics reflects how cyclones are perceived by the people in the culture that tell the tall tale. Nature sometimes seemed like a thinking being that was intent on harming them. The way the characteristics are described adds to the humor of the tale. Humor might have helped the people of the culture deal with the anxiety and fear that cyclones evoked.

10 Reading Check

Answer: The cyclone is angry because Bill is not afraid of it and because Bill has taken over its position as the most powerful thing in the land.

Differentiated Instruction for Universal Access

Strategy for Less Proficient Readers
Students may have difficulty imagining some of the wild, exaggerated events that take place in "Pecos Bill: The Cyclone." Suggest that each student work with a partner to read aloud the story. Each partner should read a section and then stop so that the listening partner can summarize what has happened. Then, partners should switch roles. Encourage students to draw or act out the events as well as describe them orally.

EL Strategy for English Learners
Students may have trouble with words that relate to the American Old West. As students read, have them list unfamiliar words and phrases. Students may identify words such as *posthole, prairie dog, mountain lion, mustang,* and *quirt.* Have each student use a dictionary and work with a partner who is proficient in English to determine the meanings of the words. Encourage the proficient speaker to use gestures and draw pictures that illustrate the terms.

⓫ Literature in Context

Science Connection The word *cyclone* used to be applied only to a tornado, the funnel-shaped storm that is popularly called a "twister." In the movie *The Wizard of Oz,* for example, the tornado that lifts Dorothy's house and carries it away is called a "cyclone." Visualizing Pecos Bill's storm as a tornado probably does make it easier to imagine how he would be able to "ride" it, and Bill's cyclone is also called a "tornado."

The term *cyclone,* however, actually includes all classes of storms, from local thunderstorms to devastating typhoons and hurricanes. The word *cyclone* itself comes from the Greek word *kyklon,* meaning a circle or the coil of a snake. Today, "cyclone" is usually applied only to the destructive tropical storms that are called hurricanes in the Atlantic Ocean and typhoons in the Western Pacific.

Connect to the Literature Have students read the Literature in Context feature, and present the additional background information above. Remind students of the destructive nature of cyclones. Then **ask** the Connect to the Literature question: Why might a literary character like Bill be especially beloved by people who lived in areas affected by cyclones?

Possible response: They might appreciate imagining a cyclone being rendered helpless by a person

LITERATURE IN CONTEXT

Science Connection

Cyclones

A cyclone is an area of rapidly spinning winds that is associated with severe thunderstorms. The rotating winds can reach speeds of 250 miles per hour and are capable of lifting even very heavy objects into the column of circulating air. Cyclones develop when warm and cold masses of air collide, causing abrupt changes in wind speed and direction. Cyclones that were over a mile wide and that have spread damage along a fifty-mile path have been recorded. Unlike Pecos Bill, most people are smart enough to take shelter underground when they see a cyclone coming.

Connect to the Literature

Why might a literary character like Bill be especially beloved by people who live in areas affected by cyclones?

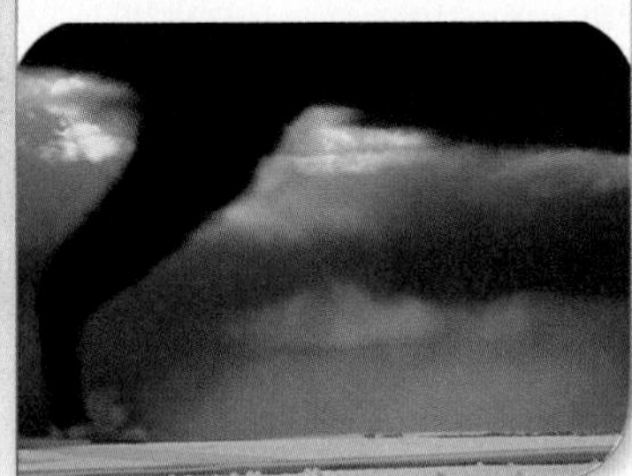

get its left in shape, that was not its best side. Bill gave rein to his mount. Widow Maker wheeled and turned on a dime which Pecos had, with great foresight and accuracy, thrown to the ground to mark the exact spot for this maneuver. It was the first time that anyone had thought of turning on a dime. Then he urged the great horse forward. The cyclone, filled with surprise, lost its balance and rushed forward at an increased speed. It went so fast that it met itself coming back. This confused the cyclone, but it did not confuse Pecos Bill. He had expected that to happen. Widow Maker went into his twenty-first gait and edged up close to the whirlwind. Soon they were running neck and neck.

At the proper instant Bill grabbed the cyclone's ears, kicked himself free of the stirrups and pulled himself lightly on its back. Bill never used spurs on Widow Maker. Sometimes he wore them for show and because he liked the jingling sound they made. They made a nice accompaniment for his cowboy songs. But he had not been singing, so he had no spurs. He did not have his rattlesnake for a quirt.[6] Of course there was no bridle. It was man against monster! There he was! Pecos Bill astride a raging cyclone, slick heeled and without a saddle!

The cyclone was taken by surprise at this sudden turn of events. But it was undaunted. It was sure of itself. Months of training had given it a conviction that it was invincible. With a mighty heave, it twisted to its full height. Then it fell back suddenly, twisting and turning violently, so that before it came back to earth, it had turned around a thousand times. Surely no rider could ever withstand such an attack. No rider ever had. Little wonder. No one had ever ridden a cyclone before. But Pecos Bill did! He fanned the tornado's ears with his hat and dug his heels into the demon's flanks and yelled, "Yipee-ee!"

The people who had run for shelter began to come out. The audience further enraged the cyclone. It was bad enough to be disgraced by having a man astride it. It was unbearable not to have thrown him. To have all the people see the failure was too much! It got down flat on the ground and rolled over and over. Bill retained his seat throughout this ruse. Evidence of this desperate but futile stratagem[7] remains today. The great Staked Plains, or as the Mexicans call it, Llano Estacado is ⓫

6. **quirt** (kwurt) *n.* riding whip with a braided lash and a short handle.
7. **futile** (fyo͞ot′'l) **stratagem** (strat′ ə jəm) useless or hopeless plan.

Vocabulary Development

CCSS Language 6

Word Forms

Expand students' vocabulary by helping them learn related forms of the selection vocabulary words. Two of the selection vocabulary words for "Pecos Bill: The Cyclone" and "Perseus" have related forms. Give students a blank **Word Form Chart** (***Professional Development Guidebook,*** p. 42), with *skeptics* and *mortified* in the correct columns. Work with the class, or have students work with a partner, to determine the related forms. The final chart should look like the one shown. Hold students accountable for integrating the related forms of the words into their speaking and writing.

Noun	Verb	Adjective	Adverb
skeptics		skeptical	skeptically
mortification	mortify	**mortified**	

the result. Its small, rugged mountains were covered with trees at the time. The rolling of the cyclone destroyed the mountains, the trees, and almost everything else in the area. The destruction was so complete, that part of the country is flat and treeless to this day. When the settlers came, there were no landmarks to guide them across the vast unmarked space, so they drove stakes in the ground to mark the trails. That is the reason it is called "Staked Plains." Here is an example of the proof of the events of history by careful and painstaking research. It is also an example of how seemingly inexplicable geographical facts can be explained.

12 It was far more dangerous for the rider when the cyclone shot straight up to the sky. Once there, the twister tried the same thing it had tried on the ground. It rolled on the sky. It was no use. Bill could not be unseated. He kept his place, and he didn't have a sky hook with him either.

As for Bill, he was having the time of his life, shouting at the top of his voice, kicking his opponent in the ribs and jabbing his thumb in its flanks. It responded and went on a wild bucking rampage over the entire West. It used all the bucking tricks known to the wildest broncos as well as those known only to cyclones. The wind howled furiously and beat against the fearless rider. The rain poured. The lightning flashed around his ears. The fight went on and on. Bill enjoyed himself immensely. In spite of the elements he easily kept his place. . . .

The raging cyclone saw this out of the corner of its eye. It knew then who the victor was. It was twisting far above the Rocky Mountains when the awful truth came to it. In a horrible heave it disintegrated! Small pieces of cyclone flew in all directions. Bill still kept his seat on the main central portion until that rained out from under him. Then he jumped to a nearby streak of lightning and slid down it toward earth. But it was raining so hard that the rain put out the lightning. When it fizzled out from under him, Bill dropped the rest of the way. He lit in what is now called Death Valley. He hit quite hard, as is apparent from the fact that he so compressed the place that it is still two hundred and seventy-six feet below
13 sea level. The Grand Canyon was washed out by the rain, though it must be understood that this happened after Paul Bunyan had given it a good start by carelessly dragging his ax behind him when he went west a short time before.

The cyclones and the hurricanes and the tornadoes nowadays are the small pieces that broke off of the big cyclone Pecos Bill rode. In fact, the rainstorms of the present day came into being in the same way. There are always skeptics, but even they will recognize

Literary Analysis
Tall Tale and Myth In his encounter with the cyclone, which details show Bill's physical strength and lack of fear?

Vocabulary
skeptics (skep´ tiks) *n.* people who doubt accepted ideas

Literary Analysis
Tall Tale and Myth According to the tale, how does Bill create a natural phenomenon?

14 

What unusual feat does Bill complete with the cyclone?

12 Literary Analysis
Tall Tale and Myth

1. **Ask** students to name some qualities that they think would have been valued by cowboys or frontiersmen.

   Possible responses: Cowboys and frontiersmen would have valued physical strength, endurance, fearlessness, and horsemanship.

2. Have students reread the first bracketed text, which begins on p. 1222. **Ask** the first Literary Analysis question: In his encounter with the cyclone, which details show Bill's physical strength and lack of fear?

   Answer: Not only does Bill not run away, but he is able to ride the cyclone and not be thrown. In fact, Bill actually enjoys the ride, displaying his fearlessness.

3. **Ask** students what Bill's way of dealing with the cyclone tells about the values of the culture of the American West.

   Answer: In this encounter, Bill is the hero who embodies the strength, fearlessness, and horsemanship that were prized by his culture.

13 Literary Analysis
Tall Tale and Myth

1. Remind students that one purpose of tall tales and myths is to explain natural phenomena.
2. Read the second bracketed passage aloud. **Ask** the second Literary Analysis question: According to the tale, how does Bill create a natural phenomenon?

   Answer: Bill creates Death Valley.

14 Reading Check

Answer: Bill rides the cyclone.

Differentiated Instruction for Universal Access

Strategy for Special-Needs Students
Because the events in "Pecos Bill: The Cyclone" are episodic and not necessarily in chronological order, students may have some trouble following the tale. Suggest that students adapt the tale to a comic-strip format, using frames or boxes for each episode. Have students work in pairs to figure out how many episodes are in the story and then draw or sketch one scene in each frame. Assure students that their drawings do not have to be perfect or even realistic; they can use simple stick figures.

Strategy for Advanced Readers
Suggest that each student write an updated version of the Pecos Bill story that includes contemporary cultural references and explains at least one event that could take place in modern life. Students can update the character of Pecos Bill, changing his occupation from cowboy to any contemporary occupation. Challenge students to use exaggeration and understatement in their stories. Invite volunteers to read aloud their stories to the class.

15 Literary Analysis

Tall Tale and Myth

1. Read the bracketed text aloud. **Ask** the Literary Analysis question: Which details in this paragraph are examples of humorous exaggeration?

   Answer: Bill's six-shooters were changed into a water pistol and a popgun, and his bowie knife became a penknife.

Concept Connector

Have students return to their **Anticipation Guides** and respond to the statements in the After Reading column. Then lead a discussion about students' responses. In addition, have students compare their Writing About the Big Question responses before reading the selection with their ideas afterwards.

ASSESS

Answers

Critical Thinking

Before students respond, you may wish to have them write a brief objective summary of the selection. As they answer the questions below, remind them to support their answers with evidence from the text.

1. (a) He calls them "'fraid holes." (b) It is clear that Bill does not experience fear at all.
2. (a) Bill will not say the word *afraid* aloud. (b) Bill's fearlessness is in part what makes him a folk hero.
3. (a) **Possible response:** The cyclone is jealous, angry, and threatened. (b) **Possible response:** Like Bill, the cyclone is bold, strong, and powerful.
4. **Possible responses:** (a) He defeats the cyclone that threatened to destroy Independence Day. (b) Students are likely to say that Bill has a responsibility to use his power and strength for the good of the community.

PHLit Online!

This selection is available in interactive format in the **Enriched Online Student Edition,** at **www.PHLitOnline.com**, which includes an interactive graphic organizer.

---

the logic of the proof of this event. They will recall that even now it almost always rains on the Fourth of July. That is because the rainstorms of today still retain some of the characteristics of the giant cyclone that met its comeuppance at the hands of Pecos Bill.

Bill lay where he landed and looked up at the sky, but he could see no sign of the cyclone. Then he laughed softly as he felt the warm sand of Death Valley on his back. . . .

Literary Analysis
Tall Tale and Myth
Which details in this paragraph are examples of humorous exaggeration?

15 It was a rough ride though, and Bill had resisted unusual tensions and pressures. When he got on the cyclone he had a twenty-dollar gold piece and a bowie knife in his pocket. The tremendous force of the cyclone was such that when he finished the ride he found that his pocket contained a plugged nickel[8] and a little pearl-handled penknife. His two giant six-shooters were compressed and transformed into a small water pistol and a popgun.

It is a strange circumstance that lesser men have monuments raised in their honor. Death Valley is Bill's monument. Sort of a monument in reverse. Sunk in his honor, you might say. Perhaps that is as it should be. After all, Bill was different. He made his own monument. He made it with his hips, as is evident from the great depth of the valley. That is the hard way.

8. **plugged nickel** fake nickel.

Critical Thinking

Cite textual evidence to support your responses.

1. **Key Ideas and Details** **(a)** What term does Bill use to refer to the cyclone cellars? **(b) Interpret:** What do you learn about the character of Pecos Bill from his reaction to the cellars?
2. **Key Ideas and Details** **(a)** What word is Bill unwilling to say aloud? **(b) Draw Conclusions:** How does his resolve never to say this word explain, in part, why he is a folk hero?
3. **Key Ideas and Details** **(a) Interpret:** What are three human characteristics of the cyclone? **(b) Compare:** How does the cyclone resemble Pecos Bill himself?
4. **Integration of Knowledge and Ideas** **(a)** How does Pecos Bill ultimately show responsibility to his community? Explain. **(b)** Do you think Bill has a responsibility to use his special abilities to help his community, or can he choose not to? Explain. *[Connect to the Big Question: Do heroes have responsibilities?]*

Vocabulary Development

Word Analysis

Bill's two six-shooters are *transformed* into a water pistol and popgun—that is, they cross over into other forms. Tell students that the prefix *trans-* means "across" or "over." Have students define each of the following words and explain how each word incorporates the idea of "across" or "over."

transport—to carry across
transatlantic—across the Atlantic Ocean
transfer—to carry or move over from one place to another
transgress—to cross over a line, to break a law
transition—crossing over from one stage or form to another
translate—to change over from one language to another

16 17 18

Perseus

Edith Hamilton

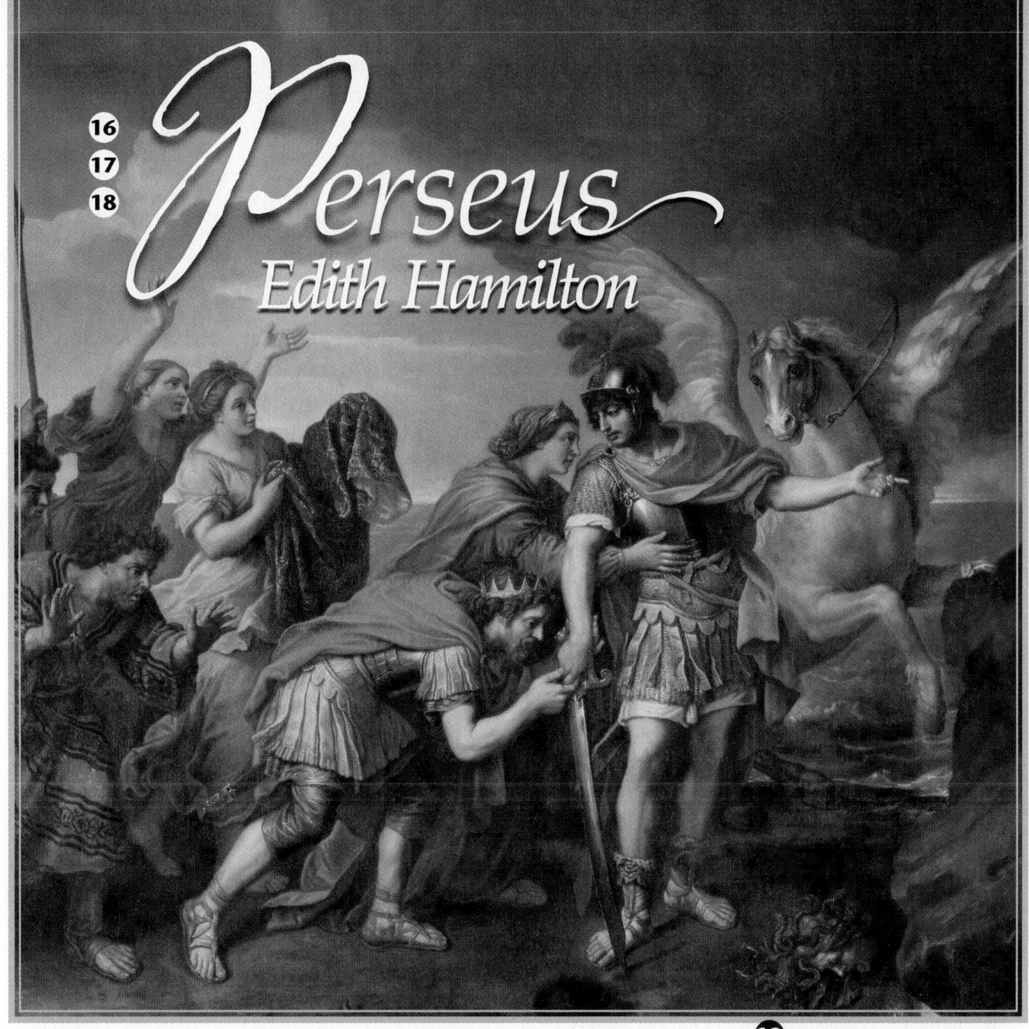

King Acrisius [a kris′ ē əs] of Argos had only one child, a daughter, Danaë [dan′ ā ē]. She was beautiful above all the other women of the land, but this was small comfort to the King for not having a son. He journeyed to Delphi to ask the god if there was any hope that some day he would be the father of a boy. The priestess told him no, and added what was far worse: that his daughter would have a son who would kill him.

The only sure way to escape that fate was for the King to have Danaë instantly put to death—taking no chances, but seeing to it himself. This Acrisius would not do. His fatherly affection was not strong, as events proved, but his fear of the gods was. They visited with terrible punishment those who shed the blood of kindred.

19 ▲ **Critical Viewing** The man with the sword is Perseus as an adult. Judging from this painting, how do you think others perceive him? **[Interpret]**

16 Background

Greek Gods

Zeus, chief of all the Greek gods, rules over the earth. His two brothers, Poseidon and Hades, rule over the seas and the underworld. Athena is Zeus' daughter; she has no mother. She sprang full grown and armed from Zeus' head. Hermes, the son of Zeus and Maia, is a messenger of the gods. The medical insignia students can see on doctors' diplomas depicts the staff of Hermes.

17 Activating Prior Knowledge

Engage students' interest by reading this passage from "Perseus":

He stood up before them all and did exactly what the King had hoped he would do, declared that he would give him a present better than any there. He would go off and kill Medusa and bring back her head as a gift. . . . No one in his senses would have made such a proposal. Medusa was one of the Gorgons.

Ask students to imagine what type of creature Medusa might be. What would make her so terrifying? Have each student write or draw a description of what Medusa might look like.

18 About the Selection

In "Perseus," when the oracle prophesies that Acrisius will die by the hand of his grandson, Acrisius shuts his daughter Danaë away to prevent her from meeting men. However, Zeus disguises himself and visits Danaë, and she conceives a son. Acrisius sets her and baby Perseus adrift in a wooden chest, but they are rescued. Eventually, Perseus kills the Gorgon, kills a sea monster, sets the princess Andromeda free, and marries her.

19 Critical Viewing

Answer: Perseus is treated with respect, gratitude, and admiration.

Text Complexity Rubric

Perseus	
Qualitative Measures	
Context/ Knowledge Demands	Modern retelling of ancient Greek myth 1 2 3 (4) 5
Structure/ Language Clarity	Challenging, formal vocabulary 1 2 3 (4) 5
Levels of Meaning	Challenging concepts (allusions to Greek myth) 1 2 3 (4) 5
Quantitative Measures	
Text Length	Word Count: 3,022
Lexile	1060L

Reader and Task Suggestions

Preparing to Read the Text

- Using the Background information on TE p. 1225, discuss Greek mythology and the Greek gods.
- Discuss the universal themes exhibited by Greek myths.
- Guide students to use Multidraft Reading strategies (TE p. 1217).

Leveled Tasks

Knowledge Demands If students will have difficulty with knowledge demands, have them first read the story and list each character. Then, have them reread, noting how each character influences the story's outcome.

Synthesizing If students will not have difficulty with knowledge demands, have them identify the theme of the story and take notes on main details that develop the theme.

20 Literary Analysis

Tall Tale and Myth

1. Remind students of the common characteristics of a hero, including a semi-divine birth.
2. Have students reread the bracketed passage. **Ask** the Literary Analysis question: Which elements of Perseus' story so far suggest that he will be a mythic hero?

   Answer: He is the subject of a prophecy, the result of a miraculous birth, and most importantly, the son of Zeus.
3. **Ask** students to speculate on any superhuman powers that Perseus might have, based on his parentage.

   Possible response: Perseus may have tremendous strength and fearlessness, and he can probably expect to be aided by various immortals.

PHLit Online!

This selection is available in interactive format in the **Enriched Online Student Edition,** which includes an interactive graphic organizer.

Acrisius did not dare slay his daughter. Instead, he had a house built all of bronze and sunk underground, but with part of the roof open to the sky so that light and air could come through. Here he shut her up and guarded her.

So Danaë endured, the beautiful,
To change the glad daylight for brass-bound walls,
And in that chamber secret as the grave
She lived a prisoner. Yet to her came
Zeus in the golden rain.

As she sat there through the long days and hours with nothing to do, nothing to see except the clouds moving by overhead, a mysterious thing happened, a shower of gold fell from the sky and filled her chamber. How it was revealed to her that it was Zeus who had visited her in this shape we are not told, but she knew that the child she bore was his son.

20 **Literary Analysis**
Tall Tale and Myth
Which elements of Perseus' story so far suggest that he will be a mythic hero?

For a time she kept his birth secret from her father, but it became increasingly difficult to do so in the narrow limits of that bronze house and finally one day the little boy—his name was Perseus—was discovered by his grandfather. "Your child!" Acrisius cried in great anger. "Who is his father?" But when Danaë answered proudly, "Zeus," he would not believe her. One thing only he was sure of, that the boy's life was a terrible danger to his own. He was afraid to kill him for the same reason that had kept him from killing her, fear of Zeus and the Furies who pursue such murderers. But if he could not kill them outright, he could put them in the way of tolerably certain death. He had a great chest made, and the two placed in it. Then it was taken out to sea and cast into the water.

In that strange boat Danaë sat with her little son. The daylight faded and she was alone on the sea.

When in the carven chest the winds and waves
Struck fear into her heart she put her arms,
Not without tears, round Perseus tenderly
She said, "O son, what grief is mine.
But you sleep softly, little child,
Sunk deep in rest within your cheerless home,
Only a box, brass-bound. The night, this darkness visible,
The scudding waves so near to your soft curls,
The shrill voice of the wind, you do not heed,
Nestled in your red cloak, fair little face."

Through the night in the tossing chest she listened to the waters that seemed always about to wash over them. The dawn came, but with no comfort to her for she could not see it. Neither could she see that around them there were islands rising high above the sea, many islands. All she knew was that presently a wave seemed to lift

Vocabulary Development

CCSS Language 6

Word Analysis

Point out to students that human beings are described as *mortals* and that gods are called *immortals.* The root *-mort-* is from the Latin word for death. Mortals are subject to death; immortals never die. The nouns derived from these words are *mortality* and *immortality.* Note also that when Perseus appears without a gift, he is keenly *mortified. Mortified* also shares this root. It may help students to think of mortified as being "embarrassed to death."

them and carry them swiftly on and then, retreating, leave them on something solid and motionless. They had made land; they were safe from the sea, but they were still in the chest with no way to get out.

Fate willed it—or perhaps Zeus, who up to now had done little for his love and his child—that they should be discovered by a good man, a fisherman named Dictys. He came upon the great box and broke it open and took the pitiful cargo home to his wife who was as kind as he. They had no children and they cared for Danaë and Perseus as if they were their own. The two lived there many years, Danaë content to let her son follow the fisherman's humble trade, out of harm's way. But in the end more trouble came. Polydectes [pol i dek´ tēz], the ruler of the little island, was the brother of Dictys, but he was a cruel and ruthless man. He seems to have taken no notice of the mother and son for a long time, but at last Danaë attracted his attention. She was still radiantly beautiful even though Perseus by now was full grown, and Polydectes fell in love with her. He wanted her, but he did not want her son, and he set himself to think out a way of getting rid of him.

22 There were some fearsome monsters called Gorgons who lived on an island and were known far and wide because of their deadly power. Polydectes evidently talked to Perseus about them; he probably told him that he would rather have the head of one of them than anything else in the world. This seems practically certain from the plan he devised for killing Perseus. He announced that he was about to be married and he called his friends together for a celebration, including Perseus in the invitation. Each guest, as was customary, brought a gift for the bride-to-be, except Perseus alone. He had nothing he could give. He was young and proud and keenly mortified. He stood up before them all and did exactly what the King had hoped he would do, declared that he would give him a present better than any there. He would go off and kill Medusa and bring back her head as his gift. Nothing could have suited the King better. No one in his senses would have made such a proposal. Medusa was one of the Gorgons,

And they are three, the Gorgons, each with wings
And snaky hair, most horrible to mortals.
Whom no man shall behold and draw again
The breath of life,

21

▲ **Critical Viewing**
Which scene in the story does this art illustrate? **[Connect]**

Vocabulary
mortified (môrt´ ə f īd´) *adj.* extremely embarrassed

23

What does Perseus promise to give the king as a gift?

21 Critical Viewing

Answer: The art illustrates the scene in which Dictys finds Danaë and her baby inside the chest. The man cannot be Acrisius setting them adrift, because he is not wearing a crown.

22 Connecting to the Big Question

1. Remind students of the Big Question by asking if they think people in positions of high status have the same responsibilities as "ordinary" people. Discuss if students' answers should apply to mythical heroes as well.
2. Direct students' attention to the bracketed passage. **Ask:** What obligation does Perseus feel toward Polydectes? What heroic task does Perseus have to complete to meet this obligation?

   Answer: He feels that he must bring a gift for Polydectes' bride-to-be, who is Perseus' mother. He has to kill a monster and bring back her head.
3. **Ask:** Do you agree that Perseus has a responsibility to risk his life in order to bring a gift to the wedding? Is it possible for a hero to meet his or her responsibilities without acting heroically? Explain.

   Possible response: No; He needs to bring a gift but it need not be obtained at such a cost.

23 Reading Check

Answer: Perseus promises the head of Medusa as a gift.

Differentiated Instruction for Universal Access

Strategy for Special-Needs Students
Edith Hamilton's formal, academic style may prove a barrier to some students. Prepare them by reading them parts of "The Gorgon's Head" in Nathaniel Hawthorne's *A Wonder Book,* or use another retelling for children.

As students listen to or read the story, have them list the names and identifications of the characters and write the basic events of the plot.

Culturally Responsive Instruction
Culture Focus Point out that in the culture of the myth, it is customary for guests to give gifts to brides-to-be. Most cultures have some custom of gift-giving to brides or couples about to be married. Invite students to share customs from their home culture or family's country of origin. Discuss different rationales for the customs, such as to supply items needed in a new home.

24 Critical Viewing

Answer: Students should recognize the Gorgon Medusa from the snakes that wreathe her face.

24 ▼ **Critical Viewing** Who is portrayed in this art? Explain how you know. **[Connect]**

for the reason that whoever looked at them were turned instantly into stone. It seemed that Perseus had been led by his angry pride into making an empty boast. No man unaided could kill Medusa.

But Perseus was saved from his folly. Two great gods were watching over him. He took ship as soon as he left the King's hall, not daring to see his mother first and tell her what he intended, and he sailed to Greece to learn where the three monsters were to be found. He went to Delphi, but all the priestess would say was to bid him seek the land where men eat not Demeter's golden grain, but only acorns. So he went to Dodona, in the land of oak trees, where the talking oaks were which declared Zeus's will and where the Selli lived who made their bread from acorns. They could tell him, however, no more than this, that he was under the protection of the gods. They did not know where the Gorgons lived.

When and how Hermes and Athena came to his help is not told in any story, but he must have known despair before they did so. At last, however, as he wandered on, he met a strange and beautiful person. We know what he looked like from many a poem, a young man with the first down upon his cheek when youth is loveliest, carrying, as no other young man ever did, a wand of gold with wings at one end, wearing a winged hat, too, and winged sandals. At sight of him hope must have entered Perseus' heart, for he would know that this could be none other than Hermes, the guide and the giver of good.

This radiant personage told him that before he attacked Medusa he must first be properly equipped, and that what he needed was in the possession of the nymphs of the North. To find the nymphs' abode, they must go to the Gray Women who alone could tell them the way. These women dwelt in a land where all was dim and shrouded in twilight. No ray of sun looked ever on that country, nor the moon by night. In that gray place the three women lived, all gray themselves and withered as in extreme old age. They were strange creatures, indeed, most of all because they had but one eye for the three, which it was their custom to take turns with, each

Vocabulary Development

CCSS Language 6

Thematic Vocabulary: The Big Question

As students are discussing "Perseus," encourage them to use the thematic vocabulary presented in Introducing the Big Question, pp. 1028–1029. You might encourage them with sentence starters like these:

1. For King Acrisius the prophecy meant that he faced a *choice* to . . .
2. Perseus announced his *intentions* to . . .
3. The *involvement* of the gods helped Perseus to . . .
4. Perseus brought *justice* to the island when he . . .
5. Despite his strong *morality*, in the end Perseus does . . .

removing it from her forehead when she had had it for a time and handing it to another.

25 All this Hermes told Perseus and then he unfolded his plan. He would himself guide Perseus to them. Once there Perseus must keep hidden until he saw one of them take the eye out of her forehead to pass it on. At that moment, when none of the three could see, he must rush forward and seize the eye and refuse to give it back until they told him how to reach the nymphs of the North.

He himself, Hermes said, would give him a sword to attack Medusa with—which could not be bent or broken by the Gorgon's scales, no matter how hard they were. This was a wonderful gift, no doubt, and yet of what use was a sword when the creature to be struck by it could turn the swordsman into stone before he was within striking distance? But another great deity was at hand to help. Pallas Athena stood beside Perseus. She took off the shield of polished bronze which covered her breast and held it out to him. "Look into this when you attack the Gorgon," she said. "You will be able to see her in it as in a mirror, and so avoid her deadly power."

26 Now, indeed, Perseus had good reason to hope. The journey to the twilight land was long, over the stream of Ocean and on to the very border of the black country where the Cimmerians dwell, but Hermes was his guide and he could not go astray. They found the Gray Women at last, looking in the wavering light like gray birds, for they had the shape of swans. But their heads were human and beneath their wings they had arms and hands. Perseus did just as Hermes had said, he held back until he saw one of them take the eye out of her forehead. Then before she could give it to her sister, he snatched it out of her hand. It was a moment or two before the three realized they had lost it. Each thought one of the others had it. But Perseus spoke out and told them he had taken it and that it would be theirs again only when they showed him how to find the nymphs of the North. They gave him full directions at once; they would have done anything to get their eye back. He returned it to them and went on the way they had pointed out to him. He was bound, although he did not know it, to the blessed country of the Hyperboreans [hī per bō′ rē anz], at the back of the North Wind, of which it is said: "Neither by ship nor yet by land shall one find the wondrous road to the gathering place of the Hyperboreans." But Perseus had Hermes with him, so that the road lay open to him, and he reached that host of happy people who are always banqueting and holding joyful revelry. They showed him great kindness: they welcomed him to their feast, and the maidens dancing to the sound of flute and lyre paused to get for him the

Literary Analysis
Tall Tale and Myth
Which details in this paragraph show Perseus' special status as a mythic hero?

Literary Analysis
Tall Tale and Myth
What heroic qualities does Perseus reveal in his encounter with the Gray Women?

Vocabulary
revelry (rev′ əl rē) *n.* noisy merrymaking

27 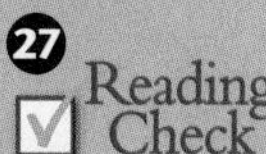

Who comes to Perseus' aid?

25 Literary Analysis
Tall Tale and Myth

1. **Ask** students what act of "folly" Perseus has committed.

   Answer: He has promised to perform an impossible feat—killing the Medusa.

2. Point out to students that great heroes are sometimes propelled into crises by the same fearless recklessness that helps them perform the very feats that make them heroes. This is one of the factors that makes their characters interestingly human.

3. Have students reread the bracketed passage. **Ask** the Literary Analysis question: Which details in this paragraph show Perseus' special status as a mythic hero?

   Answer: He has the guidance of Hermes, a god.

4. **Ask** students how they think a modern hero, facing a battle with a terrible monster, would differ from a mythological hero.

   Possible response: A modern hero would not receive supernatural help. He or she would have to find a natural or technological way to win the battle.

26 Literary Analysis
Tall Tale and Myth

1. Point out to students that, even though the mythological hero receives supernatural aid, he must be wise enough to accept it, brave enough to use it, and smart enough to use it correctly.

2. Have students read the bracketed passage, which continues onto p. 1230. **Ask** the Literary Analysis question: What heroic qualities does Perseus reveal in his encounter with the Gray Women?

   Answer: He follows the directions given to him by the divine Hermes. He is brave enough to snatch the eye away, and he is fair enough to give it back as soon as he has the information he needs.

27 Reading Check

Answer: Hermes and Athena come to Perseus' aid.

Differentiated Instruction for Universal Access

Strategy for Gifted/Talented Students
It is an ancient human custom to build monuments to honor heroes, often by erecting statues and plaques in public places. Ask students to design a monument for Perseus. Have students work in teams to decide which particular deed or deeds to emphasize and which physical details to include. Students can then draw plans for their monument or create an actual model.

Strategy for Advanced Readers
Challenge students to create a brief encyclopedia of mythology that informs readers about all the places and characters alluded to in the story of Perseus. Students can look in reference books or collections of myths to find out who the Seli are, where Dodona is, and so on. Each page of the encyclopedia can give an explanation and show an illustration of the place or the character.

Spiral Review

Universal Theme

1. Remind students that they studied the concept of universal theme in the Unit 6 Literary Analysis workshop (pp. 1030–1039).
2. **Ask** students the Spiral Review question.

   Possible response: The gifts are significant because the hero in most cultures has some superhuman talent, skill, or ability. These gifts will give Perseus superhuman powers on his quest.

28 Literary Analysis

Tall Tale and Myth

1. Remind students that mythological heroes possess more than brute strength. They are usually great in body, mind, and heart. Perseus has physical prowess, but the gods give him great knowledge, too.
2. Have students read the second bracketed passage. **Ask** the Literary Analysis question: What special knowledge helps Perseus kill Medusa?

   Answer: Athena and Hermes tell Perseus which of the Gorgons is Medusa, the only one who can be killed.
3. **Ask** students to speculate about what other kinds of special knowledge the gods might give a mythological hero.

   Possible response: The gods might tell a hero the meaning of a mysterious oracle, where to go on a quest, or how to rescue a loved one. They might also reveal the secret of the hero's identity, parentage, or destiny.

Spiral Review
Universal Theme
What is significant about the gifts Perseus receives? 26

gifts he sought. These were three: winged sandals, a magic wallet which would always become the right size for whatever was to be carried in it, and, most important of all, a cap which made the wearer invisible. With these and Athena's shield and Hermes' sword Perseus was ready for the Gorgons. Hermes knew where they lived, and leaving the happy land the two flew back across Ocean and over the sea to the Terrible Sisters' island.

By great good fortune they were all asleep when Perseus found them. In the mirror of the bright shield he could see them clearly, creatures with great wings and bodies covered with golden scales and hair a mass of twisting snakes. Athena was beside him now as well as Hermes. They told him which one was Medusa and that was important, for she alone of the three could be killed; the other two were immortal. Perseus on his winged sandals hovered above them, looking, however, only at the shield. Then he aimed a stroke down at Medusa's throat and Athena guided his hand. With a single sweep of his sword he cut through her neck and, his eyes still fixed on the shield with never a glance at her, he swooped low enough to seize the head. He dropped it into the wallet which closed around it. He had nothing to fear from it now. But the two other Gorgons had awakened and, horrified at the sight of their sister slain, tried to pursue the slayer. Perseus was safe; he had on the cap of darkness and they could not find him.

Literary Analysis
Tall Tale and Myth
What special knowledge helps Perseus kill Medusa? 28

> So over the sea rich-haired Danaë's son,
> Perseus, on his winged sandals sped,
> Flying swift as thought.
> In a wallet of silver,
> A wonder to behold,
> He bore the head of the monster,
> While Hermes, the son of Maia,
> The messenger of Zeus,
> Kept ever at his side.

On his way back he came to Ethiopia and alighted there. By this time Hermes had left him. Perseus found, as Hercules was later to find, that a lovely maiden had been given up to be devoured by a horrible sea serpent. Her name was Andromeda and she was the daughter of a silly vain woman,

> That starred Ethiop queen who strove
> To set her beauty's praise above
> The sea-nymphs, and their power offended.

She had boasted that she was more beautiful than the daughters of Nereus, the Sea-god. An absolutely certain way in those days to draw down on one a wretched fate was to claim superiority

Think Aloud

Vocabulary: Using Context

Direct students' attention to the word *vain* near the bottom of this page. Using a think-aloud process, model how to use context to infer the meaning of an unknown word. Say to students:

> I'm going to think aloud to show you how I would figure out the meaning of vain from its context.
>
> Andromeda was the daughter of a "silly vain woman" who boasted that she was more beautiful than the daughters of the sea-god. So being *vain* has something to do with boasting. This woman also "claim[s] superiority" based on her beauty, and she is punished for her "arrogance." So being *vain* means "being arrogant or boastful about a personal quality such as beauty."

in anything over any deity[1]; nevertheless people were perpetually doing so. In this case the punishment for the arrogance the gods detested fell not on Queen Cassiopeia [kas´ ē ō pē´ ə], Andromeda's mother, but on her daughter. The Ethiopians were being devoured in numbers by the serpent; and, learning from the oracle that they could be freed from the pest only if Andromeda were offered up to it, they forced Cepheus [sē fəs], her father, to consent. When Perseus arrived the maiden was on a rocky ledge by the sea, chained there to wait for the coming of the monster. Perseus saw her and on the instant loved her. He waited beside her until the great snake came for its prey; then he cut its head off just as he had the Gorgon's. The headless body dropped back into the water; Perseus took Andromeda to her parents and asked for her hand, which they gladly gave him.

With her he sailed back to the island and his mother, but in the house where he had lived so long he found no one. The fisherman Dictys' wife was long since dead, and the two others, Danaë and the man who had been like a father to Perseus, had had to fly and hide themselves from Polydectes, who was furious at Danaë's refusal to marry him. They had taken refuge in a temple, Perseus was told. He learned also that the King was holding a banquet in the palace and all the men who favored him were gathered there. Perseus instantly saw his opportunity. He went straight to the palace and entered the hall. As he stood at the entrance, Athena's shining buckler on his breast, the silver wallet at his side, he drew the eyes of every man there. Then before any could look away he held up the Gorgon's head; and at the sight one and all, the cruel King and his servile courtiers, were turned into stone. There they sat, a row of statues, each, as it were, frozen stiff in the attitude he had struck when he first saw Perseus.

When the islanders knew themselves freed from the tyrant it was easy for Perseus to find Danaë and Dictys. He made Dictys king of the island, but he and his mother decided that they would go back with Andromeda to Greece and try to be reconciled to Acrisius, to

1. **deity** (dē´ ə tē) *n.* a god.

29

30 ▲ **Analyze Representations** In what ways does this painting emphasize Perseus' physical strength and bravery? What other details in the myth are suggested in the painting? **[Interpret]**

31

Reading Check

Who does Perseus rescue from the sea serpent?

29 Humanities

Greek Gods

Perseus and Andromeda (detail), by Paolo Veronese

Paolo Veronese ("Paolo of Verona") (1528–1588), Tintoretto, and Titian are three great painters of the end of the Italian Renaissance. All are known for their brilliant colors and the epic sweep of their historical, religious, and mythological scenes. This detail from Veronese's painting shows Perseus in the act of slaying the sea monster. Use the following questions for discussion:

1. What details of Perseus' equipment does the artist include?

   Answer: Students should recognize the sword, magic cap, winged sandals, and magic wallet.

2. How does color contribute to the drama of the scene?

   Answer: The blood-red colors of Perseus' clothing flow toward the gaping red mouth of the monster. The vivid colors highlight the two combatants.

30 Critical Viewing

Answer: The hero's strong arm and his focus on the beast emphasize his strength and bravery. The winged sandals also indicate that he has received divine help.

31 Reading Check

Answer: Perseus rescues Andromeda, an Ethiopian princess.

Differentiated Instruction for Universal Access

Strategy for Special-Needs Students

Have students discuss their opinions of Perseus as a hero. Do they find him heroic? Why or why not? How does Perseus compare to students' personal heroes or to heroes they admire from movies, television, or other stories? Does Perseus seem more heroic as the story progresses, or does he seem heroic right from the beginning? Have students defend their opinions with specific details from the myth.

EL Pronunciation for English Learners

To help students distinguish short *o* and long *o*, post these words: *not, note, clock, cloak, rob, robe,* and *mop, mope*. Pronounce each word, stressing the vowel sound. Have students echo. Call out words at random as students draw, point to, or pantomime them. Have students compare and discuss results. Discuss incorrect choices and clarify.

32 Literary Analysis

Tall Tale and Myth

1. Have students **restate** the prophecy that led to Danaë's imprisonment.

   Answer: The oracle prophesied that Danaë's son would kill Acrisius.

2. **Ask** the Literary Analysis question.

   Answer: When Perseus accidentally kills Acrisius with a discus, he fulfills the prophecy made at the beginning of the story.

Concept Connector

Have students return to the **Activating Prior Knowledge** activity and revise their descriptions of Medusa. In addition, have students compare their Writing About the Big Question responses before reading the selection with their ideas afterwards.

ASSESS

Answers

Critical Thinking

Remind students to support their answers with evidence from the text.

1. (a) He is embarrassed because he has no gift for the King. (b) They are all Zeus' children.
2. (a) He hovers with the sandals, looks only at the shield, cuts off Medusa's head with the sword, puts the head in the wallet, and escapes from the other Gorgons with the aid of the cap of invisibility. (b) He might never have found Medusa and might have wandered forever. Or, he may have found Medusa and been killed.
3. (a) First audiences may have learned to respect their gods and to accept their fates. (b) Students may suggest that people still need to accept situations that are beyond their power to change.
4. **Possible responses:** (a) Perseus' connection with the gods gives him stature because the gods respect him. (b) His plans are extremely ambitious and he delivers on them, showing that he acknowledges heroic responsibility.

Literary Analysis
Tall Tale and Myth
How do the events at the end of the story relate to situations described at the beginning?

see if the many years that had passed since he had put them in the chest had not softened him so that he would be glad to receive his daughter and grandson. When they reached Argos, however, they found that Acrisius had been driven away from the city, and where he was no one could say. It happened that soon after their arrival Perseus heard that the King of Larissa, in the North, was holding a great athletic contest, and he journeyed there to take part. In the discus-throwing when his turn came and he hurled the heavy missile, it swerved and fell among the spectators. Acrisius was there on a visit to the King, and the discus struck him. The blow was fatal and he died at once.

So Apollo's oracle was again proved true. If Perseus felt any grief, at least he knew that his grandfather had done his best to kill him and his mother. With his death their troubles came to an end. Perseus and Andromeda lived happily ever after. Their son, Electryon, was the grandfather of Hercules.

Medusa's head was given to Athena, who bore it always upon the aegis, Zeus's shield, which she carried for him.

Critical Thinking

Cite textual evidence to support your responses.

1. **Key Ideas and Details** **(a)** Why does Perseus set out to kill Medusa? **(b) Infer:** What detail of Perseus' background might have led Athena and Hermes to help Perseus in his quest?
2. **Key Ideas and Details** **(a) Summarize:** Explain the weapons Perseus uses and the actions he takes to kill Medusa. **(b) Hypothesize:** What might have happened to Perseus if he had not received help from the gods?
3. **Integration of Knowledge and Ideas** **(a) Interpret:** What lesson do you think this ancient myth taught its first audiences? **(b) Extend:** In what ways is this myth still relevant today? Explain.
4. **Integration of Knowledge and Ideas** **(a)** How does Perseus' connection with the gods contribute to his stature as a hero? **(b)** How do his plans and deeds reflect his heroic responsibilities? *[Connect to the Big Question: Do heroes have responsibilities?]*

Vocabulary Development

Vocabulary Knowledge Rating

When students have completed reading and discussing "Pecos Bill: The Cyclone" and "Perseus," have them take out their **Vocabulary Rating Chart.** Read the words aloud once more and have students rate their knowledge of the words again in the After Reading column. Clarify any words that are still problematic. Have students write their own definition and example or sentence in the appropriate column. Then have students complete the Vocabulary Practice activities on the next page. Encourage students to use the words in further discussion and written work about the selections. Remind them that they will be accountable for these words on the **Selection Test, *Unit 6 Resources*** (pp. 177–179 or 181–183.)

After You Read

Pecos Bill: The Cyclone • Perseus

Comparing Tall Tale and Myth

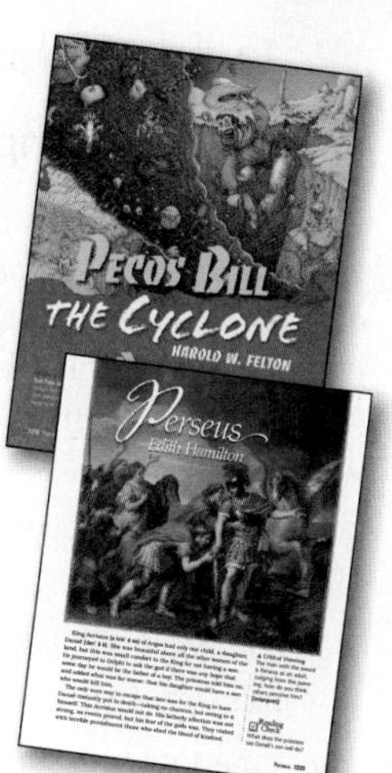

1. **Craft and Structure** Use a chart like the one shown to identify the **tall tale** elements in "Pecos Bill: The Cyclone."

Larger-than-life hero	Far-fetched situations	Amazing feats	Humor	Hyperbole

2. **Craft and Structure** **(a)** What divine actions does the **myth** of Perseus describe? **(b)** In what ways is Perseus a typical **mythic hero**?
3. **Key Ideas and Details** **(a)** What weapons, skills, and knowledge does Pecos Bill use to defeat the cyclone? **(b)** What weapons, skills, and knowledge does Perseus use to defeat Medusa? **(c)** In what ways are Pecos Bill's and Perseus' achievements similar and different?
4. **Integration of Knowledge and Ideas** **(a)** What makes Pecos Bill a hero? **(b)** What makes Perseus a hero?

Timed Writing

Explanatory Text: Essay

The heroes of tall tales and myths usually represent aspects of the cultures that create them. At the same time, every hero embodies some universal qualities—traits that are valued in all cultures. In an essay, compare and contrast the values that Pecos Bill and Perseus represent. **(40 minutes)**

5-Minute Planner

1. Read the prompt carefully and completely.
2. Think about these questions and jot down ideas for your essay.
   - Whom does each hero respect? What does each one fear?
   - What does each hero desire? What does each one accomplish?
   - Does the hero act primarily on his own behalf or on behalf of others?
   - How does each hero reflect the culture that created him?
3. List the main ideas you want to include in your essay. Then, number the ideas in the order you will discuss them.
4. Reread the prompt. Then, refer to your notes as you draft your essay.

ASSESS

Answers

Comparing Tall Tale and Myth

1. **Sample answers: hero;** Bill; **situations:** postholes blown away, resentful cyclone; **feats:** riding and taming cyclone; **humor:** prairie dogs digging postholes, badgers digging wells, six-shooters become popgun and water pistol; **hyperbole:** always raining on Fourth of July, horse learning 27 gaits, creating Death Valley.

   Other sample answers appear in ***Graphic Organizer Transparencies,*** **Comparing Tall Tales and Myths Graphic Organizer A (After You Read)**, p. 210, and in the **Additional Answers** section.
2. (a) Divine actions include Zeus' visit to Danaë as a shower of gold, and the gifts and guidance of Athena and Hermes. (b) Perseus has a divine parent, gets help from the gods, defeats monsters, and fulfills an oracle.
3. (a) Bill's "weapon" is his horse Widow Maker. His skills include strength, speed, endurance, and horsemanship. (b) Perseus uses a sword, shield, winged sandals, magic wallet, and cap of invisibility. He is skilled, resourceful, and listens to the gods. (c) Both men defeat inhuman monsters and rescue the defenseless. Perseus, though headstrong, is fulfilling the will of the gods, while Bill is following his own wild impulses.
4. (a) Bill is brave, tough, energetic, resourceful, and optimistic. (b) Perseus is the son of a god, slays a monster, and rescues a princess.

Timed Writing

1. Review the prompt with students.
2. Have students use the 5-Minute Planner to structure their time. Guide them in answering the bulleted questions. For example, guide students to connect their responses to the first three bullets to the archetype of a cultural hero. How do each hero's motivations, actions, and skills reflect the universal themes related to heroes?
3. Allow students 40 minutes to complete the assignment.
4. As students prewrite and draft, have them refer to their completed Graphic Organizer.

Six Traits Focus

✓	Ideas	Word Choice
✓	Organization	Sentence Fluency
	Voice	Conventions

Assessment Resources

Unit 6 Resources

L1 L2 EL **Selection Test A,** pp. 177–179.
L3 L4 EL **Selection Test B,** pp. 180–182.
L3 L4 **Open-Book Test,** pp. 174–176.

PHLit Online! All assessment resources are available at **www.PHLitOnline.com**

PREACH

Common Core State Standards

- Writing 2, 2.a, b, c, d; 5
- Language 1.b

Introducing the Writing Assignment

Review the assignment and the criteria, using the instruction on the student page.

Dean Smith and John Kilgo on Word Choice

Show students Segment 3 on Dean Smith and John Kilgo on ***See It!* DVD** or from this page in the **Enriched Online Student Edition** at **www.PHLitOnline.com.** Discuss using comparison-and-contrast skills to determine which events to include in a piece.

Writing Workshop
Work in Progress

If students have completed the Work-in-Progress assignments on pp. 1191 and 1207, suggest that they examine their recorded ideas as they begin prewriting. They may wish to develop these ideas in a comparison-and-contrast essay.

What Do You Notice?

1. Have a volunteer read the passage.
2. **Ask:** What do you notice about the passage? **Possible response:** It describes the use of cars in Texas in the early twentieth century.
3. **Ask** students what is compared and contrasted in the passage. **Possible response:** The presence of cars in 1911 is contrasted to that of the past.
4. **Ask:** What accurate, factual details make the contrast clear? **Possible response:** The use of specific numbers of autos and of dollars invested in them makes the contrast clear.
5. Urge students to use accurate, factual details to support their comparisons and contrasts.

Writing Workshop

Common Core State Standards

Writing

2. Write informative/explanatory texts to examine and convey complex ideas, concepts, and information clearly and accurately through the effective selection, organization, and analysis of content.

5. Develop and strengthen writing as needed by planning, revising, editing, rewriting, or trying a new approach, focusing on addressing what is most significant for a specific purpose and audience.

Write an Explanatory Text

Exposition: Comparison-and-Contrast Essay

Defining the Form A **comparison-and-contrast essay** is a written exploration of the similarities and differences between or among two or more things. You may use elements of this type of writing in essays on historical figures and events, consumer reports, or essays on works of art, literature, or music.

Assignment Write a comparison-and-contrast essay about two events, ideas, or historical leaders. Include these elements:

✓ an *analysis* and *discussion* of the similarities and differences between two things, people, places, or ideas

✓ *accurate, factual details* about each subject

✓ a *purpose* for comparing and contrasting

✓ a *balanced presentation* of each subject using either *subject-by-subject* or *point-by-point organization*

✓ error-free grammar, including *varied sentence structure and length*

To preview the criteria on which your comparison-and-contrast essay may be judged, see the rubric on page 1241.

Writing Workshop: *Work in Progress*

Review the work you did on pages 1191 and 1207.

Reading-Writing Connection

To get a feel for comparison-and-contrast writing, read "The News" by Neil Postman on page 478.

WRITE GUY
Jeff Anderson, M.Ed.

What Do You Notice?

Methods of Comparing and Contrasting

The following passage is from the 1911 Texas Almanac's "Automobiles in Texas." Read the passage several times.

Ten years ago an automobile was a curiosity in the leading cities of Texas. Five years ago the people in many counties had never seen what was then known as the horseless carriage. Today it is estimated that the number of automobiles in actual service in Texas will reach nearly 30,000 and that over $40,000,000 is invested in the machines.

Jot down what you notice about this passage and share your thoughts with a partner. Consider how you can use methods of comparing and contrasting in your essay.

Teaching Resources

The following resources can be used to enrich or extend the instruction.

- All *Unit 6 Resources*
  Writing Workshop, pp. 183–184
- All *Common Core Companion,* pp. 190–201, 220–221
- All *Professional Development Guidebook*
  Rubrics for Self-Assessment: Comparison-and-Contrast Essay, pp. 234–235
- All *Graphic Organizer Transparencies*
  Rubric for Self-Assessment: Comparison-and-Contrast Essay, p. 212
- All *See It!* DVD
  Dean Smith and John Kilgo, Segments 3 and 4

All resources, including print and video, are also available at **www.PHLitOnline.com.**

Prewriting/Planning Strategies

Explore categories. Working with a group, make a list of categories that your intended audience would find interesting, such as famous athletes, famous artists, vacation spots, or favorite foods. Then, choose one category and discuss it in greater depth. Identify specific topics within the category that present clear similarities and differences.

Find related pairs. Explore topics in terms of clear opposites, clear similarities, or close relationships. Start with names of people, places, objects, or ideas. Note related subjects that come to mind, as well as relationships that interest you. Choose one of these idea pairs to develop.

Specify your purpose. To identify a purpose for your essay, consider the following possibilities:

- To persuade—You may want readers to accept your opinion that one subject is preferable to another.
- To explain—You may want readers to understand something special about the subjects.
- To describe—You may want readers to understand the basic similarities and differences between your subjects.

Use specific criteria. When you compare and contrast, you should examine specific criteria as a basis for your writing. Use a three-column chart like the one shown to identify criteria and the similarities and differences between subjects.

Criteria	Reading Literature	Listening to Music
Entertainment value	Very entertaining, requires you to use your imagination	Entertaining, helping change your mood or making you feel like dancing
Attention needed	Requires your full attention and concentration	Allows listener to do other things
Portability/ Necessary materials	Extremely portable, books and e-readers can fit in most bags, light is always needed, batteries needed if flashlight is used	Portable if using a CD or MP3 player, batteries or electricity may be needed

PHLit Online!
www.PHLitOnline.com
- Author video: Writing Process
- Author video: Rewards of Writing

TEACH

Prewriting Strategies

1. Introduce the prewriting strategies.
2. Have students apply the strategies.

Teaching the Strategies

1. Help students explore categories by writing the following on the board: *sports, movies, music.* Invite students to suggest two other general categories.
2. Help students identify a purpose for their essays by providing these examples: *Will they want to* **persuade** *the reader that the Vietnam War was as divisive as the Civil War? Will they want to* **explain** *the similarities and differences of letters written by soldiers in the Union and Confederate Armies? Will they want to* **describe** *the similarities and differences of parades given for returning soldiers in WWII and Vietnam?*
3. Provide students with a copy of the Three-column Chart in ***Graphic Organizer Transparencies***, p. 222.

Think Aloud: Model Finding Related Pairs

Model the strategy, using the following "think aloud":

To find related pairs, I'll first think of one idea, the baseball player *Babe Ruth.* That makes me think of other baseball players like *Ted Williams, Lou Gehrig,* and *Carl Yastrzemski.* I think I'll choose *Gehrig* and *Ruth* to write about because I'm most interested in those two players.

Six Traits Focus

✔ Ideas	Word Choice
✔ Organization	Sentence Fluency
Voice	Conventions

PH WRITING COACH Grade 9

Students will find additional information on writing a comparison-and-contrast essay in Chapter 8.

Applying Understanding by Design Principles

Clarifying Expected Outcomes: Using Rubrics

- Before students begin working on this assignment, have them preview the Rubric for Self-Assessment (p. 1241) to learn what qualities their essays must have.
- Review the criteria in the Rubric with the class. Before students use the Rubric to assess their writing, work with them to rate the Student Model (p. 1240) using the Rubric.
- If you wish to assess students' essays with either a 4-point or a 6-point scoring rubric, see **Professional Development Guidebook**, pp. 234–235.

Drafting Strategies

1. Introduce the drafting strategies, using the instruction on the student page.
2. Have students apply the strategies as they draft.

Teaching the Strategies

1. Provide students with a copy of a Venn Diagram in ***Graphic Organizer Transparencies,*** p. 226. Tell them that their essays should use the most important points of similarities and differences from their Venn diagrams.
2. Note that students might use point-by-point organization if their information is detailed. This structure will help the reader keep track of complicated ideas or numerous names.
3. Tell students that they might use subject-by-subject organization if the information can be easily remembered and understood.
4. Have students make an outline with their points as the topics and their details as the subtopics. Have students make sure that every topic has at least one subtopic.

   *Refer students to the **Outline** in **Graphic Organizer Transparencies,** p. 219.*
5. Remind students that they can support their generalizations with quotations from people who know about the subject.

Think Aloud: Model Supporting Generalizations with Specifics

Model the strategy, using the following "think aloud":

Let's say that I'm contrasting the U.S. public's response to World War II with its response to the Vietnam War. In my essay, I make this general statement: *Most people supported the war effort in the 1940s.* Then I give details that led me to that generalization: *People planted Victory gardens, bought war bonds, and cheerfully accepted food rationing.*

Six Traits Focus

	Ideas	✓	Word Choice
✓	Organization		Sentence Fluency
✓	Voice		Conventions

Drafting Strategies

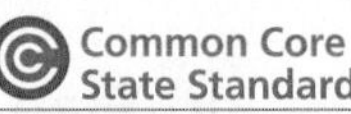

Writing

2.a. Organize complex ideas, concepts, and information to make important connections and distinctions.

2.b. Develop the topic with well-chose, relevant, and sufficient facts.

2.c. Use appropriate and varied transitions to link the major sections of the text, create cohesion, and clarify the relationships among complex ideas and concepts.

Prepare to compare. Look at your Criteria chart. Use the details from your chart to fill in a Venn diagram, separating it into similarities and differences, helping you prepare to organize your essay. Record similarities in the space where the circles overlap, and note differences in the outer sections of the circles.

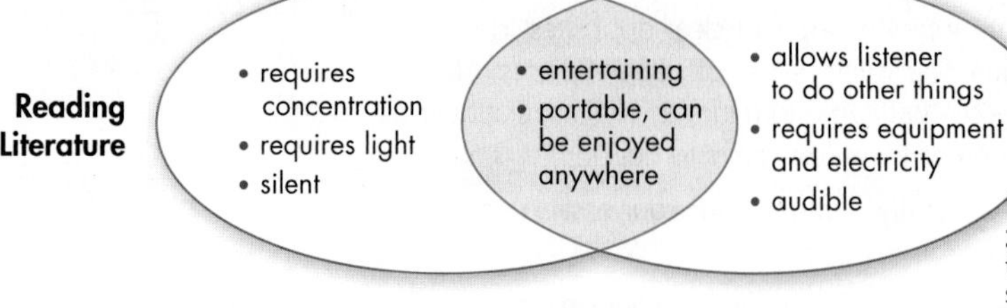

Choose an organization. Select an organization that suits your topic. Point-by-point and subject-by-subject plans are the most common types of organization used in comparison-and-contrast writing.

- **Point-by-point organization:** Move between your subjects as you discuss points of comparison. First, compare one element (or criterion) of both subjects, and then address another element of both subjects. Continue this process until you have covered all the features. This method allows you to sharpen your points of similarity and difference.
- **Subject-by-subject organization:** Compare your subjects as complete units. First, discuss all the features of one subject; then, discuss all the features of the other. This format allows you to focus on one subject at a time, but be sure to address the same features and devote equal time to each subject.

Point-by-Point Plan

Point 1
- Subject A
- Subject B

Point 2
- Subject A
- Subject B

Subject-by-Subject Plan

Subject A
- Point 1
- Point 2

Subject B
- Point 1
- Point 2

Add transitions. For either type of organization, use transitional words or phrases to connect your ideas. To make comparisons, use words such as *similarly, in comparison,* or *likewise.* If you are contrasting ideas, use transitions such as *on the other hand, in contrast,* or *however.*

Support generalizations with specifics. Whether your purpose in comparing and contrasting two subjects is to describe, to persuade, or to explain, provide enough detail to fully develop your points. Support your statements about similarities and differences with a sufficient number of facts, examples, and other forms of evidence that clearly relate to your ideas and are well suited to your audience.

Differentiated Instruction for Universal Access

Strategy for Less Proficient Writers
After students have chosen an organization for their topics, have them make outlines to map their essay layout. Have students mirror the outline offered in the Point-by-Point Plan Graphic or the Subject-by-Subject Plan Graphic. As students draft, have them check off the details as they include them in their essays.

*Refer students to the **Outline** in **Graphic Organizer Transparencies,** p. 219.*

Strategies for Advanced Writers
Have students examine the strength of their supporting details by asking themselves the following questions: *How can I make my details more specific? Have I supported my points with enough details? Have I used varied forms of evidence? Do my details reinforce my purpose?* Answering the questions will help students shape their writing.

Writers on Writing

Coach Dean Smith with John Kilgo
On Word Choice

Dean Smith and John Kilgo are the co-authors of the excerpt from *The Carolina Way* (p. 1037).

John Kilgo, my co-author, took notes of our conversations related to this book and put my ideas into written form. I have strong feelings about what I want my words to convey, which means we did extensive rewriting and revising. When we finally signed off on a chapter, it was always shorter, sharper in focus, and less repetitive than the original.

Professional Model:

from *"The Carolina Way"*

A steady focus on taking care of the little things, attending diligently to the many details involved with building a team, helped us produce a mind-set that enhanced our ability to handle the big things. . . . Here are some of the so-called little things that we integrated into our program:

Punctuality: Players knew I arrived early for meetings and practices, and I expected everyone to be there and ready to go. . . . Tardiness is the ~~definition~~ *height of* arrogance. In effect, you're saying, "My time is more important than yours." Being on time is being considerate of others. . . .

Swearing: We discouraged it in our program. When a player cursed in practice, the entire team ran for him. . . . This is not an easy subject to talk about because it can sound ~~sanctimonious~~ *pious*. . . . However, I believe that anger can be expressed without using profanity.

Top priority: We checked on the class attendance of our players, as well as their grades and academic progress.

We used the phrase "produce a mind-set," because it's important for readers to know that our program had a strong philosophy concerning team-building techniques that we instilled in our players beginning with the first day they stepped on campus.

We first wrote that tardiness is the "definition" of arrogance, but changed it to "height of arrogance" on the rewrite. Using "height of arrogance" seemed to more strongly emphasize how unacceptable tardiness was in our program.

We first used "sanctimonious" in describing the difficulty in even discussing the subject of swearing, but changed it to "pious," which sounds less "preachy," or at least we thought so at the time. Also, words have a rhythm, and "pious" just seemed to fit better here.

Dean Smith with John Kilgo on Word Choice

Review the passage on the student page with the class, using Smith and Kilgo's comments to deepen students' understanding of the process of choosing words.

Teaching From the Professional Model

1. Show students Segment 3 on Dean Smith and John Kilgo on ***See It! DVD*** or from this page in the **Enriched Online Student Edition.** Discuss their emphasis on the importance of revision.
2. Ask students to define the word *mind-set* and to explain what this word conveys to the reader.

   Possible response: If your mind is set, you carry the attitude with you at all times. It becomes a part of you. This word conveys that the coach took his program very seriously.
3. Explain to students that using precise words to convey meaning is critical to the reader's understanding. The word "sanctimonious" is an excellent word; it's just not the right word for the sentence.
4. Have students go through their essays and highlight any words that do not fit into the context of their writing. Have students use a thesaurus to find more suitable wording.

Show or assign the video online at **www.PHLitOnline.com.**

Revising Strategies

1. Introduce the revision strategies, using the instruction on the student page.
2. Have students apply the strategies as they revise their essays.

Teaching the Strategies

1. Supply each student with two different-colored pencils or highlighters, and have them follow the instructions in the text.
2. Ask students for examples of transitional words or phrases.

   Possible responses: *conversely, similarly, on the contrary, instead, in contrast*
3. When students review each other's essays, have them look for vague, weak verbs. Write on the board the following example:

   She went *into the room.*

   She stormed *into the room.*

   She floated *into the room.*

   She stomped *into the room.*

   Ask students to determine which is the vague verb and which are the vivid, precise verbs. Ask them what images the stronger verbs communicate.

   Answer: *Went* is a vague verb. *Stormed, floated,* and *stomped* are vivid, precise verbs. *Stormed* and *stomped* suggest anger, and *floated* suggests happiness or dreaminess.
4. Have student pairs work together to identify stronger words and constructions to replace the circled items in each other's essays.

   For more on revising, see Coach Dean Smith and John Kilgo's comments on p. 1237.

Six Traits Focus

✔	Ideas	✔	Word Choice
✔	Organization	✔	Sentence Fluency
✔	Voice		Conventions

Revising Strategies

Common Core State Standards

Writing

2.c. Use appropriate and varied transitions to link the major sections of the text, create cohesion, and clarify the relationships among complex ideas and concepts.

2.d. Use precise language and domain-specific vocabulary to manage the complexity of the topic.

Language

1.b. Use various types of phrases and clauses to convey specific meanings and add variety and interest to writing or presentations.

Revise to make comparisons and contrasts clear. Using two different colors, mark your draft to distinguish between the two subjects you discuss. Whether you have used point-by-point or subject-by-subject organization, this color coding will clearly reveal if you have organized a balanced presentation of both subjects. If necessary, you can expand or reduce coverage of one of your subjects to achieve balance. Next, evaluate the places where the two colors—and subjects—meet. Add transitional words to make the shifts clear.

Model: Revising for Clarity

Reading literature and listening to music are two of my favorite pastimes.
^Reading literature is an excellent source of entertainment, taking me to worlds away from today. Listening to music is also fun. I can dance around the house while I do my chores.
Both
^~~R~~eading and listening to music can be enjoyed most anywhere.
However,
^~~I~~t is better to have quiet when I try to read.

The author uses the transitions "both" and "however" to move more fluidly from one idea to the next.

Revise to add specifics. To achieve your purpose and to help your readers understand the comparisons you make, add enough detail to explain the differences and similarities you see. Look for places where you can add related information that strengthens your description or analysis, such as well-chosen facts, quotations, definitions, or examples.

Peer Review

Exchange drafts with a partner. As you read each other's essays, circle any vague language that you find. Consider choices that will convey the meaning more precisely. Then, discuss with your reader specific details that would make your comparisons more vivid. Incorporate these details into your draft.

Vague: In contrast to literature, popular music forms a soundtrack for our lives.

Specific: In contrast to literature that we must read to enjoy, popular music, like the Top 40 tunes we hear on the radio, forms a soundtrack for our lives. We can enjoy it as we drive, shop, or even fall asleep at night.

Strategies for Using Technology in Writing

If students are using word-processing software to draft and revise their comparison-and-contrast essays, suggest that they use the *Find* feature of the software to locate conjunctions such as *and, but,* and *yet.* When they find a conjunction, have them examine the sentence to determine whether it is a compound sentence. If it is, have students be sure that they have a comma before the conjunction.

Students can also use features of the **Writing and Grammar Interactive Textbook Online** at **www.pearsonsuccessnet.com** to draft or revise their essays.

Varying Sentence Structure and Length

A sequence of sentences of the same length and structural pattern can have a tedious effect on readers. You can make your paragraphs more interesting and readable by varying sentence length, introducing new sentence beginnings, and inverting subject-verb order.

Vary Sentence Length If you find an unbroken series of long sentences, look for an opportunity to include a short sentence. Since the short sentence will draw the reader's attention, use it to emphasize an important detail or idea. Be sure that it is a complete thought and not a fragment.

Original: Memories of long hours of practice, the brutal weather, the aches and bruises of an endless season were erased by the single fact that we had won the championship.

Revised: Memories of long hours of practice, the brutal weather, the aches and bruises of an endless season were erased by a single fact. We had won the championship.

Vary Sentence Beginnings If you have written a series of sentences beginning with a noun or pronoun, look for opportunities to start sentences with different parts of speech. Look at these techniques:

Adverb clause: *Anywhere you go*, you will still find most people care about others.

Prepositional phrase: *After a long Saturday of work*, Sarah did not feel like going out.

Complement: *Most interesting to me* was an electronic display of the battlefield. (complement of the verb *was*)

Direct object: *Our report* I gave to the editor; my opinion I kept to myself. (object of the verb *gave*)

Vary Subject-Verb Order You can vary sentence beginnings by reversing the usual subject-verb order.

Original: The mystery guest is here at last.

Inverted: Here at last is the mystery guest.

Grammar in Your Writing

As you review the three longest paragraphs in your draft, examine the length and pattern of each sentence to look for ways to improve variety. Change sentence lengths, alter sentence beginnings, and invert subject-verb order to add interest to your writing.

PH WRITING COACH

Further instruction and practice are available in *Prentice Hall Writing Coach*.

Varying Sentence Structure and Length

1. Introduce the writing skill, using the instruction on the student page.
2. Discuss the examples and the strategies for varying sentence length and structure.
3. Have students follow the instruction under Grammar in Your Writing to correct errors in their drafts.

Teaching the Grammar Skill

1. Have students read aloud their essays to listen for sentence patterns.
2. Write this example on the board to show students how to revise a series of long sentences:

   Original: *When you speak to Elvis fans today, they talk about Elvis in a reverent tone, and they reminisce about what a force he was, proving that, in some ways, Elvis will always be alive.*

   Revision: *When you speak to Elvis fans today, they talk about Elvis in a reverent tone, and they reminisce about what a force he was. In some ways, Elvis will always be alive.*
3. Write the following sentence on the board, and have students use alternate beginnings for it. Suggest that they use adverb clauses, participles, and prepositional phases.

   Elvis Presley was the King of Music.

   Possible response: Adverb clause: *When my grandmother was a teenager, Elvis Presley was the King of Music.* Participle: *Looking back, I understand why Elvis Presley was called the King of Music.* Prepositional phrase: *After all this time, Elvis Presley remains the King of Music.*
4. Write on the board the following sample of varying subject-verb order:

   Original: *The King of Music is here.*
   Revised: *Here is the King of Music.*
5. Have students exchange papers, look over the three paragraphs, and suggest sentence improvements.

Student Model

Review the Student Model with the class, using the annotations to analyze the writer's use of the elements of a comparison-and-contrast essay.

Teaching From the Student Model

1. Explain that the Student Model is a sample, and comparison-and-contrast essays may be longer.
2. Direct students' attention to the first sentence in the Student Model. **Ask** students how this thesis statement sets the tone of the essay.

   Possible response: The thesis statement sets up a playful tone by casually placing the words *love* and *hate* together and by comparing the town with Mayberry, a fictional town in a television comedy.
3. **Ask** students to identify the second point that Lauren addresses.

   Answer: Her second point is the size of the town.
4. **Ask** students to identify details that develop the paragraph on size. Which details reflect her love? Which details reflect her hate?

   Possible response: Love: fifteen cars is a traffic jam; has tab at the grocery and drug stores; knows everyone's first, middle, and last names; has made trustworthy friends. Hate: has to drive sixteen miles to the nearest major store; knows everyone's first, middle, and last names; everybody knows her dating history, height, weight, and age; paper reports visits to nursing homes.
5. **Ask** students how Lauren's humor helps her reflect on her ideas.

   Possible response: Lauren's humor allows her to make light of her annoyances, showing that her pet peeves are trivial in comparison to what she loves about the town.

Connecting to Real-Life Writing

Explain that students can use their comparing and contrasting skills to help them list pros and cons when they are considering important decisions in life. Point out that researchers also write comparison-and-contrast essays to answer questions such as these: *How is this newly discovered dinosaur similar to and different from those that we already know about? How does this form of medical treatment differ from previous treatments?*

Student Model: Lauren De Loach, Bernice, LA

Ambivalence

When I consider my conflicting feelings about my hometown, I see that there are things that I love and hate about living in Bernice, Louisiana, a nineties version of Mayberry. I love the security of a small town, and I hate it. I love the way that my town is not clouded by the smog of a city, and I hate it too. I love it and I hate that I love it.

Lauren's essay will compare two feelings: what she loves and what she hates about her hometown.

I love and hate the security in my town for a number of reasons. I love it because I know that it is my dog scratching at my door at 5:30 in the morning and not some dangerous stranger. In my town, a fifteen-car traffic jam is front-page news. On the other hand, I hate that it gets a little boring sometimes. I don't want criminals at my door, but a little excitement would be nice.

Using a point-by-point organization, Lauren addresses the first contrast in her attitudes about her town: She feels ambivalence about its security.

I am fond of the size of Bernice and I detest it, too. I'm glad that only fifteen cars is a major traffic jam. But I hate that I have to drive sixteen miles to the nearest major store. I love and hate that my town is so small that I know everybody's first, middle, and last names. I like it because I have a "tab" at the grocery store and the drug store, so that eliminates the necessity of carrying money. I hate that everybody knows me because that means that everybody finds out about whom I'm dating, whom I once dated, my height, weight, and age. I also hate that we all know each other so well that the most entertaining news we can come up with to put in the *Bernice Banner* is that Peggy Jane and her brother JC visited their Aunt Goosey Lou in the nursing home. But by knowing everyone so well, I've made friends who are trustworthy because we know all of one another's deepest secrets.

These facts support Lauren's ideas and opinions.

Even though I say that I detest some things, home wouldn't be home without these silly quirks. I love that my parents and their friends are known as the "elite group" because they have traveled beyond Texas, Arkansas, and Mississippi. I love saying that I have read the *Iliad* to people who think I would not read such a book. I know that it sounds like I love the provincialism that small towns can impose, but the smells of fresh-cut grass and the gardenia bush outside my door are what make my home my home.

This is what I love and what I hate, but I don't really. The overall feeling I get from living in Bernice is ambivalence. I love it and I hate that I love such goofy things. But the parts of home that seem so trivial are the ones that make you who you are. That makes a place your home.

Lauren's comparison allows her to be funny, but it also helps her reflect on her ideas.

Strategies for Test Taking

Remind students of the distinction between *compare* (show the similarities) and *contrast* (show the differences). Point out that keeping these meanings in mind when a standardized test question focuses on comparison and contrast will help them select or organize their answers.

Editing and Proofreading

Check your draft to correct errors in spelling, grammar, and punctuation.

Focus on compound sentences. Comparison-and-contrast essays often contain compound sentences—those with two independent clauses joined by a semicolon or a coordinating conjunction, such as *or, and,* or *but.* Check that you have correctly punctuated these sentences.

Conjunction: I liked the chili, but it was spicy.

Semicolon: I rushed out; I was late for the bus.

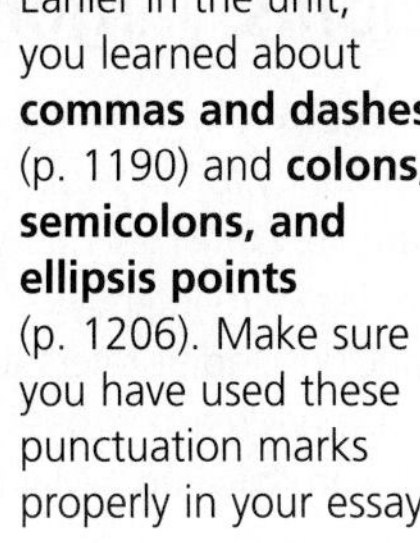

Spiral Review

Earlier in the unit, you learned about **commas and dashes** (p. 1190) and **colons, semicolons, and ellipsis points** (p. 1206). Make sure you have used these punctuation marks properly in your essay.

Publishing and Presenting

Consider one of the following ways to share your writing:

Deliver an oral presentation. Read your comparison-and-contrast essay aloud to an audience of your classmates. If possible, include props or visuals to enhance the reading.

Make a poster. Present your comparison-and-contrast findings visually in a poster. Use a graphic organizer, such as a Venn diagram, to show the similarities and differences of your subjects. If possible, add photographs and illustrations to show the distinctive elements of your subjects.

Reflecting on Your Writing

Writer's Journal Jot down your answers to this question:
How did writing about your topic help you understand it?

Rubric for Self-Assessment

Find evidence in your writing to address each category. Then, use the rating scale to grade your work.

Criteria	Rating Scale (not very – very)
Focus: How clear is your purpose for comparing and contrasting?	1 2 3 4 5
Organization: How balanced is your organization?	1 2 3 4 5
Support/Elaboration: How accurate and factual are the details you use to support your ideas?	1 2 3 4 5
Style: How effectively do you use transitions to clarify ideas?	1 2 3 4 5
Conventions: How correct is your grammar, especially related to your use of varied sentence structure and length?	1 2 3 4 5

Editing and Proofreading

1. Introduce the editing and proofreading focus, using the instruction on the student page.
2. Have students edit and proofread their essays, correcting grammar, spelling, punctuation, and word choice. Make sure they look for errors of the type noted in the lesson focus and the Spiral Review.

Teaching the Editing Focus

1. Have students go through their essays and underline every compound sentence. Tell students to make sure that each sentence has two independent clauses and is punctuated by a comma and a coordinating conjunction or by a semicolon.
2. Tell students to make sure that sentences with semicolons contain two independent clauses with related ideas.

Six Traits Focus

	Ideas		Word Choice
	Organization		Sentence Fluency
	Voice	✔	Conventions

ASSESS

Publishing and Presenting

1. If students are preparing to deliver oral presentations, have them practice in pairs. Partners should offer each other suggestions about delivery and should ask questions about each other's topics.
2. Have students review posters and discuss what was helpful. Ask students what techniques they found the most creative and informational.

Reflecting on Your Writing

Suggest that students respond to the following questions in their journals: Do you believe that you achieved your purpose? Explain your answer. Were you satisfied with how you organized your essay?

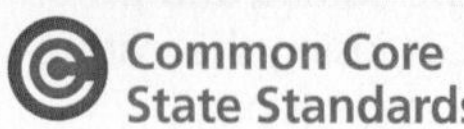

EXTEND

Common Core State Standards

- Language 4.c, 5.a

Idioms, Jargon, and Technical Terms

1. Introduce the skill, using the instruction on the student page.
2. Review the examples in the chart.

Think Aloud: Model the Skill

Use this "think aloud" to model the skill of interpreting idioms. Say to students:

Sometimes I can interpret an idiom the way I would interpret a metaphor. Let's say I read that "Jen is a back-seat driver." You can't actually drive a car from the back seat, so I know this is not meant to be taken literally. I can infer that a **back-seat driver** must be someone who is trying to control the car without actually driving it. One way to do that would be to sit in the back and tell the driver what to do. **Back-seat driver** must mean "a passenger who tells the driver how to drive."

Practice A

Sample answers:

1. black eye
2. screen
3. clarinet
4. car-washer
5. new sidewalks

Vocabulary Workshop

Idioms, Jargon, and Technical Terms

Common Core State Standards

Language

4.c. Consult general and specialized reference materials, both print and digital, to find the pronunciation of a word or determine or clarify its precise meaning, its part of speech, or its etymology.

5.a. Interpret figures of speech in context and analyze their role in the text.

An **idiom** is an expression that is characteristic of a language, region, community, or class of people. It cannot be understood literally. For example, *I'm all ears* does not mean "I am made of ears" but rather "I'm listening intently." "Throw in the towel" has nothing to do with fabric; instead, it refers to a boxer's act of forfeiting a match. Now, the phrase has reached past sports to become an idiom that is understood to mean "give up." Many dictionaries list idioms at the end of the entry for the main word in the idiom.

Many fields of study, work, and play have **technical terms.** These are words that may be familiar, but they have specialized meanings in the particular field. Examples from the field of computers include *software, hard drive, Internet,* and *USB port.* Technical terms help people who share knowledge of the field communicate more effectively.

Like technical terms, **jargon** is the specialized words and phrases used in a specific field. While it is frequently useful, jargon can sometimes appear to be scientific or technical but instead is vague and meaningless.

Jargon	Meaning
The vehicle's internal combustion engine became depleted of its distilled mixture of hydrocarbons.	The car ran out of gas.
This moisturizing cleansing bar is hot off the shelf.	This soap is brand new.
Stakeholders in our school environment need new text resources.	Students in our school need new textbooks.

Practice A Match the definition in the box with the underlined jargon in each sentence. Use context clues to figure out the meanings.

screen	clarinet	new sidewalks
car-washer	black eye	

1. When the baseball hit me in the face, I ended up with a <u>periorbital hematoma.</u>
2. On the large <u>monitor</u>, I can see more of the document at once.
3. The jazz musician put his <u>licorice stick</u> to his lips and played.

Teaching Resources

Unit 6 Resources

Idioms, Jargon, and Technical Terms, pp. 185–186

Vocabulary Central, featuring definitions, audio pronunciations. Word Families, and activities, is online at **www.PHLitOnline.com.**

4. The vehicle appearance operative washed and dried the car.
5. Public infrastructure upgrades are needed so people can walk around more safely.

Practice B Identify the idiom in each sentence and write a definition for each. If you are unsure of the meaning of the word or phrase, check your definition in a print or online dictionary.

1. She let us down by not showing up for the game.
2. I am up to my ears in homework.
3. Marvin, please cool it and sit down over there.
4. It's been a long day, so I'm going to turn in.
5. Jurors must try to keep an open mind during the trial.
6. Let's just nip this problem in the bud.
7. What are you driving at?
8. Your question has put the salesperson on the spot.
9. If you cheat in that game, I will blow the whistle on you.
10. I'm going to whip this team into shape.

PHLit Online!
www.PHLitOnline.com
- Illustrated vocabulary words
- Interactive vocabulary games
- Vocabulary flashcards

Activity Prepare five note cards like the one shown. Write each of the following words and its definition on a card. Look the word up in a dictionary and find both a common and a technical meaning. Write the technical meaning on the card and identify the professional field in which that meaning is commonly used.

mouse spare snake key single

Word:

Common Definition:

Field:

Technical Definition:

Comprehension and Collaboration

Education is a specialized field. Work with several classmates and create a glossary of technical terms that apply to education. You might begin with words like *computer lab, activity bus,* and *hall pass.* Discuss how these terms may not be familiar to people outside of education.

ASSESS/EXTEND

Answers

Practice B

Sample answers:

1. Idiom: let us down; definition: disappointed
2. Idiom: up to my ears in; definition: overwhelmed by
3. Idiom: cool it; definition: calm down
4. Idiom: turn in; definition: go to bed
5. Idiom: keep an open mind; definition: be open to changing their opinions
6. Idiom: nip this problem in the bud; definition: end the problem just as it is beginning
7. Idiom: driving at; definition: making a point about
8. Idiom: on the spot; definition: in a difficult or embarrassing situation
9. Idiom: blow the whistle; definition: report to the authorities
10. Idiom: whip into shape; definition: bring to a desired condition

Activity

Provide each student with five note cards and a dictionary or list of reliable Web sites. Set a time limit for students to complete the activity. When time is up, have students share their responses and discuss the different meanings of the words.

Comprehension and Collaboration

Assign groups and have members work together to brainstorm for technical terms from the field of education. Have students write their own technical definitions for their terms. Have groups discuss how these technical terms could be confusing for people outside the field of education. Finally, have each group create a glossary of their terms, including definitions, pronunciations, and illustrations for each. Have groups share their glossaries with the class.

Differentiated Instruction for Universal Access

Support for English Learners

Explain that one way to understand idioms is to picture what is described and think about what the picture implies. For instance, **my hands are tied** does not mean that the speaker's hands are actually tied, but picturing a person with her hands tied can help students recognize that such a person is helpless. Guide students to picture the following idioms and use their mental pictures to understand what each idiom means: *give a hand, hit the nail on the head,* and *put one's foot down.* Encourage students to create idiom dictionaries that they can refer to.

Enrichment for Advanced Students

Challenge students to write one or two paragraphs that include jargon and idioms. Paragraphs should be interpretable. When students are finished, have them exchange papers with partners and translate one another's paragraphs into plain English.

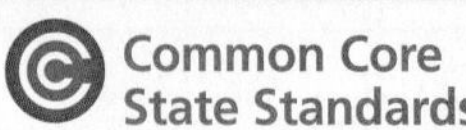

Common Core State Standards

- Reading Informational Text 7

Learn the Skills

1. Introduce the workshop, including the activity on page 1245.
2. Explain that visual images may include photographs, illustrations, charts, diagrams, or film footage.
   - Discuss the kinds of information that non-visual texts can provide. Help students recognize how texts present a sequence of events, explain cause and effect, and provide background information.
   - Point out ways in which texts can show the importance of ideas. **Ask:** What are some examples of words that call attention to certain ideas and minimize others? **Possible responses:** *most importantly, besides, in addition,* and *easily overlooked.*
   - Discuss the kinds of information that can be conveyed by images. Images can, for example, convey emotions or show how something works.
   - Explain that while images do not lie, the photographer or the editor choosing the image can manipulate an image by cropping it or taking the picture from an angle that emphasizes certain details.
3. Help students compare and contrast the article and the photograph on page 1244.

   Ask: Which treatment, the text or visual, has more impact? Why?

   Possible response: The photograph of the panda has more emotional impact because the animal looks tiny and sick.

MEDIA LITERACY

Communications Workshop

Comparing Media Coverage

Both visual images and non-visual texts present events and communicate information. Comparing and contrasting how the media uses images and text to communicate will help you to develop your media literacy skills.

Common Core State Standards

Reading Informational Text
7. Analyze various accounts of a subject told in different mediums, determining which details are emphasized in each account.

Learn the Skills

Analyze and then compare and contrast the ways in which events and information are conveyed in various types of media.

Comparing and Contrasting Presentation News events can be described with words or with images, or both. As you look at media coverage, compare and contrast the way in which text and/or images such as graphics, illustrations, and photographs bring events to life for readers.

- *When examining non-visual texts, ask:* In what order are the events described? What event, if any, is identified as most important or critical? What words or phrases indicate the importance of the event?
- *When viewing visual images, ask:* What event does the image capture? Why was this particular image chosen? What point of view does the image reveal?

Comparing and Contrasting Communication Once you have analyzed the presentation of events, compare and contrast the ways in which the information is communicated. Ask these questions:

- In what ways is the information in the text and the visual similar and different?
- Which treatment, the text or visual, gives more detailed information?
- Which treatment, the text or visual, has more impact? Why?

Twin Pandas Reach Critical Milestone

Veterinarians at the Beijing Zoo have announced that twin pandas born in September are now expected to survive. Their mother, Yong Yong, was unable to nurse them from birth. The zoo staff quickly intervened, but the future of the young pandas was uncertain. Now that the pandas have survived their first seven weeks, veterinarians are optimistic that the pandas will survive.

When asked how long the pandas will require care

▲ **1.** This article describes an event. Compare and contrast how this article and the photograph present the event.

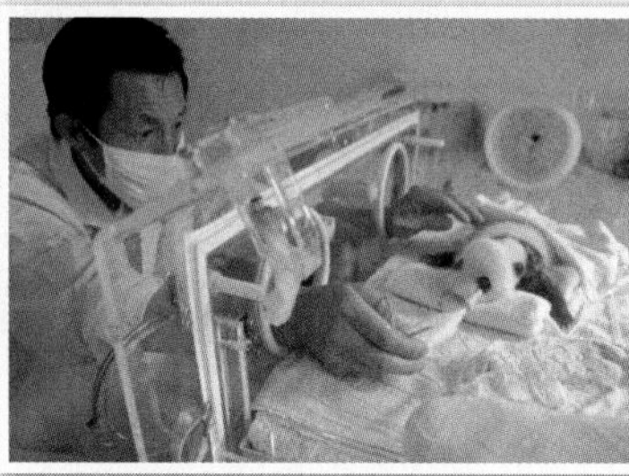

▲ **2.** This photograph shows a scene that is part of the event the text describes. Compare and contrast how the photograph and the text communicate information.

Strategies for Comparing Media Coverage

Model the skill of comparing media coverage. Say to students:

In looking at the picture of the panda, I'm immediately struck by the clinical setting. I feel sorry for the panda and want to know what's wrong with it. It looks so pathetic and vulnerable.

Now, I read the text, and I begin to understand. The text explains that the mother couldn't nurse the pandas, so that helps me understand what's happening in the picture: The baby panda is in critical condition and vets have intervened to help the panda survive. Because the vets have given the pandas care like that shown in the picture, the pandas will probably survive.

The text and the photograph give different information and evoke different feelings. Together, they give me a more complete understanding of the story.

Practice the Skills

Apply what you have learned and use the discussion guide below to complete the activity.

ACTIVITY: Compare and Contrast Text and Visuals

With a partner, analyze two pairings of image and text that report on the same subject. Use the encyclopedia entry shown below as your first pairing. Then, research print and online sources to locate another example of text and images addressing the same subject. Take notes on both pairings as you analyze ways in which the visual and the text present events and communicate information. Discuss similarities and differences between the texts and the visuals using the discussion guide below. Then, write and present a summary of your findings to your class.

San Francisco Earthquake

Damage from the San Francisco Earthquake

The San Francisco earthquake of 1906 had its epicenter near San Francisco, but the effects of the quake reached from southern Oregon to Los Angeles. Those who experienced the quake described it as about a minute of forceful shaking and powerful shocks.

The conditions of the earthquake challenged the views of contemporary scientists and resulted in extensive studies by scientists of the time. The insights that resulted from their research are the basis for

Use a **discussion guide** like this to compare and contrast how events are presented and information is communicated in visual images and non-visual texts.

1. **Compare:** What event is depicted both in the visual and in the text?
2. **Contrast:** What aspect of the event does the text describe that the visual does not? What aspect of the event does the visual bring to life that the text does not?
3. **Compare and contrast:** What overall information, or main idea, is communicated by the visual alone? What overall information is communicated by the text alone?
4. **Evaluate:** Would the encyclopedia entry be as effective if it contained text only? Would your second example be as effective as text only? Why or why not?
5. **Generalize:** What generalizations might you make about the kinds of information that are best conveyed with visuals and the kinds of information that seem better suited to text?

Practice the Skills

1. Review the assignment with students. Make sure they understand that their summaries should discuss both similarities and differences between the image and text. Encourage them to think about which form has more emotional impact and which form contains more information.
2. Explain to students that they should use a copy of the Presentation Checklist to evaluate their own presentation and the presentations made by classmates.
3. Before students give their presentations to the class, remind listeners to ask questions if any points are unclear. To maintain order, encourage them to raise their hands and wait to be acknowledged by the presenter before stating their questions. Suggest that students making presentations scan the classroom from time to time so they will notice any students who have questions.

Evaluate the Activity

1. Evaluate students' presentations on the basis of the accuracy of their summaries and their use of details to support their claims.
2. When the class discusses the presentations that were easiest to follow, encourage students to make note of the features of those presentations that made them effective and to incorporate those techniques in their future presentations.

Differentiated Instruction for Universal Access

Support for English Learners

Students may have difficulty with the vocabulary in media broadcasts. As they listen to the media reports, have students write down any unfamiliar words in the broadcast. After they identify difficult words, have them look the words up in a dictionary. Suggest that students also carefully observe the images shown and the body language and tone of voice of the reporters and those interviewed to help them in their comparisons.

Strategy for Advanced Learners

Suggest that students gather information from a news incident and create a video that presents the material from two different perspectives. Have students analyze how each perspective requires them to report. When they finish, have them share their work with the class and write a reflection of how each perspective affected their reporting.

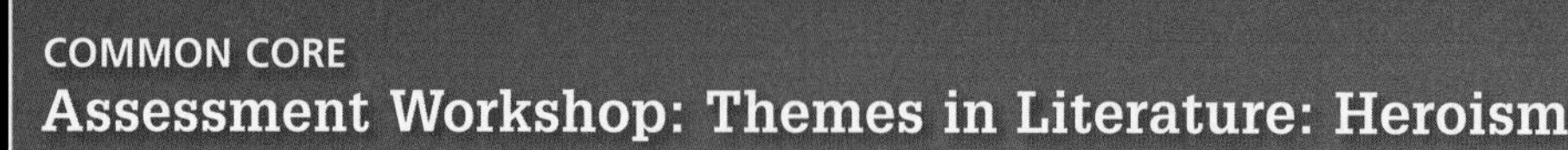

Cumulative Review

In this Common Core Assessment Workshop (pp. 1246–1251), students apply and reinforce their mastery of the Common Core State Standards and the skills taught in Unit 6. The practice is divided into four sections, including a section of Performance Tasks addressing CCS Reading standards.

1. Before assigning each section, review the relevant Common Core State Standards and unit skills with students.
2. Set a time limit for the multiple-choice items in each section, allowing a little over one minute per question. Allow twenty minutes for any Timed Writing questions.
3. Administer each of the first three sections of the Cumulative Review (pp. 1246–1249).
4. Use the Performance Tasks on pages 1250–1251 to assess the depth of students' mastery of standards taught in the unit. Follow the suggestions on teacher pages 1250–1251 for assigning tasks and for supporting and evaluating student performance.

Reteaching Skills

1. For each practice use the Reteach chart on the same page as the answers to determine which skills require reteaching, based on which items students answered incorrectly.
2. Reteach these skills prior to assigning the **Benchmark Test** for the second half of Unit 6 (**Unit** ***6 Resources***, pp. 188–193).

Cumulative Review

Common Core State Standards

RL.9-10.2, RL.9-10.6; L.9-10.4.a, L.9-10.5.a

[For the full wording of the standards, see the standards chart in the front of your textbook.]

I. Reading Literature

Directions: *Read the passage. Then, answer each question that follows.*

Dimitri's hands held tight to the rocks around him as Aeolus, the god of winds, pummeled him from all angles. As he clung to the side of the volcano with a lion's courage, he remembered his visit to the oracle.

His journey to the oracle had taken eight long days of traveling through the Greek countryside. When he arrived, he felt his journey must have been a mistake. Deaf in one ear, he thought he could never be a hero. He should leave before the priestesses serving the oracle laughed at his question.

Dimitri was about to turn around and return home when a priestess with hair as black as night spotted him. "Come with me," she said. "You have a question that must be asked." She led him into a large room.

"I want to silence the volcano next to my village. People are dying. I must help. How can I do it?" he said abruptly to the priestess.

"I will ask the oracle for you," she said. Moments later, she returned. "I have your answer. You must scale the volcano and listen for the magma to sing its song. When it sings, and not before, you must drop this stone into it. Then will the volcano rest." As the priestess spoke, she rested a flaming red crystal in Dimitri's palm.

"I. . . " he stuttered, "I cannot hear in one ear. How can I hear the volcano's song?"

"You will," she said. "The oracle is never wrong. Go and be brave."

Now, has he struggled to hold on to the side of the volcano, he felt himself strengthened by her words. With a lion's courage, he lifted one foot, then the other, against the raving of the mad wind until he stood at the top of the volcano. Opening before him, the gaping mouth of the volcano seemed ready to swallow anyone who came near. The sides of the volcano poked out like huge lips, and the magma inside lashed from side to side as a tongue would in an angry mouth. The wind blew louder around him, and Dimitri felt a moment's hesitation. Then, with a lion's courage, he rested his head against the rock and leaned forward into the volcano. It seemed all he could hear was the howling of the wind. Then, dimly, he could make out what sounded like the notes of a long-forgotten song. It seemed to be calling his name, begging him to stop holding on to the rocks and to lean just a little further over the side.

Before the hypnotic song could befuddle his reason and make him fall into the volcano, Dimitri stood against the wind and took out the red crystal. He dropped it into the volcano, and suddenly the noise stopped.

Differentiated Instruction for Universal Access

Strategy for English Learners

Review skills and warm up for the test by walking students through item 3 on p. 1247. Ask a volunteer to read item 3 aloud. Help students define *antagonist* (a character who opposes the protagonist, or hero). Next, guide students in eliminating incorrect answer choices.

- **A**—While true, this does not state the opposition of Aeolus to Dimitri. A powerful god could try to help Dimitri. (Eliminate.)
- **B**—Aeolus does not appear when Dimitri is at the oracle, but when he is at the volcano. (Eliminate.)
- **C**—While true, this does not say anything about his behavior toward Aeolus. (Eliminate.)
- **D**—Aeolus buffets Dimitri with strong winds, trying to prevent him for completing his task.

Guide students in seeing that **D** is the best choice. Have them complete the remaining items, encouraging them to apply a similar strategy. First, define key terms in the prompt and then eliminate incorrect choices.

1. Which of the following could be considered the **theme** of this selection?

A. Only take a risk if you know what will happen.
B. Slow and steady wins the race.
C. If you believe in yourself, you will succeed.
D. Nature is too powerful to overcome.

2. Which traditional quality of an **epic hero** does Dimitri demonstrate?

A. bravery
B. superhuman intelligence
C. disrespect for the gods
D. self-doubt

3. In what way is Aeolus, the god of winds, an **antagonist** in this selection?

A. Aeolus is a powerful god.
B. Aeolus obviously hates the oracle and will do anything to destroy it.
C. Readers do not learn a great deal about Aeolus.
D. Aeolus tries to stop the hero Dimitri from completing his mission.

4. What purpose is not fulfilled the **flashback**?

A. to give information about Dimitri's mission
B. to introduce another character
C. to make readers doubt Dimitri's chance for success
D. to teach readers more about Greek religion

5. Which of the following is not a characteristic of myths and is not present in the selection?

A. a basis in historical truth
B. a role played by gods
C. a protagonist who teaches values
D. a significant role for natural phenomena

6. **Epics** usually include all of the following except—

A. a heroic central character.
B. humor.
C. adventures.
D. adversity, or challenges to be overcome.

7. **Vocabulary** Which word is closest in meaning to the underlined word *befuddle*?

A. strengthen
B. identify
C. imitate
D. confuse

8. What is the significance of the **epic simile** in this selection?

A. It emphasizes the size and power of the volcano.
B. It shows the beauty of the priestess's hair.
C. It demonstrates how far Dimitri journeyed to get to the oracle.
D. It helps the reader get a mental picture of the red crystal.

9. **Repetition** of the phrase "with a lion's courage" emphasizes—

A. Dimitri's bravery.
B. the strength of the gods.
C. the frightening challenges Dimitri faces.
D. the ferociousness of the volcano.

Timed Writing

10. **Write** a five-line **epic simile** comparing an occurrence in your life to a natural event. Use "like" or "as" to state the comparison. Develop your **simile** fully.

GO ON

I. Reading Literature

Answers With Explanations

1. C—The priestess persuades Dimitri to believe in himself. *Incorrect answers:* A—Dimitri takes a risk without knowing what will happen. B—No race takes place. D—The ending shows that nature can be overcome.
2. A—Epic heroes are always brave. *Incorrect answers:* B—The gods have superhuman intelligence. C—Epic heroes have respect for the gods. D—Epic heroes do not necessarily doubt themselves.
3. D—Aeolus tries to block Dimitri's effort. *Incorrect answers:* A—A powerful god could help Dimitri. B—Aeolus has nothing to do with the oracle. C—Extensive detail about a character is not a prerequisite for the character being an antagonist.
4. C—The words of the priestess suggest that Dimitri will succeed. *Incorrect answers:* A—The flashback reveals Dimitri's purpose. B—Readers meet the priestess. D—The flashback reveals that Greek religion contains oracles and priestesses.
5. A—The passage does not reflect any historical truth. *Incorrect answers:* B—The god Aeolus plays a role. C—Dimitri's success teaches readers to trust themselves. D—The volcano and the wind are natural phenomena.
6. B—Humor is not a characteristic of epics. *Incorrect answers:* A—The heroic central character is a necessary part of an epic. C—Epic heroes always have adventures. D—Like Dimitri, epic heroes face challenges.
7. D—If the noise could affect Dimitri's reason and make him fall into the volcano, it could confuse him. *Incorrect answers:* A—If his reason were strengthened, Dimitri would not fall into the volcano. B—This meaning makes no sense in the sentence. C—same explanation as for B.
8. A—The mouth of the volcano is made to seem like a powerful and hungry beast. *Incorrect answers:* B—The simile about the priestess' hair is descriptive, rather than an epic simile. C—There is no simile in this description. D—There is no simile in involving the red crystal.

Continued from right column

9. A—Lions are considered to be brave. *Incorrect answers:* B—The repetition does not refer to the gods. C—The repetition does not refer to Dimitri's challenges, but to his character. D—The repetition does not refer to the volcano.

Timed Writing

10. Students' similes should reflect the characteristics of the epic simile and bring to mind the full power of a natural event.

Reteach

Question	Instructional Pages to Reteach
2	1041
3	1145
4	1041
5	1216
6	1041
8	1087
10	1087

II. Reading Informational Text

Answers With Explanations

1. C—*Ratification* means "official approval." *Incorrect answers:* A—Investment is a commitment of time or effort. B—A *proponent* is a supporter. D—*Designation* is an appointment or a distinguishing name.
2. A—The biography would have more detail about Madison's life. *Incorrect answers:* B—The Constitution itself would tell nothing about Madison's life. C—An encyclopedia might have more about Madison's life, but a biography of him would have far greater detail. D—A history text may or may not describe Madison's life.
3. C—The amendment states that "Congress shall make no law. . . abridging the freedom of speech, or of the press." *Incorrect answers:* A—The First Amendment does not address the right to bear arms, which is the subject of the Second Amendment. B—The First Amendment says nothing about the freedom of dress. D—The First Amendment does not address protection from unnecessary search, which is the subject of the Fourth Amendment.
4. A—Both sources are written after the historical fact. *Incorrect answers:* B—A public document is a primary source. C—same explanation as for B. D—Both an encyclopedia and a biography are secondary sources.

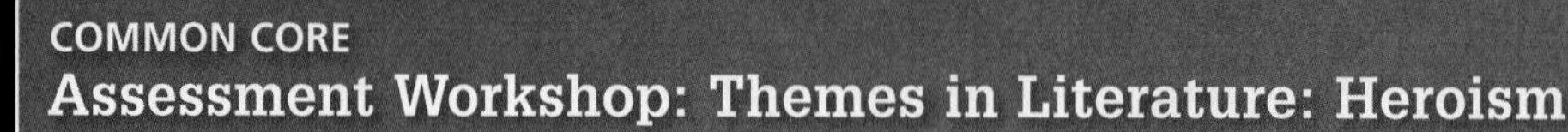

COMMON CORE
Assessment Workshop: Themes in Literature: Heroism

II. Reading Informational Text

Common Core State Standards

RI.9-10.2; L.9-10.1, L.9-10.2, L.9-10.3

[For the full wording of the standards, see the standards chart in the front of your textbook.]

Directions: *Read the passage. Then, answer each question that follows.*

Encyclopedia Entry

Bill of Rights The Bill of Rights is the list of the first ten amendments added to the Constitution of the United States of America. Some delegates at the Constitutional Convention believed that our Constitution was missing the limitation put on government to guarantee certain individual rights. The Bill of Rights was adopted in 1791. James Madison played a crucial role in the process of creation and ratification, or confirmation, of the document.

Biography

James Madison (1751–1836) was born in Port Conway, Virginia. He attended the College of New Jersey, which is now Princeton. After he graduated in 1771, he began his political career. Madison eventually went on to become the fourth president of the United States. However, his major contribution to the country came before his presidency. He served as a delegate to the Constitutional Convention of 1787, drafting much of the document of the Constitution. In addition, he was a proponent and author of the Bill of Rights, which eventually tipped the scale for ratification of the Constitution.

Public Document

Bill of Rights

Amendment I: Congress shall make no law respecting an establishment of religion, or prohibiting the free exercise thereof; or abridging the freedom of speech, or of the press; or the right of the people peaceably to assemble, and to petition the government for a redress of grievances.

1. **Vocabulary** What is the best definition for *ratification?*
   A. investment in
   B. proponent of
   C. approval of
   D. designation of

2. Which text should you consult to learn more about the author of the Bill of Rights?
   A. biography
   B. the Constitution
   C. encyclopedia
   D. history text

3. What rights are protected by Amendment I of the Bill of Rights?
   A. freedom to bear arms
   B. freedom of dress
   C. freedom of speech and press
   D. protection from unnecessary search

4. Which two texts are secondary sources?
   A. encyclopedia entry and biography
   B. encyclopedia entry and public document
   C. biography and public document
   D. none of the above

Reteach

Question	Instructional Pages to Reteach
2	1120
3	1120
4	1120

Benchmark

Reteach skills as indicated by students' performance, following the Reteach charts on pages 1247–1249. Then, administer the end-of-unit **Benchmark Test** (*Unit 6 Resources,* pp. 1188–1193.) Follow the **Interpretation Guide** for the test (*Unit 6 Resources,* pp. 194–199) to assign reteaching pages as necessary in the **Reading Kit.** Use **Success Tracker** online to assign these pages automatically.

III. Writing and Language Conventions

Directions: *Read the passage. Then, answer each question that follows.*

Recording Meeting Minutes

(1) How could anyone copy down every single word said at a meeting? (2) Although some people may say you need to do it. (3) It is impossible! (4) To take meeting minutes, you only need to worry about getting the basic ideas. (5) Follow these guidelines to take appropriate meeting minutes.

(6) Make sure that the notes you write are brief and direct. (7) When taking notes be sure to use clear abbreviations. (8) Use a highlighter or underlining to indicate important topics or decisions that have been made. (9) Recording meeting minutes may sound as tough as climbing Mount Everest, but it is not. (10) If everyone can understand your minutes, you have done an excellent job.

1. What is the *best* correction of the sentence **fragment** in sentence 2?

- **A.** Although some people may say you need to do it, it is impossible!
- **B.** Though some people may say you need to do it.
- **C.** Although it is impossible, although some people say you need to do it.
- **D.** Though you may need to, impossible!

2. Where in sentence 7 should a **comma** be added?

- **A.** after "taking"
- **B.** after "notes"
- **C.** after "sure"
- **D.** no comma needed

3. Which **transitional word** could be added to the beginning of sentence 6 for clarity?

- **A.** First,
- **B.** Finally,
- **C.** Afterward,
- **D.** Often,

4. To improve the organization of these instructions, the author may want to—

- **A.** delete sentence 4.
- **B.** include an illustration.
- **C.** create a new paragraph beginning at sentence 9.
- **D.** switch the order of sentences 9 and 10.

5. In what way should sentence 9 be revised to create a more formal **tone**?

- **A.** Replace "as tough as climbing Mount Everest" with "challenging."
- **B.** Remove "recording."
- **C.** Replace "but it is not" with "but it never is."
- **D.** Replace "it is not" with "but it is more like hiking up a hill."

ASSESS/RETEACH

Answers

III. Writing and Language Conventions

Answers With Explanations

1. A—This is a complete sentence that combines the dependent clause with an independent clause. *Incorrect answers:* B—This result remains a sentence fragment. C—This result is still a sentence fragment. D—This lacks an independent clause with a complete predicate.
2. B—The pause should come after the introductory phrase. *Incorrect answers:* A—This choice would incorrectly separate the predicate *taking* from the object *notes.* C—A comma should not be used between a verb and the following infinitive. D—The sentence is not correct as it is.
3. A—The selection has just said to follow these guidelines, and this sentence is the first guideline. *Incorrect answers:* B—This is not the final guideline. C—Since the sentence states the first step, it is part of the process, not something that is done later. D—This is not an appropriate word to introduce the first step.
4. C—Sentence 9 begins a new major thought, so it should begin a new paragraph. *Incorrect answers:* A—Sentence 4 conveys important information. B—An illustration would not be particularly useful. D—These sentences are already in the correct order.
5. A—Using a reference to Mount Everest is informal. *Incorrect answers:* B—This word is used in formal writing. C—"But it is not" is appropriate. D—"But it is more like hiking up a hill" is as informal as "climbing Mount Everest."

Reteach

Question	Instructional Pages to Reteach
1	1141
2	1190
3	1141
4	1140
5	—

Differentiated Instruction for Universal Access

Strategy for Less Proficient Readers

Review skills and warm up for the test by walking students through item 1 on page 1249. Help students define *fragment* (a statement that lacks a subject or a predicate, or a dependent clause). Next, guide students in eliminating incorrect answer choices.

- A—This sentence joins a dependent clause with an independent clause. (Possible answer.)
- B—This statement remains a fragment; it does not make sense on its own. (Eliminate.)
- C—This statement has only dependent clauses and no independent clause, meaning it is still a fragment. (Eliminate.)
- D—This statement has a dependent clause and an interjection. Without an independent clause, it is still a fragment. (Eliminate.)

Guide students in seeing that **A** is the best choice. Have them complete the remaining items, encouraging them to apply a similar strategy. First, define key terms in the prompt and then eliminate incorrect choices.

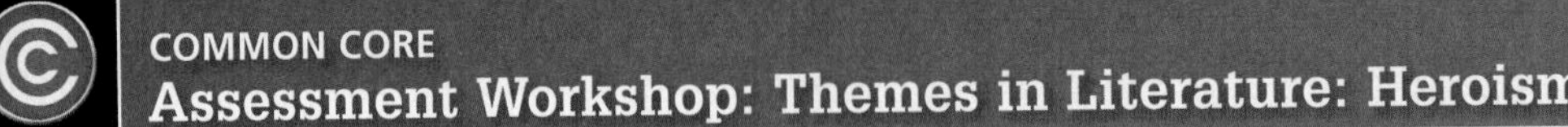

Performance Tasks

Assigning Tasks/Reteaching Skills

Use the chart below to choose appropriate Performance Tasks by identifying which tasks assess lessons in the textbook that you have taught. Use the same lessons for reteaching when students' performance indicates a failure to fully master a standard. For additional instruction and practice, assign the *Common Core Companion* pages indicated for each task.

Task	Where Taught/ Pages to Reteach	*Common Core Companion* Pages
1	1193	137–149, 255–262
2	1210	69–75, 190–201, 314–315
3	1033, 1034	55–61, 255–262
4	1030–1031, 1032, 1034	28–34, 293–299
5	1032, 1034	15–27, 293–299
6	426, 428, 429, 441	110–116, 293–301

Assessment Pacing

In assigning the Writing Tasks on this student page, allow a class period for the completion of a task. As an alternative, assign tasks as homework. In assigning the Speaking and Listening Tasks on the facing page, consider having students do any required preparation as a homework assignment. Then, allow a class period for the presentations.

Evaluating Performance Tasks

Use the rubric at the bottom of this Teacher Edition page to evaluate students' mastery of the standards as demonstrated in their Performance Task responses. Review the rubric with students before they begin work so they know the criteria by which their work will be evaluated.

Performance Tasks

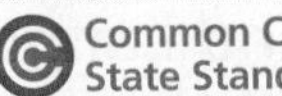
Common Core State Standards

RL.9-10.2, RL.9-10.3, RL.9-10.6, RL.9-10.9; RI.9-10.3, RI.9-10.6; W.9-10.9.a–b; SL.9-10.3, SL.9-10.4; L.9-10.2.a

[For the full wording of the standards, see the standards chart in the front of your textbook.]

Directions: *Follow the instructions to complete the tasks below as required by your teacher.*

As you work on each task, incorporate both general academic vocabulary and literary terms you learned in this unit.

Writing

Task 1: Informational Text [RI.9-10.6; W.9-10.9.b]

Analyze the Author's Purpose and Rhetoric

Write an essay in which you determine the author's purpose and analyze his or her use of rhetoric in a nonfiction work from this unit.

- State which work you chose. Briefly explain who the author is and the circumstances under which he or she wrote the work.
- Identify the author's main purpose by explaining the goals he or she wanted to achieve in writing the work. Explain whether the author states his or her purpose explicitly or merely suggests it. Cite details from the work to support your ideas.
- Identify at least two words, phrases, sentences, or other uses of language that you think help advance the author's purpose for writing. Explain your position.
- Provide a concluding statement that supports the ideas you expressed earlier in your essay.

Task 2: Literature [RL.9-10.9; L.9-10.2.a]

Analyze an Author's Interpretation of Source Material

Write an essay in which you analyze how an author from this unit draws on and transforms a theme or topic from an older work.

- Select a work from this unit that interprets, draws upon, or makes an allusion to an older work of literature.
- Organize your ideas in an outline that compares the two works.
- Begin your essay by introducing the selection you chose and briefly summarizing its content. Then, explain the source work, summarizing its content and explaining how it is used in the later work.
- Explain how the source material enriches the modern selection. In particular, analyze how the material influences the plot, character, meaning, or tone of the work you chose.
- Cite strong and thorough textual evidence from both works to support your ideas.
- Provide a strong conclusion that summarizes how references to the older work make your chosen selection more understandable and enjoyable.
- Use punctuation such as colons and semicolons correctly.

Task 3: Literature [RL.9-10.6; W.9-10.9.a]

Analyze Cultural Perspective

Write an essay in which you analyze the cultural perspective conveyed in a literary work from this unit. The work must have been written outside the United States.

- State which work you chose and briefly summarize it. Explain the cultural perspective the work expresses.
- Analyze how the cultural experience or perspective influences the selection's content and contributes to the overall meaning and tone of the work.
- Explain the theme or message of the work and show with specific examples how that message is influenced by the author's cultural perspective.
- Establish and maintain a formal style and objective tone.
- Provide a concluding statement that follows from and supports the explanation you have presented.

Performance Task Rubric: Standards Mastery	Rating Scale (*not very* – *very*)
Critical Thinking: How clearly and consistently does the student pursue the specific mode of reasoning or discourse required by the standard, as specified in the prompt (e.g., comparing and contrasting, analyzing, explaining)?	1 2 3 4 5
Focus: How well does the student understand and apply the focus concepts of the standard, as specified in the prompt (e.g., development of theme or of complex characters, effects of structure, and so on)?	1 2 3 4 5
Support/Elaboration: How well does the student support points with textual or other evidence? How relevant, sufficient, and varied is the evidence provided?	1 2 3 4 5
Insight: How original, sophisticated, or compelling are the insights the student achieves by applying the standard to the text(s)?	1 2 3 4 5
Expression of Ideas: How well does the student organize and support ideas? How well does the student use language, including word choice and conventions, in the expression of ideas?	1 2 3 4 5

Speaking and Listening

Task 4: Literature [RL.9-10.3; SL.9-10.4]

Analyze a Complex Hero

Deliver an oral report in which you analyze a heroic character in a work of literature from this unit.

- Introduce the character and explain how the character's actions, dialogue, and interactions with other characters convey heroic qualities.
- Show how the character develops over the course of the work, analyzing how events and relationships with other characters reinforce the character's heroism.
- Cite specific examples from the work to show whether the character's actions suggest a hero's quest or a universal theme.
- Present your information and supporting evidence clearly, concisely, and logically so that your audience can understand your ideas.
- Employ correct grammar and an appropriate speaking style.

Task 5: Literature [RL.9-10.2; SL.9-10.3, SL.9-10.4]

Analyze Theme

Deliver a presentation in which you analyze the theme in a literary work from this unit and consider whether it is universal.

- Explain which work you chose and provide at least two interesting facts about its author or the culture it represents.
- Briefly summarize the work, and state the theme it expresses. Cite specific details from the work that support your interpretation.
- Discuss whether the theme the work expresses is universal—one shared by people across time and from different cultures. Cite specific details.
- Add interest to your presentation by including visuals, such as photographs or drawings.
- Explain or define terms with which your audience may not be familiar. Present information clearly, concisely, and logically so that listeners can follow your reasoning.
- Conclude with a summarizing statement.

Task 6: Informational Text [RI.9-10.3; SL.9-10.3, SL.9-10.4]

Analyze the Structure of a Work

Deliver an oral presentation in which you demonstrate how an author organizes ideas in a nonfiction work from this unit.

- Explain which work you chose and briefly summarize the author's main purpose and central idea.
- Identify the order in which the author unfolds his or her ideas. Cite specific methods the author uses to introduce and develop ideas.
- Demonstrate how the author makes connections among ideas. Identify transitional words and phrases, examples, or repetition.
- Use a visual aid to make your ideas clear to your audience. Options include a handout with an annotated outline, a series of note cards or posters, or the use of display technology.
- Present your information clearly, concisely, and logically so your listeners can follow your reasoning.

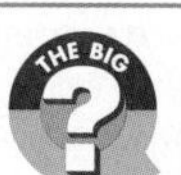

Do heroes have responsibilities?
At the beginning of Unit 6, you participated in a discussion of the Big Question. Now that you have completed the unit, write a response to the question. Discuss how your initial ideas have either changed or been reinforced. Cite specific examples from the literature in this unit, other subject areas, and your own life to support your ideas. Use Big Question vocabulary words (see p. 1029) in your response.

Differentiated Instruction for Universal Access

Strategy for Less Proficient Readers
Assign a Performance Task, and then have students meet in groups to review the standard assessed in that task. Remind students of the selections or independent readings to which they have previously applied the standard. Have groups summarize what they learned in applying the standard and then present their summaries. Discuss, clarifying any points of confusion. After students have completed their tasks, have groups meet again to evaluate members' work. Encourage members to revise their work based on the feedback they receive.

Strategy for English Learners
For each assigned Performance Task, review the instructions with students. Clarify the meaning of any unfamiliar vocabulary, emphasizing routine classroom words such as *purpose*, *content*, and *message* and academic vocabulary such as *demonstrate*. Next, have students note ideas for their responses. Pair students and have them review each other's notes, asking questions to clarify meaning and suggesting improvements. Encourage students to ask for your assistance in supplying English words or expressions they may require.

Supporting Speaking and Listening

1. Consider having students work with partners or in groups to complete Performance Tasks involving listening and speaking. For tasks that you assign for individual work, you may still wish to have students rehearse with partners, who can provide constructive feedback.
2. As students rehearse, have them keep in mind these tips:
   - Present findings and evidence clearly and concisely.
   - Observe conventions of standard English grammar and usage.
   - Be relaxed and friendly but maintain a formal tone.
   - Make eye contact with the audience, pronounce words clearly, and vary your pace.
   - When working with a group, respond thoughtfully to others' positions, modifying your own in response to new evidence.

Linking Performance Tasks to Independent Reading

If you wish to cover the standards with students' independent reading, adapt Performance Tasks of your choice to the works they have selected. (Independent reading suggestions appear on the next page).

Do heroes have responsibilities?

1. Remind students that the unit Big Question is "Do heroes have responsibilities?"
2. Have students complete their responses to the prompt on the student page. Point out that they have read selections in this unit about the responsibilities with which heroes are burdened and that they should draw on these selections in their responses. Remind them that they can also draw on their own experiences and what they have learned in other subject areas in formulating their answers.

Independent Reading

Titles featured on the Independent Reading pages at the end of each unit represent a range of reading, including stories, dramas, and poetry, as well as literary nonfiction and other types of informational text. Throughout, labels indicate the works that are CCSS Exemplar Texts. Choosing from among these featured titles will help students read works at increasing levels of text complexity in the grades 9–10 text complexity band.

Independent Reading and Pacing

See the Unit Overview and Pacing Plan, pp. 1028a–1028b, for suggestions on integrating independent reading with work in the Student Edition.

Using Literature Circles

A literature circle is a temporary group in which students independently discuss a book.

Use the guidance in the *Professional Development Guidebook*, pp. 47–49, as well as the teaching notes on the facing page, for additional suggestions for literature circles.

Meeting Unit 6 CCS Focus Standards

Students can use books listed on this page to apply and to reinforce their mastery of the CCS Focus Standards covered in this unit. (The Focus Standards are introduced on pp. 1030–1033.)

Introducing Featured Titles

Have students choose a book or books for independent reading. Assist them by previewing the titles, noting their subject matter and level of difficulty. **Note:** Before recommending a work to students, preview it, taking into account the values of your community as well as the maturity of your students.

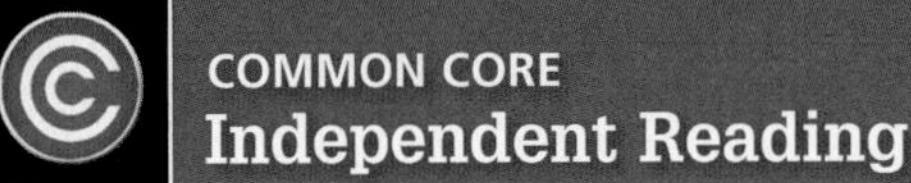

Featured Titles

In this unit, you have read a wide variety of thematically related literary works. Continue to explore thematic connections in literature. Select works that you enjoy, but challenge yourself to explore new writers and works of increasing depth and complexity. The titles suggested below will help you get started.

Literature

Fathers and Sons
by Ivan Turgenev — EXEMPLAR TEXT

This 1862 **novel** set in Russia delves into the gap that has grown between a generation of parents and children who differ greatly in their philosophies. As the young demand social change, the old cling desperately to tradition.

Revolutionary Petunias and Other Poems
by Alice Walker — EXEMPLAR TEXT

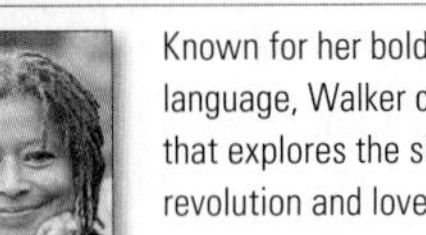

Known for her bold honesty and poetic language, Walker crafts a collection of **poetry** that explores the similarities between revolution and love.

The War of the Worlds
by H. G. Wells
Signet, 1986

This classic **science-fiction novel** is the book that launched a thousand Hollywood alien invasion movies. It imagines that Martians, intent on obliterating the human race, land on Earth. As the Martians mow down everything in their path, readers are left to wonder who, if anyone, can defend the planet against these seemingly invincible foes.

The Odyssey
by Homer
Translated by Robert Fagles — EXEMPLAR TEXT

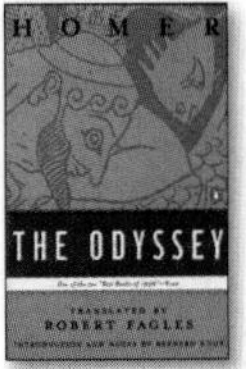

When the hero Odysseus begins his voyage home after the Trojan War, he has no idea his travels will lead him to seductive goddesses, man-eating monsters, and vengeful gods. Read this **epic tale** to decide for yourself if Odysseus is the ultimate hero.

Informational Texts

Joan of Arc
by Mary Gordon

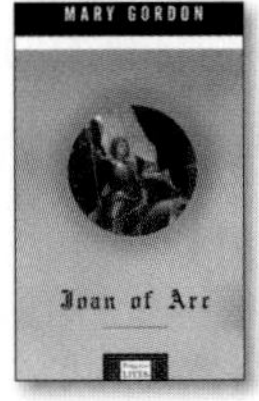

This **biography** tells the remarkable story of the short life of a peasant named Joan. After hearing a voice she believed was God's, she left her family and home behind to lead the French army to victory over the British.

The Carolina Way
by Dean Smith and Gerald Bell with John Kilgo

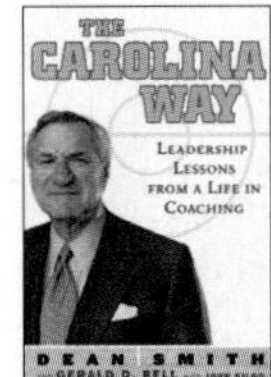

Dean Smith, the coach of the University of North Carolina men's basketball team for almost 40 years, shares his strategies for leadership, teamwork, and winning with integrity in this **nonfiction** book.

The Story of Science: Newton at the Center
by Joy Hakim — EXEMPLAR TEXT

An examination of the accomplishments and lives of several scientists, this work of **nonfiction** includes interesting stories and facts that present some engaging aspects of science.

Nelson Mandela
by Laaren Brown and Lenny Hort

This **biography** of Nelson Mandela describes his struggles against an unjust government and how he survived 27 years as a political prisoner as South Africa emerged out of the dark ages of apartheid.

Text Complexity: Aligning Texts With Readers and Tasks

TEXTS	READERS AND TASKS
• *Joan of Arc* • *The Carolina Way*	**Below-Level Readers** Allow students to focus on reading for content, and challenge them to interpret multiple perspectives.
• *The Story of Science: Newton at the Center* • *Nelson Mandela* (Lexile: 1000L) • *Fathers and Sons*	**Below-Level Readers** Challenge students as they read for content. **On-Level Readers** Allow students to focus on reading for content, and challenge them to interpret multiple perspectives. **Advanced Readers** Allow students to focus on interpreting multiple perspectives.
• *Revolutionary Petunias and Other Poems* • *The Odyssey* (Lexile: 1050L) • *The War of the Worlds* (Lexile: 1170L)	**On-Level Readers** Challenge students as they read for content. **Advanced Readers** Allow students to focus on reading for content, and challenge them to interpret multiple perspectives.

Preparing to Read Complex Texts

Attentive Reading As you read literature on your own, bring your imagination and questions to the text. The questions shown below and others that you ask as you read will help you learn and enjoy literature even more.

Common Core State Standards

Reading Literature/Informational Text

10. By the end of grade 9, read and comprehend literature, including stories, dramas, poems, and literary nonfiction in the grades 9–10 text complexity band proficiently, with scaffolding as needed at the high end of the range.

When reading texts from the oral tradition, ask yourself...

- What type of text is this? Is it an epic, a myth, a tale, or a legend? What types of characters, events, and ideas do I expect to find in this text?
- From what culture does this text come? What do I know about that culture?
- Does my knowledge of the culture lead me to expect certain qualities in this text? If so, what are my expectations?
- Does the text meet my expectations? Why or why not?
- What elements of the culture do I see in the text? For example, do I notice beliefs, foods, or settings that have meaning for the people of this culture?
- Does the text express a moral or theme that has meaning for modern readers? Why or why not?

Key Ideas and Details

- Is this text a retelling by a modern author? If so, does the author change the text for modern readers?
- How do I think the text on the page is different from the text when it was originally related, sung, or performed? Which parts of the text might a performer have exaggerated or altered?
- Does the text include characters and tell a story? If so, are the characters and plot interesting?
- What do I notice about the language, including descriptions and dialogue? How does the language compare to that of modern texts?
- Does the text include symbols? If so, do they have special meanings in the original culture of the text? Do they also have meanings in modern life?
- Does the text include patterns of events or repetitions of statements or images? If so, which ones? What is the effect?

Craft and Structure

- How does this text round out the picture of the culture I might get from a nonfiction source, such as an encyclopedia entry?
- Does this text express universal ideas or values—those that are common to people in many different cultures and time periods?
- Does this text seem like others I have read or heard? Why or why not?
- Do I know of any modern versions of this text? How are they similar to or different from this one?
- If I were researching this culture for a report, would I include passages from this text? If so, what would those passages show?
- Do I enjoy reading this text and others like it? Why or why not?

Integration of Ideas

Text Complexity: Reader and Task Support Suggestions

INDEPENDENT READING

Increased Support Suggest that students choose a book that they feel comfortable reading and one that is a bit more challenging. Pair a more proficient reader with a less proficient reader and have them work together on the more challenging text. Partners can prepare to read the book by reviewing questions on this student page. They can also read difficult passages together, sharing questions and insights. They can use the questions on the student page to guide after-reading discussion.

Increased Challenge Encourage students to integrate knowledge and ideas by combining the Big Question and the Unit Focus concepts in their approach to two or more featured titles.

For example, students might identify the responsibilities of heroes in *The Odyssey* and *Joan of Arc*. In addition, students can focus on the similarities and differences in the ways storytellers and authors develop historical and cultural context in works of literature.

Preparing to Read Complex Texts

1. Tell students they can be attentive readers by bringing their experience and imagination to the texts they read and by actively questioning those texts. Explain that the questions they see on the student page are examples of questions to ask about texts from the oral tradition.
2. Point out that, like writing, reading is a "multidraft" process, involving several readings of complete works or passages, revising and refining one's understanding each time.

Key Ideas and Details

3. As an example, review and amplify the first bulleted item. **Ask:** What key ideas and details could you use to determine the type of text you are reading?

   Possible response: You could examine the traits of characters that appear in the text. For example, an epic might focus on one strong character. A myth might feature magical creatures.

Craft and Structure

4. **Ask:** What details of craft and structure would you cite as evidence that a text includes symbols?

   Possible response: You might point to the author's effective use of an object to stand for an idea.

Integration of Ideas

5. **Ask:** How would you compare and contrast traditional and modern versions of the same text?

   Possible response: You would examine the texts for similarities and differences between characters, plots, themes, and styles.
6. Finally, explain to students that they should cite key ideas and details, examples of craft and structure, or instances of the integration of ideas as evidence to support their points during a book discussion. After hearing the evidence, the group might reach a consensus or might agree to disagree.

Resources

Glossary

Big Question vocabulary appears in **blue type**. High-utility Academic vocabulary is **underlined.**

A

abash (uh BASH) *v.* embarrass

abdicated (AB duh kayt uhd) *v.* gave up formally

absurdity (ab SUR duh tee) *n.* something ridiculous or nonsensical

accentuated (ak SEHN chu ayt uhd) *v.* emphasized; heightened the effect of

accept (ak SEHPT) *v.* take something that is given

accumulated (uh KYOO myuh layt uhd) *v.* piled up, collected, or gathered together, especially over a period of time

acquiesced (ak wee EHST) *v.* agreed or consented quietly without protest, but without enthusiasm

adversary (AD vuhr sehr ee) *n.* person who opposes or fights against another

afflicted (uh FLIHKT ihd) *v.* suffering or sickened

allotment (uh LOT muhnt) *n.* share; portion

aloofness (uh LOOF nehs) *n.* emotional distance

ambiguities (am buh GYOO uh teez) *n.* statements or events whose meanings are unclear

ambiguous (am BIHG yoo uhs) *adj.* having more than one meaning

amicably (AM uh kuh blee) *adv.* in a friendly manner

amid (uh MIHD) *prep.* among; in the middle of

analysis (uh NAL uh sis) *n.* careful examination by studying something's elements or parts

anguish (ANG gwihsh) *n.* great pain or suffering

anonymous (uh NON uh muhs) *adj.* without a known or acknowledged name

antagonize (an TAG uh nyz) *v.* make an enemy of

apex (AY pehks) *n.* highest point; peak

appreciate (uh PREE shee ayt) *v.* be aware of the value of

archaic (ahr KAY ihk) *adj.* from an earlier time; ancient

ardor (AHR duhr) *n.* passion; enthusiasm

arduous (AHR joo uhs) *adj.* difficult; laborious

argument (AHR gyuh muhnt) *n.* discussion in which there is disagreement

articulate (ahr TIHK yuh layt) *v.* express an idea clearly

articulate (ahr TIHK yuh liht) *adj.* able to express oneself clearly

assiduous (uh SIHJ oo uhs) *adj.* done with constant and careful attention; diligent

assimilated (uh SIHM uh layt uhd) *v.* took in or absorbed

assimilated (uh SIHM uh layt uhd) *adj.* having been taken in fully

assuage (uh SWAYJ) *v.* calm; pacify

assumption (uh SUHMP shuhn) *n.* something taken for granted

atonement (uh TOHN muhnt) *n.* act of making up for a wrongdoing or an injury

attributes (AT rihb yoots) *n.* characteristics or qualities of a person or thing

augmenting (awg MEHNT ihng) *v.* increasing; enlarging

authentic (aw THEHN tihk) *adj.* genuine; true

aware (uh WAIR) *adj.* knowing something because you have experienced it or have been informed of it

awestruck (AW struhk) *adj.* filled with wonder

awry (uh RY) *adj.* not straight or in the right direction

azure (AZH uhr) *adj.* blue

B

background (BAK grownd) *n.* facts that cause or explain something

bafflement (BAF uhl muhnt) *n.* puzzlement; bewilderment

balmy (BAHL mee) *adj.* having the qualities of balm; soothing, mild, pleasant

barren (BAR uhn) *adj.* empty; having little or no vegetation

battle (BAT uhl) *n.* a fight between two opposing forces

battle (BAT uhl) *v.* fight or struggle

beguiling (bih GY lihng) *v.* tricking; charming

belief (bih LEEF) *n.* something accepted to be true

bemusing (bih MYOOZ ihng) *v.* stupefying; muddling

benevolently (buh NEHV uh luhnt lee) *adv.* in a well-meaning way

bereft (bih REHFT) *adj.* deprived

bias (BY uhs) *n.* mental leaning or inclination; partiality

bilingual (by LIHNG gwuhl) *adj.* using two languages

blight (blyt) *n.* something that destroys or prevents growth

bulging (BUHLJ ihng) *adj.* swelling

C

candor (KAN duhr) *n.* sharp honesty or frankness in expressing oneself

cascade (kas KAYD) *n.* small steep waterfall; anything suggesting such a waterfall

censure (SEHN shuhr) *n.* strong disapproval

character (KAR ihk tuhr) *n.* qualities that make a person unique

choices (choys uhz) *n.* variety of things someone can choose from

circumstance (SUR kuhm stans) *n.* situation; event

clarify (KLAR uh fy) *v.* make something more clear or understandable

clasps (klasps) *v.* grips

collective (kuh LEHK tihv) *adj.* put together as a group; gathered into a whole

communication (kuh myoo nuh KAY shuhn) *n.* sharing information

compensation (kom puhn SAY shuhn) *n.* anything that makes up for a loss, damage, or debt

compete (kuhm PEET) *v.* try to win against an opponent

competition (kom puh TIHSH uhn) *n.* rivalry; act of competing

comprehend (kom prih HEHND) *v.* understand

comprehension (kom prih HEHN shuhn) *n.* act of understanding something

conceded (kuhn SEED uhd) *v.* admitted as true or valid; acknowledged

concept (KON sehpt) *n.* idea; notion

concessions (kuhn SEHSH uhnz) *n.* things given or granted as privileges

condolences (kuhn DOH luhns uhz) *n.* expressions of sympathy with another in grief

confer (kuhn FUR) *v.* give; bestow upon

confines (KON fynz) *n.* boundaries or bounded region; border; limit

conformity (kuhn FAWR muh tee) *n.* being in agreement with customs or rules

connection (kuh NEHK shuhn) *n.* joining of two or more things or ideas

conspicuous (kuhn SPIHK yoo uhs) *adj.* attracting attention by being unexpected, unusual, outstanding, or egregious; striking

contempt (kuhn TEHMPT) *n.* disdain or scorn

context (KON tehkst) *n.* parts of a sentence immediately next to or surrounding a word that determine its exact meaning

controversy (KON truh vur see) *n.* discussion of a question in which opposing opinions clash; debate; argument

convince (kuhn VIHNS) *v.* persuade by argument or evidence

cooperate (koh OP uh rayt) *v.* work together to achieve something

countenance (KOWN tuh nuhns) *n.* face

covenant (KUHV uh nuhnt) *n.* agreement or contract, especially a sacred one

credible (KREHD uh buhl) *adj.* believable

creed (kreed) *n.* statement of belief

culture (KUHL chuhr) *n.* ideas, customs, skills and arts of a group of people in a specific time in history

cunning (KUHN ihng) *adj.* skilled in deception

curtailed (kur TAYLD) *v.* cut short; reduced

D

daunting (DAWNT ihng) *adj.* intimidating

defaulted (dih FAWLT uhd) *v.* failed to do something or be somewhere when required or expected; failed to make payment when due

defend (dih FEHND) *v.* support a position with evidence or justifications

deferred (dih FURD) *adj.* put off until a future time

defiance (dih FY uhns) *n.* open, bold resistance to authority

defrauded (dih FRAWD uhd) *v.* cheated

degenerate (dih JEHN uh rayt) *v.* grow worse

dejection (dih JEHK shuhn) *n.* lowness of spirits; depression

deleterious (dehl uh TIHR ee uhs) *adj.* harmful to health or well-being

demonstrative (dih MON struh tihv) *adj.* showing feelings openly

demure (dih MYUR) *adj.* modest

depravity (dih PRAV uh tee) *n.* crookedness; corruption

depreciate (dih PREE shee ayt) *v.* reduce in value

derisive (dih RY sihv) *adj.* showing contempt or ridicule; mocking

desolate (DEHS uh liht) *adj.* forlorn; wretched

despotic (dehs POT ihk) *adj.* like an absolute ruler or tyrant

desultory (DEHS uhl tawr ee) *adj.* aimless; random

determination (dih tur muh NAY shuhn) *n.* firm intention

determine (dih TUR muhn) *v.* cause something to happen in a certain way; control

differences (DIHF uhr uhns uhz) *n.* qualities that make things not the same; ways in which things are not the same

differentiate (dihf uh REHN shee ayt) *v.* see or express what makes two or more things different from each other

diffused (dih FYOOZD) *v.* spread out

dilapidated (duh LAP uh day tihd) *adj.* broken down

diminution (dihm uh NOO shuhn) *n.* lessening

discerning (duh ZUR nihng) *adj.* having good judgment or understanding

discipline (DIHS uh plihn) *n.* training that develops self-control, character, or orderliness and efficiency

disclosed (dihs KLOHZD) *v.* revealed; made known

disconsolately (dihs KON suh liht lee) *adv.* very unhappily

discreet (dihs KREET) *adj.* careful about what one says or does; prudent; keeping silent or preserving confidences when necessary

discreetly (dihs KREET lee) *adv.* without drawing attention

discriminate (dihs KRIHM uh nayt) *v.* see the differences between things; to act against someone because of prejudice

discuss (dihs KUHS) *v.* consider a topic in writing or speaking

disgrace (dihs GRAYS) *n.* loss of respect, honor, or esteem; shame

disheveled (dih SHEHV uhld) *adj.* untidy

dishevelment (dih SHEHV uhl muhnt) *n.* disorder; messiness

dismal (DIHZ muhl) *adj.* causing gloom or misery

dispatched (dihs PACHT) *v.* finished quickly

disperse (dihs PURS) *v.* break up and scatter in all directions; spread about; distribute widely

disputed (dihs PYOOT uhd) *adj.* contested; argued about

dissemble (dih SEHM buhl) *v.* conceal under a false appearance; disguise

distinguished (dihs TIHNG gwihsht) *adj.* having an air of distinction; celebrated for excellence; eminent; famous

distort (dihs TAWRT) *v.* twist out of shape

distraught (dihs TRAWT) *adj.* very troubled or confused

diverged (duh VURJD) *v.* branched out in different directions

droll (drohl) *adj.* funny in an odd or understated way

duration (du RAY shuhn) *n.* the time that a thing continues or lasts

E

elation (ih LAY shuhn) *n.* feeling of exultant joy; pride; high spirits

eloquence (EHL uh kwuhns) *n.* speech or writing that is graceful and persuasive

embellish (ehm BEHL ihsh) *v.* decorate or improve by adding details; ornament; adorn

emerge (ih MURJ) *v.* come into existence; become visible or known

emitting (ih MIHT ihng) *v.* sending out

empathy (EHM puh thee) *n.* ability to understand and share someone else's feelings

emulate (EHM yuh layt) *v.* imitate (a person or thing admired)

enamored (ehn AM uhrd) *v.* filled with love and desire; charmed

encroaching (ehn KROHCH ihng) *adj.* intruding in a sneaky way

endeavor (ehn DEHV uhr) *n.* an earnest attempt or effort

endeavored (ehn DEHV uhrd) *v.* made an earnest attempt to achieve or succeed; tried

endurance (ehn DUR uhns) *n.* ability to withstand hardship over time

enigma (ih NIHG muh) *n.* mystery

enjoined (ehn JOYND) *v.* ordered

entailed (ehn TAYLD) *v.* caused or required as a necessary consequence; involved; necessitated

enthralled (ehn THRAWLD) *v.* held as in a spell; captivated

enumerated (ih NOO muh rayt ihd) *v.* named one by one; specified, as in a list

equity (EHK wuh tee) *n.* quality of being fair; fairness; justice

esteem (ehs TEEM) *n.* favorable opinion; high regard; respect

evanescent (ehv uh NEHS uhnt) *adj.* temporary; tending to disappear

evidence (EHV uh duhns) *n.* proof

exchange (ehks CHAYNJ) *n.* act of trading something

exchange (ehks CHAYNJ) *v.* trade

exile (EHG zyl) *v.* banish

explicit (ehk SPLIHS iht) *adj.* clearly stated

extrapolating (ehk STRAP uh layt ihng) *v.* arriving at a conclusion by inferring from known facts

F

fact (fakt) *n.* a thing that has actually happened or that is true

faltered (FAWL tuhrd) *v.* acted hesitantly; showed uncertainty; wavered; flinched

feasible (FEE zuh buhl) *adj.* capable of being done or carried out; practicable; possible

feeling (FEE lihng) *n.* emotion that a person is aware of

feisty (FYS tee) *adj.* full of spirit; energetic

fertile (FUR tuhl) *adj.* rich in nutrients that promote growth

fester (FEHS tuhr) *v.* become infected; form pus

feud (fyood) *n.* bitter, protracted, and violent quarrel, especially between clans or families

fickle (FIHK uhl) *adj.* changeable

forebears (FAWR bairz) *n.* ancestors

forgo (fawr GOH) *v.* do without; abstain from; give up

formality (fawr MAL uh tee) *n.* attention to established rules or customs

formidable (FAWR muh duh buhl) *adj.* awe-inspiring

fortitude (FAWR tuh tood) *n.* the strength to bear misfortune and pain calmly and patiently

fray (fray) *n.* noisy fight

furtive (FUR tihv) *adj.* sneaky; hidden

futile (FYOO tuhl) *adj.* useless; hopeless

G

gallant (GAL uhnt) *adj.* brave and noble

grievance (GREE vuhns) *n.* something that is thought to be unjust and a reason to feel resentment; complaint

grotesque (groh TEHSK) *adj.* having a strange, bizarre design; shocking or offensive

H

hallowed (HAL ohd) *adj.* sacred

haughty (HAW tee) *adj.* arrogant

hero (HIHR oh) *n.* someone who is admired for brave or noble actions

honesty (ON uh stee) *n.* quality of being truthful

humble (HUHM buhl) *adj.* modest; having humility

humbly (HUHM buh lee) *adv.* in a manner that is not proud or arrogant; modestly

I

identify (y DEHN tuh fy) *v.* say who someone or something is

ignorance (IHG nuhr uhns) *n.* lack of knowledge or education

illuminate (ih LOO muh nayt) *v.* light up; make something clearer

imitate (IHM uh tayt) *v.* copy the actions of another

immaculate (ih MAK yuh liht) *adj.* perfectly correct; without a flaw, fault or error

imminent (IHM uh nuhnt) *adj.* likely to happen soon

impassive (ihm PAS ihv) *adj.* showing no emotion

impenetrable (ihm PEHN uh truh buhl) *adj.* that cannot be passed through; that cannot be solved or understood; unfathomable

implications (ihm pluh KAY shuhnz) *n.* indirect results

imposition (ihm puh ZIHSH uhn) *n.* introduction of something such as a rule, tax, or punishment

incessantly (ihn SEHS uhnt lee) *adv.* continuing in a way that seems endless; continually; unceasingly

incognito (ihn kog NEE toh) *adj.* with true identity unrevealed or disguised; under an assumed name

incredulity (ihn kruh DOO luh tee) *n.* unwillingness or inability to believe

individuality (ihn duh vihj oo AL uh tee) *n.* state of being one of a kind

indolently (IHN duh luhnt lee) *adv.* lazily; idly

induction (ihn DUHK shuhn) *n.* installation; initiation

inevitability (ihn ehv uh tuh BIHL uh tee) *n.* quality of being certain to happen

inevitable (ihn EHV uh tuh buhl) *adj.* unavoidable; certain

infallibility (ihn fal uh BIHL uh tee) *n.* condition of not being likely to fail

information (ihn fuhr MAY shuhn) *n.* facts or knowledge about something

informed (ihn FAWRMD) *v.* gave someone information

informed (ihn FAWRMD) *adj.* having much knowledge, information, or education

inscrutable (ihn SKROO tuh buhl) *adj.* baffling; mysterious

insidious (ihn SIHD ee uhs) *adj.* characterized by craftiness and betrayal

insight (ihn syt) *n.* ability to have a deep understanding of something

insinuatingly (ihn SIHN yu ayt ihng lee) *adv.* suggesting indirectly; implying

insolent (IHN suh luhnt) *adj.* boldly disrespectful

instigates (IHN stuh gayts) *v.* urges on; stirs up

instinct (IHN stihngkt) *n.* behavior or response that one is born with

intentions (ihn TEHN shuhnz) *n.* aims or purposes of an action

intercession (ihn tuhr SEHSH uhn) *n.* act of pleading on another's behalf

interlopers (ihn tuhr LOHP erz) *n.* people who meddle in others' affairs; trespassers

interminably (ihn TUR muh nuh blee) *adv.* endlessly

intermission (ihn tuhr MIHSH uhn) *n.* any kind of break; more specifically, a break during a performance

interpret (ihn TUR priht) *v.* understand or explain the meaning of something

interpretation (ihn tur pruh TAY shuhn) *n.* explanation of the meaning of something

intimately (IHN tuh miht lee) *adv.* in a close manner; with a special or close knowledge; closely; jointly; familiarly

introspective (ihn truh SPEHK tihv) *adj.* having to do with looking into one's own thoughts and feelings

involvement (ihn VOLV muhnt) *n.* state of being included in something

iridescent (ihr uh DEHS uhnt) *adj.* showing colors that seem to change in different lights

issue (IHSH oo) *n.* subject for debate or discussion

J

jibed (jybd) *v.* changed direction

judicious (joo DIHSH uhs) *adj.* showing good judgment

justice (JUHS tihs) *n.* quality of fairness and impartiality

L

ladle (LAY duhl) *n.* long-handled, cuplike spoon for dipping out liquids

lament (luh MEHNT) *v.* express deep sorrow; mourn

lamentable (LAM uhn tuh buhl) *adj.* distressing; sad

languid (LANG gwihd) *adj.* drooping; weak

legacy (LEHG uh see) *n.* something handed down from an ancestor

lithe (lyth) *adj.* flexible

loathsome (LOHTH suhm) *adj.* disgusting; detestable

lofty (LAWF tee) *adj.* very high; noble

longing (lawng ihng) *n.* strong, persistent desire or craving, especially for something unattainable or distant; yearning

lurched (lurcht) *v.* moved awkwardly and suddenly

M

maladies (MAL uh deez) *n.* diseases

malodorous (mal OH duhr uhs) *adj.* having a bad smell

mammoth (MAM uhth) *adj.* enormous

manipulate (muh NIHP yuh layt) *v.* handle or control

martial (MAHR shuhl) *adj.* military; warlike

maudlin (MAWD luhn) *adj.* tearfully and foolishly sentimental

meaning (MEE nihng) *n.* what is referred to or understood

mediate (MEE dee ayt) *v.* bring about agreement between people who disagree

medium (MEE dee uhm) *n.* particular way of communicating information and news to people, such as a newspaper or a television broadcast

melancholy (MEHL uhn kol ee) *adj.* sad; gloomy

menacing (MEHN his ihng) *v.* threatening

metaphysical (meht uh FIHZ uh kuhl) *adj.* spiritual; beyond the physical

meticulously (muh TIHK yuh luhs lee) *adv.* very carefully and precisely

miraculously (muh RAK yuh luhs lee) *adv.* in an amazing way; as though by a miracle

momentous (moh MEHN tuhs) *adj.* very important

monotone (MON uh tohn) *n.* uninterrupted repetition of the same tone; utterance of successive syllables or words without change of pitch or key

monotonous (muh NOT uh nuhs) *adj.* going on in the same tone without variation

morality (muh RAL uh tee) *v.* principles that someone uses to decide if behavior is right or wrong

moribund (MAWR uh buhnd) *adj.* slowly dying

mortified (MAWR tuh fyd) *adj.* extremely embarrassed

multitude (MUHL tuh tood) *n.* large number of persons or things, especially when gathered together or considered as a unit

muted (myoot ihd) *adj.* weaker; less intense

N

naive (nah EEV) *adj.* unsophisticated; innocent

novice (NOV ihs) *adj.* new to an activity; inexperienced

nurturing (NUR chuhr ihng) *n.* the raising or promoting the development of; training, educating, fostering

O

obligation (ob luh GAY shuhn) *n.* something that must be done

oblivion (uh BLIHV ee uhn) *n.* forgetfulness; the state of being unconscious or of not noticing what is happening

obstinacy (OB stuh nuh see) *n.* stubbornness

ominous (OM uh nuhs) *adj.* threatening

oppression (uh PREHSH uhn) *n.* act of being weighed down or held back by worries or problems; keeping others down by the unjust use of power.

P

pallid (PAL ihd) *adj.* pale

pallor (PAL uhr) *n.* unnatural paleness

palpable (PAL puh buhl) *adj.* able to be felt; easily perceived

palpitating (PAL puh tayt ihng) *adj.* beating rapidly; throbbing

pandemonium (pan duh MOH nee uhm) *n.* any place or scene of wild disorder, noise, or confusion; chaos

paradoxical (PAR uh DOK suh kuhl) *adj.* seemingly full of contradictions

penetrated (PEHN uh trayt uhd) *v.* broke through

pensive (PEHN sihv) *adj.* thinking deeply or seriously; thoughtful

penury (PEHN yuhr ee) *n.* extreme poverty

perceive (puhr SEEV) *v.* become aware of

perennial (puh REHN ee uhl) *adj.* happening over and over; perpetual

permeate (PUR mee ayt) *v.* spread or flow throughout

pernicious (puhr NIHSH uhs) *adj.* causing great injury or ruin; destructive

perplexes (pehr PLEHKS uhz) *v.* confuses or puzzles

perspective (puhr SPEHK tihv) *n.* point of view

pertinent (PUR tuh nuhnt) *adj.* having some connection with the matter at hand; relevant; to the point

perverse (puhr VURS) *adj.* different from what is considered right or reasonable

picturesque (pihk chuh REHSK) *adj.* like or suggesting a picture; lovely to look at; attractive and interesting

pious (PY uhs) *adj.* having or showing religious devotion

placidly (PLAS ihd lee) *adv.* calmly; quietly

plundered (PLUHN duhrd) *v.* took goods by force; looted

poignant (POY nuhnt) *adj.* emotionally touching

pondered (PON duhrd) *v.* thought deeply about

ponderously (PON duhr uhs lee) *adv.* in a labored and dull way; in a boring and serious way

potential (puh TEHN shuhl) *n.* possibility

precariously (prih KAIR ee uhs lee) *adv.* insecurely

preceded (pree SEED uhd) *v.* came before in time, place, order, rank, or importance

precipitous (prih SIHP uh tuhs) *adj.* steep; sheer

precluded (prih KLOOD ihd) *v.* prevented

predominant (prih DOM uh nuhnt) *adj.* having dominating influence over others

preliminaries (prih LIHM uh nehr eez) *n.* steps or events before the main one

preposterous (prih POS tuhr uhs) *adj.* so contrary to nature, reason, or common sense as to be laughable; absurd; ridiculous

presumed (prih ZOOMD) *adj.* taken for granted; accepted as true, lacking proof to the contrary; supposed

pretentious (prih TEHN shuhs) *adj.* grand in a showy way

prevail (prih VAYL) *v.* gain the advantage or mastery; be victorious; triumph

procure (pruh KYUR) *v.* get; obtain

prodigious (pruh DIHJ uhs) *adj.* enormous

prodigy (PROD uh jee) *n.* person who is amazingly talented or intelligent, especially a child of highly unusual talent or genius

profound (pruh FOWND) *adj.* deep; intense

profoundly (pruh FOWND lee) *adv.* deeply

provisions (pruh VIHZH uhnz) *n.* something provided, prepared, or supplied for the future

prudence (PROO duhns) *n.* a sensible and careful attitude; economy

pungent (PUHN juhnt) *adj.* producing a sharp smell

purged (purjd) *v.* cleansed

R

raggedy (RAG uh dee) *adj.* somewhat ragged and torn; tattered

rancor (RANG kuhr) *n.* bitter hate

ravenous (RAV uh nuhs) *adj.* wildly hungry

react (ree AKT) *v.* do something in response to something else

reciprocate (rih SIHP ruh kayt) *v.* return

reckless (REHK lihs) *adj.* careless; rash

recoiling (rih KOYL ihng) *v.* staggering back

reconciliation (rehk uhn sihl ee AY shuhn) *n.* the settling of a conflict or argument; agreement; compromise

reels (reelz) *n.* frames or spools on which thread, wire, tape, film, or a net is wound

refrain (rih FRAYN) *v.* hold back

relationship (rih LAY shuhn shihp) *n.* connection between two or more people or things

remnants (REHM nuhnts) *n.* what is left over; remainders

renegade (REHN uh gayd) *adj.* disloyal; traitorous

research (rih SURCH) *n.* careful study in some field of knowledge

research (rih SURCH) *v.* perform careful study

resolution (rehz uh LOO shuhn) *n.* part of a narrative in which the plot is unraveled

respite (REHS piht) *n.* rest; relief

resplendent (rih SPLEHN duhnt) *adj.* shinning brightly

respond (rih SPOND) *v.* reply or react

responsibility (rih spon suh BIHL uh tee) *n.* having to answer to someone or something else; being accountable for success or failure

retort (rih TAWRT) *n.* sharp or clever reply

retribution (reht ruh BYOO shuhn) *n.* payback; punishment for a misdeed

revelry (REHV uhl ree) *n.* noisy merrymaking

revered (rih VIHRD) *adj.* regarded with great respect and awe

reverie (REHV uhr ee) *n.* dreamy thinking and imagining

revival (rih VY vuhl) *n.* a bringing or coming back into use, attention, or being after a decline

riddled (RIHD uhld) *adj.* affected throughout by something unpleasant

rifled (RY fuhld) *v.* ransacked and robbed; searched quickly through a cupboard or drawer

rueful (ROO fuhl) *adj.* feeling sorrow or regret

S

sallow (SAL oh) *adj.* of a sickly, pale-yellowish color

scarred (skahrd) *adj.* marked or dented

scourge (skurj) *n.* instrument for inflicting punishment

scruples (SKROO puhlz) *n.* misgivings about something one feels is wrong

segment (SEHG muhnt) *n.* division or section

seizure (SEE zhuhr) *n.* sudden and brief loss of consciousness and body control

senses (SEHNS uhz) *n.* physical ways in which a person or animal learns about the world: sight, hearing, touch, taste, and smell

sensory (SEHN suhr ee) *adj.* relating to the senses of sight, sound, taste, touch, or smell

serve (surv) *v.* work for; to be useful for

shriveled (SHRIHV uhld) *adj.* shrunken and wrinkled

siege (seej) *n.* encirclement of a fortified place by an opposing armed force intending to take it

similarity (sihm uh LAR uh tee) *n.* state of being alike

skeptics (SKEHP tihks) *n.* doubters; disbelievers

solitude (SOL uh tood) *n.* the state of being solitary, or alone; seclusion, isolation, or remoteness

sources (SAWRS uhz) *n.* places where things begin or are found

speculate (SPEHK yuh layt) *v.* think about or make up theories about a subject; guess at

spurn (spurn) *v.* reject with contempt or disdain

stalks (stawks) *v.* walks in a stiff, haughty, or grim manner

standard (STAN duhrd) *n.* idea to which other things are compared

standard (STAN duhrd) *adj.* normal; average

statistics (stuh TIHS tihks) *n.* science of collecting, analyzing, and using mathematical data

stout (stowt) *adj.* sturdy

stranded (STRAN dihd) *adj.* in a place or situation from which one needs help to leave

submerged (suhb MURJD) *adj.* covered with water or the like

subsided (suhb SYD ihd) *v.* settled down; became less active or intense

subverting (suhb VURT ihng) *v.* overthrowing or destroying something established

succumbed (suh KUHMD) *v.* gave way; yielded

suffice (suh FYS) *v.* be enough

surreal (suh REE uhl) *adj.* strange, like something from a dream

survival (suhr VY vuhl) *n.* the state of continuing to exist

T

tantalizingly (tan tuh LY zihng lee) *adv.* in a teasing way

telegraph (TEHL uh graf) *n.* an apparatus or system that converts a coded message into electric impulses and sends it to a distance receiver

temporal (TEHM puhr uhl) *adj.* having to do with time

tenacious (tih NAY shuhs) *adj.* holding firmly to beliefs; persistent; stubborn; adamant

tenement (TEHN uh muhnt) *n.* apartment house, often run-down

transgression (trans GREHSH uhn) *n.* wrongdoing; sin

treble (TREHB uhl) *n.* high-pitched voice or sound

trundle (TRUHN duhl) *v.* roll along

truth (trooth) *n.* corresponding with reality or fact

tumultuous (too MUHL chu uhs) *adj.* greatly disturbed; in an uproar

U

understanding (uhn duhr STAN dihng) *n.* ability to get the meaning of something; ability to think or learn

unique (yoo NEEK) *adj.* one of a kind

unpalatable (uhn PAL uh tuh buhl) *adj.* distasteful; unpleasant

unrequited (uhn rih KWY tuhd) *adj.* not returned or repaid

unwieldy (uhn WEEL dee) *adj.* awkward; clumsy

usurped (yoo SURPT) *v.* took power or position without right

V

values (VAL yooz) *n.* beliefs accepted by an individual

venture (VEHN chuhr) *n.* risky action

verify (VEHR uh fy) *v.* make sure something is true; confirm

vex (vehks) *v.* annoy

vial (vyl) *n.* small bottle containing medicine or other liquids

vigilant (VIHJ uh luhnt) *adj.* watchful

vile (vyl) *adj.* evil; wicked

volumes (VOL yuhmz) *n.* sets of the issues of a periodical over a fixed period of time, usually a year; books

voluminously (vuh LOO muh nuhs lee) *adv.* fully; in great volume

W

wail (wayl) *n.* lament; cry of deep sorrow

war (wawr) *n.* armed conflict between people

warp (wawrp) *v.* twist; distort

wayward (WAY wuhrd) *adj.* headstrong

wheezed (hweez) *v.* breathed hard with a breathy sound

wisdom (WIHZ duhm) *n.* ability to make good judgments based on knowledge and experience

woeful (WOH fuhl) *adj.* full of sorrow

woes (wohz) *n.* great sorrows

writhing (RYTH ihng) *v.* twisting; turning

Spanish Glossary

El vocabulario de Gran Pregunta aparece en **azul**. El vocabulario academico de alta utilidad esta **subraydo**.

A

abash / avergonzar *v.* apenar

abdicated / abdicó *v.* renunció formalmente

absurdity / absurdo *s.* algo ridículo o un disparate

accentuated / acentuó *v.* enfatizó; realzó el efecto de

accept / aceptar *v.* recibir algo que se da

accumulated / acumuló *v.* amontonado, recopilado o reunido, especialmente durante algún lapso de tiempo

acquiesced / accedió *v.* consintió o se doblegó calladamente sin protestar, pero sin entusiasmo

adversary / adversario *s.* persona que se opone o lucha contra otra

afflicted / afligió *v.* que sufrió o padeció de

allotment / asignación *s.* parte; porción

aloofness / retraimiento *s.* calidad de estar distante o apartado

ambiguities / ambigüedades *s.* declaraciones o eventos cuyos significados no son claros

ambiguous / ambiguo *adj.* que tiene más de un significado

amicably / amigablemente *adv.* de manera amistosa

amicably / amistosamente *adv.* de manera amigable

amid / entre *prep.* en medio de; rodeado por

anguish / angustia *s.* gran dolor o sufrimiento

anonymous / anónimo *adj.* sin nombre conocido o reconocido

antagonize / contrariar *v.* enemistar

apex / cima *s.* punto más alto; cumbre

appreciate / apreciar *v.* reconocer el valor de algo

archaic / arcaico *adj.* de épocas pasadas; antiguo

ardor / ardor *s.* pasión; entusiasmo

arduous / arduo *adj.* difícil; laborioso

argument / discusión *s.* intercambio de ideas cuando hay un desacuerdo

articulate / articulado *adj.* capaz de expresarse con claridad

articulate / elocuente *adj.* que se expresa con claridad y facilidad

assiduous / asiduo *adj.* hecho con atención constante y cuidadosa; diligente

assimilated / asimiló *v.* ingirió o absorbió

assimilated / asimilado *adj.* algo o alguien que ha sido completamente absorbido

assuage / apaciguar *v.* calmar; sosegar

assumption / suposición *s.* algo que se da por sentado

atonement / desagravio *s.* acción de enmendar algún agravio o perjuicio

attributes / atributos *s.* características o cualidades de una persona o cosa

augmenting / aumentando *v.* incrementando; haciendo más grande

authentic / auténtico *adj.* genuino; verdadero

aware / consciente *adj.* saber algo por haberlo experimentado o por haber sido informado de ello

awestruck / pasmado *adj.* maravillado

awry / ladeado *adj.* estar mal puesto o torcido

azure / azur *adv.* azul celeste

B

background / antecedentes *s.* hechos que causan o explican algo

bafflement / desconcierto *s.* perplejidad; dificultad de comprensión

balmy / balsámico *adj.* que tiene las cualidades del bálsamo; apacible, suave, agradable

battle / batalla *s.* pelea entre fuerzas armadas

battle / combatir *v.* pelear o luchar

barren / árido *adj.* desértico; que tiene poca o ninguna vegetación

beguiling / cautivar *v.* engañar; encantar

belief / creencia *s.* algo que se acepta como cierto

bemusing / aturdiendo *v.* confundir; desconcertar

benevolently / benévolamente *adv.* de manera bien intencionada

bereft / desprovisto *adj.* despojado, privado de

bias / predisposición *s.* inclinación o tendencia mental; parcialidad

bilingual / bilingüe *adj.* que usa dos idiomas

blight / plaga *s.* algo que destruye o impide el crecimiento

bulging / protuberante *adj.* abultado

C

candor / franqueza *s.* marcada honestidad o sinceridad al expresarse

cascade / cascada *s.* pequeño salto de agua empinado; cualquier cosa que se asemeje a un salto de agua

censure / censura *s.* firme desaprobación

character / carácter *s.* cualidades que hacen única a una persona

choices / elecciones *s.* variedad de cosas de donde uno puede seleccionar

circumstance / circunstancia *s.* situación; evento

clarify / aclarar *v.* hacer que algo sea más claro y comprensible

clasps / agarra *v.* sujeta con firmeza

collective / colectivo *adj.* conformado como grupo; reunido en uno solo

communication / comunicación *s.* intercambio de información

compensation / compensación *s.* cualquier cosa que sirve para subsanar una pérdida, daño o deuda

compete / competir *v.* tratar de ganar contra un adversario

competition / competencia *s.* rivalidad; acción de competir

comprehend / comprender *v.* entender

comprehension / comprensión *s.* acción de entender algo

comprehension / comprensión *s.* entendimiento

conceded / concedió *v.* admitió como cierto o válido; reconoció

concept / concepto *s.* idea; noción

concessions / concesiones *s.* cosas otorgadas o cedidas como privilegios

condolences / condolencias *s.* manifestaciones de compasión hacia otra persona que sufre

confer / conferir *v.* conceder; otorgar

confines / confines *s.* fronteras o zona fronteriza; borde; límite

conformity / conformidad *s.* estar de acuerdo con costumbres o normas

connection / conexión *s.* unión de dos o más cosas o ideas

conspicuous / conspicuo *adj.* que atrae la atención por ser inesperado, inusual, sobresaliente o notorio; impresionante

contempt / desprecio *s.* desdén o menosprecio

context / contexto *s.* partes de una oración cercanas a una palabra que determinan su significado exacto

controversy / controversia *s.* discusión de un asunto en el que chocan las opiniones divergentes

countenance / semblante *s.* rostro

covenant / pacto *s.* convenio o acuerdo, especialmente uno sagrado

convince / convencer *v.* persuadir mediante argumentos o evidencia

cooperate / cooperar *v.* trabajar conjuntamente para lograr algo

credible / creíble *adj.* verosímil

creed / credo *s.* declaración de creencias

culture / cultura *s.* ideas, costumbres, destrezas y arte de un grupo de personas de una época específica en la historia

cunning / astuto *adj.* hábil en el engaño

curtailed / restringió *v.* acortó; redujo

D

daunting / amedrentador *adj.* intimidante

defaulted / incumplió *v.* dejó de hacer algo o no compareció en alguna parte cuando era requerido o esperado; faltó a un pago a su vencimiento

defend / defender *v.* proteger contra ataques

deferred / difirió *v.* postergó a una fecha futura

defiance / desafío *s.* franca y descarada resistencia a la autoridad

defrauded / estafó *v.* engañó

degenerate / degenerar *v.* empeorar

dejection / desaliento *s.* desánimo; depresión

deleterious / nocivo *adj.* perjudicial para la salud o el bienestar

demonstrative / expresivo *adj.* que demuestra abiertamente los sentimientos

demure / reservado *adj.* modesto

depravity / depravación *s.* deshonestidad; corrupción

depreciate / depreciar *v.* disminuir su valor

derisive / burlón *adj.* que muestra desprecio o ridiculiza; mofador

desolate / desolado *adj.* afligido; desconsolado

despotic / despótico *adj.* como un gobernante absoluto o tirano

desultory / vago *adj.* sin rumbo; aleatorio

determination / determinación *s.* firme intención

determine / determinar *v.* ocasionar que algo ocurra de cierta forma

differences / diferencias *s.* características que hacen que las cosas sean disímiles; maneras en que las cosas no son iguales

differentiate / diferenciar *v.* ver o expresar lo que hace que dos o más cosas sean diferentes entre sí

diffused / difundió *v.* diseminó

dilapidated / desmoronado *adj.* ruinoso

diminution / disminución *s.* reducción

discerning / perspicaz *adj.* tener buen juicio o comprensión

discipline / disciplina *s.* entrenamiento que desarrolla el dominio de sí mismo, carácter, o el orden y eficiencia

disclosed / divulgó *v.* reveló; hizo público

disconsolately / desconsoladamente *adv.* muy desdichadamente

discreet / discreto *adj.* cuidadoso con lo que dice o hace; prudente; que calla o mantiene confidencias cuando es necesario

discreetly / discretamente *adv.* sin llamar la atención

discriminate / discriminar *v.* distinguir las diferencias entre las cosas; actuar en contra de alguien por prejuicio

discuss / discutir *v.* hablar sobre algo

disgrace / deshonra *s.* pérdida del respeto, honor, o estima; vergüenza

disheveled / desordenado *adj.* desarreglado

dishevelment / desorden *s.* desarreglo; desaseo

dismal / melancólico *adj.* que ocasiona tristeza o desolación

dispatched / despachó *v.* terminó con prontitud

disperse / dispersar *v.* romper y desparramar en todas direcciones; esparcir; distribuir ampliamente

disputed / disputado *adj.* en litigio; contencioso

dissemble / disimular *v.* ocultar bajo una falsa apariencia; disfrazar

distinguished / distinguido *adj.* que tiene un aire de distinción; reconocido por su excelencia; eminente; famoso

distort / distorsionar *v.* enredar hasta perder la forma original

distraught / afligido *adj.* muy alterado o confundido

diverged / bifurcó *v.* ramificó en diferentes direcciones

droll / gracioso *adj.* divertido de manera comedida

duration / duración *s.* el tiempo en que algo continúa o permanece

E

elation / entusiasmo *s.* sentimiento de júbilo; orgullo; alborozo

eloquence / elocuencia *s.* elegancia y persuasión en el discurso o la escritura

embellish / embellecer *v.* decorar o mejorar agregando detalles; ornamentar; adornar

emerge / surgir *v.* nacer como algo nuevo o mejorado; tornarse visible o conocido

emitting / emitir *v.* despedir

empathy / empatía *s.* capacidad de comprender y compartir los sentimientos de otra persona

emulate / emular *v.* imitar (a una persona o cosa que se admira)

enamored / enamoró *v.* lleno de amor y deseo; encantado

encroaching / de manera usurpadora *adj.* invadir de manera furtiva

endeavor / intento *s.* tentativa o esfuerzo formal

endeavored / intentó *v.* hizo un esfuerzo formal para conseguir o lograr algo; trató

endurance / resistencia *s.* capacidad para soportar adversidades

enigma / enigma *s.* misterio

enjoined / impuso *v.* exigió

entailed / implicó *v.* causó o requirió como consecuencia necesaria; involucró; obligó

enthralled / embelesó *v.* mantuvo como hechizado; cautivó

enumerated / enumeró *v.* nombró uno a uno; especificó, como en una lista

esteem / estima *s.* opinión favorable; aprecio; respeto

evanescent / evanescente *adj.* temporal; tendiente a desaparecer

evidence / evidencia *s.* prueba

exchange / intercambio *s.* acción de comerciar algo

exchange / intercambiar *v.* comerciar

exile / exiliar *v.* desterrar

explicit / explícito *adj.* expresado con claridad

extrapolating / extrapolando *v.* llegando a una conclusión por deducción de hechos conocidos

F

fact / hecho *s.* algo que realmente ocurrió o que es cierto

faltered / titubeó *v.* actuó de forma vacilante; mostró incertidumbre; flaqueó; se acobardó

feasible / factible *adj.* capaz de hacerse o realizarse; viable; posible

feeling / sentimiento *s.* emoción de la que están conscientes las personas

feisty / determinado *adj.* lleno de coraje; vigoroso

fertile / fértil *adj.* rico en nutrientes que promueven el crecimiento

fester / enconar *v.* infectar; formar pus

feud / lucha encarnizada *s.* amargas, prolongadas y violentas disputas, especialmente entre clanes o familias

fickle / voluble *adj.* cambiante

forebears / antepasados *s.* ascendientes

forgo / privar *v.* contenerse de; abstenerse de; renunciar a

formality / formalidad *s.* atención a normas o costumbres establecidas

formidable / formidable *adj.* impresionante

fortitude / fortaleza *s.* fuerza para soportar el infortunio y el dolor con calma y paciencia

fray / refriega *s.* pelea escandalosa

furtive / furtivo *adj.* a hurtadillas; oculto

futile / fútil *adj.* inútil; sin remedio

G

gallant / gallardo *adj.* valiente y noble

grotesque / grotesco *adj.* que tiene un diseño extraño, raro; extraño o inusual de manera tal que resulta repugnante u ofensivo

H

hallowed / santificado *adj.* sagrado

haughty / altanero *adj.* arrogante

hero / héroe *s.* alguien a quien se admira por sus acciones valientes o nobles

honesty / sinceridad *s.* calidad de ser veraz

humble / humilde *adj.* modesto; que tiene humildad

humbly / humildemente *adv.* de tal manera que no es soberbio ni arrogante; modestamente

I

identify / identificar *v.* describir lo que es una persona o cosa

ignorance / ignorancia *s.* falta de conocimiento o educación

illuminate / iluminar *v.* alumbrar; aclarar

imitate / imitar *v.* copiar las acciones de otro

immaculate / impecable *adj.* en perfectas condiciones; sin defectos, faltas o errores

imminent / inminente *adj.* que probablemente ocurrirá pronto

impassive / impasible *adj.* que no muestra emoción alguna

impenetrable / impenetrable *adj.* que no se puede atravesar; que no puede ser resuelto o entendido; insondable

implications / implicaciones *s.* consecuencias indirectas

imposition / imposición *s.* introducción de algo como una norma, impuesto o castigo

incessantly / incesantemente *adv.* que sigue de forma que pareciera interminable; continuamente; constantemente

incognito / incógnito *adj.* sin revelar la verdadera identidad; bajo un nombre ficticio

incredulity / incredulidad *s.* renuencia o incapacidad para creer

individuality / individualidad *s.* condición de ser único

indolently / indolentemente *adv.* con pereza; ociosamente

induction / instalación *s.* inclusión; iniciación

inevitability / inevitabilidad *s.* calidad de que ciertamente ocurrirá

inevitable / inevitable *adj.* ineludible; con seguridad

infallibility / infalibilidad *s.* condición de que no puede fallar

information / información *s.* hechos o conocimientos sobre algo

informed / informado *adj.* que tiene mucho conocimiento, información o educación

informed / informó *v.* le dio información a alguien

insight / perspicacia *s.* capacidad de tener una profunda comprensión sobre algo

inscrutable / inescrutable *adj.* desconcertante; misterioso

insidious / insidioso *adj.* que se caracteriza por su astucia y traición

insinuatingly / de manera insinuante *adv.* que sugiere indirectamente; que implica

insolent / insolente *adj.* descaradamente irrespetuoso

instigates / instiga *v.* fomenta; promueve

instinct / instinto *s.* conducta o respuesta con la que se nace

intentions / intenciones *s.* objetivos o propósitos de una acción

intercession / intercesión *s.* acción de abogar por otra persona

interlopers / intrusos *s.* personas que interfieren en los asuntos de otros; invasores

interminably / interminablemente *adv.* que no tiene fin

intermission / intermedio *s.* cualquier tipo de interrupción; más específicamente, el entreacto durante una función de teatro

interpret / interpretar *v.* entender o explicar el significado de algo

interpretation / interpretación *s.* explicación del significado de algo

intimately / íntimamente *adv.* de forma cercana; con conocimiento especial o estrecho; celosamente; conjuntamente; familiarmente

introspective / introspectivo *adj.* que tiene que ver con el análisis de sus propios pensamientos y sentimientos

involvement / participación *s.* condición de estar incluido en algo

iridescent / iridiscente *adj.* que muestra colores que parecen cambiar de acuerdo a los diferentes tipos de luz

issue / asunto *s.* tema para debate o discusión

J

jibed / viró *v.* cambió de dirección

judicious / juicioso *adj.* que muestra buen juicio

justice / justicia *s.* calidad de equidad e imparcialidad

L

ladle / cazo *s.* cucharón hondo de mango largo usado para servir líquidos

lament / lamentar *v.* expresar profunda tristeza; penar

lamentable / lamentable *adj.* angustioso; penoso

languid / lánguido *adj.* flojo; débil

legacy / legado *s.* algo heredado de un antepasado

lithe / ágil *adj.* flexible

loathsome / odioso *adj.* repugnante; detestable

lofty / elevado *adj.* muy alto; noble

longing / añoranza *s.* fuerte y persistente deseo o antojo, particularmente por algo inalcanzable o distante; nostalgia

lurched / sacudió *v.* se movió torpe y repentinamente

M

maladies / dolencias *s.* enfermedades

malodorous / maloliente *adj.* que tiene mal olor

mammoth / gigante *adj.* enorme

manipulate / manipular *v.* manejar o controlar

martial / marcial *adj.* de corte militar

maudlin / llorón *adj.* lloroso y tontamente sentimental

meaning / significado *s.* de qué trata o qué se entiende por algo

mediate / mediar *v.* interceder para que las partes que están en desacuerdo lleguen a un acuerdo

SPANISH GLOSSARY

medium / medio *s.* manera particular de comunicar información y noticias a la gente, como un periódico o un programa de televisión

melancholy / melancolía *s.* tristeza; pesimismo

menacing / amenazar *v.* intimidar

metaphysical / metafísico *adj.* espiritual; que traspasa lo físico

meticulously / meticulosamente *adv.* de manera muy cuidadosa y precisa

miraculously / milagrosamente *adv.* de manera sorprendente; como por milagro

momentous / trascendental *adj.* muy importante

monotone / monotonía *s.* repetición ininterrumpida de un mismo tono; pronunciación de sílabas o palabras sucesivas sin cambiar el tono o tonalidad

monotonous / monótono *adj.* seguir en el mismo tono sin variación

morality / moralidad *v.* principios que sirven para decidir si el comportamiento es correcto o incorrecto

moribund / moribundo *adj.* que muere lentamente

mortified / avergonzado *adj.* extremadamente humillado

multitude / multitud *s.* gran cantidad de personas o cosas, especialmente cuando se juntan o se consideran una unidad

muted / silencioso *adj.* más débil; menos intenso

N

naive / ingenuo *adj.* poco sofisticado; inocente

novice / novato *adj.* nuevo en cualquier actividad; sin experiencia

nurturing / formación *s.* crianza o fomento del desarrollo; capacitación, educación, crianza

O

obligation / obligación *s.* algo que se debe hacer

oblivion / olvido *s.* falta de memoria; condición de estar inconsciente o inadvertido de lo que ocurre

obstinacy / obstinación *s.* terquedad

ominous / siniestro *adj.* amenazante

oppression / opresión *s.* sensación de estar agobiado o reprimido por preocupaciones, problemas o el uso injusto del poder

P

pallid / pálido *adj.* lívido

pallor / palidez *s.* lividez poco natural

palpable / palpable *adj.* capaz de sentirse; percibido con facilidad

palpitating / palpitante *adj.* que late rápidamente; que pulsa

pandemonium / pandemonio *s.* cualquier lugar o escena de desorden, ruido o confusión desenfrenada; caos

paradoxical / paradójico *adj.* aparentemente lleno de contradicciones

penetrated / penetró *v.* traspasó

pensive / pensativo *adj.* que reflexiona profunda o seriamente

penury / penuria *s.* extrema pobreza

perceive / percibir *v.* darse cuenta de

perennial / perenne *adj.* que ocurre una y otra vez; perpetuo

permeate / penetrar *v.* extenderse o fluir a través

pernicious / pernicioso *adj.* que causa gran perjuicio o ruina; destructivo

perplexes / desconcierta *v.* confunde o deja perplejo

perspective / perspectiva *s.* punto de vista

pertinent / pertinente *adj.* que tiene alguna conexión con el asunto entre manos; relevante; al grano

perverse / perverso *adj.* distinto de lo que se considera correcto o razonable

picturesque / pintoresco *adj.* que sugiere o que se parece a una pintura; hermoso a la vista

pious / piadoso *adj.* que tiene o muestra fervor religioso

placidly / plácidamente *adv.* tranquilamente; sosegadamente

plundered / saqueó *v.* que tomó mercancías por la fuerza; robó

poignant / conmovedor *adj.* que suscita emociones

pondered / sopesó *v.* consideró profundamente

ponderously / pesadamente *adv.* de manera forzada y monótona; de forma aburrida y seria

potential / potencial *s.* posibilidad; habilidades que se necesitan para triunfar

precariously / precariamente *adv.* de manera insegura

preceded / precedió *v.* que estaba antes en tiempo, lugar, orden, rango o importancia

precipitous / escarpado *adj.* abrupto; vertical

precluded / impidió *v.* imposibilitó

predominant / predominante *adj.* que tiene influencia dominante sobre otros

preliminaries / preparativos *s.* pasos o eventos antes del principal

preposterous / absurdo *adj.* tan contrario a la naturaleza, la razón o el sentido común que es irrisorio; ilógico; ridículo

presumed / supuesto *adj.* dado por sentado; aceptado como cierto, a falta de prueba de lo contrario; asumido

pretentious / pretencioso *adj.* magnífico de manera ostentosa

prevail / prevalecer *v.* obtener la ventaja o el dominio; salir victorioso; triunfar

procure / procurar *v.* lograr; obtener

prodigious / prodigioso *adj.* enorme

prodigy / prodigio *s.* persona que es increíblemente talentosa o inteligente, particularmente un niño de talento extraordinario; genio

profound / profundo *adj.* hondo; intenso

profoundly / profundamente *adv.* intensamente

provisions / suministros *s.* algo que se provee, prepara o suple para el futuro

prudence / prudencia *s.* actitud racional y cuidadosa; economía

pungent / acre *adj.* que produce un olor penetrante

purged / depuró *v.* purificó

R

raggedy / andrajoso *adj.* bastante harapiento y roto; hecho jirones

rancor / rencor *s.* odio implacable

ravenous / voraz *adj.* con hambre desmesurada

react / reaccionar *v.* hacer algo en respuesta a otra cosa

reciprocate / corresponder *v.* devolver

reckless / temerario *adj.* descuidado; descabellado

recoiling / retrocediendo *v.* dando marcha atrás

reconciliation / reconciliación *s.* resolución de un conflicto o disputa; acuerdo; compromiso

reels / carretes *s.* marcos o rollos en los que se arrolla hilo, alambre, cinta o red

refrain / abstener *v.* contenerse

relationship / relación *s.* conexión entre dos o más personas o cosas

remnants / remanentes *s.* sobrantes; restos

renegade / renegado *adj.* desleal; traicionero

research / investigación *s.* estudio profundo en algún campo del conocimiento

research / investigar *v.* realizar estudio profundo

resolution / resolución *s.* parte de una narrativa en la que se desenmaraña la trama

respite / respiro *s.* descanso; alivio

resplendent / resplandeciente *adj.* radiantemente iluminado

respond / responder *v.* contestar o reaccionar

responsibility / responsabilidad *s.* tener que responder ante alguien o algo; tener que rendir cuentas por el éxito o el fracaso

retort / réplica *s.* respuesta cortante o astuta

retribution / castigo *s.* restitución; escarmiento por una falta cometida

revelry / parranda *s.* fiesta ruidosa

revered / venerado *adj.* tratado con gran respeto y admiración

reverie / ensueño *s.* pensamiento e imaginación soñadora

revival / restablecimiento *s.* traer o devolver al uso, atención o naturaleza después de un descenso

riddled / plagado *adj.* afectado completamente

rifled / desvalijó *v.* saqueó y robó; buscó rápidamente en un armario o gaveta

rueful / arrepentido *adj.* que siente tristeza o remordimiento

S

sallow / amarillento *adj.* de color enfermizo, pálido macilento

scarred / cicatrizado *adj.* marcado o abollado

scourge / azote *s.* instrumento para imponer un castigo

scruples / escrúpulos *s.* dudas sobre algo que uno siente que es incorrecto

segment / segmento *s.* división o sección

seizure / ataque *s.* breve y repentina pérdida del conocimiento y del control corporal

senses / sentidos *s.* formas físicas con las que una persona o animal aprende sobre el mundo: vista, oído, tacto, gusto y olfato

sensory / sensorial *adj.* relativo a los sentidos de la vista, oído, gusto, tacto y olfato

serve / servir *v.* trabajar para; ser útil para

shriveled / marchito *adj.* seco y arrugado

siege / sitio *s.* cercamiento de un lugar fortificado por fuerzas armadas opositoras con el fin de tomarlo

similarity / similitud *s.* condición de ser parecidos

skeptics / escépticos *s.* aquéllos que dudan; aquéllos que no creen

skeptics / escépticos *s.* personas que dudan y cuestionan las ideas generalmente aceptadas

solitude / soledad *s.* condición de estar solitario o solo; reclusión, aislamiento o alejamiento

sources / fuentes *s.* lugares en donde comienzan o se encuentran las cosas

speculate / especular *v.* pensar o inventar teorí**as sobre un tema; adivinar**

spurn / desdeñar *v.* rechazar con desprecio o desdén

stalks / taconea *v.* que camina de manera arrogante, ceremoniosa y severa

standard / norma *s.* concepto contra el que se comparan otras cosas

standard / estándar *adj.* normal; promedio

statistics / estadísticas *s.* ciencia de recoger, analizar y usar datos matemáticos

stout / sólido *adj.* robusto

stranded / varado *adj.* desamparado en un lugar o situación donde se necesita ayuda para salir

submerged / sumergido *adj.* cubierto con agua o algo similar

subsided / disminuyó *v.* se calmó; se volvió menos activo o intenso

subverting / trastornando *v.* derribando o destruyendo algo establecido

succumbed / sucumbió *v.* se rindió; cedió

suffice / bastar *v.* ser suficiente

surreal / surrealista *adj.* extraño, como algo salido de un sueño

survival / supervivencia *s.* condición de continuar existiendo

T

tantalizingly / tentadoramente *adv.* de manera provocativa

telegraph / telégrafo *s.* aparato o sistema que convierte un mensaje codificado en impulsos eléctricos y lo envía a un receptor distante

temporal / temporal *adj.* que tiene que ver con el tiempo

tenacious / tenaz *adj.* que se mantiene firme en sus creencias; persistente; terco; decidido

tenement / casa de vecindad *s.* vivienda, a menudo en malas condiciones

transgression / transgresión *s.* infracción; pecado

treble / tiple *s.* voz o sonido muy agudo

trundle / rodar *v.* ir rodando

truth / verdad *s.* que corresponde a realidades o hechos

tumultuous / tumultuoso *adj.* muy agitado; en un alboroto

U

understanding / entendimiento *s.* capacidad de comprender el significado de algo; capacidad para pensar o aprender

unique / único *adj.* exclusivo

unpalatable / desagradable *adj.* repugnante; molesto

unrequited / no correspondido *adj.* no reciprocado ni devuelto

unwieldy / abultado *adj.* incómodo; torpe

usurped / usurpó *v.* tomó el poder o posición sin derecho

V

values / valores *s.* convicciones aceptadas por una persona

venture / ventura *s.* acción riesgosa

verify / verificar *v.* asegurarse de que algo es cierto; corroborar

vex / fastidiar *v.* irritar

vial / frasco *s.* envase pequeño que contiene medicamento u otros líquidos

vigilant / vigilante *adj.* alerta

vile / vil *adj.* malévolo; malvado

volumes / volúmenes *s.* conjuntos de ejemplares de periódicos que abarcan un lapso de tiempo fijo, generalmente un año; libros

voluminously / voluminosamente *adv.* completamente; de gran volumen

W

wail / gemido *s.* lamento; grito de profundo dolor

war / guerra *s.* conflicto armado entre pueblos

warp / torcer *v.* retorcer; distorsionar

wayward / avieso *adj.* caprichoso

wheezed / resolló *v.* respiró con silbido

wisdom / sabiduría *s.* capacidad de emitir buenos juicios con base en el conocimiento y la experiencia

woeful / afligido *adj.* lleno de dolor

woes / aflicciones *s.* grandes tristezas

writhing / retorcer *v.* contorsionar; serpentear

Literary Terms

ACT See ***Drama.***

ALLEGORY An ***allegory*** is a story or tale with two or more levels of meaning—a literal level and one or more symbolic levels. The events, setting, and characters in an allegory are symbols for ideas and qualities.

ALLITERATION ***Alliteration*** is the repetition of initial consonant sounds. Writers use alliteration to give emphasis to words, to imitate sounds, and to create musical effects. In the following line from Edgar Allan Poe's "The Raven" (p. 710), there is alliteration of the *w* sound: Once upon a midnight dreary, while I pondered weak and weary, . . .

ALLUSION An ***allusion*** is a reference to a well-known person, place, event, literary work, or work of art. In O. Henry's "The Gift of the Magi" (p. 260), the title and details of the story refer to the biblical account of the Magi, wise men who brought gifts to the baby Jesus.

ANALOGY An ***analogy*** makes a comparison between two or more things that are similar in some ways but otherwise unalike.

ANECDOTE An ***anecdote*** is a brief story about an interesting, amusing, or strange event told to entertain or to make a point. In the excerpt from "A Lincoln Preface" (p. 500), Carl Sandburg tells anecdotes about Abraham Lincoln. See also ***Narrative***.

ANTAGONIST An ***antagonist*** is a character or force in conflict with a main character, or protagonist.

ANTICLIMAX Like a climax, an ***anticlimax*** is a turning point in a story. However, an anticlimax is always a letdown. It's the point at which you learn that the story will not turn out the way you had expected. In Thayer's "Casey at the Bat" (p. 696), the anticlimax occurs when Casey strikes out instead of hitting a game-winning run.

ARCHETYPE An ***archetype*** is a type of character, detail, image, or situation that appears in literature throughout history. Some critics believe that archetypes reveal deep truths about human experience.

ARGUMENT See ***Persuasion.***

ASIDE An ***aside*** is a short speech delivered by a character in a play in order to express his or her true thoughts and feelings. Traditionally, the aside is directed to the audience and is presumed to be inaudible to the other actors.

ASSONANCE ***Assonance*** is the repetition of vowel sounds followed by different consonants in two or more stressed syllables. Assonance is found in the phrase "weak and weary" in Edgar Allan Poe's "The Raven" (p. 710).

ATMOSPHERE See ***Mood.***

AUTOBIOGRAPHY An ***autobiography*** is a form of nonfiction in which a writer tells his or her own life story. An autobiography may tell about the person's whole life or only a part of it. An example of an autobiography is the excerpt from *A White House Diary* (p. 104).

See also ***Biography*** and ***Nonfiction.***

See also ***Oral Tradition.***

BIOGRAPHY A ***biography*** is a form of nonfiction in which a writer tells the life story of another person. Biographies have been written about many famous people, historical and contemporary, but they can also be written about "ordinary" people. An example of a biography is the excerpt from *Arthur Ashe Remembered* (p. 508).

See also ***Autobiography*** and ***Nonfiction.***

BLANK VERSE ***Blank verse*** is poetry written in unrhymed iambic pentameter lines. This verse form was widely used by William Shakespeare.

See also ***Meter.***

CHARACTER A ***character*** is a person or an animal that takes part in the action of a literary work. The main character, or protagonist, is the most important character in a story. This character often changes in some important way as a result of the story's events. In Richard Connell's "The Most Dangerous Game" (p. 214), Rainsford is the main character and General Zaroff is the antagonist, or character who opposes the main character.

Characters are sometimes classified as round or flat, dynamic or static. A ***round character*** shows many different traits—faults as well as virtues. A *flat character* shows only one trait. A *dynamic character* develops and grows during the course of the story; a static character does not change.

See also ***Characterization*** and ***Motivation.***

CHARACTERIZATION ***Characterization*** is the act of creating and developing a character. In ***direct characterization,*** the author directly states a character's traits.

For example, at the beginning of "The Necklace" (p. 332), Maupassant directly characterizes Madame Loisel: "She was one of those pretty, charming young women. . . ."

In ***indirect characterization,*** an author provides clues about a character by describing what a character looks like, does, and says, as well as how other characters react to him or her. It is up to the reader to draw conclusions about the character based on this indirect information.

The most effective indirect characterizations usually result from showing characters acting or speaking.

See also ***Character.***

CLIMAX The ***climax*** of a story, novel, or play is the high point of interest or suspense. The events that make up the rising action lead up to the climax. The events that make up the falling action follow the climax.

See also ***Conflict, Plot,*** and ***Anticlimax.***

COMEDY A ***comedy*** is a literary work, especially a play, that has a happy ending. Comedies often show ordinary characters in conflict with society. These conflicts are resolved through misunderstandings, deceptions, and concealed identities, which result in the correction of moral faults or social wrongs. Types of comedy include *romantic comedy,* which involves problems among lovers, and the *comedy of manners,* which satirically challenges the social customs of a sophisticated society. Comedy is often contrasted with tragedy, in which the protagonist meets an unfortunate end.

COMIC RELIEF ***Comic relief*** is a technique that is used to interrupt a serious part of a literary work by introducing a humorous character or situation.

CONFLICT A ***conflict*** is a struggle between opposing forces. Characters in conflict form the basis of stories, novels, and plays.

There are two kinds of conflict: external and internal. In an ***external conflict,*** the main character struggles against an outside force. This force may be another character, as in Richard Connell's "The Most Dangerous Game" (p. 214), in which Rainsford struggles with General Zaroff. The outside force could also be the standards or expectations of a group, such as the family prejudices that Romeo and Juliet struggle against. Their story (p. 806) shows them in conflict with society. The outside force may be nature itself, a person-against-nature conflict. The two men who are trapped by a fallen tree in Saki's "The Interlopers" (p. 270) face such a conflict.

An ***internal conflict*** involves a character in conflict with himself or herself. In "Checkouts" (p. 82), two young people who meet by chance in a supermarket agonize over whether they should speak to each other.

See also ***Plot.***

CONNOTATION The ***connotation*** of a word is the set of ideas associated with it in addition to its explicit meaning.

See also ***Denotation.***

CONSONANCE ***Consonance*** is the repetition of final consonant sounds in stressed syllables with different vowel sounds, as in *hat* and *sit.*

CONTEMPORARY INTERPRETATION A ***contemporary interpretation*** is a literary work of today that responds to and sheds new light on a well-known, earlier work of literature. Such an interpretation may refer to any aspect of the older work, including plot, characters, settings, imagery, language, and theme. Edna St. Vincent Millay's poem "An Ancient Gesture" (p. 1128), for example, provides a modern perspective on the characters Penelope and Odysseus in the *Odyssey.*

COUPLET A ***couplet*** is a pair of rhyming lines, usually of the same length and meter. In the following couplet from a poem by William Shakespeare, the speaker comforts himself with the thought of his love:

> For thy sweet love remember'd such wealth brings
> That then I scorn to change my state with kings.

See also ***Stanza.***

DENOTATION The ***denotation*** of a word is its dictionary meaning, independent of other associations that the word may have. The denotation of the word *lake,* for example, is an inland body of water. "Vacation spot" and "place where the fishing is good" are connotations of the word *lake.*

See also ***Connotation.***

DESCRIPTION A ***description*** is a portrait in words of a person, a place, or an object. Descriptive writing uses sensory details, those that appeal to the senses: sight, hearing, taste, smell, and touch. Description can be found in all types of writing. Rudolfo Anaya's essay "A Celebration of Grandfathers" (p. 444) contains descriptive passages.

DIALECT ***Dialect,*** the form of language spoken by people in a particular region or group, may involve changes to the pronunciation, vocabulary, and sentence structure of standard English. An example from Mark Twain's "The Invalid's Story" (p. 362) is a character's use of the term *yourn* for *yours.*

DIALOGUE A ***dialogue*** is a conversation between characters that may reveal their traits and advance the action of a narrative. In fiction or nonfiction, quotation marks indicate a speaker's exact words, and a new paragraph usually indicates a change of speaker. Following is an exchange between the narrator and his frail younger brother, Doodle, in "The Scarlet Ibis" (p. 384):

> "Aw, come on Doodle," I urged. "You can do it. Do you want to be different from everybody else when you start school?"
>
> "Does it make any difference?"

Quotation marks are not used in a *script,* the printed copy of a play. Instead, the dialogue follows the name of the speaker, as in this example from Chekhov's *The Inspector General* (p. 970):

> **DRIVER.** Oh, yes, he's a good one, this one.

DICTION ***Diction*** refers to an author's choice of words, especially with regard to range of vocabulary, use of slang and colloquial language, and level of formality. These lines from Ernest Lawrence Thayer's poem "Casey at the Bat" (p. 696) are an example of colloquial, informal diction: "It looked extremely rocky for the Mudville nine that day; / The score stood two to four; with but an inning left to play."

See also ***Connotation*** and ***Denotation.***

DIRECT CHARACTERIZATION
See ***Characterization.***

DRAMA A ***drama*** is a story written to be performed by actors. The script of a drama is made up of ***dialogue***—the words the actors say—and ***stage directions,*** which are comments on how and where action happens.

The drama's ***setting*** is the time and place in which the action occurs. It is indicated by one or more sets, including furniture and backdrops, that suggest interior or exterior scenes. *Props* are objects, such as a sword or a cup of tea, that are used onstage.

At the beginning of most plays, a brief ***exposition*** gives the audience some background information about the characters and the situation. Just as in a story or novel, the plot of a drama is built around characters in conflict.

Dramas are divided into large units called ***acts,*** which are divided into smaller units called scenes. A long play may include many sets that change with the ***scenes,*** or it may indicate a change of scene with lighting.

See also ***Dialogue, Genre, Stage Directions,*** and ***Tragedy.***
Romeo and Juliet (p. 806) is a long play in five acts.

DRAMATIC IRONY See ***Irony.***

DRAMATIC MONOLOGUE A ***dramatic monologue*** is a poem in which a character reveals himself or herself by speaking to a silent listener.

DRAMATIC POETRY ***Dramatic poetry*** is poetry that utilizes the techniques of drama. The dialogue used in Edgar Allan Poe's "The Raven" (p. 710) makes it dramatic dialogue. A ***dramatic monologue*** is a poem spoken by one person, addressing a silent listener.

END RHYME See ***Rhyme.***

EPIC An ***epic*** is a long narrative poem about the deeds of gods or heroes. Homer's *Odyssey* (p. 1044) is an example of epic poetry. It tells the story of the Greek hero Odysseus, the king of Ithaca.

An epic is elevated in style and usually follows certain patterns. The poet begins by announcing the subject and asking a Muse—one of the nine goddesses of the arts, literature, and sciences—to help. An *epic hero* is the larger-than-life central character in an epic. Through behavior and deeds, the epic hero displays qualities that are valued by the society in which the epic originated.

See also ***Epic Simile*** and ***Narrative Poem.***

EPIC SIMILE An ***epic simile,*** also called ***Homeric simile,*** is an elaborate comparison of unlike subjects. In this example from the *Odyssey* (p. 1044), Homer compares the bodies of men killed by Odysseus to a fisherman's catch heaped up on the shore:

> Think of a catch that fishermen haul in to a
>   half-moon bay
> in a fine-meshed net from the whitecaps of the sea:
> how all are poured out on the sand, in throes
>   for the salt sea,
> twitching their cold lives away in Helios' fiery air:
>   so lay the suitors heaped on one another.

See also ***Figurative Language*** and ***Simile.***

EPIPHANY An ***epiphany*** is a character's sudden flash of insight into a conflict or situation. At the end of Judith

Ortiz Cofer's story "American History" (p. 240), for example, the central character experiences an epiphany.

ESSAY An ***essay*** is a short nonfiction work about a particular subject. While classification is difficult, four types of essays are sometimes identified.

A *descriptive essay* seeks to convey an impression about a person, place, or object. In "A Celebration of Grandfathers" (p. 444), Rudolfo Anaya describes the cultural values that his grandfather and other "old ones" from his childhood passed down.

A *narrative essay* tells a true story. In "The Washwoman" (p. 26), Isaac Bashevis Singer tells of his childhood in Poland.

An *expository essay* gives information, discusses ideas, or explains a process. In "Single Room, Earth View" (p. 468), Sally Ride explains what it is like to be in outer space.

A *persuasive essay* tries to convince readers to do something or to accept the writer's point of view. Pete Hamill's "Libraries Face Sad Chapter" (p. 530) is a persuasive essay.

See also ***Description, Exposition, Genre, Narration, Nonfiction,*** and ***Persuasion.***

EXPOSITION ***Exposition*** is writing or speech that explains a process or presents information. In the plot of a story or drama, the exposition is the part of the work that introduces the characters, the setting, and the basic situation.

EXTENDED METAPHOR In an ***extended metaphor,*** as in regular metaphor, a writer speaks or writes of a subject as though it were something else. An extended metaphor sustains the comparison for several lines or for an entire poem.

See also ***Figurative Language*** and ***Metaphor.***

EXTERNAL CONFLICT See ***Conflict.***

FALLING ACTION See ***Plot.***

FANTASY A ***fantasy*** is highly imaginative writing that contains elements not found in real life. Examples of fantasy include stories that involve supernatural elements, stories that resemble fairy tales, and stories that deal with imaginary places and creatures.

See also ***Science Fiction.***

FICTION ***Fiction*** is prose writing that tells about imaginary characters and events. The term is usually used for novels and short stories, but it also applies to dramas and narrative poetry. Some writers rely on their imaginations alone to create their works of fiction. Others base their fiction on actual events and people, to which they add invented characters, dialogue, and plot situations.

See also ***Genre, Narrative,*** and ***Nonfiction.***

FIGURATIVE LANGUAGE ***Figurative language*** is writing or speech not meant to be interpreted literally. It is often used to create vivid impressions by setting up comparisons between dissimilar things.

Some frequently used figures of speech are ***metaphors, similes,*** and ***personifications.***

See also ***Literal Language.***

FLASHBACK A ***flashback*** is a means by which authors present material that occurred earlier than the present tense of the narrative. Authors may include this material in a character's memories, dreams, or accounts of past events.

FOIL A ***foil*** is a character who provides a contrast to another character. In *Romeo and Juliet* (p. 806), the fiery temper of Tybalt serves as a foil to the good nature of Benvolio.

FOOT See ***Meter.***

FORESHADOWING ***Foreshadowing*** is the use in a literary work of clues that suggest events that have yet to occur. This technique helps create suspense, keeping readers wondering about what will happen next.

See also ***Suspense.***

FREE VERSE ***Free verse*** is poetry not written in a regular pattern of meter or rhyme. Like Whitman's "I Hear America Singing" (p. 750), however, it may use parallelism and various sound devices.

GENRE A ***genre*** is a category or type of literature. Literature is commonly divided into three major genres: poetry, prose, and drama. Each major genre is in turn divided into smaller genres, as follows:

1. Poetry: Lyric Poetry, Concrete Poetry, Dramatic Poetry, Narrative Poetry, and Epic Poetry
2. Prose: Fiction (Novels and Short Stories) and Nonfiction (Biography, Autobiography, Letters, Essays, and Reports)
3. Drama: Serious Drama and Tragedy, Comic Drama, Melodrama, and Farce

See also ***Drama, Poetry,*** and ***Prose.***

HAIKU The ***haiku*** is a three-line verse form. The first and third lines of a haiku each have five syllables. The second line has seven syllables. A haiku seeks to convey a single vivid emotion by means of images from nature.

HOMERIC SIMILE See ***Epic Simile.***

HYPERBOLE A ***hyperbole*** is a deliberate exaggeration or overstatement. In Mark Twain's "The Notorious Jumping Frog of Calaveras County," the claim that Jim Smiley would follow a bug as far as Mexico to win a bet is a hyperbole. As this example shows, hyperboles are often used for comic effect.

IAMB See ***Meter.***

IDIOM An ***idiom*** is an expression that is characteristic of a language, region, community, or class of people. *Idiomatic expressions* often arise from figures of speech and therefore cannot be understood literally. In "The Invalid's Story" (p. 362), for example, a character uses the idiom *throw up the sponge,* meaning "surrender."

See also ***Dialect.***

IMAGE An ***image*** is a word or phrase that appeals to one or more of the five senses—sight, hearing, touch, taste, or smell. Writers use images to re-create sensory experiences in words.

See also ***Description.***

IMAGERY ***Imagery*** is the descriptive or figurative language used in literature to create word pictures for the reader. These pictures, or images, are created by details of sight, sound, taste, touch, smell, or movement.

INDIRECT CHARACTERIZATION
See ***Characterization.***

INTERNAL See ***Conflict.***

INTERNAL RHYME See ***Rhyme.***

IRONY ***Irony*** is the general term for literary techniques that portray differences between appearance and reality, or expectation and result. In ***verbal irony,*** words are used to suggest the opposite of what is meant. In ***dramatic irony,*** there is a contradiction between what a character thinks and what the reader or audience knows to be true. In *irony of situation,* an event occurs that directly contradicts the expectations of the characters, the reader, or the audience.

LEGEND See ***Oral Tradition.***

LITERAL LANGUAGE ***Literal language*** uses words in their ordinary senses. It is the opposite of ***figurative language.*** If you tell someone standing on a diving board to jump in, you speak literally. If you tell someone on the street to jump in a lake, you are speaking figuratively.

See also ***Figurative Language.***

LYRIC POEM A ***lyric poem*** is a highly musical verse that expresses the thoughts, observations, and feelings of a single speaker.

MAIN CHARACTER See ***Character.***

METAPHOR A ***metaphor*** is a figure of speech in which one thing is spoken of as though it were something else. Unlike a simile, which compares two things using *like* or *as,* a metaphor implies a comparison between them. In "Dreams" (p. 621), Langston Hughes uses a metaphor to show what happens to a life without dreams:

> . . . if dreams die
>
> Life is a broken-winged bird
>
> That cannot fly.

See also ***Extended Metaphor*** and ***Figurative Language.***

METER The ***meter*** of a poem is its rhythmical pattern. This pattern is determined by the number and types of stresses, or beats, in each line. To describe the meter of a poem, you must scan its lines. Scanning involves marking the stressed and unstressed syllables, as shown with the following two lines from "I Wandered Lonely as a Cloud" by William Wordsworth (p. 622):

> Ĭ wán|dĕred lóne|lŷ ás| ă clóud
>
> Thăt floáts | ŏn hígh| o'ĕr váles| ănd hílls.

As you can see, each strong stress is marked with a slanted line (´) and each unstressed syllable with a horseshoe symbol (˘). The stressed and unstressed syllables are then divided by vertical lines (|) into groups called ***feet.*** The following types of feet are common in English poetry:

1. *Iamb:* a foot with one unstressed syllable followed by a stressed syllable, as in the word "again"
2. *Trochee:* a foot with one stressed syllable followed by an unstressed syllable, as in the word "wonder"
3. *Anapest:* a foot with two unstressed syllables followed by one strong stress, as in the phrase "on the beach"
4. *Dactyl:* a foot with one strong stress followed by two unstressed syllables, as in the word "wonderful"
5. *Spondee:* a foot with two strong stresses, as in the word "spacewalk"

LITERARY HANDBOOK

Depending on the type of foot that is most common in them, lines of poetry are described as ***iambic, trochaic, anapestic,*** and so forth.

Lines are also described in terms of the number of feet that occur in them, as follows:

1. *Monometer:* verse written in one-foot lines
   All things
   Must pass
   Away.
2. *Dimeter:* verse written in two-foot lines
   Thomas | Jefferson
   What do | you say
   Under the | gravestone
   Hidden | away?

   —Rosemary and Stephen Vincent Benét,
   "Thomas Jefferson, 1743–1826"
3. *Trimeter:* verse written in three-foot lines
   I know | not whom | I meet
   I know | not where | I go.
4. *Tetrameter:* verse written in four-foot lines
5. *Pentameter:* verse written in five-foot lines
6. *Hexameter:* verse written in six-foot lines
7. *Heptameter:* verse written in seven-foot lines

Blank verse, used by Shakespeare in *Romeo and Juliet* (p. 806), is poetry written in unrhymed iambic pentameter.

Free verse, used by Walt Whitman in "I Hear America Singing" (p. 750), is poetry that does not follow a regular pattern of meter and rhyme.

MONOLOGUE A ***monologue*** in a play is a speech by one character that, unlike a ***soliloquy,*** is addressed to another character or characters. An example from Shakespeare's *Romeo and Juliet* (p. 806) is the speech by the Prince of Verona in Act 1, Scene i, lines 72–94.

See also ***Soliloquy.***

MONOMETER See ***Meter.***

MOOD ***Mood,*** or ***atmosphere,*** is the feeling created in the reader by a literary work or passage. The mood is often suggested by descriptive details. Often the mood can be described in a single word, such as lighthearted, frightening, or despairing. Notice how this passage from Edgar Allan Poe's "The Cask of Amontillado" (p. 60) contributes to an eerie, fearful mood:

> "The niter!" I said; "see, it increases. It hangs like moss upon the vaults. We are below the river's bed. The drops of moisture trickle among the bones. Come, we will go back ere it is too late."

See also ***Tone.***

MORAL A ***moral*** is a lesson taught by a literary work, especially a fable—many fables, for example, have a stated moral at the end. It is customary, however, to discuss contemporary works in terms of the themes they explore, rather than a moral that they teach.

MOTIVATION ***Motivation*** is a reason that explains or partially explains why a character thinks, feels, acts, or behaves in a certain way. Motivation results from a combination of the character's personality and the situation he or she must deal with. In "Checkouts" (p. 82), the main character is motivated by conflicting feelings.

See also ***Character*** and ***Characterization.***

MYTH A ***myth*** is a fictional tale that describes the actions of gods and heroes or explains the causes of natural phenomena. Unlike legends, myths emphasize supernatural rather than historical elements. Many cultures have collections of myths, and the most familiar in the Western world are those of the ancient Greeks and Romans. "Perseus" (p. 1225) is a retelling of a famous ancient Greek myth.

See also ***Oral Tradition.***

NARRATION ***Narration*** is writing that tells a story. The act of telling a story in speech is also called narration. Novels and short stories are fictional narratives. Nonfiction works—such as news stories, biographies, and autobiographies—are also narratives. A narrative poem tells a story in verse.

See also ***Anecdote, Essay, Narrative Poem, Nonfiction, Novel,*** and ***Short Story.***

NARRATIVE A ***narrative*** is a story told in fiction, nonfiction, poetry, or drama.

See also ***Narration.***

NARRATIVE POEM A ***narrative poem*** is one that tells a story. "Casey at the Bat" (p. 696) is a humorous narrative poem about the last inning of a baseball game. Edgar Allan Poe's "The Raven" (p. 710) is a serious narrative poem about a man's grief over the loss of a loved one.

See also ***Dramatic Poetry, Epic,*** and ***Narration.***

NARRATOR A ***narrator*** is a speaker or character who tells a story. The writer's choice of narrator determines the story's ***point of view,*** which directs the type and amount of information the writer reveals.

When a character in the story tells the story, that character is a *first-person narrator.* This narrator may be a major character, a minor character, or just a witness. Readers see only what this character sees, hear only what he or she hears, and so on. The first-person narrator may or may not be reliable. We have reason, for example, to be suspicious of the first-person narrator of Edgar Allan Poe's "The Cask of Amontillado" (p. 60).

When a voice outside the story narrates, the story has a *third-person narrator.* An omniscient, or all-knowing, third-person narrator can tell readers what any character thinks and feels. For example, in Guy de Maupassant's "The Necklace" (p. 332), we know the feelings of both Monsieur and Madame Loisel. A limited third-person narrator sees the world through one character's eyes and reveals only that character's thoughts. In James Thurber's "The Secret Life of Walter Mitty" (p. 128), the narrator reveals only Mitty's experiences and feelings.

See also ***Speaker.***

NONFICTION ***Nonfiction*** is prose writing that presents and explains ideas or that tells about real people, places, ideas, or events. To be classified as nonfiction, a work must be true. "Single Room, Earth View" (p. 468) is a nonfictional account of the view of Earth from space.

See also ***Autobiography, Biography,*** and ***Essay.***

NOVEL A ***novel*** is a long work of fiction. It has a plot that explores characters in conflict. A novel may also have one or more subplots, or minor stories, and several themes.

NOVELLA A ***novella*** is a work of fiction that is longer than a short story but shorter than a novel.

OCTAVE See ***Stanza.***

ONOMATOPOEIA ***Onomatopoeia*** is the use of words that imitate sounds. *Whirr, thud,* and *hiss* are examples.

ORAL TRADITION The ***oral tradition*** is the passing of songs, stories, and poems from generation to generation by word of mouth. Many folk songs, ballads, fairy tales, legends, and myths originated in the oral tradition.

See also ***Myth.***

OXYMORON An ***oxymoron*** is a combination of words, or parts of words, that contradict each other. Examples are "deafening silence," "honest thief," "wise fool," and "bittersweet." This device is effective when the apparent contradiction reveals a deeper truth, as in Act 2, Scene ii, line 184, of *Romeo and Juliet* (p. 806) when Juliet bids goodbye to Romeo: "Parting is such *sweet sorrow.*"

PARADOX A ***paradox*** is a statement that seems contradictory but actually may be true. Because a paradox is surprising, it catches the reader's attention.

PARALLELISM See ***Rhetorical Devices.***

PENTAMETER See ***Meter.***

PERSONIFICATION ***Personification*** is a type of figurative language in which a nonhuman subject is given human characteristics. William Wordsworth personifies daffodils when he describes them as "Tossing their heads in sprightly dance" (p. 626).

See also ***Figurative Language.***

PERSUASION ***Persuasion*** is writing or speech that attempts to convince the reader to adopt a particular opinion or course of action. An ***argument*** is a logical way of presenting a belief, conclusion, or stance. A good argument is supported with reasoning and evidence.

PLOT ***Plot*** is the sequence of events in a literary work. In most novels, dramas, short stories, and narrative poems, the plot involves both characters and a central conflict. The plot usually begins with an ***exposition*** that introduces the setting, the characters, and the basic situation. This is followed by the ***inciting incident,*** which introduces the central conflict. The conflict then increases during the ***development*** until it reaches a high point of interest or suspense, the ***climax.*** All the events leading up to the climax make up the ***rising action.*** The climax is followed by the ***falling action,*** which leads to the ***denouement,*** or ***resolution,*** in which a general insight or change is conveyed.

POETRY ***Poetry*** is one of the three major types of literature, the others being prose and drama. Most poems make use of highly concise, musical, and emotionally charged language. Many also make use of imagery, figurative language, and special devices of sound such as rhyme. Poems are often divided into lines and stanzas and often employ regular rhythmical patterns, or meters. However, some poems are written out just like prose, while others are written in free verse.

See also ***Genre.***

POINT OF VIEW See ***Narrator.***

PROSE ***Prose*** is the ordinary form of written language. Most writing that is not poetry, drama, or song is considered prose. Prose is one of the major genres of literature and occurs in two forms: fiction and nonfiction.

See also ***Fiction, Genre,*** and ***Nonfiction.***

PROTAGONIST The protagonist is the main character in a literary work.

See also ***Antagonist*** and ***Character.***

PUN A ***pun*** is a play on words involving a word with two or more different meanings or two words that sound alike but have different meanings. In *Romeo and Juliet* (p. 806), the dying Mercutio makes a pun involving two meanings of the word *grave,* "serious" and "burial site": "Ask for me tomorrow, and you shall find me a grave man" (Act 3, Scene i, lines 92–93).

QUATRAIN A ***quatrain*** is a stanza or poem made up of four lines, usually with a definite rhythm and rhyme scheme.

REPETITION ***Repetition*** is the use of any element of language—a sound, a word, a phrase, a clause, or a sentence—more than once.

Poets use many kinds of repetition. Alliteration, assonance, rhyme, and rhythm are repetitions of certain sounds and sound patterns. A refrain is a repeated line or group of lines. In both prose and poetry, repetition is used for musical effects and for emphasis.

See also ***Alliteration, Assonance, Rhyme,*** and ***Rhythm.***

RESOLUTION See ***Plot.***

RHETORICAL DEVICES ***Rhetorical devices*** are special patterns of words and ideas that create emphasis and stir emotion, especially in speeches or other oral presentations. ***Parallelism,*** for example, is the repetition of a grammatical structure in order to create a rhythm and make words more memorable. In his "I Have a Dream" speech (p. 542), Martin Luther King, Jr., uses parallel statements beginning, "I have a dream that . . ."

Other common rhetorical devices include *restatement,* expressing the same idea in different words, and *rhetorical questions,* questions with obvious answers.

RHYME ***Rhyme*** is the repetition of sounds at the ends of words. ***End rhyme*** occurs when the rhyming words come at the ends of lines, as in "The Desired Swan Song" by Samuel Taylor Coleridge:

> Swans sing before they die—'twere no bad thing
> Should certain persons die before they sing.

Internal rhyme occurs when the rhyming words appear in the same line, as in the first line of Edgar Allan Poe's "The Raven" (p. 710):

> Once upon a midnight *dreary,* while I pondered, weak and *weary,*

Exact rhyme involves the repetition of words with the same vowel and consonant sounds, like *ball* and *hall. Slant rhyme* involves the repetition of words that sound alike but do not rhyme exactly, like *grove* and *love.*

See also ***Repetition*** and ***Rhyme Scheme.***

RHYME SCHEME A ***rhyme scheme*** is a regular pattern of rhyming words in a poem. The rhyme scheme of a poem is indicated by using different letters of the alphabet for each new rhyme. In an *aabb* stanza, for example, line 1 rhymes with line 2 and line 3 rhymes with line 4. William Wordsworth's poem "I Wandered Lonely as a Cloud" (p. 622) uses an *ababcc* rhyme pattern:

> I wandered lonely as a cloud a
> That floats on high o'er vales and hills, b
> When all at once I saw a crowd, a
> A host, of golden daffodils; b
> Beside the lake, beneath the trees, c
> Fluttering and dancing in the breeze. c

Many poems use the same pattern of rhymes, though not the same rhymes, in each stanza.

See also ***Rhyme.***

RHYTHM ***Rhythm*** is the pattern of *beats,* or *stresses,* in spoken or written language. Some poems have a very specific pattern, or meter, whereas prose and free verse use the natural rhythms of everyday speech.

See also ***Meter.***

RISING ACTION See ***Plot.***

ROUND CHARACTER See ***Character.***

SATIRE A ***satire*** is a literary work that ridicules the foolishness and faults of individuals, an institution, society, or even humanity in general.

SCENE See ***Drama.***

SCIENCE FICTION ***Science fiction*** is writing that tells about imaginary events involving science or technology. Many science-fiction stories are set in the future. Arthur C. Clarke's "If I Forget Thee, Oh Earth . . ." (p. 162) is set on the moon after a nuclear disaster on Earth.

See also ***Fantasy.***

SENSORY LANGUAGE ***Sensory language*** is writing or speech that appeals to one or more of the senses.

See also ***Image.***

SESTET See ***Stanza.***

SETTING The ***setting*** of a literary work is the time and place of the action. Time can include not only the historical period—past, present, or future—but also a specific year, season, or time of day. Place may involve not only the geographical place—a region, country, state, or town—but also the social, economic, or cultural environment.

In some stories, setting serves merely as a backdrop for action, a context in which the characters move and speak. In others, however, setting is a crucial element.

See also ***Mood.***

SHORT STORY A *short story* is a brief work of fiction. In most short stories, one main character faces a conflict that is resolved in the plot of the story. Great craftsmanship must go into the writing of a good story, for it has to accomplish its purpose in relatively few words.

See also ***Fiction*** and ***Genre.***

SIMILE A ***simile*** is a figure of speech in which the words *like* or *as* are used to compare two apparently dissimilar items. The comparison, however, surprises the reader into a fresh perception by finding an unexpected likeness. In "Dream Deferred" (p. 620), Langston Hughes uses the simile "Does it dry up/like a raisin in the sun?" to discuss a dream deferred.

SOLILOQUY A ***soliloquy*** is a long speech expressing the thoughts of a character alone on stage. In William Shakespeare's *Romeo and Juliet* (p. 806), Romeo gives a soliloquy after the servant has fled and Paris has died (Act V, Scene iii, lines 74–120).

See also ***Monologue.***

SONNET A ***sonnet*** is a fourteen-line lyric poem, usually written in rhymed iambic pentameter. The *English,* or *Shakespearean,* sonnet consists of three quatrains (four-line stanzas) and a couplet (two lines), usually rhyming *abab cdcd efef gg.* The couplet usually comments on the ideas contained in the preceding twelve lines. The sonnet is usually not printed with the stanzas divided, but a reader can see distinct ideas in each. See the Sonnet 30 by William Shakespeare on page 754.

The *Italian,* or *Petrarchan,* sonnet consists of an octave (eight-line stanza) and a sestet (six-line stanza). Often, the octave rhymes *abbaabba* and the sestet rhymes *cdecde.* The octave states a theme or asks a question. The sestet comments on or answers the question.

See also ***Lyric Poem, Meter,*** and ***Stanza.***

SOUND DEVICES A ***sound device*** is a technique used by a poet to emphasize the sound relationships among words in order to create musical and emotional effects and emphasize a poem's meaning. These devices include ***alliteration, consonance, assonance, onomatopoeia,*** and ***rhyme.***

SPEAKER The ***speaker*** is the imaginary voice assumed by the writer of a poem. In many poems, the speaker is not identified by name. When reading a poem, remember that the speaker within the poem may be a person, an animal, a thing, or an abstraction. The speaker in the following stanza by Emily Dickinson is a person who has died:

> Because I could not stop for Death—
>
> He kindly stopped for me—
>
> The Carriage held but just Ourselves—
>
> And Immortality.

STAGE DIRECTIONS ***Stage directions*** are notes included in a drama to describe how the work is to be performed or staged. These instructions are printed in italics and are not spoken aloud. They are used to describe sets, lighting, sound effects, and the appearance, personalities, and movements of characters.

See also ***Drama.***

STANZA A ***stanza*** is a repeated grouping of two or more lines in a poem that often share a pattern of rhythm and rhyme. Stanzas are sometimes named according to the number of lines they have—for example, a ***couplet,*** two lines; a ***quatrain,*** four lines; a ***sestet,*** six lines; and an ***octave,*** eight lines.

STATIC CHARACTER See ***Character.***

STYLE ***Style*** refers to an author's unique way of writing. Elements determining style include diction; tone; characteristic use of figurative language, dialect, or rhythmic devices; and syntax, or typical grammatical structures and patterns.

See also ***Diction*** and ***Tone.***

SURPRISE ENDING A ***surprise ending*** is a conclusion that violates the expectations of the reader but in a way that is both logical and believable.

O. Henry's "The Gift of the Magi" (p. 260) and Guy de Maupassant's "The Necklace" (p. 332) have surprise endings. Both authors were masters of this form.

SUSPENSE ***Suspense*** is a feeling of uncertainty about the outcome of events in a literary work. Writers create suspense by raising questions in the minds of their readers.

SYMBOL A ***symbol*** is anything that stands for something else. In addition to having its own meaning and reality, a symbol also represents abstract ideas. For example, a flag is a piece of cloth, but it also represents the idea of a country. Writers sometimes use conventional symbols like flags. Frequently, however, they create symbols of their own through emphasis or repetition. In James Hurst's "The Scarlet Ibis" (p. 384), for example, the ibis symbolizes the character named Doodle. Both are beautiful and otherworldly.

TALL TALE A ***tall tale*** is a type of folk tale that contains some or all of these features: humor, hyperbole, far-fetched situations, highly imaginative language, and a hero who performs outrageous feats. Tall tales originated during the development of the American frontier and are a particularly American form of folk tale. "Pecos Bill: The Cyclone" (p. 1218) is an example of a tall tale.

THEME A ***theme*** is a central message or insight into life revealed through a literary work.

The theme of a literary work may be stated directly or implied. When the theme of a work is implied, readers think about what the work suggests about people or life.

Archetypal themes are those that occur in folklore and literature across the world and throughout history. Ill-fated love, the theme of *Romeo and Juliet* (p. 806), is an example of such a theme.

TONE The ***tone*** of a literary work is the writer's attitude toward his or her audience and subject. The tone can often be described by a single adjective, such as *formal* or *informal, serious* or *playful, bitter* or *ironic.* When O. Henry discusses the young couple in "The Gift of the Magi" (p. 260), he uses a sympathetic tone.

See also ***Mood.***

TRAGEDY A ***tragedy*** is a work of literature, especially a play, that results in a catastrophe, a disaster or great misfortune, for the main character, or *tragic hero.* In ancient Greek drama, the main character was always a significant person—a king or a hero—and the cause of the tragedy was a *tragic flaw,* or weakness, in his or her character. In modern drama, the main character can be an ordinary person, and the cause of the tragedy can be some evil in society itself. Tragedy not only arouses fear and pity in the audience but also, in some cases, conveys a sense of the grandeur and nobility of the human spirit.

Shakespeare's *Romeo and Juliet* (p. 806) is a tragedy. Romeo and Juliet both suffer from the tragic flaw of impulsiveness. This flaw ultimately leads to their deaths.

See also ***Drama.***

UNDERSTATEMENT An ***understatement*** is a figure of speech in which the stated meaning is purposely less than (or "under") what is really meant. It is the opposite of ***hyperbole,*** which is a deliberate exaggeration.

UNIVERSAL THEME A ***universal theme*** is a message about life that can be understood by most cultures. Many folk tales and examples of classic literature address universal themes such as the importance of courage, the effects of honesty, or the danger of greed.

VERBAL IRONY See ***Irony.***

VILLANELLE A ***villanelle*** is a nineteen-line lyric poem written in five three-line stanzas and ending in a four-line stanza. It uses two rhymes and repeats two refrain lines that appear initially in the first and third lines of the first stanza. These lines then appear alternately as the third line of subsequent three-line stanzas and, finally, as the last two lines of the poem.

VISUAL ESSAY A ***visual essay*** is an exploration of a topic that conveys its ideas through visual elements as well as language. Like a standard essay, a visual essay presents an author's views of a single topic. Unlike other essays, however, much of the meaning in a visual essay is conveyed through illustrations or photographs.

VOICE ***Voice*** is a writer's distinctive "sound" or way of "speaking" on the page. It is related to such elements as word choice, sentence structure, and tone. It is similar to an individual's speech style and can be described in the same way—fast, slow, blunt, meandering, breathless, and so on.

Voice resembles ***style,*** an author's typical way of writing, but style usually refers to a quality that can be found throughout an author's body of work, while an author's voice may sometimes vary from work to work.

See also ***Style.***

Tips for Discussing Literature

As you read and study literature, discussion with other readers can help you understand, enjoy, and develop interpretations of what you read. Use the following tips to practice good speaking and listening skills while participating in group discussions of literature.

• Understand the purpose of your discussion

When you discuss literature, your purpose is to broaden your understanding and appreciation of a work by testing your own ideas and hearing the ideas of others. Stay focused on the literature you are discussing, and keep your comments relevant to that literature. Starting with one focus question will help keep your discussion on track.

• Communicate effectively

Effective communication requires thinking before speaking. Plan the points that you want to make, and decide how you will express them. Organize these points in logical order, and cite details from the work to support your ideas. Jot down informal notes to help keep your ideas focused.

Remember to speak clearly, pronouncing words slowly and carefully so that others can understand your points. Also, keep in mind that some literature touches readers deeply—be aware of the possibility of counterproductive emotional responses, and work to control them. Negative emotional responses can also be conveyed through body language, so work to demonstrate respect in your demeanor as well as in your words.

• Encourage everyone to participate

While some people are comfortable participating in discussions, others are less eager to speak up in groups. However, everyone should work to contribute thoughts and ideas. To encourage the entire group's participation, try the following strategies:

- If you enjoy speaking, avoid monopolizing the conversation. After sharing your ideas, encourage others to share theirs.
- Try different roles. For example, have everyone take turns being the facilitator or host of the discussion.
- Use a prop, such as a book or gavel. Pass the prop around the group, allowing whomever is holding the prop to have the floor.

• Make relevant contributions

Especially when responding to a short story, a poem, or a novel, avoid simply summarizing the plot. Instead, consider *what* you think might happen next, *why* events take place as they do, or *how* a writer provokes a response in you. Let your ideas inspire deeper thought or discussion about the literature.

• Consider other ideas and interpretations

A work of literature can generate a wide variety of responses in different readers—and that can make your discussions exciting. Be open to the idea that many interpretations can be valid. To support your own ideas, point to the events, descriptions, characters, or other literary elements in the work that produced your interpretation. To consider someone else's ideas, decide whether details in the work support the interpretation he or she presents. Be sure to convey your criticism of the ideas of others in a respectful and supportive manner.

- ## Ask questions and extend the contributions of others

Get in the habit of asking questions to help you clarify your understanding of another reader's ideas. You can also use questions to call attention to possible areas of confusion, to points that are open to debate, or to errors.

In addition, offer elaboration of the points that others make by providing examples and illustrations. To move a discussion forward, pause occasionally to summarize and evaluate tentative conclusions reached by the group members. Then, continue the discussion with a fresh understanding of the material and ideas you have already covered.

- ## Manage differing opinions and views

Each participant brings his or her own personality, experiences, ideas, cultural background, likes and dislikes to the experience of reading, making disagreement almost inevitable. As differences arise, be sensitive to each individual's point of view. Do not personalize disagreements, but keep them focused on the literature or ideas under discussion.

When you meet with a group to discuss literature, use a chart like the one shown to analyze the discussion.

Work Being Discussed:	
Focus Question:	
Your Response:	Another Student's Response:
Supporting Evidence:	Supporting Evidence:

Literary Criticism

Criticism is writing that explores the meaning and techniques of literary works, usually in order to evaluate them. Writing criticism can help you think through your experience of a work of literature and can also help others deepen their own understanding. All literary criticism shares similar goals:

- ***Making Connections*** within or between works, or between a work of literature and its context
- ***Making Distinctions*** or showing differences between elements of a single work or aspects of two or more works
- ***Achieving Insights*** that were not apparent from a superficial reading
- ***Making a Judgment*** about the quality or value of a literary work

Critics use various ***theories of literary criticism*** to understand, appreciate, and evaluate literature. Some theories focus on the context of the work while others focus on the work itself. Sometimes critics combine one or more theories. These charts show a few examples of the many theories of criticism:

Focus on Contexts	
Human Experience	**Mythic Criticism** Explores universal situations, characters, and symbols called archetypes as they appear in a literary work.
Culture and History	**Historical Criticism** Analyzes how circumstances or ideas of an era influence a work
Author's Life	**Biographical Criticism** Explains how the author's life sheds light on the work

Focus on the Work Itself
Formal Criticism Shows how the work reflects characteristics of the genre, or literary type, to which it belongs

Examples of Literary Theories in Action

- ***Mythic Criticism:*** discussing how Robert Frost's "The Road Not Taken," p. 724, explores the archetypal situation of choice at a fork in the road
- ***Historical Criticism:*** showing how American frontier life led to the use of exaggeration in "Pecos Bill: The Cyclone," p. 1218
- ***Biographical Criticism:*** showing that Edgar Allan Poe's loss of his parents at an early age influenced the theme of "The Raven," p. 710
- ***Formal Criticism:*** showing how "The Scarlet Ibis," p. 384, displays short-story elements like plot, setting, character, symbol, and theme

Literary Movements

Our literary heritage has been shaped by a number of literary movements, directions in literature characterized by shared assumptions, beliefs, and practices. This chart shows, in chronological order, some important literary movements. While these movements developed at particular historical moments, all of them may still influence individual writers working today.

Movement	Beliefs and Practices	Examples
Classicism Europe during the Renaissance (c. 1300–1650)	• Looks to classical literature of ancient Greece and Rome as models • Values logic, clarity, balance, and restraint • Prefers "ordered" nature of parks and gardens	the clarity and restraint of Robert Frost's verse ("The Road Not Taken," p. 724)
Romanticism Europe during the late 1700s and the early 1800s	• Rebels against Classicism • Values imagination and emotion • Focuses on everyday life	the celebration of the natural world in Rachel Carson's writings ("Silent Spring," p. 167)
Realism Europe and America from the mid–1800s to the 1890s	• Rebels against Romanticism's search for the ideal • Focuses on everyday life	the faithful rendering of Pueblo life in Leslie Marmon Silko's fiction ("The Man to Send Rain Clouds," p. 292)
Naturalism Europe and America during the late 1800s and early 1900s	• Assumes people cannot choose their fate but are shaped by psychological and social forces • Views society as a competitive jungle	the portrayal of characters as victims of social pressures and psychology in Guy de Maupassant's fiction ("The Necklace," p. 332)
Modernism Worldwide between 1890 and 1945	• In response to WWI, questions human reason • Focuses on studies of the unconscious and the art of primitive peoples • Experiments with language and form	the experiments with language in E. E. Cummings's poetry ("maggie and milly and molly and may," p. 732)
Post-Modernism Worldwide after 1945; still prevalent today	• Includes an eclectic mix of styles, such as parody, magical realism, and dark humor. • Often rebels against reason.	the magical realism in Isabel Allende's fiction ("Uncle Marcos," p. 138)

Tips for Improving Reading Fluency

When you were younger, you learned to read. Then, you read to expand your experiences or for pure enjoyment. Now, you are expected to read to learn. As you progress in school, you are given more and more material to read. The tips on these pages will help you improve your reading fluency, or your ability to read easily, smoothly, and expressively.

Keeping Your Concentration

One common problem that readers face is the loss of concentration. When you are reading an assignment, you might find yourself rereading the same sentence several times without really understanding it. The first step in changing this behavior is to notice that you do it. Becoming an active, aware reader will help you get the most from your assignments. Practice using these strategies:

- Cover what you have already read with a note card as you go along. Then, you will not be able to reread without noticing that you are doing it.
- Set a purpose for reading beyond just completing the assignment. Then, read actively by pausing to ask yourself questions about the material as you read.
- Use the Reading Strategy instruction and notes that appear with each selection in this textbook.
- Stop reading after a specified period of time (for example, 5 minutes) and summarize what you have read. To help you with this strategy, use the Reading Check questions that appear with each selection in this textbook. Reread to find any answers you do not know.

Reading Phrases

Fluent readers read phrases rather than individual words. Reading this way will speed up your reading and improve your comprehension. Here are some useful ideas:

- Experts recommend rereading as a strategy to increase fluency. Choose a passage of text that is neither too hard nor too easy. Read the same passage aloud several times until you can read it smoothly. When you can read the passage fluently, pick another passage and keep practicing.
- Read aloud into a tape recorder. Then, listen to the recording, noting your accuracy, pacing, and expression. You can also read aloud and share feedback with a partner.
- Use the *Prentice Hall Listening to Literature* audiotapes or CDs to hear the selections read aloud. Read along silently in your textbook, noticing how the reader uses his or her voice and emphasizes certain words and phrases.

Understanding Key Vocabulary

If you do not understand some of the words in an assignment, you may miss out on important concepts. Therefore, it is helpful to keep a dictionary nearby when you are reading. Follow these steps:

- Before you begin reading, scan the text for unfamiliar words or terms. Find out what those words mean before you begin reading.
- Use context—the surrounding words, phrases, and sentences—to help you determine the meanings of unfamiliar words.
- If you are unable to understand the meaning through context, refer to the dictionary.

Paying Attention to Punctuation

When you read, pay attention to punctuation. Commas, periods, exclamation points, semicolons, and colons tell you when to pause or stop. They also indicate relationships between groups of words. When you recognize these relationships you will read with greater understanding and expression. Look at the chart below.

Punctuation Mark	Meaning
comma	brief pause
period	pause at the end of a thought
exclamation point	pause that indicates emphasis
semicolon	pause between related but distinct thoughts
colon	pause before giving explanation or examples

Using the Reading Fluency Checklist

Use the checklist below each time you read a selection in this textbook. In your Language Arts journal or notebook, note which skills you need to work on, and chart your progress each week.

Reading Fluency Checklist

- ❑ Preview the text to check for difficult or unfamiliar words.
- ❑ Practice reading aloud.
- ❑ Read according to punctuation.
- ❑ Break down long sentences into the subject and its meaning.
- ❑ Read groups of words for meaning rather than reading single words.
- ❑ Read with expression (change your tone of voice to add meaning to the word).

Reading is a skill that can be improved with practice. The key to improving your fluency is to read. The more you read, the better your reading will become.

Types of Writing

Good writing can be a powerful tool used for many purposes. Writing can allow you to defend something you believe in or show how much you know about a subject. Writing can also help you share what you have experienced, imagined, thought, and felt. The three main types of writing are argument, informative/explanatory, and narrative.

Argument

When you think of the word *argument*, you might think of a disagreement between two people, but an argument is more than that. An argument is a logical way of presenting a belief, conclusion, or stance. A good argument is supported with reasoning and evidence.

Argument writing can be used for many purposes, such as to change a reader's point of view or opinion or to bring about an action or a response from a reader.

There are three main purposes for writing a formal argument:

- to change the reader's mind
- to convince the reader to accept what is written
- to motivate the reader to take action, based on what is written

The following are some types of argument writing:

Advertisements An advertisement is a planned message meant to be seen, heard, or read. It attempts to persuade an audience to buy a product or service, accept an idea, or support a cause. Advertisements may appear in print, online, or in broadcast form.

Several common types of advertisements are public-service announcements, billboards, merchandise ads, service ads, and political campaign literature.

Persuasive Essay A persuasive essay presents a position on an issue, urges readers to accept that position, and may encourage a specific action. An effective persuasive essay

- Explores an issue of importance to the writer
- Addresses an issue that is arguable
- Uses facts, examples, statistics, or personal experiences to support a position
- Tries to influence the audience through appeals to the readers' knowledge, experiences, or emotions
- Uses clear organization to present a logical argument

Forms of persuasion include editorials, position papers, persuasive speeches, grant proposals, advertisements, and debates.

Informative/Explanatory

Informative/explanatory writing should rely on facts to inform or explain. Informative/explanatory writing serves some closely related purposes: to increase readers' knowledge of a subject, to help readers better understand a procedure or process, or to provide readers with an enhanced comprehension of a concept. It should also feature a clear introduction, body, and conclusion. The following are some examples of informative/explanatory writing:

Cause-and-Effect Essay A cause-and-effect essay examines the relationship between events, explaining how one event or situation causes another. A successful cause-and-effect essay includes

- A discussion of a cause, event, or condition that produces a specific result
- An explanation of an effect, outcome, or result
- Evidence and examples to support the relationship between cause and effect
- A logical organization that makes the explanation clear

Comparison-and-Contrast Essay A comparison-and-contrast essay analyzes the similarities and differences between or among two or more things. An effective comparison-and-contrast essay

- Identifies a purpose for comparison and contrast
- Identifies similarities and differences between or among two or more things, people, places, or ideas
- Gives factual details about the subjects
- Uses an organizational plan suited to the topic and purpose

Descriptive Writing Descriptive writing creates a vivid picture of a person, place, thing, or event. Most descriptive writing includes

- Sensory details—sights, sounds, smells, tastes, and physical sensations
- Vivid, precise language
- Figurative language or comparisons
- Adjectives and adverbs that paint a word picture
- An organization suited to the subject

Types of descriptive writing include descriptions of ideas, observations, travel brochures, physical descriptions, functional descriptions, remembrances, and character sketches.

Problem-and-Solution Essay A problem-and-solution essay describes a problem and offers one or more solutions to it. It describes a clear set of steps to achieve a result. An effective problem-and-solution essay includes

- A clear statement of the problem, with its causes and effects summarized for the reader
- The most important aspects of the problem
- A proposal of at least one realistic solution
- Facts, statistics, data, or expert testimony to support the solution
- A clear organization that makes the relationship between problem and solution obvious

Research Writing Research writing is based on information gathered from outside sources. A research paper—a focused study of a topic—helps writers explore and connect ideas, make discoveries, and share their findings with an audience. An effective research paper

- Focuses on a specific, narrow topic, which is usually summarized in a thesis statement
- Presents relevant information from a wide variety of sources
- Uses a clear organization that includes an introduction, body, and conclusion
- Includes a bibliography or works-cited list that identifies the sources from which the information was drawn

Other types of writing that depend on accurate and insightful research include multimedia presentations, statistical reports, annotated bibliographies, and experiment journals.

Workplace Writing Workplace writing is probably the format you will use most after you finish school. In general, workplace writing is fact-based and meant to communicate specific information in a structured format. Effective workplace writing

- Communicates information concisely
- Includes details that provide necessary information and anticipate potential questions
- Is error-free and neatly presented

Common types of workplace writing include business letters, memorandums, résumés, forms, and applications.

Narrative

Narrative writing conveys experience, either real or imaginary, and uses time to provide structure. It can be used to inform, instruct, persuade, or entertain. Whenever writers tell a story, they are using narrative writing. Most types of narrative writing share certain elements, such as characters, a setting, a sequence of events, and, often, a theme. The following are some types of narration:

Autobiographical Writing Autobiographical writing tells a true story about an important period, experience, or relationship in the writer's life. Effective autobiographical writing includes

- A series of events that involve the writer as the main character
- Details, thoughts, feelings, and insights from the writer's perspective
- A conflict or an event that affects the writer
- A logical organization that tells the story clearly
- Insights that the writer gained from the experience

Types of autobiographical writing include autobiographical sketches, personal narratives, reflective essays, eyewitness accounts, and memoirs.

Short Story A short story is a brief, creative narrative. Most short stories include

- Details that establish the setting in time and place
- A main character who undergoes a change or learns something during the course of the story
- A conflict or a problem to be introduced, developed, and resolved
- A plot, the series of events that make up the action of the story
- A theme or message about life

Types of short stories include realistic stories, fantasies, historical narratives, mysteries, thrillers, science-fiction stories, and adventure stories.

Writing Friendly Letters

A friendly letter is much less formal than a business letter. It is a letter to a friend, a family member, or anyone with whom the writer wants to communicate in a personal, friendly way. Most friendly letters are made up of five parts:

- ✔ the heading
- ✔ the salutation, or greeting
- ✔ the body
- ✔ the closing
- ✔ the signature

The purpose of a friendly letter is often one of the following:

- ✔ to share personal news and feelings
- ✔ to send or to answer an invitation
- ✔ to express thanks

Model Friendly Letter

In this friendly letter, Betsy thanks her grandparents for a birthday present and gives them some news about her life.

11 Old Farm Road
Topsham, Maine 04011

April 14, 20—

The **heading** includes the writer's address and the date on which he or she wrote the letter.

Dear Grandma and Grandpa,

Thank you for the sweater you sent me for my birthday. It fits perfectly, and I love the color. I wore my new sweater to the carnival at school last weekend and got lots of compliments.

The weather here has been cool but sunny. Mom thinks that "real" spring will never come. I can't wait until it's warm enough to go swimming.

School is going fairly well. I really like my Social Studies class. We are learning about the U.S. Constitution, and I think it's very interesting. Maybe I will be a lawyer when I grow up.

When are you coming out to visit us? We haven't seen you since Thanksgiving. You can stay in my room when you come. I'll be happy to sleep on the couch. (The TV is in that room!!)

Well, thanks again and hope all is well with you.

The **body** is the main part of the letter and contains the basic message.

Love,

Betsy

Some common **closings** for personal letters include "Best Wishes," "Love," "Sincerely," and "Yours Truly."

Writing Business Letters

Formatting Business Letters

Business letters follow one of several acceptable formats. In **block format,** each part of the letter begins at the left margin. A double space is used between paragraphs. In **modified block format,** some parts of the letter are indented to the center of the page. No matter which format is used, all letters in business format have a heading, an inside address, a salutation or greeting, a body, a closing, and a signature. These parts are shown and annotated on the model business letter below, formatted in modified block style.

Model Business Letter

In this letter, Yolanda Dodson uses modified block format to request information.

Students for a Cleaner Planet
c/o Memorial High School
333 Veteran's Drive
Denver, CO 80211

January 25, 20—

Steven Wilson, Director
Resource Recovery Really Works
300 Oak Street
Denver, CO 80216

Dear Mr. Wilson:

Memorial High School would like to start a branch of your successful recycling program. We share your commitment to reclaiming as much reusable material as we can. Because your program has been successful in other neighborhoods, we're sure that it can work in our community. Our school includes grades 9–12 and has about 800 students.

Would you send us some information about your community recycling program? For example, we need to know what materials can be recycled and how we can implement the program.

At least fifty students have already expressed an interest in getting involved, so I know we'll have the people power to make the program work. Please help us get started.

Thank you in advance for your time and consideration.

Sincerely,

Yolanda Dodson

Yolanda Dodson

The **heading** shows the writer's address and organization (if any) and the date.

The **inside address** indicates where the letter will be sent.

A **salutation** is punctuated by a colon. When the specific addressee is not known, use a general greeting such as "To whom it may concern:"

The **body** of the letter states the writer's purpose. In this case, the writer requests information.

The **closing** "Sincerely" is common, but "Yours truly" or "Respectfully yours" are also acceptable. To end the letter, the writer types her name and provides a **signature.**

Writing a Résumé

Writing a Résumé

A résumé summarizes your educational background, work experiences, relevant skills, and other employment qualifications. It also tells potential employers how to contact you. An effective résumé presents the applicant's name, address, and phone number. It follows an accepted résumé organization, using labels and headings to guide readers.

A résumé should outline the applicant's educational background, life experiences, and related qualifications using precise and active language.

Model Résumé

With this résumé, James, a college student, hopes to find a full-time job.

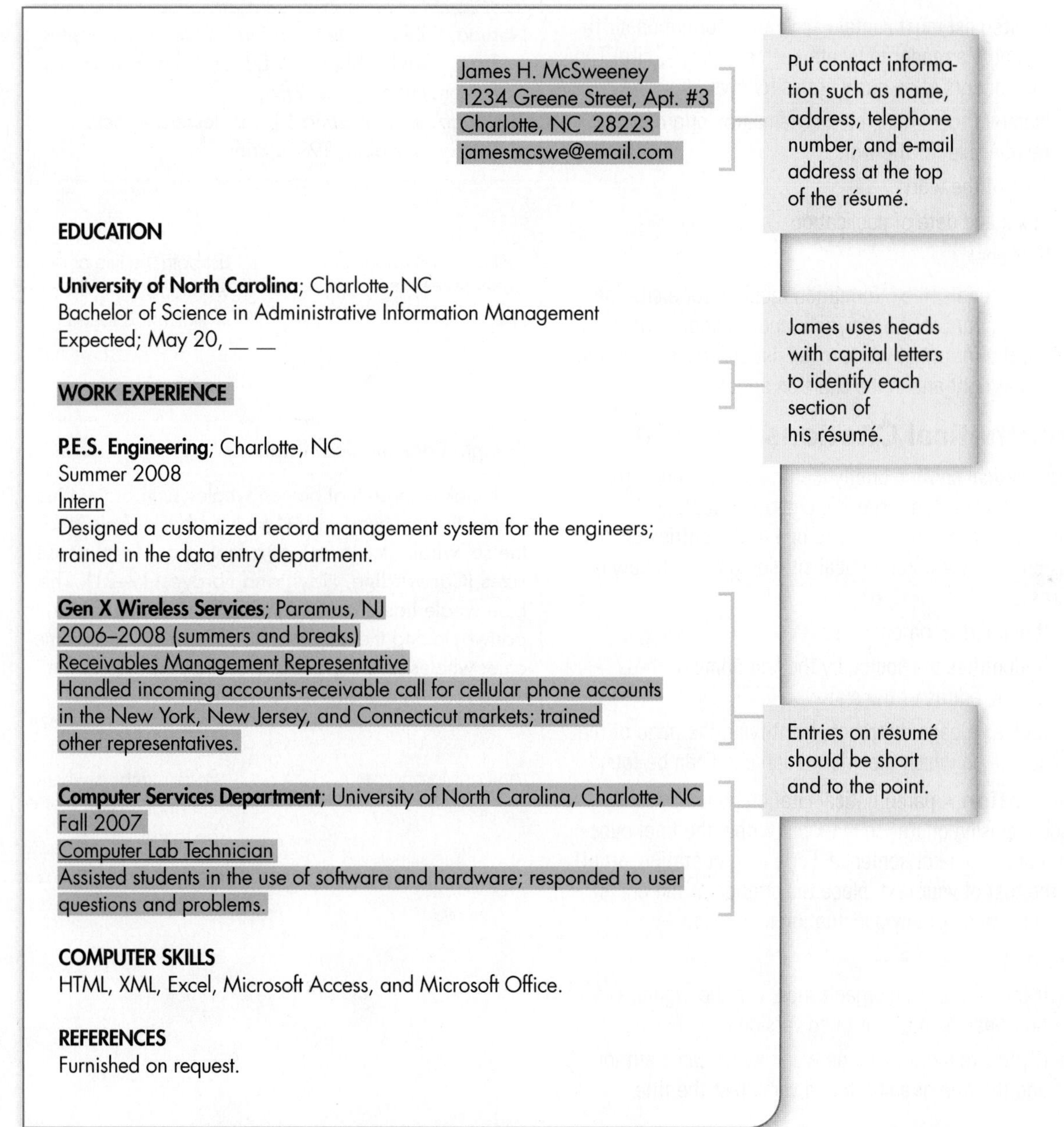

James H. McSweeney
1234 Greene Street, Apt. #3
Charlotte, NC 28223
jamesmcswe@email.com

EDUCATION

University of North Carolina; Charlotte, NC
Bachelor of Science in Administrative Information Management
Expected; May 20, _ _

WORK EXPERIENCE

P.E.S. Engineering; Charlotte, NC
Summer 2008
<u>Intern</u>
Designed a customized record management system for the engineers; trained in the data entry department.

Gen X Wireless Services; Paramus, NJ
2006–2008 (summers and breaks)
<u>Receivables Management Representative</u>
Handled incoming accounts-receivable call for cellular phone accounts in the New York, New Jersey, and Connecticut markets; trained other representatives.

Computer Services Department; University of North Carolina, Charlotte, NC
Fall 2007
<u>Computer Lab Technician</u>
Assisted students in the use of software and hardware; responded to user questions and problems.

COMPUTER SKILLS
HTML, XML, Excel, Microsoft Access, and Microsoft Office.

REFERENCES
Furnished on request.

Put contact information such as name, address, telephone number, and e-mail address at the top of the résumé.
James uses heads with capital letters to identify each section of his résumé.
Entries on résumé should be short and to the point.

Citing Sources and Preparing Manuscript

In research writing, cite your sources. In the body of your paper, provide a footnote, an endnote, or a parenthetical citation, identifying the sources of facts, opinions, or quotations. At the end of your paper, provide a bibliography or a works-cited list, a list of all the sources you cite. Follow an established format, such as Modern Language Association (MLA) Style.

Works-Cited List (MLA Style)

A works-cited list must contain accurate information sufficient to enable a reader to locate each source you cite. The basic components of an entry are as follows:

- Name of the author, editor, translator, or group responsible for the work
- Title of the work
- Place and date of publication
- Publisher

For print materials, the information required for a citation generally appears on the copyright and title pages of a work. For the format of works-cited list entries, consult the examples at right and in the chart on page R37.

Parenthetical Citations (MLA Style)

A parenthetical citation briefly identifies the source from which you have taken a specific quotation, factual claim, or opinion. It refers the reader to one of the entries on your works-cited list. A parenthetical citation has the following features:

- It appears in parentheses.
- It identifies the source by the last name of the author, editor, or translator.
- It gives a page reference, identifying the page of the source on which the information cited can be found.

Punctuation A parenthetical citation generally falls outside a closing quotation mark but within the final punctuation of a clause or sentence. For a long quotation set off from the rest of your text, place the citation at the end of the excerpt without any punctuation following.

Special Cases

- If the author is an organization, use the organization's name, in a shortened version if necessary.
- If you cite more than one work by the same author, add the title or a shortened version of the title.

Sample Works-Cited Lists (MLA 7th Edition)

Carwardine, Mark, Erich Hoyt, R. Ewan Fordyce, and Peter Gill. *The Nature Company Guides: Whales, Dolphins, and Porpoises.* New York: Time-Life, 1998. Print.

"Discovering Whales." *Whales on the Net.* 1998. Whales in Danger Information Service. Web. 18 Oct. 1999.

Neruda, Pablo. "Ode to Spring." *Odes to Opposites.* Trans. Ken Krabbenhoft. Ed. and illus. Ferris Cook. Boston: Little, 1995. Print.

The Saga of the Volsungs. Trans. Jesse L. Byock. London: Penguin, 1990. Print.

List an anonymous work by title.

List both the title of the work and the collection in which it is found.

Sample Parenthetical Citations

It makes sense that baleen whales such as the blue whale, the bowhead whale, the humpback whale, and the sei whale (to name just a few) grow to immense sizes (Carwardine, Hoyt, and Fordyce 19–21). The blue whale has grooves running from under its chin to partway along the length of its underbelly. As in some other whales, these grooves expand and allow even more food and water to be taken in (Ellis 18–21).

Author's last name

Page numbers where information can be found

MLA Style for Listing Sources

Book with one author	Pyles, Thomas. *The Origins and Development of the English Language.* 2nd ed. New York: Harcourt, 1971. Print.
Book with two or three authors	McCrum, Robert, William Cran, and Robert MacNeil. *The Story of English.* New York: Penguin, 1987. Print.
Book with an editor	Truth, Sojourner. *Narrative of Sojourner Truth.* Ed. Margaret Washington. New York: Vintage, 1993. Print.
Book with more than three authors or editors	Donald, Robert B., et al. *Writing Clear Essays.* Upper Saddle River: Prentice, 1996. Print.
Single work in an anthology	Hawthorne, Nathaniel. "Young Goodman Brown." *Literature: An Introduction to Reading and Writing.* Ed. Edgar V. Roberts and H. E. Jacobs. Upper Saddle River: Prentice, 1998. 376–385. Print. [Indicate pages for the entire selection.]
Introduction to a work in a published edition	Washington, Margaret. Introduction. *Narrative of Sojourner Truth.* By Sojourner Truth. Ed. Washington. New York: Vintage, 1993. v–xi. Print.
Signed article from an encyclopedia	Askeland, Donald R. "Welding." *World Book Encyclopedia.* 1991 ed. Print.
Signed article in a weekly magazine	Wallace, Charles. "A Vodacious Deal." *Time* 14 Feb. 2000: 63. Print.
Signed article in a monthly magazine	Gustaitis, Joseph. "The Sticky History of Chewing Gum." *American History* Oct. 1998: 30–38. Print.
Newspaper	Thurow, Roger. "South Africans Who Fought for Sanctions Now Scrap for Investors." *Wall Street Journal* 11 Feb. 2000: A1+. Print. [For a multipage article that does not appear on consecutive pages, write only the first page number on which it appears, followed by the plus sign.]
Unsigned editorial or story	"Selective Silence." Editorial. *Wall Street Journal* 11 Feb. 2000: A14. Print. [If the editorial or story is signed, begin with the author's name.]
Signed pamphlet or brochure	[Treat the pamphlet as though it were a book.]
Work from a library subscription service	Ertman, Earl L. "Nefertiti's Eyes." *Archaeology* Mar.–Apr. 2008: 28–32. *Kids Search.* EBSCO. New York Public Library. Web. 18 June 2008 [Indicate the date you accessed the information.]
Filmstrips, slide programs, videocassettes, DVDs, and other audiovisual media	*The Diary of Anne Frank.* Dir. George Stevens. Perf. Millie Perkins, Shelley Winters, Joseph Schildkraut, Lou Jacobi, and Richard Beymer. 1959. Twentieth Century Fox, 2004. DVD.
CD-ROM (with multiple publishers)	Simms, James, ed. *Romeo and Juliet.* By William Shakespeare. Oxford: Attica Cybernetics; London: BBC Education; London: Harper, 1995. CD-ROM.
Radio or television program transcript	"Washington's Crossing of the Delaware." *Weekend Edition Sunday.* Natl. Public Radio. WNYC, New York. 23 Dec. 2003. Television transcript.
Internet Web page	"Fun Facts About Gum." NACGM site. 1999. National Association of Chewing Gum Manufacturers. Web. 19 Dec. 1999 [Indicate the date you accessed the information.]
Personal interview	Smith, Jane. Personal interview. 10 Feb. 2000.

All examples follow the style given in the *MLA Handbook for Writers of Research Papers,* seventh edition, by Joseph Gibaldi.

Guide to Rubrics

What is a rubric?

A rubric is a tool, often in the form of a chart or a grid, that helps you assess your work. Rubrics are particularly helpful for writing and speaking assignments.

To help you or others assess, or evaluate, your work, a rubric offers several specific criteria to be applied to your work. Then, the rubric helps you or an evaluator indicate your range of success or failure according to those specific criteria. Rubrics are often used to evaluate writing for standardized tests.

Using a rubric will save you time, focus your learning, and improve the work you do. When you know what the rubric will be before you begin writing a persuasive essay, for example, you will be aware as you write of specific criteria that are important in that kind of essay. As you evaluate the essay before giving it to your teacher, you will focus on the specific areas that your teacher wants you to master—or on areas that you know present challenges for you. Instead of searching through your work randomly for any way to improve it or correct its errors, you will have a clear and helpful focus on specific criteria.

How are rubrics constructed?

Rubrics can be constructed in several different ways.

- Your teacher may assign a rubric for a specific assignment.
- Your teacher may direct you to a rubric in your textbook.
- Your teacher and your class may construct a rubric for a particular assignment together.
- You and your classmates may construct a rubric together.
- You may create your own rubric with criteria you want to evaluate in your work.

How will a rubric help me?

A rubric will help you assess your work on a scale. Scales vary from rubric to rubric but usually range from 6 to 1, 5 to 1, or 4 to 1, with 6, 5, or 4 being the highest score and 1 being the lowest. If someone else is using the rubric to assess your work, the rubric will give your evaluator a clear range within which to place your work. If you are using the rubric yourself, it will help you make improvements to your work.

What are the types of rubrics?

- A **holistic rubric** has general criteria that can apply to a variety of assignments. See p. R-40 for an example of a holistic rubric.
- An **analytic rubric** is specific to a particular assignment. The criteria for evaluation address the specific issues important in that assignment. See p. R-39 for examples of analytic rubrics.

Sample Analytic Rubrics

Rubric With a 4-point Scale

The following analytic rubric is an example of a rubric to assess a persuasive essay. It will help you evaluate focus, organization, support/elaboration, and style/convention.

	Focus	Organization	Support/Elaboration	Style/Convention
4	Demonstrates highly effective word choice; clearly focused on task.	Uses clear, consistent organizational strategy.	Provides convincing, well-elaborated reasons to support the position.	Incorporates transitions; includes very few mechanical errors.
3	Demonstrates good word choice; stays focused on persuasive task.	Uses clear organizational strategy with occasional inconsistencies.	Provides two or more moderately elaborated reasons to support the position.	Incorporates some transitions; includes few mechanical errors.
2	Shows some good word choices; minimally stays focused on persuasive task.	Uses inconsistent organizational strategy; presentation is not logical.	Provides several reasons, but few are elaborated; only one elaborated reason.	Incorporates few transitions; includes many mechanical errors.
1	Shows lack of attention to persuasive task.	Demonstrates lack of organizational strategy.	Provides no specific reasons or does not elaborate.	Does not connect ideas; includes many mechanical errors.

Rubric With a 6-point Scale

The following analytic rubric is an example of a rubric to assess a persuasive essay. It will help you evaluate presentation, position, evidence, and arguments.

	Presentation	Position	Evidence	Arguments
6	Essay clearly and effectively addresses an issue with more than one side.	Essay clearly states a supportable position on the issue.	All evidence is logically organized, well presented, and supports the position.	All reader concerns and counterarguments are effectively addressed.
5	Most of essay addresses an issue that has more than one side.	Essay clearly states a position on the issue.	Most evidence is logically organized, well presented, and supports the position.	Most reader concerns and counterarguments are effectively addressed.
4	Essay adequately addresses issue that has more than one side.	Essay adequately states a position on the issue.	Many parts of evidence support the position; some evidence is out of order.	Many reader concerns and counterarguments are adequately addressed.
3	Essay addresses issue with two sides but does not present second side clearly.	Essay states a position on the issue, but the position is difficult to support.	Some evidence supports the position, but some evidence is out of order.	Some reader concerns and counterarguments are addressed.
2	Essay addresses issue with two sides but does not present second side.	Essay states a position on the issue, but the position is not supportable.	Not much evidence supports the position, and what is included is out of order.	A few reader concerns and counterarguments are addressed.
1	Essay does not address issue with more than one side.	Essay does not state a position on the issue.	No evidence supports the position.	No reader concerns or counterarguments are addressed.

WRITING HANDBOOK

Sample Holistic Rubric

Holistic rubrics such as this one are sometimes used to assess writing assignments on standardized tests. Notice that the criteria for evaluation are focus, organization, support, and use of conventions.

Points	Criteria
6 Points	• The writing is strongly focused and shows fresh insight into the writing task. • The writing is marked by a sense of completeness and coherence and is organized with a logical progression of ideas. • A main idea is fully developed, and support is specific and substantial. • A mature command of the language is evident, and the writing may employ characteristic creative writing strategies. • Sentence structure is varied, and writing is free of all but purposefully used fragments. • Virtually no errors in writing conventions appear.
5 Points	• The writing is clearly focused on the task. • The writing is well organized and has a logical progression of ideas, though there may be occasional lapses. • A main idea is well developed and supported with relevant detail. • Sentence structure is varied, and the writing is free of fragments, except when used purposefully. • Writing conventions are followed correctly.
4 Points	• The writing is clearly focused on the task, but extraneous material may intrude at times. • Clear organizational pattern is present, though lapses may occur. • A main idea is adequately supported, but development may be uneven. • Sentence structure is generally fragment free but shows little variation. • Writing conventions are generally followed correctly.
3 Points	• Writing is generally focused on the task, but extraneous material may intrude at times. • An organizational pattern is evident, but writing may lack a logical progression of ideas. • Support for the main idea is generally present but is sometimes illogical. • Sentence structure is generally free of fragments, but there is almost no variation. • The work generally demonstrates a knowledge of writing conventions, with occasional misspellings.
2 Points	• The writing is related to the task but generally lacks focus. • There is little evidence of organizational pattern, and there is little sense of cohesion. • Support for the main idea is generally inadequate, illogical, or absent. • Sentence structure is unvaried, and serious errors may occur. • Errors in writing conventions and spellings are frequent.
1 Point	• The writing may have little connection to the task and is generally unfocused. • There has been little attempt at organization or development. • The paper seems fragmented, with no clear main idea. • Sentence structure is unvaried, and serious errors appear. • Poor word choice and poor command of the language obscure meaning. • Errors in writing conventions and spelling are frequent.
Unscorable	The paper is considered unscorable if: • The response is unrelated to the task or is simply a rewording of the prompt. • The response has been copied from a published work. • The student did not write a response. • The response is illegible. • The words in the response are arranged with no meaning. • There is an insufficient amount of writing to score.

Student Model

Persuasive Writing

This persuasive letter, which would receive a top score according to a persuasive rubric, is a response to the following writing prompt, or assignment:

With the increased use of technology in the workplace, the skills that high-school graduates must possess have changed. Write a letter to your principal advocating new technology courses that could give high-school graduates a competitive edge.

Dear Principal:

I am writing to alert you to an urgent need in our school's curriculum. We need computer graphics courses!

> The letter begins with an engaging introduction that clearly states the persuasive focus.

Although you would have to find funds to buy the equipment, I've concluded that setting up this course would well be worth it. By adding this course, you would be adding many high paying career options for students. Computer graphics is a type of art, and businesses all around us involve art in some form. You see computer graphics in commercials, movies, news broadcasts, weather broadcasts, architectural design, and business presentations. Workers with computer graphics skills are well paid because they are in such high demand.

You may argue that the school already has computer science classes. Good point! I'm in a computer science class and it is mainly programming. Once we did have an assignment to design a graphic of a pumpkin. You wouldn't believe how much coding it takes to get a simple, animated drawing. In order to get a really creative image with definite lines, shading, lifelike colors, and texture, you need to use computer graphics software designed especially for that purpose. With software, you can make images that move and talk smoothly and environments with realistic colors and lighting. This is the same graphics software that businesses use for commercials, movies, and brochures. Students should be learning how to use this software.

> The author effectively counters an opposing argument to increase the persuasive power of her own argument.

Most important, computer graphics is a subject area that allows students to express their creativity. Adding a computer graphics course would have a positive effect on students. Course participants would enjoy doing their assignments, so they would earn good grades and turn in creative work. The energy and enthusiasm they would bring to their projects would catch the attention of the community at large. As a result, they would make the school and the principal look good.

> A positive argument that is well supported enhances the letter's persuasive appeal.

As you can see, adding a computer graphics course could be a very profitable idea for you, the students, and the community. You would be ensuring the success of the students who desire an art or computer career. You would be opening hundreds of different career pathways. Wouldn't it be great to know you were the reason for these students' success? Thanks for your time and consideration.

Sincerely,
Dawn Witherspoon

21st-Century Skills

New technology has created many new ways to communicate. Today, it is easy to contribute information to the Internet and send a variety of messages to friends far and near. You can also share your ideas through photos, illustrations, video, and sound recordings. *21st-Century Skills* gives you an overview of some ways you can use today's technology to create, share, and find information. Here are the topics you will find in this section.

- ✔ Blogs
- ✔ Multimedia Elements
- ✔ Social Networking
- ✔ Podcasts
- ✔ Widgets & Feeds
- ✔ Wikis

BLOGS

A **blog** is a common form of online writing. The word *blog* is a contraction of *Web log*. Most blogs include a series of entries known as *posts*. The posts appear in a single column and are displayed in reverse chronological order. That means that the most recent post is at the top of the page. As you scroll down, you will find earlier posts.

Blogs have become increasingly popular. Researchers estimate that 75,000 new blogs are launched every day. Blog authors are often called *bloggers*. They can use their personal sites to share ideas, songs, videos, photos, and other media. People who read blogs can often post their responses with a comments feature found in each new post.

Because blogs are designed so that they are easy to update, bloggers can post new messages as often as they like, often daily. For some people blogs become a public journal or diary, in which they share their thoughts about daily events.

Types of Blogs

Not all blogs are the same. Many blogs have a single author, but others are group projects. These are some common types of blog:

- ✔ Personal blogs often have a general focus. Bloggers post their thoughts on any topic they find interesting in their daily lives.
- ✔ Topical blogs focus on a specific theme, such as movie reviews, political news, class assignments, or health-care opportunities.

Web Safety

Always be aware that information you post on the Internet can be read by everyone with access to that page. Once you post a picture or text, it can be saved on someone else's computer, even if you later remove it.

Using the Internet safely means keeping personal information personal. Never include your address (e-mail or real), last name, or telephone numbers. Avoid mentioning places you can be frequently found. Never give out passwords you use to access other Web sites and do not respond to e-mails from people you do not know.

Anatomy of a Blog

Here are some of the features you can include in a blog.

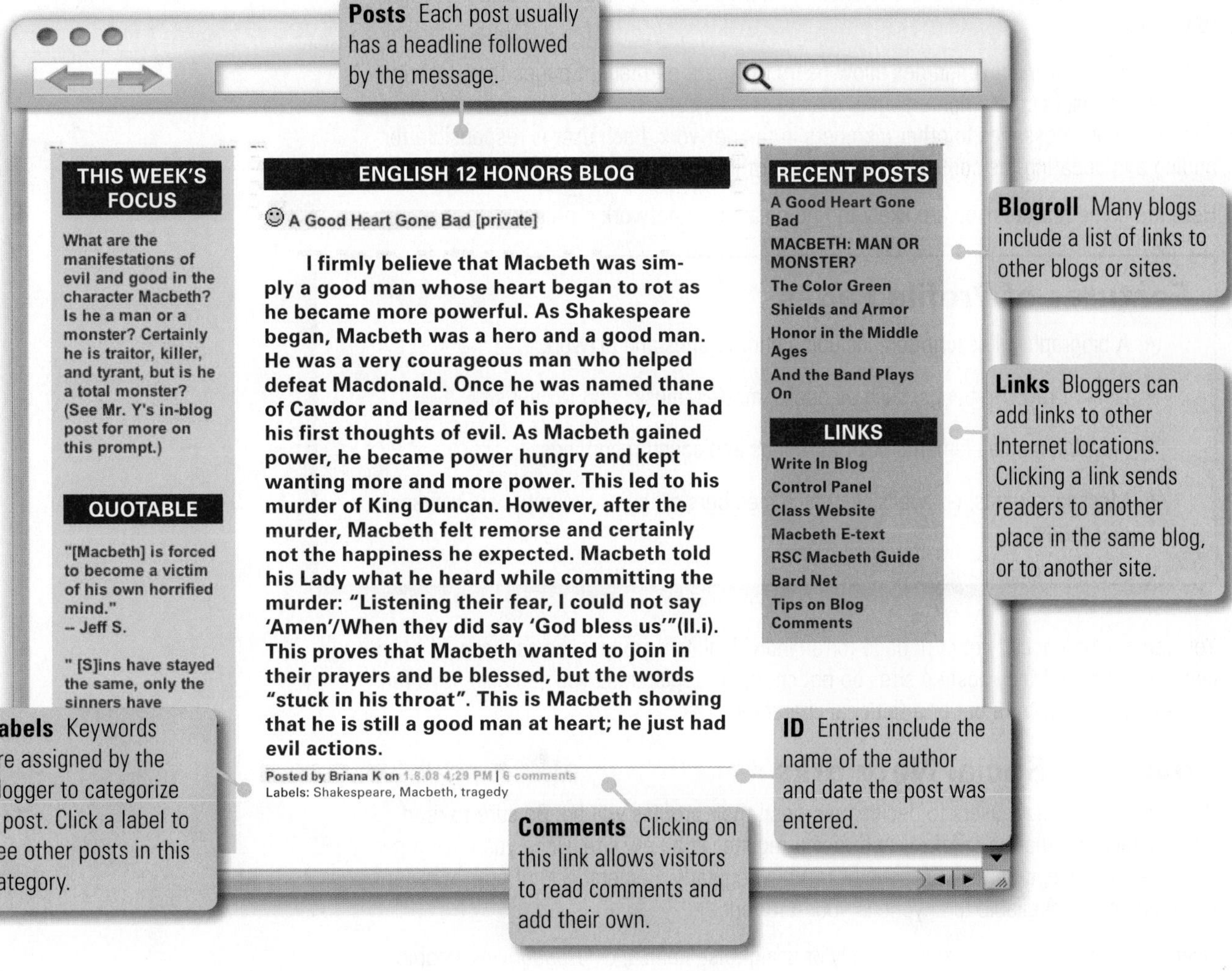

Posts Each post usually has a headline followed by the message.
THIS WEEK'S FOCUS
What are the manifestations of evil and good in the character Macbeth? Is he a man or a monster? Certainly he is traitor, killer, and tyrant, but is he a total monster? (See Mr. Y's in-blog post for more on this prompt.)
QUOTABLE
"[Macbeth] is forced to become a victim of his own horrified mind." -- Jeff S.
" [S]ins have stayed the same, only the sinners have
ENGLISH 12 HONORS BLOG
A Good Heart Gone Bad [private]
I firmly believe that Macbeth was simply a good man whose heart began to rot as he became more powerful. As Shakespeare began, Macbeth was a hero and a good man. He was a very courageous man who helped defeat Macdonald. Once he was named thane of Cawdor and learned of his prophecy, he had his first thoughts of evil. As Macbeth gained power, he became power hungry and kept wanting more and more power. This led to his murder of King Duncan. However, after the murder, Macbeth felt remorse and certainly not the happiness he expected. Macbeth told his Lady what he heard while committing the murder: "Listening their fear, I could not say 'Amen'/When they did say 'God bless us'"(II.i). This proves that Macbeth wanted to join in their prayers and be blessed, but the words "stuck in his throat". This is Macbeth showing that he is still a good man at heart; he just had evil actions.
Posted by Briana K on 1.8.08 4:29 PM | 6 comments
Labels: Shakespeare, Macbeth, tragedy
RECENT POSTS
A Good Heart Gone Bad
MACBETH: MAN OR MONSTER?
The Color Green
Shields and Armor
Honor in the Middle Ages
And the Band Plays On
LINKS
Write In Blog
Control Panel
Class Website
Macbeth E-text
RSC Macbeth Guide
Bard Net
Tips on Blog Comments
Blogroll Many blogs include a list of links to other blogs or sites.
Links Bloggers can add links to other Internet locations. Clicking a link sends readers to another place in the same blog, or to another site.
Labels Keywords are assigned by the blogger to categorize a post. Click a label to see other posts in this category.
ID Entries include the name of the author and date the post was entered.
Comments Clicking on this link allows visitors to read comments and add their own.

Creating a Blog

Keep these hints and strategies in mind to help you create an interesting and fair blog:

- ✔ Focus each blog entry on a single topic.
- ✔ Vary the length of your posts. Sometimes, all you need is a line or two to share a quick thought. Other posts will be much longer.
- ✔ Choose font colors and styles that can be read easily.
- ✔ Many people scan blogs rather than read them closely. You can make your main ideas pop out by using clear or clever headlines and boldfacing key terms.
- ✔ Give credit to other people's work and ideas. State the names of people whose ideas you are quoting or add a link to take readers to that person's blog or site.
- ✔ If you post comments, try to make them brief and polite.

SOCIAL NETWORKING

Social networking means any interaction between members of an online community. People can exchange many different kinds of information, from text and voice messages to video images.

Many social network communities allow users to create permanent pages that describe themselves. Users create home pages to express themselves, share ideas about their lives, and post messages to other members in the network. Each user is responsible for adding and updating the content on his or her profile page.

Here are some features you are likely to find on a social network profile:

Features of Profile Pages

- A biographical description, including photographs and artwork.
- Lists of favorite things, such as books, movies, music, and fashions.
- Playable media elements such as videos and sound recordings.
- Message boards, or "walls" in which members of the community can exchange messages.

You can create a social network page for an individual or a group, such as a school or special interest club. Many hosting sites do not charge to register, so you can also have fun by creating a page for a pet or a fictional character.

Privacy in Social Networks

Social networks allow users to decide how open their profiles will be. Be sure to read introductory information carefully before you register at a new site. Once you have a personal profile page, monitor your privacy settings regularly. Remember that any information you post will be available to anyone in your network.

Users often post messages anonymously or using false names, or *pseudonyms*. People can also post using someone else's name. Judge all information on the net critically. Do not assume that you know who posted some information simply because you recognize the name of the post author. The rapid speed of communication on the Internet can make it easy to jump to conclusions—be careful to avoid this trap.

Tips for Sending Effective Messages

Technology makes it easy to share ideas quickly, but writing for the Internet poses some special challenges, as well. The writing style for blogs and social networks is often very conversational. In blog posts and comments, instant messages, and e-mails, writers often express themselves very quickly, using relaxed language, short sentences, and abbreviations. However, in a conversation, we get a lot of information from a speaker's tone of voice and body language. On the Internet, those clues are missing. As a result, Internet writers often use italics or bracketed labels to indicate emotions. Another alternative is using emoticons—strings of characters that give visual clues to indicate emotion:

:-) smile (happy)	**:-(** frown (unhappy)	**;-)** wink (light sarcasm)

Use these strategies to communicate effectively when using technology:

- ✔ Reread your messages. Before you click *Send,* read your message through and make sure that your tone will be clear to the reader.
- ✔ Do not jump to conclusions—ask for clarification first. Make sure you really understand what someone is saying before you respond.
- ✔ Use abbreviations your reader will understand.

WIDGETS & FEEDS

A **widget** is a small application that performs a specific task. You might find widgets that give weather predictions, offer dictionary definitions or translations, provide entertainment such as games, or present a daily word, photograph, or quotation.

A **feed** is a special kind of widget. It displays headlines taken from the latest content on a specific media source. Clicking on the headline will take you to the full article.

Many social network communities and other Web sites allow you to personalize your home page by adding widgets and feeds.

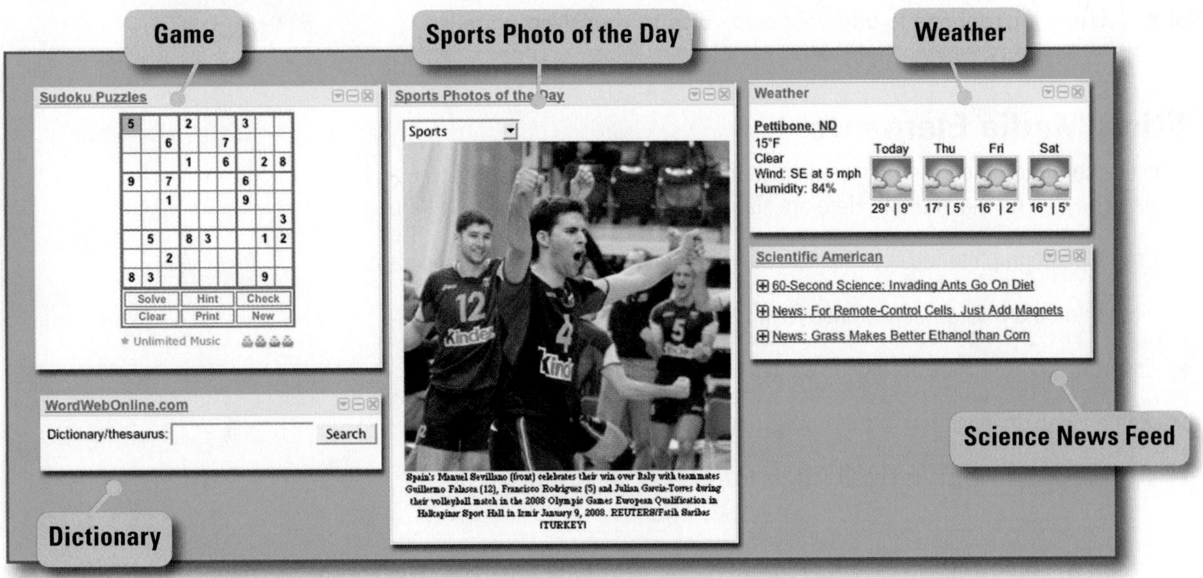

MULTIMEDIA ELEMENTS

One of the great advantages of communicating on the Internet is that you are not limited to using text only. When you create a Web profile or blog, you can share your ideas using a wide variety of media. In addition to widgets and feeds (see page R45), these media elements can make your Internet communication more entertaining and useful.

Graphics	
Photographs	You can post photos taken by digital cameras.
Illustrations	Artwork can be created using computer software. You can also use a scanner to post a digital image of a drawing or sketch.
Charts, Graphs, and Maps	Charts and graphs can make statistical information clear. Use spreadsheet software to create these elements. Use Internet sites to find maps of specific places.

Video	
Live Action	Digital video can be recorded by a camera or recorded from another media source.
Animation	Animated videos can also be created using software.

Sound	
Music	Many social network communities make it easy to share your favorite music with people who visit your page.
Voice	Use a microphone to add your own voice to your Web page.

Editing Media Elements

You can use software to customize media elements. Open source software is free and available to anyone on the Internet. Here are some things you can do with software:

- ✔ Crop a photograph to focus on the subject or brighten an image that is too dark.
- ✔ Transform a drawing's appearance from flat to three-dimensional.
- ✔ Insert a "You Are Here" arrow on a map.
- ✔ Edit a video or sound file to shorten its running time.
- ✔ Add background music or sound effects to a video.

PODCASTS

A **podcast** is a digital audio or video recording of a program that is made available on the Internet. Users can replay the podcast on a computer, or download it and replay it on a personal audio player. You might think of podcasts as radio or television programs that you create yourself. They can be embedded on a Web site or fed to a Web page through a podcast widget.

Creating an Effective Podcast

To make a podcast, you will need a recording device, such as a microphone or digital video camera, as well as editing software. Open source editing software is widely available and free of charge. Most audio podcasts are converted into the MP3 format. Here are some tips for creating a podcast that is clear and entertaining:

- ✔ Listen to several podcasts by different authors to get a feeling for the medium. Make a list of features and styles you like and also those you want to avoid.
- ✔ Test your microphone to find the best recording distance. Stand close enough to the microphone so that your voice sounds full, but not so close that you create an echo.
- ✔ Create an outline that shows your estimated timing for each element.
- ✔ Be prepared before you record. Rehearse, but do not create a script. Podcasts are best when they have a natural, easy flow.
- ✔ Talk directly to your listeners. Slow down enough so they can understand you.
- ✔ Use software to edit your podcast before publishing it. You can edit out mistakes or add additional elements.

WIKIS

A **wiki** is a collaborative Web site that lets visitors create, add, remove, and edit content. The term comes from the Hawaiian phrase *wiki wiki,* which means "quick." Web users at a wiki are both the readers and the writers of the site. Some wikis are open to contributions from anyone. Others require visitors to register before they can edit the content.

All of the text in these collaborative Web sites was written by people who use the site. Articles are constantly changing, as visitors find and correct errors and improve texts.

Wikis have both advantages and disadvantages as sources of information. They are valuable open forums for the exchange of ideas. The unique collaborative writing process allows entries to change over time. However, entries can also be modified incorrectly. Careless or malicious users can delete good content and add inappropriate or inaccurate information.

You can change the information on a wiki, but be sure your information is correct and clear before you add it. Wikis keep track of all changes, so your work will be recorded and can be evaluated by other users.

Rules of Debate

A **debate** is a structured contest based on a formal discussion of opinion. In essence, it is a battle of intellect and verbal skill. The goal is mastering the art of persuasion. Who can best express, argue, and support opinions on a given topic? Who can best refute an argument, showing that the opponent's points are invalid? Which team, in the end, can convince the judges that their argument is the most sound?

Teams

A **formal debate** is conducted with two teams—an Affirmation team and a Negative team. As the names suggest, the Affirmation team is responsible for presenting the "pro" side of an issue, while the Negative team presents the "con" side of the issue. Each team has a main purpose and will offer both constructive and rebuttal speeches, practicing the art of persuasion and debate.

Affirmation team The Affirmation team as a whole carries the burden of proof for the debate. They must prove there is a problem. To do so, they need to cite credible sources, include relevant details, and present and support valid points. Each team member has a specific job. The first speaker has the most responsibility. He or she must

- define the issue or problem
- introduce the team line—a one-line summary of the team's position on the issue
- identify the point of the argument each speaker will discuss

The remaining team members have the job of presenting and supporting the main points of the argument.

Negative team Though the Negative team does not carry the burden of proof, the team must show that there is no problem or that the Affirmation team's solutions are invalid. Though their purpose is to rebut an argument, the rebuttal technique calls for a formation of their own argument. They must argue against the Affirmation team. To construct their argument, they must use—like the Affirmation team—credible sources, relevant details, and valid points. They should incorporate any available statistics, pertinent facts, or applicable testimonies to bolster their argument. Even though the first speaker of the Affirmation team lays out each point of the argument, the Negative team speakers cannot address points that have not been thoroughly discussed by an Affirmation team member.

Structure

Just like most other contests, debates have a set structure. Debates are divided into halves. The first half begins with the constructive speeches from both teams, which last ten minutes each.

After the first half, there is a short intermission. Then, the second half begins with the Negative team. This half is reserved for the rebuttal speeches, which last five minutes each and include rebuttals and refutations. This is each team's chance to rebuild their arguments that the other team broke down (rebuttal), and put forth evidence to show the other team is wrong (refutation). Although the Negative team begins the argument in the second half, every debate begins and ends with the Affirmation team.

Structure of Debate

1st Half: Constructive Speeches (10 minutes each)	2nd Half: Rebuttal Speeches (5 minutes each)
1st Affirmative Team Speaker	1st Negative Team Speaker
1st Negative Team Speaker	1st Affirmative Team Speaker
2nd Affirmative Team Speaker	2nd Negative Team Speaker
2nd Negative Team Speaker	2nd Affirmative Team Speaker
3rd Affirmative Team Speaker	3rd Negative Team Speaker
3rd Negative Team Speaker	3rd Affirmative Team Speaker

Speeches—Content, Organization, and Delivery

Debate speeches are the result of practicing the art of persuasion. To be effective, speakers must include pertinent content, use clear and logical organization, and have a powerful delivery. These combined elements make a strong speech.

Content Debates often focus on concrete issues that can be proved or disproved. The basis for a debate speech is its content. The Affirmation team should first determine their position. They should be sure to include any facts and/or statistics that concretely support the argument. Speech writers should cite specific instances and occurrences that solidify their position. Writers might also include testimonies or ideas from professionals. Finally, the Affirmation team needs to propose possible solutions to the problem or issue and examine the costs and effects of those solutions.

Though the Negative team does not have to state a position—their position is automatically the opposing position—they still need to include facts, statistics, testimony, and descriptions of specific instances or occurrences to make their counterpoints. They need to analyze the Affirmation team's proposed solutions and explain why they will not work. In essence, the Negative team must construct an argument around the Affirmation team's argument.

Organization Debate speeches are organized like other speeches and essays. They should have an introduction, transitions, body, and conclusion. The speeches should have clear main points and supporting details for those points. Because a debate is a structured discussion, there will be a specific order of points and the speakers who present them must be identified. Speakers can use note cards to help them stick to the planned organization, but they should only use brief notes, never reading directly from the cards.

Delivery The manner in which a speech is delivered can make or break the argument. The impression the speaker makes on the audience, including the judges, is key. To make a good impression, the speaker must present the material with confidence. He or she can portray confidence by forming a connection with the audience through eye contact, glancing away only briefly to consult notes. A speaker should focus on his or her voice, varying the tone, volume, and pace appropriately. Body movements should not include fidgeting or nervous movement. They should only be used if they are deliberate and help express or underscore a point. Finally, speakers should be concise, focusing on vivid and clear word choice and using words that emphasize the point.

Scoring

Debates are scored much like other contests. Each side is judged on the content and delivery of their speeches. Judges contemplate different elements of content and delivery in order to determine the number of points to give each team. They might ask themselves the questions in the chart below in order to determine the score.

Finally, judges look at the observation of debate etiquette. Speakers are expected to be mature and respectful of their opponents. Speakers should never attack an opponent, but instead should attack the argument. Judges will deduct points for personal attacks.

Scoring Criteria

Content	Delivery
Were arguments convincing?	Were speakers able to speak extemporaneously?
Were arguments supported with credible, valid and relevant reasons?	Were body movements deliberate and effective?
Were refutations and rebuttals effective?	Did speakers make a connection with the audience?
Were speakers confident and knowledgeable?	Did speakers stay within their time limits?

Parts of Speech

Nouns A noun names a person, place, or thing. Common nouns name any one of a class of people, places, or things. Proper nouns name specific people, places, or things.

Common Noun	***Proper Noun***
city	Washington, D.C.

Use *apostrophes* with nouns to show ownership. Add an apostrophe and *s* to show the **possessive case** of most singular nouns. Add just an apostrophe to show the possessive case of plural nouns ending in *s* or *es*. Add an apostrophe and s to show the possessive case of plural nouns that do not end in *s* or *es*.

Pronouns A **pronoun** is a word that stands for a noun or for a word that takes the place of a noun.

A **personal pronoun** refers to (1) the person speaking, (2) the person spoken to, or (3) the person, place, or thing spoken about.

	Singular	***Plural***
First Person	I, me, my, mine	we, us, our, ours
Second Person	you, your, yours	you, your, yours
Third Person	he, him, his, she, her, hers, it, its	they, them, their, theirs

A **reflexive pronoun** ends in *-self* or *-selves* and adds information to a sentence by pointing back to a noun or pronoun earlier in the sentence.

As I said these words I busied *myself* among the pile of bones of which I have before spoken.
—"The Cask of Amontillado," p. 60

An **intensive pronoun** ends in *-self* or *-selves* and simply adds emphasis to a noun or a pronoun in the same sentence.

The best playground, however, was the dark alley *itself*.
—"Rules of the Game," p. 316

Demonstrative pronouns (*this, these, that,* and *those*) direct attention to a specific person, place, or thing.

These are the juiciest pears I have ever tasted.

A **relative pronoun** begins a subordinate (relative) clause and connects it to another idea in the sentence.

The poet *who* wrote "Fire and Ice" is Robert Frost.

The poet *whom* I admire is Frost.

An **interrogative pronoun** is used to begin a question. The five interrogative pronouns are *what, which, who, whom, whose*.

An **indefinite pronoun** refers to a person, place, or thing, often without specifying which one.

Some of the flowers were in bloom.

Everybody chose something.

Verbs A **verb** is a word that expresses time while showing an action, a condition, or the fact that something exists.

An **action verb** indicates the action of someone or something. An action verb is **transitive** if it directs action toward someone or something named in the same sentence.

Marcos accepted their bouquets . . .
—"Uncle Marcos," p. 138

An action verb is **intransitive** if it does not direct action toward something or someone named in the same sentence.

"He nodded and smiled a lot."
—"American History," p. 240

A **linking verb** is a verb that connects the subject of a sentence with a noun or pronoun that renames or describes the subject. All linking verbs are intransitive.

Life *is* a broken-winged bird . . .
—"Dreams," p. 621

A **helping verb** is a verb that can be added to another verb to make a verb phrase.

Nor *did* I suspect that these experiences could be part of a novel's meaning.

Adjectives An **adjective** describes a noun or a pronoun or gives a noun or a pronoun a more specific meaning. Adjectives answer these questions:

What kind?	*blue* lamp, *large* tree
Which one?	*this* table, *those* books
How many?	*five* stars, *several* buses
How much?	*less* money, *enough* votes

The articles *the, a,* and *an* are adjectives. *An* is used before a word beginning with a vowel sound.

A noun may sometimes be used as an adjective.

diamond necklace   *summer* vacation

Adverbs An **adverb** modifies a verb, an adjective, or another adverb. Adverbs answer the questions *Where? When? In what way?* or *To what extent?*

He could stand *there*. (modifies verb *stand*)

He was *blissfully* happy. (modifies adjective *happy*)

It ended *too* soon. (modifies adverb *soon*)

Prepositions A **preposition** relates a noun or a pronoun that appears with it to another word in the sentence.

the scene *before* the end   stood *near* me

Conjunctions A **conjunction** connects other words or groups of words. A **coordinating conjunction** connects similar kinds or groups of words.

mother *and* father   simple *yet* stylish

Correlative conjunctions are used in pairs to connect similar words or groups of words.

both Sue *and* Meg   *neither* he *nor* I

A **subordinating conjunction** connects two complete ideas by placing one idea below the other in rank or importance.

You would know him *if* you saw him.

Interjections An **interjection** expresses feeling or emotion and functions independently of a sentence.

"*Oh,* my poor, poor, Mathilde!"
—"The Necklace," p. 332

Sentences, Phrases, and Clauses

Sentences A **sentence** is a group of words with a subject and a predicate. Together, these parts express a complete thought.

I closed my eyes and pondered my next move.
— "Rules of the Game," p. 316

A **fragment** is a group of words that does not express a complete thought.

The Swan Theater in London

A **run-on** is two or more complete sentences run together without punctuation.

A **direct object** is a noun or pronoun that receives the action of a transitive verb.

An **indirect object** is a noun or pronoun that appears with a direct object and names the person or thing that something is given to or done for.

The Four Structures of Sentences There are two kinds of clauses: independent and subordinate. These can be used to form four basic sentence structures: *simple, compound, complex,* and *compound-complex.*

A **simple sentence** consists of a single independent clause.

A **compound sentence** consists of two or more independent clauses.

The clauses in a compound sentence can be joined by a comma and a coordinating conjunction (*and, but, for, not, or, so, yet*) or by a semicolon (;).

A **complex sentence** consists of one independent clause and one or more subordinate clauses.

The independent clause in a complex sentence is often called the *main clause* to distinguish it from the subordinate clause or clauses.

A **compound-complex sentence** consists of two or more independent clauses and one or more subordinate causes.

Phrases A **phrase** is a group of words, without a subject and a verb, that functions in a sentence as one part of speech.

A **prepositional phrase** is a group of words that includes a preposition and a noun or a pronoun that is the object of the preposition.

outside my window   below the counter

An **adjective phrase** is a prepositional phrase that modifies a noun or a pronoun by telling *what kind* or *which one.*

The wooden gates *of that lane* stood open.

An **adverb phrase** is a prepositional phrase that modifies a verb, an adjective, or an adverb by pointing out *where, when, in what way,* or *to what extent.*

". . . I could sleep without closing my eyes . . ."
—"The Most Dangerous Game," p. 215

An **appositive phrase** is a noun or pronoun with modifiers, placed next to a noun or a pronoun to add information and details.

"It is a very great pleasure and honor to welcome Mr. Sanger Rainsford, *the celebrated hunter,* to my home."
—"The Most Dangerous Game," p. 215

A **participial phrase** is a participle with its modifiers or complements. The entire phrase acts as an adjective.

"Try the settee," said Holmes, *relapsing into his armchair . . .*
—"The Red-headed League," p. 1166

A **gerund phrase** is a gerund with modifiers or a complement, all acting together as a noun.

The baying of the hounds drew nearer, . . .
—"The Most Dangerous Game," p. 215

An **infinitive phrase** is an infinitive (*to* and a verb) with modifiers, complements, or a subject, all acting together as a single part of speech.

I continued, as was my wont, *to smile in his face,* . . .
—"The Cask of Amontillado," p. 60

Clauses A **clause** is a group of words with a subject and a verb.

An **independent clause** has a subject and a verb and can stand by itself as a complete sentence.

A **subordinate clause** has a subject and a verb but cannot stand by itself as a complete sentence; it can only be part of a sentence.

An **adjective clause** is a subordinate clause that modifies a noun or a pronoun by telling *what kind* or *which one.*

Walter Mitty stopped the car in front of the building *where his wife went to have her hair done.*
—"The Secret Life of Walter Mitty," p. 128

An **adverb clause** modifies a verb, an adjective, an adverb, or a verbal by telling *where, when, in what way, to what extent, under what condition,* or *why.*

The hunter shook his head several times, *as if he was puzzled.*

—"The Most Dangerous Game," p. 215

A **noun clause** is a subordinate clause that acts as a noun.

. . . I discovered *that the intoxication had worn off* . . .

—"The Cask of Amontillado," p. 60

Parallelism involves using similar grammatical structures to express similar ideas. Sentences with parallel structure contain repeated grammatical patterns or repeated types of phrases or clauses within a sentence.

Marguerite has a great love *for art, for children,* and *for teaching.*

The Four Principal Parts of Verbs

Tenses are formed from principal parts and helping verbs.

A verb has four **principal parts:** the present, the present participle, the past, and the past participle.

Pronoun Case The **case** of a pronoun is the form it takes to show its use in a sentence. There are three pronoun cases: nominative, objective, and possessive.

The **nominative case** is used to rename the subject of the sentence. The nominative case pronouns are *I, you, he, she, it, we, you, they.*

As the subject: *She* is brave.

Renaming the subject: The leader is *she.*

The **objective case** is used as the direct object, indirect object, or object of the preposition. The objective case pronouns are *me, you, him, her, us, you, them.*

As a direct object: Our manager praised her.

As an indirect object: Give him the new product.

As an object of the preposition: The coach gave pointers to me.

The **possessive case** is used to show ownership. The possessive pronouns are *my, you, his, her, its, our, their, mine, yours, his, hers, its, ours, theirs.*

Subject and Verb Agreement A singular verb must be used with a singular subject; a plural verb must be used with a plural subject.

Reegan is going home now.

Many *storms are* the cause of beach erosion.

In a sentence with combined singular and plural subjects, the verb should agree with the subject closest to it.

Either the *cats* or the *dog is* hungry.

Neither *Angie* nor her *sisters were* present.

Antecedents are the nouns (or the words that take the place of nouns) to which pronouns refer.

A personal pronoun must agree with its antecedent in number and gender. *Number* indicates whether a pronoun is singular or plural.

Some pronouns and nouns also indicate one of three *genders:* masculine, feminine, or neuter.

Use a singular personal pronoun to refer to two or more singular antecedents joined by *or* or *nor.*

Use a plural personal pronoun to refer to two or more antecedents joined by *and.*

Degrees of Comparison Most adjectives and adverbs have different forms to show degrees of comparison.

The three degrees of comparison are the *positive,* the *comparative,* and the *superlative.*

Use the comparative degree to compare two people, places, or things. Use the superlative degree to compare three or more people, places, or things.

Use *more* or *most* to form the comparative and superlative degrees of all modifiers with three or more syllables.

Memorize the irregular comparative and superlative forms of certain adjectives and adverbs.

The most commonly used irregular modifiers are listed in the following chart. Notice that some modifiers differ only in the positive degree. For instance, the modifiers *bad, badly,* and *ill* all have the same comparative and superlative forms (*worse, worst*).

Capitalization and Punctuation

Capitalization Capitalize the first word of a sentence and also the first word in a quotation if the quotation is a complete sentence.

I said to him, "My dear Fortunato, you are luckily met."

—"The Cask of Amontillado," p. 60

Capitalize all proper nouns and adjectives.

O. Henry Ganges River Great Wall of China

Capitalize a person's title when it is followed by the person's name or when it is used in direct address.

Madame Dr. Mitty General Zaroff

Capitalize titles showing family relationships when they refer to a specific person, unless they are preceded by a possessive noun or pronoun.

Uncle Marcos Granddaddy Cain

Capitalize the first word and all other key words in the titles of books, periodicals, poems, stories, plays, paintings, and other works of art.

Odyssey "I Wandered Lonely as a Cloud"

Punctuation

End Marks Use a **period** to end a declarative sentence, an imperative sentence, an indirect question, and most abbreviations.

Mr. Jabez Wilson laughed heavily.

—"The Red-headed League," p. 1166

Use a **question mark** to end a direct question, an incomplete question, or a statement that is intended as a question.

"What do you expect me to do with that?"

—"The Necklace," p. 332

Use an **exclamation mark** after a statement showing strong emotion, an urgent imperative sentence, or an interjection expressing strong emotion.

Free at last! Free at last!

Thank God almighty, we are Free at last!

—"I Have a Dream," p. 542

Commas Use a **comma** before the coordinating conjunction to separate two independent clauses in a compound sentence.

All at once . . . she came upon a superb diamond necklace, and her heart started beating with overwhelming desire.

—"The Necklace," p. 332

Use commas to separate three or more words, phrases, or clauses in a series.

My brothers and I would peer into the medicinal herb shop, watching old Li dole out onto a stiff sheet of white paper the right amount of insect shells, saffron-colored seeds, and pungent leaves for his ailing customers.

—"Rules of the Game," p. 316

Use commas to separate adjectives of equal rank. Do not use commas to separate adjectives that must stay in a specific order.

The big cottonwood tree stood apart from a small group of winterbare cottonwoods which grew in the wide, sandy arroyo.

—"The Man to Send Rain Clouds," p. 292

His present turned out to be a box of intricate plastic parts.

—"Rules of the Game," p. 316

Use a comma after an introductory word, phrase, or clause.

When Marvin was ten years old, his father took him through the long, echoing corridors . . .

—"If I Forget Thee, Oh Earth . . . ," p. 162

Use commas to set off parenthetical and nonessential expressions.

An evil place can, so to speak, broadcast vibrations of evil.

—"The Most Dangerous Game," p. 215

Use commas with places, dates, and titles.

Poe was raised in Richmond, Virginia.

On September 1, 1939, World War II began.

Dr. Martin Luther King, Jr., was born in 1929.

Use a comma to set off a direct quotation, to prevent a sentence from being misunderstood, and to indicate the omission of a common verb in a sentence with two or more clauses.

Michele said, "I'm going to the game tonight."

Faulty: She stifled the sob that rose to her lips and lay motionless.

Revised: She stifled the sob that rose to her lips, and lay motionless.

In the *Odyssey,* the Cyclops may symbolize brutishness; the Sirens, knowledge.

Semicolons Use a **semicolon** to join independent clauses that are not already joined by a conjunction.

The lights of cities sparkle; on nights when there was no moon, it was difficult for me to tell the Earth from the sky. . . .

—"Single Room, Earth View," p. 468

Use a semicolon to join independent clauses separated by either a conjunctive adverb or a transitional expression.

Edward Way Teale wrote nearly thirty books; moreover, he was also an artist and a naturalist.

Use semicolons to avoid confusion when independent clauses or items in a series already contain commas.

Unable to afford jewelry, she dressed simply; but she was as wretched as a *déclassée,* for women have neither caste nor breeding—in them beauty, grace, and charm replace pride of birth.

—"The Necklace," p. 332

Colons Use a **colon** in order to introduce a list of items following an independent clause.

The authors we are reading include a number of poets: Robert Frost, Lewis Carroll, and Emily Dickinson.

Use a colon to introduce a formal quotation.

I have a dream that one day this nation will rise up and live out the true meaning of its creed: "We hold these truths to be self-evident; . . ."

—"I Have a Dream," p. 542

Quotation Marks A **direct quotation** represents a person's exact speech or thoughts and is enclosed in quotation marks.

"This great nation will endure as it has endured, will revive and will prosper," said President Franklin D. Roosevelt.

—"First Inaugural Address," p. 552

GRAMMAR, USAGE, AND MECHANICS HANDBOOK

An **indirect quotation** reports only the general meaning of what a person said or thought and does not require quotation marks.

I went up to her, put my arms around her, and said something to her.

—from *A White House Diary,* p. 104

Always place a comma or a period inside the final quotation mark.

"There," he said, "there's something for you."

—"The Necklace," p. 332

Place a question mark or an exclamation mark inside the final quotation mark if the end mark is part of the quotation; if it is not part of the quotation, place it outside the final quotation mark.

"That pig will devour us, greedily!"

—"The Golden Kite, the Silver Wind," p. 396

Have you ever read the poem "Dreams"?

Use single quotation marks for a quotation within a quotation.

" 'But,' said I, 'there would be millions of red-headed men who would apply.' "

—"The Red-headed League," p. 1067

Use quotation marks around the titles of short written works, episodes in a series, songs, and titles of works mentioned as parts of a collection.

"I Hear America Singing"   "Pride"

Dashes Use **dashes** to indicate an abrupt change of thought, a dramatic interrupting idea, or a summary statement.

The streets were lined with people—lots and lots of people—the children all smiling, placards, confetti, people waving from windows.

—from *A White House Diary,* p. 104

Parentheses Use **parentheses** to set off asides and explanations only when the material is not essential or when it consists of one or more sentences.

One last happy moment I had was looking up and seeing Mary Griffith . . . (Mary for many years had been in charge of altering the clothes which I purchased) . . .

—from *A White House Diary,* p. 104

Hyphens Use a **hyphen** with certain numbers, after certain prefixes, with two or more words used as one word, and with a compound modifier coming before a noun.

seventy-six   Post-Modernist

Apostrophes Add an **apostrophe** and *-s* to show the possessive case of most singular nouns.

Thurmond's wife   the playwright's craft

Add an apostrophe to show the possessive case of plural nouns ending in *-s* and *-es.*

the sailors' ships   the Wattses' daughter

Add an apostrophe and *-s* to show the possessive case of plural nouns that do not end in *-s* or *-es.*

the children's games   the people's friend

Use an apostrophe in a contraction to indicate the position of the missing letter or letters.

You'll be lonely at first, they admitted, but you're so nice you'll make friends fast.

—"Checkouts," p. 82

Glossary of Common Usage

among, between: *Among* is usually used with three or more items. *Between* is generally used with only two items.

Among the poems we read this year, Margaret Walker's "Memory" was my favorite.

Mark Twain's "The Invalid's Story" includes a humorous encounter *between* the narrator and a character named Thompson.

around: In formal writing, *around* should not be used to mean *approximately* or *about.* These usages are allowable, however, in informal writing or in colloquial dialogue.

Shakespeare's *Romeo and Juliet* had its first performance in *approximately* 1595.

Shakespeare was *about* thirty when he wrote this play.

as, because, like, as to: The word *as* has several meanings and can function as several parts of speech. To avoid confusion, use *because* rather than *as* when you want to indicate cause and effect.

Because Cyril was interested in the history of African American poetry, he decided to write his report on Paul Laurence Dunbar.

Do not use the preposition *like* to introduce a clause that requires the conjunction as.

Dorothy Parker conversed *as* she wrote—wittily.

The use of *as to* for *about* is awkward and should be avoided.

Rosa has an interesting theory *about* E. E. Cummings's unusual typography in his poems.

Index of Skills

Boldface numbers indicate pages where terms are defined.

Literary Analysis

Reading

Reading Skills

Vocabulary

Word Origins (Etymology)

Writing

Writing Applications

Writing Strategies

Prewriting:

Drafting:

Revising:

Student Models:

Professional Models:

Writer's Toolbox:

Editing/Proofreading:

More Skills

Critical Thinking

Critical Viewing

LISTENING AND SPEAKING

Activities:

Steps/Tips:

Research and Technology

Activities:

INDEX OF SKILLS

Media Literacy

Index of Features

Boldface numbers indicate pages where terms are defined.

Literary Analysis Workshops

Literature in Context

Reading for Information

Vocabulary Workshop

Writing Workshop: Work in Progress

Index of Authors and Titles

Notes: Page numbers in *italics* refer to biographical information; nonfiction and informational text appear in red.

Acknowledgments

Grateful acknowledgment is made to the following for copyrighted material:

The Academy of American Poets "Pablo Neruda Poetfans" by Alberto Meza from *http://poets.org/viewmedia.php/prmMID/19607.* "Emily Dickinson Poetfans" by Sharyn Moore from *http://poets.org/viewmedia.php/prmMID/19605.* Copyright © 1997-2007 by The Academy of American Poets. Used by permission of the Academy of American Poets.

American Broadcasting Companies, Inc. "No. 42 Jackie Robinson" by John Nadel from *http://abcnews.go.com/Sports/wireStory?id=3044174.* Copyright © 2007 ABCNews Internet Ventures. Used courtesy of ABC News.

Arte Publico Press, Inc. "A Voice" by Pat Mora from *Communion* by Pat Mora. Copyright © 1991 Arte Publico Press—University of Houston. Used by permission of the publisher.

Ballantine Books "New Road Chicken Pies" from *The Book Lover's Cookbook* by Shaunda Kennedy Wenger and Janet Kay Jensen. Copyright © 2003 by Shaunda Kennedy Wenger and Janet Kay Jensen. Used by permission of Ballantine Books, a division of Random House, Inc.

Bantam Doubleday Dell Publishing "Tell Me a Riddle" by Tillie Olsen from *Delta Book, Doubleday.* "Things Fall Apart" by Chinua Achebe from *Anchor Books, Doubleday.* All rights reserved.

Susan Bergholz Literary Services "Twister Hits Houston" from *My Wicked Wicked Ways* by Sandra Cisneros. Copyright © 1987 by Sandra Cisneros. Published by Third Woman Press and in hardcover by Alfred A. Knopf. From *A Celebration of Grandfathers* by Rudolfo Anaya. Copyright © 1983 by Rudolfo Anaya. First published in New Mexico Magazine, March 1983. "My English" by Julia Alvarez from *Something to Declare* by Julia Alvarez. Published by Plume, an imprint of Penguin Group (USA), in 1999 and originally in hardcover by Algonquin Books of Chapel Hill. Copyright © 1998 by Julia Alvarez. Used by permission of Third Woman Press and Susan Bergholz Literary Services, New York, NY and Lamy, NM. All rights reserved.

Gary I. Blackwood From *The Shakespeare Stealer* by Gary I. Blackwood. Copyright © 2003 by Gary I. Blackwood. Used by permission of the author.

Tyroneca Booker "The Day of the Storm" by Ty Booker from *Katrina, In Their Own Words* edited by Richard Louth. All works copyrighted © 2006 by the individual authors. Southeastern Louisiana Writing Project, Publisher. Southeastern Louisiana University, Hammond, Louisiana, 70402. Used by permission of Tyroneca Booker.

Georges Borchardt, Inc. "The Glass Menagerie" by Tennessee Williams. Copyright © 1945, renewed 1973 by The University of the South. Reprinted by permission.

Brandt & Hochman Literary Agents, Inc. "The Most Dangerous Game" from *The Most Dangerous Game* by Richard Connell. Copyright © 1924 by Richard Connell. Copyright renewed © 1952 by Louise Fox Connell. "Sonata For Harp and Bicycle" from *The Green Flash and Other Tales of Horror* by Joan Aiken. Copyright © 1957, 1958, 1959, 1960, 1965, 1968, 1969, 1971 by Joan Aiken. Used by permission of Brandt & Hochman Literary Agents, Inc. Any copying or redistribution of the text is expressly forbidden.

Curtis Brown, Ltd. "Uncoiling" by Pat Mora. First appeared in *Daughters of the Fifth Sun*, published by Riverhead Press. Copyright © 1995. Used by permission of Curtis Brown, Ltd.

The Bukowski Agency "The Jade Peony" by Wayson Choy. First published in the *UBC Alumni Chronicle*, Vol. 34, No. 4, Winter 1979. Copyright by Wayson Choy 1977. The novel The Jade Peony, based on this story, is published in the United States by The Other Press. Used by permission of The Bukowski Agency.

California State Parks Railtown 1897 State Historic Park, Filming on Location: The Movie Railroad from *www.csrmf.org/railtown/doc.asp?id=13.* Copyright © 2001 California State Railroad Museum Foundation. All rights reserved. Used by permission of California State Parks.

Jonathan Clowes Ltd. "The Red-headed League" from *The Adventures of Sherlock Holmes* by Sir Arthur Conan Doyle. Copyright © 1996 Sir Arthur Conan Doyle Copyright Holders. Used by kind permission of Jonathan Clowes Ltd., London, on behalf of Andrea Plunket, the Administrator of the Sir Arthur Conan Doyle Copyrights.

Don Congdon Associates, Inc. "The Golden Kite, the Silver Wind" by Ray Bradbury from *Epoch*, February 1953. Copyright © 1953 by Epoch Associates; renewed 1981 by Ray Bradbury. Used by permission of Don Congdon Associates, Inc.

Catherine Costello "There is No Word For Goodbye" by Mary Tall Mountain from *There Is No Word for Goodbye: Poems by Mary Tall Mountain.* Copyright © 1994 by Tall Mountain Estate. Used by permission of Catherine Costello. All rights reserved.

Dell Publishing, a div of Random House, Inc. From *The Giant's House* by Elizabeth McCracken, copyright © 1996 by Elizabeth McCracken. Used by permission of The Dial Press/Dell Publishing, a division of Random House, Inc.

Dunow Carlson Lerner Agency "Desiderata" by Elizabeth McCracken from *http://www.randomhouse.com/boldtype/0397/mccracken/.* Copyright © 1996 by Elizabeth McCracken. Used by permission of Dunow Carlson Lerner Agency.

Stephen Edwards "Rock Climbing Equipment and Techniques" by Stephen Edwards from *http://alumnus.caltech.edu/~sedwards/climbing/techniques.html.* Used by permission of Stephen Edwards.

eSchool News "Georgia School Displays iPod Ingenuity" by eSchool News Staff and wire service reports from *http://www.eschoolnews.com/news/showStory.cfm?ArticleID=6211.* Copyright © 2007 eSchool News. All rights reserved. Used by permission of eSchool News.

Faber and Faber Limited "The Horses" by Edwin Muir from *Collected Poems by Edwin Muir*, copyright © 1960 by Willa Muir. "Macavity: The Mystery Cat" by T. S. Eliot from *Old Possum's Book of Practical Cats* by T. S. Eliot. Copyright © 1939 by T. S. Eliot and renewed 1967 by Esme Valerie Eliot. Used by permission of Faber and Faber Limited.

Farrar, Straus & Giroux, LLC "Prologue and Epilogue" by Derek Walcott from *The Odyssey: A Stage Version* by Derek Walcott. Copyright © 1993 by Derek Walcott. "The Washwoman" by Isaac Bashevis Singer from *A Day of Pleasure* by Isaac Bachevis Singer. Copyright © 1969 by Isaac Bashevis Singer. "Part 1: The Adventures of Odysseus" and "Part 2: The Return of Odysseus" from *The Odyssey* by Homer, translated by Robert Fitzgerald. Copyright © 1961, 1963 by Robert Fitzgerald. Copyright renewed 1989 by Benedict r. C. Fitzgerald, on behalf of the Fitzgerald children. Used with permission of Farrar, Straus and Giroux, LLC.

Florida Railroad Museum, Inc. Florida Gulf Coast Railroad Museum from *www.frrm.org/information.html*. Copyright © 2006 Florida Railroad Museum, Inc. Used by permission of Florida Railroad Museum, Inc.

Fresno State University Communications "iPods Join Educational Toolkit at Fresno State" by Megan Jacobsen from FresnoStateNews January 17, 2007, *www.fresnostatenews.com/2007/01/podcasts.htm*. Used courtesy of FresnoStateNews.com.

Professor Anthony I. Gooch From *Cassell's Spanish-English English-Spanish Dictionary* by Anthony Gooch and Angel Garcia de Paredes. Copyright © 1978 by Macmillan Publishing Company, a division of Macmillan, Inc. Used by permission of Professor Anthony I. Gooch.

Graywolf Press "Fifteen" from *The Way It Is: New and Selected Poems* by William Stafford. Copyright © 1966, 1998 by the Estate of William Stafford. Used by permission of Graywolf Press, Saint Paul, MN.

Harcourt Education Limited "The Girl Who Can" by Ama Ata Aidoo from *Opening Spaces: An Anthology of Contemporary African Women's Writing*, edited by Yvonne Vera. Used by permission of Harcourt Education.

Harcourt, Inc. "The Writer" from *The Mind-Reader* by Richard Wilbur. Copyright © 1971 by Richard Wilbur. "Women" by Alice Walker from *Revolutionary Petunias & Other Poems*, copyright © 1970 and renewed 1998 by Alice Walker. From *A Lincoln Preface*, copyright 1953 by Carl Sandburg and renewed 1981 by Margaret Sandburg, Janet Sandburg, and Helga Sandburg Crile. "Macavity: The Mystery Cat" from *Old Possum's Book of Practical Cats* by T. S. Eliot. Copyright 1939 by T. S. Eliot and renewed 1967 by Esme Valerie Eliot. "Ithaca" by Constantine Cavafy from *The Complete Poems of Cavafy*. English translation copyright © 1961 and renewed 1989 by Rae Dalven. Used by permission of Harcourt, Inc. This material may not be reproduced in any form or by any means without the prior written permission of the publisher.

HarperCollins Publishers, Inc. "Summer" from *Brown Angels: An Album of Pictures and Verse* by Walter Dean Myers. Copyright © 1993 by Walter Dean Myers. Used by permission of HarperCollins Publishers.

Harvard University Press "Much madness is divinest sense" from *The Poems of Emily Dickinson*, Thomas H. Johnson, ed., Cambridge, Mass.: The Belknap Press of Harvard University Press, Copyright © 1951, 1955, 1979, 1983 by the President and Fellows of Harvard College. Used by permission of the publishers and the Trustees of Amherst College. Reprinted by permission of the publishers and the Trustees of Amherst College from *The Poems of Emily Dickinson*, Thomas H. Johnson, ed., Cambridge, Mass.: The Belknap Press of Harvard University Press, Copyright (c) 1951, 1955, 1979, 1983 by the President and Fellows of Harvard College.

Hawaiian Lifeguard Association "Beach and Ocean Safety Signs" by Staff from *www.aloha.com*. Copyright © 1986, 2001 Hawaiian Lifeguard Association. All rights (and lefts) reserved. Used with permission.

David Hilbun "Hope" by David Hilbun from *Katrina, In Their Own Words* edited by Richard Louth. All works copyrighted © 2006 by the individual authors. Southeastern Louisiana Writing Project, Publisher. Southeastern Louisiana University, Hammond, Louisiana, 70402. Used by permission of David Hilbun.

Helmut Hirnschall "There is a Longing . . ." by Chief Dan George & Helmut Hirnschall from *My Heart Soars*. Copyright © 1974 by Chief Dan George and Helmut Hirnschall. Used by permission of Helmut Hirnschall.

The Barbara Hogenson Agency, Inc. "The Secret Life of Walter Mitty" by James Thurber from *My World-And Welcome To It*. Copyright © 1942 by James Thurber. Copyright © renewed 1970 by Rosemary A. Thurber. Used by permission from The Barbara Hogenson Agency, Inc.

Henry Holt and Company, Inc. "Talk" by Harold Courlander and George Herzog from *The Cow-Tail Switch and Other West African Stories* by Harold Courlander and George Herzog, © 1947, 1974 by Harold Courlander. "Fire and Ice" by Robert Frost from *The Poetry of Robert Frost*, edited by Edward Connery Lathem. Copyright © 1951 by Robert Frost. Used by permission of Henry Holt and Company, LLC.

Houghton Mifflin Company, Inc. "Siren Song" from *Selected Poems, 1965-1975* by Margaret Atwood. Copyright © 1976 by Margaret Atwood. Excerpt from "A Fable for Tomorrow" from *Silent Spring* by Rachel Carson. Copyright © 1962 by Rachel I. Carson, renewed 1990 by Roger Christie. "All Watched Over by Machines of Loving Grace" from *The Pill Versus the Springhill Mine Disaster* by Richard Brautigan. Copyright © 1968 by Richard Brautigan. Used by permission of Houghton Mifflin Company. All rights reserved.

HowStuffWorks, Inc. "How Podcasting Works" by Stephanie Watson from *http://computer.howstuffworks.com/podcasting.htm*. Copyright © 1998-2007 HowStuffWorks, Inc. Courtesy of How Stuff Works.com.

James r. Hurst "The Scarlet Ibis" by James Hurst, published in *The Atlantic Monthly*, July 1960. Copyright © 1988 by James Hurst. Used by permission of the author.

International Creative Management, Inc. "Libraries Face Sad Chapter" by Pete Hamill from *www.petehamill.com*. Copyright © 2002 by Pete Hamill. Used by permission of International Creative Management, Inc.

Japan Publications, Inc. "Temple bells die out" by Basho; and "Dragonfly catcher" and "Bearing no flowers" by Chiyojo, translated by Daniel C. Buchanan, from *One Hundred Famous Haiku* by Daniel C. Buchanan. Copyright © 1973 by Japan Publications. Used by permission of Japan Publications, Inc.

Lyndon b. Johnson Library From *A White House Diary* by Lady Bird Johnson. Used with permission of the Lyndon b. Johnson Library.

The Estate of Dr. Martin Luther King, Jr. c/o Writer's House LLC "I Have a Dream" by Dr. Martin Luther King, Jr. from *The Words Of Martin Luther King, Jr.* Copyright © 1963 Martin Luther King Jr., copyright renewed © 1991 Coretta Scott King. Used by arrangement with The Heirs to the Estate of Martin Luther King Jr., c/o Writers House as agent for the proprietor New York, NY.

Alfred A. Knopf, a division of Random House, Inc. "Pecos Bill: The Cyclone" from *Pecos Bill: Texas Cowpuncher* by Harold W. Felton, illustrated by Aldren A. Watson, copyright © 1949 by Alfred A. Knopf, a division of Random House, Inc. Copyright © renewed 1976 by Harold W. Felton. "Dreams" from *The Collected Poems of Langston Hughes* by Langston Hughes. Copyright © 1994 by The Estate of Langston Hughes. "The News" from *Conscientious Objections* by Neil Postman, copyright © 1988 by Neil Postman. "Dream Deferred" from *The Collected Poems of Langston Hughes* by Langston Hughes. Copyright © 1994 by The Estate of Langston Hughes. "Uncle Marcos" by Isabel Allende, translated by Magda Bogin, from *The House of the Spirits* by Isabel Allende, copyright © 1985 by Alfred A. Knopf, a division of Random House, Inc. Used by permisson of Alfred A. Knopf, a division of Random House, Inc.

Learned Hand "I Am An American Day" address by Learned Hand. New York City, May 21, 1944.

Liberty Travel, Inc. "Italy Travel Guide" from *Liberty Travel Brochure.* Copyright © 2006 Liberty Travel, Inc. Used by permission of Liberty Travel, Inc.

Little, Brown and Company, Inc. "Pyramus and Thisbe" and "Perseus" from *Mythology* by Edith Hamilton. Copyright © 1942 by Edith Hamilton; Copyright © renewed 1969 by Dorian Fielding Reid and Doris Fielding Reid. Used by permission of Little Brown & Company.

Liveright Publishing Corporation "maggie and milly and molly and may" by E. E. Cummings from *Complete Poems, 1904-1962* by E.E. Cummings, edited by George J. Frimage. Copyright © 1956, 1984, 1991 by the Trustees for the E. E. Cummings Trust. Used by permission of Liveright Publishing Corporation.

Andrew MacAndrew "The Necklace" by Guy de Maupassant, translated by Andrew MacAndrew, from *Boule de Suif and Selected Stories* by Guy de Maupassant, New York, NAL, 1964, pp. 143-151. Translation copyright © 1964 by Andrew MacAndrew. Used by permission of Marie-Christine MacAndrew.

Massachusetts Institute of Technology "Team Builds 'Sociable' Robot" by Elizabeth A. Thomson from *Massachusetts Institute of Technology News Office February 14, 2001, http://web.mit.edu/news-office/2001/kismet-0214.html.* Copyright © 2001. Used by permission of MIT News Office.

John McPhee "Arthur Ashe Remembered" by John McPhee, first published in *The New Yorker*, March 1, 1993. Used by permission of the author.

Methuen Publishing, Ltd. "The Inspector-General" from *The Sneeze: Plays and Stories* by Anton Chekhov, translated and adapted by Michael Frayn, published by Methuen Drama. Originally from An Awl in a Sack by Anton Chekhov, 1885. Used by permission of Methuen Publishing, Ltd.

Edna St. Vincent Millay Society "An Ancient Gesture" by Edna St. Vincent Millay from *Collected Poems*, HarperCollins. Copyright © 1954, 1982 by Norma Millay Ellis. All rights reserved. Used by permission of Elizabeth Barnett, literary executor.

NASA Johnson Space Center "Space Shuttle Basics" by Staff from *www.nasa.gov.* "Launch Schedule 101/ NASA's Shuttle and Rocket Missions" from *www.nasa.gov/missions/highlights/schedule101.html.* "Robotics Education Project" by Staff from *http://robotics.arc.nasa.gov/.* Copyright © National Aeronautics and Space Administration.

Charles Neider "The Invalid's Story" by Mark Twain from *The Complete Sketches and Tales of Mark Twain*, edited by Charles Neider: Copyright © 1977 by Charles Neider. Used by permission of Charles Neider.

The New York Times Syndication Sales Corp. Headquarters "World Trade Center Movie Review" by Rebecca Murray from *http://movies.about.com/od/worldtradecenter/fr/wtcreview080806.htm.* Copyright © 2007 by Rebecca Murray. Used with permission of About, Inc., a part of The New York Times Company. All rights reserved.

NJ TRANSIT Port Jervis & Pascack Valley Lines from *MTA Train Schedule: Metro-North Railroad.* Copyright © 2006 NJ Transit. Used by permission of NJ TRANSIt.

Northwestern University Press "Sonnets on Love XIII" from *Sonnets on Love and Death* by Jean de Sponde translated by David r. Slavitt. English translation copyright © 2001 by David r. Slavitt. Published 2001. Evanston: Northwestern University Press, 2001. Used by permission of Northwestern University Press. All rights reserved. http://www.nupress.northwester.edu.

W. W. Norton & Company, Inc. "The War Against the Trees" from *The Collected Poems* by Stanley Kunitz. Copyright © 2000 by Stanley Kunitz. Used by permission of W.W. Norton & Company, Inc.

Naomi Shihab Nye "Daily" by Naomi Shihab Nye from *Hugging The Jukebox* by Naomi Shihab Nye. Copyright © 1982 All rights reserved. Used by permission of the author.

Orchard Books, an imprint of Scholastic Inc. "Checkouts" adapted from *A Couple of Kooks and Other Stories About Love* by Cynthia Rylant. Published by Scholastic Inc./Orchard Books. Copyright © 1990 by Cynthia Rylant. Used by permission of Scholastic, Inc.

Oxford University Press, Canada "Siren Song" by Margaret Atwood from *Selected Poems 1966-1984.* Copyright © Margaret Atwood 1990. Used by permission of Oxford University Press Canada.

Oxford University Press, Inc. "The Horses" by Edwin Muir from *Collected Poems* by Edwin Muir. Copyright © 1960 by Willa Muir. Used by permission of Oxford University Press, Inc.

Penguin Group (USA) Inc. & Wallace Literary Agency, Inc. "Rama and Ravana in Battle," from *The Ramayana* by R.K. Narayan, copyright © 1972 by R.K. Narayan. Used by permission.

The Penguin Press "Play Hard; Play Together; Play Smart" by Dean Smith and Gerald D. Bell with John Kilgo from *The Carolina Way: Leadership Lessons From A Life In Coaching.* Copyright © 2004 by Dean E. Smith. Used by permission of The Penguin Press, a division of Penguin Group (USA) Inc.

Playbill Magazine "On Summer" by Lorraine Hansberry, reprinted from *Playbill Magazine*, June 1960. Copyright © Playbill, Inc. All rights reserved. Used by permission of Playbill, Inc.

Portfolio (A Penguin Company) "The Only Thing We Have to Fear" from *Nothing to Fear: Lessons in Leadership from FDR*, by Alan Axelrod. Copyright © 2003 by Alan Axelrod. Used by permission of Portfolio, an imprint of Penguin Group (USA) Inc.

G.P. Putnam Sons From "Rules of the Game" from *The Joy Luck Club* by Amy Tan. Copyright © 1989 by Amy Tan. Used by permission of G.P. Putnam Sons, a division of Penguin Putnam, Inc.

Random House Group, Ltd. & Simon & Schuster, Inc. "Blues Ain't No Mockin Bird" from *Gorilla, My Love* by Toni Cade Bambara. Copyright © 1971 by Toni Cade Bambara. "New Directions" from *Wouldn't Take Nothing For My Journey Now* by Maya Angelou. Copyright © 1993 by Maya Angelou. Used by permission of Random House, Inc. From *The Complete Short Stories of Ernest Hemingway* by Ernest Hemingway. Copyright renewed © 1966 by Mary Hemingway. All rights reserved.

Dr. Sally K. Ride c/o The Washington Speakers Bureau "Single Room, Earth View" by Sally Ride, published in the April/May 1986 issue of *Air & Space/Smithsonian Magazine*, published by The Smithsonian Institution. Used by permission of Dr. Sally K. Ride.

Riverhead Books "Carry Your Own Skis" by Lian Dolan, from *Satellite Sisters' Uncommon Sense* by Julie, Liz & Sheila Dolan and Monica & Lian Dolan. Copyright © 2001 by Satellite Sisters LLC. Used by permission of Riverhead Books, an imprint of Penguin Group (USA) Inc.

Scovil Chichak Galen Literary Agency, Inc. "If I Forget Thee, Oh Earth…" from *Expedition to Earth* by Arthur C. Clarke. Copyright © 1953, 1970 by Arthur C. Clarke; Copyright 1951 by Columbia Publications, Inc. Used by permission of the author and the author's agents, Scovil Chichak Galen Literary Agency, Inc.

Southeastern Railway Museum Southeastern Railway Museum: Georgia's Official Transportation History Museum from *www.srm-duluth.org/Exhibits/diesel.htm.* Copyright © 1997-2006 Southeastern Railway Museum. All Rights Reserved. Used by permission of Southeastern Railway Museum.

St. Petersburg Times "New iPod mix: Jay-Z, Beyonce, Econ Lecture" by Shannon Colavecchio-Van Sickler from *http://www.sptimes.com/2006/08/05/Tampabay/New_iPod_mix__Jay_Z__.shtml.* Copyright © 2007 St. Petersburg Times. All rights reserved. Used by permission of St. Petersburg Times.

The State of Florida, Department of Management Services State of Florida Job Application from *www.myflorida.com/dms/hrm/jobsdirect/app.pdf.* Copyright © The State of Florida, Department of Management Services. Used by permission of The State of Florida, Department of Management Services.

State Personnel Administration State of Georgia Application for Employment from *www.psc.state.ga.us/jobopenings/stateapp.doc.* Copyright © 1999 by the Georgia Merit System. Used by permission of the State Personnel Administration (formerly the Georgia Merit System).

The Supreme Court of Ohio "A Hero in Our Midst" by Justice Paul E. Pfeifer from *www.sconet.state.oh.us/Justices/pfeifer/column/2006/jp091306.asp.* Copyright © 2006 The Supreme Court of Ohio. Used by permission of The Supreme Court of Ohio.

Literary Estate of May Swenson "Analysis of Baseball" by May Swenson from *American Sports Poems* by r.r. Knudson and May Swenson. Copyright © 1989. Orchard Press. Used with permission of The Literary Estate of May Swenson.

University of California, Davis "Poultry Fact Sheet No. 35: Incubating Eggs in Small Quantities" by Ursula K. Abbott, Ralph A. Ernst, and Francine A. Bradley from *http://animalscience.ucdavis.edu/Avian/pubs.htm.* Used by permission of University of California, Davis.

The University of Georgia Press "American History" from *The Latin Deli: Prose and Poetry* by Judith Ortiz Cofer. Copyright © 1992 by Judith Ortiz Cofer. Used by permission of The University of Georgia Press.

University Press of New England "The Talk" by Gary Soto from *A Summer Life* by Gary Soto. Copyright © 1990 by University Press of New England, Hanover, NH. Reprinted with permission.

Viking Penguin, Inc. "Old Man of the Temple" from *Under The Banyan Tree* by r. K. Narayan. Copyright © 1985 by r. K. Narayan. Used by permission of Viking Penguin, a division of Penguin Group (USA) Inc.

Villard Books From *Big Kiss* by Henry Alford, copyright © 2000 by Henry Alford. Used by permission of Villard Books, a division of Random House, Inc.

Vital Speeches of the Day "Glory and Hope" by Nelson Mandela, from *Vital Speeches of the Day*, June 1, 1994. Used by permission of Vital Speeches of the Day.

Wesleyan University Press "Slam, Dunk, & Hook" from *Magic City* by Yusef Komunyakaa. Copyright © 1992 by Yusef Komunyakaa. Used by permission of Wesleyan University Press.

Wikipedia.org "Hurricanes" retrieved from *http://en.wikipedia.org/wiki/Hurricane accessed on 07/23/07.* "Earthquakes" retrieved from http:*//en.wikipedia.org/wiki/Earthquake accessed on 07/23/07.* "Wikipedia: Verifiability" retrieved from *http://en.wikipedia.org accessed on 07/23/07.*

Writer's House, LLC "Meciendo" by Gabriela Mistral ("Rocking"), translated by Doris Dana from *Selected Poems Of Gabriela Mistral*, translated and edited by Doris Dana. Copyright © 1961, 1964, 1970, 1971 by Doris Dana. Used by permission of Writer's House, LLC.

The Wylie Agency, Inc. "The Man to Send Rain Clouds" from *Storyteller* by Leslie Marmon Silko. Copyright © 1981 by Leslie Marmon Silko. Used by permission of The Wylie Agency, Inc.

Note: Every effort has been made to locate the copyright owner of material reproduced on this component. Omissions brought to our attention will be corrected in subsequent editions.

Credits

Photo Credits

xii–xiii: Sean Davey/CORBIS; **xiv–xv:** Sean Davey/CORBIS; **xvi–xvii:** Images.com/CORBIS; **xviii–xix:** Images.com/CORBIS; **xx–xxi:** Images.com/CORBIS; **xxii–xxiii:** Images.com/CORBIS; **xxvi–xxvii:** © Diana Ong/SuperStock; **xxviii–xxix:** Nice One Productions/CORBIS; **xxx–xxxi:** Nice One Productions/CORBIS; **xlviii** Thomas Owen Jenkins/Shutterstock; **Gr09 U1** **1:** © Catherine Cabrol/Kipa/CORBIS; **2:** © Dave Cutler/Images.com; **3:** © Johner/ Johner Images/ Getty Images; **5:** Images.com/CORBIS; **6:** CALVIN AND HOBBES © 1994 Watterson. Reprinted with permission of UNIVERSAL PRESS SYNDICATE. All rights reserved.; **9:** Alberto Giacometti, *Man Pointing,* 1947. Bronze, 70 1/2 x 40 3/4 x 16 3/8". The Museum of Modern Art/Licensed by Scala-Art Resource, NY. Gift of Mrs. John D. Rockefeller 3rd. © 2004 Artists Rights Society (ARS), New York/ADAGP, Paris.; **10:** © Lisa Haney /Images.com; **12:** Christooph Wilhelm/Getty Images; **13:** © Bob Winsett/CORBIS; **15:** *Library,* 2003 (acrylic on wood), Crook, P.J. (b. 1945) /Private Collection, /The Bridgeman Art Library International; **17:** Michael S. Lewis/CORBIS; **17:** bkgrnd. Nick Belton/ istockphoto.com; **18:** Maria Ferrari/SuperStock; **18–19:** bkgrnd. Nick Belton/ istockphoto.com; **20:** akg-images; **20:** bkgrnd. Nick Belton/ istockphoto.com; **25:** t. Robert Maass/CORBIS; **25:** b. Lee Snider/CORBIS; **26:** *The Oldest Inhabitant,* 1876, Julian Alden Weir, oil on canvas, 65 1/2 x 32" Signed, upper left. Butler Institute of American Art, Youngstown, Ohio; **26:** bkgrnd. Lee Snider/CORBIS; **29:** Erich Lessing/Art Resource, NY; **30:** The Washerwomen, from the 'Tableau de Paris' series, engraved by C. Motte, c.1830–40 (colour litho), Delarue, Fortune (b. 1794) (after)/Musee de la Ville de Paris, Musee Carnavalet, Paris, France, Archives Charmet/The Bridgeman Art Library International; **31:** Lee Snider/CORBIS; **32:** *The Oldest Inhabitant* (detail), 1876, Julian Alden Weir, oil on canvas, 65 1/2 x 32" Signed, upper left. Butler Institute of American Art, Youngstown, Ohio; **35:** t. Getty Images; **35:** b. © Ashok Rodrigues/istockphoto.com; **36:** t. istockphoto.com; **36:** b. © Ashok Rodrigues/istockphoto.com; **37:** CORBIS; **48:** Royalty Free © Vladimir Piskunov/Dreamtime.com; **49:** John Heseltine/© Dorling Kindersley; **49:** bkgrnd. istockphoto.com; **50:** Canberra Bicycle Museum and Resource Centre, Australia; **52:** © Dorling Kindersley; **54:** Royalty Free/ PhotoDisc/ Getty Images; **55:** tl. © Dorling Kindersley; **55:** tr. istockphoto.com; **55:** b. Canberra Bicycle Museum and Resource Centre, Australia; **56:** rt. istockphoto.com; **56:** tl. Royalty Free/ C Squared Studios/PhotoDisc/Getty Images; **56:** rb. istockphoto.com; **59:** t. Bettmann/CORBIS; **60–61:** © Held Collection/The Bridgeman Art Library International; **62:** istockphoto.com; **62–63:** border. istockphoto.com; **64:** RF Digital Vision/ Getty Images; **64–65:** border. istockphoto.com; **66:** t. istockphoto.com; **66:** b. istockphoto.com; **67:** l. © Holton Collection/SuperStock; **67:** r. istockphoto.com; **68:** l. istockphoto.com; **68:** r. istockphoto.com; **75:** Barnabas Kindersley/© Dorling Kindersley; **76:** © Foodfolio/ Image State/ Jupiter Images; **77:** t. © GK Hart/Vikki Hart/ Getty Images; **77:** b. © Peter Kubal/Photographers Direct; **78:** t. © GK Hart/Vikki Hart/ Getty Images; **78:** b. © C.Fleurent/ photocuisine/ CORBIS; **81:** b. Ama Ata Aidoo; **82–83:** istockphoto.com; **84:** istockphoto.com; **85:** RF © Tim Jones/ Digital Vision/ Getty Images; **86:** © Ron Giling/Peter Arnold, Inc.; **88:** © Ron Giling/Peter Arnold, Inc.; **90:** Barnabas Kindersley/© Dorling Kindersley; **91:** l. Corel Professional Photos CD-ROM™; **91:** r. Corel Professional Photos CD-ROM™; **92:** © Ron Giling/Peter Arnold, Inc.; **103:** © Archive Photos; **104:** Bettmann/CORBIS; **104:** bkgrnd. istockphoto.com; **105:** l. Art Rickerby/Time & Life Pictures/Getty Images; **105:** m. © CORBIS; **105:** r. © Bettmann/ CORBIS; **106:** tl. Audio Visual Archives at the John F. Kennedy Library; **106:** tm. istockphoto.com; **106:** tr. CORBIS Sygma; **106:** m. Courtesy of The Peace Corps; **106:** b. Bettmann/CORBIS; **107:** l. © Randy Faris/ CORBIS; **107:** m. © Bettmann/CORBIS; **107:** r. © Bettmann/ CORBIS; **108:** t. Loretta Hostettler/istockphoto.com; **108:** bl. Art Rickerby/ Time & Life Pictures/Getty Images; **108:** bm. Bettmann/CORBIS; **108:** br. © Wally McNamee/CORBIS; **109:** l. Bettmann/CORBIS; **109:** m. Keystone/ Hulton Archive/ Getty images; **109:** r. Lisa Svara/istockphoto.com; **110:** istockphoto.com; **113:** Copyright© by Julia Alvarez/Bill Eichner. Reprinted by permission of Susan Bergholz Literary Services, NY. All Rights reserved.; **114:** t. istockphoto.com; **114:** b. RF Terry Vine/Blend Images/Getty Images; **114–115:** istockphoto.com; **116:** RF Medioimages/Photodisc/Getty Images; **119:** l. istockphoto.com; **119:** r. RF George Marks/Retrofile/Getty Images; **120:** RF Terry Vine/Blend Images/Getty Images; **127:** CORBIS; **128–129:** istockphoto.com; **129:** istockphoto.com; **130:** © Ufuk Zivana/ istockphoto.com; **131:** l. RF Tetra Images/Getty Images; **131:** r. RF Joshua Ets-Hokin/ PhotoDisc/Getty Images; **132:** l. Hulton-Deutsch/CORBIS; **132:** r. Comstock Select/CORBIS; **132:** inset. RF Rubberball/ Getty Images; **133:** RF Joshua Ets-Hokin/ PhotoDisc/Getty Images; **134:** istockphoto.com; **137:** t. AFP/Getty Images; **137:** m. RF © Brownie Harris/CORBIS; **137:** b. RF PhotoDisc/Jules Frazier/ Getty Images; **138:** Images.com/CORBIS; **139:** RF© Tom Grill/ CORBIS; **140:** istockphoto.com; **141:** istockphoto.com; **142:** Bettmann/CORBIS; **142–143:** istockphoto.com; **145:** Bettmann/CORBIS; **147:** l. RF © Brownie Harris/ CORBIS; **147:** r. RF PhotoDisc/ Jules Frazier/Getty Images; **148:** Images.com/CORBIS; **156:** Courtesy of NJ Transit; **157:** l. istockphoto.com; **157:** r. istockphoto.com; **157:** br. © Ted Streshinsky/ CORBIS; **157:** istockphoto.com; **157:** t. courtesy of the Florida Railroad Museum; **157:** t. Randy Mayes/ istockphoto.com; **158:** mr. © NRM/SSPL/The Image Works; **158:** br. © Wolfgang Kaehler/CORBIS; **158:** istockphoto.com; **158:** mr. courtesy of SouthEastern Railway Museum; **158:** b. courtesy of SouthEastern Railway Museum; **161:** t. AP/Wide World Photos; **161:** b. Photofest; **162:** NASA; **164:** t. NASA; **164:** b. NASA; **165:** © RF - ER Productions; **166:** © RF - Natphotos/DigitalVisions/ Getty Images; **167:** © Momatiuk - Eastcott/ CORBIS; **168–169:** © Ed Freeman/Stone/Getty Images; **175:** Prentice Hall; **182:** © Michael Newman/Photo Edit; **190** (CL) ©Sophie Bassouls/Sygma/Corbis, (BR) ©The Granger Collection, NY, (TR) Getty Images **Gr09 U2** **192–193:** Sean Davey/ CORBIS; **194:** Associated Press; **197:** © Images.com/CORBIS; **198:** www.CartoonStock.com; **199:** 20th Century Fox/Photofest; **201:** © David Forbert/SuperStock; **201:** border. istockphoto.com; **202:** © Andrew Gunners/ Digital Vision/ Getty Images; **206:** Pearson Education/PH School Division; **208:** Alan Carey/Photo Researchers, Inc.; **213:** t. The New York Times/Redux Pictures; **221:** Sovfoto/Eastfoto; **233:** bkgrnd. Hulton Archive/Getty Images Inc.; **233:** t. Getty Images; **233:** m. The Imperial War Museum London; **233:** b. Jane Burton/© Dorling Kindersley; **239:** Miriam Berkely/Authorpix; **240:** Ralph Fasanella, "Sunday Afternoon - Stickball Game" (1953). 40 X 36, oil on canvas. Courtesy A.C.A. Galleries, N.Y.; **249:** CORBIS; **252:** Robert Harding World Imagery; **259:** t. Bettmann/CORBIS; **259:** b. Corel Professional Photos CD-ROM™; **260:** © Christie's Images; **262:** *Hairdresser's Window,* 1907, John Sloan, oil on canvas, 1947.240, Wadsworth Atheneum, Hartford, Ct. The Ella Gallup Sumner and Mary Catlin Sumner Collection Fund; **263:** Corel Professional Photos CD-ROM™; **269:** t. E.O. Hoppe/Stringer/Time Life Pictures/Getty Images; **269:** b. © Ingram Publishing/SuperStock; **270–271:** © Ghislain & Marie David de Lossy/ Getty Images; **272:** © Mel Curtis/ Stockbyte/ Getty Images; **273:** © PhotoAlto/Ale Ventura/ Getty Images; **274–275:** © Ken Redding/CORBIS; **276:** © Ingram Publishing/SuperStock; **285:** istockphoto.com; **287:** © Adam Woolfitt/CORBIS; **290:** istockphoto.com; **291:** t. © Nancy Crampton; **291:** b. © Marilyn Silverstone /Magnum Photos; **295:** *Feast Day,* San Juan Pueblo, 1921, William Penhallow Henderson, National Museum of American Art, Smithsonian Institution; Given in Memory of Joshua C. Taylor/Art Resource, New York; **298–299:** © Steve Allen/ TIB/ Getty images; **299:** border. istockphoto.com; **300–301:** border. istockphoto.com; **301:** Sheldon Collins/CORBIS; **302:** Historical Picture Archive/CORBIS; **302–303:** border. istockphoto.com; **304:** border. istockphoto.com;

315: © Gary Rhijnsburger/Masterfile; 316–317: Courtesy of Ryan Eastman; 318: ©1999, 2007 Kaihsu Tai; 321: © Gary Rhijnsburger/ Masterfile; 322: Getty Images; 323: © Bob Krist/CORBIS; 325: Mary Grace Long /Asia Images/Getty Images; 326: Red Chopsticks/ Getty Images; 328: David Muir/digital vision/Getty Images; 331: Time Life Pictures/Getty Images; 332–333: © SuperStock, Inc./SuperStock; 333: border. istockphoto.com; 333: istockphoto.com; 334–335: border. istockphoto.com; 337: © Christie's Images/SuperStock; 338: © SuperStock, Inc./SuperStock; 349: Nikky Finney; 350: Elizabeth Catlett, American, born 1915, *Sharecropper,* 1952, printed 1970, Color linocut on cream Japanese paper, 450 x 431 mm (block); 544 x 513 mm (sheet), Restricted gift of Mr. and Mrs. Robert S. Hartman, 1992.182, The Art Institute of Chicago. Photography © The Art Institute of Chicago.; 353: *The Vegetable Garden,* Coombe, 1988, Riley, Paul (b. 1944) (Contemporary Artist)/Private Collection, © Chris Beetles, London, U.K./The Bridgeman Art Library International; 354: t. Frank Greenaway/© Dorling Kindersley; 354: b. Jim Zipp/Photo Researchers, Inc.; 361: t. Bettmann/CORBIS; 361: b. istockphoto.com; 362: *Duchess in Defiance* (oil on canvas), Parrish, Kevin (Contemporary Artist) Guild of Railway Artist/Private Collection,/The Bridgeman Art Library International; 364: © Corey Hochachka/Design Pics/CORBIS; 368: Foodpix; 369: North Wind Picture Archives; 370: istockphoto.com; 383: t. Photo Courtesy James Hurst; 383: b. Bassouls Sophie/CORBIS; 384: © Biosphoto/BIOS; Bios - Auteurs (droits geres); Huguet Pierre;/Peter Arnold Inc.; 384–385: © Panoramic Images/ Getty Images; 386: © Robin Chittenden; Frank Lane Picture Agency/CORBIS; 387: © Biosphoto/BIOS; Bios - Auteurs (droits geres); Huguet Pierre;/Peter Arnold Inc.; 389: Two Boys in a Punt, 1915 - Cover Illustration, Popular Magazine N.C. Wyeth (1882–1945) Oil on Canvas, 37-1/2 x 26 1/2, Private Collection, Photography courtesy of Brandywine River Museum; 392: © GERARD LACZ/Animals Animals - Earth Scenes; 394: © Biosphoto/BIOS; Bios - Auteurs (droits geres); Huguet Pierre;/Peter Arnold Inc.; 396: Portrait of a Mandarin (w/c) by Chinese School (19th century) Stapleton Collection, UK/ The Bridgeman Art Library; 398: border. istockphoto.com; 398: © Photographer:Rosmizan Abu Seman/ Agency: Dreamstime.com; 400: istockphoto.com; 402: © Pierre Tremblay/Masterfile; 405: Eric Cator; 410: Associated Press; 412: © Robert Recker/zefa/CORBIS; 420 (CL) ©Bettmann/Corbis, (CR) ©Marc Brasz/Corbis, (TL) National Portrait Gallery, London 422–423: Images.com/CORBIS; Gr09 U3 428: PEANUTS reprinted by permission of United Feature Syndicate, Inc.; 429: © Ryan McVay/ PhotoDisc/ Getty Images; 431: tl. © aleksandar velasevic/ istockphoto.com; 431: t. © Luis Bellagamba/ istockphoto. com; 433: tr. © Manik Ratan/ istockphoto.com; 433: t. istockphoto.com; 434: © Brandon Laufenberg/ istockphoto.com; 434: t. istockphoto.com; 437: tr. istockphoto.com; 437: tr. © Alexander Yakovlev/ istockphoto. com; 437: t. istockphoto.com; 438: b. istockphoto.com; 438: b. © Sylwia Nowik/istockphoto.com; 443: Courtesy of the author; 444: © Prisma/ SuperStock; 447: Tom Lea, Wood cutter and Burro ("El Lenador"), 1934, Oil on Canvas 29"x42". on Long term loan to the New Mexico Museum of Art from the U.S. General Services Administration, Works Project Administration. Photograph by Blair Clark (2833.23P); 448–449: border. istockphoto.com; 448–449: Three Reds, courtesy of Patrick Coffaro, Photography courtesy of Joan Cawley Licensing, Ltd.; 455: CORBIS; 467: b. Bettmann/CORBIS; 467: m. NASA; 468–469: NASA; 470: istock-photo.com; 471: istockphoto.com; 472: © Dorling Kindersley; 473: istockphoto.com; 474: NASA; 477: t. AP/Wide World Photos; 477: b. Cartesia/ Photodisc/ Getty Images; 478: Cartesia/ Photodisc/ Getty Images; 479: istockphoto.com; 480: t. istockphoto.com; 480: t. Cartesia/ Photodisc/ Getty Images; 482: t. istockphoto.com; 486: istockphoto. com; 495: border. © Josh Westrich/zefa/CORBIS; 495: r. NASA; 496: t. NASA; 496: border. © Josh Westrich/zefa/CORBIS; 499: b. Thomas Victor; 499: r. Time Life Pictures/Getty Images; 500–501: Courtesy of The Lincoln Museum, Fort Wayne, Indiana, (#983)- *Lincoln Proclaiming Thanksgiving,* Dean Cornwell; 502: *Peculiarsome Abe,* N.C. Wyeth, Courtesy of Children's Literature Research Collection, The Free Library of Philadelphia, Photography courtesy of the Brandywine River Museum; 505: Courtesy of the Library of Congress; 506: © CORBIS; 508: Focus on Sport/Getty Images; 509: istockphoto.com; 510: istockphoto. com; 521: t. Photo Courtesy of ABC Radio Networks; 521: b. Lambert/ Hulton Archive/ Getty Images; 522: © Mike Powell/CORBIS; 524: © Anthony Marsland/The Image Bank/ Getty Images; 526: Lambert/Hulton Archive/Getty Images; 529: t. AP/Wide World Photos; 529: b. © Prisma/ SuperStock; 530: © Prisma/SuperStock; 532: © George Steinmetz/ CORBIS; 533: The Granger Collection, New York; 534: © Richard T. Nowitz/ CORBIS; 541: Bettmann/CORBIS; 542: Bettmann/CORBIS; 544: CORBIS; 545: © Flip Schulke/CORBIS; 547: © Bob Adelman/Magnum Photos; 551: t. CORBIS; 551: b. Underwood & Underwood/CORBIS; 552: CORBIS; 553: Underwood & Underwood/CORBIS; 554: Getty Images; 555: Underwood & Underwood/CORBIS; 557: t. Bettmann/CORBIS; 557: b. National Collection of Fine Arts, Washington, DC; 558: © Bettmann/ CORBIS; 560: © Bettmann/ CORBIS; 569: t. © Bettmann/ CORBIS; 569: b. © CORBIS; 570: © Bettmann/ CORBIS; 573: t. Courtesy of the Author. Photo by Carolyn Soto.; 573: m. © 1966 by Michael Courlander; 573: b. Courtesy of Archives of Traditional Music; 574: © Images.com/CORBIS; 577: t. Images.com; 578: l. istockphoto.com; 579: r. istockphoto.com; 580: r. istockphoto.com; 582: b. Jose Luiz Pelaez, Inc. /CORBIS; 585: Marion Ettlinger; 602–603: Images.com/CORBIS; 600 (BR) James McGoon Photography Gr09 U4 605: © Colin Young-Wolff/Photo Edit; 607: © Images.com/CORBIS; 608: LUCKY COW ©2003 Mark Pett. Dist. By UNIVERSAL PRESS SYNDICATE. Reprinted with permission. All rights reserved.; 609: © Bob Daemmrich/ PhotoEdit Inc.; 611: Paul & Lindamarie Ambrose/Getty Images; 612: Paul & Lindamarie Ambrose/ Getty Images; 613: t. Photo courtesy of Pat Mora; 614: b. Photo courtesy of Pat Mora; 619: ml. Bettmann/CORBIS; 619: t. Time Life Pictures/Getty Images; 619: b. Getty Images; 619: akg-images; 620: t. Lawrence, Jacob (1917–2000), *Street Shadows,* 1959. Egg tempera on hardboard, 24 x 30". © ARS, NY/ Photo courtesy of: The Jacob and Gwendolyn Lawrence Foundation/Art Resource, NY; 621: istockphoto.com; 622: akg-images; 624: t. Kathleen Brown/CORBIS; 625: t. Kathleen Brown/ CORBIS; 626: © Ian Mckinnell/ Getty Images; 631: m. Hulton Archive/ Getty Images Inc.; 631: b. Getty Images; 631: t. Roger Ressmeyer/ CORBIS; 632: Charles O'Rear/CORBIS; 634: b. McDonald Wildlife Photog./Animals Animals; 635: m. Reza Estakhrian/ Getty Images; 636: © Alamy Images; 645: m. Alfred Lord Tennyson, © 1840, S. Laurence, by courtesy of the National Portrait Gallery, London; 645: b. Oscar White/CORBIS; 645: t. Miriam Berkley/Authorpix; 646: b. Stewart Cohen/ Digital Vision by Getty Images; 647: t. © Antar Dayal/Illustration Works/ CORBIS; 648–649: © Lance Richbourg/SuperStock; 650: t. © Lance Richbourg/SuperStock; 653: m. Photo by Mandy Sayer; 653: t. Bettmann/ CORBIS; 653: b. Bettmann/CORBIS; 654: *The Bells of Rostov,* 1983 (oil on canvas), Chepik, Sergei (b. 1953)/Private Collection, Roy Miles Fine Paintings/The Bridgeman Art Library International; 657: © Christie's Images/SuperStock; 658: The Bells, Edmund Dulac, New York Public Library; Astor, Lenox and Tilden Foundations; 660: © Images. com/CORBIS; 662–663: Illustrations copyright ©1977 by Jane Breskin Zalben from Jabberwocky. Published by Caroline House, Boyds Mills Press, Inc. Reprinted by permission.; 664: Illustrations copyright ©1977 by Jane Breskin Zalben from Jabberwocky. Published by Caroline House, Boyds Mills Press, Inc. Reprinted by permission.; 671: tl. © Tetra Images/ CORBIS; 671: mi. Stockbyte/Alamy; 672: Michelangelo Gratton/ Photo Researchers, Inc.; 677: rm. Photo by Robert Pedley; Courtesy of Kitty Costello; 677: b. photo by James Evans; 677: mb. © Bill Barksdale/ CORBIS; 677: mb. © Paul Buck/epa/CORBIS; 678: bl. SuperStock; 680: © Bill Barksdale/CORBIS; 682: © Paul Buck/epa/CORBIS; 695: t. Bettmann/ CORBIS; 695: m. AP/Wide World Photos; 695: b. AP/Wide World Photos; 696: The Granger Collection, New York; 699: © Cocoro Photos/CORBIS; 700: Reuters/CORBIS; 705: t. Mark Gerson Photography; 705: m. Oscar White/CORBIS; 705: b. The Granger Collection, New York; 707: Corel Professional Photos CD-ROM™; 708: © Flip De Nooyer/Foto Natura/ Minden Pictures, Inc.; 709: Tony Cordoza/Alamy; 710: Aaron/Horowitz/ CORBIS; 713: © Ed Reschke/Peter Arnold, Inc.; 723: t. Eric Schaal/Time Life Pictures/Getty Images; 723: m. Courtesy of the Library of Congress;

723: b. The Granger Collection, New York; **724:** © Alan Goldsmith; **728:** *Bubbles,* watercolor, 39" x 29", Courtesy of Scott Burdick; **731:** t. Courtesy of the Library of Congress; **731:** m. SuperStock; **731:** b. Eric Schaal/Time Life Pictures/Getty Images; **736:** tl. Corel Professional Photos CD-ROM™; **736:** tr. Corel Professional Photos CD-ROM™; **742:** Photo courtesy of NASA, Ames Research Center; **743:** © George Steinmetz/ CORBIS; **744:** Sam Ogden/Photo Researchers, Inc.; **749:** The Granger Collection, New York; **749:** AP/Wide World Photos; **749:** t. Bettmann/CORBIS; **749:** b. SuperStock; **750:** Ron Brown/SuperStock; **752:** *The Quiltmakers,* Paul Goodnight, 22 11/16" x 24" Color Circle Art Publishing Inc.; **756:** Jose Luiz Pelaez, Inc./Getty Images; **759:** t. Cheron Bayna; **766:** m. © Superstock; **766:** b. © image100/ CORBIS; **774** (TCL) ©Bettmann/Corbis, (BR) ©Najlah Feanny/Corbis, (BCL) ©The Granger Collection, NY; **776–777:** © Diana Ong/SuperStock; **Gr09 U5** **781:** istockphoto.com; **782:** IN THE BLEACHERS © 1999 Steve Moore. Reprinted with permission of UNIVERSAL PRESS SYNDICATE. All rights reserved.; **783:** © Inti St Clair/ Digital Vision/ Getty Images; **785:** Chris Bennion/Seattle Children's Theatre; **787:** Chris Bennion/Seattle Children's Theatre; **789:** tm. Michael Newman/PhotoEdit Inc.; **789:** tr. Getty Images; **793:** b. Chris Bennion/Seattle Children's Theatre; **794:** Chris Bennion/Seattle Children's Theatre; **798A** Scala/Art Resource, NY **798B** ©Lebrecht Music and Arts Photo Library/Alamy Images **798:** t. 20TH CENTURY FOX/THE KOBAL COLLECTION/MORTON, MERRICK; **798:** b. © Andrea Pistolesi/ Getty Images; **799** ©DK Images; **802:** Jon Arnold Images/Masterfile Corporation; **805** (T) 20TH CENTURY FOX/ MORTON, MERRICK/The Kobal Collection, (B) 20TH CENTURY FOX/The Kobal Collection; **805:** b. 20TH CENTURY FOX/THE KOBAL COLLECTION/MORTON, MERRICK; **806:** border. istockphoto.com; **806:** 20TH CENTURY FOX/THE KOBAL COLLECTION/MORTON, MERRICK; **810:** Alinari/Art Resource, NY; **814:** TM and Copyright © 20th Century Fox Film Corp. All rights reserved. Courtesy: Everett Collection; **823:** TM and Copyright © 20th Century Fox Film Corp. All rights reserved. Courtesy: Everett Collection; **826:** 20TH CENTURY FOX/THE KOBAL COLLECTION/ MORTON, MERRICK; **827:** 20TH CENTURY FOX/THE KOBAL COLLECTION/MORTON, MERRICK; **829:** 20th Century Fox/Photofest; **834:** 20TH CENTURY FOX/THE KOBAL COLLECTION/MORTON, MERRICK; **838:** 20th Century Fox/Photofest; **841:** 20th Century Fox/ Photofest; **842:** br. Michael Melford/Getty Images; **842:** m. akg-images; **848:** © Araldo de Luca/CORBIS; **851:** TM and Copyright © 20th Century Fox Film Corp. All rights reserved. Courtesy: Everett Collection; **857:** 20TH CENTURY FOX/THE KOBAL COLLECTION/MORTON, MERRICK; **862:** 20TH CENTURY FOX/THE KOBAL COLLECTION/MORTON, MERRICK; **865:** TM and Copyright © 20th Century Fox Film Corp. All rights reserved. Courtesy: Everett Collection; **866:** TM and Copyright © 20th Century Fox Film Corp. All rights reserved. Courtesy: Everett Collection; **867:** 20TH CENTURY FOX/THE KOBAL COLLECTION/ MORTON, MERRICK; **872:** Private Collecton/Bridgeman Art Library, London/New York; **876:** l. © Mary Evans Picture Library/The Image Works; **876:** m. © Mary Evans Picture Library/MARK FURNESS/The Image Works; **876:** r. THE KOBAL COLLECTION/ Picture- Desk; **877:** l. The Everett Collection; **877:** m. © MGM/ Photofest; **877:** r. © Paramount Pictures/ Photofest; **878:** l. © ArenaPal/Topham/The Image Works; **878:** m. © ArenaPal/Topham/The Image Works; **878:** r. © Royal Shakespeare Theatre/Lebre/Lebrecht Music & Arts; **879:** ml. © Tristram Kenton/ Lebrecht Music/Lebrecht Music & Arts; **879:** br. © Neale Osborne/ Lebrecht Music &/Lebrecht Music & Arts; **879:** bl. © Royal Shakespeare Theatre/Lebre/Lebrecht Music & Arts; **879:** br. © Maremagnum/ Getty Images; **883:** Rod Planck/Photo Researchers, Inc.; **889:** 20th Century Fox/Photofest; **894:** 20th Century Fox/Photofest; **902:** 20th Century Fox/ Photofest; **907:** CORBIS; **909:** TM and Copyright © 20th Century Fox Film Corp. All rights reserved. Courtesy: Everett Collection; **914:** 20TH CENTURY FOX/THE KOBAL COLLECTION/MORTON, MERRICK; **916:** TM and Copyright © 20th Century Fox Film Corp. All rights reserved. Courtesy: Everett Collection; **918:** The Granger Collection, New York; **923:** 20TH CENTURY FOX/THE KOBAL COLLECTION/MORTON, MERRICK; **924:** 20TH CENTURY FOX/THE KOBAL COLLECTION/ MORTON, MERRICK; **937:** © Michael Maslan Historic Photographs/ CORBIS; **938:** © Michael Maslan Historic Photographs/ CORBIS; **939:** Rainer Jahns; **939:** © Dorling Kindersley; **942:** t. Peter Phipp/ Travelshots; b. © Mel Lindstrom/Mira; **945:** t. Archivo Iconografico, S.A/ CORBIS; **945:** b. SuperStock; **946:** *Thisbe,* John William Waterhouse/The Bridgeman Art Library, London/New York; **946:** bkgrnd. © Helmut Meyer zur Capellen/zefa/CORBIS; **948:** *Thisbe and the Lioness,* from 'The Children's Hour: Stories from the Classics', published by the Waverley Book Company (colour litho), Brock, Charles Edmund (1870–1938)/Private Collection/The Bridgeman Art Library International; **949:** © Helmut Meyer zur Capellen/zefa/CORBIS; **950:** The Everett Collection, Inc; **951:** istockphoto.com; **952:** The Granger Collection, New York; **954:** The Everett Collection, Inc.; **956:** © CORBIS Sygma; **969:** Bettmann/ CORBIS; **970:** Valmondois Sous La Neige, Maurice de Vlaminck, Superstock; **973:** White Night, 1901, Edvard Munch, Photo: Scala/Art Resource, NY/©2010 The Munch Museum/The Munch-Ellingsen Group/ Artists Rights Society (ARS), NY; **981:** © noneAA/CORBIS; **987:** t. Bettmann/CORBIS; **987:** b. Courtesy Henry Alford; **988:** bkgrnd. istockphoto.com; **988:** The Everett Collection, Inc; **989:** istockphoto.com; **990:** Photofest; **993:** Camera Press/Retna, LTD; **996:** Photofest; **998:** Photofest; **999:** tr. Toho Company/Photofest; **999:** m. Lynton Gardiner/© Dorling Kindersley, Courtesy of The American Museum of Natural History; **999:** rm. Colin Keates/© Dorling Kindersley; **999:** mi. Paul Van Reil/Robert Harding World Imagery; **1002:** Kwame Zikomo/SuperStock; **1007:** Prentice Hall; **1016:** istockphoto.com; **1024** (BR) Photo by Charles Barry/Santa Clara University; **1026–1027:** Nice One Productions/ CORBIS; **1030:** istockphoto.com; **Gr09 U6** **1031:** © Gerald Bustamante/ Stock Illustration Source, Inc.; **1032:** CORNERED © 2004 Mike Baldwin. Reprinted with permission of UNIVERSAL PRESS SYNDICATE. All rights reserved.; **1037:** Getty Images; **1038:** Getty Images; **1040A** (T) ©Masterfile Royalty-Free, (B) Robert Harding Images/Masterfile Corporation; **1040C** adv/Shutterstock; **1040D** Clara/Shutterstock; **1040E** Georgy Markov/Shutterstock; 1040F Panos Karapanagiotis/Shutterstock **1043:** Wunson/Shutterstock; **1043:** l. © Kevin Fleming/CORBIS; **1043:** bkgrnd. istockphoto.com; **1043:** bkgrnd. istockphoto.com; **1044–1045:** l. © Kevin Fleming/CORBIS; **1044–1045:** bkgrnd. istockphoto.com; **1046:** Mary Evans Picture Library/EDWIN WALLACE/Everett Collection; **1055:** Mary Evans Picture Library/EDWIN WALLACE/Everett Collection; **1058:** Mary Evans Picture Library/EDWIN WALLACE/Everett Collection; **1061:** Polyphemus, The Cyclop from Homer's The Odyssey, N.C. Wyeth; **1066:** Odysseus in the Land of the Dead from Homer's The Odyssey, N.C. Wyeth, Brandywine River Museum; **1069:** Réunion des Musées Nationaux/Art Resource, NY; **1070:** Circe Meanwhile Had Gone Her Ways..., 1924, William Russell Flint, Collection of the New York Public Library; Astor, Lenox and Tilden Foundations; **1075:** Mary Evans Picture Library; **1080:** © Stapleton Collection/CORBIS; **1089:** © Kevin Fleming/ CORBIS; **1089:** bkgrnd. istockphoto.com; **1089:** b. istockphoto.com; **1091:** Eumaeus, the Swineherd from Homer's The Odyssey, N.C. Wyeth, The Museum of Texas Tech University; **1095:** Scala/Art Resource, NY; **1096:** © Araldo de Luca/CORBIS; **1099:** Mary Evans Picture Library/ EDWIN WALLACE/Everett Collection; **1102:** The Trial of the Bow from Homer's The Odyssey, N.C. Wyeth, Brandywine River Museum; **1104:** Bridgeman Art Library, London/New York; **1106:** The Slaughter of the Suitors from Homer's The Odyssey, N.C. Wyeth, Licensed by ASaP Worldwide. Photo courtesy of the Archives of the American Illustrators Gallery, NYC. © Copyright 2000 National Museum of American Illustration, Newport, RI. www.americanillustration.org; **1113:** Erich Lessing/Art Resource, NY; **1119:** PARAMOUNT PICTURES/THE KOBAL COLLECTION; **1120:** b. AP/Wide World Photos; **1120:** bkgrnd. Frank Schwere/Getty Images; **1121:** m. PARAMOUNT PICTURES/THE KOBAL COLLECTION/DUHAMEL, FRANCOIS; **1121:** b. PARAMOUNT PICTURES/ THE KOBAL COLLECTION/DUHAMEL, FRANCOIS; **1121:** bkgrnd. Photo by Keystone/ J.Byrnes; **1121:** tl. PARAMOUNT PICTURES/THE KOBAL COLLECTION; **1122:** t. PARAMOUNT PICTURES/THE KOBAL

COLLECTION/DUHAMEL, FRANCOIS; **1122:** b. PARAMOUNT PICTURES/ THE KOBAL COLLECTION/DUHAMEL, FRANCOIS; **1122:** bkgrnd. Photo by Keystone/ J.Byrnes; **1127:** bl. The Granger Collection, New York; **1127:** tl. © Bassouls Sophie/CORBIS Sygma; **1127:** br. Getty Images; **1127:** Time Life Pictures/Getty Images; **1128:** *Penelope and the Suitors,* 1912, J.M. Waterhouse, 51 1/2 x 75 in. (131 x 191 cm) City of Aberdeen Art Gallery and Museums Collections, Scotland; **1130:** Herve Lewandowski/Reunion de Musees Nationaux/Art Resource; **1132:** Perry Mastrovito/CORBIS; **1134–1135:** John Miller/Robert Harding Picture Library/Alamy; **1139:** Jason Lewis/© Dorling Kindersley; **1147:** t. © Agnew's, London, UK/ The Bridgeman Art Library; **1147:** b. istockphoto.com; **1148–1149:** Paul Hardy/CORBIS; **1149:** inset. istockphoto.com; **1150:** istockphoto.com; **1151:** © Agnew's, London, UK/ The Bridgeman Art Library; **1153:** istockphoto.com; **1154:** istockphoto.com; **1156–1157:** Denis Scott/CORBIS; **1159:** istockphoto.com; **1160:** istockphoto.com; **1165:** t. Getty Images; **1165:** b. The Granger Collection, New York; **1166:** The Granger Collection, New York; **1168:** The Granger Collection, New York; **1170:** Simon Jauncey/Getty Images; **1171:** The Granger Collection, New York; **1174:** The Granger Collection, New York; **1175:** The Granger Collection, New York; **1177:** The Granger Collection, New York; **1179:** The Granger Collection, New York; **1180:** The Granger Collection, New York; **1181:** Historical Picture Archive/CORBIS; **1183:** The Granger Collection, New York; **1186:** The Granger Collection, New York; **1195:** Bettmann/CORBIS; **1196–1197:** *We the People,* Kathy Morrow, Original scratchboard painting with hand-loomed beadwork, Courtesy of the artist; **1201:** t. AP/Wide World Photos; **1201:** b. © Tibor Bognar/CORBIS; **1202:** l. © BRAUCHLI DAVID/CORBIS SYGMA; **1202:** r. © Tibor Bognar/ CORBIS; **1204:** © Reuters/ CORBIS; **1209:** AP/Wide World Photos; **1209:** bkgrnd. AP/Wide World Photos; **1210:** Photo File/ MLB Photos via Getty Images; **1210:** bkgrnd. AP/Wide World Photos; **1211:** t. Mary Evans Picture Library/The Image Works; **1211:** b. Photo by Elaine Rosner; **1211:** bkgrnd. Masterfile (Royalty-Free Div.); **1212:** Photo by Alberto Meza; **1212:** b. Photo by Connie Herrera; **1212:** bkgrnd. Masterfile (Royalty-Free Div.); **1217:** t. Falls Village-Canaan Historical Society; **1217:** b. Time Life Pictures/Getty Images; **1218:** Illustration by Tim Raglin; **1220–1221:** border. istockphoto.com; **1222:** Jim Zuckerman/CORBIS; **1224:** Franck Fotos/Alamy; **1225:** *Andromeda Liberated,* Pierre Mignard, Louvre, Paris, France, Erich Lessing/Art Resource, NY; **1227:** Danae with young Perseus arriving on the island of Seripo, Museo Archeologico, Ferrara, Italy. Scala/Art Resource, NY; **1228:** Scala/Art Resource, NY; **1231:** Perseus and Andromeda (detail), Ca.1580, Paolo Veronese, Musee des Beaux-Arts, Rennes, France, Erich Lessing/Art Resource, NY; **1234:** Jose Luiz Pelaez, Inc. /CORBIS; **1237:** Getty Images; **1252** (CL) ©Associated Press, (TL) ©INTERFOTO/Alamy Images

CREDITS

Staff Credits

The people who made up the Pearson Prentice Hall Literature team—representing design, editorial, editorial services, education technology, manufacturing and inventory planning, market research, marketing services, planning and budgeting, product planning, production services, project office, publishing processes, and rights and permissions—are listed below. Boldface type denotes the core team members.

Tobey Antao, Margaret Antonini, Rosalyn Arcilla, Penny Baker, James Ryan Bannon, Stephan Barth, **Tricia Battipede**, Krista Baudo, Rachel Beckman, Julie Berger, Lawrence Berkowitz, Melissa Biezin, **Suzanne Biron**, Rick Blount, **Marcela Boos**, **Betsy Bostwick**, Kay Bosworth, Jeff Bradley, Andrea Brescia, Susan Brorein, Lois Brown, **Pam Carey**, Lisa Carrillo, **Geoffrey Cassar**, Patty Cavuoto, Doria Ceraso, Jennifer Ciccone, Jaime Cohen, Rebecca Cottingham, Joe Cucchiara, Jason Cuoco, **Alan Dalgleish**, **Karen Edmonds**, **Irene Ehrmann**, Stephen Eldridge, **Amy Fleming**, Dorothea Fox, Steve Frankel, Cindy Frederick, Philip Fried, Diane Fristachi, Phillip Gagler, **Pamela Gallo**, Husain Gatlin, **Elaine Goldman**, Elizabeth Good, John Guild, Phil Hadad, Patricia Hade, Monduane Harris, Brian Hawkes, Jennifer B. Heart, Martha Heller, John Hill, Beth Hyslip, Mary Jean Jones, Grace Kang, Nathan Kinney, Roxanne Knoll, **Kate Krimsky**, Monisha Kumar, Jill Kushner, Sue Langan, Melisa Leong, Susan Levine, Dave Liston, **Mary Luthi**, **George Lychock**, **Gregory Lynch**, **Joan Mazzeo**, **Sandra McGloster**, Eve Melnechuk, Kathleen Mercandetti, Salita Metha, Artur Mkrtchyan, Karyn Mueller, Alison Muff, Christine Mulcahy, Kenneth Myett, Elizabeth Nemeth, Stefano Nese, Carrie O'Connor, April Okano, Kim Ortell, Sonia Pap, Raymond Parenteau, Dominique Pickens, Linda Punskovsky, **Sheila Ramsay**, Maureen Raymond, Mairead Reddin, **Erin Rehill-Seker**, **Renée Roberts**, **Laura Ross**, Bryan Salacki, Sharon Schultz, Jennifer Serra, **Melissa Shustyk**, Rose Sievers, Christy Singer, Yvonne Stecky, **Cynthia Summers**, Steve Thomas, Merle Uuesoo, Roberta Warshaw, Patricia Williams, Daniela Velez

Additional Credits

Lydie Bemba, Victoria Blades, Denise Data, Rachel Drice, Eleanor Kostyk, Jill Little, Loraine Machlin, Evan Marx, Marilyn McCarthy, Patrick O'Keefe, Shelia M. Smith, Lucia Tirondola, Laura Vivenzio, Linda Waldman, Angel Weyant